The Directory of British Associations can't be right all the time.

We publish DBA every two years and contact every single body to verify their details, but every day, associations merge, or close, or change their names, or simply move.

And one day your letter comes back marked "Gone Away", or your e-mail bounces, or the "number you have dialled has not been recognised". Or perhaps the one association you really want to find isn't in DBA at all.

Infuriating isn't it? What do you do then?

You could search in other association directories, although none list as many British & Irish associations as DBA does. You could buy a directory that comes out annually, but that would simply work out to be more expensive in the long term. Or…

You could simply ask us!

Although we publish every two years, we update our data every day. Just contact us at CBD Research Ltd, by letter, phone, e-mail or fax, and you could have the information you need instantly – completely free of charge – whether you've bought the Directory of British Associations or not.

CBD Research Ltd is a small company, which means that whoever answers your call will at least understand your question, and may well be able to answer it. And if we don't immediately know the answer to your question, we'll work hard to track it down for you.

If it's not in DBA… Just ask CBD!

Tel: 020 8650 7745

Email: cbd@cbdresearch.com

www:cbdresearch.com

We welcome your enquiries.

Directory of British Associations

& Associations in Ireland

Edition 20

CBD Research Ltd

Tel: 020 8650 7745
Email: cbd@cbdresearch.com www.cbdresearch.com

062
DIR

First Published   1965

Edition 20   2012

Copyright ©   2012 CBD Research Ltd

Published by   CBD Research Ltd

Telephone: 020 8650 7745   E-mail: cbd@cbdresearch.com
Internet: www.cbdresearch.com
UK Registered Company No. 700855

ISBN   978-0-955451-46-1

Price   £248.00   US$400.00

No payment is either solicited or accepted for the inclusion of entries in this publication. Every possible precaution has been taken to ensure that the information it contains is accurate at the time of going to press and the publishers cannot accept any liability for errors or omissions however caused.

CBD Research Ltd   founder members of the Data Publishers Association (DPA) and the European Association of Directory Publishers, and are pledged to a strict code of professional practice designed to protect against fraudulent directory publishing and dubious selling methods.

Printing and binding: Polestar.

CONTENTS

*NOTE: the explanations of abbreviations are repeated inside
the front and back covers.

Councils Committees & Boards

a handbook of advisory, consultative, executive, regulatory & similar bodies in British public life including government agencies & authorities

giving their:

- address
- telephone
- fax
- e-mail
- web site
- names of chairman & other senior officials
- date of formation
- authority for establishment
- constitution
- terms of reference

- geographical area of competence
- responsibilities, duties & activities
- publications

_____

- index of officials
- abbreviated names index
- index of activities & interests fields

We welcome your enquiries

CBD Research Ltd

Tel: 020 8650 7745

E-mail: cbd@cbdresearch.com

www.cbdresearch.com

INTRODUCTION

1.   This book provides information on national associations, societies, institutes, and similar organisations – in all fields of activity – which have a voluntary membership. Regional and local organisations concerned with important industries and trades (e.g. Birmingham Metallurgical Association) are included, as are local chambers of commerce and county agricultural, archaeological, historical, natural history, and similar organisations which are the principal sources of information and contacts in their areas.

Particular attention has been given to the inclusion in DBA of national federations of local organisations and of 'controlling bodies' of various sports and interest which can usually provide a means of contact with local or specialised units. A complete listing of voluntary organisations in the British Isles, including all social, political, sports, young people's clubs and all specialised societies with major hobbies and interests would require a library of volumes the size of DBA.

Excluded are friendly societies, building societies, benevolent societies in aid of specific trades or professions, advice centres, trusts, and certain other categories; but a number of organisations strictly outside our definition of 'associations' are listed because the user of DBA might, from the wording of their names, expect to find them listed (e.g. British Malignant Hyperthermia Association) – such entries are marked § and generally contain an explanation of their status.

All entries are FREE, no payment is sought or accepted for entries in the Directory, nor are entries made conditional on the purchase of the book. The publishers reserve the right to edit information supplied, and to exclude any organisation considered to be outside the scope of the Directory, for any reason.

2. AREA

'British' in the title has been used in the sense of relating to the British Isles: England, Wales, Scotland, Northern Ireland, the Irish Republic, the Isle of Man and the Channel Islands. Some British organisations overseas (e.g. British Chamber of Commerce in Mexico) are also included.

3. BASIS OF COMPILATION

(a)   Questionnaires or revision documents were sent to all of the organisations listed and the courtesy of those who responded is acknowledged by the symbol ■ preceding their addresses. The abbreviation NR shows that the organisation failed to return our questionnaire, but that its validity has been checked by telephone or e-mail.

(b)   Entries for associations in the Republic of Ireland are distinguished by the letters IRL and are limited to name, abbreviation, date of formation and contact details. Most of them are included in DBA by courtesy of the Institute of Public Administration, Dublin, whose publication 'Administration Yearbook and Diary' contains extensive information about most associations and many other organisations in Ireland. Copies of the Yearbook are available from the Institute at 57–61 Lansdowne Road, Dublin 4; telephone (from UK) 00 353 (1) 240 3600, fax 00 353 (1) 668 9135, e-mail information@ipa.ie.

(c)   Associations which we believe to exist, but for which we have not been able to find or validate the address, or from whose last known address our questionnaires have been returned marked 'Gone Away' are listed by name only, prefixed by two ** in the main directory. Any information regarding the existence and whereabouts of these organisations will be welcomed by the editors.

4. ARRANGEMENT AND ALPHABETISATION

DBA is arranged in four parts:

(a)   The main directory, in the alphabetisation of which prepositions, articles and conjunctions are ignored, thus:

> Society of Antiquaries of London
> Society for Applied Philosophy
> Society of the Irish Motor Industry
> Society for the Promotion of New Music

(b)   abbreviations index – an index to the initials, acronyms or other forms of abbreviation by which organisations are generally known.

(c)   publications index – an index to the titles of publications notified by associations

(d)   subject index – an index to the activities, professions, groups or interests served by associations

SPECIAL NOTE

In the indexes names of associations are shortened to the words which govern their arrangement in the main directory, abbreviated as shown on page xiii and inside the back cover.

5. FORM OF ENTRY

Each entry in the main directory consists of:

Name of organisation – the full name as stated in Articles, Constitution or Rules

Abbreviation (in parentheses) by which the organisation is known

Date of formation (not necessarily the date of incorporation, which in many cases is later)

Validity indicator (see paragraph 3(a) above)

Address of headquarters, secretary or person to contact

Telephone number

Fax number

E-mail address

Website address

Letters (in parentheses) indicating whether the address is that of the organisation's permanent
   headquarters (hq), the honorary secretary's business or private address (hsb) or (hsp),
   registered office (regd off), official secretariat (asa) or other

Name of the organisation's secretary or other officer, with designation of office held

© CBD Research Ltd · Beckenham · BR3 5JS · Tel 020 8650 7745 · E-mail cbd@cbdresearch.com · www.cbdresearch.com

Legal Status of Organisation (prefixed ▲)

Branches: number of branches in UK, number or location of branches elsewhere

Type of organisation and sphere of interest (prefixed ○): the symbol followed by a code letter (see Abbreviations 1) indicate the type of organisation, a brief note amplifying or explaining the purpose of the organisation may follow

Groups: details of specialist groups, sections, divisions, committees etc.

Activities (prefixed ●): a series of abbreviations – in a set order – indicating the types of activity within the organisation, followed by notes of any special activities

Affiliations (prefixed <): especially international; in most cases this information is printed exactly as received – often in the form of abbreviations or acronyms

Affiliations (prefixed >): bodies affiliated to the organisation

Membership data (prefixed M): indicating whether individuals (i), firms (f) or other organisations (org) form the membership. "Firms" is used in the colloquial sense, to denote all forms of commercial enterprise. Wherever received for publication, the number of members in each category in the UK and overseas is shown (e.g. 250 i, 32 org UK/17 org o'seas) but in many cases, a total has been received without analysis; thus 2,250 i, f & org = total membership 2,250 made up of unspecified numbers of individuals, firms and other organisations.

Publications (prefixed ¶): title, frequency (number of issues a year) and supply data. Titles such as "Journal of the Society of Fireback Collectors" containing the whole name of the issuing body are abbreviated to Jnl, Proceedings, etc. Other abbreviations used in this heading are shown on page xi and inside front cover

Thus: Backfire – 4; ftm, £9.50 yr nm. NL – 12; ftm only

indicates that the society publishes a quarterly periodical called "Backfire" distributed free to members and on sale to non-members at £9.50 per annum; and a free monthly newsletter distributed to members only.

Previous names (prefixed ✕): if the name of the organisation has been changed within the last 5 years the former name or names and the date of the change are given. Names of organisations which have been absorbed are also entered here

6. OTHER SOURCES

Users of DBA are reminded of standard sources for certain categories excluded from this book. Advisory, consultative, executive and similar bodies, including Government agencies and authorities, in Great Britain and Northern Ireland are listed, described and indexed in COUNCILS, COMMITTEES AND BOARDS (CBD Research Ltd – see advert). Certain organisations which used to appear in DBA have been transferred to our publication CENTRES, BUREAUX AND RESEARCH INSTITUTES (see advert). Full details of building societies are given in the Building Societies Yearbook (Building Societies Association) and of charitable organisations in the Charities Digest (Wilmington Publishing). Friendly societies are to be found in the lists available from the Registrar of Friendly Societies (Financial Services Authority).
A complete list of livery companies in the City of London is contained in the City of London Directory (City Press Ltd, Colchester) and in Whitaker's Almanack.

For national associations in Europe we recommend our other publications: DIRECTORY OF EUROPEAN INDUSTRIAL & TRADE ASSOCIATIONS and DIRECTORY OF EUROPEAN PROFESSIONAL & LEARNED SOCIETIES (see adverts).

7. ENQUIRIES AND SUGGESTIONS

The greatest care is taken in the compilation of DBA and every effort is made to ensure the inclusion of all organisations which purchasers may reasonably expect to find listed; some associations have been omitted because the editors have doubts about their bona fides; certain others have been left out at the specific and reasonable request of their secretaries. The publishers have records of several thousand associations which, for various reasons, are not listed in DBA – these records are constantly under review and we are always glad to assist enquirers seeking to trace organisations not listed.

Secretaries of unlisted associations or of those marked "unverified and lost" are invited to use the questionnaire reproduced in this volume (or to write or telephone for another) so that their organisations can be recorded in readiness for the next edition.

8. ACKNOWLEDGEMENTS

We have benefited, as usual, from the helpful response of countless secretaries, and the advice of many users of the Directory who tell us of associations newly formed or recently defunct. Editors' names are not shown on the title page; the reason is simple: everyone in the 'CBD' team has been involved in all the tasks of mailing, verification, preparation of entries...
To all who have helped in any way we express our thanks.

© CBD Research Ltd · Beckenham · BR3 5JS · Tel 020 8650 7745 · E-mail cbd@cbdresearch.com · www.cbdresearch.com

ABBREVIATIONS: 1 – IN MAIN ALPHABETICAL DIRECTORY

Validity indicators:

■	entry based on questionnaire, or other document, returned by organisation
NR	No reply received for this edition
IRL	Irish entry - see introduction 3(b)
§	Organisation outside normal scope of DBA but included for convenience of users
**	Organisation unverified or lost

Address:

asa	official secretariat		hsp	honorary secretary's private address
hq	organisation's permanent headquarters		sb/p	secretary's business or private address
hsb	honorary secretary's business address		regd off	registered office

Name of secretary or chief executive, with designation of office held:

Chmn	Chairman	Sec	Secretary	Org Sec	Organising Secretary
Dir	Director	Gen Sec	General Secretary	Pres	President
Exec	Executive	Hon Sec	Honorary Secretary	Hon Treas	Honorary Treasurer
Mgr	Manager	Mem Sec	Membership Secretary	PRO	Public Relations Officer

▲   Legal Status of Organisation

Br   Branches

○   Type of organisation & sphere of interest: indicated by one or more of the following letters, with an amplification or explanation only where necessary; if an organisation's interests are obvious from its name, only the starred letter is given

*A	Art & Literature		*N	Co-ordinating bodies
*B	Breed Societies		*P	Professional
*C	Chambers of Commerce Industry or Trade		*Q	Research Organisations
			*R	Religious Organisations
*D	Dance, Music & Theatre		*S	Sports
*E	Educational		*T	Trade
*F	Farming & Agriculture		*U	Trade Unions
*G	General Interest & Hobbies		*V	Veterinary & Animal Welfare
*H	Horticultural		*W	Welfare Organisations
*K	Campaigns & Pressure Groups		*X	International Friendship
*L	Learned, Scientific & Technical Socs		*Y	Youth Organisations
*M	Medical Interest		*Z	Political Organisations

Gp(s)   Groups

●   Activities:

Comp	Competitions		LG	Liaison with Government
Conf	Conference(s)		Lib	Library
Empl	Negotiations of pay & conditions of employment		Mtgs	Regular Meetings
ET	Education &/or training for professional or other qualifications		PL	Picture Library
Exam	Examinations for professional or other qualifications		Res	Scientific or other systematic research
Exhib	Exhibitions & Shows		SG	Study Groups
Expt	Export promotion		Stat	Collection of Statistics
Inf	Information service available		VE	Visits & Excursions

<   Affiliations to international & other organisations
>   Bodies affiliated to the organisation

M   Membership Data

    i=individuals   f=firms   org=organisations

¶   Publications

AR	Annual Report		m	members
ftm	free to members		NL	Newsletter
hbk	Handbook		nm	non-members
Jnl	Journal		Ybk	Year book
LM	List of members		yr	per annum

X   Former name or names of organisation if changed during past five years (preceded by date of change, if known)

ABBREVIATIONS 2 – IN INDEXES

Advy	Advisory	Gp	Group
Agricl	Agricultural	H'capped	Handicapped
Amal	Amalgamated	Hist	History
Amat	Amateur	Histl	Historical
Amer	American	Hortl	Horticultural
Archaeol	Archaeological	Inc	Incorporated
Assd	Associated	Ind	Industry
Assn	Association	Indep	Independent
Bd(s)	Board(s)	Indl	Industrial
Bldg	Building	Inf	Information
Brit	British	Inst	Institute
C'ee	Committee	Instn	Institution
Cent	Central	Intl	International
Cham	Chamber	Ir	Irish
Chart	Chartered	(IRL)	Republic of Ireland
Co	Company	Jt	Joint
Coll	College	Lond	London
Comm	Commerce	Manch	Manchester
Comml	Commercial	Mchts	Merchants
Conf	Conference	Med	Medical
Confedn	Confederation	Mfrg	Manufacturing
Consvn	Conservation	Mfrs	Manufacturers
Contrs	Contractors	Mgrs	Managers
Corpn	Corporation	Mgt	Management
Coun	Council	Mid	Midland
C'wealth	Commonwealth	Mult	Multiple
Dept	Department	N	North
Devt	Development	Nat	National
Distbn	Distribution	NI	Northern Ireland
Distbrs	Distributors	Nthn	Northern
E	East	Org	Organisation
Eastn	Eastern	Presvn	Preservation
Educ	Education	Profl	Professional
Educl	Educational	Pubr	Publisher
Emplr	Employer	R	Royal
Engg	Engineering	Res	Research
Engl	English	Rly	Railway
Engr	Engineer	S	South
Envt	Environment	Scot	Scottish
Envtl	Environmental	Soc	Society
Eqpt	Equipment	Sthn	Southern
Eur	European	Tr(s)	Trade(s)
Expt	Export	TV	Television
Fac	Faculty	U	Union
Fed	Federated	UK	United Kingdom
Fedn	Federation	Utd	United
GB	Great Britain	W	West
Gen	General	Whls	Wholesale
Gld	Guild	Wld	World
Govt	Government	Wstn	Western

© CBD Research Ltd · Beckenham · BR3 5JS · Tel 020 8650 7745 · E-mail cbd@cbdresearch.com · www.cbdresearch.com

A1 Motor Stores Ltd   (AIMS)   1983

NR   Unit 20 Waterfield Way, Sketchley Industrial Estate, Sketchley
Meadows, HINCKLEY, Leics, LE10 3ER.   (hq)
01455 637031
email admin@a1motorstores.co.uk
http://www.a1motorstores.co.uk
Chief Exec: Derrick Lawton
▲   Company Limited by Guarantee
○   *T; voluntary group of independent automotive accessory &
spare parts retailers. The association offers marketing &
purchasing support
●   Conf - Mtgs - ET - Exhib - Comp - Stat - Inf - Lib - VE - Empl -
LG
M   115 f
¶   Newstime - 24; ftm only.

A-T Society
see **Ataxia-Telangiectasia Society**

AAA - Action against Allergy   (AAA)   1978

■   PO Box 278, TWICKENHAM, Middx, TW1 4QQ.   (hq)
020 8892 2711 + 4949   fax 020 8892 4950
email aaa@actionagainstallergy.freeserve.co.uk
http://www.actionagainstallergy.co.uk
Exec Dir: Patricia Schooling
▲   Company Limited by Guarantee; Registered Charity
○   *G, *K, *W; to provide information & advice to all those who
have allergies or allergy-related illness & those who care for
them; to campaign for the improvement of NHS resources
for treatment of these conditions
●   Conf - Inf - Workshops for parents of allergic children
<   The Allergy Alliance
M   1,000 i
(Sub: £15)
¶   Allergy (NL) - 3; ftm, £15 yr nm.

Abbeyfield Society   1956

§   Abbeyfield House, 53 Victoria St, ST ALBANS, Herts, AL1 3UW.
01727 857536   fax 01727 846168
email post@abbeyfield.com
http://www.abbeyfield.com
Provision of housing, support and companionship to older
people in their local communities.

Aberdeen-Angus Cattle Society   1879

■   Pedigree House, 6 King's Place, PERTH, PH2 8AD.   (regd off)
01738 622477   fax 01738 636436
email info@aberdeen-angus.co.uk
http://www.aberdeen-angus.com
Chief Exec: Ron McHattie
▲   Company Limited by Guarantee
○   *B
●   Mtgs - Res - Exhib - Stat - Expt - Inf
<   Nat Beef Assn
M   1,100 i, f & org
¶   Aberdeen Angus Review - 1.
Aberdeen-Angus Herdbook - 1.   AR.

Aberdeen Fish Curers' & Merchants' Association Ltd   (AFCMA)   1944

NR   South Esplanade West, ABERDEEN, AB11 9FJ.   (hq)
01224 897744   fax 01224 871405
▲   Company Limited by Guarantee
○   *T; to promote & protect the interests of fish merchants in
Aberdeen & district
●   Conf - Mtgs - ET - Inf - Empl
M   60 f
¶   Ybk & Diary; free.
LM - 1;   Information circulars - 52;   AR; all ftm only.

Aberdeen & Grampian Chamber of Commerce   (AGCC)   1877

■   Greenhole Place, Bridge of Don, ABERDEEN, AB23 8EU.   (hq)
01224 343900   fax 01224 343943
email info@agcc.co.uk   http://www.agcc.co.uk
Chief Exec: Robert Collier
▲   Company Limited by Guarantee
○   *C
Gp   UK West Africa Action; Aberdeen Freight Agents' Association;
Business Gateway International Trade
●   Conf - Mtgs - ET - Stat - Expt - Inf - VE - LG
<   Scot Chams Comm; Brit Chams Comm
>   Chambers of Commerce in: Moray, Cairngorms, Caithness,
Sutherland, Inverness, Orkney, Western Isles
M   1,200 f
¶   Business Bulletin - 10; ftm, £30 yr nm.   AR; ftm.
Scottish National Directory - 1; ftm, £50 nm.
Members Listing (LM) - as required; £150.

Abertay Historical Society   1947

■   c/o Matthew Jarron, Museum Services, University of Dundee,
DUNDEE, DD1 4HN.   (hsb)
email museum@dundee.ac.uk
Sec: Matthew Jarron
○   *L; to promote the study & discussion of local history in
Dundee, Angus, Tayside & Fife
●   Conf - Workshops - VE - Lectures
M   i
¶   NL.
Annual publication on specific aspects of the area.

Abortion Rights   1936

NR   18 Ashwin St, LONDON, E8 3DL.   (hq)
020 7923 9792
▲   Un-incorporated Society
○   *K; to realise, in law & in practice, a woman's right to choose
on abortion
M   i

Absorbent Hygiene Products Manufacturers Association   (AHPMA)   1995

■   46 Bridge St, GODALMING, Surrey, GU7 1HL.   (hq)
01483 418221
Dir Gen: Tracy Stewart
▲   Company Limited by Guarantee
○   *T; to represent the non-competitive interests of UK companies
involved in the manufacture of tampons, feminine hygiene
products, disposable nappies & adult continence care
products
●   Mtgs
M   9 f

ABTA - the Travel Association   (ABTA)   1950

NR 30 Park St, LONDON, SE1 9EQ.   (hq)
    020 3117 0500
    http://www.abta.com
    Sec: Riccardo Nardi
▲ Company Limited by Guarantee
○ *T; interests of travel agents and tour operators in GB and
    Ireland; administration of codes of conduct; administration of
    tour operators' bonds & their utilisation as public protection
    in the event of financial failure; administration of fund for
    compensation of holidaymakers in case of financial failure by
    a retail travel agent
Gp Airways; Railways; Roadways; Shipping;
    Codes of conduct; Finance; Insurance; Technology; UK tourism
    ABTA National Training Board
● Conf - Mtgs - ET - Res - Inf - LG
< Confedn of Brit Ind (CBI), Assn of Travel Agents & Tour
    Operators in the EU (ECTAA)
M 2,700 f
¶ ABTA Magazine - 12; ftm only.
× 2008 (Association of British Travel Agents
    (Federation of Tour Operators (merged 1 July)

ACADEMI - Welsh National Literature Promotion Agency (ACADEMI)   1959

■ Mount Stuart House, Mount Stuart Square, CARDIFF,
    CF10 5FQ.   (hq)
    029 2047 2266   fax 029 2049 2930
    email post@academi.org   http://www.academi.org
    Chief Exec: Peter Finch
○ *L; to promote the literature of Wales & its authors
● Conf - Mtgs - ET - Comp - Lib
M 516 i
¶ Taliesin (Jnl) - 4.
    New Welsh Review.   A470 - 6.

Academic Paediatrics Association of Great Britain & Ireland (APA(GBI))   1976

■ c/o Prof N J Bishop, Academic Unit of Child Health, Sheffield
    Children's NHS Foundation Trust, SHEFFIELD, S Yorks,
    S10 2TH.   (hsb)
    0114-271 7228   fax 0114-275 5364
    email n.j.bishop@sheffield.ac.uk
    Hon Sec: Prof N J Bishop
▲ Un-incorporated Society
○ *M, *P
● Mtgs - ET
< Fedn Clinical Professors
M 93 i
× 2007 Association of Clinical Professors of Paediatrics

Academic & Professional Publishers
    a group of the **Publishers Association**

Academy of Culinary Arts

NR 53 Cavendish Rd, LONDON, SW12 0BL.
    020 8673 6300   fax 020 8673 6543
    email info@academyofculinaryarts.org.uk
    http://www.academyofculinaryarts.org.uk
    Dir: Sara Jayne-Stanes
○ *P

Academy of Curative Hypnotherapists   (ACH)

NR Central Buildings, 15 Station Rd, CHEADLE HULME, Cheshire,
    SK8 5AE.
    0161-485 4009   fax 0161-485 4009
    email admin@ach.co.uk   http://www.ach.co.uk
○ *M

Academy of Executives & Administrators   (AEA)   2002

■ Warwick Corner, 42 Warwick Rd, KENILWORTH, Warks,
    CV8 1HE.   (hq)
    01926 259342
    email info@academyofexecutivesandadministrators.org.uk
    http://www.academyofexecutivesandadministrators.org.uk
    Exec Admin: Lynne Sykes
○ *P
● ET - Exam
< Fac of Profl Business & Technical Mgt; Inst of Mgt Specialists;
    Inst of Mfrg
¶ Jnl - 2; ftm, £7 nm.

Academy of Experts   1987

■ 3 Gray's Inn Square, LONDON, WC1R 5AH.   (hq)
    020 7430 0333   fax 020 7430 0666
    email ara@atlas.co.uk
    http://www.academy-experts.org/
    Sec Gen: Nicola Cohen
○ *P; to promote a more effective use of experts in all professions
    & trades; to maintain & develop the excellence already
    achieved; to provide a cost efficient service to facilitate the
    quick resolution of disputes
Gp Register of experts; Register of mediators
● Conf - Mtgs - ET - Exam - Exhib - SG - Inf - VE
M [not for publication]
¶ The Expert (Jnl) - 4.
    NL - 12;   Hbk; both ftm only.

Academy of Medical Sciences   1998

■ 41 Portland Place, LONDON, W1B 1QH.   (hq)
    020 3176 2150
    email info@acmedsci.ac.uk   http://www.acmedsci.ac.uk
    Exec Dir: Dr Helen Munn
▲ Company Limited by Guarantee; Registered Charity
○ *P; to promote advance in medical science & campaign to
    ensure these are converted as quickly as possible into
    healthcare benefits for society
Gp specialist working groups created for specific studies &
    publications
● Conf - SG - LG
M c 850 i
¶ Fellows' Directory - 1; ftm only.   Review - 2 yrly.
    Miscellaneous Reports - see on website.

Academy of Multi-Skills   (AMS)   1995

■ 219 Bow Rd, LONDON, E3 2SJ.   (hq)
    07092 012910
    email info@academyofmultiskills.org.uk
    http://www.academyofmultiskills.org.uk
○ *P; to bring recognition to multi-skilled personnel, skilled
    trades, crafts & professions

Academy of Pharmaceutical Sciences   (APSGB)   2001

■ 840 Melton Rd, Thurmaston, LEICESTER, LE4 8BN.   (asa)
    0116-269 2299   fax 0116-264 0141
    email aps@associationhq.org.uk
    http://www.apsgb.org
    Sec: Robert Seager
▲ Company Limited by Guarantee
○ *L, *M, *Q
● ET - Res - SG
M 310 i
¶ NL - 4; ftm only.

© CBD Research Ltd · Beckenham · BR3 5JS · Tel 020 8650 7745 · E-mail cbd@cbdresearch.com · www.cbdresearch.com

Academy of Social Sciences   (AcSS)   1982
■ 30 Tabernacle St, LONDON, EC2A 4UE.   (hq)
   020 7330 0898
   email administrator@acss.org.uk   http://www.acss.org.uk
   Exec Dir: Stephen Anderson
▲ Company Limited by Guarantee; Registered Charity
○ *L, *N; the voice of the social sciences in the UK
● Conf - Mtgs - Res - SG - Inf - LG
M 469 i, 35 org
   (Sub: £50 i, £500 corporate)
¶ Contemporary Social Science (Jnl) - 3.
✕ 2007 (5 July) Academy of Learned Societies for the Social
   Sciences

access CINEMA   1977
IRL The Studio Building, Meeting House Sq, DUBLIN 2, Republic of
   Ireland.
   353 (1) 679 4420   fax 353 (1) 679 4166
   email info@accesscinema.ie
   Director: Maretta Dillon
○ *N

Access Flooring Association   (AFA)   1987
NR PO Box 386, HULL, HU9 5WX.   (sb)
   0845 120 0068
▲ Company Limited by Guarantee
○ *T; for manufacturers &/or contractors of access flooring
● Mtgs - SG - Inf
M 8 f

Accident Management Association
   2010 merged with the National Association of Credit Hire Operators
   to form the **Credit Hire Organisation**

Account Planning Group   (APG)   1978
■ 16 Creighton Ave, LONDON, N10 1NU.   (hq)
   020 8444 3692
   email mail@apg.org.uk   http://www.apg.org.uk
   Chmn: Sarah Newman
▲ Un-incorporated Society
○ *P; to promote excellence in creative thinking in account
   planning & communications strategy in the advertising
   industry & business
● Conf - Mtgs - ET
M 700 i, UK / 100 i, o'seas

Accounting Technicians Ireland   (ATI)
IRL 47-49 Pearse St, DUBLIN 2, Republic of Ireland.
   353 (1) 649 8100   fax 353 (1) 633 6846
   email info@iati.ie   http://www.iati.ie
   Chief Exec: Gay Sheehan
○ *P
✕ 2008-09 Institute of Accounting Technicians in Ireland

ACCU: professionalism in programming   (ACCU)   1987
NR [Contact by email only]
   email webeditor@accu.org   http://www.accu.org
▲ Un-incorporated Society
○ *P; 'a community of programmers who care about
   programming'
● Conf - Mtgs - Lectures
M i & f
   (Sub: £35 i, £120+ f)
¶ C Vu - 6;   Overload - 6; Hbk - 1; all ftm only.
✕ 2006 Association of C & C++ Users

Ace Credit Union Services   1999
NR 185-189 Shields Rd, Byker, NEWCASTLE upon TYNE,
   NE6 8DP.   (hq)
   0191-276 3737
   http://www.acecus.org
   Gen Mgr: Barbara S Hann
▲ Un-incorporated Society
○ *N; training & support for credit unions
● Conf - ET - Inf - LG - Provision of credit union stationery -
   Model rules for credit unions - Advice & support: computer
   specialist software, insurance, banking
M 44 credit unions

ACFO Ltd   (ACFO)   1970
NR c/o Fleet Audits Ltd, 35 Lavant St, PETERSFIELD, Hants,
   GU32 3EL.   (dir/b)
   01730 266666
   http://www.acfo.org
   Dir: Stewart Whyte
▲ Company Limited by Guarantee
Br 9 regions
○ *T; to represent all fleet operators to all levels of government,
   motor manufacturers, suppliers & insurance companies; to
   improve the professionalism of fleet managers
Gp Motor cars & light vans up to 7.5 tonnes GVW; Fleet
   consultancy; Defect reporting
● Conf - Mtgs - LG
M 12 i, 750 f
¶ Fleet Operator - 6;   NewsFax - 52; both ftm only.

ACT TravelWise   2008
NR 1 Vernon Mews, Vernon St, LONDON, W14 0RL.   (regd/off)
   020 7348 1970
   http://www.acttravelwise.org
○ *K; 'to drop the level of pollution caused by traffic; to reduce
   the use of cars for inappropriate journeys'
✕ 2008 (Association for Commuter Transport
   (National TravelWise Association

Action4   2011
NR Elite House, 179 Kings Road, READING, Berks, RG1 4EX.   (hq)
   0844 496 3333   fax 0844 496 3334
   email info@action4.org.uk   http://www.action4.org.uk
▲ Company Limited by Guarantee
○ *T; for companies involved in the premium rate telephone
   industry
● Mtgs - Res - LG - Liaison with regulators (ICSTIS, OFCOM)
M 35 f
¶ NL - 4.
✕ 2011 Premium Rate Association (successor)

Action against Allergy
   see **AAA - Action against Allergy**

Action with Communities in Rural England   (ACRE)   1987
■ Somerford Court, Somerford Rd, CIRENCESTER, Glos,
   GL7 1TW.   (hq)
   01285 653477   fax 01285 654537
   email acre@acre.org.uk   http://www.acre.org.uk
   Chief Exec: Sylvia Brown
▲ Company Limited by Guarantee; Registered Charity
○ *N, *W; to support sustainable rural community development
● Conf - Mtgs - ET - Res - Inf - Lib - LG
M 38 rural community councils
¶ Publications list available on website:
   acre.org.uk/DOCUMENTS/resources/publicationlist/pdf

Action on Dementia
   see **Alzheimer Scotland - Action on Dementia**

Action on Hearing Loss
   the trading name of the **RNID**

Action for Homeopathy   1982
NR   11 Wingle Tye Rd, BURGESS HILL, W Sussex, RH15 9HR.   (hsp)
        01444 236848
        http://www.actionforhomeopathy.org.uk
        Nat Admin: Mrs Mary Mitchell
▲   Un-incorporated Society
○   *K, *M, *N
M   20 i, 10 org
✕   2009 National Association of Homeopathy Groups

Action for ME   1987
NR   PO Box 2778, BRISTOL, BS1 9DJ.   (mail/address)
        0117-927 9551   fax 0117-927 9552
        email admin@actionforme.org.uk
        http://www.actionforme.org.uk
▲   Registered Charity
○   *K; working to improve the lives of people with ME (Myalgic
        Encephalomyelitis), CFS (Chronic Fatigue Syndrome) &
        PVFS (Post Viral Fatigue Syndrome)
●   Inf - Fundraising - Provision of services for people with ME -
        Campaigning
        lo-call 0845 123 2380
M   8,000 i
¶   Interaction - 4; ftm only.

Action against Medical Accidents   (AvMA)   1982
NR   44 High St, CROYDON, Surrey, CR0 1YB.   (hq)
        fax 020 8667 9065
        email admin@avma.org.uk   http://www.avma.org.uk
        Chief Exec: Peter Walsh
▲   Registered Charity
○   *K, *W; to offer advice & information to anyone who has been
        the victim of a medical accident; this can include referral to a
        specialist medical negligence solicitor
●   Mtgs - Inf - Co-ordination of the Support Network
        Helpline: 0845 123 2352
M   [not stated]

Action on Pre-Eclampsia   (APEC)   1991
NR   2C The Halfcroft, SYSTON, Leics, LE7 1LD.   (hq)
        0116-260 8088 (admin only)   fax 020 8424 0653
        email info@apec.org.uk   http://www.apec.org.uk
        Chief Exec: Mike Rich
▲   Company Limited by Guarantee; Registered Charity
Br   Australia, New Zealand
○   *W; to inform & educate parents & health professionals about
        pre-eclampsia; to support sufferers; to campaign for better
        care & promote research into all aspects of the condition
●   Conf - ET - Inf
        Helpline: 020 8863 3271 (Mon-Fri 0900-1700)
<   Australian Action on Pre-Eclampsia (AAPEC); Stichting Hellp
        Syndroom
M   800 i, UK / 40 i, o'seas
¶   NL - 3;   AR - 1; both free.
        Information pack; ftm, £5 nm.

Action for Prisoners' Families   1990
■   Unit 21 Carlson Court, 116 Putney Bridge Rd, LONDON,
        SW15 2NQ.   (hq)
        020 8812 3600   fax 020 8871 0473
        email info@actionpf.org.uk
        http://www.prisonersfamilies.org.uk
        Dir: Deborah Cowley
▲   Company Limited by Guarantee; Registered Charity
Br   2
○   *K; to promote the development of a nationwide network of
        support groups for prisoners' families
●   Conf - Mtgs - ET - Res - Inf - LG
M   122 org
¶   NL - 4;   AR - 1.
        Danny's Mum - 1;   Tommy's Dad - 1; both £2 m, £3 nm.
        Finding Dad - 1; £3.50 m, £4.50 nm.

Action on Rights for Children
        see **ARCH - Action on Rights for Children**

Action for Sick Children   (ASC/NAWCH)   1961
NR   32 Buxton Rd, High Lane, STOCKPORT, Cheshire, SK6 8BH.
        (hq)
        01663 763004
▲   Registered Charity
○   *W; to raise awareness of the psychosocial & emotional needs
        of sick children at home & in hospital
●   Conf - Mtgs - Res - Stat - Inf - Lib - LG - Parents advice service
        (free)
        Helpline: 0800 074 4519
M   800 i, 150 f, UK / 10 i, o'seas
¶   Cascade (Jnl) - 4; ftm.
        Leaflets & other publications.

Action on Smoking & Health   (ASH)   1971
NR   144-145 Shoreditch High St (1st floor), LONDON, E1 6JE.
        (hq)
        020 7739 5902   fax 020 7729 4732
○   *K

Active Retirement Ireland
IRL 124 The Capel Building, St Mary's Abbey, DUBLIN 7, Republic
        of Ireland.
        353 (1) 873 3836
        http://www.activeirl.ie
○   *W
✕   c 2009 Federation of Active Retirement Associations

Acuity   1935
NR   5 St Vincent St, EDINBURGH, EH3 6SW.   (hsb)
        0131-220 4542
        http://www.acuityscotland.org
        Chmn: Ian Rough
▲   Un-incorporated Society
○   *P; represents interests of optometrists in Scotland
●   Conf - Mtgs - ET - Res - LG
<   General Optical Coun; Brit Coll Optometrists; Assn
        Optometrists; Eyecare Information Service
M   740 i
¶   Look North - 4; free.
✕   2010 Scottish Committee of optometrists

Acupuncture Society   (AS)   1992
NR   27 Cavendish Drive, EDGWARE, Middx, HA8 7NR.   (hsp)
        0773 466 8402
        email acusoc@yahoo.co.uk
        http://www.acupuncturesociety.org.uk
        Chmn: Paul Robin
▲   Company Limited by Guarantee
○   *P; for professional acupuncturists & chinese herbal
        practitioners
Gp   Acupuncture; Chinese herbal medicine
●   Mtgs - ET - Exam - Res - SG - LG
<   College of Chinese Medicine
M   50 i, UK / 10 i, o'seas

Addisons Disease Self Help Group   (ADSHG)
NR   PO Box 1083, GUILDFORD, Surrey, GU1 9HX.
        http://www.addisons.org.uk
        Mem Sec: Deana Kenward
▲   Registered Charity
○   *W

© CBD Research Ltd · Beckenham · BR3 5JS · Tel 020 8650 7745 · E-mail cbd@cbdresearch.com · www.cbdresearch.com

Additional Curates Society (ACS) 1837
§   Gordon Browning House, 8 Spitfire Rd, BIRMINGHAM,
     B24 9PB.   (hq)
     0121-382 5533   fax 0121-382 6999
     email info@additionalcurates.co.uk
     http://www.additionalcurates.co.uk
     Gen Sec: Fr Darren Smith
○   *R; enables the placement of curates in parishes needing
     financial help
     To ensure that the Christian faith is proclaimed to poor and
     populous parishes, by funding assistant priests and
     encouraging vocations to the priesthood.

Additive Manufacturing Association   (AMA)
NR c/o Institution of Mechanical Engineers, 1 Birdcage Walk,
     LONDON, SW1H 9JJ.
     020 7304 6837
○   *T; to stimulate the adoption of rapid product design &
     manufacturing technologies
M   250 i

ADEPT (ADEPT) 1885
■   Director of Development Services, Shropshire Council, The Shire
     Hall, Abbey Foregate, SHREWSBURY, Shropshire, SY2 6ND.
     (hsb)
     01743 255008
     email adept@shropshire.gov.uk
     http://www.adeptnet.org.uk
     Hon Sec: Tom McCabe
▲   Un-incorporated Society
Br 3
○   *P; to represent local authority chief officers, closely involved in
     crucial transport, waste management, environment,
     planning, energy & economic development issues
Gp C'ees: Engineering, Environment, Finance, Planning &
     regeneration, Transport
●   Conf - Mtgs - ET - Res - SG - Stat - LG
M   116 i, 221 honorary members, 43 special honorary members
¶   A wide variety of technical reports.
✕   2009 CSS
     2010 Association of Directors of Environment, Economy,
               Planning & Transport

ADFAM (ADFAM) 1986
§   25 Corsham St, LONDON, N1 6DR.   (hq)
     020 7553 7640   fax 020 7253 7991
     http://www.adfam.org.uk
     Chief Exec: Vivienne Evans
○   *W; works with & for families affected by alcohol & drugs
     National organisation working with and for families affected by
     drug and alcohol misuse.

Adhesive Tape Manufacturers' Association (ATMA) 1950
■   7 Newman Rd, BROMLEY, Kent, BR1 1RJ.   (asa)
     020 8464 0131   fax 020 8464 6018
     email tradeassn@craneandpartners.com
     Secs: Crane & Partners
▲   Un-incorporated Society
○   *T; to promote the sale of all types of pressure sensitive tape; to
     promote & undertake research into all forms of technical
     development in pressure sensitive adhesive tape
●   Conf - Mtgs - LG
<   Assn des Fabricants Européens de Rubans Auto-adhesifs
     (AFERA)
M   2 f
¶   LM - irreg; free.

ADI Federation 1996
NR Kingsmith House, 63a Marshalls Rd, RAUNDS, Northants,
     NN9 6EY.   (hq)
     01933 461821
     email info@theadifederation.org.uk
○   *P; for approved driving instructors

**Adlerian Society UK - Institute for Individual Psychology
(ASIIP) 1952**
■   73 South Ealing Rd, LONDON, W5 4QR.   (hq)
     020 8567 8360   fax 020 8567 8360
     email admin@asiip.org   http://www.asiip.org
     Chmn: Margaret Wadsley
▲   Registered Charity
Br 5; Latvia
○   *L; to promote the understanding, application & development
     of the Individual Psychology of Alfred Adler (1870-1937)
●   Conf - Mtgs - ET - Inf - Lib - Training counsellors in private
     practice - Parent education
<   Intl Assn of Individual Psychology (IAIP); Brit Assn of Counselling
     & Psychotherapy (BASP); Parenting Educ & Support Forum
M   220 i, UK / 7 i, o'seas
     (Sub: £35 UK / £45 o'seas)
¶   NL - 4;   AER - 1; both ftm only.   Ybk - 1.

Adoption UK 1971
■   Linden House 55 The Green, South Bar St, BANBURY, Oxon,
     OX16 9AB.   (hq)
     01295 752240
     email admin@adoptionuk.org.uk
     http://www.adoptionuk.org.uk
     Dir: Jonathan Pearce
▲   Registered Charity; Adopotion Support Agency
Br coordinators in most counties
○   *W; self-help group for prospective & existing adoptive families
     giving information, advice & support through all stages of
     adoption
●   Conf - Mtgs - ET - Inf - Lib
<   Brit Assn for Adoption & Fostering; Nat Foster Care Assn;
     Natural Parents Support Gp; Nat Org for Counselling
     Adoptees & their Parents
M   4,500 i, adoption agencies
¶   Adoption Today - 6; ftm only.
     Publications list available.

Adrian Bell Society 1996
■   28 Skelton Rd, DISS, Norfolk, IP22 4PW.   (treas/p)
     01379 641494
     Hon Treas: M A Flynn
▲   Un-incorporated Society
○   *A; for those interested in the writing of Adrian Bell (1901-
     1980), who was born in London but lived & wrote mainly in
     Suffolk
●   Mtgs - Inf - VE
M   c 250 i, 2 org, UK / 3 i, o'seas
¶   Jnl - 2; ftm only.

**ADS Group Ltd (Advancing UK aerospace defence & security
industries) (ADS) 2009**
NR Salamanca Square, 9 Albert Embankment, LONDON,
     SE1 7SP.   (hq)
     020 7091 4500   fax 020 7091 4545
     email enquiries@adsgroup.org.uk
     http://www.adsgroup.org.uk
     Chmn: Ian Godden,   Chief Exec: Rees Ward
▲   Company Limited by Guarantee
Br 3; France, India, Middle East
○   *T; to advance the interests of the British aerospace, defence,
     security & space industries
Gp ADS supports & facilitates 56 boards, committees & groups
●   Conf - Exhib - Expt - Inf - Lib - VE - LG
<   AeroSpace & Defence Inds Assn of Europe; Trade Assn Forum
M   2,600 f
¶   Advance - 4.
✕   2009 (Association of Police & Public Security Suppliers
               (Defence Manufacturers Association
               (Society of British Aerospace Companies
                    (merged 1 October)
     Note: Also encompasses the British Aviation Group

ADSET
No longer a membership organisation, continues as a training body

Adult Education Officers' Association
IRL Adult Education Officer, Mayo VEC Adult Education Service, Cavendish House, CASTLEBAR, Co Mayo, Republic of Ireland.
353 (94) 902 3159
Hon Sec: Pat Higgins
○ *P
× 2005 Adult Education Organisers' Assn

Adult Industry Trade Association (AITA) 2003
NR 77 Beak St (suite 14), LONDON, W1F 9DB. (hq)
0845 500 AITA (2482)
http://www.aita.co.uk/
○ *T; for all in the trade - video & magazine producers, advertising, artists, bondage, condoms, cosmetic surgery, entertainers, fetish, furniture, models, piercing, sex shops etc
● Inf (on regulation & legislation) - LG
M i, f

Adult Residential Colleges Association (ARCA) 1983
NR 6 Bath Rd, FELIXSTOWE, Suffolk, IP11 7JW. (hsp)
01394 278161 fax 01394 271083
http://www.arca.uk.net
▲ Un-incorporated Society
○ *E; to promote & disseminate knowledge of the opportunities for adult learning, in short-term residential situations, to central & local government, other institutions & the general public
● Conf - ET - SG - Inf - Lib
M 32 colleges
¶ ARCA Short breaks - 1. Leaflets.

Adults Affected by Adoption - NORCAP (AAA-NORCAP) 1982
NR 112 Church Rd, WHEATLEY, Oxon, OX33 1LU. (hq)
01865 875000 (Mon-Thurs 0930-1600)
email enquiries@norcap.org http://www.norcap.org.uk
▲ Registered Charity
○ *W; to support adults affected by adoption who want to find out more about their families
M i & org
× 2008 Supporting Adults affected by Adoption

Advantage 1978
NR 21 Provost St, LONDON, N1 7NH.
020 7324 3930
▲ Company Limited by Guarantee
○ *T; for independent travel agents

Advertising Association (AA) 1926
NR Artillery House (7th floor North), 11-19 Artillery Row, LONDON, SW1P 1RT. (hq)
020 7340 1100 fax 020 7222 1504
email aa@adassoc.org.uk http://www.adassoc.org.uk
Chief Exec: Tim Lefroy
○ *N, *T; to represent the common interests of all sides of the UK advertising business
● Conf - Mtgs - Res - Stat - Inf - Lib - LG - Educational material
< Intl Advertising Assn; Intl Cham Comm; Advertising Inf Gp
M 6 f, 24 org
¶ Quarterly Survey of Advertising Expenditure - 4; £590 yr m, £715 yr nm.
Advertising Statistics Ybk - 1; £170 (2005).
Long Term Advertising Expenditure Forecast - 1; £535 m, £995 nm.
The European Advertising & Media Forecast; £730 yr m, £1,365 yr nm.
The Marketing Pocket Book (2006); £34.95. AR; free.
List of constituent organisations on website.
publications list available from the Information Centre or website.

Advertising Producers Association (APA) 1978
NR 47 Beak St, LONDON, W1F 9SE. (hq)
020 7434 2651 fax 020 7434 9002
Chief Exec: Stephen Davies
▲ Un-incorporated Society
○ *T; to represent the interests of commercial film production companies
● Mtgs - ET - Inf
< Comml Film Producers of Europe (CFP/E)
M 110 f

Advertizing Rule Collectors' Society
NR 81 Park View, Collins Rd, Islington, LONDON, N5 2UD.
○ *G; for collectors of rulers bearing advertizing logos
M 14 i

Advice NI (AIAC) 1995
NR 1 Rushfield Avenue, BELFAST, BT7 3FP. (hq)
028 9064 5919 fax 028 9049 2313
email info@adviceni.net http://www.adviceni.net
Dir: Bob Stronge
▲ Registered Charity
○ *N; to develop an independent advice sector that provides the best possible advice to those that need it most
● Conf - Mtgs - ET - Res - Exhib - Stat - Inf - LG
< Fedn of Indep Advice Centres; AdviceUK
M 4 i, 74 f, 8 org
¶ NL - 4; AR - 1; both free.
× Association of Independent Advice Centres

Advice Services Alliance (ASA) 1980
NR 63 St Mary Axe (6th floor), LONDON, EC3A 8AA. (hq)
020 7398 1470 fax 020 7398 1471
email admin@asauk.org.uk http://www.asauk.org.uk
Dir: Richard Jenner
▲ Company Limited by Guarantee
○ *N; brings together Citizens Advice Bureaux, Law Centres & a wide range of local & national independent advice agencies
● Conf - Mtgs - ET - Res - Inf - LG
M 10 org (& 16 associate members):
Advice UK
Age Concern England
Citizens Advice
Citizens Advice Scotland
Dial UK
Law Centres Federation
Scottish Association of Law Centres
Shelter
Shelter Cymru
Youth Access
¶ 'We produce regular briefings for our members & occasional policy reports'

© CBD Research Ltd · Beckenham · BR3 5JS · Tel 020 8650 7745 · E-mail cbd@cbdresearch.com · www.cbdresearch.com

AdviceUK   1979

■   63 St Mary Axe (6th floor), LONDON, EC3A 8AA.   (hq)
    020 7469 5700   fax 020 7469 5701
    email general@adviceuk.org.uk
    http://www.adviceuk.org.uk
    Chief Exec: Steve Johnson
▲   Company Limited by Guarantee; Registered Charity
○   *N; to promote the provision of independent advice centres
    across the UK; to provide services to support centres
    delivering independent advice to the public
Gp East Midlands, Eastern, London, Scotland, Wales; BME (Black &
    Ethnic Minority); Money & Debt
●   Conf - Mtgs - ET - Exhib - Stat - Inf - LG - Case management
    software - Consultancy - Insurance - Recruitment advertising
<   Advice Services Alliance
M   900 org
    (Sub: £100-£460)
¶   Independent Adviser - 4; ftm, £20-£30 nm.
    Jobs in Advice email - 52; free.
    Members E-Bulletin - 52; ftm only.
    Money Advice E-Bulletin - 26; ftm only.

aeroBILITY   (BDFA)

NR Blackbushe Airport, CAMBERLEY, Surrey, GU17 9LQ.
    0303 303 1230
    email info@aerobility.com   http://www.aerobility.com
    Chief Exec: Mike Miller-Smith
▲   Registered Charity
○   *W; flying for the disabled in the form of lessons or 'rides' for
    the seriously ill
✕   2012 British Disabled Flying Association

The Aeroplane Collection Ltd   (TAC)   1972

■   7 Mayfield Avenue, Stretford, MANCHESTER, M32 9HL.   (hsp)
    0161-866 8255
    email aeroplanecol@aol.com
    Chmn: Edward Sherratt
▲   Company Limited by Guarantee; Registered Charity
○   *G; preservation, restoration & display of aircraft & associated
    artifacts
●   Mtgs - ET - Res
<   Brit Aviation Presvn Coun
M   24 i
¶   TAC NL - 12.

Aerosol Society   1986

■   PO Box 34, Portishead, BRISTOL, BS20 7FE.   (hq)
    01275 849019 (Tues-Thurs 0930-1430)
    fax 01275 844877
    email admin@aerosol-soc.org.uk
    http://www.aerosol-soc.org.uk
    Admin: Shelia Coates
○   *P; to promote: all scientific branches of aerosol research (the
    study of particles suspended in a gas); the spread of
    information on an interdisciplinary basis; to make available a
    pool of expert knowledge; to assist in training; to encourage
    investment in aerosol research
●   Conf - Mtgs - ET - Res - Exhib
¶   (Sub: £15 i, £200 corporate)

Aerospace Composites Group
    a group of **Composites UK Ltd**

Aetherius Society   1955

■   757 Fulham Rd, LONDON, SW6 5UU.   (hq)
    020 7736 4187   fax 020 7731 1067
    email info@aetherius.co.uk   http://www.aetherius.org
    European HQ Exec Sec: Dr Richard Lawrence
▲   Un-incorporated Society
Br 2; Ghana, New Zealand, Nigeria
○   *R; a metaphysical organisation dedicated to the service of
    mankind in numerous ways - world & individual healing,
    service to God through humankind, cooperation with higher
    intelligences on earth & from other planets
Gp The Inner Potential Centre - an educational centre run by the
    Society in the UK
●   Mtgs - ET - Exhib - SG - Divine services - Cosmic missions -
    Pilgrimages - Spiritual healing
M   i
    (Sub: £15, £45 full associate membership)
¶   Cosmic Voice - 4;   NL - 12.

Afasic   (Afasic)   1968

■   20 Bowling Green Lane, LONDON, EC1R 0BD.   (hq)
    020 7490 9410   fax 020 7251 2834
    email info@afasic.org.uk   http://www.afasic.org.uk
    Chief Exec: Mrs Linda Lascelles
▲   Registered Charity
○   *E, *W; to represent children & young adults with speech,
    language & communication impairments; to work for their
    inclusion in society; to support their parents & carers
●   Conf - ET - Res - Inf
    Helpline: 0845 355 5577
M   2,000 i, 65 org, UK / 20 i, o'seas
    (Sub: £15 family, £20 profl, £35 instns, £5 benefits/pension)
¶   NL - 3; on website.   AR.
    Publications list available.

**African Studies Association of the United Kingdom   (ASAUK)
1963**

NR Royal African Society, 36 Gordon Sq, LONDON, WC1H 0PD.
    (hq)
    020 3073 8335   fax 020 3073 8340
    email secretary@asauk.net   http://www.asauk.net
    Hon Sec: Gemma Haxby
○   *L, *Q; advancement of African studies in the UK
●   Conf - Symposia - Inf
<   R African Soc
M   278 i, 6 libraries, UK / 304 i, 9 libraries, o'seas
¶   African Affairs (Jnl of Royal African Society) - 4; ftm.
    AR; free.

Against Legalised Euthanasia - Research & Teaching
    see **ALERT**

Age & Employment Network   (taen)

NR Tavis House, 1-6 Tavistock Square, LONDON, WC1H 9NA.
    (hq)
    020 3033 1507   fax 020 3033 1510
    email info@taen.org.uk   http://www.taen.org.uk
    Chief Exec: Chris Ball
○   *K; help remove age barriers to employment

AgeCare
    the operating name of the **Royal Surgical Aid Society**

Agents' Association (Great Britain)   1927

NR 54 Keyes House, Dolphin Sq, LONDON, SW1V 3NA.   (hq)
    020 7834 0515
○   *P; for entertainment agents representing performers, celebrities
    & musicians

Agricultural Consultants Association   (ACA)
IRL   Bank House, Main St, CARRICK-on-SUIR, Co Tipperary,
         Republic of Ireland.
         353 (51) 645705
         email acaservices@som.ie
○   *P
M   c 70 f

Agricultural Economics Society   (AES)   1926
NR   Holtwood, Red Lion St, Cropredy, BANBURY, Oxon,
         OX17 1PD.   (hsb)
         01295 750182
         email aes@cingnet.org.uk   http://www.aes.ac.uk
         Secretariat
▲   Company Limited by Guarantee
○   *L; study & teaching of all disciplines relevant to agricultural
         economics as they apply to the agricultural, food & related
         industries & rural communities
●   Conf - Comp
<   Intl / Eur / Amer Assn[s] of Agricl Economics
M   300 i, 50 org, UK / 100 i, 600 org, o'seas
¶   Jnl of Agricultural Economics - 3; ftm.
         EuroChoices - 3; £12 m.
            (Sub: £48).

Agricultural Economics Society of Ireland   1967
IRL   c/o Rural Economy Research Centre (Teagasc), Kinealy,
         DUBLIN 15, Republic of Ireland.   (h/treas/b)
         email fiona.thorne@teasagc.ie
         Hon Treas: Fiona Thorne
○   *F, *L

Agricultural Engineers' Association   (AEA)   1875
■   Samuelson House, 62 Forder Way, Hampton,
         PETERBOROUGH, Cambs, PE7 8JB.   (hq)
         0845 644 8748   fax 01733 314767
         email ab@aea.uk.com   http://www.aea.uk.com
         Dir Gen: Roger Lane-Nott
▲   Company Limited by Guarantee
○   *F, *H, *T; for manufacturers and importers of agricultural
         machinery & outdoor power equipment (horticulture,
         professional & leisure grass care, & forestry)
Gp   Farm Equipment Council; Outdoor Power Equipment Council
●   Conf - Mtgs - ET - Exhib - Stat - Expt - Inf - LG
M   157 f, UK / 3 f, o'seas
¶   OPE Price Guide - 2; £30 (for 2 editions).   AR - 1.

Agricultural Industries Confederation   (AIC)   2003
■   Confederation House, East of England Showground,
         PETERBOROUGH, Cambs, PE2 6XE.   (hq)
         01733 385230   fax 01733 385270
         email enquiries@agindustries.org.uk
         http://www.agindustries.org.uk
         Chief Exec: David Caffall
▲   Company Limited by Guarantee
○   *F, *T; to promote the benefits of modern commercial
         agriculture in the UK; to support collaboration throughout the
         food chain
Gp   Animal feed; Crop protection; Crop marketing; Fertilisers; Seed
●   Conf - ET - Stat - LG
M   300 f
         AIS is the scheme manager of the Feed Materials Assurance
         Scheme (FEMAS), Fertiliser Industry Assurance Scheme (FIAS),
         Trade Assurance Scheme for Combinable Crops (TASCC)
         and Universal Feed Assurance Scheme (UFAS)

Agricultural Law Association   (ALA)   1975
NR   Kimblewick Cottage, Prince Albert Rd, WEST MERSEA, Essex,
         CO5 8AZ.   (contact/p)
         01206 383521   fax 01206 385943
         email enquiries@ala.org.uk   http://www.ala.org.uk
         Consultant & Adviser: Geoff Whittaker
▲   Un-incorporated Society
○   *F, *P; 'to promote the study, knowledge & understanding of the
         law & practice relating to agriculture, the environment,
         farming, forestry & the rural community . . . in the United
         Kingdom of Great Britain & Northern Ireland & the European
         Union'
Gp   C'ees: European affairs, Land & property, Litigation & dispute
         resolution, Planning & environment, Taxation, Tenancies
●   Conf - Mtgs - ET - Res - LG
<   Comité Européen Droit de Rural (CEDR)
M   881 i, UK / 6 i, o'seas
¶   The Bulletin - 4; ftm only.

Agricultural Lime Association
         is a product group of the **Mineral Products Association**

Agricultural Manpower Society
         no longer exists

Agricultural Science Association
IRL   Irish Farm Centre, Bluebell, DUBLIN 12, Republic of Ireland.
         353 (1) 460 3682   fax 353 (1) 456 5415
         email msasa@gofree.indigo.ie
         http://www.asaireland.ie
         Pres: James Fitzgerald
○   *F, *P

**AHS: the National Federation of Atheist, Humanist & Secular
Student Societies   (AHS)   2008**
NR   1 Gower St, LONDON, WC1E 6HD.
         email secretary@ahsstudents.org.uk
         http://www.ahsstudents.org.uk
         Sec: Nicola Young Jackson
○   *N; to act as the umbrella organisation for all non-religious
         student societies in every institute of higher education in the
         UK; to be a shared voice in public life
●   Conf - Mtgs - Inf
M   org
¶   NL - 52.   Directories.

Aid for Children with Tracheostomies   (ACT)   1983
■   Lammas Cottage, Stathe, BRIDGWATER, Somerset, TA7 0JL.
         (sp)
         01823 698398
         email support@actfortrachykids.com
         http://www.actfortrachykids.com
         Sec: Amanda Saunders
▲   Registered Charity
○   *W; a self-help group run by parents to give support & help to
         other parents with children with a tracheostomy; to promote
         knowledge nationally about the needs involved in the care of
         a child with a tracheostomy
●   Conf - Mtgs - Stat - Inf - Hire of medical equipment - Holiday
         caravan - Seminars for professionals in the medical field
<   Contact a Family
M   250 i
¶   NL - 4; ftm only.

© CBD Research Ltd · Beckenham · BR3 5JS · Tel 020 8650 7745 · E-mail cbd@cbdresearch.com · www.cbdresearch.com

Air-Britain (Historians) Ltd   1948
■ 74 High Ridge Rd, Apsley, HEMEL HEMPSTEAD, Herts,
   HP3 0AU.   (hsp)
   01442 267883
   http://www.air-britain.com
   Sec: Ronald A Webb
▲ Company Limited by Guarantee
Br 17; Holland & France
○ *G; for those interested in all aspects of current & historical
   aviation
Gp Specialists & groups cover the whole spectrum of aviation
   worldwide
● Res - Inf - Lib - PL - VE
< Amer Aviation Histl Soc
M 3,500 i, 10 f, UK / 120 i, 7 f, o'seas
¶ News - 12;   Aeromilitaria - 4;   Archive;
   (rates vary according to magazine(s) subscriptions).
   (2)+(3); £33(a) £38(b) £41(c).
   (1)+(3); £53(a) £62(b) £69(c).
   (1)+(2)+(3); £62(a) £72(b) £79(c).
   Membership only; £18(a) £20(b) £22(c).

Air Conditioning Group
   a group of the **Heating, Ventilating & Air Conditioning
   Manufacturers' Association**

**Air Conditioning & Refrigeration Industry Board   (ACRIB)
1994**
NR Kelvin House, 76 Mill Lane, CARSHALTON, Surrey, SM5 2JR.
   (hq)
   020 8254 7842   fax 020 8773 0165
   email acrib@acrib.org.uk
   Chief Exec: M J Horlick
▲ Company Limited by Guarantee
○ *N; for representative organisations with a direct interest in the
   provision or use of air conditioning, refrigeration &
   mechanical ventilation
Gp Working groups: Environment (incl energy efficiency); Education
   & training (incl implementation of NVQs); Food safety (incl
   de-regulation); Building regulations
M 3 org (Full members):
   Federation of Environmental Trade Associations
   Heating & Ventilating Contractors Association
   Institute of Refrigeration
   6 org (Associate members):
   Associated Air Conditioning & Refrigeration Contractors
   Association of Manufacturers of Domestic Appliances
   British Frozen Food Federation
   Cambridge Refrigeration Technology
   Chartered Institution of Building Services Engineers
   Food Storage & Distribution Federation

Air League   1909
■ Broadway House, Tothill St, LONDON, SW1H 9NS.   (hq)
   020 7222 8463   fax 020 7222 8462
   email exec@airleague.co.uk
   http://www.airleague.co.uk
   Dir: Edward Cox
▲ Company Limited by Guarantee
○ *P; to promote the cause of British aviation
Gp The Air League Educational Trust (air education - awards flying
   scholarships & bursaries & engineering scholarships);
   Associate Parliamentary Aerospace Group
● Mtgs - ET - Comp - Inf - VE - LG
< Flight Safety Foundation
M 950 i, 115 f, 95 org, UK / 1 org, o'seas
¶ NL - 6; ftm only.

Air Safety Group   (ASG)   1964
NR 51 Wellington Way, HORLEY, Surrey, RH6 8JL.   (hsp)
   email secretary@airsafetygroup.org
   http://www.airsafetygroup.org
   Hon Sec: Robin Boning
▲ Un-incorporated Society
○ *K; 'a voluntary effort to promote greater safety for air
   travellers'
Gp Accident investigation; Certification requirements; Engineering;
   Medical; Operations
● Mtgs - Res - SG - Inf - LG
M 30 i

Air Transport Auxiliary Association   (ATA Assn)   1946
■ 40 Goldcrest Rd, CHIPPING SODBURY, S Glos, BS37 6XG.
   (hsp)
   01454 319175   fax 01454 319175
   Hon Sec: Mrs M Viles
○ *G; for retired war-time ferry pilots
● Social gatherings only
< RAFA
M i
¶ NL - 1.

Aircraft Owners & Pilots Association   (AOPA)   1965
NR 50a Cambridge St, LONDON, SW1V 4QQ.   (hq)
   020 7834 5631   fax 020 7834 8623
▲ Company Limited by Guarantee
○ *P, *T; 'to further the cause of pilots, instructors & flying training
   organisations; fighting for legislation etc to protect the rights
   of individuals in general aviation, keeping costs to a
   minimum'
● Conf - ET - Exhib - Inf
< Intl Coun of Aircraft Owner & Pilot Assns (IAOPA)
M i
¶ Light Aviation - 4; ftm only.

**Aircraft Owners & Pilots Association of Ireland   (AOPA
Ireland)**
IRL Curramore, Kiltoom, ATHLONE, County Roscommon, Ireland.
   353 (87) 127 3369
   email info@aopaireland.com
   Hon Sec: Kitty Cronin
○ *P, *T
< Intl Coun of Aircraft Owner & Pilot Assns (IAOPA)

Aircraft Research Association Ltd   (ARA)   1952
■ Manton Lane, BEDFORD, Beds, MK41 7PF.   (hq)
   01234 350681   fax 01234 328584
   http://www.ara.co.uk
   Chief Exec: D Hunter,   Sec: K J Rentle
▲ Company Limited by Guarantee
○ *Q; aerodynamic wind-tunnel testing & ancillary services
Gp Research
● Conf - Res - Inf - Lib
< AIRTO
M 4 f
¶ Research Reports.

Aircrete Products Association
   an product association of the **British Precast Concrete Federation**

Aircrew Association
   the decision was taken on 25 September 2010 that this
   association should be dissolved in 2011.

Aircrewman's Association (ACA) 1977
■ Glencairn, 82 Heywood Rd, Mapperley, NOTTINGHAM, NG3 6AE. (hsp)
http://www.aircrewman.org.uk
Sec: Ian Williams
○ *P; membership is restricted to non-commissioned rating aircrew gaining flying wings whilst serving in the Royal Navy; all members fly, or have flown, in all types of naval helicopters; honorary membership is offered to widows of members, & associate membership to interested parties
M i

Airline Public Relations Organisation (APRO) 1965
NR c/o Romanski Ltd, 2 Archie St (No 4), LONDON, SE1 3JT. (asa)
020 7260 2999
email apro@romanski.co.uk   http://www.airlinepr.org
Secretariat: Pauline Kirkman
○ *P; an informal body open to membership of any airline with an office in the UK to enable public relations staff or PR consultants of that airline to meet to exchange views
M i & f
¶ APRO Handbook - 1; ftm only.

Airport Operators Association (AOA) 1934
NR 3 Birdcage Walk, LONDON, SW1H 9JJ. (hq)
020 7222 2249   fax 020 7976 7405
http://www.aoa.org.uk
Chief Exec: Keith Jowett
▲ Company Limited by Guarantee
○ *T; the trade association that speaks for British airports - representing all of the nation's international hub & major regional airports as well as many of those serving community, business & leisure aviation
Gp Operations & safety; Environment & planning; Security; Government & industry affairs; General aviation; Finance
● Conf - Mtgs - ET - Res - Inf - LG
< Airports Coun Intl (ACI)
M 71 airports, 150 f (associates)
¶ Airport Operator (Jnl) - 5; free.

Airship Association 1971
NR PO Box 715, FOLKESTONE, Kent, CT20 9ER. (h/treas/p)
01303 277650
email treas@airship-association.org
http://www.airship-association.org
▲ Company Limited by Guarantee
○ *G, *K, *L; a forum for those interested in the technology of airships
● Conf - ET - Res - Exhib - Inf - LG
M 336 i, UK / 313 i, o'seas
(Sub: £25).
¶ Airship (Jnl) - 4.
Airships Today & Tomorrow, by Oliver Netherclift; £8.90.

Airship Heritage Trust
NR 65 South Avenue, Elstow, BEDFORD, MK42 9YS. (archivist/p)
email aht.ndirect.co.uk
Archivist: Den Burchmore
○ *G; for all interested in the study of lighter-than-air travel (airships)
● Mtgs
< Brit Aviation Presvn Coun (BAPC)
M i
¶ Dirigible - 3; ftm.

AIRTO Ltd: Association of Independent Research & Technology Organisations (AIRTO) 1986
■ c/o Karen Barlow, National Physical Laboratory, Hampton Rd, TEDDINGTON, Middx, TW11 0LW. (hq)
020 8943 6600   fax 020 8614 0470
email enquiries@airto.co.uk   http://www.airto.co.uk
Dir of Operations: Peter Russell
▲ Company Limited by Guarantee
○ N; to represent the contract research & knowledge transfer sector
Gp Finance & contracts; Marketing; Personnel; Secretaries; Health & safety; Testing & accreditation; Environment
● Conf - Res - LG
M 34 f
¶ AIRTO Review - 2;   Policy Papers - 2/3; both free.

Akhal-Teke UK 2007
NR Great Mistleigh Farm, Doddiscombsleigh, EXETER, Devon, EX6 7RF. (founder/b)
01647 253187
email contact@akhaltekeuk.com
http://www.akhaltekeuk.com
Co-founders: Maria Baverstock,   Darya Hannigan
▲ Company Limited by Guarantee
○ *B; the Akhal-Teke horse breed
● Inf - VE to stud farms - help wit studbook registration

Al-Anon Family Groups UK & Eire (Al-Anon) 1960
§ 61 Great Dover St, LONDON, SE1 4YF. (hq)
020 7403 0888   fax 020 7378 9910
email enquiries@al-anonuk.org.uk
http://www.al-anonuk.org.uk
Provides understanding, strength and hope to anyone whose life is, or has been, affected by someone else's drinking.

Al Bowlly Circle 1968
■ Memory Lane, PO Box 1939, LEIGH-on-SEA, Essex, SS9 3UH. (hsb)
email ray@memorylane.org.uk
http://www.memorylane.org.uk
Sec: Ray Pallett
▲ Un-incorporated Society
○ *D, *G; to promote interest in the life & works of 1930s crooner Al Bowlly (1899-1941) & interest in the popular music of that time
● Mtgs - Res - Inf - PL
M 1,700 i, UK / 300 i, o'seas
(Sub: £15)
¶ Memory Lane - 4; ftm, £4 nm UK (£5 o'seas).

ALARM: the National Forum for Risk Management in the Public Sector (ALARM)
NR Ashton House, Weston, SIDMOUTH, Devon, EX10 0PF. (hq)
0333 123 0007   fax 0333 456 0007
email admin@alarm-uk.com
http://www.alarm-uk.com
Chief Exec: Dr Lynn Drennan
▲ Company Limited by Guarantee
○ *P; 'to advise, encourage & represent public sector organisations in the development of risk management strategies to address the risks which might threaten the successful achievement of their objectives'
● Conf - Mtgs - ET - Res - Exhib - Lib
M 1,635 i, 117 f, UK / 13 i, o'seas

Albinism Fellowship (AF) 1979
■ PO Box 77, BURNLEY, Lancs, BB11 5GN.   (mail/address)
01282 771900
email info@albinism.org.uk   http://www.albinism.org.uk
Pres: Mark Sanderson
▲ Registered Charity
○ *W; to provide advice & support for people with Albinism, their
family & those with a professional interest in Albinism
● Conf - Mtgs
M 350 i
(Sub: £15)
¶ Albinism Life - 2.
Real Lives; by Archie Roy & Robin Spinks (2005).
(ISBN 0955 0344 0 X).

Alcohol Beverage Federation of Ireland   (ABFI)   2007
IRL   Confederation House, 84-86 Lower Baggot St, DUBLIN 2,
Republic of Ireland.   (hq)
353 (1) 605 1500   fax 353 (1) 638 1500
email rosemary.garth@ibec.ie   http://www.abfi.ie
Dir: Rosemary Garth
○ *T; to promote the many positive contributions the industry
makes to the Irish Exchequer, balance of trade, employment
& society as a whole
Gp Irish Brewers Association; Irish Cider Association; Irish Spirits
Association; Irish Wine Association
< Ir Business & Emplrs Confedn (IBEC)
M 18 f

Alcohol Concern   1984
■ 64 Leman St, LONDON, E1 8EU.   (hq)
020 7264 0510   fax 020 7488 9213
email contact@alcoholconcern.org.uk
http://www.alcoholconcern.org.uk
Chief Exec: Don Shenker
▲ Company Limited by Guarantee; Registered Charity
○ *K; to reduce the incidence & costs of alcohol abuse; to
develop the range & quality of services to people with alcohol
related problems; to support specialist & non-specialist
service providers tackling alcohol problems at local level
● Conf - Stat - Inf - Bookshop
Drinkline: 0800 917 8262 (for those concerned with their own
or another's drink problems)
M c 1,000 i
¶ Straight Talk - 4;   Leaflets & Reports; prices on application.
A series of books on aspects of alcohol; c £2.75-£16 (available
from the online bookshop, pre-paid)

Alcoholics Anonymous (Great Britain) Ltd   (AA)   1947
■ PO Box 1, 10 Toft Green, YORK, YO1 7NJ.
01904 644026   fax 01904 629091
http://www.alcoholics-anonymous.org.uk
▲ Registered Charity
Br 2,800; Worldwide
○ *K; 'primary purpose is to stay sober & help other alcoholics
achieve sobriety'
● Mtgs - Inf
Helpline: 0845 769 7555
M 40-45,000 i, UK / c 1,750,000 i, o'seas
¶ AA News.
List of publications.

Alcuin Club   1897
■ 5 Saffron St, ROYSTON, Herts, SG8 9TR.   (hsp)
01763 248676
email alcuinclub@gmail.com
http://www.alcuinclub.org.uk
Sec: The Revd Dr Gordon Jeanes
▲ Registered Charity
○ *L; to promote study of Christian liturgy & worship - especially
the Anglican Communion
● Conf - Res - Inf - Lib
M 350 i, 50 org, UK / 130 i, 50 org, o'seas
¶ Liturgical Studies - 2.
Collections - 1; ftm, prices vary nm.   AR; ftm.

ALERT   (ALERT)   1991
■ 27 Walpole St, LONDON, SW3 4QS.   (hsp)
020 7730 2800   fax 020 7730 0818
email info@alertuk.org   http://www.alertuk.org
Hon Sec: Mrs Elspeth Chowdharay-Best
▲ Company Limited by Guarantee
○ *K; to defend vulnerable people's right to live; is against
legalised euthanasia
Gp Carers
● Mtgs - Exhib - Inf
< Care not Killing
M 600 subscribers
¶ Various pamphlets; 3/4.   Mailings to supporters; irreg.
[subscription to mailings £5 yr (£1 un-waged)]
Note: Also known as ALERT against Euthanasia, the
organisation takes its name from 'Against Legalised
Euthanasia - Research & Teaching'

*ALES (UK) - association of amusement & leisure equipment suppliers of the
United Kingdom*
**see Association of Amusement & Leisure Equipment
Suppliers of the UK**

Alexander Thomson Society   1991
NR   7 Walmer Crescent, GLASGOW, G51 1AT.
email info@greekthomson.org.uk
http://www.greekthomson.org.uk
○ *A, *G; to promote the life & work of the Glasgow architect
Alexander 'Greek' Thomson (1817-1875)
M i & f
¶ NL - 3/4.

Alfred Williams Heritage Society   (AWHS)   2009
NR   Great Western Hospital, Marlborough Rd, SWINDON, Wilts,
SN3 6BB.   (chmn/b)
email committee@alfredwilliams.org.uk
http://www.alfredwilliams.org.uk
Chmn: Dr John Cullimore
▲ Registered Charity
○ *A, *G; to make more people aware of the Wiltshire poet &
writer Alfred Williams (1877-1930), who was known as the
Hammerman poet; to create a permanent exhibition of his
life & works
● Mtgs - Exhib - Inf - Digitising works to be available online
< The Friends of Alfred Williams
M 4 i
¶ see website.
for newcomers to the works of Alfred Williams

Alkan Society   1977
■ 42 St Albans Hill, HEMEL HEMPSTEAD, Herts, HP3 9NG.   (hsp)
01442 262895
email secretary@alkansociety.org
http://www.alkansociety.org
Hon Sec: Nicholas King
▲ Un-incorporated Society
○ *D; to encourage the knowledge, understanding & appreciation
of the life & works of the French pianist & composer Charles-
Valentine Alkan (1813-1888)
● Mtgs - Inf - Lib - 1-day lectures & recitals
M 90 i, UK / 50 i, o'seas
¶ Bulletin - 3.   Discography & Library Catalogue - irreg;
both ftm.

All England Netball Association Ltd   1926
NR   Netball House, 9 Paynes Park, HITCHIN, Herts, SG5 1EH.   (hq)
01462 442344   fax 01462 442343
email info@englandnetball.co.uk
http://www.englandnetball.co.uk
Co Sec: Paul Smith
○ *S; to promote the game of netball in England for women of all
ages
M i, clubs
Note: the association is known as England Netball

All Styles Martial Arts Association   (ASMAA)   2000
NR   18 Marshall Close, ROTHERHAM, S Yorks, S62 6DB.   (hsp)
       07843 736787
       email info@asmaa.org.uk   http://www.asmaa.org.uk
       Hon Sec: Dave Turton
○   *G; for all interested in various methods of self-defence
M   c 3,000 i, 30 clubs

All Terrain Boarding Association   (ATBA-UK)   1997
NR   16 Churchill Way, CARDIFF, CF10 2DX.
       email info@atbauk.org   http://www.atbauk.org
○   *S; the enjoyment & promotion of the sport of boarding

**All Wheel Drive Club (Britain's Cross Country Vehicle
Association)   (AWDC)   1968**
NR   c/o Vallance Lodge & Co, Units 082-086, 555 White Hart Lane,
       LONDON, N17 7RN.   (regd off)
       http://www.awdc.co.uk
       Co Sec: Hesketh Emden
▲   Company Limited by Guarantee
○   *G; for owners of 4x4 & other off-road vehicles interested in
       off-road driving
●   VE
M   2,000 i
¶   All Wheel Driver - 6.

Allergy UK   1991
NR   Planwell House, LEFA Business Park, Edgington Way, SIDCUP,
       Kent, DA14 5BH.   (hq)
       01322 470341   fax 01322 430330
       http://www.allergyuk.org
       Chmn: Mrs Muriel Simmons
▲   Registered Charity
○   *W; to provide information, support & advice for all people with
       allergies, their families & carers
●   Conf - ET - Inf - National allergy masterclasses
       Helpline: 01322 619898
<   Brit Soc for Allergy & Clinical Immunology (BSACI)
M   6,000 i, 42 f, 135 org, UK / 35 i, 4 f, o'seas
¶   Publications list available.
       Note: Allergy UK is the operational name of the British Allergy
       Foundation.

Alliance for Better Food & Farming
       see **Sustain**

**Alliance for Beverage Cartons & the Environment   (ACE UK)
1986**
NR   Webber House, 26-28 Market St, ALTRINCHAM, Cheshire,
       WA14 1PF.   (hq)
       01869 353600
       Chmn: Richard Hands
▲   Un-incorporated Society
○   *T; to represent manufacturers of liquid food/beverage cartons;
       to address environmental issues (recovery, re-cycling,
       renewability)
<   Alliance for Beverage Cartons & the Envt (Brussels) [this is the
       umbrella organisation for marketing activities]
M   3 f
¶   Alliance NL - 4; free.
       The Alliance for Beverage Cartons & the Environment
       (brochure); free.
×   2007 Liquid Food Carton Manufacturers' Association

Alliance of Business Consultants
NR   24 The Street, Lydiard Millicent, SWINDON, Wilts, SN5 3NU.
       (mem/sec/b)
       01793 772920
       email pete@anaconn.com
       Mem Sec: Peter Jones
○   *P
●   Mtgs
M   i
       (Sub: £100)

Alliance for Health Professionals
       has asked to be removed from the directory since it 'no longer
       exists in the format that would make inclusion appropriate'

Alliance of Independent Retailers
       Company dissolved 2009

Alliance of Industry Associations
       The AIA, formed in 1991, is an alliance of trade associations
       representing companies operating in many sectors of the chemical
       industry supply chain (http://www.aiabusiness.org)

Alliance against Intellectual Property Theft
NR   c/o BPI - Riverside Building, County Hall, Westminster Bridge
       Rd, LONDON, SE1 7JA.   (hq)
       020 7803 1324   fax 020 7803 1310
       email info@allianceagainstiptheft.co.uk
       http://www.allianceagainstiptheft.co.uk
       Dir Gen: Susie Winter
○   *N; trade enforcement organisations concerned to prevent
       intellectual property theft, counterfeiting & copyright

Alliance of Literary Societies   (ALS)   1973
NR   59 Bryony Rd, BIRMINGHAM, B29 4BY.   (chmn/p)
       0121 475 1805
       email l.j.curry@bham.ac.uk
       http://www.allianceofliterarysocieties.org.uk
       Chmn: Linda Curry
▲   Un-incorporated Society
○   *N; to act as a liaison / spokesman for literary societies; to
       assist in any way with advice on anything concerning the
       societies; to promote interest in their work
●   Conf - Mtgs - Res - Comp
>   over 100 societies
M   c 100 org UK / 3 org, o'seas
       (Sub: £10-£25 according to number of members)
¶   NL - 2;   Open Book - 1; both ftm.

Alliance for Natural Health   (ANH)   2002
■   The Atrium, Curtis Rd, DORKING, Surrey, RH4 1XA.   (hq)
       01306 646600   fax 01306 646552
       email info@anhcampaign.org
       http://www.anhcampaign.org
       Exec Dir: Dr Robert Verkerk
▲   Company Limited by Guarantee
○   *K, *W; to support the development of natural & sustainable
       healthcare; to positively shape EU & international legislation
       affecting natural health
Gp   Complementary healthcare practitioners; Health food
       manufacturers; Health food retailers; Organic food
       producers/retailers; Health-conscious consumers
●   Conf - Mtgs - ET - Res - Stat - Inf - LG
<   Amer Assn for Health Freedom; Nat Health Fedn (USA): New
       Zealand Health Trust; Fritt Helsevalg (Norway)
M   i & f
¶   Information by email to subscribers - irreg.

Alliance of Private Sector Chiropody & Podiatry Practitioners
NR   7 Wynnstay Rd, COLWYN BAY, Conwy, LL29 8NB.
       (regd/office)
       01492 534333
       http://www.thealliancepsp.com
       Managing Dir: Janet Taylor
○   *M, *P

© CBD Research Ltd · Beckenham · BR3 5JS · Tel 020 8650 7745 · E-mail cbd@cbdresearch.com · www.cbdresearch.com

Alliance of Registered Homeopaths   (ARH)   2001
- ■ Millbrook, Millbrook Hill, NUTLEY, E Sussex, TN22 3PJ.   (hq)
     01825 714506   fax 01825 712242
     email info@a-r-h.org   http://www.a-r-h.org
     Co Sec: June Sayer,   Dir: Karin Mont
- ▲ Company Limited by Guarantee
- ○ *P; to provide a register of practitioners competent to practice
     safely & effectively; to ensure homeopathy is available to all;
     to raise public awareness of the potential of homeopathy
- Gp Homeopathy; Healthcare; Complementary medicine
- ● Conf - ET - Res - SG - Inf - LG
- < Eur Coun for Classical Homeopathy
- M 700 i, UK / 60 i, o'seas
- ¶ Homeopathy in Practice - 4; ftm, £32 yr UK , £40 yr o'seas.

Alliance of Religions & Conservation   (ARC)   1995
- NR The House, Kelston Park, BATH, BA1 9LE.
     01225 758004
     http://www.arcworld.org
     Sec Gen: Martin Palmer
- ▲ Company Limited by Guarantee
- ○ *K; to promote for the public benefit the protection and
     preservation of the natural environment throughout the
     world, in accordance with the religious teachings and beliefs
     which encourage respect for nature

Alliance of UK Virtual Assistants   (AUKVA)   2000
- NR Walnut Trees, 4 Southwall Rd, DEAL, Kent, CT14 9QA.
     01304 389338
     email enquiries@v-sec.co.uk
     http://www.allianceofukvirtualassistants.org.uk
     Founder: Jo Johnston
- ▲ Un-incorporated Society
- ○ *P; to link to clients, freelance workers with office skills who
     work from their own premises
     Note: uses working name of UKVA

Alliance against Urban 4x4s   2004
- NR The Hub, 5 Torrens St, LONDON, EC1V 1NQ.   (hq)
     email info@stopurban4x4s.org.uk
     http://www.stopurban4x4s.org.uk
- ▲ a non-profit organisation
- ○ *K; a campaign for the increase of taxes & congestion charges
     on big 4-wheel drive vehicles & a ban on advertising in the
     mainstream media
- Gp We are Futureproof
- M [a non-membership body]
- ¶ [website only]

Allied Health Professions Federation   (AHPF)
- ■ 2 White Hart Yard, LONDON, SE1 1NX.   (hq)
     020 7378 3022
     http://www.ahpf.org.uk
     Dir: Paul Hitchcock
- Br 3
- ○ *P; to provide collective leadership & representation on
     common issues that impact on its member professions
- M British Association of Art Therapists; British Association of
     Dramatherapists; British Association for Music Therapy;
     British Association of Occupational Therapists; British
     Association of Prosthetists & Orthotists; British Dietetic
     Association; British & Irish Orthoptic Society; Chartered
     Society of Physiotherapy; College of Paramedics; Royal
     College of Speech & Language Therapists; Society of
     Chiropodists & Podiatrists; Society & College of
     Radiographers

ALLMI Ltd   (ALLMI)   1978
- ■ Prince Maurice House (Unit 7b), Cavalier Court, Bumpers
     Farm, CHIPPENHAM, Wilts, SN14 6LH.   (hq)
     01249 659150   fax 01249 464675
     email enquiries@allmi.com   http://www.allmi.com
     Chmn: Mark Rigby,   Dir: Tom Wakefield
- ▲ Company Limited by Guarantee
- ○ *T; is the only association devoted exclusively to the lorry loader
     industry; to promote the safe use of lorry loaders; to ensure it
     is involved in the formulation of any legislation which affects
     the industry's interests; to promote compliance with training
     requirements embodied in current legislation
- ● Conf - Mtgs - ET - Exhib - Stat - Inf - Lib - PL - Work with BSI for
     development of standards - Produce technical &/or training
     literature
- M 40 mfrs & service companies, 40 fleet owners
     (Sub: £350-£1,350)
- ¶ ALLMI Code of Practice; £15 m, £33 nm.
     ALLMI Lorry Loader Operator's Manual; £32.50 ftm only.
     ALLMI Slinger/Signaller Manual; £32.50 ftm only.
     ALLMI Thorough Examinations Manual; £32.50 ftm only.
     ALLMI Guidance Notes;   ALLMI Membership Book;
     both ftm only.
- × 2008 (Association of Lorry Loader Manufacturers & Importers
     (ALLMI Training Ltd (merged 1 February)

Allotments & Gardens Council (UK)
- ■ 7 Mattingly Rd, Hempshill Vale, NOTTINGHAM, NG6 7BD.
     (chmn/p)
     0115 927 6860
     Chmn: Reginald B Knowles
- ▲ Un-incorporated Society
- ○ *G, *H; to represent allotment holders & societies in all areas

Almshouse Association
  see **National Association of Almshouses**

Alopecia Patients' Society
  seef **Hairline International: the Alopecia Patients' Society**

Alpha-1 Awareness Alliance   1997
- NR 39 Smelter Wood Drive, SHEFFIELD, S Yorks, S13 8RJ.
     0114-239 7232   fax 0114-239 7232
     email kama@kama.u-net.com
     http://www.kama.u-net.com
     Nat Co-ordinator: Kathleen Mallinder
- ○ *M, *W; to raise awareness in the medical field of Alph 1
     Antitriypsin Deficiency (A1AD)

Alpine Club   (AC)   1857
- NR 55-56 Charlotte Rd, LONDON, EC2A 3QT.   (hq)
     020 7613 0755
     http://www.alpine-club.org.uk
     Hon Sec: Martin Scott
- ▲ Un-incorporated Society
- ○ *S; mountaineering in alpine & greater ranges (including ski
     mountaineering)
- ¶ Alpine Jnl.

Alpine Garden Society (AGS) 1929
■ AGS Centre, Avon Bank, PERSHORE, Worcs, WR10 3JP. (hq)
  01386 554790   fax 01386 554801
  email ags@alpinegardensociety.net
  http://www.alpinegardensociety.net
  Dir: Chris McGregor
▲ Registered Charity
Br 60
○ *H; promotion of knowledge & cultivation of all plants suitable
  for rock gardens, frame or alpine house
Gp Androsace; Frit
● Conf - Mtgs - ET - Comp - SG - Inf - Lib - PL - VE - Seed
  distribution scheme
< R Horticl Soc
M 11,500 i, 15 f, 5 org, UK / 2,500 i, 3 f, 3 org, o'seas
¶ Bulletin - 4;   NL - 4; both ftm.
  Gardens Open Directory - 1;   Show Hbk - 1; both free.
  Monographs & alpine titles.
  Publications list available on request.

Alström Syndrome UK   (AS UK)
§ 49 Southfield Avenue, PAIGNTON, S Devon, TQ3 1LH. (hq)
  01803 524328
  email info@alstrom.org.uk   http://www.alstrom.org.uk
  Chief Exec: Kay Parkinson
▲ Registered Charity
  a support group for children & adults with a rare genetic
  condition affecting various organs of the body - the first
  symptom noted is usually an extra-sensitivity to light.
  The group provides information, advice & support to
  individuals, families & professionals; runs specialist clinics &
  organises research & raises awareness of this rare condition.

Alternative Operators in the Communications Market
    see **ALTO - Alternative Operators in the Communications
    Sector**

ALTO - Alternative Operators in the Communications Market
(ALTO)
IRL Clifton House, Lower Fitzwilliam St, DUBLIN 2, Republic of
  Ireland.
  353 (01) 661 3788
  email info@alto.ie   http://www.alto.ie
  Chmn: Liam O'Halloran
○ *T

Altrincham & Sale Chamber of Commerce   1909
NR 1 Kingsway, ALTRINCHAM, Cheshire, WA14 1PN. (hq)
  0161-941 3250   fax 0161-941 1909
  email info@altrinchamchamber.co.uk
  http://www.altrinchamchamber.co.uk
  Chief Exec: Barbara Hallwood
▲ Un-incorporated Society
○ *C; for the business community within South Trafford
● Mtgs - ET - Inf - LG & local & regional bodies - Advice service -
  Networking
< Brit Chams Comm; Chams Comm NW; also local societies etc
M 15 i, 405 f, 10 org
¶ Altruism - 6; ftm, £18 nm.   Diary (incl LM) - 1.
  Annual Accounts - 1.

Aluminium Alloy Manufacturing and Recycling Association
(AAMRA)   1958
■ National Metalforming Centre, 47 Birmingham Rd,
  WEST BROMWICH, W Midlands, B70 6PY. (hq)
  0121-601 6363   fax 0870 138 9714
  email alfed@alfed.org.uk   http://www.alfed.org.uk
  Sec: Will Savage
○ *T; an independent organisation promoting the production of
  unwrought light alloys (aluminium) made in general from
  secondary light metals; the extension of the trade in products
  manufactured from the alloys
● Mtgs - Stat - Inf
< a member association of the Aluminium Federation
M 24 f

Aluminium Extruders Association   (AEA)
■ National Metalforming Centre, 47 Birmingham Rd,
  WEST BROMWICH, W Midlands, B70 6PY.
  0121-601 6363   fax 0870 138 9714
  email alfed@alfed.org.uk   http://www.alfed.org.uk
  Sec: Will Savage
○ *T
< a member association of the Aluminium Federation
M 11 f

Aluminium Federation Ltd   (ALFED)   1962
■ National Metalforming Centre, 47 Birmingham Rd,
  WEST BROMWICH, W Midlands, B70 6PY. (hq)
  0121-601 6363   fax 0870 138 9714
  email alfed@alfed.org.uk   http://www.alfed.org.uk
  Sec Gen: Will Savage
○ *T; interests of those engaged in reduction, smelting, rolling,
  extrusion, drawing, casting, forging & flaking of aluminium &
  aluminium alloys
● Conf - Mtgs - ET - Exhib - Stat - Inf - Lib (technical enquiries &
  other queries) - LG
< Eur Aluminium Assn
M 200+ f
¶ AR.

Aluminium Finishing Association   (AFA)
■ National Metalforming Centre, 47 Birmingham Rd,
  WEST BROMWICH, W Midlands, B70 6PY. (hq)
  0121-601 6363   fax 0870 138 9714
  email alfed@alfed.org.uk   http://www.alfed.org.uk
  Sec: T Siddle
○ *T; aluminium coatings & anodising
< a member association of the Aluminium Federation
M 28 f

Aluminium Packaging Recycling Organisation   (Alupro)
1989
■ 1 Brockhill Court, Brockhill Lane, REDDITCH, Worcs,
  B97 6RB. (hq)
  01527 597757   fax 01527 594140
  email info@alupro.org.uk   http://www.alupro.org.uk
○ *T; to promote recycling of aluminium foil & cans working with
  local authorities & private sector companies
● Conf - Mtgs - ET - Res - Comp - Stat - PL - Provision of
  educational materials to schools, groups etc to set up a
  recycling initiative
M 21 f
¶ Campaign NL - 4; ftm, on application nm.
✕ UK Aluminium Packaging Recycling Organisation

Aluminium Powder & Paste Association
■ National Metalforming Centre, 47 Birmingham Rd,
  WEST BROMWICH, W Midlands, B70 6PY. (hq)
  0121-601 6363   fax 0870 138 9714
  email alfed@alfed.org.uk   http://www.alfed.org.uk
  Sec: T Siddle
○ *T
< a member association of the Aluminium Federation
M f

Aluminium Primary Producers Association   (APPA)
■ National Metalforming Centre, 47 Birmingham Rd,
  WEST BROMWICH, W Midlands, B70 9PY. (hq)
  0121-601 6363   fax 0870 138 9714
  email alfed@alfed.org.uk   http://www.alfed.org.uk
  Sec: Will Savage
○ *T
< a member association of the Aluminium Federation
M f

© CBD Research Ltd · Beckenham · BR3 5JS · Tel 020 8650 7745 · E-mail cbd@cbdresearch.com · www.cbdresearch.com

Aluminium Rolled Products Manufacturers Association (ARPMA)

■ National Metalforming Centre, 47 Birmingham Rd, WEST BROMWICH, W Midlands, B70 9PY. (hq)
  0121-601 6363   fax 0870 138 9714
  email alfed@alfed.org.uk   http://www.alfed.org.uk
  Sec: Will Savage
○ *T
● Stat - Inf - Lib
< a member association of the Aluminium Federation
M 4 f
¶ Various booklets.

Aluminium Stockholders Association   (ASA)   1962

■ National Metalforming Centre, 47 Birmingham Rd, WEST BROMWICH, W Midlands, B70 9PY. (hq)
  0121-601 6363   fax 0870 138 9714
  email asa@alfed.org.uk
  Sec: Will Savage
▲ Un-incorporated Society
○ *T; representative body for UK aluminium, stainless steel & non-ferrous stockholders & distributors
● Conf - Mtgs - ET - Inf - VE
< Aluminium Fedn
M 19 f, 12 associates
¶ Review - 2;   NL - 6; free.

Alzheimer Scotland - Action on Dementia   1994

NR 22 Drumsheugh Gardens, EDINBURGH, EH3 7RN. (hq)
  0131-243 1453   fax 0131-243 1450
  email alzheimer@alzscot.org   http://www.alzscot.org
  Chief Exec: Henry Simmons
▲ Company Limited by Guarantee
○ *K, *W; to be the national & local voice in Scotland, for people with dementia & their carers; to improve public policies & secure provision of high quality services; to provide high quality services
● Conf - ET - Res - Care service provision - Campaigning
  Helpline: 0808 808 3000
< Alzheimer's Disease Intl; Alzheimer's Europe
M 2,541 i, 35 f, 59 org
¶ Dementia in Scotland (NL) - 4; ftm, £1 nm.   AR; ftm.

Alzheimer's Society   (AS)   1979

NR Devon House, 58 St Katharine's Way, LONDON, E1W 1JX. (hq)
  020 7423 3500   fax 020 7423 3501
  email enquiries@alzheimers.org.uk
  http://www.alzheimers.org.uk
  Dir: Neil Hunt
▲ Company Limited by Guarantee; Registered Charity
Br c 200
○ *W; the leading care & research charity for people with dementia; to provide information, education & support for carers as well as day & home care
● Conf - Res - Inf - Lib
  Helpline: 0845 300 0336 (Mon-Fri 0830-1830); charged at local rates
M c 24,000 i
¶ NL - 12.
  Publications list available.

Amateur Boxing Association of England Ltd   (ABAE)   1880

NR English Institute of Sport, Coleridge Rd, SHEFFIELD, S Yorks, S9 5DA. (hq)
  0114-223 5654
  http://www.abae.co.uk
  Chief Exec: Paul King
▲ Company Limited by Guarantee
Br 10 regions
○ *S; to further the sport of amateur boxing in England
Gp Commissions: Coaching & performance, Development, Ethics, Medical, Referees & judges, Technical & rules
● Mtgs - ET - Exam - Comp - Inf
< Intl Amat Boxing Assns (IABA); Eur Amat Boxing Assns (AEBA
M 10,330 i, 638 clubs

Amateur Boxing Scotland   (ABS)   1908

NR 5 Nasmyth Court, Houston Industrial Estate, LIVINGSTON, EH54 5EG.
  0845 241 7016
  http://www.amateurboxingscotland.co.uk
▲ Company Limited by Guarantee
○ *S; the governing body of amateur boxing in Scotland
< Amat Intl Boxing Assn (AIBA); Eur Amat Boxing Assn (EABA)

Amateur Entomologists' Society   (AES)   1935

NR PO Box 8774, LONDON, SW7 5ZG.   (mail address)
  email enquiries@amentsoc.org   http://www.amentsoc.org
  Registrar: Nick Holford
▲ Registered Charity
○ *L; to promote the study of entomology (insects) particularly amongst amateurs & young people
Gp AES Bug Club (for those aged 13 & under)
● Exhib - SG - Inf
< R Entomological Soc London (RES)
> R Entomological Soc London (RES)
M 1,200 i, 20 org, UK / 100 i, 6 org, o'seas
¶ Bulletin - 6; free.
  Various handbooks & pamphlets.

Amateur Football Alliance   (AFA)   1907

NR 7 Wenlock Rd (Unit 3), LONDON, N1 7SL. (hq)
  020 8733 2613
  email info@amateur-fa.com
  Chief Exec: Mike Brown
○ *S; administration of Association Football clubs, referees & competitions (primarily in the Greater London area)

Amateur Jockeys Association of Great Britain Ltd   (AJA)   1995

■ Crews Hill House, Alfrick, WORCESTER, WR6 5HF. (hq)
  01886 884488   fax 01886 884068
  email sph.oliver@btinternet.com
  http://www.amateurjockeys.org.uk
  Chief Exec: Mrs Sarah Oliver
▲ Company Limited by Guarantee
○ *S; to protect & promote the role of amateur jockey
● Conf - Mtgs - ET - Stat - Inf
< Intl Fedn of Gentlemen Riders & Lady Riders (FEGENTRI)
M 500 i, UK / 25 i, o'seas
  (Sub: £75)
¶ NL - 4; ftm only.

Amateur Martial Association   (AMA)   1971

NR 169 Cotswold Crescent, Walshaw Park, BURY, Lancs, BL8 1QL. (hq)
  0161-763 5599   fax 05601 502065
  email office@amauk.co.uk   http://www.amauk.co.uk
▲ Un-incorporated Society
○ *S; martial arts
● ET - Res - Comp
< Sport & Recreation Alliance
M 90,000 i

Amateur Motor Cycle Association Ltd   (AMCA)   1932
■ 28 Navigation Way, Mill Park, CANNOCK, Staffs,
WS11 7XU.   (hq)
01543 466282   fax 01543 466283
email office@amca.uk.com   http://www.amca.uk.com
Sec: Carol Davis
▲ Company Limited by Guarantee
○ *S; to promote off road motor cycle sporting events
● Conf - Mtgs - Res - Inf - LG
< Intl Motor Sport Band for Amateurs (IMBA); Land Access &
Recreation Assn (LARA)
M 5,000 i
¶ Off Road Rider - 8; ftm, £2 nm.

Amateur Rose Breeders Association   (ARBA)   1975
■ 48 Shrewsbury Fields, SHIFNAL, Shropshire, TF11 8AN.   (hsp)
01952 461333
Hon Sec: Derrick Everitt
▲ Un-incorporated Society
○ *H; to protect & further the interests, knowledge & status of
amateur rosebreeders by the best, honest means including a
willingness by members to share their expertise & to
cooperate with other organisations (amateur or professional),
& a common interest in the rose
● Mtgs - Res - Exhib - Comp - VE
< R Nat Rose Soc (a specialist interest gp)
M 125 i, UK / 20 i, o'seas
¶ NL - 2/4.   ARBA Annual - 1.
Specialist publications - irreg.

Amateur Rowing Association Ltd   (ARA)   1882
NR 6 Lower Mall, Hammersmith, LONDON, W6 9DJ.   (hq)
020 8237 6700   fax 020 8237 6749
email info@britishrowing.org
http://www.britishrowing.org
Sec: Liz O'Flaherty
▲ Company Limited by Guarantee
○ *S; the governing body for the sport of rowing
M i & clubs

Amateur Swimming Association   (ASA)   1869
■ SportPark, 3 Oakwood Drive, LOUGHBOROUGH, Leics,
LE11 3QF.   (hq)
01509 618700   fax 01509 618701
email chiefexecutive@swimming.org
Chief Exec: David Sparkes
Br 8 regions
○ *S; to promote the teaching & practice of swimming, diving,
synchronised swimming & water polo; to stimulate public
opinion in favour of provision of facilities for them; to enforce
laws for the control of the four disciplines in England
Gp Swimming; Diving; Water polo; Synchronised swimming;
Education
● Conf - Mtgs - ET - Exam - Comp
< Fédn Intle de Natation Amateur (FINA); Ligue Eur de
Natation (LEN)
M 194,443 i, 1,584 clubs, 30 org
¶ Hbk - 1; £6.   AR; free.

Amateur Swimming Federation of Great Britain Ltd
since 2008 **British Swimming**

Amateur Yacht Research Society Ltd   (AYRS)   1955
NR BCM AYRS, LONDON, WC1N 3XX.   (hs)
01727 862268   fax 0870 052 6657
email office@ayrs.org   http://www.ayrs.org
Hon Sec: Sheila Fishwick
▲ Company Limited by Guarantee; Registered Charity
○ *G, *Q; to improve yachts & equipment through research &
development
● Conf - Mtgs - Exhib
M 352 i, 29 org, UK / 281 i, 10 org, o'seas
¶ NL - 4; ftm.

Ambulance Service Association
on 14 January 2008 merged with the NHS Confederation to form the
Ambulance Service Network

Ambulance Service Institute   (ASI)   1976
NR Maddison House (Suite 183), 226 High St, CROYDON, Surrey,
CR9 1DF.
email enquiries@asi-international.com
http://www.asi-international.com
Nat Admin & Sec: Graham Sleight
▲ Company Limited by Guarantee; Registered Charity
Br 20; Hong Kong, Canada
○ *P; to promote, advance & encourage the education & training
of ambulance service employees & to extend the training to
the general public
● Conf - Mtgs - ET - Exam - Comp - SG - LG
< Inst of Ambulance Officers Australia (& N Zealand); Ambulance
Service Assn
M i
¶ NL - 4.

Ambulance Service Network   1997
NR 29 Bressenden Place (3rd floor), LONDON, SW1E 5DD.   (hq)
020 7074 3200
Dir: Sue Slipman
▲ Registered Charity
○ *N; to represent the interests of all NHS bodies across the UK;
includes over 95% of NHS trusts, health authorities & boards
✕ 2008 (Ambulance Service Association
(NHS Confederation

American Civil War Round Table (UK)   (ACWRT(UK))   1953
■ 34 Linden Rd, Muswell Hill, LONDON, N10 3DH.   (msp)
020 8883 3552
email tonybrown@americancivilwar.org.uk
http://www.americancivilwar.org.uk
Mem Sec: Tony Brown
▲ Un-incorporated Society
○ *L; serious & impartial study of the War Between The States
1861-1865
● Mtgs - SG - Inf - Lib - Historical research
< Civil War Round Table Associates (USA)
M c 170 i, UK / 10 i, o'seas
¶ Crossfire - 3; free.

American Quarter Horse Association UK Ltd   (AQHA-UK)
1974
■ 63 Laughton Rd, Lubenham, MARKET HARBOROUGH, Leics,
LE16 9TE.   (treas/p)
0870 609 1654
email accounts@aqha.uk.com   http://www.aqha.uk.com
Treas: Mrs P A M Dyke
▲ Company Limited by Guarantee; Registered Charity
Br USA
○ *B; to promote, record & preserve the Quarter horse breed in
the UK
● Mtgs - Comp - LG
< Brit Horse Soc
M 650 i
¶ AQHA.UK Jnl - 4; ftm; £3 nm.

American Saddlebred Association of GB   (ASAoGB)   1985
NR 24 Coton Grove, Shirley, SOLIHULL, W Midlands, B90 1BS.
0121-430 4281
▲ Un-incorporated Society
○ *B; to promote the breed in Great Britain
M i

Amusement & Gaming Industry Forum
Advised as no longer in existence, but we would appreciate
confirmation.

© CBD Research Ltd · Beckenham · BR3 5JS · Tel 020 8650 7745 · E-mail cbd@cbdresearch.com · www.cbdresearch.com

An Óige   (Irish Youth Hostel Association)   (IYHA)   1931
IRL   61 Mountjoy St, DUBLIN 7, Republic of Ireland.   (hq)
        353 (1) 830 4555   fax 353 (1) 830 5808
        email mailbox@anoige.ie   http://www.anoige.ie
Br   13 An Óige hostels & 12 franchise hostels
○   *Y; to help all, but especially young people, to a love &
        appreciation of the countryside, particularly by providing
        sample hostel accommodation for them whilst on their travels
<   Intl Youth Hostel Fedn (IYHF)
        Note: 'An Óige' is Gaelige for 'The Youth'

Anaerobic Digestion and Biogas Association   (adba)
NR   Room 318 Canterbury Court, Kennington Park, 1-3 Brixton Rd,
        LONDON, SW9 6DE.   (hq)
        020 3176 0503
        http://www.adbiogas.co.uk
○   *T; for all in the biogas & anaerobic digestion industries
●   Inf - LG

Anaesthetic Research Society   (ARS)   1958
NR   c/o Dr J G Hardman, University Division of Anaesthesia &
        Intensive Care, Queen's Medical Centre, NOTTINGHAM,
        NG7 2UH.   (hsb)
        0115-823 1002
        http://www.ars.ac.uk
        Hon Sec: Dr Jonathan G Hardman
▲   Registered Charity
○   *L; forum for discussion of current research in anaesthesia
●   Conf
M   650 i, UK / 75 i, o'seas
¶   Proceedings of Conferences - 3. (in British Jnl of Anaesthesia).

Anaphylaxis Campaign   1994
NR   PO Box 275, FARNBOROUGH, Hants, GU14 6SX.   (hq)
        01252 546100
        http://www.anaphylaxis.org.uk
        Dir: David Reading
▲   Registered Charity
○   *K; to offer support & guidance to those affected by potentially
        fatal food allergies; it is dedicated to raising awareness in the
        food industry; it is seeking to ensure that the medical
        profession at every level offers the best possible advice &
        treatment
¶   Anaphylaxis Campaign (NL) - 4.

Anatomical Society of Great Britain & Ireland   (ASGBI)   1887
■   c/o Dept of Anatomy & Human Sciences, King's College
        London, Room 41N Hodgkin Building (Guy's Campus),
        LONDON, SE1 1UL.   (sb)
        020 7848 8234   fax 020 7848 8234
        email maryanne.piggott@kcl.ac.uk
        http://www.anatsoc.org.uk
        Exec Admin: Mary-Anne Piggott
▲   Registered Charity
○   *L, *Q; the promotion, study, development & advancement of
        research & education in the anatomical & related sciences
●   Conf - Mtgs - ET - Res
<   Eur Fedn for Experimental Morphology; Intl Fedn Assns
        Anatomists
M   c 700 i
        Subs: £35 (without Jnl), £65 (with Jnl)
¶   Jnl of Anatomy - 12;   Aging Cell;
        Anastomosis (NL) - 4; prices on application.

Ancient Cattle of Wales
        see **Gwartheg Hynafol Cymrumt Cattle of Wales)**

Ancient Egypt & Middle East Society   (AEMES)   1987
■   2 Seathorne Crescent, SKEGNESS, Lincs, PE25 1RP.   (hsp)
        01754 765341   fax 01754 765341
        email sue.kirk12@btinternet.com
        http://www.aemes.co.uk
        Hon Sec: Mrs Sue Kirk
▲   Un-incorporated Society
○   *G; the history, archaeology & cultures of the ancient Near East
●   Conf - Mtgs - ET - Res - Exhib - SG - Inf - Lib (members only) -
        VE
M   90 i, UK / 2 i, o'seas
        (Sub: £14.50 i, £20,50 family, UK / on request o'seas)
¶   AEMES Jnl - 3; ftm, on application nm.

Ancient & Honourable Guild of Town Criers   (AHGTC)   1978
■   10 Weston Rd, GUILDFORD, Surrey, GU2 8AS.   (hsp)
        01483 532796   fax 01483 833489
        email secretary@ahgtc.org.uk   http://www.ahgtc.org.uk
        Sec: David Peters
▲   Company Limited by Guarantee
Br   Australia, Bahamas, Belgium, Canada, Germany, Netherlands,
        New Zealand, Poland, USA
○   *P; promotion & regulation of town-crying; preservation of
        ancient art of town-crying
●   Conf - Mtgs - Comp - LG
>   Gld of Eur Town Criers; Gld of Australian Town Criers
M   c 120 i, UK / c 25 i, o'seas
¶   The Crier - 4; ftm only.

Ancient Monuments Society   (AMS)   1924
■   St Ann's Vestry Hall, 2 Church Entry, LONDON, EC4V 5HB.
        (hq)
        020 7236 3934
        email office@ancientmonumentssociety.org.uk
        http://www.ancientmonumentssociety.org.uk
        Chmn: Giles Quarme,   Sec: Matthew Saunders
▲   Registered Charity
○   *K; study & conservation of ancient monuments, historic
        buildings & fine old craftsmanship
●   Conf - Res - Inf - VE - Comments to local authorities on the
        demolition of listed buildings - Dissemination of methods &
        techniques of preservation - Advice to planning authorities on
        listed buildings
<   Jt C'ee of the Nat Amenity Socs; Friends of Friendless Churches
M   2,000 i, 200 libraries, UK / c 100 i, 50 libraries, o'seas
¶   Transactions - 1; ftm.   NL - 3.

Ancient Tree Forum
■   c/o Woodland Trust, Autumn Park, Dysart Rd, GRANTHAM,
        Lincs, NG31 6LL.
        01476 581135
        http://www.woodland-trust.org.uk/ancient-tree-forum
▲
        ancient-tree-forum@woodland-trust.org.uk
○   *K; conservation of ancient trees

Androgen Insensitivity Syndrome Support Group   (AISSG)
NR   [Contact via website only]
        http://www.aissg.org
○   *W; for those with androgen resistance syndrome - disorders of
        sex development in either gender
        Note: Address changes frequently - check website for contact

Angela Thirkell Society   1980
■   24 Park St, SALISBURY, Wilts, SP1 3AU.   (hsp)
        email member@salisbury75.freeserve.co.uk
        http://www.angelathirkellsociety.com
        Hon Sec: Jane Davies
Br   Eire, USA
○   *A, *G; to honour the memory of Angela Thirkell (1890-1961)
        as a writer & to make her works available to new generations
●   Mtgs - VE
<   Alliance Literary Socs
M   150 i, UK / 500 i, o'seas
¶   Jnl - 1; ftm, £5 nm.

Anglers' Conservation Association
    since 2009 Fish Legal, the legal branch of the **Angling Trust**

Anglesey Agricultural Society   1886
■   Ty Glyn Williams, The Showground, Gwalchmai, HOLYHEAD,
    Anglesey, LS65 4RW.   (hq)
    01407 720072   fax 01407 720880
    email info@angleseyshow.org.uk
    http://www.angleseyshow.org.uk
    Show Admin: Aled W Hughes
▲   Company Limited by Guarantee; Registered Charity
○   *F; to promote agriculture, horticulture & forestry
Gp Poultry; Rabbits; Goats; Pigs; Sheep; Dairy & beef cattle; Shire
    & heavy horses; Light horses; Show jumping; Cookery;
    Produce; Horticultural; Shearing; Dry stone walling
●   Mtgs - ET - Exhib - Comp - Expt - Inf - LG
<   Assn of Shows & Agricl Orgs
M   1,100 i
¶   Show Catalogue - 1.   AR - 1.
    Winter Show Catalogue - 1.
    Schedules of Events & Classes; - 1.

Anglesey Antiquarian Society & Field Club   (AAS)   1911
■   1 Fronheulog, Sling, TREGARTH, Caernarfonshire, LL57 4RD.
    (hsp)
    01248 600083
    http://www.hanesmon.org.uk
    Hon Sec: Siön C G Caffell
▲   Registered Charity
○   *L; archaeology, natural science, art & literature of Anglesey
●   Mtgs - Inf - Lib - VE
M   900 i, 118 org
¶   Transactions - 1; £6 m, £10 nm.   NL - 2; ftm.
    Studies in Anglesey History - irreg.

Angling Trades Association Ltd   (ATA)
■   Federation House, STONELEIGH PARK, Warks, CV8 2RF.   (hq)
    024 7641 4999   fax 024 7641 4990
    email ata@sportsandplay.com
    http://www.anglingtradesassociation.com
    Chief Exec: David Pomfret
○   *T; to represent manufacturers, wholesalers & distributors; to
    defend angling
●   Mtgs - Exhib - Stat - Expt - Inf - LG
<   a group of the Fedn of Sports & Play Assns (FSPA)
M   c 50 f

Angling Trust
NR Eastwood House, 6 Rainbow St, LEOMINSTER, Herefords,
    HR6 8DQ.
    0844 770 0616
    email admin@anglingtrust.net
○   *S; to represent all game, coarse & sea anglers in England
Gp Fish Legal
M   i, org
¶
    (Sub: £20 i, £50-£250 org)
×   2009 (Anglers Conservation Association
        (Fisheries & Angling Conservation Trust
        (National Association of Fisheries & Angling Consultatives
        (National Federation of Anglers
        (National Federation of Sea Anglers
        (Specialist Anglers Alliance

Anglo-Argentine Society   1948
■   Canning House, 2 Belgrave Sq, LONDON, SW1X 8PJ.   (hq)
    020 7235 9505 (Mon-Thurs 1330-1630)   fax 020 7235
    9505
    email info@angloargentinesociety.co.uk
    http://www.angloargentinesociety.org.uk
    Chmn: Barney Miller,   Hon Sec: Claudia Morales
▲   Registered Charity
○   *X; to advance the education of the people of GB about
    Argentinian people, history, language, institutions & culture
    (& vice-versa)
●   Conf - Mtgs - Exhib - Social gatherings
M   i & f
¶   AR.

Anglo-Austrian Society   1954
NR 60 Brimmers Hill, Widmer End, HIGH WYCOMBE, Bucks,
    HP15 6NP.   (hq)
    01494 711116
    email info@angloaustrian.demon.co.uk
    http://www.angloaustrian.org.uk
    Sec: Peter Gieler
○   *X; promotion of friendship & understanding between peoples
    of GB & Austria
M   2,500 i

Anglo-Belgian Society   (ABS)   1918
■   5 Hartley Close, BICKLEY, Kent, BR1 2TP.   (hsp)
    020 8467 8442   fax 020 8467 8442
    http://www.anglo-belgiansoc.co.uk
    Hon Sec: Patrick Bresnan
▲   Un-incorporated Society
Br Belgium
○   *X; maintain & develop friendship between the British & Belgian
    peoples through cultural & social relations
●   Conf - Mtgs - VE - Cultural & social activities
M   480 i, 17 f, UK / 40 i, 5 f, o'seas
¶   LM - 5 yrly.   AR - 1.

Anglo-Brazilian Society   1943
NR 32 Green St, LONDON, W1K 7AU.   (hq)
    020 7493 8493
    http://www.anglobraziliansociety.org
○   *X; to promote friendly relations between Brazil & the UK

Anglo-Catalan Society   (ACS)   1954
■   c/o Dr Montserrat Roser i Puig, School of European Culture &
    Languages, University of Kent, CANTERBURY, CT2 7NF.
    (hsb)
    email jill@faura.me.uk   http://www.anglo-catalan.org
    Hon Sec: Dr Jill Buckenham
▲   Un-incorporated Society
○   *L, *X; the promotion of Catalan language & culture, Catalan
    studies & Anglo-Catalan relations
●   Conf - Mtgs - ET - Res - Inf
<   Institut Ramon Llull; Fundació Congrés de Cultura Catalana
>   NACS
M   200 i, 4 f, UK / 80 i, 5 f, o'seas
¶   NL - 2; free.   Annual Lecture - 1.
    Publications available at www.kent.ac.uk/acsop/

Anglo-Central American Society   (ACAS)   1982
NR Flat 6 Lanark Mansions, 12 Lanark Rd, LONDON, W9 1DB.
    (mem/sp)
    Sec: Sylvia Ugalde
▲   Registered Charity
○   *X; to promote knowledge about Central America in the UK
    and vice versa
●   Mtgs - ET - Exhib - VE
M   140 i, 1 f

© CBD Research Ltd · Beckenham · BR3 5JS · Tel 020 8650 7745 · E-mail cbd@cbdresearch.com · www.cbdresearch.com

Anglo-Chilean Society   1944
NR   12 Devonshire St, LONDON, W1N 2DS.   (hq)
        020 7580 1271
○   *X

Anglo-Colombian Society   1960
NR   Flat 3H Grove End House, Grove End Rd, LONDON, NW8 9HP.
        020 7266 4116
        email anglocols@hotmail.com
        Sec: Myriam Martinez
○   *X; promotion of friendly relations between UK & Colombia
●   Mtgs - VE
M   c 200 i & f

Anglo-Côte d'Ivoire Society
      has closed

Anglo-Danish Society   (A-DS)   1924
NR   43 Maresfield Gardens, LONDON, NW3 5TF.   (sp)
        020 7794 8781
        http://www.anglo-danishsociety.org.uk
        Sec: Birger Jensen
▲   Registered Charity
○   *X; to promote understanding between the two countries
●   Mtgs - VE - Award of scholarships to post-graduates for Danes
        to study in the UK & for British students to study in Denmark
        for a maximum of 6 months & worth £200 per month
<   Confedn of Scandinavian Socs of GB & Ireland (CoSCAN)
M   380 i, 40 f, UK / 10 i, Denmark
¶   News & Views Magazine - 4; ftm only.
        NL with visits & meetings programme - 4; ftm only.

Anglo-Ecuadorian Society
NR   29 Chantry Hurst, EPSOM, Surrey, KT19 7BW.   (treas/p)
        Contact: Mr Simpson
▲   Un-incorporated Society
○   *X; to encourage & promote friendly relations between Ecuador
        & the UK; proceeds from cultural & social events provide
        funds for children-in-need charities in Ecuador
●   Mtgs - Annual dinner (Autumn) - Fiesta Latina (May in London)
M   [not stated]
¶   NL - 4; ftm only.

Anglo-Finnish Society
NR   44 Elfort Rd, LONDON, N5 1AZ.   (hs)
        email honsec@anglofinnishsociety.org.uk
        http://www.anglofinnishsociety.org.uk
        Hon Sec: Paulus Thomson
○   *X
¶   Finn-Niche - 4; ftm.
        (Sub: £10)

Anglo-German Family History Society   1987
NR   Tresco 26 Haddon Way, Carlyon Bay, ST AUSTELL, Cornwall,
        PL25 3QG.   (hsp)
        01628 524384
        http://www.agfhs.org.uk
        Publicity Officer: Eluned Eidmans
▲   Un-incorporated Society
○   *G; family history for those wishing to research their German
        ancestors
●   Mtgs - Res - Inf - Lib - VE
<   Fedn of Family History Socs
M   1,500 i, UK / 150 i, o'seas
¶   Mitteilungsblatt - 4.

Anglo-Hellenic League   1913
■   The Hellenic Centre, 16-18 Paddington St, LONDON,
        W1U 5AS.   (hq)
        020 7486 9410
        email info@anglohellenicleague.org
        http://www.anglohellenicleague.org
        Chmn: Sir David Dain, KCVO, CMG
        Admin: Dr Sophia B Economides
▲   Registered Charity
○   *X; to strengthen ties between GB & Greece; to spread
        information & encourage travel, social & cultural relations
        between the peoples of the two countries
●   Mtgs - VE - Administers the Runciman Literary Award, the Katie
        Lentakis Award (for students)
M   320 i, 29 f, 2 org, UK / 50 i, o'seas
        (Sub: £25 i, £150 f, UK / £25 i, o'seas)
¶   The Anglo-Hellenic Review - 2; ftm, £6 (£7.50 o'seas) nm.
        AR.

Anglo-Indonesian Society   (AIS)   1956
■   Church Cottage, Pedlinge, HYTHE, Kent, CT21 4JL.   (hsp)
        01303 260541   fax 01303 238058
        email info@angloindonesiansociety.org
        http://www.angloindonesiansociety.org
        Chmn & Hon Sec: Christopher Scarlett
▲   Un-incorporated Society
○   *X; a non-political society fostering friendship & understanding
        between the people in Britain interested in Indonesia &
        people of Indonesian nationality resident in Britain; to
        encourage cultural, literary & social relations between the two
        countries
●   Mtgs - VE
M   250 i, 20 f
¶   NL - 26;   AR & Accounts - 1; both ftm only.

Anglo-Israel Association   (AIA)   1949
NR   PO Box 47819, LONDON, NW11 7WD.   (hq)
        020 8458 1284
▲   Registered Charity
○   *X; to foster understanding between GB & Israel
M   i & f

Anglo-Jewish Association   (AJA)   1871
NR   Haskell House, 152 West End Lane, LONDON, NW6 1SD.
        (hq)
        020 7443 5169
        email info@anglojewish.co.uk
        http://www.anglojewish.co.uk
        Pres: Neil Miron
▲   Registered Charity
○   *W; administration of charitable educational funds for Jewish
        students in financial need in higher education in the UK
●   Mtgs - ET - Arrangement of lectures
<   Conf on Jewish Material Claims
>   CCJO
M   500 i

Anglo-Jordanian Society   (AJS)   1981
■   PO Box 840, RICHMOND, Surrey, TW9 9AN.   (hsb)
        020 8940 0474
        http://www.a-j-s.org.uk
        Hon Sec: Emma Bodossian
▲   Registered Charity
○   *X
Gp   Youth
●   Mtgs - Exhib - Expt - VE
<   Jordan British Society
M   677 i, 39 f, UK / 53 i, o'seas
¶   Jordaniana - 3/4.

Anglo-Malagasy Society   1961
■   1 Golding Crescent, STANFORD le HOPE, Essex, SS17 7AZ.
      (chmn/p)
      01375 677138
      http://www.anglo-malagasysociety.co.uk
      Chmn: Stuart Edgill
▲   Un-incorporated Society
○   *X; to further friendship between GB & Madagascar; to
      promote business with & visits to the Republic
●   Conf - Mtgs - Exhib
M   300 i, 20 f
      (Sub: £20 i, £100 f, UK)
¶   NL - 4.   AR; both ftm only.

Anglo-Netherlands Society   1920
NR PO Box 68, Unilever House, LONDON, EC4P 4BQ.   (hq)
      020 7767 6959
○   *X; to promote friendship between British & Dutch subjects by
      organising events (in Britain) at which they can meet

Anglo-Norman Text Society   (ANTS)   1938
■   c/o Dept of European Cultures & Languages, Birkbeck College,
      Malet St, LONDON, WC1E 7HX.   (hsb)
      020 7631 6170 & 020 8239 9424
      email ishort@bbk.ac.uk
      Hon Sec: Prof Ian Short
▲   Registered Charity
○   *L; the publication of Anglo-Norman texts of literary, linguistic,
      historical & legal value & interest
●   Publication - Compilation of an Anglo-Norman Dictionary
M   74 i, 48 f, universities, UK / 114 i, 96 f, o'seas
¶   1 volume of Anglo-Norman text - 1.
      Prospectus (incl LM).   Occasional volumes.

Anglo-Norse Society   1918
■   25 Belgrave Sq, LONDON, SW1X 8QD.   (hq)
      020 7235 9529   fax 020 7235 9529
      email secretariat@anglo-norse.org.uk
      Sec: Irene Garland
▲   Registered Charity
Br Norway
○   *X; promotion of better understanding/knowledge of Norway in
      the UK
Gp Bursaries for study of a 'Norwegian' subject
●   Mtgs - Selling books for language study, & Norwegian literature
M   c 400 i
¶   Anglo Norse Review - 2; ftm.

**Anglo North Irish Fish Producers Organisation   (ANIFPO)
1984**
NR The Harbour, KILKEEL, Co Down, BT34 4AX.
      028 4176 2855   fax 028 4176 4904
      email info@anifpo.com   http://www.anifpo.com
      Admin: Lynda McCall
○   *T

Anglo-Nubian Breed Society   1972
NR 3 Wadehouse Lane, Draxhales, Drax, SELBY, N Yorks, YO8 8PN.
      01757 618756
      http://www.anglo-nubian.org.uk
      Sec: Mrs Margaret Edginton
○   *B; Nubian goats

Anglo-Omani Society   1976
NR 34 Sackville St, LONDON, W1S 3ED.
      020 7851 7439
      Sec: Richard R Owens
▲   Company Limited by Guarantee; Registered Charity
○   *X
●   Mtgs - VE - LG
M   600 i, 12 f

Anglo-Peruvian Society   1961
NR PO Box 494, WEMBLEY, Middx, HA9 8ZB.   (hq)
      020 8908 1916
▲   Registered Charity
○   *X; to advance the education of the people of Great Britain
      about Peru, its people, history, language & literature,
      institutions, folklore & artistic & economic life
●   Conf - Mtgs - ET - Lectures - Concerts - Seminars - Fundraising
      - Cultural events
M   i & f

Anglo-Polish Society   1832
NR c/o The Polish Institute, 20 Princes Gate, LONDON,
      SW7 1PT.   (mail/address)
○   *X; to promote friendship & understanding between British &
      Polish people; to protect the interests of the Poles in Britain
M   i

Anglo-Portuguese Society   1938
NR Canning House, 2 Belgrave Sq, LONDON, SW1X 8PJ.   (hq)
      020 7245 9738
      Sec: Miss Ann Waterfall
○   *X; the education of the people of the United Kingdom about
      Portugal, its people & its culture

Anglo-Scottish Fishermen's Association
      a member association of the **Scottish Fishermen's Federation**

Anglo-Spanish Society   1958
■   102 Eaton Square, LONDON, SW1W 9AN.   (hsp)
      07903 801576
      email info@anglospanishsociety.org
      http://www.anglospanishsociety.org
      Hon Sec: Dorothy H McLean
▲   Registered Charity
○   *X; to promote friendship between the peoples of Britain &
      Spain through a knowledge of each other's customs,
      institutions, history & way of life
●   Mtgs - VE
M   300 i, 11 f, UK / 40 i, 1 f, o'seas
¶   Anglo-Spanish Quarterly Review - 4.

Anglo-Swedish Society of Great Britain & Ireland   1919
NR 6a Oakfield St, LONDON, SW10 9JB.
      020 7352 0599   fax 020 7352 0599
      email info@angloswedishsociety.org.uk
      http://www.angloswedishsociety.org.uk
      Hon Sec: Mrs Kari Hedly
▲   Registered Charity
○   *X; to promote good relations & awareness between the
      peoples of GB & Sweden in the fields of culture, science, art,
      literature, music, history, economics & philosophy
●   VE - Scholarship scheme
M   283 i, 11 f
¶   NL - 3;   AR; both ftm only.

Anglo-Thai Society   1962
■   Southwood, 62a Dore Rd, SHEFFIELD, S Yorks, S17 3NE.
      (hsp)
      0114-236 8129
      email info@anglothaisociety.org
      http://www.anglothaisociety.org
      Hon Sec: T J Knox
▲   Un-incorporated Society
○   *X
●   Mtgs
M   250 i, 10 f, UK / 20 i, o'seas

© CBD Research Ltd · Beckenham · BR3 5JS · Tel 020 8650 7745 · E-mail cbd@cbdresearch.com · www.cbdresearch.com

Anglo-Turkish Society   1953
■   72 New Park Avenue, LONDON, N13 5NB.   (mem/sp)
     http://www.anglo-turkish-society.co.uk
     Mem Sec: Mrs Aysen Timms
▲   Company Limited by Guarantee; Registered Charity
○   *X; a social & cultural society
●   Lectures, social gatherings & outings
M   400 i, 2 f, UK / 10 i, o'seas

Anglo-Venezuelan Society   1976
NR PO Box 930, ST ALBANS, Herts, AL1 9GE.   (sp)
     email secretary@angloven.org   http://www.angloven.org
     Sec: Valerie Lucien
▲   Un-incorporated Society
○   *X; to promote informed discussion on Venezuelan issues,
     particularly those relating to British investment & trade
●   Conf - Mtgs - Lectures - Concerts - Annual dinner
M   90 i, 38 f, UK / 5 i, 1 f, o'seas

Animal Consultants & Trainers Association   (ACTA)   1989
■   147 Coppermill Rd, WRAYSBURY, Berks, TW19 5NX.
     01753 683773
     http://www.acta4animals.com
     Sec: Jill Clark
○   *V; training & provision of animals for the film, television &
     advertising industries; provision of expert & professional
     advice; members must hold a valid licence under the
     Performing Animals (Regulation) Act 1925 & hold an
     adequate public liability insurance policy
M   30 i, 24 f, UK / 1 i, o'seas

**Animal Health Distributors Association (UK) Ltd   (AHDA)
1985**
■   Belmesthorpe Grange, Newstead Lane, STAMFORD, Lincs,
     PE9 4JJ.   (sp)
     01780 767757   fax 01780 767221
     email ian@ahda.org.uk   http://www.ahda.org.uk
     Sec Gen: Ian Scott
▲   Company Limited by Guarantee
○   *T; 'interests of distributors of animal health products -
     particularly those who distribute animal medicines to farmers
     (in order to try to prevent EU legislating members out of
     business)'
●   Conf - Mtgs - Exhib - LG
M   148 f, UK / 2 f, o'seas
¶   NL - 12.   Animal Medicines Record Book.

**Animal Medicines Training Regulatory Authority   (AMTRA)
1983**
■   Unit 1c Woolpit Business Park, Windmill Avenue, Woolpit, BURY
     ST EDMUNDS, IP30 9UP.   (hsb)
     01359 245801   fax 01359 242569
     email info@amtra.org.uk   http://www.amtra.org.uk
     Sec Gen: Stephen Dawson
▲   Company Limited by Guarantee
○   *N; independent regulatory body ensuring that the distribution
     of animal medicines in the UK is undertaken in a responsible
     manner by qualified persons
●   ET - Exam (for the staff of manufacturers) - LG - Register of
     those licensed to hold medicines & those qualified to
     distribute them
M   c 3,500 i
¶   AMTRA News - c 2-yrly.   AR.
     Syllabus & examination course leaflet.

Animal & Plant Health Association   (APHA)
IRL 8 Woodbine Park, BLACKROCK, Co Dublin, Republic of
     Ireland.
     353 (1) 260 3050   fax 353 (1) 260 3021
     email info@apha.ie   http://www.apha.ie
     Dir: Brendan Barnes
○   *F, *T, *V; manufacturers & sole distributors of veterinary
     medicines & plant protection products/agrochemicals
M   c 30 f

Animal Welfare Filming Federation   (AWFF)   1998
§   11 Hobshill Rd, GREAT MISSENDEN, Bucks, HP16 0BW.   (hsp)
     01494 442750
     email info@awff.com   http://www.mytvpetstar.com
     for those concerned with the welfare of animals used in film &
     TV

Anorchidism Support Group   (ASG)
■   PO Box 3025, ROMFORD, Essex, RM3 8GX.
     01708 372597
     email contact.asg@virgin.net
     Contact: Mrs Lorraine Bookless
○   *W; to support men & boys with anorchidism (congenital or
     acquired absence of the testes) & their families

Anrhydeddus Gymdeithas y Cymmrodorion
     Welsh name of the **Honourable Society of Cymmrodorion**

Anthony Powell Society   2000
■   76 Ennismore Avenue, GREENFORD, Middx, UB6 0JW.   (hsp)
     020 8864 4095   fax 020 8020 1483
     email secretary@anthonypowell.org
     http://www.anthonypowell.org.uk
     Hon Sec: Dr Keith C Marshall
▲   Registered Charity
Br 2 o'seas
○   *G; to advance for the public benefit, education & interest in
     the life & works of the English author Anthony Dymoke
     Powell (1905-2000)
●   Conf - Mtgs - ET - Res - Inf - VE
<   Alliance of Literary Socs
M   160 i UK / 100 i, o'seas
     (Sub: £22 UK / £28 o'seas)
¶   Secret Harmonies (Jnl) - 1; ftm, £7.50 nm.
     NL - 4; ftm, £3.50 nm.
     Anthony Powell & Oxford of the 1920s; £7 m, £11 nm.
     Dance Music: a guide to musical references in Anthony Powell's
     'A Dance to the Music of Time' (2010); £7 m, £11 nm.
     Other publications; all with postage charged to nm.

Anthroposophical Society in Great Britain   (ASinGB)   1923
■   Rudolf Steiner House, 35 Park Rd, LONDON, NW1 6XT.   (hq)
     020 7723 4400   fax 020 7724 4364
     email rsh-office@anth.org.uk
     http://www.anthroposophy.org.uk
▲   Registered Charity
○   *L; philosophy, art & education, based on the work of Rudolf
     Steiner - 'a union of human beings who desire to further the
     life of the soul, both in the individual & in society at large,
     based on a true knowledge of the spiritual world'
<   General Anthroposophical Soc (Switzerland)

Anti Academies Alliance
NR PO Box 14412, BIRMINGHAM, W Midlands, B11 9DZ.
     0752 820 1697
     http://www.antiacademies.org.uk
     Contact: Pete Jackson
○   *K; campaign against Academy schools as setting up a two-tier
     system in education

Anti Copying in Design Ltd   (ACID)   1996
NR PO Box 5078, GLOUCESTER CENTRAL, GL19 3YB.   (hq)
     0845 644 3617   fax 0845 644 3618
     email help@acid.uk.com   http://www.acid.uk.com
     Chief Exec: Dids Macdonald
▲   a not-for-profit organisation
○   *K; for all designers & manufacturers; to fight copyright theft; to
     raise awareness of intellectual property right
Gp Exhibitions & shows; Information service
●   Conf - Exhib - Inf

Anti Counterfeiting Group   (ACG)   1980
NR   PO Box 578, HIGH WYCOMBE, Bucks, HP11 1YD.   (hq)
    01494 449165   fax 01494 465052
    email admin@a-cg.com   http://www.a-cg.com
    Dir Gen: Ruth Orchard
▲   Company Limited by Guarantee
○   *T; to combat counterfeiting of branded products
Gp   Affiliates; Clothing & footwear; International; Public policy;
    Watches
●   Conf - Mtgs - ET - Res - Exhib - Comp - Stat - Inf - LG
<   Assn des Inds Marques (AIM); Alliance against Counterfeiting &
    Piracy (AACP)
M   130 f, UK / 44 f, o'seas
¶   NL - 5/6;   Enforcement Guides;
    Hbk;   AR - 1; all ftm only.

Anti-Graffiti Association
NR   Kemp House, 152-160 City Road, LONDON, EC1V 2NX.
    email info@theaga.org.uk   http://www.theaga.org.uk
○   *K, *T; 'to promote best practice in the management of graffiti,
    vandalism & related crime'

**Antiquarian Booksellers Association (International)   (ABA)
1906**
■   Sackville House, 40 Piccadilly, LONDON, W1J 0DR.   (hq)
    020 7439 3118   fax 020 7439 3119
    email admin@aba.org.uk   http://www.aba.org.uk
    Sec: John Critchley,   Pres: Robert Frew
▲   Company Limited by Guarantee (without a share capital)
○   *T; for dealers of rare books, manuscripts, maps, prints &
    ephemera in the British Isles
●   Lib - Books fairs - Benevolent fund
<   Intl League Antiquarian Booksellers
M   230 f, UK / 40 f, o'seas
¶   NL - 8;   AR - 1; both ftm only.
    LM (with geographical index & list of specialities); on request &
    on website.
    Book Fair Guide.

Antiquarian Horological Society   (AHS)   1953
■   New House, High St, Ticehurst, WADHURST, E Sussex,
    TN5 7AL.   (hq)
    01580 200155   fax 01580 201323
    email secretary@ahsoc.org   http://www.ahsoc.org
    Sec: Mrs Wendy B Barr
▲   Registered Charity
Br   6; Canada, USA
○   *L; to promote the study & conservation of timepieces
Gp   Electrical horology; Turret clock
●   Conf - Mtgs - ET - Res - Exhib - SG - Lib - VE
M   2,000 i, 100 f, 100 org
    (Sub: £44)
¶   Antiquarian Horology - 4; ftm, £40 nm.

Antique Metalware Society   (AMS)   1991
■   The Secretary AMS, Metalwork Section, Victoria & Albert
    Museum, Cromwell Rd, LONDON, SW7 2RL.   (hsb)
    020 7942 2079
    email s.seavers@vam.ac.uk
    http://www.oldcopper.org.uk/ams.htm
    Chmn: Tony North,   Sec: Stephanie Seavers
▲   Un-incorporated Society
○   *G; to study artifacts, mainly domestic, made of non-precious
    metals & their alloys, their manufacture & history
●   Mtgs - Res - VE
M   146 i, UK / 35 i, o'seas
    (Sub: £20 single, £28 joint)
¶   Jnl - 1;   Base Thoughts (NL) - 1; both ftm only.

Antiquities Dealers Association   (ADA)   1982
NR   Faustus Ancient Art & Jewellery, 67A Greencroft Gardens,
    LONDON, NW6 3LJ.   (hsb)
    020 7624 5908
    http://www.theada.co.uk
    Sec: Mrs Susan Hadida
○   *T; for dealers, professionals & collectors of antiquities
Gp   Dealers; Collectors (associates)
●   ET - Exhib - Inf - LG - International fairs
<   Museums Association; Brit Art Market Fedn (BAMF)
M   61 i, UK / 38 i (dealers) o'seas, 35 i associates (collectors)
¶   LM.

Anxiety UK   1970
§   Zion Community Resource Centre, 339 Stretford Rd, Hulme,
    MANCHESTER, Lancs, M15 4ZY.   (hq)
    0844 477 5774   fax 0161-227 9862
    email info@anxietyuk.org.uk
    http://www.anxietyuk.org.uk
▲   Registered Charity
    A registered charity supporting persons suffering with anxiety
    disorders; originally known as the National Phobics Society

Apostrophe Protection Society   2001
NR   23 Vauxhall Rd, BOSTON, Lincs, PE21 0JB.
    01205 350056
    email chairman@apostrophe.org.uk
    http://www.apostrophe.org.uk
    Chmn: John Richards
○   *K; to preserve the correct usage of the apostrophe in written
    English

Applied Earth Sciences Division
    a group of the **Institute of Materials, Minerals & Mining**

Applied Vision Association   1995
■   c/o Prof T Troscianko, Department of Experimental Psychology,
    University of Bristol, 12a Priory Road, BRISTOL, BS8 1TU.
    (sec/b)
    0117 928 8565
    email tom.troscianko@bristol.ac.uk
    http://www.theava.net
    Sec: Prof Tom Troscianko
○   *P; promoting vision research and its applications
●   Mtgs
M   c 450 i

**Approved Driving Instructors National Joint Council
(ADINJC)   1974**
NR   47 Sweetman's Road, SHAFTESBURY, Dorset, SP7 8EH.
    01747 855091
○   *N; a consortium of driving instructors associations representing
    the members in negotiations with official bodies likely to
    influence the sphere of their activities
●   Conf - Mtgs - ET - SG - VE - LG
M   6,500 i, 3 f
¶   Report of Annual Conference - 1; free.

Arab-British Chamber of Commerce   (ABCC)   1975
NR   43 Upper Grosvenor St, LONDON, W1K 2NJ.   (hq)
    020 7235 4363
    http://www.abcc.org.uk
○   *C

© CBD Research Ltd · Beckenham · BR3 5JS · Tel 020 8650 7745 · E-mail cbd@cbdresearch.com · www.cbdresearch.com

Arab Horse Society   1918

NR   Windsor House, Ramsbury, MARLBOROUGH, Wilts,
        SN8 2PE.   (hq)
        01672 521411
        email membership@arabhorsesociety.com
        http://www.arabhorsesociety.com
        Office Mgr: Maggie Court
▲   Company Limited by Guarantee; Registered Charity
○   *B, *S; breeding & importation of Arabian horses; encouraging
        the wider use of Arab blood in light horse breeding; welfare
        of horses; education of equestrian skills
<   Assn of Show & Agricl Orgs

Arboricultural Association   (AA)   1964

■   Ullenwood Court, Ullenwood, CHELTENHAM, Glos,
        GL53 9QS.   (hq)
        01242 522152   fax 01242 577766
        email admin@trees.org.uk   http://www.trees.org.uk
        Dir: Nick Eden
▲   Company Limited by Guarantee; Registered Charity
Br 9
○   *H, *P; to promote excellence in tree care to government,
        professionals & society
Gp Registered consultants; Approved contractors
●   Conf - ET - Exhib - LG - Publishing information - Promotion of
        competent consultants & specialists
<   Soc for the Envt (SocEnv)
M   1,600 i, 200 f, UK / 60 i, 25 f, o'seas
¶   Jnl - 4.   NL - 4.
        Directory of Approved Contractors; free.
        Directory of Registered Consultants; free.
        Guidance Note(s); all £12.50:
            1. Trees & Bats;
            3. Planting & Managing Amenity Woodlands;
            4. Amenity Valuation of Trees & Woodland.
        12 leaflets on maintenance of trees & hedges; £3 a set.
        publications list available.

ARCH - Action on Rights for Children   (ARCH)

NR   62 Wallwood Road, LONDON, E11 1AZ.
        020 8558 9317
○   *K

Archaeology Abroad   1972

■   31-34 Gordon Sq, LONDON, WC1H 0PY.   (mail/address)
        020 8537 0849
        email arch.abroad@ucl.ac.uk   http://www.britarch.ac.uk/
        archabroad
        Hon Sec & Editor: Wendy Rix Morton
▲   Un-incorporated Society
○   *G; to list opportunities for volunteers & staff to work on
        archaeological excavations outside the UK
●   Inf
M   427 i, 90 f, UK / 100 i, 10 f, o'seas
¶   Archaeology Abroad - 2; £20-£24 i, £30-£34 instns.
        Factsheets; free for large sae, (general guidance & information
        for those interested in fieldwork in countries from which few
        entries are received).

Archaeology Scotland   1988

NR   Stuart House (suite 1a), Eskmills, Station Rd, MUSSELBURGH,
        EH21 7PB.   (hq)
        0845 872 3333   fax 0845 872 3334
        email info@archaeologyscotland.org.uk
        http://www.archaeologyscotland.org.uk
        Dir: Eila Macqueen
▲   Company Limited by Guarantee; Registered Charity
○   *G; to promote the conservation, management, understanding
        & enjoyment of Scotland's heritage
Gp Education & outreach; Promoting our heritage; Supporting
        communities
●   Conf - Mtgs - VE
M   693 i, 96 org
¶   Archaeology Scotland - 3; ftm.
        Discovery & Excavation in Scotland - 1; ftm.
✕   2010 Council for Scottish Archaeology

Archery UK
        the trading name of the **Grand National Archery Society**

Archibald Knox Society

NR   c/o The Centre for Manx Studies, University of Liverpool,
        Stable Building, Old Castletown Rd, DOUGLAS, Isle of Man,
        IM2 1QB.   (mail/address)
        01624 695777
        email info@archibaldknowxsociety
        http://www.archibaldknoxsociety
        Dir: Liam O'Neill
▲   Company Limited by Guarantee; Registered Charity (IoM)
○   *A, *G; to promote the artistic life & works of Archibald Knox
        (1864-1933), water colourist & designer of art nouveau
        household articles as well as war memorials in the Isle of
        Man
M   i

Archif Menywod Cymru (Women's Archive of Wales)   1998

NR   7 Rhianfa Gardens, SWANSEA, Glam, SA1 6DH.   (hsp)
        01792 468237
        email info@womensarchivewales
        http://www.womensarchivewales.org
        Contact: Lesley Hulonce
▲   Registered Charity
○   *G; to raise the awareness of the history of women in Wales; to
        identify, rescue & preserve materials relevant to women's
        lives in Wales, past & present
●   Conf - ET - Res - Exhib
M   150 i, 20 org, UK / 3 i, o'seas
¶   NL - 4;   AR; both ftm.

Architectural & Archaeological Society for the County of Buckinghamshire   1847

■   County Museum, Church St, AYLESBURY, Bucks, HP20 2QP.
        (hq)
        01296 387341 (Wed: 1000-1600 only)
        email bucksas@buckscc.gov.uk
        http://www.bucksas.org.uk
        Hon Sec: Maureen Brown
▲   Registered Charity
○   *L
Gp Natural history section
●   Mtgs - Res - Lib - VE
<   Coun Brit Archaeol
M   500 i, 14 org, UK / 6 i, o'seas
¶   Records of Buckinghamshire - 1; ftm, £16 nm.
        NL - 2; ftm.

Architectural & Archaeological Society of Durham & Northumberland   (AASDN)   1861

- ■ Broom Cottage, 29 Foundry Fields, CROOK, Co Durham, DL15 9JY.   (hsp)
  01388 762620
  email belindalburke@aol.com   http://www.dur.ac.uk/archandarch.dandn
  Hon Sec: Mrs Belinda Burke
- ▲ Registered Charity
- ○ *G, *L; to stimulate interest in all aspects of the archaeology & architecture of North East England
- ● Mtgs - ET - Inf - VE
- M 124 i, 27 f
- ¶ Durham Archaeological Jnl - 1; ftm, £19 nm.

Architectural Association

- NR 34-36 Bedford Sq, LONDON, WC1B 3EG.
  020 7887 4000
- ○ *P

Architectural Cladding Association
  a product association of the **British Precast Concrete Federation**

Architectural Heritage Society of Scotland   (AHSS)   1956

- ■ The Glasite Meeting House, 33 Barony St, EDINBURGH, EH3 6NX.   (hq)
  0131-557 0019   fax 0131-557 0049
  email headoffice@ahss.org.uk   http://www.ahss.org.uk
  Chmn: Peter Drummond
- ▲ Company Limited by Guarantee; Registered Charity
- Br 6
- ○ *A, *G, *L; the protection, preservation, study & appreciation of Scotland's buildings
- ● Conf - Mtgs - Inf - VE - LG - Representations on applications for listed building consent
- < Soc Protection Ancient Bldgs; Georgian Gp; Victorian Soc; Nat Trust for Scotland; Scot Civic Trust; Twentieth Century Soc
- M 1,000 i
- ¶ Architectural Heritage Jnl - 1;   Magazine - 2.

Architectural & Specialist Door Manufacturers Association (ASDMA)   1989

- ■ 3 Coates Lane, HIGH WYCOMBE, Bucks, HP13 5EY.   (hsb)
  01494 447370   fax 01494 462094
  email specialdoors@gmail.com
  http://www.asdma.com
  Sec: Mrs L A Parry
- ○ *T; for specialists in timber doors & doorsets; to promote quality assured doors which meet all British & European standards of fire resistance & safety
- Gp Full membership open to manufacturers, fabricators & suppliers of doorsets;
  Associate membership open to companies providing associated components & services;
  Sponsor membership open to providers of relevant testing &/or certification services
- ● Mtgs - Inf - LG
- M 15 f (full), 11 f (associate), 1 sponsor
- ¶ The Facts on the Performance of Timber Doors & Doorsets.
  LM - 2;   Leaflet on ASDMA - 1; both free.
  Best Practice Guide to Timber Fire Doors (free download from website).

Architecture & Surveying Institute
  a specialist group of the **Chartered Institute of Building**

Archives & Records Association (GB & Ireland)   2010

- ■ Prioryfield House, 20 Canon St, TAUNTON, Somerset, TA1 1SW.   (hq)
  01823 327030   fax 01823 271719
  email societyofarchivists@archives.org.uk
  Admin: Lorraine Logan
- ○ *P
- ✕ 2010 (Association of Chief Archivists in Local Government
  (National Council on Archives
  (Society of Archivists

Aristotelian Society for the systematic study of philosophy   1870

- NR Stewart House (room 281), Russell Square, LONDON, WC1E 6BT.   (admin)
  020 7862 8685
  email mail@aristoteliansociety.org.uk
  http://www.aristoteliansociety.org.uk
  Exec Admin: Mark Cortes Favis
- ▲ Registered Charity
- ○ *L; to advance systematic study of philosophy
- ● Conf - Mtgs - Res
- < Brit Philosophical Assn
- M 500 i, UK / 150 i, o'seas
- ¶ Proceedings - 3 pts a yr (or 1 vol bound).
  Supplementary volume - 1;   Various other publications.

Arkwright Society   1971

- NR Cromford Mill, Mill Lane, CROMFORD, Derbys, DE4 3RQ.   (hq)
  01629 823256
  Chief Exec: Sarah McLeod
- ▲ Company Limited by Guarantee; Registered Charity
- ○ *L; the restoration of Sir Richard Arkwright's Cromford Mill; to preserve & promote conservation of buildings, monuments & machinery of industrial archaeological & historical interest
- ● Conf - Mtgs - ET - Res - Exhib - Inf - VE
- < Regeneration through Heritage; Nat Coun Civic Trust Socs
- M 250 i, 2 f
- ¶ NL - 4.   Cromford Venture Centre - 1.
  Lecture Programmes - 2.   AR & Accounts - 1.
  Cromford Venture Centre Prospectus - 1.

ARLIS/UK & Ireland: the Art Libraries Society   (ARLIS)   1969

- NR National Art Library, Victoria & Albert Museum, Cromwell Rd, LONDON, SW7 2RL.
  020 7942 2317
  email arlis@vam.ac.uk   http://www.arlis.org.uk
  Business Mgr: Natasha Held
- ▲ Registered Charity
- ○ *A, *L; for people & organisations with an interest in the documentation of art & design and the promotion of library & information services to artists, designers & architects
- ● Conf - Mtgs - ET - SG - Stat - VE
- < Library Assn; IFLA section of art libraries
- ¶ Art Libraries Jnl - 4.

Arms & Armour Society   1950

- NR PO Box 10232, LONDON, SW19 2ZD.   (hsb)
  01323 844278
  Hon Sec: Anthony Dove
- ○ *L, *Q; the study of arms & armour from the earliest times to the present day; to conserve specimens of arms & armour for the future
- ● Mtgs - Res - Inf - VE
- M i, f & org
- ¶ Jnl - 2 (Mar & Sep).   NL - 4.

© CBD Research Ltd · Beckenham · BR3 5JS · Tel 020 8650 7745 · E-mail cbd@cbdresearch.com · www.cbdresearch.com

Army Cadet Force Association (ACFA) 1930

- Holderness House, 51-61 Clifton St, LONDON, EC2A 4OW. (hq)
  020 7426 8377   fax 020 7426 8378
  email acfa@armycadets.com
  http://www.armycadets.com
  Gen Sec: Brig M Wharmby
▲ Company Limited by Guarantee; Registered Charity
Br 1,754
○ *Y; a voluntary youth organisation for 12-18 year old young
  men & women; to provide a challenging & stimulating
  environment & develop self respect & confidence through
  citizenship & service
● Conf - Mtgs - ET - Exhib - Comp - Inf - LG
< St John Ambulance; Heartstart; Duke of Edinburgh Award
> Nat Coun Voluntary Youth Orgs
M 50,000 i, 80 f, 20 orgs
¶ Jnl - 4; ftm, £20 nm.   AR - 1; ftm only.

Army Parachute Association (APA) 1963

NR Airfield Camp, Netheravon, SALISBURY, Wilts, SP4 9SF.   (hq)
  01980 628250
Br Cyprus, Germany
○ *S; runs courses of basic sports parachuting for members of all
  three services
Gp AFF (Accelerated Free Fall to gain competency in a quicker
  time); Tandem (the method of introducing non parachutists to
  sky diving with the minimum of instruction - approximately
  3/4 hour)
● ET - Res - Comp
< Brit Parachute Assn

Army Records Society 1983

NR School of ESPaCH, Crescent House, SALFORD,
  Greater Manchester, M5 4WT.   (hsb)
  email j.m.beach@salford.ac.uk
  http://www.armyrecordssociety.org.uk
  Hon Sec: Dr Jim Beach
▲ Registered Charity
○ *L; publication of original records concerning the history of the
  British Army
● Res - Annual lecture
M 350 i, 30 org UK / 100 i, 30 org, o'seas
¶ Annual Volume - 1; ftm only.

Arnold Bennett Society 1955

- 4 Field End Close, Trentham, STOKE-on-TRENT, Staffs,
  ST4 8DA.   (hsp)
  01782 641337
  http://www.arnoldbennettsociety.org.uk
  Hon Sec: Carol Gorton
▲ Un-incorporated Society
○ *A; to promote the study & appreciation of the life, works &
  times of Arnold Bennett (1867-1931) & other provincial
  writers with particular reference to North Staffordshire
● Mtgs
< Alliance of Literary Socs
M 250 i, UK / 25 i, o'seas
¶ NL - 3; ftm, £1 nm.

Aromatherapy & Allied Practitioners Association (AAPA) 1994

NR 14 Orleans Rd, Upper Norwood, LONDON, SE19 3TA.
  (chmn/p)
  020 8653 9152
  email enquiries@aapa.org.uk   http://www.aapa.org.uk
  Chmn: Joyce West
○ *P; to develop the profession & support therapists
< Aromatherapy Coun

Aromatherapy Trade Council (ATC) 1993

- PO Box 387, IPSWICH, Suffolk, IP2 9AN.   (mail/address)
  01473 603630   fax 01473 603630
  email info@a-t-c.org.uk   http://www.a-t-c.org.uk
  Admin: Sylvia Baker,   Chmn: Geoff Lyth
▲ Company Limited by Guarantee
○ *T; to act as the authoritative body for the specialist
  aromatherapy essential oil industry; to promote consumer
  safety through safe usage of essential oils; to offer advice on
  the responsible marketing of aromatherapy products
● Conf - Mtgs - Res - Exhib - Expt - Inf - LG
< Eur Fedn of Essential Oils (EFEO); Parliamentary Gp for
  Alternative & Complementary Medicine
M 58 f
¶ Guidelines on the Regulation, Labelling, Advertising &
  Promotion of Aromatherapy Products - irreg; £50 m,
  £100 nm.
  General Information Booklet.   LM.

Arrhythmia Alliance (A-A)

- PO Box 3697, STRATFORD-upon-AVON, Warks, CV37 8YL.
  (hq)
  01789 450787 (24-hour)
  email info@heartrhythmcharity.org.uk
  http://www.heartrhythmcharity.org.uk
  Chief Exec: Mrs Trudi Lobban
▲ Registered Charity
○ *W; a patient support group for those with heart rhythm
  disorders; aims to promote better understanding, diagnosis,
  treatment & quality of life for individuals with cardiac
  arrhythmia. Members include medical professionals, industry,
  patients, carers & parent groups
● Conf - Mtgs - ET - Exhib - Inf - LG - Parent support helpline
< Brit Cardiovascular Soc
> Arrhythmia Alliance Portugal; APPCC (Italy): Brit Cardiovascular
  Soc
M [not stated]

Art & Architecture (A&A) 1972

NR 70 Cowcross St, LONDON, EC1M 6EJ.   (mail/address)
  http://www.artandarchitecture.co.uk
▲ Un-incorporated Society
○ *A, *K; promotes collaboration between artists, crafts people &
  architects in the interests of a better environment; campaigns
  for the Percent for Art scheme & for the employment of art &
  artists in architecture & construction; acts as a network for all
  concerned with public art
M i, f & org

The Art Fund
see **National Art Collections Fund** (the Art Fund)

Art Libraries Society
see **ARLIS/UK & Ireland (the Art Libraries Society)**

Art Metalware Manufacturers' Association
has closed

Art Workers Guild (AWG) 1884

NR 6 Queen Sq, LONDON, WC1N 3AT.   (hq)
  020 7713 0966   fax 020 7713 0967
  email monica@artworkersguild.org
  http://www.artworkersguild.org
  Sec: Monica Grose-Hodge
○ *A; a society of artists, craftsmen & designers with a common
  interest in the interaction, development & distribution of
  creative skills

Arthritic Association (AA) 1942
■ 1 Upperton Gardens, EASTBOURNE, E Sussex, BN21 2AA.
   01323 416550   fax 01323 639793
   email info@arthriticassociation.org.uk
   http://www.arthriticassociation.org.uk
   Mgr: Bruce Hester
▲ Company Limited by Guarantee; Registered Charity
○ *M; to relieve symptoms of arthritis by natural methods
● Res - Inf
M 3,900 i, UK / 100 i, o'seas
¶ Rheumatic Review - Jnl.   Treating Arthritis Naturally.
   A Balanced View: Practical Tips for a Healthy Diet.
   Recipes Compiled for the Arthritic Association.
   [subscription £6].

Arthritis Care 1947
NR 18 Stephenson Way, LONDON, NW1 2HD.   (hq)
    020 7380 6500
    email info@arthritiscare.org.uk
    http://www.arthritiscare.org.uk
    Interim Chief Exec: Susie Parsons
▲ Company Limited by Guarantee; Registered Charity
Br 6
○ *W; a national voluntary organisation working with & for
   people with arthritis
● ET - Publishing - Campaigning
   Helpline: 0808 800 4050
M i
¶ Arthritis News - 6;   Information & advisory leaflets.
   Publications list available.

Arthritis & Musculoskeletal Alliance (ARMA) 1972
NR Bride House, 18-20 Bride Lane, LONDON, EC4Y 8EE.   (hq)
    020 7842 0910
▲ Registered Charity
○ *N; an umbrella organisation of professional & user groups
   working together to ensure high quality services are
   maintained for people with arthritis

Arthrogryposis Group (TAG) 1984
■ PO Box 5336, STOURPORT-on-SEVERN, Worcs, DY13 3BE.
   (hq)
   0800 028 4447
   email info@taguk.org.uk
   Chmn: Emmeline McChieery
▲ Registered Charity
○ *W; to offer support, contact & information for the families,
   children & adults affected with arthrogryposis, & those
   involved in their care; also known as Arthrogryposis Multiplex
   Congenita, is congenital disorder that causes joint
   contractures, muscle weakness & fibrosis
● Conf - Mtgs - Res - Inf - VE - Activity camps for young people
   aged 10-15
M 800 i, 12 org, UK / 40 i, o'seas
¶ Tag Talk - 4; ftm.

Arthur Findlay Society
NR 5 Muirfield, Bushmead, LUTON, Beds, LU2 7SB.
    01582 512184
    http://www.arthurfindlay.com
    Founder: Peter George Wakeham
○ *A; The works and writings of James Arthur Findlay (1883-
   1964)

Arthur Ransome Society Ltd (TARS) 1990
■ Abbot Hall, Kirkland, KENDAL, Cumbria, LA9 5AL.
   (regd/office)
   01539 722464
   email tarsinfo@arthur-ransome.org
   http://www.arthur-ransome.org
   Co Sec: Peter Hyland
▲ Company Limited by Guarantee
Br 5; Australia, Canada, Japan, New Zealand, USA
○ *A; to promote the works of Arthur Ransome (1884-1967) &
   support research into his life & writings; to encourage
   children in the reading of his books & to participate in
   outdoor activities
● Conf - Mtgs - Res - Lib - VE
< Alliance of Literary Socs
M 1,200 i, UK / 260 i, o'seas
¶ Mixed Moss (Jnl) - 1;   Outlaw (junior magazine) - 2;
   Signals (NL) - 3;   all ftm only.

Arts & Business 1976
NR Nutmeg House, 60 Gainsford St, LONDON, SE1 2NY.   (hq)
    020 7378 8143
    http://www.aandb.org.uk
▲ Company Limited by Guarantee; Registered Charity
Br 13
○ *A, *T; to promote & encourage partnership between business
   & the arts
Gp Development forum
● Conf - Mtgs - ET - Res - Stat - Inf - Lib - LG
< Coun for Business & the Arts in Canada; CEREC; Foundation
   for Business in Support of the Arts (Hong Kong); Assn for
   Corporate Support of the Arts (Japan)
M c 350 f, 700 org
¶ Re-creating Communities: business, the arts & regeneration.
   AR (incl LM) - 1.

Arts Centre Group (ACG) 1971
■ The Menier Chocolate Factory (1st floor), 51-53 Southwark St,
   LONDON, SE1 1BU.   (hq)
   0845 458 1881; 020 7407 1881
   email info@artscentregroup.org.uk
   http://www.artscentregroup.org.uk
   Sec: Susanne Scott
▲ Company Limited by Guarantee; Registered Charity
○ *A; to provide a network & support for Christians professionally
   involved in the arts, media & entertainment business
Gp Actors; Architects; Arts admin; Dancers; Designers;
   Entertainment; Fashion & Textiles; Graphics; Media;
   Musicians; Photographers; Teachers; Visual artists; Writers
● Mtgs - ET - Exhib - Comp
M 500 i, 15 f, 20 org, UK / 30 i, 5 f, 10 org, o'seas
   (Sub: £50 profl, £35 friend)
¶ E-info - 12; ftm only.

Arts Development UK 1997
■ Oak Villa (off Amman Rd), Lower Brynamman, AMMANFORD,
   Carmarthenshire, SA18 1SN.   (hq)
   01269 824728   fax 01269 824728
   http://www.artsdevelopmentuk.org
▲ Registered Charity
○ *A, *P; for logal government arts officers & those in the creative
   industries sector
Gp Local authority arts officers &those working in the creative
   industries sector
● Conf - Mtgs - ET - Res - SG - Stat - Inf - VE - LG
M 45 i, 333 f, 34 org
¶ NL - 3; ftm only.
× 2010 National Association of Local Government Arts Officers

© CBD Research Ltd · Beckenham · BR3 5JS · Tel 020 8650 7745 · E-mail cbd@cbdresearch.com · www.cbdresearch.com

Arts Marketing Association   (AMA)   1993

■ 7A Clifton Court, CAMBRIDGE, CB1 7BN.   (hq)
  01223 578078
  email info@a-m-a.co.uk   http://www.a-m-a.org.uk
  Dir: Julie Aldridge
▲ Company Limited by Guarantee
○ *P; professional development in arts marketing
Gp Freelancers
● Conf - ET - Inf
M c 1,800 i
¶ Jnl of Arts Marketing - 4.   Ybk.   Books.

Arts Society of Ulster   (RUA)

NR 5 Church Close, Ballylesson, BELFAST, BT8 8JX.   (sp)
  028 9032 0819
  email liz.shanks@ntlworld.com
  http://www.artssocietyofulster.com
  Sec: Liz Shanks
○ *A, *P
M 130 i

ArtWatch UK

NR 15 Capel Rd, EAST BARNET, Herts, EN4 8JD.
  020 8216 3492
  email information@artwatch.org.uk
  Dir: Michael Daley
○ *A, *K; to preserve the integrity of works of art from over-
  ambitious restoration
M c 150 i
¶ NL - 4.

ASBCI - the Forum for Clothing & Textiles   (ASBCI)   1974

■ Unit 5, 25 Square Rd, HALIFAX, W Yorks, HX1 1QG.   (hq)
  01422 354666   fax 01422 381184
  email info@asbci.co.uk   http://www.asbci.co.uk
  Co Sec: Stephanie Ingham,   Chmn: Malcolm Ball
▲ Company Limited by Guarantee
○ *T; 'a recognised centre of excellence where companies at the
  forefront of their specific sectors can discuss, share & develop
  practices, processes & initiatives that will benefit their
  organisations & the UK clothes & textile supply chain as a
  whole'
Gp C'ees: Ball, Conference, Marketing, Student membership,
  Technical
● Conf - Mtgs - ET - Comp - Inf - VE
< Soc of Dyers & Colourists (SDC); Textile Inst
> Soc of Dyers & Colourists; Textile Inst
M 10 i, 80 f, 3 org
¶ Technical booklets available - details on website; £10 m,
  £15 nm.
  Conference Proceedings booklets; £30.

Asbestos Removal Contractors Association   (ARCA)   1980

■ Unit 1 Stretton Business Park 2, Brunel Drive, BURTON upon
  TRENT, Staffs, DE13 0BY.   (hq)
  01283 566467   fax 01283 568228
  email info@arca.org.uk   http://www.arca.org.uk
  Chief Exec: Stephen Sadley
▲ Company Limited by Guarantee
○ *T; for HSE licensed contractors & UKAS accredited asbestos
  testing & inspection laboratories
● Conf - Mtgs - ET - Exam - Inf - LG
M 30 i, 320 f
¶ ARCA News - 4; ftm, £20 yr nm.   AR - 1.

Asbestos Testing & Consultancy Association   (ATaC)

NR Unit 1 Stretton Business Park 2, Brunel Drive, BURTON UPON
  TRENT, Staffs, DE13 0BY.   (hq)
  01283 566467
  http://www.atac.org.uk
○ *T; for asbestos testing & consultancy specialists

ASET, the Work-based & Placement Learning Association   (ASET)   1982

NR Broomgrove, 59 Clarkehouse Rd, SHEFFIELD, S Yorks,
  S10 2LE.   (hq)
  0114-221 2902   fax 0114-221 2903
  email aset@asetonline.org   http://www.asetonline.org
  Admin: Keith Fildes
▲ Company Limited by Guarantee; Registered Charity
○ *E; to develop, promote & implement the concept of higher
  education courses that integrate periods of relevant work in
  an employing organisation
● Conf - Mtgs - Res - Exhib - Comp - Stat - LG
M 47 i, 110 f & universities, UK / 2 i, 2 f, o'seas
¶ ASET Directory of Sandwich Courses - 1.
✕ 2008 Association for Sandwich Education & Training

Ashmolean Natural History Society of Oxfordshire   (ANHSO)   1828

NR Oxford University Museum of Natural History, Parks Rd,
  OXFORD, OX1 3PW.   (mtgs)
  http://www.anhso.org.uk
▲ Un-incorporated Society
○ *L; natural science
Gp Education; Fritillary; Rare plants; Verge survey
● Mtgs - Comp - Lib - VE - Survey of rare plants
M 100 i
¶ Fritillary (Jnl) - 4; (produced in conjunction with the Berks,
  Bucks & Oxon Naturalists' Trust).

Asian Business Association
  a special interest group of the **London Chamber of Commerce &
  Industry**

Aslib: The Association for Information Management   (aslib)   1924

NR Howard House, Wagon Lane, BINGLEY, W Yorks, BD16 1WA.
  (hq)
  01274 777700
  email aslib@aslib.com   http://www.aslib.com
▲ Registered Charity
○ *L, *P, *Q; to promote better management & provision of
  information in information centres & libraries
M i, f & org

Asparagus Growers' Association

■ PVGA House, Nottingham Rd, LOUTH, Lincs, LN11 0WB.
  (asa)
  01507 602427   fax 01507 600689
  email jayne.dyas@pvga.co.uk
  http://www.british-asparagus.co.uk
  Sec: Mrs Jayne Dyas
○ *T; to provide technical, commercial & marketing information
  for growers
● Conf - Mtgs - Res - Exhib - Stat - Inf - LG
M 120 f

Asphalt Industry Alliance   2000

NR 14a Eccleston St, LONDON, SW1W 9LT.   (hq)
  020 7730 1100   fax 020 7730 2213
  email asphalt@hmpr.co.uk
  http://www.asphaltindustryalliance.com
▲ Un-incorporated Society
○ *T; to promote adequate funding of road maintenance
● Conf - Mtgs - Res - Stat - Inf - LG
M 2 org:
  Mineral Products Association
  Refined Bitumen Association
¶ Asphalt Now - 2;
  Annual Local Authority Road Maintenance Survey - 1; both free.

Asset Based Finance Association   (ABFA)   1996

NR   20 Hill Rise (3rd floor), RICHMOND, Surrey, TW10 6UA.   (hq)
   020 8332 9955   fax 020 8332 2585
   http://www.factors.org.uk
   Chief Exec: Kate Sharp
▲   Company Limited by Guarantee; Registered Charity
○   *P; an association of British & Irish companies in business to
   business financial services
●   Conf - Mtgs - ET - Exam - Stat - Inf - LG
M   42 f
¶   NL - 4; ftm & limited associated companies
✕   2007 Factors & Discounters Association

Asset Disposal & Information Security Alliance   (ADISA)

NR   The Ice House, 124 Walcot Street, BATH, Somerset,
   BA1 5BG.   (hq)
   0845 833 1600
   http://www.adisa.org.uk
○   *T; 'for professionals to operate for & between asset owners,
   data controllers & providers of data destruction & IT
   recycling services'

Associated National Electrical Wholesalers   (ANEW)   1993

NR   Titmore Court (suite 3), Titmore Green, Little Wymondley,
   HITCHIN, Herts, SG4 7JT.   (hq)
   email office@anew.co.uk   http://www.anew.co.uk
   Chief Exec: Neal Wilcox
▲   Company Limited by Guarantee
○   *T; a buying consortium of electrical wholesalers
●   Mtgs
M   31 f totalling 331 branches
¶   LM - on website.

Associated Train Crew Union   (ATCU)   2005

NR   PO Box 647, BARNSLEY, S Yorks, S72 8XU.
   01226 16417
   email admin@atcu.org.uk   http://www.atcu.org.uk
   Chmn of Formation C'ee: Steven Trumm
▲   Un-incorporated Society
Br   9
○   *U; non-affiliated, non-political
Gp   Crew section; Driver section
●   Representation - Legal cover
M   50 i

Association for Accountancy & Business Affairs   (AABA)

NR   PO Box 5874, BASILDON, Essex, SS16 5FR.
   http://www.aabaglobal.org
▲   Company Limited by Guarantee
○   *K; to broaden public choices & to advance public policy
   reform
M   i
   (Sub: £10)

Association of Accounting Technicians   (AAT)   1980

NR   140 Aldersgate St, LONDON, EC1A 4HY.
   020 7397 3000
   http://www.aat.org.uk
   Chief Exec: Miss Jane Scott Paul
▲   Registered Charity
○   *E, *P; a vocational training body awarding NVs/SVQs levels 2,
   3 & 4 in accounting
M   22,000 i, UK / 3,000 i, o'seas

Association for Achievement and Improvement through Assessment   (AAIA)

NR   2 Laneside Drive, HINCKLEY, Leics, LE10 1TG.   (mem/sp)
   Mam Sec: Elizabeth Lewin
○   *P; to 'promote pupil achievment through the processes of
   effective assessment, recording & reporting'

Association of Advertisers in Ireland Ltd   (AAI)   1951

IRL   Fitzwilliam Business Centre, 26 Upper Pembroke St, DUBLIN 2,
   Republic of Ireland.
   353 (1) 637 3950   fax 353 (1) 637 3954
   email info@aai.ie   http://www.aai.ie
   Hon Sec: Catherine Bent
○   *T

Association of Air Ambulances   (AAA)

NR   East of England Ambulance Service, Bedford Locality Office,
   Hammond Rd, BEDFORD, Beds, MK41 0RG.   (chmn/b)
   01234 408974
   email info@airambulanceassociation.co.uk
   http://www.airambulanceassociation.co.uk
   Chmn: Hayden Newton
○   *N; to be the representative body for all air ambulance services
   in the UK; to ensure close cooperation between the services,
   the ambulance service & charities
M   c 32 centres

Association of Alabaster Importers & Wholesalers   (AAI)   1977

■   Kingswey House, Wrootham Rd, Meopham, GRAVESEND, Kent,
   DA13 0AU.   (hsp)
○   *T; interests of importers of unworked alabaster & articles made
   of alabaster
●   Mtgs - Inf - Lib - Stat - VE
M   7 f

Association of American Dancing   (AAD)   1936

■   Aspenshaw Hall, THORNSETT, High Peak, Derbys,
   SK22 1AU.   (hq)
   01663 744986
   Dir: Miss Anna Scott
▲   Un-incorporated Society
○   *D; an examining body promoting all forms of dance
   movement amongst professionals, teachers & the public
Gp   Modern art group (for younger people)
●   ET - Exam - Inf - Scholarships & awards
<   Coun for Dance Educ & Training
M   i (through examination qualification)
¶   Text books covering the five disciplines of dance within the
   syllabus.

Association of Amusement & Leisure Equipment Suppliers of the UK   (ALES(UK))

■   c/o TSI Ltd, 74 Kilbury Drive (1st floor), WORCESTER,
   WR5 2NG.   (sb)
   01905 360169   fax 01905 360172
   email ales@alesuk.org   http://www.alesuk.org
   Hon Sec: Gerry Robinson
▲   Un-incorporated Society
○   *T; the interests of UK registered manufacturers & suppliers of
   non-gambling amusement & related leisure equipment &
   services
Gp   Inflatable manufacturers & suppliers; Safety
●   Conf - ET - Res - Exhib - Expt - Inf - LG
<   World Water Park Assn; Associazione Nazionale Costruttori
   Attrezzature Spettacoli Viaggienti (Italy); Asociación de
   Fabricantes Exportadores Maquinas de la Foia de
   Bunyol (Spain)
M   48 f
   (Sub: £100)
¶   NL (email) - 6 weekly; free.
✕   2010 (July) Inflatable Play Manufacturers Association (merged)

© CBD Research Ltd · Beckenham · BR3 5JS · Tel 020 8650 7745 · E-mail cbd@cbdresearch.com · www.cbdresearch.com

Association of Anaesthetists of Great Britain & Ireland (AAGBI) 1932

NR 21 Portland Place, LONDON, W1B 1PY. (hq)
    020 7631 1650
▲ Company Limited by Guarantee
○ *L, *Q; to promote & support the speciality of anaesthesia
● Conf - ET - Exhib - Inf - Lib - Seminars
< R Coll Anaesthetists
M c 5,200 i
¶ Publications list available.

Association of Anatomical Pathology Technology

NR 12 Coldbath Square, LONDON, EC1R 5HL. (sb)
    020 7278 2151
    email mail@aaptuk.org   http://www.aaptuk.org
    Sec: Christian Burt
○ *P

Association of Applied Biologists (AAB) 1904

NR Warwick Enterprise Park, Wellesbourne, WARWICK,
    CV35 9EF. (hq)
    01789 472020   fax 01789 470234
    email carol@aab.org.uk   http://www.aab.org.uk
    Hon Gen Sec: A J Keys
▲ Registered Charity
○ *L, *Q; 'to promote the study & advancement of all branches of
    biology & in particular (but without prejudice to the generality
    of the foregoing) to foster the practice, growth &
    development of applied biology, incl the application of
    biological sciences for the production & preservation of food,
    fibre & other materials for the maintenance & improvement
    of the environment'
Gp Applied micrology & bacteriology; Biological control; Cropping
    & the environment; Food systems; Nematology; Pesticide
    application; Plant physiology & crop improvement; Post
    harvest biology; Virology
● Conf - Mtgs - ET - Publication of scientific research
< Assn of Learned & Profl Soc Publishers; Inst Biology
M 800 i, UK / 100 i, o'seas
¶ Annals of Applied Biology (Jnl) - 6.   NL - 3; ftm only.
    Aspects of Applied Biology (proceedings of conferences) - irreg.
    Descriptions of Plant Viruses (CD-ROM) - irreg.

Association of Aquarists

■ 21 Oakdene, Chobham, WOKING, Surrey, GU24 8PS.
    http://www.fishkeepers.org
    Mem Sec: Ruth Kinder
○ *G

Association of Archaeological Illustrators & Surveyors (AAI&S) 1978

■ c/o IFA/SHES, University of Reading, Whiteknights, PO Box 227,
    READING, Berks, RG6 6AB. (mail/address)
    email admin@aais.org.uk   http://www.aais.org.uk
    Hon Sec: Lesley Collett
○ *P; to set standards & promote best practice within the
    profession
● Conf - Production of special technical reports on special
    material or technique
M c 254 i, UK & o'seas
¶ Graphic Archaeology (Jnl) - 2.   AAI&S NL - 4.
    Technical Papers (1-13) - irreg.

Association of Art & Antique Dealers Ltd (LAPADA) 1974

NR 535 Kings Rd, LONDON, SW10 0SZ. (hq)
    020 7823 3511   fax 020 7823 3522
    email lapada@lapada.co.uk   http://www.lapada.co.uk
    Chief Exec: John Newgas
▲ Company Limited by Guarantee
○ *T; for professional art & antiques dealers
Gp Antiques dealers; Art dealers; Specialist shippers; Art &
    antiques valuers & restorers
● Conf - Stat - Expt - Inf - LG - Fairs
< Confédn Intle des Négociants en Oeuvres d'Art (CINOA); other
    local associations
M 700 f, UK / 25 f, o'seas
¶ LAPADA Views (NL) - 2; ftm.   LM - 1; free.

Association of Art Historians (AAH) 1974

NR 70 Cowcross St, LONDON, EC1M 6EJ. (hq)
    020 7490 3211   fax 020 7490 3277
    email admin@aah.org.uk   http://www.aah.org.uk
    Chmn: Colin Cruise
▲ Registered Charity
○ *P; to promote the study of art history & visual culture; to ensure
    a wider public recognition of the field.
    Is the national organisation for professional art historians &
    researchers (including academics, teachers, students &
    museum & gallery professionals)
Gp Independent & freelance art historians; Museum & gallery
    professionals; School teachers; University & college
    academics; Students
● Conf - Mtgs - Res - Comp - VE - Empl - LG
< Comité Intl d'Histoire de l'Art (CIHA); College Art Assn
    (CAA)(USA); Intl Assn of Art Critics (AICA)
M c 1,200 i
¶ Art History (Jnl) - 5;   The Art Book (Jnl) - 4;
    Bulletin (NL) - 3; details on application.

Association for Astronomy Education (AAE) 1980

NR c/o Royal Astronomical Society, Burlington House, Piccadilly,
    LONDON, W1J 0BQ. (mail/address)
    http://www.aae.org.uk
    Sec: Dr Anne Urquhart-Potts
▲ Registered Charity
○ *E; to promote & advance public education in the science of
    astronomy; to support the teaching of astronomy at all levels
    of education
● Conf - Mtgs - ET
M i & org
¶ Gnomon (NL) - 4; ftm.

Association of ATOL Companies (AAC) 1995

■ Regal House (5th floor), 70 London Rd, TWICKENHAM, Middx,
    TW1 3QS. (secretariat)
    020 8607 9539   fax 020 8944 2993
    email secretariat@aac-uk.org   http://www.aac-uk.org
    Contact: Ian Hawkes
○ *T
● Mtgs - LG
M 65 f

Association of Authorised Public Accountants Ltd (AAPA) 1978

■ 10 Lincoln's Inn Fields, LONDON, WC2A 3BP. (hq)
    020 7059 5916
    http://www.aapa.co.uk
    Sec: Ros Leah
▲ Company Limited by Guarantee
○ *P; 'a recognised Supervisory Body under the provisions of the
    Companies Act 1989.   No student membership or
    examinations are held as all members must already be fully
    qualified under the provisions of the Companies Act 1985
    section 389(1)(b) or section 389(2)'
● Conf - LG
< is part of the Association of Chartered Certified Accountants
M c 200 f, UK / 50 f, o'seas
¶ Accounting Business (Jnl) - 10.   NL   LM.   AR.

Association of Authors' Agents   (AAA)   1974
NR   Watson, Little Ltd, 48-56 Bayham Place, LONDON,
     NW1 0EU.   (hsb)
     020 7388 7529
     email jw@watsonlittle.com
     http://www.agentsassoc.co.uk
     Sec: James Wills
▲   Un-incorporated Society
○   *T; to act as a forum for authors' agents
M   f

Association for Automatic Identification & Mobile Data Capture   (AIMUK)   1984
■   The Old Vicarage, All Souls Rd, HALIFAX, W Yorks, HX3 6DR.
     (hq)
     01422 368368
     http://www.aimuk.org
     Business Devt Mgr: Neil G Smith
○   *T; for automatic data capture industry - bar codes, radio
     frequency identification & communication, optical character
     recognition, magnetic strip cards, voice recognition
✕   2007-08 Automatic Identification Manufacturers & Suppliers
     Association

Association of Average Adjusters   (AAA)   1869
NR   c/o The Baltic Exchange, St Mary Axe, LONDON, EC3A 8BH.
     (sb)
     020 7623 5501   fax 020 7369 1623
     email AAA@balticexchange.com
     http://www.Average-Adjusters.com
     Chmn: Nigel Rogers
▲   Un-incorporated Society
○   *P
●   ET - Exam
M   450 i
¶   AR; ftm.

Association of Aviation Medical Examiners   (AAME)
NR   The Tollgate, Staverton Rd, DAVENTRY, Northants, NN11 4NN.
     email enquiries@aame.org.uk
     Hon Sec: Dr Kevin Herbert
○   *P

Association of Bakery Ingredient Manufacturers   (ABIM)   1917
NR   6 Catherine St, LONDON, WC2B 5JU.   (asa)
     020 7420 7113   fax 020 7836 0580
     email geraldine.albon@fdf.org.uk
     http://www.abim.org.uk
     Exec Sec: Geraldine Albon
▲   Company Limited by Guarantee
○   *T; to represent the interests of manufacturers & suppliers of
     ingredients & mixes to the baking industry
●   Mtgs - Inf
<   EEC Assn of Suppliers of Raw Materials to the Baking
     Ind (FEDIMA); Food & Drink Fedn; UK Baking Ind
     Consultative C'ee (UKBICC)
M   17 f

Association of Basic Science Teachers in Dentistry   (ABSTD)   1978
■   Oral Biology, Leeds Dental Institute, Clarendon Way, LEEDS,
     W Yorks, LS2 9LU.   (hsb)
     0113-343 6170
     email r.c.shore@leeds.ac.uk   http://www.abstd.org
     Hon Sec: Roger Shore
▲   Registered Charity
○   *E, *P; university lecturers concerned with education in dentistry
●   Conf - Mtgs
M   110 i
¶   NL - 2/3; free.

Association of Bee Appliance Manufacturers of Great Britain   1960
NR   Beehive Works, WRAGBY, Lincs, LN8 5LA.   (hsb)
     01673 858555
     Contact: Paul Smith
○   *T; to represent the trade at exhibitions, shows & in meetings
     with Defra & BBKA

Association of Biomedical Andrologists   (ABA)
NR   Fertility Unit, Queen's Medical Centre, NOTTINGHAM,
     NG7 2UH.   (reg/add)
     0114-226 8290
     http://www.aba.uk.net
○   *P

Association of Blind Piano Tuners   (ABPT)   1953
■   31 Wyre Crescent, Lynwood, DARWEN, Lancs, BB3 0JG.   (hsp)
     01254 776148   fax 01254 773158
     email abpt@uk-piano.org   http://www.uk-piano.org/
     abpt
     Sec: Barrie Heaton
▲   Registered Charity
Br   4; 9 o'seas
○   *P; to give all possible assistance to blind piano tuners in
     carrying out their work
●   Conf - ET
M   80 i
¶   ABPT NL - 4 (on cassette).

Association of Block Paving Contractors
     see Interlay, an affiliated association of the **British Precast
     Concrete Federation**

Association for Boarding School Survivors   1990
NR   6 Chester Court, Lissenden Gardens, LONDON, NW5 1LY.
     020 7267 7098
     http://www.boardingschoolsurvivors.co.uk
○   *K, *W; to raise public consciousness about the psychological
     effects of sending children to boarding school

Association of Boat Safety Examiners   (ABSE)
■   89 Higher Lane, Rainford, ST HELENS, Merseyside,
     WA11 8BQ.   (chmn/p)
     01744 882856
     http://www.abse.org.uk
     Chmn: John Bromilow
▲   Un-incorporated Society
○   *P
●   Mtgs - Inf - Lib
M   132 i
¶   The Examiner - 4; ftm only.

Association of Breast Surgery   (ABS)   2010
NR   c/o Royal College of Surgeons, 35-43 Lincoln's Inn Fields,
     LONDON, WC2A 3PE.
     020 7869 6853
     email office@asgbi.org.uk
○   *P; 'to advance the practice of breast surgery for the benefit of
     patients with benign & malignant breast disease'
●   Mtgs
M   i
✕   until March 2010 was a specialist group of BASO ~ the
     Association for Cancer Surgery

© CBD Research Ltd · Beckenham · BR3 5JS · Tel 020 8650 7745 · E-mail cbd@cbdresearch.com · www.cbdresearch.com

Association of Breastfeeding Mothers   (ABM)   1980
■   Woodpecker House, Henny Rd, Lamarsh, BURES, Suffolk,
      CO8 5EX.   (mail/add)
      0844 412 2948
      email info@abm.me.uk   http://www.abm.me.uk
      Sec: Nyree Davis
▲   Registered Charity
○   *W; to provide education in the techniques & benefits of
      breastfeeding; to train breastfeeding counsellors
●   Conf - ET - Inf
M   600 i, UK / 50 i, o'seas
      (Sub: £18)
¶   ABM Magazine - 3; ftm.
      Breastfeeding Leaflets.   AR.
      List of publications available.

Association of Brickwork Contractors Ltd   (ABC)   2004
NR   The Building Centre, 26 Store St, LONDON, WC1E 7BT.   (hq)
      020 7323 7036   fax 020 7580 3795
      email info@brickworkcontractors.info
      http://www.brickworkcontractors.info
      Chief Exec: Michael Driver
▲   Company Limited by Guarantee
○   *T; to promote quality brickwork by training of operatives &
      health & safety of site workers
●   Mtgs - Inf - LG
M   24 f, 10 associates
¶   [NL - 2; free. To come]

Association of British Bookmakers Ltd   2002
NR   Warwick House, 25 Buckingham Palace Rd, LONDON,
      SW1W 0PP.   (hq)
      020 7434 2111
      http://www.abb.uk.com
▲   Company Limited by Guarantee
○   *T; for off-course bookmakers
Gp   Racing security; Technical
M   f

Association for British Brewery Collectables   (ABBC)   1983
■   47 Peartree Avenue, Bitterne, SOUTHAMPTON, Hants,
      SO19 7JN.   (ed/p)
      email mike.breweriana@gmail.com
      http://www.abbclist.info
      Newsletter Editor: Mike Peterson
▲   Un-incorporated Society
○   *G; to promote the hobby of collecting brewery memorabilia
●   Mtgs - Res - Inf
M   150 i
¶   What's Bottling - 6; £7 m only.

Association of British Certification Bodies   (ABCB)   1984
NR   Sandover Centre, 129a Whitehorse Hill, CHISLEHURST, Kent,
      BR7 6DQ.   (hq)
      020 8295 1128   fax 020 8467 8095
      http://www.abcb.org.uk
▲   Company Limited by Guarantee
○   *T; the UK's centre of excellence for product, quality
      management & environmental certification
●   Mtgs - SG - Inf - LG
M   f

Association of British Choral Directors   (ABCD)   1986
■   15 Granville Way, SHERBORNE, Dorset, DT9 4AS.   (sp)
      01935 389482
      email rachel.greaves@abcd.org.uk
      http://www.abcd.org.uk
      Gen Sec: Rachel Greaves
▲   Registered Charity
Br   11; 1
○   *P; to promote the education, training & development of choral
      directors from all choral sectors; to encourage the
      composition of choral music
●   Conf - Mtgs - ET - SG - Inf - VE - Workshops
<   Intl Fedn for Choral Music (IFCM); Inc Soc of Musicians; Music
      Educ Coun
M   700 i, 50 f
      (Sub: £45 i)
¶   Mastersinger - 4; ftm.   Membership Annual - 1; m only.

Association of British Civilian Internees Far East Region
      no longer in existence

Association of British Climbing Walls   (ABC)   1994
NR   c/o Mile End Climbing Wall, Haverfield Rd, LONDON,
      E3 5BE.   (chmn/b)
      020 8980 0289
      email andrew.reid@mileendwall.org.uk
      Chmn: Andrew Reid
▲   Company Limited by Guarantee
○   *S, *T; for owners of climbing walls in centres, leisure centres &
      schools
M   c 45 walls

Association of British Clinical Diabetologists   (ABCD)   1997
NR   Red Hot Irons Ltd, PO Box 2927, MALMESBURY, Wilts,
      SN16 0WZ.   (asa)
      01666 850589
      email eliseharvey@redhotirons.com
      http://www.diabetologist-abcd.org.uk
      Secretariat: Elise Harvey
○   *P; for consultant physicians specialising in diabetes mellitus

Association of British Concert Promoters
      see **British Association of Concert Halls**

Association of British Conifer Growers
      a group of the **Horticultural Trades Association**

Association of British Correspondence Colleges   (ABCC)   1956
■   PO Box 17926, LONDON, SW19 3WB.   (hq)
      020 8544 9559
      email info@homestudy.org.uk
      http://www.homestudy.org.uk
      Sec: Heather Owen
▲   Company Limited by Guarantee
○   *E, *T; to represent the major private correspondence colleges
      in the UK
●   ET - Inf - LG - Advice on correspondence education in Britain
M   21 f

Association of British Counties (ABC) 1989

■ 28 Alfreda Rd, Whitchurch, CARDIFF, Glamorgan, CF14 2EH. (chmn/p)
029 2033 3728
email mailman@abcounties.co.uk
http://www.abcounties.co.uk
Hon Sec: J M Bradford
▲ Un-incorporated Society
○ *K; to promote an awareness of the continuing existence of all the historic, traditional counties of Britain, as distinct from administrative counties
Gp Campaign for True Identity; County of Middlesex Trust; Friends of Real Lancashire; Historic Counties Trust; Huntingdonshire Society; North Riding Society; Saddleworth White Rose Society; Staffordshire Society
● Mtgs - Inf
< Historic Counties Trust
M 1,000 i
(Sub: £5 i)
¶ The Counties (Jnl) - 2; ftm only.
Gazetteer - showing traditional counties & local government areas; on website: gazetteer.co.uk

Association of British Credit Unions Ltd (ABCUL) 1979

■ Holyoake House, Hanover St, MANCHESTER, M60 0AS. (hq)
0161-832 3694   fax 0161-832 3706
email info@abcul.org   http://www.abcul.coop
Chief Exec: Mark Lyonette
▲ Industrial & Provident Society
Br 3
○ *N; the principal trade association for credit unions in Britain with members in England, Scotland & Wales
Gp 35 study groups
● Conf - Mtgs - ET - Res - SG - Inf - LG
< Wld Coun of Credit Us (WOCCU); Co-operatives UK
M 385 credit unions
¶ Credit Union News - 4;   AR - 1; both ftm.

Association of British Cycling Coaches (ABCC)

NR 1 Small Drove, Weston, SPALDING, Lincs, PE12 6HS.
Contact: Malcolm Smith
○ *P

Association of British Designer Silversmiths
since 2008 **Contemporary British Silversmiths**

Association of British Dispensing Opticians (ABDO) 1986

■ 199 Gloucester Terrace, LONDON, W2 6LD. (hq)
020 7298 5100   fax 020 7298 5111
email general@abdo.org.uk   http://www.abdo.org.uk
Gen Sec: Sir Anthony Garrett
▲ Company Limited by Guarantee
○ *P
● Conf - ET - Exam
< Optical Confedn
M 7,396 i, UK / 909 i, o'seas
¶ Dispensing Optics - 9; ftm, £10 m   AR - 1; free.
Bifocals without Tears (L E Swift).
Practical Ophthalmic Lenses (M Jalie/Ray).
Principles of Ophthalmic Lenses (M Jalie).
Optics (A H Tunnicliffe & J G Hurst).
Other publications available.

Association of British Drivers (ABD) 1992

NR PO Box 2228, KENLEY, Surrey, CR8 5ZT. (hsp)
07000 781544   fax 0870 136 2370
email enquiries@abd.org.uk   http://www.abd.org.uk
Mem Sec: Susan Newby-Robson
▲ Company Limited by Guarantee
○ *G, *K; to provide an active, reasonable voice & lobby for the British driver
● Mtgs - Exhib
< Amer Auto Enthusiast Club; Fiat Motor Club; Nat Assn of Street Clubs
M 1,600 i, 3,775 affiliates, UK / 5 i, o'seas
¶ On the Road (NL) - 6; ftm, £2 nm.
Note: The Association of British Drivers is the operating name of Pro-Motor (a Company Limited by Guarantee).

Association of British Fire Trades Ltd
2007 merged with the British Fire Protection Systems Association, the Fire Extinguishing Trades Association & the Fire Industry Confederation to form the **Fire Industry Association**

Association of British Fungus Groups (ABFG) 1996

NR Harveys, Alston, AXMINSTER, Devon, EX13 7LG.
01460 221788   fax 01460 221788
email enquiries@abfg.org   http://www.abfg.org
Contacts: Michael Jordan & Hazel Malcolm
○ *G; for those interested in mushrooms & toadstools
M i

Association of British Hammer Throwers   (The Hammer Circle)
see **Hammer Circle**

Association of British Healthcare Industries (ABHI) 1988

■ 111 Westminster Bridge Rd, LONDON, SE1 7HR. (hq)
020 7960 4360   fax 020 7960 4361
email enquiries@abhi.org.uk   http://www.abhi.org.uk
Dir Gen: John Wilkinson
▲ Company Limited by Guarantee
○ *T; for the medical technology industry - manufacturers & distributors of products ranging from plasters to pacemakers
● Mtgs - Expt - LG
< Eucomed
M 226 f, 5 trade assns
¶ Health-Care Focus - 6.   In Focus - 6.   Primed - 24.   AR.

Association of British Independent Oil Exploration Companies (BRINDEX) 1974

■ 55 Riddlesdown Rd, PURLEY, Surrey, CR8 1DJ. (hsp)
020 8668 3359   fax 020 8668 3359
http://www.brindex.co.uk
Admin: Jackie Steer
○ *T; to develop & promote the British independent oil industry
Gp North Sea taxation
● Conf - Mtgs - SG

Association of British Insurers (ABI) 1985

NR 51 Gresham St, LONDON, EC2V 7HQ. (hq)
020 7600 3333
http://www.abi.org.uk
○ *T; for insurers authorised to transact any class of insurance business in the UK
M f

© CBD Research Ltd · Beckenham · BR3 5JS · Tel 020 8650 7745 · E-mail cbd@cbdresearch.com · www.cbdresearch.com

Association of British Introduction Agencies   (ABIA)   1981
NR   315 Chiswick High Rd (suite 109), LONDON, W4 4HH.
    (chmn/b)
    020 8742 0386
    email hhepercy@aol.com   http://www.abia.org.uk
    Chmn: Heather Heber-Percy
▲   Un-incorporated Society
○   *T; 'assisting consumer & agency with advice; monitoring
    industry & trying to persuade agencies to a set minimum
    standard of service'
●   Conf - Mtgs - ET - Res - Stat - Inf - LG
M   35 f
¶   LM - (updated); free.

Association of British Investigators   (ABI)   1913
■   295-297 Church St, BLACKPOOL, Lancs, FY1 3PJ.   (hsb)
    0871 474 0006; 01253 297502   fax 0871 474
    0007; 01253 752185
    email info@theabi.org.uk   http://www.theabi.org.uk
    Gen Sec: Eric Shelmerdine
▲   Company Limited by Guarantee
Br   4
○   *P; for private investigators & process servers (many members
    are certified bailiffs)
●   Conf - Mtgs - ET - Exam - Inf - LG
<   Intle Kommission der Detektiv-Verbände (IKD)
M   369 i, UK / 61 i, o'seas
¶   Investigate - 4.   LM - 1.

Association of British & Irish Showcaves   (ABIS)
NR   c/o Peak Cavern, Castleton, HOPE VALLEY, Derbys, S33 8WS.
    01433 620285
    email info@visitcaves.com   http://www.visitcaves.com
    Chmn: John Harrison
○   *T; underground tourist attractions across the British Isles
M   12 f

**Association of British & Irish Wild Animal Keepers   (ABWAK)
1974**
NR   The Aviary, Leeds Castle, MAIDSTONE, Kent, ME17 1PL.   (hsb)
    01622 765400
    http://www.abwak.co.uk
    Hon Sec: Laura Gardner
▲   Un-incorporated Society
○   *P, *V; captive husbandry of exotic animals in zoos & private
    collections
●   Conf - Mtgs
<   Intl Congress of Zoo Keepers (ICZ)
M   298 i, UK / 16 i, o'seas
    (Sub: £25 i, UK / £45 i, o'seas)
¶   RATEL (Jnl) - 4; £20 yr UK, £30 yr o'seas.
    Conference Proceedings (CD) - 1; £5 m, £7 nm.
×   2007 Association of British Wild Animal Keepers

Association of British Jazz Musicians   (2azz)   1987
NR   c/o Jazz Services Ltd, 132 Southwark St (1st floor), LONDON,
    SE1 0SW.   (hsb)
    020 7928 9089   fax 020 7401 6870
    email touring@jazzservices.org.uk
    http://www.jazzservices.org.uk
    Hon Sec: Chris Hodgkins
▲   Un-incorporated Society
○   *D; interests of jazz musicians in the UK
●   Conf - Mtgs - Inf - LG
M   i
¶   ABJM News - 4.

Association of British Kart Clubs   (ABKC)   1990
■   Stoneycroft, Godsons Lane, Napton, SOUTHAM, Warks,
    CV47 8LX.   (sp)
    01926 812177   fax 01926 812177
    email secretary@abkc.org.uk   http://www.abkc.org.uk
    Sec: Graham Smith
▲   Un-incorporated Society
○   *N, *S; provision of technical & procedural regulations for
    competition kart racing in the UK
●   Conf - Mtgs - Comp - Stat - Inf - Organisation of national
    championships - Setting technical regulations for kart racing
<   Motor Sports Assn
M   31 clubs
¶   ABKC News - 4; free.

Association of British Language Schools   (ABLS)   1993
NR   PO Box 315, GREAT YARMOUTH, Norfolk, NR30 9EN.
    01493 393471
    email info@abls.co.uk   http://www.abls.co.uk
    Sec: Joanne Adcock
▲   Un-incorporated Society
○   *E, *P; accreditation body for establishments teaching English
    as a foreign language (TEFL)
●   Conf - Mtgs - ET - Expt - Inf - LG - Lobbying embassies abroad
    - Networking for members
M   c 30 f
¶   LM - 1; free.

**Association of British Mining Equipment Companies
(ABMEC)   1967**
NR   Unit 1 Thornes Office Park, Monckton Rd, WAKEFIELD, W Yorks,
    WF2 7AN.   (hq)
    01924 360200   fax 01924 380553
    email ruth.bailey@abmec.org.uk
    http://www.abmec.org.uk
    Dir Gen: Ruth Bailey
▲   Un-incorporated Society
○   *T; to promote the UK mining equipment manufacturers
●   Conf - Mtgs - ET - Exhib - Expt - Inf - LG
M   33 f
¶   Buyers' Guide - 1. free.

Association of British Naturist Clubs   (ABNC)
NR   45A Lye Lane, Bricket Wood, ST ALBANS, Herts, AL2 3TD.
    0795 268 0091
    http://www.britishnaturistclubs.org
○   *G, *N;

Association of British Neurologists   (ABN)   1933
■   Ormond House, 27 Boswell St, LONDON, WC1N 3JZ.   (hq)
    020 7405 4060   fax 020 7405 4070
    email info@theabn.org   http://www.abn.org.uk
    Admin: Karen Reeves
▲   Registered Charity
○   *P; to promote education in, & the advancement of, the
    neurological sciences including the practice of neurology in
    the UK & Ireland
●   Conf - ET - Res - Stat - LG
M   1,000 i

Association of British Offshore Industries   (ABOI)   1983
NR   28-29 Threadneedle St, LONDON, EC2R 8AY.   (hq)
    020 7628 2555   fax 020 7638 4376
    email info@maritimeindustries.org
    http://www.maritimeindustries.org
    Dir: Ken Gibbons
○   *T; 'companies who develop specialist offshore systems &
    provide worldwide services & facilities for oil & gas
    exploration, production, transportation & conversion'
●   Conf - Mtgs - Exhib - SG - Expt - LG
<   Soc of Maritime Inds
M   f

Association of British Orchestras   (ABO)   1947
- ■   20 Rupert St, LONDON, W1D 6DF.   (hq)
   020 7287 0333   fax 020 7287 0444
   email info@abo.org.uk   http://www.abo.org.uk
   Dir: Mark Pemberton
- ▲   Company Limited by Guarantee
- ○   *N, *T; to support, develop & advance the interests & activities
   of orchestras in the UK
- ●   Conf - Mtgs - ET - Res - Stat - Inf - Lib - Empl - LG - Seminars -
   Public symposia
- <   Intl Alliance of Orchestral Assns (IAOA); Performing Arts
   Employers Assns League Europe (PEARLE); American
   Symphony Orchestra League (ASOL); Inc Soc of
   Musicians (ISM); Nat Campaign for the Arts (NCA); Sound
   Sense
- M   11 i, 47 f, 89 org, UK / 4 f, 5 org, o'seas
   (Sub: £260 f, UK)
- ¶   ABO Update (email NL) - 12; ftm.
   A Sound Ear; A Wright Reid (2001); £10.
   Knowing the Score 2; A Lewis-Crosby & R Moon (2002); £20.
   Review of the Year.
   Publications list available.

Association of British Paediatric Nurses   (ABPN)   1938
- NR   100 Forest Rd, LISS, Hants, GU33 7BP.   (hsp)
   http://www.abpn.org.uk
   Hon Sec: Katrina Macnamara-Goodger
- ▲   Registered Charity
- ○   *P; to promote the development of children's nursing through
   evidence based information about practice & education
- Gp   Children nurse education
- ●   Conf - Mtgs - Exhib - LG - Policy influence - Scholarships
- M   1,000 i, UK / 20 i, o'seas
   (Sub: c £35).
- ¶   Jnl of Child Health Care - 4.   NL - 4;   AR - 1; all free.

Association of British Pewter Craftsmen   (ABPC)   1971
- NR   10 Edmund Rd Business Centre, 135 Edmund Rd, SHEFFIELD,
   S Yorks, S2 4ED.   (asa)
   0114-252 7550   fax 0114-252 7555
   email enquiries@abpcltd.co.uk
   http://www.britishpewter.com
   Co Sec: Mrs C T Steele
- ▲   Company Limited by Guarantee
- ○   *T; the promotion of pewter
- ●   Mtgs - Exhib - Inf
- <   Worshipful Company of Pewterers
- M   35 f

**Association of the British Pharmaceutical Industry   (ABPI)
   1930**
- NR   12 Whitehall, LONDON, SW1A 2DY.   (hq)
   0870 890 4333   fax 020 7747 1414
   http://www.abpi.org.uk
- ▲   Un-incorporated Society
- ○   *T
- M   [not stated]

Association of British Philatelic Societies Ltd   (ABPS)   1994
- NR   c/o Royal Philatelic Socety London, 41 Devonshire St,
   LONDON, W1G 6JY.
   Sec: Colin Searle
- ▲   Company Limited by Guarantee
- ○   *N; to promote philately in the UK; to represent philatelic
   societies
- ●   Conf - Comp - SG - Inf
- <   Fédn Intle de Philatélie; FEPA
- M   c 400 org
- ¶   ABPS News (NL) - 4; ftm, £10 yr nm.
   National & Specialists Society Hbk - 1.
   ABPS Directory - 2 yrly; ftm, £15 nm.

Association of British Physiotherapists
   see **SMAE Fellowship (Association of British Physiotherapists)**

**Association of British Professional Conference Organisers
   (ABPCO)   1981**
- NR   11 Hawthorn Manor, Carryduff, BELFAST, BT8 8SR.   (hq)
   07840 5015835
   email info@abpco.org   http://www.abpco.org
   Exec Dir: Lesley Maltman
- ▲   Company Limited by Guarantee
- ○   *P; to develop & enhance the professional status of conference
   & event organisers
- ●   Conf - Mtgs - ET - Exhib - Inf
- <   Business Tourism Partnership
- M   72 i

Association of British Riding Schools   (ABRS)   1954
- ■   Queen's Chambers, 38-40 Queen St, PENZANCE, Cornwall,
   TR18 4BH.   (hq)
   01736 369440   fax 01736 351390
   email office@abrs-info.org   http://www.abrs-info.org
   Chmn: Julian Marczak
- ▲   Company Limited by Guarantee
- ○   *P, *S; to raise the standards of riding instruction &
   horsemanship
- ●   Conf - ET - Exam - Exhib - LG
- <   Cent Coun for Physical Recreation (CCPR); Brit Equestrian Fedn
   (BEF); Lantra; Brit Equestrian Tr Assn (BETA); Nat Equine
   Forum
- M   450 i, 350 f, UK / 20 i, 16 f, o'seas
- ¶   NL - 3/4; ftm only.
   Locations leaflet - 1; free.

Association of British Sailmakers   (ABS)   1984
- NR   15 Chapel St, ABERFELDY, Perthshire, PH15 2AS.   (hsp/b)
   01887 829310
- ○   *T; to provide technical support for sailmakers

Association of British Science Writers   (ABSW)   1947
- NR   The Dana Centre, 165 Queen's Gate, LONDON, SW7 5HD.
   (hsb)
   0870 770 3361
   http://www.absw.org.uk
- ○   *P; to encourage & improve science writing in the UK
- ●   Mtgs - VE
- <   Eur U of Science Journalists' Assns (EUSJA); Creators' Rights
   Alliance
- M   900 i
- ¶   NL - 12; ftm only.

Association of British Scrabble Players   (ABSP)   1986
- NR   8 Glen Cova Place, KIRKCALDY, Fife, KY2 6UL.   (hsp)
   email secretary@absp.org.uk   http://www.absp.org.uk
   Mem Sec: Anne Ramsay
- ○   *G; to promote matchplay scrabble tournaments
- ●   Comp
- <   Wld Engl Speaking Scrabble Players Asn
- M   c 700 i
- ¶   The Last Word - 6; £15 yr m.

Association of British Tennis Officials   (ABTO)   2000
- NR   Officiating Dept, The Lawn Tennis Association, The National
   Tennis Centre, 100 Priory Lane, Roehampton, LONDON,
   SW15 5JQ.   (hq)
   020 8487 7000   fax 020 8487 7301
- ○   *P; to officiate at tennis events & apply & uphold rules &
   regulations in force; to promote advancement of high
   standards for tennis officials

© CBD Research Ltd · Beckenham · BR3 5JS · Tel 020 8650 7745 · E-mail cbd@cbdresearch.com · www.cbdresearch.com

Association of British Theatre Technicians   (ABTT)   1961
NR   55 Farringdon Rd, LONDON, EC1M 3JB.   (hq)
         020 7242 9200
         email office@abtt.org.uk   http://www.abtt.org.uk
▲   Registered Charity
○   *A, *P; 'to act as a forum for theatre technicians & express their
         corporate view on matters affecting the industry; to collect &
         disseminate technical information; to advise on the planning
         of new theatres & the conversion of existing buildings'
M   i

**Association of British Theological & Philosophical Libraries
   (ABTAPL)   1956**
NR   c/o Dr Carol Reekie, Cambridge Theological Federation,
         Wesley House, Jesus Lane, CAMBRIDGE, CB5 8BJ.   (hsb)
         01223 741043
         http://www.abtapl.org.uk
         Hon Sec: Dr Carol Reekie
○   *P; to promote bibliographical work & common interests
         among librarians specialising in theology, religious studies &
         philosophy
●   Conf - ET - inf
<   Bibliothèques Européenes de Théologie
M   97 i, 75 f, 5 org, UK / 29 i, 44 f, o'seas
¶   Bulletin - 3; ftm.

**Association of British Tour Operators to France Ltd   (ABTOF)
   1993**
NR   Bencewell Business Centre, Oakley Road, BROMLEY, Kent,
         BR2 8HG.   (hq)
         020 8315 8674   fax 020 8315 8675
         email info@abtof.org.uk
         Chief Exec: Richard Brierly
▲   Company Limited by Guarantee
○   *T
Gp   French & UK affiliate members who are suppliers of services to
         ABTOF members
●   Conf - Mtgs - ET - Exhib - SG - Stat - Inf - VE - LG - PR Service
M   150 f, UK / 70 f, o'seas
¶   ABTOF News Update - 12; ftm only.

**Association of British Transport & Engineering Museums
   (ABTEM)   1962**
■   c/o Tim Bryan, Heritage Motor Centre, Banbury Rd, GAYDON,
         Warks, CV35 0BJ.   (hsb)
         01926 645105   fax 01926 645111
         email tbryan9@landrover.com   http://www.abtem.co.uk
         Hon Sec: Tim Bryan
▲   Un-incorporated Society
○   *N; to act as a forum for the discussion of matters of common
         interest to transport & engineering museums; to provids a
         means of representing their views on matters of inportance
●   Conf - VE
M   c 20 i, c 50 org
         (Sub £10 i, £22 f)
¶   NL - 4.

Association of British Travel Agents Ltd
         on 1 July 2008 merged with the Federation of Tour Operators to form
         ABTA - the Travel Association

Association of British Veterinary Acupuncturists
         a group of the **British Small Animal Veterinary Association**

Association of British Wild Animal Keepers
         since 2007 **Association of British & Irish Wild Animal Keepers**

Association of Broadcasting Doctors   (ABD)   1988
■   1 Lark Bank, Prickwillow, ELY, Cambs, CB7 4SW.   (hq)
         01353 687966
         email jackiepetts@oneservice.co.uk
         http://www.broadcasting-doctor.org
         Dir: Jacqueline Petts
▲   Un-incorporated Society
○   *P; to represent practising clinicians who also broadcast on
         radio & TV
Gp   Dentists' media
●   Conf - Mtgs - ET - Inf - Lib - LG
<   GP Writers Assn
M   760 i
¶   NL - 12.

Association of Brokers & Yacht Agents   (ABYA)
■   The Glass Works, Penns Rd, PETERSFIELD, Hants, GU32 2EW.
         (hq)
         01730 266430   fax 01730 710423
         email info@ybdsa.co.uk   http://www.abya.co.uk
         Chief Exec: Jane Gentry
▲   Company Limited by Guarantee
Br   Spain
○   *P; for yacht brokers, agents & dealers
●   Conf - Mtgs
M   85 i, UK / 15 f, o'seas
¶   NL - 4; ftm only.
         Note: The Yacht Brokers, Designers & Surveyors Association is
         the management company for the ABYA & the Yacht
         Designers & Surveyors Association

**Association of Building Cleaning Direct Service Providers
   (ABCD)   1989**
■   PO Box 137, NORTHAMPTON, NN3 6AD.   (hsp)
         01604 705934   fax 01604 705934
         email abcd@wherton.freeserve.co.uk
         http://www.abcdsp.org.uk
         Exec Gen Sec: Patricia Wherton
▲   Un-incorporated Society
Br   3
○   *T; to support managers of direct service cleaning provision in
         local authorities throughout the UK
●   Conf - Mtgs - Exhib - Stat - LG
<   Asset Skills; Brit Cleaning Coun; Assn of Public Service
         Excellence; Brit Brit Inst of Cleaning Science
M   75 local authorities, 20 suppliers
         (Sub: £205)

Association of Building Engineers   (ABE)   1925
■   Lutyens House, Billing Brook Rd, Weston Favell,
         NORTHAMPTON, NN3 8NW.   (hq)
         01604 404121   fax 01604 784220
         email building.engineers@abe.org.uk
         http://www.abe.org.uk
         Chief Exec: David R Gibson
▲   Company Limited by Guarantee
○   *P; to promote & advance the study & practice of the arts &
         sciences concerned with building technology, planning,
         design, construction, maintenance & repair of the built
         environment
Gp   ABE Assess - home inspector reaining; Fire safety engineering
●   Conf - ET - Exam - Inf - Lib - LG
<   Assn d'Experts Eur du Bâtiment et de la Construction (AEEBC);
         Construction Ind Coun; Fedn of Brit Fire Orgs; Soc for the
         Envt
M   5,000 i, 200 f, UK / 400 i, o'seas
         (Sub: from £45 for students to £200 for fellows)
¶   Building Engineer - 12; ftm, £40 yr nm.
         AR; free.
×   2008 (April) Institute of Maintenance & Building
         Management (merged)

Association of Burial Authorities Ltd   (ABA)   1993

- ■ Waterloo House, 155 Upper St, LONDON, N1 1RA.   (hq)
  020 7288 2522   fax 020 7288 2533
  email aba@burials.org.uk   http://www.burials.org.uk
  Chief Exec & Hon Sec: Deborah Powton
  Dir: John Clark
- ▲ Company Limited by Guarantee
- ○ *T; to promote & protect the interests of organisations engaged in the management & operation of burial grounds
- ● Conf - Res - Comp - Inf - Lib - VE - LG - Advice on planning, designing & layout of burial grounds & extensions, & on acquisitions of burial grounds (incl churchyards, municipal & private cemeteries) - Legal advice
- < Fédn Intle des Assns Thanatologues FIAT/IFTA); Assn Significant Cemeteries Europe (ASCE); Eur Fedn of Funeral Services (EFFS); Coun Brit Funeral Services
- M 9 i, 23 f, 315 local authorities
  (Sub: £20 i, £175 f, £90-£335 local authorities
- ¶ ABA Info (NL) - 4.
  ABA Informatives - factsheets.
  Cemetery & Churchyard Regulations.
  Planning for Memorials.
  Planning for Memorials after Cremation.
  Guide to Funerals & Bereavement.
  ABA/ZM Guide to Safety in Burial Grounds.

Association of Business Administration   (ABA)   1984

- NR PO Box 70, LONDON, E13 0UU.   (hq)
  email info@theaba.org.uk   http://www.theaba.org.uk
- ○ *P; to encourage professional business administration especially in education, training & professional practice
- ● ET - Exam - SG
- M [not stated]
- ¶ ABA Jnl - 4; ftm, £25 nm.   Membership Hbk; ftm, £5 nm.
  Dictionary of Business Administration.
  Directory of Business Administration - 1.

Association of Business-to-Business Agencies   (ABBA)   1985

- ■ Clarence Mill, Clarence Rd, BOLLINGTON, Cheshire, SK10 5JZ.   (hq)
  01625 578511   fax 01625 578579
  email info@abba.co.uk   http://www.abba.co.uk
  Chmn: John Stanton
- ▲ Un-incorporated Society
- ○ *P; to establish professional standards of service & competence in business to business marketing; to encourage a strategic, business-focussed, integrated approach
- Gp Business to business marketing & communications
- ● Conf - Mtgs - ET - Res - Exhib - Stat
- M 26 f
  (Sub: £1,250)

Association of Business Executives   (ABE)   1973

- ■ CI Tower (5th floor), St Georges Sq, NEW MALDEN, Surrey, KT3 4TE.   (hq)
  020 8329 2930   fax 020 8329 2945
  email info@abeuk.com   http://www.abeuk.com
  Founder/Chmn: Lyndon Jones
- ▲ Company Limited by Guarantee
- Br 11 countries
- ○ *P; examination board setting professional qualifications & advanced diplomas in business nominations, business information systems, travel, tourism & hospitality resource management
- ● Conf - ET - Exam
- M 4,000 i, UK / 18,000 i, o'seas
- ¶ Business Executives - 2; ftm, £20 nm.

Association of Business Management Academics   (ABMA)

- ■ Bristol Broad Quay, Broad Quay House, Prince St, BRISTOL, BS1 4DJ.   (hq)
  email info@abma.org.uk   http://www.abma.org.uk
- ○ *P

Association of Business Managers & Administrators   (ABMA)   1975

- ■ Venture House, 42 London Rd, STAINES, Middx, TW18 4HF.   (hq)
  020 8733 7000   fax 020 8733 7033
  email info@abma.uk.com   http://www.abma.uk.com
  Senior Exec: Alan Hodson
- ▲ Company Limited by Guarantee
- ○ *T; a non-profit making, independent examinations board, recognised worldwide for providing a unique solution in terms of British qualifications; offers customised courses to suit the needs of both institutions & students as direct entry requirements for bachelor courses in the UK & USA
- ● ET - Exam
- M c 12,000 i, 89 f, affiliated universities in UK & USA

Association of Business Psychologists   (ABP)   2000

- ■ 180 Piccadilly, LONDON, W1J 9ER.   (hsb)
  020 7917 1733
  email admin@theabp.org.uk   http://www.theabp.org.uk
  Gen Administrator: Richard Taylor
- ▲ Company Limited by Guarantee
- ○ *P; for practitioners in business psychology
- ● Conf - Mtgs - ET - Res - Inf - LG
- M 900 i, UK / 10 i, o'seas
- ¶ NL - 3 [email].

Association of Business Recovery Professionals   (R3)

- NR 120 Aldersgate St (8th floor), LONDON, EC1A 4JQ.   (hq)
  020 7566 4200
  http://www.r3.org.uk
- ▲ Company Limited by Guarantee
- ○ *P; for all those who deal with Britain's underperforming businesses & individuals in financial trouble
- M 3,400 i
- ¶ Recovery - 4; ftm only.

Association of Business Schools   (ABS)   1992

- NR 137 Euston Rd, LONDON, NW1 2AA.   (hq)
  020 7388 0007   fax 020 7388 0009
  http://www.associationofbusinessschools.org
  Chmn: Prof Angus Laing
- ○ *P; the representative body & authoritative voice for all the business schools of UK universities, higher education institutions & independent management colleges
- M 100 f, 6 org

Association of Button Merchants   1928

- ■ Southernhay (suite 7), 207 Hook Rd, CHESSINGTON, Surrey, KT9 1HJ.   (asa)
  020 8391 2266   fax 020 8391 4466
  email abm@sleat.co.uk
  Sec: David M Hart
- ▲ Company Limited by Guarantee
- ○ *T; interests of button merchants in the UK
- ● Mtgs - Inf
- < Brit Button Coun
- M 15 f
- ¶ NL - irreg;   AR; both m only.

Association for Cancer Surgery
   styles itself **BASO ~ the Association for Cancer Surgery**

Association of Cannibals' Equipment Suppliers   (ACES)   2000

- ■ 76c The Avenue, BECKENHAM, Kent, BR3 2ES.   (hq)
- ○ *T
- Gp Vegetarian
- ● Conf - Mtgs - Exhib - Expt - Lib - Stat - VE - LG
- M f
- ¶ Eat You - 4; ftm only.
  Note: this is a control entry

© CBD Research Ltd · Beckenham · BR3 5JS · Tel 020 8650 7745 · E-mail cbd@cbdresearch.com · www.cbdresearch.com

Association of Caravan & Camping Exempted Organisations (ACCEO)   1985
- ■ PO Box 5191, RUGELEY, Staffs, WS15 9BS.   (hq)
  0845 419 1520
  http://www.acceo.org.uk
  Sec: Mick Holmes
- ○ *N, *T; for camping & caravanning clubs holding meetings of not more than 5 days; site licences are not required if the site is under the supervision of an organisation holding the Certificate of Exemption from the Dept for Environment, Food & Rural Affairs; ACCEO is one of 5 organisations permitted, in conjunction with member clubs, to hold meetings of up to 28 days
- M c 45,000 i in c 200 clubs

Association of Cardiothoracic Anaesthetists   (ACTA)   1985
- NR c/o Royal College of Anaesthetists, Churchill House, Red Lion Square, LONDON, WC1R 4SG.   (hsb)
  020 7092 1726
  http://www.acta.org.uk
  Sec: Mrs Carol Bunnell   (acta@rcoa.ac.uk)
- ▲ Company Limited by Guarantee
- ○ *M, *P; promotion education, training, taching & research in the field of cardiothoracic anaesthesia & intensive care
- ● Conf - Mtgs - ET - Exam - Res - Stat - Inf
- < Eur Assn of Cardiothoracic Anaesthesia
- M 470 i
- ¶ ACTA News - 2; ftm only.

Association for Careers Education & Guidance   (ACEG)   1969
- ■ 9 Lawrence Leys, Bloxham, BANBURY, Oxon, OX15 4NU.   (hsp)
  01295 720809   fax 01295 720809
  email info@aceg.org.uk   http://www.aceg.org.uk
  Hon Sec: Alan Vincent
- ▲ Company Limited by Guarantee
- ○ *E, *P; to promote excellence & innovation in careers education & guidance for all young people
- ● Conf - ET - Res - Inf - LG
- < Intl Assn Educl & Vocational Guidance; Fedn of Profl Assns in Guidance; Guidance Coun; Profl Assns Res Network
- M 1,750 i
- ¶ Careers Education & Guidance (Jnl) - 4; ftm, £10.50 nm.

Association of Casualty & Health Emergency Simulators
- ■ 293 Lonsdale Drive, GILLINGHAM, Kent, ME8 9JT.   (hsp/b)
  01634 235760   fax 01634 235760
  email gwildridge@blueyonder.co.uk
  Sec: Mrs Sylvia Wildridge
- ▲ Company Limited by Guarantee; Registered Charity
- ○ *P; to provide trained, simulated casualties whenever & wherever first aid medicine & rescue are taught &/or practised
- ● ET - Exam - Comp
- M 40 i

Association of Catering Excellence   (ACE)   1937
- ■ Bourne House, Horsell Park, WOKING, Surrey, GU21 4LY.   (hq)
  01483 765111   fax 01483 751991
  email admin@acegb.org   http://www.acegb.org
  Admin: Vic Laws
- ▲ Company Limited by Guarantee
- Br 8
- ○ *P; provision of catering services - comprising managers, executives, contract caterers, etc
- ● Conf - Mtgs - ET - Exhib - Comp - Inf - Lib - VE - Book service
- < Eur Catering Assn
- M 200 i, 30 f

Association of Celebrity Assistants (UK)   (ACA (UK))   2003
- NR 206 Canalot Studios, 222 Kensal Rd, LONDON, W10 5BN.   (hq)
  email hello@aca-uk.com   http://www.aca-uk.com
  Sec: Carlene Findlay
- ○ *P; personal assistants who work for high profile individuals in the worlds of film, TV, theatre, music, fashion & beauty, charity, business and politics

Association of Cereal Food Manufacturers   (ACFM)   1955
- NR 6 Catherine St, LONDON, WC2B 5JJ.   (hq)
  020 7420 7113   fax 020 7836 0580
  email geraldine.albon@fdf.org.uk
  http://www.fdf.org.uk
  Exec Sec: Geraldine Albon
- ▲ Un-incorporated Society
- ○ *T; manufacturers of breakfast cereal products
- ● Mtgs - Inf
- < Eur Breakfast Cereal Assn (CEEREAL); Food & Drink Fedn
- M 8 f

Association of Certificated Field Archaeologists   (ACFA)   1987
- ■ 12 Struan Gardens,GLASGOW, G44 3BW.   (hsp)
  email acfacommittee@gmail.com
  http://www.acfabaseline.info
  Hon Sec: Janie C Munro
- ▲ Registered Charity
- ○ *P; members undertake field surveys in Scotland in a voluntary capacity; members are holders of the certificate in field archaeology from DACE, Glasgow University
- ● ET - Res
- M 77 i
  (Sub: @20)
- ¶ Baseline (NL) - 3; ftm only.
  Occasional papers - irreg; prices vary (see website).

Association of Certified Commercial Diplomats   (ACCD)   2006
- ■ PO Box 50561, LONDON, E16 3WY.   (hq)
  0870 321 9481   fax 0870 321 9437
  email enquiries@chartereddiplomats.org
  http://www.chartereddiplomats.org
  Mem Sec: Miss Debbie Bailey
- ▲ Company Limited by Guarantee
- Br Brunei, Cambodia, North Borneo, Saudi Arabia, UAE
- ○ *P; an independent, global institution providing training & accreditation for commercial & economic diplomats in government ministries, parastatals, corporations, diplomatic missions, educational institutions & intergovernmental organisations
- Gp Council on Commercial Diplomacy is the oversight regulator for the profession
- ● Conf - Mtgs - ET - Exam - Res - SG - Lib - VE - LG - Accreditation
- < United Nations Global Compact; OECD; UN Office on Drugs & Crime; Inst for Tr & Comml Diplomacy; UN Principles for Responsible Mgt Educ
- > Eur Diplomatic Acad; Eur Inst Campus Stellae; Instn of Comml Diplomats
- M [not stated]

Association of Certified IT Professionals
- NR Wolverton Park, WOLVERTON, Hants, RG26 5RU.   (hq)
  0845 060 3456   fax 01494 483581
  http://www.acitp.org
  Chief Exec: Garry Carter
- ▲ Company Limited by Guarantee
- M 10,000 i

Association of Certified Public Accountants   (CPA UK)   1989
NR   Onward Buildings, 207 Deansgate, MANCHESTER,
        M3 3NW.   (hq)
        0161-834 5998   fax 0161-833 1422
        email admin@acpa.org.uk   http://www.acpa.org.uk
        Chmn: Bill Annand
Br   14; Canada, Egypt, Malaysia, Singapore, Thailand, UAE
○   *P; to offer a British version of the CPA qualification in the UK
<   Brit Accounting Assn; Eur Accounting Assn; Eur Inst for
        Advanced Studies in Mgt; Intl Assn of Accounting & Educl
        Res; Confedn of Indep Accountancy Bodies
M   i
        also known as the Certified Public Accountants Association

Association of Charitable Foundations   (ACF)   1989
NR   Central House, 14 Upper Woburn Place, LONDON,
        WC1H 0AE.   (hq)
        020 7255 4499   fax 020 7255 4496
        email acf@acf.org.uk   http://www.acf.org.uk
        Chief Exec: David Emerson
▲   Company Limited by Guarantee; Registered Charity
○   *N; to promote & support the work of charitable grant-making
        trusts & foundations
Gp   Alcohol & drugs; Arts; Children & young people; Disability;
        Education; Environment; Health; Housing; Individuals in
        need; International; Neighbourhood issues; Northern
        Ireland; Penal affairs; Race equality; Rural issues; Scotland;
        Strategic issues in the voluntary sector; Wales; Women's
        issues
●   Conf - Mtgs - Inf - LG
M   300 org
¶   Trust & Foundation News - 4; ftm.   NL.   AR.
        A Guide to Giving (2nd ed); £20.
        Monitoring & Evaluation; a practical guide for grant-making
        trusts; £10.
        SORP Made Simple: a guidance for grant-making
        charities (2006).
        Why Rich People Give; £15.
        Various other publications.

Association for Charities   (AfC)   1999
NR   83 Priory Gardens, LONDON, N6 5QU.   (hsb/p)
        020 8348 9114
▲   Un-incorporated Society
○   *K; to support & protect charities, trustees & beneficiaries
        affected by the actions of Charity Commission for England &
        Wales; to campaign for a fairer system of charity regulation
        & a more accountable Commission

Association of Charity Independent Examiners   (ACIE)   1999
■   The Gatehouse, White Cross, LANCASTER, LA1 4QX.   (asa)
        01524 34892
        email info@acie.org.uk   http://www.acie.org.uk
        Dir: Fiona Gordon (director@acie.org.uk)
▲   Company Limited by Guarantee; Registered Charity
○   *P; to promote the greater effectiveness of UK charities by
        providing support & encouraging professional standards for
        all persons acting as independent examiners of charity
        accounts
●   Conf - ET - Exam - Inf - LG
M   570 i
¶   Independent Examiner (NL) - 3; ftm, £40 yr nm.
        ACIE Hbk - 1; ftm, £10 nm.
        AR & Financial Statement - 1; free.

Association of Charity Officers   (ACO)   1946
■   Central House, 14 Upper Woburn Place, LONDON,
        WC1H 0NN.   (hq)
        020 7255 4480
        email info@aco.uk.net   http://www.aco.uk.net
        Dir: Mrs Valerie J Barrow
        Chmn: Mike Carter
▲   Registered Charity
○   *N, *W; to promote efficiency & encourage liaison &
        cooperation between charities
Gp   Forums: Residential care - dealing with all matters relating to
        residential & nursing home care; Grant making - dealing
        with all matters relating to grant aid for individuals /
        benevolence & the interface with Social Security; special work
        on occupational benevolent funds; Under 5's group for very
        small charities
●   Mtgs - Res - LG
<   Age Concern; NCVO; HELPLINES for members
M   250 charities (giving non-contributory relief)
¶   NL - 4/5.   AR.
        Various other publications - irreg.

Association of Charity Shops   (ACS)   1999
■   Central House, 14 Upper Woburn Place, LONDON,
        WC1H 0AE.   (hq)
        020 7255 4470   fax 020 7255 4475
        email mail@charityshops.org.uk
        http://www.charityshops.org.uk
        Exec Sec: Lekha Klouda
▲   Company Limited by Guarantee
○   *N; to promote & support charities, that run shops as part of
        their fund-raising activities, by pooling expertise to enable
        them to run their shops as effectively as possible
●   Conf - Mtgs - ET - Res - Exhib - Stat - LG
<   Brit Retail Consortium
M   c 250 charities, c 30 associate m (commercial interests)
¶   Bulletin - 10;   AR - 1; both free.
        Note: uses the trading name of Charity Retail Association

**Association of Charter Trustee Towns & Charter Town Councils
(ACTCTC)   1975**
■   Barratts Court, Rectory Lane, Rock, KIDDERMINSTER, Worcs,
        DY14 9RR.   (hsb/hsp)
        01299 832797
        email charles@talbotkidder.demon.co.uk
        Hon Sec: Charles Ellis Talbot
▲   Un-incorporated Society
○   *N; to preserve & enhance the status & traditions of charter
        trustee cities, towns & charter town councils
●   Conf - Mtgs - Inf - LG
M   16 towns

Association of Chartered Certified Accountants   (ACCA)   1904
■   29 Lincoln's Inn Fields, LONDON, WC2A 3EE.   (hq)
        020 7059 5000   fax 020 7059 5959
        email info@accaglobal.com
        http://www.accaglobal.com
        Sec: Michael Sleigh
▲   Incorporated by Royal Charter
Br   3; Botswana, China, Ethiopia, Ghana, Ireland, Malaysia,
        Mauritius, Pakistan, Singapore, UAE, Vietnam
○   *P
●   Mtgs - ET - Exam - Inf - LG
<   Intl Fedn of Accountants; Intl Accounting Standings Bd
M   58,000 i, UK / 68,000 i, o'seas
        (Sub: £175 UK & o'seas)
¶   Jnl - 12; ftm, £10 nm.
        Rulebook - 1; £20 (+available online).   AR - 1; ftm.

Association of Chief Archivists in Local Government
        merged in 2010 with the National Council on Archives & the Society
        of Archivists to form the **Archives & Records Association (UK &
        Ireland)**

© CBD Research Ltd · Beckenham · BR3 5JS · Tel 020 8650 7745 · E-mail cbd@cbdresearch.com · www.cbdresearch.com

Association of Chief Corporate Property Officers in Local Government   (COPROP)
NR   Beaufort West Associates Ltd, 5 Elston Meadow, Westwood, CREDITON, Devon, EX17 3SZ.   (hsb)
       01363 776108
       http://www.coprop.org.uk
       Hon Sec: Tony Gale
○   *P; development & implementation of policy affecting community assets & the management of local authority property estates
●   Mtgs
M   60 local authorities

Association of Chief Estates Surveyors & Property Managers in the Public Sector   (ACES)   1908
■   23 Athol Rd, BRAMHALL, Cheshire, SK7 1BR.   (sb)
       0161-439 9589
       email secretary@aces.org.uk   http://www.aces.org.uk
       Consultant Sec: Tim Foster
▲   Un-incorporated Society
Br   10
○   *P; to provide a forum for debate about public property; sharing of best practice in property asset management
Gp   Best Value; Compensation; Housing; PFI; Regeneration; Rural affairs; Town centre management
●   Conf - Mtgs - Res - LG
<   Fedn of Property Socs
M   390 i
¶   The Terrier - 4; free,   Per Annum (Ybk) - 1; ftm only.
×   2008 Association of Chief Estates Officers & Property Managers in Local Government

Association of Chief Executives of State Agencies
IRL   c/o IPA, 57-61 Lansdowne Rd, Dublin 4, Republic of Ireland.
       353 (87) 243 6591
       email acesa@eircom.net   http://www.acesa.ie
       Secretariat: Mary Rose Tobin
○   *P

Association of Chief Executives of Voluntary Organisations (ACEVO)   1988
NR   1 New Oxford St, LONDON, WC1A 1NU.   (hq)
       020 7280 4960
       email info@acevo.org.uk   http://www.acevo.org.uk
       Chief Exec: Stephen Bubb
▲   Company Limited by Guarantee
Br   Leeds
○   *P; for chief executives of voluntary organisations in England & Wales
●   Conf - Mtgs - ET - Res - Exhib - LG
M   1,500 i, 125 f, 40 org
¶   NoticeBoard (NL) - 9;   Hbk - 1;   Annual Review; all ftm only.
       Basic Guides to Good Practice [20 published]; £5 each.
       Replacing the State?; £12.50.
         Publications list available.

Association of Chief Officers of Scottish Voluntary Organisations (ACOSVO)
■   Thorn House, 5 Rose St, EDINBURGH, EH2 2PR.
       0131-243 2755
       email office@acosvo.org.uk   http://www.acosvo.org.uk
       Exec Dir: Pat Armstrong
○   *P: to promote excellence in leadership & management in the voluntary sector

Association of Chief Police Officers of England, Wales & Northern Ireland   (ACPO)   1948
NR   10 Victoria St (1st floor), LONDON, SW1H 0NN.   (hq)
○   *P
M   i

Association of Chief Police Officers in Scotland   (ACPOS) 1870
■   26 Holland St, GLASGOW, G2 4NH.   (hsb)
       0141-435 1230
       email secretariat@acpos.pnn.police.uk
       http://www.acpos.police.uk
       Hon Sec: Sir William Rae
○   *N; to oversee the direction & development of the Scottish Police Service
Gp   Crime; Finance; General policing; Road policing; Information management; Personnel & training; Professional standards; Diversity; Criminal justice; Performance; Management
●   Conf - Mtgs - Empl - LG
M   i
¶   AR - 1.

Association of Child Abuse Lawyers   (ACAL)
NR   Claremont House (suite 13), 22-24 Claremont Rd, SURBITON, Surrey, KT6 4QU.   (asa)
       020 8390 4701 (1000-1300 + 1400-1600 Tues & Thurs only)   fax 020 8399 1152
       http://www.childabuselawyers.com
○   *P

Association for Child & Adolescent Mental Health   (ACAMH) 1956
NR   St Saviour's House, 39-41 Union St, LONDON, SE1 1SD.   (hq)
       020 7403 7458   fax 020 7403 7081
       email acamh@acamh.org.uk
       http://www.acamh.org.uk
       Exec Dir: Ingrid King
▲   Registered Charity
Br   2
○   *L; to further the study of the mental health of children, young people & their families, through the media of meetings & publications
●   Mtgs - ET - Res - SG - Inf
M   2,410 i, UK / 300 i, o'seas
¶   Jnl of Child Psychology & Psychiatry - 8.
       Child & Adolescent Mental Health - 4.

Association of Child Psychotherapists   (ACP)   1949
NR   120 West Heath Rd, LONDON, NW3 7TU.   (hq)
       020 8458 1609   fax 020 8458 1482
       email admin@acp-uk.eu   http://www.acp.uk.net
○   *P
●   Mtgs - Lectures
M   693 i

Association for Children with Hand or Arm Deficiency
       see **REACH: Association of Children with Hand or Arm Deficiency**

Association of Children's Hospices
NR   Bridge House (4th floor), 4852 Baldwin St, BRISTOL, BS1 1QB.
       0117-989 7820
       email info@childhospice.org.uk
▲   Registered Charity
○   *M
       Uses working name of Children's Hospices UK

Association for Children with Life-Threatening or Terminal Conditions & their Families
       since June 2006 **Association for Children's Palliative Care**

Association for Children's Palliative Care   (ACT)   1993
NR   Brunswick Court, Brunswick Square,BRISTOL, BS2 8PE.
       0117-916 6422(admin)   fax 0117-916 6430
       email info@act.org.uk   http://www.act.org.uk
       Chief Exec Officer: Lizzie Chambers
▲   Company Limited by Guarantee
○   *K, *M, *W; campaigns for the provision of locally coordinated
       palliative care services for terminally ill children; to provide
       information on services available to families caring for a
       child with a life-threatening or terminal condition
Gp   ACT Council (Chmn: Heather Wood),
       Children's palliative care (Chmn: Dr Angela Thompson)
●   Conf - Mtgs - ET - Inf - Lib - LG
       Helpline: 0845 108 2201
<   Inst of Child Health (Bristol)
M   [not stated], over 800 families
       (Sub:from £50 i, £60-£150 f UK / £70 i, £80-170 f o'seas)
¶   Act Now (NL) - 5; ftm, £20 yr nm.
       Act for Families - 5; ftm, £20 yr nm.
       Transition Care Pathway; ftm, £10 nm.
       Voice for Change (2003).
       Other publications.
×   2006 (June) Association for Children with Life-Threatening
               or Terminal Conditions & their Families

Association of Christian Teachers   (ACT)   1971
NR   23 Billing Rd, NORTHAMPTON, NN1 5AT.   (hq)
       01604 632046
       http://www.christian-teachers.org.uk
▲   Company Limited by Guarantee; Registered Charity
○   *E, *R; to support Christians employed in education
M   i

Association of Christian Teachers Scotland
NR   2 Oxgangs Path, EDINBURGH, EH13 9LX.
       0755 765 2785
       email actscotland@btinternet.com
       http://www.actscotland.org.uk
       Chmn: Bernard Bowers
○   *E, *R; supporting and serving Christian teachers in Scotland

Association for Church Editors   (ACE)
NR   Carousel, 1 Barrow Slade, Keyworth, NOTTINGHAM,
       NG12 5JQ.   (mem/sp)
       0115-914 2930   fax 0115-914 2960
       http://www.churcheditors.org
       Mem Sec: Margaret Wood
○   *P; for all editors of church magazines
M   i

Association of Circulation Executives   (ACE)   1951
NR   1 Warwick Row, LONDON, SW1E 5ER.
       07545 018388
       http://www.acecirculation.com
       Marketing Mgr: Mark Farris
▲   Un-incorporated Society
○   *P, *T; for senior executives responsible for circulation,
       marketing & distribution of newspapers, magazines,
       periodicals (national & regional); for the dissemination of
       information & promotion of goodwill between publishers
       (members) & the wholesalers & retailers who handle their
       publications

Association of Circus Proprietors of Great Britain   (ACP)   1932
■   PO Box 131, BLACKBURN, Lancs, BB1 9GA.   (hsp)
       01254 814789   fax 01254 814789
       email malcolmclay@talk21.com
       http://www.circus-uk.co.uk
       Sec: Malcolm S Clay
▲   Un-incorporated Society
○   *T; the conduct of the circus industry in GB; the welfare of
       animals in circuses
●   Conf - Mtgs - Inf - LG
M   20 f

Association for Citizenship Teaching
NR   63 Gee St, LONDON, EC1V 3RS.   (regd/address)
       020 7253 0051   fax 020 7566 4131
       email info@teachingcitizenship.org.uk
       http://www.teachingcitizenship.org.uk
       Devt Officer: Millicent Scott
▲   Registered Charity
○   *P; to educate pupils & help them understand the happenings
       in the world around them
●   Conf - ET - Inf
M   i
       (Sub: £35)

Association of Civic Hosts
       in 2006 merged with the **Association for Public Service
       Excellence**

Association of Civil Enforcement Agencies
       in January 2011 merged with the Enforcement Services Association to
       form the **Civil Enforcement Association**

Association of Classic Trials Clubs Ltd   (ACTC)   1979
■   10 Beechwood, ROSS-on-WYE, Herefords, HR9 7QE.   (hsp)
       01989 763403
       http://www.actc.org.uk
       Hon Sec: Stuart R Harrold
▲   Company Limited by Guarantee
Br   22
○   *K, *S; to promote grass-roots motorsport through national
       classic reliability trials championships for cars & motorcycles
Gp   Technical panel; Public relations; Rights of way; Championships
●   Mtgs - Exhib - Comp - PL - LG
<   Motor Sports Assn UK; Byways & Bridleways Trust Coun
M   c 3,000 i, 22 org
¶   Restart - 4.

Association for Clinical Biochemistry   (ACB)   1953
NR   130-132 Tooley St, LONDON, SE1 2TU.   (hq)
       020 7403 8001   fax 020 7403 8006
       email admin@acb.org.uk   http://www.acb.org.uk
       Chmn: Dr I D Watson,   Hon Sec: Dr G McCreanor
▲   Company Limited by Guarantee
○   *L; advancement of clinical biochemistry in the UK
Gp   C'ees: Education, Scientific, Publications, Workforce advisory
●   Conf - Mtgs - ET - Res - Exhib - Empl - LG
<   Intl Fedn of Clinical Chemistry (IFCC)
M   1,835 i, 56 f, UK / 306 i, o'seas
¶   Annals of Clinical Biochemistry - 6; ftm, £136 yr nm.

Association of Clinical Biochemists in Ireland
IRL   c/o Clinical Biochemistry Dept, St Vincent's University Hospital,
       Elm Park, DUBLIN 4, Republic of Ireland.   (sb)
       email president@acbi.ie   http://www.acbi.ie
       Sec: Ms Orla Maguire
○   *P

Association for Clinical Cytogenetics
       a group of the **British Society for Human Genetics**

Association for Clinical Data Management   (ACDM)
NR   105 St Peter's St, ST ALBANS, Herts, AL1 3EJ.   (hq)
       01727 896080
       http://www.acdm.org.uk
       Sec: Angela Ison
▲   Company Limited by Guarantee
○   *P; data management in the pharmaceutical industry
<   Conf - Mtgs - ET - Exam - Exhib
M   1,438 i, UK / 259 i, o'seas

Association of Clinical Embryologists
- ■ Kelmer Court House, 102 Sale Lane, MANCHESTER, M29 8PZ. (hsb)
  0161-790 2020   http://www.embyologists.org.uk
  Sec: Mike Hooper
- ○ *P

Association of Clinical Pathologists   (ACP)   1927
- NR 189 Dyke Rd, HOVE, E Sussex, BN3 1TL. (hq)
  01273 775700   fax 01273 773303
  email info@pathologists.org.uk
  http://www.pathologists.org.uk
  Gen Admin: Alison Martin
- ▲ Company Limited by Guarantee; Registered Charity
- Br 12
- ○ *L, *P; the study & practice of clinical pathology
- ● Conf - Mtgs - ET
- M 2,200 i, UK & o'seas
- ¶ ACP News - 3;   ACP Ybk - 1.

Association of Clinical Professors of Paediatrics
  since 2007 **Academic Paediatrics Association of Great Britain & Ireland**

Association for Coaching   (AC)
- NR 66 Church Rd, LONDON, W7 1LB.
  http://www.associationforcoaching.com
  Chmn: Katherine Tulpa
- ○ *P; lifestyle coaching

Association for Cognitive Analytic Therapy   (ACAT)
- NR PO Box 6793, DORCHESTER, Dorset, DT1 9DL.
  0844 800 9496
  http://www.acat.me.uk
  Admin: Susan van Baars
- ○ *P

Association of Collaborative Family Lawyers
  a group of the **Law Society of Northern Ireland**

Association for College Management   (ACM)   1987
- NR 35 The Point, MARKET HARBOROUGH, Leics, LE16 7QU. (admin)
  01858 461110   fax 01858 461366
  email administration@acm.uk.com
  http://www.acm.uk.com
  Chief Exec & Gen Sec: Peter Pendle
- Br 110
- ○ *P, *U; a trade union for college managers (principals, vice-principals & other senior college managers)
- Gp Many connected with vocational education & training
- ● Conf - Mtgs - ET - SG - Empl - LG
- M 3,500 i, UK / 10 i, o'seas
- ¶ NL - 10;   Information & Briefing Sheet - irreg; both ftm only.

Association of Colleges   (AoC)   1893
- ■ 2-5 Stedham Place, LONDON, WC1A 1HU. (hq)
  020 7034 9900   fax 020 7034 9950
  email debra-stych@aoc.co.uk   http://www.aoc.co.uk
  Chief Exec: Martin Doel,   Co Sec: Debra Stych
- ▲ Company Limited by Guarantee
- ○ *E, *N; 'leading body in the UK on further education'
- ● Conf - Mtgs - ET - Empl - LG
- M 332 colleges
  (Sub: varies, c £4,000,000 in total)

Association of Coloproctology of Great Britain & Ireland   1990
- ■ at the Royal College of Surgeons, 35-43 Lincoln's Inn Fields, LONDON, WC2A 3PE. (hq)
  020 7973 0307   fax 020 7430 9235
  email acpgbi@asgbi.org.uk   http://www.acpgbi.org.uk
  Hon Sec: Karen Nugent
- ▲ Company Limited by Guarantee; Registered Charity
- ○ *P; the advancement of the science & practice of coloproctology (treatment of patients with diseases of the colon & rectum; to practice high standards in training & research
- ● Conf - Mtgs - ET - Res - Exhib
- M 1,200 i, UK / 100 i, o'seas
- ¶ Colorectal Disease - 9; prices vary (published by Blackwell Publishing).

Association of Commercial Specials Manufacturers
- NR Rosemont House, Yorkdale Industrial Park, Braithwaite St, LEEDS, W Yorks, LS11 9XE. (hq)
  http://www.acsm.uk.com
  Sec: Jen Postlethwaite
- ○ *T; suppliers of unlicensed, tailor-made, medicines prescribed by a doctor when a licensed product is not available
- ● ET - LG
- M 13 f

Association of Commonwealth Universities   (ACU)   1913
- NR Woburn House, 20-24 Tavistock Sq, LONDON, WC1H 9NF. (hq)
  020 7380 6700
  http://www.acu.ac.uk
- ▲ Registered Charity
- ○ *E; a Commonwealth body, governed & financed by the membership throughout the Commonwealth which promotes contact & cooperation between universities

Association of Community & Comprehensive Schools   1982
- IRL 10H Centrepoint Business Park, Oak Drive, DUBLIN 12, Republic of Ireland.
  353 (1) 460 1150   fax 353 (1) 460 1203
  email office@accs.ie   http://www.accs.ie
  Hon Sec: Ciarán Flynn
- ○ *E
- M 92 schools

** ** Association for Community-based Maternity Care**
  organisation lost; see Introduction paragraph 3

Association of Community Rail Partnerships   (ACoRP)   1999
- ■ Rail & River Centre, Canal Side, Civic Hall, 15a New St, Slaithwaite, HUDDERSFIELD, W Yorks, HD7 5AB. (hq)
  01484 847790   fax 01484 847877
  http://www.acorp.uk.com
  Sec: Philip Jenkinson
- ▲ Company Limited by Guarantee
- ○ *K; to encourage local communities to become actively involved with their local railway station/train service, predominantly in the rural sector
- Gp Rolling stock; Station design
- ● Conf - Res - Exhib - SG - Inf - Lib - VE - LG
- < Community Transport Assn
- > Community Transport Assn; Heritage Rly Assn; Sustrans
- M 7 i, 7 f, 57 org
- ¶ Train Times - 4; ftm, £70 nm (includes discounts at conferences, specialist advice; email NL - ftm only).
  Research/consultancy Reports - 2/3; ftm.   AR.

Association for Commuter Transport
  merged in 2008 with the National TravelWise Association to form **ACT TravelWise**

Association of Company Registration Agents Ltd   (ACRA)   1978

NR   14-18 City Rd, CARDIFF, CF24 3DL.   (hsb)
      email phil.vibrans@acra-uk.org   http://www.acra-uk.org
      Hon Sec: M R Chettleburgh
▲   Company Limited by Guarantee
○   *P; 'to promote the interests of those using the facilities of the
      Companies Registration Office; to maintain a high standard
      among members'
●   LG
<   Law Services Assn
M   13 f

Association for Comparative Legal Studies   (ACLS)

§   20 Park Hill Road, WALLINGTON, Surrey, SM6 0SB.
      A body consisting of legal experts to publish the Journal of
      Comparative Law

Association of Composite Door Manufacturers   (ACDM)

NR   4 Brookside, Stretton-on-Dunsmore, RUGBY, Warks,
      CV32 9LY.   (mem/sec)
      http://www.acdm.co.uk
      Sec: Loretta Curtis
      Technical Officer: Paul Curtis (0798 917 3546)
○   *T; for manufacturers of doors made from composite materials
      - steel-faced, thermoplastic-faced (PVCu, ABS) & thermoset-
      faced (fibreglass, carbon fibre)
M   17 f

Association of Computer Cable Manufacturers   (ACCM)   1993

■   Kingsway House, Wrotham Rd, GRAVESEND, Kent,
      DA13 0AU.   (asa)
○   *T
●   Conf - Mtgs - LG - Lib
M   f

Association of Computer Engineers & Technicians   (ACET)

NR   Association House, St David's Rd, CRANBROOK, Kent,
      TN17 3HL.
      01580 712744   fax 01580 712281
      email info@acet-uk.org   http://www.acet-uk.org
○   *P

Association of Computer Professionals   (ACP)   1984

■   Chilverbridge House, ARLINGTON, E Sussex, BN26 6SB.   (hq)
      01323 871874   fax 01323 871875
      email admin@acpexamboard.com
      http://www.acpexamboard.com
      Sec Gen: Mrs N Keats
○   *P; to provide high standards of efficiency throughout the
      industry; to prepare candidates, through examinations, for a
      successful career in computing
●   Exam (for: Certificate in information technology &
      programming; Diploma in information systems analysis &
      design; Advanced diploma in computer science
M   i

Association of Concrete Industrial Flooring Contractors (ACIFC)   1994

■   Royal London House, 22-25 Finsbury Square, LONDON,
      EC2A 1DX.   (asa)
      0844 249 9176   fax 0844 249 9177
      email info@acifc.org   http://www.acifc.org
      Secretariat: S Doshi,   Chmn: David Harvey
▲   Un-incorporated Society
○   *T; interests of specialist contractors & the development of
      concrete floors
Gp   Technical - all aspects of slab construction
●   Conf - Mtgs - Inf - Liaison with technical & trade bodies
<   ACIFC (France)
M   40 f, UK / 10 f, o'seas
¶   Technical publications, published through the Concrete Society:
      Concrete Mix Design.   Dry Shake Topping.
      Admixtures.   Steel Fibre Reinforcement.

Association for Conferences & Events   (ACE)   1971

■   CreativeXchange, Longsands Campus, Longsands Rd,
      ST NEOTS, Cambs, PE19 1TE.   (hq)
      01480 223484
      email ace@aceinternational.org
      http://www.aceinternational.org
      Mem Mgr: John Thompson
▲   Company Limited by Guarantee
○   *N, *P, *T; information centre & forum for member
      organisations involved in the organising, marketing,
      accommodating & servicing of events
●   ET - Inf - VE - LG
>   Business Visits & Events Partnership (BVEP)
M   150 f, UK / 2 f, o'seas
¶   NL - 12;   AR; both ftm only.
      Conference & Exhibition Fact Finder - 12; ftm, £36 nm.
      ACE Ybk - Who's Who in the Meetings Industry - 1; ftm,
      £14.99 nm.
      ACE Guide to a Career in Conferences (Hbk); ftm, £2.50 nm.

Association for the Conservation of Energy   (ACE)   1981

NR   Westgate House, 2a Prebend St, LONDON, N1 8PT.   (hq)
      020 7359 8000   fax 020 7259 0863
      http://www.ukace.org
      Dir: Andrew Warren
▲   Company Limited by Guarantee
○   *K, *T; to encourage a positive national awareness of the
      benefits & need for energy conservation
●   Res
<   EUROACE
M   16 f
¶   The Fifth Fuel (NL) - 2; free.
      Publications list available on website.

Association for Consultancy & Engineering   (ACE)   1913

NR   Alliance House, 12 Caxton St, LONDON, SW1H 0QL.   (hq)
      020 7222 6557   fax 020 7222 0750
      email consult@acenet.co.uk   http://www.acenet.co.uk
      Chief Exec: Nelson Ogunshakin
▲   Company Limited by Guarantee
○   *T
M   750 f, UK / 10 f, o'seas

Association of Consultant Approved Inspectors   (ACAI)   1996

NR   c/o Teaselwood Barn, Lamberhurst Vineyard, Furnace Lane,
      LAMBERHURST, Kent, TN3 8LA.
      http://www.acai.org.uk
      Hon Sec: David Allen
▲   Un-incorporated Society
○   *P; to promote the role & development of private sector
      building control by approved inspectors instead of the use of
      local authorities in England & Wales.   Approved Inspectors
      are statutory appointees under Part II of the Building
      Act 1984, such appointees being made by the Secretary of
      State for Local Government & the Regions, or the
      Construction Industry Council

Association of Consultant Architects   (ACA)   1973

NR   60 Godwin Rd, BROMLEY, Kent, BR2 9LQ.   (hq)
      020 8325 1402   fax 020 8466 9079
      email office@acarchitects.co.uk
      http://www.acarchitects.co.uk
      Sec Gen: Alison Low
▲   Company Limited by Guarantee
○   *T; for architects in private practice
Gp   Planning advisory; Conservation; Small business
●   Conf - Mtgs - Res - Exhib - Comp - SG - VE - LG
M   250 f
¶   NL - 4; ftm only.
      ACA Specialist Services Directory - 1; ftm, £10 nm.
      ACA Form of Building Agreement (Contract
      document); £7.87 m, £10.50 nm.

© CBD Research Ltd · Beckenham · BR3 5JS · Tel 020 8650 7745 · E-mail cbd@cbdresearch.com · www.cbdresearch.com

Association of Consulting Actuaries   (ACA)   1951
NR   St Clement's House, 27-28 St Clement's Lane, LONDON,
     EC4N 7AE.   (hq)
     020 3207 9380   fax 020 3207 9134
     http://www.aca.org.uk
     Hon Sec: Andrew Vaughan
○   *P; to advise individuals, institutions, the government &
     corporate bodies on pensions, life & general insurance &
     other financial issues

Association of Consulting Engineers of Ireland   (ACIE)   1938
IRL   46 Merrion Sq, DUBLIN 2, Republic of Ireland.
     353 (1) 642 5588   fax 353 (1) 642 5590
     http://www.acei.ie
     Pres: Eamon Timoney
○   *P; to represent the business & professional interests of firms &
     individuals engaged in Consulting Engineering
<   Electro-Technical Coun of Ireland
M   205 i, 106 f

Association of Consulting Scientists   (ACS)   1958
■   5 Willow Heights, CRADLEY HEATH, W Midlands, B64 7PL.
     (hsb)
     0121-602 3515
     http://www.consultingscientists.co.uk
     Hon Sec: Dr Stuart Guy
▲   Company Limited by Guarantee
○   *P; to make known the services of consulting scientists; to
     promote scientific & technical research through contracts with
     member firms; to ascertain & make known the views of
     independent scientists on matters of wider interest
Gp   Forensic & expert witness; Testing laboratories
●   Conf - Mtgs - Res - Inf - LG
M   42 f
¶   NL - 4; free.
     Directory of Members & Services - on website.

Association of Contact Lens Manufacturers Ltd   (ACLM)   1962
NR   PO Box 735, DEVIZES, Wilts, SN10 3TQ.   (sec-gen/b)
     01380 860418   fax 01380 860863
     email info@aclm.org.uk   http://www.aclm.org.uk
     Sec Gen: Simon Rodwell
▲   Company Limited by Guarantee
○   *T; to promote the wearing of contact lenses
Gp   EDI; Ethics; EDI; Hygienic management; Labelling; Packaging
     waste; Technical working
●   Conf - Mtgs - ET - Exhib - Stat - LG - Regulatory [activities] in
     connection with CE marking
<   Optical Confedn
     Eur Fedn Nat Assns Contact Lens Mfrs (Euromcontact);
     Eyecare UK (E-UK)
M   3 i, 30 f
¶   ACLM Contact Lens Ybk - 1; £17.

Association for Contemporary Iberian Studies   (ACIS)   1968
■   c/o Dr Mark Gant, Languages Dept, University of Chester,
     CHESTER, CH1 4BJ.   (hsb)
     01244 513049   fax 01244 511311
     email m.gant@chester.ac.uk
     http://www.iberianstudies.net
     Sec: Dr Mark Gant
▲   Un-incorporated Society
○   *L; the study of social, economic & political affairs of the
     Iberian area, together with its languages
●   Conf - ET - Res
M   180 i, 30 f, UK / 20 i, o'seas
     (Sub: £40 UK / £54 o'seas)
¶   International Jnl of Iberian Studies - 3; ftm, £33 i, £90 instns.
     [see: www.intellectbooks.co.uk]

Association for Contemporary Jewellery   (ACJ)   1997
■   PO Box 37807, LONDON, SE23 1XJ   (admin/p)
     020 8291 4201   fax 020 8291 4452
     email enquiries@acj.org.uk   http://www.acj.org.uk
     Admin: Sue Hyams,   Chmn: Frances Julie Whitelaw
○   *G, *P, *T
●   Conf - ET - Exhib - Inf - VE
¶   Findings - 4.

Association for Continence Advice   (ACA)   1981
■   Fitwise Management Ltd, Drumcross Hall, BATHGATE,
     W Lothian, EH48 4JT.   (asa)
     01506 811077   fax 01506 811477
     http://www.aca.uk.com
▲   Company Limited by Guarantee; Registered Charity
Br   10
○   *P; a multi-professional membership organisation, open to all
     interested in the promotion of continence & who have a
     concern for the better management of incontinence
Gp   Special interest: Bowel, Pelvic floor
●   Conf - Mtgs - ET - Res - Exhib - SG
<   Works closely with: Incontact; PromoCon
M   c 600 i, 35 f, UK / 29 i, o'seas
     (Sub: £45 i, £450 f, UK / £60 o'seas)
¶   NL - 4; ftm, £22 yr nm.
     Notes for Good Practice; on-line (annual updates).
     Resource Pack for Care Homes; ftm, £15 nm.
     Directory of members - 2 yrly; ftm, £587.50 nm.

Association of Contractors & Temporary Workers   2003
NR   The Frieslawn Centre, Hodsoll Street, SEVENOAKS, Kent,
     TN15 7LH   (hq)
     0870 720 0259
     http://www.actw.co.uk
○   *T; a non-profit organisation to represent temporary workers in
     the UK

The Association of Controls Manufacturers
    a sector group of **BEAMA**

Association of Convenience Stores   (ACS)   1994
■   Federation House, 17 Farnborough St, FARNBOROUGH,
     Hants, GU14 8AG.   (hq)
     01252 515001
     http://www.acs.org.uk
     Chief Exec: James Lowman
▲   Company Limited by Guarantee
○   *T; to represent convenience stores across the UK; to foster the
     development of the whole of the professional convenience
     store sector, for the benefit of retailers, wholesalers &
     suppliers; to optimise the benefit to the sector of legislation
     emanating from UK & EU parliaments & by anticipating
     demand for information & training required by the sector
Gp   Association of News Retailing
●   Conf - Mtgs - Res - Inf - VE - LG
<   Intl Fedn of Grocers' Assns
M   33,000 stores
¶   ACS News - 12; ftm.

**Association of Copyright Infringement Investigators   (ASCII)
2000**
■   81 Park View, Collins Rd, Islington, LONDON, N5 2UD.   (hq)
○   *P
●   Mtgs - Stat - LG
M   i & f
×   2007 Association of Copyright Investigators

Association of Corporate Treasurers   (ACT)   1979
NR   51 Moorgate, LONDON, EC2R 6BH.   (hq)
         020 7847 2540   fax 020 7374 8744
         http://www.treasurers.org
         Chief Exec: Stuart Siddall
Br   16; Belgium, Eire, Hong Kong
○   *P; the management of financial risk, liquidity, corporate
         finance, the balance sheet
●   Conf - Mtgs - ET - Exam - Res - Exhib - SG - Lib - LG
M   c 4,000 i
¶   The Treasurer - 12;   The Treasurers Hbk - 1; both ftm.

Association of Corporate Trustees   (TACT)   1974
NR   3 Brackerne Close, Cooden, BEXHILL-on-SEA, E Sussex,
         TN39 3BT.   (hsb)
         01424 844144   fax 01424 844144
         http://www.trustees.org.uk
         Sec: W J Stephenson
▲   Un-incorporated Society
○   *P; to consider & act on items of mutual interest in the fields of
         law, taxation, investment & related technical & practical
         subjects
Gp   Pensions; Loan capital; Private trusts; Charities
●   Mtgs - ET
M   70 f, UK / 1 f, o'seas
¶   TACT Review - 2; free.

Association of Cost Engineers Ltd   (ACostE)   1962
NR   Lea House, 5 Middlewich Rd, SANDBACH, Cheshire,
         CW11 1XL.   (hq)
         01270 764798   fax 01270 766180
         email enquiries@acoste.org.uk
         http://www.acoste.org.uk
▲   Company Limited by Guarantee
○   *P; to represent the professional interests of those with
         responsibility for the prediction, planning & control of
         resources & cost for activities that involve engineering,
         manufacturing & construction
M   i

Association of Cost Management Consultants   (ACMC)   1999
NR   Blays House, Churchfield Rd, CHALFONT ST PETER, Bucks,
         SL9 9EW.   (hsb)
         01753 891313
         http://www.theacmc.co.uk
         Hon Sec: Tony Gibson
▲   Un-incorporated Society
○   *P; business cost reduction specialists
M   7 f

Association of Council Secretaries & Solicitors   (ACSeS)   1974
NR   64 Smithbrook Kilns, CRANLEIGH, Surrey, GU6 8JJ.   (hq)
         01305 836328
         http://www.acses.org.uk
○   *P; local government administration, law & management

Association of Countryside Voluntary Wardens   (ACVW)   1967
NR   1 Ballinbreich Farm, Newburgh, CUPAR, Fife, KY14 6HJ.   (hsp)
         01337 842704
         Sec: Jay Burkinshaw
▲   Un-incorporated Society
○   *P; to promote effective wardening by volunteers throughout the
         countryside
●   Conf - SG - LG
<   Coun for Nat Parks; LANTRA NTO
M   380 i
¶   NL - 2;   Newssheet - 2; both ftm only.

Association of County Chief Executives   (ACCE)   1974
■   Office of the Chief Executive, County Hall, TROWBRIDGE,
         Wilts, BA14 8JF.   (hsb)
         01225 713101   fax 01225 713092
         email jeanpotter@wiltshire.gov.uk
         Hon Sec: M Lloyd
▲   Un-incorporated Society
○   *P
●   Conf - Mtgs - LG
<   County section of the Society of Local Authority Chief Executives
M   38 i
¶   ACCE Members' Hbk; ftm.

Association of County & City Councils   (ACCC)   1899
IRL   Rathcloghen House, GOLDEN, Tipperary, Republic of Ireland.
         353 (1) 062 72136
         email councillors@gmail.com   http://www.councillors.ie
         Pres: Michael Fitzgerald
○   *N
×   2007 General Council of County Councils

Association of County Cricket Scorers   (ACCS)   1993
■   14 Briery Avenue, BOLTON, Lancs, BL2 4AJ.   (chmn/p)
         Hon Sec: Alan West
○   *P; to improve the standards of cricket scoring; 'to cooperate &
         cultivate good relations with all bodies associated with cricket
         for the betterment of the game'
●   AGM; Annual lunch
M   47 i
¶   The Scorer (NL) - 4; ftm only.

Association of Cricket Officials
         see **England & Wales Cricket Board Association of Cricket
         Officials**

Association of Cricket Statisticians & Historians   (ACS)   1973
NR   Archives Dept, Glamorgan Cricket, Sophia Gardens, CARDIFF,
         CF11 9XR.   (hsb)
         029 2041 9383
         email office@acscricket.com   http://www.acscricket.com
         Hon Sec: Andrew Hignell
▲   Un-incorporated Society
Br   Victoria (Australia)
○   *S; cricket history & statistics
●   Mtgs - Res - SG - Stat - Inf - Compilation of records of feats &
         matches worldwide
M   1,000 i, UK / 250 i, o'seas
¶   The Cricket Statistician - 4; ftm. 4.
         ACS International Cricket Ybk - 1.
         Various other annual publications.

Association of Cricket Umpires & Scorers
         on 1 January 2008 merged with the ECB Officials Association to form
         the **England & Wales Cricket Board Association of Cricket
         Officials**

Association of Cruise Experts   (ACE)   1958
NR   41-42 Eastcastle St (1st floor), London, W1W 8DU.   (hq)
         020 7436 2449   fax 020 7636 9206
         http://www.cruiseexperts.org
▲   Company Limited by Guarantee
○   *T; for cruise lines & ferry operators
●   Mtgs - ET - Inf - VE
M   54 f
¶   Get Cruisewise - 4; ftm only.
×   2007 Passenger Shipping Association

**Association for Cultural Advancement through Visual Art
(ACAVA) 1983**
NR 54 Blechynden St, LONDON, W10 6RJ.   (hq)
       020 8960 5015
       http://www.acava.org
       Artistic Dir: Duncan Smith
▲ Company Limited by Guarantee; Registered Charity
Br 6
○ *A; promotion of the visual arts by provision of facilities
       (including studios & galleries) & organisation of programmes
       for their production & access as well as education
● ET - Exhib
M 300 i
¶ NL - 4; free.

Association for Cushing's Treatment & Help   (ACTH)   1993
NR 54 Powney Rd, MAIDENHEAD, Berks, SL6 6EQ.
       (coordinator/p)
       01628 670389   fax 01628 415603
       email cushingsacth@btinternet.com
       http://www.cushingsacth.co.uk
       Coordinator: Mrs Elaine Eldridge
Br Regional coordinators
○ *W; a self-help group of offering experience, help & advice to
       sufferers of Cushing's Sydrome (over production of
       cortocisterid hormones) & their carers
● Mtgs (small & informal)
M C 170 i
¶ Cushy (NL) - 3; ftm only.   LM.
       Information booklets: for -
       Newly diagnosed patients;   Post surgery.

Association of Cycle Traders   (ACT)   1982
NR PO Box 5110, HOVE, E Sussex, BN52 9EB.   (hq)
       0870 428 8404   fax 0870 428 8403
       Nat Sec: Anne Killick
▲ Company Limited by Guarantee
Br 30
○ *T; to promote the interests of the independent cycle trader
● Conf - Mtgs - ET - Exam - Exhib - Inf - LG - Operation of a
       national cycle technicians accreditation programme
< Eur Twowheel Retailers Assn; Bicycle Assn GB; Indep Retailers
       Consortium
M 30 i, 800 f
¶ The Independent - 4; ftm only.

Association of Dance & Freestyle Professionals   (ADFP)   1981
NR 13 Phoenix House, Hyssop Close, CANNOCK, Staffs,
       WS11 7GA.   (regd off)
       01922 419531
       http://www.adfp.co.uk
       Chmn: Denise Baker;   Chief Exec: Diane Corbett
Br 6
○ *D; to promote & advance the teaching of freestyle dancing
       (formerly disco dancing)
● Conf - Mtgs - Comp

**Association for Dance Movement Therapy UK Ltd   (ADMT
UK) 1982**
■ 32 Meadfoot Lane, TORQUAY, Devon, TQ1 2BW.
       (mail address)
       email queries@admt.org.uk   http://www.admt.org.uk
       Co Sec & Administrator: Andrew Clements
▲ Company Limited by Guarantee
○ *P; to promote mental & physical health by the use of dance
       movement therapy; to ensure that proper standards of
       professional competence & ethics are maintained
● Conf - Mtgs - ET - Inf - LG - Courses & accreditation of
       practitioners
< Eur Dance Movement Assn
M 200 i
¶ E-Motion (NL) - 4; ftm, £16 nm.   AR.

Association of Deer Management Groups   (ADMG)   1992
■ c/o Finlay Clark, Bidwells, Carn Dearg House, North Rd,
       FORT WILLIAM, Inverness-shire, PH33 6PP.   (asa)
       01397 702433   fax 01397 702010
       email finlay.clark@bidwells.co.uk
       http://www.deer-management.co.uk
       Sec: Finlay Clark
▲ Un-incorporated Society
○ *N, *T, *V; coordination & representation of deer management
       groups in Scotland; also representation of the Scottish wild
       venison industry
● Conf - Mtgs - LG
M 30 groups
¶ NL - 2; free.

**Association of Denominational Historical Societies & Cognate
Libraries 1993**
NR 33 Addison Rd, CATERHAM, Surrey, CR3 5LU.   (sp)
       email secretary@adhscl.org.uk
       Sec: Mrs Pauline Jones
▲ Un-incorporated Society
○ *P, *R; to encourage research into the traditions of the various
       Christian denominations
● Conf - Mtgs - Res - Inf
M 21 soc & libraries
¶ NL - 1; ftm.

Association of Dental Anaesthetists   (ADA)   1977
■ 21 Portland Place, LONDON, W1B 1PY.   (hq)
       020 7631 1650   fax 020 7631 4352
       email info@aagbi.org
       http://www.dentalanaesthesia.org.uk
       Pres: Dr Ken Ruiz,   Hon Sec: Diana Terry
▲ Registered Charity
○ *P; to promote management of highest standards in the
       conduct of sedation & anaesthesia for dentistry
● Conf - Mtgs - ET
< Assn of Anaesthetists of GB & Ireland
M 350 i
       (Sub: £10)
¶ Proceedings - 1;   NL - 2/3; both ftm.

**Association of Dental Hospitals of the United Kingdom
(ADH) 1948**
■ c/o Jane Luker, Bristol Dental Hospital, Chapter House, Lower
       Maudlin St, BRISTOL, BS1 2LY.
       0117-342 4301
       Sec: Jane Luker
Br 14
○ *N; for dental teaching hospitals
● Mtgs
M 28 i

Association of Dental Implantology UK   (ADI)   1986
■ 98 South Worple Way, LONDON, SW14 8ND.   (hq)
       020 8487 5555   fax 020 8487 5566
       email office@adi.org.uk   http://www.adi.org.uk
       Hon Sec: Dr Steve Byfield,   Chief Exec: Cherry Wilson
▲ Company Limited by Guarantee; Registered Charity
○ *P; to provide post graduate education in dental implantology
       profession
Gp Dentists; Dental technicians; Hygienists; Max-Fax surgeons;
       Nurses; Restorative consultants
● Conf - Mtgs - ET - Res - Exhib - SG - Inf
M 1,500 i, 30 f, UK / 25 i, o'seas
       (Sub: £35-£222)
¶ Dental Implant Summaries - 6;
       European Jnl for Dental Implantologists - 4; both ftm.

Association of Diocesan and Cathedral Architects   (ADCA)
NR c/o Oxford Archaeology, James House, Osney Mead,
       OXFORD, OX2 0ES.   (hsb)
       http://www.britarch.ac.uk/adca
       Hon Sec: J Munby
○ *P

**Association of Directors of Adult Social Services   (ADASS)
2007**
NR   ADASS Business Unit, Local Government House, Smith Sq,
     LONDON, SW1P 3HZ.   (hsb)
     020 7072 7433
     http://www.adass.org.uk
     Admin: Marinda Oosthuizen
▲   Registered Charity
Br   11
○   *P; promotion of a comprehensive social service for families,
     individuals & communities
●   Conf - Mtgs - Res - Stat - Inf - LG
M   135 i
¶   ADSS News - 4/5.   AR - 1.   Hbk (incl LM).
     Directory of Contracting Officers.
     Abuse of Older People.   Towards Community Care.
     Training for the Caring Business.
✕   2007 Association of Directors of Social Services - adult element

Association of Directors of Children's Services   (ADCS)   2007
NR   The Triangle (3rd floor), Exchange Square, MANCHESTER,
     M4 3TR.   (hq)
     0161-838 5757   fax 0161-838 5756
     http://www.adcs.org.uk
     Sec: Sarah Caton
○   *P
●   Conf - Mtgs - Res - LG - Representation to government & other
     bodies on educational matters
M   950 i
✕   2007 (Confederation of Children's Services Managers
         (Association of Directors of Social Services - children's
     element

**Association of Directors of Education in Scotland   (ADES)
1920**
NR   Lochan House, Birse, ABOYNE, AB34 5FP.   (hsb)
     01339 887160
     email jstodter@freeserve.co.uk
     http://www.adescotland.org.uk
     Sec Gen: John Stodter
○   *E, *P
M   ['not applicable']

Association of Directors of Environment, Economy, Planning and Transport
     since 2010 **ADEPT**

Association of Directors of Public Health   (ADPH)   1856
NR   Lockton House (2nd floor), Clarendon Rd, CAMBRIDGE,
     CB2 8FH.   (hq)
     01223 725308   fax 01223 725401
     email enquiries@adph.org.uk   http://www.adph.org.uk
     Chief Exec: Nicola Close
○   *M, *P; 'to maximise the effectiveness and impact of Directors
     of Public Health & public health leaders'
M   i

Association of Directors of Social Services
     in 2007 split to become the **Association of Directors of Adult
     Social Services** & the **Association of Directors of Children's
     Services**

Association of Directors of Social Work   (ADSW)   1969
NR   Verity House, 19 Haymarket Yards, EDINBURGH, EH12 5BH.
     (hq)
     0131-474 9220
     email sophie.mills@adsw.org.uk   http://www.adsw.org.uk
     Sec: Jim Dean, Admin: Sophie Mills
○   *P; for senior social workers working in Scottish local
     government
<   Conf - Mtgs
M   140 i

Association of Disabled Professionals   (ADP)   1971
■   BCM ADP, LONDON, WC1N 3XX.   (mail/address)
     01204 431638   fax 01204 431638
     email adp.admin@ntlworld.com
     http://www.adp.org.uk
     Chmn: Jane Hunt
▲   Registered Charity
○   *W; improvement of rehabilitation, education, training &
     employment opportunities of the disabled
●   Conf - Res - Inf - LG
M   c 240 i, 3 f, UK / 3 i, o'seas
¶   Quarterly - 4.

**Association of Distributors, Coaters & Converters of Adhesive
Tapes**
     we have been informed that this organisation is dormant -
     confirmation is required please

Association of Dogs & Cats Homes   (ADCH)   1985
■   c/o MGFT Animal Sanctuary, Church Knowle, WAREHAM,
     Dorset, BH20 5NQ.   (hsb)
     01929 480474
     email mgft.trustees@btopenworld.com
     http://www.adch.org.uk
     Sec: Matt Devereux
▲   Un-incorporated Society
○   *N; to provide a forum for people in dog & cat rescue
     organisations to discuss common issues
●   Conf - Mtgs
M   51 org, UK / 3 org, o'seas
¶   Code of Practice - 1; ftm, on website.

Association of Domestic Management
     since 2007 the **Association of Healthcare Cleaning
Professionals**

Association of Drainage Authorities   (ADA)   1937
NR   1 Claremont Rd (1st floor), SURBITON, Surrey, KT6 4QS.   (hsb)
     020 8399 7350   fax 020 8390 9368
     email admin@ada.org.uk   http://www.ada.org.uk
     Chief Exec: Dr Jean Venables
▲   Un-incorporated Society
Br   9
○   *N, *T; for those involved in water level management, including
     Internal Drainage Boards, RFDSs, local authorities &
     suppliers
Gp   Finance & administration; Publicity; Technical & environmental
●   Conf - Mtgs - Exhib - Stat - Inf - VE - Demonstration of land
     drainage eqpt & products (3 yrly)
<   Eur U of Water Mgt Assns (EUWMA)
M   157 f, 90 associates
     (Sub: IDBds varies according to size, £209.15 Associates)
¶   ADA Gazette - 4; ftm.

Association of Drama Adjudicators - Ireland   (ADA)
IRL   70 Riverside, PORTARLINGTON, Co Offaly, Republic of
     Ireland.   (sp)
     353 (87) 297 5275
     email pollywol@eircom.net   http://www.ada.ie
     Sec: Paula Dempsey
○   *D

Association of Ductwork Contractors & Allied Services   (ADCAS)
■   2 Waltham Court, Milley Lane, Hare Hatch, READING, Berks,
     RG10 9TH.
     0118-940 3416   fax 0118-940 6258
     email adcas@feta.co.uk   http://www.feta.co.uk
     Pres: Malcolm Moss
○   *T; dedicated to ductwork contractors, allied suppliers &
     manufacturers of equipment for ventilation & air conditioning
     systems
M   68 f

Association of Dunkirk Little Ships   (ADLS)   1966
■ 35 Finians Close, UXBRIDGE, Middx, UB10 9NW.   (hsp)
   01895 254193   fax 01895 813788
   email info@adls.org.uk   http://www.adls.org.uk
   Hon Sec: M Cormack
○ *G; to commemorate the Little Ships' rescue mission to Dunkirk
   in 1940, & to keep them afloat
● Mtgs:
   Afloat: Trip from Dover/Ramsgate to Dunkirk every 5 yrs -
   Annual commemorative cruise
   Ashore: AGM - Annual Fitting-out & Laying-up Supper
M 130 privately owned boats (not people)
¶ NL - 2; ftm only, appropriate advertising accepted

Association of Early Pregnancy Units   (AEPU)   1999
NR St Michael's Hospital (ward 78), Southwell St, BRISTOL,
   BS2 8EG.   (hsb)
   0117-342 5174   fax 0117-342 5776
   email enquiries@earlypregnancy.org.uk
   http://www.earlypregnancy.org.uk
   Sec: Mrs Caroline Overton
▲ Company Limited by Guarantee
○ *M; to provide accessible information to help patient choice &
   allow access their local EPU when needed
● Conf - Info
M 200+ EPUs

Association for Education & Ageing   (AEA)   1985
■ 132 Dawes Rd, LONDON, SW6 7EF.   (hsp)
   020 7385 4641
   email infoaea.allen1@gmail.com
   http://www.associationforeducationandageing.org
   Hon Sec: Carol Allen
▲ Registered Charity
Br 1
○ *E, *P; promotion of education in later life
● Conf - Mtgs - ET - Res
M c 50 i, c 10 org
¶ AEA Digest (NL) - 4; ftm & to potential members only.
   Educational Gerontology (Jnl); £50 m, £200+ nm.

Association for the Education & Guardianship of International Students   (AEGIS)   1994
■ 66 Humphreys Close, Randwick, STROUD, Glos, GL5 4NY.
   (regd off)
   01453 755160   fax 01453 755160
   email secretary@aegisuk.net   http://www.aegisuk.net
   Sec: Janet Bowman
▲ Company Limited by Guarantee; Registered Charity
○ *W; to promote the welfare & well-being of international
   students at UK boarding schools
● Conf - Mtgs - ET
M 17 org, 65 schools
¶ NL - 2;   LM - continuous; both free.

Association for Education Welfare Management   (AEWM)   1917
NR Education Welfare Service, Civic Centre, Stickwell Close,
   BROMLEY, Kent BR1 3UH.   (pres/b)
   http://www.aewmweb.com/
   Pres: Jenny Clarke
▲ Un-incorporated Society
○ *P; managers of education welfare & social work services; to
   help children & young people maximise their educational
   opportunities through regular attendance at school
● Conf - Mtgs - ET
M 150 i

Association of Educational Development & Improvement Professionals in Scotland   (Aedips)   2005
NR c/o East Dunbartonshire County Council, Tom Johnstone
   House, Civic Way, KIRKINTILLOCH, G66 4TJ.
   0300 123 4510
   email edith.girvaneastdunbarton.gov.uk
   http://www.aedips.org.uk
   Sec: Edith Girvan
○ *E

Association of Educational Psychologists   (AEP)   1962
■ 4 The Riverside Centre, Frankland Lane, DURHAM,
   DH1 5TA.   (hq)
   0191-384 9512   fax 0191-386 5287
   email enquiries@aep.org.uk   http://www.aep.org.uk
   Sec: Eric Page
▲ Un-incorporated Society
○ *E, *P, *U; to promote educational psychology as a profession;
   to liaise with government, local authorities & others
   concerned with the development of children & young people
● Conf - Mtgs - ET - Res - Stat - Empl - LG
< TUC; GFTU; IPSA; Nat Children's Bureau
M 3,386 i
¶ Educational Psychology in Practice - 4; ftm, £67 i, £200 instns,
   £190 online, nm.

Association of Electoral Administrators   (AEA)
NR PO Box 201, South Eastern, LIVERPOOL, L16 5HH.   (hsb)
   0151-281 8246
   http://www.aea-elections.co.uk
   Exec Dir: Gina Armstrong
○ *P; for the consistent & efficient administration of electoral
   registration & the conduct of elections
M i
¶ Arena (NL) - 4.

Association of Electrical Contractors (Ireland)   (AECI)
IRL Woodview Centre, Main St, CELBRIDGE, Co Kildare, Republic
   of Ireland.   (hq)
   353 (1) 610 2715   fax 353 (1) 610 2692
   email aeci@indigo.ie   http://www.aeci.ie
   Exec Sec: Chris Lundy
○ *T; to project & promote the interests of electrical contractors
< Electro-Technical Coun of Ireland
M 360 f

Association of Electrical & Mechanical Trades   (AEMT)   1945
NR St Saviour's House, St Saviour's Place, YORK, N Yorks,
   YO1 7PJ.   (regd/office)
   01904 674899
   http://www.aemt.org.uk
▲ Company Limited by Guarantee
○ *T; interests of electrical motor apparatus repairers &
   manufacturers (electric motors, pumps & rotating plant,
   controls & electronic equipment)
M f

Association of Electricity Producers   (AEP)   1987
■ Charles House, 5-11 Regent St, LONDON, SW1Y 4LR.   (hq)
   020 7930 9390   fax 020 7930 9391
   email enquiries@aepuk.com   http://www.aepuk.com
   Chief Exec: David Porter
▲ Company Limited by Guarantee
○ *T; to promote & protect the interests of privately owned
   companies producing electricity
Gp C'ees: Electricity & gas, Electricity trading, Environment,
   European, Health & safety, Renewable energy, Scottish
● Conf - Mtgs - Res - SG - Expt - Inf - Lib - VE - LG
M 6 i, 97 f, 3 org

Association of Endoscopic Surgeons of Great Britain & Ireland
   a group of the **Association of Surgeons of Great Britain & Ireland**

Association of English Cathedrals   (AEC)   1990
Hon Sec: Sarah King
▲   Company Limited by Guarantee; Registered Charity
○   *N; to represent the 42 English Anglican cathedrals in dealing
        with government departments & agencies, national church
        institutions & other agencies; to encourage best practice
        between cathedrals & support their mission activities
Gp Cathedrals liturgy & music; Cathedrals as partners in adult
        learning
●   Conf - Res - Inf LG
M   42 cathedrals
        (Sub: £250)

Association of English Singers & Speakers   (AESS)   1913
■   Melin-y-Grogue, Llanfair Waterdine, KNIGHTON, Powys,
        LD7 1TU.   (chmn/p)
        01547 510327   fax 01547 510327
        email graham.trew@virgin.net
        http://www.aofess.org.uk
        Chmn: Graham Trew
▲   Registered Charity
○   *D, *P; to encourage the communication of English words in
        singing & speech, with clarity, understanding & imagination
●   Mtgs - ET - Comp - Master classes - Concerts
<   Inc Soc of Musicians
M   170 i
¶   NL - 3; ftm only.

Association for Environment Conscious Building   (AECB)   1989
■   PO Box 32, LLANDYSUL, Ceredigion, SA44 5ZA.   (hq)
        0845 456 9773
        email info@aecb.net   http://www.aecb.net
        Chief Exec: Andy Simmonds
▲   Company Limited by Guarantee
○   *K, *T; to facilitate environmentally responsible practices within
        building
Gp Passivhaus Trust
●   Mtgs - ET - Res - Exhib - Inf - Lib - VE - LG
M   c 1,500 f & org
¶   Green Building Magazine - 4; ftm, prices vary nm.

Association for Environmental Archaeology   (AEA)   1979
NR Fort Cumberland, Fort Cumberland Rd, Eastney,
        PORTSMOUTH, PO4 9LD.   (sb)
        02392 856789
        email far.worley@english-heritage.org.uk
        http://www.envarch.net
        Sec: Fay Worley
▲   Un-incorporated Society
○   *L, *Q; to study the human use of & effects on the environment
        in the past
●   Conf - Mtgs - Res
M   c 400 i
¶   Environmental Archaeology: Jnl of Human Palaeoecology - 2;
        £38 m.

Association of Erotic Artists   (AEA)   2003
■   Flat 3 / 50 Britannia St, LONDON, WC1X 9JH.
        (co-founder/sp)
        020 7837 7049
        email admin@associationoferoticartists.co.uk
        http://www.associationoferoticartists.co.uk
        Co-Founders: Christopher J Ball,   Paul Woods
○   *A; to promote positive interest within the public & media with
        regard to the erotic arts; to generate debate & fight
        censorship of the production & display of erotic arts made by
        consenting adults
Gp Body painting/painters; Comic book artists; Dancers; Erotic art:
        galleries, collectors, publications; Film makers; Illustrators;
        Models (as muse); Multi-media artists; Musicians; Painters;
        Photographers; Pin-up artists; Poets; Printmakers; Sculptors;
        Videographers; Writers
●   Mtgs - Res - Exhib - Comp - SG - Inf - VE - Awards
M   58 i, 3 f, UK / 9 i, o'seas
¶   [membership £35 i, £60 org]
        Note: membership is available by invitation, after submission of
        a panel of work which is viewed by all the members, & on its
        receiving a simple majority in favour

Association of European Trade Mark Owners
        see **MARQUES the Association of European Trade Mark
        Owners**

Association of Event Organisers   (AEO)   1921
■   119 High St, BERKHAMSTED, Herts, HP4 2DJ.   (hq)
        01442 285810   fax 01442 875551
        email info@aeo.org.uk
        Chief Exec: Austen Hawkins
▲   Company Limited by Guarantee
○   *T; exhibition organisers working in partnership with contractors
        & venues to raise the profile of exhibitions as a medium
●   Conf - Mtgs - ET - Res - Inf - LG
<   Events Ind Alliance
M   184 f, UK / 20 f, o'seas
¶   Exhibition Standard - 6; ftm.
✕   2008 Association of Exhibition Organisers Ltd

Association of Event Venues   (AEV)   2004
■   119 High St, BERKHAMSTED, Herts, HP4 2DJ.   (hq)
        01442 285811   fax 01442 875551
        email info@aev.org.uk   http://www.aev.org.uk
        Dir: Chris Sketh
▲   Company Limited by Guarantee
○   *T; venues working in partnership with organisers & contractors
        to promote quality & value for exhibitors, thus raising the
        profile of exhibitions as a medium
●   Conf - Mtgs - ET - Res - Inf - LG
M   24 f, UK / 15 f, o'seas
¶   Exhibition Standard - 6; ftm.

Association for Events Management Education   (AEME)   2004
NR UK Centre for Events Management, Leeds Metropolitan
        University, Brontë Hall Room 225, Headingley Campus,
        LEEDS, W Yorks, LS6 3QS.   (sb)
        0113-812 3484
        http://www.aeme.org
        Chmn: Glenn Bowdin
○   *P

Association of Exhibition Contractors
        in January 2008 merged with the British Exhibition Contractors'
        Association to form the **Event Supplier & Services Association**

Association of Exhibition Organisers Ltd
        since 2008 the **Association of Event Organisers**

© CBD Research Ltd · Beckenham · BR3 5JS · Tel 020 8650 7745 · E-mail cbd@cbdresearch.com · www.cbdresearch.com

Association of External Verifiers   (AEV)   1999
NR   PO Box 97, WIRRAL, Cheshire, CH63 0QX.
　　 0151-327 5007
　　 http://www.ava.org.uk
○   *P; 'to provide professional services for people working in
　　 quality assurance in learning & development & for those
　　 working as external verifiers for awarding or regulator
　　 bodies'

**Association for Families who have Adopted from Abroad
(AFAA)   1987**
■   30 Bradgate, CUFFLEY, Herts, EN6 4RL.   (hsp)
　　 01707 872129   fax 01707 872129
　　 email information.afaa@ntlworld.com
　　 http://www.afaa.org.uk
　　 Gen Sec: Patricia Wordley
▲   Registered Charity
○   *W; to help adopted children to grow up happy & well
　　 adjusted, proud of their birth country and well integrated into
　　 their country of adoption
●   Conf - Mtgs - ET - Inf - VE - LG
M   400 i, 20 org, UK / 6 i, o'seas
¶   NL - 2/3;   LM - 1;   AR - 1; all free.

**Association of Family History Societies of Wales   (AFHSW)
1981**
■   c/o Adran Casgliadau, National Library of Wales,
　　 ABERYSTWYTH, Ceredigion, SY13 3BU.   (hsb)
　　 http://www.fhswales.info
　　 Hon Sec: Menna Evans
▲   Un-incorporated Society
○   *G, *N; to coordinate the activities of Welsh family history
　　 societies
●   Mtgs - Inf
M   'not applicable'
　　 Note: When writing to the association, if a reply is required,
　　 please enclose an s.a.e. or 2 International Reply Coupons

Association for Family Therapy   (AFT)   1976
NR   7 Executive Suite, St James Court, Wilderspool Causeway,
　　 WARRINGTON, WA4 6PS.   (hq)
　　 01925 444414
　　 email s.kennedy@aft.org.uk   http://www.aft.org.uk
　　 Exec Officer: Sue Kennedy
▲   Company Limited by Guarantee
○   *N, *P; to promote & bring together professional disciplines
　　 involved in family therapy, training, research, family law &
　　 practice
M   i & org
¶   Jnl of Family Therapy - 4; ftm.   NL - 4.

Association of Festival Organisers   (AFO)   1987
NR   PO Box 296, MATLOCK, Derbys, DE4 3XU.   (hq)
　　 01629 827014   fax 01629 821874
　　 email info@folkarts-england.org
　　 http://www.folkarts-england.org
　　 Dir: Steve Heap
▲   Registered Charity
○   *D; to act as a channel of communication bewtween festivals &
　　 events in the folk, roots, traditional & acoustic music world,
　　 or community events
●   Conf - Mtgs - ET - Res - Inf - LG
>   Folk Arts England; Folk Arts Network; Shooting Roots Youth
　　 Project
M   4 i, 30 f, 150 org
¶   Folk Arts England News - 4; free.   LM - continuous.

Association of Financial Controllers & Administrators   2002
NR   Akhtar House, 2 Shepherds Bush Rd, LONDON, W6 7PJ.
○   *P
●   Conf - Mtgs - ET - Exam - SG - LG
　　 international organisation

Association for Financial Markets in Europe   (AFME)
NR   St Michael's House, 1 George Yard, LONDON, EC3V 9DH.
　　 (hq)
　　 020 7743 9300
　　 http://www.afme.eu
　　 Chief Exec: Simon Lewis
Br   Brussels
○   *T; advocates stable, competitive and sustainable European
　　 financial markets that support economic growth and benefit
　　 society
Gp   Divisions
●   Conf - Mtgs
M   f
×   (London Investment Banking Association
　　 (SIFA

Association of Financial Mutuals   (AFM)   2010
NR   7 Castle Hill, CAISTOR, Lincs, LN7 6QL.   (hq)
　　 0844 879 7863
　　 email martin@financialmutuals.org
　　 Chief Exec: Martin Shaw,   Chmn: John Reeve
○   *T
M   57 f
¶   Mutually Yours - online.
×   2010 (Association of Friendly Societies
　　 (Association of Mutual Insurers (merged 1 January)

Association of Fire Consultants
NR   20 Park St, PRINCES RISBOROUGH, Bucks, HP27 9AH.
　　 0870 011 4514
　　 http://www.afc.eu.com
○   *P, *T; for fire safety professional consultants, independent of
　　 any commercial interests, offering advice on the prevention
　　 of fire in buildings or any other structure
M   i

Association of First Aiders   (AoFA)
NR   24 Thomas Drive, NEWPORT PAGNELL, Bucks, MK16 8TH.
　　 (hq)
　　 01908 610093   fax 01908 610808
　　 email admin@aofa.org   http://www.aofa.org
　　 Chmn: David Arnold
○   *P; to be the independent authoritative body representing &
　　 supporting a membership of all persons & organisations
　　 involved in the training, provision & practice of first aid
M   2,000 i

Association of Football Statisticians   (AFS)   1978
■   53a St Philip St, LONDON, SW8 3SR.   (regd/office)
　　 020 7720 5079
　　 email enquiries@11v11.com   http://www.11v11.com
　　 Chief Exec: Mark Baker
○   *S; research & publishing of football statistics from 1860
●   Mtgs - Res - Stat - Inf - Lib
M   1,100 i, UK / 400 i, o'seas

Association of Foreign Banks   (AFB)   1947
■   1 Bengal Court, LONDON, EC3V 9DD.   (hq)
　　 020 7283 8300
　　 http://www.foreignbanks.org.uk
　　 Managing Dir: John Treadwell
○   *T; foreign banks operating in the UK
●   Mtgs - ET - SG - Inf
M   f

Association of Former MPs

NR   1 Parliament St (Room G13), House of Commons, LONDON,
        SW1A 2NE.   (hq)
        020 7219 8207
        email grocotts@parliament.uk   http://www.epolitix.com
        Exec Officer: Sally Grocott
○   *Z; to keep in touch with all ex-MPs
●   Mtgs
M   c 300 i
¶   Order Order - 3; ftm.

Association of Franchised Distributors of Electronic Components Ltd   (AFDEC)   1970

■   The Manor House, High St, BUNTINGFORD, Herts,
        SG9 9AB.   (hq)
        01763 274748   fax 01763 273255
        email enquiries@afdec.org.uk   http://www.afdec.org.uk
        Sec: Jill Waite
○   *T
M   100 f

Association of Freelance Editors, Proofreaders & Indexers

IRL   11 Clonard Rd, Sandyford, DUBLIN 16, Republic of Ireland.
        353 (1) 295 2194
        http://www.afepi.ie
        Chmn: Brenda O'Hanlon
○   *P; to act as a point of contact between members & publishers

Association of Freelance Writers

NR   Sevendale House, 7 Dale St, MANCHESTER, M1 1JB.
        0161-228 2362   fax 0161-228 3533
        http://www.freelancemarketnews.com
        Contact: Angela Cox

Association for French Language Studies   (AFLS)   1981

NR   c/o Marie Noëlle Guillot, School of Language Studies,
        University of East Anglia, NORWICH, Norfolk, NR4 7TJ.   (sb)
        01603 592136
        http://www.afls.net
        Sec: Marie-Noëlle Guillot
▲   Registered Charity
○   *L
●   Conf - Mtgs - ET - Res - SG - Inf - LG - Workshops
M   50 i, UK / 50 i, o'seas
¶   Journal of French Language Studies - 3.
        Cahiers (NL) - 2.

Association of Friendly Societies
        On 2010 merged with the Association of Mutual Insurers to form the
        Association of Financial Mutuals

Association of Friends of the Waterloo Committee   1972

NR   Hillcrest, 23A Wylde Green Rd, SUTTON COLDFIELD,
        B72 1HD.   (hsp)
        0121-240 9030
        http://www.waterloocommittee.org.uk
        Hon Sec: John S White
▲   Registered Charity
○   *L; to promote study & research into the events of the
        Napoleonic Wars, during 1789-1815, & the Battle of
        Waterloo & the campaigns of the Duke of Wellington
●   Conf - Mtgs - Res - SG - Inf - VE
<   Waterloo C'ee in Belgium; The Wellington Museum at Waterloo
M   500+ i, 10 f, 15+ org, UK / 150+ i, o'seas
¶   The Waterloo Jnl - 3; ftm only.

Association of Fundraising Consultants   (AFC)

NR   Linen Hall (suite 316), 162-168 Regent St, LONDON,
        W1B 4JN.
        01582 762446   fax 01582 461489
        http://www.afc.org.uk
○   *P

Association of Garage Door Specialists
        in 2008 became the garage door installer group of the **Door &
        Hardware Federation**

Association of Gardens Trusts   (AGT)   1992

■   70 Cowcross St, LONDON, EC1M 6EJ.   (hq)
        020 7251 2610   fax 020 7251 2610
        email gardenstrusts@agt.org.uk   http://www.agt.org.uk
        Chmn: Sally Walker
▲   Registered Charity
○   *N; a national organisation representing gardens trusts in
        counties of England & Wales, which are actively engaged in
        researching, documenting, protecting & caring for designed
        landscapes
●   Conf - ET - Res - SG - Inf - Lib - LG
M   34 county gardens trusts
¶   NL - 2; ftm only.

Association of GB Athletics Clubs   (ABAC)   2005

■   19 Sheephouse Green, Wotton, DORKING, Surrey,
        RH5 6QW.   (hsp)
        01306 888886
        email mandy@white1966.freeserve.co.uk
        http://www.britishathleticsclubs.com
        Sec: Michael White
▲   Company Limited by Guarantee
○   *S; to protect & advance the interests of Britain's athletic clubs
M   97 clubs
        (Sub: £25)

Association of Genealogists & Researchers in Archives   (AGRA)   1968

■   43 Bowes Wood, New Ash Green, LONGFIELD, Kent,
        DA3 8QL.   (sp)
        email agra@agra.org.uk   http://www.agra.org.uk
        Hon Sec: Craig Nimmo
▲   Company Limited by Guarantee
○   *P; to promote high standards of research amongst members
●   Conf - Res
<   Fedn of Family History Socs
M   100 i, 2 f
¶   NL - 2.   LM - 1.

Association of Genetic Nurses & Counsellors
        a group of the **British Society for Human Genetics**

Association for Geographic Information   (AGI)   1989

■   5 St Helen's Place, Bishopsgate, LONDON, EC3A 6AU.   (hq)
        020 7036 0430   fax 020 7036 0301
        email info@agi.org.uk   http://www.agi.org.uk
        Chief Operating Officer: Angel Baker
▲   Company Limited by Guarantee
Br   3
○   *L, *P; to maximise the use of geographic information for the
        benefit of the citizen, good governance & commerce
Gp   Address geography; Crime & disorder; Environmental; Land &
        emgergency; Local public services; Marine & coastal zone;
        System & service suppliers; Technical; Utilities &
        telecommunications
●   Conf - Mtgs - ET - Exhib - Inf - Lib
M   1,788 i, 322 f
¶   enewsletter - 26;   AR - 1; both free online.

© CBD Research Ltd · Beckenham · BR3 5JS · Tel 020 8650 7745 · E-mail cbd@cbdresearch.com · www.cbdresearch.com

Association of Geotechnical & Geoenvironmental Specialists (AGS) 1988
■ 83 Copers Cope Rd, BECKENHAM, Kent, BR3 1NR.   (asa)
020 8658 8212   fax 020 8663 0949
email ags@ags.org.uk   http://www.ags.org.uk
Admin: Dianne Jennings
▲ Company Limited by Guarantee
○ *T; site investigation, geotechnics, engineering geology &
related disciplines of environmental engineering &
contaminated land assessment & remediation
● Conf - Mtgs - LG
< Ground Forum
M 24 i, 85 f
¶ Geoenvironmental Site Assessment: guide to the model report.
Electronic Transfer of Geotechnical Data from Ground
Investigations; available as download from Internet.
Collateral Warranties (2nd ed).
Guide to Laboratory Testing.
Guidelines for Combined Geoenvironmental & Geotechnical
Investigation.

Association for German Studies in Great Britain & Ireland
NR Dept of German, University of Leeds, LEEDS, W Yorks,
LS2 9JT.   (hsb)
http://www.cutg.ac.uk/
Pres: Prof Frank Finlay
▲ Registered Charity
○ *P; to promote the discipline of German studies in higher
education

Association for Glycogen Storage Disease (UK)   (AGSD(UK)) 1984
■ Old Hambledon Racecourse, Sheardley Lane, DROXFORD,
Hants, SO32 3QY.   (hq)
0300 123 2790
http://www.agsd.org.uk
Gen Sec: Mrs Ann Phillips
▲ Registered Charity
Br 6 countries o'seas
○ *W; to provide support for all persons affected with some form
of glycogen storage disease (which occurs when there is an
absence or deficiency of the enzymes needed to produce or
break down glycogen in the body).   It primarily affects the
liver & muscles
Gp McArdles Clinic (Oswestry); Pompe's Research Fund
Project II - to establish centres for collating treatment of children
& adults
● Conf - ET - Res - Exhib - SG - Inf - Lib - VE
< Assn Glycogen Storage Disease (USA) & other countries o'seas
M 200 families, 100 professionals, libraries & health centres, UK /
8 i, o'seas
¶ NL - 2; ftm, £1.50 nm (incl all back numbers).
Special Reports & AR.   Workshop Reports; on website.

Association of Golf Club Secretaries
since 2007 the **Golf Club Managers' Association**

Association of Golf Writers   (AGW)   1938
■ 1 Pilgrim's Bungalow, Mulberry Hill, CHILHAM, Kent,
CT4 8AH.   (hsp)
01227 732496   fax 01227 732496
email andyfarrell292@btinternet.com
http://www.agwgolf.org
Admin: Andy Farrell
▲ Un-incorporated Society
○ *P, *S; to liaise with governing bodies of golf for improved
working conditions
● Liaison with golfing bodies
M 109 i, UK / 48 i, o'seas
¶ NL - 10; ftm only.   Members' Hbk - 1; free.

Association of Governing Bodies of Independent Schools (AGBIS)   1941
NR The Grange, 3 Codicote Rd, WELWYN, Herts, AL6 9LY.   (hq)
01438 840730
email gensec@agbis.org.uk   http://www.agbis.org.uk
Gen Sec: Stuart Westley
▲ Registered Charity
○ *E; to support governing bodies of independent schools; to
promote good school governance in the independent sector
● Conf - Mtgs - ET - Inf - LG
< Indep Schools Coun
M independent day & boarding schools
¶ NL - 2;   AR; both ftm.

Association of Government Veterinarians
a group of the **British Veterinary Association**

Association of Graduate Careers Advisory Services   (AGCAS) 1967
NR Millennium House, 30 Junction Rd, SHEFFIELD, S Yorks,
S11 8XB.   (hq)
0114-251 5750
http://www.agcas.org.uk
▲ Company Limited by Guarantee; Registered Charity
○ *E, *P; to support the work of careers services in higher
education
< Fedn of Profl Assns in Guidance
M i

Association of Graduate Recruiters   (AGR)   1968
NR Innovation Centre, Warwick Technology Park, Gallows Hill,
WARWICK, CV34 6UW.   (hq)
01926 623236   fax 01926 623237
email info@agr.org.uk   http://www.agr.org.uk
Chief Exec: Carl Gilleard
▲ Company Limited by Guarantee
○ *T; to provide a forum for the discussion of issues relevant to
graduate recruitment
M 551 f

Association for Group & Individual Psychotherapy   (AGIP) 1974
NR 1 Fairbridge Rd, LONDON, N19 3EW.   (hq)
020 7272 7013
http://www.agip.org.uk
▲ Registered Charity
○ *P; to promote education in psychotherapy; to make
psychotherapy more widely available
M i

Association of Guernsey Banks   (AGB)
NR c/o EFG Private Bank (CI) Ltd, PO Box 603, EFG House, St
Julian's Avenue, ST PETER PORT, Guernsey, GY1 4NN.
01481 723432
email stephen.watts@efgci.com
Chmn: Steve Watts
▲ Un-incorporated Society
○ *T; to represent all licensed Guernsey banks
● Mtgs - LG
< Guernsey Intl Bankers Assn
M 48 f

Association of Guilds of Weavers, Spinners & Dyers 1955
- ■ 17 St Mary's Close, HENLEY-on-THAMES, Oxon, RG9 1RD. (hsp)
  email info@wsd.org.uk   http://www.wsd.org.uk
  Sec: Mrs Matty Smith
- ▲ Registered Charity
- Br 102; France, Japan, New Zealand, Serbia, South Africa, USA
- ○ *A, *G; to preserve & improve craftsmanship in handweaving, spinning & dyeing; to promote public awareness & education in such craftsmanship
- ● Conf - Mtgs - ET - Exam - Exhib - Inf
- M 4,500 i, 102 org, UK / i, 9 org, o'seas
  (Sub: £3.75)
- ¶ The Jnl for Weavers, Spinners & Dyers - 4; ftm, £5 nm.

Association of Head Teachers in Scotland
   since March 2006 the **Association of Headteachers & Deputes in Scotland**

** **Association of Heads of Independent Schools**
   Organisation lost: see Introduction paragraph 3

Association of Heads of Outdoor Education Centres   (AHOEC) 1963
- NR Woodlands OEC, Glasbury-on-Wye, via HEREFORD, HR3 5LP.   (chmn/b)
  01497 847272
  http://www.ahoec.org
  Chmn: Kevin Jackson
- ▲ Un-incorporated Society
- ○ *S; to encourage all-round personal development through residential experience & the use of the outdoors; to develop, establish & maintain safe practice in outdoor activities
- ● Conf - Mtgs - ET
- < Engl Outdoor Coun
- M 120 i, UK / 1 i, o'seas

Association of Headteachers & Deputes in Scotland   (AHDS) 1975
- ■ PO Box 18532, INVERURIE, Aberdeenshire, AB51 0WS. (mail/address)
  0845 260 7560
  email info@ahds.org.uk   http://www.ahds.org.uk
  Gen Sec: Greg Dempster
- ▲ Un-incorporated Society
- ○ *U; to represent the interests & perspectives of Scotland's headteachers & deputes from nursery, primary & special schools
- Gp Headteachers; Depute headteachers
- ● Conf - Mtgs - ET - Empl - LG
- < Eur School Heads Assn
- M 1,400 i
- ¶ Head to Head - 4; ftm only.
- × 2006 (March) Association of Head Teachers in Scotland

Association of Healthcare Cleaning Professionals   (AHCP)
- ■ Prospect House, 148 Lawrence St, YORK, YO10 3EB.   (reg off)
  07866 632330
  email chair@ahcp.co.uk   http://www.ahcp.co.uk
  Chmn: Denise Foster
- ▲ Company Limited by Guarantee
- Br 10
- ○ *P; for managers in the cleaning & support services, suppliers of goods for these services, & students & lecturers in colleges & universities
- Gp Cleaning
- ● Conf - Mtgs - ET - Exhib - SG - Inf - VE
- < Brit Cleaning Coun
- M c 300 i, c 50 f
- ¶ Excel (NL) - 4; ftm.   Annual Programme. Conference Report.   Guidance Booklets.   AR. Standards of Environmental Cleanliness in Hospitals.
- × 2007 Association of Domestic Management

Association of Healthcare Communications & Marketing (AHC) 1997
- ■ PO Box 4277, DUNSTABLE, Beds, LU6 2WU.   (admin/p)
  01525 222155   fax 01525 222155
  email katherine.baldwin@virgin.net
  http://www.ahcm.org.uk
  Admin: Kate Baldwin
- Br 2
- ○ *P; for healthcare communications professionals working in, or mainly with, the NHS
- ● Conf - ET - Inf
- M 350 i
  (Sub: £60 i, £200 gp)
- ¶ AHCM News (NL) - 4; ftm only.
- × Association of Healthcare Communicators

Association of Healthcare Technology Providers for Imaging, Radiothgerapy & Care
   since 2009 **AXrEM: Association of Healthcare Technology Providers for Imaging, Radiotherapy & Care**

Association for Heritage Interpretation   (AHI) 1975
- NR 54 Balmoral Rd, GILLINGHAM, Kent, ME7 4PG.   (hq)
  0560 274 7737
  email mail@ahi.org.uk   http://www.ahi.org.uk
  Contact: The Administrator
- ▲ Registered Charity
- ○ *L; to encourage excellence in the presentation & management of our natural & cultural environments
- ● Conf - ET - Res - Inf - Lib - VE
- M 300 i, 250 f & org
- ¶ Jnl - 3;   NL - 6; both ftm only.

Association of Higher Civil & Public Servants
- IRL Fleming's Hall, 12 Fleming's Place, DUBLIN 4, Republic of Ireland.
  353 (1) 668 6077   fax 353 (1) 668 6380
  email info@ahcps.ie   http://www.ahcps.ie
  Gen Sec: Dave Thomas
- ○ *P

Association of Hispanists of Great Britain and Ireland (AHGBI) 1955
- NR School of Modern Languages, Old Library Bldg, Newcastle University, NEWCASTLE UPON TYNE, NE1 7RU.   (mem/sb)
  email Ann.Davies@newcastle.ac.uk
  http://www.hispanists.org.uk
  Mem Sec: Dr Ann Davies
  Sec: Dr Jean Andrews (Jean.Andrews@nottingham.ac.uk)

Association of History & Computing UK   (AHC-UK) 1997
- NR c/o Derek Harding, Centre for Learning & Quality Enhancement, University of Teesside, MIDDLESBROUGH, Tees Valley, TS1 3BA.   (hsb)
  email derek.harding@tees.ac.uk   http://www.ahc.ac.uk
  Sec: Derek Harding
- ▲ Un-incorporated Society
- ○ *L; to promote the use of computers in historical research & training

© CBD Research Ltd · Beckenham · BR3 5JS · Tel 020 8650 7745 · E-mail cbd@cbdresearch.com · www.cbdresearch.com

Association for the History of Glass (1977)   (AHG)   1977

- ■ c/o Society of Antiquaries, Burlington House, Piccadilly, LONDON, W1J 0BE.   (regd/office)
  http://www.historyofglass.org.uk
  Hon Sec: Sandra Davidson
- ▲ Company Limited by Guarantee; Registered Charity
- ○ *L; to advance the education of the public in the historical, archaeological, aesthetic & technological study of glass, for all periods of history & all parts of the world; the problems of conservation & presentation
- ● Conf - Mtgs
- < Assn Intle pour l'Histoire du Verre
- M 154 i, instns
  (Sub: £10)
- ¶ Glass News (NL) - 2; ftm, £5 nm.

Association of Holistic Biodynamic Massage Therapists (AHBMT)   1992

- NR 4 St Peters House, Windmill St, MACCLESFIELD, Cheshire, SK11 7HS.   (memsec/p)
  01625 615754
  email enquiries@ahbmt.org   http://www.ahbmt.org
  Chmn & Sec: Pam Billinge;   Mem Sec: Hayley Merron
- ▲ Un-incorporated Society
- ○ *P; to promote biodynamic massage, encourage high standards in its practice & support its members in establishing & maintaining appropriate practices in the UK
- ● Inf - Mtgs
- < Gen Coun for Massage Therapies
- M 40 i
- ¶ Biodynamic Massage (Jnl) - 2; ftm.

Association of Home Information Pack Providers
Closed July 2010

Association of Hot Foil Printers   (AssHFP)   1991

- NR 15 Hunt St, Atherton, MANCHESTER, M46 9JF.   (hq)
  01942 873574   fax 0845 166 8396
  email association@hotfoilprinting.org
  http://www.hotfoilprinting.org
  Sec: Paul Forshaw
- ▲ Un-incorporated Society
- ○ *T; to promote the benefits of hot foil printed products
- ● ET - Inf
- M [not available]
- ¶ Monthly Magazine - 12; £25 yr m only.
  Hot Foil Printing: a guide to the whole business; £25.

Association for Humanistic Psychology in Britain   (AHP(B))   1968

- NR BM Box 3582, LONDON, WC1N 3XX.   (mail/add)
  0845 707 8506
  email admin@ahpb.org.uk   http://www.ahpb.org.uk
- ▲ Registered Charity
- ○ *L; to encourage interest in humanistic psychology
- ● Conf - Mtgs - ET - SG - Inf
- M 1,000 i, 30 f
- ¶ Self & Society - 6.

Association of Illustrators   (AoI)   1973

- ■ Back Building (2nd floor), 150 Curtain Rd, LONDON, EC2A 3AT.   (hq)
  020 7613 4328   fax 020 7613 4417
  email info@theaoi.com   http://www.theaoi.com
  Chmn: Russell Cobb
- ▲ Company Limited by Guarantee
- ○ *P; to advance & protect illustrators' rights; to raise the profile of illustration & the standard of practice within the industry
- ● Conf - ET - Exhib - Comp - Inf - Empl - LG
- < Eur Illustrators Forum (EIF); Brit Copyright Coun; Creators' Rights Alliance
- > Soc of Artists Agents
- M 1,300 i, 20 f, 50 colleges, UK / 20 i, o'seas
  (Sub: £150 i, £185 f, £100 colleges)
- ¶ Varoom [Jnl] - 3; ftm, £30 nm.
  Survive; £17.50 m, £27.50 nm.   Pricing; £7.50 m, £10 nm.
  Illustrators Guide to Law & Business Practice; £19.95, £24.95 nm.
  Images; £29.95 m, £39.95 nm.
  Publishing Directory;   Editorial Directory;   Advertising Directory; all £25 m, £33 nm.

Association for Improvements in the Maternity Services (AIMS)   1960

- NR 5 Ann's Court, Grove Rd, SURBITON, Surrey, KT6 4BE.   (chmn/p)
  020 8390 9534
  http://www.aims.org.uk
  Chmn: Beverley Beech
- ▲ Un-incorporated Society
- ○ *K; a pressure group providing information to new parents on rights & choices in the maternity services; supports midwives as practitioners in their own right
- Gp VBAC (Vaginal birth after Caesarean Section) support; Home birth support
- ● Conf - Inf
- M 1,000 i
- ¶ AIMS Quarterly Jnl - 4.
  Wide range of books & leaflets.

Association of Independent Advice Centres
since 2007 **Advice NI**

Association of Independent Care Advisers   (AICA)   1994

- NR Orchard House, Albury, GUILDFORD, Surrey, GU5 9AG.   (hq)
  01483 203066   fax 01483 202535
  email info@aica.org.uk   http://www.aica.org.uk
  Chmn: Christopher Cain
- ▲ Un-incorporated Society
- ○ *P; to represent private organisations who offer independent advice to older people, their families & carers, to help find appropriate care at home or in residential care or nursing homes
- ● Conf - Mtgs - LG
- M 250 i, 12 f

Association of Independent Computer Specialists   (AICS)   1972

- ■ Honeyhill, Bismore, Eastcombe, STROUD, Glos, GL6 7DG.   (hsp)
  0845 123 5399   fax 0845 130 5812
  email honsec@aics.org.uk   http://www.aics.org.uk
  Hon Sec: R K Brooks
- ▲ Company Limited by Guarantee
- ○ *T; the provision of specialist computer related services by individual practitioners & owner-directed firms
- ● Conf - Networking
- M 40 i, 30 f
- ¶ NL - 4; ftm, £10 yr nm.

Association of Independent Construction Adjudicators   (AICA)
NR   Royal London House, 22-25 Finsbury Square, LONDON,
      EC2A 1DX.
      0844 249 5353   fax 0844 249 5354
      email enquiries@aica-adjudication.co.uk
      http://www.aica-adjudication.co.uk/
      Chmn: Peter Shiells
▲   Company Limited by Guarantee
○   *P; nomination body for appointment of adjudicators to resolve
      construction disputes
●   Conf - Mtgs - ET - Inf
M   136 i

Association of Independent Crop Consultants   (AICC)   1980
■   Agriculture Place, Drayton Farm, East Meon, PETERSFIELD,
      Hants, GU32 1PN.   (hq)
      01730 823881   fax 01730 823882
      email aicc@farmline.com   http://www.aicc.org.uk
      Chief Exec: Sarah Cowlrick
▲   Company Limited by Guarantee
○   *F, *P; for independent crop consultants
●   Conf - Mtgs - ET - Inf - LG
M   230 i, 1 f
¶   NL - 4; ftm only.   LM - 1; free.

Association of Independent Financial Advisers   (AIFA)   1999
NR   2-6 Austin Friars House, Austin Friars, LONDON,
      EC2N 2HD.   (hq)
      020 7628 1287
      http://www.aifa.net
▲   Company Limited by Guarantee
○   *P
●   Conf - Mtgs - ET - Res - Stat - Inf - Lib - LG
M   13,364 i, 5,069 f, 1 org (CBI)

Association of Independent First Aid at Work Training Organisations
     since 2008 **First Aid Council for Training**

Association of Independent Inventory Clerks   (AIIC)   1996
■   PO Box 1288, West End, WOKING, Surrey, GU24 9WE.
      01276 855388   fax 01276 855388
      email centraloffice@theaiic.co.uk
      http://www.theaiic.co.uk
      Hon Sec: Holly Doole
▲   Un-incorporated Society
○   *P
●   ET - Inf
M   220 i
¶   The Declaration.

Association of Independent Jewellery Valuers   (AIJV)
NR   Algo Business Centre, Glenearn Rd, PERTH, PH2 0NJ.   (hq)
      01738 450477
○   *T

Association of Independent Libraries   (AIL)   1989
NR   The Leeds Library, 18 Commercial St, LEEDS, W Yorks,
      LS1 6AL.   (chmn/b)
      0113-245 3071
      http://www.independentlibraries.co.uk
      Contact: Catherine Levy
○   *A; subscription libraries founded between c 1690 & 1841
      before the creation of the public library service; to care for
      their historic collections & buildings; to supply the latest
      books, periodicals & a personal service to their members
M   28 libraries

Association of Independent Meat Suppliers   (AIMS)   2001
NR   PO Box 125, NORTHALLERTON, N Yorks, DL6 2YG.
      01609 761547   fax 01609 761548
      http://www.aims2001.co.uk
○   *T; small & medium-sized abattoirs

Association of Independent Museums   (AIM)   1977
NR   4 Clayhall Rd, GOSPORT, Hants, PO12 2BY.   (admin/p)
      023 9258 7751
      email admin@aim-museums.co.uk
      http://www.aim-museums.co.uk
      Administrator: Roger Hornshaw
▲   Company Limited by Guarantee
○   *L, *N; to comnnect, support & represent independent
      museums (those not supported by government)
●   Conf - Mtgs - ET - Stat - Inf - VE - LG
M   100 i, 100 f, 500 org
¶   AIM Bulletin - 5; free.

Association of Independent Music   (AIM)   1999
NR   Lamb House, Church Street, LONDON, W4 2PD.   (hq)
      020 8994 5599
      http://www.musicindie.org
▲   Company Limited by Guarantee
○   *D, *T; independent record companies
●   LG - Negotiating - Advising - Networking
<   IMPALA
M   700 f
¶   AR; free.

Association of Independent Organ Advisers   (AIOA)   1996
■   [communication via website only]
      http://www.aioa.org.uk
▲   Un-incorporated Society
○   *P; to offer independent, professional advice on new pipe
      organs & pipe organ restoration
●   Mtgs - Accreditation of advisers
M   7 i

Association of Independent Practitioners
     a group of the **British Association for Counselling &
     Psychotherapy**

Association of Independent Research & Technology Organisations
     see **AIRTO Ltd: Association of Independent Research &
     Technology Organisations**

**Association of Independent Specialist Medical Accountants
(AISMA)   1995**
■   48 St Leonards Rd, BEXHILL-on-SEA, E Sussex, TN40 1JB.
      01424 730345   fax 01424 730330
      email aisma@honeybarrett.co.uk
      http://www.aisma.org.uk
      Sec: Liz Densley
▲   Un-incorporated Society
○   *P
●   Conf - Mtgs - Stat
M   75 f
¶   NL - 4; ftm only.
      Medical Practitioners' Financial Hbk - 3 yrly.

Association of Independent Tobacco Specialists   (AITS)   1976
■   12-14 Wyndham Arcade, CARDIFF, Glamorgan, CF10 1FJ.
      (hq)
      029 2066 4114
      Sec: Donald C Higgins
Br   103
○   *T; to keep the tobacconist in the high street
●   Conf - Mtgs - Exhib - SG - Inf - VE
M   73 i, 103 f
¶   NL - 12.   Tobacco Index - 1.
      National Tobacconists Trade Exhibition Catalogue.

© CBD Research Ltd · Beckenham · BR3 5JS · Tel 020 8650 7745 · E-mail cbd@cbdresearch.com · www.cbdresearch.com

Association of Independent Tour Operators   (AITO)   1976
■ 133a St Margaret's Rd, TWICKENHAM, Middx, TW1 1RG.
    (hq)
    020 8744 9280   fax 020 8744 3187
    email info@aito.co.uk   http://www.aito.co.uk
    Chmn: Derek Moore
○ *T; includes small & specialist tour operators
M c 150 f

Association for Industrial Archaeology   (AIA)   1973
NR The Ironbridge Institute, Ironbridge Gorge Museum,
    Coalbrookdale, TELFORD, Shropshire, TF8 7DX.   (hq)
    01740 656280
    email aia-enquiries@contacts.bham.ac.uk
    http://www.industrial-archaeology.org
    Sec: Davis de Haan
▲ Registered Charity
○ *L; to promote the study, preservation & presentation of Britain's
    industrial heritage; a national organisation for people who
    share an interest in Britain's industrial past
< Nat Assn Mining History Assns (NAMHO)

Association of Industrial Laser Users
    since 14 April 2007 the **Association of Laser Users**

Association of Industrial Road Safety Officers   (AIRSO)   1965
■ 68 The Boulevard, WORTHING, W Sussex, BN13 1LA.   (hsb)
    01903 506095   fax 01903 506095
    email airso@talk21.com   http://www.airso.org.uk
    Sec: Graham Feest
▲ Registered Charity
○ *P; to promote road safety within vehicle fleet undertakings;
    exchange of information on accident prevention schemes,
    driver training techniques & vehicle construction & usage
● Conf - Mtgs - ET - LG
M 500 i, UK / 10 i, o'seas
¶ Directory of Members - 1; ftm only.

Association of Industrial Truck Trainers   (AITT)   1985
NR Unit 20 The Springboard Centre, Mantle Lane, COALVILLE,
    Leics, LE67 3DW.   (hsb)
    01530 277857   fax 01530 810231
    email sueaitt@aol.com   http://www.aitt.co.uk
    Sec: Mrs Susan Finney
▲ Un-incorporated Society
○ *P; research into methods of training, operation & maintenance
    of equipment
Gp Independent Training Standards Scheme & Register Ltd (ITSSAR
    Ltd) - provides standards & monitoring of training of fork lift
    truck operators & maintains a register of tutors, trainers &
    operators of fork lift trucks
● Conf - Mtgs - ET - Exam - Res - Exhib - Inf - LG
< Brit Indl Truck Assn (BITA)
M i & f
¶ NL - 2;   LM - 1;   AR; all ftm only.

Association for Infant Mental Health UK   (AIMH UK)
NR 27 Old Gloucester St, LONDON, WC1N 3AX.
    email info@aimh.org.uk   http://www.aimh.org.uk
    Chmn: Dr Shirley Gracias
▲ Company Limited by Guarantee
○ *P; to bring together professionals to promote the mental health
    of infants

Association of Inflatable Manufacturers, Operators, Designers & Suppliers
    a group of the **Performance Textiles Association**

Association for Information Management
    see **Aslib: the Association for Information Management**

Association of Information Security Auditors & Business
Executives   (AISABE)   2010
NR Coventry House (suite 2.2), Coventry Rd, ILFORD, Essex,
    IG1 4QR.   (hq)
    0844 809 9220
○ *P; a UK awarding body & examination board overseeing
    assessment for the higher level vocational qualifications to
    the information & business management sectors

Association of Inland Navigation Authorities   (AINA)   1996
NR Fearns Wharf, Neptune St, LEEDS, W Yorks, LS9 8PB.   (hq)
    0113-243 3125   fax 0113-245 8394
    email info@aina.org.uk   http://www.aina.org.uk
    Contact: The Executive Director
▲ Un-incorporated Society
○ *T; to develop, share & promote good practice in the
    management & use of the UK's inland waterways; to
    represent the views of owners & operators of the waterways
    to government & its agencies, local authorities, policy
    makers, funders & stakeholders
● Conf - Mtgs - LG
M 30 org
¶ [Publications on website].

Association of Inner Wheel Clubs in Great Britain & Ireland
1934
NR 51 Warwick Sq, LONDON, SW1V 2AT.   (hq)
    020 7834 4600 (Mon-Fri 0930-1630)
Br 1,057
○ *W; 'friendship & service', membership is limited to the
    womenfolk of Rotarians
● Conf - Mtgs
< Intl Inner Wheel; Women's Nat Commission
M 29,500 i
¶ Inner Wheel - 3; m only.

*Association of Installers of Unvented Hot Water Systems (Scotland &
    N Ireland)*
    a group of the **Scottish & Northern Ireland Plumbing
    Employers' Federation**

Association of Insurance & Risk Managers   (AIRMIC)   1963
NR 6 Lloyd's Ave, LONDON, EC3N 3AX.   (hq)
    020 7480 7610   fax 020 7702 3752
    http://www.airmic.com
    Exec Dir: David Gamble
▲ Company Limited by Guarantee
○ *P; to provide a forum for the exchange of data & opinion
    concerning risk management in industry, commerce & local
    government
M i

Association of Insurance Surveyors Ltd   (AIS)
NR 4 Napier Drive, CAMBERLEY, Surrey, GU15 3UD.   (mem/sb)
    http://www.insurancesurveyors.org
    Mem Sec: Andy Grieve
○ *P; research into methods of burglary protection; cooperation
    with security organisations

Association of Integrative Sandplay Therapists   (AIST)
NR Cliff Cottage, Sussex Steps, West Hill Rd, ST LEONARDS-ON-
    SEA, E Sussex, TN38 0NF.   (Regd off)
    01424 440775
    email info@sandplaytherapy.co.uk
    http://www.sandplaytherapy.co.uk
    Sec: John Daly
▲ Company Limited by Guarantee
○ *P; to promote, support & develop integrative approaches to
    sandplay & associated creative arts therapies
● Et - Exam
M 13 i

Association of Inter-Varsity Clubs   (AIVC)   1946
NR   c/o Manchester IVC, 94-96 Grosvenor St, MANCHESTER,
        M1 7HL.   (forwarding/add)
        0870 321 0482
        http://www.ivc.org.uk
▲   Un-incorporated Society
Br   46; Bermuda
○   *N; coordinating body for member clubs; to provide cultural,
        social & sporting activities within the British Isles, for
        graduates & others of like interests
●   Conf - Mtgs - ET - Inf - VE
M   c 6,000 i, 46 clubs, UK / 20 i, 1 club, o'seas
¶   Newslines - 12;   LM - 2; both ftm only.
        (Each club publishes a monthly bulletin with a list of social
        events).

**Association for Interactive Media and Entertainment   (AIME)
2008**
■   28 Foundry St(ground floor), BRIGHTON, E Sussex, BN1 4AT.
        (hq)
        01273 685328   fax 01273 6860094
        email info@aimelink.org   http://www.aimelink.org
        Sec: Toby Padgham
▲   Compnay Limited by Guarantee
○   *T; interactive media & entertainment, premium rate services,
        Mobile/fixed link
●   Conf - Mtgs - Res - Exhib - Comp - Stat - LG
M   82 f
¶   AIMR Monthly Knowledge & Networking NL - 12; free.
✕   2008 Network for Online Commerce

Association of Interchurch Families   (AIF)   1968
NR   27 Tavistock Square, LONDON, WC1H 9HH.   (hq)
        020 3384 2947
        email info@interchurchfamilies.org.uk
        http://www.interchurchfamilies.org.uk
        Chief Exec: Keith Lander
▲   Registered Charity
○   *E, *R; offers a support network for interchurch families (usually
        a Roman Catholic married to a Christian of another
        communion) & a voice for such families as they seek to
        contribute to the growing together of their churches; works in
        England, Scotland & Wales
●   Conf - Mtgs - Res - Inf - VE
<   Interchurch Families Intl Network; (sister assns in Australia,
        Austria, Canada, France, Germany, Italy, N Zealand,
        N Ireland, Switzerland, USA)
M   940 i (mostly couples/families)
¶   AIF News - 3; ftm only.
        Issues, Reflections, News [internet bulletin]; 1/3; free.
        Annual Review - 1; free.

Association of Interior Specialists   (AIS)   1998
■   Olton Bridge, 245 Warwick Rd, SOLIHULL, W Midlands,
        B92 7AH.   (hq)
        0121-707 0077   fax 0121-706 1949
        email info@ais-interiors.org.uk
        http://www.ais-interiors.org.uk
        Chief Exec: David Frise
▲   Company Limited by Guarantee
○   *T; to represent companies involved in the manufacture, supply
        & installation of all aspects of interior fit-outs &
        refurbishment; members operate in retail & commercial
        offices, the public sector, banks, hotels, hospitals, schools
        factories etc (including access floors, ceilings, lighting,
        movablewalls, partitioning)
●   Conf - Mtgs - ET - Res - Exhib - Stat - Inf - LG - website features
        an interactive directory search
<   Nat Specialist Contrs Coun; Construction Products Assn
M   430 f, UK / 4 f, o'seas
¶   Interiors Focus - 2; ftm, free to specifiers nm.
        Interior Insight (NL) - 4; ftm only.
        LM - 2; ftm & specifiers.

Association of International Accountants Ltd   (AIA)   1928
■   Staithes 3, The Watermark, Metro Riverside,
        NEWCASTLE upon TYNE, NE11 9SN.   (hq)
        0191-493 0277   fax 0191-493 0278
        email aia@aiaworldwide.com
        http://www.aiaworldwide.com
        Chief Exec: Philip J J Turnbull
▲   Company Limited by Guarantee
Br   9; China, Cyprus, Ghana, Greece, Hong Kong, Ireland,
        Malaysia, Singapore
○   *P; to offer a recognised professional accountancy qualification
●   Conf - Mtgs - ET - Exam - Exhib - Comp - Expt - Inf - Lib
M   i
¶   International Accountant - 6; ftm, £40 yr nm.
        Student Focus - 2;   AR - 1; both ftm.

Association for International Cancer Research   (AICR)   1979
NR   Madras House, South St, ST ANDREWS, Fife, KY16 9EH.   (hq)
        01334 477910   fax 01334 478667
        http://www.aicr.org.uk
        Chief Exec: Norman Barrett
▲   Company Limited by Guarantee; Registered Charity
○   *Q; a charity which endeavours to support & fund basic (as
        opposed to clinical) research into the basic mechanisms
        which are involved in the development of those diseases
        commonly known as cancer
Gp   Scientific advy c'ee (determines research direction)

**Association of International Courier & Express Services
(AICES)   1977**
NR   Unit 6 Poyle 14, Newlands Drive, COLNBROOK, Berks,
        SL3 0DX.   (hq)
        01753 680550
        http://www.aices.org
        Contact: Exec Sec
○   *T; for companies handling international express documents &
        packages
M   45 f

Association of International Property Professionals   (AIPP)
NR   St Clements House, 27028 Clements Lane, LONDON,
        EC4N 7AE.   (hq)
        020 3207 9095
        email enquiries@aipp.org.uk   http://www.aipp.org.uk
○   *P; to protect the interests of UK citizens buying property abroad
M   c 380 i

Association of Investment Companies   (AIC)   1932
NR   24 Chiswell St (9th floor), LONDON, EC1Y 4YY.   (hq)
        020 7282 5555   fax 020 7282 5556
        email info@theaic.co.uk   http://www.theaic.co.uk
        Dir Gen: Daniel Godfrey
▲   Company Limited by Guarantee
○   *T; to work with member investment trust companies to add
        value to their shareholders over the long-term; to provide a
        coordinated response to any new developments in regulation
        or tax & initiate favourable legislative changes
●   Conf - Mtgs - ET - Exhib - Stat - Inf - LG
        Information line: 0800 085 8520
M   246 f
¶   Monthly Information Service - 12.
        IT Hbk - 1.
        Information packs & Factsheets.

Association of Irish Choirs   1980
IRL   University Concert Hall, Foundation Building,
        University of Limerick, LIMERICK, Republic of Ireland.
        353 (61) 234823
        email aoic@ul.ie   http://www.aoic.ie
        Chmn: Kevin O'Callaghan
○   *D; to promote choral music and singing in Ireland

Association of the Irish Dental Industry Ltd
IRL   Roscrea Rd, Shinrone, BIRR, Co Offaly, Republic of Ireland.
      353 (86) 400 2030
      http://www.aidi.ie
○   *T

Association of Irish Musical Societies Ltd   (AIMS)   1965
IRL   Slieve Bloom, Kavanagh Place, THURLES, Co Tipperary,
      Republic of Ireland.   (sp)
      353 (5o4) 22364
      email mary.butler@aims.ie   http://www.aims.ie
      Sec: Mary Butler
○   *D

Association of Irish Racecourses Ltd
IRL   63 Fitzwilliam Square, Dublin 2, Republic of Ireland
      353 (1) 676 0911
      email air@iol.ie   http://www.air.ie
      Chief Exec: Paddy Walsh

Association of Jewish Ex-Servicemen & Women   (AJEX)   1930
NR   Shield House, Harmony Way, LONDON, NW4 2BZ.   (hq)
     020 8202 2323   fax 020 8202 9900
     email headoffice@ajex.org.uk   http://www.ajex.org.uk
     Gen Sec: S J Weisser
▲   Registered Charity
Br   60
○   *W; to assist ex-service men & women & their dependents; to
     observe remembrance of the fallen; to combat religious &
     racial intolerance
Gp   Public relations; Remembrance Jewish military museum;
     Welfare & social services
●   Conf - Mtgs - Res - Exhib - SG - Inf - Lib & museum - VE
<   Intl Congress of Jewish War Veterans
M   c 5,000 i

Association of Jungian Analysts   1977
NR   7 Eton Ave, LONDON, NW3 3EL.
     020 7794 8711   fax 020 7794 8711
     http://www.jungiananalysts.org.uk
○   *P

Association des Juristes Franco-Britanniques
     see **Franco-British Lawyers Society**

Association of Labour Providers   (ALP)   2004
■   102 Frimley House, 5 The Parade, High Street, FRIMLEY, Surrey,
     GU16 7JQ.   (mail/address)
     01276 5093066   fax 01276 7610769
     email info@labourproviders.org.uk
     http://www.labourproviders.org.uk
     Chmn: Mark Boleat
▲   Un-incorporated Society
○   *T; for organisations that provide workers within the food
     agricultural & other Gangmasters Regulated Licensing
     Authority sectors to produce, pick & pack food
●   Res - LG
M   120 f
¶   NL - 12; ftm only.   AR - 1; free.

Association for Land Based Colleges
     since 2008 **Landex - Land Based Colleges Aspiring to
     Excellence**

Association of Land Rover Clubs Ltd   (ALRC)   1983
NR   1a Duncan Avenue, HUNCOTE, Leics, LE9 3AN.   (hsp)
     email tonybirch@btopenworld.com   http://www.alrc.co.uk
     Hon Sec: Simone Birch
○   *G, *S; renovation & restoration of all Rover vehicles; Rover
     marque enthusiasts clubs
M   org

**Association of Landscape Contractors of Ireland (Northern
Ireland)   (ALCI)   1971**
NR   22 Summerhill Park, BANGOR, Co Down, BT20 5QQ.   (hsp)
     028 9127 2823   fax 028 9127 2823
     http://www.alci.org.uk
     Admin Coordinator: Lyn Sherriff
▲   Un-incorporated Society
○   *T; to represent the landscape industry in Northern Ireland
Gp   General landscaping; Grounds maintenance; Sportsground
     construction; Tree surgery
●   Conf - Mtgs - ET - Exhib - Comp - Inf - Lib - VE - LG
<   Brit Assn Landscape Inds
M   10 i, 50 f, 4 org
¶   ALCI Directory - 2 yrly; free.

Association for Language Learning   (ALL)   1990
■   University of Leicester, University Road, LEICESTER, LE1 7RH.
     (hq)
     0116-229 7453   fax 0116-229 7454
     email yvonneh@all-languages.org.uk
     http://www.all-languages.org.uk
     Office Mgr: Yvonne Hogben
▲   Registered Charity
Br   21
○   *N, *P; 'the major professional organisation for language
     teachers in the UK; the teaching, learning & use of
     languages in education & society as a whole'
Gp   C'ees: Dutch, French, German, Italian, Russian, Spanish &
     Portuguese, Asian languages, Publications, Policy
●   Conf - Mtgs - ET - Exhib - Inf - LG
¶   Language Learning Jnl - 2; £78 (£95 EU) (£107 o'seas).
     Language World (NL) - 4; free.
     Francophonie - 2; £60 (£72 EU) (£82 o'seas).
     Deutsch: Lehren und Lernen (the German Jnl) - 2; £60
     (£72 EU) (£82 o'seas).
     Vida Hispánica (the Spanish & Portuguese Jnl) - 2; £60 (£72 EU)
     (£82 o'seas).
     Tuttitalia (the Italian Jnl) - 2; £60 (£72 EU) (£82 o'seas).
     Russistika (the Russian Jnl) - 1; £32 (£37 EU) (£42 o'seas).
     All seven titles; £203 (£253 EU) (£300 o'seas).
     Onze Taal - 10; ftm only.

Association of Laparoscopic Surgeons   (ALS)   1994
NR   at The Royal College of Surgeons, 35-43 Lincoln's Inn Fields,
     LONDON, WC2A 3PE.   (mail/add)
     020 7973 0305
     email jtreglohan@asgbi.org.uk   http://www.alsgbi.org
     Exec Officer: Jenny Treglohan
     Hon Sec: Mr Mark Vipond
○   *P; to foster developments in laparoscopic surgery, to provide a
     structure for training
●   Mtgs - ET - Courses
<   Eur Assn of Endoscopic Surgeons (EAES)
M   i

Association of Laser Safety Professionals   (ALSP)   2004
■   PO Box 513, ABINGDON, Oxon, OX14 9AY.   (hq)
     http://www.laserprotectionadviser.org.uk
○   *P; for those active in the field of laser safety in any area of
     laser application
M   13 i

Association of Laser Users   (AILU)   1995
■ Oxford House, 100 Ock St, ABINGDON, Oxon, OX14 5DH. (hq)
  01235 539595   fax 01235 550499
  email info@ailu.org.uk   http://www.ailu.org.uk
  Sec: Dr J M Green
▲ Company Limited by Guarantee
○ *T; to foster cooperation & collaboration on non-competitive technical matters relating to the commercial use of lasers & laser-related research
Gp Additive layer manufacturers; Job shop; Market development; Medical; Micro:Nano; Product & process innovation
● Mtgs - ET - Res - Inf
< Eur Laser Applications Network (ELAN); Laser Inst of America (LIA)
M 50 i, 198 f, UK / 12 i, 12 f, o'seas
  (Sub: £70 i, £295 f, £25 students, all + VAT)
¶ The Laser User - 4; ftm only.
✕ 2007 (14 April) Association of Industrial Laser Users

Association for Latin Liturgy   (ALL)   1969
■ 16 Brean Down Avenue, BRISTOL, BS9 4JF.   (hsp)
  email enquiries@latin-liturgy.org
  http://www.latin-liturgy.org
  Sec: Christopher Francis
▲ Registered Charity
○ *R; to promote understanding of the theological, pastoral & spiritual quality of the liturgy in Latin; to preserve the sacredness & dignity of the Roman rite; to secure, for the present & future generations, the Church's unique inheritance of liturgical music
● Mtgs - ET - Res - Inf - Liturgical celebrations - Talks by scholars
< Latin Liturgy Assn (USA); Vereniging voor Latijnse Liturgie (Netherlands); Association pro Liturgia (France)
M 340 i, UK / 30 i, o'seas
¶ NL - 3; ftm only.
  New Approach to Latin for the Mass; £12.
  New Latin-English Sunday Missal; £12 (paperback).
  Latin CD; £12.   A Voice for all Time; £6.
  Various musical publications.

Association for Latin Teaching   (ARLT)   1911
■ c/o Mrs Elizabeth Scott, The Westgate School, Cheriton Rd, WINCHESTER, Hants, SO22 5AZ.   (hsb)
  http://www.arlt.co.uk
  Hon Sec: Mrs E Scott
▲ Registered Charity
○ *E; to promote by discussion, cooperation & experiment, the teaching of classics in schools
● Conf - ET - Inf - Resources service to members
< Jt Assn Classical Teachers (JACT)
M 2,000 i
¶ The Jnl of Latin Teaching (published jointly with JACT) - 3;
  NL [email] - 6; both ftm only.

Association of Law Costs Draftsmen   (ALCD)   1977
NR Church Cottage, Church Lane, Stuston, DISS, Norfolk, IP21 4AG.
  01379 741404   fax 01379 742702
  email enquiries@alcd.org.uk   http://www.alcd.org.uk
  Admin Sec: Sheila Chapman
▲ Voluntary Professional Association
○ *P; 'specialists in the law who operate by advising upon & applying laws & directions which relate to the evaluation & recovery of solicitors' fees'
  Members are based throughout England & Wales
● Conf - Mtgs - ET - Exam - Lib
M 900 i, UK / 2 i, o'seas
¶ ALCD NL - 6; ftm only.

Association of Law Teachers   (ALT)   1965
NR 4 Gray's Inn Place, LONDON, WC1R 5DX.   (hsb)
  020 7404 5787 ext 368
  http://www.lawteacher.ac.uk
  Hon Sec: Amanda Fancourt
▲ Un-incorporated Society
○ *E, *L; to study understanding & reform of the educational aspects of law & the teaching of law; to research into legal education systems & methods
● Conf - ET - Res - SG - LG
< UK Assn for Eur Law
M 800 i, UK / 50 i, o'seas
¶ The Law Teacher (Jnl) - 3.
  The Bulletin - 3.   LM - 1.

Association of Lawyers for Children   (ALC)   1993
■ PO Box 283, EAST MOLESEY, Surrey, KT8 0WH.   (hsp)
  020 8224 7071
  email admin@alc.org.uk   http://www.alc.org.uk
  Admin: Julia Higgins
○ *P; to promote justice for children & young people within the justice system; for lawyers involved in work relating to children
● Conf - Mtgs - ET - SG - LG
M 1,200 i
¶ ALC NL - 4; ftm only.

** Association of Lawyers & Legal Advisors
Organisation lost: see Introduction paragraph 3

Association for Leaders in Nursing
NR 9 Prescot St (3rd floor), LONDON, E1 8PR.   (hq)
  020 7480 4738
  http://www.leadersinnursing.co.uk
○ *P; to represent nurse directors, & senior nurses working in the armed forces, the independent sector, the NHS & other voluntary & charitable organisations in the UK
¶ NL.
✕ 2008 Nurse Directors Association

Association of Leading Visitor Attractions   (ALVA)   1990
■ 4 Westminster Palace Gardens, LONDON, SW1P 1RL.   (hq)
  020 7222 1728   fax 020 7222 1729
  email email@alva.org.uk   http://www.alva.org.uk
  Dir: Robin Broke
▲ Company Limited by Guarantee
○ *T; to represent the country's major visitor attractions on matters which concern the effectiveness of the tourism industry
Gp Museums & galleries; Cathedrals; Heritage organisations; Large leisure attractions; Gardens & conservation sites
● Conf - Mtgs - ET - Stat - VE - LG
M 42 org
¶ LM.   AR.

Association of Learned & Professional Society Publishers (ALPSP)   1972
NR 1 Abbey Cottages, The Green, Sutton Courtenay, ABINGDON, Oxon, OX14 4AF.   (hsp)
  01235 847776
  http://www.alpsp.org
  Chief Exec: Ian Russell
▲ Company Limited by Guarantee
Br Australia, N America, New Zealand
○ *N; to represent not-for-profit publishers & those who work with them
Gp C'ees: Copyright, Professional development
● Conf - Mtgs - ET - Res - Exhib - Stat - Inf - VE - LG - Professional development
< Intl Fedn of Scholarly Publishers
M 216 f, UK / 124 f, o'seas
¶ Learned Publishing - 4; ftm (extra copies £60 yr), £75 (i), £145 (instns), £115/60 email only.
  ALPSP Alert - 12; ftm only.

© CBD Research Ltd · Beckenham · BR3 5JS · Tel 020 8650 7745 · E-mail cbd@cbdresearch.com · www.cbdresearch.com

Association for Learning Languages en Famille   (ALLEF UK)
- ■ 7 Lucas Court, Biddenham, BEDFORD, MK40 4RN.   (hq)
  01892 543212
  http://www.allef.org.uk
  Contact: Penny Dauncey
- ○ *X; arranges mutual exchanges between children in the UK, France & Germany

Association of Learning Providers   (ALP)
- NR Colenso House, 46 Bath Hill, Keynsham, BRISTOL, BS31 1HG.   (hq)
  0117-986 5389
  email enquiries@aelp.org.uk   http://www.aelp.org.uk
  Chief Exec: Graham Hoyle
- ▲ Company Limited by Guarantee
- ○ *E, *T; providers of work-based learning
- ● ET
- M 400 f

Association for Learning Technology   (ALT)   1993
- NR Gipsy Lane, Headington, OXFORD, OX3 0BP.   (hq)
  01865 484125   fax 01865 484165
  email alt@brookes.ac.uk   http://www.alt.ac.uk
  Dir: Rhonda Riachi
- ▲ Registered Charity
- ○ *P; promotion of good practice in the use of learning technology in education & industry
- ● Conf - ET - Res - Inf
- M 426 i, 38 f, 104 universities, 52 colleges, UK / 38 i, o'seas
- ¶ Alt-J (Jnl) - 3; £10/£15.   Alt-N (NL) - 4; free.
  Conference Abstracts - 1; £5.   AR; free.

Association of Leasehold Enfranchisement Practitioners   (ALEP)   2003
- ■ Financial House, 14 Barclay Rd, CROYDON, Surrey, CR0 1JN.   (hsp)
  0845 225 2277   fax 0870 225 2287
  email info@alep.org.uk   http://www.alep.org.uk
  Hon Sec: Alex Greenslade
- ○ *P; to foster best practice & integrity & maintain professional standards in leasehold enfranchisement
- M 2 i, 1 f

Association of Leisure Industry Professionals   (ALIP)   2001
- NR 2A The Drove Estate, Avis Way, NEWHAVEN, E Sussex, BN9 0EB.   (hq)
  01273 612300   fax 01273 612812
- ▲ Un-incorporated Society
- ○ *P; tourism industry
- ● Conf - ET - SG - Inf
- > Intl Work Experience Program
- ¶ Lipservice (NL) - 4; ftm only.

Association of Library Equipment Suppliers   (TALES)   1980
- ■ Forge Cottage, 3 Church End, Sandridge, ST ALBANS, Herts, AL4 9DL.   (hsb)
  01727 837507
  email john@newtondavies.plus.com
  http://www.tales.org.uk
  Mem Sec/Hon Treas: John Newton-Davies
- ▲ Un-incorporated Society
- ○ *T; 'providing representation for suppliers into the library & information marketplace'
- Gp Automation; AV & other media supply; Books, journals & other print material; Conservation, large print; Human resources & other professional services; ICT & Security; Shelving, furniture & associated equipment
- ● Mtgs - Exhib - Inf - LG
- < The British Library
- M 1 i, 46 f

Association of Licensed Aircraft Engineers (1981)   (ALAE)   1981
- NR Bourn House, 8 Park St, BAGSHOT, Surrey, GU19 5AQ.   (hq)
  01276 474888
  http://www.alae.org
- ▲ Un-incorporated Society
- ○ *U; for licensed aircraft maintenance engineers & flight engineers
- M i

Association of Licensed Deep Sea Pilots
  see Europilots - the Association of Licensed Deep Sea Pilots

Association of Licensed Multiple Retailers   (ALMR)   1992
- ■ 9b Walpole Court, Ealing Studios, LONDON, W5 5ED.   (hq)
  020 8579 2080   fax 020 8579 7579
  email info@almr.org.uk   http://www.almr.org.uk
  Chief Exec: Nick Bish
- ▲ Un-incorporated Society
- ○ *T; to promote members' interests; to be a positive influence for the future of licensed retailing
- Gp Operator members: pub companies or other licensed retailers having at least 2 units
  Supplier members: suppliers of foods & services to the licensed trade
- ● Conf - Mtgs - Exhib - SG - Stat - Inf - VE - LG
- M 205 f
- ¶ NL - 12;   Political Digest - 12;
  On Trade Media Review - 1; all ftm only.

Association of Light Touch Therapists   (ALTT)   1988
- ■ 22 Baldock St, WARE, Herts, SG12 9DZ.   (hsb)
  01920 485265
  email info@altt.org   http://www.altt.org
  Chmn: Peter Collins
- ▲ Un-incorporated Society
- ○ *P; to assist in the establishment of light touch therapies within the normal health-care provision of the nation
- Gp Biomobility; Body mechanics; Bowen technique; Cranio-sacral therapy; Emotional freedom technique; Health kinesiology; Light touch healing; Lymph drainage; Metamorphic technique; Muscle release therapy; Orthobionomy; Polarity therapy; Pulsing; Rejuvanessence; Reflexology; Reharmonisation; Reiki; Spontaneous muscle release; Spinal touch therapy; Touch for health; Therapeutic touch
- ● Conf - Mtgs - Inf
- < Brit Complementary Medicine Assn (BCMA)
- M 73 i, UK / 1 i, o'seas
- ¶ NL - 4;   Register of Members - 1; both free.

Association of Lighthouse Keepers   (ALK)   1988
- ■ 116 Abbeyfield Drive, FAREHAM, Hants, PO15 5PQ.   (hsp)
  01329 843883   fax 01329 843883 (on request)
  email secretary@alk.org.uk   http://www.alk.org.uk
  Hon Sec: Keith W Morton
- ▲ Registered Charity
- ○ *G; the advancement of education of the public in pharology - the history & current practice of coastal & inland aids to navigation
- ● ET - Res - Exhib - Inf - Lib - PL - VE - Archive of artifacts
- < Wld Lighthouse Soc (WLS)
- M 550 i, UK / 20 i, o'seas
  (Sub: £16 UK / 30, $50 o'seas)
- ¶ Lamp (Jnl) - 4.

Association of Lighting Designers   (ALD)
- NR PO Box 680, OXFORD, OX1 9DG.   (sb)
  07817 060189
  email office@ald.org.uk   http://www.ald.org.uk
  Admin Sec: Geoff Spain
- ▲ Un-incorporated Society
- ○ *P; for lighting designers in the entertainment field
- ● Conf - Mtgs - ET - Exhib - SG - Stat - Inf - Lib - VE - Empl
- M 486 i, 24 f, 29 org, UK / 45 i, 3 f, o'seas
- ¶ Focus (Jnl) - 6; ftm only.   Ybk - 1; ftm, £7.50 nm.

Association of Lightweight Campers
  a group of the **Camping & Caravanning Club**

Association of Liner Producers
  a group of **Horticultural Trades Association**

Association of Lipspeakers   (ALS)   1992
NR   5 Furlong Close, Upper Tean, STOKE-ON-TRENT, Staffs,
       ST10 4LB.   (inf offr/p)
       01538 722482
       http://www.lipspeaking.co.uk
       Inf Officer: Dilys Palin
▲   Un-incorporated Society
Br   Regional gps
○   *P; for lipspeakers (providers of communication services for
       deaf & hard of hearing people who lipread)
●   Conf - Mtgs - ET - Exhib - Inf - Workshops
<   R Nat Inst for Deaf People (RNID); Coun for the Advancement
       of Communication with Deaf People (CACDD); UK Coun on
       Deafness (UKCOD)
M   115 i
¶   ALS News - 2.
       Leaflets: General, Legal, For Users, For Agencies.
       NOTE: please enclose SAE if an answer is required

Association of Lloyd's Members   (ALM)   1983
■   100 Fenchurch St, LONDON, EC3M 5LG.   (admin/dir)
       020 7488 0033   fax 020 7488 7555
       email mail@alm.ltd.uk
       http://www.association-lloyds-members.co.uk
       Snr Admin: Linda Evans
○   *P, *T; 'trade association for Names' - the underwriting
       members of Lloyd's of London (insurance market)
M   c 6,750 i, UK / c 2,250 i, o'seas
¶   ALM News (NL) - 6.
       Members' Agents' Profiles - 1.

**Association of Loading & Elevating Equipment Manufacturers
(ALEM)   1973**
■   Airport House, Purley Way, CROYDON, Surrey, CR0 0XZ.
       (asa)
       020 8253 4501   fax 020 8253 4510
       email alem@admin.co.uk   http://www.alem.org.uk
▲   Un-incorporated Society
○   *T; safety & good design of lift tables, dock levellers, platform
       lifts, tailboard lifts
●   Mtgs - Exhib - SG - Inf - LG
<   Brit Materials Handling Fedn; Fédn Eur de la Manutention
M   29 f
¶   LM & Product Guide; free.

Association of Local Authority Chief Executives   (ALACE)   1974
NR   c/o Waverley Borough Council, The Burys, GODALMING,
       Surrey, GU7 1HR.   (hsb)
       01483 523208
       http://www.alace.org.uk
       Hon Sec: Mary Orton
Br   2
○   *U; to represent the chief executives of local authorities in
       England, Wales, Scotland & Northern Ireland. The Council of
       ALACE forms the 'staff side' of the Joint Negotiating
       Committee for Chief Executives (the body responsible for the
       salary & terms/conditions of employment & regulations which
       affect the role of the 'head of the paid service' together with
       issues such as reorganisation of local government)
●   Mtgs - LG
M   330 i
¶   NL - 4.

Association of Local Bus Company Managers   (ALBUM)   1984
NR   41 Redhills, ECCLESHALL, Staffs, ST1 6JW.
       01785 859414
       http://www.album-bus.co.uk
       Hon Sec: Thomas Knowles
▲   Un-incorporated Society
○   *P, *T
●   Conf - Mtgs - LG
¶   NL - irreg; ftm only.

**Association of Local Environmental Records Centres   (ALERC)
2008**
NR   c/o ERCCIS, Five Acres, Allet, TRURO, Cornwall, TR4 9DJ.
       (hq)
       01872 240777
       http://www.alerc.org.uk
       Sec: Darwyn Sumner
○   *N; to represent the interests of local records centres in the UK

**Association of Local Government Archaeological Officers
(ALGAO)   1996**
NR   Cornerstone, Forbes, ALFORD, Aberdeenshire, AB33 8QH.
       01975 564071
       email admin@algao.org.uk   http://www.algao.org.uk
       Contact: Caroline Ingle
▲   Un-incorporated Society
○   *P; to represent archaeologists working in local government
       throughout the UK
Gp   Countryside; European; Historic environment records; Historic
       buildings;Maritime; Planning & legislation; Urban
●   Mtgs - ET - Res - Exhib - Stat - LG
<   Eur Assn Archaeologists
M   115 local authorities

**Association of Local Government Communications
(LGcommunications)   1971**
NR   Communications Unit, City Hall (17th floor), 64 Victoria St,
       LONDON, SW1E 6QP.   (sb)
       020 7641 2575
       email lgcommunications@westminster.gov.uk
       http://www.lgcomms.org.uk
       Sec: Alex Aiken
▲   Un-incorporated Society
○   *P; to enhance the reputation of local government; to provide a
       united voice to public relations & communications functions
       in all UK principal local authorities
●   Conf - Mtgs - Res - Comp - Stat - VE - LG
M   158 local authorities
¶   NL - 12 (email based distribution); ftm only.

Association of Local History Tutors
  in 2008 merged with **British Association for Local History**

Association of London Clubs   (ALC)
■   c/o White's, 37 St James's St, LONDON, SW1A 1JG.   (sb)
       020 7493 6671
       http://www.alclubs.org.uk
       Sec: Mrs June M Aitken
○   *N; to provide a forum for matters of common interest to
       member clubs
●   Mtgs - ET - Comp - Empl - LG
M   55 London clubs

Association of London Government
  since October 2006 **London Councils**

Association of Lorry Loader Manufacturers & Importers of Great Britain
  since 1 February 2008 **ALLMI Ltd**

© CBD Research Ltd · Beckenham · BR3 5JS · Tel 020 8650 7745 · E-mail cbd@cbdresearch.com · www.cbdresearch.com

Association for Low Countries Studies in Great Britain & Ireland (ALCS)
NR Dept of Germanic Studies, University of Sheffield, Jessop West, SHEFFIELD, S Yorks, S3 7RA.   (pres/b)
0114-222 4396   fax 0114-222 2160
email alcs@sheffield.ac.uk
http://www.alcs.group.shef.ac.uk
Pres: Dr Nicola McLelland
▲ Un-incorporated Society
○ *L, *X; 'to promote the scholarly study of the language, culture, history & society of the Low Countries; to increase public awareness of the Low Countries, especially the Dutch language & Dutch & Flemish culture, history & society
● Conf - Mtgs - ET - Res - Inf - LG - Postgraduate training days - Undergraduate days
< Intle Vereniging voor Neerlandistiek
M 65 i, UK / 40 i, o'seas
¶ Dutch Crossing: a journal of Low Countries studies - 2; £15 yr m, £25 yr nm.
Crossways: a series of books & collections of papers - irreg.

Association of Mainframe Operators & Network Administrators (AMONO)   1992
■ 1 Caryl House, Windlesham Grove, LONDON, SW19 6AH.   (hsp)
○ *T; operation & maintenance of large computer systems
M 879 i, 53 f, UK / 38 i, 4 f, o'seas

Association for Management Education & Development (AMED)   1960
NR PO Box 7578, DORCHESTER, DT1 9GD.   (hq)
0300 365 1247
email office@amed.org.uk   http://www.amed.org.uk
Contact: Linda Williams
▲ Company Limited by Guarantee; Registered Charity
○ *E, *P; a professional network for people in individual & organisational development (trainers, HR directors, management consultants & business school lecturers)
Note: also known as the AMED Network.

Association of Managerial & Professional Staffs
an autonomous professional body within **Unite the Union**

Association of Manufacturers of Domestic Appliances (AMDEA)   1969
■ Rapier House, 40-46 Lamb's Conduit St, LONDON, WC1N 3NW.   (hq)
020 7405 0666   fax 020 7405 6609
email info@amdea.org.uk   http://www.amdea.org.uk
Chief Exec: Douglas Herbison
▲ Company Limited by Guarantee
○ *T; interests of manufacturers of electric domestic appliances, and/or their components
● Mtgs - Stat - LG
< Eur C'ee of Domestic Appliance Mfrs (CECED)
M [depending on annual turnover]
¶ NL - 12;   AR - 1; both free.   LM - printout on request.
AMDEA Technical News - 12; ftm only.

Association of Manufacturers of Power generating Systems (AMPS)   1977
■ Samuelson House, 62 Forder Way, Hampton, PETERBOROUGH, Cambs, PE7 8JB.   (hq)
0845 644 8748   fax 01733 314767
email ab@amps.org.uk   http://www.amps.org.uk
Dir-Gen: Roger Lane-Nott
▲ Company Limited by Guarantee
○ *T; for manufacturers of power generation equipment & their suppliers
Gp Statistics; Technical
● Conf - Mtgs - Exhib - Stat - Expt - Inf - VE - LG
< Eur Generating Set Assn (EUROPGEN); Electrical Generating Systems Assn (EGSA)(USA); BEAMA
M 80 f
¶ Amps Power - 4.

Association of Marine Scientific Industries   (AMSI)
NR 28-29 Threadneedle St, LONDON, EC2R 8AY.
020 7628 2555   fax 020 7638 4376
email info@maritimeindustries.org
http://www.maritimeindustries.org
Chmn: Richard Burt
○ *T; to support companies in the marine science & technology sector
< Soc of Maritime Inds

Association for Marketing & Development in Independent Schools   (AMDIS)   1993
■ 2 St Michael's St, MALTON, N Yorks, YO17 7LJ.   (hq)
0700 062 3347
http://www.amdis.co.uk
Admin: Victoria Gillingham
▲ Un-incorporated Society
○ *P; 'to promote good marketing practice in independent education'
● Conf - Mtgs - ET - Stat
< ADAPA (Australia)
M 430 schools

Association of Master Herbalists   1995
NR 3 Maple Cottages, Broadgate, BEVERLEY, E Yorks, HU17 8RW.
01482 862277
http://www.associationofmasterherbalists.co.uk
Gen Sec: David Blackwell
○ *P

Association of Master Upholsterers & Soft Furnishers Ltd (AMUSF)   1947
■ Francis Vaughan House, Q1 Capital Point, Capital Business Park, Parkway, CARDIFF, CF3 2PU.   (hq)
029 2077 8918
http://www.upholsterers.co.uk
Chief Exec: Michael B Spencer
▲ Company Limited by Guarantee
Br 11
○ *T
● Conf - Mtgs - Exhib - Inf - Li - PL - LG
< Fedn of Small Businesses; Assn of Soft Furnishers Ltd
M c 550 f
¶ Upholsterer & Soft Furnisher - 12; ftm, £35 yr nm.
CFC Contract Furnishing Concepts - 6; ftm, £21.50 yr nm.
Note: incorporates the Chair Frame Manufacturers' Association.

Association of Masters of Harriers & Beagles   (AMHB)   1891
NR Langley House, Winchcombe, CHELTENHAM, Glos, GL54 5AB.   (dir/p)
01242 602564
email director@amhb.org.uk   http://www.amhb.org.uk
Dir: Lizzie Salmon
○ *F: to oversee the promotion & proper management of harrier & beagle hunts
● Peterborough Festival of Hunting
< Coun of Hunting Assns
M 600 i

Association of MBAs Ltd   1967
NR 25 Hosier Lane, LONDON, EC1A 9LQ.   (hq)
020 7246 2686
http://www.mbaworld.com
▲ Company Limited by Guarantee; Registered Charity
○ *E; for holders of the MBA degree; to promote management education in order to maximise its contribution to British industry
M c 10,000 i, 70 f, 5 org, UK / 1,000 i o'seas

Association for Measurement & Evaluation of Communication (AMEC)

NR Communications House, 26 York St, LONDON, W1U 6PZ. (hsp)
020 8675 4442
email jacquelinemilton@amecorg.com
http://www.amecorg.com
Admin: Jacqueline Milton
▲ Un-incorporated Society
○ *T; to represent the interest of media evaluation companies
● Mtgs - Promotion of media evaluation
M 11 f, UK / 4 f, o'seas
✕ 2006 Association of Media Evaluation Companies

Association of Meat Inspectors GB Ltd   (AMI)   1960

■ 25 Central Rd, Downfield, STROUD, Glos, GL5 4HQ. (hsb)
01453 756487
http://www.meatinspectors.co.uk
Gen Sec: Ian D Robinson
▲ Un-incorporated Society
Br 7 divisions
○ *P; meat inspection & hygiene in abattoirs, meat curing premises & cold stores; to promote research & publish the results; to promote high standards of meat inspection & hygiene
Gp Technical, Legislative; Educational trust
● Conf - Mtgs - ET - Lib - LG
M 1,200-1,400 i
(Sub: £70)
¶ Meat Hygienist - 4; ftm; £75 nm.

Association for Media Education in Scotland   (AMES)   1983

■ 24 Burnett Place, ABERDEEN, AB24 4QD. (hsp)
01224 277113
email desmurphy47@gmail.com
http://www.mediaedscotland.org.uk
Sec: Des Murphy
▲ Registered Scottish Charity
○ *P; to advance media education & media literacy in education & in society
● Conf - Mtgs - ET - Res - SG - LG
< Eur Network of Media Educators (EUROMEDUC) (www.euromedialiteracy.eu)
M 150 i, UK / 6 i, o'seas
¶ The Media Education Jnl - 2; £20 i, £35 instns m, £15 i, £30 instns, nm.
NL - 2/3; ftm only.

Association of Media Evaluation Companies
since 2006 the **Association for Measurement & Evaluation of Communication**

Association of Media Practice Educators
see **Media, Communication & Cultural Studies Association**

Association of Medical Advisers to British Orchestras (AMABO)   1990

NR Totara Park House (4th floor), 34-36 Gray's Inn Rd, LONDON, WC1X 8HR. (hq)
020 7404 5888   fax 020 7404 3222
email amabo@bapam.org.uk
http://www.bapam.org.uk/amabo
Sec: Dr Penny Wright
▲ Registered Charity
Br 19
○ *M, *P; for doctors attached to major British orchestras; research & training in performing arts medicine
● Mtgs - ET - Res - SG
< Brit Assn for Performing Arts Medicine
M 21 i

Association of Medical Insurance Intermediaries   (amii)   1998

NR Colchester Business Centre (suite 23-24), 1 George Williams Way, COLCHESTER, Essex, CO1 2JS. (hsb)
01206 731181   fax 01206 367580
http://www.amii.org.uk
Chmn: Mike Izzard,   Treas: Wayne Pontin
○ *T; to offer specialist independent advice on health issues
● Conf - Mtgs - ET - Exhib
M c 98 f

Association of Medical Microbiologists
2009 merged with the British Infection Society to form the **British Infection Association**

Association of Medical Reporting Organisations   (AMRO)

NR Melford House, 30 Rookwood Park, HORSHAM, West Sussex, RH12 1UB.
01403 271232
http://www.amro-uk.co.uk
○ *N; is 'dedicated to the promotion of professional standards in medical reporting & in the preparation & use of medical reports & the conduct of medical experts in the course of legal proceedings'
M 16 f

Association of Medical Research Charities   (AMRC)   1987

NR Charles Darwin House, 12 Roger St, LONDON, WC1N 2JU. (hq)
020 7685 2620
email info@amrc.org.uk   http://www.amrc.org.uk
Chief Exec: Simon Denegri
▲ Company Limited by Guarantee; Registered Charity
○ *K, *M, *Q; to further medical interests in the UK generally & the effectiveness of charities whose principal activity is medical research
● ET - LG
M 112 charities
¶ NL - 6/8; ftm only.   AR - 1; free.

Association of Medical Secretaries, Practice Managers, Administrators & Receptionists   (AMSPAR)   1964

NR Tavistock House North, Tavistock Sq, LONDON, WC1H 9LN. (hq)
020 7387 6005
http://www.amspar.co.uk
Chief Exec: Tom Brownlie
▲ Company Limited by Guarantee; Registered Charity
○ *P
● Conf - Mtgs - ET - Exam - Inf
< Eur Fedn of Med Secretary Assns
M 5,500 i, UK / 90 i, o'seas
¶ AMSPAR Magazine - 4.   NL - 4.
Professional Guidelines.   Careers leaflets.

Association of Member-Directed Pension Schemes   (AMPS) 1979

■ c/o Barnett Waddingham LLP, Port of Liverpool Building, Pier Head, LIVERPOOL, L3 1BW. (hsb)
0151-235 6600   fax 0151-235 6640
http://www.ampsonline.co.uk
Hon Sec: Andrew Roberts
▲ Un-incorporated Society
○ *P; to represent small self-administered pension schemes & self-invested personal pensions
● Conf - Mtgs - ET - Inf - LG
M 193 f
(Sub: £200)
¶ NL - 12; ftm only.

© CBD Research Ltd · Beckenham · BR3 5JS · Tel 020 8650 7745 · E-mail cbd@cbdresearch.com · www.cbdresearch.com

Association of Members of Independent Monitoring Boards (AMIMB) 1981
■ 3 Forsham Cottages, Forsham Lane, Sutton Valence, MAIDSTONE, Kent, ME17 3WQ. (v-chmn/p)
01622 844481
email info@amimb.co.uk   http://www.amimb.co.uk
Chmn: Helen Boothman,   V-chmn: Mrs Angela Clay
▲ Registered Charity
○ *W; independent monitoring of every prison & immigration removal in the UK
● Conf - Mtgs - ET - Res - SG - Stat - Inf - VE - LG
< Criminal Justice Alliance
M 400 i
(Sub: £20 i, c £300 org)
¶ The Independent Monitor - 3; free.

Association of Men of Kent & Kentish Men (MKKM) 1897
NR Cantium Lodge, Terrace Rd, MAIDSTONE, Kent, ME16 8HU. (hq)
01622 758722
Sec: Mrs T M Robinson
Br 19
○ *G, *K; to foster a sense of pride in the County of Kent; to protect the county's heritage & the beauty of the countryside
● Conf - Mtgs - Inf - Lib - VE
M 3,000 i
¶ Kent - 3.

Association of Meter Operators (AMO) 1996
NR c/o Gemserv, 10 Fenchurch St, LONDON, EC3M 3BE.
020 7090 1032
http://www.meteroperators.org.uk
Sec: Ryan Perry
▲ Un-incorporated Society
○ *T; for meter operators in the UK electricity & gas markets
● Mtgs - Inf (to members only)
M 14 f
¶ LM on website.

Association of Miniature Engine Manufacturers (AMEM) 1975
■ Kingsway House, Wrotham Rd, MEOPHAM, Kent, DA13 0AV. (mail address)
○ *T; includes petrol, diesel & bio fuel, battery & solar powered units
● Conf - Mtgs - SG - Inf - LG
¶ Mini-motion - 3/4; ftm only.

Association of Mining Analysts (AMA)
NR c/o Bankside plc, 1 Frederick's Place, LONDON, EC2R 8AE. (mail add)
http://www.ama.org.uk
Sec: Louise Mason (020 7367 8872)
▲ Un-incorporated Society
○ *P; for fund managers, bankers & analysts
● Mtgs - VE
M 251 i, UK / 24 i, o'seas

Association of Model Agents (AMA) 1974
■ 11-19 Fashion St, LONDON, E1 6PX. (hq)
020 7422 0699   fax 020 7247 9230
email amainfo@btinternet.com
○ *T; to protect the reputation of models & model agents
● Mtgs - Inf
M 22 f

Association of Model Railway Societies in Scotland (AMRSS) 1966
NR Model Rail Scotland, PO Box 19564, JOHNSTONE, PA6 7YP. (mail/address)
0845 226 3061
▲ Un-incorporated Society
○ *G; to promote 'Modelrail Scotland', the national model railway exhibition held at the SECC Glasgow, on the last weekend in February
● Exhib
M 34 clubs

Association of Mortgage Intermediaries (AMI)
NR 2-6 Austin Friars House, Austin Friars, LONDON, EC2N 2HD. (hq)
020 7628 1288
http://www.a-m-i.org.uk
Dir Gen: Chris Cummings
○ *P

Association of Motion Picture Sound (AMPS) 1989
NR 28 Knox St, LONDON, W1H 1FS. (hq)
020 7723 6727   fax 020 7723 6727
email admin@amps.net   http://www.amps.net
Hon Sec: Brian Hickin
▲ Un-incorporated Society
○ *P; to promote & encourage the science, technology & creative application of all aspects of motion picture sound recording & reproduction
Gp Sound for film & television
● Mtgs - Private film screenings
M 340 i, 35 f, UK / 23 i, 1 f, o'seas
¶ AMPS Jnl - 4.

Association of Motor Racing Circuit Owners Ltd (AMRCO) 1962
■ c/o BARC Ltd, Thruxton Circuit, ANDOVER, Hants, SP11 8PN. (sb)
01264 882200   fax 01264 882233
email amrco@barc.net
http://www.motorsportsuk.co.uk
Sec: Mrs A J Curley
▲ Company Limited by Guarantee
○ *T; to represent the interests of motor racing licensed circuit owners
● Mtgs
M 17 f, UK / 1 f, o'seas

Association of Mountaineering Instructors
NR Siabod Cottage, CAPEL CURIG, Conwy, LL24 0ES.
01690 720314   fax 01690 720248
http://www.ami.org.uk
Devt Officer: Ed Chard (07721 620428)
○ *P

Association of Municipal Authorities of Ireland
IRL AMAI House, 63 Ormond St, NENAGH, Co Tipperary, Republic of Ireland.
353 (67) 42222
email director@amai.ie
Dir: Tom Ryan
○ *N

Association of Mutual Insurers
On 2010 merged with the Association of Friendly Societies to form the **Association of Financial Mutuals**

Association of Nanny Agencies   (ANA)
NR   7 Water's Edge, Bois Hall Rd, ADDLESTONE, Surrey,
       KT15 2HW.   (hsp)
       email angela@anauk.org   http://www.anauk.org
       Chmn: Angela Spencer
▲   Un-incorporated Society
○   *T; to raise the standards of nanny agencies in the UK
●   Mtgs - Inf
<   VOICE
M   50 i
       (Sub: £120)
¶   NL - 3; free.

**Association of National Driver Improvement Scheme Providers
   (ANDISP)   1998**
NR   c/o Alan Prosser, TTC Group, Hadley Park East, Hadley,
       TELFORD, Shropshire, TF1 6QJ.
       01952 602621
       http://www.driver-improvement.co.uk
       Sec: Alan Prosser
▲   Un-incorporated Society
○   *T; organisation & practice of driver improvement courses on
       behalf of police constabularies. The association manages
       these courses on behalf of the Dept of Transport (DFT) &
       Association of Chief Police Officers (ACPO)
●   Mtgs - ET - LG
M   42 f & local authorities

Association of National Park Authorities   (ANPA)   1992
NR   126 Bute St, Cardiff Bay, CARDIFF, CF10 5LE.   (hq)
       029 2049 9966
       email info@anpa.gov.uk
       http://www.nationalparks.gov.uk
       Co-ordinator: Kathryn Cook
▲   Un-incorporated Society
○   *N; for the national park authorities of England, Wales &
       Scotland
●   Conf - Mtgs - Res - Comp - SG - LG - Public relations of NPA's
       at national level
M   15 National Park Authorities
¶   Annual Review - 1;   Technical papers - irreg.

Association of National Specialist Colleges   (NATSPEC)
NR   Derwen College, OSWESTRY, Shropshire, SY11 3JA.
       (reg/office)
       01691 661234
       http://www.natspec.org.uk
       Chief Exec: Alison Boulton (0117-923 2830)
○   *E; colleges providing further education, or training, for persons
       with learning difficulties or disabilities

**Association of National Tourist Office Representatives
   (ANTOR)   1953**
■   39 Pennington Close, Colden Common, WINCHESTER, Hants,
       SO21 1UR.   (mail/address)
       0870 241 9084
       http://www.antor.com
       Exec Sec: Esther C Smith
▲   Company Limited by Guarantee
○   *T; 'the principal lobbying organisaton for the world's tourist
       offices'
●   Mtgs - Exhib - Inf - LG
M   60 overseas tourist offices represented in the UK
¶   LM - 1; free.

Association of Natural Burial Grounds   (ANBG)   1994
NR   12A Blackstock Mews, Blackstock Rd, LONDON, N4 2BT.   (hq)
       0871 288 2098
       email office@anbg.co.uk   http://www.anbg.co.uk
       Contact: Michael Jarvis
▲   Registered Charity
○   *K; 'to promote 'natural' burial, where trees or flowers are
       planted on the grave instead of having headstones'
●   Conf - ET - Res - Exhib - Stat - Inf - LG
<   Natural Death Centre
M   50 f
¶   The Natural Death Hbk - 3 yrly; £14.99.
       Living Will + Forms; £7.

Association of Natural Medicine   (ANM)   1983
■   27 Braintree Rd, WITHAM, Essex, CM8 2DD.   (hq)
       01376 502762   fax 01376 502762
       email a-nm@hotmail.co.uk
       http://www.associationnaturalmedicine.co.uk
       Chief Exec: Martin Duncombe
▲   Registered Charity
○   *P; training courses for professional practice of natural
       medicine & therapies
●   Mtgs - ET - Exam - Res - Exhib - SG - Inf
<   Parliamentary Gp for Integrated & Complementary Medicine
M   c 300 i
¶   Natural Medicine (Jnl) - 4.

**Association for Neuro-Linguistic Programming (UK) Ltd
   (ANLP)   1985**
NR   Apsley Mills Cottage, Stationers Place, HEMEL HEMPSTEAD,
       Herts, HP3 9RH.   (admin/p)
       fax 020 3355 0705
       http://www.anlp.org
       Contact: Karen
▲   Company Limited by Guarantee; Registered Charity
○   *E
●   Conf - Mtgs - ET - SG - Inf
M   750 i, 40 f, UK / 50 i, o'seas
¶   Rapport (Jnl) - 4.   Information booklet - 1.
       Directory of Members.   AR; free.

Association of Neurophysiological Scientists   (ANS)   1949
NR   EBS, City Wharf, Davidson Rd, LICHFIELD, Staffs, WS14 9DZ.
       (asa)
       0845 226 3068
       http://www.ansuk.org
       Admin: Lindsey Sevier-White
▲   Company Limited by Guarantee
○   *P; to promote a high standard of training & education in the
       field of neurophysiology
●   Conf - Mtgs - Exam - Exhib - SG - Empl
M   c 600 i
¶   Jnl of Electro-physiology & Technology - 4.
×   2007 Electro-physiological Technologists' Association

Association of New Age Industries   (ANAIS)   1995
■   c/o Honeybees, Milkhouse Water, PEWSEY, Wilts, SN9 5JX.
▲   Un-incorporated Society
○   *T
Gp   Water power; Wind power
M   i, f & org

Association of News Retailing
       a group of the **Association of Convenience Stores**

© CBD Research Ltd · Beckenham · BR3 5JS · Tel 020 8650 7745 · E-mail cbd@cbdresearch.com · www.cbdresearch.com

Association of Newspaper & Magazine Wholesalers (ANMW) 1917
NR Wakefield House, Pipers Way, SWINDON, Wilts, SN3 1RF.
       (hq)
       01793 563692
       email howard.birch@smithsnews.co.uk
       Contact: Howard Birch
▲   Un-incorporated Society
○   *T
●   Mtgs - ET - Inf - LG
M   29 f

Association of Noise Consultants (ANC) 1964
■   The Old Pump House, 1A Stonecross, ST ALBANS, Herts,
       AL1 4AA.   (asa)
       020 8253 4518
       email anc@kingstonsmith.co.uk   http://www.theanc.co.uk
       Manager: Robert Osborne
▲   Company Limited by Guarantee
○   *P; to represent & support noise & consultancy companies
●   Conf - Mtgs - Res
M   100 f

Association of North East Councils (ANEC) 1986
NR The Guildhall, Quayside, NEWCASTLE upon TYNE, NE1 3AF.
       (hq)
       0191-261 7388   fax 0191-232 4558
       http://www.northeastcouncils.gov.uk
       Chief Exec: Melanie Laws
▲   Un-incorporated Society
○   *N; an association of the local councils (county councils, district
       councils & metropolitan district councils) in the counties
       forming the North East Region of England - Durham,
       Northumberland, Tyne & Wear & Tees Valley; to promote the
       economic & social wellbeing of the people of the region.
       Is the Joint Directorate for the North East Assembly

Association of Northern Ireland Colleges (ANIC)
§   Millennium Community Outreach Centre, Springfield
       Educational Village, 400 Springfield Rd, BELFAST, BT12 7DU.
       028 9090 0060
       http://www.anic.ac.uk
       Chief Exec: John D'Arcy
○   *E; further education in Northern Ireland

Association of Northern Ireland Education & Library Boards
       replaced in 2010 by the Education & Skills Authority for
       Northern Ireland, which is listed in the companion volume
       Councils, Committees & Boards

Association of Northumberland Local History Societies (ANLHS) 1966
■   c/o The Black Gate, Castle Garth, NEWCASTLE upon TYNE,
       NE1 1RQ.   (hsb)
       0191-284 0555
       email mark@anlhs.org.uk   http://www.anlhs.org.uk
       Hon Sec: Mrs Patricia Hix
▲   Registered Charity
○   *L; to stimulate interest & research in the local history of the
       ancient county of Northumberland
Gp Projects (incl research)
●   Conf - Mtgs - ET - Res - Exhib - SG - Inf - VE
<   Brit Assn for Local History
M   82 i, 15 instns, 53 org, UK / 4 i, o'seas
       (Sub: £10.50 i, £11.50 instns, UK / £11.50 i o'seas)
¶   Tyne & Tweed (Jnl) - 1; ftm, £4.50 yr nm.   AR; free.

Association for Nurse Prescribing (ANP) 1998
■   PO Box 2078, Rayleigh, Essex, SS6 9YA.   (hq)
       01245 327763   fax 01245 327763
       email admin@anp.org.uk   http://www.anp.org.uk
       Hon Sec: Dr Barbara Stuttle
▲   Registered Charity
○   *P; to support non-medical prescribers, recotgnised by the Dept
       of Health as a leading organisation for extended prescribing
       rights
●   Conf - ET (for effective prescribing)
M   i
       (Sub: £25)

Association of Nursery Training Colleges Ltd (ANTC) 1934
NR Chiltern College, 16 Peppard Rd, Caversham, READING,
       Berks, RG4 8JZ.   (regd/off)
▲   Registered Charity
○   *E; promotion of nursery nurse training
●   Mtgs - ET - LG

Association of Nurses in Substance Abuse (ANSA) 1983
NR 37 Star St, WARE, Herts, SG12 7AA.
       0870 241 3503   fax 01920 462730
       http://www.ansauk.org

Association of Nursing Religious
       closed 2008

Association of Occupational Health Nurse Practitioners (UK) (AOHNP (UK)) 1992
■   PO Box 11785, PETERHEAD, Aberdeenshire, AB42 5YG.
       (mail/address)
       0845 225 5937   fax 0845 255 5937
       email admin@aohnp.co.uk   http://www.aohnp.co.uk
       Admin: Linda Riseborough
▲   Un-incorporated Association
○   *P; to increase representation & raise the profile of
       occupational health nurses
●   Conf - Mtgs - SG - LG (DoH, NMC) - Networking - Job
       introduction scheme
M   350 i, UK / 6 i, o'seas
¶   OH Today (NL) - 6; ftm.

Association of Occupational Therapists of Ireland (AOTI)
IRL PO Box 11555, Ground floor office, Bow Bridge House,
       Bow Lane, Kilmainham, DUBLIN 8, Republic of Ireland.
       353 (1) 633 7222
       email aoti@eircom.net   http://www.aoti.ie
       Chmn: Yvonne Finn-Orde
○   *P

Association of Occupational Therapists in Mental Health
       a specialist section of the **British Association of Occupational
       Therapists**

Association for Off Road Driving Centres
       see **British Off Road Driving Association**

Association of Old Vehicle Clubs in Northern Ireland (AOVC) 1973
■   38 Ballymaconnell Rd, BANGOR, Co Down, BT20 5PS.   (hsb)
       028 9146 7886   fax 028 9146 3211
       email secretary@aovc.co.uk   http://www.aovc.co.uk
       Dir & Co Sec: Trevor Mitchell
▲   Company Limited by Guarantee
○   *G; the restoration & use of all types of historic vehicles in
       Northern Ireland
Gp Car clubs; Vintage clubs
●   Mtgs - Exhib - VE
<   Fedn of Brit Historic Vehicle Clubs
M   i, 28 clubs
¶   Ybk - 1; free to affiliated clubs.

Association of On-Track Labour Suppliers
  since January 2006 **Rail Industry Contractors Association**

Association of Online Publishers   (AOP)   2002
NR Queens House, 55-56 Lincoln's Inn Fields, LONDON,
      WC2A 3LJ.   (hq)
      020 7404 4166   fax 020 7404 4167
○ *T; for interactive (online) publishers from all sectors of media,
      whether from newspaper, magazine or broadcasting
      industries, or solely online. The primary purpose of AOP is to
      raise standards & revenue across all sectors of online
      publishing, & to raise the credibility & profile of the industry

Association of Operating Department Practitioners
  in 2007 was incorporated into the **College of Operating
  Department Practitioners**

Association of Optometrists   (AOP)   1946
■ 61 Southwark St, LONDON, SE1 0HL.   (hq)
      020 7261 9661
      http://www.assoc-optometrists.org
      Chief Exec: Bob Hughes
▲ Company Limited by Guarantee
○ *P; to represent the interests of optometrists
Gp Hospital optometrists
● Conf - Mtgs - ET - Inf - Empl - LG - Professional indemnity
      insurance - Provision of representation of individual members
      in legal & disciplinary cases
< Optical Confedn
      Eur Coun of Optometry & Optics; Jt Optical C'ee on the EU
M 11,000 i, UK / 100 i, o'seas
¶ OT (Optometry Today/OpticsToday) - 26;   Blink (NL) - 4; both
      ftm.

Association of Optometrists: Ireland
IRL Kevin Culliton Rooms, 18 Greenmount House,
      Harolds CrossRd, DUBLIN 6W.
      353 (1) 453 8850   fax 353 (1) 453 8867
      email info@optometrists.ie
      Sec: Peter Coleman
○ *P

Association of Organics Recycling   (AOR)   1995
■ 3 Burystead Place, WELLINGBOROUGH, Northants,
      NN8 1AH.   (hq)
      01993 446440
      email enquiries@organics-recycling.org.uk
      http://www.organics-recycling.org.uk
      Acting Chief Exec: Jeremy Jacobs
▲ Company Limited by Guarantee
○ *Q; to promote the sustainable management of biodegradable
      resources & the use of biological treatment techniques
● Conf - Mtgs - ET - Stat - Inf - Lib - VE - LG
M 20 i, 550 f, 10 org, UK / 2 i, o'seas
¶ Composting News (Jnl) - 4; ftm only.
      Technical Manuals:
      A Guide to Anerobic Digestion + Directory of Suppliers;
      £25 m,
        £50 nm.
      A Guide to In-Vessel Composting + Directory of Suppliers;
      £45 nm, £65 nm.
      Health & Safety at Composting Sites - a guide for managers;
      £45 m, £65 nm.
      Standardised Protocol for the Sampling & Enumeration of
      Airborne Microorganisms at Composting Facilities (1999);
      £5 m, £25 nm.
      Hazard Analysis & Critical Control Point for Composting;
      £35 m, £55 nm.
× 2008 Composting Association

Association of Paediatric Anaesthetists (Great Britain & Ireland)   (APAGBI)   1973
■ 21 Portland St, LONDON, W1B 1PY.   (hsb)
      020 7631 8887
      Hon Sec: Dr Kathleen Wilkinson
▲ Un-incorporated Society
○ *L, *P; education & research in paediatric anaesthesia
Gp Clinical trials; Guidelines; Peer review
● Conf - ET - Res - SG - LG - Liaison with medical royal colleges
< Fedn of Eur Assns in Paediatric Anaesthesia; Assn of
      Anaesthetists
M 450 i, UK / 180 i, o'seas
¶ NL - 12; free.

Association Paediatric Emergency Medicine
  a group of the **Royal College of Paediatrics & Child Health**

Association for Paediatric & Palliative Medicine
  a group of the **Royal College of Paediatrics & Child Health**

Association of Paediatric Resuscitation Officers   (APRO)
NR Flat 3 Marlborough House, Marlborough Hill, BRISTOL,
      BS2 8EZ.
      email enquiries@apro.org.uk
      Contact: Mrs Gillian Alexander,   Sec: Tanya Ralph
○ *P;

Association of Painting Craft Teachers   (APCT)   1921
■ Shrewsbury College of Art & Technology, London Rd,
      SHREWSBURY, Shropshire, SY2 6PR.   (hsb)
      o1743 342501
      email barrym@shrewsbury.ac.uk   http://www.apct.co.uk
      Nat Sec: Barry Mason
○ *E; 'craft skills throughout the painting & decorating industry'
● Mtgs - ET - Exhib - Comp
M 265 i, 5 f, UK / 2 i, o'seas

Association for Palliative Medicine of Great Britain & Ireland   (APM)   1985
NR Peterkin House, 76 Botley Rd, SOUTHAMPTON, Hants,
      SO31 1BA.   (hq)
      01489 565665
      http://www.apmonline.org
      Pres: Dr Bee Wee   Hon Sec: Dr Andrew Davies
▲ Registered Charity
○ *P
● Conf - Mtgs - ET - Res - SG
< Eur Assn for Palliative Care
M 500 i, UK / 10 i, o'seas
¶ NL - 2; ftm only.

Association of Past Rotarians   1960
■ 11 Highgate Place, West Park, LYTHAM ST ANNES, Lancs,
      FY8 4QJ.   (hsp)
      01253 732342   fax 01253 732342
      email jonandkateha8852@aol.com
      http://www.pastrotarians.com
      Hon Sec: John Harrop
▲ Un-incorporated Society
Br 24
○ *G; a fellowship of member clubs of former Rotarians
● Conf - Mtgs - VE
M 374 i
¶ Proclaim - 4;   AR; both free.
      Pioneers & Pathfinders (1948) [&] Forty Years On (2000) by
      W R Braide, (histories of the Past Rotarian movement).

Association for Pastoral Care in Mental Health   (APCMH)   1986
NR   c/o St Paul's Church, 5 Rossmore Rd, LONDON, NW1 6NJ.
(hsb)
020 3397 2497
email apcmh@pastoral.org.uk
http://www.pastoral.org.uk
Mem & Co Sec: Mark Dodds
▲   Company Limited by Guarantee; Registered Charity
Br   4
○   *W; to support & facilitate groups who wish to seek advice on
setting up projects for people with mental health problems -
mainly in the churches
●   Conf - Mtgs - ET - Drop in centres - Befriending schemes -
Awareness raising conferences
Helpline: 01483 538936
<   Gld of Health; Nat Schizophrenia Fellowship
M   200 i, 20 org
¶   NL - 6; ftm only.
uses the operating name Being Alongside

Association for Pastoral & Spiritual Care & Counselling
a group of the **British Association for Counselling &
Psychotherapy**

Association for Payment Clearing Services
since April 2009 **UK Cards Association**

Association of Pension Lawyers   (APL)   1984
NR   20 Gresham St, LONDON, EC2V 7JE.   (mail add)
Chmn: Pauline Sibbit
○   *P; to promote awareness of the importance of the role of law
in the provision of pensions; to afford opportunities for
discussion & consideration of matters of interest as well as
education
Gp   Education & seminars; International; Investment; Leigislative &
parliamentary; Litigation
●   Conf - Mtgs - LG
M   c 950 i
¶   Pension Lawyer - 4.

Association for Perioperative Practice   (NATN)   1964
■   Daisy Ayris House, 6 Grove Park Court, HARROGATE, N Yorks,
HG1 4DP.   (hq)
01423 508079   fax 01423 531613
email hq@afpp.org.uk   http://www.afpp.org.uk
Chief Exec: Alison Tait
▲   Company Limited by Guarantee; Registered Charity
Br   15
○   *P; for those working in & around operating theatres
●   Conf - Mtgs - ET - Res - Exhib - SG - Inf - Lib - VE
M   8,500 i, 10 f, UK / 250 i, o'seas
¶   Jnl of Perioperative Practice - 12; ftm, £65 yr nm.

Association of Personal Injury Lawyers   (APIL)   1989
NR   11 Castle Quay, NOTTINGHAM, NG7 1FW.   (hq)
0115-958 0585   fax 0115-958 0885
http://www.apil.org.uk
Sec: Frances Swaine,   Chief Exec: Denise Kitchener
▲   Company Limited by Guarantee
○   *P; to promote full & prompt compensation for all types of
personal injury; to promote wider redress for personal injury
in the legal system; to campaign for improvements in
personal injury law for the public good
Gp   Special interest: Procedure, Brain injury, Child abuse, Child
injury, Clinical negligence, Costs & funding, Damages,
Environment, International, Military, Multi party actions,
Occupational health, Product liability, Spinal cord injury,
Transport
●   Conf - Mtgs - ET - Exam - Res - Exhib - Stat - Inf - LG
M   5,213 i, UK / 62 i, o'seas + 150 f
¶   Jnl - 4.
Focus (NL) - 6;   Agenda - 12; both ftm only.
Rehab Directory - 1; ftm, £20 nm.
Membership Directory - 1; ftm, £100 nm.   AR; free.

Association of Pet Behaviour Counsellors   (APBC)   1989
NR   PO Box 46, WORCESTER, WR8 9YS.   (mail address)
01386 751151   fax 01386 750743
http://www.apbc.org.uk
○   *P; for practising pet behaviour therapists who work exclusively
on referral from veterinary practitioners, to treat behaviour
problems in dogs & cats primarily, but also horses, rabbits,
parrots & occasionally, exotic species
M   practices

Association of Pet Dog Trainers   (APDT)   1995
■   PO Box 17, KEMPSFORD, Glos, GL7 4WZ.   (hq)
01285 810811
email apdtoffice@aol.com   http://www.apdt.co.uk
Chmn: Val Harvey
▲   Un-incorporated Society
○   *P; to promote kind, fair & effective dog training
●   ET - Inf - Lib
M   500 i
(Sub: £45)
¶   Dog Trainer - 3; free.

**Association for Petroleum & Explosives Administration
(APEA)   1958**
■   PO Box 106, SAFFRON WALDEN, Essex, CB11 3XT.   (hq)
0845 603 5507   fax 0845 603 5507
email admin@apea.org.uk   http://www.apea.org.uk
Business Mgr: Jane Mardell
▲   Company Limited by Guarantee
○   *P; to represent all sides of the petroleum industry (incl:
national & local government, oil companies, equipment
manufacturers & suppliers, service & installation
organisations & training establishments)
●   Conf - Mtgs - ET - Exhib - Inf - VE - LG - Publication
M   630 i, 321 f, UK / 32 i, 24 f, o'seas
¶   Guidance for the Design, Construction & Maintenance of Petrol
Filling Stations - 1; £30 m, £90 nm.

Association of Pharmacy Technicians   1952
NR   1 Mabledon Place (4th floor), LONDON, WC1H 9AJ.
020 7551 1551
http://www.aptuk.org
○   *P; dispensing prescriptions for doctors at doctors' surgeries

Association of Photographers Ltd   1968
■   81 Leonard St, LONDON, EC2A 4QS.   (hq)
020 7739 6669
Managing Dir: Kingsley Martin
▲   Company Limited by Guarantee
Br   3
○   *P, *T; for professional photographers working in fashion,
advertising & editorial fields
●   Conf - Mtgs - ET - Exhib - Comp - Inf - Lib - Copyright advice
service
<   Pyramide Europe; Pyramide GB
M   1,000 i, 10 f, 18 org, UK / 21 i, o'seas
¶   Image - 12;   The Annual Awards - 1;
Business Info Beyond the Lens; all ftm.

Association for Physical Education   (AfPE)   1899
NR   Bredon (Room 117), University of Worcester, Henwick Grove,
        WORCESTER, WR2 6AJ.   (hq)
        01905 855584   fax 01905 855594
        email enquiries@afpe.org.uk   http://www.afpe.org.uk
     Sec: John Matthews
▲   Company Limited by Guarantee; Registered Charity
Br   2
○   *E, *P; to promote & maintain high standards & safe practice in
        all aspects of physical education
●   Conf - Mtgs - ET - Res - SG
<   Intl Coun of Sport Science & Physical Educ (ICSSPE); Eur
        Physical Educ Assn EUPEA)
M   2,000 i, 50 f, UK / 50 i, 10 f, o'seas
¶   Physical Education Matters - 4;
     Physical Education & Sports Pedagogy - 3;
     Members Ybk - 1; all ftm.

Association of Physical & Natural Therapists   (APNT)   1980
NR   27 Old Gloucester St, LONDON, WC1N 3XX.   (mail)
        0845 345 2345
        email info@apnt.org   http://www.apnt.org
     Chmn: Albie McMahon
○   *P; to represent practitioners of complementary medicine in
        educational, professional & political matters
<   Aromatherapy Coun; Gen Coun for Massage Therapies

Association of Pioneer Motor Cyclists   (APMC)   1928
NR   Heather Bank, May Close, Headley, BORDON, Hants,
        GU35 8LR.   (hsp)
        01428 712666
     Hon Sec: Mrs J McBeath
Br   Counties; Belgium, Holland, USA
○   *G; for all who contributed to the establishment of the sport,
        pastime & industry of motorcycling. 'Companion'
        membership available to those having held a licence for 40+
        years, 'Pioneer' membership for those licensed for 50+ years
●   Mtgs - Comp - VE - Social activities
M   550 i, UK / 20 i, o'seas
¶   NL - 4;   Rules & register of members - 2; ftm only.

Association of Play Industries   (API)
■   Federation House, STONELEIGH PARK, Warks, CV8 2RF.   (hq)
        024 7641 4999   fax 024 7641 4990
        http://www.api-play.org
     Co Sec: Deborah Holt
▲   Company Limited by Guarantee
○   *T; manufacturers & suppliers of play equipment & impact
        absorbing surfaces (incl inflatable structures)
●   Mtgs - Exhib - Inf - LG
<   a group of the Fedn of Sports & Play Assns (FSPA)
M   c 60 f

Association of Pleasure Craft Operators
     a group association of the **British Marine Federation**

Association of Plumbing & Heating Contractors   (APHC)   1925
NR   12 The Pavilions, Cranmore Drive, SOLIHULL, W Midlands,
        B90 4SB.   (hq)
        0121-711 5030   fax 0121-705 7871
        email info@aphc.co.uk   http://www.aphc.co.uk
     Chief Exec: Clive Dickin
▲   Company Limited by Guarantee
○   *T; for employers in the plumbing & heating industry in England
        & Wales
Gp   Major Contractors Group
●   Conf - Mtgs - ET - Exam - Exhib - Empl - LG
M   1,200 f
¶   Hot & Cold - 6; free.

Association of Polelathe Turners & Greenwood Workers   1990
NR   Little Malt House, Ockham Road North, EAST HORSELY, Surrey,
        KT24 6PU.   (mem/sp)
        http://www.bodgers.org.uk
     Mem Sec: David Reeve
○   *G, *T; 'for anyone interested in pole-lathes & greenwood (un-
        seasoned timber) crafts
●   ET - Inf
M   i
        (Sub £15)
¶   Bodgers Gazette.

Association of Police Authorities   (APA)   1997
■   15 Greycoat Place, LONDON, SW1P 1BN.
        020 7664 3096
○   *N; to form a link between police authorities, chief constables &
        the Home Office

Association of Police & Court Interpreters   (APCI)   1974
■   The Octagon, Exchange Tower, 2 Harbour Exchange Square,
        LONDON, E14 9GE.   (hq)
        email secretary@apciinterpreters.org.uk
        http://www.apciinterpreters.org.uk
     Sec: Alan P M Thompson
▲   Un-incorporated Society
○   *P; for independent, freelance interpreters working within the
        Criminal Justice System
●   Mtgs - ET - Empl - LG
M   100 i
¶   The Interrupter - 2;   Membership Directory - irreg; both free.

Association of Police & Public Security Suppliers
     on 1 October 2009 merged with the Defence Manufacturers
     Association & the Society of British Aerospace Companies to form
     ADS Group Ltd

Association of Policy Market Makers   (APMM)   1992
■   PO Box 6717, STURMINSTER NEWTON, Dorset, DT10 9AR.
        (hq)
        0845 643 6381
        email compliance@apmm.org   http://www.apmm.org
     Dir: Tim Villiers
▲   Company Limited by Guarantee
○   *T; 'to promote the business of policy market makers in the
        acquisition & disposal of traded (second-hand) endowment
        policies'
●   Mtgs - Stat - Inf - LG
M   f
¶   AR - 1; ftm only.

Association of Port Health Authorities   (APHA)   1899
■   Walbrook Wharf (3rd floor), 79-83 Upper Thames St,
        LONDON, EC4R 3TD.   (hq)
        0870 744 4505   fax 020 7248 2114
     Exec Sec: Mike Young
▲   Company Limited by Guarantee
○   *T; health control of ships & aircraft & the people & cargo
        landed from them on arrival in the UK
Gp   C'ees: Imported food; Environmental health & hygiene; Border
        inspection post
●   Conf - Mtgs - Inf - LG
M   70 port health & local authorities
¶   Port Health Hbk - 1;   AR; both free.

Association for Postnatal Illness   (APNI)   1979
NR   145 Dawes Rd, LONDON, SW6 7EB.   (hq)
      020 7386 0868   fax 020 7386 8885
      email info@apni.org   http://www.apni.org
      Hon Sec: Mrs Diane Nehmé
▲   Registered Charity
○   *W; to offer advice & support to women suffering from
      postnatal depression; support is offered by volunteers who
      are all ex-sufferers
●   Inf
M   4,455 i
¶   Baby Blues & Post Natal Depression;   Post Natal
      Depression;   Puerperal Psychosis; all free.

Association of Practising Accountants   (APA)   1987
■   105 St Peter's St, ST ALBANS, Herts, AL1 3EJ.   (hq)
      01727 896067   fax 01727 896026
      email ksam@kingstonsmith.co.uk
      http://www.apa-uk.co.uk
      Chmn: Michael J Snyder
▲   Un-incorporated Society
○   *P; for medium sized firms of chartered accountants
●   Mtgs - Inf
M   16 f
¶   Becoming a Chartered Accountant - training with a medium
      sized firm.
      Medium sized firms of Chartered Accountants - the vital link
      between businesses & the City.
      Research document: challenge & opportunity for medium sized
      accountancy firms; ftm, £70 nm.

Association of Primary Care Groups & Trusts
      since 2006 the **NHS Trusts Association**

Association of Print Specialists & Manufacturers
      see **Prism - association of print specialist & manufacturers**

Association of Printing Machinery Importers
      in 2007-08 merged with **Picon Ltd**

**Association of Private Client Investment Managers &
Stockbrokers   (APCIMS)   1990**
NR   22 City Rd, Finsbury Square, LONDON, EC1Y 2AJ.   (hq)
      020 7448 7100
      email info@apcims.co.uk   http://www.apcims.co.uk
      Chief Exec: David Bennett
▲   Company Limited by Guarantee
○   *T; for wealth management & banking firms which provide
      services to private investors
Gp   UK & European financial regulation; Corporate governance;
      Clearing & settlement; Indices
●   Conf - Mtgs - Res - Stat - Inf - LG
M   200 f, UK / 20 f, o'seas
¶   APCIMS Update - 12;   Q Review - 4;   LM - 1;
      AR - 1; all free.

Association of Private Crematoria & Cemeteries   (APCC)   1944
NR   37 The Meadows, Cherry Burton, BEVERLEY, E Yorks,
      HU17 7RL.   (sp)
      01964 503055
      http://www.apcandc.co.uk
▲   Un-incorporated Society
○   *T; interests of proprietary cemeteries & crematoria
●   Mtgs - Stat - Inf - LG
<   Fedn Brit Cremation Authorities; Cremation Soc; Inst of Burial &
      Cremation Administration
M   15 crematoria, 7 cemeteries

Association of Private Market Operators
      in 2007 became part of the **National Association of British
      Market Authorities**

**Association of Private Pet Cemeteries & Crematoria   (APPCC)
1993**
NR   Nunclose, Armathwaite, CARLISLE, CA4 9TJ.
      01697 472232   fax 01697 472260
      email contact@appcc.org.uk   http://www.appcc.org.uk
      Chmn: N J Ricketts
▲   Company Limited by Guarantee
○   *T; to provide a post death pet care service; to educate pet
      owners, vets & others in the pet world, to the advantages of
      giving pet animals a decent, dignified departure
●   Conf - Mtgs - Res - LG - Keeping abreast of the deluge of EU
      legislation which threatens the livelihood of members
      Helpline 01252 844478
<   Coun of Brit Funeral Services
M   41 f
¶   Chairman's Update - irreg; free.

Association of Private Railway Wagon Owners   (APRO)
NR   Homelea, Westland Green, Little Hadham, WARE, Herts,
      SG11 2AG.   (hsp)
      01279 843487
      email geoffrey.pratt@btconnect.com
      Sec Gen: Geoffrey Pratt
○   *T

**Association of Professional Ambulance Personnel   (APAP)
1981**
NR   PO Box 1102, WOODHALL SPA, Lincs, LN10 6WL.   (hq)
      0843 289 1256
      email enquiries@apap.org.uk   http://www.apap.org.uk
○   *U; for ambulance services personnel
M   i

**Association of Professional Astrologers International   (APAi)
1990**
■   Quince Cottage, 26 Marden Way, Herne Farm, PETERSFIELD,
      Hants, GU31 4PW.   (sp)
      0800 074 6113
      Sec: Jennifer Scott
○   *P; to provide a forum for professional discussion of astrology
      on all levels; to promote astrology as a serious subject,
      counter the star-sign image of the astrologer & take active
      steps to correct misinterpretation in the press
M   69 i, UK / 5 i, o'seas
¶   NL - 4;   Consultants list - updated;
      Minutes of AGM & all meetings; all free.
×   2003 Association of Professional Astrologers

**Association of Professional Clay Target Shooting Grounds
(APCTSG)**
NR   c/o Sporting Targets Ltd, Knotting Lane, RISELY, Beds,
      MK44 1BX.
      01234 708893   fax 01234 708886
      Sec: Andrew Clifton
○   *T

**Association of Professional De-clutterers & Organisers   (APDO-
UK)   2004**
NR   The Rectory, Weston Longville, NORWICH, Norfolk, NR9 5JU.
      01603 880563
      http://www.apdo-uk.co.uk
      Admin: Cassie Tillett
○   *P
M   i
      (Sub: £100)

Association of Professional Genealogists in Ireland   (APGI)   1987

IRL   30 Harlech Crescent, Clonskeagh, DUBLIN 14, Republic of
     Ireland.   (hsb)
     http://www.apgi.ie
     Hon Sec: Hilda McGauley
○   *G; the promotion of genealogical research by members using
     records for the whole of Ireland
M   i (NI), i (Republic of Ireland)
¶   LM - 1; free.

Association for Professional Hypnosis & Psychotherapy   (APHP)   2002

NR   15 Clarence Rd, SOUTHEND-ON-SEA, Essex, SS1 1AN.
     (admin/p)
     01702 434431   fax 01702 434432
     email aphp@aphp.net   http://www.aphp.co.uk
     Administrator: Wendy Pilkington
○   *P; to maintain a high standard of professionalism amongst its
     members
<   Complementary & Natural Healthcare Coun; UK Confedn of
     Hypnotherapy Orgs
M   321 i, UK / 152 i, o'seas

Association of Professional & Independent Chimney Sweeps   (APICS)   2002

■   Bryallen Henger Rd, St Tudy, BODMIN, Cornwall, PL9 3PL.
     (hsp)
     0845 604 4327
     email ryanandpeggy@tiscali.co.uk
     http://www.apics.org.uk
     Dir: Bryan Metters,   Admin: Mrs Peggy Metters
▲   Company Limited by Guarantee
○   *T; to ensure the competence & uphold the status of chimney
     sweeps; to educate the public about regular sweeping, the
     dangers of carbon monoxide & the risk of chimney fires
Gp   Chimney: Sweeps, Inspections, Insulations
●   Mtgs
<   Heating Eqpt Testing & Approval Scheme (HETAS); Nat Assn of
     Chimney Engrs (NACE)
M   37 i

Association of Professional Landscapers
     a specialist group of the **Horticultural Trades Association**

Association of Professional Music Therapists
     merged 6 April 2011 with the British Society for Music Therapy to
     form the **British Association for Music Therapy**

Association of Professional Political Consultants   (APPC)   1995

■   PO Box 55486, LONDON, SW4 4AY.   (hsb)
     0773 918 8753
     email mail@appc.org.uk   http://www.appc.org.uk
     Sec: Mary Shearer
▲   Company Limited by Guarantee
○   *P; the representative & regulatory body for professional
     political consultants
●   Mtgs - ET - LG
M   58 f
¶   Register of Members' Interests; on request.

Association of Professional Recording Services Ltd   (APRS)   1947

■   PO Box 22, TOTNES, Devon, TQ9 7YZ.   (hq)
     01803 868600   fax 01803 868444
     email info@aprs.co.uk   http://www.aprs.co.uk
     Chief Exec: Peter Filleul
▲   Company Limited by Guarantee
○   *T; for all commercially involved in professional sound
     recording & associated fields
Gp   Consultancies, education & hire; Individuals - freelance &
     industry professionals; Manufacturers & distributors;
     Mastering & music services; Sound recording studios & post-
     production facilities; Students
●   ET - Expt - Inf - LG
M   250 i, 200 f, 8 educational org, UK / 10 i, o'seas
¶   NL.   LM.   Hbk.   AR; all ftm.

Association of Professional Sales Agents (Sports & Leisure Industries)   (APSA)

■   Federation House, STONELEIGH PARK, Warks, CV8 2RF.   (hq)
     024 7641 4999   fax 024 7641 4990
     email apsa@sportsandplay.com
     http://www.sportsandplay.com
     Assn Mgr: Mrs Jane Montgomery
▲   Company Limited by Guarantee
○   *T
●   Mtgs - Exhib - Inf
<   a group of the Fedn of Sports & Play Assns (FSPA)
M   55 i

Association of Professional Shooting Instructors   (APSI)   1997

NR   24 Nobles Close, Grove, WANTAGE, Oxon, OX12 0NR.
     01235 768280
     email apsi@totalshooting.com
     http://www.apsishooting.co.uk
     Sec: Paul Bentley

Association of Professional Staffing Companies   (APSCo)   1999

NR   1 Sycamore Court, Royal Oak Yard, Bermondsey St, LONDON,
     SE1 3TR.   (hq)
     0845 899 7388   fax 0845 899 7389
     email info@apsco.org   http://www.apsco.org
     Chief Exec: Ann Swain
▲   Company Limited by Guarantee
○   *T; to represent, promote & support the professional recruitment
     industry
●   Conf - Inf - LG - Mtgs
M   261 f
¶   Short List - 4.
×   2009 (Association of Technology Staffing Companies
     (Forum of Professional Recruiters (merged 1 January)

Association of Professional Staffs in Colleges of Education & Humanities   (APSCEH)

IRL   c/o Irish Federation of University Teachers, 11 Merrion Sq,
     DUBLIN 2, Republic of Ireland.
     353 (1) 661 0910   fax 353 (1) 661 0909
     email ifut@eircom.net   http://www.ifut.ie
○   *E, *P

Association of Professional Stress Managers & Life Support Managers
     see **Society of Stress Managers (the Association of
     Professional Stress Managers & Life Support Managers)**

Association of Professional Tourist Guides (APTG) 1987
NR 128 Theobald's Rd, LONDON, WC1X 8TN. (hq)
      020 7611 2545 fax 020 7611 2500
      email aptg@aptg.org.uk
      http://www.touristguides.org.uk
      Admin: Annie Simpson,   Chmn: Robina Brown
○ *P; for London registered blue badge tourist guides
● Conf - SG - VE - Walking tours - Tours with private car & guide
      - General sightseeing tours
< ICOMOS; Wld Fedn of Tourist Guides Assns; Fedn of Eur
      Tourist Guides Assns
M 465 i
¶ Tourist Guides' Directory - 1.

Association of Professional Videomakers
      has ceased trading

**Association of Professionals in Education & Children's Trusts
(ASPECT) 1919**
NR Woolley Hall, Woolley, WAKEFIELD, W Yorks, WF4 2JR. (hq)
      01226 383428 fax 01226 383427
      email info@aspect.org.uk   http://www.aspect.org.uk
      Gen Sec: John Chowcat
○ *P, *U; to represent professionals working in children's services
Gp National Association of Youth & Community Education Officers
< TUC
M 4,161 i

Association for Professionals in Services for Adolescents
      has become a Foundation & is therefore outside the scope of
      this directory

Association for Project Management (APM) 1972
NR Ibis House, Regent Park, Summerleys Rd,
      PRINCES RISBOROUGH, Bucks, HP27 9LE. (hq)
      01844 271640 fax 01844 274509
      email info@apm.org.uk   http://www.apm.org.uk
      Chief Exec: Andrew Bragg,   Co Sec: John Salisbury
▲ Company Limited by Guarantee; Registered Charity
Br 12; Hong Kong
○ *P; run by project managers for project managers
Gp Contracts & procurement; Earned value; Governance of project
      management; People; Programme management; Project &
      programme excellence; Value management; Women in
      project management
● Conf - Mtgs - ET - Exam - Res - Exhib - Comp - Stat - Inf - LG
< Intl Project Mgt Assn (IPMA); Engg Coun UK
M 13,630 i, 355 f, UK / 673 i, 8 f, o'seas
¶ Project (Jnl) - 10.   Network (NL) - 10; Ybk - 1;   AR - 1;
      all ftm only.
      International Jnl of Project Management - 8; £35 m, 217 nm.

Association for Project Safety (APS) 1995
■ Stanhope House, 12 Stanhope Place, EDINBURGH,
      EH12 5HH. (hq)
      0845 612 1290 fax 0845 612 1291
      email info@aps.org.uk   http://www.aps.org.uk
      Chief Exec: Brian B Law
▲ Company Limited by Guarantee
Br 16
○ *P; to provide support, guidance & development for all those
      involved in construction health & safety & risk management
      in terms of the Construction (Design & Management)
      Regulations 2007
Gp CDM co-ordinators
● Conf - Mtgs - ET - Exam - Stat - Inf - LG
< Intl Safety & Health Construction Coordinators Org;
      Construction Ind Coun (CIC)
M 5,000 i, 600 f, UK / 31 i, o'seas
      (Sub: £129 i, £240 f, UK / £129 i, o'seas)
¶ NL - 6.   Practice Notes - 6.   AR; all ftm.
      Design Risk Management Guide (book+CD-ROM); £35 m,
      £45 nm.
      Management of CDM Coordination (book+CD-ROM); £76 m,
      £95 nm.
      Pre-construction Information (guide+CD-ROM); £80 m,
      £140 nm.
      H+S File (CD-ROM); £95 m, £155 nm.
      Form of Appointment; £8.50.

Association for Promoting Retreats (APR) 1913
NR Kerridge House, 42 Woodside Close, AMERSHAM, Bucks,
      HP6 5EF. (hq)
      01494 433004
      email apr@retreats.org.uk
      Admin: Alison MacTier
▲ Registered Charity
○ *R; promoting retreats; to provide a national network of those
      able to advise on the subject
● Conf - ET - Exhib - Inf
M 1,700 i, 300 org
¶ Retreats - 1.

Association for the Promotion of Preconceptual Care
      see **Foresight (Association for the Promotion of Preconceptual
      Care)**

**Association for the Promotion of Quality in TESOL Education
(QuiTE)**
NR The Language Centre, Middlesex University, The Burroughs,
      LONDON, NW4 4BT. (sb)
      020 8511 5376
      email c.o'domoghue@mdx.ac.uk
      http://www.quality-tesol-ed.org.uk
      Co-Secs: Claire O'Donoghue, Susan Jaine
○ *E; for teacher educators, course providers & all working in
      areas relating to the training, education & development of
      teachers of English to speakers of other languages
● Seminars

Association of Property Bankers (APB) 1991
NR c/o DG Hyp, 10 Aldersgate St, LONDON, EC1A 4HJ.
      020 7776 7611
      http://www.theapb.co.uk
      Mem Sec: Sally Hurst
○ *T; to foster a better understanding of property finance within
      the banking & property sections
M c 350 i & f

Association of Property & Fixed Charge Receivers   (NARA) 1995
■ PO Box 629, OLDHAM, Lancs, OL1 9HH.   (admin/sb)
    0870 600 1925   fax 0870 600 1925
    http://www.nara.org.uk
    Admin: Dag Smith
○ *P; to promote the interests of receivers who are NOT
    administrative receivers; incl LPA & fixed charge receivers
    (agricultural receivers, receivers of book debt & court
    appointed receivers)
✕ 2008 Non-Administrative Receivers Association
    Note: uses the trading name NARA

Association for the Protection of Rural Scotland   (APRS)   1926
NR Gladstone's Land (3rd floor), 483 Lawnmarket, EDINBURGH,
    EH1 2NT.   (hq)
    0131-225 7012
    email info@ruralscotland.org
    http://www.ruralscotland.org
    Contact: Walter Simpson
▲ Charitable Company; Limited by Guarantee
○ *G; to improve, protect & preserve the rural scenery &
    amenities of country districts, towns & villages in Scotland for
    the benefit of the public
M i, f & org

Association for Psychoanalytic Psychotherapy in the NHS (APP) 1981
NR Unit 7, 19-23 Wedmore St, LONDON, N19 4RU.   (hq)
    020 7272 8681   fax 020 7561 9005
    email app-nhs@btconnect.com
    http://www.app-nhs.org.uk
    Admin Sec: Janaki Hemaratne
▲ Registered Charity
○ *M; to promote psychoanalytic psychotherapy in the NHS
Gp Adult psychiatry; Child & adolescent; Group section; Nursing;
    Older adults; Primary care
● Conf - Mtgs - Res
< Eur Fedn for Psychoanalytic Psychotherapy (EFPP); Brit
    Psychoanalytic Coun; Assn Child Psychotherapists (ACP)
M 800 i, UK / 20 i, o'seas
¶ Psychoanalytic Psychotherapy (Jnl) - 4; ftm, £71 yr nm.
    APP NL - 2.   AR.

Association for Psychological Therapies   (APT)
NR 1-3 Saxby St, LEICESTER, LE2 0ND.   (mail/address)
    0116-255 5963
○ *P
< Mtgs

Association of Psychosexual Nursing   1998
NR PO Box 2762, LONDON, W1A 5HQ.   (mail/address)
▲ Registered Charity
○ *M, *P; training for nurses concerned to develop clinical skills to
    address the sexual anxieties or distress presented by patients
¶ NL - 2; ftm.

Association of Public Analysts   (APA)   1953
NR Burlington House, Piccadilly, LONDON, W1J 0BG.   (regd/add)
▲ Company Limited by Guarantee
○ *P; to coordinate the activities of public analysts in the provision
    of scientific advice to local authorities on matters concerning
    food, water, animal feeds, consumer safety & the
    environment

Association of Public Analysts of Scotland   (APAS)   1897
■ c/o Edinburgh Scientific Services, 4 Marine Esplanade,
    EDINBURGH, EH6 7LU.   (hsb)
    0131-555 7980   fax 0131-555 7987
    Hon Sec: Dr Andrew Mackie
▲ Un-incorporated Society
○ *P; analysis of food, waters, environmental materials, consumer
    products, & agricultural products for public protection;
    interpretation of public protection legislation
Gp Sub-gps: Chemistry, Microbiology, Quality & IT
● Mtgs - ET - LG
< Assn Public Analysts
M 9 i

Association of Public Health Observatories   2000
NR Innovation Centre, York Science Park, Heslington, YORK,
    N Yorks, YO10 5DG.   (hq)
    01904 567658
    Chmn: Prof Brian Ferguson
○ *W; 'working across England, Scotland, Wales, Northern
    Ireland & the Republic of Ireland on the production of
    information, data & intelligence on people's health & health
    care for practitioners & policy makers'
● Inf
M 12 org
¶ Reports

Association for Public Service Excellence   (APSE)   1981
NR Washbrook House (2nd floor), Lancastrian Office Centre,
    32 Talbot Rd, Old Trafford, MANCHESTER, M32 0FP.   (hq)
    0161-772 1810   fax 0161-772 1811
    email enquiries@apse.org.uk   http://www.apse.org.uk
▲ Un-incorporated Society
Br 2
○ *N, *T; the networking organisation which consults, develops,
    promotes & advises on best practice in the delivery of local
    authority services
Gp Advisory groups for local authority service areas; Best value
    consultancy; Life long learning; Performance networks
● Conf - Mtgs - ET - Res - Exhib - SG - Stat - Inf - Lib - LG
M 3 f, 244 local authorities
¶ Direct News - 6;   Briefing Notes - 1; both ftm only.
    AR (incl LM) - 1; ftm.   Publications - 2; at cost.
✕ 2006 Association of Civic Hosts (merged)

Association of Publishing Agencies   (APA)   1993
NR Queens House (3rd floor), 55-56 Lincoln's Inn Fields,
    LONDON, WC2A 3LJ.   (hq)
    020 7404 4166   fax 020 7404 4167
    email info@apa.co.uk   http://www.apa.co.uk
    Chief Exec: Patrick Fuller
○ *T; to promote the customer magazine publishing industry; to
    promote awareness of the effectiveness of such magazines as
    a marketing tool
● Mtgs - Res - Inf - Marketing - Awards
< Periodical Publishers Assn (PPA)
M 29 f, UK / 5 f, o'seas
¶ NL - 4;   A Guide to Customer Publishing - 1;
    Case Studies - 2; all free.
    The Case for Customer Magazines;   Membership pack;
    Info Pack; all on request.

Association of Qualified Graphologists   1995
NR 50 Crediton Hill, LONDON, NW6 1HR.
    020 7435 1271
    http://www.aqg.org.uk
    Sec: Ivana Vojnovic
○ *P

© CBD Research Ltd · Beckenham · BR3 5JS · Tel 020 8650 7745 · E-mail cbd@cbdresearch.com · www.cbdresearch.com

Association for Qualitative Research   (AQR)   1980
- Davey House, 31 St Neots Rd, Eaton Ford, ST NEOTS, Cambs, PE19 7BA.   (hq)
  01480 407227   fax 01480 211267
  email info@aqr.org.uk   http://www.aqr.org.uk
  Sec: Rose Molloy
- ▲ Company Limited by Guarantee
- ○ *P, *T; for qualitative research
- ● Conf - ET
- M 1,000 i, UK / 100 i, o'seas
- ¶ In Brief (Jnl) - 6; ftm, subject to availability nm.
  Directory - 1; free.

Association for Quality Education
- NR Unit 3, Weavers Court Business Park, BELFAST, BT12 5GH.
  028 9022 4002
  email aqeoffice1@yahoo.co.uk   http://www.aqe.org.uk
  Head of Office: Miss N Morrison
- ○ *E

Association of Racecourse Bookmakers
see **Federation of Racecourse Bookmakers**

Association of Racing Kart Schools Ltd   (ARKS)   1994
- Stoneycroft, Godsons Lane, Napton, SOUTHAM, Warks, CV47 8LX.   (sp)
  01926 812177   fax 01926 812177
  email secretary@arks.co.uk   http://www.arks.co.uk
  Sec: Graham Smith
- ▲ Company Limited by Guarantee
- Br 13; Dubai
- ○ *T
- ● Conf - ET - Exam - Stat - Inf
- < Motor Activities Training Coun (MATC)
- M 13 f, UK / 1 f, o;seas

Association for Radiation Research   (ARR)   1958
- NR c/o Dr Tracy Robson, Reader in Molecular Pharmacology, Experimental Therapeutics, School of Pharmacy, Queen's University Belfast, Medical Biology Centre, 97 Lisburn Rd, BELFAST, BT9 7BL.
  028 9097 2360   fax 028 9024 7794
  email marie.boyd@strath.ac.uk   http://www.le.ac.uk/cm/arr/home.html
  Hon Sec: Dr Marie Boyd
- ○ *L; promotion of learning & education in the field of radiation research
- M i

Association of Radical Midwives   (ARM)   1976
- 16 Wytham St, OXFORD, OX1 4SU.   (sp)
  01865 248159
  email sarahmontagu@gmail.com
  Admin Sec: Sarah Montagu
- ▲ Registered Charity
- Br 50 local contacts
- ○ *K, *P; to preserve & increase the choices in childbirth for women; to restore & strengthen the role of midwife
- ● Conf - Mtgs - LG
- < Intl Confedn of Midwives; Eur Midwives Liaison C'ee
- M 1,200 i, 140 orgs & colleges, UK / 80 i, o'seas
- ¶ Midwifery Matters - 4; ftm, £2 each nm.

Association of Railway Training Providers   (ARTP)   1997
- 22 Headfort Place, LONDON, SW1X 7RY.   (asa)
  020 7201 0778   fax 020 7235 5777
  email info@artp.co.uk   http://www.artp.co.uk
  Secretariat: Peter Loosley
- ▲ Company Limited by Guarantee
- ○ *T; for training, development & competence management services to the railway industry
- Gp Audit protocols (Achilles); Communications; Competence management; Rule book / standards / documentation; Track safety assessment; Track safety plans
- ● Conf - Mtgs - ET - Res - Wxhib - Inf
- < Rly Ind Assn
- M 100 f
- ¶ E-NL - 4; ftm only.

Association for Rational Emotive Behaviour Therapy   (AREBT)   1973
- c/o PO Box 177, FAVERSHAM, Kent, ME13 8WB.   (hsp)
  http://www.arebt.org
  Chmn: Irene Tubbs
- ▲ Company Limited by Guarantee
- Br New Zealand, USA
- ○ *P, *W; for those offering behavioural therapy to clients; to counsel clients on how their belief systems largely determine how they feel about & act towards situations & life events
- ● Conf - ET - Res- LG - Continuing professional development programmes
- < UK Coun of Psychotherapists (UKCP); Brit Assn of Behavioural & Cognitive Psychotherapists (BABCP)
- M 167 i, 2 org, UK / 10 i, o'seas
  (Sub:£40 i, £60 org)
- ¶ Jnl - 1;   NL - 3; both ftm only.

Association of RE Inspectors, Advisors & Consultants   (AREIAC)
- NR c/o Schools Team - Diocesian Office, 41 Holywell Hill, ST ALBANS, Herts, AL1 1HE.
  01727 818175
  email chair@areiac.org.uk   http://www.areiac.org.uk
  Chmn: Jane Chipperton
- ○ *P, for teachers supporting multi-faith education in schools & colleges

Association for Real Change   (ARC)   1976
- ARC House, Marsden St, CHESTERFIELD, Derbys, S40 1JY.   (hq)
  01246 555043   fax 01246 555045
  email contact.us@arcuk.org.uk
  http://www.arcuk.org.uk
  Chief Exec: James Churchill
- ▲ Company Limited by Guarantee; Registered Charity
- Br 8
- ○ *T, *W; to support providers of services for people with a learning disability
- ● Conf - Mtgs - ET - Inf - Lib - LG
- < Eur Assn for Service Providers for Persons with a Disability (EASPD); Nat Coun for Voluntary Orgs (NCVO); Assn Chief Execs of Voluntary Orgs (ACEVO); Brit Inst of Learning Disabilities (BILD); Indep Care Orgs Network (IVCON); Learning Disability Coalition
- M 350 f
- ¶ Basic Steps; £55 m, £75 nm.
  Getting Started: the common induction standards in adult social care; £45 m, £80 nm.
  Banking Matters to Me; £10 m, £15 nm.
  Moving on Up: a short guide for professionals; £10.
  Moving on Up: young people & families guide; £20 m, £25 nm.

Association of Real Estate Funds   (AREF)   1970

NR   65 Kingsway, LONDON, WC2B 6TD.   (hq)
020 7269 4577
email info@aref.org.uk   http://www.aref.org.uk
Chief Exec: John Cartwright
O   *T; to develop the interests of property unit trusts
M   64 f

Association of Reflexologists   (AoR)   1984

■   5 Fore St, TAUNTON, Somerset, TA1 1HX.   (hq)
01823 351010   fax 01823 336646
email info@aor.org.uk   http://www.aor.org.uk
Chief Exec: Doreen Baker
▲   Company Limited by Guarantee
Br   62
O   *P; to promote the knowledge & understanding of reflexology;
to set standards for qualifications
●   Conf - Mtgs - ET - Res - Inf - LG
<   Reflexology in Europe Network; Reflexology Forum
>   Intl Inst of Reflexologists
M   6,674 i, UK / 171 i, o'seas
(Sub: £71, £63 friends)
¶   Reflexions (Jnl) - 4; ftm only.

Association of Regional City Editors   1969

NR   1 Fern Dene, Templewood, LONDON, W13 8AN.   (hsp)
020 8997 6868
email john.heffernan@virgin.net
Hon Sec: John Heffernan
O   *P; interests of those concerned with economic & financial news
(incl London-based wire service correspondents, & radio)
M   22 i

Association of Registrars of Scotland   (AROS)   1865

■   Council Offices, 15 Ednam St, ANNAN, Dumfriesshire,
DG12 5EF.   (hsb)
01461 204914
email alison.quigley@dungal.gov.uk
Hon Sec: Alison Quigley
▲   Un-incorporated Society
O   *P; to promote the registration service in Scotland on behalf of
registrars & the legislation which may affect them
●   Conf - Mtgs - ET - Exam
M   250 i
¶   Informant (NL) - 2; ftm only.

Association for Rehabilitation of Communication & Oral Skills (ARCOS)   1992

NR   Whitbourne Lodge, 137 Church St, MALVERN, Worcs,
WR14 2AN.   (hq)
01684 576795   fax 01684 576895
email arcos@globalnet.co.uk   http://www.arcos.org.uk
▲   Registered Charity
O   *W; provision of specialist help for children & adults with voice,
speech, language & eating (swallowing) problems, & for their
families & those working with them
●   ET - Lib
¶   AR - 1.

Association of Relocation Professionals   (ARP)   1986

■   PO Box 189, DISS, Norfolk, IP22 1PE.   (hq)
0870 073 7475   fax 0870 071 8719
email info@relocationagents.com
http://www.relocationagents.com
Chief Exec: Tad Zurlinden
▲   Company Limited by Guarantee
O   *P; to promote the services & benefits of using relocation agents
●   Conf - Mtgs - ET - Res - Exhib - Stat - Inf - LG
<   US Employee Relocation Coun; Eur Relocation Assn; CBI;
Relocation Network (Australia)
M   140 f, UK / 15 f, o'seas
¶   Directory of Members - 1; free.
Guide to the United Kingdom - 2 yrly; £5 m, £9.95 nm.
Guide to Homesearch (for those starting a business) - 1; ftm,
£75 nm.

Association of Research Centres in the Social Sciences (ARCISS)   1997

NR   Gill Clisham,c/o NIESR, 2 Dean Tench St, LONDON,
SW1P 3HE.   (admin/b)
020 7222 7665
http://www.arciss.ac.uk
Admin: Gill Clisham,   Hon Sec: Deborah Cox
▲   Registered Charity
O   *Q; promotion, management & dissemination of independent
social science research
●   Conf - Res
M   c 45 non-profit independent university-based centres

Association for Research in the Voluntary & Community Sector (ARVAC)   1978

NR   c/o Steven Howlett, Southlands College, 80 Roehampton Lane,
LONDON, SW15 5SL.   (hq)
020 8392 3862
http://www.arvac.org.uk
Contact: Dr Steven J Howlett
▲   Company Limited by Guarantee; Registered Charity
O   *P, *N; to promote effective community action through research;
to help community groups carry out their own research

Association of Researchers in Medicine & Science Ltd

has closed

Association of Residential Letting Agents   (ARLA)   1981

■   Arbon House, 6 Tournament Court, Edgehill Drive, WARWICK,
CV34 6LG.   (hq)
01926 496800   fax 01926 417788
email info@arla.co.uk   http://www.arla.co.uk
Operations Mgr: Ian Potter
▲   Company Limited by Guarantee
O   *P; for agents letting residential property
●   Conf - Mtgs - ET - Exam - Stat - LG
<   a division of the National Federation of Property Professionals
M   1,500 i, 2,250 f
(Sub: £175 i, varies f)
¶   Agreement (NL) - 6; ftm, £54 nm.

Association of Residential Managing Agents Ltd   (ARMA) 1991

■   178 Battersea Park Rd, LONDON, SW11 4ND.   (hq)
020 7978 2607   fax 020 7498 6153
email info@arma.org.uk   http://www.arma.org.uk
Contact: The Executive Secretary
▲   Company Limited by Guarantee
O   *P; members focus exclusively on matters relating to block
management of leasehold property (at least 60% of the flats
are lessee-owned properties)
●   Conf - Mtgs - ET - LG
M   200+ f
¶   [publications available to nm are on website]

Association of Respiratory Technology & Physiology   (ARTP) 1972

■   Executive Business Support Ltd, City Wharf, Davidson Road,
LICHFIELD, Staffs, WS14 9DZ.   (hq)
0845 226 8200
email admin@artp.org.uk   http://www.artp.org.uk
▲   Registered Charity
O   *P
Gp   Education; Manufacturers liaison
●   Conf - Mtgs - ET - Exam - Res - Inf - Empl - LG
<   Brit Thoracic Soc; Assn of Clinical Scientists; Registration Coun
for Clinical Physiology
M   530 i, 25 f (affiliated), UK / 5 i, 5 f (affiliated), o'seas
¶   Inspire - 3; ftm only.

© CBD Research Ltd · Beckenham · BR3 5JS · Tel 020 8650 7745 · E-mail cbd@cbdresearch.com · www.cbdresearch.com

Association of Retirement Housing Managers   (ARHM)   1991
NR   Southbank House, Black Prince Rd, LONDON, SE1 7SJ.   (hq)
       020 7463 0660
▲   Company Limited by Guarantee
○   *P; to represent managers of private sheltered housing
M   f

Association of Revenue and Customs   (ARC)   2005
NR   8 Leake St, LONDON, SE1 7NN.   (hq)
       0845 470 1111
       email info@arc-union.org.uk
       http://www.arc-union.org.uk
       Sec Gen: Jonathan Baume
○   *P, *U; the union of choice for senior managers & professionals
       in HM Revenue & Customs
●   Conf - Mtgs - Empl - LG
<   FDA
M   2,600 i

Association of Rivers Trusts   2004
■   10 Exeter St, LAUNCESTON, Cornwall, PL15 9EQ.   (hq)
       0870 774 0689
       email arlin@associationofriverstrusts.org.uk
       http://www.associationofriverstrusts.org.uk
       Dir: Arlin Rickard,   Sec: Alan Hawken
▲   Company Limited by Guarantee; Registered Charity
○   *K; to improve the rivers of England & Wales; to advance the
       education of the public in the management of water &
       environmental protection, conservation, rehabilitation &
       improvement, & the understanding of rivers & their basins,
       fauna & flora
●   Conf - ET - Res - LG
M   6 i, 6 org
¶   e-newsletters; free.

**Association for Road Traffic Safety & Management   (ARTSM)
1933**
NR   Shepstone, Holmesdale Rd, SOUTH NUTFIELD, Surrey,
       RH1 4JE.   (hq)
       01737 823360
       http://www.artsm.org.uk
▲   Un-incorporated Society
○   *T; interests of makers & suppliers of road traffic signs, portable
       traffic signals, variable message signs, vehicle & pedestrian
       detectors, sign luminaires, fittings, fixings & components, sign
       design software & related products & services
M   f

Association for Roman Archaeology   (ARA)   1966
NR   75 York Rd, SWINDON, Wilts, SN1 2JU.   (hsp)
       01793 534008   fax 01793 534008
       Dir: Bryn Walters
▲   Company Limited by Guarantee
○   *K, *L; free access to Roman archaeology events & venues
●   Conf - Mtgs - Inf - VE
<   Coun Brit Archaeology (CBA)
M   2,500 i
¶   ARA News Bulletin - 2.

Association of Royal Navy Officers   (ARNO)   1925
NR   70 Porchester Terrace, LONDON, W2 3TP.   (hq)
       020 7402 5231
▲   Registered Charity
○   *W; to give general & financial assistance to members, their
       widows & families (membership is open to serving & retired
       officers of the RN, RM, WRNS, QARNNS & their Reserves)
●   Inf - VE
<   Officers' Assn
M   8,500 i, UK / 300 i, o'seas
¶   Ybk - 1; ftm only.

Association of Run-off Companies   (ARC)
NR   47 Bury St, STOWMARKET, Suffolk, IP14 1HD.   (hq)
       020 3362 4233
       http://www.arclegacy.eu
       Sec: Mark Everiss
▲   Company Limited by Guarantee
○   *P; for insurance & re-insurance legacy management
       professionals

Association of Running Clubs   (ARC)   2007
■   19 Sheephouse Green, Wotton, DORKING, Surrey,
       RH5 6QW.   (hsp)
       01306 888886
       email mandy@white1966.freeserve.co.uk
       http://www.runningclubs.org.uk
       Hon Sec: Michael White
▲   Company Limited by Guarantee
○   *S; the governing body for road running, cross country running,
       trail running & fell running
M   135 org
       (Sub: varies)

Association of Safety Fencing Contractors
       a group of the **Fencing Contractors' Association**

Association of Salmon Fishery Boards   (ASFB)   1932
■   CBC House, 24 Canning St, EDINBURGH, EH3 8EG.   (hsb)
       0131-272 2797   fax 0131-272 2800
       http://www.asfb.org.uk
       Dir: Andrew Wallace
▲   Un-incorporated Society
○   *F, *N; to protect, preserve & develop salmon & sea trout
       fisheries in Scotland; to coordinate the work of the 41 District
       Salmon Fishery Boards
●   LG - Mtgs

Association for Sandwich Education & Training
       since 2008 **ASET, the Work-Based & Placement Learning
       Association**

Association of School & College Leaders   (ASCL)   1975
■   130 Regent Rd, LEICESTER, LE1 7PG.   (hq)
       0116-299 1122   fax 0116-299 1123
       email info@ascl.org.uk
       Gen Sec: Dr John Dunford
Br   c150
○   *E, *P, *U; for leaders of schools & colleges
●   Conf - Mtgs - ET - Res - Exhib - Empl - LG - Legal support -
       Provision of professional publications
M   14,000 i
×   2006 Secondary Heads Association

Association for Science Education   (ASE)   1963
■   College Lane, HATFIELD, Herts, AL10 9AA.   (hq)
       01707 283000   fax 01707 266532
       http://www.ase.org.uk
       Chief Exec: Annette Smith
▲   Registered Charity
○   *E; improvement of the teaching of science in schools
●   Conf - Mtgs - ET - Res - Exhib - SG - Stat - Inf
M   14,000 i
¶   School Science Review - 4;   Education in Science - 5.
       Primary Science Review - 5;   all ftm.

Association for the Scientific Study of Anomalous Phenomena (ASSAP) 1981
- ■ PO Box 371, STROUD, Glos, GL6 1EL. (hsb)
  0845 652 1648
  email enquiries@assap.org   http://www.assap.org
  Hon Sec: Nicky Sewell
- ▲ Company Limited by Guarantee; Registered Charity
- ○ *G, *Q; to investigate reports of anomalous phenomena & to analyse & publish the results of such investigations.
- Gp The subject area breaks down into broadly four categories: Psychic phenomena (telepathy, ghosts, premonitions, etc); Fortean phenomena (fish falling from the sky, out-of-place animals); Earth mysteries (alignment of ancient monuments, etc); & UFOs.
- ● Conf - Mtgs - Lib
- M 350 i
- ¶ Anomaly (Jnl) - 2.   ASSAP News (NL) - 12.

Association of Scintigraphers 1994
- ■ 76 May's Hill Road, BROMLEY, Kent, BR2 0HT.   (hsp)
- ▲ Un-incorporated Society
- ○ *P; veterinary radiology
- ● Conf - Mtgs - ET - LG
- M i

Association of Scotland's Colleges   (ASC)
- NR Argyll Court, The Castle Business Park, STIRLING, FK9 4TY. (hq)
  01786 892010
  http://www.ascol.org.uk
  Admin: Marian McMorland
- ▲ Company Limited by Guarantee; Registered Charity
- ○ *E; to support Scottish further education, advance its interests & represent the views of colleges
- M org
- ✕ 2006 Association of Scottish Colleges

Association in Scotland to Research into Astronautics Ltd (ASTRA) 1953
- NR 96 Bloomfield Rd, AIRDRIE, Lanarkshire, ML6 9LX. (pres/p)
  01236 602076
  email info@astra.org.uk   http://www.astra.org.uk
  Pres: George McCue
- ▲ Company Limited by Guarantee
- Br 2
- ○ *L; all aspects of space research & related subjects; to stimulate public interest
- Gp Airdrie public observatory; Amateur rocketry; Exhibitions; Publications; Waverider aerodynamic study programme
- ● Conf - Mtgs - ET - Res - Exhib - PL - VE - Amateur astronomy & rocketry
- < Scot Astronomers Gp; Fedn of Astronomical Socs; Scot Coun for Voluntary Orgs
- M 65 i, UK / 5 i, o'seas
- ¶ Spacereport - 4;   ASGARD - irreg; both ftm only.

Association of Scotland's Self-Caterers (ASSC) 1978
- ■ PO Box 23, TAYNUILT, Argyll, PA35 1WX. (hq)
  01866 822122
  email secretary@assc.co.uk   http://www.assc.co.uk
  Sec: Jenifer Moffat
- ▲ Un-incorporated Society
- ○ *T; representation, services & marketing for owners of holiday properties; 'the only trade association to represent the self-catering industry in Scotland'
- ● Conf - Mtgs - Res - Inf - LG
- < Fedn of Nat Self-Catering Assns (FoNSCA); Scot Tourism Forum (STF)
- M 560 f
- ¶ The Standard (NL) - 2.

Association of Scottish Colleges
    since 2006 the **Association of Scotland's Colleges**

Association of Scottish Community Councils   (ASCC) 1993
- NR PO Box 5099, GLASGOW, G79 9AL. (hq)
  0845 644 5153
  email info@ascc.org.uk   http://www.ascc.org.uk
  Sec: Douglas Murray
- ▲ Un-incorporated Society
- ○ *N; to provide advice & information to Community Councils in Scotland; to promote their role, effectiveness & status through liaison with local & national governments
- ● Conf - Mtgs - Res - SG - Stat - Inf - Lib - LG
- M 625 community councils
- ¶ ASCC NL - 4; ftm.

Association of Scottish Genealogists & Researchers in Archives (ASGRA) 1981
- NR 22 Marjory Place, BATHGATE, W Lothian, EH48 2TR. (hsp)
  01506 653654
  http://www.asgra.co.uk
  Sec: Margaret Hubble
- ▲ Un-incorporated Society
- ○ *G; genealogical & family history research in Scotland
- ● Res
- < Scot Assn of Family History Socs
- M 25 i

Association for Scottish Literary Studies   (ASLS) 1970
- ■ Dept of Scottish Literature, 7 University Gardens, GLASGOW, G12 8QH. (hq)
  0141-330 5309   fax 0141-330 5309
  email office@asls.org.uk   http://www.asls.org.uk
  Gen Mgr: Duncan Jones
- ▲ Registered Charity
- ○ *A, *L; to promote the study, teaching & writing of Scottish language & literature
- ● Conf - Comp
- < Scot Arts Coun
- M 343 i, 91 f, UK / 121 i, 55 f, o'seas
- ¶ Scottish Studies Review (Jnl) - 2;   Scotlit - 2;
  Scottish Language (Jnl) - 1; all ftm only.
  New Writing Scotland (Anthology) - 1; ftm, £6.95 nm.
  Scotnotes (study guides); £3.60 m, £4.50 nm.
  ScotLit (NM); ftm.
  Annual Volume (book); ftm, £25 nm.

Association of Scottish Philatelic Societies   (ASPS) 1924
- ■ 44 Rennie St, FALKIRK, Stirlingshire, FK1 5AL. (hsp)
  01324 415558
  email scottishphilately@hotmail.com
  http://www.scottishphilately.co.uk
  Hon Sec: Alan Watson
- ▲ Un-incorporated Society
- ○ *N; to promote philately & allied areas within Scotland
- ● Conf - Exhib - Comp
- < Assn of Brit Philatelic Socs
- M 41 societies
- ¶ Scottish Philately (NL) -6; ftm, postage nm.

Association of Scottish Police Superintendents   (ASPS) 1924
- NR Milngavie Police Station, 99 Main St, E Dunbartonshire, G62 6JH. (asa)
  0141-532 4016
  http://www.scottishpolicesupers.co.uk
  Gen Sec: Carol Forfar
- ○ *P
- < Intl Assn Chiefs Police (IACP)
- M i
- ¶ NL - 4;   AR; both free.

© CBD Research Ltd · Beckenham · BR3 5JS · Tel 020 8650 7745 · E-mail cbd@cbdresearch.com · www.cbdresearch.com

Association of Scottish Schools of Architecture   (ASSA)   1983
NR   c/o Gordon Murray Architects, Breckenridge House, 274
        Sauchiehall St, GLASGOW, G2 3EH.   (chmn/b)
        0141-331 2926
        Hon Chmn: Gordon Murray
▲   Un-incorporated Society
○   *N; to maintain & improve the education provision for
        architecture in Scotland; to foster areas of collaboration
        between the schools

Association of Scottish Shellfish Growers   (ASSG)   1983
NR   c/o Muckairn Mussels Ltd, Achnacloich, CONNEL, Argyllshire,
        PA37 1PR.   (chmn/b)
        01631 710653
        http://www.assg.org.uk
        Chmn: Walter Speirs
▲   Company Limited by Guarantee
○   *T; interests of Scottish shellfish farmers
Gp   Mussels; Scallops; Oysters
●   Conf - Mtgs - ET - Res - Exhib - Inf - LG
<   Shellfish Assn of GB
M   200 f, 25 org
¶   The Grower - 4; ftm, £2 nm.   Ybk - 1; £5 m.

Association of Scottish Visitor Attractions   (ASVA)   1989
NR   Epic House, 28-32 Cadogan St, GLASGOW, G2 7LP.   (hq)
        01441-229 0923
        email info@asva.co.uk   http://www.asva.co.uk
▲   Company Limited by Guarantee
○   *T; concerned with the improvements at, & marketing of, visitor
        attractions in Scotland
Gp   covering each of the first 9 activities below
●   Conf - Mtgs - ET - Exhib - SG - Stat - Inf - VE - LG -
        Consultancy
M   500 org
¶   Scotland's Finest Visitor Attractions - 1.

Association of Scottish Yacht Charterers   (ASYC)   1980
NR   Camusdarach, KILMELFORD, Argyll, PA34 4XA.   (sp)
        01852 200258
        email info@asyc.co.uk   http://www.asyc.co.uk
        Sec: Robert Fleck
▲   Un-incorporated Society
○   *T; to represent the major yacht charter companies operating in
        the west of Scotland
●   Conf - Mtgs - Exhib - Inf - LG
<   Sail Scotland Ltd
M   18 f
¶   LM - irreg; free.

**Association of Sea Fisheries Committees of England & Wales
(ASFCEW)   1919**
■   6 Ashmeadow Rd, Arnside, CARNFORTH, Lancs, LA5 0AE.
        (hsp)
        01524 761616
        Chief Exec: Peter Winterbottom
○   *N; regulation & development of inshore fisheries (within
        territorial limits)
●   Mtgs
M   12 sea fisheries' committees

Association of Sea Training Organisations   (ASTO)   1971
NR   Unit 10 North Meadow, Royal Clarence Yard, GOSPORT,
        Hants, PO12 1PB.   (hq)
        023 9250 3222
        http://www.asto.org.uk
○   *Y; to further personal development of young people & adults
        by seamanship training under sail
●   Mtgs - ET - Exhib - Comp - Inf
M   18 org
¶   Sail to Adventure - 1; free.

Association of Sealant Applicators Ltd   (ASA)   1986
NR   Grovedell House, 15 Knightswick Rd, CANVEY ISLAND, Essex,
        SS8 9PA.   (asa)
        01268 696878   fax 01268 511247
        email arichardson@rowlandhall.co.uk
        http://www.associationofsealantapplicators.org
        Sec: A E Richardson
▲   Company Limited by Guarantee
○   *T; for sealant applicators & manufacturers
●   Mtgs - ET
<   Nat Specialist Contrs Coun
M   51 f

Association of Search & Rescue Hovercraft
        since 2008 **Hovercraft Search & Rescue UK**

Association of Secondary Teachers, Ireland   (ASTI)   1909
IRL   Thomas MacDonagh House, Winetavern St, DUBLIN 8,
        Republic of Ireland.
        353 (1) 604 0160   fax 353 (1) 671 9280
        email info@asti.ie   http://www.asti.ie
        Gen Sec: John White
○   *E, *P

Association of Secondary Ticket Agents   (ASTAUK)   2005
NR   Buckingham Court (suite G1 ground floor), 78 Buckingham
        Gate, LONDON, SW1E 6PE.   (hq)
        020 7183 0777
        email enquiries@asta-uk.org   http://www.asta-uk.org
○   *T; to represent companies selling tickets to entertainment &
        sporting events
M   21 f

Association of Security Consultants   (ASC)   1990
NR   42 Amis Avenue, New Haw, ADDLESTONE, Surrey,
        KT15 3ET.   (sb)
        07071 224865   fax 01923 345033
        email info@securityconsultants.org.uk
        http://www.securityconsultants.org.uk
        Sec: Maurice Parsons
▲   Company Limited by Guarantee
○   *P; for independent security consultants having no allegiance to
        specific suppliers of goods or services; to stay in the forefront
        of work on security methods, technology & applications; to
        contribute to the development of national & international
        standards
●   Conf - Mtgs - ET - Exhib - LG
<   Jt Security Ind Coun
M   59 i
¶   NL.   Consultancy Resources Directory - 1; free.
        Your Introduction to the ASC - 1; free.

Association of Separated & Divorced Catholics   (ASDC)   1981
■   c/o 250 Chapel St, SALFORD, M3 5LL.   (hq)
        http://www.asdcengland.org.uk
Br   19
○   *W; to provide mutual help and spiritual support to those who
        have experienced the pain of marriage failure
●   Conf - Mtgs
        Helpline: 0113-264 0638
M   c 200 i
¶   New Vision - 6; £6 yr.

Association of Service Providers   (ASP)   1985
NR   Edgcott House, Lawn Hill, Edgcott, AYLESBURY, Bucks,
        HP18 0QW.   (sb)
        01296 770458   fax 01296 770423
        email bc@aspfm.cc
        Sec: Brian Copsey
○   *T; the agency for radio licensing outside of the UK
●   Inf - LG
M   i & f
¶   NL - irreg.

Association of Serviced Apartment Providers (ASAP) 2002
NR   88-90 Hatton Garden, LONDON, EC1N 8PN.   (hq)
        020 7193 7104
        email office@theasap.org.uk   http://www.theasap.org.uk
     Sec: Joyce Cawthorpe
○   *T; operates in the UK & Ireland
M   44 f

Association of Sewing Machine Distributors (ASMD) 1992
■   Sheaf House, Holland Fen, LINCOLN, LN4 4QH.   (secretariat)
        01205 280094
     Sec: Mike Houldershaw
▲   Un-incorporated Society
○   *T; importers & suppliers of domestic sewing machines &
        overlockers
●   Mtgs - Stat - LG
M   6 f

Association for Shared Parenting 1993
■   1 Kendal Drive, Crofton Hackett, BIRMINGHAM, W Midlands,
        B45 8QA.   (sp)
        0121-445 3665
     Hon Sec: Jim Rowan
▲   Registered Charity
Br   5
○   *K; to promote the right of children to continue to receive love
        & nurture from both their parents after separation or divorce
●   Conf - Mtgs - ET - Advice & support sessions open to the public
        - Telephone helpline - Child contact centre (where children
        can meet the parent they no longer live with)
M   100 i

Association of Show & Agricultural Organisations (ASAO) 1923
■   PO Box 1201, WINCANTON, Somerset, BA9 8YD.   (hq)
        01749 814086   fax 01749 812655
        http://www.asao.co.uk
     Sec: Paul Hooper
▲   Company Limited by Guarantee
Br   10 regions
○   *F; to promote improvement of agriculture, kindred shows &
        allied industries
●   Conf - Stat - LG - Agricultural shows
M   199 org
¶   Official List of Shows & Events - 1; ftm, £5 nm.

Association of Signals, Lighting & other Highway Electrical Connections (ASLEC) 1952
■   Highdown House, Littlehampton Rd, FENNING, W Sussex,
        BN12 6PG.   (hq)
        01903 705140
        email aslec@highwayelectrical.org.uk
        http://www.highwayelectrical.org.uk/aslec
     Chief Exec: Gareth Pritchard
▲   Company Limited by Guarantee
○   *T; contractors operating in the highway electrical industry, in
        particular street lighting
●   Conf - Mtgs - ET - Res - Exhib - Inf - LG
M   c 70 f
✕   2007 Association of Street Lighting Electrical Contractors

Association for Skeptical Enquiry (ASKE) 1997
■   10 Woodholm Rd, SHEFFIELD, S Yorks, S11 9HT.
        email aske1@talktalk.net
        http://www.aske-skeptics.org.uk
     Chmn: Dr Michael Heap
▲   Un-incorporated Society
○   *L; to promote rational, objective & scientific methods in the
        investigation & understanding of ideas, claims & practices,
        especially those of an extraordinary or paranormal nature
M   i
        (Sub: £10)
¶   The Skeptical Intelligencer - 1; ftm.
     The Skeptical Adversaria (NL) - 4; ftm only.

Association of Small Direct Wine Merchants (ASDW)
■   3 Park Steps, St Georges Fields, LONDON, W2 2YQ.
        020 7724 4606
     Contact: Warren Edwardes
○   *T

Association of Small Historic Towns & Villages of the United Kingdom (ASHTAV) 1988
■   2 Warwick Court, Abbey Rd, GREAT MALVERN, Worcs,
        WR14 3HU.   (hsp)
        01684 566543   fax 0870 136 0926
        email mail@ashtav.org.uk   http://www.ashtav.org.uk
     Hon Sec: Dan Wild
▲   Registered Charity
○   *K, *N; uniting amenity societies & groups, parish & town
        councils in small historic towns & villages in a common effort
        for the preservation, protection & where appropriate,
        sensitive adaptation of their features of historic & public
        interest; to encourage high standards of architecture &
        planning; to stimulate the public interest & care for the
        beauty, character & fabric of small historic towns & villages in
        the context of an understanding of the social & economic
        changes which affect them
●   Conf - Mtgs - ET - Res - SG - Inf - VE
<   Coun for the Protection of Rural England
M   35 i, 2 f, 85 amenity org & parish / town councils
¶   ASHTAV News - 4; ftm.

Association of Social Anthropologists of the UK & the Commonwealth (ASA) 1946
■   PO Box 5233, BRIGHTON, E Sussex, BN50 9YW.   (hq)
        email admin@theasa.org   http://www.theasa.org
     Admin: Rohan Jackson,   Hon Sec: Dr Catherine Alexander
▲   Un-incorporated Society
○   *L; to promote the study & teaching of social anthropology
●   Conf - ET
<   Academy of the Learned Socs in the Social Sciences (ALSISS)
M   452 i, UK / 134 i, o'seas
¶   Annals - 1;   LM - 2-yearly; both ftm, £50 together nm.

Association of Soft Furnishers (ASF) 2007
NR   Francis Vaughan House, Q1 Capital Point, Capital Business
        Park, Parkway, CARDIFF, CF3 2PU.
        029 2077 8918   fax 029 2079 3508
        email susan.spencer@thefurnishinggroup.co.uk
        http://www.associationofsoftfurnishers.org
     Mgr: Sue Spencer
○   *T; for curtain makers, drapery specialists, track fitters, loose
        cover makers, quilters & others associated with the craft of
        soft furnishing

Association of Solicitor Notaries in Greater London (ASN) 1996
■   15 William Mews, LONDON, SW1X 9HF.   (asa)
        020 7235 7216   fax 020 8681 8183
     Dir: Hans J Hartwig
○   *P; representation of notaries in the Greater London region who
        are also qualified solicitors &/or foreign lawyers
●   Conf - Mtgs - ET - Res - SG - LG - Devt of 'best standards' for
        international documentation & translations
M   30 i
¶   Membership Register - 1; ftm.

Association of Solicitors & Investment Managers   (ASIM) 1993

NR   Riverside House, River Lawn Rd, TONBRIDGE, Kent, TN9 1EP.
        (hq)
        01732 783548
        email admin@asim.org.uk
        Sec: Elaine Reilly
▲   Company Limited by Guarantee
○   *P, *T; to encourage the wider provision of portfolio investment
        services by solicitors' firms
●   Conf - Mtgs - ET - Stat - VE - LG
M   51 f
¶   NL - 4.   LM - 1.   AR.

Association of South-East Asian Studies in the United Kingdom (ASEASUK)

■   Centre for South-East Asian Studies, SOAS, Thornhaugh St,
        LONDON, WC1H 0XG.   (hsb)
        020 7352 9890
        email sc66@soas.ac.uk   http://www.aseasuk.org
        Sec: Dr Susan Conway
○   *L; 'to facilitate cooperation & coordination between individual
        scholars & institutions in the development of South-East Asian
        studies & research programmes... the circulation of
        professional information amongst scholars with South East
        Asian interests & the projection of South East Asia as an
        important field of study within the UK generally'
●   Conf - Res
<   Eur South-East Asian Studies (ASEASUK-EUROSEAS); UK
        Coordinating Coun of Area Studies Assns (UKCCASA)
M   180 i, UK / 20 i, o'seas
        (Sub: £12 (full mems), £5 students)
¶   Aseasuk News - 2; ftm only.

Association of Speakers Clubs   (ASC)   1972

NR   36 Pemberton Rd, Winstanley, WIGAN, Lancs, WN3 6DA.
        (nat/sp)
        email nationalsecretary@the-asc.org.uk
        http://www.the-asc.org.uk
        Nat Sec: Mrs Gwyneth Millard
▲   Un-incorporated Society
Br   141
○   *G; promotion of the art of public speaking, chairmanship &
        the proper conduct of meetings
●   Conf - Mtgs - ET - Comp - SG
M   2,000 i, 141 clubs
¶   The Speaker - 3.

Association of Special Constabulary Chief Officers   (ASCCO) 2008

NR   Denise Maynard, c/o Essex Police HQ, PO Box 2, Springfield,
        CHELMSFORD, Essex, CM2 6DA.   (admin)
        email denise.maynard@ascco.org.uk
        Admin: Denise Maynard
○   *G; to act as the federation for all special constables

Association for Specialist Fire Protection   (ASFP)   1975

■   Kingsley House, Ganders Business Park, Kingsley, BORDON,
        Hants, GU35 9LU.   (asa)
        01420 471612   fax 01420 471611
        email info@associationhouse.org.uk
        http://www.asfp.org.uk
        Sec: John Fairley
▲   Company Limited by Guarantee
○   *T; all questions affecting the fire protection of structural
        steelwork & buildings
Gp   Assessment of fire tests; BSI representation; Contracting
        conditions; European harmonisation; Fire testing &
        standards; Health & safety; Intumescent materials; Spray
        applied materials; Technical matters
●   Conf - Mtgs - ET - Res - Exhib - Inf
<   Eur Assn for Structural Fire Protection; BSI; Construction
        Products Assn; Fedn of Brit Fire Orgs
M   54 f, UK / 4 f, o'seas
¶   Fire Protection for Structural Steel in Buildings, 2nd ed; £30.
        Supplement to 2nd ed; £5.
        Ybk & Directory of Members - 1; free.
        Other publications & guidance notes; list available.

Association of Specialist Technical Organisations for Space (ASTOS)   1988

■   c/o Mr J Barrington-Brown, Nohmia Ltd, 79 Larksway,
        BISHOP'S STORTFORD, Herts, CM23 4DG.   (chmn/b)
        01279 505047
        Chmn: James Barrington-Brown
▲   Company Limited by Guarantee
○   *T; aims to promote & support the interests of UK small &
        medium enterprises in the space industry
●   Mtgs - Res - Inf - VE - LG - Guest Speaker programme
M   20 f

Association of Speech & Language Therapists in Independent Practice   (ASLTIP)   1989

■   Woodside, Coleheath Bottom, Speen, PRINCES RISBOROUGH,
        Bucks, HP27 0SZ.   (asa)
        http://www.helpwithtalking.com
        Chmn: Robyn Johnson,   Sec: Julie Andrews
▲   Un-incorporated Society
○   *P; the only database of speech & language therapists working
        independently
Gp   Medico legal; Sendist Tribunal (Special Educational Needs &
        Disability Tribunal)
●   Conf - Mtgs - ET - Exhib - SG - Inf
<   R Coll of Speech & Language Therapists (RCSLT)
M   700 i
        (Sub: £150)
¶   Independent Talking Pages - 4; ftm only.

Association for Spina Bifida & Hydrocephalus   (ASBAH)   1966

NR   42 Park Rd, PETERBOROUGH, Cambs, PE1 2UQ.   (hq)
        01733 555988   fax 01733 555985
        email info@asbah.org   http://www.asbah.org
        Exec Dir: Andrew Russell
▲   Registered Charity
Br   5 regional
○   *W; provides information & advice to people with spina bifida
        &/or hydrocephalus & their carers.   Team of area advisers
        is backed by specialist advisers in education, continence,
        hydrocephalus etc
●   LG - Study days
        Helpline: 0845 450 7755
<   Nat Coun for Voluntary Orgs (NCVO); Assn Med Res Charities;
        R Assn for Disability & Rehabilitation (RADAR); Disabled Living
        Foundation; Neurological Alliance
M   14,000 i
¶   Link (Jnl) - 6.
        AR.   Various booklets (list available).

Association for Spinal Injury Research, Rehabilitation &
Reintegration (ASPIRE) 1983
■ Wood Lane, STANMORE, Middx, HA7 4AP. (hq)
020 8420 6700 fax 020 8420 6352
email info@aspire.org.uk http://www.aspire.org.uk
Chief Exec: Brian Carlin
▲ Registered Charity
○ *Q; works with the 40,000 people with spinal cord injury, &
offers practical support to them throughout the UK, so that
they can lead fulfilled & independent lives
● Res - Specialist IT facilities - Integrated leisure centre
M c 40,000 i
¶ Aspirations! (NL) - 2; free.

Association of Stainless Fastener Distributors
since 2010 the Stainless Steel Fastners Group of the **British**
Association of Fastener Distributors

Association of Stillwater Game Fishery Managers (ASGFM)
1983
NR Fishery Lodge, Maxstoke Lane, MERIDEN, Warks, CV7 7HR.
(hq)
01676 522754
Sec: Mrs Penny Wigley
○ *T; for owners &/or managers of stillwater fishery businesses
● Conf - Mtgs - ET - Exhib - LG
< Country Landowners Assn
M 100 i & f
¶ Newsline - 2/3; ftm only.

Association of Street Lighting Electrical Contractors
since 2007 the **Association of Signals, Lighting & other**
Highway Electrical Connections

Association of Stress Therapists (AST) 1991
■ c/o Snowsfields Wellness, 41 Snowsfields, LONDON,
SE1 3SU. (contact/p)
020 7407 9910
email relax@turquoiseray.com
Contact: Tracy Tutty
▲ Un-incorporated Society
○ *M, *P; to establish a network of therapists to alleviate the
physical & mental symptoms caused by stress
● ET - Exam - SG
< Crystal Healing Fedn (CHF)
M 50 i, UK / 3 i, o'seas
¶ NL; ftm.

Association for Student Residential Accommodation (ASRA)
1997
■ Accommodation Office, King's College, Strand, LONDON,
WC2R 2LS. (sb)
020 7848 2332
email secretary@asra.ac.uk http://www.asra.ac.uk
Sec: Susannah Stringer
▲ Un-incorporated Society
○ *P; concerned with student housing - institutionally owned,
managed or private sector
● Conf - Mtgs - ET - Exhib - LG
< Assn for College & University Housing Officers (ACUHOI)
M 580 i, 12 f
¶ NL (website); m only.

Association for Studies in the Conservation of Historic Buildings
(ASCHB) 1968
■ c/o 77 Cowcross St, LONDON, EC1M 6EJ. (mail/address)
020 7720 4764 fax 020 7720 4764
email info@aschb.org.uk http://www.aschb.org.uk
Hon Sec: Jackie Heath
▲ Registered Charity
○ *L; to provide a forum to keep members informed on all
aspects of building conservation
● Conf - Mtgs - VE
< ICCROM; ICOMOS UK; COTAC; UPKEEP; IHBC
M 350 i, UK / 4 i, o'seas
(Sub:£35)
¶ Transactions - 1; ftm, £25 nm. NL - 6; ftm only.

Association of Studio & Production Equipment Companies Ltd
(ASPEC) 1993
■ 17 Ember Farm Way, EAST MOLESEY, Surrey, KT8 0BH. (sb)
email contact@aspec-uk.com http://www.aspec-uk.com
Sec: John Rendall
▲ Company Limited by Guarantee
○ *T; to represent the interests of all film facility companies
providing their services to the film & television production
industry
Gp Lighting; Studio; Camera
● Mtgs - ET - Empl
< Production Eqpt Rental Assn (PERA) (USA)
M 25 f

Association for the Study of Ethnicity & Nationalism (ASEN)
1990
NR London School of Economics, Houghton St, LONDON,
WC2A 2AE. (hq)
020 7955 6801 fax 020 7955 6218
email ASEN@lse.ac.uk http://www.lse.ac.uk/ASEN
Chief Exec: Mitchell Young
▲ Un-incorporated Society
○ *Q; an academic association fostering research into the areas
of ethnicity & nationalism
● Conf - Res - SG
< London School of Economics
M 180 i, 3 university research centres, UK / 120 i, o'seas
¶ Nations & Nationalism (Jnl) - 4.
Studies in Ethnicity & Nationalism [SEN] - 2.

Association for the Study of German Politics
2010 merged with the US German Politics Association to form
the International Association for the Study of German Politics
& is therefore outside the scope of this directory.

Association for the Study of Medical Education (ASME) 1957
■ 12 Queen St, EDINBURGH, EH2 1JE. (hq)
0131-225 9111 fax 0131-225 9444
email info@asme.org.uk http://www.asme.org.uk
Chief Exec: Nicky Pender
▲ Registered Charity
○ *E, *P, *Q; to bring together doctors, behavioural scientists &
educationalists with interests & responsibilities in medical
education
Gp Research c'ee
● Conf - Mtgs - ET - Res - Exhib - Inf
M c 850 i, UK / c 350 i, o'seas, 90 corporate
(Sub: £133 i)
¶ Bulletin - 6; AR - 1; both free.
(a) Medical Education - 12.
(b) The Clinical Teacher - 4.
(access online (a+b) £100, (a) £85, (b) £60)
Understanding Medical Education - a series of extended papers
designed to meet the needs of all newcomers, whether
under- or post-graduate.
Books on various aspects of medical education; £5.99 m,
£9.99 nm.
List of publications available.

© CBD Research Ltd · Beckenham · BR3 5JS · Tel 020 8650 7745 · E-mail cbd@cbdresearch.com · www.cbdresearch.com

Association for the Study of Modern & Contemporary France (ASMCF) 1979

■ 1 West North 4.2A, Dept of European Studies & Modern Languages, University of Bath, BATH, BA2 7AY. (hsb)
01225 385195
email secretary@asmcf.org   http://www.asmcf.org
Hon Sec: Dr Steve Wharton
▲ Registered Charity
Br Oxford, S Wales & W of England
○ *L; to promote research & scholarship into all aspects of modern French history, politics, society & culture, as well as relations between France & other countries, including those in the French-speaking world
● Conf - Mtgs - ET - Res - SG
M [not stated]
(Sub: £47)
¶ Modern & Contemporary France - 4; ftm, £78 nm.
Annual Conference Proceedings.

Association for the Study of Modern Italy (ASMI) 1982

■ c/o Department of Italian, University College London, Gower St, LONDON, WC1E 6BT. (hsb)
email l.rinaldi@ucl.ac.uk   http://www.asmi.org.uk
Hon Sec: Lucia Rinaldi
▲ Registered Charity
○ *L; the study of modern & contemporary Italian history, society, politics, culture & economy in the period between 1780 & the present
● Conf - Mtgs - Comp
M 61 i, UK / 2 i, o'seas
(Sub: £36 (waged) £20 (unwaged), Online £365, Print & online £385)
¶ Jnl of Modern Italy - 4; ftm, (enquiries to: (Taylor & Francis/Routledge: www.informaworld.com)

Association for the Study of Obesity (ASO) 1967

NR PO Box 410, DEAL, Kent, CT14 4AP. (hsb)
01304 367788
email helen.thorn@aso.org.uk   http://www.aso.org.uk
Dir: John Tabor
▲ Registered Charity
○ *L, *Q; study of causes, treatment & prevention of human obesity
● Conf - Res - Stat - Inf
< Intl Assn for the Study of Obesity; Eur Assn for the Study of Obesity
M 520 i, UK / 24 i, o'seas

Association for the Study & Preservation of Roman Mosaics (ASPROM) 1978

NR 3 Ramsholt Close, North Waltham, BASINGSTOKE, Hants, RG25 2DG. (hsp)
http://www.asprom.org
Hon Sec: Dr Janet Huskinson
▲ Registered Charity
○ *G, *L; study & preservation of Roman mosaics, principally from Britain
M i & f

Association for the Study of Primary Education (ASPE) 1987

■ The Swallow Barn, Brandon Court, Station Rd, LONG MARSTON, Herts, HP23 4RA. (hsb)
email mary@swallowbarn.fsnet.co.uk
http://www.aspe-uk.eu
Hon Sec: Mary Woodcock
▲ Registered Charity
○ *P; dedicated to the belief that good primary school practice should be based on best scholarship & research evidence available
● Conf - Mtgs - Res - SG
< Brit Educl Res Assn (BERA)
M 135 i
¶ Education 3-13 (Jnl) - 3.

Association of Subscription Agents & Intermediaries (ASA) 1934

NR Field Cottage, School Lane, BENHALL, Suffolk, IP17 1HE. (sp)
01728 633196
http://www.subscription-agents.org
Sec Gen: Sarah Durrant
▲ Un-incorporated Society
○ *T; interests of periodical subscription agents & intermediaries worldwide
● Conf - Mtgs - Discussion groups
M 4 f, UK / 36 f, o'seas
¶ NL - irreg; ftm.   LM - irreg; free.
The Work of Subscription Agents - irreg; free.

Association of Supervisors of Midwives (ASM) 1912

NR James Paget Healthcare NHS Trust, Lowestoft Rd, Gorleston, GREAT YARMOUTH, Norfolk, NR31 6LA. (hsb)
01493 452269
email elayne.guest@jpaget.nhs.uk
Hon Sec: Mrs Elayne Guest
▲ Un-incorporated Society
○ *P; to promote a high standard of supervision of midwives in the practice & teaching of midwifery
● Conf - Mtgs
< Intl Confedn of Midwives
M 350 i

Association of Suppliers to the Furniture Industry

has closed

Association for Supported Living (ASL)

NR Heritage Care Ltd, Connaught House, 112-120 High Rd, LOUGHTON, Essex, IG10 4HJ. (hq)
020 8502 3933
http://www.a-s-l.org.uk
Chmn: Kim Foo
○ *W; to provide a central source of support & information for the improvement of supported living services for those with learning disabilities

Association of Surgeons of Great Britain & Ireland (ASGBI) 1920

■ at the Royal College of Surgeons, 35-43 Lincoln's Inn Fields, LONDON, WC2A 3PE. (hq)
020 7973 0300
▲ Company Limited by Guarantee; Registered Charity
○ *P; advancement of science & art of surgery - general surgery to include GI, vascular, endocrine, breast, transplant, endoscopic
Gp Association of Coloproctology GB&I; Association of Endoscopic Surgeons GB&I; Association of Surgeons in Training; Association of Upper Gastro Intestinal Surgeons; British Association of Endocrine & Thyroid Surgeons; Vascular Society Great Britain & Ireland
● Conf - ET - Exhib - LG
M i
¶ LM - 1; ftm only.

Association of Surgeons in Training (ASiT) 1976

NR at the Royal College of Surgeons, 35-43 Lincoln's Inn Fields, LONDON, WC2A 3PE. (hq)
020 7973 0300   fax 020 7430 9235
email asit@asgbi.org.uk   http://www.asit.org
▲ Registered Charity
○ *M, *P; surgical training
● Conf - Mtgs - ET
M 768 i
¶ Ybk; ftm.

Association for Survey Computing   1971
- ■   PO Box 76, BERKELEY, Glos, GL13 9WU.
  01453 511511   fax 01453 511512
  email admin@asc.org.uk   http://www.asc.org.uk
  Admin: Christine Jenkins
- ○   *T; the application of computing & software technology to market research & government surveys
- ●   Conf
- M   450 i & f
- ¶   Survey Computing - NL.

Association of Systematic Kinesiology   (ASK)   1988
- NR   104A Sedlescombe Rd North, ST LEONARDS-on-SEA, E Sussex, TN37 7EN.   (hq)
  0845 020 0383
  http://www.systematic-kinesiology.co.uk
  Chief Exec: Mrs Marie Cheshire
- ▲   Registered Charity
- ○   *M, *P; applied systematic kinesiology (muscle testing) enables holistic functional analysis of nutritional sensitivities/needs & structural imbalances; helps resolve emotional problems
- ●   Mtgs - ET - Exam - Exhib
- M   160 i

Association of Tank & Cistern Manufacturers   (ATCM)   1965
- ■   22 Grange Park, St Arvans, CHEPSTOW, Monmouthshire, NP16 6EA.   (hsp)
  01291 623634   fax 01291 623634
  email imcc@atcmtanks.org.uk
  http://www.atcmtanks.org.uk
  Chmn & Sec: Ian McCrone
- ○   *T; for manufacturers of vessels for storing drinking water, waste water & other liquids (incl domestic heating oil & chemicals); to promote good practice in the manufacture of tank & cistern products
- Gp   GRP tanks & cisterns; Plastic oil tanks; Plastic chemical tanks; Steel tanks & cisterns; Thermoplastic tanks & cisterns
- ●   Mtgs - Inf
- <   Inst of Plumbing (as industrial associate)
- M   11 f
- ¶   ATCM News Update - 12; free.

Association of Taxation Technicians   (ATT)   1989
- NR   Artillery House (1st floor), 11-19 Artillery Row, LONDON, SW1P 1RT.   (hq)
  0844 251 0830   fax 0844 251 0831
  email info@att.org.uk   http://www.att.org.uk
  Sec: Andrew R Pickering
- ▲   Company Limited by Guarantee; Registered Charity
- Br   27; Europe, Hong Kong, Singapore
- ○   *P; to provide an appropriate qualification for individuals working in taxation on a day-to-day basis
- ●   Conf - Mtgs - ET - Exam - Lib
- <   Chart Inst of Taxation
- M   5,406 i
- ¶   Tax Adviser - 12.   LM - 2 yrly.   Annotated Finance Act - 1.
  Tax Advisers Practice Hbk.
  Professional Rules & Practice Guidelines.   AR.
  Note: the association is sponsored by the Chartered Institute of Taxation

Association of Teachers & Lecturers   (ATL)   1884
- NR   7 Northumberland St, LONDON, WC2N 5RD.   (hq)
  020 7930 6441   fax 020 7930 1359
  email info@atl.org.uk   http://www.atl.org.uk
  Gen Sec: Dr Mary Bousted
- ○   *P, *U; to defend the pay, conditions & career development of teachers, supply teachers, heads, lecturers, managers & support staff in maintained & independent sector schools & colleges
- <   TUC
- M   125,778 i

Association of Teachers of Lipreading to Adults   (ATLA)   1976
- NR   c/o Hearing Link, 27-28 The Waterfront, EASTBOURNE, E Sussex, BN23 5UZ.   (mail)
  email atla@lipreading.org.uk
  http://www.lipreading.org.uk
  Sec: Carol Riley
- ▲   Registered Charity
- ○   *P; to maintain & develop standards of lipreading teaching to adults; to promote understanding of the needs of adults with any level of acquired hearing loss
- Gp   Deaf; Deafened; Hard of hearing
- ●   Conf - Mtgs - ET - Exhib - LG
- <   UK Coun on Deafness (UKCOD)
- M   300+ i, 4 org, UK / 6+ i, o'seas
- ¶   Catchword - 2;   NL - 2; both ftm only.

Association of Teachers of Mathematics   (ATM)   1952
- NR   Unit 7 Prime Industrial Park, Shaftesbury St, DERBY, DE23 8YB.   (hq)
  01332 346599
  http://www.atm.org.uk
- ▲   Company Limited by Guarantee; Registered Charity
- ○   *E, *P; to support the teaching & learning of mathematics teaching by encouraging increased understanding & enjoyment of maths, understanding how people learn maths, the exploration of new ideas & practices
- M   i & instns

Association of Teachers of Singing   (AOTOS)   1975
- NR   23 Spring Valley, Upper Milton, WESTON-super-MARE, Somerset, BS22 9AS.   (hsp)
  01934 412921
  http://www.aotos.org.uk
  Hon Sec: Margaret Hopes
- ▲   Registered Charity
- ○   *E, *P; to promote the understanding of aspects of the teaching of singing
- ●   Conf - ET (teacher training course) - Inf
- <   Eur Voice Teachers Assn; Inc Soc Musicians
- >   Assn of English Singers & Speakers; Vocal Faculty Birmingham Conservatoire; R Coll of Music; Napier University
- M   435 i, 5 f, UK / 18 i, o'seas
  (Sub: £40 i, £80 f)
- ¶   Voice - 2; ftm, £4 nm.

Association for Teaching Psychology   (ATP)   1971
- NR   School of Health & Social Sciences, Napier University, EDINBURGH, EH9 2TB.   (hsb)
  0131-455 6010
  email m.williamson@napier.ac.uk   http://www.theatp.org
  Hon Sec: Morag Williamson
- Br   Scotland
- ○   *E, *L, *P; to further the study & teaching of psychology
- ●   Conf - Mtgs - ET - Exam - LG
- <   Brit Psychological Soc
- M   38,485 i, UK / 3,705 i, o'seas
- ¶   Psychology Teaching (Jnl) - 1; ftm, £5 nm.
  ATP NL - 3; ftm only.
  Various other publications.

Association for the Teaching of the Social Sciences   (ATSS)   1965
- NR   c/o British Sociological Association, Palatine House, Belmont Business Park, DURHAM, DH1 1TW.   (regd/office)
  0191 383 0839
  email atss@britsoc.org.uk   http://www.atss.org.uk
  Chmn: Pam Burrage
- ▲   Company Limited by Guarantee; Registered Charity
- ○   *P; dissemination of good teaching practices in the field of social science
- ●   Conf - ET - LG
- <   Brit Sociological Assn (BSA)
- >   General Teaching Coun
- M   c 500 i
- ¶   Social Science Teacher (Jnl) - 3; ftm only.

© CBD Research Ltd · Beckenham · BR3 5JS · Tel 020 8650 7745 · E-mail cbd@cbdresearch.com · www.cbdresearch.com

Association of Technical Lighting & Access Specialists (ATLAS)   1946
■ 6-8 Bonhill St, LONDON, EC2A 4BX.   (hq)
   0844 249 0026   fax 0844 249 0027
   email info@atlas.org.uk   http://www.atlas.org.uk
   Contact: The Secretary
○ *T; interests of steeplejacks & firms involved in the erection & maintenance of lightning conductors
Gp Chimney steeplejacks; Lightning conductor engineers; Training
● Mtgs - ET - Inf - Empl
M 59 f
¶ LM - 1; free.   Codes of Practice.

Association of Technology Staffing Companies
   on 1 January 2009 merged with the Forum of Professional Recruiters
   to form the **Association of Professional Staffing Companies**

Association of Thallophyte Treatment Plants   (ATTP)   1997
■ 1 Caryl House, Windlesham Grove, LONDON, SW19 6AH.
   (sb)
○ *T;
● Conf - Mtgs - LG - VE
M 6 f

Association of Therapeutic Communities   (ATC)   1972
NR Barns Centre, Church Lane, Toddington, CHELTENHAM, Glos, GL54 5DQ.   (mail/add)
   01242 620077   fax 01242 620077
   email post@therapeuticcommunities.org
   http://www.therapeuticcommunities.org
▲ Registered Charity
○ *W; to further implementation of the therapeutic community approach & ideology in the psychiatric hospital & social services for the psychiatric patient & appropriate related fields
● Conf - ET - Res
M 87 i, 49 f, UK / 37 i, 3 f, o'seas
¶ Therapeutic Communities Jnl - 4.
   NL - 4.

Association for Therapeutic Healers   (ATH)   1983
NR 110a Alexander Rd, LONDON, N19 4JN.   (memsec/p)
   020 7263 5266
   email enquiries@ath.org.uk   http://www.ath.org.uk
   Mem Sec: Jane Robertson
▲ Un-incorporated Society
○ *P; for professional healers who combine healing with other therapies; to promote health, wellbeing & self wisdom
● Mtgs - Clinic (at above address) - Professional liability service for members
< Confedn of Healing Orgs; UK Healers
M 70 i, UK / 2 i, o'seas
¶ NL - 3.

Association for Therapeutic Philosophy
   since 2010 **Institute of Management & Technology**

Association of Therapy Lecturers
   a group of the **Federation of Holistic Therapists**

Association of Timber Growers & Forestry Professionals
   since 2006 the **Confederation of Forest Industries**

Association of Tourism Teachers & Trainers
   a specialist section of the **Tourism Society**

Association of Town Centre Management   (ATCM)   1991
NR 1 Queen Anne's Gate, LONDON, SW1H 9BT.   (hq)
   020 7222 0120
   email info@atcm.org   http://www.atcm.org
   Chief Exec: Simon Quin
▲ Company Limited by Guarantee
○ *T; to promote the long term survival of the town centre as a place to live, work, shop & find entertainment
< Markets Alliance
M f

** Association of Town Clerks of Ireland
   Organisation lost: see Introduction paragraph 3

Association for Toy Importers
   since 2006 **Equitoy: the association for toy importers**

Association of Traditional Chinese Medicine   (ATCM)   1994
NR 5 Grosvenor House, 1 High St, EDGWARE, Middx, HA8 7TA.
   (hq)
   020 8951 3030   fax 020 8951 3030
   http://www.atcm.co.uk
   Gen Sec: Jidong Wu (020 8411 2647)
○ *P; for practitioners of Chinese medicine - herbal, cupping, therapeutic massage & Qi Gong; promotes proper professional qualifications
M i

Association of Train Operating Companies   (ATOC)   1994
NR 40 Bernard St (3rd floor), LONDON, WC1N 1BY.   (hq)
   020 7841 8000
   http://www.atoc.org
○ *T; for the passenger rail industry
M 27 f
¶ [In-house only]

Association of Translation Companies   (ATC)   1976
■ Unit 28 Level 6 North, New England House, New England St, BRIGHTON, E Sussex, BN1 4GH.   (hq)
   01273 676777   fax 0845 058 2590
   email info@atc.org.uk   http://www.atc.org.uk
   Gen Sec: Geoffrey Bowden
▲ Company Limited by Guarantee
○ *T; to encourage use of professionally produced translations by industry, commerce, public sector organisations & government depts
● Conf - Mtgs - ET - Res - LG
< Eur U of Assns of Translation Companies (EUATC)
M 178 f, UK / 22 f, o'seas
¶ Communicate - 4; online.

Association of Transport Co-ordinating Officers   (ATCO)   1974
NR Hermes House, TUNBRIDGE WELLS, Kent, TN4 9UZ.
   0844 209 6556
   http://www.atco.org.uk
▲ Un-incorporated Society
Br 8
○ *P; to secure nationwide a better transport service for passengers
Gp Sub-c'ees: Best value; Bus; Community health & social transport; Education transport; Information & ticketing; Performing management: Rail
● Conf - Mtgs - ET - Res - Exhib - Stat - LG
< Assn County Councils; Convention Scot Local Authorities; County Surveyors Soc
M 290 i
¶ ATCO News - 4;   Membership Directory - 1; both ftm only.

Association of Tutors   (AoT)   1958

- ■ Sunnycroft, 63 King Edward Rd, NORTHAMPTON, NN1 5LY. (hsp)
  01604 624171   fax 01604 624718
  http://www.tutor.co.uk/aot.htm
  Hon Sec: Dr D J Cornelius
- ▲ Un-incorporated Society
- ○ *E; *P; for independent private tutors; the Association is registered with the Criminal Records Bureau & has stringent vetting procedures
- ● Conf - Mtgs - Inf
- M i
- ¶ NL - 2;   LM - 1; both ftm only.
  Information Leaflets; free.

Association of UK Media Librarians   (AUKML)   1986

- NR PO Box 14254, LONDON, SE1 9WL.   (mail address)
  email chair@aukml.org.uk   http://www.aukml.org.uk
- ▲ Un-incorporated Society
- ○ *P; for librarians & information specialists in the media industry
- ● Conf - Mtgs - ET - VE
- M 70 i, UK / 30 i, o'seas
- ¶ Deadline (NL) - 4; ftm only.

Association of United Kingdom Oil Independents
    since 2010 **Downstream Fuel Association**

Association of United Recording Artists
    in 2007 merged with **Phonographic Performance Ltd**

Association of Universal Healers & Spiritualists
    see **Universal Spiritualists Association**

Association of University Administrators   (AUA)   1993

- NR Sackville Street Building, The University of Manchester, Sackville St, MANCHESTER, M60 1QD.   (hq)
  0161-275 2063
  http://www.aua.ac.uk
  Exec Dir: Alison Robinson
- ▲ Registered Charity
- Br 180
- ○ *E, *P; for all with administrative & managerial responsibilities in higher education incl the Republic of Ireland
- Gp Corporate planning forum; Equal opportunities working group; Quality assurance network; S/NVQ national support & focus
- ● Conf - Mtgs - ET - Exhib - SG - VE - LG
- M 4,000 i, UK / 52 i, o'seas
- ¶ Perspectives (Jnl) - 4; ftm, £120 nm.
  Newslink (NL) - 4;   AR - 1; both ftm only.

Association for University & College Counselling
    a group of the **British Association for Counselling & Psychotherapy**

Association of University Language Centres in the UK & Ireland

- NR Caroline Campbell, The Language Centre, University of Leeds, LEEDS, W Yorks, LS2 9JT.   (hsb)
  0113-343 3250
  http://www.aulc.org
  Sec: Caroline Campbell
- ▲ Registered Charity
- ○ *N, *P
- Gp Management & teaching; Technical & resources

Association of University Professors & Heads of French   (AUPHF)

- NR Dept of French, University of Leeds, LEEDS, W Yorks, LS2 9JT. (sb)
  0113 343 3495   fax 0113 343 3477
  Sec: Prof Russell Goulbourne
- ○ *P; to defend the specifity of French within the general advocacy for languages'

Association of University Radiation Protection Officers   (AURPO)   1961

- NR Corporate Assurance Team, National Physical Laboratory, TEDDINGTON, Middx, TW11 0LW.   (hsb)
  020 8943 6480   fax 020 8614 0487
  email john.makepeace@npl.co.uk
  http://www.aurpo.org
  Sec: John Makepeace
- ▲ Un-incorporated Society
- ○ *P; radiation protection from ionizing & non-ionizing radiations
- ● Conf - Mtgs - ET - Res - LG
- < Intl Radiation Protection Assn
- M 208 i, 13 f, UK / 3 i, o'seas
- ¶ NL - 4; ftm only.

Association of University Research & Industry Links   (AURIL)   1994

- NR c/o Queen's University, Lanyon North, University Rd, BELFAST, BT7 1NN.   (hq)
  028 9097 2589   fax 028 9097 2570
  http://www.qub.ac.uk/auril
  Exec Dir: Dr Philip Graham
- ▲ Company Limited by Guarantee
- ○ *N, *P; to support universities in the UK & Eire in the development of mutually beneficial partnerships with industry & other sectors, in the field of research, technology & knowledge transfer, consultancy & related activities

Association of Unpasteurised Milk Producers & Consumers   (AUMPC)   1989

- NR Hardwick Estate Office, Whitchurch-on-Thames, READING, Berks, RG8 7RE.
  0118-984 2955
  Founders: Sir Julian Rose,   Marwood Yeatman
- ▲ Un-incorporated Society
- ○ *F, *K, *T; for producers & consumers of unpasteurised milk; to keep small producers in business & allow consumers freedom of choice
- ● Inf - LG
- ¶ The Case for Untreated Milk.
  Note: The association was first formed to fight a 1989 attempt to ban the sale of unpasteurised milk. It was reactivated, to mobilise public opinion again, to fight another move to ban the milk in 1997.

Association of Upper Gastro Intestinal Surgeons
    a group of the **Association of Surgeons of Great Britain & Ireland**

Association of Users of Research Agencies   (AURA)   1965

- NR 51 Dalkeith Rd, HARPENDEN, Herts, AL5 5PP.   (admin/p)
  01582 620331
  http://www.aura.org.uk
  Admin: Peter Goudge
- ▲ Company Limited by Guarantee
- ○ *P; forum for clientside researchers to exchange information
- Gp General Insurance Market Research Association
  Advertising; Database marketing; International research
- ● Mtgs - Res - Networking
- M 240 i, UK / 135 i, o'seas

Association of Valuers of Licensed Property   (AVLP)   1894

- ■ c/o Fleurets, Wellesley House, 96 East St, SUDBURY, Suffolk, CO10 2TP.   (hsb)
  01787 378050   fax 01787 880292
  email bob.whittle@fleurets.com   http://www.avlp.com
  Hon Sec: R Whittle
- ○ *P; for auctioneers, surveyors & valuers whose sole or main business is concerned with the sale & valuation of hotels, public houses & licensed property generally
- M c 120 i

© CBD Research Ltd · Beckenham · BR3 5JS · Tel 020 8650 7745 · E-mail cbd@cbdresearch.com · www.cbdresearch.com

Association of Vehicle Recovery Operators Ltd   (AVRO)   1977
- ■   1 Bath St, RUGBY, Warks, CV21 3JF.   (hq)
  01788 572850   fax 01788 567320
  email info@avrouk.com   http://www.avrouk.com
  Chief Exec: Gary Satchwell
- ▲   Company Limited by Guarantee
- ○   *T
- Gp   AVRO show; Finance; Insurance; Legal; Magazine, Directory,
  Website; Membership; Motoring organisations; Police
  schemes; Standards & safety
- ●   Mtgs - Inf - LG
- <   Intl Fedn Recovery Services
- M   500 f
- ¶   Recovery Operator Magazine - 6; ftm, £2.40 nm.
  Members NL - 6; ftm only.   AR; free.
  Members Directory - 1; ftm, £15 nm.

Association of Veterinarians in Industry
  a group of the **British Veterinary Association**

Association of Veterinary Anaesthetists
  a group of the **British Small Animal Veterinary Association**

Association of Veterinary Clinical Pharmacology & Therapeutics
  a group of the **British Small Animal Veterinary Association**

Association of Veterinary Soft Tissue Surgeons
  a group of the **British Small Animal Veterinary Association**

Association of Veterinary Students
  a group of the **British Veterinary Association**

Association of Veterinary Teaching & Research Work
  a group of the **British Veterinary Association**

**Association of Visitors to Immigration Detainees   (AVID)
1997**
- NR   Archway Resource Centre, 1b Waterlow Rd, LONDON,
  N19 5NJ.   (mail/address)
  020 7281 0533
  email coordinator@aviddetention.org.uk
  http://www.aviddetention.org.uk
- ▲   Registered Charity
- ○   *N, *W; an umbrella organisation supporting visiting groups,
  individual visitors & immigration detainees held in removal,
  reception & holding centres by the Immigration Service; to
  advocate for improved conditions in detention
- ●   Conf - ET - Res - Stat - Inf - LG
- M   350 i, 25 gps
- ¶   Hbk; ftm, £5 nm.   AR.

Association of Voluntary Services Managers
- NR   Ian Rennie Hospice at Home, CHALFONT St GILES, Bucks,
  HP8 4LS.   (sb)
  01494 877200
  Sec: Rozina Ahmad
- ○   *W; to manage volunteers in palliative care
- M   i

Association of Volunteer Managers   (AVM)   2007
- NR   9 Stamford Rd, WATFORD, Herts, WD17 4QS.
  http://www.volunteermanagers.org.uk
- ○   *P; for those coordinating or administering volunteers
- M   i

Association of Waterways Cruising Clubs   (AWCC)
- NR   c/o 49 Alcester Rd, STUDLEY, WArks, B80 7NJ.   (hq)
  email secretary@awcc.org.uk   http://www.awcc.org.uk
  Sec: Brian Rich
- ○   *G
- <   Nat Navigation Users Forum (NNUF)
- M   i

Association of Welding Distribution   (AWD)   1973
- NR   Secure Hold Business Centre, Studley Rd, REDDITCH, Worcs,
  B98 7LG.   (hq)
  01952 290036   fax 01952 290037
  email info@awd.org.uk   http://www.awd.org.uk
  Chmn: Dave Ellwood
- ▲   Un-incorporated Society
- ○   *T; for the welding supply industry - distributors, manufacturers,
  wholesalers & importers with a UK operational base
- ●   Conf - Mtgs - ET - Exhib - Stat - Inf - Lib - VE - LG (through
  METCOM)
- <   Mechanical & Metal Trades Confedn (METCOM)
- M   161 f
- ¶   NL - 12; m only.
  AWD Business Bulletin - 4; free.
- ✕   Association of Welding Distributors

**Association of Well Head Equipment Manufacturers
(AWHEM)   1961**
- NR   c/o Aker Solutions, Howe Moss Avenue, Kirkhill Industrial
  Estate, Dyce, ABERDEEN, AB21 0NA.   (chmn/b)
  North Sea Committee Chmn: Simon Vaughan
- ▲   Un-incorporated Society
- ○   *T; repair & manufacture of well control equipment used within
  the Continental shelf

Association of Wheelchair Children
- NR   6 Woodman Parade, North Woolwich, LONDON, E16 2LL.
  (hq)
  0870 121 0050
- ▲   Registered Charity
  uses the name Go Kids Go!

**Association of Wholesale Electrical Bulk Buyers Ltd   (AWEBB)
1975**
- NR   AWEBB House, 2 Kensington Works, Hallamfields Rd,
  ILKESTON, Derbys, DE7 4BR.   (hq)
  0115-944 3334
  http://www.awebb.org.uk
- ○   *T
- M   59 f

Association of Wine Educators   (AWE)
- ■   Scots Firs, 70 Joiners Lane, CHALFONT ST PETER, Bucks,
  SL9 0AU.   (admin/p)
  01753 882320   fax 01753 882320
  email admin@wineeducators.com
  http://www.wineeducators.com
  Admin: Andrea Warren;   Hon Sec: Laura Clay
- ▲   Un-incorporated Society
- ○   *P; to inform, educate & inspire the general public on the
  subject of wines
- M   60 i
- ¶   AWE Inspiring News

Association of Woodturners of GB   (AWGB)   1987
- NR   Brimbles, 114 Slough Rd, Datchet, Berks, SL3 9AF.   (treas/p)
  01753 593771
  http://www.woodturners.co.uk
  Treas: Adrian Needham,   Sec: Mike Collas
  Sec: Mike Collas 020 8894 6759
- ○   *P, *G; to provide education, information & organisation to
  those interested in woodturning, whether as hobbyists,
  professionals, gallery owners or collectors; also wood & tool
  suppliers

Association of X-ray Equipment Manufacturers
  in 2009 became **AXrEM: Association of Healthcare Technology
  Providers for Imaging, Radiotherapy & Care**

Association of Young Medical Scientists
  a group of the **Medical Research Society**

Association of Young People with ME   (AYME)   1996
- ■ 10 Vermont Place, Tongwell, MILTON KEYNES, Bucks,
    MK15 8JA.   (hq)
    0845 123 2389
    email info@ayme.org.uk   http://www.ayme.org.uk
    Chair of Trustees: Jill Moss
- ▲ Company Limited by Guarantee; Registered Charity
- ○ *M, *W, *Y; 'cheerful support, friendship & information to
    children & young people aged 0 to 25 with ME. Free
    membership to eligible applicants living in the UK'
- ● Inf - Lib - Peer support
    Helpline: 0845 123 2389
- M 2,000 i
- ¶ NL - 6.
    Books:
       A Ray of Hope; £10.99.   Three Villains?; £6.50.
       My Daughter & ME; £7.50.
    Videos:
       Education DVD; £9.00.
    Numerous other publications for sufferers, schools & doctors.

Assurance Medical Society
    2011 merged with the Association of Medical Underwriters to form
    the **Assurance Medical & Underwriting Society.**

Assurance Medical & Underwriting Society   (AMUS)   1893
- ■ Lettsom House, 11 Chandos St, LONDON, W1G 9EB.   (hq)
    020 7636 6308
    Exec Sec: Col Richard Kinsella-Bevan
- ○ *L; life assurance medicine
- ● Mtgs
- < Intl Congress Life Assurance Medicine
- M 450 i, 70 f
- ¶ Transactions - 2; ftm only.
- × 2011 (Association of Medical Underwriters
    (Assurance Medical Society

Asthma Society of Ireland
- IRL 43 Amiens St, DUBLIN 1, Republic of Ireland.
       353 (1) 817 8886   fax 353 (1) 817 8878
       email office@asthmasociety.ie
       http://www.asthmasociety.ie
       Chmn: Angela Edghill
- ○ *W

Asthma UK   1927
- ■ Summit House, 70 Wilson St, LONDON, EC2A 2DB.   (hq)
    020 7786 4900   fax 020 7256 6075
    email info@asthma.org.uk   http://www.asthma.org.uk
    Chief Exec: Neil Churchill
- ▲ Registered Charity
- Br Scotland, Wales, Northern Ireland
- ○ *K, *W; to research into asthma & related allergy; to give
    information & advice for people with asthma, their relatives,
    carers & health professionals
- Gp Carers; Healthcare professionals; Parents of children with
    asthma; People with asthma; Researchers & scientists
- ● ET - Res - Stat - Inf
    Helpline: 0845 710 0203
- < Assn Medical Res Charities
- M 20,000 i
- ¶ all publications on website

Astrological Association of Great Britain   (AAGB)   1958
- ■ BCM 450, LONDON, WC1N 3XX.   (hq)
    020 8625 0098
    email office@astrologicalassociation.com
    http://www.astrologicalassociation.com
    Chmn: Wendy Stacey
- ▲ Un-incorporated Society
- ○ *G; for people interested in western & Vedic astrology
- ● Conf - Inf - Lib - VE
- M 1,200 i, UK / 500 i, o'seas
- ¶ Astrological Jnl - 6.   Transit Magazine - 6.
    Correlation (research jnl) - 2.   Cosmos & Culture - 4.
    Astrology & Medicine - 3.

Astrological Lodge of London   (ALL)   1915
- NR PO Box 57743, LONDON, NW11 1EW.   (mem/sec)
    Sec: Gill Dorren
- ○ *P; the study of astrology in all its branches
- ● Mtgs (Mondays 50 Gloucester Place, W1U 8AE) - ET - Comp -
    SG - Lib
- M 400 i, UK / 90 i, o'seas
- ¶ Astrology - 4.

Astronomical Society of Edinburgh   (ASE)   1924
- NR 105-19 Causewayside, EDINBURGH, EH9 1QG.   (hq)
    0131-208 1924
    Sec: Graham Rule
- ▲ Registered Charity
- ○ *L; to promote interest in astronomy in Edinburgh
- M i

ASUCplus   (ASUCplus)   1991
- NR Kingsley House, Ganders Business Park, Kingsley, BORDON,
    Hants, GU35 9LU.   (asa)
    01420 471613   fax 01420 471611
    email admin@asuc.org.uk   http://www.asuc.org.uk
    Sec: John G Fairley
- ○ *T; 'specialists in subsidence repair techniques & engineered
    foundation solutions, including new build foundations &
    basement development'
- ● Conf - Mtgs - ET - Exhib
- M 20 f

Ataxia-Telangiectasia Society   (A-T Society)   (ATS)   1989
- ■ c/o IACR-Rothamsted, HARPENDEN, Herts, AL5 2JQ.   (hq)
    01582 760733   fax 01582 760162
    email atsociety@btconnect.com
    http://www.atsociety.org.uk
    Hon Sec: Mrs Maureen Poupard
- ▲ Company Limited by Guarantee; Registered Charity
- ○ *M, *W; the relief of suffering caused by A-T
- ● Mtgs - Inf - 2 specialist clinics - Support for families
- < Assn Med Res Charities; Genetic Interest Gp; Contact a Family
- M 120 families, UK / 30 families, o'seas
- ¶ NL - 2; free.
    What is A-T?   A-T: an overview.
    Ataxia-Telangiectasia [guides for/to]: Therapies; Parents;
    Teachers.

© CBD Research Ltd · Beckenham · BR3 5JS · Tel 020 8650 7745 · E-mail cbd@cbdresearch.com · www.cbdresearch.com

Ataxia UK (ATAXIA) 1964
NR Lincoln House, 1-3 Brixton Rd, LONDON, SW9 6DE. (hq)
     020 7582 1444   fax 020 7582 9444
     email office@ataxia.org.uk   http://www.ataxia.org.uk
     Chief Exec: Alastair MacDougall
▲ Registered Charity
Br 8
○ *W; to provide advice, support & information to sufferers & their
     families; to finance research into Friedreich's, cerebellar &
     other ataxias; to offer information for health-care & social
     service professionals
● Conf - Inf
     Helpline: 0845 644 0606
< Neurological Alliance; Genetic Interest Gp
M 1,854 i, f & org, UK / 51 i, f & org, o'seas
¶ The Ataxia - 4;   AR - 1; both ftm only.
     Freidreichs Ataxia / Cerebellar (leaflets); free.

Atheism 2009
■ 11 Thoresby Place, CLEETHORPES, Lincs, DN35 9AL. (hsp)
     07722 708324
     email pjwatheist@hushmail.com
     Sec: P J Wain
▲ Un-incorporated Society
○ *G; the spread of atheism (the reasoning that God does not &
     cannot exist); suppression of all religious influence &
     propaganda
● Mtgs - ET - Inf
M i

Æthelflæd
■ 1a Auckland Rd, LONDON, SW11 1EW.
     020 7924 5868
     email c.maddern@gold.ac.uk
     Hon Sec: Dr Carole Maddern
○ *L; research & scholarly activities relating to Alfred the Great's
     daughter Æthelflæd, the Lady of the Mercians; and to studies
     of manuscripts in Old English
● Conf - Res
M 12 i

Athletics Northern Ireland 1989
NR Athletics House, Old Coach Road, BELFAST, BT9 5PR. (hq)
     028 9060 2707   fax 028 9030 9939
     email info@niathletics.org   http://www.niathletics.org
     Gen Sec: John Allen
○ *S; the governing body for the sport of athletics in Northern
     Ireland
< UK Athletics
M 60 clubs

Atlantic Council of the United Kingdom
NR 130 City Rd, LONDON, EC1V 2NW. (hq)
     020 7251 6111
     http://www.atlanticcounciluk.org
▲ Registered Charity
○ *K; 'to explain, in simple & lucid terms to schools, universities &
     public opinion generally, the implications of the momentous
     changes that have taken place in Europe since the end of the
     Cold War'
M i

Attend 1949
NR 11-13 Cavendish Square, LONDON, W1G 0AN. (hq)
     0845 450 0285
     email info@attend.org.uk   http://www.attend.org.uk
     Chief Exec: David Wood
▲ Registered Charity
○ *N, *W; supporting volunteering to enhance health & social
     care for local communities
M 750 org
¶ Friends Connect - 4.
     AR.   Training publications.
× 2006 (April) National Association of Hospital & Community
     Friends

Aubrac Cattle Society of the UK Ltd 1990
NR Gore Farm, Ashmore, SALISBURY, Wilts, SP5 5AR. (hsp)
     01747 811157   fax 01747 811157
     Sec: Mrs Jennifer Biles,   Pres: Sir John Eliot Gardiner
○ *B; promotion, registration & import of registered Aubrac beef
     cattle
M 2 i

Audax United Kingdom 1976
NR 26 Naseby Rd, BELPER, Derbys, DE56 0ER. (mem/sec)
     http://www.aukweb.net
     Mem Sec: Ian Hobbs
○ *S; the organisation of long-distance cycling in the UK
M i
     (Sub: £19)

Audio Engineering Society (British Section) (AES) 1970
NR PO Box 645, SLOUGH, Berks, SL1 8BJ. (hq)
     01628 663725   fax 0870 7626137
     email uk@aes.org   http://www.aes.org
     Sec: Mrs Heather Lane
○ *L, *P
M i & f
¶ Jnl - 10.

Audio Visual Association
     a specialist group of the **British Institute of Professional
     Photography**

Audiobook Publishing Association
     has closed

Audiovisual Federation (AF)
IRL Confederation House, 84-86 Lower Baggot St, DUBLIN 2,
      Republic of Ireland. (hq)
      353 (1) 660 1011   fax 353 (1) 660 1717
      email tommy.mccabe@ibec.ie   http://www.ibec.ie/avf
      Dir: Tommy McCabe
○ *T; to promote the interests of the audiovisual sector as a whole
< Ir Business & Emplrs Confedn (IBEC)

Australia & New Zealand Chamber of Commerce
     since 2006 **Australian Business**

Australian Business 1910
NR Australia Centre, Strand, LONDON, WC2B 4LG. (hq)
     0870 890 0720   fax 0870 890 0721
     email enquiries@australianbusiness.co.uk
     http://www.australianbusiness.co.uk
     Dir: Melissa Brown
▲ Non-profit organisation
○ *C; to promote & facilitate bilateral trade between Australia/
     New Zealand & the UK
Gp UK, Australia/New Zealand Business
● Inf - Lib - Events & functions relevant to business involving
     Australasia & the UK
< Australian Brit Cham Comm
M 500 i, 2300 f, 3,000 org UK / 10 i, 10 f, 1,000 org, o'seas
¶ Up & Under Updates - 6; ftm.
× 2006 Australia & New Zealand Chamber of Commerce

Australian Finch Society (AFS) 1971
NR 15 Skeifs Row, Benwick, MARCH, CAmbs, PE15 0XB. (sp)
     http://www.australianfinchsociety.co.uk
     Sec: Joy Mitchell
○ *G

Austro-British Chamber (ABC) 1963
NR Ebendorferstrasse 3, A-1010 WIEN, Austria.
     43 (1) 404 43 3950   fax 43 (1) 404 43 93950
     email info@abchamber.org   http://www.abchamber.org
○ *C

Authors' Licensing & Collecting Society   (ALCS)   1977
NR   The Writers' House, 13 Haydon St, LONDON, EC3N 1DB.
        (hq)
        020 7264 5700
        Admin: Dawn Ryan
○   *T; the British rights management society for all writers; to
        distribute fees to writers whose work has been copied,
        broadcast or recorded
M   i

**Autism Independent UK (Society for the Autistically
        Handicapped)   (SFTAH)   1987**
■   199-203 Blandford Avenue, KETTERING, Northants,
        NN16 9AT.   (hq)
        01536 523274   fax 01536 523274
        email autism@autismuk.com
        http://www.autismuk.com
        Dir: Keith Lovett
▲   Registered Charity
○   *W; to promote the understanding & awareness of autism; to
        provide support for families and carers; training for
        professionals
●   Conf - ET - Res - Lib - LG
<   TEACCH (USA)
M   209 i, 850 org, UK / 20 i, o'seas
¶   Autism News - 4.   AR.   (both on web).

Auto-Cycle Union Ltd   (ACU)   1903
NR   ACU House, Wood St, RUGBY, Warks, CV21 2YX.   (hq)
        01788 566400   fax 01788 573585
        email admin@acu.org.uk   http://www.acu.org.uk
        Gen Sec: Gary Thompson
▲   Company Limited by Guarantee
○   *S; governing body of British motorcycle sport & leisure
●   Conf - Mtgs - ET - Exhib - Comp - Inf
<   Fédn Intle Motocyclisme (FIM)
M   29,415 i, 650 clubs
¶   Motorcycling GB - 4.   ACU Hbk - 1.

Auto Locksmiths Association   (ALA)   1997
NR   PO Box 66, SAXMUNDHAM, Suffolk, IP17 3WA.   (sb)
○   *T; to enhance & develop the auto locksmith industry
●   Conf - Mtgs - ET - Res - Exhib - Inf - Lib - VE - LG
M   50 i
¶   NL - 6; ftm only.

Autograph Club of Great Britain   (ACOGB)   1996
■   12 Duxmore Way, Dawley, TELFORD, Shropshire, TF4 2RD.
        (hsp)
        01952 410332
        email contactacogb@blueyonder.co.uk
        http://www.acogb.co.uk
        Chmn: Robert Gregson
▲   Un-incorporated Society
○   *G; to keep autograph collectors in touch with each other; to
        raise money for charities
●   Mtgs - Exhib - Inf - Help & advice - Collections bought & sold
M   c 200 i
        (Sub: Free membership)
¶   [website forum only].

**Automated Material Handling Systems Association Ltd
        (AMHSA)   1986**
NR   PO Box 7113, LEICESTER, LE7 9XX.   (hq)
        0116-259 8518
▲   Company Limited by Guarantee
○   *T; to promote the use of automated material handling & unit
        load conveyor systems in the UK
M   f

Automatic Door Suppliers Association   (ADSA)   1985
■   411 Limpsfield Rd, The Green, WARLINGHAM, Surrey,
        CR6 9HA.   (hq)
        01883 624961   fax 01883 626841
        http://www.adsa.org.uk
        Contact: Anne Saxby
○   *T; safety standards for automatic door installations
●   Mtgs - Exam - Stat - Inf - LG
M   13 f

Automatic Identification Manufacturers & Suppliers Association
        since 2007-08 **Association for Automatic Identification &
        Mobile Data Capture**

Automatic Vending Association   (AVA)   1929
■   1 Villiers Court, 40 Upper Mulgrave Rd, CHEAM, Surrey,
        SM2 7AJ.   (hq)
        020 8661 1112   fax 020 8661 2224
        http://www.ava-vending.co.uk
        Dir: Jonathan Hilder
▲   Company Limited by Guarantee
Br   5
○   *T; for the automatic refreshment industry
Gp   Coinage; Commodities; Technical
●   Conf - Mtgs - Res - Exhib - Stat - Inf - Lib - LG - Preparation of
        technical standards - Sales promotion & publicity
<   Eur Vending Assn; Brit Retail Consortium; CBI
M   29 i, 264 f, UK / 6 f, o'seas
¶   VENDinform - 6.   LM - 1.   Census - 1.
        Explaining Vending;   Vending Quality Standards.

Automobile Association   (AA)   1905
NR   Contact Centre, Lambert House, Stockport Rd, CHEADLE,
        Cheshire, SK8 2DY.   (hq)
        0161-488 7544
        email customer.services@theaa.com
        http://www.theaa.com
        Chief Exec: Andrew Strong
▲   Un-incorporated Society
○   *G
●   Insurance services - Motoring services - Publishing
M   c 12,000,000 i
¶   AR.

Automotive Distribution Federation
        since 2010 **Independent Automotive Aftermarket Federation**

Automotive Division
        a group of the **Institute of Materials, Minerals & Mining**

Aviation Environment Federation   (AEF)   1975
NR   Broken Wharf House, 2 Broken Wharf, LONDON, EC4V 3DT.
        (hq)
        020 7248 2223   fax 020 7329 8160
        email info@aef.org.uk   http://www.aef.org.uk
        Chief Exec: Tim Johnson
▲   Company Limited by Guarantee
○   *K; 'UK-based association concerned exclusively with the
        environmental impacts of aviation'
●   Conf - ET - Res - SG - Stat - Inf - Lib - LG
<   Intl Coalition for Sustainable Aviation (ICSA); Eur Fedn for
        Transport & Envt (T&E)
M   120 i, f & org
¶   NL - 4.

© CBD Research Ltd · Beckenham · BR3 5JS · Tel 020 8650 7745 · E-mail cbd@cbdresearch.com · www.cbdresearch.com

Aviation Preservation Society of Scotland   (APSS)   1973
NR   c/o National Museum of Flight, East Fortune Airfield,
        NORTH BERWICK, E Lothian, EH39 5LF.   (hq)
            email secretary@apss.org.uk   http://www.apss.org.uk
        Hon Sec: Frank Fiddes
▲   Registered Charity
○   *G; to preserve the history of aviation & associated skills; to
        support the National Museum of Flight
Gp   Slingsby T53 Glider; Sopwith 1½ Strutter
●   Mtgs
<   Brit Aviation Presvn Coun (BAPC)
M   100 i

Aviation Society   (TAS)   1973
NR   c/o The Aviation Shop, Terminal One Arrivals, MANCHESTER
        AIRPORT, M90 1QX.   (hq)
        0161-489 2443
        email admin@tasmanchester.com
        http://www.tasmanchester.com
        Chmn: Peter Hampson
▲   Un-incorporated Society
○   *G; all aspects of aviation for enthusiasts
Gp   Civil & military; Aviation; Manchester airport
●   Mtgs - Res - Exhib - Comp - SG - Stat - Inf - VE - Coach tours &
        flights to airports in the UK & o'seas
M   2,000 i
¶   Winged Words (NL) - 12; ftm.

Avicultural Society   (AS)   1894
■   Sheraton Lodge, Station Rd, SOUTHMINSTER, Essex,
        CM0 7EW.   (hsp)
        Sec: Peter Stocks
▲   Un-incorporated Society
○   *L; study of British & foreign birds in freedom & captivity
●   VE
<   Nat Coun Aviculture
M   200 i, 10 instns, UK / 50 i, 66 instns, o'seas
¶   The Avicultural Magazine - 4.

**AXrEM: Association of Healthcare Technology Providers for
    Imaging, Radiotherapy & Care   (AXrEM)   1974**
NR   Broadwall House, 21 Broadwall, LONDON, SE1 9PL.   (hq)
        020 7207 9660   fax 020 7642 8096
        email peter.lawson@axrem.org.uk
        Dir: Peter J Lawson
▲   Un-incorporated Society
○   *T; medical X-ray diagnostic & radiotherapy equipment
●   Mtgs - Stat - LG
<   Eur Coordination C'ee of the Radiological & Electromedical
        Ind (COCIR)
M   7 f
×   2009 Association of X-ray Equipment Manufacturers

Ayrshire Agricultural Association   (AAA)   1836
NR   Oswald Hall, Auchincruive, AYR, KA6 5HW.   (hsp)
        0845 201 1460   fax 01292 525939
        email lorrainem@ayrcountyshow.co.uk
        Sec & Treas: Mrs Lorraine Murdoch
▲   Registered Charity
○   *F; to promote agriculture in Ayrshire
●   Exhib
<   Assn of Agricl Shows
M   i

**Ayrshire Archaeological & Natural History Society   (AANHS)
    1947**
NR   27 Marchmont Road, AYR, KA7 2SB.   (memsec/p)
        email info@aanhs.org.uk   http://www.aanhs.org.uk
        Mem Sec: Mrs Merry Graham
▲   Un-incorporated Society
○   *L, *Q; to promote interest in the archaeology, history & natural
        history of Ayrshire
●   Conf - Mtgs - VE
<   Coun Scot Archaeology
M   260 i
¶   Ayrshire Monographs - 2; ftm.   Ayrshire Notes - 2; ftm.

Ayrshire Cattle Society of Great Britain & Ireland   1887
NR   17 Barns St, AYR, KA7 1XB.   (hq)
        01292 267123   fax 01292 611973
        email society@ayrshirescs.org
        http://www.ayrshirescs.org
        Office Mgr: Irene Kirkpatrick
▲   Registered Charity
○   *B; to promote & register Ayrshire dairy cows
●   Conf - Mtgs - Promotion of breed - Register cattle
<   Nat Cattle Assn (Dairy)
M   1,100 i, UK / 30 i, o'seas
¶   Ayrshire Jnl - 2.
        Ayrshire Dairyman (NL) - 2.   AR.

Ayrshire Chamber of Commerce & Industry   (ACCI)   1992
NR   Suite 1005, Glasgow Prestwick International Airport,
        PRESTWICK, Ayrshire, KA9 2PL.   (hq)
        01292 678666   fax 01292 678667
        email enquiries@ayrshire-chamber.org
        http://www.ayrshire-chamber.org
        Chief Exec: Martin Cheyne
▲   Company Limited by Guarantee
○   *C
<   Scot Chams Comm
M   f

Ayurvedic Medical Association UK
        closed in 2008.

Baby Equipment Hirers Association (BEHA) 2000
■ 8 Anselm Rd, HATCH END, Middx, HA5 4LJ.
020 8621 4378
http://www.beha.co.uk
Contact: Juliette Morrison
○ *T; to supply members with insurance & equipment through buyers
● Conf - Res
M 10 i
¶ BEHA News - 6; AR; both ftm only.

Baby Milk Action 1979
■ 34 Trumpington St, CAMBRIDGE, CB2 1QY. (hq)
01223 464420 fax 01223 464417
email info@babymilkaction.org
http://www.babymilkaction.org
Office Mgr: Sarah Hansen
▲ Company Limited by Guarantee
○ *K; 'to save infant lives & to end the avoidable suffering caused by inappropriate infant feeding by working within a global network (IBFAN); to strengthen independent, transparent & effective controls on the marketing of the baby feeding industry worldwide; the Independent Baby Food Action Network is a coalition of more than 200 citizen & health worker groups in more than 100 countries working for better child health & nutrition through the promotion of breastfeeding & the elimination of irresponsible marketing of infant foods, bottles & teats
● Conf - ET - Exhib - LG
< Intl Baby Food Action Network (IBFAN)
M 2,000 i
¶ Update NL - 2; ftm, £15 nm.

Baby Products Association (BPA) 1945
■ 2 Carrera House, Merlin Court, Gatehouse Close, AYLESBURY, Bucks, HP19 8DP. (hq)
0845 456 9570 fax 0845 456 9573
email info@b-p-a.org http://www.thebpa.eu
▲ Company Limited by Guarantee
○ *T; for manufacturers & importers of baby & nursery goods, including wheeled goods, nursery furniture, baby walkers, soft goods, child restraints, toys & early learning
● Conf - Mtgs - Exhib - Comp - Inf - Lib - LG - Organises BPA Baby & Child Trade Fair
< Eur C'ee for Standardization (CEN); Brit Standards Instn (BSI); Tr Assn Forum (TAF)
M 80 f, UK / 10 f, o'seas
¶ NL - 4; LM - 4; both ftm only.
BPA Ybk - 1; ftm, £35 nm. AR - 1.
BPA Baby & Child Exhibition Catalogue - 1; free to exhibitors & visitors, £6 non-exhibitors.

BackCare
see **National Backpain Association (BackCare)**

Backpackers Club (BPC) 1972
NR 56 The Leys, CHIPPING NORTON, Oxon, OX7 5HH. (memsec/p)
http://www.backpackersclub.co.uk
Mem Sec: Geoff Gafford
▲ Un-incorporated Society
Br County groups; Canada, Holland
○ *G; lightweight camping travelling on foot, by bicycle, canoe or ski
● Mtgs - Inf - Lib - Informal weekends
M 1,150 i, UK / 24 i, o'seas
¶ Backpack (Jnl) - 4; ftm only.

Badge Collectors Circle (BCC) 1980
NR 57 Middleton Place, LOUGHBOROUGH, Leics, LE11 2BY. (sp)
01509 569270
email f.setchfield@ntlworld.com
Editor: Frank Setchfield
○ *G; collecting non-military, enamel & tin lapel badges as a hobby
Gp Badges: Button, Enamel
● Mtgs - Res - SG - Inf - Swapping badges
M 450 i, 2 f, UK / 6 i, o'seas
¶ The Badger (NL) - 6; £15 yr (£2.50 each).

Badger Face Welsh Mountain Sheep Society (Cymdeithas Defaid Torddu Cymreig Torwen) (BFWMSS) 1976
NR Llanarithon, Howey, LLANDRINDOD WELLS, Powys, LD1 5PP. (hsp)
01597 823238
http://www.badgerfacesheep.co.uk
Sec: Peter Weale
▲ Un-incorporated Society
○ *B
● Mtgs - Exhib - Comp
< Nat Sheep Assn
M 250 i, UK / 2 i, o'seas
¶ NL - 4; ftm only. Flockbook - 1; ftm, £5 nm.

Badger Trust 1986
NR PO Box 708, EAST GRINSTEAD, W Sussex, RH19 2WN. (hq)
0845 828 7878
email enquiries@badgertrust.org.uk
http://www.badgertrust.org.uk
▲ Registered Charity
○ *K, *V; to develop & support a network of badger protection groups in the UK; to campaign for the protection of badgers & against persecution, including snares
Gp Badgers & TB; Badgers & roads; Badgers' rehabilitation & welfare
● Conf - Mtgs - Inf
M 80 groups
¶ NL - 2. AR.
Report of Annual Conference - 1.
Occasional papers & guidance notes - irreg; ftm.
× 2005 National Federation of Badger Groups

Badminton Association of England
since 2006 **Badminton England**

Badminton England 1893
NR National Badminton Centre, MILTON KEYNES, Bucks, MK8 9LA. (hq)
01908 268400
http://www.badmintonengland.co.uk
Chief Exec: Adrian Christy
▲ Company Limited by Guarantee
Br 41 assns
○ *S; the governing body for the game of Badminton in England, the Channel Islands and the Isle of Man
Gp Badminton Umpires Association; English Schools' Badminton Association; Regional coaching scheme
● Conf - Mtgs - ET - Exam - Exhib - Comp - Stat - Inf - VE - LG
< Intl Badminton Fedn; Eur Badminton U
M 45,000 i, 2,000 clubs
¶ Badminton Magazine - 4. Coaches Register - 4.
ESBA Post - 10. Ybk. AR & Accounts.
× 2006 Badminton Association of England

Badminton Ireland   (BI)   1899
IRL   Baldoyle Badminton Centre, Baldoyle Industrial Estate,
          Grange Rd, DUBLIN 13, Republic of Ireland.   (hq)
          353 (1) 839 3028
          http://www.badmintonireland.com
          Chmn: Ronan Rooney
▲   Un-incorporated Society
○   *S; national body responsible for the administration of the sport
          in the 32 counties of Ireland
●   Conf - Mtgs - ET - Exhib - Comp - Stat - Inf - LG
<   Intl Badminton Fedn; Eur Badminton U
M   5,100 i & clubs
¶   Handbook - 1; ftm.
×   Badminton Union Ireland

Badminton Umpires Association
      a group of **Badminton England**

Badminton Union of Ireland
      see **Badminton Ireland**

BadmintonScotland
      the trading name of the **Scottish Badminton Union**

Bagot Goat Society   1988
NR   Pen-Twyn, Llangenny, CRICKHOWELL, Powys, NP8 1HD.
          01873 810547   fax 01873 810547
          email info@bagotgoats.co.uk
          http://www.bagotgoats.co.uk
          Sec: Mrs Rosemary Kent
○   *B

Bagpipe Society   1985
NR   11 Queens Place, OTLEY, W Yorks, LS21 3HY.   (mem/sp)
          email bagpipes@snozz.com
          http://www.bagpipesociety.org.uk
          Mem Sec: Michael Ross
▲   Un-incorporated Society
○   *D; to promote the playing & music of bagpipes, including
          English, Scottish, French, Spanish & Balkan bagpipes
●   Workshops
M   250 i, UK / 100 i, o'seas
¶   Chanter - 4; ftm, £3 on request nm.

Bahrain Society   1972
■   Manor Cottage, Bredon, TEWKESBURY, Glos, GL20 7EG.
          (hsp)
          01684 772293
          http://www.bahrainsociety.com
          Hon Sec: H V Whittingham
▲   Un-incorporated Society
○   *X; to promote friendship & close understanding between
          Bahrainis & British citizens
●   Mtgs - VE - LG
M   380 i, 4 f, 1 embassy
¶   NL - irreg; free.

Bakers, Food & Allied Workers Union   (BFAWU)   1849
NR   Stanborough House, Great North Rd, Stanborough,
          WELWYN GARDEN CITY, Herts, AL8 7TA.   (hq)
          01707 260150   fax 01707 261570
          email info@bfawu.org   http://www.bfawu.org
          Gen Sec: Ronnie Draper
Br   7
○   *U
<   TUC
M   29,325 i, UK / 1,025 i, o'seas
¶   Foodworker - 4; ftm.

Balint Society   1969
■   Tollgate Medical Centre, 220 Tollgate Rd, LONDON, E6 5JS.
          (hsb)
          020 7473 9399   fax 020 7473 9388
          email david.watt@gp-f84093.nhs.uk
          http://www.balint.co.uk
          Hon Sec: Dr David E Watt
▲   Registered Charity
○   *L; an organisation of general practitioners seeking to promote
          the study of the healer-patient relationship, particularly in
          general practice, as first investigated by the psychoanalyst
          Dr Michael Balint
●   Conf - Mtgs - ET - Res - Comp - SG
<   Intl Balint Fedn
>   Assn Psychosexual Nursing
M   140 i, UK / 50 i, o'seas
¶   Jnl - 1; ftm, £8 nm.

Ball & Roller Bearing Manufacturers Association   (BRBMA)
■   35 Calthorpe Rd, Edgbaston, BIRMINGHAM, B15 1TS.   (asa)
          0121-454 4141   fax 0121-207 7002
          email info@brbma.org   http://www.brbma.org
          Sec: Sharon Parker
▲   Un-incorporated Society
○   *T; to promote, assist & represent the interests of member ball
          & roller bearing manufacturers
Gp   Standards
●   Conf - Mtgs - Stat - Standards
<   Fedn of Eur Bearing Mfrs Assn (FEBMA)
M   4 f

Balloon Association
      see **NABAS (the Balloon Association)**

Ballroom Dancers Federation   (BDF)   1956
■   4 Magnolia Drive, BANSTEAD, Surrey, SM7 1AW.   (sp)
          Sec: Graham Oswick
▲   Un-incorporated Society
○   *D; competitive ballroom & Latin American dancing

Baltic Air Charter Association   (BACA)   1949
NR   c/o The Baltic Exchange, St Mary Axe, LONDON, EC3A 8BH.
          (hsb)
          020 7623 5501   fax 020 7369 1623
          http://www.baca.org.uk
          Contact: W van der Pol
▲   Un-incorporated Society
○   *T; chartering, sale, purchase & lease of aircraft
●   Conf - Mtgs - Inf
M   86 f, UK / 14 f, o'seas
¶   LM - 1;   AR; both ftm only.   Diaries - 1; £7.50.

Balwen Welsh Mountain Sheep Society (Cymdeithas Defaid
**   Mynydd Cymreig Balwen)   1985**
NR   Swffryd Farm, Harodyrynys, CRUMLIN, Gwent, NP11 5HY.
          (hsp)
          01495 247869
          email enquiries@balwensheepsociety.com
          http://www.balwensheepsociety.com
          Sec: Mrs Anne Groucott
○   *B
●   Mtgs - Exhib - Comp
<   Nat Sheep Assn
M   150 i

Bamboo Society   1985
NR   Chapel House, Brough Park, RICHMOND, N Yorks,
      DL10 7PJ.   (mem/sp)
      01748 811452
      email secretary@bamboo-society.org.uk
      http://www.bamboo-society.org.uk
      Mem Sec: Janet Lord,   Sec: Greville Worthington
▲   Un-incorporated Society
○   *H; to study the distribution of bamboo plants & seeds grown in
      the UK
●   Mtgs - ET - VE
<   Eur Bamboo Soc (EBS)
M   163 i, 6 org, UK / 4 i, o'seas
¶   NL - 4; ftm only.

Banbury & District Chamber of Commerce   1947
NR   Colin Sanders Innovation Centre, Mewburn Rd, BANBURY,
      Oxon, OX16 9PA.   (hq)
      01295 817642 (Mon-Fri: 1000-1330)
      fax 01295 8177601
      email bcoc@banburychamber.com
      http://www.banburychamber.com
▲   Company Limited by Guarantee
○   *C; business interests of Banbury & the surrounding area
Gp   Business & professional; Industrial; Retail
●   Mtgs
M   3 i, 150 f, 1 org
¶   NL - 6.   AR.

Bankruptcy Association   1983
NR   FREEPOST LA1118, 4 Johnson Close, LANCASTER, LA1 5BR.
      (hq)
      01524 782713 (Mon-Fri: 1000-1230)
      email johnmcqueen@theba.org.uk
      http://www.theba.org.uk
      Chief Exec: John McQueen
▲   Un-incorporated Society
○   *K, *W; to provide help & advice to bankrupts & debtors; to
      campaign for reform of insolvency legislation
●   Mtgs - Res - Inf - LG
M   c 1,500 i
¶   NL - 3; free.
      Bankruptcy Explained.
      List of books available.

Baptist Historical Society   1908
NR   PO Box 44, 129 Broadway, DIDCOT, Oxon, OX11 8RT.
      (regd/office)
      01235 517700
      email stephen.bhs@dial.pipex.com
      http://www.baptisthistory.org.uk
      Sec: Revd Stephen Copson
▲   Registered Charity
○   *L, *Q; study of Baptist history in the UK
●   Conf - Mtgs - Res - Inf - Lib
M   600 including 150 libraries, churches & colleges
¶   Baptist Quarterly - 4.

Baptist Union of Great Britain   (BU)   1812
NR   PO Box 44, 129 Broadway, DIDCOT, Oxon, OX11 8RT.   (hq)
      01235 517700   fax 01235 517715
      http://www.baptist.org.uk
      Gen Sec: Rev Jonathan Edwards
○   *R
Gp   Christian education; Christian missionary; Current affairs;
      Pensions; Sociological; Theological; Trusts & property;
      Women; Young people
●   Conf - Mtgs - Exhib - SG - Stat - Inf - Lib - VE
<   Baptist Wld Alliance; Free Church Federal Coun; Conf of Eur
      Churches; Eur Baptist Fedn; Coun of Churches for Britain &
      Ireland; Churches Together in England
M   c 140,000 i in 2,000 churches, 6 theological colleges
¶   Baptist Times - 52.
      Baptist Union Directory - 1.   AR - 1.

**Bar Association for Commerce, Finance & Industry   (BACFI)
1965**
NR   PO Box 4352, Edlesborough, DUNSTABLE, Beds, LU6 9EF.
      (mail address)
      01525 222244
○   *L, *P; to represent the interests of members of The Bar who are
      employed in commerce, finance & industry
M   i

**Bar Association for Local Government & the Public Service
(BALGPS)   1945**
■   Chief Legal Officer, Birmingham City Council, Ingleby House,
      11-14 Cannon St, BIRMINGHAM, B2 5EN.   (chmn/treas/b)
      0121-303 9991
      email chairman@balgps.org.uk
      http://www.balgps.org.uk
      Chmn/Treas: M F N Ahmad
▲   Un-incorporated Society
○   *P; for barristers employed in local government & the public
      sector
●   Conf - ET - Inf - LG - Representation on Bar Council
M   c 110 i
¶   NL;   (publications on website).

Bar Entertainment & Dance Association   (BEDA)   2008
NR   5 Waterloo Rd, STOCKPORT, Cheshire, SK1 3BD.
      0161-476 8380
      http://www.beda.org.uk
      Exec Dir: Amy Wright
○   *T; for owners & operators of late licensed property -
      discotheques, clubs, bars, & live music venues, as well as
      suppliers & product manufacturers for the industry
¶   Night.
×   2008 British Entertainment & Discotheque Association
      2011 Noctis

Barbara Pym Society   1994
NR   c/o Eileen Roberts, Development & Alumnae Office, St Hilda's
      College, OXFORD, OX4 1DY.
      01865 276828   fax 01865 276820
      http://www.barbara-pym.org
      Contact: Eileen Roberts
○   *A; for those interested in the life & works of the novelist
      Barbara Mary Crampton Pym (1913-1980)
●   Mtgs
¶   Green Leaves (NL) - 2.

Barbirolli Society   1972
■   2 Cedar Close, UTTOXETER, Staffs, ST14 7NP.   (chmn p)
      01889 564562   fax 01889 564562
      http://www.barbirolli.co.uk
      Hon Chmn: Miss R P Pickering
▲   Registered Charity
○   *D; to advance knowledge, understanding & appreciation of
      music in general & of the work of Sir John Barbirolli in
      particular
M   400 i, UK / 50 i, o'seas
¶   Jnl - 2;   NL - irreg; both ftm only.

Barema   (BAREMA)   1977
■   The Stables, Sugworth Lane, RADLEY, Oxon, OX14 2HX.   (hq)
      01865 736393   fax 01865 736393
      email barema@btinternet.com
      http://www.barema.org.uk
      Chmn: M F Freeman,   Sec: Harrie Cooke
▲   Company Limited by Guarantee
○   *T: to promote the interests of suppliers to the NHS/private
      sector for anaesthetic & respiratory products
●   Mtgs - Inf - LG
<   Eur Med Device Tr Assn (EUROM VI); Assn of Brit Health Care
      Inds (ABHI)
M   31 f
¶   Barema Hbk - updated; ftm, £10 nm.

© CBD Research Ltd · Beckenham · BR3 5JS · Tel 020 8650 7745 · E-mail cbd@cbdresearch.com · www.cbdresearch.com

Barge Association
see **DBA - the Barge Association**

Barking & Dagenham Chamber of Commerce   1995
NR   Roycraft House (ground floor), 15 Linton Rd, BARKING, Essex,
    IG11 8HE.   (hq)
    020 8591 6966
▲   Company Limited by Guarantee
○   *C
<   London Cham Comm & Ind
M   f

Barn Owl Conservation Network
a group of the **Hawk & Owl Trust**

Barnsley & Rotherham Chamber of Commerce   2006
NR   Innovation Centre, Innovation Way, Wilthorpe, BARNSLEY,
    S Yorks, S75 1JL.   (hq)
    0844 414 5100   fax 0844 846 5102
    email info@brchamber.co.uk
    http://www.brchamber.co.uk
    2 Genesis Park, Sheffield Rd, Templeborough,
    ROTHERHAM, S Yorks, S60 1DX.
    Exec Dir: Andrew Denniff
▲   Company Limited by Guarantee
○   *C
<   Brit Chams Comm
M   f

BaseballSoftballUK   (BSUK)   1890
NR   Ariel House (5th floor), 74A Charlotte St, LONDON,
    W1T 4QJ.   (hq)
    020 7453 7055   fax 020 7453 7007
    email info@baseballsoftballuk.com
    http://www.baseballsoftballuk.com
    Chief Operations Dir: John Boyd
▲   Company Limited by Guarantee
○   *S; to promote the games of Baseball & Softball in Britain
Gp   Scorers; Umpires; Coaching; Old Timers; Players
●   Conf - Mtgs - ET - Comp - Stat - Inf - PL
<   Brit Olympic Assn (BOA); Intl Baseball Assn (IBA); Confedn of
    Eur Amat Baseball; CCPR
M   c 1,500 i, 50 teams (baseball); c 3,000 i, 240 teams (softball)
¶   Baseball & Softball Bulletins - 12;
    Information booklets; all free.

Basketball Ireland   1945
IRL   National Basketball Arena, Tymon Park, Tallaght, DUBLIN 24,
    Republic of Ireland.
    353 (1) 459 0211   fax 353 (1) 459 0212
    email info@basketballireland.ie
    http://www.basketballireland.ie
    Chief Exec: Debbie Massey
○   *S

Basketball Scotland Ltd   1947
NR   Caledonia House, South Gyle, EDINBURGH, EH12 9DQ.   (hq)
    0131-317 7260   fax 0131-317 7489
    email enquiries@basketball-scotland.com
    http://www.basketball-scotland.com
    Chief Exec: Kevin Pringle
▲   Company Limited by Guarantee
○   *S; to develop, promote & facilitate the playing of basketball; to
    encourage interest in the sport in Scotland

BasketballWales   (BW)   1956
NR   c/o Welsh Institute for Sport, Sophia Gardens, CARDIFF,
    CF11 9SW.   (hq)
    Chmn: Ieuan Jones (01656 861982)
○   *S; governing body for basketball in Wales
✕   Basketball Association of Wales

Basketmaker's Association   (BA)   1975
■   64 Lakes Lane, Newport Pagnell, MILTON KEYNES, Bucks,
    MK16 8HR.   (hsp)
    0845 201 1936
    email honsec@basketassoc.org
    http://www.basketassoc.org
    Hon Sec: Ruth Salter
○   *T; to promote the knowledge of basketry, chairseating & allied
    crafts, their making, study, collecting, teaching & use
●   ET - Exam - Exhib - Inf - PL
M   800 i, UK / 100 i, o'seas
¶   NL - 4; ftm, £20 nm.

Basking Shark Society
has closed

**BASO ~ the Association for Cancer Surgery   (BASO-ACS)
1973**
■   at the Royal College of Surgeons, 35-43 Lincoln's Inn Fields,
    LONDON, WC2A 3PE.   (hq)
    020 7405 5612   fax 020 7404 6574
    email lucydavies@baso.org.uk   http://www.baso.org.uk
    Hon Sec: Zenon Rayter
▲   Registered Charity
○   *P; to advance the practice of surgical oncology for surgeons
    involved with cancer
Gp   Association of Breast Surgery at BASO
●   Conf - Mtgs - ET
M   740 i, UK / 20 i, o'seas
¶   European Jnl of Surgical Oncology - 6; ftm.
    Note: this organisation deals with enquiries from professional
    members ONLY & does not answer queries from the general
    public.

Bat Conservation Trust   (BCT)   1990
NR   Unit 2 / 15 Cloisters House, 8 Battersea Park Rd, LONDON,
    SW8 4BG.   (hq)
    020 7627 2629
    email enquiries@bats.org.uk   http://www.bats.org.uk
    Chief Exec: Julia Hanmer
▲   Company Limited by Guarantee; Registered Charity
○   *K; the conservation of bats & their habitats; to stop further
    declines in populations & aid the recovery of threatened
    species
●   Conf - ET - Res - Exhib
    Helpline: 0845 130 0228
M   c 4,000 i in 90 gps
¶   Bat News - 4;   Young Batworker - 4;
    Bat Monitoring Post - 4; all ftm.
    Books & educational leaflets.

Bates Association for Vision Education   (BAVE)   1989
NR   95 Brodrick Rd, EASTBOURNE, E Sussex, BN22 9NY.   (hsp)
    0800 055 6130
    email info@seeing.org   http://www.seeing.org
▲   Un-incorporated Society
○   *P; to advance the knowledge & practice of the methods of
    visual re-education developed by William H Bates
●   Mtgs - ET
M   20 i
    (Sub: £100)

Bath Chamber of Commerce   1902
■   Trimbridge House, Trim St, BATH, Somerset, BA1 2DP.   (hq)
    01275 333128
    email info@bathchamber.co.uk
    http://www.businesswest.co.uk
    Exec Dir: Ian Bell
▲   Company Limited by Guarantee
○   *C
<   GWE Business West Ltd
    Note: trades as Bath Chamber of Commerce & Initiative

Bath & West
>short name of the **Royal Bath & West of England Society**

Bathroom Manufacturers Association   (BMA)   2001
NR   Innovation Centre 1, Keele Science & Business Park,
>NEWCASTLE-UNDER-LYME, Staffs, ST5 5NB.   (hq)
>01782 631619   fax 01782 630155
>email info@bathroom-association.org.uk
>http://www.bathroom-association.org
>Chief Exec: Yvonne Orgill

▲   Un-incorporated Society
○   *T; interests of bathroom manufacturers trading in the UK
<   Construction Products Assn
M   56 f

Batik Guild   1986
NR   6 Grove House, Huntingdon Rd, REDHILL, Surrey, RH1 1HP.
>(hsp)
>01737 213274
>email secretary@batikguild.org.uk
>http://www.batikguild.org.uk
>Sec: Sue Cowell

○   *G; for professional artists, amateur artists, teachers, students &
>those that simply enjoy doing batik
●   Exhib
M   200 i
¶   NL - 3.

Batten Disease Family Association   (BDFA)   1998
■   PO Box 504, FLEET, Hants, GU51 9GE.   (mail/address)
>01252 416110
>http://www.bdfa-uk.org.uk
>Mgr: Andrea West

▲   Registered Charity
○   *M, *W; a supportive, informative national networking
>organisation for the families, carers & professionals, giving
>care to children & adults with Batten Disease; to promote
>awareness of, & research into, the disease
●   Conf - ET - Res - Direct family liaison
<   Batten Disease Support & Res Assn (BDSRA); GOLD; GIG;
>CLIMB
M   c 200 i, associates
¶   NL - 2; ftm.   AR.

Battery Vehicle Society   (BVS)   1973
■   Peter Croft, Sunbank Lane, ALTRINCHAM, Cheshire,
>WA15 0PS   (chmn/p)
>0845 094 2173
>http://www.batteryvehiclesociety.org.uk
>Chmn: Mary Perkins

▲   Un-incorporated Society
Br   3
○   *K; the exchange of information on battery-powered vehicles
●   Mtgs - Exhib - Comp - Inf - Lib - VE
>01874 730320 (for road vehicle coordinator & competitions)
<   Transport Trust
M   361 i, UK / 20 i, o'seas
¶   Battery Vehicle Review - 6; ftm, £12 yr nm (subscription).

Battle of Britain Historical Society
NR   Greenfields, Gunthorpe, MELTON CONSTABLE, Norfolk,
>NR24 2NS.
>0845 130 0588   fax 01263 861483
>email billatBOBHS@aol.com
>http://www.battleofbritain1940.net
>Chief Exec: Bill Bond

▲   Registered Charity
○   *L; 'education of the young regarding the Battle of Britain'
●   Conf - Mtgs - ET
M   c 1,500 i
¶   Scramble (NL) - 6.
>Battle of Britain Remembered - 1.

Battlefields Trust   1993
NR   60 Seymour Rd, ST ALBANS, Herts, AL3 5HW.   (coor/p)
>01727 831413
>email nationalcoordinator@battlefieldtrust.com
>http://www.battlefieldstrust.com
>Coordinator: Peter Burley

▲   Company Limited by Guarantee; Registered Charity
○   *K; preservation, interpretation & presentation of battlefields
>worldwide
●   Conf - ET - Res - Inf - VE
M   380 i, 5 f, 15 org, UK / 10 i, o'seas
¶   NL - 4; ftm only.

BCS, the Chartered Institute for IT   (BCS)   1957
NR   North Star House (Block D 1st floor), North Star Avenue,
>SWINDON, Wilts, SN2 1FA.   (hq)
>01793 417417
>http://www.bcs.org.uk

▲   Registered Charity
○   *P; 'to promote wider social and economic progress through
>the advancement of information technology science and
>practice'
●   Conf - Mtgs - ET - Exam - Comp - Lib
M   70,000 i
×   2008-09 British Computer Society
>Note: 'is the only Chartered Engineering Institution for
>Information Systems Engineering'

Bead Society of Great Britain   (BSGB)   1989
■   1 Casburn Lane, Burwell, CAMBRIDGE, CB25 0ED.
>(memsec/p)
>01638 742024   fax 01638 742024
>email bead.society@ntlworld.com
>http://www.beadsociety.org.uk
>Mem Sec: Dr Carole Morris

▲   Un-incorporated Society
○   *G; for all interested, either privately or professionally, in beads
>ancient & modern, of all shapes, sizes, materials & colours,
>their techniques of manufacture & their application
●   Mtgs - Exhib - Workshops - Annual fair
M   800 i, UK / 50 i, o'seas
¶   Jnl - 4; ftm only.

BEAMA Capacitor Manufacturers Association
>an association of **BEAMA Ltd**

BEAMA Electric Vehicle Infrastructure Project
>an association of **BEAMA Ltd**

BEAMA Ltd   (BEAMA)   1905
- ■ Westminster Tower, 3 Albert Embankment, LONDON, SE1 7SL.   (hq)
  020 7793 3000   fax 020 7793 3003
  email info@beama.org.uk   http://www.beama.org.uk
  Chief Exec: Dr Howard Porter
- ○ *N, *T; the national grouping of trade associations serving the electrotechnical industries of the United Kingdom
- Gp Energy sector:
  The Association of Controls Manufacturers (TACMA)
  BEAMA Smart Metering Association (BSMA)
  Domestic Heat Pump Association
  Domestic Water Treatment Association DWTA)
  The Electric Heating & Ventilation Association (TEHVA)
  Thermostatic Mixing Valve Manufacturers' Association (TMVA)
  Underfloor Heating Manufacturers' Association (UHMA)
  Installation sector:
  Cable Management Products Group (CMPG)
  Cut-out & Feeder Pillar Group (COFPG)
  Engineered Systems Product Group (ESPG)
  Industrial & Single Phase Products Group (ISPPG)
  Power sector:
  Conductor accessories & fittings
  Instrument transformers
  Overhead transmission line contractors
  Power generation contractors
  Principal products (switchgear & transformers)
  Protective gear & relays
  Associations:
  BEAMA Capacitor Manufacturers Association (BCMA)
  BEAMA Electric Vehicle Infrastructure Project (BEVIP)
  Rotating Electrical Machines Association (REMA)
  Smart Housing
  Welding Manufacturers Association (WMA)
  Companies:
  BEAMA Foundation for Disabled People
  BEAMA Recycling Company Ltd
- ● Conf - Exhib - Stat - LG
- < Construction Products Assn
- M [see groups above]
- ¶ BEAMA Bulletin - 4; ftm only.   AR; free.

BEAMA Smart Metering Association
  an association of **BEAMA Ltd**

Bean Curd & Tofu Canners & Preservers Group   1976
- ■ 32 Coombe End, CROWBOROUGH, E Sussex, TN6 1NH. (mail address)
- ○ *T
- Gp Freeze drying
- ● Conf - Mtgs - Stat - LG
- M 17 f
- ¶ NL; ftm only.

Beat
  working name of the **Eating Disorders Association**

Beatrix Potter Society   1980
- NR The Lodge, Salisbury Avenue, HARPENDEN, Herts, AL5 2PS. (admin/p)
  01582 769755
- ▲ Registered Charity
- ○ *L; to promote the study & appreciation of the life & works of Beatrix Potter (1866-1943) author, artist, diarist, farmer & conservationist
- M i
- ¶ NL - 4.   LM - 1.   Books.

Beaumont Society   (BS)   1966
- ■ 27 Old Gloucester St, LONDON, WC1N 3XX.   (mail address)
  01582 412220
  email enquiries@beaumontsociety.org.uk
  http://www.beaumontsociety.org.uk
  Pres: Shirley Keel
- ○ *W; self-help group for those that cross-dress, or who are transsexual; support for partners & families
- Gp Transvestite; Transsexual
- ● Conf - Mtgs - ET - Res - Lib - VE
- < Beaumont Trust
- M 852 i, UK / 22 i, o'seas
- ¶ Beaumont Magazine - 4; ftm.

Beauty Companies Association   (BCA)   2010
- NR 2 Old College Court, 29 Priory St, WARE, Herts, SG12 0DE. (asa)
  0844 482 7275   fax 0845 612 2061
  email info@beautycosassn.com   http://www.thebca.co
- ○ *T; to provide an influential & coherent voice of the professional beauty industry
- M 12 f

Beckford Society   1995
- ■ The Timber Cottage, Crockerton, WARMINSTER, Wilts, BA12 8AX.   (hsp)
  01985 213195
  email sidney.blackmore@btinternet.com
  Hon Sec: Sidney Blackmore
- ▲ Un-incorporated Society
- ○ *A; to promote interest in the life & work of William Beckford, writer & art collector (1760-1844)
- ● Conf - Mtgs - SG - VE
- M 151 i, 5 f, UK / 101 i, o'seas
- ¶ The Beckford Jnl - 1; ftm, £10 nm.   NL - 2; ftm only.

Beckwith-Wiedemann Support Group   (BWS Support)   1987
- ■ The Drum & Monkey, HAZELBURY BRYAN, Dorset, DT10 2EE. (hsp)
  01258 817573
  email rbaker5165@aol.com
  http://www.bws-support.org.uk
  Co-ordinator: Robert Baker
- ▲ Un-incorporated Society
- ○ *W; to provide information for parents of Beckwith Syndrome children - an overgrowth disorder present at birth
- ● Inf
- < Genetic Alliance; Contact-a-Family
- M 180 i, UK / 20 i, o'seas
- ¶ Fact sheets: What is BWS; Genetics of BWS; both free.

Bedford Architectural, Archaeological & Local History Society 2008
- NR 7 Lely Close, BEDFORD, MK41 7LS.   (sp)
  01234 365095
  Sec: Sylvia Woods
- ▲ Registered Charity
- ○ *A
- ● Mtgs -
- M i
  (Sub: £10-£12)
- × 2008 (Bedford Archaeological & Local History Society (Bedford Society

Bedfordshire Historical Record Society   (BHRS)   1912
- ■ 48 St Augustine's Rd, BEDFORD, MK40 2ND.   (hsp)
  - 01234 309548
  - email rsmart@ntlworld.com
  - http://www.bedfordshirehrs.org.uk
  - Hon Sec: Dr Richard Smart
- ▲ Company Limited by Guarantee; Registered Charity
- ○ *L; the publication of sources & monographs relating to the history of Bedfordshire
- ● Res
- M 150 i, 50 org, UK / 50 i, 50 org, o'seas
- ¶ Vauxhall Motors & the Luton Economy 1900-2002 - 1; £12 m, £25 nm.
  - The Bousfield Diaries; £12 m, £25 nm.

Bedfordshire & Luton Chamber of Commerce   1998
- NR Business Competitiveness Centre, Kimpton Rd, LUTON, Beds, LU2 0SX.
  - 01582 522448   fax 01582 522450
  - email info@chamber-business.com
  - http://www.chamber-business.com
- ▲ Company Limited by Guarantee
- ○ *C
- ✕ 2010 The Chamber

Bee Farmers Association of the United Kingdom   (BFA)
- NR 8 Olivers Close, West Totton, SOUTHAMPTON, Hants, SO40 8FH.   (hsp/b)
  - 023 8090 7850
  - http://www.beefarmers.co.uk
  - Gen Sec: John Howat
- ○ *P, *T
- M i

Bee Improvement & Bee Breeders Association   (BIBBA)   1964
- NR 75 Newhall Rd, DONCASTER, S Yorks, DN3 1QQ.   (me/sp)
  - http://www.bibba.com
  - Mem Sec: David Allen
- ▲ Registered Charity
- ○ *B, *G; conservation, restoration, study, selection & improvement of our native honeybees of GB & Ireland
- ● Conf - Mtgs - Inf
- M i

Beef Shorthorn Cattle Society   1936
- ■ 4th Street, Stoneleigh Park, KENILWORTH, Warks, CV8 2LG.   (hq)
  - 024 7669 6549   fax 024 7669 6729
  - email shorthorn@shorthorn.co.uk
  - http://www.shorthorn.co.uk
  - Sec: Frank Milnes
- ▲ Registered Charity
- ○ *B
- ● Conf - Mtgs - Res - Exhib - Comp - SG - Stat - Expt - Inf - PL - VE - Empl
- < Nat Beef Assn
- M 330 i, UK / 30 i, o'seas
- ¶ Shorthorn Jnl - 1.   Coates Herd Book - 1.

Bees, Wasps & Ants Recording Society   (BWARS)
- NR Nightingales, Haslemere Rd, MILFORD, Surrey, GU8 5BN.   (memsec/treas)
  - 01483 421154
  - email david@tiphia.eu   http://www.bwars.com
  - Mem Sec & Treas: David Baldock
- ○ *G; for all interested in identifying bees & wasps - all enquiries should be addressed to the BWARS Forum & NOT to individual officers
  - Please note all questions relating to honeybees should be addressed to the British Beekeepers Association
- M c 450 i
  - Note: Operates under the ægis of the UK Biological Records Centre.

Behçet's Syndrome Society   1983
- ■ 8 Abbey Gardens, EVESHAM, Worcs, WR11 4SP.   (dir/p)
  - 01386 47920
  - email info@behcetsdisease.org.uk
  - http://www.behcets.org.uk
  - Dir: Chris Phillips
- ▲ Registered Charity
- ○ *M, *W; a charity providing a contact support network, information & financial aid for sufferers of the disease (a vasculitic disorder with orogenital ulceration, uveitis & arthritis)
- ● Inf
- < Longterm Medical Conditions Alliance (LMCA); UK Rare Diseases Assn; Nat Coun for Voluntary Orgs
- M 1,200 i, UK / 100 i, o'seas
- ¶ NL - 2; ftm, £2.50 nm.

Being Alongside
   the operating name of the **Association of Pastoral Care in Mental Health**

Belgian-Luxembourg Chamber of Commerce in Great Britain (BLCC)
- ■ Westwood House, Annie Med Lane, South Cave, BROUGH, North Humbersde, HU15 2HG.
  - 020 7127 4282   fax 0870 429 2148
  - email info@blcc.co.uk   http://www.blcc.co.uk
  - Chief Exec: Michel Van Hoonacker
- ▲ Company Limited by Guarantee
- ○ *C; to help Belgian & Luxembourg companies exporting to the UK, & British companies wishing to do business with Belgian & Luxembourg exporters
- ● Conf - Mtgs - ET - Res - Exhib - Comp - SG - Expt - Inf - VE - Empl - LG
- < Coun of Foreign Chams Comm; Belgian Fedn of Chams Comm
- M 12 i, 68 f, UK / 49 f, o'seas
- ¶ BELUX (NL) - 3; ftm.

Belted Galloway Cattle Society   1922
- NR Rock Midstead, ALNWICK, Northumberland, NE66 2TH.   (hsp)
  - 07891 245870   fax 01665 579326
  - email info@beltedgalloways.co.uk
  - http://www.beltedgalloways.co.uk
  - Sec: Ian Sutherland
- ○ *B
- < Nat Beef Assn
- M i

Beltex Sheep Society   1989
- ■ Shepherds View, Barras, KIRKBY STEPHEN, Cumbria, CA17 4ES.   (hsp)
  - 01768 341124   fax 01768 341124
  - email info@beltex.co.uk   http://www.beltex.co.uk
  - Sec: Rachel Buckle
- ▲ Company Limited by Guarantee; Registered Charity
- ○ *B; to promote the Beltex breed of sheep
- ● Mtgs - ET - Res
- < Nat Sheep Assn
- M 465 i
- ¶ Ybk - 1;   NL - 4; both free.

Benesh Institute
   a group of the **Royal Academy of Dance**

© CBD Research Ltd · Beckenham · BR3 5JS · Tel 020 8650 7745 · E-mail cbd@cbdresearch.com · www.cbdresearch.com

Bereavement Services Association (BSA) 2005
- ■ PO Box 105, Bereavement Care, Addenbrooke's Hospital, CAMBRIDGE, CB2 2QQ. (hsb)
  01223 217769
  Vice-Chmn: Revd Dr Derek Fraser,   Dr Dawn Chaplin
- ▲ Un-incorporated Society
- ○ *W; to provide a national network for all those who work in providing bereavement services, primarily within the NHS
- ● Conf - ET - LG
- M 100 i, 10 org
- ¶ NL - 3.

Berkshire Archaeological Society 1871
- ■ 19 Challenor Close, WOKINGHAM, Berks, RG40 4UJ.   (hsp)
  0118-973 2882
  email andrew_hutt@talktalk.net
  http://www.berksarch.co.uk
  Hon Sec: Dr Andrew Hutt
- ▲ Registered Charity
- ○ *L; to advance the education of the public in the fields of archaeology & history in the past & present County of Berkshire
- ● Conf - Mtgs - Res - Lib - VE
- M 100 i, 15 f
  (Sub: £10 i, £15 f)
- ¶ Berkshire Archaeological Jnl - irreg; ftm, £15 nm.
  NL - 4.

Berkshire Archaeology Research Group (BARG) 1958
- ■ 48 Hawkesbury Drive, Calcot, READING, Berks, RG31 7ZR. (chmn/p)
  0118-942 9712
  email mail@barg-online.org   http://www.barg-online.org
  Chmn: G C Johnson
- ▲ Un-incorporated Society
- ○ *L; to provide an opportunity for people to partake in the practical investigation, understanding & publication of archaeology in Berkshire
- Gp Archive research; Excavation; Fieldworking; Geophysical surveying; Hedgerow dating; Post-excavation analysis; Site monitoring
- ● Mtgs - ET - Res - Exhib - Inf - Lib - VE
- M 65 i, UK / 1 i, o'seas
- ¶ In the Field (NL) - 4.

Berkshire Pig Breeders Club 1983
- NR Eastbourne, Moss House Lane, Westby-with-Plumpton, PRESTON, Lancs, PR4 3PE. (hsp)
  01772 673245
  http://www.berkshirepigs.org.uk
  Sec: Mrs Tracey Bretherton
- ○ *B; for breeders of the Berkshire pig
- ● mtgs - EXhib - Inf
- M i
- ¶ NL.

Berlioz Society 1952
- NR 450b Lea Bridge Rd, LONDON, E10 7DY.   (hsp)
  020 8359 9122
  email sqing@btinternet.com
  http://www.theberliozsociety.org.uk
  Sec: Simon Jones
- ▲ Registered Charity
- ○ *D; to promote & increase knowledge of the great French composer Hector Berlioz (1803-1869)
- ● Mtgs - Inf
- M 46 i, UK / 66 i, 20 libraries, o'seas
  (Sub: £15, UK)
- ¶ The Bulletin - 3; both ftm only.

Berwickshire Agricultural Association 1885
- ■ The Cottage, Nabdean Farm, PAXTON, Berwickshire, TD15 1SZ. (hsb)
  01289 386412   fax 01289 386852
  email dunsshow@btopenworld.com
  Sec: Natalie Cormack
- ▲ Registered Charity
- ○ *F; to promote the interests of agriculture primarily through the organisation of the Berwickshire County Show
- ● Exhib - Comp
- M 250 i, 75 f
- ¶ Show Schedule & Catalogue.   AR.

Berwickshire Naturalists' Club (BNC) 1831
- ■ c/o The Borough Museum, The Barracks, BERWICK-upon-TWEED, TD15 1DQ. (hq)
  01289 330933
- ▲ Registered Charity
- ○ *L; all matters connected with the natural history & antiquities of Berwickshire & North Northumberland
- ● Mtgs - Res - Exhib - Stat - Inf - Lib - VE
- < Coun Brit Archaeology
- M 360 i, 39 org
- ¶ History of the Berwickshire Naturalists' Club - 1; ftm, £10 nm.

BESA New Educational Technologies Group
  a group of the **British Educational Suppliers Association**

BESA Special Needs Group
  a group of the **British Educational Suppliers Association**

Best Western Dance Academy (BWDA) 1989
- NR PO Box 1848, SHEFFIELD, S Yorks, S6 5YA.   (hq)
  http://www.tulsashuffle.co.uk/bwda/
- ▲ Un-incorporated Society
- ○ *D, *K; to promote Country Western Line & Partner dancing
- ● Mtgs - ET - Exam - Inf
- M 400 i, UK / 6 i, o'seas
- ¶ The Western Dancer Magazine - 6; ftm only.
- ✕ 2001 British Western Dance Association

Betjeman Society 1988
- NR 386 Hurst Rd, BEXLEY, Kent, DA5 3JY.   (mem/sec)
  email johnbetjeman.com/society.html
  Mem Sec: Martin H Revill
- ▲ Un-incorporated Society
- Br 7
- ○ *A; 'to advance the education of the public in the works of Sir John Betjeman by promoting the knowledge, appreciation & study of his life & works'
- ● Mtgs - ET - Res - Exhib - VE
- M 878 i, 4 f, UK / 17 i, 2 f, o'seas
- ¶ The Betjemanian (Jnl) - 1.

Better Brickwork Alliance (BBA) 1999
- NR The Building Centre, 26 Store St, LONDON, WC1E 7BT.   (hsb)
  020 7323 7030   fax 020 7580 3795
  email brick@brick.org.uk
  Sec: Michael Driver
- ▲ Un-incorporated Society
- ○ *N, *T; an alliance of organisations interested in the development of all aspects of masonry, with special interest in the training / recruitment of craftspeople
- ● Mtgs - ET
- M 15 f

Better Off Out
  a campaign (to leave the EU) of the **Freedom Association**

Beverage Council of Ireland

IRL Unit 19a Naas Road Business Park, DUBLIN 12, Republic of
Ireland.
353 (1) 460 0811   fax 353 (1) 460 0814
email bci@esatlink.com
Dir: Bernard J Murphy
○ *T; interests of producers & distributors of non-alcoholic
beverages

Beverage Standards Association   (BSA)   1996

■ PO Box 6244, READING, Berks, RG19 9HR.   (hq)
01364 645761
http://www.beveragestandardsassociation.com
Chmn: Martyn Herriot
○ *T
× 2009 Beverage Service Association

Bewick Society   1985

■ c/o The Hancock Museum, NEWCASTLE upon TYNE,
NE2 4PT.   (hsb)
email bewick.society@ncl.ac.uk
http://www.bewicksociety.org
Hon Mem Sec: Mrs J Holmes
▲ Un-incorporated Society
○ *L; to study the life & work of Thomas Bewick (naturalist &
wood engraver, 1753-1828); to encourage wood engraving
● Mtgs - VE
M 140 i, UK / 10 i, o'seas
¶ Cherryburn Times - 2; ftm only.

BFM Ltd (British Furniture Manufacturers)   (BFM)   1943

NR Wycombe House, 9 Amersham Hill, HIGH WYCOMBE, Bucks,
HP13 6NR.   (hq)
01494 523021   fax 01494 474270
email info@bfm.org.uk   http://www.bfm.org.uk
Managing Dir: Roger Mason
▲ Company Limited by Guarantee
○ *T; the manufacture, sale & export of furniture
● ET - Res - Exhib - Stat - Expt - Inf - Empl - LG
M 378 f
¶ Export Directory - 1;   UK Directory of Members - 1; both free.

Biblical Creation Society   (BCS)   1976

■ PO Box 22, RUGBY, Warks, CV22 7SY.   (mail address)
01788 810633
http://www.biblicalcreation.org.uk
▲ Registered Charity (Scotland)
○ *L, *R; a Christian society that advances & defends biblical
teaching on creation; to think through issues related to
origins from a biblical & scientific standpoint; to challenge
Christians who have accepted the evolutionary theory
● Mtgs - ET - Lectures
M c 500 i
¶ Origins (Jnl) - 2.
The Creation Manifesto (a systematic overview of the
implications of the Genesis account of the Creation).

Bibliographical Society   1892

■ c/o Institute of English Studies, University of London,
Senate House, Malet St, LONDON, WC1E 7HU.   (hsb)
020 7862 8679
email admin@bibsoc.org.uk   http://www.bibsoc.org.uk
Sec: Margaret Ford
▲ Registered Charity
○ *L; promotion of study & research of historical, analytical,
descriptive & textual bibliography; the history of the book
(printing, publishing, collecting & bookbinding)
● Mtgs - Res - Lib - Awards grants to support bibliographical
research
M 400 i, 100 f, UK / 400 i, 100 f, o'seas
¶ The Library - 4; £33 m.   AR; ftm.
Monographs - irreg; prices vary.

Bicycle Association of Great Britain Ltd   1973

NR 3 The Quadrant, COVENTRY, Warks, CV1 2DY.   (hq)
024 7655 3838
email office@ba-gb.com
Sec: Mrs Patricia Morris
○ *T
Gp Mfrs: Bicycles, components & accessories; Concessionaires
(bicycles); Ancillary members
● Mtgs - Exhib - Stat - LG
< Comité de Liaison des Fabricants de Pièces et Equipements de
Deux-Roues (COLIPED)
M 50 f
¶ AR.   LM.

Big Brother Watch   2009

NR 55 Tufton St, LONDON, SW1P 3QL.
020 7340 6030
email info@bigbrotherwatch.org.uk
http://www.bigbrotherwatch.org.uk
Chief Exec: Matthew Elliott
○ *K; to fight intrusion on privacy & to protect civil liberties
● Campaigning
M i
¶ NL.

Bingo Association   (BAGB)   1998

NR Lexham House, 75 High St North, DUNSTABLE, Beds,
LU6 1JF.   (hq)
01582 860921   fax 01582 860925
email info@bingo-association.co.uk
http://www.bingo-association.co.uk
▲ Un-incorporated Society
○ *T; to promote & develop the interests of the licensed bingo
industry; to represent members' interests in contact with third
parties
M 77 f

Biochemical Society   1911

NR Charles Darwin House, 12 Roger St, LONDON, WC1N 2JU.
(hq)
020 7685 2400   fax 020 7685 2470
email genadmin@biochemistry.org
http://www.biochemistry.org
Chief Exec: Dr Chris Kirk
▲ Registered Charity
Br 2
○ *L; to advance the science of biochemistry in the context of
cellular & molecular life sciences as a seamless continuum
Gp Theme panels: Bioenergetics & metabolism, Biotechnology &
informatics, Cell biology, Development & disease, Genes,
Molecular structure
● Conf - Mtgs - ET - Res - Exhib - Stat - Inf
< Fedn Eur Biochemical Socs; Intl U Biochemistry
M 6,000 i
¶ Biochemical Jnl - 24.   Clinical Science - 12.
Transactions - 6.   Symposia - 1.
Biotechnology & Applied Biochemistry - 6.
Essays in Biochemistry - 2.

© CBD Research Ltd · Beckenham · BR3 5JS · Tel 020 8650 7745 · E-mail cbd@cbdresearch.com · www.cbdresearch.com

Biodynamic Agricultural Association   (BDAA)   1928
■   Painswick Inn Project, Gloucester St, STROUD, Glos,
    GL5 1QG.   (hq)
    01453 759501   fax 01453 759501
    email office@biodynamic.org.uk
    http://www.biodynamic.org.uk
    Chmn: Sebastian Parsons
▲   Registered Charity
○   *F, *H, *Q; to support, promote & develop biodynamic farming,
    gardening & forestry; part of a worldwide movement inspired
    by the insights of Rudolf Steiner (1861-1925) Austrian
    philosopher, scientist & social reformer
Gp Biodynamic seed; Demeter (organic certification UK6) scheme;
    Training
●   Conf - ET - Exhib - Inf - Lib - LG - Training apprenticeships -
    Res & devt of seeds suited to organic & biodynamic systems
<   Intl Fedn of Organic Agricl Movements (IFOAM);
    Anthroposophical Soc (GB); GM Freeze; Sustain; Agricl Dept
    of the School of Spiritual Science
M   800 i, UK / 50 i, o'seas
¶   Star & Furrow - 2; £4.50.   Newssheet - 4; free.

BioIndustry Association   (BIA)   1985
NR Southside (7th floor), 105 Victoria St, LONDON, SW1E 6QT.
    (hq)
    020 7630 2180   fax 020 7900 2443
    email admin@bioindustry.org
    http://www.bioindustry.org
    Chief Exec: Nigel Gaymond
○   *T; to promote the human health benefits of new bioscience
    technologies, encouraging the commercial success of the
    bioscience industry by focusing on emerging enterprise and
    the related interests of companies with whom such enterprise
    trades
M   f & org

Biological Recording in Scotland   (BRISC)
■   140 Pitcorthie Drive, DUNFERMLINE, Fife, KY11 8BJ.
    (mem/sp)
    http://www.brisc.org.uk
    Mem Sec: Duncan Davidson
▲   Registered Charity
○   *P; to promote best practise in biological recording methods; to
    provide liaison between local records centres
●   Conf - ET - Inf
M   100 i, 30 f
¶   Recorder News - 4.

Biomedical Applications Division
    a group of the **Institute of Materials, Minerals & Mining**

Biosciences Federation
    merged in 2009 with the Institute of Biology to form the **Society of
    Biology**

BiPolar Organisation
    see **MDF - the BiPolar Organisation**

Birdcare Standards Association
NR Market Link, 30 St George's Square, WORCESTER, WR1 1HX.
    01905 726575
    email enquiries@birdcare.org.uk
○   *T; suppliers of bird care products
M   10 f

Birmingham Chamber of Commerce   (BCCI)   1813
NR 75 Harborne Rd, Edgbaston, BIRMINGHAM, B15 3DH.   (hq)
    0121-454 6171   fax 0121-455 8670
    email info@birmingham-chamber.com
    http://www.bci.org.uk
▲   Company Limited by Guarantee
○   *C
●   Conf - Mtgs - ET - Expt - Inf - LG
M   4,000 f

Birmingham Metallurgical Association   (B MET A)   1903
NR c/o School of Metallurgy & Materials, University of Birmingham,
    Edgbaston, BIRMINGHAM, B15 2TT.   (hsb)
    0121 414 5222
    http://www.eng.bham.ac.uk/metalurgy/bmeta.shtml
    Hon Sec: Prof Rex Harris
▲   Company Limited by Guarantee
○   *L; to promote the science & application of engineering
    materials
●   Conf - Mtgs - ET - Comp - VE
<   Inst of Materials (IOM)
M   c 120 i
¶   AR & Accounts; ftm only.

Birmingham & Midland Institute   (BMI)   1854
■   9 Margaret St, BIRMINGHAM, B3 3BS.   (hq)
    0121-236 3591   fax 0121-212 4577
    email admin@bmi.org.uk   http://www.bmi.org.uk
    Admin & Gen Sec: Philip A Fisher
▲   Registered Charity
○   *A, *L; the diffusion & advancement of science, art & literature
Gp Birmingham & Midland Society for Genealogy & History;
    Society for the History of Astronomy
●   Conf - Mtgs - ET - Res - SG - Lib
<   Assn of Indep Libs
M   300 i
¶   BMI Insight - 1; ftm, £3.50 nm.   AR; free.

Birmingham & Midland Society for Genealogy & History
    is a group of the **Birmingham & Midland Institute**

Birmingham Natural History Society   (BNHS)   1858
■   23 Crosbie Rd, Harborne, BIRMINGHAM, B17 9BG.   (hsp)
    0121-427 1010
    http://www.clareh3.webspace.virginmedia.com/bnhs.htm
    Hon Sec: Dr Peter Jarvis
▲   Registered Charity
○   *L; all aspects of natural history
Gp Entomology; Mycology [with the Warwickshire Fungus Survey -
    http://freespace.virgin.net/william.moodie/wfs.htm]
●   Mtgs - Res - Inf - Lib - Supervision of Edgbaston Nature
    Reserve (SSSI)
M   120 i, 4 org
¶   Proceedings - 2 yrly; ftm, £5 nm.   NL - 3; ftm.
    Programmes - 2; ftm.

Birmingham Transport Historical Group   (BTHG)   1963
■   21 The Oaklands, DROITWICH SPA, Worcs, WR9 8AD.   (hsp)
    01905 778243
    Hon Sec: Peter Jaques
▲   Un-incorporated Society
○   *G; research into public passenger transport in Birmingham &
    the West Midlands from its commencement to the present
    day
●   Mtgs - Res - Inf
M   21 i, 1 org
¶   A Comprehensive History - vol 1.   Various booklets.

**Birmingham & Warwickshire Archaeological Society   (BWAS)
1870**
NR c/o Birmingham & Midland Institute, 3 Margaret St,
    BIRMINGHAM, B3 3BS.   (hq)
    http://www.birminghamandwarwickshirearchaeological
    society.co.uk
    Hon Sec: Mick Bridgman
▲   Registered Charity
○   *L; study of archaeology in Birmingham, Warwickshire & West
    Midlands
Gp Field
●   Mtgs - VE - Field study - Publishing
<   Birmingham & Midland Inst
M   c 150 i, c 75 org
¶   Transactions - 1; price varies nm.   NL;   AR; all ftm only.

Birth Trauma Association   (BTA)   2004
- ■   PO Box 671, IPSWICH, Suffolk, IP1 9AT.   (mail/address)
     http://www.birthtraumaassociation.org.uk
     Sec: Maureen Treadwell,   Chmn: Julie Orford
- ▲   Company Limited by Guarantee; Registered Charity
- ○   *W; a non-professional organisation (of mothers) supporting
     women suffering Post Natal Post Traumatic Stress Disorder, or
     birth trauma; the only organisation in the UK which deals
     solely & specifically with this issue
- ●   Conf - ET - Res - Inf - LG
- M   800 i
- ¶   BTA NL - 2/3 (available on web:
     www.birthtraumaassociation.org.uk/publications.htm)

Birthmark Support Group   (BSG)   1998
- ■   BM The Birthmark Support Group, LONDON, WC1N 3XX.
     (mail/address)
     0845 045 4700
     email info@birthmarksupportgroup.org.uk
     http://www.birthmarksupportgroup.org.uk
     Sec: Lindsay Weinstein
- ▲   Registered Charity
- ○   *G; to provide information & advice to people affected by
     birthmarks
- Gp Sub-Groups:
     Teenagers (teentalk@birthmarksupportgroup.org.uk)
     Adults (faceittogether@birthmarksupportgroup.org.uk)
- ●   Conf - Res - Fun-days - Support network available to all
- M   voluntary membership
- ¶   NL - 3; free.

BKSTS - the Moving Image Society   (BKSTS)   1933
- NR Pinewood Studios, IVER HEATH, Bucks, SL0 0NH.   (hq)
     01753 656656
     http://www.bksts.com
     Hon Sec: P Rutter
- ▲   Company Limited by Guarantee
- ○   *L; to support those who creatively or technologically are
     involved in the production of moving images & associated
     sound
- M   i, f & org

Black & Asian Studies Association   (BASA)   1992
- ■   Institute of Commonwealth Studies, Room 236, University of
     London, Senate House, Malet Street, LONDON,
     WC1E 7HU.   (hsp)
     email sean.creighton@btinternet.com
     http://www.blackandasianstudies.org/
     Sec: Jonah Albert
- ▲   Un-incorporated Society
- ○   *L; to encourage study, publishing, teaching & research into the
     history of African, Asian & Caribbean peoples in Britain; to
     foster the collection & preservation of archives & artifacts
- Gp Newsletter editorial board
- ●   Conf - Mtgs - EDiscussion forum - Lobbying
- M   i, f & org
- ¶   NL - 3; ftm, £1.25 nm.

Black Country Chamber of Commerce   2001
- NR Chamber of Commerce House, Ward St, WALSALL,
     W Midlands, WS1 2AG.   (hq)
     0845 002 1234   fax 01922 645721
     email info@blackcountrychamber.co.uk
     http://www.blackcountrychamber.co.uk
     Chief Exec: Margaret Corneby
- ▲   Company Limited by Guarantee
- Br Dudley, Sandwell, Walsall, Wolverhampton
- ○   *C
- ●   Mtgs - Expt - Inf - Lib - VE - LG
- M   3,380 f
- ¶   Prosper - 4.   Chamber Directory - 1; ftm.

Black Country Society   (BCS)   1967
- ■   PO Box 71, KINGSWINFORD, W Midlands, DY6 9YN.   (hsb)
     http://www.blackcountrysociety.co.uk
     Hon Sec: Judith Watkin
- ▲   Un-incorporated Society
- Br 4
- ○   *G; to promote interest in the past, present & future of the Black
     Country
- Gp Indl Archaeology Branch
- ●   Mtgs - Res - Exhib - Inf - VE
- <   Civic Trust; Assn Indl Archaeology; Family Hist Soc
- M   c 2,000 i, f & org, UK / 32 i, o'seas
- ¶   The Blackcountryman - 4; ftm, £2.75 each nm.
     Publications list available.

Black Simmental Society   1997
- NR Grove Farm, Felbrigg, NORWICH, Norfolk, NR11 8PL.   (hsb)
     01263 512028   fax 01263 515617
     Sec: Mrs Zoe Hall,   Chmn: Brian Filby
- ▲   Un-incorporated Society
- ○   *B; British Black Simmental cattle
- ●   Mtgs - Res - Expt
- M   i
     (Sub: £20)

Black Welsh Mountain Sheep Breeders' Association   1920
- ■   Strathearn, Ruthwell, DUMFRIES, DG1 4NN.   (hq)
     01387 870653
     email fiona.sloan@blackwelshmountain.org.uk
     http://www.blackwelshmountain.org.uk
     Sec: Fiona Sloan
- ▲   Company Limited by Guarantee; Registered Charity
- ○   *B
- ●   Mtgs - ET - Exhib - Comp - SG - Stat - Inf - LG
- <   Nat Sheep Assn
- M   250 i, UK / 15 i, o'seas
- ¶   NL - 2/3; ftm only.   LM - 1; free.
     Ybk (Flock Book); ftm, £5 nm.

Blackface Sheep Breeders' Association   1901
- NR Woodhead of Mailer, PERTH, PH2 0QA.
     01738 634018   fax 01738 634018
     email aileen@scottish-blackface.co.uk
     http://www.scottish-blackface.co.uk
     Sec: Aileen McFadzean
- ○   *B; incl matters relevant to hill & upland farming
- ●   Mtgs - Exhib - Inf
- <   Nat Sheep Assn
- M   1,600 i
- ¶   Jnl - 1; free.

Blacksmiths Guild
- NR Six Arches, Bridge End, KINGSBRIDGE, Devon, TQ7 4NU.
     (memsec/p)
     email courses@blacksmithsguild.com
     http://www.blacksmithsguild.com
     Mem Sec: Eric White
- ▲   Un-incorporated Society
- ○   *P, *T; to provide training for the traditional & developing skills
     of the blacksmith's craft, & to promote the craft by supporting
     members & providing outlets for their products at many
     shows throughout the country
- ●   Comp - ET - Exhib - Mtgs
- M   i
- ¶   NL.

© CBD Research Ltd · Beckenham · BR3 5JS · Tel 020 8650 7745 · E-mail cbd@cbdresearch.com · www.cbdresearch.com

Bladder & Bowel Foundation   1989
■   SATRA Innovation Park, Rockingham Rd, KETTERING,
     Northants, NN16 9JH.   (hq)
     01536 533255   fax 01536 533240
     http://www.bladderandbowelfoundation
     Communications Mgr: Gill Turton
▲   Company Limited by Guarantee; Registered Charity
○   *G, *K,*W; campaigns for people living with bladder & bowel
     control problems; to raise awareness & improve the
     understanding of continence issues
●   Res - Inf - LG
     Advice Line: 0800 011 4623
¶   E-Newletters.
✕   2008 (June) Incontact

Blair Bell Research Society   (BBRS)   1962
■   c/o RCOG, 27 Sussex Place, LONDON, NW1 4RG.   (hq)
     020 7772 6200
     Sec: Dr F Denison
▲   Registered Charity
○   *P, *Q; to promote research by clinicians & scientists into
     women's health & obstetrics & gynaecology; named after
     William Blair Bell the first president of the Royal College of
     Obstetricians & Gynaecologists
●   Conf - Mtgs - ET - Res - Comp
<   R Coll of Obstetricians & Gynaecologists
M   335 i
     [Sub: £20]
¶   Abstracts (of papers presented at meetings) are published in the
     British Jnl of Obstetrics & Gynaecology - 1; free.

Blake Society at St James's   1986
NR St James's Church, 197 Piccadilly, LONDON, W1J 9LL.
     (mail/address)
     020 7495 5654
     email secretary@blakesociety.org.uk
     http://www.blakesociety.org.uk
     Hon Sec: Dr Keri Davies
▲   Registered Charity
○   *A; to celebrate the life work of William Blake (1757-1827)
     poet, printer, visionary
Gp 250th anniversary celebration
●   Conf - Mtgs - VE
M   300 i, UK / 40 i, o'seas
¶   Blake Jnl - 1; ftm.

BLC, Leather Technology Centre Ltd   (BLC)   1984
NR Leather Trade House, King's Park Rd, Moulton Park,
     NORTHAMPTON, NN3 6JD.   (hq)
     01604 679999
     http://www.blcleathertech.com
▲   Limited Company
○   *Q, *T; servicing leather manufacturing & related industries
<   a subsidiary of BLC Research
M   f & org

BLISS   (BLISS)   1979
NR 9 Holyrood St, London Bridge, LONDON, SE1 2EL.   (hq)
     020 7378 1122   fax 020 7403 0673
     email information@bliss.org.uk   http://www.bliss.org.uk
     Chief Exec: Andy Cole
▲   Company Limited by Guarantee; Registered Charity
Br 40
○   *K, *W; to campaign for improved neonatal services; to support
     nurse training; to support families
Gp Befriending service for parents of babies born too soon, too
     small, too sick
●   Conf - Mtgs - ET - Exhib - SG - Stat - Inf - Lib - PL - Provision of
     specialist equipment - Funds research
     Family support helpline: 0500 618 140
M   1,000 i
¶   Little Bliss - 4; free.   AR - 1.

Blood Pressure Association   2000
NR 60 Cranmer Terrace, LONDON, SW17 0QS.
     020 8772 4994 (0930-1730 Mon-Fri)
     fax 020 8772 4999
     http://www.bpassoc.org.uk
     Exec Dir: Michael Rich
▲   Registered Charity
○   *M, *W; for people whose lives are affected by their blood
     pressure

Blue Albion Cattle Society
     closed 2011

Blue Badge Network   (BBN)   1991
NR 11 Parson's St, DUDLEY, W Midlands, DY1 1JJ.   (hq)
     01384 257001
     http://www.bluebadgenetwork.org
     Admin: Jacquie Russell
▲   Registered Charity
Br 44
○   *W; 'to help disabled people integrate more effectively with
     people in the community at large'
●   Exhib - Inf - LG - Advocacy
M   c 10,500 i
¶   Blue Badge Network NL - 4; ftm.

Bluebell Railway Preservation Society   (BRPS)   1960
NR Sheffield Park Station, UCKFIELD, E Sussex, TN22 3QL.   (hq)
     01825 720800   fax 01825 720804
     Hon Sec: Gavin Bennett
▲   Un-incorporated Society
○   *G; railway preservation & running 'The Bluebell Line' (part of
     the Lewes & E Grinstead Railway)
●   Conf - Mtgs - ET - Exhib - Lib - VE
<   Heritage Rly Assn
M   c 10,000 i
¶   Bluebell News - 4; ftm, £2 nm.

**Bluefaced Leicester Sheep Breeders Association   (BLSBA)
1962**
■   Riverside View, Warwick Rd, CARLISLE, Cumbria, CA1 2BS.
     (2q)
     01228 598022
     email info@blueleicester.co.uk
     http://www.blueleicester.co.uk
     Sec: Helen Carr-Smith
▲   Registered Charity
○   *B
●   Mtgs - Exhib - Inf - VE
<   Nat Sheep Assn
M   c 1,400 i
¶   Looking Ahead - 1; November News - 1; both ftm.
     Flock Book - 1; ftm.

Boarding Schools Association   (BSA)   1966
■   Grosvenor Gardens House, 35-37 Grosvenor Gdns,
     LONDON, SW1W 0BS.   (hq)
     020 7798 1580   fax 020 7798 1581
     email bsa@boarding.org.uk
     http://www.boarding.org.uk
     Nat Dir: Mrs Hilary Moriarty
▲   Company Limited by Guarantee
○   *E; to promote the qualities of boarding education; to
     encourage the highest standards of welfare in boarding
     schools
Gp State Boarding Schools' Association
●   Conf - Mtgs - ET - Res - Inf - LG
M   500 schools, UK / 50 schools, o'seas
¶   Boarding School Magazine.
     Good Practice in Boarding Schools: a resource handbook for
     all those working in boarding.
     Parents' Guide to Maintained Boarding Schools.
     Choosing a Boarding School: a guide for parents.
     Briefing Paper(s) 1-23.
          Other publications available.

Boat Jumble Association   (BJA)   1987
NR   Compass Marine, Compass Cottage, DARTMOUTH, Devon,
      TQ6 0JN.   (sb/p)
      01803 835915
      Sec: Tim Mear
▲   Un-incorporated Society
○   *G, *T; organisation & regulation of boat jumbles
Gp   Stallholders; Event organisers
●   Exhib
M   1,350 i, 650 f
¶   Boat Jumble Fixtures List - 1.

Boat Retailers & Brokers Association
      a group of the **British Marine Federation**

Boating Alliance
NR   RYA House, Ensign Way, HAMBLE, Hants, SO31 4YA.
      023 8060 4223
      http://www.boatingalliance.org.uk
○   *N, *S; to promote responsible boating; to offer a co-ordinated
      approach to the boating industry & boat users; to represent
      the member organisations to government
●   Mtgs - Inf - LG
M   4 org:
      British Canoe Union
      British Marine Federation
      Inland Waterways Association
      Royal Yachting Association

Body Control Pilates Association   1997
■   35 Little Russell St, LONDON, WC1A 2HH.
      020 7636 8900   fax 020 7636 8898
      http://www.bodycontrol.co.uk
      Dir: Lynne Robinson
○   *S; exercise similar to the Alexander technique
      Note: send sae for details

Bodyshop Services Division
      a division of the **Retail Motor Industry Federation**

Boiler & Radiator Manufacturers Association Ltd   (BARMA)
1941
NR   The Archways, Back Lane, SHIRLEY, Derbys, DE6 3AS.
      (regd/office)
▲   Company Limited by Guarantee
○   *T
Gp   Commercial boiler; Technical c'ee
●   Mtgs - Stat - LG
<   Eur Heating Ind (EHI); Eur Radiator Assn (EURORAD)
M   8 f
¶   LM; free.

Bonded Warehousekeepers' Association   (BWA)   1885
■   PO Box 29089, DUNFERMLINE, Fife, KY11 9WB.   (hsb)
      07736 633162
      http://www.thebwa.com
      Hon Sec: John Tripp
▲   Un-incorporated Society
○   *T; (incl implementation of UK & EC legislation as it effects HM
      Customs & Excise & related documentation issues)
Gp   Health & safety; HM Customs & Excise
●   Conf - Mtgs - ET - Inf - VE - LG
<   Scotch Whisky Assn; Road Haulage Assn; Freight Transport
      Assn; Wine & Spirit Assn; Gin & Vodka Assn
M   65 i, 45 f
¶   NL - 4.   LM - 1.   Minutes of meetings.

Bone Research Society   (BRS)   1950
■   c/o Prof Eugene McCloskey, Academic Unit of Bone
      Metabolism, Metabolic Bone Centre, University of Sheffield,
      Sorby Wing, Northern General Hospital, Herries Rd,
      SHEFFIELD, S Yorks, S5 7AU.   (sb)
      http://www.brsoc.org.uk
      Sec: Prof Eugene McCloskey
▲   Registered Charity
○   *L, *Q; to advance basic & clinical research into the calcified
      tissues
●   Conf - Mtgs - ET - Res - Inf - PL - LG
<   Intl Osteoporosis Foundation; Brit Endocrine Socs
M   c 250 i, UK / 10 i, o'seas
      (Sub: £50)
¶   Meeting abstracts published in Calcified Tissue International - 1.

Bookmark Society   1991
NR   53 Victoria Rd, Horwich, BOLTON, Lancs, BL6 5ND.   (hsp)
      01204 692458
      Contact: Joe Stephenson
○   *G; collecting & research into bookmarks
●   Mtgs - Res - Inf - VE
M   i
¶   Bookmark - 4; ftm.
      Note: please enclose an SAE with any enquiries requiring a
      reply.

Bookplate Society   1983
■   Yarkhill, Upper Bucklebury, READING, Berks, RG7 6QH.   (hsp)
      01635 862226
      email geoffreyvevers2@tiscali.co.uk
      http://www.bookplatesociety.org
      Hon Sec: Geoffrey Vevers
▲   Registered Charity
○   *A, *G; to promote the study & collecting of bookplates; to
      publish material & arrange exhibitions
●   Mtgs - Res - Exhib - VE
<   Fédn Intle des Sociétés d'Amateurs d'Exlibris
M   250 i
      (Sub: £30 UK / £34 o'seas)
¶   The Bookplate Jnl - 2; ftm.
      NL - 2; ftm only.   Book - 2 yrly; ftm, prices vary nm.

Booksellers Association of the United Kingdom & Ireland
(BA)   1895
NR   Minster House, 272 Vauxhall Bridge Rd, LONDON,
      SW1V 1BA.   (hq)
      020 7802 0802   fax 020 7802 0803
      email mail@booksellers.org.uk
      http://www.booksellers.org.uk
      Chief Exec: T E Godfray
▲   Company Limited by Guarantee
Br   15
○   *T
Gp   Academic bookselling; Children's bookselling; Christian
      bookselling; Internet bookselling; Library supply; School
      supply; Small business forum
●   Conf - Mtgs - Exhib - Stat - Inf - LG
M   1,282 f, UK / 165 i, o'seas
¶   Bookselling Essentials - 4/5;   AR; both free.
      Directory of Booksellers - 1; ftm, £34 nm.
      Directory of Book Publishers - 1; £58.75 m, £76.38 nm.
      The Complete Guide to Starting & Running a Bookshop; £28.

Booktrust   2004
§   Book House, 45 East Hill, LONDON, SW18 2QZ.   (hq)
      020 8516 2977   fax 020 8516 2978
      email query@booktrust.org.uk
      http://www.booktrust.org.uk
      Dir: Viv Bird
      An independent national charity that encourages people of all
      ages and cultures to discover and enjoy reading.

© CBD Research Ltd · Beckenham · BR3 5JS · Tel 020 8650 7745 · E-mail cbd@cbdresearch.com · www.cbdresearch.com

Boot & Shoe Manufacturers' Association   (BASMA)   1882
NR   24-25 Bloomsbury Sq, LONDON, WC1A 2PL.   (hq)
         020 7612 7757
▲   Company Limited by Guarantee
○   *T; to provide credit management services (including debt
      recovery, credit reporting & credit insurance) to the footwear
      manufacturing sector in the UK & overseas
M   c 380 f
¶   BASMA News - 4; free.

Border Stick Dressers Association   (1951)
NR   18 Crumstone Court, Killingworth, NEWCASTLE upon TYNE,
         NE12 6SZ.
         0191-268 2224
         http://www.bsda.eu
         Sec: Wilf Laidler
○   *G; makers of shepherd's crooks and walking sticks

Border Union Agricultural Society   (BUAS)   1813
NR   Showground Office, Springwood Park, KELSO, Roxburghshire,
         TD5 8LS.   (hq)
         01573 224188   fax 01573 226778
         email enquiries@buas.org   http://www.buas.org
         Contact: Ronald Wilson
▲   Registered Charity
○   *F; organisation of events & competitions; to promote interest in
      agriculture
<   Assn of Show & Agricl Orgs
M   1,000 i

Borreliosis & Associated Diseases Awareness UK   (BADA-UK)
§   PO Box 544, Wath upon Dearne, ROTHERHAM, S Yorks,
      S63 3DW.   (mail/address)
      0845 519 0813
      http://www.bada-uk.org
      a charity formed to give information on the treatment &
      dangers of bites from ticks received when walking in the
      country & woodland

BOSS Federation
      an alternative name for the **British Office Supplies & Services
      Federation**

Boston Area Chamber of Commerce   1930
NR   Boston Business Centre, Norfolk St, BOSTON, Lincs,
         PE21 9HH.   (hq)
         01205 358800
▲   Company Limited by Guarantee
○   *C; for Boston & South Holland areas
M   f
×   Boston Chamber of Commerce & Industry

Botanical Society of the British Isles   (BSBI)   1836
■   c/o Dept of Botany, Natural History Museum, Cromwell Rd,
         LONDON, SW7 5BD.
         020 7942 5002 (answerphone)
         http://www.bsbi.org.uk
         Hon Gen Sec: Miss L Farrell
▲   Registered Charity
○   *L; study of flowering plants, cryptogams & charophyta of the
      British Isles & of the problems of their conservation
Gp   Meetings; Publications; Records; Science & research; Training &
      education
●   Conf - Mtgs - Res - Exhib - SG - Inf - Surveys
M   2,800 i, 60 libraries, UK / 150 i, o'seas
¶   BSBI News - 3; ftm only.
      Watsonia - 2;   Abstracts - 1; both ftm, prices on
      application nm.
      (to Mr R G Ellis, 41 Marlborough Rd, Roath, CARDIFF,
      CF23 5BU)

Botanical Society of Scotland   (BSS)   1836
■   c/o Royal Botanic Garden Edinburgh, 20A Inverleith Row,
         EDINBURGH, EH3 5LR.   (hsb)
         0131-552 7171
         http://www.botanical-society-scotland.org.uk
         Gen Sec: Dr Barbra Harvie
▲   Registered Scottish Charity
○   *L; all branches of botanical science
Gp   Cryptogamic; Alpine plants; Conservation
●   Conf - Mtgs - Exhib - Conf - VE
M   280 i, 1 school, UK / 16 i, o'seas
¶   BSS News - 2; ftm only.
      Plant Ecology & Diversity - 2, ftm.

Bournemouth Chamber of Trade & Commerce   (bctc)   1916
NR   8 Lansdowne Rd, BOURNEMOUTH, Dorset, BH1 1SD.   (hq)
         01202 372437
         email info@bournemouthchamber.org.uk
         http://www.bournemouthchamber.org.uk
         Chief Exec: Peter J Goodson
▲   Un-incorporated Society
○   *C
Gp   C'ees: Local government affairs; Executive
●   Mtgs - Inf - VE - LG
<   Dorset Cham Comm & Ind
M   180 f
¶   [emails to members]

Bourton-on-the-Water Chamber of Commerce
NR   PO Box 5, BOURTON-ON-THE-WATER, Glos, GL54 2YJ.   (hq)
         01451 821478
         email admin@bourtoninfo.com
         http://www.bourtoninfo.com
         Sec: Janet Prout
○   *C
<   Gloucestershire Cham of Commerce & Ind

Bowen Association UK   1997
NR   PO Box 210, BOSTON, Lincs, PE21 1DD.   (hq)
         01205 319100
         email office@bowen-technique.co.uk
         http://www.bowen-technique.co.uk
○   *P; to provide support, training & information to members & to
      promote awareness of the Bowen Technique (re-alignment &
      balance of the body) to the public & health professionals

Bowls England   1903
■   Lyndhurst Rd, WORTHING, W Sussex, BN11 2AZ.   (hq)
         01903 820222   fax 01903 820444
         email enquiries@bowlsengland.com
         http://www.bowlsengland.com
         Chief Exec: Anthony Allcock
▲   Company Limited by Guarantee
○   *S; governing body of flat green lawn bowls in England
Gp   Greens maintenance; Coaching scheme; Child protection
      panel; Youth development
●   Mtgs - ET - Comp
<   World Bowls; Brit Isles Bowling Coun; Brit Isles Womens
      Bowling; Eur Bowls U
M   135,000 i, 4,201 clubs
      (Sub: £4.50)
¶   Ybk - 1; £3.50,
×   2007 (English Bowling Association
            (English Women's Bowling Association

Bowls Group
      in 2006 merged with the **Sporting Goods Industry Association**

Bowls Scotland   2010

NR National Centre for Bowling, Hunters Avenue, AYR, KA8 9AL.
    (hq)
    01292 294623   fax 01292 266556
    email info@bowlsscotland.com
    http://www.bowlsscotland.com
    Chief Exec: Alan J G McMillan
○   *S; to control & foster the level green game of bowls
●   Comp
<   Brit Isles Bowls Coun (BIBC); Eur Bowls U (EBU); Wld Bowls
M   c 90,000 i in c 894 clubs
¶   Bowls for the Beginner - 1.
    Ybk - 1.   Laws of the Game - 1.
✕   2010 (Scottish Bowling Association
        (Scottish Women's Bowling Association (merged)

Box Culvert Association
    a product association of the **British Precast Concrete Federation**

Boys' Brigade   (BB)   1883

NR Felden Lodge, HEMEL HEMPSTEAD, Herts, HP3 0BL.   (hq)
    01442 231681   fax 01442 235391
    email enquiries@boys-brigade.org.uk
    http://www.boys-brigade.org.uk
    Brigade Sec: Steven Dickinson
▲   Company Limited by Guarantee; Registered Charity
Br 1,650; 70 o'seas
○   *Y; Christian youth work with boys & young people aged 4-18
<   Global Fellowship of Christian Youth
M   75,000 i, UK / 600,000 i, o'seas
¶   The Boys' Brigade Gazette - 4.

Boys' & Girls' Clubs of Northern Ireland
    since 2007 **Clubs for Young People (NI)**

Boys' & Girls' Clubs of Scotland
    since 2007 **Clubs for Young People Scotland**

BPI (British Recorded Music Industry) Ltd   (BPI)   1973

■   Riverside Building, County Hall, Westminster Bridge Rd,
    LONDON, SE1 7JA.   (hq)
    020 7803 1300   fax 020 7803 1310
    email general@bpi.co.uk   http://www.bpi.co.uk
    Chief Exec: Geoff Taylor
▲   Company Limited by Guarantee
○   *T; for British record companies
●   Mtgs - Res - Stat - Inf - Lib - LG
<   Intl Fedn of the Phonographic Ind (IFPI)
M   c 370 f
¶   BPI Statistical Hbk - 1.   LM - website.
✕   2007 British Phonographic Industry Ltd

Bracknell Forest Chamber of Commerce
    a local chamber of **Thames Valley Chamber of Commerce &
    Industry**

Bradford Chamber of Commerce & Industry   (BCofC)   1851

NR Devere House, Vicar Lane, Little Germany, BRADFORD,
    W Yorks, BD1 5AH.   (hq)
    01274 772777   fax 01274 771081
    email info@bradfordchamber.co.uk
    http://www.bradfordchamber.co.uk
    Chief Exec: Sandy Needham
▲   Company Limited by Guarantee
○   *C
●   Conf - Mtgs - ET - Res - Exhib - Stat - Expt - Inf - Lib - VE - LG
<   Brit Chams Comm
M   1,000 f
¶   Business Plus - 6; ftm, £2.50 nm.   M Dir - 1; ftm, £125 nm.

Braid Society   1993

■   Spring House, Old Stone Trough Lane, KELBROOK, Lancs,
    BB18 6UE.   (hsp)
    email secretary@braidsociety.com
    http://www.braidsociety.com
    Hon Sec: Debbie Richardson
▲   Un-incorporated Society
○   *G; education & practice of the art & craft of making
        constructed or embellished braids & narrow bands
●   Mtgs - Exhib - Comp - SG - VE
M   200 i
    (Sub: £18.50 i)
¶   Strands (Jnl) - 1; ftm, £3.75 nm.
    NL - 4.

Braille Authority UK
    merged on 1 January 2009 with the Confederation of Transcribed
    Information Services to form **United Kingdom Association for
    Accessible Formats**

Brain Injury Association
    see **Headway**

Brain Tumour UK   1997

NR Tower House, Latimer Park, CHESHAM, Bucks, HP5 1TU.   (hq)
    0845 450 0386
    email enquiries@braintumouruk.org.uk
    http://www.braintumouruk.org.uk
    Inf & Support Services Mgr: Jane Stephens
▲   Registered Charity
○   *M; all aspects of brain tumours, their treatment & effects of
        treatment
●   Conf - Res
<   NCVO; Assn of Chief Execs for Voluntary Orgs
M   2,800 i
¶   Magazine - 4; free.

Brainwave, the Irish Epilepsy Association   1967

IRL 249 Crumlin Rd, DUBLIN 12, Republic of Ireland.
    353 (1) 455 7500   fax 353 (1) 455 7013
    email info@epilepsy.ie
    Chief Exec: Mike Glynn
○   *W

Brake   1995

§   PO Box 548, HUDDERSFIELD, W Yorks, HD1 2XZ.
    01484 559909   fax 01484 559983
    email brake@brake.org.uk   http://www.brake.org.uk
    a non-membership charity campaigning for road safety &
    offering advice to road users
    Victim helpline: 0845 603 8570

Branch Line Society   (BLS)   1955

■   73 Norfolk Park Avenue, SHEFFIELD, S Yorks, S2 2RB.   (hsp)
    0114-275 2303   fax 0114-275 2303
    email BLS.Sales@tesco.net
    http://www.branchline.org.uk
    Hon Gen Sec: N J Hill
▲   Un-incorporated Society
○   *G; study of branch & minor railway lines, principally in the
        British Isles, but also throughout the world
●   Mtgs (annual) - Inf - VE
M   1,000 i, 4 org, UK / 20 i, o'seas
¶   Branch Line News - 24;   AR; both ftm only.

© CBD Research Ltd · Beckenham · BR3 5JS · Tel 020 8650 7745 · E-mail cbd@cbdresearch.com · www.cbdresearch.com

Brassica Growers Association   (BGA)
- ■ PVGA House, Nottingham Rd, LOUTH, Lincs, LN11 0WB. (asa)
   01507 602427   fax 01507 607689
   email jayne.dyas@pvga.co.uk
   http://www.loveyourgreens.co.uk
   Sec: Mrs Jayne Dyas
- ▲ Company Limited by Guarantee
- ○ *T; marketing information, research & development
- Gp British Sprout Growers Association
- ● Conf - Mtgs
- M 25 f

Brazilian Chamber of Commerce in Great Britain
- NR 32 Green St, LONDON, W1K 7AT.
   020 7399 9281   fax 020 7499 0186
   email pavlova@brazilianchamber.org.uk
   http://www.brazilianchamber.org.uk
   Sec: Valentina Ravagni
- ▲ Company Limited by Guarantee
- ○ *C; bilateral trade between Brazil & the UK
- Gp Brazilian exporters to the UK; British investors in Brazil
- ● Conf - Mtgs - Expt - Inf - LG
- M i, f & org
- ¶ Brazil Business Brief - 3; ftm only.

BRE Trust   (BRE)   1946
- NR Bucknalls Lane, WATFORD, Herts, WD25 9XX.   (regd off)
   01923 664000
   email secretary@bretrust.org.uk
   http://www.bretrust.org.uk
- ▲ Company Limited by Guarantee; Registered Charity
- ○ *L, *P; to advance knowledge, innovation & communication in all matters concerning the built environment for public benefit

Breast Implant Information Society   (BIIS)   1998
- ■ Highway Farm, Horsley Rd, Downside, COBHAM, Surrey, KT11 3JZ.   (founder/p)
   07041 471225   fax 07041 471225
   email info@biis.org   http://www.biis.org
   Founder: Maxine Heasman
- ▲ Un-incorporated Society
- ○ *G; to provide comprehensive information & advice &/or guidance to women who have, or are considering, breast implant surgery
- ● ET - Res - Stat - Inf - Lib - LG
   Helpline: 07041 471255 (weekdays 1800-2000 hours, not Bank Holidays)
- M c 350 i, UK / 20 i, o'seas
- ¶ B-Plus - 1; m only.
   The Ultimate Cleavage: a complete practical guide to cosmetic breast enlargement surgery.

Brecknock Hill Cheviot Sheep Society
- NR 13 Lion St, BRECON, Powys, LD3 7HY.   (hq)
   01874 622488
   email info@brecknockhillcheviotsheep.co.uk
   http://www.brecknockhillcheviotsheep.co.uk
   Sec: Peter Francis
- ○ *B
- < Nat Sheep Assn

Brecknockshire Agricultural Society   (Brecon County Show) 1755
- NR Plas Gwyn, Saron, LLANDYSUL, Carmarthenshire, SA44 5DZ.   (hq)
   01599 371557
   email breconshow@btinternet.com
   Admin: Barbara Green
- ▲ Registered Charity
- ○ *F; interests of farming & breed societies
- ● Mtgs - ET - Exhib - Comp - Brecknock Show
- < Assn of Show & Agricl Orgs
- M 500 i, 15 f, 10 org
- ¶ LM;   AR.

Brewery History Society   1972
- ■ Manor Side East, Mill Lane, Byfleet, WEST BYFLEET, Surrey, KT14 7RS.   (chmn/p)
   01932 341084
   email chairman@breweryhistory.com
   http://www.breweryhistory.com
   Chmn: Jeff Sechiari
- ○ *L; research into the history of the British brewing & related industries
- ● Conf - Mtgs - Res - Exhib - Lib - PL - VE
- > Engl Heritage; Assn for Indl Archaeology
- M 400 i, 32 f, 40 org, UK / 12 i, 6 f, o'seas
   (Sub: £18 i, £60 f, £27 org, UK / £25 i, £60 f, o'seas)
- ¶ Jnl - 4; ftm, £4.50 each nm.   NL - 4; ftm only.
   County Directories -1; c £12.

Brewing, Food & Beverage Industry Suppliers Association (BFBi)   1907
- ■ 3 Brewery Rd, WOLVERHAMPTON, W Midlands, WV1 4JT. (hq)
   01902 422303   fax 01902 795744
   email info@bfbi.org.uk   http://www.bfbi.org.uk
   Chief Exec: Ruth Evans
- ▲ Un-incorporated Society
- Br 5
- ○ *T; companies supplying raw materials, engineering components, process control & consultancy to the brewing, food & beverage industries
- ● Conf - Mtgs - ET - Res - Exhib - SG - Inf - VE - LG
- M 156 i, 350 f, UK / 8 f, o'seas
- ¶ Directory - 1; ftm, £95 nm.

Brick Development Association Ltd   (BDA)   1954
- NR The Building Centre, 26 Store St, LONDON, WC1E 7BT.   (hq)
   020 7323 7030   fax 020 7580 3795
   email brick@brick.org.uk   http://www.brick.org.uk
   Chief Exec: Simon Hay
- ▲ Company Limited by Guarantee
- ○ *T; interests of clay brick & paver manufacturers of the UK & Ireland
- ● Mtgs - ET - Exhib - Comp - Stat - Inf - Lectures - Symposia
- < Fédn Européenne des Fabricants de Tuiles et de Briques; Construction Products Assn; Brit Ceramic Res Ltd
- M 24 f, UK / 2 f, Ireland
- ¶ Brick Bulletin - 2; £10 yr.   Technical literature.
- ✕ 2006-07 (amalgamated) National Brickmakers Federation

Brickish Association
- NR 25 Carmichael Way, BASINGSTOKE, Hants, RG22 4NJ. (mem/sp)
   http://www.brickish.org
- ○ *G; for adult fans of Lego
- M i
   (Sub: £12)
- ¶ The Brick Issue

Bridge Deck Waterproofing Association   (BWA)   1990
NR   PO Box 4174, CROWTHORNE, Berks, RG42 9LE.   (hsb)
     01344 775576   fax 01344 775576
     email enquiry@bdwa.org.uk   http://www.bdwa.org.uk
▲   Company Limited by Guarantee
○   *T; for those concerned with the waterproofing of bridges
     (highway, railway & waterway)
M   i & f

Bridlington Chamber of Trade
     a local chamber of the **Hull & Humber Chamber of Commerce**

Bristol Chamber of Commerce & Initiative   1823
NR   Leigh Court, Abbots Leigh, BRISTOL, BS8 3RA.   (hq)
     01275 373373
     email info@gwebusinesswest.co.uk
     http://www.businesswest.co.uk
▲   Company Limited by Guarantee
○   *C
<   GWE Business West Ltd

**Bristol & Gloucestershire Archaeological Society   (BGAS)
1876**
■   Stonehatch, Oakridge Lynch, STROUD, Glos, GL6 7NR.   (hsp)
     01285 760460
     email john@loosleyj.freeserve.co.uk
     http://www.bgas.org.uk
     Hon Gen Sec: John Loosley
▲   Registered Charity
○   *L; to promote the study of the history, archaeology &
     antiquities of Bristol & Gloucestershire; to encourage
     conservation
Gp   Sections: Bristol, Gloucester
●   Mtgs - Lib - VE - Publications of historical records of
     Gloucestershire
M   700 i, 70 org, UK / 10 i, 60 org, o'seas
¶   NL - 2; ftm only.   Transactions - 1; ftm, £12 nm.
     Record Series - 1; £12 m, £30 nm.

Bristol Industrial Archaeological Society   (BIAS)   1967
NR   8 Northfield Rd, Portishead, BRISTOL, BS20 8LE.   (sec/p)
     01225 847522
     http://www.b-i-a-s.org.uk
     Sec: Roger Davis,   Chmn: Geoff Sheppard
○   *L; research into industrial archaeology of the Bristol region
<   Assn for Indl Archaeol
M   i, f & org

Bristol Junior Chamber of Commerce
NR   c/o Veale Wasbrough Vizards, Orchard Court, Orchard Lane,
     BRISTOL, BS1 5WS.   (pres/b)
     0117-314 5382
     email david.bird@bristoljuniorchamber.co.uk
     http://www.bristoljuniorchamber.co.uk
     Pres: David Bird
○   *C
<   GWE Business West Ltd

Britain-Australia Society   (B-AS)   1937
NR   Swire House, 59 Buckingham Gate, LONDON, SW1E 6AJ.
     (hq)
     020 7630 1075   fax 020 7828 2260
     email britaus@britain-australia.org.uk
     http://www.britain-australia.org.uk
     Nat Dir: Kim Hemmingway
▲   Un-incorporated Society
Br   10
○   *X
●   Mtgs - VE
M   1,200 i, 30 f
¶   Brit Oz Bulletin - 3; ftm only.

Britain's Cross Country Vehicle Association
     see **All Wheel Drive Club (Britain's Cross Country Vehicle
     Association)**

Britain-Nepal Chamber of Commerce   (BNCC)   1995
■   Tamesis House, 33 St Philip's Avenue, WORCESTER PARK,
     Surrey, KT4 8JS.   (asa)
     020 8330 6446   fax 020 8330 7447
     email bncc@tamgroup.co.uk
     http://www.nepal-trade.org.uk
     Sec: N Barry Jaynes
▲   Un-incorporated Society
○   *C; to encourage import & export trade between UK & Nepal
●   Mtgs - Exhib - LG
M   f

Britain Nepal Society   (BNS)   1960
■   33 Abbey St, Ickleton, SAFFRON WALDEN, Essex, CB10 1SS.
     (chmn/p)
     http://www.britain-nepal-society.org.uk
     Chmn: Lt-Col Gerry D Birch
▲   Un-incorporated Society
○   *X; to promote good relations between the peoples of the UK &
     Nepal; & in particular between UK citizens with an interest in
     Nepal & Nepalese citizens resident in the UK
●   Mtgs - VE
>   Britain Nepal Cham Comm; R Nepalese Embassy in UK; Britain
     Nepal Otology Service
M   450 i, 20 f, UK / 50 i, o'seas
¶   BNS Jnl - 1; ftm only.
     Note: also at the same address is the Britain Nepal Otology
     Service - a charity dedicated to the prevention & treatment of
     deafness in Nepal.

Britain Nigeria Business Council   (BNBC)   1977
■   The Africa Centre, 38 King St, Covent Garden, LONDON,
     WC2E 8JT.   (hq)
     Exec Vice Chmn: Clive Carpenter
▲   Company Limited by Guarantee
○   *C; to promote trade & investment between Britain & Nigeria
●   Conf - Mtgs - Inf - LG
<   Business Coun Africa UK
M   c 80 f
     (Sub: £355)
¶   Nigeria News Report - 12;   AR - 1; both ftm only.

Britain-Nigeria Educational Trust   (BNA)   1961
■   The Africa Centre, 38 King St, Covent Garden, LONDON,
     WC2E 8JT.   (hq)
     020 7240 8950   fax 020 7828 5251
     http://www.britain-nigeria.org
     Hon Sec: G Clark
▲   Registered Charity
○   *X
●   Mtgs - LG - Social gatherings & receptions
<   Nigeria-Britain Assn, Nigeria
M   c 850 i & f
¶   BNA NL - 3; ftm only.

Britain-Tanzania Society   (BTS)   1975
NR   24 Oakfield Drive, REIGATE, Surrey, RH2 9NR.   (memsec/p)
     01737 210532   fax 01737 210532
     http://www.btsociety.org
     Mem Sec: Ann Brumfit
▲   Un-incorporated Society
Br   2; Tanzania
○   *X; to increase mutual knowledge, understanding & respect
     between the peoples of the two countries
●   Conf - Mtgs - Exhib - Inf - VE - LG
<   BOND
M   750 i, UK / 100 i, o'seas, & 20 org
¶   Tanzanian Affairs - 3; ftm, £7.50 nm.
     NL;   AR; ftm only.

© CBD Research Ltd · Beckenham · BR3 5JS · Tel 020 8650 7745 · E-mail cbd@cbdresearch.com · www.cbdresearch.com

Britain Zimbabwe Society   (BZS)   1981
- ■ 63 The Mall, SWINDON, Wilts, SN1 4JA.   (mem/sp)
    email mutsai@tinyworld.co.uk
    http://www.britain-zimbabwe.org.uk
    Mem Sec: Mutsai Hove
- ▲ Un-incorporated Society
- ○ *X; to foster friendship & understanding between the peoples of
    Zimbabwe & Britain; to encourage open discussion about
    Zimbabwean affairs; to inform the British & Zimbabwe public
    about Zimbabwean culture & economy
- ● Annual research day - email network - Networking support -
    AGM
- M 260 i, 2 f, 8 org, UK / 13 i, 1 embassy, o'seas
    (Sub: £18 i, £40 instns)
- ¶ Zimbabwe Review [with NL] - 4; prices vary.

Britannia Naval Research Association   (BNRA)
- NR 40 Hermitage Rd, ABINGDON, Oxon, OX14 5RW.   (sp)
    http://www.britannia-naval-research-association.org
    Contact: The Secretary
- ○ *G; to preserve, promote, research from Drake to Dreadnought
    & beyond
- ● Conf - Mtgs - SG - VE
- M i
- ¶ Jnl.

British Abrasives Federation   (The BAF)   1968
- ■ Toad Hall, Hinton Rd, HURST, Berks, RG10 0BS.   (hsp)
    0845 612 1380   fax 0845 612 1380
    email info@thebaf.org.uk   http://www.thebaf.org.uk
    Sec: Stuart Lane
- ▲ Un-incorporated Society
- ○ *N, *T; to represent manufacturers & producers of abrasives in
    the UK
- Gp Safe use of abrasive; Technical standards; Training
- ● ET - Stat - Inf - Safety codes - Standards
- < Fedn of Eur Producers of Abrasives (FEPA) (Paris)
- M 22 f

British Academy   1902
- ■ 10 Carlton House Terrace, LONDON, SW1Y 5AH.   (hq)
    020 7969 5200   fax 020 7969 5300
    email secretary@britac.ac.uk   http://www.britac.ac.uk
    Sec: Robin Jackson
- ▲ Registered Charity
- ○ *L; is the UK's national academy for the humanities & social
    sciences.   Scholars are elected for distinction in their area
    of study
- Gp Classical antiquity; Theology & religious studies; African &
    oriental studies; Linguistics & philology; Early modern
    languages & literature; Modern languages, literature & other
    media; Archaeology; Medieval studies: history & literature;
    Early modern history to c 1800; Modern history from c 1800;
    History of art & music; Philosophy; Law; Economics &
    economic history; Social anthropology & geography;
    Sociology, demography & social statistics; Political studies:
    political theory, government & international relations;
    Psychology
- ● Conf - Mtgs - Res - Comp - LG - Awards to support
    fundamental research - Symposia
- M c 800 i
- ¶ Proceedings;   Review (monographs) - irreg; ftm, prices
    vary nm.
    Directory - 1; ftm only.   AR - 1; free.
- × 2005-06 British Academy for the Promotion of Historial,
    Philosophical & Philological Studies

British Academy of Audiology   (BAA)   1985
- ■ Kingston Smith Association Management, Chester House, 68
    Chestergate, MACCLESFIELD, Cheshire, SK11 6DY.   (hq)
    01625 664545
    email admin@baaudiology.org
    http://www.baaudiology.org
    Pres: Mark Lutman
- ▲ Company Limited by Guarantee
- ○ *P; the professional body for audiologists in the UK
- ● Conf - ET - Exam - Exhib - Inf - LG

British Academy of Composers & Songwriters
   since 2009 **British Academy of Songwriters, Composers &
Authors**

British Academy of Dramatic Combat   (BADC)   1969
- NR [communication by e-mail only]
    email kevin.rowntree@badc.co.uk
    http://www.badc.co.uk
    Chmn: Kevin Rowntree
- ○ *D, *P; to advance the art of stage combat in all forms of
    performance media
- M 91 i

British Academy of Film & Television Arts   (BAFTA)   1963
- NR 195 Piccadilly, LONDON, W1J 9LN.   (hq)
    020 7734 0022   fax 020 7734 1792
    email reception@bafta.org   http://www.bafta.org
    Chief Exec: Amanda Berry
- ▲ Registered Charity
- ○ *A; to support, develop & promote the art forms of the moving
    image
- Gp Film; Games; Television
- ● Awards - Events - Archive
- M c 5,000 i, UK / 1,500 i, o'seas

British Academy of Forensic Sciences   (BAFS)   1959
- NR PO Box 6314, LONDON, N1 0DL.   (hsb)
    020 7837 0069
    Admin: Mrs Sandra Dawson
- ○ *L; to encourage the study, improve the practice & advance the
    knowledge of legal medicine & forensic science
- M i
- ¶ Medicine, Science & the Law (Jnl) - 4.

**British Academy of Songwriters, Composers & Authors
(BASCA)   1999**
- ■ British Music House, 26 Berners St, LONDON, W1T 3LR.   (hq)
    020 7636 2929   fax 020 7636 2212
    email info@basca.org.uk   http://www.basca.org.uk
    Chief Exec: Chris Green
- ▲ Company Limited by Guarantee
- ○ *P; the interests of composers & songwriters across all genres
- ● Mtgs - Comp - Inf - LG - Administration of the Ivor Novello &
    the Gold Badge Awards
- < Creators' Rights Assn; Brit Music Rights; MCPS; PRS
- M 2,500 i
- ¶ The Works - 2;   Four Four - 4; both ftm only.
- × 2008-09 British Academy of Composers & Songwriters

British Accounting Association   (BAA)   1984
- NR c/o The Management School, University of Sheffield, 9 Mappin
    St, SHEFFIELD, S Yorks, S1 4DT.   (admin/b)
    0114-222 3462
    Admin: Kathryn Hewitt
- ▲ Registered Charity
- ○ *E; *Q; advancement of education & encouragement of
    research in accounting
- M i

British Acoustic Neuroma Association   (BANA)   1992
NR   Oak House, Ransom Wood Business Park, Southwell Road
         West, MANSFIELD, Notts, NG21 0HJ.   (hq)
         01623 632143
▲   Registered Charity
○   *W; for people with acoustic neuromas (brain tumours), their
         families & interested medical personnel
M   i

British Activity Holiday Association   (BAHA)   1986
■   The Hollies, Oak Bank Lane, Hoole Village, CHESTER,
         CH2 4ER.   (hq)
         01244 301342
         email info@baha.org.uk   http://www.baha.org.uk
         Sec: Jane Tomlin
▲   Company Limited by Guarantee
○   *T; for providers of activity & special-interest holidays & courses
●   Conf - Mtgs - ET - Inf - LG
<   English Outdoor Coun; Skills Active
M   32 f
         (Sub: £75-£1,000)
¶   Publications; m only.

British Actors' Equity Association   (Equity)   1930
NR   Guild House, Upper St Martin's Lane, LONDON,
         WC2H 9EG.   (hq)
         020 7379 6000   fax 020 7379 7001
         email info@equity.org.uk   http://www.equity.org.uk
         Gen Sec: Christine Payne
▲   Un-incorporated Society
Br   7
○   *U; for performers, stage managers, choreographers, directors,
         stunt arrangers & professional broadcasters in theatre,
         television, radio, film & variety
<   Trades U Congress (TUC)
M   36,525 i

British Acupuncture Council   (BAcC)   1995
■   63 Jeddo Rd, LONDON, W12 9HQ.   (hq)
         020 8735 0400   fax 020 8735 0404
         email info@acupuncture.org.uk
         http://www.acupuncture.org.uk
○   *P; to represent acupuncturists; to maintain standards of
         education, methods & practice in the acupuncture profession
         in the UK
Gp   Admissions; Code of practice, ethics & disciplinary procedures;
         Conference; Education; Finance; PR & marketing; Research;
         Regulation; Safe practice
●   Mtgs - ET - Res - Inf - LG
<   Wld Fedn of Acupuncture Socs; Brit Acupuncture Accreditation
         Bd
M   2,600 i
¶   LM - 1.   AR.
         List of Local Practitioner Members - daily.

British Adhesives & Sealants Association   (BASA)   1983
■   5 Alderson Rd, WORKSOP, Notts, S80 1UZ.   (sb)
         01909 480888   fax 01909 473834
         email secretary@basaonline.org
         http://www.basaonline.org
         Sec: John Murdoch
▲   Un-incorporated Society
○   *T; interests of British manufacturers of sealants & adhesives
●   Conf - ET - SG - Stat - Inf - LG
<   Assn of Eur Adhesives Mfrs (FEICA); Alliance of Ind Assns
M   82 f
¶   BASA Bulletin - 3; ftm only.   AR; free.
         BASA Members Hbk - 1; ftm, £50 nm.
         Manuals:
              Guide to Reach; free.
              Manual of Sealant Practice; ftm, POA nm.

British Aerobatic Association   (BAeA)   1974
NR   c/o West London Aero Club, White Waltham Airfield,
         MAIDENHEAD, Berks, SL6 3NJ.   (hq)
         01628 6377732
         email info@aerobatics.org.uk
         http://www.aerobatics.org.uk
         Chmn: Alan Cassidy
▲   Company Limited by Guarantee
○   *S; for all interested in aerobatic flying
●   ET - Comp - Arranging contests
<   R Aero Club
M   200 i, 5 f, UK / 10 i, o'seas
¶   Aerobatics News Review - 6; ftm only.

British Aerobiology Federation   (BAF)   1990
NR   B148 Natural Resources Institute, University of Greenwich at
         Medway,Central Avenue, CHATHAM, Kent, ME4 4TB.   (hsb)
▲   Registered Charity
○   *P; aerobiology, pollen counts, pollen spores, hayfever, asthma
●   Conf - Mtgs - ET
<   Intl Assn for Aerobiology
M   15 i, 30 f
¶   NL - 2; ftm only.

British Aerophilatelic Federation
         since May 2007 **British Air Mail Society**

British Aerosol Manufacturers Association   (BAMA)   1961
■   Kings Buildings, Smith Sq, LONDON, SW1P 3JJ.   (hq)
         020 7828 5111
         Dir: Sue Rogers
▲   Company Limited by Guarantee
○   *T; to promote & protect the aerosol industry & its products
●   Mtgs - Stat - Inf - LG
<   Alliance of Ind Assns; Chemical Inds Assn
M   c 75 f
¶   Volatile Substance Abuse - be aware.
         BAMA Code of Practice.
         BAMA Electrostatic Guidelines.
         BAMA Guide to Safety in the Laboratory.
         Aerosol Product Recall Guide.
         Other similar publications.

British African Business Association
         since 2009 **Business Council for Africa UK**

British Aggregates Association   (BAA)   1999
■   10 Brookfields, Calver, HOPE VALLEY, Derbys, S32 3XB.   (hsp)
         01433 639879   fax 01433 639879
         email phuxtable@british-aggregates.com
         http://www.british-aggregates.co.uk
         PO Box 99, LANARK, ML11 8WA.
         Sec: Peter Huxtable
▲   Company Limited by Guarantee
○   *T; to represent the independent, privately owned SME quarry
         operator in the UK minerals industry in consultation with
         government, EU regulators, officials & politicians
●   Conf - Mtgs - ET - Inf - LG
<   Confedn of Brit Ind (CBI); Construction Products Assn (CPA);
         Mineral Ind Res Org (MIRO)
M   52 f (indep), 24 associates

© CBD Research Ltd · Beckenham · BR3 5JS · Tel 020 8650 7745 · E-mail cbd@cbdresearch.com · www.cbdresearch.com

British Agricultural & Garden Machinery Association (BAGMA) 1917
- ■ Middleton House, 2 Main Rd, Middleton Cheney, BANBURY, Oxon, OX17 2TN. (hq)
  01295 713344 fax 01295 711665
  email info@bagma.com http://www.bagma.com
  Pres: John Barrett
- ▲ Un-incorporated Society
- ○ *F, *H, *T; agricultural, ground care & garden machinery dealers
- ● Empl - ET - Inf - LG - Mtgs
- < Brit Indep Retailers Assn
- M 900 f
- ¶ BAGMA Bulletin - 6; free.

British Agricultural History Society (BAHS) 1952
- NR Dept of Humanities (History Study Group), Sheffield Hallam University, Howard St, SHEFFIELD, S Yorks, S1 1WB. (hsb)
  0114 225 3693
  email n.verdon@shu.ac.uk http://www.bahs.org.uk
  Hon Sec: Dr Nicola Verdon
- ▲ Registered Charity
- ○ *L; to promote the study of agricultural history & the history of the rural economy & society
- ● Conf - Mtgs - Res
- M c 500 i, 450 f, UK & o'seas
- ¶ Agricultural History Review - 2.
  Rural History Today (NL) - 2.

British Aikido Board (BAB) 1977
- NR 6 Halkingcroft, Langley, SLOUGH, Berks, SL3 7AT. (hsp)
  http://www.bab.org.uk
  Sec: Shirley Timms
- ○ *S; to further the advancement of all styles of aikido in the UK & to establish & monitor standards, safety & behaviour conducive to the safety of practitioners of aikido
- < Sport England
- M 50 org
  BAB is recognised by Sport England as the national governing body for aikido in the UK

British Air Line Pilots Association (BALPA) 1937
- NR BALPA House, 5 Heathrow Blvd, 278 Bath Rd, WEST DRAYTON, UB7 0DQ. (hq)
  020 8476 4000 fax 020 8476 4077
  email balpa@balpa.org http://www.balpa.org
  Gen Sec: Jim McAusnan
- ▲ Un-incorporated Society
- ○ *U; the representation of British commercial airline pilots & flight engineers to their employers & aviation authorities
- < TUC
- M 8,400 i

British Air Mail Society (BAMS) 1985
- ■ 97 Albany Park Avenue, ENFIELD HIGHWAY, Middx, EN3 5NX. (mem/sp)
  http://www.britishairmailsociety.co.uk
  Hon Sec: Peter Lister
- ▲ Un-incorporated Society
- ○ *G; to encourage & contribute to the advancement & study of all material relating to the carriage of mail by air
- ● Conf - Mtgs - Res - Exhib - Comp - SG - Lib - VE
- < Assn of Brit Philatelic Socs
- M 280 i, UK / 50 i, o'seas
- ¶ Airmail News - 4; free.
- ✕ 2007 (May) British Aerophilatelic Federation

British Air Transport Association (BATA) 1976
- ■ Artillery House, 11-19 Artillery Row, LONDON, SW1P 1RT. (hq)
  020 7222 9494 fax 020 7222 9595
  email info@bata.uk.com http://www.bata.uk.com
  Sec Gen: Roger Wiltshire
- ▲ Company LImited by Guarantee
- Br 1
- ○ *T; to be the voice of UK airlines
- Gp Aviation security; Flight operators; Security; Technical
- ● Mtgs - ET - LG
- M 12 f

British Airgun Shooters' Association (BASA)
- NR 3 The Courtyard, Denmark St, WOKINGHAM, Berks, RG40 2AZ.
  0118-977 1677
  Sec: Nigel Allen
- ○ *G
- M c 4,500 i

British Airport Services & Equipment Association (BASEA) 1988
- NR Pine Court Business Centre (Suite 4), 36 Gervis Rd, BOURNEMOUTH, Dorset, BH1 3DH. (hq)
  01202 585505
- ▲ Un-incorporated Society
- ○ *T; to promote the British suppliers to the airport industry & their products in the UK & overseas; to serve as a bureau for purchasers of airport equipment & services worldwide; to offer members a wide range of marketing support services
- M i, f, 2 org (Airport Owners Assn & Jt Security Ind Coun)

British Allergy Foundation
  see **Allergy UK**

British Alliance of Healing Associations (BAHA)
- ■ PO Box 856, BOGNOR REGIS, W Sussex, PO21 9HQ. (sec/b)
  01243 840989
  email bahasecretary@gmail.com
  http://www.britishalliancehealingassociations.com
  Sec: Maurice Burns
- ▲ Registered Charity
- ○ *N; an unbrella organisation for independent healing groups & centres throughout the UK; to promote spiritual healing & healer training
- ● Conf - Mtgs - ET - Res - Exhib - Inf
- < Eur Confedn of Healing Orgs; Confedn of Healing Orgs (COHO); UK Healers
- M 15,000 i in 60 orgs
- ¶ Alliance Review - 2.

British Allied Trades Federation (BATF) 1970
- ■ Federation House, 10 Vyse St, BIRMINGHAM, B18 6LT. (hq)
  0121-236 2657 fax 0121-236 3921
- ▲ Company Limited by Guarantee
- ○ *N, *T; to support 6 trade associations in the jewellery, giftware, leathergoods & metal finishing industries
- Gp Giftware; Home enhancement; Jewellery; Surface engineering; Travel goods & accessories
- ● Conf - Mtgs - Exhib - SG - Expt - Inf - Lib - LG
- M 1,800 f, UK / 50 f, o'seas, 721 others
- ¶ Export News - 4.
- ✕ 2011 British Jewellery, Giftware & Finishing Federation

British Alpaca Society (BAS) 1997
■ PO Box 251, EXETER, Devon, EX2 8WX.   (hq)
   01382 437788   fax 01392 270421
   email info@bas-uk.com   http://www.bas-uk.com
   Admin: Elizabeth Henson
▲ Company Limited by Guarantee
○ *B; for owners & breeders of alpacas
Gp Fibre production; Welfare; Shows; Education
● Conf - Mtgs - ET - Res - Exhib - Comp - SG - Stat - Expt - Inf -
   PL - VE - LG
M 1,000 i, UK / 30 i, o'seas
   (Sub: £70, £25 (magazine))
¶ Alpaca - 4;   Members Handbook - 1; both ftm only.

British Alpine Racing Ski Clubs   (BARSC)
■ 4 The Beeches, Calderstones, LIVERPOOL, L18 3LT.
   http://www.barsc.net
○ *S

British Amateur Boxing Association (BABA) 2008
§ English Institute of Sport, Coleridge Rd, SHEFFIELD, S Yorks,
   S9 5DA.   (hq)
   0114-223 5613
   Sec: Matt
   A company established in 2008 to manage the World Class
   Programme, with the 3 home nations (England, Scotland &
   Wales) as shareholders.   Initially for men only, women were
   invited to compete in August 2009

British Amateur Gymnastics Association (British Gymnastics)
see **British Gymnastics**

British Amateur Rugby League Association (BARLA) 1973
NR 4 New North Parade, HUDDERSFIELD, W Yorks, HD1 5JP.   (hq)
   01484 544131   fax 01484 519985
   email info@barla.org.uk   http://www.barla.org.uk
   Sec: Nigel Hollingsworth
▲ Un-incorporated Society
○ *S; the governing body of amateur Rugby League football in
   Great Britain
● Conf - Mtgs - ET - Exam - Res - Exhib - Comp - Stat - Inf - PL -
   VE - LG
< BARLA is the amateur section of the Rugby Football League
M 1,400 teams, 900 youth & junior sides
¶ BARLA Bulletin - 6.   Hbk - 1.

British Amateur Television Club (BATC) 1949
■ 9 Prior Croft Close, CAMBERLEY, Surrey, GU15 1DE.   (hsp)
   0774 029 1191 (1830-2100)
   email secretary@batc.org.uk   http://www.batc.org.uk
   Hon Sec: Brian Summers
▲ Un-incorporated Society
○ *G; all technical aspects of television & radio, computing
● Conf - Mrtgs - Lib - Internet television streaming
< Radio Soc of Great Britain (RSGB)
M [not stated]
¶ CQ-TV (Jnl) - 4; ftm only.

British Ambulance Association
NR PO Box 100, PAIGNTON, Devon, TQ3 1YE.
   01803 843966
   email info@baa999.com
○ *T; for private ambulance providers

British Ambulance Society (BAS) 1977
NR 21 Victoria Rd, HORLEY, Surrey, RH6 9BN.   (sp)
   http://www.b-a-s.org.uk
   Chmn: Roger Leonard,   Gen Sec: Graham Andrews
▲ Un-incorporated Society
○ *G; compilation & storage of ambulance history: vehicles,
   uniforms, badges, equipment & photographs & any other
   artifacts concerning ambulance manufacture, services etc
M i, f & org

British American Business Council (BABC) 1954
NR 703 Market Street (suite 1314), SAN FRANCISCO, CA 94103,
   USA.   (hq)
   1 (415) 296 8645   fax 1 (415) 296 9649
   email info@babcsf.org   http://www.babcsf.org
   Exec Dir: Zoe Matthews
▲ Company Limited by Guarantee
○ *C; to provide a forum for information, networking &
   identification of business opportunities, trade & investment in
   Northern California & the UK
● Conf - Mtgs - Expt - Inf - Lib - LG
< Brit Amer Business Coun
M 85 i, 165 f, o'seas
¶ Membership Directory - 1; ftm only.

British-American Business Inc (BABi) 1920
■ 75 Brook St, LONDON, W1K 4AD.   (hq)
   020 7290 9888   fax 020 7491 9172
   http://www.babinc.org
   Dir: Peter Hunt
▲ Company Limited by Guarantee
Br New York
○ *C; to promote the growth & development of trade between
   British & American companies in both Britain & USA
● Conf - Mtgs - Stat - Expt - Inf - Lib - LG
< Eur Coun of Amer Chams Comm; Brit-Amer Cham Comm
M 700 f
¶ Network London - 4;   Network New York - 4; both free.
   British American Business, the UK Hbk - 1; ftm; £60 nm.
   American British Business - 1; ftm, £60 nm.
   Membership Directory - 1; ftm only.

British American Football Association   (BAFA) 1987
NR West House, Hedley-on-the-Hill, STOCKSFIELD,
   Northumberland, NE43 7SW.   (chmn/p)
   01661 843179
   email chairman@bafa.org.uk
   Chmn: Gary Marshall
▲ Company Limited by Guarantee
○ *S; to act as the governing body for amateur American football
   in GB
M c 4,500 i

**British Amusement Catering Trades Association   (BACTA)
1974**
NR Alders House, 133 Aldersgate St, LONDON, EC1A 4JA.   (hq)
   020 7726 9826
   http://www.bacta.org.uk
   Chief Exec: Leslie Macleod-Miller
Br 10
○ *T; to represent the pay-to-play leisure machine industry
   including manufacturers, suppliers & amusement centre
   owners
Gp Inland amusement arcades; Seaside amusement centres;
   Manufacturers, importers, distributors of amusement
   machines; Operators of amusement machines
● Conf - Mtgs - ET - Exhib - SG - Stat - Expt - Inf - Lib - VE - LG
< Fedn of Coin Machine Trade Assns of Europe (EUROMAT);
   Music Users' Coun of Europe; Nat Amusements Coun; Music
   Users' Coun
M i & f
¶ NL - 10 ftm only.   AR; free.
   Hbk (LM) - 1; ftm.

British Andrology Society (BAS) 1975
NR GlaxoSmithKline (Bldg 4), Park Rd, WARE, Herts, SG12 0DP.
   (hsb)
   01920 882828
   email jacqui.a.piner@gsk.com
   Sec: Dr Jacqui A Piner
○ *Q; promotion of research & professional training in male
   infertility & reproduction research
M i

British Angora Goat Society   1981
NR   5 The Langlands, HAMPTON LUCY, Warks, CV35 8BN.   (hq)
       01789 841930
       email secretary@angoragoat.fsnet.co.uk
       http://www.britishangoragoats.org.uk
○   *B
M   i & groups
¶   NL - 3.   Ybk - 1.

British Anti-Vivisection Association   (BAVA)
NR   PO Box 73, CHESTERFIELD, Derbys, S41 0YZ.
○   *K

British Antique Dealers' Association   (BADA)   1918
■   20 Rutland Gate, LONDON, SW7 1BD.   (hq)
       020 7589 4128   fax 020 7581 9083
       email info@bada.org   http://www.bada.org
       Sec Gen: Mrs Elaine J Dean
▲   Company Limited by Guarantee
○   *T; for the leading antique dealers in the UK - the association
       was incorporated in 1951
●   ET - Exhib - Stat - Inf - LG
<   Confédn Intle des Négociants en Oeuvres d'Art (CINOA)
M   400 f
¶   LM - 2; free.

**British Antique Furniture Restorers' Association   (BAFRA)
1979**
■   The Old Rectory, Warmwell, DORCHESTER, Dorset,
       DT2 8HQ.   (hq)
       01305 854822   fax 01305 854822
       email headoffice@bafra.org.uk
       http://www.bafra.org.uk
       Chief Exec: Michael Barrington
▲   Company Limited by Guarantee
○   *P; to promote study & research in furniture conservation &
       restoration; to maintain high professional standards among
       members
Gp   Carving & gilding; Marble & stone; Metalware; Oriental
       lacquerwork & japanning; Persian carpets; Upholstery
●   Conf - ET - Res - Exhib - Inf - Workshop seminars
M   101 i, 1 f, UK / 10 i, o'seas
       (Sub: £350 i, £600 f, £50 BAFRA Friends)
¶   BAFRA Jnl - 3; ftm, £16-£21 nm.
       The BAFRA Directory - 1; ftm, £8-£20 nm.

British Aphasiology Society   (BAS)   1987
NR   c/o Fiona Stewart, Speech & Language Therapy Dept,
       Sunderland Royal Hospital, Kayll Rd, SUNDERLAND,
       SR4 7TP.   (sec/b)
       0191-565 6256
       http://www.bas.org.uk
       Sec: Fiona Stewart
▲   Un-incorporated Society
○   *L; to foster the study of aphasia (language disorder following
       brain injury); to promote professional & scientific work on
       aphasia
M   i

British Appaloosa Society   (BApS)   1976
NR   Homestead House, Peel Green, Hellifield, SKIPTON, N Yorks,
       BD23 4LD.   (chmn/p)
       01729 850730
       http://www.appaloosa.org.uk
       Chmn: Brian Entwistle,
       Sec: Suzanne Entwistle
▲   Registered Charity
○   *B; to provide a registry for Appaloosa horses; to preserve &
       improve the breed
●   Conf - Mtgs - Comp - Expt
<   Brit Horse Soc
M   750 i
¶   NL - 4; ftm only.   Register of Horses - 1.
       Stallion Directory - 2.

British Apparel & Textile Confederation   (BATC)   1992
NR   3 Queen Sq, Bloomsbury, LONDON, WC1N 3AR.   (hq)
       020 7843 9460   fax 020 7843 9478
       http://www.ukft.org
       Dir Gen: John Wilson
▲   Company Limited by Guarantee
○   *T; representation of the apparel & textile industry in the UK to
       government, the press & others
●   Mtgs - Stat - Inf - LG
<   Eur Apparel & Textile Org (EURATEX)
M   7 f, 2 org, 13 trade org

British Approvals for Fire Equipment   (BAFE)   1984
NR   Bridges 2, The Fire Service College, London Rd, MORETON-IN-
       MARSH, Glos, GL56 0RH.   (hq)
       0844 335 0897
       email info@bafe.org.uk   http://www.bafe.org.uk
▲   Company Limited by Guarantee
○   *P; registration & certification of providers of active fire
       protection equipment & services
●   Mtgs - LG - Certification & registration
M   c 100 f, UK / 4 f, o'seas
¶   BAFE Brochure;   BAFE Supplement;
       BAFE List of Approved Registered Organisations; all free.

British Arachnological Society   (BAS)   1963
NR   31 Duxford Close, REDDITCH, Worcs, B97 5BY.   (hsp)
       01527 544952
       http://www.britishspiders.org.uk
       Hon Sec: John Partridge
▲   Registered Charity
○   *L, *Q; distribution, behaviour, taxonomy etc of spiders
       (araneae), harvestmen (opilionidae), & pseudoscorpions
       (pseudoscorpionidae)
●   Conf - Mtgs - ET - Res - SG - Stat - Inf - Lib - PL
M   c 300 i, 20 libraries & universities, UK / 275 i, 100 libraries &
       universities, o'seas
¶   Bulletin - 3.   NL - 3.   Hbk.

British Archaeological Association   (BAA)   1843
NR   18 Stanley Rd, OXFORD, OX4 1QZ.   (hsp)
       01865 724378
       http://www.britarch.ac.uk/baa   (hsb)
       Hon Sec: John McNeill
○   *L; study of archaeology & the preservation of national
       antiquities

British Argentine Chamber of Commerce   (BACC)   1995
NR   65 Brook St, LONDON, W1K 4AH.   (hq)
       020 7495 8730
       http://www.britargcham.co.uk
       Chmn: Peter Edbrooke
▲   Company Limited by Guarantee
○   *C; trade & investment promotion
●   Conf - Exhib - Stat - Expt - VE - LG
¶   Bulletin.

British Armwrestling Federation   (BAF)
NR   13 Westland Avenue, DARWEN, Lancs, BB3 2ST.   (mem/sp)
       http://www.armwrestling.co.uk
       Pres: Neil Pickup
○   *S

British Art Market Federation   (BAMF)   1996
NR   10 Bury St, LONDON, SW1Y 6AA.   (hq)
       020 7389 2148
       Chmn: Anthony Browne,   Sec: Christopher Battiscombe
▲   Un-incorporated Society
○   *T; to represent the various elements of the British art trade
M   3 f, 8 org

British Art Medal Society (BAMS) 1982

- ■ Dept of Coins & Medals, British Museum, Great Russell St, LONDON, WC1B 3DG. (hsb)
  020 7323 8568   fax 020 7323 8171
  http://www.bams.org.uk
  Sec: Miss Janet Larkin
- ○ *A; study of the history of the medal
- ● Conf - Mtgs - Exhib - Comp
- M c 370 i, f & org
- ¶ The Medal - 2

British Artist Blacksmiths Association (BABA) 1978

- ■ Anwick Forge, 62 Main Rd, Anwick, SLEAFORD, Lincs, NG34 9SU. (hsb)
  01526 830303
  email babasecretary@baba.org.uk
  http://www.baba.org.uk
  Hon Sec: Tim Mackereth
- ▲ Un-incorporated Society
- ○ *P, *T; to encourage a greater awareness of the blacksmiths' art amongst architects, interior designers & the general public
- ● Conf - Mtgs - ET - Exhib - Comp - SG - Inf - PL
- M 638 i, UK / 30 i, o'seas
- ¶ Artist Blacksmith - 4;
  Members' Address Book - 1; both ftm only.

British Arts Festivals Association (BAFA) 1970

- NR 1 Goodwins Court, LONDON, WC2N 4LL. (hq)
  020 7240 4532
  email info@artsfestivals.co.uk
  Admin: Kim Hart
- ▲ Registered Charity; Un-incorporated Society
- ○ *A, *N; the meeting point of arts festivals in the UK. It aims to strengthen the arts festivals; to raise their profit & status; to provide a centre for information
- ● Conf - Mtgs - ET - Res - Inf
- < Eur Festivals Assn
- M c 100 festivals
- ¶ Arts Festivals Calendar & Directory - 1; free.

British Association of Academic Phoneticians (BAAP) 1982

- ■ Dept of English Language, The University, GLASGOW, G12 8QQ. (archivist b)
  0141-330 4596   fax 0141-330 3531
  email m.macmahon@englang.arts.gla.ac.uk
  http://www.baap.ac.uk
  Hon Sec & Archivist: Prof M K C MacMahon
- ▲ Un-incorporated Society
- ○ *P; for people with a teaching or research post in phonetics in an institute of higher education in the UK or the Republic of Ireland
- ● Colloquium (2 yrly)
- M 150 i, UK / c 50 i, o'seas
  Note: The Convenorship changes every 2 years.

British Association for Adoption & Fostering (BAAF) 1980

- NR Saffron House, 6-10 Kirby St, LONDON, EC1N 8TS. (hq)
  020 7421 2600
  email mail@baaf.org.uk   http://www.baaf.org.uk
  Dir: Felicity Collier
- ▲ Registered Charity
- Br 6
- ○ *N, *W; to promote the interests of children separated from their parents
- ● Conf - Mtgs - ET - Inf - Lib - LG (Dept of Health)
- < R Coll Paediatrics & Child Health
- M 1,250 i, 210 agencies, 80 associate members
- ¶ Adoption & Fostering (Jnl) - 4.
  Adoption & Fostering News - 8.
  List of Agency Members.   Legal Member Directory.
  Medical Member Directory.
  Be My Parent Newspaper - 6.
  Focus on Fives NL - 26.   AR - 1.

British Association for the Advancement of Science
since 2009 British Science Association

British Association of Aesthetic Plastic Surgeons (BAAPS) 1985

- ■ at the Royal College of Surgeons, 35-43 Lincoln's Inn Fields, LONDON, WC2A 3PE. (hq)
  020 7430 1840   fax 020 7242 4922
  email secretariat@baaps.org.uk
  http://www.baaps.org.uk
  Pres: Fazel Fatah
- ▲ Company Limited by Guarantee; Registered Charity
- ○ *P; teaching & research of aesthetic plastic surgery
- ● Conf - Mtgs - ET - Res - Exhib - Stat - Inf - PL
- < Intl Soc of Aesthetic Plastic Surgeons (ISAPS); Brit Assn of Plastic Surgeons (BAPS); Intl Confedn of Plastic & Reconstructive Surgery
- M 170 i, UK / 5 i, o'seas
- ¶ Factsheets on Aesthetic Surgery.
  Syllabus for Surgeons.   LM; all free.

British Association of American Square Dance Clubs (BAASDC) 1953

- NR 87 Brabazon Rd, HESTON, Middx, TW5 9LL. (hsp)
  020 8897 0723
  http://www.uksquaredancing.com
  Sec: Mrs Patricia Connett-Woodcock
- ▲ Un-incorporated Society
- Br 230
- ○ *D; promotion of modern American square dancing for fun & friendship
- Gp Square Dance Clubs; Round Dance Clubs
- ● Mtgs
- M c 5,000 i
- ¶ Let's Square Dance - 10.

British Association for American Studies (BAAS) 1955

- ■ c/o Dr Catherine Morley, Dept of English, University of Leicester, University Rd, LEICESTER, LE1 7RH. (hsb)
  07841 288478
  email catherine.morley@baas.ac.uk
  http://www.baas.ac.uk
  Hon Sec: Dr Catherine Morley
- ▲ Registered Charity
- Br 2
- ○ *L; to promote serious study of the United States of America
- ● Conf - Mtgs - ET - Res - Comp - Inf
- < Eur Assn for Amer Studies; Amer Studies Assn; Canadian Assn for Amer Studies; Ir Assn for Amer Studies
- M 500 i, UK / 30 i, o'seas
  (Sub: £14-£48)
- ¶ Jnl of American Studies - 3.   NL - 2.
  American Studies (book series) - 3.

British Association of Anger Management (BAAM) 2001

- ■ 4 The Bothy, Plawhatch Hall, Plawhatch Lane, Sharpthorne, EAST GRINSTEAD, W Sussex, RH19 4JL. (hq)
  0845 130 0286   fax 01342 811513
  email info@angermanage.co.uk
  http://www.angermanage.co.uk
  Dir: Mike Fisher
- ▲ Un-incorporated Society
- ○ *G, *P; all issues concerning anger, conflict & stress management for people, education, organisations & government bodies; training for those wishing to move into anger management
- ● Conf - ET - SG - Inf - Programmes in anger management & conflict management - One-to-one therapy - Bespoke anger management courses
- < Codes & practices of the British Association for Counselling & Psychotherapy & the UK Council for Psychotherapy
- M i, f, org
- ¶ NL - 4.
  Beating Anger (published by Rider Books); £7.99 m, £7.55 nm.

© CBD Research Ltd · Beckenham · BR3 5JS · Tel 020 8650 7745 · E-mail cbd@cbdresearch.com · www.cbdresearch.com

British Association for Applied Linguistics (BAAL) 1967
- ■ PO Box 6688, LONDON, SE15 3WB.   (asa)
  020 7639 0090   fax 020 7635 6014
  email admin@baal.org.uk   http://www.baal.org.uk
  Chmn: Prof Guy Cook,   Hon Sec: Dr Paul Thompson
- ▲ Registered Charity
- ○ *L; to promote the study of language in use; to foster
  interdisciplinary collaboration; to provide a common forum
  for those engaged in the theoretical study of language & for
  those whose interest is in the practical applications of such
  work
- ● Conf - Mtgs - ET - Res
- < Assn Intl de Linguistique Appliquée (AILA)
- M 737 i, 20 f, UK / 201 i, o'seas
- ¶ NL - 3;   LM - 1;   Annual Proceedings - 1; all ftm only.
  Publications of the International Association:
  AILA News - 2/3;   AILA Review - 1; both ftm.

British Association of Art Therapists Ltd   (BAAT)   1991
- ■ 24-27 White Lion St, LONDON, N1 9PD.   (hq)
  020 7686 4216   fax 020 7837 7945
  email info@baat.org   http://www.baat.org
  Chief Exec: Val Huet
- ▲ Company Limited by Guarantee
- ○ *U; to promote art therapy in hospitals, clinics & special
  schools; to support therapists
- Gp Art therapy &: Autism & spectrum disorder, Education,
  Forensics, Learning disabilities, Neurology, Older people
- ● Conf - Mtgs - ET - SG - Inf - Empl - LG
- < Allied Health Professions Fedn
- M i & org
- ¶ Inscape - International Jnl of Art Therapy - 2; ftm, £25 nm.
  Newsbriefing Magazine (NL) - 4;
  Newsbulletin (jobs & news) - 12; both ftm only.

**British Association of Audiovestibular Physicians   (BAAP)
1977**
- NR Dept of Audiovestibular Medicine, Queen Alexander Hospital,
  Southwick Hill Rd, Cosham, PORTSMOUTH, Hants,
  PO6 3LY.   (admin)
  email adminsec@baap.org.uk   http://www.baap.org.uk
  Admin Sec: Mrs Carol Bishop
- ○ *M, *P; for consultant & trainee physicians & paediatricians
  practising audiovestibular medicine

British Association of Aviation Consultants   (BAAC)   1972
- NR c/o Jacobs Consultancy, 16 Connaught Place, LONDON,
  W2 2ES.   (asa)
  email committee@baac.org.uk   http://www.baac.org.uk
  Co Sec: Peter Mackenzie-Williams
- ▲ Company Limited by Guarantee
- Br Australia, New Zealand
- ○ *P, *T; to ensure that all services provided by its registered
  Aviation Consultants are subjected to definite standards of
  professional competence with the interests of the customer
  paramount
- ● Consultancy services - Training - Personnel selection - Social
  events
- < Academy of Experts; Farnborough Aerospace Consortium
- M c 80 i
- ¶ NL - 2/3; ftm only.   Register (LM) - 1; free.

British Association of Balloon Operators   (BABO)   1993
- NR 195 Moor Rd, CROSTON, Lancs, PR26 9HP.   (chmn/p)
  0845 643 6016
  email chairman@babo.org.uk   http://www.babo.org.uk
  Chmn: John Fenton (01772 601525)
- ▲ Company Limited by Guarantee
- ○ *T; to represent UK Balloon Air Operators Certificate holders
  (passenger carrying hot air balloons)
- ● Mtgs - ET - Inf
- < Brit Balloon & Airship Club
- M c 70 f
- ¶ NL - 12; ftm only.

British Association of Barbershop Singers   (BABS)   1974
- ■ Druids Lea, Upper Stanton Drew, BRISTOL, BS39 4EG.   (hsp)
  01275 332778   fax 01275 332778
  email babs@crbennett.co.uk
  http://www.singbarbershop.com
  Admin Dir & Co Sec: Colin Bennett
- ▲ Company Limited by Guarantee; Registered Charity
- Br 50+
- ○ *D; to encourage barbershop singing in the UK
- Gp Convention; Directorate of music services (education); Guild of
  Judges; Harmony Foundation
  Colleges: Harmony, Directors
- ● Conf - ET - Comp - Inf
- < Barbershop Harmony Soc (USA); Making Music (UK)
- M 2,000 i
  (Sub: £23-£160)
- ¶ Harmony Express - 6; ftm.   AR - 1.

**British Association of Beauty Therapy & Cosmetology Ltd
(BABTAC)   1977**
- NR Ambrose House, Meteor Court, Barnett Way, Barnwood,
  GLOUCESTER, GL4 3GG.   (hq)
  01452 623115
  email enquiries@babtac.com   http://www.babtac.com
  Gen Mgr: Julie Speed
- ○ *P

**British Association for Behavioural & Cognitive
Psychotherapies   (BABCP)   1972**
- NR Imperial House, Hornby St, BURY, Lancs, BL9 5BN.   (hq)
  0161-705 4304   fax 0161-705 4306
  email babcp@babcp.com   http://www.babcp.com
  Hon Sec: Helen Macdonald
- ▲ Registered Charity
- Br 12
- ○ *K; to advance the theory & practice of the psychotherapies; in
  particular the application of experimental methodology &
  learning techniques to the assessment & modification of
  behaviour in a wide variety of settings
- ● Conf - Mtgs - ET - SG - Inf - Accreditation & registration of
  psychotherapists
- < Eur Assn for Behaviour & Cognitive Therapy (EABCT); Ir Assn for
  Behaviour & Cognitive Therapies (IABCP); UK Coun
  Psychotherapy (UKCP)
- M 6,000 i
- ¶ Behavioural & Cognitive Psychotherapy - 4.
  BABCP News - 4.
  Directory of Accredited Behavioural / Cognitive & REBT
  Psychotherapists - 1.

British Association for Biofuels & Oils
  in 2006 merged with **Renewable Energy Association**

**British Association of Biological Anthropology &
Osteoarchaeology**
- NR Leverhulme Centre for Evolutionary Studies, Henry
  Wellcome Bldg, Fitzwilliam St, CAMBRIDGE, CB2 1QH.
  (hsb)
  01223 7647006
  http://www.babao.org.uk
  Sec: Piers Mitchell
- ○ *P; for those interested in all areas of the analysis of human
  remains

British Association for Canadian Studies (BACS) 1975
NR South Block Senate House (room 212), University of London,
Malet St, LONDON, WC1E 7HU. (hq)
020 7862 8687 (1000-1600 Tues-Fri)   fax 020 7117
1875
email canstuds@gmail.com
http://www.canadian-studies.net
Admin Sec: Jodie Robson
▲ Registered Charity
○ *L; to encourage & support research & teaching concerning
Canada across the whole of the educational community in
the UK; the dissemination of knowledge & understanding of
Canada to the public of the UK
Gp Groupe des Récherche et d'études sur le Canada francophone
Aboriginal studies circle; Business & economic stuies; Canada/
UK cities research; History & politics; International studies;
Legal studies; Library resources; Literature
● Conf - ET - SG - Inf
< Intl Coun for Canadian Studies; Eur Canadian Studies Network;
UK Coun for Area Studies Assns
M 280 i, 120 org, UK / 50 i, o'seas
(Sub: £30 i)
¶ British Jnl of Canadian Studies - 2;   NL - 2.
BACS E-news (electronic bulletin - 12.

British Association for Cancer Research (BACR) 1960
■ c/o Leeds Institute of Molecular Medicine, Clinical Sciences
Building, St James's University Hospital, Beckett St, LEEDS,
W Yorks, LS9 7TF.   (hq)
0113-206 5611
email bacr@leeds.ac.uk   http://www.bacr.org.uk
Hon Sec: Prof Sue Burchill
▲ Registered Charity
○ *P, *Q; clinical & basic researchers interested in cancer
● Conf - Mtgs - ET
M 1,589 i

British Association for Cemeteries in South Asia (BACSA) 1977
■ 135 Burntwood Lane, LONDON, SW17 0AJ.   (hsp)
email rosieljai@clara.co.uk
Hon Sec: Dr Rosie Llewellyn-Jones
▲ Registered Charity
Br India
○ *K; preservation of historical cemeteries; conversion of those
dilapidated beyond repair to social use; recording &
publishing information relating to Europeans in Asia
● Mtgs - Res - Exhib - SG - Inf - VE - Collecting monumental
inscriptions from UK churches, or churchyards, with
references to S Asia
< Fedn Family History Socs; Indian Nat Trust of Art & Cultural
Heritage (INTACH); Assn for Presvn of Histl Cemeteries in
India (APHCI)
M c 1,900 i, f & org
¶ Chowkidar (Jnl) - 2.
Publications list available.

British Association for Chemical Specialities (BACS) 1983
■ Simpson House, Windsor Court, Clarence Drive, HARROGATE,
N Yorks, HG1 2PE.   (hq)
01423 700249   fax 01423 520297
email enquiries@bacsnet.org   http://www.bacsnet.org
Sec: John Reid
▲ Company Limited by Guarantee
○ *T; manufacturers & formulators of speciality chemicals &
intermediates (incl maintenance products for consumer &
industrial use), disinfectants & industrial biocides (incl water
treatment chemicals & services) & speciality surfactants
Gp Biocides forum; COSRAM; Speciality surfactants; Water
treatment
● Conf - Mtgs - LG
< Alliance Ind Assns; Brit Business Bureau; Confedn Brit Ind;
M 135 f
¶ AR - 1; free.

British Association for Chinese Studies (BACS) 1976
NR School of East Asian Studies, University of Sheffield,
Western Bank, SHEFFIELD, S Yorks, S10 2TN.   (pres/b)
0114-222 8400
http://www.bacsuk.org.uk
Pres: Prof Tim Wright
▲ Registered Charity
○ *L; to promote & support Chinese studies in the UK
● Conf - Mtgs - Inf - VE - LG
< Eur Assn of Chinese Studies; Coordinating Coun Area Studies
Assns; Jt E Asian Studies Conf/C'ee
M c 200 i & org
¶ Bulletin - 1; ftm only.

British Association of Clinical Anatomists (BACA) 1977
■ School of Medicine, Health Policy & Practice, University of East
Anglia, NORWICH, NR4 7TJ.   (hsb)
01603 591104
email d.heylings@uea.ac.uk
Hon Sec: Dr David Heylings
▲ Registered Charity
○ *E, *M, *P
● Mtgs - Res
< Amer Assn of Clinical Anatomists (AACA); Australian & New
Zealand Assn of Clinical Anatomists (ANZACA)
> Amer Assn of Clinical Anatomists (AACA); Australian & New
Zealand Assn of Clinical Anatomists (ANZACA)
M 171 i, UK / 69 i, o'seas
¶ Clinical Anatomy - 8.

British Association of Clinical Dental Technology (BACDT) 2009
NR 44-46 Wollaton Rd, Beeston, NOTTINGHAM, NG9 2NR.   (hq)
0115-957 5370
email info@bacdt.org.uk   http://www.bacdt.org.uk
▲ Company Limited by Guarantee
○ *T;
● Mtgs - Res - ET - Inf
M i

British Association of Cold Pressed Oil Producers (BACPOP)
NR PO Box 259, BECKENHAM, Kent, BR3 3YA.
020 8776 2644
http://www.bacpop.org.uk
○ *T; to represent British farmers producing cold pressed oils for
use in everything from mayonnaise to face creams
M 11 f

British Association of Colliery Management - Technical, Energy, Administrative & Management (BACM-TEAM) 1947
NR 17 South Parade, DONCASTER, S Yorks, DN1 2DR.   (hq)
01302 815551   fax 01302 815552
email gs@bacmteam.org.uk
http://www.bacmteam.org.uk
Gen Sec: Patrick Carragher
Br 7
○ *U; it represents employees within numerous sections of
industry, with members in information technology, finance,
pensions administration, distribution, manufacturing &
utilities, as well as its traditional areas of mining &
professional engineering
● Lib - Empl - LG
< TUC
M 2,537 i
¶ Focus NL - 4;   AR - 1; both ftm only.

British Association of Communicators in Business Ltd
since 2010 **Institute of Internal Communication**

British Association for Community Child Health
a group of the **Royal College of Paediatrics & Child Health**

© CBD Research Ltd · Beckenham · BR3 5JS · Tel 020 8650 7745 · E-mail cbd@cbdresearch.com · www.cbdresearch.com

British Association of Community Doctors in Audiology
as the British Association of Paediatricians in Audiology it is now a special interest group of the **Royal College of Paediatrics & Child Health**

British Association of Concert Halls   1989
■ Cadogan Hall, 5 Sloane Terrace, LONDON, SW1X 9DQ. (hsb)
○ *T; a forum for discussion between concert promoters of classical music
● Conf - Mtgs - SG - Inf
M 38 f
✕ Association of British Concert Promoters

British Association of Conference Destinations
merged on 1 January 2009 with **Eventia**

British Association of Construction Heads
NR 25 Glenore Rd, WEYMOUTH, Dorset, DT4 0PG.
01305 835583
http://www.bach.uk.com
○ *P; for university & college managers of construction training departments; training organisations & educational consultants

British Association of Cosmetic Doctors
NR Shorne Village Surgery, Crown Lane, SHORNE, Kent, DA12 3DY.
01474 823900
email info@cosmeticdoctors.co.uk
http://www.cosmeticdoctors.co.uk
○ *P

British Association of Cosmetic Surgeons   (BACS)   1980
NR 10 Harley St, LONDON, W1G 9PF.   (hsb)
0800 783 5614
email cajano@onetel.net   http://www.b-a-c-s.co.uk
Hon Sec: Paulo Cajano
○ *M; to teach, expound, promote & propagate the theory & practice & develop the science of cosmetic surgery for the benefit of the public & the profession as a whole
● Conf - ET - Inf - Mtgs
M 28 i
¶ Basic Account of Plastic Surgery; £9.99

British Association for Counselling & Psychotherapy   (BACP)   1977
■ BACP House, 15 St John's Business Park, LUTTERWORTH, Leics, LE17 4HB.   (hq)
01455 883300   fax 01455 550243
email bacp@bacp.co.uk   http://www.bacp.co.uk
Chief Exec: Laurie Clarke
▲ Company Limited by Guarantee; Registered Charity
○ *P; to lead the effort to make counselling & psychotherapy widely recognised as a profession whose purpose & activity is understood by the general public; to be the professional body for counselling & psychotherapy
Gp Association of Independent Practitioners; Association for Pastoral & Spiritual Care & Counselling (APSCC); Association for University & College Counselling (AUCC); BACP Coaching; BACP Healthcare; BACP Workplace; Counselling Children & Young People (CCYP)
● Conf - Mtgs - ET - Res - Exhib - Inf - Lib - LG
M 24,500 i, 1,000 f, UK / 326 i, 12 f, o'seas
¶ Therapy Today - 10; ftm, £69 nm.
Counselling & Psychotherapy Research (CPR) - 4; ftm, £54 nm.
Healthcare Counselling & Psychotherapy Jnl - 4; ftm, £30 nm.
Counselling at Work (Jnl of the Assn for Counselling at Work) - 4; free to ACW members, £30 nm.
AUCC (Jnl of the Assn for University & College Counselling) - 4; free to AUCC members, £30 nm.

British Association of Crystal Growth   (BACG)   1969
■ c/o Dr Tim Joyce, George Holt Bldg, University of Liverpool, LIVERPOOL, L69 3GH.   (hsb)
0151-794 5369
email t.joyce@liverpool.ac.uk   http://www.bacg.co.uk
Hon Sec: Dr Tim Joyce
▲ Registered Charity
○ *L; to encourage discussion of the theory & practice of crystal growth in industry, government laboratories & universities in the UK including all types of inorganic & organic crystalline materials including metals, ceramics, polymers & electronic device materials
Gp Materials: Biological / chemical, Optical, Oxide, Semi-conductor
● Conf - Mtgs - ET - Exhib - Comp
< Intl Org Crystal Growth (IOCG)
M 400 i, UK / 50 i, o'seas
¶ NL - 2; ftm only.

British Association of Day Surgery   (BADS)   1989
NR at the Royal College of Surgeons, 35-43 Lincoln's Inn Fields, LONDON, WC2A 3PE.   (hq)
020 7973 0308   fax 020 7973 0314
email bads@bads.co.uk   http://www.bads.co.uk
Admin: Mrs V Hall   Hon Sec: Douglas McWhinnie
▲ Registered Charity
○ *P; to promote good practice in day surgery
● Conf - Mtgs - ET - Res - Exhib - VE - LG
< Intl Assn of Ambulatory Surgery
M c 750 i
¶ Jnl of One-Day Surgery - 4.

British Association of Dental Nurses   (BADN)   1940
■ PO Box 4/ Room 200, Hillhouse International Business Centre, THORNTON-CLEVELEYS, Lancs, FY5 4QD.   (hq)
01253 338360
email admin@badn.org.uk   http://www.badn.org.uk
Chief Exec: Pamela Swain
○ *P
Gp National gps for Dental nurses in: Armed forces, Conscious sedation, Education, Orthodontics, Practice management, Reception
Special care (for dental nurses working with patients with special needs); Orthodontic (for dental nurses working in ortho conscious sedation / anaesthesia) [in process of formation]
● Conf - SG - Empl - LG
M c 5,600 i
(Sub: £70 (rates vary for students, retired etc)
¶ British Dental Nurses' Jnl - 4; ftm.

British Association of Dental Therapists   (BADT)   1961
■ Providence House, 11 The Broadway, SANDHURST, Berks, GU47 9AB.
07800 728082
email secretary@badt.org.uk   http://www.badt.org.uk
Br c 8
○ *P
● Conf - Mtgs - ET - SG - Inf - Empl - LG
M 300 i
¶ Dental Therapy Update - 4.   Contact Point (NL) - 2.

British Association of Dermatologists   (BAD)   1921
- ■   Willan House, 4 Fitzroy Sq, LONDON, W1T 5HQ.   (hq)
     020 7383 0266   fax 020 7388 5263
     email admin@bad.org.uk   http://www.bad.org.uk
     Chief Exec: Miss Marilyn Benham
- ▲   Registered Charity
- ○   *P; study & teaching of dermatology (diseases of the skin); to promote high quality care for sufferers
- Gp   British Cosmetic Dermatology Group; British Dermatological Nursing Group; British Epidermo-Epidemiology Society; British Photodermatology Group; British Society for Cutaneous Allergy; British Society for Dermatological Surgery; British Society for Dermatopathology; British Society for Investigative Dermatology; British Society for Paediatric Dermatology; British Society for the Study of Vulval Disease; British Teledermatology Society; Dowling Club; Primary Care Dermatology Society; Scottish Dermatological Society; The Skin Investigation Society (THESIS)
- ●   Conf - Mtgs - Exhib
- M   741 i, UK / 202 i, o'seas
- ¶   British Jnl of Dermatology - 12.   NL - 4.
     Clinical & Experimental Dermatology - 6.

British Association of Dramatherapists   (BADth)   1976
- ■   Waverley, Battledown Approach, CHELTENHAM, Glos, GL52 6RE.   (postal/address)
     01242 235515
     email enquiries@badth.org.uk   http://www.badth.org.uk
     Chmn: Madeline Andersen-Warren
- ▲   Company Limited by Guarantee
- ○   *P; to promote, maintain, improve & advance the education of the public about the benefits, theory & practice of dramatherapy
- ●   Conf - ET - Res - Inf
- <   Allied Health Professions Fedn
- M   'varies'
- ¶   The Prompt - 4;   The Dramatherapy Jnl - 3; both ftm.

British Association for Early Childhood Education   (Early Education)   1923
- ■   136 Cavell St, LONDON, E1 2JA.   (hq)
     020 7539 5400   fax 020 7539 5409
     email office@early-education.org.uk
     http://www.early-education.org.uk
     Operations Mgr: Jenny Rabin
- ▲   Company Limited by Guarantee; Registered Charity
- Br   52
- ○   *E, *K, *W; to promote the right of all children to education of the highest quality; to provide a multi-disciplinary network of support & advice for everyone concerned with the care & education of children from birth to eight
- ●   Conf - Mtgs - ET - Res - Exhib - Inf
- M   6,000 i, UK / 25 i, o'seas
- ¶   Early Education (Jnl) - 3;   NL - 3;   AR - 1; all ftm only.

British Association for Emergency Medicine
     in 2008 merged with the **College of Emergency Medicine**

British Association of Endocrine & Thyroid Surgeons   (BAETS)   1980
- NR   at the Royal College of Surgeons, 35-43 Lincoln's Inn Fields, LONDON, WC2A 3PE.   (hsb)
     020 7304 4771
     http://www.baes.info
     Sec: Greg Sadler
- ▲   Registered Charity
- ○   *M, *P; to promote the dissemination of education & information about endocrine & thyroid diseases particularly insofar as they may be treated by surgeons; to promote research
- <   Assn Surgeons GB & I
- M   i
- ×   2007 British Association of Endocrine Surgeons

British Association of Equine Dental Technicians   2001
- NR   Higher Longwood, Highhampton, BEAWORTHY, Devon, EX21 5LF.
     01409 231686
     http://www.equinedentistry.org.uk
     Hon Sec: G Spinney
- ○   *V

British Association of European Pharmaceutical Distributors   (BAEPD)   1984
- NR   4 Connaught Rd, Chingford, LONDON, E4 7DL.   (sb)
     020 8529 3646
     Sec: Catherine Evans
- ▲   Company Limited by Guarantee
- ○   *T; the importation of licensed pharmaceutical products from within the EU & their distribution into the supply chain in the UK
- M   20 i, 6 f, UK / 1 i, 1 f, o'seas

British Association for Fair Trade Shops   (BAFTS)   1996
- NR   66 Longstomps Avenue, CHELMSFORD, Essex CM2 9LA.   (hq)
     0786 675 9201
     email info@bafts.org.uk   http://www.bafts.org.uk
     Contact: Chris Davis
- ▲   Company Limited by Guarantee
- ○   *K, *T; to develop fair trade retailing; to raise profile of fair trade shops; to campaign on fair trade issues
- ●   Conf - Inf
- <   Intl Fedn for Alternative Trade (IFAT); Network of Eur Wld Shops (NEWS)
- M   c 80 org
- ¶   NL;   AR; both ftm only.

British Association of Fastener Distributors   (BAFD)
- ■   35 Calthorpe Rd, Edgbaston, BIRMINGHAM, B15 1TS.   (asa)
     0121-454 4141   fax 0121-207 7002
     email info@bafd.org   http://www.bafd.org
     Sec: Sharon Parker
- ▲   Company Limited by Guarantee
- ○   *T; to represent the interests of, & provide services & support to, leading UK distributors & wholesalers of fasteners, fixings & related products
- Gp   Stainless steel fasteners
- ●   Conf - Mtgs - ET - Exhib - Stat - Lib
- <   Eur Fastener Distbr Assn (EFDA)
- M   75 f
- ¶   News from BAFD - 2;   LM - 1; both ftm.

British Association of Feed Supplement & Additives Manufacturers   (BAFSAM)   1968
- NR   238 Chester Rd, Hartford, NORTHWICH, Cheshire, CW8 1LW.   (hsb)
     01606 783314   fax 01606 783314
     email hwebafsam@onetel.com
     Sec Gen: Harry Evans
- ▲   Company Limited by Guarantee
- ○   *T; manufacturers of animal feed
- ●   Mtgs - Consultees to Food Standrads Agency, DEFRA, Veterinary Medicines Directive in all legislative matters in relation to animal nutrition
- <   EU Food Additives & Premixtures Assn (FEFANA)
- M   20 f

British Association of Flower Essence Producers   (BAFEP)   2000
- ■   PO Box 100, Exminster, EXETER, Devon, EX6 8YT.   (hsp)
     01392 832005
     email info@bafep.com   http://www.bafep.com
     Hon Sec: Sue Lilly
- ▲   Un-incorporated Society
- ○   *T; for producers of Bach flower remedies & other types of essences
- <   Brit Flower & Vibrational Essences Assn
- M   55 f
- ¶   Guidelines on Essence Production; free.

© CBD Research Ltd · Beckenham · BR3 5JS · Tel 020 8650 7745 · E-mail cbd@cbdresearch.com · www.cbdresearch.com

British Association in Forensic Medicine   (BAFM)   1951
NR   Dept of Forensic Medicine & Science, University College of
       Glasgow, GLASGOW, G12 8QQ.   (hsb)
       0141-330 4145
       http://www.bafm.org
       Hon Sec: Dr J Clark
▲   Un-incorporated Society
○   *P; to advance the study & practice of forensic pathology; to act
       as a negotiating & advisory body when required
●   Conf
M   135 i, UK / 35 i, o'seas

British Association of Forensic Odontology
NR   Morialta, Palmerston Rd, NEWHAVEN, E Sussex, BN9 0NS.
       01539 720923   fax 01539 737589
       http://www.bafo.org.uk
       Sec: Dr S Sampson

**British Association of Former United Nations Civil Servants
(BAFUNCS)   1977**
NR   Rydal House, 36 Manor Park Ave, PRINCES RISBOROUGH,
       Bucks, HP27 9AS.   (ed/p)
       01844 343652
       email tony.loftas@btinternet.com
       Newsletter Editor: Tony Loftas
▲   Un-incorporated Society
Br   10 regions
○   *W; comradeship, fellowship and associated social activities
●   Mtgs - VE
<   Fedn of Assns of Former UN Civil Servants (FAFICS)
M   769 i, UK /c 76 i, o'seas
¶   NL - 2;   LM; both ftm.

British Association of Friends of Museums   (BAFM)   1973
■   7 Northbrook House, Free St, BISHOP'S WALTHAM, Hants,
       SO23 1NP.   (hq)
       email admin@bafm.org.uk   http://www.bafm.org.uk
       Hon Sec: Sue Hall
▲   Registered Charity
Br   330
○   *A, *N; 'the only national independent organisation for friends,
       volunteers & supporters of museums, galleries, archives,
       libraries, historic house gardens & parks, churches & other
       institutions preserving the UK's cultural heritage'
●   Conf - Mtgs - SG - Inf - Lib - VE - LG
       Central source of inf: 'about Friends for Friends'
<   Wld Fedn of Friends of Museums
M   97 i, 30 museums etc, 330 Friends gps (representing
       200,000 i)
¶   NL - 3.   Hbk for Friends.   Information Sheets 1-15 - irreg.
       Charter & Hbk for Volunteer Managers & Administrators.

British Association of General Paediatrics
       a group of the **Royal College of Paediatrics & Child Health**

**British Association of Golf Course Constructors   (BAGCC)
1981**
■   Savannah, 32 New Rd, RINGWOOD, Hants, BH24 3AU.
       (chmn/p)
       01425 475584   fax 01425 475643
       email secretary@bagcc.org.uk
       http://www.bagcc.org.uk
       Chmn: Brian D Pierson
▲   Un-incorporated Society
○   *T; golf course construction, remodelling & renovation
Gp   Golf course constructors (full members); Suppliers (associate
       members)
●   Conf - Mtgs - Exhib - Inf
M   18 members
¶   Folder of brochures of BAGCC members; free.

British Association of Green Crop Driers Ltd   (BAGCD)   1950
■   March Hares, Montagu Rd, Canwick, LINCOLN, LN4 2RW.
       (asa)
       01522 523322   fax 01522 568539
       email info@bagcd.org   http://www.bagcd.org
       Sec: Mrs Elizabeth Harding
▲   Company Limited by Guarantee
○   *T; to promote use of dried green crops for animal feed (grass
       & lucerne)
●   Conf - Mtgs - Inf - VE - LG
<   Commission Intersyndicale des Déshydrateurs Européens
M   [not stated]

**British Association of Head & Neck Oncologists   (BAHNO)
1968**
NR   PO Box 85, MIDHURST, W Sussex, GU29 9WS.   (asa)
       01730 813700
       Secretariat: Mrs Jill McFarland
▲   Registered Charity
○   *P; to advance the understanding & treatment of head & neck
       cancer. Members are surgeons, oncologists, pathologists &
       other interested medical staff involved in the care &
       management of patients with head & neck cancer
●   Conf - Mtgs - Res - SG
M   c 450 i, UK / 50 i, o'seas
¶   Abstracts of meetings incl in Clinical Oncology - 1.

**British Association of Health Services in Higher Education
(BAHSHE)   1947**
■   35 Hazelwood Rd, Bush Hill Park, ENFIELD, Middx, EN1 1JG.
       (hq)
       020 8482 2412   fax 010 8482 2412
       email S.Furmston@mdx.ac.uk
       http://www.bahshe.co.uk
       Admin Officer: Sandra Furmston
▲   Registered Charity
○   *W; health of students studying in universities & colleges in UK
●   Conf

British Association of Homoeopathic Manufacturers   (BAHM)
■   65 Church St, Langham, OAKHAM, Leics, LE15 7JE.
       (secretariat)
       01572 771115
       Sec: Penny Viner
▲   Un-incorporated Society
○   *T; to advance the knowledge & practice of homoeopathy; to
       maintain standards, research, quality control & development
       of homoeopathic medicines
<   Homoeopathic Devt Foundation
M   6 f
       NOTE: is active only in a crisis; eg with a change of the
       licensing law

**British Association of Homoeopathic Veterinary Surgeons
(BAHVS)   1981**
NR   Glenbrae Veterinary Clinic, 49-51 Stockiemuir Avenue,
       Bearsden, GLASGOW, G61 3JJ.   (hsb)
       http://www.bahvs.com
       Mem Sec: Wendy McGrandles
○   *L, *P, *V; to promote veterinary homoeopathy amongst the
       veterinary profession
●   Conf - ET - Res (clinical only) - SG - Inf
<   Intl Assn for Veterinary Homoeopathy
M   c 140 i
¶   NL - 2; ftm only.

British Association of Hospitality Accountants   (BAHA)   1969
■   The Hollies, Oak Bank Lane, Hoole Village, CHESTER,
      Cheshire, CH2 4ER.   (hq)
      01244 301342
      http://www.baha-uk.org
○   *P; interests of financial managers in the hotel, catering &
      leisure industry
●   Conf - Mtgs - ET - Exam - Advice
<   Chart Inst Mgt Accountants (CIMA) - for BAHA's training
      programme
M   550 i, UK / 150 i, o'seas
¶   BAHA Times (NL) - 10;   AR - 1; both ftm only.

British Association of Hotel Representatives   (BAHREP)
NR   127 New House Park, ST ALBANS, Herts, AL1 1UT.   (hsb)
      01727 812722
      Sec: Diana Hall
▲   Un-incorporated Society
○   *P
●   Mtgs - ET - Exhib - Inf - LG
M   60 i, 60 f

British Association for Human Identification   (BAHID)   2001
NR   2 Market Square, STONEHAVEN, Kincardineshire, AB39 2BT.
      (asa)
      01569 760022
      email info@bahid.org   http://www.bahid.org
      Treas: Mr Black
▲   Un-incorporated Society
○   *P; to bring together forensic practitioners & academics
      involved in the field of human identification & address
      common problems & develop research & communication
Gp   Forensic: Anthropology, Archaeology, Entomology, Pathology,
      Podiatry, Radiology
      Facial analysis; Molecular genetics; Police; Anatomy
●   Conf - ET - Res - Current information on up-dated website
M   c 300 i, UK / c 60 i, o'seas
¶   Forensic Human Identification.

British Association for Immediate Care   (BASICS)   1977
■   Turret House, 2 Turret Lane, IPSWICH, Suffolk, IP4 1DL.   (hq)
      01473 218407   fax 01473 280585
      email admin@basics.org.uk   http://www.basics.org.uk
      Hon Sec: Anthony Kemp,   Chief Exec: Mrs Ruth Lloyd
▲   Registered Charity
Br   41 affiliated schemes
○   *W; to promote & improve all aspects of immediate care
      (provision of skilled medical help at the site of accidents,
      major incidents & other emergencies)
Gp   BASICS Education Ltd (provides courses on pre-hospital
      emergency care, Extrication, Paediatic & others); International
      directorate
●   Conf - Mtgs - ET - Exam - Exhib - Stat - Inf - Lib - LG
M   c 1,300 i
      (Sub: £88)
¶   NL - 3;   AR - 1; both ftm only.   Monographs; £10.

**British Association for Information & Library Education &
Research   (BAILER)   1962**
■   c/o Dr Paul Matthews, Dept of Information Science & Digital
      Media, Faculty of the Environment & Technology, University
      of the West of England, Frenchay Campus, BRISTOL,
      BS16 1QY.   (sb)
      0117-328 3353
      http://www.bailer.org.uk
      Sec: Dr Paul Matthews
○   *E, *P; information & library studies education & research in the
      UK
Gp   Information policy; Information management; Records
      management
●   Conf - Mtgs - ET - Res
M   220 i
¶   Directory of Courses in Library & Information Studies in the
      UK - 1; free.

**British Association of International Mountain Leaders
(BAIML)   2008**
NR   Siabod Cottage, Capel Curig, BETWS-y-COED, Conwy,
      LL24 0ES.   (hq)
      01690 720272
      email baiml.office@baiml.org   http://www.baiml.org
      Contact: Susan Doyle
○   *P; for those leading walking parties through remote mountain
      areas where the full alpine climbing & teaching skills of a
      mountian guide are not necessary
●   ET
<   U of Intl Mountain Leaders Assns
M   i

British Association for Irish Studies   (BAIS)   1985
NR   School of English Literature, Languages & Linguistics, University
      of Sheffield, Sir William Empson House, Shearwood Rd,
      SHEFFIELD, S Yorks, S10 2TD.   (sb)
      email m.campbell@sheffield.ac.uk   http://www.bias.ac.uk
      Sec: Dr Matthew Campbell
▲   Registered Charity
○   *E; promotion & support for Irish studies in the UK
●   Conf - ET - LG - Organisation of public lectures
M   c 300 i & f, UK / 30 i, o'seas
¶   Irish Studies Review - 3.   NL - 4.

British Association of Japanese Studies   (BAJS)   1974
NR   BAJS Secretariat, University of Essex, COLCHESTER, Essex,
      CO4 3SQ.
      01206 872543 (answerphone)   fax 01206 873408
      Exec Sec: Mrs Lynn Baird
○   *L
¶   NL -3;   Japan Forum - 3.

British Association of Journalists
■   89 Fleet St, LONDON, EC4Y 1DH.   (hq)
      020 7353 3003   fax 020 7353 2310
      email office@bajunion.org.uk
      Gen Sec: Steve Turner
○   *P, *U; raising the status & rewards of journalists: seeks to
      protect & improve fees for freelance members & pay,
      conditions & pensions for staff members
M   1,000 i, UK / 25 i, o'seas
¶   BAJ News (NL) - 4.

British Association of Korean Studies   (BAKS)   1983
■   47 Willowtree Avenue, Gilesgate Moor, DURHAM, Co Durham,
      DH1 1EA.   (sp)
      fax 0191-374 3242
      email k.l.pratt@yahoo.co.uk   http://www.baks.org.uk
      Sec: Prof Keith Pratt
▲   Un-incorporated Society
○   *L, *X; to promote, in the UK, the study & understanding of
      Korea
●   Conf
<   UK Area Studies Assn
M   59 i, UK / 8 i, o'seas
¶   Papers - 1-2 yrly; prices vary.

British Association of Landscape Industries   (BALI)   1972
- ■ Landscape House, STONELEIGH PARK, Warks, CV8 2LG.   (hq)
  024 7669 0333   fax 024 7669 0077
  email contact@bali.org.uk   http://www.bali.org.uk
  Chief Exec Officer: Sandra Loton-Jones
- ▲ Company Limited by Guarantee
- Br 9
- ○ *T; to represent UK firms undertaking landscaping, both interior
  & exterior, & a wide range of associated suppliers
- Gp Affiliates; Designers; Domestic; Grounds; Interiors;
  Maintenance; Students
- ● Mtgs - ET - Exhib - Comp - Inf - VE - LG - Annual awards
  ceremony
- < Eur Landscape Contrs Assn (ELCA)
- > Assn of Landscape Contrs Ireland (Northern & Southern) (ALCI)
- M 54 i, 687 f, UK / 9 f, o'seas
- ¶ Landscape News - 4.   Business News - 4;
  Awards Brochure - 1; all ftm only.
  Who's Who Directory - 1; ftm, £40 nm.

British Association of Leisure Parks, Piers & Attractions (BALPPA)   1936
- NR 37 Tanner St (suite 12), LONDON, SE1 3LF.   (hq)
  020 7403 4455
  http://www.balppa.org
- ▲ Company Limited by Guarantee
- ○ *T; for British private sector leisure parks, piers, attractions &
  suppliers to the industry
- M f

British Association for Literacy in Development   (BALID)
- NR c/o Park Place, 12 Lawn Lane, LONDON, SW8 1UD.   (hq)
  email admin@balid.org.uk   http://www.balid.org.uk
  Admin: Sarah Snow
- ▲ Un-incorporated Society
- ○ *E, *K, to promote literacy & numeracy for adults as an integral
  part of human development; to increase awareness of the
  relationship between literacy & numeracy & economic
  development & social change
- ● Conf - Mtgs - Res
- < UNESCO; Universities of: Pennsylvania, Brighton, London, East
  Anglia & Sussex
- > Education Action Intl; Nat Res & Devt Centre; Nottingham
  University
- M [not stated]
- ¶ Reports [on website].

British Association for Local History   (BALH)   1982
- NR PO Box 6549, Somersal Herbert, ASHBOURNE, Derbys,
  DE6 5WH.   (hq)
  01283 585947
  http://www.balh.co.uk
  Business Mgr: A Jones
- ▲ Registered Charity; Un-incorporated Society
- ○ *L, *P; to promote the advancement of public education
  through the study & teaching of local history
- ● Conf - SG - Inf - VE
- M c 2,300 i
- ¶ The Local Historian - 4.   Local History News - 4.
- × 2008 Association Local History Tutors

British Association for Lung Research   (BALR)   1982
- NR c/o National Heart & Lung Institute, Dept of Respiratory
  Pharmacology in Airway Diseases, Imperial College London,
  South Kensington Campus, LONDON, SW7 2AZ.   (hsb)
  020 7589 5111
  email deborah.clarke@imperial.ac.uk
  http://www.balr.co.uk
  Sec: Dr Deborah Clarke
- ▲ Registered Charity
- ○ *P
- ● Conf - Mtgs
- M c 350 i
- ¶ NL - 3; ftm only.   LM.

British Association for Martial Arts   (BAMA)   2009
- NR Unit 1 Bradley Mills, Bradley Lane, NEWTON ABBOT, Devon,
  TQ12 1LZ.   (hq)
  01626 360999
  email info@karateassociation.co.uk
  http://www.karateassociation.co.uk
  Sec: John Burke
- ○ *S; practitioners of karate, judo, iaido, aikido, kickboxing, kung
  fu & tai chi chuan
- ● ET - Exam - Facebook
- M 11 org

British Association of Medical Hypnosis   2001
- NR 45 Hyde Park Square, LONDON, W2 2JT.   (sb)
  020 7402 9037
  email rnp@medicalhypnotherapy.co.uk
  Organising Sec: Dr Rumi Peynovska
- ○ *P
- ¶ European Journal of Clinical Hypnosis.

British Association of Medical Managers
has closed

British Association of Mountain Guides   (BMG)   1975
- ■ Siabod Cottage, CAPEL CURIG, Conwy, LL24 0ES.
  (regd/office)
  01690 720386   fax 01690 720248
  email guiding@bmg.org.uk   http://www.bmg.org.uk
  Hon Sec: Libby Peter
- ▲ Company Limited by Guarantee
- ○ *P, *S; professional mountaineering services, mountain guiding,
  rock climbing, ice climbing, alpine guiding, ski
  mountaineering
- ● Mtgs - ET - Exam
- < Intl Fedn of Mountain Guide Assns (IFMGA)
- M 125 i, UK / 52 i, o'seas
- ¶ NL - 3;   AR; both ftm.
  Members' Directory; free (also available on website).

British Association for Music Therapy   (BAMT)   2011
- ■ 24-27 White Lion St, LONDON, N1 9PD.   (hq)
  020 7837 6100   fax 020 7837 6142
  email info@bamt.org   http://www.bamt.org
  Admin: Grace Walter
- ▲ Company Limited by Guarantee; Registered Charity
- ○ *D, *P; to promote for the public benefit the art & science of
  music therapy, & its use & development for children & adults
  with a wide range of needs; to advance education in music
  therapy; & to promote understanding of music therapy for
  the general public
- ● Conf - Mtgs - ET - Res - Exhib - Inf
- < Allied Health Professions Fedn
- ¶ British Jnl of Music Therapy - 2.
  Leading Note (NL) - 2.
- × 2011 (Association of Professional Music Therapists
  (British Society for Music Therapy (merged 6 April)

British Association of Nature Conservationists   (BANC)   1997
- NR 41 Winchester Rd, NORTHAMPTON, NN4 4NZ.   (contact/b)
  email enquiries@banc.org.uk   http://www.banc.org.uk
  Contact: Ruth Boogert
- ▲ Company Limited by Guarantee, Registered Charity
- ○ *K; to advance nature conservation in the UK; to act as a
  network for conservationists & people who care about the
  natural world
- M i & org
- ¶ Ecos: a review of conservation - 3; ftm.

British Association of Numismatic Societies (BANS) 1953
- ■ c/o Bush Boake Allen Ltd, Blackhorse Lane, LONDON, E17 5QP. (hsb)
  020 8523 6351
  email phil.mernick@bushboakeallen.com
  http://www.coinclubs.freeserve.co.uk
  Hon Sec: P Mernick
- ▲ Un-incorporated Society
- Br 60
- ○ *N; to promote & coordinate interest & research by local & regional societies
- ● Conf - Res - SG - Inf - PL - VE
- M c 2,000 i
- ¶ Doris Stockwell Memorial Papers - irreg; price varies.

British Association for Nutritional Therapy (BANT) 1997
- NR 27 Old Gloucester St, LONDON, WC1N 3XX.   (mail address)
  0870 606 1284   fax 0870 606 1284
  email theadministrator@bant.org.uk
  http://www.bant.org.uk
  Sec: Susan McGinty
- ▲ Company Limited by Guarantee
- ○ *P; the application of nutrition science in the promotion of optimum health & peak performance, disease prevention & patient care
- ● Conf - ET
- M c 1,500 i
- ¶ The BANT Membership NL - 4.

British Association of Occupational Therapists Ltd (BAOT/ COT) 1932
- NR 106-114 Borough High St, LONDON, SE1 1LB.   (hq)
  020 7357 6480   fax 020 7450 2299
  http://www.cot.org.uk
  Sec: Julia Scott
- ▲ Company Limited by Guarantee; Registered Charity
- ○ *P, *U; for all occupational therapy staff & students in the UK
- Gp College of Occupational Therapists; Association of Occupational Therapists in Mental Health
  Housing; HIV/AIDS oncology, palliative care & education; Neurology; Rapid intervention; Paediatric; Rheumatology; Work practice & productivity; Working with people with learning disabilities; Independent practice; Older people; Trauma & orthopaedics
- ● Conf - Mtgs - ET - Comp - Res - Exhib - SG - Lib - Empl - LG
- < Wld Fedn of Occupational Therapists (WFOT); Coun of Occupational Therapists for the Eur Countries (COTEC); Allied Health Professions Fedn (AHPF)
- M 27,000 i, UK / 500 i, o'seas
- ¶ British Journal of Occupational Therapy - 12; ftm, £153 nm. Occupational Therapy News - 12; ftm.   AR; free. Publications list on website.

British Association of Oral & Maxillofacial Surgeons (BAOMS) 1962
- NR at the Royal College of Surgeons, 35-43 Lincoln's Inn Fields, LONDON, WC2A 3PE.   (hq)
  020 7405 8074   fax 020 7430 9997
- ○ *L, *P; mouth, jaws, face & neck surgery
- ● Conf - Mtgs - ET - Res - SG
- M 797 i, UK / 303 i, o'seas
- ¶ British Journal of Oral & Maxillofacial Surgery - 6; ftm.

British Association of Otorhinolaryngologists - Head & Neck Surgeons ENT.UK (BAO-HNS) 1943
- ■ at the Royal College of Surgeons, 35-43 Lincoln's Inn Fields, LONDON, WC2A 3PE. (hq)
  020 7404 8373   fax 020 7404 4200
  email entuk@entuk.org   http://www.entuk.org
  Hon Sec: Prof Janet A Wilson,
  Admin Mgr: Nechama Lewis
- ▲ Registered Charity
- ○ *L, *M, *P; to promote education research & audit & works to achieve the highest standards of medical & surgical practice in otology, laryngology, rhinology & head & neck surgery
- ● Conf - Mtgs - ET - Exhib - Inf - LG
- > Brit Otology, Hearing & Balance Gp
- M 1,404 i, UK / 26 i, o'seas
- ¶ NL - 6;   AR;   LM & Constitution - irreg; all ftm only.

British Association for Paediatric Nephrology
     a group of the **Royal College of Paediatrics & Child Health**

British Association of Paediatric Otorhinolaryngology (BAPO) 1990
- ■ c/o Michael Kuo, Birmingham Children's Hospital, Steelhouse Lane, BIRMINGHAM, W Midlands, B4 6NH. (hsb)
  0121-333 8113
  http://www.bapo.org.uk
  Hon Sec from October 2011: Mr Neil Bateman, Sheffield Children's Hospital, Western Bank, SHEFFIELD, S Yorks, S10 2TH.
  Hon Sec: Michael Kuo
- ▲ Un-incorporated Society
- ○ *P; paediatric ear, nose & throat surgery
- ● Conf - Mtgs - ET - Res
- < Eur Soc for Paediatric Otolaryngology; ENT-UK
- M c 200 i, UK / c 20 i, o'seas

British Association of Paediatric Surgeons (BAPS) 1954
- NR at the Royal College of Surgeons, 35-43 Lincoln's Inn Fields, LONDON, WC2A 3PE.   (hq)
  020 7312 6638
  Sec: Richard Stewart
- ○ *P
- ● Conf - Mtgs - Exhib - Inf
- M 140 i, UK / 460 i, o'seas
- ¶ Jnl of Paediatric Surgery - 6;   NL - 4;   LM - 1; all ftm.

British Association of Paediatricians in Audiology
     is a special interest group of the **Royal College of Paediatrics & Child Health**

British Association of Paintings Conservator-Restorers (BAPCR) 1943
- ■ 42 Oaken Lane, Claygate, ESHER, Surrey, KT10 0RG.   (sp)
  01372 468143
  email secretary@bapcr.org.uk   http://www.bapcr.org.uk
  Sec: Samantha Robinson
- ▲ Un-incorporated Society
- ○ *A, *P; conservation & restoration of paintings
- ● Conf - Mtgs - ET - Exam - Exhib - Comp - VE
- < Intl Inst for Consvn (IIC); Scot Soc for Consvn & Restoration (SSCR); Inst of Paper Consvn (IPC)
- M 400 i, UK / 30 i, o'seas
  (Sub: £45)
- ¶ The Picture Restorer (Jnl) - 2; ftm, £3.50 each nm. Conference pre-prints.

British Association of Paper Historians   (BAPH)   1989
- ■ Smithy Cottage, Hilton, BLANDFORD FORUM, Dorset, DT11 0DB.   (memsec/p)
  01665 577988
  http://www.baph.org.uk
  Sec: Shulla Jaques
- ▲ Un-incorporated Society
- ○ *L; to promote all aspects of the study of paper & papermaking history
- ● Conf - Mtgs - VE
- M 170 i, 37 f, UK / 40 i, 18 f, o'seas
- ¶ The Quarterly (Jnl) - 4.   LM - 1.
  BAPH News (NL) - 4.   Conference Report - 1.

British Association of Parenteral & Enteral Nutrition   (BAPEN)
- ■ Secure Hold Business Centre, Studley Road, REDDITCH, Worcs, B98 7LG.   (asa)
  01527 457850   fax 01527 458718
  email bapen@sovereignconference.co.uk
  http://www.bapen.org.uk
  Hon Chmn: Dr Mike Stroud
- ▲ Registered Charity
- ○ *M; to help ensure that those suffering from malnutrition, or other nutritional problems, are appropriately recognised & managed
- ● Conf - Mtgs - ET - Res - Exhib
- M i, f & org
  (Sub: £40 i, £60 f, £20 org)
- ¶ Home Economic Report - the cost of disease-related malnutrition in the UK & economic considerations for the use of nutritional supplements in adults; £27.
  Combatting Malnutrition: recommendations for action; £22.
  Screening for Malnutrition in Sheltered Housing; £22.
  Publications list available.

British Association for Performing Arts Medicine   (BAPAM)   1984
- NR Totara Park House (4th floor), 34-36 Gray's Inn Rd, LONDON, WC1X 8HR.   (hq)
  020 7404 5888   fax 020 7404 3222
  email admin@bapam.org.uk
  http://www.bapam.org.uk
  Chief Exec: Naomi Wayne
- ▲ Registered Charity
- ○ *K, *P; to ensure the highest standards of medical care for those involved in the performing arts; to monitor the incidence of performing arts injuries & to record the way in which they are treated
- ● Conf - ET - Res
- M 350 i, 5 f, UK / 5 i, o'seas
- ¶ Jnl - 2;   NL - 4; both ftm only.

British Association of Perinatal Medicine   (BAPM)   1976
- ■ c/o Dr Alan Fenton, Royal Victoria Infirmary, NEWCASTLE UPON TYNE, NE1 4LP.   (hq)
  0191-282 5034
  email a.c.fenton@ncl.ac.uk   http://www.bapm.org
  Hon Sec: Dr Alan Fenton
- ▲ Registered Charity
- ○ *M, *P; to support newborn babies & their families by providing services that help all those involved in perinatal practice; to improve the standards of perinatal care in the British Isles
- Gp Dietitians; Midwives; Neonatologists; Nurses; Obstetricians
- ● Conf - Mtgs - ET - SG - LG
- < R Coll Paediatrics & Child Health; R Coll Obstetricians & Gynaecologists
- M 850 i, UK / 50 i, o'seas
  (Sub: £100 medical, £50 non-medical)
- ¶ NL - 3;   AR - 1; both ftm.

British Association for the Person-Centred Approach   (BAPCA)   1989
- NR PO Box 143, ROSS-on-WYE, Herefs, HR9 9AH.
  01989 763863
  email enquiries@bapca.org.uk   http://www.bapca.org.uk
- ○ *P

British Association of Pharmaceutical Physicians   (BrAPP)
- NR Royal Station Court, Station Rd, Twyford, READING, Berks, RG10 9NF.
  0118-934 1943
  Assn Mgr: Elizabeth Langley
- ○ *P
- ¶ Jnl - 6.

British Association of Pharmaceutical Wholesalers   (BAPW)   1966
- ■ 90 Long Acre, LONDON, WC2E 9RA.   (hq)
  020 7031 0590   fax 020 7031 0591
  email mail@bapw.net   http://www.bapw.net
  Sec: Kayleigh Ross
- ▲ Company Limited by Guarantee
- ○ *T; to secure the safest & most cost effective distribution of a comprehensive range of healthcare products & related services; to advance efficient healthcare management
- ● Conf - SG - Inf - LG
- < Intl Fedn of Pharmaceutical Wholesalers; Groupement Intl de la Réparation Pharmaceutique des Pays de la CE; Assn of the Brit Pharmaceutical Ind
- M 11 f (full), 43 f (associate), 3 f (affiliate)

British Association for Physical Training
inactive since 2006

British Association of Picture Libraries & Agencies   (BAPLA)   1975
- NR 59 Tranquil Vale, LONDON, SE3 0BS.   (hq)
  020 8297 1198
- ▲ Company Limited by Guarantee
- ○ *T, *P; issues relevant to the picture library industry: copyright laws & rights, technology, standards, digital imagery, archiving
- Gp Collective management; Copyright; Technology - digital images
- ● Conf - Mtgs - ET - Res - Exhib - SG - PL - VE - LG
- < Creators' Rights Alliance
- M 4 i, 450 f, UK / 2 f, o'seas
- ¶ Lightbox - 4.   Weekly NL - 52.
  BAPLA Directory of Picture Libraries & Agencies - 1.

British Association of Plastic, Reconstructive & Aesthetic Surgeons   (BAPRAS)   1946
- ■ at the Royal College of Surgeons, 35-43 Lincoln's Inn Fields, LONDON, WC2A 3PE.   (hq)
  020 7831 5161   fax 020 7831 4041
  email secretariat@bapras.co.uk
  http://www.bapras.co.uk
  Hon Sec: D J Coleman
- ▲ Company Limited by Guarantee, Registered Charity
- ○ *L, *M, *P, *Q; promotion & development of plastic surgery; to advance education in the field
- Gp Breast special interest; Head & neck; Overseas training service
- ● Conf - Mtgs - ET - Res
- < Brit Assn of Aesthetic Plastic Surgeons (BAAPS)
- M 570 i, UK / 160 i, o'seas
- ¶ Jnl of Plastic, Reconstructive & Aesthetic Surgery - 12; ftm.

British Association of Play Therapists   (BAPT)   1992
■   1 Beacon Mews, South Rd, WEYBRIDGE, Surrey, KT13 9DZ.
      (admin/asst/p)
      01932 828638
      email info@bapt.uk.com   http://www.bapt.uk.com
      Chmn: Mary Carden
○   *P; to promote & develop standards of training in play therapy
●   Conf - Mtgs - Res - SG - Inf
M   c 350 i
¶   NL - 4; ftm only.   Jnl for Play Therapy - 1.
      What is Play Therapy? (leaflet for parents & carers).
      What is Play Therapy? (booklet for children).
      A Guide to Play Therapy.

British Association of Pool Table Operators   (BAPTO)   1975
NR   Silverdale, Oakfield Close, SHREWSBURY, Shropshire,
      SY3 8AB.   (chmn/p)
      01743 464232
      http://www.bapto.org.uk
      Chmn: Alan Boswell
▲   Company Limited by Guarantee
○   *T; to promote the game of pool
●   Conf - Mtgs - ET - Exam - Comp - Stat - Inf
M   43 f, UK / 3 f, o'seas

British Association for Print & Communication   (BAPC)   1979
■   Catalyst House / 720 Centennial Court, Centennial Park,
      ELSTREE, Herts, WD6 3SY.   (hq)
      020 8736 5862   fax 020 8224 9090
      email info@bapc.org.uk   http://www.bapc.co.uk
      Dir: Tony Honnor,   Chmn & CEO: Sidney Bobb
▲   Company Limited by Guarantee
○   *T; for the creative industry, including graphic arts, print &
      communication sectors
●   Conf - Mtgs - ET - Res - Exhib - Stat
M   3,800 f
¶   Bulletin [NL] - 6; free.

British Association of Prosthetists & Orthotists   (BAPO)   1994
■   Sir James Clark Building, Abbeymill Business Centre, PAISLEY,
      Renfrewshire, PA1 1TJ.   (hq)
      0141-561 7217   fax 0141-561 7218
      email enquiries@bapo.com   http://www.bapo.com
      Chmn: Steve Mottram
▲   Un-incorporated Society
○   *M, *P; Prosthetics: healthcare involved in fitting prostheses
      (artificial limbs); Orthotics: healthcare in fitting orthoses
      (braces, splints & other devices externally / to the human
      body)
●   Conf - Mtgs - ET - Exhib - SG - Inf - LG
<   Allied Health Professions Fedn
M   734 i, UK / 22 i, o'seas
¶   BAPOMAG - 4; ftm, £20 yr nm.

British Association for Psychological Type   (BAPT)   1989
■   17 Royal Crescent, CHELTENHAM, Glos, GL50 3DA.   (sp)
      01242 282990
      email office@bapt.org.uk   http://www.bapt.org.uk
      Sec: Bill Davies
▲   Registered Charity
○   *L; for all interested in Jungian psychological type theory

British Association for Psychopharmacology   (BAP)   1974
■   36 Cambridge Place, Hills Rd, CAMBRIDGE, CB2 1NS.   (hq)
      01223 358395   fax 01223 321268
      email susan@bap.org.uk   http://www.bap.org.uk
      Exec Officer: Mrs Susan Chandler (01223 358428)
▲   Registered Charity
○   *L; to advance education & research in the science of
      psychopharmacology both clinical & experimental
●   Conf - Mtgs - ET
M   850 i, UK / 150 i, o'seas
¶   Jnl of Psychopharmacology - 4.   NL - 4; ftm.

British Association of Psychotherapists   (BAP)   1951
NR   37 Mapesbury Rd, LONDON, NW2 4HJ.   (hq)
      020 8452 9823   fax 020 8452 0310
      email mail@bap-psychotherapy.org
      http://www.bap-psychotherapy.org
      Chief Exec: Mrs Elise Ormerod
      Publicity Officer: Dr Tim Fox
▲   Registered Charity
○   *E, *P; a training organisation for adult, child & adolescent
      psychoanalytic & Jungian analytic psychotherapy; to offer
      assessment & where appropriate, treatment for people
      seeking individual psychotherapy.
      The BAP aims to provide information to the public & to the
      caring professions, to make psychotherapy more widely
      available; to maintain standards in training & clinical practice
      & professional conduct
Gp   Jungian analytic; Psychoanalytic (adult); Psychoanalytic (child &
      adolescent)
●   Conf - Mtgs - ET - Res - SG - Lib - Assessment for, & provision
      of, psychotherapy
<   Assn Child Psychotherapists (ACP); Brit Confedn of
      Psychotherapists (BCP); Intl Assn of Analytical
      Psychology (IAAP)
M   500 i, UK / 12 i, o'seas
¶   Jnl - 2; ftm, £27 i, £55 instns, nm.

**British Association of Public Safety Communications Officers
(BAPCO)   1994**
NR   PO Box 374, LINCOLN, LN1 1FY.
      01522 548325
      http://www.bapco.org.uk
      Chief Exec: Ken Mott
○   *P; the development of communications & supporting
      information technologies to enhance delivery of public safety
      & civil contingency services
M   i, f & org

**British Association for the Purebred Spanish Horse   (BAPSH)
1982**
NR   Tybrith, MEISOD, Powys, SY22 6YG.   (hsp)
      01938 500708
      http://www.bapsh.co.uk
      Sec: Anita Ashworth
○   *B
●   Exhib
<   Jefatura de Cria Caballar; FICCE
M   c 400 i
¶   Pura Raza Española - 4; ftm.

British Association of Record Dealers
      since July 2006 the **Entertainment Retailers Association**

British Association of Rehabilitation Companies   (BARC)   2009
NR   Chartis Medical & Rehabilitation Ltd, The Chartis Building (7th
      floor), 58 Fenchurch St, LONDON, EC3M 4AB.   (chmn/b)
      email info@thebarc.co.uk   http://www.thebarc.co.uk
      Chmn: Melanie Summers
○   *T; for rehabilitation case management companies, treatment
      providers & their agencies, healthcare & vocational
      practitioner companies, specialist rehabilitation practitioners
      & prosthetic providers 'to name but a few'
●   LG
      The Association was officially launched in the House of
      Commons in May 2009

© CBD Research Ltd · Beckenham · BR3 5JS · Tel 020 8650 7745 · E-mail cbd@cbdresearch.com · www.cbdresearch.com

British Association for Reinforcement   (BAR)
- ■ Riverside House, 4 Meadows Business Park, Station Approach, Blackwater, CAMBERLEY, Surrey, GU17 9AB.   (hq)
  07802 747031
  http://www.uk-bar.org
  Chmn: Graham Mackenzie
- ○ *T; to provide an industry & marketing champion for the UK's steel reinforcement products industry
- Gp Codes of practice; Health & safety; Marketing; Technical
- M 16 f
- ¶ Re:View - 1.

British Association of Remote Sensing Companies   (BARSC) 1985
- NR c/o Vega Group plc, 2 Falcon Way, Shire Park, WELWYN GARDEN CITY, Herts, AL7 1TW.   (hsb)
  01707 391999
  http://www.barsc.org.uk
  Exec Sec: Gareth Davies
- ▲ Un-incorporated Society
- ○ *T; companies undertaking activities directly connected with remote sensing (the collection of information about physical objects & the environment from remote platforms - aircraft & satellites)
- Gp Applications working gp - focus on commercial opportunities to exploit earth observation data
- ● Conf - Mtgs - Exhib - Expt - LG - Liaison European agencies
- M 18 f

British Association of Removers   (BAR)   1900
- NR Tangent House, 62 Exchange Rd, WATFORD, Herts, WD18 0TG.   (hq)
  01923 699480   fax 01923 699481
  email info@bar.co.uk   http://www.bar.co.uk
  Gen Sec: Robert D Syers
- ▲ Company Limited by Guarantee
- ○ *T; for the professional moving industry; to maintain standards for the benefit of members & their customers
- Gp Commercial; National & European domestic moves; Overseas
- ● Conf - Mtgs - ET - Exam - Exhib - Comp - SG - Inf - VE - LG
- < Fedn Eur Moving Assns (FEDEMAC); Fedn Intl Movers (FIDI)
- M 650 f, UK / 250 f, o'seas
- ¶ Removals & Storage - 12.

British Association for Research Quality Assurance   (BARQA) 1977
- NR 3 Wherry Lane, IPSWICH, Suffolk, IP4 1LG.   (hq)
  01473 221411
  Assn Mgr: David Weller
- ▲ Company Limited by Guarantee
- ○ *P; to evaluate & appraise the quality assurance aspects of regulations, guidelines & principles, both national & international, related to studies conducted on chemicals, biologicals & devices which affect humans, animals & the environment known as good laboratory practice (GLP), good clinical practice (GCP) & good manufacturing practice (GMP)
- Gp C'ees: Animal health, Computing, Education & training, Field studies, Good clinical practice, Good laboratory practice, Good manufacturing practice, Meetings, Publications
- ● Conf - Mtgs - ET - Exam - Comp - SG - Inf
- < Eur Quality Assurance Soc (EQAS); US Soc of Quality Assurance (SQA); Japan Soc of Quality Assurance (JSQA)
- M 1,100 i, UK / 500 i, o'seas
- ¶ Quasar Magazine - 4;   AR - 1;
  Members' Directory - 1;   all ftm only.

British Association of Rose Breeders   (BARB)   1973
- ■ 17 Wren Centre, Westbourne Rd, EMSWORTH, Hants, PO10 7SU.   (hq)
  01243 389532   fax 01243 389509
  email info@barbuk.org.uk   http://www.rosesuk.com/barb/
  Gen Mgr: Ian Kennedy
- ▲ Un-incorporated Society
- ○ *H, *T; to encourage, improve & extend the introduction & growing of roses & other ornamental plants under Plant-Breeders' Rights
- Gp Plant breeders; Roses, Rose growers
- ● Mtgs - Exhib - Stat - Inf - Rose trials - International liaison
- M 17 f
- ¶ Ybk (listing protected plants available through BARB) - 1; free.
- × 2006 British Association Representing Breeders

British Association of Seating Equipment Suppliers   (BASES)
- ■ Federation House, STONELEIGH PARK, Warks, CV8 2RF.   (hq)
  024 7641 4999   fax 024 7641 4990
  email bases@sportsandplay.com
  http://www.basesuk.com
- ▲ Company Limited by Guarantee
- ○ *T; manufacturers & suppliers of various types of audience seating
- ● Mtgs - Inf - LG
- < a group of the Fedn of Sports & Play Assns (FSPA)
- M 6 f

British Association of Seed Analysts   (BASA)   1923
- ■ Confederation House, East of England Showground, PETERBOROUGH, Cambs, PE2 6XE.   (hq)
  01733 385230   fax 01733 385270
  email info@britseedanalysis.org.uk
  http://www.britseedanalysis.org.uk
  Sec: Paul Rooke
- ○ *T; advancement of seed testing & seed testing laboratories
- ● Conf - Mtgs - Inf - VE
- < Agricl Inds Condfedn
- M 80 i
- ¶ e-newsletters

British Association of Seed Producers
- NR 99 Rhoshendre, Waunfawr, ABERYSTWYTH, SY23 3PX.
  01970 623977
  Contact: Owen Davies
- ○ *T

British Association for Service to the Elderly   (BASE)   1974
- NR c/o James Lewis, Community Sciences Centre, Northern General Hospital NHS Trust, Herries Rd, SHEFFIELD, S Yorks, S5 7AU.   (hq)
  0845 130 0675
  email enquiries@base.org.uk   http://www.base.org.uk
- ▲ Registered Charity
- Br 4
- ○ *W; to provide education & training for all those working with older people, vulnerable adults & their carers in health & social care
- ● ET
- M 720 i, 100 f
- ¶ Quality in Agency - 4; £55 m.

British Association of Settlements & Social Action Centres   (BASSAC)   1920
- NR 33 Corsham St, LONDON, N1 6DR.   (hq)
  0845 241 0375
- ▲ Company Limited by Guarantee; Registered Charity
- ○ *W; 'is a national organisation of multi-purpose urban centres committed to helping local communities to bring about social change'
- M c100 centres
- ¶ Monthly ENews - 10; ftm.   BASSAC Directory - 1.

British Association for Sexual Health & HIV (BASHH) 1922

■ c/o Royal Society of Medicine, 1 Wimpole St, LONDON,
   W1G 0AE.   (hq)
   020 7290 2968   fax 020 7290 2989
   email bashh@rsm.ac.uk   http://www.bashh.org
   Hon Sec: Dr Janette Clarke
▲ Registered Charity
Br 17
○ *L, *M; to promote the study of the art & science of diagnosing
   & treating sexually transmitted infections, including HIV &
   other sexual health problems
Gp British Co-operative Clinical Group; Genito-Urinary Physicians
   Colposcopy Group
   Special interest: Adolescence, Bacterial, Herpes simplex virus,
   HIV, HPV, Sexual dysfunction
● Conf - Mtgs - ET - Res - Lib - LG
M 900 i, UK / 72 i, o'seas
¶ NL -3/5.
   Guidelines - irreg;   AR;   both free.

British Association for Sexual & Relationship Therapy
   see **College of Sexual & Relationship Therapists**

British Association of Ship Suppliers (BASS) 1906

NR The Moorings, Heron Lakes, Routh, BEVERLEY, E Yorks,
   HU17 9SL.   (sp)
   01964 544554
   email britship@gmx.co.uk   http://www.bassweb.co.uk
   Sec: Mrs E A Marchant
○ *T
● Mtgs - SG - Inf - VE
< Intl Ship Suppliers Assn
M 55 f
¶ LM - 1; ftm, £5 nm.

British Association for Shooting & Conservation (BASC) 1908

■ Marford Mill, Rossett, WREXHAM, Denbighshire, LL12 0HL.
   (hq)
   01244 573000   fax 01244 573013
   email enq@basc.org.uk   http://www.basc.org.uk
   Chief Exec: John Swift
▲ Industrial & Provident Society
Br 8
○ *S; national representative body for sporting & shooting
Gp Firearms; Gamekeeping & gameshooting; Land management
   & conservation; Research; Shooting standards; Stalking;
   Wildfowling
● Conf - Et - Exam - Res - Exhib - Inf - Lib - PL - LG
< F Assn des Chasseurs Eur (FACE)
M 127,000 i
   (Sub: £62)
¶ Shooting & Conservation (Jnl) - 6; ftm, £4.25 nm.
   The Custodian (for Gamekeepers) - 4, ftm, £3 nm.
   Wildfowling - 2; ftm, £2 nm.

British Association of Ski Patrollers (BASP) 1978

■ 20 Lorn Drive, GLENCOE, Argyll, PH49 4HR.   (regd off)
   01855 811443
   email skipatrol@basp.org.uk   http://www.basp.org.uk
   Company Sec: Fiona Gunn
▲ Company Limited by Guarantee (BASP UK Ltd)
○ *P; ski patrol & rescue; exchange of knowledge & information
   internationally with other patrollers
Gp First aid training in the outdoors; Training & grading of ski
   patrollers
● ET - Stat
< Fédn Intl Patrouilles de Ski (FIPS); Brit Assn of Snowsport
   Instructors (BASI)
M 125 i, UK / 5 i, o'seas
¶ NL - 4.   BASP Outdoor First Aid & Safety Manual; £10.

British Association of Skin Camouflage (BASC) 1986

NR PO Box 3671, CHESTER, CH1 9QH.   (asa)
   01254 703107
   email basc9@hotmail.com
   http://www.skin-camouflage.net
▲ Registered Charity
○ *P; to promote, support & further the remedial technique of skin
   camouflage, for the relief of those who need to be restored
   to confidence in a normal appearance, by means of
   prescribable camouflage creams
● Conf - Mtgs - ET - Inf
M c 60 i, UK
¶ The Cover (NL) - 4; free.

British Association for Slavonic & East European Studies (BASEES) 1953

NR c/o Dr Birgit Beumers, SML, University of Bristol,
   17 Woodland Rd, BRISTOL, BS8 1TE.   (inf officer/b)
   Inf Officer: Dr Birgit Beumers
▲ Registered Charity
○ *L; study of language & literature, history, politics, economics &
   society of the former USSR & Eastern Europe
M c 650 i
¶ NL - 3; ftm only.

British Association of Snowsport Instructors (BASI) 1913

NR Morlich House, 17 The Square, GRANTOWN-on-SPEY,
   Morayshire, PH26 3HG.   (hq)
   01479 861717   fax 01479 873657
   email basi@basi.org.uk   http://www.basi.org.uk
   Chief Exec: Peter Kuwall
▲ Company Limited by Guarantee
○ *P, *S; the UK authority for training & grading professional
   snowsport instructors
Gp Skiing: Alpine, Nordic, Telemark, Adaptive (disabled);
   Snowboarding
● ET - Exam
M c 4,000 i
¶ BASI News (Jnl) - 2;   BASI Manual - 1;
   BASI Alpine Manual - 2 yrly; all ftm only.

British Association of Social Workers (BASW) 1970

■ 16 Kent St, BIRMINGHAM, B5 6RD.   (hq)
   0121-622 3911   fax 0121-622 4860
   email info@basw.co.uk   http://www.basw.co.uk
   Chief Exec: Ian Johnston
▲ Company Limited by Guarantee; Registered Charity
○ *P; to promote an active involvement of members who share a
   commitment to good social work practice & uphold the code
   of ethics of the association
● Conf - Mtgs - ET - Exhib - SG - Policy reports - Professional
   publications
< Intl Fedn of Social Work
M 11,200 i
¶ British Jnl of Social Work - 8.   Practice (Jnl) - 4.
   Professional Social Work - 12; ftm, corporate subscription
   only nm.

British Association for South Asian Studies (BASAS) 1972

NR 14 Stephenson Way, LONDON, NW1 2HD.   (hq)
   020 7388 5490
   email basas@basas.org.uk   http://www.basas.org.uk
   Sec: Dr Lawrence Saez
▲ Registered Charity
○ *L; to promote & support South Asian studies in Britain
● Conf - Mtgs - Res
< British Academy
¶ BASAS Bulletin (NL) - 1
× 2007 (1 October) Society for South Asian Studies (merged)

British Association of Spinal Surgeons
   a specialist society of the **British Orthopaedic Association**

© CBD Research Ltd · Beckenham · BR3 5JS · Tel 020 8650 7745 · E-mail cbd@cbdresearch.com · www.cbdresearch.com

British Association of Sport & Exercise Medicine   (BASEM) 1952

NR Hutton Business Centre (suite 1C), Bentley Rd, DONCASTER,
S Yorks, DN5 9QP. (hq)
01302 822300 fax 01302 822300
email basemcentral@basem.co.uk
http://www.basem.co.uk
Mgr: Katy Jones

▲ Company Limited by Guarantee; Registered Charity

Br 9 regions in England; Scotland, Wales

○ *S; for sports orientated consultants & dental surgeons, GPs,
chartered physiotherapists, educationalists, osteopaths,
podiatrists (sports medics & paramedics), veterinary
surgeons, chiropodists, pure & applied scientists

● Conf - ET

< Intl Fedn of Sports Medicine; Eur Fedn of Sports Medicine

M 1,000 i, UK / 100 i, o'seas

¶ British Jnl of Sports Medicine - 6.

British Association of Sport & Exercise Sciences   (BASES) 1985

■ BASES - GO7-GO8 Leeds Metropolitan University, Carnegie
Faculty of Sport & Education, Fairfax Hall, Headingley
Campus Beckett Park, LEEDS, LS6 3QS. (hq)
0113-812 6162 fax 0113-812 6162 (tel first)
email info@bases.org.uk http://www.bases.org.uk
Chmn: Prof Craig Mahoney
Hon Sec: Prof Edward Winter

▲ Company Limited by Guarantee

○ *P, *S; to promote excellence in sport & exercise sciences
through evidence-based practice

Gp Bio-mechanics; Interdisciplinary; Psychology; Physiology; Bio-
mechanics

● Conf - Mtgs - ET - Res - Exhib - Stat

M 3,300 i

¶ The Sport & Exercise Scientist - 4; m only [various rates].

British Association for Sports & Law Ltd   (BASL)   1992

NR c/o Charles Russell, 5 Fleet Place, LONDON, EC4M 7RD.
(regd/office)
0795 797 0289
email basl@britishsportslaw.org
http://www.britishsportslaw.org
Admin: Lorraine Stylianou,   Hon Sec: Jason Saiban

▲ Company Limited by Guarantee

○ *P

● Conf

M i & f
(Sub: £164.50 i, £822.50 f)

¶ Sport & the Law Jnl - 3; ftm only.

British Association of Steelbands   (BAS)   1995

■ 20 Queensbury Road, WEMBLEY, Middx, HA0 1LR. (hsp)
07956 546724
email debi@panpodium.com
http://www.panpodium.com

▲ Company Limited by Guarantee

○ *D

● Conf - Mtgs - ET - Comp - Acts as booking agency

M 10 i, 43 org, UK / 2 org, o'seas

¶ Panpodium (Jnl) - 2; ftm, £3 yr nm.

British Association for the Study of Community Dentistry (BASCD)   1974

NR c/o Kamnini Shah, Stockton-on-Tees Teaching PCT, Tower
House, Teesdale South, Thornaby Place, Thornaby,
STOCKTON-on-TEES, TS17 6SF. (hsb)
01642 3526700
email kamini.shah@northteespct.nhs.uk
http://www.bascd.org
Hon Sec: Dr Liana Zoitopoulos

○ *L, *M; study, research & teaching of all aspects of dentistry in
the community

Gp Community clinical practice; Education; Epidemiology

● Conf - ET - Res

< Eur Assn Dental Public Health

M 500 i

¶ Community Dental Health - 4; £50 m, £88 nm (EU).

British Association for the Study of Headache   (BASH)   1992

■ Dept of Neurology, Hull Royal Infirmary, Anlaby Rd, HULL,
E Yorks, HU3 2JZ. (regd off)
http://www.bash.org.uk
Vice Chmn: Dr Fayyaz Ahmed

▲ Company Limited by Guarantee; Registered Charity

○ *M; to relieve persons suffering from headache by the
advancement of scientific study into that condition

Gp Management guidelines writing c'ee
Working gps: Education, Organisation of headache services

● Conf - ET - Res - LG

< Intl Headache Soc; Eur Headache Fedn

British Association for the Study of the Liver   (BASL)

■ Suite 24 Level 6, New England House, BRIGHTON E Sussex,
BN1 4GH. (hq)
0845 521 0272
email info@basl.org.uk http://www.basl.org.uk
Secretariat Dircector: Geoffrey Bowden

○ *P; knowledge and understanding of the biology and pathology
of the liver for the optimum care of patients.

Gp British Viral Hepatitis Gp

British Association for the Study & Prevention of Child Abuse & Neglect (BASPCAN)   1975

■ 17 Priory St, YORK, YO1 6ET. (hq)
01904 613605 fax 01904 642239
email baspcan@baspcan.org.uk
http://www.baspcan.org.uk
Chmn: Jonathan Picken
Nat Office Mgr: Judy Sanderson

▲ Registered Charity

Br 10

○ *P

● Conf - ET - Res - SG - Inf - LG

< Intl Soc for the Study & Prevention of Child Abuse & Neglect

M 1,590 i, 50 f, UK / 38 i, 3 f, o'seas

¶ Child Abuse Review - 6; ftm.
BASPCAN News - 4; ftm.

British Association for the Study of Religions   (BASR)   1954

NR School of Theology, Religious Studies & Islamic Studies,
University of Wales, Trinity St David, LAMPETER, Ceredigion,
SA48 7ED. (hsb)
email b.schmidt@tsd.ac.uk http://www.tsd.ac.uk
Hon Sec: Dr Bettina Schmidt

▲ Registered Charity

○ *L; to promote the academic study of religions

● Conf

< Intl Assn for the History of Religions; Eur Assn for the Study of
Religions

M 230 i, UK / 7 i, o'seas

¶ DISKUS [online Jnl] - 1; free.
Bulletin - 3; ftm only.

British Association for Supported Employment (BASE) 2006
NR   Unit 4 / 200 Bury Rd, TOTTINGTON, Lancs, BL8 3DX.
        (regd/office)
        0844 561 7445   fax 0844 561 7441
        email admin@base-uk.org   http://www.base-uk.org
        Org Sec: Christopher Wise
▲   Company Limited by Guarantee; Registered Charity
○   *K; promotion & development of supported employment in
        order to enable people with a disability to be able to succeed
        in employment
Gp Supported business interest group
●   Conf - Mtgs - ET - SG - Inf
<   Eur U of Supported Employment
M   200 f
        (Sub: £250)

British Association for Surgery of the Knee
        a specialist society of the **British Orthopaedic Association**

**British Association of Symphonic Bands & Wind Ensembles
(BASBWE) 1981**
■   Fron, LLANSADWRN, Anglesey, LL59 5SL.   (memsec/p)
        01248 811285
        http://www.basbwe.org
        Mem Sec: Richard Edwards
▲   Un-incorporated Society
○   *D; to advance the status of symphonic wind bands &
        ensembles & to educate the general public
M   35 f; 146 org
¶   Winds - 4; ftm.   LM - 1; ftm only.
        Leaflets Series - 1; ftm.

** **British Association of Teachers of Conservative Dentistry**
        Organisation lost; see Introduction paragraph 3.

British Association of Teachers of Dancing (BATD) 1892
NR   Upper Level (Pavilion 8), Watermark Business Park,
        315 Govan Rd, GLASGOW, G51 2SE.   (hq)
        0141-427 3699   fax 0141-419 9783
        email enquiries@batd.co.uk   http://www.batd.co.uk
        Gen Sec: Mrs Katrina Allan
▲   Registered Friendly Society
Br   8; Canada, USA
○   *D, *P; all forms of dancing
●   Conf - Mtgs - ET - Exam - Exhib - Comp - Stat - Inf - VE
<   Stage Dance Council Intl; Brit Dance Council; Scot Official Bd
        of Highland Dancing; Cent Coun Physical Recreation (CCPR)
M   2,000 i, UK / 1,500 i, o'seas
¶   Conference Guide - 1;   Conference Report - 1;
        December Bulletin - 1; all ftm only.

British Association of Teachers of the Deaf (BATOD) 1976
■   175 Dashwood Ave, HIGH WYCOMBE, Bucks, HP12 3DB.
        01494 464190   fax 01494 464190
        email secretary@batod.org.uk
        http://www.batod.org.uk
        Sec: Paul A Simpson
▲   Un-incorporated Society
Br   7 regions
○   *P; to promote the interests of all hearing impaired children &
        young people; to safeguard the interests of their teachers
Gp Audiology; Conference; GCSE; Education & research; Pre-
        school; Publications; Teacher training for teachers of the
        deaf; Transition & post-16
●   Conf - Mtgs - ET - Res - Exhib - Stat - Inf - LG
M   1,750 i, UK / c 25 i, o'seas
¶   Deafness & Education (Jnl) - 4; ftm, £50 yr nm.
        Association Magazine - 5; ftm only.

British Association of Tennis Supporters (BATS) 1979
NR   178 Roebuck St, Ashton, PRESTON, Lancs, PR2 2JN.
        http://www.britishtennisfans.info
        Mem Sec: Linda Biscomb
        Contact: Pat Case (patmcase@tiscali.co.uk)
○   *S; to provide an information service for people interested in
        British tennis players & in attending tournaments to support
        them
●   Conf - Mtgs - Comp - Inf - VE
M   600 i, UK / 5 i, o'seas
¶   NL - 4; £5 yr m.

**British Association of Therapeutical Hypnotists & NLP
Practitioners (BAThH) 1951**
NR   Brogdale Farm, Brogdale Rd, FAVERSHAM, Kent, ME13 8XZ.
        (sic/b)
        01344 421481
        email jane@countrypractice.co.uk
        http://www.bathh.co.uk
        Sec: Jane Clark
○   *P; to seek official & public recognition of qualified practitioners
        of therapeutic hypnosis; the promotion, development,
        research & practice of therapeutic hypnosis for the benefit of
        all
<   UK Confedn of Hypnotherapy Orgs

British Association for Tissue Banking   (BATB)
NR   c/o Society of Biology, Charles Darwin House, 12 Roger St,
        LONDON, WC1N 2JU.
        http://www.batb.org.uk
○   *M

5 British Association of Urological Nurses (BAUN) 1995
■   Fitwise Management Ltd, Drumcross Hall, BATHGATE,
        W Lothian, EH48 4JT.   (asa)
        01506 811077   fax 01506 811477
        email info@fitwise.co.uk   http://www.bun.co.uk
        Pres: Lucinda Poulton
▲   Company Limited by Guarantee
○   *P; to promote & maintain the highest standards in the practice
        & development of urological nursing & urological patient
        care
Gp Benign; Oncology; Male & female sexual dysfunction
●   Conf - Inf
<   Brit Assn of Urological Surgeons (BAUS)
¶   NL - 4; ftm.

British Association of Urological Surgeons (BAUS) 1945
NR   at the Royal College of Surgeons, 35-43 Lincoln's Inn Fields,
        LONDON, WC2A 3PE.   (hq)
        020 869 6950
        http://www.baus.org.uk
▲   Registered Charity
○   *P

British Association for Vedic Astrology (BAVA) 1996
NR   108 Tyrone Rd, THORPE BAY, Essex, SS1 3HB.   (hq)
        http://www.bava.org
        Mem Sec: Dr K Chidambaram
○   *P

British Association of Veterinary Emergency Care
        a group of the **British Small Animal Veterinary Association**

British Association of Veterinary Ophthalmologists
        a group of the **British Small Animal Veterinary Association**

British Association of Women Entrepreneurs   (BAWE)   1953
■   Unit 3 Ninian Park, Ninian Way, TAMWORTH, B77 5ES.
    (pres/b)
    01827 312812
    http://www.bawe-uk.org
    Nat Pres: Deb Leary
▲   Company Limited by Guarantee
Br   4; 50
○   *P; to bring together all women who are qualified to be called
    'Heads of Business', whether they operate alone, with co-
    directors, or with members of their families; to confine
    activities to economic matters; to explore & advise on the
    means by which the rights & duties of women in business,
    industry & domestic spheres may be reconciled & improved
●   Conf - Mtgs - ET - Exhib - Comp - SG - Expt - Inf - VE - Empl -
    LG
<   Les Femmes Chefs d'Entreprises Mondiales (FCEM); Amer
    Cham Comm; CBI; IoD; London Cham Comm
M   150 i
¶   BAWE National NL - 4;   BAWE West NL - 4; FCEM News
    International - 4; all ftm only.

British Astrological & Psychic Society   (BAPS)   1976
■   26 Second Avenue, LONDON, W3 7RX.   (reg/office)
    020 8932 1145
    email lauraboyle@ymail.com   http://www.baps.uk.com
    Sec: Laura Boyle
▲   Company Limited by Guarantee
Br   3
○   *G, *P; astrology & all esoteric/psychic disciplines - tarot, runes,
    palmistry, astrology, numerology, psy cards, crystal
    divination, psychic perception, mediumship, clairvoyance,
    aura readings etc
Gp   BAPS School of: Astrology (1995) / Palmistry, runes, tarot
    (1996) / Numerology (correspondence courses)
●   ET - Exhib - Workshops
M   257 i, 100 vetted counsellors, UK / 10 i, o'seas
¶   Mercury (Jnl) - 4; ftm, £3.50 each nm.
    National Register of Consultants; ftm, cover price nm.

British Astronomical Association   (BAA)   1890
NR   Burlington House, Piccadilly, LONDON, W1J 0DU.   (hq)
    020 7734 4145   fax 020 7439 4629
    http://www.britastro.org
▲   Company Limited by Guarantee; Registered Charity
Br   Australia (New South Wales)
○   *L; organisation of observers in the work of astronomical
    observation, encouragement of popular interests in
    astronomy
Gp   Solar; Lunar; Mercury & Venus; Mars; Asteroids & remote
    planets; Jupiter; Saturn; Comet; Variable star; Meteor;
    Aurora; Deep sky; Computing; Instruments & imaging
●   Mtgs - ET - Res - Exhib - Comp - SG - Inf - Lib - VE
M   c 3,500 i, c 100 org
¶   Jnl - 6.   Hbk - 1.

British Audio-Visual Dealers Association   (BADA)   1982
NR   33 High St, Hampton Wick, KINGSTON-UPON-THAMES,
    Surrey, KT1 4DA.   (hq)
    020 8150 6714
    email info@bada.co.uk   http://www.bada.co.uk
    Operations & Marketing Mgr: Phil Hansen
▲   Company Limited by Guarantee
○   *T; to promote, raise & monitor the standards of retail practice
    in the UK Hi Fi industry
●   Mtgs - ET - Stat
M   75 f

British Autogenic Society   (BAS)   1984
NR   c/o Royal London Homoeopathic Hospital, Gt Ormond Street,
    LONDON, WC1N 3HR.   (hq)
    020 7391 8908
    email admin@autogenic-therapy.org.uk
    http://www.autogenic-therapy.org.uk
    Sec: Mrs Jane Bird,   Chmn: Mr Chris Perrin
▲   Company Limited by Guarantee; Registered Charity
○   *P; 'the professional & regulatory body for autogenic therapists
    & psychotherapists in the UK; sets training standards, runs
    training courses & provides information for the public.
    Autogenic therapy is self-help for mind & body. Therapists
    teach easy mental exercises over 8-10 weeks; allows switch-
    off of stress response, helps many problems & also helps
    realise potential in many areas'
●   Mtgs - ET - SG
<   Intl C'ee for Autogenic Therapy (ICAT); Eur Assn for
    Psychotherapy (EAP)
M   94 i, UK / 12 i, o'seas
¶   NL - 2; ftm only.

**British Automatic Fire Sprinkler Association Ltd   (BAFSA)
1974**
NR   Richmond House, Broad St, ELY, Cambs, CB7 4AH.   (hq)
    01353 659187   fax 01353 666619
    email info@bafsa.org.uk   http://www.bafsa.org.uk
    Sec Gen: Stewart Kidd
▲   Company Limited by Guarantee
○   *T; to promote the use of automatic sprinkler & other systems
    using water as a means of controlling & extinguishing fires in
    all types of premises
Gp   Contractual; Marketing & promotion; Technical
●   Conf - Exhib - LG
<   Fedn of Brit Fire Orgs; Fire Ind Confedn; Fire Ind Coun (Trade
    Enterprises) Ltd
M   96 f, 3 org
¶   LM & affiliates;   Sprinkler Systems: the facts; both free.
    Sprinklers for Safety; ftm, £25 nm.
    Sprinklers in:
    Schools; Heritage Buildings; Retail Premises; Warehouses.
    Sprinkler Facts (CD-ROM).   Domestic Sprinkler Systems.
    Joint Code of Practice for Sprinklers in Schools; £5.
✕   2005 British Automatic Sprinkler Association Ltd

British Automation & Robot Association Ltd   (BARA)   1977
NR   c/o PPMA Ltd, New Progress House, 34 Stafford Rd,
    WALLINGTON, Surrey, SM6 9AA.   (hq)
    020 8773 8111   fax 020 8773 0022
    email bara@bara.org.uk   http://www.bara.org.uk
    Pres: Mike Wilson,   CEO: Chris Buxton
▲   Company Limited by Guarantee
○   *T; the development & application of automation in British
    industry; suppliers of robotics & automation
Gp   Advanced robotics; Aerospace, control systems security; Safety
●   Conf - Mtgs - Res - Exhib - Stat - Inf - LG
<   Intl Fedn of Robotics (IFR); EAMA
M   30 f
¶   Quartermation (email NL) - 4; free.

British Automobile Racing Club   (BARC Ltd)   1912
■   Thruxton Circuit, ANDOVER, Hants, SP11 8PN.   (hq)
    01264 882200   fax 01264 882233
    email info@barc.net   http://www.barc.net
    Chief Exec: Dennis Carter
▲   Company Limited by Guarantee
Br   7; Canada
○   *S; organisation of circuit motor racing, hill climbs & sprints
●   Mtgs - Social events
M   4,000 i, UK / 100 i, o'seas
¶   Startline - 6; ftm, £2.75 nm.
    Programme of events - 1; free.

British Aviation Archaeological Council   (BAAC)   1978
NR   Coupland Bell Ltd, The TechnoCentre, Puma Way, COVENTRY,
       CV1 2TT.   (hsb)
       email baac3@couplandbell.com
       http://www.aviationarchaeology.org.uk
       Sec: Mark Evans
○   *N; coordination of recovery, restoration & research of historic
       aircraft wrecks & aviation history by groups & individuals
●   Inf - LG - Mtgs - Res - VE
M   8 i, 36 org, UK / 4 org, o'seas
¶   Aviation Archaeologist - 4; ftm only.

British Aviation Enthusiasts Society   (BAES)   2001
■   28a Frogmore Lane, Lovedean, WATERLOOVILLE, Hants,
       PO8 9QL.   (hsp)
       023 9242 1903   fax 023 9242 1903
       email mail@baes.org.uk   http://www.baes.org.uk
       Sec: Deryn Hawkins
▲   Un-incorporated Society
○   *G; to visit aviation facilities worldwide (airports, airfields, air
       forces, museum collections); to experience, photograph &
       record details of aircraft & historic aviation buildings
●   Mtgs - VE (an experienced tour escort is provided)
M   180 i, UK / 23 i, o'seas
¶   NL - 4; ftm only.

British Aviation Preservation Council   (BAPC)   1967
■   19 Acton Place, High Heaton, NEWCASTLE UPON TYNE,
       NE7 7RL.   (hsp)
       0191-266 2049   fax 0191-266 2049
       email secretarybapc@btconnect.com
       http://www.bapc.org.uk
       Chmn: Steve Hague, Sec: Brian Dixon
▲   Un-incorporated Society
○   *N; coordinating body for all aviation museums & collections
       working for the advancement of aviation preservation &
       promotion of aviation heritage
Gp   National Aviation Heritage Registers; Stopping the Rot
       conferences
●   Conf - Mtgs - ET - Res - Inf
<   Eur Aviation Presvn Coun
M   135 org, UK / 10 org, o'seas
¶   Update (NL) - 4; ftm only.

British Badge Collectors Association   1980
■   PO Box 1362, LICHFIELD, Staffs, WS13 7YD.   (mem/sp)
       01543 256486
       email badgecollectorsassociation@yahoo.co.uk
       http://www.thebbca.tripod.com
       Mem Sec: Peter Duffen
▲   Un-incorporated Society
○   *G; for collectors of any type & every description of badge
●   Mtgs - Exhib
M   i
       (Sub: £5 i, UK / £7 i, o'seas)
¶   NL - 6.   The Badge Mag - 1.

British Ballet Organization Ltd   (BBO)   1930
■   Woolborough House, 39 Lonsdale Rd, Barnes, LONDON,
       SW13 9JP.   (hq)
       020 8748 1241
       http://www.bbo.org.uk
       Dir: John Travis
▲   Company Limited by Guarantee
Br   Australia, New Zealand
○   *D, *G; ballet, tap, jazz & modern dancing examinations; ballet
       & tap teaching qualifications
●   Conf - Mtgs - ET - Exam - Lib
<   Regd by Coun for Dance Education & Training (UK) (CDET)
M   c 300 teachers, UK / 135 teachers, o'seas
¶   The Dancer - 1.

British Balloon & Airship Club   (BBAC)   1965
■   c/o Cameron Balloons, St John St, Bedminster, BRISTOL,
       BS3 4NH.   (pro/b)
       email information@bbac.org   http://www.bbac.org
       Inf Officer: Hannah Cameron,   Chmn: Ian Hooker
▲   Company Limited by Guarantee
Br   regional clubs
○   *S; to promote all aspects of lighter than air flight, including hot
       air ballooning, gas ballooning & airship flying; to serve
       sporting & commercial interests equally
Gp   Clubs: Regional in UK, Competitions
●   Conf - Mtgs - ET - Exam - Comp - Inf - LG
       BBAC carries delegated authority from the CAA for
       airworthiness & pilot training
<   UK Civil Aviation Authority
>   British Balloon Museum & Library
M   c 2,000 i, 20 f, UK / 100 i, o'seas
¶   Aerostat - 6.

British Bankers' Association   (BBA)   1919
NR   Pinners Hall, 105-108 Old Broad St, LONDON, EC2N 1EX.
       (hq)
       020 7216 8800   fax 020 7216 8811
       http://www.bba.org.uk
       Chief Exec: Angela Knight
○   *T; for banks carrying out business in the UK
Gp   Press Office (020 7216 8989)
●   Conf - Stat - LG
M   300 f
¶   NL; ftm.

British Banking History Society   (BHSS)   1980
■   71 Mile Lane, Cheylesmore, COVENTRY, CV3 5GB.   (hsp)
       024 7650 3245
       email info@banking-history.co.uk
       http://www.banking-history.co.uk
       Hon Sec: John Purser
▲   Un-incorporated Society
○   *G; to encourage & popularise the collection of cheques,
       banknotes & memorabilia relating to banking; to promote
       the study of the history of banking
●   Mtgs - Res - Inf
M   110 i, 10 f, UK / 30 i, o'seas
¶   Counterfoil - 4; subscription only.

British Barometer Makers Association   (BBMA)   2006
■   c/o Barometer World Ltd, Quicksilver Barn, Merton,
       OKEHAMPTON, Devon, EX20 3DS.   (hsb)
       01805 603443   fax 01805 603344
       email prc@barometerworld.co.uk
       Sec: Phillip Collins
▲   Un-incorporated Society
○   *G, *K; to lobby support for mercury barometers
●   Stat - Inf - Lobbying in the EU
<   Eur Barometer Makers Assn
M   3 i

British Basketball Federation   (BBF)   2005
NR   PO Box 3971, SHEFFIELD, S Yorks, S9 9AZ.
       email info@british-basketball.co.uk
       http://www.british-basketball.co.uk
○   *N, *S; represents the national basketball associations of
       England, Scotland & Wales on the national Olympic
       Committee
<   Brit Olympic Assn
M   3 org: England Basketball   basketballscotland   Basketball
       Wales

© CBD Research Ltd · Beckenham · BR3 5JS · Tel 020 8650 7745 · E-mail cbd@cbdresearch.com · www.cbdresearch.com

British Battery Industry Federation (BBIF) 1991
■ 3 Blakeley Dene, Raby Mere, WIRRAL, Cheshire, CH63 0QE.
   (hsp)
   0151-334 2040   fax 0151-334 2040
   email jgferris@tesco.net   http://www.ibda.co.uk
   Hon Sec: J Godfrey Ferris
▲ Un-incorporated Society
○ *T; for battery manufactures & independent distributors of
   automotive & industrial batteries in the UK
● Conf - Mtgs - ET - Inf - LG
< Automotive Aftermarket Liaison Gp
× 2011 (Independent Battery Distributors Association
   (Society of the British Battery Industry

British Battery Manufacturers Association (BBMA) 1986
NR 3 The Registry, Royal Mint Court, LONDON, EC3N 4QN.
   (regd/off)
▲ Company Limited by Guarantee
○ *T; manufacturers of primary (non-rechargeable) & secondary
   (re-chargeable) portable consumer batteries - NOT
   automotive lead-acid
● Mtgs - Stat - Inf - LG
< Eur Portable Battery Assn (EPBA)

British Bazadaise Cattle Society 1989
■ Unthank Farm, Constable Burton, LEYBURN, N Yorks,
   DL8 5LX. (hsp)
   01677 451852
   email enquiry@bazadaise.org.uk
   http://www.bazadaise.org.uk
   Sec: Rachel Loadman
▲ Company Limited by Guarantee; Registered Charity
○ *B; a beef breed originating in South West France
< Nat Beef Assn
M 44 i
   (Sub: £30)

British Bedding & Pot Plant Association
   since 2007 **British Protected Ornamentals Association**

British Bee-Keepers' Association (BBKA) 1874
■ National Beekeeping Centre, NAC, Stoneleigh Park,
   KENILWORTH, Warks, CV8 2LG. (hq)
   024 7669 6679
   Gen Sec: Mike Harris
▲ Registered Charity
Br 61
○ *G, *T; to further the craft of keeping bees
Gp Appliance trade; Bee health; Bee disease; Insurance; Research;
   Education; Bee breeding; Protection against spray &
   pesticides
● Conf - ET - Exam - Res - Exhib - LG
< Cent Assn of Beekeepers; Bee Improvement & Bee Breeders
   Assn; Assn of Beekeeping Appliance Mfrs
M 9,824 i, 5 org
¶ BBKA News - 5; ftm.

British Beer & Pub Association (BBPA) 1904
NR Brewers' Hall (ground floor), Aldermanbury Square, LONDON,
   EC2V 7HR. (hq)
   020 7627 9191   fax 020 7627 9123
   email enquiries@beerandpub.com
   http://www.beerandpub.com
   Chief Exec: Brigid Simmonds
▲ Company Limited by Guarantee
Br Scottish Beer & Pub Association
○ *T; to represent the beer & pub industry when dealing with
   government & government bodies in the UK & EU; to
   enhance the reputation of the brewing & pub sector
● Conf - Mtgs - ET - Res - Comp - Stat - Expt - LG
< Hotels, Restaurants & Cafés in Europe (HOTREC); The Brewers
   of Europe (BoE); Confedn of Brit Ind (CBI)
M 72 f
¶ Digest - 11; ftm only.
   Statistical Hbk - 1; £27.75 m, £47.50 nm.   AR; ftm.
   Publications list available from: Brewing Publications Ltd, at
   above address.

** British Beermat Collectors' Society
   Organisation lost: see Introduction paragraph 3

British Belgian Blue Cattle Society
   since 2008 **British Blue Cattle Society**

British Berrichon du Cher Sheep Society 1986
NR Tregwynt, Three Ashes, HEREFORD, HR2 8LY. (sp)
   01989 770071
   email berrichom@btconnect.com
   http://www.berrichonsociety.com
   Sec: Sue Powell
▲ Company Limited by Guarantee
○ *B
● Exhib - Inf
< Nat Sheep Assn
M 97 i
¶ NL - 4;   Magazine - 1;   Flock Book - 1;   all free.

British Biathlon Union
NR Bryn Siriol, Old Rd, Bwlch, BRECON, LD3 7RZ.
   01874 730562   fax 01874 730049
   http://www.britishbiathlon.com
   Sec Gen: Mark Goodson
○ *S the national governing body for the Olymic sport

British Big Cats Society (BBCS) 2001
NR PO Box 28, PLYMOUTH, Devon, PL1 1AA.
   0845 230 2329   fax 01752 664547
   email sightings@britishbigcats.org
   http://www.britishbigcats.org
   Founder: Danny Bamping
○ *G, *V; to scientifically identify, quantify, catalogue & protect the
   big cats that freely roam the British countryside
M c 500 i

** British Biomagnetic Association
   Organisation lost: see Introduction paragraph 3

British Biophysical Society (BBS) 1966
NR c/o Prof J M Seddon, Dept of Chemistry, Imperial College,
   LONDON, SW7 2AZ. (hq)
   020 7594 5797
   Hon Sec: Prof John M Seddon
▲ Registered Charity
○ *L; advancement of science of biophysics - 'the study of the
   functioning & structure of living organisms viewed from a
   physical standpoint, & the application of physical & physio-
   chemical techniques to biological problems'

British Bird Council
   a group of the **National Council for Aviculture**

British Bison Association   (BBA)   1991
- ■ Bush Farm, West Knoyle, WARMINSTER, Wilts, BA12 6AE.
  (hsp/b)
  01747 830263
  email info@bisonfarm.co.uk   http://www.bisonfarm.co.uk
  Hon Sec: Lord Seaford
- ▲ Un-incorporated Society
- ○ *B; to promote the interests of bison & bison farmers & meat
  producers
- ● Conf - Mtgs - Inf - VE - LG
- < Nat Bison Assn (USA)
- M 40 i, UK / 4 i, o'seas
  (Sub: £25)
- ¶ NL - 2;   Bison Hbk; £12 nm.   AR.

British Bleu du Maine Sheep Society   1982
- NR Long Wood Farm, Trostrey, USK, Monmouthshire, NP15 1LA.
  (hsp)
  01291 673816
  email jane@bleudumaine.co.uk
  http://www.bleudumaine.co.uk
  Breed Sec: Mrs Jane Smith
- ▲ Registered Charity
- ○ *B
- ● Mtgs - Res - Exhib - SG
- < Nat Sheep Assn
- M 250 i, 10 f
- ¶ NL - 4;   Flock Book - 1; ftm only.
  Breeder's Directory [LM] - 2/3 years; free.

British Blind & Shutter Association   (BBSA)   1919
- NR PO Box 232, STOWMARKET, Suffolk, IP14 9AR.   (hq)
  01449 780444
  email info@bbsa.org.uk   http://www.bbsa.org.uk
  Sec: A D Skelding
- ▲ Company Limited by Guarantee
- ○ *T; represents leading UK manufacturers of interior & exterior
  window blinds, security shutters & grilles
- ● Mtgs - Exhib - ET - Inf - VE
- M 350 f, UK / 8 f, o'seas
- ¶ Blinds & Shutters - 4.

British Blonde Society   2002
- ■ Avenue M, Stoneleigh Park, KENILWORTH, Warks, CV8 2RG.
  (hq)
  024 7641 9058   fax 024 7641 9082
  email secretary@britishblondesociety.co.uk
  http://www.britishblondesociety.co.uk
  Sec: Rachel Foley
- ▲ Registered Charity
- Br 9
- ○ *B
- Gp Farmers; Abattoirs; Agricultural
- ● Mtgs - Exhib - Comp - Stat - Expt - VE
- < Nat Beef Assn
- M 530 i
- ¶ Blonde (Jnl) [incl LM] - 1;   Blonde News {NL} - 1; both free.

British Blood Transfusion Society   (BBTS)   1983
- NR Enterprise House, Manchester Science Park, Lloyd Street North,
  MANCHESTER, M15 6JJ.   (hq)
  0161-232 7999   fax 0161-232 7979
  email bbts@bbts.org.uk   http://www.bbts.org.uk
  Hon Sec: Mrs Joan Jones
- ▲ Registered Charity
- ○ *M, *P; for those engaged in transfusion medicine & transfusion
  science in hospitals & blood centres
- ● Conf - Mtgs - ET - Exam - Res - SG
- M 1,400 i & f, UK / 300 i, o'seas
- ¶ Transfusion Medicine (Jnl) - 6.
  NL - 4; ftm only.

British Blue Cattle Society
- NR Fell View, Blencarn, PENRITH, Cumbria, CA10 1TX.
  01768 88775   fax 01768 88779
  email info@britishbluecattle.org
  http://www.belgianblue.co.uk
  Sec: John Fleming
- ○ *B
- < Nat Beef Assn
- × 2008 British Belgian Blue Cattle Society

British Bluegrass Music Association   (BBMA)   1990
- NR 26 Martin Rd, PORTSMOUTH, Hants, PO3 6JZ.   (mem/sp)
  023 9265 1265
  email membership@britishbluegrass.co.uk
  http://www.britishbluegrass.co.uk
  Mem Secs: David & Clare Rozzell
- ▲ Un-incorporated Society
- ○ *D; promotion of bluegrass music & associated traditions in UK
- ● Mtgs - Inf - Organising tours - Producing CDs - Sponsoring
  events - Teaching / tuition - Publicising concerts & tours
- < Intl Bluegrass Music Assn
- M c 600 i, UK / c 20 i, o'seas
- ¶ British Bluegrass News - 4; ftm, £2 yr nm.

British Bob Skeleton Association
- NR Dept of Sports Development, University of Bath,
  Claverton Down, BATH, BA2 7AY.
  01225 383696
  http://www.bobskeleton.org.uk
  Gen Sec: Phil Searle
- ○ *S

British Bobsleigh Association Ltd   (BBA)   1956
- ■ Invision House, Wilbury Way, HITCHIN, Herts, SG4 0TW.
  (regd off)
  07590 851082
  http://www.bobteamgb.org
  Company Sec: Helen Smyth
- ▲ Company Limited by Guarantee
- ○ *S; to promote British bobsleighing; to attain world prominence
  in championships
- M i
- ¶ The British Bobsleigh Annual - 1; ftm.

British Body Piercing Association   (BBPA)
- NR Dalton House, 60 Windsor Rd, LONDON, SW19 2RR.
  http://www.bbpa.org.uk
- ○ *P

British Bodyboard Club   (BBC)   1993
- NR 3 Quintet Close, EXETER, Devon, EX1 3HZ.   (hsb)
  07594 705475
  email matt@britishbodyboardclub.co.uk
  http://www.britishbodyboardclub.co.uk
  Hon Sec: Matt Hawken
- ○ *S; a form of surfing
- M i

British Bodyguard Association   (BBA)
- NR 58 Lower Friar St (suite 27), NEWCASTLE UPON TYNE,
  NE1 5UE.   (mail/address)
  email admin@the-bba.org.uk
- ○ *P; for security professionals
- M c 49 f
- ¶ The Circuit (Jnl) - 4; ftm.
  Directory [of services].

© CBD Research Ltd · Beckenham · BR3 5JS · Tel 020 8650 7745 · E-mail cbd@cbdresearch.com · www.cbdresearch.com

British Boomerang Society (BBS) 1980

■   36 Fox Dene, GODALMING, Surrey, GU7 1YG.   (chmn/p)
01483 417236
email mckennaslade@inbox.com
http://www.boomerangs.org.uk
Gen Sec: Seán McKenna-Slade
▲   Un-incorporated Society
○   *S; to promote boomerang throwing as a sport; to provide
designs of boomerangs & the materials to make
boomerangs from; to research the history of boomerangs &
the physics of their flight
●   Mtgs - Res - Comp - Talks on various aspects of boomerangs
<   Fedn of Intl Boomerang Assns
M   50 i, 3 f, UK / 5 i, c 20 org, o'seas
(Sub: £5 i, free reciprocal exchange org)
¶   Jnl - irreg; ftm only.

British Bottlers' Institute (BBI) 1953

NR   c/o Binsted Group, 53 Basepoint, Caxton Close, ANDOVER,
Hants, SP10 3FG.   (hsp)
01246 326480
email secretary@bbi.org.uk   http://www.bbi.org.uk
Gen Sec: John Yates
▲   Un-incorporated Society
○   *T; a forum for those concerned with the bottling, canning &
packaging of beverages, food & other products, enabling
them to share their experience & problems
●   Conf - Mtgs - Exhib - Comp - VE
M   40 i, 70 f, UK / 2 i, 2 f, o'seas

British Brands Group (BBG) 1994

■   100 Victoria Embankment, London, EC4Y 0DH.   (hq)
07020 934250   fax 07020 934252
email info@britishbrandsgroup.org.uk
http://www.britishbrandsgroup.org.uk
Dir: John Noble
▲   Company Limited by Guarantee
○   *K, *N; to speak out authoritatively on behalf of brands & to
represent them collectively when commercial & regulatory
issues threaten both their value & their ability to be a positive
force in society
●   Mtgs - ET - Res - Exhib - Inf - PL - VE - LG
<   Eur Brands Assn (AIM)
M   25 f
¶   NL - 4.

British Brewery Playing Card Society (BBPCS) 1996

■   65 Chandlers, Orton Brimbles, PETERBOROUGH, Cambs,
PE2 5YW.   (hsp)
email mikle@bbpcs.co.uk   http://www.bbpcs.co.uk
Sec: Mike Johnson
▲   Un-incorporated Society
○   *G; for playing card collectors of cards advertising products
such as breweries, whisky, tobacco, shipping etc interest on
their backs
●   Mtgs
M   80 i, 3 org, UK / 10 i, o'seas
¶   NL - 4.
Catalogues of playing cards: Brewery, Tobacco, Spirits; prices
on application.

British Brick Society (BBS) 1972

■   19 Woodcroft Avenue, STANMORE, Middx, HA7 3PT.   (hsp)
email micksheila67@hotmail.com
http://www.britishbricksoc.free-online.co.uk
Hon Sec: Mick Oliver
▲   Un-incorporated Society
○   *G, *L; to study & record all aspects of the archaeology &
history of brick, brickmaking & brick building
●   Inf - VE - Coordinating records of brickmaking sites &
manufacturers' names in the British Isles
<   Brit Archaeological Assn (Brick section)
M   c 300 i, c 20 f, UK / c 20 i, o'seas
¶   BBS Information (NL) - 3; ftm, back issue prices on
application nm.

British Bridalwear Association (BBA) 1995

NR   11 Boldmere Road, SUTTON COLDFIELD, W Midlands,
B73 5UY.
0121-321 3939
http://www.bbabridalwear.com
○   *P, *T;

British Brush Manufacturers Association
has amalgamated with the **British Home Enhancement Trade
Association**

British Bryological Society (BBS) 1896

NR   6 Darnford Close, Parkside, STAFFORD, ST16 1LR.   (mem/sp)
http://www.rbg-web2.rbge.org.uk/bbs/bbs.htm
Mem Sec: M F Godfrey
▲   Registered Charity
○   *L, *Q; study & conservation of mosses & liverworts, especially
those in the British Isles
Gp   Reading circle; Tropical bryology
●   Conf - Mtgs - ET - Res - Exhib - SG - Stat - Inf - Lib - VE
<   N Western Naturalist U
M   382 i, UK / 215 i, o'seas
¶   Jnl of Bryology - 4; ftm.
Bulletin - 2; ftm.

British Buddhist Association (BBA) 1974

■   11 Biddulph Rd, LONDON, W9 1JA.   (hq)
020 7286 5575
Dir: A Haviland-Nye
▲   Registered Charity
○   *R
●   Conf - Mtgs - ET (courses & weekends) - SG - VE - Courses for
teachers of religious education in schools
M   'confidential'

British Bulgarian Chamber of Commerce (BBCC) 1993

■   PO Box 123, BROMLEY, Kent, BR1 4ZX.   (hq)
020 8464 5007
email info@bbcc.bg   http://www.bbcc.bg
Exec Dir: Mrs Christine Booth
▲   Company Limited by Guarantee
Br   8 Charles Darwin Str, Sofia 1113, Bulgaria
○   *C; promotion of business between Britain & Bulgaria
●   Conf - Mtgs - Expt - Inf - LG - Business missions
M   80 f, UK / 70 f, o'seas
¶   NL - 52 [email only]; ftm only.

British Bulgarian Friendship Society (BBFS) 1952

NR   22 Modena Rd, HOVE, E Sussex, BN3 5QG.   (hsb)
01273 726433   fax 01273 726433
email bbfs@care4free.net   http://www.bbfs.org.uk
Hon Sec: K Barker
▲   Un-incorporated Society
○   *X; to promote friendship between British & Bulgarian peoples
●   Mtgs - Exhib - Inf - Lib - VE
M   c 300 i,
¶   NL - 3/4; ftm.

British Burn Association (BBA) 1967

■   Faculty of Life Sciences, University of Manchester, Brunswick St,
MANCHESTER, Lancs, M13 9PL.   (chmn/b)
0161-275 6765
email mamta.shah@manchester.ac.uk
http://www.britishburnassociation.org
Chmn: Mamta Shah
▲   Registered Charity
○   *P; to promote burn prevention, treatment, care & rehabilitation
●   Conf - Mtgs - Exhib
<   Intl Soc for Burn Injuries
M   c 400 i

British Business Angels Association   (BBAA)   2005
- ■ 100 Pall Mall, LONDON, SW1Y 5NQ.   (hq)
  020 7321 5669
  email info@bbaa.org.uk   http://www.bbaa.org.uk
  Chief Exec: Anthony Clarke
- ▲ Company Limited by Guarantee
- ○ *T; the national trade body for the UK's Business Angel
  networks & their associates
- Gp Accountants; Banks; Business Angel networks; Business support
  services; Early stage funds; Lawyers; Regional Development
  Agencies
- ● Conf - ET - Res - Stat - Inf - LG
- < Eur Business Angels Network (EBAN)
- M 500-750 f
- ¶ NL - 12;   Directory - 1;   Research - 1.

British Business Awards Association   (BBAA)   1993
- § Highfield Park, Creaton, NORTHAMPTON, NN6 8NT.
  01604 505480   fax 01604 505861
  email info@bbaa.co.uk   http://www.bbaa.co.uk
  Designs and organises awards programmes for leading
  publishing groups throughout the UK.

**British Business & General Aviation Association   (BBGA)
1975**
- ■ 19 Church St, Brill, AYLESBURY, Bucks, HP18 9RT.   (hq)
  01844 238020   fax 01844 238087
  email info@bbga.aero   http://www.bbga.aero
  Chief Exec: Guy Lachlan
- ▲ Company Limited by Guarantee
- ○ *T; to represent companies operating & trading in the industry -
  including manufacturers, business aviation operators,
  organisations in repair & overhaul, training & aircraft &
  helicopter sales, also spares stockists & supporting
  organisations in finance, insurance & publishing
- Gp Air transport; Airport working; Engineering; Flying training;
  Sales & service
- ● Conf - Mtgs - Res - Exhib - SG - Stat - Inf - LG
- M 180 f
- ¶ BBGA Industry Directory - 18 months; free.

British Button Society   (BBS)   1976
- ■ 346 Avebury Avenue, TONBRIDGE, Kent, TN9 1TQ.   (hsp)
  01732 364309
  email angelaclarkbuttons@btinternet.com
  http://www.britishbuttonsociety.org
  Hon Sec: Mrs A Clark
- ▲ Un-incorporated Society
- ○ *G; the collection & preservation of antique & modern buttons
- ● Mtgs - Res - Lib - VE - Publication of articles on, & photographs
  of, buttons
- M 300 i, 10 f, UK / 50 i, o'seas
- ¶ Button Lines - 4; ftm only.

British Cables Association   (BCA)   1965
- NR Flat 7, 11 The Grange, LONDON, SW19 4PT.   (hq)
  020 8946 6978
  email peter.smeeth@btconnect.com
  http://www.bcauk.org
  Sec Gen: Peter Smeeth
- ▲ Un-incorporated Society
- ○ *T; manufacturers of insulated cables and wires and associated
  products
- Gp Accessories; Communications cables; Covered conductors;
  Energy cables; Supertension cables
- ● Conf - Mtgs - Res - SG - Stat - Expt - LG
- < Eur Confedn Assns Mfrs Insulated Wires & Cables
  (EUROPACABLE); CBI
- M 18 f

British Cactus & Succulent Society   (BCSS)   1945
- ■ 49 Chestnut Glen, HORNCHURCH, Essex, RM12 4HL.   (hsp)
  01708 447778   fax 01444 454061
  email bcss@cactus-mall.com   http://www.bcss.org.uk
  Hon Sec: E A Harris
- ▲ Registered Charity
- Br 94; Republic of Ireland
- ○ *H; study & conservation of cacti & succulent plants
- Gp Robins
- ● Conf - Mtgs - Res - Exhib - Comp - LG
- < Cactus & Succulent Soc of America, German Cactus &
  Succulent Soc; Succulent Soc S Australia; R Horticl Soc
- M 3,500 i, UK / 500 i, o'seas
- ¶ Cactus World (Jnl) - 4; £15 m (£20 or 38 o'seas).
  Bradleya (Ybk) - 1; £16 m, (£20 o'seas)

British Calcium Carbonates Federation   (BCCF)   1943
- NR Omya UK Ltd, Omya House, Stephensons Way, Wyvern
  Business Park, Chaddesden, DERBY, DE21 6LY.   (hsb)
  01332 887435
  Sec: Mike Nocivelli
- ▲ Un-incorporated Society
- ○ *T; to foster & develop the manufacture & sale of calcium
  carbonates
- ● Mtgs - Stat - Inf
- M 5 f
- ¶ LM; ftm only.

British Camargue Horse Society   (BCHS)   1991
- ■ The Cottage - Valley Rd, Wickham Market, WOODBRIDGE,
  Suffolk, IP13 0ND.   (hq)
  01728 746916
  http://www.valleyfarmonline.co.uk
  Sec: Sarah Ling
- ○ *B; to promote the Camargue horse & educate children
- ● ET - VE
- M 40 i

British Camelids Association
  A charity concerned with the welfare, general promotion,
  education & research on Camelids.
  For membership bodies see **British Alpaca Society** & the
  British Llama Society

British Canadian Chamber of Trade & Commerce   1951
- ■ Toronto-Dominion Centre, 77 King St West (suit2 2401),
  TORONTO ON, Canada, M5K 1G8.   (hq)
  1 (416) 502 0847   fax 1 (416) 502 9319
  Exec Dir: Idalia Obregon
- ○ *C; to foster bi-lateral trade between Britain & Canada
- M i & f

British Candlemakers Federation   1995
- NR c/o Tallow Chandlers Hall, 4 Dowgate Hill, LONDON,
  EC4R 2SH.
  020 7248 4726
- ▲ Un-incorporated Society
- ○ *T; to ensure that the skills & arts of candlemaking in Britain are
  continued along with modern methods & future development
- ● Mtgs - Exhib - Stat
- < Eur Candlemakers Fedn
- M 33 f, UK / 1 f, o'seas

© CBD Research Ltd · Beckenham · BR3 5JS · Tel 020 8650 7745 · E-mail cbd@cbdresearch.com · www.cbdresearch.com

British Canoe Union   (BCU)   1936
NR   18 Market Place, Bingham, NOTTINGHAM, NG2 5AS.   (hq)
    0845 370 9500   fax 0845 370 9501
    email info@bcu.org.uk   http://www.bcu.org.uk
    Sec: Paul Owen
▲   Company Limited by Guarantee
Br   10 regions
○   *S; the national body governing the sport of canoeing
Gp   Canoe polo; Canoe sailing; Freestyle; Marathon; Sea
    canoeing; Slalom; Surf; Wild water racing
    Coaching; Lifeguards; Touring
●   ET - Exhib - Comp - SG - Stat - Inf - Lib - VE
<   Intl Canoe Fedn; Eur Canoe Assn; Brit Olympic Assn; C'wealth
    Games Coun for England; Sport & Recreation Alliance;
    Boating Alliance; Nat Navigation Users Forum
M   21,430 i, 420 org
¶   Canoe Focus - 6; ftm, £2 each nm.
    Canoeing Hbk - 1; £15.95.

British Caravanners' Club
    a group of the **Camping & Caravanning Club Ltd**

**British Cardiac Patients Association   (Zipper Club)   (BCPA)
1982**
NR   15 Abbey Rd, BINGHAM, Notts, NG13 8EE.   (hq)
    01949 837070
    email admin@bcpa.co.uk   http://www.bcpa.co.uk
    Chmn: Keith Jackson
▲   Registered Charity
Br   20
○   *W; to offer practical advice, support & reassurance to all heart
    patients & families, particularly those awaiting or who have
    undergone investigations, procedures or heart surgery
●   Mtgs
M   4,000 i, UK / 20 i, o'seas
¶   Zipper News - 6; ftm, £1.00 each nm.

British Cardiac Society
    since 2006 **British Cardiovascular Society**

British Cardiovascular Society   (BCS)   1922
NR   9 Fitzroy Sq, LONDON, W1T 5HW.   (hq)
    020 7383 3887   fax 020 7388 0903
    email enquiries@bcs.com   http://www.bcs.com
    Chief Exec: Steven Yeats
▲   Company Limited by Guarantee; Registered Charity
○   *L; advancement of knowledge of diseases of the heart &
    circulation
M   1,400 i
×   2006 (April) British Cardiac Society

British Carillon Society   (BCS)   1976
NR   2 Abnalls Lane, LICHFIELD, Staffs, WS13 7BN.
    (treas/mem/sp)
    email secretary@carillons.org   http://www.carillons.org
    Treas & Mem Sec: Lucy Smith
▲   Un-incorporated Society
○   *D; to promote the art of the carillon in the British Isles (a
    musical instrument of 23 or more cast bronze bells played
    from a baton keyboard & pedal-board); to propagate music
    for the same
●   Mts - Exhib - Lib - VE
<   Wld Carillon Fedn
M   2 org, 1 f, UK / 19 i, 1 f, 1 org, o'seas
¶   NL - 3.
    Music Albums (anthologies) for Carillon of 2 or 3 octaves; irreg.

British Carrot Growers' Association
NR   Fresh Growers Ltd, Inkersall Grange Farm, BILSTHORPE, Notts,
    NG22 8TN.   (chmn/p)
    020 8892 5033
    email info@mustardcommunications.co.uk
    http://www.britishcarrots.co.uk
    Sec: John Birkenshaw
○   *T; for commercial carrot & parsnip growers

British Cartographic Society   (BCS)   1963
■   at the Royal Geographical Society, 1 Kensington Gore,
    LONDON, SW7 2AR.   (mail/address)
    0115-932 8684
    email admin@cartography.org.uk
    http://www.cartography.org.uk
    Hon Sec: Dr Tim Rideout
▲   Registered Charity
○   *E, *L, *P, *Q; to promote all aspects of cartography &
    geographical information science; its structure & members
    reflect maps in all their forms & the art & science of
    cartography as a whole
Gp   Map Curators; Map Design; Historical Military Mapping;
    Corporate members forum
●   Conf - ET - Exhib - SG - Lib - VE
<   Intl Cartographic Assn (ICA); Intl Map Trade Assn (IMTA); UK
    Geoforum: Assn for Geographic Inf (AGI)
M   466 i, 53 f, UK / 86 i, 4 f, o'seas
    (Sub: £35 i, £75-£195 f)
¶   The Cartographic Jnl - 4; ftm, £61 i UK+EU ($144 USA),
    £232 instns UK+EU ($415 USA).
    Maplines (NL) - 3; ftm only.
    Cartographiti (NL) - 3; ftm, £10 UK (£15 airmail).
    Maps & Surveys (NL) - 2; ftm, £10 UK (£15 airmail).

British Cartoonists' Association   1966
■   Mead Cottage, 77 Woodfield Rd, Hadleigh, BENFLEET, Essex,
    SS7 2ES.   (hsp)
    01702 557205
    email collinscartoons@aol.com
    Hon Sec: Clive Collins
○   *P; to aid cartoonists & young cartoonists
Gp   Animators; Caricaturists; Cartoonists; Designers; Editors;
    Illustrators; Painters; Writers for cartoons
●   Conf - Exhib - Comp - Inf - VE
<   Cartoon Arts Trust & Museum
M   100 i
    (Sub: £20)
¶   NL - irreg.   Ybk;   AR - 1; all ftm.

British Casino Association Ltd
    since 1 April 2009 **National Casino Industry Forum**

British Catapult Association
NR   2 Brookside Terrace, Kilmington, WARMINSTER, Wilts,
    BA12 6RQ.   (chmn/p)
    Chmn: J Sanford,   Treas: Mrs S Sanford
○   *G; sport of (hand) catapult shooting

British Cattle Breeders' Club   (BCBC)   1947
■   Lake Villa, Bradworthy, HOLSWORTHY, Devon, EX22 7SQ.
    01409 241579
    email lesley.lewin@cattlebreeders.org.uk
    http://www.cattlebreeders.org.uk
    Sec: Mrs Lesley Lewin
▲   Company Limited by Guarantee; Registered Charity
○   *B; improvements in sphere of cattle breeding; dissemination of
    information & new ideas
●   Conf - Publication of proceedings
M   238 i
¶   Digest - 1; ftm, £25 nm.   NL - irreg; ftm only.

British Cattle Veterinary Association
    a group of the **British Veterinary Association**

British Cave Rescue Council   (BCRC)   1967
- ■ Pearl Hill, Dent, SEDBERGH, Cumbria, LA10 5TG.   (hsp)
  01539 625412; 07803 028830 (mobile)
  email secretary@caverescue.org.uk
  http://www.caverescue.org.uk
  Hon Sec: Pete Allwright
- ▲ Registered Charity; Un-incorporated Society
- ○ *G, *W; representation & coordination of voluntary cave rescue throughout the UK
- ● Conf - Mtgs - ET - Stat - Inf - LG
- < UK Search & Rescue (UKSAR); Mountain Rescue England & Wales; Brit Caving Assn
- > Mountain Rescue England & Wales
- M 16 member teams
- ¶ Information & Briefing CD; ftm only.
  Incident Report - 1 [on website, donation appreciated].

British Cave Research Association   (BCRA)   1973
- ■ The Old Methodist Chapel, Great Hucklow, BUXTON, Derbys, SK17 8RG.   (hq)
  01298 873810
  email bcra-enquiries@bcra.org.uk
  http://www.bcra.org.uk
  Chmn: David Checkley
- ▲ Registered Charity
- ○ *L; all aspects of sciences & technology associated with caves, caving & karst: geology, hydrology, archaeology, biology, surveying, photography, cave exploration, etc
- Gp Cave radio & electronics; Cave surveying; Hydrology; Speleohistory; Explosives users
- ● Conf - Mtgs - ET - Res - SG - Lib
- < U Intl de Speleologie (UIS); Brit Caving Assn (BCA)
- M 212 i, 53 org
  (Sub: £18)
- ¶ Cave & Karst Science - 3; ftm, price on application nm.

British Caving Association   (BCA)   2004
- NR The Old Methodist Chapel, Great Hucklow, BUXTON, Derbys, SK17 8RG.   (hq)
  email secretary@british-caving.org.uk
  http://www.british-caving.org.uk
  Sec: Damian Weare
- ▲ Un-incorporated Society
- ○ *N, *S; to act as the governing body of the sport in the UK; to act as the umbrella organisation on behalf of 9 constituent bodies in respect of Sports Council aid
- Gp British Cave Rescue Council; British Cave Research Association; National Association of Mining History Organisations; William Pengelly Cave Studies Trust Ltd & 5 regional Caving Councils (Southern, Northern, Cambrian, Derbyshire, Devon & Cornwall)
- ● Mtgs - ET - Inf - LG
- < Intl Speleological U (UIS)
- M 4,000 i, 10 f, 250 org, UK / 500 i, 10 org, o'seas
- ¶ NL; Hbk; Speleology; all ftm only.

British Cement Association
  merged in June 2009 with the Quarry Products Association to form
  the **Mineral Products Association**

British Ceramic Confederation   (BCC)   1986
- ■ Federation House, Station Rd, STOKE-ON-TRENT, Staffs, ST4 2SA.   (hq)
  01782 744631   fax 01782 744102
  email bcc@ceramfed.co.uk   http://www.ceramfed.co.uk
  Chief Exec: Dr Laura Cohen
- ▲ Un-incorporated Society
- ○ *T; to represent the collective interests of all sectors of the UK ceramics industry
- Gp Bricks, clay roof tiles & drainage pipes; Sanitaryware, wall & floor tiles; Tableware & giftware; Industrial ceramics & refractories; Materials suppliers
- ● Conf - Mtgs - Comp - SG - Stat - Expt - Inf - VE - Empl - LG
- < Cerame Unie; CBI; Conctruction Products Assn
- M 100 f
- ¶ Bulletin - 6;   Briefing Documents - irreg; both ftm only.

British Ceramic Gift & Tableware Manufacturers' Association (BCGTMA)
- ■ Federation House, Station Rd, STOKE-ON-TRENT, Staffs, ST4 2SA.   (hq)
  01782 744631   fax 01782 744102
  email bcc@ceramfed.co.uk
  Sec: C P Hall
- ▲ Un-incorporated Society
- ○ *T
- ● Mtgs - SG - Stat - Expt - Inf - LG
- < Brit Ceramic Confedn (BCC); Fédn Eur des Inds de Porcelaine et de Faïence de Table et d'Ornementation (FEPF)
- M 26 f

British Ceramic Research Ltd
  see subsidiary **CERAM Research Ltd**

British Cervical Spine Society
  a specialist society of the **British Orthopaedic Association**

British Chamber of Business in Southern Africa   (SABRITA)   1965
- NR P O Box 66, Parklands, JOHANNESBURG 2121, South Africa.   (hq)
  27 (72) 992 2685
  email info@britishchamber.co.za
  PRO: Adam Ginster
- ○ *C; promotion of trade & investment between UK & South Africa
- < SABA (UK)
- M i, f & org

British Chamber of Commerce for Belgium   (BCCB)   1898
- ■ Boulevard Buschoffsheim 11, 1000 BRUXELLES, Belgium.   (hq)
  32 (02) 540 9030   fax 32 (02) 512 8263
  email britcham@britcham.be   http://www.britcham.be
  Exec Dir: Glenn Vaughan
- ▲ Company Limited by Guarantee
- Br Belgium
- ○ *C; to encourage business contacts between Belgium & the UK; to influence the development of public policy & facilitate networking
- Gp C'ees: Business development, EU, ICT
- ● Conf - Mtgs - ET - Inf - LG (EU institutions)
- < Coun Brit Chams Comm Continental Europe (COBCOE)
- M 20 i, 260 f, Belgium
- ¶ BCC NL - 10.   Trade & Membership Directory - 1.

© CBD Research Ltd · Beckenham · BR3 5JS · Tel 020 8650 7745 · E-mail cbd@cbdresearch.com · www.cbdresearch.com

British Chamber of Commerce in China - Beijing   (BCCC) 1993
NR   The British Centre (Room 1001), China Life Tower,
       16 Chaoyangmenwai Dajie, BEIJING 100020, China.   (hq)
       86 (10) 8525 1111   fax 86 (10) 8525 1100
       email information@pek.britcham.org
       http://www.pek.britcham.org
       Exec Dir: Christopher Baron
○   *C
¶   British Business in China (Jnl) - 4.

British Chamber of Commerce in China - Shanghai   1995
NR   5F Marks & Spencer Building, 863 Nanjing Xi Lu,
       SHANGHAI 200041, China.   (hq)
       86 (21) 6218 5022   fax 86 (21) 6218 5066
       email admin@sha.britcham.org
       http://www.sha.britcham.org
       Exec Dir: Ian Crawford
○   *C; to promote & deepen the relationship between China & the
       UK; to support the increasing number of business interests in
       Shanghai & the East China region; to act as a central source
       of information, including a contract data-base, on issues
       facing foreign companies operating in China
●   Conf - Mtgs - Inf - LG
M   86 i, 535 f
¶   The Beat - 12; free.
       British Business in China Directory.
×   British Chamber of Commerce Shanghai (Britcham Shanghai)

British Chamber of Commerce in the Czech Republic   (BCC CR)
■   Richtrův dům, Malé Náměstí 11, 110 00 PRAHA 1, Czech
       Republic.
       420 224 835 161   fax 420 224 835 162
       http://www.britishchamber.cz
       Exec Dir: Simon Rawlence
○   *C

British Chamber of Commerce in Germany e.V.   (BCCG)   1960
■   Friedrichstrasse 140, D-10117 BERLIN, Germany.   (hq)
       49 (30) 206 70 80
       email info@bccg.de   http://www.bccg.de
       Pres: Norbert Strohschen
▲   Eingetragener Verein
Br   London; 8 in Germany
○   *C; to further British-German trade, business contacts &
       cooperation
M   900 i, f & org, UK & Germany
¶   NL - 3-4; E-NL - 52; both ftm.
       LM - 1; Ybk; both ftm, 200 nm.

British Chamber of Commerce in Hong Kong   1987
NR   Emperor Group Centre (room 1201), 288 Hennessy Rd,
       WAN CHAI, Hong Kong.   (hq)
       (852) 2824 2211   fax (852) 2824 1333
       email info@britcham.com   http://www.britcham.com
       Exec Dir: Christopher Hammerbeck
▲   Company Limited by Guarantee
○   *C
Gp   C'ees: General, China, Education, Environment, IT, Marketing
       & communications, Real estate; Gps: Construction industry,
       Financial services focus, Logistics, Scottish business, Small &
       medium enterprise, YNetwork (Young executives); Business
       policy unit: Women in business
●   Conf - Mtgs - ET - Inf - VE - LG
M   500 f
¶   British Business in China (LM) - 1.
       The British Directory (LM) - 1.

British Chamber of Commerce in Hungary   (BCCH)   1991
■   Szt István krt 24 IV/3, H-1137 BUDAPEST, Hungary.   (hq)
       36 (1) 302 5200   fax 36 (1) 302 3069
       email bcch@bcch.com   http://www.bcch.com
▲   Un-incorporated Society
○   *C; 'to represent British business values & promote trade &
       investment flows between the UK & Hungary
Gp   Communications; CSR (Corporate Social Responsibility);
       Education; Government relations; Hospitality & tourism; HR
       (Human resources); IT; Membership; SME (Small & Medium
       Enterprises); Tax & Legal
●   Conf - Mtgs - Res - SG - Inf - LG
M   c 170 f
¶   Business News (NL) - 4; free.
       BCCH Trade & Membership Directory - 1; ftm.
       CSR brochure - occasional;
       Electronic NL - 12; both free.

British Chamber of Commerce & Industry in Brazil   (BCCIB) 1916
NR   Rua Ferreira de Araújo 741-1 andar, Pinheiros,
       SÃO PAULO SP 05428-002, Brazil.   (hq)
       55 (11) 3819 0265
       http://www.britcham.com.br
       Exec Dir: Philip Hamer
▲   Registered Charity
Br   Rio de Janeiro
○   *C; to encourage the growth of trade & commercial
       relationships between Great Britain & Brazil
Gp   Foreign investment; Foreign trade; Events; Legal; Seminar; Tax
●   Conf - Mtgs - ET - Expt - Inf - Lib
<   Eurochambres; Brit Cham Comm in Latin-America; London
       Cham Comm & Ind
M   2 f, UK / 5 f, o'seas
¶   Britain Brasil - 6.   Doing Business in Brazil - 1.   Ybk - 1.

British Chamber of Commerce for Italy, Inc   (BCCI)   1904
■   via Dante 12, I-20121 MILANO, Italy.   (hq)
       39 (02) 877 798   fax 39 (02) 8646 1855
       email bcci@britchamitaly.com
       http://www.britchamitaly.com
       Chief Exec: Kelly Ben Frech
▲   Incorporated Society
Br   London: 020 7222 7040
○   *C
Gp   Business examinations; Consultancy services; English courses in
       tbe UK; English language consultancy service; Events (cultural
       events, seminars)
●   Conf - Mtgs - ET - Exam - Res - Inf - Debt & VAT recovery -
       Company searches
<   Maintains ties with UK Dept for Business, Enterprise &
       Regulatory Reform; Coun of Brit Chams Comm in
       Continental Europe (COBCOE), U of Foreign Chams Comm
       & Italo-Foreign Chams Comm (UNIONESTERE)
M   i, f
¶   Britaly (NL online) - 12;   Focus on Italy - 1;
       Speak to the World - 1; all free.
       Trade Directory - 2 yrly; ftm, 25.

British Chamber of Commerce in Japan   (BCCJ)   1948
■   3F Kenkyusha Eigo Centre Building, 1-2 Kagurazaka, Shinjuku-
       ku, TOKYO 162-0825, Japan.   (hq)
       81 (3) 3267 1901   fax 81 (3) 3267 1903
       email info@bccjapan.com   http://www.bccjapan.com
       Chief Exec: Ian de Stains
○   *C; to promote Anglo-Japanese commercial relations
Gp   C'ees: British Industry Centre; Finance; Membership; Property
       Forum; Technology Centre
●   Conf - Mtgs - Stat - Expt - Inf - LG

British Chamber of Commerce in Korea   1981
NR Regus Business Centre (20th floor), Korea First Bank Bldg, 100
        Gongpyong-dong, Jongro-gu, SEOUL 110 702,
        South Korea.   (hq)
        82 (2) 720 9407
        Dir Gen: Ms Jeongmi Seo
○   *C
●   Mtgs - Stat - Inf
M   c 200 f
¶   NL - 12; free.

British Chamber of Commerce in Latvia   (BCCL)   1996
■   Kr Valdemara 33 (office 33), LV-1010 RIGA, Latvia.   (hq)
        371 6724 9043   fax 371 6721 8045
        email info@bccl.lv   http://www.bccl.lv
        Exec Dir: Juris Benkis
▲   Un-incorporated Society
○   *C; promoting trade & partnership in British-Latvian business
●   Conf - Mtgs - Expt - Inf - VE - LG
<   Foreign Investors' Coun in Latvia
M   17 i, 99 f, 3 org
¶   British Latvian Trade (Jnl) - 6; free.

British Chamber of Commerce for Luxembourg   (BCC)   1992
■   6 rue Antoine de Saint Exupéry, L-1432 LUXEMBOURG.   (hq)
        00 352 (-) 465466   fax 00 352 (-) 220384
        email mail@bcc.lu   http://www.bcc.lu
        Mgr: Sophie Kerschen
○   *C
●   Conf - Mtgs - LG
¶   LM - 2 yrly; free.

British Chamber of Commerce in Mexico
    see **Cámara de Comercio Británica AC (British Chamber of
    Commerce in Mexico**

British Chamber of Commerce for Morocco   (BCCM)   1923
■   65 avenue Hassan Seghir, 20000 CASABLANCA, Morocco.
        (hq)
        212 (22) 44 88 60/61/65   fax 212 (22) 44 88 68
        email britcham@casanet.net.ma
        http://www.bccm.co.ma
        Pres: Barry Marsh
○   *C; to promote bi-lateral trade between the UK & Morocco
●   Conf - Mtgs - Exhib - Expt - Inf - Lib - VE
<   Moroccan Brit Business Coun (MBBC); Assn des Chambres de
        Commerce et d'Industrie Européenne au Maroc (ACCIEM)
M   10 f, UK / 400 f, Morocco
¶   Business Link - 4;   Annual Review - 1; both ftm only.

British Chamber of Commerce Singapore   (BritCham)   1954
■   138 Cecil St, 11-01 Cecil Court, SINGAPORE 069538.   (hq)
        00 (65) 6222 3552   fax 00 (65) 6222 3556
        email info@britcham.org.sg
        http://www.britcham.org.sg
        Exec Dir: Brigitte Holtschneider
○   *C
Gp Consumer; Education; Energy & utilities; Financial services;
        Hospitality, tourism & entertainment; Media & marketing;
        Professional services; Science & technology; Shipping; SME
●   Conf - Mtgs - Inf
M   750 i, 300 f
¶   Orient - 6.
        Membership Directory - 1.

British Chamber of Commerce in the Slovak Republic
■   Sedlárska 5 (3rd floor), 811 01 BRATISLAVA, Slovakia.   (hq)
        421 (2) 5292 0371   fax 421 (2) 5292 0371
        email director@britcham.sk   http://www.britcham.sk
        Exec Dir: Lívia Eperjesiová
▲   Un-incorporated Society
○   *C; to support its members & their business relations between
        Slovakia & the UK
Gp Action groups: EU funds, Events, Government relations, Small /
        medium enterprises
●   Conf - Mtgs - Res - Expt - Inf - LG
<   Brit Chams Comm; COBCOE
M   1 i, 3 f, UK / 6 i, 107 f, o'seas
¶   E-Digest - 12; free.
        Bridges (Jnl).
        UK-Slovakia Trade Guide.
        Membership Directory.   AR.

**British Chamber of Commerce in Spain   (Cámara de Comercio
    Británica en España)   1908**
NR c/ Bruc 21 - 1° 4a, E-08010 BARCELONA, Spain.
        34 933 173 220
        email britchamber@britchamber.com
        http://www.britishchamberspain.com
        Dir: Charlotte Fraser-Prynne
○   *C

British Chamber of Commerce in Taipei   (BCCT)
■   26F President International Tower, 9-11 Song Gao Rd,
        TAIPEI 11073, Taiwan.   (hq)
        00 (02) 2720 1919   fax 00 (02) 2720 9200
        http://www.bcctaipei.com
        Chmn: Paul Burke,   Exec Dir: Lee Ting
▲   Company Limited by Guarantee
○   *C; to promote & develop trade & investment between Britain &
        Taiwan; to provide members in both countries with a forum
        to express their views on commercial & trade related issues
        affecting the two countries
●   Mtgs - Res - Inf - VE - LG
<   Britain in Asia Pacific (BIAP)
M   10 i, 100 f, (Taiwan)
¶   Effective Business in Taiwan - 1; ftm, £30 nm.
        LM - 1; ftm, £120 nm.

British Chamber of Commerce Thailand   (BCCT)   1946
■   208 Wireless Rd (7th floor), Lumphini, Pathumwan,
        BANGKOK 10330, Thailand.   (hq)
        66 (2) 651 5350-3   fax 66 (2) 651 5354
        email greg@bccthai.com   http://www.bccthai.com
        Exec Dir: Greg Watkins
○   *C
●   Conf - Mtgs - ET - Exam - Exhib - SG - Stat - Expt - Inf - Lib - VE
        - LG
M   c 620 f
¶   The Brief - 6;   The Digest - 12;   Partners in Progress;
        Monthly Industry Sector Reports;   Annual Hbk;
        Annual Expatriate Cost of Living Survey (online);
        Annual Compensation & Benefits Survey (online);
        LM (online);   all ftm only.

British Chamber of Commerce of Turkey (Association)   (BCCT)
NR Mešrutiyet Caddesi 18, Asli Han Kat 6, Galatasaray, TR-
        80050 ISTANBUL, Turkey.   (hq)
        90 (212) 249 0420   fax 90 (212) 252 5551
        email buscenter@bcct.org.tr   http://www.bcct.org.tr
        Sec Gen: Ida Akalin
○   *C; to promote Anglo-Turkish trade
●   Conf - Mtgs - Exhib - Expt - Inf - Lib - VE
<   Assn Brit Cham Comm
M   51 i, UK / 410 i, Turkey – under Turkish law, only individuals
        can be members
¶   Trade Journal [in English] - 4; ftm.
        Trade Journal [in Turkish] - 6; ftm.
        Trade Fairs & Exhibitions in Turkey - 1; free.

© CBD Research Ltd · Beckenham · BR3 5JS · Tel 020 8650 7745 · E-mail cbd@cbdresearch.com · www.cbdresearch.com

British Chambers of Commerce   (BCC)   1890
NR   65 Petty France, LONDON, SW1H 9EU.   (hq)
　　020 7654 5800   fax 020 7654 5819
　　email info@britishchambers.org.uk
　　http://www.britishchambers.org.uk
　　Dir Gen: David Frost
▲　Company Limited by Guarantee
○　*C; business representation, international, national & local
M　130,000 i, f & org

British Charolais Cattle Society Ltd   1962
■　Avenue M, Stoneleigh Park, KENILWORTH, Warks, CV8 2RG.
　　(hq)
　　024 7669 7222   fax 024 7669 0270
　　email charolais@charolais.co.uk
　　http://www.charolais.co.uk
　　Chief Exec: David Benson
▲　Company Limited by Guarantee; Registered Charity
○　*B
●　Conf - Mtgs - Exhib - Comp - Expt - Inf - VE - Empl - LG
<　Nat Beef Assn
M　3,000 i, UK / 100 i, o'seas
¶　Charolais News - 3; free.

British Charollais Sheep Society Ltd   (BCSS)   1977
NR   Crogham Farm, Youngmans Rd, WYMONDHAM, Norfolk,
　　NR18 0RR.   (hq)
　　01953 603335   fax 01953 607626
　　email office@charollaissheep.com
　　http://www.charollaissheep.com
　　Chf Exec: Jonathan Barber
▲　Company Limited by Guarantee; Registered Charity
○　*B
Gp　Charollais Lamb Marketing Organisation
　　Trials: Crossbred lamb; Halfbred ewe; Ram
●　Conf - Mtgs - ET - Res - Exhib - SG - Stat - Expt - Inf - VE
<　UPRA Mouton Charollais (France); Nat Sheep Assn
M　1,100 i
¶　Flock Book - 1.   LM.   NL - 3.   AR.

British Chauffeurs Guild
NR   13 Stonecot Hill, SUTTON, Surrey, SM3 9HB.
　　020 8641 1740   fax 020 8644 1945
　　http://www.britishchauffersguild.co.uk
○　*P; to improve & promote the interests & reputation of
　　chauffeuring
●　Mtgs - ET (courses)
M　i, f
　　Note: The Guild is not a recognised union nor employee
　　organisation; it is a licensing registration authority issuing
　　accepted members with a personalised chauffers permit, a
　　cap & lapel badge.

British Cheerleading Association   (BCA)   1984
NR   54c High St, NORTHWOOD, Middx, HA6 1BL.   (chmn)
　　01923 825527
　　http://www.cheerleading.org.uk
▲　Un-incorporated Society
○　*G; to act as the governing body for cheerleading in Britain
M　i in clubs

British Chelonia Group   (BCG)   1976
NR   47 Hill Corner Rd, CHIPPENHAM, Wilts, SN15 1DP.   (hsp)
　　01249 462375
　　http://www.britishcheloniagroup.org.uk
　　Gen Sec: Diana Scott
▲　Registered Charity
○　*G, *L; the study, conservation & welfare of tortoises, terrapins
　　& turtles worldwide
M　i

**British Chemical Engineering Contractors Association
(BCECA)   1966**
■　1 Regent St, LONDON, SW1Y 4NR.   (hq)
　　020 7839 6514
　　http://www.bceca.org.uk
　　Dir: Rod Dean
▲　Un-incorporated Society
○　*T; interests of the principal companies in the UK which provide
　　engineering, procurement, construction & project
　　management services to the process industries
M　22 f

British Cheque & Credit Association   (BCCA)   1994
■　PO Box 3414, CHESTER, CH1 9BF.   (hq)
　　01244 505904   fax 01244 505909
　　email info@bcca.co.uk   http://www.bcca.co.uk
　　Chief Exec: Geoff Holland
▲　Company Limited by Share
○　*T; for companies in the UK offering third party cheque
　　encashment services & pay day advances (consumer credit)
●　Conf - Mtgs - ET - Res - Inf - LG - Liaison with orgs in the
　　finance sector
<　Tr Assn Forum; Confedn Brit Ind (CBI); MALG
M　1,250 f
¶　Cheque This Out (NL) - 2;   AR - 1;
　　Money Laundering Guidelines - irreg; all ftm only.
　　Code of Practice; free.
×　2008 British Cheque Cashers Association

British Chilean Chamber of Commerce
　　see **Cámara Chileno Británica de Comercio (British Chilean
　　Chamber of Commerce**

British Chiropody & Podiatry Association   (BChA)   1959
NR   New Hall, 149 Bath Rd, MAIDENHEAD, Berks, SL6 4LA.
　　(pres/b)
　　01628 632440   fax 01628 674483
　　http://www.bcha-uk.org
　　Hon Pres: Michael J Batt
▲　Un-incorporated Society
○　*P; for fully trained chiropodists & podiatrists
M　i

British Chiropractic Association   (BCA)   1925
■　59 Castle St, READING, Berks, RG1 7SN.   (hq)
　　0118-950 5950   fax 0118-958 8946
　　email enquiries@chiropractic-uk.co.uk
　　http://www.chiropractic-uk.co.uk
　　Exec Dir: Susan Wakefield
▲　Company Limited by Guarantee
○　*P; the registration body for chiropractors; an independent
　　branch of medicine which specialises in mechanical disorders
　　of the joints (particularly those of the spine) & their effect on
　　the nervous system
●　Conf - Mtgs - ET - Res - Exhib - Stat - Inf - LG
<　Eur Chiropractic U; Wld Fedn of Chiropractic
M　1,073 i, UK / 36 i, o'seas
¶　Contact (NL) - 4;   In Touch - 12; both ftm only.

British Christmas Tree Growers Association   (BCTGA)   1980
■　13 Wolrige Rd, EDINBURGH, EH16 6HX.   (hq)
　　0131-664 1100   fax 0131-664 2669
　　http://www.christmastree.org.uk
　　Sec: Roger Hay
▲　Un-incorporated Society
○　*T; to provide marketing assistance & technical advice to
　　growers of live Christmas trees
●　Conf - Mtgs - Stat - Inf
<　Timber Growers Assn; Christmas Tree Growers Assn of Western
　　Europe; Amer Nat Christmas Tree Assn
M　300 i, 50 f, 1 org, UK / 1 i, o'seas
¶　NL - 2; ftm.   LM.   AR; ftm.

British Civil Engineering Test Equipment Manufacturers Association   (CTMA)   1968
■　c/o Andrew Robertson, Capco Test Equipment, Unit 10 Farthing Road Industrial Estate, IPSWICH, Suffolk, IP1 5AP.   (chmn/b)
　　01473 748144　fax 01473 748179
　　email andrew@capco.co.uk
　　Chmn: Andrew Robertson
▲　Un-incorporated Society
○　*T; for manufacturers & suppliers of test equipment for the construction industry (civil engineering & building)
●　Mtgs - BSI Standards Development (Test Methods) C'ees
M　8 f

British Classification Society   (BCS)   1986
■　c/o Dr Fionn Murtagh, Dept of Computer Science, Royal Holloway College, University of London, EGHAM, Surrey, TW20 0EX.   (sb)
　　01784 443429
　　http://www.thames.cs.rhul.ac.uk/~bcs
　　Sec: Dr Jo Padmore
▲　Un-incorporated Society
○　*L; to encourage the cooperation & exchange of views & information amongst those interested in the principles & practice of classification in any discipline where they are used
●　Conf - Mtgs - Res - Stat
<　Intl Fedn of Classification Socs (ICFS)
M　c 50 i

British Cleaning Council (BCC Ltd)   (BCC)   1982
■　478-480 Salisbury House, London Wall, LONDON, EC2M 5QQ.   (hsb)
　　020 7920 9640　fax 020 7638 6990
　　email info@britishcleaningcouncil.org
　　http://www.britishcleaningcouncil.org
　　Co Sec: Andrew Large
▲　Company Limited by Guarantee
○　*N, *T; interests of the cleaning industry in general
●　Conf - Mtgs - ET - Exhib - LG - Voice of Industry - Council of Associations
M　18 org
¶　The Voice - 4; free.

British Clematis Society   1991
NR　2 Ravensbourne Avenue, BROMLEY, Kent, BR2 0BP.   (chmn/p)
　　http://www.britishclematis.org.uk
　　Chmn: Denise Macdonald
▲　Registered Charity
○　*H; to promote the cultivation & preservation of clematis
●　Mtgs - Exhib - Inf - Slide library - VE - Seed exchange - Plant sales
<　R Horticl Soc
M　750 i
¶　The Clematis (Jnl) - 1.

British Clothing Industry Association
　　since 2009 **United Kingdom Fashion & Textile Association**

British Coal Utilisation Research Association   (BCURA)   1938
■　Gardner-Brown Ltd, Calderwood House, 7 Montpellier Parade, CHELTENHAM, Glos, GL50 1UA.   (regd off)
　　01242 224886　fax 01242 577116
　　email john@gardnerbrown.co.uk
　　http://www.bcura.org
　　Co Sec: John Gardner
▲　Company Limited by Guarantee; Registered Charity
○　*Q; to promote research & other activities concerned with the production, distribution & use of coal & its derivitives
<　Nat Assn Mining History Orgs (NAMHO)
M　f

British Coalition of Heritable Disorders of Connective Tissue   1990
■　Rochester House, 5 Aldershot Rd, FLEET, Hants, GU51 3NG.
　　Founder/Coordinator: Mrs Diane L Rust
○　*M, *W; to promote contact & cooperation between voluntary organisations working with connective tissue disorder
M　Independent support groups representing patients with rheumatological & orthopaedic symptoms
¶　Leaflet.

British Coatings Federation Ltd   (BCF)   1993
NR　The Stables, Thorncroft Manor, Thorncroft Drive, LEATHERHEAD, Surrey, KT22 8JB.   (hq)
　　01372 700848　fax 01372 700851
　　email enquiry@bcf.co.uk　http://www.bcf.co.uk
　　Chief Exec: Tony Mash
▲　Company Limited by Guarantee
○　*T; interests of UK manufacturers of surface coatings, printing inks, wallcoverings & solvents
Gp　Sector councils: Decorative coatings; Industrial coatings; Powder coatings; Printing ink; Wallcoverings
<　Alliance of Ind Assns (AIA)
M　130 f
¶　Covered (NL) - 3; ftm

British Coffee Association   2001
NR　PO Box 5, CHIPPING NORTON, Oxon, OX7 5UD.   (hq)
　　01608 644995　fax 01608 644996
　　email info@britishcoffeeassociation.org
　　http://www.britishcoffeeassociation.org
　　Exec Dir: Dr Euan Paul
▲　Un-incorporated Society
○　*T; the representative voice for all of the UK coffee trade & industry, promoting & safeguarding members' interests in all matters relating to the growth, preparation, shipment, warehousing, transport, insurance, manufacturing, distribution & consumption of coffee
●　Mtgs - Inf
<　Assn EEC Soluble Coffee Mfrs (AFCASOLE); Food & Drink Fedn
M　8 f

British & Colombian Chamber of Commerce   (B&CCC)   1996
NR　2 Belgrave Sq, LONDON, SW1X 8PJ.   (hq)
　　020 7235 2106　fax 020 7235 0933
　　email director@britishandcolombianchamber.com
　　http://www.britishandcolombianchamber.com
　　Chmn: Alexander Kennedy,　Exec Dir: Tania Hoxos
▲　Company Limited by Guarantee
Br　Colombia
○　*C; to promote commercial links between Colombia & the United Kingdom
●　Conf - Mtgs - ET - Expt - Inf - VE - LG
M　20 i, 60 f, UK / 15 f, o'seas
¶　Colombian Correspondent (NL) - 52; ftm, £30 nm.

British Colombian Chamber of Commerce
　　see **Cámara de Comercio Colombo Británica (British Colombian Chamber of Commerce)**

British Colour Makers Association   (BCMA)   1932
■　19 Wyatville Avenue, BUXTON, Derbys, SK17 6WJ.   (sp)
　　01298 27028
　　email info@bcma.org.uk　http://www.bcma.org.uk
　　Sec: P D Johnson
▲　Un-incorporated Society
○　*T; represents manufacturers & suppliers of pigments in the UK
Gp　Standing technical c'ee
●　Mtgs - ET - Inf - LG
<　Eurocolour; Colour Pigment Makers of America; Ecological & Toxicological Assn of Dyes & Organic Pigments Mfrs (ETAD); Alliance of Ind Assns (AIA)
M　12 f

British Coloured Sheep Breeders Association   1985
NR   Daren Uchaf, Cwmyoy, ABERGAVENNY, Monmouthshire,
      NP7 7NR.   (sp)
      01873 890712
      Mem Sec: Sarah Stacey
○   *B; to promote coloured sheep & use of their fleece & by-
      products
●   Inf - Demonstrations
M   120 i
¶   Coloured Sheep News - 4.

British Comedy Society   (BCS)   1991
■   37 Langbourne Avenue, LONDON, N6 6PS.   (regd/office)
      020 8347 0115   fax 020 8347 0115
      email johngatenby@yahoo.com
      Treas: John Gatenby
▲   Company Limited by Guarantee
○   *G; to preserve & foster the tradition of British Comedy
●   Plaque unveilings - Charity fundraising - Celebrity luncheons -
      Pinewood Studio Hall of Fame - Elstree Wall of Fame
M   150 i
¶   NL - irreg.

British Commercial Boatbuilders Association
      a group of the **British Marine Federation**

British Committee for Standards in Haematology
      a group of the **British Society for Haematology**

British Compact Collectors' Society   (BCCS)   1994
■   PO Box 64, Langford, BIFGGLESWADE, Beds, SG18 9BF.
      (hsp)
      http://www.compactcollectors.co.uk
      Mem Sec: Amalia Ramsay
○   *G; for collectors of ladies' powder compacts & related vintage
      glamour items
●   Conf - Res - Exhib
M   c 400 i
¶   Face Facts - 3; ftm only.
      Note: Please enclose sae on initial contact

British Comparative Literature Association   (BCLA)   1975
NR   Dept of French Studies, University of Manchester, Oxford Rd,
      MANCHESTER, M13 9PL.   (hsb)
      Sec: Mrs Penny Brown
○   *A; to promote the scholarly study of literature without
      confinement to national or linguistic boundaries
●   Conf - Mtgs - Comp
<   Intl Comparative Literature Assn
M   150 i
¶   New Comparison - 2; ftm.
      Comparative Criticism - 3.

British Complementary Medicine Association   (BCMA)   1992
NR   PO Box 5122, BOURNEMOUTH, Dorset, BH8 0WG.   (hq)
      0845 345 5977
      email info@bcma.co.uk   http://www.bcma.co.uk
      Admin: Tracy Smith
▲   Un-incorporated Society
○   *M, *P; complementary medicine & healthcare; to make
      available public efficacious & safe complementary medicine
Gp   Professional organisations; Practitioners register
●   Mtgs - ET - Res - Exhib - SG - Inf - LG - Maintaining the register
      of practitioners
<   Indep Care Org Coun
M   20,000 i, 40 assns, 30 colleges/schools
¶   NL;   AR; both ftm only.

British Composites Society
      a group of the **Institute of Materials, Minerals & Mining**

British Compressed Air Society   (BCAS)   1930
NR   33-34 Devonshire St, LONDON, W1G 6PY.   (hq)
      020 7935 2464   fax 020 7935 3307
      email info@britishcompressedairsociety.co.uk
      http://www.britishcompressedairsociety.co.uk
      Exec Dir & Co Sec: C P Dee
▲   Company Limited by Guarantee
○   *T; manufacturers & distributors of compressed air products &
      services in the UK; to represent members to UK government
      & European institutions; to provide a forum for the
      manufacturers & the broad distribution, supply & installation
      interests in the compressed air, vacuum & pneumatics
      industry
Gp   Industrial process compressors; Industrial tools; Portable
      compressors & contractors' tools; Pneumatic control & air
      treatment; Service industries equipment;
      C'ees: Air treatment & pneumatic control, Compressor &
      vacuum, Distributors, Tools
●   Mtgs - ET - Stat - Inf - LG
<   Eur C'ee of Mfrs of Compressors, Vacuum Pumps & Pneumatic
      Tools PNEUROP
M   5 i, 105 f, UK / 7 f, o'seas
¶   NL - 12; ftm [email].   AR - 1; free.
      Air treatment & general services:
      Installation Guide.   Pipe Joint Guide.
      Compressed Air Condensate.
      Air Treatment Contamination & Purity Classes &
      Measurement Methods.

British Compressed Gases Association   (BCGA)   1971
NR   1 Gleneagles House, Vernongate, DERBY, DE1 1UP.   (hq)
      01332 225120   fax 01332 225101
      http://www.bcga.co.uk
      Dir: Doug Thornton
▲   Company Limited by Guarantee
○   *T; interests of companies engaged in the manufacture,
      distribution & safe use of gases, cylinders & equipment
●   Conf - Mtgs - Exhib - Inf - LG - Representation on BSI, CEN &
      ISO C'ees - Advice on use & application of gases
<   Eur Indl Gases Assn (EIGA); Engg Eqpt & Materials Users Assn;
      CBI; BSI; Tr Assn Forum; Instn Mechanical Engrs
M   57 i, 3 associate members
¶   Codes of Practice & Guidance Notes;   Technical Reports;
      Leaflets - all 3-yrly; prices vary.

British Computer Association of the Blind
NR   58-72 John Bright St, BIRMINGHAM, B1 1BN.
      0845 430 8627
      http://www.bcab.org.uk
      Chmn: Derek Naysmith
○   *G; visually impaired computer professionals & users

British Computer Society
      see **BCS, the Chartered Institute for IT**

British Concrete Pumping Group
      a special interest group of the **Construction Plant-hire
      Association**

British Confectioners Association   (BCA)   1905
NR   Unit 4 Home Farm Business Centre, BRIGHTON, E Sussex,
      BN1 9HU.   (hsb)
      01273 601404
      Hon Sec: Tim Cutress
▲   Un-incorporated Society
○   *T; to promote craftsmanship & good training in the flour
      confectionery trade (not sugar confectionery sweets)
M   26 i

British Congenital Cardiac Association
      a group of the **Royal College of Paediatrics & Child Health**

British Conifer Society (BCS) 2003
NR Bedgebury National Pinetum, GOUDHURST, Kent, TN17 2SL.
    (sb)
    01580 211044   fax 01580 212423
    http://www.britishconifersociety.org.uk
    Sec: Daniel Luscombe
○ *H; to bring together people interested in conifers from keen
    gardeners to experts
M i

British Connemara Pony Society (BCPS) 1947
NR 1 Lansdowne Cottages, Ilsley Rd, Compton, NEWBURY, Berks,
    RD20 7PQ. (sb)
    0845 604 9690
    email secretary@britishconnemaras.co.uk
    http://www.britishconnemaras.co.uk
    Sec: Mrs Sandra Parkington
○ *B
< Connemara Pony Breeders Soc (Republic of Ireland)
× 2003-04 English Connemara Pony Society

British Constructional Steelwork Association Ltd (BCSA) 1906
NR 4 Whitehall Court, LONDON, SW1A 2ES. (hq)
    020 7839 8566 fax 020 7976 1634
    http://www.steelconstruction.org
    Dir Gen: Dr Derek Tordoff
▲ Company Limited by Guarantee
○ *T; fabricators of constructional steelwork & suppliers of
    components & services to the steel construction industry
Gp Register of qualified steelwork contractors scheme; Steel
    construction certification scheme;
● Conf - Mtgs - ET - Res - Comp - SG - Stat - Expt - Inf - VE - LG
< Eur Convention for Constructional Steelwork (ECCS)
M 150 f
¶ Directory for Specifiers & Buyers - 1;
    Steel Construction News [incl LM] - 3;
    New Steel Construction [incl LM] - 6;   Annual Review; all free.
    Various technical publications: list available.

British Contact Dermatitis Society (BCDS) 2002
NR c/o Dr David Orton, Amersham Hospital, Wheldon St,
    AMERSHAM, Bucks, HP7 0JD. (hsb)
    email david.orten@bucks.nhs.uk
    C'ee Sec: Dr David Orton
○ *P; to promote research & education in dermatitis
● Conf - Mtgs
M i
¶ NL; Abstracts. *Publications.*
× 2002 British Contact Dermatitis Group

British Contact Lens Association (BCLA)
NR 7-8 Market Place, LONDON, W1W 8AG.
    020 7580 6661 fax 020 7580 6669
    http://www.bcla.org.uk
▲ Registered Charity
○ *T
Gp Dispensing; Medical; Optometric; Technical; Student
    membership; Overseas
M i
¶ Jnl.

British Contract Furnishing Association Ltd (BCFA) 1970
NR Project House, 25 West Wycombe Rd, HIGH WYCOMBE,
    Bucks, HP11 2LQ. (hq)
    01494 896790 fax 01494 896799
    email enquiries@bcfa.org.uk   http://www.thebcfa.com
    Contact: Trudy Pearce
▲ Company Limited by Guarantee
○ *T
● Mtgs - ET - Exhib - Stat - Inf
M 300 f
¶ UK Contract Furnishing Directory - 1; ftm, £85 nm.

British Contract Manufacturers & Packers Association (BCMPA)
NR St Mary's Court, The Broadway, OLD AMERSHAM, Bucks,
    HP7 0UT.
    01494 582013 fax 01494 778147
    email info@bcmpa.org.uk   http://www.bcmpa.org.uk
    Chief Exec: Rodney Steel
○ *T; members outsource services in chemical, agrochemical,
    pharmaceutical, medical, cosmetics, toiletries, food,
    beverage & general packaging
M 90 f

British Cooperative Clinical Group
    a specialist group of the **British Association for Sexual Health &**
    HIV

British Correspondence Chess Association (BCCA) 1906
NR 65 Newman Way, Rubery, BIRMINGHAM, B45 9LU.
    (memsec/p)
    http://www.bcca.info
    Mem Sec: Stan Grayland
○ *G
< Brit Fedn for Correspondence Chess (BFCC)
¶ Correspondence Chess (Jnl); ftm.

British Costume Association (BCA) 1986
NR PO Box 136, ASHINGTON, Northumberland, NE62 5ZX.
    (chmn/p)
    0845 230 0515
    http://www.incostume.co.uk
    Chmn: Peter Denton
▲ Un-incorporated Society
○ *T; costume & fancy dress suppliers
● ET - Exhib - Inf - LG
M 300 f
¶ In Costume - 4; ftm.

BRITISH COUNCIL ...
    For details of British Councils, other than those below, see the
    companion volume **'Councils, Committees & Boards'**

British Council for Chinese Martial Arts (BCCMA) 1973
■ c/o 110 Fensham Drive, Stockingford, NUNEATON, Warks,
    CV10 9QL. (mail)
    024 7639 4642
    email enquiries@bccma.com info@bccma.com
    Gen Sec: Bob Weatherall
○ *N, *S; the governing body for Chinese martial arts in the UK
    recognised by the Sports Council since 1980
< Intl Wushu Fedn; Eur Wushu Fedn; Sports Coun
M 75 org (10,000 i)

British Council for Offices (BCO) 1990
■ 78-79 Leadenhall St, LONDON, EC3A 3DH. (hq)
    020 7283 0125 fax 020 7626 1553
    email mail@bco.org.uk   http://www.bco.org.uk
    Chief Exec: Richard Kauntze
▲ Company Limited by Guarantee
○ *N, *T; to research, develop & communicate best practice in all
    aspects of the office sector; to provide a forum for discussion
    & debate of relevant issues; members are organisations
    involved in creating, acquiring & occupying office space
● Conf - Mtgs - Res - Awards programme
M c 1,500 i & f, UK & o'seas
¶ Publications list available.

© CBD Research Ltd · Beckenham · BR3 5JS · Tel 020 8650 7745 · E-mail cbd@cbdresearch.com · www.cbdresearch.com

British Council of Shopping Centres (BCSC) 1983
NR   1 Queen Anne's Gate, LONDON, SW1H 9BT.   (hq & regd
      office)
      020 7222 1122
      http://www.bcsc.org.uk
▲   Company Limited by Guarantee
○   *T; for those engaged in the development, design &
      management of shopping centres & the retailing & other
      functions therein
M   i & f

British Country Music Association
      The association's activities ceased in 2008.
      Any correspondence should be sent to Jim Marshall,
      3 Chester Terrace, Brighton, BN1 6BG.   01273 559750.
      jimars@globalnet.co.uk.

British Crown Green Bowling Association (BCGBA) 1907
NR   94 Fishers Lane, Pensby, WIRRAL, Merseyside, CH61 8SB.
      (chief/exec/p)
      0151-648 5740
      http://www.crowngreenbowls.org
      Chief Exec: John Crowther
○   *S; the governing body of crown green bowling

British Cryogenics Council (BCC) 1997
NR   PO Box 227, WANTAGE, Oxon, OX12 2DP.   (mail/address)
      01372 376544   fax 01372 376544
      http://www.bcryo.org.uk
      Hon Sec: Charles Monroe
▲   Registered Charity
○   *P; to promote knowledge & interest in cryogenics (low
      temperature science & technology); to foster development &
      application of cryogenics for public benefit
●   Conf - Mtgs - ET
M   70 i
¶   Low Temperature News - 4; ftm only.
✕   2006 British Cryoengineering Society

British Crystallographic Association (BCA) 1982
NR   Northern Networking Events Ltd, Glenfinnan Suite, 9/11
      Braeview Place, EAST KILBRIDE, G74 3XH.   (admin)
      01355 244966   fax 01355 249959
      email admin@crystallography.org.uk
      http://www.crystallography.org.uk
▲   Registered Charity
○   *L; for those interested in study & research into crystallography
      - of biological structures, chemical, industrial & physical
      applications
Gp   Biological structure; Chemical crystallography; Industrial;
      Physical crystallography
●   Conf - Mtgs - ET - Awarding bursaries for students
<   Intl U of Crystallography (IUCr)
M   c 875 i
¶   Crystallography News - 4.

British Culinary Federation   2005
NR   PO Box 10532, ALCESTER, Warks, B50 4ZY.
      01789 491218
      http://www.britishculinaryfederation.co.uk
      Admin: Jayne Mottram
○   *P

British Cutlery & Silverware Association   (BCSA)
NR   10 Edmund Rd Business Centre, 135 Edmund Rd, SHEFFIELD,
      S Yorks, S2 4ED.   (hq)
      0114-252 7550   fax 0114-252 7555
      Chief Exec: Mrs C T Steele
○   *T; promotion of cutlery & silverware
●   Conf - Mtgs - Inf
M   f

British Cycling Federation (BCF) 1959
NR   National Cycling Centre, Stuart St, MANCHESTER,
      M11 4DQ.   (hq)
      0161-274 2060   fax 0161-274 2001
      email info@britishcycling.org.uk
      http://www.britishcycling.org.uk
      Chief Exec: Peter King
▲   Un-incorporated Society
○   *S; to act as the governing body of UK cycle sport
M   i & clubs
      Note: uses the trading name British Cycling

British Czech & Slovak Association (BCSA) 1990
NR   643 Harrow Rd, WEMBLEY, Middx, HA20 2EX.   (hsp)
      020 8902 0328
      email secretary@bcsa.co.uk
      Hon Sec: Blanka Shrimpton
▲   Registered Charity
○   *X; to raise awareness in Britain of Czeck & Slovak life, history,
      arts etc

British Dam Society (BDS) 1950
NR   Institution of Civil Engineers, One Great George St, LONDON,
      SW1P 3AA.   (hq)
      020 7665 2234
      email bds@ice.org.uk
      Sec: Tim Fuller,   Chmn: Dr Andy Hughes
▲   Registered Charity
○   *P; to stimulate interest & encourage improvements in the
      design, construction, maintenance, operation & safety of
      dams & reservoirs
●   Conf - Mtgs - ET - Res - Exhib - Comp - Inf - LG
<   Intl Commission Large Dams (ICOLD)
M   i & f
¶   Dams & Reservoirs (NL) - 4.

British Damage Management Association (BDMA) 1999
■   Willow Business Centre, Connect House, 21 Willow Lane,
      MITCHAM, Surrey, CR4 4NA.   (hq)
      0700 0843 2362   fax 0700 0236 2329
      email info@bdma.org.uk   http://www.bdma.org.uk
      Chmn: Don Pringle
▲   Company Limited by Guarantee
○   *P, *T
Gp   Damage management; Fire & flood restoration
●   Conf - Mtgs - Exam
M   1,110 i, 600 f
¶   Recovery - 4; free.

British Darts Organisation Ltd (BDO) 1973
■   2 Pages Lane, Muswell Hill, LONDON, N10 1PS.   (hq)
      020 8883 5544
      Hon Sec: O A Croft
▲   Company Limited by Guarantee
Br   66
○   *S; promoting the sport of darts
●   Comp
<   Wld Darts Fedn
M   25,000 i in 66 member counties, 60 affiliated national darts
      bodies
¶   Ybk.

British Deaf Association   (BDA)   1890
- ■ Coventry Point (10th floor), Market Way, COVENTRY, W Midlands, CV1 1EA.   (hq)
024 7655 0936
http://www.bda.org.uk
Chief Exec: Simon Wilkinson-Blake
- ▲ Registered Charity
- Br 5
- ○ *W; a democratic, membership-led body campaigning on behalf of deaf sign language users in the UK; to increase deaf people's access to lifestyles that most hearing people take for granted
- ● Conf - ET - Inf
Textphone: 024 7655 0393
- M 3,500 i, UK / 15-20 i, o'seas
- ¶ Sign Matters; £25 yr (annual sub).
BDN British Deaf News - 12.

British Deaf Sports Council   (BDSC)   1930
- NR Suffolk House, 2 Wharfdale Rd, IPSWICH, Suffolk, IP1 4JP.
(hq)
http://www.britishdeafsportscouncil.org.uk
Sec: Mike Webster
- ▲ Company Limited by Guarantee; Registered Charity
- Br 115
- ○ *S; national governing body for sport for deaf people locally, regionally, nationally (England, Scotland, Wales) & internationally
- ● Mtgs - Comp
- < Comité Intl de Sport de Sourds (CISS); Eur Deaf Sports Org EDSO)
- M 3,000 i, 115 clubs

British Decoy Wildfowl Carvers Association   (BDWCA)   1990
- ■ 26 Shendish Edge, HEMEL HEMPSTEAD, Herts, HP3 9SZ.
(hsp)
01442 247610
http://www.bdwca.org.uk
Sec: Janet Nash
- ▲ Un-incorporated Society
- Br 8
- ○ *A; for decoy (bird) & wildfowl carvers & collectors
- ● Mtgs - ET - Res - Exhib - Comp - SG - Inf - VE
- M 174 i, 4 f, UK / 8 i, o'seas
- ¶ NL - 4; free.

British Deer Farms & Parks Association   (BDFPA)   1978
- NR PO Box 7522, MATLOCK, Derbys, DE4 9BR.   (hq)
0845 634 4758   fax 0845 634 4759
email info@bdfpa.org   http://www.bdfpa.org
Sec: Claire Parkinson
- ▲ Un-incorporated Society
- ○ *F, *T; to promote deer farming & the interests of deer farmers & venison producers
- ● Conf - ET - Inf - VE - LG
- M f
- ¶ Deer Farming (Jnl) - 4.   Deer News (NL) - 6.
- ✕ British Deer Farmers Association

British Deer Society   (BDS)   1963
- ■ The Walled Garden, Burgate Manor, FORDINGBRIDGE, Hants, SP6 1EF.   (hq)
01425 655434   fax 01425 655433
email h.q@bds.org.uk   http://www.bds.org.uk
Sec: Mrs Sue Williams (suebdsnwest@aol.co.uk)
- ▲ Company Limited by Guarantee; Registered Charity
- ○ *L, *V; to promote & conserve the 6 species of wild deer within the UK
- Gp Northern Ireland
- ● Mtgs - ET - Res - Exhib - Comp - Stat - Inf - VE - LG
- M c 6,000 i, UK & o'seas
- ¶ Deer (Jnl) - 4; ftm, £5 nm.   Annual Review; ftm, postage nm.

British Dental Association   (BDA)   1880
- ■ 64 Wimpole St, LONDON, W1G 8YS.   (hq)
020 7935 0875   fax 020 7487 5232
email enquiries@bda.org   http://www.bda.org
Sec: Peter Ward
- ▲ Company Limited by Guarantee
- Br 21
- ○ *P, *U; to represent dentists in the UK
- Gp Armed forces dentists; Community; Dental services; Hospital; University dental teachers & research workers
- ● Conf - Mtgs - SG - Stat - Inf - Lib - Empl - LG
- < Fédn Dentaire Intl; C'wealth Dental Assn
- M 20,500 i, UK / 600 i, o'seas
- ¶ British Dental Jnl - 24.   BDA News (NL) - 12.
Hbk - 1;   AR.

British Dental Hygienists Association
since 2008 **British Society of Dental Hygiene & Therapy**

British Dental Practice Managers Association   (BDPMA)   1993
- NR 3 Kestrel Court, Waterwells Drive, Waterwells Business Park, GLOUCESTER, GL2 2AT.   (hq)
01452 886364   fax 01452 886468
email info@bdpma.org.uk   http://www.bdpma.org.uk
Chmn: Miss Bridget M Crump
- ▲ Un-incorporated Society
- Br 7
- ○ *P; to promote a payscale & job description; to offer job opportunities
- ● Conf - Mtgs - ET - Res - Exhib - Inf - Empl
- M 460 i
- ¶ Networking (NL) - 4; ftm only.

British Dental Trade Association   (BDTA)   1923
- ■ Mineral Lane, CHESHAM, Bucks, HP5 1NL.   (hq)
01494 782873   fax 01494 786659
email admin@bdta.org.uk   http://www.bdta.org.uk
Exec Dir: A H Reed
- ▲ Company Limited by Guarantee
- ○ *T; to promote the dental industry & trade
- Gp Computer services; Dental dealers; Financial services; Importers / exporters; Manufacturers; Publishers; Wholesalers
- ● Conf - ET - Exam - Exhib - Stat - Inf - LG
- < Fedn of the Eur Dental Ind (FIDE); Assn of Dental Dealers in Europe (ADDE); Assn Brit Health Care Inds (ABHCI)
- M 123 f, UK / 4 f, o'seas
- ¶ The Dental Trader (Jnl) - 4;   NL;   LM;
Exhibition Catalogue - 1;   AR; all ftm.

British Dermatological Nursing Group
a group of the **British Association of Dermatologists**

British Dietetic Association   (BDA)   1936
- ■ Charles House (5th floor), 148/149 Great Charles St Queensway, BIRMINGHAM, B3 3HT.   (hq)
0121-200 8080   fax 0121-200 8081
email info@bda.uk.com   http://www.bda.uk.com
Chief Exec: Andy Burman
- ▲ Company Limited by Guarantee; Registered Charity
- ○ *P; to advance the science & practice of dietetics & associated subjects, to promote training & education, & to regulate relations between dietitians & their employers
- Gp Community nutrition; Diabetes management & education; Dietitians in HIV/Aids; Mental health; Metabolic & research; Nutrition advice for the elderly; Parenteral & enteral nutrition; Paediatric; Renal analysis
- ● Conf - Mtgs - ET - Res - Empl
- < Allied Health Professions Fedn; TUC
- M 6,540 i
- ¶ Jnl of Human Nutrition & Dietetics - 6; Dietetics Today (NL) - 12;   all ftm.   AR - 1.

British Disabled Flying Association
see **aeroBILITY**

© CBD Research Ltd · Beckenham · BR3 5JS · Tel 020 8650 7745 · E-mail cbd@cbdresearch.com · www.cbdresearch.com

British Disc Golf Association   (BDGA)
NR   c/o InFlight Magazine, 3 Aston St, OXFORD, OX4 1EW.
    email secretary@bdga.org.uk   http://www.bdga.org.uk
    Communications Dir: Richard Wood (0788 158 5379)
    Sec: Tom Lowes
▲   Un-incorporated Society
○   *S; the national governing body for the sport of disc golf; to be
    responsible for coordination of competitive disc golf; to
    promote disc golf
●   Comp - Inf
<   Wld Flying Disc Fedn; Profl Disc Golf Assn
M   80 i
¶   In Flight Magazine - 4; ftm only.

British Display Society Ltd   (BDS)   1943
NR   14-18 Heralds Way, Town Centre, SOUTH WOODHAM
    FERRERS, Essex, CM3 5TQ.   (regd/office)
    020 8856 2030   fax 0870 421 5589
    http://www.britishdisplaysociety.co.uk
    Sec: Elaine Fisher
▲   Registered Charity
○   *P; for visual merchandising, display, point-of-sale, exhibition
    design & training
●   ET - Exam - Comp
M   [not disclosed]
¶   BDS NL - 11; free.   AR; ftm only.

British Dog Groomers' Association
    a group of the **Pet Care Trade Association**

British Domesticated Ostrich Association   (BDOA)   1992
■   33 Eden Grange, Little Corby, CARLISLE, Cumbria,
    CA4 8QW.   (hsp)
    01228 562532   fax 01228 562187
    email craig@bdoa.info   http://www.ostrich.org.uk
    Sec: Craig Culley
▲   Un-incorporated Society
○   *B, *F; promotion of ostrich farming in the UK
M   i, f

British Double Reed Society   (BDRS)   1988
■   5 North Avenue, Stoke Park, COVENTRY, Warks, CV2 4DH.
    (hsp)
    024 7665 0322
    email secretary@bdrs.org.uk   http://www.bdrs.org.uk
    Hon Sec: Mrs Maxine Moody
▲   Registered Charity
○   *D; for practitioners & enthusiasts of the bassoon, oboe & other
    double reed instruments; to improve the standards of
    teaching; to encourage research into design & to encourage
    the writing of new music
●   Conf - ET - Comp - Inf - Annual convention to promote all
    double reed players & activities
<   Intl Double Reed Soc (IDRS)
M   c 1,000, UK & o'seas
    (Sub: £25)
¶   Double Reed News (Jnl) - 4; ftm, £3.95 nm.

British Dragon Boat Racing Association   (BDA)   1987
■   13 The Prebend, Northend, ROYAL LEAMINGTON SPA, Warks,
    CV47 2TR.   (hsp)
    01295 770734
    Co Sec: David A Cogswell
▲   Company Limited by Guarantee
○   *S; governing body for Chinese Dragon Boat racing in the UK
●   Conf - Mtgs - Comp
<   Intl Dragon Boat Fedn (IDBF); Eur Dragon Boat Fedn (EDBF);
    C'wealth Dragon Boat Fedn (CDBF)
M   800 i, 35 clubs, UK / 50 i, o'seas
¶   Dragon Line NL - 12; ftm only.

British Dragonfly Society   (BDS)   1983
NR   23 Bowker Way, Whittlesey, PETERBOROUGH, Cambs,
    PE7 1PY.   (hsp)
    01733 204286
    email bdssecretary@dragonflysoc.org.uk
    http://www.british-dragonflies.org.uk
    Hon Sec: Henry Curry
▲   Registered Charity
○   *L; to promote & encourage the study & conservation of
    dragonflies & their natural habitats
Gp Conservation
●   Mtgs - ET - Inf - Lib - PL - VE - LG
<   Soc Intle Odontologica; Wld Dragonfly Assn
M   1,400 i, 15 f, UK / 75 i, o'seas
¶   Jnl - 2;   Dragonfly News - 2; both ftm only.

British Dressage
    a discipline member of the **British Equestrian Federation**

British Dried Flowers Association
    is not currently active.

British Drilling Association Ltd   (BDA)   1976
NR   Wayside, London End, Upper Boddington, DAVENTRY,
    Northants, NN11 6DP.   (hq)
    01327 264622   fax 01327 264623
    email office@britishdrillingassociation.co.uk
    http://www.britishdrillingassociation.co.uk
    Nat Sec: Brian Stringer
▲   Company Limited by Guarantee
○   *T; to group together companies engaged in all aspects of
    ground drilling
●   Conf - Mtgs - ET - Exhib - SG - Stat - Inf
M   115 f
¶   BDA NL - 6.   LM - 1.

British Driving Society   (BDS)   1957
NR   83 New Rd, Helmingham, STOWMARKET, Suffolk, IP14 6EA.
    (hsp)
    01473 892001   fax 01473 892005
    email email@britishdrivingsociety.co.uk
    http://www.britishdrivingsociety.co.uk
    Co Sec: Mrs T K Styles
▲   Company Limited by Guarantee
○   *S; to encourage & assist those interested in the driving of
    horses & ponies
Gp Carriage Foundation
●   Conf - Mtgs - ET - Exam - Exhib - Comp - Inf - VE
M   75 driving clubs
¶   NL - 4.   Ybk.

British Drug Free Powerlifting Association   (BDFPA)   1989
■   Oakfield Cottage, Bromley Lane, KINGSWINFORD,
    W Midlands, DY6 8JP.   (sp)
    01384 270270
    http://www.bdfpa.co.uk
    Gen Sec: Pat Reeves
○   *S
●   Mtgs
M   i
¶   Raw Power - 4; ftm, £24 nm.

British Dyslexia Association   (BDA)   1972
■   Unit 8 Bracknell Beeches, Old Bracknell Lane, BRACKNELL,
    Berks, RG12 7BW.   (hq)
    0845 251 9003   fax 0845 251 9005
    http://www.bdadyslexia.org.uk
    Chief Exec: Judi Stewart
▲   Registered Charity
○   *N; to represent all with dyslexia; to work towards early
    identification & appropriate remediation, teacher training &
    support
●   Helpline: 0845 251 9002
M   8,000 i, 75 f

British Ecological Society   (BES)   1913
NR   Charles Darwin House, 12 Roger St, LONDON, WC1N 2JU.
    (hq)
    020 7685 2500
    email info@britishEcologicalSociety.org
    Hon Sec: Dave Hodgson
▲   Registered Charity
○   *L; promotion of the study of ecology through research
M   i

British Edible Pulse Association   (BEPA)   1975
NR   Bumblebee Cottage, 37 Hays Lane, HALIFAX, W Yorks,
    HX2 8UL.   (mail/address)
    01422 246438
    email barry.reed@msn.com   http://www.bepa.co.uk
    Sec: Barry Reed
▲   Registered Charity
○   *T; 'to promote the uses of edible pulses (dried pea & bean)
    from farmer to the housewife'
●   Conf - Mtgs - Exhib - Comp - Stat - Expt - Inf - LG
M   48 f
¶   Monthly Member Report - 12; free.

British Educational Furniture Manufacturers Group
    a group of the **British Educational Suppliers Association**

British Educational Leadership, Management & Administration Society   (BELMAS)   1971
NR   Victoria Hall (room 50), Norfolk St, SHEFFIELD, S Yorks,
    S1 2JB.   (hq)
    0114-279 9926   fax 0114-279 6868
    email info@belmas.org.uk   http://www.belmas.org.uk
    Hon Sec: Nigel Bennett
▲   Registered Charity
○   *E; development of practice, teaching, training & research in
    educational administration
Gp   Research in education management; Teachers of education
    management
●   Conf - Mtgs - Res
<   Eur Forum on Educ Admin (EFEA); C'wealth Coun for Educl
    Admin & Mgt (CCEAM)
M   c 550 i, c 50 org UK / c 30 i, o'seas
¶   Education Management & Administration - 4.
    Management in Education - 5.
    Books on related subjects.

British Educational Research Association   (BERA)   1974
■   Institute of Education, 20 Bedford Way, LONDON,
    WC1H 0AL.   (asa)
    020 7612 6987
    email enquiries@bera.ac.uk   http://www.bera.ac.uk
    Chief Exec: Jeremy Hoad
▲   Registered Charity
○   *E, *L, *Q; to further education research & in particular, the link
    between education policy & practice of teachers, lecturers,
    teachers' assistants & researchers
Gp   Assessment; Comparative & international education; Creativity
    in education; Early childhood; Educational research & policy-
    making; Educational effectiveness & improvement; Higher
    education; Inclusive education; Leading & managing schools
    & colleges; Learning in the professions; Literacy &
    languages; Mathematics education; Mentoring & Coaching;
    Neuroscience & education; New researchers; New
    technologies in education; Philosophy of education; Physical
    education & sports pedagogy; Post-compulsory & lifelong
    learning; Practitioner research; Primary school teachers'
    work; Race, ethnicity & education; Religious & moral
    education; Research methodology in education; Science
    education; Sexualities; Social justice; Social theory &
    education; Social-cultural history activity theory; Teacher
    education & development
●   Conf - Mtgs - ET - Res - Comp - SG - Inf - Lib - LG
<   Eur Educl Res Assn
M   1,700 i, UK / 400 i, o'seas
    (Sub: £65)
¶   British Educational Research Jnl - 6; ftm.
    Research Intelligence (NL) - 4; free.
    Occasional Publications - see website.

British Educational Suppliers Association   (BESA)   1933
■   20 Beaufort Court, Admirals Way, LONDON, E14 9XL.   (hq)
    020 7537 4997   fax 020 7537 4846
    email besa@besa.org.uk   http://www.besa.org.uk
    Dir Gen: Dominic Savage
▲   Company Limited by Guarantee
○   *T; for the British educational supply industry; to represent
    manufacturers & distributors of educational equipment,
    materials, consumables, books, furniture, technology, ICT
    hardware & software related services in the UK & to
    international markets
Gp   BESA New Educational Technologies Group (BNETG); British
    Educational Furniture Manufacturers Group (BEFMG); British
    Educational Special Needs Group (BSNG); Educational
    Software Publishers Association (ESPA); Engineering Training
    Equipment Manufacturers Association (ETEMA)
●   Conf - Mtgs - Res - Expt - Inf - LG
M   300 f
¶   BESAbook - 1; free.   ICT in State Schools - 1; ftm, £350 nm.
    UK Schools Survey on Budget & Resource Provision - 1; ftm,
    £350 nm.

British Educational Travel Association   (BETA)   2003
■   PO Box 182, CARSHALTON, Surrey, SM5 2XW.   (hq)
    020 8669 1444
    email info@betauk.com   http://www.betauk.com
    Exec Dir: Emma English
▲   Company Limited by Guarantee
○   *T; to promote youth, student & educational travel to, from &
    within the UK
●   Conf - Mtgs - ET - Res - Exhib - SG - Stat - Inf - VE - LG
<   Intl Student Travel Confedn; Fedn of Intl Youth Travel Orgs;
    English UK
M   120 f, UK / 20 f, o'seas
¶   NL - free.

British Egg Association   (BEA)   1961
NR   52A Cromwell Rd, LONDON, SW7 5BE.   (hq)
         020 7052 8899
         http://www.britegg.co.uk
         Sec: Louisa Platt
▲   Company Limited by Guarantee
○   *F, *T
●   Mtgs - ET - Res - Stat - Inf - VE - LG
<   Eur U of Whlsrs with Eggs, Egg Products, Poultry &
         Game (EUWEP); Brit Egg Ind Coun
M   26 i, 30 f
¶   Quarterly Report;   LM;   AR; all ftm only.

British Egg Products Association   (BEPA)   1971
■   89 Charterhouse St (2nd floor), LONDON, EC1M 6HR.   (hq)
         020 7608 3760   fax 020 7608 3860
         http://www.bepa.org.uk
         Chmn: Clive Frampton
▲   Company Limited by Guarantee
○   *T; to maintain & improve the high quality of egg products
●   Mtgs - Res - Stat - Inf - LG
<   Intl Egg Commission (IEC); Brit Egg Ind Coun (BEIC)
M   10 f
¶   Import & Export Statistics - 10;
         Breaking & Production - 10; both ftm only.

British Elastic Rope Sports Association   (BERSA)   1989
■   33a Canal St, OXFORD, OX2 6BQ.   (hq)
         01865 311179   fax 01865 426007
         email info@bersa.org
         Chmn: David Boston
▲   Company Limited by Guarantee
Br   10; Eire, Greece, Spain
○   *S; promotion & safety regulation of bungee jumping & other
         elastic rope sports
●   Mtgs - Exam - Res - Comp - Stat - Inf - Lib - PL - LG
<   RoSPA; Brit Standards Inst
M   30,888 i, 10 f, 7 org, UK / 3,069 i, 3 f, o'seas
¶   Code of Safe Practice.
         Guidelines for Local Safety Officers.

British Elbow & Shoulder Society
         a specialist society of the **British Orthopaedic Association**

British Electroless Nickel Society
         a division of the Metal Finishing Association which is a group of the
         Surface Engineering Association

British Electrostatic Control Association   (BECA)
■   35 Calthorpe Rd, Edgbaston, BIRMINGHAM, B15 1TS.   (asa)
         0121-454 4141   fax 0121-207 7002
         email spaarker@cvdfk.com
         http://www.becaonline.co.uk
         Sec: Sharon Parker
○   *T; suppliers, manufacturers & users of equipment, materials &
         services for the UK electrostatic control industry
M   7 f

British Endodontic Society   (BES)   1963
NR   PO Box 707, GERRARDS CROSS, Bucks, SL9 0DR.   (admin/p)
         01494 581542   fax 01494 581542
         Hon Sec: Annabel Thomas
▲   Registered Charity
○   *L; to promote and advance the study of all endodontic
         procedures; to improve dental services to the public
●   Conf - Mtgs - ET - Res - SG - LG
<   Amer Assn Endodontics; Eur Soc Endodontology
M   760 i, UK / 40 i, o'seas
¶   International Endodontic Jnl - 6; ftm, £60 yr nm.

British Energy Association
         on 1 January 2010 merged with the Energy Institute to form
         UKWEC - the UK member committee of the World Energy
         Council & is now outside the scope of this directory

**British Engineering Manufacturers' Association Ltd   (BEMA)
1936**
NR   BEMA House, Unit 1 Millers Court, Windmill Rd, Kenn,
         CLEVEDON, Somerset, BS21 6UL.   (hq)
         01275 335870   fax 01275 335871
         email enquiries@bema.co.uk   http://www.bema.co.uk
         Dir: John Whitlow
▲   Company Limited by Guarantee
○   *T; for engineering companies operating nationally
●   Mtgs - ET - Exhib - Expt - Inf - Lib - VE - LG
M   120 f
¶   Handbook - 12; ftm, on request nm.

British Entertainment & Discotheque Association
         in February 2008 merged with the Bar Entertainment & Dance
         Association to form Noctis & in 2011 Noctis reverted to original title
         of **Bar Entertainment & Dance Association**

**British Entomological & Natural History Society   (BENHS)
1872**
NR   The Pelham-Clinton Building, Dinton Pastures Country Park,
         Davis St, Hurst, READING, Berks, RG10 0TH.   (hq)
         http://www.benhs.org.uk
▲   Registered Charity
○   *L; study of natural history, particularly entomology & insect
         conservation; principally in the British Isles, but extends into
         Europe as a whole
M   i

British Epicure Society
■   58 Redcliffe Square, LONDON, SW10 9BN.
         020 7244 0494
         http://www.britishepicuresociety.org.uk
         Sec: Maureen Bebb
○   *G; 'the knowledge, appreciation & enjoyment of good food &
         wine in congenial company'

British Epidermo-Epidemiology Society
         a group of the **British Association of Dermatologists**

British Epigraphy Society   1996
■   19 Purcell Rd, Marston, OXFORD, OX3 0EZ.   (hsp)
         http://www.csad.ox.ac.uk/BES/
         Sec: Dr Peter Haarer
▲   Registered Charity
○   *L; the study of Greek, Roman & other inscriptions, texts &
         historical documents
Gp   Conf - ET
<   l'Assn Intle d'Epigraphie grecque et latine (AIEGL)
M   125 i, UK / 22 i, o'seas
         (Sub: £9)
¶   NL - 2; ftm only.

British Epilepsy Association   (BEA)   1950
NR   New Anstey House, Gate Way Drive, Yeadon, LEEDS, W Yorks,
         LS19 7XY.   (hq)
         0113-210 8800
         email epilepsy@epilepsy.org.uk
         http://www.epilepsy.org.uk
▲   Registered Charity
○   *W; to provide care in the community for those with epilepsy
●   Helpline: freephone 0808 800 5050 (Mon-Thurs 0900-1630,
         Fri 0900-1600)
M   21,000 i
¶   Epilepsy Today - 4.   AR.   Other publications.
         Note: uses the working name of Epilepsy Action.

British Equestrian Federation   (BEF)   1972
NR   Stoneleigh Park, KENILWORTH, Warks, CV8 2RH.   (hq)
   024 7669 8871   fax 024 7669 6484
   email info@bef.co.uk   http://www.bef.co.uk
   Chmn: Keith Taylor
▲   Company Limited by Guarantee
○   *N, *S; acts as the international secretariat on behalf of
   member disciplines & represents their interests in all matters
   concerned with the Fédération Equestre Internationale (FEI)
Gp   Discipline members: Association of British Riding Schools;
   British Dressage; British Equestrian Trade Association; British
   Equestrian Vaulting Association; British Eventing; British
   Grooms Association; British Horse Driving Trials Association;
   British Horse Society; British Horseball Association; British
   Reining; British Showjumping; Endurance GB; Horsescotland;
   Mounted Games Association of GB; The Pony Club; Riding
   for the Disabled; UK Polocrosse Association
●   Mtgs - Comp - SG - Stat - Inf - LG
<   Fédn Equestre Intle; a member of the Brit Horse Ind Confedn
M   6 org (discipline members),
   affiliates: British Horse Society, Pony Club

British Equestrian Trade Association   (BETA)   1979
■   East Wing, Stockeld Park, WETHERBY, W Yorks, LS22 4AW.
   (hsb)
   01937 587062   fax 01937 582728
   email info@beta-uk.org   http://www.beta-uk.org
   Chief Exec: Claire Williams
▲   Company Limited by Guarantee
○   *T; to promote the British equestrian industry from retailers to
   manufacturers, associated services & dealers; to promote
   riding as a sport
Gp   Dealers; Equestrian organisations; Feed merchants; Mobile
   retailers; Pharmaceutical; Saddlers; Safety equipment
●   Mtgs - ET - Exam - Res - Exhib - Stat - Expt - Inf - LG -
   Administration of VAT second hand scheme for horses &
   ponies on behalf of HM Customs & Excise - BETA Body
   Protector Standard
<   Brit Equestrian Fedn; Brit Horse Soc; Countryside Alliance; Soc
   of Master Saddlers; Horse & Pony Taxation C'ee
M   700 f, 5 org, UK / 5 org, o'seas
¶   Equestrian Trade News - 12; free to retailers
   (£59 manufacturers).
   British Equestrian Directory - 1; £9.95 m.
   Trade Suppliers Directory - 1; £16 m.
   What to Wear - 2 yrly; £5.50.

British Equestrian Vaulting Association
   a discipline member of the **British Equestrian Federation**

British Equine Veterinary Association
   a group of the **British Veterinary Association**

British Essence Manufacturers' Association   (BEMA)   1917
■   PO Box 172, CRANLEIGH, Surrey, GU6 8WU.   (hq)
   01483 275411   fax 01483 275411
   email secretariat@bemaorg.org
   http://www.bemaorg.org
   Exec Sec: Julie Young
▲   Un-incorporated Society
○   *T; interests of manufacturers & blenders of flavours for food &
   drink
●   Mtgs - Inf
<   Intl Org Flavour Ind (IOFI); Eur Flavour Assn (EFFA)
M   33 f

British Essential Oils Association Ltd   (BEOA)   1978
NR   15 Exeter Mansions, Exeter Rd, LONDON, NW2 3UG.   (sec/p)
   020 8450 3713
   email secretariat@beoa.co.uk   http://www.beoa.co.uk
   Sec: Malcolm Irvine
▲   Company Limited by Guarantee
○   *T; to promote the essential oil, oleoresin & aromatic chemical
   trade
Gp   Technical c'ee
●   Conf - Mtgs - ET - Res - SG - Inf - Lib - LG
<   Eur Fedn for Essential Oils (EFEO); Eur Flavour & Fragrance
   Org (EFFA)
M   53 f, UK / 3 f, o'seas
¶   NL - 3; free.   Hbk & LM - 1; ftm only.

British Estonian Association
NR   c/o Estonian Embassy, 16 Hyde Park Gate, LONDON,
   SW7 5DG.
   020 7589 3428
○   *X
●   Mtgs - Concerts - Talks
M   i
¶   LENNUK - 2; ftm.

British-Estonian Chamber of Commerce
NR   Ahtri 6, 10151 TALLINN, Estonia.   (hq)
   372 56 622-623
   email becc@becc.ee   http://www.becc.ee
   Contact: Garry Parker
○   *C

British & European Geranium Society
   since 2008 **Pelargonium & Geranium Society**

British Eventing
   a discipline member of the **British Equestrian Federation**

British Exhibition Contractors' Association
   in January 2008 merged with the Association of Exhibition
   Contractors to form the **Event Supplier & Services Association**

British Exporters Association   (BExA)   1940
■   Broadway House, Tothill St, LONDON, SW1H 9NQ.   (hq)
   020 7222 5419   fax 020 7799 2468
   email hughbailey@bexa.co.uk   http://www.bexa.co.uk
   Dir: Hugh W Bailey
▲   Un-incorporated Society
○   *T; to lobby on behalf of members on export, export credit
   insurance & trade finance issues
●   Mtgs - VE - LG
M   70 f
¶   AR.

British Falconers' Club   (BFC)   1924
■   Westfield, Meeting Hill, Worstead, NORTH WALSHAM, Norfolk,
   NR28 9LS.   (hsb)
   01692 404057
   http://www.britishfalconersclub.co.uk
   Sec: Jacqui Morris
▲   Un-incorporated Society
Br   9 regions
○   *G; the promotion of practical falconry in the British Isles; to
   promote the captive breeding of birds of prey
●   Mtgs - Lib
<   Intl Assn for Falconry & Consvn of Birds of Prey (IAF); Fedn of
   Field Sports Assns of the EEC (FACE); Countryside Alliance
M   1,270 i, UK / 79 i, o'seas
   (Sub: £42)
¶   Falconer (Jnl) - 1; ftm.   NL - 2; ftm.

© CBD Research Ltd · Beckenham · BR3 5JS · Tel 020 8650 7745 · E-mail cbd@cbdresearch.com · www.cbdresearch.com

British False Memory Society   (BFMS)   1993
■   Newtown, BRADFORD-on-AVON, Wilts, BA15 1NF.
      01225 868682   fax 01225 862251
      Dir: Madeline Greenhalgh
▲   Registered Charity
○   *K; a support group for accused parents
●   Conf - Mtgs - Res - Stat - Inf - Lib
      Helpline: 01225 868682

British Fantasy Society   (BFS)   1971
■   23 Mayne St, Hanford, STOKE-on-TRENT, Staffs, ST4 4RF.   (sp)
      email secretary@britishfantasysociety.org
      http://www.britishfantasysociety.org
      Sec: Helen Hopley
▲   Un-incorporated Society
○   *A, *G; to promote interest in the fields of horror & fantasy
      literature, media & art
●   Conf - Mtgs
M   350 i, UK / 50 i, o'seas
      (Sub: £30 UK / £45-60 o'seas)
¶   Prism NL - 4;   Dark Horizons - 6;   New Horizons;
      all ftm only.

British Federation of Audio Ltd   (BFA)   1994
NR   PO Box 365, FARNHAM, Surrey, GU10 2BD.   (hq)
      01428 714616
      Sec: C I C Cowan,   Chmn: S N Harris
▲   Company Limited by Guarantee
○   *T; to promote the use of domestic audio equipment & the
      interests of the UK audio manufacturers & the British high
      fidelity audio industry
Gp   BTI sponsorship to overseas exhibitions
●   Mtgs - Exhib - Stat - LG
<   Intellect
M   c 45 f

British Federation of Brass Bands   (BFBB)   1968
■   Unit 12 Maple Estate, Stocks Lane, BARNSLEY, S Yorks,
      S75 2BL.   (hq)
      01226 771015   fax 01226 732630
      email natoffice@bfbb.co.uk   http://www.bfbb.co.uk
      Chmn: Robert Morgan,   Mem Sec: Terry Luddington
▲   Registered Charity
○   *D; to promote brass bands; to develop bands & youth bands
●   Conf - Mtgs - ET - Lib
<   Eur Brass Band Assn (EBBA)
M   300 bands
      (Sub: £100)
¶   Forum - 1; ftm only.

British Federation for Correspondence Chess   (BFCC)
NR   Flat 3, 17 Wenlock Terrace, YORK, YO10 4DU.
      http://www.bfcc-online.org.uk
      Sec: Duncan Chambers
○   *G; to encourage the playing of correspondence chess
<   Intl Correspondence Chess Fedn (ICCF)
M   7 org
¶   Information Circular - 4; ftm.

British Federation of Film Societies   (BFFS)   1945
NR   Unit 315 The Workstation, 15 Paternoster Row, SHEFFIELD,
      S Yorks, S1 2BX.   (hq)
      0845 603 7278
      email info@bffs.org.uk
      Chief Exec: David Phillips
○   *A, *N; a national body which promotes voluntary film
      exhibition & represents the interests of film societies
●   Technical & legal advice
M   171 societies

British Federation for Historical Swordplay   (BFHS)   1998
NR   41 Wythan View, Eynsham, WITNEY, Oxon, OX29 4LX.   (sp)
      email secretary@bfhs.org   http://www.bfhs.org
      Sec: Mark Hillyard
▲   Un-incorporated Society
Br   16
○   *G, *N; for individual groups & societies studying & practising
      fencing & European martial arts
●   Conf - Mtgs - ET - Exam - Res - Inf
M   16 org

**British Federation of Sand & Land Yacht Clubs   (British
Landsailing)   (BFSLYC)   1962**
■   Y Bwthyn, Druidston Cross, BROAD HAVEN, Pembrokeshire,
      SA62 3ND.   (hsp)
      01437 781458
      email secretary@bfslyc.org.uk   http://www.bfslyc.org.uk
      Sec: Andy Parr
▲   Un-incorporated Society
Br   18
○   *S; to regulate, administer & promote land yachting in the UK
Gp   Kite buggying; Landsailing; Landyachting; Parakarting;
      Sandyachting
●   Mtgs - ET - Res - Comp - Inf - LG
<   Fedn Intl of Sand & Land Yachting
M   800 i, 18 org
¶   Land Sailor (Jnl) - 4; ftm.

**British Federation against Sexually Transmitted Diseases
(BFSTD)   1948**
NR   c/o BMA House, Tavistock Square, LONDON, WC1H 9JP.
      (hsb)
      Hon Sec: Dr Jean Tobin
▲   Registered Charity
○   *L, *M; issues relating to sexually transmitted infections
      including HIV/AIDS
Gp   representatives from main UK organisations working in the field
      of sexual & reproductive health
●   Mtgs - ET - Inf - LG
<   EUROPAP
M   21 org
¶   AR; free.

British Federation of Women Graduates   (BFWG)   1907
NR   4 Mandeville Courtyard, 142 Battersea Park Rd, LONDON,
      SW11 4NB.   (hq/regd office)
      020 7498 8037   fax 020 7498 5213
      email office@bfwg.org.uk   http://www.bfwg.org.uk
      Exec Sec: Mrs A B Stein
▲   Company Limited by Guarantee; Registered Educational
      Charity
Br   35
○   *E, *P, *X
●   Conf - Mtgs - Comp - SG - Stat - Lib - VE - LG
<   Intl Fedn of University Women (Geneva)
M   180,000 i, UK & o'seas
¶   NL;   LM;   AR; all ftm.

**British Federation of Youth Marching Brass Bands   (BFYMBB)
2000**
NR   The Pavilion on the Park, 1 Kingfisher Rd, EASTLEIGH, Hants,
      SO50 9LH.   (regd/address)
      023 8027 3772
      email marchbands@aol.com
      http://www.marchingbands.org.uk
      Contact: Jim Vaughan
▲   Registered Charity
○   *D, *N
      NOTE: as a totally voluntary organisation the telephone can
      only be staffed occasionally

British Fencing Association   1902
NR   1 Baron's Gate, 33-35 Rothschild Rd, LONDON, W4 5HT.
    (hq)
    020 8742 3032   fax 020 8742 3033
    email headoffice@britishfencing.com
    http://www.britishfencing.com
▲   Company Limited by Guarantee
○   *S; governing body for the sport of fencing in the UK

British Fertility Society   (BFS)   1974
■   22 Apex Court, Woodlands, Bradley Stoke, BRISTOL,
    BS32 4JT.   (asa)
    01454 642217
    http://www.fertility.org.uk
▲   Company Limited by Guarantee
○   *M; to promote the knowledge & study of fertility & infertility
Gp   Counsellors; Doctors; Nurses; Scientists
●   Conf - Mtgs - ET
<   Intl Fedn of Fertility Socs
M   760 i, 12 f
¶   Human Fertility (Jnl) - 3.   NL - 3.

British Film Designers Guild   (BFDG)   1946
NR   Pinewood Studios, Pinewood Rd, IVER HEATH, Bucks,
    SL0 0NH.   (hq)
    01753 509013
    email enquiries@filmdesigners.co.uk
    http://www.filmdesigners.co.uk
    Chmn: Kevin Phipps
○   *P; for all working in film art & costume departments
●   Mtgs - Exhib - Inf - Empl - Film screenings
<   Cine Glds of GB (CGGB)
M   117 i, 35 f, UK / 3 i, o'seas
¶   NL - 12; ftm only.

British Film Institute   (BFI)   1933
NR   21 Stephen St, LONDON, W1T 1LN.   (hq)
    020 7255 1444
    http://www.bfi.org.uk
    Dir: Amanda Nevill
▲   Registered Charity
○   *A, *Q; to promote understanding & appreciation of Britain's
    rich film & television & culture
M   i, f & org
¶   Sight & Sound - 12.

British Fire Consortium   (BFC)   1983
NR   38b Thornleigh Trading Estate, Blowers Green Rd, DUDLEY,
    DY2 8UB.   (hsb)
    0333 123 5306
    email secretary@britishfireconsortium.org.uk
    http://www.britishfireconsortium.org.uk
▲   Company Limited by Guarantee
○   *T; for nationally based independent fire protection companies
Gp   Fire: Alarms, Extinguisher mfrs, Extinguisher suppliers,
    Protection service companies
    Training; Consultants; Signs; Intumescent materials; Health &
    safety
●   Conf - Mtgs - ET - Exam - Res - Exhib - Lib
<   BSI
M   200 f
¶   NL - 4; ftm only.

British Fire Protection Systems Association Ltd
    in 2007 merged with the Association of British Fire Trades, the Fire
    Extinguishing Trades Association & the Fire Industry Confederation to
    form the **Fire Industry Association**

British Fire Services Association   (BFSA)   1950
NR   8 Clover House, Boston Rd, SLEAFORD, Lincs, NG34 7HD.
    (hq)
    01526 830255
    Gen Sec: Derrick Crouch
▲   Registered Charity
○   *T; for fire fighters
M   10,000 i, 1,000 f, 200 org

British Fireworks Association
NR   25 Belmot Rd, Tutbury, BURTON on TRENT, Staffs, DE13 9NL.
    (sp)
    01283 813344
    http://www.b-f-a.org
    Sec: John Park
○   *T; firework manufacturers
M   16 f

British Flat Roofing Council
    no longer in existence

British Florist Association Ltd   (BFA)   1979
■   PO Box 674, WIGAN, Lancs, WN1 9LL.   (mail/address)
    0844 800 7299
    email info@britishfloristassociation.org
    http://www.britishfloristassociation.org
    Co Sec: Carl Hodgkinson
▲   Company Limited by Guarantee
○   *N, *T; to represent professional retail florists
Gp   Training & Education C'ee
●   Conf - Mtgs - ET - Exhib - Comp - Inf - LG
    Helpline: 0870 240 3208
<   Fédn Europeénne Unions Professionelles de Fleuristes
>   Teleflorist; Flowergram; Masterflorist
M   180 i, 5 f, UK / 1 f, o'seas
    (Sub: £10,500 i, £53,000 f, UK / £500 f o'seas)
¶   NL - 12; ftm only.

British Flower Bulbs Association   1945
■   Springfield Gardens, Camelgate, SPALDING, Lincs,
    PE12 6ET.   (hq)
    01775 724843   fax 01775 711209
    Sec: David Norton
▲   Un-incorporated Society
○   *T; all connected in the sale & distribution of flower bulbs,
    corms etc in the UK
●   Mtgs - Inf
M   40 f
×   2006 Bulb Distributors' Association

**British Flower & Vibrational Essences Association   (BFVEA)
1997**
■   BM BFVEA, LONDON, WC1N 3XX.   (mail/address)
    01305 760295
    email info@bfvea.com   http://www.bfvea.com
    Chmn: Jan Stewart,   Sec: Emma le Monnier
▲   Un-incorporated Society
○   *T; to stimulate interest in & standards for, training in flower &
    vibrational essences
●   Conf - Mtgs - ET - Res - Inf - LG
<   Brit Assn of Flower Essence Producers
M   120 i, UK / 40 i, o'seas
    (Sub: £35 UK / £40 o'seas)
¶   Essence - 3/4; ftm, £20 yr nm.   E-NL - 4; free.

British Flue & Chimney Manufacturers' Association   (BFCMA) 1977
- ■ 2 Waltham Court, Milley Lane, Hare Hatch, READING, Berks, RG10 9TH.   (hq)
    0118-940 3416   fax 0118-940 6258
    email info@feta.co.uk   http://www.feta.co.uk/
    Dir Gen: C Sloan
- ○ *T; natural draught flues & chimneys
- ● Mtgs - SG - Representation on standards c'ees
- < Fedn Envtl Tr Assns (FETA)
- M 11 f, 6 associates

British Fluid Power Association (incorporating AHEM)   (BFPA) 1959
- ■ Cheriton House, Cromwell Park, CHIPPING NORTON, Oxon, OX7 5SR.   (hq)
    01608 647900   fax 01608 647919
    email enquiries@bfpa.co.uk   http://www.bfpa.co.uk
    Chief Exec: Ian Morris
- ▲ Company Limited by Guarantee
- ○ *T; engineering, hydraulic & pneumatic fluid power equipment systems
- Gp Commercial & promotions; Component performance; Connectors; Contamination control; Control components; Cylinders; Education & training; Electrohydraulic control systems; Fluids; Market forecasting & statistics; Pneumatic equipment; Quality assurance; Research; Seals
- ● Conf - Mtgs - ET - Exhib - SG - Stat - Expt - Inf - Lib
- < Comité Eur des Transmissions Oléohydraulique et Pneumatique (CETOP); CBI; BSI; METCOM
- M 100 f
- ¶ NL - 10; ftm only.   Directory - irreg;   Product list - 1;   LM;   AR; all free.
    Publications lists BFPA/CETOP.

British Fluid Power Distributors' Association   (BFPDA)   1989
- ■ Cheriton House, Cromwell Park, CHIPPING NORTON, Oxon, OX7 5SR.   (hq)
    01608 647900   fax 01608 647919
    email bfpda@bfpa.org.uk   http://www.bfpa.co.uk
    Chief Exec: Ian Morris
- ▲ Company Limited by Guarantee
- ○ *T; for British distributors of oil-hydraulic & pneumatic equipment
- ● Conf - Mtgs - ET - Exhib - SG - Stat - Expt - Inf - Lib
- < Brit Fluid Power Assn
- M 100 f
- ¶ NL - 4; ftm only.   Directory - irreg;   Product list;   LM; AR; all free.
    Publications lists BFPA.

British Fluoridation Society   1969
- NR Ashton Leigh & Wigan PCT, Bryan House, Standishgate, WIGAN, Lancs, WN1 1AH.   (hq)
    01942 483099
    email bfs@bfsweb.org   http://www.bfsweb.org
    Inf & Res Officer: Sheila Jones
- ▲ Company Limited by Guarantee
- ○ *K; 'to promote fluoridation of the public water supplies for the benefit of dental health'
- ● Conf - ET - Res - Inf - Lib - LG
- ¶ Briefings on various aspects of fluoridation & dental health statistics - irreg.

British Flute Society   (BFS)   1983
- NR 27 Eskdale Gardens, PURLEY, Surrey, CR8 1ET.   (hsp)
    020 8668 3360
    email secretary@bfs.org.uk
    Hon Sec: Anna Munks
- ▲ Registered Charity
- ○ *D; furtherance & enjoyment of playing the flute
- Gp Junior Section
- ● Mtgs - ET - Comp - SG - Inf - Concerts - Flute Festivals
- M c 1,800 i
- ¶ Pan - 4.

British Flyball Association   (BFA)   1993
- NR PO Box 990, DONCASTER, S Yorks, DN1 9FY.   (sp)
    0776 726 6916
    email rachel.child@flyball.org.uk
    http://www.flyball.org.uk
    Sec: Rachel Child
- ▲ Un-incorporated Society
- ○ *G, *S; to promote flyball - a team sport for dogs & dog owners
- ● Conf - ET - Exam - Exhib - Comp - Internet information
- < Assns in Australia, Netherlands, N America, S Africa; Belgian Flyball Fedn
- M 1,500 i
- ¶ Flyball Record - 4; ftm only.

British Food Importers & Distributors Association   (BFIDA) 1997
- ■ Crescent House, 34 Eastbury Way, SWINDON, Wilts, SN25 2EN.   (asa)
    01793 727387   fax 01793 726486
    email foodimporters@aol.com
    Sec: Walter J Anzer
- ○ *T; to represent the interests of food importers in the UK
- ● LG
- < FRUCOM
- M 22 f

British Foosball Association
- ■ c/o 100 Park Rd, Hindley, WIGAN, Lancs, WN2 3RX.
    fax 01942 204158
    email bfa@britfoos.com   http://www.britfoos.com
    Chmn: Joe Bundy,   Gen Sec: Jonathan May
- ○ *S; for players of bar (or table) football

British Footwear Association   (BFA)   1996
- ■ 3 Burystead Place, WELLINGBOROUGH, Northants, NN8 1AH.   (hq)
    01933 229005   fax 01933 225009
    email info@britfoot.com   http://www.britfoot.com
    Chief Exec: Richard Kottler
- ▲ Company Limited by Guarantee
- ○ *T; to promote & protect the interests of the UK footwear industry
- ● Conf - Mtgs - Stat - Empl
- < Eur Footwear Mfrs Confedn (CEC)
- M 80 f
- ¶ NL; ftm only.

British Fragrance Association
    see **International Fragrance Association - United Kingdom**

British Franchise Association Ltd   (BFA)   1977
- NR Centurion Court, 85f Milton Park, ABINGDON, Oxon, OX14 4RY.   (hq)
    01235 820470
    email mailroom@thebfa.org   http://www.thebfa.org
    Dir-Gen: Brian Smart
- ▲ Company Limited by Guarantee
- ○ *T; promoting ethical franchising, voluntary self-regulatory body for franchisors, providing advice to potential franchisees / franchisors, education in franchising, lobbying on behalf of franchise community
- ● Conf - Mtgs - ET - Res - Exhib - Stat - Inf - LG
- < Wld Franchise Coun; Eur Franchise Assn
- M 250 f
- ¶ Members Newsline (NL) - 12; ftm only.
    Franchise Link - 2; ftm, part of infopacks for nm.
    Franchisee Guide.   Franchisor Guide.

British Free Range Egg Producers Association   (BFREPA)   1991

- ■ PO Box 3425, Ashton Keynes, SWINDON, Wilts, SN6 6WR.   (admin)
  01285 869913
  email admin@bfrepa.co.uk   http://www.bfrepa.co.uk
  Admin: Alison Bone
- ▲ Un-incorporated Society
- ○ *F, *T
- ● Conf - Mtgs - ET - Res - Exhib - Stat - Inf - PL - VE - LG
- < Brit Egg Assn; Brit Egg Ind Coun; Nat Farmers U
- M 271 i, 41 f
- ¶ Ranger - 12; ftm, £35 (+VAT) yr nm.

British Friction Materials Council

November 2011, in the process of being wound up

British Friesland Sheep Society   1980

- ■ Weir Park Farm, Waterwell Lane, Christow, EXETER, Devon, EX6 7PB.   (hsp)
  01647 252549
  Hon Sec: Peter Baber
- ▲ Un-incorporated Society
- ○ *B; to promote the use of British Friesland sheep as a supreme dairy animal & as a crossing sire to produce profitable cross-bred ewes for prime lamb production
- ● Mtgs (AGM)
- < Nat Sheep Assn
- M 48 i
- ¶ NL - irreg.   Hbk;   LM - updated.

British Frozen Food Federation   (BFFF)   1951

- NR Warwick House (Unit 7), Long Bennington Business Park, Main Rd, Long Bennington, NEWARK, NG23 5JR.   (hq)
  01400 283090   fax 01400 293097
  http://www.bfff.co.uk
  Dir-Gen: Brian Young
- ○ *T
- M f

British Fruit Juice Association   (BFJA)   1947

- ■ Shoelands House, Seale, FARNHAM, Surrey, GU10 1HL.   (hsp)
  01483 811433   fax 01483 811433
  email clive@clivewebster.co.uk   http://www.bfja.co.uk
  Exec Sec/Treas: Clive Webster
- ▲ Un-incorporated Society
- ○ *T; interests of companies & organisations which have dealings in fruit juices
- Gp Handlers; Importers; Laboratories; Manufacturers/packers
- ● Conf - Mtgs - Inf - LG
- < Brit Soft Drinks Assn
- > Brit Soft Drinks Assn
- M 52 f
  (Sub: £130)

British Fuchsia Society   (BFS)   1938

- ■ PO Box 8177, READING, Berks, RG6 9PH.   (hsp)
  http://www.thebfs.org.uk
  Hon Sec: Geoffrey Oke
- ▲ Registered Charity
- ○ *H; to further interest in the cultivation & understanding of Fuchsias
- Gp Special interest: Hybridising, Pre-1914 cultivars, Species Show organisation & exhibiting; Fuchsia (collecting fuschsia memorabilia); Photography
- ● Conf - ET - Exam - Exhib - Comp - Inf
- < Fuchsia Res Intl; Eurofuchsia; R Horticl Soc
- > Fuchsia Res Intl
- M 3,800 i, 280 org, UK / 325 i, 20 org, o'seas
- ¶ Spring [& Autumn] Bulletin(s) - 1; ftm, £3 nm.
  Annual publication - 1; ftm, £4 nm.

British Fur Trade Association Inc   (BFTA)   1964

- ■ Brookstone House, 6 Elthorne Rd, LONDON, N19 4AG.   (hq)
  020 7281 9299   fax 020 7281 1374
  email info@britishfur.co.uk   http://www.britishfur.co.uk
  Contact: The Executive Officer
- ▲ Company Limited by Guarantee
- ○ *T
- ● Mtgs - Exhib - Comp - Expt - Inf - Empl
- M 50 f

British Furniture Confederation

- NR c/o FIRA International Ltd, Maxwell Rd, STEVENAGE, Herts, SG1 2EW.   (hq)
  01438 777700   fax 01438 777800
  http://www.britishfurnitureconfederation.org.uk
  Chmn: Martin Jourdan
- ○ *T
- M f

British Furniture Manufacturers
  see **BFM Ltd (British Furniture Manufacturers)**

British Gear Association   (BGA)   1986

- ■ Suite 59 Imex Business Centre, Shobnall Rd, BURTON upon TRENT, Staffs, DE14 2AU.   (hq)
  01283 515521   fax 01283 515841
  email admin@bga.org.uk   http://www.bga.org.uk
  Technical Exec: Andrew Harry
- ▲ Company Limited by Guarantee
- ○ *E, *Q, *T; to promote technical, economic, educational, training & research activities in the interest of the mechanical power transmission sector
- Gp C'ees: Technical, Education & training; Marketing; Research Foundation
- ● Conf - Mtgs - ET - Res - Exhib - SG - Stat - Expt - Inf - Lib - VE - LG
- < Eur C'ee of Assns of Mfrs of Gears & Transmission Parts (EUROTRANS); Mechanical & Metal Trs Confedn (METCOM)
- M 6 i, 82 f, 8 org
- ¶ BGA NL - 4; free.
  Technical Bulletin - 12;   Technical Literature Survey - 12;
  AR - 1; all ftm only.
  Buyers Guide - 2 yrly; ftm, £10 nm.

British Gelbvieh Cattle Society   1972

- NR Upper Old Wheatley Farm, Pocombe Bridge, EXETER, Devon, EX4 2HA.   (hsp)
  01392 434056
  Hon Sec: Sally Turner
- ▲ Registered Charity
- ○ *B
- ● Conf - Exhib - Comp - VE - Shows
- M c 20 i
- ¶ NL - 4;   AR - 1; both ftm.   LM - 1; free.

British Generic Manufacturers' Association   (BGMA)   1989

- NR The Registry, Royal Mint Court, LONDON, EC3N 4QN.   (hq)
  020 7457 2018   fax 020 7866 7900
  email info@britishgenerics.co.uk
  http://www.britishgenerics.co.uk
  Sec: Alex Harris
- ▲ Company Limited by Guarantee
- ○ *T; for UK manufacturers & suppliers of generic medicines; to promote the industry
- ● Mtgs - LG
- < Eur Generic Medicines Assn (EGA)
- M 14 f

© CBD Research Ltd · Beckenham · BR3 5JS · Tel 020 8650 7745 · E-mail cbd@cbdresearch.com · www.cbdresearch.com

British Geomembrane Association   (BGA)   1999
NR   c/o Naue Geosynthetics Ltd, The Genesis Centre, Birchwood,
      WARRINGTON, Cheshire, WA3 7BH.   (hsb)
      01925 810280   fax 01925 810284
      email info@bga.uk.net   http://www.bga.uk.net
      Sec: Chris Quirk
▲   Un-incorporated Society
○   *T
●   Conf- Mtgs - ET - Exam
M   1 i, 20 f

British Geophysical Association
      a group of the **Geological Society**

British Geotechnical Association   (BGA)   1949
NR   Institution of Civil Engineers, 1 Great George St, LONDON,
      SW1P 3AA.   (hq)
▲   Registered Charity
○   *P; promotion of cooperation among engineers & scientists for
      the advancement of knowledge in the fields of soil & rock
      mechanics & engineering geology & their application to
      engineering
M   i

British Geriatrics Society   (BGS)   1947
NR   Marjory Warren House, 31 St John's Square, LONDON,
      EC1M 4DN.   (hq)
      020 7608 1369   fax 020 7608 1041
      email info@bgs.org.uk   http://www.bgs.org.uk
      Hon Sec: Dr David Beaumont
▲   Registered Charity
○   *P; to improve standards of health; to put the case for a well-
      funded health & community care service for elderly people
Gp   Bladder & bowel; Cardiovascular; Cerebral ageing & mental
      health; Diabetes; Drugs & prescribing; Falls & bone health;
      Gastroenterology & nutrition; Health services research;
      Medical ethics; New technology in elderly care; Parkinson's
      disease; Primary & continuing care; Respiratory
●   Conf - Mtgs - ET - Res
<   Intl Assn of Gerontology
M   c 2,000 i, UK / 500 i, o'seas
¶   Age & Ageing (Jnl) - 6; ftm.

British-German Association   (BGA)   1951
NR   34 Belgrave Square, LONDON, SW1X 8QD.   (hq)
      020 7235 1922   fax 020 7235 1902
      email info@britishgermanassociation.org
      http://www.britishgermanassociation.org
      Exec Sec: Martina Schmidt
▲   Company Limited by Guarantee; Registered Charity
○   *X; promotion of understanding between British & German
      peoples, their culture & history
●   Conf - Mtgs - Annual Nutcracker Ball
<   Deutsch-Englische Gesellschaft (Berlin)
M   c 700 i
¶   British-German Review - 4; ftm.

British-German Jurists' Association   (BGJA)   1970
NR   14 New St, LONDON, EC2M 4HE.   (chmn/b)
      020 7972 9727   fax 020 7972 9721
      http://www.bgja.org.uk
○   *P

British Gestalt Society
      reported as wound-up 2010

British Gladiolus Society   (BGS)   1926
■   197 Aston Clinton Rd, AYLESBURY, Bucks, HP22 5AD.   (hsp)
      01296 630360
      email duckglads@aol.com   http://www.britglad.com
      Hon Sec: Mrs Susan Fawcett
▲   Un-incorporated Society
○   *H; the cultivation, breeding & exhibition of all types of
      gladiolus
Gp   3 test grounds for cultivars supplied for trial from UK & o'seas,
      in South of England, Midlands & Scotland
●   Conf - Mtgs - Res - Exhib - Stat - Inf - Lib - PL - Regional
      annual show
<   N Amer Gladiolus Coun (NAGC)
M   275 i, 55 affiliated socs, UK / 22 i, o'seas
¶   NL - 3.   Ybk.

**British Glass Manufacturers' Confederation   (British Glass)
1988**
■   9 Churchill Way, SHEFFIELD, S Yorks, S35 2PY.   (hq)
      0114-290 1850   fax 0114-290 1851
      email info@britglass.co.uk   http://www.britglass.org.uk
      Chief Exec: Dave Dalton,   Inf Officer: Theresa Green
▲   Company Limited by Guarantee
○   *T; to represent the interests of members to government at EU,
      national & local level; to provide technical & consultancy
      services to members & non members
Gp   Glass Technology Services (the technical arm of British Glass
      offering specialist services in consultancy, project
      management, environmental monitoring & all types of glass
      analysis)
●   Conf - Mtgs - ET - Res - Stat - Inf - Lib - LG
<   FGUE; CPIV; EDGA; EDG; CBI; CETUE; CEN; Packaging Fedn
M   95 f, UK / 2 f, o'seas
¶   NL - 2;   Legislative Update;   Digest of Information - 4;
      Various NL;   AR - 1; all ftm.

British Gliding Association Ltd   (BGA)   1929
■   8 Merus Court, Meridian Business Park, LEICESTER, LE19 1RJ.
      (hq)
      0116-289 2956
      email office@gliding.co.uk   http://www.gliding.co.uk
      Chief Exec: Peter Stratten
▲   Company Limited by Guarantee
○   *S; promotion of every aspect of gliding & soaring
M   c 11,000 i

British Glove Association   (BGA)   1998
■   Sussex House, 8-10 Holmesdale Rd, BROMLEY, Kent,
      BR2 9LZ.   (asa)
      020 8464 0131
      email info@gloveassociation.org
      http://www.gloveassociation.org
○   *T; to promote glove sales; to encourage designers; to bring
      together manufacturers & retailers
M   30 f

British Go Association   (BGA)   1953
■   30 Market St, ST ANDREWS, Fife, KY16 9NS.   (contact/p)
      01334 470585
      email bga@britgo.org   http://www.britgo.org
      Contact: Edwin Brady,
      Sec: Jonathan Chin (secretary@britgo.org)
▲   Un-incorporated Society
Br   68 clubs
○   *G, *S; to promote the playing of the ancient oriental board
      game of Go
●   Conf Mtgs - ET - Comp - SG
<   Intl Go Fedn; Eur Go Fedn
M   c 600 i, UK; 50 i, o'seas
¶   British Go Jnl - 4; ftm, £3.50 nm.
      BGA NL - 6; ftm only.

British Goat Society   (BGS)   1879
NR   Gibshiel, Tarset, HEXHAM, Northumberland, NE48 1RR.   (hq)
    email secretary@allgoats.com   http://www.allgoats.com
    Sec: Jane Wilson
▲   Registered Charity
○   *B; to increase supply & consumption of goats' milk; to improve
    the various breeds of goats; to safeguard against cruelty;
    production of cashmere & cashgora fibre, hides & leather
Gp   Working party on the composition & utilisation of goats milk;
    Caprine & Ovine Breeding Services Ltd (artificial
    insemination)
●   Conf - Mtgs - ET - Res - Exhib - SG - Stat - Expt - Inf - Sales of
    products allied to goat keeping & dairy work, production of
    butter, cheeses & yoghurt
<   Breed Societies: Anglo-Nubian, Brit Alpine, Brit Saanen, Brit
    Toggenburg, Golden Guernsey, Soanen, Toggenberg
    Harness Goat Soc; Regional Goat Socs
M   3,000 i, 15 f, 100 org, UK / 50 i, o'seas
¶   Jnl - 11.   Ybk.   Herdbook - 1.   AR.

British Goldpanning Association   1988
■   2 Spout Cottages, The Spout, ELLESMERE, Shropshire,
    SY12 0NE.   (treas/p)
    01691 623954
    http://www.britishgoldpanningassociation.com
    Treas: Barbara Copley
○   *G; for British goldpanners
<   Wld Goldpanning Assn
M   c 45 i

British Golf Collectors' Society   (BGCS)   1987
NR   20 Druim Avenue, INVERNESS, IV2 4LG.   (mem/sp)
    01463 231145
    http://www.golfcollectors.co.uk
    Mem Sec: Hamish Ewan
○   *G; to promote interest in the history & traditions of golf & the
    collecting of items connected with that history
●   Mtgs - Inf
M   c 600 i
¶   Through the Green - 4.
    LM - on website.

British Golf Industry Association   (BGIA)   1919
■   Federation House, STONELEIGH PARK, Warks, CV8 2RF.   (hq)
    024 7641 7141   fax 024 7641 4990
    email bgia@sportsandplay.com
    http://www.bgia.org.uk
    Sec: Mrs Jacqui Baldwin
▲   Company Limited by Guarantee
○   *T; manufacturers & distributors of golf equipment
●   Conf - Mtgs - Res - Stat - Expt - Inf - LG
<   Eur Golf Ind Assn; Fedn of Sports & Play Assns (FSPA)
M   70 f

British Gotland Sheep Society   (BGSS)   1990
■   Whitehall Farm, Luppitt, HONITON, Devon, EX14 4TR.   (hsp)
    01404 42141
    http://www.gotlandsheep.com
    davidbarlo@aol.com   (chmn)
    Sec: Mrs A E Barlow
▲   Un-incorporated Society
○   *B
●   Mtgs - ET - Exhib - LG - Promotion & breed registration of
    British Gotland Sheep
<   Nat Sheep Assn
M   26 i
¶   NL - 4;   Flock Book - 1; both ftm only.
    Breed Hbk - 2 yrly; ftm, £2 nm.

British Grassland Society   (BGS)   1945
NR   Unit 32C Stoneleigh Deer Park, Stareton, KENILWORTH, Warks,
    CV8 2LY.   (hq)
    024 7669 6600
    email office@britishgrassland.com
    http://www.britishgrassland.com
    Dir: Jessica Buss
▲   Registered Charity
○   *A, *L; grass & forage production, study & research
●   Conf - Mtgs - ET - EXhib - SG - Inf - VE - LG - Networking -
    Knowledge transfer
M   600 i, 69 org, UK / 100 i, o'seas
    (Sub: £30 (farmer) 40 (non-farmer)i, £45 org)
¶   Grass & Forage Science - 4.   Grass & Forage Farmer - 4.

British Grooms Association   (BGA)   2007
NR   PO Box 592, LONDON, KT12 9ER.
    0845 331 6039
    email info@britishgrooms.org.uk
    http://www.britishgrooms.org.uk
    Chief Executive: Lucy Katan
▲   Company Limited by Guarantee
○   *P; representation and support for grooms working in the
    equine industry
●   ET - Res - Inf
<   Brit Equestrian Fedn
M   150 i, UK / 2 i, o'seas
¶   British Grooms - 4, ftm, £2.50 nm.

British Group of Altimeter Specialists
    a group of the **Challenger Society for Marine Science**

British Growers Association   (BGA)   1969
■   PVGA House, Nottingham Rd, LOUTH, Lincs, LN11 0WB.   (hq)
    01507 602427   fax 01507 600689
    email postbox@britishgrowers.org
    http://www.britishgrowers.org
    Chief Exec: Martin Riggall
▲   Company Limited by Guarantee
○   *F, *H; to provide leadership, representation, co-ordination &
    support services to British growers, their marketing
    organisations & specialist crop associations
Gp   Yes Peas
●   Mtgs - Res - Stat - Expt - Inf - LG - Provision of administration &
    secretarial services - Contract negotiation support
×   2011 (December) Processed Vegetable Growers' Association

British Guild of Beer Writers   1988
■   Woodcote, 2 Jury Rd, DULVERTON, Somerset, TA22 9DU.
    (hsp)
    01398 324314
    email tierneyjones@btinternet.com
    http://www.beerwriters.co.uk
    Hon Sec: Adrian Tierney-Jones
▲   Un-incorporated Society
○   *P; to improve the standards of beer writing; to extend public
    knowledge of beers & brewing
●   Conf - Mtgs - Res - Comp - Inf
<   Intl Fedn of Beer Writers
M   132 i, 21 f, UK / 10 i, o'seas
¶   BGBW NL - 10; ftm.

British Guild of Travel Writers   (BGTW)   1960
NR   335 Lordship Rd, LONDON, N16 5HG.   (hsp)
    020 8144 8713
    Sec: Antonia Cunningham
○   *P; for specialist travel writers, broadcasters, producers, editors
    & photographers
●   Mtgs - Res - Inf - VE
<   all members are also members of Eur Fedn of Tourism
    Journalists (FEDAJT)
M   220 i
¶   Globe Trotter - 12; ftm only.

© CBD Research Ltd · Beckenham · BR3 5JS · Tel 020 8650 7745 · E-mail cbd@cbdresearch.com · www.cbdresearch.com

British Gymnastics (BG) 1888
NR Ford Hall, Lilleshall National Sports Centre, NEWPORT,
    Shropshire, TF10 9NB. (hq)
    0845 129 7129
    http://www.british-gymnastics.org
▲   Company Limited by Guarantee
○   *S; governing body for gymnastics in GB
M   103,000 i
✕   British Amateur Gymnastics Association

British Haiku Society (BHS) 1990
■   Longholm, East Bank, Winglands, SUTTON BRIDGE, Lincs,
    PE12 9YS. (hsp)
    http://www.britishhaikusociety.org
▲   Registered Charity
○   *A; to promote the appreciation & writing of haiku & related
    forms (Japanese poetry & prose)
●   Conf - Mtgs - Comp - SG - Inf - Lib - VE
M   c 200-500 i
¶   Blithe Spirit (Jnl) - 4; ftm.

British Handball Association
    see **England Handball Association**

British Hang Gliding & Paragliding Association (BHPA) 1974
■   8 Merus Court, Meridian Business Park, LECICESTER,
    LE19 2RJ. (hq)
    0116-289 4316
    email office@bhpa.co.uk   http://www.bhpa.co.uk
▲   Company Limited by Guarantee
Br 120
○   *S; control & development of the sport of hang gliding &
    paragliding
Gp Over land towed ascent; Self launched (unassisted) flight
●   Conf - ET - Exhib - Comp - Stat
<   R Aero Club; CCPR; Fédn Aéronautique Intle
M   8,000 i, 120 clubs
¶   Skywings (Jnl) - 12; ftm, £2.50 nm.

British Hanoverian Horse Society (BHHS) 1992
■   Hawkins Stud, Stanbrook Farm, STAUNTON, Glos,
    GL19 3QR. (hsp)
    01452 841101
    email info@hanoverian-gb.org.uk
    http://www.hanoverian-gb.org.uk
    Hon Sec: Judith Davis
▲   Company Limited by Guarantee
○   *B; breeding the Hanoverian horse for competition
●   Licensing of stallions - Maintaining UK studbook
<   Verband Hannoverscher Warmblützüchter eV
M   120 i
¶   NL - 3; ftm only.

**British Hardmetal & Engineers' Cutting Tool Association
(BHECTA) 2004**
■   c/o 62 Bayswater Rd, LONDON, W2 3PS. (MTA/hq)
    020 7298 6400   fax 020 7298 6430
    email bhecta@mta.org.uk
    Dir Gen (MTA): Graham Dewhurst
▲   Un-incorporated Society
○   *T; to act as the national organisation representing the interests
    of manufacturers within the hardmetal & cutting tool industry
Gp Research & development (hardmetal)
●   Conf - Mtgs - ET - Res - Exhib - SG - Stat - Expt - Inf - VE - LG -
<   World Cutting Tool Conf; Eur Cutting Tool Assn
M   30 f
    Note: in April 2006 was incorporated into the Manufacturing
    Technologies Association

British Hardware Federation (BHF) 1899
NR 225 Bristol Rd, Edgbaston, BIRMINGHAM, B5 7UB. (hq)
    0121-446 6688   fax 0121-446 5215
    email info@bira.co.uk   http://www.bira.co.uk/bhf/
    Chmn: Richard Rowlatt
▲   Un-incorporated Society
○   *T; retailers of hardware, ironmongery, tools, DIY & allied
    products
●   Empl - ET - Inf - LG - Mtgs
<   Brit Indep Retailers Assn
M   f
    BHF & the British Shops & Stores Association (BSSA) merged in
    September 2009 as BSSA-BHF, renamed British Independent
    Retailers Association (BIRA) in May 2011. BHF & BSSA now
    function as divisional trade associations within BIRA.

British Hardware & Housewares Manufacturers' Association
    since 2007 **British Home Enhancement Trade Association**

British Harness Racing Club (BHRC) 1963
NR Burlington Crescent, GOOLE, E Yorks, DN14 5EG.
    (regd/office)
    01405 766877   fax 01405 766878
    email harnessgb@aol.com   http://www.bhrc.org.uk
    Sec: Miss Geraldine Berry
▲   Company Limited by Guarantee
○   *S; governing body for harness racing in GB
●   Mtgs - Comp - Inf - Race meetings - Issuing of licences
<   Wld Trotting Assn
M   1,500 i (licence holders)
¶   Calendar - 6; £12.   Fixtures List (Jan).
    Record Book - 1; £14.

British Hat Guild
    is dormant

British Hawking Association (BHA) 1967
NR 43 Amherst Crescent, HOVE, E Sussex, BN3 7EP. (chmn/p)
    0870 755 0211
    Contact: Brian Morris
▲   Un-incorporated Society
Br 6
○   *G
●   Mtgs - ET - Apprenticeship scheme - campaign to licence raptor
    keepers in the UK
<   3 Spanish falconry clubs
M   'Unable to disclose due to constitution'
¶   Yarak Jnl - 1;   Yarak NL - 4; both ftm.

British Hay & Straw Merchants' Association (BHSMA) 1917
■   Northfields Farm, Clayhithe Rd, HORNINGSEA, Cambs,
    CB25 9JA. (sp)
    0777 053 3488
    email aprilgingel@googlemail.com
    http://www.hay-straw-merchants.co.uk
    Sec: Mrs April Gingell
○   *T; interests of those involved in growing, processing or trading,
    in all types of forage
Gp Technical
●   Mtgs - ET - EXhib - SG - Inf - VE - LG
<   Eur Hay & Straw Merchants (CIPF)
M   50 f
    (Sub: £150)
¶   LM.

British Health Care Association   (BHCA)   1931
NR   PO Box 6752, ELGIN, Morayshire, IV30 9BN.   (hq)
         01343 544841
         email info@bhca.org.uk   http://www.bhca.org.uk
▲   Un-incorporated Society
○   *P; represents not for profit health care organisations, including
         health cash plan providers
●   Conf - Mtgs - SG - Stat - Inf - Lib - LG
M   13 f
¶   NL - 4; ftm only.   AR (incl LM) - 1; free.
         Caring for the Nation's Health (brochure) - 1; free.

British Health Professionals in Rheumatology   (BHPR)   1985
NR   Bride House, 18-20 Bride Lane, LONDON, EC4Y 8EE.   (hq)
         020 7842 0900   fax 020 7842 0901
         email bhpr@rheumatology.org.uk
         http://www.rheumatology.org.uk
         Chief Exec: Samantha Peters
▲   Registered Charity
○   *P; to encourage & emphasise the multi-disciplinary approach
         to the management of people with rheumatic diseases; to
         provide a forum for health professionals to exchange
         knowledge, skills & experience
●   Conf - Mtgs - ET - Res - Annual clinical prize - Annual Spring
         meeting
<   Brit Soc for Rheumatology (BSR); Arthritis & Musculoskeletal
         Alliance (ARMA)
M   600 i, UK / 3 i, o'seas
¶   BHPR NL - 2;   BHPR Hbk - 2 yrly, both ftm only.

British Healthcare Business Intelligence Association   (BHBIA)
NR   105 St Peter's St, ST ALBANS, Herts, AL1 3EJ.
         01727 896085
         email admin@bhbia.org.uk   http://www.bhbia.org.uk
○   *P

British Healthcare Trades Association   (BHTA)   1917
■   New Loom House, 101 Backchurch Lane, LONDON, E1 1LU.
         (hq)
         020 7702 2141
         email bhta@bhta.com   http://www.bhta.com
         Dir Gen: Ray Hodgkinson
▲   Company Limited by Guarantee
○   *T; to represent companies providing healthcare & assistive
         technology products & services
Gp   Beds & support services; Dispensing appliance contractors; First
         aid medical equipment; Health & safety training
         organisations; Infection control; Mobility access & stairlifts;
         Mobility vehicles (manufacturers, distributors); Orthotics;
         Postural control; Prosthetics; Rehabilitation products; Seating
         & positioning; Stoma & continence; Visual impairment
         products & services
●   Conf - Mtgs - ET - Stat - Inf - LG
M   350 f
¶   Friday Morning at BHTA (NL) - 52;   Bulletin; both ftm only.

British Heather Growers Association
NR   John Hall Plants Ltd, Red Lane (Churt Rd), Headley Down,
         BORDEN, Hants, GU35 8SR.
         01428 715505
         Chmn: John Hall
○   *T
         a specialist group of the **Horticultural Trades Association**

British Hedgehog Preservation Society   (BHPS)   1982
■   Hedgehog House, Dhustone, LUDLOW, Shropshire, SY8 3PL.
         (hq)
         01584 890801   fax 01584 891313
         email info@britshhedgehogs.org.uk
         http://www.britishhedgehogs.org.uk
         Chief Exec: Fay Vass
▲   Registered Charity
○   *K, *V; to encourage & give advice to the public on the care of
         hedgehogs, particularly when injured, sick, orphaned or in
         any other danger; to fund research into behavioural habits in
         order to assist their survival; to encourage the younger
         generation to value and respect our natural wildlife & to
         foster their interest in hedgehogs
●   Conf - ET - Res - Exhib - Inf - Lib
M   11,000 i, UK & o'seas
         (Sub: £7.50 i, UK / £10 i o'seas, £200 life)
¶   NL - 2; ftm, 60p nm.   Catalogue - 1; free.

British Helicopter Advisory Board Ltd   (BHAB)   1969
NR   Graham Suite West Entrance, Fairoaks Airport, Chobham,
         WOKING, Surrey, GU24 8HX.   (hq)
         01276 856100   fax 01276 856126
         email info@bhab.org   http://www.bhab.org
         Chief Exec: Peter Norton
○   *T; 'to promote the use of helicopters in the UK; to help
         helicopter operations to be conducted safely & responsibly'
Gp   Heliport & environmental matters; Offshore operations;
         Onshore operations; Technical matters
●   Mtgs - Inf - Lib - LG
<   Eur Helicopter Assn (EHA)
M   i, f & org
¶   The Rotorhead - 4; ftm only.   Leaflets.
         BHAB Information Hbk - 1; ftm.

British Hellenic Chamber of Commerce   (BHCC)   1945
■   25 Vas Sophias Avenue, GR-106 74 ATHENS, Greece.   (hq)
         30 (210) 72 10 361   fax 30 (210) 72 12 119
         email info@bhcc.gr   http://www.bhcc.gr
         Jt Pres: Harilaos Goritsas & Irene Watson
▲   Un-incorporated Society
○   *C; to serve the business world in Greece & Britain
●   Conf - Mtgs - Exhib - Inf - Social events
M   2 i, 21 f, UK / 85 i, 307 f, o'seas
¶   BH Magazine - 4; free.
         Business Directory of Members - 1; ftm, £50 nm.

British Herb Trade Association   (BHTA)   1976
■   PVGA House, Nottingham Rd, LOUTH, Lincs, LN11 0WB.
         (asa)
         01507 602427   fax 01507 600689
         email tim.mudge@pvga.co.uk   http://www.bhta.org.uk
         Sec: Tim Mudge
▲   Un-incorporated Society
○   *T; for herb growers, processors & retailers in the UK
●   Conf - Mtgs - Res - LG
<   Nat Farmers U
M   80 f
¶   Herbnews - 4; ftm only.

British Herbal Medicine Association   (BHMA)   1964
- ■ PO Box 583, EXETER, Devon, EX1 9GX.   (mail)
   0845 680 1134   fax 0845 680 1136
   email secretary@bhma.info   http://www.bhma.info
   Sec: Roberta Hutchins
- ▲ Company Limited by Guarantee
- ○ *K, *T; to advance the science & practice of herbal medicine in the UK; to ensure its continued statutory recognition at a time when all medicines are becoming subject to greater regulatory control
- Gp Advertising; Code of advertising practice; Database; Pharmacopoeia; Scientific
- ● Conf - Mtgs - Res - Inf
- < Eur Scientific Cooperative on Phytotherapy (ESCOP); Nat Inst of Med Herbalists; Natural Medicine Gp
- M c 300 i, f & org
- ¶ BHMA Post - 4.
   The British Herbal Pharmacopoeia.
   British Herbal Compendium, Vols 1 & 2.
   A Guide to Traditional Herbal Medicines.

British Herpetological Society   (BHS)   1948
- NR 11 Strathmore Place, MONTROSE, Angus, DD10 8LQ.   (hsp)
   email info@thebhs.org
   Sec: Trevor Rose
- ▲ Registered Charity
- ○ *L; to promote the study, protection, captive breeding, research & conservation of amphibians & reptiles
- Gp Captive breeding; Conservation
- ● Mtgs - Res - Inf - Lib
- M c 450 i, UK / 350 i, o'seas
- ¶ Jnl - 4;   Natterjack (NL) - 3;   Bulletin - 4.

British Hip Society
   a specialist society of the **British Orthopaedic Association**

British Hire Cruiser Federation
   a group association of the **British Marine Federation**

British Historical Games Society   (BHGS)   1996
- ■ The White Cottage, 8 West Hill Avenue, EPSOM, Surrey, KT19 8LE.
   01372 812132   fax 01372 800005
   email bhgs@slitherine.co.uk   http://www.bhgs.co.uk
   Chmn: J D McNeil
- ▲ Un-incorporated Society
- ○ *G; to organise & run table top wargaming with miniature figurines on a tournament basis; to liaise with other national bodies to organise tournaments internationally
- ● Exhib - Comp
- < Intl Wargames Fedn
- M 500 i

British HIV Association   (BHIVA)
- ■ c/o Mediscript Ltd, 1 Mountview Court, 310 Friern Barnet Lane, LONDON, N20 0LD.   (hq)
   020 8369 5380   fax 020 8446 9194
   email bhiva@bhiva.org   http://www.bhiva.org
- ▲ Registered Charity
- ○ *M, *P; for professionals in the treatment of HIV & related illnesses; to act as a national advisory body to the profession & other organisations on all aspects of HIV care
- ● Conf - ET - Res - Promotion of graduate & continuing medical education within HIV care
- < Intl AIDS Soc; Fedn of Infection Socs
- M 566 i, UK / 8 i, o'seas
- ¶ HIV Medicine - 4; ftm.

British Holiday & Home Parks Association   (BH&HPA)   1952
- ■ 6 Pullman Court, Great Western Rd, GLOUCESTER, GL1 3ND.   (hq)
   01452 526911   fax 01452 508508
   email enquiries@bhhpa.org.uk
   http://www.ukparks.com
   Dir-Gen: Mrs Ros Pritchard
- Br 22
- ○ *T; for owners of caravan holiday parks, touring parks, mobile home parks, chalets & all types of self-service holiday accommodation
- ● Conf - Mtgs - ET - Exhib - SG - PL - LG
- < Eur Fedn of Camping/Caravanning Orgs
- M 2,500 i, 3,000 f
- ¶ Jnl - 6;   Ybk - 1;   NL - irreg; all ftm only.

British Holistic Medical Association   (BHMA)   1983
- NR 5 Sea Lane Close, EAST PRESTON, W Sussex, BN16 1NQ.   (hq)
   Chmn: Craig K Brown
- ▲ Registered Charity
- ○ *L; education of doctors & medical students to the principles & practice of holistic medicine & dissemination of information to the public
- M i

British Home Enhancement Trade Association   (BHETA)   1958
- ■ Federation House, 10 Vyse St, BIRMINGHAM, B18 6LT.   (hq)
   0121-237 1130   fax 0121-237 1133
   email info@bheta.co.uk   http://www.bheta.co.uk
   Chief Exec: David French
- ▲ Company Limited by Guarantee
- ○ *T
- Gp Brush; Cookware; DIY; Hardware; Housewares
- ● Conf - Mtgs - Exhib - Stat - Expt - Inf - LG
- < Brit Allied Trs Fedn (Jewellery, Giftware, Home & Finishing) (BATF); Intl Housewares Assn (USA); Fedn of Eur DIY Mfrs (FEDIYMA)
- M 300 f, 10 affiliate org
- ¶ NL - 12; free.   Membership Directory - 1; ftm, £75 nm.
- ✕ 2011 (amalgamated) British Brush Manufacturers Association 2007 British Hardware & Housewares Manufacturers' Association

British Homeopathic Dental Association   1991
- ■ Menehey, Shawbury Lane, Shustoke, Coleshill, BIRMINGHAM, B46 2LA.
   01675 481535
   email brianteall@bhda.co.uk   http://www.bhda.co.uk
   Hon Sec: Brian Teall
- ▲ Registered Charity
- ○ *P; to encourage dentists & ancillaries to use homoeopathic remedies in their work
- ● Conf - ET - Exam - Res - SG - Inf
- M 143 i
   (Sub: £40)
- ¶ NL.

British Homoeopathic Association   (BHA)   1902
- NR Hahnemann House, 29 Park Street West, LUTON, Beds, LU1 3BE.   (hq)
   0870 444 3950   fax 0870 444 3960
   email info@trusthomeopathy.org
   http://www.trusthomeopathy.org
   Chief Exec: Sally Penrose
- ▲ Registered Charity
- ○ *P, *Q; to provide an information service to the public; to campaign for more homeopathy in the NHS; to fund research & training in homeopathy
- Gp Supporters' scheme - Friends of the BHA
- ● Inf - LG - Provides list of homeopathic doctors, dentists, pharmacists, vets & podiatrists
- M 3,000 i
- ¶ Health & Homeopathy - 4.

British Horn Society (BHS) 1980
NR The Cottage, Ramsdell Rd, Monk Sherborne, TADLEY, Hants,
RG26 5HS. (chmn/p)
01256 855066
▲ Registered Charity
○ *D; promotion & knowledge of the art, craft & fun of horn &
horn playing - the French Horn & Wagner Tuba
M i

British Horological Federation
in 2010 amalgamated with the **British Jewellers' Association**

British Horological Institute (BHI) 1858
■ Upton Hall, Upton, NEWARK, Notts, NG23 5TE. (hq)
01636 813795   fax 01636 812258
email clocks@bhi.co.uk   http://www.bhi.co.uk
The Secretary
▲ Company Limited by Guarantee
Br 20; 6 area representatives o'seas
○ *P; promotion of the art & science of horology to cover both the
professional & the amateur member
● Conf - Mtgs - ET - Exam - Exhib - Inf - Lib - LG
M c 3,000 i, UK / 500 i, o'seas
¶ Horological Journal - 12; ftm only.

British Horse Driving Trials Association (BHDTA) 1925
NR East Overhill, Stewarton, KILMARNOCK, Ayrshire, KA3 5JT.
(hq)
0845 643 2116   fax 0845 643 9474
email bhdta@horsedrivingtrials.co.uk
http://www.horsedrivingtrials.co.uk
Co Sec: Peter Bridson
○ *S; carriage driving
< Brit Equestrian Fedn
¶ Carriage Driving Magazine - 12.   Ybk - 1.

British Horse Society (BHS) 1947
NR Abbey Park, Stareton, KENILWORTH, Warks, CV8 2XZ.   (hq)
02476 840500   fax 02476 840501
email enquiry@bhs.org.uk   http://www.bhs.org.uk
Chief Exec: Graham Cory
▲ Registered Charity
○ *B, *V; to promote the welfare, care & use of the horse & pony;
to encourage horsemanship & the improvement of horse
management & breeding
Gp Access & rights of way; Riding clubs; Riding & road safety;
Training & education; Welfare
● Conf - ET - Exam - Exhib - Comp - Inf - LG
M c 100,000 (with those in affiliated riding clubs)
¶ British Horse - 6;   Ybk - 1; both ftm only.   AR; free.

British Horseball Association (BHA) 1991
■ Arkenfield Stables, Lowdham Rd, Gunthorpe, NOTTINGHAM,
NG14 7ER.   (hsp)
0115-966 4574
email mary.pettifor1@btinternet.com
http://www.horseball.org.uk
Chief Exec: David Pettifor
▲ Company Limited by Guarantee
Br 10
○ *S; to promote & regulate the sport of horseball
● Mtgs - ET - Exam - Comp
< Fedn Intl Horseball (FIHB); Brit Equestrian Fedn
M 200 i, 10 org, UK / 7,000 i, o'seas
¶ BHA NL - 4; free (on website).   BHA Ybk - 1; ftm, £2.50 nm.

British Hospitality Association (BHA) 1910
■ Queen's House, 55-56 Lincoln's Inn Fields, LONDON,
WC2A 3BH.   (hq)
020 7404 7744   fax 020 7404 7799
email bha@bha.org.uk   http://www.bha.org.uk
Chief Exec: Ufi Ibrahim
▲ Company Limited by Guarantee
○ *T; to be 'the effective voice of the national hotel & food service
industry'
● Conf - Mtgs - ET - Stat - Inf - LG
< Intl Hotel & Restaurants Assn (IH&RA); Eur Hotel, Restaurant &
Catering Assn (HOTREC); Eur Fedn of Contract Caterers
(FERCO)
M 25,000 f
¶ Hospitality Matters (Jnl) 3-6; ftm, £40 yr nm.
Contract Catering Survey - 1; ftm, £60 nm.
Trends & Statistics - 1; ftm, £195 nm.

British Hosta & Hemerocallis Society (BHHS) 1980
■ 29 Southdown Rd, HARPENDEN, Herts, AL5 1PF.   (hsp)
01582 713798
email msturman@waitrose.com
http://www.hostahem.org.uk
Hon Sec: Marjorie Sturman
▲ Registered Charity
Br 2
○ *H; to promote the breeding & growing of hosta & hemerocallis
Gp Hosta; Hemerocallis
● Mtgs - Res - Exhib - SG - Inf - Lib - VE - Lectures
< R Horticl Soc; Hardy Plant Soc
M 360 i, 18 f, UK / 28 i, 8 f, 2 org, o'seas
¶ British Hosta & Hemerocallis Society Bulletin - 1; ftm, £5 nm.
NL - 3; ftm, £1 nm.

**** British Housewives' League**
Organisation lost: see Introduction paragraph 3

British Humanist Association (BHA) 1963
■ 1 Gower St, LONDON, WC1E 6HD.   (hq)
020 7079 3580   fax 020 7079 3588
email info@humanism.org.uk
http://www.humanism.org.uk
Exec Dir: Hanne Stinson
▲ Company Limited by Guarantee; Registered Charity
Br 50
○ *K; 'to promote humanism & campaign against religious
privilege & discrimination on grounds of religion or belief'
Gp Ceremonies; Education
● Conf - Mtgs - ET - Res - Inf - Lib
< Intl Humanist & Ethical U
M 7,000 i, UK / 100 i, o'seas
(Sub: £35)
¶ BHA News - 6.
Books on non-religious ceremonies:
Funerals without God; £4.50.
New Arrivals; £4.
Sharing the Future; £5.
Booklets & leaflets on humanism & ethical issues.

British-Hungarian Society 1990
NR PO Box 130, HENLEY-on-THAMES, Oxon, RG9 5YU.
01491 641435
http://www.british-hungarian.co.uk
Sec: Ilona Esterhazy
○ *X
● Mtgs

© CBD Research Ltd · Beckenham · BR3 5JS · Tel 020 8650 7745 · E-mail cbd@cbdresearch.com · www.cbdresearch.com

British Hydrological Society   (BHS)   1983
NR   Institution of Civil Engineers, 1 Great George St, LONDON,
        SW1P 3AA.   (hq)
        020 7222 7722   fax 020 7222 7500
        email bhs@ice.org.uk   http://www.hydrology.org.uk
        Sec: Tim Fuller,   Hon Sec: Dr Tim Jolley
▲   Registered Charity
Br   6
○   *L; to promote interest & scholarships in both scientific &
        applied aspects of hydrology
●   Conf - Mtgs - VE - LG
<   Instn of Civil Engrs; Inst of Hydrology
M   736 i, UK / 68 i, o'seas
¶   Circulation (NL) - 4.

British Hydropower Association   (BHA)   1975
■   Unit 6B Manor Farm Business Centre, Gussage St Michael,
        WIMBORNE, Dorset, BH21 5HT.   (hq)
        01258 840934
        email info@british-hydro.org
        http://www.british-hydro.org
        Chief Exec: David Williams
▲   Company Limited by Guarantee
○   *G, *K; to represent the interests of the UK Hydropower industry
        & its associated stakeholders
Gp   Exporters
●   Conf - Mtgs - ET - Res - Exhib - Stat - Expt - Inf - VE - LG
<   Intl Hydropower Assn; Eur Small Hydro Assn (ESHA); Scot
        Renewables Forum
M   20 i, 80 f, 5 org
¶   NL - 4.

British Hypertension Society   (BHS)   1981
■   Hampton Medical Conferences Ltd, 113-119 High St,
        HAMPTON HILL, Middx, TW12 1NJ.   (meetings/sb)
        020 8979 8300   fax 020 8979 6700
        email hmc@hamptonmedical.com
        http://www.bhsoc.org
        BHS Information Service, c/o Jackie Howarth:
        Clinical Sciences Wing, Glenfield Hospital, Groby Rd,
        LEICESTER, LE3 9QP.   07717 467973.
        email bhs@le.ac.uk
        Meetings Sec: Caroline Phelan
▲   Registered Charity
○   *L, *M, *P; the pathophysiology, epidemiology, detection,
        investigation & treatment of arterial hypertension & related
        vascular diseases
●   Conf - ET - Res - Inf - LG
>   Nurses' Hypertension Assn
M   226 i, UK / 20 i, o'seas

British Hypnotherapy Association   (BHA)   1958
■   30 Cotsford Ave, NEW MALDEN, Surrey, KT3 5EU.   (hq)
        020 8942 3988
        http://www.hypnotherapy-association.org
▲   Un-incorporated Society
○   *P; for psychotherapists using hypnotherapy (when appropriate)
        in the treatment of nervous disorders, relationship difficulties,
        emotional problems
●   Mtgs - ET - Exam - Res - SG - Inf - Lib - LG - Provision of
        speakers for seminars & lectures
M   368 i, UK / 16 i, o'seas
¶   Publications list available (prices £1 - £20).

British Icelandic Sheep Breeders Group   (BISGBG)   1994
■   Cefn Maen Isaf, Saron, DENBIGH, LL16 4TH.   (hsp)
        01745 550515
        http://www.icelandicsheepbreedersofbritain.co.uk
        Hon Sec: Mrs Jill Tyrer
▲   Un-incorporated Society
○   *B; promotion of the Icelandic sheep in Britain & of the
        products from the fleece
●   ET - Exhib - Inf - LG - eGroup - Maintaining a register of
        pedigree Icelandic sheep born in Britain
<   Nat Sheep Assn
M   34 i, UK / 2 i, o'seas
        (Sub: £10 UK / £15 o'seas)
¶   Icenews & Ramblings - 2;   Flock Book - 1; both ftm only.
        Note: also known as Icelandic Sheep Breeders of Britain

British Ile de France Sheep Society
NR   6 Fort Rd, Kilroot, CARRICKFERGUS, Co Antrim, BT38 9BS.
        (hsp)
        07711 071209
        http://www.iledefrancesheep.co.uk
        Sec: Edward Adamson
▲   Un-incorporated Society
○   *B
●   Mtgs - Exhib - Comp - VE
<   Nat Sheep Assn
M   50 i

**British In Vitro Diagnostics Association Ltd   (BIVDA Ltd)
1992**
■   1 Queen Anne's Gate, LONDON, SW1H 9BT.   (hq)
        020 7957 4633   fax 020 7957 4644
        email enquiries@bivda.co.uk
        http://www.bivda.co.uk   or www.medicallab.org.uk
        Dir Gen: Doris-Ann Williams
▲   Company Limited by Guarantee
○   *T; for UK manufacturers & suppliers of in-vitro diagnostic
        products
Gp   Diabetes; Market audit; Interest groups; Point of care testing;
        Procurement; Public affairs; Regulatory affairs
●   Mtgs - ET - Exhib - Stat - Expt - Inf - LG
<   Eur Diagnostic Mfrs Assn (EDMA)
M   130 f
¶   Diagnostics in Healthcare - 3;   Annual Review - 1; both free.

British Independent Fruit Growers Association   (BIFGA)
■   Aylsham, Broad Oak, Brenchley, TONBRIDGE, Kent,
        TN12 7NN.   (contact/p)
        01892 722080
        Contact: Mrs Perry
○   *T

British Independent Motor Trade Association   (BIMTA)   1998
NR   Kenwood House, 1 Upper Grosvenor, TUNBRIDGE WELLS,
        Kent, TN1 2EL.   (hq)
        01892 779615
        email queries@bimta.org   http://www.bimta.org
        Gen Sec: Richard Moore
▲   Un-incorporated Society
○   *T; for all sectors of the independent motor trade
Gp   Importers of European & Japanese vehicles; Parts suppliers &
        servicing agents; Professional PR & lobbying
●   Conf - Mtgs - Inf - LG
<   Eur Assn of Indep Vehicle Traders (EAIVT); Eur Parallel Import
        Coalition (EPIC)
M   c 140 fUK / 4 f, o'seas
¶   LM; free for sae.

British Independent Retailers Association   (BIRA)   2009
NR   225 Bristol Rd, Edgbaston, BIRMINGHAM, B5 7UB.   (hq)
          0121-446 6688   fax 0121-446 5215
          email info@bira.co.uk   http://www.bira.co.uk
          Middleton House, 2 Main St, Middleton Cheney, BANBURY,
          Oxon, OX17 2TN.
          Chief Exec: Alan Hawkins
▲   Un-incorporated Society
Br   15
○   *K; to provide first class support, business services & specialist
          representation for member associations
Gp   British Agricultural & Garden Machinery Association
          British Hardware Federation
          British Shops & Stores Association
          Cookshop & Housewares Association
          Home Decoration Retailers Association
          Pet Product Retail Association
●   Conf - ET - LG - Mtgs - Business services
M   6 org (7,500 f)
✕   2009 (British Hardware Federation
          (British Shops & Stores Association (merged September)

British Indoor Cricket Association
          since 2009 **Indoor Cricket England**

**British Industrial Furnace Construction Association   (BIFCA)
1946**
NR   National Metalforming Centre, 47 Birmingham Rd,
          WEST BROMWICH, W Midlands, B70 6PY.   (hq)
          0121-601 6350   fax 0121-601 6387
          email enquiry@bifca.org.uk   http://www.bifca.org.uk
          Sec: David B Corns
▲   Company Limited by Guarantee
○   *T; to represent the interests of leading manufacturers of
          industrial furnaces & component suppliers
●   Mtgs - Exhib - LG - Seminars - Tech course
<   METCOM; Eur C'ee Indl Furnace & Heating Eqpt Mfrs (CECOF)
M   17 f

British Industrial Truck Association Ltd   (BITA)   1942
NR   5-7 High St, Sunninghill, ASCOT, Berks, SL5 9NQ.   (hq)
          01344 623800   fax 01244 291197
          http://www.bita.org.uk
          Sec Gen: James Clark
○   *T; industrial fork lift trucks industry
Gp   Finance houses; Importers; Major mfrs; Smaller mfrs; Suppliers
●   Conf - Mtgs - ET - Exhib - SG - Inf - LG
M   c 70 f
¶   LM & their products; free.   AR; ftm.
          Operators Safety Code for Powered Industrial Trucks.
          List of publications available.

British Infection Association   1974
NR   Hartley Taylor Ltd, Henderson House, New Rd, PRINCES
          RISBOROUGH, Bucks, HP27 0JN.   (hsb)
          01844 275650
          http://www.britishinfection.org
          Vice-Pres: Dr Peter Moss
▲   Registered Charity
○   *V, *P, *Q; to relieve sickness by the study of all aspects of
          infection; to promote the wide dissemination of relevant
          knowledge
●   Conf - Mtgs - ET - Res
<   Fedn of Infection Socs
M   c 600 i, UK / 100 i, o'seas
¶   Jnl of Infection - 6.
✕   2009 (Association of Medical Microbiologists
          (British Infection Society

British Infection Society
          2009 merged with the Association of Medical Microbiologists to form
          the **British Infection Association**

British Infertility Counselling Association   (BICA)   1988
NR   c/o S Fisher, Nuffield Health Woking Hospital, Shore's Rd,
          WOKING, Surrey, GU21 4BY.   (mail/address)
          01483 227800
          email info@bica.net   http://www.bica.net
          Chmn: Suze Fisher
▲   Registered Charity
○   *P, *W; to promote highest standards of counselling for those
          considering, or undergoing, fertility investigations & treatment
●   Conf - Mtgs - ET - SG - Inf - LG
M   c 170 i
¶   Jnl of Infertility Counselling - 3; ftm.

British Inflatable Boat Owners Association   (BIBOA)   1990
NR   Mewstone Cottage, Back Lane, Sway, LYMINGTON, Hants,
          SO41 6BU.
          http://www.biboa.com
○   *S; for owners of rigid inflatable boats; to encourage cruising,
          racing & expeditions; to stimulate design & cosntruction
¶   Riblines - 5.

British Inflatable Hirers Alliance   (BIHA)   2000
NR   130 Moordale Avenue, BRACKNELL, Berks, RG42 1TH.   (hq)
          07880 540201
          email jerram@ntworld.com   http://www.biha.org.uk
○   *T; for all businesses involved in the hire of bouncy castles &
          inflatable play equipment in the UK
M   1,600 f
¶   NL.

British Inherited Metabolic Disease Association
          a group of the **Royal College of Paediatrics & Child Health**

British Inline Puck Hockey Association   (BIPHA)
NR   PO Box 641, ROTHERHAM, S Yorks, S60 9BU   (mail)
          email secretary@bipha.co.uk   http://www.bipha.co.uk
          Chmn: Sarah Finney
○   *S; inline puck hockey is a sport with players on inline roller
          skates, played in indoor rinks with a smooth plastic surface
<   Intl Fedn of Roller Sports (FIRS); Confedn of Eur Roller
          Skating (CERS); Brit Roller Sports Fedn (BRSF)

British Inline Skater Hockey Association   (BiSHA)   1984
NR   Cumberland House, 24-28 Baxter Avenue, SOUTHEND-ON-
          SEA, Essex, SS2 6HZ.   (regd off)
          http://www.bishahockey.co.uk
          Co Sec: Elizabeth Ann Jeffries
▲   Company Limited by Guarantee (Bishahockey Ltd)
Br   12
○   *S; national governing body for inline skater hockey in Britain
●   Comp - ET - LG
<   Intl Inline-Skaterhockey Fedn (ISHF)
M   8,500 i, 500 f, UK / 10,000 i, o'seas

British Institute of Agricultural Consultants   (BIAC)   1957
■   Portbury House, Sheepway, PORTBURY, Somerset, BS20 7TE.
          (hq)
          01275 375559
          email info@biac.co.uk   http://www.biac.co.uk
          Chief Exec: C Anthony Hyde
Br   1
○   *F, *H, *P; independent qualified specialists in agriculture,
          horticulture, forestry & related sciences which have
          application in the countryside; members work in the UK &
          overseas
Gp   Business management; Engineering; Environmnet; Expert
          opinion; International; Livestock; Rural planning
●   Conf - Mtgs - ET - Exhib
<   Brit Consultants Bureau
M   c 300 i
¶   NL - 12;   LM - 1; both free.

British Institute for Allergy & Environmental Therapy   1987

- Ffynnonwen, Llangwyryfon, ABERYSTWYTH, Ceredigion, SY23 4EY.   (hq)
  01974 241376   fax 01974 241795
  email allergy@onetel.com   http://www.allergy.org.uk
  Dir: Donald M Harrison
- ▲ Un-incorporated Society
- ○ *M, *P; is concerned with the development of techniques & dissemination of information to & from health professionals in the diagnosis & treatment of food, chemical & environmental allergy; to maintain a register of therapists working in this field
- ● SG - Inf
- M 308 i, UK / 6 i, o'seas

British Institute & Association of Electrolysis Ltd   1956

- NR 40 Parkfield Rd, ICKENHAM, Middx, UB10 8LW.   (sb)
  0844 544 1373
  email sec@electrolysis.co.uk
  Sec: Nicky Wilsher
- ▲ Company Limited by Guarantee
- ○ *P
- Gp some members offer specialised treatment of broken veins, removal of warts, moles & skin tags
- ● Conf - Mtgs - ET - Exam - Exhib - Comp - Inf
- M c 320 i
- ¶ The BIAE Probe - 6;   AR; both ftm only.
  LM - up-dated; free.

British Institute of Cleaning Science   (BICSc)   1960

- NR 9 Premier Court, Boarden Close, Moulton Park, NORTHAMPTON, NN3 6LF.   (hq)
  01604 678710   fax 01604 645988
  email info@bics.org.uk   http://www.bics.org.uk
- ○ *P; training, education, qualification & certification for the cleaning industry

British Institute of Dental & Surgical Technologists   (BIDST)   1935

- 4 Thompson Green, SHIPLEY, W Yorks, BD17 7PR.   (sp)
  0845 644 3726
  http://www.bidst.org
  Sec: Beryl Dawe
- ▲ Company Limited by Guarantee
- ○ *P
- ● Conf - ET - SG

British Institute of Embalmers   (BIE)   1927

- 21c Station Rd, Knowle, SOLIHULL, W Midlands, B93 0HL. (hq)
  01564 778991   fax 01564 770812
  email info@bioe.co.uk   http://www.bioe.co.uk
  Admin Sec: I Grainger
- ○ *P; to encourage & promote the practice of embalming
- M i
- ¶ The Embalmer - 4; ftm.

British Institute of Energy Economics   (BIEE)   1976

- Stars Cottage, Stars Lane, DINTON, Bucks, HP17 8UL.   (hq)
  01296 747916
  http://www.biee.org
  Admin: Debbie Heywood
- ▲ Registered Charity
- ○ *L, *P; the study & exchange of information about energy economics

British Institute of Facilities Management Ltd   (BIFM)   1993

- NR Number One Building, The Causeway, BISHOP'S STORTFORD, Herts, CM23 2ER.   (hq)
  0845 058 1356   fax 01279 712669
  Chief Exec: Ian Fielder
- ▲ Company Limited by Guarantee
- Br 10 regions
- ○ *P; to promote & develop the science & understanding of facilities management (planning & designing office premises, buying office equipment & furniture); the institute provides a national qualification & continuing professional development (CPD) through presentations, meetings & visits
- Gp C'ees; Special interest
- ● Conf - Mtgs - ET - Exam - Res - Exhib - Inf - VE - LG
- M 9,900 i, 375 f, UK / 100 i, o'seas

British Institute of Funeral Directors   (BIFD)   1981

- NR High Oak House (suite 1), Collet Rd, WARE, Herts, SG12 7LY. (sp)
  0800 032 2733   fax 01332 225101
  email admin@bifd.org.uk   http://www.bifd.org.uk
  Chief Exec: John M G Payne
- ▲ Un-incorporated Society
- ○ *P; a professional organisation for individual qualified funeral directors
- ● Conf - Mtgs - ET - Exhib - LG - Diploma in funeral directing
- < Coun of Brit Funeral Services
- M 1,657 i, UK / 10 i, o'seas
- ¶ Jnl - 4; ftm, £12.50 yr nm.
  LM - 1;   Membership Hbk - 1; both ftm only

British Institute of Graphologists   (BIG)   1983

- PO Box 3060, GERRARDS CROSS, Bucks, SL9 9XP.   (admin/p)
  01753 891241   fax 01753 886412
  email elaine.quigley@britishgraphology.org
  http://www.britishgraphology.org
  Admin: Mrs Elaine Quigley
- ▲ Registered Charity
- ○ *P; to promote the use of graphology as a scientific tool in understanding the behavioural patterns & potential of people
- Gp Career advice; Counselling; Recruitment; Team building
- ● Conf - Mtgs - ET - Exam - Res - SG
- M 109 i, UK / 30 i, o'seas
- ¶ The Graphologist - 4; ftm, £4 nm.

British Institute of Hypnotherapy & NLP   1984

- NR 12 Heycroft Rd, LEIGH-ON-SEA, Essex, SS9 5SW.
  01702 524484
  email bih@globalnet.co.uk
  http://www.britishinstituteofhypnotherapy-nlp.com
  Contact: Mary & Peter Lawrance
- ○ *P; for hypnotherapists/psychotherapists & NLP (neuro linguist programming) practitioners
- < UK Confedn of Hypnotherapy Orgs
- M 440 i, UK / 12 i, o'seas

British Institute of Innkeeping   (BII)   1981

- NR Wessex House, 80 Park St, CAMBERLEY, Surrey, GU15 3PT. (hq)
  01276 684449
- ○ *P; the education & training of persons concerned with the day-to-day running of premises having a Justice's full licence for the sale of intoxicating liquor
- ● Conf - Mtgs - ET - Exam - Res - Exhib - Comp - SG - LG
- M 17,500 i

British Institute of International & Comparative Law   (BIICL) 1958
NR   Charles Clore House, 17 Russell Square, LONDON,
       WC1B 5JP.   (hq)
       020 7862 5151
       http://www.biicl.org
       Dir: Prof Robert McCorquodale
▲   Registered Charity
○   *L, *Q; an established independent centre with unique focus on
       linking academics & legal practitioners in the understanding
       & development of international law including the law of
       Human Rights, the Commonwealth & the European Union.
       Our mission is to understand & influence the development of
       law as this applies to an increasingly international
       community.
       This mission is fulfilled by serving as: a research organisation;
       the publisher of academic volumes; a training & advice
       centre
M   i

British Institute for Learning & Development   (BILD)
NR   Trym Lodge, 1 Henbury Rd, Westbury on Trym, BRISTOL,
       B9 3HQ.
       0117-959 6517   fax 0117-959 6518
       email info@thebild.org   http://www.thebild.org
       Manager: Sarah Wills
▲   Company Limited by Guarantee; Registered Charity
○   *E; a dynamic community, with a global reach, committed to
       innovation, best practice & excellence in innovative & well
       established techniques & technologies for learning
●   Conf - Mtgs - Res - Exhib - Inf - LG
M   314 i & org (a network of 600 i)
¶   Connect (Jnl) - 4;
       Learning Blitz (NL) [online] - 26; both ftm only.
×   2007 British Learning Association

British Institute of Learning Disabilities   (BILD)   1972
NR   Campion House, Green St, KIDDERMINSTER, Worcs,
       DY10 1JL.   (hq)
       01562 723010   fax 01562 723029
       email enquiries@bild.org.uk   http://www.bild.org.uk
       Chief Exec: Keith Smith
▲   Registered Charity
○   *W; to contribute towards quality lifestyles for people with
       learning disabilities
Gp   People with learning disabilities; People with profound &
       multiple disabilities
●   Conf - ET - Res - Inf - Lib - Publishing
<   University of Birmingham
M   c 1,300 i, f & org
¶   British Jnl of Learning Disabilities - 4;
       Learning Disability Bulletin - 4;
       Journal of Applied Research in Intellectual Disabilities - 4;
       Current Awareness Service - 12; all ftm.

British Institute of Musculoskeletal Medicine   (BIMM)   1992
NR   PO Box 1116, BUSHEY, Herts, WD23 9BY.   (hsp)
       020 8421 9910
       email info@bimm.org.uk   http://www.bimm.org.uk
       Chief Exec: Deena Harris
▲   Registered Charity
○   *E, *M, *P; dissemination of knowledge & increase of expertise
       in musculoskeletal medicine within the medical profession
●   Conf - Mtgs - ET - Res
<   Brit League against Rheumatism (BLAR); Intl Fedn Manual
       Medicine (FIMM)
M   300 i, UK / 60 i, o'seas
¶   Jnl of Orthopaedic Medicine - 4; ftm.

British Institute of Non-Destructive Testing   (BInstNDT)   1954
NR   Newton Building, St George's Avenue, NORTHAMPTON,
       NN2 6JB.   (hq)
       01604 893811
       email info@bindt.org   http://www.bindt.org
▲   Company Limited by Guarantee; Registered Charity
○   *L; 'to promote the advancement of the science & practice of
       non-destructive testing & all other associated materials
       testing disciplines'
M   i

British Institute of Organ Studies   (BIOS)   1976
■   Ashcroft 10 Ridgegate Close, REIGATE, Surrey, RH2 0HT.   (hsp)
       01737 241355
       http://www.bios.org.uk
       Hon Sec: Melvin Hughes
▲   Registered Charity
○   *L; promotion of scholarly research into the history of organs
       (particularly British organs); preservation & conservation of
       historic organs; information sources & materials
Gp   Brit Organ Archive; National Pipe Organ Register; Historic
       organs certificate scheme
●   Conf - Mtgs - Res - SG - VE - LG
M   671 i
¶   Jnl - 1;   Reporter - 4; both ftm.

British Institute of Persian Studies   (BIPS)   1961
NR   c/o The British Academy, 10 Carlton House Terrace, LONDON,
       SW1Y 5AH.   (hq)
       020 7969 5203
       http://www.bips.ac.uk
       Sec: Mariam Emamy
▲   Registered Charity
○   *L; promotion of Iranian studies including language, history, art
       history & archaeology
M   i

British Institute of Professional Dog Trainers   (BIPDT)   1974
■   Bowstone Gate, DISLEY, Cheshire, SK12 2AW.   (regd/office)
       01663 762772
       email info@bipdt.org.uk   http://www.bipdt.org.uk
       Contact: General Secretary
▲   Company Limited by Guarantee
○   *P; to compile a register of qualified trainers of working dogs;
       to raise the standard of training, management, welfare &
       usage of working dogs
Gp   Security
●   ET - Exam - Inf - Seminars
M   750 i, 27 f, 37 org, UK / 40 i, o'seas
¶   Training & Education Jnl - 3.

British Institute of Professional Photography   (BIPP)   1901
NR   1 Prebendal Court, Oxford Rd, AYLESBURY, Bucks, HP19 8EY.
       (hq)
       01296 718530   fax 01296 336367
       email info@bipp.com   http://www.bipp.com
       Chief Exec: Chris Harper
▲   Company Limited by Guarantee
○   *P
Gp   Advertising; Architectural; Audio Visual Association; Cine;
       Commercial/Industrial; Education; Medical; Photo-science;
       Portraiture; Theatre; Wedding
●   Conf - Mtgs - ET - Exam - Exhib - Comp - SG - Inf - LG
<   Wld Coun Profl Photographers; Fedn Eur Photographers; Profl
       Photographers of America; Brit Copyright Coun; BSI; Photo
       Imaging Coun
M   3,673 i, UK / 260 i, o'seas
¶   The Photographer - 12; ftm, £4,25 nm.   AR; ftm only.

British Institute of Radiology   (BIR)   1897
NR   36 Portland Place, LONDON, W1B 1AT.   (hq)
         020 7307 1400
         http://www.bir.org.uk
▲   Registered Charity
○   *L; an independent forum to bring together all the professions
      in radiology; to share medical & scientific knowledge to
      detect & treat disease
M   i

British Institute of Verbatim Reporters   (BIVR)   1887
NR   73 Alicia Gardens, Kenton, HARROW, Middx, HA3 8JD.   (regd
         off)
         fax 020 8907 5820
         email sec@bivr.org.uk   http://www.bivr.org.uk
         Sec: Mary Sorene
▲   Company Limited by Guarantee
○   *P; to promote the more efficient practice of the art of machine
      & pen shorthand in connection with legal & other
      proceedings
M   179 i
¶   NL - 3; free.

British Insurance Brokers' Association   (BIBA)   1977
■   John Stow House (8th floor), 18 Bevis Marks, LONDON,
         EC3A 7JB.   (hq)
         0844 770 0266   fax 020 7626 9676
         email enquiries@biba.org.uk   http://www.biba.org.uk
         Chief Exec: Eric Galbraith
▲   Company Limited by Guarantee
○   *T; representing insurance brokers & independent
      intermediaries
●   Conf - Mtgs - ET - Inf - LG
M   2,100 f
¶   The Broker (Jnl) - 4;
         BIBA Membership Directory - 1; both ftm only.

British Insurance Law Association   (BILA)   1964
■   47 Bury St, STOWMARKET, Suffolk, IP14 1HD.   (hsb)
         07776 115795   fax 01449 770941
         email secretariat@bila.org.uk   http://www.bila.org.uk
         Secretariat: Doug Jordan
▲   Un-incorporated Society
○   *P; to consider & discuss matters of general interest arising out
      of the law, (both statutory & common, including tax law &
      regulations & current revenue practice) in so far as it affects
      any branch of insurance
●   Conf - Mtgs - Res - SG
<   Assn Intle de Droit des Assurances (AIDA)
M   225 i, 485 f, UK / 20 i, 23 f, o'seas
¶   BILA Jnl - 3; ftm.

British Interactive Group
NR   148 Taff Embankment, CARDIFF, CF11 7BJ.   (admin/b)
         email admin@big.uk.com   http://www.big.uk.com
         Admin: Sarah Vining
○   *G; 'the skills sharing network for individuals involved in the
      communication of science, technology, engineering & maths'

British Interactive Media Association   (BIMA)   1984
NR   The Lightwell, 12-16 Laystall St, Clerkenwell, LONDON,
         EC1R 4PF.   (hq)
         020 7843 6797
         email info@bima.co.uk   http://www.bima.co.uk
○   *T; to promote the use of interactive media in commerce &
      industry
●   Conf - Mtgs - ET - Exhib - Comp - SG - Expt - Inf - LG - BIMA
      Awards
M   i & f
¶   E-Newsletter - 12; m only.

British Interior Design Association   (BIDA)   1966
NR   109-111 The Chambers, Chelsea Harbour, LONDON,
         SW10 0XF.   (hq)
         020 7349 0800   fax 020 7349 0500
         email enquiries@bida.org
         Exec Mgr: Joy Whittaker
▲   Company Limited by Guarantee
○   *P, *T; to support the interior decorator/designer member & the
      corporate member
●   Mtgs - ET - Exhib - PL - VE
<   Intl Fedn of Interior Architects (IFI)
M   c 1,100 i & f
¶   Review - 4; ftm, £117.50 nm.
         Directory of Members & Associates - 1; ftm.

British Interior Textiles Association   (BITA)   1987
NR   3 Queen Sq, Bloomsbury, LONDON, WC1N 3AR.   (hq)
         020 7843 9460   fax 020 7843 9478
         email enquiries@interiortextiles.co.uk
         http://www.interiortextiles.co.uk
         Sec: Adam Mansell
○   *T
●   Mtgs - Exhib - Comp - Stat - Expt - LG
<   Brit Apparel & Textile Confedn
M   f

British Interlingua Society   (BIS)   1955
NR   14 Ventnor Court, Wostenholm Rd, SHEFFIELD, S Yorks,
         S7 1LB.   (hsp)
         0114-258 2931
         Sec: Brian C Sexton
▲   Un-incorporated Society
○   *K; to inform as many people as possible, mainly in GB, of the
      existence & character of the international auxiliary language
      'Interlingua'; to promote & coordinate its use
<   U Mundial pro Interlingua
M   c 20 i
¶   Lingua e Vita - 3.   Contacto - 3.

**British & International Federation of Festivals for Music, Dance &
Speech   1921**
NR   Festivals House, 198 Park Lane, MACCLESFIELD, Cheshire,
         SK11 6UD.   (hq)
         0870 774 4290
▲   Company Limited by Guarantee
○   *G; headquarters of the amateur competitive festival movement
M   i & f

British International Freight Association   (BIFA)   1944
■   Redfern House, Browells Lane, FELTHAM, Middx, TW13 7EP.
         (hq)
         020 8844 2266   fax 020 8890 5546
         email bifa@bifa.org   http://www.bifa.org
         Dir Gen: Peter Quantrill
▲   Company Limited by Guarantee
○   *T; for the international transport sector
Gp   Freight forwarders; Logistics services supplies; Supply chain
         management; International traders; General sales agents;
         Transit shed operators; Export packers
●   Conf - Mtgs - ET - Exhib - LG - Political lobbying - Promotion &
      advice
<   Intl Fedn of Freight Forwarders Assns (FIATA); Intl Air Transport
      Assn (IATA); Eur Org for Forwarding & Logistics (CLECAT)
M   1,203 f
¶   Bifalink (NL) - 12; ftm.   AR - 1; both ftm.
         Freight Services Directory - 1; ftm, £95 nm.

**British & International Golf Greenkeepers' Association
(BIGGA)   1987**
NR   BIGGA House, Aldwark, Alne, YORK, YO61 1UF.   (hq)
         01347 833800
         Chief Exec Dir: John Pemberton
▲   Un-incorporated Society
○   *P; to represent golf greenkeepers throughout the UK
M   6,580 i, 20 f, UK / 400 i, o'seas

British International Studies Association   (BISA)   1975
NR   International Politics Bldg, Aberystwyth University, Penglais,
       ABERYSTWYTH, SY23 3FE.   (admin/b)
       01970 628672
○   *P; to promote the study of international relations & related
       subjects through teaching, research & facilitating contact
       between scholars

British Internet Publishers Alliance
       has closed

British Interplanetary Society   (BIS)   1933
NR   27-29 South Lambeth Rd, LONDON, SW8 1SZ.   (hq)
       020 7735 3160
○   *L; promotion of the science, engineering & technology of
       astronautics
M   i

British Iris Society   (BIS)   1922
■   Mill House, Woodlands Lane, CHICHESTER, W Sussex,
       PO19 3PA.   (memsec/p)
       http://www.britishirissociety.org.uk
       Mem Sec: Mrs J Christianson
▲   Registered Charity
○   *H; irises, in the wild & in cultivation & other members of the
       Iridaceae
Gp   Crocus; Remontant; Species; Siberian; Spuria & Japanese
●   Conf - Mtgs - Exhib - Comp - SG - Inf - Lib - PL (& slides) -
       Registration & trials for new cultivars
<   R Horticl Soc; American Iris Soc
M   300 i, UK / 100 i, 20 org, o'seas
       (Sub: £14 i, £7, students)
¶   NL - 2;   Ybk - 1; both ftm only.

British & Irish Association of Law Librarians   (BIALL)   1969
NR   Box 123, 12 South Bridge, EDINBURGH, EH1 1DD.   (hsb)
       07788 443817
       email admin@biall.org.uk   http://www.biall.org.uk
       Hon Sec: Elaine Bird
▲   Un-incorporated Society
○   *P; to promote the better administration & exploitation of law
       libraries & legal information units; to encourage
       bibliographical study & research in law & librarianship, &
       cooperation with other organisations & societies
Gp   Marketing; Academic; Law libraries
●   Conf - ET - Exhib
<   Amer Assn of Law Libs (AALL); Canadian Assn of Law
       Libs (CALL)
M   680 i, 162 f
¶   Legal Information Management - 4; ftm, £98 nm.
       BIALL NL - 6; ftm only.

**British & Irish Association of Zoos & Aquariums   (BIAZA)
1966**
NR   Regent's Park, LONDON, NW1 4RY.   (hq)
       020 7449 6351   fax 020 7449 6359
       http://www.biaza.org.uk
       Dir: Dr Miranda Stevenson,   Admin: Gwen Manning
▲   Registered Charity
○   *P, *V; to represent the zoo community in Britain & Ireland; to
       maintain the world's biodiversity, the welfare of animals in
       zoos & the advancement of scientific knowledge
●   Conf - Mtgs - ET - Inf - LG
<   Wld Assn Zoos & Aquaria (WAZA); Wld Consvn U (IUCN); Eur
       Assn Zoos & Aquaria (EAZA)
>   Wld Assn of Zoos & Aquariums (WAZA); Eur Assn of Zoos &
       Aquaria (EAZA)
M   66 i, 69 zoos
¶   Zoo Federation News - 3;   LM; both ftm only.

**British & Irish Legal Education Technology Association
(BILETA)   1986**
NR   c/o UK Centre for Legal Education, University of Warwick,
       COVENTRY, Warks, CV4 7AL.   (hq)
       024 7652 3117   fax 024 7652 3290
○   *P; promoting technology in legal education & improving
       contacts between academics & practising professionals in UK
       & Ireland
M   i

British & Irish Ombudsman Association   (BIOA)   1993
■   PO Box 308, TWICKENHAM, Middx, TW1 9BE.   (hq)
       020 8894 9272
       email secretary@bioa.org.uk   http://www.bioa.org.uk
       Sec: Ian Pattison
○   *P; the role of ombudsmen in both public & private sectors
●   Conf - Mtgs - SG - Inf - LG
M   112 i, 45 org, UK / 11 i, 6 org, o'seas
¶   NL - 3/4;   Reports of Conferences - 2 yrly; both ftm only.
       Directory of Ombudsmen - up-dated; on Internet.

British & Irish Orthoptic Society   (BIOS)   1937
■   62 Wilson St, LONDON, EC2A 2BU.   (hq)
       01353 665541   fax 07050 659103
       email membership@orthoptics.org.uk
       http://www.orthoptics.org.uk
       Business Mgrs: Anita McCallum,   Hamish McCallum
▲   Company Limited by Guarantee; Registered Charity
Br   6
○   *M, *P, *U; to encourage, study & improve practice of orthoptics
Gp   Glaucoma; Low vision; Special learning difficulties; Stroke &
       rehabilitation
●   Conf - Mtgs - ET - Stat - Inf - Empl - LG
<   Allied Health Professions Fedn; Intl Orthoptic Assn (IOA);
       Orthoptistes de la Communauté Européenne (OCE); TUC
M   869 i
¶   British Orthoptic Jnl; ftm, £50 nm.
       Parallel Vision - 12; ftm only.

British & Irish Spa & Hot Tub Association
NR   4 Eastgate House, East St, ANDOVER, Hants, SP10 1EP.
       01264 356211
       http://www.bishta.co.uk
○   *T

British Isles Backgammon Association   (BIBA)   1989
NR   2 Redbourne Drive, LINCOLN, LN2 2HG.   (hq)
       01522 888676   fax (telephone first)
       Dir: Michael Crane
▲   Un-incorporated Society
○   *S; to promote the game of backgammon
●   Conf - Mtgs - ET - Comp - Stat - Inf
M   1,200 i, clubs
¶   Bibafax (NL) - 6; free.

British Isles Baton Twirling Association   (BIBTA)
NR   208 Horninglow Rd, Firth Park, SHEFFIELD, S Yorks, S5 6SG.
       (hq)
       0114-220 4010
       email bibta@ymail.com   http://www.bibta.co.uk
▲   Registered Charity
Br   3
○   *G
●   Mtgs - ET - Exhib - Comp - Inf - VE

© CBD Research Ltd · Beckenham · BR3 5JS · Tel 020 8650 7745 · E-mail cbd@cbdresearch.com · www.cbdresearch.com

British Isles Bowls Council (BIBC) 1903

■ 12/1 Oxgangs Avenue, EDINBURGH, Midlothian, EH13 9JB. (hsp)
0131-455 5838
email michaelswatland@btinternet.com
http://www.britishislesbowls.com
Hon Sec: Duncan McClaren
▲ Un-incorporated Society
○ *S; the game of flat green bowls
● Comp - Organisation of British Isles championships; & the Senior & Junior International series
< World Bowls Ltd
> English / Scottish / Irish / Welsh / Jersey / Guernsey Bowling Assns
M 265,000 i

British Isles Indoor Bowls Council (BIIBC)

NR 25 Saltford Close, Gedling, NOTTINGHAM, NG4 4BD. (hsp)
0115-961 9831 fax 01656 849160
email trevor-costall@sky.com http://www.biibc.org.uk
Hon Sec & Treas: Trevor Costall
▲ Un-incorporated Society
Br 5
○ *S; to promote the game of indoor bowls & to be responsible for the promotion of all British Isles-run championships
● Mtgs - Comp - Inf
< Wld Indoor Bowls Coun
> English / Welsh / Scot / Guernsey Indoor Bowling Assn[s]; Assn of Irish Indoor Bowls; Brit Wheelchair Bowling Assn
M 13,781 i, 6 f, 435 org

British-Italian Society (BIS) 1941

NR 7 Hanover Rd, LONDON, NW10 3DJ. (gen/sec)
020 8150 9167
email info@british-italian.org
http://www.british-italian.org
▲ Registered Charity
○ *X; to increase knowledge & understanding in the UK of Italian culture in terms of history, institutions, way of life, language & contribution to civilisation; to promote the traditional friendship between UK & Italy
● Mtgs - Exhib - Inf - VE - Archive
< Associazione Cultivale Italia-Inghilterra (Sardinia); St Peter's Italian Church (London)
M 445 i, 9 f, 1 org, UK / 17 i, 1 org, o'seas
¶ Rivista - 3/4; free.

British Jewellers' Association (BJA) 1887

■ Federation House, 10 Vyse St, BIRMINGHAM, B18 6LT. (hq)
0121-237 1110 fax 0121-237 1113
http://www.bja.org.uk
Chief Exec: Simon Rainer
○ *T; to promote & protect the growth & prosperity of UK jewellery & silverware suppliers; BJA represents manufacturers, bullion suppliers, casting houses, diamond & gem dealers, designer jewellers, craftsmen & -women, equipment suppliers, wholesalers, galleries, internet retailers & traders
< Brit Allied Trs Fedn (BATF)
M 1,000 f
× 2010 British Horological Federation (merged)

British Jewellery, Giftware & Finishing Federation Ltd
since 2011 **British Allied Trades Federation**

British Jigsaw Puzzle Library (BJPL) 1933

■ Clarendon, Parsonage Rd, HERNE BAY, Kent, CT6 5TA. (hsp)
01227 742222
http://www.britishjigsawpuzzlelibrary.co.uk
Owner: Dave Cooper
○ *G; lending library of wooden jigsaws operated on a postal basis to private individuals who join by subscription; (personal callers by appointment only)
● Lib
M c 350 i, UK / 10 i, o'seas

British Ju Jitsu Association GB (BJJAGB) 1960

NR 5 Avenue Parade, ACCRINGTON, Lancs, BB5 6PN.   (chmn/p)
01254 396806 fax 01254 391234
email chairman@bjjagb.com   http://www.bjjagb.com
Chmn: Martin Dixon
○ *S; the national governing body, providing instruction & governance in the martial art of ju jitsu
● Comp - ET - Exam
< Intl Ju Jitsu Fedn (JJIF); Sport & Recreation Alliance

British Judo Association (BJA) 1948

NR Loughborough Technology Park (suite B), Epinal Way, LOUGHBOROUGH, Leics, LE11 3GE.   (hq)
01509 631670 fax 01509 631680
email bja@britishjudo.org.uk
http://www.britishjudo.org.uk
Chief Exec: Scott McCarthy
▲ Company Limited by Guarantee
○ *S; the governing body to control, foster & develop the practice & spirit of judo
< Intl Judo Fedn; Eur Judo U; Judo Confedn of the Eur U; Brit Olympic Assn; Cent Coun for Physical Recreation; C'wealth Judo Assn; C'wealth Games Coun
M 30,000 i

British Kennel & Cattery Association
a group of the **Pet Care Trade Association**

British Kerry Cattle Society

NR Windle Hill Farm, Sutton on the Hill, ASHBOURNE, Derbys, DE6 5JH. (hsp)
01283 732377
Hon Sec: Mrs Joan Lennard
▲ Registered Charity
○ *B
● Inf
M c 40 i
¶ NL - irreg.

British Kidney Patient Association (BKPA) 1975

NR 3 The Windmills, St Mary's Close, Turk St, ALTON, Hants, GU34 1EF. (hq)
01420 541424
Chmn: Sally Taber
▲ Company Limited by Guarantee; Registered Charity
○ *W; benefit & welfare of kidney patients & their families; to lobby for more & improved facilities & increased government funding so that all patients may benefit from improvements in technology & pharmaceutical achievements
● Inf
M i
¶ Silver Lining Appeal Brochure - 1; free.

British Kite Surfing Association (BKSA) 1999

NR Manor Barn, Stottingway St, Uppway, WEYMOUTH, Dorset, DT3 5QA. (hq)
01305 8135552
email info@bksaonline.org
http://www.britishkitesurfingassociation.co.uk
Chmn: Richard Gowers
○ *S

British Kodály Academy   (BKA)   1981
- ■ c/o 10 Lapwing Close, SOUTH CROYDON, Surrey,
  CR2 8TD.   (sp)
  020 8651 3728
  email enquiries@britishkodalyacademy.org
  http://www.britishkodalyacademy.org
  Sec: Cyrilla Rowsell
- ▲ Registered Charity
- ○ *E; a music education charity, using the voice as the main
  instrument; to improve British music education through
  courses for anyone wanting to develop their own, or others,
  musical skills, using Kodály's principles
- Gp Courses: Certificate in early years music education; Certificate
  in primary education; Intermediate & advanced diplomas in
  Kodály's musicianship; Elementary & foundation courses,
  early years & SEN
- ● Conf - ET - Exam - Res - Exhib - Inf - Lib
- < Intl Kodály Soc (IKS)
- M 210 i
- ¶ NL - 3; ftm.
  How Can I Keep from Singing (songbook for ages 8-11);
  £20 including double CD.

British Korfball Association   (BKA)   1946
- NR 3 Mill Lane, Blue Bell Hill, CHATHAM, Kent, ME5 9RB.
  (finance offr/p)
  01634 864053
  email fiannce@korfball.co.uk   http://www.korfball.co.uk
  Finance officer: David Hubbard
  Gen Sec: Jackie Hoare (07814 004135)
- ▲ Un-incorporated Society
- ○ *S; governing body of the sport of Korfball in the UK
- Gp Area associations; Competitions; Exams
- ● Mtgs - ET - Exam - Comp
- < Intl Korfball Fedn (IKF)
- M 51 clubs
- ¶ Korfball - 3; ftm, £1.50 each nm.

British Kune Kune Pig Society   (BKKPS)   1993
- NR Llanbister, LLANDRINDOD WELLS, Powys, LD1 6TW.   (sp)
  01597 840321
  email alison212@aol.com
  http://www.britishkunekunepigsociety.co.uk
  Sec: Alison Shinn
- ▲ Un-incorporated Society
- ○ *B
- ● Mtgs - ET - Expt - Inf - PL
- < New Zealand Kune Kune Pig Soc
- M c 300 i

British Lace Federation   (BLF)   1914
- NR c/o Lemans, 29 Arboretum St, NOTTINGHAM, NG1 4JA.
  (asa)
  0115-978 7291
  email davidm@lemans.co.uk
  Gen Sec: Jane Whitfield,   Contact: David Marshall
- ○ *T; all aspects of lace manufacture
- M f

British Ladder Manufacturers Association
    since 2010 **Ladder Association**

British Laminate Fabricators Association
- ■ PO Box 775, BROSELEY WOOD, Shropshire, TF7 9FG.
  0845 056 8496
  http://www.blfa.co.uk
  Contact: Christopher D Thomas
- ○ *T

British Land Speedsail Association   (BLSA)   1989
- ■ 103 Mead Vale, Worle, WESTON-super-MARE, Somerset,
  BS22 8XE.   (sp)
  01934 511780
  email chris@theblsa.com   http://www.theblsa.com
  Mem Sec: Chris Moore
- ○ *S; to promote blokarting & land speedsailing in the UK; to
  organise racing in the UK
- Gp Blokarting; Land speedsailing
- ● Comp - Provision of 3rd party liability insurance
- < Land Yachting Assn
- M 180 i
  (Sub: £40)

British Landsailing
    see **British Federation of Sand & Land Yacht Clubs**

British Lawn Mower Racing Association   (BLMRA)   1973
- ■ Hunt Cottage, Wisborough Green, BILLINGSHURST, W Sussex,
  RH14 0HN.   (hsp)
  email info@blmra.co.uk   http://www.blmra.co.uk
  Pres & Hon Sec: Jim Gavin
- ▲ Company Limited by Guarantee
- ○ *G; organisation of lawn mower races
- ● Mtgs - ET - Comp - Inf - VE - Film shows
- < R Automobile Club
- M c 300 i, UK & o'seas
- ¶ Cuttings (NL) - 12; ftm.

British Leafy Salads Association   (BLSA)
- ■ PVGA House, Nottingham Rd, LOUTH, Lincs, LN11 0WB.
  (asa)
  01507 602427   fax 01507 600689
  email jayne.dyas@pvga.co.uk
  http://www.britishleafysalads.co.uk
  Sec: Mrs Jayne Dyas
- ▲ Company Limited by Guarantee
- ○ *T; to commercially increase consumption of UK salad product
- ● Conf - Mtgs - Res - Exhib - Stat - Inf - LG
- M 120 f

British Learning Association
    since 2007 **British Institute for Learning & Development**

British Lebanese Association
- NR 1 Hyde Park Gate, LONDON, SW7 5EW.
  020 7370 2572
  Dir: Lenia Tannous
- ○ *X

British Legal Association   (BLA)   1964
- NR c/o Stanley Best, Barnstaple Chambers, WINKLEIGH, Devon,
  EX19 8ED.   (hq)
  01837 83763
  Chmn: Stanley Best
- ○ *P; to look after the interests of solicitors in general
- M 1,700 i

British Legion
    see **Royal British Legion**

British Lichen Society   (BLS)   1958
- NR c/o Botany Dept, Natural History Museum, Cromwell Rd,
  LONDON, SW7 5BD.   (mail/address)
  Royal Botanic Garden Edinburgh, 20A Inverleith Row,
  EDINBURGH, EH3 5LR   (sb)
  Sec: Dr Chris Ellis
- ▲ Registered Charity
- ○ *L; to promote the study of lichens
- ● Mtgs - ET - Res - Exhib - Inf - Lib
- M c 600 i, 160 institutions
- ¶ The Lichenologist - 6.   Bulletin - 2.

British Limb Reconstruction Society
  a specialist society of the **British Orthopaedic Association**

British Limbless Ex-Service Men's Association   (BLESMA) 1932
■ Frankland Moore House 185-187 High Rd, Chadwell Heath, ROMFORD, Essex, RM6 6NA.   (hq)
    020 8590 1124   fax 020 8599 2932
    email headquarters@blesma.org
    http://www.blesma.org
    Gen Sec: J W Church
▲ Company Limited by Guarantee; Registered Charity
Br 36
○ *W; to promote the welfare of all those, of either sex, who have lost limb(s) or eye(s), or the use of limb(s) or sight, after or as a result of service in any branch of HM Forces (incl their needy dependents)
Gp Amputee counselling; Residential homes
● Conf - Mtgs - Res - Inf - VE - LG - Counselling service for amputees - Welfare visiting service - Residential homes - Grants
< Wld Veterans Fedn; Intl Soc of Prosthetics & Orthotics; Confedn of British Service & Ex-service Orgs; NCVO; RADAR
M 4,720 i, UK / 95 i, o'seas
¶ BLESMAG - 3; ftm, £1 each nm.
    Out on a Limb [history of association] (1982); £2 m, £5 nm.
    Making the Best of Amputation (2003); ftm, 20p + postage nm.
    Driving after Amputation (1991); postage.
    Amputees Guide; £1.   AR; free.

British Lime Association
  is a product group of the **Mineral Products Association**

British Limousin Cattle Society Ltd   (BLCS)   1970
■ Avenue Q, National Agricultural Centre, STONELEIGH, Warks, CV8 2RA.   (hq)
    024 7669 6500   fax 024 7669 6716
    email info@limousin.co.uk   http://www.limousin.co.uk
    Chief Exec: Iain Kerr
▲ Registered Charity
○ *B; pedigree beef cattle society
● Mtgs - Expt - VE
< Intl Limousin Coun; Eurolim; Nat Beef Assn
M 2,500 i, 10 f, 10 org
¶ News Magazine - 3.   Studbook - 1.   AR.
    Herdbook - 1.   Sire & Dam Summary - 1.

British Lingual Orthodontic Society   (BLOS)
NR BLOS Office, British Orthodontic Society, 12 Bridewell Place, LONDON, EC4V 6AP.
    020 7353 8680   fax 020 7353 8682
    http://www.blos.co.uk
M i
    (Sub: £150 i, £75 (postgraduate))

British Lithuanian Society   1994
■ 34 Thurleigh Road, LONDON, SW12 8UD.   (hsp)
    http://www.britishlithuaniansociety.org.uk
    Sec: Aleksas Vilčinskas
○ *X
¶ Tiltas - 2; ftm

British Livestock Genetics Consortium Ltd
NR Brackenford, Fernhill Lane, Fen End, KENILWORTH, Warks, CV8 1NU.
    0778 955 3449
    http://www.britishlivestockgenetics.com
    Contact: Caroline Hadley
○ *T; the development & maintenance of profitable long-term business generated by exports of British livestock & genetics; to create a positive, favourable image in international markets & promote Britain as a supplier of high quality animals & germplasm

British Llama Society   2005
NR Nutfield Park Farm, SOUTH NUTFIELD, Surrey, RH1 5PA.
    01737 823375
    email secretary@britishllamasociety.org
    http://www.britishllamasociety.org
    Enquiries: Liz Butler
○ *B

British Locksmiths & Keycutters Association   (BLKA)
NR 3 Murrow Lane, Parson Drove, WISBECH, Cambs, PE13 4JH.   (hq)
    0845 644 5397   fax 01945 701552
    email enquire@blka.co.uk   http://www.blka.co.uk
    Mem Sec: Denise Mace (Adenash@aol.com)
○ *P

British Long Distance Swimming Association   (BLDSA)   1956
■ 1 Cairns Rd, MURTON SEAHAM, Co Durham, SR7 9TD.   (mem/sp)
    0191-526 4215
    http://www.bldsa.org.uk
    Mem Sec: Vince Classen
▲ Un-incorporated Society
○ *S; to further & promote the sport of open water, long distance (below 25km) & marathon (25km & above) swimming
● Mtgs - ET - Exam - Comp - Stat
M c 450 i, c 20 org
¶ Hbk - 1.

British Longevity Society   (BLS)   1993
NR PO Box 4202, DUNSTABLE, Beds, LU5 5WU.   (mail/address)
    fax 07092 350063
    http://www.thebls.org
○ to further public education on issues connected with the means of counteracting the processes, causes and effects of ageing

British Lop Pig Society   (BLPS)   1920
■ Farm Five, The Moss, WHIXALL, Shropshire, SY13 2PF.   (hsp)
    01948 880243; 07759 487469
    email secretary@britishloppig.org.uk
    http://www.britishloppig.org.uk
    Hon Sec: Frank Miller
▲ Un-incorporated Society
○ *B
● Mtgs
< Rare Breeds Survival Trust
M c 40 i
¶ Herd Book - 1; £3.

British Lymphology Society   (BLS)   1985
■ The Garth House, Rushey Lock, Tadpole Bridge, Buckland Marsh, Nr FARINGDON, Oxon, SN7 8RF.   (hq)
    01452 790178
    http://www.thebls.co.uk
    Chmn: Alex Munnoch
▲ Registered Charity
○ *P; for health care professionals & other interested parties involved in the management of lymphoedema; to raise awareness of oedema amongst all health professionals
● Conf - Mtgs - ET - Res - Exhib - Sg - Inf - LG - Writing protocols
< Intl Soc of Lymphologists (ISL); Eur Soc of Lymphologists (ESL); Intl Lymphoedema Framework (ILF); Lymphoedema Support Network
M 350 i, 8 f, UK / 10 i, o'seas
    (Sub £48 i, £1,500 f, UK / £15 o'seas)
¶ BLS News & Views - 6; ftm, £5 nm.   AR - 1; free.

British Machine Vision Association & Society for Pattern Recognition   (BMVA)   1990
■   c/o Dr Andrew Fitzgibbon, Microsoft Research Ltd,
      7 JJ Thomson Avenue, CAMBRIDGE, CB3 0FB.   (chmn/b)
      01223 479899
      http://www.bmva.ac.uk
      Chmn: Dr Andrew Fitzgibbon
▲   Company Limited by Guarantee; Registered Charity
Br 3
○   *L; to promote knowledge & application of machine vision &
      pattern recognition
Gp Computer vision, image analysis; Machine vision education &
      training
●   Conf - Mtgs - ET - Res - Exhib - SG - Stat - Inf - PL - VE - LG
<   Intl Assn for Pattern Recognition (IAPR); Mammographic Image
      Analysis Soc
M   c 400 i, UK / c 50 i, o'seas
¶   BMVA News - 4; free.
      Proceedings of the British Machine Vision Conference - 1; free
      to delegates, £25 (sales).

British Magical Society   (BMS)   1905
NR The Selly Oak Ex-Servicemen's Club, 8 Selly Hill Rd, Selly Oak,
      BIRMINGHAM, B29 7DL.   (hsp)
      0121-451 3944
      Hon Sec: Paul Cadley
▲   Un-incorporated Society
○   *G, *P; the furtherance of the art of magic
Gp Junior section (ages 10-16)
●   Mtgs - Comp - Lib
M   107 i, UK / 4 i, o'seas
¶   BMS News - 6; ftm only.

British Malaysian Society   (BMS)   1983
NR Kemp House, 152-160 City Rd, LONDON, EC1V 2NX.   (sb)
      020 7307 5454
      email info@thebritishmalaysiansociety.org
      Hon Sec: Anthony Cooper
▲   Un-incorporated Society
○   *X; bi-lateral friendship society
M   i & f

British Malignant Hyperthermia Association   (BMHA)   1983
§   MH Investigation Unit, St James Hospital, Beckett St, LEEDS,
      W Yorks, LS9 7TF.
      01773 717901
      email helpline@bmha.co.uk   http://www.bmha.co.uk
      Sec: Mrs Alison Winks
▲   Registered Charity
○   *M, *W; help & advice to persons & families affected by
      malignant hyperthermia (very high body temperature) during
      a general anaesthesia
●   Helpline: 01773 717901
      To provide medical and medico-social support for individuals
      affected by malignant hyperthermia (progressive raising of
      body temperature during general anaesthesia).

British Manual Lymph Drainage Association   (BMLDA)   2000
■   PO Box 309, SUTTON, Surrey, SM1 9DE.   (hsp)
      020 8133 5686
      http://www.bmlda.org.uk
      Contact: Nina Pearson
▲   Company Limited by Guarantee
Br Regional
○   *M, *P; to advance education & knowledge & develop the
      standards of practice of therapists in the treatment of manual
      lymph drainage; membership is open to those who have
      qualified
●   Conf - Mtgs - ET - Exam - Res - Exhib - Inf
<   Inst of Complementary Medicine; Brit Lymphology Soc
M   c 50 i & f
¶   Networks (NL) - 6; ftm only.

British Marine Aggregates Producers Association
      is a product group of the **Mineral Products Association**

British Marine Electronics Association
      a group association of the **British Marine Federation**

British Marine Equipment Association   (BMEA)   1966
NR 28-29 Threadneedle St, LONDON, EC2R 8AY.   (hq)
      020 7628 2555   fax 020 7638 4376
      email bmea@maritimeindustries.org
      http://www.maritimeindustries.org
      Dir: John Southerden
▲   Company Limited by Guarantee
○   *T; 'representing the interests of suppliers of marine equipment
      & associated services for every type of merchant vessel, from
      low tonnage work-boats through every class of cargo-
      carrying ship, including container carriers & tankers,
      specialist ships, passenger-car ferries, Ro-Ro's, up to the
      largest cruise liners'
●   Conf - Mtgs - Exhib - Expt - Inf - LG - Trade missions
<   Soc of Maritime Inds
M   200 f
¶   Directory - 1.

British Marine Federation   (BMF)   1913
NR Marine House, Thorpe Lea Rd, EGHAM, Surrey, TW20 8BF.
      (hq)
      01784 473377   fax 01784 439678
      email info@britishmarine.co.uk
      http://www.britishmarine.co.uk
      Chief Exec: Rob Stevens
▲   Company Limited by Guarantee
Br 12 regions
○   *T; for the leisure marine industry
Gp Association of Pleasure Craft Operators (APCO); BMF
      Sailmakers Association; BMF Thames Valley; Boat Retailers &
      Brokers Association (BRBA); British Commercial Boatbuilders
      Association (BCBA); British Hire Cruiser Federation (BHCF);
      British Marine Electronics Association (BMEA); British
      Sailing (BS); British Small Boatbuilders Association (BSBA);
      Broads Hire Boat Federation (BHBF); Canal Boatbuilders
      Association (CBA); Insurance Financial & Legal Services
      Association (ILFSA); Leisure Boat Builders Association (LBBA);
      Marine Engine & Equipment Association (MEEMA); Marine
      Leisure Association (MLA); Marine Trades Association (MTA);
      Superyacht UK; Yacht Harbour Association (TYHA)
●   Conf - Mtgs - ET - Res - Exhib - Stat - Expt - Inf - Lib - PL - Empl
      - LG
<   Boating Alliance
M   c 1,500 f
¶   BM News - 12; ftm only.
      Membership Hbk & Classified Buyers' Guide - 1; ftm.
      Industry Statistics - 1; ftm.
      Publications list available.

British Marine Finfish Association
      has closed

British Marine Life Study Society   (BMLSS)   1990
NR Glaucus House, 14 Corbyn Crescent, SHOREHAM-BY-SEA,
      W Sussex, BN43 6PQ.   (hsb)
      01273 465433
      email glaucus@hotmail.com   http://www.glaucus.org.uk
      Chief Exec: Andy Horton
▲   Un-incorporated Society
○   *G, *L; the study of the wildlife & ecology of the marine
      environment of the British Isles; for the layman, amateur &
      professional naturalist
Gp Aquariology (aquaria); Scuba diving; Rockpooling (seashore
      study); Marine biology; Biological recording
●   Exhib - SG - Inf - Lib - PL
<   Inst of Biology; Nat Fedn of Biological Recording
M   349 i
¶   Glaucus (Jnl) - irreg; m only.
      Shorewatch (NL) - irreg.
      Torpedo (electronic NL) - 12.

© CBD Research Ltd · Beckenham · BR3 5JS · Tel 020 8650 7745 · E-mail cbd@cbdresearch.com · www.cbdresearch.com

British Maritime Law Association   (BMLA)   1908
- ■ c/o Reed Smith LLP The Broadgate Tower, 20 Primrose St, LONDON, EC2A 2RS.   (asa)
  020 3116 3000   fax 020 3116 3999
  email adtaylor@reedsmith.com
  http://www.bmla.org.uk
  Sec & Treas: Andrew Taylor
- ▲ Un-incorporated Society
- ○ *P; to coordinate the contributions of members, who operate within the shipping & support industries, to national & international shipping related legislation
- ● Conf - Mtgs - ET - Res - SG - Inf - Lib - LG
- < Comité Maritime Intl (CMI)
- M 260 i, 52 f
- ¶ AR & Accounts; ftm.

British Masonry Society
     since 1 January 2008 **International Masonry Society**

British Matchbox, Label & Booklet Society   (BML&BS)   1945
- ■ 122 High St, MELBOURN, Cambs, SG8 6AL.   (hsp)
  01763 260399
  email secretary@phillumeny.com
  http://www.phillumeny.com
  Hon Sec: Arthur Alderton
- ▲ Un-incorporated Society
- ○ *G; for collectors of match-boxes, labels, bookmatch covers, containers, strikers & associated ephemera
- ● Mtgs - Res - Exhib - Inf - Lib
- M 480 i, UK / 110 i, o'seas
- ¶ Match Label News (Jnl) - 6; ftm, £3.50 nm.

British Materials Handling Federation   (BMHF)   1964
- NR National Metalforming Centre, 47 Birmingham Rd, WEST BROMWICH, W Midlands, B70 6PY.   (hq)
  0121-601 6350   fax 0121-601 6387
  email enquiry@bmhf.org.uk   http://www.bmhf.org.uk
- ▲ Company Limited by Guarantee
- ○ *N; 'constitutes the British national committee of FEM & is the UK's voice in Europe on materials handling matters'
- ● Mtgs - Exhib - Stat - Inf - LG - Intl Handling & Storage Exhibition (3 yrly)
- < Fédn Eur'nne de la Manutention
- M 5 associations:
  Association of Loading & Elevating Equipment Manufacturers
  Automated Material Handling Systems Association
  British Industrial Truck Association
  International Powered Access Federation
  Storage Equipment Manufacturers' Association
- ¶ Ybk & Dir - 1; ftm.

British Maternal & Fetal Medicine Society   (BMFMS)
- NR c/o RCOG, 27 Sussex Place, LONDON, NW1 4RG.
  email bmfms@rcog.org.uk   http://www.bmfms.org.uk
  Coordinator: Sabi Proctor
- ○ *P

British Measurement & Testing Association   (BMTA)   1990
- ■ East Malling Enterprise Centre, New Rd, EAST MALLING, Kent, ME19 6BJ.   (hq)
  0845 644 4603   fax 01732 897453
  email enquiries@bmta.co.uk   http://www.bmta.co.uk
  Sec: Peter Russell
- ▲ Company Limited by Guarantee
- ○ *T; interests of the measurement & testing laboratory community to government, UK Accreditation Service, BSI & other official bodies & UK laboratories in Europe through EUROLAB
- Gp Accredited laboratories
- ● Conf - Mtgs - Exhib - Inf - LG
- < EUROLAS
- M 5 i, 75 f
- ¶ Electronic NL - 4; free.

British Meat Processors Association   (bMPA)   2003
- NR 12 Cock Lane, LONDON, EC1A 9BU.   (hq)
  020 7329 0776   fax 020 7329 0653
  email info@bmpa.uk.com   http://www.bmpa.uk.com
  Dir: Stuart Roberts
- ▲ Company Limited by Guarantee
- ○ *T; slaughtering, processing, manufacturing, wholesale distribution & packaging sectors of the meat industry
- ● Conf - Mtgs - Inf - LG
- M f

British Medical Acupuncture Society   (BMAS)   1980
- ■ BMAS House, 3 Winnington Court, NORTHWICH, Cheshire, CW8 1AQ.   (hq)
  01606 786782   fax 01606 786783
  email admin@medical-acupuncture.org.uk
  http://www.medical-acupuncture.org.uk
  c/o Royal London Hospital for Integrated Medicine, 60 Great Ormond St, LONDON, WC1N 3HR.
  020 7713 9437.
  Gen Mgr: Jane Llewellyn
- ▲ Registered Charity
- Br London: 020 7713 9437
- ○ *L; training for doctors, dentists, vets & registered health professionals in medical acupuncture
- ● Conf - Mtgs - ET - Exam - Res - SG - LG
- < Intl Coun of Med Acupuncture & Related Techniques (ICMART)
- > Acupuncture Assn of Chart Physiotherapists (AACP); Brit Academy of Wstn Acupuncture (BAWA)
- M 2,100 i, UK / 120 i, o'seas
- ¶ Acupuncture in Medicine - 4; ftm, £11 each nm.

British Medical Association   (BMA)   1832
- ■ BMA House, Tavistock Square, LONDON, WC1H 9JP.   (hq)
  020 7387 4499
  http://www.bma.org.uk
  Chief Exec/Sec: Tony Bourne
- ▲ Company Limited by Guarantee
- Br Offices in the 3 national capitals, a regional network
- ○ *E, *P, *U; to promote the medical & allied sciences, to maintain the honour & interests of the medical profession; to promote the achievement of high quality health care
- Gp C'ees on: Equal opportunities, International affairs; Medical ethics, Medical education; Science
  Practice c'ees: Central consultants & specialists, General practitioners, Junior doctors, Medical academic staff, Medical students, Public health medicine & community health, Staff & associate specialists
- ● Conf - Mtgs - ET - Res - Stat - Inf - Lib - Empl - LG
- M 115,512 i, 19.053 students, UK / 3.060 i, o'seas
- ¶ British Medical Jnl.   Specialist Jnls.   AR.
  Branch of Practice Committees ARs.
  Various other reports on health & health policy.

British Medical Laser Association   (BMLA)   1983
- ■ Photobiology Unit, University of Dundee, Ninewells Hospital & Medical School, DUNDEE, DD1 9SY.   (hq)
  01382 496227
  email h.moseley@dundee.ac.uk   http://www.bmla.co.uk
  Pres: Prof Harry Moseley
- ▲ Registered Charity
- ○ *L, *M, *P; medical uses of lasers & associated technology
- ● Conf - Mtgs - ET - LG
- < Eur Laser Assn
- M 120 i, UK / 20 i, o'seas
- ¶ Lasers in Medical Science (Jnl) - 4; ftm.

British Medical Ultrasound Society   (BMUS)   1984
- ■ 36 Portland Place, LONDON, W1B 1LS.   (hq)
  020 7636 3714   fax 020 7323 2175
  email secretariat@bmus.org   http://www.bmus.org
  Gen Sec: Mrs Joy Whyte
- ▲ Company Limited by Guarantee
- ○ *L; the advancement of the science & technology of ultrasonics as applied in medicine; the maintenance of the highest standards
- ● Conf - Mtgs - ET - Exhib - Comp - SG - Lib
- < Eur Fedn Socs for Ultrasound in Medicine & Biology
- M c 2,500 i
- ¶ Jnl of Ultrasound - 4.

British Menopause Society   (BMS)   1989
- NR 4-6 Eton Place, MARLOW, Bucks, SL7 2QA.   (hq)
  01628 890199
  Chief Exec: Sara Moger
- ▲ Company Limited by Guarantee; Registered Charity
- ○ *L; the advancement of knowledge, interest & study of all matters connected with the menopause; to promote high standards of training for those involved in advising women
- M i

British Menswear Guild Ltd   (BMG)   1959
- NR 3 Queen Sq, Bloomsbury, LONDON, WC1N 3AR.   (hq)
  020 7843 9460
  http://www.british-menswear-guild.co.uk
  Dir: David Challinor
- ○ *T; for manufacturers of high quality men's clothing & accessories, luggage, leathergoods & umbrellas; to promote & increase export worldwide
- M 16 f

British Metallurgical Plant Constructors' Association (BMPCA)   1963
- ■ c/o NAMTEC, Swinden House, Moorgate Rd, ROTHERHAM, S Yorks, S60 3AR.   (hq)
  01709 362288
  email enquiries@bmpca.org.uk
  Dir: R W Welburn
- ○ *T; the design & manufacture of systems, plant & equipment for the metals industry worldwide
- ● Mtgs - Exhib - Stat - Expt - Inf - VE - LG
- < EEF; UK Steel
- M 30 f
- ¶ List of Member Companies & Product Range; free.

British Metals Recycling Association   (BMRA)   1919
- ■ 16 High St, Brampton, HUNTINGDON, Cambs, PE28 4TU. (hq)
  01480 455249   fax 01480 453680
  email admin@recyclemetals.org
  http://www.recyclemetals.org
  Dir Gen: Lindsay Millington
- ▲ Company Limited by Guarantee
- ○ *T; to represent metal recyclers
- Gp Exporters; Shredders division
- ● Conf - Mtgs - ET - Exhib - SG - Stat - Expt - Inf - LG
- < Bureau Intl de la Récupération (BIR); Eur Ferrous Recovery & Recycling Fedn (EFR); Freight Transport Assn (FTA); CBI
- M 350 f, UK / 30 f, o'seas
- ¶ Recycling Health & Safety Manual - 4; ftm only.

British Mexican Society   (BMS)   1942
- NR PO Box 251, MORPETH, Northumberland, NE61 9DH.
  0870 922 0679
  http://www.britishmexicansociety.co.uk
  4
- ▲ Registered Charity
- ○ *X
- M i & f

British Microcirculation Society   (BMS)   1963
- NR School of Biomedical Sciences, University of Nottingham, NOTTINGHAM, NG7 2UH.   (hsb)
  0115-823 0175
  email lopa.leach@nottingham.ac.uk
  Hon Sec: Dr Lopa Leach
- ▲ Registered Charity
- ○ *L; study of microvascular structure, function & disease & related vascular phenomena
- M i

British Microlight Aircraft Association   (BMAA)   1979
- NR The Bullring, Deddington, BANBURY, Oxon, OX15 0TT.   (hq)
  01869 338888   fax 01869 337116
  email general@bmaa.org   http://www.bmaa.org
- ▲ Company Limited by Guarantee
- Br 100; France, Gambia, Portugal, Spain
- ○ *S; to foster & safeguard the interests of microlight flying in the UK
- Gp Flying schools (training of students up to PPL(A) microlights standard)
- ● ET - Exam - Exhib - Comp - Inf
- < Fédn Aéronautique Intle; R Aero Club of GB
- M 4,300 i, 100 clubs & schools
- ¶ Microlight Flying - 6; ftm only.

British Milksheep Society   1983
- NR St Kenelms, Broad Lane, Tanworth-in-Arden, SOLIHULL, W Midlands, B94 5HX.   (hsp)
  01564 742398
  email whopkins@britishmilksheep.com
  http://www.britishmilksheep.com
  Sec: William Hopkins
- ▲ Un-incorporated Society
- Br France, Hungary
- ○ *B; registration, promotion & export of British milksheep
- ● Mtgs - Exhib - Expt
- < Nat Sheep Assn
- M 26 i, 4 f, UK / 1 i, 2 f, o'seas

British Miniature Horse Society   (BMHS)   1992
- NR Stretcholt Farm, Stretcholt, BRIDGWATER, Somerset, TA6 4SR. (hsb)
  01278 685943 (Mon-Thurs 1400-1700)
  Chmn: Wendy Edgar
- ○ *B
- ● Comp
- < Brit Central Prefix Registry; Brit Horse Soc
- M 400 i, UK / 200 i, o'seas

British Model Flying Association   (BMFA)   1922
- ■ Chacksfield House, 31 St Andrews Rd, LEICESTER, LE2 8RE. (hq)
  0116-244 0028   fax 0116-244 0645
  email admin@bmfa.org   http://www.bmfa.org
  Chief Exec: David Phipps
- ▲ Company Limited by Guarantee (as Society of Model Aeronautical Engineers)
- ○ *G, *S; the promotion, protection, organisation & encouragement of model aircraft building, flying & development in all its aspects in the UK
- Gp Control line; Free flight; Gas turbines; Indoor; Model rocketry; Radio control power (fixed wing & rotary wing); Radio control silent flight (thermal, slope soaring, electric)
- ● Conf - Mtgs - ET - Exam - Res - Exhib - Comp - Stat - Inf - VE - LG
- < Fédn Aéronautique Intle (FAI); R Aero Club (RAC); Cent Coun of Physical Recreation (CCPR)
- M 37,000 i, 740 clubs
- ¶ BMFA News - 6; ftm, £1.50 nm.   AR - 1; ftm only.
  Members Hbk - 3 yrly; ftm, £3 nm.
  Note: is also known as the Society of Model Aeronautical Engineers

© CBD Research Ltd · Beckenham · BR3 5JS · Tel 020 8650 7745 · E-mail cbd@cbdresearch.com · www.cbdresearch.com

British Model Soldier Society (BMSS) 1935
- ■ 12 Savay Lane, Denham Green, DENHAM, Bucks, UB9 5NH. (hsp)
  01895 832757   fax 01895 832757
  Hon Sec: Julie Newman
- ▲ Un-incorporated Society
- Br 22
- ○ *E, *G, *Q; to promote research & scholarship in all aspects of military history, weaponry, uniforms etc, through the media of military models & the portraying of historical events
- Gp American civil war; Artillery; Britain's figures; Conversions; Indian army; Military aircraft; Military bands; Military vehicles; Yeomanry
- ● Mtgs - ET - Res - Exhib - Comp - SG - Inf
- M 425 i, UK / 50 i, o'seas
- ¶ Bulletin - 4;   Bulletin Extra - 4;   Hbk - irreg; all ftm only.

British Morgan Horse Society (BMHS) 1975
- ■ 9 First Avenue, Astley, Tyldesley, MANCHESTER, M29 7JH. (hq)
  01942 886141
  email admin@morganhorse.org.uk
  http://www.morganhorse.org.uk
  Exec Officer: Dawn Sharif
- ○ *B; to promote the Morgan horse in Britain
- ● Conf - Exhib - Comp - Inf
- < Amer Morgan Horse Assn (AMHA)
- M 85 i (adult), 33 i (youth)
- ¶ NL - 6.
  European Morgan Horse Magazine - 1.

British Moroccan Society (BMS) 1976
- NR Dartmouth House, Dartmouth Place, LONDON, W4 2RH. (v-chmn/b)
  0783 126 1830
  email admin@british-moroccansoc.org
  http://www.british-moroccansoc.org
  Hon Sec: Benedicte Clarkson
- ▲ Un-incorporated Society
- ○ *X; to foster links between the Kingdoms of Great Britain & Morocco through commercial, cultural & social contacts; to promote events to raise money for Moroccan charitable institutions
- ● Mtgs - VE - Social events - Dinner (November) to raise money for the most needy in Morocco
- M 400 i, UK / 2 i, o'seas
- ¶ NL - 8; free.

British Motor Cycle Racing Club Ltd (BMCRC) 1909
- ■ Unit 85 Seedbed Centre, Davidson Way, ROMFORD, Essex, RM7 0AZ. (hq)
  01708 720305   fax 01708 720235
  email mikedommett@hotmail.com
  http://www.bemsee.net
  Sec: Eddie Bellas   Chief Exec: Mike Dommett
- ▲ Company Limited by Guarantee
- ○ *S; organising motor cycle racing events
- ● Comp
- < Auto-Cycle U
- > Brit Motorcycle Club Marshals Assn
- M 1,000 i
  (Sub: £30)

British Motor Sprint Association
- NR 52 Brendon Rd, Portishead, BRISTOL, BS20 6DH. (co-ord/p)
  01275 843478
  email britshsprint@paulparker.f9.co.uk
  http://www.britishsprint.org
  Championship Co-ordinator: Paul Parker
- ○ *G, *S
- ● Mtgs - Organisers of British Sprint Championship
- M i in 5 clubs
- ¶ Blue Book.

British Motorcyclists' Federation (BMF) 1960
- NR 3 Oswin Rd, Brailsford Industrial Estate, Braunstone, LEICESTER, LE3 1HR.   (hq)
  0116-279 5112
  Press & PR Mgr: Jeff Stone
  Chief Exec Officer: Simon Wilkinson-Blake
- ▲ Company Limited by Guarantee
- ○ *K, *S; to pursue, protect & promote the interests of motorcyclists
- ● Mtgs - ET - Res - Exhib - SG - Stat - Inf - VE - LG - Attendance at exhibitions & rallies - Legal & insurance advice - European lobbying - Preservation of green lanes
- < Eur Motorcyclists U (EMU); CCPR; RAC; Motorcycle Inds Assn (MCIA); Nat Motorcycle Coun (NMC); Fedn Eur Motorcyclists (FEM)
- M 25,000 i, 115,000 i (affiliates), 100 f, 330 clubs, UK / 40 i, o'seas
- ¶ Motorcycle Rider - 6.

British Motorsport Marshals Club (BMMC) 1957
- NR Ballaugh, 27 Dollicott, HADDENHAM, Bucks, HP17 8JL. (chmn/p)
  0778 920 6909
  email bmmc.chair@marshals.co.uk
  http://www.marshals.co.uk
  Nat Chmn: Chris Hobson
- ▲ Company Limited by Guarantee
- Br 7
- ○ *S; to bring together, train & organise marshals for all types of motor sport events
- ● Mtgs - ET - Exhib - Comp
- < RAC Motor Sport Assn (RACMSA)
- > Brit Rally Marshals Club
- M 1,500 i
- ¶ Trackside - 4; ftm, £2 nm.

British Mountaineering Council (BMC) 1944
- NR The Old Church, 177-179 Burton Rd, West Didsbury, MANCHESTER, M20 2BB.   (hq)
  0161-445 6111   fax 0161-445 4500
  email office@thebmc.co.uk   http://www.thebmc.co.uk
  Chief Exec: Dave Turnbull
- ▲ Company Limited by Guarantee
- ○ *S; to protect the freedoms & promote the interests of climbers, hill walkers & mountaineers including ski-mountaineers
- M 14,000 i, 330 org

British Mule Society (BMS) 1978
- ■ 2 Boscombe Rd, SWINDON, Wilts, SN25 3EY.   (hsp)
  01793 615478
  http://www.britishmulesociety.org.uk
  Hon Sec: Mrs Ann Hunter
- ▲ Company Limited by Guarantee; Registered Charity
- ○ *B; to encourage the breeding of good quality mules
- ● Conf - Mtgs - ET - Res - Exhib - Comp - Stat - Inf - Lib - VE
- < Brit Driving Soc; Amer Donkey & Mule Soc
- M 150 i, 2 org, UK / 19 i, 5 org, o'seas
- ¶ The Mule - 4; ftm only.

British Museum Friends (BMS) 1968
- ■ c/o The British Museum, Great Russell St, LONDON, WC1B 3DG. (hq)
  020 7323 8195
  email friends@britishmuseum.org
  Chmn: Prof Sir Barry Cunliffe
  Head of Friends: Carolyn Young
- ▲ Registered Charity
- ○ *G; to support the British Museum
- ● Exhib - Inf
- M 17,500 i
- ¶ British Museum Magazine - 3.

British Music Hall Society   (BMHS)   1963
- ■ 45 Mayflower Rd, Park St, ST ALBANS, AL2 3QN.   (hsb)
  01727 768878
  http://www.music-hall-society.com
  Hon Sec: Mrs Daphne Masterton
- ○ *D; to preserve the history of music hall & variety; to recall the artistes who were part of the scene; to support the entertainers of the present
- ● Conf - Mtgs - Res - Exhib - SG - Inf - VE - 5 shows a year at the Concert Artistes Association, 20 Bedford St, London, WC2E 9HP
- M 900 i, UK / 50 i, o'seas
- ¶ The Call Boy - 4; ftm, £3 each nm.

British Music Rights   1996
- NR British Music House, 26 Berners St, LONDON, W1T 3LR.   (hq)
  020 7306 4446   fax 020 7306 4449
  email britishmusic@bmr.org   http://www.bmr.org
  Dir Gen: Frances Lowe
- ○ *N, *P, *T; an umbrella organisation representing the interests of composers, songwriters & music publishers

British Music Society   (BMS)   1978
- ■ 7 Tudor Gardens, UPMINSTER, Essex, RM14 3DE.   (treas/p)
  01708 224795
  http://www.britishmusicsociety.co.uk
  Hon Treas: Stephen Trowell
- ▲ Registered Charity
- ○ *D; to promote the music of neglected British composers who do not have a society, or trust, to champion their cause
- ● Mtgs - Res - Exhib - Comp - Inf - Lib - VE - Concert promotion - Recordings - Publications
- M 525 i, 5 f, 15 org, UK / 77 i, 7 org, o'seas
- ¶ Jnl - 1; ftm, £5 nm.   NL - 4; ftm only.

British Music Writers' Council
   a group of the **Musicians' Union**

British Mycological Society   (BMS)   1896
- ■ City View House, 5 Union St, Ardwick, MANCHESTER, M12 4JD.
  email admin@britmycolsoc.info
  http://www.britmycolsoc.org.uk
- ▲ Registered Charity
- ○ *L, *Q; to promote all aspects of mycology (fungi, ecology, molecular biology, biodiversity, conservation, pathogens, biocontrol, systematics, physiology, secondary metabolites)
- M c 2,000 i

British Myriapod & Isopod Group   (BMIG)
- ■ 2 Egypt Wood Cottages, Egypt Lane, FARNHAM COMMON, Bucks, SL2 3LE.   (hsp)
  01753 646699   fax 01753 646699
  email helen.read@dsl.pipex.com
  Sec: Helen Read
- ▲ Un-incorporated Society
- ○ *L; the study of myriapods (millipedes, centipedes) & isopods (woodlice, water-slaters)
- ● Conf - Res - SG - Lib - VE
- < Brit Entomological & Natural History Soc
- M 240 i, UK / 36 i, o'seas
- ¶ Bulletin - 1; £10.   NL - 2; free.

British Narrow Fabrics Association   (BNFA)
- NR 9 Romway Rd, LEICESTER, LE5 5SD.   (hsp)
  0116-273 7866   fax 0116-273 9633
  email directorate@knitfed.co.uk
  Sec: Mrs Anne Carvell
- ▲ Un-incorporated Society
- ○ *T; to promote the narrow fabrics industry in the UK - is a non-profit making organisation (manufacturers of ribbon, tapes, woven labels & webbing etc)
- ● Mtgs - ET (of technical textiles technicians) - Inf - Empl
- < Knitting Inds Fedn
- M f
- ¶ NL - 12;   AR - 1; both ftm only.

British National Carnation Society   (BNCS)   1948
- ■ Linfield, Duncote, TOWCESTER, Northants, NN12 8AH.   (hsp)
  01327 351594
  email blinnell723@btinternet.com
  http://www.blog.carnations.org.uk
  Hon Sec: Mrs B M Linnell
- ▲ Un-incorporated Society
- ○ *H; cultivation, breeding & exhibition of the Dianthus family of carnations & pinks
- ● Competitive shows & displays
- < R Horticl Soc
- M c 370 i
- ¶ NL - 2; ftm only.   Carnation Ybk - 1; ftm.

British National Martial Arts Association
   closed 2006 - members invited to join the **National Association of Karate & Martial Art Schools**

British National Temperance League   (BNTL)   1834
- ■ 30 Keswick Rd, WORKSOP, Notts, S81 7PT.   (hq)
  01909 477882
  email bntl@btconnect.com   http://www.bntl.org
  Chief Exec & Co Sec: Mrs Barbara Briggs
- ▲ Company Limited by Guarantee; Registered Charity
- ○ *E, *K, *Y; an initiative of the League is to offer children & young people the options to not drink alcohol, or take illegal drugs, solvents or other addictive substances, through educational resources & training
- ● ET
- M 35 i, 1,000 i (associates)
- ¶ Freeway (NL) - 4.   AR - 1; both free.
  Note: uses the abbreviated title of BNTL Freeway

British Natural Bodybuilding Federation
- NR c/o The Body Academy, 40 South William St, PERTH, PH2 8LS.
  email info@bnbf.co.uk   http://www.bnbf.co.uk

British Natural Hygiene Society   (BNHS)   1956
- ■ Shalimar, 3 Harold Grove, FRINTON-on-SEA, Essex, CO13 9BD.   (hsp)
  01636 682941
  http://www.bnhs.ms11.net
  Pres & Hon Sec: Dr K R Sidhwa
- ▲ Un-incorporated Society
- ○ *K; to propagate the message of natural healthy living in accordance with natural law
- Gp Diet; Fasting for health; Nutrition
- ● Conf - Inf
- < Intl Assn of Profl Natural Hygienists; Amer Natural Hygiene Soc
- M c 400 i
- ¶ The Hygienist - 4.

British Naturalists' Association   (BNA)   1905
- NR PO Box 5682, CORBY, Northants, NN17 2ZW.
  0844 892 1917
  http://www.bna-naturalists.org
- ▲ Company Limited by Guarantee; Registered Charity
- ○ *K; the education of the public in natural history areas & sanctuaries

© CBD Research Ltd · Beckenham · BR3 5JS · Tel 020 8650 7745 · E-mail cbd@cbdresearch.com · www.cbdresearch.com

British Naturism
    is the trading name of the **Central Council for British Naturism**

British Naturopathic Association   (BNA)   1992
NR   1 Green Lane Ave, STREET, Somerset, BA16 0QS.   (hsb)
         01458 840072
         Sec: M W F Szewiel
▲   Company Limited by Guarantee
○   *P; for qualified & registered naturopaths
●   Conf - Mtgs - Res - Inf
M   310 i, UK / 19 i, o'seas
¶   British Naturopathic Jnl - 4.

British Naval Equipment Association   (BNEA)   1973
NR   28-29 Threadneedle St, LONDON, EC2R 8AY.   (hq)
         020 7628 2555   fax 020 7638 4376
         email info@maritimeindustries.org
         http://www.maritimeindustries.org
         Dir: Christopher McHugh
○   *T; 'dedicated to the needs of companies in the British naval
         industrial sector which build, refit & modernise warships,
         supply operations & weapons systems & other equipment;
         also dedicated to the needs of the companies providing
         related services in design, consultancy & finance'
●   Conf - Mtgs - ET - Exhib - SG - Expt - LG
<   Soc of Maritime Inds
M   f

British Neuropathological Society   (BNS)   1950
NR   c/o Dr A Chakrabarty, Level 5 Bexley Wing, St James University
         Hospital, LEEDS, W Yorks, LS9 7TF.   (hsb)
         0113 206 7505
         Hon Sec: Dr Aruna Chakrabarty
▲   Registered Charity
○   *L; to promote research, education & clinical practice relating
         to neuropathy (study of brain, nerve & muscle disorders)
●   Conf - Mtgs - ET - Res
<   Intl Soc Neuropathology
M   c 200 i
¶   Neuropathology & Applied Neurobiology - 10.

British Neuropsychiatry Association   (BNPA)   1987
NR   Lion House, 51 Sheen Lane, LONDON, SW14 8AB.
         (admin/p)
         0560 114 1307   fax 020 8878 0573
         email admin@bnpa.org.uk   http://www.bnpa.org.uk
         Admin: Jackie Ashmenall,   Hon Sec: Dr Hugh Rickards
○   *M, *P; to provide a forum for cross-disciplinary discussion
         among psychiatrists, neurologists, neuropsychologists &
         workers in the related sciences, as well as qualified persons
         with an interest in brain function in relation to behaviour
●   Mtgs
M   c 400 i

British Neuropsychological Society   (BNS)   1989
NR   School of Psychological Sciences (Room T7D),
         Zochonis Building, University of Manchester, Brunswick St,
         MANCHESTER, M13 9PL.   (pres/b)
         http://www.the-bns.org
         Pres: Prof Matt Lambon Ralph
○   *M

British Neuroscience Association   (BNA)   1965
NR   Department of Experimental Psychology, University of
         Cambridge, CAMBRIDGE, CB2 3EB.
         01223 766450
         http://www.bna.org.uk
         Exec Dir: Yvonne Allen
▲   Registered Charity
○   *L, *P; to promote an understanding of the structure, function &
         development of the nervous system in health & disease
●   Conf - Mtgs - ET - Res
<   Intl Brain Res Org (IBRO); Fedn of Eur Neuroscience
         Socs (FENS)
M   c 1,900 i, 9 f, UK / c 1,000 i, o'seas
¶   BNA NL - 4; free.
         National Meeting Book of Abstracts - 2 yrly; ftm.

**British/New Zealand Trade Council (Incorporated)   (BNZTC)
1917**
■   PO Box 55305, Mission Bay, AUCKLAND 1744, New
         Zealand.   (hq)
         64 (9) 578 1312
         http://www.bnztc.co.nz
         Contact: Damon Butler
▲   Incorporated society
Br   2 o'seas
○   *C; to foster trade & investment between UK & New Zealand
●   Conf - Mtgs - Expt - Inf - VE - LG - Promotion of investment in
         UK
<   NZ Europe Business Council (NZEUBC)
M   20 i, 50 f

British Non-Ferrous Metals Federation   (BNFMF)
■   c/o CDA, 5 Grovelands Business Centre, Boundary Way,
         HEMEL HEMPSTEAD, Herts, HP2 7TE.   (hq)
         01442 275705   fax 01442 275716
         email bnfmf@copperuk.org.uk
         Exec Sec: Carol Godfrey
▲   Un-incorporated Society
○   *T; fabricators of copper & copper-based alloy wire, tube, sheet
         & strip, & rods & profiles
●   Mtgs
<   Construction Products Assn
M   14 f
¶   LM.

British North American Research Association   (BNARA)
NR   St Clement's House, 27-28 St Clement's Lane, LONDON,
         EC4N 7AE.   (hq)
         020 3207 9432
         http://www.bnac.org
▲   Registered Charity
Br   Canada; USA
○   *X; promotion of Anglo-North American trade, commercial &
         political relations
●   Conf - Mtgs - ET - Res - SG
M   45 i, UK / 30 i, o'seas

British Nuclear Energy Society
         on 1 January 2009 merged with the Institution of Nuclear Engineers
         to form the **Nuclear Institute**

British Nuclear Medicine Society   (BNMS)   1969
■   Regent House, 291 Kirkdale, LONDON, SE26 4QD.   (hq)
         020 8676 7864   fax 020 8676 8417
         email suehatchard@bnms.org.uk
         http://www.bnms.org.uk
         Pres: Dr Gillian Vivian
         Chief Exec: Mrs Susan Hatchard
▲   Registered Charity
○   *P; to advance the science & public education in nuclear
         medicine
●   Conf - ET - Exhib
M   c 700 i
¶   Nuclear Medicine Communications - 12.

British Nuclear Test Veterans Association (BNTVA) 1983
- ■ BM 5657, LONDON, WC1N 3XX.   (mail/address)
    020 8144 3080
    email secretary@bntva.com   http://www.bntva.com
    Nat Sec: J R Liddiatt
- ▲ Registered Charity
- ○ *K, *W; seeking recognition & compensation from Ministry of
    Defence for damages to health of men who took part in
    Britain's Nuclear Test Programme 1952-1958
- ● Conf - Mtgs - ET - Res - Exhib - LG
- M 1,600 i, UK / 300 i, o'seas
- ¶ Campaign - 4; free.

British Number Plate Manufacturers Association   (BNMA)
- ■ Oakley Cottage, Oakley Drive, FLEET, Hants, GU51 3PP.
    (liaison/officer)
    Liaison Officer: Bill Shouler
- ▲ Un-incorporated Society
- ○ *T
- ● Mtgs - Res - LG
- M 9 f

British Numismatic Society   (BNS)   1903
- ■ c/o Warburg Institute, Woburn Sq, LONDON, WC1H 0AB.
    (hsb)
    01223 332915
    email secretary@britnumsoc.org
    http://www.britnumsoc.org
    Hon Sec: Richard Kelleher
- ▲ Registered Charity
- ○ *L; promotion of numismatic science with regard to the coins,
    tokens & medals of Great Britain, our Empire &
    Commonwealth, & the English speaking world
- ● Mtgs - Inf - Lib
- < Brit Assn of Numismatics Socs
- M 393 i, 50 org, UK / 112 i, 62 org, o'seas
- ¶ British Numismatic Jnl - 1; ftm only.
    Specialist numismatic publications; at cost m.

British Numismatic Trade Association Ltd   (BNTA)   1973
- ■ PO Box 2, RYE, E Sussex, TN31 7WE.   (hq)
    01797 229988   fax 01797 229988
    email bnta@lineone.net   http://www.bnta.net
    Gen Sec: Mrs Rosemary Cooke
- ▲ Company Limited by Guarantee
- ○ *T; to ensure a high standard of ethical conduct within the
    numismatic trade
- ● Coin fairs
- < Fedn of Eur Numismatic Trade Assns (FENAP)
- M 73 i & f

British Nutrition Foundation   (BNF)   1967
- ■ High Holborn House, 52-54 High Holborn, LONDON,
    WC1V 6RQ.   (hq)
    020 7404 6504   fax 020 7404 6747
    email postbox@nutrition.org.uk
    http://www.nutrition.org.uk
    Co Sec: T Barclay,   Admin Officer: Nicholas Baldwin
- ▲ Company Limited by Guarantee; Registered Charity
- ○ *L; to provide unbiased information; to encourage education;
    to foster research concerned with human nutrition
- Gp School education; Publishing
- ● Conf - Mtgs - ET - Inf
- M 42 f
- ¶ BNF Bulletin - 4; £67 yr.   AR - 1; £10.

British Oat & Barley Millers' Association   (BOBMA)   1978
- ■ 6 Catherine St, LONDON, WC2B 5JJ.   (hq)
    020 7420 7109   fax 020 7836 0580
    email harriet.green@fdf.org.uk
    Exec Sec: Harriet Green
- ▲ Un-incorporated Society
- ○ *T; interests of UK millers of oat & barley for human
    consumption
- ● Mtgs
- < Eur Breakfast Cereal Assn (CEEREAL); Food & Drink Fedn (FDF)
- M 8 f

British Obesity & Metabolic Surgery Society   (BOMSS)   2000
- ■ c/o Association of Upper Gastrointestinal Surgeons, Royal
    College of Surgeons of England, 35-43 Lincoln's Inn Fields,
    LONDON, WC2A 3PE.   (asa)
    020-7304 4786
    http://www.bomss.org.uk
    Specialty Mgrs: Harriet Innes, Sarvjit Madhar
- ▲ Un-incorporated Society
- ○ *L, *P; to promote awareness of obesity surgery; to advise on
    training & accreditation
- ● Conf - ET
- < Intl Fedn for the Surgery of Obesity (IFSO); Assn for the Study of
    Obesity (ASO); Assn of Upper GI Surgeons (AUGIS)
- M 70 i
- ¶ NL - 2/3; free.
- × 2009-10 British Obesity Surgery Society

British Obesity Surgery Patient Association   (BOSPA)   2003
- NR PO Box 805, TAUNTON, Somerset, TA4 9DU.
    0845 602 0446
    email enquiries@bospa.org   http://www.bospa.org
- ▲ Registered Charity
- ○ *K, *M; to provide support & information to patients for whom
    obesity surgery can provide an enormous benefit

British Obesity Surgery Society
    since 2009-10 **British Obesity & Metabolic Surgery Society**

British Occupational Hygiene Society   (BOHS)   1953
- NR 5-6 Melbourne Business Court, Millennium Way, Pride Park,
    DERBY, DE24 8LZ.   (hq)
    01332 298101
    email admin@bohs.org
    Hon Sec: Heather Jackson
- ▲ Company Limited by Guarantee; Registered Charity
- Br 8 regions
- ○ *L; to promote the good practice of occupational hygiene; to
    prevent workplace conditions affecting the health & wellbeing
    of workers
- Gp Chemical hazard & risk; Environmental; Management;
    Microbiology; NHS; Offshore; Radiation; Sampling &
    analytical methods; Standards; Technology
- ● Conf - Mtgs - ET - Res - SG
- < Intl Occupational Hygiene Assn
- M c 1,200 i
- ¶ Annals of Occupational Hygiene - 8.   NL - 4.
    Abstracts of Conference Papers - 1.   AR.

British Off Road Driving Association   (BORDA)   1995
- NR Leisure House, Salisbury Rd, ANDOVER, Hants, SP11 7DN.
    (hq)
    01264 710080
    email info@borda.org.uk   http://www.borda.org.uk
    Sec: David Heaton
- ▲ Un-incorporated Society
- ○ *T; to encourage best practice in the organisation of events
    among member operators; to develop technical guidance for
    off road driving
    Note: also uses title Association of Off Road Driving Centres

British Office Supplies & Services Federation   (BOSS Federation)   1987
- ■ Farringdon Point, 29-35 Farringdon Rd, LONDON, EC1M 3JF.   (hq)
  0845 450 1565   fax 020 7405 7784
  http://www.bossfederation.com
  Chief Exec: Michael Gardner
- ▲ Company Limited by Guarantee
- Br 13
- ○ *T; to represent manufacturers, importers, wholesalers, distributors, mail order, resellers, retailers, dealers, superstores & commercial contract dealers
- Gp Rubber Stamp Manufacturers' Guild; Writing Instruments Association
- ● Conf - Mtgs - ET - Exam - Exhib - Comp - SG - Stat - Expt - Inf - LG
- < Eur Stationery & Office Products Trade Assn
- M f

British Olive Oil Buyers' Association   (BOOBA)
- ■ Kingsway House, Wrotham Rd, Meopham, GRAVESEND, Kent, DA13 0AU.   (asa)
- ○ *T
- ● Conf - Mtgs - Stat - LG
- M 7 f

British Olympic Association   (BOA)   1905
- NR 60 Charlotte St, LONDON, W1T 2NU.   (hq)
  020 7842 5700
  email boa@boa.org.uk   http://www.olympics.org.uk
  Chmn: Colin Moynihan
- ▲ Company Limited by Guarantee
- ○ *S; to provide services to elite sport in the UK; to promote the Olympic movement in the UK; to prepare & manage the Great Britain Olympic team for the games
- ● Conf - ET - Res - Inf - Lib - LG
- < Intl Olympic C'ee
- M 2,289 i
- ¶ Cutting Edge (NL) - 4;   Inside Track (NL) - 4.   AR - 1.

British Oncological Association   (BOA)   1985
- NR Royal Marsden Hospital, Orchard House, Downs Rd, SUTTON, Surrey, SM2 5PT.   (sb)
  020 8661 3063   fax 020 8661 3470
  http://www.boanet.org
  Sec: Romayne McMahon
- ▲ Registered Charity
- ○ *L, *P, *Q; for clinicians & scientists working in oncology specialities
- ● Conf - Mtgs - ET - Comp
- M c 400 i
- ¶ BOA News - 4; ftm only.

British Oncology Patients Association   (BOPA)   1996
- NR c/o Essex Cancer Network, Hedgerow Business Park, Colchester Rd, CHELMSFORD, Essex, CM2 5PF.   (sb)
  01245 397626
  Hon Sec: Netty Wood
- ○ *P; 'to promote excellence in the care of patients with cancer'
- M i

British Onion Producers' Association   (British Onions)   1986
- ■ PVGA House, Nottingham Rd, LOUTH, Lincs, LN11 0WB.   (asa)
  01507 602427   fax 01507 600689
  email jayne.dyas@pvga.co.uk
  http://www.britishonions.org.uk
  Sec: Mrs Jayne Dyas
- ○ *F, *T

British Ophthalmic Anaesthesia Society   (BOAS)   1998
- ■ Dept of Anaesthesia, City Hospital, Dudley Rd, BIRMINGHAM, B18 7QH.   (hsb)
  0121-507 4343   fax 0121-507 4349
  http://www.boas.org
  Sec: Dr K-L Kong
- ○ *P; for anaesthetists, ophthalmologists & other clinicians who are committed to sharing information & education that will enable them to provide the highest level of anaesthetic management during ophthalmic surgery
- ● Conf - Mtgs - ET - Comp - Inf
- < Wld Congress of Ophthalmic Anaestheia; Ophthalmic Anesthesia Soc
- M c 200 i
  (Sub: £25)
- ¶ BOAS NL - 2; free.

British Orchid Council   (BOC)   1971
- ■ Hall Farm House, Shelton, NEWARK, Notts, NG23 5JG.   (hsp)
  email bocsecretary@tiscali.co.uk
  http://www.british-orchid-council.info
  Hon Sec: Richard Baxter
- ▲ Registered Charity
- ○ *H; to provide a single forum for amateur & commercial orchid growers & orchid scientists; to broaden the knowledge of orchids; to promote & encourage excellence in their culture
- Gp Judging scheme; Lecturers panel; Slide library
  C'ees: Conservation, Congress, Communications
- ● Conf - Mtgs - Exhib - SG - Inf - PL
- < Eur Orchid Coun
- M 47 org
- ¶ A Grower's & Buyer's Guide - 1; ftm, £1 nm.

British Orchid Growers Association   (BOGA)   1949
- NR 61 Stanwell Lea, Middleton Cheney, BANBURY, Oxon, OX17 2RF.   (hsb)
  01295 712159
  email peter@orchidsbypeterwhite.co.uk
  http://www.boga.org.uk
  Chmn & Sec: Peter White
- ○ *H, *T; 'for orchid growers & sundries traders to promote & maintain the highest standards of our trade'
- ● Conf - Mtgs - Exhib - Inf - LG re CITES (Convention for International Trade of Endangered Species)
- < Brit Orchid Coun
- M 17 f
- ¶ Grower's & Buyer's Guide (LM) - 1; ftm, 50p or 2 1st class stamps nm.

British Organ Archive
   a group of the **British Institute of Organ Studies**

British Organ Donor Society
   has closed

British Oriental Rug Dealers Association   (BORDA)   1993
- ■ c/o Rug Gallery Ltd, 42 Verulam Rd, ST ALBANS, Herts, AL3 4DQ.   (hsb)
  01727 841046
  Sec: Richard H Mathias
- ▲ Un-incorporated Society
- ○ *T
- Gp Exhibitions; Information
- ● Mtgs - Inf - PL
- M 20 f

British Orienteering Federation Ltd   (BOF)   1967
- ■ 8A Stancliffe House, Whitworth Rd, Darley Dale, MATLOCK, Derbys, DE4 2HJ.   (hq)
  01629 734042   fax 01629 733769
  email info@britishorienteering.org.uk
  http://www.britishorienteering.org.uk
  Chief Exec: Mike Hamilton
- ▲ Company Limited by Guarantee
- ○ *S; national governing body for the sport of orienteering
- Gp Federated regional & home national associations & affiliated clubs
- ● Conf - Mtgs - ET - Comp - LG
- < Intl Orienteering Fedn (IOF)
- M 8,500 i, 140 clubs
- ¶ Focus Magazine (NL) - 4;   Fixtures List - 4; both ftm only. Leaflets & posters.

British Origami Society   (BOS)   1967
- ■ 2a The Chestnuts, COUNTESTHORPE, Leics, LE8 5TL. (mem/sp)
  Mem Sec: Mrs P A Groom
- ▲ Registered Charity
- ○ *A; the development of Origami (folding paper) & related techniques of manipulation of paper as a form of art, education, therapy & recreation
- ● Conf - Mtgs - ET - Exhib
- < Origami associations worldwide
- M 350 i, UK / 350 i, o'seas
- ¶ British Origami - 6; ftm only.

British Ornithologists' Club   (BOC)   1892
- NR c/o Natural History Museum, Cromwell Rd, LONDON, SW7 5BD.   (hsb)
  020 7942 5000
  Sec: Dr Robert Prys-Jones
- ○ *L; to promote scientific discussion & facilitate publication & dissemination of scientific information connected with ornithology; to maintain a special interest in avian systematics, taxonomy & distribution
- M i

British Ornithologists' Union   (BOU)   1858
- ■ PO Box 417, PETERBOROUGH, Cambs, PE7 3FX.   (mail)
  01733 844820
  email bou@bou.org.uk   http://www.bou.org.uk
  Admin: Steve P Dudley
- ▲ Registered Charity
- ○ *L; promoting the understanding of avian biology & conservation
- Gp BOU Records C'ee (BOURC)
- ● Conf - Res - Publishing - Grants
- M c 1,000 i
  (Sub: £35)
- ¶ Ibis (Jnl) - 4; ftm (ibis.ac.uk)
  BOU Checklist Series - irreg: prices vary.

British Orthodontic Society   (BOS)   1994
- ■ 12 Bridewell Place, LONDON, EC4V 6AP.   (hq)
  020 7353 8680   fax 020 7353 8682
  email ann.wright@bos.org.uk   http://www.bos.org.uk
  Sec: Ann Wright
- ▲ Company Limited by Guarantee; Registered Charity
- ○ *P; a branch of dentistry concerned with developmental abnormalities of the teeth & face
- Gp Consultant orthodontists; Community; Practitioners; Specialist practitioners; Training grades; University teachers
- ● Conf - Mtgs - Res - LG
- < Orthodontic Technicians Assn; Orthodontic Nat Gp for Dental Burses; Brit Lingual Orthodontic Soc
- M 1,700 i, UK / 150 i, o'seas
- ¶ British Jnl of Orthodontics - 4.   BOS NL - 4.

British Orthopaedic Association   (BOA)   1918
- ■ 35-43 Lincoln's Inn Fields, LONDON, WC2A 3PE.   (hq)
  020 7405 6507   fax 020 7831 2676
  email secretary@boa.ac.uk   http://www.boa.ac.uk
  Chief Exec: D C Adams,   Hon Sec: Joseph Dias
- ▲ Company Limited by Guarantee; Registered Charity
- ○ *P; science, art & practice of orthopaedic surgery
- Gp Specialist societies:
  British Association of Spinal Surgeons; British Association for Surgery of the Knee; British Cervical Spine Society; British Elbow & Shoulder Society; British Hip Society; British Limb Reconstruction Society; British Orthopaedic Foot & Ankle Surgery Society; British Orthopaedic Oncology Society ; British Orthopaedic Research Society; British Orthopaedic Specialists Association; British Orthopaedic Sports Trauma & Arthroscopy Association; British Orthopaedic Trainees Association; British Scoliosis Society; British Society for Children's Orthopaedic Surgery; British Trauma Society; Rheumatoid Arthritis Surgical Society; Society for Back Pain Research; World Orthopaedic Concern
- ● Conf - ET - Exhib - Stat - Inf - LG
- M c 4,220 i
- ¶ Jnl of Bone & Joint Surgery - 24.
  British Orthopaedic News - 3.
  Hbk & LM - 1; ftm only.   AR - 1; free.

British Orthopaedic Foot & Ankle Surgery Society
   a specialist society of the **British Orthopaedic Association**

British Orthopaedic Oncology Society
   a specialist society of the **British Orthopaedic Association**

British Orthopaedic Research Society
   a specialist society of the **British Orthopaedic Association**

British Orthopaedic Specialists Association
   a specialist society of the **British Orthopaedic Association**

British Orthopaedic Sports Trauma & Arthroscopy Association
   a specialist society of the **British Orthopaedic Association**

British Orthopaedic Trainees Association
   a specialist society of the **British Orthopaedic Association**

British Osteopathic Association   (BOA)   1998
- ■ 3 Park Terrace, Manor Rd, LUTON, Beds, LU1 3HN.   (hq)
  01582 488455   fax 01582 481533
  email boa@osteopathy.org   http://www.osteopathy.org
  Chief Exec: Michael Watson
- ▲ Company Limited by Guarantee
- ○ *M, *P; to provide independent representation, care & support for osteopaths
- ● Conf - Res - Inf
- M c 2,600 i
- ¶ Osteopathy Today - 10.

British Othello Federation   (BOF)   1984
- ■ 1 Beaconsfield Terrace, Victoria Rd, CAMBRIDGE, CB4 3BP. (chmn/p)
  01223 366197
  email atc12@mole.bio.cam.ac.uk
  http://www.britishothello.org.uk
  Chmn: Geoff Hubbard,   Mem Sec: Adelaide Carpenter
- ○ *S; to promote the playing & understanding of the game of Othello - a board game of pure skill sometimes known as 'Reversi'
- ● Comp
- < US Othello Assn; Fédn Française d'Othello; Japan Othello Assn
- M 50 i, UK / 50 i, o'seas
- ¶ NL - 2; ftm, £3 nm.

© CBD Research Ltd · Beckenham · BR3 5JS · Tel 020 8650 7745 · E-mail cbd@cbdresearch.com · www.cbdresearch.com

British Outdoor Professionals Association (BOPA) 1993
NR   1 Ash Drive, Rhosgoch, BUILTH WELLS, Powys, LD2 3LU.   (hq)
          0707 122 5853   fax 01479 851279
          email info@the-bopa.co.uk   http://www.the-bopa.co.uk
          Gen Sec: Chris Charters
○   *P; to encourage professionalism in providing the best training
       in outdoor activities (incl abseiling, archery, ballooning,
       caving, gliding, golf, horse-riding, orienteering, sailing, etc)
●   ET - Database providing activities available, instructors & their
       qualifications - Workshops & seminars
M   1,200 i (associate membership for trainees)
¶   NL - 12; free.

British Packaging Association (BPA) 1908
NR   24 Grange St, KILMARNOCK, Ayrshire, KA1 2AR.   (hq)
          01563 570518   fax 01563 572728
          email office@britishpackagingassociation.com
          http://www.britishpackagingassociation.com
          Exec Dir: Allan Glen
▲   Un-incorporated Society
○   *T; (members are mainly small to medium sized owner-run
       boxmakers)
●   Conf - Mtgs - Comp - Inf - Empl
<   CITPA
M   70 f, UK / 3 f, o'seas

British Paediatric & Adolescent Bone Group
       a group of the **Royal College of Paediatrics & Child Health**

British Paediatric Allergy, Immunology & Infection Group
       a group of the **Royal College of Paediatrics & Child Health**

British Paediatric Cardiac Association
       now called the British Congenital Cardiac Association, it is a group of
       the **Royal College of Paediatrics & Child Health**

British Paediatric Mental Health Group
       a group of the **Royal College of Paediatrics & Child Health**

British Paediatric Neurology Association
       a group of the **Royal College of Paediatrics & Child Health**

British Paediatric Pathology Association
       a group of the **Royal College of Paediatrics & Child Health**

British Paediatric Respiratory Society
       a group of the **Royal College of Paediatrics & Child Health**

British Pain Society (the British Chapter of IASP) 1968
NR   Churchill House (3rd floor), 35 Red Lion Square, LONDON,
          WC1R 4SG.   (hq)
          Secretariat: Jenny Duncan (020 7296 7844)
▲   Registered Charity
Br   14 regional
○   *P; to relieve the suffering of pain by promotion of education,
       research & training; to increase professional & public
       awareness of the prevalence of pain & the facilities available
       for its management
Gp   (deal with specific aspects of pain - acute, in children, etc)
●   Conf - ET - Res - Exhib - Inf - LG
<   Intl Assn for the Study of Pain (IASP)
M   1,387 i, 5 f
¶   NL; ftm only.   Information for Patients; free.
       Desirable Criteria for Pain Management Programmes.

British Palomino Society   (BPS)
■   Penrhiwllan, LLANDYSUL, Cardiganshire, SA44 5NZ.   (hq)
          01239 851387   fax 01239 851040
          email britpal@lineone.net
          http://www.britishpalominosociety.co.uk
          Hon Sec: Mrs Peter Howell
▲   Company Limited by Guarantee
○   *B
●   Annual show
M   i
¶   Palomino - 3; ftm, £3 nm.

British Paper Machinery Suppliers Association
       a division of **Picon Ltd**

British Parachute Association (BPA) 1962
■   5 Wharf Way, Glen Parva, LEICESTER, LE2 9TF.   (hq)
          0116-278 5271   fax 0116-247 7662
          email skydive@bpa.org.uk   http://www.bpa.org.uk
          Sec-Gen: Martin Shuttleworth,   Chmn: John Smyth
▲   Company Limited by Guarantee
Br   25; Cyprus, Germany
○   *S; governing body of sport parachuting in the UK
Gp   Competitions (international & national); Development; Safety &
       training
●   Mtgs - ET - Exam - Exhib - Comp
<   Fédn Aéronautique Intle; Sports Coun; CCPR; R Aero Club; UK
       Sport
M   5,100 i, 33,000 i (students)
¶   Skydive, the British Mag - 6; ftm, £22 nm.

British Paralympic Association (BPA) 1989
NR   60 Charlotte St, LONDON, W1T 2NU.   (hq)
          020 7842 5789   fax 020 7842 5777
          email info@paralympics.org.uk
          http://www.paralympics.org.uk
          Chief Exec: Tim Hollingsworth
▲   Company Limited by Guarantee; Registered Charity
○   *S; to support & manage British Paralympic team
●   Mtgs - Comp - Organisation of teams for the winter & summer
       Paralympic Games
<   Intl Paralympic C'ee
M   78 org
       uses title of Paralympics GB

British Parking Association (BPA) 1970
NR   Stuart House, 41-43 Perrymount Rd, HAYWARDS HEATH,
          W Sussex, RH16 3BN.   (hq)
          01444 447300   fax 01444 454105
          email info@britishparking.co.uk
          http://www.britishparking.co.uk
          CEO: Patrick Troy
▲   Company Limited by Guarantee
○   *T; to promote the advancement of knowledge & standards in
       the management, planning, design, improvement, regulation
       & maintenance of all types of parking facilities on & off-street
●   Conf - Mtgs - ET - Exhib - Inf - Lib - LG
M   c 700 i, f & local authorities
¶   Parking News (Jnl) - 11; ftm only.

British Parthenais Cattle Society 1988
NR   Willow Creek Farm, TETNEY, Lincs, DN36 5JZ.   (hsp)
          01472 816974   fax 01472 816974
          email info@parthenais.co.uk
          http://www.parthenais.co.uk
          Sec: Peter Wesley
▲   Company Limited by Guarantee
○   *B; to promote the Parthenais breed for pedigree & beef
       production
●   Agricultural shows - Beef events
<   Nat Beef Assn
M   30 i, UK / 1 i, o'seas
¶   NL - 5/6;   Promotional leaflets; both free.

British Peanut Council   (BPC)   1967
- ■ 20 St Dunstan's Hill (1st floor), LONDON, EC3R 8NQ.   (hq)
     020 7283 2707   fax 020 7623 1310
     http://www.peanuts.org.uk
     Sec: Stuart Logan
- ▲ Company Limited by Guarantee
- ○ *T; to protect & promote the interests of the British peanut
     industry
- Gp Manufacturers; Packers; Importers & distributors; Traders
- ● Mtgs - Inf - LG
- M 34 f, 1 org, UK / 5 f, o'seas
- ¶ BPC NL - 4; ftm only.   BPC Hbk - 1.

British Pelargonium & Geranium Society
   since 2008 **Pelargonium & Geranium Society**

**British Pensioners & Trade Union Action Association
(BP&TUAA)   1972**
- NR 30 Wareham Green, Walsgrave, COVENTRY, Warks,
     CV2 2JL.   (hsp)
     Gen Sec: Alan Wilkins
- ▲ Un-incorporated Society
- Br 150
- ○ *K; active campaigning over pensions, health & social services,
     transport & other issues affecting OAPs
- ● Conf - Mtgs - Res - VE - LG
- M c 5,000 i
- ¶ British Pensioner Jnl - 4; 35p each.

British Percheron Horse Society   (BPHS)   1919
- NR 3 Field Barn Cottages, North Charford, Breamore,
     FORDINGBRIDGE, Hants, SP6 2DW.   (hsp)
     01725 511047
     email secretary@percheron.org.uk
     http://www.percheron.org.uk
     Sec: Mrs Rowena McDermott
- ▲ Company Limited by Guarantee
- ○ *B
- ● Mtgs - Res - VE - Progress Days - Open Days - Marathons -
     Trials
- M c 270 i
- ¶ NL - 4; ftm only.   Studbook, Vol XIV.

British-Peruvian Chamber (Cámara Peruano Británica)   1988
- ■ Torre Parque Mar (piso 22), Av José Larco 1301, MIRAFLORES-
     LIMA 18, Perú.   (hq)
     51 (1) 617 3090   fax 51 (1) 617 3095
     email bpcc@bpcc.org.pe   http://www.bpcc.org.pe
     Pres: Charles Fyfe
- ▲ Registered Charity
- Br Peru
- ○ *C; a bilateral chamber which seeks to promote investment &
     commerce between Peru & the UK as well as corporate social
     responsibility amongst its members
- ● Conf - Mtgs - Comp - Stat - Expt - Inf - VE - LG
- < Assn Bilateral Brit Chams Latin America (BRITLAN)
- M 10 i, 92 f
- ¶ Opportunities (Jnl) - 4; free.
     Members Directory - 2; free.
     Online bulletin - 12; ftm only.

British Pest Control Association   (BPCA)   1942
- ■ 4A Mallard Way, Pride Park, DERBY, DE24 8GX.   (hq)
     01332 294288   fax 01332 295904
     email enquiry@bpca.org.uk   http://www.bpca.org.uk
     Admin: Sofja Halliday (01332 225111)
- ▲ Company Limited by Guarantee
- ○ *T; for servicing companies & others engaged in the control of
     food, hygiene or nuisance pests, or having a close interest in
     industrial pest control; it includes control of pests in food
     storage & preparation areas in domestic premises, factories,
     hospitals, hotels, restaurants, shops & transport; BPCA also
     represents manufacturers & distributors of the pesticides &
     equipment used by the servicing companies & responsible &
     safe use of pesticides in the interests of the general public
- ● Mtgs - ET - Exam - Exhib - Inf - LG
- M 22 i, 229 f, UK / 38 f, o'seas
- ¶ Professional Pest Controller (Jnl) - 4; free.

British Pharmacological Society   (BPS)   1931
- NR 16 Angel Gate, City Rd, LONDON, EC1V 2SG.   (hq)
     020 7239 0171   fax 020 7417 0114
     email ml@bps.ac.uk   http://www.bps.ac.uk
     Exec Officer: Sarah-Jane Stagg
- ▲ Company Limited by Guarantee; Registered Charity
- ○ *L; to promote & advance the science of pharmacology; to
     research into drugs & the way in which they work
- Gp Clinical pharmacology; Pharmacology
- ● Conf - Mtgs - ET - Exam - Res - Exhib
- < Intl U of Pharmacology; Fedn of Eur Pharmacological Socs; Eur
     Assn for Clinical Pharmacology & Therapeutics
- M 1,700 i, UK / 8060 i, o'seas
- ¶ British Jnl of Pharmacology - 12; £103 m.
     British Jnl of Clinical Pharmacology - 12; £55 m.
     PA2 (NL) - 4; ftm only.   AR; free.

British Phonographic Industry Ltd
   since 2007 **BPI (British Recorded Music Industry) Ltd**

British Photodermatology Group
   is a group of the **British Association of Dermatologists**

British Photovoltaic Association
   on 1 April 2006 merged with the **Renewable Energy Association**

British Phycological Society   1952
- NR Union Place, Upgang Lane, WHITBY, N Yorks, YO21 3DT.
     (hsp)
     01947 605501
     email j.pottas@hull.ac.uk
     Sec: Dr Jane Pottas
- ▲ Registered Charity
- ○ *L; study of algae (seaweed and related forms)
- ● Conf - Res - SG - VE
- < Biosciences Fedn
- M 613 i, UK & o'seas
- ¶ European Jnl of Phycology - 4.   NL - 3.

British Piemontese Cattle Society Ltd   1988
- ■ 33 Eden Grange, Little Corby, CARLISLE, Cumbria,
     CA4 8QW.   (hsp)
     01228 562946   fax 01228 562187
     email craig@piemontese.info
     http://www.piemontese.org.uk
     Sec: Craig Culley
- ▲ Company Limited by Guarantee; Registered Charity
- ○ *B
- < Nat Beef Assn
- M i & f

© CBD Research Ltd · Beckenham · BR3 5JS · Tel 020 8650 7745 · E-mail cbd@cbdresearch.com · www.cbdresearch.com

British Pig Association (BPA) 1884
NR Trumpington Mews, 40b High St, Trumpington, CAMBRIDGE,
       CB2 2LS.   (hq)
       01223 845100
       email bpa@britishpigs.org   http://www.britishpigs.org
▲   Company Limited by Guarantee; Registered Charity
○   *B, *V; to represent the pig industry
M   i, f & org

British Plant Gall Society (BPGS) 1986
NR 2 The Dene, NETTLEHAM, Lincs, LN2 2LS.   (hsp)
       01522 875939
       http://www.british-galls.org.uk
       Hon Sec: Graeme Clayton
○   *L; to encourage & co-ordinate the study of cecidology (plant
       galls - an abnormal growth produced by a plant or other
       host under the influence of another organism) with particular
       reference to the British Isles

British Plastics Federation (BPF) 1933
NR 6 Bath Place, Rivington St, LONDON, EC2A 3JE.   (hq)
       020 7457 5000   fax 020 7457 5020
       email reception@bpf.co.uk   http://www.bpf.co.uk
       Dir Gen: Peter Davis
○   *T; for all sectors of the plastics industry; to carry out
       commercial studies & provide commercial trade &
       information services
Gp Additives; Bio-based & degradable; Cellular PVC-U;
       Composites; Equipment; Expanded polysterene; Flexible
       foam; Industrialised plastics welding & fabrication;
       Masterbatch & technical compounds; Moulders & specialist
       processors; Packaging; Plastic pipes; Polymer distributors &
       compounders; Recyclers; Rotational moulding; Sheet &
       coated fabrics; Small plastics processors; Vinyls; Windows
<   Alliance of Ind Assns; Construction Products Assn

British Polarological Research Society
       Organisation lost; see Introduction paragraph 3

British Polio Fellowship (BPF) 1939
NR Unit A (ground floor), Eagle Office Centre, The Runway,
       SOUTH RUISLIP, Middx, HA4 6SE.   (hq)
       0800 018 0586
       email info@britishpolio.org.uk
▲   Registered Charity
○   *W; welfare of people in the UK & Ireland who are disabled by
       poliomyelitis
M   9,000 i

British-Polish Chamber of Commerce (BPCC)
NR 43045 Portman Square, LONDON, W1H 6HN.   (hq)
       020 7969 2789
       http://www.bpcc.org.pl
       Chief Operating Officer: Suzy Adcock
Br 3
○   *C; to develop British business links with Poland
●   Conf - Res - Expt - Inf
<   the British office of BPCC in Warsaw
M   2 i, 30 f, UK / 10 i, 350 f, o'seas
¶   Contact - 6; free.   Membership Directory - 1; ftm, £45 nm.

British-Polish Chamber of Commerce (BPCC)
NR ul Fabryczna 16-22, PL-00-446 WARSAW, Poland.   (hq)
       48 (22) 320 01 00   fax 48 (22) 621 19 37
       Exec Dir: Barbara Stachowiak
▲   Company Limited by Guarantee
Br London
○   *C
Gp C'ees: Banking, Energy, Environment, Human resources &
       management training, Privatisation, Tax
●   Conf - Mtgs - ET - Res - Inf - Lib - LG
<   Confedn Brit Chams Comm Continental Europe (COBCOE);
       Assn Brit Chams Comm
M   5 i, 24 f, UK / 16 i, 301 f, Poland
¶   Contact (NL) - 6.
       Membership Directory - 1.

British Polling Council (BPC) 2004
NR c/o Nick Moon, GfK NOP Social Research, 245 Blackfriars Rd,
       LONDON, SE1 9UL.   (hsb)
       020 7890 9830
       email nick.moon@gfk.com
       http://www.britishpollingcouncil.org
       Hon Sec: Nick Moon
▲   Un-incorporated Society
○   *N, *T; for associations that publish polls; to ensure the highest
       standards of disclosure; designed to ensure that consumers
       of survey results which enter the public domain have an
       adequate basis for judging the reliability & validity of the
       results
●   Conf - Mtgs - Res - Inf - LG - Apply rules of disclosure to
       published polls & investigate alleged breaches
M   12 f

British Polyolefin Textiles Association
       has closed

British Porphyria Association (BPA) 1998
■   136 Devonshire Rd, DURHAM, DH1 2BL.   (regd/address)
       01474 369231
       email helpline@porphyria.org.uk
       http://www.porphyria.org.uk
       Chmn: John Chamberlayne,   Admin: Sarah Pepperdine
▲   Registered Charity
○   *W; to encourage research & improve understanding of
       Porphyria; to offer help & advice to sufferers & their families
●   Mtgs - ET - Res - Inf
<   Eur Porphyria Initiative; Amer (& Canadian) Porphyria Assn(s)
>   Porphyria Interest Gp; Genetic Interest Gp (GIG)
M   c 300 families
¶   NL - 2.
       Patients booklets & drugs list.

British Ports Association (BPA) 1992
■   Carthusian Court (4th floor), 12 Carthusian St, LONDON,
       EC1M 6EZ.   (hq)
       020 7260 1780   fax 020 7260 1784
       email info@britishports.org.uk
       http://www.britishports.org.uk
       Dir: David Whitehead,   Sec: Richard Ballantyne
▲   Un-incorporated Society
○   *T; to represent the interests of member ports in the UK &
       Europe
●   Conf - Mtgs
M   110 f & org
¶   Monthly Update - 12; m only.

British-Portuguese Chamber of Commerce (Câmara de Comércio Luso-Británica) (BPCC) 1911

- ■ Rua da Estrela 8, 1200-669 LISBOA, Portugal. (hq)
  351 213 942 020   fax 351 213 942 029
  email info@bpcc.pt   http://www.bpcc.pt
  Chief Exec: Christopher Barton
- ▲ Un-incorporated Society
- ○ *C; to promote Anglo-Portuguese trade relations; to provide services for members
- ● Conf - ET - Res - Expt - Inf
- < Coun Brit Cham Comm Continental Europe (COBCOE)
- M 23 f, UK / 469 f, Portugal
- ¶ Members Directory - 1; ftm, 56 nm.

British Postmark Society (BPS) 1958

- ■ 12 Dunavon Park, STRATHAVEN, Lanarks, ML10 6LP. (hsp)
  01357 522430
  email johlen@stracml10.freeserve.co.uk
  http://www.britishpostmarksociety.org.uk
  Hon Sec: John A Strachan
- ▲ Registered Charity
- ○ *G; 'to promote & to co-ordinate the study & collection of British postal markings, particularly of the 20th century & subsequently, & the means & methods by which they are applied; to publish & disseminate the results of such study for the education of the public'
- Gp Printed Postage Impression Study Circle
- ● Mtgs - Res - Comp - SG - Lib - Yearly auction - Yearly sale - Circulating exchange packets
- M 222 i, UK / 18 i, o'seas
  (Sub: £12 UK / £17 o'seas)
- ¶ Jnl - 4; ftm, £12 yr nm.
  PPI News & Junk Mail (NL) - irreg; ftm, £3 yr nm.
  LM - 3 yrly; ftm only.   Library List; on website.

British Potato Trade Association (NASPM) 1940

- NR 12 Buckstone Hill, EDINBURGH, EH10 6TH. (regd/off)
  0131-623 0183
  http://www.bpta.org.uk
  Sec: Charlie Greenslade
- ▲ Un-incorporated Society
- ○ *T
- ● Mtgs - ET - SG - Inf - VE - LG
- < Brit Eur Potato Assn; Jt Potato Trade Coun; Nat Inst Agricl Botany
- × 2006 (National Association of Seed Potato Merchants (Scottish Potato Trades Association

British Poultry Council (BPC) 2002

- NR 5-11 Lavington St, LONDON, SE1 0NZ. (hq)
  0772 555 4944
  email info@britishpoultry.org.uk
  http://www.britishpoultry.org.uk
  Chief Exec: Peter Bradnock
- ▲ Company Limited by Guarantee
- ○ *T; to promote the interest of the British poultry meat production (all species - chicken, turkeys, ducks & geese are represented)
- ● LG
- < avec (Association of Poultry Processors & Poultry Import & Export Trade in the EU)
- M 95% of the sector

British Power Kitesports Association (BPKA) 1994

- NR PO Box 4015, SMETHWICK, W Midlands, B67 6HJ.
  email admin@bpka.co.uk   http://www.bpka.co.uk
- ○ *S; Kite buggying, kite surfing, kite landboarding, snow kiting & power kiting
- M 4,121 i
  (Sub: £15)
- × 2006 British Buggy Club

British Precast Concrete Federation Ltd (BPCF) 1964

- ■ 60 Charles St, LEICESTER, LE1 1FB. (hq)
  0116-253 6161   fax 0116-251 4568
  email info@britishprecast.org
  http://www.britishprecast.org
  Chief Exec: Martin Clarke
- ▲ Company Limited by Guarantee
- ○ *T; promoting the interests of the precast concrete industry; provision of central services; (is structured on product associations, see below)
- Gp 9 product associations:
  Architectural Cladding Association
  Box Culvert Association
  Concrete Pipeline Systems Association
  Concrete Sleeper Manufacturers' Association
  Construction Packed Products Association
  Interpave, the Precast Concrete Paving & Kerb Association
  Precast Flooring Federation
  Prestressed Concrete Association
  Structural Precast Association
  6 affiliated associations:
  Aircrete Products Association
  Concrete Block Association
  Concrete Tile Manufacturers Association
  Interlay, the Association of Block Paving Contractors
  Modern Masonry Alliance
  Traditional Housing Bureau
- ● Mtgs - Inf - Empl - LG
- < Bureau Intl du Beton Manufacture; Construction Products Assn
- M 106 f, UK / 5 f, o'seas

British Precision Pilots Association (BPPA) 1975

- ■ 1 Lavender Way, BOURNE, Lincs, PE10 9TT.
  01778 421346
  email chairman@rallyflyingclub.org
  http://www.rallyflyingclub.org
  Chmn: Martin Reynolds
- ▲ Company Limited by Guarantee
- ○ *P, *S; to promote the sport of precision & rally flying; to represent GB in international competitions
- ● Comp
- < R Aero Club
- M 30 i
  (Sub: £50)

British Printing Industries Federation (BPIF) 1900

- NR Farringdon Point, 29-35 Farringdon Rd, LONDON, EC1M 3JF. (hq)
  020 7915 8300
  http://www.britishprint.com
  Chief Exec: Michael Johnson
- ▲ Company Limited by Guarantee
- Br 6
- ○ *T; to encourage efficiency & profitability in the printing industry
- Gp Book production, Cartons, Digital, Direct marketing special products, Engraved stationery, Finishers, In-house & corporate print services, Labels, Operational print suppliers, Promotional finishers, Web offset
- M f

© CBD Research Ltd · Beckenham · BR3 5JS · Tel 020 8650 7745 · E-mail cbd@cbdresearch.com · www.cbdresearch.com

British Printing Society (BPS) 1944
NR 2A Chatsworth Rd, Parkstone, POOLE, Dorset, BH14 0QL.
  (hsp)
    email enquiries@bpsnet.org.uk
    Sec: S Hubbard
▲ Un-incorporated Society
Br 20; Germany, Italy, Japan, N Zealand, South Africa, Spain,
    USA
○ *G; to unite full-time, part-time & hobby printers in friendly
    association; to improve the standards of craftsmanship of its
    members; to encourage printing as a hobby
Gp Blockmaking; Bookbinding; Letterpress; Printing (25 specialist
    printers); Publishing
● Conf - Mtgs - Exhib - Inf - Lib - VE
M 400 i, UK / 30 i, o'seas
    (Sub: £24 UK / £30 o'seas)
¶ Small Printer - 12.   Small Printing - 1.
    Basic Letterpress for Beginners (Jubilee issue):
      1: History of Printing Ink.
      2: Glossary of Printing Terms.
      3: Index to ISPA News & Small Printer (Pt 1) 1954-82.
      4: The Adana Collection: a history of the Adana Company &
        its machines.

British Private Equity & Venture Capital Association
    see **BVCA (British Private Equity & Venture Capital
    Association**

British Professional Pool Players Association
    has closed.

British Professional Toastmasters Authority
    is no longer in existence

British Promotional Merchandise Association (BPMA) 1965
NR 52-53 Russell Square, LONDON, WC1B 4HP.   (hq)
    020 7631 6960   fax 020 7831 6944
    email enquiries@bpma.co.uk   http://www.bpma.co.uk
    Co Sec: Colin Levine
▲ Company Limited by Guarantee
○ *T; to bring together buyers & sellers within the promotional
    merchandise industry
● ET - Res - Exhib - Inf - LG
< Marketing Assn Alliance
M 700 f
    (Sub: £375-£750)
¶ Promotions Buyer - 12; free.
    bpma Directory: the authoritative guide for buyers of
    promotional merchandise.
    Promotions Buyer [Ybk] - 1; free.

British Property Federation (BPF) 1974
NR St Albans House (5th floor), 57-59 Haymarket, LONDON,
    SW1Y 4QX.   (hq)
    020 7828 0111   fax 020 7834 3442
    email info@bpf.org.uk   http://www.bpf.org.uk
○ *T; to represent the views of the property industry, both
    commercial & residential

British Protected Ornamentals Association (BPOA) 1980
NR PO Box 691, CHICHESTER, W Sussex, PO19 9NA.   (hq)
    01243 784699
    email bpoa@btconnect.com
    http://www.bpoaonline.co.uk
    Sec: David Fox
○ *H, *T; 'to represent bedding & pot plant growers in aspects of
    promotion, political & technical issues relating to their
    business'
● Conf - Mtgs - ET - Res - Exhib - SG - Stat - Inf - PL - VE - Empl -
    LG - Social events
< Nat Farmers U
M 180+ i, 100 f, 25 org
    (Sub: £50 - £600)
¶ NL - 12;   News & Views - 4; both ftm only.
× 2007 British Bedding & Pot Plant Association

British Psychoanalytic Council (BPC) 1993
NR 19-23 Wedmore St (suite 7), LONDON, N19 4RU.   (hq)
    020 7561 9240
    email mail@psychoanalytic-council.org
    http://www.psychoanalytic-council.org
    Hon Sec: James Johnston
▲ Company Limited by Guarantee
○ *N; an association of training institutions & professional
    associations of psychoanalysts, Jungian analysts,
    psychoanalytic psychotherapists & child psychotherapists
● Conf - Mtgs - ET - Res - LG
< Eur Fedn of Psychoanalytic Psychotherapists (EFPP)
> Soc of Analytical Psychology; Brit Psychoanalytical Soc; Brit Assn
    of Psychotherapists; Scot Assn of Psychoanalytic
    Psychotherapists; NI Assn for the Study of Psychoanalysis
M 1,700 i
    (Sub: £98)
¶ Register of Psychotherapists - 1; ftm, £35 nm.
    NL - 2;   AR - 1; both ftm only.
    Brochures:
      What is Psychoanalytic Psychotherapy? free.
      Making sense of Psychotherapy and Psychoanalysis; £1.50.

British Psychoanalytical Society 1913
NR Byron House, 112A Shirland Rd, LONDON, W9 2EQ.
    020 7563 5000   fax 020 7563 5001
    http://www.psychoanalysis.org.uk
    Pres: David Bell
▲ Registered Charity
○ *P; promotion & dissemination of the theory & practice of
    Freudian psychoanalysis
● Conf - Mtgs - ET - Inf - Lib - VE
< Intl Psychoanalytical Assn; Brit Psychoanalytic Coun
M 439 i, UK
¶ International Jnl of Psychoanalysis - 6.

British Psychodrama Association (BPA) 1984
NR 33 Prince's Rd, CHELTEMHAM, Glos, GL50 2TX.   (treas/p)
    0758 284 2231
▲ Company Limited by Guarantee
○ *L, *P; to promote & encourage the use of psychodrama
M i & org

British Psychological Society   (BPS)   1901
- ■ St Andrews House, 48 Princess Rd East, LEICESTER, LE1 7DR. (hq)
  0116-254 9568   fax 0116-227 1314
  email enquiries@bps.org.uk   http://www.bps.org.uk
  Hon Sec: Prof Pam Maras
- ▲ Registered Charity
- Br 7
- ○ *L, *P; advancement of knowledge of psychology both pure & applied
- Gp Sections: Cognitive, Consciousness, Developmental, Education, History & philosophy, Lesbian & gay, Mathematical, Psychobiology, Psychotherapy, Social, Sports & exercise, Statistical & computing, Transpersonal, Women
  Divisions: Clinical, Counselling, Educational, Forensic, Health, Neuropsychology, Occupational, Teachers & researchers;
  Special groups: Social services
- ● Conf - Mtgs - ET - Exam - LG
- < Eur Fedn of Psychological Assns
- M 38, 485 i, UK / 3,705 i, o'seas
- ¶ The Psychologist - 12; ftm, £66 yr nm.
  British Jnl of Psychology - 4; £17 m.
  British Jnl of Clinical Psychology - 4.
  British Jnl of Developmental Psychology - 4.
  British Jnl of Educational Psychology - 4.
  British Jnl of Health Psychology - 4.
  British Jnl of Mathematical & Statistical Psychology - 2.
  Jnl of Occupational & Organisational Psychology - 4.
  Psychology & Psychotherapy - 4.
  Legal & Criminological Psychotherapy - 2.

British Pteridological Society   (BPS)   1891
- NR c/o Dept of Botany, Natural History Museum, Cromwell Rd, LONDON, SW7 5BD.   (mail/address)
  020 8850 3218   fax 010 8850 3218
  email secretary@ebps.org.uk   http://www.ebps.org.uk
  Gen Sec: Dr Yvonne C Golding
- ▲ Registered Society
- ○ *H, *L, *Q; study, growing & conservation of ferns & other pteridophytes
- Gp Tree-ferns
- ● Conf - Mtgs - ET - SG - Inf - VE - Spore & plant exchange
- < Nat Coun Consvn Plants & Gardens; Plantlife; R Horticl Society
- M 478 i, UK / 248 i, o'seas
- ¶ Fern Gazette - 1;   Pteridologist - 1;   Bulletin - 1; all ftm only.
  Special publications series - irreg.

British Pugwash Group   1959
- ■ Ground floor flat, 63A Great Russell St, LONDON, WC1B 3BJ.   (hq)
  020 7405 6661
  email pugwash@mac.com   http://www.pugwash.org/uk
  Sec: Dr Christopher Watson
- ▲ Un-incorporated Society
- ○ *L; social implications of development of science & technology, especially in military area (international relations, nuclear weapons, peace research, science policy); education & dissemination of information
- ● Conf - Mtgs - ET - Res
- < Pugwash Conferences on Science & World Affairs
- M 240 i, UK / 10 i, o'seas
- ¶ Pugwash NL - 2.   BPG Reports - irreg;   Occasional Reports.

British Pump Manufacturers' Association   (BPMA)   1941
- NR National Metalforming Centre, 47 Birmingham Rd, WEST BROMWICH, W Midlands, B70 6PY.   (hq)
  0121-601 6350   fax 0121-601 6373
  email admin@bpma.org.uk   http://www.bpma.org.uk
  Dir: Brian Huxley
- ○ *T; suppliers of liquid pumps & pumping equipment
- Gp C'ees: Marketing/commercial; Marketing data; Small firms; Technical; Training
- ● Conf - Mtgs - ET - Res - Expt - Inf - LG
- < C'ee Eur Pump Assns (EUROPUMP); Mechanical & Metal Trs Confedn (METCOM)
- M c 80 f
- ¶ Pumps from Britain - 2 yrly.

British Puppet & Model Theatre Guild   (BPMTG)   1925
- ■ 65 Kingsley Ave, LONDON, W13 0EH.   (chmn/p)
  020 8997 8236   fax 020 8997 8236
  email peter@peterpuppet.co.uk
  http://www.puppetguild.org.uk
  Hon Chmn: Peter Charlton
- ○ *D; to advocate the use of puppets & model theatres; to encourage the art & practice of puppetry
- ● Mtgs - Inf - Shows
- M c 270 i & org
- ¶ Puppet Master - 1;   NL - 12; both ftm.

British Pyrotechnists Association   (BPA)   1980
- ■ 8 Aragon Place, Kimbolton, HUNTINGDON, Cambs, PE28 0JD.   (hsb)
  01480 861975   fax 01480 861108
  email enquiries@bpa-fmg.org.uk
  http://www.pyro.org.uk
  Sec: Dr Tom Smith
- ▲ Registered Charity
- ○ *T; a non-commercial organisation promoting the safe manufacture, handling & use of pyrotechnics
- ● Mtgs - Exam - Stat - Inf - LG
- < Eur Fireworks Assn (EUFIAS)
- M 36 f
  (Sub: £450)

British Quadrathlon Association   (BQA)   1995
- ■ 2 Stockton Cottages, Oldcastle Heath, MALPAS, Cheshire, SY14 7AE.   (hsp)
  email press@britishquadrathlon.org.uk
  http://www.britishquadrathlon.org.uk
  Sec: Jean Ashley
- ▲ Un-incorporated Society
- ○ *S; to promote & suport the sport of quadrathlon (swimming, cycling, kayaking & running)
- ● Comp
- < Wld Quadrathalon Fedn
- M 50 i
  (Sub: £12 - £25)

British Quality Foundation   (BQF)   1993
- NR 32-34 Great Peter St, LONDON, SW1P 2QX.   (hq)
  020 7654 5000
- ▲ Company Limited by Guarantee
- ○ *T; 'total quality management & business excellence'
- Gp Automotive; Construction; Education & training; Engineering, projects & operations; Financial services; Food & drink; Founder members; Health; IT & telecommunications; Insurance; Local authorities; Printing, paper, packaging & media; Social care; T Q professionals; Tourism & hospitality
- ● Conf - Mtgs - ET - Res - SG - Inf - Lib
- M f
- ¶ UK Excellence - 6.

British Quilt Study Group
   a group of the **Quilters' Guild of the British Isles**

British Rabbit Council (BRC) 1918
■ Purefoy House, 7 Kirkgate, NEWARK, Notts, NG24 1AD.   (hq)
  01636 676042   fax 01636 611683
  email info@thebrc.org   http://www.thebrc.org
  Co Sec: Mrs Susan Mason,   Hon Treas: J F Fletcher
▲ Un-incorporated Society
○ *B; the governing body for fur & fancy rabbits & cavies
● Conf - Mtgs - Exhib - Comp - Inf - Lib
M 2,436 i, 220 org
  (Sub: varies c £22.50)
¶ Fur & Feather (inc Rabbits) - 12; £3.50 m only.

British Racing & Sports Car Club   (BRSCC)   1946
NR Homesdale Business Centre, Platt Industrial Estate,
  Maidstone Rd, BOROUGH GREEN, Kent, TN15 8JL.   (hq)
  01732 780100
○ *S; organisation of motor racing
M i

British Radio Car Association   (BRCA)   1972
■ Park View, Uffculme, CULLOMPTON, Devon, EX15 3DN.
  (mem/sp)
  01884 840158   fax 01884 840158
  email membership@brca.org   http://www.brca.org
  Mem Sec: Jacquie Rowcliffe
○ *G; to organise all aspects of radio controlled model car racing
  in Britain
● Organising races
< RAC
M 9,500 i, 230 clubs
¶ Circuit Chatter (NL) - 4;   BRCA Hbk - 1; both ftm only.

British Ready-Mixed Concrete Association
  is a product group of the **Mineral Products Association**

British Rebirth Society   (BRS)
NR 41/6 The Causeway, EDINBURGH, EH15 3QA.   (mem/sp)
  0131-661 2039
  http://www.rebirthingbreathwork.co.uk
  Mem Sec: Jo Tait
  Gen Sec: Clare Gabriel (0845 330 8214)
○ *P; 'The Society for Transformation through Breathwork'.   To
  educate people in the techniques of conscious connected
  breathing & its benefits
● ET - Workshops
M i
¶ Books.

British Record Society Ltd   1888
NR Department of Economic History, LSE, Houghton St, LONDON,
  WC2A 2AE.   (hsb)
  email p.h.wallis@lse.ac.uk
  http://www.britishrecordsociety.org
  Hon Sec: Patrick Wallis
○ *L
● Compilation & publication of indexes to historical records,
  particularly testamentary records

British Recorded Music Industry Ltd
  see **BPI (British Recorded Music Industry) Ltd**

British Records Association   (BRA)   1932
■ c/o Finsbury Library, 245 St John Street, LONDON,
  EC1V 4NB.   (hq)
  020 7833 0428   fax 020 7833 0416
  email britrecassoc@hotmail.com
  http://www.britishrecordsassociation.org.uk
  Hon Sec: Catherine Taylor
▲ Registered Charity
○ *L; to encourage & assist the preservation, care, study &
  publication of records; acts as a clearing-house & rescue
  body for historic documents
Gp Records preservation
● Conf - Mtgs - ET - Exhib - SG - Inf - Storage - Preservation
M 551 i, 416 f (incl museums, galleries, libraries, universities)
  (Sub: £25 i, £55 f, £20 org, UK / £35 i, £65 f,
  £30 org, o'seas)
¶ Archives (Jnl) - 2; ftm, £55 yr nm.   NL - 2; ftm only.
  Archives & User Series (guides to source material for research).
  Guidelines 1-5; on website.

British Red Cross Society   (BRCS)   1870
NR 44 Moorfields, LONDON, EC2Y 9AL.   (hq)
  020 7877 7000   fax 020 7562 2000
  email information@redcross.org.uk
  http://www.redcross.org.uk
  Chief Exec: Sir Nicholas Young
▲ Registered Charity
Br 70; 8 o'seas
○ *W; an officially recognised organisation for humanitarian aid;
  disaster preparedness & response; refugees & asylum
  seekers; overseas development; first aid training & health
  activities; supporting statutory authorities in UK; community
  services, education / youth & schools
● Conf - Mtgs - ET - Res - Exhib - SG - Stat - Inf - Lib - PL - LG
< Intl Red Cross; Red Crescent Movement
M 40,000 i
¶ Lifeline (Jnl).   Information pack.
  Annual Review.   Trustees' Report & Accounts.

British Reed Growers' Association   (BRGA)   1967
NR c/o Brown & Co, Old Bank of England Court, Queen St,
  NORWICH, Norfolk, NR2 4TA.   (hsb)
  01603 629871   fax 01603 760756
  email info@brga.org.uk   http://www.brga.org.uk
  Sec: I D Lonsdale,   Chmn: R Buxton
▲ Un-incorporated Society
○ *T; promotion of reed & sedge growing; coordination of supply
  to thatchers, monitoring supply & demand; promotion of
  research into improved production
● Mtgs - Res - Stat - Inf - LG
M 16 i, 5 f, 15 org
¶ Reedbed Management for Commercial & Wildlife
  Interests; £14.95 (published by RSPB).
  Norfolk Reed Roofing Today;   Buying & Selling Reed;
  Reedbed Management for Bitterns;
  New Wetland Harvests - New Life for the Broads Fens; all free.

British Reflexology Association   (BRA)   1985
■ Monks Orchard, Whitbourne, WORCESTER, WR6 5RB.   (hq)
  01886 821207   fax 01886 822017
  email bra@britreflex.co.uk   http://www.britreflex.co.uk
  Chmn: Miss Nicola Hall
▲ Company Limited by Guarantee
○ *P; to promote the practice of reflexology
● Conf - Mtgs - Res - Inf
< Reflexology in Europe Network (RIEN)
M 700 i
¶ Footprints (NL) - 4; £10 yr (UK) (£13 Europe).

British Refractories & Industrial Ceramics Association
  a group of the **British Ceramic Confederation**

British Refrigeration Association   (BRA)   1940
- ■ 2 Waltham Court, Milley Lane, Hare Hatch, READING, Berks, RG10 9TH.   (hq)
  0118-940 3416   fax 0118-940 6258
  email info@feta.co.uk   http://www.feta.co.uk/
  Dir Gen: C Sloan
- ○ *T; the interests of the refrigeration & air conditioning plant & equipment industry
- Gp Cabinet & cold store; Components; Contractors; Education & training; Refrigeration machinery & air conditioning; Statistics; User & suppliers
- ● Conf - Mtgs - ET - Exhib - SG - Stat - Inf - Lib - VE - Empl
- < Fedn Envtl Tr Assns (FETA)
- M 84 f
- ¶ NL - 4; ftm.   LM - 1;   AR; both free.

British Register of Complementary Practitioners
administered by the **Institute for Complementary & Natural Medicine**

British Reining
a discipline member of the **British Equestrian Federation**

British Renal Society   (BRS)   2001
- NR 26 Oriental Rd, WOKING, Surrey, GU22 7AW.   (hq)
  01483 764114   fax 01483 727816
  http://www.britishrenal.org
  Secretariat: Patti & John Monkhouse
- ▲ Registered Charity
- ○ *K, *W; 'to promote effective patient-centred multi professional care to improve the quality of life for people with kidney failure'
- ● Conf - Inf
- M i
- ¶ Abstracts - 1.

British Resorts & Destinations Association   (BRADA)   1921
- ■ Crown Buildings, 9-11 Eastbank St, SOUTHPORT, Merseyside, PR8 1DL.   (hsb)
  0151-934 2286   fax 0151-934 2287
  email bresorts@sefton.u-net.com
  http://www.britishresorts.co.uk
  Hon Sec: Mr G Haywood   Dir: Peter Hampson
- ○ *T; interests of UK inland & seaside resorts & tourist regions
- ● Conf - Mtgs
- M 60 local authorities, 8 tourist boards
- ¶ AR; m only.
- ✕ 2006 (1 April) British Resorts Association

British Retail Consortium   (BRC)   1992
- ■ 21 Dartmouth St, LONDON, SW1H 9BP.   (hq)
  020 7854 8900   fax 020 7854 8901
  email info@brc.org.uk   http://www.brc.org.uk
  Dir Gen: Stephen Robertson
- ▲ Company Limited by Guarantee
- Br Edinburgh; Belgium
- ○ *T; 'represents over 90% of the retail industry'
- < EUROCOMMERCE (retail, wholesale & international trade representation to the European Community)
- M 10,000 f

British Retinitis Pigmentosa Society   (BRPS)   1975
- ■ PO Box 350, BUCKINGHAM, MK18 1GZ.   (hsp)
  01280 821334 (office)   fax 01280 815900
  email info@brps.org.uk   http://www.brps.org.uk + fightingblindness.org.uk
  Chief Exec: David Head
- ▲ Registered Charity
- Br 30 & o'seas
- ○ *W; to raise funds for scientific research; to provide treatments leading to a cure for RP; to provide a welfare support & guidance service to members & their families
- ● Res - Inf - Provision of a welfare & guidance service to members
  Helpline: 0845 123 2354 - helpline@brps.org.uk
- < Retina Intl; Assn Med Res Charities (AMRC); Genetic Interest Gp (GIG)
- M c 3,000 i
  (Sub: £20)
- ¶ NL - 4.   e-bulletin - 12.
  Publications list available.

British Rig Owners' Association   (BROA)   1983
- ■ Carthusian Court, 12 Carthusian St, LONDON, EC1M 6EZ.   (hq)
  020 7417 2827   fax 020 7726 2080
  email postmaster@broa.org   http://www.broa.org
  Mgr: Adrian Lester
- ○ *T; promote & protect the interests of British oil rig owners & managers
- ● Mtgs - SG - Inf - LG
- M 9 f

British Rigid Urethane Foam Manufacturers' Association Ltd   (BRUFMA)   1967
- ■ 12a High St East, GLOSSOP, Derbys, SK13 8DA.   (hq)
  01457 855884
  http://www.brufma.co.uk
- ▲ Company Limited by Guarantee
- ○ *T; interests of manufacturers, raw materials & chemicals suppliers & machinery manufacturers of rigid urethane foam
- Gp Technical; Building applications; Environmental health & safety
- ● Conf - Mtgs - LG
- < PU Europe; Construction Products Assn
- M 18 f
- ¶ LM - on change of details.   AR.
  Information Documents - irreg.

British Roller Sports Federation   (BRSF)   1998
- NR PO Box 68966, LONDON, NW26 9FD.   (hq)
  020 8838 1171
  email secretary@brsf.co.uk   http://www.brsf.co.uk
  Gen Sec: Kathy Morris
- ○ *S; the national governing body for all roller sports in the UK
- Gp Artistic; Freestyle; Hockey (inline, roller & skater); Roll ball; Roller derby; Speed
- < Intl Fedn of Roller Sports (FIRS); Confedn of Eur Roller Skating (CERS)
- M i, clubs

British Rootzone & Top Dressing Manufacturers Association   (BRTMA)   2000
- NR Federation House, STONELEIGH PARK, Warks, CV8 2RF.   (hq)
  024 7641 4999   fax 024 7641 4990
  email brtma@sportsandplay.com
  http://www.brtma.com
  Sec: Jacqui Baldwin
- ▲ Un-incorporated Society
- ○ *T; 'manufacture of quality construction mixes & top dressings'
- ● Mtgs - ET - Res - Stat - Inf
- < a group of the Fedn of Sports & Play Assns (FSPA)
- M 11 f
- ¶ Ybk - 1; free.

British Rope Skipping Association   (BRSA)
NR   39 Riverside, STUDLEY, Warks, B80 7SD.
         01527 854194
         http://www.brsa.org.uk
         Sec: Sue Dale
○   *G, *S

British Rose Group
         a specialist group of the **Horticultural Trades Association**

British Rose Growers Association
         is now the British Rose Group of the **Horticultural Trades Association**

British Rouge Sheep Society
NR   Marston Mill Farm, Priory Road, Wolston, COVENTRY, CV8 3FX.
         024 7654 1766   fax 024 7654 1766
         email secretary@rouge-society.co.uk
         http://www.rouge-society.co.uk
         Sec: Mrs Sue Archer
▲   Company Limited by Guarantee; Registered Charity
○   *B
<   Nat Sheep Assn
M   c 120 i

British Rubber & Polyurethane Products Association   (BRPPA) 2006
NR   5 Berewyk Hall Court, White Colne, COLCHESTER, Essex, CO6 2QD.
         01787 226995   fax 0845 301 6583
         http://www.brppa.co.uk
○   *T; to represent the British rubber & polyurethane product manufacturers, & the suppliers of new materials & services
<   Alliance of Ind Assns

British Saddleback Breeders Club   1995
■   Freepost (GL442), CIRENCESTER, Glos, GL7 5BR.   (mail)
         01285 860229   fax 01285 860229
         email mail@saddlebacks.org.uk
         http://www.saddlebacks.org.uk
         Hon Sec: Richard Lutwyche
▲   Un-incorporated Society
○   *B
●   Mtgs - Comp - Workshops
M   120 i, 5 f, UK / 2 i, o'seas
¶   NL.
✕   2007 British Saddleback Pig Breeders Club

British Safety Industry Federation   (BSIF)   1994
■   93 Bowen Court, St Asaph Business Park, ST ASAPH, Denbighs, LL17 0JE.   (asa)
         01745 585600   fax 01745 585800
         email b.s.i.f@virgin.net   http://www.bsif.co.uk
         Sec Gen: Geoff Hooke
▲   Company Limited by Guarantee
○   *T
Gp   Personal Safety Manufacturers Association
         Pipe manufacturers; Safety distributors; Safety products manufacturers; Safety professionals; Testing & certification organisations
●   Conf - Mtgs - Exam - Res - Exhib - Expt - Inf - Lib - LG
<   Eur Safety Fedn
M   162 f
¶   BSIF Guide - 1;   Health & Safety Matters - 6; both free.

British Sailing
         a group association of the **British Marine Federation**

British Sandwich Association   (BSA)   1990
NR   Association House, 18c Moor St, CHEPSTOW, Monmouthshire, NP16 5DB.   (hq)
         01291 636331   fax 01291 630402
         email admin@sandwich.org.uk
         http://www.sandwich.org.uk
         Dir: Jim Winship
○   *T; to raise standards in the UK sandwich industry
●   Conf - Mtgs - Res - Comp - Inf - VE - LG
M   1,450 i & f, UK / 87 i & f, o'seas
¶   Sandwich & Snack News - 8; ftm, £55 yr nm.

British Sausage Appreciation Society   (BSAS)   1992
NR   BPEX (AHDB), Stoneleigh Park, KENILWORTH, Warks, CV8 2TL.   (hq)
         024 7669 2051   fax 024 7641 9071
         http://www.britishsausageweek.com
▲   Un-incorporated Society
○   *G; to promote interest in British sausage eating & the range of sausages available in Britain
●   ET - Comp - Inf - Promotional roadshow
M   7,396 i
¶   The Missing Link - 1.

British Science Association   1831
NR   Wellcome Wolfson Building, 165 Queen's Gate, LONDON, SW7 5HD.   (hq)
         0870 770 7101   fax 020 7581 6587
         email help@the-ba.net
         http://www.britishscienceassociation.org
         Chief Exec: Dr Roland Jackson
▲   Registered Charity
○   *L; 'to connect science with people, making science itself & the ways in which it is applied accessible to all'
Gp   16 sections covering the main areas of science: engineering, mathematics, medicine, social science
●   Conf - Mtgs
M   3,000 i, 100 f, 200 org, UK / 100 i, o'seas
¶   Science & Public Affairs.
✕   2010 British Association for the Advancement of Science

British Science Fiction Association Ltd   (BSFA)   1958
■   Flat 4 Stratton Lodge, 79 Bulwer Rd, BARNET, Herts, EN5 5EU.   (msp)
         http://www.bsfa.co.uk
         Mem Sec: Peter Wilkinson
▲   Company Limited by Guarantee
○   *A, *G; promotion of science fiction & related genre in all media
Gp   Orbiter: postal writers' workshops
●   Inf - Publishing
M   550 i, UK / 50 i, o'seas
¶   Vector (Jnl) - 6;   Matrix (NL) - 6;
         Focus (Writers' Jnl) - 2; all ftm.

British Scoliosis Society
         a specialist society of the **British Orthopaedic Association**

British Scooter Sport Organisation   (BSSO)   1969
NR   82 Broadlands Way, COLCHESTER, Essex, CO4 0AR. (mem/sb)
         email info@scooterracing.org.uk
         http://www.scooterracing.org.uk
         Mem Sec: Scott Chapman
○   *S; to promote scooter road racing
Gp   Road racing: Scooter cross (off road, on grass)
●   Mtgs - Comp
<   Auto-Cycle U
>   Lambretta Club of GB; Vespa Club of GB
M   100 i, 500 org
¶   NL - 12; ftm only.

British Security Industry Association Ltd   (BSIA)   1967
- ■ Kirkham House, John Comyn Drive, WORCESTER, WR3 7NS. (hq)
  0845 389 3889   fax 0845 389 0761
  email info@bsia.co.uk   http://www.bsia.co.uk
  Chief Exec: James Kelly
- ▲ Company Limited by Guarantee
- ○ *T; to represent the security sector; members have to adhere to British standards & codes of practice
- Gp Cash & property marking; Cash & valuables in transit; Closed circuit television; Export council; Information destruction; Physical security; Security guarding; Security systems
- ● Conf - Mtgs - Res - Exhib - Comp - Stat - Expt - Inf - LG - Formation of technical standards & codes of practice
- < Eurosafe; Euralarm; CoESS
- M 450 f, UK / 10 f, o'seas
- ¶ Spectrum (NL) - 2;   Security Direct (directory) - 1; both free. LM - 6; free (& on website).
  Publications list on website.

British Sedimentological Research Group
    a group of the **Geological Society**

British Shakespeare Association   (BSA)   2003
- NR 15 Appold St, LONDON, EC2A 2HB.
  http://www.britishshakespeare.ws
- ○ *A
- ¶ Shakespeare (Jnl) - 4.

British Sheep Dairying Association   (BSDA)   1983
- NR c/o High Weald Dairy, Tremains Farm, Treemans Rd, HORSTED KEYNES, W Sussex, RH17 7EA.   (hsp)
  01825 791636
  email office@sheepdairying.co.uk
  http://www.sheepdairying.co.uk
- ○ *T; to sponsor the improvement of dairy sheep in the UK; to promote the marketing of sheep milk
- Gp Milk products; Sheep milk marketing
- ● Conf - Comp - SG - Expt - Inf - VE - LG
- < Schweiz Milchschafzucht-Genossenschaft; N Amer Sheep Dairying Soc
- M c 300 i
- ¶ Sheep Dairy News (Jnl) - 3; ftm.
  (Sub: £50)

British Shell Collectors Club   (BSCC)   1972
- ■ Higher Marsh Farm, HENSTRIDGE, Somerset, BA8 0NQ. (hsp)
  01963 363715
  http://www.britishshellclub.org
  Hon Sec: Tom Walker
- ○ *G, *L; to promote the study of all aspects of shells, both land & marine, British & foreign, & of the molluscs which produce them
- ● Exhib - Comp
- M c 230 i
- ¶ Pallidula (NL) - 2; ftm only.

British Shippers Council
    a group of the **Freight Transport Association**

British Shogi Federation   (BSF)
- NR 12 Garston Rd, CORBY, Northants, NN18 8NH.   (hsp)
  01536 460655
  Sec/Treas: Stuart Patterson
- Br 3
- ○ *S; the play & study of Shogi (Japanese chess) & its variants
- ● Comp - British Shogi championship
- < Fedn of Eur Shogi Assns (FESA); Nihon Shogi Renmai (Japanese Shogi Assn)
- M c 60 i

British Shooting   1988
- ■ 40 Bernard St, LONDON, WC1N 1ST.   (admin)
  020 7211 5189
  email admin@britishshooting.org.uk
  http://www.britishshooting.org.uk
- ▲ Un-incorporated Society
- ○ *N, *S; a coordinating body for services & international events undertaken by target shooting associations
- M 4 org & 4 national bodies (England, Scotland, Wales & N Ireland)
- × 2007 Great Britain Target Shooting Federation

British Shooting Sports Council   (BSSC)   1978
- ■ PO Box 53608, LONDON, SE24 9YN.   (hsb)
  020 7095 8181
  email djpbssc@btconnect.com   http://www.bssc.org.uk
  Sec: David Penn
- ▲ Un-incorporated Society
- ○ *S; to promote shooting sports & firearms legislation
- ● Conf - Mtgs - Res - Inf - LG
- < Wld Forum on the Future of Sports Shooting Activities (WFSA)
- M 12 affiliated org:
  Association of Professional Clay Target Shooting Grounds
  Association of Professional Shooting Instructors
  British Association for Shooting & Conservation
  Countryside Alliance
  Clay Pigeon Shooting Association
  Gun Trade Association
  Institute of Clay Shooting Instructors
  Muzzle Loaders Association of GB
  National Rifle Association
  National Small-bore Rifle Association
  Sportsman's Association of GB & NI
  UK Practical Shooting Association
- ¶ AR; ftm, £5 nm (free from website).

British Shops & Stores Association   (BSSA)   1989
- ■ Middleton House, 2 Main Rd, Middleton Cheney, BANBURY, Oxon, OX17 2TN.   (hq)
  01295 712277   fax 01295 711665
  email info@bira.co.uk   http://www.bira.co.uk/bssa/
  Chmn: Bruce McLaren
- ▲ Un-incorporated Society
- ○ *T; core merchantise areas are department stores, men's, women's & children's fachions, furniture, beds, floor coverings & general merchandise
- ● Empl - ET - Inf - LG - Mtgs
- < Brit Indep Retailers Assn
- M 4,000 f
  BSSA & the British Hardware Federation (BHF) merged in September 2009 as BSSA-BHF, renamed British Independent Retailers Association (BIRA) in May 2011. BSSA & BHF now function as divisional trade associations within BIRA.

British Shorinji Kempo Federation   (BSKF)   1974
- NR 864 Harrow Rd, WEMBLEY, Middx, HA0 2PX.
  020 8908 6265   fax 020 8385 1821
  email skmizuno@freeuk.com   http://www.bskf.org
  Chief Instructor: Sensei Tameo Mizuno
- ▲ Un-incorporated Society
- ○ *S; Shorinji Kempo (a Japanese martial art incorporating punching, kicking & blocking techniques with releases, pins & throws, combined with meditation, therapeutic massage & basic philosophy)

British Show Horse Association   (BSHA)   1936
NR   Suite 16, Intech House, 34-35 The Cam Centre, Wilbury Way, HITCHIN, Herts, SG4 0TW.   (hq)
  01462 437770   fax 01462 437776
  email admin@britishshowhorse.org
  http://www.britishshowhorse.org
  Gen Sec: Charles Wilkerson
▲   Company Limited by Guarantee
○   *S; to promote the showing & breeding of the ridden hack, cob & riding horse; to promote equine welfare
●   Conf - Mtgs - ET - Comp
M   c 1,500 i
¶   NL - 4.
×   2008 British Show Hack, Cob & Riding Horse Association

British Show Pony Society   (BSPS)   1949
■   124 Green End Rd, Sawtry, HUNTINGDON, Cambs, PE28 5XS.   (hq)
  01487 831376   fax 01487 832779
  email info@bsps.com   http://www.bsps.com
  Exec Officer: Mrs Joy Hall
▲   Company Limited by Guarantee
○   *S; to promote & encourage the showing of children's ponies via classes & competitions for show ponies, show hunter ponies, working hunter ponies, & mountain & moorland, for riders between the ages of 3 and 25 & ponies up to 15.2hh
●   Mtgs
<   Assn of Show & Agricl Orgs
M   4,601 i, 20 f
¶   News Review - 10; £20.   Ybk - 1; £25.   Rule Book; free.

British Showjumping
  is a discipline member of the **British Equestrian Federation**

British Sign & Graphics Association Ltd   (BSGA)   1977
■   5 Orton Enterprise Centre, Bakewell Rd, Orton Southgate, PETERBOROUGH, Cambs, PE2 6XU.   (hq)
  01733 230033   fax 01733 230993
  email info@bsga.co.uk   http://www.bsga.co.uk
  Dir/Co Sec: David Catanach
▲   Company Limited by Guarantee
Br   1
○   *T; interests of sign manufacturers & traders in the UK
Gp   Publicity items - banners, bunting; flags, plaques etc
  Sign manufacture - illuminated & non-illuminated; Sign writing
●   Mtgs - ET - Exhib - LG
<   Eur Sign Fedn; Inst of Assn Mgt
M   240 f, UK / 14 f, o'seas
¶   BSGA News - 4; ftm.

British Simmental Cattle Society Ltd   (BSCS)   1971
■   Stoneleigh Park, KENILWORTH, Warks, CV8 2LG.   (hq)
  024 7669 6513   fax 024 7669 6724
  email information@britishsimmental.co.uk
  http://www.britishsimmental.co.uk
  Breed Sec: Neil Shand
▲   Registered Charity
○   *B
<   Nat Beef Assn
M   1,400 i, UK / 200 i, o'seas
¶   Review - 1; ftm, £12 nm.

British Sjogren's Syndrome Association   (BSSA)   1987
NR   PO Box 15040, BIRMINGHAM, B31 3DP.   (hq)
  0121-455 6532
  email kate@bssa.uk.net   http://www.bssa.uk.net
  Office Mgr: Kate Endacott
▲   Company Limited by Guarantee; Registered Charity
Br   15 regional groups
○   *W; to provide information on Sjogren's Syndrome (an auto-immune disorder in which the body's immune system turns against itself, destroying the mucous-secreting glands as though they were foreign bodies); to spread information on alleviation of the symptoms; to support medical research
●   Mtgs - Res - Inf
M   c 2,500 i, UK & o'seas
¶   Sjogren's Today - 4; ftm, £2.50 per back issue nm.
  New Sjogren's Hbk (3rd ed 2005); £17.50 m, £18.50 nm.
  Advisory Guide for Patients & Doctors; ftm, £2.50 nm (£3.50 o'seas).

British Skeet Shooting Association   (BSSA)   1985
NR   c/o Lakenheath Clay Target Centre, Brandon Rd, Eriswell, BRANDON, Suffolk, IP27 9FB.   (sb)
  01638 533353   fax 01638 532037
  email info@mynssa.co.uk   http://www.mynssa.co.uk
  Custodian Sec: Peter Usher
○   *S

British Skewbald & Piebald Association   (BSPA)   1989
NR   Stanley House, Silt Drove, Tipps End, Welney, WISBECH, Cambs, PE14 9SL.
  01354 638226   fax 01354 638238
  http://www.bspaonline.com
  Sec: Sandra Lawrence
○   *B
<   Assn of Show & Agricl Orgs

British Ski Slope Operators Association   (BSSOA)
NR   Barbour Associates, PO Box 2195, GLOUCESTER, GL3 9BH.   (chmn/b)
  01452 618095
  email bssoa@bssoa.co.uk   http://www.bssoa.co.uk
  Chmn: Richard Barbour
○   *T
M   26 f

British Ski & Snowboard Federation
  closed in February 2010, replaced by **British Ski & Snowboard Ltd**

British Ski & Snowboard Ltd   (BSS)   2010
■   60 Charlotte St, LONDON, W1T 2NU.
  020 7842 5764   fax 020 7842 5777
  email bss@teamGB.com   http://www.teambss.org.uk
  Chief Exec: Dave Edwards
▲   Company Limited by Guarantee
○   *S; to support British skiers & snowboarders to achieve outstanding results; to promote participation in FIS disciplines; to select, manage & lead British teams to international events
Gp   Alpine Skiing; Freestyle; Nordic Skiing; Snowboarding; Telemark
<   Intl Ski Fedn (FIS); Brit Olympic Assn (BOA)
  Note: has been set up by the British Olympic Association to replace the British Ski & Snowboard Federation

British Slate Association
  a group of **Stone Federation Great Britain**

British Sleep Society (BSS) 1989
- ■ PO Box 247, Colne, HUNTINGDON, Cambs, PE28 3UZ.   (hq)
  - fax 01480 840618
  - email bssoffice@btopenworld.com
  - http://www.sleeping.org.uk
  - Hon Sec: Andrew Hall
- ▲ Registered Charity
- ○ *L, *Q; to promote knowledge & research in sleep & its disorders & treatment
- ● Conf - Mtgs - ET - Res - SG
- < Wld Fedn of Sleep Res Socs; Eur Sleep Res Soc
- M 500 i, 10 f, UK / 30 i, o'seas
- ¶ NL - 2; ftm, £5 nm.   Conference Papers Abstracts - 1.

British Slot Car Racing Association (BSCRA) 1964
- ■ 48 Wiltshire Gardens, Bransgore, CHRISTCHURCH, Dorset, BH23 8BJ.   (hsp)
  - 01425 672060
  - email info@bscra.co.uk   http://www.bscra.org.uk
  - Hon Sec: C M Frost
- ▲ Un-incorporated Society
- Br 64; 13 countries o'seas
- ○ *G, *S; controlling body for slot car racing in the UK; the cars are controlled by a guide running in a slot in the track, (NOT radio-controlled)
- ● Conf - Mtgs - Exhib - Comp - Inf - Promotion of national & international championships
- < Intl Slot Racing Assn (ISRA)
- M 300 i, 64 org, UK / 13 org, o'seas
- ¶ Slot Car Racing News - 4; ftm, £20 yr nm.
  Members Handbook - 2 yrly; ftm, £3 nm.
  [subscription,£20 yr].

British-Slovene Society 1993
- NR c/o Howard Kennedy (Solicitors), 19 Cavendish Square, LONDON, W10 0PN.
  - 020 7636 1616
- ▲ Registered Charity
- ○ *X; operates in England, Wales & Slovenia

British Small Animal Veterinary Association (BSAVA) 1956
- ■ Woodrow House, 1 Telford Way, Waterwells Business Park, Quedgeley, GLOUCESTER, GL2 2AB.   (hq)
  - 01452 726700   fax 01452 726701
  - email administration@bsava.com
  - http://www.bsava.com
  - Hon Sec: Patricia Colville
- ▲ Registered Charity
- Br 13 regions; 1
- ○ *P; to foster & promote high scientific & educational standards in small animal medicine & surgery
- Gp Association of British Veterinary Acupuncturists; Association of Veterinary Anaesthetists; Association of Veterinary Clinical Pharmacology & Therapeutics; Association of Veterinary Soft Tissue Surgeons; British Association of Veterinary Emergency Care; British Association of Veterinary Ophthalmologists; British Veterinary Dental Association; British Veterinary Dermatology Study Group; British Veterinary Neurology Study Group; British Veterinary Oncology Study Group; British Veterinary Orthopaedic Association; Companion Animal Behaviour Therapy Study Group; European Association of Veterinary Diagnostic Imaging; International Society of Feline Medicine; Small Animal Medical Society; Veterinary Cardiovascular Society
- ● Conf - Mtgs - ET - Res - Exhib - SG - Stat - Inf - LG
- < Wld Small Animal Veterinary Assn (WSAVA); Fedn of Eur Companion Animal Veterinary Assns (FECAVA); Brit Veterinary Assn (BVA)
- M c 5,600 i
- ¶ Jnl of Small Animal Practice - 12; ftm.
  Manuals & CD-ROMs:
    Practice Resource Manual.
    Client Information leaflets.

British Small Boatbuilders Association
a group of the **British Marine Federation**

British Snoring & Sleep Apnoea Association (BSSAA) 1991
- § Castle Court, 41 London Rd, REIGATE, Surrey, RH2 9RJ.   (hq)
  - 01737 245638   fax 0870 052 9212
  - email info@britishsnoring.co.uk
  - http://www.britishsnoring.co.uk
  - Dir: Marianne Davey
  - A not-for-profit organisation dedicated to helping snorers and their bed partners improve their sleep, returning them to peaceful nights together

British Society of Aesthetics (BSA) 1963
- NR PO Box 271, Cheadle, STOCKPORT, Cheshire, SK8 9BU. (hsb)
  - http://www.british-aesthetics.org
  - Admin: Caroline Auty
- ▲ Company Limited by Guarantee; Registered Charity
- ○ *A, *L; to promote study, research & discussion of the fine arts & related types of experience from a philosophical, sociological, historical, critical & educational standpoint
- ● Conf
- < Intl Assn of Aesthetics; Amer Soc for Aesthetics
- M 170 i
- ¶ British Jnl of Aesthetics - 4.   NL - 2.

British Society for Allergy & Clinical Immunology (BSACI) 1947
- NR Elliott House, 10-12 Allington St, LONDON, SW1E 5EH.   (hq)
  - 020 7808 7135   fax 020 7808 7139
  - email info@bsaci.org   http://www.bsaci.org
  - Co Sec: Mrs Fiona Rayner
- ▲ Registered Charity
- ○ *L; to advance & encourage the study of allergy & clinical immunology & their recognition as specialised branches of medicine
- Gp Anaphlaxis; Dermatology; ENT allergy; Gastroenterology; Occupational allergy; Ophthalmology; Paediatrics; Primary health care
- ● Conf - Mtgs - Res
- < Intl Union Immunological Socs; Intl Assn Allergy & Clinical Immunology; Eur Academy Allergology & Clinical Immunology; Allergy UK; Brit Soc Immunology
- M 400 i, UK / 80 i, o'seas
- ¶ Clinical & Experimental Allergy (Jnl) - 12;
  Allergy Update (NL)- 3;   both ftm only.
  UK Allergy Clinic Database available on website.

British Society of Animal Science (BSAS) 1943
- NR PO Box 3, PENICUIK, Midlothian, EH26 0RZ.   (hq)
  - 0131-445 4508   fax 0131-535 3120
  - email bsas@sac.ac.uk   http://www.bsas.org.uk
  - Chief Exec: Mike Steele
- ▲ Registered Charity
- ○ *E, *L; to enhance the understanding of animal sciences & to promote its integration into economic & ethical systems
- ● Conf - Mtgs - ET - Res - SG - LG
- < Eur Assn Animal Production; Biosciences Fedn; Genesis Faraday; Assn of Learned & Profl Soc Publishers
- M 600 i, UK / 300 i, o'seas
- ¶ Animal Science - 6.   BSAS Annual Proceedings; ftm, £50 nm.

British Society for Antimicrobial Chemotherapy (BSAC) 1972
- NR Griffin House, 53 Regent Place, BIRMINGHAM, B1 3NJ.   (hq)
  - 0121-236 1988
  - http://www.bsac.org.uk
- ▲ Registered Charity
- ○ *L, *Q; to facilitate the acquisition & dissemination of knowledge in the field of antimicrobial chemotherapy
- Gp Microbiology; Mycology; Virology
- < Fedn of Infection Socs
- M i

British Society of Audiology (BSA) 1967
- ■ 80 Brighton Rd, READING, Berks, RG6 1PS.   (hq)
  - 0118-966 0622   fax 0118-935 1915
  - email bsa@thebsa.org.uk   http://www.thebsa.org.uk
  - Admin Sec: Jan Deevey,   Hon Sec: Dr David Furness
- ▲ Registered Charity
- ○ *P; for professionals working in hearing & balance
- Gp Hearing
  - Interest groups: Auditory process, Balance, Paediatric
- ● Conf - Mtgs - ET - SG - Inf
- M 1,169 i, 24 f, UK / 226 i, o'seas
- ¶ International Jnl of Audiology - 12.
  - BSA News - 3.

British Society of Blood & Marrow Transplantation   (BSBMT)
- NR c/o Dr Jenny Byrne, City Hospital, Hucknall Rd, NOTTINGHAM, NG5 1PB.
  - 0115-969 1169
  - email mail@bsbmt.org
  - Sec: Dr Jenny Byrne
- ○ *L, *P; for those with a professional interest in haematopoietic cell transplantation
- ● Mtgs - Inf
- M i
- ¶ NL.

British Society for Cell Biology (BSCB)   1959
- NR Dept of Biological Science, Firth Court, University of Sheffield, SHEFFIELD, S10 2TN.   (hsb)
  - 0114-222 4635
  - http://www.bscb.org
  - Hon Sec: Prof Elizabeth Smythe
- ○ *L; cell biology including: cell membranes, cell secretions, cytoskeleton, nuclei, growth factors, cell differentiation, cell matrix & cell motility etc

British Society for Children's Orthopaedic Surgery
  a specialist society of the **British Orthopaedic Association**

British Society of Cinematographers Ltd (BSC)   1949
- ■ PO Box 2587, GERRARDS CROSS, Bucks, SL9 7WZ.   (hq)
  - 01753 888052   fax 01753 891486
  - email office@bscine.com   http://www.bscine.com
  - Sec: Frances Russell
- ▲ Company Limited by Guarantee
- ○ *P; to promote & encourage the highest standards in the art & craft of cinematography
- Gp Full members: Directors of photography;
  - Honorary members: Retired DoPs & camera operators;
  - Associate members: Top [film] camera operators;
  - Patron members: Companies closely associated with motion picture photography
- ● Mtgs - ET - Exhib - Awards
- < Eur Fedn of Cinematographers (IMAGO); Cine Glds of GB (CGGB)
- M 260 i, UK / 41 i, o'seas
- ¶ BSC NL - 4; ftm only.
  - British Cinematographer Magazine - 6; £16.80 yr (£3.50 each).

British Society of Clinical & Academic Hypnosis
  see **BSCAH - British Society of Clinical & Academic Hypnosis**

British Society for Clinical Cytology (BSCC) 1962
- NR 12 Coldbath Square, LONDON, EC1R 5HL.   (hsb)
  - 020 7278 6907
  - http://www.clinicalcytology.co.uk
- ▲ Registered Charity
- ○ *L, *P; promotion of the growth & practice of cytopathology
- < Eur Fedn Cytology Socs
- M i

British Society of Clinical Hypnosis (BSCH) 1987
- ■ 125 Queensgate, BRIDLINGTON, E Yorks, YO16 7JQ.   (hq)
  - 01262 403103
  - email sec@bsch.org.uk   http://www.bsch.org.uk
  - Sec: Tom Connelly
- ▲ Un-incorporated Society
- Br 2
- ○ *P; to maintain a register of properly trained therapists; to set & maintain the standard for hypnotherapy in the UK
- ● Inf - Liaison between the public & the body of therapists
- M 1,435 i

British Society of Clinical Neurophysiology (BSCN) 1942
- ■ c/o Dr Nick Kane, Ward 17 Frenchay Hospital, Frenchay Park Rd, BRISTOL, BS16 1LE.   (sb)
  - 0117-970 1212 ext 03643
  - http://www.bscn.org.uk
  - Sec: Dr Nick Kane
- ▲ Registered Charity
- ○ *M, *P; 'education & scientific advancement in the field of electrodiagnostic medicine & physiological investigation of the human nervous system'
- Gp Electroencephalography; Infra-operative monitoring
- ● Conf - Mtgs - ET
- < Intl Fedn for Clinical Neurophysiology (IFCN)
- M c 400 i
- ¶ Abstracts of presentations to society scientific meetings - 3; NL - 1; both free.

British Society of Comedy Writers (BSCW) 1999
- ■ 61 Parry Rd, WOLVERHAMPTON, W Midlands, WV11 2PS.   (pres/p)
  - 01902 722729
  - email info@bscw.co.uk   http://www.bscw.co.uk
  - Pres: Kenneth Rock
- Br 5
- ○ *P; to develop & promote the work of comedy writers & the art of comedy writing
- Gp Corporate videos; Films; Quiz shows; Publications; Radio; Situation comedy; Sketch shows; Soap operas; Speeches; Stage
- ● Conf - Mtgs
- M c 100 i
- ¶ NL - 4; ftm only.

British Society of Criminology (BSC)
- NR 2-6 Cannon St, LONDON, EC4M 6YH.   (hq)
  - 07908 966543
  - http://www.britsoccrim.org
  - Exec Sec: Dr Kate Williams
- ▲ Company Limited by Guarantee, Registered Charity
- Br 7
- ○ *L, *P; promotion of criminological knowledge
- ● Conf - Mtgs - ET - Comp - Inf - LG
- M 850 i, UK / 80 i, o'seas
- ¶ NL - 4; ftm only.

British Society of Dental Hygiene & Therapy (BSDHT) 1949
- NR 3 Kestrel Court, Waterwells Drive, Waterwells Business Park, GLOUCESTER, GL2 2AT.   (admin/b)
  - 0870 243 0752
  - http://www.bsdht.org.uk
  - Admin: Mrs Ann Craddock
- ○ *L, *P; study & practice of oral hygiene
- M i
- × 2008 British Dental Hygienists' Association

British Society of Dental & Maxillofacial Radiology   (BSDMFR)   1958
- ■ c/o Alison Menhinick: Clinical Radiology, Dundee Dental Hospital, 2 Park Place, DUNDEE, DD1 4HR.   (s/b)
  http://www.liv.ac.uk/~ppnixon/
  Hon Sec: Alison Menhinick
- ▲ Registered Charity
- ○ *L; to promote study & research into all aspects of dental & maxillofacial radiology & radiography
- ● Conf - Mtgs - Comp - SG - LG
- M 110 i, UK / 20 i, o'seas
- ¶ NL - 2; ftm only.

British Society for Dental Research
   since 2009 **British Society for Oral & Dental Research**

British Society for Dermatological Surgery
   a group of the **British Association of Dermatologists**

British Society for Dermatopathology
   a group of the **British Association of Dermatologists**

British Society for Developmental Biology   (BSDB)   1964
- NR Cardiff School of Biosciences, Cardiff University Main Building, Park Place, CARDIFF, CF10 3TL.   (hsb)
  029 2087 5881
  email secretary@bsdb.org   http://www.bsdb.org
  http://www.bms.ed.ac.uk/services/webspace/bsdb/people/taylor.htm
  Sec: Mike Taylor
- ▲ Registered Charity
- ○ *L; research in developmental biology (concerned with the mechanisms of embryonic development, growth & regeneration in animals & plants)
- ● Conf - ET - Res
- < Eur Developmental Biology Org; Biological Sciences Fedn; Company of Biologists
- M c 900 i, UK / c 300 i, o'seas
- ¶ NL - 2; ftm only.

British Society for Disability & Oral Health   (BSDH)   1976
- NR 19 Hazelmere Avenue, Melton PArk, GOSFORTH, Tyne & Wear, NE3 5QL.   (hsb)
  http://www.bsdh.org.uk
  Hon Sec: Kathy Wilson
- ▲ Registered Charity
- ○ *P; to improve, preserve & protect the oral health of peoples of all ages with disabilities
- M i

British Society of Dowsers   (BSD)   1933
- NR 4/5 Cygnet Centre, Worcester Rd, Hanley Swan, WORCESTER, WR8 0EA.   (hq)
  01684 576969
  email info@britishdowsers.org
  http://www.britishdowsers.org
  Pres: Grahame Gardner
- ▲ Company Limited by Guarantee; Registered Charity
- ○ *L; to encourage & support the study & practice of dowsing & its application in every field of human interest
- Gp Archaeological dowsing; Earth energies; Health; Water divining
- ● Conf - Mtgs - ET - Res - Exhib - SG - Lib - VE - LG
  Office hours: Mon-Fri 1030-1500
- M 1,600 i
- ¶ NL - 3;   Dowsing Today (Jnl) - 3; both ftm.

British Society of Echocardiography   (BSE)   1990
- ■ Dockland Business Centre, 10-19 Tiller Rd, Docklands, LONDON, E14 8PX.
  email info@bsecho.org   http://www.bsecho.org
- ○ *P;
- < Brit Cardiac Soc

British Society for Ecological Medicine   (BSEM)   1981
- NR BSEM c/o New Medicine Group, PO Box 3AP, LONDON, W1A 3AP.   (hq)
  020 7100 7090
  email info@ecomed.org.uk
- ▲ Registered Charity
- ○ *P; to promote the study of allergy, environmental & nutritional medicine
- M i

British Society of Enamellers   (BSOE)   1985
- NR 16 West End, BRASTED, Kent, TN16 1HT.   (memsec/p)
  01959 569721
  email treasurer@enamellers.org
  http://www.enamellers.org
  Treas: Penny Davis
- ▲ Un-incorporated Society
- ○ *P; to promote excellence in British enamelling & professional enamellers worldwide
- ● Conf - ET - Exhib - Lib - PL
- < societies in: Australia, France, Germany, Holland, Spain, USA
- M 49 i, 51 i (associates)
- ¶ NL - 4; ftm only.

British Society of Experimental & Clinical Hypnosis
   in May 2007 merged with the British Society of Medical & Dental Hypnosis to form **BSCAH - British Society of Clinical & Academic Hypnosis**

British Society of Flavourists   (BSF)   1960
- ■ 1 Wansford Close, BRENTFORD, Essex, CM14 4PU.   (hsp)
  01277 224587
  email christogoddard@aol.com   http://www.bsf.org.uk
  Sec: Christopher A Goddard
- ▲ Un-incorporated Society
- ○ *L, *P, *Q; the technology & application of flavours
- ● Conf - Mtgs - ET - Exhib - VE
- < American Flavour Soc; Brit Soc Perfumers
- M c 500 i, UK / c 150 i, o'seas
- ¶ News & Views - 4;   LM;   AR; all ftm.

British Society of Gastroenterology   (BSG)   1937
- ■ 3 St Andrews Place, LONDON, NW1 4LB.   (hq)
  020 7387 3534   fax 020 7487 3734
  email c.romaya@bsg.org.uk   http://www.bsg.org.uk
  Exec Sec: Mrs Chris Romaya
- ▲ Registered Charity
- ○ *L; advancement of gastroenterology (incl endoscopy, pathology, radiology, basic science, liver disease, colorectal disease)
- Gp Basic science; Endoscopy; Liver; Nutrition; Oesophagus; Paediatrics; Pancreas; Pathology; Radiology; Small bowel; Surgery
- ● Conf - ET - Exhib
- M 1,500 i, UK / 300 i, o'seas
- ¶ Gut - 12; ftm, £260 nm.

British Society for Gene Therapy   (BSGT)
- NR PO Box 2181, BUCKINGHAM, MK18 9AX.
  email info@bsgt.org   http://www.bsgt.org
  Secretariat: Clare Beach
- ○ *M; *Q; to accelerate scientific progress & promote ethical & efficient transfer gene- & cell-based technologies from the laboratory to the clinic

British Society for General Dental Surgery **(BSGDS)** **1981**

NR Comberstone, Ware Lane, LYME REGIS, Dorset, DT7 3EJ.
    (hsb)
    01297 446009
    email chrisandjenny@hotmail.com
    http://www.bsgds.com
    Hon Sec: Chris James
▲ Registered Charity
○ *P; quality of care in general dental practice; training of dentists
    in primary care
● Conf - ET - Res
M 359 i, UK / 15 i, o'seas
    (Sub: £45)
¶ NL - 4; free.

British Society for Geomorphology
    a group of the **Geological Society**

British Society of Gerodontology

NR Dental Dept, Ringland Health Centre, NEWPORT, Gwent,
    NP19 9PS. (hsb)
    01633 283190
    http://www.gerodontology.com
    Hon Sec: Vicki Jones
○ to protect, maintain and improve the oral health of older
    people

British Society of Gerontology **(BSG)** **1973**

NR PO Box 607, YORK, YO26 0EQ. (hsb)
    07532 248835
    http://www.britishgerontology.org
    Admin: Rachel Hazelwood
▲ Registered Charity
○ *L, *Q; to promote research & study of human ageing & later
    life
● Conf - Mtgs - Res
< Intl Assn of Gerontology (Eur Region); Academy of Learned
    Socs for the Social Sciences
M 441 i, 19 org, UK / 34 i, o'seas
¶ Generations Review - 4; ftm.   Ageing & Society - 6; £29 m.
    Directory of Members' Research - 2 yrly; ftm only.

British Society of Gynaecological Endoscopy **(BSGE)** **1989**

NR c/o RCOG, 27 Sussex Place, LONDON, NW1 4RG. (asa)
    020 7772 6474   fax 020 7772 6410
    http://www.bsge.org.uk
▲ Registered Charity
○ *M, *P, *Q; to promote endoscopic gynaecological surgery &
    research; to coordinate training & teaching programmes; to
    advise on safety in diagnostic & operative hysteroscopy &
    laparoscopic surgery
Gp Gynaecologists; Laparoscopic surgeons
● Conf - Mtgs - ET - Res - SG
< Eur Soc of Gynaecological Endoscopy; Amer Assn of
    Gynaecological Laparoscopists
M c 450 i

British Society of Habromaniacs

NR 81 Park View, Collins Rd, LONDON, N5 2UD.
○ *G; 'for mutual appreciation of morbid gaiety'
● Exhib - Mtgs - PL - VE
M ['confidential']
¶ Happy Talk (NL) - irreg.

British Society for Haematology **(BSH)** **1960**

■ 100 White Lion St, LONDON, N1 9PF. (hq)
    020 7713 0990   fax 020 7837 1931
    email info@b-s-h.org.uk   http://www.b-s-h.org.uk
    Sec: Dr Patrick Carrington
▲ Company Limited by Guarantee; Registered Charity
○ *L; to advance the practice & study of haematology
Gp Brit C'ee for Standards in Haematology (BCSH);
    Sub-c'ees: Clinical science (CSHF); Paediatric (PHF)
● Conf - Mtgs - ET - Res - Exhib
< Intl Soc for Haematology; Intl Coun for Standardisation in
    Haematology
M 993 i, 28 f, UK / 113 i, o'seas
¶ British Jnl of Haematology - 16; (price on application).
    [www.bloodmed.com]
    BSH Bulletin - 3; ftm only.
    Guidelines Documents - irreg; ftm only. (Published in
    haematology jnls). [www.bcshguidelines.com].

British Society of Hearing Aid Audiologists Ltd **(BSHAA)**
1954

■ 9 Lukins Drive, GREAT DUNMOW, Essex, CM6 1XQ. (sp)
    01371 876623   fax 01371 876623
    email secretary@bshaa.com   http://www.bshaa.com
    Sec: Jill Humphreys,
    Pres: M Georgevic
▲ Company Limited by Guarantee
○ *P; to represent the interests of the private hearing aid
    dispenser; to provide ongoing education
● Conf - Mtgs - ET - Exhib
M 1,100 i, UK / 50 i, o'seas
¶ BSHAA News - 4; ftm.

British Society for the History of Mathematics **(BSHM)** **1971**

NR 21 Bowerland Avenue, Barton, TORQUAY, Devon,
    TQ2 8QH. (admin)
    http://www.bshm.org
▲ Registered Charity
○ *L; to provide a forum for all interested in the history &
    development of mathematics & related disciplines
● Conf - Mtgs - SG - VE
M 282 i, 3 org, UK / 142 i, o'seas
¶ NL - 2/3;   AR - 1; both ftm only.

British Society for the History of Medicine **(BSHM)** **1965**

■ 24 Foxes Dale, LONDON, SE3 9BQ. (sp)
    020 8852 6245
    email drfdavidson@yahoo.co.uk
    http://www.bshm.org.uk
    Sec: Dr Fiona Davidson
▲ Un-incorporated Society
Br 17
○ *N; to foster interest & research in the history of medicine &
    bring together various smaller societies
● Conf - Mtgs
< Intl Soc for the History of Medicine
M 24 org
¶ NL - 1; free on website.

British Society for the History of Paediatrics & Child Health
    a group of the **Royal College of Paediatrics & Child Health**

British Society for the History of Pharmacy (BSHP) 1967
NR 840 Melton Rd, Thurmaston, LEICESTER, LE4 8BN. (asa)
0116-264 0083   fax 0116-264 0141
email bshp@associationhq.org.uk
http://www.bshp.org
Hon Sec: Peter G Homan
▲ Registered Charity
○ *L; to act as a focus for the development of all areas of the history of pharmacy, from the works of the ancient apothecary to today's ever changing role of the community, hospital, wholesale or industrial chemist
● Conf - Mtgs - Res - VE
< Intl Soc for the History of Pharmacy; R Pharmaceutical Soc of GB
M 250 i, 4 org, UK / 24 i, 4 org, o'seas
¶ The Pharmaceutical Historian (NL) - 4; ftm, £1.50 each nm.

British Society for the History of Philosophy (BSHP) 1984
NR Dept of Philosophy, University of York, YORK, YO10 5DD. (hsb)
01904 433254
email jac505@york.ac.uk
Sec: Dr James Clarke
▲ Registered Charity
○ *P; to promote & foster all aspects of the study of the history of philosophy
● Conf - Mtgs
M 100 i
¶ British Jnl for the History of Philosophy - 4.

British Society for the History of Science (BSHS) 1947
■ PO Box 3401, NORWICH, Norfolk, NR7 3JF. (exec/s)
01603 516236
http://www.bshs.org.uk
Exec Sec: Lucy Tetlow
▲ Registered Charity
○ *L; to further the study of the history of science, technology & medicine
Gp Education (to promote the wider use of the history of science in the teaching of both science & history in schools)
● Conf - Mtgs - Publication
M 850 i
¶ British Jnl for the History of Science - 4.   NL - 3.
List of theses in history of science in British universities in progress, or recently catalogued.
Guide to History of Science Courses in Britain.

British Society for Human Genetics (BSHG) 1996
■ Clinical Genetics Unit, Birmingham Women's Hospital, Edgbaston, BIRMINGHAM, B15 2TG. (hq)
0121-627 2634   fax 0121-623 6971
email bshg@bshg.org.uk   http://www.bshg.org.uk
Gen Sec: Prof Diana Eccles
▲ Registered Charity
○ *P; to advance the science of human genetics; to promote research relating to health & disease; to promote public awareness of human genetics
Gp Association for Clinical Cytogenetics; Association of Genetic Nurses & Counsellors; Cancer Genetics Group; Clinical Genetics Society; Clinical Molecular Genetics Society; Society for Genomics, Policy & Population Health
● Conf - Mtgs - ET - Res - SG - Inf - LG
< Intl Fedn of Human Genetics Socs
M i
¶ BSHG NL - 3.

British Society of Hypnotherapists (1950) (BSH) 1950
■ 37 Orbain Rd, LONDON, SW6 7JZ. (hsp/b)
020 7385 1166   fax 020 7385 1166
email enquiries@britishhypnotherapists.org.uk
http://www.britishhypnotherapists.org.uk
Hon Sec: S C Young
▲ Un-incorporated Society
○ *P; the application of hypnosis for therapeutic purposes - phobias, anxiety & other emotional problems - behaviour change public
● Mtgs - Inf
< Hypnotherapy Training Inst of Britain
M [not stated]
¶ AR / AGM Minutes - 1; ftm only.

British Society for Immunology (BSI) 1956
NR Vintage House, 37 Albert Embankment, LONDON, SE1 7TL. (hq)
020 3031 9800   fax 020 7582 2882
http://www.immunology.org
Chief Exec: Judith Willetts
▲ Registered Charity
Br 18
○ *P; to advance the science of immunology
Gp Autoimmunity; Biochemistry; Cellular signalling; Clinical immunology; Comparative & veterinary immunology; Developmental immunology; Histocompatibility & immunogenetics; Infection & immunity; Lymphocyte Immunosenescence & differentiation; Mucosal; Neuroimmunology; Nutritional immunology; Parasitology; Reproductive immunology; Tumour immunology; Vaccines
● Conf - Mtgs - ET - Exhib - Inf - LG
< Intl U Immunological Socs; Eur Fedn Immunological Socs; UK Life Sciences C'ee
M c 3,500 i, UK / 500 i, o'seas
¶ Immunology - 12.   Immunology News - 6.
Clinical & Experimental Immunology - 12.
Directory - 1; ftm only.   AR - 1; ftm.

British Society for Investigative Dermatology
is a group of the **British Association of Dermatologists**

British Society of Magazine Editors (BSME) 1960
■ c/o Gill Branston Associates, 137 Hale Lane, EDGWARE, Middx, HA8 9QP. (hq/admin)
020 8906 4664   fax 020 8959 2137
email admin@gillbranston.com   http://www.bsme.com
Admin: Gill Branston
○ *P; for magazine editors in the UK

British Society of Master Glass Painters (BSMGP) 1921
NR PO Box 15, MINEHEAD, Somerset, TA24 8ZX. (hsp)
01643 862807
email secretary@bsmgp.org.uk
http://www.bsmgp.org.uk
Hon Sec: Chris Wyard
▲ Company Limited by Guarantee
○ *A, *L; to promote & encourage high standards in the art & craft of stained glass painting & staining; to act as a focus for the exchange of information & ideas within the stained glass craft; to preserve the invaluable stained glass heritage of Britain
● Conf - Mtgs - ET - Res - Exhib - Inf - Lib - VE
M c 600 (incl 50 instns, libraries etc)
¶ Jnl of Stained Glass - 1.
Stained Glass (NL) - 4; ftm.

British Society of Medical & Dental Hypnosis
in May 2007 merged with the British Society of Experimental & Clinical Hypnosis to form **BSCAH - British Society of Clinical & Academic Hypnosis**

British Society for Medical Mycology   (BSMM)   1965
■ Mycology - St John's Institute of Dermatology, St Thomas' Hospital, LONDON, SE1 7EH.   (hsb)
  020 7188 6400
  http://www.bsmm.org
  Hon Sec: Sue Howell
▲ Registered Charity
○ *P; to advance research into fungal infections in humans & animals, the pathogenesis & virulence of fungal infections, diagnosis & treatment, agents & mechanics of resistance
Gp Diploma working party; Standards of care working party
● Conf - ET - Grant funding (travel grants)
< Intl Soc for Human & Animal Mycology; Biosciences Fedn; Inst Biology
M 212 i, UK / 75 i, o'seas
¶ BSNN News (NL) - 2;   LM; both ftm only.

British Society for Mental Health & Deafness   (BSMHD)   1996
NR Deaf Access, Community House, South Street, BROMLEY, Kent, BR1 1RH.
  email info@bsmhd.org.uk   http://www.bsmhd.org.uk
○ *W; to promote the mental health in deaf people, particularly those who use sign language
● Conf - Mtgs
M i, org
  (Sub: £35)
¶ NL

British Society for Mercury Free Dentistry   (BSMFD)   1984
NR The Weathervane, 22A Moorend Park Rd, CHELTENHAM, Glos, GL53 0JY.   (hq)
  01242 226918
  http://www.mercuryfreedentistry.org.uk
  Contact: Dr Gareth Rhidian
▲ Registered Charity
○ *P; the investigation of potential side-effects of dental materials, particularly mercury; to identify patients affected
● Conf - Mtgs - ET - Res - SG - Inf

British Society for Microbial Technology   (BSMT)
NR Microbiology Dept (F Floor), Royal Hallamshire Hospital, Glossop Rd, SHEFFIELD, S Yorks, S10 2JF.   (chmn/b)
  0114-271 3121   fax 0114-278 9376
  email tgwinstanley@hotmail.com
  http://www.bsmt.org.uk
  Chmn: Trevor Winstanley
○ *P; for microbiologists working as healthcare scientists & medical microbiologists

British Society for Middle Eastern Studies   (BRISMES)   1973
NR Institute for Middle Eastern & Islamic Studies, University of Durham, Elvet Hill Rd, DURHAM, DH1 3TU.   (admin)
  0191-334 5179   fax 0191-334 5661
  email a.l.haysey@durham.ac.uk
  http://www.brismes.ac.uk
  Admin: Louise Haysey
▲ Registered Charity
○ *L; to promote the study of the Middle Eastern region, its culture, languages, literature, history & politics
● Conf - ET
< Middle East Studies Assn of America (MESA); Eur Assn of Middle Eastern Studies (EURAMES)
M 400 i, 2 f, 18 org, UK / 200 i, o'seas
¶ British Jnl of Middle Eastern Studies - 2; ftm, £64 nm. Business NL - 3; ftm, £20 nm

British Society of Miniaturists   (BSM)   1895
NR 13 Manor Orchards, KNARESBOROUGH, N Yorks, HG5 0BW.   (hsp/b)
  01423 540603
  email info@britpaint.co.uk   http://www.britpaint.co.uk
  Dir: Margaret Simpson
○ *A; to promote excellence in the art of miniature painting; to promote the sale of miniature paintings
● Exhib - Comp - Inf - Free entry to view exhibitions
< Intl Gld Artists; Brit Watercolour Soc; Brit Soc of Painters (in oil, pastel & acrylic)
M 40 i, 4 org, UK / 10 i, o'seas
¶ Exhibition Catalogues - 2; £1.

British Society for Music Therapy
  merged 6 April 2011 with the Association of Professional Music Therapists to form the **British Association for Music Therapy**

British Society for Neuroendocrinology   (BSN)   1985
■ c/o Neil Evans, Institute of Biodiversity, Animal Health & Comparative Medicine, College of Medical, Veterinary & Life Sciences, University of Glasgow, Bearsden Rd, GLASGOW, G61 1QH.   (hsb)
  0141 330 5795
  email neil.evans@glasgow.ac.uk
  http://www.neuroendo.org.uk
  Sec: Prof Neil Evans
▲ Registered Charity
○ *L; to promote research into the interplay between the endocrine & nervous systems that control so many important body processes & to provide therapies for the many neuroendocrine diseases & disorders
● Conf - ET - Res - LG - Research funding
< Intl Neuroendocrine Fedn
¶ Jnl of Euroendocrinology - 12; £75 m, £157 nm.

British Society of Neuroradiologists   (BSNR)   1970
NR c/o Dr M Gawne-Cain, Southampton General Hospital, SOUTHAMPTON, Hants, SO16 6YD.   (sb)
  023 8079 6641
  email bsnr.sec@googlemail.com   http://www.bsnr.co.uk
  Sec: Dr M Gawne-Cain
▲ Un-incorporated Society
○ *P; all matters relating to neuroradiology
● Conf - LG
< Wld Fedn of Neuroradiological Socs
M 190 i, UK / 10 i, o'seas

British Society for Oral & Dental Research   (BSDR)   1950
NR c/o Dr A S High, Diagnostic Services Dept, Level 6, Medical & Dental School, University of Leeds, LEEDS, LS2 9LU.   (sb)
  0113 343 6115   fax 0113 343 6264
  http://www.bsomp.co.uk
  Sec: Dr A S High
▲ Registered Charity
○ *L, *Q; to advance research & increase knowledge for the improvement of oral health worldwide
Gp Behavioural sciences & health services; Dental materials; Implant research; Mineralised tissue research; Oral biology; Oral microbiology & immunology
● Conf - Res - Exhib - SG - LG
< Intl Assn of Dental Res (USA)
M 898 i, 3 org, UK / 14 i, o'seas
¶ Jnl of Dental Research - 12.   NL - 1.
✕ 2009 British Society for Dental Research

British Society for Oral & Maxillofacial Pathology (BSOP) 1967
NR Diagnostic Services / Level 6, Medical & Dental School,
University of Leeds, LEEDS, W Yorks, LS2 9LU.   (hsb)
0113-343 6115   fax 0113-343 6264
email a.s.high@leeds.ac.uk   http://www.bsomp.org
Hon Sec: Dr Alec S High
▲ Un-incorporated Society
○ *L, *M, *P; to promote & encourage the study & practice of
head & neck histopathology; to facilitate communication
between pathologists with an interest in head, neck, oral &
dental disease
Gp Council; Members; Overseas members; Teachers
● Conf - ET - Res
M 110 i, UK / 20 i, o'seas

British Society for Oral Medicine (BSOM) 1976
NR c/o Professor Crispian Scully, Eastman Dental Hospital, 256
Gray's Inn Road, LONDON, WC1X 1LD.   (sb)
020 3456 7899
http://www.bsom.org.uk
Sec: Prof Crispian Scully
○ *L; oral soft tissue disease
● Conf - ET - Comp - Inf - Devt of higher training programmes
M c 180 i
¶ NL - 1; free.

British Society for Paediatric & Adolescent Rheumatology
a group of the **Royal College of Paediatrics & Child Health**

British Society of Paediatric Dentistry
NR 12 Bridewell Place, LONDON, EC4V 6AP.
020 7353 2072
http://www.bspd.co.uk
▲ Registered Charity
Br 13
○ *P; dental care of children
Gp Consultants; Teachers
● Conf - Mtgs - ET - Res - LG
< Intl Assn of Paediatric Dentistry
M c 800 i
¶ Intl Jnl of Paediatric Dentistry - 4.

British Society for Paediatric Dermatology
a group of the **British Association of Dermatologists** & of the
Royal College of Paediatrics & Child Health

British Society of Paediatric Endocrinology & Diabetes
a group of the **Royal College of Paediatrics & Child Health**

British Society for Paediatric Gastroenterology & Nutrition
a group of the **Royal College of Paediatrics & Child Health**

British Society of Paediatric Radiology
a group of the **Royal College of Paediatrics & Child Health**

British Society of Painters (in Oil, Pastels & Acrylic)
NR 13 Manor Orchards, KNARESBOROUGH, N Yorks,
HG5 0BW.   (dir b/p)
01423 540603
email info@britpaint.co.uk   http://www.britpaint.co.uk
Dir: Leslie Simpson
○ *A; to promote excellence in the field of painting
● Exhib - Comp - Free entry to exhibitions
M 50 i, UK / 3 i, o'seas
¶ Catalogue; £1.

British Society for Parasitology (BSP) 1962
NR 87 Gladstone St, BEDFORD, MK41 7RS.   (asa)
01234 211015
http://www.bsp.uk.net
Secretariat: Cathy Fuller
○ *L; to advance the study of parasitology; to promote wider
dissemination of advances in the subject

British Society of Perfumers (BSP) 1963
NR 15 Underwood Close, CANTERBURY, Kent, CT4 7BS.   (gen/sp)
http://www.bsp.org.uk
Gen Sec: Roger Duprey
▲ Un-incorporated Society
○ *P; the art, craft & science of creative perfumery

British Society of Periodontology (BSP) 1949
NR PO Box 228, Bubwith, SELBY, W Yorks, YO8 1EY.   (admin/mgr)
0844 335 1915
email bspadmin@btinternet.com
http://www.bsperio.org.uk
Admin Mgr: Helen Clough
▲ Registered Charity
○ *P; to promote the art & science of dentistry & in particular the
art & science of periodontology
Gp Teachers; General practitioners
● Conf - Mtgs - ET - Comp
< Eur Fedn of Periodontology
M 775 i, UK / 125 i, o'seasas
(Sub: £30-158)
¶ The Jnl of Clinical Periodontology - 12; ftm.   NL - 1; ftm.

British Society for Phenomenology (BSP) 1967
NR 3 Gibsons Rd, STOCKPORT, Cheshire, SK4 4JX.   (mem/sp)
0161-432 4010
email jacksonpub@aol.com
http://www.britishphenomenolgy.co.uk
Mem Sec: Brian Jackson,   Sec: Dr David Webb
○ *L; the study of phenomenology & continental philosophy
● Conf - SG
M i
¶ Jnl - 3;

British Society for the Philosophy of Science (BSPS) 1959
■ c/o Dr C Timpson, Brasenose College, OXFORD, OX1 4AJ.
(hsb)
http://www.thebsps.org
Hon Sec: Dr C Timpson
▲ Registered Charity
○ *L; to study the logic, methods & the philosophy of science, as
well as those of the various special sciences, incl the social
sciences
● Conf - Mtgs - Res - Inf
M i
¶ British Jnl for the Philosophy of Science - 4.

British Society of Plant Breeders Ltd (BSPB) 1966
NR Woolpack Chambers, Market St, ELY, Cambs, CB7 4ND.   (hq)
01353 653200   fax 01353 661156
email enquiries@bspb.co.uk   http://www.bspb.co.uk
Chief Exec: Dr Penny Maplestone
▲ Company Limited by Guarantee
○ *T; to license and collect royalties on plant varieties; to promote
the interests of plant breeders
Gp British Sugar Beet Seed Producers Association
● LG
< Intl Seed Fedn; Eur Seed Assn
M 50 f, UK / 1 i, 2 f, o'seas

British Society for Plant Pathology   (BSPP)   1981
NR   RHS Wisley, WOKING, Surrey, GU23 6QB.   (hsb)
      01483 212330
      email secretary@bspp.org.uk   http://www.bspp.org.uk
      Sec: Dr Roger Williams
▲   Company Limited by Guarantee; Registered Charity
○   *L; advancement of plant pathology (study & control of plant
      disease)
¶   Plant Pathology - 6; Molecular Plant Pathology - 9; both ftm
      NL - 3; ftm

British Society for Population Studies   (BSPS)   1973
NR   PS201, London School of Economics, Houghton St, LONDON,
      WC2A 2AE.   (hq)
      020 7955 7666   fax 020 7955 6831
      email pic@lse.ac.uk   http://www.bsps.org.uk
▲   Registered Charity
○   *L, *P; to further the study of biological, economic, historical,
      medical, social & other disciplines connected with human
      populations; to contribute to public awareness of these
      problems; to provide facilities for study & research
●   Conf - Mtgs - Inf
M   250 i, 10 f, UK / 50 i, o'seas
¶   BSPS News - 4; free.

British Society for Proteome Research   (BSPR)   1984
NR   c/o Dr Kathryn Lilley, Dept Biochemistry, Bldg O - Downing Site,
      CAMBRIDGE, CB2 3DZ.   (hsb)
      01223 765255   fax 01223 333345
      email k.s.lilley@bioc.cam.ac.uk   http://www.bspr.org
      Hon Sec: Dr Kathryn Lilley
▲   Registered Charity
○   *L; to promote the study of proteomics - the study of proteins as
      a system group
●   Conf - ET - Res - Exhib - SG - Inf - LG
<   Biosciences Fedn
M   165 i
¶   NL - 2/3; ftm only.

**British Society of Psychosomatic Obstetrics, Gynaecology &
Andrology   (BSPOGA)   1988**
NR   c/o Dr Mira Lal, Dept of Obstetrics & Gynaecology, Russells
      Hall Hospital, DUDLEY, DY1 2QH.   (chmn/b)
      http://www.bspoga.org
      Chmn: Dr Mira Lal
▲   Registered Charity
○   *L, *M; to promote & increase knowledge & research into
      psychological problems related to all aspects of reproductive
      medicine incl pre & post menopause
●   Conf - ET
<   Intl Soc of Psychosomatic Obstetrics & Gynaecology
M   100 i
¶   NL - 2.

British Society of Rehabilitation Medicine   (BSRM)   1984
NR   c/o Royal College of Physicians, 11 St Andrews Place,
      LONDON, NW1 4LE.   (mail/address)
      01992 638865
      Exec Sec: Sandy Weatherhead (01992 638865)
▲   Registered Charity
○   *M, *P; to promote the development, understanding &
      management of acute & chronic disabling diseases & injuries
M   i

British Society for Research on Ageing   (BSRA)   1947
NR   c/o Dr Matthew Hardman, Faculty of Life Sciences,
      AV Hill Building, University of Manchester, MANCHESTER,
      M13 9PT.   (hsb)
      Hon Sec: Dr Sian Henson
▲   Registered Charity
○   *L, *Q; promotion of teaching & research on the biology of
      ageing
M   i

British Society for Restorative Dentistry   (BSRD)   1968
NR   83 Aylesbury End, BEACONSFIELD, Bucks, HP9 1LS.
      (admin/s)
      http://www.bsrd.org
      Hon Sec: Mr Matthew Garrett
▲   Registered Charity
○   *M, *P; to promote study & high standards of restorative
      dentistry
●   Conf - ET
<   Brit Prosthodontic Conference
M   704 i
¶   European Jnl of Prosthodontics & Restorative Dentistry - 4; ftm,
      £60 nm.
      NL - 1; ftm only.

British Society of Rheology   (BSR)   1940
■   c/o Prof Simon Cox, Inst of Mathematics & Physics, Aberystwyth
      University, ABERYSTWYTH, Ceredigion, SY23 3BZ.   (hsb)
      01970 622764
      email sxc@aber.ac.uk   http://www.bsr.org.uk
      Hon Sec: Prof Simon Cox
▲   Registered Charity
○   *L, *Q; to promote science & disseminate knowledge in pure &
      applied rheology - defined as the science of the flow &
      deformation of matter.   Rheology finds application in
      engineering, materials processing, physics, chemistry,
      applied maths & biological / medical systems
●   Conf - Mtgs - Lib - Awards - Student sponsorships
<   Intl C'ee of Rheology; Eur Soc of Rheology
M   400 i, UK / 200 i, o'seas
      (Sub: £25)
¶   Rheology Reviews (Jnl) - 1; £20 m, £35 nm.
      Rheology Bulletin - 3.   Rheology Abstracts - 4; both ftm only.

British Society for Rheumatology   (BSR)   1984
■   Bride House, 18-20 Bride Lane, LONDON, EC4Y 8EE.   (hq)
      020 7842 0900   fax 020 7842 0901
      email bsr@rheumatology.org.uk
      http://www.rheumatology.org.uk
      Chief Exec: Samantha Peters
▲   Registered Charity
○   *L, *P; to advance the knowledge & practice in the field of
      rheumatology; to work for high standards of care for patients
      with rheumatic disorders
●   Conf - Mtgs - ET - Res - Stat - Lib
<   Arthritis & Musculoskeletal Alliance (ARMA); Brit Health Profls in
      Rheumatology (BHPR)
M   950 i, UK / 450 i, o'seas
¶   Rheumatology (Jnl) - 12; ftm, prices vary nm.
      BSR News - 3;   Hbk - 2 yrly;   AR; all ftm only.

British Society of Scientific Glassblowers   (BSSG)   1960
■   Glassblowing Workshop, Bedson Building, University of
      Newcastle, NEWCASTLE UPON TYNE, NE1 7RU.   (hsb)
      0191-222 7100
      http://www.bssg.co.uk
      Hon Sec: Willie McCormack
▲   Un-incorporated Society
○   *P
●   Conf - Mtgs - Exam - Comp - Inf - Lib
<   Amer Soc Scientific Glassblowers; Soc Glass Technology; Glass
      Mfrs Confedn
M   200 i, 5 f, UK / 40 i, 1 f, o'seas
¶   Jnl - 4; £5 m, £6 nm.

British Society for Sexual Medicine   (BSSM)   1997
NR   Holly Cottage, Fisherwick, LICHFIELD, Staffs, WS14 9JL.
      01543 432757   fax 01543 433303
      http://www.bssm.org.uk
      Sec: Mrs Sally Hackett
○   *M; 'for the purpose of promoting research & exchange of
      knowledge of impotence & other aspects of sexual function &
      dysfunction'

British Society of Soil Science   (BSSS)   1947
- ■ Cranfield University, Building 53, CRANFIELD, Beds, MK43 0AL.   (sb)
  http://www.soils.org.uk
- ▲ Un-incorporated Society
- ○ *L; to promote the study of soils & increase awareness of the importance of soils in many aspects of life
- ● Conf - ET - Exhib
- < Intl Soc of Soil Science
- M 750 i, UK / 250 i, o'seas
- ¶ European Jnl of Soil Science.
  Soil Use & Management - 4.

British Society of Sports History
- ■ c/o Dr Carol A Osborne, University of Cumbria, Bowerham Rd, LANCASTER, LA1 3JD.
  01524 384578
  email carol.osborne@cumbria.ac.uk
  http://www.sportinhistory.org
  Web Services Mgr: Richard Cox
- ○ *G, *P; to stimulate, promote & coordinate interest in the historical study of sport, physical education, recreation & leisure; to encourage & assist in the preservation & cataloguing of historical records

British Society for Strain Measurement   (BSSM)   1965
- ■ TechniMeasure, Alexandra Buildings, 59 Alcester Rd, STUDLEY, Warks, B80 7NU.   (hq)
  01525 712779   fax 01525 712779
  email info@bssm.org   http://www.bssm.org
  Hon Sec: Ian Ramage
- ▲ Company Limited by Guarantee
- Br 11
- ○ *L; engineering strain measurement & associated measurement
- Gp C'ees: Centrification, Technical
- ● Conf - Mtgs - ET - Exam - Exhib - Comp - Inf
- < Soc of Experimental Mechanics (USA)
- M 100 i, 100 f, UK / 20 i, o'seas
- ¶ Strain (Jnl) - 4; ftm, £50 yr nm.

British Society for the Study of Prosthetic Dentistry   (BSSPD)   1953
- NR School of Dental Sciences, Newcastle University, Framlington Place, NEWCASTLE upon TYNE, NE2 4BW.   (admin)
  0191-222 8140
  Admin: Mrs Linda Erickson
- ▲ Registered Charity
- ○ *L; the study & development of prosthetic dentistry (the artificial replacement of teeth)
- M c 500 i
- ¶ NL - 2;   Proceedings of the Annual Conference - 1; ftm.

British Society for the Study of Vulval Diseases   (BSSVD)
- NR c/o Dr Laurence Brown, Dept of Histopathology, Leicester Royal Infirmary, LEICESTER, LE1 5WW.   (hsb)
  http://www.bssvd.org
  Sec: Dr P Munday
- ○ *M, *P; promotes research into the causes of vulval disease
- ● Mtgs
- M c 160 i

British Society for Surgery of the Hand   (BSSH)   1968
- ■ at the Royal College of Surgeons, 35-43 Lincoln's Inn Fields, LONDON, WC2A 3PE.   (hq)
  020 7831 5162   fax 020 7831 4041
  email secretariat@bssh.ac.uk   http://www.bssh.ac.uk
  Hon Sec: R Eckersley
- ▲ Company Limited by Guarantee, Registered Charity
- ○ *M, *P; to promote & direct development of hand surgery; to foster & co-ordinate education, study & research
- ● Conf - Mtgs - ET - Res
- < Intl Fedn of Socs for the Surgery of the Hand
- M 520 i, UK / 150 i, o'seas
- ¶ Jnl of Hand Surgery (European volume) - 6; ftm only.

British Society of Toxicological Pathologists   (BSTP)   1985
- ■ PO Box 6356, ISLE of SKYE, IV41 8WZ.   (admin)
  07894 123533
  email bstpostoffice@aol.com   http://www.bstp.org.uk
  Secretariat
- ▲ Registered Charity
- ○ *P; to advance education in toxicological pathology for the public benefit
- ● Conf - Mtgs - ET
- M 105 i, UK / 67 i, o'seas
- ¶ BSTP NL - 1; ftm only.

British Society of Underwater Photographers   (BSoUP)   1967
- NR 12 Coningsby Rd, SOUTH CROYDON, Surrey, CR2 6QP.   (hsp)
  020 8668 8168
  http://www.bsoup.org
  Pres: Brian Pitkin
- ▲ Un-incorporated Society
- ○ *P; underwater photography, cinematography & video
- ● Mtgs - Exhib - Comp
- M c 300 i
- ¶ In Focus (NL) - 6.

British Sociological Association   (BSA)   1951
- ■ Palatine House (Bailey suite), Belmont Business Park, DURHAM, DH1 1TW.   (hq)
  0191-383 0839   fax 0191-383 0782
  email judith.mudd@britsoc.org.uk
  http://www.britsoc.co.uk
  Chief Exec: Judith Mudd
- ▲ Company Limited by Guarantee; Registered Charity
- ○ *P; promotion of interest in sociology & advancement of its study & application in the UK
- Gp over 30 specialist study groups
- ● Conf - Mtgs - ET - Res - Exhib - Comp - SG - Stat - Inf - LG
- < Intl Sociological Assn; Foundation for Science & Technology; Standing Conf of Arts & Social Sciences; Amer/ Australian / Indian Sociological Assn(s); Canadian Sociological & Anthropological Assn
- M 2,127 i, UK / 180 i, o'seas
- ¶ Sociology (Jnl) - 6; ftm, £82 yr nm.
  Work, Employment & Society (Jnl) - 4; ftm, £66 yr nm. [1st copy to m, free; 2nd copy, £35].
  Network (NL) - 3;   AR; both ftm only.

British Soft Drinks Association   (BSDA)   1987
- ■ 20-22 Stukeley St, LONDON, WC2B 5LR.   (hq)
  020 7430 0356   fax 020 7831 6014
  email bsda@britishsoftdrinks.com
  http://www.britishsoftdrinks.com
  Dir Gen: Jill Ardagh
- ▲ Company Limited by Guarantee
- ○ *T; for all manufacturers of soft drinks, fruit juices & bottled waters; cover packaging, dispensing & vending machines & environmental concerns
- Gp Various specialist c'ees
- ● Conf - ET - Inf - PL - LG
- < UNESDA; EFBW; AIJN
- M 47 f, 47 f (associates)
- ¶ Publications list available.

British Soluble Coffee Packers & Importers Association (BSCPIA) 1994
- ■ Crescent House, 34 Eastbury Way, SWINDON, Wilts, SN25 2EN. (sb)
  01793 723387   fax 01793 726486
  email bscpia@aol.com
  Sec: Walter J Anzer
- ▲ Company Limited by Guarantee
- ○ *T; to represent the needs of the soluble coffee packers & importers on an international basis supplying the British & EU markets
- ● LG
- M 10 f
- ¶ Code of Practice for the Soluble Coffee Industry in the UK; ftm, £5 nm.

British Sound Recording Association (BSRA) 1958
- ■ 42 Lewis Rd, CHIPPING NORTON, Oxon, OX7 5JS. (hsp)
  email bsra@soundhunters.com
  http://www.soundhunters.com/bsra/
  Hon Sec: Peta Simmons
- ○ *G; all aspects of amateur sound recording, including video with creative sound
- ● Conf - Mtgs - Comp - VE
- < Fédn Intle des Chasseurs de Sons (Intl Fedn Soundhunters)
- M 65 i, 2 f, 4 org
- ¶ Recording News - 4;
  Sound Track Audio Magazine - 4; both ftm only.

British Specialist Nutrition Association Ltd (BSNA) 1986
- NR 6 Catherine St, LONDON, WC2B 5JJ. (hq)
  020 7836 2460
  email info@bsna.co.uk   http://www.bsna.co.uk
  Dir Gen: Roger Clarke
- ▲ Company Limited by Guarantee
- ○ *T; to represent the manufacturers of products designed to meet the nutritional needs of individuals at different lifestages or with specific health requirements
- Gp Complementary feeding (weaning); Formula; Gluten free foods; Medical foods; Slimming foods; Sports foods
- ● Mtgs - Res - SG - Inf - LG
- < Intl Soc for Dietetic Foods (ISDI); Assn of Infant & Dietetic Foods in the EEC (IDACE); Food & Drink Fedn
- M 14 f
- ✕ 2010 (May) Infant & Dietetic Foods Association Ltd

British Speedway Promoters' Association (BSPA) 1965
- NR ACU House, Wood St, RUGBY, Warks, CV21 2YX. (hq)
  01788 560648   fax 01788 546785
  email office@speedwaygb.com
  http://www.speedwaygb.com
- ○ *S; organisation of British speedway racing
- M 25 f

British Spotted Pony Society (BSpPS) 1946
- ■ Heiffers Farm, Rackenford, TIVERTON, Devon, EX16 8EW. (hsp)
  01884 881258   fax 01884 881258
  http://www.britishspottedponysociety.co.uk
  Chmn & Sec: Miss Marlyn Pollard
- ▲ Company Limited by Guarantee; Registered Charity
- ○ *B; to encourage the breeding of quality spotted ponies & to foster interest in & promote the breed
- ● Mtgs - Exhib - Comp - Inf - PL - LG - Breed show
- M i
- ¶ NL - 2;   AR - 1; both ftm only.

British Sprouts Growers Association
  a group of the **Brassica Growers Association**

British Stainless Steel Association (BSSA) 1992
- ■ Broomgrove, 59 Clarkehouse Rd, SHEFFIELD, S Yorks, S10 2LE. (hq)
  0114-267 1260   fax 0114-266 1252
  email enquiry@bssa.org.uk   http://www.bssa.org.uk
  Dir: Nigel Ward
- ▲ Un-incorporated Society
- ○ *T; to promote & develop the use of stainless steel in all regions of the UK
- Gp Architecture & building construction; Finishing section; Industry forum; Rebar
- ● Conf - Mtgs - ET - Exhib - Stat - Inf - LG
- < Intl Stainless Steel Forum; Euro-Inox
- > Nickel Inst
- M 100 f
- ¶ Stainless Steel Industry (Jnl) - 6; ftm, £105 nm (UK & Europe)
  NL (email).

British Stammering Association (BSA) 1978
- ■ 15 Old Ford Rd, LONDON, E2 9PJ. (hq)
  020 8983 1003
  email mail@stammering.org   http://www.stammering.org
  Chief Exec Officer: Norbert Lieckfeldt
- ▲ Registered Charity
- ○ *W; to promote awareness of stammering; to offer support for all whose lives are affected by stammering; to identify & promote effective therapies; to initiate & support research into stammering
- Gp Helping stammering pupils project
- ● Conf - ET - Inf - Lib - Counselling & information service on speech therapy
  Counselling & information service on speech therapy provision & self-help groups for the whole of the UK
  Helpline: 0845 603 2001
- < Intl Fluency Assn; Intl Stuttering Assn
- M 1,600 i
- ¶ Speaking Out - 4; ftm only.

British Standards Institution
  see **BSI**

British Standards Society (BSS) 1960
- NR c/o BSI, 389 Chiswick High Rd, LONDON, W4 4AL. (hq)
- ○ *K; to promote techniques & benefits of standardisation; to help standards users in their understanding & use of standards
- M i
  Note: is a part of BSI

British Starch Industry Association (BSIA) 1989
- NR 6 Catherine St, LONDON, WC2B 5JJ. (hq)
  020 7420 7109   fax 020 7836 0580
  email harriet.green@fdf.org.uk
  Exec Sec: Harriet Green
- ▲ Un-incorporated Society
- ○ *T
- ● Mtgs - LG
- < Eur Starch Assn; Food & Drink Fedn
- M 6 f

British Stickmakers Guild (BSG) 1984
- ■ Ebbisham, 19 Woodmancote Rd, WORTHING, W Sussex, BN14 7HT. (hsp)
  01903 205015
  http://www.thebsg.org.uk
  Hon Sec: Charles Hutcheon
- ▲ Un-incorporated Society
- ○ *G; for all interested in the history, making, collection, stickdressing & uses of walking sticks, canes & crooks
- ● Exhib - Comp
- M 1,940 i, UK / 41 i, o'seas
- ¶ The Stickmaker - 4.

British Stock Car Drivers Association (BSCDA) 1956
NR PO Box 662, HALIFAX, W Yorks, HX3 0WZ.   (hsp)
    Hon Sec: Barry Tempest
▲ Un-incorporated Society
○ *P

British Streptocarpus Society 1999
NR 72 Coopers Rd, Handsworth Wood, BIRMINGHAM,
    W Midlands, B20 2JX.   (htreas/p)
    01543 672938
    http://www.streptocarpussociety.org.uk
    Treas: Peter Pinches
○ *G, *H; for all interested in the flower species
● Mtgs - Exhib - Inf

British Structural Waterproofing Association (BSWA) 1992
NR Westcott House, Catlins Lane, PINNER, Middx, HA5 2EZ.
    020 8866 8339   fax 0871 522 7442
    email enquiries@bswa.org.uk   http://www.bswa.org.uk
○ *T; waterproofing contractors, consultants, manufacturers &
    distributors
M 58 f

British Sub-Aqua Club (BSAC) 1953
NR Telford's Quay, South Pier Rd, ELLESMERE PORT, Cheshire,
    CH65 4FL.   (hq)
    0151-350 6200
    email info@bsac.com   http://www.bsac.com
▲ Company Limited by Guarantee
○ *S; the governing body for the sport of sub-aqua in the UK
M i

British Sugar Beet Seed Producers Association
    a group of the **British Society of Plant Breeders**

British Sugarcraft Guild (BSG) 1983
■ Wellington House, Messeter Place, LONDON, SE9 5DP.   (hq)
    020 8859 6943
    email nationaloffice@bsguk.org   http://www.bsguk.org
    Sec: Jacky Buckley
▲ Un-incorporated Society
Br 225; Japan
○ *G; to promote & stimulate interest in sugarcraft as an art form
● Conf - Mtgs - ET - Exam - Res - Exhib - Comp - SG - Expt - Inf
M 6,700 i, UK / 1,500 i, o'seas
¶ The British Sugarcraft News - 4; ftm only.

British Summer Fruits
NR PVGA House, Nottingham Rd, LOUTH, Lincs, LN11 0WB.
    (asa)
    01507 602427   fax 01507 600689
    email tim.mudge@pvga.co.uk
    http://www.britishsummerfruits.co.uk
    Sec: Tim Mudge
○ *T; to promote British-grown soft & stone fruits
Gp Seasonal Berries

British Sundial Society (BSS) 1989
NR 4 Sheardhall Avenue, Disley, STOCKPORT, Cheshire,
    SK12 2DE.   (hsp)
    01663 762415
    email graham@sheardhall.co.uk
    http://www.sundialsoc.org.uk
    Hon Sec: Graham Aldred
▲ Registered Charity
○ *G, *L; to promote the science of gnomonics & knowledge of
    all types of sundial; research & advice on the restoration &
    preservation of old sundials in the British Isles & the
    construction of new ones
Gp Education; Mass dials; Recording; Restoration
● Conf - Mtgs - ET - Res - SG - Inf - Lib - PL - VE - Cataloguing
    the dials which still exist in the British Isles
< N Amer Sundial Soc; R Astronomical Soc
M 500 i, 12 f, 25 org, UK / 150 i, o'seas
¶ The Bulletin (Jnl) - 4; ftm, £6.50 nm.
    Make a Sundial (book for schools); £7.
    Sets of Slides for lectures (6 sets); £5.50 each.
    Listing of Dials in UK - 3 yrly; m only.
    Sundial Makers.

British Superkart Association 1998
NR 2 Lion Close, NORWICH, Norfolk, NR5 0UQ.
    01603 743563
    http://www.superkart.org.uk
    Series Mgr: Ian Rushforth
○ *S

British Surface Treatment Suppliers Association
    a group of the **Surface Engineering Association**

British Surfing Association
    is in liquidation - activities now taken up by **Surfing GB**

British Suzuki Institute (BSI) 1980
NR Unit 1.01 The Lightbox, 111 Power Rd, LONDON, W4 5PY.
    (hq)
    020 3176 4172
    email info@britishsuzuki.com
    http://www.britishsuzuki.org.uk
    Admin: Minette Joyce
▲ Registered Charity
○ *D; to advance education in the Suzuki method of teaching for
    violin, cello, flute, piano & recorder
Gp Music education
● Conf - Mtgs - ET - Exam - Inf - Teacher training - Concerts
< Eur Suzuki Assn
M 2,000 i, UK / 100 i, o'seas
¶ Ability - 4; ftm, £3 nm.

**British Swedish Chamber of Commerce in Sweden (BSCC)
1954**
NR Jakobs Torg 3 (4th floor), Box 16050, SE-103 21
    STOCKHOLM, Sweden.   (hq)
    46 (8) 555 100 00
    Sec Gen: Ingrid Berggren
▲ Company Limited by Guarantee
○ *C
M c 120 f

© CBD Research Ltd · Beckenham · BR3 5JS · Tel 020 8650 7745 · E-mail cbd@cbdresearch.com · www.cbdresearch.com

British Swimming

- ■ SportPark, 3 Oakwood Drive, LOUGHBOROUGH, Leics, LE11 3QF.   (hq)
  01509 618700   fax 01509 618701
  email chiefexecutive@swimming.org
  Chief Exec: David Sparkes
- ○ *N, *S; determination of policies for participation in world events
- Gp Diving; Swimming; Synchronised swimming; Water polo
- ● Comp - Determination of policies for participation in world championships
- < Fédn Intle de Natation Amateur (FINA); Ligue Eur de Natation (LEN)
- M 5,000 i, 5,000 org
- ¶ AR - 1; ftm.
- X 2008 Amateur Swimming Federation

British Swimming Pool Federation   (BSPFA)   1961

- ■ 4 Eastgate House, East St, ANDOVER, Hants, SP10 1EP.   (hq)
  01264 356210   fax 01264 332628
  email admin@bspf.org.uk   http://www.bspf.org.uk
  Managing Dir: Chris Hayes
- ○ *N; umbrella organisation for the Swimming Pool & Allied Trades Association, the British & Irish Spa & Hot Tub Association, the Swimming Teachers' Association, & SPATEX (the annual trade exhibition for the industry)
- M 4 org

British-Swiss Chamber of Commerce   (BSCC)   1920

- ■ Bellerivestrasse 209, CH-8008 ZRICH, Switzerland.   (hq)
  41 44 422 31 31   fax 41 44 422 32 44
  email info@bscc.co.uk   http://www.bscc.co.uk
  London Office: 14 New St, London, EC2M 4HE.
  020 7650 3802
  Mgr: Carolyn Helbling
- Br 8 regional chapters
- ○ *C; to support the development of Anglo Swiss business relations; to assist individual entrepreneurs & businesses in advancing their own commercial interests
- Gp Business technology; Legal & tax chapter; Public affairs commission
- ● Conf - Business luncheons - Seminars
- < Coun of Brit Chams Comm in Continental Europe (COBCOE)
- M f
- ¶ NL (email) - 6;   Perspectives (NL) - 1; both free.

British Syrian Society   2003

- NR Bury House, 33 Bury St, LONDON, SW1Y 6AX.
  020 7839 1637   fax 020 7839 1638
  http://www.britishsyriansociety.org
- ▲ Company Limited by Guarantee
- ○ *X; to strengthen relations between the two countries

British Tapestry Group   (BTG)   2005

- NR 141 West Stirling St, ALVA, Clackmannanshire, FK12 5EL.
  (honsec/p)
  email britishtapestry@yahoo.com
  http://www.thebritishtapestrygroup.co.uk
  Hon Sec: Louise Martin
- ○ *A; to promote the art of tapestry weaving

British Tarantula Society   (BTS)   1984

- NR 3 Shepham Lane, POLEGATE, E Sussex, BN26 6LZ.   (hsp)
  Hon Sec: Angela Hale
- ▲ Un-incorporated Society
- ○ *B, *G; to educate & provide information on captive husbandry of theraphosid spiders & associated fauna (scorpions etc)
- Gp Captive breeding directory
- ● Mtgs - Res - Exhib - SG - Inf - Lib
- M c 700 i
- ¶ Jnl - 4.

British Technion Society   (BTS)   1951

- NR 62 Grosvenor St, LONDON, W1K 3JF.   (hq)
  020 7495 6824
  http://www.britishtechnionsociety.org
- ▲ Registered Charity
- ○ *K; to promote the Technion (Israel Institute of Technology); to ensure research by introducing active partners; to fundraise for various projects
- M i

British Teledermatology Society
    a group of the **British Association of Dermatologists**

British Tennis Coaches Associaton

- NR 124 Main St, Burnley in Wharfdale, ILKLEY, W Yorks, LS29 7JP.   (hq)
  01943 865810
  Admin: Sharon Lockley, Jo Dakin
- ○ *P, *S
- ¶ Coachline - 6.
  Note: uses the trading name of TenniscoachUK

British Tenpin Bowling Association   (BTBA)   1961

- NR 114 Balfour Rd, ILFORD, Essex, IG1 4JD.   (hq)
  020 8478 1745   fax 020 8514 3665
  email admin@btba.org.uk   http://www.btba.org.uk
- ○ *S; to act as the governing body for tenpin bowling in the UK; to promote the sport
- M c 30,000 i

British Tensional Strapping Association   (BTSA)   1950

- NR 5 Church Mews, Barlby, SELBY, N Yorks, YO8 5LL.   (hq)
  01757 708555
  Sec: Graham Cooper
- ▲ Un-incorporated Society
- ○ *T; strapping equipment & materials
- ● Mtgs - SG - Stat
- M 7 f
- ¶ An Introduction to Tensional Strapping.
  Health & Safety guides:
      Steel strapping.   Non-metallic strapping.
      Strapping machines.
  Hazard Data Sheets.

British Tersk Society

- NR Drummond, Dores, INVERNESS, IV2 6TX.
  01463 751251   fax 01463 751240
  email candy@dores.demon.co.uk
  Contact: Candy Cameron
- ○ *B; for breeders of the Russian horses

British Texel Sheep Society Ltd   (BTSS)   1974

- NR National Agricultural Centre, Stoneleigh Park, KENILWORTH, Warks, CV8 2LG.   (hq)
  024 7669 6629   fax 024 7669 6472
  email office@texel.co.uk   http://www.texel.co.uk
  Chief Exec: John Yates
- ▲ Company Limited by Guarantee; Registered Charity
- ○ *B
- ● Exhib - Comp - Expt - Inf
- < Nat Sheep Assn
- M 2,500 i, 1 f, 19 breeders' clubs
- ¶ Jnl - 1;   Texel Bulletin - 4; both free.

British Textile Machinery Association   (BTMA)   1940
- ■ Glazebrook Lane, Glazebrook, WARRINGTON, Lancs, WA3 5BN.   (hq)
   0161-775 5710   fax 0161-775 5485
   email btma@btma.org.uk   http://www.btma.org.uk
   Dir: Alan Little
- ▲ Company Limited by Guarantee
- ○ *T
- Gp Sub-c'ees: Executive, Exhibitions, Technical
- ● Mtgs - Exhib - Stat - Expt - Inf - LG
- < Eur C'ee Textile Machinery Mfrs (CEMATEX)
- M 100 f
- ¶ Monthly Circular - 12;   Export Financing & Insurance;
   Outfitter conditions;   AR; all ftm only.
   BTMA Directory - 1; free.

British Textile Technology Group   (BTTG)   1988
- NR Wira House, West Park Ring Rd, LEEDS, W Yorks, LS16 6QL.
   (hq)
   0113-259 1999
   Chmn: William Laidlaw
- ▲ Company Limited by Guarantee
- Br 4
- ○ *Q; a centre of excellence in textile & materials related testing,
   investigation & evaluation
- Gp BCTC (British Carpet Technical Centre; CASE (coatings,
   adhesives, sealant & encapsulate testing); Certification; Fire
   technology services; Shirley technologies; Spinning &
   nonwovens; Wiratec
- ● Conf - ET - Res - Inf - Exhib
- M 143 f, UK / 19 f, o'seas
- ¶ Independent - 4.

British Theatre Dance Association   (BTDA)   1973
- ■ The International Arts Centre, Garden St, LEICESTER, LE1 3UA.   (hq)
   0845 166 2179   fax 0845 166 2189
   Gen Sec: Helen Mence
- ▲ Company Limited by Guarantee
- ○ *P; to support followers of all types of dance - teacher, student
   or supporter
- ● Mtgs - ET - Exam - Comp
- M 1,800 i, UK / 100 i, o'seas
- ¶ Danceworld - 2.

British Thoracic Society
- NR 17 Doughty St, LONDON, WC1N 2PL.   (HQ)
- ○ *P; to develop & maintain the highest standards of care for
   patients with respiratory disease
   NOTE: The society has no patient information service & is
   unable to deal with direct enquiries from the public.
   We have omitted contact details at their request.

British Throwsters Association   1934
- NR 3 Queen Sq, Bloomsbury, LONDON, WC1N 3AR.   (hq)
   020 7843 9460   fax 020 7843 9478
   Dir: Adam Mansell
- ○ *P; to promote & protect the UK throwing & texturising industry
   (both stages in yarn production)

British Thyroid Association   (BTA)
- NR c/o Dr Amil Allahabadia, Dept of Endocrinology, Royal
   Hallamshire Hospital, Glossop Rd, SHEFFIELD, S Yorks,
   S10 2JF.
   http://www.british-thyroid-association.org
   Sec: Dr Amit Allahabadia
- ○ *W

British Tinnitus Association   (BTA)   1979
- ■ Unit 5 Acorn Business Park, Woodseats Close, SHEFFIELD,
   S Yorks, S8 0TB.   (hq)
   0114-250 9922 freephone: 0800 018 0527   fax 0114-
   258 2279
   email info@tinnitus.org.uk   http://www.tinnitus.org.uk
   Operations Mgr: Mrs Val Rose
- ▲ Company Limited by Guarantee; Registered Charity
- Br 80 self-help groups
- ○ *M, *W; to support people with information & advice; to fund
   tinnitus research projects in order to find a cure; to promote
   awareness & understanding of the condition
- ● Conf - Mtgs - ET - Res - Pen pal register
- M c 10,000 i, UK / c 300 i, o'seas
- ¶ Quiet (Jnl) - 4.
   Leaflets;   Audio cassette relaxation tapes.

British Titanic Society   (BTS)   1986
- NR PO Box 401, Hope Carr Way, LEIGH, Lancs, WN7 3BB.
   Hon Dec: Nigel Wright
- ▲ Un-incorporated Society
- ○ *G; to research & preserve the memory of RMS Titanic & her
   passengers & crew

British Toilet Association   (BTA)   1999
- ■ PO Box 847, HORSHAM, W Sussex, RH12 5AL.   (hq)
   01403 258779
   email enquiries@britloos.co.uk   http://www.britloos.co.uk
   Managing Dir: Mike Bone
- ▲ Company Limited by Guarantee
- ○ *K; pressure group campaigning for more & better public
   lavatories
- ● Conf - Mtgs - Res - Stat - Inf - Lib - LG - Awards: Loo of the
   Year & Attendant of the Year
- M i, f, org

British Tomato Growers Association   (TGA)   1997
- ■ Pollards Nursery, Lake Lane, BARNHAM, W Sussex, PO22 0AD.
   01243 554859   fax 01243 554645
   email tga@britishtomatoes.co.uk
   http://www.britishtomatoes.co.uk
   Sec: Mrs Julie Woolley
- ▲ Company Limited by Guarantee
- ○ *H, *T; represents British growers; marketing information,
   research & development
- ● Conf - Mtgs - ET - Res - Exhib - LG
- M 45 f

British Tortoise Society
- NR PO Box 75, MANCHESTER, M26 4WZ.
   http://www.britishtortoisesociety.com
- ○ *G; offers help & advice on the keeping of tortoise
- ● Inf - Re-homing register - Sanctuary for injured, sick &
   unwanted tortoise
- M i
- ¶ NL - 4.

British Town Criers Authority
   no longer in existence

© CBD Research Ltd · Beckenham · BR3 5JS · Tel 020 8650 7745 · E-mail cbd@cbdresearch.com · www.cbdresearch.com

British Toxicology Society   (1TS)   1979
NR   PO Box 10371, COLCHESTER, Essex, CO1 9GL.   (hq)
   01206 226059
   email secretariat@thebts.org
   Sec: Dr H Wallace,   Meetings Sec: Dr S Price
▲   Registered Charity
○   *L; to advance the science & education of toxicology & the
   safety of chemicals for people & the environment
Gp   Biotechnology; Human toxicology; Immunotoxicology;
   Neurotoxicology; Occupational toxicology; Regulatory
   toxicology; Risk Assessment
●   Conf - Mtgs - Specialist working parties on scientific topics
<   Intl U of Toxicology; Fedn of Eur Socs of Toxicology; Biological
   Coun
M   692 i, UK / 158 i, o'seas

British Toy & Hobby Association Ltd   (BTHA)   1944
■   80 Camberwell Rd, LONDON, SE5 0EG.   (hq)
   020 7701 7271   fax 020 7708 2437
   email admin@btha.co.uk   http://www.btha.co.uk
   Dir Gen & Sec: David L Hawtin
○   *T
●   Mtgs - Res - Exhib - Stat - Expt - Inf
M   180 i & f
¶   Buyers Guide - 1; ftm, £15 nm.
   NTC leaflets; free.

British Toy Importers Association
   since 2006 **Equitoy: the association for toy importers**

British Toymakers Guild   (BTG)   1955
■   PO Box 4498, BRADFORD-on-AVON, BA15 5BB.   (hq)
   0845 474 7905
   email info@toymakersguild.co.uk
   http://www.toymakersguild.co.uk
   Mgr: Robert Nathan
▲   Un-incorporated Society
○   *T; to promote excellence in toy design & manufacture
Gp   Craft toy making
●   Mtgs - Exhib - Stat - Inf - LG
M   35 i, 140 f
¶   The Toymaker - 4.   Directory - 1.

British Traditional Molecatchers Register   (BTMR)   2007
NR   Ashbrooke, Littlethorpe, RIPON, N Yorks, HG4 3LJ.
   http://www.britishmolecatchers.co.uk
   Sec: Brian Alderton
○   *P; promotion of British molecatchers throughout the UK

British Transplantation Society   (BTS)   1971
NR   Chester House, 60 Chestergate, MACCLESFIELD, Cheshire,
   SK11 6DY.   (hq)
   01625 504060   fax 01625 267879
   http://www.bts.org.uk
   Sec: Dr Chris Dudley
▲   Company Limited by Guarantee; Registered Charity
○   *L; to advance the study of the biological & clinical problems of
   tissue & organ donation; to facilitate contact between persons
   interested in transplantation; to make new knowledge
   available for the general good of the community
Gp   Clinical trials; Standards; Training
●   Mtgs - ET - Res
M   c 650 i
¶   NL - 2.

British Trauma Society
   a specialist society of the **British Orthopaedic Association**

British Travel Health Association   (BTHA)   1999
NR   PO Box 336, SALE, M33 3UU.   (hq)
   0845 003 9197   fax 0870 005 3521
   email info@byha.org   http://www.btha.org
   Hon Sec: Dr George Kassianos
▲   Registered Charity
○   *K, *M; to promote a multi-disciplinary approach to travel
   health; to increase public awareness of travel health hazards
●   Conf - Mtgs - ET - Res - SG - Inf
M   c 530 i
¶   Jnl - 2;   Travelwise - 4; both ftm only.

British Travelgoods & Accessories Association   (BTAA)   1918
NR   Federation House, 10 Vyse St, BIRMINGHAM, B18 6LT.   (hq)
   0121-237 1107
   http://www.btaa.org.uk
   Sec: Diana Fiveash
▲   Company Limited by Guarantee
○   *T; representing manufacturers, distributors & importers of
   luggage, handbags & small leathergoods
●   Conf - Mtgs - Exhib - Expt - Inf - LG
<   Brit Allied Trs Fedn (BATF)
M   90 f
¶   Buyer's Guide - amended as necessary.

British Trials & Rally Drivers Association   (BTRDA)
NR   Woodlands, Anthony's Cross, NEWENT, Glos, GL18 1JF.   (hsp)
   01531 820761
   email simonharris@lineone.net   http://www.btrda.com
   Contact: Simon Harris

British Triathlon Federation   1984
NR   PO Box 25, LOUGHBOROUGH, Leics, LE11 3WX.   (hq)
   01509 226161   fax 01509 226165
   email info@britishtriathlon.org
   http://www.britishtriathlon.org
   Chief Exec: Zara Hyde Peters
▲   Company Limited by Guarantee
○   *N, *S; to manage a number of services (British & international
   events, anti-doping, international representation, age group
   teams) on behalf of its three home nation members, Triathlon
   England, TriathlonScotland & Welsh Triathlon
M   3 org
×   2007 British Triathlon Association Ltd

British Trolleybus Society   (BTS)   1961
■   2 Josephine Court, Southcote Rd, READING, Berks,
   RG30 2DG.   (hsp)
   0118-958 3974
   http://www.britishtrolley.org.uk
   Hon Sec: A J Barton
▲   Registered Charity
○   *G; to study the history & development of the trolley bus &
   trolley bus networks
●   Mtgs - VE
M   320 i, UK / 10 i, o'seas
¶   Trolleybus - 12.   Bus Fare - 12.   Wheels - 12.

British Trombone Society   (BTS)   1983
■   7 Sandy Lodge Court, 20 Sandy Lodge Way, NORTHWOOD,
   Middx, HA6 2AN.   (hsp)
   0844 445 7931
   email secretary@britishtrombonesociety.org
   http://www.britishtrombonesociety.org
   Sec: Geoff Wolmark
▲   Un-incorporated Society
○   *D; to promote the trombone & trombone-related issues in the
   UK
●   Conf - ET - Comp - Inf - Commissioning of compositions
<   Intl Trombone Assn
M   700 i, UK / 300 i, o'seas
   (Sub: £24, UK / £30, o'seas)
¶   The Trombonist - 4.

British Trout Association Ltd (BTA) 1982

- ■ The Rural Centre, West Mains, INGLISTON, Midlothian, EH28 8NZ. (hq)
  0131-472 4080   fax 0131-472 4083
  email mail@britishtrout.co.uk
  http://www.britishtrout.co.uk
  Chief Exec: David Bassett
- ▲ Company Limited by Guarantee
- ○ *T; to represent the UK trout aquaculture industry; research relating to trout health & welfare
- Gp British Trout Farmers Restocking Association
- ● Conf - Mtgs - Res - Stat - Inf - VE - LG - Marketing - PR - Technical advice - QA scheme
- < Fedn of Eur Aquaculture Producers (FEAP); Fedn of Scot Aquaculture Producers (FSAP)
- M 100 f
- ¶ NL - 4;   AR - 1; both ftm.
  Code of Practice;   QTUK Standards;   Technical Briefing Notes; all ftm only.

British Trout Farmers Restocking Association
a group of the **British Trout Association**

British Truck Racing Association (BTRA) 1985

- NR Roughwood, Thibet Rd, SANDHURST, Berks, GU47 9AR. (sp)
  01344 762774
  http://www.britishtruckracing.co.uk
  Sec: Terry Cox
- ○ *S; to further interest in motoring & motor sport with trucks

British Trust for Conservation Volunteers (BTCV) 1959

- NR Sedum House, Mallard Way, Potteric Carr, DONCASTER, S Yorks, DN4 8DB. (hq)
  01302 388883
  email information@btcv.org.uk   http://www.btcv.org
- ▲ Registered Charity
- ○ *K; to ensure that the potential for voluntary action for the environment is fully realised; to ensure that people of the world value their environment & take practical action to improve it
- M 130,000 i, 1,950 org, 1,358 other

British Trust for Ornithology (BTO) 1933

- ■ The Nunnery, THETFORD, Norfolk, IP24 2PU. (hq)
  01842 750050   fax 01842 750030
  email general@bto.org   http://www.bto.org
  Dir: Dr Andy Clements,   Sec: Andrew T Scott
- ▲ Company Limited by Guarantee; Registered Charity
- Br BTO Scotland, Stirling
- ○ *L; 'to promote & encourage wider understanding, appreciation & conservation of birds through scientific studies. . . by members, other birdwatchers & staff'
- Gp Habitats research: Coastal & wetlands, Terrestrial
  Populations research: Ringing, Censuses, Nest records
  Administration; Membership & development
- ● Conf - Mtgs - ET - Res - SG - Stat - Inf - Lib - LG - Research & monitoring consultancy
- M 9,000 i, 300 org, UK / 500 i, 20 org, o'seas
- ¶ Bird Table - 4.
  Bird Study - 3.   BTO News (NL) - 6.
  Ringing Migration - 2.   AR.

British Tugowners Association (BTA) 1934

- ■ Carthusian Court, 12 Carthusian St, LONDON, EC1M 6EZ. (hq)
  020 7417 2828
  email info@britishtug.org   http://www.britishtug.org
  Sec-Gen: Saurabh Sachdeva
- ▲ Un-incorporated Society
- ○ *T; 'members own/operate tugs for shiptowage services in ports of the UK, coastal & ocean towage & salvage'
- ● Conf - Mtgs - ET - Stat - Inf - LG
- < Eur Tugowners Assn
- M 18 f, UK / 1 f, o'seas

British Tunnelling Society (BTS) 1971

- ■ Institution of Civil Engineers, 1 Great George St, LONDON, SW1P 3AA. (hq)
  http://www.britishtunnelling.org.uk
- ▲ Registered Charity
- ○ *L, *Q; to develop the art, science & techniques of tunnelling
- ● Conf - Mtgs - Comp - Inf
- < Intl Tunnelling Assn
- M 780 i, 40 f, UK / 165 i, o'seas
- ¶ Tunnels & Tunnelling International - 12.
  NL - 3.   AR.

British Turf & Landscape Irrigation Association (BTLIA) 1978

- NR 41 Pennine Way, Great Eccleston, PRESTON, Lancs, PR3 0YS. (sp)
  01995 670675   fax 01995 670675
  email info@btlia.org.uk   http://www.btlia.org.uk
  Sec: Martyn T Jones
- ▲ Company Limited by Guarantee
- ○ *T; to promote the proper & responsible installation of turf & landscape irrigation schemes; to provide eduational opportunities to fulfil these criteria
- Gp Consultants; Equipment manufacturers; Installation contractors; Irrigation
- ● Conf - Mtgs - ET - Exam - Exhib - Inf
- < Irrigation Assn (USA); Eur Irrigation Assn; UK Irrigation Assn
- M c 50 f
- ¶ LM - 1; ftm, on request nm.

British Turned Parts Manufacturers Association (BTMA) 1920

- ■ 77 Greyhound Lane, STOURBRIDGE, W Midlands, DY8 3AD. (dir/p)
  01789 730877   fax 01789 730899
  email chrisgladwin@btma.org   http://www.btma.org
  Dir: Chris Gladwin
- ○ *T: for UK manufacturing companies producing precision turned parts & machined components
- ● Conf - Mtgs - ET - Exhib - SG - Stat - Inf - VE - LG
- M 75 f
- ¶ BTMA Buyer's Guide (LM) - 1; free.

British Tyre Manufacturers' Association Ltd (BTMA) 1968

- NR 5 Berewyk Hall Court, White Colne, COLCHESTER, Essex, CO6 2QD. (hq)
  0845 310 6852   fax 0845 301 6853
  email mail@btmauk.com   http://www.btmauk.com
  Dir: A J Dorken,   Admin: Christine Joyce
- ▲ Company Limited by Guarantee
- ○ *T; to promote & protect the interests of the rubber manufacturing industry in the UK
- Gp Geeral rubber goods (GRG); Tyre management c'ee (TNC)
- ● Conf - Mtgs - ET - Stat - Inf - LG
- < Eur Rubber Assn (BLIC); Tyre Ind Coun (TIC)
- M 61 f

British UFO Research Association (BUFORA) 1963

- § Clarendon House, 117 George Lane, South Woodford, LONDON, E18 1AN. (hsp)
  0844 567 4694
  email enquiries@bufora.org.uk
  http://www.bufora.org.uk
- ▲ Company Limited by Guarantee
- ¶ [all publications on website].
  Originally named the British Unidentified Flying Object Research Association, BUFORA Ltd assumed dormancy status in 2007 and now exists solely as a non-membership organisation researching unidentified flying phenomena throughout the UK; disseminating & collating evidence & cooperating with others doing similar research throughout the world.

© CBD Research Ltd · Beckenham · BR3 5JS · Tel 020 8650 7745 · E-mail cbd@cbdresearch.com · www.cbdresearch.com

British Union for the Abolition of Vivisection **(BUAV)** **1898**
- ■ 16a Crane Grove, LONDON, N7 8NN. (hq)
  020 7700 4888 fax 020 7700 0252
  email info@buav.org http://www.buav.org
  Chief Exec: Michelle Thew
- ▲ Company Limited by Guarantee
- ○ *K; campaigning to end all animal experiments
- ● Conf - Res - Exhib - Comp - Stat - Inf - Lib - PL - LG - Lobbying
  UK/EU legislation - Undercover investigations
- < Intl Coun for Animal Protection in OECD Programmes; Eur
  Coalition to End Animal Experiments
- ¶ BUAV Action (NL) - 3 (email - 6); BUAV Update (NL) - 4; AR -
  1; all free.

British Union of Social Work Employees
  in 2008 merged with **Community**

British Universities & Colleges Sport Ltd **(BUCS)** **2008**
- NR 20-24 King's Bench St, LONDON, SE1 0QX. (hq)
  020 7633 5080 fax 020 3268 2120
  http://www.bucs.org.uk
  Chief Exec: Karen Rothery
- ▲ Company Limited by Guarantee; Registered Charity
- ○ *S, *K; organisation & promotion of sport to students in higher
  education through organisation of championships
  representing fixtures & British teams for international events
- ● Conf - Mtgs - ET - Comp
- M 161 org
- ¶ Hbk - 1; AR - 1; both free.
- × 2008 (British Universities Sports Association
  (University College Sport (merged June)

British Universities Film & Video Council **(BUFVC)** **1948**
- NR 77 Wells St, LONDON, W1T 3QJ. (hq)
  020 7393 1500
  email ask@bufvc.ac.uk http://www.bufvc.ac.uk
  Chief Exec: Murray Weston
- ▲ Company Limited by Guarantee; Registered Charity
- ○ *E; to foster the production, study & use of film & related audio-
  visual media (incl TV, video & computer-based multi media)
  for higher education & research
- M c 220 universities, insts etc

British Universities Industrial Relations Association **(BUIRA)**
1950
- NR c/o MMU Business School, Aytoun Building, Aytoun St,
  MANCHESTER, M1 3GH. (sb)
  0161-247 6160
  Contact: Ann Marie McDonald
- ○ *P; the academic study of industrial relations & allied areas in
  Britain & internationally
- ● Conf - Res - SG - Specialist bibliographies research register
- < Intl Indl Relations Assn; Academy of Learned Socs for the Social
  Sciences
- M i

British Universities Snowsports Council **(BUSC)** **1992**
- NR Edinburgh University Sports Union, 48 Pleasance, EDINBURGH,
  EH8 9TJ. (hq)
  email info@buscevents.com http://www.buscevents.com
  Sec: Alex Collins
- ▲ Company Limited by Guarantee
- ○ *S

British Universities Sports Association
  in June 2008 merged with University College Sport to form **British
  Universities & Colleges Sport Ltd**

British Urban Regeneration Association
  went into liquidation 14 August 2010 and relaunched as UK
  Regeneration, a non-membership online database resource

British Urban & Regional Information Systems Association
(BURISA) **1972**
- NR Royal Statistical Society, 12 Errol St, LONDON, EC1Y 8LX.
  (asa)
  email secretary@burisa.org.uk http://www.burisa.org.uk
  Sec: Mark Pearson
- ▲ Un-incorporated Society
- ○ *P; to promote better communication between people
  concerned with information & information systems in local &
  central government, the health services, utilities & the
  academic world
- ● Conf - Mtgs
- < R Statistical Soc
- ¶ BURISA (NL) - 6.

British Urethane Foam Contractors Association **(BUFCA Ltd)**
1980
- ■ PO Box 12, HASLEMERE, Surrey, GU27 3AH. (hq)
  01428 654011 fax 01428 651401
  email info@bufca.co.uk http://www.bufca.co.uk
  Co Sec: Leonie Onslow
- ▲ Company Limited by Guarantee
- ○ *T; contractors & suppliers in the sprayed urethane foam
  industry for thermal insulation of buildings & plant
- Gp Health & safety; Fire hazards; Coatings; Foam specification
- ● Conf - Mtgs - Exhib - SG - Stat - Inf
- M f
- ¶ NL; Technical Bulletin; Technical Guidelines; all ftm only.

British-Uruguayan Chamber of Commerce
  see **Cámara de Comercio Uruguayo Británica (Brtitish-
  Uruguayan Chamber of Commerce)**

British Uruguayan Society **1945**
- NR 18 Longland Drive, LONDON, N20 8HE. (sp)
  020 8445 2462
- ▲ Registered Charity
- ○ *X; to advance the knowledge of Britons about Uruguay &
  Uruguayans about the UK
- ● Mtgs - Exhib - Inf - Lib (at Hispanic Council, Canning House) -
  VE
- M c 250 i, UK / c 30 i, o'seas
- ¶ El Hornero - 2.
  Tales of Uruguay (members' reminiscences of Uruguay),
  (1988);
  A History of the Society 1945-1985, (1997);
  The Uruguayan Short Story, (2007); all £5.

British Used Printing Machinery Suppliers Association
(BUPMSA) **1993**
- ■ 20 Spencer Bridge Rd, NORTHAMPTON, NN5 5EZ. (hq)
  01604 756100 fax 01604 750910
  email info@bupmsa.org.uk http://www.bupmsa.org.uk
  Chmn: Michael Steele
- ▲ Company Limited by Guarantee
- ○ *T; for dealers of used print related equipment who buy & sell
  worldwide
- ● Exhib - Expt - Inf

British Vacuum Council **(BVC)** **1965**
- NR 76 Portland Place, LONDON, W1B 1NT. (hq)
  020 7470 4838 fax 020 7470 4848
  http://www.british-vacuum-council.org.uk
  Sec: Dr Mark Bowden
- ▲ Registered Charity
- ○ *L; to promote & advance the understanding & teaching of
  vacuum science, technology & its applications
- M 2 org:
  Institute of Physics
  Royal Society of Chemistry

British Valve & Actuator Association Ltd   (BVAA)   1939
- ■ 9 Manor Park, BANBURY, Oxon, OX16 3TB.   (hq)
     01295 221270   fax 01295 268965
     email enquiry@bvaa.org.uk   http://www.bvaa.org.uk
     Dir: Rob Bartlett
- ▲ Company Limited by Guarantee
- ○ *T; to represent interests of British manufacturers, distributors & repairers of industrial valves & actuators
- Gp Actuator; Executive; Manufacturing & quality; Marketing; Technical; Training
- ● Conf - Mtgs - ET - Exhib - Stat - Expt - Inf - VE - Journal
- < CBI Trade Assn Forum
- M 100 f (annual)
- ¶ NL - 4;   Buyers Guide - 1 yrly;   AR; all free.
     Valve Users Manual (Technical Handbook); £10.

British Vehicle Rental & Leasing Association Ltd   (BVRLA)   1967
- NR River Lodge, Badminton Court, AMERSHAM, Bucks, HP7 0DD.   (hq)
      01494 434747   fax 01494 434499
      email info@bvrla.co.uk   http://www.bvrla.co.uk
      Dir Gen: John Lewis
- ▲ Company Limited by Guarantee
- ○ *T; to represent the interests of operators of daily rental, leasing, contract hire & fleet management for cars, minibuses & light & heavy commercial vehicles
- Gp Vehicle leasing & contract hire; Vehicle rental
- M f

British Vehicle Salvage Federation   (BVSF)   1998
- ■ Flint Research Institute, 132 Heathfield Rd, KESTON, Kent, BR2 6BA.   (hq)
     01689 855583
     email email@bvsf.org.uk   http://www.bvsf.org.uk
     Chmn & Sec Gen: Alan W Greenouff
- ▲ Un-Incorporated Society
- ○ *T; representative body for the UK vehicle salvage industry
- Gp Management c'ee
- ● Conf - Mtgs - LG
- < Assn of Brit Insurers; Motor Repair Res Centre (Thatcham)
- M 98 f
- ¶ Vehicle Salvage Professional - 4; free.   AR.

British Vendéen Sheep Society   1984
- ■ Darkes House, Conderton, TEWKESBURY, Glos, GL20 7PP. (hsp)
     01386 725229   fax 01386 725229
     email info@vendeen.co.uk   http://www.vendeen.co.uk
     Sec: Andrew John
- ▲ Registered Charity
- ○ *B; the promotion & improvement of British Vendéen sheep
- Gp Sire reference scheme
- ● Comp - Inf
- < Nat Sheep Assn
- M 80 i
- ¶ Flock Book - 1; £10.

British Veterinary Association   (BVA)   1881
- NR 7 Mansfield St, LONDON, W1G 9NQ.   (hq)
      020 7636 6541
      email bvahq@bva.co.uk   http://www.bva.co.uk
      Co Sec: Henrietta Alderman
- ▲ Company Limited by Guarantee
- Br Scottish, Welsh, Northern Ireland & territorial divns
- ○ *P, *V; standards of animal health; veterinary surgeons' working practices; profl standards of quality of service; relations with external bodies; policy development; service provision
- Gp Association of Government Veterinarians; Association of Veterinarians in Industry; Association of Veterinary Students; Association of Veterinary Teaching & Research Work; British Cattle Veterinary Association; British Equine Veterinary Association; British Small Animal Veterinary Association; British Veterinary Hospitals Association; British Veterinary Poultry Association; British Veterinary Zoological Society; Fish Veterinary Society; Goat Veterinary Society; Laboratory Animal Science Association; Pig Veterinary Society; Royal Army Veterinary Corps Division; Sheep Veterinary Society; Society of Greyhound Veterinarians; Society of Practising Veterinary Surgeons; Society for the Study of Animal Breeding; Veterinary Deer Society; Veterinary Public Health Association
- ● Conf - Mtgs - ET - SG - Inf - Empl - LG
- < Fedn of Veterinarians in Europe; Commonwealth Veterinary Assn; Wld Veterinary Assn
- M c 10,000 i UK & o'seas
- ¶ The Veterinary Record - 52.   In Practice - 10.
     Off the Record - 12;   Ybk.   Annual Review.
     Other publications.

British Veterinary Camelid Society   (BVCS)   1994
- NR Foxes Grove - Spring Hill, Punnetts Town, HEATHFIELD, E Sussex, TN21 9PE.   (hsp)
      01435 864422
      email secretary@camelidvets.org
      http://www.camelidvets.org
      Sec: Janet Nuttall
- ▲ Un-incorporated Society
- ○ *V; to stimulate knowledge of diseases & management of South American camelids (alpaca, llama, guanaco & vicuña); to promote interest in these fascinating animals with respect to their management, breeding, feeding, health & disease
- ● Conf - Mtgs - ET - Inf - LG
- M c 110 i, f & org
- ¶ Proceedings of Conference - 1.

British Veterinary Dental Association
     a group of the **British Small Animal Veterinary Association**

British Veterinary Dermatology Study Group
     a group of the **British Small Animal Veterinary Association**

British Veterinary Forensic & Law Association   (BVFLA)   1992
- NR The Beeches, Rickerby, CARLISLE, Cumbria, CA3 9AA.   (hsp)
      01228 521450
      http://www.veterinaryexpertwitnesses.co.uk
      Hon Sec: Graham D Cawley
- ▲ Un-incorporated Society
- ○ *P; to promote the study of all aspects of jurisprudence, arbitration & Alternative Dispute Resolution (ADR) within the veterinary profession; to assist with training for members
- Gp [all specialities]
- ● Conf - Mtgs - ET - Inf
- < Forensic Science Soc; Inst of Biology
- M 90 i, UK / 10 i, o'seas
- ¶ Proceedings - 2; ftm, £25 nm.   NL - irreg; free.
- × 2008 Veterinary Association for Arbitration & Jurisprudence

© CBD Research Ltd · Beckenham · BR3 5JS · Tel 020 8650 7745 · E-mail cbd@cbdresearch.com · www.cbdresearch.com

British Veterinary Hospitals Association (BVHA) 1960
- ■ c/o Station Bungalow, Main Rd, STOCKSFIELD, Northumberland, NE43 7HJ. (office/mgr/p)
  0796 690 1619   fax 0781 391 5954
  email office@bvha.org.uk   http://www.bvha.org.uk
  Office Manager: Christine Shield,   Hon Sec: Ian Harris
- ▲ Un-incorporated Society
- ○ *P, *V; to promote the highest standards of excellence in animal treatment through the design, construction & equipping of veterinary hospitals
- ● Conf - ET - Exhib - Comp - Inf - VE
- < a division of the Brit Veterinary Assn
- M 108 i, 116 f
- ¶ Bulletin - 4; ftm only.

British Veterinary Neurology Study Group
  a group of the **British Small Animal Veterinary Association**

British Veterinary Nursing Association Ltd (BVNA) 1965
- NR 82 Greenway Business Centre, Harlow Business Park, HARLOW, Essex, CM19 5QE. (hq)
  01279 408644   fax 01279 408645
  email bvna@bvna.co.uk   http://www.bvna.co.uk
- ▲ Company Limited by Guarantee
- ○ *P, *V; for veterinary nurses
- ● Conf - ET - Exam - Exhib - Inf
- < Intl Veterinary Nurses & Technicians Assn (IVNTA)
- M 4,020 i, UK / 59 i, o'seas
- ¶ Veterinary Nursing Jnl - 12; free.

British Veterinary Oncology Study Group
  a group of the **British Small Animal Veterinary Association**

British Veterinary Orthopaedic Association
  a group of the **British Small Animal Veterinary Association**

British Veterinary Poultry Association
  a group of the **British Veterinary Association**

British Veterinary Zoological Society
  a group of the **British Veterinary Association**

British Video Association (BVA) 1980
- NR 167 Great Portland St, LONDON, W1W 5PE. (hq)
  020 7436 0041   fax 020 7436 0043
  email general@bva.org.uk   http://www.bva.org.uk
  Dir Gen: Mrs Lavinia Carey
- ▲ Company Limited by Guarantee
- ○ *T; to represent the interests of publishers and rights owners of pre-recorded video home entertainment
- ● Conf - Mtgs - Res - Exhib - Stat - Inf - LG
- M 46 f (26 full, 20 associate)
- ¶ NL - 12.   LM - 12.   Ybk - 1.

British Vintage Wireless Society (BVWS) 1976
- NR AOPP, Clarendon Laboratory, Parks Rd, OXFORD, OX1 3PU. (hq)
  01865 247971
  http://www.bvws.org.uk
  Sec: Dr Guy Peskett
- ▲ Un-incorporated Society
- ○ *G; the history & preservation of vintage wireless & television equipment
- ● Mtgs - Res - Exhib - Comp - Inf - Lib - PL
- M 1,400 i, 55 org, UK / 200 i, 16 org, o'seas
- ¶ Bulletin (incorporating 405 Alive) - 4; ftm only.

British Violin Making Association (BVMA) 1995
- NR 16 Coombe Lane, Bowlish, SHEPTON MALLET, Somerset, BA4 5XD.
  01749 343912
  email secretary@bvma.org.uk   http://www.bvma.org.uk
  Sec: Kai-Thomas Roth
- ▲ Un-incorporated Society
- ○ *P, *T; to raise the standards & skills of violin & bow makers & restorers; to encourage dissemination of information amongst them
- ● Conf - ET - Exhib - Comp
- M 479 i, 20 org
- ¶ [Jnl] - 4

British Viral Hepatitis Group
  a group of **British Association for the Study of the Liver**

British Voice Association (BVA) 1991
- ■ 330 Gray's Inn Rd, LONDON, WC1X 8EE. (hq)
  020 7713 0064   fax 020 7915 1388
  email bva@dircon.co.uk
  http://www.british-voice-association.com
  Co Sec: Kristine Carroll-Porczynski
- ▲ Company Limited by Guarantee; Registered Charity
- ○ *P; for all professionals interested in the human voice
- Gp Laryngology; Phonetics; Singing; Singing teaching; Speech therapy; Voice teaching
- ● Conf - Mtgs - ET - Res - Comp - Inf - Professional standards in related medical groups
- < Intl Assn of Logopedics & Phoniatrics
- M 470 i, UK / 30 i, o'seas
  (Sub: £55 UK / £65 o'seas)
- ¶ Logopedics, Phoniatrics & Vocology - 4;
  NL - 3;   LM - 1; all ftm only.

British Volleyball Federation (BVF) 1981
- NR English Institute of Sport, Coleridge Rd, SHEFFIELD, S Yorks, S9 5DA. (hq)
  0114-223 5731   fax 0114-223 5660
  http://www.britishperformancevolleyball.org
  Programme Mgr: Kenny Barton
- ▲ Un-incorporated Society
- ○ *N, *S; umbrella organisation to coordinate activities of the English, Northern Ireland, Scottish & Welsh Volleyball Associations
- Gp Volleyball Association(s): English / Northern Ireland / Scottish / Welsh;
  Great Britain National Volleyball Teams
- M 4 org

British Walking Federation (BWF) 1983
- NR 2 Test Cottages, St Mary Bourne, ANDOVER, Hants, SP11 6BX. (hsp)
  01264 738569
  email info@bwf-ivv.org.uk   http://www.bwf-ivv.org.uk
  Sec: Peter Denison
- ▲ Un-incorporated Society
- ○ *G, *S; walking for health
- ● Conf - Mtgs - LG - Monitoring of non-competitive walks
- < Intl Fedn of Popular Sports (IVV)
- M i & org
- ¶ Footprint - 6.

British Warm Air Hand Drier Association (BWAHDA) 1981
- ■ Technology House, Oakfield Industrial Estate, EYNSHAM, Oxon, OX29 4AQ. (regd/off)
  01865 882330   fax 01865 881647
  Sec: Graham Davies
- ▲ Company Limited by Guarantee
- ○ *T; promotion of warm air hand driers
- ● Mtgs - Inf - LG
- M 5 f, UK / 1 f, o'seas

British Warm-Blood Society
since January 2008 the **Warmblood Breeders' Studbook - UK**

British Watch & Clock Makers' Guild   (BWCMG)   1907
■   PO Box 2368, ROMFORD, Essex, RM1 2YZ.   (hsp)
      01708 750616   fax 01708 750616
      email sec@bwcmg.org   http://www.bwcmg.org
      Hon Sec: P Craddock
▲   Company Limited by Guarantee
○   *P, *T; for those professionally engaged in the manufacture,
      restoration or repair of watches & clocks
●   Inf
M   1,000 i, UK / 15 i, o'seas
¶   NL - 2; ftm only.

British Water   1993
■   1 Queen Anne's Gate, LONDON, SW1H 9BT.   (hq)
      020 7957 4554   fax 020 7957 4565
      email info@britishwater.co.uk
      http://www.britishwater.co.uk
      Chief Exec: David Neil-Gallacher
▲   Company Limited by Guarantee
○   *N, *T; to represent the collective interests of the supply chain of
      the UK water & waste water industry in relation to
      government, regulators, trade promotion, industry standards,
      legislative & regulatory affairs. Membership includes civil &
      process contractors, management, engineering & IT
      consultants, equipment manufacturers & suppliers, law firms,
      financial institutions & specialist research & training
      organisations
Gp International Forum; Technical forum & specialist focus groups;
      UK forum
      Overseas (Asia-Pacific, Europe, Middle East)
●   Conf - Mtgs - ET - Exhib - Expt - Inf - LG
<   Intl Water Assn (IWA); Aqua Europa; Mechanical & Metal Trs
      Confedn (METCOM)
M   175 f
¶   Codes of Practice; prices vary.   AR; both free.

British Water Cooler Association   (BWCA)   1991
■   PO Box 276, RICKMANSWORTH, Herts, WD3 0HR.   (asa)
      01923 775770
      email info@bwca.org.uk   http://www.bwca.org.uk
      Secretariat: Phillipa Atkinson-Clow
○   *T; all aspects of chain of supply from water source to
      satisfaction & health of consumers
●   Mtgs - ET - Res - SG - Stat - Inf - LG
M   f
¶   Handbooks.

British Water Ski & Wakeboard   1951
NR Unit 3 The Forum, Hanworth Lane, CHERTSEY, Surrey,
      KT16 9JX.   (hq)
      01932 560007
      email info@bwsf.co.uk   http://www.britishwaterski.org.uk
      Chief Exec: Patrick Donovan
▲   Company Limited by Guarantee
Br 2
○   *S; the governing body for water skiing in the UK
Gp Wakeboard UK
●   ET - Exam - Comp - Inf
<   Intl Water Ski & Wakeboard Fedn (IWWF); Eur Boating Fedn
M   c 11,000 i, 150 clubs
¶   Waterski & Wakeboard - 5; free.

British Waterbed Association   (BWA)   1984
■   Manchester Waterbed Centre, 7a Victoria Lane, Whitefield,
      MANCHESTER, M45 6BL.   (sb)
      0161-766 8333
      http://www.waterbed.org
      Sec: Michael Hand
▲   Un-incorporated Society
Br 35; Belgium, Denmark, Netherlands
○   *T; to promote quality waterbed products; to advance sleep
      research; to increase consumer awareness & advise
      waterbed users
Gp Manufacturers; Retailers; Wholesalers
●   Exhib - Annual trade show
<   Speciality Sleep Assn (USA)
M   35 f, UK / 4 f, o'seas
¶   Waterbeds - the facts.   Fact & Fiction.
      Backaches & Waterbeds.   Arthritis & Waterbeds.
      Waterbed Owners Manual.

British Watercolour Society   (BWS)   1985
NR 13 Manor Orchards, KNARESBOROUGH, N Yorks,
      HG5 0BW.   (hq)
      01423 540603
      email info@britpaint.co.uk   http://www.britpaint.co.uk
      Dir: Leslie Simpson
○   *A; to promote excellence in the field of watercolours, both in
      the UK & internationally
M   i
¶   Catalogue - 2.

British Waterfowl Association   (BWA)   1887
■   PO Box 163, OXTED, Surrey, RH8 0WP.   (mail/add)
      01892 740212
      email info@waterfowl.org.uk
      http://www.waterfowl.org.uk
      Sec/Treas: Mrs Sue Schubert
▲   Registered Charity
○   *B, *G; to promote the conservation, education & preservation
      of wildfowl & domestic waterfowl; to assist breeders
●   Mtgs - Exhib - Inf - LG - Open days
<   Nat Coun for Aviculture
>   Call Duck Assn; Indian Runner Duck Assn
M   750 i, 6 f, UK / 30 i, o'seas
¶   Waterfowl - 3; ftm, £3.50 nm.
      The Breeders Directory - 1.   Ybk - 1.

British Wave Ski Association
NR Trevellian, Ham Lane South, LLANTWIT MAJOR, Glamorgan,
      CF61 1RP.
      http://www.waveski.co.uk
      Chmn: Neil Sutch
○   *S

British Weight Lifting   (BWLA)   1904
NR 10 Cavendish, Leeds Metropolitan University Headingley
      Campus, LEEDS, W Yorks, S6 3QS.   (hq)
      0113-812 7098
      http://www.britishweightlifting.org
      Admin: Lorraine Fleming
▲   Company Limited by Guarantee
○   *S; promotes & controls all aspects of weight lifting, power
      lifting & weight training
M   15,000 i in 450 clubs
¶   The British Weightlifter - 6.
✕   British Weight Lifting Association

© CBD Research Ltd · Beckenham · BR3 5JS · Tel 020 8650 7745 · E-mail cbd@cbdresearch.com · www.cbdresearch.com

British Weights & Measures Association   (BWMA)   1995
■   EG8 Panther House, Mount Pleasant, LONDON, WC1X 0AN.
      (hsb)
      email bwma@email.com   http://www.bwmaonline.com
      Pres: Vivian Thornton Linacre (01738 783936)
      Dir: John Gardner
▲   Un-incorporated Society
○   *K; preservation & promotion of imperial weights & measures;
      to oppose compulsory metrication & the repeal of EEC/EU
      directives as enforced by UK government
Gp   Educational; Historical & cultural; International; Technical
      research
●   Conf - Mtgs - ET - Res - LG - Political representation
M   [not given]
      (Sub: £12)
¶   The Yardstick - 4; ftm.

British Westerners Association   (BWA)   1973
NR   103 St Nicholas Drive, WybersWood, GRIMSBY, N Lincs,
      DN37 9QE.   (sp)
      014272 883564
      Sec: David Smithson
▲   Un-incorporated Society
○   *G; for anyone interested in all aspects of the American West
●   Conf - Mtgs - Res - Exhib - Comp - Inf - VE
<   Westerners Intl (USA)
M   1,200 i, 30 f, 40 org, UK / 20 i, o'seas
¶   Round-Up - 4; ftm.

British Wheel of Yoga   (BWY)   1965
NR   25 Jermyn St, SLEAFORD, Lincs, NG34 7RU.   (hq)
      01529 306851   fax 01529 303233
      email office@bwy.org.uk   http://www.bwy.org.uk
▲   Registered Charity
Br   11
○   *G; to further the practice & teaching of yoga
●   Conf - Mtgs - ET - Exam - Exhib - SG - Inf
<   Eur U of Fedns of Yoga
M   c 8,500 i
¶   Spectrum - 4;   Yoga the World Over - 4; both ftm only.

British Wheelchair Athletics Association   (BWAA)
NR   30 Grape Lane, Croston, Leyland, Lancs, PR26 9HB.   (hsp)
      email barbarahoole@hotmail.com
      16 Poole Hey Lane, SCARISBRICK, Lancs, PR8 5HS.
      Contacts: Barbara Hoole,   Ernie Gould
○   *S; for wheelchair athletes entering shot, discus, javelin, club &
      pentathlon events
●   Mtgs - Inf
M   i

British Wheelchair Bowls Association   (BWBA)   1984
NR   Kerria, Station Rd, EAST PRESTON, W Sussex, BN16 3AJ.
      (chmn/b)
      http://www.bwba.org.uk
      Chmn: Ian Blackmore
▲   Registered Charity
○   *S
●   ET - Comp - Inf
<   Brit Wheelchair Sports Foundation, Brit Isles Indoor Bowls Assn,
      Brit Paralympic Assn, English Bowling Assn, English Indoor
      Bowls Assn
M   150 i, 20 bowls clubs
¶   The Shot - 4; ftm only.

British Wheelchair Pool Players' Association
■   No postal address.   (pres/p)
      07968 966042
      email matthew@bwppa.org   http://www.bwppa.org
      Pres: Matthew Gleaves
○   *S

British Wheelchair Racing Association   (BWRA)
NR   Ballasalla, The Avenue, Eaglescliffe, STOCKTON-on-TEES,
      TS16 9AS.   (hsp)
      01642 769262
      http://www.bwra.co.uk
      Sec: Dr Ian Thompson
○   *S

British Whippet Racing Association   (BWRA)   1967
NR   186 Byerley Rd, SHILDON, Co Durham, DL4 1HW.   (sp)
      01388 776307
      http://www.thebwra.co.uk
      Sec: Mrs Alison Armstrong
▲   Un-incorporated Society
Br   8
○   *S; to promote & control all issues to do with non-pedigree
      whippet racing, breeding, registering & welfare
●   Race mtgs
M   c300 i, 23 clubs
¶   [pages in Whippet News - 12].

British White Cattle Society   (BWCS)   1918
NR   Meadow View, Kelby, GRANTHAM, Lincs, NG32 3AJ.   (hsp)
      01400 230142
      email breedsecretary@britishwhitecattle.co.uk
      http://www.britishwhitecattle.co.uk
      Sec: Mrs Ruth Mawer
▲   Un-incorporated Society
○   *B; to encourage the breeding of British White cattle & establish
      & publish a Herd Book for them
●   Mtgs - Expt - Inf - Lib (archive) - VE
<   Nat Cattle Assn; Rare Breeds Survival Trust
M   291 i
¶   Ybk (incl Herdbook) - 1; ftm.
      NL - 4; ftm.   Leaflet.

British Wind Energy Association
      since 21 Decenber 2009 **Renewable UK Association**

British Women Pilots Association   (BWPA)   1955
■   Brooklands Museum, Brooklands Rd, WEYBRIDGE, Surrey,
      KT13 0QN.   (mail/address)
      http://www.bwpa.co.uk
      Hon Sec: Lesley Roff,   Chmn: Tricia Nelmes
▲   Un-incorporated Society
○   *G, *P; to encourage & help women who have an interest in
      aviation, either as a private pilot or commercially
●   Mtgs - ET - Comp - VE - LG
<   Fedn of Eur Women Pilots; R Aero Club; Aircraft Owners &
      Pilots Assn; Air League
M   c 300 i
¶   NL - 5; free.   Careers Book - irreg; ftm.

British Wood Preserving & Damp-proofing Association
      in 2003 this association formed 2 divisions - the **Property Care
      Association** and the **Wood Protection Association;** in 2006 these
      two divisions became independent bodies & the PCA absorbed the
      BWPA

British Wood Pulp Association   (BWPA)   1896
■   Penrallt, Copthill Lane, KINGSWOOD, Surrey, KT20 6HL.
      (hsp)
      01737 358444   fax 01737 363069
      email bwpasec@tiscali.co.uk   http://www.bwpa.org.uk
      Sec: Michael D Hobday
▲   Un-incorporated Society
○   *T; to further the interest of the pulp selling industries to the UK
●   Conf - Mtgs - Stat
<   Europulp
M   34 i, 17 f, UK / 20 i, 7 f, o'seas
      (Sub: £75 i, £225 f)
¶   AR - 1; £50.

British Wood Turners Association   (BWTA)   1946
- ■ c/o The Old Sawmills, Wetmore Rd, BURTON-on-TRENT, Staffs, DE14 1QN.   (hsb)
  01283 563455   fax 01283 511526
  email secretary@britishwoodturners.co.uk
  http://www.britishwoodturners.co.uk
  Hon Sec: Mike Cherry
- ▲ Un-incorporated Society
- ○ *T; to promote British wood turners & their production capabilities
- ● Mtgs - LG
- < Brit Woodworking Fedn
- > Brit Woodworking Fedn
- M 35 f
- ¶ Members Directory - 2/3 yrly.

British Woodcarvers Association   (BWA)   1987
- ■ Hall Rigg, Rebels Lane, Great Wakering, SOUTHEND-on-SEA, Essex, SS3 0QE.   (mem/sp)
  01453 833131
  http://www.britishwoodcarversassociation.co.uk
- ▲ Un-incorporated Society
- Br Australia, Canada, France, Netherlands, Russia, S Africa, USA
- ○ *A, *P
- Gp Chainsaw; Lovespoons; Netsuke; Sticks (walking)
- ● Conf - Mtgs - ET - Exhib - Comp - Inf - VE
- M c 600 i, UK / c 20 i, o'seas
- ¶ The Woodcarver Gazette; ftm only.

British Woodworking Federation   (BWF)   1976
- NR Royal London House, 22-25 Finsbury Square, LONDON, EC2A 1DX.   (hq)
  0844 209 2610   fax 0844 209 2611
  email bwf@bwf.org.uk   http://www.bwf.org.uk
  Chief Exec: Richard Lambert
- ○ *T; joinery & woodworking including timber frame construction & timber engineering, architectural & general joinery, windows, doors & kitchen furniture
- < Construction Products Assn
- M i, f & org

British Wrestling Association   (BWA)   2001
- NR 12 Westwood Lane, Brimington, CHESTERFIELD, Derbys, S43 1PA.   (admin/p)
  01246 236443
  email admin@britishwrestling.org
  http://www.britishwrestling.org
  Admin: Yvonne Ball
- ▲ Company Limited by Guarantee
- ○ *S; to develop Olympic freestyle wrestling in the UK

British Youth Band Association   (BYBA)   1974
- NR 64 Moor Rd, Queensbury, BRADFORD, W Yorks, BD13 2EA. (sp)
  http://www.byba.org.uk
  Sec: Elaine Thurtle
- ▲ Registered Charity
- Br regions
- ○ *D, *G; to raise the profile of bands nationally; to encourage the playing of all forms of wind & percussion instruments
- ● Mtgs - ET - Comp - Marching bands
- M 1,500 i

British Zeolite Association   (BZA)   1977
- NR c/o Prof Craig Williams, School of Applied Sciences, University of Wolverhampton, Wulfruna St, WOLVERHAMPTON, WV1 1LY.   (sec/b)
  01902 322159   fax 01902 322714
  http://www.bza.org
  Sec: Prof Craig Williams
- ▲ Registered Charity
- ○ *L; the study & research into the technology & applications in the fields of chemistry, geology, chemical engineering & other branches of science & engineering of zeolites (aluminosilicate minerals)
- ● Conf - Mtgs - ET
- < Intl Zeolite Assn; Fedn of Eur Zeolite Assns
- M 117 i, UK / 88 i, o'seas
- ¶ Template - 1; free.

Britpave (British In-situ Concrete Paving Association) (Britpave)   1991
- NR Atrium Court, The Ring, BRACKNELL, Berks, RG12 1BW.   (hq)
  01344 393300
  email djones@britpave.org.uk
  http://www.britpave.org.uk
  Dir & Co Sec: D P Jones
- ▲ Company Limited by Guarantee
- ○ *T; the authoritative voice of the in-situ concrete paving industry
- Gp Airfields; Environment; Rail; Roads; Specialist applications
- ● Conf - Mtgs - ET - Res - Exhib - VE - LG
- M 50 f, UK / 2 f, o'seas
- ¶ NL - 3; free.   Technical Guidance Sheets - 12; ftm only. Videos & CD-ROMs.

Brittle Bone Society   (BBS)   1972
- ■ 30 Guthrie St, DUNDEE, DD1 5BS.   (hq)
  0800 028 2459   fax 01382 206771
  email bbs@brittlebone.org   http://www.brittlebone.org
  Chief Exec: Raymond Lawrie
- ▲ Registered Charity
- Br 6
- ○ *K; to promote research into the causes, inheritance & treatment of osteogenesis imperfecta & similar disorders; to provide advice, encouragement & practical help for patients & their families
- ● Conf - Mtgs - Inf
- M 1,000 i, UK / 300 i, o'seas
- ¶ NL - 4; free.   Factsheets.

Broadcasting Entertainment Cinematograph & Theatre Union (BECTU)   1991
- NR 373-377 Clapham Rd, LONDON, SW9 9BT.   (hq)
  020 7346 0900   fax 020 7346 0901
  email info@bectu.org.uk   http://www.bectu.org.uk
  Gen Sec: Gerry Morrissey
- ▲ Un-incorporated Society
- Br 5
- ○ *U; for workers (not performers) in broadcasting, film, theatre & other areas of the entertainment & media industry
- ● Conf - Mtgs - Inf - Empl - LG
- < Fedn of Entertainment Us; Gen Fedn Tr Us; Labour Party; STUC; TUC; U Network Intl
- M 25,045 i
- ¶ Stage Screen & Radio (Jnl) - 10.
  Directories of Members (freelance) - irreg; prices vary.
  AR - 1; ftm.

Broads Hire Boat Federation
  a group association of the **British Marine Federation**

© CBD Research Ltd · Beckenham · BR3 5JS · Tel 020 8650 7745 · E-mail cbd@cbdresearch.com · www.cbdresearch.com

Brontë Society   1893

NR   Brontë Parsonage Museum, Haworth, KEIGHLEY, W Yorks,
      BD22 8DR.   (hq)
      01535 642323   fax 01535 647131
      http://www.bronte.ork.uk
      Hon Council Sec: Lyn C Glading
      Mem Sec: Hedley Hickling
▲   Registered Charity
Br   1; 7 countries
○   *L; preservation of the history, home & literature of the Brontë
      family
●   Conf - Mtgs - ET - Res - Exhib - SG - Inf - Lib - VE
M   2,000 i, UK / 900 i, o'seas
¶   Transactions - 2;   Gazette - 2; both ftm.

Brooklands Society Ltd   1967

■   Culverden, Azalea Drive, HASLEMERE, Surrey, GU27 1JR.
      (hsp)
      01428 645724   fax 01428 645724
      http://www.brooklands.org.uk
      Hon Sec: Len Battyll
▲   Company Limited by Guarantee
○   *G; to perpetuate the story, history & preservation of the
      Brooklands Motor course & site
●   Disseminating Brooklands motor course history
<   Fedn Brit Historic Vehicle Clubs; Motor Sports Assn
M   1,150 i
¶   Gazette - 4; with NL - 4; £30.

Brown Swiss Cattle Society (UK)   1973

NR   Barhouse Farm, Elmore, GLOUCESTER, GL2 3NT.   (hsp)
      01452 883063
      email office@brownswiss.org   http://www.brownswiss.org
      Sec: Jenni Hobbs
▲   Registered Charity
○   *B; Brown Swiss dairy cattle
●   Mtgs - SG - VE - Open farm days
<   Nat Cattle Assn (Dairy)
M   130 i
¶   Swiss Chimes Jnl - 4; ftm only.

Browning Society   1970

■   Dept of English Literature, 5 University Gardens, University of
      Glasgow, GLASGOW, G12 8QQ.   (hsb)
      0141-330 1897
      email r.williams@englit.arts.ac.uk
      http://www.browningsociety.org
      Hon Sec: Dr Rhian Williams
▲   Registered Charity
○   *A; to promote appreciation of the poetry of Robert & Elizabeth
      Barrett Browning
●   Mtgs
<   Browning Institute Inc (New York); Friends of Casa Guidi; Assn
      of Literary Socs
M   65 i, UK / 30 i, o'seas
      (Sub: £15 UK / $38.50 o'seas)
¶   Browning Society Notes - 1; ftm only.

**BSCAH - British Society of Clinical & Academic Hypnosis
(BSCAH)   2007**

■   Inspiration House, Redbrook Grove, SHEFFIELD, S20 6RR.
      (hq)
      0844 884 3116   fax 0844 884 3116
      email bscah@btinternet.com   http://www.bscah.com
      Nat Sec: Mrs Christine Henderson
▲   Company Limited by Guarantee; Registered Charity
Br   7
○   *L; to promote the study, teaching & use of hypnosis in the
      fields of medicine, dentistry, psychology & other clinical
      applications; to support the academic research into hypnosis
Gp   Academic professionals involved in research; Counsellors &
      other health professionals; Dentists; Doctors; Nurses;
      Physios; Psychologists
●   Conf - Mtgs - ET - Res - Inf
<   Intl Soc of Hypnosis (ISH); Eur Soc of Hypnosis & Psychosomatic
      Medicine (ESH)
M   490 i, UK / 6 i, o'seas
      (Sub: £60)
¶   NL - 3;   Membership Directory - 1; both ftm only.
      Contemporary Hypnosis - 4; ftm, (price nm via Wiley,
      publishers).
×   2007 (British Society of Medical & Dental Hypnosis
      (British Society of Experimental & Clinical Hypnosis

BSES Expeditions   (BSES)   1932

NR   at the Royal Geographical Society, 1 Kensington Gore,
      LONDON, SW7 2AR.   (hq)
      020 7591 3141
      Exec Dir: William Taunton-Bornet
▲   Company Limited by Guarantee; Registered Charity
○   *E; to foster the spirit of exploration & self-reliance in young
      people, through expeditions with a scientific purpose
M   c 4,000 i, 120 schools
¶   NL - 3; ftm.   AR; ftm.
      Note: BSES - British Schools Exploring Society

BSI   1901

NR   389 Chiswick High Rd, LONDON, W4 4AL.   (hq)
      020 8996 9000
      http://www.bsigroup.com
▲   Royal Charter
○   *G, *T; the development & promulgation of standards
M   f

BSRIA Ltd
      the trading company of **Building Services Research &
      Information Association**

BTC Testing Advisory Group   (BTC)   1963

■   Lynk House, 17 Peckleton Lane, DESFORD, Leics, LE9 9JU.
      (regd/address)
      01455 821921   fax 01455 821921
      email btc@interlynk.co.uk   http://www.btctag.org
      Co Sec: Mrs Lyn Dearling
▲   Company Limited by Guarantee
○   *Q; for technical & procedural consultation between
      organisations conducting vehicle &/or engine dynamometer
      based testing & research
Gp   Engine coolants; Laboratory managers; Technician training;
      Vehicle & engine emissions
●   Mtgs - ET - Res - SG - VE - Training for technicians engaged in
      testing activities in motor, petroleum & chemical industries
M   20 f
      (Sub: £2,500)

Buckinghamshire Chamber of Commerce
      a local chamber of **Thames Valley Chamber of Commerce &
      Industry**

**Bucks County Agricultural Association   (Bucks County Show)
1840**
- ■ The Old Barn, Wingbury Courtyard Business Village,
  Leighton Rd, WINGRAVE, Bucks, HP22 4LW.   (hq)
  01296 680400   fax 01296 680445
  email alison@buckscountyshow.co.uk
  http://www.buckscountyshow.co.uk
  Sec: Mrs Alison Baylis
- ▲ Company Limited by Guarantee, Registered Charity
- ○ *F, *H; agricultural county show promoting agriculture, farming
  & country life
- ● Comp - County show
- < Assn of Show & Agricl Orgs; Brit Show Jumping Assn; Nat
  Show Pony Soc; all horse, cattle & sheep breed socs
- M 800 i

Buddhist Society   1924
- ■ 58 Eccleston Sq, LONDON, SW1V 1PH.   (hq)
  020 7834 5858   fax 020 7976 5238
  email info@thebuddhistsociety.org
  http://www.thebuddhistsociety.org
  Registrar: Louise Marchant
- ▲ Registered Charity
- ○ *R; to publish & make known the principles of Buddhism; to
  encourage the study & practice of Buddhism
- Gp Pure Hand; Theravada; Tibetan; Zen
- ● Mtgs - ET - SG - Inf - Lib - Lectures - Summer schools
- < Wld Fellowship of Buddhists
- M 2,000 i, UK / 500 i, o'seas
- ¶ The Middle Way (Jnl) - 4; ftm, £4.50 each nm.
  The Buddhist Directory; 2004-06; £12 m, £14 nm.
  [subscription; £18].

Budgerigar Society   (BS)   1925
- ■ Davies House, Spring Gardens, NORTHAMPTON, NN1 1DR.
  01604 624549   fax 01604 627108
  http://www.budgerigarsociety.com
  Sec: David Whittaker
- ▲ Un-incorporated Society
- ○ *B, *G; to promote the breeding & development of the
  budgerigar in all parts of the world
- ● Conf - Exhib - Comp
- < Wld Budgerigar Org
  is a group of the National Council for Aviculture
- M 4,500 i
- ¶ The Budgerigar - 6; ftm only.

Buglife - the Invertebrate Conservation Trust   2000
- NR 90 Bridge St (1st floor), PETERBOROUGH, Cambs, PE1 1DY.
  01733 201210
  email info@buglife.org.uk   http://www.buglife.org.uk
  Sec: Helen Boothman
- ▲ Registered Charity
- ○ *G; devoted to the conservation of all invertebrates (slugs,
  snails, bees, wasps, ants, spiders, beetles & many more)

Builders' Conference   1935
- ■ Crest House, 19 Lewis Rd, SUTTON, Surrey, SM1 4BR.   (hq)
  020 8770 0111
  email info@buildersconf.co.uk
  http://www.buildersconference.co.uk
  Chief Exec: Neil Edwards
- ▲ Registered Charity; Un-incorporated Society
- Br 3
- ○ *T; to reduce industry insufficiencies in construction industry; to
  provide market analysis of construction industry at tender &
  contract stage
- ● Conf - Mtgs - ET - Stat - Inf - LG
- M professionals, main contractors, sub-contractors
  (Sub: as above categories - on application, up to £2,000 yr,
  £1,185 yr)
- ¶ List of Contractors - 1; ftm.   AR; ftm only.

Builders Merchants Federation   (BMF)   1901
- ■ 15 Soho Sq, LONDON, W1D 3HL.   (hq)
  020 7439 1753   fax 020 7734 2766
  email info@bmf.org.uk   http://www.bmf.org.uk
  Managing Dir: Chris Pateman
- ○ *T; for wholesale distributors of building materials in the UK
- ● Mtgs - ET - Inf - LG
- < Eur Assn Nat Builders Merchants Assns (UFEMAT); Eur Fedn
  Heating & Sanitary Wholesalers (FEST); Construction Products
  Assn (CPA)
- M 300 f (with 3,000 outlets)
- ¶ Internal NL - 12;   LM - 1;   Ybk - 1; all ftm only.

Building Controls Industry Association   (BCIA)   2004
- ■ 2 Waltham Court, Milley Lane, Hare Hatch, READING, Berks,
  RG10 9TH.
  0118-940 3416   fax 0118-940 6258
  email bcia@feta.co.uk   http://www.feta.co.uk
- ○ *T; to establish & maintain the highest standards in product &
  system development, application & customer service
- M 34 f, 4 associates

Building Cost Information Service   (BCIS)   1962
- NR 12 Great George St, LONDON, SW1P 3AD.   (hq)
  020 7695 1500   fax 020 7695 1501
  email contact@bcis.co.uk   http://www.bcis.co.uk
  Gen Mgr: Andrew Thompson
- ▲ Company Limited by Guarantee
- ○ *T; to publish information services relating to cost of
  construction & occupancy & maintenance of buildings
- Gp Building Maintenance Information (BMI)
- < is a trading division of RICS (Royal Institution of Chartered
  Surveyors)

Building & Engineering Services Association
  from 1 March 2012 the trading name of the **Heating & Ventilating
  Contractors' Association**

Building Maintenance Information (BMI)
  a group of the **Building Cost Information Service**

Building Materials Federation   (BMF)   1969
- IRL Confederation House, 84-86 Lower Baggot St, DUBLIN 2,
  Republic of Ireland.   (hq)
  353 (1) 605 1621   fax 353 (1) 638 1621
  email mark.mcauley@ibec.ie   http://www.ibec.ie/bmf/
  Dir: Mark McAuley
- ○ *T; manufacturers of adhesives, bricks, cement, chimney
  systems, cladding products, concrete products, insulation
  products, plasterboard, plastic pipes & roofing products
- < Coun of Eur Producers of Materials for Construction (CEPMC);
  Ir Business & Emplrs Confedn (IBEC)
- M 35 f

**Building Services Research & Information Association
(BSRIA)   1955**
- NR Old Bracknell Lane West, BRACKNELL, Berks, RG12 7AH.   (hq)
  01344 465600
  http://www.bsria.co.uk
  Dir: Andrew Eastwell
- ▲ Company Limited by Guarantee
- ○ *T, *Q; 'provision of collaborative research programmes;
  supply of information & expertise'
- Gp Building energy management systems; Energy utilisation;
  Information centre; Instrument hire; Market intelligence
  centre; Operations & management; Quality; Systems design;
  Test; Ventilation & air movement
- ● Mtgs - ET - Res - SG - Inf - Lib
- M c 1,000 f
- ¶ 'too numerous'.
  Note: has a wholly owned subsidiary & trading company BSRIA
  Ltd

© CBD Research Ltd · Beckenham · BR3 5JS · Tel 020 8650 7745 · E-mail cbd@cbdresearch.com · www.cbdresearch.com

Building Societies Association   (BSA)   1869
- ■ York House (6th floor), 23 Kingsway, LONDON, WC2B 6UJ. (hq)
020 7520 5900   fax 020 7240 5290
email information@bsa.org.uk   http://www.bsa.org.uk
Dir Gen: Adrian Coles
- ▲ Un-incorporated Society
- ○ *T; for the building industry sector
- ● Conf - Mtgs - ET - Res - Stat - Inf - Lib - LG
- M 59 org
- ¶ Society Matters - 4;   AR - 1; both free.
Building Societies Ybk - 1; ftm, £20 nm.

Building Societies Members Association   (BSMA)   1982
- ■ 49 Clifford Ave, TAUNTON, Somerset, TA2 6DL.   (hsp)
01823 321304
email alandebenham@hotmail.com
Hon Sec: Alan Debenham
- ▲ Un-incorporated Society
- ○ *K; 'our field of interest is the maintenance of the principles of mutuality in building societies; we campaign against them in converting to PLCs;... to advocate that building societies' rules are framed to allow & encourage the maximum participation by members in their societies' affairs...; to defend & expand members' rights & fair treatment generally'
- ● Mtgs
- M 200 i
- ¶ BSMA NL - 4; free.

Buildings Archaeology Group
a group of the **Institute of Field Archaeologists**

Buildings Energy Efficiency Federation   (BEEF)   1997
- NR The Centre for Sustainable Design, University for the Creative Arts, Falkner Rd, FARNHAM, Surrey, GU9 7DF.   (dir/b)
01252 892772
Dir: Martyn Charter
- ▲ Un-incorporated Society
- ○ *N, *T; to act as a coordination body for the energy efficiency industry & for liaison purposes between the industry & the Energy Efficiency Office; to stimulate the market for products & processes used in buildings (predominantly domestic)
- ● Mtgs - LG
- M 17 org

Bulb Distributors' Association
since 2006 **British Flower Bulbs Association**

Bumblebee Conservation Trust   (BBCT)
- ■ School of Biological & Environmental Sciences, University of Stirling, STIRLING, FK9 4LA.
http://www.bumblebeeconservationtrust.co.uk
Dirs: Prof David Goulson,   Dr Ben Darvill
- ○ *K

Bureau of Engineer Surveyors
a professional sector of the **Society of Operations Engineers**

Burgon Society   2000
- NR Oxford University Computing Laboratory, Wolfson Building, Parks Rd, OXFORD, OX1 3QD.   (sb)
email registrar@burgon.org.uk
http://www.burgon.org.uk
Registrar: Dr Thornsten Hauler
- ▲ Registered Charity
- ○ *G; 'the study of academical dress & its design, history & practice; to preserve details of the practices of institutions; to act in an advisory capacity to film, TV companies & others, in its correct usage'
- ● Mtgs - Inf - Lib
- M i, f & org
(Sub: £30 i, £50 org)
- ¶ Transactions - 1.
Note: 'The society is named after Dean Burgon, the only person to have a shape of academic hood named after him'

Burney Society   1990
- ■ Chawton House Library, Chawton, ALTON, Hants, GU34 1SJ. (hsp)
email jacqui.grainger@chawton.net
http://www.burneysociety-uk.net
Hon Sec: Jacqui Grainger
- ▲ Un-incorporated Society
- ○ *A; for all interested in the life & times of of the writer Fanny Burney d'Arblay (1752-1840)
- ● Conf
- M 75 i, UK / 90 i, o'seas
- ¶ Burney Letter - 2; ftm, £5 nm.   Burney Jnl - 1; ftm, £10 nm.

Burton & District Chamber of Commerce
- ■ First Avenue, Centrum 100, BURTON UPON TRENT, Staffs, DE14 2WE.   (hq)
01283 526210
email info@burton-chamber.com
http://www.burton-chamber.com
- ▲ Company Limited by Guarantee
- ○ *C
- ● Mtgs - ET - Res - Stat - Expt - Inf - Lib - VE - LG
- < Birmingham Cham Comm; Brit Chams Comm
- ¶ Chamberlink - 10;   AR; both ftm.

Bury St Edmunds Chamber of Commerce & Industry   1938
- NR 90 Guildhall St (2nd floor), BURY ST EDMUNDS, Suffolk, IP33 1PR.   (hq)
01284 700800 (Mon-Fri 1000-1500)
http://www.burystedmundschamber.co.uk
Sec: Robert Bourne
- ▲ Company Limited by Guarantee
- ○ *C
- ● Mtgs - Inf - VE - Lobbying
The Chamber is open: Mon-Fri 1000-1500
- M 200 f
- ¶ NL - 12; free.

Bus Users UK   (BUUK)   1985
- ■ PO Box 119, SHEPPERTON, Middx, TW17 8UX.   (hq)
01232 232574
email enquiries@bususers.org   http://www.bususers.org
Chmn: Gavin Booth,   Pres: Dr Caroline Cahm
- Br 18
- ○ *K; to campaign for better services for bus users; to increase the influence of bus users in public transport issues; to improve communication between bus users & providers
- ● Conf - Mtgs - Comp - Bus appeals body
- < Campaign for Better Transport; Pedestrians' Assn
- M 725 i, 110 f, 82 org
- ¶ Bus User (NL) - 4; £10 yr m, £1 each nm.
Welcome Aboard: good practice - 2; free (send sae).

Business Analysts Association of Ireland
- IRL 2 Lakelands Rd, STILLORGAN, Co Dublin, Republic of Ireland.
353 086 819 6283

Business Application Software Developers Association (BASDA) 1993
- ■ 92 High St, GREAT MISSENDEN, Bucks, HP16 0AN. (chmn/b)
  01494 868030   fax 01494 868031
  email info@basda.org   http://www.basda.org
  Chief Exec: Dennis Keeling
- ▲ Company Limited by Guarantee
- ○ *T; to bring together people & organisations with an interest in the accreditation, development & marketing of business & accounting software products
- Gp eCommerce-business-to-business (eBIS); EMU - the introduction of the Euro; VAT-specification
- ● Conf - Mtgs - Exhib - SG - Stat - Inf - LG
- ¶ BASDA News (NL) - 3. ftm only.
  eBusiness Booklet;   IFRS White Paper;
  Sarbanes Oxley White Paper;
  Selecting a Business System & Selecting a Reseller - 1; all free.

Business Archives Council (BAC) 1934
- ■ c/o Lloyds TSB Group Archives, 48 Chiswell St (2nd floor), LONDON, EC1Y 4XX. (hq)
  020 7860 5762
  email karen.sampson@lloydstsb.co.uk
  Hon Sec: Karen Sampson
- ▲ Registered Charity
- ○ *L; promoting the efficient management, preservation & use of business records
- M i, f & org
- ¶ Jnl - 2;   NL - 4;   Ybk - 1; all ftm.

Business Centre Association (bca) 1988
- ■ ECC London City, 3 Bunhill Row, LONDON, EC1Y 8YZ. (hq)
  020 7847 4018   fax 020 7847 4081
  email info@bca.uk.com   http://www.bca.uk.com
  Exec Dir: Jennifer Brooke
- ▲ Company Limited by Guarantee
- ○ *T; for owners & operators of business centres & managed workspaces
- ● Conf (& exhibition showcase) - Inf - LG - Annual industry awards gala dinner
- M 700+ business centres / managed workspaces
- ¶ bca News (NL) - 4; ftm only.

Business Continuity Institute (BCI) 1994
- NR 10 Southview Park, Marsack St, Caversham. READING, Berks, RG4 5AF. (hq)
  0118-947 8215   fax 0118-947 6237
- ▲ Company Limited by Guarantee
- ○ *P; promotion of the art & science of business continuity management
- M i

Business Council for Africa UK
- NR 2 Vincent St, LONDON, SW1P 4LD.
  020 7828 5511   fax 020 7828 5251
  http://www.bcafrica.co.uk
- ○ *N
- M c 400 f
- ✕ 2009 British African Business Association

Business Council for Africa West & Southern (BCA) 1956
- NR The Africa Centre, 38 King St, Covent Garden, LONDON, WC2E 8JT. (hq)
  020 7836 3854
  http://www.bcafrica.co.uk
- ▲ Un-incorporated Society
- Br Cote d'Ivoire, Ghana, Nigeria, Gambia, Senegal, Guinea, Sierra Leone, S Africa
- ○ *T; to represent & sustain overseas investment in the Anglophone & Francophone countries of West Africa
- ● Conf - Mtgs - Res - Expt - VE - LG
- < W African Enterprise Network; Business Coun Europe - Africa, Mediterranean; Brit African Business Assn
- M c 200 i & f
- ¶ London NL - 12;   Country Reports - 12; both ftm only.
- ✕ West Africa Business Association

Business English UK
    a group of **English UK**

Business Management Association 1981
- ■ Coburn House, Docklands, LONDON, E3 2DA. (hq)
  0871 231 1689
  email info@businessmanagement.org.uk
  http://www.businessmanagement.org.uk
- ○ *P; with specific reference to small business to improve the performance of business management at every level in terms of management skills, education & planning

Business for New Europe (BNE) 2006
- NR Tenter House, 45 Moorfields, LONDON, EC2Y 9AE.
  020 7256 6575   fax 020 7256 6582
  email info@bnegroup.org   http://www.bnegroup.org
  Dir: Zaki Cooper
- ○ K; independent coalition of business leaders articulating a possible case for reform in Europe

Business & Professional Women UK Ltd (BPW UK Ltd) 1938
- ■ 74 Fairfield Rise, BILLERICAY, Essex, CM12 9NU. (hq)
  01277 623867
  email hq@bpwuk.co.uk   http://www.bpwuk.co.uk
- ▲ Company Limited by Guarantee
- Br 45
- ○ *K, *P; 'for all working women to discuss, develop, network, influence & participate in issues affecting women'
- Gp Carers; Computers; Criminal justice; Finance; Health; Lawyers; Marketing & media; Property; Science; Training; Women in business
- ● Conf - Mtgs - ET - LG
- < Intl Fedn Business & Profl Women; Eur Fedn of Business & Profl Women
- ¶ BPW News - 4;   Annual Review; both ftm only.

Business Services Association Ltd (BSA) 1993
- ■ 130 Fleet St (2nd floor), LONDON, EC2A 2BH. (hq)
  020 7822 7420
  email mark.fox@bsa-org.com   http://www.bsa-org.com
  Chief Exec: Mark Fox
- ▲ Company Limited by Guarantee
- ○ *T; represents companies providing business & outsourced services in the public & private sectors - driving innovation, training, efficiency & raising professional standards & improving productivity
- ● Res - Events - Publications
- < Confedn Brit Ind
- M 15 f, 14 associates
  (Sub: £2,500 associates)
- ¶ NL - 12; on website.

© CBD Research Ltd · Beckenham · BR3 5JS · Tel 020 8650 7745 · E-mail cbd@cbdresearch.com · www.cbdresearch.com

Business Software Alliance   (BSA)   1988
§   2 Queen Anne's Gate Buildings, Dartmouth St, LONDON,
        SW1H 9BP.   (hq (Europe))
        020 7340 6080   fax 020 7340 6090
        email europe@bsa.org   http://www.bsa.org
        an international organisation with headquarters in Washington
            DC, formed to eradicate software piracy

Business in Sport & Leisure   (BISL)   1985
NR   46 Fieldsend Rd, LONDON, SM3 8NR.
        020 8255 3782
        email amanda.fry@bisl.org   http://www.bisl.org
        Exec Assistant: Amanda Fry
○   the hospitality, sport and leisure industry

Butterfly Conservation   1968
■   Manor Yard, East Lulworth, WAREHAM, Dorset, BH20 5QP.
        (hq)
        01929 400209   fax 01929 400210
        email info@butterfly-conservation.org
        http://www.butterfly-conservation.org
        Chief Exec: Dr Martin Warren
▲   Company Limited by Guarantee; Registered Charity
Br   31
○   *B, *L, *Q; conservation of British wild butterflies, moths & their
            habitats; to research into their life needs; to set up reserves
            for the rare species
●   Conf - Mtgs - ET - Res - Exhib - Stat - Inf - PL
>   Butterfly Consvn Europe
M   12,000 i
            (Sub: £28)
¶   Local branch & regional NLs - irreg.   AR - 1; m only.

Buttonhook Society   1979
■   PO Box 1089, MAIDSTONE, Kent, ME14 9BA.   (hq)
        01622 752949
        email buttonhooksociety@tiscali.co.uk
        http://www.thebuttonhooksociety.com
        Chmn: Paul Moorehead
▲   Un-incorporated Society
Br   USA
○   *G; to encourage the research into, collection & preservation of
            buttonhooks & ancillary articles; to build up archives on the
            50,000 known buttonhooks researched
●   Mtgs - Res - Exhib - Inf - Lib - PL
M   c 230 i, UK / 140 i, o'seas
            (Sub: £18.50 UK / £26 Europe / £24 o'seas)
¶   The Boutonneur (NL) - 6.
        Compendium of Buttonhooks - in parts; priced individually.

**BVCA (British Private Equity & Venture Capital Association)
(BVCA)   1983**
NR   Brettenham House (1st Floor North), Lancaster Place,
            LONDON, WC2E 7EN.   (hq)
        020 7420 1800   fax 020 7420 1801
        email bvca@bvca.co.uk   http://www.bvca.co.uk
        Chief Exec: Simon Walker
▲   Company Limited by Guarantee
○   *T; 'the public face of the industry providing services to its
            members, investors & entrepreneurs, as well as government
            & media'
●   Conf - Mtgs - ET - Res - Exhib - Stat - Expt - Inf - LG
M   180 f, 175 f (associate)
¶   Directory (LM) - 1; ftm, £10 nm.
        A Guide to Private Equity; free.
        Report of Investment Activity - 1; ftm, £50 nm.

Byron Society   1971
NR   Bay Trees, 35 Blackbrook Rd, FAREHAM, Hants, PO15 5DQ.
            (dir/p)
        01329 287336
        Hon Dir: Miss Maureen O'Connor
▲   Registered Charity
Br   2; 36
○   *A; to promote research into the life & work of the English poet
            Lord Byron (1788-1824)
M   i
¶   The Byron Jnl - 1.

Cable Management Products Group
a product group of **BEAMA Ltd**

Caernarvonshire Historical Society   (Cymdeithas Hanes Sir Caernarfon) (CHS) 1939
NR   County Offices, Shirehall St, CAERNARFON, LL55 1SH.   (hsb)
01286 679088   fax 01286 679637
Hon Sec: Ann Rhydderch
▲   Registered Charity
○   *L; to collect & preserve the history relating to the county of Caernarfon
●   Mtgs - VE
M   460 i, 10 org, UK / 20 i, o'seas
¶   Transactions (Jnl) - 1.

Café Society   (CS)   1992
NR   Association House, 18c Moor St, CHEPSTOW, Monmouthshire, NP16 5DB.   (hq)
01291 636331   fax 01291 630402
Sec: Jim Winship
▲   Company Limited by Guarantee
○   *T; to promote quality standards in the coffee market in the UK
●   Conf - Mtgs - ET - Inf - LG - Promotion - Awards dinner
M   14 i, 68 f
¶   Café Culture Magazine - 4; ftm, £25 yr nm.

Cairngorms Chamber of Commerce
NR   Inverdruie House, Inverdruie, AVIEMORE, Inverness-shire, PH22 1QH.
01479 780539
email info@cairngormschamber.com
http://www.cairngormschamber.com
Dir: Debbie Strang
○   *C; to be a single voice for business in the whole of the Cairngorms National Park & adjacent areas
<   Scot Chams Comm

Caithness Agricultural Society   (CAS)   1830
■   Eilean Donan, East May, THURSO, Caithness, KW14 8XL.   (hsp)
01847 851997
email enquiries@caithnessshow.co.uk
http://www.caithnessshow.co.uk
Sec: Kerry Mackenzie
▲   Registered Charity
○   *F
●   Mtgs - Exhib - Comp - Agricultural show
<   Assn of Show & Agricl Orgs; Clydesdale Horse Soc; Highland Pony Soc; Shetland Pony Stud-Book Soc
M   c 400 i
(Sub: £10 adult, £5 child)

Caithness Chamber of Commerce
NR   66 Princes St, THURSO, Caithness, KW14 7DH.   (hq)
01847 890076
http://www.caithnesschamber.com
Chief Exec: Trudy Morris
○   *C; to work with & lead its members & key partners to create a vibrant economy within Caithness that is successful, sustainable & diverse
<   Scot Chams Comm
✕   Caithness & Sutherland Chamber of Commerce

Caithness Paperweight Collectors Club   (CPCC)   1976
NR   Caithness Glass Ltd, Muthill Rd, CRIEFF, Perthshire, PH7 4HQ.   (hq)
01738 637373   fax 01738 492300
http://www.caithnessglass.co.uk
Mgr: Caroline Clark
○   *G; for collectors of paperweights in traditional, contemporary, limited & open editions
M   c 6,500 i

Caledonian Railway Association   (CRA)   1983
NR   63 Andrew Drive, CLYDEBANK, Dunbartonshire, G81 1BU.   (hsp)
0141-952 7162
http://www.crassoc.org.uk
Sec: Douglas Hind
▲   Un-incorporated Society
Br   2
○   *G; to study the former Caledonian Railway Company
●   Mtgs - Res - Exhib - Inf - Lib - VE
M   310 i, 12 f, 7 org, UK / 16 i, o'seas
¶   The True Line (Jnl) - 4; ftm, £5 nm.   LM - 1; £3 m only.

Call Centre Management Association (UK) Ltd   (CCMAUK)   1995
NR   PO Box 125, SANDBACH, Cheshire, CW11 2FF.   (hqa)
01477 500826
http://www.ccma.org.uk
Sec: Roy Bailey
○   *P
●   Mtgs - ET
M   350 i, UK / 20 i, o'seas
¶   NL

Calligraphy & Lettering Arts Society   (CLAS)   1994
NR   54 Boileau Rd, LONDON, SW13 9BL.
020 8741 7886
email info@clas.co.uk   http://www.clas.co.uk
Admin: Sue Cavendish
▲   Registered Charity
○   *A
Gp   Copperplate; Little book makers; Palaeography
●   Exhib - Mtgs - SG
M   1,500 i
¶   The Edge - 5, ftm.

Camanachd Association   (CA)   1893
■   Alton House, 4 Ballifeary Rd, INVERNESS, IV3 5PJ.   (hq)
01463 715931   fax 01463 226551
email admin@shinty.com   http://www.shinty.com
Chief Exec: Gill McDonald
▲   Un-incorporated Society
○   *S; governing body for the sport of shinty
Gp   Coaching; Development; Youth development
●   ET - Comp
>   Glasgow Celtic Soc; MacAulay Assn; Camanachd Referees' Assn
M   3,000 i, clubs
(Sub: £12 i, £5 youth)

© CBD Research Ltd · Beckenham · BR3 5JS · Tel 020 8650 7745 · E-mail cbd@cbdresearch.com · www.cbdresearch.com

Cámara Chileno Británica de Comercio (British Chilean Chamber of Commerce)   1917
NR   Av El Bosque Norte 0125, Las Condes, SANTIAGO, Chile. (hq)
     56 (2) 370 4175   fax 56 (2) 370 4164
     http://www.britcham.cl
     Gen Mgr: Andrew Robshaw
○   *C
●   Mtgs - Comp - Expt - Inf - Lib
M   24 i, 130 f (in Chile)
¶   NL - 12; ftm.   Economic Report - 4; ftm.
     Directory of Members; ftm, £10.

Cámara de Comercio Argentino-Británica   (CCAB)   1914
■   Av Corrientes 457 (Piso 10), CP (C1043AAE), BUENOS AIRES, Argentina.   (hq)
     54 (11) 4394 2762   fax 54 (11) 4326 3860
     email info@ccab.com.ar   http://www.ccab.com.ar
     Chief Exec: Mónica Mesz
▲   Registered Charity
○   *C; to promote general trade & commerce between the UK & Argentina
Gp   HHRR & IT; Executive education; Lawyers
●   Conf - Mtgs - ET - Exhib - Expt - Inf - LG
M   140 f, Argentina
¶   NL - 26; ftm only.

Cámara de Comercio Británica AC (British Chamber of Commerce in Mexico)   1921
NR   Rio de la Plata 30, Col Cuauhtémoc, 06500 MEXICO DF, Mexico.   (hq)
     52 (5) 256 09 01   fax 52 (5) 211 54 51
     email britcham@infoabc.com
     Dir Gen: Teresa de Lay
○   *C; to promote trade & investment between the UK & Mexico

Cámara de Comercio Británica en España
     see **British Chamber of Commerce in Spain   (Cámara Comercio Británica en España**

Cámara de Comercio Colombo Británica   (British Colombian Chamber of Commerce)   (CCCB)   1981
NR   Calle 104 No 14A-45, Oficina 301, BOGOTÁ DC, Colombia.   (hq)
     57 (1) 256 2833
     email comunicaciones@colombobritanica.com
     http://www.colombobritanica.com
     Exec Dir: Patricia Tovar
○   *C; to promote commerce & investment between Colombia & GB
●   Conf - Mtgs - Exhib - Expt - Inf - Lib - VE - LG
¶   NL - 6; ftm.

Câmara de Comércio Luso-Británica
     see **British-Portuguese Chamber of Commerce   (Câmara Comércio Luso-Británica)**

Cámara de Comercio Uruguayo Británica (British-Uruguayan Chamber of Commerce)   1969
NR   Av Libertador Juan A Lavalleja 1641, Piso 2 Oficina 201, CP 11.100, MONTEVIDEO, Uruguay.   (hq)
     598 (2) 908 0349   fax 598 (2) 900 0936
     email camurbri@netgate.com.uy
     http://www.camurbri.com.uy
     Sec: Armando Barrios
○   *C; to promote Anglo-Uruguayan commercial relations

Cámara Peruano Británica
     see **British-Peruvian Chamber (Cámara Peruano Británica)**

Cámara Venezolana Británica de Comercio   (CVBC)   1951
NR   Torre Britanica (piso 11), Altamira Sor (PO Box 69102), CARACAS 1062a, Venezuela.   (hq)
     58 (2) 267 3112   fax 58 (2) 263 0362
     http://www.britcham.com.ve
     Gen Mgr: Helen Wadham
○   *C; to improve commercial relations between UK & Venezuela
Gp   Commercial dept; Events dept; Young executive section (to help develop business & English language skills in both a business & social environment)
●   Conf - Mtgs - Res - Comp - Expt - Inf - Lib - VE - Overseas missions
M   2 i, 22 f, UK / 55 i, 107 f, o'seas, 20 i (young execs section)
¶   Directory - 1.

Cambrian Archaeological Association   (Cymdeithas Hynafiaethau Cymru)   1846
NR   Braemar, Llangunnor Rd, CARMARTHEN, SA31 2PB.   (hsp)
     email h.james44@btinternet.com
     http://www.orchardweb.co.uk/cambrians
     Gen Sec: Mrs Heather James
▲   Registered Charity
○   *L; to examine, preserve & illustrate the ancient monuments & remains of the history, language, manners, customs, arts & industries of Wales & the Marches
Gp   Research; Meetings
●   Conf - Mtgs - Res - Comp - Lib - VE - LG
<   Coun for Brit Archaeology (CBA)
M   600 i, 140 org, UK / 30 i, 30 org, o'seas
¶   Archaeologia Cambrensis - 1.   LM - 2 yrly.

Cambrian Railways Society
■   Oswald Rd, OSWESTRY, Shropshire, SY11 1RE.   (hq)
     01691 671749
     email information@cambrian-railways-soc.co.uk
     http://www.cambrian-railways-soc.co.uk
     Sec: A M Hignett
▲   Company Listed by Guarantee, Registered Charity
○   *G; to acquire, preserve & restore any & all of the Cambrian Railways Company's infrastructure, buildings, lines & artifacts
●   Mtgs - ET - Res - Exhib - Inf - VE
M   488 i, UK / 5 i, o'seas
¶   Cambrian Line Magazine - 4; ftm, £1 nm.

Cambridge Antiquarian Society   (CAS)   1840
NR   86 Harvey Goodwin Court, French's Rd, CAMBRIDGE, CB4 3JR.   (hsb)
     http://www.camantsoc.org
     Hon Sec: Chris Michaelides
▲   Registered Charity
○   *L; archaeology & history of the city & county of Cambridge
●   Conf - Mtgs - ET - Inf - Lib - VE - LG (local)
<   Coun Brit Archaeology
M   465 i, 52 affiliated socs, 85 subscribing org
¶   Proceedings - 1; ftm, £14.50 nm.   The Conduit - 1; ftm only.

Cambridge Bibliographical Society   1949
■   University Library, West Rd, CAMBRIDGE, CB3 9DR.   (hsb)
     01223 333000   fax 01223 333160
     email nas1000@cam.ac.uk
     Hon Sec: N Smith
▲   Registered Charity
○   *L; to promote the study of bibliographical & palaeographical research
●   Mtgs - VE
M   150 i, 10 f, 50 org, UK / 45 i, 15 f, 120 org, o'seas
¶   Transactions - 1; £12.   Monographs - irreg; price varies.

Cambridge Philosophical Society (CPS) 1819
NR Central Science Library, Arts School, Bene't St, CAMBRIDGE,
      CB2 3PY. (hq)
      01223 334743
      email philosoc@hermes.cam.ac.uk
      http://www.cambridgephilosophicalsociety.org
      Exec Sec: Mrs B Larner
▲ Registered Charity
○ *L; promotion of scientific enquiry
● Conf - Mtgs - Participation in upkeep & management of
      Scientific Periodicals Library of the University of Cambridge
      Office hours: Mon-Fri 0800-1615, Sat 0900-1300
M 1,900 i
¶ Mathematical Proceedings [articles on original research] - 6.
      Biological Reviews [long reviews on the state of research in a
      particular field of Biology - NOT book reviews] - 4.

Cambridge Refrigeration Technology (CRT) 1945
■ 140 Newmarket Rd, CAMBRIDGE, CB5 8HE. (hq)
      01223 365101   fax 01223 461522
      email crt@crtech.co.uk   http://www.crtech.co.uk
▲ Company Limited by Guarantee
○ *Q; research, development, testing, consultancy & information
      services relating to all types of refrigerated transport &
      storage
Gp Refrigerated Transport Information Society
● Conf - ET - Res - Exhib - Inf - Lib - PL
< Intl Inst Refrigeration (IIR); Amer Soc Heating, Refrigerating &
      Air-Conditioning Engrs Inc (ASHRAE); Assn Indep Res &
      Technology Orgs (AIRTO); BSRIA; Inst Refrigeration; Brit
      Refrigeration Assn
M 5 i, 10 f, 10 org, UK / 6 i, 30 f, 2 org, o'seas
¶ NL - 4; ftm only.
      The Transport of Perishable Foodstuffs; £6.50.
      Cargo Companion (3 vol); ftm, £155 nm.

Cambridge Sheep Society 1978
■ Pharm House, Neston Rd, Willaston, NESTON, Cheshire,
      CH64 2TL. (hsp)
      0151-327 5699
      email d.a.r.davies@liverpool.ac.uk
      Hon Sec: Alun Davies
▲ Registered Charity
○ *B
● Conf - Mtgs - Res - Exhib - SG - Stat - Expt - Inf
< Nat Sheep Assn
M 20 i
      (Sub: £15)
¶ NL - 3/4;   LM - 1;   AR - 1; all free.

Cambridge Society for the Application of Research (CSAR) 1956
■ 10 Trumpington St, CAMBRIDGE, CB2 1QA. (organising s)
      01223 333543   fax 01223 332988
      email barrythompson@enterprise.cam.ac.uk
      http://www.csar.org.uk
      Organising Sec: Dr Richard Freeman
▲ Un-incorporated Society
○ *L; to bring together & promote cooperation within & between
      the University of Cambridge & industry of all kinds with a
      view to the expeditious use of resources & research
● Mtgs - VE
M 150 i, 16 f, 9 university colleges & depts
      (Sub: £25 i, £150 f & colleges/depts)

Cambridgeshire Association for Local History (CALH) 1951
NR PO Box 1112, Basham, CAMBRIDGE, CB21 4WP. (hsp)
      01223 892430
      Hon Sec: Andrew Westwood-Bate
▲ Company Limited by Guarantee; Registered Charity
○ *L, *N; to encourage the study of local history & impart
      information on it
Gp Photographic recording
● Conf - Mtgs - Res - Exhib - VE
< Cambridge Antiquarian Soc
M 160 i, 10 org
¶ Review - 1.
× 2006 Cambridgeshire Local History Society

Cambridgeshire Chambers of Commerce (CCC) 1918
NR Enterprise House, Chivers Way, Histon, CAMBRIDGE,
      CB24 9ZR. (hq)
      01223 237414   fax 01223 237405
      email enquiries@cambscci.co.uk
      http://www.cambridgeshirechamber.co.uk
      6 The Forum, Minerva Business Park, Lynch Wood,
      PETERBOROUGH, Cambs,PE2 6FT.   01733 370809
      Chief Exec: John Bridge
▲ Company Limited by Guarantee
Br Cambridge, Ely, Fenland, Huntingdonshire, Peterborough
○ *C
Gp Policy; Professional; Retail; Technology
● Conf - Mtgs - ET - Exhib - Stat - Expt - Inf - Lib - Export
      documentation - Advice skills training
< Brit Chams Comm
M f

Cambridgeshire Local History Society
      since 2006 **Cambridgeshire Association for Local History**

Cambridgeshire Records Society (CRS) 1972
NR c/o Cambridgeshire Archives, Box RES 1009, Shire Hall,
      CAMBRIDGE, CB3 0AP. (hsb)
      01223 717281   fax 01223 718823
      Hon Sec: Mrs Francesca Ashburner
▲ Un-incorporated Society
○ *L; to publish documentary sources relating to the history of
      Cambridgeshire & neighbouring areas
M c 100 i, UK / c 20 i, o'seas
¶ Source material - 1.

Camera Club 1885
NR 16 Bowden St, LONDON, SE11 4DS. (hq)
      020 7587 1809
      http://www.thecameraclub.co.uk
      The Hon Secretary
▲ Un-incorporated Society
○ *G; to foster the art & science of photography by provision of
      affordable, high quality darkrooms & studio, exhibition
      gallery & courses
● Mtgs - ET - Exhib - SG - Inf - Lib
M 320 i, 10 f, UK / 4 i, o'seas
¶ Club News - 12; free.

Campaign for Angling
      a campaign of the **Countryside Alliance**

Campaign against Arms Trade (CAAT) 1974
■ 11 Goodwin St, LONDON, N4 3HQ. (hq)
      020 7281 0297   fax 020 7281 4369
      email enquiries@caat.org.uk   http://www.caat.org.uk
      Coordinators (different people for enquiries)
▲ Un-incorporated Society
○ *K; information & campaigning about the arms trade
● Mtgs - Res - Exhib - Inf - Lib - Day schools
M 15,000 i
¶ CAATnews; ftm, £1 nm.

© CBD Research Ltd · Beckenham · BR3 5JS · Tel 020 8650 7745 · E-mail cbd@cbdresearch.com · www.cbdresearch.com

Campaign for Better Transport   1973
- ■ 16 Waterside, 44-48 Wharf Rd, LONDON, N1 7UX.   (hq)
  020 7566 6480
  email info@bettertransport.org.uk
  http://www.bettertransport.org.uk
  Exec Dir: Stephen Joseph
- ▲ Company Limited by Guarantee; Registered Charity
- ○ *K, *N; to develop sustainable transport policies reducing dependence on private cars & road-based transport modes; to campaign for their implementation
- Gp Road Block (a project to support groups campaigning against road building)
- ● Res - Inf
- ✕ 2007 Transport 2000 Ltd

Campaign against Censorship   (CAC)   1968
- ■ 25 Middleton Close, FAREHAM, Hants, PO14 1QN.   (hsp)
  01329 284471
  http://www.dlas.org.uk
  Hon Sec: Mrs Mary M Hayward
- ▲ Un-incorporated Society
- ○ *K; to uphold freedom of speech & publication; to oppose censorship in all fields
- ● Inf - Lobbying
- M [not available]
- ¶ NL - irreg.

Campaign against Climate Change
- NR 5 Caledonian Rd (top floor), LONDON, N1 9DX.
  020 7837 4473
- ○ *K

Campaign for Community Banking Services   1997
- ■ 50 Roundwood Park, HARPENDEN, Herts, AL5 3AF.   (dir/p)
  01582 764760   fax 01582 764760
  http://www.communitybanking.org.uk
  Hon Dir: Derek P G French
- ▲ Un-incorporated Society
- ○ *K; 'to promote the continued existence of convenient access to banking services within communities in order to sustain local commercial activity; to combat financial & social exclusion & assist the vulnerable, disabled & elderly'
- ● Res - Stat - Inf - LG - Lobbying financial service providers - Publicity
- M 25 org

Campaign for Courtesy
  see **National Campaign for Courtesy**

Campaign for Dark Skies   (CfDS)   1990
- NR c/o Burlington House, Piccadilly, LONDON, W1J 0DU.   (hq)
  email info@dark-skies.org
  Coordinator: Bob Mizon
- Br 118 local officers
- ○ *K; a scientific (astronomical) pressure group set up to counter the increasing threat to the visibility of the night sky from waste upward artificial light
  Note: this is a campaign of the British Astronomical Association.

Campaign for the Defence of the Traditional Cathedral Choir
  since 2006 **Campaign for the Traditional Cathedral Choir**

Campaign against Drinking & Driving   (CADD)   1986
- NR PO Box 62, BRIGHOUSE, W Yorks, HD6 3YY.   (hq)
  0845 123 5543
  http://www.cadd.org.uk
- ▲ Company Limited by Guarantee; Registered Charity
- ○ *K, *W; to support victims & families of those killed & injured by drunk & irresponsible drivers; to work for a reduction of deaths & injuries on the road
- M i & f
- ¶ NL - 4.

Campaign for an English Parliament   (TheCEP)   1998
- ■ The Poplars, 18 Leicester Rd, MARKET HARBOROUGH, Leics, LE16 7AU.   (mail/address)
  0845 634 6108
  email admin@thecep.org.uk   http://www.thecep.org.uk
  Co Sec: Edward Higginbottom
- ▲ Company Limited by Guarantee
- ○ *K, *Z; to campaign for an English Parliament
- ● Conf - Mtgs - Res - Exhib - Inf - LG
- M 1,700 i, UK / 30 i, o'seas
  (Sub: £15-£25)
- ¶ Publicity leaflets - irreg.

Campaign against Euro-federalism   (CAEF)   1991
- ■ PO Box 46295, LONDON, W5 2UG.
  email caef@caef.org.uk   http://www.caef.org.uk
- ▲ Un-incorporated Society
- ○ *K; the campaign is based on the rights of states to self-determination & national democracy.   The campaign opposes: Britain's membership of the European Union, joining the single currency, the EU constitution & charter of fundamental rights including a common foreign policy & European army
- ● Conf - Public mtgs
- < Intl Alliance of Euro-critical Movements & Orgs (TEAM); Campaign for an Indep Britain; Anti Maastricht Alliance
- M [not stated]
- ¶ The Democrat - 12.
  Democratic Broadsheet - irreg.
  Various pamphlets & leaflets.

Campaign for the Farmed Environment   (CFE)   2009
- § Agriculture House, Stoneleigh, Warks, CV8 2TZ.   (hq)
  024 7685 8892
  http://www.cfeonline.org.uk
  A campaign of the NFU, working with 12 other organisations to promote the work that farmers & managers do to protect & benefit the soil, water resources & the environment, whilst ensuring profitable food production & the protection of wildlife

Campaign for Freedom of Information   1984
- § 16 Baldwins Gardens (suite 102), LONDON, EC1N 7RJ.   (hq)
  020 7831 7477   fax 020 7831 7461
  email admin@cfoi.demon.co.uk   http://www.cfoi.org.uk
  Dir: Maurice Frankel
  Campaigns against unnecessary official secrecy and for an effective Freedom of Information Act; presses for more disclosure in the private sector if the information is of public interest.

Campaign for Freedom from Piped Music   (Pipedown)   1992
- ■ 1 The Row, Berwick St James, SALISBURY, Wilts, SP3 4TP.   (mail address)
  01722 790622
  email newpipedown@btinternet.com
  http://www.pipedown.info
  Hon Sec: Nigel Rodgers
- ▲ Un-incorporated Society
- Br Germany (associated), USA
- ○ *K; 'to campaign for the freedom in public spaces (shops, hospitals, doctors' surgeries, rail/bus stations, airports, trains, buses) from piped music (muzak), meaning music (of any sort) relayed nonstop around a room, building etc'
- ● Conf - Mtgs - Stat - Inf - LG - Co-ordinated letter writing campaigns - Lobbying Parliament for a bill - Handing out protest cards - Peaceful demonstrations - Listing muzak-free places
- M 1,800 i, UK / 50 i, o'seas
- ¶ Newsletter - 4; ftm, £2 nm.

Campaign for Homosexual Equality (CHE) 1969
NR   c/o LGBT Consortium, J111 Tower Bridge Business Complex,
       100 Clements Rd, LONDON, SE16 4DG.   (mail address)
       020 7064 6510
       email secretary@c-h-e.org.uk
▲   Un-incorporated Society
○   *K; 'promotion of equality in law & society for lesbians, gays &
       bisexuals'
●   ET - Inf
M   150 i & affiliates
¶   Publications list available.

**Campaign against Hysterectomy & Unnecessary Operations on
Women (CAH) 1995**
■   The Maltings, 99 Saunders Lane, WOKING, Surrey,
       GU22 0NR.   (mail/add)
       01483 715435
       email sandra.simkin@virgin.net
       Dir: Sandra Simkin
▲   Un-incorporated Society
Br 4
○   *K; to campaign for legal protection against unnecessary
       surgery; to raise women's awareness of their right to choose
       what happens to their bodies; to provide women with
       information which will enable them to challenge ignorant
       decisions; to research into the consequences of unnecessary
       surgery
Gp Information; Informed consent; Legal
●   Conf - Res - Inf
<   Rights of Women
M   i
¶   Information Sheets
       The Case against Hysterectomy.

Campaign for an Independent Britain (CIB) 1989
NR   Morton House, 3 Stamford Drive, GROBY, Leics, LE6 0YD.
       07092 857684
       http://www.eurosceptic.org.uk
       Hon Sec: Mrs Petrina Holdsworth
▲   Un-incorporated Society
Br 20
○   *K; to halt the drive to political, economic & monetary union in
       the EC; to regain for Britain the rights, freedoms & powers of
       an independent nation
●   Conf - Mtgs - ET - Res - Stat - Inf
<   Anti-Common Market League; Campaign against Euro
       Federalism; Cheaper Food League; Labour Euro-Safeguards
       Campaign; Conservatives against a Federal Europe
M   3,000 i
¶   Independence - 4.   Leaflets.
       Common Fisheries Policy - End or Mend?
       There is an Alternative.   A Price not worth Paying.
       From Rome to Maastricht - a reappraisal of Britain's
       membership of the EC.

Campaign for Independent Food
       a campaign of the **Countryside Alliance**

Campaign for Learning 1997
§   19 Buckingham Street (basement), LONDON, WC2N 6EF.
       (hq)
       020 7930 1111   fax 020 7930 1551
       http://www.campaign-for-learning.org.uk
▲   Company Limited by Guarantee; Registered Charity
       An independent voluntary organisation working for an inclusive
       society in which learning is valued, understood & freely
       available & accessible to everyone as a right; to stimulate
       learning which will sustain people for life

Campaign for National Parks
§   6-7 Barnard Mews, LONDON, SW11 1QU.   (hq)
       020 7924 4077
       http://www.cnp.org.uk
       A campaign to protect, stand-up for & expand the national
       parks of England & Wales

Campaign for Nuclear Disarmament (CND) 1958
NR   162 Holloway Rd, LONDON, N7 8DQ.   (hq)
       020 7700 2393   fax 020 7700 2357
       email enquiries@cnduk.org   http://www.cnduk.org
▲   Un-incorporated Society
○   *K; works for international peace & disarmament & a world in
       which the vast resources now devoted to militarism are
       dedicated to the real needs of the human community
M   45,000 i, 627 org

Campaign for Philosophical Freedom (CFPF) 1985
■   12a Westover Rise, BRISTOL, BS9 3LU.   (hsp)
       http://www.cfpf.org.uk
       Hon Sec: Michael Roll
○   *K; a non-membership body campaigning to obtain a balance
       on all media & educational outlets; to disestablish the Church
       & make the second House of Parliament an elected chamber;
       to give a secular balance to all religious affairs departments;
       to challenge orthodox scientific thinking
●   Res - Inf
¶   The Mode of Future Existence by Sir Oliver Lodge;
       free, please send sae.

Campaign against Political Correctness
NR   Trevose House, Orsett St, LONDON, SE11 5PN.
       0709 204 0916   fax 0709 204 0916
       email info@capc.co.uk   http://www.capc.co.uk
       Co-founders: Laura & John Midgley
○   *K

Campaign for Press & Broadcasting Freedom (CPBF) 1979
■   23 Orford Rd (2nd floor), LONDON, E17 9NL.   (hq)
       020 8521 5932   fax 020 8521 5932
       email freepress@cpbf.org.uk   http://www.cpbf.org.uk
       Nat Sec: Jonathan Hardy
Br 2
○   *K; to campaign for diverse, democratic & representative
       media; to carry out research & generate debate on
       alternative forms of media free from state control or business
       domination
●   Conf - Mtgs - ET - Res - Exhib - SG - Stat - Inf - LG
M   1,500 i, 50 org, UK / 50 i, o'seas
¶   Free Press - 6.

Campaign to Protect Rural England (CPRE) 1926
NR   128 Southwark St, LONDON, SE1 0SW.   (hq)
       020 7981 2800   fax 020 7981 2899
       email info@cpre.org.uk   http://www.cpre.org.uk
       Chief Exec: Shaun Spiers
○   *G, *K; campaigning for the beauty, tranquility & diversity of the
       countryside
Gp Farming & food; Housing & urban policy; Landscape; Natural
       resources; Planning; Stop the drop; Transport
M   i

**Campaign for the Protection of Rural Wales   (Ymgyrch Diogelu
Cymru Wledig) (CPRW/TDCW) 1928**
■   Tŷ Gwyn, 31 High St, WELSHPOOL, Powys, SY21 7YD.   (hq)
       01938 552525   fax 01938 552741
       email info@cprwmail.org.uk   http://www.cprw.org.uk
       Dir: Peter Ogden
▲   Registered Charity
Br 17
○   *G; to protect & improve the rural scenery & amenities in Wales
●   Inf - Lib
¶   Rural Wales / Cymru Wledig - 3; ftm.

Campaign for Qualified Politicians
       see **Cognition: Campaign for Qualified Politicians**

Campaign for Real Ale Ltd   (CAMRA)   1971
■   230 Hatfield Rd, ST ALBANS, Herts, AL1 4LW.   (hq)
    01727 867201   fax 01727 867670
    email camra@camra.org.uk   http://www.camra.org.uk
    Chief Exec: Mike Benner
▲   Company Limited by Guarantee
Br   200
○   *K; to promote quality, choice & value for money; to support
    the public house as a focus for community life; to maintain
    consumer rights & increase the appreciation of traditional
    beers & ciders
●   Conf - Mtgs - Res - Exhib - Comp - Stat - Lib - VE - LG
<   Eur Beer Consumers U (EBCU); Sustain; Nat Coun for Voluntary
    Orgs (NCVO)
M   79,000 i, UK / 1,000 i, o'seas
¶   What's Brewing - 12; ftm only.
    Good Beer Guide - 1; £10 m, £13.99 nm.
    Good Bottled Beer Guide - 1; £7.99 m, £9.99 nm.
    CAMRA's Good Cider Guide - 2/3 yrly; £8.99 m, £10.99 nm.
    Good Beer Guide to Germany; £10.99 m, £12.99 nm.

Campaign for Real Education   (CRE)   1987
■   12 Pembroke Sq, LONDON, W8 6PA.   (hsp)
    020 7937 2122   fax 020 7938 1638
    email cred@cre.org.uk   http://www.cre.org.uk
    18 Westlands Grove, Stockton Lane, YORK, YO31 1EF.
    01904 424134   (chmn/p).
    Hon Sec: Dr Vera Dalley,   Chmn: Nick Seaton
○   *E, *K; an association of parents, teachers & academics which
    campaigns for higher standards in state schools & colleges;
    to support individuals & groups with similar interests; to
    promote educational research & the dissemination of
    information
M   c 3,000 i, UK / c 30 i, o'seas

Campaign for Real Recycling
NR   57 Prince St, BRISTOL, BS1 4QH.
    0117-942 0142   fax 0117-934 9944
    email info@realrecycling.org.uk
    http://www.realrecycling.org.uk
    Coordinator: Andy Moore
○   *K; to improve the quality of materials collected for recycling

Campaign for Science & Engineering in the UK   (CASE)   1986
NR   Gordon House, 29 Gordon Square, LONDON, WC1H 0PP.
    (hq)
    020 7679 4995
▲   Un-incorporated Society
○   *K; to communicate to the public, parliament & the government
    a proper appreciation of the economic & cultural benefits of
    scientific & technological research & development, with the
    consequent importance to the nation of adequate funding of
    research by government & industry
M   i, f & org

Campaign for Shooting
    a campaign of the **Countryside Alliance**

Campaign against Stage Hypnosis   (CASH)   1994
■   62 Station Rd, Hesketh Bank, PRESTON, Lancs, PR4 6SP.
    (hsp/b)
    01772 813052
    Jt Secs: Connell Harper,   Nora Harper
○   *K; to inform the public of the abuse & dangers of stage
    hypnosis
●   Inf - LG
M   [not stated]

Campaign for State Education   (CASE)   1961
NR   98 Erlanger Rd, LONDON, SE14 5TH.
    07932 149942
    http://www.campaignforstateeducation.org.uk
▲   Un-incorporated Society
○   *E, *K; to campaign for a fully comprehensive & locally
    accountable education system which enables all children to
    achieve their personal best in all areas of learning in a
    happy & secure environment; high quality early years
    education for all whose parents want it

Campaign for the Traditional Cathedral Choir   (CTCC)   1996
NR   49 Cambridge Rd, Oakington, CAMBRIDGE, CB24 3BG.
    (chmn/p)
    email ctcc@ctcc.org.uk   http://www.ctcc.org.uk
    Chmn: David Blumlein
▲   Un-incorporated Society
○   *K; to champion the ancient tradition of the all-male choir in
    cathedrals, chapels royal, collegiate churches, university
    chapels & similar ecclesiastical foundations; to encourage
    parish churches which maintain, or seek to establish, all-
    male voice choirs
●   Mtgs - Res - Campaigning
M   i
¶   Bulletin - 2; ftm, £2 nm.   NL - 2; ftm only.
×   2006 Campaign for the Defence of the Traditional Cathedral
    Choir

Campden BRI   1919
NR   Station Rd, CHIPPING CAMPDEN, Glos, GL55 6LD.   (hq)
    01386 842000
    http://www.campden.co.uk
    Co Sec: Clare Cairns
▲   Company Limited by Guarantee
○   *Q; research & services for the food & allied industries (food
    packaging, machinery, manufacturers, distributors, retailers
    & growers, drink, cereals processing)
●   Conf - Mtgs - ET - Res - Exhib - SG - Stat - Inf - Lib - LG
M   800 f, UK / 200 f, o'seas
¶   Campden & Chorleywood NL - 12; free.
    Research Reports;   Guidelines;   Specifications;   Reviews;
    Symposium Proceedings - all irreg; prices vary.
×   2008 (Brewing Research International
    (Campden & Chorleywood Food Research Association

Campden & Chorleywood Food Research Association
    2008 merged with Brewing Research International to form **Campden
    BRI**

Camping & Caravanning Club Ltd   1901
NR   Greenfields House, Westwood Way, COVENTRY, CV4 8JH.
    (hq)
    0845 130 7631
    http://www.campingandcaravanningclub.co.uk
    Dir Gen: Robert Louden
▲   Company Limited by Guarantee
○   *G; 'the promotion & servicing of the pastime of mobile
    recreational camping & caravanning'
Gp   Association of Lightweight Campers; Boating Group; British
    Caravanners' Club; Camping Club Youth; Canoe Camping
    Club; Folk Song & Dance Group; Motor Caravan Section;
    Mountain Activity Section; Photographic Group; Trailer Tent &
    Folding Camper Group
●   Inf
<   Fédn Intl de Camping et de Caravanning (FICC)
M   c 400,000 i
¶   Camping & Caravanning Magazine - 12;
    Your Place in the Country (site guide) - 1;
    Your Big Sites Book (site guide) - 2 yrly; all ftm only.
    Carefree Camping & Caravanning Guide to Europe - 1.

Camping Club Youth
    a group of the **Camping & Caravanning Club**

Can Makers   1981
- ■ c/o One Chocolate Communications, 10 Frith Street, LONDON, W1D 3JF.   (hq)
  020 7437 0227   fax 020 7440 0941
  http://www.canmakers.co.uk
- ○ *T; promotion of beverage cans & can recycling
- ● Conf - Res - Stat - Inf (on beverage cans, beer & soft drinks market)
- < Beverage Can Makers Europe (BCME)
- M 8 f
- ¶ Thirst Choice - 2 yrly; free.

Canada-United Kingdom Chamber of Commerce   1921
- NR 38 Grosvenor St, LONDON, W1K 4DP.   (hq)
  020 7258 6576   fax 020 7258 6594
  email info@canada-uk.org   http://www.canada-uk.org
  Exec Dir: Nigel Bacon
- ▲ Company Limited by Guarantee
- ○ *C, promotion of trade & investment between Canada & the UK in both directions
- ● Conf - Mtg - Res - Inf
- < Canadian High Commission; Coun of Foreign Chams Comm
- M c 200 i, f & org
- ¶ NL - 6;   Membership Book - 1; both ftm only.

Canal Boatbuilders Association
a group association of the **British Marine Federation**

Canal Card Collectors Circle   (CCCC)   1978
- ■ 18 Kilpatrick Way, Yeading, HAYES, Middx, UB4 9SX.   (hsp)
  020 8841 3788
  email ianjwilson@uwclub.net   http://www.gongoozler.org
  Hon Sec/Treas & Mem Sec: Ian J Wilson
  mobile: 0788 518 9765
- ▲ Un-incorporated Society
- ○ *G; the collection of post cards of canals & inland navigations
- ● Mtg (Annual in June) - VE
- < Inland Waterways Assn
- > Shardlow Heritage Centre
- M 55 i, 1 org, UK / 3 i, o'seas
- ¶ Gongoozler - 4; ftm, 50p nm.

Canary Council
a group of the **National Council for Aviculture**

Cancer Genetics Group
a group of the **British Society for Human Genetics**

Canine & Feline Behaviour Association   (CFBA)
- NR Applewood House, Ringshall Rd, Dagnall, BERKHAMSTED, Herts, HP4 1RN.
  0845 644 5993 (Mon-Fri 1000-1600)
  email mail@cfba.co.uk
- ○ *G; provides dog training & behaviour courses

Canoe Association of Northern Ireland   (CANI)
- NR Unit 2 River's Edge, 13-15 Ravenhill Rd, BELFAST, BT6 8DN.
  0870 240 5065
  http://www.cani.org.uk
  Sec: Mary Doyle
- ○ *S
- ● Mtgs - Comp

Canoe Camping Club
a group of the **Camping & Caravanning Club**

Canoe Wales
- NR National White Water Centre, Frongoch, BALA, Gwynedd, LL23 7NU.   (hq)
  01678 521199   fax 01678 521158
  email admin@canoewales.com
  http://www.canoewales.con
  Admin: Pat Holmes
- ○ *S; to manage canoeing in Wales
- M 1,800 i; 53 affil clubs (2,000 i)
- × 2009 Welsh Canoeing Association

Canterbury & York Society   1904
- ■ Borthwick Institute, University of York, Heslington, YORK, YO10 5DD.   (hsb)
  email cf13@york.ac.uk
  http://www.canterburyandyork.org
  Hon Sec: Dr C Fonge
- ▲ Registered Charity
- ○ *L; publication of the records of the medieval English church
- ● Publishing
- M 101 i, 141 libraries
- ¶ Annual Volume; prices vary (c £15 i, c £20 instns).

Capability Scotland   1946
- NR Westerlea, 11 Ellersly Rd, EDINBURGH, EH12 6HY.
  0131-337 9876   fax 0131-346 7864
  email ascs@capability-scotland.org.uk
  http://www.capability-scotland.org.uk
  Chief Exec: Dana O'Dwyer
- ▲ Company Limited by Guarantee; Registered Charity
- ○ *W; to support children, young people & adults with a range of disabilities, providing a diverse range of services including community living, day & residential services, employment, respite/short breaks, therapy, education & learning, family support & activities

Capel: the Chapels Heritage Society   (CAPEL)   1986
- ■ 5 Cuffnell Close, Liddell Park, LLANDUDNO, LL30 1UX.   (hsp)
  01492 860449
  email obadiah1@btinternet.com
  http://www.capeli.org.uk
  Hon Sec: Rev Peter Jennings
- ▲ Registered Charity
- ○ *G, *L, *R; the study & preservation of the non-conformist heritage in Wales, with particular regard to chapel buildings & their records
- ● Conf - Mtgs - Exhib - Inf - VE
- M c 300 i
- ¶ Capel NL - 2; ftm, £1 nm.

Captive Animals' Protection Society   (CAPS)   1957
- ■ PO Box 4186, MANCHESTER, M60 3ZA.   (hq)
  0845 330 3911
  email info@captiveanimals.org
  http://www.captiveanimals.org
  Chief Exec: Pat Simpson
- ▲ Company Limited by Guarantee
- ○ *K; is opposed to the use of animals in entertainment; campaigns to end the captivity of animals in zoos, circuses & the exotic pet trade
- ● ET - Inf
- M i
  (Sub: £12 , UK / £15, o'seas)
- ¶ Release - 2; ftm, £1.50 nm.

Car Park Appreciation Society (CPAS) 2005

- ■ 8 The Limes, Evesham Rd, Astwood Bank, REDDITCH, Worcs, B96 6AA. (hsp)
    email kevin@beresfordB96.freeserve.co.uk
    Sec/Pres: Kevin Beresford
- ▲ Un-incorporated Society
- ○ *G; to collect photographs & interesting data on car parks throughout Britain & the Irish Republic
- ● Mtgs - VE
- < AA Insurance
- M 2 i
- ¶ Car Parks of GB Calendar - 1; £8.
    Get Carter Calendar (the Gateshead car park) - 1; £6 m, £8 nm.

Car Rental Council of Ireland

- IRL 5 Upper Pembroke St, DUBLIN 2, Republic of Ireland.
    353 (1) 676 1690   fax 353 (1) 661 9213
    email predmond@simi.ie
    http://www.carrentalcouncil.ie
    Chief Exec: Paul Redmond
- ○ *T

Caravan Club Ltd   1907

- NR East Grinstead House, EAST GRINSTEAD, W Sussex, RH19 1UA. (hq)
    01342 326944   fax 01342 410258
    http://www.caravanclub.co.uk
- ○ *G; for touring caravanners; providing sites, travel & information services
- < Fédn Intle de Camping et Caravanning (FICC); Alliance of Intl Tourism (AIT); Fédn Intle Automobile (FIA); Soc of Motor Mfrs & Traders (SMMT)
- M 323,000 i, UK / 1,000 i, o'seas

Carbon Capture & Storage Association   (CCSA)

- NR 35-37 Grosvenor Gardens (suites 142-152), LONDON, SW1W 0BS.
    020 7821 0528   fax 020 7828 0310
    email info@ccsassociation.org
    http://www.ccsassociation.org
    Chief Exec: Jeff Chapman
- ○ *T; the capture & geological storage of carbon dioxide

Carbon Monoxide & Gas Safety Society   1995

- § Lorien, Common Lane, CLAYGATE, Surey, KT10 0HY.
    01372 466135
    email office@co-gassafety.co.uk
    http://www.co-gassafety.co.uk
    Pres: Stephanie Trotter
    Known as **CO-Gas Safety,** the society campaigns to reduce accidents from carbon monoxide (CO) poisoning and other gas dangers.

Cardiff Chamber of Commerce, Trade & Industry
was liquidated in 2008 & is now within the area covered by the
South Wales Chamber of Commerce

Cardiff Naturalists' Society (CNS) 1867

- NR 36 Rowan Way, Lisvane, CARDIFF, CF14 0TD. (hsp)
    029 2075 6869
    http://www.cardiffnaturalists.org.uk
    Sec: Mike Dean
- ▲ Un-incorporated Society
- ○ *E, *L; to promote the study of the natural sciences & the conservation of the natural environment, with special reference to the counties of Glamorgan
- M i

Cardigan County Agricultural Society

- NR Pensarn, Brynberian, CRYMYCH, Pembrokeshire, SA41 3TG. (hq)
    01239 891637
    email alwyn.evans@btconnect.com
    http://www.cardigancountyshow.co.uk
    Contact: Alwyn Evans
- ○ *F
- ● Cardiganshire County Show
- < Assn of Show & Agricl Orgs

Cardiomyopathy Association   (CMA)   1989

- ■ Unit 10 Chiltern Court, Asheridge Rd, CHESHAM, Bucks, HP5 2PX. (hq)
    01494 791224   fax 01494 797199
    email info@cardiomyopathy.org
    http://www.cardiomyopathy.org
    Chmn: Peter McBride
- ▲ Registered Charity
- Br 1
- ○ *K, *W; to provide accurate & up-to-date information about cardiomyopathy (a heart muscle disease) to patients, family members, doctors & medical staff
- ● Conf - Mtgs - ET - Inf - Support through groups & individuals (one to on on telephone)
- < Children's Heart Fedn; GIG; Heart Transplant Families Together; NVCO
- M 900 i, 5 org, UK / 21 i, o'seas
- ¶ NL - 2;   AR; both ftm.

Care not Killing Alliance
    since 2007 **CNK Alliance Ltd (Care not Killing)**

Care Leavers Association   (CLA)

- NR Phase 1 Express Networks (Unit 27), 1 George Leigh St, MANCHESTER, M4 5DL. (hq)
    0845 308 2755
    email info@careleavers.org   http://www.careleavers.org
    Sec: Jim Goddard
- ▲ Company Limited by Guarantee
- ○ *K, *W; 'to protect, promote & strengthen rights for care leavers; to challenge negative public perceptions of care leavers & children in care; to ensure care leavers receive the support services they require'
- ● Conf - Mtgs - ET - Res - Inf - LG
- M 50 i, 2 org, UK / 1 i, o'seas
- ¶ The Grapevine (NL) - 4; free.

Care Management Group

- NR The Pointe, 89 Hartfield Rd, Wimbledon, LONDON, SW19 3TJ.
    020 8544 8900
    http://www.cmg.co.uk
    Managing Dir: Peter Kinsey
- ○ *W; 'to support people with learning disabilities, physical disabilities, chronic & enduring mental health needs, sensory & communication impairments & associated complex needs including challenging behaviours'

Careers Development Group   1895

- ■ c/o CILIP, 7 Ridgmount St, LONDON, WC1E 7AE. (hsb)
    020-7811 3131 (Mon-Fri 0830-1630)
    http://www.careerdevelopmentgroup.org.uk
    Hon Sec: Lorna Robertson
- ▲ Registered Charity
- Br 15 regional gps
- ○ *P
- ● Conf - Mtgs - ET - Res - Exhib
- < Library Assn
- M 5,000 i
- ¶ Impact - 10; £34 yr m (£39 o'seas, £98 USA).

Careers Writers' Association (CWA) 1978

- ■ 32 Leyborne Avenue, LONDON, W13 9RA. (hsp)
  020 8567 0796
  email sarah.marten@btinternet.com
  http://www.careerswriting.co.uk
  Sec: Sarah Marten
- ▲ Un-incorporated Society
- ○ *P; to promote the values of accuracy, clarity, impartiality, creativity & integrity in written & other forms of careers information
- ● Mtgs - ET
- M 28 i
- ¶ Booklet - 1.

CArers Association 1974

- ■ 33-35 Cathedral St (3rd floor), CARDIFF, CF11 9HB.
  0845 450 0350   fax 029 2022 8859
  email communications@crossroads.org.uk
  http://www.crossroads.org.uk
  10 Regent Place, RUGBY, Warks, CV21 2PN.   (regd/office).
  Chief Exec: Anne Roberts
- ▲ Company Limited by Guarantee; Registered Charity
- Br 126 (England & Wales)
- ○ *W; to provide practical support for carers; to supply trained support workers to relieve carers for essential breaks
- M [not stated]
- ¶ AR & Accounts - 1.
  Note: uses the working title of Crossroads: caring for carers

Carers Association

- IRL Market Square, TULLAMORE, Co Offaly, Republic of Ireland.
  353 (057) 932 2920
  email ceo@carersireland.com
  http://www.carersireland.com
  Chmn: Frank Goodwin
- ○ *W

Carers UK 1965

- ■ 20 Great Dover St, LONDON, SE1 4LX.   (hq)
  020 7378 4999   fax 020 7378 9781
  email info@carersuk.org   http://www.carersuk.org
  Chief Exec: Imelda Redmond
- ▲ Company Limited by Guarantee; Registered Charity
- Br 80
- ○ *W; to campaign for the rights of carers & to advise carers about their rights & entitlements to support
- ● ET - Inf - LG
  Helpline: 0808 808 7777 (Wed & Thurs 1000-1200 + 1400-1600)
- M 10,000 i, 569 f
- ¶ Caring (Jnl) - 4; m only.
  Publications list.

Caribbean-British Business Council (CBBC) 1974

- NR 2 Belgrave Sq, LONDON, SW1X 8PJ.   (hq)
  020 7235 9484   fax 020 7823 1370
  email admin@caribbean-council.org
  http://www.caribbean-council.org
  Exec Dir: David Jessop
- ▲ Un-incorporated Society
- Br Brussels
- ○ *T; to promote & support trade & investment between Britain & the Caribbean
- ● Conf - Mtgs - Exhib - Expt - Inf - LG
- M 8 i, 87 f, 3 org, UK / 3 f, o'seas
- ¶ Caribbean Briefing - 52; ftm, £210 yr nm.
  Caribbean Airline News - 6;   The Week in Europe;
  Weekly NL - 52; all ftm only.

Caring for Carers
  see **Crossroads: Caring for Carers**

Carlyle Society 1929

- ■ c/o Prof Ian Campbell, University of Edinburgh, David Hume Tower, George Sq, EDINBURGH, EH8 9JX.   (pres/b)
  0131-650 4284   fax 0131-650 6898
  email ian.campbell@ed.ac.uk
  Pres: Prof Ian Campbell
- ○ *A, *L; the study & encouragement of knowledge & information on the life & writing of the Carlyles - Thomas (1795-1881) & Jane (1801-1866)

Carmarthenshire Antiquarian Society 1905

- NR 63 Oaklands, Swiss Valley Park, LLANELLI, SA14 8DH.
  01554 773468
  http://www.carmants.org.uk
  Sec: Mrs Molly Rees
- ○ *G; all things related to the history, antiquities & natural history of Carmarthenshire & West Wales

Carnival Band Secretaries League
  since 2009 **Marching Display Bands Association**

Carnival Glass Society (CGS) 1982

- ■ PO Box 14, HAYES, Middx, UB3 5NU.   (mail/address)
  email pmphyllis@aol.com   http://www.thecgs.co.uk
  Sec: Phyllis Atkinson
- ▲ Company Limited by Guarantee
- ○ *G; for collectors of carnival glass & its accurate documentation; (Carnival Glass is mostly press moulded & sprayed, whilst hot, with metallic salts suspended in oil)
- M 300 i, UK / 6 i, o'seas
  (Sub: £18 UK / £24 o'seas)
- ¶ NL - 4; ftm only.

Carnival Guild
  see **National Carnival Guild - the National Federation of Carnival Associations (Carnival Guild)**

Carnivorous Plant Society (CPS) 1978

- ■ 100 Lambley Lane, Burton Joyce, NOTTINGHAM, NG14 5BL.   (hsp)
  07528 342224
  email derek.c.petrie@btinternet.com
  http://www.thecps.org.uk
  Show Sec: Derek Petrie
- ▲ Registered Charity
- ○ *H; to promote the growing & conservation of carnivorous plants
- ● Conf - Mtgs - ET - Exhib - Lib - PL - VE
- < R Horticl Soc

Carp Society 1983

- NR Horseshoe Lake, Burford Rd, LECHLADE, Glos, GL7 3QQ.   (hq)
  01367 253959   fax 01367 252450
  email info@thecarpsociety.com
  Commercial Mgr: David Mannall
- ○ *G; for those interested in fishing for carp
- ● Conf - Exhib
- M c 3,500 i
- ¶ Various.

Carpenters' Fellowship (CF)

- NR PO Box 2823, CORSHAM, Wilts, SN13 8WZ.   (mail)
  email bill@carpentersfellowship.co.uk
  http://www.carpentersfellowship.co.uk
  Chmn: Bill Keir
- ▲ Company Limited by Guarantee
- ○ *P; to promote communication, training & sharing of knowledge amongst those interested in historic & contemporary timber framed structures
- ● Conf - ET - Exam
- M i
  (Sub: £45)
- ¶ Mortice & Tenon (Jnl) - 4.

Carpet Foundation   2001
- MCF Complex, 60 New Rd, KIDDERMINSTER, Worcs, DY10 1AQ.   (hq)
  01562 755568   fax 01562 865405
  email info@carpetfoundation.com
  http://www.carpetfoundation.com
  Chief Exec: Mike H Hardiman
- ▲ Company Limited by Guarantee
- ○ *T; British carpet industry; Registered Specialists (qualified independent retailers) & manufacturers
- ● Mtgs - Res - Stat - Inf - LG - Promoting public awareness of the benefits of carpet through the Quality Mark & media campaigns
- M 14 mfrs, 1,244 retailers, 5 associates
- ¶ NL - 4; ftm.

Carrier Bag Consortium
- Gothic House (3rd floor), Barker Gate, NOTTINGHAM, NG1 1JU.
  0115-958 0403   fax 0115-948 3098
  email opinion@carrierbagtax.com
  http://www.carrierbagtax.com
  Contact: Peter Woodall
- ○ *K, *N, *T; a group of major UK carrier bag suppliers fighting the possibility of a carrier bag tax being imposed in the UK
- M f

Cartoonists' Club of Great Britain   (CCGB)   1960
- 17 Eliot Rd, WORCESTER, WR3 8DP.   (mem/sp)
  http://www.ccgb.org.uk
  Contact: The Membership Secretary
- ▲ Un-incorporated Society
- ○ *P, *G; to champion the art & craft of the cartoon; to provide contact between members
- ● Conf - Mtgs - Exhib - Comp - PL - VE
- < Fedn Eur Cartoonist Orgs (FECO)
- M 200 i, UK / 10 i, o'seas
- ¶ The Jester (NL) - 12; ftm only.
  LM - 1; ftm, free on request nm.

Cartophilic Society of Great Britain Ltd   1938
- NR Ivy House, Ivy Farm, School Lane, Lower Heath, PREES, Shropshire, SY13 2BU.   (hsp)
  http://www.csgb.co.uk
  Gen Sec: Robin Short
- ▲ Company Limited by Guarantee
- Br 12
- ○ *G; 'propagating, enhancing & preserving the hobby of cigarette & trade card collecting'
- ● Conf - Mtgs - Res - Inf - Lib
- M 900 i, UK / 100 i, o'seas
- ¶ Cartophilic Notes & News - 6.

Casino Operators' Association of the UK   (COA(UK))   2001
- 15 Livesey St, SHEFFIELD, S Yorks, S6 2BL.   (sb)
  0114-281 6209   fax 0114-281 6199
  email gensec@coa-uk.org.uk
  http://www.casinooperatorsassociation.org.uk
  Gen Sec: Phil Lowther
- ▲ Company Limited by Guarantee
- ○ *T; formed from companies who felt the the British Casino Association was unable to represent adequately other than large company views. Those smaller companies have fundamentally different perspectives of the casino industry through experience & usually, a risk to their own capital
- ● Mtgs - Inf - LG
- M f

Caspari Foundation for Educational Therapy & Therapeutic Teaching   2000
- NR Angel Wharf, 53 Eagle Wharf Rd, LONDON, N1 7ER.   (hq)
  020 7704 1977
  email casparihouse@btconnect.com
  http://www.caspari.org.uk
  Admin: Anne Casimir
- ▲ Registered Charity
- ○ *E; to develop theory & practice of educational therapy as a treatment for those with learning difficulties; to promote the psychological insight of teachers in general into the emotional factors in learning & failing to learn
- ● Conf - Mtgs - ET - Inf - Lib - LG - Educational therapy - Lectures
- < Nat Children's Bureau
- M 80 i, 30 f, UK / 10 i, 5 f, o'seas, school services in corporate membership
- ¶ Educational Therapy & Therapeutic Teaching - 1; ftm, £10 nm.

Caspian Breed Society   (CBS(UK))   1999
- Sparrow Farm, Lanhill, CHIPPENHAM, Wilts, SN14 6LX.   (hsp)
  01249 782246   fax 0871 251 3199
  email uk.caspian.society@virgin.net
  http://www.caspianbreedsociety.co.uk/
  Sec: Ronald J Scott
- ▲ Company Limited by Guarantee
- ○ *B; the promotion & preservation of the Caspian horse, an ancient breed from 3,000 BC
- Gp Horse breeding; Miniature horse
- ● Mtgs - Exhib - Breed show - Agricultural show promotion
- < Brit Horse Soc; Brit Assn of Equine Socs; Central Prefix Register
- M 102 i, UK / 30 i, o'seas
- ¶ CBS News (NL) - 6;   AR - 1; both free.

Caspian Horse Society   (CHS)   1987
- Eglentyne, 6 Nuns Walk, VIRGINIA WATER, Surrey, GU25 4RT.   (hsp)
  01344 843352
  email rlharris@talk21.com
  http://www.caspianhorsesociety.org.uk
  Sec: Dr Rosemary Harris
- ▲ Company Limited by Guarantee; Registered Charity
- ○ *B
- ● Conf - Mtgs - Comp - Expt - LG
- < Intl Caspian Soc; Brit Horse Soc (Breeds C'ee); Central Prefix Register; Nat Equine Forum
- M 95 i
- ¶ The Caspian (Jnl) - 4; ftm.

Cast Iron Drainage Development Association
has closed

Cast Metals Federation   (CMF)   2001
- NR National Metalforming Centre, 47 Birmingham Rd, WEST BROMWICH, W Midlands, B70 6PY.   (hq)
  0121-601 6397   fax 0121-601 6391
  email admin@cmfed.co.uk
  http://www.castmetalsfederation.com
  Chief Exec: John Parker
- ▲ Company Limited by Guarantee
- ○ *T; for the UK metal casting industry
- Gp Sections: Costs, Health & safety, Raw materials
  Gps: Iron castings, brass & bronze; Investment castings; Light metals; Steel; Suppliers; Zinc
- ● Conf - Mtgs - Inf - LG
- < C'ee of Assns of Eur Foundries (CAEF); METCOM
- M c 200 f

Casting Division
a group of the **Institute of Materials, Minerals & Mining**

Castle Studies Group
NR 4 Cotley Place, Heytesbury, WARMINSTER, Wilts, BA12 0HT.
      (mem/sp)
      http://www.castlestudiesgroup.org.uk
      Mem Sec: David Bartlett,   Sec: Dr Pamela Marshall
○ *G; for all interested in the study of castles in all their forms
● Conf - Mtgs - Study tours
M i
      (Sub: £25)
¶ CSG Jnl - 1.   Bibliography - 1.

Castlemilk Moorit Sheep Society   1973
NR Hillcrest Farm, Coventry Rd, Berkswell, COVENTRY, CV7 7AZ
      (hsp)
      01676 535242
      http://www.castlemilkmoorit.co.uk
      Hon Sec: Sheila Cooper
○ *B; conservation & promotion of Britain's rarest sheep breed
● Mtgs - Exhib - Livestock shows - Workshops
< Nat Sheep Assn; Rare Breeds Survival Trust
M 60 i
¶ NL - 3; ftm only.

Casualties Union   (CU)   1942
■ PO Box 1942, LONDON, E17 6YU.   (hsp)
      0870 007 0590   fax 0870 078 0590
      email hq@casualtiesunion.org.uk
      http://www.casualtiesunion.org.uk
      Hon Gen Sec: Caroline Thomas
▲ Registered Charity
Br 42; 2 o'seas
○ *W; to supply trained casualties for the training of first aid,
      nursing & rescue
Gp Acting; Make-up; Staging
● Conf - Mtgs - ET - Exam - Res - Comp - SG
M 440 i, UK / 8 i, o'seas
¶ Casualty Simulation - 4; ftm only.

Cat Fancy
      see **Governing Council of the Cat Fancy**

Catalogue Exchange
NR 155 High St, ILFRACOMBE, Devon, EX34 9EZ.
      01271 855545   fax 01271 866281
      http://www.catalogueexchange.co.uk
○ *T; to support businesses in all areas of catalogue & online
      retailing
● Mtgs - Inf
M f

Catch 22 in Action   1988
NR Churchill House, 142-146 Old St, LONDON, EC1V 9BW.   (hq)
      020 7336 4800   fax 020 7336 4801
      http://www.catch-22.org.uk
      Chief Exec: Joyce Moseley
▲ Registered Charity
○ *K; to specialise in issues involving youth crime - criminality,
      high crime neighbourhoods, business & town centre crime, &
      rural crime, as well as hospital, passenger, school & women's
      safety
● Conf - ET - Res - Exhib - Comp - Inf - Lib - LG
< Eur Forum for Urban Security; Intl Centre for the Prevention of
      Crime
M 25 f
¶ Various publications.
× 2008 Crime Concern

Catenian Association   1908
NR Copthall House (2nd floor), Station Sq, COVENTRY, Warks,
      CV1 2FY.   (hq)
      024 7622 4533
      http://www.thecatenians.com
▲ Company Limited by Guarantee; Registered Charity
Br 255; Australia, Eire, Hong Kong, Malta, S Africa, Zambia,
      Zimbabwe
○ *R; Catholic business & professional men
Gp Benevolent & children's fund; Bursary fund
● Conf - Mtgs - VE
M 9,500 i, UK / 1,000 i, o'seas
¶ Catena - 12.

Catering Equipment Association   (CEA)   1965
IRL Confederation House, 84-86 Lower Baggot St, DUBLIN 2,
      Republic of Ireland.   (hq)
      353 (1) 605 1669   fax 353 (1) 638 1669
      email info@cea.ie   http://www.cea.ie
      Contact: Neil McGowan
○ *T; manufacturers, suppliers & distributors involved in all
      aspects of the catering & hospitality industry
< Eur Fedn of Catering Eqpt Mfrs (EFCEM); Food & Drink Ind
      Ireland (FDII)
M 42 f

**Catering Equipment Distributors Association of Great Britain
(CEDA)   1972**
NR PO Box 683, INKBERROW, Worcs, WR7 4WQ.   (dir/b)
      01387 793911
      email robinmcknight@ceda.co.uk   http://www.ceda.co.uk
      Dir: Robert McKnight (07557 432952)
▲ Un-incorporated Society
○ *T; design, supply, installation & after-sales service of
      commercial kitchens & all catering equipment
Gp CEDACARE (a catering equipment service initiative)
● Conf - Mtgs - ET - Exhib - Stat - Inf - LG
M 80 f
¶ CEDA News - 4; free.

Catering Equipment Suppliers' Association   (CESA)   1994
NR Westminster Tower (ground floor), 3 Albert Embankment,
      LONDON, SE1 7SL.   (hq)
      020 7793 3030   fax 020 7793 3031
      email enquiries@cesa.org.uk   http://www.cesa.org.uk
▲ Company Limited by Guarantee
○ *T; to promote cooperation between those engaged in the food
      service equipment industry
M f

** **Catering Managers Association of Great Britain & the Channel
Islands**
      Organisation lost: see Introduction paragraph 3

Cathedral Architects Association   (CAA)   1948
■ St Ann's Gate Architects, The Close, SALISBURY, Wilts,
      SP1 2EB.   (hsb)
      01722 555200   fax 01722 555201
      email antony@stannsgate.com
      Hon Sec: Anthony Feltham-King
▲ Un-incorporated Society
○ *P; sharing sharing in relation to aesthetic, liturgical & technical
      issues particular to cathedrals & church buildings of similar
      status
● Conf - VE - LG
M 80 i, UK / 10 i, o'seas
¶ Conference Notes & Proceedings - 1/2 yrly; ftm only.

© CBD Research Ltd · Beckenham · BR3 5JS · Tel 020 8650 7745 · E-mail cbd@cbdresearch.com · www.cbdresearch.com

Cathedral & Church Shops Association   (CCSA)
NR   c/o Sue Kastner, Glastonbury Abbey Shop Ltd, The Abbey
       Gatehouse, Magdalene St, GLASTONBURY, Somerset,
       BA6 9EL.   (hsb)
       email ccsa.sec@btinternet.com
       http://www.ccshops.org.uk
       Hon Sec: Sue Kastner
▲   Un-incorporated Society
○   *T; 'to extend the ministry of the church through the sale of
       Christian books & cards; by providing a presence in a church
       or cathedral; by making a 'bridge' into the worship building'
●   Conf - Mtgs - ET - Exhib
M   cathedrals & churches

Cathedral Libraries & Archives Association   (CLAA)
NR   c/o The Librarian, Norwich Cathedral, 12 The Close,
       NORWICH, NR1 4DH.   (hsb)
       01603 218327
       Hon Sec: Mrs Gudrun Warren
○   *L; to preserve & protect cathedral libraries & archives in the
       UK & Ireland
●   Mtgs
M   i

Cathedral Organists' Association   (COA)   1946
■   19 The Close, SALISBURY, Wilts, SP1 2EB.   (hsb)
       Hon Sec: T Hone
▲   Un-incorporated Society
○   *P; interests & training of cathedral & collegiate church
       organists in the UK
●   Conf - Mtgs - ET - SG - VE - Empl - Liaison with the Church of
       England
M   127 i

CATHOLIC...
       for Catholic organisations, other than those listed below, please refer
       to the **Catholic Directory** published by Gabriel Communications.

Catholic Archives Society   (CAS)   1979
■   50A Gordon Rd, FAREHAM, Hants, PO16 7SP.   (hsp)
       http://www.catholic-history.org
       Hon Sec: Sarah Stanton,   Chmn: Judith Smeaton
▲   Un-incorporated Society
○   *L; to promote the care & preservation of archives of dioceses,
       religious orders, & other institutions of the Catholic Church in
       the UK & Ireland
●   Conf - ET - Inf - VE
M   200-250 i
       (Sub: £20)
¶   Catholic Archives - 1; ftm, £7 nm.   Bulletin - 1; ftm only.
       Occasional Papers - 1; £3-£5.
       Advice leaflets (see website) - 1/2; free to download.

Catholic Family History Society   (CFHS)   1983
■   14 Sydney Rd, ILFORD, Essex, IG6 2ED.   (mem/sp)
       020 8550 5543
       email kathmar247@btinternet.com
       http://www.catholic-history.org.uk/cfhs
       Mem Sec: Kathleen Black
▲   Registered Charity
Br   2
○   *G; to encourage research into the history of Catholic families
       in England, Wales & Scotland from the 16th to the 19th
       centuries
●   Conf - Mtgs
<   Fedn of Family History Socs
M   329 i, 15 f, 6 org, UK / 19 i, 2 f, 4 org, o'seasUK / 35 i, o'seas
       (Sub: £10 i & org, £15 f UK / £14 o'seas)
¶   Catholic Ancestor (Jnl) - 3; ftm.
       Publication - 1; on CD-ROM.

Catholic Medical Association (UK)   (SMA)   1923
■   39 Eccleston Square, LONDON, SW1V 1BX.   (hq)
       020 7901 4895   fax 020 7901 4819
       http://www.catholicmedicalassociation.org.uk
▲   Registered Charity
Br   29
○   *P; professional support in medical ethics; informed opinion
       about implications of developments in medicine & social
       policy
●   Conf - Mtgs - SG - Inf - LG
<   Intl Fedn of Catholic Doctors (FIAMC); Eur Fedn of Catholic
       Doctors (FEAMC); Eur Doctors U
M   1,000 i, UK / 10 i, o'seas
¶   Catholic Medical Quarterly - 4.
×   2008 Guild of Catholic Doctors

Catholic Record Society   (CRS)   1905
NR   12 Melbourne Place, WOLSINGHAM, Co Durham,
       DL13 3EH.   (hsp)
       01388 527747
○   *L; publication of original documents & occasional
       monographs relating to the English Catholics from the
       Reformation to the end of the 19th century (but NOT
       genealogical)
M   350 i, 350 org
¶   Recusant History - 2.   Records & Monograph.

Catholic Truth Society   (CTS)   1868
§   40-46 Harleyford Rd, LONDON, SE11 5AY.
       020 7640 0042
       email info@cts-online.org.uk
       http://www.cts-online.org.uk
       A non-membership body of the Roman Catholic Church
       publishing & distributing books & tracts

Catholic Union of Great Britain   (CU)   1870
NR   St Maximilian Kolbe House, 63 Jeddo Rd, LONDON,
       W12 9EE.   (hsb)
       020 8749 1321   fax 020 8735 0816
       email info@catholicunion.org
       http://www.catholicunion.org
       Sec: Peter H Higgs
▲   Un-incorporated Society
○   *R; non-political association of Roman Catholic laity seeking to
       promote the common good & to uphold the Christian
       standpoint in public life
●   Conf - Inf - LG
M   1,700 i
¶   NL - 4; free.   AR; ftm only.

Cats Protection   (CP)   1927
NR   Chelwood Gate, HAYWARDS HEATH, Sussex, RH17 7TT.   (hq)
       0870 770 8650
       email cpl@cats.org.uk   http://www.ncac.cats.org.uk
       Chief Exec: Helen Ralston
▲   Registered Charity
○   *V; to rescue stray & unwanted cats & kittens to rehabilitate &
       re-home them; to encourage the neutering of all cats &
       kittens; to inform the public on their care
●   Helpline: 01403 221919
M   79,000 i

CEDIA UK Ltd   (CEDIA)   1986
■ Unit 2 Phoenix Park, ST NEOTS, Cambs, PE19 8EP.   (hq)
      01480 213744   fax 01480 213469
      email info@cedia.co.uk   http://www.cedia.co.uk
      Exec Dir: Wendy Griffiths
○ *T; for designers & installers of residential, custom integrated
      electronics that reflect people's lifestyles
● Conf -ET - Exam - Res - Exhib - Stat - Inf
< CEDIA Americas; CEDIA Asia Pacific
M companies & manufacturers
      (Sub: £411.25 companies, £850 manufacturers)
¶ LM - ftm only.
      Red Book CEDIA Guide - every 18 months; £10 m only.
      Red Book (handout); 40p.

Cement Admixtures Association Ltd   (CAA)   1963
■ 38a Tilehouse Green Lane, KNOWLE, W Midlands, B93 9EY.
      (sp)
      01564 776362   fax 01564 776362
      http://www.admixtures.org.uk
▲ Company Limited by Guarantee
○ *T; to encourage responsible use of admixtures in concrete,
      mortar & cement mixes
< Eur Fedn of Cement Admixture Assns (EFCA)
M 12 f

Cement Manufacturers Ireland   (CMI)   2003
IRL Confederation House, 84-86 Lower Baggot St, DUBLIN 2,
      Republic of Ireland.   (hq)
      353 (1) 605 1652
      email info@cement.ie   http://www.cement.ie
      Dir: Mark McAuley
○ *T; manufacturers of cement products for the construction sector
< Eur Cement Assn (CEMBUREAU); Ir Business & Emplrs
      Confedn (IBEC)
M 4 f

Cementitious Slag Makers Association   (CSMA)   1985
NR The Coach House, West Hill, OXTED, Surrey, RH8 9JB.   (hq)
      01708 682439
      email standards@ukcsma.co.uk
      http://www.ukcsma.co.uk
      Dir Gen: Denis Higgins
▲ Un-incorporated Society
○ *T; to promote the use of GGBS, ground granulated
      blastfurnace slag (a cementitious material widely used in
      concrete)
● Conf - Res
M 4 f

Central Association of Agricultural Valuers   (CAAV)   1910
NR Market Chambers, 35 Market Place, COLEFORD, Glos,
      GL16 8AA.   (hq)
      01594 832979   fax 01594 810701
      email enquire@caav.org.uk   http://www.caav.org.uk
      Sec & Adviser: Jeremy Moody
▲ Company Limited by Guarantee
Br 27
○ *P; representation & qualification of agricultural valuers dealing
      withtenancy matters, sales of farms & land, taxation &
      compulsory purchase
● Conf - Mtgs - ET - Exam - Stat - LG
M 2,400 i
¶ NL - 4;   Hbk - 1;   AR; all ftm only.
      LM; on website.
      Tenanted Farm Survey - 1; £10.
      Costings of Agricultural Operations - 1; ftm, £20 nm.
      Other professional publications.

Central Council for British Naturism   (CCBN)   1964
NR 30-32 Wycliffe Rd, NORTHAMPTON, NN1 5JF.   (hq)
      01604 620361   fax 01604 230176
      email headoffice@british-naturism.org.uk
      http://www.british-naturism.org.uk
○ *G; promotion of physical, moral & mental wellbeing through
      indoor & outdoor recreation without clothes, either
      individually or socially in private grounds, premises or on
      official beaches
M 25,000 i
      Note: trades as British Naturism

Central Council of Church Bell Ringers   1890
■ 11 Bullfields, SAWBRIDGEWORTH, Herts, CM21 9DB.   (hsp)
      01279 726159
      http://www.cccbr.org.uk
      Hon Sec: I H Oram
▲ Registered Charity
○ *G, *R; the ringing of bells for Christian worship, their
      maintenance & standards of change ringing
Gp Education; Peal compositions; Publications; Public relations;
      Records; Redundant bells; Restoration funds; Towers &
      belfries
● Conf - ET - Res - Exhib - Stat - Inf - Lib
M 27 i, 61 org, UK / 6 org, o'seas
¶ The Ringing World - 52; £1.60.

Central Dredging Association   (CEDA)
■ Institution of Civil Engineers, 1 Great George St, LONDON,
      SW1P 3AA.   (hsb)
      020 7665 2262   fax 020 7799 1365
      email adam.kirkup@ice.org.uk
      http://www.dredging.org
      Sec: Adam Kirkup
▲ Registered Charity
Br Africa, Belgium, Holland
○ *P; an independent, non-governmental society providing a
      forum for all those involved in activities related to dredging &
      who live or work in Europe, Africa, or the Middle East; it does
      not represent the interests of any particular industry sector
● Conf - Mtgs
< is a member of the World Org of Dredging Assns (WODA)
M i
      (Sub: 71 i, 615-8120 f, by turnover)

Central Organisation for Maritime Pastimes & Support Services
(COMPASS)   1990
■ 178 Woodfield Park, Cool Oak Lane, LONDON, NW9 7ND.
      (hq)
      020 8205 4492   fax 020 8200 6792
      Sec: Cmdr Gerald F Beck
▲ Registered Charity
○ *G; to promote character development of girls & boys through
      adventure & education using the practice of seafaring &
      seamanship
M c 3,000 i

Central Scotland Aviation Group   (CSAG)   1965
NR 102 Criagmount Brae, EDINBURGH, EH12 8XN.
      Contact:Ian Gibson
○ *G
¶ Scottish Air News.
      Scottish Register [of aircraft based in Scotland]; £5.95

CENTRE ...
see 'Centres, Bureaux & Research Institutes' (Introduction 6)

© CBD Research Ltd · Beckenham · BR3 5JS · Tel 020 8650 7745 · E-mail cbd@cbdresearch.com · www.cbdresearch.com

CERAM Research Ltd (CERAM) 1920
NR Queens Rd, Penkhull, STOKE-on-TRENT, Staffs, ST4 7LQ.   (hq)
     0845 025 0902
     email enquiries@ceram.com   http://www.ceram.com
▲ Company Limited by Guarantee
○ *Q; research, development, consultancy, testing, environmental
     & information services, materials & materials processing
     development, technology transfer
M f
     CERAM is the trading name of CERAM Research Ltd, a
     subsidiary of British Ceramic Research Ltd

Ceramics Society
    a group of the **Institute of Materials, Minerals & Mining**

Cereal Ingredient Manufacturers' Association (CIMA) 1986
NR 6 Catherine St, LONDON, WC2B 5JJ.   (hq)
     020 7420 7106   fax 020 7836 0580
     email martin.turton@fdf.org.uk
     Exec Sec: Martin Turton
▲ Un-incorporated Society
○ *T; to represent the interests of UK manufacturers of cereal-
     based food ingredients, including rusk, breadcrumb & batter
● Mtgs
< Food & Drink Fedn
M 6 f

Ceredigion Historical Society
    see **Cymdeithas Hanes Ceredigion (Ceredigion Historical**
    Society)

Ceretas (ceretas) 1988
NR 21 Regent St, NOTTINGHAM, NG1 5BS.   (hsp)
     0115-959 6130   fax 0115- 959 6148
     email admin@ceretas.org.uk
     http://www.ceretas.org.uk
     Chief Exec: Mary Bryce
▲ Company Limited by Guarantee
○ *P; *W; for people who work in home care
● Conf - Mtgs - ET - Workshops - Seminars
M 600 i, 50 f
¶ NL - 4; ftm.
     Good Practice Guidelines; £5 each or £60 for complete pack.
       Handling Service Users' Finances & Valuables.
       Caring for Staff.   Dementia.   Elder Abuse.
       Food Hygiene.   Managing Absence.   Medication.
       Personal & Professional Boundaries;   Personal Safety.
       Safe Hygiene Practice.   Staff Support, Supervision &
       Appraisal.

Certified Public Accountants Association
    see **Association of Certified Public Accountants**

CFA Society of the UK (CFA) 1956
■ 135 Cannon St (2nd floor), LONDON, EC4N 5BP.   (hq)
     020 7280 9620   fax 020 7280 9636
     email cfaukstaff@cfauk.org   http://www.cfauk.org
     Chief Exec: Will Goodhart
▲ Company Limited by Guarantee
○ *P; for investment professionals; [CFA = Chartered Financial
     Analyst]
● Conf - Mtgs - Exam - SG - Inf - VE
< CFA Inst
M 7,500 i
¶ Professional Investor - 4.   Report - 1; ftm.
     Headline Earnings Definition.
✕ 2007 (30 November) UK Society of Investment Professionals

Chair Frame Manufacturers' Association (CFMA) 1940
■ Francis Vaughan House, Q1 Capital Point, Capital Business
     Park, Parkway, CARDIFF, CF3 2PU.   (hq)
     029 2077 8918   fax 029 2079 3508
     Chief Exec: Michael Bennett Spencer
○ *T; interests of manufacturers of upholstery frames & associated
     components
● Conf - Mtgs - Exhib - Inf - Lib - VE - LG
< Fedn of Small Businesses
M 18 f
¶ CFC Contract Furnishing Concepts - 6; ftm, £21.50 yr nm.
     Note: This association is incorporated into the Association of
     Master Upholsterers.

Challenger Society for Marine Science 1903
■ National Oceanography Centre (Rm 346/10), Waterfront
     Campus, European Way, SOUTHAMPTON, Hants,
     SO14 3ZH.   (hsb)
     023 8059 5106   fax 023 8059 5107
     email jxj@noc.soton.ac.uk
     http://www.challenger-society.org.uk
     Exec Sec: Mrs Jennifer Jones
▲ Company Limited by Guarantee; Registered Charity
○ *L; to advance the study of marine science through research &
     education; to encourage a wider interest in the study of the
     seas & an awareness of their proper management
Gp Special interest groups:
     British Group of Altimeter Specialists; Biophysical interactions;
       Marine biogeochemistry; Marine optics; Marine technologies;
       Ocean modelling; Physics & chemistry of sea ice
● Conf - Mtgs - ET - SG
< Eur Fedn of Marine Science & Technology Socs (EFMS)
M 400 i, UK / 50 i, o'seas
     (Sub: £40 i, £20 student/retired)
¶ Ocean Challenge (Jnl) - 3;
     Challenger Wave (NL) - 12; 3; both ftm only.

The Chamber
    see **Bedfordshire & Luton Chamber of Commerce**

Chamber of Commerce East Lancashire 1991
■ Red Rose Court, Clayton Business Park, ACCRINGTON, Lancs,
     BB5 5JR.   (hq)
     01254 356400   fax 01254 388900
     email info@chamberelancs.co.uk
     http://www.chamberelancs.co.uk
     Chief Exec: Michael Damms
▲ Company Limited by Guarantee
○ *C; business support
Gp Business support; ICT; International trade; Supply train; Training
● Conf - Mtgs - ET - Res - Exhib - Stat - Expt - Inf - LG
< Brit Chams Comm; Chams Comm NW
M 1,000 f
¶ Lancashire Business View - 6.

Chamber of Commerce - Pembrokeshire 1990
NR Booth House, Llys Y Fran, Pembrokeshire, SA63 4RS.   (hq)
     01437 532533
○ *C
Gp various sub-c'ees
● Conf - Mtgs - ET - Res - Exhib - SG - Expt - Inf - VE - LG - Web
     sites/pages for members
M f

Chamber of Shipping Ltd   1975
- ■ Carthusian Court, 12 Carthusian St, LONDON, EC1M 6EZ.
  020 7417 2800   fax 020 7726 2080
  email stewart.conacher@british-shipping.org
  http://www.british-shipping.org/
  Sec: Stewart Conacher
- ▲ Company Limited by Shares
- ○ *T; to protect & promote the interests of the British owners & managers of merchant ships
- ● Mtgs - Stat - LG
- < Intl Cham of Shipping; Intl Shipping Fedn; EC Shipowners' Assn
- M 120 f
- ¶ AR; ftm.

Chambers of Commerce of Ireland
  see **Chambers Ireland**

Chambers of Commerce North West Ltd
- NR International Business Centre, Delta Crescent, Westbrook, WARRINGTON, Cheshire, WA5 7WQ.
  01925 715166   fax 01925 715159
  http://www.chambersofcommercenw.org.uk
- ○ *C; to champion the regional chamber of commerce network as the voice of business at regional, national and international level

Chambers Ireland
- IRL 17 Merrion Square, DUBLIN 2, Republic of Ireland.   (hq)
  353 (1) 400 4300
  email info@chambers.ie
- ○ *C; represents 60 member chambers with over 13,000 businesses throughout Ireland

Chambre de Commerce Française de Grande-Bretagne (CCFGB)   1883
- NR Lincoln House (4th floor), 300 High Holborn, LONDON, WC1V 7JH.   (hq)
  020 7092 6600   fax 020 7092 6601
  email mail@ccfgb.co.uk   http://www.ccfgb.co.uk
  Managing Dir & Co Sec: Stéphane Bossavit
- ▲ Company Limited by Guarantee
- Br 2; France
- ○ *C; business development between France & Britain
- Gp Business consultancy; Finance & administration; Public relations
- ● Conf - Mtgs - ET - Exam - Res - Exhib - Comp - SG - Stat - Expt - Inf - VE
- < U des Chambres de Commerce et de l'Industrie Françaises à l'Etranger; Franco-Scottish Business Club
- M 531 f, UK / 70 f, o'seas
- ¶ Info (Jnl) - 6; ftm, £45 yr nm.
  The Franco-British Trade Directory - 1; ftm, £100 nm.
  The List of French Investments in the UK - 1:
    (book) £85 m, £120 nm.   (CD) £450 m, £700 nm.
  A range of practical & professional guides to daily & business life in Britain & France; ftm, £5-£30 nm.

Champagne Agents' Association   1908
- ■ c/o Mentzendorff & Co Ltd, Prince Consort House, 27-29 Albert Embankment, LONDON, SE1 7TJ.
  020 7840 3600
  Chmn: Andrew Hawes
- ○ *T
- M f

Channel Chamber of Commerce
- NR Shearway Business Park, Shearway Rd, FOLKESTONE, Kent, CT19 4RH.
  01303 270022   fax 01303 270476
  email info@shepwaybc.co.uk
  http://www.shepwaybc.co.uk
  Chief Exec: Peter Hobbs
- ○ *C

Channel Crossing Association   2001
- NR 103 Station Rd, LYDD, Kent, TN29 9LJ.   (hsp/b)
  01797 329479
  email channelcrossings@aol.com
  http://www.channelcrossingassociation.com
  Sec: Andy King
- ▲ Company Limited by Guarantee
- ○ *S; to promote, organise & support Channel crossings by unorthodox craft & assisted Channel swims; to record & ratify successful attempts
- M i

Channel Swimming Association Ltd   (CSA)   1927
- NR 381 New Ashby Rd, LOUGHBOROUGH, Leics, LE11 4ET.
  (hsp/b)
  01509 554137
  email swimsecretary@channelswimmingassociation.com
  http://www.channelswimmingassociation.com
  Hon Sec: Dr Julie Bradshaw
- ▲ Company Limited by Guarantee
- ○ *S; the governing body for English Channel swimming
- ● Inf - LG - Observing Channel swim attempts during Summer - Annual dinner
- M 100 i, UK / 100 i, o'seas
- ¶ NL - 3.   Info pack - 1;   Hbk; both price on application.

Channel Swimming & Piloting Federation   (CSPF)
- NR 21 Spielplatz, Lye Lake, Bricket Wood, ST ALBANS, Herts, AL2 3TD.   (hsp)
  01843 852858
  email secretary@cspf.co.uk
  http://www.channelswimming.net
  Hon Sec: Kevin Murphy
- ○ *S; is the governing body for Cross-Channel swimming; it promotes, as well as Cross-Channel swimming, all long distance swimming & crossing the Channel by other methods (rowing, canoeing, paddle-boarding); to assist in any way in making such attempts possible
- ● Mtgs - ET - Provision of pilot boats, advice & guidelines
- < Amat Swimming Assn

Chapels Heritage Society
  see **Capel: the Chapels Heritage Society**

Chapels Society   1988
- ■ 1 Newcastle Avenue, BEESTON, Notts, NG9 1BT.   (hsp)
  0115-922 4930
  email website@adhscl.org.uk   http://www.britarch.ac.uk/chapelsoc
  Hon Sec: Robin Phillips
- ▲ Registered Charity
- ○ *K, *L; to foster the understanding, study & preservation of nonconformist (ie non-Anglican) places of worship & related buildings in the UK (includes Roman Catholic, Orthodox & Jewish)
- ● VE - LG
- < Capel: the Chapels Heritage Soc; Coun for Brit Archaeology; Heritage Link
- M 286 i, 1 f, 22 org, UK / 6 i, 1 org, o'seas
  (Sub: £8 i, £12 f & org)
- ¶ NL - 2; ftm.   LM; ftm.   AR; on website.
  Occasional publications.

Charcuterie Guild
  a training programme of the **Guild of Fine Food**

© CBD Research Ltd · Beckenham · BR3 5JS · Tel 020 8650 7745 · E-mail cbd@cbdresearch.com · www.cbdresearch.com

CHARGE Family Support Group   1987
NR   59 Elmer Rd, LONDON, SE6 2HA.
    020 8265 3604
    email si_howardhotmail.com
    http://www.chargesyndrome.org.uk
    Contact: Simon Howard
○   *W; for families of children with birth defects - Coloboma,
    Heart defects, Atresia of the choanae, Retarded growth,
    Genital anomalies, Ear anomalies

Charities' Property Association   (CPA)   1976
■   Church House, Great Smith St, LONDON, SW1P 3AZ.   (hq)
    020 7222 1265   fax 020 7222 1250
    email info@charity-property.org
    http://www.charity-property.org.uk
    Chmn: The Lord Cameron of Dillington
▲   Un-incorporated Association
○   *K; to monitor legislation, or changes in policy of public bodies,
    that may affect the property investments of charities
●   Conf - Mtgs - Inf - LG
M   100 charities
¶   NL - 4.

Charities' Tax Reform Group
    since 2007 **Charity Tax Group**

Charity Christmas Card Council   (4C)   1966
NR   4c for Charity, 114 High St, STEVENAGE, Herts, SG1 3DW.
    (hq)
    0845 230 0046   fax 0845 230 0048
    email 4c@charitycards.org   http://www.charitycards.org
    Chief Exec: Neville C Bass
▲   Company Limited by Guarantee
○   *K; to raise funds for member charities by the design,
    publishing & marketing of charity Christmas cards to the
    corporate sector & abroad
Gp Depts: Design & publishing, Marketing
●   Conf - Exhib - Stat - Design & publishing
M   96 charities
¶   Executive Range Catalogue - 1;   AR; both free.

Charity Fairs Association   1994
NR   64 Erpingham Rd, LONDON, SW15 1BG.   (chmn/p)
    020 8785 0757
    email lindaweldon1@aol.com
    Chmn: Mrs Linda Weldon
    Admin: Anne Assheton (020 3021 213541)
    admin@charityfairsassociation.co.uk
○   *T; to promote a closer understanding between organisers &
    stallholders
●   Seminars - Advice - Arranging insurance
M   466 stallholders, 139 fair organisers
¶   Guides to stallholding

Charity Finance Directors' Group   (CFDG)   1988
NR   CAN Mezzanine, 49-51 East Rd, LONDON, N1 6AH.   (hq)
    0845 345 3192   fax 0845 345 3193
    email info@cfdg.org.uk   http://www.cfdg.org.uk
    Dir: Shirley Scott
▲   Company Limited by Guarantee; Registered Charity
○   *T; to assist in improving financial standards in the charity
    sector; to provide an additional focal point within the charity
    world to which others can refer for an informed view
●   Conf - Mtgs - ET - LG
M   900 i, 850 org
¶   Charity Finance Ybk - 1; ftm.

Charity Law Association   1992
NR   c/o Hempsons, The Exchange, Station Parade, HARROGATE,
    N Yorks, HG1 1DY.   (sb)
    01423 724105
    http://www.charitylawassociation.org.uk
    Sec: Catherine Rustomji
○   *P; 'to advance the understanding of charity law; to act as a
    forum for charity law specialists to consult & be consulted in
    the field'
Gp Working parties: Responding to consultative documents;
    Examining areas of charity law in need of development
●   Mtgs - Joint project with NCVO & Liverpool University on the
    development of new legal structure for charities
M   600 f (solicitors, barristers, accountants, charities)

Charity Retail Association
    the trading name since 4 November 2010 of the **Association of
    Charity Shops**

Charity Tax Group   (CTG)   1980
■   Church House, Great Smith St, LONDON, SW1P 3AZ.   (hq)
    020 7222 1265   fax 020 7222 1250
    email info@ctrg.org.uk   http://www.ctrg.org.uk
    Chmn: Mike Parkinson
▲   Un-incorporated Society
○   *K; to campaign to relieve the tax burden on charities,
    particularly VAT
●   Conf - Mtgs - Res - Inf - LG
<   Eur Charities' C'ee on VAT [ECCVAT]
M   350 charities
×   2007 Charities' Tax Reform Group

**Charles Close Society for the Study of Ordnance Survey Maps
1980**
■   Sycamore Cottage, Chapel Lane, Harmston, LINCOLN,
    LN5 9TB.   (hsp)
    http://www.charlesclosesociety.org.uk
    Official address (not for normal correspondence):
    c/o Map Library, British Library, 96 Euston Rd, LONDON,
    NW1 2DB.
    Hon Sec: Rob Wheeler
▲   Registered Charity
○   *L; to promote interest in, & research into, the maps, plans &
    other activities of the Ordnance Surveys of Great Britain &
    Ireland.
    The Society is named after Col Sir Charles Close, Director of
    the Ordnance Survey 1911-1922
●   Mtgs - Res - Exhib - SG - Inf - VE
M   477 i, 6 f, 14 org, UK / 10 i, o'seas
¶   Sheetlines (Jnl/NL) - 3; ftm.
    Publications mainly on the 1 inch Ordnance Survey maps.

Charles Lamb Society   1935
■   28 Grove Lane, LONDON, SE6 8ST.
    Chmn: Nicholas Powell
○   *L; to study the life, works & times of Charles Lamb (Elia) & his
    circle; to stimulate the Elian spirit of friendliness & humour

Charles Rennie Mackintosh Society   (CRM Soc)   1973
■   The Mackintosh Church, 870 Garscube Rd, GLASGOW,
    G20 7EL.   (hq)
    0141-946 6600   fax 0141-946 7276
    email info@crmsociety.com   http://www.crmsociety.com
    Dir: Stuart Robertson
▲   Company Limited by Guarantee
Br 4
○   *G, *L; the conservation & improvement of the buildings &
    artifacts designed by Mackintosh & his contemporaries; the
    society's address is that of the only church designed by
    Mackintosh to be built
●   ET - Exhib - SG - Inf - Lib - VE
<   l'Assn Charles Rennie Mackintosh en Rousillon (Port Vendres)
M   1,257 i, UK / 311 i, o'seas
¶   Jnl - 2; ftm, £5 nm.

Charles Williams Society   1976
- ■ 35 Broomfield, Stacey Bushes, MILTON KEYNES, Bucks, MK12 6HA.   (hsp)
  01908 316779
  email charles_wms_soc@yahoo.co.uk
  http://www.charleswilliamssociety.org.uk
  Hon Sec: Dr R L Sturch
- ▲ Registered Charity
- ○ *A; research into, & encouragement of the study of, the life & work of the author, lay theologian & poet Charles Walter Stansby Williams (1886-1945)
- ● Conf - Mtgs - SG - Lib
- < Alliance of Literary Socs
- M 92 i, UK / 37 i, 3 org, o'seas
- ¶ Charles Williams Quarterly - 4.

Charlotte M Yonge Fellowship   (CMYF)   1995
- ■ 8 Anchorage Terrace, DURHAM, DH1 3DL.   (hsp)
  0191-384 7857
  email c.e.schultze@durham.ac.uk
  http://www.cmyf.org.uk
  Mem Sec: Dr Clemence E Schultze
- ▲ Un-incorporated Society
- Br USA
- ○ *A; to provide a forum for all who enjoy reading the work of Charlotte M Yonge; to offer opportunities to learn more about her life & writings
- ● Conf - Mtgs - Res
- < Alliance of Literary Socs
- M 160 i, UK / 30 i, o'seas
- ¶ Review - 2; ftm.   Jnl - 1; £9.

Charmoise Hill Sheep Society
- NR Llandinam Hall, LLANDINAM, Powys, SY17 5DN.   (hsp)
  01686 688234
  http://www.charmoisesheep.co.uk
  Hon Sec: David Trow
- ○ *B
- < Nat Sheep Assn
- M 17 i

Chart & Nautical Instrument Trade Association   (CNITA)   1918
- NR Luther Pendragon, Priory Court, Pilgrim St, LONDON, EC4V 6DR.
  020 7618 9178
  email info@cnita.com   http://www.cnita.com
- ○ *T; suppliers of equipment & information to national & merchant navies
- Gp Admiralty chart agents; Magnetic compass manufacturers; Magnetic compass adjusters; Nautical publishers; Nautical instrument manufacturers & stockists
- ● Conf - Mtgs - Exam
- < Brit Standards Instn
- M 9 i, 14 f, UK / 19 f, o'seas
- ¶ LM - 1; ftm.

Charter 88
   see **Unlock Democracy (incorporating Charter 88)**

Chartered Accountants Ireland   1888
- IRL Chartered Accountants House, 47-49 Pearse St, DUBLIN 2, Republic of Ireland.   (hq)
  353 (1) 637 7200   fax 353 (1) 668 0842
  email charteredaccountants.ie
- Br 11 Donegall Square South, Belfast, BT1 5JE.
  028 9032 1600
- ○ *P
- ✕ 2009 Institute of Chartered Accountants in Irelamd

Chartered Banker Institute
   the trading name of the **Chartered Institute of Bankers of Scotland**

Chartered Institute of Arbitrators   (CIArb)   1915
- ■ International Arbitration & Mediation Centre, 12 Bloomsbury Sq, LONDON, WC1A 2LP.   (hq)
  020 7421 7444   fax 020 7404 4023
  email info@ciarb.org   http://www.ciarb.org
  Dir Gen: Michael Forbes-Smith
- ▲ Registered Charity
- Br 13; 18
- ○ *P; promote & facilitate the determination of disputes by arbitration & alternate forms of dispute resolution
- M i
- ¶ Arbitration (Jnl) - 4; ftm.
  NL - 4;   LM - 1; both ftm.   AR - 1; free.

Chartered Institute of Architectural Technologists   (CIAT)   1965
- ■ 397 City Rd, LONDON, EC1V 1NH.   (hq)
  020 7278 2206   fax 020 7837 3194
  email info@ciat.org.uk   http://www.ciat.org.uk
  Chief Exec: Mrs Francesca Berriman
- ▲ Company Limited by Guarantee
- Br 15; Republic of Ireland, Hong Kong
- ○ *P; qualifying body for professionals in architectural technology
- ● Conf - Mtgs - ET - Res - Exhib - Comp - Inf - LG
- < Soc for the Envt (SocEnv)
- M 6,500 i, UK / 500 i, o'seas
- ¶ Architectural Technology (Jnl) - 6; ftm, £2 nm.
  Directory of Practices - 1;   Membership Booklet - 1;
  The Architectural Technology Careers Hbk - 1;   AR - 1;
  all free.
- ✕ 2005 British Institute of Architectural Technologists

Chartered Institute of Bankers in Scotland   1875
- NR Drumsheugh House, 38b Drumsheugh Gardens, EDINBURGH, EH3 7SW.   (hq)
  0131-473 7777   fax 0131-473 7788
  http://www.charteredbanker.com
- ○ *L, *P
- M 12,500 i, 4 f
  Note: uses the trading name Chartered Banker Institute

Chartered Institute of Building   (CIOB)   1834
- ■ Englemere, Kings Ride, ASCOT, Berks, SL5 7TB.   (hq)
  01344 630700   fax 01344 630777
  email reception@ciob.org.uk   http://www.ciob.org.uk
  Chief Exec: Chris Blythe
- ▲ Incorporated by Royal Charter; Registered Charity
- Br 8; Australia, China, Hong Kong, Ireland, Malaysia, South Africa
- ○ *P; promotion of the science & practice of building
- Gp Architecture & Surveying Institute; FM Society
- ● Mtgs - ET - Exam - Res - Exhib - Comp - Inf - Lib - LG
- < Soc for the Envt (SocEnv)
- M 33,500 i, 470 f, UK / 7,650 i, o'seas
- ¶ Construction Manager - 10; ftm, £50 nm.   AR; free.
  Construction Information Quarterly - 4; £38 (£44 o'seas) m, £88 nm.
  Contact (NL) - 6; ftm only.

Chartered Institute of Educational Assessors   (CIEA)   2005
- NR c/o 55-56 Butts Rd, COVERNTRY, Warks, CV1 3BH.
  fax 020 7788 3456
  http://www.ciea.org.uk
- ▲ Registered Charity
- ○ *P
- ✕ 2008 (2 April) Institute of Educational Assessors

© CBD Research Ltd · Beckenham · BR3 5JS · Tel 020 8650 7745 · E-mail cbd@cbdresearch.com · www.cbdresearch.com

Chartered Institute of Environmental Health   (CIEH)   1883
NR   Chadwick Court, 15 Hatfields, LONDON, SE1 8DJ.   (hq)
        020 7928 6006
        http://www.cieh.org
▲   Registered Charity
○   *P; the promotion of environmental health & dissemination of
        knowledge about environmental issues
M   8,700 i

Chartered Institute of Housing   (CIoH)   1965
NR   Octavia House, Westwood Way, COVENTRY, Warks, CV4 8JP.
        (hq)
        024 7685 1700   fax 024 7669 5110
        email customer.services@cih.org   http://www.cih.org
        Chief Exec: Sarah Webb
▲   Registered Charity
○   *P; to promote the provision & management of good quality
        housing for all through education & continuing professional
        development
●   Conf - Mtgs - ET - Exam - SG - LG
M   c 10,500 i, UK / c 1,000 i, o'seas
¶   Housing - 12; ftm.

Chartered Institute of Internal Auditors   (IIA)
NR   13 Abbeville Mews, 88 Clapham Park Rd, LONDON,
        SW4 7BX.   (hq)
        020 7498 0101   fax 020 7978 2492
        email info@iia.org.uk   http://www.iia.org.uk
        Chief Exec: Ian Peters
○   *P; to promote the role & value of internal audit
M   i
¶   Internal Auditing & Business Risk - 12.
        Various other publications.
✕   2010 Institute of Internal Auditors

Chartered Institute for IT
        see **BCS, the Chartered Institute for IT**

Chartered Institute of Journalists   (IOJ)   1890
NR   2 Dock Offices, Surrey Quays Rd, LONDON, SE16 2XU.   (hq)
        020 7252 1187   fax 020 7232 2302
▲   Un-incorporated Society
○   *P; for all journalists - freelance, national & provincial
        newspaper, press & public relations, international,
        parliamentary & broadcasting
<   Creators' Rights Alliance
M   i
¶   The Jnl - 6; ftm only.

Chartered Institute of Library & Information Professionals
        see **CILIP**

Chartered Institute of Linguists   (IoL)   1910
■   Saxon House, 48 Southwark St, LONDON, SE1 1UN.   (hq)
        020 7940 3100   fax 020 7940 3101
        email info@iol.org.uk   http://www.iol.org.uk
        Chief Exec: John Hammond
▲   Company Limited by Guarantee
○   *P
Gp   National Register of Public Service Interpreters
●   ET - Exam - Interpreting - Translating - Production
M   5,000 i, UK / 1,500 i, o'seas
¶   The Linguist - 6; ftm, £39 yr nm.

Chartered Institute of Logistics & Transport Ireland
IRL   1 Fitzwilliam Place, DUBLIN 2, Republic of Ireland.
        353 (1) 676 3188   fax 353 (1) 676 4099
        email info@cilt.ie   http://www.cilt.ie
        Chief Exec: Colm Holmes
○   *P; to advance & promote the science & art of logistics &
        transport

**Chartered Institute of Logistics & Transport in the UK
(CILT(UK))   1990**
NR   Earlstrees Court, Earlstrees Rd, CORBY, Northants,
        NN17 4AX.   (hq)
        01536 740100
▲   Company Limited by Guarantee; Registered Charity
○   *P; to promote & develop the concept of logistics & transport
M   2,1450 i, 284 f, UK / 1,767 i, o'seas
        Note: in 2004 the individual members of the British
        International Freight Association became the CILT(UK) Freight
        Forwarding Forum

Chartered Institute of Loss Adjusters   (CILA)   1942
NR   Warwick House, 65-66 Queen St, LONDON, EC4R 1EB.   (hq)
        020 7337 9960
        http://www.cila.co.uk
        Exec Dir: Graham Cave
▲   Un-incorporated Society
Br   Australia
○   *P
●   Conf - ET - Exam - SG - Lib
M   2,600 i, UK / 400 i, o'seas
¶   Jnl;   NL;   AR;   Books & Technical Bulletins - all irreg;
        prices vary.

**Chartered Institute of Management Accountants   (CIMA)
1919**
NR   26 Chapter St, LONDON, SW1P 4NP.   (hq)
        020 8849 2251
        http://www.cimaglobal.com
○   *P; to promote the science of financial management & cost
        accounting
M   137,000 i

Chartered Institute of Marketing   (CIM)   1911
■   Moor Hall, Cookham, MAIDENHEAD, Berks, SL6 9QH.   (hq)
        01628 427120   fax 01628 427158
        http://www.cim.co.uk
        Chief Exec: Rod Wilkes
▲   Incorporated by Royal Charter; Registered Charity
Br   12; Australia, Ghana, Hong Kong, Kenya, Malawi, Malaysia,
        Malta, New Zealand, Poland, Singapore, Sri Lanka
○   *P; 'the world's largest organisation for professional marketers,
        play[s] a key role in training, developing & representing [the]
        profession'
Gp   Hotel Marketing Association
●   Conf - Mtgs - ET - Exam - Res - Exhib - Stat - Inf - Lib
<   World Marketing Assn (WMA); Eur Marketing Coun (EMC); The
        CAM Foundation
>   CAM Foundation
M   39,175 i, 75 f, org, UK / 16,035 i, o'seas
¶   the marketer - 10.

Chartered Institute of Patent Attorneys   (CIPA)   1882
NR   95 Chancery Lane (3rd floor), LONDON, WC2A 1DT.   (hq)
      020 7405 9450
         email mail@cipa.org.uk   http://www.cipa.org.uk
      Press & PR: Peter Prowse
▲   Incorporated by Royal Charter
○   *P; protection of industrial property - patents, trade marks,
      designs, copyright
●   Conf - Mtgs - ET - Exam - Inf
M   2,800 i, UK / 220 i, o'seas
¶   CIPA (Jnl) - 12.   LM.
      Register of Patent Agents - 1.
      CIPA Directory of Patent Agents.
×   2006 Chartered Institute of Patent Agents

Chartered Institute of Payroll Professionals   (IPP)   1985
■   Shelly House, Farmhouse Way, Monkspath, SOLIHULL,
      W Midlands, B90 4EH.   (hq)
      0121-712 1000   fax 0121-712 1001
         email info@cipp.org.uk   http://www.cipp.org.uk
      Chief Exec: Lindsay Melvin
▲   Company Limited by Guarantee
○   *P
Gp   CIPP Consult; Representations to government by the Pay &
      Policy Team
●   Conf - Mtgs - ET - Exam - Res - Exhib - SG - LG - Advisory
      service for members
M   5,000 i, UK / 300 i, o'seas
      (Sub: £116 UK / £142 o'seas)
¶   Payroll Professional - 10; ftm, £100 nm.
×   2010 Institute of Payroll Professionals
      2006 Institute of Payroll & Pensions Management

Chartered Institute of Personnel & Development   (CIPD)   1913
■   151 The Broadway, LONDON, SW19 1JQ.   (hq)
      020 8612 6200   fax 020 8612 6201
         email cipd@cipd.co.uk   http://www.cipd.co.uk
      Chief Exec: Geoff Armstrong
Br   48; Ireland
○   *P; promotion of the art & science of the management &
      development of people for the public benefit
●   Conf - Mtgs - ET - Exam - Res - Exhib - Inf - Lib - LG
<   Intl Fedn of Training & Devt Orgs; Wld [& Eur] Fedn of
      Personnel Mgt Assns; Eur Training & Devt Fedn
M   119,784 i, 5,046 f, UK / 4,000 i, o'seas
¶   People Management - 12.   AR.

**Chartered Institute of Plumbing & Heating Engineering
(CIPHE)   1906**
NR   64 Station Lane, HORNCHURCH, Essex, RM12 6NB.   (hq)
      01708 472791
      Chief Exec & Sec: Blane Judd
▲   Company Limited by Guarantee; Registered Charity
○   *L, *P, *T; to advance the science & practice of plumbing &
      heating engineering in the public interest
M   1,3647 i, 278 f, UK / 526 i, 10 f, o'seas

Chartered Institute of Public Finance & Accountancy
      see **CIPFA - the Chartered Institute of Public Finance &
      Accountancy**

Chartered Institute of Public Relations   (CIPR)   1948
■   Public Relations Centre, 52-53 Russell Square, LONDON,
      WC1B 4HP.   (hq)
      020 7631 6900   fax 020 7631 6944
         email info@cipr.co.uk   http://www.cipr.co.uk
      Chief Exec: Jane Wilson
▲   Incorporated by Royal Charter
Br   13 regional
○   *P; to represent the PR industry
Gp   Construction & property; Corporate & financial; Education &
      skills; Government affairs; Health & medical; Internal
      comunications; International PR; Marketing &
      communications; Motor industry; Science, engineering &
      technology; Voluntary sector; Women in PR
●   Conf - ET - Exam - Res - Exhib - Lib
<   Global Alliance for PR & Communication Mgt; Confédn Eur de
      Relations Publiques (CERP)
M   7,800 i, UK / 377 i, o'seas
¶   Profile (Jnl) - 6; ftm, £55 yr nm.
      Annual Review; ftm, free online nm.

Chartered Institute of Purchasing & Supply   (CIPS)   1932
■   Easton House, Easton on the Hill, STAMFORD, Lincs,
      PE9 3NZ.   (hq)
      01780 756777   fax 01780 751610
         email info@cips.org   http://www.cips.org
      Chief Exec: Simon Sperryn
▲   Registered Charity
Br   40; 16
○   *L, *P; raising standards in purchasing & supply chain
      management
●   Conf - ET - Exam - Res - EXhib - Inf - LG
M   27,600 i, UK / 18,100 i, o'seas
      (Sub: £125 UK / £88 o'seas)
¶   Supply Management - 26; ftm, £110 nm.

Chartered Institute for Securities & Investment   1992
NR   8 Eastcheap, LONDON, EC3M 1AE.   (hq)
      020 7645 0600   fax 020 7645 0601
      http://www.cisi.org
      Chief Exec: Simon Culhane
▲   Company Limited by Guarantee; Registered Charity
○   *P; for qualified & experienced practitioners of good standing in
      securities, derivatives & related areas of investment business;
      to set & improve standards through training & qualifications
●   Conf - Mtgs - ET - Exam - Res - Lib - LG
M   16,000 i, UK / 1,000 i, o'seas
¶   Securities & Investment Review (Jnl) - 6; ftm.
      LM - 2; ftm.   Report & Accounts - 1; free.
×   2008-09 Securities & Investment Institute

Chartered Institute of Taxation   (CIOT)   1930
NR   Artillery House (1st floor), 11-19 Artillery Row, LONDON,
      SW1P 1RT.   (hq)
      020 7340 0550
      http://www.tax.org.uk
▲   Registered Charity
○   *P; for tax advisers
M   1,000 i, UK & o'seas

**Chartered Institution of Building Services Engineers   (CIBSE)
1897**
NR   222 Balham High Rd, LONDON, SW12 9BS.   (hq)
      020 8675 5211   fax 020 8675 5449
      http://www.cibse.org
      Chief Exec: Julian Amey
▲   Registered Charity
○   *P; the art, science & practice of engineering services
      associated with the built environment (incl heating,
      ventilating, air conditioning, lighting, public health, internal
      transportation, electrical services)
M   12,000 i, UK / 3,000 i, o'seas
¶   Building Services Jnl - 12.
      Lighting Research & Technology - 4.
      Building Services Engineering Research & Technology - 4.
      AR.   Publications list available.

Chartered Institution of Civil Engineering Surveyors   (ICES) 1969

NR   Dominion House, Sibson Rd, SALE, Cheshire, M33 7PP.   (hq)
        0161-972 3100   fax 0161-972 3118
        email admin@cices.org   http://www.cices.org
        Admin: Simeon Payne & Serena Ronan
▲   Company Limited by Guarantee; Registered Charity
○   *P; the qualification & regulation of geospatial engineering
        surveyors (land surveyors) & commercial managers (quantity
        surveyors)
●   Conf - Mtgs - ET - Exam - Res - Exhib - Stat - Inf - Lib
<   Intl Fedn Surveyors (FIG); Construction Ind Coun; Instn Civil
        Engrs
M   3,100 i, UK / 400 i, o'seas
¶   Civil Engineering Surveyor (Jnl) - 12.
        Construction & Law Review - 1.   .
        Reference Manual for Construction Plant - 3/4 yrly.
×   2009 Institution of Civil Engineering Surveyors

Chartered Institution of Highways & Transportation   (CIHT) 1930

■   119 Britannia Walk, LONDON, N1 7JE.   (hq)
        020 7336 1550
        http://www.ciht.org.uk
        Chief Exec: Sue Percy
▲   Company Limited by Guarantee; Registered Charity
Br   18; Hong Kong, Malaysia, Republic of Ireland, United Arab
        Emirates
○   *P; to advance for the public benefit the science & art
        associated with highways & transportation in all their aspects;
        to promote the education, training & research & development
        of the said science & art
●   Conf - Mtgs - ET - Exhib - Expt - Inf - VE - LG
M   12,000 i
¶   Transportation Professional - 10; ftm, £67.
×   7 December 2009 Institution of Highways & Transportation

Chartered Institution of Wastes Management   (CIWM)   1898

NR   9 Saxon Court, St Peter's Gardens, NORTHAMPTON,
        NN1 1SX.   (hq)
        01604 620426   fax 01604 621339
        email ciwm@ciwm.co.uk   http://www.ciwm.co.uk
        Chief Exec: Steve Lee
▲   Company incorporated by Royal Charter; Registered Charity
Br   10
○   *L, *P; promotion of scientific, technical & practical aspects of
        wastes management
Gp   Reclamation; Recycling; Regulation; Street cleansing; Treatment
        & disposal; Waste collection
●   Conf - Mtgs - ET - Exhib - Inf - Lib - VE - LG
<   Eur C'ee Waste Mgt Org; WHO; Inst of Solid Wastes
        Assn (ISWA); Waste Mgt Ind Training & Advy Bd (WAMITAB);
        Soc for the Envt (SocEnv)
M   6,123 i, 346 f, UK / 390 i, 8 f, o'seas
¶   Wastes Management (Jnl) - 12, ftm, £84 yr nm.
        News On-line (NL on Web page) - 52;   AR; both free.
        CIWM Register of Consultants - 1; ftm, £15 nm.
        Technical publications, Codes of practice, Advice notes.
        Note: The Institution administers a Registered Environmental
        Body - CIWM(EB)

Chartered Institution of Water & Environmental Management (CIWEM) 1895

■   15 John St, LONDON, WC1N 2EB.   (hq)
        020 7831 3110   fax 020 7405 4967
        email admin@ciwem.org   http://www.ciwem.org
        Exec Dir: Nick Reeves
▲   Registered Charity; Incorporated by Royal Charter
Br   14 in UK; Hong Kong; Republic of Ireland
○   *P; to advance the science & practice of water & environmental
        management & sustainable development
Gp   Environment; Rivers & coastal; Scientific
●   Conf - Mtgs - ET - Exam - Exhib - SG - Inf - VE
<   Water Envt Fedn (WEF); Eur Water Assn (EWA); Soc for the
        Envt (SocEnv)
M   9,900 i, UK / 1,300 i, o'seas
¶   Jnl - 4; ftm, £165 yr nm.
        Water & Environment Manager - 10; ftm, £98 yr nm.
        Manuals & handbooks - list available.

Chartered Insurance Institute   (CII)   1912

■   42-48 High Rd, South Woodford, LONDON, E18 2JP.   (hq)
        020 8989 8464   fax 020 8530 3052
        email customer.serv@cii.co.uk   http://www.cii.co.uk
        Dir: Sandy Scott
○   *P; for those working in the insurance & financial services
        industry
●   Conf - Mtgs - ET - Exam - Res - SG - Stat - Inf - Lib - LG
M   79,000 i, UK / 13,000 i, o'seas

Chartered Management Institute   (CMI)   1992

NR   Management House, Cottingham Rd, CORBY, Northants,
        NN17 1TT.   (hq)
        01536 204222   fax 01536 201651
        email membership@managers.org.uk
        http://www.managers.org.uk
        Chief Exec: Ruth Spellman
▲   Company Limited by Guarantee; Registered Charity
Br   90; Hong Kong, Malaysia, Singapore, Sri Lanka
○   *P; to promote the art & science of management
Gp   Institute of Consulting; Police Professional Network; Women in
        Management Network (WiMN)
●   ET - Res - Inf - Lib - LG
<   Eur Foundation for Mgt Devt; Conseil Eur du Comité Intl de
        l'Org Scientifique (CECIOS)
M   65,000 i, 300 f, UK / 5,500 i, o'seas
¶   Professional Manager - 6; ftm, £3.60 nm.   AR; free.

Chartered Quality Institute   (CQI)   1919

■   12 Grosvenor Crescent, LONDON, SW1X 7EE.   (hq)
        020 7245 6722   fax 020 7245 6844
        email info@thecqi.org   http://www.thecqi.org
        Chief Exec: Simon Feary
▲   Company Limited by Guarantee; Registered Charity
Br   29; Australia, Hong Kong, Singapore
○   *L, *P; 'to promote the benefits of quality generally throughout
        the UK & international marketplace by being an active &
        vocal advocate of quality, by developing & disseminating
        quality knowledge & practices & through the competent
        quality professionals who are our members. We believe that
        quality approaches are a fundamental prerequisite for
        sustainable business where survival & success requires
        innovation in product & service, combined with reduction in
        cost & a socially responsible approach'
Gp   Defence industry; Deming; Digital; Engineering; Integrated
        management; Medical technologies; Nuclear;
        Pharmaceuticals; Quality; Standards development;
●   Conf - Mtgs - ET - Exam - Exhib - Res - Inf - Lib - LG
<   Brit Quality Fedn; Inst of Customer Services; London Excellence;
        Eur Org for Quality (EOQ)
M   4,091 i (members), 2,801 i (associates), 1,029 i (fellow), 144 f
        (Subs: £123 (members), £101 (associates), £142 (fellows))
        (Subs for f: on request)
¶   Quality World - 12; ftm, £66 nm.
        Pharmaceutical quality group publications:
            A: Good Quality Control Laboratory Practice;
            B: Pharmaceutical Auditing;
            C: Pharmaceutical Distribution;
            D: Elements & Philosophy of Pharmaecutical QA;
            E: Pharmaceutical Manufacturing;
            F: Pharmaceutical Premises & Environment;
            G: Cleaning Validation;
            H: Pharmaceutical Packaging Validation;
            I: Pharmaceutical Documentation;
            J: Pharmaceutical Contract Manufacture; all £30.
        Forward (e-newsletter).
        Pocket guides; further information available on website.
×   2006 Institute of Quality Assurance

Chartered Society of Designers (CSD) 1930

- ■ 1 Cedar Court, Royal Oak Yard, Bermondsey St, LONDON, SE1 3GA. (hq)
  020 7357 8088   fax 020 7407 9878
  email info@csd.org.uk   http://www.csd.org.uk
  Chief Exec: Frank Peters
- ▲ Registered Charity
- Br Regional Gps; Hong Kong
- ○ *P
- Gp Design: Exhibition, Fashion, Graphic, Interactive, Interior, Product, Textile
  Design education; Design management
- ● Mtgs - ET - Res - Comp - SG - Expt - Inf - LG
- < Design Assn
- > Design Assn
- M 3,000 i, UK / 250 i, o'seas
- ¶ The Designer - 4; ftm, £5 nm.
  Various professional publications - list available.

Chartered Society of Physiotherapy (CSP) 1894

- ■ 14 Bedford Row, LONDON, WC1R 4ED.   (hq)
  020 7306 6666   fax 020 7306 6611
  email enquiries@csp.org.uk   http://www.csp.org.uk
  Chief Exec: Phil Gray
- ▲ Registered Charity; Un-incorporated Society
- Br 4
- ○ *E, *P, *U; for chartered physiotherapists, students & assistants
- Gp 35 clinical interest groups
- ● Conf - Mtgs - ET - Res - Exhib - Expt - Inf - Lib - Empl - LG
- < Wld Confedn Physical Therapy (WCPT); Trades U Congress (TUC); Allied Health Professions Fedn (AHPF)
- M 36,101 i
- ¶ Physiotherapy - 4; ftm, rates vary nm.   AR - 1; free.
  Frontline - 26; ftm, £74.90 (UK), £110.20 o'seas.

Chase Chamber of Commerce

- ■ Point East, Park Plaza, Hayes Way, CANNOCK, Staffs, WS12 2DB. (hq)
  0845 071 0191
  email info@chase-chamber.com
  http://www.chase-chamber.com
- ▲ Company Limited by Guarantee
- ○ *C
- ● Mtgs - ET - Res - Stat - Expt - Inf - Lib - VE - LG
- < Birmingham Cham Comm; Brit Chams Comm
- ¶ Chamberlink - 10;   AR; both ftm.

Chatham House
the registered name of the **Royal Institute of International Affairs**

Cheltenham Chamber of Commerce

- NR 2 Trafalgar St, CHELTENHAM, Glos, GL50 1UH. (hq)
  01242 252626
  email info@cheltenhamchamber.org.uk
  http://www.cheltenhamchamber.org.uk
  Chief Exec: Michael Ratcliffe
- ○ *C
- < Gloucestershire Cham of Comm & Ind

Chemical Business Association (CBA) 1923

- ■ Lyme Building, Westmere Drive, Crewe Business Park, CREWE, Cheshire, CW1 6ZD. (hq)
  01270 258200   fax 01270 258444
  email cba@chemical.org.uk
  http://www.chemical.org.uk
  Dir: Peter Newport
- ○ *T; interests of chemical distributors & specialist service companies
- ● Conf - Mtgs - ET - Exhib - Stat Inf - LG
- < Fédn Européenne du Commerce Chimique (FECC); Alliance of Ind Assns (AIA)
- M 120 f
- ¶ Outlook (technical document) - 12; Outlook (NL) - 3; both ftm only.
  Where to Buy Directory - 1.
- × 2006 (September) British Chemical Distributors & Traders Association

Chemical Distribution Ireland (CDI) 1994

- IRL Confederation House, 84-86 Lower Baggot St, DUBLIN 2, Republic of Ireland.   (hq)
  353 (1) 605 1625   fax 353 (1) 638 1625
  email nessa.moyles@ibec.ie   http://www.ibec.ie
  Contact: Nessa Moyles
- ○ *P; to promote, support & encourage the development of the multinational & indigenous chemical distribution sector in Ireland
- < Eur Assn of Chemical Distbrs (FECC); Ir Business & Emplrs Confedn (IBEC)
- × 2009 Irish Chemical Marketers Association

Chemical Hazards Communication Society (CHCS) 1994

- ■ PO Box 222, LYMINGTON, Hants, SO42 7GY.   (chmn/p)
  0844 636 2427   fax 0844 636 2428
  email chcs@chcs.org.uk   http://www.chcs.org.uk
  Chmn & Mem Sec: Desmond Waight
- ▲ Un-incorporated Society
- ○ *P; to promote awareness of chemical hazards & improvements in their identification & communication; to provide a forum for sharing experiences, views & information; to promote the need for specific training & aim toward setting of competency standards
- ● Conf - Mtgs - Exhib - SG
- M 450 i, UK / 20 i, o'seas
- ¶ NL - 3/4;   LM - 1; both ftm only.

Chemical & Industrial Consultants Association (CICA) 1988

- ■ Rosemead, Proffits Lane, FRODSHAM, Cheshire, WA6 9JX.   (hsp)
  01928 722095
  email secretary@chemical-consultants.co.uk
  http://www.chemical-consultants.co.uk
  Hon Sec: Dr P Smallwood
- ▲ Un-incorporated Society
- ○ *L, *T; a networking group of independent, self-employed consultants serving the chemical & industrial community
- ● Mtgs - Res - Exhib - Inf
- M 40 i
  (Sub: £40)
- ¶ LM; on website.

Chemical Industries Association Ltd (CIA) 1965

■ Kings Buildings, Smith Sq, LONDON, SW1P 3JJ.   (hq)
  020 7834 3399   fax 020 7834 4469
  email enquiries@cia.org.uk   http://www.cia.org.uk
  Chief Exec: Steve Elliott
▲ Company Limited by Guarantee
○ *T; to represent UK chemical & allied industries to relevant
  shareholders; to support members in achieving economic,
  social & environmental sustainability, labour & technical
  fields affecting interests of members
Gp GOSIP; Hydrogen fluoride, Speciality biocides
● Conf - Mtgs - Stat - Expt - LG
< Eur Chemistry Ind C'ee (CEFIC);
> Food Additives & Ingredients Assn; Nat Sulphuric Acid Assn
M 135 f, 20 org
¶ CIA Matters - 10;   CIA Bulletin (email) - 52; both ftm only.
  AR & Accounts - 1; free.

Chemical Recycling Association (CRA) 1998

■ 62 Lower St, STANSTED, Essex, CM24 8LR.   (hsp)
  01279 814035   fax 01279 814035
  email chemrecycass@aol.com
  Hon Sec: Roger Creswell
○ *T; to promote, protect, represent & otherwise assist the
  members engaged in the recovery, recycling &/or re-use of
  contaminated chemicals, including secondary fuels
● Mtgs - Stat - Inf - LG
M 5 f
¶ NL - 4; ftm only.

Chemists' Defence Association
  since 2007 is NPA Insurance Ltd, a section of the **National
  Pharmacy Association**

Cherished Numbers Dealers Association
  a group of the **Retail Motor Industry Federation**

Cheshaght Ghailckagh (the Manx Gaelic Society) 1899

■ 16 Hilary Rd, DOUGLAS, Isle of Man, IM2 3EG.   (hsp)
  01624 623821
  email bstowell@mcb.net   http://www.ycg.iofm.net
  Hon Sec: Dr T Brian Stowell
▲ Company Limited by Guarantee
Br 102; Isle of Man
○ *K, *L; preservation & revival of Manx Gaelic
● Conf - Mtgs - ET - Inf - LG - Publishing books
M 140 i, UK (incl 102 i, Isle of Man) / 13 i, o'seas
¶ Dhooraght (NL) - ftm only.

Cheshire Agricultural Society (CAS) 1838

NR Clay House Farm, Flittogate Lane, Tabley, KNUTSFORD,
  Cheshire, WA16 0HJ.   (hq)
  01565 650200   fax 01565 650540
  email nevans@cheshirecountyshow.org.uk
  http://www.cheshirecountyshow.org.uk
  Exec Dir: Nigel Evans
▲ Registered Charity
○ *F, *H; to encourage agricultural enterprise; to improve the
  breeding, rearing & health of livestock
● Exhib - Comp
< Assn Show & Agricl Orgs
M 1,300 i
¶ Schedule of Classes - 1; free.   AR; ftm only.
  Show Catalogue of Entries - 1; £3.
  Programme of Events - 1; £2.

Chess Arbiters' Association (CAA) 1990

NR 11 Lilford St, LEIGH, Lancs, WN7 4JN.   (hsp)
  01942 604262
  email chessarbiters@googlemail.com
  http://www.chessarbiters.co.uk
  Sec: Geoff Jones
○ *P; to encourage a high standard of arbiting at all chess events;
  to review & standardise the rules for various types of
  competition
● ET - Exam

Chess Scotland (CS) 2001

■ 60 Baberton Crescent, Juniper Green, EDINBURGH,
  EH14 5BP.   (memsec/p)
  email membership@chessscotland.com
  http://www.chessscotland.com
  Mem Sec: Dick Heathwood
▲ Registered Charity; Un-incorporated Society
○ *G; to foster & promote the game of chess throughout Scotland
  among players of all ages
● Comp - ET - Inf - Mtgs
< Eur Chess U (ECU); Wld Chess Fedn (FIDE)
M 575 i
¶ Scottish Chess - 6.

Chester Archaeological Society (CAS) 1849

NR 20 The Yonne, City Walls Rd, CHESTER, CH1 2NH.   (hsb)
  01244 327750
  http://www.chesterarchaeolsoc.org.uk
  Hon Sec: Alan Williams (01244 310563)
▲ Registered Charity
○ *L; study of archaeology, history & architecture of Chester,
  Cheshire & N Wales

Chester, Ellesmere Port & North Wales Chamber of Commerce
  see **West Cheshire & North Wales Chamber of Commerce**

Chesterfield Canal Trust Ltd (CCT) 1998

NR 18 Barncliffe Crescent, Lodge Moor, SHEFFIELD, S Yorks,
  S10 4DA.   (sp)
  0114-229 5355
  http://www.chesterfield-canal-trust.org.uk
  Sec: Martin Bloomfield
▲ Company Limited by Guarantee; Registered Charity
○ *G; to make the Chesterfield canal fully navigational
M i, f & org

Chesterton Society (GKCSoc) 1964

■ 6 Sunningwell Rd, OXFORD, OX1 4SX.   (hsp)
  Treas: The Revd Simon Heans
▲ Registered Charity
○ *A; to promote interest & study of the works of G K Chesterton
  (1874-1936), critic, novelist & poet
● Lib
M 250 i, UK / 50 i, o'seas
¶ G K Quarterly - 4; £2.

Chetham Society for the Publication of Remains Historical & Literary Connected with the Palatinate Counties of Lancaster & Chester 1843

NR Alnwick Castle, ALNWICK, Northumberland, NE66 1NQ.
  (hsp)
  Hon Sec: Chris Hunwick
○ *L; to publish documents & monographs on the history of
  Lancashire & Cheshire
● Annual Mtg - Publication of records & monographs
< Brit Records Assn
M c 150 i, 100 universities & libraries, UK / 100 universities &
  libraries, o'seas
¶ Monograph / Record - c 1.

Cheviot Sheep Society 1891
- ■ Holm Cottage, LANGHOLM, Dumfriesshire, DG13 0JP. (sp)
  01387 380222
  email info@cheviotsheep.org
  http://www.cheviotsheep.org
  Sec: Isobel J McVittie
- ▲ Registered Charity
- ○ *B
- ● Mtgs
- < Nat Sheep Assn
- M 122 i
  (Sub: £15 + £20)
- ¶ Flock Book 1. NL. AR.

Chichester Chamber of Commerce & Industry (CCCI)
- ■ 3 Chapel St, CHICHESTER, W Sussex, PO19 1BU.
  01243 531765
  email office@chichestercci.org.uk
  http://www.chichestercci.org.uk
  Sec: Carylyn Webber-Walton
- ○ *C

Chief Building Surveyors Society 1975
- NR Property Services Client Support Unit, County Hall,
  WORCESTER, WR5 2NP. (sb)
  01905 766476
  email jburton@worcestershire.gov.uk
  Hon Treas: John Burton
- ○ *P; to share knowledge & experience & promote awareness of
  property maintenance & management within local
  government
- ● Mtgs - Stat - LG
- < Fedn Property Socs
- M c 80 i

Chief Cultural & Leisure Officers Association (CLOA) 1976
- NR Park Farm, HETHERSETT, Norfolk, NR9 3DL. (hq)
  0759 200 8710
  email sarahfoulkes@cloa.org.uk http://www.cloa.org.uk
  Policy Officer: David Albutt
  Admin: Sarah Gilvey (sarahgilvey@cloa.org.uk)
- ▲ Un-incorporated Society
- ○ *P; interest of arts, sports & recreation management; to
  represent chief leisure officers in England & Wales
- M 320 i & local authorities

Chief Fire Officers' Association (CFOA) 1974
- ■ 9-11 Pebble Close, Amington, TAMWORTH, Staffs, B77 4RD.
  (hq)
  01827 302300 fax 01827 302399
  email info@cfoa.org.uk http://www.cfoa.org.uk
  Gen Mgr: Steve Currey
- ▲ Company Limited by Guarantee
- ○ *P; 'to reduce the loss of life, personal injury & damage to
  property & the environment by improving the quality of
  firefighting, rescue, fire protection & fire prevention in the UK'
- Gp Policy c'ees: Appliances, equipment & uniform;
  Communications & computing; Fire safety; Health & safety;
  Operations; Personnel & training
- ● Conf - Mtgs - ET - Res - Exhib - Comp - Inf - LG - Serving on
  standards groups (BSI, CEN & ISO)
- < Fedn of Brit Fire Orgs (FBFO); Metrochiefs
- M 186 i

Chief Fire Officers Association Ireland
- IRL Limerick County Council, DOORADOYLE, Limerick, Republic of
  Ireland.
  353 (44) 943 1794
  http://www.cfoa.net
  Sec: Carmel Kirby
- ○ *P
- M i

Child Growth Foundation (CGF) 1977
- ■ 2 Mayfield Ave, LONDON, W4 1PW. (chmn/p)
  020 8995 0257 fax 020 8995 9075
  email info@childgrowthfoundation.org
  http://www.childgrowthfoundation.org
  Chmn: Tam Fry
- ▲ Registered Charity
- ○ *W; to seek regular growth assessment for every UK child; to
  ensure that every growth-related abnormality is immediately
  referred to an endocrine specialist for care of treatment
- ● Conf - Res
- M 1,100 i, UK / 25 i, o'seas
- ¶ NL - 2; ftm only.
  Publications list available.

Child Protection Special Interest Group
  a group of the **Royal College of Paediatrics & Child Health**

Child & Public Health Special Interest Group
  a group of the **Royal College of Paediatrics & Child Health**

Children 1st
  the working title of the **Royal Scottish Society for Prevention of
  Cruelty to Children**

Children's Books History Society (CBHS) 1969
- ■ 26 St Bernard's Close, BUCKFAST, S Devon, TQ11 0EP.
  (chmn/p)
  01364 643568
  email cbhs@abcgarrett.demon.co.uk
  Chmn: Mrs Pat Garrett
- ○ *G; to promote an appreciation of children's books; to study
  their history, bibliography & literary content
- ● Conf - Mtgs - Exhib - VE - Biennial Harvey Darton Award
- < Library Assn; Osborne Collection (Toronto, Canada)
- M Libraries & Universities
- ¶ NL - 3. Occasional papers - 1.

Children's Cancer & Leukaemia Group
  a group of the **Royal College of Paediatrics & Child Health**

Children's Chronic Arthritis Association (CCAA) 1990
- ■ Amber Gate, City Walls Rd, WORCESTER, WR1 2AH. (hq)
  01905 745595 fax 01905 745703
  email info@ccaa.org.uk http://www.ccaa.org.uk
  Gen Sec: Mrs Caroline Cox
- ▲ Registered Charity
- ○ *M, *W; to provide help & information for children with arthritis,
  their families & professionals involved in their care; to raise
  awareness of arthritis of childhood in the community
- ● Conf - Mtgs - ET - Inf - Annual support weekend for children
  with arthritis & their families
- M 2,000 i
- ¶ Joint Report (NL) - 2.
  Chat; Chat 2; Chat for Teachers; free on joining.

Children's Heart Association (CHA) 1973
- NR 22 Hesketh Drive, HESWALL, Wirral, CH60 5SP.
  01706 221988
  http://www.heartchild.info
- ▲ Registered Charity
- Br 7 in Scotland
- ○ *W; to give support & understanding in everyday care & welfare
  to parents & families of children with heart disorders; to raise
  money for research into congenital heart disorders; to
  improve facilities & maintain improvements in hospitals
- ● Mtgs - Inf - Family, teenage & young adult weekends - Fund
  raising
- < Heart Care
- M families
- ¶ Heart Beat - 2; free.
  Information pack; free for parents of a heart child.

Children's Hospices UK
    the working title of **Association of Children's Hospices**

Children in Hospital Ireland
IRL Carmichael Centre, Coleraine House, Coleraine St, DUBLIN 7,
     Republic of Ireland.
     353 (1) 878 0448   fax 353 (1) 873 5283
     email info@childreninhospital.ie
     Chief Exec: Mary O'Connor
○   *W

**Children Living with Inherited Metabolic Diseases   (CLIMB)
2000**
■   Climb Building, 176 Nantwich Rd, CREWE, Cheshire,
     CW2 6BG.   (hq)
     0845 241 2173
     email adm.vcs@climb.org.uk   http://www.climb.org.uk
     Chief Exec: Steve Hannigan
▲   Company Limited by Guarantee; Registered Charity
Br   5
○   *W; to.provide information & support, on over 700 metabolic
     diseases, to families & professionals
Gp   Metabolic
●   Conf - Mtgs - ET - Res - Inf
M   857 i, 52 org, UK / 64 i, 7 org, o'seas
¶   CLIMB Update - 4; £22 m.
     CLIMB book 100 metabolic diseases; £23.

Children's Rights Alliance for England   (CRAE)
NR   94 White Lion St, LONDON, N1 9PF.   (regd office)
     020 7278 8222   fax 020 7278 9552
     email info@crae.org.uk   http://www.crae.org.uk
○   *K

Children in Scotland   1983
■   Princes House, 5 Shandwick Place, EDINBURGH, EH2 4RG.
     (hq)
     0131-228 8484   fax 0131-228 8585
     email info@childreninscotland.org.uk
     http://www.childreninscotland.org.uk
     Chief Exec: Bronwen Cohen
○   *N, *W; Scotland's national agency for voluntary, statutory &
     professional organisations & individuals working with
     Scotland's children & their families
●   Conf - Mtgs - Res - SG - Stat - Inf - LG
<   Nat Children's Bureau; Children in Wales; Children in Northern
     Ireland
M   91 i, 373 org
¶   NL;   AR; both ftm.   Factsheets.
     List of publications on aspects of child & family policy.

Chilled Beam & Ceiling Association   (CCA)   1996
■   2 Waltham Court, Milley Lane, Hare Hatch, READING, Berks,
     RG10 9TH.   (hq)
     0118-940 3416   fax 0118-940 6258
     email info@feta.co.uk   http://www.feta.co.uk
     Dir Gen: C Sloan
○   *T; to promote the use of chilled beams & chilled ceilings &
     encourage best practice in their development & application
●   Mtgs
<   Heating, Ventilating & Air Conditioning Mfrs' Assn (HEVAC);
     Fedn Envtl Trade Assns (FETA)
M   14 f
¶   Chilled Ceilings (leaflet); free.
×   2008 Chilled Ceilings Association

Chilled Ceilings Association
    since 2008 **Chilled Beam & Ceiling Association**

Chilled Food Association Ltd   (CFA)   1989
■   PO Box 6434, KETTERING, Northants, NN15 5XT.   (hsb)
     01536 514365
     email cfa@chilledfood.org   http://www.chilledfood.org
     Sec Gen: Miss Kaarin Goodburn
▲   Company Limited by Guarantee
○   *T; to develop & promote common standards of safety & quality
     in the production & distribution of chilled prepared foods; to
     represent the key interests of manufacturers of chilled
     prepared foods
●   Mtgs - ET - Res - SG -LG
<   Eur Chilled Food Fedn (ECFF); Food & Drink Fedn; Food
     Northwest
>   North West Food Alliance
M   17 f
¶   Best Practice Guidelines for the Production of Chilled Foods -
     irreg; £80 m, £100 nm.
     Handwash (training poster) - irreg; £10 m, £25 nm.
     Water Quality Management - irreg; £40, £55 nm.
     Regulatory Guidance - irreg.

Chillingham Wild Cattle Association Ltd   1939
■   Warden's Cottage, Chillingham, ALNWICK, Northumberland,
     NE66 5NP.   (sp)
     01668 215250
     http://www.chillingham-wildcattle.org.uk
     Sec: Mrs A E Widdows
▲   Company Limited by Guarantee; Registered Charity
○   *B; a registered charity set up to ensure the survival of the
     Chillingham wild cattle in their own environment at
     Chillingham Park, Northumberland
●   Conservation - Open to visitors
M   400 i, UK / 30 i, o'seas
     (Sub: £15)
¶   NL - 3;   AR - 1; both ftm, sae nm.
     History leaflet - 1; £1.

China-Britain Business Council   (CBBC)   1991
■   Portland House (3rd floor), Bressenden Place, LONDON,
     SW1E 5BH.   (hq)
     020 7802 2000   fax 020 7802 2029
     email enquiries@cbbc.org   http://www.cbbc.org
     Chief Exec: Stephen Phillips
▲   Company Limited by Guarantee
Br   7; China
○   *T; to promote British business in China through seminars,
     missions to & from China & offices in China
●   Conf - Mtgs - Res - Exhib - Expt - Inf - Lib - LG
<   Dept for Business Enterprise & Regulatory Reform (BERR)
M   426 i, 447 f
     (Sub: £427 i, £705-£2,937.50)
¶   China-Britain Trade Review - 10; ftm, £100 nm.

Chinese Takeaway Association (UK)
    closed 2010

Chippendale Society   1963
NR   Last Cawthra Feather, 128 Sunbridge Rd, BRADFORD, W Yorks,
     BD1 2AT.   (hsb)
     01274 848800
     http://www.thechippendalesociety.co.uk
     Hon Sec: Simon Stell
▲   Registered Charity
○   *A, *L; to promote appreciation of the work of Thomas
     Chippendale (1718-1790) & the art of woodcarving
●   Mtgs - Exhib - Inf - VE to country houses - Lectures
M   400 i, 3 f, 2 org
¶   NL - 3/4; ftm.   Occasional publications.

Chiropractic Patients' Association (CPA) 1966
- ■ 8 Centre One, Lysander Way, Old Sarum Park, SALISBURY, Wilts, SP4 6BU. (hq)
  01722 415027   fax 01722 415028
  email cpa@centreonesarum.com
  http://www.chiropatients.org.uk
  Sec: Nastasya Blissett
- ▲ Registered Charity
- Br 1
- ○ *K, *W; to support chiropractic; to advance knowledge & increase awareness of chiropractic treatment
- ● Mtgs
- < Eur Fedn of Pro-Chiropractic Assns
- M 923 i
- ¶ Back Chat (NL) - 3; ftm only.

Chocolate, Confectionery & Biscuit Council of Ireland
a group of **Food & Drink Industry Ireland**

Chocolate Society 1987
- ■ Unit B1 Southgate, Commerce Park, FROME, BA11 2RY. (hq)
  01373 473335
  email info@chocolate.co.uk   http://www.chocolate.co.uk
  Chmn: Alan Porter
- ▲ Company Limited by Guarantee
- Br 3
- ○ *G; to promote awareness of & make available fine chocolate
- ● ET - Exhib - Inf
- M 5,000 i, UK / 500 i, o'seas
- ¶ NL.

Choice in Personal Safety (CIPS) 1983
- ■ Mount House, Urra, Chop Gate, MIDDLESBROUGH, TS9 7HZ. (chmn/p)
  01642 778302
  Chmn: Don Furness
- ▲ Un-incorporated Society
- ○ *G, *K; campaigning to repeal the seatbelt compulsion legislation, which our research has shown to be actuallly inimical to personal safety & is thereby a malign interference with freedom of choice
- ● Mtgs - LG
- < Soc for Individual Freedom; Assn of Brit Drivers
- M 40 i, UK / 3 i, o'seas
- ¶ Minutes of Meetings - 5; free.

Choir Schools Association (CSA) 1919
- NR Windrush, Church Rd, Market Weston, DISS, Norfolk, IP22 2NX. (inf/officer)
  01359 221333
  email info@choirschools.org.uk
  http://www.choirschools.org.uk
  Information Officer
- ▲ Registered Charity
- ○ *A, *E
- Gp Bursary trust (to ensure that no child is denied a choristership on financial grounds)
- ● Conf - Mtgs
- M 44 schools, UK / 4 schools, o'seas
- ¶ Choir Schools Today - 1; ftm.

Chopin Society 1971
- NR 44 Bassett Rd, LONDON, W10 6LJ. (hsp)
  020 8960 4027
  email info@chopin-society.org.uk
  http://www.chopin-society.org.uk
  Sec: Gillian Newman
- ▲ Registered Charity
- ○ *D; the promotion & appreciation of the music of Chopin & of piano music in general; to support the development of young pianists
- ● Mtgs - Exhib
- < Warsaw Chopin Soc (Poland); Chopin Foundation of the US (Miami, USA)
- M 230 i
- ¶ NL - 4; free.

Christian Education (CE) 2001
- ■ 1020 Bristol Rd, Selly Oak, BIRMINGHAM, W Midlands, B29 6LB. (hq)
  0121-472 4242   fax 0121-472 7575
  email enquiries@christianeducation.org.uk
  http://www.christianeducation.org.uk
  Chief Exec: Peter Fishpool
- ▲ Company Limited by Guarantee
- Br 25
- ○ *P; 'to promote Christian concerns in education generally & religious education in schools particularly'
- Gp Study & research
- ● Conf - ET - Res - Exhib - Comp - LG
- M 4,500 i, 6,500 associated schools
- ¶ Publications list available.

Christian Evidence Society (CES) 1870
- ■ 5 Vicarage Lane, CHELMSFORD, Essex, CM2 8HY. (hsp)
  01245 478038
  http://www.christianevidencesociety.org.uk
  Admin: Canon Harry Marsh
- ▲ Company Limited by Guarantee; Registered Charity
- ○ *R; a non-membership body for 'the proclamation, defence & study of the Christian Faith'
- ¶ Booklets; details available on website.
  Note: The Christian Evidence Society does not provide grants.

Christian Social Order (CSO) 1965
- ■ 157 Vicarage Rd, LONDON, E10 5DU. (hq)
  020 8539 3876   fax 020 8539 3876
  email keys@fsmail.net
  Sec: Ronald King
- ▲ Un-incorporated Society
- ○ *K, *R; to oppose organised naturalism by promoting a Christian social order
- Gp Pugin Gild
- ● Mtgs - Res - SG - Stat - Inf - Lib - PL
- M [not given]
- ¶ The Keys of Peter - 6; £5 (£6 o'seas).

Christmas Prepayment Association (CPA)
- NR Unit 4 Alpha Court, Monks Drive, Huntington, YORK, YO32 9WN.
  0845 460 1060
  http://www.cpa-advice.co.uk
- ○ *T; for all in the Christmas savings industry

Chromatographic Society
- NR c/o Meeting Makers, Jordanhill Campus, 76 South Brae Drive, GLASGOW, G13 1PP. (hq)
  0141-434 1500   fax 0141-434 1519
  http://www.chromsoc.com
- ▲ Registered Charity
- ○ *L, *Q; to promote & disseminate knowledge on chromatography & separation techniques - gas, liquid, thin-layer & column liquid chromatography & capillary electrophoresis, supercritical fluids & HPLC
- M i

© CBD Research Ltd · Beckenham · BR3 5JS · Tel 020 8650 7745 · E-mail cbd@cbdresearch.com · www.cbdresearch.com

Church of England Guild of Vergers (CEGV) 1932
- ■ 70B The Close, SALISBURY, Wilts, SP1 2EN.
  07946 387616
  email berryberry50@hotmail.com
  http://www.cofegv.org.uk
  Gen Sec: Mrs Amanda Berry
- ○ *R
- M c 750 i, UK / 100 i, o'seas
- ¶ The Verger - 4; ftm.

Church of England Record Society 1991
- ■ c/o Dr Michael Snape, Dept of Modern History, University of Birmingham, Edgbaston, BIRMINGHAM, W Midlnds, B15 2TT. (sb)
  email m.f.snape@bham.ac.uk   http://www.coers.org
  Hon Sec: Dr Michael Snape
- ▲ Registered Charity
- ○ *L; to promote interest & knowledge of the Church of England, from the 16th century onwards, by the publication of primary sources of information
- ● Mtgs - Publication (1 vol a year)
- M c 450 i & org
- ¶ Annual Volume - 1.

Church Lads' & Church Girls' Brigade (CL&CGB) 1891
- NR 2 Barnsley Rd, Wath-upon-Dearne, ROTHERHAM, S Yorks, S63 6PY. (hq)
  01709 876535   fax 01709 878089
  email brigadesecretary@clcgb.org.uk
  http://www.clcgb.org.uk
  Brigade Sec: A Millward
- ▲ Company Limited by Guarantee; Registered Charity
- ○ *R; 'a uniformed voluntary organisation which, through a wide range of recreational, cultural & spiritual activities, seeks to equip young people & children for life & encourages them to be faithful members of the Church of England'
- ● Mtgs - ET - Comp - VE
- < Nat Coun of Voluntary Orgs; Nat Coun of Volunteer Youth Services
- M 5,000 i
- ¶ NL - 3;   AR; both ftm only.

Church Monuments Society (CMS) 1979
- ■ c/o National Maritime Museum, LONDON, SE10 9NF. (hsb)
  020 8312 6724
  email churchmonuments@aol.com
  http://www.churchmonumentssociety.org
  Sec: Barbara Tomlinson
- ▲ Registered Charity
- ○ *L; to promote the study & conservation of all church monuments both in the UK & abroad
- ● Conf - Mtgs - SG - Inf - VE
- M 398 i, 5 f, 43 org, UK / 18 i, 1 f, 25 org, o'seas
- ¶ Church Monuments (Jnl) - 1; ftm, £15 nm.
  NL - 2; ftm, £1.50 nm.

Churchill Society London 1990
- ■ Ivy House, 18 Grove Lane, IPSWICH, Suffolk, IP4 1NR. (hq)
  01473 413533
  email secretary@churchill-society-london.org.uk
  http://www.churchill-society-london.org.uk
  Chmn: Mrs Pamela Timms,   Gen Sec: Mrs Judith O'Hanlon
- ▲ Un-incorporated Society
- ○ *G; the education re the causes & consequences of war, history of Churchill's life, & the encouragement of all the fine arts & crafts
- ● ET - Res - SG
- < www.englishadviser.co.uk
- M [not stated]
- ¶ All publications on website.

CIC Association CIC (CIC)
- NR c/o Bates Wells & Braithwiate, 2-6 Cannon St, LONDON, EC4M 6YH. (asa)
  020 3262 3044
  email john@cicassociation.org.uk
- ○ *T; 'the association believe the community interest company legislation (CIC) is an evolution, a legislation, brand & structure that will change the way people do business in the UK'

CIFE - Council for Independent Education (CIFE) 1973
- NR 1 Knightsbridge Green, LONDON, SW1X 7NW. (hsp)
  020 8767 8666   fax 020 8767 9444
  email enquiries@cife.org.uk   http://www.cife.org.uk
  Hon Sec: Dr Norma R Ball
- ▲ Un-incorporated Society
- ○ *E, *P; for academic sixth form & tutorial colleges in the UK
- ● Conf - Mtgs - ET - Exam - Comp - Inf - LG - Provider of first attempt & retake GCSE & A+A/S level courses
- < Brit Accreditation Coun
- M 17 colleges
- ¶ LM & Guide to Courses - 1; free.
- × 2006 Council for Independent Further Education

Cigarette Packet Collectors' Club of Great Britain 1980
- ■ 9 Regent Place, HEATHFIELD, E Sussex, TN21 8TJ. (hsp)
  01435 865427
  email bkrussell@sky.com
  http://www.cigarettepacket.com
  Hon Sec: Barry Russell
- ▲ Un-incorporated Society
- ○ *G; preservation of, & research into, the history of cigarette packets, tins & boxes; the collection of ephemera connected with the tobacco trade - packets of cigarette rolling papers (Rizla), tobacco trade price lists etc
- ● Mtgs - Lib - Auctions (qtrly)
- M 215 i, UK / 35 i, o'seas
  (Sub: £14 i, UK / £17 o'seas)
- ¶ The Cigarette Packet - 4; ftm; £14 (25 EU) ($30 USA).
  Auction lists - 4; ftm.
  [subscription £14].

CILIP: Chartered Institute of Library & Information Professionals (CILIP) 1877
- ■ 7 Ridgmount St, LONDON, WC1E 7AE. (hq)
  020 7255 0500   fax 020 7255 0501
  email info@cilip.org.uk   http://www.cilip.org.uk
  Chief Exec: Bob McKee
- ▲ Registered Charity
- Br 12
- ○ *P; for librarians & information managers
- Gp Divisions: Scottish Library Association, Welsh Library Association
  Special interest: Professional development, Subject interests, Employment sectors
  Online User Group
- ● Conf - Mtgs - ET - Exam - Inf - Empl - LG
- M 22,830 i, 461 f, UK / 999 i, 178 f, o'seas
- ¶ Update (Jnl) - 12.   Gazette (NL) - 12.

Cine Guilds of Great Britain (CGGB) 1988
- ■ 72 Pembroke Rd, LONDON, W8 6NX. (hsp)
  0560 294 2610
  email cineguilds@cineguilds.org
  http://www.cineguilds.org
  Sec: Sally Fisher
- ▲ Un-incorporated Society
- ○ *P; maintaining levels of excellence in UK film-making crafts
- Gp CineMasters; Movie Crew UK
- ● Mtgs - ET - Res - LG
- M 7 org (1,500 i)

Cinema Advertising Association Ltd   (CAA)   1953
NR   279 Tottenham Court Rd, LONDON, W1T 7RJ.   (hq)
    020 7199 2433
▲   Company Limited by Guarantee
○   *T; for cinema advertising contractors in the UK & Eire
M   f

Cinema Exhibitors Association   (CEA)   1912
NR   22 Golden Sq, LONDON, W1F 9JW.   (hq)
    020 7734 9551
    Chief Exec: John Wilkinson
▲   Un-incorporated Society
Br   6
○   *T; interests of cinema exhibitors
Gp   Independent cinemas; Specialist exhibition
●   Conf - Mtgs - ET - Stat - Inf - VE - LG - Liaison with production
    & distribution in UK & overseas
<   U Intle Cinémas; Media-Salles
M   c 180 f, UK / 5 f, o'seas
¶   NL - 6;   Guidance notes on operations;   AR; all free.

Cinema Organ Society   (COS)   1952
NR   Dolby House, Barrington Gate, Holbeach, SPALDING, Lincs,
    PE12 7DA.   (memsec/p)
    http://www.cinema-organs.org.uk
    Mem Sec: David Shepherd
    (david.shepherd@cinema-organs.org.uk)
○   *G; for those interested in the cinema (theatre) organ for
    entertainment
M   i

Cinema Theatre Association   (CTA)   1967
■   44 Harrowdene Gardens, TEDDINGTON, Middx, TW11 0DJ.
    (hsp)
    020 8977 2608
    http://www.cta-uk.org
    Hon Sec: Adam Unger
▲   Company Limited by Guarantee; Registered Charity
Br   2
○   *D, *G, *K; promotes serious interest in all aspects of cinema
    buildings (architecture, lighting, film projection & stage
    facilities); promotes their study in terms of the history of
    entertainment, social & architectural history; campaigns for
    the preservation & continued use of cinemas for their original
    purpose
●   Mtgs - Res - Inf - Lib - PL - VE - Lectures, talks & shows -
    Archive available for public research
M   1,500 i
¶   Picture House - 1; ftm, £4.50 nm.
    CTA Bulletin - 6; ftm, £2 nm.

**CIPFA - The Chartered Institute of Public Finance & Accountancy
(CIPFA)   1885**
NR   3 Robert St, LONDON, WC2N 6RL.   (hq)
    020 7543 5600   fax 020 7543 5700
    http://www.cipfa.org.uk
▲   Registered Charity
○   *P; professional accountancy body for public services (both
    public & private sectors) providing education & training in
    accountancy & financial management; to set & monitor
    professional standards
M   13,500 i

Circle of Wine Writers   (CWW)   1960
■   Scots Firs, 70 Joiners Lane, CHALFONT ST PETER, Bucks,
    SL9 0AU.   (admin/p)
    01753 882320
    email administrator@winewriters.org
    http://www.winewriters.org
    Admin: Andrea Warren
▲   Un-incorporated Society
○   *P; to improve the standard of writing, broadcasting & lecturing
    about wines & spirits; to promote wines & spirits of good
    quality & to comment adversely on faulty products & dubious
    practices; the Circle is open to all currently being published,
    including photographers
●   Mtgs - ET - Comp - VE - Wine tastings
M   195 i, UK / 83 i, o'seas
¶   Circle Update - 5.   LM (email only) - 12 ftm, £95 nm.
    [subscription £60].

Circus Friends Association of Great Britain   (CFA)   1934
■   Flat 3 / 24 Devonshire Road, HASTINGS, E Sussex,
    TN34 1NE.   (mem/sec/p)
    07812 647678
    email joditimmscfa@aol.com
    http://www.circusfriends.co.uk
    Mem Sec: Jodi Timms
▲   Un-incorporated Society
○   *G; to support traditional circus as a popular entertainment &
    valuable part of British culture
●   Mtgs - Inf - Lib - VE - Video archive - Rallies to shows
M   700 i, UK / 150 i, o'seas
¶   King Pole - 5; £27 yr.

Circus Society   1983
NR   6 Sherwood Court, 372 London Rd, Langley, SLOUGH, Berks,
    SL3 7HX.   (mem/sp)
    01753 547081
    Mem Sec: R Bartlett
▲   Un-incorporated Society
Br   9 areas
○   *P, *T; promotion of circus & circus artistes; to oppose anti-
    circus activities by various animal rights groups & local
    authorities
Gp   Circus: proprietors, artistes, artistes agents, friends &
    supporters, clowns, staff
●   Inf
M   100 i
¶   Circus News - 4.
    (Sub: £17)
    Note: any request for information should be accompanied by
    an sae.

Citizens Advice
    see **National Association of Citizens Advice Bureaux**

Citizens Advice Scotland   (CAS)   c 1940
NR   Spectrum House, 2 Powderhall Rd, EDINBURGH, EH7 4GB.
    (hq)
    0131-550 1000   fax 0131-550 1001
    email info@cas.org.uk   http://www.cas.org.uk
▲   Company Limited by Guarantee
○   *N, *W; supporting Scottish Citizens Advice Bureaux; provision
    of free, confidential & impartial information, guidance,
    counselling & support to all individuals

City Information Group
    closed July 2009

© CBD Research Ltd · Beckenham · BR3 5JS · Tel 020 8650 7745 · E-mail cbd@cbdresearch.com · www.cbdresearch.com

City Property Association   (CPA)   1904
NR   1 Warwick Row (7th floor), LONDON, SW1E 5ER.   (hq)
         020 7630 1782   fax 020 7630 8344
         http://www.londoncpa.com
▲   Un-incorporated Society
○   *T; interests of owners of property in the City of London
●   Mtgs - Inf - LG
<   Brit Property Fedn Ltd
M   125 f
¶   NL.   AR (incl LM).

Civil Court Users Association   (CCUA)
NR   Warwick House, Birmingham New Rd, STRATFORD-upon-
         AVON, Warks, CV37 0BP.   (hq)
         0845 052 5336   fax 0845 052 5337
         http://www.ccua.org.uk
○   *K; to liaise with debt collection companies & the Lord
         Chancellor's office; to encourage the updating of laws to
         benefit both debt collectors & debtors
●   LG

Civil Defence Association
NR   24 Paxton Close, MATLOCK, Derbys, DE4 3TD.
         01629 55738
         http://www.civildefenceassociation.org.uk
         Sec: Tim Essex-Lopresti
○   *G; for all former members of the Civil Defence Corps,
         Auxiliary Fire Service, Civil Defence, search & rescue groups
         & similar organisations

Civil Enforcement Association   (CIVEA)   2011
NR   513 Bradford Rd, BATLEY, W Yorks, WF17 8LL.   (hq)
         0844 893 3922   fax 0844 854 6322
         email admin@civea.co.uk   http://www.civea.co.uk
         Dir Gen: Dr Steven Everson
▲   Company Limited by Guarantee
○   *P; to represent all private certificated bailiffs (enforcement
         agents) in England & Wales
●   ET - Exam - Empl -Inf - LG - Mtgs - Res
M   84 i, 61 f
×   2011 (Association of Civil Enforcement Agencies
         (Enforcement Services Association

Civil Engineering Contractors' Association   (CECA)
NR   1 Birdcage Walk, LONDON, SW1H 9JJ.
         020 7340 0450
         http://www.ceca.co.uk
         Dir: Rosemary Beales
○   *T
●   Mtgs - Seminars
M   i & f
¶   [see website]

Claims Standards Council   (CSC)   2004
NR   11 Poland Street, LONDON, W1F 8QA.   (hq)
         0870 444 6454
         email info@claimscouncil.org
         http://www.claimscouncil.org
         Chmn: Darren Werth
○   *T; to represent claims management businesses; to ensure that
         the claims management sector is fairly promoted to lawyers,
         insurers & the government
●   Mtgs - Inf
M   53 f
¶   CSC Industry Directory

Clarice Cliff Collectors Club   (CCCC)   1982
NR   PO Box 2706, STAFFORD, Staffs, ST21 6WY.   (hq)
         email information@claricecliff.com
         http://www.claricecliff.com
         Hon Sec: Leonard Griffin
▲   Un-incorporated Society
○   *G; for collectors of ceramics designed by Clarice Cliff between
         1927-1964
Gp   Websites: (1) public, (2) members only
●   Conf - Mtgs - Res - Exhib - SG - PL - VE
M   [confidential]
¶   NL - 4; ftm only.   NL [email] - 4; £25 yr.

Clarinet Heritage Society   (CHS)   1945
■   25 Hambalt Rd, LONDON, SW4 9EQ.   (hsp/b)
         020 8675 3877
         email chs@chello.se
         Hon Sec: Stephen Bennett
▲   Un-incorporated Society
Br   USA
○   *D, *K; to encourage the literature, repertoire, research, study &
         playing of clarinet music
Gp   Research (music, history, evolution & development); Recording
         & music publishing; Commissions; Teaching & study; Public
         relations & promotion
●   ET - Res - SG - Expt - Inf - Lib
M   500 i, UK / 400 i, Library of Congress, o'seas
¶   Sheet music, records, cassettes & CDs; £12-£15.

**Clarinet & Saxophone Society of Great Britain   (CASS GB)
1976**
■   12 Hanbury Close, Ingleby Barwick, STOCKTON-on-TEES,
         Cleveland, TS17 0UQ.   (mem/sp)
         0845 644 0187
         email membership@cassgb.org   http://www.cassgb.org
         Mem Sec: Andrew Smith
▲   Company Limited by Guarantee
○   *D, *Q; all aspects of the music for, & playing of, clarinet &
         saxophone
●   Conf - ET - Comp - Inf - Lib
M   1,410 i, UK / 120 i, o'seas
         (Sub: £35 i, UK / £30 i, o'seas)
¶   Clarinet & Saxophone - 4; ftm.

Clarsach Society
      see **Comunn na Clàrsaich (the Clarsach Society)**

Classic Motor Boat Association of Great Britain   (CMBA)   1998
NR   c/o Unit 1c Deacon Estate, Forstal Rd, AYLESFORD, Kent,
         ME20 7SP.
         01628 524169
         email jarretts@tiscali.co.uk   http://www.cmba-uk.com
         Contacts: Merle & Keith Jarrett
○   *G, *S; for clasic motor boat enthusiasts
●   Mtgs

Classic Rally Association
NR   PO Box 633, NEWPORT, Monmouthshire, NP20 5ZX.   (hq)
         01633 263366
○   *S; for competitors in classic (car) rallies
M   i

Classical Association   (CA)   1904
- ■   Senate House, Malet St, LONDON, WC1E 7HU.   (hq)
    020 7862 8706   fax 020 7255 2297
    email office@classicalassociation.org
    http://www.classicalassociation.org
    Hon Sec: Prof D Cairns,   Admin: Miss Clare L Roberts
- ▲   Registered Charity
- ○   *E, *L; promotion of awareness of, & education in, the Classics
    & the ancient world
- ●   Conf - Publishing
- <   Jt Assn of Classical Teachers
- M   3,875 i, 70 f, UK / 700 i, 170 f, o'seas
- ¶   Classical Review (Jnl) - 2; £31 m, £88 nm.
    Classical Quarterly - 2; £29 m, £81 nm.
    Greece & Rome - 2; £25 m, £69 nm.

Clay Pigeon Shooting Association Ltd   (CPSA)   1928
- NR   Edmonton House, Bisley Camp, Brookwood, WOKING, Surrey,
    GU24 0NP.   (hq)
    01483 485400   fax 01483 485410
    email info@cpsa.co.uk   http://www.cpsa.co.uk
    Chief Exec Officer: Phil Boakes
- ▲   Company Limited by Guarantee
- ○   *S; national governing body for the sport of clay target shooting
    in England
- ●   Mtgs - ET - Exam - Exhib - Comp - Inf - LG
- <   Intl Clay Target Shooting Coun (ICTSC); Intl Shooting U (UIT);
    C'wealth Shooting Fedn (CSF); Fédn Intle de Tir aux Armes
    Sportives de Chasse; Brit Shooting Sports Coun
- M   26,065 i, 170 f, 380 clubs, UK / 2,000 i, 30 org, o'seas
    (Sub: £59 i)
- ¶   Pull! - 10; ftm, £2 nm.

Clay Pipe Development Association Ltd   (CPDA)   1965
- NR   Tree Tops, Bellingdon, CHESHAM, Bucks, HP5 2XL.   (hq)
    01494 791456   fax 01494 791456
    email cpda@aol.com   http://www.cpda.co.uk
- ▲   Company Limited by Guarantee
- ○   *T; to foster the design, manufacture & sale of vitrified clay
    sewer & drain pipes & fittings, ducts for services & related
    products through research, representation, technical literature
    & direct advice
- ●   ET - Res - Inf - LG
- <   Eur Fedn Vitrified Clay Ind (FEUGRES); Construction Products
    Assn (CPA)
- M   15 f
- ¶   Technical publications on clay pipes, relevant standards, design
    & construction of drains & sewers; list available.

Clay Roof Tile Council   (CRTC)   1981
- NR   Federation House, Station Rd, STOKE-ON-TRENT, Staffs,
    ST4 2SA.   (hq)
    01782 744631   fax 01782 744102
    email chrish@ceramfed.co.uk
    http://www.clayroof.co.uk
    Sec: Christopher Hall
- ▲   Un-incorporated Society
- ○   *T
- ●   Mtgs - Exhib - Inf
- <   Brit Ceramic Confedn; Construction Products Assn
- M   5 f
- ¶   Promotional matter.

CLÉ - Irish Book Publishers' Association
    since 2008 **Publishing Ireland**

Cleaning & Hygiene Suppliers' Association Ltd   (CHSA)   1979
- ■   PO Box 770, MARLOW, Bucks, SL7 2SH.   (sb)
    01628 478273   fax 01628 478286
    email secretary@chsa.co.uk   http://www.chsa.co.uk
    Gen Sec: Graham G Fletcher
- ▲   Company Limited by Guarantee
- ○   *T; to represent manufacturers & distributors / suppliers to the
    cleaning industry
- ●   Mtgs - Res - Stat - Inf
- <   Intl Sanitary Supply Assn; Brit Cleaning Coun
- M   200 f
- ¶   AR; free.

Cleaning & Support Services Association   (CSSA)   1967
- NR   478-480 Salisbury House, London Wall, LONDON,
    EC2M 5QQ.   (hq)
    020 7920 9632   fax 020 7256 9630
    http://www.cleaningindustry.org
    Chief Exec: Andrew Large
- ▲   Company Limited by Guarantee
- ○   *T
- Gp   Employment; Marketing; Membership; Standards
- ●   Conf - Mtgs - Exhib - Comp - SG - Stat - Inf - LG
- <   Wld Fedn of Bldg Services Contrs (WFBSC); Eur Fedn of
    Cleaning Inds (EFCI)
- M   250 f, UK / 6 f, o'seas
- ¶   The Supporter (NL) - 12;   LM - 1; both ftm only.
    Code of Practice;   Membership Benefits;
    How to Profit from Contracting out;
    It Makes Sense to Choose a Member of the CSSA; all free.

Cleft Lip & Palate Association   (CLAPA)   1979
- NR   Green Man Tower (1st floor), 332 Goswell Rd, LONDON,
    EC1V 7LQ.   (hq)
    020 7833 4883
    http://www.clapa.com
    Chief Exec: Rosanna Preston
- ▲   Registered Charity
- ○   *W; to provide advice & support to the parents of cleft lip &/or
    palate children & subsequently to the children themselves; to
    encourage research into craniofacial abnormalities
- M   [not stated]

Cleveland Agricultural & Horticultural Society
    the Cleveland Show is now organised by a committee of
    unpaid volunteers

Cleveland Bay Horse Society   (CBHS)   1884
- ■   Regional Agricultural Centre, The Great Yorkshire Showground,
    HARROGATE, N Yorks, HG2 8NZ.   (hq)
    01423 546168
    http://www.clevelandbay.com
    Chmn: David Anderson
- ▲   Registered Charity
- ○   *B; preservation & promotion of Britain's only clean legged
    native breed of horse
- <   sister socs in Australia & North America
- M   c 250 i, 1 f, UK / c 50 i, o'seas
- ¶   NL - 3/4; ftm only.   Magazine - 1; ftm, £5 nm.
    Stud Book - 3 yrly; £15-£25.

Clinical Contract Research Association   (CCRA)   1988
- NR   PO Box 1055, OADBY, Leics, LE2 4XZ.   (admin/b)
    0116-271 9727   fax 0116-271 3155
- ○   *T; clinical research organisations
- M   f

Clinical Genetics Group
    a group of the **Royal College of Paediatrics & Child Health**

Clinical Genetics Society
    a group of **British Society for Human Genetics**

© CBD Research Ltd · Beckenham · BR3 5JS · Tel 020 8650 7745 · E-mail cbd@cbdresearch.com · www.cbdresearch.com

Clinical Molecular Genetics Society
a group of the **British Society for Human Genetics**

Cloth Insignia Research & Collectors Society
see **Military Heraldry Society (the Cloth & Insignia Research & Collectors Society)**

Cloth Merchants Association   1934
- ■ c/o H Lesser & Sons (London) Ltd, Unit A, 43-53 Markfield Rd, LONDON, N15 4QA.   (sb)
  020 8275 6400   fax 020 8275 6401
  Sec: David Lesser
- ▲ Company Limited by Guarantee
- ○ *T
- ● Conf - Mtgs - Exhib - Expt - Inf - LG
- M 10 f

Cloud Appreciation Society   2004
- NR PO Box 81, SOMERTON, Somerset, TA11 9AY.
  http://www.cloudappreciationsociety.org
  Founder: Gavin Pretor-Pinney
- ○ *G
- ¶ Cloudspotters Guide.

Club Cricket Conference   (CCC)   1915
- NR 24-26 High St (top floor), HAMPTON HILL, Middx, TW12 1PD.   (hq)
  020 8973 1612   fax 0870 143 2824
  email enquiries@club-cricket.co.uk
  http://www.club-cricket.co.uk
  Hon Operations Mgr: Simon Dyson
- ○ *N, *S; 'wide ranging representational, advisory, procurement, legal & other support services for over 1,500 recreational cricket clubs & league members throughout the south / south-east / Home Counties of England & Wales'

Clubs for Young People   (CYP)   1925
- ■ 371 Kennington Lane, LONDON, SE11 5QY.   (hq)
  020 7793 0787   fax 020 7820 9815
  email office@clubsforyoungpeople.org.uk
  http://www.clubsforyoungpeople.org.uk
  Chief Exec: Helen Marshall
- ▲ Registered Charity
- ○ *Y; to enable young men & young women to achieve their potential by providing them with opportunities to develop their personal & social education from activities delivered through a network of affiliated clubs
- ● ET - LG - Postitive activities incl Sports, arts, leadership training for young PPU
- < Clubs for Young People (Wales; Scotland; N Ireland)
- M 400,000 i, 3,500 clubs
- ¶ Annual review.   NL - 4.
  Various booklets & leaflets.

Clubs for Young People (NI)   (CYP)   1940
- ■ 22 Stockmans Way, Musgrave Park Industrial Estate, BELFAST, BT9 7JU.   (hq)
  028 9066 3321   fax 028 9066 3306
  email post@cypni.net   http://www.cypni.net
  Chief Exec: Paul Curran
- ▲ Registered Charity; Un-incorporated Society
- ○ *Y; the headquarters for youth clubs & youth organisations in Northern Ireland
- Gp Youth sports: Boxing, Soccer, Swimming etc
- ● Mtgs - Comp - VE
- < Clubs for Young People (UK; Scotland; Wales)
- M 150 clubs
- × 2007 Boys' & Girls' Clubs of Northern Ireland

Clubs for Young People Scotland   (CYP)   1928
- NR 88 Giles St, EDINBURGH, EH6 6BZ.   (hq)
  0131-555 1729   fax 0131-555 5921
  email info@cypscotland.com
  http://www.cypscotland.com
  Chief Officer: Tom Leishman
- ▲ Company Limited by Guarantee
- Br 5 local federations
- ○ *Y; to create & offer opportunities to young people
- ● Mtgs - Comp - SG - Lib - LG
- < Eur Fedn of Youth Service Orgs (EFYSO); Clubs for Young People (UK; Wales; N Ireland)
- M 15,000 i
- × 2007 Boys' & Girls' Clubs of Scotland

Clubs for Young People Wales   (CYP)
- NR Western Business Centre, Riverside Terrace, Ely Bridge, CARDIFF, CF5 5AS.
  029 2057 5705   fax 029 2057 5715
  email office@cypwales.org.uk
  http://www.cypwales.org.uk
  Admin: Shirley Higgins
- ▲ Registered Charity
- ○ *Y; to enable young men & young women to achieve their potential by providing them with opportunities to develop their personal & social education from activities delivered through a network of affiliated clubs
- < Clubs for Young People (UK; Scotland; N Ireland)

Clun Forest Sheep Breeders Society Ltd   1925
- ■ Wollerton Farm, Wollerton, MARKET DRAYTON, Shropshire, TF9 3NA.   (hsp)
  01630 685981
  email sandrahw@yahoo.co.uk
  http://www.clunforestsheep.co.uk
  Sec: Sandra Williams
- ▲ Registered Charity
- ○ *B
- < Nat Sheep Assn
- M 180 i, UK / 2 i, o'seas
- ¶ Flock Book - 1; ftm.   Hbk - 3/4 yrly; free.

Clydesdale Horse Society   (CHS)   1877
- NR Kinclune, Kingoldrum, KIRRIEMUIR, Angus, DD8 5HX.   (hsp)
  01575 570900
  email secretary@clydesdalehorsesociety.com
  http://www.clydesdalehorsesociety.com
  Sec: Mrs Marguerite Osborne
- ○ *B
- M i

CMT United Kingdom   1986
- ■ 98 Broadway, Southborne, BOURNEMOUTH, Dorset, BH6 4EH.   (hsp)
  0800 652 6316 (0900-1500)
  email secretary@cmt.org.uk   http://www.cmt.org.uk
  Sec: Mrs Karen Butcher
- ▲ Company Limited by Guarantee; Registered Charity
- Br 10
- ○ *W; to offer support, advice & information to people affected by CMT (Charcot-Marie-Tooth Disease), a condition which affects the nerves in the arms and legs
- ● Conf - Inf
- < Wld Muscle Soc; LTCA; Neurological Alliance
- M 1,200 i, UK / c 100 i, o'seas
  (Sub: £20 UK / £25 o'seas)
- ¶ Comment (NL) - 3   AR - 1; both ftm.

CNK Alliance Ltd (Care not Killing) (CNK) 2006
- ■ PO Box 56322, LONDON, SE1 8XW.   (hq)
  020 7234 9680   fax 0871 900 4745
  email info@carenotkilling.org.uk
  http://www.carenotkilling.org.uk
  Co Sec: Charles Wookey
- ▲ Limited Liability Partnership
- ○ *K; a UK alliance of individuals & organisations bringing
  together groups concerned with human rights, healthcare,
  palliative care, as well as faith based organisations, with the
  aim of 1) promoting more & better palliative care;
  2) opposing euthanasia & assisted suicide; 3) influencing the
  balance of public opinion
- ● Conf - Mtgs - ET - Res - Exhib - Inf - Lobbying & campaigning
- < Care Not Killing Scotland
- M 400 +, 18 org, UK / 30 org, o'seas
  (Sub: £10 i, £1,500 org, UK / £50 org o'seas)
- ¶ NL - 4; free (on website).

Co-operatives UK Ltd 1869
- NR Holyoake House, Hanover St, MANCHESTER, M60 0AS.   (hq)
  0161-246 2900   fax 0161-831 7684
  email enquiries@cooperatives-uk.coop
  http://www.cooperatives-uk.coop
  Chief Exec: Dame Pauline Green
- ▲ An Industrial & Provident Society
- Br 3
- ○ *T; national representational, promotional & advisory body for
  consumer co-operatives in the UK
- ● Conf - ET - Exhib - Stat - Inf - LG - Legal registration of co-
  operatives & other social enterprises & charities
- < Intl Co-op Alliance
- M 50 i, 450 f, 100 org
- ¶ Co-operatives - 3;   AR; both free.
  Co-operatives UK Briefing - 12; ftm only.

Coach Operators Federation (COF) 1955
- ■ 64 Brookside, Paulton, BRISTOL, BS39 7YR.
  01761 415456   fax 01761 415456
  http://www.cofed.net
  Sec: Tim Jennings
- ▲ Un-incorporated Society
- ○ *T
- ● Mtgs - VE - Empl - LG
- M 5 i, 42 f, UK / 1 i, o'seas

Coach Tourism Council (CTC) 1989
- NR 10 Bermondsey Exchange, 179-181 Bermondsey St, LONDON,
  SE1 3UW.   (hq)
  0870 850 2839
  email admin@coachtourismcouncil.co.uk
  http://www.coachtourismcouncil.co.uk
  Chief Exec: Graham Beacom
- ▲ Un-incorporated Society
- ○ *T; promotion of travel & tourism by coach
- ● Conf - Mtgs - ET - Res - Exhib - VE
- < Confedn of Passenger Transport; Visit Britain / London /
  England; Tourism Alliance
- M 400 f, UK / 23 f, o'seas
- ¶ NL - 6; ftm only.   Ybk - 1; ftm, £40 nm.

**Coal Merchants Association of Scotland Ltd (CMAS Ltd)
1913**
- ■ PO Box 9224, KILMACOLM, Renfrewshire, PA13 4YP.
  (mail/address)
  01505 874389   fax 01505 874389
  email norrie.johnstone@btinternet.com
  Sec: Norman Johnstone
- ▲ Company Limited by Guarantee
- ○ *T
- ● Mtgs - SG
- < Solid Fuel Assn; Coal Merchants Fedn (GB) Ltd
- M 130 i
- ¶ AR.

Coal Merchants Federation (Great Britain) Ltd   (CMF) 1934
- ■ 7 Swanwick Court, ALFRETON, Derbys, DE55 7AS.   (hq)
  01773 835400   fax 01773 834351
  email cmf@solidfuel.co.uk
  http://www.coalmerchants.co.uk
  Gen Sec: Jim Lambeth
- ▲ Company Limited by Guarantee
- Br 13
- ○ *T
- ● Mtgs - ET - Res - Stat - Inf - LG
- < Solid Fuel Assn
- M 850 f
- ¶ Coal Trader - 4; free.

Coalition for Medical Progress
  2008 merged with the Research Defence Society to form
  Understanding Animal Research

Coalition for the Removal of Pimping (CROP) 1996
- NR 34 York Rd, LEEDS, W Yorks, LS9 8TA.
  0113-240 3040
  email info@cropuk.org.uk   http://www.cropuk.org.uk
  Sec: Alan Mastin Suggate
- ○ *K; to end the sexual exploitation of children and young people
  by pimps and traffickers

Coastguard Association 1976
- § 34 Beacons Park, BRECON, LD3 9BR.
  01874 611859
  email victory@tinyworld.co.uk
  http://www.coastguardassoc.demon.co.uk
  Sec: Mrs M Miller
  provides help & financial support for coastguards in need

Coaters Group
  a group of the **Performance Textiles Association**

Coble & Keelboat Society (CKS) 1987
- ■ 20 The Green, SALTBURN-by-the-SEA, N Yorks, TS12 1NF.
  (hsp)
  01287 623661
  email ae@readman1.plus.com
  http://www.coble-keelboatsociety.org
  Hon Gen Sec: A Edgar Readman
- ▲ Registered Charity
- ○ *G; preservation of traditional working boats of the North East
  coast of England
- Gp Preservers; Historians; Researchers
- ● Mtgs - Inf
- < Sailing Smack Assn; 40+ Fishing Boat Assn; Bridlington Sailing
  Coble Presvn Soc; Sunderland Marine Sports Club; W Wales
  Maritime Heritage Soc
- M 180 i, 400 org, 1 assn, UK / 6 i, o'seas
- ¶ The Coble & Keelboat Society (Jnl) - 2; ftm, 50p nm.
  Coblegram (NL) - 4; ftm only.

Cockburn Association - The Edinburgh Civic Trust 1875
- NR Trunk's Close, 55 High St, EDINBURGH, EH1 1SR.   (hq)
  0131-557 8686   fax 0131-557 9387
  http://www.cockburnassociation.org.uk
  Dir: Moira Tasker
- ○ *K; protection of the beauty of Edinburgh by the
  encouragement of enlightened planning & the preservation
  of good buildings of all ages
- M c 1,200 i

Coeliac Society of Ireland
- IRL Carmichael House, 4 North Brunswick St, DUBLIN 7, Republic
  of Ireland.
  353 (1) 872 1471   fax 353 (1) 873 5737
  email coeliac@iol.ie   http://www.coeliac.ie
  Sec: Mary Thowig-Murray
- ○ *W

© CBD Research Ltd · Beckenham · BR3 5JS · Tel 020 8650 7745 · E-mail cbd@cbdresearch.com · www.cbdresearch.com

Coeliac UK   1968
- ■ Apollo Centre (3rd floor), Desborough Rd, HIGH WYCOMBE, Bucks, HP11 2QW.   (hq)
  01494 437278   fax 01494 474349
  email info@coeliac.org.uk   http://www.coeliac.org.uk
  Contact: Jean Christopher
- ▲ Registered Charity
- ○ *W; to support the health, welfare & rights of coeliacs & those with dermatitis herpetiformis (DH); to promote & commission research into causes, alleviation, treatment, care & cure of these conditions; to educate the public & those in the appropriate sectors of health, government, commerce & industry
- ● Helpline: 0870 444 8804 (Mon-Fri 1000-1600)
- M 50,000 i
- ¶ Crossed Grain Magazine - 3.
  Food & Drinks Directory of the United Kingdom - 1.
  Publications list available.

Coffee Industry Association of Ireland
  a group of **Food & Drink Industry Ireland**

Cognition: Campaign for Qualified Politicians   (Cognition) 1998
- ■ 3 Hughes Stanton Way, MANNINGTREE, Essex, CO11 2HQ. (asa)
- ○ *K; 'we believe that a new political qualification, covering business & financial studies, national & international current affairs & general knowledge, should become compulsory for all those wishing to stand for Parliament - such a qualification only being obtainable through involvement in the foregoing'
- ● Mtgs - Stat - Lib
- M i, f & org
- ¶ Re: Cognition (NL) - 3.

Coir Association   1956
- ■ 1 Gate Lodge Way, Noak Bridge, LAINDON, Essex, SS15 4AR.   (sp)
  01268 532797   fax 01268 272549
  email coirassociation@tiscali.co.uk
  Sec: David G Sunderland
- ○ *T; coir & allied products
- ● Mtgs
- M 4 f, UK / 7 f, o'seas
  (Sub: £95)
- ¶ LM - 1;   Panel of arbitrators;   AR; all ftm.

Coke Oven Managers Association   (COMA)   1915
- NR c/o Dave Willmott, Otto Simon Ltd, Churchfield House, 5 The Crescent, CHEADLE, Cheshire, SK8 1PS.   (hsb)
  0161-491 7447   fax 0161-491 3369
  email dwillmott@ottosimon.co.uk
  http://www.coke-oven-managers.org
  Hon Gen Sec: Dave Willmott
- ▲ Un-incorporated Society
- Br 3 sections UK; 1 o'seas
- ○ *P; the science & technology of coal carbonisation, the recovery & chemical processing of by-products & peripheral technologies
- Gp Editorial c'ee
- ● Conf - Mtgs - Stat - Inf
- M i & f
- ¶ Bulletin - 2; ftm.   COMA Ybk (incl LM); ftm.
  Technical publications; prices vary.

Cold Rolled Sections Association   (CRSA)   1946
- NR National Metalforming Centre, 47 Birmingham Rd, WEST BROMWICH, W Midlands, B70 6PY.   (sb)
  0121-601 6350   fax 0121-601 6373
  http://www.crsauk.com
- ○ *T; to sponsor research & promote use of cold rolled sections
- ● Mtgs - Res - Inf

Cold Storage & Distribution Federation
  since March 2008 **Food Storage & Distribution Federation**

Cold War Research Group
  a group of **Subterranea Britannica**

Collections Trust   1977
- NR CAN Mezzanine, Downstream Building, 1 London Bridge, LONDON, SE1 9BG.   (hq)
  020 07022 1889
  email office@collectionstrust.org.uk
  http://www.collectionstrust.org.uk
  Chief Exec: Nick Poole
- ▲ Company Limited by Guarantee
- ○ *T; to support education by promoting standards & best practice in museums
- ● Mtgs - ET - Res - Inf - Standards
- M 671 i & f, 5 org
- ¶ Collections News - 4;   AR - 1; both free.
- ✕ 2008 MDA Europe

College of Emergency Medicine   (CEM)   1993
- ■ Churchill House, 35 Red Lion Square, LONDON, WC1R 4SG.   (hq)
  020 7404 1999   fax 020 7067 1267
  email cem@emergencymedicine.uk.net
  http://www.collemergencymed.ac.uk
  Registrar: Dr Ruth Brown
- ▲ Company Limited by Guarantee; Registered Charity
- ○ *E, *M; the college has responsibility for the training & academic standards of the speciality of emergency medicine
- Gp Emergency Medicine Trainees Association
- ● Conf - ET - Exam - Res - LG
- M 1,700 i, UK / 200 i, o'seas
- ✕ 2008 British Association for Emergency Medicine (merged)

College of Occupational Therapists
  part of the **British Association of Occupational Therapists**

College of Operating Department Practitioners   (CODP)   1945
- NR 1 Mabledon Place, LONDON, WC1H 9AJ.   (hq)
  0870 746 0984   fax 0870 746 0985
  http://www.aodp.org
- ○ *P; those qualified in operating department practice; to protect patients by self regulation & maintaining & improving standards of practice & education in theatre practice
  2007 incorporated the Association of Operating Department Practitioners

College of Optometrists   (BCO)   1980
- NR 41-42 Craven St, LONDON, WC2N 5NG.   (hq)
- ▲ Registered Charity
- ○ *P; 'awards the sole registrable qualification in optometry in the UK'
- M i

College of Paramedics   (CoP)   2001
- ■ The Exchange, Express Park, Bristol Rd, BRIDGWATER, Somerset, TA6 4RR.
  01278 420014
  email help@collegeofparamedics.co.uk
  http://www.collegeofparamedics.co.uk
  Chief Exec: Dave Hodge
- ▲ Company Limited by Guarantee
- Br 14
- ○ *M, *P; to develop the scope & practice of paramedic science & related subjects in the ambulance profession for the benefit of its practitioners & the general public
- < Allied Health Professions Fedn

College of Piping   1944
NR   16-24 Otago St, GLASGOW, G12 8JH.   (hq)
        0141-334 3587   fax 0141-587 6068
        Principal: Robert Wallace
▲   Registered Charity
○   *D, *E; the teaching of the Highland Bagpipe; dissemination of
        information on piping
●   Conf - Mtgs - ET - Exam - Res - Comp - Inf - Lib
M   200 i, UK / 100 i, o'seas
¶   The Piping Times - 12.

College of Psychiatry of Ireland   2009
IRL   5 Herbert St, DUBLIN 2, Republic of Ireland.   (hq)
        353 (1) 661 8450   fax 353 (1) 661 9835
        email info@irishpsychiatry.ie
        http://www.irishpsychiatry.ie
        Senior Admin: Grace Smyth
○   *L, *M, *P
M   600 i
✕   2009 (Irish College of Psychiatry
        (Irish Psychiatric Association
        (Irish Psychiatric Training Committee

College of Radiographers
        a group of the **Society of Radiographers**

College of Sexual & Relationship Therapists   (BASRT)   1972
■   PO Box 13686, LONDON, SW20 9ZH.   (mail address)
        020 8543 2707   fax 020 8543 2707
        email info@basrt.org.uk   http://www.basrt.org.uk
        Chief Exec Officer: Corinna Furse
▲   Company Limited by Guarantee; Registered Charity
○   *P; for clinicians & therapists who treat sexual & relationship
        problems
●   Conf - ET - Res - Approves training courses in sex therapy -
        Provides list of local therapists
M   700 i, UK / 30 i, o'seas
¶   Sexual & Relationship Therapy - 3; ftm.
✕   2008-10 British Association for Sexual & Relationship Therapy

College of Teachers   1849
NR   Institute of Education, 20 Bedford Way, LONDON,
        WC1H 0AL.   (hq)
        020 7911 5536   fax 020 7631 4865
        email info@cot.ac.uk   http://www.cot.ac.uk
        Chief Exec & Registrar: Prof Ray Page
▲   Registered Charity
○   *E, *P; to promote sound learning & advance the interests of
        education
Gp   Primary education; Secondary education; F/HE
●   Conf - Mtgs - ET - Exam
M   2,000 i, 100 schools, 20 org, UK / 200 i, 2 f, 12 org, o'seas
¶   Education Today (Jnl) - 4; ftm, from £110 yr nm.
        NL - 4; ftm only (incl AR).

College of Vibrational Medicine Practitioner Association
NR   1 Rectory Rd, Tivetshall St Mary, NORWICH, Norfolk,
        NR15 2AL.
        0845 478 6373
        http://www.collegeofvibrationalmedicine.org.uk
○   *P; for trained practitioners using pure vibrational, natural
        frequencies to create balance, harmony & unity in body,
        mind & spirit
●   ET - Workshops
M   i

Colloquium for Scottish Medieval & Renaissance Studies
        see **Scottish Medievalists (Colloqium for Scottish Medieval &
        Renaissance Studies)**

Colonel Stephens Society   1985
NR   10 Cedar Court, Farrand Rd, HEDON, E Yorks, HU12 8LX.
        01482 897645
        email secretary@colonelstephenssociety.co.uk
        http://www.colonelstephenssociety.co.uk
        Sec: Kerry Baylis
○   *G; for enthusiasts of the light and narrow gauge railways of
        Colonel Holman F Stephens (1868-1931)

Colour Group (Great Britain)   (CGGB)   1940
■   c/o Applied Vision Research Centre, Tate Building, The City
        University, Northampton Square, LONDON, EC1V 7DD.
        (mail/address)
        email colourgroupgb@city.ac.uk
        http://www.colour.org.uk
        Hon Sec: Prof Lindsay MacDonald
▲   Registered Charity
○   *L; to encourage the study of colour in all its aspects; to
        promote education of the public in the field of colour; to
        further research into the uses of colour in art & science
●   Conf - Mtgs - ET - Res - Exhib - Comp - Inf - Travel awards for
        those studying colour - Mtgs are at the above address
<   Assn Intle de la Couleur (AIC); Commission Intle de
        l'Eclairage (CIE); Intl Soc of Colour Couns (ISCC)
M   162 i, 14 f, UK / 19 i, o'seas
¶   NL - 12; ftm only.

Coloured Horse & Pony Society   (CHAPS(UK))   1983
■   1 McLaren Cottages, Abertysswg, Rhymney, TREDEGAR, Gwent,
        NP22 5BH.   (hsp)
        01685 845045   fax 01685 845045
        email admin@chapsuk.datanet.co.uk
        http://www.chapsuk.com
        Sec: Miss Lorraine Amor
▲   Company Limited by Guarantee
○   *B
●   Shows - Issuing passports to horses - Studbook - Performance
        award scheme
<   Brit Horse Soc; Central Prefix Register
M   1,200 i, UK / 12 i, o'seas
¶   A World of Colour - 3.

Comann Each nan Eilean
        see **Eriskay Pony Mother Studbook Society**

Combined Cadet Force Association   (CCFA)   1952
■   Holderness House, 51-61 Clifton St, LONDON, EC2A 4OW.
        (hq)
        020 77426 8377   fax 020 7426 8378
        email acfa@armycadets.com
        http://www.armycadets.com
        Sec: Brig M Wharmby
▲   Company Limited by Guarantee; Registered Charity
Br   280
○   *Y; a national youth organisation working in schools to develop
        leadership, citizenship & self belief; for young men & women
        aged 13-18
●   Comp - Mtgs - ET - Comp - Stat - Inf - LG
M   50,000 i
¶   Ybk - 1;   AR - 1; both free.

Combined Edible Nut Trade Association   (CENTA)   1970
■   18 Lichfield Rd, WOODFORD GREEN, Essex, IG8 9ST.   (asa)
        020 8506 2391   fax 020 8506 2391
        email treenuts@centa.uk.com
        http://www.centa.uk.com
        Sec: David G Sunderland
○   *T
Gp   Almonds; Brazil nuts; Cashews; Hazelnuts; Pistachios; Walnuts
M   28 f, UK / 10 f, o'seas
        (Sub: £520)
¶   LM - 1;   Trade Reports;   AR - 1; all ftm.
        Terms & Conditions of Trading - on joining; ftm, £15 nm.
        Panel of Arbitrators - 1;
        List of Defaulters to Arbitration Awards - as arising; both ftm.

© CBD Research Ltd · Beckenham · BR3 5JS · Tel 020 8650 7745 · E-mail cbd@cbdresearch.com · www.cbdresearch.com

Combined Heat & Power Association   (CHPA)   1968
NR   Grosvenor Gardens House, 35-37 Grosvenor Gardens,
        LONDON, SW1W 0BS.   (hq)
        020 7828 4077   fax 020 7828 0310
        email info@chpa.co.uk   http://www.chpa.co.uk
        Dir: Graham Meeks
▲   Company Limited by Guarantee
○   *T; to promote energy efficiency & environmental improvement
        through the provision of integrated energy services & the
        wider use of combined heat, power & community heating;
        the use of waste incineration
●   Conf - Mtgs - Inf - Lib - LG
M   15 i, 100 f
¶   CHPA Ybk; £35.
        Publications list available.

Combustion Engineering Association   (CEA)   1932
NR   1a Clarke St, Ely Bridge, CARDIFF, Glamorgan, CF5 5AL.   (hq)
        029 2040 0670   fax 029 2055 5542
        http://www.cea.org.uk
▲   Registered Charity
○   *L, *Q; to further the cause of combustion engineering
M   i & f

Comedy Writers' Association UK   (CWAUK)   1981
NR   44 Cherry Ave, SWANLEY, Kent, BR8 7DU.
        01322 410742
        Contact: Mark Nicholson
○   *P

Comics Creators Guild   (CCG)   1977
NR   22 St James' Mansions, West End Lane, LONDON,
        NW6 2AA.   (mail address)
        Sec: Ben Counter
▲   Un-incorporated Society
○   *P; for those working in the comic strip or graphic narrative
        medium; to promote this medium as an art form
M   i

Commemorative Collectors Society   (CCS)   1972
■   Lumless House, 77 Gainsborough Rd, Winthorpe, NEWARK,
        Notts, NG24 2NR.   (hsp)
        01636 671377
        http://www.commemorativescollecting.co.uk
        Hon Sec: Steven N Jackson
▲   Un-incorporated Society
○   *A, *G; to research, publish & offer advice & information to
        members & manufacturers, on the design & issuing of all
        'popular' commemorative items made from glass, ceramics,
        metal, wovens, paper & all printed materials etc
●   Mtgs - ET - Res - Exhib - Stat - Inf - Lib - LG
M   3,821 i, UK / 747 i, o'seas
        (Sub: £14 UK / £16 o'seas)
¶   Jnl - 4; ftm.   Review - irreg.

Commemoratives Museum Trust   (CMT)   2003
■   Lumless House, 77 Gainsborough Rd, Winthorpe, NEWARK,
        Notts, NG24 2NR.   (hq)
        01636 671377
        Chief Exec: Steven N Jackson
▲   Registered Charity
○   *A; to maintain & display a collection of commemorative items
        for information of private collectors, designers & historians
●   ET - Res - Exhib - Inf
M   489 i, UK / 218 i, o'seas

Comment on Reproductive Ethics   (CORE)
NR   PO Box 4593, LONDON, SW3 6XE.
        020 7581 2623   fax 020 7581 3868
        http://www.corethics.org

Commerce & Industry Group   (C&I)
NR   Woodbank House, 80 Churchgate, STOCKPORT, Cheshire,
        SK1 1YJ.
        0161-480 2918   fax 0161-968 1851
        email info@cigroup.org.uk   http://www.cigroup.org.uk
        Chmn: Sapna Bedi FitzGerald
○   *P; in-house solicitors
<   The Law Soc
        Commercial arm: C&I Group Services Ltd

Commercial Bar Association   (COMBAR)   1989
NR   3 Verulam Buildings, LONDON, WC1R 5NT.
        020 7404 2022   fax 020 7404 2088
○   *P
M   598 i

Commercial Boat Operators Association   (CBOA)   1989
■   PO Box 38479, LONDON, SE16 4WX.   (hs)
        0778 550 2478
        http://www.cboa.org.uk
        Sec: David Lowe
▲   Un-incorporated Society
○   *T; the maintenance & furtherance of cargo carrying by inland
        waterway
●   Mtgs - ET - Inf - LG - Trade furtherance
M   130 i, 20 f
¶   NL - 4; ftm only.
×   1999 Commercial Narrowboat Operators Association

Commercial Farmers Group   (CFG)   1998
■   Hurn Hall, Holbeach Hurn, SPALDING, Lincs, PE12 8JF.   (hsb)
        01406 422230
        email info@commercialfarmers.co.uk
        http://www.commercialfarmers.co.uk
        Sec: Henry Fell
▲   Un-incorporated Society
○   *F; 'agricultural lobbying'
●   Mtgs - Res - SG
M   22 i

Commercial Horticultural Association   (CHA)   1978
■   The White House, High St, Brasted, SEVENOAKS, Kent,
        TN16 1JE.   (asa)
        01959 565995
        email info@cha-hort.com   http://www.cha-hort.com
        Hon Sec: Dr Chris Wood,   Expt Promoter: Peter Grimbly
▲   Un-incorporated Society
○   *T; for manufacturers & suppliers of equipment, products &
        services to the commercial horticultural industry worldwide
●   Conf - Exhib - Expt - Lib - LG
M   120 f
¶   NL - 5; ftm only.
        Buyers' Guide: association details, members & what they
        provide - 1; free (also on website).

Commercial Radio Companies Association   (CRCA)   1973
NR   77 Shaftesbury Avenue, LONDON, W1D 5DU.   (hq)
        020 7306 2603   fax 020 7470 0062
        email info@crca.co.uk   http://www.crca.co.uk
        Chmn: Lord John Eatwell
▲   Company Limited by Guarantee
○   *T; for commercial radio, representing UK commercial radio to
        government, the Regulator & the media
●   Conf - Mtgs - Res - LG - Negotiation with copyright bodies
<   Assn Eur des Radios
M   255 f
¶   Bulletin - 26; ftm only.   LM - updated; free.

Commercial Trailer Association   (CTA)   1980
NR   Forbes House, Halkin St, LONDON, SW1X 7DS.   (hq)
        020 7235 7000
○   *T; represents the interests of manufacturers of trailers over 3.5
        tonnes gross weight
M   f

Commissioning Specialists Association   (CSA)   1990
■   The Old House (2nd floor office suite), 24 London Rd,
      HORSHAM, W Sussex, RH12 1AY.   (hq)
      01403 754133   fax 01403 754134
      email office@csa.org.uk   http://www.csa.org.uk
      Sec: Julie Parker
▲   Un-incorporated Society
○   *T; for commissioning specialists within the construction industry
Gp   Commissioning for: Air conditioning, Heating & ventilating,
      Refrigeration
●   ET - Inf
M   208 i, 54 f, UK / 20 i, 4 f, o'seas
¶   Index (NL) - 4.   LM.   Guidance Notes.
      Commissioning Engineers Compendium; £12.50 m, £16 nm.
      Technical Memoranda; £7.50 m, £10 nm.

COMMITTEE ...
      For details of official & non-official committees, other than the
      following, see the companion volume
      'Councils, Committees & Boards'

Committee on the Administration of Justice   (CAJ)   1981
■   Sturgen Building (2nd floor), 9-15 Queen St, BELFAST,
      BT1 6ES.   (hq)
      028 9031 6000   fax 028 9031 4583
      email info@caj.org.uk   http://www.caj.org.uk
      Dir: Mike Ritchie
▲   Company Limited by Guarantee
○   *G, *K; works for a just & peaceful society in Northern Ireland
      where the human rights of all are protected
●   Conf - ET - Res - Inf - Lib - Campaigning, lobbying & advising
<   Intl Fedn for Human Rights
M   180 i, 40 org, UK / 120 i, o'seas
¶   AR - 1.
      Publications list available.

Committee of Registered Clubs Associations   (CORCA)   1983
■   253-254 Upper St, LONDON, N1 1RY.   (hq)
      020 7226 0221   fax 020 7354 1847
      Gen Sec: Mick McGlasham
○   *N; 'for separate club organisations who meet regularly for
      mutual benefit'
●   Mtgs - Stat - Empl - LG
M   8,000,000 i, 6 org
¶   CORCA-NJIC Wages Booklet - 1; 20p m, £2 nm.
      All Parliamentary Party Progress Report - 1; £2.

Commons, Open Spaces & Footpaths Preservation Society
(Open Spaces Society)   1865
■   25a Bell St, HENLEY-on-THAMES, Oxon, RG9 2BA.   (hq)
      01491 573535   fax 01491 573051
      email hq@oss.org.uk   http://www.oss.org.uk
      Gen Sec: Miss Kate Ashbrook
▲   Registered Charity
○   *K; to create & conserve common land, village greens, open
      spaces & rights of public access, in town & country, in
      England & Wales
●   Inf
M   2,460 i, local & national org, amenity groups, etc
¶   Open Space (Jnl) - 3; ftm only.
      Our Common Land (book); £14 m, £25 nm.
      Various other leaflets & publications.
      Note: the registered title of this organisation is Commons,
      Open Spaces & Footpaths Preservation Society; it is now
      better known under the title of Open Spaces Society

Communication Workers Union   (CWU)   1995
NR   150 The Broadway, LONDON, SW19 1RX.   (hq)
      020 8971 7200   fax 020 8971 7300
      http://www.cwu.org
      Gen Sec: Billy Hayes
○   *U; for people working in the postal & telecommunications
      industries
●   Conf - ET - Res - Stat - Lib - Empl - LG
<   U Network Intl; Labour Party; Trades U Congress
M   217,807 i
¶   Voice - 10; ftm.

Communications Management Association   (CMA)   1958
■   North Star House (Block D 1st floor), North Star Avenue,
      SWINDON, Wilts, SN2 1FA.   (hq)
      01793 417605
      email cma@thecma.com   http://www.thecma.com
      Chief Exec: Glenn Powell
▲   Registered Charity
○   *P; for professionals & organisations focused on
      communications, networks & ICT, for business advantage
●   Conf - ET - Res - Exhib - SG - Stat - Inf - LG
<   BCS, the Chartered Institute for IT
M   452 i, 75 f
      (Sub: £119.15 i, £595 f)
¶   Newsline (email) - 12;   Update (email) - 12; both free.
×   2007 Telecommunications Users' Association (merged October)
      Note: The CMA is part of BCS, the Chartered Institute of IT.

Community   2004
■   67-68 Long Acre, Covent Garden, LONDON, WC2E 9FA.
      (hq)
      020 7420 4000
      email info@community-tu.org
      http://www.community-tu.org
      Gen Sec: Michael Leahy
Br   480
○   *U
Gp   Steel, wire & domestic appliances; Betting shop workers; Social
      & voluntary workers; Textile, leather & garment workers;
      Equality;
      National League for the Blind & Disabled
●   Conf - Mtgs - ET - Res - Stat - Inf - Empl - LG
<   Trades U Congress (TUC)
M   67,488 i

Community Composting Network   (CCN)
NR   67 Alexandra Rd, SHEFFIELD, S Yorks, S2 3EE.
      0114-258 0483
      http://www.communitycompost.org.uk
○   *H, *K, *N; promotes community composting at a national level
      & through local groups
●   Conf - Inf - Lib - LG
M   230 org
¶   The Growing Heap - 4.   Guide to Community Composting.

Community Development Finance Association   (cdfa)   2001
NR   Hatton Square Business Centre (Room 101), 16-16a Baldwins
      Gardens, LONDON, EC1N 7RJ.
      020 7430 0222
      email info@cdfa.org.uk   http://www.cdfa.org.uk
      Chief Exec: Bernie Morgan
▲   Company Limited by Guarantee
○   *T; for community development finance institutions -
      sustainable, independent financial institutions that provide
      capital & support to enable individuals to develop & create
      wealth in disadvantaged communities or under-served
      markets
●   Conf - Mtgs - ET - LG
M   5 i, 104 f
¶   Inside Out (survey of sector) - 1; £15, £15 +postage nm.
      Enterprise Communities (wealth beyond welfare); free.
      Money-go-Round: recycling finances, realising capital.
      Community Investment Relief Guide; £10 m, £12.50 nm.
      Guide to Building a CDFI; £200 m, £200+postage nm.

Community & District Nursing Association UK (CDNA) 1971
NR 22-24 Worple Rd, Wimbledon, LONDON, SW19 4DD. (hq)
  020 8971 4268
  http://www.cdna-online.org.uk
  Dir: Anne Duffy
Br 40
○ *P, *U
● Conf - Mtgs - ET - Exhib - SG - Empl - LG
M 5,090 i
¶ Nursing Care - 4; ftm, £1.20 nm. Nurse Prescribing; £3.
  Key Issues in District Nursing 1, 2 & 3; £4. AR.
  Innovations in Primary Health Care Nursing; £5.

Community Foundation Network 1991
NR 12 Angel Gate, 320-326 City Rd, LONDON, EC1V 2PT. (hq)
  020 7713 9326 fax 020 7713 9327
  email network@communityfoundations.org.uk
  http://www.communityfoundations.org.uk
  Dir: Stephen Hammersley
▲ Company Limited by Guarantee; Registered Charity
○ *N; 'a support organisation for community trusts & foundations
  & those wishing to establish them in the UK'
● Conf - Mtgs - Res - Stat - Inf - Lib - VE - LG
M 56 trusts / foundations
¶ NL - 4; ftm.
  Giving Shares & Securities: information pack for financial
  advisers; ftm.
  A Guide to European Funding; ftm.
  Community Foundations & Community Needs Assessment; ftm.
  Tackling Multiple Disadvantage; ftm.
  Changing the Future; ftm.
  Publications list available.

Community Hospitals Association (CHA) 1969
NR Meadow Brow, Broadway, ILMINSTER, Somerset, TA19 9RG.
  (hsb)
  01460 55951 fax 01460 53207
  Chief Exec: Mrs Barbara Moore
▲ Un-incorporated Society
○ *K, *M; promotion of community hospitals
● Conf - Res - Stat - Inf - VE - LG
< Assn for GP Maternity Care; Scot Assn of GP Community
  Hospitals
M 25 i, 10 org, 250 hospitals
¶ NL - 4; ftm.

Community Housing Cymru
NR Fulmar House, Beignon Close, Ocean Park, CARDIFF,
  CF24 5HF.
  0300 303 1073 fax 029 2055 7415
  email enquiries@chcymru.org.uk
  http://www.chcymru.org.uk
  Chief Exec: Nick Bennett
○ *N,*W; housing associations
< Comité Européen Co-ordination de l'Habitat Social
  (CECODHAS Housing Europe)
M c 70 assns

Community Matters
  see **National Federation of Community Organisations
  (Community Matters)**

Community Media Association (CMA) 1983
NR 15 Paternoster Row, SHEFFIELD, S Yorks, S1 2BX. (hq)
  0114-279 5219 fax 0114-279 8976
  email cma@commedia.org.uk
  http://www.commedia.org.uk
  Dir: Diane Reid
▲ Company Limited by Guarantee
○ *K, *N; to represent community media in the UK to
  government, regulators & industry
● Conf - Lib - LG
< Wld Assn of Community Radio Broadcasters (AMARC)
M 200 i, 300 f, UK / 10 i, 10 f, o'seas
¶ Airflash (Jnl) - 4; ftm only (subscription £5-£60).

Community Pharmacy Scotland
NR 42 Queen St, EDINBURGH, EH2 3NH. (hq)
  0131-467 7766 fax 0131-467 7767
  email enquiries@communitypharmacyscotland.org.uk
  http://www.communitypharmacyscotland.org.uk
  Chief Exec: Harry McQuillan
○ *T; to represent community pharmacy owners throughout
  Scotland
M 1,117 i
✕ 2006 Scottish Pharmaceutical Federation (merged)
  2007 Scottish Pharmaceutical General Council

Community Recycling Network UK (CRN UK)
NR The Grayston Centre, 28 Charles Square, LONDON, N1 6HT.
  020 7324 4705
  email info@crn.org.uk http://www.crn.org.uk
○ *K; to promote community based sustainable waste
  management

Community Service Volunteers (CSV) 1962
■ 237 Pentonville Rd, LONDON, N1 9NJ. (hq)
  020 7278 6601 fax 020 7833 0149
  email information@csv.org.uk http://www.csv.org.uk
  Chief Exec: Elisabeth Hoodless
▲ Company Limited by Guarantee; Registered Charity
Br 120
○ *W; to create opportunities for people to take an active part in
  the life of their community through volunteering, training &
  community action; Please note that CSV is NOT able to offer
  sponsorship or grants
Gp Education consultancy; Employee volunteering; Full-time
  volunteering, social care up to 12 moinths; Retired & senior
  volunteers programme; Social action broadcasting;
  Vocational training
● Conf - ET - Res - Exhib - Inf
M 229,000 i (per year)

Community Transport Association UK (CTA) 1982
NR Highbank, Halton St, HYDE, Cheshire, SK14 2NY.
  0870 774 3586 fax 0870 774 3581
  email ctauk@communitytransport.com
  http://www.ctauk.org
  Chief Exec: Keith Halstead
▲ Company Limited by Guarantee; Registered Charity
Br 7
○ *W; any form of non-profit transport provision for people with
  mobility problems
Gp Community car scheme; Dial-a-Ride; Rural transport; Training
● Conf - Mtgs - ET - Exhib - Inf - Lib - PL - LG - Vehicle purchase
  scheme - Issue of minibus permits
< NCVO
M 1,250 org, UK / 10 org, o'seas
¶ Community Transport - 6; ftm, £21 nm. AR; free.
  Publications list available.

Community & Youth Workers' Union (CYWU) 1971
NR Transport House, 211 Broad St, BIRMINGHAM, B15 1AY. (hq)
  0121-643 6221
  http://www.cywu.org.uk
  Nat Sec: Doug Nicholls
○ *U; trade union for full & part-time youth, community & play
  workers in the statutory or voluntary sector
< Unite, the Union
¶ Rapport - 6.

Companion Animal Behaviour Therapy Study Group
  a group of the **British Small Animal Veterinary Association**

Company Chemists' Association Ltd   (CCA)   1898
- ■ Garden Studios, 11-15 Betterton St, London, WC2H 9BP.   (hq)
  020 7470 8775   fax 020 7470 8776
  http://www.thecca.org.uk
  Chief Exec: Robert Darracott
- ▲ Company Limited by Guarantee
- ○ *T; for corporate bodies operating community pharmacy
  businesses
- ● Mtgs - LG
- M   9 f

Company of Goldsmiths of Dublin   1637
- IRL   Assay Office, Dublin Castle, DUBLIN 2, Republic of Ireland.
  353 (1) 475 1286; 478 0323   fax 353 (1) 478 3838
  email hallmark@assay.ie
- ○ Controls & conducts the Assay Office

Compassionate Friends   (TCF)   1969
- ■ 53 North St, BRISTOL, BS3 1EN.   (hq)
  0845 120 3785   fax 0845 120 3786
  email info@tcf.org.uk   http://www.tcf.org.uk
  Chmn: Diana Youdale
- ▲ Company Limited by Guarantee; Registered Charity
- Br   Australia, Europe, New Zealand, USA
- ○ *W; to offer support & friendship to bereaved parents & their
  families through 250 local contacts
- Gp   Childless parents; POMC - parents of murdered children;
  Shadow of suicide; SIBBS - support in bereavement for
  brothers & sisters
- ● Mtgs - Inf - Lib - Annual weekend gathering - Personal &
  telephone support
  Helpline: 0845 123 2304
- M   10,000 families, 100 f, 100 org, UK / 50 families, o'seas
- ¶ TCF NL - 4; £30 m only.

Competing Pipers Association   (CPA)   1976
- NR   Drumcairn, Cawdor Crescent, DUBNBLANE, Stirlingsire,
  FK15 9JJ   (sp)
  email secretary@competingpipers.com
  http://www.competingpipers.com
  Sec: Peter McCalister
- ○ *D; to represent the world's competitive solo piping community
  in Scotland (highland bagpipes)
- ● Mtgs - Comp
- M   i

Complementary Medical Association   (CMA)   1995
- NR   Blackcleuch, Teviothead, HAWICK, Roxburghshire, TD9 0PU.
  (hq)
  0845 129 8434
  http://www.the-cma.org.uk
- ▲ Un-incorporated Society
- Br   2; Bulgaria, Georgia, India, Nepal, Portugal, S Africa
- ○ *P; a register of complementary medical practitioners & training
  organisations
- ● Conf - ET - Exam - Res - Exhib - Comp - SG - Inf - VE - LG -
  Educational programmes to PhD level
- M   15,000 i (worldwide), 10 f, 3 org, UK / 3 f, o'seas
- ¶ With Our Complements - 4.

Complementary Therapists Association   (CTA)
- NR   Chiswick Gate (2nd floor), 598-608 Chiswick High Rd,
  LONDON, W4 5RT.   (hq)
  0845 202 2941   fax 0844 779 8898
  email info@ctha.com   http://www.ctha.com
- ○ *P; for therapists in the UK & Ireland
- <   Aromatherapy Coun
- M   c 9,000 i

Component Obsolescence Group   (COG)   1997
- ■ Curo Park (Unit 3), St ALBANS, Herts, AL2 2DD.   (asa)
  01727 876029   fax 01727 871336
  email info@cog.org.uk   http://www.cog.org.uk
  Contact: Ian Blackman
- ▲ Company Limited by Guarantee
- ○ *G; to provide a forum for industry professionals concerned
  with obsolescence of electronic, mechanical & software
  components in industries where equipment life is long
- Gp   Standardisation & guidance; Wensite maintenance
- ● Conf - Mtgs - ET - Exhib - Inf - LG
- M   135 f, UK / 60 f, o'seas

Composites UK Ltd   1989
- NR   4A Broom Business Park, CHESTERFIELD, Derbys, S41 9DG.
  (hq)
  01246 266245   fax 01246 266249
  email info@compositesuk.org
  http://www.compositesuk.org
  Techynical enquiries: Dr Sue Halliwell
- ▲ Company Limited by Guarantee
- ○ *T; to enhance & promote the safe & effective use of
  composites
- Gp   Aerospace Composites Group
- ● Conf - ET - Exhib - Lib - LG
- <   American Composites Mfrs' Assn
- M   90 f
- ¶ Composites UK Bulletin - 4; free.
- ×   2007 (March) Composites Processing Association Ltd

Composting Association
  since 2008 **Association of Organics Recycling**

Composting Association of Ireland   (CR/Ea/)
- IRL   PO Box 13, DUNDALK, Co Louth, Republic of Ireland.
  email info@cre.ie   http://www.compostireland.ie
  Chief Exec: Percy Foster
- ○ *T

Compulsory Annuity Purchase Protest Alliance   (CAPPA)   1999
- NR   85 Oldfield Rd, SHEFFIELD, S Yorks, S6 6DU.   (mem/s/p)
  http://www.cappa.org.uk
  Mem Sec: Tony Davies
- ▲ Un-incorporated Society
- ○ *K; to seek reform of Finance Acts which compel private
  pension fund holders to buy an annuity at age 75

Computer Conservation Society   (CCS)   1988
- NR   25 Comet Close, Ash Vale, ALDERSHOT, Hants, GU12 5SG.
  (hsp)
  http://www.computerconservationsociety.org
  Sec: Kevin Murrell
- ▲ Un-incorporated Society
- Br   2
- ○ *G; conservation & restoration of historic computers; collection
  of archive material in history of computing, including
  hardware, software, publications & reminiscences
- Gp   Working parties: DEC, Elliott 401, Elliott 803, Ferranti Pegasus,
  S100 BUS, Turing bombe
- ● Mtgs - Working parties to restore historic computers
- <   Parent Org: Brit Computer Soc, Science Museum South
  Kensington, Museum of Science & Ind in Manchester
- M   c 700 i, 1 f, UK / c 25 i, o'seas
- ¶ Computer Resurrection (Jnl) - 3/4; ftm.

Comunn na Clàrsaich   (the Clarsach Society)   1931
NR   Out of the Blue Drill Hall (studio G43), 36 Dalmeny St,
        EDINBURGH, EH6 8RG.   (hq)
        0131-554 0212
        email clarsachs@blueyonder.co.uk
        http://www.clarsachsociety.co.uk
     11 Granby Rd, EDINBURGH, EH16 5NP.   (hsp)
        0131-667 4645
        Hon Sec: Mary Scott
▲   Registered Charity
Br   11
○   *D; to encourage the playing of the clarsach (Celtic harp); to
        preserve its place in the national life of Scotland, particularly
        among Gaelic speaking people
Gp   Wire strung harp
●   ET - Comp - Inf - Harp hire service to members - Organisation
        of the Edinburgh Harp Festival
<   An Comunn Gaidhealach
M   900 i, UK / 50 i, o'seas
¶   Branch newsletters - irreg; ftm only.
        Folios of Music (detailed catalogue on request).
        AR (incl list of harp makers).
        Diary of Events - 2; free to branches.

An Comunn Gaidhealach [The Highland Association]   1891
NR   109 Church St, INVERNESS, IV1 1EY.   (hq)
        01463 709705   fax 01463 715557
        http://www.ancomunn.co.uk
○   *L; promotion of the Gaelic language, literature, arts & music
M   c 2,500 i

Concert Artistes' Association   (CAA)   1897
■   20 Bedford St, LONDON, WC2E 9HP.   (hq)
        020 7836 3172   fax 020 7836 3172
        email office@thecaa.org   http://www.thecaa.org
        Sec: Malcolm Knight,   Pres: Chris Emmett
○   *A, *D; for all those interested in the entertainment profession
        with particular reference to concerts, cabarets, radio,
        television & West End productions
        The association has its own West End club - the Club for Acts &
        Actors
Gp   General committee & several sub-committees; Trustees of the
        benevolent fund
●   Mtgs - ET - Exam - Exhib - Comp - SG - VE - Rehearsals, shows
        - Theatrical productions
<   Catholic Stage Gld
M   998 i, 1 guild, UK / 50 i, o'seas
¶   NL - 3;   Chairman's Report -1;   LM - 2 yrly; all ftm only.
        But - What do you do in the Winter? (book by Larry Parker); £8.

Concert Promoters Association   (CPA)   1986
NR   6 St Mark's Rd, HENLEY-on-THAMES, Oxon, RG9 1LJ.   (sp)
        01491 575060   fax 01491 414082
        email carolesmith.cpa@virgin.net
        Sec: Carole Smith
▲   Company Limited by Guarantee
○   *T; the interests of promoters of contemporary music concerts/
        tours in the UK
M   [not given]

**Conchological Society of Great Britain & Ireland   (CSGBI)
1876**
■   447B Wokingham Rd, Earley, READING, Berks, RG6 7EL.
        (hsp)
        Hon Sec: Rosemary Hill
▲   Registered Charity
○   *L; to promote the study of the mollusca in all its aspects;
        actively engaged in biographical distribution of marine &
        non-marine molluscs
●   Conf - Mtgs - Res - Stat
<   Brit Trust Consvn Volunteers; Coun Nature
M   280 i, 20 org, UK / 100 i, 20 org, o'seas
¶   Journal of Conchology - 2; ftm, £40 nm.
        Mollusc World - 3; ftm, £3 nm.
        Other occasional publications.

Concrete Block Association
        a product association of the **British Precast Concrete Federation**

Concrete Bridge Development Group   (CBDG)   1992
NR   Riverside House, 4 Meadows Business Park, Station Approach,
        Blackwater, CAMBERLEY, Surrey, GU17 9AB.   (hq)
        01276 33777   fax 01276 38899
        email enquiries@cbdg.org.uk   http://www.cbdg.org.uk
        Sec: Alan Tovey
▲   Company Limited by Guarantee
○   *T; to enhance the design, construction & management of
        concrete bridges
M   80 f & org

Concrete Manufacturers Association of Ireland   (CMAI)
IRL   Confederation House, 84-86 Lower Baggot St, DUBLIN 2,
        Republic of Ireland.   (hq)
        353 (1) 605 1621   fax 353 (1) 638 1621
        email mark.mcauley@ibec.ie   http://www.ibec.ie/cmai/
        Dir: Mark McAuley
○   *T; companies engaged in the manufacture of ready mixed
        concrete & concrete blocks
<   Ir Business & Emplrs Confedn (IBEC)

Concrete Pipeline Systems Association
        a product association of the **British Precast Concrete Federation**

Concrete Repair Association   (CRA)   1988
■   Kingsley House, Ganders Business Park, Kingsley, BORDON,
        Hants, GU35 9LU.   (asa)
        01420 471615
        email admin@cra.org.uk   http://www.cra.org.uk
        Sec: John G Fairley
▲   Company Limited by Guarantee
○   *T; to promote the practice of concrete repair
●   Conf - Mtgs - ET - Exhib - Inf - Seminars - Quality assurance &
        control system implementation
M   38 f
¶   LM - 3; free.
        Standard Method of Measurement; £5 m, £10 nm.
        Application & Measurement of Protective Coatings; free.
        Route to a Successful Concrete Repair; £2.50 m, £5 nm.

Concrete Sleeper Manufacturers' Association
        a product association of the **British Precast Concrete Federation**

Concrete Society   1966
■   Riverside House, 4 Meadows Business Park, Station Approach,
        Blackwater, CAMBERLEY, Surrey, GU17 9AB.   (hq)
        01276 607140   fax 01276 607141
        email enquiries@concrete.org.uk
        http://www.concrete.org.uk
        Chief Exec: Richard England
▲   Company Limited by Guarantee
Br   20
○   *L, *T; to bring together all who are interested in concrete to
        exchange information, to encourage innovation, to promote
        excellence in design, construction, appearance &
        performance
Gp   Design; Construction; Materials
●   Conf - Mtgs - ET - Res - Inf - Lib - PL - LG - Annual awards -
        Advisory service
<   Fédn Intle du Beton; Eur Concrete Soc Network
M   1,000 i, 500 f
¶   Concrete (Jnl) - 10.
        Concrete Engineers International Jnl - 4.

Concrete Structures Group Ltd
        see **Construct: Concrete Structures Group**

Concrete Tile Manufacturers' Association
        an affiliated association of the **British Precast Concrete
        Federation**

Confederation of Aerial Industries Ltd   (CAI)   1978
NR   41A Market St, WATFORD, Herts, WD18 0PN.   (hq)
    01923 803030   fax 01923 803203
    email office@cai.org.uk   http://www.cai.org.uk
    Sec: Mrs Beverley K Allgood
▲   Company Limited by Guarantee
○   *T; for the aerial & satellite industry
●   ET - Exam - Exhib - LG
M   c 750 f
¶   Feedback - 4;   LM - 1;   Ybk - 1; Codes of practice; all free.

Confederation of British Industry   (CBI)   1965
NR   Centre Point, 103 New Oxford St, LONDON, WC1A 1DU.
    (hq)
    020 7379 7400
    http://www.cbi.org.uk
    Dir Gen: John Cridland
○   *T; employers organisation promoting the prosperity of British
    industry
<   Businesseurope
M   250,000 f

Confederation of British Metalforming   (CBM)
NR   National Metalforming Centre, 47 Birmingham Rd, WEST
    BROMWICH, W Midlands, B70 6PY.   (hq)
    0121-601 6350   fax 0121-601 6373
    email info@britishmetalforming.com
    http://www.britishmetalforming.com
    Dir Gen: John Houseman
○   *T; manufacturers of fasteners, forgings & pressings
●   Conf - Mtgs - Inf
M   300 f

Confederation of British Service & Ex-Service Organisations
(COBSEO)   1982
■   c/o GVAMP, The Baird Medical Centre, Gassiott House,
    St Thomas' Hospital, Lambeth Palace Rd, LONDON,
    SE1 7EP.   (hsb)
    020 7202 8322   fax 020 7928 0435
    email sec.cobseo@btconnect.com
    http://www.cobseo.org.uk
    Co Sec: Michael Bray
▲   Company Limited by Guarantee
○   *N, *W; to represent, promote & further the interest of service &
    ex-service personnel of all ranks & their spouses &
    dependents
●   Conf - Mtgs - Inf - LG
M   140 org
    (Sub: £50)
¶   Bulletin - 4; ftm;   AR - 1.

Confederation of British Wool Textiles Ltd
    closed 2009

Confederation of Children's Services Managers
    in 2007 merged with the children's element of the Association of
    Directors Social Services to form the **Association of Directors of**
    Children's Services

Confederation of Co-operative Housing   1993
■   18 Devonshire Rd, LIVERPOOOL, L8 3TX.
    0151-726 2228
    http://www.cch.coop
    Chmn: Nic Bliss
▲   Company Limited by Guarantee
○   *N; for all housing co-operatives & tenant controlled housing
    bodies

Confederation of Construction Specialists   (CCS)   1983
■   1 Walpole House, 2 Pickford St, ALDERSHOT, Hants,
    GU11 1TZ.   (hq)
    01252 312122   fax 01252 343081
    email info@constructionspecialists.org
    http://www.constructionspecialists.org
    Group Dir: A R Gibbs
▲   Un-incorporated Society
○   *N, *T; central representative body for specialist building & civil
    engineering firms
●   Conf - Mtgs - ET - Res - SG - Stat - Inf - Lib - LG - Advisory &
    consultancy service - Commercial intelligence service
<   Construction Specialists Gp
M   f & affiliated trade assns
¶   NL - 10; ftm.
    Performance Bond; £10.   Certificate of vesting; £10.
    Standard forms of contract & sub-contract; £5-£10.

Confederation of Dental Employers   (CODE)   1978
■   Elm Tree House, Bodmin St, HOLSWORTHY, Devon,
    EX22 6BB.   (hq)
    01409 254354   fax 01409 254364
    email info@codeuk.com   http://www.codeuk.com
    Chief Exec: Dr Paul Mendlesohn
▲   Incorporated Society
○   *P; to represent the interests of practice owners in the UK
●   Conf - ET - Res - Exhib - Inf - LG - Management services -
    Helpline
M   450 i, 8 f
¶   face2face - 4; ftm.

Confederation of English Fly Fishers   (CEFF)   1974
NR   23 Smithson Close, Talbot Village, POOLE, Dorset,
    BH12 5EY.   (hsp)
    01202 537321   fax 07754 091923
    email secretary@ceff.org.uk   http://www.ceff.org.uk
    Hon Sec: Malcolm Price
○   *G; to foster all aspects of fly fishing; to promote the sport
    including respect for the environment
M   c 5,000 i

Confederation of Forest Industries   (ConFor)   1959
■   59 George St, EDINBURGH, EH2 2JG.
    0131-240 1410   fax 0131-240 1411
    email stuart.goodall@confor.org.uk
    http://www.confor.org.uk
    Chief Exec: Stuart Goodall
▲   Company Limited by Guarantee
○   *T; to represent the whole wood supply chain - growers,
    woodland managers, contractors, harvesters & primary &
    secondary processors
●   Conf - Mtgs - Exhib - VE - LG
M   400 i, 1,300 f, 50 org
    (Sub: varies)
¶   Forestry & Timber News - 6; ftm, £32 yr nm.
×   2006 Association of Timber Growers & Forestry Professionals

Confederation of Healing Organisations   (CHO)   1981
■   c/o 18A Littleham Rd, EXMOUTH, Devon, EX8 2QG.   (asa)
    01584 890662
    email diane.schooley@btinternet.com
    http://www.confederation-of-healing-organisations.org
    Sec: Mrs Diane Schooley
▲   Company Limited by Guarantee; Registered Charity
○   *K, *N; to advance public education in methods of healing; to
    promote research into the methods & effects of healing; to
    coordinate & represent member organisations
●   Mtgs - Res - Inf
M   8,000 i in 12 org

Confederation of Long Distance Racing Pigeon Unions of Great Britain & Ireland

NR 20 Gorsey Lane, Banks, SOUTHPORT, PR9 8EH.   (hq)
01704 232164
Hon Sec: Brian Newsome
○ *N, *S

Confederation of Paper Industries Ltd   (CPI)   1999

NR 1 Rivenhall Rd, SWINDON, Wilts, SN5 7BD.   (hq)
01793 889600   fax 01793 878700
email cpi@paper.org.uk   http://www.paper.org.uk
Dir Gen: David Workman
▲ Company Limited by Guarantee
○ *N; the authoritative & effective voice of the UK's paper-related industries
Gp Corrugated; Papermaking; Recovered paper; Tissue
● Conf - Mtgs - ET - Stat - Inf - Empl - LG
< Confedn of Eur Paper Inds (CEPI); Fédn Eur des Fabricants de Carton Ondulé (FEFCO); Eur Recovered Paper Assn (ERPA)
M 100 f
¶ CPI News - 26;   Daily Data - daily;   MP's NL - 4;   statistics (various); all ftm only.
Annual Review - 1; free.

Confederation of Passenger Transport UK   (CPT)   1974

NR Drury House, 34-43 Russell St, LONDON, WC2B 5HA.   (hq)
020 7240 3131   fax 020 7240 6565
email cpt@cpt-uk.org   http://www.cpt-uk.org
Dir Gen: Brian Nimick
▲ Company Limited by Guarantee
○ *T; representing bus & coach operators
● Conf - Mtgs - ET - Res - Exhib - SG - Stat - Inf - PL - LG
M 1,200 f
¶ Newsline (NL) - 10;   Annual review;   Bulletins - irreg;   Hbk - 1; all ftm.

Confederation of Roofing Contractors Ltd   (CRC)   1985

NR 22D Victoria Place, BRIGHTLINGSEA, Essex, CO7 0bx.   (hq)
01206 306600   fax 01206 306200
email enquiries@corc.co.uk   http://www.corc.co.uk
Chief Exec: Allan Buchan
▲ Company Limited by Guarantee
Br 4
○ *T; 'the main consumer protection organisation in the roofing industry'
● ET - Inf - Lib - LG
M 625 i, 625 f
¶ The Roofing Trades Jnl - 6; free.

Confederation of Transcribed Information Services
merged on 1 January 2009 with the Braille Authority UK & the United Kingdom Association of Braille Producers to form **United Kingdom Association for Accessible Formats**

Confederation of UK Coal Producers   (COALPRO)   1991

■ Confederation House, Thornes Office Park, Denby Dale Rd, WAKEFIELD, W Yorks, WF2 7AN.   (hq)
01924 200802   fax 01924 200796
email db@coalpro.co.uk   http://www.coalpro.co.uk
Dir Gen: David Brewer,   Gen Mgr: Mrs A Fellows
▲ Company Limited by Guarantee
○ *T; represents the majority of UK companies engaged in coal extraction
Gp British Standards; Deep mining; Marketing & development; Opencast mining; Safety & Health
● Conf - Mtgs - Exhib - Stat - Inf - Lib - PL - LG - Liaison with European Commission - Liaison with associate organisations worldwide
< Worls Coal Inst; Euriscoal (Brussels); Combined Heat & Power Assn; Confedn of Brit Ind
M 21 f
¶ LM - 1.   Mines Database.
Technical Information - 12.   AR.   NL - 12.

Confederation of West Midlands Chambers of Commerce   2002

NR 75 Harborne Rd, BIRMINGHAM, W Midlands, B15 3DH.
0845 074 3515
http://www.wmchambers.co.uk
M 7 org
¶ Economic Survey - 4.
LM.

Conference Centres of Excellence   (CCE)

NR Innovation Centre, Warwick Technology Park, Gallows Hill, WARWICK, CV34 6UW.
0845 230 1414   fax 01926 419280
http://www.cceonline.co.uk
Exec Dir: Anthony Lishman
○ *T; specialist conference, meeting & training providers
M 37 centres

Conference of Drama Schools   (CDS)   1969

■ PO Box 34252, LONDON, NW5 1XJ.   (hsp)
020 7692 0032   fax 020 7692 0032
email info@cds.drama.ac.uk   http://www.drama.ac.uk
Exec Sec: Saul Hyman
▲ Company Limited by Guarantee
○ *P; to provide a voice for drama trainers; to give advice to prospective students
● Conf - Mtgs - ET - Res - Comp - Inf
< Nat Coun for Drama Training
M 21 f
¶ CDS Guide to Professional Training in Drama & Technical Theatre 1; free.
CDS Guide to Careers Back Stage; free.

Conference Interpreters Group   (CIG)   1979

NR 46 Oakfield Court, Haslemere Rd, LONDON, N8 9QY.   (hq)
020 8341 5891
email ciglondon@aol.com
http://www.cig-interpreters.com
Exec Sec: Amanda Carrara
▲ Company Limited by Guarantee
○ *P; cooperative grouping of simultaneous interpreters
M 22 i

Conference of Professional Dance Schools
a group of the **Council for Dance Education & Training (UK)**

Conflict Research Society   (CRS)   1963

■ 28 Severn Drive, NEWPORT PAGNELL, Bucks, MK16 9DQ.   (chmn/p)
01908 611296
http://www.conflictresearchsociety.org.uk
Chmn: Gordon John Burt
▲ Registered Charity
○ *L, *Q; to promote research into, & the extension of knowledge about, conflict processes at all levels
M c 80 i
¶ Jnl of the Conflict Research Society - 1; ftm, £10 nm (£15 o'seas).

Confraternity of Saint James (CSJ) 1983
- ■ 27 Blackfriars Rd, LONDON, SE1 8NY.
  020 7928 9988   fax 020 7928 2844
  email office@csj.org.uk   http://www.csj.org.uk
  Sec: Marion Marples
- ▲ Registered Charity
- ○ *G; a nondenominational organisation for all interested in the pilgrimage to Santiago de Compostela; to promote research into the history of the pilgrimage in Britain; to identify & safeguard works of art connected with St James & the pilgrimage
- Gp Research working party
- ● Conf - Mtgs - Res - Exhib - SG - Inf - Lib - PL - VE - Concerts
- < European Assn Friends Road to St James
- M 2,500 i, 15 org, UK / 300 i, 3 org, o'seas
- ¶ Bulletin - 4; ftm, £2.50 nm.
  Pilgrim Guides & other publications: list on application.

Congenital CMV Association 1986
- ■ 111 Windmill Hill Lane, Kingsway, DERBY, DE22 3BN.   (hsp)
  01332 365528
  email congenitalcmv.association@ntlworld.com
  http://www.cmvsupport.org
  Coordinator: Mrs Carmen Burton
- ○ *W; the welfare & support of families with congenital cytomegalovirus (of the herpes virus group); to support research to aid medical staff & professionals
- ● Res - Stat - Inf - Lib
- M 80 i, 10 f, UK / 25 i, 10 f, o'seas
- ¶ NL - 4; ftm, free email nm.
  Information leaflets on Congenital CMV; free email.

CONNECT
since 2010 is the Connect sector of **Prospect**

Connemara Pony Breeders Society
- IRL The Showgrounds, Hospital Rd, CLIFDEN, Co Galway, Republic of Ireland.
  353 (95) 21863
  email enquiries@cpbs.ie   http://www.cpbs.ie
- ○ *B

Conservatoires UK   (CBC)
- ■ c/o John Wallace, Royal Scottish Academy of Music & Drama, 100 Renfrew St, GLASGOW, G2 3DB.   (chmn/b)
  Chmn: John Wallace
- ○ *D, *E; music education & training
- ● Conf - Mtgs - SG - LG
- < Assn of Eur Conservatoires
- M 7 conservatoires

Conservatory Association
a specialist division of **Glass & Glazing Federation**

Consortium of Caterers in Education Hospitality & Leisure
- NR c/o Head of Catering Services, Calderdale College, Francis St, HALIFAX, W Yorks, HX1 3UZ.   (sp)
  01422 357357 (enquiries)
  http://www.cca-education.com.uk
  Sec: Tom Griffiths
- ○ *P

Consortium of Lesbian, Gay & Bisexual Transgendered Voluntary & Community Organisations   (LGBT Consortium)
- NR J111 Tower Bridge Business Complex, 100 Clements Rd, LONDON, SE16 4DG.   (hq)
  020 7064 8383   fax 020 7064 8382
  email paul.roberts@lgbtconsortium.org.uk
  http://www.lgbtconsortium.org.uk
  Chief Exec: Paul Roberts
- ▲ Company Limited by Guarantee; Registered Charity
- ○ *N
- Gp Bisexual; Gay; Lesbian; Transgendered
- ● Conf - Res - Inf - Lib
- M c 400 i in 300 org

Consortium of Research Libraries in the British Isles
since 2008 **RLUK: Research Libraries UK**

Consortium of University Research Libraries
in 2004 was renamed CURL (Consortium of Research Libraries) & in 2008 became **RLUK: Research Libraries UK**

Constitutional Monarchy Association
part of the **Monarchist League**

Construct: Concrete Structures Group Ltd   (Construct)   1993
- ■ Riverside House, 4 Meadows Business Park, Station Approach, Blackwater, CAMBERLEY, Surrey, GU17 9AB.   (hq)
  01276 38444   fax 01276 38899
  email enquiries@construct.org.uk
  http://www.construct.org.uk
- ▲ Company Limited by Guarantee
- ○ *T; for all specialist concrete contractors (concrete frame & other structures); to improve the efficiency of the concrete industry & thereby widening the market for concrete
- Gp Health & safety
- ● Mtgs - ET - Inf
- M 3 i, 76 f, 2 org (by negotiation)
  (Sub: £75-£3,500)
- ¶ Framework (NL); on website.   Ybk - 1; free.
  In-Situ Concrete Frames: a report; £5.
  Best Practice Guides (8); on website.
  Other publications; £10 - £60.

Construction Confederation
wound up

Construction Employers Federation Ltd   (CEF)   1945
- ■ 143 Malone Rd, BELFAST, BT9 6SU.   (hq)
  028 9087 7143   fax 028 9087 7155
  email mail@cefni.co.uk   http://www.cefni.co.uk
  Dir: J Armstrong
- ▲ Company Limited by Guarantee
- ○ *T
- Gp Private housing; Public authority housing; General contracting; Export; Civil engineering
- ● Conf - Mtgs - ET - Exhib - Stat - Expt - Inf - VE - Empl - LG
- M 500 f
- ¶ Bulletin - 12;   AR; both ftm.

Construction Equipment Association   (CEA)   1942
- ■ Airport House, Purley Way, CROYDON, Surrey, CR0 0XZ.   (asa)
  020 8253 4502   fax 020 8253 4510
  email cea@admin.co.uk   http://www.coneq.org.uk
  Secs: Administration Services Ltd
- ▲ Un-incorporated Society
- ○ *T; to serve construction equipment manufacturers, their component & accessory suppliers & service providers
- ● Conf - Mtgs - Exhib - Stat - Expt - Inf - VE - LG
- < C'ee for Eur Construction Eqpt (CECE); Fédn Eur de la Manutention (FEM)
- M 120 f
- ¶ Newsline - 4; ftm.

© CBD Research Ltd · Beckenham · BR3 5JS · Tel 020 8650 7745 · E-mail cbd@cbdresearch.com · www.cbdresearch.com

Construction Fixings Association   (CFA)   1977

■   65 Deans St, OAKHAM, Rutland, LE15 6AF.   (asa)
    01664 823687   fax 01664 823687
    email info@fixingscfa.co.uk
    http://www.fixingscfa.co.uk
    Gen Mgr: Mark Salmon
▲   Company Limited by Guarantee
○   *T; ensuring 'best fixings practice' among specifiers, distributors
    & installers of construction fixings
Gp Manufacturers (full members); Sellers within the UK (approved
    distributors); Sellers overseas (international members)
●   Conf - Mtgs - ET - Inf
<   Comité Eur de l'Outillage (CEO); Eur Tools C'ee
M   6 full members, 21 approved distbrs, UK; 2 f, o'seas
¶   Guidance Notes on the Correct Selection & Application of
    Fixings (a series of 10) - download from website; free.

Construction History Society   1981

■   c/o CIB Information Services Manager, Englemere, Kings Ride,
    ASCOT, Berks, SL5 8TB   (sb)
    01344 630741   fax 01344 630764
    email michael.tutton@virgin.net
    http://www.constructionhistory.co.uk
    Exec Sec & Admin: Michael Tutton
▲   Registered Charity; Un-incorporated Society
○   *L; to focus attention on the problems of historical information
    about the construction process becoming lost by default; to
    undertake a survey to establish the records available & their
    accessibility
●   Conf - Mtgs - Lib
M   300 i
    (Sub: £25)
¶   Construction History Jnl - 1; ftm, price on application nm.
    NL - 4; ftm only.

Construction Industry Computing Association

    closed in 2008

Construction Industry Council   (CIC)   1987

NR The Building Centre, 26 Store St, LONDON, WC1E 7BT.   (hq)
    020 7399 7400   fax 020 7399 7425
    email cic@cic.org.uk   http://www.cic.org.uk
    Chief Exec: Graham Watts
▲   Company Limited by Guarantee
○   *N, *T; to represent organisations in the built environment & to
    provide a forum for discussion, particularly for professional
    bodies
●   Conf - Mtgs - Res - Inf - LG
M   34 full, 15 associate, 17 affiliate
¶   AR.   Publications list available on website.

Construction Industry Federation

IRL Construction House, Canal Rd, DUBLIN 6, Republic of Ireland.
    353 (1) 406 6000   fax 353 (1) 496 6953
    email cif@cif.ie   http://www.cif.ie
    Dir Gen: Tom Parlon
Br 13
○   *T
M   c 3,000

Construction Industry Information Group   (CIIG)   1962

■   1 Ridgewood Drive, SUTTON COLDFIELD, W Midlands,
    B75 6TR.   (mem s/p)
    0121-308 1631
    http://www.ciig.org.uk
    Mem Sec: Paul James
○   *N, *P; to promote good practice in construction libraries &
    information services
Gp Freelance librarians
●   Conf - VE
M   180 i
¶   NL - 12;   Review - irreg;   LM - 1; all ftm only.

Construction Industry Research & Information Association (CIRIA)   1960

NR Classic House, 174-180 Old St, LONDON, EC1V 9BP.   (hq)
    020 7549 3300   fax 020 7253 0523
    email enquiries@ciria.org   http://www.ciria.org
▲   Company Limited by Guarantee
○   *Q; 'best practice research into issues relating to construction &
    the environment'
Gp Construction Ind Envt Forum (CIEF); Construction Productivity
    Network (CPN)
●   Conf - Mtgs - ET - Res
M   70 f, 500 subscribers
¶   Publications list available.

Construction Industry Trade Alliance   (CITA)

NR PO Box 97, CARMARTHEN, SA31 1WT.
    0870 066 4404   fax 0870 066 4405
    email enquiries@cita.co.uk   http://www.cita.co.uk
    Gen Mgr: Tony Crosbie
○   *T; for builders & allied tradesmen within the contruction
    industry

Construction Packed Products Association
    a product association of the **British Precast Concrete Federation**

Construction Plant-hire Association   (CPA)   1941

■   27-28 Newbury St, Barbican, LONDON, EC1A 7HU.   (hq)
    020 7796 3366   fax 020 7796 3399
    email enquiries@cpa.uk.net   http://www.cpa.uk.net
    Chief Exec: Colin Wood
▲   Un-incorporated Society
○   *T; to represent the interests of plant hirers nationally
Gp Rail Plant Association
    Special Interest Groups: Concrete pumping; Construction hoist;
    Crane; Powered access; Road sweepers; Shoring technology;
    Tower crane
●   Conf - Mtgs - Stat - Inf - LG
<   Intl Powered Access Fedn; Construction Confedn; Freight
    Transport Assn
>   Intl Powered Access Fedn
M   1,410 f
¶   The Bulletin - 4; free.   Plant Finder - 1; ftm, £30 nm.

Construction Products Association   (CPA)   2000

■   The Building Centre, 26 Store St, LONDON, WC1E 7BT.   (hq)
    020 7323 3770   fax 020 7323 0307
    email enquiries@constructionproducts.org.uk
    http://www.constructionproducts.org.uk
    Chief Exec: Michael Ankers
▲   Company Limited by Guarantee
○   *N, *T; to represent the manufacturers & suppliers of
    construction products
●   Conf - Mtgs - Res - Exhib - Stat - Inf - LG
<   Coun of Eur Producers of Materials for Construction (CEPMC);
    CBI
M   22 f, 40 trade assns, 7 associates, 7 affiliates
¶   Construction Industry Forecasts - 2.
    Construction Markets Trends - 12.
    Construction Products Trade Survey - 4.
    Construction Products Briefing - 6.
    Weekly Notes - 52.   AR.

Construction Specialists Group

    is no longer in existence

Consumer Credit Association   (CCA)   1978
NR   Queens House, Queens Rd, CHESTER, CH1 3BQ.   (hq)
     01244 312044
     email cca@ccauk.org   http://www.ccauk.org
     Dir: Jack Bennett
▲   Company Limited by Guarantee
○   *T; 'main representative trade association for the home credit
     industry'
●   Conf - Mtgs - ET - SG - Inf - VE - LG - Provide regulated credit
     agreements & other documentation
<   Consumer Credit Assn (Republic of Ireland)
M   500 f
¶   CCA News - 4; ftm, £7.50 nm.   LM - 1; ftm only.   AR; free.
     Distributors of PSI Report.
     Note: Credit Consumer Association & CCA are trading names
     of CCA (UK) Advisory Services Ltd

Consumer Credit Trade Association   (CCTA)   1891
■   The Wave (suite 4), 1 View Croft Rd, SHIPLEY, W Yorks,
     BD17 7DU.   (hq)
     01272 714959
     email info@ccta.co.uk   http://www.ccta.co.uk
     Chief Exec: Greg Stevens
▲   Company Limited by Guarantee
○   *T; to support businesses involved in consumer credit
●   Conf - Mtgs - ET - Res - Inf - LG
<   Eur Fedn of Finance House Assns (EUROFINAS)
M   20 i, 450 f
¶   Consumer Credit - 6; £24 m, £39 yr nm.
     Information leaflet - 6.

Consumer Electronics Distributors Association   (CEDA)
IRL   Confederation House, 84-86 Lower Baggot St, DUBLIN 2,
     Republic of Ireland.   (hq)
     353 (1) 605 1582   fax 353 (1) 638 1582
     email paul.sweetman@ibec.ie   http://www.ibec.ie/ceda
     Dir: Paul Sweetman
○   *T; to promote the development & represent the interests the
     major distributors of consumer electronic goods in Ireland
<   Ir Business & Emplrs Confedn (IBEC)
M   10 f

Consumer Finance Association   (CFA)
NR   46 Brook St, CHESTER, Cheshire, CH1 3DZ.   (hq)
     01244 505545
     http://www.cfa-uk.co.uk
     Chief Exec: John Lamidey
▲   Company Limited by Guarantee
○   *T; for business offering short term, unsecured loans (pay-day
     loans)
M   c 9 f

Consumer Focus
NR   Artillery House (4th floor), Artillery Row, LONDON, SW1P 1RT.
     020 7799 7900

Consumer Foods Council
     a group of **Food & Drink Industry Ireland**

Consumer Protection Association   (CPA)
NR   CPA House, 11 North Bridge St, SHEFFORD, Beds,
     SG17 5DQ.   (hq)
     01462 850062   fax 01462 817161
     email helpline@thecpa.co.uk   http://www.thecpa.co.uk
▲   Company Limited by Guarantee
○   *T; consumer protection; insurance backed guarantees

Consumers' Association   (CA)   1957
■   2 Marylebone Rd, LONDON, NW1 4DF.   (hq)
     020 7770 7000   fax 020 7770 7600
     email editor@which.co.uk   http://www.which.co.uk
     Chief Exec: Peter Vicary-Smith,   Co Sec: Andrew Reading
▲   Registered Charity
○   *K, *Q; independent research & testing of consumer products &
     services; results published by CA's trading subsidiary Which?
     Ltd; campaigning on behalf of consumers
●   Res - Inf - Comparative testing of consumer goods & services
     Helpline: 01992 822800
<   Consumers Us Intl; Bureau Européen des Unions de
     Consommateurs (BEUC)
M   982,000 i
¶   Which? - 12.   Which? Holiday - 4.
     Which? Gardening - 10.
     Which? Money - 12.   Which? Money - 6.
     Consumer Policy Review - 6.
     Note: trades as Which?

Consumers Association of Ireland Ltd   1966
IRL   43-44 Chelmsford Rd, Ranelagh, DUBLIN 6, Republic of
     Ireland.
     353 (1) 497 8600
     email cai@consumerassociation.ie
     http://www.consumerassociation.ie
     Chief Exec: Dermott Jewell
○   *K

Consumers for Health Choice   1995
■   Southbank House, Black Prince Rd, LONDON, SE1 7SJ.
     020 7463 0690
     http://www.consumersforhealthchoice.org.uk
     Chmn: M J Peet
○   *K; for the right of consumers to have ready access to a wide
     range of natural health products, including vitamin & mineral
     supplements and health remedies.
M   i & f

Contact the Elderly   1965
■   15 Henrietta St, LONDON, WC2E 8QG.   (hq)
     020 7240 0630   fax 020 7379 5781
     email info@contact-the-elderly.org.uk
     http://www.contact-the-elderly.org.uk
     Dir: Roderick Sime
▲   Registered Charity
Br   280
○   *W; to alleviate the loneliness & isolation in people over 75 by
     promoting volunteer-led social groups meeting monthly
●   Mtgs
M   4,500 i
¶   Contact News (NL) - 2; free.   AR - 1.

**Container Handling Equipment Manufacturers' Association
(CHEM)   1969**
■   3 Berry Close, FARINGDON, Oxon, SN7 7FL.
     01367 244992
     email enquiries@chem.uk.com   http://www.chem.uk.com
     Technical Sec: David H Buxton
▲   Un-incorporated Society
○   *T; 'vehicles & equipment for the collection, transportation &
     handling of dry waste: to create standards for the interface of
     equipment with containers & to promote safe operations; to
     participate in the drafting of standards for equipment used in
     the collection & transportation of dry waste'
Gp   Technical c'ees for refuse collection vehicles (RCVs) of all types -
     skip loaders, hook loaders, static compactors
●   Mtgs - LG (DTI & Dept of Transport) - Liaison with standards
     institutes BSI & CEN
M   26 f

Contemporary Art Society (CAS) 1910
NR 11-15 Emerald St, LONDON, WC1N 3QL.   (hq)
020 7831 1243   fax 020 7831 1214
email cas@contempart.org.uk
http://www.contempart.org.uk
Dir: Gill Hedley
▲ Company Limited by Guarantee; Registered Charity
○ *A; to acquire works of art by living artists for gift to public art
galleries & museums; to promote collecting by individuals &
companies
● Exhib - VE
M 700 i, 96 org, UK / 100 i, o'seas
¶ NL - 2;   Events NL - 2;   AR - 1.

Contemporary Art Society for Wales (CASW) 1937
■ Mulberry Lodge, 3 Pencisely Rd, CARDIFF, CF5 1DG.
(memsec/p)
http://www.casw.org.uk
Mem Sec: Dr D Evans
▲ Registered Charity
○ *A; the purchase of contemporary art for free distribution to
public galleries & museums throughout Wales
M i, f, org

Contemporary British Silversmiths (ABDS) 1996
■ PO Box 42034, LONDON, E5 9WG.   (admin)
0794 478 6011
http://www.contemporarybritishsilversmiths.com
Chmn: Julie Chamberlain
○ *P, *T; to act as forum for silversmiths throughout the country; to
promote the highest standards in design & craftsmanship
Gp Full: full-time silversmith (by selection);
Graduate: all graduates up to 3 years from leaving a course;
Student; Friend - anyone interested in the field
● Mtgs - Exhib
M 81 i, 12 f, 30 org
¶ NL - 4; ftm.
× 2008 Association of British Designer Silversmiths

Contemporary Glass Society (CGS) 1997
NR c/o Broadfield House Glass Museum, Compton Drive,
KINGSWINFORD, W Midlands, DY6 9NS.   (mail address)
01379 741120   fax 01379 741120
email admin@cgs.org.uk   http://www.cgs.org.uk
Admin: Pam Reekie
▲ Company Limited by Guarantee
○ *A; to encourage excellence in glass as a creative medium; to
develop a greater awareness & appreciation of contemporary
glass world wide
Gp Glass makers
● Conf - Mtgs - ET - Exhib
M 450 i/f
¶ Glass Networks (NL) - 4; ftm only.

Contract Bridge Association of Ireland
see **Irish Bridge Union**

Contract Flooring Association Ltd (CFA) 1974
■ 4c St Mary's Place, The Lace Market, NOTTINGHAM,
NG1 1PH.   (hq)
0115-941 1126   fax 0115-941 2238
email info@cfa.org.uk   http://www.cfa.org.uk
Chief Exec: Richard Catt,   Office Mgr: Mrs Helen Tidmarsh
Br 10
○ *T; for flooring contractors, manufacturers, distributors &
consultants across a wide range of flooring finishes including
carpets, underlays, vinyls, rubber, timber, adhesives &
flooring accessories
Gp Distributors; Environmental; Manufacturers
● Conf - Mtgs - ET - Res - Exhib - Inf - Lib - Empl
< Construction Products Assn (CPA); Nat Specialist Contrs
Coun (NSCC)
M 500 f, UK / 5 f, o'seas
¶ The Contract Flooring Jnl - 10; ftm, £30 yr nm.

Contract Heat Treatment Association
a group of the **Surface Engineering Association**

Contractors Mechanical Plant Engineers (CMPE) 1957
■ 1 Milton Ave, WELLINGBOROUGH, Northants, NN8 3RD.
(asa)
07796 138979
http://www.cmpe.co.uk
Nat Sec: Giovanna Papp
▲ Un-incorporated Society
Br 15
○ *L; all aspects of mechanical plant used in the construction &
building industries
● Conf - Mtgs - ET
M [not stated]

*Controls Manufacturers Association incorporating the Domestic Heating
Controls Group*
see **Association of Controls Manufacturers, a group in the
Energy sector of BEAMA Ltd**

Convenience Stores & Newsagents Association (CSNA) 1988
IRL Market Square, KILDARE TOWN, Co Kildare, Republic of
Ireland.
353 (45) 535051   fax 353 (45) 530016
email info@csna.ie   http://www.csna.ie
Chief Exec: Vincent Jennings
○ *T
× 2006 (May) Irish Retail Newsagents Association

Convention of Scottish Local Authorities (COSLA) 1975
NR Rosebery House, 9 Haymarket Terrace, EDINBURGH,
EH12 5XZ.   (hq)
0131-474 9200   fax 0131-474 9292
email enquiries@cosla.gov.uk   http://www.cosla.gov.uk
○ *N; the association for local authorities in Scotland
M Councils in Scotland

Cookshop & Housewares Association (CHA)
NR 225 Bristol Rd, Edgbaston, BIRMINGHAM, B5 7UB.   (hq)
0121-446 6688   fax 0121-446 5215
email info@bira.co.uk   http://www.bira.co.uk/cha/
Chmn: Lyn Wiltshire
▲ Un-incorporated Society
○ *T; kitchenware retailers
● Empl - ET - Inf - LG - Mtgs
< Brit Indep Retailers Assn
¶ Cookshop, Housewares & Tabletop (Jnl).

Copper Development Association (CDA) 1933
■ 5 Grovelands Business Centre, Boundary Way,
HEMEL HEMPSTEAD, Herts, HP2 7TE.   (hq)
fax 01442 275716
email mail@copperdev.co.uk
http://www.copperinfo.co.uk
Dir & Co Sec: Angela Vessey
▲ Company Limited by Guarantee
○ *T; promotion of the correct use of copper & copper alloys
Gp Brass Advisory Service; Copper Club; Copper in Architecture;
Power Quality Partnership; UK Copper Board
● Conf - Exhib - Comp - Inf - PL
< Intl Copper Assn; Eur Copper Inst
M 8 f, UK / 2 f, o'seas

Coracle Society   1990
NR   8 Barnetts Close, Comberton Green, KIDDERMINSTER, Norfolk,
        Worcs, DY10 3DG.   (msp)
        http://www.coracle-fishing.net
        Mem Sec: Nina Grove
▲   Un-incorporated Society
○   *G, *L; to promote the knowledge of coracles & allied craft,
        their making, use & study; to support the continuance of
        coracle fishing; to encourage the craft of coracle building
●   ET (courses) - Exhib - Comp - VE - Demonstrations - Seaboat
        construction - Use of hides as 'skin'
M   120 i, UK / 10 i, o'seas
¶   NL - 1; ftm only.

Cork Industry Federation   (CIF)   1966
■   13 Felton Lea, SIDCUP, Kent, DA14 6BA.   (hsp)
        020 8302 4801   fax 020 8302 4801
        http://www.cork-products.co.uk
        Hon Sec: Mrs Joy Bell
○   *N, *T; the umbrella organisation for all aspects of cork in the
        UK; decorative cork for floors & walls; industrial &
        construction materials (cork based); cork closures for wine &
        drinks industry
●   Mtgs - Res
<   Confédn Européenne du Liège
M   16 f
¶   LM.

Cornish Chamber of Mines & Minerals   (CCMM)   1917
■   Old Mine Offices, Wheal Jane, Baldhu, TRURO, Cornwall,
        TR3 6EE.   (regd/office/hsb)
        01872 560200   fax 01872 562000
        Sec: B J Ballard
▲   Company Limited by Guarantee
○   *T; to promote & protect mining (incl china clay & stone) in
        Cornwall & Devon
Gp   Legislation
●   Mtgs
<   CBI
M   15 i, 6 f, 2 org
¶   AR; ftm.

Cornish Language Board
        see **Kesva an Taves Kernewek**

Cornish Language Partnership
        see **Mala, the Cornish Language Partnership**

Cornish Mining Development Association   (CMDA)   1948
NR   Roundway, Sennen, PENZANCE, Cornwall, TR19 7AW.   (hsp)
        Hon Gen Sec: Dr Keith Russ
○   *T; to encourage, develop & protect the metalliferous mining
        industry of GB particularly in Devon & Cornwall
M   c 150 i, f & org
¶   AR.

Cornish Pasty Association   (CPA)   2002
NR   c/o Cornwall Development Company, The Old Dry, South
        Wheal Crofty, Station Road, Pool, REDRUTH, Cornwall,
        TR15 3QG.
        01209 6160970
        http://www.cornishpastyassociation.co.uk
        Chmn: Alan Adler
○   *T; Cornish pasty manufacturers & bakers
M   54 f

Cornwall Archaeological Society   (CAS)   1961
■   18 St Sulien, Luxulyan, BODMIN, Cornwall, PL30 5EB.   (hsp)
        01726 850792
        http://www.cornisharchaeology.org.uk
        Hon Sec: Roger Smith
▲   Registered Charity
○   *E, *L
Gp   Cornwall branch of Young Archaeolgists Club
●   Conf - Mtgs - ET - Res - VE
M   520 i, 2 org, UK / 20 i, o'seas
¶   Cornish Archaeology (Jnl) - 1; ftm, £20 nm.
        NL - 3; ftm only.

Cornwall Chamber of Commerce & Industry   (CCCI)   1988
■   Chamber Office, Stanley Way, Cardrew, REDRUTH, Cornwall,
        TR15 1SP.   (hq)
        01209 216006   fax 01209 216007
        email chamber@ccci.org.uk   http://www.ccci.org.uk
        Chief Executive: Richard Glover
▲   Company Limited by Guarantee
○   *C; to support Cornish industry
Gp   Export; Training courses; Information provision
●   Conf - Mtgs - ET - Expt - Inf - Lib - LG
<   Brit Chams Comm
M   160 f
¶   NL - 4; free.

**Coronary Artery Disease Research Association   (CORDA)
1975**
■   Chelsea Square, LONDON, SW3 6NP.   (hq)
        020 7349 8686   fax 020 7349 9414
        email corda@rbht.nhs.uk   http://www.corda.org.uk
        Exec Dir & Sec: Jennifer Jenks
▲   Company Limited by Guarantee; Registered Charity
○   *Q; to support high quality clinical research into the prevention
        of heart attacks & strokes through non-invasive techniques
●   Res

Coroners' Society of England & Wales   1846
NR   HM Coroner's Court, The Cotton Exchange, Old Hall St,
        LIVERPOOL, L3 9UF.   (hsb)
        0151-233 4708
        http://www.coroner.org.uk
        Hon Sec: André J A Rebello
▲   Un-incorporated Society
○   *P
●   Conf - Mtgs - Empl - LG
¶   Annual Report & Directory; m only.

Corporate Responsibility Coalition   (CORE)
NR   26-28 Underwood St, LONDON, N1 7JQ.
        020 7566 1665   fax 020 7490 0881
        http://www.corporate-responsibility.org
○   *K, *N; a coalition of voluntary bodies, trade unions &
        companies who are 'calling on the UK government to enact
        laws that will ensure making profits is done within the context
        of businesses' responsibilities to their stakeholders ... are
        sustainable long-term'
M   170 i, f & org

Corporation of Insurance, Financial & Mortgage Advisers Ltd
        dissolved 2008

Corps of Drums Society   1977
- ■ 103 Clare Lane, EAST MALLING, Kent, ME19 6JB.   (hsp)
   01732 845207
   email info@corpsofdrums.com
   http://www.corpsofdrums.com
   Hon Sec: Mrs Christine Fairfax
- ▲ Registered Charity
- ○ *D; to promote & preserve the tradition of drum & fife/flute music as demonstrated in the infantry of the British Army
- ● Mtgs - ET
- M 250 i, 2 f, 34 org, UK / 17 i, o'seas
- ¶ Drummers Call (Jnl) - 2; ftrm, £3 nm.   NL - irreg; ftm.

Corrosion Prevention Association   (CPA)   1992
- ■ Kingsley House, Ganders Business Park, Kingsley, BORDON, Hants, GU35 9LU.
   01420 471614   fax 01420 471611
   email cpa@associationhouse.org.uk
   http://www.corrosionprevention.org.uk
   Sec: John G Fairley
- ▲ Company Limited by Guarantee
- ○ *P
- ● Seminars - Workshops
- M 27 f
- ¶ Brochure;   LM (with areas of expertise);
   Special Feature Supplement;   all free.
   Reinforced Concrete: History, Properties & Durability; £5.
   Cathodic Protection of Reinforced Concrete: Status Report; £35.

COSCA (Counselling & Psychotherapy in Scotland)   (COSCA) 1990
- NR 16 Melville Terrace, STIRLING, FK8 2NE.   (hq)
   01786 475140
   email info@cosca.org.uk   http://www.cosca.org.uk
   Chief Exec: Brian Magee
- ▲ Company Limited by Guarantee; Registered Charity
- ○ *N, *W; to coordinate & promote development of training & good practice in counselling in Scotland; to encourage communication & cooperation between agencies & individuals engaged in similar activities
- Gp Gps who perform counselling services; Gps whose work includes some counselling skills
- ● Conf - Mtgs - ET - LG
- < Eur Assn for Counselling
- M org
- ¶ Counselling in Scotland - 4; ftm, subscription nm.

Cosmetic, Toiletry & Perfumery Association Ltd   (CTPA)   1945
- ■ Josaron House, 5-7 John Princes St, LONDON, W1G 0JN. (hq)
   020 7491 8891   fax 020 7493 8061
   email info@ctpa.org.uk   http://www.ctpa.org.uk
   Sec: Joyce Traylen
- ▲ Company Limited by Guarantee
- ○ *T; to represent manufacturers & distributors of cosmetic, toiletry & perfumery products (full members) & suppliers of raw materials & contract services (associate members) in the UK
- Gp Scientific Advisory Committee; Packaging Committee; Communications Advisory Group
- ● Conf - Mtgs - Expt - LG
- < Eur Cosmetic Tr Assn (COLIPA); Alliance Ind Assns; CBI
- M 99 f (full), 38 f (associate)
- ¶ NL - 12; ftm only.   Join Us;   AR; both free.
   Publications list available.

Costume Society   1966
- ■ 28 Eburne Rd, LONDON, N7 6AU.   (chmn/p)
   http://www.costumesociety.org.uk
   Chmn: Sylvia Ayton
- ▲ Registered Charity
- ○ *L; to promote every aspect of the study of clothing & textiles
- Gp Sub-c'ees: Programme, Symposium
- ● Conf - VE - Awards
- M 700 i, 100 libraries, UK / 150 i, 200 org, o'seas
- ¶ Costume (Jnl) - 1; £24.   NL - 2; ftm only.

Costume Society of Scotland   (CSS)   1965
- ■ 16 Muirpark, DALKEITH, Midlothian, EH22 3JE.   (hsp)
   0131-663 0967
   email costumescotland@hotmail.co.uk
   http://www.costumesocietyofscotland.org
   Sec: Dorie Wilkie
- ▲ Un-incorporated Society
- ○ *G, *L; to promote interest in, & study of, costume
- ● Mtgs - Exhib - VE
- < Costume Soc; Canadian Costume Museum & Archives of BC; Northern Soc of Costume & Textiles; Textile Soc; Cymdeithas Gwisgoedd a Thecstilau Cymru
- M 89 i, 6 museums etc, UK / 3 i, o'seas
- ¶ Bulletin - 1; ftm only.

Costume & Textile Society of Wales   (Cymdeithas Gwisgoedd a Thecstliau Cymru)
- NR c/o National History Museum, St Fagans, CARDIFF, CF5 6XB. (mtgs/address)
   029 2057 3500
   http://www.costumeandtextilesocietyofwales.org.uk
- ○ *L; to promote & encourage the study, preservation & documentation of costume & textiles in the region of Wales & the Marches, & to further research into these subjects
- ● Exhib - Mtgs -Inf - VE
- M i

Cotswold Sheep Society   1891
- ■ Hampton Rise, 1 High St, MEYSEY HAMPTON, Glos, GL7 5JW.   (hsb)
   01285 851197
   email info@cotswoldsheepsociety.co.uk
   http://www.cotswoldsheepsociety.co.uk
   Sec: Mrs Lucinda Foster
- ▲ Registered Charity
- ○ *B; conservation of the rare breed
- ● Mtgs - Exhib - Stat - Inf - Breeder workshops
- < Nat Sheep Assn
- M 170 i, 8 org, UK / 5 i, o'seas
- ¶ NL - 4; ftm.   AR.
   Flock Book (incl LM) - 1; ftm, £3.50 nm.

Cottage Garden Society   (CGS)   1982
- NR Brandon, Ravenshall, Betley, CREWE, Cheshire, CW3 9BH. (admin/p)
   01270 820940
   Admin: Clive Lane
- ▲ Un-incorporated Society
- ○ *H; to promote interest in cottage gardens & cottage garden plants
- M 8,500 i, UK / 500 i, o'seas

COUNCIL ...
For details of official & non-official councils, other than those listed below, see our companion volume **Councils, Committees & Boards** (note in introduction paragraph 6)

Council for the Advancement of Arab-British Understanding (CAABU)   1967

NR   1 Gough Square, LONDON, EC4A 3DE.   (hq)
      020 7832 1310   fax 020 7832 1329
      email caabu@caabu.org   http://www.caabu.org
      Dir & Chief Exec: Chris Doyle
▲   Company Limited by Guarantee
○   *X; 'Arab-British relations, Israel-Palestine, Iraq, War on Terror'
Gp   Education section (gives talks to schools); Parliamentary;
      Membership
●   Conf - Mtgs - ET - Res - Exhib - Inf - LG
¶   Jnl - 6; £12 yr m, £20 yr nm.
      AR - 1; both free.

Council for Aluminium in Building   (CAB)   1995

■   Bank House, Bond's Mill, STONEHOUSE, Glos, GL10 3RF.
      (hq)
      01453 828851   fax 01453 828861
      email enquiries@c-a-b.org.uk   http://www.c-a-b.org.uk
      Chief Exec: Justin Ratcliffe
▲   Company Limited by Guarantee
○   *T; to promote the use of aluminium in building by being the
      recognised voice of the sector
●   Conf - Mtgs - ET - Inf - LG
<   Construction Products Assn
M   114 f
¶   NL.   LM - updated.
      Technical publications; £10 m, £20 nm.

Council of British Archaeology   (CBA)   1944

■   St Mary's House, 66 Bootham, YORK, YO30 7BZ.   (hq)
      01904 671417   fax 01904 671384
      email info@britarch.ac.uk   http://www.britarch.ac.uk
      Dir: Dr Mike Heyworth
▲   Company Limited by Guarantee; Registered Charity
Br   13
○   *G, *L, *N; to advance the study & care of Britain's historic
      environment; to improve public awareness of Britain's past
Gp   Education; Industrial archaeology panel; Publication; Research
      & conservation; Young archaeologists' club
●   Conf - Mtgs - ET - Res - Exhib - Comp - Inf - Lib - VE - LG
<   Eur Forum of Heritage Assns; Jt C'ee of the Nat Amenity Socs
M   6,000 i, 505 org, UK / 300 i, o'seas
¶   British Archaeology - 6; ftm, £25 yr nm.
      British & Irish Archaeological Bibliography - 2; free.
      Publications catalogue available.

Council of British Druid Orders   (CoBDO)   1989

NR   Attention: Liz Murray, BM Oakgrove, LONDON, WC1N 3XX.
      (mail/add)
      http://www.cobdo.org.uk
      Liaison Officer: Liz Murray
○   *N; to bring together the heads & representatives of all Druid
      groups
●   Mtgs - Inf
M   21 orders

Council of British International Schools   (COBIS)   1981

■   Pembroke House, 8 St Christopher's Place, FARNBOROUGH,
      Hants, GU14 0NH.   (gen/sb)
      01252 513930   fax 01252 516000
      email admin@cobis.org.uk   http://www.cobis.org.uk
      Exec Dir: Colin Bell
▲   Company Limited by Guarantee
○   *E, *N; 'is a global membership association of quality British
      schools with member & affiliate schools in more tha 40
      countries worldwide; benefits include professional
      development for school staff & quality assurance'
●   Conf - ET - Exam - Res - Exhib - Stat - Expt - VE - Empl - LG
M   i, 55 f, UK / i, 94 schools, o'seas
¶   e-NL - 12;   e-Directory - 2; both ftm.

Council on Commercial Diplomacy
      a group of the **Association of Certified Commercial Diplomats**

Council of Cricket Societies   (CofCS)   1969

NR   2 Jodrell Rd, WHALEY BRIDGE, High Peak, Derbys,
      SK23 7AN.   (hsp)
      01663 732866
      http://www.councilcricketsocieties.com
      Hon Sec: Bob Wood
Br   25; Australia, New Zealand, South Africa, Zimbabwe
○   *S; to maintain interest in cricket during the 'off-season' period
●   Mtgs - Inviting speakers to address societies
M   c 3,000 i, UK / 1,000 i, o'seas
¶   NL - 1; ftm only.   NL of individual socs - irreg; free.

Council for Dance Education & Training (UK)   (CDET)   1978

■   Old Brewer's Yard, 17-19 Neal St, LONDON, WC2H 9UY.
      (hq)
      020 7240 5703   fax 020 7240 2547
      email info@cdet.org.uk   http://www.cdet.org.uk
      Dir: Sean Williams
▲   Company Limited by Guarantee; Registered Charity
○   *D; 'to advance the education of all persons & principally
      children, young people & students, in the art, practice &
      appreciation of the cultural significance of dance; to promote
      high standards in dance education & training'
Gp   Conference of Professional Dance Schools
      Negotiation Board; Teaching society c'ee
●   Conf - Mtgs - ET - Res - Stat - Inf - LG - Accreditation &
      assessment service
M   20 i, 30 org
¶   UK Directory of Registered Dance Teachers - 1; ftm.
      Information sheets on dance education & training.
      AR - 1; ftm only.

Council of Docked Breeds

      Since the passing of the law banning the docking of dogs' tails
      in 2007 (in England from 6 April, Wales 28 March &
      Scotland 20 April) membership has closed for new applicants
      & no renewals are sought from current members.
      The Council insists that the tail docking option should be
      legally available for all traditionally docked breeds.
      The Council has no telephone line, but can be contacted on
      help@cdb.org

Council of Gas Detection & Environmental Monitoring (COGDEM)   1975

■   Unit 11 Theobald Business Park, Knowle Piece, Wilbury Way,
      HITCHIN, Herts, SG4 0TY.   (hq)
      01462 434322   fax 01462 434488
      email cogdem@aol.com   http://www.cogdem.org.uk
      Admin: Leigh Greenham
▲   Company Limited by Guarantee
○   *T; to safeguard the standards of, & expand the market for, gas
      detection, gas analysis & environmental monitoring
      equipment & services
Gp   Sub-groups: Carbon monoxide, Industrial
●   Mtgs - ET - Exam - Exhib - SG - Stat - Inf - Lib - LG
M   33 f, 2 org, UK / 2 f, o'seas

Council of Hunting Associations   (CHA)   2001

NR   The Hunting Office, Overley Barn, Daglingworth,
      CIRENCESTER, Glos, GL7 7HX.   (hq)
      01285 653001   fax 01285 653559
      http://www.council-of-hunting-associations.co.uk
      Sec: Alastair Jackson
○   *K; to promote & protect the interests of those who hunt with
      dogs within the law
M   11 org

Council for Independent Archaeology   1989

NR   2 The Watermeadows, Swarkestone, DERBY, Derbys,
　　　 DE73 7FX.   (hsp)
　　　 01332 704148
　　　 email skfoster@btopenworld.com
　　　 http://www.independents.org.uk
　　　 Hon Sec: Keith Foster
▲　Registered Charity; Un-incorporated Society
○　*L; the promotion of archaeology independent of government,
　　　 especially amateur archaeology
●　Conf - Mtgs - ET - Res - Inf - VE - LG
M　200 i, UK / 20 i, o'seas
¶　NL - 4; ftm only.

Council for Independent Education
　　　 see **CIFE: Council for Independent Education**

Council for Independent Further Education
　　　 see **CIFE - Council for Independent Education**

Council of Mortgage Lenders   (CML)   1989

NR   North West Wing, Bush House, Aldwych, LONDON,
　　　 WC2B 4PJ.   (hq)
　　　 0845 373 6771　fax 0845 373 6778
　　　 http://www.cml.org.uk
▲　Un-incorporated Society
○　*T; interests of the UK residential mortgage market
●　Conf - Mtgs - ET - Res - Stat - Inf - Lib - LG
　　　 Consumer information: 020 7438 8956
M　151 f
¶　[all on website]

Council of Property Search Organisations   (CoPSO)

NR   The Old Rectory, Church Lane, THORNBY, Northants,
　　　 NN6 8SN.
　　　 0870 950 7739
　　　 http://www.copso.org.uk
　　　 Chief Exec: Mike Ockenden
▲　Company Limited by Guarantee
○　*T; for companies providing property information - local
　　　 searches, environmental reports, water & drainage searches
　　　 & other specialist services
¶　NL.　Factsheets & Briefing Papers.
　　　 Home Information Packs.　Guides.

Council for Registered Gas Installers   (CORGI)   1991

NR   Unit 7 Prisma Park (1st floor), Berrington Way, BASINGSTOKE,
　　　 Hants, RG24 8GT.   (hq)
　　　 01256 372300
　　　 email enquiries@corgi-group.com
　　　 http://www.corgi-gas-safety.com
　　　 Chief Exec: Mike Thompson,　Co Sec: Philippa Caine
▲　Company Limited by Guarantee
○　*T; the national watchdog for gas safety
●　Inf - LG - Inspection of registered businesses - Dealing with
　　　 customer complaints regarding gas safety - Gas safety
　　　 publicity - Nationally accredited certification scheme for
　　　 individual gas fitting operatives
M　52,000 f
¶　Gas Installer Magazine - 11; ftm.
　　　 AR; free.

**Council for the Registration of Schools Teaching Dyslexic Pupils
(CReSTeD)   1993**

■　Old Post House, Castle St, WHITTINGTON, Shropshire,
　　　 SY11 4DF.   (regd/office)
　　　 0845 601 5013
　　　 email lesley@crested.org.uk　http://www.crested.org.uk
　　　 Admin: Lesley Farrar
▲　Registered Charity
○　*W; to register schools & other educational institutions
　　　 providing facilities for & care of dyslexic pupils (those with
　　　 learning difficulties)
●　Mtgs - Inf
<　Brit Dyslexia Assn; Dyslexia Action
M　85 schools
¶　Register of Schools that help Dyslexic Children - 1; free.

Council for Scottish Archaeology
　　　 2010 **Archaeology Scotland**

Counselling   1998

■　5 Pear Tree Walk, WAKEFIELD, W Yorks, WF2 0HW.   (regd/off)
　　　 email trustees@counselling.ltd.uk
　　　 http://www.counselling.ltd.uk
▲　Company Limited by Guarantee; Registered Charity
○　*W; to provide free counselling to those on low income
　　　 throughout the UK; to maintain a website of counselling
　　　 colleges & counselling related matters
●　ET - Exam - Res - Stat - Inf
M　2,500 i, c 250 f
¶　Counselling NL - 12;　LM (website);　AR - 1; all free.

Counselling Children & Young People
　　　 a group of the **British Association for Counselling &
　　　 Psychotherapy**

Counselling & Psychotherapy in Scotland
　　　 see **COSCA (Counselling & Psychotherapy in Scotland)**

Country Doctors Association   (CDA)   1998

NR   17 Symonds Rd, HITCHIN, Herts, SG5 2JJ.   (chmn/p)
　　　 01462 434515
　　　 http://www.countrydoctor.co.uk
　　　 Chmn: Dr David Roberts
○　*M; education & welfare & promotion of country doctors & their
　　　 staff

Country Gentlemen's Association Ltd   (CGA)   1893

§　Chalke House, Station Rd, Codford, WARMINSTER, Wilts,
　　　 BA12 0JX.   (hq)
　　　 01985 850706　fax 01985 850378
　　　 email enquiries@thecga.co.uk
　　　 http://www.thecga.co.uk
　　　 Chief Exec: William Harrison-Allan
　　　 supplies goods and materials for estates, households, farms
　　　 and gardens; advisor on agricultural, tax, financial and
　　　 insurance matters.

Country Land & Business Association   (CLA)   1907

NR   16 Belgrave Sq, LONDON, SW1X 8PQ.   (hq)
　　　 020 7235 0511　fax 020 7235 4696
　　　 email mail@cla.org.uk　http://www.cla.org.uk
▲　Un-incorporated Society
○　*P; the national association of owners of rural land &
　　　 businesses in England & Wales
<　Access to Farms Partnership
M　40,000 i

Country Markets
NR Dunston House, Dunston Rd, Sheepbridge, CHESTERFIELD,
    Derbys, S41 9QD.   (hq)
    01246 261508 (Mon-Fri 1000-1600)
    email info@country-markets.co.uk
○   *T; a membership cooperative enabling members to sell their
    home-based produce direct to the general public
<   Markets Alliance
M   i

Countryside Alliance   1997
NR The Old Town Hall, 367 Kennington Rd, LONDON,
    SE11 4PT.   (hq)
    020 7840 9200
    email info@countryside-alliance.org
    http://www.countryside-alliance.org
    Chief Exec: Alice Barnard
▲   Company Limited by Guarantee
○   *K; to champion & campaign for country sports, the countryside
    & the rural way of life
Gp Specialist campaigns for: Angling, Coursing, Falconry,
    Fisheries, Hunting, Rural issues, Shooting
    Honest Food - the Campaign for Independent Food
●   ET - Res - Stat - Inf - VE - LG
<   Fedn Eur Field Sports Gps (FACE)
M   80,000 i, 1,500 f, 320,000 org
¶   Country Sports - 4; ftm.

Countryside Alliance Ireland
NR Larchfield Estate, Bailliesmills Road, LISBURN, Co Antrim,
    BT27 6XJ.
    028 9263 9911   fax 028 9263 9922
    http://www.caireland.org
○   *K; campaigning for the countryside, country sports and the
    rural way of life

Countryside Ireland   1970
IRL Courtlough Shooting Grounds, BALBRIGGAN, Co Dublin,
    Republic of Ireland.
    353 (1) 690 3610
    email secretary@countrysideireland.com
    http://www.countrysideireland.com
    Hon Sec: Philip E de N Lawton
○   *S

Countryside Management Association   (CMA)   1966
■   Writtle College, Lordship Rd, Writtle, CHELMSFORD, Essex,
    CM1 3RR.   (hq)
    01245 424116   fax 01245 420456
    http://www.countrysidemanagement.org.uk
    Admin: Mike Anderson
○   *P; to promote professional & sustainable management of the
    countryside & urban greenspace
●   Conf - Mtgs - ET - LG
M   i
¶   Ranger - 4; ftm, £5 nm.

County Antrim Agricultural Association   (CAAA)   1898
■   Ballymena Showgrounds, Warden St, BALLYMENA, Co Antrim,
    BT43 7DR.   (hq)
    028 2565 2666   fax 028 2565 2666
    email secretary@ballymenashow.co.uk
    http://www.ballymenashow.co.uk
    Sec: Mrs Jane Lamont
▲   Registered Charity
○   *F; to encourage the breeding of all classes of farm stock; the
    cultivation of farm crops & products; to encourage cottage
    industries, agricultural & horticultural education
●   Ballymena Show
<   Assn Show & Agricl Orgs; NI Shows' Assn
M   450 i

County Armagh Wildlife Society   (CAWS)   1952
■   13 Enniscrone PArk, PORTADOWN, Co Armagh, BT63 5DQ.
    (hsp)
    028 3833 3927
    email info@armaghwild.org.uk
    http://www.armaghwild.org.uk
    Hon Sec: Ian Rippet
▲   Un-incorporated Society
○   *L; the study of the natural history, botany, zoology & geology
    of County Armagh & Ireland
Gp Butterfly & moth recording on behalf of Ulster Wildlife Trust in
    local nature reserve
●   Mtgs - Stat - Lib - VE
M   c 80 i, 1 org
¶   AR; ftm.   LM.

County Education Officers of Two Tier Authorities
■   c/o Graham Badman, Kent County Council, Sessions House,
    County Hall, MAIDSTONE, Kent, ME14 1XQ.
    01622 696550
○   *E

Coventry & District Archaeological Society   (CADAS)   1965
NR c/o 14 Ventnor Close, COVENTRY, Warks, CV2 5AS.   (sp)
    http://www.covarch.org.uk
▲   Un-incorporated Society
○   *L; to promote archaeology in the Coventry area; to care for
    Coventry heritage

Coventry & Warwickshire Chamber of Commerce   1997
■   Chamber House, Innovation Village, Cheetah Rd, COVENTRY,
    Warks, CV1 2TL.   (hq)
    024 7665 4321   fax 024 7645 0242
    email info@cw-chamber.co.uk
    http://www.cw-chamber.co.uk
    Chief Exec: Louise Bennett
▲   Company Limited by Guarantee
Br Rugby, Coventry & South, Mid & Northern Warwickshire
○   *C
Gp Building & construction; Education; Engineering &
    manufacturing; Hotel & leisure; Professional & commercial;
    Retail; Transport
●   Conf - Mtgs - ET - Exams - Res - Exhib - Stat - Expt - Inf - Lib -
    LG
<   BCC
M   2,300 f
¶   C & W In Business - 6;   Update - 6; both ftm.
    AR - 1; free.

CP Sport England & Wales
■   Unit 5 Heathcoat Bldg, Nottingham Science & Technology Park,
    University Boulevard, NOTTINGHAM, NG7 2QJ.   (hq)
    0115-925 7027   fax 0115-922 4666
    http://www.cpsport.org
○   *S; for sportspeople with cerebral palsy

Crabbet Organisation   2002
NR Binley House Farm, Binley, ANDOVER, Hants, SP11 6HA.
    01264 738343
    http://www.crabbet.org.uk
    Contact: Caroline Sussex
Br Australia, Netherlands, USA
○   *B; to promote & perpetuate the influence of Arabian horses
    descended from those bred by Lady Anne & Wilfrid Scawen
    Blunt & their daughter at Crabbet Park
●   Inf - Shows
M   i, 16 studs
    (Sub: £15-£22)
¶   Jnl - 2.   Stud Directory

© CBD Research Ltd · Beckenham · BR3 5JS · Tel 020 8650 7745 · E-mail cbd@cbdresearch.com · www.cbdresearch.com

Craft Brewing Association   1995
NR   26 Hawkesley Mill Lane, Northfield, BIRMINGHAM,
        W Midlands, B31 2RL.   (mem/sec/p)
        0121-475 3842
        Mem Sec: Greg Pittaway
○   *P, *T; to uphold the tradition of private brewing to the highest
        standards
M   i & f

Craft Guild of Chefs   (CFA)   1965
NR   1 Victoria Parade, by 331 Sandycombe Rd, RICHMOND,
        Surrey, TW9 3NB.   (hq)
        020 8948 3870   fax 020 8948 3944
        http://www.craftguildofchefs.com
        Sec: Suzanne Barshall
○   *P; to increase standards of professional cooking through
        greater awareness, education & training
M   i
✕   2009 Food Development Association (merged)

Craft Guild of Traditional Bowyers & Fletchers   (CGTBF)   1986
■   29 Batley Court, OLDLAND, S Glos, BS30 8YZ.   (clerk/p)
        0117-932 3276   fax 0117-932 3276
        email guildclerk@btinternet.com
        http://www.bowyersandfletchersguild.org
        Clerk: Veronica-Mae Soar
▲   Un-incorporated Society
○   *P; to provide a forum for all concerned with the manufacture
        of quality traditional archery equipment; to encourage,
        maintain & improve the standard of bow & arrow making &
        other associated activity
Gp   Bows; Arrows; Arrow Heads; Sundries
●   Conf - ET (incl apprentices) - Exam (for apprentices &
        established craftsmen before membership)
M   27 i
¶   NL - irreg; ftm only.

Craft Potters' Association of Great Britain   (CPA)   1957
NR   63 Great Russell St, LONDON, WC1B 3BF.   (hq)
        020 3137 0750
        email admin@cpaceramics.co.uk
        http://www.cpaceramics.co.uk
        Sec: Tony Ainsworth
▲   Company Limited by Guarantee; Registered Charity
○   *A; promotion of high quality, hand-made ceramics,
        particularly work of original design & individual character
        made by members
●   Conf - Mtgs - Exhib - VE
M   150 fellows, 600 associates, 200 professional, UK /
        50 associates, o'seas
¶   Ceramic Review - 6.
        CPA News - 6.   Potters - 2 yrly.

Cranio Sacral Society
NR   6 Clinton Rd (lwr gd floor), REDRUTH, Cornwall, TR15 2QE.
        01209 211078
        email mail@cranio-sacral.org.uk
        http://www.cranio-sacral.org.uk
        Hon Pres: Dr John E Upledger
○   *P; for practitioners of the Upledger CranioSacral therapy
M   c 130 i

Craniofacial Society of Great Britain   1970
NR   c/o Faculty of Dental Surgery, Royal College of Surgeons, 35-
        43 Lincoln's Inn Fields, LONDON, WC2A 3PE.   (hsb)
        020 7869 6802
        email honsec@craniofacialsociety.org.uk
        http://www.craniofacialsociety.org.uk
        Hon Sec: Mark Devlin
▲   Company Limited by Guarantee; Registered Charity
○   *M, *P; for those concerned with cleft lip & palate & other
        craniofacial anomalies
Gp   Maxillofacial surgeons; Nurses; Orthodontists; Plastic
        surgeons; Speech therapists
●   Conf - Mtgs - ET - Res
M   300 i, UK / 20 i, o'seas

Craniofacial Support Group
    see **Headlines, the Craniofacial Support Group**

Craniosacral Therapy Association of the UK   (CSTA)   1990
■   Monomark House, 27 Old Gloucester St, LONDON,
        WC1N 3XX.   (mail/address)
        07000 784735
        email secretary@craniosacral.co.uk
        http://www.craniosacral.co.uk
        Sec: Roger R James
▲   Un-incorporated Society
○   *P; to disseminate information about craniosacral therapy; to
        regulate training organisations
●   Conf - Mtgs - ET - Res - Inf - Maintain a register of qualified
        members
M   450 i, 5 org
¶   The Fulcrum - 3; ftm, £18.50 yr nm.

Creators' Rights Alliance   (CRA)   2000
NR   Headland House, 308 Gray's Inn Rd, LONDON, WC1X 8DP.
        (hq)
        http://www.creatorsrights.org.uk
        Chmn: David Ferguson
▲   Un-incorporated Society
○   *N; an alliance of the major organisations representing
        copyright creators & content providers throughout the media,
        particularly television, radio & the press
●   Conf - Mtgs - Inf - LG
M   14 orgs
¶   Between a Rock & a Hard Place (the problems facing freelance
        creators in the media market place).
        Creators Have Rights (Video).

Credit Hire Organisation   (CHO)   2010
NR   Hampden House, 1 Hampden Hill, WARE, Herts, SG12 7JT.
        (asa)
        email thetonybaker@gmail.com   http://www.thecho.co.uk
        Dir Gen: Tony Baker
▲   Company Limited by Guarantee
○   *T
●   Mtgs - Inf - LG
✕   2010 (Accident Management Association
        (National Association of Credit Hire Operators

Credit Protection Association plc   (CPA)   1914
■   CPA House, 350 King St, LONDON, W6 0RX.   (hq)
        020 8846 0000   fax 020 8741 7459
        email info@cpa.co.uk   http://www.cpa.co.uk
        Hon Sec: O M Holmes
        Chmn & Managing Dir: David S Baber
Br   Bolton, Bristol, Birmingham, Knaresborough, Newmarket,
        Falkirk
○   *T; for credit management services & debt recovery online
●   Inf
<   American Collectors Assn (USA); Credit Services Assn (UK)
M   3,500 f
¶   Business Informer - irreg; free.

Credit Services Association (CSA) 1902

■ Wingrove House (2nd floor east), Ponteland Rd,
NEWCASTLE upon TYNE, NE5 3AJ.   (hq)
0191-286 5656   fax 0191-286 0900
email info@csa-uk.com   http://www.csa-uk.com
Exec Dir: Kurt Obermaier
○ *T
Gp Debt buyers & sellers
● Conf - Mtgs - ET - Exhib - LG - City & Guilds diploma course
for the debt collection industry
< Fedn Eur Nat Collection Assns (FENCA)
M 260 f, UK / 46 f, o'seas
¶ NL - 6;   AR - 1; both ftm.
Inside the Industry Report; £125 m, £250 nm.

Cremation Society of Great Britain   1874

■ Brecon House, 16-16a Albion Place (2nd floor), MAIDSTONE,
Kent, ME14 5DZ.   (hq)
01622 688292/3
email info@cremation.org.uk
http://www.cremation.org.uk
Sec: R N Arber
▲ Registered Charity
○ *L; promotion of cremation; supply of technical & other
information on every aspect of cremation & crematorium
administration (including pets)
● Conf - Stat - Inf - Lib - LG
< Intl Cremation Fedn
M i
¶ Pharos International (Jnl) - 4; £30.
Directory of British Crematoria - 1; £23 (inserts)(£27 with
binder).
British Crematoria in Public Profile; £4.13.
Directory of Pet Crematoria; £2.50.
May Catholics choose Cremation?; 35p.
AR & Accounts - 1; ftm only.
Other prices on application.

Cri du Chat Syndrome Support Group

NR Administration Office, PO Box 3408, NORWICH, NR3 3WE.
0845 094 2725
email admin@criduchat.co.uk
http://www.criduchat.co.uk
Nat Co-ordinator: Angela Stokes

Cricket & Hockey Association
in 2006 merged with the **Sporting Goods Industry Association**

Cricket Memorabilia Society (CMS) 1987

■ 4 Stoke Park Court, Stoke Rd, Bishops Cleve, CHELTENHAM,
Glos, GL52 8US.   (hsp)
01242 677102
email cms87@btinternet.com
http://www.cricketmemorabilia.org
Hon Sec: Steve Cashmore
▲ Un-incorporated Society
○ *G; the preservation of cricket memorabilia
● Mtgs - Res - Exhib - Inf - Valuations
M 850 i
(£20-£10)
¶ Jnl - 4; free.
Directory of Collectors Interests - 2 yrly; ftm only.

Cricket Scotland   1908

NR National Cricket Academy, Ravelston, EDINBURGH,
EH4 3NT.   (hq)
0131-313 7420
▲ Un-incorporated Society
○ *S; governing body of cricket in Scotland
M i, clubs

Cricket Society   1945

NR PO Box 6024, LEIGHTON BUZZARD, Beds, LU7 2ZS.   (hsp)
01525 370204
email davidwood@cricketsociety.com
http://www.cricketsociety.com
Hon Sec: David Wood
▲ Un-incorporated Society
Br 3
○ *S; to encourage a love of cricket in all its spheres - for all ages
& interests - playing, watching, reading or listening
● Mtgs - Lib
M 1,900 i, UK / 100 i, o'seas
¶ Jnl - 2; ftm, £3 nm.   News Bulletin - 8; ftm only.

Crime Concern
since 2008 **Catch 22 in Action**

** Crime Reporters Association

organisation lost; see Introduction paragraph 3

Crime Writers Association (CWA) 1953

■ PO Box 273, BOREHAMWOOD, Herts, WD6 2XA.   (hsb)
email info@thecwa.co.uk   http://www.thecwa.co.uk
Sec: Liz Evans
▲ Company Limited by Guarantee
○ *P; for all involved in crime writing (authors, publishers, agents,
booksellers)
● Conf - Mtgs - Comp - Inf - Administration of: CWA Cartier
Diamond Dagger,CWA Non-fiction Gold Dagger, New Blood
Dagger, Ian Fleming Steel Dagger, Duncan Lawrie Dagger
(International Dagger) - Ellis Peters Award - Debut Dagger
< Mystery Writers of America
M 400 i, UK / 100 i, o'seas
¶ Red Herrings - 12;   LM - 1; both ftm only.

Crimean War Research Society   1983

■ 4 Castle Estate, RIPPONDEN, W Yorks, HX6 4JY.   (hsp)
01422 823529
http://www.crimeanwar.org/
Hon Sec: David Cliff
▲ Un-incorporated Society
○ *L, *G; to encourage research into all aspects of the Crimean
War, 1853-1856
● Conf - Mtgs - Res - Exhib - SG - Inf - Lib
M 250 i, UK / 100 i, o'seas
¶ The War Correspondent (Jnl) - 4; £15 UK (£20 o'seas) m only.

Criminal Bar Association (CBA) 1969

NR 289-293 High Holborn, LONDON, WC1V 7HZ.   (hq)
020 7242 1289   fax 020 7242 1107
email jbradley@barcouncil.org.uk
http://www.criminalbar.com
Admin: Julian Bradley
▲ Un-incorporated Society
○ *P; practising members of the Bar of England & Wales
● Conf - Mtgs - ET - Res - SG - Inf - Lib - Empl - LG
M c 3,000 i
¶ NL - 4; free.   Brochure.

Criminal Justice Alliance   (CJA)   1994
NR   Park Place, 10-17 Lawn Lane, LONDON, SW8 1UD.   (hq)
    020 7091 1298
    http://www.criminaljusticealliance.org
○   *N; an alliance of organisations committed to improving the
    criminal justice system & to reduce prison overcrowding; it
    includes most of the charities working in this sector as well as
    the Prison Officers Association & the Prison Governors
    Association
●   Mtgs
M   65 org
¶   NL - 52 (email).

Criminal Law Solicitors' Association   1990
NR   New England House (Suite 2 Level 6), New England St,
    BRIGHTON, E Sussex, BN1 4GH.   (hq)
    01273 676725
    Admin: Sue Johnson
▲   Un-incorporated Society
○   *P
M   i

Critics' Circle   1913
NR   50 Finland Rd, LONDON, SE4 2JH.   (hsp)
    020 7732 9696
    http://www.criticscircle.org.uk
    Hon Gen Sec: William Russell
○   *P; critics of the performing arts

Crohn's in Childhood Research Association   (CICRA)   1978
■   Parkgate House, 356 West Barnes Lane, MOTSPUR PARK,
    Surrey, KT3 6NB.   (hq)
    020 8949 6209   fax 020 8942 2044
    email support@cicra.org   http://www.cicra.org
    Chmn Bd of Trustees: Mrs Margaret Lee
▲   Registered Charity
○   *K, *W; to create wider awareness & understanding of Crohn's
    disease & ulcerative colitis, particularly as it affects children &
    young adults; to raise funds to support medical research
    aimed at finding more effective treatments & eventual cure
Gp   Children & youth; Health
●   Conf - Mtgs - Res
M   3,000 i
¶   The Insider - 4.

Cromwell Association   1935
NR   c/o The Cromwell Museum, Grammar School Walk,
    HUNTINGDON, Cambs, PE29 3LF.   (mail address)
    01480 375830
    http://www.olivercromwell.org
▲   Un-incorporated Society
○   *L; to commemorate Oliver Cromwell (1599-1658); to
    stimulate interest in Cromwell & the general history of the
    British Isles & dependent territories from the birth of
    Cromwell to the Restoration; to encourage scholarly study of
    the period
●   Conf - ET - Comp - Lib
M   c 600 i, 6 libraries, UK / c 30 i, 1 library, o'seas
¶   Cromwelliana - 1; ftm.   NL - 2; ftm only.

Crop Circle Connector   1995
NR   11 Richmond Terrace, Clifton, BRISTOL, BS8 1AB.
    http://www.cropcircleconnector.com
○   *G; for all interested in crop circles
M   i
    (Sub: £21, $31, 24)
¶   NL.

Crop Protection Association   (CPA)   1928
■   2 Swan Court, Cygnet Park, Hampton, PETERBOROUGH,
    Cambs, PE7 8GX.   (hq)
    01733 355370   fax 01733 355371
    email info@cropprotection.org.uk
    http://www.cropprotection.org.uk
    Chief Exec: Dominic Dyer
▲   Company Limited by Guarantee
○   *T; to represent members engaged in the manufacture,
    formulation & supply of crop protection products for use in
    agriculture, horticulture, forestry, home gardening, industrial,
    amenity & local authority outlets
●   Mtgs - Exam - Exhib - Stat - Inf
<   CropLife Intl; Eur Crop Protection Assn (ECPA)
M   40 f
¶   Annual Review;   Hbk; both free.
    Publications & other resources.

Croquet Association   (CA)   1897
■   c/o Cheltenham Croquet Club, Old Bath Rd, CHELTENHAM,
    Glos, GL53 7DF.   (hq)
    01242 242318
    email caoffice@croquet.org.uk
    http://www.croquet.org.uk
    Mgr: Elizabeth Larsson
▲   Un-incorporated Society
Br   9
○   *S; the governing body for the sport of croquet
●   Conf - ET - Exam - Res - Comp - Stat - Inf - LG
<   Wld Croquet Fedn; Eur Croquet Fedn
M   1,600 i, 160 clubs
    (Sub: £37 i, UK / £32 i, £6.70 per mem clubs)
¶   The Croquet Gazette - 6.

Crossroads: Caring for Carers
   see Crossroads Association

Crossword Club   1978
■   Coombe Farm, Awbridge, ROMSEY, Hants, SO51 0HN.   (hsb)
    01794 524346   fax 01794 514988
    email bh@thecrosswordclub.co.uk
    http://www.thecrosswordclub.co.uk
    Sec: Brian Head
▲   Registered Business Name
○   *G; promotion of the art of the crossword - especially the
    setting & solving of puzzles of a high level of construction &
    difficulty
    NOTE: 'we do not offer non-members free advice on selling
    crosswords'
M   c 700 i, 2 f, UK / c 50 i, 2 org, o'seas
¶   Crossword - 12; ftm only.   Hbk - irreg; free.
    Crossword Club Guide to Playfair; £1.25.

Croydon Chamber of Commerce & Industry   1891
■   Lansdowne Building, 2 Lansdowne Rd, CROYDON, Surrey,
    CR9 2ER.   (hq)
    020 8263 2345   fax 020 8263 2352
    email info@croydonchamber.org.uk
    http://www.croydonchamber.org.uk
    Gen Mgr: Matthew Sims
▲   Company Limited by Guarantee
○   *C
●   Mtgs - Exhib - Expt - Inf
<   since 1 April 2003 a branch of London Cham Comm &
    Ind (LCCI)
M   400 i, f & org
¶   Business South - 10; ftm, £1.50 nm.
    Directory of Members - 1;   AR; both ftm only.

Croydon Natural History & Scientific Society Ltd (CNHSS) 1870
- ■ 96A Brighton Rd, SOUTH CROYDON, Surrey, CR2 6AD. (hq)
  020 8688 3593
  Hon Sec: Brian Lancaster,   Co Sec: Paul W Sowan
- ▲ Company Limited by Guarantee; Registered Charity
- ○ *L; covering NE Surrey, NW Kent & southern London boroughs
- Gp Archaeology; Botany & mycology; Entomology; Geology;
  Industrial studies; Local history; Meteorology; Ornithology
- ● Conf - Mtgs - Res - Exhib - SG - Inf - Lib - VE - Museums
  The library may be visited by appointment only, contact Paul W
  Sowan 020 8688 3593
- < Botanical Soc of the Brit Isles; Brit Assn for Local History; Coun
  for Brit Archaeology; Geologists' Assn
- M 344 i, 16 org
  (Sub: £13, £8 associates)
- ¶ Proceedings - irreg;   Bulletin - 2; ftm, prices vary nm.
  Croydon Church Townscape; £4.50.
  The River Wandle:
    Distribution of its flora; £1;
    The Non-conformist experience in Croydon; £1.
  From Palace to Washhouse: a study of the Old Palace,
    Croydon, from 1780 to 1887; £3.50.
  The Archbishop's town: the making of mediaeval
    Croydon; £2.95.
  Many other publications on Croydon & its history.

Cruising Association (CA) 1908
- NR CA House, 1 Northey St, Limehouse Basin, LONDON,
  E14 8BT. (hq)
  020 7537 2828   fax 020 7537 2266
  email office@cruising.org.uk
  http://www.cruising.org.uk
  Hon Sec: Desmond Scott
- ▲ Company Limited by Guarantee
- ○ *S; an amateur organisation encouraging cruising in yachts &
  boats; protection of the interests of yachtsmen

Crusaders
  since 2006 **Urban Saints**

Cruse Bereavement Care (CRUSE) 1959
- ■ PO Box 800, RICHMOND, Surrey, TW9 1RG. (hq)
  020 8939 9530
  email info@cruse.org.uk   http://www.cruse.org.uk
  Chief Exec: Debbie Kerslake
- ▲ Registered Charity
- Br 138 in UK (not Scotland)
- ○ *W; offers help to people bereaved by death, in any way,
  whatever their age, nationality or belief; also free counselling
  service, advice on practical matters & opportunities for
  contact with others through support groups
- ● Conf - ET - Res - Stat - Inf - Lib - LG
  Helpline: 0844 477 9400
- M 5,500 i (volunteers)
- ¶ Bereavement Care Jnl - 4; £19 m only.

Crystal & Healing Federation (CHF) 1998
- ■ c/o 6 Buer Rd, LONDON, SW6 4LA. (hsp)
  020 7736 0283
  email vhflondon@aol.com
  http://www.crystalandhealing.com
  Hon Sec: Henriette Maasdijk
- ○ *N; an umbrella organisation for crystal healing schools &
  graduates; also spiritual healing, stress therapy & Bach
  flower remedies
- ● Mtgs - ET
- < Brit Crystal Healers (BCH); Complementary Med Assn (CMA)
- M 115 i, 6 org
- ¶ Crystals & Healing for Everyone [book]; £5 m, £6 nm.
  Crystals Strong & Beautiful; £16 m.

Crystal Palace Foundation (CPF) 1979
- ■ Crystal Palace Museum, Anerley Hill, LONDON, SE19 2BA.
  (hq)
  0788 933 8812   fax 0870 133 7920
  email crystalpalacefoundation@hotmail.com
  http://www.crystalpalacefoundation.org.uk
  Sec: David Britton,   Chmn: Melvyn Harrison
- ▲ Registered Charity
- ○ *G; to support the Crystal Palace Museum
- ● ET - Res - Exhib - SG - Inf - Lib - PL - VE - Promotes education
  & research - Publishing work concerned with Crystal Palace
- < Assn Indep Museums (AIM); Brit Assn Friends of Museums;
  Urban Parks Forum (UPF)
- M 700 i, 10 org, UK / 50 i, o'seas
- ¶ Crystal Palace Foundation News - 4; ftm only.
  New Crystal Palace Matters - 4; ftm, £1 nm.

CSS
  since 2009 **Association of Directors of Environment, Economy,
  Planning and Transport**

CTC 1878
- ■ Parklands, Railton Rd, GUILDFORD, Surrey, GU2 9JX. (hq)
  0844 736 8450   fax 0844 736 8454
  email cycling@ctc.org.uk   http://www.ctc.org.uk
  Dir: Kevin Mayne
- ▲ Company Limited by Guarantee; Registered Charity
- ○ *K, *S; campaigns for the rights of all cyclists - membership
  includes 3rd party insurance & legal aid
- ● ET - Res - Comp - Inf - LG
- M 54,000 i, 200 orgs, UK / 1,000 i, o'seas
- ¶ Cycle - 6; ftm only.
- × 2007 Cyclists' Touring Club

Cucumber Growers Association (CGA) 2000
- NR c/o Growco Ltd, Park Lane, COTTINGHAM, East Yorks,
  HU16 5RX.
  01482 841139   fax 01482 841139
  email info@cucumbergrowers.co.uk
  http://www.cucumbergrowers.co.uk
  Chmn: Steve Clarkson
- ○ *T
- M 70 f

Cue Sports Association
  in 2006 merged with the **Sporting Goods Industry Association**

Cued Speech Association UK (CSAUK) 1980
- ■ 9 Jawbone Hill, DARTMOUTH, Devon, TQ6 9RW. (hq)
  01803 832784   fax 01803 835311
  email info@cuedspeech.co.uk
  http://www.cuedspeech.co.uk
  Chief Exec: Anne Worsfold
- ▲ Company Limited by Guarantee; Registered Charity
- ○ *W; to provide information & training in cued speech - an exact
  visual representation of spoken language by using 8 hand
  shapes in 4 positions to clarify the lip patterns of speech.
  Its use allows deaf children to think in English and so
  improve their literacy, lip-reading & speech; it can also help
  deafened & deaf adults
- ● Conf - ET - Exam - Exhib - Inf
- < UK Coun on Deafness (UKCoD)
- M 70 i
- ¶ NL - 4;   AR - 1; both free.
  The Cued Speech Research Book; £29.99
  Cued Speech Instructional Booklet; £6.
  Parents Booklet; £6.
  Cued Speech Explained by People who use it (DVD); £5.
  Cued Speech Instructional Video; £10.
  Application for membership; £10.

Cumann na Scríbheann nGaedhilge
  see **Irish Texts Society (Cumann na Scríbheann Gaedhilge)**

Cumberland Agricultural Society 1836
■ Warcarr, Greenhead, BRAMPTON, Cumbria, CA8 7HY. (hsp)
  01697 747397   fax 01697 747397
  email secretary@cumberlandshow.co.uk
  http://www.cumberlandshow.co.uk
  Sec: Donella Rozario
▲ Un-incorprated Society with charitable status
○ *F
● Mtgs - Exhib (Cumberland Agricultural Show) - Comp - Inf
< Assn of Show & Agricl Orgs
M c 1,000 i
¶ Catalogue - 1; £2.50.   Schedule - 1; free.

**Cumberland & Westmorland Antiquarian & Archaeological
   Society (CWAAS) 1866**
NR Westlands, Westbourne Drive, LANCASTER, LA1 5EE. (hsp)
  01524 675234
  email eajones@skynow.net   http://www.cwaas.org.uk
  Hon Sec: Mrs M E MacClintock
▲ Registered Charity
○ *L; the study of the archaeology, history, genealogy, customs &
  traditions of the old counties of Cumberland, Westmorland &
  Lancashire north of the sands
Gp C'ees: Industrial archaeology, Parish registers, Regional,
  Research
● Mtgs - Res - Inf - Lib - VE
< Coun of Brit Archaeology
M c 850 i, c 120 org
¶ Transactions - 1; ftm, £15 nm.   NL - 3; ftm only.
  Research series, Record series & Extra series - all irreg;
    prices vary.

Cumbria Chamber of Commerce (CCC) 1999
NR Broadacre House (3rd floor), 16-20 Lowther St, CARLISLE,
  Cumbria, CA3 8DA. (hq)
  0845 226 0040   fax 0845 226 0050
  email info@cumbriachamber.co.uk
  http://www.cumbriachamber.co.uk
  Chief Exec: Rob Johnston
▲ Un-incorporated Society
Br Barrow, Carlisle, Kendal, Whitehaven
○ *C; support & services for the Cumbrian business community
< Brit Chams Comm; Chams Comm NW
M f & org

*CURL: Consortium of Research Libraries in the British Isles
  since 2008 **RLUK: Research Libraries UK***

Curtain Walling Association
  see **Glass & Glazing Federation**

Curwen Institute 1972
■ 56 Creffield Rd, COLCHESTER, Essex, CO3 3HY. (hsp)
  email admin@johncurwensociety.org.uk
  http://www.johncurwensociety.org.uk
  Hon Sec: Yvonne Lawton
○ *E; to develop & extend the teaching of music in schools by
  means of a modern version of John Curwen's Tonic Sol-fa
  system
  The Institute is funded by the John Curwen Society.

Customer Contact Association (CCA) 1996
■ 20 Newton Place, GLASGOW, G3 7PY. (hq)
  0141-564 9010   fax 0141-564 9011
  email cca@cca.org.uk   http://www.cca.org.uk
  Chief Exec: Anne Marie Forsyth
▲ Company Limited by Guarantee
○ *T; development & promotion of customer contact expertise
Gp Foundation partners; Industry council; Standards council
● Conf - Mtgs - ET - Res - Exhib - Stat - Inf - Lib - LG
M 800 f UK, 20 f o'seas
  (Sub: £20)
¶ In Touch - 4; ftm only.

Customs Practitioners Group (CPG) 1988
NR 12 Ascot Drive, PORT TALBOT, SA12 8YL. (hsb)
  01639 778988   fax 01639 778988
  http://www.customspractitioners.org
  Hon Sec: Gary Charles
○ *P; to further the interests of importers & exporters who are
  concerned with the impact of non-VAT customs & excise
  regimes
● LG - Mtgs
< UK Jt Customs Consultative C'ee
M 70 i

Cut-out & Feeder Pillar Group
  a product group of **BEAMA Ltd**

Cut the VAT Coalition 2008
NR Gordon Fisher House, 14-15 Great James St, LONDON,
  WC1N 3DP. (hq)
  020 7242 7583   fax 020 7405 0854
  http://www.cutthevat.co.uk
○ *K; to reduce VAT on all maintenance & home improvement
  work

Cutlery & Allied Trades Research Association (CATRA) 1952
NR Henry St, SHEFFIELD, S Yorks, S3 7EQ. (hq)
  0114-276 9736   fax 0114-272 2151
  email info@catra.org   http://www.catra.org
  Dir of Research: R C Hamby
▲ Company Limited by Guarantee
○ *Q; research & technology organisation, specialising in all
  aspects of domestic & industrial tools, blades, knives, cutters,
  surgical instruments, razors & shaving systems, kitchen
  gadgets & cookware
Gp Blade manufacturing technology; Cutting technology; Shaving
● Res - Inf - Testing & product evaluation - Commercial
  consultancy
M 15 f
¶ [numerous publications].

Cutty Sark Trust 1969
■ 2 Greenwich Church St, LONDON, SE10 9BG. (hq)
  020 8858 2698   fax 020 8858 6976
  email enquiries@cuttysark.org.uk
  http://www.cuttysark.org.uk
  Hon Sec: Richard Doughty,   Admin: Gail Smith
▲ Registered Charity
○ *G; preservation & conservation of the Cutty Sark clipper ship
M c 600 i
¶ NL - 1;   AR; both ftm only.
  This replaces the Maritime Trust which is now dormant

Cyclamen Society 1977
NR Little Orchard, Church Rd, WEST KINGSDOWN, Kent,
  TN15 6LG. (h/mem/p)
  http://www.cyclamen.org
  Mem Sec: Arthur Nicholls
▲ Registered Charity
○ *H; the study of the cyclamen species
● Conf - Res - Exhib - Comp - Inf - Lib - VE - Seed distribution
M 1,200 i, UK / 200 i, o'seas
¶ Cyclamen Jnl - 2; ftm, c £2 nm.

Cycle Engineers' Institute (CEI) 1896
■ 28 King St, SANDWICH, Kent, CT13 9BT. (sp/b)
  01304 617161   fax 01304 617161
  Sec: Arthur H Lock
▲ Un-incorporated Society
○ *L; for the highest standards of design & manufacture of
  custom-built & made to measure bicycles
Gp Building; Designing; Engineering methods
● Conf - Res - Inf
< League Intl (cycle racing); Eur Inst of Cycle Engg
M c 50 i, UK / 10 i, o'seas
¶ Proceedings - 6;   LM - 1;   Rules - irreg; all ftm only.

Cyclical Vomiting Syndrome Association UK

- ■ 77 Wilbury Hills Road, LETCHWORTH, Herts, SG6 4LD.   (hsp)
  0151-342 1660
  email info@cvsa.org.uk   http://www.cvsa.org.uk
  Chmn of Trustees: Dr Robin Dover
- ▲ Registered Charity
- ○ *W; 'cyclical vomiting syndrome: promotion of education,
  research, & offering support to sufferers & their families'
- ● Mtgs - ET - Inf
- M 300 i, UK / 20+ f, o'seas
- ¶ Bi-Annual NL - 2; ftm.

Cycling Ireland

- IRL Kelly Roche House, 619 North Circular Rd, DUBLIN 1, Republic
  of Ireland.   (hq)
  353 (1) 855 1522
- ○ *S; the national governing body for cycling in Ireland

Cycling Time Trials   (CTT)   2002

- ■ Moor End, Etherley Moor, BISHOP AUCKLAND, Co Durham,
  Dl14 0JU.   (hq/hsp)
  01388 609824
  email andy.cosgrove@cyclingtimetrials.org.uk
  http://www.cyclingtimetrials.org.uk
  Nat Sec: Andy Cosgrove
- ▲ Company Limited by Guarantee
- Br 21
- ○ *S; governing body for road cycling time trials in UK (England,
  Wales, Channel Islands, Isle of Man)
- ● Conf - Mtgs - LG
- < Cent Coun for Physical Recreation
- M 998 clubs
- ¶ CTT Hbk - 1; £7.   AR - 1.

Cyclists' Touring Club
  since 2007 **CTC**

Cymdeithas Alawon Gwerin Cymru
  see **Welsh Folk Song Society (Cymdeithas Alawon Gwerin
  Cymru)**

Cymdeithas Amaethyddol Frenhinol Cymru Cyf
  see **Royal Welsh Agricultural Society Ltd (Cyndeithas
  Amaethyddol Frenhinol Cymru Cyf)**

Cymdeithas Cymru-Ariannin   1939

- ■ Rhos Helyg, 23 Maesyrefail, Penrhyn-coch, ABERYSTWYTH,
  Ceredigion, SY23 3HE.   (hsp)
  01970 828017
  email rhoshelyg@btinternet.com
  Sec: Ceris Gruffudd
- ▲ Registered Charity
- ○ *X; to form a link between Wales & the Welsh community in
  Chubut, Argentina; to organise & sponsor exchange visits for
  Welsh teachers, students & ministers of religion, &
  Argentinian students wishing to go to Wales to expand their
  educational horizon
- ● Mtgs - Exhib - Inf - Annual celebration to mark the landing of
  the first Welsh settlers in Chubut - Sponsorship of annual
  literary competition (in the Welsh lanuguage) at the National
  Eisteddfod of Wales
- < Wales Intl
- M 231 i, 1 org, UK / 6 i, o'seas
- ¶ AR; free.

Cymdeithas Ddawns Werin Cymru (Welsh Folk Dance Society) (CDdWC/WFDS)   1949

- ■ Ffynnonlwyd, Trelech, CAERFYRDDIN, SA33 6QZ.   (sec/p)
  01994 484496
  email dafydd.evans@ic24.net
  http://www.welshfolkdance.org.uk
  Sec: Dafydd M Evans
- ▲ Registered Charity
- Br 27; Australia, New Zealand, USA
- ○ *D; promoting Welsh folk dancing & music through the
  medium of Welsh language & English
- ● Conf - Mtgs - ET - Exam - Res - Exhib - Comp - SG - Inf - Lib -
  VE - Dancing displays - Publishing dance notations, records
  & tapes
- < Welsh Amat Music Fedn (WAMF)
- M 196 i, 67 families, 29 groups, UK / 21 i, o'seas
- ¶ Dawns (Jnl) - 1.   NL - 1.   Hbk.   AR (incl LM).
  Dance notations, records, tapes, CDs, videos & DVDs

Cymdeithas Ddrama Cymru
  see **Drama Association of Wales (Cymdeithas Ddrama
  Cymru)**

Cymdeithas Defaid Llanwenog
  the Welsh title for the **Llanwenog Sheep Society**

Cymdeithas Defaid Torddu Cymreig Torwen
  see **Badger Face Welsh Mountain Sheep Society (Cymdeithas
  Defaid Torddu Cymreig Torwen)**

Cymdeithas Gwisgoedd a Thecstilau Cymru
  see **Costume & Textile Society of Wales**

Cymdeithas Hanes Ceredigion (Ceredigion Historical Society) 1909

- ■ Penygeulan, Abermagwr, ABERYSTWYTH, Ceredigion,
  SY23 4AR.   (hsb)
  01974 261222
  email nonbaskerville@onetel.com
  Hon Sec: Mrs Eirionedd A Baskerville
- ▲ Registered Charity
- ○ *L; local history, antiquities & folklore of Ceredigion
- Gp Archaeological
- ● Mtgs - VE
- M 500+ i
- ¶ Ceredigion (Jnl) - 1.
  County History, 3 vol; in course of publication.

Cymdeithas Hanes Sir Caernarfon
  see **Caernarvonshire Historical Society (Cymdeithas Hanes
  Sir Caernarfon)**

Cymdeithas Hanes Sir Ddinbych - Denbighshire Historical Society   1950

- NR Ysgubor Isa, Llanfair Dyffryn Clwyd, RUTHIN, Denbighshire,
  LL15 2UN.   (treas)
  01824 702747
  http://www.glyndwr.ac.uk
  Treas: Arthur Wyn Lloyd
- ▲ Registered Charity
- ○ *L; study of the history of the old county of Denbighshire,
  including family history, folklore & archaeology
- ● Mtgs - VE
- M c 410 i & org
- ¶ Transactions - 1.

Cymdeithas Hynafiaethau Cymru
>see **Cambrian Archaeological Association (Cymdeithas Hynafiaethau Cymru)**

Cymdeithas yr Iaith Gymraeg   (Welsh Language Society) 1962
NR   Ystafell 5, Y Cambria, Rhodfa'r Môr, ABERYSTWYTH, Ceredigion, SY23 2AZ.   (hq)
01970 624501   fax 01970 627122
email swyddfa@cymdeithas.org
Contact: Dafydd Morgan Lewis
○   *K, *Z; 'a socialist organisation to ensure the future of the Welsh language'
M   [not given]

Cymdeithas Melinau Cymru
>see **Welsh Mills Society (Cymdeithas Melinau Cymru)**

Cyngor Gweithredu Gwirfoddol Cymru
>see **Wales Council for Voluntary Action (Cyngor Gweithredu Gwirfoddol Cymru)**

Cystic Fibrosis Association of Ireland   1963
IRL   24 Lower Rathmines Rd, DUBLIN 6, Republic of Ireland.
353 (1) 496 2433   fax 353 (1) 496 2201
email 09>cfireland.ie
Sec: Kay Cannon
○   *W

Cystic Fibrosis Trust   1964
NR   11 London Rd, BROMLEY, Kent, BR1 1BY.   (hq)
020 8464 7211   fax 020 8313 0472
http://www.cftrust.org.uk
Chief Exec: Rosie Barnes
▲   Registered Charity
Br   97
○   *Q, *W; to fund hospital & university research into improved detection & treatment of cystic fibrosis; to provide a comprehensive support & advice network for people with cystic fibrosis & their families
●   Conf - Mtgs - ET - Res - Exhib - Helpline 0845 859 1000
<   Intl Cystic Fibrosis (Mucoviscidosis) Assn (ICF(M)A)
M   16,000 i
¶   CF Today;   CF Talk; both free.   Annual Review. Books, information leaflets, videos - list available.

Cystitis & Overactive Bladder Foundation   (COB Foundation) 1994
■   Kings Court, 17 School Rd, BIRMINGHAM, W Midlands, B28 8JD.   (hq)
0121-702 0820
email info@cobfoundation.org
http://www.cobfoundation.org
▲   Registered Charity
Br   35
○   *W; support for sufferers & their families; information dissemination to the medical profession on causes & treatments of, & research into, all forms of cystitis & overactive bladder
●   Mtgs - Stat - Inf
<   Interstitial Cystitis Assn of America
M   2,000 i
¶   A Wee Ray of Hope (NL) - 4.
×   2003 Interstitial Cystitis Support Group

Czech British Chamber of Commerce
NR   Quadrant House, 4 Thomas More Square, LONDON, E1W 1YW.
020 7216 4623
http://www.cbcc.org.uk
○   *C

D&AD   (D&AD)   1962
NR   9 Graphite Sq, Vauxhall Walk, LONDON, SE11 5EE.   (hq)
      020 7840 1120   fax 020 7840 0840
      email info@dandad.co.uk   http://www.dandad.org
      Chief Exec: Michael Hockney
▲   Registered Charity
○   *A, *P; to work on behalf of the design & advertising industries;
      to set standards of creative excellence & educate & inspire
      the next creative generation; to promote good design &
      advertising to the business area

D H Lawrence Society   1974
■   1 Church St, SWEPSTONE, Leics, LE67 2SA.   (hsp)
      Hon Sec: Mrs Brenda Sumner
▲   Registered Charity
○   *A; promotion of interest in the life & work of D H Lawrence
      (1885-1930) novelist, poet & essayist
Gp   1
●   Conf - Mtgs - Inf - Lib - VE
<   Assn of Literary Socs; societies in Australia, France, Italy, Japan,
      USA
M   126 i, UK / 75 i, o'seas
¶   Jnl - 1; ftm, £7 nm.   NL - 2; ftm, £2 nm.

Dad's Army Appreciation Society   (DAAS)   1993
■   41 Borough Close, Kings Stanley, STONEHOUSE, Glos,
      GL10 3LJ.   (hsp)
      email info@dadsarmy.co.uk   http://www.dadsarmy.co.uk
      Hon Sec (members): Tony Pritchard,
      Hon Sec (articles): Paul Carpenter
▲   Un-incorporated Society
○   *G; to promote & research the television series & share with
      like-minded people rare footage, photographs & information
Gp   Archives; Filming locations; Rare videos & photographs
●   Mtgs - Exhib - Inf - PL
M   1,700 i
¶   Permission to Speak Sir! [NL] - 4; £8; UK m only.
      Dad's Army Companion (all the facts about the
      programme); £12 m, £14 nm.

Daffodil Society   1898
NR   105 Derby Rd, Bramcote, NOTTINGHAM, NG9 3GZ.   (hsp)
      0115-925 5498
      email rogerbb@lineone.net
      http://www.thedaffodilsociety.com
      Hon Sec: Mrs Terry Braithwaite
▲   Registered Charity
○   *H; cultivation & exhibition of the genus narcissus
●   Exhib - Regional meetings
<   R Horticl Soc
M   670 i, 220 org, UK / 123 i, o'seas
¶   Jnl - 1; NL - 1; ftm only.

Dairy Executives Association
IRL   33 Kildare St, DUBLIN 2, Republic of Ireland.
      353 (1) 676 1989   fax 353 (1) 676 7162
      email dairyexe@indigo.ie
      Gen Sec: Michael B McCann
○   *P; executives & managers in the dairy industry & agribusiness

Dairy UK   1933
NR   93 Baker St, LONDON, W1U 6QQ.   (hq)
      020 7486 7244   fax 020 7847 4734
      email info@dairyuk.org   http://www.dairyuk.org
      110A Maxwell Avenue, Westerton, Bearsden, GLASGOW,
      G81 1HU.
      Director General: Jim Begg
○   *T; body dealing with matters relating to manufacture &
      distribution of milk & milk products, & relating to wages &
      conditions of employees in the industry

Daisy Network   1995
■   PO Box 183, ROSSENDALE, Lancs, BB4 6WZ.   (mail/address)
      email daisy@daisynetwork.org.uk
      http://www.daisynetwork.org.uk
      Hon Sec: Mrs J Banks
▲   Registered Charity
○   *W; to support & inform those who have gone through a
      premature menopause, & their families
●   Conf - Inf
M   c 350 i, UK / 3 i, o'seas
      (Sub: £20)
¶   NL -4;   AR - 1; both ftm only.

Dalcroze Society UK (Inc)   1926
■   7 Canada Rise, Market Lavington, DEVIZES, Wilts,
      SN10 4AD.   (admin/p)
      01380 813198
      email admin.dalcroze@googlemail.com
      http://www.dalcroze.org.uk
      Admin: Greta Price,   Chmn: Nicola Gaines
▲   Registered Charity
○   *D; musical education through movement
●   ET - Exam
<   Institut Jaques Dalcroze (Geneva)
M   150 i, UK / i, o'seas
¶   NL - 2; ftm.   Publications list available.

Dales Pony Society   (DPS)   1916
■   Greystones, Glebe Avenue, Great Longstone, BAKEWELL,
      Derbys, DE45 1TY.   (hsp)
      01629 640439   fax 01629 640439
      email dpssecretary@googlemail.com
      http://www.dalespony.org
      Hon Sec: Mrs J C Ashby
▲   Company Limited by Guarantee; Registered Charity
Br   Canada, France, USA
○   *B
●   Conf - Comp - Inf
<   Nat Pony Soc; Brit Horse Soc
M   600 i, UK / 25 i, o'seas
      (Sub: £20)
¶   Dales Despatch - 2; ftm only.

Dalesbred Sheep Breeders Association Ltd   1930
■   Brackenber Lane Farm, Brackenber Lane, Giggleswick, SETTLE,
      N Yorks, BD24 0EB.   (hsp)
      01729 822228
      http://www.dalesbredsheep.co.uk
      Sec: Mrs Jean Bradley
○   *B
●   Mtgs - Res - Exhib - Comp
<   Nat Sheep Assn
M   200 i
      (Sub: varies)
¶   Jnl - 5.   Flock Book - 1.

© CBD Research Ltd · Beckenham · BR3 5JS · Tel 020 8650 7745 · E-mail cbd@cbdresearch.com · www.cbdresearch.com

Dance UK Ltd   1982
NR   The Urdang, Old Finsbury Town Hall, Rosebery Avene,
      LONDON, EC1R 4QT.   (hq)
      020 7713 0730   fax 020 7833 2363
      email info@danceuk.org   http://www.danceuk.org
      Dir: Caroline Miller
▲   Company Limited by Guarantee; Registered Charity
○   *D, *W; 'the lead organisation for the dance profession; we
      work to create a diverse, dynamic & healthy future for dance
      & to build a stronger sense of a UK-wide dance community'
Gp   National Choreographers Forum
      Communication & advocacy; Healthier dance practice;
      Professional development; Support & development of African
      dance
●   Conf - Mtgs - ET - Res - Stat - Inf
M   800 i, 130 f, UK / 50 i, 10 f, o'seas
¶   Dance UK News (Jnl) - 4.   Your Body Your Risk.
      Look Before You Leap.   Choreography as Work.
      Dance Teaching Essentials.
      Warm up Cool down (posters).
      Information sheets.   Poster series.

Dancesport Scotland   1945
NR   93 Hillfoot Drive, Bearsden, GLASGOW, G61 3QG.   (hsp)
      0141-563 2001
      http://www.dancesportscotland.org
      Exec Admin: Mrs Margo Fraser
○   *S; the governing body for ballroom & Latin American dancing
      in Scotland

Danish-UK Chamber of Commerce   (DUCC)   1989
■   55 Sloane St, LONDON, SW1X 9SR.   (hq)
      020 7259 6795
      email info@ducc.co.uk   http://www.ducc.co.uk
      Chief Exec: Martin Mortensen
▲   Company Limited by Guarantee
○   *C; to promote & assist the Anglo-Danish business community
      in both UK & Denmark
Gp   Managing Directors Network; Young Professionals
      Network (YPN); The Junior Chamber
●   Mtgs
M   150 i, 250 f
¶   Trade Directory - 1; free.

Daresbury Lewis Carroll Society   1970
■   Blue Grass, Clatterwick Lane, Little Leigh, NORTHWICH,
      Cheshire, CW8 4RJ.   (hsp)
      01606 891303 & 781731 (evgs)
      Hon Sec: Kenneth N Oultram
○   *L; to honour & promote the work of C L Dodgson (Lewis
      Carroll)
●   Mtgs (in Daresbury, Carroll's birthplace)

Dartmoor Pony Society   (DPS)   1946
NR   Swn Yr Afon, Thornhill Rd, CWMGWILI, SA14 6PT.   (hsp)
      01269 844303
      http://www.dartmoorponysociety.com
      Hon Sec: Mrs Viv Brown
▲   Company Limited by Guarantee
○   *B
●   Conf - Res - Exhib - Comp - Expt - Inf - Compilation of history
      of breed
<   Nat Pony Soc
M   550 i, UK / 100 i, o'seas
¶   NL - 4.   Dartmoor Diary.

Dartmoor Preservation Association   (DPA)   1883
■   Old Duchy Hotel, Princetown, YELVERTON, Devon,
      PL20 6QF.   (pt/time hq)
      01822 890646
      email info@dartmoorpreservation.com
      http://www.dartmoorpreservation.com
      Chief Exec: James Paxman
▲   Registered Charity
○   *G, *K; protection, preservation & enhancement in the public
      interest of landscape, antiquities, flora & fauna, natural
      beauty & scientific interest of Dartmoor; preservation of
      Dartmoor Commons
●   Mtgs - ET - Res - Exhib
<   Coun Protection Rural England (CPRE); Coun Nat Parks (CNP);
      Open Spaces Soc (OSS)
M   2,400 i, UK / 30 i, o'seas
¶   Dartmoor Matters (NL) - 3; free.

Dartmoor Sheep Breeders Association   (DSBA)   1909
■   Lower Stockadon Farm, St Mellion, SALTASH, Cornwall,
      PL12 6QF.   (hsp)
      01579 350920
      email secretary@greyface-dartmoor.org.uk
      http://www.greyface-dartmoor.org.uk
      Sec: Patrick Aubrey-Fletcher
▲   Registered Charity
○   *B; for breeders of the Greyface Dartmoor, also known as the
      Dartmoor or 'improved' Dartmoor
●   Inf
<   Nat Sheep Assn
M   250 i
¶   Flock Book - 1; ftm.

Darts Association
      in 2006 merged with the **Sporting Goods Industry Association**

Data Federation
      a group of the **Federation of Copyright Theft**

Data Publishers Association   (DPA)   1970
NR   Queens House, 28 Kingsway, LONDON, WC2B 6JR.   (hq)
      020 7405 0836   fax 020 7404 4167
      email christine@dpa.org.uk   http://www.dpa.org.uk
      Sec: Christine Scott
▲   Company Limited by Guarantee
○   *T; to represent data & directory publishers in the UK; to
      promote the interests of the industry both in print & electronic
      media
●   Conf - Mtgs - Stat - LG
<   Eur Assn of Directory & Database Pubrs (EADP); Advertising
      Assn; Periodical Pubrs Assn; Digital Content Forum
>   Periodical Pubrs Assn
M   80 f
¶   News in Brief - 12;   Members' Hbk - 1; both ftm, on
      request nm.
      AR; free.

David Hume Institute   1985
NR   26 Forth St, EDINBURGH, EH1 3LH.   (hq)
      0131-550 3746
      http://www.davidhumeinstitute.com
      Dir: Jeremy Peat
○   *L, *Q; to promote discourse & research on economic & legal
      aspects of public policy questions

David Jones Society   1996
■   22 Gower Rd, Sketty, SWANSEA, SA2 9BY.   (hq)
    01792 206144   fax 01792 470385
    Sec: Kirsty Black,   Dir: Dr Anne Price-Owen
▲   Un-incorporated Society
○   *A; to promote interest in the life & works of the painter-poet
    David Jones (1895-1974) & his sense of unity within the
    world & its people
Gp Literature; Theology; Visual arts
●   Conf - Mtgs - ET - Res - Exhib - Inf - Lib - PL - VE - Poetry
    readings - Seminars
M   250 i, 8 f, UK / 50 i, 4 f, o'seas
    (Sub: £20 i, £35 f)
¶   The David Jones Jnl - 2; £7.50 m, £10 nm.
    NL - 4.

Dawn Duellists' Society   (DDS)   1994
NR 3F2, 8 Thirlstane Rd, Marchmont, EDINBURGH, EH9 1AN.
    (hsp)
    email secretary@dawnduellists.co.uk
    http://www.dawnduellists.co.uk
    Sec: Matt Noel
▲   Un-incorporated Society
○   *S; revival of historically accurate swordplay from c1300-1900;
    to research teaching & practice of duelling techniques
●   Mtgs - ET - Res - Demonstrations
M   20 i, UK / 3 i, o'seas
¶   Information leaflets.

DBA - the Barge Association   (DBA)   1992
■   Cormorant, Spade Oak Reach, Cookham, MAIDENHEAD,
    Berks, SL6 9RQ.   (mail)
    07000 227437 (07000 BARGES)   fax 0870 706 4033
    email info@barges.org   http://www.barges.org
    Hon Sec & Treas: Paul Whitehouse
▲   Company Limited by Guarantee
○   *G; support group for barge owners
Gp Continental cruising; Sailing barge; Thames
●   ET - Inf - LG - Liaison with navigation authorities, trade assns &
    other clubs - Arrangement of member discounts for goods &
    services
<   Eur Boating Assn; Nat Navigation Users Forum (NNUF)
M   1,200 i, UK / 300 i, o'seas
    (Sub: £25 (Eur), £35 RoW)
¶   Blue Flag - 6; ftm.   Barge Buyers' Hbk.
×   2006-08 Dutch Barge Association

De Vere Society   1989
■   The Courtyard, 45 Royal York Crescent, Clifton, BRISTOL,
    BS8 4JS.   (hsp)
    0117-923 8993
    email malim@btinternet.com
    http://www.deveresociety.co.uk
    Hon Sec: R C W Malim
▲   Registered Charity
○   *A, *L, *Q; Shakespeare authorship question with 2
    propositions:
    a) that William Shakespeare (1564-1616) did not write any
    (or any significant part) of the works now attributed to him
    b) that Edward de Vere, 17th Earl of Oxford (1550-1604) is
    substantially the best candidate for (or plays a major role in)
    such authorship
●   Conf - Mtgs - ET - Res - Exhib - Inf - Lib - VE
<   Shakespeare Oxford Soc (USA)
M   150 i, UK / 60 i, o'seas
¶   NL - 3/4; ftm only.   Occasional study papers - irreg.
    Great Oxford Collection of Newsletter Essays 1996-2004;
    £12 m, £14 nm.

Deaf Broadcasting Council
    has closed

Deaf Education through Listening & Talking   (DELTA)   1980
■   The Con Powell Centre, Alfa House, Molesey Rd, WALTON-on-
    THAMES, Surrey, KT12 3PD.   (hq)
    0845 108 1437
    email enquiries@deafeducation.org.uk
    http://www.deafeducation.org.uk
▲   Company Limited by Guarantee; Registered Charity
○   *W; a support group of teachers & parents of deaf & hearing-
    impaired children, providing information, advice & support to
    guide parents in helping their children develop normal
    speech & live independently in a hearing society
Gp Deaf children & families; Professionals who support them
●   Conf - Mtgs - ET - Res - Exhib - Stat - Inf
<   Alexander Graham Bell Assn Deaf & Hard of Hearing; Brit
    Academy Audiology; Brit Assn Educ Audiologists; Brit
    Cochlear Implant Users Assn; Elizabeth Foundation; Ewing
    Foundation
M   258 i
¶   Chat - 4;   Good Practice Guide; both ftm.

Deafblind UK   1928
NR National Centre for Deafblindness, John & Lucille van Geest
    Place, Cygnet Rd, Hampton, PETERBOROUGH, Cambs,
    PE7 8FD.   (hq)
    01733 358100 (voice & minicom)   fax 01733 358356
    email info@deafblind.org.uk
    http://www.deafblind.org.uk
    Chief Exec: Jeff Skipp
▲   Registered Charity
○   *W; to further the interests of deafblind people by offering the
    full range of support services, education & training
●   Conf - ET - Exhib - Stat - Inf - VE
<   Brit Assn Disabled People
M   3,520 i
¶   Open Hand Magazine - 4.   Snippets (NL) - 52.
    Both publications are available in Braille, Moon, large print,
    tape or disk format.   Annual Review; free.

DeafHear   1963
IRL 35 North Frederick St, DUBLIN 1, Republic of Ireland.
    353 (1) 817 5700   fax 353 (1) 878 3629
    email nad@iol.ie   http://www.deafhear.ie
    Chief Exec: Niall Keane
○   *W
×   2007 National Association for Deaf People

Debt Management Standards Association   (DEMSA)   2000
NR West Point, Westland Square, LEEDS, W Yorks, LS11 5SS.
    (chmn/b)
    0113-277 7610
    email info@demsa.co.uk   http://www.demsa.co.uk
    Chmn: Michael Land
○   *T
●   Mtgs - Inf
M   4 f

Defence Industry Security Association   (DISA)   1963
NR c/o CGP Associates Ltd, 2 Maple Park, Enigma Business Park,
    MALVERN, Worcs, WR14 1GQ.
    0870 458 9636
    http://www.thedisa.org.uk
○   *P; for those responsible for security in the defence industry,
    offering advice & training to organisations working with
    government, the Ministry of Defence & their contractors
    advice on such matters to organisations working with
    government, the Ministry of Defence & their contractors
●   Mtgs - Inf
M   f

Defence Manufacturers Association
    on 1 October 2009 merged with the Association of Police & Public
    Security Suppliers & the Society of British Aerospace Companies to
    form **ADS Group Ltd**

Delphinium Society 1928

■ 35 Ringstead Rd, SUTTON, Surrey, SM1 4SJ. (sec/p)
  email jmwooll@blueyonder.co.uk
  http://www.delphinium.org.uk
  Gen Sec: Mrs Jean Woolley
▲ Registered Charity
Br 3
○ *H; the study of delphiniums in all their aspects - botanical,
  horticultural, genetic, physiological & general interest for
  non-specialists; investigation of species & their ecology; is
  also a forum for the more scientifically minded
Gp Species & Breeders Communications Forum
● ET - Exhib - Comp - Inf - VE
< R Horticl Soc Jt Delphinium C'ee
M c 600 i, c 20 affiliates, UK / c 150 i, o'seas
¶ Autumn Bulletin - 1 (Oct).   Delphiniums (Ybk) - 1.
  The Delphinium Garden; published on the 75th anniversary.

Democracy Movement

NR 72 Hammersmith Rd, LONDON, W14 8TH.   (hq)
  020 7603 7796   fax 020 7602 9699
  email mail@democracymovement.org.uk
  http://www.democracymovement.org.uk
Br 160
○ *K; a non-party campaign to keep the pound & stop the EU
  superstate
M c 320,000 i

Denbighshire & Flintshire Agricultural Society Ltd   1839

■ 1 Cross St, HOLYWELL, Flintshire, CH8 7LP. (hq)
  01352 712131   fax 01352 712098
  email denbandflintshow@ukonline.co.uk
  http://www.denbighandflintshow.com
  Sec: Liz Turner
▲ Company Limited by Guarantee; Registered Charity
○ *F, *H; the encouragement of agriculture & horticulture by
  education, scientific research, experimental work & the
  holding of shows
Gp Bantams; Cattle; Classic cars & motorcycles;; Eggs; Floral art;
  Honey; Horses; Horticulture; Merched y Wawr; Poultry;
  Pigeons; Rabbits; Sheep; WI; Vintage machinery & cars
● Mtgs - Comp - VE - Show
< Assn of Show & Agricl Orgs; Various breed socs
M 1,200 i, 20 f
¶ Show Day Catalogue - 1.
  Show Schedule - 1.   AR.

Denbighshire Historical Society
   see **Cymdeithas Hanes Sir Ddinbych (Denbighshire Historical Society)**

Dental Laboratories Association Ltd (DLA) 1961

NR 44-46 Wollaton Rd, Beeston, NOTTINGHAM, NG9 2NR. (hq)
  0115-925 4888   fax 0115-925 4800
  http://www.dla.org.uk
  Chief Exec: Richard Daniels
▲ Company Limited by Guarantee
Br 16
○ *T; interests of proprietors of dental laboratories; to represent
  views of dental technology to professional bodies &
  government
Gp Business development; Education; Materials & technical
  standards
● Conf - Mtgs - ET - Res - Exhib - SG - Stat - Inf - Empl
< Fédn Eur des Patrons Prosthétistes Dentaires (FEPPD); Brit
  Dental Health Foundation (BDHF)
M c 1,000 i
¶ Dental Laboratory (Jnl) - 12; ftm, £28 yr nm.
  DLA Directory - 1; ftm, £20 nm.   Year Planner - 1; free.

Dental Professionals Association (DPA) 1954

■ 61 Harley St, LONDON, W1G 8QU.   (hq)
  020 7193 7240   fax 020 7636 1086
  email info@uk-dentistry.org   http://www.uk-dentistry.org
  Chief Exec: Derek Watson
▲ Un-incorporated Society
○ *P, *U; the promotion of the welfare & interests of general
  dental practitioners, especially those working in high street
  practice
● Conf - Mtgs - Stat - Inf - Empl - LG
< Eur U of Dentists (EUD)
M 3,000 i, UK / 3 f, o'seas
¶ General Dental Practitioner - 6; ftm only.

Dental System Suppliers Association (DSSA) 1990

NR c/o Geoff Emery, Elopak House, Rutherford Close, STEVENAGE,
  Herts, SG1 2EF. (chmn/b)
  01438 245000
  Chmn: Geoff Emery
▲ Un-incorporated Society
○ *P, *T; promotion of & setting standards for management
  computer systems for dental surgeries
Gp Dental surgeons; Suppliers of computer systems for dental
  surgeons & allied trades
● Exhib - Inf - LG
M 5 f, 3 associates
¶ LM - updated; free.

Dental Technologists Association   (DTA)

NR 3 Kestrel Court, Waterwells Drive, Waterwells Business Park,
  GLOUCESTER, GL2 2AT.
  0870 243 0753
  http://www.dta-uk.org
○ *P

Depression Alliance (DA) 1979

■ 20 Geat Dover St, LONDON, SE1 4LX.   (hq)
  0845 123 2320
  email information@depressionalliance.org
  http://www.depressionalliance.org
  Sec: Paul Lanham
▲ Company Limited by Guarantee; Registered Charity
Br 3
○ *W; information & understanding for anyone affected by
  depression
● Inf - Co-ordination of self-help groups, correspondence
  schemes & e-mail group
M 2,500 i, UK & o'seas
¶ Various Booklets & Leaflets.

Depression UK (D-UK) 1973

■ c/o Self Help Nottingham, Ormiston House, 32-36 Pelham St,
  NOTTINGHAM, NG1 2EG.   (mail/address)
  email info@depressionuk.org
  http://www.depressionuk.org
  Hon Sec: Katie Wilkins
▲ Registered Charity
○ *W; support & encouragement for people with depression, &
  for their relatives & friends
● Conf - Res - Inf - Pen / phone friend schemes - Self help group
  support
M 350 i, 1 org (NCVO), UK / 4 i, o'seas
  (Sub: £10)
¶ NL - 6; ftm, £1.50 each nm.   AR; free.
✕ 2007 (September) Fellowship of Depressives Anonymous

Derby Porcelain International Society   (DPIS)   1984
- ■ PO Box 6997, COLESHILL, Warks, B46 2LF.   (hsp)
      01675 481293
      email a.varnam@farming.co.uk
      http://www.derby-porcelain.org.uk
      Hon Sec: Anthony Varnam
- ▲ Registered Charity
- ○ *G, *L; the history & research of Derbyshire ceramics from
      1748 to date
- ● Res - VE
- M 250 i, UK / 25 i, o'seas
      £25 UK / £35 o'seas)
- ¶ Jnl - 3; ftm, £10 nm.   NL - 2; ftm, £5 nm.

**Derbyshire Agricultural & Horticultural Society Ltd   (DAHS)
1860**
- ■ 5 Willow Park Way, Aston on Trent, DERBY, DE72 2DF.   (hsp)
      01332 793068   fax 01332 793068
      email info@derbyshirecountyshow.org.uk
      http://www.derbyshirecountyshow.org.uk
      Gen Sec: Mrs Anne James
- ▲ Registered Charity
- ○ *F, *H; farming & agriculture, horticulture & staging the
      Derbyshire County Show
- ● Derbyshire County Show
- < Assn of Show & Agricl Orgs
- M 592 i
- ¶ Show Catalogue - 1; price varies.

Derbyshire Archaeological Society   (DAS)   1878
- NR 2 The Watermeadows, Swarkestone, DERBY, DE73 1JA.   (hsp)
      01332 704148
      email barbarafoster@talk21.com
      http://www.derbyshireas.org.uk
      Hon Sec: Barbara Foster
- ▲ Registered Charity
- ○ *L; to promote the study of archaeology & history of Derbyshire
- M 502 i, 60 org
- ¶ Derbyshire Archaeological Jnl - 1; ftm, varies nm.
      Derbyshire Miscellany - 2; £4 m, £5 nm.
      Gazeteers of Industrial Archaeology - irreg.
        [subscription, £15].

Derbyshire Chamber & Business Link
      in 2008 merged with the Nottinghamshire Chamber of Commerce &
      Industry to form the **Derbyshire & Nottinghamshire Chamber of
      Commerce**

Derbyshire Gritstone Sheepbreeders Society   (DGSS)   1906
- NR 5 Bridge Close, Waterfoot, ROSSENDALE, Lancs, BB4 9SN.
      (hsp)
      01706 228520
      email susan@pmcoppack.com
      http://www.derbyshiregritstone.org.uk
      Hon Sec: Mrs Susan Coppack
- ▲ Registered Charity
- ○ *B
- < Nat Sheep Assn
- M 160 i
- ¶ NL - 1;   Booklet; both ftm only.

**Derbyshire & Nottinghamshire Chamber of Commerce
(DNCC)   1899**
- ■ Commerce Centre, Canal Wharf, CHESTERFIELD, Derbys,
      S41 7NA.   (hq)
      0844 443 2150   fax 01246 233228
      email info@dncc.co.uk   http://www.dncc.co.uk
      Chief Exec: George Cowcher
- ▲ Company Limited by Guarantee
- Br 2
- ○ *C; business support services incl training, business
      development & networking
- Gp Forums: International trade, Engineering, Skills
      Councils: Derbyshire members, Nottinghamshire members
- ● Conf - Mtgs - ET - Exam - Res - Exhib - Expt - Inf - LG
- < Brit Chams Comm; E Midlands Cham Comm
- > Derbyshire Enterprise Agency
- M 3,600 f
- ¶ In Business - 12; ftm, £2.95 nm.
- × 2008 (Derbyshire Chamber & Business Link
            (Nottinghamshire Chamber of Commerce & Industry

Derbyshire Record Society   (DRS)   1977
- ■ School of History, University of Nottingham, University Park,
      NOTTINGHAM, NG7 2RD.   (hsb)
      Hon Sec: Philip Riden
- ▲ Registered Charity
- ○ *L; publication of historical records relating to Derbyshire
- ● Res
- M 300 i, 15 org, UK / 15 i, o'seas
- ¶ NL - 2; ftm only.

Derry Chamber of Commerce
      see **Londonderry Chamber of Commerce**

Design & Artists Copyright Society Ltd   (DACS)   1983
- ■ 33 Great Sutton St, LONDON, EC1V 0DX.   (hq)
      020 7336 8811   fax 020 7336 8822
      email info@dacs.org.uk   http://www.dacs.org.uk
      Chief Exec: Joanna Cave
- ▲ Company Limited by Guarantee
- ○ *A, *T; the copyright & collecting society for the visual arts in the
      UK; to administer & protect the rights of visual creators;
      membership is open to all artists & photographers
- Gp Artists copyright
- ● ET - Inf - LG - Collecting society
- < Eur Visual Artists (EVA); IFRRO; CISAC; Brit Copyright Coun
- M c 60,000 i
- ¶ AR - 1; free.

Design Association   (DA)   2001
- ■ 1 Cedar Court, Royal Oak Yard, Bermondsey St, LONDON,
      SE1 3GA.   (hq)
      020 7357 8282   fax 020 7407 9878
      email info@design-association.org
      http://www.design-association.org
      Chief Exec: Frank Peters
- ▲ Company Limited by Guarantee
- ○ *T; accreditation of design businesses
- ● ET - Stat - Expt
- < Chart Soc of Designers
- M f
- ¶ Various professional publications & practice documents.

Design Business Association   (DBA)   1986
- NR 35-39 Old St, LONDON, EC1V 9HX.   (hq)
      020 7251 9229   fax 020 7251 9221
      email deborah.dawton@dba.org.uk
      http://www.dba.org.uk
      Chief Exec: Deborah Dawton
- ▲ Company Limited by Guarantee
- ○ *T; 'to demonstrate the contribution that design makes to
      society & to promote professional excellence in bringing
      together creativity & commerce'
- ● Conf - Mtgs - ET - Res - Exhib - Comp - Expt - Inf - LG
- M 200 f, UK / 2 f, o'seas

© CBD Research Ltd · Beckenham · BR3 5JS · Tel 020 8650 7745 · E-mail cbd@cbdresearch.com · www.cbdresearch.com

Design History Society (DHS) 1977
- ■ School of Humanities, Faculty of the Arts, University of Brighton, Grand Parade, BRIGHTON, E Sussex, BN2 0JY.   (hsp)
  01273 600900
  email nicklas@brighton.ac.uk
  http://www.designhistorysociety.org
  Hon Sec: Charlotte Nicklas
- ▲ Registered Charity
- ○ *A; to promote the study of & research into, design history; to disseminate & publish the useful results; to exchange information with other bodies & individuals concerned with design history
- ● Conf - Mtgs - ET - Exhib - SG - Inf - VE
- M 200 i, 100 libraries & colleges, UK / 30 i, o'seas
- ¶ Jnl of Design History - 4;   NL - 4; both ftm.

Design & Industries Association (DIA) 1917
- NR c/o Derek Rothera & Co, Unit 15-16, 7 Wenlock Rd, LONDON, N1 7SL.
- ▲ Registered Charity
- ○ *P; to provide a forum for those engaged in education, design & industry with the common aim of raising the standards of design & the public awareness of the value of good design

Design Research Society (DRS) 1966
- NR International Digital Laboratory, Warwick University, COVENTRY, Warks, CV4 7AL.
  024 7652 75951
  http://www.designresearchsociety.org
  Hon Sec: Dr Rebecca Cain
- ○ *P; for all involved with design research in all its forms
- Gp Special interest: Experiential knowledge; Health & well-being; Objects, practices, experiences, networks; Pedagogy
- ¶ Design Research NL - 12 (electronic).
  Design Research Quarterly - 4.

Design & Technology Association (DATA) 1989
- NR 16 Wellesbourne House, Walton Rd, WELLESBOURNE, Warks, CV35 9JB.   (hq)
  01789 470007   fax 01789 841955
  email data@data.org.uk   http://www.data.org.uk
  Chief Exec: Richard Green
- ▲ Company Limited by Guarantee; Registered Charity
- ○ *E, *P; for all those involved in design & technology education & associated subject areas; to promote the advancement of education & in particular, but not exclusively, to support, encourage, promote, develop & maintain design & technological education in all its branches
- Gp Advisory groups: Initial teacher education, Primary, Secondary, Special educational needs
- ● Conf - Mtgs - ET - Res - Exhib - Stat - Inf (members only) - Lib - LG
- M 5,423 i, 54 f, UK / 118 i, o'seas
- ¶ DATA News - 3;   DATA Jnl - 3;   MODUS - 6; all ftm only.
  Designing Magazine - 3; £18 m, £21 nm.

Designer Bookbinders (DB) 1951
- NR 24 Junction Rd, BATH, Somerset, BA2 3NH.   (hsp)
  01225 342793
  email secretary@designerbookbinders.org.uk
  http://www.designerbookbinders.org.uk
  Hon Sec: Wendy Hood
- ▲ Registered Charity
- ○ *A; devoted to the craft of fine bookbinding
- ● Comp - ET - Exhib
- M 41 i (fellows & licentiates)
- ¶ The New Bookbinder - 1;   DB Newsletter - 4, both ftm.

Designer Jewellers Group (DJG) 1975
- NR 24 Rivington St, LONDON, EC2A 3DU.   (chmn/b)
  01728 861669
  email info@michaelcarpenterjewellery.co.uk
  http://www.designerjewellersgroup.co.uk
  Chmn: Michael Carpenter
- ○ *P; to promote individuality in design & professional craftsmanship
- ● Exhib
- M 34 i

Despatch Association (DA) 1985
- NR 2A Brownlow Mews, LONDON, WC1N 2LA.   (hq)
  020 7685 1132
  email phil@despatch.co.uk   http://www.despatch.co.uk
  Chief Exec: Phillip Stone
- ▲ Un-incorporated Society
- ○ *T; to represent the despatch & courier industry
- ● Res - Inf - LG
- < Eur Express Assn
- M 250 f
- ¶ Despatches Magazine - 6; ftm, £1.10 nm.
  Despatches Magazine - online; ftm.

Deutsch-Britische Industrie- und Handelskammer
   see **German-British Chamber of Industry & Commerce (Deutsche-Britische Industrie- und Handelskammer**

Development Education Association (DEA) 1993
- NR CAN Mezzanine, 32-36 Loman St, LONDON, SE1 0EH.   (hq)
  020 7922 7930   fax 020 7922 7929
  email dea@dea.org.uk   http://www.dea.org.uk
  Office Mgr: Dean Weston
- ▲ Company Limited by Guarantee; Registered Charity
- ○ *E, *N; an umbrella body working to support & promote greater awareness & understanding of global & international development issues in the UK; member organisations work within schools & education, youth organisations, community groups etc to bring a global perspective to learning at all ages
- ● Conf - Mtgs - ET - Res - Inf - Lib - LG
- M 60 centres, 230 org
- ¶ Development Education (Jnl) - 3.
  DEA Bulletin - 10;   Schools News (NL) - 2;
  Global Youth Work (NL) - 2;   AR;
  Worldlywise (adult education) (NL) - 2; all ftm only.
  Note: Uses the title Think Global

Development Studies Association (DSA) 1978
- NR PO Box 108, BIDEFORD, Devon, EX39 6ZQ.   (admin/b)
  0845 519 3372
  email admin@devstud.org.uk   http://www.devstud.org.uk
  Exec Dir: Frances Hill
- ▲ Registered Charity
- ○ *G, *K; to connect & promote the development research community in the UK & Ireland
- Gp DSA Scotland
  Study groups: Ageing & development; Agriculture & rural development; Bridging research & policy, Conflict & human security, Corporate social responsibility, Design & development, Development ethics, Development management, Disasters & development, Economics, finance & trade, Environment, resources & sustainable development, European development policy, History & development, HIV/AIDS, Information technology & development, Livestock, Media & development, Multi-dimensional poverty, NGOs in development, Public engagement in development, Research students, Tourism & development, Urban policy, Women in development
- ● Conf - Mtgs - ET - SG - Inf - LG
- < Brit O'seas NGOs for Devt; Devt Educ Assn; Eur Assn Devt Training Insts
- M 1,000 i, 80 f, UK / 250 i, o'seas
- ¶ Jnl of International Development - 8; £52 yr m, £340 yr nm.

Development Trusts Association   (DTA)   1992
NR   33 Corsham St, LONDON, N1 6DR.   (hq)
  0845 458 8336   fax 0845 458 8337
  email info@dta.org.uk   http://www.dta.org.uk
  Dir: Steve Wyler
▲   Company Limited by Guarantee; Registered Charity
○   *N; to support existing development trusts & the creation of new
  ones

Development Trusts Association Scotland   2003
NR   54 Manor Place, EDINBURGH, EH3 7EH.
  0131 220 2456   fax 0131 220 3777
  email info@dtascot.org.uk   http://www.dtascot.org.uk
○   *K

Devon Archaeological Society   (DAS)   1929
■   Royal Albert Memorial Museum, Queen St, EXETER, Devon,
  EX4 3RX.   (hsb)
  http://www.groups.ex.ac.uk/das/
▲   Registered Charity
○   *L, *Q; archaeological promotion & conservation within Devon
●   Conf - Mtgs - ET - Res - Exhib - SG - Inf - Lib - VE
M   940 i, 52 org, UK / 20 i, o'seas
¶   Proceedings - 1; ftm, £18 nm.   NL - 3; ftm only.
  Devon Archaeology - 1; ftm, from £1.50 nm (as available).

Devon Cattle Breeders' Society   (DCBS)   1884
■   Wisteria Cottage, Iddesleigh, WINKLEIGH, Devon,
  EX19 8BG.   (sp)
  01837 810942   fax 01837 810942
  email dcbs@btconnect.com
  http://www.redrubydevon.co.uk
  Sec: Andy Lane
▲   Company Limited by Guarantee; Registered Charity
○   *B; to further the breeding of the Red Ruby Devon breed of
  cattle
●   Mtgs - Comp - Stat - Expt - Inf - Lib
<   Nat Beef Assn; Devon Cattle Breeder Socs in: Australia, Brazil,
  New Zealand, & USA
M   c 400 i
¶   NL - 4;   AR; both ftm only.
  Davy's Devon Herd Book - 1.

Devon Closewool Sheep Breeders' Society   1923
■   c/o Holtom & Thomas, The Elms Office, Bishops Tawton,
  BARNSTAPLE, Devon, EX32 0EJ.   (hsb)
  01271 326900
  email ron@holtomandthomas.co.uk
  http://www.devonclosewool.co.uk
  Sec: Ron Smith
▲   Un-incorporated Society
○   *B
●   Comp
<   Nat Sheep Assn
M   65 i, 2 f
¶   Flock Book - 1; ftm, £2 nm.

Devon & Cornwall Longwool Flock Association   1977
NR   Pelkham View, Kentisbeare, CULLOMPTON, Devon, EX15 2EY.
  01884 266201
  http://www.devonandcornwalllongwool.co.uk
  Sec: Melvyn Britton
▲   Registered Charity
○   *B; breeding of pedigree longwool sheep; production of good
  lustre wool
●   Mtgs - Comp
<   Nat Sheep Assn
M   60 i
¶   Flock Book - 1.

Devon & Cornwall Record Society   (DCRS)   1904
■   c/o Devon & Exeter Institution, 7 Cathedral Close, EXETER,
  Devon, EX1 1EZ.   (hsb)
  01392 274727
  http://www.genuki.cs.ncl.ac.uk/DEV/DCRS
  Admin: Mrs E Franceschini
▲   Registered Charity
○   *L; publication of local records, promotion of local historical
  studies & genealogical research
●   Res - Lib - Collection of transcripts of parish registers & other
  source material
M   500 i, 50 org, UK / 15 i, 40 org, o'seas, (org are libraries &
  institutions)
¶   Publications list available.

Devon County Agricultural Association   (DCAA)   1872
NR   Westpoint, Clyst St Mary, EXETER, Devon, EX5 1DJ.   (hq)
  01392 446000   fax 01392 444808
  email info@dcshow.co.uk
  http://www.devoncountyshow.co.uk
  Sec: Ollie Allen
▲   Registered Charity
○   *F; promotion of agriculture, forestry, horticulture & commerce
  in Devon
●   Agricultural shows, exhibitions & events
<   Assn of Show & Agricl Orgs
M   2,212 i, f & org
¶   Devon County Show Catalogue - 1.   DCAA Ybk; ftm only.
  Devon County Show Programme - 1.

Dexter Cattle Society   1892
■   Charolais Pavilion, STONELEIGH PARK, Warks, CV8 2RG.   (hq)
  024 7669 2300   fax 024 7669 2400
  email secretary@dextercattle.co.uk
  http://www.dextercattle.co.uk
  Sec: Mrs Sue Archer
▲   Company Limited by Guarantee; Registered Charity
Br   14; France, Germany, Ireland
○   *B; to promote the development of the breed & its markets
  (niche beef)
●   Conf - Mtgs - ET - Res - SG - Stat - Expt
M   1,400 i, UK / 50 i, o'seas
¶   The Dexter Bulletin - 3;   Dexter NL - 3; both ftm only.

Diabetes Federation of Ireland
IRL   76 Lower Gardiner St, DUBLIN 1, Republic of Ireland.
  353 (1) 836 3022
  email info@diabetes.ie   http://www.diabetes.ie
  Hon Chmn: Dr Tony O'Sullivan
○   *W
●   Helpline: 353 (1) 850 909909

Diabetes UK   1934
■   Macleod House, 10 Parkway, LONDON, NW1 7AA.   (hq)
  020 7424 1000   fax 020 7424 1001
  email info@diabetes.org.uk
  http://www.diabetes.org.uk
  Chief Exec: Douglas Smallwood
▲   Registered Charity
Br   6
○   *W; to fund research into diabetes; to raise awareness of the
  seriousness of the condition; to provide information to people
  with diabetes, their families, healthcare professionals & the
  general public
Gp   Healthcare professionals
●   Conf - ET - Res - Exhib - Stat - Inf - Lib - PL - VE - LG
<   Intl Diabetes Fedn (IDF)
M   180,000 i
¶   Balance - 6; ftm, £2.95 nm.
  Diabetic Medicine - 12.
  Diabetes Update (for healthcare professionals) - 4; ftm.

© CBD Research Ltd · Beckenham · BR3 5JS · Tel 020 8650 7745 · E-mail cbd@cbdresearch.com · www.cbdresearch.com

Diaconal Association of the Church of England   1988
§   55 Vicarage Lane, Marton, BLACKPOOL, Lancs, FY4 4EF.
    0870 321 3260
    email secretary@dace.org   http://www.dace.org
    Sec: Revd Ann Wren
    An association of deacons in the Church of England working in
    the community to make links between the church & the
    world.

Dickens Fellowship   1902
■   48 Doughty St, LONDON, WC1N 2LX.   (hq)
    020 7405 2127   fax 020 7831 5175
    email postbox@dickensfellowship.org
    http://www.dickensfellowship.org
    Jt Hon Gen Secs: Mrs Lee Ault, Mrs Joan Dicks
▲   Un-incorporated Society
Br 15; 33 o'seas
○   *L; literary society for lovers of the works of Charles Dickens;
    preservation of buildings & objects associated with him
●   Conf - Mtgs - Res - SG - Inf - VE
M   i (branches are autonomous, numbers unknown)
¶   The Dickensian - 3; £12 m.

Diecasting Society   (DCS)   1966
■   National Metalforming Centre, 47 Birmingham Rd,
    WEST BROMWICH, W Midlands, B70 6PY.   (hq)
    0121-601 6365   fax 0870 138 9714
    email dcs@alfed.org.uk
    Sec: Will Savage
▲   Company Limited by Guarantee; Registered Charity
Br 3
○   *P; to advance the study of diecasting, the technology &
    methods, to promote research & disseminate the results
●   Conf - Mtgs - ET - Exhib - SG - Inf - Lib - VE
M   153 i, 90 f, UK / 5 i, o'seas
¶   NL - 3; ftm only.
    Conference Proceedings - 2 yrly; £20.

** Digital Content Forum
    Organisation lost: see Introduction paragraph 3

Digital & Screen Printing Association
    since 23 April 2008 **Prism: Association of Print Specialists &
    Manufacturers**

Dignity in Dying   1935
NR 181 Oxford St, LONDON, W1D 2JT.   (hq)
    020 7479 7730
    email info@dignityindying.org.uk
    http://www.dignityindying.org.uk
    Chief Exec: Deborah Annetts
▲   Un-incorporated Society
○   *K; to make it legal for a competent adult, who is suffering
    unbearably from an incurable illness, to receive medical help
    to die at their own considered & persistent request.
    The VES distributes forms for living wills in order to refuse
    unwanted life-prolonging treatment & advises on their usage
    (which is legally enforceable)
●   LG
M   15,000 i
¶   NL - 4; ftm only.   Living Wills; £15.
✕   2006 Voluntary Euthanasia Society

Dinosaur Society UK   1993
■   PO Box 20, HEATHFIELD, E Sussex, TN21 8GY.   (mem/sp)
    01462 626686
    email enquiries@dinosaursociety.com
    http://www.dinosaursociety.com
▲   Registered Charity
○   *K; to raise the awareness & to advance public interest in
    dinosaur palaeontology
●   Conf - ET - Exhib
M   purely web-based; free.
¶   web-based.

Diplomatic Service Families Association   (DSFA)
NR Foreign & Commonwealth Office, King Charles St, LONDON,
    SW1A 2AH.
    020 7008 1500
    email dsfa.enquiries@fco.gov.uk
    Chmn: Tina Attwood
○   *W

Dipterists Forum - the Society for the Study of Flies   1993
NR c/o BENHS, The Pelham-Clinton Building, Dinton Pastures
    Country Park, Hurst, READING, RG10 0TH.
    http://www.dipteristsforum.org.uk
○   *P, *G
<   Brit Entomological & Natural History Soc
¶   Dipterists Digest.

Direct Marketing Association (UK) Ltd   (DMA)   1992
NR DMA House, 70 Margaret St, LONDON, W1W 8SS.   (hq)
    020 7291 3300
    http://www.dma.org.uk
▲   Company Limited by Guarantee
○   *T; 'to raise the stature of the direct marketing industry, giving
    the consumer trust & confidence in direct marketing'

Direct Selling Association Ltd   (DSA)   1965
■   c/o Enterprise House, 30 Billing Rd, NORTHAMPTON,
    NN1 5DQ.   (hq)
    01604 635700
    http://www.dsa.org.uk
    Dir: Richard M Berry
▲   Company Limited by Guarantee
○   *T; to represent companies who use independent salespeople to
    sell their products, by party plan or person to person, &
    whose marketing plans are legal & who have agreed to
    abide by the DSA codes of practice
●   Conf - Mtgs - Res - Stat - Inf - Lib - LG
<   Wld Fedn of Direct Selling Assns (USA); Fedn of Eur Direct
    Selling Assns (FEDSA)
M   41 f, 12 prospective f, 40 associates (suppliers of services)
¶   Shopping at Home: consumer guide including the DSA Code of
    Practice;
    A guide to earnings opportunities in direct selling (containing
    DSA Code of Business Conduct);
    Report - Independent Code Administration - 1; all free.
    Direct Selling, Consumer Goods in the UK (survey) - 1; ftm,
    £25 nm.
    Direct Selling: from door to door to network marketing; £17.99.

Directors Guild of Great Britain   (DGGB)   1983
■   Studio 24, Royal Victoria Patriotic Building, John Archer Way,
    LONDON, SW18 3SX.   (hq)
    020 8871 1660
    http://www.dggb.org
    Gen Sec: Piers Haggard
○   *P, *U; represents the interests of directors in all media: theatre,
    film, TV, ballet, opera, commercials, videos etc
Gp Recorded media: Film, Television, Video, Radio
    Live media: Theatre, Opera, Dance
●   Conf - Mtgs - Res - Inf - Empl - LG - Events - Networking -
    Masterclasses
<   Fedn of Eur Film Directors (FERA), Informal Eur Theatre Meeting
    (IETM), Nat Campaign for the Arts (NCA)
M   1,000 i, 50 f, 22 org, UK / 20 i, o'seas
¶   Direct (NL) - 4.   LM - 2 yrly.
    Rates Cards (Schedule of rates of pay) - 1.
    Contract Guide - 1.
    Monitoring Report on Theatre Directors.

Disability Alliance   1974
- ■ Universal House, 88-94 Wentworth St, LONDON, E1 7SA. (hq)
  020 7247 8776 (1000-1600 hrs)   fax 020 7247 8765
  email office.da@dial.pipex.com
  http://www.disabilityalliance.org
  Chief Exec: Vanessa Stanislas,   Sec: David Fletcher
- ▲ Company Limited by Guarantee; Registered Charity
- ○ *K, *W; to break the link between poverty & disability by providing information to disabled people about their entitlements; to campaign for improvements to the social security system & for increases in benefits
- ● ET - Inf - LG
- M 380+ org
  (Sub: in price bands)
- ¶ Disability Rights Hbk 2008-09 - 1; £21 (£14.50 for individuals in receipt of benefits).
  Employment & Support Alliance Guide 2008-09; £7 or (£2 concessionary rate)

Disability Federation of Ireland   (DFI)
- IRL Fumbally Court, Fumbally Lane, DUBLIN 8, Republic of Ireland.
  353 (1) 454 7978   fax 353 (1) 454 7981
  email info@disability-federation.ie
  http://www.disability-federation.ie
  Chief Exec: John Dolan
- ○ *N, *W

Disabled Motorcyclists Association
  has closed

Disabled Motoring UK   1922
- ■ Ashwellthorpe, NORWICH, Norfolk, NR16 1EX.   (hq)
  01508 489449   fax 01508 488173
  email info@disabledmotoring.org
  http://www.disabledmotoring.org
  Dir: Helen Dolphin
- ▲ Registered Charity
- Br 50 area representatives
- ○ *W; to promote & protect the interests & welfare of physically disabled drivers; assistance regarding car conversions, ferry concessions, reduced RAC subscriptions, general information
- ● Mtgs - ET - Exam - LG
- M 14,500 i, 7 f
- ¶ Mobilise - 6; ftm, £2.50 each nm.
- ✕ 2011 (April) Mobilise Organisation

Disabled Motorists Federation   (DMF)   1955
- ■ Chester-le-Street CVS Volunteer Centre, Clarence Terrace, CHESTER-LE-STREET, Co Durham, DH3 3DQ.   (hsp)
  0191-416 3172   fax 0191-416 3172
  http://www.dmfed.org.uk
  Hon Sec: J E Killick
- ▲ Registered Charity
- Br 11 affiliated clubs; Russia
- ○ *W; to provide motoring information to the disabled & their carers on all matters of disabled travel; to run social clubs & to negotiate with national bodies on all matters connected with disabled travel, not specialising in motoring
- ● Mtgs - Inf - LG
- M c 2,000 i, 11 affiliated clubs
- ¶ The Way Ahead - 4; ftm, £1.25 nm.
  Publications list available.

Disablement Income Group Scotland
  dissolved 2009

Discovery Award England   (DAE)
- ■ St Mary's Church Hall, Wollaton Hall Drive, NOTTINGHAM, NG8 1AF.   (hq)
  0115-978 6988
  http://www.discoveryawardengland.co.uk
  Discovery Award Scotland, Ancrum Outdoor Education Centre, 10 Ancrum Rd, DUNDEE, DD2 2HZ.
- ▲ Un-incorporated Society
- Br 100; Australia, Malta
- ○ *G; as part of the Discovery Award Federation, fosters & encourages the development of people over the age of 50, physically, mentally & spiritually - enables & encourages people to make choices about their own lives & increase their contribution to life by meeting personal challenges
- ● Conf - Mtgs - VE
- M 525 i, UK / 5 i, o'seas
  (Sub: £5)
- ¶ AR; free.

Discrimination Law Association   (DLA)   1995
- ■ PO Box 63576, LONDON, N6 9BB.   (hq)
  0845 478 6375
  email info@discriminationlaw.org.uk
  http://www.discriminationlaw.org.uk
  Admin: Chris Atkinson
- ▲ Company Limited by Guarantee
- ○ *P; to promote good community relations by improving assistance & support to victims of discrimination; to advance education & training in the field of legal representation
- ● Conf - Mtgs - ET - Inf LG
- M 233 i, 41 f, 133 org
- ¶ Discrimination Law Briefings - 4; ftm, £20 each nm.
  Directory of Members - on-going; ftm only.
  Directory of Trainers - 2; free.
  NL - 4; ftm.   AR; ftm, £1 nm.

Dispensing Doctors Association Ltd   (DDA)   1997
- ■ Low Hagg Farm, Starfitts Lane, KIRKBYMOORSIDE, N Yorks, YO62 7JF.   (hsb)
  01751 430835   fax 01751 430836
  email office@dispensingdoctor.org
  http://www.dispensingdoctor.org
  Chief Exec: Dr David Baker
  Sec: Jeff Lee
- ▲ Company Limited by Guarantee
- ○ *P; for doctors providing pharmaceutical services in rural areas
- Gp Financial; Publicity
- ● Conf - ET - Inf - LG
- M c 2,400 i, 25 f
- ¶ Jnl - 4.

** District Auditors Society
  Organisation lost; see Introduction paragraph 3

District of Wigtown Chamber of Commerce   2006
- NR WRDC Business Centre, Queen St, NEWTON STEWART, Wigtownshire, DG8 6JL.
  01671 403875
  http://www.dwchamber.wigtownshirechamberofcommerce.org.uk
  Sec: Bobbie Jeal
- ○ *C

Doctor E F Schumacher Society   (Schumacher UK)   1978
- ■ The Create Environment Centre, Smeaton Rd, BRISTOL, BS1 6XN.   (hq)
  0117-903 1081   fax 0117-903 1081
  email admin@schumacher.org.uk
  http://www.schumacher.org.uk
  Dir: Richard St George
- ▲ Company Limited by Guarantee
- Br 3; Germany, India, Ireland, USA
- ○ *G; to promote the philosophy of Dr E F Schumacher; to promote human scale sustainable development in the UK & abroad
- Gp Schumacher book service
- ● Conf - ET - Res - Inf - VE - Presentation of annual Schumacher award
- < Members of the Schumacher Circle:
  Centre for Alternative Technology; Intermediate Technology; New Economics Foundation; Soil Association
- > Schumacher College
- M 500 i, 5 f, 5 org, UK / 50 i, o'seas
- ¶ Schumacher NL - 2; ftm, £2 nm.
  Schumacher Briefings - 2/3; ftm, £6-£8 nm.

Dogs Trust   1891
- ■ 17 Wakley St, LONDON, EC1V 7RQ.   (hq)
  020 7837 0006   fax 020 7833 2701
  email info@dogstrust.org.uk
  http://www.dogstrust.org.uk
  Chief Exec: Clarissa Baldwin
- ▲ Registered Charity
- Br 15
- ○ *V; 'working towards the day when all dogs can enjoy a happy life, free from the threat of unnecessary destruction'
- ● Conf - Mtgs - ET - Res - Exhib - Comp - Stat - Expt - Inf - PL
- M 15,825 i, 826 f, 262,775 supporters, UK / 96 i, 808 supporters, o'seas
- ¶ NL - 3; free.   AR; ftm only.
  Educational literature.

Doll Club of Great Britain
- NR 2 Palace Green, ELY, Cambs, CB7 4EW.   (mail/address)
  email dollclubgb@yahoo.co.uk
- ▲ Un-incorporated Society
- ○ *G; the study & appreciation of dolls, dolls' houses & other nursery bygones of the past
- ● Mtgs - Comp - SG - VE
- M 150 i, UK / 20 i, o'seas
- ¶ Plangon - 4; ftm only.

Dolmetsch Historical Dance Society   (DHDS)   1970
- ■ 17 Well Lane, Stock, INGATESTONE, Essex, CM4 9LT.   (hsp)
  01277 840473   fax 01277 840473
  email secretary@dhds.org.uk   http://www.dhds.org.uk
  Hon Sec: Mrs Jo Saunders
- ▲ Registered Charity
- ○ *A, *D, *G, *L, *Q; conducting & promoting original research into & practice of dance, from the 14th-19th centuries & allied subjects of music, literature, art, costume & social history
- ● Conf - Mtgs - Res - Inf
- M 94 i, UK / 21 i, o'seas
- ¶ Historical Dance (Jnl) - 2/3 yrly; ftm, £8 nm.
  NL - 3; ftm only.   Teaching Resource Packs.
  Summer School Booklets & CDs (dance instructions & music) - 1; prices vary.
  Conference Proceedings - 2 yrly; prices vary.

Domestic Appliance Service Association   (DASA)   1978
- ■ 145-157 St John St, LONDON, EC1V 4PY.   (asa)
  0870 224 0343   fax 0870 224 0358
  email dasa@dasa.org.uk   http://www.dasa.org.uk
  Chmn: W Russell
- ▲ Un-incorporated Society
- ○ *T; repair & servicing of domestic appliances
- ● Mtgs - ET - Exhib - LG
- < Brit Quality Foundation; Electrical & Electronics Servicing Training Coun;Trade Assn Forum
- M 100 i, 30 f
- ¶ Orbit (NL) - 6; ftm only.   LM [website].

Domestic Fowl Trust   1974
- NR Station Rd, Honeybourne, EVESHAM, Worcs, WR11 7QZ.   (hq)
  01386 833083   fax 01386 833364
  email dlf@domesticfowltrust.co.uk
  http://www.domesticfowltrust.co.uk
  Chief Exec: Mrs Bernie Landshoff
- ○ *B; conservation of the domestic fowl & rare breeds of farm animals; marketing of poultry housing & equipment, hybrid & traditional breeds of poultry, books & gifts
- ● ET
- M 350 i, UK / 30 i, o'seas

Domestic Heat Pump Association
  as association of **BEAMA Ltd**

Domestic Water Treatment Association
  an association in the Energy section of **BEAMA Ltd**

Doncaster Chamber of Commerce & Enterprise   (DCCE)   1941
- ■ Doncaster Business Innovation Centre, Ten Pound Walk, DONCASTER, S Yorks, DN4 5HX.   (hq)
  01302 341000   fax 01302 328382
  email enquiries@doncaster-chamber.co.uk
  http://www.doncaster-chamber.co.uk
  Chief Exec: Stephen Shore
- ▲ Company Limited by Guarantee
- ○ *C
- ● Conf - Mtgs - ET - Res - Exhib - Comp - Stat - Expt - Inf - Lib - VE - Empl - LG
- < Brit Chams Comm
- M 1,000 f
- ¶ Chamber News - 6;   Chamber Link - 6; both free.
- × Doncaster Chamber

Donizetti Society   1973
- ■ 146 Bordesley Rd, MORDEN, Surrey, SM4 5LT.   (hsp)
  020 8648 9364
  http://www.donizettisociety.com
  Hon Sec: J P Clayton
- ○ *D; to promote interest in the works of Gaetano Donizetti (1797-1848) & the music of his period
- M i

Donkey Breed Society   (DBS)   1967
- NR The Hermitage, Pootings, EDENBRIDGE, Kent, TN8 6SD.   (hsb)
  01732 864414   fax 01732 864414
  email carol@morse.freeserve.co.uk
  http://www.donkeybreedsociety.co.uk
  Sec: Carol Morse
- ○ *B; to encourage the use, appreciation, well being & protection of the donkey

Donor Watch   1995
- ■ Turner House, 153 Cromwell Road, LONDON, SW5 0TQ. (hsp)
  020 7373 5560   fax 020 7373 5560
  email selbywhittingham@hotmail.com
  Sec-Gen: Dr Selby Whittingham
- ▲ Un-incorporated Society
- ○ *L; campaigning in support of fidelity to the conditions on which money, or objects, are given or bequeathed for the benefit of the public
- ● Campaigning
- M [not stated]
- ¶ NL - 2/3; ftm only.

Door & Hardware Federation   (DHF)   1970
- ■ 42 Heath St, TAMWORTH, Staffs, B79 7JH.   (hq)
  01827 52337   fax 01827 310827
  email info@dhfonline.org.uk
  http://www.dhfonline.org.uk
  Sec: Michael Skelding
- ▲ Company Limited by Guarantee
- ○ *T; to represent the interests of manufacturers & installers of industrial, pedestrian & garage doors; also manufacturers of locks & building hardware. It provides professionals in all sectors of the building industry with a single source for technical expertise to assure progress & maintenance of standards throughout the industry
- Gp 7 specialist groups: Garage door; Garage door installer; Gate; Hardware; Industrial door; Metal doorset; Timber doorset
- ● Conf - Mtgs - ET - Res - Exhib - Inf - LG
- < Construction Products Assn
- M 320 f
  (Sub: varies)
- ¶ Best Practice Guide (series) on [eg]: Thief resistant locks; Exit devices; Door & window bolts; Lock cylinders.
  Code of Practice on: Hardware for fire & escape doors; Rolling shutters; Repair & maintenance; FR metal doorsets
  List available.

Dorchester Agricultural Society   (DAS)   1841
- NR Acland Rd, DORCHESTER, Dorset, DT1 1EF.   (hq)
  01305 264249   fax 01305 251643
  email secretary@dorsetcountyshow.co.uk
  http://www.dorsetcountyshow.co.uk
  Dir: Sam Mackenzie-Green
- ▲ Company Limited by Guarantee; Registered Charity
- ○ *F
- ● Dorset County Show
- < Assn of Show & Agricl Orgs
- M 1,500 i, 20 f

Dorothy Dunnett Society   2001
- NR Weedy End Cottage, 41 High Street, SILVERTON, Devon, EX5 4JD.   (treas/p)
  email anne.buchanan@ddra.org   http://www.ddra.org
  Treas: Olive Millward,   Sec: Anne Buchanan
- ▲ Registered Charity
- ○ *G; for all interested in the writings of Dorothy Dunnett (1923-2001) & the historical periods in which they were set
- ● Conf - Mtgs - Inf - History prize
- M i
  (Sub: £24.50, £28 o'seas)
- ¶ Whispering Gallery - 4.

Dorothy L Sayers Society   1976
- ■ Rose Cottage, Malthouse Lane, HURSTPIERPOINT, W Sussex, BN6 9JY.   (chmn/p)
  01273 833444   fax 01273 835988
  email jasmine@sayers.org.uk
  http://www.sayers.org.uk/
  Chmn: Christopher J Dean
- ▲ Registered Charity
- ○ *A; study of the life & works of Dorothy L Sayers; encouragement & advice on production & research of her works
- ● Conf - Res - SG - Inf
- M 260 i, UK / 255 i, o'seas
- ¶ DLS Bulletin - 6; ftm.   Sidelights on Sayers - 2; £3.
  Annual Proceedings - 1; £3.

Dorset Chamber of Commerce & Industry   (DCCI)   1949
- NR Chamber House, Ling Rd, POOLE, Dorset, BH12 4NZ.   (hq)
  01202 714800   fax 01202 747862
  email contact@dorsetbusiness.net
  http://www.dcci.co.uk
  Chief Exec: Peter Scott
- ▲ Company Limited by Guarantee
- ○ *C
  Note: is known as Dorset Business.

Dorset Down Sheep Breeders' Association   (DDSBA)   1906
- ■ Havett Farm, Dobwalls, LISKEARD, Cornwall, PL14 6HB.   (hsp)
  01579 320273
  email secretary@dorsetdownsheep.org.uk
  http://www.dorsetdownsheep.org.uk
  Breed Sec: Carolyn Opie
- ▲ Company Limited by Guarantee; Registered Charity
- ○ *B
- ● Mtgs - Exhib - Comp - Stat - Expt - Inf - VE - Annual breed sale
- < Nat Sheep Assn
- M 84 i, UK / 1 i, o'seas
- ¶ NL - 3/4; ftm only.   Breed Flock Book - 1; ftm, £5 nm.

Dorset Horn & Poll Dorset Sheep Breeders' Association   (DHSBA)   1891
- ■ Agriculture House, Acland Rd, DORCHESTER, Dorset, DT1 1EF.   (hq)
  01305 262126   fax 01305 262126
  email mail@dorsetsheep.org
  http://www.dorsetsheep.org
  Sec: Mrs Marguerite Cowley
- ▲ Registered Charity
- ○ *B; for breeders of the Dorset Horn & the Poll Dorset
- ● Mtgs - Comp - Expt - Inf - Breed show & sales
- < Nat Sheep Assn
- M 300 i
- ¶ Flock Book - 1; ftm, £20 nm.

Dorset Natural History & Archaeological Society   (DNHAS)   1875
- ■ 66 High West St, DORCHESTER, Dorset, DT1 1XA.   (hq)
  01305 262735
  email enquiries@dorsetcountymuseum.org
  http://www.dorsetcountymuseum.org
  Dir: Judy Lindsay
- ▲ Registered Charity
- ○ *A, *L; archaeology, local history, natural history & geology, art & literature (including Thomas Hardy) of Dorset
- Gp Archaeology; Geology; Natural history; Junior members
- ● Conf - Mtgs - ET - Res - Exhib - Comp - SG - Inf - Lib - PL - VE - Conservation
- M 1,900 i, 100 org
- ¶ Proceedings - 1.   AR.
  Archaeological Monographs.   Dorset Series.
  Note: The Dorset Record Society is a committee of DNHAS.

Dorset Record Society
  a committee of the **Dorset Natural History & Archaeological Society**

© CBD Research Ltd · Beckenham · BR3 5JS · Tel 020 8650 7745 · E-mail cbd@cbdresearch.com · www.cbdresearch.com

Dover District Chamber of Commerce & Industry   1850
NR   White Cliffs Business Centre, Honeywood Rd, Whitfield,
       DOVER, Kent, CT16 3EH.
       01304 824955   fax 01304 822354
       http://www.doverchamber.co.uk
       Mgr: Julia Chambers
○   *C

Down's Syndrome Association   (DSA)   1970
NR   Langdon Down Centre, 2A Langdon Park, TEDDINGTON,
       Middx, TW11 9PS.   (hq)
       0845 230 0372   fax 020 8682 4012
       email info@downs-syndrome.org.uk
       http://www.downs-syndrome.org.uk
▲   Company Limited by Guarantee; Registered Charity
○   *W; to help people with Down's syndrome to live full &
       rewarding lives; to provide information, counselling &
       support as well as being a resource to interested
       professionals
●   Helpline: 0845 230 0372 (Mon-Fri 1000-1600)
M   7,500 i, 900 f, 900 org

Down's Syndrome Scotland   1982
■   158-160 Balgreen Rd, EDINBURGH, EH11 3AU.   (hq)
       0131-313 4225   fax 0131-313 4285
       email info@dsscotland.org.uk
       http://www.dsscotland.org.uk
       Dir: Pandora J Summerfield
▲   Registered Charity
Br   6
○   *W; a national support group giving information & support to
       people with Down's Syndrome & their families in Scotland
●   Conf - ET - Inf - Lib - Local group activities
M   1,200 i, 500 professionals
¶   Publications list available; 50p - £5.

Downstream Fuel Association   (AUKOI)   1976
NR   Woodcroft, Broomhill Lane, REEPHAM, Norfolk, NR10 4QY.
       (hsb)
       01603 870296
       email ros.attridge@downstreamfuelassociation.org.uk
       Sec: Ros Attridge
▲   Un-incorporated Society
○   *T; to represent & protect within the UK & the EEC the common
       interests of independent oil importers &/or distributors
Gp   Oil: distribution, importation, wholesaling, retailing
●   Mtgs - LG - Liaison in EU
<   Union Pétrolière Européenne Indépendante (UPEI)
M   11 f
×   2010 Association of UK Oil Independents

Dozenal Society of Great Britain   (DSGB)   1960
■   32 Lansdowne Crescent, CARLISLE, Cumbria, CA3 9EW.
       (gen/sp)
       01228 596834
       http://www.dozenalsociety.org.uk
       Gen Sec: Shaun Ferguson
▲   Un-incorporated Society
○   *K; 'following the introduction of place-value arithmetic it was
       recognised calculations to a divisible scale of twelve
       numerals would not only simplify the operations but allow a
       precise representation of the basic ratios required to define
       the physical world or manage our material affairs.
       The Society affirms this view with the object of unifying scientific
       & social practices'
Gp   Arithmetic & mathematics; Historical metrology; Metrication
●   Res - Inf - Lib - Publishing - Cooperation with the British
       Weights & Measures Association providing technical
       information & informed criticism of attempts to impose
       decimal-metric methods in areas where they are
       inappropriate
<   Dozenal Soc of America (NY); Brit Weights & Measures Assn
M   200 i, UK / 15 i, o'seas
¶   The Dozenal Jnl - 1.
       T.G.M. a coherent dozenal metrology.
       Booklets & reprints of salient articles.

Dracula Society   1973
■   PO Box 30848, LONDON, W12 0GY.   (mail address)
       http://www.thedraculasociety.org.uk
       Chmn & Treas: Julia Kruk
○   *G; 'since it is named after the most evocative title in the entire
       genre, the Society naturally devotes a good deal of its
       attention to the book & its author, Bram Stoker. However
       vampires, werewolves, mummies & all the other monsters
       spawned by the Gothic genre fall within its field of interest,
       which also embraces stage & screen, adaptations & the
       sources of inspiration in myth & folklore; The society is not
       concerned with psychic research or occult ceremony of any
       kind'
●   Mtgs - VE
<   The Vampire Empire (NY)
M   c 90 i, UK / c 20 i, o'seas
¶   Voices from the Vaults (NL) - 4; ftm only.

Drake Exploration Society   (DES)   1996
■   7 Rosewood Ave, BURNHAM-on-SEA, Somerset, TA8 1HD.
       (hsp)
       01278 783519
       email sfdsociety@aol.com
       http://www.indrakeswake.co.uk/Society
       Founder: Michael Turner
▲   Un-incorporated Society
○   *G; to perpetuate the memory of Sir Francis Drake through
       research, fieldwork, lectures & publications
●   Mtgs - Res - Exhib - SG - Inf - Lib - PL - VE - Illustrated lectures
       & fieldwork
<   Drake Navigator's Guild (USA)
M   26 i, 2 f, 3 org, UK / 6 i, o'seas
       (Sub: £15)
¶   The Drake Broadside - 1;   The Drake NL - 1; both ftm.

**Drama Association of Wales   (Cymdeithas Ddrama Cymru)
(DAW)   1973**
- ■ The Old Library, Singleton Rd, Splott, CARDIFF, CF24 2ET.   (hq)
  029 2045 2200   fax 029 2045 2277
  email aled.daw@virgin.net   http://www.amdram.co.uk/
  daw/
  Admin: Gary Thomas
- ▲ Registered Charity
- ○ *A; to promote amateur theatre in Wales & worldwide; to
  encourage new writing
- ● Mtgs - ET - Res - Comp - SG - Inf - Lib (world's largest
  collection of playscripts) - LG - Publishing
- < Intl Amat Theatre Assn; Cent Coun for Amat Theatre; Nat Assn
  Youth Theatre; Wales Assn for the Performing Arts
- M 221 i, 16 f, 267 org, UK / 11 i, 1 f, 6 org, o'seas
- ¶ Dawn (NL) - 4; ftm.

Drama League of Ireland
- IRL The Mill Theatre, Dundrum, DUBLIN 14, Republic of Ireland.
  353 (1) 296 9343
  email dli@eircom.net   http://www.dli.ie
  Sec: Maura Lucey
- ○ *D; to promote amateur drama & theatre in Ireland

Draught Proofing Advisory Association Ltd   (DPAA)   1980
- ■ PO Box 12, HASLEMERE, Surrey, GU27 3AH.   (hq)
  01428 654011   fax 01428 651401
  email dpaaassociation@aol.com
  http://www.dpaa-association.org.uk
  Dir: Gillian Allder
- ▲ Company Limited by Guarantee
- ○ *T; representing the draught proofing industry
- ● Mtgs - Inf - LG
- M f
- ¶ NL; m only.   LM.

Drawing Society
the alternative title for the **Society of Graphic Fine Art**

Dress & Textile Specialists   (DATS)
- NR Furniture, Textiles & Fashion, Victoria & Albert Museum,
  LONDON, SW7 2RL.   (hsb)
  020 7942 2673
  http://www.dressandtextilespecialists.org.uk
  Hon Sec: Edwina Ehrman
- ▲ Un-incorporated Society
- ○ *P; to support museum professionals working with costume &
  textile collections
- ● Conf - Mtgs - ET
- < Museums Assn
- M 88 i, 44 f
- ¶ NL - 2; ftm only.

Driffield Agricultural Society
- NR The Showground, Kellythorpe, DRIFFIELD, E Yorks,
  YO25 9DN.   (hq)
  01377 257494   fax 01377 257464
  email david@driffieldshow.co.uk
  http://www.driffieldshow.co.uk
  Dir: David Tite
- ○ *F, *H
- ● Driffield Show
- < Assn of Show & Agricl Orgs
- M i & f

Drilling & Sawing Association Ltd   (DSA)   1984
- ■ Unit 3 Brand St, NOTTINGHAM, NG2 3GW.   (asa)
  0115 986 7029   fax 0115 985 0341
  email dsa@drillandsaw.org.uk
  http://www.drillandsaw.org.uk
- ▲ Company Limited by Guarantee
- ○ *T; concrete drilling & sawing industry
- Gp Specialist drilling & sawing contractors; Suppliers of drilling &
  sawing equipment
- ● Mtgs - ET - Exhib - Inf - VE
- < Intl Assn of Concrete Drillers & Sawers
- M 100 f, UK / 5 org, o'seas
- ¶ Concrete Cutter (Jnl) - 2.   LM.   Brochure.

Drinking Fountain Association
see **Metropolitan Drinking Fountain & Cattle Trough
Association**

Drinks Industry Group of Ireland
- IRL Anglesea House, Anglesea Rd, Ballsbridge, DUBLIN 4, Republic
  of Ireland.
  353 (1) 668 0215   fax 353 (1) 668 0448
  http://www.drinksindustry.ie
  Chmn: Kieran Tobin
- ○ *T

Drivers' Alliance
- NR e-Innovation Centre SE209, University of Wolverhampton,
  Priorslee, TELFORD, Shropshire, TF2 9FT.
  01952 288338
  http://www.driversalliance.org.uk
  Dir: Peter Roberts
- ○ *K

Driving Instructors Association   (DIA)   1978
- NR Safety House, Beddington Farm Rd, CROYDON, Surrey,
  CR0 4XZ.   (hq)
  020 8665 5151   fax 020 8665 5565
  http://www.driving.org
  Sec: Tina Tutton
- ▲ Registered Charity
- ○ *P; to raise the standard of driver education & improve road
  safety by means of professional training
- Gp Holders of Diploma in Driving Instruction; Specialist LGV & PCV
  instructors
- ● Conf - Mtgs - ET - Exam - Res - Exhib - Comp - SG - Stat - Inf -
  Lib - VE
- < Soc of Motor Mfrs & Traders; Parliamentary Advy Coun for
  Traffic Safety; Intl Assn for Driver Education (IVV)
- M 10,000 i, UK / 180 i, o'seas
- ¶ Driving Magazine - 6.   Driving Instructor - 6.

Drum Corps of the United Kingdom   1980
- NR 3 Eridge Rd, HOVE, E Sussex, BN3 7QD.
  0845 688 8906   fax 0870 706 5608
  email admin@dcuk.org.uk   http://www.dcuk.org.uk
- ○ *D
- M c 1,500 i

© CBD Research Ltd · Beckenham · BR3 5JS · Tel 020 8650 7745 · E-mail cbd@cbdresearch.com · www.cbdresearch.com

Dry Stone Walling Association of Great Britain   (DSWA)   1968
- ■ Westmorland County Showground, Lane Farm, Crooklands, MILNTHORPE, Cumbria, LA7 7NH.   (mail address)
  01539 567953
  http://www.dswa.org.uk
  Admin: Alison Shaw
- ▲ Registered Charity
- Br 19
- ○ *G; to foster an interest in dry stone walling & dyking; to ensure that the best craftsmanship of the past is preserved
- ● Mtgs - ET - Exam - Comp - Inf (send sae) - LG
- M 1,200 i, 15 f, UK / 10 i, o'seas
- ¶ Waller & Dyker (Jnl) - 3; ftm, £2.50 nm.
  Register of Certificated Wallers/Dykers; free with sae.
  Building & Repairing Dry Stone Walls; £1.50.
  In There Somewhere; £5.   [all plus p&p].

Dublin Chamber of Commerce   1783
- IRL 7 Clare St, DUBLIN 2, Republic of Ireland.
  353 (1) 644 7200   fax 353 (1) 676 6043
  email info@dublinchamber.ie
  http://www.dublinchamber.ie
  Chief Exec: Gina Quin
- ○ *C

Duchenne Family Support Group   (DFSG)   1987
- ■ 6 Laburnum Rd, SANDY, Beds, SG19 1HQ.   (hsp)
  01767 680644   Office 0870 241 1857   fax 0870 241 1857
  email info@dfsg.org.uk   http://www.dfsg.org.uk
  Hon Sec: Mrs Ann Patterson
- ▲ Registered Charity
- ○ *W; is run by families for families affected by Duchenne muscular dystrophy (a severely disabling & life-limiting muscle wasting condition)
- ● Conf - Mtgs - Inf - VE - National support network of parents, their families & professionals
  Helpline: 0800 121 4518 (Mon-Fri 0900-1200)
- M 2,000 i, 230 org, UK / 40 i, 10 org, o'seas
- ¶ Duchenne News - 4; free.

Dugdale Society   1920
- ■ The Shakespeare Centre, Henley St, STRATFORD-upon-AVON, Warks, CV37 6QW.   (hq/hsb)
  01789 204016   fax 01789 296083
  email records@shakespeare.org.uk
  http://www.shakespeare.org.uk/dugdale
  Chmn: Prof C C Dyer,   Hon Sec: Mrs Cathy Millwood
- ▲ Registered Charity
- ○ *L; publication of original documents on history of Warwickshire (named after Sir William Dugdale, antiquary 1605-1680)
- ● Res
- M 250 i, 70 org, UK / 50 org, o'seas
- ¶ Volumes & Occasional Papers - irreg; ftm, varies nm.   AR.

Dumfries & Galloway Chamber of Commerce   (DGCC)   1987
- ■ Hillhead House, The Crichton, Bankend Rd, DUMFRIES, DG1 4UQ.   (hq)
  01387 270866
  email admin@dgchamber.co.uk
  http://www.dgchamber.co.uk
  Chief Exec: Gordon Mann
- ▲ Company Limited by Guarantee
- ○ *C
- ● Mtgs - Inf - Seminars
- < Scot Chams Comm; Glasgow Cham Comm
- M 2,400 i, 90 f

Dumfries & Lockerbie Agricultural Society
- NR 15 Fruid's Park Ave, ANNAN, Dumfriesshire, DG12 6AY.   (hsp)
  01461 201199   fax 01461 206261
  email ebicket@talktalk.net
  http://www.dumfriesshow.co.uk
  Sec: Esther Bicket
- ○ *F
- ● Dumfries Agricultural Show
- < Assn of Show & Agricl Orgs

Dumfriesshire & Galloway Natural History & Antiquarian Society   (DGNHAS)   1862
- NR Merkland, Kirkmahoe, DUMFRIES, DG1 1SY.   (hsp)
  01387 710274
  http://www.dgnhas.org.uk
  Hon Sec: John L Williams
- ▲ Registered Charity
- ○ *L
- ● Mtgs - VE
- M 300 i, 50 org, UK / 50 i, o'seas
- ¶ Transactions - 1.

Dun Horse & Pony Society   (DHAPS)   1999
- NR 4 Elderfield Rd, Kings Norton, BIRMINGHAM, W Midlands, B30 3PE.   (chmn/p)
  0121-451 3479
  http://www.dhaps-online.co.uk
  Chmn: Andrew Ward
- ○ *B; for those interested in dun horses & ponies (Palomino coloured, but with black mane & tail); to promote dun horses in all spheres of the horse industry
- ● Comp - Horse show sponsorship
- M 100 i
- ¶ The Dun Thing - 4;   The Dun Thing Update - 2/3;   Hbk - 1; all ftm only.

Dundee & Angus Chamber of Commerce   1835
- NR 11 City Quay, Camperdown St, DUNDEE, DD1 3JA.   (hq)
  01382 228545   fax 01382 228441
  http://www.dundeeandanguschamber.co.uk
  Chief Exec: Alan Mitchell
- ○ *C
- ● Mtgs - Exhib - Expt - Inf - LG (local) - Business support
- < Brit Chams Comm; Scot Chams Comm
- M 750 f
- ¶ The Business - 6;   Annual Diary.
- ✕ 2008 Dundee & Tayside Chamber of Commerce & Industry

Dundee & Tayside Chamber of Commerce & Industry
    since 2008 **Dundee & Angus Chamber of Commerce**

Durham County Agricultural Society
    reported as believed to have closed - we would appreciate confirmation

Durham County Local History Society   (DCLHS)   1964

- 21 St Mary's Grove, Tudhoe, SPENNYMOOR, Co Durham,
  DL16 6LR.   (hsp)
  01388 816209
  email johnbanham@tiscali.co.uk
  http://www.durhamweb.org.uk/dclhs
  Sec: Dr J D Banham
- ▲ Registered Charity
- ○ *L; to encourage & promote interest in the study of the history
  of County Durham, and of the North East in general
- < Brit Assn for Local History
- M 232 i, 33 org, UK / 7 i, o'seas
  (Sub: £10 i, £20 org)
- ¶ Jnl - 2; ftm, £5 nm.
  Documentary series; prices vary.
  Durham Biographies (edited by Batho) vol 1-5; £25 set of 5.
  The Durham Crown Lordships (Reid).
  Durham City and its MPs (Heesom).
  Joseph Bouet's Durham; £10.
  The Lost Hills - history of papermaking in County
  Durham; 10.

Durham Wildlife Trust   (DWT)   1971

- Rainton Meadows, Chilton Moor, HOUGHTON-le-SPRING,
  Tyne & Wear, DH4 6PU.   (hq)
  0191-584 3112   fax 0191-584 3934
  email mail@durhamwt.co.uk
  http://www.durhamwt.co.uk
  Dir: James Cokill
- ▲ Company Limited by Guarantee; Registered Charity
- ○ *K; protection of wild life & natural beauty of Durham County &
  Tyne & Wear south of the Tyne; management of the Trust's
  nature reserves
- Gp 10 local groups; 26 nature reserves; 3 visitor centres
- ● Conf - Mtgs - ET - Exhib - SG - Inf - VE
- < R Soc of Wildlife Trusts (UK Office)
- M 8,500 i, 55 f
- ¶ Durham Wildlife - 3; tm, £1.50 nm.

Dutch Barge Association
    see **DBA - the Barge Association**

Dvořák Society for Czech & Slovak Music   1974

- NR 13 Church Lane, Knutton, NEWCASTLE-under-LYME, Staffs,
  ST5 6DU.   (sp)
  http://www.dvorak-society.org
  Hon Sec: Dave Roberts
- ▲ Registered Charity
- ○ *D; 'to educate the public in the arts & sciences & in particular,
  the music of the Czech Republic & Slovakia'
- M 400 i, 7 f, 2 org, UK / 140 i, 9 f, 5 org, o'seas
- ¶ Czech Music - 1.
  NL - 4/5.   Ybk.

Dwarf Sports Association United Kingdom   (DSAUK)   1993

- PO Box 4269, DRONFIELD, Derbys, S18 9BG.
  01246 414238
  email office@daauk.org   http://www.daauk.org
- ○ *S; to make regular sporting opportunity accessible & enjoyable
  to anyone & everyone of restricted growth in the UK
- × Dwarf Athletic Association

Dying Matters Coalition
    is part of the National Council for Palliative Care (020 7697 1520)
    Note: For further information about the National Council see
    our companion volume 'Councils, Committees & Boards'

Dylan Thomas Society of Great Britain   1977

- Fernhill, 24 Chapel St, Mumbles, SWANSEA, Glam,
  SA3 4NH.   (chmn p)
  01792 363785
  Chmn: Mrs Cecily Hughes
- Br Australia, Canada
- ○ *G; to foster & stimulate interest in the work of Dylan Marlais
  Thomas (1914-1953) & the literature of Anglo-Welsh writers
- ● Mtgs - VE
- M 240 i, UK / 20 i, o'seas
- ¶ NL - 2; ftm, £1 nm.
  I Sang in My Chains, essays & poems in tribute to Dylan
  Thomas; £10. (2003 commemorative publication).

Dyslexia Action   1974

- Egham Centre, Park House, Wick Rd, EGHAM, Surrey,
  TW20 0HH.   (hq)
  01784 222300   fax 01784 222333
  email info@dyslexiaaction.org.uk
  http://www.dyslexiaaction.org.uk
  Chief Exec: K Geeson
- ▲ Company Limited by Guarantee; Registered Charity
- Br 27 dyslexia institutes
- ○ *E, *W; assessment of children & adults; teaching of dyslexic
  children & adults; teacher training
- Gp Assessment; Teaching
- ● Conf - ET - Exhib - Comp - Inf - LG - Fund raising
- < Brit Dyslexia Assn
- M 'friends'
- ¶ As We See It (NL) - 1; free.   Leaflets.
- × 2006 (Dyslexia Institute
            (Hornsby Dyslexia Charity (merged July)

Dyslexia Association of Ireland   1972

- IRL Suffolk Chambers, 1 Suffolk St, DUBLIN 2, Republic of Ireland.
  353 (1) 679 0276   fax 353 (1) 679 0273
  email info@dyslexia.ie   http://www.dyslexia.ie
  Dir: Ann Hughes
- ○ *K, *W

Dyslexia Institute
    since 2006 **Dyslexia Action**

Dyslexia Scotland   1968

- Unit 10 Stirling Business Centre, Wellgreen, STIRLING,
  FK8 2DZ.   (hq)
  01786 446650   fax 01786 471235
  email info@dyslexiascotland.org.uk
  http://www.dyslexiascotland.org.uk
  Chief Exec: Cathy Magee
- ▲ Company Limited by Guarantee; Registered Charity (Scotland)
- Br 13 (Scotland)
- ○ *K, *W; 'to enable & encourage dyslexic people, regardless of
  their age & abilities, to reach their potential in education,
  employment & life'
- ● Conf - Mtgs - ET - Stat - Inf - Lib - LG
  Resource centre of books, teaching materials, computer
  software, audio & visual aids
  Helpline: 0844 800 8484 (1000-1300, 1400-1600)
- M 700 i, 20 f

© CBD Research Ltd · Beckenham · BR3 5JS · Tel 020 8650 7745 · E-mail cbd@cbdresearch.com · www.cbdresearch.com

Dyspraxia Foundation   1987

■   8 West Alley, HITCHIN, Herts, SG5 1EG.   (hq)
01462 455016   fax 01462 455052
email dyspraxia@dyspraxiafoundation.org.uk
http://www.dyspraxiafoundation.org.uk
Admin: Mrs Eleanor Howes

▲   Registered Charity

Br   2

○   *W; to support individuals & families affected by dyspraxia
(clumsy child syndrome); to promote better diagnosis &
treatment facilities; to help professionals in health &
education to assist those with dyspraxia

Gp   Adults with dyspraxia

●   Conf - Mtgs - Res - Exhib - Stat - Inf - LG
Helpline: 01462 454986 (Mon-Fri 1000-1300)

M   c 2,000 i

¶   Praxis Makes Perfect.   Information pack.
Books & guides for parents; leaflets, booklets.

Dystonia Society   (TDS)   1983

■   Camelford House (1st floor), 89 Albert Embankment,
LONDON, SE1 7TP.   (hq)
0845 458 6211   fax 0845 458 6311
email info@dystonia.org.uk
http://www.dystonia.org.uk
Chief Exec: Philip Eckstein

▲   Registered Charity

Br   24

○   *M, *W; to raise awareness of dystonia, a neurological
movement disorder; to support those affected by dystonia &
provide information

Gp   Young Dystonia - support group for families

●   Conf - Mtgs - Inf
Helpline: 0845 458 6322

<   Eur Dystonia Fedn; Neurological Alliance

M   3,000 i, UK / 115 i, o'seas

¶   NL - 4; free.

**Dystrophic Epidermolysis Bullosa Research Association
(DebRA)   1978**

NR   13 Wellington Business Park, Duke's Ride, CROWTHORNE,
Berks, RG45 6LS.   (hq)
01344 771961   fax 01344 762661
email debra@debra.org.uk   http://www.debra.org.uk

○   *W; to help all people with Epidermolysis Bullosa (blistering of
the skin) & their families; to fund research

●   Conf - Res - SG - Inf

<   DEBRA Intl; DEBRA Europe

¶   NL - 4;   AR; both free.

E A Bowles of Myddleton House Society
NR   2(A) Plough Hill, Cuffley, POTTERS BAR, Herts, EN6 4DR.
    http://www.eabowlessociety.org.uk
    Treas: A Pettitt
○   *G, *H; to commemorate the life & work of E A Bowles (1965-1954)

E F Benson Society   1984
■   The Old Coach House, High St, RYE, E Sussex, TN31 7JF.
    (hsp)
    01797 223114
    http://www.efbensonsociety.org
    Sec: Allan V Downend
▲   Un-incorporated Society
○   *A; furtherance of the knowledge & appreciation of the Benson family & particularly E F Benson (the author) & his works
●   Mtgs - Exhib - VE - Walks
M   200 i, UK / 30 i, o'seas
¶   Dodo (Jnl) - 1; ftm, £4 nm.   NL - 4; ftm only.

EADA: the voice of English amateur dancers   (EADA)   1969
NR   Four Winds, Old Potbridge Rd, WINCHFIELD, Hants, RG27 8BT.
    fax 01252 843887
    http://www.eada.org.uk
▲   Un-incorporated Society
○   *S; the governing body for dancesport in England incl Modern, Latin-American, Sequence & Freestyle
●   Mtgs - Comp
<   Intl Dancesport Fedn
M   3,000 i, 5 specialist clubs
¶   AR - 1; ftm only.
×   2008 English Amateur Dancesport Association

Ealing Chamber of Commerce   1901
NR   Grove Mews, 42 The Grove, LONDON, W5 5LH.
    020 8840 6332   fax 020 8579 0685
    email info@ealingchamber.org
    http://www.ealingchamber.org
    Gen Mgr: Matthew Sims
Br   Hammersmith & Fulham Chamber of Commerce
○   *C
<   since 2004 a branch of London Cham Comm & Ind (LCCI)

Early Childhood Ireland   2011
IRL   Unit 4 Broomhill Business Complex, Broomhill Rd, Tallaght, DUBLIN 24, Republic of Ireland.   (hq)
    353 (1) 463 0010   fax 353 (1) 463 0045
    email info@ippa.ie
    http://www.earlychildhoodireland.ie
    Chief Exec: Irene Gunning
○   *E, *P, *W; to enable the provision of quality early childhood care & education in Ireland with positive outcomes for children
M   3,200 i & org
×   2011 (IPPA - the Early Childhood Organisation (National Children's Nurseries Association

Early Dance Circle   (EDC)   1984
■   Hunter's Moon, Orcheston, SALISBURY, Wilts, SP3 4RP.
    (chmn/p)
    01980 620339
    email dianacruic@aol.com
    http://www.earlydancecircle.co.uk
    Chmn: Diana Cruickshank
▲   Un-incorporated Society
○   *D; to promote & foster the knowledge, understanding & appreciation of dance & its context in European society up to the beginning of the 20th century
●   Conf - Mtgs - ET - Res - SG - Inf - Advisory service
<   Nat Early Music Assn (NEMA); Nat Resource Centre for Historical Dance (NRCHD)
M   166 i
¶   NL - 4; ftm only.   Publications list available.

Early Education
    see **British Association for Early Childhood Education**

Early English Text Society   (EETS)   1864
■   c/o Prof V A Gillespie, Lady Margaret Hall, OXFORD, OX2 6QA.   (exec/sb)
    01865 284066
    http://www.eets.org.uk
    Exec Sec: Prof Vincent A Gillespie
▲   Un-incorporated Society
○   *L; printing of English texts earlier than 1558
M   i, f & org
¶   1 or 2 books per yr.

Early Mines Research Group   (EMRG)   1988
§   96 Victoria Rd, CAMBRIDGE, CB4 3DU.
    01223 329737
    email timberlake@mcmail.com
    This group has no formal membership & 'exists solely to carry out excavation & research into the origins of metal mining & metallurgy in Britain & to disseminate these findings through refereed academic journals & other forms of media'

Earth Science Teachers' Association   (ESTA)   1968
■   81A Birches Lane, Lostock Green, NORTHWICH, Cheshire, CW9 7SN.   (hsp)
    email rostodhunter@aol.com   http://www.esta-uk.net
    Hon Sec: Dr Rosalind Todhunter
▲   Registered Charity
Br   3
○   *E, *P; to encourage & support the teaching of earth science & geology at all levels as part of science & geography courses
Gp   Education: Primary, Secondary, Teacher, Higher; Fieldwork
●   Conf - Et - SG - Stat
M   740 i, UK / 60 i, o'seas
    (Sub: £32)
¶   Teaching Earth Sciences (Jnl) - 2; ftm only.

Earthworm Society of Britain   (ESB)   2009
NR   c/o Soil Biodiversity Group, Dept of Entomology, Natural History Museum. LONDON, SW7 5BD.
    http://www.earthwormsoc.org.uk
○   *G, *K; to increase the knowledge & understanding of earthworms & the important work they do in the soil
●   Res
M   i

East Cheshire Chamber of Commerce & Enterprise   2009
- Riverside Mill, Mountbatten Way, CONGLETON, Cheshire, CW12 1DY.
  01260 540570   fax 0845 676 6376
  email info@eastcheshirechamber.co.uk
  http://www.eastcheshirechamber.co.uk
  Chief Exec: David Watson
- ○ *C
- < Brit Chams Comm; Chams Comm NW

East of England Agricultural Society   1797
- East of England Showground, PETERBOROUGH, Cambs, PE2 6XE.   (hq)
  01733 234451   fax 01733 370038
  email info@eastofengland.org.uk
  http://www.eastofengland.org.uk
  Chmn: Mr A Sharpley
- ○ *F
- ● Conf - Exhib - Comp - SG - Inf - E of England Show
- < Assn of Show & Agricl Orgs
- M c 8,000 i
- ¶ NL.   Show Catalogue.

East Hampshire Chamber of Commerce & Industry
    merged in 2010 to form the **Hampshire Chamber of Commerce**

East Herts Archaeological Society   (EHAS)   1898
- 11 St Leonards Close, Bengeo, HERTFORD, SG14 3LL.   (hsp)
  Hon Sec: Mrs G Pollard
- ▲ Registered Charity
- ○ *L; to promote interest in, & preservation of, archaeology in the county, old buildings & local history
- Gp Old buildings survey
- ● Exhib - Inf - Lib - VE
- < Coun Brit Archaeology; Hertfordshire Archaeol Trust
- M 130 i
- ¶ Hertfordshire Archaeology - irreg; ftm, £15 nm.
  NL.   AR.
  A Century of Archaeology in East Herts; £9.95 (£4.95 paperback).

East Lancashire Chamber of Commerce & Industry
    see **Chamber of Commerce East Lancashire**

East Lothian Antiquarian & Field Naturalists' Society (ELAFNS)   1924
- NR 3 Stories Park, EAST LINTON, E Lothian, EH40 8BN.   (hsp)
  email allison1314@gmail.com
  http://www.eastlothianantiquarians.org.uk
  Sec: Allison Cosgrove
- ▲ Registered Charity
- ○ *L; antiquities, archaeology & natural history of the county
- ● Mtgs - Exhib - VE
- M 264 i, 11 org, UK / 1 org, o'seas
- ¶ Transactions (incl LM) - 3 yrly; ftm.   AR - 1; free.

East Yorkshire Local History Society   (EYLHS)   1950
- NR 5 John Gray Court, Main St, WILLERBY, E Yorks, HU10 6XZ.
  (memsec/p)
  01482 671009
  http://www.eylhs.org.uk
  Mem Sec: Patricia Aldabella
- ▲ Registered Charity
- ○ *L; study & appreciation of local history & the preservation of local records & objects of historical interest
- ● Mtgs - VE
- < Brit Assn for Local History
- M c 350 i, f, org
- ¶ Bulletin - 2; ftm only.
  Booklets on various subjects of local interest.

Eastbourne & District Chamber of Commerce Ltd   (EDCC) 1892
- 7 Hyde Gardens, EASTBOURNE, E Sussex, BN21 4PN.   (hq)
  01323 641144   fax 01323 730454
  email info@eastbournechamber.co.uk
  http://www.eastbournechamber.co.uk
  Co Sec: Mrs Christine Purkess
- ▲ Company Limited by Guarantee
- ○ *C
- ● Conf - Mtgs - ET - Exhib - Inf - LG
- M 600+ f
- ¶ NL - 12;   Directory - 1;   both ftm only.

Eastern Africa Association   (EAA)   1964
- Equity House, Old Market St, HARLOW, Essex, CM17 0AH.
  (hq)
  01279 400441   fax 01279 422334
  email jcsmall@eaa-lon.co.uk
  http://www.eaa-lon.co.uk
  Chief Exec: John C Small
- ▲ Company Limited by Guarantee
- Br Kenya, Uganda
- ○ *T; to facilitate the participation of firms & companies from other countries in the economic development of Kenya, Eritrea, Ethiopia, Burundi, Rwanda, Seychelles, Tanzania & Uganda
- ● Conf - Mtgs - Inf - LG
- < Brit African Business Assn
- M 30 i, 272 f, UK & o'seas
- ¶ The Eastern Africa NL - 8; m only.

Easy Care Sheep Society   2003
- NR Glantraeth, BODORGAN, Anglesey, LL62 5EU.   (hsp)
  01407 840250
  http://www.easycaresheep.com
  Sec: R Iolo Owen
- ○ *B; a hardy, hornless breed developed predominately from crossing the Wiltshire Horn sheep with other breeds
- ● Mtgs - Expt - Sales
- M c 22 i
- ¶ NL.

Eating Disorders Association   (beat)   1989
- 103 Prince of Wales Rd, NORWICH, Norfolk, NR1 1DW.   (hq)
  0300 123 3355 (admin); 01603 619090
  email info@b-eat.co.uk   http://www.b-eat.co.uk
  Chief Exec: Mrs Susan Ringwood
- ▲ Company Limited by Guarantee; Registered Charity
- Br UK-wide network of local help goups
- ○ *M, *W; to provide help & support for people affected by eating disorders, especially anorexia & bulimia nervosa; to provide training & help for professionals
- ● Conf - ET - Res - LG - Service specifications guidelines for treatment
  Helpline: 0845 634 1414 (Mon-Fri 1030-2030 / Sat 1300-1630)
  Youthline (up to age 18): 0845 634 7650 (Mon-Fri 1600-2030)
  Text Service: 07786 201820
- ¶ Upbeat (Jnl) - 4; ftm.   Lists of treatment by area.
  European Eating Disorders Review (professional jnl).
  Note: uses the working name 'beat'

ECB Association of Cricket Officials
    see the **England & Wales Cricket Board Association of Cricket Officials**

ECB Coaches Association
    see **England & Wales Cricket Board Coaches Association**

Ecclesiastical Architects & Surveyors Association   (EASA)   1872
NR   Thomas Ford & Partners, 177 Kirkdale, LONDON,
       SE26 4QH.   (hsb)
       020 8659 3250   fax 020 8659 3146
       email john.bailey@thomasford.co.uk
       http://www.easanet.co.uk
       Hon Sec: John Bailey
○   *P; to promote good standards of design & repair of
       ecclesiastical buildings, be they churches, chapels, halls,
       parsonage houses or similar buildings, across all
       denominations
●   Mtgs
M   500 i
¶   EASA Journal - 4.

Ecclesiastical History Society   (EHS)   1962
NR   32 Highfield Avenue, Great Sankey, WARRINGTON, Cheshire,
       WA5 2TW.   (hsp)
       email stella@ravenna123.freeserve.co.uk
       http://www.ehsoc.org.uk
       Hon Sec: Dr Stella Fletcher
▲   Registered Charity
○   *L; study of ecclesiastical history & maintenance of relations
       between British historians & scholars abroad
●   Conf - Res
<   Commission Intle d'Histoire Ecclésiastique Comparée (CIHEC)
M   700 i, 35 colleges & Libraries, UK / 200 i, o'seas
¶   Studies in Church History - 1.

Ecclesiological Society   1879
■   38 Rosebery Ave, NEW MALDEN, Surrey, KT3 4JS.   (chmn/p)
       email info@ecclsoc.org   http://www.ecclsoc.org
       Chmn: Trevor Cooper
▲   Registered Charity
○   *A, *L; the study of the arts, architecture & liturgy of the
       Christian church
●   Conf - Mtgs - Inf - Lib - PL - VE
M   1,000 i, 20 org, UK / 20 i, o'seas
¶   Ecclesiology Today - 2; ftm.
       Standalone publications - irreg; ftm.

Eckhart Society   1987
■   Summa, 22 Tippings Lane, Woodley, READING, Berks,
       RG5 4RX.   (hsp)
       0118-969 0118
       email ashleyyoung@aysumma.demon.co.uk
       http://www.eckhartsociety.org
       Hon Sec & Exec Dir: Ashley Young
       Chmn: Christopher Glover (cgg@cgglover.com)
▲   Registered Charity
○   *G, *R; to promote understanding & appreciation of the
       writings of Meister Eckhart (1260-1327, a Dominican
       preacher) & their importance for Christian thought &
       practice; to facilitate scholarly research into Eckhart's life &
       works; to promote the study of Eckhart's teaching as a
       contribution to religious dialogue
●   Conf - SG
M   200 i, UK / 130 i, o'seas
       (Sub: £25)
¶   The Eckhart Review - 1; ftm, £9.50 nm.
       Tapes from annual conference - 1; £7.25 each.
       CDs from annual conference - 1; £8.50 each.
       Publications list available.

Economic History Society   1927
NR   Dept of Economic & Social History, University of Glasgow,
       Lilybank House, Bute Gardens, GLASGOW, G12 8RT.   (hq)
       0141-330 4662   fax 0141-330 4889
       email ehsocsec@arts.gla.ac.uk   http://www.ehs.org.uk
       Hon Sec: Mrs Maureen Galbraith
▲   Registered Charity
○   *L; to promote the study of economic & social history; to
       publish & sponsor publications
Gp   Urban; Financial; Transport
●   Conf - Mtgs - ET - Res - Inf
<   Intl Historical Congress; Intl Economic History Assn
M   1,500 i, libraries & colleges
¶   Economic History Review - 4; ftm only.   NL - 4.   AR.

Economic Research Council   (ERC)   1943
■   55 Tufton St, LONDON, SW1P 3QL.   (hq)
       020 7340 6016
       http://www.ercouncil.org
       Hon Sec: James Y Bourlet
▲   Registered Charity
○   *L; to promote education in the science of economics with
       particular reference to monetary practice
●   Mtgs - Res - Comp - SG - Dinners with talks
M   c 400 i, c 20 f, UK / c 30 i, o'seas
¶   Britain & Overseas - 4; £20.   Occasional Research Papers.

Economic & Social History Society of Ireland   (ESHSI)   1970
IRL   Dept of Modern History, Trinity College, DUBLIN 2, Republic of
       Ireland.   (mail)
       email eshsireland@gmail.com   http://www.eh.net/eshsi/
○   *L

Economic & Social Research Institute   (ESRI)   1960
IRL   Whitaker House, Sir John Rogerson's Quay, DUBLIN 2, Republic
       of Ireland.
       353 (1) 863 2000   fax 353 (1) 863 2100
       email admin@esri.ie   http://www.esri.ie
       Dir: Brendan J Whelan
○   *L

Economics, Business & Enterprise Association   (EBEA)   1946
■   The Forum, 277 London Rd, BURGESS HILL, W Sussex,
       RH15 9QU.   (hq)
       01444 240150   fax 01444 240101
       email office@ebea.org.uk   http://www.ebea.org.uk
       Chief Exec: Duncan Cullimore
▲   Registered Charity
○   *E, *L; supporting teachers & lecturers of economics, business
       studies & enterprise
Gp   Business studies; Economics; Enterprise
●   Conf - Mtgs - ET - Inf
M   1,410 i, 210 org
¶   Teaching Business & Education (Jnl) - 3; ftm, only.
       EBEA News - monthly in term-time & online only; free.
×   2008 (June) Economics & Business Education Association

ECR Ireland - Efficient Consumer Response   (ECR)
IRL   The Nutley Building, Merrion Rd, DUBLIN 4, Republic of
       Ireland.
       353 (1) 208 0676
○   *T; to educate the Irish business community about efficient
       consumer response & the resultant benefits

Ectodermal Dysplasia Society (EDS) 1984
- ■ Unit 1 Maida Vale Business Centre, Leckhampton, CHELTENHAM, Glos, GL53 7ER.
  01242 261332
  email diana@ectodermaldysplasia.org
  http://www.ectodermaldysplasia.org
  Sec: Diana Perry
- ▲ Registered Charity
- ○ *M, *W; to promote the health of people affected by ectodermal dysplasia & any related condition, & to support their families & carers; 'ectodermal dysplasias are heritable conditions in which there are abnormalities of two or more ectodermal structures such as the hair, teeth, nails, sweat glands, cranial-facial structure, digits & other parts of the body'
- ● Conf - Mtgs - Res - Inf
- M 332 i, UK / 79 i, o'seas
- ¶ NL - 4; ftm.

Edinburgh Bibliographical Society (EBS) 1890
- ■ c/o Rare Books Collections, National Library of Scotland, George IV Bridge, EDINBURGH, EH1 1EW. (sb)
  email h.vincent@nls.uk   http://www.mcs.qmuc.ac.uk/ebs/
  Sec: Helen Vincent
- ▲ Registered Charity
- ○ *L; study of books & manuscripts, particularly those of Scottish interest
- ● Mtgs (at above address) - VE
- M c 200 i & org
- ¶ Transactions - 1; £15, UK / £20, o'seas.

Edinburgh Chamber of Commerce 1785
- ■ Capital House, 2 Festival Sq, EDINBURGH, EH3 9SU. (hq)
  0131-221 2999   fax 0131-221 2998
  email info@edinburghchamber.co.uk
  http://www.edinburghchamber.co.uk
  Chief Exec: Ron Hewitt
- ○ *C
- Gp Leith Chamber of Commerce
- ● Conf - Mtgs - ET - Expt
- < Scot Chams Comm
- M 1,400 f

Edinburgh Civic Trust
  see **Cockburn Association**

Edinburgh Geological Society 1834
- NR 23 Summerfield Place, EDINBURGH, EH6 8AZ. (hsp)
  0131-555 5488
  email secretary@edinburghgeolsoc.org
  http://www.edinburghgeolsoc.org
  Hon Sec: Angus Miller
- ○ *L; to stimulate public interest in geology; advancement of geological knowledge

Edinburgh Highland Reel & Strathspey Society (EHRSS) 1881
- ■ 12 Comely Bank Terrace, EDINBURGH, EH4 1AS. (sp)
  0131-343 1923
  http://www.ehrss.org.uk
  Sec: Nicola Foy
- ▲ Registered Charity
- ○ *D; to improve taste in traditional Scottish music, especially highland reels & strathspeys by performing concerts
- ● Mtgs - Comp - Public concerts
- M 50 i
  (Sub: £20)

Edinburgh Mathematical Society (EMS) 1883
- ■ James Clerk Maxwell Building, Mayfield Rd, EDINBURGH, EH9 3JZ. (hsb)
  0131-650 5040
  email edmathsoc@maths.ed.ac.uk
  http://www.maths.ed.ac.uk/~ems/
  Hon Sec: Dr A D Gilbert
- ▲ Registered Charity
- ○ *L; advancement of mathematics, especially in Scotland
- ● Conf - Mtgs - Res - Lib
- < Eur Mathematical Soc
- M 360 i, UK / 60 i, o'seas
- ¶ Proceedings - 3; £18 yr m, £208 yr nm.

Edinburgh Sir Walter Scott Club 1894
- NR 4 Lonsdale Terrace, EDINBURGH, EH3 9HN. (hsp)
  0131-228 2430
  email honsec@walterscottclub.org.uk
  http://www.eswsc.com
  Hon Sec: Prof Peter Garside
- ▲ Un-incorporated Society
- ○ *A; to keep alive & cherish the memory of Sir Walter Scott
- ● Mtgs
- M 300 i, UK / 40 i, o'seas
- ¶ Bulletin - 1; free.

Edith Nesbit Society 1996
- ■ 26 Strongbow Rd, Eltham, LONDON, SE9 1DT. (treas/p)
  http://www.edithnesbit.co.uk
  Hon Treas: Mrs M Kennett
- ▲ Un-incorporated Society
- ○ *A; to promote interest in the life & works of author Edith Nesbit (1858-1924) & her friends
- Gp Archives
- ● Mtgs - Res - Exhib - SG - VE
- M 81 i, 2 org, UK / 3 i, o'seas
- ¶ NL - 4; ftm only.

Education Law Association (ELAS)
- NR 33 College Rd, READING, Berks, RG6 1QE. (sp)
  0118-966 9866
  http://www.educationlawassociation.org.uk
  Sec: Catherine Croft
- ○ *P
- M c 320 i

Education Otherwise Association Ltd (EO) 1977
- ■ PO Box 3761, SWINDON, Wilts, SN2 9GT. (mail)
  email enquiries@education-otherwise.net
  http://www.education-otherwise.net
  Admin: Shena Deuchars
- ▲ Company Limited by Guarantee; Registered Charity
- Br local groups
- ○ *E, *K; self-help organisation offering support, advice & information to families practising, or contemplating, home-based education as an alternative to schooling.
  EO takes its name from the Education Act which states that parents are responsible for their children's education, 'either by regular attendance at school or otherwise'
- ● Conf - Mtgs - Exhib - Comp - Inf - VE - Liaison with LEA's
- M 4,500 families
- ¶ NL - 6;   Hbk - 1;   School is not Compulsory;
  Contact list - 1; all ftm only.
  Publications list available [see website].

Educational Centres Association (ECA) 1920
- Henderson Business Centre, Ivy Rd, NORWICH, Norfolk, NR5 8BF. (regd off)
  0844 249 5594   fax 01603 469292
  email info@e-c-a.ac.uk   http://www.e-c-a.ac.uk
  Chmn & Chief Exec: Bernard Godding
- ▲ Registered Charity
- ○ *E; promotion of lifelong learning
- ● Conf - Mtgs - Inf - LG
- < Eur Assn Educ Adults; Community Sector Coalition; SEBDA; Nat Inst Adult Continuing Educ
- > engage; Nat Inst Adult Continuing Educ
- M i, f & org
- ¶ NL - 3;   AR; both ftm.

Educational Institute of Scotland (EIS) 1847
- 46 Moray Place, EDINBURGH, EH3 6BH. (hq)
  0131-225 6244   fax 0131-220 3151
  email enquiries@eis.org.uk   http://www.eis.org.uk
  Gen Sec: Ronald A Smith
- ▲ Un-incorporated Society
- Br 38
- ○ *E, *U; promotion of sound learning & the interests & welfare of teachers
- ● Conf - Mtgs - ET - Empl
- < Education Intl; Eur Trade U C'ee on Educ; TUC; STUC
- M 60,170 i
- ¶ Scottish Educational Jnl - 6; ftm, £12 yr nm.

Educational Publishers Council
  a group of the **Publishers Association**

Educational Software Publishers Association
  a group of the **British Educational Suppliers Association**

Edward Thomas Fellowship 1980
- 1 Carfax, Undercliff Drive, ST LAWRENCE, Isle of Wight, PO38 1XG. (hsp)
  01983 853366
  Hon Sec: Colin G Thornton
- ▲ Un-incorporated Society
- ○ *L; to perpetuate the memory of the writer Edward Thomas (1878-1917); to preserve the countryside known to him; to further interest in his life & work
- ● Conf - Mtgs - Res - VE
- < Alliance of Literary Socs
- M 450 i, 2 colleges, 1 museum, UK / 25 i, 1 library, o'seas
- ¶ NL - 2; ftm, £2 nm.

EEF Ltd - the manufacturers' organisation (EEF) 1896
- NR EEF House, Queensway North, Team Valley Trading Estate, GATESHEAD, Tyne & Wear, NE11 0NX. (hq)
  0191-497 3240
  http://www.eef.org.uk
  Chief Exec: Terry Scuoler
- ▲ Company Limited by Guarantee
- ○ *T; to help manufacturing businesses evolve, innovate & compete in a fast-changing world
- M f 'around a quarter of all the UK's manufacturing businesses'
  Note: Prior to rebranding in November 2003, the organisation was known as the Engineering Employers' Federation

Egg Crafters Guild of Great Britain 1979
- The Studio, 7 Hylton Terrace, NORTH SHIELDS, Tyne & Wear, NE29 0EE. (memsec/b)
  0191-258 3648   fax 0191-258 3648
  http://www.freewebs.com/eggcraftersguild/
  Chief Exec: Joan Cutts
- ▲ Un-incorporated Society
- Br 30; 10 o'seas
- ○ *A, *G; to promote & encourage the craft of egg decoration
- ● Conf - Mtgs - ET - Exhib - SG
- M 1,500 i, UK / 500 i, o'seas
- ¶ The Egg Crafter (NL) - 4; ftm.

Egypt Exploration Society (EES) 1882
- 3 Doughty Mews, LONDON, WC1N 2PG. (hq)
  020 7242 1880   fax 020 7404 6118
  email contact@ees.ac.uk   http://www.ees.ac.uk
  Sec: Dr Patricia A Spencer
- ▲ Company Limited by Guarantee; Registered Charity
- Br London, Manchester
- ○ *L; promotion of the study of the history & archaeology of ancient Egypt
- ● Conf - Mtgs - Res - Lib - PL - VE - Archaeological excavations
- M 2,608 i, 281 libraries
- ¶ Jnl of Egyptian Archaeology - 1; £40 m, £50 nm.
  Egyptian Archaeology - 2; £4.95.   AR; ftm.

Egyptian British Chamber of Commerce (EBCC) 1981
- 299 Oxford St, LONDON, W1A 4EG. (hq)
  020 7499 3100   fax 020 7499 1070
  email info@theebcc.com
  Sec-Gen: T Sherif
- ▲ Company Limited by Guarantee
- ○ *C; to promote commercial, industrial & tourist relations between Egypt & the UK
- ● Conf - Mtgs - Exhib - Stat - Expt - Inf - Lib - LG
- ¶ Egyptian-British Trade - 4; free.
  Bulletin - trade opportunities - 26; ftm only.

EIS Association (EISA) 1990
- Erico House, 93-99 Upper Richmond Rd, LONDON, SW15 2TG. (hq)
  020 8785 5560   fax 020 8785 5561
  email members@eisa.org.uk   http://www.eisa.org.uk
  Dir: Susan Phillips
- ▲ Company Limited by Guarantee
- ○ *T; to stimulate investment in the smaller company economy in the broadest sense but also specifically through the EIS (Enterprise Investment Scheme)
- Gp EISA Council; Tax c'ee
- ● Inf - LG
- M 80 f
- ¶ LM; [website].

Ekbom Support Group
  see **RLS-UK / Ekbom Syndrome Association**

eLearning Network (eLN) 1989
- NR Thrift Cottage, Common Rd, HADLOW, Kent, TN11 0JE. (admin/b)
  01732 850650
  email info@elearningnetwork.org
  http://www.elearningnetwork.org
  Admin: Pat Straughan
- ▲ Un-incorporated Society
- ○ *G; to provide leadership in the application of technologies to learning; to provide an independent perspective on the issues
- ● Conf - Mtgs - ET - Res - Inf
- M 15 i, 84 f, 10 org

© CBD Research Ltd · Beckenham · BR3 5JS · Tel 020 8650 7745 · E-mail cbd@cbdresearch.com · www.cbdresearch.com

Electoral Reform Society Ltd   (ERS)   1884
- ■ 6 Chancel St, LONDON, SE1 0UU.   (hq)
  020 7928 1622   fax 020 7401 7789
  email ers@electoral-reform.org.uk
  http://www.electoral-reform.org.uk
  Chief Exec: Katie Ghose
- ▲ Company Limited by Guarantee
- ○ *K; to campaign for the introduction of the single transferable vote for all UK public elections & elections within common interest bodies; to provide election monitoring & voter education for emerging democracies internationally
- Gp Subsidiaries: Electoral Reform Ballot Services Ltd, Electoral Reform International Services Ltd; McDougall Trust (educational charity)
- ● Conf - Mtgs - ET - Res - Exhib - SG - Stat - Inf - Lib - VE - LG - Votes At 16 Campaign
- < UNESCO; CVD (USA); NLGN; NCVO; Make Votes Count
- M 2,300 i, 2 f, 6 org, UK / 40 i, 2 org, o'seas
- ¶ Representation: jnl of democracy & electoral systems - 4; ftm, £25 yr nm.
  ERS News - 4;   AR; both free.

Electric Boat Association   (EBA)   1982
- ■ 150 Wayside Green, Woodcote, READING, Berks, RG8 0QJ. (hsp)
  01491 681449
  email secretary@eboat.org.uk   http://www.eboat.org.uk
  Hon Sec: Barbara Penniall
- ▲ Un-incorporated Society
- ○ *G; to promote electric boating throughout the UK; to represent the interests of electric boat owners with the inland waterways authorities & government departments
- Gp User group (boat owners)
- ● Conf - Res - Exhib - Comp - SG - Stat - Expt - Inf - LG
- M c 400 i, 50 f
- ¶ Electric Boat News - 3; ftm, on application nm.

The Electric Guitar Appreciation Society   (TEGAS)
- NR 65 Stapleton Lane, Barwell, LEICESTER, LE9 8HE.   (pres/p)
  01455 457928
  http://www.tegas.co.uk
  Founder & Pres: John Williams
- ○ *G, *D

The Electric Heating & Ventilation Association
  an association of **BEAMA Ltd**

Electric Railway Society   (ERS)   1946
- ■ 48 Oakways, LONDON, SE9 2PD.   (hsp)
  email jhforrester@btinternet.com
  http://www.electric-rly-society.org.uk
  Hon Sec: John Forrester
- ▲ Un-incorporated Society
- Br 2
- ○ *G; to study the history, development & practice of electric railways incl rapid transit metro lines; to evaluate their effectiveness in public transport in major cities throughout the world
- ● Mtgs - Exhib - SG - PL - VE
- < Rly Soc Sthn Africa; Asociación Uruguaya Amigos Riel; Pacific Railroad Soc; Scot Intl Tramway Assn; Australian Electric Traction Assn
- M 271 i, 7 f, 4 org, UK / 105 i, 2 f, 3 org, o'seas
- ¶ The Electric Railway - 6; ftm, £13.00 nm.
  [subscription £13.50].

Electric Security Fencing Federation
  a group of the **Fencing Contractors' Association**

Electric Steel Makers' Guild   (ESMG)   1956
- ■ 193 Fitzwilliam St, Swinton, MEXBOROUGH, S Yorks, S64 8RW.   (hsp)
  01709 584135
  Assistant Sec: John Kitchen
- ○ *T; improving steelmaking in electric arc furnaces (commercial quantities only)
- ● Conf - Mtgs
- M 51 i, UK / 3 i, o'seas

Electric Trace Heating Industry Council   (ETHIC)   1988
- ■ Oak Tree Lodge, 49 Biddulph Rd, CONGLETON, Cheshire, CW12 3LQ.   (hsp)
  01260 274701
  http://www.ethic-global.com
  Hon Sec: J W Young
- ▲ Un-incorporated Society
- ○ *T; communication between manufacturers, designers & installers of electric trace heating equipment & the specifiers & users of the equipment; the correct use of approved quality equipment & industry specifications, standards & codes of practice
- ● Mtgs - ET - Preparation of International Standards
- < Energy Ind Coun; Electricity Assn; Brit Nat C'ee for Electroheat; BSI
- M 7 f

Electric Vehicle Network   (EV Network)
- NR 5 Egerton Drive, Langdon Hills, BASILDON, Essex, SS16 6EE. (hq)
  0845 095 1357
  email admin@ev-network.org.uk
  http://www.ev-network.org.uk
- ○ *G; to establish & maintain the most comprehensive listing of publically available charge points in the UK
- M i, f, public charge points

Electrical Contractors' Association   (ECA)   1901
- NR Esca House, 34 Palace Court, LONDON, W2 4HY.   (hq)
  020 7313 4800   fax 020 7221 7344
  email info@eca.org.uk   http://www.eca.co.uk
  Chief Exec: Steve Bratt
- ○ *T; to represent the interests of contractors who design, install, inspect, test & maintain electrical & electronic equipment & services
- Gp Electrical Contractors Insurance Company; ELECSA
- ● Conf - Mtgs - ET - Inf - Empl
- M 3,000 f

Electrical Distributors Association   (EDA)   1914
- ■ Union House, Eridge Rd, ROYAL TUNBRIDGE WELLS, Kent, TN4 8HF.   (hq)
  01892 619990   fax 01892 619991
  email info@eda.org.uk   http://www.eda.org.uk
  Dir: Nigel Ellis
- ▲ Company Limited by Guarantee
- ○ *T. to promote the interests of the electrical wholesale distribution industry
- ● Mtgs - ET - Stat
- < Eur U of Electrical Whlsrs (EUEW)
- M 30 f
- ¶ Ybk - 1; ftm, £59.50 nm.

Electrical & Electronic Retailers Association of Ireland
  has closed

Electrical & Engineering Staff Association
  an autonomous professional body within **Unite the Union**

Electrical Insulation Association   (EIA)   1911
- ■ PO Box 2462, STAFFORD, ST16 9AE.   (hq)
    01785 661306
    email jcgwheeler@tiscali.co.uk   http://www.eiauk.org
    Sec: Dr Jeremy C G Wheeler
- ▲ Un-incorporated Society
- ○ *T; to represent companies that manufacture or supply
    insulation materials & products used in electrical equipment
- Gp C'ees: Activities; Insucon (international conference)
- ● Conf - Mtgs - ET - VE
- M 24 f
    (Sub: £720)

Electricity Arbitration Association   (EAA)   1990
- ■ 5 Meadow Rd, Great Gransden, SANDY, Beds, SG19 3BD.
    (hq)
    01767 677043   fax 01767 677043
    Sec: Donald H J Lester
- ○ *T; to provide dispute resolution services for the UK electricity
    industry
- M f

Electro-Technical Council of Ireland   (ETCI)   1972
- IRL Unit H12 Centrepoint Business Park, Oak Rd, DUBLIN 12,
    Republic of Ireland.
    353 (1) 429 0088   fax 353 (1) 429 0090
    email admin@etci.ie   http://www.etci.ie
    Chief Exec: Patrick Hession
- ▲ Company Limited by Guarantee
- ○ *N; for organisations representative of all aspects of electro-
    technology in Ireland
- Gp Technical Management Committee
- M 19 org

Electro-physiological Technologists' Association
     since 2008 **Association of Neurophysiological Scientists**

Electronic Applications Division
     a group of the **Institute of Materials, Minerals & Mining**

Elgar Society   1951
- NR 29 Badgers Close, HORSHAM, W Sussex, RH12 5RU.
    (memsec/p)
    email membership@elgar.org   http://www.elgar.org
    Mem Sec: David Young
- ▲ Registered Charity
- Br 10; Canada
- ○ *A; to promote the study, performance & appreciation of the
    works of Sir Edward Elgar & research into his life & music
- Gp Elgar Enterprises (trading company)
- ● Conf - Mtgs - ET - SG - Inf - VE - Awards to young composers -
    Sponsorship of CDs & concerts - Grants for the hire of
    orchestral parts
- M 1,700 i, UK / 50 i, o'seas
- ¶ The Elgar Jnl - 3;   The Elgar News - 3; both ftm only.

T S Eliot Society   2006
- ■ Ferrar House, Little Gidding, HUNTINGDON, Cambs,
    PE28 5RJ.
    01832 293383
    email info@ferrarhouse.co.uk
    http://www.eliotsociety.org.uk
    Sec: Dr Kathy Radley
- ○ A; for all interested in the life & works of Thomas Stearns Eliot
    (1888-1965)
- ¶ NL.

**Elsie Jeanette Oxenham Appreciation Society   (EJO Society)
1989**
- ■ 32 Tadfield Rd, ROMSEY, Hants, SO51 5AJ.   (memsec/p)
    01794 517149
    email abbeybufo@gmail.com
    http://www.sites.google.com/site/ejosociety/
    Mem Sec/Treas: Ruth Allen,   Editor: Fiona Dyer
- ▲ Un-incorporated Society
- Br Canada & USA, Australia & New Zealand
- ○ *A; to provide a postal meeting point for all who are interested
    in the work & collect the books of Elsie J Oxenham (1880-
    1960); to investigate the settings used for the books & the
    folk dances which form the backdrop to many of her titles
- ● Inf - Lib - VE - Web pages with discussion board
- < Alliance of Literary Socs
- M 470 i, 2 org, UK / 64 i, o'seas
- ¶ The Abbey Chronicle (Jnl) - 3; ftm only, £2-£3 back issues.
    LM (suppt to Jnl) - 1; ftm only.

Embroiderers' Guild   1906
- NR 1 Kings Rd, WALTON-ON-THAMES, Surrey, KT12 2RA.   (hq)
    01932 2607389
    email administrator@embroiderersguild.com
    http://www.embroiderersguild.com
    Dir: Jane Sweet
- ▲ Registered Charity
- Br 210
- ○ *A; to promote an understanding of embroidery history, design
    & technique to ensure the long-term future of the craft
- Gp Young Embroiderers (under 18s)
- ● Conf - Mtgs - ET - Res - Exhib - Comp - Lib - PL - VE
- M 25,000 i
    (Sub: £20 i, £8 young embroiderers, UK / £28.50 o'seas)
- ¶ Embroidery - 6.   NL - 2.   Ybk.
    Stitch with the Embroiderers' Guild - 6.
    Textile Ideas - 3; £8 m, £20 nm.   The Workbook.
    Various other publications.

EMC Industry Association   (EMCIA)   2002
- ■ c/o Nutwood UK Ltd, Eddystone Court, De Lank Lane,
    St Breward, BODMIN, Cornwall, PL30 4NQ.   (asa)
    01208 851530   fax 01208 850871
    email emcia@emcia.org   http://www.emcia.org
    Sec: Alan Hutley
- ▲ Un-incorporated Society
- ○ *P, *T; for EMC (electromagnetic compatibility) product & service
    providers; EMC is defined as 'the ability of an equipment or
    system to function satisfactorily in its electromagnetic
    environment without introducing intolerable electromagnetic
    disturbances to anything in that environment'
- ● Conf - Mtgs - Exhib - Expt - Inf - LG
- M 35 i, 35 f

EMDP: moving together   (EMDP)
- NR 1 Grove House, Foundry Lane, HORSHAM, W Sussex,
    RH13 5PL.
    01403 266000
    http://www.emdp.org
    Chief Exec: Darran Bennett
- ○ *D; the national governing body for the development of
    exercise, movement & dance provision, throughout the UK,
    so that people enjoy good health & wellbeing
- M 49 county sports partnerships
- × Exercise, Movement & Dance Partnership

Emergency Medicine Trainees Association
     a group of the **College of Emergency Medicine**

© CBD Research Ltd · Beckenham · BR3 5JS · Tel 020 8650 7745 · E-mail cbd@cbdresearch.com · www.cbdresearch.com

Emergency Planning Society   (EPS)   1993
■   The Media Centre, Culverhouse Cross, CARDIFF, CF5 6XS.
      (hq)
      0845 600 9587   fax 029 2059 0397
      email accounts@the-eps.org   http://www.the-eps.org
      Co Sec: John Liddell,   Operational Mgr: Dan Taylor
▲   Company Limited by Guarantee
Br   14
○   *P; to promote emergency planning & management in the UK
      (all functions relating to the preparation for the assessment of
      a response to emergencies for the benefit of people, property
      & the environment)
Gp   Professional issues; Society issues
●   Conf - Mtgs - ET - Exhib - SG - Inf - LG
<   Soc of Indl Emergency Services Officers (SIESO)
M   2,000 i
¶   Blue Print Magazine - 4; ftm only.

**Emergency Response & Rescue Vessel Association   (ERRVA)
1979**
■   56-58 Bon Accord St, ABERDEEN, Aberdeenshire, AB11 6EL.
      (hq)
      01224 857970
      http://www.errva.org.uk
      Chmn: David Kenwright,   Sec: Marie Brown
▲   Company Limited by Guarantee
○   *N, *T; for owners & operators of the UK continental shelf
      emergency response & rescue vehicles (ERRVs), which recover
      people employed on offshore installations in case of
      emergencies & to warn other vessels of collison hazards
●   ET - Liaison with other industry bodies - To conduct trials & tests
      on any relevant equipment

Emergency Social Services Association   (ESSA)   1997
■   PO Box 6466, BRIDPORT, Dorset, DT6 3US.   (hsb)
      http://www.essauk.com
      Hon Sec: Terri Goodwin,   Treas: Sylvia Watkin
○   *P; to promote high standards in (& the significance of) out-of-
      hours social work
●   Conf - Mtgs
M   c 100 authorities
¶   ESSA News (NL) - 3; ftm only.

Employers Forum on Age   (EFA)   1996
NR   32-36 Leman St, LONDON, SE1 0EH.   (hq)
      020 7922 7790
      email efa@efa.org.uk   http://www.efa.org.uk
○   *N; to support member organisations in achieving an age-
      diverse workforce
M   f & org

Employers' Forum on Disability
§   Nutmeg House, 60 Gainsford St, LONDON, SE1 2NY.
      020 7403 3020   fax 020 7403 0404
      email enquiries@efd.org.uk   http://www.efd.org.uk
      Chief Exec: Susan Scott-Parker
      A unique network of organisations that share best practice on
      disability; to create a society where business and the public
      sector promote the economic and social inclusion of disabled
      people.

Employment Lawyers Association   (ELA)   1992
NR   PO Box 353, UXBRIDGE, Middx, UB10 0UN.
      01895 256972   fax 01895 256972
○   *P

ENABLE Scotland   (ENABLE)   1954
NR   146 Argyle St (2nd floor), GLASGOW, G1 8BL.   (hq)
      0141-226 4541   fax 0141-204 4398
      email enable@enable.org.uk
      http://www.enable.org.uk
▲   Registered Charity; Un-incorporated Society
Br   57
○   *W; to support people with learning difficulties & their families
      in Scotland; to achieve equal opportunities & better services
Gp   ACE - national advisory committee of people with learning
      disabilities
●   Conf - Mtgs - Inf - Lib - LG
<   Inclusion Intl; Inclusion Europe; Disability Agenda Scotland;
      Learning Disability Alliance Scotland
M   c 4,000 i
¶   Newslink (NL) - 4.   AR.

ENCAMS
      on 1 June 2009 reverted to its original name of **Keep Britain Tidy**

Encephalitis Society   1994
■   7b Saville St, MALTON, N Yorks, YO17 7LL.   (hq)
      01653 699599   fax 01653 604369
      email mail@encephalitis.info
      http://www.encephalitis.info
      Resource Centre Mgr: Elaine Dowall
▲   Company Limited by Guarantee; Registered Charity
○   *M, *W; to provide support, everyday advice & general
      information to families & carers of children or adults with
      encephalitis; to raise public awareness & gather more
      information to aid research into encephalitis.
      Contact between families in similar situations is encouraged so
      mutual experiences can be shared
●   Conf - Mtgs - ET - Res - Inf
<   Eur Org for Rare Disorders (EURORDIS); Children's Acquired
      Brain Injury Interest Gp (CABIIG); Contact-a-Family; Long-
      term Medical Conditions Alliance (LMCA); Neurological
      Alliance; Rare Disorders Alliance; R Assn for Disability &
      Rehabilitation (RADAR); UK Acquired Brain Injury
      Forum (UKABIF)
M   800 i
¶   NL - 3;   Annual Review; free.
      Note: Encephalitis Society is the operating name of the
      Encephalitis Support Group

Encephalitis Support Group
      operates as the **Encephalitis Society**

Endometriosis UK   1981
■   Suites 1 & 2, 46 Manchester St, LONDON, W1U 1RR.   (hq)
      020 7222 2781   fax 020 7222 2786
      http://www.endometriosis-uk.org
      Chief Exec: Robert Music
▲   Company Limited by Guarantee
Br   50+
○   *K; support for women suffering from endometriosis; raising
      money for research into the disease; information to health
      professionals
●   Conf - Mtgs - Res - Inf
      Helpline: 0808 808 2227
M   c 2,500 i
¶   NL - 4;   AR - 1; both ftm only.
      Publications list available.
×   2010 National Endometriosis Society

Endurance GB (EGB) 2001

NR National Agricultural Centre, Stoneleigh Park, KENILWORTH, Warks, CV8 2RP. (hq)
024 7669 8863 fax 024 7641 8429
email enquiries@endurancegb.co.uk
http://www.endurancegb.co.uk
Chmn: Wendy Dunham
▲ Company Limited by Guarantee
Br 22
○ *S; to promote & enhance the sport of endurance (competitive long distance) riding in the UK for all levels of rider
● Conf - Mtgs - ET - Exhib - Comp
< Brit Equestrian Fedn
M 2,200 i, UK / 100 i, o'seas
¶ Magazine - 4; ftm;
Branch Group NL - 12; AR - 1; all ftm only.

Energy Industries Council (EIC) 1943

NR 89 Albert Embankment, LONDON, SE1 7TP. (hq)
020 7091 8600 fax 020 7091 8601
email info@the-eic.com http://www.the-eic.com
Chief Exec: Mike Major
▲ Company Limited by Guarantee
○ *T; manufacturers, contractors & financial institutions serving the oil, petrochemical, natural gas, coal, power & process industries
● Conf - Mtgs - Exhib - Expt - Inf - VE
< Fedn of Eur Petroleum & Gas Eqpt Mfrs
M 600 f
¶ NL - 17; m only.
Catalogue of British Suppliers - 2 yrly; ftm, £45 nm.
Technical publications, specification & datasheets.

Energy Institute (EI) 1924

■ 61 New Cavendish St, LONDON, W1G 7AR. (hq)
020 7467 7100
email info@energyinst.org http://www.energyinst.org
Chief Exec: Louise Kingham
▲ Registered Charity; Un-incorporated Society
○ *N; to promote the sustainable supply & use of energy for the greatest benefit of all people
● Conf - Mtgs - Inf - LG
< Utd Nations (cat 3); Wld Coal Inst; Wld Nuclear Assn; Wld Renewable Energy Congress; Soc for the Envt
M 15 i, 19 f, 6 org
(Sub: £100 i, £2,900 f, £475 org)
× 2009 (British Energy Association (Energy Institute

Energy Intensive Users Group

NR Broadway House, Tothill St, LONDON, SW1H 9NQ. (hq)
020 7654 1536 fax 020 7222 2782
http://www.eiug.org.uk
○ *K; campaigning for secure industrial energy supplies at internationally competitive prices
M f & org

Energy Networks Association

NR Dean Bradley House (6th floor), 52 Horseferry Rd, LONDON, SW1P 2AF.
020 7706 5100
Chief Exec: David Smith
○ *T; UK gas & electricity transmission & distribution licence holders

Energy Retail Association (ERA) 2003

NR 1 Hobhouse Court, Suffolk St, LONDON, SW1Y 4HH.
020 7104 4150 fax 020 7104 4180
email info@energy-retail.org.uk
http://www.energy-retail.org.uk
Chief Operating Offr: Lawrence Slade
○ *T; represents the six main electricity & gas suppliers; focuses on finding ways to continually improve all customers' experiences with their electricity & gas suppliers

Energy Services & Technology Association
see **ESTA Energy Services & Technology Association**

Energy Systems Trade Association
since 2010 **ESTA Energy Services & Technology Association**

Enforcement Services Association
in January 2011 merged with the Association of Civil Enforcement Agencies to form the **Civil Enforcement Association**

engage: National Association of Gallery Education 1988

NR Rich Mix, 35-47 Bethnal Green Rd, LONDON, E1 6LA. (hq)
020 7729 5858 fax 020 7729 3688
email info@engage.org http://www.engage.org
Dir: Jane Sillis
▲ Registered Charity
○ *A, *E, *G, *P; to promote greater understanding & enjoyment of the visual arts by engaging with the public, artists, galleries & educators
M i, f & org
¶ engage review - 2; ftm. engagements - 4; ftm only.

Engineered Panels in Construction (EPiC) 1991

NR 29 High St, EWELL, Surrey, KT17 1SB. (hq)
020 8786 3619 fax 020 8786 8887
email info@epic.uk.com http://www.epic.uk.com
○ *T; to represent the rigid urethane insulated panel industry
< Construction Products Assn
M 5 f

Engineered Systems Product Group
a product group of **BEAMA Ltd**

Engineering Construction Industry Association (ECIA) 1994

■ Broadway House (5th floor), Tothill St, LONDON, SW1H 9NS. (hq)
020 7799 2000 fax 020 7233 1930
email ecia@ecia.co.uk http://www.ecia.co.uk
Managing Dir: Michael Hockey
▲ Un-incorporated Society
Br 6 regions
○ *T
● Mtgs - ET - Stat - Inf - Empl - LG
< CBI; EEF; Eur Construction Inst
M 270 f
¶ Publications list on website.

Engineering Equipment & Materials Users' Association (EEMUA) 1949

■ 10-12 Lovat Lane, LONDON, EC3R 8DN. (hq)
020 7621 0011 fax 020 7621 0022
email info@eemua.org http://www.eemua.org
Exec Dir: C Tayler
▲ Company Limited by Guarantee
○ *L; for companies that use engineering equipment & materials in the construction, operation & management of chemical & petrochemical process plants, offshore rigs, power generation, storage & distribution & transport systems & similar industrial & production assets
Gp Electrical; Inspection; Instruments & control; Materials technology; Mechanical (pressure equipment, storage tanks, piping & valve systems, rotating machinery)
● Mtgs - ET - SG - Inf - LG
> Eur C'ee User Inspectorates
M 17 f, UK / 2 f, o'seas
¶ c 60 technical guides & handbooks. Price List; free.

Engineering Industries Association   (EIA)   1940
■   62 Bayswater Rd, LONDON, W2 3PS.   (hq)
     020 7298 6455   fax 020 7298 6456
     email head.office@eia.co.uk   http://www.eia.co.uk
     Pres: Sir Ronald Halstead
▲   Company Limited by Guarantee
Br   3 regions
○   *T; representation & promotion of the interests of the
     engineering manufacturing sector in UK, European & global
     markets
●   Conf - Mtgs - Exhib - Expt - Inf - VE - LG
M   400 f
¶   NL - 12;   Trade Leads - 12;   Buyers' Guide - 1; all ftm.

Engineering Integrity Society   (EIS)   1985
NR   18 Oak Close, BEDWORTH, Warks, CV12 9AJ.   (regd off)
     024 7673 0126   fax 024 7673 0126
     email eis@e-i-s.org.uk   http://www.e-i-s.org.uk
     Chmn: Dr Peter Blackmore
▲   Registered Charity
○   *P; 'to advance the education of persons working in the field of
     engineering by providing a forum for the interchange of
     ideas & information on integrity of engineering practice'
Gp   Durability & fatigue; Noise, vibration & human perception;
     Simulation, test & measurement
●   Conf - Mtgs - ET - Exhib
M   100 i, 37 f, UK / 26 i, o'seas
¶   Engineering Integrity (Jnl) - 2; ftm, £50 yr nm.
     EIS News (NL) - 2; free.

Engineering & Machinery Alliance   (EAMA)   2001
■   62 Bayswater Rd, LONDON, W2 3PS.   (hq)
     020 7298 6450   fax 020 7298 6430
     email eama@mta.org.uk   http://www.eama.info
     Sec: Rupert Hodges,   Chmn: Martin Walder
▲   Company Limited by Guarantee
○   *N, *T; for the engineering, production machinery, components
     & tooling manufacturing sectors in the UK
●   Res - Stat - LG
M   9 associations:
     British Automation & Robot Association
     British Paper Machinery Suppliers Association
     British Plastics Federation
     British Turned Parts Manufacturers Association
     Confederation of British Metalforming
     Gauge & Tool Makers Association
     Manufacturing Technologies Association
     Picon Ltd
     Processing & Packaging Machinery Association
¶   Hbk - irreg; free.

Engineering Training Equipment Manufacturers' Association
     a group of the **British Educational Suppliers Association**

Engineers for Disaster Relief
     see **RedR - Engineers for Disaster Relief**

Engineers Ireland
     see **Institution of Engineers of Ireland**

England Athletics   2005
■   Wellington House, Starley Way, Birmingham International Park,
     SOLIHULL, W Midlands, B37 7HE.   (hq)
     0121-781 7271   fax 0121-781 7371
     email info@englandathletics.org
     http://www.englandathletics.org
     Exec Chmn: John Graves
▲   Company Limited by Guarantee
○   *S; governing body for athletics in England; to control, promote
     & provide athletic competitions, coaching & training
<   UK Athletics; Sport England
M   clubs

England Basketball   (EBBA)   1936
NR   PO Box 3971, SHEFFIELD, S Yorks, S9 9AZ.   (hq)
     0114-284 1060
     http://www.englandbasketball.co.uk
     Chief Exec: Keith Mair
▲   Company Limited by Guarantee
○   *S; to govern & promote the game of basketball
M   30,000 i, 1,000 clubs
¶   Zone Press - 6.   Competitions Hbk - 1.   AR.
     Note: Also known as the English Basketball Association

England Golf   (EG)   1924
■   National Golf Centre, The Broadway, WOODHALL SPA, Lincs,
     LN10 6PU.   (hq)
     01526 354500   fax 01526 354020
     email info@englishgolfunion.org
     http://www.englishgolfunion.org
▲   Company Limited by Guarantee
○   *S; to promote, administer & encourage amateur golf in
     England; to maintain a uniform system of handicapping
●   ET - Comp - Inf - Development - Coaching
M   i
×   2012 (English Golf Union
          (English Women's Golf Association (merged 1 Jan)

England Handball Association   (EHA)   1968
NR   Unit G3 Barton Hall Estate, Hardy St, Eccles, MANCHESTER,
     M30 7NB.   (hq)
     0161-707 8983   fax 0161-707 0782
     http://www.englandhandball.com
○   *S; national governing body for the sport
M   i, schools & org
     Note: Registered as the British Handball Association.

England Hockey   2003
NR   Bisham Abbey National Sports Centre, MARLOW, Bucks,
     SL7 1RR.   (hq)
     01628 897500   fax 01628 897544
     http://www.englandhockey.co.uk
▲   Company Limited by Guarantee
○   *S; the national governing body for hockey in England
<   Intl Hockey Fedn (IHF); Eur Hockey Fedn (EHF)
M   1,050 clubs

England Netball
     see **All England Netball Association**

England Squash & Racketball   (ESR)   2009
■   National Squash Centre, Sportcity, MANCHESTER, M11 3FF.
     (hq)
     0161-231 4499   fax 0161-231 4231
     email enquiries@englandsquashandracketball.com
     http://www.englandsquashandracketball.com
     Chief Exec: Nick Rider
▲   Company Limited by Guarantee
○   *S; the governing body for squash & racketball in England
<   Wld Squash Fedn; Eur Squash Fedn
M   25,000 i, 1,000 clubs, UK / 10 i, o'seas
×   2009 (Squash Rackets Association
          (English Racketball

England & Wales Cricket Board Association of Cricket Officials
ECB Association of Cricket Officials   (ECB ACO)   2008
■   Lord's Cricket Ground, LONDON, NW8 8QZ.   (hq)
     020 7432 1240   fax 020 7289 5619
     email ecbaco@ecb.co.uk   http://www.ecb.co.uk/
     ecbaco
     Member Services Mgr: Sam Greaves
Br 39; ICC Europe
○   *S; all aspects of cricket officiating from playground to the test
     area, nationally & internationally
●   Conf - Mtgs - ET - Exam
<   England & Wales Cricket Bd (ECB); Marylebone Cricket
     Club (MCC)
M   5,654 i, UK / 200 i, o'seas
     (Sub: £5-£22 UK / £10-£15 o'seas)
¶   NL - 6; ftm, website nm.
     MCC Open Learning Manual - 1; £10 m, £15 nm.
×   2008 (Association of Cricket Umpires & Scorers
     (ECB Officials Association (merged 1 January)

England & Wales Cricket Board Coaches Association   (ECB
Coaches Association)   (ECB CA)   2002
NR Warwickshire County Cricket Ground, Edgbaston,
     BIRMINGHAM, B5 7QX.   (hq)
     0121-440 4332   fax 0121-440 7605
     email coaches.association@ecb.co.uk
     http://www.ecb.co.uk
○   *S; to support the ECB's Coach Education & Development
     programmes & its member coaches
●   Conf - Mtgs - ET - Exhib - Inf - LG
M   9,000 i, UK / 599 i, o'seas

Ða Engliscan Gesíðas   (the English Companions)   1966
■   Bottom Lane Farm, Bottom House, near LEEK, Staffs,
     ST13 7QL.   (hsp)
     01538 266440
     http://www.tha-engliscan-gesithas.org.uk
     Hon Sec: Harry Ball
▲   Company Limited by Guarantee
Br 16; Australia, Canada, New Zealand, Republic of Ireland, USA
○   *G; to encourage interest in the history & other aspects of Old
     English or the Anglo-Saxon period, its language, culture &
     traditions
Gp Living history; Local shire (scir) gps; Old English
     correspondence course
●   Mtgs - ET - Res - Exhib - Comp - SG - Lib - VE - Lectures
M   544 i, UK / 42 i, o'seas
¶   Wiðowinde (Bindweed) (Jnl) - 3;
     Hrafnes Wisprung (Raven's Whisper) (NL) - 3; both ftm only.

English Amateur Dancesport Association
     since 2008 **EADA**

English Apples & Pears Ltd   (EAP)   1990
■   Bradbourne House, East Malling, WEST MALLING, Kent,
     ME19 6DZ.   (hq)
     01732 529781   fax 01732 529783
     http://www.englishapplesandpears.co.uk
▲   Company Limited by Guarantee
○   *H, *K, *T; 'to further the interests of shareholder members who
     are top fruit (apples & pears) growers in UK'
●   Inf - PL
M   280 i

English Association   (EA)   1906
■   University of Leicester, University Rd, LEICESTER, LE1 7RH.
     (hq)
     0116-252 3982   fax 0116-252 2301
     email engassoc@le.ac.uk   http://www.le.ac.uk/
     engassoc
     Sec: Helen Lucas
▲   Company Limited by Guarantee; Registered Charity
Br Australia, South Africa
○   *L; promotion of knowledge & appreciation of English
     language & literature
Gp Graduate students
●   Conf
M   i & org
¶   NL - 3.   English - 3;   English 4-11 - 3.
     The Use of English - 3.
     Year's Work in English Studies - 1.
     Essays & Studies - 1.
     Year's Work in Critical & Cultural Theory - 1.

English Association of American Bond & Shareholders
     ceased to trade in 2007

English Association of Self Catering Operators   (EASCO)
1985
■   PO Box 567, HAYES, Middx, UB3 9EW.   (mail)
     020 7078 7329   fax 0870 136 6638
     email info@englishselfcatering.co.uk
     http://www.englishselfcatering.co.uk
     Chief Exec: Martin Sach
▲   Un-incorporated Society
○   *T; to represent owners of self-catering accommodation
     businesses
●   Mtgs - Res - Inf - LG
<   Fedn of Nat Self Catering Assns; Tourism Alliance
M   25 i, 15 f

English Association for Snooker & Billiards   (EASB)
NR Cedar House, Cedar Lane, FRIMLEY, Surrey, GU16 7HY.
     0808 129 4040
     email info@englishsnooker.com
     http://www.englishsnooker.com
     Sec: Peter Ainsworth
○   *S

English Baseball Association   (EBA)   1892
■   7 Vanbrugh Rd, LIVERPOOL, L4 7TT.
     0151-476 1940
     http://www.englishbaseballassociation.co.uk
     Treas: H Ashcroft
○   *S

English Basketball Association
     see **England Basketball**

English Boccia Association   (EBA)   1999
■   Unit 5 Heathcoat Bldg, Nottingham Science & Technology Park,
     University Boulevard, NOTTINGHAM, NG7 2QJ.   (hq)
     0115-925 7027
     http://www.cpsport.org
○   *S; to develop quality opportunities for players of all disabilities
     to participate in the sport of Boccia under the regulations of
     the International Boccia Commission (Boccia is a game akin
     to indoor bowls)
●   ET - Res - Inf - Lib - Referee courses - Level 1 training courses
<   Intl Boccia Commission
M   i & org

English Bowling Association
     in 2007 merged with the English Women's Bowling Association to
     form **Bowls England**

© CBD Research Ltd · Beckenham · BR3 5JS · Tel 020 8650 7745 · E-mail cbd@cbdresearch.com · www.cbdresearch.com

English Bowling Federation
■ 14 Field Close, WORKSOP, Notts, S81 0PF. (hsp)
  01909 474346
  email j.heppel@btinternet.com
  Sec: John Heppel
○ *S

English Bridge Union (EBU) 1936
NR Broadfields, Bicester Rd, AYLESBURY, Bucks, HP19 8AZ. (hq)
  01296 317200   fax 01296 317220
  email postmaster@ebu.co.uk   http://www.ebu.co.uk
  Gen Mgr & Co Sec: Barry Capal
▲ Un-incorporated Society
○ *S; governing body for the game of duplicate contract bridge
Gp Bridge for All (learn & play programme)
● Conf - Mtgs - ET - Comp - SG - Stat - Inf - Lib
< Wld Bridge Fedn; Eur Bridge League
M 30,000 i, 1,100 clubs
¶ English Bridge - 6.   Club NL - 6.   County NL - 4.   .
  Really Easy. . . (7 titles).

English Carp Heritage Organisation (ECHO) 2001
NR 16 The Parade, YATELEY, Hants, GU46 7UN.
  01252 861955
  email info@echocarp.co.uk   http://www.echocarp.co.uk
○ *G; for carp anglers

English Chess Federation (ECF) 1904
■ The Watch Oak, Chain Lane, BATTLE, E Sussex, TN33 0YD.
  (hq)
  01424 775222   fax 01424 775904
  email office@englishchess.org.uk
  http://www.englishchess.org.uk
  Admin: Cynthia Gurney
▲ Un-incorporated Society
○ *S; the governing body for chess in England
● ET - Comp - Inf
< Fédn Intl des Echecs
> County assns
M 1,600 i
¶ Chess Moves (NL) - 6.   Ybk.

English Civil War Society Ltd (ECWS) 1980
■ Flat 11 The Stables, Milton Park, PETERBOROUGH, PE6 7AF.
  (hsb)
  01733 380177   fax 01733 380072
  http://www.english-civil-war-society.org
▲ Company Limited by Shares
○ *G; to further interest in 17th century English history; to
  organise & perform re-enactments of the English Civil War
Gp The King's Army; The Roundhead Assn; Friends of the English
  Civil War Soc (supporting gp)
● Mtgs - Res - SG
M c 3,000 i
¶ King's Army NL - 6;   Friends of the ECWS NL - 4;
  Roundhead Association NL; all ftm only.

English Clergy Association (ECA) 1938
■ The Old School House, Norton Hawkfield, BRISTOL,
  BS39 4HB. (chmn/p)
  01275 830017 (Mon-Thur 1100-1300)
  email benoporto-eca@yahoo.co.uk
  http://www.clergyassoc.co.uk
  Chmn: Rev J W Masding
▲ Registered Charity; Un-incorporated Society
○ *P, *R; a professional organisation for the clergy of the Church
  of England, & lay members supportive of the traditional
  place of the clergy
● Conf - Mtgs - Nominations for Clergy Holiday Grants -
  Monitoring the processes of legislation & other changes
M 'no reliable figures available'
¶ Parson & Parish - 2; ftm, £6 yr nm.

English Community Care Association (ECCA) 2004
■ Monmouth House (2nd floor), 38-40 Artillery Lane, LONDON,
  E1 7LS. (hq)
  0845 057 7677   fax 0845 057 7678
  email info@ecca.org.uk   http://www.ecca.org.uk
  Chief Exec: Martin Green
▲ Company Limited by Guarantee; Registered Charity
○ *T; representative body for providers of continuing care homes
  registered under the 1984 Registered Homes Act; seeks to
  protect & promote high standards of treatment & care in the
  independent sector
Gp Medical & rehabilitation units; Nursing homes; Residential
  homes
● Conf - Mtgs - Res - Stat - Inf
M Care homes
¶ Bulletin;   AR;   both ftm.

English Companions
  see **Engliscan Gesíðas**

English Cross Country Association (ECCA) 1883
■ 22 Denham Drive, BASINGSTOKE, Hants, RG22 6LR. (hsp)
  01256 328401   fax 01256 328401
  email admin@englishcrosscountry.co.uk
  Sec: Ian S Byett
○ *S; to encourage & support cross-country running for men &
  women & organise national championships
M clubs

English Curling Association (ECA) 1971
NR 14 Donnelly Drive, BEDFORD, Beds, MK41 9TU. (hsp)
  email development@englishcurling.co.uk
  http://www.englishcurling.co.uk
▲ Un-incorporated Society
Br 3
○ *S; the sport of curling in England
● Mtgs - Comp - VE
< Wld Curling Fedn; Eur Curling Fedn
M c 130 i (England)
¶ Ybk - 1.

English Draughts Association (EDA) 1897
■ 54 Mayfield Rd, RYDE, Isle of Wight, PO33 3PR. (chmn/p)
  01983 565484
  email iancaws@draughts.fsnet.co.uk
  http://www.englishdraughts.co.uk
  Chmn: Ian H Caws
▲ Un-incorporated Society
○ *G, *S; to promote the game of draughts (checkers)
● Conf - Mtgs - Comp
< Fédn Mondiale du Jeu de Dames; World Checkers/Draughts
  Fedn
> County Draughts Associations
M 200 i, UK / 35 i, o'seas
¶ English Draughts Jnl - 4; ftm, (50p back issues, nm).

English Federation of Disability Sport (EFDS)
NR SportPark, Loughborough University, 3 Oakwood Drive,
  LOUGHBOROUGH, Leics, LE11 3QF.
  01509 227750
  http://www.efds.co.uk
○ *S

English Folk Dance & Song Society   (EFDSS)   1932
- ■ Cecil Sharp House, 2 Regent's Park Rd, LONDON, NW1 7AY.   (hq)
  020 7485 2206   fax 020 7284 0534
  email info@efdss.org   http://www.efdss.org
  Chief Exec: Katy Spicer
- ▲ Company Limited by Guarantee; Registered Charity
- ○ *D, *G; 'putting English traditions into the hearts & minds of the people of England'
- ● ET - Res - Inf - Lib - PL
- M 3,500 i, 562 affiliates, UK & o'seas
- ¶ EDS (English Dance & Song) - 4; ftm.
  Folk Music Jnl - 1; ftm.
  Members' Quarterly; ftm only.

English Goat Breeders Association   (EGBA)   1978
- ■ Ivy Cottage, Whitchurch Lane, Oving, AYLESBURY, HP22 4EU.   (hsp)
  01296 640842
  http://www.egba.org.uk
  Hon Sec: Mrs Annette Monument
- ▲ Registered Charity
- ○ *B; preservation & promotion of English goats
- ● Mtgs - Exhib - Inf - LG
- < Brit Goat Soc
- M c 90 i
- ¶ Jem - 6; ftm, 75p nm.

English Goethe Society   (EGS)   1886
- NR c/o Dept of German, King's College London, Strand, LONDON, WC2R 2LS.   (hsb)
  020 7848 2131   fax 020 7848 2089
  email matthew.bell@kcl.ac.uk
  http://www.englishgoethesociety.org
  Hon Sec & Treas: Dr Matthew Bell
- ▲ Registered Charity
- ○ *L; to promote the work & thought of Goethe, as well as other 18th century German writers & some later writers, notably Thomas Mann
- ● Conf - Mtgs - ET - Res - Comp
- < Goether-Gesellschaft (Weimar)
- M 150 i, UK / 20 i, o'seas
- ¶ Publications of the English Goethe Society - 1; ftm, £20 nm.

English Golf Union Ltd
merged on 1 Jan 2012 with the English Women's Golf Association to form **England Golf**

English Guernsey Cattle Society   (EGCS)   1884
- NR Scotsbridge House, Scots Hill, RICKMANSWORTH, Herts, WD3 3BB.   (hq)
  01923 695204   fax 01923 695215
  email info@guernseycattle.com
  http://www.guernseycattle.com
  Chmn: Duncan Vincent
- ▲ Company Limited by Guarantee; Registered Charity
- ○ *B
- ● Conf - Mtgs - SG
- M 280 i, UK / 20 i, o'seas
- ¶ Guernsey Breeders NL - 3; ftm.

English Historic Towns Forum
since 1 January 2009 **Historic Towns Forum**

English Ice Hockey Association
a branch of **Ice Hockey UK**

English Indoor Bowling Association   (EIBA)   1971
- ■ David Cornwell House, Bowling Green, MELTON MOWBRAY, Leics, LE13 0FA.   (hq)
  01664 481900   fax 01664 482888
  email enquiries@eiba.co.uk   http://www.eiba.co.uk
  Co Sec: Steve Rodwell
- ▲ Company Limited by Guarantee
- ○ *S; national governing body for indoor level green bowls in England
- M 340 org
- ¶ Woods & Jack (NL) - 5.   Ybk; £3 m.
- × 2008 English Women's Indoor Bowling Association (merged 1 December)

English Lacrosse Association   (ELA)   1996
- NR The Belle Vue Centre, Pink Bank Lane, MANCHESTER, M12 5GL.   (hq)
  0161-227 3626
  email info@englishlacrosse.co.uk
  Chief Exec: David Shuttleworth
- ▲ Company Limited by Guarantee
- ○ *S; the governing body for men's & women's lacrosse in Britain
- M c 4,000 i, c 100 org

English Pétanque Association   (EPA)
- NR 41 Warwick Rd, SOUTHAM, Warwickshire, CV47 0HW.   (pres/p)
  email mike.pegg@fipjp.com
  http://www.englishpetanque.org.uk
  Nat Pres: Mike Pegg
- ○ *S; the governing body in England for the playing of pétanque
- < Fédn Intle de Pétanque et Jeu Provençal (FIPJP)

English Place-Name Society   (EPNS)   1923
- ■ School of English Studies, University of Nottingham, NOTTINGHAM, NG7 2RD.   (hq)
  0115-951 5919   fax 0115-951 5924
  email name-studies@nottingham.ac.uk
  http://www.nottingham.ac.uk/english/ins
  Hon Dir: Prof Richard Coates,   Hon Sec: Prof Turville-Petre
- ▲ Registered Charity
- ○ *L; to survey the place-names & field-names of England, county by county, & publish the results of the survey
- ● Annual Meeting - Res - Inf - Lib
- M 625 i
- ¶ The Place Names of [county] - 1.   Jnl - 1; ftm.   AR.

English Playing-Card Society   (EPCS)   1984
- NR Little Paddock, Charlton Mackrell, SOMERTON, Somerset, TA11 7BG.   (hsp)
  01458 223812
  email secretary@epcs.org   http://www.wopc.co.uk
  Sec: Barney Townshend
- ▲ Un-incorporated Society
- ○ *G; to provide information for collectors & researchers of English playing cards & children's card games
- ● Mtgs - Res - SG - Inf
- < Ephemera Soc
- M 130 i
- ¶ NL (incl LM) - 3; £20 m.

English Poetry & Song Society   (EPSS)   1983
- NR 76 Lower Oldfield Park, BATH, Somerset, BA2 3HP.   (hsp)
  email menistral@yahoo.co.uk
  Chief Exec: Richard Carder
- ○ *D; the promotion of English art song by performance, publication & recording
- ● Mtgs - Res - Comp - Lib
- < Nat Fedn of Music Socs
- M 50 i, UK / 2 i, o'seas
- ¶ NL & Song List - 2; £12 m.

English Pool Association (EPA) 1979
NR 88 Crescent Rd, Hadley, TELFORD, Shropshire, TF1 4JX.
    (gensec/p)
    01952 641682
    email ivor.edwards22@blueyonder.co.uk
    http://www.epa.org.uk
    Gen Sec: Ivor Edwards
Br 46
○ *S; to organise, administer the game of pool in England
Gp English Pool Referees Association
● Mtgs - Exhib - Comp - LG - selection of national teams -
    organisation of fixtures & inter-league events
< Wld Eight Ball Pool Fedn; Eur Eight Ball Pool Fedn
M 18,000 i
¶ Hbk - 1; ftm; £5 nm.

English Pool Referees Association
    a group of the **English Pool Association**

English Racketball
    in 2009 merged with the Squash Rackets Association to form
    England Squash & Racketball

English School [sport] Association
    no school sports associations are included in this directory - see
    controlling body for the sport concerned

English Schools' Badminton Association
    a group of **Badminton England**

English Short Mat Bowling Association (ESMBA) 1984
NR 27 Southfield, NEWARK ON TRENT, Notts, NG24 3QB.
    (gensec/p)
    01636 702067
    email enquiries@esmba.co.uk   http://www.esmba.co.uk
    Gen Sec: Vic Jones
Br 35
○ *S; to promote, foster & regulate the sport of short mat bowls in
    England
● Exhib - Comp
M i

English Ski Council Ltd (ESC) 1979
■ Area Library Bldg, Queensway Mall, The Cornbow,
    HALESOWEN, W Midlands, B63 4AJ.   (hq)
    0121-501 2314   fax 0121-585 6448
    email info@snowsportengland.org.uk
    http://www.snowsportengland.org.uk
    Chief Exec: Tim Fawke
▲ Company Limited by Guarantee
○ *S; governing body of the sport in England; to promote &
    develop the sport within England & for English skiers
● Conf - Mtgs - ET - Exam - Exhib - Comp - Inf - VE - National
    Coaching Scheme (training & coaching instructors, officials &
    competitors) - Responsibility for standards, rules &
    regulations for the sport within England
< Snowsport GB
M 3,000 i, 15 f, 150 org
    Note: trades as Snowsport England

English-Speaking Union of the Commonwealth (ESU) 1918
NR Dartmouth House, 37 Charles St, LONDON, W1J 5ED.   (hq)
    020 7529 1550   fax 020 7495 6108
    email esu@esu.org   http://www.esu.org
    Dir Gen: Peter Kyle
▲ Registered Charity
Br 40; 38 o'seas
○ *X; to promote the use of English as a common language in
    nurturing dialogue & the exchange of ideas & opinions
● Conf - Mtgs - ET - Exhib - Comp - Inf - Lib - VE - Public
    speaking & debates - Youth exchange & work experience
    schemes - Cultural & literary events
< English-Speaking U (USA)
M 5,193 i, 57 f, UK / 449 i, o'seas
¶ Concord (Jnl) - 2;   ESU NL - 10; both ftm.

The English Spelling Society (TESS) 1908
NR 20 Silhill Rd, SOLIHULL, W Midlands, B91 1JU.   (memsec/p)
    email membership@spellingsociety.org
    http://www.spellingsociety.org
    Mem Sec: Stephen Linstead
○ *K; to raise awareness of the problems caused by the
    irregularity of English spelling; to promote remedies to
    improve literacy, including spelling reform
× 2007 Simplified Spelling Society

English Subbuteo Table Football Association (ESTFA)
NR 17 Bromwich Close, Thorpe Astley, LEICESTER, LE3 3RT.   (hsp)
    07756 748230
    email jeremybradley49@yahoo.co.uk
    http://www.estfa.com
    Pres: Mike Parnaby,   Sec: Jeremy Bradley
○ *S; to play & promote Subbuteo at national & international level
< Intl Fedn of Subutteo Table Football (FISTF)
M 23 clubs

English Table Tennis Association (ETTA) 1926
■ Queensbury House (3rd floor), Havelock Rd, HASTINGS,
    E Sussex, TN34 1HF.   (hq)
    01424 722525   fax 01424 422103
    email admin@etta.co.uk   http://www.etta.co.uk
    Gen Sec: R H Sinclair,   Chief Exec: Richard Yule
▲ Company Limited by Guarantee
○ *S; governing body for the sport in England
● Conf - Organisation of national championships
< Intl Table Tennis Fedn; Eur Table Tennis U
M 40,000 i, 4,500 clubs
¶ Table Tennis News - 8; £2.75.

English Tiddlywinks Association (ETwA) 1958
■ 47 Swansholme Gardens, SANDY, Beds, SG19 1HL.   (chmn/p)
    01767 225744
    email ajdean47@msn.com   http://www.etwa.org
    Chmn: Alan Dean,   Sec: Miss Sarah Knight
▲ Un-incorporated Society
○ *S; to promote the game of tiddlywinks throughout the UK
● Comp
< Intl Fedn Tiddlywinks Assns
M 80 i, UK / 5 i, o'seas
    (Sub: £6 UK / £10 o'seas)
¶ Winking World - 2; ftm, £3 nm.

English UK   2004
- ■ 219 St John St, LONDON, EC1V 4LY.   (hq)
     020 7608 7960   fax 020 7608 7961
     email info@englishuk.com   http://www.englishuk.com
     Chief Exec: Tony Millns
- ▲ Registered Charity
- ○ *E, *P; British Council accredited English language teaching
     providers
- Gp Business English UK; Work Experience UK
- ● Conf - ET - Res - Exhib - Inf - LG
- < Eur Fedn of Nat Assns for Teaching Mother Tongues to Foreign
     Students (ELITE); Assn of Language Teaching Orgs (ALTO)
- M 330 f
- ¶ English UK News - 4;   English in the UK - 1; both free.

English Volleyball Association   (EVA)   1971
- NR SportPark, Loughborough University, 3 Oakwood Drive,
     LOUGHBOROUGH, Leics, LE11 3QF.   (hq)
     01509 227722   fax 01509 227733
     email info@volleyballengland.org
     http://www.volleyballengland.org
- ○ *S; governing body for volleyball, beach volleyball and sitting
     volleyball
- M c 18,000 i
     Note: operates under the title Volleyball England

English Westerners Society   (EWS)   1954
- NR 76 Millfield Rd, West Kingsdown, SEVENOAKS, KENT,
     TN15 6BU.   (chmn/p)
     email keg.cagb@btinternet.com
     http://www.english-westerners-society.org.uk
     Chmn: Robert Wybrow
- ▲ Un-incorporated Society
- ○ *G; study of the history of the American West, incl ethnological
     & cultural background
- ● AGM only
- < Westerners Intl (USA)
- M 150 i, UK / 55 i, o'seas
     (Sub: £12.50)
- ¶ Tally Sheet - 3;   Brand Book - 1/3;
     Special publication - irreg; all ftm, prices vary nm.
     AR - 1; free.

English Wine Producers   (EWP)   1992
- ■ PO Box 5729, MARKET HARBOROUGH, Leics, LE16 8WX.
     (mail)
     01536 772264   fax 01536 772263
     email info@englishwineproducers.com
     http://www.englishwineproducers.com
     Contact: Julia Trustram Eve
- ○ *T
- < UK Vineyards Assn
- M c 20 i

English Women's Bowling Association
     in 2007 merged with the English Bowling Association to form **Bowls England**

English Women's Golf
     merged on 1 Jan 2012 with the English Golf Union to form **England Golf**

English Women's Indoor Bowling Association
     on 1 December 2008 merged with the **English Indoor Bowling Association**

Enid Blyton Society   1995
- NR 93 Milford Hill, SALISBURY, Wilts, SP1 2QL.   (mail)
     http://www.enidblytonsociety.co.uk
- ○ *A; for Enid Blyton collectors & enthusiasts
- ● Enid Blyton Day
- ¶ Jnl - 3.

Entertainment & Leisure Software Publishers Association Ltd
     since 2010 **United Kingdom Interactive Entertainment Association**

Entertainment Retailers Association   (ERA)   1988
- ■ Colonnade House, 2 Westover Rd, BOURNEMOUTH, Dorset,
     BH1 2BY.   (hq)
     01202 292063   fax 01202 292067
     email admin@eraltd.org   http://www.eraltd.org
     Dir Gen: Kim Bayley
- ▲ Company Limited by Guarantee
- ○ *T; for the physical & digital retail & wholesale sectors of the
     music, video & videogames industries
- ● Conf - Mtgs - Res - Stat - Inf - LG
- M 150 f
- × 2006 (July) British Association of Record Dealers

Environment & Planning Law Association
     a group of the **Law Society of Northern Ireland**

Environmental Communicators' Organisation   (ECO)   1972
- ■ 8 Hooks Cross, Watton-at-Stone, HERTFORD, SG14 3RY.
     (chmn/p)
     01920 830527
     email alanmassam@btinternet.com
     Chmn: Alan Massam
- ▲ Un-incorporated Society
- ○ *K; promotion of conservationist ideas among professional
     journalists & broadcasters
- ● Res - Inf - PR support for green orgs
- < Brit Naturalists Assn
- M 300 i
- ¶ NL - irreg.

Environmental Health Officers' Association   1949
- IRL Heraghty House, 4 Carlton Terrace, Novara Avenue, BRAY,
     Co Wicklow, Republic of Ireland.
     353 (1) 276 1211   fax 353 (1) 276 4665
     http://www.ehoa.ie
- ○ *P

Environmental Industries Commission Ltd   (EIC)   1995
- NR 45 Weymouth St, LONDON, W1G 8ND.   (hq)
     020 7935 1675   fax 020 7486 3455
     email info@eic-uk.co.uk   http://www.eic-uk.co.uk
     Chief Exec: Adrian Wilkes
- ○ *N, *T; to represent the UK's environmental technology sector
- ● Conf - Mtgs - Res - Exhib - Expt - Inf - Lib - LG
- M 295 f, UK / 5 f, o'seas
- ¶ Envirotech News EU - 4;   Envirotech News UK - 12;
     both ftm, £135 nm.

Environmental Noise Barrier Association
     a group of the **Fencing Contractors' Association**

© CBD Research Ltd · Beckenham · BR3 5JS · Tel 020 8650 7745 · E-mail cbd@cbdresearch.com · www.cbdresearch.com

Environmental Protection UK   1898
■   44 Grand Parade, BRIGHTON, E Sussex, BN2 9QA.   (hq)
      01273 878770   fax 01273 606626
      email admin@environmental-protection.org.uk
      http://www.environmental-protection.org.uk
      Chief Exec: James Grugeon
▲   Registered Charity
Br 10
○   *K; to provide expert policy analysis & advice on air quality,
      land quality, waste & noise & their effects on people &
      communities in terms of a wide range of issues including
      public health, planning, transport, energy & climate
●   Conf - Mtgs - ET - Res - Inf - Lib - LG
<   Intl U of Air Pollution Prevention & Envtl Protection Assns
      (IUAPPA); Eur Envt Bureau (EEB)
M   344 i, 337 f & org
      (Sub: £60 i - £2,750 corporate, variable f & org)
¶   Briefing (NL) - 12;   AR - 1; both ftm only.
      Pollution Control Hbk - 1;   Reports - irreg.
      Information leaflets & booklets; £12-£20.
✕   2007 (October) National Society for Clean Air & Environmental
      Protection

Environmental Services Association   (ESA)   1969
■   154 Buckingham Palace Rd, LONDON, SW1W 9TR.   (hq)
      020 7824 8882   fax 020 7824 8753
      email info@esauk.org   http://www.esauk.org
      Chief Exec: Dirk Hazell
▲   Company Limited by Guarantee
○   *T; for the waste management industry (including collection,
      treatment, disposal, recovery, recycling, & use of waste in the
      commercial & industrial sectors), specialist equipment
      manufacturers, & consultants
Gp Affilates; Consultants; Overseas; Plant & equipment
      manufacturers
●   Conf - Mtgs - ET - Res - Exhib - SG - Expt - Inf - Lib - VE - LG -
      Annual lunch & AGM
<   Fedn Waste Mgt & Envtl Services (FEAD); Confedn of Brit Ind
      (CBI); UN GlobalCompact
M   250 f
¶   Guidelines; ftm, prices vary nm.   AR; free.

**Environmental & Technical Association for the Paper Sack
Industry   (ETAPS)**
NR 24 Grange St, KILMARNOCK, Ayrshire, KA1 2AR.   (hq)
      01563 570518   fax 01563 572728
      Sec: Allan Glen
▲   Un-incorporated Society
○   *T; for paper sack producing companies
●   Mtgs - Exhib - Inf
M   6 f, UK / 2 f, o'seas

Ephemera Society   1975
NR PO Box 112, NORTHWOOD, Middx, HA6 2WT.   (mail)
      01923 829079
      email info@ephemera-society.org.uk
      http://www.ephemera-society.org.uk
      Sec: Graham Hudson
▲   Un-incorporated Society
Br 1; Australia, Austria, Canada, USA
○   *G; the conservation, study & presentation of printed &
      handwritten ephemera (the minor transient documents of
      everyday life)
●   Mtgs - Inf - VE - Bazaars
<   Foundation for Ephemera Studies
M   700 i, f & org
      (Sub: £20 UK, £25 Eur, £30 RoW)
¶   The Ephemerist - 4;   Members' Hbk - updated; both ftm only.

Epilepsy Action
      see **British Epilepsy Association**

Epilepsy Scotland   (ES)   1954
NR 48 Govan Rd, GLASGOW, G51 1JL.   (hq)
      0141-427 4911   fax 0141-419 1709
      email enquiries@epilepsyscotland.org.uk
      http://www.epilepsyscotland.org.uk
      Chief Exec: Lesslie Young
▲   Company Limited by Guarantee; Registered Charity
Br 10
○   *W; to work with people living with epilepsy to ensure their
      voice is heard
●   Conf - Mtgs - ET - Exam - Exhib - Inf - LG
      Helpline: 0808 800 2200
<   Intl Bureau for Epilepsy; Mobility Intl; Jt Epilepsy Coun (UK &
      Ireland)
M   632 i
¶   Epilepsy News (NL) - 2.   Factsheets;   AR.

Epiphytic Plant Study Group   (EPSG)   1968
NR 31 Ribble Drive, Barrow-upon-Soar, LOUGHBOROUGH, Leics,
      LE12 8LJ.   (hsp)
      http://www.epiphytes.co.uk
      Sec: John F Horobin
▲   Un-incorporated Society
○   *H; to foster an interest in epiphytic plants; to circulate
      information about such plants that would not otherwise be
      readily available
M   175 i, UK & o'seas
¶   Epiphytes (Jnl) - 4.

Eppynt Hill & Beulah Speckled Face Sheep Society
NR The Firs, 63 Garth Rd, BUILTH WELLS, Powys, LD2 3NH.   (hsp)
      01982 553726   fax 01982 553726
      http://www.beulahsheep.co.uk
      Sec: Dennis J Jones
○   *B
<   Nat Sheep Assn

Equestrian Federation of Ireland
      merged 2007 with the Irish Horse Board to form **Horse Sport
      Ireland**

Equiano Society   1996
NR 15 Bramdean Gardens, LONDON, SE12 0NT.   (hsp)
      Sec: Arthur Torrington
○   *G; to celebrate & promote the life & work of the abolitionist,
      Olaudah Equiano (c1745-1797)
●   The Equiano Project (with Birmingham Museums & Art Gallery)

Equine Behaviour Forum   (EBF)   1978
■   Sea View Cottage, 41 New Rd, SHOREHAM-BY-SEA, W Sussex,
      BN43 6RB.   (memsec/p)
      http://www.gla.ac.uk/external/ebf/
      Mem Sec: Wendy Hardy
▲   Un-incorporated Society
○   *L; to exchange information on the behaviour of horses in all
      situations
●   Lib (advice)
M   c 300 i, UK / c 50 i, o'seas
¶   Equine Behaviour - 4.

Equine Shiatsu Association   (tESA)   2002
NR The Cottage, 1 East Heads Steading, NEWMILNS, Ayrshire,
      KA16 9LG.   (chmn/p)
      07961 925411
      email andrea.hibbert4@btinternet.com
      http://www.equineshiatsu.org
      Chmn: Andrea Hibbert
○   *V; to publicise the benefits of shiatsu on horses
M   30 i, UK & Ireland / 2 i, o'seas
¶   Shiatsu Practitioners Register (on website)

Equine Sports Massage Association   (ESMA)
NR   Haycroft Barn, Lower Wick, DURSLEY, Glos, GL11 6DD.   (hsp)
      01453 511814
      http://www.equinemassageassociation.co.uk
      Hon Sec: Merran McLachlan
○   *V; to ensure the client receives services from a fully trained &
      qualified equine sports masseur; to maintain a high standard
      of practice & code of conduct by all its members
●   ET - Exam
M   88 i, UK & Ireland / 2 i, o'seas

Equitoy: the association for toy importers   1950
■   Somers, Mounts Hill, BENENDEN, Kent, TN17 4ET.   (asa)
      01580 240819   fax 01580 241109
      Sec: Alan Milne
▲   Un-incorporated Society
○   *T
●   Conf - Mtgs - Exhib - LG - Lobbying European Commission -
      Advice on toy safety
M   c 2 i, 100 f, UK / 1 f, o'seas
¶   LM - updated.
      Advice on toy safety & importing quality procedures - updated
      on law or regulations change.
×   2006 British Toy Importers Association

Ergonomics Society   (ES)   1949
■   Elms Court, Elms Grove, LOUGHBOROUGH, Leics,
      LE11 1RG.   (hq)
      01509 234904   fax 01509 235666
      email ergsoc@ergonomics.org.uk
      http://www.ergonomics.org.uk
      Chief Exec: David O'Neill
▲   Company Limited by Guarantee; Registered Charity
○   *L; promotes ergonomics & the work of ergonomists, whose
      anatomical, physiological & psychological knowledge can
      help solve problems that arise between people, their working
      environment & the things they use
Gp   Professional affairs board; Regional & special interest groups
●   Conf - Mtgs - Exhib - Inf - VE - LG
      Providing ergonomics information to young people through
      www.ergonomics4schools.com
<   Intl Ergonomics Assn
M   1,100 i, 59 f, UK / 300 i, o'seas
¶   The Ergonomist NL - 12; ftm only.
      Consultancy Register.
      Applied Ergonomics - 6; £80 m.
      Behaviour & Information Technology - 6; £50 m, £192 nm.
      Ergonomics - 15; £50 m, £805 nm.
      Ergonomics in design - 4; £29 m.
      International Jnl of Injury Control & Safety Promotion - 4;
         £51.50 m, £60 nm.
      Jnl of Sports Sciences - 12; £60.
      Theoretical Issues in Ergonomics - 6; £50 m, £166 nm.
      Work & Stress - 4; £50 m, £13 nm.

**Eriskay Pony Mother Studbook Society   (Comann Each nan
Eilean Ltd)   1972**
NR   Talle Chidhe, Lochboisdale, SOUTH UIST, HS8 5TJ.   (regd off)
      01878 700828
      email eriskaypony@btinternet.com
      http://www.eriskaypony.com
      Chmn: Sheila McIntosh
▲   Registered Charity
○   *B

Eriskay Pony Society
NR   Carsaig, Gauls of Murthly, nr DUNKELD, Perthshire,
      PH1 4HT.   (hsp)
      01350 728063
      http://www.eriskaypony.com
      Sec: Jeanette Seaman
○   *B
M   c 130 i

Esperanto-Asocio de Skotlando
   see **Scottish Esperanto Association**

**Esperanto Association of Britain   (Esperanto-Asocio de Britio)
(EAB)   1904**
■   Esperanto House, Station Rd, Barlaston, STOKE-ON-TRENT,
      Staffs, ST12 9DE.   (hq)
      0845 230 1887   fax 01782 372229
      email eab@esperanto-gb.org
      http://www.esperanto-gb.org
      Hon Sec: Tim Owen
▲   Registered Charity
○   K; to advance the education of the public in the international
      language Esperanto in the furtherance of international
      communication without discrimination & of the natural right
      of all people & peoples, their languages & cultures to be
      treated equally
●   Conf - ET - Exam - Res - SG - Inf - Lib - LG
<   Universala Esperanto-Asocio (UEA)
M   460 i
¶   La Brita Esperantisto (Jnl) - 2; ftm, £2.40 nm.
      EAB Update (NL) - 4; ftm only.

**Essential Role of Sheltered Housing National Consortium
(ERoSH)   1997**
■   PO Box 2616, CHIPPENHAM, Wilts, SN15 1WZ.   (mail)
      01249 654249
      email info@shelteredhousing.org
      http://www.shelteredhousing.org
      Hon Sec: Linda Milton
▲   Registered Charity
○   *W; to raise awareness & illustrate the viability & benefits of the
      range of sheltered housing & related support services
●   Conf - ET - Comp - Inf

Essex Agricultural Society   1858
■   Writtle Agricultural College, Lordships Rd, CHELMSFORD,
      Essex, CM1 3RR.   (hq)
      01245 424113
      email heather.tarrant@essexag.co.uk
      http://www.essexag.co.uk
      Sec: Heather Tarrant
▲   Company Limited by Guarantee; Registered Charity
○   *F; to promote & advance agriculture for the benefit of the
      public through education & publicity; sponsorship of the
      County Farms competition & County Ploughing
      Championship (not the Essex Show)
●   ET - Exhib - Comp
M   350 i
¶   NL - 4;   AR; both free.

Essex Archaeological & Historical Congress   (EAHC)   1964
■   101 Farmleigh Avenue, CLACTON-ON-SEA, Essex,
      CO15 4UL.   (hsp)
      Hon Sec: N Jacobs
▲   Registered Charity
○   *L; to advance the education of the public in archaeology,
      history & conservation in Essex
●   Conf - Mtgs - Res - Exhib - Inf
<   Brit Assn for Local History (BALH); Coun Brit Archaeology
M   95 org
¶   Essex Jnl - 2; £10 yr (£5 each).   NL - 3;   AR; both ftm.

Essex Chambers of Commerce   (ECCI)   1997
NR   8-9 St Peter's Court, COLCHESTER, Essex, CO1 1WD.   (hq)
       01206 765277   fax 01206 578073
       email enquiries@essexchambers.co.uk
       http://www.essexchambers.co.uk
       Viscount House (2nd floor), London Southend Airport,
       Essex, SS2 6YF.   01702 560100
       Chief Exec: Denise Rossiter
▲   Company Limited by Guarantee
○   *C, *N
●   Conf - Mtgs - ET - Exam - Res - Exhib - Comp - Expt - Inf - Lib -
       VE - LG
<   Brit Chams Comm
M   2,500 f including affiliated chambers
¶   Business Plus - 12; ftm & enquirers.
       Essex Chambers Directory (incl LM/firms) - 1; ftm, £30 nm.

Essex Society for Archaeology & History   (ESAH)   1852
■   2 Landview Gardens, ONGAR, Essex, CM5 9EQ.   (hsp)
       01277 363106
       email leach1939@yahoo.co.uk   http://www.essex.ac.uk/
       history/esah
       Hon Sec: Dr Michael Leach
▲   Registered Charity
○   *L; study of, & promotion of interest in, archaeology & history of
       the historic County of Essex
Gp   Essex Place-names Project
●   Conf - Mtgs - ET - Res - Lib - VE
<   Coun Brit Archaeology; Scole C'ee; Stdg Conf on London
       Archaeology; Brit Assn for Local History
>   various local history societies
M   380 i, 60 academic bodies, UK / 20 academic bodies, o'seas
       (Sub: £20 i, £25 academic bodies)
¶   Essex Archaeology & History - 1; ftm, £18 nm.
       Essex Archaeology & History News - 3; ftm, £1 nm.

Essex Wildlife Trust Ltd   (EWT)   1959
■   Abbotts Hall Farm, Great Wigborough, COLCHESTER, Essex,
       CO5 7RZ.   (hq)
       01621 862960   fax 01621 862990
       email admin@essexwt.org.uk
       http://www.essexwt.org.uk
       Sec: Valerie M Crookes
▲   Company Limited by Guarantee; Registered Charity
○   *G; nature conservation
●   ET - VE
<   The Wildlife Trusts
M   17,500 i, 470 f, UK / 9 i, o'seas
¶   Essex Wildlife - 3; free.

ESTA Energy Services & Technology Association   (ESTA)   1982
NR   PO Box 77, BENFLEET, Essex, SS7 5EX.   (mail/address)
       01268 569010   fax 01268 569737
       http://www.esta.org.uk
       Exec Dir: Alan Aldridge
▲   Company Limited by Guarantee
○   *T; for companies that supply products & services covering
       energy efficiency monitoring, control, operation &
       management of buildings, building services & process
       services; to help businesses design, construct, operate &
       manage their facilities at a lower energy cost, while
       improving sustainability & reducing CO2 emissions
M   100 f
✕   2010 Energy Systems Trade Association

Estuarine & Coastal Sciences Association   (ECSA)   1971
NR   c/o Dr Mark Fitzsimons, Biogeochemistry Research Centre
       (SoGEES), University of Plymouth, PLYMOUTH, Devon,
       PL4 8AA.   (sb)
       email mfitzsimons@plymouth.ac.uk
       http://www.ecsa-news.org
       Sec: Dr Mark Fitzsimons
▲   Registered Charity
○   *L, *P, *Q; to promote knowledge & understanding of estuaries
       & brackish waters in order to prevent environmental
       deterioration; to encourage resource management for the
       public benefit
M   i & f

Ethical Trading Initiative   (ETI)   1998
■   8 Coldbath Square, LONDON, EC1R 5HL.   (hq)
       020 7841 4350   fax 020 7833 1569
       email eti@eti.org.uk   http://www.ethicaltrade.org
       Dir: Dan Rees
▲   Company Limited by Guarantee
○   *K; an alliance of companies, NGOs & trade unions committed
       to working together to identify & promote good practice in
       the implementation of codes of labour practice
●   Conf - Mtgs - ET - Res - Inf - LG
M   c 50 orgs
¶   Various occasional publications.

Eton Fives Association   (EFA)   1930
■   3 Bourchier Close, SEVENOAKS, Kent, TN13 1PD.   (hsp)
       01732 458775
       email efa@etonfives.co.uk   http://www.etonfives.co.uk
       Hon Sec: Mike Fenn
▲   Company Limited by Guarantee
○   *S; to promote & encourage the playing of Eton Fives both at
       school & adult level
●   Comp - Inf
M   550 i, 70 org, UK / 25 i, 8 org, o'seas
¶   NL - 1.   AR - 1; both ftm only.

EURISOL-UK Ltd
       see **Mineral Wool Insulation Manufacturers Association**

European Association of Veterinary Diagnostic Imaging
       a group of the **British Small Animal Veterinary Association**

European-Atlantic Group   (E-AG)   1954
■   4 St Pauls Way, LONDON, N3 2PP.   (hq)
       020 8632 9253   fax 020 8343 3532
       email info@eag.org.uk   http://www.eag.org.uk
       Dir: Justin Glass
▲   Registered Charity
○   *K; to promote closer relations between the European & Atlantic
       countries by providing a regular forum in Britain for informed
       discussion of their problems & possibilities for better
       economic & political cooperation with each other & the rest
       of the world
●   Conf - Mtgs - ET - LG
M   1,000 i, 20 f
       Subs: £29 i, £250 f.
¶   European-Atlantic Jnl - 2.   NL - 2.
       Elma Dangerfield Prize - 1.

The European Atlantic Movement (TEAM) 1958
NR   Cloverdown, Green Hill, HIGH WYCOMBE, Bucks,
      HP13 5QH.   (hq)
      01494 436636
      email info@european-atlantic.org.uk
      http://www.european-atlantic.org.uk
      Chmn: Laurence Smy
▲   Registered Charity
○   *E; to promote an understanding & discussion of world affairs
      which empowers young people to be active global citizens &
      to aspire to leadership roles within their communities
●   Conf - SG - VE
<   Atlantic Coun
M   95 i, 25 schools, UK / 35 i, o'seas

European Information Association (EIA) 1991
NR   PO Box 28, MOLD, Flintshire, CH7 6FE.   (hq)
      01352 700051
      email eric@eia.org.uk   http://www.eia.org.uk
      Coordinator: Eric Davies
▲   Registered Charity
○   *P; to develop, coordinate & improve access to European Union
      information
●   Conf - Mtgs - ET - Exhib - Inf - Liaison with EU instns
M   i, f & org
¶   Publications on various subjects linked to EU information.
      'The EIA committee has decided that the Association should be
      dissolved at the end of 2012'

European Liquid Waterproofing Association
      see **LRWA, the Liquid Roofing & Waterproofing Association**

European Movement of the United Kingdom Ltd   1948
NR   Southbank House (room 203), Black Prince Rd, LONDON,
      SE1 7SU.   (hq)
      020 3176 0543
      email info@euromove.org.uk
      http://www.euromove.org.uk
▲   Company Limited by Guarantee
Br   50
○   *K; to campaign for support for, & understanding of, the
      European Union & other European institutions
●   Conf - Mtgs - SG - Inf
M   2,500 i

European Window Film Association
      see **Glass & Glazing Federation**

Europilots - the Association of Licensed Deep Sea Pilots   1972
■   2 Dormy Avenue, Mannamead, PLYMOUTH, Devon,
      PL3 5BY.   (hsp)
      01752 262845   fax 01752 262845
      email secretary@europilots.org.uk
      http://www.europilots.org.uk
      Sec: Captain John Hunt
▲   Un-incorporated Society
○   *P; for licensed pilots of port & estuaries
●   Liaison with maritime authorities
M   30 i
      (Sub: £84)

Eurythmy Association of Great Britain & Ireland   2006
NR   BCM Eurythmy Association of GB & Ireland, LONDON,
      WC1N 3XX.   (mail)
      01924 255281 (241323 evgs)
      http://www.eurythmyassociation.org.uk
      Sec: Lynda Abrahams
○   *P; to further the work of eurythmy & eurythmists throughout the
      British Isles
●   ET - Exhib - Mtgs
M   i
¶   NL.

Evacuees Reunion Association (ERA) 1995
NR   The Mill Business Centre, Mill Hill, Gringley-on-the-Hill,
      DONCASTER, DN10 4RA.   (hq)
      01777 816166
      email era@evacuees.org.uk   http://www.evacuees.org.uk
      Chief Exec: James Roffey
▲   Registered Charity
○   *G; to ensure that the true story of the evacuation of children
      during the Second World War become better known &
      preserved for future generations
●   Conf - Mtgs - ET - Res - Exhib - SG - Inf - VE
M   3,500 i, UK / 100 i, o'seas
¶   The Evacuee - 6.

Evaluation International (EI) 1963
■   East Malling Enterprise Centre, New Rd, EAST MALLING, Kent,
      ME19 6BJ.   (hsb)
      0845 644 4602   fax 01732 897453
      email info@evaluation-international.com
      http://www.evaluation-international.com
      Mgr: Peter Russell,   Sec: Dr Derek Cornish
▲   Company Limited by Guarantee
○   *T; to commission independent evaluations of instruments, for
      measurement & control, on behalf of member companies
      who are instrument users
Gp   Technical panel
●   Conf - Mtgs - Res - Exhib - Stat - Inf - Lib - LG - Preparation of
      instrumentation guides
<   Intl Instrument Users' Assn; WIB (Netherlands); EXERCA
      (France)
M   10 f, UK / 75 f, o'seas
¶   Electronic NL - 6; free.
      Instrument Evaluation Reports - 20; ftm only.
      Instrument Selection Guides - 20; ftm, £50-£200 each nm.

Evangelical Alliance UK (EAUK) 1846
NR   186 Kennington Park Rd, LONDON, SE11 4BT.   (hq)
      020 7207 2100 (Mon-Fri 0900-1700)   fax 020 7207
      2150
      email info@eauk.org   http://www.eauk.org
      Gen Dir: Rev Joel Edwards
▲   Registered Charity
Br   England, Wales, Northern Ireland
○   *N, *R; providing a voice for evangelical Christians to
      government, the media & society
Gp   Alliance commission on unity & truth among evangelicals;
      Reaching older people; Stewardship forum; Evangelical
      coalition on drugs;
      Networks: Care for pastors, Disability; EA youth & children
●   Conf - Inf - LG
<   Wld Evangelical Fellowship; Eur Evangelical Alliance
M   38,000 i, 6,000 churches, 725 org
¶   idea (Jnl) - 6;
      Leaders-digest.com - 6 (online); both ftm only.

Event Horse Owners Association (EHOA) 1998
NR   Wolfhamcote Barn, Flecknoe, RUGBY, Warks, CV23 8AU.   (hq)
      email chris.gillespie@fsmail.net   http://www.ehoa.org
      Sec: Chris Gillespie
▲   Company Limited by Guarantee
○   *S; to encourage participation in the sport of eventing
●   Comp - ET - Mtgs - VE
M   1,000 i
¶   NL - irreg.

Event Riders Association   (ERA)
NR   The Annexe, Home Idover Farm, Dauntsey, CHIPPENHAM,
      Wilts, SN15 4JJ.   (asa)
      email secretary@eventridersassociationuk.org
      http://www.eventridersassociationuk.org
      Hon Sec: John Foden
○   *S; for British-based event riders

© CBD Research Ltd · Beckenham · BR3 5JS · Tel 020 8650 7745 · E-mail cbd@cbdresearch.com · www.cbdresearch.com

The Event Services Association (TESA) 1991

NR   Association House, 18c Moor St, CHEPSTOW, Monmouthshire,
        NP16 5DB.   (hq)
        01291 636331   fax 01291 630402
        email info@tesa.org.uk   http://www.tesa.org.uk
        Dir: Jim Winship
○   *T; to promote good practice in the event industry & to
        represent the interests of event organisers, promoters &
        suppliers
Gp   Electrics; Event organisers & venues; Fireworks; Mobile units;
        Security
●   Mtgs - Inf - LG
M   20 i, 180 f, UK / 4 f, o'seas
¶   Event Organiser - 6; ftm, £48 nm.

Event Supplier & Services Association (ESSA) 2008

■   119 High St, BERKHAMSTED, Herts, HP4 2DJ.   (hq)
        01442 285812,   0845 122 1880   fax 01442 875551
        email info@essa.uk.com   http://www.essa.uk.com
        Dir: Chris Sketh
▲   Un-incorporated Society
○   *T; for contractors working in partnership with organisers &
        venues to promote quality & value for exhibitors thus raising
        the profile of exhibitions as a medium
●   Conf - Mtgs - ET - Res - Exhib - Inf - LG
<   Events Ind Alliance (EIA)
×   2008 (Association of Exhibition Contractors
        (British Exhibition Contractors' Association

Eventia Ltd (EVENTIA) 2006

■   Galbraith House (5th floor), 141 Great Charles St,
        BIRMINGHAM, B3 3LG.   (hq)
        0121-212 1400   fax 0121-212 3131
        email info@eventia.org.uk   http://www.eventia.org.uk
        Exec Dir: Izania Downie;   Project Dir: Tony Rogers
▲   Company Limited by Guarantee
○   *T; for organisations providing events, business meetings &
        conferences, motivational experiences, training &
        communications activity, incentive travel programmes,
        celebratory functions, corporate hospitality
Gp   Education; CSR; Awards; Regulations & representation;
        Membership
●   Conf - Mtgs - ET - Exhib - LG - Annual awards ceremony &
        dinner
<   Business Visits & Events Partnership
M   14 i, 206 f, UK / 51 f, o'seas
        (Sub: £100 enrolment, £75 i, & by turnover c £350-£1.000)
¶   Ybk - 1.
×   2008 British Association of Conference Destinations

Events Sector Industry Training Organisation (ESITO) 1995

NR   Tetford House, East Road, Tetford, HORNCASTLE, Lincs,
        LN9 6QQ.   (admin/p)
        01507 533639
        15 Osborne Gdns, THORNTON HEATH, Surrey, CR7 8PA.
        [regd off]
        Admin: Peggy Glendinning
▲   Company Limited by Guarantee
○   *N; forum for training & development in the events sector:
        which comprises conferences, meetings, exhibitions, outdoor
        events, events services, incentive & business travel & venues.
        Also acts as the coordinating body for pursuing these issues
        & the development of occupational standards & NVQs with
        government departments, educational bodies, NTOs & other
        organisations
●   ET - Exam - SG - Inf - LG
<   Business Tourism Partnership (BTP); Association for Conferences
        & Events (ACE)
M   6 org, UK / 3 org, o'seas
¶   AR; ftm.

Examining Officers Association (EOA) 2001

NR   London Road Campus (G11-Bldg L11), University of Reading,
        READING, Berks, RG1 5AQ.   (hq)
        0118-975 8552   fax 0118-975 8512
        email info@examofficers.org.uk
        http://www.examofficers.org.uk
        Chief Exec: Andrew Harland
▲   Registered charity
○   *P; an independent non-union organisation supporting the
        professional development of exam office personnel working
        in centres throughout the UK
●   Inf - LG - Mtgs
M   i
¶   NL - by email; ftm.

Excellence Ireland Quality Association (EIQA) 1969

IRL   9 Appian Way, Ranelagh, DUBLIN 6, Republic of Ireland.   (hq)
        353 (1) 660 4100   fax 353 (1) 660 4280
        email info@eiqa.com   http://www.eiqa.com
        Managing Dir: Irene Collins
○   *P; offers solutions to customers that are committed to
        improving their hygiene & quality standards

Executive Research Association (ERA) 1986

NR   Unit 28, The Old Silk Mill, Brook St, TRING, Herts, HP23 5EF.
        (hq)
        01442 828846
        email sarah@theera.org   http://www.theera.org
        Mem Sec: Sarah El-Rasoul
○   *P; to provide an awareness of & an interest in executive search
        generally, & the research function specifically, within the
        industry as a whole
●   Conf - Mtgs
M   92 i

Executives' Association of Great Britain Ltd (EAGB) 1929

NR   PO Box 965, UXBRIDGE, Middx, UB8 9JN.   (hq)
        01375 893414
        http://www.eagb.co.uk
        Contact: Andrea Matyszczyk
Br   4; Canada, South Africa, USA
○   *P; business contacts & opportunities for networking
●   Conf - Mtgs
<   Intl Coordinators' Conf of Executives Assns
M   250 f, UK / 5,000 f, o'seas
¶   Bulletin - 12;   NL - 4;   Ybk - 1; all ftm only.

Exercise, Movement & Dance Partnership
see EMDP: moving together

Exeter Chamber of Commerce (1992) Ltd 1992

■   10 Southernhay West, EXETER, Devon, EX1 1JG.   (mail)
        01392 431133   fax 01392 278804
        email enqiries@exeterchamber.co.uk
        http://www.exeterchamber.co.uk
        Hon Sec: Michael Martin
▲   Company Limited by Guarantee
○   *C
●   Mtgs - Inf
M   350 f
¶   LM - 1;   AR - 1; both ftm.

Exhibition Study Group (ESG) 1980

NR 46 Thorncliffe Rd, Norwood Green, SOUTHALL, Middx,
   UB2 5RQ. (memsec/p)
   email wembleymad@btinternet.com
   http://www.studygroup.org.uk
   Mem Sec: Alan Sabey
▲ Un-incorporated Society
○ *G; for collectors of memorabilia (souvenirs, books,
   commemorative china, postcards etc) of national &
   international exhibitions, from the 1851 Great Exhibition
   onwards
● Conf - Res - Exhib - SG - Book publishing
M 100 i, UK / 5 i, o'seas
¶ Jnl - 4.

Exit

■ 17 Hart St, EDINBURGH, EH1 3RN. (hq)
   0131-556 4404
   http://www.euthanasia.cc
   Dir: Chris Docker
▲ Un-incorporated Society
○ *K; campaigns for a change in British law to promote individual
   choice in end of life matters such as voluntary euthanasia,
   assisted suicide & living wills.
● Conf - Res - Inf
M i
   (Sub: £20-£30)
¶ NL - 1; £20 m.   Five Last Acts (book); £10 m.
   Departing Drugs (booklet); £8 m.   all prices for UK.
✕ 2000 Voluntary Euthanasia Society of Scotland

Exmoor Horn Sheep Breeders' Society 1906

■ Cornercott, Oldways End, East Anstey, TIVERTON, Devon,
   EX16 9JQ. (hsp)
   01398 341372
   email info@exmoorhornbreeders.co.uk
   http://www.exmoorhornbreeders.co.uk
   Sec: Mrs Jan Brown
○ *B; to further the breeding of Exmoor sheep & their crosses
● Mtgs - Exhib - Inf - VE
< Nat Sheep Assn
M 152 i
¶ NL - 4;   Flock Book - 1; £2.

Exmoor Pony Society 1921

■ Woodmans, Brithem Bottom, CULLOMPTON, Devon,
   EX15 1NB. (hsp)
   01884 839930
   email secretary@exmoorponysociety.org.uk
   http://www.exmoorponysociety.org.uk
   Sec: Sue McGeever
▲ Company Limited by Guarantee; Registered Charity
○ *B
● Comp - Inf
M 600 i, UK / 25 i, o'seas
¶ NL - 1; ftm only.

Exmouth Chamber of Trade & Commerce 1896

NR c/o Tourist Information Bureau, Alexandra Terrace, EXMOUTH,
   Devon, EX8 1NZ. (mail)
   01395 275133
   email secretary@exmouthchamber.co.uk
   http://www.exmouthchamber.co.uk
   Sec: Robin Adams
▲ Un-incorporated Society
○ *C
● Exhib - Mtgs
M c 150 i & f
¶ The Town Guide - 1.

Experimental Food Society 2010

NR c/o apr consultancy, 14 Great Jubilee Wharf, 78-80 Wapping
   Wall, LONDON, E1W 3TH. (asa)
   020 3051 8784
   http://www.experimentalfoodsociety.com
   Founder: Alexa Perrin
○ *G; for culinary creatives
M 47 i & f

Experimental Psychology Society (EPS) 1946

■ Dept of Experimental Psychology, University of Bristol,
   12a Priory Rd, BRISTOL, BS8 1TU. (hsb)
   http://www.eps.ac.uk
   Hon Sec: Dr Helen Cassaday
▲ Registered Charity
○ *P; for the furtherance of scientific enquiry within the field of
   psychology & cognate subjects
● Mtgs - Res - Inf
M c 600 i
¶ Quarterly Jnl of Experimental Psychology - 12.

Expert Witness Institute (EWI) 1996

NR 7 Warwick Court (1st floor), LONDON, WC1R 5DJ. (hq)
   0870 366 6367
   email info@ewi.org.uk   http://www.ewi.org.uk
▲ Company Limited by Guarantee
○ *P; the support of the proper administration of justice & the
   early resolution of disputes through fair & unbiased expert
   evidence; to encourage the use by lawyers of experts
● Conf - Mtgs - ET - Inf - LG - Helpline
M c 1,200 i & org
¶ NL - 3/4; ftm only.

Explosives Industry Group (EIG)

NR Centrepoint, 103 New Oxford St, London, WC1A 1DU. (hq)
   020 7395 8063   fax 020 7836 1972
   email info@eig.org.uk   http://www.eig.org.uk
   Sec: Brig Charles Smith
○ *T

Extruded Sealants Association

NR 18 Furness Avenue, Simonstone, BURNLEY, Lancs, BB12 7SU.
   (sp)
   01282 771260
   Sec: Paul Liles
○ *T
M f

© CBD Research Ltd · Beckenham · BR3 5JS · Tel 020 8650 7745 · E-mail cbd@cbdresearch.com · www.cbdresearch.com

Fabian Society   1884
NR   11 Dartmouth St, LONDON, SW1H 9BN.   (hq)
020 7227 4900
email info@fabians.org.uk   http://www.fabians.org.uk
Gen Sec: Andrew Harrop
○   *Q; political think tank
Gp   Fabian Women; Young Fabians
●   Conf - Mtgs - Res - SG
M   7,000 i
¶   Fabian Review (Jnl) - 4; £4.95
See website for publications list

Fabricated Access Covers Trade Association   (FACTA)   1995
■   42 Heath St, TAMWORTH, Staffs, B79 7JH.   (hq)
01827 52337   fax 01827 310627
email info@facta.org.uk   http://www.facta.org.uk
Sec: Michael Skelding
○   *T; for manufacturers of fabricated access (manhole) covers
●   Mtgs - Res - Inf - British & European Standards
M   11 f
(Sub: £750)
¶   FACTA Specification.

Face Painting Association   (FACE)   1995
NR   207 Guildford Rd, Bisley, WOKING, Surrey, GU24 9DL.
(chmn/p)
01483 851155
email angelfaces1@virginmedia.com
http://www.facepaint.co.uk
Chmn: Denise Mountstephens
○   *P; to improve standards & raise the profile of face painting
●   Conf - Mtgs
M   200 i
¶   Face to Face (Jnl) - 4; ftm, £25 nm.

Facilities Management Association   (FMA)   1995
NR   c/o Cripps Dransfield, 206 Upper Richmond Rd West,
LONDON, SW14 8AH.   (mail)
07974 357042
email info@fmassociation.org.uk
http://www.fmassociation.org.uk
Chief Exec: Chris Hoar
○   *T; for companies engaged in the provision of facility
management services
Gp   Young Managers Forum
M   f

Factors & Discounters Association
since 2007 **Asset Based Finance Association**

Faculty of Actuaries in Scotland
on 1 August 2010 merged with the Institute of Actuaries to form the
Institute & Faculty of Actuaries

Faculty of Advocates   1682
NR   Advocates' Library, Parliament House, EDINBURGH, EH1 1RF.
(hq)
0131-226 5071   fax 0131-225 3642
http://www.advocates.org.uk
○   *P; the practice of Scots law in all its aspects
M   i

Faculty of Astrological Studies   1948
NR   BM Box 7470, LONDON, WC1N 3XX.   (mail)
07000 790143   fax 07000 790143
http://www.astrology.org.uk
○   *P; study of basic natal astrology
M   c 2,000 i

Faculty of Dental Surgery   1947
NR   at the Royal College of Surgeons, 35-43 Lincoln's Inn Fields,
LONDON, WC2A 3PE.   (hq)
020 7405 3474
http://www.rcseng.ac.uk/fds
○   *E, *L; advancement of science & art of dentistry

Faculty of Family Planning & Reproductive Healthcare of the RCOG
since 2007 **Faculty of Sexual & Reproductive Healthcare**

Faculty of Forensic & Legal Medicine   (FFLM)   2006
■   116 Gt Portland St (3rd floor), LONDON, W1W 6PJ.   (hq)
020 7580 8490
email info@fflm.ac.uk   http://www.fflm.ac.uk
Registrar: Dr George Fernie
▲   Registered Charity
○   *M, *P; forensic and legal medicine
M   i
¶   Jnl.   Books.

Faculty of General Dental Practice (UK)   (FGDP(UK))   1992
NR   at the Royal College of Surgeons, 35-43 Lincoln's Inn Fields,
LONDON, WC2A 3PE.   (hq)
020 7869 6754   fax 020 7869 6765
http://www.fgdp.org.uk
Registrar: Ian Pocock
Br   21
○   *M, *P; to promote excellence in primary care dentistry
●   ET - Mtgs - Res - SG
M   5,000 i
¶   Team in Practice - 4;   Primary Dental Care - 4; both ftm.

Faculty of Homeopathy   1950
■   Hahnemann House, 29 Park Street West, LUTON, Beds,
LU1 3BE.   (hq)
0870 444 3955   fax 0870 444 3960
http://www.faculyofhomeopathy.org
Chief Exec: Sally Penrose
▲   Un-incorporated Society
Br   20
○   *L, *M, *P; to promote the academic & scientific development of
homeopathy; to regulate the education, training & practice of
homeopathy by doctors, veterinary surgeons, dentists, nurses,
midwives, pharmacists & other statutorily regulated
healthcare professionals
●   Conf - Mtgs - ET - Exam - Res - Exhib - SG - Inf - Lib - LG
<   Liga Medicorum Homoeopathica Internationalis (LIGA); Eur
C'ee for Homeopathy
M   800 i, UK / 300 i, o'seas
¶   Homeopathy Jnl - 4;   Simile (LM) - 4;
Membership Directory - 18 months; all ftm only.

Faculty of Occupational Medicine   (FOM RCP)   1978
■   New Derwent House (3rd floor), 69-73 Theobalds Rd,
LONDON, WC1X 8TA.   (hq)
020 7242 8698   fax 020 3116 8900
email fom@facoccmed.ac.uk
http://www.facoccmed.ac.uk
Chief Exec: Nichola Wilkins
▲   Registered Charity
○   *L, *P; to promote high standards in the training & practice of
occupational medicine
●   Conf - Mtgs - ET - Exam - Exhib - LG
<   EU of Med Specialities/section of Occupational Medicine; R
Coll of Physicians of London
M   1,700 i
¶   NL;   eletters;   Periodicals;   AR - 1.
Guidance on Ethics for Occupational Physicians; £25 nm.
Guidance on Alcohol & Drug Misuse in the Workplace; £26 nm.

Faculty of Pharmaceutical Medicine of the Royal Colleges of Physicians of the United Kingdom   (FPM)   1989
NR   30 Furnival St (3rd floor), LONDON, EC4A 1JQ.   (hq)
       020 7831 7662   fax 020 7831 3513
       email fpm@fpm.org.uk   http://www.fpm.org.uk
       Pres: Dr Richard Tiner
▲   Company Limited by Guarantee; Registered Charity
○   *M; to advance the science & practice of pharmaceutical
       medicine by working to develop & maintain competence,
       ethics & integrity & the highest professional standards in the
       specialty for the benefit of the public
Gp   Advocacy; Education; Ethical issues; International; Professional
       standards
M   910 i, UK / 490 i, o'seas
¶   NL - 4; ftm

Faculty of Professional Business & Technical Management   (PBTM)   1983
■   Warwick Corner, 42 Warwick Rd, KENILWORTH, Warks,
       CV8 1HE.   (hq)
       01926 259342
       email info@pbtm.org.uk   http://www.pbtm.org.uk
       Exec Admin: Lynne Sykes
○   *P; to support lifelong learning & encourage education in
       management, business & technology; to give professional
       recognition to the knowledge & skills of members
<   Academy of Execs & Administrators; Inst of Mfrg; Inst of Mgt
       Specialists
×   Professional Business & Technical Management

Faculty of Public Health   (FPH)   1972
NR   4 St Andrews Place, LONDON, NW1 4LB.   (hq)
       020 7935 0243   fax 020 7224 6973
       http://www.fph.org.uk
       Chief Exec: Paul Scourfield
○   *M, *N; is a joint faculty of the Royal Colleges of Physicians in
       the UK & shares in their efforts for the advancement of
       medical knowledge & care in the field of public health &
       medicine (the prevention of disease & the prolonging of life)

Faculty of Royal Designers for Industry   1936
NR   8 John Adam St, LONDON, WC2N 6EZ.   (hq)
       020 7930 5115   fax 020 7839 5805
       email melanie.andrews@rsa.org.uk
○   *P; 'the distinction of Royal Designer for Industry (RDI) was
       established by the Royal Society of Arts in 1936, to be
       conferred on persons who have achieved sustained
       excellence in aesthetic & efficient design for industry. Persons
       holding the distinction are members of the Faculty'

Faculty of Sexual & Reproductive Healthcare of the Royal College of Obstetricians & Gynaecologists   (FSRH)   1993
■   27 Sussex Place, LONDON, NW1 4RG.   (hq)
       020 7724 5524
       http://www.fsrh.org
       Co Sec: Corin Jones
▲   Company Limited by Guarantee; Registered Charity
○   *P; to maintain & develop standards of care & training of all
       providers of sexual & reproductive healthcare; to advance
       knowledge in the dsicipline & encourage research; to give
       academic status to the discipline
●   Conf - ET - Exam - Res - Inf (m only) - Essay competition for
       medical undergraduates
<   R Coll of Obstetricians & Gynaecologists
M   11,000 i, UK / 300 i, o'seas
¶   Journal of Family Planning & Reproductive Healthcare - 4;
       President's NL - 4;   AR;
       Recommendations for Clinical Practice - 1/2; all ftm.
×   2007 Faculty of Family Planning & Reproductive Healthcare

Fair Organ Preservation Society   (FOPS)   1958
NR   Gaythorpe, Blacketts Wood Drive, CHORLEYWOOD, Herts,
       WD3 5QQ.   (memsec/p)
       email memsec@fops.org
       Mem Sec: Norman Rogers
▲   Un-incorporated Society
Br   Australia, USA
○   *D, *G; promotion & encouragement of all forms of interest in,
       & the preservation of, fairground organs & other mechanical
       musical instruments
●   Conf - Mtgs - Res - Stat - Inf - VE - Register of organs available
       for events, nationwide
       Archives held within the National Fairground Archive at the
       University of Sheffield, (email: fairground@sheffield.ac.uk)
M   650 i, UK / 85 i, o'seas
       (Sub: £17 i)
¶   The Key Frame - 4; ftm only.   On Display (205 photos).

Fair Play for Children Association   (FPFC)   1972
■   32 Longford Rd, BOGNOR REGIS, W Sussex, PO21 1AG.
       (hsp)
       0845 330 7635
       email fairplay@arunet.co.uk   http://www.arunet.co.uk/
       fairplay/
       Hon Sec: Jan Cosgrove
▲   Company Limited by Guarantee; Registered Charity
○   *K; a campaign for more, safer & better play facilities &
       services for children. The FPFC Charitable Trust (same
       address) provides information on training in play & safety for
       children
●   Conf - ET - Inf - LG
¶   Playaction - 4; ftm, £4 nm.
       Playaction Guides - irreg; ftm, 3 1st class stamps+SAE nm.

Fairground Association of Great Britain   (FAGB)   1976
NR   5 Crooks Lane, STUDLEY, Warks, B80 7QX.   (chmn/p)
       Chmn: Graham Downie
▲   Un-incorporated Society
○   *G; to record, study & publish history & current information on
       the British fairground industry

Fairground Society   1962
■   66 Carolgate, RETFORD, Notts, DN22 6EF.   (chmn/b)
       01777 702872
       http://www.fairgroundsociety.co.uk
       Chmn: Jack Schofield
▲   Un-incorporated Society
○   *G; to promote interest in the British fairground heritage &
       history of fairs
●   Mtgs - Exhib - Inf - VE - Archive
M   c 800 i
¶   The Platform - 4; ftm.

Falkland Islands Association   1976
NR   c/o Falkland House, 14 Broadway, LONDON, SW1H 0BH.
       (mail)
       0845 260 4884
       http://www.fiassociation.com
▲   Un-incorporated Society
Br   2
○   *K, *W; 'to support the wish of the people of the Falkland
       Islands to decide their own future for themselves without
       being subjected to pressure direct, or indirect, from any
       quarter'
M   c 850 i & f, UK / c 120 i & f, o'seas
¶   NL - 2.

Falklands Conservation   1979

NR   1 Princes Avenue, LONDON, N3 2DA.   (hq)
020 8343 0831   fax 020 8343 0831
http://www.falklandsconservation.com
▲   Registered Charity
Br   Falkland Islands
○   *Q; research & study of the flora & fauna of the Falkland
Islands; to protect & preserve the sites of scientific importance
& outstanding natural beauty in the islands & surrounding
seas

Fall Arrest Safety Equipment Training   (FASET)   2000

■   PO Box 138, WHITCHURCH, Shropshire, SY13 3AD.   (hq)
01948 780652
email enquiries@faset.org.uk   http://www.faset.org.uk
Sec: Stephen Kennefick
▲   Company Limited by Guarantee
○   *T; a trade association & training body for the safety net rigging
& fall arrest industry
●   Mtgs - ET - Stat - LG
<   Nat Access & Scaffolding Confedn (NASC)
M   32 f
¶   [publications on website].

Falsely Accused Carers & Teachers   (FACT)   2000

■   PO Box 3074, CARDIFF, CF3 3WZ.   (hsp)
029 2077 7499
email info@factuk.org   http://www.factuk.org
Hon Sec: Michael Barnes
Br   10
○   *K; 'we support carers & teachers (& their families) who have
been falsely accused or wrongly convicted of child abuse; we
also campaign for justice, lobby for change in the criminal
justice system, & seek to raise awareness of issues relating to
false allegations of abuse'
●   Conf - Mtgs - Inf - LG - Prison support - Lobbying
M   500 i, UK / 100 i, o'seas
¶   FACTion - 12; ftm only.

Families Anonymous   (FA)   1980

■   Doddington & Rollo Community Association, Charlotte Despard
Avenue, LONDON, SW11 5HD.   (hq)
0845 120 0660   fax 020 7498 1990
email office@famanon.org.uk
http://www.famanon.org.uk
▲   Un-incorporated Society
○   *W; to support families & friends of drug abusers by weekly
meetings
●   Mtgs (totally confidential)
M   c 750 i
¶   The FA NL - 4.   Publications list available.

Families Need Fathers   (FNF)   1974

■   134 Curtain Rd, LONDON, EC2A 3AR.   (hq)
0870 760 7111   fax 020 7739 3410
email fnf@fnf.org.uk   http://www.fnf.org.uk
Chief Exec: Jon Davies,   Sec: Ian Julian
▲   Company Limited by Guarantee; Registered Charity
Br   29
○   *K; to provide support, advice & information on children's
issues to parents, following separation / divorce
●   Conf - Mtgs - ET - Res - Inf - LG
M   2,750 i, UK / 30 i, o'seas
¶   McKenzie Magazine (Jnl) - 6; ftm, £25 nm.

Family Doctor Association   (FDA)   2007

■   FDA House, 9 York St, HEYWOOD, Lancs, OL10 4NN.   (hq)
01706 620920   fax 01706 691880
email admin@family-doctor.org.uk
http://www.family-doctor.org.uk
Chief Exec: Moira Auchterlonie
▲   Registered Charity
○   *M, *P; to improve he quality of care provided for patients in
family doctor practices in the UK
●   Conf - Mtgs ET - Inf - LG
M   i
×   2007 (September) Small Practices Association

Family Farmers' Association   (FFA)   1979

■   Osborne Newton, Aveton Gifford, KINGSBRIDGE, Devon,
TQ7 4PE.   (chmn/p)
01548 852794   fax 01548 852794
Chmn: Mrs Pippa Woods
▲   Un-incorporated Society
○   *F, *K; to represent the family farmer; to prevent the decline of
rural areas; to make farming more accessible to new
entrants
●   LG
M   250 i
¶   NL - 4; ftm.

Family Holiday Association   (FHA)   1975

§   3 Gainsford St, LONDON, SE1 2NE.   (hq)
020 3117 0650
http://www.fhaonline.org.uk
Dir: John McDonald
Charity specialising in helping provide holidays for families and
children in need.

Family Law Association of Scotland   (FLA)   1989

NR   T F Reid & Donaldson, 48 Causeyside St, PAISLEY,
Renfrewshire, PA1 1YH.   (hsb)
0141-889 7531
email enquiries@fla-scotland.co.uk
http://www.familylawassociation.org
Sec: Graham A Fordyce
▲   Un-incorporated Society
○   *P; for solicitors involved in family law
●   Conf - Mtgs - ET - Inf
M   300 i

Family Law Bar Association   (FLBA)   1947

NR   289-293 High Holborn, LONDON, WC1V 7HZ.   (admin/b)
020 7242 1289   fax 020 7831 7144
http://www.flba.co.uk
Admin: Carol Harris
▲   Un-incorporated Society
○   *P; for members of the Bar practising in the field of family law
& cases involving children
M   c 1,300 i

Family Matters Institute   (FMI)   1998

§   Park Rd, Moggerhanger, BEDFORD, MK44 3RW.   (hq)
01767 641002   fax 01767 641515
email family@familymatters.org.uk
http://www.familymatters.org.uk
Chief Exec: Matt Buttery
An educational charity specialising in research & training
programmes to strengthen marriage & family life in Britain.

Family Mediation Scotland
on 1 April 2008 merged with Relate Scotland to form **Relationships
Scotland**

Family Mediators' Association   (FMA)   1988
- Grove House, Grove Rd, BRISTOL, BS6 6UN.   (hq)
  0117-946 7062   fax 0117-946 7181
  email info@fmassoc.co.uk   http://www.fmassoc.co.uk
  Chmn: Linda Glees
▲ Registered Charity
○ *P; to provide assistance through mediation for adults & children who are affected by family breakdown
Gp Family mediators; Family mediator professional consultants; Family mediation training faculty
● Conf - Mtgs - ET - Res
  Helpline: 0808 200 0033
< UK Coll of Family Mediators
> ADR [alternative dispute resolution] Gp
M 250 i
¶ NL - 4;   LM; both free.

Family Planning Association   (FPA)   1930
- 50 Featherstone St, LONDON, EC1Y 8QU.   (hq)
  020 7608 5240   fax 0845 123 2349
  http://www.fpa.org.uk
  Contact: Julie Bentley
▲ Registered Charity
Br 6
○ *W; to improve the sexual health & reproductive rights of all people throughout the UK
● ET - Res - Inf - Lib - LG - Sexual Health Direct
  SHD Helpline: 0845 122 8690 (Mon-Fri 0900-1800)
< Intl Planned Parenthood Fedn
M 1,000 i
¶ Publications catalogue available.

Family Rights Group   (FRG)   1974
- The Print House, 18 Ashwin St, LONDON, E8 3DL.   (hq)
  020 7923 2628   fax 020 7923 2683
  http://www.frg.org.uk
  Chief Exec: Cathy Ashley
▲ Company Limited by Guarantee; Registered Charity
○ *W; to promote policies which fully involve families in decisions about their own children; to advise parents & relations whose children are known to social services; to promote good practice by social workers & solicitors working with families
● Conf - ET - Res - LG
  Advice line: 0800 731 1696 (Mon-Fri 1000-1200 + 1330-1530)
¶ Family Matters - 2;   Conference NL - 3;   AR; all ftm.

Family Welfare Association   (FWA)   1869
§ 501-505 Kingsland Rd, LONDON, E8 4AU.   (hq)
  020 7254 6251
  http://www.fwa.org.uk
  Chief Exec: Helen Dent
  Tackles some of the most complex & difficult issues facing families, including domestic abuse, mental health problems, learning disabilities & severe financial hardship; works with whole families to help them find solutions to their problems.

Fan Manufacturers' Association   (FMA)   1979
- 2 Waltham Court, Milley Lane, Hare Hatch, READING, Berks, RG10 9TH.   (hq)
  0118-940 3416   fax 0118-940 6258
  email info@feta.co.uk   http://www.feta.co.uk/
  Dir Gen: C Sloan
○ *T; interests of fan manufacturers, irrespective of the final application of their products. The association covers fans & similar air moving devices of any type & size & for any application, including: heating, ventilating, air conditioning, industrial processing, fume & dust removal, pneumatic conveying, combustion, heat transfer, drying, mines & tunnel ventilation, power generation or any other purpose involving movement & control of air or other gases as defined in Eurovent Terminology Document ref 1/1 paragraph 2 & within the scope of British Standard 848/1979
Gp C'ees: Economic, Technical
● Mtgs - ET - Res - Exhib - Stat - Expt - Inf
< HEVAC; BSI; Fedn Envtl Tr Assns (FETA)
M 30 f

Fanderson: the official Gerry Anderson Appreciation Society 1981
- PO Box 12, BRADFORD, W Yorks, BD10 0YE.   (mail)
  http://www.fanderson.org.uk
  Sec: Nick Williams
▲ Un-incorporated Society
○ *G; to promote the appreciation & preservation of Gerry Anderson productions - Thunderbirds & UFO & other TV series
● Conf - ET - Res - Exhib - Comp - Inf - PL
M 1,000 i, UK / 400 i, o'seas
¶ FAB - 4; ftm only.

Farm Equipment Council
a division of the **Agricultural Engineers' Association**

Farm Machinery Preservation Society Ltd   (FMPS)   1968
- 6 Lordship Rd, Writtle, CHELMSFORD, Essex, CM1 3EH.   (chmn/p)
  01245 420168
  email fmps@btinternet.com   http://www.fmps.org.uk
  Chmn: Bill Preston
▲ Company Limited by Guarantee
○ *G; to promote interest in & knowledge of vintage agriculture & horticulture machinery
● Mtgs - Exhib - VE
< Fedn of Brit Historic Vehicle Clubs
M 330 i
¶ Jnl - 4; free.

Farm Tractor & Machinery Trade Association   (FTMTA)   1912
IRL Tougher's Business Park (Unit 3/Rd D), Newhall, NAAS, Co Kildare, Republic of Ireland   (hq)
  353 (45) 409309   fax 353 (45) 409308
  email info@ftmta.ie   http://www.ftmta.ie
  Pres: Garry Daly
▲ Company Limited by Guarantee
○ *F, *T; manufacturers, importers, distributors & retail dealers of farm machinery
● ET - Exhib - Inf - LG - Sem
< AGRITECHNICA
M 200 f
¶ NL; ftm.

Farmers for Action   (FFA)   2000
NR Old Llanishen Farm, Llangovan, MONMOUTH, NP25 4BU.   (hq)
  01291 690224   fax 01291 690984
  email secretary@farmersforaction.org
  http://www.farmersforaction.org
  Chmn & Sec: David Handley
○ *F, *K; grassroots fighting force of British agriculture
● Protests

© CBD Research Ltd · Beckenham · BR3 5JS · Tel 020 8650 7745 · E-mail cbd@cbdresearch.com · www.cbdresearch.com

Farmers Club 1842

■ 3 Whitehall Court, LONDON, SW1A 2EL.   (hq)
020 7930 3557   fax 020 7839 7864
http://www.thefarmersclub.com
Chief Exec & Sec: Air Commodore Stephen Skinner
▲ a not-for-profit organisation
○ *F; social club for those interested in agriculture; furthers
knowledge of agriculture by educational activities
● Mtgs - Inf
M 5,700 i
¶ Jnl - 6; ftm, £20 yr nm.

Farmers' Union of Wales   (Undeb Amaethwyr Cymru)
(FUW) 1955

NR Llys Amaeth, Plas Gogerddan, ABERYSTWYTH, Ceredigion,
SY23 3BT.   (hq)
01970 820820   fax 01970 820821
http://www.fuw.org.uk
Pres: Emyr Jones
○ *F; to represent the interests of Welsh agriculture & rural Wales
M 12,000 i

Farming & Countryside Education   (FACE)   2001

NR Arthur Rank Centre, STONELEIGH PARK, Warks, CV8 2LZ.
(hq)
0845 838 7192   fax 024 7641 4808
email enquiries@face-online.org.uk
http://www.face-online.org.uk
Exec Dir: Bill Graham
▲ Company Limited by Guarantee; Registered Charity
○ *E, *F; to educate children & young people about food &
farming in a sustainable countryside
< Access to Farms Partnership; R Agricl Soc of England (RASE)
M 80 f & org

Farming & Wildlife Advisory Group

in administration 18 November 2011

Farms for Schools   (FfS)

NR Unit 4F Top Land Country Business Park, Cragg Rd,
MYTHOLMROYD, W Yorks, HX7 5RW.   (hq)
01422 885566   fax 01422 885533
email info@farmsforschools.org.uk
http://www.farmsforschools.org.uk
Chief Exec: Gary Richardson
▲ Registered Charity
○ *E, *F; to ensure that school trips to farms are safe, enjoyable &
educationally worthwhile
● Conf - Mtgs - ET - Inf
< Access to Farms Partnership
M 99 farms
¶ NL - 4; free.

Farnborough Air Sciences Trust Association   (FASTA)

NR Trenchard House, 85 Farnborough Rd, FARNBOROUGH,
Hants, GU14 6TF.   (hq)
01252 375050
email manager@farnboroughairsciences.org.uk
http://www.airsciences.org.uk
▲ Registered Charity
○ *G; to support & promote the activities of FAST
● Mtgs - ET - Res - Inf - Lib - PL - LG
M 700+ i, 5 f
Farnborough Air Sciences Trust (FAST) was established in 1993
to save the main factory site of the Royal Aircraft
Establishment, then threatened with destruction, & to
safeguard the location's aerospace heritage

Fastener Engineering & Research Association   (FERA)

NR National Metalforming Centre, 47 Birmingham Road, WEST
BROMWICH, W Midlands, B70 6PY.   (hq)
0121-601 6350   fax 0121-601 6373
email generalsec@fera.org.uk   http://www.fera.org.uk
○ *P; for engineers & designers involved in the specification of
fasteners, the installation of mechanical fasteners, the use of
adhesives & involvement in application joint design
< Confedn of Brit Metalforming

Fawcett Society 1866

NR 1-3 Berry St, LONDON, EC1V 0AA.   (hq)
020 7253 2598   fax 020 7253 2599
http://www.fawcettsociety.org.uk
Chief Exec: Ceri Goddard
▲ Registered Charity
○ *K; campaigns on women's representation in politics & public
life; on equal pay, on pensions & poverty; on valuing caring
work; & on the treatment of women in the justice system
● Conf - Res - LG
M 2,000 i, 100 org
¶ Towards Equality - 4.   Campaign Reports.   AR.

FCA Membership Ltd   (FCA)   1992

■ PO Box 1, LAIRG, Sutherland, IV27 9AA.   (hq)
0870 042 7999
email members@fcauk.com   http://www.fcauk.com
Chmn: Donald Maclean
▲ Company Limited by Guarantee
Br 3
○ *T; for businesses & individuals involved or interested in the
contracting sector of the UK forestry & wood related
industries
● Conf - Mtgs - ET - Res - Exhib - Inf
M 967 i, 382 f
¶ FCA News - 6; ftm only.
FCA Membership Ltd is the registered company name of the
Forestry Contracting Association

Federation of Active Retirement Associations
see **Active Retirement Ireland**

Federation of Aerospace Enterprises in Ireland   (FAEI)   1994

IRL Confederation House, 84-86 Lower Baggot St, DUBLIN 2,
Republic of Ireland.   (hq)
353 (1) 605 1652   fax 353 (1) 638 1652
email mark.mcauley@faei.ie   http://www.faei.ie
Dir: Mark McAuley
○ *P; to ensure that the importance of the Irish aerospace industry
is recognised by policy makers & that national policies take
into account the needs of the industry
< AeroSpace & Defence Inds Assn of Europe (ASD); Ir Business &
Emplrs Confedn (IBEC)

Federation of Archaeological Managers & Employers   (FAME)
1975

NR c/o Wessex Archaeology, Portway House, Old Sarum Park,
SALISBURY, Wilts, SP4 6EB.   (asa)
01722 326887   fax 01722 337562
email info@famearchaeology.co.uk
http://www.famearchaeology.co.uk
Chief Exec: Adrian Tindall
○ *P; to represent the views of archaeological managers &
employers within the profession & beyond
● Conf - Inf - LG - Mtgs - Stat
M 50 f
✕ 2008 Standing Conference of Archaeological Unit Managers

** Federation of Artistic & Creative Therapy

Organisation lost: see Introduction paragraph 3

Federation of Artistic Roller Skating   (FARS)
NR   Terence House, 24 London Rd, THATCHAM, Berks,
        RG18 4QL.   (hq)
        01635 877322   fax 01635 877323
        email office@fars.co.uk   http://www.fars.co.uk
        Pres: Ron Gibbs
○   *S; to encourage people of all ages to roller skate, to become
        proficient enough to enjoy the sport of artistic roller skating,
        & eventually compete in artistic roller skating events
●   Comp - ET

**Federation of Associations for Country Sports in Europe
(FACE(UK))   1977**
NR   c/o Countryside Alliance, The Old Town Hall,
        367 Kennington Rd, LONDON, SE11 4PT.   (mail)
        020 7840 9200   fax 020 7793 8899
        Sec: Col T P B Hoggarth
▲   Un-incorporated Society
○   *K; to support, maintain & promote the rights of all field
        sportsmen in the UK; it assists authorities by providing expert
        advice & information & monitors subsequent proposals &
        decisions
        This is the UK branch, the FACE hq is in Brussels
●   Mtgs - Inf - LG - Political lobbying in Europe
<   FACE-Europe
M   19 org
¶   Brochure.

Federation of Astronomical Societies   (FAS)   1974
NR   Chegwyn House, 6 Broomcroft Drive, PYFORD, Surrey,
        GU22 8NS.   (memsec/p)
        01932 341036
        http://www.fedastro.org.uk
        Mem Sec: John Axtell
▲   Un-incorporated Society
Br   Gibraltar
○   *N; to help & advise local astronomical societies
●   Inf - Conventions
<   Assn for Astronomy Educ
M   170 org
¶   FAS NL - 4; ftm only.   Hbk - 1; ftm, £4 nm.
        Astrocalendar - 1.

**Federation of Automatic Transmission Engineers   (FATE)
1978**
NR   Chester Automatic Transmission Centre, Factory Rd, Sandycroft,
        DEESIDE, CH5 2QJ.   (chmn/b)
        01244 537070
        http://www.fedauto.co.uk
        Chmn: Steve Taylor
○   *T; for rebuilders of automatic transmissions
●   Conf - Mtgs - ET - Res - Exhib - Expt - Inf - Lib
M   c 50 f

Federation of Awarding Bodies   (FAB)   2000
NR   75 Westminster Bridge Rd, LONDON, SE1 7HS.   (hq)
        020 7921 4417
        email enquiries@awarding.org.uk
        http://www.awarding.org.uk
        Admin: Jacques Wood
▲   Company Limited by Guarantee
○   *N; for Ofqual recognised bodies that award vocational
        qualifications in the UK
Gp   14-19 policy; Regulation policy; Skills policy
●   Conf - LG - Mtgs
M   118 f
¶   NL - 26 (email).

Federation of Bakers   (FOB)   1942
■   6 Catherine St, LONDON, WC2B 5JW.   (hq)
        020 7420 7190   fax 020 7379 0542
        email info@bakersfederation.org.uk
        http://www.bakersfederation.org.uk
        Dir: Gordon Polson
▲   Un-incorporated Society
○   *T; representation of the UK's leading bakeries manufacturing
        sliced & wrapped bread, bakery snacks & other bread
        products
●   Conf - Mtgs - ET - Stat - Inf - LG
<   Assn Intle de la Boulangerie Industrielle (AIBI); Food & Drink
        Fedn; CBI
M   8 f operating 46 bakeries
¶   LM;   AR.
        Information Sheets 1-21 (on aspects of bread & bread-
        making).
        Health & Safety publications:
            Breathe Easy: a training video; £49.34.
            Federation Safety Memoranda; £96.44 (the set).
            Safety Information Notes; ftm.
        Publications list available.

Federation of Bloodstock Agents (GB) Ltd   (FBA)   1978
NR   9 Paddocks Drive, NEWMARKET, Suffolk, CB8 9BE.   (hsb)
        01638 561116   fax 01638 560332
        http://www.bloodstock-agencies.com
○   *T; to represent bloodstock agents in Great Britain
●   Mtgs - Liaison with horseracing industry through British
        Horseracing Board
M   f

**Fédération Britannique des Alliances Françaises   (FBAF)
1905**
NR   1 Dorset Sq, LONDON, NW1 6PU.   (hq)
        020 7223 6439
        http://www.alliancefrancaise.org.uk
▲   Registered Charity
○   *X; to widen access to French language & culture by offering
        French classes & social & cultural events about France
<   Alliance Française
M   8,000 i, 60 org, UK / 130,000 i, 1,300 org, o'seas

Federation of British Aquatic Societies   (FBAS)   1938
NR   8 Acacia Avenue, BRENTFORD, Middx, TW8 8NR.   (chmn/p)
        020 8847 3586
        http://www.fbas.co.uk
        Chmn: Joe Nethersell
▲   Un-incorporated Society
○   *N; all aspects of fishkeeping, breeding, & showing

Federation of British Artists   (FBA)   1961
■   17 Carlton House Terrace, LONDON, SW1Y 5BD.   (hq)
        020 7930 6844   fax 020 7839 7830
        http://www.mallgalleries.org.uk
        Co Sec: John Sayers
▲   Company Limited by Guarantee; Registered Charity
○   *A; to provide exhibition facilities for member societies
●   Conf - Mtgs - Exhib - Comp - SG - Commissions bureau
M   9 org:
        Hesketh Hubbard Art Society
        New English Art Club
        Pastel Society
        Royal Institute of Oil Painters
        Royal Institute of Painters in Water Colours
        Royal Society of British Artists
        Royal Society of Marine Artists
        Royal Society of Portrait Painters
        Society of Wildlife Artists
¶   NL.   Catalogues of each society's exhibitions.

© CBD Research Ltd · Beckenham · BR3 5JS · Tel 020 8650 7745 · E-mail cbd@cbdresearch.com · www.cbdresearch.com

Federation of British Bonsai Societies   (FOBBS)   1962
NR   The Woodlands, New Hall Drive, SUTTON COLDFIELD,
      W Midlands, B76 1QX.   (chmn/p)
      0121-378 4837
      email mkhughes567@btintrnet.com
      http://www.fobbsbonsai.co.uk
      Chmn: Malcolm Hughes
▲   Company Limited by Guarantee
○   *H, *N; to educate & promote the ancient art of bonsai
      (training of miniature trees in pots)
Gp   Friends of the National Bonsai Collection
●   ET - Exhib - Comp - Inf - PL
<   Eur Bonsai Assn (EBA); R Horticl Soc
M   45 org
¶   NL -6 (published by the EBA).

Federation of British Cremation Authorities
      since 2007 **Federation of Burial & Cremation Authorities**

**Federation of British Engineers' Tool Manufacturers   (FBETM)
1943**
■   c/o MTA, 62 Bayswater Rd, LONDON, W2 3PS.   (hq)
      020 7298 6400   fax 020 7298 6430
      http://www.britishtools.com
      Sec Gen: M A Ponikowski
○   *T
●   Conf - Mtgs - Exhib - Stat - Expt - Inf - LG - Standardisation
<   ECTA; BSI; ISO
M   80 f
¶   News Bulletin - 4; ftm.

Federation of British Fire Organisations   (FOBFO)   1963
NR   BDS Consultants, 6 Nicholas St, CHESTER, CH1 2NX.
      (chmn/b)
      01244 323171   fax 01244 323171
      email firstfirecall@aol.com   http://www.fobfo.org
      Chmn: Dennis Davis
○   *N, *T; to promote the services of constituent member
      organisations, both nationally & internationally, in the fight
      against fire
M   4 f, 13 org

**Federation of British Greyhound Owners Associations
(FBGOA)**
NR   95 Grosvenor Avenue, CARSHALTON, Surrey, SM5 3EN.   (hsp)
      020 8647 6547
      http://www.cagro-greyhounds.co.uk
      Sec: John Waldron
○   *S; to represent owners of greyhounds at race tracks & on the
      committee of the Greyhound Board of Great Britain
●   Mtgs - Inf - Help with homing retired dogs
<   Combined Associates Greyhound Racing Org (CAGRO)
M   i

**Federation of British Hand Tool Manufacturers   (FBHTM)
1944**
■   c/o MTA, 62 Bayswater Rd, LONDON, W2 3PS.   (asa)
      020 7298 6400   fax 020 7298 6430
      email fbhtm@mta.org.uk   http://www.mta.org.uk
      Dir Gen (MTA): Graham Dewhurst
▲   Un-incorporated Society
○   *T; interests of manufacturers of hand tools
●   Conf - Mtgs - ET - Res - Exhib - Stat - Expt - Inf - LG
<   Comité Eur de l'Outillage (CEO);
M   9 f

Federation of British Herpetologists   (FBH)   1996
NR   C-View Media, PO Box 1006, SOUTHAMPTON, Hants,
      SO19 7TS.   (chmn/b)
      023 8044 0999   fax 023 8044 0666
      http://www.fbh.org.uk
      Chmn: Chris Newman
○   *K; to represent the legitimate interests of herpetologists &
      herpetoculture in the UK, including breeders, importers &
      keepers
●   Conf - LG
M   org only

**Federation of British Historic Vehicle Clubs Ltd   (FBHVC)
1988**
■   Stonewold, Berrick Salome, WALLINGFORD, Oxon,
      OX10 6JR.   (regd off)
      01865 400845   fax 01865 400845
      email secretary@fbhvc.co.uk   http://www.fbhvc.co.uk
      Sec: Rosy Pugh
▲   Company Limited by Guarantee
○   *G, *K; to uphold the freedom to use old vehicles on the roads
      without any undue restriction
●   Conf - Res - Inf - LG
<   Fédn Intle des Véhicles Anciens (FIVA)
M   500 org
      (Sub: £13.25 i, £54 f, £59.25 museums/collections, £0.38
      per mem (£25 min) clubs/assns
¶   NL - 6; ftm only.

Federation of British Port Wholesale Fish Merchants Associations
      has closed

Federation of Building Specialist Contractors   (FBSC)   1970
NR   Unit 9 Lakeside Industrial Estate, STANTON HARCOURT, Oxon,
      OX29 5SL.   (hq)
      01865 883558   fax 01865 884467
      http://www.fbsc.org.uk
▲   Un-incorporated Society
○   *T; for specialist sub-contractors in the building industry
M   f

Federation of Burial & Cremation Authorities   (FBCA)   1924
■   41 Salisbury Rd, CARSHALTON, Surrey, SM5 3HA.   (hsb)
      020 8669 4521
      http://www.fbca.org.uk
      Sec: Rick Powell
○   *T; practice of cremation & administration & operation of
      crematoria
●   Conf - Mtgs - Res - ET - Exhib - Stat - Inf
M   18 f, 183 org (mainly local authorities)
¶   Resurgam - 4; ftm.   Code of practice.
      Technical leaflets & booklets.   AR.
×   2007 Federation of British Cremation Authorities

Federation of Chefs Scotland   (FCS)   1994
■   8 Gosford Place, EDINBURGH, EH6 4BJ.   (memsec/p)
      0131-529 5395
      http://www.scottishchefs.com
      Mem Sec: Marie-Claire James
▲   Un-incorporated Society
○   *P; promoting excellence in the art of professional cookery
●   Conf - Exhib - Comp
<   Wld Assn Chefs Socs (WACS)
M   250 i, 10 f
      (Sub: £25 i, £5,000 f)
¶   Sizzle - 4; free.

Federation of Children's Book Groups   (FCBG)   1968
■   2 Bridge Wood View, Horsforth, LEEDS, W Yorks, LS18 5PE.
      (hq)
      0113-258 8910
      email info@fcbg.org.uk   http://www.fcbg.org.uk
      Hon Secs: Sinead & Martin Kromer
▲   Registered Charity
Br 40
○   *A; to bring children & good books together; to foster a love of
      books & reading in children
●   Conf - Mtgs - Exhib - Comp - Inf - Children's Book Award
M   110 i, 125 f (libraries, schools, publishers etc), 40 groups, UK /
      3 i, o'seas
¶   NL - 3; 50p m only.
      Booklists; ftm, 15p nm.

**Federation of City Farms & Community Gardens   (FCFCG)
1980**
■   The GreenHouse, Hereford St, Bedminster, BRISTOL,
      BS3 4NA.   (hq)
      0117-923 1800   fax 0117-923 1900
      email admin@farmgarden.org.uk
      http://www.farmgarden.org.uk
      Dir: Jeremy Iles
▲   Company Limited by Guarantee; Registered Charity
○   *F, *H, *V; supports, promotes & represents city farms,
      community gardens & similar organisations across the UK
●   Conf - Exhib - Inf - Lib - LG
<   Eur Fedn City Farms; CEE; NCVO; Soil Assn; Thrive; Nat Soc of
      Allotment & Leisure Gardens; HDRA; Greenspace; Access to
      Farms Partnership
M   300 org
¶   Growing Places (Members NL) - 4; ftm only.
      Public NL - 2;   AR; both free.

Federation of Clinical Scientists   (FCS)
NR c/o ACB, 130-132 Tooley St, LONDON, SE1 2TU.   (hq)
      020 7403 8001   fax 020 7403 8006
      email admin@acb.org.uk   http://www.acb.org.uk
○   *U; represents the Trade Union interests of clinical scientists in
      the NHS & other related areas
M   i

Federation of Clothing Designers & Executives   (FCDE)   1943
■   London College of Fashion, 100 Curtain Rd, LONDON,
      EC2A 3AA.   (gensec/b)
      http://www.fcde.org.uk
      Gen Sec: Alan Cannon-Jones
▲   Un-incorporated Society
Br 3
○   *T; technical federation for the garment industry (working &
      independent members) covering manufacture, IT, retail,
      design technology, & utilities
●   Conf - Mtgs - VE - Social
M   130 i, London College of Fashion, UK / 10 i, o'seas

Federation of Cocoa Commerce Ltd   (FCC)   1929
NR Cannon Bridge House, 1 Cousin Lane, LONDON, EC4R 3XX.
      (hq)
      020 7379 2884   fax 020 7379 2389
      email fcca@liffe.com   http://www.cocoafederation.com
      Secretariat: Silde Lauand
▲   Company Limited by Guarantee
○   *T; to promote, protect & regulate the cocoa trade
●   Conf - Mtgs - ET - Res - SG - Inf - Arbitration system for
      settlement of disputes without resort to the courts
<   Intl Cocoa Trade Fedn (ICTF); Eur Community Cocoa Trade
      Org (ECCTO)
M   c 100 f
¶   News Reports - ftm daily via email.   Contract Book.

**Federation of Commercial Audiovisual Libraries Ltd   (FOCAL)
1985**
NR 79 College Rd, HARROW, Middx, HA1 1BD.   (hq)
      020 3178 3535
      email info@focalint.org   http://www.focalint.org
      Gen Mgr: Julie Lewis
▲   Company Limited by Guarantee
○   *T; for audio-visual libraries, researchers, producers & facility
      houses, promoting the use of library footage, stills & sound in
      programming, advertising, corporate videos, multi media
      projects etc.
●   Conf - Mtgs - ET - Res - Stat - Inf - Informing users of footage
      where to go for footage & advice - Helping to find film
      researchers
M   100 i, 100 f, UK / 25 i, 75 org, o'seas
¶   Archive Zones - 4; ftm, £50 yr nm.
      LM - 1; ftm, £25 nm.
      Note: Also uses the name FOCAL International Ltd

Federation of Commodity Associations   (FCA)   1943
NR 9 Lincoln's Inn Fields, LONDON, WC2A 3BP.   (hq)
      020 7814 9666   fax 020 7814 8383
      http://www.fcassoc.co.uk
      Sec: Mrs Pamela Kirby Johnson
▲   Company Limited by Guarantee
○   *N, *T; to protect the interests of European commodity
      associations
Gp C'ees: Legal & arbitration; Shipping; Taxation
●   Mtgs - ET - SG - Expt - Inf
<   Intl Cham of Comm; Freight Transport Assn
M   7 org
¶   Book of Rules & Regulations (incl LM); m only.

Federation of Communication Services   (FCS)   1981
■   Provident House, Burrell Row, BECKENHAM, Kent, BR3 1AT.
      (hq)
      020 8249 6363   fax 0844 870 5927
      email fcs@fcs.org.uk   http://www.fcs.org.uk
      Chief Exec: Jacqui Brookes
▲   Company Limited by Guarantee
○   *T; communication service providers delivering telephony
      services & products via fixed, mobile, IP & radio
Gp Business radio; Critical national infrastructure; DECT Guard
      band licensees; Fixed service provision; Installers; Mobile
      Ireland; Mobile takeback; Number portability; Numbering;
      VOIP
●   Conf - Mtgs - Inf - LG
<   Trade Assn Forum
>   Eur Mobile Messaging Assn; Onsite Communications Assn;
      Direct Marketing Assn
M   350 f, 2 org
      (Sub: £500 f, £315 org)
¶   FCS Bulletin - 3.

© CBD Research Ltd · Beckenham · BR3 5JS · Tel 020 8650 7745 · E-mail cbd@cbdresearch.com · www.cbdresearch.com

Federation for Community Development Learning   (FCDL)   1977

NR   The Circle (3rd floor), 33 Rockingham Lane, SHEFFIELD,
        S Yorks, S1 4FW.   (hq)
        0114-253 6770   fax 0114-253 6771
        email info@fcdl.org.uk   http://www.fcdl.org.uk
        Head of Agency: Janice Marks
▲   Company Limited by Guarantee; Registered Charity
○   *E; to support the development of communities through the
        advancement & promotion of community development
        learning at local, regional & national levels; to create
        relevant opportunities for good quality training &
        qualifications
Gp   Support for Ubuntu - the national training network for Black
        Minority Ethnic practitioners who share an interest in
        promoting & developing community development from Black
        perspectives
●   Conf - Mtgs - ET - Res - Inf - Lib
M   43 i, 133 f
¶   Federation News (NL) - 4; ftm only.
        Resource Packs for the Community Development
        Programme; £54 m, £60 nm.
        Get Accredited (guidance pack); £9 m, £10 nm.
        [see website for other publications].

Federation against Copyright Theft   (FACT)   1982

NR   Europa House, Church Street, OLD ISLEWORTH, Middx,
        TW7 6DA.   (hq)
        020 8568 6646   fax 020 8560 6364
        email bc@fact-uk.org.uk   http://www.fact-uk.org.uk
▲   Company Limited by Guarantee
○   *N; copyright protection of motion pictures
Gp   Data Federation
<   Motion Picture Assn
M   20 f

Federation of Crafts & Commerce   (FCC)   1983

■   4, 5 & 6 Quaypoint, Northarbour Rd, PORTSMOUTH, Hants,
        PO6 3TD.   (hq)
        0844 371 9757   fax 0844 375 9609
        email mail@fcc.org.uk   http://www.fcc.org.uk
        Gen Sec: David Pinnock
▲   Company Limited by Guarantee
○   *T; provision of management services for small & medium sized
        businesses
Gp   Credit management; Debt recovery; Advisory services; Status
        checks etc
●   Inf - Status enquiry - Debt recovery - Legal advisory services &
        many other similar services
M   1,000 i & f

Federation for Detached Youth Work   (FDYW)

NR   c/o NYA, Eastgate House, 19-23 Humberstone Rd, LEICESTER,
        LE5 3GJ.   (mail)
        0116-242 7490
        http://www.detachedyouthwork.info
○   *P; work in which both the initial contact & building of
        relationships are developed on the street, free from the
        constraints of centre-based work

Federation of Dredging Contractors   1950

NR   c/o Alliotts, Imperial House, 15 Kingsway, LONDON,
        WC2B 6UN.   (asa)
        Sec: N Armstrong
○   *T; to further the interests of the UK dredging industry
M   3 f

Federation of Drug & Alcohol Professionals   (FDAP)   1984

NR   Unit 11A Cannon Wharf Business Centre, 35 Evelyn St,
        LONDON, SE8 5RT.   (hq)
        020 7237 3399; 01636 612590
        http://www.fdap.org.uk
▲   Company Limited by Guarantee
○   *P, *W; to contribute to the relief of poverty, sickness & distress
        among persons suffering from addiction to drugs of any
        kind; to develop alcohol & drug abuse counselling as a
        professional specialism
●   Conf - Mtgs - ET - Inf - LG
<   Nat Assn of Alcohol & Drug Abuse Counsellors (USA)
M   c 1,000 i

Federation of Education Business Link Consortia   (FEBL)

NR   Links4Learning, 26-32 Oxford Rd, BOURNEMOUTH, Dorset,
        BH8 9EZ.   (hsb)
        01202 589595   fax 01202 589596
        http://www.feblc.org
        Sec: Jane Manning
○   *N; to promote the recognition of EBLCs as key strategic
        partners in the planning & provision of education business
        link activities
●   LG - Mtgs
M   47 org
        An Education Business Link Consortium (EBLC) provides
        strategic coherence across a local Learning & Skills Council
        (LSC) area in the support of links between schools/colleges &
        local employers

Federation of Engine Re-Manufacturers   (FER)   1937

NR   18 Livonia Rd, SIDMOUTH, Devon, EX10 9JB.   (hq)
        01395 513232   fax 01395 519192
        email enquiries@fer.co.uk   http://www.fer.co.uk
○   *T; for engine reconditioners & their suppliers; to discourage
        unscrupulous traders
●   Mtgs - ET - Exhib - Comp - VE - LG
M   f

Federation of Entertainment Unions   (FEU)   1990

■   c/o NUJ, Headland House, 308-312 Gray's Inn Rd, LONDON,
        WC1X 8DP.   (mail)
        email info@feutraining.org   http://www.feutraining.org
○   *U, *N
Gp   C'ees: European, Film & electronic media, Training & equal
        opportunites
●   Mtgs - LG
M   4 org

Federation of Environmental Trade Associations   (FETA)   1977

■   2 Waltham Court, Milley Lane, Hare Hatch, READING, Berks,
        RG10 9TH.   (hq)
        0118-940 3416   fax 0118-940 6258
        email info@feta.co.uk   http://www.feta.co.uk
        Dir Gen: C Sloan
○   *N, *T; 'common action concerning environmental control in
        buildings'
M   11 assns:
        Association of Ductwork Contractors & Allied
            Services
        British Flue & Chimney Manufacturers' Association
        British Refrigeration Association
        Building Controls Industry Association
        Chilled Beam & Ceiling Association
        Fan Manufacturers' Association
        Heat Pump Association
        Heating, Ventilating & Air Conditioning Manufacturers'
            Association
        Hose Manufacturers & Suppliers Association
        Residential Ventilation Association
        Smoke Control Association

Federation of Ethical Stage Hypnotists (FESH) 1979
NR   The Maltings, Old Malton Rd, Staxton, SCARBOROUGH,
      N Yorks, YO12 4SB.   (chmn/p)
      07515 355747
      http://www.fesh.co.uk
      Chmn: Ken Webster
○   *P

Federation of Family History Societies (FFHS) 1974
■   PO Box 8857, LUTTERWORTH, Leics, LE17 9BJ.   (mail)
      01455 203133
      email info@ffhs.org.uk   http://www.ffhs.org.uk
      Jt Admin: Maggie Loughran,   Philippa McCray
▲   Company Limited by Guarantee; Registered Charity
○   *G, *L, *N; to bring together societies with a common interest in
      genealogy, heraldry & allied subjects
●   Conf - ET
M   163 org, UK / 54 org, o'seas

Federation of Garden & Leisure Manufacturers
   see **GARDENEX: the Federation of Garden & Leisure
   Manufacturers**

Federation for Healthcare Science (FHCS) 2002
NR   12 Coldbath Sq, LONDON, EC1R 5HL.   (hsb)
      020 7833 5807   fax 020 7436 4946
      email mail@fedhcs.net   http://www.fedhcs.net
      Hon Sec: Derek Bishop
○   *M, *N; to provide a collective voice for professional
      organisations representing healthcate scientists
Gp   Life sciences; Physiological sciences; Physical sciences & clinical
      engineering
M   38 org
¶   eNewsletter

Federation of Heating Spares Stockists (FHSS) 1981
NR   PO Box 672, SHIFNAL, Shropshire, TF11 8YH.   (admin)
      01952 460760
      email enquiry@heat-spares.co.uk
      http://www.heat-spares.co.uk
○   *T; a nationwide membership network of specialist heating
      stockists & suppliers of gas, oil & solid fuel spares & controls
M   16 f

Federation of Holistic Therapists (FHT) 1962
NR   18 Shakespeare Business Centre, Hathaway Close, EASTLEIGH,
      Hants, SO50 4SR.   (hq)
      023 8062 4350   fax 023 8062 4386
      email info@fht.org.uk   http://www.fht.org.uk
▲   Company Limited by Guarantee
○   *P; to promote & maintain the highest standards of
      professionalism in holistic therapies (aromatherapy,
      reflexology, massage) & health, fitness & beauty therapies
Gp   Association of Therapy Lecturers; Health & Beauty Employers
      Federation; International Council of Health Fitness & Sports
      Therapists; International Council of Holistic Therapists;
      International Federation of Health & Beauty Therapists;
      Professional Association of Clinical Therapists
●   Conf - ET
M   21,000 i
¶   The International Therapist - 6; ftm only.

Federation of Image Consultants Ltd (FIPI) 1988
■   4 Chase Side, ENFIELD, Middx, EN2 6NF.   (regd off)
      email admin@fipigroup.com   http://www.fipigroup.org
      Pres: Carol Collins
▲   Company Limited by Guarantee
○   *P; to support, develop, promote & regulate the personal image
      profession
●   Conf - Mtgs - Exam - Exhib - Inf
M   152 i, UK & o'seas
      Note: trades as the Federation of Image Professionals
      International

Federation of Image Professionals International
   trading name of the **Federation of Image Consultants Ltd**

Federation of Independent Advice Centres
   see **AdviceUK**

Federation of Independent Detectorists (FID) 1982
NR   44 Heol Dulais, Birchgrove, SWANSEA, W Glam, SA7 9LT.
      (hsp)
      01792 814615   fax 01792 814615
      email fid.pro@detectorists.net
      http://www.fid.newbury.net
      Hon Sec: Colin Hanson
▲   Un-incorporated Society
Br   2
○   *G; for those interested in recreational metal detecting
Gp   Emergency call out for veterinary tranquilliser dart recovery
●   Conf - Exhib - Comp - Inf - LG - Insurance - Advice line - Free
      recovery service (metal items)
M   5,000 i, UK / 750 i, o'seas
¶   NL - 4; ftm only.

**Federation of Independent Mines of Great Britain (FIM)
1948**
■   14 Moorland Avenue, BARNSLEY, S Yorks, S70 6PQ.   (hsp)
      01226 244437
      email d7l7b7@gmail.com
      Hon Sec: Douglas Bulmer
▲   Un-incorporated Society
○   *T; to represent the interests of coal producers & associated
      industry
●   Mtgs - ET - Exam - Stat - Expt - Inf - LG - Advice on legal
      matters (common, employment & mining law)
>   Coal Pro, Wakefield
M   12 f, 2 museums

**Federation of Independent Practitioner Organisations (FIPO)
2000**
NR   14 Queen Anne's Gate, LONDON, SW1H 9AA.
      020 7222 0975
      email info@fipo.org   http://www.fipo.org
      Contact: Linda Hulks
○   *M, *N; to represent medical professional organisations in
      Britain that have private practice committees

Federation of Infection Societies (FIS)
NR   c/o Hartley Taylor Ltd, Henderson House, New Rd,
      PRINCES RISBOROUGH, Bucks, HP27 0JN.   (mail)
      http://www.fis-infection.org.uk
○   *N
M   6 org

Federation of Inline Speed Skating (FISS)
NR   c/o BRSF, PO Box 68966, LONDON, NW26 9FD.   (mail)
      020 8338 1171
      email secretary@inlinespeed.co.uk
      http://www.inlinespeed.co.uk
      Sec: Hannah Wilkes
○   *S; governing body of speed skating in Great Britain
<   Fédn Intle de Roller Sports (FIRS); Confédn Européenne de
      Roller-Skating (CERS); Comité Européen de Course (CEC); Brit
      Roller Sports Fedn (BRSF)

Federation of International Banks in Ireland (FIBI)
IRL   Nassau House, Nassau Street, DUBLIN 2, Republic of
      Ireland.   (hq)
      353 (1) 671 5311   fax 353 (1) 679 6680
      email info@ibf.ie   http://www.ibf.ie
      Chief Exec: Pat Farrell
○   *P; to ensure that the policy priorities of the international
      banking community in Ireland are identified & addressed
<   Ir Banking Fedn (IBF)
M   50 f

Federation of Internet Traders
company dissolved 24 May 2006

Federation of Irish Beekeepers' Associations   (FIBKA)
IRL   Ballinakill, ENFIELD, Co Meath, Republic of Ireland.   (hsb)
       353 (46) 954 1433
       email mgglee@eircom.net
       http://www.irishbeekeeping.ie
       Hon Sec: Michael Gleeson
○   *F

Federation of Irish Fishermen   (FIF)   2007
IRL   Fitzwilliam Business Centre, 26-27 Upper Pembroke St,
       DUBLIN 2, Republic of Ireland.   (hq)
       353 (1) 637 3937   fax 353 (1) 662 0635
       email info@fif.ie   http://www.fif.ie
○   *T
M   4 orgs

Federation of Irish Nursing Homes
       in January 2008 merged with the Irish Nursing Homes Organisation
       to form **Nursing Homes Ireland**

Federation of Irish Societies   (FIS)   1973
NR   95 White Lion St, LONDON, N1 9PF.   (hq)
       020 7833 1226   fax 020 7833 3214
       email info@irishinbritain.org
       http://www.irishsocieties.org
○   *N; to promote the interests of the Irish people through
       community care, education, culture & arts, youth & sports
       activities & information provision; FIS is a national umbrella
       organisation which draws together Irish clubs & societies in
       Britain

**Federation of Jewellery Manufacturers of Ireland   (FJMI)
1963**
IRL   10 Johnstown Court, DÚN LAOGHAIRE, Co Dublin, Republic of
       Ireland.   (hq)
       353 (1) 284 0172
       email info@fjmi.com   http://www.fjmi.com
○   *T; to coordinate the manufacture of jewellery in Ireland
●   ET
M   20 f

Federation of Licensed Victuallers Associations   (FLVA)   1992
■   126 Bradford Rd, BRIGHOUSE, W Yorks, HD6 4AU.   (hq)
       01484 710534   fax 01484 718647
       email enquiries@flva.co.uk   http://www.flva.co.uk
       Chief Exec: Tony Payne
○   *T; to offer help & advice to members with any problems
       arising from the day-to-day running of their business,
       whether as tenants, free traders or lessees
●   Conf - Mtgs - Inf - LG
<   UK & Ireland Licensed Trade Assn
M   700 i, 9 f
¶   NL - 4; free.
       Publicans Guide to the Health & Safety Act; ftm only
       Guidance Notes:
           Employment Law
           General Food Hygiene Regulations
           Disability Audit
           Contracts of Employment; all ftm only.

Federation of Local History Societies
IRL   Winter's Hill, KINSALE, Co Cork, Republic of Ireland.   (sp)
       http://www.homepage.eircom.net/~localhist/index.html
       Sec: Dermot Ryan
○   *G

Federation of Manufacturing Opticians   (FMO)   1917
■   199 Gloucester Terrace, LONDON, W2 6LD.   (hq)
       020 7298 5123   fax 020 7298 5120
       email info@fmo.co.uk   http://www.fmo.co.uk
       Chief Exec: Malcolm Polley
▲   Company Limited by Guarantee
○   *N, *T; a federation for the ophthalmic optical manufacturing &
       distributing industry consisting of 4 trade associations each
       concerned with a separate branch of the industry
Gp   Optra Exhibitions UK; Optical Equipment Manufacturers' &
       Suppliers' Association; Optical Frame Importers' &
       Manufacturers' Association; Ophthalmic Lens Manufacturers'
       & Distributors' Association
●   Conf - Mtgs - Exhib
<   Optical Confedn; EUROM
M   152 f, UK / 1 f, o'seas
¶   In-Focus (NL) - 3;   AR (incl LM) - 1; both ftm only.

Federation of Master Builders   (FMB)   1941
■   Gordon Fisher House, 14-15 Great James St, LONDON,
       WC1N 3DP.   (hq)
       020 7242 7583   fax 020 7404 0296
       email central@fmb.org.uk   http://www.fmb.org.uk
       Dir Gen: Richard Diment
▲   Company Limited by Guarantee
Br   11
○   *T; for the construction industry
●   Conf - Mtgs - ET - Exhib - Inf - Lib - VE - Empl - LG
<   Eur Bldrs Fedn
M   13,000 f
¶   Masterbuilder - 12; ftm, £3.50 each nm.

Federation of Museums & Art Galleries of Wales
■   c/o Esther Roberts, Gwynedd Museum & Art Gallery, BANGOR,
       Gwynedd, LL57 1DT.   (hsb)
       01248 353368
       http://www.welshmuseumsfederation.org.uk
       Hon Sec: Esther Roberts
▲   Un-incorporated Society
○   *P; to encourage the highest professional standards within the
       museum profession in Wales
●   Mtgs - ET
<   Museums Assn
M   30 i, 20 f
¶   Y Mag - 2; ftm.

Federation of Music Services   (FMS)   1996
NR   7 Courthouse St, OTLEY, W Yorks, LS21 3AN.   (hq)
       01943 463311   fax 01943 461188
       email info@federationmusic.org.uk
       http://www.thefms.org
       Chief Exec: Virginia Haworth-Galt
▲   Company Limited by Guarantee; Registered Charity
○   *D; the national voice of music services representing the
       interests of 500,000 music students & 10,000 music teachers
●   Conf - Inf - LG - Mtgs
M   157 org

**Federation of National Self Catering Associations   (FoNSCA)
1996**
■   c/o EASCO, PO Box 567, HAYES, Middx, UB3 9EW.   (mail)
       020 7078 7329
       http://www.fonsca.org.uk
○   *T; furthering the interests of self catering holiday
       accommodation providers; promoting the use of self catering
       accommodation & maintaining standards within the sector
●   Mtgs - Inf - LG
M   4 org

Federation of Oils, Seeds & Fats Associations Ltd   (FOSFA)   1970

■ 20 St Dunstan's Hill, LONDON, EC3R 8NQ.   (hq)
   020 7283 5511
   http://www.fosfa.org
   Chief Exec: Stuart Logan
▲ Company Limited by Guarantee
○ *N, *T
Gp Oils & fats; Oilseeds & HPS groundnuts
● Mtgs - ET - Res - Inf - LG
< African Groundnut Coun (AGC); Amer Oil Chemists
   Soc (AOCS); AOAC Intl; Argentine Oil Ind Chamber (CIARA);
   Deutscher Verband des Grosshandels mit Ölen, Fetten und
   Ölrohstoffen eV (GROFOR); Eur Oleochemicals & Allied
   Products Gp (APAG); Intl Assn of Seed Crushers (IASC);
   Fishmeal & Fish Oil Org (IFFO); Intl Margarine Assn
   Countries Europe (IMACE); Malayan Edible Oil Mfrs
   Assn (MEOMA); Nat Inst Oilseed Products (NIOP); Nat
   Renderers Assn (NRA); Netherlands Oils, Fats & Oilseeds Tr
   Assn (NOFOTA); Palm Oil Refiners Assn Malaysia (PORAM);
   Seed Crushers & Oil Processors Assn (SCOPA)
M 800 f
¶ NL - 4.   FOSFA International Manual.   Contracts.
   Rules of Arbitration.   Codes of Practice.

Federation of Ophthalmic & Dispensing Opticians   (FODO)   1985

■ 199 Gloucester Terrace, LONDON, W2 6LD.   (hq)
   020 7298 5151   fax 020 7298 5111
   email optics@fodo.com   http://www.fodo.com
   Chief Exec: David Hewlett
▲ Company Limited by Guarantee
○ *T; representation of optical employers & businesses including
   both dispensing & ophthalmic practices; 'FODO represents
   all of the high street companies & most of the large groups'
Gp FODO educational charity
● Mtgs - SG - Stat - Empl - LG
< Optical Confedn; Eur Coun of Optometry & Optics
M 140 f
¶ Optics at a Glance - 1;   Vouchers at a Glance - 1;
   Opticians in Business - 12;
   Hbk (inc AR & accounts) - 1; all free.

Federation of Overseas Property Developers, Agents & Consultants
   in 2008 was incorporated into the **National Association of Estate Agents**

Federation of Petroleum Suppliers Ltd   (FPS)   1979

■ 6 Royal Court, Tatton St, KNUTSFORD, Cheshire, WA16 6EN.
   (hq)
   01565 631313   fax 01565 631314
   email info@fpsonline.co.uk   http://www.fpsonline.co.uk
   Chief Exec: Susan Hancock
▲ Company Limited by Guarantee
Br 9; Republic of Ireland
○ *T; interests of oil distribution industry (including heating oil &
   delivery to commercial sites for agricultural, marine &
   industrial use)
Gp FPS Forecourt Division
● Conf - Mtgs - Comp - ET - Exhib - Stat - Inf - LG
M 3 i, 230 f, UK / 30 f, o'seas
¶ Publication - 5; ftm, single complimentary copies only nm.

Federation of Piling Specialists   (FPS)   1964

■ 83 Copers Cope Rd, BECKENHAM, Kent, BR3 1NR.   (asa)
   020 8663 0947   fax 020 8663 0949
   email fps@fps.org.uk   http://www.fps.org.uk
   Sec: Dianne Jennings
▲ Company Limited by Guarantee
○ *T; specialist subcontractors carrying out all aspects of
   foundation construction & design
● Mtgs
< Eur Fedn of Foundation Contrs; Nat Specialist Contrs Coun;
   Ground Forum
M 18 f
¶ LM.

Federation of Plastering & Drywall Contractors   (FPDC)   1950

■ 61 Cheapside (4th floor), LONDON, EC2V 6AX.   (hq)
   020 7634 9480   fax 020 7248 3685
   email admin@fpdc.org   http://www.fpdc.org
   Chief Exec: Emma Tomlin
▲ Company Limited by Guarantee
○ *T
● Conf - Mtgs - ET - Res - Stat - LG
< Nat Specialist Contrs Coun
M 250 f
¶ Specialist Building Finisher - 6; free.

Federation of Private Residents' Associations   (FPRA)   1971

■ PO Box 10271, EPPING, Essex, CM16 9DB.   (hq)
   0871 200 3324   fax 020 8989 3153
   email info@fpra.org.uk   http://www.fpra.org.uk
   Chief Exec: Robert Levene
▲ Company Limited by Guarantee
○ *K; advice to members on leasehold & freehold management
   issues
● Mtgs - Inf - LG
M 500 org
¶ NL - 4; ftm only.
   Information pack (advice on forming a residents'
   association); £10.

Federation of Professional Associations in Guidance   (FedPAG)   2000

■ 19 Lawrence Leys, Bloxham, BANBURY, Oxon, OX15 4NU.
   (hsp)
   01295 720809   fax 01295 720809
   email alan@aceg.org.uk
   Hon Sec: Alan Vincent
○ *N, *P; for professionals working in career guidance

Federation of Racecourse Bookmakers   2003

NR 19 Culm Valley Way, UFFCULME, Devon, EX15 3XZ.   (hq)
   01884 841859   fax 01184 841859
   email comments@frb.org.uk   http://www.frb.org.uk
   Sec: B Newland
▲ Company Limited by Guarantee
○ *N; to act on behalf of the Association of Racecourse
   Bookmakers, the National Association of Bookmakers, and
   the Rails Bookmakers Association on matters of mutual
   interest
M 3 org:
   Association of Racecourse Bookmakers
   National Association of Bookmakers
   Rails Bookmakers Association

© CBD Research Ltd · Beckenham · BR3 5JS · Tel 020 8650 7745 · E-mail cbd@cbdresearch.com · www.cbdresearch.com

Federation of Recorded Music Societies (FRMS) 1936

- ■ 18 Albany Rd, Hartshill, STOKE-ON-TRENT, Staffs, ST4 6BB. (hsp)
  01782 251460
  http://www.thefrms.co.uk
  Hon Sec: Tony Baines
- ▲ Company Limited by Guarantee
- Br 210 affiliated societies
- ○ *D, *N; to promote the development & extension of societies or organisations using recorded music as part of their activities
- ● Conf - Mtgs
- M 12,000 i, UK / 80 i, o'seas
- ¶ Bulletin - 2; £1.75.

Federation of the Retail Licensed Trade Northern Ireland (FRLTNI) 1872

- NR 91 University St, BELFAST, BT7 1HP. (hq)
  028 9032 7578   fax 028 9032 7578
  email enquiries@pubsofulster.org
  http://www.pubsofulster.org
  Chief Exec: Nicola Carruthers
- ▲ Un-incorporated Society
- ○ *T; promotion of the licensed trade; advice & information for members
- ● Conf - Mtgs - ET - Res - Inf - LG
- < UK & Ireland Licensed Trade Assn
- M 1,200 i
- ¶ Federation section within Catering & Licensing Review - 12; ftm.
  Note: trades as Pubs of Ulster

Federation of Road Racing Motorcyclists

closed in March 2010

Federation of Road Surface Treatment Associations (FoRSTA) 2008

- NR PO Box 986, CHESTER, CH4 8XD.   (mail)
  01244 677648   fax 01244 680141
  http://www.rsda-gb.co.uk/forsta.htm
  Sec: Alistair Jack
- ○ *N, *T; to raise the profile of the road surface rtreatments industry
- × 2008 (High Friction Surfacing Association
  (Road Surface Dressing Association
  (Slurry Surfacing Comtractors Association

Federation of Scottish Aquaculture Producers

has closed

Federation of Scottish Theatre Ltd (FST)

- NR c/o Royal Lyceum Theatre, 30B Grindlay St, EDINBURGH, EH3 9AX.   (hq)
  0131-248 4842
  email fst@scottishtheatre.org
  Dir: Jon Morgan
- ○ *N, *P; to act as the voice of theatre in Scotland; to work with unions, the Scottish Arts Council, local authorities & other organisations to further interests & development of the theatre industry in Scotland
- M f

Federation of Sidecar Clubs (FOSC) 1958

- NR 107 Silverweed Rd, Walderslade, CHATHAM, Kent, ME5 0RF. (memsec/p)
  email EddieCheer@aol.com   http://www.sidecars.org.uk
  Mem Sec: Ted Cheer
- ○ *N, *G; sidecars & motorcycle combinations
- ● Conf - Mtgs - Exhib - Stat - Inf - Lib - Rallies
- M c 400 i
- ¶ Outlook.

Federation of Small Businesses (FSB) 1974

- ■ Press & Parliamentary Office, 2 Catherine Place, LONDON, SW1E 6HF.
  020 7592 8100   fax 020 7828 5919
  http://www.fsb.org.uk
- ▲ Company Limited by Guarantee
- Br 200; Belgium, Gibraltar
- ○ *K, *T; lobby organisation for small businesses
- ● Conf - Mtgs - Stat - Inf - Lib - LG
- < Eur Alliance for Small Businesses (ESBA)
- M 215,000 f
- ¶ First Voice - 6.

Federation against Software Theft (FAST) 1984

- NR York House, 18 York Rd, MAIDENHEAD, Berks, SL6 1SF.   (hq)
  01628 622121
  http://www.fastiis.org
- ▲ Company Limited by Guarantee
- ○ *T; protecting the interests of member companies from copyright infringement; to counter software piracy & increase public awareness of the damage to investment & innovation from unauthorised copying - to promote the legal use of software

Federation of Specialist Restaurants (FSR) 2006

- ■ PO Box 416, SURBITON, Surrey, KT1 9BJ.   (hq)
  020 8399 4831
  email groveint@aol.com   http://www.fedrest.com
  Sec: Colleen Grove
- ▲ Un-incorporated Society
- ○ *T; to publicise & further the interests of UK restaurants offering a specialist cuisine
- ● Res - Stat - Inf - PL
- > Gld of Bangladeshi Restarateurs
- M 1,000 f
- ¶ Mood Food Magazine - 12; ftm only.
  Publications on www.moodfoodmag.com

Federation of Sports & Play Associations (FSPA) 1919

- ■ Federation House, STONELEIGH PARK, Warks, CV8 2RF.   (hq)
  024 7641 4999   fax 024 7641 4990
  email admin@sportsandplay.com
  http://www.sportsandplay.com

  Head of Membership & Communications: Jane Montgomery
- ▲ Company Limited by Guarantee
- ○ *N, *S, *T; to represent the sports goods & play industries
- Gp Specialist:
  Angling Trades Association Ltd
  Association of Play Industries
  Association of Professional Sales Agents (Sports & Leisure Industries)
  British Association of Seating Equipment Suppliers
  British Golf Industry Association
  British Rootzone & Top Dressing Manufacturers Association
  European Golf Industry Association
  Golf Consultants Association
  Motorsports Industry Association
  Play Providers Association
  Professional Coarse Fisheries Association
  Professional Darts Players Association
  Sporting Goods Industry Association
  Sports & Fitness Equipment Association
  Sports & Play Construction Association
  UK Golf Course Owners Association
  Wheeled & Urban Sports Association
  General:
  Register of Play Inspectors International Ltd
- ● Conf - Mtgs - ET - Exam - Res - Exhib - Stat - Expt - Inf - Lib - LG
- < Wld Fedn of the Sporting Goods Ind (WFSGI); Fedn of the Eur Sporting Goods Ind
- > Profl Darts Corporation (PDC)
- M 400 f in 18 assns
- ¶ Sportslife - 4; ftm, £1.75 each nm.
  Membership Directory - 1; free.

Federation of Stadium Communities (FSC) 1991
NR Vale Park Enterprise Centre (suite 20), Hamil Rd, Burslem,
STOKE-ON-TRENT, Staffs, ST6 1AW.   (hq)
01782 831900
http://www.stadiumcommunities.org
Chief Exec: Judy Crabb
▲ Company Limited by Guarantee; Registered Charity
○ *K; to improve the quality of life of those communities that exist
in the shadow of sports stadia; to encourage & assist the
formation of constructive partnerships between sports clubs,
local communities, local authorities & other interested parties
● Conf - Mtgs - ET - Res - Inf - LG - Advocacy - Representation -
Consultancy
M 245 community groups
¶ The Shadow NL - 4;   AR; both free.

Federation of Street Traders Unions
NR Unit 1 Balmoral Trading Estate, River Rd, BARKING, Essex,
IG11 0EG.   (hq)
020 8591 1004
Hon Sec: Wally Watson
○ *T

Federation of Surgical Speciality Associations (FSSA)
NR 35-43 Lincoln's Inn Fields, LONDON, WC2A 3PE.   (asa)
020 7611 1731
email secretariat@fssa.org.uk   http://www.fssa.org.uk
Pres: Ian Martin
○ *M; to represent & coordinate the views, aims & policies of
surgeons from across the UK & Ireland
● LG - Mtgs
M 15,000 i in 9 org

Federation of Swiss Societies in the UK (FOSSUK) 1949
NR Swiss Embassy, 16-18 Montagu Place, LONDON, W1H 2BQ.
020 7616 6000   fax 020 7724 7001
email info@swiss-societies.co.uk
http://www.swiss-societies.co.uk
○ *X
M 25 org

Federation of Synagogues 1887
NR 65 Watford Way, LONDON, NW4 3AQ.   (hq)
020 8202 2263   fax 020 8203 0610
email info@federationofsynagogues.com
http://www.federationofsynagogues.com
Chief Exec: Dr Eli Kienwald
▲ Registered Charity
○ *R; to provide services to Orthodox rabbis; to assist
congregations in erection, reconstruction or redecoration of
synagogues; to assist in maintenance of Orthodox religious
instruction.   Is also a burial society providing an orthodox
Jewish funeral to its members & others of the Jewish faith

Federation of Tax Advisers (FTA) 1997
■ Burford House, 44 London Rd, SEVENOAKS, Kent,
TN13 1AS.   (hq)
01626 891222   fax 01732 455848
email admin@fta.co.uk   http://www.fta.uk.com
Managing Dir & Sec: P T Harmsworth
▲ Company Limited by Guarantee
○ *P; to offer support to tax advisers
● ET - Exam - Inf - LG
M 720 i
¶ NL - 12; ftm only

Federation of Technological Industries
dissolved May 2010

Federation of Tour Operators
merged 1 July 2008 with the Association of British Travel Agents to
form **ABTA**

Federation for Ulster Local Studies Ltd (FULS) 1975
■ 18 Ardmore Avenue, DOWNPATRICK, Co Down, BT30 6JU.
(hsp)
028 4461 2986
email info@fuls.org.uk   http://www.fuls.org.uk
Hon Sec: William Devlin
▲ Company Limited by Guarantee; Registered Charity
○ *G, *N; to promote the study & recording of the history,
antiquities & folk life of Ulster; to develop co-operation &
communications between local historical groups & between
the groups & relevant voluntary organisations
● Conf - Mtgs - ET - SG - VE - LG
< Fedn of Local History Socs (Republic of Ireland)
M 94 org
(Sub: £30)
¶ Due North - 2; £1.50 m, £3 nm.

Federation of Wholesale Distributors (FWD) 1918
NR 9 Gildredge Rd, EASTBOURNE, E Sussex, BN21 4RB.   (hq)
01323 724952   fax 01323 732820
email nikki@fwd-uk.com   http://www.fwd.co.uk
Chief Exec: Chris Etherington
▲ Un-incorporated Society
○ *T; for UK wholesalers operating in the grocery & foodservice
markets supplying independent retailers & caterers
● Conf - Inf - LG - Mtgs
M 15 f

Federation of Window Cleaners (FWC) 1947
■ Summerfield House, Harrogate Rd, STOCKPORT, Cheshire,
SK5 6HQ.   (hq)
0161-432 8754   fax 0161-947 9033
email info@f-w-c.co.uk   http://www.f-w-c.co.uk
Gen Sec: Beryl Murray
▲ Un-incorporated Society
○ *T; to support & improve the window cleaning industry
● Mtgs - ET - Exhib - Comp - Inf - LG
< Intl Window Cleaning Assn (IWCA)
M 1,600 f
¶ Window Talk (Jnl) - 4; free.
× 2006 (1 January) National Federation of Master Window &
General Cleaners

**Federation of Women's Institutes of Northern Ireland
(FWINI) 1932**
■ Federation House, 209-211 Upper Lisburn Rd, BELFAST,
BT10 0LL.   (hq)
028 9030 1506 & 028 9060 1781   fax 028 9043 1127
email wini@btconnect.com   http://www.wini.org.uk
Gen Sec: Irene Sproule
▲ Registered Charity
Br 190
○ *W; 'confidence building: encouraging women to reach their
potential, giving opportunities to meet other women, learn
new skills & provide new opportunities'
● Conf - Mtgs - Exhib - Comp
< Associated Countrywomen of the Wld (ACWW)
M 7,000+ i
¶ Ulster Countrywoman - 10; 85p.

Fèisean nan Gàidheal 1991
NR Meall House, PORTREE, Isle of Skye, IV51 9BZ.   (hq)
01478 613355   fax 01478 613399
http://www.feisean.org
Taigh a'Mhill, PORT RIGH, An t-Eilean Sgitheanach, IV51
9BZ.
Chief Exec: Arthur Cormack
▲ Company Limited by Guarantee; Registered Charity
○ *A, *D; to support the development of community-based Gaelic
arts tuition festivals throughout Scotland
M i & org

© CBD Research Ltd · Beckenham · BR3 5JS · Tel 020 8650 7745 · E-mail cbd@cbdresearch.com · www.cbdresearch.com

Fell Pony Society (FPS) 1898
■ Ion House, Great Asby, APPLEBY-IN-WESTMORLAND, Cumbria, CA16 6HD. (hsp)
01768 353100 fax 01768 353100
http://www.fellponysociety.org
Sec: Elizabeth Parkin
▲ Company Limited by Guarantee
Br Germany, Netherlands
○ *B
● Mtgs - Exhib - Comp - Inf
< Brit Assn Equine Socs; Nat Pony Soc; Brit Horse Soc; Brit Central Prefix Register
M 1,020 i, UK / 80 i, o'seas
¶ Stud Book - 1; price varies.

Fell Runners Association (FRA) 1970
■ 6 Westville Ave, ILKLEY, W Yorks, LS29 9AH. (hsp)
01943 600439
email morgan@morganwilliams.org
http://www.fellrunner.org.uk
Sec: Morgan Williams
▲ Un-incorporated Society
○ *S; the governing body of fell running in England; to encourage & promote fell running; to provide services to competitors; to establish regulations for the conduct of clubs, competitors & race organisers
● Comp
< UK Athletics; Wld Mountain Running Assn
M 6,500 i & org
¶ The Fell Runner - 3; Hbk & Fixtures Calendar - 1; both ftm only.

Fellowship of Cycling Old-Timers (FCOT) 1965
■ 5 Avocet Close, Oulton Broad, LOWESTOFT, Suffolk, NR33 8PU. (gensec/p)
01502 563262
email fcot.uk@virgin.net
Gen Sec: Sian Charlton
▲ Un-incorporated Society
○ *G; for cyclists of age 50 & up who wish to stay cycling or return to it; to keep in touch with old cycling friends
● Mtgs
M 1,160 i, UK / 60 i, o'seas
¶ Fellowship News - 4; ftm, £2 nm.

Fellowship of Depressives Anonymous
since September 2007 **Depression UK**

Fellowship of Independent Evangelical Churches (FIEC) 1922
■ 39 The Point, Rockingham Rd, MARKET HARBOROUGH, Leics, LE16 7QU. (hq)
01858 434540 fax 01858 411550
email admin@fiec.org.uk http://www.fiec.org.uk
Gen Sec: Richard J Underwood
▲ Registered Charity
Br 495
○ *R; to establish & strengthen independent evangelical churches; to uphold & proclaim the Christian gospel
Gp Pastors' Association - supporting, equipping & setting standards for ministers & their churches
Prepared for Service - a training course for Christian ministry
● Conf - Mtgs - ET - Inf
< Affinity
M 23,000 i, 495 churches, UK / 700 i, o'seas
¶ Together - 2; ftm only.   Churches Hbk - 3 yrly; £10.
FIEC Directory - 2 yrly; £6 m, £9 nm.

Fellowship of Makers & Researchers of Historical Instruments (FoMRHI) 1975
NR Southside Cottage, Brook Hill, Albury, GUILDFORD, Surrey, GU5 9DJ. (hsp)
01483 202159 fax 01483 203088
email secretary@fomrhi.org http://www.fomrhi.org
Hon Sec: Christopher Goodwin
○ *L; to promote authenticity in the making, restoration & use of historical musical instruments
● Conf - Res - SG - Inf
M 700 i, UK & o'seas
¶ FoMRHI Quarterly - 4; ftm only.   LM - 1 (updates - 4).
Note: Information is only given to persons writing theses if they are members.

Fellowship of Postgraduate Medicine (FPM) 1919
■ 12 Chandos St, LONDON, W1G 9DR. (hq)
020 7636 6334 fax 020 7436 2535
email fpm.chandos@qmail.com
http://www.fpm-uk.org
Hon Sec: Dr Timothy R J Nicholson
▲ Registered Charity
○ *E, *M; to promote postgraduate medical education & research
● Comp - Conf - Mtgs
M c 60 i
¶ Postgraduate Medical Jnl - 12.
Health Policy & Technology (Jnl) - launch issue March 2012

Fellowship of the White Boar
see **Richard III Society: Fellowship of the White Boar**

Fencing Contractors' Association Ltd (FCA) 1942
■ Warren Rd, Trellech, MONMOUTH, NP25 4PQ. (hq)
07000 560722 fax 01600 860888
email info@fencingcontractors.org
http://www.fencingcontractors.org
Chief Exec: Wendy A Baker
▲ Incorporated under the Industrial & Provident Societies Act.
○ *T; contracting, supplying & manufacturing for fencing & safety barriers
Gp Incorporating:
Association of Safety Fencing Contractors
Electric Security Fencing Federation
Environmental Noise Barrier Association
Gate Automation & Access Barrier Association
● Conf - Mtgs - Inf - Empl - LG
M 230 f
¶ NL - 4; ftm only.   LM; free.

Feng Shui Society (FSS) 1993
NR 123 Mashiters Walk, ROMFORD, Essex, RM1 4BU. (asa)
email info@fengshuisociety.org.uk
http://www.fengshuisociety.org.uk
Sec: Rosie Francis
▲ Un-incorporated Society
Br 12
○ *P; to promote the highest standards of feng shui practice
● Conf - Mtgs - ET - Exam - Res - Exhib - SG - Inf - Lib - PL - VE - LG
M 68 i
¶ Feng Shui News; ftm only.

FeRFA: the Resin Flooring Association (FeRFA) 1969
■ 16 Edward Rd, FARNHAM, Surrey, GU9 8NP. (hq)
01252 714250
email secretariat@ferfa.org.uk http://www.ferfa.org.uk
Hon Sec: Lisa Hennessey
▲ Company Limited by Guarantee
○ *T; UK manufacturers, contractors & associated companies involved in industrial resin systems
Gp Technical working parties
● Conf - Mtgs - Exhib - Comp - LG
M 82 f
¶ Technical Guidance Notes.

Fertility Care Scotland   1976
- ■ 196 Clyde St, GLASGOW, G1 4JY.   (hq)
  0141-221 0858
  email info@fertilitycare.org.uk
  http://www.fertilitycare.org.uk
- ▲ Registered Charity
- Br 16
- ○ *M, *W; to promote the Billings ovulation method of natural family planning
- Gp Educational presentations & resourcing; Fertility / infertility awareness; Natural family planning tuition; Teaching Billings ovulation method
- ● Mtgs - ET - Exam - Inf
- < Wld Org Ovulation Method Billings (WOOMB)
- M 70 i

Fertilizer Association of Ireland   1968
- IRL c/o Grassland Fertilizers Ltd, Carrigrohane Rd, CORK, Co Cork, Republic of Ireland.   (mail)
  353 (87) 275 5625
  http://www.fertilizer-assoc.ie
  Pres: Kieran Murphy
- ○ *T; to promote the efficient use of fertiliser to produce quality food in an economical & environmentally sustainable manner

Ffederasiwn Cerddoriaeth Amatur Cymru
> see **Welsh Amateur Music Federation (Ffederasiwn Cerddorieath Amatur Cymru)**

Ffestiniog Railway Society Ltd   (FRSL)   1954
- NR Harbour Station, PORTHMADOG, Gwynedd, LL49 9NF.   (hq)
  01766 516035
- ○ *G; conservation of the Ffestiniog Railway
- M i
  This is not the same organisation as the Ffestiniog Railway Company.

Fibre Bonded Carpet Manufacturers' Association
> has closed

Fibre Cement Manufacturers' Association Ltd
> is no longer active

Fibre Technology Association   (FTA)   1995
- § PO Box 420, DURHAM, DH1 9WY.
  07836 796000   fax 0870 137 0369
  email fta.services@btinternet.com
  Senior Consultant: Barry Read
- ▲ Company Limited by Guarantee
  a company offering technical support, consultancy & contract research & development services to the recovered paper industry

Fibreoptic Industry Association   (FIA)   1990
- ■ The Manor House, High St, BUNTINGFORD, Herts, SG9 9AB.   (hq)
  01763 273039   fax 01763 273255
  email secretary@fia-online.co.uk
  http://www.fia-online.co.uk
  Co Sec: Jane Morrison
- ▲ Company Limited by Guarantee
- ○ *T; to facilitate the development & professionalism of the UK's fibre optic industry; to represent end users of fibre optics, installers, distributors, training providers, consultants & component manufacturers
- ● Mtgs - ET - SG - Inf
- M 5 i, 210 f, UK / 5 i, o'seas
- ¶ NL - 6;   Members' Guide to Products & Services (2000); both free.
  Technical publications; ftm (website password); prices vary nm.

Fibromyalgia Association UK   (FMA UK)   1994
- ■ PO Box 206, STOURBRIDGE, W Midlands, DY9 8YL.   (hq)
  0845 345 2322   fax 01384 895005
  email charity@fmauk.org   http://www.fmauk.org
  Chmn: Pam Stewart
- ▲ Registered Charity
- Br 90
- ○ *W; to raise awareness of fibromyalgia & its effects, to both the public at large & to the health professionals responsible for diagnosing & treating people with the condition
- ● Conf - Mtgs - Res - Comp - Inf - LG
  Fibromyalgia benefits helpline: 0845 345 2343 (Mon-Fri 1000-1600)
- > Local support groups in UK & NI
- M 8,000 i, 65 org, UK / 100 i, o'seas
- ¶ Family Magazine - 12; £16.50 yr.

Field Studies Council   (FSC)   1943
- ■ Preston Montford, SHREWSBURY, Shropshire, SY4 1HW.   (hq)
  01743 852100   fax 01743 852101
  email enquiries@field-studies-council.org
  http://www.field-studies-council.org
  Chmn: Prof Timothy Burt
- ▲ Company Limited by Guarantee; Registered Charity
- Br 17
- ○ *E, *L; to help people of all ages to discover, explore & be inspired by the natural environment
- ● ET - Res - SG - VE
- M 4,000 i, UK / 250 i, o'seas
- ¶ Field Studies Magazine - 2; ftm only.   AR; free.
  Catalogue of publications; on request.

Fields in Trust
> see **National Playing Fields Association**

Fife Agricultural Association   (FAA)
- NR Chesterhill, Boarhills, ST ANDREWS, Fife, KY16 8PP.   (hsp)
  01334 880518
  email louise.roger@scotland.gsi.gov.uk
  http://www.fifeshow.com
  Sec: Louise Roger
- ▲ Registered Charity
- ○ *F
- ● Fife Show
- < Assn of Show & Agricl Orgs
- M 600 i

Fife Chamber of Commerce & Enterprise Ltd   1988
- NR Evans Business Centre, 1 Begg Rd, John Smith Business Park, KIRKCALDY, Fife, KY2 6HD.   (hq)
  01592 647740
  email info@fifechamber.co.uk
  http://www.fifechamber.co.uk
  Chief Exec: Alan Russell
- ▲ Company Limited by Guarantee
- ○ *C
- < Scot Chams of Comm
- M f

Film Distributors' Association   (FDA)   1915
- ■ 22 Golden Sq, LONDON, W1F 9JW.   (hq)
  020 7437 4383   fax 020 7734 0912
  http://www.launchingfilms.com
  Chief Exec & Sec: Mark Batey
- ▲ Company Limited by Guarantee
- ○ *T
- ● Mtgs - Inf - LG - Liaison with all industry & other bodies where distributor interests are concerned
- < Intl Fedn Film Distributor Assns (FIAD)
- M 13 f

Film & Video Institute
> see **Institute of Amateur Cinematographers**

© CBD Research Ltd · Beckenham · BR3 5JS · Tel 020 8650 7745 · E-mail cbd@cbdresearch.com · www.cbdresearch.com

Filtration Society   1964

■ The Well House, West Hill Rd, West Hill, OTTERY St MARY, Devon, EX11 1UZ.   (hsp)
  01404 814947   fax 01404 814947
  email richard@richardwakeman.co.uk
  http://www.filtsoc.org
  Sec: Prof Richard Wakeman
▲ Registered Charity
Br 8 o'seas
○ *L; filtration, separation & related processes; design, manufacture & use of filtration equipment & processes
● Conf - Mtgs - ET - Res - Exhib - Lib - VE
M 400 i, UK / 870 i, o'seas
¶ Jnl - 4.

Finance Industry Standards Association

dissolved 16 March 2010

Finance & Leasing Association   (FLA)   1992

NR Imperial House, 15-19 Kingsway, LONDON, WC2B 6UN.
  (hq)
  020 7836 6511   fax 020 7420 9600
  email info@fla.org.uk   http://www.fla.org.uk
  Dir Gen: Stephen Sklaroff
▲ Company Limited by Guarantee
○ *T; to represent companies providing consumer credit, business finance & leasing & motor finance
Gp Divns: Asset finance & leasing, Consumer finance, Motor finance
● Conf - Mtgs - ET - Exam - Stat - LG
< Eur Fedn of Finance House Assns (EUROFINAS); Eur Fedn Eqpt Leasing Co Assns (LEASEUROPE)
M 100 f, 56 associates
¶ Annual Survey of Business Finance.
  Code of Practice.   AR; free.
  Early Settlement Rebate (leaflet).

Financial Services Ireland   (FSI)   1984

IRL Confederation House, 84-86 Lower Baggot St, DUBLIN 2, Republic of Ireland.   (hq)
  353 (1) 605 1565   fax 353 (1) 638 1565
  email fsi@ibec.ie   http://www.fsi.ie
  Dir: Brendan Bruen
○ *T; banks, building societies, insurance companies, fund administrators & managers, investment companies, leasing companies, stockbrokers, treasury companies & other providers of financial services
< IBEC
M 150 f

Fine Art Trade Guild   1910

■ 16-18 Empress Place, LONDON, SW6 1TT.   (hq)
  020 7381 6616   fax 020 7381 2596
  email info@fineart.co.uk   http://www.fineart.co.uk
  Chief Exec: Louise Hay
▲ Company Limited by Guarantee
○ *T; for the picture trade & fine art publishing
Gp Art galleries; Suppliers to the fine arts; Picture framers; Picture restorers; Fine art printers; Artists
● Conf - Mtgs - ET - Exam - Exhib - Comp - Expt - Inf - Lib - LG
¶ Art Business Today (Jnl) - 5; ftm, £25 yr nm.
  The Directory - 1; ftm, £52.50 nm.
  LM (on disk); £141 m only.
  The Artist's Guide to Selling Work; ftm, £9.99 nm.
  Starting up a Gallery & Frame Shop; £14.99 nm.

Fingerprint Society   1974

■ Fingerprint Bureau, Humberside Police HQ, Priory Rd, HULL, HU5 5SF.   (chmn/b)
  01482 220518   fax 01482 220545
  email robert.doak@humberside.pnn.police.uk
  http://www.fpsociety.org.uk
  Chmn: Robert Doak
▲ Un-incorporated Society
○ *P; to advance the study & application of fingerprints & to facilitate the co-operation among persons interested in this field of personal identification
● Conf - Mtgs - ET
M 291 i, 10 f, 7 universities, UK / 260 i, o'seas
¶ Fingerprint Whorld - 4; ftm.

Finnish-British Chamber of Commerce   2001

NR Lyric House (5th floor), 149 Hammersmith Rd, LONDON, W14 0QL.   (hq)
  020 7602 5405
  email info@fbcc.co.uk   http://www.fbcc.co.uk
  Gen Mgr: Mrs Hely Abbondati
▲ Company Limited by Guarantee
○ *C; to promote & develop trade & other economic relations between Finland & Great Britain; to retain direct contacts with & express the views of members to both the Finnish & British governments
● Mtgs - Expt - Inf - VE - Junior Chamber of Commerce
M f

Fire Brigade Society   (FBS)   1963

■ 4 Campion Close, Scalby, SCARBOROUGH, N Yorks, YO13 0QJ.   (admin)
  http://www.thefirebrigadesociety.co.uk
  Pres: Tony McGuirk
Br 14; worldwide
○ *G; to promote & foster interest in fire & rescue services, their organisation, stations & appliances
● Mtgs - Lib - VE
M 800 i, 12 orgs, UK / 100 i, o'seas
¶ Fire Cover - 4; ftm only.

Fire Brigades Union   (FBU)   1918

■ Bradley House, 68 Coombe Rd, KINGSTON UPON THAMES, Surrey, KT2 7AE.   (hq)
  020 8541 1765   fax 020 8546 5187
  email office@fbu.org.uk   http://www.fbu.org.uk
  Gen Sec: Matt Wrack
○ *U; for all uniformed fire service personnel
< Trades U Congress (TUC)
M 43,896 i

Fire Extinguishing Trades Association
in 2007 merged with the Association of British Fire Trades, the British Fire Protection Systems Association & the Fire Industry Confederation to form the **Fire Industry Association**

Fire Fighting Vehicles Manufacturers' Association   (FFVMA)   1970

NR 25 Westfield Rd, GUILDFORD, Surrey, GU1 1RR.   (sec/b)
  01483 506678
  http://www.ffvma.org.uk
○ *T; interests of manufacturers of fire appliances & pumps
M f

Fire Industry Association (FIA) 2007
NR Tudor House, Kingsway Business Park, Oldfield Rd, HAMPTON,
　　Middx, TW12 2HD.   (hq)
　　020 3166 5001   fax 020 8941 0972
　　email info@fia.uk.com   http://www.fia.uk.com
▲ Company Limited by Guarantee
○ *T; manufacturers & specialist distributors of fire extinguishers
　　of all types, incl portable fire fighting eqpt & fittings
Gp Mfrs: Fire extinguisher, Fittings & hose; Servicing companies
● Conf - Mtgs - ET - Exam - Exhib - Inf - LG - Standards
< Eur C'ee of Mfrs of Fire Protection Eqpt & Fire Fighting Vehicles
　　(EUROFEU); Fire Ind Coun; Fire Protection Assn; Fedn of Brit
　　Fire Orgs; BSI
M 85 f, UK / 5 f, o'seas
¶ LM; free.
　　Guide to the servicing of portable fire extinguishers.
× 2007 (Association of British Fire Trades
　　　(British Fire Protection Systems Association
　　　(Fire Extinguishing Trades Association
　　　(Fire Industry Confederation

Fire Industry Confederation
　　in 2007 merged with the Association of British Fire Trades, the British
　　Fire Protection Systems Association & the Fire Extinguishing Trades
　　Association to form the **Fire Industry Association**

Fire Mark Circle (FMC) 1934
NR Flint Hall, Market Hill, BRANDON, Suffolk, IP27 0AA.
　　(chmn/p)
　　http://www.firemarkcircle.com
　　Chmn: Pat Baldwin
▲ Un-incorporated Society
○ *G; for persons interested in the origin & history of fire
　　insurance companies, their fire marks, fire brigades & all that
　　pertains to the past of fire insurance
● Conf - Mtgs - Res - Inf - Lib - Valuation of collections
< Fire Mark Circle of America
M 200 i, UK / 2 i, o'seas
¶ FMC News - 2;
　　Membership List, Rarity Guide, both 2 yrly; all ftm.

Fire Officers' Association (FOA) 1994
NR London Rd, MORETON-IN-MARSH, Glos, GL56 0RH.   (hq)
　　01608 652023
　　email foa@fireofficers.org.uk
　　http://www.fireofficers.org.uk
　　Chief Exec: Glyn Morgan
○ *U; the efficiency & status of the fire service; to maintain the
　　conditions of service of its employees
● LG
M 2,500 i
¶ Magazine - 4; ftm only.

Fire Protection Association (FPA) 1946
NR London Rd, MORETON-IN-MARSH, Glos, GL56 0RH.   (hq)
　　01608 812500   fax 01608 812501
　　email fpa@thefpa.co.uk   http://www.thefpa.co.uk
　　Managing Dir: Jonathan O'Neill
▲ Company Limited by Guarantee
○ *L, *P; the UK's national fire safety organisation, providing
　　authoritative advice, information & training on all aspects of
　　fire safety
● ET - Res - Exhib - Stat - Inf - Lib - LG
< Confedn of Fire Protection Assn Europe (CFPA-Europe); Fedn of
　　Brit Fire Orgs (FBFO)
M 3,500 i, UK / 1,500 f, o'seas
¶ Fire Prevention (Jnl) - 12.
　　Fire Protection Ybk.   Handbooks - 1.
　　Technical publications & CDs on aspects of fire fighting;
　　catalogue available.

Fire & Rescue Suppliers Association (FIRESA) 2005
NR Tudor House, Kingsway Business Park, Oldfield Rd, HAMPTON,
　　Middx, TW12 2HD.   (hq)
　　020 3166 5002   fax 020 8941 0972
　　email dsmith@fia.uk.com   http://www.firesa.org.uk
　　Sec: Dave Smith
○ *T; to contribute positively to the growth & development of the
　　fire & rescue service market, thereby improving its
　　effectiveness & playing an association role in protecting life,
　　property & the environment.
● LG - Mtgs
< Fedn of Brit Fire Orgs (FOBFO); Fire Ind Assn (FIA)
M 49 f
¶ NL

Fire Service Preservation Group (FSPG) 1968
■ 50 Old Slade Lane, IVER, Bucks, SL0 9DR.   (treas/p)
　　01753 652207
　　email Secretary@f-s-p-g.org   http://www.f-s-p-g.org
　　Treas: Andrew Scott
▲ Un-incorporated Society
Br 12
○ *G; for those interested in the history of the fire service, the
　　preservation of fire engines & associated equipment.
　　Appliances owned by the group & its members date from
　　1730 to 1987
● Mtgs
< Fedn Brit Historic Vehicles Clubs
M c 600 units, UK / 6 units, o'seas
¶ Off the Run - 12; ftm only.

Fire Sprinkler Association Ltd
　　since March 2007 **Residential Sprinkler Association**

First Aid Association (FAA) 1995
■ Hamilton House, 4 The Avenue, Highams Park, LONDON,
　　E4 9LD.   (hq)
　　020 8281 4289
　　email info@firstaidassociation.co.uk
　　http://www.firstaidassociation.co.uk
　　Founder: Tahir Parkar
▲ Un-incorporated Society
○ *G, *W; to promote the profile & status of those engaged in
　　professional first aid industry
● Conf - Mtgs - ET - Exam - Res - LG

First Aid Council for Training (FACT) 1994
NR 178 Marlborough Way, ASHBY DE LA ZOUCH, Leics,
　　LE65 2QL.   (asa)
　　020 8798 0767
　　email info@firstaidcounciloftraining.org.uk
　　http://www.aifawto.co.uk
　　Secretariat: Ian Irwin
○ *G; members run first aid courses in various parts of the
　　country
● ET
× 2008 Association of Independent First Aid at Work
　　　Training Organisations

First Division Association (FDA) 1918
NR 8 Leake St, LONDON, SE1 7NN.   (hq)
　　020 7401 5555   fax 020 7401 5550
　　email info@fda.org.uk   http://www.fda.org.uk
　　Gen Sec: Jonathan Baume
○ *P, *U; the union of choice for senior managers & professionals
　　in public service
Gp Association of Revenue & Customs
● Conf - Mtgs - Res - Empl - LG
< Trades U Congress (TUC)
M 17,466 i
¶ Public Service Magazine - 6; ftm, £22.95 yr nm.
× Association of First Division Civil Servants

© CBD Research Ltd · Beckenham · BR3 5JS · Tel 020 8650 7745 · E-mail cbd@cbdresearch.com · www.cbdresearch.com

Fish Veterinary Society
a group of the **British Veterinary Association**

Fisheries & Angling Conservation Trust
in 2009 merged with the Anglers Conservation Association, the National Association of Fisheries & Angling Consultatives, the National Federation of Anglers, the National Federation of Sea Anglers to form the **Angling Trust**

Fisheries Society of the British Isles   (FSBI)   1967
NR College of Life Sciences, University of Dundee, DUNDEE, Angus, DD1 4HN.
01382 282000
email secretary@fsbi.org.uk   http://www.fsbi.org.uk
Sec: Prof Brian Eddy
○   *L; to promote the interests of fish biology & fisheries management

Fishermen's Association (Scotland) Ltd
a member association of the **Scottish Fishermen's Federation**

Fitness Industry Association   (FIA)   1991
NR Castlewood House, 77-91 New Oxford St, LONDON, WC1A 1PX.   (hq)
020 7420 8560   fax 020 7420 8561
email info@fia.org.uk   http://www.fia.org.uk
Chief Exec: Andrée Deane
▲   Company Limited by Guarantee
○   *T; for the health & fitness industry
Gp Educational establishments; Operators; Sports centres; Suppliers; Students & individuals
●   Conf - Mtgs - ET - Res - Exhib - Comp - SG - Stat - Expt - Inf - Lib - VE - Empl - LG
<   Intl Health, Racquet & Sportsclubs Assn
M   1,600 clubs
¶   Leisure Management - 12;   Health Club Management - 12;
    Leisure Opportunities - 24;   CBI - 12;
    On Track Magazine - 4;   all ftm.

Fitness League   1930
NR 6 Station Parade, SUNNINGDALE, Berks, SL5 0EP.   (hq)
01344 874787
http://www.thefitnessleague.com
▲   Registered Charity
○   *G; the provision of exercise & movement to music classes for all ages & abilities
M   14,000 i

Fitness Northern Ireland   1952
NR The Robinson Centre, Montgomery Rd, BELFAST, BT6 9HS.   (hq)
028 9070 4080
email fitnessni@aol.com   http://www.fitnessni.org
▲   Company Limited by Guarantee
○   *G; governing body for fitness & exercising training
●   ET
M   9,000 i

Fitness Products Association
in 2006 merged with the **Sporting Goods Industry Association**

Fjord Horse National Stud Book Association of Great Britain (FHNSAofGB)   1984
■   Cilyblaidd Manor, Pencarreg, LLANYBYDDER, Carmarthenshire, SA40 9QL.   (hsb)
01570 480090
email info@fjord-horse.co.uk
http://www.fjord-horse.co.uk
Sec: Lyn D Moran
▲   Company Limited by Guarantee
○   *B; to promote, preserve & verify the fjord horse in GB in accordance with the Mother Stud Book in Norway; to act as the official Passport Issuing Authority in the UK
●   Mtgs - Res - Exhib - Stat - Inf
<   Fjordhesteavlen i Danmark; Brit Horse Soc
M   106 i, UK / 24 i, o'seas
¶   Jnl - 1.
×   Fjord Horse Society of GB

Flag Institute   1971
■   38 Hill St, LONDON, W1J 5NS.   (gensec/p)
email membership@flaginstitute.org
http://www.flaginstitute.org
Gen Sec: Mike Kearsley
▲   Un-incorporated Society
○   *L; research & publication of information on flags of all countries, periods & kinds
●   Mtgs - Res - Inf - Lib
<   Fédn Intle des Assns Véxillologiques
M   c 500 i, f & org
¶   Flagmaster - 4; ftm.

Flat Glass Council
a group of the **Glass & Glazing Federation**

Flat Glass Manufacturers Association   (FGMA)
■   Alexandra Business Park, Prescot Rd, ST HELENS, Merseyside, WA10 3TT.   (gensec/b)
01744 28882   fax 01744 692660
Sec Gen: Phil Brown
▲   Un-incorporated Society
○   *T; to support & promote interests of flat glass manufacturers in the UK
●   LG
<   Glass & Glazing Fedn
M   1 f

Flat Roofing Alliance
since 2009 a division of the **National Federation of Roofing Contractors**

Flecker & Firbank Society   (FFS)   2010
■   144c Southwark Park Rd, LONDON, SE16 3RP.   (hsp)
020 7237 5912
email walht@aol.com
http://www.fleckerandfirbanksociety.org
Hon Sec: Heather Walker
▲   Un-incorporated Society
○   *A; to further interest in the life & works of James Elroy Flecker (1884-1914) & Arthur Annesley Ronald Firbank (1886-1926)
●   Mtgs - Res - Inf
M   6 i, UK / 1 i, o'seas
¶   [NL + Jnl; to come]

** Fleece Washers & Dyers Association
Organisation lost: see Introduction paragraph 3

Flexible Packaging Association
in 2007 merged with the Packaging & Industrial Films Association which in 2009 became the **Packaging & Films Association**

Flintshire Historical Society (FHS) 1911
- 69 Pen-y-Maes Avenue, RHYL, Denbighshire, LL18 4ED. (hsp)
  01745 332220
  http://www.flintshirehistory.org.uk
  Hon Sec: Norma P Parker
- ▲ Registered Charity
- ○ *L; archaeology & history of Flintshire
- ● Mtgs - VE - 6 winter lectures
- < Coun of Brit Archaeology
- M 382 i, 34 org, UK / 4 i, 12 org, o'seas
- ¶ Jnl; £7.50 m, £21 nm.

Floatation Tank Association of the UK & Eire (FTA) 1988
- NR Floatopia, 97 Devonshire Rd, LONDON, W14 2HU. (mail)
  020 8994 0708
  http://www.floatationtankassociation.net
- ▲ Un-incorporated Society
- Br USA
- ○ *G; to promote & disseminate information on floatation (a method of deep relaxation & stress management) & on accredited public float centres
- ● Stat - Inf
- M 20 f

Flood Protection Association (FPA)
- NR Salisbury House, The Square, MAGOR, Monmouthshire, NP26 3HY. (hq)
  0844 335 8457 fax 01633 881637
  http://www.floodprotectionassoc.co.uk
  Chmn: Mary Dhonau
- ○ *T; to promote the interests of manufacturers & installers of flood protection equipment & requirements
- ● LG - Mtgs
- M 16 f

Flooring Industry Training Association (FITA) 1998
- § 4c St Mary's Place, The Lace Market, NOTTINGHAM, NG1 1PH. (hq)
  0115-950 6836 fax 0115-941 2238
  email info@fita.co.uk http://www.fita.co.uk
  FITA is a joint venture by the Contract Flooring Assn & the Nat Inst of Carpet & Floorlayers

Flower Import Trade Association
- ■ 68 First Avenue, Mortlake, LONDON, SW14 8SR. (asa)
  020 8939 6473 fax 020 8878 9983
  email info@fitauk.com http://www.fita-uk.com
- ○ *T; to promote flowers from Colombia
- ● LG
- M 10 f

Flowers & Plants Association Ltd (F&PA) 1984
- NR 68 First Avenue, Mortlake, LONDON, SW14 8SR. (hq)
  020 8939 6472
  email info@flowers.org.uk http://www.flowers.org.uk
  Chief Exec: Andrew Caldecourt
- ▲ Company Limited by Guarantee
- ○ *H, *T; to promote commercially grown cut flowers & houseplants; to work on behalf of the horticulture industry
- ● ET - Res - Exhib - Comp - Stat - Inf - Lib - PL
- < Links with equivalent orgs worldwide
- M c 200 f, UK & o'seas
- ¶ NL - 4; ftm only.
  Leaflets & Factsheets - irreg; ftm, (nm please send sae).

Flydressers Guild 1967
- ■ WorYem, Blackgate Lane, HENFIELD, E Sussex, BN5 9HA. (hsp)
  01273 493473
  email chairman@the-fgd.org http://www.the-fdg.org
  Chmn: A Middleton
- ▲ Un-incorporated Society
- ○ *G, *T; 'teaching the art of tying artificial flies for fishing'
- ● Mtgs - ET - Exhib - Comp
- M 2,200 i, UK / 200 i, o'seas
- ¶ The Flydresser - 4; ftm, £3 nm.

Flying Farmers Association (FFA) 1974
- NR Moor Farm, West Heslerton, MALTON, N Yorks, YO17 8RU. (hsb)
  01944 738281 fax 01944 738240
  http://www.ffa.org.uk
  Hon Sec: Paul A Stephens
- ▲ Company Limited by Guarantee
- ○ *P; to safeguard members' special interests as aircraft, or airstrip, owners by representation on the General Aviation Safety Council
- ● Mtgs - Inf - VE - LG (Civil Aviation Authority) - Insurance
- M c 370 i
- ¶ NL; LM; Map of Members' Airstrips; all m only.

FM Society
  a specialist group of the **Chartered Institute of Building**

FOCAL International Ltd
  see **Federation of Commercial Audiovisual Libraries Ltd**

Folio Society 1947
- § 44 Eagle St, LONDON, WC1R 4FS.
  020 7400 4200
  http://www.foliosociety.com
  Run by booklovers for booklovers, creating beautiful editions of the world's greatest books.

Folk Music Society of Ireland
  has closed

FolkArts England
- NR PO Box 296, MATLOCK, Derbys, DE4 3XU. (mail)
  01629 827014 fax 01629 821874
  email info@folkarts-england.org
  http://www.folkarts-england.org
- ○ *G; music: folk, acoustic, roots & traditional

Folklore of Ireland Society 1927
- IRL UCD School of Irish Celtic Studies, Newman Building, Belfield, DUBLIN 4, Republic of Ireland. (hq)
  353 (1) 716 8216 fax 353 (1) 716 1144
  email eolas>bealoideas.ie http://www.bealoideas.ie
  Hon Sec: Rónán Ó Gealbháin
- ○ *L; to collect, preserve & publish the folklore of Ireland

Folklore Society 1878
- ■ c/o The Warburg Institute, Woburn Sq, LONDON, WC1H 0AB. (hq)
  020 7862 8564 fax 020 7862 8565
  http://www.folklore-society.com
  Sec: Prof James Grayson
- ○ *L; systematic comparative study of oral traditions & cultures - trsditional music, song, dance, drama, narrative arts & crafts, customs & beliefs
- ● Conf - Mtgs - Res - Exhib - Inf - Lib
- M c 500 i, c 600 org
- ¶ Folklore - 3. FLS News - 3; ftm.
  New Books in Folklore - 2. Current Folklore - 2.

© CBD Research Ltd · Beckenham · BR3 5JS · Tel 020 8650 7745 · E-mail cbd@cbdresearch.com · www.cbdresearch.com

Followers of Rupert   1983
■   29 Mill Rd, LEWES, E Sussex, BN7 2RU.   (hsp)
     01273 480339   fax 01273 480339
     email rupertsecretary@btinternet.com
     http://www.rupertthebear.org.uk
     Hon Sec: John Beck
▲   Un-incorporated Society
Br   5
○   *A, *G; for all interested in the literature concerning Rupert
     Bear, his artists & storytellers
●   Annual meeting
M   1,150 i, UK / 100 i, o'seas
     (Sub: £25 UK / £30 Europe / £35 rest of world)
¶   NL (+ special issues) - 4;   Rupert Calendar - 1; all ftm only.

Folly Fellowship   1988
NR   1 Keble House, Manor Fields, LONDON, SW15 3LS.   (regd
     off)
     email webmaster@follies.org.uk
     http://www.follies.org.uk
▲   Company Limited by Guarantee; Registered Charity
Br   6; Netherlands
○   *K; to preserve, protect & promote follies, grottoes & garden
     buildings
●   Conf - Mtgs - ET - Res - Exhib - Comp - Inf - Lib - PL - VE
<   Fountain Soc
M   c 850 i, f & org, UK / c 250 i, f & org, o'seas
¶   Follies - 3;   Follies Jnl - 1; both ftm.
     e-Bulletin

Food Additives & Ingredients Association   (FAIA)   1977
■   10 Whitchurch Close, MAIDSTONE, Kent, ME16 8UR.
     (execsec/p)
     01622 682119   fax 01622 682119
     email rbr1@btconnect.com   http://www.faia.org.uk
     Exec Sec: Richard Ratcliffe
○   *T; 'to encourage a positive attitude [to food additives], through
     clear understanding of food additives & ingredients among
     identified key audiences including manufacturers, retailers,
     health professionals, regulatory authorities & consumers'
●   Mtgs - Inf (members only) - LG
<   Fedn Eur Food Additives & Food Enzymes Inds (ELC)
M   25 f

Food & Chemical Allergy Association   1976
§   27 Ferringham Lane, Ferring, WORTHING, W Sussex,
     BN12 5NB.   (chmn/p)
     Chmn: Mrs Ellen Rothera
     An advisory service - not a membership body. Offers advice to
     people on food allergies & chemical sensitivity. Publishes a
     booklet 'Understanding Allergies'; £2 with A5, or medium
     sized, sae.

Food Development Association
     in 2009 merged with the **Food Development Association**

Food & Drink Federation   (FDF)   1973
■   6 Catherine St, LONDON, WC2B 5JJ.   (hq)
     020 7836 2460   fax 020 7836 0580
     http://www.fdf.org.uk
     Dir Gen: Melanie Leech
▲   Company Limited by Guarantee
○   *M, *T; to represent, promote & further the interests of the UK
     food manufacturing industry with government, EU institutions
     & other decision making bodies
Gp   Biscuit, cake, chocolate & confectionery; Frozen food; Meat;
     Organics; Out of home; Sales directors; Seafood; Vegetarian
     & meat-free; Yogurt & chilled desserts
●   Conf - Mtgs - SG - Stat - Lib
<   FoodDrinkEurope; CBI
M   150 f, 19 trade associations

Food & Drink Industry Ireland   (FDII)   1968
IRL Confederation House, 84-86 Lower Baggot St, DUBLIN 2,
     Replublc of Ireland.   (hq)
     353 (1) 605 1621   fax 353 (1) 638 1621
     email paul.kelly@ibec.ie   http://www.fdii.ie
     Dir: Paul Kelly
○   *T; food, drink & non-food grocery manufacturers & suppliers
Gp   Catering Equipment Association; Chocolate, Confectionery &
     Biscuit Council of Ireland; Consumer Foods Council; Food
     Processors & Suppliers Group; Irish Association of Pigmeat
     Processors; Irish Bread Bakers Association; Irish Breakfast
     Cereals Association; Irish Coffee Council; Irish Cold Storage
     Federation; Irish Dairy Industries Association; Meat Industry
     Ireland; Snack Food Association
<   FoodDrinkEurope, Ir Business & Emplrs Confedn (IBEC)
M   150 f

Food Processors Association   (FPA)   2001
NR   6 Catherine St, LONDON, WC2B 5JJ.   (hq)
     020 7420 7106   fax 020 7836 0580
     email martinturton@fdf.org.uk   http://www.fdf.org.uk
     Exec Sec: Martin Turton
○   *T; set up as an umbrella group for four sector associations of
     the Food & Drink Federation which integrated into the FDF in
     2008, the FPA now holds only one formal meeting a year.

Food Processors & Suppliers Group
     a group of **Food & Drink Industry Ireland**

Food Storage & Distribution Federation   (FSDF)   1911
■   7 Diddenham Court, Lamb Wood Hill, Grazeley, READING,
     Berks, RG7 1JS.   (hq)
     0118-988 4468   fax 0118-988 7035
     email info@fsdf.org.uk   http://www.fsdf.org.uk
     Chief Exec: John Hutchings
▲   Company Limited by Guarantee
○   *T; represents & covers all aspects of food storage & distribution
     in the UK; it includes frozen, chilled & ambient sectors
●   Conf - Inf - LG
M   150 f
¶   NL - 4; free.   Information Broadsheet - 12; ftm only.
     Guide/Directory - 2 yrly; ftm, £35 nm.
     RFIC Fire Prevention Guide; ftm, £43 nm.
     RFIC Storage & Handling of Frozen Foods; ftm, £12 nm.
     RFIC Guidance on the Assessment of Fire Risk; ftm, £17 nm.
     CSDF Material Handling Safety Guide; ftm, £50 nm.
     CSDF Fire Risk Minimisation Guidance; ftm, £75 nm.
     CSDF Business Continuity Guide; ftm, £50 nm.
×   2008 (March) Cold Storage & Distribution Federation

**Foodservice Consultants Society International (UK & Ireland)
(FCSI)**
NR   Bourne House, Horsell Park, WOKING, Surrey, GU21 4LY.
     (hq)
     01483 761122   fax 01483 750991
     email admin@fcsi.org.uk   http://www.fcsi.org.uk
     Chmn: Richard Wedgbury
▲   Un-incorporated Society
○   *P; for catering consultants - designers of kitchens, restaurants,
     retail food concepts; hygiene, foodservice, & project
     management
●   Conf - Mtgs - ET - Exam - Exhib - Comp - VE
M   136 i

Foodservice Packaging Association (FPA) 1969
NR The Old Rectory, BLETCHINGTON, Oxon, OX5 3DH.
   (admin/p)
   01869 351139   fax 01869 350231
   email admin@foodservicepackaging.org.uk
   http://www.foodservicepackaging.org.uk
   Admin: Martin Kersh
▲ Un-incorporated Society
○ *T; to promote both the concept & the marketing of disposables
   manufactured in the UK for use in industry, public service &
   the home
Gp Technical c'ees
● Mtgs - Exhib - Inf
M 60 f
   (Sub: £200-£700)
¶ NL - 3/4;
   Booklets on: Drinking vessels, Napkins, Plates & bowls;
   Serviettes; Straws; all free.

Football Association of Ireland (FAI) 1923
IRL National Sports Campus, Abbotstown, DUBLIN 15, Republic of
   Ireland.   (hq)
   353 (1) 899 9500   fax 353 (1) 899 9501
   http://www.fai.ie
   Chief Exec: John Delaney
▲ Limited Liability Company
○ *S; the governing body of football in Ireland

Football Association Ltd (FA) 1863
NR Wembley Stadium, PO Box 1966, LONDON, SW1P 9EQ.   (hq)
   0844 980 8200
   email info@thefa.com   http://www.thefa.com
   Chmn: Richard Burden
▲ Company Limited by Guarantee
○ *S; the governing body for English football; to promote, control,
   organise & administer Association Football in England
● Conf - Exam - Comp - Stat - PL - LG
< U des Assns Eur de Football (UEFA); Fédn Intle de Football
   Assns (FIFA)
> County Football Assns; Football Clubs
M 30 org
¶ The FA Ybk - 1. The FA Hbk - 1.
   The FA Annual Review; free.

Football Association of Wales Ltd (FA of Wales) 1876
NR 11-12 Neptune Court, Vanguard Way, CARDIFF, CF24 5PJ.
   (hq)
   029 2043 5830   fax 029 2049 6953
   email dcollins@faw.co.uk   http://www.faw.org.uk
   Chief Exec: Jonathan Ford
○ *S; administration of Association Football in Wales

Football League Ltd 1888
NR Edward VII Quay, Navigation Way, PRESTON, Lancs, PR2 2YF.
   (hq)
   0844 463 1888   fax 0844 826 5188
   email enquiries@football-league.co.uk
   http://www.football-league.co.uk
   Chief Operating Officer: Andy Williamson
▲ Company Limited by Guarantee
Br 2
○ *S; to administer & regulate the nPower Football League,
   Carling Cup & Johnstone's Paint Trophy as well as reserve &
   youth football
Gp FL Interactive; Football League Trust
● Comp
M 72 clubs

Football Safety Officers Association (FSOA) 1992
NR PO Box 7482, ALFRETON, Derbys, DE55 8BJ.   (hq)
   0114 288 3366
   email fsoaoffice@btconnect.com   http://www.fsoa.org.uk
   Gen Sec: Chris Patzelt
○ *P

Football Supporters' Federation (FSF) 2002
NR The Fans' Stadium, 422A Kingston Rd,
   KINGSTON UPON THAMES, Surrey, KT1 3PB.   (hsb)
   0870 277 7777
   http://www.fsf.org.uk
   Sec: Mike Williamson
▲ Un-incorporated Society
Br England national; Welsh national
○ *S; representing to the Government & football authorities the
   views & concerns of football supporters at all levels of the
   game; information interchange between member clubs on
   best practice & crisis management
Gp Insurance scheme offered for personal accident & late
   cancellation of matches
● Conf - Mtgs - Res - Exhib - LG
> Nat Assn of Disabled Supporters; The Football Programme
   Directory
M 110,000 in 120 supporters clubs UK / 75 i, o'seas
¶ FSF News - 4.
   FSF Members NL - 4.

Football Writers' Association
■ 28 Adelaide Rd, BRAMHALL, Cheshire, SK7 1LT.   (chmn/p)
   07771 933242
   email paul.hetherington@footballwriters.co.uk
   http://www.footballwriters.co.uk
   Chmn: Paul Hetherington
○ *P

Forecourt Equipment Federation (FEF) 1969
■ PO Box 35084, LONDON, NW1 4XE.   (asa)
   020 7935 8532   fax 07006 065950
   email office@fef.org.uk   http://www.fef.org.uk
   Sec: Crispin Dunn-Meynell
○ *T; equipment manufacturers & servicing divisions in the UK
   retail petroleum market, includes liaising with government
   departments on safety, weights & measures legislation &
   regulation
● Mtgs - Res - Inf - LG
M 11 f

Foreign Bird Association (FBA)
NR 29 Mildred Close, DARTFORD, Kent, DA1 1XP.   (patsec/p)
   email alnjanralph@aol.com
   http://www.foreignbirdassociation.org.uk
   Patronage Sec: Mrs J Ralph
○ *G; for UK breeders of foreign birds
● Comp - Exhib - Mtgs
< Foreign Bird Fedn
¶ Beak & Claw - 3.

Foreign Bird Federation 1984
NR 4 St Andrews Drive, Tividale, OLDBURY, W Midlands,
   B69 1PR.   (hsp)
   01384 258154
   http://www.foreignbirdfederation.co.uk
   Hon Sec: Bryan Reed
○ *G; umbrella organisation for foreign bird specialist societies
● Mtgs - Exhib - Comp - VE
< Nat Coun for Aviculture
M 13 org
   (Sub: £25).
¶ Foreign Birds - 4; ftm.

Foreign Press Association in London (FPA) 1888
■ 25 Northumberland Avenue, LONDON, WC2N 5AP.   (hq)
   020 7930 0445   fax 020 7925 0469
   email secretariat@foreign-press.org.uk
   http://www.foreign-press.org.uk
   Dir: Christopher Wyld
▲ Un-incorporated Society
○ *P; to assist foreign correspondents based in the UK in their
   work by arranging briefings, visits etc
● Mtgs - ET - VE - LG
M 200 i, UK / 500 i, o'seas

Forensic Science Society   (FSSoc)   1959
- ■ Clarke House, 18a Mount Parade, HARROGATE, N Yorks, HG1 1BX.   (hq)
  01423 506068   fax 01423 566391
  email info@forensic-science-society.co.uk
  http://www.forensic-science-society.co.uk
  Chief Exec: Dr Carol Ostell
- ▲ Registered Charity
- ○ *L,*P; to advance the study, application & standing of forensic science
- ● Conf - Mtgs - ET - Exam - Inf
- < California Assn of Criminalists
- M 1,750 i, 83 f, UK / 405 i, 13 f, o'seas
- ¶ Science & Justice - 4;   Interfaces - 4; ftm.

Foresight   (Association for the Promotion of Preconceptual Care)   1978
- NR 178 Hawthorn Rd, BOGNOR REGIS, W Sussex, PO21 2UY.   (hq)
  01243 868001   fax 01243 868180
  email emailus@foresight-preconception.org.uk
  http://www.foresight-preconception.org.uk
  Dir: Nim Barnes
- ▲ Registered Charity
- ○ *W; to provide preconceptual care by way of hair analysis; to promote the maximum health & fitness in the body; to enable a healthy pregnancy & healthy babies
- ● Conf - Mtgs - ET - Res - Exhib - SG - Stat - Inf - Lib - LG
- M 2,500 i
- ¶ NL - 3; ftm only.

Forestry Contracting Association
   see **FCA Membership Ltd**

Forestry & Timber Association
   was the trading name of the Association of Timber Growers & Forestry Professionals which in 2006 became the **Confederation of Forest Industries**

Fork Lift Truck Association   (FLTA)   1972
- ■ Manor Farm Buildings, Lasham, ALTON, Hants, GU34 5SL.   (hq)
  01256 381441   fax 01256 381735
  email mail@fork-truck.org.uk
  http://www.fork-truck.org.uk
  Chief Exec: David Ellison
- ▲ Company Limited by Guarantee
- ○ *T; to promote the industry for customers, dealers, manufacturers & suppliers; to raise standards of education, training & health & safety; to provide advice & guidance on operational & related matters
- ● Conf - Mtgs - ET - Exhib - Inf - VE - LG
- < Consolidated Fork Truck Services (CFTS); Fork Lift Apprentices Trust (FLAT)
- M 380 f, UK / 10, o'seas
  (Sub: varies)
- ¶ Uplift (NL) - 4; free.
  Manuals on:
    Health & Safety; Legislation & Registration; Personal Policies & Procedures; Technical Bulletins.
  List of publications available + CDs & DVDs & other items.

Formula Air Racing Association   (FARA)   1972
- ■ c/o Chadwick International, 137 High Holborn, LONDON, WC1V 6PW.   (hsb)
  020 7269 0920   fax 020 7269 0929
  email chadwick@chadwick-international.com
  Contact: Andrew Chadwick
- ▲ Company Limited by Guarantee
- ○ *S; promotion & management of formula air racing in the UK
- ● Comp - LG - Races in UK & Europe
- < Fédn Aeronautique Intle (PAKIS); R Aero Club, London
- M 6 i

Fort Cumberland & Portsmouth Militaria Society   (FC&PMS)   1964
- ■ 5 Herne Rd, Cosham, PORTSMOUTH, Hants, PO6 3PB.   (hsp)
  023 9242 3649
  Sec: Allan Dickenson
- ▲ Registered Charity
- ○ *G; preservation of historical buildings; popularising local military history; maintaining Fort Cumberland Guard
- Gp Fort Cumberland Guard: display group which re-enacts Royal Marines drill of 1803/4 & 1860, incl musket & cannon firing & drum corps drill
- ● Mtgs - ET - Res - Exhib - Inf - Lib - PL - VE
- M 40 i, 2 f

Fort William Chamber of Commerce
- NR West Highland College UHI, An Aird, FORT WILLIAM, PH33 6FF.   (mail)
  01397 874402
  email secretary@fortwilliamchamber.co.uk
  http://www.fortwilliamchamber.co.uk
  Chmn: Robert Hawkes
- ○ *C
- < Scot Chams Comm

Fortress Study Group   (FSG)   1975
- ■ 15 West Park Ave, Roundhay, LEEDS, W Yorks, LS8 2HG.   (hsp)
  email secretary@fsgfort.com   http://www.fsgfort.com
  Hon Sec: Alistair Fyfe
- ▲ Registered Charity
- ○ *L; to encourage the research, study & recording of fortifications of all periods
- ● Conf - Res - SG - Inf - Lib
- < Intl Fortress Coun
- M c 750 i, 50 f
- ¶ Fort (Jnl) - 1;   Casemate (NL) - 3; both ftm only.

Forty Plus (40+) Fishing Boat Association   1995
- ■ 63 Birch Hill Crescent, ONCHAN, Isle of Man, IM3 3DA.   (hsp)
  01624 627568
  email mike.craine@mcb.net
  Hon Sec: Michael Craine
- ○ *G; to encourage research into the historical & social elements of fishing boats; to represent their owners; to encourage liaison between boat owners, museums, heritage centres, trusts, businesses & other organisations in the promotion of the importance of our islands' fishing boat heritage
- ● Res - Exhib - Stat - Inf - PL - LG - Compiling register of all boats over 40 years old
- M 520 i, 50 f, 20 org, UK / 10 i, o'seas
- ¶ Fishing Boats (NL) - 3.

Forum for Clothing & Textiles
   see **ASBCI - the Forum for Clothing & Textiles**

Forum of Private Business   (FPB)   1977
- ■ Ruskin Chambers, Drury Lane, KNUTSFORD, Cheshire, WA16 6HA.   (hq)
   01565 634467   fax 0870 241 9570
   email info@fpb.org   http://www.fpb.org
   Chief Exec: Philip Orford
- ▲ Company Limited by Guarantee
- Br 2
- ○ *K; business support organisation, working with small & medium-sized privately-owned businesses
- Gp Asset finance; Business insurance; Business monitoring; Card processing; D+O insurance; Invoice finance; Legal expenses insurance; Members helpline; Non-core purchasing; Payroll; Telecoms; 24-hour legal helpline; Utilities
- ● Conf - Res - Exhib - Stat - Inf - LG
- < Eur Assn of Small & Medium-sized Enterprises (UEAPME)
- > Brit Cheque Cashers Assn; Garden Centre Assn; Health Food Mfrs' Assn; Nat Soc Allied & Indep Funeral Dirs; etc
- M 600,000 i, 25,000 f, 21 org
- ¶ eNewsletter - 52.   Referendum [NL] - 4.   AR - 1; all ftm.
   Employment Guide - 1; £185 m, £415 nm.
   Health & Safety Guide - 1; £105 m, £205 nm.
   Costs, Controls & Profit (guide); £95 m, £155 nm.

Forum of Professional Recruiters
   on 1 January 2009 merged with the Association of Technology Staffing Companies to form the **Association of Professional Staffing Companies**

Fostering Network   1974
- NR 87 Blackfriars Rd, LONDON, SE1 8HA.   (hq)
   020 7620 6400   fax 020 7620 6401
   email info@fostering.net   http://www.fostering.net
   Chief Exec: Robert Tapsfield
- ▲ Registered Charity
- Br 46 local groups
- ○ *W; to improve the quality of service given to children in care; to bring together representatives of organisations & authorities concerned with fostering
- Gp Assessment of foster carers; Relatives & friends as foster carers
- ● Conf - Mtgs - ET - Res - SG - Stat - Inf - Lib - LG - Advice & mediation service
- M 21,500 i, 213 local authorities, 145 org
- ¶ Foster Care - 4.   AR.
   Publication & resources catalogue available.

Foundation, Aided Schools & Acadamies National Association (FASNA)   1992
- ■ Landau Forte College, Fox St, DERBY, DE1 2LF.   (hq)
   01332 386769
   email fasna@fasna.org.uk   http://www.fasna.org.uk
   Contacts: Sue Ferdinando, Lynne Hoptroff
- ▲ Company Limited by Guarantee; Registered Charity
- ○ *E, *P; to represent the interests & views of self-governing schools (foundation, foundation with trust, voluntary-aided & academies)
- ● Conf - ET
- M 800 schools
- ¶ NL - 3; ftm only.

Foundation for the Study of Infant Deaths   (FSID)   1971
- ■ 11 Belgrave Rd, LONDON, SW1V 1RB.   (hq)
   020 7802 3200
   email office@fsid.org.uk   http://www.fsid.org.uk
   Chief Exec: Joyce Epstein
- ▲ Registered Charity
- Br 8 regional devt offices
- ○ *K, *M, *Q; to raise funds for research into the causes & prevention of cot death; to support bereaved parents; to disseminate information about cot death & infant care
- ● Conf - Res - SG - Stat - Inf - LG
   Helpline: 0808 802 6868 (Mon-Fri 0900-1800)
- < Assn of Med Res Charities (AMRC)
- > SIDS Intl; Eur Soc for Preventing Infant Death (ESPID)
- M 12,000 i on mailing list
- ¶ FSID (NL) - 1; free.
   Various information books & leaflets; see website.

Foundry Equipment Supplies Association Ltd   (FESA)   1925
- ■ National Metalforming Centre, 47 Birmingham Rd, WEST BROMWICH, W Midlands, B70 6PY.   (hsb)
   0121-601 6976
   email secretary@fesa.org.uk   http://www.fesa.org.uk
   Sec: Andrew Turner
- ▲ Company Limited by Guarantee
- ○ *T
- ● Conf - Exhib - Expt
- < Comité Européen des Matériels et Produits pour la Fonderie (CEMAFON)
- M 28 f

Fountain Society   1986
- ■ High House, BUCKNELL, Shropshire, SY7 0AA.   (hsp)
   01547 530750
   email fs-secretary@fountainsoc.org.uk
   http://www.fountainsoc.org.uk
   Hon Sec: Ian Hay-Campbell
- ▲ Registered Charity
- ○ *K; to promote the provision, conservation & restoration of fountains, cascades & water features in both the public & private sector
- ● Conf - Mtgs - Res - Comp - VE
- M 290 i, 10 f, 12 org, UK / 12 i, o'seas
- ¶ NL - 4;   Bibliography - 3 yrly; both ftm only.
   Creating a Fountain - 2 yrly; ftm, £3 nm.   AR; free.

4Children
- NR City Reach, 5 Greenwich View Place, LONDON, E14 9NN.   (hq)
   020 7512 2112
   email info@4children.org.uk
   http://www.4children.org.uk
- ▲ Registered Charity
- ○ *W; to deliver & support innovative children's services ensuring that all children & families get the support they need in their community
- M org

Fragile X Society   1990
- ■ Rood End House, 6 Stortford Road, GREAT DUNMOW, Essex, CM6 1DA.   (hq)
   01371 875100
   email info@fragilex.org.uk   http://www.fragilex.org.uk
   Dir: Amanda Cherry
- ▲ Registered Charity
- ○ *W; to provide support & information to families affected by Fragile X syndrome; to raise awareness & assist & encourage research
- ● Conf - Inf
- M 1,490 families, 155 associates, UK / 100 families, o'seas
   Subs: associates, £15 / families £30, o'seas
- ¶ NL - 3;   AR; free.   Various publications.

Francis Bacon Society Inc   1886
- ■ 6 Arlingford Rd, LONDON, SW2 2SU.   (editor/p)
  http://www.baconsocietyinc.org
  Editor: James North
- ▲ Company Limited by Guarantee; Registered Charity
- ○ *L; to promote the study of the works of Francis Bacon, (Baron Verulam of Verulam) 1561-1626, as a philosopher, statesman & poet; to examine evidence of his authorship of the plays ascribed to Shakespeare; to investigate his connection with other works of the Elizabethan period
- ● Mtgs - Res - Lib
- M 90 i, UK / 50 i, o'seas
- ¶ Baconiana (Jnl) - irreg; on website.

Francis Brett Young Society   (FBY Soc)   1979
- ■ 92 Gower Road, HALESOWEN, W Midlands, B62 9BT.   (hsp)
  0121-422 8969
  http://www.fbysociety.co.uk
  Hon Sec: Mrs J Hadley
- ▲ Registered Charity
- ○ *A; to collate research done on the life & work of Francis Brett Young; to promote his works & the work of promising writers born in Halesowen
- ● Mtgs - ET - Res - Inf - VE - Speakers on Brett Young provided on request
- < Alliance Literary Socs
- M 189 i, 8 org, 6 org, UK / 10 i, o'seas
- ¶ Jnl - 2; ftm.

Franco-British Chamber of Commerce & Industry   (FBCCI)   1872
- NR 31 rue Boissy d'Anglas, F-75008 PARIS, France.
  33 (1) 53 30 81 30   fax 33 (1) 53 30 81 35
  email information@francobritishchamber.com
  http://www.francobritishchamber.com
  Chief Exec: Catherine Le Yaouanc
- ○ *C; 'to assist companies to promote & develop their activities from both sides of the channel'
- ● Conf - Mtgs - ET - Exam - Res - Expt - Inf - Lib - LG
  The Chamber is open Mon-Fri 1400-1700
- < Coun Brit Chams Comm Continental Europe (COBCOE)
- M 750 f
- ¶ NL - 3; ftm only.

Franco-British Lawyers Society / Association des Juristes Franco-Britanniques   (FBLS/AJFB)
- NR 10-11 Dacre St, LONDON, SW1H 0DJ   (hq)
  020 7222 3860
  email yfb31@dial.pipex.com
  http://www.franco-british-law.org
  Hon Sec: Marie-Blanche Camps
- Br France, Scotland
- ○ *P; to advance public education & training in the practice of French, Scottish & English law generally & in particular in the context of the EU & its constitutive treaties
- M i
- ¶ [mem only]

Franco-British Society   1944
- NR 3 Dovedale Studios, 465 Battersea Park Rd, LONDON, SW11 4LR.   (hq)
  020 7924 3511   fax 020 7924 3511
  email execsec@francobritishsociety.org.uk
  http://www.francobritishsociety.org.uk
  Chmn: The Rt Hon The Baroness Shepherd of Northwold
  Exec Sec: Mrs Kate Brayn
- ▲ Company Limited by Guarantee; Registered Charity
- ○ *X; an educational charity for the encouragement of British understanding of French artistic, scientific, social & economic achievements, through travel, personal contacts & meetings
- M i

Franco-Scottish Society   1895
- ■ 21 Lindsay Drive, GLASGOW, G12 0HD   (hsp)
  email rosalynemf@yahoo.co.uk
  http://www.franco-scottish.org.uk
  Nat Sec: Rosalyn Faulds
- ▲ Registered Charity
- Br 7; Canada, France
- ○ *X; promotion of knowledge of all matters of Franco-Scottish interest & of Franco-Scottish friendship & understanding through cultural, educational & social activities & personal contacts
- ● Mtgs - ET - Comp - VE
- < Assn Franco-Ecossaise (France); Franco-Scottish Soc (Canada)
- M c 300 i, UK / c 200 i, o'seas
  (Sub: £18-£20)
- ¶ Bulletin - 1; ftm.

Free Trade League   (FTL)   1905
- ■ 1 Fern Dene, Templewood, LONDON, W13 8AN.   (hsp)
  020 8997 6868
  email john.heffernan@virgin.net
  http://www.freetradeleague.org.uk
  Hon Sec: John Heffernan
- ▲ Un-incorporated Society
- ○ *K; to promote the economic & political case for unilateral UK trade policy of dismantling protection
- ● Mtgs - VE
- M i, f & org
- ¶ The Free Trader - 1.

The Freedom Association   (TFA)   1975
- ■ Richwood House, 1 Trinity School Lane, CHELTENHAM, Glos, GL52 2JL.   (hq)
  0845 833 9626
  email mail@tfa.net   http://www.tfa.net
  Dir: Simon Richards
- ▲ Company Limited by Guarantee
- ○ *K, dedicated to fighting for individual liberty & freedom of expression. Its 7 Principles of a Free Society are: Individual freedom; Personal & family responsibility; The rule of law; Limited government; Free market economy; National parliamentary democracy; & Strong national defences
- Gp Better Off Out
- ● Conf - Mtgs - Political lobbying
- M 4,000 i, UK / 1,000 i, o'seas
- ¶ Freedom Today (Jnl) - 6; ftm, £3 nm.

Freedom2Choose   2004
- NR 22 Glastonbury House, Lindisfarne Rd, Priestfields, MIDDLESBROUGH, TS3 0LF.   (hq)
  0845 643 9469   fax 0845 643 9469
  email office@freedom2choose.info
  http://www.freedom2choose.info
  Co-Chmn: Dave Atherton & Phil Johnson
- Br Scotland
- ○ *K; to promote freedom of choice & oppose any coercive restraints upon that freedom by any lawful means & with reference to the negative effects of smoking bans on individuals, groups, businesses & organisations; & to advance public education in all such matters
- M i
  (Sub: £10)

Freedom Organisation for the Right to Enjoy Smoking Tobacco (FOREST)   1981
- NR Sheraton House, Castle Park, CAMBRIDGE, CB3 0AX.   (hq)
  01223 370156
  email contact@forestonline.org
  http://www.forestonline.org
  Dir: Simon Clark
- ▲ Company Limited by Guarantee
- ○ *K; to promote equal rights for smokers
- ● Res - Inf - LG - Media lobbying
- M i, uk & o'seas
- ¶ Various research papers & information sheets.

Freelance Hair & Beauty Federation Ltd   (FHBF)   1993
■   The Business Centre, Kimpton Rd, LUTON, Beds, LU2 0LB.
      (hq)
      01582 431783
      email enquiries@fhbf.org.uk   http://www.fhbf.org.uk
      Dir: Sheila Abrahams
○   *T; for freelance, self-employed operators
●   Conf - ET - Inf
¶   Highlights (NL) - 4; ftm only.

Freemen of England & Wales   (FEW)   1964
■   Richmond House, Beech Close, Oversley Green, ALCESTER,
      Warks, B49 6PP.   (hsp)
      01789 762574
      Hon Sec: Ronald E Leek
▲   Registered Charity
○   *N; interests of the freemen of the cities & boroughs of England
      & Wales; to advance the knowledge of the history & legal
      custom of the boroughs & the legal institution of freedom
Gp   Freemen's Guilds; Groups of freemen of towns & cities in
      England & Wales
●   Mtgs - ET - Res - LG
M   425 i, 41 guilds
¶   Freemen of England & Wales (NL) - 4; ftm only.

Freemen & Guilds of the City of Chester
NR   The Guildhall, Watergate St, CHESTER, CH1 2LA.   (hq)
      01244 320431
▲   Un-incorporated Society
○   *N; founded in the 14th century the guild upholds & promotes
      the history of the individual craft companies; to support the
      Lord Mayor & Chester Council by participating in their civic &
      cultural duties
M   i

Freight Transport Association   (FTA)   1889
■   Hermes House, St John's Rd, TUNBRIDGE WELLS, Kent,
      TN4 9UZ.   (hq)
      01892 526171   fax 01892 534989
      email enquiries@fta.co.uk   http://www.fta.co.uk
      Chief Exec: Theo de Pencier
▲   Company Limited by Guarantee
Br   5; Brussels (Belgium)
○   *T; interests of companies in the transport industry
Gp   British Shippers Council; Utilities Group
●   Conf - Mtgs - ET - Res - Exhib - Stat - Inf - VE - LG - Support
      services
<   Intl Road Transport U (IRU)
M   14,000 f
¶   Freight - 12; ftm, £25 yr nm.   Ybk - 1; ftm, £34 nm.
      International Manual - 1; ftm, £60 nm.

French Chamber of Commerce in Great Britain
      see **Chambre de Commerce Française de Grande-Bretagne**

Fresh Produce Consortium (UK)   (FPC)   1993
NR   Minerva House, Minerva Business Park, Lynch Wood,
      PETERBOROUGH, PE2 6FT.   (hq)
      01733 237117   fax 01733 237118
      email info@freshproduce.org.uk
      http://www.freshproduce.org.uk
      Chief Exec: Nigel R Jenney
▲   Company Limited by Guarantee
○   *T; to develop the competitive performance of the produce &
      floral industries of the UK
Gp   Divisions: Importers, Wholesale, Floral, Technical, Business
      services, Retail, Freshfel, Growers & potato packers
●   Conf - Mtgs - ET - Res - Exhib - VE - LG - Promotion of
      consumption of fresh produce through education in schools
      & the wider community
<   Freshfel Europe; Produce Marketing Assn (USA)
M   1,000 f
¶   Hbk - 1.

Freshwater Biological Association   (FBA)   1929
■   The Ferry Landing, Far Sawrey, AMBLESIDE, Cumbria,
      LA22 0LP.   (hq)
      01539 442468   fax 01539 446914
      email info@fba.org.uk   http://www.fba.org.uk
      Dir: Dr Michael Dobson
▲   Company Limited by Guarantee; Registered Charity
Br   2
○   *L, *Q; to advance freshwater science & encourage as many
      people as possible to adopt it as the best way to understand,
      protect & manage our precious water resources
Gp   Cooperative Research Partnership; FBA NE regional group
●   Conf - ET - Res - Inf - Lib
<   Eur Fedn of Freshwater Science (EFFS); Inst of Biology
M   1,550 i & f
      (Sub: £20 students, £35 i, £300 f)
¶   Freshwater Reviews (Jnl) - 2; free online, £22 print m,
      £40 online, £65 online & print nm.
      Scientific & Special Publications - irreg.
      Publications list available.

Friedreichs Ataxia Society Ireland   (FASI)
IRL   4 Leopardstown Business Centre, Ballyogan Avenue, DUBLIN
      18, Republic of Ireland.   (hq)
      353 (1) 299 9033   fax 353 (1) 299 9055
      email info@ataxia.ie   http://www.ataxia.ie
      Chmn: Susan Creedon
▲   Registered Charity
○   *W; to support people & families living with a genetic ataxia
¶   NL

Friends of Alan Rawsthorne   1989
■   30 Florida Avenue, Hartford, HUNTINGDON, Cambs,
      PE29 1PY.   (hsp)
      01480 456931
      email apkmusicprom@ntlworld.com
      http://www.musicweb-international.com/rawsth/
      Sec: Andrew P Knowles
▲   Un-incorporated Society
○   *D; promotion of music by Alan Rawsthorne, British composer
      1905-1971
●   Mtgs - Inf - Lib - Concerts
M   70 i, 5 org
¶   The Creel (Jnl) - 1.   The Sprat (NL) - irreg.

Friends of Alfred Williams   1970
NR   Great Western Hospital, Marlborough Rd, SWINDON, Wilts,
      SN3 6BB.   (chmn/b)
      email committee@alfredwilliams.org.uk
      http://www.alfredwilliams.org.uk
      Chmn: Dr John Cullimore
○   *A; to celebrate the life & works of Alfred Williams (1877-1930)
      - Wiltshire author, poet & collector of folk songs
M   40 i

Friends of Arthur Machen   1986
NR   Stable Cottage, Priest Bank Rd, Kildwick, KEIGHLEY, N Yorks,
      BD20 9BH.   (hsp)
      http://www.machensoc.demon.co.uk
▲   Company Limited by Guarantee; Registered Charity
○   *A; to honour the life & work of writer Arthur Machen (1863-
      1947); to support research students, publishers, writers etc
      interested in Machen's work
M   i, libraries & universities

© CBD Research Ltd · Beckenham · BR3 5JS · Tel 020 8650 7745 · E-mail cbd@cbdresearch.com · www.cbdresearch.com

Friends of Blue (FOB) 1973
■ PO Box 122, DIDCOT D O, Oxon, OX11 0YN. (hsp)
01235 816266
http://www.fob.org.uk
Sec: Arthur C Roberts
▲ Un-incorporated Society
○ *G; to promote study & interest of ceramics with under-glaze blue decoration, made by transfer print, a technique developed in Britain during the last two decades of the eighteenth century
● Res
M 407 i, UK / 53 i, o'seas
¶ Bulletin - 4; ftm only.
True Blue (1998); £9.50 m, £11.50 nm.

Friends of Cathedral Music (FCM) 1956
■ 27 Old Gloucester St, LONDON, WC1N 3XX. (hq)
01727 856087
email info@fcm.org.uk   http://www.fcm.org.uk
Hon Sec: Roger Bishton
▲ Registered Charity
○ *D, *R; to safeguard the heritage of cathedral music; to increase public knowledge & appreciation of cathedral music; to encourage high standards in choral & organ music
● Mtgs - Exhib - Inf - Awards of grants to cathedral authorities to assist in maintaining choral services
M 2,700 i, 30 org, UK / 300 i, o'seas
¶ Cathedral Music Singing in Cathedrals: a listing of choral services in the UK - 2; ftm, £3.50 nm.

Friends of Classics (FoC)
■ 51 Achilles Rd, LONDON, NW6 1DZ. (hsp)
020 7431 5088   fax 020 7431 5129
email classics@friends-classics.demon.co.uk
http://www.friends-classics.demon.co.uk
Exec Sec: Jeannie Cohen
▲ Registered Charity
○ *G; to encourage the teaching of classical languages, history & culture in schools
● Mtgs - Fundraising events
M 1,000 i
¶ Ad Familiares (Jnl); ftm.

Friends of Coleridge 1986
■ 11 Castle St, NETHER STOWEY, Somerset, TA5 1LN. (hsp)
01278 733338
http://www.friendsofcoleridge.com
Hon Sec: Mrs Shirley M Watters
▲ Registered Charity
Br Canada, USA (Mems worldwide)
○ *A, *L; to promote the work of Samuel Taylor Coleridge (1772-1834); to support Coleridge Cottage with the National Trust
● Conf - Mtgs - SG - VE
M 250 i, 3 org, UK / 65 i, 2 org, o'seas
¶ The Coleridge Bulletin - 2; ftm.
Conference brochure - 2 yrly (even yrs); free.

Friends of Dr Watson (FDW) 1996
NR 13 Crofton Avenue, ORPINGTON, Kent, BR6 8DU. (memsec/p)
Mem Sec: R J Ellis
Br Belgium
○ *G; to promote interest in the life, times & work of Dr John H Watson MD (from the Sherlock Holmes stories by Arthur Conan Doyle) & the society of the period; to study the medical aspects of Conan Doyle's work
● Res - Comp - Inf - VE - Annual dinner - Maiwand luncheon - Dr Watson Day
< Franco-Midland Hardware Co (an international Sherlock Holmes study group)
M 33 i, 2 f, UK / 19 i, 1 f, o'seas
¶ The Formulary (Jnl) - 2.   The London Practice.
Watson's Wanderings;   Watson's Wanderings Again.
The Maiwand Luncheon Monograph;   Watson's Weapons;
The Maiwand Dispatch No 1;   From Netley to Maiwand;
Birthday Annual; ftm.   AR; free.

Friends of the Dymock Poets (FDP) 1993
NR 122 Preston New Rd, BLACKBURN, Lancs, BB2 6BU. (memsec/p)
01254 662923
email jeff@jeffcooper.me.uk
http://www.dymockpoets.co.uk
Mem Sec: Jeff Cooper
○ *A; to foster an interest in the group of poets associated with the Dymock area in Gloucestershire before the First World War (Lascelles Abercrombie, Rupert Brooke, John Drinkwater, Robert Frost, Wilfrid Gibson & Edward Thomas)
● Conf - Mtgs
< Alliance of Literary Socs
M 325 i, UK / 25 i, o'seas
¶ NL - irreg;   Dymock Poets & Friends - 1; both ftm only.

Friends of the Earth (FOE) 1971
§ 26-28 Underwood St, LONDON, N1 7JQ. (hq)
020 7490 1555   fax 020 7490 0881
email info@foe.co.uk   http://www.foe.co.uk
a network of national organisations campaigning on environmental issues

Friends of Friendless Churches (FFC) 1957
■ St Ann's Vestry Hall, 2 Church Entry, LONDON, EC4V 5HB. (hq)
020 7236 3934
email office@ancientmonumentssociety.org.uk
http://www.friendsoffriendlesschurches.org.uk
Chmn: Roger Evans,   Hon Dir: Matthew Saunders
▲ Company Limited by Guarantee; Registered Charity
○ *K; to campaign for & rescue redundant historic churches threatened by demolition & decay; FFC owns over 40 former places of worship, half in England, half in Wales
● Inf
< Ancient Monuments Soc (working partnership)
M 2,000 i
¶ AR;   Appeals.

Friends Historical Society (FHS) 1903
NR c/o The Quakers Library, 173-177 Euston Rd, LONDON, NW1 2BJ. (mail)
http://www.quaker.org.uk
Clerk, Treas & Mem Sec: Brian Hawkins
▲ Un-incorporated Society
○ *L; history of the Quakers
● Conf - Mtgs
¶ Jnl - 1; ftm, £6 nm.   NL - 2; ftm only.
Meeting Houses in Britain (1999); David Butler.

Friends of the Lake District (FLD) 1934

NR Murley Moss, Oxenholme Rd, KENDAL, Cumbria, LA9 7SS.
    (hq)
    01539 720788   fax 01539 730355
    Exec Dir: Andrew Forsyth
▲ Registered Charity
○ *K; protect & cherish the landscape & natural beauty of the
    Lake District & Cumbria
● Conf - Mtgs - Exhib - Inf - VE - Joint action with other societies
    for protection of the environment
< CPRE; Nat Trust; Ramblers' Assn; Coun Nat Parks
M 6,580 i, 50 org, UK / 70 i, o'seas
¶ NL - 2;   Conserving Lakeland - 2; both ftm only.

Friends of Medieval Dublin (FMD) 1975

IRL c/o Medieval History Dept, Trinity College, DUBLIN 2, Republic
    of Ireland.   (hsb)
    353 (1) 608 1801   fax 353 (1) 608 3995
    http://www.fmd.ie
    Hon Sec: Stuart Kinsella
○ *L

Friends of Mendelssohn (F of M) 1995

■ 35 Northcourt Avenue, READING, Berks, RG2 7HE.   (hq)
    0118-987 1479
    Founder & Dir: Mrs Pam Gulliver
▲ Un-incorporated Society
○ *D; to promote the music of Felix Mendelssohn & his
    contemporaries; to campaign for higher standards in
    performances & recordings of such work
Gp Team Mendelssohn (sporting events for charity)
● Mtgs - Res - SG - Inf - Lib - VE
M 20 i

Friends of the National Bonsai Collection
    a group of the **Federation of British Bonsai Societies**

Friends of the National Collections of Ireland (FNCI) 1924

IRL PO Box 11481, DUBLIN 4, Republic of Ireland.   (mail)
    353 (1) 496 5413
    email info@fnci.ie
    http://www.thefriendsofthenationalcollectionsofireland.ie
    Hon Archivist: A H O'Flanaghan
▲ Registered Charity
○ *A

Friends of the National Libraries (FNL) 1931

■ c/o Dept of Manuscripts, The British Library, 96 Euston Rd,
    LONDON, NW1 2DB.   (hsb)
    020 7412 7559
    http://www.friendsofnationallibraries.org.uk
    Hon Sec: Michael Borrie
▲ Registered Charity
○ *G; to promote the acquisition by national libraries of printed
    books, manuscripts & records of historical, literary, artistic,
    architectural, musical or suchlike interest by grants for
    purchases, channelling benefactions & legacies & public
    appeals
● Mtgs - VE
M c 700 i, 100 f
¶ AR.

Friends of the Pianola Institute (FPI) 1985

■ 111A Station Rd, WEST WICKHAM, Kent, BR4 0PX.   (asa)
    http://www.pianola.org
    Chmn: Keith Daniels
▲ Un-incorporated Society
○ *D; for supporters of the Institute, which exists to promote
    pianolas & music for pianolas
Gp Pianola roll production
● Mtgs - Res - Concerts - Roll & record production
M 65 i, UK / 15 i, o'seas
¶ Jnl - 1; ftm, £10 nm.   NL - 4; ftm only.

Friends of Real Lancashire (FoRL) 1992

■ 1 Belvidere Park, GREAT CROSBY, Lancs, L23 0SP.   (chmn/p)
    0151-928 2770
    email csd@forl.co.uk   http://www.forl.co.uk
    Chmn: C S Dawson
○ *G; to promote the true identity of the ancient & geographical
    county of Lancashire
● Inf - LG
< Assn of Brit Counties
M 660 i, 13 f, 8 org
¶ The Lancastrian - 1; ftm, £150 nm.   NL - 3; free (sae nm).

Friends of the Red Squirrel 2002

§ c/o Northumberland Wildlife Trust, The Garden House, St
    Nicholas Park, Gosforth, NEWCASTLE UPON TYNE,
    NE3 3XT.   (mail)
    0191-284 6884;   0845 347 7375
    http://www.rsne.org.uk/friends-red-squirrel
    Supporters of Red Squirrel North East (RSNE), a partnership
    project working to conserve red squirrels in northern England

Friends of St Bride Library   (FSBL)

■ c/o St Bride Library, Bride Lane, Fleet St, LONDON,
    EC4Y 8EE.   (hq)
    020 7353 4660   fax 020 7583 7073
    email friends@stbride.org   http://www.stbride.org
    Hon Sec: Stephen Lubell
▲ Registered Charity (as pt of the St Bride Foundation)
○ *G, *K; to promote, support, improve, & raise money to
    safeguard the future of the St Bride Library (contains
    collections on printing & allied subjects - paper, binding,
    design, typography, typefaces, calligraphy, illustration &
    printmaking)
● Conf - Mtgs - Exhib - Lectures
< St Bride Foundation
M c 2,000 i
¶ The Ravilious Notebook; Caroline Archer & Robert Harling.
    The Nymph and the Grot; James Mosley.
    Typefounders London A-Z; Justin Howes & Nigel Roche.

Friesian Horse Association of Great Britain & Ireland (FHAGBI) 1995

■ Harbours Hill Farm, Hanbury Rd, STOKE PRIOR, Worcs,
    B60 4AG.   (treas/p)
    01527 821276
    email fhagbi.events@btinternet.com
    http://www.fhagbi.co.uk
    Treas: Julian Atkins
▲ Company Limited by Guarantee
○ *B
● ET -Exam - Comp - Annual horse inspections - Show &
    dressage/driving events
< Het Friesch Paarden-Stamboek (Netherlands) (mother studbook)
M c 200 i,
    (Sub: £50)
¶ Phrysko - 12;   NL - 4; both ftm only.

Frontier
    the operating name of the **Society for Environmental Exploration**

Frozen & Chilled Potato Processors' Association
    see **Potato Processors' Association**

Fulke Greville Society 2006

■ 6 Mellors Court, The Butts, WARWICK, CV34 4ST.   (hsp)
    01926 492086
    Hon Sec: Anthony Astbury
○ *G; for those interested in the poetry, plays & other writings of
    Fulke Greville, 1st Baron Brooke (1554-1628)

© CBD Research Ltd · Beckenham · BR3 5JS · Tel 020 8650 7745 · E-mail cbd@cbdresearch.com · www.cbdresearch.com

Fund for the Replacement of Animals in Medical Experiments (FRAME) 1969
■ Russell & Burch House, 96-98 North Sherwood St, NOTTINGHAM, NG1 4EE. (hq)
　　0115-958 4740　fax 0115-950 3570
　　email frame@frame.org.uk　http://www.frame.org.uk
　Chmn of the Trustees: Prof Michael Balls
　Admin Mgr: Dr David Vowles
▲ Registered Charity
○ *K; to promote, research & develop the use of alternative methods in medical & related research, which refine, reduce or replace the use of laboratory animals
● Conf - ET - Res - Inf
M 500 i, 50 f org, UK / 5 f, o'seas
¶ ATLA Jnl - 6; £126 yr.　AR - 1; ftm.
　Frame News - 3 (with) Friends of Frame - 3; £15.

Funeral Furnishing Manufacturer's Association (FFMA) 1939
■ 11 Fentham Close, Hampton in Arden, SOLIHULL, W Midlands, B92 0BE. (hsp)
　01675 443718
　　email bullocksuee@gmail.com　http://www.ffma.co.uk
　Sec: Sue Bullock
▲ Un-incorporated Society
○ *T; to ensure that quality goods are produced & that the traditional high standards are maintained within the profession
Gp Autopsy equipment; Coffins & caskets; Coffin fittings & linings; Funeral planning; Hearses & limousines; Publications; Shrouds & gowns; Stretchers & trollies; Urns & memorials; Veneered board
● Conf - Mtgs - Exhib - LG
M 33 f

Funerary Monuments Group
　a group of the **National Federation of Cemetery Friends**

Furniture History Society (FHS) 1964
■ 1 Mercedes Cottages, St John's Rd, HAYWARDS HEATH, W Sussex, RH16 4EH. (memsec/p)
　01444 413845　fax 01444 413845
　　email furniturehistorysociety@hotmail.com
　　http://www.furniturehistorysociety.org
　Mem Sec: Dr Brian Austen
▲ Registered Charity
○ *L; the study of the history of furniture & furnishings on a worldwide basis
● Conf - Mtgs - ET - Res - SG - VE
M 1,200 i, 30 f, 80 org, UK / 300 i, 30 f, 70 org, o'seas
¶ Furniture History - 1;　NL - 4;　AR; all ftm.

Furniture Industry Research Association (FIRA) 1949
■ Maxwell Rd, STEVENAGE, Herts, SG1 2EW. (hq)
　01438 777700　fax 01438 777800
　　email info@fira.co.uk　http://www.askfira.co.uk
　Managing Dir: Hayden Davies
▲ Company Limited by Guarantee
Br China, Malaysia
○ *Q; research, consultancy & commercial services for the furniture industry including testing, customer care, lean manufacturing & the furniture ombudsman'
● Conf - Mtgs - ET - Res - Exhib - Inf - VE - LG - Testing - Consultancy
M 340 f, UK / 20 f, o'seas
¶ Ask FIRA News - 4;　Ybk;
　Club Green News - 2　AR; all free.

Further Education Research Association (FERA) 1973
NR External Affairs Office, University of Worcester, Henwick Grove, WORCESTER, WR2 6AJ. (chmn/b)
　01905 855145　fax 01905 855132
　　email g.elliott@worc.ac.uk　http://www.fera.uk.net
　Chmn: Prof Geoffrey Elliott
▲ Un-incorporated Society
○ *E, *L, *Q; research within & about further education (post 16)
● Conf - Mtgs - ET - Res - Inf
✕ 2007 National Association for Staff Development in the Post-16 Sector (merged)

Futon Association of Britain (FAB) 1994
NR 24 Beauchamp Rd, LONDON, SW11 1PQ. (hsb)
　020 7223 7212
　　http://www.futonsonline.co.uk
　Sec: Keith Holleyman
▲ Un-incorporated Society
○ *T; promotion & education on all matters concerning futon furniture
● ET - Stat - Inf - Lib
< Futon Assn Intl (FAI)
M 20 i, 15 f

Futures & Options Association (FOA) 1993
NR 36-38 Botolph Lane (2nd floor), LONDON, EC3R 8DE. (hq)
　020 7929 0081　fax 020 7621 0223
　　http://www.foa.co.uk
　Chief Exec: Anthony Belchambers
○ *T; for the derivatives industry; to monitor & respond to regulatory & tax changes; to heighten industry & product awareness
M f

Gaelic Athletic Association   1884
IRL   Croke Park, DUBLIN 3, Republic of Ireland.
    353 (1) 836 3222   fax 353 (1) 836 6420
    email info@gaa.ie   http://www.gaa.ie
○   *S; promotion of Gaelic football, hurling, handball and
    rounders

Gallipoli Association   1969
■   PO Box 26907, LONDON, SE21 8WB.   (hsp)
    http://www.gallipoli-association.org
▲   Un-incorporated Society
○   *G; to keep alive the memory of the Gallipoli campaign of
    1915; for those interested in the campaign
●   Mtgs - VE - 2 lunches a year - Tour to Dardanelles
M   c 1,000 i, UK & o'seas
¶   The Gallipolian - 3; ftm.

Galloway Cattle Society of Great Britain & Ireland   1877
■   15 New Market St, CASTLE DOUGLAS, Kirkcudbrightshire,
    DG7 1HY.   (hq)
    01556 502753   fax 01556 502753
    email info@gallowaycattlesociety.co.uk
    http://www.gallowaycattlesociety.co.uk
    Sec: Dorothy Goldie
▲   Registered Charity
○   *B; to promote & keep pure Galloway cattle
Gp   Farmers; Small holding-farms; Farmers' markets
●   Exhib
<   Nat Beef Assn
M   500 i, UK / 150 i, o'seas
¶   Jnl - 1; free.   Herd Book - 1; £10.

Galpin Society   1946
■   37 Townsend Drive, ST ALBANS, Herts, AL3 5RF.   (admin/p)
    http://www.galpinsociety.org
    Admin: Maggie Kilbey
▲   Registered Charity
○   *L, *Q; the study of the history, construction, development & use
    of musical instruments
●   Conf - Mtgs - Res
M   400 i, UK / 600 i, o'seas, c 300 universities & libraries
    worldwide
¶   Jnl - 1; ftm.   NL - 3; ftm only.

Galton Institute   1907
■   19 Northfields Prospect, Northfields, LONDON, SW18 1PE.
    (hq)
    020 8874 7257
    email betty.nixon@talk21.com
    http://www.galtoninstitute.org.uk
    Gen Sec: Betty Nixon
▲   Company Limited by Guarantee; Registered Charity
○   *L, *Q; to study the effects of hereditary & environmental
    factors on inborn human qualities; to promote a responsible
    attitude to parenthood; population problems
●   Conf - ET - Res
<   Inst Biology
M   300 i, UK / 100 i, o'seas
¶   NL - 4; m only.
    Proceedings of Conference (book) - 1; ftm, £5 nm.

Galvanizers Association   (GA)   1949
■   56 Victoria Rd, Wren's Court, SUTTON COLDFIELD,
    W Midlands, B72 1SY.   (hq)
    0121-355 8838   fax 0121-355 8727
    email ga@hdg.org.uk   http://www.galvanizing.org.uk
    Gen Mgr: David M Baron
▲   Company Limited by Guarantee
○   *T; to provide technical & marketing services for the hot dip
    galvanizing industry in the UK & Ireland
●   Conf - Mtgs - ET - Res - Exhib - Stat - Inf - Lib - VE
M   37 f, UK / 48 f, o'seas
¶   Hot Dip Galvanizing (Jnl) - 4; free (1st 10 copies ftm).
    Brochure: Engineers' & Architects' Guide to Hot Dip
    Galvanizing (2001); £1.50 m, £5 nm.

GAMBICA Association Ltd   1981
■   Broadwall House, 21 Broadwall, LONDON, SE1 9PL.   (hq)
    020 7642 8080   fax 020 7642 8096
    email assoc@gambica.org.uk
    http://www.gambica.org.uk
    Chief Exec: Geoff C Young
○   *T; 'for instrumentation, control, automation'
Gp   Product areas: Environmental analysis & monitoring equipment;
    Industrial control & power electronics components & systems;
    Laboratory technology; Laboratory based analytical &
    measuring equipment; Process measurement & control
    equipment & systems; Test measurement equipment
●   Conf - Mtgs - ET - Exhib - Stat - Expt - Inf
M   150 f
¶   Product Guide - 1;   AR;   Brochure; all free.

Game Conservancy Trust
    since 2007 **Game & Wildlife Conservation Trust**

Game Farmers' Association   (GFA)   1918
■   PO Box 3629, WOKINGHAM, Berks, RG40 9LG.   (hsp)
    0118-979 7255
    email secretarygfa@gmail.com   http://www.gfa.org.uk
    Sec: Harriet Robbins
▲   Un-incorporated Society
○   *F; dedicated to the production of quality gamebirds for the UK
    shooting industry
●   Mtgs - ET - Seminars
<   in close co-operation with the Nat Gamekeepers Assn
M   179 i, 29 f, UK / 3 f, o'seas
¶   Game Farming NL - 4; ftm only.

Game & Wildlife Conservation Trust   1980
■   Burgate Manor, FORDINGBRIDGE, Hants, SP6 1EF.   (hq)
    01425 652381   fax 01425 655848
    email info@gwct.org.uk   http://www.gwct.org.uk
    Chief Exec: Teresa Dent
▲   Company Limited by Guarantee; Registered Charity
○   *Q; research & advice into conservation & habitat of all game
    species.   Associated research in agriculture, arable insects,
    songbirds & pesticides/herbicides
M   24,000 i, 2,000 f, 500 org, UK / 1,000 i, 50 f, 25 org, o'seas
×   2007 Game Conservancy Trust

© CBD Research Ltd · Beckenham · BR3 5JS · Tel 020 8650 7745 · E-mail cbd@cbdresearch.com · www.cbdresearch.com

Garage Equipment Association (GEA) 1945
■ 2-3 Church Walk, DAVENTRY, Northants, NN11 4BL. (hq)
01327 312616 fax 01327 312606
email name@gea.co.uk http://www.gea.co.uk
Chief Exec: Dave Garratt
▲ Company Limited by Guarantee
○ *T; represents the interests of all sectors of the garage
equipment industry; manufacturing, servicing, installation,
selling & distribution of garage equipment & provision of
training
Gp Code of Practice; Distributors; Exhibitions; Manufacturers; MOT
Liaison; Service
● Mtgs - Exhib - Stat - LG
< Eur Garage Eqpt Assn (EGEA)
M 115 f
¶ The World of Emissions (on emission testing).

Garda Representative Association (GRA) 1978
IRL Phibsboro Tower (floor 5), Dublin 7, Republic of Ireland (hq)
353 (1) 830 3533 fax 353 (1) 830 3331
email mail@gra.ie http://www.gra.ie
Gen Sec: P J Stone
○ *U; to pursue the best interests of all members of Garda rank
in the areas of pay, welfare, conditions & services
● Empl - LG
M 11,500 i

Garden Centre Association Ltd (GCA) 1979
■ Leafield Technical Centre, Leafield, WITNEY, Oxon,
OX29 9EF. (hq)
01993 871000 fax 01993 871458
email info@gca.org.uk http://www.gca.org.uk
▲ Company Limited by Guarantee
○ *T
● Conf - Comp - SG - Inf
< Intl Garden Centre Assn
M 165 f
¶ GCA Ybk - 1; ftm, £50 nm

Garden Club
part of the **Gardening for Disabled Trust**

Garden History Society (GHS) 1965
NR 70 Cowcross St, LONDON, EC1M 6EJ. (hq)
020 7608 2409
email enquiries@gardenhistorysociety.org
http://www.gardenhistorysociety.org
Hon Sec: Elizabeth Cairns
▲ Registered Charity
Br 2
○ *H, *L; to promote study into the history of gardening &
horticulture in all aspects; to protect historic gardens
Gp Conservation
● Conf - Exhib - Inf - Lib - Mtgs - Res - Stat - VE - Advising on
restoration & preservation of historic gardens
< Intl Coun on Monuments & Sites (ICOMOS); Civic Trust;
Campaign to Protect Rural England (CPRE); Jt C'ee of the Nat
Amenity Socs; Brit Assn for Local History
M 1,800 i, UK / c 250 i, o'seas, also university & civic libraries
¶ Garden History (Jnl) - 2. NL - 3.

Garden Industry Manufacturers' Association (GIMA) 1977
NR 225 Bristol Rd, Edgbaston, BIRMINGHAM, B5 7UB. (hq)
0121-446 5213 fax 0121-446 5215
email info@gima.org.uk
Hon Sec: Fiona Carrington
▲ Company Limited by Guarantee
○ *T; to promote & protect the commercial, trading & industrial
interests of UK & EU based companies supplying the UK
garden industry
● Conf - Mtgs - ET - Res - SG - Stat
M 147 f
¶ NL; LM; both m only. AR; ftm.

Garden & Landscape Designers Association (GLDA) 1995
IRL PO Box 10954, DUBLIN 18, Republic of Ireland. (hq)
353 (1) 294 0092 fax 353 (1) 283 8043
email info@glda.ie http://www.glda.ie
Admin: Annette McCoy
○ *G, *P; qualified & experienced garden designers & landscape
architects who are also plant experts
¶ Compass (Jnl) - 4; ftm.

Garden Media Guild (GMG) 1991
■ Katepwa House, Ashfield Park Ave, ROSS-ON-WYE, Herefs,
HR9 5AX. (asa)
01989 567393 fax 01989 567676
email info@gardenmediaguild.co.uk
http://www.gardenmediaguild.co.uk
Hon Sec: Michael Howes, Admin: Gill Hinton
▲ Un-incorporated Society
○ *P; to raise the quality of garden writing, photography &
broadcasting
Gp Professional Garden Photographers' Association
Book editors; Journalists; Lecturers; TV & radio broadcasters;
Writers
● Comp - ET - Annual awards ceremony
< Creators' Rights Alliance
M 312 i, + 35 associates, 14 probationary, 19 retired
(Sub: £60 full, £85 associates, £45 probationary, £18 retired)
¶ News - 4; ftm only; Ybk - 1; ftm, £150 nm.
✕ 2007 Garden Writers' Guild

Garden Organic
working name of the **Henry Doubleday Research Association**

Garden Writers' Guild
since 2007 the **Garden Media Guild**

**GARDENEX: the Federation of Garden & Leisure Manufacturers
Ltd (GARDENEX) 1961**
NR The White House, High St, BRASTED, Kent, TN16 1JE. (hq)
01959 565995 fax 01959 565885
email info@gardenex.com http://www.gardenex.com
Chief Exec: Amanda Sizer Barrett
▲ Company Limited by Guarantee
○ *T; to promote the export of British manufactured products,
services, plants etc in international markets
M f

Gardening for Disabled Trust 1973
■ PO Box 285, TUNBRIDGE WELLS, Kent, TN2 9JD. (hq)
http://www.gardeningfordisabledtrust.org.uk
▲ Registered Charity
○ *G, *H; the Trust gives grants to people in order that they may
continue to garden despite advancing age, illness or
disability; membership of the Club gives access to advice on
garden design, answers to horticultural questions & grants
from the Trust
Gp Garden Club
M i & org
¶ NL - 1.

Gas Forum 1994
NR 10 Fenchurch St, LONDON, EC3M 3BE. (hq)
020 7090 1015
http://www.gasforum.co.uk
▲ Company Limited by Guarantee
○ *T; for companies shipping gas through the national gas
pipeline system & those supplying gas to industrial,
commercial & domestic customers

Gascon Cattle Society   1990
NR   Granish Farm, AVIEMORE, Inverness-shire, PH22 1QD.   (hsp)
        01479 810225
        email kirsteenrankin@btinternet.com
        http://www.gascon.org.uk
        Sec: Kirsteen Rankin
▲   Un-incorporated Society
○   *B; promotion of the Gascon breed of beef cattle
●   Mtgs - Res - Exhib
<   Nat Beef Assn; UPRA Gasconne (France)
M   10 i, UK / 300 i, o'seas
¶   NL - 4;   Ybk - 1; both free.

Gaskell Society   1985
■   10 Dale Rd, New Mills, HIGH PEAK, Derbys, SK22 4NW.   (hsp)
        01663 744233
        email janetrallen@googlemail.com
        http://www.gaskellsociety.co.uk
        Contact: Janet Allen
▲   Registered Charity
Br   2; Japan
○   *A; to promote interest in Mrs Elizabeth Cleghorn Gaskell's life
        & writings
●   Conf - Mtgs - SG
<   Alliance of Literary Socs
M   500 i, UK / 120 i, o'seas
¶   Jnl - 1.   NL - 2.

Gasket Cutters' Association   (GCA)   1993
NR   2 Old College Court, 29 Priory St, WARE, Herts, SG12 0DE.
        (asa)
        0844 873 2957   fax 0844 822 5215
        email info@gcassociation.co.uk
        http://www.gcassociation.co.uk
▲   Un-incorporated Society
○   *T; the commercial & professional interests of companies
        engaged in the cutting of gaskets & in the conversion &
        application of suitable meterials as gaskets & joint sealants
●   Conf - Mtgs - SG - Inf - LG
M   28 f
¶   Cutting Edge - 4; ftm only.

Gate Automation & Access Barrier Association
        a group of the **Fencing Contractors' Association**

Gauchers Association   1991
NR   Evesham House Business Centre, 48-52 Silver St, DURSLEY,
        Glos, GL11 4ND.   (hq)
        01463 549231   fax 01463 549231
        email ga@gaucher.org.uk   http://www.gaucher.org.uk
        Chief Exec: Tanya Collin-Histed
▲   Company Limited by Guarantee; Registered Charity
○   *M, *W; to promote awareness & research, to provide general
        & specific information, & to establish a support network for
        those affected by Gaucher disease (abnormal storage of
        lipids)
●   Conf - Mtgs - Res - Inf - LG
M   494 i, 454 f, UK / 30 i, 272 f, o'seas
¶   Gauchers News - 2; free.

Gauge & Tool Makers Association   (GTMA)   1942
■   National Metalforming Centre, 47 Birmingham Rd,
        WEST BROMWICH, W Midlands. B70 6PY.   (hq)
        0121-601 6350   fax 0121-601 6378
        email admin@gtma.co.uk   http://www.gtma.co.uk
        Chief Exec: Julia Moore
▲   Un-incorporated Society
○   *T
Gp   Metrology; Mould & die; Press tool; Special purpose machinery;
        Tool & workholding equipment
●   Conf - Mtgs - ET - Exhib - Stat - Expt - Inf - Lib - VE
<   Intl Special Tooling Assn
M   320 f
¶   GTMA Directory of Gauging & Toolmaking Products &
        Services - 1; ftm.

Gemmological Association of Great Britain   (Gem-A)   1925
NR   27 Greville St, LONDON, EC1N 8TN.   (hq)
        020 7404 3334
        http://www.gem-a.info
        Chief Exec: Jack Ogden
▲   Company Limited by Guarantee; Registered Charity
○   *L, *P; to promote the study of gemmology & provide
        continuous professional development to members

Gender Trust   1990
NR   Community Base, 113 Queens Rd, BRIGHTON, E Sussex,
        BN1 3XG.   (hq)
        01273 234024
        email info@gendertrust.org.uk
        http://www.gendertrust.org.uk
        Trust Admin: Rosemary Turner
▲   Registered Charity
Br   12
○   *W; information & support for transsexual people, their families
        & partners
Gp   Gender; Transsexual
●   Conf - ET - Inf - Telephone service
        Helpline: 0845 231 0505
M   450 i, 2 f, 20 org, UK / 6 i, o'seas
¶   Membership magazine - 4; £29 yr m only.
        Gender Trust Guide.   Employers Guide.
        Standards of Care.   Sex Reassignment Surgery.

General Council of County Councils
        since 2007 the **Association of County & City Councils**

General Council for Massage Therapies   (GCMT)   2002
■   27 Old Gloucester St, LONDON, WC1N 3XX.   (hsb)
        0870 850 4452
        email gcmt@btconnect.com   http://www.gcmt.org.uk
        Sec: Maggie Brooks-Carter
▲   Un-incorporated Society
○   *N, *P; to promote the adoption of high standards of practice in
        massage therapies & all bodyworks & soft tissue techniques.
●   Mtgs - ET - Res - SG - Inf - LG
<   Complementary & Natural Health Coun
>   Assn of Holistic Biodynamic Massage Therapists (AHBMT); Assn
        of Physical & Natural Therapists (APNT); Inst for
        Complementary & Natural Medicine (ICNM); LCSP Register
        of Remedial Masseurs & Manipulative Therapists; Nat Assn of
        Massage & Manipulative Therapists (NAMMT); Oxford
        Natural Therapists Assn (ONTA); Scottish Massage Therapists
        Org (SMTO); Sports Massage Association (SMA)
M   670 i, 8 org

General Council & Register of Consultant Herbalists
        trading name of the **International Register of Consultant
        Herbalists & Homoeopaths**

General Council & Register of Naturopaths   (GCRN)   1967
NR   1 Green Lane Ave, STREET, Somerset, BA16 0QS.   (hsb)
        01458 840072
        http://www.naturopathy.org.uk
        Sec: M W F Szewiel
▲   Company Limited by Guarantee
○   *L, *P; to register suitably qualified naturopathic practitioners; to
        set minimum standards for the training of practitioners for
        the benefit of the public
●   Conf - ET - LG
M   310 i, UK / 19 i, o'seas
¶   Register of Practitioners Members - 1.

© CBD Research Ltd · Beckenham · BR3 5JS · Tel 020 8650 7745 · E-mail cbd@cbdresearch.com · www.cbdresearch.com

General Federation of Trade Unions (GFTU) 1899

■ Headland House (4th floor), 308-312 Grays Inn Rd, LONDON,
  WC1X 8DP. (hq)
  020 7520 8340   fax 020 7520 8350
  email gftuhq@gftu.org.uk   http://www.gftu.org.uk
  Gen Sec: Michael Bradley
▲ Un-incorporated Society
○ *N; a federation of unions providing benefits & services to
  affiliates
● Conf - Mtgs - ET - Res - Stat - Inf - Lib - LG
M 35 unions
¶ Federation Jnl - 2/3;   Federation News - 2/3;
  Report - 2 yrly; all free.

General Insurance Market Research Association
  a group of the **Association of Users of Research Agencies**

Genetic Alliance UK 1989

NR Unit 4D Leroy House, 436 Essex Rd, LONDON, N1 3QP. (hq)
  020 7704 3141   fax 020 7359 1447
  http://www.geneticalliance.org.uk
  Dir: Alastair Kent,   Public Affrs Offr: Stephen Nutt
▲ Company Limited by Guarantee; Registered Charity
○ *M; to improve the lives of people affected by genetic
  conditions by ensuring that high quality services &
  information are available to all who need them
Gp Rare Disease UK
● Conf - ET - Inf - LG - Mtgs
< Eur Genetic Alliance Network (EGAN); EURORDIS
M 140 org
✕ 2010 Genetic Interest Group

Genetic Interest Group
  since 2010 **Genetic Alliance UK**

Genetics Society 1919

NR Roslin Biocentre, Wallace Building, ROSLIN, Midlothian,
  EH25 9PP. (hq)
  0131-200 6391   fax 0131-200 6394
  email mail@genetics.org.uk
  http://www.genetics.org.uk
  Exec Officer: Christine Fender
▲ Registered Charity
○ *L; Gene structure, function & regulation; Cell & development
  genetics; Evolutionary, ecological & population genetics;
  Genomics; Applied & quantitative genetics; Corporate
  genetics & biotechnology
● Conf - Mtgs - Inf
< Intl Genetics Fedn (IGF); Fedn Eur Genetics Socs (FEGS);
  Inst Biology (IoB); BioSciences Fedn (BSF)
M 2,000 i, UK / 300 i, o'seas
¶ Heredity - 12; £28 m, £138 nm.
  Genes & Development - 24; £128 m.

GeneWatch UK

NR 60 Lightwood Rd, BUXTON, Derbys, SK17 7BB. (hq)
  01298 24300   fax 01298 24300
  email mail@genewatch.org   http://www.genewatch.org
  Exec Dir: Dr Helen Wallace
○ *K; to monitor developments in genetic technologies from a
  public interest, human rights, environmental protection &
  animal welfare perspective

Genito-Urinary Physicians Colposcopy Group
  a special interest group of the **British Association for Sexual
  Health & HIV**

GeoConservationUK (GCUK) 1999

■ The Studios, 53 High St, STOURBRIDGE, Worcs, DY8 1DE.
  (hq)
  01384 443644
  email info@geoconservationuk.org
  http://www.gcuk.org.uk
  Hon Sec: Lesley Dunlop
▲ Un-incorporated Society
○ *N; to encourage the appreciation, conservation & promotion
  of regionally important geological & geomorphological sites
  for education & public benefit
● Conf - ET - Res - Inf - VE - LG
M 50 org (local geoconservation groups)
  (Sub: £5)
¶ NL - 4; free.
✕ 2009 National Association of United Kingdom RIGS Groups

Geographical Association (GA) 1893

■ 160 Solly St, SHEFFIELD, S Yorks, S1 4BF. (hq)
  0114-296 0088   fax 0114-296 7176
  email info@geography.org.uk
  http://www.geography.org.uk
  Chief Exec: Dr David Lambert
▲ Registered Charity; Un-incorporated Society
Br 39
○ *E, *L, *P; to further the learning & teaching of geography
Gp Phase c'ees: Early years & primary, Secondary, Post-16 & HE
  Working gps: Assessment & examinations, Citizenship,
  Education for sustainable development, ICT, Independent
  schools, International, Learning outside the classroom,
  Physical geography, Teacher education
● Conf - Mtgs - ET - Res - Exhib - Comp - SG - Inf - VE - LG
< Coun of Brit Geography; Coun for Subject Teaching Assns
M 3,155 i, 3,271 groups (schools, universities, etc)
  (Sub: according to number of journals received; £28.50 -
  £139).
¶ Geography - 3;   Primary Geography - 3;
  Teaching Geography - 3;   GA Magazine - 3; all ftm.

Geographical Society of Ireland 1934

IRL NUI Maynooth, MAYNOOTH, Co Kildare, Republic of
  Ireland. (hsb)
  http://www.geographicalsocietyireland.ie
  Sec: Dr Adrian Kavanagh
○ *L; to promote the status & study of geography
● Conf - Mtgs - VE
¶ Irish Geography (Jnl) - 3;   Geonews (NL) - 2.

Geological Society 1807

■ Burlington House, Piccadilly, LONDON, W1J 0BG. (hq)
  020 7434 9944   fax 020 7439 8975
  http://www.geolsoc.org.uk
  Exec Sec: Edmund Nickless
○ *L; furtherance of all aspects of geological science
Gp British Geophysical Association; British Society for
  Geomorphology; Joint Association for Quaternary Research;
  Joint Association of Geoscientists for International
  Development
  Gps: Borehole research, Coal geology, Engineering,
  Environment, Environmental & industrial geophysics, Forensic
  geoscience, Gaia: earth systems science, Geochemistry,
  Geological curators, Geological remote sensing, Geoscience
  information, History of geology, Hydrogeological, Marine
  studies, Metamorphic studies, Mineral deposits studies,
  Petroleum, Tectonic studies, Volcanic & magmatic studies

Geologists' Association (GA) 1858

NR Burlington House, Piccadilly, LONDON, W1J 0DU. (hq)
  020 7434 9298   fax 020 7287 0280
  http://www.geologistsassociation.org.uk
  Exec Sec: Mrs Sarah Stafford
▲ Registered Charity
○ *G, *L; to promote awareness of our geological heritage; to
  promote interest in & the study of geology & its allied
  sciences, at all levels

George Borrow Society   1991
- ■ St Mary's College, 61 Thame Rd, Warborough,
  WALLINGFORD, Oxon, OX10 7EA.   (chmn/b)
  email ann@soutter.orangehome.co.uk
  Chmn: Dr Ann Ridler
- ▲ Un-incorporated Society
- ○ *A; to promote the knowledge of the life & works of the English
  author George Borrow (1803-81), best known for his novels
  'Lavengro', 'The Romany Rye', 'The Bible in Spain' & 'Wild
  Wales'
- ● Conf - Mtgs - Res - Annual memorial lecture
- < Alliance of Literary Socs; Centre of East Anglian Studies;
  Friends of Brompton Cemetery
- M 128 i, 11 libraries, UK / 33 i, 2 orgs, o'seas
- ¶ George Borrow Bulletin - 2; ftm, £4 nm.

George Eliot Fellowship   1930
- ■ 12 Fair Isle Drive, NUNEATON, Warks, CV10 7LJ.   (hsp)
  email blueyorkshirecat@yahoo.co.uk
  http://www.george-eliot-fellowship.com
  Hon Sec: Elizabeth Mellor
- ▲ Registered Charity
- Br Japan, USA
- ○ *A; to honour George Eliot (1819-80) & to promote interest in
  her life & writings; to encourage collection of her books &
  manuscripts & other ephemera connected with her
- ● Mtgs - Res - Comp - SG - Inf - VE
- < Alliance of Literary Socs
- M 357 i, 6 org, UK / 243 i, 1 org, o'seas
- ¶ George Eliot Review - 4; ftm, £10 nm.   NL - 4; ftm only.
  Those of Us Who Loved Her: the men in George Eliot's
  life; £7.50 m.
  Pitkin Guide to George Eliot; £3.50.

George Formby Society   (GFS)   1961
- NR 52 Windrush Drive, HINCKLEY, Leics, LE10 0NY.   (memsec/p)
  http://www.georgeformby.co.uk
  Mem Sec: Andrew Gatherer
- ▲ Un-incorporated Society
- Br 16; Australia
- ○ *G; to perpetuate the music & memory of George Formby
  (1904-61)
- ● Conf - Mtgs
- M c 850 i
- ¶ Vellum - 4; ftm only.

George MacDonald Society   1981
- NR 10 Appian Court, Parnell Rd, LONDON, E3 2RS.   (regd off)
  http://www.george-macdonald.com
  Sec: Roger Bardet
- ▲ Registered Charity
- ○ *A; to promote public interest & knowledge in the life & works
  of the poet, novelist & Christian fantasy writer George
  MacDonald (1824-1905)
- ● Conf - Mtgs - Res - Exhib - Inf - Lib - VE
- M 74 i, 16 org, UK / 78 i, org, o'seas
- ¶ North Wind - 1.   Orts (NL).

Georgian Group   1937
- NR 6 Fitzroy Sq, LONDON, W1T 5DX.   (hq)
  020 7529 8920   fax 020 7529 8938
  email info@georgiangroup.org.uk
  http://www.georgiangroup.org.uk
  Sec: Robert Bargery
- ▲ Registered Charity; Un-incorporated Society
- ○ *K; to protect & preserve buildings, monuments & gardens of
  the Georgian period (broadly 1700-1837)
- ● Educ - Lib - Awards - Grants
- < Jt C'ee of the Nat Amenity Socs
- M 3,300 i & f
  The Group is a statutory consultee in the planning system in
  England & Wales & reviews around 7,000 planning
  applications a year.

Geotechnical Society of Ireland
   a group of the **Institution of Engineers of Ireland**

German-British Chamber of Industry & Commerce   1971
- ■ 16 Buckingham Gate, LONDON, SW1E 6LB.   (hq)
  020 7976 4100   fax 020 7976 4101
  email mail@ahk-london.co.uk
  http://www.grossbritannien.ahk.de
  Dir-Gen: Ulrich Hoppe
  Contact: Thesy Lobitzer (020 7976 4112)
- ▲ Company Limited by Guarantee
- ○ *C; promotion of trade & investment between Germany & the
  United Kingdom
- Gp Business: Information, Partner search, Promotion
  Green Dot; Legal; Marketing services; Trade Fairs; VAT refund
- ● Conf - Res - Exhib - Expt - Inf
- < AHK Deutsche Auslandshandelskammern (Germany)
- M 640 f, 60 org (chambers of commerce), UK / 140 f, 60 org,
  o'seas
- ¶ Publication details by request.
  Note: the German title is - Deutsch-Britische Industrie- und
  Handelskammer.

German History Society   1979
- NR c/o Annika Mombauer, Dept of History, Open University,
  Walton Hall, MILTON KEYNES, Bucks, MK7 6AA.   (hsb)
  http://www.germanhistorysociety.org
  Sec: Annika Mombauer
- ▲ Un-incorporated Society
- ○ *L; academic research on German history
- ● Conf - Res
- M c 200 i, UK / c 50 i, o'seas
- ¶ German History - 4.

German Railway Society   (GRS)   1980
- ■ 3 Reynolds St, Elvetham Heath, FLEET, Hants, GU51 1LG..
  (memsec/p)
  email memsec@grs-uk.org   http://www.grs-uk.org
  Mem Sec: Kevin Patching
- ▲ Un-incorporated Society
- Br 6 groups
- ○ *G; for enthusiasts & modellers of German & Austrian railways
- ● Mtgs - Exhib - Lib
- M c 500 i
- ¶ Merkur - 4; ftm only.

Gerry Anderson Appreciation Society
   see **Fanderson**

Giftware Association   (The GA)   1947
- ■ Federation House, 10 Vyse St, BIRMINGHAM, B18 6LT.   (hq)
  0121-236 2657   fax 0121-236 3921
  http://www.ga-uk.org
  Chief Exec: Isabel Martinson
- ○ *T; promotion & provision of supporting business services to
  British manufacturers, importers & distributors of giftware
- ● Conf - Res - Comp - Expt - Inf - LG
- < Brit Allied Trs Fedn (BATF)
- M 1,500 i, f & org
- ¶ Newsline - 2.

Gilbert & Sullivan Society   (G&SS)   1924
- NR 7 Mace Walk, CHELMSFORD, Essex, CM1 2GE.   (memsec/p)
  http://www.gilbertandsullivansociety.org.uk
  Mem Sec: John Tritton
- ▲ Registered Charity
- Br 11; Australia, Canada, Israel, South Africa, USA
- ○ *D; to inform, educate & entertain all who are interested in the
  works of Gilbert & Sullivan & the Savoy operas
- Gp Appreciation society; Music; Opera; Theatre
- ● Conf - Mtgs - ET - Res - Inf - Lib
- < Nat Fedn Music Socs
- M 1,000 i, UK / 500 i, o'seas
- ¶ Gilbert & Sullivan News - 3.

© CBD Research Ltd · Beckenham · BR3 5JS · Tel 020 8650 7745 · E-mail cbd@cbdresearch.com · www.cbdresearch.com

Gin & Vodka Association of Great Britain (GVA) 1991

- ■ Cross Keys House, Queen St, SALISBURY, Wilts, SP1 1EY.   (hq)
  01722 415892   fax 01722 415840
  http://www.ginvodka.org
  Dir Gen: Edwin Atkinson
- ▲ Company Limited by Guarantee
- ○ *T; to protect & promote the interests of the gin & vodka trades
  generally both at home & abroad; to prevent any
  malpractices or abuses that might arise in connection with
  the production, importation or sale of gin or vodka
- ● Stat - Inf - LG
- < Confédn Eur des Producteurs de Spiritueux (Brussels)
- M 29 f
- ¶ NL - 4;   AR; both ftm.

Gingerbread
  see registered title **National Council for One Parent Families**

Girlguiding UK 1910

- ■ 17-19 Buckingham Palace Rd, LONDON, SW1W 0PT.   (hq)
  020 7834 6242   fax 020 7828 8317
  email chq@girlguiding.org.uk
  http://www.girlguiding.org.uk
  Chief Exec: Denise King
- ▲ Registered Charity
- Br 7
- ○ *Y; to help girls & young women to develop emotionally,
  mentally, physically & spiritually so that they can make a
  positive contribution to the community & the wider world
- Gp Rainbow Guides (5-7 yrs) (in Ulster 4-7); Brownie Guides (7-10
  yrs); Guide (10-14 yrs); Ranger Guides; Young leaders; Adult
  leaders
- ● Mtgs - ET
- < Wld Assn Girl Guides & Girl Scouts
- M 600,000 i
- ¶ Guiding - 12; ftm (16+yrs only); £2 nm.   AR - 1.
  Note: registered as the Guide Association.

Girls' Brigade England & Wales 1893

- NR PO Box 196, 129 Broadway, DIDCOT, Oxon, OX11 8XN.   (hq)
  01235 510425   fax 01235 510429
  http://www.girls.org.uk
  Nat Dir: Miss Ruth E Gilson
- ▲ Registered Charity
- Br 966; 55 o'seas
- ○ *R, *Y; acts as the National Council for England & Wales with
  regard to the spiritual & personal development of girls &
  young women
- ● Conf - Mtgs - ET - Exhib - Comp - Stat - VE
- < Girls' Brigade Intl Coun
- M 31,782 i, 996 f, UK / 55 f, o'seas
- ¶ The View - 6.   AR.

Girls' Schools Association (GSA) 1973

- NR 130 Regent Rd, LEICESTER, LE1 7PG.   (hq)
  0116-254 1619   fax 0116-255 3792
  email office@gsa.uk.com   http://www.gsa.uk.com
  Gen Sec: Sheila Cooper
- ▲ Company Limited by Guarantee
- ○ *E, *P; policy & administration of independent girls' schools
- ● Conf - Mtgs - ET - Res - Exhib - Inf - VE - LG
- M c 212 schools; c 88 associates & o'seas

Girls Venture Corps Air Cadets (GVCAC) 1964

- ■ 1 Bawtry Gate, SHEFFIELD, S Yorks, S9 1UD.   (hq)
  0114-244 8405   fax 0114-244 8419
  email gvcac@toucansurf.com   http://www.gvcac.org.uk
  Corps Dir: Mrs B Layne
- ▲ Company Limited by Guarantee; Registered Charity
- Br 30
- ○ *W, *Y; uniformed youth organisation for girls aged 11-20 who
  are interested in aviation, sport, Duke of Edinburgh Award,
  community service, & leadership skills
- ● Conf - Mtgs - Exam - Comp - VE - LG
- < Air Training Corps; Army Cadet Force; RAF WARMA; NCYVYS;
  CCPR
- M 800 i
- ¶ Circuit - 2; ftm.

GIST Support UK 2000

- ■ 67 Between Streets, COBHAM, Surrey, KT11 1AA.   (chmn/p)
  0300 400 0000
  email admin@gistsupportuk.com
  http://www.gistsupportuk.com
  Chmn: Judith K Robinson
- ▲ Un-incorporated Society
- ○ *G, *W; to promote & protect the physical & mental health of
  sufferers of gastro-intestinal stromal tumours (GISTs) & their
  carers in the UK, through provision of emotional support,
  education & practical advice; to increase awareness of the
  needs of GIST patients & their carers
- ● Conf - Mtgs - ET - Inf - LG - email, mailtalk & phone support
- < GIST Support Intl (GSI); The Liferaft Gp; Sarcoma UK
- M [not stated]
- ¶ GIST Patient guide;   GIST Support leaflet;
  Gist Patient Passport; all free.

Glamorgan History Society 1957

- NR 87 Gabalfa Rd, Sketty, SWANSEA, Glamorgan, SA2 8ND.
  (hsp)
  01792 205888
  http://www.glamorganhistory.org
  Hon Sec: Paul Reynolds
- ○ *L; promote the study of the history of Glamorgan
- M i & org

Glasgow Agricultural Society (GAS) 1898

- NR Glenside Farm, Plean, STIRLING, FK7 8BA.   (hsp)
  01786 814729
  Sec: Jacqueline Adamson
- ○ *B, *F, *G; to promote & encourage the breeding & showing of
  horses & ponies; to organise the national stallion show
  annually (for in-hand Clydesdales, Highlands, Shetlands &
  mountain & moorland horses & ponies); farrier competitions
- < Nat Pony Soc; Highland Pony Soc; Clydesdale Horse Soc;
  Shetland Pony Studbook Soc
- M 394 i

Glasgow Archaeological Society (GAS) 1856

- NR c/o Tho & J W Barty Solicitors, 61 High St, DUNBLANE, FK15
  0EH.   (asa)
  http://www.glasarchsoc.org.uk
  Vice-Pres: Prof Stephen Driscoll
- ▲ Registered Charity
- ○ *L; to promote the study of northern archaeology with a special
  emphasis on western Scotland
- ● Conf - Mtgs - Res - Exhib - Inf - VE
- < Coun Brit Archaeology
- M 325 i, 2 f, 5 org, UK / 20 i, o'seas
- ¶ Scottish Archaeological Jnl - 2; ftm, £18 nm.
  A Touch of GAS - 4; ftm.

Glasgow Chamber of Commerce   1783
■ 30 George Square, GLASGOW, G2 1EQ.   (hq)
  0141-204 2121   fax 0141-221 2336
  email chamber@glasgowchamber.org
  http://www.glasgowchamberofcommerce.com
  Chief Exec: Stuart Patrick
○ *C; interests of the business community of Glasgow & West of
  Scotland
● Mtgs - Stat - Expt - Inf - LG
< Brit Chams Comm; Scot Chams Comm
M 2,000 f
¶ Glasgow Business Jnl - 6.   Diary & Directory - 1.

Glasgow Mathematical Association   (GMA)   1927
NR Dept of Mathematics, University of Glasgow, University
  Gardens, GLASGOW, G12 8QW.   (treas/b)
  email Frances.Goldman@glasgow.ac.uk
  Hon Treas: Dr Frances H Goldman
▲ Un-incorporated Society
○ *L; to stimulate study & teaching of mathematics at all levels; to
  provide a forum for professional mathematicians, especially
  teachers, to exchange ideas
M i
¶ Jnl.

Glasgow Natural History Society   1851
NR c/o Zoology Museum, Graham Kerr Building, University of
  Glasgow, GLASGOW, G12 8QQ.   (hq)
  0141-329 1343
  http://www.glasgownaturalhistory.org.uk
  Hon Sec: Mary Child
▲ Registered Charity
○ *L; to encourage the study of natural history, prinsipally in the
  West of Scotland
¶ Glasgow Naturalist (Jnl).   NL.

Glass Association   1983
NR 150 Braemar Rd, SUTTON COLDFIELD, W Midlands,
  B73 6LZ.   (memsec/p)
  http://www.glassassociation.org.uk
  Mem Sec: Mrs Pauline Wimpory
○ *G, *P; for all interested in glass & glassmaking

The Glass Circle   1937
■ 66 Corringham Rd, LONDON, NW11 7BX.   (hsp)
  020 8455 7348
  email secretary@glasscircle.org
  http://www.glasscircle.org
  Hon Sec: Marianne Scheer
▲ Un-incorporated Society
○ *G; to promote the study, understanding, appreciation & history
  of artistic & collected glass
● Conf - Mtgs - Exhib - Lib - VE
M 405 i, 4 f, 6 org, UK / 70 i, 4 org, o'seas
¶ Glass Circle News - 4; ftm, £5 nm.
  Glass Circle Jnl - 2; ftm, £20 nm.

Glass & Glazing Federation   (GGF)   1977
■ 54 Ayres St, LONDON, SE1 1EU.   (hq)
  020 7939 9101
  email info@ggf.org.uk   http://www.ggf.org.uk
  Chief Exec & Nat Sec: Nigel Rees
▲ Company Limited by Guarantee
Br 10; Africa, Asia, Middle East, Republic of Ireland
○ *T; interests of companies engaged in glazing (glass & plastics),
  including solar control, leaded & stained glass, shopfronts,
  patent glazing, double glazing, merchanting, laminating,
  toughening, bending, conservatories, manufacturing of
  sealed units, mirrors, compounds, all flat glass processing,
  external relations with government & all other relevant bodies
Gp Conservatory Association; Curtain Walling Association;
  European Window Film Association; Flat Glass Council; plus
  numerous committees, groups & working parties
● Conf - Mtgs - ET - Exhib - Empl - LG
M 600 f
  (Sub: according to turnover)
¶ NL (email) - 10; ftm only.   AR - 1; free.
  Glazing Manual - updated; £50 m, £100 nm.
  Publications CDs & DVDs list available.

Glenn Miller Society   1950
■ 3 Pine View Close, Verwood, WIMBORNE, Dorset, BH21 6NN.
  Contact: Brenda Martin
○ *D, *G

Global Commons Institute
  An independent group concerned with the protection of the
  'global commons' (the common heritage of all humanity),
  campaigning as 'Contraction & Convergence'

Glosa Education Organisation   (GEO)   1987
■ 35 Wingfield Road, KINGSTON UPON THAMES, Surrey,
  KT2 5LR.   (hsp)
  020 8288 0257
  http://www.glosa.org
  Hon Sec: Wendy Ashby
▲ Registered Charity
Br 5 o'seas
○ *E, *X, to promote the international language Glosa; to put
  speakers & penfriends in touch with each other; to provide
  teaching materials & establish study centres worldwide
● Mtgs - ET - Inf - Penfriends service
M 180 i, 6 org, UK / 150 i, 10 org, o'seas
¶ Plu Glosa Nota - 4; £6.50 yr.
  Dictionaries & textbooks; £1 - £10.95.

Gloucester Cattle Society   1972
■ Hillfields Lodge, Lighthorne, WARWICK, CV35 0BQ.   (hsp)
  01926 651147   fax 01926 651147
  http://www.gloucestercattle.org.uk
  Sec: Yvonne Froehlich
▲ Un-incorporated Society
○ *B; recording, support & development of the breed of
  Gloucester cattle
● Inf
< Rare Breeds Survival Trust
M 120 i

Gloucester Chamber of Trade & Commerce
NR 43 Clarence St, GLOUCESTER, GL1 1EA.   (hq)
  0845 271 2844
  email info@glos-chamber-trade.com
  http://www.glos-chamber-trade.com
  Pres: Mark Boyce
○ *C
< Gloucestershire Cham of Comm & Ind

   © CBD Research Ltd · Beckenham · BR3 5JS · Tel 020 8650 7745 · E-mail cbd@cbdresearch.com · www.cbdresearch.com

Gloucestershire Chamber of Commerce & Industry   1902
- ■ 183 Westgate St, GLOUCESTER, GL1 2RN.   (hq)
  01242 308030
  email info@gloschamber.co.uk
  http://www.gloschamber.co.uk
  Dir: Suzanne Hall-Gibbins
- ▲ Company Limited by Guarantee
- ○ *C
- Gp Bourton-on-the-Water Chamber of Commerce; Cheltenham Chamber of Commerce; Gloucester Chamber of Trade & Commerce; Tetbury Chamber of Commerce & Industry; Tewkesbury Chamber of Commerce & Industry
- < GWE Business West Ltd

Gloucestershire Old Spots Pig Breeders' Club   (GOSPBC)   1992
- ■ Freepost (GL442), CIRENCESTER, Glos, GL7 5BR.   (mail)
  01285 860229   fax 01285 860229
  email mail@oldspots.org.uk
  http://www.oldspots.org.uk
  Sec: Richard Lutwyche
- ▲ Un-incorporated Society
- ○ *B
- ● ET - Expt - Inf - VE
- M 300 i, UK / 10 i, o'seas
- ¶ Spot Press (NL) - 4.

Gloucestershire Society for Industrial Archaeology   (GSIA)   1964
- ■ Oak House, Hamshill, Coaley, DURSLEY, Glos, GL11 5EH.   (hsp)
  01453 860595
  email ray.wilson@coaley.net   http://www.gsia.org.uk
  Hon Sec: Dr R Wilson
- ▲ Registered Charity
- Br 1
- ○ *L; to stimulate interest in, to record, to study & where appropriate to preserve, items of industrial archaeology especially in the county of Gloucestershire
- ● Conf - Mtgs - Res - Exhib - SG - Inf - PL - VE
- < Assn Industrial Archaeology
- M 215 i, 1 f, 7 org, UK / 1 i, o'seas
- ¶ Jnl - 1; ftm, £9 nm.   NL - 4; free.

Glued Laminated Timber Association   (GLULAM/GLTA)   1988
- ■ Chiltern House, Stocking Lane, HIGH WYCOMBE, Bucks, HP14 4ND.   (hq)
  01494 565180   fax 01494 565487
  http://www.glulam.co.uk
  Sec: Mrs P M Presland
- ○ *T; an independent trade association of manufacturers, distributors & suppliers of glulam
- ● Promotion of glued laminated timber - Publication of technical information
- M f

GM Freeze
- NR 50 South Yorkshire Buildings, Silkstone Common, BARNSLEY, S Yorks, S75 4RJ.   (hq)
  0845 217 8992
  email enquiry@gmfreeze.org   http://www.gmfreeze.org
  Campaign coordinator: Eve Mitchell
- ○ *K; campaign for a government freeze on genetically modified crops and foods

Go Kids Go!
  see **Association of Wheelchair Children**

Goat Veterinary Society
  a group of the **British Veterinary Association**

Golden Guernsey Goat Society   1986
- NR Blaen y Waen, Talog, CAMARTHEN, SA33 6PA.   (hsp)
  http://www.goldenguernseygoat.org.uk
  Sec: Mrs Emma Rose
- ○ *B

Goldfish Club   1942
- NR 24 Bridgewater Drive, Great Glen, LEICESTER, LE8 9DX.   (hsp)
  0116-259 2105
  email richardshepherd@dsl.pipex.com
  Hon Sec: Richard Shepherd
- ▲ Un-incorporated Society
- Br Australia, Canada, N Zealand, USA
- ○ *G; to advance the equipment for aircrew ditching in the sea
- ● Annual Reunion - Dinner
- M 400 i, UK / 85 i, o'seas
- ¶ The Goldfish Club (NL) - 4; ftm only.

Golf Club of Great Britain   (GCGB)   1986
- NR 338 Hook Rd, CHESSINGTON, Surrey, KT9 1NU.   (hq)
  020 8391 4666
- ○ *S; to promote golfing activities for members & their guests
- M i & org

Golf Club Managers' Association   (GCMA)   1933
- ■ 7a Beaconsfield Rd, WESTON-SUPER-MARE, Somerset, BS23 1YE.   (hq)
  01934 641166   fax 01934 644254
  email hq@gcma.org.uk   http://www.gcma.org.uk
  Chief Exec: Keith Lloyd
- ▲ Un-incorporated Society
- Br 17 regions
- ○ *N, *P, *S; to provide support & help to secretaries, secretary/managers & owners of golf clubs in the UK
- ● Conf - Mtgs - ET - Exhib - Stat - Inf - Lib - Empl
- M 2,500 i, UK / 50 i, o'seas
- ¶ Golf Club Management - 12; ftm, £5 each (£55 yr) nm. Members' Hbk - 1; ftm only.
- × 2007 Association of Golf Club Secretaries

Golf Consultants Association   (GCA)   1999
- NR Federation House, STONELEIGH PARK, Warks, CV8 2RF.   (hq)
  024 7641 4999   fax 024 7641 4990
  email gca@sportsandplay.com
  http://www.golfconsultants.org.uk
  Sec: Jacqui Baldwin
- ▲ Un-incorporated Society
- ○ *P, S; to provide a point of reference for those requiring independent professional golf consultancy services world-wide
- ● Conf - Mtgs
- < a group of the Fedn of Sports & Play Assns (FSPA)
- M 12 i

Golf Union of Wales   (GUW)   1895
- NR Catsash, NEWPORT, Gwent, NP18 1JQ.   (hq)
  01633 436040   fax 01633 430843
  email office@golfunionwales.org
  http://www.golfunionwales.org
  Chief Exec: Richard Dixon
- ○ *S; the governing body for golf in Wales
- ● Mtgs - ET - Res - Comp - SG - Stat - Inf - VE
- < Coun Nat Golf Unions; Eur Golf Assn
- M 62,000 i, 159 affiliated clubs
- ¶ Ybk; free.   Information leaflets.
- × 2007 (Welsh Golfing Union
       (Welsh Ladies' Golf Union

Golfing Union of Ireland   1891
IRL   Carton Demesne, MAYNOOTH, Co Kildare, Republic of
    Ireland.   (hq)
    353 (1) 505 4000   fax 353 (1) 505 4001
    email information@gui.ie   http://www.gui.ie
    Gen Sec: Pat Finn
○   *S; for men's golf in Ireland

Good Gardeners' Association   (gGA)   1960
NR   4 Lisle Place, WOTTON-UNDER-EDGE, Glos, GL12 7AZ.
    (hsb)
    01453 520322
    email info@goodgardeners.org.uk
    http://www.goodgardeners.org.uk
    Hon Sec: Matt Adams
▲   Registered Charity
○   *H; a membership based charity for people who want to grow
    & eat nutritious food; to promote the concept of 'moving
    beyond organic'; no dig gardening & the use of compost
●   Conf - ET - Res
M   300 i, 5 f, 10 org, UK / 5 i, o'seas
    (Sub: £21.00-35.00)
¶   NL - 4; ftm only.

Good Homes Alliance   (GHA)   2007
NR   1 Baldwin Terrace, LONDON, N1 7RU.   (hq)
    020 7704 3503
    email info@goodhomes.org.uk
    http://www.goodhomes.org.uk
    Chmn: Peter Halsall,   Dir: Jon Bootland
○   *L; a group of housing developers, building professionals &
    sustainability experts whose aim is to build & promote
    sustainable homes & communities & to transform the whole
    of mainstream UK housing into a sustainable endeavour
●   LG - Lib - Mtgs - Res - SG
M   10 f (developers), 54 f (non-developers)

Goon Show Preservation Society   (GSPS)   1972
■   114 Fountains Rd, IPSWICH, Suffolk, IP2 9TW.   (sp)
    07825 699539
    email johnrepsch@hotmail.com
    Sec: Tina Hammond,   Chief Exec: John Repsch
▲   Un-incorporated Society
Br   6; Australia, Canada, Germany, Japan, S Africa, USA
○   *G; to ensure that as many Goon Show recordings & other
    related information / recordings / articles as possible are
    archived; to meet like-minded people
Gp   Archive recordings: Audio, video & print
●   Mtgs - Res
<   Goon Appreciation Socs: Perth & Victoria (Australia)
M   456 i, UK / 92 i, o'seas
    (Sub: £10 UK / £11 o'seas)
¶   NL - 4.

Governing Council of the Cat Fancy   (GCCF)   1910
■   5 King's Castle Business Park, The Drove, BRIDGWATER,
    Somerset, TA6 4AG.   (hq)
    01278 427575
    email officemanager@gccfcats.org
    http://www.gccfcats.org
    Office Mgr: Mark Goadby
○   *V
●   Registration of pedigree cats - Licensing of cat shows for
    pedigree cats
M   143 cat clubs

Gower Society   1947
■   The Orchard, Perriswood, Penmaen, SWANSEA, Glam,
    SA3 2HN.   (hsp)
    01792 371665
    Hon Sec: Mrs Ruth Ridge
▲   Registered Charity
○   *L; promotion of knowledge of the history & conservation of the
    physical aspects of the Lordship of Gower
Gp   Planning search; Publication; Footpaths; Working party;
    Programmes
●   Conf - Mtgs - ET - Inf - VE - LG - Archives - Weekly excursions -
    Clearing footpaths
<   Nat Trust; Campaign Protection Rural Wales; Ramblers' Assn
M   1,700 i
¶   Jnl - 1; ftm, £5.95 nm.   Guide to Gower; £4.95.
    Gower Walks; £3.   Butterflies of Gower; £2.50.
    Gower Way (leaflet); 75p.   Gower in Focus; £15.
    Vernacular Gower.   The Castles of Gower.
    The Castles of Gower.   Edgar Evans of Gower.
    The Churches & Chapels of Gower.

Grain & Feed Trade Association Ltd   (GAFTA)   1971
■   9 Lincoln's Inn Fields, LONDON, WC2A 3BP.   (hq)
    020 7814 9666   fax 020 7814 8383
    email post@gafta.com   http://www.gafta.com
    Dir-Gen: Mrs Pamela Kirby Johnson
○   *T; to promote international trade in grains, animal feeding-
    stuffs, pulses & rice
Gp   Brokers; Crushers; Dealers & manufacturers; Grain, protein,
    feeding stuffs & marine & animal products; Pulses; Shippers
●   Conf - Mtgs - ET - Res - Exhib - SG - Stat - Inf - Arbitration -
    Contracts
M   c 900 f in 80 countries
¶   NL - 6; ftm, £2 nm.   Forms of Contract.
    Hbk - 1;   AR - 1; both ftm.
×   2009 International General Produce Association (merged)

**Grand Lodge of Antient Free & Accepted Masons of Scotland (The
Grand Lodge of Scotland)   1736**
NR   Freemason's Hall, 96 George St, EDINBURGH, EH2 3DH.
    (hq)
    0131-225 5577   fax 0131-225 3953
    email gladmin@grandlodgescotland.org
    http://www.grandlodgescotland.com
    Grand Sec: David M Begg
Br   658
○   *N; freemasonry
●   Mtgs - Lib - VE
<   Scot Museums Coun
M   26,000 i, UK / 12,000 o'seas
¶   Ybk - 1; £10.

Grand National Archery Society   (GNAS)   1861
■   Lilleshall National Sports Centre, NEWPORT, Shropshire,
    TF10 9AT.   (hq)
    01952 677888   fax 01952 606019
    email enquiries@gnas.org   http://www.gnas.org
    Chief Exec: David Sherratt
▲   Company Limited by Guarantee
Br   clubs
○   *S; national governing body for the sport of archery in all its
    forms; to act as the contact office for all clubs in the UK
Gp   Clubs: Clout, Compound, Field, Flight, Popinjay, Recurve,
    Target
    Bow types: Compound; Cross bow; Long bow; Olympic
●   Conf - Mtgs - Exhib - Comp
<   Fédn Intle de Tir à l'Arc (FITA); Brit Olympic Assn (BOA); Brit
    Paralympic Assn
M   25,000+ i, 1,100 clubs
¶   Archery UK - 4; ftm, £4.25 nm.
    Note: Uses the trading name of Archery UK

Grandparents Action Group (GAG) 2001

NR 7 Hilda Hook Close, Madeley, TELFORD, Shropshire,
TF7 4HU. (chmn/p)
01952 582621 fax 01952 582621
Chmn: Mrs Pamela Wilson
○ *G, *K; to help grandparents maintain & protect the
relationship between grandchildren & grandparents when
contact is an issue
● Conf - Res - Stat - Inf - LG
M 208 i

Grandparents' Association 1987

■ Moot House, The Stow, HARLOW, Essex, CM20 3AG. (hq)
01279 428040 fax 01279 428040
email info@grandparents-association.org.uk
http://www.grandparents-association.org.uk
Chief Exec: Mrs Lynn Chesterman
▲ Registered Charity
○ *K, *W; to work with all grandparents for the best interests of
children; to support those who are denied contact with their
grandchildren, who are raising their grandchildren or who
have childcare responsibilities
Gp Hearings; Information; Support groups in some areas
● Conf - Mtgs - ET - Support groups (grandparents & toddlers)
Helpline: 0845 434 9585
< Children's Rights Alliance for England; Nat Coun for Voluntary
Child Care Organisations; Nat Coun for Voluntary
Organisations
M 1,085 i, 182 f, 8 org, 20 social services
(Sub: £15 i, £225 f, £50 org, £200 social services)
¶ Grandparent Times (NL) - 3; AR; both free.
Specialist publications; £4.40 m, £5.75 nm.
Relative Values. . . Missing out on Contact?
Relative Values. . . The Best Interests of the Child?
An Evaluation of the Grandparent & Toddler Group Initiative.

Graphic Enterprise Scotland 1910

■ 112 George St, EDINBURGH, EH2 4LH. (hq)
0131-220 4353 fax 0131-220 4344
http://www.graphicenterprisescotland.org
▲ Un-incorporated Society
Br 4
○ *T
Gp Printing; Binding; Ancillary
● Conf - Mtgs - ET - Inf - Lib - Empl - LG - Legal advisory service
< Intergraf
M 100 f
¶ NL - 2; Directory (on website); AR; all free.
✕ 2010 Scottish Print Employers Federation

Great Britain Basketball
since 2006 **British Basketball Federation**

Great Britain Diving Federation (GBDF) 1993

NR 6 Derwent Ave, Wilsden, BRADFORD, W Yorks, BD15 0LY.
(admin/p)
01535 273633
http://www.diving-gbdf.com
Admin Dir: Mrs Lesley Grist
▲ Un-incorporated Society
○ *S
● Conf - ET - Comp - Inf
< Cent Coun for Physical Recreation (CCPR); Scot Amat
Swimming Assn (SASA)
M 850 i

Great Britain Luge Association

NR 61 West Malvern Rd, MALVERN, Worcs, WR14 4NF. (hq)
01684 576604
http://www.gbla.org.uk
Dir: Mark Armstrong
○ *S; luge racing

Great Britain Postcard Club (GBPCC) 1961

■ 34 Harper House, St James Crescent, LONDON, SW9 7LW.
(hsp)
020 7771 9404
email drenebrennan@yahoo.co.uk
Chief Exec: Drene Brennan
▲ Un-incorporated Society
○ *G, *X; postcard collecting; world friendship
● Conf - Res - Comp
< Clubs in USA: Disney, Duneland, Metropolitan, San Francisco;
Sunshine; Tuscan; Webfoot
M 200 i, UK / 100 i, o'seas
¶ Postcard World - 6; £10 yr m.

Great Britain Racquetball Federation (GBRF) 1984

NR 78 Suffolk Drive, WOODBRIDGE, Suffolk, IP12 2TP. (hsp)
01394 461069
▲ Un-incorporated Society
○ *S; to promote the game of racquetball

Great Britain Target Shooting Federation
since 2007 **British Shooting**

Great Bustard Group (GBG) 1998

NR 1 Down Barn Close, Winterbourne Gunner, SALISBURY, Wilts,
SP4 6JP. (hq)
01980 671466
email enquiries@greatbustard.com
http://www.greatbustard.com
Founder & Dir: David Waters
▲ Registered Charity
○ *K; to re-introduce the Great Bustard (Otis tarda) to the UK
M i
(Sub: £20)
¶ Otis - 4; ftm; NL - email.

Great North of Scotland Railway Association (GNSRA) 1964

■ 31 Brackley Lane, Abthorpe, TOWCESTER, Northants,
NN12 8QJ. (editor/p)
01327 857083
Editor: Keith Fenwick
▲ Un-incorporated Society
○ *G; study, acquisition & preservation of documents, illustrations
& information relating to the railway
Gp Specialist groups according to the research on hand
● Mtgs - Res - Exhib - Inf - VE
M 315 i, 5 org, UK / 3 i, o'seas
¶ Great North Review - 4; (Index every 5 yrs); LM - 1; all ftm.

Great Northern Railway Society (GNR Society) 1981

■ 57 North Rd, GLOSSOP, Derbys, SK13 7AU. (hsp)
01457 852851
http://www.gnrs.150m.com
Hon Sec: Peter Hall
▲ Un-incorporated Society
○ *G; historical research & study of the former Great Northern
Railway & its joint lines from inception to present day
● Mtgs - Res - Exhib - SG - Inf - PL
M c 300 i, UK / 5 i, o'seas
¶ GN News (Jnl) - 6; ftm only.
Booklets with information on coaches, wagons etc; prices vary.

Great Western Society Ltd (GWS) 1961
■ Didcot Railway Centre, DIDCOT, Oxon, OX11 7NJ. (hq)
01235 817200 fax 01235 510621
email didrlyc@globalnet.co.uk
http://www.didcotrailwaycentre.org.uk
Sec: F Cooper
▲ Company Limited by Guarantee; Registered Charity
Br 8
○ *G; study of history, equipment & operation of the former Great
Western Railway; preservation of items of interest -
locomotives, rolling stock, buildings, etc
● Conf - Mtgs - ET - Res - Exhib - SG - Inf - VE
< Assn of Independent Museums; Heritage Railways; Assn of Brit
Transport & Engineering Museums; Transport Trust
M 4,520 i, UK / 120 i, o'seas
¶ Great Western Echo - 4; ftm, £1 nm.
NL - 7; AR; both ftm only.

**Greater London Industrial Archaeology Society (GLIAS)
1968**
■ 14 Mount Rd, BARNET, Herts, EN4 9RL. (hsp)
email secretary@glias.org.uk http://www.glias.org.uk
Hon Sec: Brian James-Strong
▲ Company Limited by Guarantee; Registered Charity
○ *L; informing the public of London's industrial history, & the
preparation of photographic & documentary records of
industrial monuments in Greater London
Gp Recording
● Res - SG - Inf - VE - Lectures - Walks
< Assn Indl Archaeology (AIA); Coun for Brit Archaeology
M c 600 i, c 50 org
¶ London's Industrial Archaeology (Jnl) - irreg; ftm.
NL - 6; free.

Greater Manchester Chamber of Commerce 1820
NR Churchgate House, 56 Oxford St, MANCHESTER, M60 7HJ.
(hq)
0161-236 3210 fax 0161-237 3277
email info@gmchamber.co.uk
http://www.gmchamber.co.uk
Chief Exec: Clive Memmott
▲ Company Limited by Guarantee
○ *C; promotion of trade & industry & provision of specialist
information & representation for NW England
< Brit Chams Comm; Chams Comm NW
M 5,000 f

Greek Institute 1969
■ 34 Bush Hill Rd, LONDON, N21 2DS. (hsp)
020 8360 7968 fax 020 8360 7968
email info@greekinstitute.co.uk
http://www.greekinstitute.co.uk
Dir: Dr Kypros Tofallis
Br 20
○ *L; to promote modern Greek studies in UK
● Mtgs - Exam - Res - ET - Comp - Inf - VE
M 20 i, f
¶ Anglo-Greek Review - 4; ftm.

Green Alliance Trust 1978
NR 36 Buckingham Palace Rd, LONDON, SW1W 0RE. (hq)
020 7233 7433 fax 020 7233 9033
email ga@green-alliance.org.uk
http://www.green-alliance.org.uk
Dir: Matthew Spencer
▲ Registered Charity
○ *K; to promote sustainable development by ensuring that the
environment is at the heart of decision-making
Gp Environment
● Conf - Mtgs - Res - Inf - LG
< Eur Envt Bureau
M 450 i, 100 f, 30 org, UK
¶ Parliamentary NL - 26. Inside Track - 4. AR.

Green Lane Association (GLASS) 1995
NR 2 Stockhill Circus, Basford, NOTTINGHAM, NG6 0LS.
(membership)
0115-875 2885
email glass@glass-uk.org http://www.glass-uk.org
▲ Company Limited by Guarantee
Br 12
○ *G, *K; to research & protect vehicular rights of way on the
network of ancient unsurfaced public roads
● Mtgs - ET - Res - Exhib - SG - LG
< Brit Trust for Consvn Volunteers (BTCV); Motoring Orgs Land
Access & Recreation Assn (LARA)
M 520 i, 20 org
¶ Green Lanes - 4; Northern Bulletin - 4;
Southern Bulletin - 4; all ftm only.

Greenock Chamber of Commerce 1813
NR Business Store, 75-81 Cathcart St, GREENOCK, Renfrewshire,
PA15 1DE. (hq)
01475 715577 fax 01475 715566
email hugh@greenockchamber.co.uk
http://www.greenockchamber.co.uk
Exec Admin: Hugh Bunten
▲ Un-incorporated Society
○ *C; to promote local business, both home & export trade
● Mtgs - ET - Inf - LG - Networking events
< Brit Chams Comm; Scot Chams Comm
M 150 f
¶ Bulletin - 4; AR.

GreenSpace
see **Institute of Parks & Green Space**

Greenwich, Bexley & Lewisham Chamber of Commerce
since July 2007 **South East London Chamber of Commerce**

Greeting Card Association (GCA) 1919
■ United House, North Rd, LONDON, N7 9DP. (hq)
020 7619 0396 fax 020 7607 6411
email gca@max-publishing.co.uk
http://www.greetingcardassociation.org.uk
Admin: Sharon Little
▲ Company Limited by Guarantee
○ *T; to promote, protect & celebrate the greeting card industry
● Mtgs - ET - Inf - LG
M 320 f
¶ Progressive Greetings - 12; £50 yr.

Gregorian Association 1870
NR 26 The Grove, Ealing, LONDON, W5 5LH. (chmn/p)
020 8840 5832
http://www.beaufort.demon.co.uk/chant.htm
Chmn: Greg Macartney
○ *D; for those interested in singing the Gregorian chant

Greyhound Action 1997
NR PO Box 127, KIDDERMINSTER, Worcs, DY10 3UZ, (mail)
01562 745778 fax 0870 138 3993
email info@greyhoundaction.org.uk
http://www.greyhoundaction.org.uk
○ *K; campaigning for the abolition of greyhound racing

Greyhound Trainers Association (GTA)
NR Burhill Kennels, Turners Lane, HERSHAM, Surrey, KT12 4AW.
(chmn/b)
01932 221545
email norah.mac@btinternet.com
http://www.cagro-greyhounds.co.uk
Chmn: Norah McEllistrim
○ *P; to represent professional greyhound trainers that race under
GBGB (Greyhound Board of Greyhound Britain) rules
● Comp - ET - Inf
< Combined Associates Greyhound Racing Org (CAGRO)

© CBD Research Ltd · Beckenham · BR3 5JS · Tel 020 8650 7745 · E-mail cbd@cbdresearch.com · www.cbdresearch.com

Grieg Society of Great Britain   1992
- ■ c/o The Royal Norwegian Embassy, 25 Belgrave Sq, LONDON, SW1X 8QD.   (mail)
  01634 714434   fax 01634 714434
  http://www.griegsociety.co.uk
  Chmn: Beryl Foster
- ▲ Un-incorporated Society
- ○ *A; to promote interest & encourage appreciation of the music of Edvard Hagerup Grieg (1843-1907) & other Norwegian composers
- ● Conf - Mtgs - Res - Exhib - Inf - Lib - Recitals & concerts
- < Intl Grieg Soc (Bergen, Norway);
  Grieg Soc(s) in: Oslo (Norway), Moscow (Russia), Münster & Leipzig (Germany), Tokyo (Japan), Groningen (Netherlands), New York (USA), Tokyo (Japan)
- M 100 i, UK / 8 i, o'seas
- ¶ The Grieg Companion (Jnl) - 1.   NL - 3; ftm only.

Grimsby & Cleethorpes Chamber of Trade
  a local chamber of the **Hull & Humber Chamber of Commerce, Industry & Shipping**

Ground Forum   (GF)   1992
- ■ 83 Copers Cope Rd, BECKENHAM, Kent, BR3 1NR.   (asa)
  020 8663 0947   fax 020 8663 0949
  email gforum@ground-forum.org.uk
  http://www.ground-forum.org.uk
  Hon Sec: Dianne Jennings
- ▲ Un-incorporated Society
- ○ *T; all aspects of geotechnical engineering (site investigation, foundation construction, tunnelling, ground improvement & remediation, geoenvironmentalism)
- ● Mtgs - LG
- < Construction Ind Coun (CIC)
- M 9 org

Ground Limestone Producers Association
  presumed closed

Group-Analytic Society (London)   (GAS)   1952
- ■ 102 Belsize Lane, LONDON, NW3 5BB.   (hq)
  020 7435 6611
- ▲ Registered Charity
- ○ *P; promotion & development of group analysis as a treatment, prophylaxis & science

Group Auto Union UK & Ireland Ltd   (GROUPAUTO)   1974
- NR Roydsdale House, Roydsdale Way, Euroway Trading Estate, BRADFORD, W Yorks, BD4 6SE.   (hq)
  01274 654600   fax 01274 654610
  email jim.mazza@groupauto.co.uk
  http://www.groupauto.co.uk
  Managing Dir: Jim Mazza
- ▲ Company Limited by Guarantee
- ○ *T; a specialist business group for independent motor factors
- M 461 f

Group for Education in Museums   (GEM)   1948
- NR 54 Balmoral Rd, GILLINGHAM, Kent, ME7 4PG.   (hq)
  01634 853424   fax 01634 853424
  email office@gem.org.uk   http://www.gem.org.uk
- ▲ Company Limited by Guarantee; Registered Charity
- Br 8
- ○ *E; to promote educational work in museums & related institutions; to foster the highest standards in museum education
- M i

Group Travel Organisers Association   (GTOA)   1992
- ■ 29 Ludford Drive, Stirchley, TELFORD, Shropshire, TF3 1RD.   (memsec/p)
  01952 590484
  http://www.gtoa.co.uk
  Mem Sec: Philip Cameron
- ▲ Un-incorporated Society
- Br 6
- ○ *T; for group travel organisers & travel trade suppliers
- ● Conf - Mtgs - SG - VE - LG
- M 213 i, 370 org, UK / 2 f, o'seas
- ¶ GTOA News - 4;   Hbk - 3 yrly;   AGM Report - 1;
  NL (to the 6 branches) - 4; all ftm.

Growing Media Association   (GMA)
- ▨ Horticulture House, 19 High St, Theale, READING, Berks, RG7 5AH.   (hq)
  0118-930 3132   fax 0118-932 3453
  email info@the-hta.org.uk
  http://www.growingmedia.co.uk
  Chief Exec: Tim Briercliffe
- ▲ Un-incorporated Society
- ○ *T; the development, production, marketing & sale of growing media & soil improvers in the UK & Ireland
- ● Mtgs - Inf - LG
- M 24 f
- ¶ NL - 4; ftm only.

GS1 Ireland
- IRL The Nutley Building, Merrion Rd, DUBLIN 4, Republic of Ireland.   (hq)
  353 (1) 208 0660   fax 353 (1) 208 0670
  email info@gs1ie.org   http://www.gs1ie.org
  Chief Exec: Jim Bracken
- ○ *T; the article number industry
- < IBEC

GS1 UK   1976
- NR Staple Court, 11 Staple Inn Buildings, LONDON, WC1V 7QH.   (hq)
  020 7092 3500   fax 020 7681 2290
  email info@gs1uk.org   http://www.gs1uk.org
  Chief Exec: Steve Coussins
- ▲ Company Limited by Guarantee
- ○ *T; dedicated to the development of global data standards for the supply chain
- ● Conf - Mtgs - ET - Res
- < GS1
- M 17,000 f
- ¶ GSQ - 4; ftm.
  e-Highlights (email NL) - 4; ftm only.

Guernsey Chamber of Commerce   1808
- NR 16 Glategny Esplanade (suite 1), ST PETER PORT, Guernsey, GY1 1WN.   (hq)
  01481 727483   fax 01481 710755
  email director@chamber.guernsey.net
  http://www.chamber.guernsey.net
  Dir: Mike Collins
- ▲ Company Limited by Guarantee
- ○ *C; to link together the members of the business community so that they can speak with an authoritative voice on matters concerning the trade, industry & commerce in the Isle of Guernsey
- ● Mtgs - Inf - LG
- < Brit Chams Comm
- M c 600 f (Guernsey)
- ¶ Contact - 12; ftm (extra copies £2.50), £2.50 nm.

Guernsey Growers Association   (GGA)   1894
- ■ Landes du Marche, VALE, Guernsey, GY6 8DE.   (hq)
  01481 253713   fax 01481 254015
  Sec: Mrs V Mechem
- ○ *F; the farming & growing of crops under glass & in the open
- ● Conf - Mtgs - Exhib - Comp - Stat - Inf - VE
- M 150 i & f (mainly local growers)
- ¶ NL.   Ybk.   AR.

Guide Association
  the registered title of **Girlguiding UK**

Guide Dogs for the Blind Association   (GDBA)   1934
- NR Hillfields, Burghfield, READING, Berks, RG7 3YG.   (hq)
  0118-983 5555
  http://www.gdba.org.uk
  Chief Exec: Bridget Wall
- ▲ Registered Charity
- ○ *W; to enhance the mobility, independence & quality of life of
  sight impaired people by providing guide dogs & other
  services
- M i

Guild of Agricultural Journalists   1946
- ■ 1 Rose Villa, Anchor Rd, Spa Common, NORTH WALSHAM,
  Norfolk, NR28 9AJ.   (hsp)
  01692 402853
  http://www.gaj.org.uk
  Gen Sec: Clemmie Gleeson
- ▲ Registered Charity
- ○ *P
- ● Conf - Mtgs - ET - Comp - VE - LG
- < Intl Fedn Agricl Journalists (IFAJ)
- M 600 i, UK / 13 i, o'seas
- ¶ NL - 4.   AR.   Ybk.

**Guild of Air Pilots & Air Navigators of London   (GAPAN)
1929**
- ■ Cobham House, 9 Warwick Court, Gray's Inn, LONDON,
  WC1R 5DJ.   (hq)
  020 7404 4032
  http://www.gapan.org
  Clerk: Paul J Tacon
- ▲ Livery Company - un-incorporated association
- Br Australia, Hong Kong, N Zealand
- ○ *E, *P; a livery company of the City of London; achievement of
  air safety through the highest standards for pilots &
  navigators
- Gp C'ees: Education & training, Technical & air safety, Trophies &
  awards;
  Benevolent Fund Board of Management [for airmen & their
  dependents]
- ● Conf - Mtgs - ET - Res - SG - VE - LG
- M 1,700 i, UK / 500 i, o'seas
- ¶ Guild News (Jnl) - 6; ftm only.

Guild of Air Traffic Control Officers   (GATCO)   1954
- NR Central Admin Facility, 4 St Mary's Rd, Bingham,
  NOTTINGHAM, NG13 8DW.   (hq)
  01949 876405
  http://www.gatco.org
  Pres: Richard Dawson
- ▲ Un-incorporated Society
- Br 5
- ○ *P
- Gp C'ees: Professional, Technical
- ● Conf - Mtgs - Exhib - SG - Inf - LG
- < Intl Fedn of Air Traffic Control Assns (IFATCA); Flight Safety
  C'ee; Gen Aviation Safety Coun; Parliamentary Advy Coun
  on Transport Safety (PACTS)
- M 2,250 i, 29 f, UK / 150 i, 3 f, o'seas
- ¶ Transmit (Jnl) - 4.   LM - 8.   AR.

** Guild of Antique Dealers & Restorers
  Organisation lost: see Introduction paragraph 3

Guild of Architectural Ironmongers   (GAI)   1961
- ■ 8 Stepney Green, LONDON, E1 3JU.   (hq)
  020 7790 3431   fax 020 7790 8517
  email info@gai.org.uk   http://www.gai.org.uk
  Chief Exec: Gary Amer
- ▲ Company Limited by Guarantee
- ○ *T; the best possible materials & service for use in each project
- ● Conf - Mtgs - ET - Exam - Exhib - SG - Inf
- < Door & Hardware Inst (USA); Construction Products Assn (CPA)
- M 190 full members (distributors), 90 associates (manufacturers)
- ¶ Architectural Ironmongery Jnl - 4; ftm.   Ybk - 1.
  Guild News - 4;   Education Prospectus - 1;
  AR - 1; all ftm.

Guild of Aviation Artists   (GAvA)   1971
- NR Trenchard House, 85 Farnborough Rd, FARNBOROUGH,
  Hants, GU14 6TF.   (hq)
  01252 513123   fax 01252 510505
  email admin@gava.org.uk   http://www.gava.org.uk
  Sec: Mrs Susan Gardner
- ○ *A, *P; encouragement of Aviation Art in all its forms
- ● Conf - Mtgs - ET - Exhib - Comp - SG - Inf - PL - VE
- < R Aero Club
- M i

Guild of Battlefield Guides   2003
- NR The Woodlands, Penrhos, RAGLAN, Monmouthshire,
  NP15 2LF.   (hsp)
  07774 639023
  email secretary@gbg-international.com
  http://www.gbg-international.com
  Sec: Tony Smith
- ▲ Company Limited by Guarantee
- ○ *P; to analyse, develop & raise the understanding & practice of
  battlefield guiding; to promote the education of battlefield
  visitors & students in military heritage
- ● ET - Info - Mtgs
- M 52 i
- ¶ BATTLEguide (Jnl) - 2; ftm.

Guild of Bricklayers   1932
- ■ Kirkstede, Church St, SUTTON-IN-ASHFIELD, Notts,
  NG17 1EX.   (hsp)
  01623 554582
  email m.thorpe@guild-of-bricklayers.org.uk
  http://www.guild-of-bricklayers.org.uk
  Sec: Malcolm Thorpe
- ▲ Registered Charity
- Br 13
- ○ *T; to promote & maintain the highest standards of
  craftsmanship in brickwork
- ● Comp - Conf - ET - Mtgs
- M 500 i, 5 colleges
- ¶ Jnl - 1;   Brickline (NL) - 1; both free.

Guild of British Camera Technicians   (GBCT)   1978
- NR c/o Panavision, Metropolitan Centre, Bristol Rd, GREENFORD,
  Middx, UB6 8GD.   (hq)
  020 8813 1999   fax 020 8813 2111
  email admin@gbct.org   http://www.gbct.org
- ○ *P; for professionally recognised camera technicians with the
  film, TV & video industry
- ● Conf - ET - Exhib
- M 500 i, UK / 50 i, o'seas
- ¶ GBCT TECHS Magazine - 6; ftm, £12 yr.

© CBD Research Ltd · Beckenham · BR3 5JS · Tel 020 8650 7745 · E-mail cbd@cbdresearch.com · www.cbdresearch.com

Guild of British Coach Operators (1985)

- ■ PO Box 5657, SOUTHEND-ON-SEA, Essex, SS1 3WT.   (hq)
  email admin@coach-tours.co.uk
  http://www.coach-tours.co.uk
  Admin: Richard Delahoy
- ▲ Company Limited by Guarantee
- ○ *T; to increase public recognition of the role that coaches play in tourism & public transport; to establish working relationships with organisations & bodies involved in transport
- < Intl Motor Coach Gp (USA)
- M 21 f

Guild of British Découpeurs (GBD) 1999

- ■ Chimneys, 18 Pembridge Close, Charlton Kings, CHELTENHAM, Glos, GL52 6XY.   (chmn/p)
  01242 235302
  http://www.decoupageguild.co.uk
  Chmn: Mrs Madeleine Smith
- ○ *A, *G; to provide information & education in the art & authentic techniques of découpage (the art of applying decorative paper cut-outs to surfaces)
- ● Mtgs - ET - Inf - PL
- M 35 i, UK / 290 i, o'seas
- ¶ Shortcuts - 2; ftm only.

Guild of British Film & Television Editors (GBFTE) 1966

- ■ 72 Pembroke Rd, LONDON, W8 6NX.   (hsp)
  0560 294 2610
  email secretary@gbfte.org   http://www.gbfte.org
  Sec: Sally Fisher
- ○ *P; to raise the profile of the skill & craft of editing
- ● Conf - Res - Exhib - Inf - VE - Film shows
- < Cine Glds of GB (CGGB)
- M 91 i, UK / 8 i, o'seas
- ¶ NL - irreg.

Guild of British Tie Makers
  a group of the **British Clothing Industry Association**

Guild of Builders & Contractors (GBC) 1994

- ■ Crest House, 102-104 Church Rd, TEDDINGTON, Middx, TW11 8PY.   (hq)
  020 8977 1105   fax 020 8943 3151
  email info@buildersguild.co.uk
  http://www.buildersguild.co.uk
  Dir: E A Goddard
- ▲ Company Limited by Guarantee
- ○ *T; for individuals & firms who are actively engaged in the building industry, who are experienced & knowledgeable & trade with integrity
- ● Mtgs - Stat - Inf - LG
- M 800 i, 2,000 f
  (Sub: £75)
- ¶ NL - 6; ftm only.

Guild of Catholic Doctors
  since 2008 **Catholic Medical Association**

Guild of Church Braillists (GoCB) 1911

- ■ 5 North St, SOUTHPORT, Merseyside, PR9 9HX.   (regd off)
  01363 860141
  http://www.gocb.org
  Sec: Mary Hazlewood
- ▲ Registered Charity
- ○ *P, *R; to advance the Christian religion in particular by transcribing Christian literature from print into braille; to increase the number of Christian books in the National Library for the Blind
- ● ET - Lib
- M i (blind proof readers, Braille consultants, transcribers)
- ¶ AR - 1; free.

Guild of Church Musicians (GCM) 1888

- ■ Hillbrow, Godstone Rd, Blechingley, REDHILL, Surrey, RH1 4PJ.   (gensec/p)
  01883 743168
  http://www.churchmusicians.org
  Gen Sec: John Ewington
- ▲ Registered Charity
- Br Australia
- ○ *L; a fellowship of amateur & professional musicians who sincerely desire to offer the best in music to the service of the church
- ● Conf - Mtgs - ET - Exam (for Archbishop's certificate in church music & in public worship; Fellowship of Guild of Church Musicians)
- M 720 i, UK / 80 i, o'seas
- ¶ Laudate - 3; ftm;   Ybk - 1; both ftm.

Guild of Cleaners & Launderers (GCL) 1949

- ■ 3 Queen Sq, Bloomsbury, LONDON, WC1N 3AR.   (hq)
  020 7843 9493
  email enquiries@gcl.org.uk   http://www.gcl.org.uk
  Hon Gen Sec: Murray Simpson
- ▲ Registered Charity
- Br 9
- ○ *P; examining body of the textile care industry & joint awarding body with SVQs/NVQs
- Gp Laundry & dry cleaning
- ● Conf - Mtgs - Exam - Inf - Lib
- M 450 i, UK / 25 i, o'seas
- ¶ NL - 6.   Retail Sales Garment Cleaning. Textiles for Launderers & Drycleaners. The After Care of Silk.   Stain Removal Guide. Other publications.

Guild of Colon Hydrotherapists 2003

- NR 12 Chapel Close, Leavesden, WATFORD, Herts, WD25 7AR. (hq)
  07825 517231
  email colonic.guild@yahoo.co.uk
  http://www.colonic-association.com
  Chmn: Margaret Ann Lund
- ▲ Company Limited by Guarantee
- ○ *P; to be the lead body in colon hydrotherapy

Guild of Drama Adjudicators (GODA) 1947

- ■ 25 The Drive, Bengeo, HERTFORD, SG14 3DE.   (hsp)
  01992 581993
  email jo.godasec@talktalk.net
  http://www.amdram.co.uk/goda
  Hon Sec: Mrs Joan Crossley
- ▲ Registered Charity
- ○ *P; to supply qualified adjudicators to all organisations promoting amateur drama
- ● Conf - Mtgs - ET - Inf - Adjudication at drama festivals
- M 125 i
- ¶ News & Views - 3; ftm only.   Asides - 1; free. A Directory of Drama Adjudicators - 1; free.

Guild of Enamellers (GE) 1978

- ■ Holly Barn, Low Gill Beck, Glaisdale, WHITBY, N Yorks, YO21 2QA.   (puboffr/p)
  01947 897788
  email info@lynne-glazzard.com
  http://www.guildofenamellers.org
  Publicity Officer: Lynne Glazzard
  Hon Sec: Shirley Gore (07940 557222)
- ▲ Un-incorporated Society
- Br 7
- ○ *A; to promote the craft of enamelling on metal; to exert a progressive influence on standards of workmanship & design
- ● Conf - Mtgs - ET - Res - Exhib - Lib - PL - VE
- M 200 i, UK / 5 i, o'seas
  (Sub: £20 UK / £28 o'seas)
- ¶ Jnl - 4; ftm, on request, nm.

Guild of Erotic Artists   2002

■ The Old Barn at Beaumont Hall Studios, Beaumont Hall Lane, Redburn Rd, ST ALBANS, Herts, AL3 6RN.   (hq)
01582 791661
http://www.theguildoferoticartists.com
Sec: Colin Ballard
○ *A
Gp Artists; Models; Photographers; Sculptors & bodycasters
Corporate; Patrons
● Mtgs - ET - Exhib - SG - Inf - PL - Demonstrations of artists' skills including photography, sketching, bodycasting, shibari, life model drawing, body painting etc
M 160 i, 5 f, UK / 6 i, o'seas
¶ Jade - 6; ftm, £35 nm.

Guild of Fine Food   (GFFR)   1995

■ Guild House, Station Rd, WINCANTON, Somerset, BA9 9FE. (hq)
01963 824464   fax 01963 824651
email bob.farrand@finefoodworld.co.uk
http://www.finefoodworld.co.uk
Nat Dir: Bob Farrand
▲ Company Limited by Guarantee
○ *T; to champion the cause of speciality food retailers & producers
Gp The Guild offers 4 training programmes: UK Cheese Guild, Charcuterie Guild, Retail Ready, & School of Fine Food
● ET - Res - Exhib - Comp - LG - Cheese training to NVQ standard - Great Taste Awards - World Cheese Awards
M 1,250 i, UK / 50 i, o'seas
¶ Fine Food Digest - 10.   Good Cheese.   Taste Gold - 1.

Guild of Food Writers   (GFW)   1984

■ 255 Kent House Rd, BECKENHAM, Kent, BR3 1JQ.   (admin/p)
020 8659 0422
email admin@gfw.co.uk   http://www.gfw.co.uk
Admin: Jonathan Woods
▲ Un-incorporated Society
○ *P; to contribute to the growth of public interest in, & knowledge of, the subject of food; to campaign for improvements in the quality of food
● Conf - Mtgs - ET - Comp - VE - LG
M 360 i
¶ LM - 1; ftm, £190 nm.

Guild of Freemen of the City of London   1908

■ PO Box 1202, KINGSTON UPON THAMES, Surrey, KT2 7XB. (mail)
020 8541 1435   fax 020 8541 1455
email clerk@guild-freemen-london.co.uk
Clerk: Brig M I Keun
▲ Company Limited by Guarantee; Registered Charity
○ *G, *W; within the City of London: to support traditions & institutions, to promote fellowship & good citizenship, to help the needy & underprivileged & to support & promote education & training
● ET - VE - Charity work & benevolence
< Hon Company of Freemen of the City of London of N America
M 3,000 i, UK / 200 i, o'seas
¶ The Freeman (Jnl) - 1; ftm, £7.50 nm.   AR; ftm only.

Guild of Glass Engravers   1975

■ 87 Nether St, LONDON, N12 7NP.   (hq)
020 8446 4050
email enquiries@gge.org.uk   http://www.gge.org.uk
Sec: Mrs Christine Reyland
▲ Registered Charity
Br 9
○ *A, *G, *P; to promote the highest quality of creative design & craftsmanship among glass engravers & advance the education of the public in the art of glass engraving & other forms of surface decoration on glass
● Conf - Mtgs - ET - Exhib - Assessments
M 380 i, UK / 53 i, o'seas
¶ NL - 4; ftm only.

Guild of Hairdressers

see **Incorporated Guild of Hairdressers, Wigmakers & Perfumers**

Guild of Health Ltd   1904

■ 58 Philip Rd, FOLKESTONE, Kent, CT19 4PZ.   (mail)
01303 277399
email enquiries@gohealth.org.uk
http://www.gohealth.org.uk
Chmn: Rev Roger Hoath
▲ Company Limited by Guarantee; Registered Charity
Br 25
○ *W; to bring together Christian people (clergy, laity, health care professionals) with a concern for healing, wholeness & 'finding God in all things'
● Conf - Mtgs - Prayer & meditation - Workshops - Retreats - Seminars - Literature
< Retreat Assn
M 350 i
¶ Way of Life (Jnl) - 4; ftm, £8 yr nm.   AR - 1; ftm only.

Guild of Health Writers   1994

■ Dale Lodge, 88 Wensleydale Rd, HAMPTON, Middx, TW12 2LX.   (chmn/p)
020 8941 2977   fax 020 8941 2977
email admin@healthwriters.com
http://www.healthwriters.com
Chmn: Caroline White
○ *P; for journalists dedicated to providing accurate, broad-based information about health & related subjects to the public
Gp Ageing; Children's health; Complementary medicine; Fitness; General medicine; Health & education; Medical ethics; Mental health; Mind body medicine; Preventative medicine; Psychology & psychotherapy; Relationships; Women's health
● Mtgs - ET - Comp
M c 230 i
¶ Health Writer - 4; ftm only.

Guild of Healthcare Pharmacists   (GHP)

■ Unite Health Office, 128 Theobald's Rd, LONDON, WC1X 8TN.   (asa)
020 3371 2009
email amanda.cass@unitetheunion.com
http://www.ghp.org.uk
Admin: Amanda Cass
Br 23
○ *P; to defend the interests of individual employed pharmacists working in hospitals, primary care & other healthcare institutions for both the NHS & commercial healthcare providers
Gp Information technology; Leadership development; Procurement & distribution
< Eur Assn Hospital Pharmacists (EAHP)
Note: an autonomous professional body within Unite the Union

Guild of Horticultural Trade Display Judges   1993

NR 3 Peacock Avenue, COVENTRY, Warks, CV2 2PB.   (hsp)
024 7661 8290
email chris.arnold2@tesco.net
Hon Sec: Chris Arnold
○ *P; to ensure uniformity of a high standard in judging, following the same criteria as practised by the Royal Horticultural Society
< Assn of Show & Agricl Orgs; Horticultural Exhibitors Assn; R Horticultural Soc
M i

Guild of International Butler Administrators & Personal Assistants
no longer in existence

Guild of International Professional Toastmasters
no longer in existence

Guild of Letting & Management (GLM) 1997

■ Site 1 Building 2, St Cross Chambers, Upper Marsh Lane, HODDESDON, Herts, EN11 8LQ. (hq)
  01992 479949 fax 01992 451340
  email info@guild-let.co.uk http://www.guild-let.co.uk
  Chief Exec: Asunta Crolla
▲ Company Limited by Guarantee
Br 2
○ *P; for property management letting agents & landlords
● Conf - ET - Exam - Inf - LG
M 75 i, 400 f, 100 org

Guild of Location Managers (GLM) 1989

NR BM 2019, LONDON, WC1N 3XX. (mail)
  email admin@golm.org.uk http://www.golm.org.uk
  Admin: Leonora Sheppard
○ *P; to maintain standards of professionalism within the film, television, event & stills industries
< Cine Glds of GB (CGGB)
M 107 i (81 full, 26 associate)

Guild of Mace-Bearers 1950

NR 54 Winifred Rd, COULSDON, Surrey, CR5 3JE. (clerk/b)
  020 8668 5997 fax 020 8407 3062
  http://www.civicprotocol.com
  Guild Clerk: Peter Townsend
▲ Un-incorporated Society
○ *P; to uphold & preserve the customs of the civic & corporate life of the country & Commonwealth & the dignity of the office of mayor; to offer advice on such matters
● Conf - ET - Inf
M 260 i, UK / 1 i, o'seas
¶ The Mace-Bearer - 3; LM - 1; both ftm only.
  The Manual of the Mace; £10 m only.

Guild of Machine Knitters 1998

NR 12 Home Close, Bracebridge Heath, LINCOLN, LN4 2LP. (regd off)
  email secretary@guild-mach-knit.org.uk
  http://www.guild-mach-knit.org.uk
  Hon Sec: Diane Leverton
▲ Company Limited by Guarantee
○ *G; to promote machine as a craft for the benefit of all individual knitters, clubs, professional designers, manufacturers, suppliers, etc.
● Comp - Exhib - Mtgs
M 905 i
¶ NL.

Guild of Master Craftsmen (GMC) 1974

■ 166 High St, LEWES, E Sussex, BN7 1XU. (hq)
  01273 478449 fax 01273 478606
  http://www.guildmc.com
  Jt Secs: Jennifer & Jonathan Phillips
▲ Company Limited by Guarantee
○ *A, *P, *T; for skilled craftspeople & professionals
● Inf - Legal advice - Debt collection - Assistance to members in finding work - Promotional material Insurance & financial services - Discounts on business expenses
M 15,000 i
¶ All journals below are supplied at a discount to members:
  Woodturning. Woodcarving.
  Woodworking plans & projects.
  Furniture & Cabinetmaking. Outdoor Photography.
  Black & White Photography. Knitting.
  The Dolls' House Magazine. Healthy & Organic Living.

Guild of Motoring Writers Ltd (GOMW) 1944

■ 40 Baring Rd, BOURNEMOUTH, Dorset, BH6 4DT. (gensec/p)
  01202 422424 fax 01202 422424
  email generalsec@gomw.co.uk
  http://www.gomw.co.uk
  Gen Sec: Patricia Lodge
▲ Company Limited by Guarantee
○ *P; for automotive editorial professionals; to raise the standard of motoring journalism & encourage motoring, motorsport & road safety

Guild of Musicians & Singers 1993

NR 5 Lime Close, CHICHESTER, W Sussex, PO19 6SW. (secgen/p)
  01243 788315
  http://www.musiciansandsingers.org.uk
  Sec-Gen: Dr Michael Walsh
○ *L, *P; for professional & amateur musicians; to promote a high standard of musical performance
● Mtgs - Concerts - Lectures & talks
M c 200 i
¶ NL - 2.

Guild of Needle Laces 1983

NR 125 Cowley Hill, BOREHAMWOOD, Herts, WD6 5NA. (hsp)
  email margaret.folan@hertfordshire.nhs.uk
  http://www.guildofneedlelaces.org
  Sec: Mrs Margaret Folan
○ *G; to promote the interest, skills, teaching, conservation & history of needlemade laces
● Comp - Lib
¶ NL - 3; ftm only.

Guild of One-Name Studies (GOONS) 1979

■ 14 Charterhouse Buildings (Box G), Goswell Rd, LONDON, EC1M 7BA. (mail)
  0800 011 2182
  email guild@one-name.org http://www.one-name.org
  Sec: Mrs Kirsty Gray
▲ Registered Charity
○ *L; study of surnames & family history
● Conf - Mtgs - Lib - e-Lib - Registration of one-name studies
M 2,000 i
¶ Jnl of One-Name Studies - 1; ftm, £2 nm.
  Register of One-Name Studies - 1; ftm, £2 nm.

Guild of Pastoral Psychology (GPP) 1937

NR Sirius, Setch Rd, Blackborough End, KING'S LYNN, Norfolk, PE32 1SL. (admin/p)
  01553 849849
  http://www.guildofpastoralpsychology.org.uk
  Admin: Val Nurse
▲ Registered Charity
○ *P; for all those interested in the relation between religion & depth psychology; especially that of C G Jung & his followers
● Conf - Mtgs - SG - Lib
M 500 i, 30 org, UK / 30 i, o'seas
¶ Pamphlets - 5; List of groups - 1; both ftm only.
  Printed lectures - 3/4. Cassette recordings; AR.

Guild of Photographers UK (GP) 1988

■ 30 St Edmunds Ave, NEWCASTLE-UNDER-LYYME, Staffs, ST5 0AB. (hq)
  01782 740526
  Dir: Joan Roberts
▲ Un-incorporated Society
○ *P; training & qualifying photographers in the skills of wedding & portrait photography
● ET - Exam - Comp - Inf
< Wedding & Portrait Photographers Intl (USA)
M 300 i, UK / 4 i, o'seas
  Note: incorporates the Guild of Wedding Photographers and the Guild of Professional Photographers

Guild of Polyglots   1987
- ■ 191 Westcombe Hill, LONDON, SE3 7DR.   (mail)
- ▲ Un-incorporated Society
- ○ *G; for people interested in speaking languages other than their native tongue
- ● Mtgs - ET - Exam - SG - Lib - VE
- M 77 i, 2 f
- ¶ NL; ftm only.

Guild of Professional Beauty Therapists Ltd   (GPBT)   1994
- ■ 320 Burton Rd, DERBY, DE23 6AF.   (hq)
    0845 217 7383   fax 0845 217 7387
    email info@beautyguild.com
    http://www.beautyguild.com
    Managing Dir: Paul Archer
- ▲ Limited Company
- ○ *P; to represent the interests of professional beauty therapists & salon owners
- ● ET - Res - Exhib - Comp - Stat - Inf - LG
- M 6,000 i
- ¶ Guild Gazette - 6;   Beautyguild Bulletin (email NL) - 26.

Guild of Professional Estate Agents   (GPEA)   1993
- NR 121 Park Lane, LONDON, W1K 7AG.   (hq)
    020 7629 4141   fax 020 7629 2329
    http://www.guildproperty.co.uk
- ▲ Company Limited by Guarantee
- ○ *T; for independent estate agencies
- ● Marketing
- M 400 f
- ¶ The Property Magazine - 12.

Guild of Professional Photographers
    incorporated by the **Guild of Photographers**

Guild of Professional Teachers of Dance & Movement to Music & Dramatic Arts   (GPTD)   1973
- ■ 43 Telfer Rd, Radford, COVENTRY, CV6 3DG.   (hsp)
    024 7659 7907
    http://www.gptd.co.uk
    Gen Sec: Terry Perkins
- Br 4
- ○ *U; an independent trade union representing teachers of dancing, movement to music & dramatic arts
- Gp Aerobics; Ballroom; Dramatic arts; Indian dance; Irish dance; Keep fit; Stage; Teachers of dance & movement to music; Western Line dancing
- ● Conf - Mtgs - ET - Exhib - Comp - Inf - Empl - LG
- M 1,200 i, UK / 10 i, o'seas
- ¶ Tempo - 4; ftm only.
- × 2009 Guild of Professional Teachers of Dancing

Guild of Professional Toastmasters   1963
- ■ 32 Shearman Rd, Blackheath, LONDON, SE3 9TN.   (hsp)
    020 8852 4621
    email rgrosse@guild-of-toastmasters.co.uk
    http://www.guild-of-toastmasters.co.uk
    Hon Sec: Robert Grosse
- ▲ Un-incorporated Society
- ○ *P; for toastmasters, masters of ceremonies & compères
- Gp Profl Toastmasters' Academy
- ● Conf - Mtgs - ET - Exam
- M 25 i

Guild of Professional Videographers   (GPV)   1991
- ■ 11 Telfer Rd, Radford, COVENTRY, Warks, CV6 3DG.   (hq)
    024 7627 2548   fax 024 7627 2548
    email mail@gpv4u.co.uk   http://www.gpv4u.co.uk
    Sec: Mrs Ann Middleton
- ▲ Company Limited by Guarantee
- ○ *P; to assist members with legal problems; advise on training; advise on grants available to small/medium business
- ● Mtgs - ET - Exam - Inf
- M 140 i, 10 f, UK / 25 i, 3 f, o'seas
- ¶ NL by email; ftm.

Guild of Psychotherapists   1974
- ■ 47 Nelson Sq, Blackfriars Rd, LONDON, SE1 0QA.   (hq)
    020 7401 3260   fax 020 7401 3472
    email admin@guildofpsychotherapists.org.uk
    http://www.guildofpsychotherapists.org.uk
- ▲ Registered Charity
- ○ *P; training in psychoanalytic psychotherapy
- ● Conf - Mtgs - ET - SG - Lib - Low-cost clinic for Southwark, Lambeth & Lewisham
- < UK Coun for Psychotherapy (UKCP)
- M 260 i

Guild of Q Butchers
    has reverted to **Q Guild**

Guild of Railway Artists   1979
- ■ 45 Dickins Rd, WARWICK, CV34 5NS.   (chfexec/p)
    01926 499246
    http://www.railart.co.uk
    Chief Exec: F P Hodges
- ▲ Un-incorporated Society
- ○ *A; to forge a link between artists depicting railway subjects
- ● Mtgs - Exhib - Inf
- < Assn of Rly Presvn Socs
- M 158 i, UK / 6 i, 1 org
- ¶ Wheel & Palette - 4; ftm.

Guild of Registered Tourist Guides   (GRTG)   1950
- ■ Guild House, 52D Borough High St, LONDON, SE1 1XN.   (hq)
    020 7403 1115   fax 020 7378 1705
    http://www.blue-badge-guides.com
    Gen Mgr: Mehmet Ahmet
- ▲ Un-incorporated Society
- ○ *P; the national professional association of qualified Blue Badge tourist guides
- ● Conf - ET - Exhib - Inf - Lib - LG
- < Wld Fedn of Tourist Guides Assns(WFTGA); Fedn of Eur Guides Assns (FEG); Visit London
- M 700 i, 38 org, UK / 2 i, o'seas
    (Sub: £194 i London, £97.50 outside)
- ¶ Guide Post - 12; free.   Guild Directory - 1; ftm, £10 nm.
    Guide's Guide - 1; ftm, £8 nm.

Guild of Rocking Horse Makers   1999
- NR The Rocking Horse Shop, Main St, Fangfoss, YORK, YO41 5JH.   (hsb)
    01759 368737
    email info@rockinghorse.co.uk
    http://www.rockinghorse.co.uk
    Hon Sec: Anthony Dew
- ○ *G, *P; to promote & encourage the craft of rocking horse making
- ● Mtgs
- ¶ NL.

Guild of Shareholders
- NR The Rectory Farmhouse, 2 Church St, OXFORD, OX2 1RS.   (regd off)
    01993 811722
- ▲ Company Limited by Guarantee
- ○ *K; to enable shareholders to influence the way their companies are run

© CBD Research Ltd · Beckenham · BR3 5JS · Tel 020 8650 7745 · E-mail cbd@cbdresearch.com · www.cbdresearch.com

Guild of Straw Craftsmen   1989

NR   Higher Bejowan, Quintrell Downs, NEWQUAY, Cornwall,
    TR8 4LJ.   (memsec/p)
    01726 860296
    email guildinfo@strawcraftsmen.co.uk
    http://www.strawcraftsmen.co.uk
    Mem Sec: Gillian Nott
▲   Un-incorporated Society
○   *G; to promote straw craft in all its many facets; to bring straw
    artists & workers together to develop the craft
●   Conf - Mtgs - ET - Exam - Res - Exhib - Comp - SG - Inf - Lib -
    PL - VE
M   100 i, UK / 40 i, o'seas
¶   Guild News (NL) - 2; ftm, £1.50 nm.

Guild of Stunt & Action Co-ordinators   (SCAG)   1985

■   72 Pembroke Rd, LONDON, W8 6NX.   (hsp)
    0560 294 2610
    email stuntsuk@btinternet.com
    http://www.stuntco-ords.org.uk
    Sec: Sally Fisher
▲   Un-incorporated Society
○   *P; to maintain &, if possible, improve existing standards of
    performance & safety within the profession
●   Mtgs - ET - LG
<   Cine Glds of GB (CGGB)
M   15 i

Guild of Taxidermists   1976

■   c/o Lancashire County Museums, Stanley St, PRESTON, Lancs,
    PR1 4YP.   (mail)
    http://www.taxidermy.org.uk
    Hon Sec: Duncan Ferguson,   Chmn: Lawrence Dowson
○   *P; to raise standards & awareness of taxidermy in the UK
●   Conf - Mtgs - ET - Exam - Exhib
<   Eur Taxidermy Fedn
M   190 i, UK / 10 i, o'seas
¶   Jnl - 1; ftm, £5 nm.

Guild of Television Cameramen   1972

NR   1 Churchill Rd, Whitchurch, TAVISTOCK, Devon, PL19 9BU.
    (admin/p)
    01822 614405   fax 01822 615785
    http://www.gtc.org.uk
    Admin Officer: Sheila Lewis
○   *P; improve the art & craft of television cameramen for
    broadcast television
M   c 1,200 i

Guild of Theatre Prompters

■   191 Westcombe Hill, LONDON, SE3 7DR.
○   *P
M   i

Guild of Travel Management Companies   (GTMC)   1967

NR   Euston Fitzrovia, 85 Tottenham Court Rd, LONDON,
    W1T 4TQ.   (hq)
    020 7269 3540   fax 020 7268 3105
▲   Company Limited by Guarantee
○   *T; to speak for business travellers & the agents who act for
    them
M   f

Guild of Travel & Tourism   1995

■   Suite 193 Temple Chambers, 3-7 Temple Avenue, LONDON,
    EC4Y 0DB.   (hq)
    020 7583 6333
    email nigel.bishop@traveltourismguild.com
    http://www.traveltourismguild.com
    Chief Exec: Nigel Bishop
▲   Company Limited by Guarantee
○   *P; to promote the interests & needs of people within the travel
    industry & those organisations involved in transport, travel &
    tourism
Gp   Travel industry trade association
●   Mtgs - Seminars
M   i, f
¶   The Travel Business (NL) - 4; free.

Guild of Wedding Photographers UK
    incorporated by the **Guild of Photographers**

Guillain Barré Syndrome Support Group   (GBS)   1985

■   Heckington Business Park, Station Rd, Heckington, SLEAFORD,
    Lincs, NG34 9JH.   (hq)
    01529 469910   fax 01529 469915
    email admin@gbs.org.uk   http://www.gbs.org.uk
    Office Exec: Carolin Morrice
▲   Registered Charity
Br   4
○   *W; to support sufferers of the disease (an auto-immune system
    affecting the peripheral nervous system) & their families; to
    promote research & treatment
Gp   CIDP (Chronic Inflammatory Demyelinating Polyneuropathy);
    Diabetic; GBS; Miller Fisher & other related neuropathies;
    Pregnant; Specialists in those who are children
●   Conf - ET - Res - Inf
    Helpline: 0800 374803
<   Guillain Barré Syndrome Foundation Intl
M   1,300 i
    (Sub: £20 + £15 concessions)
¶   Reaching Out (Jnl) - 1; ftm.   In the Know (NL) - 3; free.
    Information leaflets / posters / booklets; free.

** **Gulf Veterans Association**

    Organisation lost: see Introduction paragraph 3

Gun Trade Association Ltd   (GTA)   1896

■   PO Box 43, TEWKESBURY, Glos, GL20 5ZE.   (hq)
    01684 291868   fax 01684 291864
    email enquiries@guntradeassociation.com
    http://www.guntradeassociation.com
    Dir: John Batley
▲   Company Limited by Guarantee
○   *T; interests of the sporting firearms, ammunition, accessories
    industry & those providing related services; liaison with proof
    authorities, police & other government agencies
Gp   Joint Venture C'ee - organises British Pavilion at overseas trade
    fairs
●   Conf - Mtgs - ET - Res - Exhib - Stat - Expt - Inf - LG
<   Brit Shooting Sports Coun; Standing Conf on Countryside
    Sports; Eur Inst for Hunting & Sporting Guns; Wld Forum on
    the Future of Sport Shooting Activities
M   550 i & f, UK / 10 f (associates), o'seas
¶   NL - 6; ftm only.

Gut Trust 1991
- ■ Unit 5, 53 Mowbray St, SHEFFIELD, S Yorks, S3 8EN.   (hq)
    0114-272 3253
    email info@ibsnetwork.org.uk   http://www.theguttrust.org
    Sec: P J Nunn
- ▲ Company Limited by Guarantee; Registered Charity
- ○ *K, *M, *W; a self-help organisation for people with irritable bowel syndrome
- Gp Befriender/penpal scheme; Local self-help; Media list; Reviewer list
- ● Conf - ET - Res - Exhib - Comp - Inf
    Helpline: 0872 300 4527 (1900-2100hrs)
- < Nat Coun Voluntary Orgs (NCVO); Long-term Medical Conditions Alliance (LMCA); Patients Forum
- M 3,000 i, 10 f, 18 org, UK / 50 i, o'seas
- ¶ Gut Reaction - 4; ftm only.   Factsheets; ftm, £1 each nm.
    [back copies of Gut Reaction; £2.50 m, £5 nm].
    Note: the charity is registered as IBS Network

Gwartheg Hynafol Cymru   (Ancient Cattle of Wales)   (GHC/ ACW) 1981
- ■ Croesheddig Newydd, Pentre'r Bryn, LLANDYSUL, Ceredigion, SA44 6NB.   (hsp)
    01545 560255
    http://www.colouredwelshcattle.org
    Hon Sec: Sian Ioan
- ▲ Un-incorporated Society
- ○ *B; the breeding of Welsh cattle of colours other than black
- M 30 i
- ¶ NL - irreg; free.

GWE Business West Ltd   2008
- NR Leigh Court Business Centre, Abbots Leigh, BRISTOL, BS8 3RA.   (hq)
    01275 373373
    http://www.businesswest.co.uk
- ○ *C, *N; to provide high quality support & leadership for businesses in the south west via the Chambers of Commerce & Initiative
- Gp Bath Chamber of Commerce & Initiative; Bristol Chamber of Commerce & Initiative; Bristol Junior Chamber of Commerce; Gloucestershire Chamber of Commerce & Industry (incl its member chambers); South Gloucestershire Chamber of Commerce; & the South West Chambers network
- < Nat Fedn of Enterprise Agencies
- × 2008 (Business West
       (Great Western Enterprise (merged 1 April)
    Note: trades as Business West

Gwent Wildlife Trust   (GWT) 1963
- ■ Seddon House, Dingestow Court, MONMOUTH, NP25 4DY. (hq)
    01600 740358   fax 01600 740299
    email info@gwentwildlife.org
    http://www.gwentwildlife.org
    Chief Exec: Julian Branscombe
- ▲ Registered Charity
- ○ *L
- Gp Conservation; Education; Local groups; Membership; Reserves; Volunteers
- ● ET - Inf - VE
- M 7,200 i, 10 f, 20 org, UK / 3 i, o'seas
- ¶ Local News - 3;   Supplement in Natural World - 3; AR; all free.

Gypsum Products Development Association   (GPDA)   1889
- ■ PO Box 35084, LONDON, NW1 4XE.   (asa)
    020 7935 8532   fax 07006 065950
    email admin@gpda.com   http://www.gpda.com
    Sec: Crispin Dunn-Meynell
- ○ *T
- ● Mtgs - Inf
- < Eurogypsum
- M 4 f

Gypsy Cob Society
- NR Chywoon Farm, Church Brough, KIRKBY STEPHEN, Cumbria, CA17 4EJ.   (regd off)
    01768 341319
    email carol@chywoonstud.wanadoo.co.uk
    http://www.gypsycobsociety.org
    Hon Sec: Carol Smettem
- ○ *B

H G Wells Society (HGWS) 1960
NR 1 Nackington Rd, CANTERBURY, Kent, CT1 3NU. (hsp)
    http://www.hgwellsusa.50megs.com
    Contact: Paul Allen
▲ Un-incorporated Society
○ *A, *L; to promote an interest in, & appreciation of the life, work & thought of Herbert George Wells (1866-1946)
● Conf - Lib
< Alliance of Literary Socs
M 100 i, UK / 100 i, o'seas
¶ The Wellsian (Jnl) - 1.
    NL - 2; both ftm only.

Hackney Horse Society 1883
■ Fallowfields, Little London, Heytesbury, WARMINSTER, Wilts, BA12 0ES. (hq)
    01985 840717   fax 01985 840616
    email dawn@hackney-horse.org.uk
    http://www.hackney-horse.org.uk
    Sec: Mrs Dawn Hicketts
▲ Registered Charity
○ *B; improvement of breeding of Hackney horses & ponies; harness & driving horses
● Exhib - Comp
M 650 i, 28 org, UK / 50 i, o'seas
¶ Hackney Stud Book - 5 yrly; £30.   Ybk - 1; £12.

Haemochromatosis Society 1990
■ Hollybush House, Hadley Green Rd, BARNET, Herts, EN5 5PR. (hq)
    020 8449 1363   fax 020 8449 1363
    email info@haemochromatosis.org.uk
    http://www.haemochromatosis.org.uk
    Dir: Mrs Janet Fernau
▲ Company Limited by Guarantee; Registered Charity
○ *W; to provide support, awareness & information for families affected by this iron overload genetic disorder & to the medical profession; to promote awareness at all levels as early diagnosis prevents serious complications
● Res (support) - Inf - Support for members
M 1,000 i
¶ NL - 4;   Hbk;   Venesection record card;
    Information leaflet; all free.

Haemolytic Uraemic Syndrome Help (HUSH) 1997
NR PO Box 159, HAYES, Middx, UB4 8XE. (regd off)
    0800 731 4679
    email hush@ecoli-uk.com   http://www.ecoli-uk.com
▲ Company Limited by Guarantee; Registered Charity
○ *W; to help those affected by E Coli 0157; to increase awareness within both the medical profession and general public regarding steps that can be taken to avoid infection and to speed up diagnosis of those infected
M Membership not mentioned on website, newsletter is free to read there,supporters may donate monthly, but NO MEMBERS
¶ NL

Haemophilia Society 1950
■ Petersham House (1st floor), 57a Hatton Garden, LONDON, EC1N 8JG. (hq)
    020 7831 1020   fax 020 7405 4824
    email info@haemophilia.org.uk
    http://www.haemophilia.org.uk
    Chief Exec: Chris James
▲ Registered Charity
Br 16 groups
○ *W; the relief of people suffering from haemophilia & related or associated bleeding disorders; the advancement of public education into the nature & causes of heamophilia & related or associated bleeding disorders
Gp Young Bloods
● Conf - Mtgs - Inf
    Helpline: 0800 018 6068
< Wld Fedn of Hemophilia; Eur Haemophilia Consortium
> Wld Fedn of Hemophilia; Eur Haemophila Consortium
M 4,000 i, UK / 122 i, o'seas
¶ Twitter 'HaemoSocUK'

Haflinger Society of Great Britain (HSGB) 1970
■ 11 Northumberland Place, RICHMOND, Surrey, TW10 6TS. (hsp)
    020 8948 6599
    http://www.haflingersgb.com
    Sec: Carolyn Hallett
▲ Registered Charity
○ *B; to promote the breeding of the Haflinger horse & publish the pedigrees of those in Great Britain
● Mtgs - Comp - Inf - Young stock inspections - Breed Show
< Wld Haflinger Fedn
M c 400 i
¶ Focus on Haflingers (NL) - 4; ftm only.

Hairdressing & Beauty Suppliers Association (HBSA) 1926
■ Greenleaf House, 128 Darkes Lane, POTTERS BAR, Herts, EN6 1AE. (hq)
    01707 649499   fax 01707 649497
    http://www.hbsa.uk.com
    Pres: Mike Patey
▲ Company Limited by Guarantee
○ *T; for manufacturers & suppliers of professional hair & beauty products
Gp Wig makers
● Conf - Mtgs - ET - Exhib
M 120 f
¶ HBSA News - 6; ftm only.

Hairline International: the Alopecia Patients' Society 1995
NR Lyons Court, 1668 High Street, KNOWLE, W Midlands, B93 0LY. (hq)
    http://www.hairlineinternational.com
    Dir & Founder: Elizabeth Steel
▲ Un-incorporated Society
○ *K, *W; to provide information & support for all hair loss patients, including those who have alopecia or suffer from trichotillomania (compulsive hair-pulling)
● Inf
M i
¶ NL - 4

Hakluyt Society   1846

NR   c/o Map Library, The British Library, 96 Euston Rd, LONDON,
       NW1 2DB.   (admin)
       01428 641850   fax 01428 641998
       email office@hakluyt.com   http://www.hakluyt.com
       Admin: Richard Bateman
▲   Registered Charity
○   *L; to advance knowledge & education by the publication of
       scholarly editions of primary records of voyages, travels &
       other geographical material
●   Mtgs
<   American Friends of the Hakluyt Soc
M   810 i, 350 org, UK / 1,454 i, o'seas
¶   Volumes - 2/3.   NL - 1.   AR.   LM.
       Text of Annual Lecture.
       Publications list available.
       Named after Richard Hakluyt (1552-1616), collector & editor of
       narratives of voyages & travels & other documents relating to
       English interests overseas

Hallé Concerts Society   1858

■   The Bridgewater Hall, Lower Mosley St, MANCHESTER,
       M1 5HA.   (hq)
       0161-237 7000   fax 0161-237 7029
       http://www.halle.co.uk
       Chief Exec: John Summers
▲   Company Limited by Guarantee
○   *D; promotion of Hallé orchestra, the Hallé choir & Hallé
       emsembles through management of Hallé concerts
Gp   Symphony concerts; Recitals
●   Mtgs - Lib
<   Assn of Brit Orchestras
M   i & f
¶   NL - 4;   AR - 1.

Halliwick Association of Swimming Therapy   1952

■   c/o ADKC Centre, Whitstable House, Silchester Rd, LONDON,
       W10 6SB.   (chmn/b)
       http://www.halliwick.org.uk
       Sec: Eric Dilley
▲   Registered Charity
Br   22; 2 o'seas
○   *S, *W; to teach swimming to people with disabilities using the
       Halliwick method; to provide training for volunteers &
       professionals in the basic methods of Halliwick; to organise
       galas at club, regional & national level
●   Mtgs - ET - Exam - Res - Comp
<   Intl Halliwick Assn (IHA)
M   i & org
¶   Swimming for People with Disabilities (hbk).
       Rainbow Series: Instructors & Students Guides.
       Leaflets.   Videos.

Halton Chamber of Commerce & Enterprise   1980

NR   The Heath Business & Technical Park, RUNCORN, Cheshire,
       WA7 4QX.   (hq)
       01928 516142   fax 01928 516144
       email info@haltonchamber.com
       http://www.haltonchamber.com
       Chief Exec: Paula Cain
○   *C; representing businesses in the Widnes & Runcorn area
<   Brit Chams Comm; Chams Comm NW

**Hammer Circle: the Association of British Hammer Throwers
1952**

NR   10 Pershore Close, BEDFORD, MK41 8NS.   (hsp)
       http://www.hammer-circle.co.uk
       Hon Sec: Darren Kerr
○   *S; support & promotion of British hammer throwing

Hammersmith & Fulham Chamber of Commerce
       a branch of the London Chamber of Commerce & Industry based at
       the offices of the **Ealing Chamber of Commerce**

Hampshire Chamber of Commerce   2010

NR   Regional Business Centre, Harts Farm Way, HAVANT, Hants,
       PO9 1HR.   (hq)
       023 9244 9449   fax 023 9244 9444
       email info@hampshirechamber.co.uk
       http://www.hampshirechamber.co.uk
       Chief Exec: Jimmy Chestnutt
▲   Company Limited by Guarantee
Br   5
○   *C
●   Conf - Mtgs - ET - Res - Exhib - Expt - Inf - Lib - LG -
       Networking - Commercial services
M   800 f, 100 org
¶   Business News - 10; ftm.
×   2010 (East Hampshire Chamber of Commerce & Industry
              (North East Hampshire Chamber of Comemrce
              (Portsmouth & SE Hampshire Chamber of Commerce
              (Southampton & Fareham Chamber of Commerce
                   & Industry
              (Winchester Chamber of Commerce

**Hampshire Down Sheep Breeders Association   (HDSBA)
1889**

■   Rickyard Cottage, Denner Hill, GREAT MISSENDEN, Bucks,
       HP16 0HZ.   (hsp)
       01494 488388   fax 01494 488388
       email richard@rickyard.plus.com
       http://www.hampshiredownsociety.org.uk
       Sec: Richard Davis
▲   Company Limited by Guarantee; Registered Charity
Br   4
○   *B
●   Mtgs - Res - Exhib - Inf
<   Nat Sheep Assn
M   140 i, 20 f, UK / 40 i, 4 org, o'seas
¶   NL - 6; ftm only.   Flock Book - 1; ftm, £10 nm.

Hampshire Field Club & Archaeological Society   (HFC)   1885

■   Farview, North Lane, Nomansland, SALISBURY, Wilts,
       SP5 2BU.   (hsp)
       email secretary@fieldclub.hants.org.uk
       http://www.fieldclub.hants.org.uk
       Sec: Alex Lewis
▲   Registered Charity
○   *L, *Q; archaeology, history & natural history of Hampshire
Gp   Archaeology; Historic buildings; Landscape; Local history;
       New Forest
●   Conf - Mtgs - ET - Res - Lib - VE
M   577 i, 79 org
¶   NL - 2.   Monographs - ad hoc.   Hampshire Studies - 1.

Hand Engravers Association of Great Britain

NR   PO Box 60239, LONDON, EC1P 1QQ.   (mail)
       07500 462910
       http://www.handengravers.co.uk
○   *G, *P; to raise the profile of the craft of hand engraving on
       metal & precious & semi-precious stones
●   Mtgs - ET - Exhib - Inf - Workshops - Seminars
M   30 i
       (Sub: £30-£250)
¶   NL

Handbag Liners & Repairers Association   (HLRA)   1972

■   76c The Avenue, BECKENHAM, Kent, BR3 2ES.   (mail)
○   *T
●   Mtgs - Exhib
M   13 f

Handbell Ringers of Great Britain (HRGB) 1967
- ■ 87 The Woodfields, Sanderstead, SOUTH CROYDON, Surrey, CR2 0HJ. (hsp)
  020 8651 2663   fax 020 8651 2663
  email info@hrgb.org.uk   http://www.hrgb.org.uk
  Hon Sec: Mrs Sandra Winter
- ▲ Registered Charity
- Br 8 regions
- ○ *D; to encourage & develop the art of handbell tune ringing (as distinct from change ringing); also hand-chime & belleplate ringers
- ● Concerts, rallies, workshops & seminars
- < Making Music (the Nat Fedn of Music Socs)
- M 3,500 i
- ¶ Reverberations - 2;   Regional NLs - irreg; both ftm only.

Handcycling Association UK (HCAUK) 1999
- ■ 2 Windlesham Rd, BRIGHTON, E Sussex, BN1 3AG. (chmn/p)
  01273 269274
  http://www.handcyclinguk.org.uk
  Chmn: Barry North
- ○ *G, *S; for disabled cyclists using hands for propulsion
- ● Mtgs - Comp
- M 120 i

Handley Page Association (HPA) 1979
- ■ 160 Watford Rd, ST ALBANS, Herts, AL2 3EB. (memsec/p)
  01727 863815
  http://www.thevictorassociation.org.uk
  Mem Sec
- ▲ Un-incorporated Society
- ○ *G, *L, *Q; to keep alive the memories of the Handley Page companies, their founder & their aircraft; to foster the spirit of innovation, engineering ingenuity & excellence of construction which were hallmarks of the companies
- ● Mtgs - Comp - Inf - PL - VE
- < Brit Aviation Preservation Coun (BAPC)
- M 400 i, 1 f, 2 org, UK / 20 i, o'seas
- ¶ NL - 6; ftm.   LM; £1 m.   Video; £13 m only.

Hansard Society Ltd 1944
- ■ 40-43 Chancery Lane, LONDON, WC2A 1JA. (hq)
  020 7438 1222   fax 020 7438 1229
  email hansard@hansard.lse.ac.uk
  http://www.hansardsociety.org.uk
  Chief Exec: Fiona Booth
- ▲ Registered Charity
- Br Scotland
- ○ *L, *Z; an independent, non-partisan political research & education charity; it aims to strengthen parliamentary democracy & encourage greater public involvement in politics
- Gp Programmes: Citizenship education, eDemocracy, Hansard Society Scotland, Parliament & government, Study & scholars
- ● Conf - ET - Res - LG - Public meetings - Mock elections
- M 356 i
  (Sub: £35 UK / £45 o'seas)
- ¶ Audit of Political Engagement - 1.
  No Overall Control? the impact of a 'hung parliament' on British Politics (2008).
  Other publications available.

Hardy Orchid Society (HOS) 1993
- ■ Bumbys, Fox Rd, Mashbury, CHELMSFORD, Essex, CM1 4TJ. (memsec/p)
  email m.tarrant@virgin.net
  http://www.hardyorchidsociety.org.uk
  Mem Sec: Mrs Moira Tarrant
- ○ *H; to share the pleasures & knowledge of hardy orchids as widely as possible
- ● Comp - Exhib - Mtgs - VE
- ¶ Jnl - 4; ftm.

Hardy Plant Society (HPS) 1957
- NR Little Orchard, Great Comberton, PERSHORE, Worcs, WR10 3DP. (hq)
  01386 710317   fax 01386 710117
  email admin@hardy-plant.org.uk
  http://www.hardy-plant.org.uk
  Admin: Mrs Pam Adams
- ▲ Registered Charity
- Br 45
- ○ *H; cultivation of hardy herbaceous plants (excluding rock plants)
- Gp Half hardy; Hardy geranium; Pulmonaria; Peony; Ranunculaceae; Variegated plants;
  Correspondents
- ● Conf - Mtgs - Exhib - SG - PL - VE
- M 11,000 i, 10 org, UK / 500 i, 2 org, o'seas
- ¶ The Hardy Plant (Jnl) - 2;   NL - 3;   Seed distribution list - 1; all ftm only.

Harleian Society 1869
- ■ College of Arms, Queen Victoria St, LONDON, EC4V 4BT. (hsb)
  020 7236 7728   fax 020 7248 6448
  http://www.harleian.org.uk
  Hon Sec: T H S Duke
- ▲ Registered Charity
- ○ *L; transcribing, printing & publishing heraldic visitations of counties, parish registers or any manuscripts relating to family history, genealogy or heraldry
- M 210 i & org, UK / 105 i & org, o'seas
- ¶ Publications - irreg (c 1); free to subscribers, £25 (i), £30 (instns), £35 nm.

Harness Goat Society (HGS) 1986
- ■ Meadow Court Farm, Alfrick, WORCESTER, WR6 5HY. (chmn/p)
  01886 832294
  email harnessgoatsociety.uk@virgin.net
  http://www.harnessgoats.co.uk
  Sec: Mrs Angela Rickerby
- ▲ Un-incorporated Society
- ○ *V; the driving of goats & their welfare
- ● Mtgs - Exhib
- < Brit Goat Soc
- M 60 i, UK / 6 i, o'seas
  (Sub: £15).
- ¶ Harness Goat Society - 4; ftm, £3 nm.
  Training Your Harness Goat; £2 m, £3 nm.
  Information Leaflet No 1: History;
  Information Leaflet No 2: Where to Find Harness & Carts

Harrogate Chamber of Trade & Commerce 1896
- ■ PO Box 8, HARROGATE, N Yorks, HG2 8XB. (hq)
  01423 879208   fax 01423 870025
  email info@harrogatechamber.org
  http://www.harrogatechamber.org
  Chief Exec & Hon Sec: Brian L Dunsby
- ▲ Un-incorporated Society
- ○ *C
- Gp Focus groups: Business development, Promoting Harrogate, Town centre, Traffic & transport, Waste disposal
- ● Mtgs - Exhib - VE - Liaison with local government
- M 250 f
- ¶ Review (NL) - 12; ftm, free samples to enquirers.

Harry Roy Appreciation Society   (HRAS)   1972

- ■ 43 Repton Close, LUTON, Beds, LU3 3UL.   (memsec/p)
  01582 574946
  Mem Sec: Pauline Wolsey
- ▲ Un-incorporated Society
- ○ *G; for all appreciative of the Harry Roy Dance Band (1930's & 1940's), his musicians & vocalists
- ● Mtgs - Res - Stat - Inf
- M 90 i, UK / 6 i, o'seas
  (Sub: £5)
- ¶ The Bugle Call Rag - 4; free.

Harveian Society of Edinburgh   1782

- NR Dept of Gastroenterology, Western General Hospital, EDINBURGH, EH4 2XU.   (hsb)
  0131-537 1000
  Sec: Prof Dr Kelvin Palmer
- ○ *L

Harveian Society of London   1831

- ■ Lettsom House, 11 Chandos St, LONDON, W1G 9EB.   (hq)
  020 7580 1043
  Exec Sec: Col Richard Kinsella-Bevan
- ○ *L; advancement of medical science
- ● Mtgs - VE
- M i

Hat Pin Society of Great Britain   1980

- ■ PO Box 1089, MAIDSTONE, Kent, ME14 9BA.   (mail)
  http://www.hatpinsociety.org.uk
  Chmn: Valerie Pugh
- ▲ Un-incorporated Society
- ○ *G; collecting hat pins & hat pin holders
- ● Mtgs
- < Amer Hatpin Soc
- M 196 i, UK / 34 i, o'seas
- ¶ NL - 4; ftm only.

Havergal Brian Society   (HBS)   1974

- ■ 39 Giles Coppice, LONDON, SE19 1XF.   (hsp)
  020 8761 8134
  email damian_rees@yahoo.com
  http://www.havergalbrian.org
  Sec: Damian Rees
- ▲ Registered Charity
- ○ *D; promote knowledge & appreciation of the works of William Havergal Brian (1876-1972) English composer & writer on music
- ● Publication of Brian's music, studies of Brian's work & his own writing on music - Concerts - Recordings
- M 167 i, 2 org, UK / 47 i, o'seas
  (Sub: £12 i, varies o'seas)
- ¶ NL - 6; ftm, 50p nm.
  Havergal Brian's Gothic Symphony - two studies; £10.
  The Complete Music for Solo Piano; £11.
  Havergal Brian on Music, Vol 1: British Music; £17.95 m, £19.95 nm, (paperback £8.50 m, £9.50 nm) (in association with Toccata Press).

Hawick Archaeological Society   (HAS)   1856

- NR 8 Melgund Place, HAWICK, Roxburghshire, TD9 9HY.   (hsp)
  01450 376220
  email info@airchieoliver.co.uk
  http://www.airchieoliver.co.uk
  Hon Sec: Gerald Graham
- ▲ Un-incorporated Society
- ○ *L, *Q; antiquities & natural history of Hawick & district
- M 500 i

Hawk & Owl Trust   (HOT)   1969

- NR PO Box 400, Bishops Lydeard, TAUNTON, Somerset, TA4 3WH.   (asa)
  0844 984 2824
  http://www.hawkandowl.org
  Dir: Linda Bennett
- ▲ Company Limited by Guarantee; Registered Charity
- ○ *K, *V; conservation & protection of all birds of prey, including owls in the wild & their habitats
- Gp Barn Owl Conservation Network
- ● Conf - Mtgs - ET - Res - Exhib - SG - Stat - Inf - PL - LG
- < Birdlife Intl
- M 6,000 i, 3 f, 40 org, UK / 98 i, 20 org, o'seas
- ¶ Peregrine (NL) - 2.   Adopt a Box (NL) - 2.
  Various publications.

Haydn Society of Great Britain   1979

- ■ 2 Aldcliffe Mews, LANCASTER, LA1 5BT.   (dir/p)
  01524 61553   fax 01524 61553
  email d.mccaldin@lancaster.ac.uk
  http://www.haydnsocietyofgb.co.uk
  Dir: Prof Denis McCaldin
- ▲ Un-incorporated Society
- ○ *A; to promote a wider knowledge & understanding of the music of Joseph Haydn
- ● Conf - Res - Exhib - Inf - Lib - VE
- < Burgenland Haydn Festival (Eisenstadt, Austria)
- M 240 i, 1 f, 10 org, UK / 10 i, 1 org, o'seas
- ¶ Jnl - 1; ftm, nm by arrangement.

HDRA - the Organic Organisation
  an alternative name for the **Henry Doubleday Research Association**

Headlines, the Craniofacial Support Group   1993

- NR 128 Beesmoor Rd, Frampton Cotterell, BRISTOL, BS36 2JP.   (hq)
  01454 850557
  email info@headlines.org.uk
  http://www.headlines.org.uk
  Admin: Gil Ruff
- ○ *W; to provide help & support for those affected by craniosynostosis (a condition where one, or more, plates in the skull fuses before birth)
- ● Inf

Headmasters' & Headmistresses' Conference   (HMC)   1869

- NR 12 The Point, Rockingham Rd, MARKET HARBOROUGH, Leics, LE16 7QU.   (hq)
  01858 469059
  email hmc@hmc.org.uk   http://www.hmc.org.uk
  Gen Sec: William Richardson
- ○ *P; for the heads of independent schools, to serve & support them, to represent their views & to exemplify excellence in education
- ● Conf - Mtgs - ET - Stat - Inf - LG
- < Indep Schools Coun; Secondary Heads Assn
- M 250 i, UK / 60 i, o'seas

Headteachers' Association of Scotland
  since 1 August 2008 **School Leaders Scotland**

© CBD Research Ltd · Beckenham · BR3 5JS · Tel 020 8650 7745 · E-mail cbd@cbdresearch.com · www.cbdresearch.com

Headway - the Brain Injury Association   1979
- ■ Bradbury House, 190 Bagnall Rd, Old Basford, NOTTINGHAM, NG6 8SF.   (hq)
   0115-924 0800   fax 0115-958 4446
   email info@headway.org.uk
   http://www.headway.org.uk
   Chief Exec: Peter McCabe
- ▲ Registered Charity
- Br 115
- ○ *K, *M, *W; to provide information, support & services to people with acquired brain injuries, their families, carers & related professionals
- ● Conf
   Helpline: 0808 800 2244
- < Eur Brain Injury Soc; Brain Injured & Families Eur Confedn (BIF)
- M 800 i, 11 f, UK / 40 org, o'seas
- ¶ Headway News - 4; £2.25.
   Noticeboard (NL) - 6; ftm only.
   Publications on varying aspects of head injury; list available.

Healing Trust
   the working title of the **National Federation of Spiritual Healers**

Health & Beauty Employers Federation
   a group of the **Federation of Holistic Therapists**

Health Care Supply Association   (HCSA)   1960
- NR NHSBT, Oak House, Reeds Crescent, WATFORD, Herts, WD24 4QN.   (chmn/b)
   01923 486800
   email eugene.cooke@nhsbt.nhs.uk
   http://www.healthcaresupply.org.uk
   Chmn: Eugene Cooke
- ▲ Company Limited by Guarantee
- Br 12
- ○ *P; to provide a professional network for health care purchasing & supply that encourages shared learning & promotes the commercial profession within health care
- ● Conf - Mtgs - ET - Exhib - LG - Seminars - Annual awards
- < Chart Inst of Purchasing & Supply
- M 720 i
- ¶ Official Procurement Guide - 1; ftm, £50 nm.

Health Food Institute   (HFI)   1979
- NR Gothic House, Barker Gate, NOTTINGHAM, NG1 1JU.   (hq)
   0115-941 4188
   email enquiries@healthfoodinstitute.org.uk
   http://www.healthfoodinstitute.org.uk
   Admin: Alison Collingwood
- ▲ Company Limited by Guarantee
- ○ *P; to increase knowledge & education in nutritional & health matters; to promote & maintain standards in nutrition & health food retailing
- ● Conf - Mtgs - ET - Exam - Res - Exhib - Stat - Inf - LG
- M 200 i
- ¶ Jnl - 1.
   The HFI Professional Diploma is available solely through the National Association of Health Stores

Health Food Manufacturers' Association   (HFMA)   1965
- NR 1 Wolsey Rd, EAST MOLESEY, Surrey, KT8 9EL.   (hq)
   020 8481 7100   fax 020 8481 7101
   email hfma@hfma.co.uk   http://www.hfma.co.uk
   Exec Dir: Graham Keen
- ▲ Company Limited by Guarantee
- ○ *T; interests of manufacturers of health foods & allied products
- Gp Food supplements; Health foods; Herbal
- ● Conf - Mtgs - SG - Expt - Inf - LG
- < Intl Alliance of Dietary/Food Supplement Assns (IADSA); Eur Fedn of Health Product Mfrs Assn (EHPM)
- M c 150 f
- ¶ NL;   LM; both ftm only.

Health & Safety Sign Association   (HSSA)   1994
- NR PO Box 377, REDHILL, Surrey, RH1 2YZ.   (hq)
   01883 716768
   email enquiry@hssa.co.uk   http://www.hssa.co.uk
   Sec: Charles Hardway
- ○ *T; te create greater safety through the proper use of safety & other statutory signs; to develop & maintain industry standards & act as an industry voice to those formulating industry standards & legislation internationally
- ● LG
- M f

Healthcare Communications Association   (HCA)
- NR Wyndmere House, Ashwell Rd, Steeple Morden, ROYSTON, Herts, SG8 0NZ.   (hq)
   0844 770 0145
   email info@hca-uk.org   http://www.hca-uk.org
   Chief Exec: Julia Cook
- ○ *T; to promote excellence & best practice in healthcare communications
- Gp Benchmarking & trends; Career development; Digital; Medical communications; Standards; Training
- ● Conf - ET - Info - Mtgs
- M f
   (Sub: £250-£2,000)

Healthcare Financial Management Association   (HFMA)   1950
- NR Albert House (suite 32), 111 Victoria St, BRISTOL, BS1 6AX.   (hq)
   0117-929 4789   fax 0117-929 4844
   http://www.hfma.org.uk
   Chief Exec: Mark Knight
- ▲ Registered Charity
- Br 14
- ○ *P; for accountants engaged in healthcare financial management in the UK
- ● Conf - Mtgs - ET - Res - Exhib - Inf
- < Eur Healthcare Mgt Assn; HFMA (USA)
- M 4,000 i
- ¶ Healthcare Finance - 10; ftm.   Ybk - 1.   AR - 1.

Healthcare Infection Society   (HIS)   1980
- NR 162 Kings Cross Rd, LONDON, WC1X 9DH.   (hq)
   020 7713 0273   fax 020 7713 0255
   email sue.hollinshead@his.org.uk
   http://www.his.org.uk
   Admin: Sue Hollinshead
- ▲ Registered Charity
- ○ *M; the prevention & control of hospital & other healthcare associated infections
- Gp Education; Scientific Development
- ● Conf - ET - Exam - Mtgs
- < Fedn of Infection Socs
- ¶ Jnl of Hospital Infection - 12.
- ✕ 2011 Hospital Infection Society

Healthcare People Management Association   (HPMA)   1974
- ■ Gothic House, 3 The Green, RICHMOND, Surrey, TW9 1PL.   (admin/b)
   020 8334 4530   fax 020 8332 7201
   http://www.hpma.org.uk
   Exec Dir: Alex O'Grady
- ▲ Un-incorporated Society
- Br 10
- ○ *P; to bring together healthcare professionals to enable them to develop, influence & promote high quality human resource management in the NHS
- ● Conf - Mtgs - Res - Comp - LG
- M 288 i, 320 f, UK / 1,000 f, o'seas)
   (Sub: £20 i - £350 Corporate)
- ¶ Network - 12; ftm only.

HealthWatch   1988
NR   8 Eagle Close, AMERSHAM, Bucks, HP6 6TD.   (mail)
⬛   020 8789 7813
      http://www.healthwatch-uk.org
      Sec: Prof David Bender
▲   Registered Charity
○   *K; to develop good practices in the assessment & testing of
      treatments & the conduct of clinincal trials generally; to
      promote high standards of health care by practitioners
●   Mtgs - Inf
M   141 i
¶   NL - 4.

Hearing Concern
      merged October 2008 with LINK Centre for Deafened People to form
      Hearing Link

Hearing Link   1947
⬛   27-28 The Waterfront, EASTBOURNE, E Sussex, BN23 5UZ.
      (hq)
      0300 111 1113   fax 01323 471260
      email enquiries@hearinglink.org
      http://www.hearinglink.org
      Chief Exec: Dr Lorraine Gailey
▲   Company Limited by Guarantee; Registered Charity
Br   3
○   *W; to promote the interests of & to support adults with hearing
      loss whose preferred communication is the spoken word
●   ET - Exhib - Inf - VE
<   Intl Fedn of the Hard of Hearing; UK Coun on Deafness; Nat
      Coun for Voluntary Orgs
M   1,671 i, 34 f, 90 org, UK / 5 org, o'seas
¶   Hearing Link Matters - 6; ftm.
✕   2008 (Hearing Concern
            (LINK Centre for Deafened People

Heart of England Fine Foods   (HEFF)   1998
⬛   Shropshire Food Enterprise Centre, Vanguard Way, Battlefield
      Enterprise Park, SHREWSBURY, Shrops, SY1 3TG.   (hq)
      01743 452818
      email office@heff.co.uk   http://www.heff.co.uk
      Chief Exec: Karen Davies
▲   Private Limited Company
○   *T; organisation for the promotion of West Midlands food &
      drink
●   Conf - Mtgs - Inf
M   236 f

Heart Line Association   1980
⬛   32 Little Heath, LONDON, SE7 8HU.   (hq)
      0330 022 4466
      http://www.heartline.org.uk
      Office Mgr: Pamela Lawrence
▲   Registered Charity
Br   20
○   *W; support for families with children who have heart
      conditions
●   Support groups
M   1,400 i
¶   NL - 4; free.   Heart Children: a practical handbook; £6.

Heart UK   1986
⬛   7 North Rd, MAIDENHEAD, Berks, SL6 1PE.   (hq)
      01628 777046
      http://www.heartuk.org.uk
      Chief Exec: Michael Livingston
▲   Company Limited by Guarantee; Registered Charity
○   *K, *W; support & information for people at high risk of
      premature coronary heart disease, especially families with
      inherited (genetic) blood cholesterol or triglyceride problems
Gp   Diet & Lifestyle help-line, dieticians & other health professionals
      respond to members' enquiries by phone & post
●   Conf - ET - Res - SG - Stat - Inf - LG - Publications - Lectures -
      Professional training
      Helpline: 0845 450 5988
<   Nat Heart Forum; Genetic Interest Gp; Parliamentary Food &
      Health Forum; Long Term Medical Conditions Alliance
M   c 1,500 i
¶   Digest - 6; ftm, £2.50 nm.

Heat Pump Association   (HPA)   1994
⬛   2 Waltham Court, Milley Lane, Hare Hatch, READING, Berks,
      RG10 9TH.   (hq)
      0118-940 3416   fax 0118-940 6258
      email info@feta.co.uk   http://www.heatpumps.org.uk
      Dir Gen: C Sloan
○   *T; promotes the benefits & proper use of heat pumps & heat
      pump technology by increasing the awareness of heat pumps
      as a means of using energy efficiently, cost effectively & with
      the minimum impact on the environment
●   Mtgs - Comp - Inf
<   Fedn of Envtl Tr Assns (FETA)
M   21 full members, 12 associate

Heather Society   1963
⬛   Tippitiwitchet Cottage, Hall Rd, Outwell, WISBECH, Cambs,
      PE14 8PE.   (admin p)
      01945 774077
      email admin@heathersociety.org.uk
      http://www.heathersociety.org.uk
      Admin: Dr E Charles Nelson,   Hon Sec: Jean Julian
▲   Registered Charity
Br   13; USA
○   *H; study, research & development of heather varieties
Gp   Technical c'ee responsible for trials at Harlow Carr, Harrogate
      & RHS Garden, Wisley; Compilations of the International
      Register of Heather Names
●   Conf - Res - ET - Exhib - Comp - Inf - PL (slides only) - VE
<   R Horticl Soc; Nederlandse Heidevereniging Ericultura;
      Gesellschaft der Heidefreunde; N Amer Heather Soc
M   1,500 i, 125 f, 15 university libraries, UK / 100 i, 12 f, 15
      university libraries, o'seas
      (Sub: £15-£21)
¶   News Bulletin - 3.   Ybk; ftm only.

Heating & Hot Water Industry Council
      is a section of **SBGI**

**Heating, Ventilating & Air Conditioning Manufacturers'
Association Ltd   (HEVAC)   1962**
⬛   2 Waltham Court, Milley Lane, Hare Hatch, READING, Berks,
      RG10 9TH.   (hq)
      0118-940 3416   fax 0118-940 6258
      email info@feta.co.uk   http://www.feta.co.uk
      Dir Gen: C Sloan
○   *T; interests of heating, ventilating & air conditioning equipment
      manufacturers
Gp   Air conditioning; Air curtains; Air distribution; Fan coils; Filters;
      House ventilation; Humidity; Noise & vibration control
●   Mtgs - ET - Exhib - Comp - SG - Stat - Expt - Inf
<   Fedn of Envtl Trade Assns (FETA)
M   118 f
¶   NL - 12; ftm only.

© CBD Research Ltd · Beckenham · BR3 5JS · Tel 020 8650 7745 · E-mail cbd@cbdresearch.com · www.cbdresearch.com

Heating & Ventilating Contractors' Association (HVCA) 1904

■ Esca House, 34 Palace Court, LONDON, W2 4JG. (hq)
020 7313 4900 fax 020 7727 9268
email contact@hvca.org.uk http://www.hvca.org.uk
Chief Exec: Blane Judd
Br 10
○ *T; to represent the interests of firms active in the design, installation & commissioning of heating, ventilating, air conditioning & refrigeration products & equipment
Gp Ductwork; Heating & plumbing; Refrigeration & air conditioning; Service & facilities;
Building Engineering Services Competence Accreditation Ltd (BESCA), 0800 652 5533 info@besca.org.uk
M f
¶ HVCA Newslink (NL).
Voted 8 December 2011 to adopt the trading name Building & Engineering Services Association with effect from 1 March 2012

Heavy Transport Association (HTA) 1983

■ The White House, High St, Tattenhall, CHESTER, CH3 9PX. (hq)
01829 771774 fax 01829 773109
email info@hta.uk.net http://www.hta.uk.net
Sec: John Dyne
▲ Un-incorporated Society
○ *T; to promote the interests of the heavy haulage industry
Gp Working Groups: HTA-DfT-HA liaison; Self-escorting - Strategic sites & water - Preferred policy
● Mtgs
< Eur Assn of Heavy Haulage Transport & Mobile Cranes (ESTA)
M 91 f, UK / 3 f, o'seas
¶ HeavyTalk (NL) - 4; Members' Hbk - 2 yrly; both ftm.

Hebe Society 1985

■ 20 Beech Farm Drive, MACCLESFIELD, Cheshire, SK10 2ER. (hsp)
01625 611062
http://www.hebesoc.org
Hon Sec: Tony Hayter
▲ Registered Charity
○ *H; a specialist plant society encouraging the cultivation & conservation of Hebe, Parahebe & all other New Zealand native plants
● Mtgs - Exhib - Plant collections
< New Zealand Alpine Garden Soc; R Horticl Soc; Tatton Garden Soc
M 263 i, 22 f, libraries & arboreta, UK / 21 i, o'seas
(Sub: £10 i, £17 f)
¶ Hebe News (NL) - 4; ftm, £2 nm (with Index & Author index).
Cultivation of Hebes & Parahebes; price as below -
Bibliography of books on Hebes & other New Zealand native plants (incl in new members' starter pack), ftm, £1 nm.
Cultivation of Hebes & Parahebes; ftm, £1 nm.

Hebridean Sheep Society 1986

■ Coney Grey, Gun Lane, Sherington, NEWPORT PAGNELL, Bucks, MK16 9PE. (memsec/p)
01908 611092
email info@hebrideansheep.org.uk
http://www.hebrideansheep.org.uk
Mem Sec: Helen Brewis
○ *B
● ET - Exhib - Comp - Stat - Inf
< Nat Sheep Assn
M 300 i, UK / 2 i, o'seas
¶ The Black Sheep (Ybk) - 1; NL - 4; both ftm only.

Hedge Laying Association of Ireland (HLAI) 2004

IRL 70 Bushes Lane, Rathgar, DUBLIN 6, Republic of Ireland. (hsp)
00 (353) 86 302 8790
email htai@eircom.net http://www.hedgelaying.ie
Public Limited Company
Sec: Mark McDowell
○ *G, *H; to promote the craft & profession of hedge laying; to encourage & facilitate the conservation, protection & appropriate management of hedgerows
● ET - Exhib - PL

Hedgeline 1998

NR 1 Applebees Meadow, HINCKLEY, Leics, LE10 0FL. (admin/p)
01455 890649
http://www.hedgeline.org
Admin: Max Ayriss
▲ Un-incorporated Society
Br Regional & local
○ *K; for the legislative control of hedge nuisance
● Political lobbying
M c 3,700 i
¶ Hedgeline - irreg; free.

Helensburgh & Lomond Chamber of Commerce 1997

NR Municipal Buildings (1st floor), 2 East Princes St, HELENSBURGH, G84 7QF. (hq)
01436 268085 fax 01436 831406
email info@helensburghchamber.co.uk
http://www.helensburghchamber.co.uk
Chief Exec: Brian Alexander
○ *C
< Scot Chams Comm
M 40 f

Hellenic Society
see **Society for the Promotion of Hellenic Studies**

Helplines Association (THA) 1996

■ 9 Marshalsea Rd, LONDON, SE1 1EP. (hq)
020 7089 6321 fax 020 7089 6320
email info@helplines.org.uk
http://www.helplines.org.uk
Chief Exec: Rekhha Wadhwani
▲ Company Limited by Guarantee; Registered Charity
Br 1
○ *T, *W; to promote & support the development of helpline services
● Conf - Mtgs - ET - Res - LG - Development services
M 500 f, UK / 5 f, o'seas
(Sub: according to turnover)
¶ Digital Exchange - 12; Annual Review - 1; both free.
THA Directory - 2; £22.
Quality Standard Workbook.
× 2009 Telephone Helplines Association (October)

Hemp Lime Construction Products Association (HLCPA)

NR Kingsley House, Ganders Business Park, Kingsley, BORDON, Hants, GU35 9LU. (asa)
01420 471616 fax 01420 471611
email secretary@hemplime.org.uk
http://www.hemplime.org.uk
Sec: John G Fairley
○ *T; to promote the use and development of quality controlled hemp lime products and technology in the built environment.
● ET - Res

Henkeepers' Association   2006
- ■ 19 Joy Lane, WHITSTABLE, Kent, CT5 4LT.   (hsp)
  email info@henkeepersassociation.co.uk
  http://www.henkeepersassociation.co.uk
  Sec: Francine Raymond
- ○ *G; to inform & support henkeepers who keep small flocks in their garden for pleasure
- ● Inf
- M 60 i

Henry Bradshaw Society   (HBS)   1890
- NR The British Library (Music Collections), 96 Euston Rd, LONDON, NW1 2DB.   (gensec/b)
  http://www.henrybradshawsociety.org
  Gen Sec: Dr Nicholas Bell
- ▲ Registered Charity
- ○ *L; to publish editions & facsimiles of rare liturgical texts
- ● Res - Inf
- < Alcuin Club; Societas Liturgica; Soc for Liturgical Study
- M 83 i, 59 org, UK / 68 i, 79 org, o'seas
- ¶ HBS has published 118 volumes in its main series & a series of occasional 'Subsidia' volumes

Henry Doubleday Research Association   (HDRA)   1958
- NR Garden Organic Ryton, Wolston Lane, COVENTRY, Warks, CV8 3LG.   (hq)
  024 7630 3517   fax 024 7663 9229
  email enquiry@gardenorganic.org.uk
  http://www.gardenorganic.org.uk
  Chief Exec: Myles Bremner
- ▲ Company Limited by Guarantee; Registered Charity
- Br 60
- ○ *F, *H, *Q; to research & promote organic horticulture & food
- ● Conf - ET - Res - Inf - Lib - VE
- M 30,000 i, UK / 700 i, o'seas
- ¶ NL - 4;   AR; both ftm.   Books & pamphlets; prices vary.
  Mail order catalogue - 1; free.
  Note: Garden Organic is the working name of the Henry Doubleday Research Association (also known as HDRA - the Organic Organisation)

Henry Sweet Society for the History of Linguistic Ideas
- ■ c/o Dr R Steadman-Jones, Dept of English Language & Linguistics, 5 Shearwood Rd, University of Sheffield, SHEFFIELD, S Yorks, S10 2TN.
  email r.d.steadman-jones@sheffield.ac.uk
  http://www.henrysweetsociety.group.shef.ac.uk
  Gen Sec: Dr Richard Steadman-Jones
- ○ *L

Henry Williamson Society   (HWS)   1980
- ■ 16 Doran Drive, REDHILL, Surrey, RH1 6AX.   (memsec/p)
  http://www.henrywilliamson.co.uk
  Mem Sec: Mrs Margaret Murphy
- ▲ Registered Charity
- ○ *L; to encourage interest & a deeper understanding of the life & work of the 20th century English writer Henry Williamson (1895-1977)
- ● Mtgs - Comp - SG - VE
- M 525 i, 5 libraries, UK / 21 i, o'seas
- ¶ Jnl - 1;   NL - 1; both ftm, (subn £12).

Henty Society   1977
- ■ 205 Icknield Way, LETCHWORTH, Herts, SG6 4TT.   (hsp)
  http://www.hentysociety.org
  Hon Sec: David Walmsley
- ▲ Un-incorporated Society
- ○ *A; to further study the life & work of George Alfred Henty (1832-1902), Victorian writer & war correspondent
- Gp Biographical research; Biographical study; Publications of rare work
- ● Conf - Res - Exhib - SG - Inf
- < Alliance Literary Socs
- M 90 i, UK / 55 i, o'seas
- ¶ Bulletin - 2;   Literary Supplements - occasional.
  Bibliographical Research (for UK, Canadian & American editions) - 1; all ftm only.

Heraldry Society   1950
- NR PO Box 772, GUILDFORD, Surrey, GU3 3ZX.   (hq)
  01483 237373
  email secretary@theheraldrysociety.com
  http://www.theheraldrysociety.com
  Sec: Melvyn Jeremiah
- ▲ Company Limited by Guarantee; Registered Charity
- ○ *L; heraldry, armory, chivalry & genealogy
- ● Conf - Exam - Exhib - Lib - VE
- M 900 worldwide
- ¶ The Heraldry Gazette - 4; ftm only.
  Coat of Arms - 2.

Heraldry Society of Scotland   1977
- ■ 25 Craigentinny Crescent, EDINBURGH, EH7 6QA.   (treas/p)
  0131-553 2232
  http://www.heraldry-scotland.co.uk
  Treas: Stuart G Emerson
- ▲ Registered Charity
- ○ *L; to encourage the study & practice of heraldry in Scotland, taking into account its European & international context
- ● Conf - Mtgs - Res - Inf - Lib - VE
- < Heraldry Soc (London)
- M c 300 i, UK / c 100 i, o'seas
- ¶ The Double Tressure (Jnl) - 1; ftm.
  Tak Tent (NL) - 1/2;   LM - irreg; both m only.
  Special publications - irreg.

Herb Society   1927
- ■ Sulgrave Manor, Sulgrave, BANBURY, Oxon, OX17 2SD.   (hq)
  01295 768899
  email info@herbsociety.org.uk
  http://www.herbsociety.org.uk
  Chmn: John Baylis,   Sec: Flick Kingston
- ▲ Company Limited by Guarantee; Registered Charity
- ○ *G, *H; promotion of knowledge & use of herbs
- ● Conf - Mtgs - ET - Exhib - Comp - Inf - Lib - VE
- < R Horticl Soc; Henry Doubleday Res Assn
- M 1,750 i, UK / 258 i, o'seas
  (Sub: £25, £22.50 concession)
- ¶ Herbs - 4; £20 yr m.

Herbert Howells Society   1987
- ■ 32 Barleycroft Rd, WELWYN GARDEN CITY, Herts, AL8 6JU.   (hsp)
  01707 335315
  email andrew.millinger@virgin.net
  Hon Sec: Andrew Millinger
- ▲ Un-incorporated Society
- Br USA
- ○ *D; to commemorate the life & work of Herbert Howells (1892-1983); to encourage the performance, recording & publication of his music
- ● Inf - Working with publishers, recording companies & concert promoters
- M 200 i, 2 f, UK / 100 i, o'seas
- ¶ NL - 1; ftm.

© CBD Research Ltd · Beckenham · BR3 5JS · Tel 020 8650 7745 · E-mail cbd@cbdresearch.com · www.cbdresearch.com

Herdwick Sheep Breeders' Association (HSBA) 1916
- ■ Howe Cottage, SEASCALE, Cumbria, CA20 1EQ. (hsp)
  01946 729346 (evenings)
  email amanda@herdwick-sheep.com
  http://www.herdwick-sheep.com
  Sec: Amanda Carson
- ○ *B
- < Nat Sheep Assn
- M 150 i
- ¶ Flock Book - 2 yrly.

Hereditary Spastic Paraplegia Support Group 1989
- NR 37 Wimborne Rd West, WIMBORNE, Dorset, BH21 2DQ.
  (chmn/p)
  01202 849391
  http://www.hspgroup.org
  Chmn: Ian Bennett
- ▲ Registered Charity
- ○ *W; to help & support people diagnosed with HSP, also known
  as Familial Spastic Paraparesis, a diagnosis which covers a
  range of rare genetic disorders
- ● Mtgs - Inf - Research grants
  Helpline: 01702 218184 (Stephanie Flower)
- M c 300 i
- ¶ NL - 4; ftm.

Hereford Cattle Society 1878
- ■ Hereford House, 3 Offa St, HEREFORD, HR1 2LL. (hq)
  01432 272057 fax 01432 377529
  email postroom@herefordcattle.org
  http://www.herefordcattle.org
  Sec: David Prothero
- ▲ Company Limited by Guarantee; Registered Charity
- ○ *B
- ● Conf - Exhib - Expt
- < Nat Beef Assn; 21 other Hereford Cattle Societies throughout
  the world
- M 850 i, UK / 860 i, o'seas
- ¶ Jnl - 1; ftm, £5 nm.

Herefordshire & Worcestershire Chamber of Commerce 1839
- NR Severn House, Prescott Drive, Warndon Business Park,
  WORCESTER, WR4 9NE. (hq)
  0845 641 1641 fax 0845 641 4641
  email enquiries@hwchamber.co.uk
  http://www.hwchamber.co.uk
  Chief Exec: Mike Ashton
- Br Hereford, Shrewsbury, Worcester
- ○ *C; to support its members to achieve success that enhances
  the economic sustainability of the region, by acting as a key
  influencer through communication, networking,
  representation & lobbying
- ● Conf - Mtgs - ET - Res - Stat - Expt - Inf - Lib - LG - Business
  advice - Seminars - Training & Enterprise Council (TEC)
  services
- < Brit Chams Comm
- M 1,300 f
- ¶ New Direction (Jnl) - 6.

Heritage Afloat (HA) 1994
- ■ 9 Strode St, EGHAM, Surrey, TW20 9BT. (memsec/p)
  http://www.heritageafloat.org.uk
  Mem Sec: Bernard Hales
- ○ *K, *G; to give a national voice to all those who are helping to
  preserve ships & all other aspects of Britain's maritime past.
  Membership ranges from large associations to small trusts &
  individual owners
- ● Mtgs - Inf - LG
- M 57 i, 28 org, UK / 1 i, o'seas
- ¶ NL; free.

Heritage Alliance
- NR Clutha House, 10 Storey's Gate, LONDON, SW1P 3AY. (hq)
  020 7233 0500 fax 020 7233 0600
  email mail@theheritagealliance.org.uk
  http://www.theheritagealliance.org.uk
  Chief Exec: Kate Pugh
- ▲ Company Limited by Guarantee; Registered Charity
- ○ *N; to protect & promote the voluntary heritage sector
- ● Inf - Mtgs - Res
- M 91 org
- ¶ Heritage Update - 26 (email).

Heritage Crafts Association (HCA) 2009
- NR 132 The Glade, OLD COULSDON, Surrey, CR5 1SP.
  (admin/p)
  email info@heritagecrafts.org.uk
  http://www.heritagecrafts.org.uk
  Admin: Sally Dodson
- ▲ Registered Charity
- ○ *K, *N; advocacy body for traditional heritage crafts
- ● Inf - LG - Res

Heritage Railway Association (HRA) 1996
- ■ 33 Palmerston Place, EDINBURGH, EH12 5AU. (dir/p)
  0131-225 1486 fax 0131-220 5886
  email contact@hra.gb.com
  http://www.heritagerailways.com
  Managing Dir: David Woodhouse
- ▲ Company Limited by Guarantee; Registered Charity
- ○ *N, *T; to represent the interests of the majority of heritage &
  tourist railways, tramways & railway preservation groups in
  both the UK & Ireland
- ● Conf - Mtgs - Comp - Inf - LG
- < Eur Fedn of Museum & Tourist Rlys (FEDECRAIL)
- M 250 f & org; i (friends)
- ¶ Sidelines - 6; Broadlines - 6; Guidelines - irreg;
  Information papers - irreg; all ftm only.

Herpes Viruses Association (HVA) 1983
- ■ 41 North Rd, LONDON, N7 9DP. (hq)
  0845 123 2305
  http://www.herpes.org.uk
  Dir: Marian Nicholson
- ▲ Registered Charity
- ○ *W; to supply information, advice & counselling to people with
  herpes simplex (cold sores, whitlow & genital sores)
- Gp Shingles Support Society (provides information of self-help
  therapies & drugs to patients with Post-Herpetic Neuralgia, &
  their GPs)
- ● Conf - Mtgs - Res - Stat - Inf - Lib - Counselling & advice to
  people with herpes viruses - Provision of correct information
  to the media
- < Skin Care Campaign; All Party Parliamentary Gp on Skin; Brit
  Assn for Sexual Health & HIV (BASHH)
- M 1,000 i, 12 f, 20 clinics, UK / 30 i, o'seas
- ¶ SPHERE (NL) - 4; ftm.
  Herpes Simplex - A Guide; £1 m, 30p in bulk nm.

Herring Buyers Association Ltd (HBA) 1976
- NR 36 Springfield Terrace, South Queensferry, EDINBURGH,
  EH30 9XF. (hq)
  0131-331 1222
- ○ *T; to represent pelagic buyers & processors - herring,
  mackerel, sprat & pilchards

Hertfordshire Agricultural Society   1801
- ■ The Showground, Dunstable Rd, REDBOURN, Herts, AL3 7PT. (hq)
  01582 792626   fax 01582 794027
  email office@hertsshow.com
  http://www.hertsshow.com
  Sec: Mike Harman
- ▲ Company Limited by Guarantee; Registered Charity
- ○ *F, *H; to promote a better understanding of farming, agriculture & the country way of life in Hertfordshire
- ● Hertfordshire County Show
- < Assn of Show & Agricl Orgs; Brit Show Jumping Assn; breed societies
- M 300 i
- ¶ NL - 2;   AR - 1; both ftm only.
  Show Catalogue - 1; £3.   Show Schedule - 1; free.

Hertfordshire Chamber of Commerce & Industry   1971
- NR 4 Bishops Square Business Park, HATFIELD, Herts, AL10 9NE. (hq)
  01707 398400   fax 01707 398430
  email enquiries@hertschamber.com
  http://www.hertschamber.com
  Chief Exec: Tim Hutchings
- ▲ Company Limited by Guarantee
- ○ *C

Hesketh Hubbard Art Society
a member organisation of the **Federation of British Artists**

High Friction Surfacing Association
in 2008 merged with the Road Surface Dressing Association & the Slurry Surfacing Contractors Association to form the **Road Surface Treatments Association**

High Sheriffs' Association of England & Wales   1970
- ■ Gatefield, Green Tye, MUCH HADHAM, Herts, SG10 6JJ. (hsp)
  01279 842225   fax 07092 846777
  email secretary@highsheriffs.com
  Hon Sec: James Williams
- ▲ Company Limited by Guarantee
- ○ *P; to protect, promote & strengthen the ancient Office & traditions of the High Sheriffs
- ● Conf - Mtgs - ET - Comp - SG - Inf - LG
- M 950 i, UK / 3 i, o'seas
- ¶ The High Sheriff - 2; ftm, £20 yr nm.
  Note: also known as the Shrievalty Association

Higher Education Liaison Officers' Association   (HELOA) 1990
- ■ HELOA Office, University of Essex, Wivenhoe Park, COLCHESTER, Essex, CO4 3SQ.   (hq)
  01206 873423   fax 0871 661 5779
  email heloa@essex.ac.uk   http://www.heloa.ac.uk
  Sec: Jennifer Williams
- ▲ Un-incorporated Society
- Br 9 regional groups
- ○ *P; to provide information & assistance to students, parents & careers advisers on entry to higher education in the UK; to advise government & other organisations on needs & attitudes of students & their parents to higher education
- ● Conf - ET - LG
- M 739 i

Highland Association
the English name of An **Comunn Gaidhealach**

Highland Cattle Society   (HCS)   1884
- ■ Stirling Agricultural Centre, STIRLING, FK9 4RN.   (hq)
  01786 446866   fax 01786 446022
  email info@highlandcattlesociety.com
  http://www.highlandcattlesociety.com
  Breed Sec: Hazel Baxter
- ▲ Registered Charity
- ○ *B
- ● Exhib (Society's annual shows)
- < Nat Beef Assn
- M 890 i, UK / 50 i, o'seas
  (Sub: £68.36 incl VAT)
- ¶ Jnl - 1; ftm, £5+ nm.   NL - 3; free.   AR; ftm only.

Highland Mule Breeders Association
a group of the **Highlands & Islands Sheep Health Association Ltd**

Highland Pony Society   (HPS)   1923
- ■ Grosvenor House, Shore Rd, PERTH, PH2 8BD.   (hq)
  01738 451861   fax 01738 451861
  http://www.highlandponysociety.com
  Sec: Mrs Susie Robertson
- ▲ Company Limited by Guarantee; Registered Charity
- ○ *B; to keep the purity of the breed; to promote breeding for use in farm work, forestry, riding or driving & for sporting & show purposes
- ● Conf - Mtgs - ET - Res - Comp - Expt - Inf - VE
- < Nat Pony Soc
- M 1,500 i, UK / 100 i, o'seas
- ¶ Stud Book - 1.

Highland Railway Society
- ■ Winter Field, Terrys Lane, COOKHAM, Berks, SL6 9TJ. (memsec/p)
  01963 370697   fax 01963 370697
  http://www.hrsoc.org.uk
  Mem Sec: John Fairlie
- ▲ Un-incorporated Society
- ○ *G; study & recording of all aspects of the Highland Railway Company
- ● Mtgs - Lib - PL
- M 280 i, 10 org, UK / 15 i, o'seas
- ¶ Highland Railway Jnl - 4; ftm only.

Highlands & Islands Sheep Health Association Ltd   (HISHA) 1988
- ■ Drummondhill, Stratherrick Rd, INVERNESS, IV2 4JY.   (hq)
  01463 713687   fax 01463 713687
  email info@hisha.org.uk   http://www.hisha.org.uk
  Sec: Eleanor A Fraser
- ▲ Company Limited by Guarantee
- ○ *B, *F; to create awareness of the dangers & financial implications of enzootic abortion of ewes (EAE)
- Gp Highland Mule Breeders Association
- ● Mtgs - Inf - Promotion of the availability of the EAE-free stock of members
- < Scot Agricl Org Soc (SAOS)
- M 240 i, 1 org
- ¶ HISHA NL - 3/4;   AR - 1;
  List of Accredited Flocks - 1; all ftm only.

Highway Electrical Manufacturers & Suppliers Association (HEMSA)   1998
- ■ Highdown House, Littlehampton, FERRING, W Sussex, BN12 6PG.   (hq)
  01903 705140
  email hemsa@bowden-house.co.uk
  http://www.highwayelectrical.org.uk/hemsa/
  Chief Exec: Gareth Pritchard
- ▲ Company Limited by Guarantee
- ○ *T; for manufacturers & suppliers to the highway electrical industry
- ● Conf - Mtgs - ET - Res - Exhib - Inf - LG
- M c 30 f

Hill Radnor Flock Book Society (HRFBS) 1949
NR   Montague Harris & Co, 16 Ship St, BRECON, Powys,
     LD3 9AD.   (hsb)
     01874 623200   fax 01874 623131
     email jal@montague-harris.co.uk
     http://www.hillradnor.co.uk
     Sec: John Lewis
▲   Un-incorporated Society
○   *B; to keep the rare breed alive
●   Mtgs - Annual show & sale
<   Nat Sheep Assn
M   45 i
¶   Flock Book - 1.

Hillclimb & Sprint Association Ltd (HSA) 1979
NR   11 Wellington Drive, Bowerhill, MELKSHAM, Wilts,
     SN12 6QW   (memsec/p)
     01225 700899
     http://www.hillclimbandsprint.co.uk
     Mem Sec: David Smith
○   *G, *S; hill climbing & sprinting in cars & motorcycles

Hillfort Study Group 1965
NR   Keble College, OXFORD, OX1 3PG.   (hsb)
     01978 824570
     email ian.brown@keble.ox.ac.uk
     http://www.hillfortstudygroup.org.uk
     Hon Sec: Dr Ian Brown
○   *P; to encourage the study & exchange of information relating
     to hillforts
●   Mtgs - Inf - Fieldwork - Excavation - Archives are curated at the
     Institute of Archaeology
M   80 i
     (Sub: £5)

Hilliard Society of Miniaturists 1982
NR   Priory Lodge, 7 Priory Rd, WELLS, Somerset, BA5 1SR.   (hq)
     01749 674472
     email hilliardsociety@aol.com
     http://www.art-in-miniature.org
▲   Un-incorporated Society
○   *A; to promote & inform on contemporary & modern miniature
     paintings
●   Exhib - VE
M   c 250 i
¶   NL - 2; ftm, £2 nm.

Hispanic & Luso Brazilian Council 1943
■   Canning House, 2 Belgrave Sq, LONDON, SW1X 8PJ.   (hq)
     020 7235 2303   fax 020 7838 9258
     email enquiries@canninghouse.org
     http://www.canninghouse.org
     Dir Gen: Dr Charles Goodson-Wickes
▲   Company Limited by Guarantee; Registered Charity
○   *E, *X; to stimulate understanding & engagement between
     Britain & the Hispanic & Luso-Brazilian world through
     dynamic debates, networking events & education activities
Gp   Arts & culture; Corporate; Education & outreach
●   Conf - ET - Exhib - Expt - Inf - Lib - LG
M   i, f & schools
¶   British Bulletin of Publications on Latin America, Spain &
     Portugal - 2;   NL - 52;
     Cultural Programme - 4;   AR - 1; all ftm.
     Information leaflets on special events.

Historic Aircraft Association (HAA) 1979
■   17 Ravensdale Ave, LEAMINGTON SPA, Warks, CV32 6NQ.
     (hsp)
     http://www.haa-uk.aero
     Sec: Stuart Powney
○   *G, *K; to further the preservation of historic aircraft in a flying
     condition (which involves the provision of a flight safety
     service to the public, the authorities, owners & display
     organisers)
Gp   Register of Pilots
●   Mtgs - ET - Inf
<   Eur Fedn of Light, Experimental & Vintage Aircraft (EFLEVA); R
     Aero Club; Aircraft Owners & Pilots Assn (AOPA)
M   170 i, UK / 10 i, o'seas

Historic Artillery (HA) 1987
■   23 Viewside Close, Corfe Mullen, WIMBORNE, Dorset,
     BH21 3ST.   (hsp)
     01202 690224
     email richardbarton@caving5.freeserve.co.uk
     Sec: Richard Barton
▲   Un-incorporated Society
○   *G; research into the science of artillery in history; promotion of
     historical re-enactment for educational purposes
Gp   Artillery Association GB; Computer database; Field research;
     Research into siege weapons & techniques
●   Res - SG - Inf - VE - Re-enactment
<   Siege Warfare in the Midlands; Coalhouse Fort Project
M   20 i, 2 org

Historic Canoe & Kayak Association (HCKA) 1989
■   14 Woodcroft, Crapstone, YELVERTON, Devon, PL20 7NU.
     (memsec/p)
     email hcka@btinternet.com   http://www.hcka.org.uk
     Contact: Membership Secretary
▲   Un-incorporated Society
○   *G; to promote an interest in historic canoes & kayaks
●   Res - Inf - Displaying historic craft
>   R Marines Museum
M   i
¶   Paddles Past (Jnl) - 4; ftm.   LM - 1.
     [subscription £13].

Historic Caravan Club (HCC) 1993
NR   Arwel, Victoria Rd, LLANWRTYD WELLS, Powys, LD5 4SU.
     (treas/p)
     http://www.historiccaravanclub.com
     Hon Treas: Margaret Squires
▲   Un-incorporated Society
Br   9 area coordinators
○   *G; to encourage the rescue, restoration, display & use of
     trailer caravans up to 1960, including horse-drawn ancestors
     of the touring caravan
●   Mtgs - Res - Exhib - Inf - Provision of displays at vintage rallies
<   Fedn of Brit Historic Vehicle Clubs; Assn of Caravan &
     Camping Exempted Orgs
M   210 i, UK / 3 i, 4 org, o'seas
¶   Wanderer (NL) - 8;   LM - 1;   Register of Member's
     Caravans - 1; all ftm only.
     Membership Hbk - free on joining.
     Historic Caravan Scene (Jnl) - irreg; ftm, £2.25 each nm.

Historic Commercial Vehicle Society (HCVS) 1958
■   Two Hoots, 305 Limpsfield Rd, Sanderstead, CROYDON,
     Surrey, CR2 9DJ.   (memsec/p)
     020 8651 0778
     email hcvs2011@gmail.com   http://www.hcvs.co.uk
     Mem Sec: Clive & Chrissie MacDonald
▲   Company Limited by Guarantee; Registered Charity
Br   11
○   *G; to promote the study & preservation of historic commercial
     vehicles over 20 years old
●   Mtgs - Inf - Lib - LG
M   3,500 i, UK / 60 i, o'seas
¶   Historic Commercial News - 9; ftm, £2.50 nm.   AR.

Historic Endurance Rallying Organisation (HERO) 1996
NR   Unit 13 Kenfig Industrial Estate, Margam, PORT TALBOT,
     SA13 2PE.   (hq)
     01656 740275   fax 01656 741013
     email enquiries@heroevents.eu
     http://www.heroevents.eu
     Gen Sec: Lynn Nedin
○   *G; endurance motor rallies for classic cars

Historic Farm Buildings Group (HFBG) 1985
NR   129 Hoblands, HAYWARDS HEATH, W Sussex, RH16 3SB.
     (memsec/p)
     http://www.hfbg.org.uk
     Mem Sec: Stephen Podd
○   *G; for those concerned with the past, present & future of
     historic farm buildings
●   Conf - Mtgs
M   i
¶   Review - 2.

Historic Houses Association (HHA) 1973
■   2 Chester St, LONDON, SW1X 7BB.   (hq)
     020 7259 5688
     email info@hha.org.uk   http://www.hha.org.uk
     Dir Gen: Nick Way
○   *K, *N; an association of owners & guardians of historic
     houses, parks, gardens & places of interest (& their
     associated contents) of Great Britain; formed to promote &
     safeguard their legitimate interests so far as they are
     consistent with the interests of the nation
●   Conf - Mtgs - Res - Exhib - Inf - Cooperation with art galleries
     & museums - Seminars
<   U Historic Houses
M   1,500 i, 20,000 friends
¶   Historic House - 4.   Jnl; ftm.
     Technical papers & guidelines.

Historic Libraries Forum
NR   The Library, Exeter College, Turl St, OXFORD, OX1 3DP.   (hsb)
     01865 279657
     email thomas.gordon@manchester.ac.uk
     http://www.historicallibrariesforum.org.uk
     Hon Sec: Joanna Bowring
○   *P; for all interested in historic libraries, particularly those
     without a home
●   Mtgs - Inf
M   500 i
¶   Bulletin - 3.   Bibliotheca.

Historic Society of Lancashire & Cheshire (HSLC) 1848
■   Flat 4 / 3 Bramhall Rd, Waterloo, LIVERPOOL, L22 3XA.   (hsb)
     0151-920 8213
     email rch2949@yahoo.co.uk   http://www.hslc.org.uk
     Hon Sec: Roger Hull
▲   Registered Charity
○   *L; to promote the study of any aspect of the history of
     Lancashire & Cheshire
●   Mtgs - Lib
M   266 i, 127 org
¶   Transactions - 1.

Historic Towns Forum (HTF) 1987
■   PO Box 22, BRISTOL, BS16 1RZ.   (hq)
     0117-975 0459   fax 0117-975 0460
     email ehtf@uwe.ac.uk   http://www.ehtf.org.uk
     Dir: Noël James
▲   Un-incorporated Society
○   *K; to establish & encourage contact between local authorities
     having responsibility for the management of historic towns &
     cities, & between those authorities & other public, private &
     voluntary sector agencies
Gp   Built environment; Retail; Tourism; Transport
●   Conf - Mtgs - ET - Res - Exhib - SG - Inf - VE - LG
<   Eur Assn of Historic Towns & Regions (EAHTR)
M   i, f & org
¶   NL - 4;   AR; both free.
     Membership Directory - 1; ftm only.
     Publications list available on request.
×   2009 (1 January) English Historic Towns Forum

Historical Association (HA) 1906
NR   59a Kennington Park Rd, LONDON, SE11 4JH.   (hq)
     020 7735 3901   fax 020 7582 4989
     email enquiry@history.org.uk   http://www.history.org.uk
     Chief Exec: Rebecca Sullivan
▲   Company Limited by Guarantee; Registered Charity
Br   59
○   *E, *P; to promote the study & teaching of history at all levels
●   Conf - Mtgs - ET - VE
M   5,300 i, 500 f, 2,000 schools, UK / 400 i, o'seas
¶   The Historian - 4.   History - 4.
     Teaching History - 4.   Primary History - 3.
     Annual Bulletin of Historical Literature.
     Pamphlets.   AR.

**Historical Breechloading Smallarms Association (HBSA)
1973**
■   BCM HBSA, LONDON, WC1N 3XX.   (mail)
     01376 563684
     email general.secretary@hbsa-uk.org
     http://www.hbsa-uk.org
     Gen Sec: Chris Smith
▲   Company Limited by Guarantee
Br   4
○   *G; to study the history, development, conservation,
     preservation & use of breechloading smallarms, ammunition
     & related items; to act as the national supervisory body for
     the sporting & competitive use of historical breechloading
     smallarms
●   Conf - Mtgs - ET - Res - Exhib - Comp - LG
<   Nat Rifle Assn
M   350 i, 50 affiliates
     (Sub: £35 i, £50 affiliates)
¶   Jnl - 1; ftm, £3.55 nm.   Report - 3; ftm, £2 nm.

Historical Diving Society (HDS) 1990
NR   55 Carillon Court, Oxford Rd, LONDON, W5 3SX.
     (memsec/p)
     email enquiries@thehds.com   http://www.thehds.com
     Mem Sec: Cheryl Wingert
▲   Registered Charity
○   *G; to provide a forum for all interested in the history of
     underwater descent, including all aspects of diving
     (commercial, amateur, naval, military, experimental &
     scientific)

Historical Maritime Society (HMS) 1995
■   2 Mount Zion, Brownbirks St, Cornholme, TODMORDEN,
     Lancs, OL14 8PG.
     01706 819248
     email grog@tesco.net   http://www.hms.org.uk
     Contact: Chris Jones
○   *G; historical re-enactment group that researches & portrays
     aspects of life in Horatio Nelson's Royal Navy

© CBD Research Ltd · Beckenham · BR3 5JS · Tel 020 8650 7745 · E-mail cbd@cbdresearch.com · www.cbdresearch.com

Historical Medical Equipment Society   (HMES)   1996
- ■ Medical School Museum, Stopford Building, University of Manchester, MANCHESTER, M13 9PL.   (hsp)
  0161-275 5546
  email peter.mohr@manchester.ac.uk
  Hon Sec: Peter Mohr
- ▲ Un-incorporated Society
- ○ *G; the study of old medical & surgical items & the history of medicine
- ● Conf - Mtgs - Inf - VE
- M 90 i, UK / 20 i, o'seas
- ¶ Bulletin - 2; ftm, £2 nm.

Historical Metallurgy Society Ltd   (HMS)   1962
- ■ 267 Kells Lane, Low Fell, GATESHEAD, Tyne & Wear, NE9 5HU.   (hsb)
  0191-482 1037
  email cranconsult@btinternet.com
  http://www.hist-met.org
  Hon Gen Sec: David Cranstone
- ▲ Company Limited by Guarantee; Registered Charity
- ○ *L; study, research & preservation of the historical & archaeological evidence of the extraction, smelting & working of metals & the manufacture of metal objects
- ● Conf
- < Inst Materials
- M 340 i, 31 org, UK / 170 i, 42 org, o'seas
- ¶ Historical Metallurgy (Jnl) - 2.   NL - 3.

Historical Military Mapping Group
   a group of the **British Cartographic Society**

Historical Model Railway Society   (HMRS)   1950
- NR Midland Railway Centre, Butterley Railway Station, RIPLEY, Derbys, DE5 3QZ.   (hq)
  01773 745959
  http://www.hmrs.org.uk
  Sec: P J Wilde
- ▲ Registered Charity
- ○ *G; for the study & recording of information relating to all the railways of the British Isles; public education on matters concerning these railways; construction, operation, preservation & public exhibition of models depicting them. (Nothing to do with toys)
- ● Mtgs - ET - Res - Exhib - Comp - SG - Inf - Lib - PL - VE
- M 1,900 i, UK & o'seas
- ¶ HMRS Jnl - 4;   HMRS News - 6; both ftm.
  North Eastern Record:
     Volume 1: Infrastructure;
     Volume 2: Rolling Stock;
     Volume 3: Locomotives;
  The Locomotives of the Stockton & Darlington Railway;
  British Railways Mark 1 Coaches;
     [all above; £24.95.]
  Many other publications.

History of Anaesthesia Society   (HAS)   1986
- ■ 49 Howey Lane, FRODSHAM, Cheshire, WA6 6DD. (pres-elect/p)
  01928 731888
  email gasflo@btinternet.com
  http://www.histansoc.org.uk
  Pres-Elect: Dr Anne M Florence
- ▲ Un-incorporated Society
- ○ *L; to promote interest & study in the worldwide history of anaesthesia
- ● Mtgs
- < Brit Soc for the History of Medicine (BSHM)
- M 318 i, UK / 82 i, o'seas
  (Sub: £20)
- ¶ Proceedings - 2; ftm, £6 nm.

History Curriculum Association   (HCA)   1990
- NR Windover, Punnetts Town, HEATHFIELD, E Sussex, TN21 9DS. (dir/p)
  01435 830109
  Dir: Christopher McGovern
- ▲ Un-incorporated Society
- ○ *K; to restore the history curriculum within the UK education system
- M supporters

History of Education Society (UK)   (HES(UK))   1967
- ■ Faculty of Education, University of Winchester, WINCHESTER, Hants, SO22 4NR.   (hsb)
  01962 827125
  email secretary@historyofeducation.org.uk
  http://www.historyofeducation.org.uk
  Sec: Dr Stephanie Spencer
- ▲ Registered Charity
- ○ *L; to study & research into the history of education; to support students
- ● Conf - ET - Res
- < Intl Standing Conf for History of Education (ISCHE)
- M 155 i, UK / 45 i, o'seas
  (Sub: £25)
- ¶ History of Education Jnl - 6; £50 m, £299 nm.
  History of Education Researcher - 2; ftm only.

Hitchin Chamber of Commerce & Industry   (HCCI)
- NR 7 Park St, HITCHIN, Herts, SG4 9AH.   (hq)
  01462 433652
- ▲ Un-incorporated Society
- ○ *C

HL7 UK Ltd   2000
- NR PO Box 7230, HOOK, Hants, RG27 9WX.   (hq)
  0870 011 2866   fax 0870 011 2867
  http://www.hl7.org.uk
  Sec: Andrew Hinchley
- ○ *P, *T; to support the development, promotion & implementation of HL [Health Level] healthcare standards, in order to meet the needs of healthcare organisations, professionals & healthcare software suppliers in the UK

Holiday Centres Association   (HCA)   1935
- ■ The Coppice, Rowe Close, Devonshire Park, BIDEFORD, Devon, EX39 5XX.   (hq)
  01237 421347
  email holidaycentres@aol.com
  http://www.holidaycentres.com
  Chief Exec: David Howell
- ▲ Company Limited by Guarantee
- ○ *T; interests of holiday centres
- ● Conf - Mtgs - Res - Stat - Inf - LG
- < Music Users Coun of Europe; Tourism Alliance
- M 53 f
- ¶ NL - 2; ftm only.   LM - 1; free.

Holistic Healers Association   1998
- NR 3 MacLean Grove, Stewartfield, EAST KILBRIDE, G74 4TJ.   (hq)
  01355 276410
  http://www.holistic-healers-association.co.uk
- ○ *P

Hollyhock Society, England, Scotland, Wales   1991
- ■ 29 Henrietta Street, CHELTENHAM, Glos, GL50 4AA.
  Pres & Hon Sec: Mrs Patricia A Meyrick
- ○ *H; study & protection of hollyhocks
- ● Exhib - VE
- M 9 i
  Note: also includes the Hollyhock Painting Society.

Holstein UK   1909
NR   Scotsbridge House, Scots Hill, RICKMANSWORTH, Herts,
        WD3 3BB.   (hq)
        01923 695200   fax 01923 770003
        email info@holstein-uk.org   http://www.holstein-uk.org
        Admin: Susan Boughton
○   *B
<   Assn of Show & Agricl Orgs; Nat Cattle Assn (Dairy)
M   c 10,000 i

Home Builders Federation   (HBF)   1947
NR   Byron House, 7-9 St James's St, LONDON, SW1A 1DW.   (hq)
        020 7960 1600   fax 020 7960 1601
        http://www.hbf.co.uk
        Chief Exec: Robert Ashmead
        Head of Media Relations: Pierre Williams
▲   Un-incorporated Society
Br   8
○   *T; to ensure a favourable economic, political & planning
        climate in the UK in which private housebuilders can operate
Gp   Planning; Political; Technical; Public relations; Taxation; Europe
●   Conf - Mtgs - ET - Stat - LG
<   Intl Housing Assn; Eur U Developers & Housebuilders
M   800 f
¶   House Builder Magazine - 10;   NL - 4; both ftm.

Home Business Alliance   (HBA)   1984
■   Werrington Business Centre, 86 Papyrus Rd, PETERBOROUGH,
        PE4 5BH.   (hq)
        0871 474 1015   fax 0871 474 1016
        email info@homebusiness.org.uk
        http://www.homebusiness.org.uk
        Chmn: Leonard Tondel,   Sec: Marion Owen
○   *T; for the self-employed, freelances, small family businesses &
        those wanting to set up their own home business new ones'
M   i
¶   eBOSS (email NL).

Home Decoration Retailers Association   (HDRA)
NR   225 Bristol Rd, Edgbaston, BIRMINGHAM, B5 7UB.   (hq)
        0121-446 6688   fax 0121-446 5215
        email info:bira.co.uk   http://www.bira.co.uk/hdra/
▲   Un-incorporated Society
○   *T; independent home decoration retailers & suppliers
●   Empl - ET - Inf - LG - Mtgs
<   Brit Indep Retailers Assn

Home Education Advisory Service   (HEAS)   1995
■   PO Box 98, WELWYN GARDEN CITY, Herts, AL8 6AN.   (mail)
        01707 371854   fax 01707 338467
        email enquiries@heas.org.uk   http://www.heas.org.uk
        Sec: Mrs Brenda Holliday
▲   Company Limited by Guarantee; Registered Charity
○   *E; advice & information on education at home instead of
        school
●   Conf - ET - Inf - Lib - Subscribers' advice line
¶   HEAS Bulletin - 4; ftm only.
        HEAS Introductory Information Pack; £2.50.
        HEAS Resources Book;   Home Education Hbk; both £8.75.
        Home Education Overseas; £1.50
        Maths pack; £9.75.
        Information leaflets:
            Special Education Needs; £1.50.
            Examinations;   Dyslexia; both £1.

Home Laundering Consultative Council   (HLCC)   1966
NR   3 Queen Sq, Bloomsbury, LONDON, WC1N 3AR.   (hq)
        020 7843 9460   fax 020 7843 9478
        http://www.care-labelling.co.uk
        Sec: A Mansell
○   *T; promotion & administration of a uniform system of care-
        labelling, both nationally & internationally
●   Mtgs - Inf
<   GINETEX
M   70 f, c 70 trade assns & educational bodies with an interest in
        care-labelling
¶   LM;   AR.   Other publications.

Homeless Link   2001
■   Gateway House, Milverton St, LONDON, SE11 4AP.   (hq)
        020 7840 4430   fax 020 7840 4431
        email info@homelesslink.org.uk
        http://www.homeless.org.uk
        Chief Exec: Jenny Edwards,   Co Sec: Alex Botha
▲   Company Limited by Guarantee; Registered Charity
○   *K, *N; relief of poverty, sickness & need caused by, or resulting
        in, a condition of homelessness
●   Conf - Mtgs - ET - Res - LG
M   25 i, 480 f
        (Sub: by turnover)
¶   Connect - 4; ftm, £28 yr nm.
        Members Mailing - 12; ftm only.   AR - 1; free.
        Various books & guides; listed on website.

Homeopathic Medical Association   (HMA)   1985
■   7 Darnley Rd, GRAVESEND, Kent, DA11 0RU.   (hq)
        01474 560336   fax 01474 327431
        email info@the-hma.org   http://www.the-hma.org
        Sec: Phil Hughes
▲   Company Limited by Guarantee
○   *P; to promote homoeopathy & homoeopathic education
●   Conf
M   i
¶   Homeopathy International (Jnl) - 4; £25.

Homes for Scotland
NR   5 New Mart Place, EDINBURGH, EH14 1RW.   (hq)
        0131-455 8350   fax 0131-455 8360
        email info@homesforscotland.com
        http://www.homesforscotland.com
        Exec Dir: Bruce Black
▲   Company Limited by Guarantee
Br   1
○   *T; to promote the long-term interests of the Scottish home
        building industry; to create awareness of the economic,
        social & environmental significance of home builders;
        interests include planning, water & drainage, design,
        environmental quality
Gp   Housing planning
●   Mtgs - Inf - LG
M   160 f
¶   NL - 12; ftm only.

Honest Food - the Campaign for Independent Food
a campaign run by the **Countryside Alliance**

Honey Association   (HA)   1940
■   Grayling, Portland House, Bressenden Place, LONDON,
        SW1E 5BH.   (asa)
        020 7932 1850
        email info@honeyassociation.com
        http://www.honeyassociation.com
        Sec: Walter J Anzer
▲   Company Limited by Guarantee
○   *T; interests of British honey importers & packers
●   Mtgs - PR - Technical services
<   Eur Fedn Honey Packers & Distributors (FEEDM)
M   16 f

© CBD Research Ltd · Beckenham · BR3 5JS · Tel 020 8650 7745 · E-mail cbd@cbdresearch.com · www.cbdresearch.com

Hong Kong Association   1961
- ■ Swire House, 59 Buckingham Gate, LONDON, SW1E 6AJ. (hq)
  020 7963 9447   fax 020 7828 6331
  email info@hkas.org.uk   http://www.hkas.org.uk
  Exec Dir: Capt Robert Guy
- ▲ Company Limited by Guarantee
- ○ *T, *X; to nurture the business & commercial relationship between the Hong Kong SAR & the UK
- ● Mtgs - LG
- < Hong Kong Soc
- M 100 f

Hong Kong Society   2008
- NR Swire House, 59 Buckingham Gate, LONDON, SW1E 6AJ. (hq)
  020 7963 9447   fax 020 7828 6331
  email info@hkas.org.uk   http://www.hkas.org.uk
- ○ *X
- ¶ NL.

Honorable Society of King's Inns   (HSKI)   1541
- IRL Henrietta St, DUBLIN 1, Republic of Ireland.   (hq)
  353 (1) 874 4840   fax 353 (1) 872 6048
  email info@kingsinns.ie   http://www.kingsinns.ie
- ○ *E, *P; barristers-at-law
- ● ET - Exam

Honourable Society of Cymmrodorion   (Anrhydeddus Gymdeithas y Cymmrodorion)   1751
- NR PO Box 55178, LONDON, N12 2AY.   (mail)
  http://www.cymmrodorion.org
  Sec: Peter Jeffreys
- ▲ Registered Charity
- ○ *L; seeks to address the burning question of Welsh life, past, present & future; organises an ambitious series of lectures at which speakers from academic & public life present papers in English & Welsh
- ● Mtgs - Res - Lib
- M c 800 i, c 80 org, UK / 30 i, 40 org, o'seas
- ¶ Transactions - 1; £15.
  Dictionary of Welsh Biography - online.

The Honourable The Irish Society   1613
- ■ Salters' Hall, 4 Fore St, LONDON, EC2Y 5DE.   (hq)
  020 7786 9876   fax 020 7786 9877
  email charlesf@irishsociety.co.uk
  Sec: C J H Fisher
- ▲ Charity incorporated by Royal Charter
- ○ *W; to aid & support the economic status of both institutions & individuals in County Londonderry through grant aid & charitable donations; to support cross-community self-help initiatives & educational projects, as well as individuals & small groups who apply for financial assistance
- ● Mtgs - VE - Sets up presentation meetings in the City of London for those in Northern Ireland seeking investment
- < The Corporation of the City of London
- M members are nominated by the livery companies of the City of London

Hop Merchants Association   (HMA)   1917
- ■ The Hopstore, Monksfield Lane, Newland, MALVERN, Worcs, WR13 5BB.   (pres/b)
  01905 830734   fax 01905 831790
  email paulcorbett@charlesfaram.co.uk
  Chmn: Paul Corbett
- ▲ Un-incorporated Society
- ○ *T; to promote the interests of members trading in hops grown in England

Hopkins Society   1990
- NR 35 Manor Park, Gloddaeth Avenue, LLANDUDNO, LL30 2SE.   (PRO)
  01492 875334
  Contact: Ambrose Boothby
- ▲ Un-incorporated Society
- ○ *A; for those interested in the work & life of Gerard Manley Hopkins, English poet & priest
- M i

Horatian Society   1934
- ■ St Benet's Hall, OXFORD, OX1 3LN.   (hsb)
  email john.eidinow@stb.ox.ac.uk
  Hon Sec: John S C Eidinow
- ▲ Un-incorporated Society
- ○ *A; the poet Horace & his works
- ● Annual dinner
- M 200 i
- ¶ AR (incl LM); ftm only.

Horse Rangers Association (Hampton Court) Ltd   (HRA)   1954
- ■ Royal Mews, Hampton Court Rd, EAST MOLESEY, Surrey, KT8 9BW.   (hq)
  020 8979 4196   fax 020 8941 3310
  email admin@horserangers.com
  http://www.horserangers.com
  Dir: Jackie Bryans
- ▲ Registered Charity
- Br 4
- ○ *Y; a uniformed youth organisation enabling young people to learn stable management & to ride
- Gp Riding for the Disabled - throughout the week in term time
- ● ET
- < Brit Horse Soc; Riding for the Disabled Assn
- M 400 i

Horse Sport Ireland   2007
- IRL Beech House, Millennium Park, Osberstown, NAAS, Co Kildare, Republic of Ireland.   (hq)
  353 (45) 850800   fax 353 (45) 850850
  email info@horsesportireland.ie
  http://www.horsesportireland.ie
  Chief Exec: Damian McDonald
- ○ *S; the governing body for equestrian sport in the Republic of Ireland & Northern Ireland
- < Féd Equestre Intle (FEI); Ir Sports Coun
- × 2007 (Equestrian Federation of Ireland (Irish Horse Board

Horserace Writers & Photographers Association   (HWPA)   1927
- ■ 1 North Lane, Dringhouses, YORK, YO24 2NS.   (pres/p)
  07789 983903
  email will.hayler@yahoo.com   http://www.hwpa.co.uk
  Pres: Will Hayler
- ▲ Un-incorporated Society
- Br 3
- ○ *P; to represent the interests of all racing media (TV, radio, newspapers, photographers) within the racing industry
- ● Derby awards lunch (London, 1st Monday in December)
- < Nat Turf Writers Assn (USA)
- M 303 i
- ¶ NL - 4/5.   Derby Awards brochure - 1.

Horseracing Sponsors Association   (HSA)   1993
- NR Stirling Way, BOREHAMWOOD, Herts, WD6 2AZ.   (hq)
  020 8207 4114
  http://www.horseracingsponsors.com
- ▲ Company Limited by Guarantee
- ○ *T; to provide practical help & advice for race sponsors; to work with racecourses to attract new sponsors; to represent sponsors within the industry

Horsescotland   1999
NR   Titwood Farm, Kilmaurs, KILMARNOCK, Ayrshire, KA3 2PN.
    (hq)
    01563 549802
    http://www.s-e-a.org.uk
    Chmn: Stephen MacGregor
▲   Company Limited by Guarantee
○   *N, *S; the governing body of equestrian sports & the umbrella
    body for equestrian activities & industry in Scotland
M   800 i, 17 org, 18 clubs
✕   2010 Scottish Equestrian Association (rebranded 6 May)

Horticultural Exhibitors Association   (HEA)   1946
■   The Cottage, Cow Green, Bacton, STOWMARKET, Suffolk,
    IP14 4HJ.   (hsp)
    01449 782013   fax 01449 782013
    email secretary@the-hea.freeserve.co.uk
    http://www.the-hea.co.uk
    Hon Sec: Mrs Sarah Clare
○   *T; interests of horticultural producers & suppliers who exhibit at
    horticultural & agricultural shows
Gp   Categories of membership: Floral, Sundries, Associate
●   Mtgs
M   182 f, show organisers
    (Sub: £55)
¶   NL - 4;   Hbk - 1; both ftm only.

Horticultural Trades Association   (HTA)   1899
■   Horticulture House, 19 High St, Theale, READING, Berks,
    RG7 5AH.   (hq)
    0118-930 3132   fax 0118-932 3453
    email info@the-hta.org.uk   http://www.the-hta.org.uk
    Dir Gen: David Gwyther
▲   Company Limited by Guarantee
○   *H, *T; to represent the UK garden industry; to promote the
    profitable growth of its retail & grower members
Gp   Association of British Conifer Growers; Association of Liner
    Producers (ALP); Association of Professional
    Landscapers (APL); British Rose Group; Tree & Hedging
    Group
●   Conf - Mtgs - ET - Exam - Res - Exhib - Stat - Inf - Lib - VE - LG
M   3,000 f
¶   HTA News - 12; ftm, £2 nm.   AR; free.

Hose Manufacturers' & Suppliers' Association   (HMSA)   1999
■   2 Waltham Court, Milley Lane, Hare Hatch, READING, Berks,
    RG10 9TH.   (hq)
    0118-940 3416   fax 0118-940 6258
    email info@feta.co.uk   http://www.feta.co.uk
    Dir Gen: Cedric Sloan
○   *T; the manufacture or supply of quality flexible hoses to the
    heating, ventilating & air conditioning industry
●   Mtgs - Inf
<   Heating & Ventilating Mfrs' Assn (HEVAC); Fedn Envtl Tr
    Assns (FETA)
M   4 f

Hospital Broadcasting Association
    the trading name of **National Association of Hospital
    Broadcasting Organisations**

Hospital Caterers Association   (HCA)   1948
■   Princess of Wales Community Hospital, Stourbridge Rd,
    BROMSGROVE, Worcs, B61 0BB.   (hsb)
    01527 488114
    email sewellyn.douglass-james@worcsmhp.nhs.uk
    http://www.hospitalcaterers.org
    Nat Sec: Sewellyn Douglass-James
Br   16
○   *P; to promote & improve the standards of catering in hospitals
    & healthcare establishments in Great Britain, Northern
    Ireland & elsewhere; to educate & train persons in healthcare
    catering services; to provide & improve the professional
    interests & status of those engaged in healthcare catering
    services
●   Conf - Mtgs - ET - Exhib - Comp - Inf - Lib - LG
<   Healthcare Catering Intl
M   400 i
¶   Hospital Caterer (Jnl) - 6.   Hospital Caterer Ybk - 1.
    Hygiene Good Practice Guide.
    Food Service Standards at Ward Level: good practice guide.

Hospital Consultants & Specialists Association   (HCSA)   1948
NR   1 Kingsclere Rd, Overton, BASINGSTOKE, Hants, RG25 3JA.
    (hq)
    01256 771777   fax 01256 770999
    email conspec@hcsa.com   http://www.hcsa.com
    Chief Exec: Stephen Campion
▲   Un-incorporated Society
○   *P, *U; to represent & advise senior hospital medical staff in the
    NHS & private sectors
●   Conf - Mtgs - SG - Stat - Inf - Empl
<   Trades U Congress (TUC)
M   3,336 i
¶   HCSA News.

Hospital Infection Society
    since 1 April 2011 the **Healthcare Infection Society**

Hospital & Medical Care Association   (HMCA)   1978
§   Beech Hall, KNARESBOROUGH, N Yorks, HG5 0EA.   (hq)
    01423 866985   fax 01423 866586
    email hmca@hmca.co.uk   http://www.hmca.co.uk
    HMCA/S plc, trading as the Health & Medical Care
    Association, offers health care plans to associations &
    professional, trade & industry groups to benefit their
    members

Hostelling International Northern Ireland   (HINI)   1931
■   22-32 Donegall Rd, BELFAST, BT12 5JN.   (hq)
    028 9032 4733   fax 028 9031 5889
    http://www.hini.org.uk
    Gen Sec: Ken Canavan
▲   Company Limited by Guarantee; Registered Charity
○   *Y; to promote an appreciation of the countryside among
    young people through provision of hostel accommodation
Gp   Fell walking
●   Conf - Mtgs - Exhib - Inf - VE
<   Intl Youth Hostel Fedn (IYHF)
M   6,500 i
¶   AR; free.
✕   c2007 Youth Hostel Association of Northern Ireland

Hot Water Association   (HWA)   2007
NR   17 Victoria Rd, Saltaire, SHIPLEY, W Yorks, BD18 3LQ.   (hsb)
    01274 583355   fax 01274 583355
    email info@hotwater.org.uk
    http://www.hotwater.org.uk
▲   Un-incorporated Society
○   *T; to support, drive & promote the sustained growth &
    improvement of standards within the entire domestic hot
    water industry
<   Construction Products Assn
✕   2007 (Manufacturers of Domestic Unvented Systems
    (Waterheater Manufacturers Association

Hotel Booking Agents Association   (HBAA)   1997

- ■   Chestnut Suite Office 9, Guardian House, GODALMING, Surrey, GU7 2EA.   (hq)
    0845 603 3349   fax 01483 243501
    email carolyn.peers@hbaa.org.uk
    http://www.hbaa.org.uk
    Operations Mgr: Carolyn Peers
- ▲   Company Limited by Guarantee
- ○   *T; to promote best practice for those involved in the procurement & provision of accommodation, meetings, conferences & events
- Gp   Agents; Venues
- ●   Conf - Mtgs - ET - Inf - VE - LG
- M   83 agents, 208 venues
    (Sub: £295.00 - £8,000.00)
- ¶   Code of Working Practice.

Hotel & Catering International Management Association
    since 2007 the **Institute of Hospitality**

Hound Trailing Association   (HTA)   1906

- ■   Ash Cottage, Blencow, PENRITH, Cumbria, CA11 0DB.   (hsp)
    01768 483686
    email hta.margaret@btopenworld.com
    http://www.houndtrailing.org.uk
    Sec: Margaret Baxter
- ▲   Company Limited by Guarantee
- ○   *S; Cumbrian hound trailing, in which dogs race over moorland, fields & fells following a trail made of a mixture of paraffin & oil of aniseed
- ●   Mtgs - Comp
- M   c 1,000 i
- ¶   Ybk; £2.50.   AR; free.

House Builders Association
    an association within the **National Federation of Builders**

Houses, Castles & Gardens of Ireland   (HCGI)   1971

- IRL   Ballyshemane House, RATHDRUM, Co Wicklow, Republic of Ireland.
    353 (87) 777 6428
    http://www.hcgi.ie
- ○   *G; to promote & market historic houses, castles & gardens that are open to the public in Ireland

Housing Institute of Ireland   1989

- IRL   c/o 50 Merrion Sq, DUBLIN 2, Republic of Ireland.
    353 (1) 661 8334   fax 353 (1) 661 0320
    Co-ordinator: Sally Blair
- ○   *P

Housman Society   1973

- ■   80 New Rd, BROMSGROVE, Worcs, B60 2LA.   (chmn/p)
    01527 874136
    email info@housman-society.co.uk
    http://www.housman-society.co.uk
    Chmn: J C Page
- ▲   Registered Charity
- Br   1; Japan, USA
- ○   *L; to foster interest in & promote knowledge of A[lfred] E[dward] Housman (1865-1959), his sister Clemence & brother Laurence
- ●   Mtgs - Res - Exhib - Inf - Lib - VE - Publications
- <   Alliance of Literary Socs
- M   300 i, UK / 40 i, o'seas
    (Sub: £10)
- ¶   Housman Jnl - 1; ftm, £6 nm.   NL - 2; free.
    The Name & Nature of Poetry.   Housman's Places.
    Unkind to Unicorns.   Soldier I Wish you Well.
    A Westerly Wanderer.   Three Bromsgrove Poets.

Hovercraft Club of Great Britain Ltd   (HCGB)   1966

- ■   PO Box 328, BOLTON, Lancs, BL6 4FP.   (hsp)
    01204 841248
    email info@hovercraft.org.uk
    http://www.hovercraft.org.uk
    Sec: Rev Granville Spedding,   Vice-Chmn: Chris Barlow
- ▲   Company Limited by Guarantee
- Br   7
- ○   *G, *S; construction & development of light sports hovercraft; including regulation of design & construction safety
- Gp   Competitions; Cruising & coastal events; Specialist publications
- ●   Conf - Mtgs - Comp - Inf - Lib/Archive - National hovercraft series racing - Cruising events (river & coastal) - Coastal racing
- <   Wld Hovercraft Fedn; Eur Hovercraft Fedn
- >   Hovercraft Museum
- M   700 i, 10 f, 5 org, UK / 30 i, 2 f, o'seas
- ¶   Light Hovercraft - 12; ftm, £2.50 nm.   AR - 1; free.
    Inland Racing Competition Regulation - 1; ftm; £4 nm.
    Racing Construction Regulation - 1; ftm, £4 nm.
    Cruising Construction Regulations - 1; ftm, £4 nm.
    Coastal Racing Construction Regulations - 1; ftm, £4 nm.
    Guide to Making Model Hovercraft - irreg; £6.
    Hovercraft Construction Guide - irreg; £17.
    Guideline to Safe Operation of Cruising Hovercraft; £3.
    Hover Humour; £1.50.

Hovercraft Search & Rescue UK   (HSR-UK)   1997

- ■   2 Park Court, Pyrford Rd, WEST BYFLEET, Surrey, KT14 6SD.   (hq)
    01932 340492   fax 0870 705 9541
    email info@hsr-uk.org   http://www.hsr-uk.org
    Chmn: Bill Allen
- ▲   Registered Charity
- ○   *G; to assist the emergency services & authorities in specialist search & rescue scenarios through the provision of hovercraft with pilots & trained personnel
- ●   ET - Search & rescue
- M   30 i
- ¶   NL - 4; free by email.
- ×   2008 Association of Search & Rescue Hovercraft

Hovercraft Society   1971

- NR   24 Jellicoe Avenue, Alverstoke, GOSPORT, Hants, PO12 2PE.   (memsec/p)
    email enquiries@thehovercraftsociety.org.uk
    http://www.thehovercraftsociety.org.uk
    Mem Sec: Brian Russell
- ▲   Un-incorporated Society
- ○   *G; the encouragement of invention, research & development of hovercraft & other related issues
- ●   Mtgs - VE
- M   i
- ¶   NL - 4; ftm.

Howard League for Penal Reform   1921

- NR   1 Ardleigh Rd, LONDON, N1 4HS.   (hq)
    020 7249 7373
    http://www.howardleague.org
    Dir: Frances Crook
- ▲   Company Limited by Guarantee; Registered Charity
- ○   *K; advancement of constructive penal & social policies
- ●   Conf - Mtgs - ET - Res - VE - LG
- <   John Howard Soc of: Canada / S Australia / British Columbia
- M   3,000 i, 50 f, 50 org, UK / 300 i, 10 f, 10 org, o'seas
- ¶   HLM: Howard League Magazine - 4.
    Missing the Grade: Education for Children in Prison.
    Suicide & Self Harm Prevention (4 reports).
    Children in Prison (10 reports).

HR Society Ltd   1970
NR   1-5 Stud Offices, Redmenham Park Farm, Redmenham,
      ANDOVER, Hants, SP11 9AQ.   (hq)
      01264 774004   fax 01264 774009
      email network@hrsociety.co.uk
      http://www.hrsociety.co.uk
      Sec: Lara Roberts
▲   Company Limited by Guarantee; Registered Charity
○   *L; to promote the study & advancement of education in the
      field of manpower policy (human resources) management,
      planning & utilisation
Gp   Financial services special interest
●   Conf - Mtgs - ET - Res - SG - Inf
M   63 i, 22 f
¶   Manpower News - irreg; ftm only.   AR - 1; free.
      Spotlight (NL) - 4; ftm & free to Health Service.

HS2 Action Alliance
NR   The Red House, 10 Market Square, AMERSHAM, Bucks,
      HP7 0DQ.   (regd off)
      01494 773436
      email info@hs2actionalliance.org
      http://www.hs2actionalliance.org
      Dir: Hilary Wharf
○   *K, *N; works with 70 other groups to stop the new high speed
      line from London to Birmingham & on

Huguenot Society of Great Britain & Ireland   1885
■   PO Box 444, RUISLIP, Middx, HA4 4GU.   (hq)
      email secretary@huguenotsociety.org.uk
      http://www.huguenotsociety.org.uk
▲   Registered Charity
○   *L; to collect & publish information on the history & genealogy
      of the Huguenots, particularly those who took refuge in the
      British Isles, & their influence on the culture, politics &
      economy of Britain & Ireland
Gp   Irish section (Dublin)
●   Conf - Mtgs - Res - Inf - Lib - VE
M   1,086 i, 107 libraries, UK / 245 i, o'seas
¶   Proceedings - 1; ftm, £8 nm.   NL - 2; ftm only.
      Quarto Series - irreg; £5-£11 m, £12-£24 nm.
      CDs of some of the above; £17.50 m, £19.99 nm.
      Set of CDs: £125 m, £150 nm.
      Microfiches of 1-47 of the above; £4 (each) m, £5 nm.
      New series - irreg; £10-£15 m, £15-£20 nm.

**Hull & Humber Chamber of Commerce, Industry & Shipping
1837**
■   34-38 Beverley Rd, HULL, HU3 1YE.   (hq)
      01482 324976   fax 01482 213962
      email info@hull-humber-chamber.co.uk
      http://www.hull-humber-chamber.co.uk
      Chief Exec: Dr Ian Kelly
▲   Company Limited by Guarantee
Br   Grimsby, Hull
○   *C
Gp   Chambers of Trade: Bridlington, Grimsby & Cleethorpes
●   Conf - Mtgs - ET - Res - Exhib - Expt - Inf - LG
<   Brit Chams Comm; Yorkshire & Humber Chams Comm
>   Brit Caribbean Cham Comm
M   1,440 f, UK / 100 f, o'seas
      (Sub: £99-£800 UK / £99 o'seas)
¶   Business Intelligence - 6; ftm.

Human Genetics Alert   (HGA)   2000
■   22B St Kilda's Rd, LONDON, N16 5BZ.   (hsp)
      020 7502 7516   fax 020 7502 7516
      email david.king@hgalert.org   http://www.hgalert.org
      Sec: Dr David King
▲   Company Limited by Guarantee
○   *K; an independent secular watchdog group on human
      genetics, opposed to some developments such as genetic
      discrimination, cloning & inheritable genetic engineering of
      human beings.
●   Inf
M   30 i
¶   Human Genetics NL - 6.

Humane Slaughter Association   (HSA)   1911
NR   The Old School, Brewhouse Hill, WHEATHAMPSTEAD, Herts,
      AL4 8AN.   (hq)
      01582 831919   fax 01582 831414
      email info@hsa.org.uk   http://www.hsa.org.uk
      Sec: Donald Davidson
▲   Registered Charity
○   *V; promotion of humane methods of slaughter; introduction of
      reforms in cattle markets; welfare of animals in transit
●   ET - Res - Exhib - Inf - Lib - LG
M   605 i, 30 f, UK / 20 i, o'seas
¶   AR.   NL; both ftm.
      Numerous educational booklets, technical notes, videos.

Humanist Association of Ireland   (HAI)   1993
IRL   Rose Cottage, Coach Road, Balrothery, BALBRIGGAN,
      Co Dublin, Republic of Ireland.   (hq)
      353 (1) 841 3116
      email info@humanism.ie   http://www.humanism.ie
      Chmn: Dick Spicer
▲   Company Limited by Guarantee; Registered Charity
○   *K; to promote the ideals & values of humanism

Humanist Society of Scotland   (HSS)   1989
■   272 Bath St, GLASGOW, G2 4JR.   (hq)
      0870 874 9002
      email info@humanism-scotland.org.uk
      http://www.humanism-scotland.org.uk
      Convenor: Les Mitchell
▲   Registered Charity
○   *G; seeks to represent the views of people in Scotland who wish
      to lead good & worthwhile lives guided by reason &
      compassion rather than religion & superstition
Gp   Bioethics; Ceremonies; Education; Media; Public affairs
●   Conf - Mtgs - ET - Res - Exhib - Comp - SG - Inf - LG - Legal
      weddings, funerals & namings
<   Intl Humanist & Ethical U; Eur Humanist Fedn; Humanist Coun
      of the Isles
M   6,500 i
      (Sub: £20)
¶   Humanitie - 4; ftm, £2.50 nm.

Humanities Association   (Hums)   1984
NR   Humanities Wirral Education Centre, Acre Lane,
      BROMBOROUGH, Wirral, CH62 7BZ.   (hsb)
      0151-346 6503
      http://www.hums.org.uk
      Sec: Deirdre Smith
○   *E; an independent forum for debate about major issues in all
      aspects of humanities education
●   Conf - Mtgs - Exhib - LG
<   Devt Educ Assn
M   130 i, UK / 5 i, o'seas
¶   Humanities Too;   Humanities Now; both available on website.

© CBD Research Ltd · Beckenham · BR3 5JS · Tel 020 8650 7745 · E-mail cbd@cbdresearch.com · www.cbdresearch.com

Hundred Group of Finance Directors   1975
NR   Vodafone Group plc, The Connection, NEWBURY, Berks,
       RG14 2FN.   (chmn/b)
       email thehundredgroup@kpmg.co.uk
       http://www.one-hundred-group.production.investis.com
       Chmn: Andy Halford
○   *P; represents the finance directors of the UK's largest
       companies, with membership drawn mainly from
       boardrooms of the FTSE 100
Gp   Financial reporting; Investor relations & markets; Pensions; Tax
●   LG - Mtgs
M   107 i

Hunter Archaeological Society   1912
■   Royd Farm, Carr Rd, Deepcar, SHEFFIELD, S Yorks, S36 2NR.
       (hsp)
       0114-288 2640
       http://www.shef.ac.uk/archaeology/hunter/
       Hon Sec: Dr Ruth Morgan
▲   Registered Charity
○   *L; to study & preserve the archaeology & history of S Yorkshire
       & N Derbyshire
●   Mtgs - VE - Field work
M   200 i
¶   Transactions - biennial;   NL; both ftm.

Hunterian Society   1819
NR   Lettsom House, 11 Chandos St, LONDON, W1G 9EB.
       (admin/b)
       020 7436 7363
       email info@hunteriansociety.org.uk
       http://www.hunteriansociety.org.uk
       Admin: Betty Smallwood
▲   Registered Charity
○   *L; the cultivation & promotion of the science & practice of
       medicine
       The society was formed to commemorate John Hunter (1728-
       1793), 'the father of scientific surgery'
●   Mtgs
M   490 i
¶   Transactions - 1.

Hunting Association of Ireland   (HAI)
IRL   Friarstown Lodge, KILMALLOCK, Co Limerick, Republic of
        Ireland.   (hq)
        353 (85) 110 0645
        email hunting@hai.ie   http://www.hai.ie
▲   Company Limited by Guarantee
○   *N, *S; to represent the bodies controlling hunting in Ireland
Gp   Constituent bodies:
        Irish Foot Harriers Association
        Irish Masters of Beagles Association
        Irish Masters of Foxhounds Association
        Irish Masters of Harriers Association
        Irish Masters of Mink Hounds Association
        Ward Union Staghounds

Huntingdonshire Local History Society   1959
■   2 Croftfield Rd, Godmanchester, HUNTINGDON, Cambs,
       PE29 2ED.   (memsec/p)
       01480 411202
       email huntslocalhistory@yahoo.com
       http://www.huntslhs.org.uk
       Mem Sec: Mrs Mary Hopper
▲   Registered Charity
Br   1
○   *L; to promote the advancement of public education through
       the study of local history in the former county (now district
       borough) of Huntingdonshire
●   Mtgs - Res - Exhib - SG - VE
<   Cambridge Antiquarian Soc
M   c 200 i
¶   NL - 2;   AR.
       Records of Huntingdon - 1; (special Oliver Cromwell edition
       available).

Huntington's Disease Association   (HDA)   1971
■   Neurosupport Centre, Norton St, LIVERPOOL, L3 8LR.   (hq)
       0151-298 3298   fax 0151-298 9440
       email info@hda.org.uk   http://www.hda.org.uk
       Chief Exec: Cath Stanley
▲   Company Limited by Guarantee; Registered Charity
Br   34
○   *W; to provide help & support to sufferers of the disease; to
       promote research
●   Conf - Mtgs - ET - Res - Inf - Family counselling service -
       Support groups - Films - Speakers available
<   Intl Huntington's Disease Assn
M   8,000 i
¶   NL - 2;   Factsheets; AR; all free.
       Case Notes for Professionals; £8.50.
       Physicians Guide to the Management of Huntington's
       Disease; £5.75.
       Publications list available.

Hurdy-Gurdy Society   (HGS)   1982
■   47 Tudor Gardens, STONY STRATFORD, Bucks, MK11 1HX.
       (hsp)
       01908 565339
       email michaelpmuskett@beeb.net
       Hon Sec: Michael Muskett
▲   Un-incorporated Society
Br   80
○   *D, *G; to further the knowledge of the hurdy-gurdy, its history,
       construction, playing techniques & repertoire
●   ET - Res - Inf - Regional playing days
M   80 i, 1 f, UK / 6 i, 2 f, o'seas
¶   Jnl - 4.   LM - 1.

Hurlingham Polo Association   (HPA)   1874
NR   Manor Farm, Little Coxwell, FARINGDON, Oxon, SN7 7LW.
       (hq)
       01367 242828   fax 01367 242829
       email enquiries@hpa-polo.co.uk
       http://www.hpa-polo.co.uk
       Chief Exec: David Woodd
Br   affiliated clubs in British Isles & Commonwealth
○   *S; to act as the governing body for polo in the UK
●   Inf
<   Fedn of Intl Polo
M   2,000 i, 50 org, UK / 28 org, o'seas
¶   HPA Ybk (Blue Book) - 1; ftm, £10 nm.
       HPA Arena Ybk - 1; ftm, £10 nm.

Hydrographic Society UK   2004
■   PO Box 103, PLYMOUTH, Devon, PL4 7YP.   (hq)
       01752 223512   fax 01752 223512
       email helen@ths.org.uk   http://www.ths.org.uk
       Mgr & Co Sec: Helen Atkinson
▲   Company Limited by Guarantee; Registered Charity
Br   5; Ireland, Middle East, International
○   *L; to promote the development & understanding of
       hydrography & hydrographic learning; to facilitate the
       exchange of ideas & practices
●   Conf - Mtgs - Exhib - Inf - Publications
<   Intl Fedn of Hydrographic Socs; UK GeoForum
M   c 475 i, c 60 f, UK / c 110 i, c 30 f, o'seas
¶   Soundings - 4; free. - 4; ftm, £70 yr nm.
       Conference/Seminar Proceedings - irreg; £5.
       Proceedings of seminars & symposia; & Special
       Publications; £3.50. £50.
       Publications list available; free.

Hydrotherapy Association
NR   14 Crown Street, CHORLEY, Lancs, PR7 1DX.   (hq)
       01257 262124
       email admin@thehypnotherapyassociation.co.uk
       http://www.thehypnotherapyassociation.co.uk
       Sec: Costas Lambrias
○   *P; to maintain a national register of practising hypnotherapists
<   UK Confed of Hypnotherapy Orgs

Hymn Society of Great Britain & Ireland   1936
- ■ 99 Barton Rd, Scotforth, LANCASTER, LA1 4EN.   (hsp)
  01524 66740   fax 01524 66740
  email robcanham@haystacks.fsnet.co.uk
  http://www.hymnsocietygbi.org.uk
  Hon Sec: Rev Robert A Canham
- ▲ Registered Charity
- ○ *A, *L; to promote the use of hymns in Christian worship;
  research into hymnody
- Gp Art & literature; Educational; General interest & hobbies;
  Learned, scientific & technical societies; Research
  organisations; Religious organisations
- ● Conf - Res - SG - Inf
- < Hymn Soc in the USA & Canada
- M 369 i, 54 libraries, UK / 72 i, o'seas
- ¶ Bulletin - 4; ftm, £2.50 nm.   NL - 4; free.
  Festival of Hymns (booklet) - 1; ftm, £2.50 nm.
  Occasional Papers - irreg; ftm, £2.50 nm.   AR - 1; free.

Hyperactive Children's Support Group   (HACSG)   1977
- ■ 71 Whyke Lane, CHICHESTER, W Sussex, PO19 7PD.   (hsp)
  01243 539966
  email hyperactive@hacsg.org.uk
  http://www.hacsg.org.uk
  Dir & Founder: Mrs Sally Bunday
- ▲ Registered Charity
- Br London
- ○ *K; to support,advise & provide information for parents, carers
  & professionals interested in ADHD/hyperactivity & autistic
  spectrum disorders; to promote research & disseminate
  information on the rule of diet & nutrition
- ● Conf - ET - Inf
- < Foresight; Autism Unravelled; FAB-Food & Behaviour Res;
  Sustain; Food Cmsn; Brain Bio-Centre
- M 450 i, 50 f, 10 org, UK / 12 i, o'seas
- ¶ Jnl - 3; £15 m, £2 each nm.
  ADHD / Hyperactive Children: A Guide for Parents; ftm, £6 nm.
  Introductory pack; free.

Hypermobility Syndrome Association   (HMSA)   1992
- ■ 49 Orchard Crescent, Oreston, PLYMOUTH, Devon,
  PL9 7NF.   (hsp)
  0845 345 4465
  email info@hypermobility.org
  http://www.hypermobility.org
  Admin: Donna Wicks
- ▲ Registered Charity
- ○ *W; to provide information & support for those affected by the
  inheritable syndrome; to promote knowledge &
  understanding within the medical profession & general public
- < Brit Coalition Heritable Disorders (Connective Tissue)
- M 400 i, UK / 60 i, o'seas

Hypoparathyroidism UK   (HPTH UK)
- NR 6 The Meads, EAST GRINSTEAD, W Sussex, RH19 4DF.   (hq)
  01342 316315
  http://www.hpth.org.uk
  Dir: Liz Glenister
- ▲ Registered Charity
- ○ *M, *W; to improve the diagnosis, prevention & treatment of
  hypoparathyroidism & other parathyroid conditions; to
  provide support, information & advocacy for people with all
  parathyroid conditions, their families, friends & carers
- ● Inf - Helpline
- < Genetic Alliance UK; Rare Disease UK
- ¶ NL; ftm.

Hysterectomy Association   1998
- ■ West View, West Street, Broadwindsor, BEAMINSTER, Dorset,
  DT1 3QQ.   (hq)
  0844 357 5917
  email info@hysterectomy-association.org.uk
  http://www.hysterectomy-association.org.uk
  Dir: Linda Parkinson-Hardman
- ▲ Un-incorporated Society
- ○ *M, *W; to provide impartial, clear & timely information &
  support to women who have, or who are thinking of having,
  a hysterectomy
- ● ET - Res - Inf
- < Nat Coun for Voluntary Orgs; Brit Assn for Counselling &
  Therapy
- M 1,000 i, UK / 500 i, o'seas
- ¶ The Pocket Guide to Hysterectomy; £7.
  101 Handy Hints for a Happy Hysterectomy; £7.

© CBD Research Ltd · Beckenham · BR3 5JS · Tel 020 8650 7745 · E-mail cbd@cbdresearch.com · www.cbdresearch.com

**IA the Ileostomy & Internal Pouch Support Group (IA)
1956**
■ 1-5 Mill Rd, BALLYCLARE, Co Antrim, BT39 9DR. (hsp)
   0800 018 4724   fax 028 9332 4606
   email info@iasupport.org   http://www.iasupport.org
   Nat Sec: Mrs Anne Demick
▲ Registered Charity
Br 55
○ *W; to help people return to full & active lives following surgery
   for the removal of the colon; to promote research into the
   causes of inflammatory bowel diseases (ulcerative colitis &
   Crohn's disease)
Gp Internal pouch; Trained visitors; Welfare
● Conf - Mtgs - Res - Exhib - Inf - VE - LG
   Helpline: 0800 018 4724
< Intl Ostomy Assn (IOA); Eur Ostomy Assn (EOA)
M 10,000 i, 25 f
¶ IA Jnl - 4; ftm.   The Ostomy Book; £10.
   The IA Journal, omnibus edition [Hbk]; £5.
   Leaflets on various aspects of ileostomy; free.

IBS Network
   the registered name of the **Gut Trust**

ICC United Kingdom
   see **International Chamber of Commerce - UK National
   Committee**

Ice Cream Alliance Ltd (ICA) 1945
NR 3 Melbourne Court, Pride Park, DERBY, DE24 8LZ. (hq)
   01332 203333   fax 01332 203420
   email info@ice-cream.org   http://www.ice-cream.org
   Chief Exec: Mark Gossage
▲ Company Limited by Guarantee
Br 10
○ *T; to protect, inform & represent the UK ice cream industry
● Conf - Mtgs - Res - Exhib - Comp - Inf - Lib - PL - VE - LG
M 800 i, f, 1 org, UK / 100 i, f & org, o'seas
¶ Ice Cream - 11; £110 m.

Ice Hockey UK (IHUK) 1991
NR 19 Heather Avenue, Rise Park, ROMFORD, Essex, RM1 4SL.
   (hq)
   07917 194264   fax 01708 725241
   email ihukoffice@yahoo.co.uk
   http://www.icehockeyuk.co.uk
   Chmn: Eamon Covery
▲ Company Limited by Guarantee
○ *S; national governing body for the sport of ice hockey
Gp Elite League; English Ice Hockey Association; Scottish Ice
   Hockey
● ET - Exam - Comp - Inf - PL - LG
< Intl Ice Hockey Fedn
M 10,000 i, 65 org

Icelandic Horse Society of Great Britain Ltd (IHSGB) 1986
■ 52 Burridge Rd, Burridge, SOUTHAMPTON, Hants,
   SO31 1BT. (regd off)
   email office@ihsgb.co.uk   http://www.ihsgb.co.uk
   Sec: Debbie Ede
▲ Company Limited by Guarantee; Registered Charity
○ *B; to encourage, promote & improve the breeding & use of the
   Icelandic horse
Gp Breeding; Sports; Youth
● Conf - Mtgs - ET - Exhib - Comp - EXpt - Inf - Lib - VE
< Intl Fedn of Icelandic Horse Assns (FEIF)
M 300 i
¶ Sleipnir (Jnl) - 6; £32 yr m.

Icelandic Sheep Breeders of Britain
   see **British Icelandic Sheep Breeders Group**

ICHCA International Ltd
§ 85 Western Rd (suite 2), ROMFORD, Essex, RM1 3LS.
   01708 735295
   email info@ichca.com   http://www.ichca.com
   Dir (UK): Margaret Llewellyn
   an international body promoting efficient & economic
   movement of goods from origin to destination by air, rail,
   road & sea

Ichthyosis Support Group (ISG) 1997
NR PO Box 1404, WOKING, Surrey, GU22 2LS. (hq)
   0845 602 9202
   email isg@ichthyosis.org.uk   http://www.ichthyosis.org.uk
   Sec: Sue Corbett
▲ Company Limited by Guarantee; Registered Charity
○ *W; to help & support people suffering from Ichthyosis - dry,
   thickened, flaky or scaly skin

ICOM Energy Association (ICOM) 2004
NR Camden House, Warwick Rd, KENILWORTH, Warks,
   CV8 1TH. (hq)
   01926 513748   fax 01926 855017
   email peter.mccree@icomenergyassociation.org.uk
   http://www.icomenergyassociation.org.uk
   Chief Exec: Peter McCree
▲ Company Limited by Guarantee
○ *T; manufacturers & distributors of combustion equipment
   including boilers, burners, air heaters, radiant heaters,
   controls
Gp Air heaters; Boilers (commercial); Boilers (industrial process);
   Burners; Controls; Radiant heaters; Water heaters
● Mtgs - Stat - LG
M 44 f

ICRA (formerly the Internet Content Rating Association)
   An international body & part of the Family Online Safety
   Institute, which is concerned with a safer internet

ICT Ireland (ICT) 2001
IRL Confederation House, 84-86 Lower Baggot St, DUBLIN 2,
   Republic of Ireland. (hq)
   353 (1) 605 1569   fax 353 (1) 638 1569
   email paul.sweetman@ibec.ie   http://www.ictireland.ie
   Dir: Paul Sweetman
○ *T; to represent companies in the information &
   communications technology sector
Gp Audiovisual Federation; Consumer Electronic Distributors
   Association; Irish Cellular Industry Association; Irish Software
   Association; Telecommunications & Internet Federation;
   White Goods Association
< Ir Business & Emplrs Confedn (IBEC)
M 300 f

ideasUK 1987
NR Williams House, 11-15 Columbus Walk, Atlantic Wharf,
   CARDIFF, CF10 4BZ. (hq)
   0870 902 1658   fax 029 2049 8403
   email info@ideasuk.com   http://www.ideasuk.com
▲ Company Limited by Guarantee; Registered Charity
○ *K; to promote the benefits of employee suggestion schemes to
   industry, commerce & the public sector
M i, f, government depts
¶ News - 4;   LM;   Annual Survey; all ftm only.
   Suggestion Schemes: the management tool of the 90's (1995).

Ileostomy & Internal Pouch Support Group
see **IA**

Imaginative Book Illustration Society (IBIS) 1995
NR   50 Lauderdale Mansions, Lauderdale Rd, LONDON,
       W9 1NE.   (hsp)
       http://www.bookillustration.org
       Hon Sec: Robin Greer
○   *A; to study & research imaginatively illustrated books, mainly
       in the English language
M   200 i, 80 f, UK / 80 i, 20 f, o'seas
¶   IBIS Jnl - 2 yrly.   IBIS Studies - 3.

Immigration Law Practitioners' Association (ILPA) 1984
■   Lindsey House, 40-42 Charterhouse St, LONDON,
       EC1M 6JN.   (hq)
       020 7251 8383   fax 020 7251 8384
       email info@ilpa.org.uk   http://www.ilpa.org.uk
       Gen Sec: Alison Harvey
▲   Company Limited by Guarantee
○   *P
●   Conf - Mtgs - ET - Res - LG
M   589 i, 398 f, 125 org
¶   Publications - see website

Imperial Society of Knights Bachelor (ISKB) 1908
■   1 Throgmorton Avenue, LONDON, EC2N 2BY.   (hq)
       020 7374 8974   fax 020 7374 8968
       email iskb99@supanet.com   http://www.iskb.co.uk
       Clerk to the Council: Richard L Jenkins
▲   Registered Charity
○   *W; participation by its members in the UK & Commonwealth
       in charitable work compatible with upholding the status &
       dignity of Knights Bachelor
●   Mtgs - Inf - Lib - Annual service of dedication
¶   Chivalry - 1/2; free.
       The Story of the Knights Bachelor; ftm.

Imperial Society of Teachers of Dancing (ISTD) 1904
NR   Imperial House, 22-26 Paul St, LONDON, EC2A 4QE.   (hq)
       020 7377 1577
       http://www.istd.org
       Chief Exec: Jon Singleton
▲   Registered Charity
Br   10; 37 countries o'seas
○   *D, *P; professional society for teachers of dancing & an
       examination board
Gp   Ballroom; Cecchetti ballet; Classical Greek; Dance research;
       Disco; Freestyle; Imperial ballet; Jazz; Latin American;
       Modern; National; Natural movement; Rock & roll; Scottish;
       Sequence; Tap
M   7,000 i, UK / 2,900 i, o'seas

Imported Tobacco Products Advisory Council (ITPAC) 1974
■   Rondle Wood House, Milland, LIPHOOK, Hants, GU30 7LA.
       (hsp)
       07900 197888   fax 01730 821397
       email wyndham@carverw.com
       Sec-Gen: Wyndham H Carver
▲   Un-incorporated Society
○   *T; to represent the interests of importers of cigars, tobaccos &
       cigarettes to government & other relevant bodies; to provide
       information on tobacco & the industry
●   Mtgs - Res - Inf - LG
M   11 f, UK / 1 f, o'seas

Imported Tyre Manufacturers' Association (ITMA) 1979
■   5a Pindock Mews, LONDON, W9 2PY.   (hsp)
       020 7289 1043   fax 020 7286 9859
       email prt@itma-europe.com
       http://www.itma-europe.com
       Dir: Peter Taylor
▲   Company Limited by Guarantee
○   *T; for tyre importers & manufacturers in the UK
●   Mtgs - Stat - Inf - LG
<   Tyre Ind Fedn (TIF)
M   20 f

Inclusion Ireland National Association for People with an Intellectual
       Disability   1999
IRL   Unit C2, The Steelworks, Foley St, DUBLIN 1, Republic of
       Ireland.   (hq)
       353 (1) 855 9891   fax 353 (1) 855 9904
       email info@inclusionireland.ie
       http://www.inclusionireland.ie
       Chief Exec: Deirdre Carroll
▲   Company Limited by Guarantee; Registered Charity
○   *N, *W; an umbrella group for organisations in the intellectual
       disability sector
<   Inclusion Intl; Inclusion Europe
M   160 org
×   2006 National Association for the Mentally Handicapped of
       Ireland

Incontact
       in June 2008 merged with the Continence Foundation to become the
       Bladder & Bowel Foundation

Incorporated Association of Organists (IAO) 1913
■   Pengegon, 13 St Folra's Rd, LITTLEHAMPTON, W Sussex,
       BN17 6BD.   (gensec/p)
       01903 725002
       http://www.iao.org.uk
       Gen Sec: Malcolm Hawke
▲   Company Limited by Guarantee; Registered Charity
Br   80; 10 (inc Australia, N Zealand, S Africa)
○   *D, *E; to promote the education & enjoyment of all who love
       the (pipe) organ & its music, players & listeners alike; to
       encourage training & education to improve standards at all
       levels
●   Conf - Mtgs - ET
M   6,000 i, UK / 1,000 i, o'seas
       (Sub: £22 UK / £24.10 o'seas)
¶   Organists' Review - 4; ftm.

Incorporated Association of Preparatory Schools
       since 2008-09 **Independent Association of Preparatory
       Schools**

**Incorporated Guild of Hairdressers, Wigmakers & Perfumers
(Guild of Hairdressers) 1882**
■   Unit 1e Redbrook Business Park, BARNSLEY, S Yorks,
       S75 1JN.   (hq)
       01226 786555
       http://www.hairboo.com
       Master: Bill Shaw
▲   Company Limited by Guarantee
○   *P; to promote & advise the hairdressing industry
●   Conf - Mtgs - Exam - Comp - Inf - LG
M   580 i
¶   NL - 4;   AR - 1; ftm only.
       Note: Uses the title Guild of Hairdressers

© CBD Research Ltd · Beckenham · BR3 5JS · Tel 020 8650 7745 · E-mail cbd@cbdresearch.com · www.cbdresearch.com

Incorporated National Association of British & Irish Millers Ltd (NABIM) 1878

NR   21 Arlington St, LONDON, SW1A 1RN.   (hq)
     020 7493 2521
     http://www.nabim.org.uk
     Co Sec: Nigel Bennett
▲   Company Limited by Guarantee
○   *T; for UK flour millers
●   Conf - Mtgs - ET - Exam - Stat - Inf - LG
M   32 f
¶   Facts & Figures - 1; ftm.

Incorporated Phonographic Society (IPS) 1872

■   73 Alicia Gardens, Kenton, HARROW, Middx, HA3 8JD. (chmn/p)
     020 8907 8249
     email marysorene@ntlworld.com
     http://www.the-ips.org.uk
     Chmn: Mary Sorene
▲   Company Limited by Guarantee
○   *P; for court & other verbatim reporters, journalists, teachers of shorthand & typewriting, private secretaries, & other shorthand enthusiasts
●   Mtgs - Exam - SG - Inf
M   250 i, UK / 50 i, o'seas
¶   IPS Jnl - 4; ftm, £5 yr nm.

Incorporated Society of British Advertisers Ltd (ISBA) 1900

■   Langham House, 1B Portland Place, LONDON, W1B 1PN. (hq)
     020 7291 9020
     email answers@isba.org.uk   http://www.isba.org.uk
     Dir Gen: Mike Hughes
▲   Company Limited by Guarantee
○   *T; to represent the collective interests of British advertisers to government, regulators & the media; to provide expert advice & guidance on advertising effectively & efficiently
●   Conf - Mtgs - Inf - LG
<   Wld Fedn of Advertisers; Advertising Assn
M   400 f
¶   AR - 1; free.

Incorporated Society of Musicians (ISM) 1882

■   10 Stratford Place, LONDON, W1C 1AA.   (hq)
     020 7629 4413   fax 020 7408 1538
     email membership@ism.org   http://www.ism.org
     Chief Exec: Deborah Annetts
▲   Company Limited by Guarantee
○   *P; to promote the art of music; to maintain the honour & interests of the music profession
Gp   Musicians in education; Performers & composers; Professional private music teachers education
●   Conf - Mtgs - ET - LG
<   Creators' Rights Alliance
M   4,800 i, 120 f, UK
¶   Music Jnl - 12; ftm, £32 nm.
     Register of Professional Private Music Teachers - 1; ftm, £20 nm.
     Ybk (incl LM) - 1; ftm, £40 nm.   AR; free.
     Publications list available.

Incorporated Society of Organ Builders (ISOB) 1947

NR   35 Peasehill Gait, ROSYTH, Fife, KY11 2BD.   (hq)
     email admin1@isob.co.uk   http://www.isob.co.uk
○   *P, *T
●   Conf - Mtgs - Inf - VE
M   190 i, UK / 9 i, o'seas
¶   Jnl - irreg.   LM - 1; free.   AR; ftm only.

Incorporated Society for Psychical Research (SPR) 1882

NR   49 Marloes Rd, LONDON, W8 6LA.   (hq)
     020 7937 8984
     http://www.spr.ac.uk
     Sec: Peter M Johnson
▲   Company Limited by Guarantee; Registered Charity
○   *Q; 'to further systematic, scientific investigation of certain paranormal phenomena which are apparently inexplicable on any generally recognised hypothesis - telepathy & all forms of paranormal cognition, poltergeists, apparitions, alleged movement of objects without contact; any other phenomena which appear to be paranormal. The Society does not hold or express views'
Gp   ESP C'ee; Physical phenomena; Research advisory; Publications
●   Conf - Lectures - Res - Inf - Lib
M   1,100 i
¶   Jnl - 4.   Proceedings - irreg.
     Paranormal Review Magazine - 4.
×   Incorporated Society for Psychical Research

Incorporated Society of Registered Naturopaths (ISRN) 1934

NR   70 Kingston Avenue, Liberton, EDINBURGH, EH16 5SW.   (hsp)
     0131-664 3435
     http://www.naturecuresociety.org
     Hon Sec: Mrs May Thomson
▲   Company Limited by Guarantee
○   *P; alternative therapy offering naturopathic, dietary & manipulative therapy & advice
●   Conf - ET - Exam
<   Brit Naturopathic Assn
M   40 i, UK / 5 i, o'seas
¶   Publications list available.

Incorporation of Plastic Window Fabricators & Installers (IPWFI) 1991

NR   The Media Centre, 7 Northumberland St, HUDDERSFIELD, W Yorks, HD1 1RL.   (hq)
     0844 800 4125   fax 0844 800 4185
     email ipwfi@aol.co.uk   http://www.ipwfi.co.uk
▲   Company Limited by Guarantee
○   *T; to provide member double glazing companies with insurance backed guarantees & deposit indemnity protection
●   Conf - Exhib
M   2,000 f

Independent Academies Association (IAA) 2002

NR   c/o Djanogly City Academy, Sherwood Rise, Nottingham Road, NOTTINGHAM, NG7 7AR.   (mail)
     0115-933 2200
     email iaainfo@iaa.uk.net   http://www.iaa.uk.net
     Exec Officer: Caroline Whitty
▲   Company Limited by Guarantee
○   *E; the national representative membership organisation for leaders of academies & other state-funded independent schools
●   Conf - Mtgs
M   177 academies

Independent Age
     the operating name of the **Royal United Kingdom Beneficent Association**

Independent Association of Preparatory Schools (IAPS) 1892

■ 11 Waterloo Place, LEAMINGTON SPA, Warks, CV32 5LA. (hq)
    01926 887833   fax 01926 888014
    email iaps@iaps.org.uk   http://www.iaps.org.uk
    Chief Exec: David Hanson
▲ Company Limited by Guarantee
○ *E, *P; 'independent education of boys & girls (up to 13) for entrance to independent secondary schools'
● Conf - Mtgs - ET
< Independent Schools Coun
M 540 schools, UK / 30 schools, o'seas
¶ Independent Schools Ybk.   Prep School Magazine.
✕ 2008-09 Incorporated Association of Preparatory Schools

Independent Authors Special Interest Group
    a group of the **Institute of Scientific & Technical Communicators**

Independent Automotive Aftermarket Federation (IAAF) 2010

NR Aftermarket House, 5 Marlin Office Village, 1250 Chester Rd, Castle Bromwich, BIRMINGHAM, W Midlands, B35 7AZ. (hq)
    0845 313 1506
    http://www.iaaf.co.uk
    Chief Exec: Brian Spratt
○ *T
✕ 2010 Automotive Distribution Federation

Independent Banking Advisory Service (IBAS) 1993

■ Somersham, HUNTINGDON, Cambs, PE28 3WD.   (hq)
    01487 843444   fax 01487 740607
    email helpdesk@ibas.co.uk   http://www.ibas.co.uk
    Exec Officer: Sara Cummings
▲ Un-incorporated Society
○ *K; independent advice & case investigation on all matters relating to banking, mortgage shortfall, & banking procedures & charging structures
● Res - Stat - Inf - LG
M 2,000 i, 30,000 f, 200 org, UK / 150 i, 250 f, o'seas

Independent Battery Distributors Association
    in January 2011 merged with the Society of the British Battery Industry to form the **British Battery Industry Federation**

Independent Broadcasters of Ireland (IBI) 1989

IRL Macken House, Mayor Street Upper, DUBLIN 1, Republic of Ireland. (hq)
    email lisa@ibireland.ie   http://www.ibireland.ie
    Chmn: Scott Williams
○ *T; the representative body for Ireland's independent commercial radio broadcasters
M 34 f

Independent Children's Homes Association (ICHA) 2004

■ PO Box 99, HEBDEN BRIDGE, W Yorks, HX7 9AA. (hq)
    0845 467 8152
    email admin@icha.org.uk   http://www.icha.org.uk
    Exec Officer: Roy Williamson,   Admin: Gail Williamson
○ *W; for all independent providers of social care for children; works to raise professional standards through shared work experience
● Conf - Mtgs - ET - Res - EXhib - SG - Stat - Inf - LG
M 70+ f
¶ NL - 4;   Hbk - 1; both free.
    Weekly Electronic Bulletin - 52; ftm only.

Independent Consultants Consortium

    dissolved

Independent Doctors Federation (IDF) 1989

NR 27 Nesta Rd, WOODFORD GREEN, Essex, IG9 9RG.   (hq)
    020 8090 3470
    email info@idf.uk.net   http://www.idf.uk.net
    Chmn: Dr Jack A T Edmonds
▲ Company Limited by Guarantee
○ *P; to promote excellence in the independent medical sector
Gp C'ees: Appraisal, GP, Independent sector assessment & advisory (ISAAC), IT, Professional Development, Regulation, Social, Specialists
M 800 i
✕ 2009 Independent Doctors Forum

Independent Family Brewers of Britain (IFBB) 1993

NR Spring Cottage Offices, 28 Spring Lane, GREAT HORWOOD, Bucks, MK17 0QW.   (hq)
    01296 714745
    email jo.lynch@familybrewers.co.uk
    http://www.familybrewers.co.uk
    Contact: Jo Lynch
▲ Company Limited by Guarantee
○ *N, *T; to protect the unique heritage of family brewing companies in Britain; to promote British beers, especially cask conditioned ales; to defend the structure of tied pubs by ownership
< all members are also members of the British Beer & Pub Assn
M 30 f

Independent Federation of Nursing in Scotland (IFON) 1995

NR Huntershill Village, 102 Crowhill Rd, Bishopbriggs, GLASGOW, G64 1RP.   (hq)
    0141-772 9222   fax 0141-762 3776
    email ifoninscotland@aol.com
    http://www.ifonscotland.org
    Gen Sec: Mrs Irenee F O'Neill
Br 6
○ *U; 'is a nursing union with a solely Scottish identity, run by health care professionals for health care professionals'
Gp Health care professionals: Qualified, Un-qualified
● Conf - ET - Exhib - Empl
M i
¶ Nursing Scotland - 6; ftm only.

Independent Fire Engineering & Distributors Association (IFEDA) 1989

NR Unit 203 Solent Business Centre, 343 Millbrook Rd West, SOUTHAMPTON, Hants, SO15 0HW.   (hq)
    023 8051 3326
    email info@ifeda.org   http://www.ifeda.org
    Chmn: Nigel Walton
○ *T; to promote quality standards & procedures within the fire safety industry
● ET
¶ Fire Talk (NL) - 4.

Independent Footwear Retailers Association (IFRA) 1950

■ PO Box 123, BANBURY, Oxon, OX15 6WB.   (hq)
    01295 738726   fax 01295 738275
    email ifra@shoeshop.org.uk
    http://www.shoeshop.org.uk
    Sec: Arthur Spencer-Bolland
○ *T
● Conf - Mtgs - ET - Exhib - SG - Stat - Lib - VE - Empl
< Soc of Shoe Fitters; Nat Shoe Retailers' Assn (USA)
M 250 f
¶ NL - 4; ftm only.

Independent Games Developers Trade Association
    see **Tiga- the Independent Games Developers Association**

Independent Garage Association
    a group of the **Retail Motor Industry Federation**

Independent Group of Analytical Psychologists   (IGAP)
NR   PO Box 22343, LONDON, W13 8GP.   (hq)
　　　020 8933 0353　fax 020 8933 0645
　　　email office@igap.co.uk　http://www.igap.co.uk
　　　Sec: Clare Craig
▲　Company Limited by Guarantee; Registered Charity
○　*P; Jungian analysis
●　ET - SG
M　49 i, UK / 9 i, o'seas

Independent Holiday Hostels of Ireland   (IHH)   1983
IRL   PO Box 11772, Fairview, DUBLIN 3, Republic of Ireland.   (hq)
　　　353 (1) 836 4700
　　　email info@hostels-ireland.com
　　　http://www.hostels-ireland.com
○　*T; independent hostels & budget accommodation
●　Inf - VE
M　7 f, UK / 142 f, o'seas
¶　Guide to the Independent Holiday Hostels of Ireland - 1; free.
　　Note: This is the trading name of the Independent Hostel
　　Owners' Cooperative Society Ltd.

Independent Hospitals Association of Ireland
　　an association within the **Irish Business & Employers**
　　Confederation

Independent Midwives Association
　　since 2009 **Independent Midwives UK**

Independent Midwives UK   (IMUK)   1985
■　PO Box 539, ABINGDON, Oxon, OX14 9DF.   (hq)
　　　0845 460 0185
　　　http://www.independentmidwives.org.uk
　　　Chmn: Tina Perridge
▲　Social Enterprise with Government Support
○　*P; support group for midwives working independently, giving
　　women informed choices in childbirth, home, hospital or
　　water births
●　Mtgs - Exhib - SG - Stat - Inf
<　Intl Confedn of Midwives; Assn of Radical Midwives
M　40 i
¶　Register of Independent Midwives - 2 yrly; ftm, send sae nm.
×　2009 Independent Midwives Association

Independent Motor Trade Factors Association Ltd   (IFA)   1977
NR   20 East Hill, ST AUSTELL, Cornwall, PL25 4TR.   (hq)
　　　01726 70440
　　　email gretal.taylor@imtfa.co.uk　http://www.imtfa.co.uk
　　　Sec: Gretal Taylor
○　*T; motor vehicle component distributors
M　38 f

Independent Operators Association   (IOA)
NR   c/o S E Leisure Ltd, Unit & Motorway Industrial Estate,
　　　Forstal Rd, AYLESFORD, Kent, ME20 7AF.   (chmn/b)
　　　01622 791617
　　　email john@seleisure.com　http://www.seleisure.com
　　　Chmn: John Powell,　Chief Exec: Peter Weir
○　*T; supply & testing of amusement machines
M　20 f
¶　Independent: the Voice of the IOA Group.

Independent Pilots Association   (IPA)   1992
■　The Priory, HAYWARDS HEATH, W Sussex, RH16 3LB.   (hq)
　　　01444 441149　fax 01444 441192
　　　email office@ipapilot.com　http://www.ipapilot.com
　　　Sec: Capt Noel Baker
▲　Company Limited by Guarantee
Br　1
○　*P; for aviation pilots & flight engineers
●　Conf - Mtgs - ET - Res - Inf - LG
>　Indep Pilots Fedn
M　1,230 i, UK / 330 i, o'seas
¶　Skypointer - 4; ftm only.

Independent Print Industries Association   (IPIA)   1990
■　Unit 9 Business Innovation Centre, Staffordshire
　　Technology Park, Beaconside, STAFFORD, ST18 0AR.   (hq)
　　　0844 902 0214　fax 0844 902 0215
　　　email info@ipia.org.uk　http://www.ipia.org.uk
　　　Chief Exec: Andrew Pearce
▲　Un-incorporated Society
○　*T; for print managers, brokers, distributors, & outsourcers of
　　print as well as trade manufacturers of print & print related
　　products & services
Gp　Brokers; Distributors & outsourcers; Paper makers & merchants;
　　Print managers; Software suppliers to the printing industry;
　　Suppliers of office & computer consumables; Trade printers
●　Conf - Mtgs - ET - Exhib - Inf
<　Document Mgt Inds Assn (DMIA)(USA)
M　165 f, UK / 4 f, o'seas
¶　Innovation in Print - 6; free.

Independent Publishers Advisory Council
　　a group of the **Periodical Publishers Association**

Independent Publishers Guild   (IPG)   1962
■　PO Box 12, Llain, WHITLAND, Dyfed, SA34 0WU.   (mail)
　　　01437 563335　fax 01437 562071
　　　email info@ipg.uk.com　http://www.ipg.uk.com
　　　Exec Dir: Bridget Shine
▲　Company Limited by Guarantee
○　*T; a forum for the exchange of ideas & information for
　　directors of independent publishing companies
●　Conf - Mtgs - Exhib - Inf - VE - Book industry communication
<　Nat Book C'ee
M　419 f
¶　email bulletin- 52; ftm only.

Independent Retailers Confederation
　　is no longer active

Independent Safety Consultants Association   (ISCA)   1985
NR   The Old Bakehouse, Fullbridge, MALDON, Essex, CM9 4LE.
　　　(hsb)
　　　01621 874938　fax 01621 851756
　　　email isca@isca.org.uk　http://www.isca.org.uk
　　　Sec: Mrs Caroline Head,　Chmn: Howard Hall
▲　Un-incorporated Society
○　*P, *T; for safety consultancies giving safety advice & guidance;
　　some consultancies give specialist help for asbestos,
　　construction etc
●　Mtgs
M　5 i, 11 f

Independent Schools Association   (ISA)   1895
■　Boys' British School, East St, SAFFRON WALDEN, Essex,
　　CB10 1LS.   (hq)
　　　01799 523619
　　　http://www.isaschools.org.uk
　　　Gen Sec: Mrs J Le Poidevin
▲　Company Limited by Guarantee
○　*E; promotion of interests of independent schools
●　Conf - Mtgs - Comp - SG - Inf
<　Indep Schools Jt Coun; ISIS
M　300 i (heads of independent schools), UK / 3 i, o'seas
¶　Directory - 1.

Independent Schools' Bursars Association   (ISBA)   1932
NR   Unit 11-12 Manor Farm, Cliddesden, BASINGSTOKE, Hants,
      RG25 2JB.   (hq)
      01256 330369   fax 01256 330376
      email office@theisba.org.uk   http://www.theisba.org.uk
      Gen Sec: J R B Cook
▲   Registered Charity
○   *P; the advancement of education by the promotion of efficient
      & effective administration & ancillary services at independent
      schools
●   Conf - Mtgs - ET - SG - Inf
<   Indep Schools Coun (ISC)
M   852 schools, UK / 30 schools, o'seas
¶   The Bursar's Review - 3;   Bulletin (NL) - 10; both ftm only.

Independent Schools Council   (ISC)   1974
NR   St Vincent House, 30 Orange St, LONDON, WC2H 7HH.   (hq)
      020 7766 7070   fax 020 7766 7071
      email office@isc.co.uk   http://www.isc.co.uk
      Chief Exec: David Lyscom
▲   Company Limited by Guarantee
○   *E, *N; the policy & management of independent education
●   ET - Inf & advice service
M   1,300 schools within 7 orgs:
      Association of Governing Bodies of Independent
         Schools
      Girls' Schools Association
      Headmasters' & Headmistresses' Conference
      Independent Association of Preparatory Schools
      Independent Schools Association
      Independent Schools Bursars' Association
      Society of Heads of Independent Schools

Independent Sports Retailers Association
      in 2006 merged with the **Sporting Goods Industry Association**

Independent Surveyors & Valuers Association   (ISVA)
NR   Broadbury, OKEHAMPTON, Devon, EX20 4NH.   (hq)
      01837 871700   fax 01837 871700
      email mail@surveyorsweb.co.uk
      http://www.surveyorsweb.co.uk
○   *P; qualified chartered surveyors, either partners or sole
      practitioners who run their own practices & are not owned by
      financial or corporate institutions

Independent Theatre Council Ltd   (ITC)   1974
■   12 The Leathermarket, Weston St, LONDON, SE1 3ER.   (hq)
      020 7403 1727   fax 020 7403 1745
      email admin@itc-arts.org   http://www.itc-arts.org
      Chief Exec: Charlotte Jones
▲   Company Limited by Guarantee
○   *T; management association for the performing arts
●   Conf - ET - Advice service & networking for members
M   644 i, f & org
¶   NL - 6; ftm only.   AR - 1.
      The ITC Practical Guide for Writers & Companies; £5.
      Working in Schools; £5.
      Equal Opportunities - policy into practice; £5 each (£12 the set):
      Race; Disability; Sexuality; Gender.

**Independent Training Standards Scheme & Register
   (ITSSAR)   1990**
NR   Armstrong House, 28 Broad St, WOKINGHAM, Berks,
      RG40 1AB.   (hq)
      0118-989 3229
      http://www.itssar.org.uk
      Chmn: Lynda Dobson
▲   Company Limited by Guarantee
○   *E; fork lift truck accreditation scheme
●   ET
M   3,000 i, 200 f

Independent Turner Society   1988
■   Turner House, 153 Cromwell Road, LONDON, SW5 0TQ.
      (hq)
      020 7373 5560   fax 020 7373 5560
      email selbywhittingham@hotmail.com
      http://www.jmwturner.org
      Hon Sec: Dr Selby Whittingham
▲   Un-incorporated Society
○   *K; campaigning for a proper Turner gallery for J M W Turner's
      bequest
●   Campaigning
M   [not stated]
¶   Jnl - irreg;   NL - 2/3; both ftm only.

Independent Tyre Distributors Network   (ITDN)   1985
NR   Unit 9 Cranmere Rd, Exeter Road Industrial Estate,
      OKEHAMPTON, Devon, EX20 1UE.   (hq)
      01837 658150   fax 01837 659840
      email sales@itdn.org.uk   http://www.itdn.org.uk
○   *T; a voice within the tyre industry for the completely
      independent tyre distributor
M   500 f

Independent Warranty Association   (IWA)   1990
NR   20 Billing Rd, NORTHAMPTON, NN1 5AW.   (hq)
      01604 604511   fax 01604 604512
      email enquiries@iwa.biz   http://www.iwa.biz
○   *T; provision of insurance backed guarantees for home
      improvement products such as double glazing,
      conservatories, bathrooms, loft conversions, kitchens,
      driveways & block paving
M   f

Independent Waste Paper Processors Association
      since 2009 **Recycling Association**

Indian Military Historical Society   (IMHS)   1983
■   33 High St, Tilbrook, HUNTINGDON, Cambs, PE28 0JP.   (hsp)
      01480 860437
      email imhs@mcclenaghan.waitrose.com
      Hon Sec: A N McClenaghan
▲   Un-incorporated Society
○   *G; to act as a forum for the dissemination of knowledge of
      uniforms, medals, badges, buttons & other militaria, as well
      as the history of service in India both before & after
      independence (India, Pakistan & Bangladesh)
●   Res - Inf
M   190 i, 5 org, UK / 80 i, 2 org, o'seas
¶   Durbar - 4; ftm only.

Indoor Cricket England   (ICE)   2009
NR   12 Ashdown Rd, Portishead, BRISTOL, BS20 8DP.   (dir/p)
      01275 846514   fax 01275 846156
      email gregvl@indoorcricketengland.co.uk
      http://www.indoorcricketengland.co.uk
      Managing Dir: Greg van Laun
▲   Company Limited by Guarantee
○   *S; the governing authority for 8-a-side indoor cricket in
      England
●   Comp - Inf
<   Wld Indoor Cricket Assn
✕   2009 British Indoor Cricket Association

Industrial Agents Society (IAS) 1975
NR Lambton Smith Hampton, UK House, 180 Oxford St,
LONDON, W1D 1NN. (chmn/b)
020 7198 2296
http://www.shedshifters.co.uk
Chmn: Steve Williams
▲ Un-incorporated Society
○ *P; commercial surveyors & agents whose principal business
activity is wholly or mainly the buying, selling or development
of business space, including industrial & warehouse property
● Conf - Mtgs - VE
M 900 i
¶ NL - 2.   Members Directory - 1.

**Industrial Cleaning Machine Manufacturers Association
(ICMMA)**
■ Salisbury House (suite 478-480), London Wall, LONDON,
EC2M 5QQ. (hq)
020 7920 9638   fax 020 7638 6990
http://www.icmma.org.uk
Sec: Andrew Large
○ *T; for manufacturers of industrial & commercial cleaning
equipment, including pressure washers, vacuum cleaners,
sweepers, scrubber driers & carpet cleaners
M 11 f

Industrial Commercial Energy Association
see **ICOM Energy Association**

Industrial Law Society (ILS) 1964
NR 18 Graysmead, SIBLE HEDINGHAM, Essex, CO9 3NY. (hq)
01787 463838 (0100-1300)
email ifs@dial.pipex.com
http://www.industriallawsociety.org.uk
Contact: Jean Hughes
▲ Registered Charity
○ *L, *P; to promote the understanding of labour law & industrial
relations & to stimulate debate in these fields
● Conf - Mtgs
¶ Industrial Law Journal - 4; ftm.

Industrial Locomotive Society (ILS) 1946
■ Fermain, 31 Lower Brimley Rd, TEIGNMOUTH, Devon,
TQ14 2LH. (hsp)
email enquiries@industrial-loco.org.uk
http://www.industrial-loco.org.uk
Hon Sec: W Wright
▲ Un-incorporated Society
○ *G; historical research into railways other than main line
railways (incl military railways & associated industrial
archaeology)
● Mtgs - Res - Lib - PL
M 210 i, 10 org, UK / 30 i, 4 org, o'seas
¶ The Industrial Locomotive - 4; ftm, £3 nm.

Industrial Packaging Association (IPA) 2004
■ PO Box 110, KNARESBOROUGH, N Yorks, HG5 8ZX. (hq)
07770 633320   fax 07053 642594
email info@theipa.co.uk   http://www.theipa.co.uk
Chief Exec: Phil Pease
▲ Un-incorporated Society
○ *T; for the industrial industry - kegs, drums, intermediate bulk
containers (IBCs)
Gp IBC manufacturing; Re-conditioning & re-cycling; Fibre / Plastic
/ Steel drum manufacturing; Used container Re-conditioning
& recycling
● Mtgs - ET - Inf
< Intl Plastics Packaging (ICPP); Eur Steel Drum Mfrs (SEFA); Eur
Plastics Packaging Assn (EUPC)
M 28 f, UK / 2 f, o'seas

Industrial & Power Association (IPA)
NR Brunel Building, James Watt Avenue, Scottish Enterprise
Technology Park, EAST KILBRIDE, G75 0QD. (hq)
01355 272630   fax 01355 272633
email info@ipa-scotland.org.uk
http://www.ipa-scotland.org.uk
Chief Exec: Helen Tulloch
▲ Company Limited by Guarantee
○ *L; aims to help society meet its needs for clean & affordable
energy by bringing the experience, skills & technologies of
Scotland to the world power market
Gp Environment; Fossil & CCS; Industrial; Nuclear; Oil & gas;
Power systems; Renewables
● Mtgs
M 41 f

Industrial Railway Society (IRS) 1949
NR 4 Fernbrook Drive, HARROW, Middx, HA2 7EB. (hsp)
email secretary@irsociety.co.uk
http://www.irsociety.co.uk
Hon Sec: Edward Knotwell
▲ Un-incorporated Society
○ *G; study & record all aspects of industrial railways & their uses
Gp Coal-mining railways; Ex-British Rail locomotives engaged in
industrial use; Ministry of Defence railways; Non-locomotive
worked railway lines & small mines; Rail locomotives
engaged in industrial use; Tunnelling contractors using rail
transport
● Mtgs - Res - Lib - PL - VE (many overseas)
M 950 i, UK / 50 i, o'seas
¶ Industrial Railway Record - 4.
Bulletin - 6.   Books.

Industrial Rope Access Trade Association (IRATA) 1989
■ Kingsley House, Ganders Business Park, Kingsley, BORDON,
Hants, GU35 9LU. (asa)
01252 357839   fax 01252 357831
email info@irata.org   http://www.irata.org
Sec: John G Fairley
▲ Company Limited by Guarantee
○ *T
● Conf - Mtgs - ET - Exam - Inf - LG
M 24 i, 44 f, UK / 3 i, 16 f, o'seas
¶ Directory;   Brochure; both free.
Guidelines: on the use of rope access methods for industrial
purposes; £10 m, £45 nm.
International Guidelines: on the use of rope access methods for
industrial purposes; £10 m, £45 nm.
General Requirements: for certification of personnel engaged in
industrial rope access methods; £10 m, £45 nm.

Industrial & Single Phase Products Group
a product group of **BEAMA Ltd**

Industrial Textiles Manufacturers Group
a group of the **Performance Textiles Association**

Industrial Tyre Association
closed 2009

Industry Council for Packaging & the Environment   (INCPEN) 1974
- ■ SoanePoint, 6-8 Market Place, READING, Berks, RG1 2EG. (hq)
  0118-925 5991
  email info@incpen.org   http://www.incpen.org
  Dir: Jane Bickerstaffe
- ▲ Company Limited by Guarantee
- ○ *T; to study the environmental & social impacts of packaging; members are international companies involved in all aspects of the distribution of packaged goods
- Gp Environment; Trade
- ● Conf - Mtgs - ET - Res - Exhib - Stat - Inf - LG
- < Eur Org for Packaging & the Envt (EUROPEN)
- M 25 f
- ¶ NL - 11; ftm only.
  Factsheets;   AR; both free.

Industry Research & Development Group   (IRDG)   1992
- IRL Regus Pembroke House, 28-32 Pembroke St, DUBLIN 2, Republic of Ireland.   (hq)
  353 (1) 237 4671   fax 353 (1) 234 2596
  email info@irdg.ie   http://www.irdg.ie
  Managing Dir: Denis Hayes
- ○ *T; a representative group for companies in manufacturing & services who are engaged in product & process research, development & innovation (RD&I); to ensure that RD&I remains high on the national agenda
- < IBEC
- M 400 f

Infant & Dietetic Foods Association Ltd   (IDFA)   1986
- ■ 6 Catherine St, LONDON, WC2B 5JJ.   (hq)
  020 7420 7112   fax 020 7836 0580
  email idfa@fdf.org.uk   http://www.idfa.org.uk
  Dir Gen: Roger Clarke
- ▲ Company LImited by Guarantee
- ○ *T; manufacturers & suppliers of special foods for special requirements (infant formulae, weaning, medical, sports foods & drinks, & slimming foods)
- ● Mtgs - Res - SG - Inf - LG
- < Intl Soc for Dietetic Foods (ISDI); Assn of Infant & Dietetic Foods in the EEC (IDACE); Food & Drink Fedn
- M 14 f

Infection Control Nurses Association of GB
   since 1 October 2007 **Infection Prevention Society**

Infection Prevention Society   (IPS)   1960
- ■ Fitwise Management Ltd, Drumcross Hall, BATHGATE, W Lothian, EH48 4JT.   (asa)
  01506 811077   fax 01506 811477
  email info@fitwise.co.uk   http://www.ips.uk.net
  Hon Sec: Gill Manojlovic
- ▲ Company Limited by Guarantee; Registered Charity
- Br 12
- ○ *P; to promote the advancement of infection control & prevention for the benefit of the community as a whole, & in particular the provision of training courses, accreditiation schemes, etc
- Gp Audit & surveillance; Community infection control practitioners network; Mental health interest
- ● Conf - Mtgs - ET - Res - Exhib - SG - Inf - LG
- < Intl Fedn of Infection Control (IFIC); Fedn of Infection Socs (FIS)
- M 1,320 i, 32 f, UK / 153 i, o'seas
  (Sub: £70 i)
- ¶ Community Audit Tool (booklet & CD); £25.
  [All the following are £5 m, £10 nm]:
  Hand Decontamination Guidelines.
  Guidelines for Preventing Intravascular Catheter related Infection.
  Infection Control Guidance for General Practice.
  Enteral Feeding.
  Asepsis: preventing healthcare associated infection.
  Prevention of Infection in the Home (home hygiene booklet).
- × 2007 (1 October) Infection Control Nurses Association of GB

Infertility Network UK
- ■ Charter House, 43 St Leonards Rd, BEXHILL-ON-SEA, E Sussex, TN40 1JA.   (hq)
  0800 008 7464   fax 01424 731858
  http://www.infertilitynetworkuk.com
  Chief Exec: Claire Lewis-Jones
- ▲ Company Limited by Guarantee; Registered Charity
- ○ *K, *W; to provide essential support services & information on developments in infertility research; to represent patients' views; to campaign to raise awareness of the impact of infertility & improve access to treatment
- ● Conf - Mtgs - ET - Res - Stat - Inf - LG
- ¶ Fact sheets.
  A Journey through Infertility (video).

Inflatable Play Manufacturers Association
   merged in July 2010 with the **Association of Amusement & Leisure Equipment Suppliers of the UK**

Inflatable Safety & Survival Equipment Technical Association Ltd   (ISSETA)   1973
- ■ 34 Lytchett Drive, BROADSTONE, Dorset, BH18 9LB.   (hsp)
  01202 657814   fax 01202 693005
  email secretary@issete.com   http://www.isseta.com
  Sec: Ian C Brindle
- ▲ Company Limited by Guarantee
- Br Denmark, France, Germany, Italy, Japan, Norway, USA
- ○ *T; to improve the standard & quality of inflatable safety & survival equipment used in the marine environment
- ● Mtgs - Res - LG
- M 9 f

Information Design Association   (IDA)   1991
- NR c/o Ideography, Unit 226 Station House, Greenwich Commercial Centre, 49 Greenwich High Rd, LONDON, SE10 8JL.   (mail)
  email chair@infodesign.org.uk
  http://www.informationdesignassociation.org.uk
  Admin: Ade Tayo
- ○ *P; design, planning & production of artefacts such as software manuals, wayfinding systems, business forms & utility statements etc
- ● Conf - Mtgs - Comp
- M 120 i, 2 f
- ¶ NL.

Information & Records Management Society   (IRMS)   1983

NR   Benchmark Communications, 14 Blandford Sq,
         NEWCASTLE UPON TYNE, NE1 4HZ.   (hq)
         0191-244 2839   fax 0191-245 3802
         email info@irms.org.uk   http://www.irms.org.uk
         Chmn: Matthew Stephenson
▲   Un-incorporated Society
Br   7 regional groups
○   *P; to encourage the highest standards in records
         management: the systematic control, organisation, access &
         protection of an organisation's information (whether on tape,
         disk, paper or film) from its creation, through its use to its
         permanent retention or legal destruction
Gp   Higher & further education; Public sector
●   Conf - Mtgs - ET - Exhib - SG - VE - LG
M   700 i, 250 f
¶   Bulletin - 6.   NL - 6.
✕   2010 Records Management Society of GB

Inland Waterways Association   (IWA)   1946

NR   Island House, Moor Rd, CHESHAM, Bucks, HP5 1WA.   (hq)
         01494 783453
         http://www.waterways.org.uk
         Exec Dir: Neil Edwards
▲   Company Limited by Guarantee; Registered Charity
○   *K; to ensure the restoration, conservation, retention &
         development of the navigable waterways of the British Isles &
         their fullest commercial & recreational use
<   Nat Navigation Users Forum (NNUF)
M   18,000 i, 100 f, 200 org, UK / 300 i, o'seas
¶   Waterways - 3.   Inland Waterways Guide - 1.
         Wide variety of regional, local & specialist publications.

Inland Waterways Association of Ireland   (IWAI)   1954

IRL   10 Woodlawn, Upper Chruchtown Rd, DUBLIN 14, Republic of
         Ireland.   (hsp)
         353 (87) 256 0784
         email honsecretary@iwai.ie   http://www.iwai.ie
         Hon Sec: Derry Smyth
▲   Company Limited by Guarantee; Registered Charity
Br   21
○   *G; to promote the use, maintenance, protection, restoration &
         improvement of the inland waterways of Ireland
Gp   Heritage & conservation; Boating & leisure
●   Comp - Exhib - LG - Mtgs - VE
M   4,400 i
¶   Inland Waterways News - 4.   Guide books, maps, etc.

Inland Waterways Protection Society Ltd   (IWPS)   1958

■   Top Lock House, 7 Lime Kiln Lane, Marple, STOCKPORT,
         Cheshire, SK6 6BX.   (chmn/p)
         0161-427 7402: 07710 361093
         email ian@theedgars.co.uk   http://www.brocross.com/
         iwps/index.htm
         Chmn: Ian Edgar
▲   Company Limited by Guarantee; Registered Charity
○   *K; for the restoration, preservation & development of the
         inland waterways of Great Britain
●   Waterway restoration & development (specifically the Bugsworth
         canal basin at the head of the Peak Forest Canal)
M   300 i, 20 f, 10 org
¶   174 (NL) - 4; ftm, 50p nm.
         Note: The newsletter is called 174 after the last remaining Peak
         Forest Tramway wagon

Inn Sign Society   (ISS)   1960

NR   9 Denmead Drive, Wednesfield, WOLVERHAMPTON,
         W Midlands, WV11 2QS.   (hsp)
         01902 721808
         http://www.innsignsociety.com
         Hon Sec: Alan Rose
▲   Un-incorporated Society
○   *G; the study of the inn sign (pub sign), its origin, history, the
         stories connected with individual signs
●   Inf
M   360 i, 5 f, UK / 7 i, o'seas
¶   At the Sign of [. . .] - 4; ftm only.

Insolvency Lawyers' Association   (ILA)   1989

■   Valiant House, 4-10 Heneage Lane, LONDON, EC3A 5DQ.
         (hq)
         http://www.ilauk.org
         Pres: Christopher Mallon
▲   Company Limited by Guarantee
○   *P; a special interest group providing a forum for lawyers
         specialising in insolvency administration
●   Conf - Mtgs - ET - Inf - LG
M   291 i, 21 org, UK / 4 i, o'seas
¶   Insolvency Intelligence - 12;   Bulletins [email] - 26.

Insolvency Practitioners Association   (IPA)   1961

■   Valiant House, 4-10 Heneage Lane, LONDON, EC3A 5DQ.
         (hq)
         020 7623 5108   fax 020 7623 5127
         http://www.insolvency-practitioners.org.uk
         Pres: Patrick Brazzill
▲   Company Limited by Guarantee
○   *P; to promote & maintain standards of performance &
         professional conduct among those engaged in insolvency
         practice
●   Conf - ET - Exam - Inf - Mtgs
<   Assn of Business Recovery Profls
M   2,000 i & f
¶   Insolvency Practitioner (Jnl); ftm.

Institiúid Bitheolaíochta na h'Éireann
         the Irish title for the **Institute of Biology of Ireland**

Institiúid Ceimice na h'Éireann
         the Irish title of the **Institute of Chemistry of Ireland**

INSTITUTE . . .

         Other than the bodies listed below, organisations entitled
         'Institute' that have no voluntary membership structure but
         carry out serious research or who offer courses for
         educational purposes, will be found in our publication
         Centres, Bureaux & Research Institutes

Institute of Accounting Technicians in Ireland
         since 2008-09 **Accounting Technicians Ireland**

Institute of Acoustics   (IoA)   1974

■   77a St Peter's St, ST ALBANS, Herts, AL1 3BN.   (hq)
         01727 848195   fax 01727 850553
         email ioa@ioa.org.uk   http://www.ioa.org.uk
         Chief Exec: Kevin Macan-Lind
▲   Company Limited by Guarantee
Br   10
○   *L, *P; the art, science & technology of acoustics
Gp   Acoustics: Building, Physical, Musical, Underwater
         Noise: Electro, Environmental, Industrial, Speech
●   Conf - Mtgs - ET - Exam - Exhib - Lib
<   Intl Inst Noise Control - Engg (I-INCE); Intl Congress
         Acoustics (ICA); Eur Acoustics Assn (EAA)
M   3,100 i, 30 org, UK / 300 i, o'seas
¶   Acoustics Bulletin - 6; ftm, £20 each nm.
         Register of Members - 1; ftm, £10 nm.
         Buyers Guide - 1; ftm; £15 nm.

Institute of Actuaries
> on 1 August 2010 merged with the Faculty of Actuaries in Scotland to form the **Institute & Faculty of Actuaries**

Institute of Administrative Management   (IAM)   1915

NR   6 Graphite Sq, Vauxhall Walk, LONDON, SE11 5EE.   (hq)
     020 7091 2600   fax 020 7091 2619
     email info@instam.org   http://www.instam.org
     Chief Exec: David Woodgate
▲   Registered Charity
○   *P; to promote & develop, for the public benefit, the science of administrative management in all branches
●   Conf - ET - Exam - Res - Exhib - Stat - Inf
M   4,500 i, UK / 4,500 i, o'seas
¶   Manager: the British Jnl of Administrative Management - 6; ftm, £45 yr nm.   AR - 1.
     Publications list available.

Institute of Advanced Motorists Ltd   (IAM)   1956

■   510 Chiswick High Rd, LONDON, W4 5RG.   (hq)
     020 8996 9600   fax 020 8996 9601
     email enquiries@iam.org.uk   http://www.iam.org.uk
     Chief Exec: C T Bullock
▲   Company Limited by Guarantee; Registered Charity
Br 208
○   *K; to make a major contribution to road safety through the skill, attitude & responsibility, shown by motorists & motorcyclists, in the test for membership
Gp IAM fleet training (for company personnel)
●   Exam - IAM Fleet Training Ltd (for training of company personnel) - Advanced Driving (IAM Group Services Ltd)
M   112,000 i, UK / 1,000 i, o'seas
¶   Advanced Driving - 3; ftm.
     How to be an Advanced Motorist; £7.99.
     How to be an Advanced Motorcyclist; £7.99.

Institute of Advertising Practitioners in Ireland   (IAPI)   1964

IRL 8 Upper Fitzwilliam St, DUBLIN 2, Republic of Ireland.   (hq)
     353 (1) 676 5991   fax 353 (1) 661 4589
     email info@iapi.com   http://www.iapi.ie
     Chief Exec: Sean McCrave
○   *P; to promote the highest professional & creative standards in the production of advertising across all media
●   Comp - ET - Exam - Inf - LG - Res
<   Eur Assn of Communication Agencies (EACA)
M   60 f
¶   NL - 12; ftm.

Institute of Agricultural Management   (IAgrM)   1995

NR   Portway House, Sheepway, Portbury, BRISTOL, BS20 7TE.   (hq)
     01275 743825
     email enquiries@iagrm.org.uk   http://www.iagrm.org.uk
     Chmn: Tim Brigstocke
▲   Registered Charity
Br 20
○   *F; to promote professional management in agriculture & associated rural businesses
●   Conf - ET - Mtgs - VE
<   Soc for the Envt (SocEnv)
M   i
¶   Farm Management (Jnl) - 4; ftm.

Institute of Agricultural Secretaries & Administrators   (IAgSA)   1967

■   National Agricultural Centre, Stoneleigh Park, KENILWORTH, Warks, CV8 2LG.   (hq)
     024 7669 6592   fax 024 7641 7937
     email iagsa@iagsa.co.uk   http://www.iagsa.co.uk
     Sec: Mrs Charlotte O'Kane
▲   Company Limited by Guarantee
Br 29
○   *P, *T; to promote & encourage professional excellence in rural business administration
Gp Agriculture
●   Conf - Mtgs - ET - LG
M   900 i, 20 f
¶   Jnl - 1;   Bulletin - 12; both ftm only.   Directory - 1.

Institute of Amateur Cinematographers   (IAC)   1932

■   Dorset House, Regent Park, Kingston Rd, LEATHERHEAD, Surrey, KT22 7PL.   (hq)
     01372 824350
     email admin@theiac.org.uk   http://www.theiac.org.uk
     Chmn: Ron Prosser
▲   Registered Charity
Br 7
○   *G; to encourage & support anyone from beginner to expert who makes films & AV for the love of it
Gp Film Library
●   ET - Comp - Inf - Lib
M   2,000 i
     (Sub: £37.50)
¶   Film & Video Maker - 6; ftm only.
     Note: Generally known as IAC - The Film & Video Institute

Institute of Animal Technology   (IAT)   1965

NR   5 South Parade, Summertown, OXFORD, OX2 7JL.   (regd off)
     0800 085 4380
     email secretary@iat.org.uk   http://www.iat.org.uk
▲   Company Limited by Guarantee
Br 16
○   *P, *V; to advance & promote excellence in the care & welfare of animals in science
●   Conf - ET - Exam
<   Eur Fedn of Animal Technologists (EFAT); Amer Assn of Laboratory Animal Science (AALAS)
M   2,100 i, 60 f, UK / 50 i, o'seas
¶   Jnl of Animal Technology & Welfare - 3.
     Bulletin - 12.

Institute for Archaeologists
> trading name of the **Institute of Field Archaeologists**

Institute of Archaeologists of Ireland   (IAI)   2001

IRL 63 Merrion Sq, DUBLIN 2, Republic of Ireland.   (hq)
     353 (1) 662 9517
     email info@iai.ie   http://www.iai.ie
     Chmn: Finola O'Carroll
▲   Company Limited by Guarantee
○   *L; to advance the profession of archaeology by seeking to promote development, education, contact, regulation, high standards & public dissemination of its work

Institute of Architectural Ironmongers   (IAI)

■   8 Stepney Green, LONDON, E1 3JU.   (hq)
     020 7790 3431   fax 020 7790 8517
     email info@gai.org.uk   http://www.iai.uk.com
     Chief Exec: Gary Amer
▲   Un-incorporated Society
Br 8
○   *P; interests of individual architectural ironmongers
●   Conf - Mtgs - ET
M   350 i
¶   Architectural Ironmongery Jnl (IAI has own entry).

© CBD Research Ltd · Beckenham · BR3 5JS · Tel 020 8650 7745 · E-mail cbd@cbdresearch.com · www.cbdresearch.com

Institute of Art & Law   (IAL)
NR   Pentre Moel, Crickadarn, BUILTH WELLS, Powys, LD2 3BX.
     (hq)
     01982 560666   fax 01982 560604
     email info@ial.uk.com   http://www.ial.uk.com
     Dir: Ruth Redmon-Cooper
○   *L, *P; for those interested in all aspects of transacting in art
●   Mtgs - Seminars (speakers incl academics, practitioners,
     government officials & museum directors) - Publishing
M   i, org
¶   Art Antiquity & Law [Jnl] - 4.
     Commentary on the Unidroit Convention by Lyndel V Prott.
     Art Treasures & War by Wojciech Kowalski.

Institute of Asphalt Technology   (IAT)   1966
■   PO Box 17399, EDINBURGH, EH12 1FR.   (hq)
     0131-629 5370
     email russell.hunter@instituteofasphalt.org
     http://www.instituteofasphalt.org
     Business Mgr: Russell Hunter,   Hon Sec: Anthony Morter
▲   Company Limited by Guarantee
Br 9; Republic of Ireland
○   *P; for persons working in the field of asphalt technology & for
     those interested in all aspects of the manufacture, placing,
     technology & uses of materials containing asphalt & bitumen
●   Conf - Mtgs - ET - Exam - Exhib - Lib - PL - VE
M   15,900 i UK / 88 i, o'seas
¶   Asphalt Professional - 4; ftm.

Institute of Assessors & Internal Verifiers   (IAV)   1998
NR   PO Box 1138, WARRINGTON, Cheshire, WA4 9GS.   (hq)
     01925 485786
     email office@iavltd.co.uk   http://www.iavltd.co.uk
     Chief Exec: Mr Homan
▲   Company Limited by Guarantee
○   *P; for assessors & internal verifiers involved with national
     training / national vocational qualifications (NVQs)
●   Conf - Mtgs - ET - Res - Inf - LG
M   3,500 i, 200 i
¶   Best Practice (Jnl) - 4.

Institute of Association Management   (IofAM)   1933
■   2 Old College Court, 29 Priory St, WARE, Herts, SG12 0DE.
     (asa)
     0844 822 1736   fax 0844 822 5215
     email iam@iofam.org.uk   http://www.iofam.org.uk
     Pres: Bob Roberts
▲   Company Limited by Guarantee
○   *P; to promote best practice & professional standards in
     association management & governance; to promulgate the
     role & contribution of associations in national life & the status
     & reputation of association management as a profession
Gp Forums: Affinity schemes; Corporate governance; Event
     management; Finance management
●   Conf - Mtgs - ET - Inf - VE - LG
M   370 i, 30 f, UK
¶   Association Executive - 4; ftm, £30 nm.   Hbk & LM - 1; ftm.

**Institute of Auctioneers & Appraisers in Scotland   (IAAS)
     1926**
NR   Rural Centre, West Mains, Ingliston, NEWBRIDGE, Midlothian,
     EH28 8NZ.   (hq)
     0131-472 4067   fax 0131-472 4067
     email iaas@fsmail.net
     http://www.auctioneersscotland.co.uk
     Exec Sec: W Andrew Wright
▲   Company Limited by Guarantee
○   *P; for livestock & fine arts auctioneers, agricultural valuers &
     estate agents
Gp Fine art auctioneers & valuers; Land agents
●   Conf - ET - LG
<   Eur Assn of Livestock Markets
M   290 i, 35 f

Institute of Automotive Engineer Assessors   (IAEA)   1932
■   Brooke House, 24 Dam St, LICHFIELD, Staffs, WS13 6AB.   (hq)
     01543 266906   fax 01543 257848
     http://www.iaea.org.uk
     Sec: P A Grice
▲   Company Limited by Guarantee; Registered Charity
Br 8
○   *P; to promote & develop for public benefit the science, design,
     manufacture & related technology of motor vehicles & their
     repair
●   Exam - Res - Inf
<   FIEA
M   1,250 i, UK / 50 i, o'seas
¶   NL - 6; ftm.

Institute of Bankers in Ireland   1898
IRL   1 North Wall Quay, DUBLIN 1, Republic of Ireland.   (hq)
     353 (1) 611 6500   fax 353 (1) 611 6565
     email info@bankers.ie   http://www.bankers.ie
     Chief Exec: Michael Feeney
▲   Company Limited by Guarantee
○   *P; to enhance the knowledge & skills of those working in
     banking & financial services
●   ET - Exam
M   35,000 i

Institute of Barristers' Clerks   (IBC)   1922
NR   289-293 High Holborn, LONDON, WC1V 7HZ.   (admin/b)
     020 7831 7144
     email admin@ibc.org.uk   http://www.ibc.org.uk
▲   Registered Charity
○   *P
●   Conf - Mtgs - ET - Inf
M   850 i
¶   Mailshot (with job vacancies) - 52; £10 for 6 months.

Institute of Biology
     merged in 2009 with the Biosciences Federation to form the **Society
     of Biology**

**Institute of Biology of Ireland   (Institiúid Bitheolaíochta na
     h'Éireann) of Ireland)   (IBI)   1965**
IRL   Sch of Biology & Environmental Science, University College
     Dublin, Bellfield, DUBLIN 4, Republic of Ireland.   (hq)
     email info@ibioli.net   http://www.ibioli.net
○   *P; to represent & promote the professional interests of
     biologists

Institute of Biomedical Science   (IBMS)   1912
NR   12 Coldbath Square, LONDON, EC1R 5HL.   (hq)
     020 7713 0214   fax 020 7436 4946
     email mail@ibms.org   http://www.ibms.org
     Chief Exec: Alan Potter
▲   Registered Charity
Br 48; 5 o'seas
○   *L, *P; promotes the scientific study & development of
     biomedical science; the professional body for laboratory
     personnel
●   Conf - Mtgs - ET - Exam - Res - Comp - Inf - LG
<   Eur Professions in Biomedical Science; Eur Confedn of
     Laboratory Science
M   15,000 i, 74 f, UK / 1,000 i, o'seas
¶   Biomedical Scientist - 12.
     British Jnl of Biomedical Science - 4.
     Science & educational leaflets.   AR.

Institute of Bookbinding & Allied Trades (IBAT) 1904
NR c/o Clerkenwell Conference Centre, Clerkenwell Green,
  LONDON, EC1R 0NA.   (mtgs)
  http://www.ibat.org.uk
▲ Un-incorporated Society
○ *P. *U; to promote the exchange of information within the
  bookbinding industry & improve the standards of training
● Mtgs - ET - Inf - VE
< Worshipful Company of Stationers
M 130 i
¶ Quarterly Magazine.   LM - 1;   AR; both ftm only.

Institute of Brewing & Distilling (IBD) 1886
NR 33 Clarges St, LONDON, W1J 7EE.   (hq)
  020 7499 8144   fax 020 7499 1156
  email enquiries@ibd.org.uk   http://www.ibd.org.uk
▲ Registered Charity
○ *P; for the advancement of education & professional
  development in the science & technology of brewing,
  distilling & related industries
● Conf - Mtgs - ET - Exam - Exhib - Comp - Lib
M 1,925 i, UK / 1,950 i, o'seas
¶ The Brewer & Distiller - 12; ftm, £60 (£75 o'seas) nm.
  Jnl of the Institute of Brewing - 4; ftm only.
  Brewing & Distilling Directory - 1; ftm only.

Institute of British Geographers
  with the **Royal Geographical Society**

Institute of British Organ Building (IBO)
■ 13 Ryefields, Thurston, BURY ST EDMUNDS, Suffolk, IP31 3TD.
  01359 233433   fax 01359 233433
  http://www.ibo.co.uk
  Pres: Martin Goetze
○ *T; to represent, inform, serve & assist organ builders & their
  suppliers; & to encourage the improvement of skills &
  standards
● Mtgs - VE
M 65 f
¶ Organ Building (Jnl) - 1; NL - 4; both ftm.

Institute of Broadcast Sound (IBS) 1977
■ PO Box 208, HAVANT, Hants, PO9 9BQ.   (hq)
  0300 400 8427 (option 1)   fax 0870 762 2835
  email ibs-info@ibs.org.uk   http://www.ibs.org.uk
  Co Sec: Malcolm Johnson
▲ Company Limited by Guarantee; Registered Charity
○ *P; to promote the excellence of professional sound for radio &
  television broadcasting; to provide a continuing forum for
  such objectives
● Conf - Mtgs - ET - Exhib - Inf - Lib - LG
M 750 i, 35 f, UK / 30 i, 1 f, o'seas
  (Sub: £110 i)
¶ Line Up - 5; ftm, £45 (UK), £55 (Eur), £65 (RoW), nm.

Institute of Builders' Merchants (IoBM) 1968
■ 2 Crab Apple Way, Gamlingay, SANDY, Beds, SG19 3LS.   (hq)
  01767 650662
  http://www.iobm.co.uk
  Admin: Gill Sellick
Br 6
○ *P; improvement of technical & general knowledge of persons
  engaged in the trade of builders' merchant
● ET
< Builders Mchts Fedn; Worshipful Company of Builders Mchts
M 800 i

Institute of Business Advisers
  in 2007 merged with the Institute of Management Consultancy to
  form the Institute of Business Consulting, which in 2011 was renamed
  Institute of Consulting

Institute of Business Consulting
  since 2011 **Institute of Consulting**

Institute of Business Ethics (IBE) 1986
NR 24 Greencoat Place, LONDON, SW1P 1BE.   (hq)
  020 7798 6040
  http://www.ibe.org.uk
  Dir: Philippa Foster Back
▲ Registered Charity
○ *T; to clarify ethical issues involved in business; to identify &
  promulgate best business practice
● Conf - Mtgs - ET - Res - Lib
M 25 i, 60 f, 10 org, UK / 2 f, o'seas
¶ Various publications available.

Institute of Car Fleet Management (ICFM) 1992
NR PO Box 314, CHICHESTER, W Sussex, PO20 9WZ.   (hq)
  01462 744914   fax 01462 607591
  email administration:icfm.com   http://www.icfm.com
  Chmn: Roddy Graham
○ *P; to foster & promote the profession of vehicle fleet
  management within industry & commerce
● Conf - ET - Exam - Mtgs - Res

Institute of Career Guidance Ltd   (ICG) 1922
NR Copthall House (ground floor), 1 New Rd, STOURBRIDGE,
  W Midlands, DY8 1PH.   (hq)
  01384 376464   fax 01384 440830
  email hq@icg-uk.org   http://www.icg-uk.org
  Admin: Dan Hope
▲ Company Limited by Guarantee
○ *P; to optimise the profile, visibility and impact of career
  guidance
● Conf - ET - Exhib - Lib
< Fedn of Profl Assns in Guidance
M 3,000 i, 17 f
¶ Careers Guidance Today - 6; ftm, £27.50 yr nm.
  Front-Line - 6; ftm only.
  Vacancy Bulletin (Portico) - 26; £10 m, £40 nm.

Institute of Carpenters (IOC) 1890
NR 32 High St, WENDOVER, Bucks, HP22 6EA.   (hq)
  0844 879 7696   fax 01296 620981
  email info@instituteofcarpenters.com
  http://www.instituteofcarpenters.com
  Admin: Sharon Hutchings
○ *P; to encourage the highest standards of carpentry & joinery
  work; to promote & enhance the role & status of skilled
  craftsmen & women
M 3,000 i

Institute of Cast Metals Engineers (ICME) 1904
■ National Metalforming Centre, 47 Birmingham Rd,
  WEST BROMWICH, W Midlands, B70 6PY.   (hq)
  0121-601 6979   fax 0121-601 6981
  email info@icme.org.uk   http://www.icme.org.uk
  Dir: Dr Pam Murrell
▲ Registered Charity
Br 7
○ *P; to provide professional development programmes for
  individuals employed in the global cast metal industry
Gp Working gps (technical, educational & training) investigating
  various topics
● Mtgs - ET - Inf - Lib - PL
< Wld Foundrymen Org; Engg Coun
M 1,207 i, UK / 90 i, o'seas
¶ Foundry Trade Jnl - 10; ftm, £179 (237 RoW) nm.
  Diecasting World - 2; £38 (£56 RoW).
  Foundry Ybk & Castings Buyers Guide - 1; £151.
  AR - 1; free.

Institute of Cemetery & Crematorium Management   (ICCM) 1913
■   City of London Cemetery, Aldersbrook Rd, LONDON, E12 5DQ.   (hq)
      020 8989 4661   fax 020 8989 6112
      email julie@iccm.fsnet.co.uk   http://www.iccm-uk.com
      Chief Exec: Tim Morris
▲   Company Limited by Guarantee
Br 8
○   *P; to promote professional training, education & consultancy for UK burial & cremation authorities
●   Conf - Mtgs - ET - Exam - Exhib - Lib
<   Intl Cremation Fedn
M   680 i, 305 f, UK / 10 i, o'seas
¶   The Jnl - 4; ftm, £4 yr nm.

Institute of Certified Book-Keepers   (ICB)   1996
NR 1 Northumberland Ave, LONDON, WC2N 5BW.   (hq)
      0845 060 2345
      http://www.book-keepers.org
      Chief Exec: Garry Carter
▲   Company Limited by Guarantee
Br 32; 11 countries
○   *P; to set standards in book-keeping
Gp Members in practice
●   Exam
<   ICB Intl
M   100,000 i, 5 f, 54 colleges & training org, UK / 604 i, o'seas
¶   Invoice - 4.

Institute of Certified Public Accountants in Ireland   (CPA) 1943
IRL 17 Harcourt St, DUBLIN 2, Republic of Ireland.   (hq)
      353 (1) 425 1000   fax 353 (1) 425 1001
      email cpa@cpaireland.ie   http://www.cpaireland.ie
      Chief Exec: Eamonn Siggins
Br 3 Wellington Park, Malone Rd, BELFAST, BT9 6DJ.
      028 9092 3390   fax 028 9092 3334
○   *P

Institute of Chartered Accountants in England & Wales (ICAEW)   1880
■   Chartered Accountants' Hall, Moorgate Place, LONDON, EC2R 6EA.   (hq)
      020 7920 8100   fax 020 7920 0547
      http://www.icaew.com
      Chief Exec: Michael Izza
▲   Registered Charity
○   *P
M   95,300 i, 19,209 f, 22 org, UK / 14,000 i, o'seas
¶   Accountancy (Jnl) - 12.   LM.   AR.

Institute of Chartered Accountants in Ireland
   since 2009 **Chartered Accountants Ireland**

Institute of Chartered Accountants of Scotland   (ICAS)   1854
NR 21 Haymarket Yards, EDINBURGH, EH12 5BH.   (hq)
      0131-347 0100   fax 0131-347 0105
      email enquiries@icas.org.uk   http://www.icas.org.uk
      Chief Exec & Sec: Des Hudson
Br 7 area committees
○   *P
●   Conf - Mtgs - ET - Exam - Res - SG - Inf - Lib - LG
<   Intl Fedn of Accountants (IFAC); Intl Accounting Standards C'ee (IASC); Fédn des Experts Comptables Eur (FEE); Auditing Practices Bd (APB)
M   15,208 i
¶   CA Magazine - 12; ftm.
      Directory of Insolvency Permit Holders - 1.
      Research Publications; prices vary.

Institute of Chartered Foresters   (ICF)   1925
■   59 George St, EDINBURGH, EH2 2JG.   (hq)
      0131-240 1425   fax 0131-240 1425
      email icf@charteredforesters.org
      http://www.charteredforesters.org
      Exec Dir: Shireen Chambers
▲   Registered Charity
○   *L, *P
●   Conf - ET - Exam - Res - Inf - VE - LG
<   Soc for the Envt (SocEnv)
M   i
¶   The Chartered Forester - 4;   Forestry Jnl - 5.
      Register of Consultants - 1;   AR; all ftm.
      Forestry - 4; £40 m, £230 nm.

Institute of Chartered Secretaries & Administrators   (ICSA) 1891
NR 16 Park Crescent, LONDON, W1B 1AH.   (hq)
      020 7580 4741
      http://www.icsa.org.uk
▲   Registered Charity
○   *P; law & practice of secretaryship & administration
M   23,000 i, UK / 52,000 i, o'seas

Institute of Chartered Shipbrokers   (ICS)   1920
NR 85 Gracechurch St, LONDON, EC3V 0AA.   (hq)
      020 7623 1111
      http://www.ics.org.uk
▲   Royal Charter
○   *P
M   i, f

Institute of Chemistry of Ireland   (Institiúid Ceimice na h'Éireann)   1950
IRL PO Box 9322, Cardiff Lane, DUBLIN 2, Republic of Ireland. (hq)
      email info@instituteofchemistry.org
      http://www.instituteofchemistry.org
      Hon Sec: Dr J P Ryan
○   *L; to promote chemistry & represent the profession of chemistry in Ireland
<   Eur Assn for Chemical & Molecular Sciences (EuCheMS)
M   800 i
¶   Irish Chemical News - 2; ftm.

Institute of Chiropodists & Podiatrists   (IoCP)   1938
■   27 Wright St, SOUTHPORT, Merseyside, PR9 0TL.   (hq)
      01704 546141   fax 01704 500477
      email secretary@iocp.org.uk   http://www.iocp.org.uk
      Sec: Mrs S M Kirkham
▲   Company Limited by Guarantee
Br 25
○   *P
M   i
¶   Podiatry Review.

Institute of Civil Defence & Disaster Studies
   on 1 January 2009 the Institute of Civil Defence & Disaster Studies & the Institute of Emergency Management amalgamated to form the **Institute of Civil Protection & Emergency Management**

Institute of Civil Protection & Emergency Management (ICPEM)   1938

NR   PO Box 16248, BIRMINGHAM, B30 9EJ.   (hq)
       http://www.icpem.net
       Gen Sec: Mark Parker
○   *P; advancement of civil protection, emergency management & disaster studies (natural events, terrorism, catastrophes & system failure)
●   Conf - ET - Res - Lib - LG
<   Intl Civil Defence Org
M   i & org
¶   Alert (Jnl).
×   2009 (Institute of Civil Defence & Disaster Studies (Institute of Emergency Management

Institute of Clay Shooting Instructors   (ICSI)   1987

NR   4 Holmlands Crescent, Durham Moor, DURHAM, DH1 5AR. (memsec/p)
       http://www.icsi.org.uk
○   *P, *S; for clay shooting coaches

Institute of Clayworkers   (ICW)

§   Federation House, Station Rd, STOKE-ON-TRENT, Staffs, ST4 2SA.   (hq)
       01782 744631   fax 01782 744102
       email bcc@ceramfed.co.uk
       Sec: A McRae
       A benevolent fund, awarding long service medals

Institute of Clerks of Works of Great Britain Inc   (ICW)   1882

■   28 Commerce Rd, Lynch Wood, PETERBOROUGH, PE2 6LR. (hq)
       01733 405160   fax 01733 405161
       email info@icwgb.co.uk   http://www.icwgb.org
       Gen Sec: Rachel Morris
▲   Company Limited by Guarantee
Br 20; Hong Kong
○   *P; examining & qualifying body for clerks of works in the UK & overseas
Gp Building construction
●   Conf - Mtgs - Res - Exhib - Inf - VE - LG
>   Brit Standards Inst; Construction Ind Coun
M   1,579 i, UK / 183 i, o'seas
¶   Site Recorder (Jnl) - 12;   LM - 1; both ftm.

Institute of Clinical Research   (ICR)   1978

■   Institute House, Boston Drive, BOURNE END, Bucks, SL8 5YS. (hq)
       0845 521 0056   fax 01628 530641
       http://www.icr-global.org
       Chief Exec: Dr John Hooper
▲   Company Limited by Guarantee
○   *P
●   Conf - Mtgs - ET - Exam - Exhib
M   3,980 i, UK / 1,048 i, o'seas
¶   Clinical Research Focus - 11; ftm only.   AR; free.

Institute of Commercial Management Ltd   (ICM)   1979

■   ICM House, Castleman Way, RINGWOOD, Hants, BH24 3BA.   (hq)
       01202 490555   fax 01202 490666
       email info@icm.ac.uk   http://www.icm.ac.uk
       Chief Exec: Tom Thomas
▲   Company Limited by Guarantee; Registered Charity
○   *E, *P; educational foundation supporting business, personal & professional development
Gp Provision of expert technical assistance & consultancy services in the fields of trade, tourism & professional development
●   Conf - ET - Exam
M   12,400 i

Institute for Complementary Medicine
       since 2008 **Institute for Complementary & Natural Medicine**.

Institute for Complementary & Natural Medicine   (ICNM)   1982

NR   Can-Mezzanine, 32-36 Loman St, LONDON, SE1 0EH.   (hq)
       020 7922 7980   fax 020 7922 7981
       email info@icnm.org.uk   http://www.i-c-m.org.uk
       Chief Exec: Yvonne Wilcox
▲   Registered Charity
○   *P; to provide the public with information services for the safe & appropriate choice of complementary medicine; to administer the British Register of Complementary Practitioners (BRCP)
Gp BRCP Divisions & Practices: Aromatherapy; Bowen; Bioregulatory Medicine; Colonic hydrotherapy; Colour therapy; Counselling; Energy medicine; General; Healer counsellor; Herbal medicine; Homoeopathy; Homotoxicology; Hypnotherapy; Indian medicine; Kinesiology; Massage; Metaphysical counselling; Modern acupuncture; Naturopathy; Nutrition; Oriental medicine; Osteopathy; Physical medicine; Psychotherapy; Rebirthing; Reflexology; Sound
●   Conf - ET - Inf - LG - Registration
<   Aromatherapy Coun; Gen Coun for Massage Therapies
M   i, 600 org
¶   ICNM Jnl - 4.
×   2008 Institute for Complementary Medicine

Institute of Concrete Technology   (ICT)   1972

NR   Riverside House, 4 Meadows Business Park, Station Approach, Blackwater, CAMBERLEY, Surrey, GU17 9AB.   (hq)
       01276 607140   fax 01276 607141
       http://www.ict.concrete.org.uk
       Hon Sec: Kevin Sutherland
▲   Company Limited by Guarantee
Br 1; Ireland, South Africa
○   *P; to preserve & promote concrete technology as a recognised engineering discipline & to consolidate the professional status of practising concrete technologists worldwide
●   Conf - Mtgs - ET - Exam
<   Engineering Coun
M   420 i, UK / 210 i, o'seas
¶   NL - 4.   Ybk.   Members Hbk.
       In 2007 ICT merged with the Concrete Society to become its professional wing whilst retaining its own identity

Institute of Conflict Management   (ICM)   2000

NR   840 Melton Rd, Thurmaston, LEICESTER, LE4 8BN.   (asa)
       0116-269 1049   fax 0116-264 0141
       email icm@associationhq.org.uk
       http://www.conflictmanagement.org
       Chief Exec: Stuart Hex
▲   Company Limited by Guarantee
○   *P; to develop, monitor & promote professional standards for the effective prevention & management of aggression & conflict at work
●   Conf - Mtgs - ET - Res - Exhib - Inf - LG - Training provision of the National Foundation Certificate for Managing Work-related Violence - Quality award process for training in the management of work related violence
M   350 i
¶   ICM NL - 4.

Institute of Conservation   (Icon)   2005

NR   Unit 1.5 Lafone House, The Leathermarket, Weston St,
     LONDON, SE1 3ER.   (hq)
     020 3142 6799
     email info@icon.org.uk   http://www.icon.org.uk
     Chief Exec: Alison Richmond
▲   Company Limited by Guarantee; Registered Charity
Br   2
○   *P; to advance the education of the public by research into &
     the promotion of the conservation of items & collections of
     items of cultural, aesthetic, historic & scientific value; to
     preserve & conserve such items & collections
Gp   Archaeology; Book & paper; Care of collections; Ceramics &
     glass; Ethnography; Furniture & wood; Gilding & decorative
     services; Historic interiors; Metals; Paintings; Photographic
     materials; Science; Stained glass; Stone & wall paintings;
     Textiles
M   i
¶   Jnl.   Icon News.

Institute for the Conservation of Historic & Artistic Works in Ireland   (ICHAWI)   1991

IRL   1 Lower Grand Canal St, DUBLIN 2, Republic of Ireland.   (hq)
     353 (1) 603 0904
     email ichawi@eircom.net   http://www.ichawi.org
     Hon Sec: Maighread McParland
▲   Company Limited by Guarantee; Registered Charity
○   *P; to promote the profession of conservation in Ireland; to
     educate by promoting the advancement & knowledge of
     conservation & all its disciplines

Institute of Construction Management   (ICM)   1970

NR   23 Station Rd, CORSHAM, Wilts, SN13 9EY.   (pres/p)
     01249 713115
     http://www.the-icm.com
     Pres: Mark D Rea
▲   Company Limited by Guarantee
Br   9; Hong Kong
○   P; construction & site management & knowledge of all modern
     construction methods
●   Conf - Mtgs - ET - Exam - Inf - VE
<   Construction Ind Coun
M   c 700 i & f
¶   Viewpoint (NL) - 4; ftm only.

Institute of Construction Specialists   (IOCS)   2001

■   1 Walpole House, 2 Pickford St, ALDERSHOT, Hants,
     GU11 1TZ.   (hq)
     01252 312122   fax 01252 343081
     email info@constructionspecialists.org
     http://www.constructionspecialists.org
     Group Dir: A R Gibbs
▲   Un-incorporated Society
○   *P; for managers & administrative & supervisory staff of
     specialist construction firms; to focus on training &
     accreditation
●   ET - Exam - Comp
<   Construction Specialists Gp
M   i
¶   IOCS/CCS NL - 10; ftm only.

Institute of Consulting   (IC)   2007

■   2 Savoy Court (4th floor), Strand, LONDON, WC2R 0EZ.   (hq)
     020 7497 0580   fax 020 7497 0463
     email welcome@iconsulting.org.uk
     http://www.iconsulting.org.uk
     Dir: Lynda Purser
▲   Registered Charity
Br   12 regions
○   *P; for those offering management consultancy, business
     advice, business consulting, professional standards
Gp   Consultancy purchasing; Internal business consulting
●   Conf - Mtgs - ET - Res - Exhib - Comp - SG - Stat - Inf - Lib -
     LG
<   Intl Coun of Insts of Mgt Consultancy; Chart Mgt Inst
M   i, f
¶   Professional Manager - 6; ftm, £3.60 nm.
×   2007 (Institute of Business Advisers
          (Institute of Management Consultancy
     2011 Institute of Business Consulting
     IC is an organisation within the Chartered Management
     Institute

Institute of Consumer Affairs   (ICA)   1974

NR   Corsletts Farm, Church Rd, BROADBRIDGE HEATH, W Sussex,
     RH12 3LD.   (memsec/p)
     01403 754718
     email secretary@icanet.org.uk   http://www.icanet.org.uk
     Mem Sec: Jacqui King
○   *P; a network of consumer advisers & others working in
     consumer protection & consumer affairs. To raise the quality
     of services to consumers through better information, advice &
     education; to improve consumer protection
●   Conf - Mtgs - ET - Inf
M   150 i
¶   Help & Advice - 6; m only.

Institute of Contemporary Arts   (ICA)   1947

NR   12 Carlton House Terrace, LONDON, SW1Y 5AH.   (hq)
     http://www.ica.org.uk
○   *A, *D; a centre for contemporary cultural activities, incl film,
     theatre, dance, lectures & visual arts
M   7,000 i

Institute of Continuing Professional Development   (ICPD)

NR   RICS, Parliament Square, LONDON, SW1P 3AD.   (hq)
     020 3286 5273
     email info@cpdinstitute.org   http://www.cpdinstitute.org
     Founder: Jonathan Harris
○   *E

Institute of Corrosion   (ICorr)   1975

NR   7B High St Mews, High St, LEIGHTON BUZZARD, Beds,
     LU7 1EA.   (hq)
     01525 851771
     http://www.icorr.org
     Hon Sec: Dr Steve Mabbutt
▲   Registered Charity
Br   8; Republic of Ireland
○   *L *P; study & advice concerning corrosion engineering
     problems & corrosion prevention
●   Conf - Mtgs - ET
M   1,450 i, 40 f, UK / 150 i, 1 f, o'seas
¶   Corrosion Science - 12.   Corrosion Management - 6.
     UK Corrosion (conference papers) - 1.

Institute of Cost & Executive Accountants   (ICEA)   1958

NR   Akhtar House, 2 Shepherds Bush Rd, LONDON, W6 7PJ.   (hq)
     http://www.iceaglobal.com
▲   Company Limited by Guarantee
○   *P; 'to promote the study & adoption of scientific methods in
     industrial & commercial enterprise, local government, public
     service & intenal audit streams'
●   Mtgs - ET - Exam

Institute of Couriers (IoC) 2006

NR Green Man Tower, 332 Goswell Rd, LONDON, EC1V 7LQ. (hq)
   0845 601 0245
   email mail@ioc.uk.com   http://www.ioc.uk.com
   Sec: Tracey Worth
○ *T; to encourage knowledge sharing & development of individual's own competence in the application of courier skills
● Mtgs
¶ Signpost (NL); ftm.

Institute of Credit Management (ICM) 1939

■ The Water Mill, Station Rd, South Luffenham, OAKHAM, Rutland, LE15 8NB.   (hq)
   01780 722900   fax 01780 721333
   email info@icm.org.uk   http://www.icm.org.uk
   Dir Gen: Philip King
▲ Company Limited by Guarantee; Registered Charity
Br 26
○ *P; for those employed in credit management, credit finance & ancillary services
● Conf - Mtgs - ET - Exam - Res - Exhib - Inf - Lib - LG
< Fedn of Eur Credit Mgt Assns (FECMA)
M 9,000 i, UK / 300 i, o'seas
¶ Credit Management - 12; ftm, £75 yr nm.
   AR - 1; ftm.

Institute of Customer Service (ICS) 1997

NR 2 Castle Court, St Peter's St, COLCHESTER, Essex, CO1 1EW. (hq)
   01206 571716   fax 01206 546688
   email enquiries@icsmail.co.uk
   http://www.instituteofcustomerservice.com
   Chief Exec: David Parsons
▲ Company Limited by Guarantee
Br 10
○ *P; to develop & spread authoritative knowledge & good practice, define national professional & occupational standards & provide professional recognition to individuals in the customer service industry
● Conf - Mtgs - ET - Res - Exhib - Stat - Inf - VE - LG
M 3,000 i, 180 f
¶ Customer First - 5; ftm, £4.95 nm.
   Research publications - irreg; prices vary.

Institute of Decontamination Sciences (IDSc) 2004

NR Fitwise Management Ltd, Drumcross Hall, BATHGATE, W Lothian, EH48 4JT.   (asa)
   01506 811077   fax 01506 811477
   email idsc.admin@googlemail.com
   http://www.idsc-uk.co.uk
   Dir of Admin: Kath Saxelby
▲ Un-incorporated Society
Br 8
○ *P; for staff & management in the field of decontamination & sterile services
Gp Conference c'ee; Education
● Conf - Mtgs - ET - Exhib - Promotion of research & development
< Eur Fedn of Hospital Sterile Services
> Eur Fedn of Hospital Sterile Services
M 370 i, 15 f, UK / 8 i, o'seas
¶ Jnl - 4; ftm, £25 each nm.   Ybk - 1; ftm, £55 nm.
   Technical Vocational Training Programme; £18.
   Standards & Practices; £25.

Institute of Demolition Engineers (IDE) 1971

■ 69 Poplicans Rd, Cuxton, ROCHESTER, Kent, ME2 1EJ.   (hsp)
   01634 294255   fax 01634 294255
   email info@ide.org.uk   http://www.ide.org.uk
   Sec: Mrs Valerie J Stroud
▲ Registered Charity
○ *P; to advance the science of demolition engineering, the use of effective techniques in the industry & safer methods of working; to provide a qualifying body in the industry
● Conf - Mtgs - ET - Exam - Inf - LG
M 317 i, UK / 7 i, o'seas
¶ Demolition Engineer - 3; ftm.

Institute of Designers in Ireland (IDI) 1972

IRL The Digital Hub, Roe Lane, Thomas St, DUBLIN 8, Republic of Ireland.
   353 (1) 489 3650
   email info@idi-design.ie   http://www.idi-design.ie
   Pres: Barry Sheehan
○ *P; to promote high standards of design, to foster professionalism & to emphasise designers' responsibility to society, to the client & to each other
● Mtgs
¶ Ratio (NL) - 4; ftm.

Institute of Direct Marketing (IDM) 1987

NR 1 Park Rd, TEDDINGTON, Middx, TW11 0AR.   (hq)
   020 8977 5705   fax 020 8943 2535
   email enquiries@theidm.com   http://www.theidm.com
▲ Registered Charity
○ *P; direct marketing training & education for members
● ET - Exam - Lib
< Direct Marketing Assn
M 5,000 i, UK / 200 i, o'seas
¶ Jnl of Interactive Marketing - 4.

Institute of Directors (IoD) 1903

NR 116 Pall Mall, LONDON, SW1Y 5ED.   (hq)
   020 7839 1233   fax 020 7930 1949
   http://www.iod.com
   Dir Gen: Simon Walker
○ *P; to promote for the public benefit high levels of skill, knowledge, professional competence & integrity on the part of directors, & equivalent office holders however described, of companies & other organisations
M 40,000 i, UK / 14,000 i, o'seas
¶ Director - 11; ftm.

Institute of Directors in Ireland (IoD)

IRL Europa House, Harcourt St, DUBLIN 2, Republic of Ireland.   (hq)
   353 (1) 411 0010   fax 353 (1) 411 0090
   email info@iodireland.ie   http://www.iodireland.ie
   Chief Exec: Maura Quinn
○ *P; the representative body for senior, strategic business professionals in Ireland

Institute of Domestic Heating & Environmental Engineers (IDHEE) 1964

■ PO Box 329, SOUTHAMPTON, Hants, SO40 0BT.   (hq)
   023 8066 8900   fax 023 8066 0888
   email admin@idhee.org.uk   http://www.idhee.org.uk
   Exec Chmn: Bill Bucknell
▲ Un-incorporated Society
Br Ireland, New Zealand
○ *P; to raise the standard of domestic heating & environmental engineering
Gp Renewable energy; Consulting & design engineers
● Conf - Mtgs - ET - Exam - Exhib - LG
M 781 i, 31 f, UK / 64 i, 3 f, o'seas
¶ Comfort Engineering - 4; ftm, £5 nm.
   Technical Hbk - 1; ftm, £7.50 nm.

Institute of Ecology & Environmental Management (IEEM) 1991
NR 43 Southgate St, WINCHESTER, Hants, SO23 9EH. (hq)
01962 868626   fax 01962 868625
email enquiries@ieem.net   http://www.ieem.net
Chief Exec: Sally Hayns
▲ Company Limited by Guarantee
Br 8 regional sections
○ *P; to promote & support professionalism in the fields of
ecology & environmental management
● Conf - Mtgs - ET - Res - Exhib - Comp - Stat - Lib - LG
< Intl Consvn U (IUCN); Eur Fedn of Assns of Envtl Profls (EFAEP);
Soc for the Envt (SocEnv); EUROPARC; EUROSITE
M 3,500 i, UK / 200 i, o'seas
(Sub: £130 UK / £80 o'seas)
¶ In Practice (Jnl) - 4; ftm; £30 yr nm.
Members Directory - 1; [on website].
Conference Proceedings - 2; £21.
Technical Guidance.   AR - 1.

Institute of Economic Affairs Ltd (IEA) 1957
NR 2 Lord North St, LONDON, SW1P 3LB. (hq)
020 7799 3745
http://www.iea.org.uk
Dir Gen: John Blundell
▲ Registered Charity
○ *L; extension of public understanding of economic principles in
their application to practical problems
● Conf - ET - Lib
M i & f
¶ Economic Affairs - 4; ftm.
Publications are irreg & prices vary.

Institute of Educational Assessors
on 2 April 2008 became the **Chartered Institute of Educational
Assessors**

Institute of Emergency Management
on 2 January 2009 the Institute of Emergency Management & the
Institute of Civil Defence & Disaster Studies amalgamayed to form the
Institute of Civil Protection & Emergency Management

Institute of Employment Rights (IER) 1989
■ Jack Jones House (4th floor), 1 Islington, LIVERPOOL,
L3 8EG. (hq)
0151-207 5265   fax 0151-207 5264
email office@ier.org.uk   http://www.ier.org.uk
Dir: Carolyn Jones
▲ Company Limited by Guarantee; Registered Charity
○ *Q; to act as a focal point for the spread of new ideas in the
field of the labour law
● Conf - ET - Res - Inf - Publishing
M 81 i
¶ Books on various aspects of labour law - 8; £6.50 m, £20 nm.

Institute of Entertainment & Arts Management (IEAM) 1982
■ 17 Drake Close, HORSHAM, W Sussex, RH12 4UB. (admin/p)
01403 265988
email admin@ieamltd.co.uk   http://www.ieamltd.co.uk
Admin: Shirley Carpenter
▲ Company Limited by Guarantee
Br Northern & Southern areas
○ *D; for managers & managements throughout local
government, commercial & subsidised sectors of the arts,
entertainment & related leisure interests
● Conf - Mtgs - ET - Exhib - Comp - Stat - Inf - VE
M 290 i
¶ NL - 12;   Ybk - 1; both ftm only.
✕ 2009 Institute of Entertainment & Arts Professionals

Institute of Entertainment & Arts Professionals
since 2009 the **Institute of Entertainment & Arts Management**

**Institute of Environmental Management & Assessment
(IEMA) 1999**
NR St Nicholas House, 70 Newport, LINCOLN, LN1 3DP. (hq)
01522 540069   fax 01522 540090
email info@iema.net   http://www.iema.net
Chief Exec: Russell Foster
○ *P; to promote & develop the best practice standards in
environmental management, auditing & assessment
● Conf - Mtgs - ET - Exam - Exhib - Inf - Lib
< Soc for the Envt (SocEnv)
M 7,620 i, 310 f, UK / 1,245 i, 26 f, o'seas

Institute of Equality & Diversity Practitioners (IEDP) 2009
NR 2 Old College Court, 28 Priory St, WARE, Herts, SG12 0DE.
(asa)
0844 482 7263   fax 0844 822 5215
http://www.iedp.org.uk
Chmn: Linda Bellos
○ *P; to ensure that all practitioners who work in the equality,
diversity & human rights sector have access to high quality
learning, accreditation, professional development &
networking opportunities
● Conf - Mtgs - ET - Inf
M i
¶ NL - email.

Institute of Explosives Engineers (IExpE) 1974
NR Wellington Hall 289, Cranfield University, Defence Academy of
the UK, Shrivenham, SWINDON, Wilts, SN6 8LA. (hq)
01793 785322   fax 01793 785972
email iexpe@cranfield.ac.uk   http://www.iexpe.org
Sec: Gillian Bonar
Br 13
○ *P; the qualifying body for explosives engineers
Gp Quarrying; Tunnelling & shaft sinking; Excavation & land
clearance; Demolition; Underwater work; Pyrotechnics;
Offshore oil operations; High explosives trials; Film & special
effects
● Conf - Mtgs - ET - Exam - Res - Exhib - SG - Inf - LG
< Eur Fedn Explosives Engineers
M 758 i, 31 i (company), 20 f, UK / 145 i, 4 f, o'seas
¶ Explosives Engineering - 4.

Institute of Export (IOE) 1935
■ Export House, Minerva Business Park, Lynch Wood,
PETERBOROUGH, Cambs, PE2 6FT. (hq)
01733 404400   fax 01733 404444
email institute@export.org.uk   http://www.export.org.uk
Chmn: Doug Tweddle
▲ Company Limited by Guarantee; Registered Charity
Br 8; Hong Kong
○ *P; to represent & support the interests of everyone involved in
importing, exporting & international trade
Gp Education; Training
● ET - Exam - Exhib
M 3,000 i, 100 f, UK / 500 i, o'seas
¶ Pathfinder Business - 6; ftm, £3.95 nm.

Institute & Faculty of Actuaries   1848
- ■ Staple Inn Hall, High Holborn, LONDON, WC1V 7QJ.   (hq)
   020 7632 2100   fax 020 7632 2111
   http://www.actuaries.org.uk
   Maclaurin House, 18 Dublin St, EDINBURGH, EH1 3PP.
   0131-240 1313
   Pres: Jane Curtis,   Chief Exec: Derek Cribb
- Br Edinburgh, Oxford
- ○ *P; the controlling body for the actuarial profession
- Gp Financial consumer interest group; Non-executive directors' interest group; Resource & environment interest group; Variable annuities interest group
- ● Conf - Mtgs - ET - Exam - Res - Lib - Technical guidance - Issuance of practising certificates
   The Education Executive, Careers & Library are at:
   4 Worcester St, Oxford, OX1 2AW.   01865 268200
- < Intl Actuarial Assn
- M 22,000 i
- ¶ British Actuarial Jnl - 3.
   Annals of Actuarial Science - 2.
   Professional Standards Directory - updated.
- × 2010 (Faculty of Actuaries in Scotland (Institute of Actuaries (merged 1 August)

Institute for Family Business   (IFB)   2001
- NR 32 Buckingham Palace Rd, LONDON, SW1W 0RE.   (hq)
   020 7630 6250   fax 020 7630 6251
   email info@ifb.org.uk   http://www.ifb.org.uk
   Dir Gen: Grant Gordon
- ▲ Company Limited by Guarantee
- ○ *T; to generate, stimulate, disseminate, promote & sponsor understanding & knowledge of the development of business & managerial practices relating to the position, requirements & interests of family businesses in the UK
- Gp Next Generation Forum
- ● Conf - LG - Mtgs - Res
- < Confedn of Brit Ind (CBI)
- M 220 f
- ¶ Ybk - 1; ftm.

Institute of Field Archaeologists   (IfA)   1982
- ■ SHES, University of Reading, Whiteknights, PO Box 227, READING, Berks, RG6 6AB.   (hq)
   0118-378 6446   fax 0118-378 6448
   email admin@archaeologists.net
   http://www.archaeologists.net
   Admin: Alex Llewelyn,   Chief Exec: Peter Hinten
- ▲ Company Limited by Guarantee
- ○ *L, *P; to advance the practice of archaeology & allied disciplines by the promotion of professional standards & ethics
- Gp Area: Scotland, Wales, East Midlands
   Special interest: Buildings Archaeology Group, Diggers Forum, Finds, Forum for information standards in heritage, Geophysics, Illustration & surveying, Marine affairs
- ● Conf - Mtgs - ET - Res - Exhib - Inf
- < Irish Assn Profl Archaeologists; Assn Archaeol Illustrators & Surveyors
- M 61 f
   (Sub: depends on income / turnover)
- ¶ The Archaeologist (Jnl) - 4.ftm, £5 nm.
   Ybk & Directory - 1; ftm, £30 nm.   AR - 1; ftm, £5 nm.
   Professional Practice Papers - irreg; ftm, £10 nm.
   Standards Guidance Documents; ftm, £30 nm.
   JIS - 52; £15 or email free, c£20 per month nm.
   ote: uses the trading name Institute for Archaeologists

Institute of Financial Accountants   (IFA)   1916
- NR Burford House, 44 London Rd, SEVENOAKS, Kent, TN13 1AS.   (hq)
   01732 458080   fax 01732 455848
   email mail@ifa.org.uk   http://www.ifa.org.uk
   Chief Exec: David Woodgate
- ▲ Company Limited by Guarantee
- ○ *P; for accountants in commerce, industry & private practice
- M 8,000 i, UK / 2,000 i, o'seas

Institute of Financial Planning   (IFP)   1987
- NR Whitefriars Centre, Lewins Mead, BRISTOL, BS1 2NT.   (hq)
   0117-945 2470   fax 0117-929 2214
   email enquiries@financialplanning.org.uk
   http://www.financialplanning.org.uk
   Chief Exec: Nick Cann
- ▲ Company Limited by Guarantee
- Br 12
- ○ *P; to promote understanding & recognition of the financial planning profession (those who offer objective assistance to clients in organising their personal & business affairs)
- ● Conf - Mtgs - ET - Exam - Res - Exhib - Comp - SG - Inf - Lib - LG
- < Intl CFP Coun; Financial Planning Assn (FPA) (USA)
- M 1,250 i, UK / 50 i, o'seas
- ¶ Financial Planner - 4; ftm only.

Institute of Financial Services   (ifs)   1879
- NR ifs House, 4-9 Burgate Lane, CANTERBURY, Kent, CT1 2XJ.
   (hq)
   01227 818609
   http://www.ifslearning.ac.uk
   Chief Exec: Gavin Shreeve
- ▲ Registered Charity
- Br 72 local centres; 6 o'seas
- ○ *L, *P; education & training of financial services staff
- ● Conf - Mtgs - ET - Exam - Res - Exhib - Comp - SG - Inf - Lib
- M 42,000 i
- ¶ Financial World - 12.
   ifs News - 12.   Syllabus.   Catalogue.   AR.
   Publications list available.
   Note: The parent body of the ifs is the Chartered Institute of Bankers; the ifs develops & delivers qualifications for which the CIB acts as an assessing & awarding body

Institute for Fiscal Studies   (IFS)   1969
- ■ 7 Ridgmount St, LONDON, WC1E 7AE.   (hq)
   020 7291 4800
   email mailbox@ifs.org.uk   http://www.ifs.org.uk
   Dir: Robert Chote
- ▲ Company Limited by Guarantee; Registered Charity
- ○ *Q; promotion of research & understanding of the economic & social implications of existing taxes & different fiscal systems
- ● Conf - ET - Res - SG - Stat - Inf
- M 600 i, 100 f, 100 org, UK / 100 i, 50 org, o'seas
- ¶ Fiscal Studies (Jnl) - 4; ftm, £237 nm.
   Reports & Commentaries - 15; ftm, c £40 each nm.
   Briefing Notes - 15;   NL - 4; Working Papers - 20;
   [last 3 publications online].

Institute of Fisheries Management   (IFM)   1969
- ■ PO Box 26, EXETER, Devon, EX5 2WR.   (hq)
   0845 388 7012
   email info@ifm.org.uk   http://www.ifm.org.uk
   Hon Sec: Steve Axford
- ▲ Un-incorporated Society
- Br 11
- ○ *L, *P; management of freshwater aquatic environment
- ● Conf - Mtgs - ET - Exam - LG
- < Soc for the Envt (SocEnv)
- M 900 i, 5 f, 40 org, UK / 40 i, o'seas
- ¶ Fish - 4; ftm only.

© CBD Research Ltd · Beckenham · BR3 5JS · Tel 020 8650 7745 · E-mail cbd@cbdresearch.com · www.cbdresearch.com

Institute of Food Science & Technology   (IFST)   1964
NR   5 Cambridge Court, 210 Shepherds Bush Rd, LONDON,
        W6 7NJ.   (hq)
        020 7603 6316   fax 020 7602 9936
        email info@ifst.org   http://www.ifst.org
        Chief Exec: Jon Poole
▲   Company Limited by Guarantee; Registered Charity
Br   7
○   *L, *P; application of science & technology to every aspect of
        food
●   Conf - Mtgs - ET - Exam - VE - LG
<   Intl U of Food Science & Technology (IUFOST); UK Fedn for
        Food Science & Technology (UKFFOST); Parliamentary Food
        & Health Forum; Eur Food Law Assn (UK section); Science
        Coun; Foundation for Science & Technology
M   2,221 f, UK / 335 f, o'seas
¶   International Jnl of Food Science & Technology - 10;
        £21 (£13 online) m, £936 yr nm (UK).
        Food Science & Technology - 4; ftm, £96 yr nm.
        Keynote - 11; ftm.

**Institute of Football Management & Administration   (IFMA)
1990**
■   The Camkin Suite, 1 Pegasus House, Tachbrook Park,
        WARWICK, CV34 6LW.   (hq)
        01926 831556   fax 01926 429781
        email ifma@lmasecure.com
        http://www.leaguemanagers.com
        Chmn: Andy Daykin
▲   Registered Trade Union
○   *S; for all key staff in 92 FA Premier & Football League football
        clubs
●   Conf - Mtgs - ET - Exhib - SG - Inf
M   2 assns:
        Barclays Premier League
        npower Football League
¶   Centre Circle - 4; free.

Institute of Fundraising   (IoF)   1983
■   Park Place, 12 Lawn Lane, LONDON, SW8 1UD.   (hq)
        020 7840 1000   fax 020 7840 1001
        email info@institute-of-fundraising.org.uk
        http://www.institute-of-fundraising.org.uk
        Hon Sec: John Baguley
▲   Company Limited by Guarantee; Registered Charity
Br   Scotland, Wales
○   *P; to support fundraisers through leadership, representation,
        standards-setting & education; to champion & promote
        fundraising as a career choice
●   Conf - ET - Inf
M   300 org, 5,000 i
¶   Update - 11; ftm only.   LM; m only.   Ybk; ftm.
        List of Consultants; ftm.   AR; free.

Institute of Geologists of Ireland   (IGI)   1999
IRL   c/o School of Geological Sciences, University College Dublin,
        Belfield, DUBLIN 4, Republic of Ireland.   (hq)
        353 (1) 716 2085   fax 353 (1) 283 7733
        email info@igi.ie   http://www.igi.ie
        Sec: Jonathan Derham
○   *P; to promote the interests of the geoscience professions &
        advance the science & practice of the geosciences in Ireland

Institute of Grocery Distribution   (IGD)   1909
NR   Grange Lane, Letchmore Heath, WATFORD, Herts,
        WD25 8GD.   (hq)
        01923 857141   fax 01923 852531
        email igd@igd.com   http://www.igd.com
        Chief Exec: Joanne Denney-Finch
○   *L, *P, *Q; supply chain management in the food and grocery
        industry
M   665 f

Institute of Groundsmanship   (IOG)   1934
NR   28 Stratford Office Village, Walker Avenue, Wolverton Mill East,
        MILTON KEYNES, Bucks, MK12 5TW.   (hq)
        01908 312511   fax 01908 311140
        email iog@iog.org   http://www.iog.org
        Chief Exec: Geoff Webb
▲   Company Limited by Guarantee
○   *P; to promote quality surfaces & quality services & establish the
        IOG as the leading professional organisation for grounds
        management
●   Conf - Mtgs - ET - Exam - Res - Exhib - Inf - Lib - Empl
M   i & org
¶   The Groundsman - 12.

Institute of Group Analysis   (IGA)   1971
■   1 Daleham Gardens, LONDON, NW3 5BY.   (hq)
        020 7431 2693   fax 020 7431 7246
        email iga@igalondon.org.uk
        http://www.groupanalysis.org
        Chmn: Marcus Page
▲   Company Limited by Guarantee; Registered Charity
Br   8
○   *P; a teaching institution for group-analytic psychotherapy; to
        promote group analysis; to train in group analysis
Gp   Clinical section
●   Conf - Mtgs - ET - Res - SG - Lib
M   300 i
¶   Dialogue (NL) - 3;   AR - 1; both ftm only.

Institute of Guidance Counsellors   (IGC)   1976
IRL   17 Herbert St (The Basement), DUBLIN 2, Republic of Ireland.
        (hq)
        353 (1) 676 1975   fax 353 (1) 661 2551
        email igc@eircom.net   http://www.igc.ie
        Sec: Olivia Moriarty
Br   16
○   *P; to advance the personal, social, educational & career
        development of individuals & groups through supporting
        guidance counselling practice
M   12,000 i

Institute of Health Care Management
        see **Institute of Healthcare Management**

Institute of Health Promotion & Education   (IHPE)   1962
NR   Univ of Manchester Sch of Dentistry, Coupland 3, Oxford Rd,
        MANCHESTER, M13 9PL.   (hsb)
        email honsec@ihpe.org.uk   http://www.ihpe.org.uk
        Hon Sec: Helen Draper
▲   Un-incorporated Society
○   *L; for all interested in health promotion & education
Gp   Professional educators
M   600 i, 150 f, UK / 100 i, 50 f, o'seas
¶   Jnl - 4; ftm, £36 yr nm.

**Institute of Health Record & Information Management
(IHRIM)   1948**
NR   744a Manchester Rd, ROCHDALE, Lancs, OL11 3AQ.   (hq)
        01706 868481   fax 01706 868481
        email ihrim@zen.co.uk   http://www.ihrim.co.uk
        Office Mgr: Paula Pickup
▲   Un-incorporated Society
○   *P; the promotion of excellence & professionalism in the
        management of health records & information to enable
        delivery of high quality health care professions
●   Conf - ET - Exam - Exhib - SG - Inf
<   Intl Fedn of Health Records Orgs (IFHRO); NHS Inf Authority
M   735 i, 20 f, UK / 50 i, o'seas
¶   Jnl - 4; ftm.

Institute of Healthcare Engineering & Estate Management (IHEEM) 1943

NR 2 Abingdon House, Cumberland Business Centre, Northumberland Rd, PORTSMOUTH, Hants, PO5 1DS. (hq)
023 9282 3186
http://www.iheem.org.uk
Chief Exec: John Long
▲ Company Limited by Guarantee; Registered Charity
Br 14; Hong Kong, Ireland
○ *L, *P; for all those working in the healthcare engineering & estates field; the Institute is nominated by the Engineering Council
Gp Architects; Diagnostic imaging section; Sterilisation
● Conf - Mtgs - ET - Exhib - Lib
< Intl Hospital Fedn; Intl Fedn of Hospital Engg; Engg Coun
M 2,200 i, 60 f, UK / 150 i, 5 f, o'seas
¶ Health Estate Jnl - 10. Ybk. AR.
Guide to Commissioning.

Institute of Healthcare Management (IHM) 1902

■ 18-21 Morley St, LONDON, SE1 7QZ. (hq)
020 7620 1030 fax 020 7620 1040
email enquiries@ihm.org.uk http://www.ihm.org.uk
Chief Exec: Sue Hodgetts, Sec: Roger Morris
▲ Registered Charity
Br 12
○ *M, *N, *P; to support managers whose excellence in management contributes to excellence in healthcare; to improve standards in healthcare management
Gp Armed forces; Estates & facilities management; Independent sector; Primary care
● Conf - Mtgs - ET - Exam - Res
M 8,500 i, UK / 500 i, o'seas
¶ Health Management - 6; ftm, £55-£70 nm.
✕ Institute of Health Care Management

Institute of Heraldic & Genealogical Studies (IHGS) 1961

■ 79-82 Northgate, CANTERBURY, Kent, CT1 1BA. (hq)
01227 768664 fax 01227 765617
email ihgs@ihgs.ac.uk http://www.ihgs.ac.uk
Principal: Dr Richard Baker
▲ Registered Charity
○ *E, *P, *Q; to study the history & structure of the family genealogy, heraldry & their applications for historical research; family history research for genetical inherited diseases
● ET - Exam - Res - Lib
< Intl Confedn of Genealogy & Heraldry; Fedn of Family History Socs
M 240 i, UK / 30 i, o'seas
¶ Family History (Jnl) - 4; ftm, £15 yr nm.

Institute of Highway Engineers (IHE) 1965

■ De Morgan House, 58 Russell Square, LONDON, WC1B 4HS. (hq)
020 7436 7487 fax 020 7436 7488
email secretary@theihe.org http://www.theihe.org
Contact: Stephen Palmer
▲ Company Limited by Guarantee
Br 15
○ *P; interests of engineers & technicians in landbased highways & transportation
● Conf - Mtgs - Exam - Exhib - Comp - VE
< Engg Coun; Construction Ind Coun
M 3,000 i, UK / 100 i, o'seas
¶ Highways [magazine]. AR - 1.
✕ 2009 Institute of Highway Incorporated Engineers

Institute of Highway Incorporated Engineers
since 2009 **Institute of Highway Engineers**

Institute of Historic Building Conservation (IHBC) 1981

■ Jubilee House, High St, TISBURY, Wilts, SP3 6HA. (hq)
01747 873133 fax 01747 871718
http://www.ihbc.org.uk
Dir: Seán O'Reilly
▲ Company Limited by Guarantee; Registered Charity
Br 12
○ *P; to establish, develop & maintain the highest standards of conservation practice; to support the effective protection of the historic environment; & to promote heritage-led regeneration & access to the historic environment for all
● Conf - ET - Mtgs - Res
M c 1,750 i
¶ Context - 5; ftm, £50 nm. Ybk.

Institute of Home Inspections (IHI) 2006

NR Barnard Cottage, 2 Duncote, TOWCESTER, Northants, NN12 8AH. (dir/p)
http://www.ihi.org.uk
Dir: Jacqueline Oliver
▲ Community Interest Company
Br 20
○ *P; qualified home inspectors & domestic energy assessors
M 6,000 i

Institute of Home Safety (IHS) 1976

■ 21 Tuckers Nook, Maxey, PETERBORUGH, PE6 9EH. (contact/p)
01778 344297
http://www.instituteofhomesafety.co.uk
Contact: Sheila Merrill
○ *E, *W; accident prevention in the home & its environs (inc outbuildings, gardens, ponds etc); to provide a forum & point of contact for the development, dissemination & exchange of ideas & information
● Conf - Mtgs - ET - Exhib - Comp - Inf - LG - Organisation of campaigns etc on home safety & accident prevention
< R Soc for Prevention of Accidents (RoSPA); Child Accident Prevention Trust (CAPT); London Home & Water Safety Coun (LHWSC); Inst of Safety & Public Protection (ISPP); Brit Safety Soc (BSS)
M 70 i
¶ NL - 4. AR.

Institute of Horticulture (IOH) 1985

■ Capel Manor College, Bullsmoor Lane, ENFIELD, Middx, EN1 4RQ. (hq)
01992 707025
email ioh@horticulture.org.uk
http://www.horticulture.org.uk
Admin Mgr: Angela Evans
▲ Registered Charity
Br 8
○ *P; to promote the profession of horticulture
Gp Advisory & research; Amenity horticulture; Commercial horticulture; Education
● Conf - Mtgs - ET - Comp - Inf - VE - LG
M 1,600 i, 10 f, UK / 65 i, o'seas
¶ The Horticulturist (Jnl) - 4; ftm, £84 yr nm.
Come Into Horticulture (careers booklet);
Education & Training Courses in Horticulture; AR.

Institute of Hospitality   1971
- ■ Trinity Court, 34 West St, SUTTON, Surrey, SM1 1SH.   (hq)
  020 8661 4900   fax 020 8661 4901
  http://www.instituteofhospitality.org
  Chief Exec: Philippe Rossiter
- ▲ Company Limited by Guarantee; Registered Charity
- Br 20; Australia, Cyprus, Ghana, India, Malta, New Zealand, Sri Lanka, Zambia
- ○ *P; to promote & maintain the highest professional & ethical standards for management, education & training in the international hotel & catering industry
- ● ET - Exam - Res - SG - Inf - Lib - LG
- < Eur Coun on Hotel, Restaurant & Institutional Educ (EuroCHRIE); Profl Assns Res Network (PARN); CBI; FAB; Coun for Hospitality Mgt Educ (CHME)
- M 8,500 i, 5 f, 65 colleges, UK / 1,500 i, 'o;seas
- ¶ Hospitality - 4.   Hospitality Ybk - 1;   AR - 1; Management Guides - 4; all ftm.
- × 2007 Hotel & Catering International Management Association

Institute of Hotel Security Management   (IHSM)   1983
- NR [communication via website only]
  http://www.hotelsecuritymanagement.org
  Sec: Peter Fraser
- ○ *P; to provide the hotel & catering industry with a professional approach in dealing with all matters related to security, fire, health & safety
- Gp Fraud Forum
- M 32 f

Institute of Incorporated Public Accountants   (IIPA)   1981
- IRL Heather House, Heather Rd, Sandyford, DUBLIN 18, Republic of Ireland.   (hq)
  353 (1) 206 9000
  email info@iipa.ie   http://www.iipa.ie
- ▲ Company Limited by Guarantee
- ○ *P; to maintain & develop standards in the accountancy & auditing professions
- ● ET - Exam - Mtgs
- ¶ NL by email

Institute for Independent Business   (IIB)   1984
- NR Clarendon House, Bridle Path, WATFORD, Herts, WD17 1UB. (hq)
  01923 239543
  email info@iib.org.uk   http://www.iib.org.uk
  Principal: Linden P Dyason
- ▲ Company Limited by Guarantee; Registered Charity
- Br 4; India, USA
- ○ *T; to provide practical advice to the independent business sector
- Gp Small to medium-sized businesses
- ● Conf - Mtgs - ET - Exam - Res - SG - Expt - Inf - Support for experienced executives wishing to become management consultants
- M 950 f, UK / 30 f, o'seas
- ¶ Independent Business Today - 4.

Institute of Indirect Taxation   (IIT)   1991
- ■ Suite G1 The Stables, Station Road West, OXTED, Surrey, RH8 9EE.   (hq)
  01883 730658   fax 01883 717778
  email enquiries@theiit.org.uk   http://www.theiit.org.uk
  Sec Gen: Terry Davies
- ▲ Company Limited by Guarantee
- ○ *P; to qualify, regulate & represent practitioners & research in VAT, customs, excise, stamp taxes, other indirect taxes
- ● Conf - ET - Exam - LG - Lib - Mtgs
- < Academy of Experts
- M 615 i, UK / 50 i, o'seas
- ¶ Indirect Tax Voice - 9; ftm.

Institute for Individual Psychology
   see **Adlerian Society UK & Institute for Individual Psychology**

Institute of Industrial Engineers Ireland   (IIE)   1955
- IRL 1 Boeing Avenue, Airport Business Park, DUNMORE EAST, Co Waterford, Republic of Ireland.   (hq)
  353 (1) 525 2527
  email enquiries@iie.ie   http://www.iie.ie
  Hon Sec: Daniel Vaughan
- Br 4
- ○ *P; the professional & qualifying body for those involved in industrial engineering
- < Inst of Indl Engrs (USA)

Institute of Information Security Professionals   (IISP)   2006
- NR 83 Victoria St, LONDON, SW1H 0HW.   (hq)
  0845 612 3828
  email info@instisp.com   http://www.instisp.org
  Chmn: Dr Alastair MacWillson
- ▲ Company Limited by Guarantee
- ○ *P; to raise the standard of professionalism in information security
- M 19 f

Institute of Insurance Brokers   (IIB)
- NR Higham Business Centre, Midland Rd, HIGHAM FERRERS, Northants, NN10 8DW.   (hq)
  01933 410003   fax 01933 410020
  email inst.ins.brokers@iib-uk.com
  http://www.iib-uk.com
  Dir Gen: Andrew Paddick,   Sec: Barbara Bradshaw
- ▲ Company Limited by Guarantee
- ○ *P; for independent insurance broking businesses
- ● Conf - Mtgs - ET - Exam - Res - Exhib - Comp - SG - Inf - Lib - LG
- M 1,100 f

Institute of Interim Management   (IIM)   2001
- NR Dolphins, Elmstead Rd, WEST BYFLEET, Surrey, KT14 6JB.   (hq)
  0800 030 4716   fax 01932 350775
  email info@iim.org.uk   http://www.iim.org.uk
  Hon Sec: David Pugh
- ▲ Company Limited by Guarantee
- ○ *P; to promote, support & represent professional interim managers & executives
- M i

Institute of Internal Auditors
   since 2010 **Chartered Institute of Internal Auditors**

Institute of Internal Communication   (IoIC)   1949
- NR Oak House (GA2), Breckland, Linford Wood, MILTON KEYNES, Bucks, MK14 6EY.   (hq)
  01908 313755   fax 01908 313661
  email enquiries@ioic.org.uk   http://www.ioic.org.uk
  Chief Exec: Steve Doswell
- ▲ Company Limited by Guarantee
- ○ *P; to support internat communication practitioners in their careers, promote high professional standards within the sector & raise general awareness of the value internal communication
- ● Conf - Mtgs - ET - Exhib - Comp - SG - Lib
- < Fedn Eur Indl Editors Assns (FEIEA)
- M c 20,000 i
- × 2010 British Association of Communicators in Business

Institute of International Licensing Practitioners Ltd   (IILP)   1969

- 28 Main St, Mursley, MILTON KEYNES, MK17 0RT.   (hq)
  01296 728136   fax 01296 722007
  email enquiries@iilp.net   http://www.iilp.net
  Sec: James Hunt,   Chmn: Mike Kerr
- ▲ Company Limited by Guarantee
- ○ *P; assistance to companies, or individuals, to obtain the service of a qualified licensing practitioner; to set, promote & maintain high standards of professional practice amongst those engaged in licensing, technology transfer & commercialising invention; to promote the wider understanding of the value of licensing in international business as a marketing & business development tool
- ● Conf
- M   i, f, org

Institute of International Marketing   (IIM)   2008

- NR   PO Box 70, LONDON, E13 0UU.   (hq)
  0870 042 2072   fax 0870 042 2062
  email contact@iimonline.org
  http://www.instituteofinternationalmarketing.org
- Br   Netherlands, Nigeria, South Africa, USA
- ○ *P; to promote & encourage the advancement of international marketing in all aspects
- ● Conf - ET - Exam - Res - SG - VE - Seminars
- M   85 i, 3 f, UK / 718 i, 5 f, o'seas
  (Sub: £75 i)
- ¶ Jnl of International Marketing - 1; ftm.
  NL (email) - 6; ftm.   Membership Hbk.
  Dictionary of International Marketing (4th ed); £15 m, £20 nm.
  A Guide to Marketing in Europe.
  A Guide to Marketing in North America (4th ed) £10 m, £15 nm.
  Other books available.
- ×   2008 Association of International Marketing

Institute of International Trade of Ireland   (IITI)

- IRL   28 Merrion Sq, DUBLIN 2, Republic of Ireland.   (hq)
  353 (1) 661 2182   fax 353 (1) 661 2315
  email info@iiti.ie   http://www.iiti.ie
  Dir: John F Whelan
- ○ *T

Institute of Inventors   (IoI)   1964

- NR   19-23 Fosse Way, Ealing, LONDON, W13 0BZ.   (hq)
  020 8998 3540; 020 8998 6372
  email mikinvent@aol.com
  http://www.instituteofinventors.com
  Pres: Michael V Rodrigues
- ▲ Un-incorporated Society
- ○ *L; for design engineer inventors
- Gp   Sifting c'ee;
  Depts: Online database patent research, Patent drafting, CAD design development
- ● Exam - Res - Inf - LG - Patent searching - New invention design & development - Invention investor marriage
- M   i & f
- ¶ New Invention List - 12.

Institute of IT Training
  since 2011 **Learning & Performance Institute**

Institute for Jewish Policy Research   (JPR)   1996

- NR   7-8 Market Place, LONDON, W1W 8AG.   (hq)
  020 7436 1553   fax 020 7436 7262
  email jpr@jpr.org.uk   http://www.jpr.org.uk
  Exec Dir: Jonathan Boyd
- ▲ Company Limited by Guarantee; Registered Charity
- ○ *Q; to provide organisations with data about contemporary Jewish life
- ● Conf - Res - Inf - Development & dissemination of policy proposals - Promotion of public debate
- M   i & org
- ¶ Patterns of Prejudice (Jnl) - 4.
  JPR Reports & Policy Papers.
  Antisemitism in the World Today; (Internet publication)

Institute of Leadership & Management   (ILM)   1947

- NR   1 Giltspur St, LONDON, EC1A 9DD.   (hq)
  020 7294 2470
  http://www.i-l-m.com
  Chief Exec: Penny de Valk
- ▲ Company Limited by Guarantee; Registered Charity
- Br   Lichfield (Staffs)
- ○ *P; to improve leadership & management performance through a flexible range of learning & development solutions
- ● Conf - ET - Exam - Inf
- M   24,000 i
- ¶ Modern Management - 6.

Institute for Learning   (IfL)   2002

- NR   49-51 East Rd (1st floor), LONDON, N1 6AH.   (hq)
  0844 815 3202
  email enquiries@ifl.ac.uk   http://www.ifl.ac.uk
  Chief Exec: Toni Fazaeli
- ▲ Company Limited by Guarantee
- ○ *P; professional body for teachers, trainers & student teachers in the further education & skills sector
- M   i

Institute of Legal Cashiers & Administrators
  since 2010 **Institute of Legal Finance & Management**

Institute of Legal Executives   (ILEX)   1963

- Kempston Manor, Kempston, BEDFORD, MK42 7AB.   (hq)
  01234 841000   fax 01234 853982
  email info@ilex.org.uk   http://www.ilex.org.uk
  Chief Exec: Mrs Diane Burleigh
- ▲ Un-incorporated Society
- Br   19; Bermuda, Gibraltar, Kenya
- ○ *P; for legal executives (lawyers employed by, or working for, solicitors in private practice, or employed as such in governmental, public, commercial or other departments or undertakings)
- Gp   Lawyers; Press; Colleges; MP's
- ● Conf - Mtgs - Exam - Res - Exhib - Comp
- M   24,000 i
- ¶ Legal Executive Jnl - 12; ftm.
  AR; free.

Institute of Legal Finance & Management   (ILFM)   1978

- Marlowe House (2nd floor), 109 Station Rd, SIDCUP, Kent, DA15 7ET.   (hq)
  020 8302 2867   fax 020 8302 7481
  email exec.sec@ilfm.org.uk   http://www.ilfm.org.uk
  Exec Sec: Margaret Macdonald
- ○ *P; to promote the status of the legal cashier & administrator
- ● Conf - Mtgs - ET - Exam - Res - Exhib - Comp - Inf
- <   Inst Legal Accountants Ireland
- M   3,000 i
- ¶ Legal Abacus - 6; ftm, £30 yr nm.
- ×   2010 Institute of Legal Cashiers & Administrators

© CBD Research Ltd · Beckenham · BR3 5JS · Tel 020 8650 7745 · E-mail cbd@cbdresearch.com · www.cbdresearch.com

Institute of Legal Secretaries & PAs (ILS) 1990

NR 3.08 Canterbury Court, 1-3 Brixton Rd, LONDON, SW9 6DE. (hq)
0845 643 4974; 020 7100 9210   fax 020 3384 4976
email info@institutelegalsecretaries.com
http://www.institutelegalsecretaries.com
Chief Exec: Emma Stacey
▲ Un-incorporated Society
○ *P; to provide for the professional recognition of members by the quality of their qualifications, standard, skills & expertise; to further the knowledge of law & legal procedure
Gp Legal: Secretaries, PAs, Receptionists
● Conf - ET - Exam - Res - Exhib - Inf - LG
< Nat Assn of Licensed Paralegals
M c 2,000 i
¶ Dedicated - 4; ftm only.

Institute of Leisure & Amenity Management
in 2007 merged with the National Association of Sports Development to form the Institute for Sport, Parks & Leisure, which in 2011 merged with the Institute of Sport & Recreation Management to form the **Institute for the Management of Sport & Physical Activity**

Institute of Leisure & Amenity Management Ireland Ltd (ILAM) 1989

IRL Allenwood Enterprise Park, Allenwood North, NAAS, Co Kildare, Republic of Ireland.   (hq)
353 (45) 859950
email info@ilam.ie   http://www.ilam.ie
Chief Exec: Kilian Fisher
○ *P

Institute of Licensed Trade Stock Auditors (ILTSA) 1953

NR Brockwell Heights, Brockwell Lane Triangle, SOWERBY BRIDGE, HX6 3PQ.   (hsp)
01422 833003   fax 01422 316641
email dianeswift@iltsa.co.uk   http://www.iltsa.co.uk
▲ Company Limited by Guarantee
Br 300
○ *P; to support licensed trade stock auditors in the UK
● Mtg (AGM) - ET - Exam
M 395 i
¶ The Stock Auditor - 6; ftm, £2 each nm.
Taking Stock Book; £18.   LM - 1; free.

Institute of Machine Woodworking Technology Ltd (IMWoodT) 1952

■ St Keynes, Bowl Rd, CHARING, Kent, TN27 0HB.   (hsp)
01233 713768   fax 01233 713768
email imwoodt@tesco.net   http://www.imwoodt.org.uk
Hon Sec: John Fryer
Br 4; 1
○ *E, *L; theory & practice of machine woodworking technology
Gp Health & safety
● Conf - Mtgs - ET - Exhib - Comp - Inf - VE
M i, 1 f
¶ Woodworking Technology - 1; ftm.   AR; ftm only.

Institute of Maintenance & Building Management
in April 2008 merged with the **Association of Building Engineers**

Institute of Management Consultancy
in 2007 merged with the Institute of Business Advisers to form the Institute of Business Consulting, which in 2011 was renamed **Institute of Consulting**

Institute of Management Consultants & Advisers (IMCA) 2006

IRL 19 Elgin Rd, Ballsbridge, DUBLIN 4, Republic of Ireland.   (hq)
353 (1) 634 9636   fax 353 (1) 281 5330
email info@imca.ie   http://www.imca.ie
Sec: Brian Flanagan
○ *P; to foster & promote the value, quality & benefits of business consulting & advisory services

Institute for the Management of Information Systems (IMIS) 1978

NR 5 Kingfisher House, New Mill Rd, ORPINGTON, Kent, BR5 3QG.   (hq)
07000 023456   fax 07000 023023
email central@imis.org.uk   http://www.imis.org.uk
Chief Exec: Ian M Rickwood
▲ Registered Charity
Br 6; Malta, Malaysia, Zambia, Zimbabwe
○ *P; to advance the interests of the management of information systems / information technology profession
Gp Outsourcing; Women in Technology (WIT)
● Conf - Mtgs - ET - Exam - LG
M 3,255 i, 40 f, UK / 7,411 i, 20 f, o'seas
¶ IMIS Jnl - 6; free.
IT Skills Trend Report Summary; free.

Institute of Management Services (IMS) 1978

NR Brooke House, 24 Dam St, LICHFIELD, Staffs, WS13 6AB.   (hq)
01543 266909
http://www.ims-productivity.com
▲ Registered Charity
○ *P; productivity improvement; work study; O&M & related areas
M 4,000 i

Institute of Management Specialists (IMS) 1971

■ Warwick Corner, 42 Warwick Rd, KENILWORTH, Warks, CV8 1HE.   (hq)
01926 265342
email info@instituteofmanagementspecialists.org.uk
http://www.instituteofmanagementspecialists.org.uk
Exec Admin: Lynne Sykes
○ *P; to give professional recognition to the knowledge & skills of managers & specialists
< Academy of Executives & Administrators; Fac of Profl Business & Technical Mgt; Inst of Mfrg
¶ The Management Specialist (Jnl) - 3; £2 m, £7 nm.

Institute for the Management of Sport & Physical Activity (IMSPA) 2011

NR SportPark, Loughborough University, 3 Oakwood Drive, LOUGHBOROUGH, Leics, LE11 3QF.   (hq)
01509 226474   fax 01509 226475
email info@imspa.co.uk   http://www.imspa.co.uk
Chief Exec: Sean Holt
▲ Registered Charity
Br 9; Hong Kong
○ *P; to develop a vibrant, UK wide sport and physical activity sector, led by professionals providing advocacy and leadership and working in partnership with its stakeholders to ensure the highest standards of service delivery
● Mtgs - Lectures
M i, f
× 2011 (Institute for Sport, Parks & Leisure (Institute of Sport & Recreation Management

Institute of Management & Technology   (IMT)   1983

- ■ 33 Marlborough Rd, SWINDON, Wilts, SN3 1PH.   (hq)
  07939 460013   fax 07939 460013
  email sofroniou@gmail.com
  Sec: Dr Andreas Sofroniou
- ▲ Un-incorporated Society
- ○ *P
- Gp Development of people; Engineering; Hypnotherapy;
  Information technology; Management; Political philosophy;
  Psychotherapy; Systems; Technology; Therapeutic philosophy;
  Writing
- ● Conf - Mtgs - ET - Exam - Res - SG - Inf - Lib - VE
- > Assn for Psychological Counselling & Training (USA)
- M 270 i, 2 f, 3 org, UK / 130 i, 2 f, o'seas
- ¶ Books:
  Therapeutic Philosophy for the Individual & the State.
  Philosophic Counselling for People & their Governments.
  Moral Philosophy, from Hippocrates to the 21st Aeon.
  Other publications, list available at http://www.lulu.com/
  sofroniou
- ✕ 2010 Association for Therapeutic Philosophy

Institute of Manufacturing   (IManf)   1978

- ■ Warwick Corner, 42 Warwick Rd, KENILWORTH, Warks,
  CV8 1HE.   (hq)
  01926 259342
  email info@instituteofmanufacturing.org.uk
   http://www.instituteofmanufacturing.org.uk
  Exec Admin: Lynne Sykes
- ○ *P; to give professional recognition to the knowledge & skills of
  people in all aspects of manufacturing
- < Academy of Administrators & Executives; Fac of Profl &
  Technical Mgt; Inst of Mgt Specialists

Institute of Marine Engineering, Science & Technology   (IMarEST)   1889

- NR 80 Coleman St, LONDON, EC2R 5BJ.   (hq)
  020 7382 2600   fax 020 7382 2670
  email info@imarest.org   http://www.imarest.org
  Sec: Keith Read
- ▲ Registered Charity
- Br 14; 33 o'seas
- ○ *L, *P; to promote the scientific development of marine
  engineering, science & technology: marine, offshore &
  subsea engineering, naval architecture & ship construction,
  marine science & marine technology
- Gp Marine, offshore & subsea engineering; Naval architecture &
  ship construction; Marine science & technology
- ● Conf - Mtgs - ET - Exhib - Inf - Lib - LG
- < Engg Coun (EC); Intl Maritime Org (IMO); W Eur Confedn of
  Maritime Technology Societies (WEMT)
- M 10,073 i, UK / 6,067 i, o'seas

Institute of Master Tutors of Driving   (IMTD)   1957

- ■ 56 High Bank Drive, Garston, LIVERPOOL, L19 5PG.   (hq)
  0151-280 4248
  http://www.imtd.org.uk
- ▲ Un-incorporated Society
- ○ *P; to represent trainers of drivers, & drivers of large goods
  vehicles, motorcyclists & road safety teachers
- ● Conf - Mtgs - ET - Res - SG - Inf - LG
- M 70 i, UK / 10 i, o'seas
  (Sub: £100 UK / £50 o'seas)
- ¶ Teaching Deaf People to Drive; free.

Institute of Masters of Wine   (IMW)   1953

- NR 24 Fitzroy Square, LONDON, W1T 6EP.   (hq)
  020 7383 9130   fax 020 7383 9139
  email enquiries@mastersofwine.org
  http://www.mastersofwine.org
  Exec Dir: Siobhan Turner
- Br Australia, USA
- ○ *P; to promote the attainment & maintenance of high standards
  of technical knowledge & achievement by those making their
  livelihood in the wine & spirit trade
- M 229 i
- ¶ Jnl of Wine Research - 3.   NL - 12.   LM - 1.

Institute of Materials, Minerals & Mining   (IOM3)   1869

- ■ 1 Carlton House Terrace, LONDON, SW1Y 5DB.   (hq)
  020 7451 7300   fax 020 7839 1702
  email admin@iom3.org   http://www.iom3.org
  Chief Exec: Dr Bernie Rickinson
- ▲ Registered Charity
- Br 4
- ○ *L, *P; the professional body for all involved in the field of
  materials, minerals & mining; to promote the science & study
  of all aspects of the science, technology & use of materials &
  minerals
- Gp Materials division:
  British Composites Society
  Ceramics Society (includes the International
   Clay Technology Association)
  Iron & Steel Society
  Light Metals Division
  Materials Science & Technology Division
  Polymer Society
  Minerals & Mining division:
  International Mining & Minerals Association
  Mining Technology Division
  Petroleum & Drilling Engineering Division
  Applied Earth Science Division
  Mineral Processing & Extractive
   Metallurgy Division
  Applications division:
  Automotive Division
  Biomedical Applications Division
  Casting Division
  Electronic Applications Division
  The Packaging Society
  Surface Engineering Division:
   Corrosion Committee
   IWSc: the Wood Technology Society
   IVE: Vitreous Enamellers' Society
   Society for Adhesions & Adhesives
  Multidisciplinary Groups
  Construction Materials
  Energy Materials
  Natural Materials Association
  Sustainable Development
- ● Conf - Mtgs - ET - Exam - Exhib - Comp - SG - Stat - Inf - Lib -
  VE - Empl
- < Fedn of Eur Materials Socs; Soc for the Envt (SocEnv)
- M 14,500 i, 180 f, UK / 4,000 i, o'seas
- ¶ Materials World - 12; ftm, £55 yr nm.
  The Packaging Professional - 6; ftm, £40 yr nm.
  Clay Technology - 6; ftm, £35 yr nm.   AR - 1; free.

Institute of Mathematics & its Applications   (IMA)   1964
- ■ Catherine Richards House, 16 Nelson St, SOUTHEND-ON-SEA, Essex, SS1 1EF.   (hq)
  01702 354020   fax 01702 354111
  email post@ima.org.uk   http://www.ima.org.uk
  Exec Dir: David Youdan
- ▲ Registered Charity
- Br 6
- ○ *E, *L, *P; for qualified & practising mathematicians; to promote mathematics in industry, business, the public sector, education & research
- Gp Computational fluid dynamics; Computational science & engineering education; Environment; Numerical analysis; Management
- ● Conf - Mtgs - Comp - LG
- < Eur Mathematical Soc; Eur Mechanics Soc; Coun of Mathematical Sciences
- M 4,400 i, UK / 400 i, o'seas
- ¶ Mathematics Today - 6; ftm, £90 yr nm.
  IMA Jnl of Applied Mathematics.
  IMA Jnl of Numerical Analysis.
  Mathematical Medicine & Biology: a Jnl of the IMA.
  IMA Jnl of Mathematical Control & Information.
  IMA Jnl of Management Mathematics.
  Teaching Mathematics & its Applications: an international Jnl of the IMA.
  [prices vary with print &/or online access & discounts for the number taken].

Institute of Maxillofacial Prosthetists & Technologists   (IMPT)   1962
- NR Southern General Hospital, 1345 Govan Rd, GLASGOW, G51 4TF.   (hsb)
  http://www.impt.co.uk
  Hon Sec: Fraser Walker
- ▲ Company Limited by Guarantee; Registered Charity
- ○ *L, *M, *P; to promote study & improve practising standards
- ● Conf - Mtgs - ET - Exam - Res - SG - Lib - LG
- M i
- ¶ Jnl;   NL - 4; both ftm.

Institute of Measurement & Control   (InstMC)   1944
- ■ 87 Gower St, LONDON, WC1E 6AF.   (hq)
  020 7387 4949
  email ceo@instmc.org.uk   http://www.instmc.org.uk
  Chief Exec: Peter J Martindale
- ▲ Registered Charity
- Br 20; Hong Kong
- ○ *P; to promote for the public benefit the general advancement & application of the science & practice of measurement & control technology
- Gp Aviation; Measurement science & technology; Systems & control technology; Systems & management; Safety; Standards; Weighing
- ● Conf - Mtgs - ET - Exhib - LG
- < Intl Measurement Confedn (IMEKO); UK Automatic Control Coun (UKAC); Foundation for Science & Technology
- M 3,000 i, 130 f, UK / 400 i, o'seas
- ¶ Transactions - 7.   Measurement & Control - 10.
  Interface (NL) - 2.   Ybk.

Institute of Medical Illustrators   (IMI)   1968
- ■ 12 Coldbath Square, LONDON, EC1R 5HL.   (hq)
  020 7837 2846
  email carol.fleming@bradfordhospital.nhs.uk
  http://www.imi.org.uk
  Hon Sec: Carol M Fleming (01274 365325)
- ▲ Company Limited by Guarantee; Registered Charity
- ○ *T, *P; to promote the role of the medical illustrator as a professional member of a multi-skilled team offering clinical illustrative & communication services for the benefit of patient & client
- Gp Medical: Artists, Graphic designers, Multi-media specialists, Photographers, Videographers
- ● Conf - Mtgs - ET - Exhib - Comp - LG
- < Coun for the Accreditation of Med Illustration Practitioners (CAMP); Fedn of Healthcare Science (FHCS)
- M 370 i, 25 f, UK / 25 i, o'seas
  (Sub: £110 i, £252 f)
- ¶ Jnl of Visual Communication in Medicine (Vision) - 4; ftm, 580 nm.
  IMI News - 4; ftm only.

Institute of Metal Finishing   (IMF)   1925
- NR Exeter House, 48 Holloway Head, BIRMINGHAM, B1 1NQ.   (hq)
  0121-622 7387   fax 0121-666 6316
  email exeterhouse@instituteofmetalfinishing.org
  http://www.uk-finishing.org.uk
  Business Devt Mgr: Ken Hoare
- ▲ Registered Charity
- Br 8
- ○ *L; theory & practice of all aspects of metal finishing
- Gp Aluminium; Electroforming; Organic; Printed circuit
- ● Conf - Mtgs - ET - Exam - Exhib - SG - Inf - Lib - VE
- M 1,200 i, 62 f, UK / 345 i, 3 f, o'seas
- ¶ Transactions - 6.

Institute of Money Advisers   2006
- ■ 4 Park Court, Park Cross St, LEEDS, N Yorks, LS1 2QH.   (hq)
  0113-242 0048   fax 0113-234 5711
  http://www.i-m-a.org.uk
  Admin: Carole Robertson
- ▲ Registered Charity
- ○ *P, *W; for money advisers (ie those who advise debtors); to provide a range of services
- ● Conf - Mtgs - ET - Exhib - Stat - Inf - LG
- < NCVO; ASA
- M 600 i
- ¶ Quarterly Account - 4; ftm, £30 nm.   AR - 1; ftm only.

Institute of the Motor Industry   (IMI)   1920
- ■ Fanshaws, Brickendon, HERTFORD, SG13 8PQ.   (hq)
  01992 511521   fax 01992 511548
  email imi@motor.org.uk   http://www.motor.org.uk
  Chmn: Sarah Sillars
- ▲ Company Limited by Guarantee
- Br Australia, Malaysia
- ○ *P; to raise professional standards by recognising, supporting & developing individuals who have shown their commitment to the highest level of ethical behaviour by signing the IMI's Code of Conduct
- ● Conf - Mtgs - ET - Exam - Res - Stat - Inf
- M 25,160 i, UK / 3,100 i, o'seas
- ¶ Motor Industry Magazine - 10; ftm, £4 nm.
  IMI is the Sector Skills Council for the automotive retail industry & the governing body for the Automotive Technician Accreditation (ATA) scheme.

Institute of Musical Instrument Technology (IMIT) 1961
NR 11 Kendall Avenue South, SOUTH CROYDON, Surrey,
    CR2 0QR. (hsp)
    http://www.imit.org.uk
    Hon Sec: Malcolm Dalton
▲   Company Limited by Guarantee
○   *L, *P; for those engaged in musical instrument design,
    manufacture, repair or education
●   Conf - Mtgs - Exam - Lib - VE
M   215 i, UK / 5 i, o'seas
¶   Jnl - c 1;   Soundings - 4;   LM - 1; all ftm.

Institute for Numerical Computation & Analysis (INCA) 1980
IRL 7-9 Dame Court, DUBLIN 2, Republic of Ireland.
    353 (1) 402 8535   fax 353 (1) 402 8540
    email jm@incaireland.org   http://www.incaireland.org
    Sec: Diarmuid Herlihy
▲   Company Limited by Guarantee
○   *Q; to promote research & development in scientific &
    engineering computation & analysis

Institute of Operational Risk (IOR) 2004
NR 2 Old College Court, 29 Priory St, WARE, Herts, SG12 0DE.
    (asa)
    0800 091 3750   fax 0844 822 5215
    http://www.ior-institute.org
    Exec Chmn: Asim Balouch
Br Scotland, Asia (Hong Kong), Germany, Nigeria
○   *P; to provide professional recognition & to enable members to
    maintain competency in the discipline of operational risk
    management

Institute of Operations Management (IOM) 1969
NR Earlstrees Court, Earlstrees Rd, CORBY, Northants,
    NN17 4AX. (hq)
    01536 7401056   fax 01536 7401016
    email iom@iomnet.org.uk   http://www.iomnet.org.uk
    Chief Exec: J D Tayler
▲   Company Limited by Guarantee; Registered Charity
Br 10
○   *P; operations supply chain & production management in
    manufacturing & service industries
Gp Special interest: 1) Pharmaceutical, toiletries & chemicals;
    2) Advanced planning & scheduling; 3) Lean & agile; 4)
    Product support & services; 5) Retail; 6) Health
●   Conf - Mtgs - ET - Exam - Inf - Lib - VE - Qualification
    awarding body
M   4,000 i, 15 f, UK / 100 i, o'seas
¶   Control - 8.

Institute for Optimum Nutrition (ION) 1984
■   Avalon House, 72 Lower Mortlake Rd, RICHMOND, Surrey,
    TW9 2JY. (hq)
    0870 979 1122
    http://www.ion.ac.uk
▲   Registered Charity
○   *K; to help the public achieve optimum nutrition & optimum
    health through an education programme &/or one-to-one
    consultations for advanced assessment of personal nutrition
    needs
●   Conf - ET - Exam - Res - Exhib - Inf - Lib - Courses
M   3,700 i
¶   Optimum Nutrition - 4.
    Specialised magazine on diet & health; ftm.

Institute for Outdoor Learning (IOL) 1970
■   Warwick Mill Business Centre, Warwick Bridge, CARLISLE,
    Cumbria, CA4 8RR. (hq)
    01228 564580   fax 01228 564581
    email institute@outdoor-learning.org
    http://www.outdoor-learning.org
    Chief Exec: Andy Robinson
▲   Registered Charity
Br regional groups
○   *P; to support, develop & promote learning through outdoor
    experiences
Gp Development training; Research forum
●   Conf - Mtgs - ET - Res - Exhib - SG - Stat - Inf - Lib - LG
<   CCPR; Engl Outdoor Coun; SPRITO
M   1,100 i, 140 f, 60 org, UK / 36 i, 10 f, 3 org, o'seas
¶   Jnl of Adventure Education & Outdoor Learning - 2; £22 m,
    £25 nm.
    Horizons Magazine - 4; £17.65 m, £26 nm.
    NL - 12; ftm only.
    Outdoor Sourcebook - 1; £8 95 m, £9.95 nm.
    Guide to Careers in Outdoor Learning - 1; £8 m, £9 nm.

Institute of Paper, Printing & Publishing (IP3) 1992
■   Claremont House, 70-72 Alma Rd, WINDSOR, Berks,
    SL4 3EZ. (regd off)
    0870 330 8625   fax 0870 330 8615
    http://www.ip3.org.uk
    Dir: David Pryke
○   *P; for those employed in, or closely associated with, the paper
    industry
●   Conf - Mtgs - ET - Exam - Inf - Lib - VE
M   i
¶   NL - 4; ftm only.
    Various other publications - details on request.

Institute of Paralegals 1976
NR 1 Poultry, LONDON, EC2R 8JR. (hq)
    020 7099 9122
    http://www.theiop.org
○   *P; 'for persons of education, ability & experience who desire to
    qualify as legal secretaries &/or administrators & to secure
    professional status'
●   ET - Exam - Inf - Examination Board for Legal Secretaries
M   i
¶   Examination Papers.
✕   2008-10 Institute of Paralegal Training

Institute of Parks & Green Space (IPGS) 1999
NR Caversham Court, Church Rd, READING, Berks, RG4 7AD.
    (hq)
    0118-946 9049   fax 0118-946 9061
    email info@green-space.org.uk
    http://www.green-space.org.uk
    Campaign Mgr: Tess Stackley
▲   Company Limited by Guarantee; Registered Charity
○   *P; to advance the management, maintenance & use of parks
    & green space by promoting excellence in the profession
●   Conf - ET
M   i
¶   Green Places - 10;   Bench (email NL) - 12; both ftm
    Note: IPGS campaigns as GreenSpace

Institute of Patentees & Inventors (IPI) 1919
NR PO Box 39296, LONDON, SE3 7WH. (hq)
    0871 226 2091   fax 020 8293 5920
    email ipi@invent.org.uk   http://www.invent.org.uk
▲   Company Limited by Guarantee
○   *L; assistance & advice to inventors on protection &
    commercialising of inventions, encouragement of inventive
    talent & industrial innovation
●   Mtgs - ET - Exhib - Inf
<   Intl Fedn Inventors' Assns (IFIA)
M   830 i, 12 f, UK / 28 i, o'seas
¶   Future & the Inventor - 4; ftm.

© CBD Research Ltd · Beckenham · BR3 5JS · Tel 020 8650 7745 · E-mail cbd@cbdresearch.com · www.cbdresearch.com

Institute of Payroll Professionals
since 2010 **Chartered Institute of Payroll Professionals**

Institute of Physics   (IoP)   1919
NR   76 Portland Place, LONDON, W1B 1NT.   (hq)
         020 7470 4800   fax 020 7470 4848
         email physics@iop.org   http://www.iop.org
         Chief Exec: Julia King
▲   Registered Charity
Br   13
○   *L, *P; advancement of knowledge of physics, pure & applied,
         & the elevation of the profession of physicist
Gp   44 specialist subject groups; 4 professional groups
●   Conf - Mtgs - ET - Stat - LG
M   i
¶   Jnl of Physics:
         A Mathematical & General Physics - 24.
         B Atomic, Molecular & Optical Physics - 24.
         C Condensed Matter - 51.
         D Applied Physics - 12.
         G Nuclear & Particle Physics - 12.
         Publications list on website.

Institute of Physics & Engineering in Medicine   (IPEM)   1982
NR   Fairmount House, 230 Tadcaster Rd, YORK, YO24 1ES.   (hq)
         01904 610821
         http://www.ipem.ac.uk
         Gen Sec: Robert Neilson
▲   Company Limited by Guarantee; Registered Charity
○   *L; advancement of physics & allied physical sciences applied
         to medicine & biology

Institute of Piping   (InstP)   1960
NR   16-24 Otago St, GLASGOW, G12 8JH.   (hq)
         0141-334 3587   fax 0141-587 6068
         Hon Sec: Robert Wallace
○   *D; examination & certification of pipers

Institute of Place Management   (IPM)   2007
NR   1 Queen Anne's Gate, LONDON, SW1H 9BT.   (regd off)
         020 7227 3593
         http://www.placemanagement.org
         Dir: Prof Cathy Parker
○   *P; to support people committed to developing, managing &
         making places better

Institute of Plumbing & Heating Engineering
      see **Chartered Institute of Plumbing & Heating Engineering**

Institute of Practitioners in Advertising   (IPA)   1917
■   44 Belgrave Sq, LONDON, SW1X 8QS.   (hq)
         020 7235 7020   fax 020 7245 9904
         email info@ipa.co.uk   http://www.ipa.co.uk
         Sec: Geoffrey Russell
▲   Company Limited by Guarantee
Br   2
○   *P, *T; the professional & trade organisation for UK advertising
         & marketing agencies
●   Conf - Mtgs - ET - Res - Exhib - Stat - Inf - Lib - Empl - LG
<   Eur Assn of Communications Agencies
M   272 f
¶   see website

Institute of Professional Administrators   1957
■   6 Graphite Square, Vauxhall Walk, LONDON, SE11 5EE.   (hq)
         020 7091 2606
         email info@inprad.org   http://www.inprad.org
         Mem Devt Mgr: Jackie Wood
▲   Company Limited by Guarantee
Br   11
○   *P; establishment of status of qualified secretaries &
         administrators within the professions, commerce, industry &
         colleges
●   Conf - Mtgs - ET - Exhib - Comp - Inf
<   Intl Assn Admin Profls (US)
M   1,500 i, UK / 50 i, o'seas
¶   Career Secretary (Jnl) - 4; ftm, £60 yr nm.
✕   2010 Institute of Qualified Professional Secretaries

Institute of Professional Auctioneers & Valuers   (IPAV)   1971
IRL   129 Lower Baggot St, DUBLIN 2, Republic of Ireland.   (hq)
         353 (1) 678 5685   fax 353 (1) 676 2890
         email info@ipav.ie   http://www.ipav.ie
         Chief Exec: Fintan McNamara
○   *P; to protect, advance & promote the professional standards of
         auctioneers & valuers
<   Confedn of Eur Estate Agents (CEI)
M   801 i

Institute of Professional Designers   (IPD)   1963
NR   Piccotts End Farm, 117 Piccotts End Rd, HEMEL HEMPSTEAD,
         Herts, HP1 3AU.   (hq)
         01442 245513
▲   Un-incorporated Society
○   *A, *P; environmental design incl architecture, interior design &
         website design
Gp   Architects; Designers; Graphic designers; Interior designers;
         Landscape architects
●   Inf
M   250 i, UK / 200 i, o'seas
¶   Calendar - 1; free.

Institute of Professional Goldsmiths   (IPG)   1984
■   PO Box 838, AMERSHAM, Bucks, HP6 9GP.   (hq)
         020 3004 9806   fax 07092 882157
         email info@ipgold.org.uk   http://www.ipgold.org.uk
         Admin Sec: Adrian Mohr
○   *P; to establish & maintain the highest standards of
         craftsmanship
●   Mtgs - VE
M   i

Institute of Professional Investigators Ltd   (IPI)   1976
NR   Claremont House, 70-72 Alma Rd, WINDSOR, Berks,
         SL4 3EZ.   (hq)
         0870 330 8622   fax 0870 330 8612
         email admin@ipi.org.uk   http://www.ipi.org.uk
         Sec Gen: David Pryke
○   *P; to encourage & promote its members to achieve a high
         standard of professionalism while engaged in their
         investigative activities
M   i

Institute of Professional Soil Scientists   (IPSS)   1991
NR   Building 53, Cranfield University, CRANFIELD, Beds,
         MK43 0AL.   (hq)
         01234 752983   fax 01234 752970
         email admin@soils.org.uk   http://www.soilscientist.org
         Exec Officer: Dr Kathryn Alton
○   *P; to promote & enhance the status of soil science & allied
         disciplines

Institute of Professional Sport
      since 2007 **Professional Players Federation**

Institute of Professional Willwriters (IPW) 1991
- ■ Trinity Point, New Rd, HALESOWEN, W Midlands, B63 3HY. (hq)
  0845 644 2042   fax 0845 644 2043
  email office@ipw.org.uk   http://www.ipw.org.uk
  Chmn: Paul Sharpe
- ▲ Un-incorporated Association
- ○ *P; for individuals & organisations who specialise in will-writing
- ● Conf - ET - Exam
- < Fedn of Small Businesses
- M 500 i, UK / 2 i, o'seas
- ¶ IPW Jnl - 12; ftm.

Institute of Promotional Marketing (IPM) 1933
- NR 70 Margaret St, LONDON, W1W 8SS.   (hq)
  020 7291 7730
  email enquiries@theipm.org.uk
  http://www.theipm.org.uk
  Dir-Gen: Edwin Mutton
- ▲ Company Limited by Guarantee
- ○ *P; to promote the promotional marketing industry in the UK
- Gp Coupon c'ee; Education; Legal advisory service; Promoters
- ● Conf - Mtgs - ET - Exam - Res - Exhib - Stat - Inf - Lib - LG
- < Eur Promotional Marketing Alliance; Eur Assn of
  Communication Agencies; CBI; Advertising Assn
- M 850 i, 250 f
- ¶ ISP email - 12; ftm only.   AR - 1.
- ✕ May 2010 Institute of Sales Promotion

Institute of Psychoanalysis 1924
- ■ Byron House, 112A Shirland Rd, LONDON, W9 2EQ.   (hq)
  020 7563 5000   fax 020 7563 5001
  email nick.hall@iopa.org.uk
  http://www.psychoanalysis.org.uk
  Manager: Nick Hall
- ▲ Company Limited by Guarantee; Registered Charity
- ○ *L; to be the leading centre of excellence in the UK in the
  provision of psychoanalytic training, education, publication &
  clinical practice
- Gp London Clinic of Psychoanalysis
- ● Conf - Mtgs - ET - Exam - SG - Inf - Lib - Empl - Clinic
- < Intl Psychoanalytical Assn; Brit Psychoanalytic Coun
- M 352 i, UK / 97 i, o'seas
- ¶ International Jnl of Psychoanalysis - 6.   AR.

Institute of Public Administration (IPA) 1957
- IRL 57-61 Lansdowne Rd, DUBLIN 4, Republic of Ireland.   (hq)
  353 (1) 240 3600   fax 353 (1) 668 9135
  email information@ipa.ie   http://www.ipa.ie
  Dir Gen: John Cullen
- ○ *P; Irish public sector management development agency
- ● ET - Lib - Res
- ¶ Publications list available

Institute of Public Loss Assessors (IPLA) 1965
- NR Hill House, 9-10 Ye Corner, Bushey, WATFORD, Herts,
  WD19 4BS.   (hq)
  0844 879 3244
  http://www.lossassessors.org.uk
- ▲ Company Limited by Guarantee
- ○ *P; for all qualified persons who prepare on behalf of public &
  corporate bodies claims arising from insured losses, statutory
  claims, malicious claims & third party claims
- ● Conf - Mtgs - Inf
- M 200 i, UK / 10 i, o'seas

Institute of Public Rights of Way Management   (IPROW)
- ■ PO Box 78, SKIPTON, N Yorks, BD23 4UP.   (mail/address)
  07000 782318
  email iprow@iprow.co.uk   http://www.iprow.co.uk
  Exec Offr: Mrs L S Smith
- ▲ Un-incorporated Society
- ○ *P; for all working with public rights of way
- ● Conf - ET - Inf - LG
- M 360 i
- ¶ Waymark - 4; ftm only.
- ✕ 2007 Institute of Public Rights of Way Officers

Institute of Public Sector Management (IPSM) 1997
- NR 45 Cherry Tree Rd, AXMINSTER, Devon, EX13 5GG.   (hq)
  01297 35423
  email info@ipsm.org.uk   http://www.ipsm.org.uk
  Hon Sec: Derek Wolfe
- ▲ Company Limited by Guarantee
- ○ *P; for managers working in the public services, voluntary
  bodies & community enterprises
- Gp Balanced scorecard; Risk management
- ● Conf - ET - Res - Inf - LG
- M 300 i
- ¶ Topics - 4; ftm only.

Institute of Qualified Professional Secretaries Ltd
   since 2009 **Institute of Professional Administrators**

Institute of Quality Assurance
   since 2006 the **Chartered Quality Institute**

Institute of Quarrying (IQ) 1917
- ■ 7 Regent St, NOTTINGHAM, NG1 5BS.   (hq)
  0115-945 3880   fax 0115-948 4035
  email mail@quarrying.org   http://www.quarrying.org
  Sec: Lyn Bryden
- ▲ Company Limited by Guarantee; Registered Charity
- Br 13; Australia, Malaysia, New Zealand, Hong Kong, South
  Africa,
- ○ *P; to improve the standards of business, technical &
  environmental performance in quarrying
- ● Conf - Mtgs - ET - Exam - VE
- M 2,850 i, UK / 2,500 i, o'seas
- ¶ Quarry Management - 12.

Institute of Race Relations (IRR) 1958
- NR 2-6 Leeke St, LONDON, WC1X 9HS.   (hq)
  020 7837 0041   fax 020 7278 0623
  email info@irr.org.uk   http://www.irr.org.uk
  Chmn: Colin Prescod
- ▲ Company Limited by Guarantee; Registered Charity
- ○ *Q; promotion of research, making available information &
  advice on proposals concerned with race relations & racial
  justice in Britain & internationally
- M i

Institute of Refractories Engineers (IRE) 1961
- NR 575 Trentham Rd, Blurton, STOKE-ON-TRENT, Staffs,
  ST3 3BN.   (gensec/p)
  01782 310234   fax 01782 370145
  email secretary@ireng.org   http://www.ireng.org
  Gen Sec: Jayne Woodhead
- ▲ Un-incorporated Society
- Br 3; South Africa, Australia
- ○ *P; promotion of refractories engineering & technology - high
  temperature materials required in: iron & steel, cement,
  chemical & petrochemical, glass, incineration, power,
  ceramics & domestic uses
- ● Conf - Mtgs - ET - Inf - Assessment Centre (NVQs in refractories
  installation)
- < Inst of Materials; Soc Glass Technology; Inst of Brit Foundrymen
- M c 600 i, UK / c 420 i, o'seas
- ¶ Refractories Engineer - 6.

© CBD Research Ltd · Beckenham · BR3 5JS · Tel 020 8650 7745 · E-mail cbd@cbdresearch.com · www.cbdresearch.com

Institute of Refrigeration   (IoR)   1899
NR   Kelvin House, 76 Mill Lane, CARSHALTON, Surrey, SM5 2JR.
　　　(hq)
　　　020 8647 7033   fax 020 8773 0165
　　　email ior@ior.org.uk   http://www.ior.org.uk
　　　Sec: Miriam Rodway
▲　Registered Charity
Br　8
○　*L, *P; to advance refrigeration standards & services
Gp　Intl Refrigeration C'ee; Service engineers' section
●　Mtgs - ET - Inf
<　Intl Inst Refrigeration; Amer Soc Heating Refrigerating Air
　　　Conditioning Engrs
M　1,900 i, UK / 200 i, o'seas
¶　Proceedings - 1.   NL.

Institute of Registration Agents & Dealers   (MIRAD)   1977
■　PO Box 333, SOUTHPORT, Merseyside, PR9 7GW.   (hq)
　　　030 003 1333   fax 01704 322222
　　　email enquiries@mirad.co.uk   http://www.mirad.co.uk
○　*T; dealers in vehicle registration number plates
●　Mtgs - Res - Exhib - Comp - Inf - LG
M　31 f
　　　(Sub: £184)

Institute of Residential Property Management   (IRPM)   2002
■　178 Battersea Park Rd, LONDON, SW11 4ND.   (hq)
　　　020 7622 5092   fax 020 7498 6153
　　　email info@irpm.org.uk   http://www.irpm.org.uk
　　　Chief Exec: Jeff Platt
▲　Company Limited by Guarantee
○　*P; to promote & stimulate improvements to the technical &
　　　general knowledge of individuals engaged in residential
　　　property management
●　Exam
<　Sponsors: Assn of Residential Managing Agents (ARMA), Assn of
　　　Retirement Housing Mgrs (ARHM); Property Mgrs Assn
　　　Scotland (PMAS)
M　688 i
¶　Members' NL - 3; ftm only.
　　　[LM on website].

Institute of Revenues, Rating & Valuation   (IRRV)   1882
NR   Northumberland House (5th floor), 303-306 High Holborn,
　　　LONDON, WC1V 7JZ.   (hq)
　　　020 7831 3505   fax 020 7831 2048
　　　http://www.irrv.org.uk
　　　Chief Exec: David Magor
○　*P; to support members' professional & personal development
　　　& the sharing of best practice
Gp　Benefits; Local taxation & revenues; Valuation
●　Conf - ET - Exam - Mtgs
M　5000 i, 200 org

Institute of Risk Management   (IRM)   1986
■　6 Lloyd's Ave, LONDON, EC3N 3AX.   (hq)
　　　020 7709 9808   fax 020 7709 0716
　　　email enquiries@theirm.org   http://www.theirm.org
　　　Chief Exec: Steve Fowler
▲　Company Limited by Guarantee
○　*P; education, training & development of risk professionals
Gp　Central government; Charities; Construction; Energy; Enterprise
　　　risk management; Financial services; Human factors &
　　　communication; Innovation, value creation & opportunity;
　　　Legal risk; Operational risk; Solvency II; Transport & logistics
●　Conf - Mtgs - ET - Exam - Exhib - SG - Lib
<　Intl Fedn of Risk Mgt Assns (IFRIMA)
M　3,000 i
¶　InfoRM - 6;   InfoRM e-supplement; both ftm only.
　　　AR - 1; free.

Institute of Road Safety Officers Ltd   (IRSO)   1971
NR   12 Haddon Close, WELLINGBOROUGH, Northants,
　　　NN8 5ZB.   (hq)
　　　email irso@live.co.uk   http://www.irso.org.uk
　　　Hon Sec: Steve Barber
▲　Company Limited by Guarantee
Br　13
○　*P; to receive, analyse & disseminate information to members
　　　relating to road safety education, training & publicity
　　　programmes
●　Conf - Mtgs - ET - Exam - Exhib - LG
<　Parliamentary Advisory Coun on Transport Safety
M　400 i
¶　InRoads (Jnl) - 4; ftm, £50 nm.   AR; free.

Institute of Road Transport Engineers
　　　a professional sector of the **Society of Operations Engineers**

Institute of Roofing   (IoR)   1981
NR   Roofing House, 31 Worship St, LONDON, EC2A 2DX.   (hq)
　　　020 7448 3858   fax 020 7448 3195
　　　email info@instituteofroofing.org
　　　http://www.instituteofroofing.org
　　　Chmn: Martin Adwick
▲　Company Limited by Guarantee
○　*P; for individuals working in the roofing industry
●　Conf - Mtgs - ET - Exam
M　1,086 i, UK / 3 i, o'seas
¶　IoR Bulletin (NL) - 4; ftm only.

Institute of Safety in Technology & Research   (ISTR)   1981
NR   Bocyde, Weston Rd, Loxton, AXBRIDGE, N Somerset,
　　　BS26 2XD.   (memsec/p)
　　　01934 750915
　　　email istr-secretary@istr.org.uk   http://www.istr.org.uk
　　　Mem Sec: M A Cheshire
○　*P; for safety professionals working in organisations engaged in
　　　research activities
●　Conf - Mtgs
M　204 i, UK / 1 i, o'seas
¶　ISTR Bulletin - 3;   Ybk; both ftm only.

Institute of Sales & Marketing Management   (ISMM)   1966
■　Harrier Court, Woodside Rd, Lower Woodside, LUTON, Beds,
　　　LU1 4DQ.   (hq)
　　　01582 840001   fax 01582 849142
　　　email sales@ismm.co.uk   http://www.ismm.co.uk
▲　Company Limited by Guarantee
○　*P; to represent sales people & companies with a sales force
●　Conf - Mtgs - ET - Exam - Res - Government accredited
　　　awarding body for sales qualifications
M　[not divulged]
¶　Winning Edge - 10; ftm, £95 yr nm.

Institute of Sales Promotion
　　　since May 2010 the **Institute of Promotional Marketing**

Institute of Science & Technology   (IST)   1954
■　Kingfisher House, 90 Rockingham St, SHEFFIELD, S1 4EB.   (hq)
　　　0114-276 3197   fax 0114-272 6354
　　　http://www.istonline.org.uk
　　　Hon Sec: A Taylor
▲　Company Limited by Guarantee
○　*L, *P; to advance knowledge of science laboratory techniques;
　　　to promote professional standing of laboratory technicians,
　　　technical specialists, managerial staff
●　Conf - ET - Exam - Exhib - Inf
M　1,100 i, UK / 100 i, o'seas
¶　Science Technology - 4; ftm only.

Institute of Scientific & Technical Communicators   (ISTC)   1972
NR   Airport House, Purley Way, CROYDON, Surrey, CR0 0XZ.
　　　(hsp)
　　　020 8253 4506
　　　email istc@istc.org.uk   http://www.istc.org.uk
　　　Sec: Carol Hewitt
▲   Company Limited by Guarantee
○   *P; communication & presentation of scientific & technical
　　　information
Gp Independent Authors Special Interest Gp (IASIG); Irish; Middle
　　　East
●   Conf - ET
<   Intl Coun for Technical Communication (INTECOM)
M   c 1,000 i, 21 f, UK / c 75 i, o'seas
¶   Communicator (Jnl) - 4; ftm, £35 (£40 EU, £43 RoW) nm.
　　　ISTC Hbk on Professional Communication & Information
　　　Design; £20 (available through Amazon).

Institute of Security Management   (ISecM)   1988
■   Omega House, Richmond Row, LIVERPOOL, L3 3BU.   (hq)
　　　0845 838 1818
　　　http://www.instituteofsecuritymanagement.co.uk
　　　Hon Sec: Richard A Slater
○   *P; members are from various specialist groups employed in
　　　the industry incl: Armed forces, UK police services,
　　　Commercial & industrial security, MOD, Banks, Exhibition,
　　　Electronic security alarms, PCTV, Radio
●   Conf - Mtgs - ET - LG
<   Jt Securities Ind Coun (JSIC); Security Systems & Alarms
　　　Inspection Bd (SSAIB)
M   150 i, UK / 20 i, o'seas
¶   NL - 4.

Institute of Sheet Metal Engineering   (ISME)   1946
■   102 Richmond Drive, Perton, WOLVERHAMPTON, W Midlands,
　　　WV6 7UQ.   (hq)
　　　01789 499146
　　　email ismesec@googlemail.com   http://www.isme.org.uk
　　　Hon Sec: O W Pinfold
▲   Registered Charity
○   *L; theory & practice of sheet metal forming & fabrication
Gp Education; Sheet forming technology
●   Conf - Mtgs - Exhib - Comp - SG - Inf - VE - Lectures
<   Confedn of Brit Metalforming
M   100 i, 25 f, UK / 8 i, o'seas
¶   Oracle - 4.

Institute for Small Business & Entrepreneurship   (ISBE)   1993
■   137 Euston Rd (Ground floor), LONDON, NW1 2AA.   (hq)
　　　020 7554 9941
　　　email info@isbe.org.uk   http://www.isbe.org.uk
　　　Business Devt & Events Mgr: Lorraine Reese
▲   Company Limited by Guarantee; Registered Charity
○   *Q; a network for people & organisations involved in small
　　　business & entrepreneurship research, policy, support &
　　　advice
●   Conf - Inf - Mtgs - Res
M   500 i
　　　(Sub: £65)
¶   Enterprising Matters (Jnl) - 4; free online.

Institute for Social Inventions   1985
NR   12a Blackstock Mews, Blackstock Rd, LONDON, N4 2BT.
　　　(mtgs add)
　　　020 7359 8391   fax 020 7354 3831
　　　http://www.globalideasbank.org
　　　Contact: Nick Temple
○   *K; to promote social inventions - new imaginative non-
　　　technological solutions to social problems
●   Conf - Mtgs - ET - Res - Comp - Inf - Lib - Workshop courses in
　　　state schools - £1,000 awards for best ideas
M   400 members & subscribers
¶   Social Inventions Annual Book - 1; £15 m only.
　　　Note: The Institute runs the Global Ideas Bank see -
　　　www.globalideasbank.org

Institute of Sound & Communications Engineers   (ISCE)
NR   PO Box 7966, READING, Berks, RG6 7WY.   (hq)
　　　0118-954 2175   fax 0118-954 2175
　　　http://www.isce.org.uk
　　　Secretariat: Rosalind Wigmore
▲   Company Limited by Guarantee
○   *L, *P; supports technicians, managers & designers in the
　　　performing arts & public address industries
●   Conf - Mtgs - ET - Exam - Exhib - Lib
M   250 i, 16 f, UK / 20 i, o'seas
¶   Public Address (NL) - irreg.

Institute of Specialist Surveyors & Engineers   (ISSE)   1989
NR   Essex House, High St, CHIPPING ONGAR, Essex, CM5 9EB.
　　　(hq)
　　　0800 915 6363
　　　http://www.isse.org.uk
　　　Chmn: Derek Spring
▲   Company Limited by Guarantee
○   *P; professional advice on timber infestations (woodworm and
　　　rot) and various forms of damp problems in buildings;
　　　assistance in finding reliable surveyors & treatment specialists
M   c 200 i

Institute of Spiritualist Mediums   (ISM)   1956
NR   132 Reading Rd South, Church Crookham, FLEET, Hants,
　　　GU52 6AL.   (gensec/p)
　　　email c.jones@ism.org.uk   http://www.ism.org.uk
　　　Gen Sec: Christine Jones
▲   Registered Charity
○   *E; to improve the standard of mediumship & the work of
　　　spiritualist mediums

Institute for Sport, Parks & Leisure
　　　in 2011 merged with the Institute of Sport & Recreation Management
　　　to form the **Institute for the Management of Sport & Physical
　　　Activity**

Institute of Sport & Recreation Management
　　　in 2011 merged with the Institute for Sport, Parks & Leisure to form
　　　the **Institute for the Management of Sport & Physical Activity**

Institute of Spring Technology   (IST)   1997
■   Henry St, SHEFFIELD, S Yorks, S3 7EQ.   (hq)
　　　0114-276 0771   fax 0114-252 7997
　　　email ist@ist.org.uk   http://www.ist.org.uk
　　　Managing Dir: Andrew Watkinson
▲   Company Limited by Guarantee
○   *E, *L, *P, *Q, *T; spring design, testing & consultancy
●   ET - Res - Exhib - Inf - Lib - VE
<   Intl Wire & Machinery Assn; Eur Spring Fedn; Fastener & Engg
　　　Res Assn
M   100 i, UK / 120 i, o'seas
¶   IST Technology NL - 4;   UKSMA NL - 4; both ftm only.
　　　UKSMA Member Guide - 1;   IST Member Guide - 1; both
　　　free.

Institute of Swimming   (IOS)   1975
■   SportPark, 3 Oakwood Drive, LOUGHBOROUGH, Leics,
　　　LE11 3QF.   (hq)
　　　01509 618700
　　　email ios@swimming.org   http://www.swimming.org
　　　Admin: Jane Nickerson
▲   Company Limited by Guarantee
Br 12; Eire, International
○   *P, *S; for qualified swimming teachers & coaches
●   Conf - Mtgs - ET - Res - Exhib - Inf - Lib - LG
<   Fedn of Water Fitness Profls; Amat Swimming Assn;
　　　Synchronised Swimming Coaches Assns
M   13,000 i, UK / 1,000 i, o'seas
¶   Swimming Times - 12; ftm, £1.70 nm.   LM - 2 yrly; ftm.
×   2008 Institute of Swimming Teachers & Coaches

Institute of Swimming Pool Engineers Ltd (ISPE) 1978

NR PO Box 3083, NORWICH, Norfolk, NR6 7YL.   (hq)
01603 499959
http://www.ispe.co.uk
▲ Company Limited by Guarantee
○ *P; design, construction & maintenance of swimming pools & spas, both public & private
Gp Education & training to the swimming pool industry
● Conf - ET - Exam - Exhib - SG - Inf
M 830 i, UK / 30 i, o'seas
¶ ISPE Magazine - 4; free.   Hbk.
Home study course training manuals.
Swimming Pool Industry Directory & Specifier (SPidas).
Technical Papers (20 titles to date; £6-£13) incl:
Water treatment for pool operators.
Heat pumps.   Ozone.
Domestic & commercial spas.
Heat losses from indoor & outdoor pools.

Institute of Tourist Guiding 2002

NR Coppergate House, 16 Brune St, LONDON, E1 7NJ.   (hq)
020 7953 1257   fax 020 7953 1357
email office@itg.org.uk   http://www.itg.org.uk
Co Sec: Gail Jones
○ *P; to achieve and maintain recognition of the profession of tour guiding

Institute of Trade Mark Attorneys (ITMA) 1934

■ Outer Temple (5th floor), 222-225 Strand, LONDON, WC2R 1BA.   (hq)
020 7101 6090   fax 020 7101 6099
email tm@itma.org.uk   http://www.itma.org.uk
Chief Exec: Keven Bader
▲ Company Limited by Guarantee
○ *P
● Conf - Mtgs - ET - Exam - LG
M 970 i, UK / 500 i, o'seas
¶ NL - 12;   Information - 12;   AR - 1; all ftm only.
LM - 1; ftm, £10 nm.

Institute of Traffic Accident Investigators (ITAI) 1990

NR Column House, London Rd, SHREWSBURY, Shropshire, SY2 6NN.   (hq)
0845 621 2066   fax 0845 621 2077
email admin@itai.org   http://www.itai.org
▲ Company Limited by Guarantee; Registered Charity
○ *P; representation, communication, education, & regulation in traffic accident investigation
● Conf - ET - Exam - Res - VE
M 750 i, UK / 60 i, o'seas
¶ Impact (Jnl) - 3; ftm, £10 nm.   Contact (NL) - 6; ftm only.

Institute of Training & Occupational Learning (ITOL) 2000

NR PO Box 1969, LIVERPOOL, L69 3HP.   (hq)
0845 475 1969   fax 0151-515 3001
email enquiries@itol.org   http://www.itol.org
▲ Un-incorporated Society
○ *P; for trainers & L&D professionals
● ET - Exam - Res - Inf - Lib
¶ Training & Learning - 12.

Institute of Transactional Analysis (ITA) 1977

■ Broadway House, 149-151 St Neots Rd, Hardwick, CAMBRIDGE, CB23 7QJ.   (hq)
01954 212468
email admin@ita.org.uk   http://www.ita.org.uk
Chmn: Alastair Moodie
▲ Company Limited by Guarantee; Registered Charity
○ *P; the education of the public in the study, theory & practice of transactional analysis - a theory of personality & social psychology within a humanistic tradition
Gp Counselling; Educational; Organisational; Psychotherapy
● Conf - Mtgs - ET - Exam - SG - Counselling - Therapy - Coaching
< Eur Assn Transactional Analysis; UK Coun for Psychotherapy
M 1,200 i, 20 f, UK / 40 i, o'seas
(Sub: £33-£286 i, £25-£260 f)
¶ ITA News (NL) - 6; ftm, £16.50 nm.
Transactions (Jnl) - 2; ftm only.   AR - 1; ftm only.

Institute of Translation & Interpreting (ITI) 1986

NR Fortuna House, South Fifth St, MILTON KEYNES, Bucks, MK9 2EU.   (hq)
01908 325250
email info@iti.org.uk   http://www.iti.org.uk
Chief Exec: Alan Wheatley
▲ Company Limited by Guarantee
○ *P; for translators & interpreters; has a structure of regional group, language & subject networks
Gp Subject Networks: Book translators, Construction, Finance & trade, Information technology, Insurance, Law, Media, arts & tourism, Medicine, Patents
● Conf - Mtgs - ET - Exhib - SG - Expt - Inf
< Intl Fedn of Translators (FIT)
M 2,240 i, 93 f, UK / 480 i, 5 f, o'seas
¶ ITI Bulletin - 6; ftm.   LM - 1.   AR - 1; free.
Conference Proceedings - 1.   Leaflets & factsheets - irreg.

Institute of Transport Administration (IoTA) 1944

NR The Old Studio, 25 Greenfield Rd, Westoning, BEDFORD, MK45 5JD.   (hq)
01525 634940   fax 01525 750016
email director@iota.org.uk   http://www.iota.org.uk
Pres; Dr Michael Asteris
○ *P; to improve & develop the knowledge & efficiency of members in the skills of transport management
M i
¶ Transport Management (Jnl) - 6.

Institute of Transport Management (ITM) 1977

NR 14-20 George St, BIRMINGHAM, B12 9RG.   (hq)
0121-440 3003   fax 0121-440 4644
email marketing@itmworld.com
http://www.itmworld.com
▲ Registered Charity
○ *P; to promote academic achievement, training & professionalism with the transport & logistics industry
● Conf - ET - Exam - Mtgs - Res
< Eur Inst of Transport Mgt
M 9,000 i, UK / 6,300 i, o'seas

Institute of Travel Management
since 2009 **Institute of Travel & Meetings**

Institute of Travel & Meetings   (ITM)   1956

NR Waters Green House, Waters Green, MACCLESFIELD,
      Cheshire, SK11 6LF.   (hq)
      01625 430472   fax 01625 439183
      email secretariat@itm.org.uk   http://www.itm.org.uk
      Chief Exec: Simone Buckley
▲ Company Limited by Guarantee
Br 6; Ireland
○ *P; for those involved in the planning & procurement of
     business travel services
Gp Supplier c'ee (representatives of short-haul airlines,
     international & independent hotels & surface transportation)
● Conf - Mtgs - ET - Exhib - SG - LG
< Chart Inst Purchasing & Supply (CIPS)
M 312 i, 284 f, UK / 38 i, 16 f, o'seas
¶ Newsline - 4;   ITM Ybk - 1; both ftm only.
× 2009 Institute of Travel Management Ltd

Institute of Travel & Tourism   (ITT)   1956

NR PO Box 217, WARE, Herts, SG12 8WY.   (hq)
      0844 499 5653   fax 0844 499 5654
      email enquiries@itt.co.uk   http://www.itt.co.uk
      Chmn: Dr Steven Freudmann
▲ Company Limited by Guarantee
○ *P; to raise & maintain standards throughout the travel &
     tourism industry
● Conf - ET - Exam - LG - Mtgs
M i & f

Institute of Trichologists (Inc)   (IT)   1902

NR 24 Langroyd Rd (ground floor), LONDON, SW17 7PL.
      (regd off)
      0845 604 4657
      http://www.trichologists.org.uk
      Chmn: Mrs Marilyn Sherlock
▲ Company Limited by Guarantee
○ *L, *P; the treatment & care of human hair & scalp in health &
     disease
● ET - Exam - Res
M 220 i, UK / 20 i, o'seas
¶ The Trichologists - 2.

Institute for Turnaround   (IFT)   2000

NR The Bridge, 12-16 Clerkenwell Rd, LONDON, EC1M 5PQ.
      (hq)
      020 7324 6244   fax 020 7253 5029
      email info@instituteforturnaround.com
      http://www.instituteforturnaround.com
      Chief Exec: Christine Elliott
▲ Company Limited by Guarantee
○ *P; for individuals & organisations dedicated to helping
     businesses achieve their potential in circumstances that may
     be difficult or where profound & radical change is required
× 2008 Society of Turnaround Professionals

Institute of Value Management   (IVM)   1966

■ 1-3 Birdcage Walk, LONDON, SW1H 9JJ.   (hq)
      0870 902 0905
      email secretary@ivm.org.uk   http://www.ivm.org.uk
      Exec Sec: Doug Hurst
▲ Company Limited by Guarantee
Br 6
○ *P; to develop the competence & knowledge to deliver
     sustainable value
     Value Management is concerned with improving & sustaining a
     desirable balance between the wants & needs of
     stakeholders & the resources needed to satisfy them
● Conf - Mtgs - ET - G - Inf - LG
M 180 i, 16 f, UK / 21 i, o'seas
     (Subs: £70 i, £575 f)
¶ Value Jnl - 3; ftm, £25 nm.

Institute of Vehicle Recovery   (IVR)   1984

■ Bignell House, Horton Rd, WEST DRAYTON, Middx, UB7 8EJ.
      (hq)
      01895 436426   fax 01895 736412
      http://www.theivrgroup.org
      Sec: Geoff Gatward
▲ Company Limited by Guarantee
○ *P; interests of persons engaged in motor vehicle recovery; to
     promote technical training & improve the standard of safety
     in motor vehicle recovery
Gp Rescue & Recovery Trainers Assn
● ET - Exam - Res - Exhib - SG
M 700 i, UK / 56 i, o'seas
¶ NL; ftm.

Institute of Videography   (IOV)   1985

NR PO Box 625, LOUGHTON, Essex, IG10 3GZ.   (hq)
      020 8502 3817   fax 020 8508 9211
      email info@iov.co.uk   http://www.iov.co.uk
      Exec Admin: Kevin Cook
Br 16
○ *P; video production & training
● Conf - Comp - Mtgs - SG - ET - Inf - Exhib - VideoSkills
     workshops
M 800 i, 50 f
¶ Focus Magazine - 12.

Institute of Vitreous Enamellers & Vitreous Enamel Association
    since 2010 as IVE: the Vitreous Enamellers' Society, has beome a
    group within the Surface Engineering Division of the **Institute of**
    Materials, Minerals & Mining

Institute for Volunteering Research
    an group of **Volunteering England**

Institute of Water   1946

■ 4 Carlton Court, Team Valley, GATESHEAD, Tyne & Wear,
      NE11 0AZ.   (hq)
      0191-422 0088   fax 0191-422 0087
      email info@instituteofwater.org.uk
      http://www.instituteofwater.org.uk
      Chief Exec: Mrs Lynn Cooper
Br 9
○ *P; for people working in the water industry
● Conf - Mtgs - Exhib - SG - VE
< Engg Coun; Amer Water Works Assn; Soc for the Envt
M 2,000 i, 40 f, UK / 50 i, o'seas
¶ Jnl - 4; ftm, £25 yr nm.

Institute of Welfare   (IoW)   1945

■ PO Box 5570, STOURBRIDGE, W Midlands, DY8 9BA.   (hq)
      0800 032 3725
      email info@instituteofwelfare.co.uk
      http://www.instituteofwelfare.co.uk
      Chmn: Sally Bundock
▲ Company Limited by Guarantee; Registered Charity
○ *P; for welfare officers in industry, commerce, social
     organisations, national & local government departments
● Conf - Mtgs - ET - Res
M c 2,500 i
¶ Welfare World - 4.

Institute of Welsh Affairs   (IWA)   1987
■   4 Cathedral Rd (2nd floor), CARDIFF. CF11 9LJ.   (hq)
     029 2066 0820
     email wales@iwa.org.uk   http://www.iwa.org.uk
     Dir: John Osmond
▲   Registered Charity
Br   5
○   *P; to promote the prosperity of Wales, its industry & people by
     encouraging debate upon & research into economic, social &
     cultural issues
●   Conf - Mtgs - Res
M   1,100 i, 150 f, UK / 50 i, o'seas
     (Sub: £10-£100)
¶   Agenda - 3; ftm.   Proceedings.
     Miscellaneous Research Reports;   Discussion papers.

Institute of Wood Science
     in 2009 became IWSc: the Wood Technology Society, a division of the
     Institute of Metals, Minerals & Mining

Institution of Agricultural Engineers   (IAgrE)   1938
■   The Bullock Building, University Way, Cranfield, BEDFORD,
     MK43 0GH.   (hq)
     01234 750876   fax 01234 751319
     email secretary@iagre.org   http://www.iagre.org
     Chief Exec: Christopher R Whetnall
▲   Company Limited by Guarantee; Registered Charity
Br   13
○   *L, *P; for engineers, managers, scientists & technologists in
     agriculture & allied industries (incl forestry, food processing,
     agrochemicals & amenity industries)
Gp   Agro-industrial products; Amenity & ecological engineering;
     Food technology; Forestry engineering; Horticultural
     engineering; Machinery management; Overseas
     development; Pioneering technology; Precision in farming;
     Renewable energy; Soil & water management; Vehicles;
     Young engineers
●   Conf - Mtgs - Inf - Lib
<   Intl Commission of Agricl Engg (CIGR); Eur Soc of Agricl
     Engrs (EurAgEng); Soc for the Envt (SocEnv)
M   1,700 i, 15 f, UK / 200 i, o'seas
¶   Landwards - 4; ftm, £52 nm.

Institution of Analysts & Programmers   (IAP)   1971
■   Charles House, 36 Culmington Rd, LONDON, W13 9NH.
     (hq)
     020 8434 3685
     http://www.iap.org.uk
     Dir Gen: Alastair Revell
○   *P; systems analysis & computer programming
M   c 3,000 i, UK / c 500 i, o'seas
¶   NL - 4;   LM;   AR.

Institution of Chemical Engineers   (IChemE)   1922
NR   Davis Building, 165-189 Railway Terrace, RUGBY, Warks,
     CV21 3HQ.   (hq)
     01788 578214   fax 01788 560833
     http://www.icheme.org
     Chief Exec: Dr David Brown
▲   Registered Charity
Br   Australia, Malaysia, Singapore
○   *L, *P; the professional qualifying body for process & chemical
     engineers
●   Conf - ET - Exhib - Products & services for qualified chemical
     engineers & those interested in chemical engineering as a
     career
<   Soc for the Envt (SocEnv)
M   18,168 i, UK / 7,455 i, o'seas
¶   The Chemical Engineer (tce) - 12 ftm, £165 (UK)
     (£180 RoW) nm.
     Chemical Engineering Research & Design - 12;
        (members) print & online; £120 (UK) £140 (RoW).
        (members) online only; £50 (UK+RoW).
        (non-members) print & online £721 (UK) £742 (RoW).
     Process Safety & Environmental Protection - 6;
        (members) print & online; £80 (UK) £100 (RoW).
        (members) online only; £40 (UK+RoW).
        (non-members) print & online; £448 (UK) £464 (RoW).
     Food & Bioproducts Processing - 4;
        (members) print & online; £50 (UK) £70 (RoW).
        (members) online only; £30 (UK+RoW).
        (non-members) £278 (UK) £294 (RoW).

Institution of Civil Engineering Surveyors
     since 2009 **Chartered Institution of Civil Engineering
     Surveyors**

Institution of Civil Engineers   (ICE)   1818
NR   1 Great George St, LONDON, SW1P 3AA.   (hq)
     020 7222 7722
     email secretariat@ice.org.uk   http://www.ice.org.uk
     Dir Gen: Tom Foulkes
▲   Registered Charity
○   *L, *P; to promote & progress civil engineering
Gp   British Geotechnical Association; Society for Earthquake & Civil
     Engineering Dynamics
●   Conf - Mtgs - ET - Exam - Res - Exhib - Comp - Inf - Lib - LG -
     Register of engineers for disaster relief - Dispute resolution
     service - Recruitment subsidiary - Panel for historical
     engineering works - Archives - Audio-visual collection -
     Guided tours of building available - Rooms available for
     external bookings
<   Soc for the Envt (SocEnv)
M   60,891 i, UK / 14,162 i, o'seas

Institution of Commercial & Business Agents   (ICBA)   2008
NR   Arbon House, 6 Tournament Court, Edgehill Drive, WARWICK,
     CV34 6LG.   (hq)
     0845 250 6002
     email info@icba.uk.com   http://www.icba.uk.com
○   *P; estate agents specialising in the commercial sector
<   Is a subsidiary of the National Association of Estate Agents, a
     division of the National Federation of Property Professionals

Institution of Construction Safety   (ICS)   1995
NR   Heriot-Watt Research Park, EDINBURGH, EH14 4AP.   (hq)
     0131-449 4646   fax 0131-451 5440
     email admin@instcs.org   http://www.instcs.org
     Gen Sec: Mehdi Laftavi
▲   Company Limited by Guarantee
○   *P; to improve health & safety in the construction industry
     particularly in relation to the Construction (Design &
     Management) Regulations 1994 (CDM) & to the role of
     planning supervisor
M   i
×   2006 Institution of Planning Supervisors

Institution of Diagnostic Engineers 1983
- ■ 16 Thistlewood Rd, Outwood, WAKEFIELD, W Yorks,
  WF1 3HH.   (hq)
  01924 821000   fax 01924 821200
  email admin@diagnosticengineers.org
  http://www.diagnosticengineers.org
  Admin: Karen Seiles
- ▲ Company Limited by Guarantee; Registered Charity (as Society
  of Diagnostic Engineers)
- ○ *P; engineers involved in diagnosing faults in machines, plant,
  & systems.
  Specialist areas: Vibration analysis, condition monitoring,
  engine health
- Gp Society of Diagnostic Engineers - maintains a register of
  professional engineers who are entitled to use the
  designation P.Eng.
- ● Conf - ET - Exhib - VE
- M 1,500 i, 20 f, UK / 500 i, o'seas
- ¶ Diagnostic Engineering - 6; ftm, £60 nm.

Institution of Diesel & Gas Turbine Engineers   (IDGTE)   1913
- ■ Bedford Heights, Manton Lane, BEDFORD, MK41 7PH.   (hq)
  01234 214340   fax 01234 355493
  email enquiries@idgte.org   http://www.idgte.org
  Dir Gen: Peter Tottman
- ▲ Un-incorporated Society
- Br Canada
- ○ *L; the advancement of diesel & gas engines, gas turbines &
  related products & technology
- Gp Working gps: Diesel engines, Gas turbines
- ● Conf - Mtgs - ET - Exhib - Inf - Lib - VE
- M 457 i, 60 f, UK / 101 i, 58 f, o'seas
- ¶ The Power Engineer - 4; ftm (extra copies £15), £30 nm.
  The Power Engineer (Operational Report) - 1; ftm (extra
  copies £25), £50 nm.

Institution of Economic Development Ltd   (IED)   1983
- NR PO Box 796, NORTHAMPTON, NN4 9TS.   (hq)
  01604 874613
  http://www.ied.co.uk
  Chmn: Keith Burge
- ○ *P
- M 1,000 i
- ¶ Economic Development - 4.

Institution of Electrical Engineers
  in 2006 merged with Institution of Incorporated Engineers to form the
  Institution of Engineering & Technology

Institution of Engineering Designers   (IED)   1945
- ■ Courtleigh, Westbury Leigh, WESTBURY, Wilts, BA13 3TA.   (hq)
  01373 822801   fax 01373 858085
  email ied@ied.org.uk   http://www.ied.org.uk
  Chief Exec: Libby Brodhurst
- ▲ Company Limited by Guarantee; Registered Charity
- Br 13; Malta, Hong Kong
- ○ *P; to advance education in engineering & product design;
  Licensed body of the Engineering Council
- Gp Computer aided design (CAD); Product design
- ● Conf - Mtgs - ET - Exhib - Comp - SG - Stat - Inf - Lib - VE
- < Soc for the Envt (SocEnv)
- M 4,920 i, UK / 410 i, o'seas
- ¶ The Engineering Designer - 6; ftm, £39 yr nm.

Institution of Engineering & Technology   (IET)   1871
- ■ Savoy Place, LONDON, WC2R 0BL.   (hq)
  020 7240 1871   fax 020 7497 7735
  http://www.theiet.org
  Chief Exec & Sec: Nigel Fine
- ▲ Registered Charity
- Br 47; 53 o'seas
- ○ *L, *P; to promote the advancement of science, engineering &
  technology; to act as the voice of the profession; to set
  standards of qualifications
- Gp 40 technical interest groups grouped under: Communications
  engineering, Computing & control, Electronic systems &
  software, Information professional, Management,
  Manufacturing, Power, Transport
- ● Conf - Mtgs - ET - Exhib - Comp - Inf - Lib - PL - VE - LG
- M c 150,000 i & f
- ¶ Engineering & Technology (Jnl) - 22.
  Electronic Letters
  Wiring Matters
  Flipside (for teenagers).
  Student & Graduate Magazine.
- ✕ 2006 (Institution of Incorporated Engineers
  (Institution of Electrical Engineers

Institution of Engineers of Ireland 1835
- IRL 22 Clyde Rd, Ballsbridge, DUBLIN 4, Republic of Ireland.   (hq)
  353 (1) 665 1300   fax 353 (1) 668 5508
  email info@engineersireland.ie
  http://www.engineersireland.ie
  Pres: P J Rudden
- ○ *P; to provide standards for the engineering profession & a
  community for engineers
- M 24,000 i
  Note: uses the operating name Engineers Ireland

**Institution of Engineers & Shipbuilders in Scotland   (IESIS)
1857**
- NR Clydeport, 16 Robertson St, GLASGOW, G2 8DS.   (hq)
  0141-248 3721   fax 0141-221 2698
  email secretary@iesis.org   http://www.iesis.org
  Pres: Dr Gordon Masterton
- ○ *L, *P; to provide a forum in which individual members from all
  engineering & related disciplines can discuss & exchange
  information, generate ideas, involve young engineers &, with
  kindred bodies, promote a wider understanding of the role of
  the engineering profession in society
- M i

Institution of Environmental Sciences Ltd   (IES)   1971
- ■ 34 Grosvenor Gardens (2nd floor), LONDON, SW1W 0DH.
  (hq)
  020 7730 5516
  email enquiries@ies-uk.org.uk   http://www.ies-uk.org.uk
  Hon Sec: Phil Holmes
- ▲ Company Limited by Guarantee; Registered Charity
- ○ *L, *P; to promote, sponsor, & organise research &
  interdisciplinary action, consultation & coordination into all
  matters concerning environmental sciences
- Gp Education c'ee
- ● Conf - ET - Accreditation of university courses - Publications -
  Careers advice
- < Science Coun; Soc for the Envt (SocEnv)
- M 780 i, 8 f, 6 org, UK / 65 i, o'seas
- ¶ The Environmental Scientist - 6.

© CBD Research Ltd · Beckenham · BR3 5JS · Tel 020 8650 7745 · E-mail cbd@cbdresearch.com · www.cbdresearch.com

Institution of Fire Engineers (IFE) 1918

■ IFE House, 64-68 Cygnet Court, Timothy's Bridge Rd, STRATFORD UPON AVON, Warwicks, CV37 9NW. (hq)
01789 261463
email info@ife.org.uk   http://www.ife.org.uk
Chmn: Peter Holland
▲ Company Limited by Guarantee; Registered Charity
Br 20; 18 countries o'seas
○ *L, *P; to promote, encourage & improve the science & practice of fire extinction, fire prevention & fire engineering
● Conf - Mtgs - ET - Exam - Res - Exhib - Inf
< Fedn of Brit Fire Orgs (FBFO)
M 7,000 i, UK / 4,500 i, o'seas
¶ Fire Engineers Jnl - 6; ftm.
Fire Technology - Chemistry Combustion; - Calculations.
Principles of Fire Investigation.   How did it start?
Dictionary of Fire Technology.
Hbk for Fire Engineers.
Guide to Examinations of the IFE.

Institution of Gas Engineers & Managers (IGEM) 1863

■ IGEM House, High St, KEGWORTH, Derbys, DE74 2DA.   (hq)
0844 375 4436   fax 01509 678198
email general@igem.org.uk   http://www.igem.org.uk
Chief Exec & Sec: John Williams
▲ Registered Charity
Br 10; Brazil, Hong Kong
○ *L, *P; licensed to accredit engineers to chartered, incorporated & technician levels; provides a focus & technical standards for the gas industry
Gp Sections: Information, Membership, Technical
● Conf - Mtgs - ET - Exhib - Comp - SG - Inf - Lib - PL - LG
< Intl Gas U (IGU); Accredited by Engg Coun (UK)
M 4,846 i, 114 f, UK / 394 i, 12 f, o'seas
¶ International Gas Engineering & Management (Jnl) - 10.
✕ 2001 Institution of Gas Engineers

Institution of Highways & Transportation
since 7 December 2009 **Chartered Institution of Highways & Transportation**

Institution of Incorporated Engineers
in 2006 merged with Institution of Electrical Engineers to form the **Institution of Engineering & Technology**

Institution of Lighting Engineers
since 2010 **Institution of Lighting Professionals**

Institution of Lighting Professionals (ILP) 1924

NR Regent House, Regent Place, RUGBY, Warks, CV21 2PN.   (hq)
01788 576492   fax 01788 540145
http://www.theilp.org.uk
Chief Exec: Richard Frost
▲ Company Limited by Guarantee; Registered Charity
○ *P; to promote excellence in all forms of lighting
● Conf - ET - Exhib - Inf - Lib - Mtgs
M i & f
¶ Lighting Journal - 6; ftm.
✕ 2010 Institution of Lighting Engineers

Institution of Mechanical Engineers (IMechE) 1847

NR 1 Birdcage Walk, LONDON, SW1H 9JJ.   (hq)
020 7222 7899
http://www.imeche.org
Chief Exec: Stephen Tetlow
▲ Registered Charity
○ *L, *P; 'to create the natural professional home for all involved in mechanical engineering'
< Soc for the Envt (SocEnv)
M 66,000 i, UK / 11,000 i, o'seas

Institution of Nuclear Engineers
on 1 January 2009 merged with the British Nuclear Energy Society to form the **Nuclear Institute**

Institution of Occupational Safety & Health (IOSH) 1945

NR The Grange, Highfield Drive, WIGSTON, Leics, LE18 1NN. (hq)
0116-257 3100   fax 0116-257 3101
http://www.iosh.co.uk
▲ Incorporated by Royal Charter; Registered Charity
Br 23; 2
○ *P; for those professionally involved in occupational safety & health
Gp Construction; Healthcare; Offshore; Public services
● Conf - Mtgs - ET - Res - Exhib - Inf - Lib - PL - VE - LG
M 26,500 i, UK / 2,500 i, o'seas
¶ Safety & Health Practitioner - 12.   Jnl - 2 yrly.
Various other publications.

Institution of Planning Supervisors
since 2006 **Institution of Construction Safety**

Institution of Plant Engineers
a professional sector of the **Society of Operations Engineers**

Institution of Railway Operators (IRO) 2000

NR PO Box 128, BURGESS HILL, W Sussex, RH15 0UZ.   (hq)
01444 248931   fax 01444 246392
email admin@railwayoperators.org
http://www.railwayoperators.org
Chief Exec: Fiona Tordoff
○ *P; to advance & promote the safe, reliable & efficient operation of the railways, by improving the technical & general skills, knowledge & competence of those engaged in the operation of the railways
● ET - Exam

Institution of Railway Signal Engineers (IRSE) 1912

■ 1 Birdcage Walk (4th floor), Westminster, LONDON, SW1H 9JJ.   (hq)
020 7808 1180
http://www.irse.org
Chief Exec: Colin H Porter
▲ Registered Charity
Br worldwide
○ *L, *P; railway signalling & telecommunications
● Conf - Mtgs - ET - Exam - Exhib - SG - Inf - Lib - VE
M 2,500 i, UK / 1,000 i, o'seas
¶ NL - 6.   Proceedings - 1.   Books.

Institution of Structural Engineers (IStructE) 1908

NR 11 Upper Belgrave St, LONDON, SW1X 8BH.   (hq)
020 7235 4535   fax 020 7235 4294
email mail@istructe.org.uk   http://www.istructe.org.uk
Chief Exec & Sec: Dr Keith J Eaton
▲ Incorporated by Royal Charter; Registered Charity
○ *L, *P
● Conf - Mtgs - ET - Exam - Comp - SG - Inf - Lib
M 16,300 i, UK / 6,600 i, o'seas
¶ The Structural Engineer (Jnl) - 23.
Publications list available.

Instock Footwear Suppliers' Association (IFSA) 1947

NR Marlow House, Churchill Way, Fleckney, LEICESTER, LE8 8UD.   (hq)
0116-240 3232   fax 0116-240 2762
▲ Un-incorporated Society
○ *T; those distributing footwear (from manufacturers to retailers)
● Mtgs - LG
M 10 f
¶ NL; ftm only.

Insulated Render & Cladding Association Ltd (INCA) 1981
- ■ 6-8 Bonhill St, LONDON, EC2A 4BX. (hq)
  0844 249 0040 fax 0844 249 0042
  email info@inca-ltd.org.uk http://www.inca-ltd.org.uk
- ▲ Company Limited by Guarantee
- ○ *T; for the external wall insulation industry
- Gp System designers
- ● Mtgs - Inf - LG - Seminars
- M 51 f
- ¶ NL; m only. LM. Technical literature.

Insulating Concrete Formwork Association 1992
- NR PO Box 72, BILLINGSHURST, W Sussex, RH14 0FD. (hq)
  01403 701167
  http://www.icfinfo.org.uk
- ○ *T; to promote the use of ICF in the UK & provide a focal point for technical documentation, industry news & documentation
- < Brit Plastics Fedn
- M 12 f
- ¶ NL. List of publications available.

Insurance Financial & Legal Services Association
a group of the **British Marine Federation**

Insurance Institute of Ireland (III)
- IRL 39 Molesworth St, DUBLIN 2, Republic of Ireland. (hq)
  353 (1) 645 6600
  email info@iii.ie http://www.iii.ie
  Chief Exec: Denis Hevey
- Br 5
- ○ *P; professional & educational body for the insurance industry in Ireland

Intellect 2002
- NR Russell Square House, 10-12 Russell Square, LONDON, WC1B 5EE. (hq)
  020 7331 2000 fax 020 7331 2040
  email info@intellectuk.org http://www.intellectuk.org
  Dir Gen: John Higgins
- ▲ Un-incorporated Society
- ○ *N, *T; interests of the technology sector which comprises the information & communications technologies (ICT), electronics manufacturing & design, & consumer electronics (CE) sectors; and includes defence & space related IT
- Gp Intellect runs 93 groups & committees
- ● Conf - Mtgs - Exhib - Stat - Expt - Inf - LG
- < EECA; EICTA; FRMB; EDIG; CEN; CENELEC; ETSI; NIAG; NATO
- M 800 f
- ¶ Publications list available.

Intellectual Property Lawyers' Association (IPLA) 1982
- NR Simmons & Simmons, CityPoint, 1 Ropemaker St, LONDON, EC2Y 9SS. (hsb)
  020 7628 2020
  http://www.ipla.org.uk
  Sec: Rowan Freeland
- ○ *P; for solicitors' firms in England & Wales with an established practice in intellectual property
- M 66 f

Intelligent Membrane Trade Association (IMA)
- NR PO Box 74, Stretford, MANCHESTER, M32 0XN. (hq)
  0161-865 8913 fax 0161-866 9859
  email ima.uk@icopal.com http://www.imaroofer.com
- ○ *T; for roof waterproofing contractors
- M 200 f

Intensive Care Society (ICS) 1970
- ■ Churchill House, 35 Red Lion Square, LONDON, WC1R 4SG. (hq)
  020 7280 4350 fax 020 7280 4369
  email admin@ics.ac.uk http://www.ics.ac.uk
  Head of Secretariat: Pauline Kemp
- ▲ Company Limited by Guarantee; Registered Charity
- ○ *P; to promote & develop the medical speciality of intensive care
- Gp Conferences; Education & training; Scientific or other systematic research
- ● Conf - ET - Res - Exhib
- < Eur Soc of Intensive Care (ESICCM); Ir Intensive Care Soc; ICNARC
- M 2,450 i, UK / 100 i, o'seas
  (Sub: varies)
- ¶ JICS (Jnl) - 4; ftm. AR; free.

Interactive Media in Retail Group (IMRG) 1990
- NR 90 Long Acre, Covent Garden, LONDON, WC2E 9RZ. (hq)
  020 7716 5604
  email market@imrg.org http://www.imrg.org
  Chief Exec: James Roper
- ○ *T; to maximise the commercial potential of online shopping through the promotion of best practice
- M 264 f

Interflora
an online florist (is no longer a trade association)

Interim Management Association (IMA) 2000
- NR 15 Welbeck St, LONDON W1G 9XT. (hq)
  http://www.interimmanagement.uk.com
  Chmn: Jason Atkinson
- ▲ Company Limited by Guarantee
- ○ *P; to represent established interim management recruiters
- ● Mtgs
- < Recruitment & Employment Confedn
- M 26 f

Interlay, the Association of Block Paving Contractors
an affiliated association of the **British Precast Concrete Federation**

Intermediary Mortgage Lenders Association (IMLA) 1988
- NR North West Wing (3rd floor), Bush House, Aldwych, LONDON, WC2B 4PJ. (hq)
  020 7438 8942 fax 0845 373 6778
  http://www.imla.org.uk
  Chmn: John Heron
- ▲ Company Limited by Guarantee
- ○ *T; to represent the views & interests of UK mortgage lenders involved in the generation of mortgage business via professional financial intermediaries
- ● Mtgs
- M 21 f
- ¶ LM - 1; free.

International Association of Animal Therapists (IAAT) 1991
- NR Tyringham Hall, Cuddington, AYLESBURY, Bucks, HP18 0AP. (hq)
  01844 290512 fax 01844 290474
  email therapyenquiry@aol.com http://www.iaat.org.uk
  Sec: Katie Lawrence
- ▲ Company Limited by Guarantee
- ○ *P, *V; animal physiotherapy
- ● Mtgs - ET - Exam - Expt
- M 40 i, UK / 20 i, o'seas

© CBD Research Ltd · Beckenham · BR3 5JS · Tel 020 8650 7745 · E-mail cbd@cbdresearch.com · www.cbdresearch.com

International Association of Marine Institutions (IAMI) 1993
NR c/o South Tyneside College, St George's Avenue,
    SOUTH SHIELDS, Tyne & Wear, NE34 6ET.   (hsb)
    email mmeng@stc.ac.uk
    Sec: Gary Hindmarsh
○ *N; to provide a channel of communication between the
   colleges & national bodies involved in the training &
   certification process for persons involved in the Merchant
   Navy, towing & fishing industries
● Mtgs - ET - Exam
M i, colleges

International Bond & Share Society (IBSS) 1978
■ 167 Barnett Wood Lane, ASHTEAD, Surrey, KT21 2LP.   (hsp)
   01372 276787
   email secretary@scripophily.org
   http://www.scripophily.org
   Hon Sec: Philip Atkinson
○ *G; the study, buying & selling, exchanging & promoting the
   knowledge of scripophily (collectable bond, stock & share
   certificates)
M i

**International Chamber of Commerce - UK National Committee
(ICC United Kingdom) 1920**
NR 12 Grosvenor Place, LONDON, SW1X 7HH.   (hq)
    020 7838 9363
    http://www.iccuk.net
    Dir: Andrew Hope
○ *T; to represent interests of world business to governments &
   intergovernmental organisations
Gp Air transport; Arbitration; Banking technique & practice;
    Competition law; Computing telecommunications &
    information policy; Environment; Financial services;
    Insurance; Intellectual property; International commercial
    practice; Marketing; Multinationals & investment; Sea
    Transport; Taxation; Trade policy; Trade regulations
● Conf - Mtgs - LG
M f
¶ Business Bulletin (NL) - 6:   AR; both free.
   Publications list available.

International Child Health Group
    a group of the **Royal College of Paediatrics & Child Health**

International Clay Technology Association
    a committee of the Ceramics Society, a group of the **Institute of
    Materials, Minerals & Mining**

**International Consulting Economists' Association   (ICEA)
1986**
■ 45 Sorrel Bank, Linton Glade, CROYDON, Surrey, CR0 9LW.
   (hsb)
   020 8651 1380
   email secretariat@icea.co.uk   http://www.icea.co.uk
   Secretariat: Mrs Türhan Donegan
▲ Un-incorporated Society
○ *P; international economic consultancy; economic issues;
   development aid
Gp Agricultural & rural development; Aid & evaluation;
    Construction; Education; Energy; Environment & water; EU
    integration; Finance; Health; Industry; Infrastructure;
    Irrigation; Manufacture; Migration; Private sector; Tourism;
    Trade; Transport; Urban; Other
● Mtgs
M 126 i, UK / 18 i, o'seas
¶ NL - 2;   LM - 1; both ftm only.

**International Fragrance Association - United Kingdom   (IFRA
UK) 1941**
■ PO Box 173, CRANLEIGH, Surrey, GU6 8WU.   (uk hq)
   01483 275411   fax 01483 275411
   email secretariat@ifrauk.org   http://www.ifraorg.org
   Exec Sec: Julie Young
▲ Un-incorporated Society
○ *T; for makers of fragrances for cosmetics, toiletries & perfumes
Gp Technical Committee
● Mtgs - Distribution of code of practice
< Intl Fragrance Assn (IFRA); Eur Flavours & Fragrances
   Assn (EFFA); Alliance of Ind Assns (AIA)
M 31 f
¶ NL.
X British Fragrance Association

International General Produce Association Ltd
    2009 incorporated into the **Grain & Feed Trade Association**

**International Glassfibre Reinforced Concrete Association
(GRCA) 1975**
NR Riverside House, 4 Meadows Business Park, Station Approach,
    Blackwater, CAMBERLEY, Surrey, GU17 9AB.   (hq)
    01276 607140   fax 01276 607141
    http://www.grca.co.uk
▲ Company Limited by Guarantee
○ *T; the development of GRC industry for the benefit of
   suppliers, manufacturers, users & specifiers; GRC is a
   composite of alkali resistant glass fibres & concrete/sand
   matrix (thin high strength concrete)
M 13 f, UK / 38 f, o'seas
   GRCA became part of the Concrete Society in 2005 whilst
   maintaining its own identity

International Guild of Knot Tyers 1982
■ 144 Millhouse Lane, WIRRAL, Cheshire, CH46 6DT.   (hsp)
   email secretary@igkt.net   http://www.igkt.net
   Hon Sec: Barry Mault
▲ Registered Charity
Br 16; 7
○ *G; all aspects of knot-tying & associated ropework
M 573 i, 5 f, 5 org, UK / 629 i, 1 f, o'seas
¶ Knotting Matters (NL) - 4.
   Membership Hbk - 18 months; m only.

**International Language [Ido] Society of Great Britain
(ILSGB) 1910**
■ 24 Nunn St, LEEK, Staffs, ST13 8EA.   (hsp)
   http://www.idolinguo.org.uk
   Hon Sec: David Weston
▲ Un-incorporated Society
○ *X; to promote the use of Ido as an international language
● Mtgs - Inf
< Uniono por la Linguo Internaciona Ido
M 20 i, UK / 16 i, o'seas

International Law Association (ILA) 1873
NR Charles Clore House, 17 Russell Square, LONDON,
    WC1B 5JD.   (hq)
    020 7323 2978   fax 020 7323 3580
    http://www.ila-hq.org
    Sec Gen: David Wyld
○ *L; study, elucidation & advancement of international law, both
   public & private
M c 4,000 i

International Marine Contractors Association (IMCA) 1972
- ■ 52 Grosvenor Gardens, LONDON, SW1W 0AU. (hq)
  020 7824 5520   fax 020 7824 5521
  email imca@imca-int.com   http://www.imca-int.com
  Chief Exec: Hugh Williams
- ▲ Un-incorporated Society
- Br Africa, Americas, Asia, Europe, Middle East, Pacific
- ○ *T; for offshore, marine & underwater engineering companies
- Gp Diving; Marine; Offshore survey; Remote systems & ROV
- ● Conf - Mtgs - ET - Exam - LG
- M 896 f
- ¶ IMCA NL - 4; free.

International Masonry Society (IMS) 1986
- ■ Shermanbury, Church Rd, WHYTELEAFE, Surrey, CR3 0AR.
  (hsp)
  020 8660 3633   fax 020 8668 6983
  http://www.masonry.org.uk
  Hon Sec: Dr K Fisher
- ▲ Registered Charity
- ○ *L; the science & technology of masonry materials, their
  interaction & the finished structure; covers all forms of
  masonry, mortar & ancillary components
- ● Conf - Mtgs - ET
- M 200 i, 23 f, UK / 100 i, 1 f, o'seas
- ¶ Masonry International (Jnl) - 3; £53 m, £64 nm.
  Proceedings - irreg.   AR; free.
- ✕ 2008 (1 January) British Masonry Society

International Mining & Materials Association
  a group of the **Institute of Materials, Minerals & Mining**

International Otter Survival Fund (IOSF) 1993
- ■ 7 Black Park, BROADFORD, Isle of Skye, IV49 9DE. (hq)
  01471 822487   fax 01471 822487
  email iosf@otter.org   http://www.otter.org
  Co-ordinator: Janet Wildgoose
- ▲ Company Limited by Guarantee; Registered Charity
- Br Belarus, Sri Lanka
- ○ *K, *V; to conserve all 13 species of otter by helping to support
  scientists & other workers in practical conservation,
  education, research & rescue & rehabilitation
- ● Conf - ET - Res - Inf - Lib - PL
- M 5,500 i, 25 f, 6 org, UK / 420 i, o'seas

**International Register of Consultant Herbalists & Homoeopaths
(IRCH) 1960**
- ■ 12 Woodside Avenue, CINDERFORD, Glos, GL14 2DW. (hsp)
  01594 368443   fax 01594 655886
  email office@irch.org   http://www.irch.org
  Hon Sec: Marilyn Scott
- ▲ Company Limited by Guarantee
- ○ *M, *P; to promote the interest of herbal & homoeopathic
  medicine; to be a teaching school providing secondary
  education
- ● Conf - Mtgs - ET - Exam - Res
- < Intl Assn of Distance Learning
- M 46 i, UK / 6 i, o'seas
  (Sub: £260)
- ¶ Journal of Natural Medicine - 4.
  Note: trades as the General Council & Register of Consultant
  Herbalists Ltd

International Society of Feline Medicine
  a group of the **British Small Animal Veterinary Association**

International Society of Typographic Designers (ISTD) 1928
- ■ PO Box 7002, LONDON, W1A 2TY. (hq)
  email mail@istd.org.uk   http://www.istd.org.uk
  Dep Chmn: Becky Chilcott & David Coates
- ▲ Company Limited by Guarantee
- Br Ireland, Lebanon, South Africa
- ○ *P; to establish & maintain standards in typography within the
  professional design & education communities
- ● Conf - Mtgs - ET - Exam - Exhib - SG - Inf - VE - Student
  assessment programme for direct entry
- < Intl Congress of Graphic Design Assns
- M 580 i, UK / 75 i, o'seas
- ¶ TypoGraphic - 2; ftm, £12 nm.

International Steel Trade Association (ISTA)
- ■ Broadway House, Tothill St, LONDON, SW1H 9NQ. (hq)
  020 7799 2662   fax 020 7799 2468
  email hbailey@steeltrade.co.uk
  http://www.steeltrade.co.uk
  Dir: Hugh W Bailey
- ○ *T; to look after the interests of international steel traders
- ● Mtgs - ET - VE - LG
- M 99 f
- ¶ AR.

**International Stress Management Association UK (ISMA UK)
1984**
- ■ PO Box 491, Bradley Stoke, BRISTOL, BS34 9AH. (hq)
  0845 680 7083
  email stress@isma.org.uk   http://www.isma.org.uk
  Chmn: Ann McCracken
- ▲ Company Limited by Guarantee; Registered Charity
- Br Australia, Brazil, Eire, Hong Kong, India, Netherlands, Russia,
  USA
- ○ *P; to promote sound knowledge & best practice in the
  prevention & reduction of human stress
- Gp Trainers & consultants working with organisations to carry out:
  Primary - Risk assessment
  Secondary - Workshop & training in stress awareness
    & reduction
  Tertiary - Work with people experiencing stress
- ● Conf - Mtgs - LG
- M 550 i
  (Sub: £95)
- ¶ Stress News - 4; ftm, £35 yr nm.

**International Underwriting Association of London (IUA)
1991**
- NR London Underwriting Centre, 3 Minster Court, Mincing Lane,
  LONDON, EC3R 7DD. (hq)
  020 7617 4444   fax 020 7617 4440
  email info@iua.co.uk   http://www.iua.co.uk
  Chief Exec: Dave Matcham
- ▲ Company Limited by Guarantee
- ○ *P; to promote & advance the business environment for
  international insurance & reinsurance companies operating
  in or through London
- M 65 f

Internet Advertising Bureau (IAB) 1997
- NR 14 Macklin St, LONDON, WC2B 5NF. (hq)
  020 7050 6969   fax 020 7242 9928
  http://www.iabuk.net
- ○ *T; to promote growth & best practice for advertisers, agencies
  & media owners in online & mobile advertising
- < Eur Digital Advertising Alliance
- M 600 f

© CBD Research Ltd · Beckenham · BR3 5JS · Tel 020 8650 7745 · E-mail cbd@cbdresearch.com · www.cbdresearch.com

Internet Service Providers' Association   (ISPA UK)   1995
- ■ 111 Buckingham Palace Rd, LONDON, SW1W 0SR.   (hq)
  0870 050 0710   fax 0871 594 0298
  email secretariat@ispa.org.uk   http://www.ispa.org.uk
  Sec: Nicholas Lansman
- ▲ Company Limited by Guarantee
- ○ *T; to promote the development of the internet industry
- ● Conf - Mtgs - Res - LG
- < EuroISPA; IWF
- M 159 f
- ¶ Electronic NL - 12; (hardcopy) - 2; both free.

Interpave, the Precast Concrete Paving & Kerb Association
    a product association of the **British Precast Concrete Federation**

Intumescent Fire Seals Association   (IFSA)   1982
- NR 20 Park St, PRINCES RISBOROUGH, Bucks, HP27 9AH.   (hq)
  01844 276928
  http://www.ifsa.org.uk
  Sec: Mrs Christine Barfield
- ▲ Un-incorporated Society
- ○ *T; promotion of benefits both technical & commercial arising
  from the use of intumescent fire & smoke seals
- Gp Representation on BSS, ISO & CEN standards c'ees
- ● Conf - Mtgs - ET - Res - Expt - Inf
- M c 11 f
- ¶ Technical Information Sheets 1-5 - updated.
  IFSA Code.

Inverness Chamber of Commerce   1893
- ■ PO Box 5512, INVERNESS, IV2 3ZE.   (hq)
  01463 718131   fax 01463 231523
  email info@inverness-chamber.co.uk
  http://www.inverness-chamber.co.uk
  Chief Exec: Stewart Nicol
- ▲ Company Limited by Guarantee
- ○ *C
- ● Mtgs - Exhib - LG
- < Scot Chams Comm
- M 319 f
- ¶ inbusiness - 4.   LM; ftm only.

Invertebrate Conservation Trust
    see **Buglife - the Invertebrate Conservation Trust**

Investment Management Association   (IMA)   1959
- NR 65 Kingsway, LONDON, WC2B 6TD.   (hq)
  020 7831 0898
  http://www.investmentuk.org
  Chief Exec: Richard Saunders
- ○ *T; to improve the regulatory, fiscal & legal environment for unit
  trusts & investment funds; to increase public awareness of
  collective investments
- ● Conf - Mtgs - ET - Exam - Res - Stat - Inf - LG
- M f

Investment Property Forum   (IPF)   1988
- ■ New Broad Street House, 35 New Broad St, LONDON,
  EC2M 1NH.   (hq)
  020 7194 7920   fax 020 7194 7921
  email ipfoffice@ipf.org.uk   http://www.ipf.org.uk
  Chmn: Phil Clark
- ▲ Company Limited by Guarantee
- ○ *P; to enhance the knowledge, understanding & efficiency of
  property as an invesnment
- ● Conf - Mtgs - ET - Exam - Res - Stat - Inf - VE - LG - Social
  lunches & dinners
- M 1,900 i (by invitation only)
- ¶ Investment Property Focus - 3; ftm, on special request nm.
  Annual Review, Report & Accounts - 1; free.

Investor Relations Society   (IR Society)   1980
- ■ Bedford House, 3 Bedford St, LONDON, WC2E 9HD.   (hq)
  020 7379 1763   fax 020 7240 1320
  email enquiries@irs.org.uk   http://www.irs.org.uk
  Communications Mgr: Richard Knight
- ▲ Company Limited by Guarantee
- ○ *N; to promote excellence in investor relations
- ● Conf - Mtgs - ET - Exam - Res - Exhib - Comp - SG - Stat - Inf -
  Lib - VE - LG
- M 560 i, c 370 f, UK / 60 i, o'seas
  (Sub: £350 or £500)
- ¶ Informed (Jnl) - 4; ftm, £5 nm.
  IR Essentials Guidebooks - irreg; ftm, £15 nm.

Involvement & Participation Association   (IPA)   1884
- NR 42 Colebrooke Row, LONDON, N1 8AF.   (hq)
  020 7354 8040
  http://www.ipa-involve.com
- ▲ Company Limited by Guarantee; Registered Charity
- ○ *E, *Q; improvement of business performance through
  involving employees in the operation of the organisation
- M i & f

IP Federation
    since 2009 the operating name of the **Trade Marks, Patents &
    Designs Federation**

IPPA - the Early Childhood Organisation
    in 2011 merged with the National Children's Nurseries Association to
    form **Early Childhood Ireland**

Iran Society   1936
- ■ 2 Belgrave Sq, LONDON, SW1X 8PJ.   (hq)
  020 7235 5122   fax 020 7259 6771
  email info@iransociety.org   http://www.iransociety.org
  Hon Sec: Marjon Esfandiary
- ▲ Registered Charity
- ○ *X; to promote learning & advance education in the heritage &
  culture of Iran
- ● Mtgs - Lectures
- M 396 i, 10 f
- ¶ Jnl - 1, free.

Irish Airline Pilots' Association   (IALPA)   1946
- IRL Corballis Park, DUBLIN AIRPORT, Co Dublin, Republic of
  Ireland.   (hq)
  353 (1) 844 5272   fax 353 (1) 844 6051
  email admin@ialpa.net   http://www.ialpa.net
  Admin: Ms Danni Hickey
- ○ *P, *U; to facilitate communication & dissemination of
  information among professional pilots; to monitor & act on
  technical matters which could affect pilots in the safe
  execution of their professional duties
- Gp Safety & technical committee
- < Intl Fedn of Air Line Pilot Assns (IFALPA); Eur Cockpit
  Assn (ECA); Ir Municipal, Public & Civil Tr U (IMPACT)
- M 1,200 i

Irish Amateur Boxing Association   (IABA)
- IRL National Boxing Stadium, South Circular Rd, DUBLIN 8,
  Republic of Ireland.   (hq)
  353 (1) 453 3371   fax 353 (1) 454 0777
  http://www.iaba.ie
  Hon Sec: Séan Crowley
- ○ *S

Irish Anti-Vivisection Society (IAVS) 1970
IRL PO Box 13, GREYSTONES, Co Wicklow, Republic of Ireland.
     (hq)
     353 (1) 282 0154
     email info@irishantivivisection.org
     http://www.irishantivivisection.org
     Sec: Heather Finnegan
○ *K, *V; to secure the total abolition of all experiments causing
    suffering or distress to animals

Irish Association of Art Historians (IAAH)
IRL c/o Audrey Nicholls, School of Art History & Cultural Policy -
     UCD, Newman Building, Bellfield, DUBLIN 4, Republic of
     Ireland. (sb)
     353 (1) 716 8162
     email iaahinfo@gmail.com
     Sec: Audrey Nicholls
○ *A
× 1995 Association of Irish Art Historians

Irish Association of Corporate Treasurers (IACT) 1986
IRL PO Box 10104, LUCAN, Co Dublin, Republic of Ireland. (hq)
     353 (1) 610 8574   fax 353 (1) 621 3494
     email info@treasurers.ie   http://www.treasurers.ie
     Mem Sec: Michele Fogarty
▲ Registered Charity
○ *P; to promote the treasury profession of Ireland & establish
    standards of best practice & ethics
● Conf - ET - LG - Mtgs
M 400 i
¶ Jnl; ftm.

**Irish Association for Counselling & Psychotherapy (IACP)
1981**
IRL 21 Dublin Rd, BRAY, Co Wicklow, Republic of Ireland. (hq)
     353 (1) 272 3427   fax 353 (1) 286 9933
     email iacp@iacp.ie   http://www.irish-counselling.ie
     Nat Dir: Naoise Kelly
○ *P; to identify, develop & maintain professional standards of
    excellence in counselling & psychotherapy through
    education, training & accreditation
M 3,500 i & org

Irish Association for Cultural, Economic & Social Relations 1938
NR 33 Ballyhamage, Doagh, BALLYCLARE, Co Antrim, BT39 0PZ.
     (hq)
     email info@irish-association.org
     http://www.irish-association.org
     Pres: Rev Brian Kennaway
○ *K, *X; to foster understanding between Irish people of different
    traditions

Irish Association of Distributive Trades Ltd (IADT)
IRL Rock House, Main St, BLACKROCK, Co Dublin, Republic of
     Ireland. (hq)
     353 (1) 288 7584   fax 353 (1) 283 2206
     Dir Gen: Tara Buckley
○ *T; represents food wholesalers in Ireland

Irish Association for Economic Geology (IAEG) 1973
IRL c/o Rathdowney Resources Ltd, Unit 3 Bay Road Industrial
     Estate, MOUNTMELLICK, Co LAOIS, Republic of Ireland.
     (memsec/b)
     353 (57) 869 7887
     http://www.iaeg.org
     Mem Sec: Jeremy James
○ *L; mineral exploration, mining geology & petroleum geology
M 200 i

Irish Association for Industrial Relations (IAIR) 1972
IRL c/o Dept of Employment Relations, University of Limerick,
     LIMERICK, Republic of Ireland. (hsb)
     353 (61) 202215   fax 353 (61) 338171
     email joe.wallace@ul.ie
     Hon Sec: Joseph Wallace
○ *L; to promote the study & understanding of industrial relations

Irish Association of International Express Carriers (IAIEC)
IRL c/o 28 South Frederick St, DUBLIN 2, Republic of Ireland.
     353 (1) 676 5633   fax 353 (1) 676 5641
     email michael.darcy@darcysmyth.ie
○ *T

Irish Association of Investment Managers 1986
IRL 35 Fitzwilliam Place, DUBLIN 2, Republic of Ireland. (hq)
     353 (1) 676 1919   fax 353 (1) 676 1954
     email info@iaim.ie   http://www.iaim.ie
     Chief Exec: Frank O'Dwyer
○ *P; representative body for institutional investment managers in
    Ireland
M 14 f

Irish Association of Paper Merchants
    see **National Association of Paper Merchants**

Irish Association of Pension Funds (IAPF) 1973
IRL Slane House (suite 2), 25 Lower Mount St, DUBLIN 2, Republic
     of Ireland. (hq)
     353 (1) 661 2427   fax 353 (1) 662 1196
     email info@iapf.ie   http://www.iapf.ie
     Admin: Anne Kelly
▲ Company Limited by Guarantee
○ *P; for those involved in operating, investing & advising on all
    aspects of pensions & other retirement provision
M 350 f

Irish Association of Pigmeat Processors
    a group of **Food & Drink Industry Ireland**

Irish Association of Social Workers (IASW) 1971
IRL 114-116 Pearse St, DUBLIN 2, Republic of Ireland. (hq)
     353 (1) 677 4838
     email office@iasw.net   http://www.iasw.ie
     Hon Sec: Saragh McGarrigle
○ *P; to improve the standards & quality of social work; to provide
    support for social workers in the practice of their profession

Irish Astronomical Society 1937
IRL PO Box 2547, DUBLIN 14, Republic of Ireland.
     email irishastrosoc@gmail.com
     http://www.irishastrosoc.org
○ *L; to promote interest in astronomy & allied subjects
● Mtgs

Irish Auctioneers & Valuers Institute
    2011 merged with the Society of Chartered Surveyors to form the
    Society of Chartered Surveyors Ireland

Irish Banking Federation (IBF)
IRL Nassau House, Nassau St, DUBLIN 2, Republic of Ireland.
     (hq)
     353 (1) 671 5311   fax 353 (1) 679 6680
     email ibf@ibf.ie   http://www.ibf.ie
     Chief Exec: Pat Farrell
○ *P; to foster the development of a stable, dynamic & innovative
    banking & financial services industry which contributes to the
    economic & social wellbeing of the country
Gp ACS Ireland; Federation of International Banks in Ireland; Irish
    Mortgage Council
M 59 f
× Irish Bankers' Federation

© CBD Research Ltd · Beckenham · BR3 5JS · Tel 020 8650 7745 · E-mail cbd@cbdresearch.com · www.cbdresearch.com

Irish BioIndustry Association (IBIA) 1998
IRL   Confederation House, 84-86 Lower Baggot St, DUBLIN 2,
        Republic of Ireland.   (hq)
        353 (1) 605 1584   fax 353 (1) 638 1584
        email michael.gillen@ibec.ie   http://www.ibec.ie/ibia
        Dir: Michael Gillen
○   *P; to enhance the environment in Ireland for the development
        of a successful multinational & indigenous biotechnology
        sector
<   Ir Business & Emplrs Confedn (IBEC)
M   50 f

Irish Book Publishers' Association
        since 2008 **Publishing Ireland**

Irish Bowling Association (IBA) 1904
■   2 Oronsay Crescent, LARNE, Co Antrim, BT40 2HD.   (hsp)
        028 2827 0008
        http://www.irishbowlingassociation.com
        Hon Sec: Tom McGarel
▲   Un-incorporated Society
○   *S; regulating & organising men's outdoor flat green bowls in
        Ireland
Gp   Irish Bowls Coaches Association; Irish Bowls Umpires
        Association
●   Mtgs - Comp - Inf
<   Wld Bowls; Eur Bowls U; Brit Isles Bowls Coun; NI C'wealth
        Games Coun; NI Sports Forum; NI Sports Trust
>   Bowling League of Ireland; NI Bowling Assn; NI Private Greens
        League; NI Provincial Bowling Assn; World Bowls
M   5,200 i, 125 clubs
¶   Ybk.

Irish Bowls Coaches Association
        a group of the **Irish Bowling Association**

Irish Bowls Umpires Association
        a group of the **Irish Bowling Association**

Irish Bread Bakers Association
        a group of the **Food & Drink Industry Ireland**

Irish Breakfast Cereals Association
        a group of the **Food & Drink Industry Ireland**

Irish Brewers Association
        sector association of **Alcohol Beverage Federation of Ireland**

Irish Bridge Union
IRL   11 Talbot Downs, Castleknock, DUBLIN 15, Republic of
        Ireland.   (hsp)
        353 (1) 856 3344
        email twroche1@eircom.net   http://www.cbai.ie/ibu/
        28 Laganvale Manor, Lockview Rd, Stranmills, BELFAST,
        BT9 5BE.
            07718 392819
        Jt Secs: Tomás Roche (Dublin), Harold Curran (Belfast)
○   *G
Gp   Contract Bridge Association of Ireland; Northern Irish Bridge
        Union

Irish Brokers Association (IBA) 1931
IRL   87 Merrion Sq, DUBLIN 2, Republic of Ireland.
        353 (1) 661 3067   fax 353 (1) 661 9955
        email iba@iol.ie   http://www.irishbrokers.com
○   *P

Irish Business & Employers Confederation (IBEC) 1993
IRL   Confederation House, 84-86 Lower Baggot St, DUBLIN 2,
        Republic of Ireland.   (hq)
        353 (1) 605 1500   fax 353 (1) 638 1500
        http://www.ibec.ie
        Dir Gen: Danny McCoy
○   *N, *T; to promote the interests of business & employers in
        Ireland by working to foster the continuing development of a
        competitive environment that encourages sustainable growth
        within which both enterprise & people can flourish
Gp   Alcohol Beverage Federation of Ireland; Building Materials
        Federation; Cement Manufacturers Ireland; Concrete
        Manufacturers Association of Ireland; Federation of
        Aerospace Enterprises in Ireland; Financial Services Ireland;
        Food & Drink Industry Ireland; ICT Ireland; Irish Contract
        Cleaners Association; Irish Decorative Surface Coatings
        Association; Irish Engineering Enterprises Federation; Irish
        Forestry & Forest Products Association; Irish Marine
        Federation; Irish Medical Device Association; Irish Mining &
        Exploration Group; Irish Plastic Pipe Manufacturers
        Association Irish ProShare Association; Irish Waste
        Management Association; Nutrition & Health Foundation;
        PharmaChemical Ireland; Plastics Ireland; Retail Ireland;
        Small Firms Association

Irish Cancer Society 1963
IRL   43/45 Northumberland Rd, DUBLIN 4, Republic of Ireland.
        (hq)
        353 (1) 231 0500   fax 353 (1) 231 0555
        email info@irishcancer.ie   http://www.cancer.ie
        Chief Exec: John McCormack
▲   Registered Charity
○   *W; to ensure fewer people get cancer & those that do have
        better outcomes

Irish Cattle Breeding Federation (ICBF) 1997
NR   Highfield House, SHINAGH, Co Cork, Republic of Ireland.
        (hq)
        353 (23) 882 0222   fax 353 (23) 882 0229
        email query@icbf.com   http://www.icbf.com
▲   Company Limited by Guarantee; Registered Charity
○   *P; to achieve the greatest possible genetic improvement in the
        national cattle herd for the benefit of Irish farmers, the dairy
        & beef industries & members
Gp   Artificial insemination; Herd book; Milk recording
<   Intl C'ee of Animal Recording (ICAR); Eur Forum of Farm
        Animal Breeders (EFFAB)
M   16 f, 21 org

Irish Cattle & Sheep Farmers' Association (ICSA)
IRL   3 Gandon Court, The Fairgreen, PORTLAOISE, Co Laois,
        Republic of Ireland.   (hq)
        353 (57) 866 2120   fax 353 (57) 866 2121
        email info@icsaireland.com
        http://www.icsaireland.com
        Gen Sec: Eddie Punch
○   *F; a farming lobby group, specifically for cattle & sheep
        farmers
M   10,000 i
¶   Drystock Farmer (Jnl) - 1.

Irish Cellular Industry Association (ICIA)
IRL   Confederation House, 84-86 Lower Baggot St, DUBLIN 2,
        Republic of Ireland.   (hq)
        353 (1) 605 1500   fax 353 (1) 638 1500
        email icia@ibec.ie   http://www.icia.ie
        Chmn: Catriona Costello
○   *T; an alliance of mobile operators
<   Ir Business & Emplrs Confedn (IBEC)
M   4 f

Irish Chamber of Shipping
IRL Port Centre, Alexandra Rd, DUBLIN 1, Republic of Ireland.
　　　(hq)
　　　353 (1) 855 9011　　fax 353 (1) 855 9022
　　　Dir: B W Kerr
○　　*N

Irish Chemical Marketers Association
　　　since c 2009 see **Chemical Distributors Ireland**

Irish Chiropodists/Podiatrists Organisation
　　　see **Society of Chiropodists & Podiatrists of Ireland**

Irish Cider Association
　　　sector association of **Alcohol Beverage Federation of Ireland**

Irish Clothing & Textiles Association
　　　a former sector of the **Irish Business & Employers
　　　Confederation**

Irish Co-operative Organisation Society Ltd　(ICOS)
IRL 84 Merrion Sq, DUBLIN 2, Republic of Ireland.　(hq)
　　　353 (1) 676 4783　　fax 353 (1) 662 4502
　　　http://www.icos.ie
　　　Sec: Seamus O'Donohoe
○　　*N; for the co-operative movement in Ireland

Irish Coffee Council
　　　a group of the **Food & Drink Industry Ireland**

Irish Cold Storage Federation　(ICSF)
IRL Confederation House, 84-86 Lower Baggot St, DUBLIN 2,
　　　Republic of Ireland.　(hq)
　　　353 (1) 605 1617　　fax 353 (1) 638 1617
　　　email michael.barry@ibec.ie　　http://www.ibec.ie/icsf/
　　　Contact: Michael Barry
○　　*T; to represent the interests of public cold stores in Ireland
<　　Eur Cold Storage & Logistics Assn (ECSLA); Food & Drink Ind
　　　Ireland (FDII)
M　　7 f

Irish College of General Practitioners　(ICGP)　1984
IRL 4/5 Lincoln Place, DUBLIN 2, Republic of Ireland.　(hq)
　　　353 (1) 676 3705　　fax 353 (1) 676 5850
　　　email info@icgp.ie　　http://www.icgp.ie
　　　Chief Exec: Kieran Ryan
○　　*P; to serve the patient & the general practitioner by
　　　encouraging & maintaining the highest standards og general
　　　medical practice
M　　2,515 i

Irish Computer Society　(ICS)　1972
IRL Crescent Hall, Mount Street Crescent, DUBLIN 2, Republic of
　　　Ireland.　(hq)
　　　353 (1) 644 7820　　fax 353 (1) 662 0224
　　　email info@ics.ie　　http://www.ics.ie
　　　Hon Sec: Peter Lawless
▲　　Company Limited by Guarantee
○　　*P; to advance, promote & represent the interests of ICT
　　　professionals in Ireland; to advance & promote computer
　　　literacy throughout Ireland; to advance & promote Ireland's
　　　economic, educational & cultural participation in the
　　　worldwide information society
<　　Intl Fedn of Inf Processing (IFIP); Coun of Eur Profl Informatics
　　　Socs (CEPIS)

Irish Concrete Federation　(ICF)
IRL 8 Newlands Business Park, Newlands Cross, Clondalkin,
　　　DUBLIN 22, Republic of Ireland.　(hq)
　　　353 (1) 464 0082　　fax 353 (1) 464 0087
　　　email info@irishconcrete.ie　　http://www.irishconcrete.ie
　　　Chief Exec: Gerry Farrell
○　　*T; to represent the Irish aggregates & concrete products
　　　industry
<　　Eur Aggregates Assn (UEPG); Eur Ready Mixed Concrete
　　　Org (ERMCO)
M　　100 f

Irish Concrete Society　1973
IRL Platin, DROGHEDA, Co Louth, Republic of Ireland.　(hq)
　　　353 (41) 987 6466　　fax 353 (41) 987 6400
　　　email secretary@concrete.ie　　http://www.concrete.ie
　　　Hon Sec: Richard Bradley
○　　*P; to promote excellence in the use of concrete in Ireland

Irish Congress of Trade Unions　(ICTU)　1959
IRL 31/32 Parnell Sq, DUBLIN 1, Republic of Ireland.　(hq)
　　　353 (1) 889 7777　　fax 353 (1) 887 2012
　　　email congress@ictu.ie　　http://www.ictu.ie
　　　4-6 Donegall St Place, BELFAST, BT1 2FN.
　　　028 9024 7940　　fax 028 9024 6898
　　　Gen Sec: David Begg
Br　　Northern Ireland Committee
○　　*N, *U; to achieve economic development, social cohesion &
　　　justice by upholding the values of solidarity, fairness &
　　　equality
M　　55 org
　　　Note: see ICTU website for full details of affiliated unions

Irish Contract Cleaning Association　(ICCA)　2000
IRL Confederation House, 84-86 Lower Baggot St, DUBLIN 2,
　　　Republic of Ireland.　(hq)
　　　353 (1) 605 1500　　fax 353 (1) 638 1500
　　　http://www.ibec.ie
　　　Exec Sec: Avine McNally
○　　*T; to represent mamber companies involved in the provision of
　　　cleaning services on a commercial basis in Ireland
<　　Ir Business & Emplrs Confedn (IBEC)

Irish Corrugated Packaging Association　(ICPA)
IRL Confederation House, 84-86 Lower Baggot St, DUBLIN 2,
　　　Republic of Ireland.　(hq)
　　　353 (1) 605 1574　　fax 353 (1) 638 1574
　　　email marian.byron@ibec.ie
　　　Dir: Marian Byron
○　　*T
<　　Eur Fedn of Corrugated Bd Mfrs (FEFCO)

**Irish Cosmetics, Detergent & Allied Products Association
(ICDA)　2000**
IRL Confederation House, 84-86 Lower Baggot St, DUBLIN 2,
　　　Republic of Ireland.　(hq)
　　　353 (1) 605 1624　　fax 353 (1) 638 1624
　　　email siobhan.murphy@ibec.ie　　http://www.icda.ie
　　　Dir: Siobhan Murphy
○　　*T; to represent the interests of companies in Ireland engaged
　　　in the manufacture, distribution or sales of cosmetics,
　　　toiletries, detergents & allied household products
<　　Intl Assn for Soaps, Detergents & Maintenance Products (AISE);
　　　Eur Cosmetics Assn (COLIPA); Ir Business & Emplrs
　　　Confedn (IBEC)
M　　17 f

Irish Council against Blood Sports   1966
IRL   PO Box 88, MULLINGAR, Co Westmeath, Republic of
        Ireland.   (hq)
        353 (44) 934 9848
        email icabs@eircom.net
        http://www.banbloodsports.com
        PRO: Aideen Yourell
○   *K

Irish Council for Civil Liberties   (ICCL)   1976
IRL   9-13 Blackhall Place, DUBLIN 7, Republic of Ireland   (hq)
        353 (1) 799 4504   fax 353 (1) 799 4512
        email info@iccl.ie   http://www.iccl.ie
        Dir: Mark Kelly
○   *K: to monitor, educate & campaign in order to secure full
        enjoyment of human rights for everyone
¶   Rights News (NL) - 4.

Irish Countrywomen's Association   (ICA)   1910
IRL   58 Merrion Rd, DUBLIN 4, Republic of Ireland.   (hq)
        353 (01) 668 0002
        email office@ica.ie   http://www.ica.ie
        Hon Sec: Elizabeth Wall
○   *G

Irish Creamery Milk Suppliers Association   (ICMSA)
IRL   John Feely House, Dublin Rd, LIMERICK, Republic of Ireland.
        (hq)
        353 (61) 314677   fax 353 (61) 315737
        email icmsa@eircom.net   http://www.icmsa.ie
        Gen Sec: Ciaran Dolan
○   *F; for family farms

Irish Dairy Industries Association
        a group of **Food & Drink Industry Ireland**

Irish Deaf Society   (IDS)   1981
IRL   30 Blessington St, DUBLIN 7, Republic of Ireland.   (hq)
        353 (1) 860 1878   fax 353 (1) 860 1960
        email info@irishdeafsociety.ie
        http://www.irishdeafsociety.ie
        Chief Exec: Kevin Stanley
○   *W

Irish Decorative Surface Coatings Association   (IDSCA)
IRL   Confederation House, 84-86 Lower Baggot St, DUBLIN 2,
        Republic of Ireland.   (hq)
        353 (1) 605 1652   fax 353 (1) 638 1652
        email mark.mcauley@ibec.ie   http://www.ibec.ie/idsca/
        Dir: Mark McAuley
○   *T; manufacturers of paint & coatings products
<   CEPE (Eur Coatings assn); Ir Business & Emplrs Confedn (IBEC)
M   6 f

Irish Deer Society   1975
NR   Hillview, Ballinamona, FERRYBANK, Co Waterford, Republic of
        Ireland.   (hsp)
        353 (74) 57313
        http://www.irishdeersociety.ie
        Nat Sec: Vincent Coffrey
Br   5
○   *V; the conservation of deer & their habitat in Ireland; the
        advancement of the study & the dissemination of the
        knowledge of deer, their distribution & ecology

Irish Dental Association   (IDA)   1922
IRL   Unit 2 Leopardstown Office Park, Sandyford, DUBLIN 18,
        Republic of Ireland.   (hq)
        353 (1) 295 0072   fax 113 (1) 295 0092
        email info@irishdentalassoc.ie   http://www.dentist.ie
        Sec Gen: Fintan Hourihan
○   *P
M   1,340 i

Irish Direct Marketing Association   (IDMA)
IRL   8 Upper Fitzwilliam St, DUBLIN 2, Republic of Ireland.   (hq)
        353 (1) 661 0470   fax 353 (1) 830 8914
        email info@idma.ie   http://www.idma.ie
        Sec: Mick Cummins
○   *T
M   88 f

Irish Draught Horse Society (GB) Ltd   (IDHS(GB))   1980
■   The Forge, Avenue B, 10th St, STONELEIGH PARK, Warks,
        CV8 2LG.   (hq)
        0845 230 0399
        email administrator@idhsgb.com   http://www.idhsgb.com
        Admin: Carol Malin
▲   Company Limited by Guarantee; Registered Charity
○   *B
●   Conf - Mtgs - ET - Comp - Inf
<   Brit Horse Soc; The Showing Coun
M   850 i
        (Sub: £35)
¶   NL - 4; free.   Ybk - 1; ftm, £7 nm.

Irish Educational Publishers Association
IRL   c/o Gill & Macmillan Ltd, Hume Avenue, Park West,
        DUBLIN 12, Republic of Ireland.   (hsp)
        353 (1) 500 9509   fax 353 (1) 500 9598
        email hmahony@gillmacmillan.ie
        Sec: Hubert Mahony
○   *T

Irish Engineering Enterprises Federation   (IEEF)
IRL   Confederation House, 84-86 Lower Baggot St, DUBLIN 2,
        Republic of Irelsnd.   (hq)
        353 (1) 605 1500   fax 353 (1) 638 1500
        email marian.byron@ibec.ie   http://www.ibec.ie/ieef/
        Dir: Marian Byron
○   *T; to promote & support the competitiveness & prosperity of
        the engineering sector in Ireland
<   Ir Business & Emplrs Confedn (IBEC)

Irish Epilepsy Association
        see **Brainwave**

Irish Exporters Association   (IEA)
IRL   28 Merrion Sq, DUBLIN 2, Republic of Ireland.   (hq)
        353 (1) 661 2182   fax 353 (1) 661 2315
        email iea@irishexporters.ie   http://www.irishexporters.ie
        Chief Exec: John F Whelan
○   *T

Irish Family History Society   (IFHS)   1984
IRL   PO Box 36, NAAS, Co Kildare, Republic of Ireland.   (hq)
        email ifhs@eirnet.com   http://www.ifhs.ie
        Hon Chmn: Gerry Cahill
○   *G; to promote the study of Irish family history & genealogy
<   Fedn of Family History Socs (FFHS)

Irish Family Planning Association   (IFPA)   1969
IRL   Solomons House, 42a Pearse St, DUBLIN 2, Republic of
        Ireland.
        353 (1) 607 4456   fax 353 (1) 607 4486
        email post@ifpa.ie   http://www.ifpa.ie
        Chief Exec: Niall Behan
○   *W

Irish Farmers' Association   (IFA)   1971
IRL   Irish Farm Centre, Bluebell, DUBLIN 12, Republic of Ireland.
        353 (1) 450 0266   fax 353 (1) 455 1043
        email postmaster@ifa.ie   http://www.ifa.ie
        Gen Sec: Pat Smith
Br   947
○   *F; to promote, foster & develop agriculture in all its branches
        including horticulture, mariculture & farm tourism
Gp   Aquaculture; Cattle; Dairying; Forestry; Grain.
        Animal health; Bioenergy; Climate change & renewables;
        Economics; Environment
M   87,000 f

Irish Fashion Industry Federation   (IFIF)
IRL   14 Highfield Rd, Rathgar, DUBLIN 6, Republic of Ireland.   (hq)
        353 (1) 488 1122   fax 353 (1) 412 6041
        email info@ifif-fashion.ie
        Chmn: Terry Rowan
○   *T

Irish Federation of Sea Anglers   (IFSA)   1953
IRL   Sports HQ, 13 Joyce Way, Park West Business Park, DUBLIN 12,
        Republic of Ireland.   (hsb)
        353 (1) 280 6873
        email ccifsa@yahoo.ie   http://www.ifsa.ie
        Hon Sec: Hugh O'Rorke
○   *G, *S

Irish Federation of University Teachers   (IFUT)   1965
IRL   11 Merrion Sq, DUBLIN 2, Republic of Ireland.   (hq)
        353 (1) 661 0910   fax 353 (1) 661 0909
        email admin@ifut.ie   http://www.ifut.ie
        Gen Sec: Mike Jennings
○   *P, *U

Irish Film Institute
IRL   6 Eustace St, Temple Bar, DUBLIN 2, Republic of Ireland.   (hq)
        353 (1) 679 5744   fax 353 (1) 677 8755
        email info@irishfilm.ie   http://www.irishfilm.ie
        Dir: Mark Mulqueen
○   *A
×   2003 Film Institute of Ireland

Irish Finance Houses Association Ltd
IRL   ICB House, Newstead, Clonskeagh Rd, DUBLIN 14, Republic of
        Ireland.   (hq)
        353 (1) 260 1670
        http://www.ifha.ie
        Sec Gen: Séamus Ó Tighearnaigh
○   *T

Irish Fish Processors & Exporters Association
IRL   25 Kincora Avenue, Clontarf, DUBLIN 3, Republic of Ireland.
        (hsp)
        353 (1) 833 7882
        Sec: T F Geoghegan
○   *T

Irish Fish Producers' Organisation   (IFPO)   1975
IRL   77 Sir John Rogerson's Quay, DUBLIN 2, Republic of Ireland.
        (hq)
        353 (1) 640 1850   fax 353 (1) 640 1851
        email ifpo@eircom.net   http://www.ifpo.ie
        Chief Exec: Lorcan Ó Cinneide
○   *T; to represent the owners of commercial sea-fishing vessels of
        all sizes

Irish Fishermen's Organisation Ltd   1974
IRL   c/o Irish South & West Fish Producers Organisation Ltd,
        The Pier, CASTLETOWNBERE, Co Cork, Republic of Ireland.
        353 (27) 70670
        email irishfish@eircom.net
        The IFO acts as the umbrella organisation for the 4 Irish fish
        producers associations; the chairmanship rotates between the
        4 CEOs

Irish Foot Harriers Association
        a constituent body of the **Hunting Association of Ireland**

Irish Football Association Ltd   (IFA)   1880
■   20 Windsor Ave, BELFAST, BT9 6EG.   (hq)
        028 9066 9458
        email info@irishfa.com   http://www.irishfa.com
        Chief Exec: Howard J C Wells
▲   Company Limited by Guarantee
○   *S; governing body for Association football in Northern Ireland
●   Mtgs - ET - Exam - LG
<   Fédn Intle Football Assns (FIFA); U of Eur Football Assns (UEFA)
M   [not stated]
¶   IFA Magazine - 2; £2.50.

Irish Forestry & Forest Products Association   (IFFPA)
IRL   Confederation House, 84-86 Lower Baggot St, DUBLIN 2,
        Republic of Ireland.   (hq)
        353 (1) 605 1624
        email marian.byron@ibec.be   http://www.iffpa.ie
        Dir: Marian Byron
○   *T; to achieve a vibrant, sustainable & competitive forestry &
        forest products industry for Ireland while developing a full
        awareness of the benefits & potential benefits of the industry
        sector to a wide variety of stakeholders
<   Ir Business & Emplrs Confedn (IBEC)
M   19 f

Irish Franchise Association   (IFA)
IRL   Kandoy House, 2 Fairview Strand, DUBLIN 3, Republic of
        Ireland.   (hq)
        353 (1) 813 4555   fax 353 (1) 813 4575
        email info@irishfranchiseassociation.com
        http://www.irishfranchiseassociation.com
        Chmn: David Killeen
○   *T; to develop & promote best practice franchising in Ireland &
        create an environment within which franchise businesses can
        grow

Irish Genealogical Research Society   (IGRS)   1936
NR   18 Stratford Avenue, RAINHAM, Kent, ME8 0EP.   (hq)
        http://www.igrsoc.org
        Hon Sec: Rosemary Melian E Coleby
▲   Registered Charity
Br   1; Ireland
○   *L; to promote & encourage the study of Irish genealogy & to
        collect books & manuscripts of genealogical value
●   Mtgs - Res - Lib
M   350 i, 20 org, UK / 550 i, 20 org, o'seas
¶   The Irish Genealogist - 1; £16.   NL - 2; ftm only.

Irish Geological Association   (IGA)   1959
IRL   91 Newborough, GOREY, Co Wexford, Republic of Ireland.
        (treas/p)
        email info@geology.ie   http://www.geology.ie
        Treas: Peter Lewis
○   *L; for all who are interested in geology in Ireland & beyond

---

© CBD Research Ltd · Beckenham · BR3 5JS · Tel 020 8650 7745 · E-mail cbd@cbdresearch.com · www.cbdresearch.com

Irish Georgian Society (IGS) 1958
IRL 74 Merrion Sq, DUBLIN 2, Republic of Ireland.   (hq)
        353 (1) 676 7053   fax 353 (1) 662 0290
        email info@igs.ie   http://www.igs.ie
        Exec Dir: Donough Cahill
Br   1; USA
○   *K, *L; to encourage an interest in & the preservation of
        distinguished examples of architecture & the allied arts in
        Ireland & to assist in the implementation of such objects

Irish Girl Guides
IRL Trefoil House, 27 Pembroke Park, DUBLIN 4, Republic of
        Ireland.   (hq)
        353 (1) 668 3898   fax 353 (1) 660 2779
        email info@irishgirlguides.ie
        http://www.irishgirlguides.ie
        Chief Exec: Linda Peters
○   *Y

Irish Grain & Feed Association (IGFA)
IRL 19 Carrick Hill, PORTLAOISE, Co Laois, Republic of Ireland.
        (hq)
        353 (502) 67022   fax 353 (502) 68690
        email info@eorna.ie   http://www.eorna.ie
        Dir: Deirdre Webb
○   *T; manufacturers of compound animal feed & grain importers
        & traders
<   Eur Feed Mfrs' Fedn (FEFAC)

Irish Grassland Association (IGA) 1946
IRL Cookstown, KELLS, Co Meath, Republic of Ireland.   (hq)
        353 (87) 962 6483
        email secretary@irishgrassland.com
        http://www.irishgrassland.com
        Office Mgr: Maura Callery
○   *P; to advance & spread the knowledge of modern grassland
        husbandry in all its aspects
●   Conf - Mtgs - Res - VE
<   Eur Grassland Fedn
¶   Jnl - 1;   NL - 4; both ftm.

Irish Hardware & Building Materials Association (IHBMA)
IRL Elmville, Upper Kilmacud Rd, Dundrum, DUBLIN 14, Republic
        of Ireland.   (hq)
        353 (1) 298 0969   fax 353 (1) 298 6103
        email info@ihbma.ie   http://www.ihbma.ie
        Chief Exec: Jim Copeland
○   *T; to represent the sector which includes building materials,
        hardware, DIY, home/housewares, garden & lifestyle
●   Conf - ET - Exhib - Inf - LG - Mtgs - Res - VE
<   Intl Fedn of Hardware & Housewares Assns (IHA); Eur Assn of
        Nat Builders Mchts Assns (UFEMAT)
M   600 f
¶   NL - 1; by email.

Irish Hereford Breed Society
IRL Harbour St, MULLINGAR, Co Westmeath, Republic of
        Ireland.   (hq)
        353 (44) 934 8855   fax 353 (44) 934 8949
        email irishhereford@gmail.com
        http://www.irishhereford.com
        Sec: Larry Feeney
○   *B; to promote & develop the Hereford beed of cattle in the
        Republic of Ireland
<   Ir Cattle Breeding Fedn (ICBF)

Irish Hockey Association (IHA) 1893
IRL Newstead, University College Dublin, Belfield, DUBLIN 4,
        Republic of Ireland.   (hq)
        353 (1) 716 3261   fax 353 (1) 716 3260
        email info@hockey.ie   http://www.hockey.ie
        Sec: Joan Morgan
Br   5
○   *S; the governing body for hockey in Northern Ireland & the
        Republic of Ireland

Irish Homing Union (IHU) 1895
NR   38 Ballynahatty Rd, Shaws Bridge, BELFAST, BT8 8LE.
        (gensec/p)
        028 9064 4231
        email kenmcconaghie38@btinternet.com
        http://www.irishhomingunion.com
        Gen Sec: Ken McConaghie
○   *N, *S; to regulate the sport of pigeon racing in Ireland
M   3,318 i in 121 clubs

Irish Hospital Consultants Association (IHCA)
IRL Heritage House, Dundrum Office Park, DUBLIN 14, Republic of
        Ireland.   (hq)
        353 (1) 298 9123   fax 353 (1) 298 9395
        email info@ihca.ie   http://www.ihca.ie
        Sec Gen: Martin Varley
○   *P; to promote, encourage & support the advancement of the
        practice of medicine, in all specialities & areas, & the
        improvement of the health services in Ireland; to promote &
        protect the interests of medical & dental hospital consultants
        in Ireland
M   1,800 i

Irish Hospitality Institute (IHI) 1966
IRL 8 Herbert Lane, DUBLIN 2, Republic of Ireland.   (hq)
        353 (1) 662 4790   fax 353 (1) 662 4789
        email info@ihi.ie   http://www.ihi.ie
        Chief Exec: Natasha Kinsella
○   *P; to drive professional excellence in hospitality management
        in Ireland

Irish Hotels Federation (IHF)
IRL 13 Northbrook Rd, DUBLIN 6, Republic of Ireland.
        353 (1) 497 6459   fax 353 (1) 497 4613
        email info@ihf.ie   http://www.ihf.ie
        Chief Exec: Tim Fenn
○   *T

Irish Hydro Power Association
IRL Joseph Stewart & Co, Corn Mills, BOYLE, Co Roscommon,
        Republic of Ireland.   (hsb)
        353 (71) 967 0100
        email info@irishhydro.com   http://www.irishhydro.com
        Hon Sec: Neil Stewart
○   *T; for producers of hydroelectric power; to press for its greater
        use
<   Eur Small Hydropower Assn (ESHA)
M   16 f

Irish Ice Hockey Association (IIHA) 2000
IRL Sport HQ, 13 Joyce Way, Parkwest Business Park, DUBLIN 12,
        Republic of Ireland.   (hq)
        353 (1) 625 1157   fax 353 (1) 625 1157
        email info@iiha.org   http://www.iiha.org
        Gen Sec: Dean Kelly
○   *S; the official national governing body of ice hockey & inline
        hockey in Ireland

Irish Institute of Credit Management   (IICM)   1980
IRL   17 Kildare St, DUBLIN 2, Republic of Ireland.   (hq)
          353 (1) 609 9444   fax 353 (1) 609 9445
          http://www.iicm.ie
          Chief Exec: Sean MacMahon
○   *P; to raise the status of the profession of credit management to
     a level where membership of the Institute & appropriate
     qualifications are recognised by the business community in
     Ireland as essential prerequisites for positions in credit
     management
<   Fedn of Eur Credit Mgt Assns (FECMA)

Irish Institute of Master Mariners   1968
IRL   1 Fort Villas, COBH, Co Cork, Republic of Ireland.
          email poreganportofcork.ie
          Sec: Capt Paul O'Regan
○   *P

Irish Institute of Pensions Management   (IIPM)   1989
IRL   National College of Ireland, Mayor St IFSC, DUBLIN 1, Republic
          of Ireland.   (hq)
          353 (1) 499 8591   fax 353 (1) 497 2200
          email iipm@ncirl.ie   http://www.iipm.ie
          Sec: Maurice McCann
○   *P; to promote professional standards among those working in
     the field of pensions

Irish Institute of Purchasing & Materials Management   (IIPMM)
IRL   17 Lower Mount St, DUBLIN 2, Republic of Ireland.   (hq)
          353 (1) 644 9660   fax 353 (1) 644 9661
          email iipmm@iipmm.ie   http://www.iipmm.ie
          Chief Exec: Des Crowther
○   *P; the pursuit of excellence in purchasing & materials
     management

Irish Institute of Training & Development   (IITD)   1969
IRL   4 Sycamore House, Millennium Business Park, NAAS,
          Co Kildare, Republic of Ireland.   (hq)
          353 (45) 881166   fax 353 (45) 881192
          email info@iitd.com   http://www.iitd.ie
          Pres: John Gorman
○   *P; to ensure best practice in training & development in Ireland
¶   T&D (Jnl) - 4.

Irish Institution of Surveyors   (IIS)
IRL   36 Dame St, DUBLIN 2, Republic of Ireland.
          353 (1) 677 4797
          email iissecretary@eircom.net
          http://www.irish-surveyors.ie
          Sec: Vera DeStac
▲   Company Limited by Guarantee
○   *P
M   c 320

Irish Insurance Federation   (IIF)   1986
IRL   Insurance House, 39 Molesworth St, DUBLIN 2, Republic of
          Ireland.   (hq)
          353 (1) 676 1820   fax 353 (1) 676 1943
          email fed@iif.ie   http://www.iif.ie
          Chief Exec: Michael Kemp
○   *T; the representative body for insurance companies in Ireland
<   Comité Européen des Assurances (CEA)
M   62 f

Irish International Freight Association   (IIFA)   1962
IRL   Strand House, Strand St, MALAHIDE, Co Dublin, Republic of
          Ireland.   (hq)
          353 (1) 845 5411   fax 353 (1) 845 5534
          email iifa@eircom.net   http://www.iifa.ie
          Chief Exec: Colm Walsh
○   *P; to ensure that the flow of physical trade between Ireland &
     the rest of the world is as efficient & cost-effective as possible
<   Intl Fedn of Freight Forwarders' Assns (FIATA)
M   100 f

Irish Internet Association   (IIA)   1997
IRL   The Digital Hub, 157 Thomas St, DUBLIN 8, Republic of
          Ireland.   (hq)
          353 (1) 542 4154
          email info@iia.ie   http://www.iia.ie
          Chief Exec: Joan Mulvihill
○   *P; for those conducting business via the internet from Ireland
M   300 f

Irish Kidney Association   (IKA)   1978
IRL   Donor House, Block 43A Park West, DUBLIN 12, Republic of
          Ireland.   (hq)
          353 (1) 620 5306   fax 353 (1) 620 5366
          email info@ika.ie   http://www.ika.ie
          Chief Exec: Mark Murphy
▲   Company Limited by Guarantee; Registered Charity
Br   24
○   *W; to support patients & their families who are affected by end
     stage kidney disease

Irish Ladies' Golf Union   (ILGU)   1893
IRL   103-105 Q House, 76 Furze Rd, Sandyford Industrial Estate,
          DUBLIN 8, Republic of Ireland.   (hq)
          353 (1) 293 4833   fax 353 (1) 293 4832
          email info@ilgu.ie   http://www.ilgu.ie
          Chief Exec: Sinead Heraty
Br   5
○   *S; the governing body for amateur women's golf in Ireland

Irish Landscape Institute   (ILI)   1993
IRL   PO Box 11068, DUBLIN 2, Republic of Ireland.   (hq)
          353 (1) 662 7409
          email ili@irishlandscapeinstitute.com
          http://www.irishlandscapeinstitute.com
          Sec: Tony Williams
○   *P; to set standards of excellence in the fields of landscape
     planning, landscape architecture & landscape management
<   Intl Fedn of Landscape Architects (IFLA); Eur Foundation for
     Landscape Architecture (EFLA)
M   160 i

Irish League of Credit Unions   (ILCU)   1960
IRL   33-41 Lower Mount St, DUBLIN 2, Republic of Ireland.
          353 (1) 614 6700   fax 353 (1) 614 6701
          email info@creditunion.ie   http://www.creditunion.ie
          Chief Exec: Kieron Brennan
○   *N; to promote the credit union idea & ethos
M   508 f

Irish Legal History Society   (ILHS)   1988
■   School of Law, Queens University Belfast, BELFAST, BT7 1NN.
          (hsb)
          028 9097 3250
          email n.howlin@qub.ac.uk   http://www.ilhs.eu
          Hon Sec: Dr Niamh Howlin
▲   Un-incorporated Society
Br   Republic of Ireland
○   *L; to study of the administration of law & of the development
     of law in Ireland, both pre- & post-partition
●   Conf - Mtgs -ET - Exhib - SG - Inf - Lib
<   informal links with Selden & Stair Societies
M   100 i, UK / 180 i, o'seas
¶   Books & Occasional Papers.

Irish Linen Guild   1928
§   [communication by e-mail only]
          email info@irishlinen.co.uk   http://www.irishlinen.co.uk
     to promote Irish linen

Irish Management Institute   (IMI)   1952
IRL   Sandyford Rd, DUBLIN 16, Republic of Ireland.   (hq)
　　353 (1) 207 8400   fax 353 (1) 295 5147
　　email info@imi.ie   http://www.imi.ie
　　Chief Exec: Dr Tom McCarthy
○   *P

Irish Marine Federation   (IMF)
IRL   Confederation House, 84-86 Lower Baggot St, DUBLIN 2,
　　Republic of Ireland.   (hq)
　　353 (1) 605 1652   fax 353 (1) 638 1652
　　email mark.mcauley@ibec.ie
　　http://www.irishmarinefederation.com
　　Dir: Mark McAuley
○   *T; to promote the interests of all sectors, commercial & leisure,
　　of the marine industry in Ireland & encourage its growth &
　　development
<   Ir Business & Emplrs Confed (IBEC)
M   61 f

Irish Maritime Law Association   (IMLA)   1963
IRL   Matheson Ormsby Prentice, 70 Sir John Robertson's Quay,
　　DUBLIN 2, Republic of Ireland.   (pres/b)
　　353 (1) 232 3333
　　email helen.noble@mop.ie
　　http://www.irishmaritimelaw.com
　　Pres: Helen Noble,   Hon Sec: Edmund Sweetman
○   *L; to promote a better understanding of Irish maritime law &
　　encourage its unification on an international level
<   Comité Maritime Intl (CMI)

Irish Master Printers' Association
　　in 2008 merged with the Provincial Newspaper Association of Ireland
　　to form the **Regional Newspapers & Printers Association of
　　Ireland**

Irish Masters of Beagles Association
　　a constituent body of the **Hunting Association of Ireland**

Irish Masters of Foxhounds Association
　　a constituent body of the **Hunting Association of Ireland**

Irish Masters of Harriers Association
　　a constituent body of the **Hunting Association of Ireland**

Irish Masters of Mink Hounds Association
　　a constituent body of the **Hunting Association of Ireland**

Irish Medical Devices Association   (IMDA)   1995
IRL   Confederation House, 84-86 Lower Baggot St, DUBLIN 2,
　　Republic of Ireland.   (hq)
　　353 (1) 605 1564   fax 353 (1) 638 1564
　　email sharon.higgins@ibec.ie   http://www.imda.ie
　　Dir: Sharon Higgins
○   *T; to promote & support an environment that encourages the
　　sustainable development & profitable growth of multinational
　　& indigenous medical device & diagnostic companies
<   Ir Business & Emplrs Confedn (IBEC)
M   140 f

Irish Medical Organisation   (IMO)   1936
IRL   10 Fitzwilliam Place, DUBLIN 2, Republic of Ireland.   (hq)
　　353 (1) 676 7273   fax 353 (1) 661 2758
　　email imo@imo.ie   http://www.imo.ie
　　Chief Exec: George McNeice
○   *P, *U; to represent doctors in Ireland & to provide them with all
　　relevant services; to develop a caring, efficient & effective
　　health service
<   Wld Med Assn (WMA)

Irish Mining & Exploration Group   (IMEG)   1993
IRL   Confederation House, 84-86 Lower Baggot St, DUBLIN 2,
　　Republic of Ireland.   (hq)
　　353 (1) 605 1526   fax 353 (1) 638 1526
　　http://www.imeg.ie
　　Contact: Robert O'Shea
○   *T; the representative body for the mining & exploration
　　industry in Ireland
Gp   Environment; Health & safety
<   Ir Business & Emplrs Confedn (IBEC)

Irish Mining & Quarrying Society   (IMQS)   1958
IRL   Room G16A, UCD School of Geological Sciences, Belfield,
　　DUBLIN 4, Republic of Ireland.   (hq)
　　353 (1) 716 2185   fax 353 (1) 283 7733
　　email info@imqs.ie   http://www.imqs.ie
　　Hon Sec: Siobhan Tinnelly
○   *P; to promote, safeguard & represent the best interests of the
　　natural resources & extractive industries in Ireland

Irish Moiled Cattle Society   1926
NR   Shamrock Vale, 42 Belfast Rd, Glenavy, CRUMLIN, Co Antrim,
　　BT29 4HR.   (hsp)
　　07842 185008
　　http://www.irishmoiledcattlesociety.com
　　Sec: Gillian Steele
○   *B

Irish Mortgage Council   (IMC)   2003
IRL   Nassau House, Nassau Street, DUBLIN 2, Republic of
　　Ireland.   (hq)
　　353 (1) 671 5311   fax 353 (1) 679 6680
　　email info@ibf.ie   http://www.ibf.ie
　　Chief Exec: Pat Farrell
○   *P; to promote high standards of mortgage lending
<   Ir Banking Fedn (IBF)
M   12 f

Irish Mountain Training Board
　　a group of the **Mountaineering Council of Ireland**

Irish Municipal, Public & Civil Trade Union   (IMPACT)   1991
IRL   Nerney's Court, DUBLIN 1, Republic of Ireland.   (hq)
　　353 (1) 817 1500   fax 353 (1) 817 1501
　　http://www.impact.ie
　　Gen Sec: Shay Cody
○   *U
M   63,000 i

Irish Museums Association   (IMA)   1977
IRL   St Stephen's Green House (3rd floor), Earlsfort Terrace, DUBLIN
　　2, Republic of Ireland.   (hq)
　　353 (1) 412 0939
　　email office@irishmuseums.org
　　http://www.irishmuseums.org
　　Sec: Ken Langan
▲   Company Limited by Guarantee
○   *G, *P; to promote professional practice in museum
　　management, collections & visitor services; to provide a
　　platform for anyone interested in Irish museums to provoke
　　debate on museum ideas
●   Confs - ET - Mtgs
¶   Museum Ireland (Jnl) - 1;   NL - 2; both ftm.

**Irish National Federation against Copyright Theft   (INFACT)
1982**
IRL   PO Box 5344, DUBLIN 7, Republic of Ireland.   (hq)
　　353 (1) 882 8565   fax 353 (1) 882 8594
　　http://www.infact.ie
　　Dir Gen: Brian Finnegan
○   *T

Irish National Teachers Organisation   (INTO)   1868
IRL   35 Parnell Sq, DUBLIN 1, Republic of Ireland.   (hq)
    353 (1) 804 7700   fax 353 (1) 872 2462
    email info@into.ie   http://www.into.ie
    23 College Gardens, BELFAST, BT9 6BS.
    028 9038 1455   fax 028 9066 2803
    Gen Sec: Sheila Nunan
Br   Northern Ireland
○   *U; represents teachers at primary level in the Republic of
    Ireland & at primary & post-primary level in Northern Ireland

Irish Naturist Association   (INA)   1965
IRL   PO Box 1077, Churchtown, DUBLIN 14, Republic of Ireland.
    (hq)
    353 (86) 837 0395   fax 353 (86) 5837 0395
    http://www.irishnaturism.org
    Pres: Pat Gallagher
○   *G; to promote naturism in Ireland
<   Intl Naturist Fedn (INF)
¶   Irish Naturist - 4; ftm.

Irish Nurses & Midwives Organisation   (INMO)
IRL   Whitworth Building, North Brunswick St, DUBLIN 7, Republic of
    Ireland.   (hq)
    353 (1) 664 0600   fax 353 (1) 664 0466
    email inmo@inmo.ie   http://www.inmo.ie
    Gen Sec: Liam Doran
Br   42
○   *P; for nurses & midwives working in all areas of the Irish
    healthcare system
<   Intl Coun of Nurses (ICN); Intl Confedn of Midwives (ICM); Eur
    Fedn of Nurses (EFN)
M   c 30,000
×   2010 Irish Nurses' Organisation

Irish Nursing Homes Organisation
    in January 2008 merged with the Federation of Irish Nursing Homes
    to form **Nursing Homes Ireland**

Irish Offshore Operators Association   (IOOA)   1995
IRL   Tramway House, Dartry Rd, Rathgar, DUBLIN 6, Republic of
    Ireland.   (hq)
    353 (1) 497 5716
    email info@iooa.ie   http://www.iooa.ie
    Sec: Brendan Sheehan
○   *T; to represent the Irish offshore oil & gas industry
¶   8 f

Irish Organic Farmers & Growers Association   (IOFGA)   1982
IRL   Innish Carraig (Unit 16A), Golden Island, ATHLONE,
    Co Westmeath, Republic of Ireland.   (hq)
    353 (90) 643 3680   fax 353 (90) 644 9005
    email info@iofga.org   http://www.iofga.org
    Gen Mgr: Gillian Westbrook
▲   Company Limited by Guarantee
○   *F; to certify organic produce & products throughout Ireland
M   1,100 i
¶   Organic Matters (Jnl)

Irish Peatland Conservation Council   (IPCC)   1985
IRL   Bog of Allen Nature Centre, Lullymore, RATHANGAN,
    Co Kildare, Republic of Ireland.   (hq)
    353 (45) 860133   fax 353 (45) 860481
    email bogs@ipcc.ie   http://www.ipcc.ie
    Chief Exec: Dr Catherine O'Connell
▲   Registered Charity
○   *K; to conserve a representative sample of living intact Irish
    bogs & peatlands for the benefit of the people of Ireland & to
    safeguard their diversity of wildlife
¶   Peatland News - 2; ftm.

Irish Pharmaceutical Healthcare Assn   (IPHA)
IRL   Franklin House, 140 Pembroke Rd, DUBLIN 4, Republic of
    Ireland.   (hq)
    353 (1) 660 3350   fax 353 (1) 668 6672
    email info@ipha.ie   http://www.ipha.ie
    Chief Exec: Anne Nolan
○   *T; to create a favourable economic, regulatory & political
    environment which will enable the research-based
    pharmaceutical industry in Ireland to meet the growing
    healthcare needs & expectations of patients
<   Intl Fedn of Pharmaceutical Mrfs & Assns (IFPMA); Eur Fedn of
    Pharmaceutical Inds & Assns (EFPIA); Assn of the Eur Self-
    Medication Ind (AESGP)
M   46 f

Irish Pharmaceutical Union   (IPU)   1973
IRL   Butterfield House, Butterfield Ave, Rathfarnham, DUBLIN 14,
    Republic of Ireland.   (hq)
    353 (1) 493 6401   fax 353 (1) 493 6407
    email info@ipu.ie   http://www.ipu.ie
    Pres: Darragh O'Loughlin
○   *P, *U; to promote the professional & economic interests of
    community pharmacists
¶   IPU Review - 12.

Irish Planning Institute   (IPI)   1975
IRL   The Courtyard (floor 3), 25 Great Strand St, DUBLIN 1,
    Republic of Ireland.   (hq)
    353 (1) 878 8630   fax 353 (1) 878 8682
    email contact@irishplanninginstitute.ie
    http://www.irishplanninginstitute.ie
    Hon Sec: Amy Hastings
▲   Company Limited by Guarantee
○   *P; to raise the standards of planning & to improve & promote
    the status of the planning profession
<   Eur Coun of Spatial Planners (ECTP-CEU)
M   800 i
¶   Pleanáil (Jnl);   e-zine (NL); both ftm.

Irish Plastic Pipe Manufacturers Association   (IPPMA)
IRL   Confederation House, 84-86 Lower Baggot St, DUBLIN 2,
    Republic of Ireland.   (hq)
    353 (1) 605 1500   fax 353 (1) 638 1500
    email mark.mcauley@ibec.ie
    Dir: Mark McAuley
○   *T; to promote the use of plastic pipe systems in construction
    works
<   Eur Plastic Pipes & Fittings Assn (TEPPFA); Ir Business & Emplrs
    Confedn (IBEC)
M   7 f

Irish Playwrights & Screenwriters Guild   (IPSG)   1969
IRL   Art House, Curved St, Temple Bar, DUBLIN 2, Republic of
    Ireland.   (hq)
    353 (1) 670 9970
    email info@script.ie   http://www.script.ie
    Chief Exec: David Kavanagh
▲   Company Limited by Guarantee
○   *P; the representative body for writers for the stage, screen,
    radio & digital media

Irish Printing Federation   (IPF)   1899
IRL   Confederation House, 84-86 Lower Baggot St, DUBLIN 2,
    Republic of Ireland.   (hq)
    353 (1) 605 1663
    email terry.cummins@ibec.ie
    Dir: Terry Cummins
○   *T
<   Ir Business & Emplrs Confedn (IBEC)

© CBD Research Ltd · Beckenham · BR3 5JS · Tel 020 8650 7745 · E-mail cbd@cbdresearch.com · www.cbdresearch.com

Irish Professional Conservators' & Restorers' Association (IPCRA) 1982
IRL PO Box 9185, DUBLIN 4, Republic of Ireland. (hq)
    email ipcrasecretary@gmail.com http://www.ipcra.org
    Sec: Nuala Maguire
▲ Un-incorporated Society
○ *P; to promote within Ireland the practice of conservation of
    historic & artistic material to internationally accepted
    standards; to improve public awareness & understanding of
    the need for conservation
M 150 i
¶ NL - 2

Irish Professional Photographers Association (IPPA) 1949
IRL Office 5 Unit 200, Greenogue Business Park, RATHCOOLE,
    Co Dublin, Republic of Ireland. (hq)
    353 (1) 401 6878
    email ippa@irishphotographers.com
    http://www.irishphotographers.com
    Hon Sec: Mary McCullough
○ *P; qualified, registered & insured professional photographers
< Wld Coun of Profl Photographers; Fedn of Eur Profl
    Photographers
M 350 i

Irish Property & Facility Management Association (IPFMA) 1989
IRL 38 Merrion Square, DUBLIN 2, Republic of Ireland. (hq)
    353 (1) 644 5520 fax 353 (1) 661 1797
    email info@ipfma.com http://www.ipfma.com
    Chief Exec: Fiona Barron
▲ Company Limited by Guarantee
○ *P; to promote the highest standards in the property & facility
    management profession
< Eur Coun of Real Estate Profls (CEPI); Eur Property Agents
    Gr (EPAG)

Irish ProShare Association (IPSA)
IRL Confederation House, 84-86 Lower Baggot St, DUBLIN 2,
    Republic of Ireland.
○ *P
< an associated sector of the Irish Business & Employers
    Confederation

Irish Radio Transmitters Society (IRTS) 1932
IRL PO Box 462, DUBLIN 9, Republic of Ireland. (hq)
    email info@irts.ie http://www.irts.ie
    Sec: Ger McNamara
○ *G; to promote the study of radio communications; to
    encourage radio experimentation
< Intl Amateur Radio U (IARU)

Irish Real Tennis Association (IRTA) 1999
IRL Turnberry, Carrigaline Rd, DOUGLAS, Co Cork, Republic of
    Ireland. (hsp)
    353 (87) 226 0032
    email info@irishrealtennis.ie http://www.irishrealtennis.ie
    Sec: Ted Neville
○ *S

Irish Recorded Music Association (IRMA)
IRL 1 Corrig Avenue, DUN LAOGHAIRE, Co Dublin, Republic of
    Ireland. (hq)
    353 (1) 280 6571 fax 353 (1) 280 6579
    email irma_info@irma.ie http://www.irma.ie
    Dir Gen: Dick Doyle
○ *T; record companies & associated trades
Gp IRMA manages the shareholding in the Irish chart company
    ChartTrack
● LG - Stat

Irish Red Cross Society (IRCS) 1939
IRL 16 Merrion Sq, DUBLIN 2, Republic of Ireland. (hq)
    353 (1) 642 4600 fax 353 (1) 661 4461
    email info@redcross.ie http://www.redcross.ie
    Sec Gen: Donal Forde
○ *W; to deliver aid to vulnerable people in Ireland & in countries
    around the world that have been struck by wars or natural
    disasters
< Intl Red Cross & Red Crescent Movement

Irish Road Haulage Association (IRHA) 1973
IRL Gowna Plaza (suite 6), Bracetown Business Park, CLONEE,
    Co Meath, Republic of Ireland. (hq)
    353 (1) 801 3380 fax 353 (1) 825 3080
    email info@irha.ie http://www.irha.ie
    Hon Sec: Gerry McMahon
Br 8
○ *T; to represent & promote the interests of the licensed transport
    industry in Ireland & abroad

Irish Roller Hockey Association
IRL Leisurepoint Sport & Fitness Centre, Cardiffsbridge Rd, Finglas,
    DUBLIN 11, Republic of Ireland. (hq)
    353 (86) 403 3103 fax 353 (1) 269 4836
    email info@rollerhockeyireland.com
    http://www.rollerhockeyireland.org
    Sec: Wayne McGovern
○ *S; inline puck hockey is a sport with players on inline roller
    skates, played in indoor rinks with a smooth plastic surface
< Intl Fedn of Roller Sports (FIRS); Confed of Eur Roller
    Skating (CERS)

Irish Rugby Football Union (IRFU) 1874
IRL 10/12 Lansdowne Rd, DUBLIN 4, Republic of Ireland. (hq)
    353 (1) 647 3800 fax 353 (1) 647 3801
    email info@irishrugby.ie http://www.irishrugby.ie
    Chief Exec: Philip Browne
Br 5
○ *S; to administer the game of rugby union as it governing
    body; to promote, foster & develop the game

Irish Sailing Association (ISA)
IRL 3 Park Rd, DÚN LAOGHAIRE, Co Dublin, Republic of
    Ireland. (hq)
    353 (1) 280 0239 fax 353 (1) 280 7558
    email info@sailing.ie http://www.sailing.ie
    Chief Exec: Harry Hermon
▲ Company Limited by Guarantee
○ *S; the national governing body for sailing & motorboating
< U Intle Motonautique (UIM)
¶ NL - 52.

Irish Security Industry Association (ISIA) 1972
IRL 42-44 Northumberland Rd, DUBLIN 4, Republic of Ireland.
    (hq)
    353 (1) 484 7206
    email info@isia.ie http://www.isia.ie
    Communications Dir: Sarah O'Donnell
▲ Company Limited by Guarantee
○ *T; to represent the full spectrum of the private security industry;
    to promote, develop & maintain the highest professional
    standards
M 70 f

Irish Seed Savers Association   1991

IRL   Capparoe, SCARRIFF, Co Clare, Republic of Ireland.   (hq)
      353 (61) 921866
      email info@irishseedsavers.ie
      http://www.irishseedsavers.ie
      Chmn: Tommy Hayes
▲   Registered Charity
○   *K; to grow, conserve & distribute Irish organic vegetable seeds,
      grains & fruit trees; to raise public awareness about the
      vulnerability of Irish agricultural biodiversity
¶   NL - 2; ftm.

Irish Seed Trade Association   (ISTA)   1924

IRL   Marina House, Clarence St, DÚN LAOGHAIRE, Co Dublin,
      Republic of Ireland.   (hq)
      353 (1) 663 8700   fax 353 (1) 663 8704
      email ista@irishseedtrade.ie
      http://www.irishseedtrade.ie
      Sec: Patrick O'Mara
○   *T; for multipliers, producers & distributors of certified cereal
      seed
M   16 f

Irish Ship Agents' Association   (ISAA)

IRL   Conway House, East Wall Rd, DUBLIN 2, Republic of Ireland.
      (pres/b)
      353 (1) 855 6221   fax 353 (1) 855 7234
      email info@irishshipagents.com
      http://www.irishshipagents.com
      Pres: Michael Collins
○   *T; for ship brokers & agents
<   Fedn of Nat Assns of Ship Brokers & Agents (FONASBA)

Irish Small & Medium Enterprises Association   (ISME)

IRL   17 Kildare St, DUBLIN 2, Republic of Ireland.   (hq)
      353 (1) 662 2755   fax 353 (1) 661 0517
      email info@isme.ie   http://www.isme.ie
      Chief Exec: Mark Fielding
▲   Company Limited by Guarantee
○   *T; to represent, support & promote owner/managers of small
      & medium enterprises
M   8,500 f

Irish Society
      see the **Honourable The Irish Society**

Irish Society for Archives   (ISA)   1970

IRL   c/o Special Collections, James Joyce Library, UCD, Belfield,
      DUBLIN 4, Republic of Ireland.   (memsec/b)
      email antoinette.doran@ucd.ie
      Hon Mem Sec: Antoinette Doran
○   *L

Irish Society for Autism   (ISA)   1963

IRL   Unity Building, 16/17 Lower O'Connell St, DUBLIN 1, Republic
      of Ireland.   (hq)
      353 (1) 874 4684   fax 353 (1) 874 4224
      email autism@isa.iol.ie   http://www.autism.ie
      Chief Exec: Pat Matthews
▲   Company Limited by Guarantee; Registered Charity
○   *W; to ensure that all people with autism are provided with an
      autism specific support servicethat will enhance their lives,
      develop their potential & protect their entitlement to
      participate in the development of society in accordance with
      their individual capacity & dignity as human beings

Irish Society of Chartered Physiotherapists

IRL   Royal College of Surgeons, St Stephen's Green, DUBLIN 2,
      Republic of Ireland.   (hq)
      353 (1) 402 2148   fax 353 (1) 402 2160
      email info@iscp.ie   http://www.iscp.ie
      Chief Exec: Ruaidhri O'Connor
○   *P
M   3,000 i

Irish Society of Occupational Medicine   (ISOM)

IRL   Meridian Clinic, Roselawn Shopping Centre, Blanchardstown,
      DUBLIN 15, Republic of Ireland.   (hsb)
      353 (61) 444888   fax 353 (61) 444889
      email info@isomirl.com   http://www.isomirl.com
      Hon Sec: Dr John Connolly
○   *P; for occupational physicians & doctors with an interest in
      occupational medicine
M   270 i

Irish Society for the Prevention of Cruelty to Animals   (ISPCA)
1949

IRL   Derryglogher Lodge, KEENAGH, Co Longford, Republic of
      Ireland.   (hq)
      353 (43) 332 5035   fax 353 (43) 332 5024
      email info@ispca.ie   http://www.ispca.ie
      Dir: Barbara Bent
▲   Company Limited by Guarantee; Registered Charity
○   *N, *V; to prevent cruelty to animals; to promote animal
      welfare; to pro-actively relieve animal suffering
<   Wld Soc for the Protection of Animals
M   20 org

Irish Society for the Prevention of Cruelty to Children   (ISPCC)
1956

IRL   29 Lower Baggot St, DUBLIN 2, Republic of Ireland.   (hq)
      353 (1) 676 7960   fax 353 (1) 678 9012
      email ispcc@ispcc.ie   http://www.ispcc.ie
      Chief Exec: Ashley Balbirnie
○   *W

Irish Software Association   (ISA)

IRL   Confederation House, 84-86 Lower Baggot St, DUBLIN 2,
      Republic of Ireland.   (hq)
      353 (1) 605 1582   fax 353 (1) 638 1582
      email isa@ibec.ie   http://www.software.ie
      Dir: Paul Sweetman
○   *P; to ensure that Ireland is global leader in the software sector
<   Ir Business & Emplrs Confedn (IBEC)
M   160 f

Irish Spirits Association
      sector association of **Alcohol Beverage Federation of Ireland**

Irish Sudden Infant Death Association   (ISIDA)   1976

IRL   Carmichael House, 4 North Brunswick St, DUBLIN 7, Republic
      of Ireland.   (hq)
      353 (1) 873 2711   fax 353 (1) 872 6056
      email isida@eircom.net   http://www.isida.ie
      Chmn: Kevin O'Meara
○   *W

Irish Taxation Institute   (ITI)   1967

IRL   South Block, Longboat Quay, Grand Canal Harbour,
      DUBLIN 2, Republic of Ireland.
      353 (1) 663 1700   fax 353 (1) 668 8387
      email info@taxireland.ie   http://www.taxireland.ie
      Chief Exec: Mark Redmond
○   *P; registered tax consultants
M   6,000 i

Irish Taxi Drivers' Federation

IRL   48 Summerhill Parade, DUBLIN 1, Republic of Ireland.   (hsp)
      353 (1) 855 5682   fax 353 (1) 836 4155
      Sec: Martin J Morris
○   *P

© CBD Research Ltd · Beckenham · BR3 5JS · Tel 020 8650 7745 · E-mail cbd@cbdresearch.com · www.cbdresearch.com

Irish Texts Society (Cumann na Scríbheann nGaedhilge)   (ITS) 1898

§   69a Balfour St, LONDON, SE17 1PL.   (hsp)
      email hon.secretary@irishtextssociety.org
      http://www.irishtextssociety.org
      Hon Sec: Seán Hutton
○   *A; To promote the study of Irish literature; to publish annotated
      texts in Irish with English translations & related commentaries

Irish Thoroughbred Breeders Association   (ITBA)

IRL   Greenhills, KILL, Co Kildare, Republic of Ireland.   (hq)
      353 (45) 877543   fax 353 (45) 877429
      email info@itba.ie   http://www.itba.ie
      Mgr: Shane O'Dwyer
○   *P; the representative body of the thoroughbred breeding
      industry
<   Eur Fedn of Thoroughbreed Breeders' Assns (EFTBA)

Irish Timber Growers Association   (ITGA)   1971

IRL   17 Castle St, DALKEY, Co Dublin, Republic of Ireland.
      353 (1) 235 0520   fax 353 (1) 235 0416
      email info@itga.ie   http://www.itga.ie
      Hon Sec: D Bergin
○   *T; private woodland owners

Irish Tourist Industry Confederation   (ITIC)   1984

IRL   Ground Floor Unit 5, Sandyford Office Park, DUBLIN 18,
      Republic of Ireland.   (hq)
      353 (1) 293 4950   fax 353 (1) 293 4991
      email itic@eircom.net   http://www.itic.ie
      Chief Exec: Eamonn McKeon
○   *N, *T

Irish Translators & Interpreters Association   (ITIA)   1986

IRL   c/o Irish Writers' Centre, 19 Parnell Square, DUBLIN 1,
      Republic of Ireland.   (mail)
      353 (87) 673 8386
      email itiasecretary@gmail.com
      http://www.translatorsassociation.ie
      Chmn: Máire Nic Mhaoláin
○   *P; to promote the highest standards within the professions; to
      foster an understanding among translation & interpretation
      clients of the highly-skilled & exacting nature of the
      professions
<   Eur Coun of Assns of Literary Translators (CEATL); Fédn Intle des
      Traducteurs (FIT)
¶   ITIA Bulletin - 12;   Translation Ireland - 1; both ftm.

Irish Travel Agents Association   (ITAA)   1971

IRL   8-9 Westmoreland St (4th floor), DUBLIN 2, Republic of
      Ireland.   (hq)
      353 (1) 417 9696   fax 353 (1) 417 9664
      email info@itaa.ie   http://www.itaa.ie
      Chief Exec: Pat Dawson
▲   Company Limited by Guarantee
○   *P; for travel agents & tour operators
M   170 f

Irish Tyre Industry Association   (ITIA)   1998

IRL   PO Box 5387, DUBLIN 24, Republic of Ireland.   (hq)
      353 (86) 773 9666
      email info@itia.ie   http://www.itia.ie
      Pres: Brian O'Neill
○   *T; to unite all sectors of the tyre industry: manufacturers,
      importers, remoulders, wholesalers & equipment suppliers
●   ET - Inf - LG - Mtgs

Irish Universities Association   (IUA)   1997

IRL   48 Merrion Square, DUBLIN 2, Republic of Ireland.   (hq)
      353 (1) 676 4948   fax 353 (1) 662 2815
      email iua@iua.ie   http://www.iua.ie
      Chief Exec: Ned Costello
▲   Company Limited by Guarantee; Registered Charity
○   *P; to facilitate collaboration & develop collective strategy &
      policy which advances third & fourth level education &
      research
M   7 universities

Irish Vocational Education Association   (IVEA)   1902

IRL   Piper's Hill, Kilcullen Rd, NAAS, Co Kildare, Republic of
      Ireland.   (hq)
      353 (45) 901070   fax 353 (45) 901711
      email info@ivea.ie   http://www.ivea.ie
      Gen Sec: Michael Moriaty
○   *E; to promote the development of education & training &
      youth work in Ireland
M   33 org
¶   NL - 2.

Irish Waste Management Association   (IWMA)   1999

IRL   Confederation House, 84-86 Lower Baggot St, DUBLIN 2,
      Republic of Ireland.   (hq)
      353 (1) 605 1526   fax 353 (1) 638 1526
      http://www.ibec.ie/iwma/
      Contact: Robert O'Shea
○   *T; the voice of the private waste management industry in
      Ireland
<   Eur Fedn of Waste Mgt & Envtl Services (FEAD); Ir Business &
      Emplrs Confedn (IBEC)

Irish Wheelchair Association   (IWA)   1960

IRL   Áras Chúchulainn, Blackheath Drive, Clontarf, DUBLIN 3,
      Republic of Ireland.   (hq)
      353 (1) 818 6400   fax 353 (1) 833 3873
      email info@iwa.ie   http://www.iwa.ie
      Chief Exec: Kathleen McLoughlin
○   *W; to achieve full social, economic & educational integration
      of people with disability as equal, independent &
      participative members of the community
¶   Spokeout - 4; ftm.

Irish Wine Association
      sector association of **Alcohol Beverage Federation of Ireland**

Irish Women's Bowling Association   (IWBA)   1947

■   30 Cromlyn Fold, HILLSBOROUGH, Co Down, BT26 6SD.
      (hsp)
      028 9268 8254   fax 028 9268 8808
      email jeanfleming2006@btinternet.com
      http://www.iwba.co.uk
      Hon Sec: Mrs Jean Fleming
○   *S; to encourage the sport of bowls for women
<   Wld Bowls; Eur Bowls U (EBU); Brit Isles Bowling Coun (BIBC)
M   2,400 i

Irish Writers Union   (IWU)   1986

IRL   19 Parnell Square, DUBLIN 1, Republic of Ireland.   (hq)
      353 (1) 872 1302   fax 353 (1) 872 6282
      email iwu@ireland-writers.com
      http://www.ireland-writers.com
      Hon Sec: Kate Walsh
○   *A
<   Eur Writers Coun (EWC)

Irish Youth Hostel Association
      see **An Óige**

Iron & Steel Society
      a group of the **Institute of Materials, Minerals & Mining**

Isle of Man Chamber of Commerce   1956

- Capital House (1st floor), Circular Rd, DOUGLAS, Isle of Man, IM1 1AG.   (hq)
  01624 674941
  email enquiries@iomchamber.org.im
  http://www.iomchamber.org.im
  Chief Exec: Mrs Barbara O'Hanlon
- ▲ Company Limited by Guarantee
- ○ *C
- ● Mtgs - Expt - Inf - Lib - LG - Seminars
- < Brit Chams Comm
- M 370 f, 5 org
- ¶ Members Classified Directory 2004-05; ftm, £25 nm.

Isle of Man Natural History & Antiquarian Society (IOMNHAS)   1879

- NR Ballacrye Stream Cottage, BALLAUGH, Isle of Man, IM7 5EB.
  (hsp)
  01624 897306
  email cjbryan@manx.net
  http://www.manxantiquarians.com
  Sec: Mrs C J Bryan
- ▲ Registered Charity
- ○ *L, to advance the knowledge of natural science, human history & cultural development in the Isle of Man & counties related thereto

Isle of Mull Chamber of Commerce
  see Mull & Iona Chamber of Commerce

Isle of Wight Chamber of Commerce, Tourism & Industry   1910

- NR Mill Court, Furrlongs, NEWPORT, Isle of Wight, PO30 2AA.
  (hq)
  01983 520777   fax 01983 554555
  email chamber@iwchamber.co.uk
  http://www.iwchamber.co.uk
  Chief Exec: Kevin Smith
- ▲ Company Limited by Guarantee
- ○ *C; business support services
- ● Conf - Mtgs - ET - Res - Expt - Inf - Lib - PL - VE - LG
- < Brit Chams Comm
- M 800 f
- ¶ Island Business - 12; ftm, £2.25 nm.
  Chamber Directory - 1; ftm. [TBA nm].

Isle of Wight Natural History & Archaeological Society   1919

- Unit 16 Prospect Business Centre, WEST COWES, Isle of Wight, PO31 7AD.   (hq)
  01983 855385
  email iwnhas@btinternet.com   http://www.iwnhas.org
  Hon Sec: Mrs Lorna Snow
- ▲ Registered Charity
- ○ *L; to promote the study of the natural history & archaeology of the Isle of Wight; to promote the conservation of the Island's flora & fauna & the proper preservation of all its objects of special archaeological & geological interest
- Gp Access to the countryside; Archaeology; Bat; Botany; Conservation working parties; Entomology; Geology; Mammals, reptiles & amphibians; Marine & freshwater; Ornithology
- ● Mtgs - ET - Res - Exhib - Lib - PL - VE - LG (local)
- M c 400 i, UK / 1 i, o'seas
  (Sub: £15, £20 family)
- ¶ Proceedings - 1; ftm, £12 nm.   Bulletin - 2; ftm only.
  Isle of Wight Birds - 1; ftm, £8 nm.

Islington Chamber of Commerce & Trade Ltd   (ICCT)   1924

- 222 Upper St, LONDON, N1 1XR.   (hq)
  020 7527 2709
  email admin@islchamber.org.uk
  http://www.islchamber.org.uk
  Mgr: Andrew Mortimer
- ▲ Company Limited by Guarantee
- ○ *C
- ● Mtgs - ET - Inf - LG
- M 370 f
  (Sub: £110-£500)
- ¶ NL - 12; ftm.

Italian Chamber of Commerce & Industry for the UK

- NR 1 Princes St, LONDON, W1B 2AY.   (hq)
  020 7495 8191   fax 020 7495 8194
  email info@italchamind.org.uk
  http://www.italchamind.org.uk
  Sec Gen: Helen Girgenti
- ○ *C
- M 400 f

ITP Support Association   1995

- NR Synehurste, Kimbolton Rd, Bolnhurst, BEDFORD, MK44 2EW.
  (hq)
  email info@itpsupport.org.uk
  http://www.itpsupport.org.uk
  Founder & Chief Admin: Shirley Watson
- ▲ Registered Charity
- ○ *W; to promote & improve the general welfare of people with Immune Thrombocytopenia, a disorder which causes a shortage of platelets & bruising
- ¶ The Platelet - 4; ftm.
  Leaflets;   Information Packs.

ITS United Kingdom   1993

- Tower Bridge Business Centre (suite 312), 46-48 East Smithfield, LONDON, E1W 1AW.   (hq)
  020 7709 3003   fax 020 7709 3007
  email mailbox@its-uk.org.uk   http://www.its-uk.org.uk
  Chief Exec: Mrs Jennie Martin
- ▲ Company Limited by Guarantee
- ○ *T; for UK companies involved in ITS (intelligent transport systems) - the use of electronic systems & services to provide online route guidance; to improve traffic control & the capacity of roads as an alternative to building new ones, including road charging
- Gp Education; Government consultation; Intelligent transport systems; Millennium project; Systems architecture
- ● Conf - Mtgs - ET - Res - Exhib - SG - Expt - Inf - Lib - VE - LG
- < ITS America; Eur Road Transport Informatics Coordination & Devt Org (ERTICO)
- M 80 f, 25 org, UK / 5 org, o'seas
- ¶ ITS Focus - 4; ftm.

IVE: the Vitreous Enamellers' Society
  since 2010 has beome a group within the Surface Engineering Division of the **Institute of Materials, Minerals & Mining**

IWSc: The Wood Technology Society
  was the Institute of Wood Science until 2009 when it became a division of the **Institute of Materials, Minerals & Mining**

© CBD Research Ltd · Beckenham · BR3 5JS · Tel 020 8650 7745 · E-mail cbd@cbdresearch.com · www.cbdresearch.com

J B Priestley Society   1997
■   24 St Lawrence Quay, Salford Quays, MANCHESTER,
    M50 3XT.   (hsp)
    0161-872 0332
    email m.nelson928@btinternet.com
    http://www.jbpriestley-society.com
    Hon Sec: Rod Slater,   Inf Offr: Michael Nelson
▲   Un-incorporated Society
○   *A; appreciation of the works of the English writer John Boynton
    Priestley (1894-1984)
●   Mtgs - Exhib - VE - Walks - Archive - Links with drama groups
M   205 i, 2 f, 4 org, UK / 15 i, o'seas
¶   Jnl - 1.   NL - 2.

Jacob Sheep Society Ltd   (JSS)   1969
■   Camster Fold, Aston, STAFFORD, ST18 9LJ.   (memsec/p)
    01785 282818
    email secretary@jacobsheep.org.uk
    http://www.jacobsheep.org.uk
    Interim Mem Admin: Mrs Jean Simmons
▲   Company Limited by Guarantee; Registered Charity
○   *B
●   Mtgs - Exhib - Expt - Inf - VE
<   Nat Sheep Assn
M   730 i, UK / 24 i, o'seas
¶   Jacob Jnl - 3.   Flock Book - 1; £10.

James Hilton Society   (JHS)   2000
■   49 Beckingthorpe Drive, Bottesford, NOTTINGHAM,
    NG13 0DN.   (hsp)
    http://www.jameshiltonsociety.co.uk
    Hon Sec: J R Hammond
▲   Un-incorporated Society
○   *A; to promote interest in the life & works of the novelist &
    scriptwriter James Hilton (1900-1954), author of Goodbye
    Mr Chips, Lost Horizon & Random Harvest
●   Conf - Mtgs - Res - VE
<   Alliance of Literary Socs
M   70 i, UK / 5 i, o'seas
¶   James Hilton (NL) - 4; £10 yr m only.

Jane Austen Society   1940
■   20 Parsonage Rd, HENFIELD, W Sussex, BN5 9JG.   (hsp)
    email hq@jasoc.org.uk
    http://www.janeaustensociety.org.uk
    Hon Sec: Maureen Stiller
▲   Registered Charity
Br 12; Australia, Canada, USA
○   *A; to foster the appreciation & study of the life, work & times of
    Jane Austen
●   Conf - Mtgs - ET - Res - Comp - SG - VE
<   Jane Austen Memorial Trust
M   1,700 i, UK / 300 i, o'seas
¶   NL - 2;   AR - 1; both ftm only.

Japan Society   1891
■   Swire House, 59 Buckingham Gate, LONDON, SW1E 6AJ.
    (hq)
    020 7828 6330   fax 020 7828 6331
    email info@japansociety.org.uk
    http://www.japansociety.org.uk
    Exec Dir: Captain Robert Guy
▲   Company Limited by Guarantee; Registered Charity
○   *X; to promote learning & advance education with regard to
    Japan, its culture & people; to provide resources & support to
    schools teaching about Japan
●   Mtgs - ET - Exhib - Inf - Lib - VE - LG
M   750 i, 250 f, 20 org, UK / 30 i, 30 f, o'seas
¶   Proceedings - 1; ftm only.
    Britain and the 're-opening ' of Japan: the Treaty of Yedo of
    1858 & the Elgin Mission (2008); £10.
    Biographical Portraits Vol IV.   Japan Experiences.
×   2007 Japan 21 (merged)

Japan Society of Scotland   (JSoS)   1986
■   4 Ravelston Park, EDINBURGH, EH4 3DX.   (hsp)
    email charliedmond@hotmail.co.uk
    http://www.japansocietyofscotland.org.uk
    Hon Sec: Charles Edmond
▲   Registered Charity
○   *X; to foster knowledge & understanding of Japan; to develop
    & improve relations between Japan & Scotland
●   Mtgs - VE
<   Japan Soc
M   100 i, 2 f, 40 students
    (Sub: £15 i, £200 f, £7.50 students)
¶   NL - 3; ftm only.

Japanese Chamber of Commerce & Industry in the United
Kingdom   (JCCI)   1959
■   Salisbury House, 29 Finsbury Circus, LONDON, EC2M 5QQ.
    (hq)
    020 7628 0069   fax 020 7374 2280
    email chamber@jcci.org.uk   http://www.jcci.org.uk
    Sec-Gen: M Takahashi
▲   Company Limited by Guarantee
○   *C; to promote & extend economic relations & trade between
    Japane & the UK & to promote the interests of Japanese
    business in the UK
●   Mtgs - ET - Expt - Inf - LG
<   Coun of Foreign Chams Comm in the UK
M   300 f
¶   JCCI Review (NL) - 4; free.
    Thames (NL in Japanese) - 4;   Members' Directory - 1;
    Economic Trends UK (report in Japanese) - 4; all ftm only.

Japanese Garden Society   (JGS)   1993
NR Woodzened, Longdene Rd, HASLEMERE, Surrey, GU27 2PQ.
    http://www.jgs.org.uk
    Hon Sec: Mrs Ann Dobson
○   *G; to bring together all those who are interested in Japanese-
    Style gardens
●   Exhib - Mtgs - VE
M   750 i

Japanese Knotweed Alliance   1999
NR CABI, Nosworthy Way, WALLINGFORD, Oxon, OX10 8DE.
    01491 829361
    http://www.cabi.org/japaneseknotweedalliance/
    PR Mgr: Sarah Wilson
○   *K; to highlight the problems posed by Japanese knotweed & to
    promote its control with natural predators

Jazz Piano Teachers Association   (JAPTA)   2001
NR   70 Culverden Rd, LONDON, SW12 9LS.   (hsp)
       020 8675 0335
       email info@japta.org.uk   http://www.japta.org.uk
       Hon Sec: Robert Webb
▲   Un-incorporated Society
○   *D, *P; for jazz education relating especially to piano
●   ET
M   c 300 i, c 10 f, c 5 org
¶   NL - 2; on web.

Jerome K Jerome Society   (JKJ Society)   1984
■   The Laurels, 1 Knight's Hill, Aldridge, WALSALL, W Midlands,
       WS9 0TG.   (memsec/p)
       01922 454115
       email membership@jeromekjerome.com
       http://www.jeromekjerome.com
       Mem Sec: John Shipley
▲   Registered Charity
○   *A; to research & study the life & works of Jerome Klapka
       Jerome (1859-1927)
●   VE - Annual dinner (May), Christmas concert
M   180 i, 10 f, UK / 10 i, o'seas
¶   Idle Thoughts (NL) - 2; ftm.

Jersey Cattle Society of the United Kingdom   (JCS)   1878
NR   Scotsbridge House, Scots Hill, RICKMANSWORTH, Herts,
       WD3 3BB.   (hq)
       01923 695296   fax 01923 695303
       email info@ukjerseys.com   http://www.ukjerseys.com
       Chmn: Charles Reader
▲   Company Limited by Guarantee
○   *B
<   Nat Cattle Assn (Dairy)
M   700 i

Jersey Chamber of Commerce   1768
NR   Chamber House, 25 Pier Rd, ST HELIER, Jersey,
       Channel Islands, JE1 4HF.   (hq)
       01534 724536   fax 01534 734942
       email admin@jerseychamber.com
       http://www.jerseychamber.com
       Head of Operations: Catherine Hargreaves
○   *C
M   f

Jersey Farmers' Union   (JFU)   1919
NR   22 Seale St, ST HELIER, Jersey, Channel Islands, JE2 3QG.
       (hq)
       01534 733581   fax 01534 733582
○   *F
M   c 120 i

Jet Sport Racing Association of Great Britain   (JSRA)   1995
NR   PO Box 160, BRADFORD, W Yorks, BD11 1WX   (hsb)
       07830 090045
       email info@jsra.co.uk   http://www.jsra.co.uk
       Sec: Mark Cowdell
○   *S; jet skiing on water
●   Mtgs - ET - Inf
¶   NL - email.   Rule Book.
       Definitive Guide to Racing.

Jewellery Distributors' Association of the UK   (JDA)   1970
NR   Federation House, 10 Vyse St, BIRMINGHAM, B18 6LT.   (hq)
       0121-236 3921
       email secretariat@jda.org.uk   http://www.jda.org.uk
       Sec: Lynn Snead
▲   Company Limited by Guarantee
○   *T; to represent the wholesalers, importers & distributors of
       precious & fashion jewellery & silverware who sell to high
       street jewellery shops
●   Conf - Mtgs - Exhib - Expt - Inf - LG
<   Brit Allied Trs Fedn (BATF)
M   80 f, UK / 2 f, o'seas
¶   The Distributor - 2; free.

Jewish Historical Society of England   (JHSE)   1893
NR   33 Seymour Place, LONDON, W1H 5AP.   (hq)
       020 7723 5852   fax 020 7723 5852
       email info@jhse.org   http://www.jhse.org
       Hon Sec: Dr Emma Harris
○   *L; research into Jewish history
●   Conf - Mtgs - Res - Comp - Lib
M   i
¶   Transactions - 2 yrly.
       Bulletin, AR & Accounts - 1; ftm only.

Jockeys Association of Great Britain Ltd
       since 2008 **Professional Jockeys Association**

Johann Strauss Society of Great Britain   1964
■   12 Bishams Court, Church Hill, CATERHAM, Surrey,
       CR3 6SE.   (hsp)
       01883 349681
       Hon Sec: Mrs V E Coates
▲   Un-incorporated Society
○   *D; recording, study, & appreciation of the music of the Strauss
       family & their Viennese contemporaries
●   Mtgs - Exhib - SG - Lib
<   11 sister societies worldwide
M   500 i, UK / 100 i, o'seas
¶   Vienna Music - 2; ftm.   NL - 6; ftm only.

John Bradburne Memorial Society
■   PO Box 32, LEOMINSTER, Herefords, HR6 0YB.   (hq)
       01568 760632
       email info@johnbradburne.com
       http://www.johnbradburne.com
       Dir & Sec: Celia Brigstocke
○   *G, *W; to support the Mutemwa Leprosy Settlement,
       Zimbabwe, in memory of John Bradburne (1921-1979), who
       worked at the settlement; to disseminate information on John
       Bradburne, poet, pilgrim & prophet

John Buchan Society   1979
■   The Toft, 37 Waterloo Rd, LANARK, ML11 7QH.   (hsp)
       01555 662103
       email glennismac2000@yahoo.co.uk
       http://www.johnbuchansociety.co.uk
       Hon Sec: Glennis MacClemont
▲   Registered Charity
○   *A; to promote a wider understanding & appreciation of the life
       & works of John Buchan (1875-1940)
●   Conf - Mtgs - Res - Inf - VE
<   Alliance of Literary Socs; Biggar Museum Trust
M   430 i, UK / 70 i, o'seas
¶   The John Buchan Jnl - 2; ftm, £4 nm.   NL - 2; ftm only.

© CBD Research Ltd · Beckenham · BR3 5JS · Tel 020 8650 7745 · E-mail cbd@cbdresearch.com · www.cbdresearch.com

John Clare Society   1981

- ■ 9 The Chase, ELY, Cambs, CB6 3DR.   (memsec/p)
  01353 668438
  Mem Sec: Sue Holgate
- ▲ Un-incorporated Society
- ○ *A, *G, *L; to promote the study of the life & work of the poet John Clare (1793-1864) & the collection, preservation & exchange of items of literary & biographical interest associated with him
- ● Conf - ET - Res - VE
- < Alliance of Literary Socs
- M i & org

John Curwen Society
Funding body of the **Curwen Institute**

John Hampden Society   (JHS)   1992

- NR Little Hampden, Cryers Hill, HIGH WYCOMBE, Bucks, HP15 6JS.   (hq)
  01494 562279
  email enquiries@johnhampden.org
  http://www.johnhampden.org
  Hon Sec: Mrs Anthea Coles
- ▲ Registered Charity
- Br Australia, New Zealand, USA
- ○ *G, *L; to make better known the character & achievements of the 17th century Parliamentarian John Hampden; to stimulate research into his life & times
- ● Res - Exhib - Inf - Lib - PL - VE - Lectures - Preservation & renovation of monuments & artifacts connected with John Hampden
- < English Civil War Soc; Hampden (Maine) Histl Soc
- M 130 i, UK / 12 i, o'seas
- ¶ The Patriot (NL) - 4.
  John Hampden & His Times (brochure).
  John Hampden of Buckinghamshire: the people's hero.
  The Controversy of John Hampden's Death.
  In the Steps of the Patriot (leaflet).

John Innes Manufacturers Association   (JIMA)   1975

- ■ Horticulture House, 19 Theale St, READING, Berks, RG7 5AH.   (hq)
  email johninnes@the-hta.org.uk
  http://www.johninnes.info
- ▲ Un-incorporated Society
- ○ *T; to represent the leading independent UK manufacturers of John Innes loam-based composts (or potting mixes)
- ● Mtgs - Inf - Advertising & PR - Quality standards
- M 8 f
- ¶ Benefits of John Innes loam based compost (leaflet) - 1; ftm & consumers.
  Technical Data Sheets (set of 19); ftm & trade enquirers.

John Masefield Society   1992

- ■ The Frith, LEDBURY, Herefords, HR8 1LW.   (chmn/p)
  01531 633800
  http://www.ies.sas.ac.uk/cmps/projects/masefield/society/jmsws.htm
  Chmn: Peter Carter,   Sec: Robert Vaughan
- ▲ Registered Charity
- ○ *A; to stimulate interest in the life & works of the poet & novelist John Masefield (1878-1967) Poet Laureate 1930-1967
- ● Readings - Lectures - Festivals - Screenings - Walks
- M 160 i, 2 org
- ¶ Jnl - 1; ftm, £3 nm.   NL - 2.

John Meade Falkner Society   1999

- ■ Greenmantle, 75 Main St, Kings Newton, MELBOURNE, Derbys, DE73 8BX.   (founder/p)
  01332 865315
  email nebuly@hotmail.co.uk
  http://www.johnmeadefalknersociety.co.uk
  Founder & Hon Sec: Kenneth Hillier
- ▲ Un-incorporated Society
- ○ *A; to promote a wider understanding & appreciation of the life & works of John Meade Falkner (1858-1932)
- ● Mtgs - Res - Inf - VE
- < Alliance of Literary Societies
- M 34 i, UK / 15 i, o'seas
- ¶ Jnl - 1; ftm, £2 nm.   NL - 3; ftm only.

John Moore Society   1988

- ■ 3 Normandy Close, Hampton Magna, WARWICK, CV35 8UB.   (hsp)
  01926 494368
  email phillrobbins@yahoo.co.uk
  http://www.gloster.demon.co.uk/JMCM/jmoore.html
  Mem Sec: Phillip Robbins
- ▲ Un-incorporated Society
- ○ *A; to promote the life & works of John Moore (1907-1967), the 20th century conservation pioneer & author of the 'Brensham Trilogy', who was concerned about threats to the countryside
- ● Mtgs - ET - Exhib - Inf - Lib - VE
- M 150 i, 2 org, UK / 10 i, o'seas
- ¶ Jnl - 2; ftm, £3.50 nm.

John Snow Society   1993

- NR John Snow House, 59 Mansell St, LONDON, E1 8AN.   (hq)
  020 7265 7300
  http://www.johnsnowsociety.org
  Contact: Dawn Hunter
- ○ *L; to promote knowledge of the life of John Snow (1813-1858), to encourage communication & collaboration between specialists of the many disciplines that have benefitted from Snow's work, & to ensure that Snow's memory continues to be celebrated in the pub bearing his name
- M 2,000 i
- ¶ Broad Sheet (NL) - 1.
  The Society is administered by the Royal Society for Public Health

Johnson Society   1910

- ■ Johnson Birthplace Museum, Breadmarket St, LICHFIELD, Staffs, WS13 6LG.   (hq)
  01543 264972
  email info@thejohnsonsociety.org.uk
  http://www.thejohnsonsociety.org.uk
  Hon Gen Sec: Barbara Hattersley
- ▲ Registered Society
- ○ *L, study of life, works & times of Dr Samuel Johnson, preservation of his birthplace, books, manuscripts etc
- ● Mtgs - VE
- M i & org
- ¶ Transactions - 1; ftm.

Johnson Society of London   (JSL)   1928

- ■ 16 Laurier Rd, LONDON, NW5 1SG.   (memsec/p)
  email memsec@johnsonsocietyoflondon.org
  http://www.johnsonsocietyoflondon.org
  Mem Sec: Christopher T W Ogden
- ▲ Un-incorporated Society
- ○ *L; to 'Johnsonise the land' (Boswell); to promote the study of Samuel Johnson, his works, his circle, his contemporaries & his times
- M i
- ¶ The New Rambler - 1; ftm, £5 nm.
  The New Idler - 2-4; ftm only.

Joinery Managers Association
has closed

Joint Association of Classical Teachers   (JACT)   1962
- ■ Senate House, Malet St, LONDON, WC1E 7HU.   (hq)
  020 7862 8719   fax 020 7255 2297
  email office@jact.org   http://www.jact.org
  Hon Sec: Alan Clague,   Chmn: Prof Thomas Harrison
- ▲ Registered Charity
- ○ *E, *P; to promote the teaching of the classics in schools; to
  support those who teach classics
- ● Conf - Mtgs - ET - Exam - Comp - Inf - LG
- < Classical Assn; Brit School at Athens
- > Assn for Latin Teaching (ARLT)
- M 1,308 i, UK / 93 i, o'seas
  (Sub: £40 UK / £42 o'seas)
- ¶ Jnl of Classics Teaching - 3; ftm only.
  Omnibus Magazine - 2; ftm, £8.20 (UK), £10 (RoW).

Joint Association of Geoscientists for International Development
  a group of the **Geological Society**

Joint Association for Quaternary Research
  a group of the **Geological Society**

**Joint Committee of the National Amenity Societies   (JCNAS)
1968**
- NR c/o SPAB, 37 Spital Square, LONDON, E1 6DY.   (sb)
  email secretary@jcnas.org.uk   http://www.jcnas.org.uk
  Sec: Matthew Slocombe
- ○ *N; to represent the member societies in commenting on
  applications for consent to demolish listed buildings (in
  England & Wales) under the terms of the 1968 Town &
  Country Planning Act (& by the Garden History Society in the
  case of registered gardens)
- ● Mtgs (6 a yr)
- M 7 org:
  Ancient Monuments Society
  Council for British Archaeology
  Garden History Society
  Georgian Group
  Society for the Protection of Ancient Buildings
  Twentieth Century Society
  Victorian Society

Joseph Conrad Society (UK)   1973
- NR c/o POSK, 238-246 King St, LONDON, W6 0RF.   (hq)
  020 8741 1940
  email theconradian@aol.com
  http://www.josephconradsociety.org
  Sec: Hugh Epstein
- ▲ Registered Charity
- ○ *A, *L; to promote the study of all aspects of the work & life of
  Joseph Conrad (1857-1924)
- ● Conf - Res - Comp - Lib
- < Joseph Conrad Soc(s) of America & France; Tokyo Conrad Gp
  (Japan)
- M 50 i, UK / 100 i, o'seas
- ¶ The Conradian - 2; £20.
  Note: the hq is run by the staff of the Polish Library.

Joseph Williamson Society   1989
- NR Williamson Tunnels Heritage Centre, The Old Stableyard,
  Smithdown Lane, LIVERPOOL, L7 3EE.   (hq)
  0151-709 6868   fax 0151-709 8156
  http://www.williamsontunnels.co.uk
- ▲ Company Limited by Guarantee; Registered Charity
- ○ *G; for all interested in the tunnels dug under Liverpool at the
  instigation of the millionaire Joseph Williamson during the
  early 19th century to give employment to men returning from
  the Napoleonic Wars

Josephine Butler Society   (JBS)   1869
- ■ c/o SWISH, 314-320 Gray's Inn Rd, LONDON, WC1X 8DP.
  (hq)
  http://www.jbs.webeden.co.uk
  Correspondence Sec: Mrs Jenni Paterson
- ▲ Un-incorporated Society
- ○ *K; to prevent the exploitation of prostitutes & the
  marginalisation of those who can be forced into this activity
  by poverty & abuse
- ● Conf - Mtgs - Res - SG - Inf - Lib - LG
- < Intl Abolitionist Fedn; Intl Coun Women; C'wealth Countries
  League; Nat Coun Women; Women's Coun; Nat Assn
  Women's Orgs
- M c 80 i
- ¶ News & Views - 1.

Judo Scotland   1949
- NR EICA: Ratho, South Platt Hill, Ratho, NEWBRIDGE,
  EH28 8AA.   (hq)
  0131-333 2981
  email info@judoscotland.com
  http://www.judoscotland.com
  Chief Exec: Dougi Brice
- ▲ Company Limited by Guarantee
- ○ *S; governing body for Judo in Scotland
- ● ET - Exam - Comp - Stat
- < Brit Judo Assn
- M 6,000 i, 125 org
- ¶ Judo News - 3; ftm only.

Jussi Björling Appreciation Society   (JBAS)   1988
- ■ Glenaire, 58 Mill Rd, CROWLE, Lincs, DN17 4LN.   (hsp)
  01724 710334
  email erik.wimbles@btinternet.com
  Sec: Erik Wimbles
- ▲ Un-incorporated Society
- ○ *D; the appreciation of the life & works of Swedish tenor Jussi
  Björling (1911-1960)
- ● Conf - VE - Stat - Res
- < Jussi Björling Soc, USA
- M 50 i, UK / 4 i, o'seas
- ¶ NL - 4; ftm only.

Just William Society   1995
- NR 7 Willoughby Rd, BRIDGWATER, Somerset, TA6 7LY.   (hsp)
  01278 421958
  email heardaboutwilliambrown@yahoo.co.uk
  http://www.justwilliamsociety.co.uk
  Sec: Ray Heard
- ○ *G; to celebrate Richmal Crompton's William books

Justice Awareness & Basic Support   (JABS)   1994
- ■ 1 Gawsworth Rd, Golborne, WARRINGTON, Cheshire,
  WA3 3RF.   (hq)
  01942 713565   fax 01942 713565
  email jackie@jabs.org.uk   http://www.jabs.org.uk
  Founder & Nat Co-ordinator: Jacqueline Fletcher
- ○ *K; to promote understanding about immunisations & offer
  basic support to any parent whose child has a health
  problem after vaccination; to campaign for a legal right to
  compensation for vaccine damaged children
- ● Inf

Justices' Clerks' Society
has closed

© CBD Research Ltd · Beckenham · BR3 5JS · Tel 020 8650 7745 · E-mail cbd@cbdresearch.com · www.cbdresearch.com

Kaolin & Ball Clay Association (UK) (KaBCA) 2000

■ Par Moor Centre, Par Moor, PAR, Cornwall, PL24 2SQ. (hsb)
01726 811328 fax 01726 811200
http://www.kabca.org
Sec: George Muskett
▲ Company Limited by Guarantee
○ *T; to represent the interests of both ball clay & china clay
producers
Gp Minerals searches
● Mtgs - LG
M 5 f

Karg-Elert Archive 1987

■ 38 Lyndhurst Ave, TWICKENHAM, Middx, TW2 6BX. (hsp)
020 8894 6859 fax 020 8894 6859
email anthony@caldicott247.fslife.co.uk
http://www.karg-elert-archive.org.uk
Chmn: Anthony Caldicott
○ *D; to further the appreciation, performance & recording of the
music of Sigfrid Karg-Elert (1877-1933) composer & organist
● Res - Inf - Performances
< Karg-Elert Gesellschaft (Germany)
M 45 i, UK / 15 i, o'seas
¶ NL - 2; ftm, 50p nm.   Review - 1; ftm, 50p nm.

Keats-Shelley Memorial Association (KSMA) 1903

■ Bedford House, 76a Bedford St, LEAMINGTON SPA, Warks,
CV32 5DT. (regd off)
01926 427400 fax 01926 335133
email hello@keats-shelley.co.uk
http://www.keats-shelley.co.uk
Hon Sec: David Leigh-Hunt
▲ Company Limited by Guarantee; Registered Charity
Br Italy
○ *A; to maintain & develop the Keats-Shelley Memorial House in
Rome, the building in which Keats died; to encourage interest
in the works of John Keats, Percy Bysshe Shelley & other
Romantic poets
● Conf - Mtgs - Comp - Inf - Lib
< Alliance of Literary Socs
M i
¶ Annual Review - 1; price on application.

Keep Britain Tidy

NR Elizabeth House, The Pier, WIGAN, Lancs, WN3 4EX. (hq)
01942 612621 fax 01942 824778
http://www.keepbritaintidy.org
Chief Exec: Phil Barton
○ *K; long-term improvement of local environments - the
durability of buildings & the quality of life for those who live
in them
× 2009 (1 June) ENCAMS

Keep Fit Association (KFA) 1956

NR 1 Grove House, Foundry Lane, HORSHAM, W Sussex,
RH13 5PL. (hq)
01403 266000
email kfa@keepfit.org.uk   http://www.keepfit.org.uk
Sec: Lyn Davis
Br 70
○ *G; to enable people of all ages to enjoy a total body
experience; to be able to sample the vitality, energy & variety,
improved stamina, strength & suppleness; develop balance,
agility, coordination & rhythm, to participate in the physical &
mental challenge
Gp Youth Moves (keep fit for ages 5-16)
● Conf - Mtgs - ET - Exhib - Comp
¶ Quarterly Publication - 3.   NL - 6.
Your Move Magazine - 2.

Keighley & Worth Valley Railway Preservation Society (KWVRPS) 1962

NR The Railway Station, Haworth, KEIGHLEY, W Yorks,
BD22 8NJ. (hq)
01535 645214 fax 01535 647317
http://www.kwvr.co.uk
▲ Un-incorporated Society
○ *G; preservation of the line as an operating steam passenger
railway
● Running the railway by volunteers
M i

Keith Murray Collectors Club 2000

NR PO Box 2706, STAFFORD, Staffs, ST21 6WY. (hq)
Hon Sec: Leonard Griffin
○ *G; for collectors of ceramics designed by Keith Murray

Kempe Society 1984

■ 41 York Avenue, CROSBY, Merseyside, L23 5RN. (hsp)
0151-924 6345
email info@thekempesociety.co.uk
http://www.thekempesociety.co.uk
Hon Sec: Philip Collins
▲ Un-incorporated Society
○ *A; to encourage recognition of the work of stained glass
painter, Charles Eamer Kempe (1837-1907) and his firm; to
encourage the preservation & maintenance of Kempe
windows & church furnishings
Gp County recorder section
● Conf - Res - Exhib - PL
< Ecclesiological Soc; Victorian Soc
M 300 i, UK / 20 i, o'seas
¶ Wheatsheaf (NL) - 4; ftm only.
Complete Corpus of Kempe Glass in the UK; £15.

Kennel Club (KC) 1873

■ 1-5 Clarges St, LONDON, W1J 8AB. (hq)
0844 463 3980
email info@thekennelclub.org.uk
http://www.thekennelclub.org.uk
Sec: Caroline Kisko
○ *B; to promote the general improvement of dogs, dog shows,
field trials, working trials & obedience classes
Gp Awards; Classification of breeds; Crufts Dog Show; Discipline;
Discover dogs; Publications; Registration of pedigrees &
transfers etc; Registration of societies & associations
● Mtgs - Exhib - Inf
M 700 i
¶ Kennel Gazette - 12; ftm.   Stud Book - 1;   Ybk.
Breeds Record Supplement (7 groups) - 4; ftm.

Kenneth Grahame Society 1997

NR 37 Ashtree Hill, TANDRAGEE, Co Armagh, BT62 2HP. (hq)
email admin@kennethgrahamesociey.net
http://www.kennethgrahamesociety.net
Sec: Roger Oakes
○ *G; to promote study & interest in the work of the writer
Kenneth Grahame (1859-1932), best known for his book The
Wind in the Willows
● Mtgs
M i
¶ Complete Works of Kenneth Grahame by members of the
Society; 2009; c£25.
The Wind in the Willows Short Stories; £20.

Kensington & Chelsea Chamber of Commerce   (KCCC)
NR   The Crypt, St Luke's Church, Sydney St, LONDON,
      SW3 6NH.   (hq)
      020 7795 0304   fax 020 7795 0306
      email kccc@kccc.co.uk   http://www.kccc.co.uk
      Exec Mgr: Julia Walker-Smith
○   *C

Kent Archaeological Society   (KAS)   1857
■   Lympne Hall, The Street, Lympne, HYTHE, Kent, CT21 4LQ.
     .   (hsp)
     07792 601328
     http://www.kentarchaeology.org.uk
     Hon Gen Sec: Peter Stutchbury
▲   Registered Charity
○   *L; 'study & publication of, & education in, all aspects of
     archaeology & history of the ancient county of Kent'
Gp   Buildings; Churches; Education; Fieldwork; Library; Place
     names; Records; Visual records
●   Conf - Res - Exhib - SG - Lib - PL - VE
<   to some 193 UK & overseas institutions
M   c 1,500 i & org
¶   Archaeologia Cantiana - 1; ftm.   NL - 3; ftm only.
     Kent Record Series & Monograph Series - c 1; prices vary.

Kent County Agricultural Society   (KCAS)   1923
NR   Kent Showground, Detling, MAIDSTONE, Kent, ME14 3JF.   (hq)
     01622 630975   fax 01622 630978
     email info@kentshowground.co.uk
     http://www.kentshowground.co.uk
     Chmn: George Jessel
▲   Company Limited by Guarantee; Registered Charity
○   *F, *H; improvement of agriculture, forestry, horticulture & allied
     industries: rural crafts, breeding of livestock & the
     demonstration of improved methods
Gp   Agricultural demonstrations; Bee garden; British foods; Cherry
     & soft fruit show; Crafts; English wine; Farming fayre; Flower
     show; Forestry; Livestock; Show jumping; Trade stands
●   Conf - Mtgs - ET - Exhib - Organisation of the Kent County
     Show
<   Assn Show & Agricl Orgs; breed socs
M   2,348 i, 438 f
¶   Kent View - 2; ftm, £1 nm.

Kent & East Sussex Railway Co Ltd   (K&ESR)   1961
■   Tenterden Town Station, Station Rd, TENTERDEN, Kent,
     TN30 6HE.   (hq)
     01580 765155   fax 01580 765654
     email enquiries@kesr.org.uk   http://www.kesr.org.uk
     Co Sec: N Pallant
▲   Company Limited by Guarantee; Registered Charity
○   *G; restoration & operation of vintage railway rolling stock for
     the education & benefit of others; operation of a heritage
     railway as a tourist attraction
Gp   Engineering; Maintenance, Restoration
●   Conf - Running a tourist railway - Maintenance of rolling stock
<   Heritage Rly Assn; S E England Tourist Bd; Visit Kent
>   Norwegian Locomotive Trust; Tenterden Terrier Trust
M   2,200 i
     (Sub: £23)
¶   Tenterden Terrier - 3; ftm, £2 nm.

Kent Invicta Chamber of Commerce   1900
■   Ashford Business Point, Waterbrook Avenue, Sevington,
     ASHFORD, Kent TN24 0LH.   (hq)
     01233 503838   fax 01233 503687
     email info@kentinvictachamber.co.uk
     http://www.kentinvictachamber.co.uk
     Chief Exec: Jo James
▲   Company Limited by Guarantee
Br   Ashford, Maidstone
○   *C
●   Conf - Mtgs - Exhib - Expt - Inf - VE - LG
M   600 f
¶   Chamber Update - 12; free.   Diary (inc LM).

Kentish Cobnuts Association   1991
NR   Apple Trees, Comp Lane, St Mary's Platt, SEVENOAKS, Kent,
     TN15 8NR.   (hsp)
     01732 882734
     http://www.kentishcobnutsassociation.co.uk
     Hon Sec: Alexander Hunt
▲   Un-incorporated Society
○   *T; to promote the growing & marketing of Kentish cobnuts
●   Mtgs - ET - Exhib - VE
M   150 i, UK / 10 i, o'seas
¶   The Cobweb (NL) - 4; free.   Pruning Kentish Cobnuts.
     In a Nutshell by Meg Game.   Information pack.

Kerry Hill Flock Book Society   1899
■   The Bramleys, Broadheath, PRESTEIGNE, Powys, LD8 2HG.
     (hsp)
     01544 267353   fax 01544 267353
     email kerryhillsheep@excite.co.uk
     http://www.kerryhillsheep.net
     Sec: Mrs Pam Chilman
▲   Registered Charity
○   *B; breeding and marketing of pedigree Kerry Hill sheep
●   Exhib - Inf - Mtgs
<   Nat Sheep Assn
M   32 i, UK / 2 i, o'seas
¶   Kerry Hill Flock Book - 1; £10

Kesva an Taves Kernewek (Cornish Language Board)   1967
■   16 Trelawney Rd, CALLINGTON, Cornwall, PL17 7EE.   (hsp)
     01579 382511
     email mpiercekernow@btinternet.com
     http://www.kesva.org
     Sec: Maureen Pierce
○   *L; promotion of the Cornish language
●   Mtgs - ET - Exam - Res - Inf
¶   Books, dictionaries & academic texts.

Kilvert Society   1948
NR   30 Bromley Heath Avenue, Downend, BRISTOL, BS16 6JP.
     (hsp)
     email kilvertsociety@here.communigate.co.uk
     http://www.thekilvertsociety.org.uk
     Hon Sec: Alan Brimson
▲   Un-incorporated Society
○   *L; to foster an interest in the Revd Francis Kilvert (1840-1879),
     his work, diary & the countryside he loved
●   Conf - Mtgs - Res - Inf - Lib (archives) - PL - VE - Church
     services - Conducted walks
<   William Barnes Soc; Alliance of Literary Socs; John Clare Soc
M   484 i, 3 socs, 4 libs, UK / 116 i, o'seas
¶   Jnl - 3; ftm only.

Kinesiology Federation   (KF)   1991
■   PO Box 269, GOSPORT, Hants, PO12 9FG.   (hq)
     0845 260 1094
     email admin@kinesiologyfederation.org
     http://www.kinesiologyfederation.org
▲   Company Limited by Guarantee
○   *M, *N, *P; an organisation representing the many varied types
     of kinesiology (a holistic complementary system of natural
     healing based on muscle testing to identify & facilitate the
     release of blocks in the body's vital energies, drawing on
     principles from traditional Chinese medicine)
●   Inf
<   Brit Complementary Medicine Assn
M   378 i, 5 org, UK / 7 i, 2 org, o'seas
¶   KF Today (NL); ftm only.

King's Army
     a group of the **English Civil War Society Ltd**

© CBD Research Ltd · Beckenham · BR3 5JS · Tel 020 8650 7745 · E-mail cbd@cbdresearch.com · www.cbdresearch.com

Kingston Chamber of Commerce (KCoC) 1903

NR Unilever House, 3 St James's Rd, KINGSTON upon THAMES,
      Surrey, KT1 2AH. (hq)
      020 8541 4441 fax 020 8541 4445
      email chiefexecutive@kingstonchamber.co.uk
      http://www.kingstonchamber.co.uk
      Chief Exec: Lisa Gagliani
▲ Company Limited by Guarantee
○ *C
Gp Small/medium businesses
● Mtgs - ET - Expt
M 500 i & f
¶ Eureka - 6; free.

Kipling Society 1927

■ 6 Clifton Rd, LONDON, W9 1SS. (hsp)
      020 7286 0194 fax 020 7286 0194
      email jmkeskar@btinternet.com
      http://www.kipling.org.uk
      Hon Sec: Jane Keskar
▲ Registered Charity
Br USA
○ *A, *L; to extend the knowledge of Rudyard Kipling (1865-
      1936), his life & works; for anyone interested in his prose &
      verse
● Mtgs - Inf - Lib (housed at City University London)
M 519 i, 90 universities/libraries
      (Sub: £26)
¶ The Kipling Jnl - 4; ftm.

Kitchen Bathroom Bedroom Specialists Association (KBSA) 1977

NR Unit L4A Mill 3, Pleasley Vale Business Park, MANSFIELD, Notts,
      NG19 8RL. (hq)
      01623 818808 fax 01623 818805
      email info@kbsa.co.uk   http://www.kbsa.co.uk
▲ Company Limited by Guarantee
○ *T; for the independent kitchen, bedroom & bathroom specialist
Gp Bathrooms; Bedrooms; Fitted interiors; Kitchens
● Conf - Mtgs - ET - Res - Exhib - Inf - LG
< CBI; METO; NHIC; NKBA
M i & f

Kite Society (KSGB) 1979

■ PO Box 2274, Great Horkesley, COLCHESTER, Essex,
      CO6 4AY. (hq)
      01206 271489
      email info@thekitesociety.org.uk
      http://www.thekitesociety.org.uk
▲ Un-incorporated Society
Br 5
○ *S; to promote adult kiteflying activities
● Conf - Res - Exhib - Comp - PL - VE
M 3,500 i, 40 f, UK / 400 i, 30 f, o'seas
¶ The Kiteflier (NL) - 4.

Klinefelter's Syndrome Association (KSA)

■ 56 Little Yeldham Rd, Little Yeldham, HALSTEAD, Essex,
      CO9 4QT. (coord)
      0845 230 0047
      email coordinator@ksa-uk.co.uk
      http://www.ksa-uk.co.uk
      Nat Co-ordinator: Sue Cook
▲ Registered Charity
○ *W; gives support & information to adults & parents / carers of
      children with Klinefelter's Syndrome
● Conf - Mtgs - Inf - Activity weekends
M 140 i
¶ A Guide for Adults; 42p postage.
      A Guide for Parents; 42p postage.
      NL - 4; free.

Kmoch European Bands Society (KEBS) 1973

■ 1 Keelton Close, Bicton Heath, SHREWSBURY, Shropshire,
      SY3 5PS. (hsp)
      01743 354784
      email johnbladon@uwclub.net   http://www.kmoch.org.uk
      Hon Sec: John Bladon
Br Czech Republic, Sweden
○ *D; to promote worldwide the music played Central European
      military & civilian wind bands
● Mtgs - Res - Inf - VE
M 90 i, 2 org, UK / 60 i, 4 org, o'seas
¶ Ceska Muzika (Jnl) - 1; ftm, £4 nm.
      Blasmusik Bulletin - 3.
      Note: František Kmoch (1848-1912) was a Czech bandmaster
      & composer of marches, polkas & waltzes

Knights of Royal England (National Jousting Association) 1985

NR Beechenwood Farm, Spode Lane, Cowden, EDENBRIDGE,
      Kent, TN8 7HP. (hq)
      01342 850392 fax 01342 850392
      http://www.knightsroyal.co.uk
      Pres: Jeremy Richardson
▲ Un-incorporated Society
○ *S; to promote, perform & preserve mediaeval jousting & its
      associated history by staging tournaments, educating &
      entertaining
● Mtgs - ET - Exhib - Comp - Expt - Inf - PL
M 88 i, UK / 19 i, o'seas

Knitting & Crochet Guild 1978

■ Unit 4 Lee Mills, St Georges Rd, Scholes, HOLMFIRTH, W Yorks,
      HD9 1RJ. (hq)
      01562 754367
      email info@knitting-and-crochet-guild.org.uk
      http://www.knitting-and-crochet-guild.org.uk
      Sec: Maureen Wheeler
▲ Company Limited by Guarantee; Registered Charity
Br 33; Australia, Canada, New Zealand, USA
○ *G; to advance public knowledge & appreciation of the crafts
      of knitting & crochet
● ET - Lib
M 850 i, UK / 50 i, o'seas
¶ Slip Knot - 4; Hbk - 1; Supplements - 4; all ftm only.

Knitting Industries' Federation (KIF) 1970

■ 12 Romway Rd, LEICESTER, LE5 5SD. (dir/p)
      0116-273 7866 fax 0116-273 9633
      email directorate@knitfed.co.uk
      Dir: Mrs Anne Carvell
▲ Company Limited by Guarantee
○ *T; promotion of the interests of the textile knitting & hosiery
      industry in the UK; is a non-profit making organisation
Gp Dyeing & finishing
● Mtgs - Expt - Inf - Empl - LG
< EURATEX; Brit Apparel & Textile Confedn; UK Fashion & Textile
      Assn
> Brit Narrow Fabrics Assn (BNFA)
M 280 f
¶ Bulletin - 6; IR Bulletins - 4;
      Health & Safety Bulletin - 2; all ftm only.
      Knitstats - 1; ftm. AR; free.

Knowsley Chamber of Industry & Commerce

NR Business Resource Centre, Admin Rd, KNOWSLEY, Merseyside,
      L33 7TX. (hq)
      0151-477 1356 fax 0151-549 1357
      email info@knowsleychamber.org.uk
      http://www.knowsleychamber.org.uk
      Chief Exec: Lesley Martin-Wright
○ *C
< Brit Chams Comm; Chams Comm NW

L P Gas Association
in 2008 merged with the Association for Liquid Gas Equipment & Distributors to form **UKLPG**

Laban Guild for Movement & Dance
NR 11 Sherborne Rd, BASINGSTOKE, Hants, RG21 5TH.
(memsec/p)
http://www.labanguild.org.uk
Mem Sec: Janet Harrison
▲ Registered Charity
○ *D; the promotion & advancement of the study of human movement recognising the contribution made by Rudolf Laban
Gp Action profiling; Dance; Dance in education; Dance notation; Movement analysis; Movement/dance therapy; Movement for actors
● Conf - Mtgs - ET - Exam - Exhib
< Motus Humanus (USA); Eurolab (Europe); Foundation for Community Dance (UK)
M 240 i, 35 org, UK / 60 i, 25 org, o'seas
¶ Movement, Dance & Drama - 3.

LABC (LABC) 2005
■ 66 South Lambeth Rd, LONDON, SW8 1RL.   (hq)
020 7091 6860   fax 020 7091 6879
email info@labc.uk.com   http://www.labc.uk.com
Sec & Chief Exec: Paul Everall
▲ Company Limited by Guarantee
○ *T; to represent local authority building control departments in England & Wales; to promote the design of buildings that are safe, accessible & environmentally efficient to comply with building regulations
● Mtgs - ET - LG
< Consortium of Eur Bldg Control; Construction Ind Coun; UK Green Bldg Coun; Bldg Control Alliance; Bldg Control Performance Standards Advy Gp
M c 4,000 i
¶ Sitelines - 4;   LABC Outlook (NL) - 12; both ftm. National Directory of Services (LM) - 1; ftm, £15 nm. Directory of Local Authority Building Control -1; ftm only.

Labologists Society 1958
NR 87 Cambridge Rd, BIRMINGHAM, B13 9UG.   (hsp)
http://www.labology.org.uk
Chmn/Sec: D C Adams
▲ Un-incorporated Society
○ *G; research into history of breweries & social history connected with the brewing trade. Collection of beer, wines, spirits & soft drinks labels, as well as advertising matter relating to old breweries

Laboratory Animal Science Association (LASA) 1976
■ PO Box 524, HULL, E Yorks, HU9 9HE.   (asa)
0845 671 1956
email lasa@btconnect.com   http://www.lasa.co.uk
Admin: Sue Millington
▲ Registered Charity
○ *P, *V; welfare of animals in laboratory science; to promote refinement of scientific procedures
Gp Sections: Alternatives, Animal health & nutrition, Ethics, Management, Toxocology & pathology, Transgenic animals
● Conf - Mtgs - ET - Comp - SG - LG
< Fedn of Eur Laboratory Animal Science Assns
M 289 i, 14 f, UK / 63 i, 2 f, o'seas
¶ Laboratory Animals (Jnl) - 4;   NL - 4;   AR; all ftm only.

Laboratory Animals Veterinary Association
is a group of the **British Veterinary Association**

Lace Guild 1976
NR The Hollies, 53 Audnam, STOURBRIDGE, W Midlands, DY8 4AE.   (hq)
01384 390739 (Mon-Fri 0900-1600)   fax 01384 444415
email hollies@laceguild.org   http://www.laceguild.org
Hon Chmn: Sue Dane,   Hon Sec: Sara Ruks
▲ Registered Charity
○ *G; to promote understanding of all aspects of lace & lacemaking by hand
● Conf - Mtgs - ET - Exam - Res - Exhib - Comp - SG - Inf - Lib - PL
M c 4,888 i, 30 org, UK / c 1,000 i, 20 org, o'seas
¶ Lace (NL) - 4;   Young Lacemaker - 4; AR - 1; all ftm only.

Lace Society 1968
NR PO Box 14463, HENLEY-IN-ARDEN, Warks, B95 8AQ.   (hq)
email thelacesociety@gmail.com
http://www.thelacesociety.org.uk
▲ Un-incorporated Society
○ *A; to further interest in lace & lace making
● Conf - ET - Exhib - Inf - Lib
M 850 i, UK / 36 i, o'seas
¶ Lacemaking (NL) - 4;   AR; both ftm only.

Ladder Association 1947
■ PO Box 26970, GLASGOW, G3 9DS.   (hq)
0845 260 1048   fax 0845 260 1049
http://www.ladderassociation.org.uk
○ *T; for manufacturers of access equipment in the UK
● Conf - Mtgs - LG
M 37 f
¶ Leaning Ladder & Stepladder User Guide.
✕ 2010 British Ladder Manufacturers' Association

Ladder Systems Manufacturers Association (LaSMA) 1997
NR Rojak Design Ltd, Danesmead Business Centre, 33 Fulford Cross, YORK, YO1 4PB.   (chmn/b)
01904 623555
Chmn: Barrie Weatherall
▲ Un-incorporated Society
○ *T; to further the development of safe ladder systems
● Inf - LG
M 3 f

Ladies' Association of British Barbershop Singers (LABBS) 1976
NR [communication via website only]
email membership@labbs.org.uk
http://www.labbs.org.uk
Mem Sec: Lee Westlake
▲ Un-incorporated Society
○ *A; to encourage & promote singing in 4-part harmony in the UK, through education & friendship

Ladies' Golf Union (LGU) 1893
■ The Scores, ST ANDREWS, Fife, KY16 9AT.   (hq)
01334 475811   fax 01334 472818
email info@lgu.org   http://www.lgu.org
Chief Exec: Shona Malcolm
Br 4
○ *S; the governing body for women's amateur golf in the UK, Ireland & overseas; to uphold the rules of the game
● Mtgs - Lib
< [too many to list]
M c 2,760 clubs (representing c 209,000 lady members)
¶ LGU Hbk - 1; £3.

© CBD Research Ltd · Beckenham · BR3 5JS · Tel 020 8650 7745 · E-mail cbd@cbdresearch.com · www.cbdresearch.com

Lakeland Dialect Society   (LDS)   1939

NR   Gale View, Main St, Shap, PENRITH, Cumbria, CA10 3NH.
 (hsp)
 01931 716386
 email lakespeak@galeview.freeserve.co.uk
 http://www.lakelanddialectsociety.org
 Hon Sec: Mrs Jean M Scott-Smith
▲   Un-incorporated Society
○   *L; to study origins & history of dialect, folklore & songs, local
 customs & traditions; to encourage interest in the use of
 dialect speech & writing all particular to Cumbria (the former
 counties of Cumberland & Westmorland & the Furness district
 formerly in Lancashire)
●   Mtgs - Comp - Inf - Lib - Church service conducted in dialect
 (2-yrly, next June 2012) - Talks & lectures by arrangement
>   Yorkshire Dialect Soc; Northumbrian Language Soc,
 Edwin Waugh Soc
M   264 i, 3 org, 4 colleges & libraries, UK / 9 i, 7 colleges &
 libraries, o'seas
¶   The Jnl - 1; ftm, £1.50 nm.
 Lakeland Treasury 1998; £5 m, £5.50 nm.
 Lakeland Gems 1999; (tape) £5 m, £5.50 nm, (CD) £11 m,
 £11.50 nm.
 Old Fell Side (Kendal) 1991; £5 m, £5.50 nm.
 Susannah Blamire (18th century poet) 1994; £2 m, £2.50 nm.
 Hoosta Ga'an On?, 2002; £7 m, £7.50 nm.

Lanarkshire Chamber of Commerce   2003

■   Barncluith Business Centre, Townhead St, HAMILTON, Lanarks,
 ML3 7DP.   (hq)
 01698 426882   fax 01698 424699
 email info@lanarkshirechamber.org
 http://www.lanarkshirechamber.org
 Chief Exec: Douglas Millar
○   *C
<   Scot Chams Comm

Lancashire Archaeological Society   1975

NR   12a Carleton Avenue, Fulwood, PRESTON, Lancs, PR2 6YA.
 01772 709187
 email bill_shannon@msn.com
 http://www.lancsarchsoc.org.uk
 Sec: Mrs Mavis Shannon
○   *L

Lancashire Authors' Association   (LAA)   1909

■   5 Quakerfields, Westhoughton, BOLTON, Lancs, BL5 2BJ.
 (memsec/p)
 email laaenqs@gmail.com
 http://www.lancashireauthorsassociation.wordpress.com
 Mem Sec: Mrs B Holt
▲   Un-incorporated Society
○   *L; to foster & stimulate public interest in all aspects & forms of
 literature, both Lancashire orientated & general, as well as
 preserving an interest in Lancashire history & tradition
●   Mtgs - Comp - Lib
M   c 220 i, c 30 libraries & org, UK / c 20 i, c 10 libraries &
 org, o'seas
 (Sub: £15.00 i)
¶   The Record (Jnl) - 4; ftm only.

Lancashire & Cheshire Antiquarian Society   (LCAS)   1883

■   553 Southport Rd, Scarisbrick, ORMSKIRK, Lancs, L40 9RG.
 (chmn/p)
 01704 880996
 email stevecollins009@googlemail.com
 http://www.landcas.org.uk
 Chmn: Steve Collins
▲   Un-incorporated Society
○   *L, *Q; to promote the study of the history of Lancashire &
 Cheshire, from antiquity to the twentieth century, including
 archaeology, architecture, & social, economic & industrial
 history
●   Conf - Mtgs - Res - Lib (housed at Manchester Central
 Reference Library) - VE - Making representations concerning
 listed buildings, conservation areas & major planning
 applications
M   171 i, f & org, UK / c 150 i, f & org, o'seas
¶   Transactions - 1; ftm, £18 nm.

Lancashire Parish Register Society   (LPRS)   1897

■   13 Corrie Drive, Kearsley, BOLTON, Lancs, BL4 8RG.   (treas/p)
 email jr.corrie@ntlworld.com   http://www.genuki.org.uk/
 big/eng/LAN/lprs
 Hon Treas: Mrs Jackie Roberts
▲   Registered Charity
○   *G, L; to transcribe, index & publish the pre-1837 parochial
 registers of ancient Lancashire
●   Mtgs - Transcribing & publishing parish registers
<   Fedn of Family History Socs
M   320 i, 55 libraries, UK / 35 i, 30 libraries, o'seas
 (Sub: £25 i, £35 libraries)
¶   NL - irreg; ftm only.
 Printed Parish Registers - 2; £18 to i, £28 libraries).

Lancashire & Yorkshire Railway Society   (LYRS)   1950

■   31 Enfield Close, Hilton, DERBY, DE65 5HT.   (hsp)
 01283 730544
 http://www.lyrs.org.uk
 Hon Sec: Martin Nield
▲   Un-incorporated Society
○   *G; to create a permanent record of the 75 years existence of
 The Lancashire & Yorkshire Railway
●   Mtgs - Exhib - Inf - PL - VE
M   671 i, 23 org, UK / 27 i, o'seas
¶   Focus - 3;   NL - 4; both free.

Lancashire & Yorkshire Railway Trust   (LYRPS)   1960

NR   The Railway Station, Haworth, KEIGHLEY, W Yorks,
 BD22 8NJ.   (hq)
 http://www.lyrtrust.org.uk
▲   Registered Charity
○   *G; to seek, preserve &/or restore to working order rolling
 stock & other items of the Lancashire & Yorkshire Railway, its
 connections & records
●   Mtgs

**Lancaster District Chamber of Commerce, Trade & Industry
1897**

■   Commerce House, Fenton St, LANCASTER, LA1 1AB.   (hq)
 01524 381331   fax 01524 389505
 email info@lancaster-chamber.org.uk
 http://www.lancaster-chamber.org.uk
 Chief Exec: Mrs Ann Morris
▲   Company Limited by Guarantee
○   *C
Gp   Commerce; Economic development; Economic policy; Finance;
 Industry; Retail & retail promotion; Tourism; Transport
●   Mtgs - ET - Expt - Inf - Lib - LG
<   Brit Chams Comm; Chams Comm NW
M   454 f
¶   Business Matters - 12; free.

Land Access & Recreation Association
 see **Motoring Organisations' Land Access & Recreation
 Association**

Land Based Colleges Aspiring to Excellence
see **Landex**

Land Drainage Contractors Association   (LDCA)   1985

NR   NAC Stoneleigh Park, Stoneleigh, KENILWORTH, Warks,
CV8 2LG.   (hq)
01327 263264   fax 01327 263265
email secretary@ldca.org   http://www.ldca.org
Sec: Bruce Brockway
▲   Company Limited by Guarantee
○   *T; contractors in agricultural drainage, pipeline utilities &
highway, & sports turf drainage
Gp   Consultants; Contractors; Trade manufacturers & suppliers
●   Conf - Mtgs - ET - Exhib - VE - LG - Demonstrations
M   70 f
¶   NL - 4; ftm.
Specifications (at £25 each) for:
Field drainage.
Pipeline reinstatement.
Sports turf drainage.

Land's End John O'Groats Association   1983

NR   St Anthony's, Greenhill Rd, SANDFORD, Somerset,
BS25 5PB.   (memsec/p)
01934 852110
http://www.landsend-johnogroats-assoc.com
Mem Sec: Adrian Cole
▲   Un-incorporated Society
○   *G, *K; to support, assist or organise attempts by the public to
make a continuous journey from Land's End to John
O'Groats (or vice versa), in compliance with the law & other
statutory provisions, for social or recreational purposes
●   Mtgs - Inf
M   c 200 i, UK / 8 i, o'seas
¶   Quo Vadis? (Jnl) - 2; ftm only.   LM - irreg.

Land Value Taxation Campaign

NR   19 Queen's Gardens, Brighton, E Sussex, BN1 4AR.   (hsp)
http://www.landvaluetax.org
Hon Sec: Henry Law
○   *G, *K; 'to raise public revenue by means of an annual charge
on the rental value of land (not including the value of crops
or buildings on it)'

Landex - Land Based Colleges Aspiring to Excellence
(LANDEX)   1950

■   Kingston Maurward College, DORCHESTER, Dorset,
DT2 8PY.   (cosec/b)
http://www.landex.org.uk
Company Sec: David Henley
▲   Un-incorporated Society
○   *P; to support the role & work of UK colleges engaged in the
provision of further & higher education & training in land
based & associated subjects
●   Conf - Mtgs - ET - SG - Inf - LG
<   Assn of Colleges
M   34 colls; 8 associate colls
✕   2008 Napaeo - the Association for Land Based Colleges

Landlife   1975

NR   National Wildflower Centre, Court Hey Park, LIVERPOOL,
L16 3NA.   (hq)
0151-737 1819   fax 0151-737 1820
email info@landlife.org.uk   http://www.landlife.org.uk
Chief Exec: Grant Luscombe
▲   Company Limited by Guarantee; Registered Charity
○   *K; a charity taking action for a better environment by creating
new opportunities for wildlife & encouraging people to enjoy
them
Gp   Suppliers of wildflower seeds & plants
●   Res - PL - VE
>   Lady Bird Johnson Wildflower Ctr (Texas, USA)
M   200 i
¶   Natterjack News - 2;   AR - 1;
Wildflower Seed Catalogue - 2 yrly; all free.
Wildflower Seed & Plant Catalogue - 1.

Landlords' Association of Northern Ireland   (LANI)   1989

NR   197 Lisburn Rd, BELFAST, BT9 7EJ.   (hq)
028 9082 7033
email info@lani.org.uk   http://www.lani.org.uk
○   *T; to represent landlords in the private rented sector
<   Nat Landlords Assn (NLA)

Landscape Institute   (LI)   1929

NR   Charles Darwin House, 12 Roger St, LONDON, WC1N 2JU.
(hq)
020 7685 2640
http://www.landscapeinstitute.org
Chief Exec: Alastair McCapra
▲   Registered Charity
○   *L, *P; the advancement of all aspects of the arts & sciences of
landscape architecture & management
M   i

Landscape Research Group   (LRG)   1966

■   PO Box 1482, OXFORD, OX4 9DN.   (hq)
email admin@landscaperesearch.org
http://www.landscaperesearch.org
Chmn: Dr George Revill,   Sec: Dr S Shuttleworth
Admin: Mrs Pauline Graham
▲   Company Limited by Guarantee; Registered Charity
○   *L; to promote the study of & interest in landscape, landscape
research & the human environment
●   Conf - Res
M   117 i, 40 f, 150 org, UK / 65 i, 5 f, 90 org, o'seas
¶   Landscape Research Jnl - 4; ftm, £35 nm.   LM.
Landscape Research Extra (NL) - 3; ftm only

Latex Allergy Support Group   1996

NR   PO Box 27, FILEY, N Yorks, YO14 9YH.   (hq)
07734 176426
http://www.lasg.org.uk
Vice Chmn: Lesley Fudge
▲   Company Limited by Guarantee; Registered Charity
○   *W; to raise awareness of latex allergy among the general
public & healthcare workers; to provide a national support
network for those affected by latex allergy
●   Helpline: 07071 225838 (Mon-Fri 1900-2200 hrs)
M   300 i

Latin American Association

has become the Latin American House - a charity providing
family welfare advice & a bilingual nursery predominately for
all Latin American people working or living in Greater
London

© CBD Research Ltd · Beckenham · BR3 5JS · Tel 020 8650 7745 · E-mail cbd@cbdresearch.com · www.cbdresearch.com

Latin Mass Society for the Preservation of the Tridentine Rite of Mass (LMS) 1965

■ 11-13 Macklin St, LONDON, WC2B 5NH.   (hq)
     020 7404 7284   fax 020 7831 5585
     email thelatinmasssociety@snmail.co.uk
     http://www.latin-mass-society.org
▲ Registered Charity
Br 22
○ *R; preservation & restoration of the Tridentine Rite of Mass in
     the Catholic Church
● Arranging masses
< Intl Fedn of Una Voce (Switzerland)
M 4,000 i, UK / 300 i, o'seas
¶ NL - 4; ftm only; and selected bookshops; £1.95 each.

Laurel & Hardy Appreciation Society - Sons of the Desert   1972

NR 63 Wollaston Close, GILLINGHAM, Kent, ME8 9SH.   (hsp)
     01634 371550
     http://www.laurelandhardy.org
     Pres: Robert S Lewis
▲ Un-incorporated Society
○ *G; founded (in the USA in 1965 & in the UK in 1972) to
     perpetuate the spirit & genius of Laurel & Hardy
● Conf - VE
< worldwide Laurel & Hardy Fan Club
M 6,000 i, UK / 10,000 i, o'seas
¶ The Laurel & Hardy Magazine - 4.

Laurence-Moon-Bardet-Biedl Society   (LMBBS)   1987

■ 1 Blackthorn Avenue, Southborough, TUNBRIDGE WELLS, Kent,
     TN4 9YA.   (hsp)
     01633 664163
     email kevin.julie1@btinternet.com
     http://www.lmbbs.org.uk
     Sec: Mrs Julie Sales
▲ Registered Charity
○ *W; to preserve & protect the health & promote the welfare of
     persons suffering from Laurence-Moon-Bardet-Biedl
     Syndrome (LMBBS), & to advance the education of medical &
     educational professionals & the general public on the subject
     of LMBBS
● Conf - ET
< Genetic Interest Gp; Contact-a-Family
M 200 i, UK / 50 i, o'seas
¶ NL - 2;   Conference Report - 1; both free.
     More than meets the eye (medical leaflet);
     LMBBS child at school;   Introducing LMBBS;
         Who are we & how can we help; all free.

Law Centres Federation   (LCF)   1978

■ PO Box 65836, LONDON, EC3P 4FX.   (hq)
     020 7842 0720   fax 020 7842 0721
     email info@lawcentres.org.uk
     http://www.lawcentres.org.uk
     Dir: Julie Bishop,   Chmn: John Fitzpatrick
▲ Company Limited by Guarantee; Registered Charity
Br 57
○ *N, *W; to encourage the development of publicly funded legal
     services for those most disadvantaged in society; to provide
     support & development services to Law Centres
● Conf - Inf - LG
< Advice Services Alliance; Nat Coun for Voluntary Orgs
M 51 org
¶ Law Centres providing Equal Access for All.
     LCF Promoting Equal Access for All.   AR.

The Law Society of England & Wales   (The Law Society)   1825

NR Law Society's Hall, 113 Chancery Lane, LONDON,
     WC2A 1PL.   (hq)
     020 7242 1222
     email contact@lawsociety.org.uk
     http://www.lawsociety.org.uk
○ *P; solicitors
M i & f

Law Society of Ireland   1830

IRL Blackhall Place, DUBLIN 7, Republic of Ireland.   (hq)
     353 (1) 672 4800   fax 353 (1) 672 4801
     email general@lawsociety.ie   http://www.lawsociety.ie
     Dir Gen: Ken Murphy
○ *P; the educational, representative & regulatory body of the
     solicitors' profession in Ireland
M 12,000 i

Law Society of Northern Ireland   1922

■ 96 Victoria St, BELFAST, BT1 3GN.   (hq)
     028 9023 1614   fax 028 9023 2606
     email info@lawsoc-ni.org   http://www.lawsoc-ni.org
     Chief Exec: Alan Hunter
○ *L, *P; by Royal Charter & Statute, the governing body of
     solicitors in Northern Ireland
Gp Association of Collaborative Family Lawyers; Environment &
     Planning Law Association; Solicitors' Criminal Bar Associaton
     Lawyers: Company & commercial; Employment
● Conf - Mtgs - ET - Exam - Res - Stat - Inf - Lib - Empl
< Intl Bar Assn; C'wealth Bar Assn
M 2.200 i, 575 f
¶ The Writ (NL) - 10; ftm only.
     Solicitors of the Supreme Court of Northern Ireland: List - 2 yrly;
     m only.
     Legal Aid Solicitors List (NL) - 1; free.

Law Society of Scotland   1949

NR 26 Drumsheugh Gardens, EDINBURGH, EH3 7YR.   (hq)
     0131-226 7411   fax 0131-225 2934
     email lawscot@lawscot.org.uk
     http://www.lawscot.org.uk
     Chief Exec: Lorna Jack
○ *L, *P
M i

Lawn Tennis Association   (LTA)   1888

NR The National Tennis Centre, 100 Priory Lane, Roehampton,
     LONDON, SW15 5JQ.   (hq)
     020 8487 7000   fax 020 8487 7301
     http://www.lta.org.uk
     Chief Exec: Roger Draper
○ *S; promotion of the game of lawn tennis
● Conf - Mtgs - ET - Exam - Res - Exhib - Comp - Stat - Inf
< Intl Tennis Fedn; Eur Tennis Assn; Brit Olympic Assn; Central
     Coun Physical Recreation
M 82,000 i, 2,500 clubs, 3,000 schools
¶ Ace & Volley - 11.   British Tennis - 11.
     LTA Hbk - 1; ftm.   AR.

Lawn Tennis Writers Association   (LTWA)   1950

NR Cedar Lodge, Howe Rd, WATLINGTON, Oxon, OX9 5ER.
     (hsp)
     01491 612042
     http://www.ltwa.org.uk
     Hon Sec: Henry Wancke
○ *P, *S

LCSP Register of Remedial Masseurs & Manipulative Therapists 1919

NR 38A High St, LOWESTOFT, Suffolk, NR32 1HY.   (hq)
     01502 563344   fax 01502 582220
     email lcsp@btconnect.com   http://www.lcsp.uk.com
     Admin: Stephen G Foster
○ *P
● Mtgs - ET
✕ 2009 London & Counties Society of Physiologists

Lead Contractors Association (LCA) 1984

■ Centurion House, 36 London Rd, EAST GRINSTEAD, W Sussex, RH19 1AB. (hq)
01342 317888 fax 01342 303200
email rwr@lca.gb.com http://www.lca.gb.com
Sec: R W Robertson
▲ Un-incorporated Society
○ *T; specialist leadwork contractors
Gp Quality assessment & training; Quality standards
● Conf - Mtgs - ET - Comp
< Lead Sheet Assn; Plumbing & Heating Ind Alliance; Summit Skills
M 90 f
¶ Quarterly NL; Annual Directory; both free.

Lead Sheet Association (LSA) 1926

■ Unit 10 Archers Park, Branbridges Rd, East Peckham, TONBRIDGE, Kent, TN12 5HP. (hq)
01622 872432 fax 01622 871649
email nigel@leadsheet.co.uk
http://www.leadsheet.co.uk
Chief Exec: Douglas E Weston, Gen Mgr: Nigel Johnston
▲ Company Limited by Guarantee
○ *T; for manufacturers of rolled lead sheet who supply the UK construction industry
● ET - Exam - Res - Stat - Inf - Lib
< Construction Products Assn
M 4 f
¶ The Leader (NL).

Lead Smelters & Refiners Association (LSRA) 1967

■ 17A Welbeck Way, LONDON, W1G 9YJ. (hq)
020 7499 8422 fax 020 7493 1555
email enq@ila-lead.org http://www.ldaint.org
Sec: Dr David Wilson
○ *T
< Intl Lead Assn (ILA)
M 5 f

League against Cruel Sports (LACS) 1924

NR New Sparling House, Holloway Hill, GODALMING, Surrey, GU7 1QZ. (hq)
01483 524250
email info@league.org.uk http://www.league.org.uk
Chief Exec: Douglas Batchelor
▲ Registered Charity
○ *K, *V; to expose & end the cruelty inflicted on animals for sport
M 20,000 i

League for the Exchange of Commonwealth Teachers

closed in 2011.
The Commonwealth Teacher Exchange Programme is now managed by the Commonwealth Youth Exchange Council, details of which can be found in our publication **Councils, Committees & Boards**

League Managers Association (LMA) 1990

■ The Camkin Suite, 1 Pegasus House, Tachbrook Park, WARWICK, CV34 6LW. (hq)
01926 831556 fax 01926 429781
email lma@lmasecure.com
http://www.leaguemanagers.com
Chief Exec: Richard Bevan
▲ Un-incorporated Association
○ *P; for managers at all 92 FA Premier & Football League football clubs
● Mtgs - ET - Exam - SG
< Profl Players Fedn
M 150 i
¶ Centre Circle - 4; free. LMA NL - 12; ftm only.

Learning Institute

§ Overbrook Business Centre, Poolbridge Rd, Blackford, WEDMORE, Somerset, BS28 4PA. (hq)
01934 713563
http://www.inst.org
the institute runs a series of over 25 courses, on a variety of subjects, for those wishing to study for a new career career

Learning & Performance Institute (LPI) 1995

NR Westwood House, Westwood Business Park, COVENTRY, Warks, CV4 8HS. (hq)
0845 006 8858 fax 0845 006 8871
http://www.learningandperformanceinstitute.com
Chief Exec: Colin Steed
▲ Company Limited by Guarantee
○ *P; to continuously raise standards of professionalism within the learning industry while promoting & measuring the impact of learning on organisational performance
● Conf - ET - Exam - Mtgs - Res
M 3,000 i, 400 f
× 2011 Institute of IT Training

Leasehold Enfranchisement Association (LEA) 1988

■ 52-3 Kingsway Court, 1st Avenue, HOVE, E Sussex, BN3 2LQ. (chief exec/p)
01273 705432 fax 01273 735101
email enfranchiseinfo@yahoo.co.uk
http://www.leaseadvice.org
Chief Exec: Shula Rich
▲ Un-incorporated Society
○ *K; 'abolition of leasehold ownership of flats & houses, plus easy fair access to freeholds for leaseholders'
● Conf - Mtgs - ET - Res - SG - Inf - LG
M 8,000 i
¶ Escaping the Leasehold Trap (video); £6 m, £10 nm.

Leeds Chamber of Commerce

2008 merged with the Yorkshire & North Yorkshire Chamber of Commerce to form the **Leeds, York & North Yorkshire Chamber of Commerce & Industry**

Leeds, York & North Yorkshire Chamber of Commerce & Industry 1851

NR White Rose House, 28a York Place, LEEDS, W Yorks, LS1 2EZ. (hq)
0113-247 0000 fax 0113-247 1111
email info@yourchamber.org.uk
http://www.yourchamber.org.uk
Innovation Centre, York Science Park, Innovation Way, YORK, YO10 5DG.
01904 567838
Chief Exec: Gary Williamson
▲ Company Limited by Guarantee
Br Leeds, York
○ *C
¶ ML - 1. NL - 6.
× 2008 (Leeds Chamber of Commerce (York & North Yorkshire Chamber of Commerce
Note: The Leeds Chamber was established in 1785 and was the first body in the country to bear the name 'Chamber of Commerce'. It was refounded in 1851.

The Leek Growers' Association Ltd (TLGA)

■ PVGA House, Nottingham Rd, LOUTH, Lincs, LN11 0WB. (asa)
01507 602427 fax 01507 600689
email jayne.dyas@pvga.co.uk
http://www.british-leeks.co.uk
Sec: Mrs Jayne Dyas
○ *T; to provide technical, commercial & marketing information for growers
● Conf - Mtgs - Res - Exhib - Stat - Inf - LG
M 120 f

© CBD Research Ltd · Beckenham · BR3 5JS · Tel 020 8650 7745 · E-mail cbd@cbdresearch.com · www.cbdresearch.com

Left-Handers Association (LHA) 1989
- ■ Sterling House, 18 Avenue Rd, BELMONT, Surrey, SM2 6JD. (hq)
     020 8770 3722   fax 020 8715 1220
     email enquiries@anythingleft-handed.co.uk
     http://www.anythingleft-handed.co.uk
     Organiser: Lauren Milsom
- ▲ Un-incorporated Society
- ○ *K; for improvements in product design, teaching of writing &other skills for left-handed people
- Gp Left-Handers Club
- ● ET - Res - Stat - Inf - LG
- M i & schools
- ¶ The Left-Hander (NL) - 12.

Left-Handers Club (LHC) 1990
- ■ Sterling House, 18 Avenue Rd, BELMONT, Surrey, SM2 6JD. (hq)
     020 8770 3722   fax 020 8715 1220
     email enquiries@anythingleft-handed.co.uk
     http://www.anythingleft-handed.co.uk
     Dir: Lauren Milsom
- ▲ Un-incorporated Society
- ○ *G; to provide support, advice & information for left-handers
- < Left-Handers Assn
- M 50,000 i, worldwide
- ¶ The Left-Hander (NL) - 12.

Leg Ulcer Forum
- NR PO Box 641, HUNTINGDON, Cambs, PE29 9GU.   (mail/add)
     01480 412381
     Sec: Denise Elson
- Br Ireland, Scotland
- ○ *M, *P; for all concerned with the treatment of persons with leg ulcers & related conditions
- ● Conf - Mtgs - Inf
- M i, org

Legal Aid Practitioners Group (LAPG)
- NR 242 Pentonville Rd, LONDON, N1 9UN.   (hq)
     020 7833 7431
     http://www.lapg.co.uk
     Sec: Sarah Angell
- ○ *P

Legal Defence Union (LDU)
- NR Athas House, Inchbare, By EDZELL, Angus, DD9 7QL.   (hq)
     01356 648480 (advice line)
     email david.odonnell@ldu.org.uk   http://www.ldu.org.uk
     Chief Exec: Prof David O'Donnell
- ▲ Company Limited by Guarantee
- ○ *P; to promote & protect the welfare of solicitors in Scotland

Legal Software Suppliers Association (LSSA) 1996
- ■ River Cottage, Water Lane, North Witham, GRANTHAM, Lincs, NG33 5LJ. (hq)
     01476 860417   fax 01476 737449
     email sec@lssa.co.uk   http://www.lssa.co.uk
     Sec: Roger M Hancock
- ▲ Un-incorporated Society
- ○ *T; regulatory body for suppliers of software to legal firms & businesses
- ● Conf - Mtgs - ET - Exhib - Inf
- M 25 f
- ¶ NL - 4; free on website.

Leicester Longwool Sheepbreeders Association (LLSA) 1883
- ■ White Lodge Farm, Gaddesby Lane, Frisby on the Wreake, MELTON MOWBRAY, Leics, LE14 2PA.   (hsp)
     01604 840642
     email whitelodgefrisby@aol.com
     http://www.leicesterlongwoolsheepassociation.co.uk
     Sec: Mrs Sue Hatton
- ▲ Un-incorporated Society
- Br Australia, New Zealand, America
- ○ *B; preservation & conservation of the rare breed of which 85% are scrapie resistant
- ● Mtgs - Inf - VE
- < Rare Breeds Survival Trust; Nat Sheep Assn
- > Rare Breeds Survival Trust (RBST); Nat Sheep Assn
- M 60 i, UK / 5 i, o'seas
     (Sub: £35)
- ¶ NL - 4;   Flock Book (LM) - 1;   AR - 1; all ftm only.

Leicestershire Agricultural Society Ltd (LAS) 1833
- ■ The Show Office, Dishley Grange Farm, Derby Rd, LOUGHBOROUGH, Leics, LE11 5SF.   (hq)
     01509 646786   fax 01509 646787
     email info@leicestershireshow.co.uk
     http://www.leicestershireshow.co.uk
     Show Admin: J A Hardy-Smith
- ▲ Company Limited by Guarantee; Registered Charity
- ○ *F, *G
- Gp BSJA showjumping; Cattle; Goats; Horse & pony; Sheep; Dog show; Trade stands; Pigeon & poultry; Heavy horse; Private driving; Funfair; Army
- ● Comp - ET - Leicestershire County Show
- < Various breed socs
- M c 400 i
- ¶ NL - 2;   AR - 1; both free.

Leicestershire Archaeological & Historical Society (LAHS) 1855
- NR The Guildhall, Guildhall Lane, LEICESTER, LE1 5FQ.   (hq)
     0116-270 3031
     http://www.le.ac.uk/lahs/
     Hon Sec: Dr Alan D McWhirr
- ▲ Registered Charity
- ○ *L; study of archaeological history & preservation of historical buildings in Leicestershire
- Gp Historic buildings; Archaeology
- M i & org
- ¶ NL - 2; ftm.   Transactions - 1; ftm.

Leicestershire Chamber of Commerce 1860
- ■ 1 Mill Lane, LEICESTER, LE2 7HU.   (hq)
     0116-247 1800   fax 0116-241 0430
     email leics@chamberofcommerce.co.uk
     http://www.chamberofcommerce.co.uk
     Chief Exec: Martin Traynor
- ▲ Company Limited by Guarantee
- ○ *C
- ● Mtgs - ET - Res - Stat - Expt - Inf - LG
- < Brit Chams Comm
- M 1,800 f
- ¶ Chamber News - 12.   Directory - 1.

Leisure Boat Builders Association
     a group association of the **British Marine Federation**

Leisure Management Contractors Association
     is no longer active

Leisure & Outdoor Furniture Association   (LOFA)   1967
■   PO Box 743, CHICHESTER, W Sussex, PO19 9QQ.   (hsb)
    01243 839593   fax 01243 839467
    email info@lofa.com   http://www.lofa.com
    Sec: Phil Gibbs
○   *T; for manufacturers & distributors of garden furniture,
    barbecues, outdoor play equipment, hammocks, parasols or
    soft furnishings
M   66 f

Leisure Studies Association   (LSA)   1975
NR   Chelsea School, University of Brighton, EASTBOURNE, E Sussex,
    BN20 7SP.   (mail)
    email emily.l.coates@gmail.com
    http://www.leisure-studies-association.info
    Sec: Emily Coates
▲   Registered Charity
○   *P; an independent body of researchers, planners,
    policymakers, administrators & practitioners interested in
    leisure issues

Leith Chamber of Commerce
    a branch of the **Edinburgh Chamber of Commerce**

Leopold Stokowski Society
    closed at the end of 2009.

Let's Face It   (LFI)   1984
■   72 Victoria Ave, WESTGATE-ON-SEA, Kent, CT8 8BH.   (hq)
    01843 833724   fax 01843 835695
    email chrisletsfaceit@aol.com
    http://www.lets-face-it.org.uk
    Chief Exec: Christine Piff
▲   Registered Charity
Br   26; 8 o'seas
○   *W; to give patient & family support when coping with facial
    disfigurement; to advise on surgeons, prosthetics & other
    services
    Incl the junior 'Let's Face It'
Gp   Acne; Accidents; Bell's Palsy; Burns; Congenital disfigurement;
    Dysmorphobia; Facial cancer; Facial hair
●   Mtgs - SG - Inf
M   c 1,700 i
¶   Let's Face It.   NL - 3;   Me & My Face;   Leaflets.

Letter Box Study Group   (LBSG)   1976
■   13 Amethyst Ave, CHATHAM, Kent, ME5 9TX.   (hsp)
    01634 861714
    email enquiry@lbsg.org   http://www.lbsg.org
    Hon Sec: Mrs Avice Harms
○   *G; to collect, disseminate & record information on letter boxes
    at home & abroad, particularly those of historical importance
    & rarity
●   Conf - Res - Inf
M   c 800 i
¶   NL - 4; ftm only.

Leukaemia CARE   1967
NR   1 Birch Court, Blackpole East, WORCESTER, WR3 8SG.   (hq)
    01905 755977   fax 01905 755166
    email info@leukaemiacare.org.uk
    http://www.leukaemiacare.org.uk
    Chief Exec: Tony Gavin
▲   Registered Charity
○   *W; to provide vital care & support services to those whose lives
    are affected by leukaemia & allied blood disorders, including
    the welfare of families & carers as well as the sufferers
    themselves
●   Mtgs - Inf
    Support line: 0800 169 6680
M   6,200 i, 220 f, 600 org
¶   Focus (NL) - 2;   Booklets: Insight;   Care; all free.
    Framework (AR); ftm, charged to nm.

Lewis Carroll Society   1969
■   50 Lauderdale Mansions, Lauderdale Rd, LONDON,
    W9 1NE.   (hsp)
    email alanwhite@tesco.net
    http://www.lewiscarrollsociety.org.uk
    Sec: Alan White
▲   Registered Charity
○   *A, *G; to promote interest in the life of Charles Lutwidge
    Dodgson (1832-1898); to study works produced under his
    real name & under his famous pseudonym, Lewis Carroll
●   Conf - Mtgs - ET - Res - Exhib - Comp - SG - Inf - VE
<   Lewis Carroll Socs: Australia, Canada, Japan, N America
M   250 i, UK / 150 i, o'seas
¶   The Carrollian (Jnl) - 2; ftm, £10 issue nm.
    Bandersnatch (NL) - 4; ftm, prices vary nm.
    Lewis Carroll Review - 4; ftm, £1 issue nm.

LGCommunications
    see **Association of Local Government Communications**

**Liberation - incorporating the Movement for Colonial Freedom
1954**
■   75-77 St John St, LONDON, EC1M 4NN.   (hq)
    020 7324 2498
    email info@liberationorg.co.uk
    http://www.liberationorg.co.uk
    Gen Sec: Mrs Maggie Bowden
▲   Un-incorporated Society
○   *K; an anti-racist, anti-imperialist organisation for peace &
    social justice concerned with Africa, Asia, Caribbean & Latin
    America
Gp   NGO; Racism; Somalis; Sudanese; UN; Women
●   Conf - ET - Res
M   c 1,000 i
¶   Liberation - 6; £2.   AR - 1; free.

Libertarian Alliance   (LA)   1967
NR   2 Lansdowne Row (suite 35), LONDON, W1J 6HL.   (hq)
    07956 472199
    email sean@libertarian.co.uk
    http://www.libertarian.co.uk
    Dir: Dr Sean Gabb
○   *K; 'leading radical pro-free market & civil libertarian group.
    Campaigning for social & economic freedom'
●   Conf - Mtgs - Seminars
<   Intl Soc for Individual Liberty; Libertarian Intl
¶   Free Life (Jnl) - 4.
    List available of c 700 publications in print.

Liberty: National Council for Civil Liberties   1934
■   21 Tabard St, LONDON, SE1 4LA.   (hq)
    020 7403 3888   fax 020 7407 5354
    http://www.liberty-human-rights.org.uk
    Dir: Shami Chakrabarti
▲   Registered Charity
○   *K; campaigns to extend & defend civil liberties
●   Conf - Mtgs - Res - Inf - Lib - Lobbying - Test case work in UK &
    European courts
<   Intl League of Human Rights
M   7,000 i
¶   Liberty - 4; ftm.   AR.   Publications list available.
    Note: The National Council for Civil Liberties has operated as
    Liberty since 1989

© CBD Research Ltd · Beckenham · BR3 5JS · Tel 020 8650 7745 · E-mail cbd@cbdresearch.com · www.cbdresearch.com

Librarians' Christian Fellowship   (LCF)   1976
- 34 Thurlestone Ave, ILFORD, Essex, IG3 9DU.   (hsp)
  020 8599 1310
  email secretary@librarianscf.org.uk
  http://www.librarianscf.org.uk
  Hon Sec: Graham Hedges
▲ Un-incorporated Society
Br 9
○ *R; to help members develop a Christian perspective on issues facing the library & information profession
Gp C'ee for Overseas Library Development
● Conf - Mtgs - Res - Exhib - SG - Inf - Lib - VE
< Universities' & Colleges' Christian Fellowship
M 330 i, UK / 30 i, o'seas
¶ Christian Librarian - 4; ftm, £20 nm.

Librarians of Institutes & Schools of Education
has closed

Library Association of Ireland   1928
IRL 53 Upper Mount St, DUBLIN 2, Republic of Ireland.   (hq)
  353 (1) 459 7834
  email honsec@libraryassociation.ie
  http://www.libraryassociation.ie
  Hon Sec: Kieran Swords
○ *P; to promote & develop high standards of librarianship & of library & information services in Ireland; A to secure greater co-operation between libraries

Library Campaign: supporting friends & users of libraries   1984
- 22 Upper Woburn Place, LONDON, WC1H 0TB.   (hq)
  0845 450 5946   fax 0845 450 5947
  email librarycam@aol.com
  http://www.librarycampaign.com
  Sec: Andrew Coburn
▲ Registered Charity
○ *K; to advance the lifelong education of the public by the promotion, support, assistance & improvement of libraries through the activities of friends & users' groups
● Conf - LG
> UNISON; NASUWT
M 600 i, 10 f, 50 org
  (Sub: £15 i, £100 f, on application org)
¶ The Campaigner (NL) - 2/3; ftm, £30 yr nm.

Licensed Animal Slaughterers & Salvage Association   (LASSA)   1917
NR Hopwood House, Nottingham Rd, Somercotes, ALFRETON, Derbys, DE55 4JJ.   (hq)
  01773 602212
  email sydgrotier@yahoo.co.uk
  http://www.lassamembers.com
  Sec: Syd Grotier
▲ Un-incorporated Society
○ *T; to represent & promote the interests of members engaged in the licensed animal slaughtering & knacker trades
● Mtgs - ET - SG - Inf - LG
M 40 f
¶ NL - 4; ftm only.

Licensed Taxi Drivers' Association Ltd   (LTDA)   1967
NR Taxi House, 9-11 Woodfield Rd, LONDON, W9 2BA.   (hq)
  020 7286 1046   fax 020 7286 2494
  http://www.ltda.co.uk
○ *W; the wellbeing of taxi drivers & their families
M i

Licensed Vintners' Association   (LVA)   1817
IRL Anglesea House, Anglesea Rd, Ballsbridge, DUBLIN 4, Republic of Ireland.   (hq)
  353 (1) 668 0215   fax 353 (1) 668 0448
  http://www.lva.ie
  Chief Exec: Donall O'Keeffe
○ *T; to represent the publicans of Dublin & to protect & promote their strategic business interests
M 700 f

Licensing Executives Society Britain & Ireland   (LES B&I)   1968
- Northern Networking Ltd, Braeview House (Glenfinnan Suite), 9-11 Braeview Place, EAST Kilbride, G74 3XH.   (hq)
  01355 244966   fax 01355 249959
  email les@northernnetworking.co.uk
  http://www.les-bi.org
  Hon Sec: Dr John Roe
▲ Company Limited by Guarantee
○ *P; for professionals & business people interested in licensing, the transfer of technology & the commercialisation of intellectual property rights
Gp Brands; Education; EC laws; Healthcare; IT & commerce
● Conf - Mtgs - ET - LG
< Licensing Executives Soc Intl (LESI)
M 635 i, UK/ 10,000 i, o'seas
¶ NewsXchange - 6.   Les Nouvelles - 6.
  LM (LESI) -1.   AR (LESI) - 1.

Lichfield & Tamworth Chamber of Commerce
- Point East, Park Plaza, Hayes Way, CANNOCK, Staffs, WS12 2DB.   (hq)
  0845 071 0191
  email info@lichfield-tamworth-chamber.com
  http://www.lichfield-tamworth-chamber.com
▲ Company Limited by Guarantee
○ *C
● Mtgs - ET - Res - Stat - Expt - Inf - Lib - VE - LG
< Birmingham Cham Comm; Brit Chams Comm
¶ Chamberlink - 10;   AR; both ftm.

LIFE   (LIFE)   1970
NR LIFE House, 1 Mill St, LEAMINGTON SPA, Warks, CV31 1ES.   (hq)
  01926 421587
  email sam@lifecharity.org.uk
  http://www.lifecharity.org.uk
  Chmn: Prof J J Scarisbrick
▲ Company Limited by Guarantee; Registered Charity
Br 75
○ *W; to save lives & transform the futures of some of the most disadvantaged children & young people by supporting vulnerable pregnant mothers & young families through difficult times
Gp Housing; Care; Education; FertilityCare
● Helpline: 0808 802 5433
M 15,000 i

Life Academy   1964
- 9 Chesham Rd, GUILDFORD, Surrey, GU1 3LS.   (hq)
  01483 301170   fax 01483 300981
  email info@life-academy.co.uk
  http://www.life-academy.co.uk
  Chief Exec: Stuart Royston
○ *E, *W; planning & preparation for retirement & life change; incl social circumstances, leisure, health, career development & training of trainers to assist such guidance
Gp Mid-life planning; Post retirement; Pre-retirement education; Retirement
● ET - Post-graduate certificate & Masters Programme in Pre-Retirement Education & Planning - Introduction to life-planning level 3 qualification
M i & corporate
¶ NL.   Your Retirement - 1.   AR.
  Resource lists & other publications available.

Life Saving Awards Research Society   (LSARS)   1987
NR   PO Box 248, Snettisham, KING'S LYNN, Norwich, PE31 7TA.
     (hq)
     http://www.lsars.pwp.blueyonder.co.uk
○   *G; to further research into worldwide humanitarian awards
     given for saving or perpetuating life or endeavouring to do
     so
¶   Jnl - 3; ftm.

Lifeboat Enthusiasts' Society   (LBES)   1964
■   13 West Way, Petts Wood, ORPINGTON, Kent, BR5 1LN.   (hsp)
     01689 829068
     Hon Sec: John G Francis
▲   Registered Charity
○   *G; to bring together all with a keen interest in lifeboats & the
     lifeboat service, past & present
●   Res - Stat - PL - Lifeboat modelling
<   R Nat Lifeboat Instn (RNLI)
M   744 i, UK / 29 i, o'seas
¶   NL - 3; ftm only.   Annual Hbk - 1; ftm, £5 nm.

Lift & Escalator Industry Association   (LEIA)   1997
■   33-34 Devonshire St, LONDON, W1G 6PY.   (hq)
     020 7935 3013   fax 020 7935 3321
     email enquiries@leia.co.uk   http://www.leia.co.uk
     Managing Dir: D M Fazakerley
▲   Company Limited by Guarantee
○   *T; interests of manufacturers & distributors of lifts, escalators &
     passenger conveyors & equipment therefor
Gp   Escalators; Lifts; Passenger conveyors
●   Mtgs - ET - Inf - Technical cooperation on high standard of
     design & safety - Standardisation
M   f

Lifting Equipment Engineers Association   (LEEA)   1944
■   3 Osprey Court, Kingfisher Way, Hinchingbrooke Business Park,
     HUNTINGDON, Cambs, PE29 6FN.   (hq)
     01480 432801   fax 01480 436324
     http://www.leea.co.uk
     Chief Exec: Derrick Bailes
▲   Company Limited by Guarantee
○   *T; interests of specialists engaged in design, manufacture,
     testing, examination, inspection, sale, repair, maintenance &
     hire of lifting equipment
Gp   Examination; Registration; Technical
●   Conf - Mtgs - ET - Exam - Exhib - SG - Inf - Lib
M   163 f, UK / 115 f, o'seas
     (Sub: £925 f, UK / £820 f, o'seas)
¶   Bulletin - 8;   LM;   AR - 1; all ftm only.
     Lifting Engineers Hbk; £8 m, £20 nm.
     Lifting Equipment - a user's pocket guide; £8.
     Code of Practice for Safe Use of Lifting Equipment; £81 m,
     £135 nm.
     Hand Chain Blocks & Lever Hoists in the Offshore Environment;
     £10 m, £15 nm.

Light Aircraft Association   (LAA)   1946
■   Turweston Aerodrome, BRACKLEY, Northants, NN13 5YD.
     (hq)
     01280 846786   fax 01280 846780
     email office@laa.uk.com   http://www.laa.uk.com
     Chmn: Roger Hopkinson,   Sec: Bob Littledale
▲   Company Limited by Guarantee
○   *G, *S; the representative body in the UK for amateur aircraft
     construction, recreational & sport flying; encourages amateur
     design; promotes clubs & light aviation's infrastructure
Gp   Engineering (to administer & regulate amateur aircraft
     construction)
●   Conf - Mtgs - ET - Res - Inf - Lib - LG - Annual international air
     rally
<   R Aero Club; Sports Council
M   8,500 i
¶   Light Aviation (Jnl) - 12; ftm, £5 each nm.
✕   2007 Popular Flying Association

Light Metals Division
     a group of the **Institute of Materials, Minerals & Mining**

Light Music Society   1957
■   19a Eshton Terrace, CLITHEROE, Lancs, BB7 1BQ.   (hsp)
     01220 427066
     email hilary.ashton@talk21.com
     http://www.lightmusicsociety.com
     Sec: Mrs Hilary Ashton
▲   Un-incorporated Society
○   *D; to act as the backing organisation for the Library of Light-
     Orchestral Music; this music is available for hire by members
     & provides an archive of the kind of music played by popular
     orchestras for over one hundred years
●   Mtgs - Inf - Lib
M   385 i, UK / 15 i, o'seas
¶   NL - 3/4; ftm only.

Light Rail Transit Association   (LRTA)   1938
■   c/o 138 Radnor Avenue, WELLING, Kent, DA16 2BY.   (mail)
     0117-951 7785
     email office@lrta.org   http://www.lrta.org
     Chmn: Andrew Braddock
▲   Company Limited by Guarantee
Br   18; New Zealand
○   *K; to advocate the development of public transport, especially
     light rail transit & tramway systems
●   Mtgs - Inf - Lib - VE - Duplication of books & videos on
     tramways
<   Confedn of Passenger Transport (fixed track section); UITP
M   c 1,800 i, UK / c 1,500 i, o'seas
¶   Tramways & Urban Transit - 12.

Lighting Association Ltd   (LA)   1970
NR   Stafford Park 7, TELFORD, Shropshire, TF3 3BQ.   (hq)
     01952 290905   fax 01952 290906
     email enquiries@lightingassociation.com
     http://www.lightingassociation.com
     Chief Exec: Peter Hunt
▲   Company Limited by Guarantee
○   *T; for all sectors of the lighting industry
Gp   Component manufacturers & suppliers; Lamp suppliers &
     producers; Lighting distributors; Luminaire manufacturers
●   Mtgs - ET - Exhib - Comp - SG - Stat - Expt - Inf - Lib - LG -
     Seminars - Accreditation - Certification laboratories
<   C'ee Eur Luminaire Mfrs Assn (CELMA)
>   Furniture Ind Res Assn (FIRA); Profl Lighting & Sound
     Assn (PLASA)
M   218 f, UK / 12 f, o'seas
¶   LA News & Views - 12;   Lighting News - 2;
     Buyers Guide - 1;   AR - 1; all ftm only.

Lighting Industry Federation Ltd   (LIF)   1969
NR   Westminster Tower (ground floor), 3 Albert Embankment,
     LONDON, SE1 7SL.   (hq)
     020 7793 3020   fax 020 7793 3003
     email info@lif.co.uk   http://www.lif.co.uk
     Chief Exec: Eddie Taylor
▲   Company Limited by Guarantee
○   *T; to promote & develop the UK lighting market for the benefit
     of members & all other stakeholders
<   Fedn of Nat Mfrs Assns for Luminaires & Electrotechnical
     Components for Luminaires in the Eur U (CELMA)
M   f

Limbless Association   1983
- ■ Jubilee House, 3 The Drive, Warley Hill, BRENTWOOD, Essex, CM13 3FR.   (hq)
  01277 725182   fax 01277 725001
  http://www.limbless-association.org
- ▲ Company Limited by Guarantee; Registered Charity
- ○ *W; for the welfare of people of all ages who have been born without limb(s), or who have had amputations, their carers & the professionals involved with their care; to promote policy matters & monitor NHS services for limbless people
- ● Conf - Res - Inf
- < R Assn for Disability & Rehabilitation
- M 3,000 i, 13 f, UK / 100 i, o'seas
- ¶ Step Forward - 4; ftm, amputees, carers & professionals.

Lincoln Longwool Sheep Breeders Association   1892
- NR Lincolnshire Showground, Grange de Lings, LINCOLN, LN2 2NA.   (hq)
  01522 568660
  email lincolnlongwool@yahoo.co.uk
  http://www.lincolnlongwools.co.uk
  Sec: Ruth Mawer
- ▲ Registered Charity
- ○ *B
- ● Mtgs - Exhib - Comp - Stat - Expt - Inf
- < Nat Sheep Assn
- M 87 i
- ¶ Jnl - 6.   Flock Book - 1.

Lincoln Record Society   (LRS)   1910
- ■ Lincoln Cathedral Library, Minster Yard, LINCOLN, LN2 1PX.   (treas/b)
  01522 561640
  http://www.lincoln-record-society.org.uk
  Treas: Ken Hollamby
- ▲ Registered Charity
- ○ *L; publication of historical records relating to the ancient county & diocese of Lincoln
- ● Res
- M 175 i, 70 org, UK / 9 i, 43 org, o'seas
- ¶ Lincoln Record Society - 1; £18 m, £25-£30 nm.

Lincoln Red Cattle Society   (LRCS)   1895
- NR Lincolnshire Showground, Grange de Lings, LINCOLN, LN2 2NA.   (hq)
  01522 511395
  email secretary@lincolnredcattlesociety.co.uk
  http://www.lincolnredcattlesociety.co.uk
  Sec: Jane Borrows
- ▲ Registered Charity
- ○ *B
- ● Mtgs - Exhib - Comp - Stat - Inf
- < Nat Cattle Assn
- M 108 i, 1 f, 2 org, UK / 4 i, o'seas
- ¶ Jnl - 6.   Herd Book - 1.

Lincolnshire Agricultural Society   (LAS)   1869
- NR Lincolnshire Showground, Grange de Lings, LINCOLN, LN2 2NA.   (hq)
  01522 522900   fax 01522 520345
  email mfarmer@lincs-events.co.uk
  http://www.lincolnshireshowground.co.uk
  Chief Exec: Mark Farmer
- ▲ Company Limited by Guarantee; Registered Charity
- ○ *F; the furtherance, welfare & progress of the agricultural industry & all professions, trades & crafts connected therewith
- ● Conf - Mtgs - ET - Exhib - Comp - Annual show
- < Assn of Show & Agricl Orgs
- M 3,000 i
- ¶ Show catalogue.   Programme & prize list schedule;   AR.

Lincolnshire Chamber of Commerce   1889
- NR Commerce House, Outer Circle Rd, LINCOLN, LN2 4HY.   (hq)
  01522 523333   fax 01522 546667
  email enquiries@lincs-chamber.co.uk
  http://www.lincs-chamber.co.uk
  Chief Exec: Simon Beardsley
- Br Boston, Gainsborough, Grantham, Lincoln, Sleaford, Spalding
- ○ *C
- < Brit Chams of Comm (BCC)
- M c 1,000 i, f & org

Lindsay Society for the History of Dentistry   1963
- ■ 14 Howard Rd, GREAT BOOKHAM, Surrey, KT23 4PW.   (hsp)
  http://www.bda.org.uk
  Hon Sec: Dr Brian Williams
- ▲ Un-incorporated Society
- ○ *L; to study all aspects of the history of dentistry - including oral diseases, education of dentists & other staff, economic effects in the development of dental treatments & history of leading personalities in the development of dental sciences
- ● Conf - Mtgs - ET - VE
- < Brit Dental Assn; Brit Soc for the History of Medicine
- > Henry Noble Dental Res Gp
- M 100 i, 4 f, UK / 30 i, o'seas
  (Sub: £22 i, £100 f, UK / £27 i, o'seas)
- ¶ Dental Historian (Jnl) - 3; ftm, £15 nm.

Linguistics Association of Great Britain   (LAGB)   1959
- NR c/o Dr David Willis, Selwyn College, Grange Rd, CAMBRIDGE, CB3 9DQ.   (hsb)
  http://www.lagb.org.uk
  Hon Sec: Dr David Willis
- ▲ Un-incorporated Society
- ○ *L; to promote the study of linguistics
- Gp C'ee for endangered languages; C'ee for linguistics in education
- ● Conf - Mtgs - ET - Res - LG
- M 600 i
- ¶ Jnl of Linguistics - 3.

Linking Environment & Farming   (LEAF)
- NR Stoneleigh Park, STONELEIGH, Warks, CV8 2LG.   (hq)
  024 7641 3911   fax 024 7641 3636
  http://www.leafuk.org
  Sec: Val Goldstraw
- ▲ Company Limited by Guarantee; Registered Charity
- ○ *F; to help famers & growers protect the environment
- ● Mtgs - Inf
- < Access to Farms Partnership
- M i, f & org

Linnean Society of London   1788
- NR Burlington House, Piccadilly, LONDON, W1J 0BF.   (hq)
  020 7434 4479   fax 020 7287 9364
  email info@linnean.org   http://www.linnean.org
  Exec Sec: Dr Ruth Temple
- ▲ Registered Charity
- ○ *L; the science of natural history in all its branches
- ● Conf - Mtgs - Lib
- M 1,700 i, UK / 800 i, o'seas
- ¶ The Linnean - 4; ftm, (internet; free nm).
  Biological Jnl.   Botanical Jnl.   Zoological Jnl.

Lipizzaner National Stud Book Association of Great Britain
- ■ Cilyblaidd Manor, Pencarreg, LLANYBYDDER, Carmarthenshire, SA40 9QL.   (hsb)
  0870 908 9080
  email info@lipizzanerhorse.com
  http://www.lipizzanerhorse.com
  Sec: L Moran
- ▲ Company Limited by Guarantee
- ○ *B; to register & verify the pure bred Lipizzaner in the UK
- ● Inf
- < Lipizzaner Intl Fedn (LIF); Brit Horse Soc
- M i

Lipizzaner Society of Great Britain (LSGB) 1982
■ Starrock Stud, Leopards' Lair, Homelands, Bish Mill,
    SOUTH MOLTON, Devon, EX36 4EH. (chmn/p)
    01769 551773
    email lsgb@lipizzaner.co.uk   http://www.lipizzaner.co.uk
    Chmn: Una Harley,   Hon Sec: Mary Kibblewhite
▲ Company Limited by Guarantee
○ *B; to register pure-bred & part-bred Lipizzaner horses
● Mtgs - ET - Comp - Inf - Lib - VE - LG - Issuing of EU equine
    passports -
< Intl Lipizzaner U; Brit Horse Soc (BHS); Spanish Riding School of
    Vienna
M 131 i
    (Sub: £20)
¶ NL - 2; ftm only.
    The Lipizzaner (published by J A Allen); £5.99.

Liquid Food Carton Manufacturers' Association
    since 2007 **Alliance for Beverage Cartons & the Environment**

Liquid Roofing & Waterproofing Association
    see **LWRA, the Liquid Roofing & Waterproofing Association**

Lisburn Chamber of Commerce 1961
NR 3a Bridge St, LISBURN, Co Antrim, BT28 1XZ. (hq)
    028 9266 6297   fax 028 9266 6297
    email lisburnchamber@btconnect.com
    Hon Sec: Ellen Hillen
▲ Un-incorporated Society
○ *C
● Conf - Mtgs - Inf - VE - LG
< NI Cham Comm & Ind
M 120 f
¶ News Sheet - 4; free.

List & Index Society (LIS) 1965
NR c/o The National Archives, Ruskin Avenue, Kew, RICHMOND,
    Surrey, TW9 4DU. (sec/b)
    020 8876 3444   fax 020 8878 8905
    email listandindexsociety@nationalarchives.gov.uk
    Hon Sec: B Pappalardo
▲ Un-incorporated Society
○ *L; to distribute unpublished Public Record Office search room
    lists & indexes
M 50 i, 50 org, UK / 25 i, 70 org, o'seas
¶ Lists & indexes:
    Standard series - 1;
    Special series - irreg; all prices on application.

Listed Property Owners Club (LPOC) 1994
■ Lower Dane, Hartlip, SITTINGBOURNE, Kent, ME9 7TE. (hsp)
    01795 844939   fax 01795 844862
    email info@lpoc.co.uk   http://www.lpoc.co.uk
    Managing Dir: Peter Anslow
▲ Company Limited by Guarantee
○ *G, *K; to keep listed building owners informed of their
    obligations, rights, privileges & responsibilities
● Conf - Exhib - Inf - LG
M 2,423 i, 229 f
¶ Listed Heritage - 6; ftm only.

Liszt Society 1951
NR 3 Offlands Court, MOULSFORD, Oxon, OX10 9EX.
    01491 651842
    email memsec@lisztsoc.org.uk   http://www.lisztsoc.org.uk
    Mem Sec: Jim Vincent
▲ Company Limited by Guarantee; Registered Charity
○ *D; to foster & promote interest in the music of Franz Liszt
● Res - Inf - Lib (Books, CDs, tapes) - Recitals - Talks -
    Masterclasses
M 190 i, UK / 80 i, o'seas
¶ Jnl - 1.   NL - 4.   Occasional piano scores.

Lithuanian Association UK Ltd   (Britanjos Lietuviai) 1947
NR Headley Park Club, Picketts Hill, BORDON, Hants,
    GU35 8TE. (hq)
▲ Company Limited by Guarantee
Br 12
○ *W; promotion of welfare, social & cultural activities for
    Lithuanians in Great Britain
Gp Lithuanian Youth Association
● Conf - Mtgs - Exhib - SG - Lib
< Lithuanian Wld Community
M c 800 i, 10 org
¶ Europos Lietuvis - 52.   Lynes (Youth NL) - 4.
✕ 2008 Lithuanian Association in Great Britain Ltd

Little Theatre Guild of Great Britain (LTG) 1946
NR Satley House, Satley, BISHOP AUCKLAND, Co Durham,
    DL13 4HU. (sp)
    01388 730042
    http://www.littletheatreguild.org
    Sec: Caroline Chapman
○ *D; encouragement of establishment & work of little theatres

Liverpool Chamber of Commerce (LCC) 1850
NR Number One Old Hall St, LIVERPOOL, L3 9HG. (hq)
    0151-227 1234   fax 0151-236 0121
    email chamber@liverpoolchamber.org.uk
    http://www.liverpoolchamber.org.uk
    Chief Exec: Jack Stopforth
▲ Community Interest Company Limited by Guarantee
Br 2; China
○ *C; represents, promotes & supports the business community of
    Merseyside
● Conf - Mtgs - ET - Exam - Res - Exhib - Comp - Stat - Expt - Inf
    - Lib - VE - LG
< Eurochambers; Brit Chams Comm; Chams Comm NW
M 50 i, 1,550 f
¶ Liverpool Chamber - 6; ftm, £3 nm.

Livestock Auctioneers Association (LAA) 1954
NR Cobblethwaite, Wreay, CARLISLE, Cumbria, CA4 0RZ. (hq)
    01697 475433   fax 01697 475423
    email chris.dodds@laa.co.uk   http://www.laa.co.uk
    Sec: Chris Dodds
▲ Un-incorporated Society
Br 13
○ *T; 'all matters pertaining to the sale by auction of cattle, sheep
    & pigs in England & Wales'
Gp Conditions of sale sub-c'ee; (Working parties as required)
● Mtgs - Stat - Inf - LG
< Association Européenne des Marchés aux Bestiaux (Brussels)
M 13 i (associates), 216 f
¶ NL - as required; m only.   Report - 1; ftm, postage nm.
    Directory of Markets in England, Wales & Scotland - 3 yrly; ftm,
    £25 nm.
    Conditions of sale - as required; ftm, £10 nm.

Livestock Traders Association of Great Britain Ltd (LTA) 1918
■ Coscote Farm, West Hagbourne, DIDCOTE, Oxon,
    OX11 0NP. (hsp)
    Hon Sec: Mrs J M Drewe
▲ Company Limited by Guarantee
○ *T; interests of livestock traders & cattle & sheep salesmen in
    the farming industry
● LG
M 35 i, 15 f

© CBD Research Ltd · Beckenham · BR3 5JS · Tel 020 8650 7745 · E-mail cbd@cbdresearch.com · www.cbdresearch.com

Living Streets: putting people first   1929
NR   Universal House (4th floor), 88-94 Wentworth St, LONDON,
      E1 7SA.   (hq)
      020 7377 4900
      email info@livingstreets.org.uk
      http://www.livingstreets.org.uk
      Chief Exec: Tony Armstrong
▲   Registered Charity
Br   Offices: Newcastle upon Tyne; Scotland
○   *K; to promote the interests & safety of people on foot
●   Conf - Mtgs - Res - LG
<   Intl Fedn of Pedestrians; Fedn of Eur Pedestrian Assns
M   c 1,200 i, 50 org
¶   Walk (Jnl) - 4; ftm.   AR; free.

Lizard Canary Association   (LCA)
NR   30 Glenorrin Close, Lambton, WASHINGTON, Tyne & Wear,
      NE38 0DZ.   (hsp)
      0191-416 4967
      http://www.lizardcanary.co.uk
      Sec: Dave Ross
○   *G

**Llanwenog Sheep Society   (Cymdeithas Defaid Llanwenog)
1957**
■   Preswylfa, Dihewyd, LAMPETER, Ceredigion, SA48 7PN.   (hsp)
      01570 471777
      email llanwenogsheep@hotmail.com
      http://www.llanwenog-sheep.co.uk
      Sec: Emily Addis
○   *B
●   Conf - Mtgs - Exhib - Comp - Lib - VE
<   Nat Sheep Assn
M   170 i
¶   Ybk;   NL;   LM;   AR; all ftm only.

Lleyn Sheep Society
NR   Gwyndy, Bryncroes, Sarn, PWLLHELI, Gwynedd, LL53 8ET.
      (hsp)
      01758 730366
      email office@lleynsheep.com   http://www.lleynsheep.com
      Sec: Mrs Gwenda Roberts
○   *B
<   Nat Sheep Assn
M   c 700 i

Lloyd's Market Association   (LMA)   2001
NR   Suite 358, 1 Lime St, LONDON, EC3M 7DQ.
      020 7327 3333   fax 020 7327 4443
      email lma@lmalloyds.com   http://www.lmalloyds.com
      Chief Exec: David Gittings
○   *N, *P; 'to promote the interests of the Society of Lloyds & to
      represent the interests of underwriters, managers & members
      of the Association'
Gp   4 underwriting committees: Aviation, Marine, Non-marine &
      Motor

Lloyd's Names Association
NR   Kenton House, Oxford St, MORETON in MARSH, Glos,
      GL56 0LA.

Loan Market Association   (LMA)
NR   10 Upper Bank St, LONDON, E14 5JJ.   (hq)
      020 7006 6007   fax 020 7006 3423
      email lma@cliffordchance.com
      http://www.lma.eu.com
      Exec Dir: Clare Dawson
▲   Company Limited by Guarantee
○   *T; 'embraces all aspects of the primary & secondary
      syndicated loan markets in Europe'
●   Conf - Mtgs - ET - Inf - LG (regulatory & fiscal issues) -
      Seminars - Provision of recommended standard
      documentation & secondary loan pricing data
<   Asia Pacific Loan Market Assn; Loan Syndications & Trading
      Assn Inc
M   77 f, 3 courtesy mems, UK / 122 f, 5 courtesy mems, o'seas
¶   LMA News - 2; free.

**Local Authorities Research & Intelligence Association
(LARIA)   1974**
■   1 Henderson Close, Great Sankey, WARRINGTON, Cheshire,
      WA5 3JJ.   (admin/p)
      01925 723539   fax 01925 721548
      email admin@laria.gov.uk   http://www.laria.gov.uk
      Hon Sec: Christine Collingwood,   Admin: Doris Besford
○   *P; to promote the role & practice of research within the field of
      local government; to provide a supporting network for those
      conducting or commissioning research
●   Conf - ET - Res - SG - LG
M   1,045 i, 271 local authorities
¶   Laria News - 3; ftm.
      Note: is a Registered Friendly Society.

Local Authority Caterers Association   (LACA)   1990
■   Bourne House, Horsell Park, WOKING, Surrey, GU21 4LY.
      (hq)
      01483 766777   fax 01483 751991
      email admin@laca.co.uk   http://www.laca.co.uk
      Chmn: Lynda Mitchell
▲   Company Limited by Guarantee
Br   9
○   *T; to promote professionalism in local authority catering
Gp   Representation on c'ees of relevant professional bodies
●   Conf - Mtgs - ET - Exhib - Comp - LG
M   700 i, 250 f
¶   NL - 4; ftm.   Reports & Hbk (incl LM) - 1; ftm.

Local Authority Civil Enforcement Forum   (LACEF)   2001
NR   Brighton & Hove City Council, Priory House, PO Box 2929,
      BRIGHTON, E Sussex, BN1 1PS.
      01273 291876   fax 01273 291881
      email barrie.minney@brighton-hove.gov.uk
      http://www.lacef.org.uk
      Chmn: Barrie Minney
○   *P; for those responsible for the enforcement of payment of
      debts & council tax

** Local Authority PVC-u Frame Advisory Group
      Organisation lost: see Introduction paragraph 3

*Local Authority Road Safety Officers' Association
since 30 April 2009* **Road Safety GB**

Local Government Association (LGA) 1997

NR Local Government House, Smith Sq, LONDON, SW1P 3HZ. (hq)
020 7664 3000 fax 020 7664 3030
email info@lga.gov.uk http://www.lga.gov.uk
Chief Exec: John Ransford
○ *P; 'to enable local authorities to speak with one voice & promote the cause for democratic local communities which are prosperous, safe, healthy & environmentally friendly'
Gp Sparsity Partnership for Authorities Delivering Rural Service
● Conf - Mtgs - Inf - Empl - LG
M 480 local authorities
¶ First - 52; ftm.

Local Government Technical Advisers Group (TAG) 1995

■ Bluewaters, Andurn, Down Thomas, PLYMOUTH, Devon, PL9 0AT. (hsb)
01752 863053 fax 01752 863778
email tag-1@rfconsultancy.co.uk
http://www.tagonline.co.uk
Nat Sec: Roy Fairclough
▲ Un-incorporated Society
Br 8 regions
○ *P; the provision of coordinated & comprehensive services to local & central government & its agencies in the management & operation of all areas of technical services - regeneration, environment, waste, transportation, coastal & fluvial management, climate change & operations
Gp Climate change; Coastal & fluvial management; Highways; Transportation; Waste
● Conf - Mtgs - ET - VE - LG
< Construction Ind Coun
M 200 i, 10 f, 100 local govt
¶ The Bulletin - 4/6; on website.

Local Population Studies Society (LPSS) 1973

NR 17A Romford Close, COLCHESTER, Essex, CO4 0AP. (hsp)
01206 870307
email ip[sa@herts.ac.uk
http://www.localpopulationstudies.org.uk
Contact: Dr Christine Jones
○ *G; studies local historical demography in England & Wales
● Conf - ET - Res - SG
M i & org
¶ Local Population Studies - 2.

Local Registration Services Association (LRSA) 2009

NR 1 Sylvan Court, Sylvan Way, Southfields Business Park, BASILDON, Essex, SS15 6TH. (asa)
0845 608500 fax 0845 608 9425
email natalieb@tsi.org.uk http://www.lrsa.org.uk
Chmn: Mark Rimmer
▲ Company Limited by Guarantee
○ *P; to assist & support service managers, enabling them to deliver efficient & effective registration services to their local communities, whilst continuing to develop service excellence & share best practice
● Conf - ET

Locomotive & Carriage Institution (Loco & Carr Inst) 1911

■ c/o Stuart Smith, First Great Western, 20 Clonmel Close, CAVERSHAM, Berks, RG4 5BF. (sb)
07887 998557
email smithstuart@btinternet.com
Gen Sec: Stuart Smith
▲ Un-incorporated Society
○ *L; the advancement of knowledge & information in all aspects of modern railway operation

Locomotive Club of Great Britain (LCGB) 1949

■ 58 Osprey Rd, BIGGLESWADE, Beds, SG18 8HE. (chmn/p)
01767 220271 fax 01767 220271
email p.crossman@ntlworld.com
http://www.lcgb.org.uk
Sec: P S Crossman
▲ Un-incorporated Society
Br 8
○ *G; railway history & operation & all other aspects
● Mtgs - Res - Exhib - SG - Lib - VE
M c 600 i, UK / c 200 i, o'seas
¶ Jnl - 10; free.

Locomotive 6201 'Princess Elizabeth' Society Ltd (PELS) 1963

■ PO Box 6201, MILLOM, Cumbria, LA18 4GE. (chmn/p)
01229 775215 fax 01229 775215
Chmn: Clive Mojonnier
▲ Company Limited by Guarantee
○ *G; to preserve & operate on British Rail main lines (passed for steam operation) the 'Princess Elizabeth' 6201. This locomotive was preserved because of its record non-stop runs between London-Glasgow-London, 16-17 November 1936 & was the forerunner of non-stop steam operation between the two cities; the locomotive is available for private charter
● AGM - Open days at the East Lancs Railway, Bury - Preservation of the engine
< Mainline Steam Locomotive Operators Ltd; Assn Rly Presvn Socs
M 160 i, UK / 6 i, o'seas
¶ NL - 4; ftm only.

Locus Association

■ c/o Harriet Crosthwaite, Luther Pendragon, Priory Court, Pilgrim St, LONDON, EC4V 6DR. (asa)
020 7618 9136
email harrietcrosthwaite@luther.co.uk
http://www.locusassociation.co.uk
Sec: Harriet Crosthwaite
○ *K, *T; to increase opportunities & reduce barriers to fair trade between the public & private sector, particularly in the use of PSI (public sector information)

London Anglers' Association (LAA) 1884

NR Izaak Walton House, 2A Hervey Park Rd, LONDON, E17 6LJ. (hq)
020 8520 7477 fax 020 8520 7477
email admin@londonanglers.net
http://www.londonanglers.net
Chmn/Sec: A E Hodges
▲ Un-incorporated Society
○ *S; to promote the sport of fair angling & to provide fishing facilities for members
● Comp
M 3,000 i
¶ AR - 1; free.

London Association of Recovery Operators (LARO)

NR 81 High St, Green Street Green, ORPINGTON, Kent, BR6 6BJ. (hq)
07000 781565
http://www.laro-online.co.uk
○ *T; to represent car recovery companies operating in the London area & within the M25
M i, f, org
(Sub: £350)

© CBD Research Ltd · Beckenham · BR3 5JS · Tel 020 8650 7745 · E-mail cbd@cbdresearch.com · www.cbdresearch.com

London Bullion Market Association   (LBMA)   1987
NR   13-14 Basinghall St, LONDON, EC2V 5BQ.   (hq)
         020 7796 3067   fax 020 7796 2112
         Chief Exec: Stewart Murray
▲   Company Limited by Guarantee; Registered Charity
○   *T; to promote the interests of the London (gold & silver) bullion
         market
●   Conf - ET - Stat - LG - Liaison with regulatory authority
M   63 f
¶   Alchemist (NL) - 4; free.
         Brochure; ftm, single copy free nm.

London Chamber of Commerce & Industry   (LCCI)   1881
■   33 Queen St, LONDON, EC4R 1AP.   (hq)
         020 7248 4444   fax 020 7489 0391
         email lc@londonchamber.co.uk
         http://www.londonchamber.co.uk
         Chief Exec: Colin Stanbridge
▲   Company Limited by Guarantee
Br   Docklands Business Club, East London Chamber of
         Commerce.
         See separate entries for Croydon Chamber of Commerce &
         Industry and Ealing Chamber of Commerce (inc
         Hammersmith & Fulham Chamber of Commerce)
○   *C
Gp   Defence & security; Property & construction; Women in business
         Asian Business Association
●   Conf - Mtgs - ET - Stat - Expt - Inf - Lib - LG - Networking -
         Seminars
<   Intl Chams Comm; Brit Chams Comm
M   3,000 f
¶   London Business Matters (Jnl) - 12; ftm.
         Directory of Members - 1; ftm, £155 nm.   AR & Accounts.

London Cornish Association   (LCA)   1898
■   26 Sharrow Vale, HIGH WYCOMBE, Bucks, HP12 3HB.   (hsp)
         01494 531703   fax 01494 531703
         http://www.londoncornish.co.uk
         Hon Sec: Dr Francis Dunstan
Br   19; Australia, Canada, N Zealand, South Africa, USA
○   *G; to encourage fellowship & social activities among Cornish
         people in London & the Home Counties, & to provide a link
         to Cornish associations worldwide.
Gp   Family History; 'Old Cornwall'
●   Conf - Mtgs - Research - SG - Lib - VE
<   19 in UK and Cornish Associations in Australia, Canada, N
         Zealand, S Africa, & USA
M   230 i, UK / 50 i, o'seas
¶   NL - 6; ftm.   Ybk (incl LM).

London Councils   (ALG)   1995
■   59¹/₂ Southwark St, LONDON, SE1 0AL.   (hq)
         020 7934 9999
         email info@londoncouncils.gov.uk
         http://www.londoncouncils.gov.uk
         Contact: Pauline McMahon
▲   Company Limited by Guarantee
○   *N; consultation with government & the European Union over
         matters relating to local authorities & the services provided by
         them
✕   2006 Association of London Government

London Cycling Campaign
         since 2011 **London Cyclists**

London Cyclists   (LCC)   1978
NR   2 Newhams Row, LONDON, SE1 3UZ.   (hq)
         020 7234 9310
         email office@lcc.org.uk   http://www.lcc.org.uk
         Chief Exec: Ashok Sinha
Br   33
○   *K
●   Conf - Mtgs - Exhib - Inf - Lib - LG
M   c 9,000 i
¶   London Cyclist - 6.
✕   2100 (1 May) London Cycling Campaign

London District Surveyors Association   (LDSA)   1845
NR   c/o John Jackson, Building Control, Royal Borough of
         Kensington & Chelsea, Hornton St, LONDON, W8 7NX.
         (hsb)
         020 7361 3822
         email john.jackson@rbkc.gov.uk
         http://www.londonbuildingcontrol.org.uk
         Hon Sec: Lola Majekodunmi
Br   34
○   *P; 'uniformity of interpretation & operation of the Building
         Regulations in London'
Gp   C'ees: Education & training, Electrical & mechanical, Fire safety
         & means of escape, LANTAC, Licensing, Management &
         legislation, Publications & seminars, Safety at sports grounds,
         Technical & foundations
●   Mtgs - ET - SG - Inf - LG
<   District Surveyors Assn
M   33 i

London First   1991
NR   3 Whitcomb St, LONDON, WC2H 7HA.   (hq)
         020 7665 1500   fax 020 7665 1501
         http://www.london-first.co.uk
         Chief Exec: Baroness Jo Valentine
○   *K; to make London the best city in the world in which to do
         business
M   f

London Fish Merchants (Billingsgate) Ltd   (LFMA)   1923
NR   Office 36, Billingsgate Market, Trafalgar Way, LONDON,
         E14 5ST.   (hq)
         020 7515 2655   fax 020 7538 2618
○   *T; to promote Billingsgate Market; to help merchants in any
         sphere of their business
M   f
¶   AR.

London Fish & Poultry Retailers Association
         a branch association of the **National Federation of Fishmongers**

London Food Link
         a campaign group of **Sustain**

London General Shipowners' Society
         incorporated in the **London Shipowners' & River Users' Society**

London Harness Horse Parade Society   1885
■   Oakley Farm, Merstham, REDHILL, Surrey, RH1 3QN.   (hq)
         01737 646132   fax 01737 645121
         http://www.lhhp.co.uk
         Sec: Mrs J E Shearman
▲   Company Limited by Guarantee; Registered Charity
○   *V; improvement of general condition & treatment of horses &
         ponies employed for transport
●   Annual parade on Easter Monday at the South of England
         Centre, Sussex.

London Investment Banking Association
         merged with SIFA to form **Association for Financial Markets in
         Europe**

London Library 1841

■ 14 St James's Sq, LONDON, SW1Y 4LG.   (hq)
  020 7930 7705   fax 020 7766 4766
  email membership@londonlibrary.co.uk
  http://www.londonlibrary.co.uk
  Librarian: Inez T P A Lynn
○ *G; a research library of books in the humanities, with lending service to subscribing members
● Res - Lib
M 8,200 i, 250 org
¶ AR; ftm only.

London Mathematical Society (LMS) 1865

■ De Morgan House, 57-58 Russell Sq, LONDON, WC1B 4HS. (hq)
  020 7927 0800
  email lms@lms.ac.uk   http://www.lms.ac.uk
  Gen Sec: J M E Hyland
▲ Registered Charity
○ *L; to promote & extend mathematical knowledge
● Conf - Mtgs - Stat - Inf - Lib - LG
< 19 mathematical societies in other countries
M c 1,700 i, UK / c 800 i, o'seas
  (Subs: £49.00)
¶ Proceedings - 6; £97 m.   Jnl - 6; £97 m.
  Bulletin - 6; £51 m.
  NL - 11;   Hbk - 2 yrly;   AR; all ftm only.

London Mayors' Association (LMA) 1901

■ 7 Highview Court, 57A Augustus Rd, LONDON, SW19 6LU. (hsp)
  020 8788 9656
  email helenmwatson@tscali.co.uk
  http://www.londonmayors.org.uk
  Hon Sec: Mrs Helen Watson
▲ Company Limited by Guarantee
○ *P; to represent the Mayors, Lord Mayors & former Mayors & Lord Mayors of the London Boroughs
● Mtgs - VE
M 600 i
¶ NL - 4; free.
  Mayoral Directory - 1; £55 (for 7).

London Medieval Society (LMS) 1945

■ Dept of History, Queen Mary University of London, Mile End Rd, LONDON, E1 4NS.   (pres/b)
  020 7882 7897
  email m.e.rubin@qmul.ac.uk   http://www.the-lms.org
  Pres: Prof Miri Rubin
▲ Un-incorporated Society
○ *L; promotion of research & study of the culture & civilisation of the Middle Ages
● Conf - Mtgs - Inf - Research encouragement
< Inst of Romance Studies (University of London)
M 30 i
  (Sub: £20)

London & Middlesex Archaeological Society (LAMAS) 1855

■ c/o Museum of London, London Wall, LONDON, EC2Y 5HN.   (regd address)
  020 7814 5734   fax 020 7600 1058
  http://www.lamas.org.uk
  Hon Sec: Jackie Keily
▲ Registered Charity
○ *L; to promote the study of the local history & archaeology of the metropolitan area of London
Gp C'ees: Archaeological research, Historic buildings, Local history
● Conf - Mtgs - Res - Inf - Lib - LG
M 651 i
¶ [Visit website for full information]

London Money Market Association (LMMA) 1998

NR c/o Investec Bank (UK) Ltd, 2 Gresham St, LONDON, EC2V 7QP.   (hsb)
  020 7597 4492
  Sec: Shilla Pindoria
○ *T; to monitor the liquidity of the Sterling Money Market; to consider matters of policy interest to members; to promote good relations with the Treasury & the Bank of England
● Mtgs - Inf
M c 20 f

London Motor Cab Proprietors' Association (LMCPA) 1909

■ c/o Richmond Road Cab Centre, 195 Richmond Rd, LONDON, E8 3NJ.   (hq)
  020 7275 7589
  Deputy Chmn: Eddie Crossley
▲ Un-incorporated Society
○ *T; taxi fleet proprietors operating within the licensed London taxi trade
● Mtgs - Stat - VE - LG
< London Taxi Bd
M 50 f

London Natural History Society (LNHS) 1858

■ 381B Whitton Avenue East, GREENFORD, UB6 0JU.   (hsp)
  020 8426 6621
  email davidhowdon@virgin.net   http://www.lnhs.org.uk
  Hon Sec: David Howdon
▲ Registered Charity
○ *L, *Q; conservation & study of natural history in the London area; recording of species & habitats found there
Gp Botany; Ecology; Entomology; Ornithology
● Conf - Mtgs - Res - Lib - VE
M 1,000 i, 20 org
  (Sub: £20)
¶ The London Naturalist - 1; ftm, £8 nm.
  London Bird Report - 1; ftm, £8 nm.
  Ornithological Bulletin - 6;   NL - 6;   both m only.

London Private Hire Car Association Ltd 1994

■ 56 Austins Mead, Bovingdon, HEMEL HEMPSTEAD, Herts, HP3 0LH.   (hq)
  07956 329288   fax 01442 380607
  http://www.lphca.co.uk
  Chmn: Steve Wright
○ *T; for private hire, chauffeur & mini cab companies

London Record Society 1964

■ PO Box 691, EXETER, Devon, EX1 9PH.   (hsb)
  email londonrecordsoc@btinternet.com
  http://www.londonrecordsociety.org.uk
▲ Registered Charity
○ *L; publication of an annual series of carefully edited transcripts, abstracts & lists of original sources for the history of London; stimulation of public interest in the archives of London
● Mtgs
M 126 i, 72 f & org, UK / 21 i, 85 f & org, o'seas
¶ Annual volume; £18 m, £23 instns, UK / £20 m, £25 instns, o'seas

London Rice Brokers' Association (LRBA) 1869

NR 4 St Georges Yard, FARNHAM, Surrey, GU9 7LW.   (hq)
  01252 727677
  email lrba@lrba.co.uk   http://www.lrba.co.uk
  Sec: Michael French
○ *T; establishment of contract forms on which rice business is transacted
M i & f
¶ Monthly Rice Circular - 12.

© CBD Research Ltd · Beckenham · BR3 5JS · Tel 020 8650 7745 · E-mail cbd@cbdresearch.com · www.cbdresearch.com

London Shipowners' & River Users' Society (incorporating the London General Shipowners' Society)   1811
- ■ Carthusian Court, 12 Carthusian St, LONDON, EC1M 6EZ. (hq)
  020 7417 2830   fax 020 7600 1534
  Sec: D W Chard
- ○ *T; representative body protecting & promoting the interests of London river users
- M f

London Society   1912
- ■ Mortimer Wheeler House, 46 Eagle Wharf Rd, LONDON, N1 7ED.   (hq)
  020 7253 9400
  email info@londonsociety.org.uk
  http://www.londonsociety.org.uk
  Hon Sec: Patrick Gaskell-Taylor
- ▲ Registered Charity
- ○ *K; is active in reviewing & commenting on the planning & development of London, as well as conservation; to stimulate appreciation of London; to encourage excellence in planning & development & to preserve its amenities & the best of its buildings; it reviews planning proposals & considers planning applications
- ● Res - Inf - Lib - VE
- M 812 i, 10 f, 28 org, UK & o'seas
  (Sub: £6 i & £9 f UK, £12 i & f o'seas)
- ¶ Jnl - 2; ftm only.

London Stock Exchange plc   1676
- NR 10 Paternoster Square, LONDON, EC4M 7LS.   (hq)
  020 7797 1000
  http://www.londonstockexchange.com
  Chief Exec: Mrs Clara Furse
- ○ *P; to provide a central market in securities
- M f

London Subterranean Survey Association   (LSSA)   1968
- ■ 98 Cambridge Gardens, LONDON, W10 6HS.   (hsp)
  020 8968 1360
  email wolstan-dixie@hotmail.co.uk
  Hon Sec: Roger Morgan
- ▲ Un-incorporated Society
- ○ *L; to promote the discovery & recording of natural & man-made features of subterranean London; to promote the utilisation of subterranean space & to minimise its conflict with surface developments
- ● Res - Inf - Lib - PL - VE
- < Subterranea Britannica
- M 20 i, 1 org

London Swing Dance Society   (LSDS)   1986
- ■ 22 Bessingby Rd, RUISLIP, Middx, HA4 9BX.   (hq)
  01895 613703
  email mail@swingdanceuk.com
  http://www.swingdanceuk.com
  Dir & Founder: Simon Selmon
- ▲ Company Limited by Guarantee
- ○ *D, *G; to support & promote swing dance events, classes & performances
- ● Mtgs - Exhib - Comp
- M c 400 i

London Topographical Society   (LTS)   1880
- ■ 7 Linden Avenue, DORCHESTER, Dorset, DT1 1EJ.   (hsp)
  email patfrazer@yahoo.co.uk   http://www.topsoc.org
  Hon Sec: Patrick Frazer
- ▲ Registered Charity
- ○ *L, *Q; publication of facsimiles of scarce printed or manuscript maps & views of London; research on these & other topographical subjects
- ● Res - Publication
- M c 1,100 i & f
- ¶ London Topographical Record (Jnl) - 5 yrly.   NL - 2.

London Underground Railway Society   (LURS)   1961
- ■ 54 Brinkley Rd, WORCESTER PARK, Surrey, KT4 8JF.   (sp)
  020 8330 1855
  http://www.lurs.org.uk
  Sec: Eric Felton
- ▲ Un-incorporated Society
- ○ *G; study of the railways of London Transport, its predecessors & successors & other underground railways in London
- Gp Modelling; Visits
- ● Mtgs - Inf - VE
- M c 900 i, UK / 50 i, o'seas
- ¶ Underground News - 12; ftm (on sale at the London Transport Museum).

London Vintage Taxi Association   (LVTA)   1978
- NR 51 Ferndale Crescent, Cowley, UXBRIDGE, Middx, UB8 2AY.   (mem sec)
  http://www.lvta.co.uk
  Contact: Mem Sec
- ○ *G; for collectors & enthusiasts
- ● Mtgs - Inf - Archive - Provision of vintage taxis for special events & films, TV etc
- ¶ Magazine - 6; ftm.

London Welsh Association   (LWA)   1920
- ■ 157-163 Gray's Inn Rd, LONDON, WC1X 8UE.   (hq)
  020 7837 3722   fax 020 7837 6268
  email administrator@lwcentre.demon.co.uk
  http://www.londonwelsh.org
  Hon Sec: Olwen Evans,   Admin: Huw Jackson
- ▲ Registered Charity
- ○ *D, *E; to promote Welsh culture & language
- Gp Gwalia Choir; London Welsh Chorale; London Welsh Male Voice Choir
- ● Mtgs - ET - Comp
- M 1,500 i
  (Sub: £55)
- ¶ Cymry Llundain - London Welshman - 4; ftm, £2 nm.

Londonderry Chamber of Commerce   1885
- ■ The Old Fire Station, 1a Hawkin St, LONDONDERRY, BT48 6RD.   (hq)
  028 7126 2379   fax 028 7128 6789
  email info@londonderrychamber.co.uk
  http://www.londonderrychamber.co.uk
  Chief Exec: Sinead McLaughlin
- ▲ Company Limited by Guarantee
- ○ *C; the business representation body to drive & develop economic development in the Northwest region; areas of interest - tourism, infrastructure, skills business development & information
- Gp Business Information & Guidance Service; NWCCI - Cross Border Lobby Gp
- ● Conf - Mtgs - ET - Stat - Expt - Inf - LG
- < Cham of Comm Ireland
- M 310 f
  (Sub: £90-£713.79 according to employees)
- ¶ NL - 4;   Ybk - 1;   AR - 1; all free.

Lone Twin Network   (LTN)   1989
- ■ 54 Ventnor Avenue, Hodge Hill, BIRMINGHAM, W Midlands, B36 8EF.   (mail/address)
  Chmn: Jill Deeley
- ○ *W; an informal, unfunded network for people whose twin has died
- ● Conf - Inf
- M i
  (Sub: £20 i)
- ¶ Spring Newssheet 0 1;   Autumn NL - 1;   LM ; ftm only.

Long-term Conditions Alliance
  since 2009 **National Voices**

Long Distance Walkers Association Ltd   (LDWA)   1972
- ■ 35 Gardenia Drive, WOKING, Surrey, GU24 9XG.   (hsp)
  email secretary@ldwa.org.uk   http://www.ldwa.org.uk
  Hon Sec: Fiona Cameron
- ▲ Company Limited by Guarantee
- Br 40
- ○ *G; furthering the interests of people who enjoy long distance walking
- ● Mtgs - Challenge & social walks, long distance paths
- < Ramblers Assn
- M 6,500 i
- ¶ Strider - 3; ftm only.
  Database of Long Distance Paths (on website).

Longhorn Cattle Society   1878
- ■ 3 Eastgate, Stoneleigh Park, STONELEIGH, Warks, CV8 2LG. (hq)
  0845 017 1027
  email secretary@longhorncattlesociety.com
  http://www.longhorncattlesociety.com
  Sec: Debbie Dann
- ▲ Registered Charity
- ○ *B; registration of pedigree longhorn cattle & their promotion, improvement & marketing
- ● Conf - Mtgs - ET - Exhib - Comp - SG - Expt - Inf - PL - VE
- < Nat Beef Assn (NBA); Rare Breeds Survival Trust (RBST)
- M 510 i, UK / 10 i, o'seas
- ¶ Jnl - 1;   NL - 6;   List of A1 Bulls - 2 yrly;   Rules;   AGM Report; all ftm.
  Herd Book - 1; ftm, £3 nm.

Lonk Sheep Breeders Association   (LSBA)   1905
- NR Park House Farm, Elslack, SKIPTON, N Yorks, BD23 3AT.   (hsp)
  01282 842423
  email beckertonc@aol.com   http://www.lonk-sheep.org
  Hon Sec: Christine Scrivin
- ▲ Registered Charity
- ○ *B
- ● Mtgs - Exhib - Shows & sales
- < Nat Sheep Assn
- M 78 i
- ¶ Flock Book - irreg.

LOOK: National Federation of Families with Visually Impaired Children   (LOOK)   1991
- ■ Queen Alexandra College, 49 Court Oak Rd, Harborne, BIRMINGHAM, B17 9TG.   (hq)
  0121-428 5038   fax 0121-428 5038
  http://www.look-uk.org
  Inf Officer: Jane Benham
- ▲ Registered Charity
- ○ *W; the national federation of families with visually impaired children; to support parents &/or carers of children with visual problems
- ● ET - Inf - Lib - Welfare support - Linking families with similar disabilities
- M [not stated]
- ¶ NL - 4; ftm.

Lotteries Council   1979
- NR 42 Kynaston Rd, SHREWSBURY, Shropshire, SY1 3JN. (mail/address)
  http://www.lotteriescouncil.org.uk
  Exec Officer: Tina Sandford
- ○ *T; for any person or organisation who is engaged in activities connected with the promotion of lawful lotteries
- ● Conf - Mtgs - Inf - LG
- M c 150 i, f & org
- ¶ Lottery Magazine - 4.   The Acts Combined.

Low Incomes Tax Reform Group   (LITRG)   1998
- ■ Chartered Institute of Taxation, Artillery House (1st floor), 11-19 Artillery Row, LONDON, SW1P 1RT.   (hq)
  http://www.litrg.org.uk
  Chmn: John Andrews
- ▲ Registered Charity
- ○ *K; the tax problems of those on low incomes
- ● ET - Res - LG
  Helpline (TaxHelp for Older People): 0845 601 3321
- M 20 i
- ¶ Older People on Low Incomes:
  The case for a friendlier tax system.
  The taxman's response; both irreg.

Lowe Syndrome Association (UK Contact Group)   (LSA)   1983
- ■ 29 Gleneagles Drive, Penwortham, PRESTON, Lancs, PR1 0JT.   (hsp)
  01772 745070
  email info@lowesyndrome.org
  http://www.lowesyndrome.org
  UK Contact Family: Mr David & Mrs Julie Oliver
- ▲ Un-incorporated Society
- ○ *W; to provide mutual support & information among families; Lowe Syndrome is a rare genetic condition which only affects boys, causing physical & mental handicaps & medical problems
- ● Conf - Res - Inf
- < Contact-a-Family
- M 15 i, UK / 350 i, o'seas
- ¶ NL - 3;   Family Directory - 1; both ftm only.

Loyal Company of Town Criers   (LCTC)   1994
- ■ 29 Lichfield Court, STAFFORD, Staffs, ST17 4UE.   (v/chmn)
  01785 241470
  email peter@towncrier.co   http://www.towncrier.co/999.html
  Vice-Chmn: Peter Taunton
- ○ *G; to promote & encourage the appointment of town criers; to maintain the standards & conduct of their ancient office
- ● Conf - Mtgs - Res - Exhib - Comp - Expt - Inf - VE
- < Pacific Northwest Company of Town Criers (Canada); Public Criers of Victoria (Canada)
- M 100 i, UK / 10 i, o'seas
  (Sub: £26 UK / £20 o'seas)
- ¶ The Scroll (NL) - 2; ftm only.

LRWA, the Liquid Roofing & Waterproofing Association (LRWA)   1979
- NR Roofing House, 31 Worship St, LONDON, EC2A 2DY.
  020 7448 3859
  email info@lrwa.org.uk   http://www.lrwa.org.uk
- ▲ Company Limited by Guarantee
- ○ *T; for manufacturers of liquid applied waterproofing systems
- Gp Balconies & walkways; Bridge decks; Car park decks; Roofing
- ● Mtgs - ET - Inf - Drafting industry standards & technical guidance notes
- M 21 f
- ¶ LM.
- ✕ 2010 European Liquid Waterproofing Association

Luing Cattle Society Ltd   1965
- ■ Wester Drumlochy, Lornty, BLAIRGOWRIE, Perthshire, PH10 6TD.   (sp)
  01250 873882
  email secretary@luingcattlesociety.co.uk
  http://www.luingcattlesociety.co.uk
  Sec: Johnny Mackey
- ▲ Registered Charity
- ○ *B; a native beef-breed from the Island of Luing off the west coast of Scotland
- ● Mtgs - Comp - Stat - Inf - VE
- < National Beef Assn
- M 320 i, 6 f, UK / 15 i, o'seas
- ¶ The Luing Jnl - 1;   Luing News - 3; both free.
  AR; ftm only.

© CBD Research Ltd · Beckenham · BR3 5JS · Tel 020 8650 7745 · E-mail cbd@cbdresearch.com · www.cbdresearch.com

Lupus UK   1990
NR St James House, Eastern Rd, ROMFORD, Essex, RM1 3NH.
       (hq)
       01708 731251   fax 01708 731252
       email headoffice@lupusuk.org.uk
       http://www.lupusuk.org.uk
       Dir: Chris Maker
▲ Registered Charity
Br 30 regional gps
○ *W; to support those who suffer with the disease Systemic Lupus
       Erythematosus; fundraising for research & welfare support;
       advice for members & those seeking diagnosis
● Conf - Mtgs - Res
< Eur Lupus Fedn; Long Term Medical Conditions Alliance; Brit
       League Against Rheumatism; Brit Assn of Dermatologists
M 7,500 i, UK / 100 i, o'seas
¶ Factsheets; free.   Publications list available.

Lusitano Breed Society of Great Britain   (LBSGB)   1984
NR Carreg Dressage, Abercegir, MACHYNLLETH, Powys,
       SY20 8NW.   (hsp)
       01650 511800
       http://www.lusobreedsociety.co.uk
▲ Company Limited by Guarantee
○ *B; promotion & registration of the Lusitano (Portuguese) horse
       in the UK
Gp Classical riding; Dressage; Training
● ET - Comp - Inf
< Associação Portuguesa de Craidores do Cavalo Puro Sangue
       Lusitano (Lisbon)
M 250 i, UK / 10 i, o'seas
¶ Luso News - 3; ftm, £3.50 each nm.   NL - 3/4.

Lute Society   1956
■ Southside Cottage, Brook Hill, Albury, GUILDFORD, Surrey,
       GU5 9DJ.   (hsp/b)
       01483 202159   fax 01483 203088
       email lutesoc@aol.com   http://www.lutesoc.co.uk
       Sec: Christopher Goodwin
▲ Un-incorporated Society
○ *D; to spread information on the lute, other related instruments
       & their music
● Mtgs - Res - Comp - Inf - PL - Publication of music, working
       drawings of instruments
M 350 i, 10 libraries, UK / 400 i, 50 libraries, o'seas
¶ The Lute (Jnl) - 1; with Lute News - 4; £33 (subscription only).
       Catalogue available of booklets & music.

Lutheran Council of Great Britain   (LC)   1955
NR 30 Thanet St, LONDON, WC1H 9QH.   (hq)
       020 7554 2900   fax 020 7383 3081
       http://www.lutheran.org.uk
       Gen Sec: Rev Thomas Bruch
○ *R
M 25,000 i
¶ The Lutheran Link - 3.

Lutyens Trust   1985
■ Goddards, Abinger Common, DORKING, Surrey, RH5 6JH.
       (hq)
       01306 730487
       http://www.lutyenstrust.org.uk
       Chmn: Martin Lutyens
▲ Registered Charity
○ *A; to protect the spirit & substance of the work of the architect
       Sir Edwin Lutyens
¶ NL - 3; ftm only.
       Guidebook to Goddards (the Trust's house designed by Sir
       Edwin Lutyens)

Lymphoedema Support Network   (LSN)
■ St Luke's Crypt, Sydney St, London, SW3 6NH.
       020 7351 0990   fax 020 7349 9809
       http://www.lymphoedema.org/lsn/
○ *W

Lymphoma Association   1986
NR PO Box 386, AYLESBURY, Bucks, HP20 2GA.   (hq)
       01296 619400   fax 01296 619414
       email information@lymphoma.org.uk
       http://www.lymphoma.org.uk
       Chief Exec: Melanie Burfitt
▲ Registered Charity
○ *W; to provide information & emotional support to anyone with
       Lymphatic cancer, their families, carers & friends
Gp Hodgkin lymphoma; Non-Hodgkin's lymphoma
● Conf - Exhib - Inf - Lib
       Helpline: 0808 808 5555; www.lifesite.info (for young adults)
M 2,125 i
¶ Lymphoma NL - 4;
       Lymphoma Fundraising News - 4; both ftm only.
       Booklets (designed to help patients to cope with their
           illness & treatments):
       Lymphomas (a general booklet for Hodgkin); £2.
       Low Grade Hodgkin Lymphomas; £2.
           (both - £25 for 15 copies).
       Hodgkin Lymphoma; £3 (£25 for 10 copies).
       Videos:
       Hodgkin lymphoma & its treatments; £10.
       Understanding non-Hodgkin lymphoma; £10.
       Publications list available.

Mac Technology Association
▲ Company Limited by Guarantee
in 2009 merged with the Professional Computing Association to form the Technology Channels Association, which later merged with CompTIA, an association of the USA, and is therefore outside the scope of this directory

Macclesfield Chamber of Commerce & Enterprise (MCCE) 1994
NR Churchill Chambers, Churchill Way, MACCLESFIELD, Cheshire, SK11 6AS. (hq)
01625 665940   fax 01625 665941
email info@macclesfieldchamber.co.uk
http://www.macclesfieldchamber.co.uk
Chief Exec: John Lamond
▲ Company Limited by Guarantee
○ *C
● Mtgs - Inf - LG
< Brit Chams Comm; Chams Comm NW
M 500 f
¶ Chamberlink (NL) - 6.   Directory - 1.

Macedonian Society of Great Britain 1989
NR The Hellenic Centre, 16-18 Paddington St, LONDON, W1U 5AS. (regd/office)
020 7487 5060   fax 020 7486 4254
http://www.macedonia.org.uk
○ *G; for the further education of the public in aspects of Macedonian culture, art, language & life

Machinery Ring Association of England and Wales (MRA)
NR Cadwyn Cymru Wales Link (Unit K), Henfaes Lane, Welshpool, POWYS, ST21 7BE.
01938 555600   fax 01938 555700
email gilly@walesmr.com
http://www.machineryrings.org.uk
Sec: Gill Wood
○ *F; operating in England & Wales the cooperatives act as brokers so that intensive plant & machinery is used to best economic advantage

Machinery Users' Association (Inc) (MUA) 1887
NR Warlies Park House, Horseshoe Hill, UPSHIRE, Essex, EN9 3SL. (hq)
0844 322 1200
▲ Company Limited by Guarantee
○ *P; representations to government on property rating & valuation matters
M 5 i, 60 f
¶ NL - 4; ftm only.

Macrobiotic Association of Great Britain (MBA) 1996
NR 123 Mashiters Walk, ROMFORD, Essex, RM1 4BU. (chmn)
email maria@macrobiotics.org.uk
http://www.macrobiotics.org.uk
Chmn: Maria Serrano
○ *G

Macular Disease Society (MDS) 1987
■ PO Box 1870, ANDOVER, Hants, SP10 9AD.   (hq)
01264 350551   fax 01264 350558
email info@maculardisease.org
http://www.maculardisease.org
Chief Exec: Tom Bremridge
▲ Company Limited by Guarantee; Registered Charity
○ *W; to provide information, help, support & practical advice to people with Macular Disease (loss of central vision due to scarring of the retina - the most common cause of registrable blindness in the UK), health professionals & the general public
● Conf - Mtgs - Res - Exhib - LG
Helpline: 0845 241 2041
< AMD Alliance Intl
M 17,500 i in 173 gps
¶ Side View (NL) - 4;   Digest (Jnl) - 1; both ftm only.
[subscription: i (£15 UK / £30 o'seas), professionals (eyehealth) £50-£100.]

Maga, the Cornish Language Partnership
■ Cornwall Council, Dalvenie House, County Hall, TRURO, TR1 3AY.
01872 323465
email jlowe@cornwall.gov.uk
http://www.magakernow.org.uk
Devt Mgr: Jenefer Lowe
○ *G; 'includes language organisations, local authorities & a number of other organisations who have come together with the aim of promoting Cornish & developing it further in Cornish life'

Magazines Ireland
IRL 25 Denzille Lane, DUBLIN 2, Republic of Irelnad.
353 (1) 667 5579
email grace@magazinesireland.ie
http://www.magazinesireland.ie
Chief Exec: Grace Aungier
○ *T; for publishers of magazines
✕ c 2010 Periodicals Publishers Association Ireland

The Magic Circle 1905
NR Centre for the Magic Arts, 12 Stephenson Way, LONDON, NW1 2HD.   (hq)
020 7387 2222
email enquiries@themagiccircle.co.uk
http://www.themagiccircle.co.uk
Pres: Jack Delvin
○ *D; to promote & advance the art of magic
● Mtgs - ET - Exam - Res - Comp - Exhib - Lib
M 1,500 i
¶ The Magic Circular - 12; ftm only.

Magic Lantern Society 1976
■ South Park, Galphay Rd, Kirkby Malzeard, RIPON, N Yorks, HG4 3RX.   (hsp)
email lmh.smith@magiclanternsocy.demon.co.uk
http://www.magiclantern.org.uk
Hon Sec: L M H Smith
▲ Un-incorporated Society
○ *G
● Conf - Mtgs - Res - Exhib - Inf - Lib
< Magic Lantern Soc US & Canada
M 260 i, 10 f, UK / 120 i, o'seas
¶ Jnl;   NL; both ftm.

© CBD Research Ltd · Beckenham · BR3 5JS · Tel 020 8650 7745 · E-mail cbd@cbdresearch.com · www.cbdresearch.com

Magistrates' Association 1920
NR 28 Fitzroy Sq, LONDON, W1T 6DD. (hq)
      020 7387 2353   fax 020 7383 4020
      email secretariat@magistrates-association.org.uk
      http://www.magistrates-association.org.uk
▲ Registered Charity (incorporated by Royal Charter)
Br 60
○ *P; supports magistrates in their duties; contributes towards
      their training
● Conf - Mtgs - ET - Inf - LG
M 28,500 i

Maidenhead & District Chamber of Commerce   1905
■ c/o 52 Queen St, MAIDENHEAD, Berks, SL6 1HY.
      (mail/address)
      01628 670573   fax 01628 670573
      email admin@maidenhead.org.uk
      http://www.maidenhead.org.uk
      Sec: Lynda Morten
▲ Un-incorporated Society
○ *C
M 400 i & f

** Mail Competition Forum
      Organisation lost: see Introduction paragraph 3

Mail Consolidators Association   (MCA)
NR 4 Kingsmill Business Park, Chapel Mill Rd, KINGSTON-upon-
      THAMES, Surrey, KT1 3GZ.   (chmn/b)
      020 8439 1177   fax 020 8439 1144
      email nst@imxuk.co.uk   http://www.themca.org.uk
      Chmn: Nicholas Street
○ *T; for consolidators of international mail
● Mtgs
M 25 f

Mail Order Traders' Association of Great Britain
      ceased December 2009

Mail Users' Association Ltd   (MUA)   1975
NR 70 Main Rd, EMSWORTH, Hants, PO10 8AX.   (hsb)
      01243 370840   fax 01243 370840
      http://www.mailusers.co.uk
      Sec: Jeremy Partridge
○ *T; to work on behalf of its members for improvements in the
      postal services

Maize Growers Association   (MGA)   1988
NR Town Barton Farm, Sandford, CREDITON, Devon, EX17 4LS.
      (hq)
      01363 775040
      http://www.maizegrowersassociation.co.uk
      Admin: June Howard
▲ Company Limited by Guarantee
○ *F; a farmer managed group providing technology to maximise
      the profitability of growing forage crops, particularly maize
● Conf - Res - Comp - Inf - VE
M c 900 i & f
¶ MGA Times - 12;   Maize Grower - 2;
      Technical Notes - agronomy / ruminant - 12; all ftm only.

Maize Maze Association   (MMA)   2009
NR [communication by e-mail only]
      email info@maize-maize.com
      http://www.maize-maize.com
○ *P; to help maize maze operators grow better mazes & improve
      the maize maze experience for all visitors
● Conf
M 21 f

Major Contractors Group
      part of the **UK Contractors Group**

Major Projects Association   (MPA)   1982
NR Egrove Park, Kennington, OXFORD, OX1 5NY.   (hq)
      01865 422581   fax 01865 326068
      http://www.majorprojects.org
○ *L, *P; to explore specific, mainly industrial, projects
M c 70 f

Makers Guild in Wales   1984
NR Craft in the Bay, The Flourish, Lloyd George Ave, CARDIFF,
      CF10 4QH.   (hq)
      029 2048 4611   fax 029 2049 1136
      email admin@makersguildinwales.org.uk
      http://www.makersguildinwales.org.uk
▲ Company Limited by Guarantee; Registered Charity
○ *A, *P; to bring together & promote the best Welsh craftsmen
● Exhib
M 71 i
      The Guild owns & runs the 'Craft in the Bay' gallery in Cardiff.

Making Music, the National Federation of Music Societies   1935
NR 2-4 Great Eastern St, LONDON, EC2A 3NW.   (hq)
      0870 903 3780   fax 0870 903 3785
      email info@makingmusic.org.uk
      http://www.makingmusic.org.uk
      Chief Exec: Robin M Osterley
▲ Company Limited by Guarantee; Registered Charity
Br 13
○ *D; to represent & assist the UK's voluntary music sector
Gp Choirs; Music clubs; Orchestras
● Conf - ET - Inf - LG
< Nat Music Coun, Assn Brit Orchestras, Nat Campaign for the
      Arts, Voluntary Arts Network, Scottish Arts Lobby
M c 2,300 org
¶ Making Music News - 4; free.
      Annual Review;   Guide to Member Services; both ftm.
      Orchestral Catalogue.   Choral Catalogue.
      Chamber Music Catalogue.   Information sheets; ftm only.

Malacological Society of London   (Malsoc)   1893
■ c/o Dept of Zoology, University of Cambridge, Downing St,
      CAMBRIDGE, CB2 2EJ.   (hsb)
      01223 336600
      email t.white@zoo.cam.ac.uk
      http://www.malacsoc.org.uk
      Hon Sec: Tom White
▲ Registered Charity
○ *L; study of molluscs from pure & applied aspects
● Conf - Res
M c 230 i
¶ Jnl of Molluscan Studies - 4 (with supplements); ftm.
      Bulletin - 2; ftm only.

Malcolm Muggeridge Society   2003
■ Pilgrim's Cottage, Pike Rd, EYTHORNE, Kent, CT15 4DJ.
      (sb/p)
      01304 831964
      email info@malcolmmuggeridge.org
      http://www.malcolmmuggeridge.org
      Sec: David Williams
▲ Un-incorporated Society
○ *A, *G; to promote interest in the work of the author, journalist,
      broadcaster, Christian apologist & soldier/spy, Malcolm
      Muggeridge 1903-1990
● Conf - Mtgs - Inf - Lib - VE
M 105 i, UK / 110 i, o'seas
      (Sub: £15)
¶ The Gargoyle (Jnl) - 4; ftm, £5 nm.

Malcolm Saville Society 1994

■ 33 Chapel Rd, Penketh, WARRINGTON, Cheshire, WA5 2NG. (msp)
  email mystery@witchend.com http://www.witchend.com
▲ Un-incorporated Society
○ *A, *G; to celebrate the life & work of Malcolm Saville (1901-1982) a popular children's author; to stimulate awareness of his books
● Mtgs - Lib - Themed walks based on the novels - Book search service
M 370 i, UK / 12 i, o'seas
¶ Acksherley! - 3;   Peewit! (LM) - 1; both ftm only.
  AGM Souvenir programme; price varies.

Malone Society 1906

■ Institute of English Studies, Senate House, Malet St, LONDON, WC1E 7HU. (hq)
  020 7862 8675
  email conor.wyer@sas.ac.uk http://www.ies.sas.ac.uk/malone
  Exec Sec: Prof John Creaser
▲ Registered Charity
Br Australia, Canada, Japan, Switzerland
○ *A, *D, *L; to publish editions of 16th & 17th century plays from manuscript, photographic facsimile editions of printed plays of the period, & editions of original documents relating to Renaissance theatre & drama
● ET - Inf - Lib
< Shakespeare Assn of America
M 238 i, UK / 432 i, o'seas
¶ Books - 1 or 2 yr; ftm.   AR - 1; free.

Malt Distillers Association of Scotland (MDAS) 1874

■ 1 North St, ELGIN, Moray, IV30 1UA. (asa)
  01343 544077   fax 01343 548523
  email mdas@grigor-young.co.uk
  Secs: Grigor & Young (solicitors & estate agents)
○ *T; interests of the pot still malt whisky industry
M f

Maltsters' Association of Great Britain (MAGB) 1827

NR 31b Castlegate, NEWARK, Notts, NG24 1AZ. (hq)
  01636 700781
  email info@magb.org.uk http://www.ukmalt.com
▲ Un-incorporated Society
○ *T; 'to promote & safeguard the UK malting industry'
Gp Malt exporters
● Conf - Mtgs - ET - Exam - Res - Stat - Expt - LG
< Euromalt
¶ AR; ftm only.

Malvern Spa Association (MSA) 1998

■ 24 Assarts Lane, MALVERN, Worcs, WR14 4JR. (treas/p)
  http://www.malvern-hills.co.uk/malvernspa/
  Chmn: Rose Garrard,   Treas: John Bibby
○ *G, *K; to conserve, protect and restore the springs, wells and fountains of the Malvern Hills.

Mammal Society 1954

NR 3 The Carronades, New Road, SOUTHAMPTON, Hants, SO14 0AA. (hq)
  023 8023 7874
  email enquiries@mammal.org.uk
  http://www.mammal.org.uk
  Admin Officer: Sarah Gardner
▲ Company Limited by Guarantee; Registered Charity
○ *L, *Q; to protect British mammals, halt the decline of threatened species & advise on all issues affecting British mammals; to study mammals, identify the problems they face & promote conservation & other policies based on sound science
● Conf - Mtgs - ET - Res - Inf - Study of conservation needs of threatened species - Trap loan scheme for members
< IVCN; Wildlife & Countryside Link
M 2,200 i, UK / 100 i, o'seas
¶ Mammal Review - 4.   Mammal News - 4.
  Mammalaction News [youth group NL] - 4.
  Other publications.

Mammillaria Society

NR 10 Copperkins Grove, AMERSHAM, Bucks, HP6 5QD.
  email admin@mammillaria.co.uk
  http://www.cactus.mall.com/mammsoc/
  Sec: Chris Davies
○ *H; promoting and furthering the study of the cactus genus mammillaria

Management Consultancies Association (MCA) 1956

■ 60 Trafalgar Sq, LONDON, WC2N 5DS. (hq)
  020 7321 3990   fax 020 7321 3991
  email mca@mca.org.uk   http://www.mca.org.uk
  Chief Exec: Alan Leaman
▲ Company Limited by Guarantee
○ *P, *T; to maintain standards within the UK management consultancy sector
Gp Directors: Finance, HR, Marketing
  Interest gps: Public sector, Statistics
● Conf - Mtgs - ET - Res - Exhib - Stat - Inf - LG
< Eur Fedn of Mgt Consultancy Assns (FEACO)
M 65 f
¶ Spectra (Jnl) - 4;   Electronic NL - 12;   Careers Guide; Corporate brochure; all free.
  The UK Consulting Industry Report - 1.
  MCA book series (published by Hodder & Stoughton).

Managing & Marketing Sales Association (MAMSA) 1979

■ PO Box 11, SANDBACH, Cheshire, CW11 3GE. (hq)
  01270 526339   fax 01270 526339
  email info@mamsasbp.org.uk
  http://www.mamsasbp.org.uk
  Chief Exec: M Whitaker
▲ Company Limited by Guarantee
○ *P; examination board for sales marketing; management; business studies & communications
● Exam
M 1,000 i, UK / 17,000 i, o'seas
¶ Nexus - 1.

Manchester Geographical Society 1884

■ Meadowbank, Ringley Rd, Radcliffe, MANCHESTER, M26 1FW. (hq)
  http://www.mangeogsoc.org.uk
  Hon Sec: Dr B P Hindle
▲ Registered Charity
○ *E, *L, *Q; to promote all branches of geographical science
● Mtgs - Inf - Library on permanent loan to the University of Manchester
< R Geographical Soc; Geographical Assn
M 160 i
¶ North-West Geography (Jnl) - 4; free.   AR - 1; ftm only.

© CBD Research Ltd · Beckenham · BR3 5JS · Tel 020 8650 7745 · E-mail cbd@cbdresearch.com · www.cbdresearch.com

Manchester Literary & Philosophical Society   (LIT & PHIL) 1781
NR   MMU Business School, Aytoun St, MANCHESTER, M1 3GH. (hq)
    0161-247 6774   fax 0161-247 6773
    http://www.manlitphil.co.uk
    Hon Sec: Mrs Patricia Verdin
▲   Company Limited by Guarantee; Registered Charity
○   *A, *L; 'to promote the advancement of education & the widening of public interest in, & appreciation of, any form of literature, science, the arts & public affairs...'
Gp   Sections: Arts, Science & technology, Social philosophy, Young people
●   Conf - Mtgs - Lib
M   c 500 i
¶   Manchester Memoirs - 1.   NL - 12.   AR.
    John Dalton Bibliography, Vol 2.

Manchester Medical Society   (MMS)   1834
■   John Rylands University Library, Oxford Rd, MANCHESTER, M13 9PP.   (hq)
    0161-273 6048   fax 0161-272 8046
    email admin@mms.org.uk   http://www.mms.org.uk
    Chmn: Dr R F T McMahon
▲   Registered Charity
○   *L, *M; to cultivate & promote all branches of medicine, & of all related schemes
Gp   Anaesthesia; Imaging; Medicine; Odontology; Paediatrics; Pathology; Primary care; Psychiatry; Public health medicine; Surgery
●   Mtgs - ET - Lib
M   2,100 i

Mangold Hurling Association
NR   c/o 11 Orchard Lane, Wembdon, BRIDGWATER, Somerset, TA6 7QY.
    email mail@mangoldhurling.co.uk
    http://www.mangoldhurling.co.uk
    Contact: John Ennals
○   *G, *S; the traditional Somerset sport of hurling (pitching) mangold-wurzel (or mangel-wurzel), a vegetable of the beet family

Manifesto Club
NR   Free Word Centre, 60 Farringdon Rd, LONDON, EC1R 3GA.
    Josie Appleton
○   *K; campaigning agaist the hyper-regulation of everyday life

Manila Hemp Association
    this association is currently dormant

Manorial Society of Great Britain   (MSGB)   1906
■   104 Kennington Rd, LONDON, SE11 6RE.   (hq)
    020 7735 6633   fax 020 7582 7022
    email manorial@msgb.co.uk   http://www.msgb.co.uk
    Hon Exec Chmn: Robert A Smith
○   *L; historical research, manorial rights, legal liability, insurance, estate management, genealogy, armigerous devices
●   Conf
M   i & f
¶   Bulletin - 2; ftm only.   NL - 12; m only.
    Land Tenures & Customs of Manors (1673, reprinted 1999).
    Britain & Europe (1999).
    The Land Registration Bill (2002).
    Blood Royal (2002).
    The Land Registration Act (2005).

Manufacturers' Agents' Association of Great Britain & Ireland Inc   (MAA)   1909
■   Unit 16 Thrales End, HARPENDEN, Herts, AL5 3NS.   (hq)
    01582 767618   fax 01582 766092
    email prw@themaa.co.uk   http://www.themaa.co.uk
    Sec: Paul Wakeling
▲   Company Limited by Guarantee
○   *T; independent manufacturers' (commission) agents
●   Conf - Mtgs - ET - Stat - Res - Inf - LG - Legal advice
<   Intl U of Comml Agents & Brokers (Amsterdam)
M   900 i
¶   Agents News - 12.
    The Commission Agent.   20 Legal Questions Agents Ask.

Manufacturers of Domestic Unvented Systems
    in 2007 merged with the Waterheater Manufacturers Association to form the **Hot Water Association**

Manufacturing Alliance
    Consists of EEF, Manufacturing Technologies Association, UK Steel, Chemical Industries Association, Society of Aerospace Companies, British Plastics Federation, and the Construction Products Association

Manufacturing Technologies Association   (MTA)   1919
■   62 Bayswater Rd, LONDON, W2 3PS.   (hq)
    020 7298 6400   fax 020 7298 6430
    email info@mta.org.uk   http://www.mta.org.uk
    Dir Gen: Graham Dewhurst
▲   Company Limited by Guarantee
Br   2 o'seas
○   *T; to represent companies in the machine tool sector & related technologies
Gp   Equipment importers; Equipment manufacturers
●   Mtgs - ET - Exhib - Stat - Expt - LG - Technical support
M   252 f
¶   Various technical publications.

Manx Gaelic Society
    see **Cheshaght Ghailckagh (Yn)   (Manx Gaelic Society)**

Manx Grand Prix Riders' Association   (MGPRA)
NR   Mountain View, GLEN MAYE, Isle of Man, IM5 3BJ.   (sp)
    http://www.manxgrandprix.org
    Sec: Frances Thorp
○   *S
●   Mtgs - Inf
M   i

Manx Loaghtan Sheep Breeders' Group   (MLSBG)   1988
■   Cannons, Huntley Rd, Tibberton, GLOUCESTER, GL19 3AB   (hsp)
    01452 790309
    email kempsoncannons@aol.com
    http://www.manxloaghtansheep.org
    Sec: Carol Kempson
▲   Un-incorporated Society
○   *B
●   Workshops
<   Nat Sheep Assn; Rare Breed Survival Trust
M   72 i, 3 f, 1 org, UK / 1 i, o'seas
¶   NL - 3; ftm only.

Manx National Farmers' Union   (MNFU)   1947
NR   Agriculture House, Ballafletcher Farm Rd, TROMODE, Isle of Man, IM4 4QL.   (sp)
    01624 662204   fax 01624 662204
    email manx-nfu@talk21.com   http://www.manx-nfu.org
▲   Un-incorporated Society
Br   3
○   *F
●   Mtgs - LG
M   c 360 i

Map Curators Group
  a group of the **British Cartographic Society**

Map Design Group
  a group of the **British Cartographic Society**

Marchigiana Cattle Breed Society
NR   White Cottage, Llwynhelig, COWBRIDGE, S Glam, CF71 7FF.
     (sp)
     Sec: G Bradley
○   *B

Marching Display Bands Association   (MDBA)   1936
■   9 Kingsclere Avenue, Oakwood, DERBY, DE21 2QH.   (hsp)
     01332 544876
     email j.atkins@marchingdisplaybands.co.uk
     http://www.marchingdisplaybands.co.uk
     Hon Sec: Mrs J Atkins
▲   Un-incorporated Society
○   *D; to promote the use of carnival marching showbands & the
     holding of band contests & arena displays at carnivals etc
Gp   Competitions (3-6 bands); Exhibitions (1-6 bands)
●   ET - Exhib (1-5 bands) - Comp (3-5 bands) - Massed band
     displays - Cabaret
M   [not stated]
✕   2009 Carnival Band Secretaries League

Marfan Association UK   1984
■   Rochester House, 5 Aldershot Rd, FLEET, Hants, GU51 3NG.
     (hq)
     01252 810472   fax 01252 810473
     email marfan@tinyonline.co.uk
     http://www.marfan-association.org.uk
     Chmn: Mrs Diane Rust
▲   Registered Charity
○   *W; offering support to patients with Marfan syndrome, which
     affects the cardiovascular system, causing near-sightedness &
     skeletal abnormalities; working alongside the many medical
     sectors involved in patient care; educating patients, doctors,
     the public, the Dept of Health & the Government;
     undertaking & sponsoring research projects
●   Conf - ET - Res - Exhib - Stat - Inf - LG
<   Intl Fedn of Marfan Syndrome Orgs; Eur Marfan Support
     Network
M   1,500 families
¶   In Touch (Jnl) - 2.   Publications list available.

Margarine & Spreads Association   (MSA)
■   6 Catherine St, LONDON, WC2B 5JJ.   (hq)
     020 7836 2460   fax 020 7379 5735
     email info@margarine.org.uk
     http://www.margarine.org.uk
     Sec: Juliet Howarth
▲   Un-incorporated Society
○   *T; to monitor & help shape UK, European & international
     legislation
<   Intl Fedn Margarine Assns (IFMA); Intl Margarine Assn
     Countries Europe (IMACE); Food & Drink Fedn
M   3 f
¶   AR; ftm only.

Margery Allingham Society   1987
■   28 Parkfield Avenue, AMERSHAM, Bucks, HP6 6BE.   (hon/sec)
     http://www.margeryallingham.org.uk
     Hon Sec: Jo Hesslewood
▲   Un-incorporated Society
○   *A, *G; to bring together all interested in the life & work of
     Margery Allingham, a queen of crime & one of the greatest
     detective story writers of the 'Golden Age'
●   Conf - VE
M   120 i, UK / 12 i, o'seas
¶   The Bottle Street Gazette - 2; ftm.

Margery Kempe Society   1999
NR   1a Auckland Rd, LONDON, SW11 1EW.   (hsp)
     020 7924 5868
     email c.maddern@gold.ac.uk
     Hon Sec: Dr Carole Maddern
○   *G; to further learned research into the English mystic Margery
     Kempe (c1373-c1440); to further historical & literary
     research in this field
●   Conf
M   30 i

Marie Stuart Society   1992
■   Copeland, 3 Barley Close, Little Eaton, DERBY, DE21 5DJ.
     (hsp)
     email syd@qcinternet.co.uk
     http://www.marie-stuart.co.uk
     Sec: Syd Whitehead
▲   Registered Charity
Br   3
○   *G; study & research into the life & times of Mary Queen of
     Scots (1542-1587)
●   Mtgs - Res - Exhib - Comp - Inf - Lib - PL - LG
M   134 i, UK / 30 i, o'seas
¶   Jnl - 3; ftm only.

Marine Biogeochemistry Forum
  a group of the **Challenger Society for Marine Science**

Marine Biological Association of the United Kingdom   (MBA)
   1884
■   The Laboratory, Citadel Hill, PLYMOUTH, Devon, PL1 2PB.
     (regd/office)
     01752 633207   fax 01752 633102
     email sec@mba.ac.uk   http://www.mba.ac.uk
     Dir & Sec: Prof Colin Brownlee
▲   Registered Charity
○   *L, *Q; studies in various aspects of marine biology &
     biological oceanography, pollution, taxonomy, physiology,
     molecular biology & biochemistry
Gp   Biochemists; Biologists; Library; Molecular biologists;
     Physiologists
●   Mtgs - ET - Res - Inf - Lib - SG - VE
M   808 i, 10 f, UK / 196 i, 1 f, o'seas
     (Sub: £35-£425)
¶   Jnl - 6; ftm, £95 m, £688 nm.
     IMBA Global Marine Environment (NL) - 2.

Marine Conservation Society   (MCS)   1983
NR   Unit 3 Wolf Business Park, Alton Rd, ROSS-ON-WYE,
     Herefords, HR9 5BU.   (hq)
     01989 566017   fax 01989 567815
     email info@mcsuk.org   http://www.mcsuk.org
▲   Company Limited by Guarantee; Registered Charity
○   *K, *L; 'the only UK based charity devoted exclusively to the
     protection of the marine environment; it believes that
     decisions affecting our seas & coasts should be based on
     sound scientific principles & implemented by environmentally
     sensitive management'
●   Conf - ET - Res - Inf - PL - VE - LG - Volunteer work
<   Sea at Risk; Sea Turtle Survival; Wildlife & Countryside Link
M   5,200 i, UK / 200 i, o'seas
¶   Marine Conservation (Jnl) - 4; ftm.

Marine Engine & Equipment Manufacturers' Association
  a group association of the **British Marine Federation**

Marine Industries Leadership Council
  a group of the **Shipbuilders & Shiprepairers Association**

© CBD Research Ltd · Beckenham · BR3 5JS · Tel 020 8650 7745 · E-mail cbd@cbdresearch.com · www.cbdresearch.com

Marine Institute   1941
IRL   Rinville, ORANMORE, Co Galway, Republic of Ireland.
    353 91 387 200
    email institutemail@marine.ie   http://www.marine.ie
    Pres: Desmond Branigan   (353 (1) 660 0737)
○   *G; to promote greater awareness among the people of Ireland
    of their maritime history & of the sea
✕   Maritime Institute of Ireland

Marine Leisure Association
    a group association of the **British Marine Federation**

Marine Society & Sea Cadets   (MSSC)   2004
■   202 Lambeth Rd, LONDON, SE1 7JW.   (hq)
    020 7654 7000   fax 020 7928 8914
    email info@ms-sc.org   http://www.sea-cadets.org
    Chief Exec: Jeremy Cornish
▲   Registered Charity
Br   400
○   *E, *W; to raise public awareness of the Royal & Merchant
    Navies, & the maritime world in general; to provide support
    for those who go to sea & enhance the well-being of
    professional sailors; to be responsible for the activities of the
    Sea Cadet Corps, open to young people 10-18 years old
Gp   Sea Cadet Corps
●   ET - Lib - Nautical/maritime youth training (sponsored by Royal
    Navy training ships)
<   Intl Sea Cadet Assn (ISCA)
M   16,000 i, UK / 1,200 i, o'seas
¶   The Seafarer (Jnl) - 6; £25 yr m, £3 each nm.
    AR - 1; ftm only.

Marine Trades Association
    a group association of the **British Marine Federation**

Maritime Information Association   (MIA)   1971
■   18 Durrington Avenue, LONDON, SW20 8NT.   (sec/p)
    http://www.maritime-information.net
    Sec: Roy Fenton
▲   Un-incorporated Society
○   *L; contact with marine librarians, information workers & others
    with an interest in the maritime world
●   Conf - Mtgs - VE - Lectures
¶   NL - 4;   LM - 1.
    Maritime Information: a guide to sources.

Maritime Security & Safety Group
    a group of the **Society of Maritime Industries**

Maritime Skills Alliance   (MSA)   2004
NR   1 Hillside, Beckingham, LINCOLN, LN5 0RQ.   (hq)
    http://www.maritimeskills.org
○   *T; to promote UK maritime skills development & common
    training & qualifications frameworks, in commercial sea
    fishing, the marine leisure industry, maritime search &
    rescue, Merchant Navy & in ports & harbours
●   Mtgs - ET
M   c 8 assns

Maritime UK
NR   12 Carthusian St, LONDON, EC1M 6EZ.   (hq)
    020 7417 2833   fax jonathan.roberts@british-
    shipping.org
    Chmn: Jim Stewart
    Secretariat: Jonathan Roberts
○   *T; to speak with one voice for the shipping, port & maritime
    businesss services sector in the UK
●   Inf - LG
M   7 assns

Market Research Quality Standards Association   (MRQSA)
1996
■   Pendowrick, Pendower Rd, Veryan, TRURO, Cornwall,
    TR2 5QL.   (admin/p)
    01872 501373
    email pettrevjac@aol.com
    Admin: Peter Jackson
▲   Company Limited by Guarantee
○   *P; to develop quality standards for market research services; to
    develop schemes by which organisations can be assessed to
    these standards
●   Conf - liaison with bodies in associated fields
M   5 org

Market Research Society   (MRS)   1946
■   15 Northburgh St, LONDON, EC1V 0JR.   (hq)
    020 7490 4911   fax 020 7490 0608
    email info@marketresearch.org.uk
    http://www.mrs.org.uk
    Dir Gen: David Barr
▲   Company Limited by Guarantee
Br   Scotland
○   *P, *T; for professional researchers & other engaged (or
    interested) in market, social & opinion research & for
    company partner organisations
●   Conf - Mtgs - ET - Exam - Res - Exhib - Inf - Lib - LG
<   Intl Cham Comm (UK): Eur Fedn of Assns of Market Res
    Orgs (EFAMRE); Advertising Assn
M   7,300 i, UK / 700 i, o'seas
¶   Research - 12; ftm.   MRS News - 8; ftm only.
    International Jnl of Market Research - 6; ftm.
    Research Buyers Guide - 1; ftm.   AR - 1; ftm only.

Marketing Agencies Association   (MAA)   1989
NR   4 New Quebec St, LONDON, W1H 7RF.   (hq)
    020 7535 3550   fax 020 7535 3551
    email ian.miller@marketingagencies.org.uk
    http://www.marketingagencies.org.uk
    Chmn: Ian Miller
○   *T; practitioners in promotional marketing & communication
M   c 50 f
✕   2011 Marketing Communication Consultants Association

Marketing Association Alliance   (MAA)   2009
NR   c/o IPIA, Unit 9 Business Innovation Centre, Staffordshire
    Technology Park, Beaconside, STAFFORD, ST18 0AR.
○   *N, *T; 'committed to working together, promoting best practice
    & the value of all media & disciplines within the marketing
    mix'
M   British Promotional Merchandise Association
    Direct Marketing Association
    Independent Print Industries Association
    Incorporated Society of British Advertisers
    Institute of Promotional Marketing
    Point of Purchase Advertising International
    UK Gift Card & Voucher Association

Marketing Communication Consultants Association
    since 2011 **Marketing Agencies Association**

Marketing Institute [Ireland]
IRL   South County Business Park, Leopardstown, DUBLIN 18,
    Republic of Ireland.
    353 (1) 295 2355   fax 353 (1) 295 2453
    email info@mii.ie   http://www.mii.ie
○   *P

Marketing Society [Ireland]
IRL   PO Box 58, BRAY, Co Wicklow, Republic of Ireland.
    353 (1) 276 1995
    email info@marketingsociety.ie
    http://www.marketingsociety.ie
    Chmn: Kay McCarthy
○   *P

Marketing Society Ltd   1959
NR 1 Park Rd, TEDDINGTON, Middx, TW11 0AR.   (hq)
020 8973 1700
http://www.marketing-society.org.uk
Chief Exec: Hugh Burkitt
▲ Company Limited by Guarantee
○ *P; 'for senior marketers'
● Conf - Mtgs - Inf
M 3,500 i
¶ Market Leader - 4.

Marlowe Society   1955
■ 27 Melbourne Court, Randolph Avenue, LONDON, W9 1BJ.
(hsp)
email valerie.colin-russ@marlowe-society.org
http://www.marlowe-society.org
Chmn: Valerie Colin-Russ
▲ Company Limited by Guarantee; Registered Charity
○ *A, *G; to present Christopher Marlowe in his true light as a
great poet-dramatist; to stimulate research into his life &
work, into the lives of his friends & associates & the era in
which he lived
● Mtgs - Res - Exhib - Lib - VE - Annual MArlowe Day (usually in
Canterbury) - Biennial commemoration at the Marlowe
memorial window in Poet's Corner, Westminster Abbey
M 138 i, 2 schools, UK / 46 i, o'seas
(Sub: £15 i, £200 (1-off) schools, UK / £20 i, o'seas)
¶ NL - 3; ftm, £3 (UK), £3.50 (Eur), £4 (RoW).
Note: 'this is not the same as the Marlowe [Dramatic] Society of
Cambridge which was founded by Rupert Brooke & is
devoted to performing plays'.

Marquee Hire Group
a group of the **Performance Textiles Association**

**MARQUES the Association of European Trade Mark Owners
(MARQUES)   1988**
NR 840 Melton Rd, Thurmaston, LEICESTER, LE4 8BN.   (asa)
0116-264 0080   fax 0116-264 0141
email info@marques.org   http://www.marques.org
Co Sec: Robert Seager
▲ Company Limited by Guarantee
○ *T; representing on a Pan-European basis the interests of
owners of trade marks & associated intellectual property
● Conf - Mtgs - Inf - LG
M 50 f, UK / 250 f, o'seas
¶ Marques News Sheet - 10; ftm only.
✕ Association of European Brand Owners

Marquetry Society   1952
NR 14 Buntingsdale Rd, MARKET DRAYTON, Shrops, TF9 1LT.
(hsp)
01630 656550
http://www.marquetry.org
Hon Gen Sec: Neil Micklewright
▲ Un-incorporated Society
Br 29; 8
○ *G; to foster the craft of marquetry
● Mtgs - Exhib (annual + members competitions) - Inf - PL
< Crafts Coun; Voluntary Arts Network
M c 500 i, UK / c 150 i, o'seas
¶ The Marquetarian - 4; ftm, £2 nm.

MARS   (M.A.R.S.)
NR 34 Wycliffe Road, Battersea, LONDON, SW11 5QR.
email info@mars.org.uk   http://www.mars.org.uk
○ *G; an experienced & technically qualified team interested in
amateur & high power rocketry; development of rockets for
amateur space missions
M i

Mary Rose Society   1978
NR c/o The Mary Rose Trust, College Rd, HM Naval Base,
PORTSMOUTH, Hants, PO1 3LX.   (hq)
023 9275 0521
http://www.maryrose.org
○ *G; support of the Mary Rose (King Henry VIII's flagship)

Mary Webb Society   1972
■ 8 The Knowe, Willaston, NESTON, Cheshire, CH64 1TA.   (hsp)
0151-327 5843
email suehigginbotham@yahoo.co.uk
http://www.marywebbsociety.co.uk
Sec: Sue Higginbotham
▲ Un-incorporated Society
○ *A, *G; to honour the memory of the author Mary Webb; to
further appreciation of her works & the Shropshire
countryside about which she wrote
● Mtgs - Exhib - VE
< Alliance of Literary Socs
M 157 i, UK / 9 i, o'seas
¶ Jnl - 1; ftm, £3 nm.   NL - 2/3; free.

Masham Sheep Breeders Association   (MSBA)   1986
■ Oak Bank, Bentham, LANCASTER, LA2 7DW.
01524 261606
email vallawson@tinyworld.co.uk
Sec: Mrs V J Lawson
▲ Company Limited by Guarantee
○ *B; for breeders of quality half bred grimmers; the Masham
(Teeswater ram cross Dalesbred ewe) is predominantly
produced in the North of England
● Mtgs - Exhib
< Nat Sheep Assn
M 80 i
¶ NL - 4; ftm only.   LM; ftm.

** **Massenet Society**
Organisation lost: see Introduction paragraph 3

** **Mast Action UK: the National Campaign for the Sensible Siting
of Masts**
Organisation lost: see Introduction paragraph 3

Master Carvers Association   (MCA)   1897
■ Unit 2, 15b Vandyke Rd, LEIGHTON BUZZARD, Beds,
LU7 2QD.   (hsb)
01525 851594   fax 01525 851594
email info@mastercarvers.co.uk
http://www.mastercarvers.co.uk
Hon Sec: Paul Ferguson
▲ Un-incorporated Society
○ *A, *T; promotion & protection of the interests of wood carving,
stone carving & modelling generally
● Conf - Inf - Empl
M 37 f, UK / 2 f, o'seas
¶ NL - irreg; ftm only.   LM; free.

Master Chefs of Great Britain   (MCGB)   1980
■ Woodmans, Brithem Bottom, CULLOMPTON, Devon,
EX15 1NB.   (hsp)
01884 35104   fax 01884 35105
email mcgb@masterchefs.co.uk
http://www.masterchefs.co.uk
Chmn: Gerald Roser
Sec: Susan M McGreever
○ *P; to provide a forum for the exchange of culinary ideas; to
further the profession through the training & guidance of
young chefs; to promote all that is best about British cuisine
& the produce available
● Mtgs - ET - Culinary demonstrations
M 240 i, 22 f, UK / 5 i, o'seas
¶ Masterchefs - 4; ftm, £3 nm.

© CBD Research Ltd · Beckenham · BR3 5JS · Tel 020 8650 7745 · E-mail cbd@cbdresearch.com · www.cbdresearch.com

Master Craftsmen's Association & Retail Export Group
no longer active

Master Locksmiths' Association   (MLA)   1958
NR   5d Great Central Way, Woodford Halse, DAVENTRY, Northants,
        NN11 3PZ.   (hq)
        01327 262255   fax 01327 262539
        email admin@locksmiths.co.uk
        http://www.locksmiths.co.uk
▲   Company Limited by Guarantee
○   *P, *T
Gp   Guild of Key Cutters (divn)
●   Conf - Mtgs - ET - Exam - Exhib - Inf - Lib - LG - Locktesting -
        Professional consultancy
M   1,000 i, 350 f, UK / 100 i, o'seas
¶   Keyways - 6; ftm only.

Master Photographers Association Ltd   (MPA)   1952
■   1 Chancery Lane, DARLINGTON, Co Durham, DL1 5QP.   (hq)
        01325 356555   fax 01325 357813
        email enquiries@mpauk.com   http://www.thempa.com
        Chief Exec: Colin R Buck
○   *T; represents professional photographers
M   f

Masters of Basset Hounds Association   (MBHA)   1912
■   The Hemmels, Brinkhill, LOUTH, Lincs, LN11 8RA.   (chmn/p)
        Chmn: A D Hindle
○   *S; represents masters of basset hounds used for hunting
<   Coun of Hunting Assns
M   21 i, UK / 1 i, o'seas
¶   NL - 2; free.

Masters of Deerhounds Association   (MDHA)   1951
NR   Riphay Barton, DULVERTON, Somerset, TA22 9AX.   (chmn/p)
        Chmn: T A H Yandle
▲   Company Limited by Guarantee; Registered Charity
○   *S; control & regulation of deer hunting with hounds
<   Coun of Hunting Assns
M   3 hunts in England (Devon & Somerset, Tiverton, Quantock)

Masters of Draghounds & Bloodhounds Association
NR   RMA Sandhurst - Blacklands Farm, Milford Rd, ELSTEAD,
        Surrey, GU8 6LA.   (chmn/p)
        01252 703304
        http://www.bloodhoundhunting.co.uk
        Chmn: Pat Sutton
○   *G, *S; for followers of the sport - hounds following artificial
        scent laid down by a runner or mounted rider

Masters of Foxhounds Association   (MFHA)   1881
■   Overley Barn, Daglingworth, CIRENCESTER, Glos, GL7 7HX.
        (hq)
        01285 653001   fax 01285 653559
        http://www.mfha.org.uk
        Dir: Alastair Jackson
○   *S; the governing body of foxhunting
<   Coun of Hunting Assns
M   i (masters of 186 packs of foxhounds)

Mastic Asphalt Council   (MAC)   1995
■   PO Box 77, HASTINGS, E Sussex, TN35 4WL.   (hq)
        01424 814400   fax 01424 814446
        email masphaltco@aol.com
        http://www.masticasphaltcouncil.co.uk
        Dir & Sec: John Blowers
▲   Company Limited by Guarantee
○   *T; represents mastic asphalt contractors & manufacturers
        providing a free technical service to specifiers
Gp   Specialist mastic asphalt contractors
●   Conf - Mtgs - ET - Exhib - Comp - SG - Inf - VE - Empl - LG
        (via NSCC)
<   Eur Mastic Asphalt Assn (EMAA); Construction Products
        Assn (CPA); Nat Specialist Contrs Coun (NSCC)
M   72 f (contractors), 6 f (manufacturing), 21 associates
¶   The New Technical Guide (incl Roofing, Flooring, Paving,
        Tanking); ftm, £30 nm.
        [the Guide is produced as an A4 loose-leaf ring-binder]

Materials Handling Engineers Association   (MHEA)   1938
■   2B Hills Lane, ELY, Cambs, CB6 1AY,   (hq)
        01353 666298   fax 01353 666298
        email pw@mhea.co.uk   http://www.mhea.co.uk
        Sec: Peter Webster
▲   Un-incorporated Society
○   *T; manufacturers & users of bulk & continuous handling eqpt
●   Conf - Mtgs - Expt through ISHAB - LG
<   permanent member of Intl Solids Handling Advy Bd (ISHAB)
M   27 f
¶   Online NL - 3; ftm.
        Recommended Practice for Troughed Belt Conveyors.

Materials Science & Technology Division
        a group of the **Institute of Materials, Minerals & Mining**

MatheMagic   1999
■   1 Straylands Grove, YORK, YO31 1EB.
        email info@mathemagic.org + qed@enterprise.net
        http://www.mathemagic.org
        Dir: John Bibby
▲   Un-incorporated Society
○   *E; to popularise maths & numeracy
Gp   Adult basic skills; Multicultural mathematics
●   Conf - Exhib - Comp - PL - VE - Maths Funfairs
<   Adults Learning Mathematics
M   300 i, UK / 20 i, o'seas
¶   NL

Mathematical Association   (MA)   1871
NR   259 London Rd, LEICESTER, LE2 3BE.   (hq)
        0116-221 0013   fax 0116-212 2835
        email office@m-a.org.uk   http://www.m-a.org.uk
        Admin: Marcia Murray
▲   Registered Charity
Br   20
○   *E, *P; to improve mathematical education
Gp   Careers; Diplomas; Library; Problem bureau; Publications;
        Schools & industry; Teaching; Universities
        Society of Young Mathematicians (http://www.syms.org.uk)
●   Conf - Mtgs - ET - Exam - Exhib - Comp - Lib - LG
<   Intl Congress on Mathematical Educ; Coun of Subject Teaching
        Assns; R Soc Mathematical Instruction (sub c'ee); Standing
        Conf of Assns concerned with Mathematical Education in
        Schools
M   5,000 i worldwide UK / 500 i, 300 f, o'seas
¶   [publishes a range of mathematics books & jnls].

Max Wall Society   2003

- ■ 11 Milland Rd, HAILSHAM, E Sussex, BN27 1TG.   (h/mem/sp)
  http://www.maxwall.org
  Mem Sec: Jean Barham
- ▲ Un-incorporated Society
- ○ *G; for all interested in the life & performing career of Max[well George Lorimer] Wall (1908-1990), actor & comedian & to perpetuate his memory
- ● Exhib - Lectures - Annual dinner
- M c 150 i
- ¶ Wallpaper; ftm only.

McCarrison Society   1965

- NR c/o IBCHN, London Metropolitan University, North London Campus, 166-222 Holloway Rd, LONDON, N7 8DB. (pres/b)
  020 7133 2926   fax 020 7133 2453
  email president@mccarrisonsociety.org.uk
  http://www.mccarrisonsociety.org.uk
  Pres: Prof Michael A Crawford
- ▲ Registered Charity
- Br 2
- ○ L, *P; research & dissemination of knowledge on nutrition & health; areas of interest include the rise in mortality from non-communicable diseases, mental ill-health & the widening inequality of health
- Gp Cancer; Cardiology; Comparative pathology; Dietetics; Diseases of Western & developing countries; Epidemiology; Nutrition
- ● Conf - Mtgs - ET - Res - Comp - SG - LG
- < Mother & Child Foundation
- M 250 i, UK / 50 i, o'seas
- ¶ Nutrition & Health - 4.

MCPS-PRS Alliance

- NR 29-33 Berners St, LONDON, W1T 3AB.   (hq)
  020 7580 5544   fax 020 7306 4455
  http://www.mcps-prs-alliance.co.uk
- ○ *T; collection of royalties for the music industry
- M 2 org:
  Mechanical Copyright Protection Society Ltd
  Performing Right Society Ltd

McTimoney Chiropractic Association   (MCA)   1979

- NR Crowmarsh Gifford, WALLINGFORD, Oxon, OX10 8DJ.   (hq)
  01491 829211   fax 01491 829492
  email services@mctimoney-chiropractic.org
  http://www.mctimoney-chiropractic.org
  Sec: Christine Chalmers,   Chmn: Dr Christina Cunliffe
- ○ *P; promotion of McTimoney chiropractic
- Gp Chiropractic; Private sector education (McTimoney chiropractic college)
- ● Conf - ET - Exam - Res - Exhib - Inf - PL
- M 500 i, UK / 10 i, o'seas
- ¶ Background (NL) - 4; ftm only.
  Directory of Practitioners - 1; ftm, £7.10 nm.
  Information leaflets & college prospectus.

MDA Europe
  since 2008 **Collections Trust**

MDF - the BiPolar Organisation   (MDF)   2005

- NR Castle Works, 21 St George's Rd, LONDON, SE1 6ES.   (hq)
  0845 634 0540   fax 020 7793 2639
  email mdf@mdf.org.uk   http://www.mdf.org.uk
- ▲ Company Limited by Guarantee; Registered Charity
- ○ *W; to support those with manic depression & their carers & friends; to encourage research into the illness; to educate the public & caring professions
- M c 150 self-help groups
- ¶ Pendulum - 4; ftm.   Group News.   Factsheets & Literature.

Meat Industry Ireland
  a group of **Food & Drink Industry Ireland**

MeCCSA with AMPE
  since 2008 **Media, Communications & Cultural Studies Association**

Mechanical Copyright Protection Society Ltd
  a member of the **MCPS-PRS Alliance**

Mechanical & Metal Trades Confederation
  closed 2010

Mechanical Organ Owners Society   (MOOS)   1976

- ■ Market House, Low St, Hoxne, EYE, Suffolk, IP21 5AR. (chmn/p)
  email info@moos.org.uk   http://www.moos.org.uk
  Chmn: Alan Smith
- ▲ Un-incorporated Society
- ○ *G; to promote an interest in all types of mechanical organs (fair, street & dance); to protect owners' interests regarding the playing & legislation of organ display vehicles
- ● Res - Exhib - Inf - VE - LG
- < Kring van Draaiorgelvrienden (Dutch Organ Soc); Fair Organ Presvn Soc
- M 250 i, UK / 30 i, 1 org (Nat Museum of Mechanical Musical Instruments (Netherlands)
- ¶ Vox Humana (Jnl) - c 1; ftm. (subscription £12 (£15 o'seas)).

Medau Society   1952

- NR 1 Grove House, Foundry Lane, HORSHAM, W Sussex, RH13 5PL.   (hq)
  01403 266000
  email office@medau.org.uk   http://www.medau.org.uk
  Admin: Lynda Bridges
- ▲ Company Limited by Guarantee
- ○ *G, *S; to train & support Medau Movement teachers; (for women (devised by Hinrich Medau) using hoops, clubs & balls)
- ● Mtgs - ET - SG - Inf
- < Sport England; Cent Coun of Physical Recreation (CCPR)
- M 2,200 i, UK / 7 i, o'seas
- ¶ Medau News - 2;   AR; both ftm only.

Media, Communication & Cultural Studies Association (MeCCSA)   1999

- ■ c/o Prof Peter Golding (Vice-Chancellor), Northumbria University, NEWCASTLE UPON TYNE, Northumberland, NE1 8ST.   (hsb)
  0191-243 7200
  email peter.golding@northumbria.ac.uk
  http://www.meccsa.org.uk
  Hon Sec: Prof Peter Golding
- ○ *P; for all who teach or research in higher education in media, communications & cultural studies whether in arts, humanities or social science departments
- Gp Media policy network; Media practice section; Postgraduate network; Women's media studies network
- ● Conf - Mtgs - SG - LG
- M c 70 i, c 60 instns
  Sub: c £25 i, c £100-£300 instns
- × 2008 MeCCSA with AMPE
  2006 Association of Media Practice Educators (merged)

Media Education Association   (MEA)   2006

- ■ 91 Berwick Stand St, LONDON, W1F 0BP.
  020 7609 4313
  email info@mediaedassociation.org.uk
  http://www.mediaedassociation.org.uk
  Sec: Terry Bolas
- ○ *P; to support media teachers, promote media literacy work, and raise the status of media education

© CBD Research Ltd · Beckenham · BR3 5JS · Tel 020 8650 7745 · E-mail cbd@cbdresearch.com · www.cbdresearch.com

Media Research Group   (MRG)   1964
- ■ Red Lion House, West Dean, SALISBURY, Wilts, SP5 1JF.
    (admin/p)
    01794 341337
    email sallyhiddleston@mrg.org.uk
    http://www.mrg.org.uk
    Admin: Sally Hiddleston
    Jt Chmn: David Lucas,   Keith Donaldson
- ○ *P; 'to recognise & promote importance of media research, its
    validity, directness & development'
- ● Conf - Mtgs - ET - Res
- M i
    (Sub: £45)

Media Society Ltd   (MS)   1973
- NR 29 Albert Mansions, Albert Bridge Rd, LONDON,
    SW11 4QB.   (pres/p)
    email gsn@sharpeconnections.net
    http://www.themediasociety.co.uk
    Pres: Geraldine Sharpe-Newton
- ▲ Registered Charity
- ○ *P; for people working in the media & public life
- ● Mtgs
- < Chart Inst of Journalists
- M 300 i

Mediators Institute Ireland   1992
- IRL 35 Fitzwilliam Place, DUBLIN 2, Republic of Ireland.
    353 (1) 609 9190   fax 353 (1) 493 0595
    http://www.themii.ie
    Admin: Deirdre Conway
- ○ *P

mediawatch-uk: campaigning for decency & accountability in the media   1965
- ■ 3 Willow House, Kennington Rd, ASHFORD, Kent,
    TN24 0NR.   (hq)
    01233 633936   fax 01233 633836
    email info@mediawatchuk.org
    http://www.mediawatchuk.org
    Dir: Vivienne Pattison
- ▲ Un-incorporated Society
- Br 40; Australia
- ○ *K; 'to uphold good standards of programme content in TV &
    radio; to strengthen the law against obscenity in the media'
- ● Conf - ET - Res - Inf - LG
- M 8,000 i, 175,000 org, UK / 100 i, o'seas
- ¶ newsbrief - 3; 50p.
    Children and the Media (booklet); £1.

Medical Action for Global Security   (MEDACT)   1992
- NR The Grayston Centre, 28 Charles Sq, LONDON, N1 6HT.   (hq)
    020 7324 4739
- ○ *K; for doctors & other health professionals committed to
    preventing war & promoting peace & global security

Medical Artists Association of Great Britain & Northern Ireland (MAA)   1949
- NR Medical Illustration UK Ltd, Charing Cross Hospital, LONDON,
    W6 8RF.   (hsb)
    020 8846 7165
    http://www.maa.org.uk
    Contact: Mrs Anne Wadmore
- ○ *A; to promote & facilitate the acquisition & dissemination of
    knowledge of the graphic & plastic arts as applied to the
    illustration of medicine
- M c 80 i

Medical Council on Alcohol   (MCA)   1967
- ■ 3 St Andrews Place, LONDON, NW1 4LB.   (hq)
    020 7487 4445   fax 020 7935 4479
    email mca@medicouncilalcol.demon.co.uk
    http://www.m-c-a.org.uk
    Sec & Medical Dir: Dr Guy Ratcliffe
- ▲ Registered Charity
- ○ *L, *M, *P; to improve medical understanding of alcohol related
    problems - particularly for medical students & medical
    practitioners. Members are from most, if not all, specialities
    within medicine
- Gp C'ees: Education, Executive, Journal
- ● Conf - Mtgs - ET - Comp - Inf - Lib
- < R Coll of Physicians of London; Alcohol Health Alliance
- > Eur Soc of Biomedical Res on Alcohol (ESBRA)
- M 280 i, 20 f, UK / 5 i, o'seas
    (Sub: £55 i, £105 with Jnl)
- ¶ Alcohol & Alcoholism (Jnl) - 6; £45 m, £520 nm.
    Alcoholis (NL) - 4; ftm, £3 nm.
    Alcohol & Health: a handbook for medical students &
    practitioners; free to students; £12 for qualified practitioners.

Medical Defence Union   (MDU)   1885
- NR 230 Blackfriars Rd, LONDON, SE1 8PJ.   (hq)
    020 7202 1500   fax 020 7202 1666
    http://www.the-mdu.com
    Chief Exec: Dr Michael Saunders
- ▲ Company Limited by Guarantee
- ○ *N; provision of medico-legal advice, assistance & indemnity to
    doctors, dentists, nurses & other healthcare professionals in
    the UK & Eire
- ● Conf - ET - LG - Workshops - Presentations
- M c 90,000 i
- ¶ Jnl - irreg; ftm only.   AR; free.
    Training packages; m only.

Medical & Dental Defence Union of Scotland   (MDDUS)   1902
- NR Mackintosh House, 120 Blythswood St, GLASGOW, G2 4EA.
    (hq)
    0141-221 5858   fax 0141-228 1208
    email info@mddus.com   http://www.mddus.com
    Chief Exec: Prof Gordon Dickson
- ▲ Company Limited by Guarantee
- ○ *M; professional indemnity for doctors & dentists
- Gp Education for primary care staff; Risk management
- ● Conf - ET - Inf - LG
- < Physician Insurers Assn of America (PIAA)
- M 22,000 i
- ¶ Summons (Jnl) - 4;   AR; both free.

Medical Equestrian Association   (MEA)   1984
- NR Bridge Farm, Blackford, CARLISLE, Cumbria, CA6 4EA.   (hsp)
    01228 674238
    http://www.medequestrian.co.uk
    Hon Sec & Treas: Dr Ian Mackay
- ▲ Registered Charity
- Br links with similar gps in Eire, Australia, New Zealand, Sweden,
    USA
- ○ *K, *M; to maintain & improve medical cover at equestrian
    events - Pony Club, riding clubs, British eventing, carriage
    driving, flat & jump racing
- ● Mtgs - ET - VE
- M 150 i, UK / 50 i, o'seas

** Medical Ethics Alliance
    Organisation lost: see Introduction paragraph 3

Medical Journalists' Association   (MJA)   1967
NR   Fairfield, Cross in Hand, HEATHFIELD, E Sussex, TN21 0SH.
      (hsp)
      01435 868786   fax 01435 865714
      email pigache@tiscali.co.uk   http://www.mja-uk.org
      Hon Sec: Philippa Pigache
▲   Un-incorporated Society
○   *M, *P; to improve the quality of medical journalism &
      understanding between medical healthcare professionals, the
      media & the public
●   Mtgs - ET - Awards
M   390 i, UK / 2 i, o'seas
¶   MJA News (NL) - 5; ftm only.
      Directory of Members with contacts - 1; ftm,
      £450 (commercial), £200 (charities & academics).

Medical Officers of Schools Association   (MOSA)   1884
NR   Amherst Medical Practice, 21 St Botolph's Rd, SEVENOAKS,
      Kent, TN13 3AQ.   (pres/b)
      01732 459255   fax 01732 450751
      email honsec@mosa.org.uk   http://www.mosa.org.uk
      Pres: Dr Neil Arnott
▲   Un-incorporated Society
○   *L, *P; promotion of school health
●   Conf - Mtgs - ET - Inf - Empl
<   Eur U of School & University Health & Medicine
M   c 400 i
¶   NL - 4; free.
      Handbook of School Health - 5-6 yrly.

Medical Protection Society Ltd   (MPS)   1892
NR   33 Cavendish Sq, LONDON, W1G 0PS.   (hq)
      020 7399 1300
      http://www.medicalprotection.org
▲   Company Limited by Guarantee
○   *P; a not-for-profit mutual association run exclusively for, &
      largely by, doctors, dentists & other healthcare professionals
●   ET - Inf - Wide range of medico-legal services (professional
      indemnity for adverse awards of costs & damages in medical
      negligence cases)
<   Physician Insurers Assn of America
M   100,000 i UK / 125,000 i, o'seas
¶   Casebook (Jnl) - 2;   Medico-legal booklets;   AR; all free.

Medical Research Society   (MRS)
NR   Box 118, Dialysis Centre, Addenbrooke's Hospital, Hills Rd,
      CAMBRIDGE, CB2 2QQ.   (hsb)
      http://www.medres.org.uk
      Academic Sec: Dr Afzal Chaudhry
▲   Registered Charity
○   *L; exchange of information on medical research
Gp   Association of Young Medical Scientists (AYMS)
●   Conf - Mtgs - ET - Comp - LG
<   Biological Coun

Medical Science Historical Society   (MSHS)   1982
■   117 Woodland Drive, Cassiobury, WATFORD, Herts,
      WD17 3DA.   (hsp)
      01923 231704
      Hon Sec: Hilda Taylor
▲   Registered Charity
○   *L; to further education in the history of diagnostic medical
      sciences; to provide a forum for everyone with an interest in
      the history of the medical laboratory
●   Mtgs
<   Brit Soc History Medicine
M   i
¶   Jnl - 1 (Summer);   NL - 2 (Spring & Autumn).

Medical Society of London   1773
■   Lettsom House, 11 Chandos St, LONDON, W1G 9EB.   (hq)
      020 7580 1043
      Registrar: Col Richard Kinsella-Bevan
○   *L; the advancement of medicine & surgery
●   Mtgs - Inf
M   i
¶   Transactions - 1.

Medical Women's Federation   (MWF)   1917
NR   Tavistock House North, Tavistock Sq, LONDON, WC1H 9HX.
      (hq)
      020 7387 7765   fax 020 7388 9216
      http://www.medicalwomensfederation.org.uk
○   *P; to further the careers of women doctors
M   i
¶   Medical Woman.   AR; both ftm.

Medico-Legal Society   1901
NR   c/o Portland Press Ltd (Customer Services), Commerce Way,
      COLCHESTER, Essex, CO2 8HP.   (hq)
      01206 7963518
      http://www.medico-legalsociety.org.uk
      Pres: Miss Elizabeth Pygott (020 7289 0188)
▲   Registered Charity
○   *L; the dissemination of medico-legal knowledge in all its
      aspects
¶   Medico-Legal Jnl; £50 m, £102 yr nm.

Medieval Dress & Textile Society   (MEDATS)
NR   Royal Armouries, Armouries Drive, LEEDS, W Yorks, LS10 1LT.
      (sec)
      http://www.medats.org.uk
      Sec: Karen Watts
○   *L
●   Mtgs

Medieval Settlement Research Group   (MSRG)   1986
■   School of Archaeology & Ancient History, University of Leicester,
      University Rd, LEICESTER, LE1 7RH.   (hsb)
      0116-252 2617   fax 0116-252 5005
      email njc10@le.ac.uk   http://www.britarch.ac.uk/msrg/
      Hon Sec: Dr Neil Christie
▲   Registered Charity
○   *L; to advance knowledge of settlements, especially those
      dating between the 5th & 16th centuries; to offer advice &
      information to those conducting research into settlement
      history; to influence national policy on the survey,
      conservation & excavation of medieval settlement sites; to
      encourage the preservation of settlement sites wherever
      possible.
●   Conf - Mtgs - Res - VE
M   430 i, 55 org
¶   AR - 1; ftm, back numbers to 2004; £5 each nm.

Medieval Siege Society
NR   11-12 Wrotham Rd, GRAVESEND, Kent, DA11 0PE.
      (reg/office)
      email secretary@medieval-siege-society.co.uk
      http://www.medieval-siege-society.co.uk
      Hon Sec: Peter Baldwin (0795 749 3327)
○   *G; re-enactment of medieval sieges
<   Nat Assn Re-enactment Socs

Meet-a-Mum Association
      has closed

© CBD Research Ltd · Beckenham · BR3 5JS · Tel 020 8650 7745 · E-mail cbd@cbdresearch.com · www.cbdresearch.com

Meetings Industry Association (MIA) 1991

NR PO Box 515, KELMARSH, Northants, NN6 9XW. (hq)
0845 230 5508   fax 0845 230 7708
email info@mia-uk.org   http://www.mia-uk.org
Chief Exec: Jane Evans
▲ Company Limited by Guarantee
○ *P, *T; meetings & conference industry
● Conf - Mtgs - ET - Res - Exhib
M 450 f
¶ NL - 12;   Magazine - 4; both free.
UK Conference Market Survey - 1; £135 m, £165 nm.
Buyers' Directory of Members - 1; free.   AR - 1; ftm only.

Megalithic Society (incorporating the Stonehenge Society) 1997

■ 25A Whitehill, BRADFORD-on-AVON, Wilts, BA15 1SQ. (hq)
01225 862482
email terence.meaden@stonehenge-avebury.net
http://www.stonehenge-avebury.net
Chief Exec: Dr Terence Meaden
▲ Un-incorporated Society
Br 2
○ *G, *K; to promote interest in & the preservation & security of the ancient stones of Britain; is also concerned with crop circles
Gp Avebury; Stonehenge (information: 01980 624715)
● Mtgs - ET - Res - Inf - PL - VE
< Stonehenge Soc
M 50 i
¶ The Complete Guidebook to Avebury; £8 m, £10 nm.

Meiosis Ltd 1989

■ Bradbourne House, Stable Block, EAST MALLING, Kent, ME19 6DZ. (hq)
01732 872711   fax 01732 872712
http://www.meiosis.co.uk
○ *H; to introduce new cultivars to the soft fruit industry
M 36 f

Melton Mowbray Pork Pie Association

NR PO Box 5540, MELTON MOWBRAY, Leics, LE13 1YU.
01664 569388
http://www.mmppa.co.uk
○ *T; makers of Melton Mowbray pork pies
M 7 f

Men of the Stones (MOS) 1947

NR 1 Steele's Yard, North St, STAMFORD, Lincs, PE9 2ZS. (mem/sec)
email jegiakes@aol.com
http://www.menofthestones.org.uk
▲ Registered Charity
○ *K; a society advocating the use of stone & other natural & local building materials; to encourage craftsmanship & preservation of the good architectural qualities of Stamford & other places in the limestone belt

Mencap Ltd
the operating title of the **Royal Mencap Society**

Ménière's Society 1984

■ The Rookery, Surrey Hills Business Park, Wotton, DORKING, Surrey, RH5 6QT. (hq)
01306 876883   fax 01306 876057
email info@menieres.org.uk
http://www.menieres.org.uk
Dir: Mrs Natasha Harrington-Benton
▲ Registered Charity
○ *W; to help those with the symptoms of Ménière's disease: vertigo (nausea), fluctuating & increasing deafness & tinnitus
● Conf - Mtgs - Res - Stat - Inf
Helpline: 0845 120 2975
M 5,400 i, 139 org, UK / 53 i, 10 org, o'seas
¶ NL - 4;   Contact List - 4;   Information sheets; AR; all ftm only.

Meningitis Association of Scotland 1991

NR 9 Edwin St, GLASGOW, G51 1ND.
0141-554 6680
http://www.menscot.org
Chmn: Mrs Eileen E McKiernan
○ *G, *W; support for families affected by meningitis

Meningitis Research Foundation 1989

■ Midland Way, Thornbury, BRISTOL, BS35 2BS. (hq)
01454 281811   fax 01454 281094
email info@meningitis.org   http://www.meningitis.org
Chief Exec: Christopher Head
▲ Company Limited by Guarantee; Registered Charity
Br 3; Republic of Ireland
○ *M, *Q; to promote research into the causes & treatment of all forms of meningitis & associated infections, & the dissemination of knowledge gained by such research; to advance the education of the public in the causes, treatment & prevention of meningitis & associated infections; to help relieve distress to individuals & families caused by death & damage through meningitis & associated infections
● Conf - ET - Res - Exhib - G - Stat - Inf - PL - VE
Helpline: 0808 800 3344 (24-hours)
< Assn of Med Res Charities (AMRC); Telephone Helpline Assn (THA)
M 5,500 i, UK / 100 i, o'seas
¶ Microscope (NL) - 3;   AR - 1; both free.
Awareness Literature:
Baby Watch; Get it Sussed; Race against Time; Tot Watch.
Materials for health professionals to help in the diagnosis & treatment of meningitis & septicaemia.

Mental Health Ireland

IRL 6 Adelaide St, DÚN LAOGHAIRE, Co Dublin, Republic of Ireland.
353 (1) 284 1166   fax 353 (1) 284 1736
email info@mentalhealthireland.ie
http://www.mentalhealthireland.ie
○ *W

Merchant Navy Association (MNA) 1989

NR 9 Saxon Way, Caistor, MARKET RASEN, Lincs, LN7 6SG. (hq)
01472 851130
http://www.mna.org.uk
Sec: Tim Brant
Br 32
○ *W; for both serving and retired seafarers.

Merchant Navy Locomotive Preservation Society Ltd (MNLPS) 1965

NR 12 Inglewood Ave, Heatherside, CAMBERLEY, Surrey, GU15 1RJ. (hsp)
01276 514000
http://www.clan-line.org.uk
Sec: R F Abercrombie
▲ Registered Charity
○ *G, *K; to preserve, maintain, operate & foster an interest in the ex-British Railways Southern Region 'Merchant Navy' Class locomotive no. 35028 'Clan Line'
● Mtgs - ET - Exhib - Comp - Maintenance of the locomotive - Special excursion runs
M i
¶ Southern Express (Jnl).

Mercia Cinema Society

has been wound up

Merioneth Agricultural Society (MAS) 1868
■ Tir y Dail, Cader Rd, DOLGELLAU, Gwynedd, LL40 1SG. (hsp)
  01341 422837   fax 01341 422837
  email sioesir@aol.com   http://www.sioesir.co.uk
  Hon Sec: E Douglas Powell
▲ Registered Charity
○ *F; promotion of agriculture by staging an annual county show
● Exhib - Comp - Merioneth County Show
< Assn of Show & Agricl Orgs
M 400 i
¶ Show catalogue - 1; £2.

Merseyside Archaeological Society 1976
NR 44 Oakdene Avenue, WARRINGTON, Cheshire, WA1 4NU.
  (mem/sp)
  http://www.merseysidearchsoc.weebly.com
  Mem Sec: Dr Eveline van der Steen
○ *G
● Mtgs - VE - Lectures - Fieldwork projects
M c 100 i
  (Sub: £12-£15)
¶ Jnl; ftm, £10 nm.   NL - 4.

Merseyside Industrial Heritage Society (MIHS) 1970
NR 14 Ardern Lea, Alvanley, FRODSHAM, Cheshire, WA6 9EQ.
  http://www.mihs.org.uk
▲ Un-incorporated Society
○ *K, *L; to foster an interest in the study & conservation of the
  industrial heritage of Merseyside
M i & org

Merton Chamber of Commerce 1992
NR Tuition House (5th floor), 27-37 St George's Rd, LONDON,
  SW19 4EU.
  020 8944 5501   fax 020 8286 2552
  email info@mertonchamber.co.uk
  http://www.mertonchamber.co.uk
  Chief Exec: Diana Sterck
▲ Company Limited by Guarantee
○ *C
● Mtgs - ET - Exhib - Inf - LG - Business support services
M 350 f
¶ NL - 4; free.   LM - 1; ftm, £5 nm.

Metal Cladding & Roofing Manufacturers Association Ltd (MCRMA)
NR 106 Ruskin Ave, Rogerstone, NEWPORT, Gwent, NP10 0BD.
  01633 895633
  email mcrma@compuserve.com
  http://www.mcrma.co.uk
▲ Company Limited by Guarantee
○ *T; for manufacturers in the metal roofing & cladding industry
Gp Floor/Deck Group; Independent Consultants Group
< Construction Products Assn
M 9 f

Metal Finishing Association
  a group of the **Surface Engineering Association**

Metal Gutter Manufacturers Association Ltd (MGMA) 1994
NR 106 Ruskin Ave, Rogerstone, NEWPORT, Gwent, NP10 0BD.
  01633 891584
  email mgmagutters@gmail.com   http://www.mgma.co.uk
▲ Company Limited by Guarantee
○ *T; to represent the leading UK manufacturers of metal gutters
M 10 f

Metal Packaging Manufacturers Association (MPMA) 1914
■ The Stables, Tintagel Farm, Sandhurst Rd, WOKINGHAM,
  Berks, RG40 3JD. (hq)
  0118-978 8433
  email enquiries@mpma.org.uk   http://www.mpma.org.uk
  Dir: N J Mullen
▲ Company Limited by Guarantee
○ *T; interests of companies involved directly, or indirectly, in the
  production of light metal containers, closures & components
  (including cans, & tinplate items)
Gp Business c'ees: Closures, Food contact, General line, Open top,
  Technical
  Service/advisory c'ees: Environment, Health & safety, Public
  relations
● Mtgs - Exhib - Stat - Inf
< Eur Metal Packaging (EMPAC)
M 23 f (full), 18 f (associate)

Metalforming Machinery Makers' Association Ltd (MMMA)
■ The Cottage, Down End, Hook Norton, BANBURY, Oxon,
  OX15 5LW. (hq)
  01608 737129   fax 01295 253333
  email rayjelf@mmma.org.uk
  http://www.mmma.org.uk
  Co Sec: Ray Jelf
▲ Company Limited by Guarantee
○ *N, *T; to act as the central organisation promoting the interests
  of companies involved in the manufacture & sale of
  metalforming machinery & ancillary products in the UK
● Exhib - Inf
< a METCOM organisation
M 35 f
  (Sub: £400)
¶ Hbk.

Metalworking Fluid Product Stewardship Group
  a group of the **United Kingdom Lubricants Association Ltd**

Metamorphic Association 1979
NR 159 Bembrook Rd, HASTINGS, E Sussex, TN34 3PD. (hq)
  0870 770 7984 (recorded information only)
  email metamorphicassoc@cs.com
  http://www.metamorphicassociation.org
▲ Registered Charity
○ *P; to promote awareness, understanding & use of the
  metamorphic technique - a unique & simple approach to
  self-healing & personal development through the contact with
  the spinal reflex points in the feet
● Conf - Mtgs - ET - Exhib - Inf
M c 350 i
¶ NL - 4;   Bulletin - 4; both ftm only.
  Programme of Activities - 2; ftm, on request for sae.

Metric Martyrs
NR PO Box 526, SUNDERLAND, SR1 3YS.
  0191-565 2004
  email beth@metricmartyrs.co.uk
  http://www.metricmartyrs.co.uk
  Campaign Dir: Neil Herron (0777 620 2045)
○ *K; to keep Imperial measurements

© CBD Research Ltd · Beckenham · BR3 5JS · Tel 020 8650 7745 · E-mail cbd@cbdresearch.com · www.cbdresearch.com

Metropolitan Drinking Fountain & Cattle Trough Association 1859

■ Oaklands, 5 Queenborough Gardens, CHISLEHURST, Kent, BR7 6NP. (hsp)
020 8467 1261
email ralph.baber@tesco.net
http://www.drinkingfountains.org
Sec: Ralph P Baber
▲ Registered Charity
○ *G; to promote the provision of drinking water for people & animals in the UK & overseas; to keep an archive of materials, artifacts, drinking fountains, cattle troughs & other installations
M 25 i
Note: Also known as the Drinking Fountain Association

Metropolitan Public Gardens Association   (MPGA)   1882

NR 348 London Rd, MITCHAM, Surrey, CR4 3ND.   (sp)
020 8648 9469
http://www.mpga.org.uk
Sec: Mrs Joyce K Bellamy
▲ Registered Charity
○ *G; the protection, preservation & acquiring for permanent preservation for public use of gardens, disused burial grounds, churchyards, open spaces, areas of land adjoining roads & footpaths, or any land situated within the Metropolitan Police District; the encouragement of window boxes, provision of seats & the planting of trees
● AGM - Res - Exhib - Comp (via London in Bloom) - SG - LG
< London in Bloom
M 100 i
¶ Ybk (AR) - 1; free.

Meuse Rhine Issel Cattle Society of the United Kingdom (MRI)   1971

NR Castlemoor Farm, Four Oaks, NEWENT, Glos, GL18 1LU. (sp/b)
01531 890730   fax 01531 890939
email office@mri.org.uk   http://www.mri.org.uk
Sec: Mrs Niki Ford
▲ Registered Charity
Br N Zealand
○ *B, *F
● Conf - Mtgs - Exhib - Stat - Expt - Inf - Semen sales
< R Assn Brit Dairy Farmers; Nat Cattle Assn (Dairy)
M 72 i, UK / 3 i, o'seas
¶ MRI NL - 3;   Herdbook - 1; £10; both m only.

Meyrick Society   1890

■ 38 Downs Hill, BECKENHAM, Kent, BR3 5HB.   (hsp)
020 8650 4527
email robin@peterdaleltd.com
Hon Sec: Robin Dale
○ *G, *L; promotion of the study of antiques, arms & armour
● Mtgs
M 25 i

Micro & Anophthalmic Children's Society   (MACS)   1993

■ PO Box 92, HOLYHEAD, Anglesey, LL65 9AW.   (hsp)
0800 169 8088
email enquiries@macs.org.uk   http://www.macs.org.uk
Sec: Lynda Rhodes
▲ Registered Charity
○ *W; a support group for children born with anophthalmia (absence of eyes), microphthalmia (small eyes) & coloboma (a structural defect of the eyes)
● Conf - Mtgs
< Contact a Family
M 300 i, UK / 120 i, o'seas
¶ NL;   AR; both free.

Micropalaeontological Society   (TMS)   1971

NR c/o Dr J Pike. School of Earth & Ocean Sciences, Cardiff University Main Building, Park Place, CARDIFF, CF10 3YE.
029 2087 5181
email pikej@cardiff.ac.uk
Sec: Dr Jenny Pike
▲ Registered Charity
○ *L
Gp Froaminifera; Mcrovertebrates; Nonnofossils; Ostracods; PAlynology; Silicofossils
● Mtgs - VE
M i
¶ Jnl of Micropalaeontology.

Micropower Council   2004

NR Stowe House, 1688 High Street, Knowle, SOLIHULL, W Midlands, B93 0LY.
01564 732790
http://www.micropower.co.uk
Chief Exec: Dave Sowden
○ *T; manufacturers & installers of microgeneration systems for the production of heat or electricity by individual households & small businesses businesses
< Construction Products Assn
M 63 f

Microtome Manufacturers Association   (MMA)   1976

■ 3 Hughes Stanton Way, MANNINGTREE, Essex, CO11 2HQ. (hsp)
▲ Un-incorporated Society
○ *T
● Mtgs - Stat
M 34 f
¶ Notes - 2/3;   Report - 1.

Microwave Technologies Association   (MTA)   1978

■ Norfolk Glen, Love Lane, IVER, Bucks, SL0 9QZ.   (hq)
01753 652939   fax 01753 652939
email jennipher@microwaveassociation.org.uk
http://www.microwaveassociation.org.uk
Chmn: Jennipher Marshall-Jenkinson
▲ Un-incorporated Society
○ *T; to promote & advise on all aspects of microwave & microwave related products to trade, hotels, caterers & consumers
Gp Individual membership; Corporate membership
● Mtgs - ET - Exhib - Inf
< Food Standards Authority
M 50 i, 20 f
¶ NL - 6; ftm only.

Mid-Somerset Agricultural Show Society

NR PO Box 5037, WELLS, Somerset, BA5 9AX.   (hq)
01749 870124   fax 01749 780629
email secretary@midsomersetshow.org.uk
http://www.midsomersetshow.org.uk
Sec: Lisette Smith
○ *F
● Mid-Somerset Show
< Assn of Show & Agricl Orgs

Mid Yorkshire Chamber of Commerce & Industry   (MYCCI)   1853

■ The Stable Block, Brewery Drive, HUDDERSFIELD, W Yorks, HD4 6EN.   (hq)
01484 483660   fax 01484 514199
email info@mycci.co.uk   http://www.mycci.co.uk
Exec Dir: Andrew Choi
▲ Company Limited by Guarantee
Br Halifax, Huddersfield, Wakefield
○ *C
● Conf - Mtgs - ET - Exhib - Expt - LG - Export documentation
< Brit Chamber of Commerce
M 1,500 f
¶ Close Up - 4; free.

Middle East Association   (MEA)   1961
- ■ Bury House, 33 Bury St, LONDON, SW1Y 6AX.   (hq)
  020 7839 2137   fax 020 7839 6121
  email mail@the-mea.co.uk   http://www.the-mea.co.uk
  Sec: Graham Green
- ▲ Company Limited by Guarantee
- ○ *T; to promote trade & investment between the UK & the Middle East (all Arab states, Iran, Turkey, Afghanistan, Ethiopia & Eritrea) on behalf of its members
- Gp Law sub group
- ● Conf - Mtgs - Exhib - Stat - Expt - Inf - Lib - VE - LG
- M c 70 i, 350 f
- ¶ Information Digest - 24;   Hbk - 1;   AR; free.
  Information sheets.

Middle White Pig Breeders Club   1990
- ■ Benson Lodge, 50 Old Slade Lane, IVER, Bucks, SL0 9DR.
  (hsp)
  01753 654166
  http://www.middlewhite.co.uk
  Hon Sec: Mrs Miranda M Squire
- ○ *B; promotion of the traditional breed
- ● Exhib (occasional) - Expt -Inf
- < Brit Pig Assn (BPA)
- M c 110 i
  (Sub: £15)
- ¶ NL - 4.

**Midlands Asthma & Allergy Research Association   (MAARA)
1968**
- ■ 7 Stadium Business Court, Millennium Way, Pride Park, DERBY, DE24 8HP.   (hq)
  01332 799600   fax 01332 792200
  email enquiries@maara.org   http://www.maara.org
- ▲ Registered Charity
- ○ *Q; to research into asthma & allergy
- Gp Aerobiology research
- ● Mtgs - Res
- < Intl Assn of Aerobiology; Brit Aerobiology Fedn
- M 300 i
- ¶ [see website]

Midlands Club Cricket Conference   (MCCC)   1947
- ■ 19 Pensham Croft, Monkspath, SOLIHULL, W Midlands, B90 4XT.   (hsp)
  0121-744 5263
  email william@galahospitality.co.uk
  http://www.mccc.co.uk
  Hon Sec: W George
- ▲ Un-incorporated Society
- ○ *S; to foster & maintain club cricket in the Midlands
- Gp Club insurance; Competitions for various age groups; Fixtures bureau; Tours bureau
- ● Comp - Inf
- < England & Wales Cricket Bd
- M c 500 clubs and leagues
- ¶ NL - 3;   Ybk - 1

Midlothian & East Lothian Chamber of Commerce   (MELCC)
- NR 42/3 Hardengreen Business Park, Dalhousie Rd, DALKIETH, Midlothian, EH22 3NU.   (hq)
  0131-654 1234   fax 0131-561 6259
  email info@met.org.uk   http://www.melcc.org.uk
  Exec Dir: Gregor Murray
- ▲ Company Limited by Guarantee
- ○ *C
- < Scot Chams Comm

Migraine Action Association   1958
- NR 27 East St (4th floor), LEICESTER, LE1 6NB.   (hq)
  0116 275 8317   fax 0116 254 2023
  email info@migraine.org.uk
  http://www.migraine.org.uk
- ▲ Registered Charity
- ○ *Q; promotion of research into causes & cure of migraine; information & assistance to sufferers
- ● Conf - Res - Inf - Migraine Action Week (September)
- M c 36,000 i
- ¶ NL - 4.   Various booklets & leaflets.

Milestone Society   2001
- ■ Hollywell House, Hollywell Lane, Clows Top, KIDDERMINSTER, Worcs, DY14 9NR.   (hsp)
  01299 832338
  email john113atkinson@btinternet.com
  http://www.milestonesociety.co.uk
  Hon Sec: John Atkinson
- ▲ Registered Charity
- ○ *G; to identify, record, research, conserve & interpret for public benefit the milestones & other waymarkers of the British Isles
- ● Conf - Mtgs - Res - Inf - PL
- M 500 i, 15 f, UK / 3 i, o'seas
  (Sub: £10 i, £15 f UK / £20 i, o'seas
- ¶ Milestones & Waymarkers; ftm, £5 nm.
  NL - 2; ftm, £2 nm.   On the Ground - 1; ftm, £3 nm.

**Military Heraldry Society (the Cloth Insignia Research & Collectors
Society)   (M Her S)   1951**
- ■ Windyridge, 27 Sandbrook, Ketley, TELFORD, Shropshire, TF1 5BB.   (publicityofficer)
  01952 270221
  email info@militaryheraldrysociety.com
- ▲ Un-incorporated Society
- ○ *G; collectors of cloth formation signs (shoulder sleeve insignia, shoulder titles, regimental & unit flashes & similar items)
- ● Mtgs - Res - Inf - Lib
- M 250 i, UK / 140 i, o'seas
  (Sub: £15 i, UK)
- ¶ The Formation Sign - 4; free.

Military Historical Society   (MHS)   1948
- ■ c/o National Army Museum, Royal Hospital Rd, LONDON, SW3 4HT.   (mail addr)
  020 7730 0717
  email herbert99@blueyonder.co.uk
  http://www.militaryhistsoc.plus.com
  Sec: Mike Taylor
- ▲ Registered Charity
- Br 4
- ○ *G; the study of the history of the uniformed services of the Crown, of uniforms, weapons, & all aspects of military history
- ● Conf - Mtgs - Res - Exhib - Comp - VE
- M 680 i, 20 org, UK / 20 i, 5 org, o'seas
  (Sub: £15)
- ¶ Bulletin - 4; ftm, £4 each nm.
  Special publication - irreg; ftm, £6.

Military History Society of Ireland   1949
- IRL Newman House, University College Dublin, 86 St Stephen's Green, DUBLIN 2, Republic of Ireland.
  Sec: Dr Pat McCarthy
- ○ *L

© CBD Research Ltd · Beckenham · BR3 5JS · Tel 020 8650 7745 · E-mail cbd@cbdresearch.com · www.cbdresearch.com

Military Vehicle Trust (MVT) 1970
- ■ Meadowhead Cottage, Beaumaris Avenue, BLACKBURN, Lancs, BB2 4TP. (hsp)
  01254 202253
  http://www.mvt.org.uk
  Gen Sec: Simon P Bromley
- ▲ Company Limited by Guarantee; Registered Charity
- Br 43
- ○ *G; preservation & restoration of military vehicles
- ● Mtgs - Exhib - Inf - Lib - PL - VE - LG - Shows - Film hire
- < Danish Soc Military Vehicle Presvn (FMKB), Belgian Military Vehicle Trust, MOVT, Swiss Club Romand, VHSP
- M 6,616 i, UK / 421 i, o'seas
- ¶ Windscreen - 4; ftm, £3.50 nm.
  Greensheet (NL) - 6; ftm only.

Milk Bottle News (MBN) 1984
- ■ 60 Rose Valley Crescent, STANFORD-le-HOPE, Essex, SS17 8EF. (hsp)
  01375 679527
  email mbneditor@blueyonder.co.uk
  http://www.milkbottlenews.org.uk
  Sec: Paul Luke
- ○ *G; to share information on milk botles & subjects ascertaining to the UK dairy industry past & present
- ● Mtgs - Exhib - VE
- M 108 i, 8 f, UK / 1 i, o'seas
- ¶ Milk Bottle News (NL) - 4; £15 yr.
- × Milk Bottle & Dairyana Collectors

Milking Equipment Association (MEA) 1941
- ■ Samuelson House, 62 Forder Way, Hampton, PETERBOROUGH, Cambs, PE7 8JB. (hq)
  0845 644 8748 fax 01733 314767
  email ab@aea.uk.com
  http://www.milkingequipment.uk.com
  Dir Gen: Roger Lane-Nott
- ▲ Company Limited by Guarantee
- ○ *T; for manufacturers of milking equipment, associated suppliers & distributors
- M 5 f
- × 2008 Milking Machine Manufacturers' Association

Milking Machine Manufacturers' Association
since 2008 **Milking Equipment Association**

Milton Keynes & North Bucks Chamber of Commerce 1994
- NR Brooklyn House, 9 Rillaton Walk, MILTON KEYNES, Bucks, MK9 2FZ. (hq)
  01908 259000 fax 01908 246799
  email enquiry@mk-chamber.co.uk
  http://www.mk-chamber.co.uk
  Chief Exec: Rita Spada
- ○ *C
- ● ET - Inf
- < Brit Chams Comm; TEC Nat Coun
- M 1,500 f
- ¶ Opportunity (Jnl) - 6.   AR - 1; both free.

Mind (the mental health charity) (MIND) 1946
- ■ Granta House, 15-19 Broadway, LONDON, E15 4BQ. (hq)
  020 8519 2122 fax 020 8522 1725
  email contact@mind.org.uk   http://www.mind.org.uk
  Contact: The Chief Exec
- ▲ Registered Charity
- ○ *W; works for everyone with experience of mental distress
- ● Conf - ET - Res - Exhib - Inf - Lib - LG - Advice service & legal network
  MINDinfoline: 020 8522 1728   (Outer London 0845 766 0163)
- < Wld Fedn for Mental Health
- M c 1,200 i
- ¶ Publications list available.

Mineral Industry Research Organisation (MIRO) 1974
- ■ Concorde House, Trinity Park, SOLIHULL, W Midlands, B37 7UQ. (hq)
  0121-635 5225 fax 0121-635 5226
  email mail@miro.co.uk   http://www.miro.co.uk
  Dir: A Gibbon
- ▲ Company Limited by Guarantee
- ○ *Q; technology transfer brokerage & research facilitation that identifies, promotes & manages innovative technology research projects on exploration, mining, extraction & processing of primary & secondary raw materals
- Gp Research panels
- ● Conf - Res - Inf - LG
- M 25 f, UK / 7 f, o'seas
- ¶ Miro News - 6;   AR; both ftm.

Mineral Processing & Extractive Metallurgy Division
a group of the **Institute of Materials, Minerals & Mining**

Mineral Products Association (MPA) 2009
- ■ Gillingham House, 38-44 Gillingham St, LONDON, SW1V 1HU. (hq)
  020 7963 8000 fax 020 7963 8001
  email info@mineralproducts.org
  http://www.mineralproducts.org
  Chief Exec: Nigel Jackson
- ▲ Company Limited by Guarantee
- Br 8 regional divns
- ○ *T; for quarry operators & suppliers of aggregates, asphalt, cement, concrete, lime, mortar, sand & silica
- Gp Aggregates, asphalt & industrial; British precast; Cementitious & concrete;
  Agricultural Lime Association (ALA); British Lime Association (BLA); British Marine Aggregates Producers Association (BMAPA); British Ready-Mixed Concrete Association (BRMCA); Mortar Industry Association (MIA); Silica & Moulding Sands Association (SAMSA)
- ● Conf - Mtgs - ET - Res - Exhib - Stat - Inf - Lib - PL - LG
- < Eur Asphalt Producers Assn; Eur Ready-Mixed Concrete Org; Eur Aggregates Assn; Construction Products Assn
- M c 140 f
- ¶ The Aggregates Industry at a Glance (fact file).
  Voice of the Quarrying Industry (a profile of the QPA & its work).
  General:
    What's in a Quarry (Video); £15.
    Quarrying in Depth - recycling.
  Environmental:
    Directory of Restoration: a compendium of examples.
    Shifting Ground (Video); £35.
    Managers' Guide to the video; £3.25.
  Lime:
    Lime Stabilisation Manual; £6.   Leaflets.
  Marine:
    Aggregates from the Sea (video) & (booklet); free.
  Health & Safety:
    Clearing Blocked Crushers; £6.75.
    Code of Practice for Safeguarding Machinery; £7.50.
    Record Book for the Recording of Explosives kept in:
    Quarries' Blasting Sites; £3.
    Quarries' Explosives Stores; £3.
  Safety booklets; 30p each.
  Publications list available.
- × 2009 (British Cement Association
       (Quarry Products Association

Mineral Wool Insulation Manufacturers Association   (MIMA) 1962
- ■ 57c Albany St, LONDON, NW1 4BT.   (hq)
   020 7935 8532   fax 07006 065950
   email admin@mima.info   http://www.mima.info
   Sec Gen: Crispin Dunn-Meynell
- ▲ Company Limited by Guarantee
- ○ *T; interests of manufacturers of stone & glass mineral wool; to promote the usage of mineral wool products for thermal & acoustic insulation & fire protection in building, industry & commerce
- ● Mtgs - Exhib - LG
- < Construction Products Assn
- M 5 f
- ¶ Technical publications & general guidance notes for home insulation.
- × EURISOL-UK Ltd (UK Mineral Wool Association)

Mineralogical Society of Great Britain & Ireland   (MINSOC) 1876
- NR 12 Baylis Mews, Amyand Park Rd, TWICKENHAM, Middx, TW1 3HQ.   (hq)
   020 8891 6600   fax 020 8891 6599
   email info@minersoc.org   http://www.minersoc.org
   Gen Sec: Dr Mark Hodson
- ▲ Registered Charity
- ○ *L; advancing the knowledge of the science of mineralogy & its application to other subjects including crystallography, geochemistry, petrology, environmental science & economic geology
- Gp Applied mineralogy; Clay minerals; Geochemistry; Metamorphic studies; Mineral physics; Volcanic & magmatic studies
- ● Conf - Mtgs - ET - SG - Exhib - Inf - Lib - VE - LG
- < Intl Mineralogical Assn; Eur Mineralogical U; Foundation for Science & Technology; Geological Soc; R Society
- M c 900 i
- ¶ Publications list available on request.

Minerals Engineering Society   (MES)   1958
- ■ 2 Ryton Close, Blyth, WORKSOP, Notts, S81 8DN.   (hsp)
   01909 591787   fax 01909 591940
   email hon.sec.mes@lineone.net
   http://www.mineralsengineering.org
   Hon Sec: A W Howells
- ▲ Company Limited by Guarantee; Registered Charity
- Br 3; Australia, Canada, New Zealand, South Africa, USA
- ○ *L, *P; to disseminate the science of minerals processing
- ● Conf - Mtgs
- < American Coal Preparation Soc; Australian Coal Preparation Soc
- M 410 i, 4 f, UK / 30 i, o'seas
   (Sub: £14-£20 i)
- ¶ MQR - 6; ftm.

Miners' & Industrial Lamp Manufacturers' Association
   has closed

Miniature Armoured Fighting Vehicle Association   (MAFVA) 1965
- ■ 45 Balmoral Drive, HOLMES CHAPEL, Cheshire, CW4 7JQ.   (hsp)
   01477 535373   fax 01477 535892
   email mafvahq@aol.com   http://www.mafva.net
   Pres & Sec: G E Gary Williams
- ▲ Un-incorporated Society
- Br 52; 59 o'seas
- ○ *G; for makers & collectors of model AFVs & other military vehicles & equipment
- ● Mtgs - Res - Exhib - Comp - Stat - Inf - VE
- M 4,060 i, f & org, UK / 2,600 i, f & org, o'seas
- ¶ Tankette - 6.
   NL (county groups) - 7; ftm only.

Miniature Mediterranean Donkey Association   (MMDA)   1996
- ■ Holebrook Farm, Cheriton Bishop, EXETER, Devon, EX6 6HL.   (hsp)
   01647 281642
   http://www.miniature-donkey-assoc.com
   Sec: Mrs Penny Cooke
- ▲ Company Limited by Guarantee
- ○ *B; care, welfare, education & promotion of the breed
- Gp Register & stud book of the UK
- ● ET - Stat - Expt - Inf - Lib - LG
- < Nat Miniature Donkey Assn (USA)
- M 150 i, UK / 4 i, o'seas
- ¶ Little People (NL) - 6; ftm only.

Mining Association of the United Kingdom   (MAUK)   1946
- ■ 78 Copt Heath Drive, Knowle, SOLIHULL, W Midlands, B93 9PB.   (hsb)
   01564 205079   fax 01564 205079
   email mail@mauk.org.uk   http://www.mauk.org.uk
   Sec: R A Fenton
- ▲ Company Limited by Guarantee
- ○ *T; to promote & foster the mining of metals & minerals worldwide
- ● LG
- < Euromines (Brussels); CBI Minerals C'ee
- M 3 i, 16 f, 4 org
- ¶ AR - 1; ftm.

Minor Counties Cricket Association   (MCCA)   1895
- NR Blueberry Haven, 20 Boucher Rd, BUDLEIGH SALTERTON, Devon, EX9 6JF.   (sp)
   01395 445216   fax 01395 445216
   email geoffe1@btinternet.com
   Sec: G R Evans
- ▲ Un-incorporated Society
- ○ *S
- ● Cricket matches
- < England & Wales Cricket Bd
- M 280 i, 20 county cricket clubs
- ¶ Minor Counties Cricket Annual.

Minor Metals Trade Association   1973
- NR Angel Gate, 326A City Rd, LONDON, EC1V 2PT.   (asa)
   020 8330 7456   fax 020 8330 7447
   email secretariat@mmta.co.uk   http://www.mmta.co.uk
   Sec: N Barry Jaynes
- ▲ Company Limited by Guarantee
- ○ *T; regulation of trading relationships in the trading of minor metals
- ● Conf - Mtgs - LG
- M 35 f, UK / 35 f, o'seas

MIRA Ltd   (MIRA)   1946
- NR Watling St, NUNEATON, Warks, CV10 0TU.   (hq)
   024 7635 5000   fax 024 7635 5355
   http://www.mira.co.uk
   Managing Dir: J R Wood
- ▲ Company Limited by Guarantee
- ○ *Q
- Gp Aerodynamics; Durability; Engines & transmissions; Noise; Proving ground; Ride & handling; Vehicle analysis; Vehicle safety
- ● Conf - Mtgs - Res - SG - Inf - Lib
- < Assn Indep Res & Technology Orgs
- M 85 f
- ¶ Automobile Abstracts - 12.
   Automotive Business News - 25.
   Research Reports; ftm.   AR; free.

© CBD Research Ltd · Beckenham · BR3 5JS · Tel 020 8650 7745 · E-mail cbd@cbdresearch.com · www.cbdresearch.com

Miscarriage Association (MA) 1982
- ■ c/o Clayton Hospital, Northgate, WAKEFIELD, W Yorks, WF1 3JS. (hq)
  01924 200799 (Helpline) fax 01924 298834
  email info@miscarriageassociation.org.uk
  http://www.miscarriageassociation.org.uk
  Nat Dir: Ruth Bender Atik
- ▲ Company Limited by Guarantee; Registered Charity
- Br 50+
- ○ *M, *W; to provide information & support to women & their partners who have had a miscarriage, ectopic or molar pregnancy; to promote good practice in the way pregnancy loss is managed in hospitals & the community
- Gp Special register
- ● Support group meetings - Inf
- M 200 volunteer support contacts, 45 support gps
- ¶ NL - 4; ftm. AR.
  Information leaflets; prices vary.

Mixed Wood-chip Suppliers Association (MWSA)
- ■ Kingsway House, Wrotham Rd, Meopham, GRAVESEND, Kent, DA13 0AU. (sp)
- ○ *T
- ● Mtgs - ET - Stat
- M 7 f

Mobile Data Association (MDA) 1994
- ■ PO Box 9347, SLEAFORD, Lincs, NG34 4DA. (mail/addr)
  0870 225 5632
  email info@themda.org   http://www.themda.org
  Operations Dir: Martin Ballard
- ▲ Company Limited by Guarantee
- ○ *T; to increase awareness of mobile applications
- ● Conf - Mtgs - Stat - Expt - LG
- M 65 f, UK / 15 f, o'seas

Mobile Electronics & Security Federation (MESF) 1977
- NR PO Box 3750, BRAINTREE, Essex, CM77 8DZ. (hq)
  0870 863 5210
  email advice@mesf.org.uk   http://www.mesf.org.uk
- ○ *T; for the aftermarket mobile electronics industry - security (incl electronic & mechanical devices), mobile media (incl audio & in-car entertainment), telematics (incl fleet management & tracking) & communications (incl cellular & mobile radio), van lining & racking, & towing equipment
- ● Mtgs - ET - Exam - Exhib - Comp - Inf - LG
- M i & org

Mobile Industry Crime Action Forum (MICAF) 2000
- NR PO Box 28353, LONDON, SE20 7WJ.
  020 8778 9864 fax 020 8659 9561
  email micaf@tuff.co.uk   http://www.micaf.co.uk
  Exec Sec: Jack Wraith
- ▲ Un-incorporated Society
- ○ *T; to provide a forum for the exchange of information & research in mobile handset abuse & theft
- Gp Administrative Board
  Crime prevention; Cooperation working; Mobile phone & theft technical group working group
- ● Conf - Mtgs - ET - SG - Stat - Inf - LG
- < TUFF Ltd
- M 30 i, 14 f

Mobile Media Specialist Association (MMSA) 2003
- NR Holly House, Holly Lane, SILCHESTER, Berks, RG7 2NA.
  http://www.mmsa-org.uk
  Gen Sec: Kevin O;Byrne
- ▲ COmpany Limited by Guarantee
- ○ *T; for installers of specialist aftermarket in-car electronics
- M 9 f

Mobile Messaging Forumn
  a sector of the **Irish Business & Employers Confederation**

Mobile Operators Association (MOA) 2003
- NR Russell Square House, 10-12 Russell Square, LONDON, WC1B 5EE.
  020 7331 2015 fax 020 7931 2047
  email info@ukmoa.org
  http://www.mobilemastinfo.com
  Exec Dir: John Cooke
- ○ *T; to represent the UK mobile phone network operators on radio frequency health & safety, & related town planning issues associated with the use of mobile phone technology
- M 4 f

Mobilise Organisation
  since April 2011 **Disabled Motoring UK**

Model Electronic Railway Group (MERG) 1967
- ■ Dingle Bank, Elmhurst Walk, Goring-on-Thames, READING, Berks, RG8 9DE. (chmn/p)
  01491 872566
  email chairman@merg.org.uk   http://www.merg.org.uk
  Chmn: Howard Watkins
- ▲ Un-incorporated Society
- ○ *G; to promote & foster interest in the application of electronics, including computers, to railway modelling
- ● Mtgs - ET - Exhib - Inf - Lib - VE
- M 800 i, UK / 80 i, o'seas
- ¶ Jnl - 4;   Technical Bulletins (on web); both ftm only.

Model Power Boat Association (UK) Ltd   (MPBA)   1924
- NR Furzelands FArm, Maypole Rd, LAngford, MALDON, Essex, CM9 4SZ. (treas/p)
  01621 854765
  email peter@furzelands.demon.co.uk
  Gen Treas: Peter Revill
- ○ *S; national body controlling model power boating in UK.

Model Railway Club (MRC) 1910
- ■ Keen House, 4 Calshot St, LONDON, N1 9DA. (hq)
  020 7837 2542
  http://www.themodelrailwayclub.org
  Chmn: Peter Mann
- ▲ Company Limited by Guarantee
- ○ *G; the modelling & study of railways
- ● Conf - Mtgs - ET - Exhib - SG - Inf - Lib
- < Chiltern Model Rly Assn
- M c 200 i
- ¶ Bulletin - 6; ftm only.

Model Yachting Association (MYA) 1911
- NR 5A Cuckoo Lane, Stubbington, FAREHAM, Hants, PO14 3PJ. (sp)
  01329 665880
  http://www.mya-uk.org.uk
  Sec: Chris Durant
- ▲ Un-incorporated Society
- ○ *G, *S; to promote the design, construction & racing of model sailing boats; to act as the model yacht racing authority for the UK
- ● Mtgs - Comp - Settling conditions, venues & dates for national & international competitions
- < Intl Sailing Fedn/Radio Sailing Divn (ISAF/RSD); R Yachting Assn; Cent Coun of Physical Recreation (Water Recreation Divn)
- M 1,600 i & clubs
- ¶ Acquaint - 4;   Ybk - 1; both ftm, £2.50 each nm.

Modern Churchpeople's Union (MCU) 1898

■ MCU Office, 9 Westward View, Aigburth, LIVERPOOL, Merseyside, L17 7EE. (hq)
0151-726 9730
email office@modchurchunion.org
http://www.modchurchunion.org
Gen Sec: Revd Jonathan Clatworthy
▲ Registered Charity
○ *R; an Anglican society for the study & advancement of liberal theological thought
● Conf - Mtgs - ET - SG
< Inclusive Church
M 550 i, 130 org, UK / 10 i, 90 org, o'seas
¶ Modern Believing - 4; ftm, £6 each nm.
Signs of the Times (NL) - 4; ftm, 50p each nm.

Modern Humanities Research Association (MHRA) 1920

■ 1 Carlton House Terrace, LONDON, SW1Y 5DB. (hsb)
01225 385404
email d.c.gillespie@bath.ac.uk   http://www.mhra.org.uk
Hon Sec: Prof David Gillespie
▲ Registered Charity
Br Washington (DC)
○ *L, *Q; advanced studies & research in modern & medieval languages & literature (incl English)
● Res
< Intl Fedn Modern Languages Literatures
M 200 i, 50 f, UK / 100 i, 50 f, o'seas
(Sub: £27)
¶ Modern Language Review - 4; £27 (US$51).
Publications list available on request.

Modern Masonry Alliance
an affiliated association of the **British Precast Concrete Federation**

Modern Pentathlon Association of Great Britain (MPAGB) 1948

■ Wessex House, University of Bath, Claverton Down, BATH, BA2 7AY. (hq)
01225 386808   fax 01225 386995
email admin@pentathlongb.org
http://www.pentathlongb.org
Admin Sec: Skip Peacey,   Chief Exec: Peter Hart
▲ Company Limited by Guarantee
○ *S; organisation of modern pentathlon (a compilation of 5 different events, fencing, swimming, shooting, cross-country running & riding)
● Comp
< U Intle Pentathlon Moderne (UIPM)
M 4,400 i, 80 clubs, UK / 25 i, o'seas
¶ Points per Second (NL) - 4; ftm only.
Note: uses registered name of Pentathlon GB

Modern Studies Association (MSA) 1972

NR 14 Fontstane St, MONIFIETH, Angus, DD5 4LE. (sp)
http://www.msa-scotland.net
▲ Un-incorporated Society
○ *E, *P; to promote & enhance teaching of modern studies in Scottish schools
● Conf - ET - Res - Comp
M i

Modular & Portable Building Association Ltd (MPBA) 1938

■ PO Box 99, CAERSWS, Powys, SY17 5WR. (mail/addr)
0870 241 7687   fax 01686 4304005
email mpba@mpba.biz   http://www.mpba.biz
▲ Company Limited by Guarantee
○ *T; to promote the modular & portable buildings industry & companies involved in the supply of products & services to the industry
Gp C'ees: Health & safety, Hire, Technical
● Conf - Mtgs - ET - Res - Exhib - LG
M c 110 f

Momentum - the Northern Ireland ICT Federation (MOMENTUM)

NR NiSoft House, Ravenhill Business Pk, Ravenhill Rd, BELFAST, BT6 8AW.
028 9045 0101   fax 028 9045 2123
http://www.momentumni.org

Monarchist League 1943

■ PO Box 5307, BISHOP'S STORTFORD, Herts, CM23 3DZ. (mail/address)
01279 465551   fax 01279 466111
http://www.monarchyinternational.net
Contact: The Secretary
▲ Un-incorporated Society
Br 22; Australia, USA
○ *G; to promote, support & defend the monarchical system of government in the UK & abroad
Gp Heraldry; Bulgaria; Egypt; Portugal
● Mtgs - Inf - Lib - LG
< cooperates with c 100 monarchist organisations worldwide
M 4,500 i, UK / 500 i, o'seas
¶ Monarchy (Jnl) - 4.   The Crown (Jnl) - 4.
Note: The Constitutional Monarchy Association is part of the League.

Monmouthshire Antiquarian Association 1847

NR 1 Fields Park Avenue, NEWPORT, Monmouthshire, NP20 5BG.
○ *L

Monmouthshire Show Society Ltd 1790s

NR Parclands House, Raglan, USK, Monmouthshire, NP15 2BX. (hq)
01291 691160   fax 01291 691161
email anna@monmouthshow.co.uk
http://www.monmouthshow.co.uk
Sec: Anna Williams
▲ Registered Charity
○ *F; to produce the Monmouthshire agricultural show; to promote the welfare of animals
● Mtgs - ET - Exhib - Comp
< Assn of Show & Agricl Orgs
M 350 i

Montessori Society (AMI) UK (Mont Soc) 1935

■ 26 Lyndhurst Gardens, LONDON, NW3 5NW. (hq)
020 7435 7874
email montessori.ami.uk@tiscali.co.uk
http://www.montessori-uk.org
Mem Sec: Mrs Elizabeth Hood
▲ Un-incorporated Society
○ *E; promotion of the philosophy of Dr Maria Montessori with regard to child development & general attitude to life
● Conf - Exhib - Inf
< Assn Montessori Intle (AMI)
M 300 i, UK / 50 i, o'seas
¶ Montessori Direction - 2; free.

Monumental Brass Society 1887

■ Lowe Hill House, STRATFORD ST MARY, Suffolk, CO7 6JX. (hsp)
http://www.mbs-brasses.co.uk
Hon Sec: H Martin Stuchfield
▲ Registered Charity
Br 12; 2 in USA
○ *L; study & preservation of monumental brasses, indents of lost brasses & incised slabs
● Conf - Mtgs - Res - Stat - Inf - VE - Advice & assistance to Church authorities on care & repair of brasses
M c 500 i, 50 org
¶ Portfolio - irreg;   Transactions - 1;   Bulletin - 3;
AR - 1;   LM - irreg; all ftm only.

© CBD Research Ltd · Beckenham · BR3 5JS · Tel 020 8650 7745 · E-mail cbd@cbdresearch.com · www.cbdresearch.com

Moorland Association   1987
NR   16 Castle Park, LANCASTER, LA1 1YG.   (hsb)
　　01524 846846
　　http://www.moorlandassociation.org
　　Sec: R M N Gillibrand
▲　Un-incorporated Society
○　*K; to conserve heather moorland in England & Wales
●　Conf - Mtgs - ET
M　i & f

Moray Chamber of Commerce
NR   17 Victoria St, Craigellachie, ABERLOUR-ON-SPEY, AB38 9SR.
　　01340 821226
　　email info@moraychamber.co.uk
　　http://www.moraychamber.co.uk
　　Chief Exec: Lesley Ann Parker
○　*C
<　Scot Chams Comm

Morganatic Society
NR   191 Westcombe Hill, LONDON, SE3 7DR.
○　*G; 'for mutual sympathy for the lesser-born persons in
　　morganatic relationships''
●　Mtgs - LG
M　25 i

Morris Federation   (MF)   1971
■　28 Fairstone Close, HASTINGS, E Sussex, TN35 5EZ.   (hsp)
　　01424 436052
　　email sec@morrisfed.org.uk
　　http://www.morrisfed.org.uk
　　Hon Sec: Fee Lock
▲　Un-incorporated Society
Br　400+; 6
○　*D, *G; to encourage & maintain interest in Morris dancing
Gp　Archive; Notation; Publicity; Step-dance
●　Conf - Mtgs - Res - Inf - Lib - PL - LG - Public dance displays
<　Folk Arts England; Engl Folk Dance & Song Soc
M　30 i, 350 org, UK / 2 i, 3 org, o'seas
¶　NL - 4; ftm only.

Morris Ring   1934
■　70 Greengate Lane, Birstall, LEICESTER, LE4 3DL.   (hsp)
　　Bagman: Charlie Corcoran
○　*G; practice & performance of English men's ritual dance
　　(Morris, sword-dancing & mumming)
●　Conf - Mtgs - ET - Res - Exhib - SG - Inf
M　180 clubs & 60 associates, UK / 6 o'seas
¶　Ring Directory (list of clubs) - 1.
　　List of books, tapes & equipment available.

Mortar Industry Association
　　is a product group of the **Mineral Products Association**

Mothers Apart from Their Children   (MATCH)   1979
■　BM Box No 6334, LONDON, WC1N 3XX.   (mail address)
　　email enquiries@matchmothers.org
　　http://www.matchmothers.org
　　Chmn: Penny Cross, Hon Sec: Penny Cooper
▲　Un-incorporated Society
○　*G, *W; run by & for mothers who are, or have been,
　　separated from their children in a wide variety of
　　circumstances
●　Mtgs - LG - Email support groups
M　220 i
¶　NL - 4.

Mothers' Union   (MU)   1876
§　Mary Sumner House, 24 Tufton St, LONDON, SW1P 3RB.   (hq)
　　020 7222 5533　fax 020 7222 1591
　　email mu@themothersunion.org
　　http://www.themothersunion.org
　　Chief Exec: Reg Bailey
　　A Christian organisation with over 3.6 million members
　　worldwide promoting marriage and family life.

Motor Accident Solicitors Society   (MASS)   1991
■　St Bartholomews Court, 18 Christmas St, BRISTOL, BS1 5BT.
　　(hq)
　　0117-925 9604
　　email office@mass.org.uk　　http://www.mass.org.uk
　　Exec Dir: Jane Loney
▲　Un-incorporated Society
○　*P; for solicitors who specialise in road traffic accident claims,
　　providing advice & assistance to claimants; 'MASS promotes
　　the highest standards of legal services through education &
　　representation in the pursuit of justice for the victims of road
　　traffic accidents'
●　Conf - Mtgs - ET - Inf - LG
M　170 f
¶　MASS Newsletter - 4; ftm, £50 nm.
　　Accident Advice Leaflets;　Accident Report Forms; both ftm.

Motor Caravanners' Club Ltd   1960
■　Wood Farm Estate (1st floor office), Marlbank Rd, Welland,
　　MALVERN, Worcs, WR13 6NA.   (hq)
　　01684 311677 (Mon-Thurs 0900-1700, Fri 0900-1400)
　　email info@motorcaravanners.eu
　　http://www.motorcaravanners.eu
　　Sec: Colin Reay
▲　Company Limited by Guarantee
Br　27; Europe & rest of world
○　*G; to promote & develop motor-caravanning
Gp　American motor homes; European rallies; Photography;
　　Walking
●　Mtgs - Exhib - Inf - VE - LG
<　Fédn Intle de Camping & de Caravanning
M　11,500 i, UK / 100 i, o'seas
¶　Motor Caravanner - 12;　Buyers Guide;　Sites List - 1; all ftm.

Motor Cycle Industry Association Ltd   (MCIA)   1973
■　1 Rye Hill Office Park, Birmingham Rd, Allesley, COVENTRY,
　　Warks, CV5 9AB.   (hq)
　　024 7640 8000　fax 024 7640 8001
　　http://www.mcia.co.uk
　　Chief Exec: Mark Foster
▲　Company Limited by Guarantee
○　*T
Gp　Manufacturers & importers of machines; Accessory &
　　component manufacturers; Factors; Associates
●　Conf - Mtgs - Res - Exhib - Stat - Expt - Inf - LG
<　Intl Motorcycle Mfrs Assn; Nat Motorcycle Coun; RoSPA; ACEM
M　150 f
¶　Revolutions (NL) - 4; ftm.　LM.　AR.

Motor Industry Public Affairs Association Ltd   (MIPAA)   2005
■　Little Grange, Church St, West Grimstead, SALISBURY, Wilts,
　　SP5 3RE.   (gsp)
　　01722 711295　fax 01722 711295
　　email hyaxley@supanet.com　　http://www.mipaa.com
　　Gen Sec: Heather Yaxley
▲　Company Limited by Guarantee
○　*P; for those engaged in communications in the motor industry
●　Mtgs - ET - SG - Inf - VE - Job search service - Mentoring
　　programme
M　460 i, UK / 10 i, o'seas
¶　The News (NL) - 4;　Directory - 1; both ftm.

Motor Neurone Disease Association   1979
- ■ PO Box 246, NORTHAMPTON, NN1 2PR.   (hq)
     01604 250505   fax 01604 624726
     http://www.mndassociation.org
     Chief Exec: Dr Kirstine Knox
- ▲ Registered Charity
- Br 100
- ○ *W; the support of people with MND & their carers; to research
     into the causes & treatment of the disease
- ● Conf - Mtgs - ET - Res - Inf - Lib - Loan of equipment - Helpline
     MND Connect: 0845 762 6262
- < Intl Alliance of ALS/MND Assns; Assn of Medical Res Charities
- M c 6,500 i
- ¶ Thumbprint (NL) - 4; free.
     MND Association News (NL) - 12; ftm only.   AR - 1; free.
     International Exchange (NL) - 3.

Motor Schools Association of Great Britain Ltd   (MSA)   1935
- NR 101 Wellington Rd North, STOCKPORT, Cheshire, SK4 2LP.
      (hq)
      0161-429 9669   fax 0161-429 9779
      http://www.msagb.com
- ○ *T; all aspects of learning to drive, driving, advanced driving &
     road safety
- M i

Motor Sports Association UK   (MSAUK)   1979
- NR Motor Sports House, Riverside Park, Colnbrook, SLOUGH,
      Berks, SL3 0HG.   (hq)
      01753 765000   fax 01753 682938
      http://www.msauk.org
- ▲ Company Limited by Guarantee
- ○ *S; the governing body for motor sport in the UK
- < Fédn Automobile Intle (FIA)

**Motor Vehicle Dismantlers Association of Great Britain
(MVDA)   1943**
- ■ Charrington House (office 5 top floor), 17A Market St,
     LICHFIELD, Staffs, WS13 6JX.   (hq)
     01543 254254   fax 01543 254274
     email mail@mvda.org.uk   http://www.mvda.org.uk
     Sec: Duncan Wemyss
- ▲ Un-incorporated Society
- ○ *T
- ● Conf - Mtgs - ET - Inf - LG
- < Eur Vehicle Dismantlers Assn (EGARA)
- M 217 f, UK / 8 f, o'seas
- ¶ Automotive Recycling & Disposal UK - 4; free.

Motorcycle Action Group   (MAG(UK))   1973
- ■ Central Office, PO Box 750, WARWICK, CV34 9FU.   (hq)
     01926 844064   fax 01926 844065
     http://www.mag-uk.org
- ▲ Company Limited by Guarantee
- ○ *K; to protect the rights & interests of motorcyclists; to
     safeguard the tradition & future of motorcycling in the UK; to
     promote positive aspects of motorcycling
- ● Conf - Mtgs - Res - Exhib - SG - Stat - Inf - LG
- < Intl Coalition of Motorcyclists (ICOM); Fédn Eur de
     Motocyclistes Assns (FEMA); links with other motorcycle assns
     & gps worldwide
- M 25,000 i, 40 f, 270 clubs, / 80 i, o'seas
- ¶ The Road - 6; ftm, £2 nm.
     Network for Regions (NL) - 12; ftm, £10 yr nm.

Motorcycle Retailers Association
     a group of the **Retail Motor Industry Federation**

Motorcycle Rider Training Association
     a group of the **Retail Motor Industry Federation**

**Motoring Organisations' Land Access & Recreation Association
(LARA)   1986**
- ■ PO Box 142, NEWCASTLE UPON TYNE, NE3 5YP.   (hq)
     0191-236 4086
     email admin@laragb.org   http://www.laragb.org
- ▲ Un-incorporated Society
- ○ *N, *S; an umbrella organisation of motor sport groups -
     promoting responsible use of the environment for motor
     sports & recreation
- ● Conf - Mtgs - Res - Inf - LG - Liaison with local & county
     authorities & with sporting, recreational & rights of way
     groups
- M 330,000 i, in 11 org
- ¶ Access Guide; ftm.   Conference papers.   Leaflets;
     Codes of Conduct; all free.

Motorsport Industry Association Ltd   (MIA)   1994
- NR Federation House, STONELEIGH PARK, Warks, CV8 2RF.   (hq)
      024 7669 2600   fax 024 7669 2601
      email info@the-mia.com   http://www.the-mia.com
- ○ *T; to represent, promote & protect the interests of the British
     motorsport industry
- < Fedn of Sports & Play Assns
- M f

Mountain Bothies Association   (MBA)   1965
- NR c/o Henderson Black & Co, 22 Crossgate, CUPAR, Fife,
      KY15 5HW.   (asa)
      01334 656666   fax 01334 656278
      email mba@hendersonblack.co.uk
      http://www.mountainbothies.org.uk
- ▲ Company Limited by Guarantee; Registered Charity
- Br 9 areas
- ○ *W; to maintain simple shelters in remote country for the use &
     benefit of all who love wild & lonely places
- Gp Renovation work on old & derelict buildings in remote areas
- ● Renovation & maintenance work parties
- < Scot Rights of Way & Access Soc; Mountaineering Coun
     Scotland; NE Mountain Trust
- M c 3,000 i
- ¶ NL - 4; ftm.   AR - 1; ftm, on request nm.
     Members Hbk - 1; ftm only.
     Volunteer's Hbk - 1; ft volunteers, on request nm.

Mountain Leader Training Association   (MLTA)
- ■ Siabod Cottage, CAPEL CURIG, Conwy, LL24 0ES.   (hq)
     01690 720120   fax 01690 720248
     email info@mlta.co.uk   http://www.mlta.co.uk
     Devt Officer: Phillip Thomas
- ○ *S; to provide on-going training for leaders who hold MLTUK
     leaderships awards; to provide communication between
     membership of training boards & provide leadership in the
     mountains
- Gp Leaders of mountaineering groups who have, or are engaged
     in obtaining, MLTUK leadership awards
- ● Conf - ET - Inf
- < Mountain Leader Training UK
- M 1,900 i
     (Sub: £15)
- ¶ NL (e-NL) - irreg; free.

© CBD Research Ltd · Beckenham · BR3 5JS · Tel 020 8650 7745 · E-mail cbd@cbdresearch.com · www.cbdresearch.com

Mountaineering Council of Ireland   (MCI)   1972
IRL   Sport HQ, 13 Joyce Way, Park West Business Park, DUBLIN 12,
       Republic of Ireland.   (hq)
       353 (1) 625 1115   fax 353 (1) 625 1116
       email info@mountaineering.ie
       http://www.mountaineering.ie
       Chief Officer: Stuart Garland
▲   Company Limited by Guarantee
Br   N Ireland
○   *S; to promote mountaineering, including hill walking, rock
     climbing, rambling, bouldering & alpinism; to preserve &
     maintain the mountaineering environment
Gp   Irish Mountain Training Board; Access & Conservation
     Committee; Youth Steering Group
●   Comp - Conf - ET - Inf - LG - Lib
<   U Intle des Assns d'Alpinisme; Eur Ramblers Assn
M   1,400 i, 130 clubs (7,600 i)
¶   Irish Mountain Log - 4; ftm.

Mountaineering Council of Scotland   (MCofS)   1970
■   The Old Granary, West Mill St, PERTH, PH1 5QP.   (hq)
     01738 492942   fax 01738 442095
     email info@mountaineering-scotland.org.uk
     http://www.mcofs.org.uk
     Senior Officer: David Gibson
▲   Company Limited by Guarantee
○   *S; representative body for Scotland's hill walkers, climbers &
     ski-mountaineers; the national sports governing body for
     sport climbing; to provide information on mountain safety
     matters
Gp   Mountain safety; Membership services; Environment & Access
●   ET - Comp - Inf - LG
<   UK & Ireland Mountaineering Co-ordination Gp
M   3,000 i, 35 f, 130 org
     (Sub: £27.30 i, £60 f, £13 org (per capita))
¶   The Scottish Mountaineer - 4; ftm, £3,15 nm.
     The Scottish Club Huts List - 1;   AR - 1; both free.
     Club Safety & Liability Guidance - 2 yrly; free.
     Publications on mountain safety, wild camping & environmental
     issues; free.

**Mounted Games Association of Great Britain   (MGAGB)
1984**
NR   Wyelands Cottage, 59 St Johns Rd, BUXTON, Derbys,
     SK17 6XA.   (hsb)
     01298 24292   fax 01298 24292
     email mary@mgagb.co.uk   http://www.mgagb.co.uk
     Chief Exec: Mrs Mary Worth
▲   Company Limited by Guarantee
○   *S, *Y; to organise & promote mounted games events for young
     riders
●   Mtgs - Comp
<   Intl Mounted Games Assn (IMGA); Brit Equestrian Fedn
M   1,400 i
¶   Pony Express - 4; ftm.   Hbk - 1.

Movement for Colonial Freedom
   see **Liberation**

Movers Institute (TMI)   (TMI)   1937
NR   Tangent House, 62 Exchange Rd, WATFORD, Herts,
     WD18 0TG.   (hq)
     01923 699480   fax 01923 699481
     email info@bar.co.uk   http://www.bar.co.uk
     Sec: Robert D Syers
▲   Company Limited by Guarantee
○   *T; training, educational & accreditation for the removals &
     storage industry
Gp   Commercial; National & European domestic moves; Overseas
●   Conf - Mtgs - ET - Exam - Comp - SG - Inf - VE
<   Brit Assn of Removers (BAR)
M   1,300 i
¶   Moving News - 4; ftm only.

Moving Image Society
   see **BKSTS - the Moving Image Society**

MRSA Support Group
NR   46 Great Stone Rd, Northfield, BIRMINGHAM, W Midlands,
     B31 2LS.
     0121-476 6583
     email info@mrsasupport.co.uk
     http://www.mrsasupport.co.uk
     Contact: Tony Field
○   *W; for sufferers & families of those affected by MRSA
     (Methicillin-resistant Staphylococcus aureus)

Mull & Iona Chamber of Commerce   1992
NR   Kellan Old Farm, AROS, Isle of Mull, PA72 6JY.   (sb)
       http://www.mullchamber.org
       Mem Sec: Michael Ackerley
○   *C

Multi Vintage Wine Growers Society   (MVWGS)   1985
■   191 Westcombe Hill, LONDON, SE3 7DR.   (hsp)
▲   Un-incorporated Society
○   *G; for anyone interested in wine growing techniques
●   Mtgs - Stat - VE - LG
M   23 i
¶   The Corker (Jnl) - irreg; m only.

Multiple Births Foundation   (MBF)   1988
■   Hammersmith House Level 4, Queen Charlotte's & Chelsea
     Hospital, Du Cane Rd, LONDON, W12 0HS.   (hq)
     020 8383 3519   fax 020 8383 3041
     email mbf@imperial.nhs.uk
     http://www.multiplebirths.org.uk
     Dir: Jane Denton,   Admin: Marian Patterson
▲   Registered Charity
○   *P, *W; to offer support to parents of twins, triplets & more; to
     offer advice & training to the professions concerned with
     them
Gp   Education (teachers, psycholgists); Medical (paediatricians,
     obstetricians, GPs); Nursing (midwives, health visitors)
●   Conf - Mtgs - ET - Stat - Inf - Lib - PL
¶   NL - 4; £10-£15 yr m.   AR.
     Publications list available.

Multiple Sclerosis National Therapy Centres   1993
■   PO Box 126, WHITCHURCH, Shropshire, SY14 7WL.   (hq)
     0845 367 0977
     email info@msntc.org.uk   http://www.msntc.org.uk
     Admin: Mrs V Woods
▲   Company Limited by Guarantee; Registered Charity
○   *N, *W; to administer the MS therapy centres throughout the
     country which provide therapy, support & information to all
     MS sufferers & their families
●   ET - Inf
M   35 centres
¶   NL (to all MS centres) - 2/3.

**Multiple Sclerosis Society of Great Britain & Northern Ireland
(MS Society)   1953**
NR   372 Edgware Rd, LONDON, NW2 6ND.   (hq)
       020 8438 0700   fax 020 8438 0701
       email info@mssociety.org.uk
       http://www.mssociety.org.uk
       Chief Exec: Mike O'Donovan
▲   Registered Charity
Br   360
○   *M, *W; to advise & assist anyone affected by MS
●   Conf - Mtgs - Res - Inf
     Helpline: 0808 800 8000
>   MS Trust
M   c 44,000 i
¶   MS Matters - 6; ftm.
     Publications list available.

Multiple Sclerosis Society of Ireland
IRL 80 Northumberland Rd, DUBLIN 4, Republic of Ireland.
      353 (1) 678 1600   fax 353 (1) 678 1601
      email info@ms-society.ie   http://www.ms-society.ie
      Chief Exec: Anne Winslow
○   *W

MultiService Association Ltd   (MSA)   2003
■   PO Box 9378, NEWARK, Notts, NG24 9FE.   (sp)
      01400 281298   fax 01400 282326
      email info@msauk.biz   http://www.msauk.biz
      Sec: Martyn Harvey
▲   Company Limited by Guarantee
○   *T; the only trade association representing shoe repairers &
      associated trades - key cutting, engraving & watch repairs
●   ET - Exhib - Comp - Inf - Lib
<   Cutting Edge - represents suppliers to the trade
>   Cutting Edge
M   350 i, 6 f, UK / 5 i, o'seas
¶   Shoe Service - 4; free.

Murray Grey Beef Cattle Society Ltd   1973
■   Pen-Twyn, Llangenny, CRICKHOWELL, Powys, NP8 1HD.   (hq)
      01873 810547   fax 01873 810547
      email info@murray-grey.co.uk
      http://www.murray-grey.co.uk
      Sec: Mrs Rosemary Kent
▲   Company Limited by Guarantee; Registered Charity
○   *B; to promote research into improvement of the breed; to
      maintain the purity of the breed
●   Mtgs - Exhib - Comp - VE
<   Nat Beef Assn
M   50 i, UK / 4 i, o'seas
¶   NL - 3;   Herdbook - 1;   Ybk - 1.

Muscular Dystrophy Campaign   1961
■   61 Southwark St, LONDON, SE1 0HL.   (hq)
      020 7803 4800
      http://www.muscular-dystrophy.org
▲   Company Limited by Guarantee; Registered Charity
○   *M, *W; to raise funds for & to manage medical research into
      muscular dystrophy & allied neuromuscular diseases;
      practical advice & support to affected families
<   Eur Alliance of Muscular Dystrophy Assns
M   c 2,000 i
¶   Target MD (NL) - 4; ftm.   AR; free.

Muscular Dystrophy Ireland
IRL 75 Lucan Rd, Chapelizod, DUBLIN 20, Republic of Ireland.
      353 (1) 623 6414   fax 353 (1) 620 8663
      email info@mdi.ie   http://www.mdi.ie
○   *W

Museum Ethnographers Group   (MEG)   1976
■   c/o Claire Wintle, Lecturer - History of Art & Design, School of
      Humanities, University of Brighton, 10-11 Pavilion Parade,
      BRIGHTON, E Sussex, BN2 1RA.   (hsb)
      http://www.museumethnographersgroup.org.uk
      Hon Sec: Claire Wintle
▲   Registered Charity
○   *P; to encourage good practice in the curatorship of
      ethnographic collections in the UK; to encourage research &
      the exchange of information
●   Conf - Mtgs - ET - Inf - VE
M   [not stated]
      (Sub: £30 i, £35 f, UK / £27-32 i, £37 f o'seas)
¶   Jnl of Museum Ethnography - 1; ftm (£25 back issues),
      £30 nm.
      Occasional Papers; prices vary.

Museum Professionals Group   (MPG)   1937
NR c/o David Rice, Gloucester City Museum, Brunswick Rd,
      GLOUCESTER, GL1 1HP.   (treas/b)
      http://www.museumprofessionalsgroup.org
      Treas: David Rice
▲   Un-incorporated Society
○   *P; to campaign on issues relevant to all junior museum
      professionals
●   Conf - Mtgs - ET - Res
M   100 i, 40 org, UK / 10 org, o'seas

Museums Action Movement
      see **National Heritage: the Museums Action Movement**

Museums Association   (MA)   1889
■   24 Calvin St, LONDON, E1 6NW.   (hq)
      020 7426 6950   fax 020 7426 6962
      email info@museumsassociation.org
      http://www.museumsassociation.org
      Dir: Mark Taylor
▲   Registered Charity
○   *A, *P; the interests of museum people, museums & their
      collections
●   Conf - Mtgs - ET - Inf - LG
M   5,000 i, 250 f, 600 instns, UK & o'seas
¶   Museums Jnl - 12.   Museum Practice - 4.
      Museums Ybk (a directory of museums & galleries of the British
      Isles).
      Ethics Guidelines.   Museum briefings.   AR.

Mushroom Growers' Association
      has closed

Music Education Council   (MEC)   1975
NR 10 Stratford Place, LONDON, W1C 1AA.   (hq)
      0757 096 9970
      http://www.mec.org.uk
▲   Registered Charity
○   *D, *E; promote & advance the education & training of the
      public in music
●   Conf - Inf
<   Intl Soc for Music Educ (ISME)
M   c 50 i, 170 org
¶   NL - 6.

Music Industries Association   (MIA)   1882
■   Ivy Cottage Offices, Finch's Yard, Eastwick Rd,
      GREAT BOOKHAM, Surrey, KT23 4BA.   (hq)
      01372 750600   fax 01372 750515
      email office@mia.org.uk   http://www.mia.org.uk
      Chief Exec: Paul McManus
▲   Company Limited by Guarantee
○   *D, *T; for the musical instrument industry: represents
      manufacturers, wholesalers, distributors, retailers, educators,
      publishers etc of musical instruments, accessories &
      amplification eqpt
Gp All types & genres of musical instuments & associated products
●   Conf - Mtgs - ET - Res - Exhib - Stat - Expt - Inf
<   Nat Assn of Music Merchants (USA)
M   350 f
      (Sub: £500)
¶   NL - 26; ftm only.

Music Managers Forum   (MMF)
NR British Music House, 26 Berners St, LONDON, W1T 3LR.
      0870 850 7800
○   *P

© CBD Research Ltd · Beckenham · BR3 5JS · Tel 020 8650 7745 · E-mail cbd@cbdresearch.com · www.cbdresearch.com

Music Masters' & Mistresses' Association   (MMA)   1903
■   St Edmund's School, CANTERBURY, Kent, CT2 8HU.
    (admin/b)
    01227 475600
    http://www.mma-online.org.uk
    Admin: Carol Hawkins
▲   Company Limited by Guarantee
○   *E, *P; advancement of musical education in independent
    schools; a professional forum for teachers of music
●   Conf - Mtgs - Inf
M   c 950 i, UK / c 10 i, o'seas
¶   Jnl - 3;   LM - 1; both ftm only.

Music Producers Guild UK Ltd   (MPG)   1986
■   PO Box 38134, LONDON, W10 6XL.   (hq)
    07798 621891
    http://www.mpg.org.uk
    Co Sec: Penny Ganz,   Chmn: Mike Howlett
▲   Company Limited by Guarantee
Br affiliates in 10 countries o'seas
○   *T; to represent producers, engineers, remixers & mastering
    engineers to the music industry
●   Mtgs - ET - LG
<   Eur Sound Directors Assn (ESDA); Assn ofProfl Recording
    Services (APRS); Jt Audio Media Services (JAMES)
M   400 i
¶   NL (online); free.

Music Publishers' Association Ltd   (MPA)   1881
■   British Music House (6th floor), 26 Berners St, LONDON,
    W1T 3LR.   (hq)
    020 7580 0126   fax 020 7637 3929
    email info@mpaonline.org.uk
    http://www.mpaonline.org.uk
    Chief Exec: Stephen Navin
▲   Company Limited by Guarantee
○   *T; to represent the interests of music publishers to government,
    the music industry, the media & the public
●   Conf - Mtgs - ET - Inf - LG
<   Intl Confedn of Music Publishers; Brit Music Rights
M   c 200 f
¶   Music Copyright Matters - 4; ftm only.
    Distributor's List - 1; ftm, £10 nm.
    LM - 1; ftm, £10 nm.   Code of Fair Practice.

Musical Box Society of Great Britain   (MBSGB)   1962
■   PO Box 373, WELWYN, Herts, AL6 0WY.   (hsb)
    email mail@mbsgb.org.uk   http://www.mbsgb.org.uk
○   *D, *G; preservation of musical boxes & all other forms of
    mechanical musical instruments, including automata;
    research into their history & development
●   Conf - Mtgs - Res - Exhib - SG - Inf - VE
M   c 250 i, UK / 350 i, o'seas
    (Sub: £24)
¶   The Music Box - 4; ftm only.

Musicians' Union   (MU)   1893
NR 60-62 Clapham Rd, LONDON, SW9 0JJ.   (hq)
    020 7582 5566   fax 020 7840 5505
    email info@theMU.org   http://www.theMU.org
    Gen Sec: John Smith
Br 74
○   *U
Gp British Music Writers' Council
    Sections: Folk, Jazz, Session, Theatre
    Freelance orchestral; Teachers' register
●   Conf - Mtgs - ET - Exhib - Stat - Inf - Empl - LG - Careers
    service - Lobbying
<   Intl Fedn Musicians (FIM); Creators' Rights Alliance; (TUC)
M   29,540 i
¶   Musician (Jnl) - 4; free.
    Section NL - 4;   Branch NL - 12; both ftm only.

Mutton Renaissance Campaign   2004
■   c/o Mags Barrow, Pastoral Alliance, The Sheep Centre,
    MALVERN, Worcs, WE13 6PH.
    01684 892255
    email mags@pastral.org
    http://www.muttonrenaissance.org.uk
○   *K, *F; to encourage the use of meat from traceable farm
    assured sheep that are at least two years old

Muzzle Loaders Association of GB   (MLAGB)   1952
■   PO Box 304, SEVENOAKS, Kent, TN14 6WB.   (mail/address)
    http://www.mlagb.com
    Chmn: Ken Hocking
Br 29
○   *G; for collectors, shooters & students of muzzle loading
    firearms
Gp Rifle; Pistol; Clay pigeon
●   Mtgs - Comp
<   Muzzle Loading Assns Intl C'ee (Paris); Brit Shooting Sports
    Coun; Nat Rifle Assn
M   1,900 i, 180 clubs, UK / 17 i, 3 clubs, o'seas
¶   Black Powder (NL) - 4; ftm.

MVRA Ltd
    2009 merged with the Bodyshop Services Division of the **Retail
    Motor Industry Federation**

Myalgic Encephalopathy Association   (MEA)   1976
■   7 Apollo Office Court, Radclive Road, GAWCOTT, Bucks,
    MK18 4DF.   (hq)
    01280 818968   fax 01280 821602
    email meconnect@meassociation.org.uk
    http://www.meassociation.org.uk
    Admin: Gill Briody
▲   Company Limited by Guarantee; Registered Charity
○   *W; to serve the needs of people with ME/CFS & their families
    & carers
●   Conf - Res
    Helpline 0844 576 5326
<   Nat Coun of Voluntary Orgs (NCVO); Long-Term Med
    Conditions Alliance (LMCA)
M   6,800 i
¶   Perspectives - 4.
    [subscription £18]

Myasthenia Gravis Association   (MGA)   1976
■   The College Business Centre, Uttoxeter New Rd, DERBY,
    DE22 3WZ.   (hq)
    01332 290219   fax 01332 293641
    email mg@mga-charity.org
    http://www.mga-charity.org
    Chmn: Peter Finney
▲   Registered Charity
○   *W; to provide advice & support for sufferers, carers & the
    medical profession; to fund research into improved
    treatment; (an auto-immune disease characterised by
    fluctuating, sometimes fatal, muscle weakness)
●   Conf - Mtgs - ET - Res - Exhib - Inf
    Helpline: 0800 919922
<   Neurological Alliance
M   9,000 i, UK / 270 i, o'seas
¶   MGA News - 4; free.   Medical Companion; ftm, £2.50 nm.
    AR; ftm only.   Information leaflets; free.

Myositis Support Group   1985
NR   146 Newtown Rd, Woolston, SOUTHAMPTON, Hants,
        SO19 9HR.
        023 8044 9708   fax 023 8039 6402
        email info@myositis.org.uk   http://www.myositis.org.uk
        Chmn: Les Oakley
▲   Registered Charity
○   *W; support & information to individuals & families affected by
        inflammatory myopathies - dermatomyositis, polymyositis &
        juvenile dermatomyositis
●   Mtgs - Inf
M   i
¶   NL;   Information Guides.

Myotonic Dystrophy Support Group   (MDSG)   1985
■   35a Carlton Hill, Carlton, NOTTINGHAM, NG4 1BG.
        0115-987 5869
        email mdsg@tesco.net   http://www.mdsguk.org
        Nat Co-ordinator: Margaret Bowler
▲   Registered Charity
○   *W; to give support to families & professionals concerning
        myotonic dystrophy, a form of muscular dystrophy
●   ET - Res - Exhib - Helpline
        Helpline: 0115 987 0080
<   Muscular Dystrophy Campaign; Contact-a-Family; LMCA;
        NCVO
M   35 i, UK / 20 i, o'seas
¶   NL - 3; ftm.

Naace (Naace) 1984
- ■ PO Box 6511, NOTTINGHAM, NG11 8TN.   (hq)
  0115-945 7235
  email office@naace.org   http://www.naace.co.uk
  Gen Mgr: Bernadette Brooks
- ▲ Company Limited by Guarantee; Registered Charity
- ○ *P; 'advancing education through ICT'
- ● Conf - Mtgs - ET - Res - Exhib - SG - Inf - LG
- M 3,100 i, 115 f
- ¶ NL - 52;   Jnl - 2; both ftm only.

NABAS (the Balloon Association) Ltd (NABAS) 1988
- ■ Katepwa House, Ashfield Park Ave, ROSS-ON-WYE, Herefs,
  HR9 5AX.   (asa)
  01989 762204   fax 01989 567676
  email admin@nabas.co.uk   http://www.nabas.co.uk
  Admin: Gill Hinton
- ▲ Company Limited
- ○ *T; to coordinate the party & promotional balloon decorating
  industry, both latex & foil
- Gp Decorators; Retailers; Manufacturers; Wholesalers
- ● Conf - Mtgs - ET - Exhib - Comp - Inf
- M 720 f
- ¶ Balloonies (NL) - 4;   LM - 2; both ftm.

NACRO - National Association for the Care & Resettlement of Offenders 1966
- NR Park Place, 10-12 Lawn Lane, LONDON, SW8 1UD.   (hq)
  020 7840 7200   fax 020 7840 7240
  http://www.nacro.org.uk
- ○ *W

NAEA International incorporating FOPDAC
  a group of the **National Association of Estate Agents**

NAEGA - promoting adult guidance on learning & work (NAEGA) 1982
- ■ c/o SAS Event Management, The Old George Brewery,
  Rollestone St, SALISBURY, Wilts, SP1 1DX.   (asa)
  01722 415154
  email admin@naega.org.uk   http://www.naega.org.uk
- ▲ Company Limited by Guarantee
- Br 10
- ○ *E; to promote adult career guidance & provide development
  opportunities for people who deliver it
- Gp Career guidance managers, practitioners & others
- ● Conf - Mtgs - ET - Inf - LG
- < Fedn of Profl Assns in Guidance
- M 300 i, 400 f
  (Sub: £50 i, £70 + £40 each i)
- ¶ e NL - 4; ftm only.   AR - 1;   Occasional publications;   see
  website for updates & articles; all free.
- × 2006 National Association of Educational Guidance for Adults

NAGALRO: Professional Association for Children's Guardians & Children & Family Reporters & Independent Social Workers (NAGALRO) 1989
- ■ PO Box 264, ESHER, Surrey, KT10 0WA.
  01372 818504   fax 01372 818505
  email nagalro@globalnet.co.uk
  http://www.nagalro.com
  Principal Admin: Karen Harris
- ▲ Company Limited by Guarantee
- ○ *P
- ● Conf - Mtgs - Inf - LG
- M 900 i
- ¶ Seen & Heard - 4; ftm.

Nail Patella Syndrome UK (NPS UK)
- NR PO Box 26415, East Kilbride, GLASGOW, G74 1YW.
  0800 121 8298
  http://www.npsuk.org
- ○ *W; a genetic condition affecting the nails, knees, can cause
  iliac horns & other skeletal problems

Napaeo - the Association for Land Based Colleges
  since 2008 **Landex - Land Based Colleges Aspiring to Excellence**

Napoleonic Association Ltd (NA) 1975
- ■ 7 Fair Oak Way, Baughurst, TADLEY, Hants, RG26 5NT.
  (sec/p)
  0118-981 0573
  http://www.napoleonicassociation.org
  Co Sec: Chrissy Wisken
- ▲ Company Limited by Guarantee
- ○ *G, *L; to promote interest & study in military history 1792-
  1815 & to re-enact such history
- Gp Research; Wargames; Re-enactment
- ● Res - Battle re-enactment & shows - Research conferences
- < Muzzle Loaders Assn of GB
- M 600 i, UK / 20 i, o'seas
- ¶ The Adjutant (NL).

Napoleonic Society 1969
- ■ 157 Vicarage Rd, LONDON, E10 5DU.   (hq)
  020 8539 3876   fax 020 8539 3876
  email keys@fsmail.net
  Sec: Ronald King
- ▲ Un-incorporated Society
- ○ *L, *Q; to foster interest & understanding of French history
  1756-1945
- ● Res - SG - Inf - Lib - PL
- ¶ Napoleon.
  Note: Please note this is NOT a re-enactment or fancy costume
  society.

NARA - the breathing charity (NARA) 1984
- ■ Moulton Park Business Centre, Redhouse Rd, Moulton Paark,
  NORTHAMPTON, NN3 6AQ.   (hq)
  01604 494960   fax 01604 497550
  email info@thebreathingcharity.org.uk
  http://www.naratbc.org.uk
- ○ *W; a registered charity & non-membership body offering help,
  advice & provision of medical equipment to people with
  apnoea, asthma & other respiratory conditions
- × National Association for the Relief of Apnoea

NARA - Association of Property & Fixed Charge Receivers
  see **Associaton of Property & Fixed Charge Receivers (NARA)**

Narcolepsy UK   1981
- ■ PO Box 13842, PENICUIK, Midlothian, EH26 8WX.
   (mail/address)
   0845 450 0394
   email info@narcolepsy.org.uk
   http://www.narcolepsy.org.uk
- ▲ Registered Charity
- Br 20
- ○ *W; to support research into the causes & treatment of
   narcolepsy (a sleep disorder characterised by excessive
   daytime sleepiness); to provide support & information for
   sufferers & their families; to press for recognition of
   narcolepsy as a disability by the DoE & DSS
- ● Inf - LG
- < Eur Narcolepsy Assn (ENA); Neurological Alliance; Long-term
   Med Conditions Alliance (LMCA); Genetic Interest Gp (GIG);
   Nat Coun of Voluntary Orgs (NCVO)
- M 700 i, 1 f, 4 org, UK / 50 i, o'seas
- ¶ Catnap (Jnl) - 4; ftm, 50 p each nm.
   Personal Experience; £2 m, £3 nm.
   Reports:
      1. Medication for Narcolepsy; £1.50 m, £2.25 nm.
      2. Narcolepsy: a layman's guide; £1 m, £1.50 nm.
      3. Narcolepsy: care & treatment; £1.80 m, £2.70 nm.
- ✕ 2009 (13 December) Narcolepsy Association United Kingdom

Narrow Gauge Railway Society   (NGRS)   1951
- NR 4 Park Mews, Park Gate, SOUTHAMPTON, Hants,
   SO31 1ED.   (hsp)
   http://www.ngrs.org
   Sec: Iain McCall
- ▲ Un-incorporated Society
- ○ *G
- ¶ Narrow Gauge - 4.   Narrow Gauge News - 6.

Narrow-bandwidth Television Association   (NBTVA)   1975
- ■ 1 Lucknow Ave, Mapperley Park, NOTTINGHAM, NG2 5AZ.
   (chmn/p)
   0115-962 1453
   http://www.nbtv.org
   Chmn: Jeremy Jago
- ▲ Un-incorporated Society
- ○ *G; for those interested in amateur television - construction of
   apparatus, transmission & reception & the history of
   television
- ● Conf - ET - Res - Exhib
- < Brit Amat TV Club
- M 100 i, UK / 50 i, o'seas
- ¶ NBTV (NL) - 4; £5 yr m.

nasen   (nasen)   1992
- ■ Nasen House, 4-5 Amber Business Village, Amber Close,
   Amington, TAMWORTH, Staffs, B77 4RP.   (hq)
   01827 311500   fax 01827 313005
   email welcome@nasen.org.uk
   http://www.nasen.org.uk
   Chief Exec Officer: Lorraine Peterson
- ▲ Company Limited by Guarantee; Registered Charity
- Br 65
- ○ *E, *P; to promote the development of children & young people
   with special educational needs
- ● Conf - Mtgs - ET - Res - Exhib - SG - Inf - LG
- < NCVO; COSTA; Nat Children's Bureau
- M 5,059 i, f, UK / 79 i, o'seas
   (Sub: £68 i, £88 f, UK / £110 i, £130 EU)
- ¶ British Journal for Special Education - 4; ftm.
   Support for Learning - 4; ftm.
   Special (NL) - termly; ftm, £12 nm (£15 o'seas).
   Publications list available.

National Access & Scaffolding Confederation   (NASC)   1943
- ■ 12 Bridewell Place (4th floor), LONDON, EC4V 6AP.   (hq)
   020 7822 7400
   email enquiries@nasc.org.uk   http://www.nasc.org.uk
   Managing Dir: Robin James
- ▲ Company Limited by Guarantee
- ○ *T; for the access & scaffolding industry; members provide
   products & services including the supply & erection, hire, sale
   & manufacturing of: access & scaffolding equipment,
   formwork & falsework & temporary suspended access
   systems
- ● Inf - LG
- < Nat Specialist Contrs Coun; Access Ind Forum
- > Specialist Access Engg & Maintenance Assn (SAEMA); Fall Arrest
   Safety Eqpt Training (FASET)
- M 180 f
- ¶ NASC Ybk (incl LM - 1.
   SG4:05 - Preventing falls in scaffolding & falsework; £25.
   SG4: You - User guide to SG4:05; £5.
   Guide to Good Practice for Scaffolding with Tubes &
   Fittings; £105.
   Technical & Safety Guidance Notes; prices vary.

**National Accordion Organisation of the United Kingdom
(NAO)   1947**
- ■ 17 Marsh Mill Village, THORNTON CLEVELEYS, Lancs,
   FY5 4JZ.   (hsb)
   01253 822046
   email naouk@accordions.com
   http://www.accordions.com/nao
   Hon Sec: Gina Brannelli
- ▲ Registered Charity
- ○ *D; to promote accordion playing through competition
- ● Mtgs - Exam (through the British Academy of Accordionists
   (BCA) at address above) - Comp
- < Confédn Intle des Accordéonistes (CIA)
- M 700 i
   (Sub: £18 family, £28 i)
- ¶ NL - 12;   Ybk - 1; both ftm only.

National Acquisitions Group   (NAG)   1986
- ■ 12-14 King St, WAKEFIELD, W Yorks, WF1 2SQ.   (hq)
   01924 383010   fax 01924 383010
   email nag@btconnect.com   http://www.nag.org.uk
   Admin: Judith Rhodes
- ▲ Un-incorporated Society
- ○ *P; to stimulate, coordinate & publicise developments
   concerning the acquisition of library materials; to provide a
   forum for their discussion
- ● Conf - Mtgs - ET - Res - VE
- M 5 i, 450 f, UK / 15 f, o'seas
- ¶ Directory of Acquisitions Librarians; £60 m, £80 nm.
   Publications list available.

National Acrylic Painters' Association   (NAPA)   1985
- ■ 134 Rake Lane, Wallasey, WIRRAL, Merseyside, CH45 1JW.
   (hq)
   0151-639 2980   fax 0151-639 2980
   email kjhnapa@hotmail.com   http://www.napauk.org
   Sec: Kenneth Hodgson
- ▲ Un-incorporated Society
- Br USA
- ○ *A, *G, *P; the promotion of the use of acrylic paint as a
   medium of excellence & innovation for professional fine art
   painters
- ● Exhib - PL
- < Fine Art Tr Gld
- M 100 i, UK / 300 i, ISAP, o'seas
- ¶ International (NL) - 2; ftm, £1 nm.
   Exhibition Catalogue - 1; £1.

© CBD Research Ltd · Beckenham · BR3 5JS · Tel 020 8650 7745 · E-mail cbd@cbdresearch.com · www.cbdresearch.com

**National Acupuncture Detoxification Association   (NADA)
1988**
NR   50-54 Mount Pleasant, LIVERPOOL, L3 5SD.   (hq)
        0151-702 6959
        http://www.nadauk.com
▲   Un-incorporated Society
Br   Europe, Australia, Canada, India, Mexico, Nepal, Russia,
        Trinidad, USA
○   *P; to treat substance abuse, compulsive behaviour, attention
        deficient disorder & stress management
M   1,000 i, UK / 10,000 i, o'seas
¶   NL - 2; ftm only.

National Adult School Organisation
        has closed

National Advisory Service for Parents of Children with a Stoma
        has closed

National Alcohol Producers Association   (NAPA)   1982
■   4 Stour Close, KESTON, Kent, BR2 6BX.   (hsb)
        01689 889583
        email dhw@dhward.com
        Chmn & Gen Sec: David H Ward
▲   Un-incorporated Society
○   *T; UK producers of neutral alcohol for drinks & industrial use.
        Neutral alcohol is distilled from agricultural crops, the main
        market being in the production of spirit drinks (gin & vodka)
        & a growing potential for use in biofuel production
●   Mtgs - Stat - Inf
<   ePURE; Confédn Eur des Producteurs de Spiritueux (CEPS); Gin
        & Vodka Assn; Scotch Whisky Assn
M   5 f, 7 f (associates)
✕   2008 (1 January) Neutral Alcohol Producers Association

National Alliance of Women's Organisations   (NAWO)   1989
NR   33-41 Dallington St (Ground Floor East), LONDON,
        EC1V 0BB.   (hq)
        020 7324 3045
        email info@nawo.org.uk   http://www.nawo.org.uk
▲   Registered Charity; Un-incorporated Society
○   *N; brings together widely diverse women's organisations to
        achieve equality & justice for all women
M   org

National Amateur Bodybuilders Association   (NABBA)   1950
NR   PO Box 1186, BRIERLEY HILL, W Midlands, DY5 2GL.   (hq)
        01384 898578   fax 01384 898579
        http://www.nabba.co.uk
▲   Un-incorporated Society
○   *S; the controlling body for bodybuilding contests for men &
        women; promotion of weight-training as a means of health &
        fitness
M   15,000 i, 250 org

National Ankylosing Spondylitis Society   (NASS)   1976
■   Unit 0.2, 1 Victoria Villas, RICHMOND, Surrey, TW9 2GW.
        (hq)
        020 8948 9117   fax 020 8940 7736
        email nass@nass.co.uk   http://www.nass.co.uk
        Dir: Fergus Rogers
▲   Registered Charity
Br   110
○   *W; patient education & support
●   Conf - Mtgs - ET - Res - Inf
<   Ankylosing Spondylitis Intl Fedn; Brit League against
        Rheumatism; Brit Soc of Rheumatology
M   7,000 i, UK / 400 i, o'seas
¶   AS News - 2; free.
        Guidebook for Patients - 1; free.
        Living with Ankylosing Spondylitis.
        Physiotherapy (cassette tape).
        Fight Back (physiotherapy video + DVD); £12
        Other publications available.

National Anti-Vivisection Society   (NAVS)   1875
§   Millbank Tower, Millbank, LONDON, SW1P 4QP.   (hq)
        020 7630 3340   fax 020 7828 2179
        http://www.navs.org.uk
        Chief Exec: Jan Creamer
        To promote awareness of the inequity of experiments or
        processes causing suffering or distress to living creatures and
        to obtain legislation totally prohibiting all such experiments.
        The society is affiliated to The Animal Defenders & Animal +
        World Show.

National Approved Premises Association   (NAPA)   1942
NR   PO Box 13682, CRADLEY HEATH, W Midlands, B62 2DY.
        0121-550 6444
        http://www.napbh.org.uk
        Dir: Duncan Moss
○   *W; to support and develop approved residential provision for
        offenders
M   c 300 i
✕   2007 National Association of Probation & Bail Hostels

National Arabidopsis Society   (NAS)   1999
■   81 Park View, Collins Rd, LONDON, N5 2UD.   (asa)
○   *L
●   Conf - Mtgs - VE
M   i

National Arenas Association   (NAA)   1991
NR   c/o Phil Mead, The NEC Group, National Exhibition Centre,
        BIRMINGHAM, B40 1NT.   (chmn/b)
        0121-780 4141
        http://www.nationalarenasassociation.com
        Chmn: Phil Mead
○   *T; managers of concert & event venues
M   15 f

National Art Collections Fund (The Art Fund)   1903
NR   Millais House, 7 Cromwell Place, LONDON, SW7 2JN.   (hq)
        020 7225 4800
○   *A; the UK's leading art charity; to help museums, art galleries,
        historic houses & other public collections to acquire works of
        art, either by grants or through gifts & bequests.
        The Art Fund is independent of government & receives no
        public funding
M   80,000 i
¶   Art Quarterly - 4;   Review - 1; both ftm only.

National Association for Able Children in Education   (NACE)
■   The Core Business Centre, Milton Hill, ABINGDON, Oxon,
        OX13 6AB.
        01235 828280
        email info@nace.co.uk   http://www.nace.co.uk
        Dir: Joanna Raffan
○   *E; to help education professionals to improve classroom
        practice for able, gifted & talented pupils
M   c 2,000 i

National Association of Accordion & Fiddle Clubs
■   7 Lathro Lane, KINROSS, KY13 8RX.
        01577 862337
        Sec: Lorna Mair
○   *D
M   76 clubs

National Association of Adult Placement Services (NAAPS)
- ■ 6 The Cotton Exchange, Old Hall St, LIVERPOOL, L3 9LQ. (hq)
  0151-227 3499   fax 0151-236 3590
  http://www.naaps.co.uk
  Chmn: Martin Ewing
- ▲ Registered Charity
- ○ *W; to promote & develop adult placement as a resource offering vulnerable adults the opportunity to live in a normal domestic setting, as part of a family & of a local community
- ● Conf - Mtgs - ET - Inf
- M 2,000+ i, 150+ SSDs
- ¶ Publications list available.

National Association of Advisers in English (NAAE)
- NR 63 Fort Royal Hill, WORCESTER, WR5 1BY.   (treas/p)
  01905 358649
  email macr@mervynriches.plus.com
  http://www.naae.org.uk
  Treas: Mervyn Riches
  Sec: Nicola Copitch (ncopitch@wlv.ac.uk)
- ○ *P; as advisers, inspectors & consultants, to promote the highest standards in the teaching of English in schools in England, Wales & Northern Ireland
- ● Mtgs
- M i
  (Sub: £25)

National Association of Advisers & Inspectors in Design & Technology (NAAIDT) 1992
- ■ 1 Lodge Cottage, Whilton Locks, DAVENTRY, Northants, NN11 2NH.   (hsp)
  01327 842016
  email barry.lewis@naaidt.org.uk
  http://www.naaidt.org.uk
  Co Sec: Barry Lewis
- ▲ Un-incorporated Society
- ○ *P; promotes the teaching of design & technology in schools
- < Standing Conf Schools' Science & Technology
- M 315 i & f
- ¶ NL.   Conference Report - 1.
  Safety Training for Teachers.   Occasional papers.

National Association of Advisory Officers for Special Educational Needs (NAAOSEN) 1983
- ■ 22 St Peter's St, SANDWICH, Kent, CT13 9BW.   (hsp)
  01304 620179
  email linda.samson@kent.gov.uk
  http://www.naaosen.org.uk
  64 Glossop Rd, Marple Bridge, Stockport, SK6 5EL.
    0161-427 0803.   (treas)
  Hon Sec: Linda Samson, Treas: Sue Woodgate
- ○ *P
- ● Conf - LG
- < Nat Assn Educl Inspectors, Advisers & Consultants
- M i

National Association of Aerial Photographic Libraries (NAPLIB) 1989
- ■ c/o RCAHMS, John Sinclair House, 16 Bernard Terrace, EDINBURGH, EH8 9NX.
  0131-662 1456
  Contact: Executive Secretary
- ○ *L; promote the use & preservation of aerial photography
- ● Conf - Inf - VE
- < Remote Sensing & Photogrammetry Soc
- M 47 i, 31 f, UK / 1 i, o'seas
- ¶ NAPLIB Flyer - 4; ftm only.
  NAPLIB Directory of Aerial Photographic Collections in the UK; £10 m, £15 nm.
  The Care & Storage of Photographs: recommendations for good practice; £2.50 m, £5 nm.

National Association of Agricultural Contractors (NAAC) 1893
- ■ The Old Cart Shed, Easton Lodge Farm, Old Oundle Rd, Wansford, PETERBORUGH, PE8 6NP.   (hq)
  0845 644 8750   fax 01780 784933
  email jill.hewitt@naac.co.uk   http://www.naac.co.uk
  Chief Exec: Mrs Jill Hewitt
- ▲ Company Limited by Guarantee
- ○ *F,*H, *T; for UK contractors who supply land-based services to farmers, government, local authorities, sports & recreational facilities
- Gp Crop spraying; Amenity; Livestock; Mobile feed mill+mix; Mobile seed processors
- ● Conf - Mtgs - ET - Inf & advice - LG
- < Confédn Eur des Entrepreneurs de Travaux Techniques Agricoles et Rurales (CEETAR)
- M i & f (numbers confidential)
- ¶ Contracting Bulletin - 12; ftm only.
  ProContractor - 2; free.
  Contractors Directory [Ybk] - 1; ftm only.

National Association of Almshouses   1946
- ■ Billingbear Lodge, Maidenhead Rd, WOKINGHAM, Berks, RG40 5RU.   (hq)
  01344 452922   fax 01344 862062
  email naa@almshouses.org
  http://www.almshouses.org
  Dir: A P De Ritter
- ▲ Registered Charity
- ○ *W; to advise members on any matters concerning almshouses & the welfare of the elderly
- ● Conf - Mtgs - Res - Exhib - SG - VE - LG
- < Age Concern; Charities Working Party
- M 1,800 almshouses
- ¶ The Almshouses Gazette - 4; £1;   AR - 1; £1.
  Note: Also known as the Almshouse Association.

National Association for Areas of Outstanding Natural Beauty (NAAONB)
- NR Fosse Way, NORTHLEACH, Glos, GL54 3JH.
  01451 862007
  http://www.aonb.org.uk
  Sec: Jill Smith
- ○ *G

** **National Association of Bank & Insurance Customers**
  Organisation lost: see Introduction paragraph 3

National Association for Bikers with a Disability   (NABD) 1991
- NR Unit 20 The Bridgewater Centre, Robson Avenue, Urmston, MANCHESTER, Lancs, M41 7TE.   (hq)
  0870 759 0603
  email office@thenabd.org.uk   http://www.nabd.org.uk
- ▲ Registered Charity
- Br 32; Republic of Ireland
- ○ *W; to help disabled people enjoy motorcycling to the full; to organise & finance adaptions to motorcycles, trikes & scooters to suit the disability of the rider; help with licensing, insurance & general access to motorcycling events; to ensure that when it comes to motorcycling 'a disability is not a handicap'.
- ● Conf - Mtgs - ET - Res - Exhib - Comp - Inf - VE - LG - Annual National Rally
- < Motorcycle Action Group (MAG); Brit Motorcyclist Fedn (BMF)
- M 2,000 i, 30 f, 70 org, UK / 20 i, o'seas
- ¶ Open House - 4; ftm, donation nm.

© CBD Research Ltd · Beckenham · BR3 5JS · Tel 020 8650 7745 · E-mail cbd@cbdresearch.com · www.cbdresearch.com

National Association of Boat Owners   (NABO)   1991
- ■ FREEPOST (BM8367), BIRIMNGHAM, W Midlands, B31 2BR.
 (hs/mail/address)
 0798 944 1674
 email gen.sec@nabo.org.uk   http://www.nabo.org.uk
 Gen Sec: Richard Carpenter
- ▲ Un-incorporated Society
- ○ *G; representation of private boat owners on Britain's inland
 waterways
- ● Stat - Inf - LG & representation to statutory bodies & waterway
 authorities
- < Intl Navigation Assn; Nat Navigation Users Forum (NNUF)
- M 2,500 i & org
- ¶ NABO News - 7; ftm only.

National Association of Bookmakers Ltd   (NAB)   1932
- NR 19 Culm Valley Way, UFFCULME, Devon, EX15 3XZ.   (hq)
 01884 841859
 http://www.nab-bookmakers.co.uk
- ○ *T; for on-course bookmakers
- < Fedn Racecourse Bookmakeres

**National Association of Brass Band Conductors   (NABBC)
1946**
- ■ 4 Chippendale Close, Blackwater, CAMBERLEY, Surrey,
 GU17 9DS.   (hsp)
 01276 31074
 http://www.nabbc.org.uk
 Hon Sec: Davis Ruel
- ▲ Un-incorporated Society
- Br 6
- ○ *G; the promotion of brass band music & conductors
- ● Conf - Mtgs - Comp - Lib - Assistance to members wishing to
 study adjudication & conducting
- M 300 i
- ¶ The Conductor - 4; ftm, £2.50 yr nm.

National Association of British & Irish Millers
 see the **Incorporated National Association of British & Irish
 Millers**

**National Association of British Market Authorities   (NABMA)
1919**
- NR The Guildhall, OSWESTRY, Salop, SY11 1PZ.   (hq)
 01691 680713   fax 01691 671080
 email nabma@nabma.com   http://www.nabma.com
 Chief Exec: Graham Wilson
- ○ *N, *T; to constitute a medium of communication between
 members & others in promoting & administering matters of
 common interest relating to markets, fairs, abattoirs & cold
 stores
- Gp Section c'ees: Livestock & abattoirs, Retail markets, Wholesale
 markets
- ● Conf - Mtgs - Exhib - Inf - VE - LG
- < Assn of Town Centre Mgt; Eur Assn of Livestock Markets; Wld U
 of Whls Markets;
 Is part of the Markets Alliance
- M 135 local authorities
- ¶ AR; ftm.
- × 2007 Association of Private Market Operators (merged)

**National Association of Building Co-operatives Society Ltd
(NABCO)**
- IRL 33 Lower Baggot St, DUBLIN 2, Republic of Ireland.
 353 (1) 661 2877   fax 353 (1) 661 4462
 http://www.nabco.ie
- ○ *N

National Association of Caravan Owners   (NACO)   1996
- NR Leisurefame House, 37 Clacton Rd, St OSYTH, Essex,
 CO16 8RA.
 01255 820321
 http://www.nacoservices.com
- ▲ Company Limited by Guarantee
- ○ *T; to represent the owners of static holiday caravans
- ¶ The Holiday Caravanner (Jnl) - 3.

National Association of Care Catering   (NACC)   1986
- NR Meadow Court, Faygate Lane, FAYGATE, W Sussex, RH12 4SJ.
 0870 748 0180   fax 0870 748 0181
 email info@thenacc.co.uk   http://www.thenacc.co.uk
- ○ *T; to promote & enrich the standard of catering within the care
 sector
- M c 500 i

National Association for the Care & Resettlement of Offenders
 see **NACRO - National Association for the Care &
 Resettlement of Offenders**

National Association of Catering Butchers   (NACB)   1983
- NR 224 Central Markets, LONDON, EC1A 9LH.   (hq)
 020 7248 1896   fax 020 7329 0658
 email info@nacb.co.uk   http://www.nacb.co.uk
- ○ *T; to raise the standard of catering butchery
- M c 30 f

National Association of Cattle Foot Trimmers
- NR Berthlwyd, Maestmeillion, LLANDYSUL, Ceredigion,
 SA44 4NG.   (treas/p)
 01545 590590
 http://www.nacft.co.uk
 Treas: Andrew Tyler
 Sec: Steve Jones (01829 781476)
- ○ *P; for cattle hoof trimmers

National Association of Child Contact Centres   (NACCC)   1985
- ■ 1 Heritage Mews, High Pavement, NOTTINGHAM,
 NG1 1HN.   (hq)
 0115-948 4557   fax 0845 450 0420
 email contact@naccc.org.uk   http://www.naccc.org.uk
 Chief Exec: Yvonne Kee
- ▲ Company Limited by Guarantee; Registered Charity
- ○ *N, *W; to keep over 2,000 children a week in touch with both
 parents through a network of child contact centres
- ● Helpline: 0845 450 0280 (0900-1300 Mon-Fri)
- M c 300 centres
- ¶ Ben's Story: an introduction to child contact centres (a children's
 book); £2 m, £2.50 nm.
 AR.

National Association for Child Support Action   (NACSA)   1993
- NR PO Box 4454, DUDLEY, W Midlands, DY1 9AN.
 (mail/address)
 email admin@nacsa.co.uk   http://www.nacsa.co.uk
- ▲ Company Limited by Guarantee
- ○ *K; to help & support parents who have problems with the
 Child Support Agency
- Gp Specialist advisers
- ● Res - Inf - LG
- ¶ NACSA News - 4; ftm only.

National Association for Children of Alcoholics   (NACOA)
- § PO Box 64, Fishponds, BRISTOL, BS16 2UH.
 0117-924 8005   fax 0117-924 2928
 http://www.nacoa.org.uk
- ● Helpline: 0800 358 3456 / helpline@nacoa.org.uk
 Provides information, advice and support to children of
 alcoholics and people concerned with their welfare
 Helpline: 0800 358 3456.

National Association of Chimney Engineers Ltd (NACE) 1982
- ■ PO Box 849, Metheringham, LINCOLN, LN4 3WU. (hq)
  01526 322555 (Mon-Thur 0930-1600, Fri 0930-1230)
  fax 01526 323181
  email info@nace.org.uk   http://www.nace.org.uk
  Sec: Michael Carr
- ▲ Company Limited by Guarantee
- ○ *T; to promote & develop the safe installation & construction of all types of chimney & chimney lining in domestic properties
- Gp Competent persons register; Code of practice development
- ● ET - Exhib - Inf - LG
- M 15 installers, 7 associates
- ¶ Flueways (NL) - 4; ftm only.

National Association of Chimney Sweeps (NACS) 1982
- ■ Unit 15 Emerald Way, Stone Business Park, STONE, Staffs, ST15 0SR. (hq)
  01785 811732   fax 01785 811712
  email nacs@chimneyworks.co.uk
  http://www.nacs.org.uk
  Admin: Mrs Amanda Pulfer
- ○ *T; to promote the use of professional sweeps to clean & maintain chimneys; to advise public of chimney safety
- ● Conf - Mtgs - ET - Exam - Exhib - LG
- < Europäische-Schornsteinfegermeister-Föderation; Co-Gas Safety; HETAS; OFTEC; Solid Fuel Assn; Nat Fireplace Assn; Nat Energy Foundation
- M 235 i, 16 f, UK / 2 f, o'seas
- ¶ Chimney Jnl - 3; ftm.

National Association of Choirs (NAC) 1920
- ■ 35 Hawton Crescent, Wollaton Park, NOTTINGHAM, Notts, NG8 1BZ. (hsp)
  email rhodeswf@ntlworld.com
  http://www.nationalassociationofchoirs.org.uk
  Gen Sec: Lord James Ferrabbee
- ▲ Registered Charity
- Br 25 areas
- ○ *D, *N; to promote, develop & maintain public education in, & appreciation of, the art & science of music & in particular choral music
- ● Conf - Mtgs - Inf - Lib
- < Tonsil
- M 13 i, 16 f, 500 org
- ¶ NAC News & Views - 3; ftm, £2 nm.
  NAC Ybk - 1; ftm, £2 nm.

National Association of Cider Makers (NACM) 1920
- ■ International Wine & Spirit Centre, 39-45 Bermondsey St, LONDON, SE1 3XF. (hq)
  07761 874277
  email info@cideruk.com   http://www.cideruk.com
  Sec: Gemma Keyes
- ▲ Un-incorporated Society
- ○ *T; interests of makers of cider & perry
- Gp Technical (incl manufacture, packaging & labelling)
- ● Mtgs - LG
- < Assn des Inds des Cidres et Vins de Fruits de l'EU (AICV); Food & Drink Fedn
- M 8 f, 2 affiliated org
  SW of England Cidermakers Association
  Three Counties Cider & Perry Association
- ¶ Cider - 2.   LM; on request.

National Association of Cigarette Machine Operators (NACMO) 1968
- ■ Cherwell Tobacco, Unit 2 Waymills Industrial Estate, WHITCHURCH, Shropshire, SY13 1AD. (hsb)
  01948 663322   fax 01948 663671
  Gen Sec: Michael G White
- ▲ Company Limited by Guarantee
- Br 5
- ○ *T; for cigarette vending machine operators & protection of their interests
- Gp Tobacco distribution
- ● Conf - Mtgs - Stat - Inf
- < Europäischer Tabakwaren-Grosshandels-Verband eV (ETG)
- M [not available]
- ¶ NL - 4; free.

National Association of Citizens Advice Bureaux (NACAB) 1939
- NR Myddelton House, 115-123 Pentonville Rd, LONDON, N1 9LZ. (hq)
  020 7833 2181   fax 020 7833 4371
  http://www.citizensadvice.org.uk + adviceguide.org.uk
  Chief Exec: Gillian Guy
- ▲ Registered Charity
- Br 17
- ○ *K, *N, *W; provision of free, confidential & impartial advice & information on all subjects; social policy campaigning; lobbying
- ● Conf - Mtgs - ET - Res - EXhib - Stat - Inf - Empl - LG
- M 394 bureaux
- ¶ Mid Month NL - 12; m only.   Hbk; £6 m, £12 nm.   AR.
  Social Policy Reports - irreg.
  Note: also uses the operating name of Citizens Advice

National Association of Clinical Tutors (NACT) 1969
- NR Norfolk House East, 499 Silbury Boulevard, MILTON KEYNES, Bucks, MK9 2AH.
  01908 488033   fax 01296 715255
  email office@nact.org.uk   http://www.nact.org.uk
  Hon Sec: Dr Peter Harrison
- ▲ Registered Charity
- ○ *E, *P; to support medical education in running postgraduate medical education in teaching hospitals
- Gp Clinical tutors; Foundation programme training directors
- ● Conf - Mtgs - ET
- M 480 i
- ¶ Directory of Postgraduate Medical Centres (with gazetteer) - 1; ftm, £60 nm.

National Association of Co-operative Officials (NACO) 1917
- ■ 6a Clarendon Place, HYDE, Cheshire, SK14 2QZ. (hq)
  0161-351 7900   fax 0161-366 6800
  email info@naco.coop   http://www.naco.coop
  Gen Sec: Neil Buist
- ▲ Registered Trade Union
- Br 31
- ○ *U
- ● Conf - ET - Empl - LGI - LG
- < Trades U Congress (TUC); Soc for Coop Studies; Cooperatives UK
- M 2,120 i
- ¶ Co-operative Official - 4;   Grapevine NL - irreg;
  AR - 1; all free.

National Association for Colitis & Crohn's Disease   (NACC) 1979
NR   4 Beaumont House, Sutton Rd, ST ALBANS, Herts, AL1 5HH. (hq)
        01727 830038   fax 01727 862550
        http://www.nacc.org.uk
▲   Registered Charity
○   *W; to provide support & information to patients & families with ulcerative colitis & Crohn's disease; to fund research into the cause & cure of these conditions
Gp   NACC in contact listening ear service; Welfare fund
●   Conf - Mtgs - Res - Inf
        Infoline: 0845 130 2233
M   c 30,000 i
¶   NL - 4.   AR; free.
        Note: uses the working name Crohn's & Colitis UK.

National Association of Commercial Finance Brokers (NACFB)   1993
NR   3 Silverdown Office Park, Fair Oak Close, EXETER, Devon, EX5 2UX.   (hq)
        email admin@nacfb.org   http://www.nacfb.org
▲   Company Limited by Guarantee
○   *P; for commercial mortgage, lease & asset finance, factoring & invoice discounting brokers
●   Conf - Mtgs - ET - Exhib - LG
M   500 i, 350 f
¶   Niche Commercial - 12.

National Association of Community Run Shops   (NACRS)
■   Steamer Point, 29 West St, LEWES, E Sussex, BN7 2NZ.
        01273 472153
        http://www.communityshops.co.uk
        Sec: Alan Wyle
○   *T

National Association of Councillors   (NAC)   1959
NR   Gateshead MBC, Civic Centre, GATESHEAD, Tyne & Wear, NE8 1HH.   (hsb)
        0191-433 3000   fax 0191-477 9253
        email info@nac.uk.com   http://www.nac.uk.com
        Nat Sec: Councillor Peter Mole
○   *P; to represent the interests of local government councillors
¶   The Councillor - 2.   Bulletin - 2.

National Association of Councils for Voluntary Service
        since 14 June 2006 **National Association for Voluntary & Community Action**

National Association of Counsellors, Hypnotherapists & Psychotherapists   (NACHP)   1993
■   PO Box 719, Burwell, CAMBRIDGE, CB5 0NX.   (hq)
        01638 741363   fax 01638 744190
        email mail@nachp.org   http://www.nachp.org
        Chmn: James Hammond
▲   Company Limited by Guarantee; Registered Charity
○   *P; to advance the education for the benefit of the public by the publication of knowledge & best practice in the area of clinical psychotherapy & associated health care
●   Conf - Mtgs - ET - Inf
        Helpline: 0844 381 4088
<   UK Confedn of Hypnotherapy Orgs
M   102 i, UK / 2 i, o'seas
¶   NL - 4; ftm only.

National Association of Credit Hire Operators
        June 2010 merged with the Accident Management Association to form the **Credit Hire Organisation**

National Association for Deaf People
        since May 2007 **DeafHear**

National Association of Deafened People   (NADP)   1984
■   PO Box 50, AMERSHAM, Bucks, HP6 6XB.   (mail)
        0845 055 9663; 07527 211348 (SMS)
        fax 01305 262591
        email enquiries@nadp.org.uk   http://www.nadp.org.uk
        Hon Sec: Paul Tomlinson
▲   Registered Charity
○   *W; to promote the interests & welfare of people with a profound or total acquired hearing loss
●   Conf - Exhib - Inf - Local support groups
<   UK Council on Deafness
M   500 i
        (Sub: £15)
¶   Network (NL) - 4; ftm only.
        Information Booklet; ftm, £2.50 nm.
        An Introduction to Cochlear Implants; ftm, £5 nm.

National Association of Decorative & Fine Arts Societies (NADFAS)   1968
■   NADFAS House, 8 Guilford St, LONDON, WC1N 1DA.   (hq)
        020 7430 0730   fax 020 7242 0686
        email enquiries@nadfas.org.uk
        http://www.nadfas.org.uk
        Chief Exec: Mrs Gri Harrison
▲   Company Limited by Guarantee; Registered Charity
Br   338; Belgium, France, Germany, Netherlands, New Zealand, Spain
○   *A; to educate the public in the cultivation, appreciation & study of the decorative & fine arts
Gp   Church recorders; Heritage volunteers; Young arts
●   Mtgs - ET - SG - VE
<   Assn of Australian Decorative & Fine Arts Soc
M   c 90,000 i, 370 societies
¶   NADFAS Review - 4; ftm, £2.50 nm.
        Inside Churches; £15.95.   Stained Glass + Monograms; £12.50.
        Behind the Acanthus: the NADFAS story; £20.

National Association for the Education of Sick Children
        has closed

National Association for the Education, Training & Support of Blind & Partially Sighted People
        has closed

National Association of Educational Guidance for Adults
        since 2006 **NAEGA - promoting adult guidance on learning & work**

National Association for Environmental Education (UK) (NAEE)   1960
■   University of Wolverhampton, Walsall Campus, Gorway Rd, WALSALL, W Midlands, WS1 3BD.   (hq)
        01922 631200
        email info@naee.org.uk   http://www.naee.org.uk
        Hon Sec: Sue Fenoughty
▲   Registered Charity
○   *E, *L, *P; 'for all interested in education & the environment'
●   Conf - Mtgs - ET - Res - SG - Inf
M   2,000 i, 12 local org, UK / i, o'seas
        (Sub: £25 i, £30 f, UK / £40 i, £50 f, o'seas)
¶   Environmental Education - 3; £25 yr m, £6 each nm.

National Association of Estate Agents   (NAEA)   1962

- ■ Arbon House, 6 Tournament Court, Edgehill Drive, WARWICK, CV34 6LG.   (hq)
  01926 496800   fax 01926 417788
  email info@naea.co.uk   http://www.naea.co.uk
  Hon Sec: Peter Bolton King
- ▲ Company Limited by Guarantee
- Br 48
- ○ *P; cooperation among estate agents & protection of public against fraud, misrepresentation & malpractice
- Gp Institution of Commercial & Business Agents
  National Association of Valuers & Auctioneers
  NAEA International incorporating the Federation of Overseas Property Developers, Agents & Consultants (FOPDAC)
- ● Conf - Mtgs - ET - Exam - Res - Exhib - Lib
- < Intl Consortium of Real Estate Agents (ICREA);
  Is a division of the National Federation of Property Professionals
- M 10,000 i
- ¶ The Estate Agent - 8; ftm.
- ✕ 2008 Federation of Overseas Property Developers, Agents & Consultants (incorporated into NAEA)

National Association of Farriers, Blacksmiths & Agricultural Engineers   (NAFBAE)   1902

- NR The Forge, Avenue B 10th St, STONELEIGH PARK, Warks, CV8 2LG.   (hq)
  024 7669 6595   fax 024 7669 6708
  email nafbaehq@nafbae.org   http://www.nafbae.org
- Br 28
- ○ *T
- ● Conf - Mtgs - ET - Exhib - Comp - Inf - Empl
- M 1,300 i
- ¶ Forge - 6; ftm, £5.90 nm.

National Association of Field Studies Officers   (NAFSO)   1969

- ■ CEES Stibbington Centre, Church Lane, Stibbington, PETERBOROUGH, PE8 6LP.
  01780 782386   fax 01780 783835
  email office@nafso.org.uk   http://www.nafso.org.uk
  Chmn: Chas Matthews
- ▲ Un-incorporated Society
- ○ *P; for field studies officers in education & all interested in the environment, natural history & historical sites & buildings
- Gp Ecology; Education; Environmental; Field studies; Geography; Geology; Heritage education; History; Outdoor education
- ● Conf - Mtgs - ET - Res - Exhib - SG - Stat - Inf - Lib - VE - LG
- < Outdoor Coun; Nat Assn of Envtl Educ; Inst of Outdoor Learning
- M 150 i, UK/ 5 i, o'seas
  (Sub: £35)
- ¶ Jnl - 1; ftm; £5 nm.   NL - 3 (electronic); free.
  Topical publications - 1; ftm, c £5 nm.   AR - 1.
  Note: the enquiry address is open for 1 day a week

National Association of Financial Assessment Officers (NAFAO)   1995

- ■ St Mary's House (4th floor), 52 St Leonards Rd, EASTBOURNE, East Sussex, BN21 3UU.   (hsb)
  01273 481252   fax 01273 482475
  email asc.nafao@eastsussex.gov.uk
  http://www.nafao.org.uk
  Sec: Beverley Lambert
- ▲ Un-incorporated Society
- ○ *P; members undertake the financial assessment function for residential & non-residential services provision on behalf of local authorities
- ● Conf - Mtgs - Res - LG
- M 162 local authorities in the UK

National Association of Fine Art Education   (NAFAE)

- NR Head of Painting, Northumbria University, Newcastle upon Tyne, NE1 8ST.   (admin)
  email secretary@nafae.org.uk   http://www.nafae.org.uk
  Sec: Sue Spark
- ○ *A
- M c 30 org

National Association of Fire Officers
   an autonomous professional body within **Unite the Union**

National Association of Fisheries & Angling Consultatives
   in 2009 merged with the Anglers Conservation Association, the Fisheries & Angling Conservation Trust, the National Federation of Anglers, the National Federation of Sea Anglers & Specialist Anglers Alliance to form the **Angling Trust**

National Association of Flower Arrangement Societies (NAFAS)   1959

- NR Osborne House, 12 Devonshire Square, LONDON, EC2M 4TE.   (hq)
  020 7247 5567   fax 020 7247 7232
  email flowers@nafas.org.uk   http://www.nafas.org.uk
- ▲ Registered Charity
- ○ *A; promotion of the art & practice of flower arranging
- Gp Demonstrators; Teachers; Judges & speakers
- ● Conf - Mtgs - ET - Exam - Exhib - Comp - SG - Lib - PL - VE
- < Wld Assn of Flower Arrangers (WAFA); R Horticl Soc
- M 80,000 i, UK / 500 i, o'seas
- ¶ The Flower Arranger - 4.

National Association of Funeral Directors   (NAFD)   1905

- ■ 618 Warwick Rd, SOLIHULL, W Midlands, B91 1AA.   (hq)
  0845 230 1343   fax 0121-711 1351
  email info@nafd.org.uk   http://www.nafd.org.uk
  Chief Exec: Alan Slater
- ▲ Un-incorporated Society
- ○ *T; to protect the interests of members by means of formulating policy with regard to the statutory, legal, economic, health & safety, commercial, educational & other matters affecting funeral service
- ● Conf - Mtgs - ET - Exam - Exhib - Stat - Inf - LG
- < Eur Fedn Funeral Services; Fédn Intle des Assns des Thanatologues; Coun of Brit Funeral Service
- M 3,382 f, UK / 37 f, o'seas
- ¶ The Funeral Director Monthly - 12; ftm; £48 nm, £72 (Europe), £90 row.

National Association of Gallery Education
   see **engage: National Association of Gallery Education**

National Association for Gifted Children   (NAGC)   1967

- NR Challenge House (suite 1-2), Sherwood Drive, Bletchley, MILTON KEYNES, Bucks, MK3 6DP.   (hq)
  01908 646433
  email amazingchildren@nagcbritain.org.uk
  http://www.nagcbritain.org.uk
  Dir: Denise Yates
- Br 26
- ○ *W; to help, support & encourage gifted & talented children & their families & all others involved in their education & welfare
- M c 2,000 i, 500 schools
- ¶ Gifted & Talented (Jnl) - 1.
  NL - 3;   AR - 1; both ftm only.

**National Association of Goldsmiths of GB & Ireland   (N.A.G.)
1894**
- ■   78a Luke St, LONDON, EC2A 4XG.   (hq)
  020 7613 4445   fax 020 7613 4450
  email michael@jewellers-online.org
  http://www.jewellers-online.org
  Chief Exec: Michael J Hoare
- ▲   Company Limited by Guarantee
- ○   *T; to represent the interests of retail jewellers (incl goldsmiths, silversmiths & horologists) in the UK & Ireland
- Gp   Jewellery sector
- ●   Conf - ET - Res - Exhib - Inf - Lib - LG - Promotional services
- M   3,000 f
- ¶   The Jeweller (Jnl) - 6; ftm.
  n:gauge (NL) - 12.
  Note: It is a legal requirement that this association uses full stops in its abbreviation

National Association of Head Teachers   (NAHT)   1897
- ■   1 Heath Sq, Boltro Rd, HAYWARDS HEATH, W Sussex, RH16 1BL.   (hq)
  01444 472472   fax 01444 472473
  email info@naht.org.uk   http://www.naht.org.uk
  Gen Sec: Mick Brookes
- ○   *E, *P, *U; for head teachers, deputy head teachers & leaders, principals & vice-principals, of schools & colleges in state maintained & the private sector from nursery to tertiary level
- M   c 30,500 i

National Association of Health Stores   (NAHS)   1931
- NR   PO Box 14177, TRANENT, E Lothian, EH34 5WX.   (hq)
  01875 341408
  email nahsoffice:gmail.com   http://www.nahs.co.uk
- ▲   Company Limited by Guarantee
- ○   *T; for independent health food retailers
- ●   Mtgs - ET - Stat - Inf - Empl - LG
- M   i representing retail outlets
- ¶   NL - 4/8 weekly; free.

**National Association of Healthcare Fire Officers   (NAHFO)
1973**
- ■   c/o Peter Aldridge, Estates Management Team, St James's, Beckett St, LEEDS, W Yorks, LS9 7TF.   (hsb)
  http://www.nahfo.org
  Gen Sec: Peter Aldridge
- ○   *P; to promote & encourage the highest standards of fire safety in Health Service premises
- ●   Conf - Mtgs - ET - SG - Stat - VE - LG - Liaison with NHS Estates & Fire & Local Authorities on development of legislation & all matters relating to fire safety in healthcare
- <   Brit Fire Services Assn; UNISON
- ✕   2006 National Association of Hospital Fire Officers

National Association for Healthcare Security
- ■   c/o Nick van der Bijl, Somerset Partnership NHS Trust, Bristol Rd, BRIDGWATER, Somerset, TA8 4RN.
  01278 432074
  http://www.nahs.org.uk
  Pres: Nick van der Bijl
- ○   *P
- M   c 70 i

**National Association for Higher Education in the Moving Image
(NAHEMI)   1963**
- NR   c/o Sara Jolly, ATRiuM, University of Glamorgan, Adam St, CARDIFF, CF24 2HX.   (sb)
  http://www.nahemi.org
  Sec: Sara Jolly
- ○   *A, *E

National Association of Homeopathic Groups
  since 2009 **Action for Homeopathy**

**National Association of Hospital Broadcasting Organisations
(HBA)   1970**
- ■   54 St Annes Close, WINCHESTER, Hants, SO22 4LQ.   (hsp)
  0870 321 6003
  email secretary@hbauk.com   http://www.hbauk.com
  Hon Sec: Nigel Dallard
- ▲   Company Limited by Guarantee; Registered Charity
- Br   12
- ○   *W; support & representation of hospital broadcasters
- ●   Conf - Mtgs - ET - Inf - LG - Liaison with NHS, Copyright collecting societies
- M   i, 6 f, 230 org
  (Sub: £15 i, £300 f, £37 org)
- ¶   On Air - 6;   AR - 1; both ftm only.
  Note: trades as Hospital Broadcasting Association

National Association of Hospital & Community Friends
  since April 2006 **Attend**

National Association of Hospital Fire Officers
  since 2006 **National Association of Healthcare Fire Officers**

National Association of Hospital Play Staff   (NAHPS)   1975
- ■   143 Gresham Rd, STAINES, Middx, TW18 2AG.   (inf/officer/p)
  http://www.nahps.org.uk
  Admin: Sue Pallot
- ▲   Registered Charity
- ○   *W; support & information for staff who lead therapeutic play for hospital patients under 21 years; to campaign & advise on high quality hospital play services
- ●   Conf - Mtgs - ET - Inf - Empl
- M   c 450 i
- ¶   Jnl - 2.   NL - 2.   Expert articles & reading list.
  Salary & other information; free.   AR.

National Association of Investigators & Process Servers
  has closed

**National Association of Karate & Martial Art Schools
(NAKMAS)   1990**
- ■   PO Box 262, HERNE BAY, Kent, CT6 9AW.   (hq)
  01227 370055   fax 01227 370056
  email info@nakmas.org.uk   http://www.nakmas.org.uk
  Chmn: Joe Ellis
- ▲   Un-incorporated Society
- Br   1,200; 500 clubs o'seas
- ○   *S; to act as the governing body for martial arts; to provide training courses & vocational & NVQ qualifications
- Gp   Autistic Martial Arts
- ●   Mtgs - ET - Exam - Exhib - Comp - LG
- <   Sport & Recreation Alliance
- M   73,000 i, 1,200 f, 400 org, UK / 2,000 i, o'seas
  (Sub: varies i, £99.45 f & org)
- ¶   NAKMAS Review - 6; ftm, £2.99 nm.
  NAKMAS Annual Review - 1; ftm, £2.99 nm,
  Martial Arts Code of Safety.
  Codes of Ethics & Child Protection Procedures.

**National Association of Ladies' Circles of Great Britain &
Ireland   (NALC)   1936**
- ■   29 Ridge St, Wollaston, STOURBRIDGE, DY8 4QF.   (hq)
  email victoria.perry1000@virgin.net
  http://www.ladies-circle.org.uk
  Contact: Vicky Perry
- Br   280
- ○   *W; 'non-political, non-sectarian organisation for women aged 18-45 for fun, friendship & fund-raising
- Gp   Community service projects; Fundraising; Social activities
- ●   Conf - Mtgs - VE
- <   Ladies' Circle Intl
- M   2,300 i
  (Sub: £42.50)
- ¶   The Circler - 2; ftm only.

National Association of Language Advisers   (NALA)   1969

NR   Top of the Hill, Hartest, BURY ST EDMUNDS, Suffolk,
       IP29 4ET.   (treas/p)
       http://www.nala.org.uk
       Treas: Jerry Carpenter
○   *P; for modern foreign language (MFL) advisers, consultants &
       inspectors (public & private sectors) who work with schools &
       colleges in the UK to promote the quality of MFL teaching &
       learning
●   Conf - Mtgs - ET - Res - Inf - LG
M   c 250 i
¶   NALA Update - 3; ftm only.
     Report on Members' Annual Trends Survey - 1; ftm; (from
       Centre for Information on Language Teaching & Research,
       20 Bedfordbury, London, WC2N 4LB).

National Association of Laryngectomee Clubs   (NALC)   1976

■   152 Buckingham Palace Rd, LONDON, SW1W 9TR.   (hq)
       020 7730 8585   fax 020 7730 8584
       http://www.laryngectomy.org.uk
       Gen Sec: Vivien Reed
▲   Registered Charity
Br 95
○   *W; to promote the welfare & rehabilitation of laryngectomy
       patients & their families; to be of assistance to professionals
       working in the field
Gp Cancer of the larynx
●   Conf - Mtgs - ET - Res - Inf
<   MacMillan Cancer Support
M   4,500 i, 95 clubs, UK / 500 i, o'seas
       (Sub: £20)
¶   Publications list available.

**National Association of the Launderette Industry Ltd   (NALI)
1955**

■   33 Buckland Ave, SLOUGH, Berks, SL3 7PJ.   (hq)
       01753 521463
       http://www.nali.co.uk
       Sec: Mrs J Cowan
▲   Company Limited by Guarantee
○   *T; for launderette operators & supplier companies to the trade
●   Mtgs - Exhib - SG - Stat - Inf - LG
M   586 i, 56 f
¶   Launderette & Cleaning World - 4; ftm.

**National Association for Leisure Industry Certification
(NAFLIC)   1988**

NR   PO Box 752, SUNDERLAND, Co Durham, SR3 1XX.   (hsp)
       0191-523 9498   fax 0191-523 9498
       email mccleisure@lineone.net   http://www.naflic.org.uk
       Gen Sec: Neil R McCullough
▲   Un-incorporated Society
○   *T; to promote safety in the leisure industry
●   Conf - Mtgs - Exhib - Inf - LG
M   34 f, UK / 2 f, 1 org, o'seas

National Association of Licensed Opencast Operators

     has closed

National Association of Licensed Paralegals   (NALP)   1987

■   3.08 Canterbury Court, Kennington Business Park, 1-3 Brixton
       Rd, LONDON, SW9 6DE.   (hsb)
       020 3176 0900
       email info@nationalparalegals.co.uk
       http://www.nationalparalegals.com
       Hon Sec: Amanda Hamilton
▲   Company Limited by Guarantee
○   *P; national regulatory & professional body for paralegals;
       provides educational & qualifying requirements, training,
       professional status & licensing to all those working or seeking
       to work as paralegals in solicitors' offices or within
       commerce, industry or the public sector
Gp Community & voluntary sector paralegals group; Paralegal
       advocacy group; Private paralegal practitioners; Vocational
       training
●   Conf - Mtgs - ET - Exam - Res - Exhib - SG - Inf - VE - Empl -
       LG
>   Inst Legal Secs & PAs
M   c 4,000 i, UK / c 250 i, o'seas
¶   The Paralegal (Jnl) - 4; ftm only.

**National Association of Licensing & Enforcement Officers
(NALEO)   1985**

NR   3 Tyne Close, LIVERPOOL, L4 1XP.
       0151-933 4301
       http://www.naleo.org.uk
       Hon Sec: John Thompson
○   *P; for those concerned with Hackney carriage & private vehicle
       hire legislation & licensing enforcement
●   Mtgs - ET
×   2007-08 National Association of Taxi & Private Hire Licensing &
       Enforcement Officers

**National Association for Literature Development   (NALD)
1994**

■   PO Box 243, ILKLEY, W Yorks, LS29 1AT.   (mail/address)
       01943 862107
       email director@nald.org   http://www.nald.org
       Dir: Steve Dearden
▲   Company Limited by Guarantee
○   *P; for literature professionals & those working in writng &
       reading & developing literature audiences
●   Conf - Mtgs - ET - Inf
<   The Literature Consortium
M   200 ii, 110 f
       (Sub: £30 - £50)
¶   Literature Professional (online pdf) - 4; ftm.

National Association of Local Councils   (NALC)   1947

NR   109 Great Russell St, LONDON, WC1B 3LD.   (hq)
       020 7637 1865   fax 020 7436 7451
       email nalc@nalc.gov.uk   http://www.nalc.gov.uk
▲   Un-incorporated Society
○   *N; to promote interests of parish, community & town councils;
       to assist them in the performance of their duties; to promote
       social, cultural & recreational life of parishes & villages
●   Conf - Mtgs - ET - Exhib - Inf - Empl - LG
<   Intl U Local Authorities
M   10,000 parish, community & town councils in England & Wales
¶   Local Council Review.   Various other publications.

*National Association of Local Government Arts Officers
     since 2010 **Arts Development UK***

**National Association for Managers of Student Services in
Colleges   (NAMSS)**

■   PO Box 529, WESTON-super-MARE, Somerset, BS23 9EQ.
       01934 811275   fax 01934 811275
       Admin: Tina Philp
○   *P

   © CBD Research Ltd · Beckenham · BR3 5JS · Tel 020 8650 7745 · E-mail cbd@cbdresearch.com · www.cbdresearch.com

National Association of Massage & Manipulative Therapists (NAMMT)
NR   24 Mount St, DERBY, DE1 2HH.   (hsb)
      01332 349493
      email dianne@drichardson80.orangehome.co.uk
      http://www.nammt.co.uk
      Sec: Dianne Richardson
○   *P; to promote the welfare & professional development of
      professional massage & manipulative therapists
<   Gen Coun for Massage Therapies
M   119 i

National Association of Master Bakers   (NAMB)   1887
NR   21 Baldock St, WARE, Herts, SG12 9DH.   (hq)
      01920 468061   fax 01920 461632
      http://www.masterbakers.co.uk
      Chief Exec: Gill Brooks-Lonican
○   *T; to represent craft bakery businesses in England & Wales
M   f

National Association of Master Letter Carvers   (NAMLC) 1920
■   c/o NAMM, 1 Castle Mews, RUGBY, Warks, CV21 2XL.   (hq)
      01788 542264   fax 01788 542276
      Sec: John Smith
▲   Un-incorporated Society
○   *P; to preserve & promote hand carved lettering in stone,
      marble & granite
●   Mtgs - Empl
M   50 i
¶   LM; free.

National Association of Mathematics Advisers   (NAMA)   1974
NR   PO Box 5056, WESTBURY, Wilts, BA13 9BA.   (mail/address)
      email info@nama.org.uk   http://www.nama.org.uk
      Hon Sec: Angela Easton
▲   Un-incorporated Society
○   *E, *P; to disseminate information & ideas on all subjects
      relating to maths education; to promote specific policies on
      maths education
●   Conf - ET - SG - LG
M   350 i
¶   NL - 3; ftm.

National Association for Medical Education Management (NAMEM)   1975
■   c/o Miss Corinne Trim, Kings' College Hospital, Western
      Education Centre, 10 Cutcombe Rd, LONDON, SE5 9RJ.
      (hsb)
      020 7848 5642
      http://www.namem.org.uk
      Hon Sec: Miss Corinne Trim
○   *N, *P; organisation & administration of postgraduate medical
      training for dentists & doctors
●   Conf - Mtgs - ET - SG
<   Nat Assn Clinical Tutors (NACT)
>   NAMPS; Middlesex University
M   250 i
¶   NL - 2.   LM;   Reference Hbk;   Council Hbk; all - 1.
      Training Programmw (3-yr course); £1,200.

National Association of Memorial Masons   (NAMM)   1907
■   1 Castle Mews, RUGBY, Warks, CV21 2XL.   (hq)
      01788 542264   fax 01788 542276
      email enquiries@namm.org.uk
      http://www.namm.org.uk
      Pres: Penny Lymn Rose
▲   Company Limited by Guarantee
○   *T; interests of memorial masonry industry (natural stone
      memorials)
●   Conf - Mtgs - ET - Exam - Res - Exhib - Comp - Inf - VE - Empl
      - LG
<   Intl Monument Fedn; EURO-ROC; Coun of Brit Funeral
      Services; Confedn of Burial Authorities (UK)
M   25 i, 400 f, UK / 5 i, 25 f, o'seas
¶   Review (Jnl) - 4; ftm only.

National Association for Mental After-Care in Residential Care Homes   (MARCH)   1989
■   10 Holmwood Avenue, UDDINGSTON, Lanarkshire,
      G71 7AJ.   (hq)
      0300 999 2014
      email ian@silverwellshouse.co.uk
      http://www.march.org.uk
      Sec: Ian Strachan
▲   Company Limited by Guarantee; Registered Charity
○   *W; to relieve those persons who are, or who have been,
      suffering from a mental disorder; to secure & enhance their
      quality of life & assist in the prevention of further episodes of
      acute illness
Gp   Dementia care (EMI); Respite care
●   Conf - Mtgs - ET - Res - Exhib - SG - Stat - Inf - LG
M   70 i
¶   MARCH Mental Health Circular - 4; ftm, £2.50 nm.

** **National Association of Microwave Engineers**
      Organisation lost: see Introduction paragraph 3

National Association of Mining History Organisations (NAMHO)   1979
NR   Peak District Mining Museum, The Pavilion, MATLOCK BATH,
      Derbys, DE4 3NR.   (hq)
      01629 583834
      http://www.namho.org
      Sec: Nigel Dibben
▲   Registered Charity
○   *L, *N; for learned & research organisations; to promote
      development of knowledge of mining history
●   Conf - Res - SG - Inf - VE - LG - Field meetings - Formation of
      codes of practice
<   Assn of Indl Archaeology; Brit Cave Res Assn; Nat Caving Assn
M   7 f, 73 org, UK / 1 org, o'seas
¶   NL - 3; ftm, £1 nm.   Mining Heritage Guide; £5 m, £6 nm.
      Code of Practice for: Mineral collecting, Removal of artefacts,
      Mine exploration; free for sae please.   Publicity leaflet.

** **National Association of Mortgage Victims**
      Organisation lost: see Introduction paragraph 3

National Association of Music Educators   (NAME)   1947
- ■ Gordon Lodge, Snitterton Rd, MATLOCK, Derbys, DE4 3LZ. (hq)
  01629 760791   fax 01629 760791
  email musiceducation@name.org.uk
  http://www.name.org.uk
  Business Mgr: Helen Fraser
- ▲ Company Limited by Guarantee; Registered Charity
- ○ *D, *E; for all involved in the furtherance of musical education
- Gp Music curriculum: Primary, Secondary; Initial teacher training & higher education; Advisers, inspectors, consultants; Corporate members
- ● Conf - Mtgs - ET - Res - Inf - LG
- < Music Educ Coun; Fedn of Music Services; Scot Assn of Music Educators; Welsh Music Inf Centre (CAGAC)
- M 556 i, 53 org, UK / 4 i, o'seas
- ¶ Name magazine - 3; ftm, £3.50 nm.
  Postbag (NL) - 4; ftm, £1 nm.

** National Association of Musical Instrument Repairers
  Organisation lost: see Introduction paragraph 3

** National Association of Nappy Services
  Organisation lost: see Introduction paragraph 3

National Association of NFU Group Secretaries   (NAGS) 1947
- NR Woodside Industrial Estate, Llanbadoc, USK, Monmouthshire, NP15 1SS.   (hsb)
  01291 672715   fax 01291 673835
- ▲ Un-incorporated Society
- ○ *T; 'to represent the business & welfare interests of agents of the NFU Mutual & Farming Union Secretaries to their principals, & otherwise promote the prosperity of their business'
- Gp Education; Financial services; Insurance; IT & group services
- ● Conf - Mtgs - ET - SG - Stat - Inf - Empl

National Association of Nurses for Contraception & Sexual Health
- NR 14 Nightingale Close, MIDDLEWICH, Cheshire, CW18 0SL.
  07511 639650
  email nancsh@hotmail.com
- ○ *M, *P

National Association of Official Prison Visitors   (NAOPV) 1924
- NR Eskdale 27 Collier Lane, Baildon, SHIPLEY, W Yorks, BD17 5LN.   (hsp)
  01274 583417
  Contact: Mrs Barbara M Crompton
- Br 40
- ○ *W; for official prison visitors in England & Wales
- ● Conf - Mtgs - LG (Home Office)
- M 1,400 i
- ¶ NL - 2; ftm.

National Association of Ovulation Method Instructors UK (NAOMI)   1978
- ■ The Billings Method Centre, 4 Southgate Drive, CRAWLEY, W Sussex, RH10 6RP.   (pres/p)
  01444 881744   fax 01444 881744
  http://www.billingsnaomi.org
  Pres: Dr Helen Davies
- ▲ Registered Charity
- ○ *P; to provide information & authentic literature on the Billings Ovulation Method of natural family planning to achieve, or avoid, a pregnancy
- ● ET (for qualifications to instruct) - Inf - Lib
- < Wld Org of the Ovulation Method Billings (WOOMB)
- M i

National Association of Paper Merchants   (NAPM)   1920
- NR PO Box 2850, NOTTINGHAM, NG5 2WW.   (hq)
  0115-841 2129   fax 0115-841 0831
  email info@napm.org.uk   http://www.napm.org.uk
  Dir: Tim Bowler
- ▲ Un-incorporated Society
- ○ *T; to promote the value of the UK paper & board merchant
- Gp Irish Association of Paper Merchants
- ● Conf - Mtgs - Stat - Inf - Lib - LG
- < Europäischer Verband Grosshändler Papier (EUGROPA)
- M 22 f, UK / 9 f, Ireland

National Association of Park Home Residents   (NAPHR) 1982
- ■ Flat B, 38 Abergele Rd, COLWYN BAY, LL29 7PA.   (hq)
  01492 535677
  email jim@naphr.org   http://www.naphr.org
  Treas: Jim Winchester
- ▲ Un-incorporated Society
- ○ *G; voluntary advisory group serving the interests of park home / mobile home owner occupiers on permanently licensed parks
- Gp Mobile home law
- ● Inf
- M 10,000 i
- ¶ NAPHR NL - irreg; ftm.

National Association for Pastoral Care in Education   (NAPCE) 1982
- ■ PO Box 6005, NUNEATON, Warks, CV11 9GY.   (hq)
  0753 145 3670
  email base@napce.org.uk   http://www.napce.org.uk
  Chmn: Jae Bray
- ▲ Registered Charity
- Br 13
- ○ *E, *W; 'promoting pastoral care & personal-social education'
- ● Conf - Mtgs - ET - Res - Comp - Inf
- M 800 i, 1,200 org, UK / 50 i, o'seas
- ¶ Pastoral Care in Education (Jnl) - 4; ftm;   AR; free.

National Association for Patient Participation   1978
- NR 19 Harvey Rd, WALTON-on-THAMES, Surreym KT12 2PZ.   (mail/address)
  01932 242350
  Hon Sec: Mrs Edith Todd
- ▲ Registered Charity
- ○ *W; to develop & maintain patient participation at surgeries & health care centres; to facilitate improved networking of patients within primary care groups; individuals can affiliate
- ● Conf - Mtgs - ET - LG
- M c 200 groups
- ¶ NL - 4; m only.
  Note: it is a legal requirement that this Association uses full stops in its abbreviation

National Association of Pension Funds Ltd   (NAPF)   1923
- NR Cheapside House, 138 Cheapside, LONDON, EC2V 6AE.   (hq)
  020 7601 1700   fax 020 7601 1799
  http://www.napf.co.uk
- ○ *T

National Association for People Abused in Childhood (NAPAC)   1997
- ■ 42 Curtain Rd, LONDON, EC2A 3NH.
  http://www.napac.org.uk
- ▲ Registered Charity
- ○ *W
- ● Helpline: 0800 085 3330

National Association for People with an Intellectual Disability
  see **Inclusion Ireland**

National Association of Percussion Teachers   (NAPT)   1984
- ■ 11 Mallard Close, Kempshott, BASINGSTOKE, Hants,
   RG22 5JP.   (hsp)
   01256 329009
   email wendy@waba4.co.uk   http://www.napt.org.uk
   Hon Sec: Wendy Harding
- ○ *D, *P; for teachers, instructors & players of percussion
   instruments
- Gp Percussion teachers & performers
- ● Conf - ET - Lib
- M 200 i, 8 f, UK / 10 i, o'seas
- ¶ NL - 3; ftm only.

**National Association for Pre-Paid Funeral Plans   (NAPFP)
1993**
- NR 15 Riverside Drive, SOLIHULL, W Midlands, B91 3HH.   (hq)
   0121-705 5133
   http://www.napfp.co.uk
   Sec: Nigel Burton
- ▲ Un-incorporated Society
- ○ *T; to serve the interests of members in providing pre-paid
   funeral plans for clients (incl ensuring the security of funds
   entrusted for this purpose) & maintaining a high standard of
   integrity in the marketing & selling of such plans
- ● Inf - LG
- M 9 f
- ¶ Code of Practice - 1;   AR - 1;
   Independent Chairman's Report on Adherence to Code of
   Practice - 1; all ftm.

**National Association for Premenstrual Syndrome   (NAPS)
1984**
- ■ 41 Old Rd, EAST PECKHAM, Kent, TN12 5AP.   (hq)
   0844 815 7311
   email naps@pms.org.uk   http://www.pms.org.uk
   Chief Exec: Christopher Ryan
- ▲ Registered Charity
- ○ *W; to provide support, help & information to women who
   suffer pre-menstrual syndrome & their families; works to
   promote better understanding of the condition & its treatment
- ● Conf
   Helpline: 0870 777 2177
- < Long-term Med Conditions Alliance
- M c 850 i
- ¶ NL - 12;   Understanding PMS.
   Diet books & other publications.

National Association of Press Agencies Ltd   (NAPA)   1983
- ■ c/o Mercury Press Agency, Contemporary Urban
   Centre (2nd floor), 41-51 Greenland St, LIVERPOOL,
   L1 0BS.   (asa)
   0870 609 1935
   http://www.napa.org.uk
   Contact: The Administrator
- ▲ Company Limited by Guarantee
- Br 46; 3
- ○ *T; for news & photographic agencies, established
   correspondents for all leading newspapers, magazines, TV &
   broadcasting outlets
- ● Conf - Mtgs
- M 46 f, UK / 3 f, o'seas
- ¶ NAPA Hbk - 1.

National Association of Primary Care   (NAPC)   1998
- NR Lettsom House, 11 Chandos St, Cavendish Sq, LONDON,
   W1G 9DP.   (hq)
   020 7636 7228   fax 020 7636 1601
- ○ *N; for all practices working as Primary Care Groups
- ● Helpline: 020 7636 1677 (Mon-Fri 0900-1700)
- M org

**National Association of Primary Care Educators UK   (NAPCE)
1990**
- NR DTE House, Hollins Mount, BURY, Lancs, BL9 8AT.   (hq)
   0161-796 1212
   email napce@btinternet.com   http://www.napce.net
   Chmn: Dr Stephen Holmes
- ▲ Registered Charity
- ○ *E, *M, *P
- ● Conf - Mtgs - ET
- ¶ NL - 4; free.
   List of publications available.

National Association for Primary Education   (NAPE)   1980
- ■ Moulton College Management Centre, Moulton,
   NORTHAMPTON, NN3 7RR.   (hq)
   01604 647646   fax 01604 647660
   email nationaloffice@nape.org.uk
   http://www.nape.org.uk
   Nat Sec: John Coe
- ▲ Registered Charity
- Br 4
- ○ *E; partnership between parents & teachers & any other
   interested individuals, in the promotion & provision of
   primary & pre-school education; the professional
   development of all who work with primary children
- ● Conf - Mtgs - ET - Res - Exhib - SG - Inf - Lib - LG
- < Design & Technology Assn
- M a network of c 2,500
- ¶ Newsbrief (NL) - 3;   NAPE News - 3; both ftm only.
   Primary First - 3; ftm, £5 each nm.

**National Association of Private Ambulance Services
(NAPAS)   1987**
- ■ 21 Bassenhally Rd, WHITTLESEY, Cambs, PE7 1RN.   (hq)
   01733 350916   fax 01733 350112
   email napas@ambulanceservices.co.uk
   http://www.ambulanceservices.co.uk
   Nat Dir: Peter A Littledyke
- ▲ Un-incorporated Society
- Br 53; 3 Republic of Ireland
- ○ *P; to ensure standards in the provision of independent, private
   & professional ambulance & ambulance aid in the UK &
   throughout Europe
- Gp Boxing; Club medics; Equestrian; Motor sport; NHS contracting;
   Pop concerts; Rave parties; Repatriation
   Ambulance services: Air, Ice sports; Rail, Road
   Advisory & contingency for all events & business
- ● Conf - Mtgs - ET - Res - SG - Stat - Inf - Lib - PL - LG
- < Brit Ambulance Services Panel; DTI Foresight
- M 53 f, UK / 3 f, o'seas
- ¶ NAPAS News & Views - 4; ftm only.
   NAPAS Code of Practice & Annual Members Audit - 1; ftm,
   4x1st class stamps, nm.

National Association of Probation & Bail Hostels
   since 2007 **National Approved Premises Association**

National Association of Probation Officers   (NAPO)   1912
- NR 4 Chivalry Rd, LONDON, SW11 1HT.   (hq)
   020 7223 4887   fax 020 7223 3503
   email info@napo.org.uk   http://www.napo.org.uk
   Gen Sec: Jonathan Ledger
- ○ *P, *U; for probation officers & family court staff
- < Trades U Congress (TUC)
- M 9,501 i

**National Association of Professional Inspectors & Testers
(NAPIT)   1992**
- NR Mill 3 (4th floor), Pleasey Vale Business Park, MANSFIELD,
   Notts, NG19 8RL.
   0870 444 1392   fax 0870 444 1427
   http://www.napit.org.uk
   Chief Exec: John Andrews
- ○ *U; inspectors and testers of electrical, plumbing, heating and
   ventilation systems

National Association of Professionals concerned with Language Impairment in Children   (NAPLIC)   1986
NR   29 Franklands Drive, Rowtown, ADDLESTONE, Surrey, KT15 1EG.   (chmn/p)
http://www.naplic.org.uk
Chmn: John Parrott
○   *P; teachers, speech and language therapists and other professionals

National Association for Providers of Activities for Older People (NAPA)   1997
■   Bondway Commercial Centre,(Unit 5 12 5th floor), 71 Bondway, LONDON, SW8 1SQ.   (hq)
020 7078 9375   fax 020 7735 9634
email sylvie@napa-activities.co.uk
http://www.napa-activities.co.uk
Strategic Dir: Mrs Sylvie Silver
▲   Company Limited by Guarantee; Registered Charity
○   *W; to provide activities for older people, essential to the maintenance of physical & psychological health & well-being; to provide education & training; to support individuals who provide activities, whether in home or care settings
●   ET - Res - Inf
M   660 i
¶   NAPA NL - 3; ftm.

National Association of Public & Proprietary Golf Clubs & Courses   (NAPGC)   1927
■   12 Newton Close, REDDITCH, Worcs, B98 7YR.   (hsp)
01527 542106   fax 01527 455320
email eddiemitchell@blueyonder.co.uk
http://www.napgc.org.uk
Hon Sec: Ed Mitchell
▲   Un-incorporated Society
○   *S; to represent public pay & play golf courses in the UK
M   100 clubs & members
¶   Annual Competitions Review - 1; ftm.   Ybk.

National Association of Railway Clubs   (NARC)   1952
■   2 Romsey Rd, EASTLEIGH, Hants, SO50 9FE.   (hq)
023 8032 2686   fax 023 8039 9736
email narcsrmb@aol.com
http://www.railsocialclubs.co.uk
Gen Sec: Malcolm Brown
▲   Un-incorporated Society
Br   180
○   *N; for sports & community clubs
M   [not stated]

National Association of Range Manufacturers   1933
NR   c/o Preston & Thomas Ltd, Woodville Engineering Works, Heron Rd, Rumney, CARDIFF, Glamorgan, CF3 3YF.   (sb)
029 2079 3331   fax 029 2077 9195
Sec: Simon Preston
○   *T; interests of makers & suppliers of equipment for fried fish & chip restaurants

National Association of Re-enactment Societies   (NAReS)   1991
■   Alma House, 72 Cow Close Rd, LEEDS, W Yorks, LS12 5PD.   (hsp)
0113-229 6759
email general@nares.org.uk   http://www.nares.org.uk
Contact: Des Thomas
▲   Un-incorporated Society
○   *G, *N; to represent the interests of British re-enactors
●   Conf - Mtgs - ET - Res - Exhib - SG - Inf - PL
M   4f, 27 org
¶   Retrospection - 4; ftm, £1 nm.

National Association of Reformed Offenders
    see **Unlock - National Association of Reformed Offenders**

National Association of Regional Game Councils   1968
IRL   Castle St, CLOGHAN, Co Offaly, Republic of Ireland.   (dir/p)
email nargc@iol.ie   http://www.nargc.ie
Nat Dir: Des Crofton
○   *S; for those interested in game shooting & conservation

National Association of Registered Home Inspectors
has closed

National Association of Registered Petsitters
NR   PO Box 1433, OXFORD, OX4 9AU.
0845 230 8544
email info@dogsit.com   http://www.dogsit.com
Chmn: Robin Taylor
○   *G

National Association for the Relief of Apnoea
    see **NARA - the breathing charity**

National Association for the Relief of Paget's Disease
    since 2011 **Paget's Association**

National Association of Retired Police Officers   (NARPO)   1919
NR   38 Bond St, WAKEFIELD, W Yorks, WF1 2QP.   (hq)
01924 362166   fax 01924 372088
http://www.narpo.org.uk
▲   Un-incorporated Society
Br   120
○   *P; 'to safeguard the rights of members & promote measures for their welfare with particular regard to pensions'
●   Conf - Mtgs - Inf - Pension matters - Appeals & benefits
<   Public Services Pensioners Coun
M   100,000 i
¶   Magazine - 4; ftm only.

National Association of Road Transport Museums   (NARTM)   1982
■   4 Dockroyd Lane, Oakworth, KEIGHLEY, W Yorks, BD22 7RN.   (chmn/b)
email email@nartm.org.uk   http://www.nartm.org.uk
Chmn: Dennis Talbot
▲   Company Limited by Guarantee; Registered Charity
○   *G, *N; the representative body for organisations or individuals with collections of historic buses & coaches, goods vehicles & other large road vehicles who wish to make their collections accessible to the public
●   Mtgs - Stat - Inf - VE - LG
<   Fedn Brit Historic Vehicle Clubs
M   95 org
¶   NARTM Newslink - 4; ftm only.
Bus & Coach Preservation Handbook - 1.

National Association of Rooflight Manufacturers   (NARM)   1988
■   43 Clare Croft, Middleton, MILTON KEYNES, MK10 9HD.   (hq)
01908 692325   fax 01908 692325
email admin@narm.org.uk   http://www.narm.org.uk
Sec: Lorraine Cookham
○   *T; represents manufacturers of rooflights & raw materials in the UK; to enhance & improve standards within the UK & Europe on all types of rooflight products; to provide assistance to architects & other specifiers
Gp   Technical c'ee
●   Mtgs
<   Construction Products Assn
M   7 f
¶   Publications available on website only.

© CBD Research Ltd · Beckenham · BR3 5JS · Tel 020 8650 7745 · E-mail cbd@cbdresearch.com · www.cbdresearch.com

National Association of Round Tables of Great Britain & Ireland   (RTBI)   1927
- ■ Marchesi House, 4 Embassy Drive, Edgbaston, BIRMINGHAM, B15 1TP.   (hq)
  0121-456 4402
  email hq@roundtable.org.uk
  http://www.roundtable.org.uk
  Admin: Maureen Huggins
- ○ *W, *X; service to community through cultivation of highest ideals in business, professional & civic traditions
- M c 10,000 i

National Association of School Business Management (NASBM)
- NR 140 Wood St (1st floor offices), RUGBY, Warks, CV21 2SP.   (hq)
  01788 573300   fax 01788 571812
  email bursarsassoc@btinternet.com
  http://www.nba.org.uk
  Chief Exec: William Simmonds
- ○ *P; for school bursars, business managers & senior administrative staff
- M i
- X 2008 National Bursars Association

National Association of Schoolmasters Union of Women Teachers   (NASUWT)   1919
- ■ Rose Hill, Rednal, BIRMINGHAM, B45 8RS.   (hq)
  0121-453 6150   fax 0121-457 6208
  email nasuwt@mail.nasuwt.org.uk
  http://www.nasuwt.org.uk
  Gen Sec: Chris Keates
- Br 360; Cyprus, Germany, Gibraltar, Guernsey, Jersey
- ○ *E, *P, *U; for all teachers from early years to further education, in all roles including heads & deputies
- ● Conf - Mtgs - ET - Res - Exhib - Comp - Empl - LG
- < Educ Intl; Trades U Congress (TUC)
- M 279,145 i
- ¶ Teaching Today - termly; ftm.

National Association of Screen Make-up Artists & Hairdressers (NASMAH)   2000
- ■ 68 Sarsfield Rd, Perivale, GREENFORD, Middx, UB6 7AG.   (chmn/p)
  020 8998 7494
  email info@nasmah.co.uk   http://www.nasmah.co.uk
  Chmn: Sandra Exelby
- ○ *P; to raise the standards of make-up artists & hairdressers in this country; to improve training & raise the profile of members in the media industry
- Gp Courses; Master classes; Seminars; Training
- ● ET
- < Cine Glds of GB (CGGB)
- M 200 i
- ¶ NL - 4; free.

National Association of Security Dog Users   (NASDU)   1996
- ■ Unit 11 Boundary Business Centre, WOKING, Surrey, GU21 5DH.   (mailing/address)
  01483 888588   fax 01483 486335
  email info@nasdu.co.uk   http://www.nasdu.co.uk
  Co Sec: Steve Hill
- ▲ Company Limited by Guarantee
- ○ *P; to achieve, promote & maintain national standards for all trainers, handlers & dogs within the security industry; for those who are concerned the care, health, safety & welfare of dogs within the industry
- Gp Training sub-c'ee; Detection dogs (incl drugs & explosives)
- ● Conf - Mtgs - ET - Exam - Res - Inf - LG - Annual working security dogs trials
- < Brit Inst of Profl Dog Trainers; Skills for Security
- M 200+ i, 60 f, 10 org, UK / 10 i, o'seas
- ¶ NL - 4; ftm, £2 nm.   Code of Practice; £25.
  Pocket Reference Guide; £5.
  Underpinning Knowledge Pack; £25 m, £32.50 nm.
  Trainers Pack; £150 m only.

National Association of Seed Potato Merchants in 2006 merged with the Scottish Potato Trades Association to form the **British Potato Trade Association**

National Association of Sessional GPs   (NASGP)   1997
- NR PO Box 188, CHICHESTER, W Sussex, PO19 2ZA.   (hsp)
  email info@nasgp.org.uk   http://www.nasgp.org.uk
  Chief Exec: Richard Fieldhouse
- ▲ Company Limited by Guarantee
- ○ *P; voluntary organisation supporting sessional general practitioners (locums, salaried & freelance)
- Gp GPs: salaried; Freelance/locum
- ● Inf
- M 1,500 i
- ¶ The Sessional GP - 6; ftm, £5 nm.

National Association of Shopfitters   (NAS)   1919
- ■ NAS House, 411 Limpsfield Rd, WARLINGHAM, Surrey, CR6 9HA.   (hq)
  01883 624961   fax 01883 626841
  http://www.shopfitters.org
  Dir: R Hudson
- Br 4
- ○ *T
- ● Conf - Mtgs - Comp - Stat - Expt - Inf
- < Intl Shopfitting Org; Australian Shopfitters Assn; NZ Shopfitters Assn
- M f

National Association for Small Schools   (NASS)   1978
- ■ Quarrenden, Upper Red Cross Rd, GORING-on-THAMES, Berks, RG8 9BD.   (nat/coord/p)
  0845 223 5029
  email mbenford@bigfoot.com
  http://www.smallschools.org.uk
  Sec: Barbara Taylor
- ○ *E, *K, *N; to advance the case for retaining small local schools, mainly those threatened with closure; to promote good practice in both school & community
- ● Conf - Res - Inf
- < Interskola (education in sparsely populated areas)
- > Human Scale Education; Village Retail Services Assn
- M 600 i & gps, UK / 15 i & gps, o'seas
- ¶ NL - 2.

National Association of Social Workers in Education (NASWE)   1884
- NR c/o National Children's Bureau, 8 Wakley St, LONDON, EC1V 7QE.   (sb)
  020 7843 6000
  http://www.naswe.org.uk
  Gen Sec: Jacqui Newvell
- ▲ Un-incorporated Society
- ○ *E, *P; for all education welfare officers & education social workers working for a local education authority
- ● Conf - Mtgs - ET - LG
- < UNISON
- M c 500 i
- ¶ The Education Social Worker - 3; ftm, on request nm.

National Association of Specialist Computer Retailers
has been reported to us as having closed: we should appreciate confirmation.

National Association for Spina Bifida & Hydrocephalus Ireland
- IRL National Resource Centre, Old Nangor Rd, DUBLIN 22, Republic of Ireland.
  353 (1) 457 2329
  http://www.sbhi.ie
  Chief Exec: George Kennedy
- ○ *W; to provide information, support & advice to people with spina bifida &/or hydrocephalus
  Note: Trades as Spina Bifida Hydrocephalus Ireland

National Association for Sports Development
in 2007 merged with the Institute of Leisure & Amenity Management to form the Institute for Sport, Parks & Leisure, which in 2011 merged with the Institute of Sport & Recreation Management to form the **Institute for the Management of Sport & Physical Activity**

National Association of Stable Staff   (NASS)   1975
- ■ Bretby Business Park, Ashby Rd, Bretby, BURTON UPON TRENT, Staffs, DE15 0YZ.   (hq)
  01283 211522
  email office@naoss.co.uk   http://www.naoss.co.uk
  Chief Exec: Jim Cornelius
- ○ *U; for stable staff employed by licensed racehorse trainers
- ● Conf - Mtgs - ET - Comp - SG - Stat
- < Gen Fedn Tr Us (GFTU); Trades U Congress (TUC)
- M 1,954 i
- ¶ Stable Talk - 4; free.
- × 2007 (September) Stable Lads Association

National Association for Staff Development in the Post-16 Sector
in 2007 merged with the **Further Education Research Association**

National Association of Steel Stockholders   (NASS)   1928
- ■ The Citadel (1st floor), 190 Corporation St, BIRMINGHAM, B4 6QD.   (hq)
  0121-200 2288   fax 0121-236 7444
  email info@nass.org.uk   http://www.nass.org.uk
  Dir Gen: Bryan Holden
- ○ *T
- Gp Product Gps: Bright & engineering steels, General steels, Plate & processing, Stainless steels, Strip mill coil & sheet, Tubes
  Specialist c'ee: Health & safety
- ● Conf - Mtgs - ET - Exhib - SG - Stat - Inf - VE - LG
- < EUROMETAL; is a member of Metals Forum
- M 113 f
- ¶ NASS News (NL) - 4.   LM.   AR.
  Steel & Its Distribution.
  Safety Guidelines for Steel Stockholders & Processors.
  Beating the Odds [&] Moving Steel by Crane (health & safety video).

National Association for the Support of Victims of Stalking & Harassment   (NASH)   1993
- NR PO Box 1309, KENILWORTH, Warks, CV8 2YJ.
  01926 850089
  Dir: Evonne von Heussen-Countryman
- ○ *W; to support & advise the victims of stalking & harassment, in any circumstances, & their families; to provide expert witnesses in court cases
  Note: Please enclose an SAE when writing to the Association.

** National Association of Supporting Artistes Agents
Organisation lost: see Introduction paragraph 3

National Association of Swimming Clubs for the Handicapped   (NASCH)   1965
- NR The Willows, Mayles Lane, WICKHAM, Hants, PO17 5ND.
  01329 833689
  http://www.nasch.org.uk
  Nat Coordinator: Mike O'Leary
- ○ *S; to promote swimming & swimming clubs for people with disabilities
- M 10,000 i, 102 org

National Association of Taxi & Private Hire Licensing Enforcement Officers
since 2007-08 **National Association of Licensing & Enforcement Officers**

National Association of Teachers of Dancing Ltd   (NATD)   1906
- ■ 44-47 The Broadway, THATCHAM, Berks, RG19 3HP.   (hq)
  01635 868888   fax 01635 872301
  email info@natd.org.uk   http://www.natd.org.uk
  Sec: Mrs Lyn Foster
- ▲ Company Limited by Guarantee
- Br worldwide
- ○ *D, *P; to promote & improve the art of dancing in all its forms - ballroom, theatrical & social
- Gp Acrobatic; Ballet; Ballroom; Classic & sequence; Contemporary dance; Country & Western; Dance & exercise; Disco freestyle; Latin American; Modern stage; National dance; Rock'n'roll; Street; Tap
- ● Conf - Mtgs - ET - Exam
- M 2,500 i, UK / 500 i, o'seas
- ¶ NL - 4; free.   AR - 1; ftm only.
  Mail shots - new dances etc - irreg; ftm.

National Association of Teachers of Religious Education   (NATRE)   1985
- NR 1020 Bristol Rd, Selly Oak, BIRMINGHAM, W Midlands, B29 6LB.   (hq)
  0121-472 4242   fax 0121-472 7575
  email retoday@retoday.org.uk   http://www.natre.org.uk
  Gen Sec: Peter Fishpool
- ▲ Un-incorporated Society
- ○ *E, *P, *R; for teachers of religious education in schools & colleges
- Gp Examinations & assessment
- ● Conf - Mtgs - ET - Res - Comp - LG
- < Eur Fedn Teachers of Religious Educ
- M 2,500 i
- ¶ Resource - 3; ftm only.
- × 2008 Professional Council for Religious Education

National Association of Teachers of Travellers + other Professionals   (NATT+)   1980
- NR Children's Services, Castle Hill Resource Centre, Castleton St, BOLTON, BL2 2JW.   (pres/b)
  01204 338150
  http://www.natt.org.uk
  Pres: Kath Cresswell
- ▲ Company Limited by Guarantee; Registered Charity
- ○ *E, *P; to promote access to educational opportunities for Gypsies & Travellers as a recognised ethnic group under the Race Relations Act
- ● Conf - Mtgs - Inf
- < Eur Fedn Educ Children Occupational Travellers (EFECOT)
- M 200 i
- ¶ NL - 3; free.   Information Mail Out - 3; ftm only.
- × 2008 National Association of Teachers of Travellers

National Association for the Teaching of Drama   (NATD)   1977
- ■ The Kingstone School, Broadway, BARNSLEY, S Yorks, S70 6RB.
  01226 738591
  email k.fechter@barnsley.org
  Admin: Kirsty Fechter
- ○ *A, *E; the advancement of young people through drama; to encourage & promote the development of drama at all levels of education; to provide support for all involved with drama in education
- ● Conf - Mtgs - ET - SG - LG
- < Standing Conf of Young Peoples Theatre (SCYPT)
- M c 120 i
- ¶ Jnl for Drama in Education - 2; ftm.
  Publication arising from Annual Conference.
  Other occasional publications.

National Association for the Teaching of English   (NATE)
- ■ 50 Broadfield Rd, SHEFFIELD, S Yorks, S8 0XJ.   (hq)
       0114-255 5419   fax 0114-255 5296
       email info@nate.org.uk   http://www.nate.org.uk
       Co Sec: Lyn Fairfax
- ▲ Registered Charity
- Br 13 regions
- ○ *E, *P; to improve the teaching of English at all levels of
       education; to provide a national voice on all aspects of
       education concerning English concerning English
- ● Conf - Mtgs - Exhib - SG - Inf
- M [not stated]
- ¶ English, Drama, Media - 3; ftm, £10 per issue nm.
       NATE Classroom - 3; ftm, £6.50 per issue nm.
       NATE News - 3; ftm only.

**National Association for Teaching English & other Community
    Languages to Adults   (NATECLA)   1976**
- ■ South Birmingham College (room HA205), Hall Green
       Campus, Cole Bank Rd, BIRMINGHAM, B28 8ES.   (hq)
       0121-688 8121   fax 0121-694 5062
       email co-ordinator@natecla.fsnet.co.uk
       http://www.natecla.org.uk
       Coordinator: Cathy Burns
- ▲ Un-incorporated Society
- Br 10
- ○ *E, *K, *P; campaigning, information, training for ESOL & other
       language tutors
- ● Conf - ET - Inf - LG
- M 489 i, 122 org
- ¶ NATECLA News - 3; ftm, £2 nm.
       Language Issues [Jnl] - 2; £10 m (£20 instns), £15 nm
       (£30 instns).

National Association for Therapeutic Education   (NATE)   1995
- ■ 59 Birdham Rd, CHICHESTER, W Sussex, PO19 8TB.   (hsp)
       01243 776042
       email john.tierney@virgin.net
       Dir: John Tierney
- ▲ Un-incorporated Society
- ○ *E, *P; to promote understanding of therapeutic education; to
       provide a focus for workers in the field
- ● Mtgs - Res - LG - Lobbyists
- M c 95 i

National Association of Toastmasters   (NAT)   1952
- ■ 1 Ridgeway, RAYLEIGH, Essex, SS6 7BJ.   (hsp)
       01268 779992
       http://www.natuk.com
       Hon Sec: Ted Prior
- ▲ Un-incorporated Society
- ○ *P; provision of toastmasters for all types of functions worldwide
- ● Conf - Mtgs - Exhib
- M 62 i
       (Sub: £145)

**National Association of Toy & Leisure Libraries   (Play Matters)
    (NATLL)   1972**
- NR 1A Harmood St, LONDON, NW1 8DN.   (hq)
       020 7428 2286 (helpline)
       email admin@playmatters.co.uk   http://www.natll.org.uk
- ▲ Registered Charity
- ○ *W; to promote the principle that play DOES matter for the
       developing child; to offer a supportive service to parents &
       extend the opportunity for shared play in the home;   Leisure
       libraries extend this concept to adults with special needs
- ● Conf - ET - Exhib - Inf - Making available & lending
       appropriate toys at local level, through toy libraries
- < Intl Toy Libraries Assn
- M c 1,000 libraries
- ¶ Play Matters (Jnl) - 4; ftm, £1 nm.   AR.
       Publications list available.

National Association of Tree Officers   (NATO)
- NR PO Box 734, MANCHESTER, M60 3UB.
       0161-281 6122   fax 0161-281 6122
       email admin@nato.org.uk   http://www.nato.org.uk
       Admin: David Williams
- ○ *P

National Association of Tripe Dressers   (NATD)
- NR 1 Tuscan Court, 18 The Esplanade, TELSCOMBE CLIFFS,
       E Sussex, BN10 7HF.   (hsp)
       01273 585422
       Hon Sec: Mrs Jean Beves
- ○ *T
- ● Mtgs
- M 4 f

National Association of United Kingdom RIGS Groups
    since 2009 **GeoConservationUK**

National Association of Valuers & Auctioneers   (NAVA)   1988
- ■ Arbon House, 6 Tournament Court, Edgehill Drive, WARWICK,
       CV34 6LG.   (hsb)
       0845 250 6004
       http://www.nava.org.uk
       Hon Sec: Peter Bolton King
- ▲ Company Limited by Guarantee
- ○ *P; valuers & auctioneer firms giving independent, impartial
       valuation advice & asset sales services to business & the
       public, for finance, company restructuring, insurance,
       insolvency, asset transfer & probate purposes (covers
       everything from drawing pins through antiques, plant,
       machinery to aeroplanes & house sales)
- Gp Fine arts & antiques; Insolvency; Plant & machinery
- ● Conf - Mtgs - ET - Exam - Res - Exhib - Lib
- < Intl Consortium of Real Estate Agents (ICREA);
       Is a subsidiary of the Nat Assn Estate Agents, a division of the
       Nat Fedn Property Profls
- M 279 i
- ¶ The Gavel (NL) - 4; free.

National Association of Village Shops
       has closed

**National Association for Voluntary & Community Action
    (NAVCA)   1991**
- ■ The Tower, Furnival Square, SHEFFIELD, S Yorks, S1 4QL.   (hq)
       0114-278 6636   fax 0114-278 7004
       email navca@navca.org.uk   http://www.navca.org.uk
       Chief Exec: Kevin Curley
- ▲ Company Limited by Guarantee; Registered Charity
- ○ *N, *W; to promote, support & develop an effective local
       voluntary sector; the national forum of local infrastructure
       organisations
- ● Conf - Mtgs - ET - Inf - LG
- < Nat Coun Voluntary Orgs (NCVO); Standing Conf for
       Community Devt (SCCD)
- M 350 local infrastructure org
- ¶ NACVS Circulation - 6.   AR; free.   Publications.
- × 2006 (14 June) National Association of Councils for Voluntary
       Service

National Association of Voluntary Service Managers (NAVSM) 1968
NR c/o Carol Rawlings, Room 69F, 4th floor Nuffield House, Queen Elizabeth Hospital, Edgbaston, BIRMINGHAM, B15 2TH.   (chmn/b)
    0121-371 3974
    email carol.rawlings@uhb.nhs.uk   http://www.navsm.org
    Chmn: Carol Rawlings
▲ Un-incorporated Society
○ *P, *W; for voluntary managers & volunteers in the field of health & social care
● Conf - Mtgs - ET - Stat - Inf - LG
< Volunteer Centre UK
M 135 i
¶ NL - 6; free.   AR.

National Association of Waste Disposal Officers   (NAWDO)
NR c/o Nick Tempest, Cambridgeshire County Council, Shire Hall, Castle Hill, CAMBRIDGE, CB3 0AP.
    01223 715445
    http://www.nawdo.org
    Sec: Nick Tempest
○ *P
M i

National Association of Widows   (NAW)   1971
■ 48 Queen's Rd (3rd floor), COVENTRY, Warks, CV1 3EH.   (hq)
    0845 838 2261
    email inf@nawidows.org.uk
    http://www.nawidows.org.uk
    Nat Chmn: Jean Sargent
▲ Company Limited by Guarantee; Registered Charity
Br 34
○ *W; run by & for widows & widowers; to provide friendship & support; there are local branches nationwide & headquarters membership is available where there is no local branch
● Conf - Mtgs - Comp - LG
    Office hours: Mon-Fri 0900-1600
M 3,000 i

National Association of Widows in Ireland   1967
IRL Coleraine House, Coleraine St, DUBLIN 7, Republic of Ireland.   (hq)
    353 (1) 872 8814
    email info@nawi.ie
○ *W

National Association of Wine & Beermakers (Amateur) (NAWB(A))   1961
■ 12 Callerdale Rd, BLYTH, Northumberland, NE24 5AB.   (mem/sp)
    01670 356070
    email membership@nawb.org.uk
    http://www.nawb.org.uk
    Mem Sec: Joe Lee
▲ Un-incorporated Society
○ *G; to promote the art of home wine & beermaking
● Conf - Mtgs - ET - Comp
M 237 i, 62 org
¶ News & Views (NL) - 3; ftm only.

National Association of Women's Clubs   (NAWC)   1935
NR 5 Vernon Rise, King's Cross Rd, LONDON, WC1X 9EP.   (hq)
    020 7837 1434   fax 020 7713 0727
    http://www.nawc.org.uk
Br 300
○ *E; to advance education & provide facilities for recreation or other leisure time occupations for women, without distinction of political, religious or other opinions
● Conf - Mtgs - Comp - SG
< NCVO; Nat Coun Women; Women's Nat Commission
M c 7,000 i
¶ NL - 6; ftm.   Club History.   AR.

National Association of Women Pharmacists   (NAWP)   1905
■ c/o The Office Manager, Royal Pharmaceutical Society of GB, 1 Lambeth High St, LONDON, SE1 7JN.   (mail address)
    01453 759516
    email enquiries@nawp.org.uk   http://www.nawp.org.uk
    Hon Sec: Hazel Baker
▲ Un-incorporated Society
Br 3
○ *P
● Conf - ET - VE
M c 300 i
¶ NL - 4; ftm.

National Association of Writers in Education   (NAWE)   1987
NR PO Box 1, Sheriff Hutton, YORK, YO60 7YU.   (mail/address)
    01653 618429
    email info@nawe.co.uk   http://www.nawe.co.uk
    Dir: Paul Munden
▲ Company Limited by Guarantee
○ *A; to promote & support the development of creative writing of all genres in all educational settings
● Conf - ET - Res - Inf - LG
M c 800 i, c 100 f
¶ Writing in Education - 3; ftm only.

National Association of Writers' Groups   (NAWG)   1995
NR PO Box 9891, MARKET HARBOROUGH, Leics, LE16 0FU.   (hq)
    Chmn: Mike Wilson
▲ Registered Charity, Un-incorporated Society
○ *A, *N; to support writers' groups
● Conf - Mtgs - ET - Comp - SG - Inf
M 160 i, f & org
¶ Link Magazine - 6; ftm only.

National Association of Youth & Community Education Officers is an autonomous section of the **Association of Professionals in Education & Children's Trusts**

National Association for Youth Drama   (NAYD)
IRL 7 North Great George's St, DUBLIN 1, Republic of Ireland.
    353 (1) 878 1301   fax 353 (1) 874 9816
    email info@nayd.ie   http://www.nayd.ie
    Admin Offr: Katie Martin
○ *D, *Y

National Association for Youth Justice   (NAYJ)   1995
■ 24 Manor Mount, Forest Hill, LONDON, SE23 3PZ.   (hsp)
    020 8291 2148
    email info@thenayj.org.uk   http://www.thenayj.org.uk
    Sec: Barry Anderson
○ *K; to promote the rights of, & justice for, children in trouble; to campaign for the development & implementation of policies & practice consistent with this purpose
● Conf - Mtgs - ET - Liaison with children's orgs
> Regional organisations & observers from NI, Scotland & Wales
M 200 i, associated regional orgs
¶ Youth Justice; ftm, £30 nm. (published jointly with Russell House Publishing).

National Association of Youth Orchestras
    closed 31 December 2010. For membership services contact the **Association of British Orchestras (www.abo.org.uk)**

© CBD Research Ltd · Beckenham · BR3 5JS · Tel 020 8650 7745 · E-mail cbd@cbdresearch.com · www.cbdresearch.com

National Association of Youth Theatres   (NAYT)   1982
- ■ The Arts Centre, Vane Terrace, DARLINGTON, Co Durham, DL3 7AX.   (hq)
  01325 363330   fax 01325 363313
  email nayt@btconnect.com   http://www.nayt.org.uk
  Chief Exec: Jill Adamson
- ▲ Company Limited by Guarantee; Registered Charity
- ○ *D; supports the development of Youth Theatre activity; is open to any group or individual using theatre techniques in their work with young people, outside of formal education
- ● Conf - ET - Inf - Big Youth Theatre Festival (4-day workshop & performance programme)
- < Nat Coun for Voluntary Youth Service (NCVSI); Nat Assn of Clubs for Young People (NACYP); Nat Operatic & Dramatic Assn (NODA); Nat Assn Youth Drama (NAYD); Promote Youth Theatre Scotland; Nat Coun of Voluntary Orgs (NCVO)
- M 838 i, youth theatres & groups, UK / 9, o'seas
- ¶ Bulletin - 12;   AR; both ftm only.
  The Big Youth Theatre Manual; £19.99.
  Playing a Part: a study of the impact of youth theatre on the personal, social & political development of young people; £10.

National Auricula & Primula Society (Midland & West Section)   (NAPS)   1901
- NR 9 Church St, Belton, LOUGHBOROUGH, Leics, LE12 9UG. (treas/p)
  01530 222458   fax 01530 222458
  email david.tarver@btinternet.com
  http://www.auriculaandprimula.org.uk
  Treas: David Tarver
- ▲ Un-incorporated Society
- ○ *H; to encourage & extend the cultivation of auriculas & primulas; to preserve & improve accepted standards
- ● Conf - Mtgs - Res - Exhib - Comp - Inf - PL - LG
- < R Horticl Soc
- M c 600 i
- ¶ NL - 2; 25p.   Argus [Ybk] - 1.

National Auricula & Primula Society (Northern)   1872
- ■ 3 Daisybank Drive, SANDBACH, Cheshire, CW11 4JR.   (hsp)
  email keith@leeming448.fsnet.co.uk
  http://www.auriculas.org.uk
  Hon Sec: R Taylor
- ▲ Un-incorporated Society
- ○ *H; to encourage the growing & exhibition of Auriculas & Primulas
- ¶ Ybk.

National Auricula & Primula Society (Southern)   1876
- ■ 67 Warnham Court Rd, CARSHALTON BEECHES, Surrey, SM5 3ND.   (hsp)
  http://www.southernauriculaprimula.org
  Hon Sec: L E Wigley
- ○ *H; breeding & cultivation of auriculas, primroses, polyanthuses & other hardy primula species
- ● Exhib - Comp - Inf - Plant sales
- M 400 i, UK / 10 i, o'seas
- ¶ Offsets (NL) - 1; free.   Ybk; ftm; £4 nm.

National Autistic Society   (NAS)   1962
- NR 393 City Rd, LONDON, EC1V 1NG.   (hq)
  020 7833 2299   fax 020 7833 9666
  email nas@nas.org.uk   http://www.nas.org.uk
- ▲ Company Limited by Guarantee; Registered Charity
- Br 45
- ○ *W; to provide: 1) specialist schools & adult services for people with autistic spectrum disorder, 2) supported employment; to promote awareness with central government & the public; to offer information, advice & support to people with autism & their families & carers
- ● Conf - ET - Inf - Lib - LG
  Helpline: 0845 070 4004
- M 11,600 i, 160 org, UK / 210 i, 30 org, o'seas
- ¶ Publications list available.

National Autograss Sport Association Ltd   (NASA)
- NR 53 Andrew Drive, Haywood Oaks, BLIDWORTH, Notts, NG21 0TR.
  01623 796494
  http://www.national-autograss.co.uk
  Sec: Maureen Boyd
- ○ *S; for motorsport racing on a natural soil surface
- ● Mtgs
- M i
- ¶ Fixtures list.

National Backpain Association   (BackCare)   1968
- ■ 16 Elmtree Rd, TEDDINGTON, Middx, TW11 8ST.   (hq)
  020 8977 5474   fax 020 8943 5318
  email info@backcare.org.uk
  http://www.backcare.org.uk
  Office Mgr: Helen Horton
- ▲ Company Limited by Guarantee; Registered Charity
- Br 30
- ○ *Q, *W; to educate people on how to avoid preventable back pain; to support those living with back pain; to promote research into causes & treatment of back pain
- ● ET - Res - Inf - LG
- < NCVO; Assn of Medical Res Charities (AMRC); Long-term Medical Conditions Alliance (LMCA); Arthritis & Musculo-Skeletal Alliance (ARMA)
- M 4,000 i, 200 f, UK / 100 i, o'seas
- ¶ Talkback - 4; ftm, £3.95 nm.
  Various books & leaflets.

National Baton Twirling Association (England)   (NBTA)   1982
- NR 17 Gard Close, TORQUAY, Devon, TQ2 8QU.   (hsp)
  01803 324175
  email denise.pearse568@btinternet.com
  http://www.nbta.org.uk
  Sec: Denise Pearse
- ○ *S; to promote the sport of baton twirling & associated activities
- ● Mtgs - ET - Exam - Comp
- < Nat Baton Twirling Assn Europe; Nat Baton Twirling Assn Intl (USA)
- M c 1,500 i
- ¶ News Direct (NL) - 4; ftm only.

National Bed Federation Ltd   (NBF)   1912
- ■ High Corn Mill, Chapel Hill, SKIPTON, N Yorks, BD23 1NL. (hq)
  0845 055 6406   fax 0845 055 6407
  email info@bedfed.org.uk   http://www.bedfed.org.uk
  Exec Dir: Jessica Alexander
- ▲ Company Limited by Guarantee
- ○ *T; interests of manufacturers of beds & mattresses & their suppliers
- ● Conf - Mtgs - Exhib - Stat - Inf - VE - LG
- M 112 f, UK & o'seas

National Beef Association   (NBA)   1998
- ■ The Mart Centre, Tyne Green, HEXHAM, Northumberland, NE46 3SG.   (hq)
  01434 601005   fax 01434 601008
  email info@nationalbeefassociation.com
  http://www.nationalbeefassociation.com
  Sec: Helen Dobson
- ▲ Company Limited by Guarantee; Registered Charity
- ○ *F, *T; development & sustainability of beef cattle production within the UK
- ● Conf - Mtgs - ET - Expt - LG
- M 2,600 i, 70 f
  (Sub: £50 i, £200 f)
- ¶ Beef Farmer - 4; ftm, £3 nm.   NL - 52; ftm only.

National Begonia Society (NBS) 1948
NR 7 Brabraham Rd, Sawston, CAMBRIDGE, CB22 3DQ. (hsp)
01223 834202
http://www.national-begonia-society.co.uk
Hon Sec: Alan Harris
○ *H; improved cultivation of begonias & their hybridisation
● Mtgs - ET - Comp
< R Horticl Soc
M c 500 i, f & org
¶ Bulletin - 3; ftm only.

National Bingo Game Association Ltd (NBGA) 1986
NR Lexham House, 75 High St North, DUNSTABLE, Beds,
LU6 1JF. (hq)
01582 860900
email info@nationalbingo.co.uk
http://www.nationalbingo.co.uk
Chief Exec: Paul Talboys
▲ Company Limited by Guarantee
○ *T; administration of the game
● Administration
M f
¶ AR.

National Brickmakers Federation
2006-7 amalgamated with the **Brick Development Association**

National Bursars Association
since 2008 **National Association of School Business Management**

National Campaign for the Arts (NCA) 1985
■ 1 Kingly St, LONDON, W1B 5PA. (hq)
020 7287 3777 fax 020 7287 4777
email nca@artscampaign.org.uk
http://www.artscampaign.org.uk
Dir: Louise de Winter
▲ Company Limited by Guarantee
○ *A, *D, *K; the only independent lobbying organisation which
exists to represent the interests of the whole arts sector in all
its diversity.
It is funded entirely by its members to ensure its independence
● Conf - ET - Res - ST - LG
M c 500 i, 500 org
¶ NCA News - 4; ftm; £5 nm.
Friday Briefing (email) - 52; ftm only.

National Campaign for Courtesy 1986
■ 240 Tolworth Rise South, SURBITON, Surrey, KT5 9NB. (hq)
020 8330 3707
email info@campaignforcourtesy.org.uk
http://www.campaignforcourtesy.org.uk
Chmn: Peter G Foot, Hon Sec: Mary Doyle
▲ Registered Charity
○ *K; to encourage courtesy & good manners; to encourage
respect for others & their property; to encourage respect for
themselves; to reject anti-social behaviour
● Mtgs - VE - LG - Seminars
M 1,000 i
¶ Courtesy Call (Jnl) - 4; free to subscibers to society.
× Campaign for Courtesy

National Campaign for Firework Safety (NCFS) 1969
NR 118 Long Acre, LONDON, WC2E 9PA. (hq)
020 7836 6703
email ncfs@cgsystems.co.uk
http://www.cgsystems.co.uk/ncfs
Dir: Noël Tobin
▲ Registered Charity
Br 12; N Zealand
○ *K; to amend the 1875 Explosives Act & 1976 & 1992
Fireworks Acts; to license fireworks for use by trained people
for organised displays only, to dis-allow sale of fireworks to
un-licensed individuals
Gp Fireworks; Consumers; Safety
● Conf - Mtgs - Res - Exhib - Stat - Inf - LG
< Fire Brigades U; Age Concern; Cats Protection League; Canine
Defence League; Nat Civil Defence Org
> Confedn of Brit Ind (CBI)
M 100,000 i, 15 org
¶ [see website].

National Campaign for real Nursery Education (NCNE) 1965
NR c/o Tachbrook Nursery School, Aylesford St, LONDON,
SW1V 3RN. (mail address)
email ncea@yahoo.co.uk
Treas: Tess Robson
○ *E, *K; promoting & defending state funded nursery education
nationally
M i

National Campaign for Water Justice (NCWJ) 1992
■ 25 Brooklyn Close, CARSHALTON, Surrey, SM5 2SL. (hq)
020 8773 9743 fax 020 8773 9743
Gen Sec: Tony May, Chmn: Neil Fishpool
Br 40; Canada, France, USA
○ *K; 'for the re-instatement of the core business of water supply
& sewerage services into public hands; for the lowering of all
water charges; to stop the abuses of the water industry such
as high salaries to the selected few; to campaign against the
bringing in of measured water & forced installation of water
meters where they are not wanted'
Gp Advice on: Complaints against the industry; Matters related to
people on state benefits, the retired & aged, & water matters
overseas; Political (legislative issues); Water law
● Conf - Mtgs - Res - Stat - Inf - Lib - LG
< U Associates US; Canadian Envtl Law Assn; Nat Consumer
Coun
M 38,250 i, 18 f, 36 org, UK / 14 i, o'seas
¶ Justice Bulletin - irreg; free.
Membership Joining Book - 4; free.

National Cancer Alliance (NCA) 1995
NR PO Box 579, OXFORD, OX4 1LB. (hq)
01865 241485
email nationalcanceralliance@btinternet.com
http://www.nationalcanceralliance.co.uk
Chief Exec: Dr Becky Miles
▲ Company Limited by Guarantee; Registered Charity
○ *N; an alliance of patients, carers & health professionals
working together to improve the treatment & care of all
cancer patients in Britain
M i

National Candida Society 1997
NR PO Box 151, ORPINGTON, Kent, BR5 1UJ.
01689 813039
email info@candida-society.org.uk
http://www.candida-society.org.uk
Dir: Dr Christine Tomlinson
○ *M

© CBD Research Ltd · Beckenham · BR3 5JS · Tel 020 8650 7745 · E-mail cbd@cbdresearch.com · www.cbdresearch.com

National Caravan Council Ltd   (NCC)   1939
NR   Catherine House, Victoria Rd, ALDERSHOT, Hants,
     GU11 1SS.   (hq)
     01252 318251   fax 01252 322596
     email info@nationalcaravan.co.uk
     http://www.nationalcaravan.co.uk
     Dir Gen: Graham Beacon
▲   Company Limited by Guarantee
○   *G; interests of the caravan industry
Gp   National Park Homes Council
     Holiday caravan distributors; Manufacturers; Park operators;
     Supplies & service; Traders
●   Conf - Mtgs - ET - Exhib - Stat - Inf - LG
<   Eur Caravan Fedn
M   23 i, 500 f, UK / 10 f, o'seas
¶   The Business - 4;   NL - 12; AR; all ftm.

National Care Association   (NCA)   1981
■   45-49 Leather Lane, LONDON, EC1N 7TJ.   (hq)
     020 7831 7090   fax 020 7831 7040
     email info@nationalcareassociation.org.uk
     http://www.nationalcareassociation.org.uk
     Chief Exec: Sheila Scott
▲   Company Limited by Guarantee
○   *N, *T; to represent providers of care to local & national
     government; to provide services to members to allow them to
     concentrate on the people they care for
Gp   Children's services; Domiciliary care; Nursing care; Older
     people; Younger adults
●   Conf - Mtgs - ET - Exhib - Inf - LG
M   2,000 i
¶   NL - 12;   Homeowners Manual;   Health & Safety Manual;
     Working Safely (Employees' Hbk).

**National Carnival Guild - the National Federation of Carnival
Associations   (Carnival Guild)   1964**
NR   54 Rokesly Avenue, LONDON, N8 8NR.   (hsp)
     020 8340 7339
     Chmn: Gordon P Rathbone
○   *G; promotion of carnival; cooperation between carnival
     associations

National Carpet Cleaners Association Ltd   (NCCA)   1968
NR   62c London Rd, OADBY, Leics, LE2 5DH.   (hq)
     0116-271 9550   fax 0116-271 9588
     email info@ncca.co.uk   http://www.ncca.co.uk
     Co Sec: Paul Pearce
▲   Limited Company
Br   3
○   *T; as well as carpets also incl soft furnishings (curtains &
     upholstery), fire & flood restoration
Gp   Fire & flood divn
●   Conf - ET - Exam - Res - Exhib - Inf - Lib - PL - LG
<   Brit Cleaning Coun; Carpet & Upholstery Cleaners Assn of
     Australia [& South Africa]; Assn of Specialists in Cleaning &
     Restoration (USA)
M   c 550 f
¶   NL - 12; ftm.

National Casino Industry Forum   (NCIF)   2009
■   Carlyle House, 235-237 Vauxhall Bridge Rd, LONDON,
     SW1V 1EJ.   (hq)
     020 7828 5410   fax 020 7932 0751
     email director@nci-forum.co.uk
     http://www.nci-forum.co.uk
     Dir: Tracy Damestani
▲   Company Limited by Guarantee
○   *T; representing the interests of the land-based casino industry
     in GB
●   Mtgs - LG
<   Eur Casino Assn
M   12 f
¶   NL - irreg; ftm only.
✕   2009 (1 April) British Casino Association

National Cattle Association (Dairy)
■   Brick House, Risbury, LEOMINSTER, Herefords, HR6 0NQ.
     (hq)
     01568 760632   fax 01568 760523
     email timbrigstocke@hotmail.com
     Sec: Tim Brigstocke
▲   Un-incorporated Society
○   *B, *N; to represent the interests of dairy cattle breed societies
●   Conf - Mtgs - Et - Stat - Inf - LG
M   11 breed societies

National Cavy Club   (NCC)   1890
NR   2 Woodside, Devitts Green, OLD ARLEY, Warks, CV7 8GH.
     (hsp)
     email margaret.thorpe@talktalk.net
     http://www.nationalcavyclub.co.uk
     Hon Sec: Margaret Thorpe
▲   Un-incorporated Society
○   *G, *V; to promote & encourage the breeding, keeping &
     exhibiting of all varieties of cavies (guinea pigs)
●   Mtgs - Exhib - Comp - Inf
M   c 575 i, UK / 5 i, o;seas
¶   Newsflash (NL) - 2; ftm only.   NCC Hbk - 2 yrly; ftm, £4 nm.
     Cavies (Jnl) - 12; £30 yr (the official organ for the club but not
     published by it).

National Childbirth Trust   (NCT)   1956
NR   Alexandra House, Oldham Terrace, LONDON, W3 6NH.   (hq)
     0870 770 3237 (admin), 0870 444 8707 (enquiries)
     fax 0870 770 3237
     email enquiries@national-childbirth-trust.co.uk
     http://www.nctpregnancyandbabycare.com
     Chief Exec: Belinda Phipps
▲   Registered Charity
Br   336
○   *W; 'the NCT wants all parents to have an experience of
     pregnancy, birth & early parenthood that enriches their lives
     & gives them confidence in being a parent; it runs antenatal
     classes & provides information on maternity issues,
     breastfeeding & postnatal support'
Gp   Caesarian; Home birth; Postnatal support
●   Mtgs - ET - Res - Exhib - Inf - LG
<   Intl Childbirth Education Assn; Unicef Baby Friendly Initiative;
     Baby Milk Action; Consumer Congress; Nat Alliance
     Women's Orgs; Nat Children's Bureau; Nat Coun Voluntary
     Orgs (NCVO); Nat Coun Women; Women's Nat Cmsn
M   42,000 i
¶   New Generation (Jnl) - 4;   Local NLs - varies; all ftm.
     NCT Sales Catalogue (with sales goods); free.

National Childminding Association   (NCMA)   1977
NR   Royal Court, 81 Tweedy Rd, BROMLEY, Kent, BR1 1TG.   (hq)
     0845 880 0044
     email info@ncma.org.uk   http://www.ncma.org.uk
     Chief Exec: Liz Bayram
▲   Registered Charity
Br   2 (North & South)
○   *W; promotes quality registered childminding for children,
     families & communities
●   Conf - Mtgs - ET - Res - SG - Inf - Lib - VE - LG
M   c 47,000 i
¶   Who Minds - 4; ftm.   AR.
     Publications list available.

National Children's Nurseries Association
     in 2011 merged with IPPA to form **Early Childhood Ireland**

National Childrenswear Association of Great Britain & Ireland (NCWA) 1940

NR   3 Queen Sq, Bloomsbury, LONDON, WC1N 3AR.   (hq)
     020 7483 9488   fax 020 7483 9478
     email enquiries@ncwa.co.uk   http://www.ncwa.co.uk
     Co Sec: Elizabeth Fox
▲   Company Limited by Guarantee
○   *T; all sectors of the children's wear industry
Gp   Accredited agents; Distributors; Manufacturers; Retailers
●   Conf - Mtgs - ET - Exhib - Inf - LG - Seminars
<   BKCEC; BSSA; BCIA
M   c 600 f

National Chinchilla Society (NCS) 1955

■   101 Simmondley Lane, GLOSSOP, Derbys, SK13 6LU.   (hsp)
     01457 856945
     email chillaquip@freeserve.com
     http://www.natchinsoc.co.uk
     Hon Sec: Paul S Spooner
▲   Un-incorporated Society
Br   4
○   *B; to promote good husbandry practice in the breeding of
     animals known as Chinchilla Lanigera & Chinchilla
     Brevicaudata & with any mutant form of these animals
●   Conf - Mtgs - ET - Exhib - Stat - Inf
M   c 150 i
     (Sub: £15 UK / £20 o'seas)
¶   Gazette - 6; ftm only.
     Guide to Quality Chinchilla;   Show Rules.

National Choreographers Forum
     is a group of **Dance UK Ltd**

National Chrysanthemum Society (NCS) 1846

■   317 Plessey Rd, BLYTH, Northumberland, NE24 3LJ.
     (memsec/p)
     01670 353580
     http://www.nationalchrysanthemumssociety.org.uk
     Mem Sec: Peter Fraser
▲   Registered Charity
Br   6
○   *H; to encourage the growing of chrysanthemums to the
     highest standard
●   Conf - Mtgs - Exam - Exhib - Comp - SG - National Register of
     Chrysanthemums
<   R Horticl Soc
M   4,000 i, 1,000 org, UK / 300 i, o'seas
¶   Bulletin - 2.   Ybk.
     List of specialist publications available.

National Churchwatch 1999

§   Endeavour, 8 Commercial Rd, SHEPTON MALLET, Somerset,
     BA4 5DH.
     01749 344992
     http://www.nationalchurchwatch.com
     Co-ordinator: Nick Tolson
     a non-membership body which runs seminars dealing with
     church security & personal safety of church people; it is in
     association with Ecclesiasical Insurance

National Coastwatch Institution

■   Unit 26 Basepoint Business Centre, Yeoford Way, EXETER,
     EX2 8LB.   (hq)
     0845 460 1202
     email admin01@nci.org.uk   http://www.nci.org.uk
○   *K; set up by the Sea Safety Group (UK) to re-open the coastal
     look-out stations closed by the government as a money-
     saving idea in the 'age of satellite installations'
M   15,000 i, 39 stations

National Cochlear Implant Users Association (NCIUA)

■   The Vicarage, 70 Sycamore Rd, AMERSHAM, Bucks,
     HP6 5DR.   (hsp)
     email secretary@nciua.org.uk   http://www.nciua.org.uk
     Sec: Dr Raymond Glover
▲   Registered Charity
Br   10 local support groups for parents & users
○   *K; campaigning for adequate funds for cochlear implants for
     the deaf; to support users
●   Conf - Inf
<   EURO-CIU
M   403 i, 12 f, 10 org
     (Sub: £10)
¶   NCIUA NL - 4; ftm only.
     Cochlear Implants: a collection of experiences of users of all
     ages; ftm, £2 nm.

National Community Boats Association 1985

NR   c/o The Yorkshire Waterways Museum, Dutch River Side,
     GOOLE, E Yorks, DN14 5TB.   (hq)
     0845 051 0649
     email staff@national-cba.co.uk
     http://www.national-cba.co.uk
○   *W; to provide community groups (schools, hospitals, youth
     clubs, etc) with access to the UK & European inland
     waterways

National Confederation of Parent-Teacher Associations (NCPTA) 1956

NR   39 Shipbourne Rd, TONBRIDGE, Kent, TN10 3DS.   (hq)
     01732 375460
     email info@ncpta.org.uk   http://www.ncpta.org.uk
     Chief Exec: D W Butler
▲   Company Limited by Guarantee; Registered Charity
○   *E, *K; to promote cooperation between home & school
●   Conf - ET - Res - LG
<   Eur Parents Assn
M   12,000 org
¶   PTA - 3;   News & Views - 3;   AR; all ftm only.

National Consumer Federation (NCF) 2001

■   24 Hurst House, Penton Rise, LONDON, WC1X 9ED.   (hsp)
     020 7837 8545
     email secretary@ncf.info   http://www.ncf.info
     Hon Sec: Hugh Jenkins
▲   Company Limited by Guarantee; Registered Charity
○   *K, *N; to promote grassroot consumer interests & provide a
     channel for consumer opinion & representation
Gp   Communications; Consumer affairs; Food; Personal finance;
     Utilities
●   Mtgs - ET - Res - Inf
M   130 i, 20 f, 50 org
     (Sub: £20 i, £500 f, £200 org)

National Contractors Federation
     a member federation of the **UK Contractors Group**

National Cooperage Federation (NCF) 1919

■   34 Maitland Rd, KIRKLISTON, W Lothian, EH29 9AP.   (hsp)
     0131-333 3314
     email john@gaffney113.wanadoo.co.uk
     Hon Sec: John Gaffney
▲   Un-incorporated Society
○   *T; interests of employers of coopers in the UK
●   Mtgs - Trade tests for apprentices
M   42 f
¶   AR - 1; free.

NATIONAL COUNCIL ...
     For details of bodies whose names begin thus, other than the
     following, see the companion volume **'Councils, Committees &**
     Boards' (Introduction paragraph 6)

© CBD Research Ltd · Beckenham · BR3 5JS · Tel 020 8650 7745 · E-mail cbd@cbdresearch.com · www.cbdresearch.com

National Council for Aviculture Ltd (NCA) 1955
- ■ Evenstar, Pinkuah Lane, Pentlow, SUDBURY, Suffolk, CO10 7JW. (hq)
  01787 282332
  email info@nca.uk.net   http://www.nca.uk.net
  Sec & Publicity Officer: Ghalib Al-Nasser
- ▲ Un-incorporated Society
- ○ *N; coordination body representing aviculturists in the UK
- Gp British Bird Council; Budgerigar Society; Canary Council; Foreign Bird Federation
- ● Mtgs - Exhib - Comp
- M 29,000 i
- ✕ 2007 Society for the Protection of Aviculture (merged)

National Council for Civil Liberties
  see **Liberty**

National Council for the Conservation of Plants & Gardens (NCCPG) 1978
- ■ 12 Home Farm, Loseley Park, GUILDFORD, Surrey, GU3 1HS. (hq)
  01483 447540   fax 01483 458933
  email info@nccpg.org.uk   http://www.nccpg.com
  Exec Officer: Genevieve Melbourne Webb
- ▲ Company Limited by Guarantee; Registered Charity
- Br 41
- ○ *H, *N; to conserve the heritage of our garden plants built up during the past 400 years.   This is achieved through NCCPG's 650 National Plant Collections in which some 100,000 garden plants are maintained in safe cultivation
- Gp 650+ National Plant Collections
- ● Mtgs - Res - Exhib - Inf - PL - VE
- < works closely with RBG, Kew, R Horticl Soc, NTS & Engl Heritage
- M 4,500 i, 100 f, 100 org, UK / 100 i, o'seas
- ¶ Plant Heritage (Jnl) - 2.
  The National Plant Collections Directory.
  Publications list available.
  Note: Uses the title Plant Heritage

National Council for the Divorced, Separated & Widowed (NCDS) 1974
- NR 68 Parkes Hall Rd, Woodsetton, DUDLEY, W Midlands, DY1 3SR. (hsp)
  0704 147 8120
  email info@ncds.org.uk   http://www.ncds.org.uk
- ▲ Registered Charity
- Br 75; Ireland
- ○ *W; welfare of all persons divorced, separated or bereaved
- ● Conf - Mtgs - Inf - VE
- < NCDS Trust (a charity)
- M 6,000 i
- ¶ NL - 4.
  Note: Also known as NCDS Phoenix.

National Council for Housing & Planning
  see **ROOM at RTPI**

National Council for Hypnotherapy (NCH) 1973
- NR PO Box 89, YORK, YO43 4WL. (hq)
  0845 544 0788   fax 0845 544 0821
  email admin@hypnotherapists.org.uk
  http://www.hypnotherapists.org.uk
  Company Sec: Martin Armstrong-Prior
- ▲ Company Limited by Guarantee
- ○ *P; to raise the standards of hypnotherapy; to maintain a common Code of Ethics & Practice & a Complaints & Disciplinary Procedure
- ● Conf - Mtgs - ET - Exam - Res - Inf - LG - Referrals register
- < Nat Gld of Hypnotists (USA); UK Confedn of Hypnotherapy Orgs
- M c 800 i
- ¶ Jnl - 4.   LM.   AR.

National Council on Inland Transport (NCIT) 1962
- ■ 6 Merrivale Avenue, REDBRIDGE, Essex, IG4 5PQ.   (Chmn/p)
  020 8550 2454
  email admin@ncit.org.uk   http://www.ncic.org.uk
  Chmn: Derek Leggetter
- ▲ Un-incorporated Society
- ○ *K; development of an integrated inland transport system
- ● Conf - Inf
- M c 30 i, 1 org
- ¶ AR; ftm.

National Council for Metal Detecting (NCMD) 1981
- ■ 51 Hilltop Gardens, Denaby, DONCASTER, S Yorks, DN12 4BA.   (sp)
  01709 868521
  email trevor.austin@ncmd.co.uk   http://www.ncmd.co.uk
  Gen Sec: Trevor Austin
- ▲ Un-incorporated Society
- Br 150; USA
- ○ *G; the encouragement & defence of the hobby of recreational metal detecting
- ● Mtgs - Comp - LG
- < Cent Coun Physical Recreation (CCPR)
- M 5,000 i, UK / 150 i, o'seas
- ¶ Reports of Executive Committee Meetings - 3/4; free.
  Reports of meetings with government bodies.

National Council for One Parent Families / Gingerbread 2007
- ■ 255 Kentish Town Road, LONDON, NW5 2LX.   (hq)
  020 7428 5400   fax 020 7482 4851
  http://www.gingerbread.org.uk
- ▲ Registered Charity
- Br 2
- ○ *W; to give support & help to lone parent families
- ● Mtgs
  Helpline: 0800 018 5026 (Mon-Fri 0900-1700, Wed 0900-2000)
- M 11,000 i
- ¶ NL - 4; ftm only.   e-newsletter - 12; ftm only.   AR.
  Note: Trades under the title of Gingerbread.

National Council of Psychotherapists (NCP) 1971
- ■ PO Box 7219, HEANOR, Derbys, DE75 9AG.   (hsb)
  0845 230 6072   fax 01773 711031
  email ncphq@btinternet.com   http://www.ncphq.co.uk
  Sec: Brian Jackson
- ▲ Un-incorporated Society
- Br 1; Singapore
- ○ *P; to represent & protect registered members & the general public in the field of psychotherapy & hypnotherapy
- Gp Critical incident de-briefing; Hypnotherapy; Psychotherapy
- ● Conf - ET - Exam - Res
- < Intl Coun of Psychotherapists
- M 653 i, UK / 37 i, o'seas i, o'seas
  (Sub: £70 UK / £125 o'seas)
- ¶ Fidelity (Jnl) - 4; ftm.
  AR; ftm only.

National Courier Association (NCA) 1989
- ■ 30 Woodhall Croft, PUDSEY, W Yorks, LS28 7TU.   (hsp)
  0845 603 7813
  email theadministrator@thenca.co.uk
  http://www.thenca.co.uk
  Admin: Lyn Cox,   Chmn: Mike McCartney
- ▲ Company Limited by Guarantee
- ○ *T; network of independent courier companies completing same-day work throughout the UK, which intertrade with each other
- Gp Same day courier companies
- ● Mtgs
- M 95 f

National Crossbow Federation of Great Britain   (NCFGB)   1984
NR   24 Ivy Rd, POYNTON, Cheshire, SK12 1PE.   (gensec/p)
    Gen Sec: Graeme Peatfield
▲   Un-incorporated Society
○   *S; to promote competitive amateur crossbow shooting at
    national & club level in the British Isles
●   Mtgs - ET - Comp - Inf - Lib - VE - LG
<   Wld Crossbow Shooting Assn (WCSA)
M   c 70 i
    (Sub: £22 i, 15 clubs)
¶   Crossbow UK (NL) - 4; ftm.

National Dahlia Society   (NDS)   1881
NR   48 Vickers Rd, Ash Vale, ALDERSHOT, Hants, GU12 5SE.   (sp)
    01252 693003
    Gen Sec: David Kent
▲   Registered Charity
○   *H; to encourage, improve & extend the cultivation of the
    dahlia

National Dance Teachers Association   (NDTA)   1988
■   c/o Birmingham Hippodrome, Thorp St, BIRMINGHAM,
    W Midlands, B5 4TB.   (hq)
    0121-689 1085
    email office@ndta.org.uk   http://www.ndta.org.uk
    Chmn: Veronica Jobbins
▲   Company Limited by Guarantee; Registered Charity
○   *D, *P; to support teachers in schools & colleges to deliver
    dance within the school curriculum
●   Conf - ET - Inf - LG
M   484 i, 266 f, UK / 12 i, 1 f, o'seas
    (Sub: £45 i, £90 f)
¶   Dance Matters - 3; ftm, £4 50 each nm.

National Day Nurseries Association   (NDNA)   1991
■   National Early Years Enterprise Centre, Longbow Close,
    HUDDERSFIELD, W Yorks, HD2 1GQ.   (hq)
    01484 407070   fax 01484 407060
    email info@ndna.org.uk   http://www.ndna.org.uk
    Chief Exec: Purnima Tanuku
▲   Registered Charity
○   *T; to represent children's day nurseries across the UK; to give
    information, training & support their families & communities
●   Conf - ET - EXhib - Inf
M   [not stated]
¶   Nursery News.

National Deaf Children's Society   (NDCS)   1944
NR   15 Dufferin St, LONDON, EC1Y 8UR.   (hq)
    020 7490 8656   fax 020 7251 5020
    email ndcs@ndcs.org.uk   http://www.ndcs.org.uk
    Chief Exec: Susan Daniels
▲   Company Limited by Guarantee; Registered Charity
Br   120
○   *E, W, *Y; to inform & advise deaf children & young people &
    their carers
Gp   Technology Inf Centre (London); Services delivery (London)
●   Conf - ET - Res - Exhib - Inf - Lib
    Helpline: 0808 800 8880 (Mon-Fri 0010-1700, Tues-1900)
M   14,000 i
¶   Talk - 6; £10.   AR.   Publications list available.

National Deafblind & Rubella Association
    see Sense - National Deafblind & Rubella Association

National Dog Wardens Association   (NDWA)   1987
NR   Haffield Lodge, Gloucester Rd, Corse, STAUNTON, Glos,
    GL19 3RA.
    Pres: Sue Bell
Br   12; Bermuda, France, Gibraltar, USA
○   *P; for workers in the field of animal control
●   Conf - Mtgs - ET - Res - Exhib - Stat - Inf - VE - LG
<   Nat Animal Control Assn America
M   i, f, & org
¶   Dog Warden News - 4.

National Doorwatch
NR   The Booking Office, Station Approach, Saxilby, LINCOLN,
    LN1 2HB.
○   *P; to represeent 'the interests of professional door supervisors
    (people employed to ensure guests safety during their time in
    a licensed entertainment venue'

National Drama   (ND)   1989
■   West Barn, Church Farm, Happisburgh, NORWICH, Norfolk,
    NR12 0QY.   (chmn/p)
    01692 650066
    http://www.nationaldrama.co.uk
    Chmn: Patrice Baldwin
▲   Un-incorporated Society
○   *D, *P; for people who work with young people (all ages) in
    drama & theatre
Gp   Teachers (all sectors of education); Theatre educators; Theatre
    workers; Workers with people with special needs
●   Conf - Mtgs - ET - Res - Inf - LG
M   c 650 i, UK & o'seas
¶   Drama (Jnl) - 2; ftm.   Reflections (NL) - 3; ftm only.
    Drama Research.

National Drama Festivals Association   (NDFA)   1964
■   NODA House, 58-60 Lincoln Rd, PETERBOROUGH, Cambs,
    PE1 2RZ.   (hsb)
    0870 770 2480   fax 0870 770 2490
    email secretary@ndfa.org.uk   http://www.ndfa.org.uk
    Hon Sec: Bronwen Stanway
▲   Registered Charity
○   *D; to encourage & support the amateur theatre in all its forms
    & through the organisation of drama festivals
●   Drama festivals - Play writing competitions - Representation,
    coordination & liaison
<   Nat Operatic & Dramatic Assn (NODA)
M   50 i, 44 festival organisers, 23 associate org, UK / 1 1,
    1 festival organiser, 1 org, o'seas
    (Sub: £12 i, £30 organisers, £18 org)
¶   NL - 4;   Directory (incl festival details) - 1; both ftm only.

National Dried Fruit Trade Association (UK) Ltd   (NDFTA)   1942
■   18 Lichfield Rd, WOODFORD GREEN, Essex, IG8 9ST.   (hq)
    020 8506 2379   fax 020 8506 2379
    email cathy@ndfta.co.uk   http://www.ndfta.co.uk
    Sec / Treas: Mrs Cathy Grant
▲   Company Limited by Guarantee
○   *T; all matters connected with the dried fruit trade (mainly
    currants, sultanas, raisins, apricots, peaches, pears, dates &
    prunes)
Gp   Sub-c'ees: Public relations, Technical
●   Conf - Mtgs - Res - Stat - Inf - VE - LG
<   Fédn Eur du Commerce en Fruits Secs, Conserves, Epices et
    Miel (FRUCOM);
M   22 f, UK / 14 f, o'seas

© CBD Research Ltd · Beckenham · BR3 5JS · Tel 020 8650 7745 · E-mail cbd@cbdresearch.com · www.cbdresearch.com

National Early Music Association   (NEMA)   1981
- ■ 126 Shanklin Drive, LEICESTER, LE2 3QB.   (admin/p)
  0116-270 9984
  http://www.nema-uk.org
  Admin: John Bence
- ▲ Registered Charity
- Br 11
- ○ *D, *N; to bring together organisations & individuals, both professional & amateur, involved in the whole range of early music
- Gp Dance; Music; Theatre; Coordinating bodies
- ● Conf - ET - Inf
- < UK Early Music Forum
- M c 300 i, f & org
- ¶ Early Music Performer - 2.

National Eczema Society   (NES)   1976
- ■ Hill House, Highgate Hill, LONDON, N19 5NA.   (hq)
  020 7281 3553   fax 020 7281 6395
  email info@eczema.org   http://www.eczema.org
  Chief Exec: Margaret Cox
- ▲ Company Limited by Guarantee; Registered Charity
- ○ *W; to (1) provide people with independent & practical advice about treating & managing eczema; & (2) raise awareness of the needs of eczema sufferers with healthcare professionals, teachers & the government
- ● Conf - Mtgs - ET - Res (support & fund) - Exhib - Comp - SG - Inf - VE
- M 6,000 i, 8 corporate
  (Sub: £20 i, £6,000 corporate)
- ¶ Exchange (Jnl) - 4; ftm only.
  Information Sheets 3-10, 11-25; ftm, £7 nm.
  Guides & Booklets; ftm, £2.50 nm.
  Publications order form available.

National Edible Oil Distributors Association   (NEODA)
- NR PO Box 259, BECKENHAM, Kent, BR3 3YA.   (hq)
  020 8776 2644   fax 020 8249 5402
  http://www.neoda.org.uk
  Sec: Lynda Simmons
- ▲ Un-incorporated Society
- ○ *T; of trades concerned in the supply of frying media & suchlike material
- ● Conf - Mtgs - Inf
- < Food & Drink Fedn; Fedn Oils, Seeds Fats Assns (FOSFA)
- M 70 f
- ¶ LM; ftm only.   AR.

National Egg Marketing Association Ltd   (NEMAL)   1935
- ■ 89 Charterhouse St (2nd floor), LONDON, EC1M 6HR.   (hq)
  020 7608 3760   fax 020 7608 3860
  email Louisa.Platt@britisheggindustrycouncil.com
  http://www.britegg.co.uk
  Sec: Louisa Platt
- ▲ Company Limited by Guarantee
- ○ *T; interests of those who pack & market eggs
- ● Mtgs - LG
- < Brit Egg Ind Coun
- M 53 f

National Endometriosis Society
  since 2010 **Endometriosis UK**

National Energy Action   (NEA)   1981
- NR West 1, Forth Banks, NEWCASTLE-upon-TYNE, NE1 3PA.   (hq)
  0191-261 5677   fax 0191-261 6496
  email info@nea.org.uk   http://www.nea.org.uk
- ▲ Registered Charity
- ○ *K; promotes energy efficiency services to tackle the heating & insulation problems of low-income households
- ● Conf - Mtgs - ET - Res - Lib
- < Nat Coun of Voluntary Orgs
- M 242 org
- ¶ Energy Action - 4; ftm, £25 nm.   NL - 6; ftm only.
  AR - 1; free.   Other publications.

National Enterprise Network
  a trading name of the **National Federation of Enterprise Agencies**

National Entertainment Agents Council
  in January 2010 merged with & became the Entertainment Agencies Section of the **National Outdoor Events Association**

National Exhibitors Association   (NEA)   1988
- ■ 29a Market Sq, BIGGLESWADE, Beds, SG18 8AQ.   (hq)
  01767 316255
  http://www.eou.org.uk
  Sec Gen: Peter Cotterell
- ▲ Un-incorporated Society
- ○ *T
- ● Conf - ET
- M 70 f

National Family Mediation   (NFM)   1982
- ■ Margaret Jackson Centre, 4 Barnfield Hill, EXETER, Devon, EX1 1SR.   (hq)
  01392 271610   fax 01392 271945
  email general@nfm.org.uk   http://www.nfm.org.uk
  Chief Exec: Jane Robey
- ▲ Registered Charity
- Br 50
- ○ *W; to help those involved in family breakdown to communicate better with one another & reach their own decisions about some or all of the issues arising from separation, divorce, children, property & finance
- Gp Divorce; Families; Mediation
- ● ET - Mediation
- M 60 services
- ¶ The Bulletin - 4; free.   AR - 1.

National Fancy Rat Society   (NFRS)   1976
- NR BM NFRS, LONDON, WC1N 3XX.   (hsb)
  email n_f_r_s@hotmail.com   http://www.nfrs.org
  Hon Sec: Estelle Sandford
- ▲ Un-incorporated Society
- ○ *B; to promote the care of the Fancy Rat (Domesticus Rattus Norvegicus) as a pet & exhibition animal
- ● Conf - Mtgs - ET - Res - Exhib - Comp - Inf - Lib
- < Amer Fancy Rat & Mouse Assn; Amer Rat, Mouse & Hamster Soc; Svenska Råttssällskapet; Sydsveriges Maädjursvänner; Finnish Rat Soc
- M c 800 i
- ¶ Pro-rat-a (NL) - 6.

National Farmers' Retail & Markets Association Ltd   (FARMA)   1979
- NR 12 Southgate St, WINCHESTER, Hants, SO23 9EF.   (hq)
  0845 458 8420   fax 0845 456 5156
  email justask@farma.org.uk   http://www.farma.org.uk
  Exec Sec: Rita Exner
- ▲ Co-operative under Industrial & Provident Society rules
- ○ *F, *K, *T; 'representing direct sales to customers through farm shops, pick-your-own, farmers' markets, home delivery, on-farm catering & farm entertainment'
- ● Conf - Mtgs - ET - Res - Exhib - Comp - SG - Stat - Inf - Lib - PL - VE - LG
- < Markets Alliance
- M 650 f, UK / 10 f, o'seas
- ¶ Retail Farmer - 4; ftm only.
  Note: LM for Markets, Shops, Pick your own on:
      http://www.farmersmarkets.net
      http://www.farmshopping.net
      http://www.pickyourown.info

National Farmers Union of England & Wales (NFU) 1908
■ Agriculture House, Stoneleigh Park, STONELEIGH, Warks,
  CV8 2TZ. (hq)
  024 7685 8500 fax 020 7685 8501
  http://www.nfuonline.com
  Pres: Peter Kendall, Dir Gen: Kevin Roberts
▲ Un-incorporated Society
Br 8; Brussels
○ *F, *H; to represent & promote the interests of farmers &
  growers & others with an interest in agriculture, horticulture &
  the countryside
● Conf - Mtgs - ET - Res - Exhib - Comp - SG - Stat - Inf - VE - LG
< Intl Fedn of Agricl Producers (IFAP); Gen Confedn of Agricl Co-
  operatives in the EU (COGECA); Eur Confedn of
  Agriculture (CEA); Nat Pig Assn; Taste of the West; Dairy
  Coun
M 136,573 i (incl countryside mems)
¶ British Farmer & Grower - 12; ftm, £55 yr nm.
  NFU Horticulture - 3; NFU Professional - 12;
  NFU Countryside - 12; NFU Farming Wales - 12; all ftm only.
  nfuonline.com (hosting various publications).

National Farmers Union of Scotland
  see **NFU Scotland**

National Federation of Anglers
  in 2009 merged with the Anglers Conservation Association, the
  Fisheries & Angling Conservation Trust, the National Association of
  Fisheries & Angling Consultatives, the National Federation of Sea
  Anglers & the Specialist Anglers Alliance to form the **Angling Trust**

National Federation of Atheist, Humanist & Secular Student Societies
  see **AHS: the National Federation of Atheist, Humanist &
  Secular Student Societies**

National Federation for Biological Recording (NFBR) 1985
NR Stonecroft, 3 Brookmead Close, Sutton Poyntz, WEYMOUTH,
  Dorset, DT3 6RS.
  01305 837384
  email john_newbould@btinternet.com
  http://www.nfbr.org.uk
  Sec: John Newbould
▲ Un-incorporated Society
○ *G, *P; wildlife recording - the recording of the natural world
  (species & habitats)
● Conf - Mtgs - ET - Res
M c 200 i
¶ NL - 3; Conference Proceedings - 1; both ftm.

**National Federation of the Blind of the United Kingdom
(NFBUK) 1947**
■ Sir John Wilson House, 215 Kirkgate, WAKEFIELD, W Yorks,
  WF1 1JG. (hq)
  01924 291313 fax 01924 200244
  email nfbuk@nfbuk.org http://www.nfbuk.org
▲ Registered Charity
Br 20
○ *K, *W; for the welfare of all blind people
● Conf - Mtgs - Exhib - Comp - SG - Inf
< Wld Blind U; Eur Blind U; NCVO; Disability Alliance; RNIB;
  Disabled Living Foundation
M c 1,400 i & associates
¶ Viewpoint - 2; Fedtalk tape - 4; AR; free.

National Federation of Bridleway Associations (NFBA) 1989
■ Baxenden House, Manchester Rd, ACCRINGTON, Lancs,
  BB5 2RU. (treas/p)
  email nfba@rightsofway.org.uk
  http://www.rightsofway.org.uk/nfbafront.html
  Treas: Chris Peat
▲ Un-incorporated Society
○ *K; to protect & defend existing & potential bridleways &
  byways & the rights of all bridleway & byway users
● Mtgs - Res - Inf - LG
< Rights of Way Review Committee
> Local Bridleway Assns; Local Riding Gps
M 6 i, 20 org
¶ Seminar Proceedings - 1; £5.

National Federation of Builders (NFB)
NR B & CE Building, Manor Royal, CRAWLEY, W Sussex,
  RH10 9QP. (hq)
  0845 057 8160
○ *T
Gp House Builders Association - a division
● Mtgs - ET -
¶ Brochure.

National Federation of Carnival Associations & Committees
  see **National Carnival Guild - the National Federation of
  Carnival Associations & Committees**

National Federation of Cemetery Friends (NFCF) 1986
■ 42 Chestnut Grove, SOUTH CROYDON, Surrey, CR2 7LH.
  (sec/p)
  020 8651 5090
  email gwyneth1@btinternet.com
  http://www.cemeteryfriends.org.uk
  Hon Sec: Gwyneth Stokes
▲ Un-incorporated Society
○ *N; provides a forum for the exchange of information & views
  on the conservation of cemeteries & their appropriate
  development for educational & recreational purposes
Gp Funerary Monuments Group
● Inf - Advises potential groups
M 80 groups (Friends)
¶ NL - 2; ftm only.

**National Federation of Community Organisations (Community
Matters) 1945**
NR 12-20 Baron St, LONDON, N1 9LL. (hq)
  020 7837 7887 fax 020 7278 9253
  email communitymatters@communitymatters.org.uk
  http://www.communitymatters.org.uk
  Nat Dir: David Tyler
▲ Company Limited by Guarantee; Registered Charity
○ *N, *W; to promote & support action by ordinary people in
  response to society, education & recreational needs in their
  neighbourhood & community, resulting in healthy,
  sustainable communities in which everyone can play their full
  part
Gp Local Federation of Community Organisations
● Conf - Mtgs - ET - Res - Inf - LG - Advice & consultancy
< Nat Coun for Voluntary Orgs; Charity Tax Reform Gp; Wales
  Coun for Voluntary Assns
M 1,156 org
¶ Community - 6; ftm, £15 nm.
  Community Extra; ftm, £15 nm. NL; free.
  Other publications available.

© CBD Research Ltd · Beckenham · BR3 5JS · Tel 020 8650 7745 · E-mail cbd@cbdresearch.com · www.cbdresearch.com

National Federation of Demolition Contractors   (NFDC)   1941
- ■ Resurgam House, Paradise, HEMEL HEMPSTEAD, Herts, HP2 4TF.   (hq)
  01442 217144   fax 01442 218268
  email info@demolition-nfdc.com
  http://www.demolition-nfdc.com
  Chief Exec: Howard Button
- ▲ Company Limited by Guarantee
- Br 5
- ○ *T; for the demolition & dismantling industry
- ● Conf - Mtgs - ET - Stat - Empl - LG
- < Eur Demolition Assn (EDA)
- M 167 f
  (Sub: £1,690)
- ¶ Demolition & Dismantling Jnl - 4;   Ybk - 1.

National Federation of Enterprise Agencies   (NFEA)   1993
- NR 12 Stephenson Court, Fraser Rd, Priory Business Park, BEDFORD, MK44 3WH.   (hq)
  01234 831623   fax 01234 831625
  email enquiries@nationalenterprisenetwork.org
  http://www.nationalenterprisenetwork.org
  Chief Exec: Dawn Whiteley
- ○ *N; for organisations committed to the support & development of enterprise; as well as enterprise agencies, members include chambers of commerce, local authorities, specialist enterprise providers, universities & corporate organisations
  Note: trades as National Enterprise Network.

National Federation of Families with Visually Impaired Children
   see **LOOK: National Federation of Families with Visually Impaired Children**

National Federation of Fish Friers Ltd   (NFFF)   1913
- NR New Federation House, 4 Greenwood Mount, Meanwood, LEEDS, W Yorks, LS6 4LQ.   (hq)
  0113-230 7044   fax 0113-230 7010
  email mail@federationoffishfriers.co.uk
  http://www.federationoffishfriers.co.uk
  Gen Sec: Mrs A M Kirk
- ▲ Company Limited by Guarantee
- ○ *T
- ● Conf - Mtgs - ET - Exhib - Inf - LG
- M c 2,500 i
- ¶ Fish Friers Review - 12; ftm.

National Federation of Fishermen's Organisations   (NFFO)   1977
- NR 30 Monkgate, YORK, YO31 7PF.   (hq)
  Chief Exec: Barrie C Deas
- ○ *T; to represent fishermen & their interests, locally, nationally & within the European Community
- M c 1,200 i in 40 org
- ¶ NL - 6.   NFFO Official Ybk & Diary - 1.

National Federation of Fishmongers   (NFF)   1932
- NR PO Box 9639, COLCHESTER, Essex, CO5 9WR.   (hq)
  01376 571391
  email info@fishmongersfederation.co.uk
  http://www.fishmongersfederation.co.uk
  Pres: David Ridley
- Br London Fish & Poultry Retailers Association
- ○ *T; interests of retail fishmongers

National Federation of Gateway Clubs
   a division of the **Royal Mencap Society**

National Federation of Glaziers   (NFG)   1991
- ■ 27 Old Gloucester St, LONDON, WC1N 3XX.   (hq)
  020 7404 3099
  Chmn: A C Jones
- ▲ Un-incorporated Society
- ○ *T; to provide information & assistance on glass products in relation to window & conservatory installation
- ● Inf - Vetting of individuals & companies in the field - Arrangement of insured guarantees (as introducer) of approved schemes - Helpline for members
- M 170 f
- ¶ Commitment to Good Practice.

National Federation of Inland Wholesale Fish Merchants (NFIWFM)
- NR Office 36, Billingsgate Market, Trafalgar Way, LONDON, E14 5ST.
  020 7515 2655   fax 020 7517 3531
- ○ *T; to promote inland fish merchants
- M f

National Federation of Meat & Food Traders   1888
- NR 1 Belgrove, ROYAL TUNBRIDGE WELLS, Kent, TN1 1YW.   (hq)
  01892 541412   fax 01892 535462
  email info@nfmft.co.uk
  Chief Exec: Graham Bidston
- ○ *T
- M f
- ¶ Food Trader - 10; ftm.   Ybk.

National Federation of Music Societies
   see **Making Music, the National Federation of Music Socities**

National Federation of Occupational Pensioners   (NFOP)   1930
- ■ Unit 6 Imperial Court, Laporte Way, LUTON, Beds, LU4 8FE.
  01582 721652   fax 01582 450906
  http://www.nfop.org.uk
  Gen Sec: Roger Turner
- ○ *U
- M 102,569 i, UK / 225 i, o'seas
- ¶ The Magazine - 8; ftm.
- × 2010 Unite: the National Federation of Royal Mail & BT Pensioners

National Federation of Plus Areas of Great Britain   (Plus)   1941
- NR 210 Commerce House, High St, SUTTON COLDFIELD, W Midlands, B72 1AB.   (hq)
  http://www.plusgroups.org.uk
  Hon Gen Sec: James Oliver
- Br 50 gps
- ○ *N, *Y; a multi-activity social group for ages 18-35, run by members for the members
- ● Conf - Mtgs - ET - VE
- M c 1,000 i
- ¶ Plus News - 4; ftm only.
- × 2006 National Federation of Eighteen Plus Groups
  Note: also uses title Plus

National Federation of Property Professionals
- § Arbon House, 6 Tournament Court, Edgehill Drive, WARWICK, CV34 6LG.
  Umbrella organisation for the **National Association of Estate Agents** and the **Association of Residential Letting Agents**

National Federation of Residential Landlords
   merged in 2008 with the **National Landlords' Association**

National Federation of Retail Newsagents 1919
NR Yeoman House, Sekforde St, LONDON, EC1R 0HF. (hq)
       020 7253 4225   fax 020 7250 0927
       http://www.nfrnonline.com
       Nat Pres: Parminder Singh
▲ Un-incorporated Society
Br 209; 20 o'seas (incl Republic of Ireland)
○ *T
● Conf - Mtgs - ET _ Res - Exhib - Stat - Inf - LG - CTN World
       Exhib
M 18, 603 i, UK / 469 i, o'seas
¶ Retail Newsagent - 52; £1.50.
       Retail Express - 26; free.   The FED - 12; ftm, £1.95 nm.
       Members Business Guide - 1;   AR - 1; both ftm only.

National Federation of Roofing Contractors Ltd   (NFRC) 1943
NR Roofing House, 31 Worship St, LONDON, EC2A 2DY. (hq)
       020 7638 7663   fax 020 7256 2125
       email info@nfrc.co.uk   http://www.nfrc.co.uk
       Chief Exec: Ray Horwood
▲ Company Limited by Guarantee
Br 6; Ireland
       Scottish section: PO Box 28011, Edinburgh, EH16 6WN.
       0131-448 0266   fax 0131-440 4032
       email jmckinney@support-services.fsbusiness.co.uk
       Sec: John McKinney
○ *T; for the roofing trade (includes manufacturers, suppliers &
       service providers); ensures (through its vetting procedure &
       code of practice) that high standards of workmanship & high
       quality materials are used
Gp Construction; Roofing
       Flat Roofing Alliance
● Conf - Mtgs - ET - Res - Comp - Inf - VE - Empl - LG
< Intl Fedn of Roofing Contrs (IFD); Nat Home Improvement
       Coun (NHIC); Nat Specialist Contrs Coun (NSCC);
       Constructors' Liaison Gp (CLG); Construction Products
       Assn (CPA)
M c 900 f
¶ Update (NL) - 6; ftm only.   Annual Directory - 1; ftm.
       Technical Bulletins; prices vary.   AR - 1; free.

National Federation of Royal Mail & BT Pensioners
       until 2010 was Unite: the National Federation of Royal Mail & BT
       Pensioners,which then changed name to Unite Federation & then to
       National Federation of Occupational Pensioners

National Federation of Sea Anglers
       in 2009 merged with Anglers Conservation Association, Fisheries &
       Angling Conservation Trust, National Association of Fisheries &
       Angling Consultatives, National Federation of Anglers & Specialist
       Angling Alliance to form the **Angling Trust**

**National Federation of Services for Unmarried Parents & their
Children   (Treoir) 1976**
IRL 14 Gandon House, Custom House Sq, IFSC, DUBLIN 1,
       Republic of Ireland.
       353 (1) 670 0120   fax 353 (1) 670 0199
       http://www.treoir.ie
       Chief Exec: Margaret Dromey
○ *W

National Federation of Shopmobility   (NFS) 1987
NR PO Box 6641, CHRISTCHURCH, Dorset, BH23 9DQ. (hq)
       0845 644 2446   fax 0845 644 4442
       email info@shopmobilityuk.org.uk
       http://www.justmobility.co.uk
○ *K; to assist groups to establish shopmobility schemes
       throughout the country by providing information, advice &
       contacts
       Shopmobility is a free mobility equipment loan scheme -
       equipment is loaned daily
● Conf - Mtgs - Inf
M 300 schemes representing 720,000 users
¶ NFS Review - 2;   AR; both ftm only.
       NFS Directory - 2.   NFS Guidelines - 1.

National Federation of Solo Clubs   (Solo NFSC) 1965
NR PO Box 2278, NUNEATON, Warks, CV11 5YX.   (sp)
       024 7673 6499
       Nat Sec: Mavis Marsden
▲ Registered Charity
Br 53
○ *W; to provide friendship, social activities & welfare facilities for
       widowed, divorced, separated & single people over 21; to
       offer help & comfort to the bereaved & lonely
● Mtgs - Holidays - Day trips - Dancing - Skittles - Ten pin
       bowling - Social gatherings
M 3,500 i

National Federation of Spiritual Healers   (NFSH) 1955
■ 21 York Rd, NORTHAMPTON, NN1 5QG.   (hq)
       01604 603247
       email office@nfsh.org.uk   http://www.nfsh.org.uk
▲ Registered Charity
○ *P; for potential & established spiritual healers; 'NFSH is not
       associated with any religion'
● Conf - Mtgs - Res - Exhib - SG - Inf - National Healer Referral
       Service - Distance healing
       Helpline: 0845 123 2777
M c 5,000 i
¶ Healing Today (Jnl) - 4;   Regional NLs - 4;   AR; all ftm.
       Note: Uses the working name of The Healing Trust

National Federation of Sub-Postmasters   (NFSP) 1897
NR Evelyn House, 22 Windlesham Gardens, SHOREHAM-by-SEA,
       W Sussex, BN43 5AZ.   (hq)
       01273 452324   fax 01273 465403
       email admin@nfsp.org.uk   http://www.nfsp.org.uk
       Gen Sec: George Thomson
▲ Un-incorporated Society
Br 95
○ *U
● Conf - Mtgs - ET - Res - Exhib - Inf - Empl - LG
M c 14,000 i
¶ The Subpostmaster (Jnl) - 12.   Hbk - 3 yrly.
       Branch Secretaries Circular - 24.   AR.

National Federation of SwimSchools   (NFS)
NR c/o STA, Anchor House, Birch St, WALSALL, W Midlands,
       WS2 8HZ.
       01922 645097
       http://www.nfswimschools.co.uk
○ *S
M org
       (Sub: £50)

**National Federation Terrazzo, Marble & Mosaic Specialists
(NFTMMS) 1932**
■ PO Box 2843, LONDON, W1A 5PG.   (hsp)
       0845 609 0050   fax 0845 607 8610
       email info@nftmms.co.uk   http://www.nftmms.co.uk
       Sec: Brian James
▲ Un-incorporated Society
○ *T; interests of manufacturers & fixers of terrazzo, working &
       laying of natural stone & mosaic
Gp Associate membership for suppliers of goods & services to full
       members
● Mtgs - Inf - VE - Provision of technical information (free) -
       Technical Inspection service (chargeable)
< Brit Standards Inst; Trade Assn Forum
M c 50 f
¶ Technical Specifications for Terrazzo & Marble - irreg; free.

© CBD Research Ltd · Beckenham · BR3 5JS · Tel 020 8650 7745 · E-mail cbd@cbdresearch.com · www.cbdresearch.com

National Federation of Women's Institutes   (NFWI)   1915
- ■ 104 New Kings Rd, LONDON, SW6 4LY.   (hq)
  020 7371 9300   fax 020 7736 3652
  email hq@nfwi.org.uk   http://www.thewi.org.uk
  Gen Sec: Mrs Jana Osborne
- ▲ Registered Charity
- Br c 6,500
- ○ *G; to enable women to improve & develop conditions of rural
  life; to advance their education in citizenship, cultural
  subjects, home economics & social welfare
- ● Mtgs - ET - Social & community work
- M 200,000 i
- ¶ WI Life - 8; ftm.

National Federation of Young Farmers' Clubs (England & Wales)   (NFYFC)   1932
- NR YFC Centre, 10th St, Stoneleigh Park, KENILWORTH, Warks,
  CV8 2LG.   (hq)
  024 7685 7200   fax 024 7685 7229
  email post@nfyfc.org.uk   http://www.nfyfc.org.uk
  Contact: The Chief Exec
- ▲ Registered Charity
- ○ *F, *Y; to advance knowledge of agriculture, rural life,
  countryside issues & home crafts
- ● Conf - Mtgs - Comp - LG
- M c 20, 500 i
- ¶ Ten 26 - 4; ftm only.

National Ferret Welfare Society   (NFWS)   1989
- NR 1 The Terrace, Loddiswell, KINGSBRIDGE, Devon, TQ7 4RH.
  (treas/p)
  01548 550156
  http://www.homepage.ntlworld.com/ferreter/contacts.htm
  Treas: Mrs B Lye
- ○ *V; to promote the welfare of ferrets
- ● Inf - Annual show (open)
- < Countryside Alliance (CA)
- M c 300
- ¶ NL - 3.   Information booklet - 1. .

National Field Archery Society   (NFAS)   1973
- ■ 48 Muirfield Way, MANSFIELD WOODHOUSE, Notts,
  NG19 9EH.   (m/sp)
  email membership@nfas.net   http://www.nfas.net
  Mem Sec: Richard Dobson
- ▲ Company Limited by Guarantee
- ○ *S; promotion of archery in woodland
- ● Exhib - Comp
- M c 4,500 i
- ¶ NFAS NL - 6; ftm only.

National Fillings Association
  we cannot trace any mention of this association since 2006

National Fire Sprinkler Network   (NFSN)   1998
- NR RBFRS HQ, 103 Dee Rd, Tilehurst, READING, Berks,
  RG30 4FS.   (chmn/b)
  email nfsn@btconnect.com   http://www.nfsn.co.uk
  Chmn: Iain Cox
- ○ *T; to seek reductions in the incidence of death & injury to
  persons, & damage to property & the environment, from fire
  by promoting the provision of risk specific control measures,
  especially fire sprinklers
- < Fedn of Brit Fire Orgs (FBFO)
- M 25 f, 62 org (fire services)

National Fireplace Association
  wound up 1 July 2010

National Forum of Engineering Centres   (NFEC)   1993
- ■ 1 Further Meadow, Writtle, CHELMSFORD, Essex, CM1 3LE.
  (hq)
  01245 421393
  http://www.nfec.org.uk
  Business operations: Alan Gray
- ▲ Registered Charity
- ○ *E; offers support & advice on any issues about quality learning
  in engineering & related technologies
- M f & org

National Forum for Risk Management in the Public Sector
  see **ALARM: National Forum for Risk Management in the
  Public Sector**

National Foundation for Educational Research in England & Wales   (NFER)   1946
- ■ The Mere, Upton Park, SLOUGH, Berks, SL1 2DQ.   (hq)
  01753 574123   fax 01753 691632
  email enquiries@nfer.ac.uk   http://www.nfer.ac.uk
  Chief Exec: Sue Rossiter
- ▲ Company Limited by Guarantee; Registered Charity
- Br 2
- ○ *E, *Q; provision of educational research services, information
  & results; development of assessment tests & methods
- ● Conf - Mtgs - ET - Res - Inf - Lib
- M c 200 org
- ¶ Publications list available.

National Fox Welfare Society   (NFWS)   1993
- NR 135 Higham Rd, RUSHDEN, Northants, NN10 6DS.
  (coordinators/p)
  01933 411996
- ○ *V; to rescue & rehabilitate sick & injured foxes; to provide
  advice to the public on any aspect of fox behaviour or
  problems; to recommend, or provide, an effective deterrent

National Franchised Dealers Association
  a group of the **Retail Motor Industry Federation**

** **National Fruit Wine, Mead & Liqueur Producers Association**
  Organisation lost: see Introduction paragraph 3

National Game Dealers' Association   (NGDA)   1979
- ■ Pollards Farm, Clanville, ANDOVER, Hants, SP11 9JE.
  (chmn/b)
  01264 730294   fax 01264 730780
  Chmn: Chris Chappel
- ▲ Un-incorporated Society
- Br Scotland
- ○ *T; to safeguard & promote the commercial interests of the
  members; to encourage best practice in the industry
- ● Conf - Mtgs - ET - Res - Exhib - Stat - Expt - Inf - LG
- M 1 i, 36 f, 1 org
- ¶ Various publications.

National Gamekeepers Organisation   (NGO)   1997
- ■ PO Box 246, DARLINGTON, Co Durham, DL1 9FZ.   (hq)
  01833 660869
  http://www.nationalgamekeepers.org.uk
  Mem Sec: Ann Robinson-Ruddock
- ○ *P
- Gp Moorland branch
- M 12,400 i

National Gardens Scheme Charitable Trust   (NGS)   1927
- ■ Hatchlands Park, East Clandon, GUILDFORD, Surrey,
   GU4 7RT.   (hq)
   01483 211535   fax 01483 211537
   email ngs@ngs.org.uk   http://www.ngs.org.uk
   Chief Exec: Mrs Julia Grant
- ▲ Company Limited by Guarantee; Registered Charity
- ○ *G, *H, *W; a non-membership body concerned to arrange the
   opening of gardens of quality, character & interest to raise
   money for beneficiary charities such as: 1) Queen's Nursing
   Institute, 2) Macmillan Cancer Support, 3) the careership
   scheme of the National Trust, 4) Perennial Fund, 5) the Royal
   Fund for Gardeners' Children, 6) Crossroads, 7) Help the
   Hospices, 8) Marie Curie Cancer Care; & many others
   chosen by garden owners
- ● Exhib - Arrangement of opening (to the public) of nearly 3,500,
   mostly private, gardens in England & Wales on advertised
   days to raise money
- ¶ The Yellow Book, 2008; £7.99. (formerly known as Gardens of
   England & Wales open for Charity).

National Gerbil Society   (NGS)   1971
- NR   373 Lynmouth Ave, MORDEN, Surrey, SM4 4RY.   (sp)
   020 8241 8942   fax 0870 160 0843
   email jackie@gerbils.co.uk   http://www.gerbils.co.uk
   Sec: Jackie Roswell
- ▲ Un-incorporated Society
- ○ *G; to promote Gerbils & Jirds as pets, breeding & exhibition
   animals
- ● Mtgs - Exhib - Comp - Inf - PL - VE
- < Intl Gerbil Fedn
- M   200 i, 1 f, UK / 11 i, 3 org, o'seas
- ¶ The Nibbler - 4;   Ybk; both ftm only.

National Golf Clubs' Advisory Association   (NGCAA)   1922
- NR   The Threshing Barn, Homme Castle Barns, Shelsley Walsh,
   WORCESTER, WR6 6RR.   (hq)
   01886 812943
   http://www.ngcaa.org.uk
   Sec: Michael Shaw
- ▲ Un-incorporated Society
- ○ *N, *S; provision of advice, especially legal advice, to affiliated
   golf clubs
- ● Inf
- M   1,200 golf clubs
- ¶ NL - 6;   Ybk (incl AR & LM); both ftm only.

National Governors' Association   2006
- NR   36 Great Charles St (ground Floor), BIRMINGHAM, B3 3JY.
   (hq)
   0121-237 3780
   http://www.nga.org.uk
   Chief Exec: Phil Revell
- ▲ Company Limited by Guarantee; Registered Charity
- ○ *E; to represent the governor's view
- Gp   Governing bodies of schools
- ● Publications
- M   c 6,000 i, 600 org

National Grammar Schools Association   (NGSA)   1986
- NR   18 Leomansley Rd, LICHFIELD, Staffs, WS13 8AW.   (sb/p)
   01543 251517
   http://www.ngsa.org.uk
- ○ *K; to support selective education as a parental option within
   the State education sector; to offer support & advice to
   grammar schools under threat of closure or reorganisation

National Greyhound Racing Club Ltd
   in January 2009 merged with the British Greyhound Racing
   Board to form the Greyhound Board of Great Britain & is
   therefore no longer within the scope of this directory.
   See entry in our **Councils, Committees & Boards**

National Guild of Removers & Storers   1993
- NR   PO Box 690, CHESHAM, Bucks, HP5 1WR.   (hq)
   01494 792279   fax 01494 792111
   http://www.ngrs.org.uk
   Hon Chmn: Jonathan Bramwell
- ○ *T
- ● Conf - Mtgs - LG
- < Assn Relocation Agents; Nat Register of Approved Removers &
   Storers
- M   c 200 f
- ¶ The Professional Remover - 6; free.

National Gulf Veterans and Families Association
- § Bld E Office 8 Chamberlain Business Centre, Chamberlain Rd,
   HULL, HU8 8HL.   (hq)
   0845 257 4853
   http://www.ngvfa.com
   a registered charity supporting those affected by Gulf Wars 1 &
   2 (Iraq), the on-going conflict in Afghanistan & all future
   desert conflicts

National Hairdressers' Federation   (NHF)   1942
- ■ 1 Abbey Court, Fraser Rd, Priory Business Park, BEDFORD,
   MK44 3WH.   (hq)
   0845 345 6500   fax 01234 838875
   email enquiries@nhf.info   http://www.nhf.info
   Gen Sec: Eileen Lawson
- ▲ Un-incorporated Society
- Br   52
- ○ *T; for self-employed hairdressing, beauty therapists & salon
   owners
- ● Conf - Mtgs - Comp - SG - Empl - LG
- < Org Mondiale de la Coiffure
- M   7,250 i, 30 f, UK / 30 i, o'seas
- ¶ Salon Focus - 6; ftm only.

** National Hamster Council
   Organisation lost: see Introduction paragraph 3

National Harmonica League   (NHL)   1975
- NR   112 Hag Hill Rise, Taplow, MAIDENHEAD, Berks, SL6 0LT.
   (chmn/p)
   01628 604069
   Chmn: Dr Roger Trobridge
- ▲ Registered Charity; Un-incorporated Society
- ○ *D; for anyone interested in the harmonica, whether a player or
   not
- ● Mtgs - ET - Comp - Inf
- < Intl Harmonica Org
- M   c 400 i
- ¶ Harmonica World - 6; ftm, £1.50 nm.

National Health Service Consultants' Association   1976
- NR   Hill House, Great Bourton, BANBURY, Oxon, OX17 1QH.
   (chmn p)
   01295 750407   fax 01295 750407
   email nhsca@pop3.poptel.org.uk
   http://www.nhsca.org.uk
   Pres: Peter Fisher,   Chmn: Prof Allyson Pollock
- ○ *P

© CBD Research Ltd · Beckenham · BR3 5JS · Tel 020 8650 7745 · E-mail cbd@cbdresearch.com · www.cbdresearch.com

National Hedgelaying Society (NHLS) 1978
NR Ashlands, Stocklands, HONITON, Devon, EX14 9DY.   (hsb)
    01404 861714
    email nhls.enquiries@googlemail.com
    http://www.hedgelaying.org.uk
    Hon Sec: John Vickery
▲ Registered Charity
○ *F, *K; to encourage the art of hedge laying & to keep local
    styles in existence; to encourage landowners to manage
    hedges by laying
● ET - Exhib - Comp - PL - LG
M 450 i
    (Sub: £15 i, £30 profl)
¶ NL - 3; ftm, £1 nm.

National Heritage: the Museums Action Movement (NH) 1971
■ NH Administration Centre, Rye Rd, HAWKHURST, Kent,
    TN18 5DW.   (hq)
    01580 752052   fax 01580 755670
    email liz@lizm.eclipse.co.uk
    http://www.nationalheritage.org.uk
    Admin: Liz Moore
▲ Registered Charity
○ *A, *G; to support museums & galleries in the United Kingdom;
    to represent their visitors & users
● Mtgs - Inf - Research/survey collection
M i, f, museums
¶ Museum News.   AR.

National Hillclimb Association
■ 3 Perryfield Rd, Southgate, CRAWLEY, E Sussex, RH11 8AA.
    (mem/sp)
    Mem Sec: Lin Cooper
○ *S; motor-cycle hillclimbs

National Historic Ships (NHSC) 1992
NR Park Row, Greenwich, LONDON, SE10 9NF.   (hq)
    020 8312 8558
    email martyn.heighton@nationalhistoricships.org.uk
    http://www.nationalhistoricships.org.uk
    Head of Secretariat: Martyn Heighton
○ *L; to secure the long time preservation of a sample of ships
    representing important aspects of UK maritime history
Gp Technical c'ee (people with specialist skills & knowledge in ship
    preservation)
● Conf - Mtgs - Res - Inf - PL - LG
< Nat Maritime Museum
M [not stated]
× 2006 National Historic Ships Committee

National Home Improvement Council (NHIC) 1974
■ Roofing House, 31 Worship St, LONDON, EC2A 2DY.   (hq)
    020 7448 3853   fax 020 7256 2125
    email info@nhic.org.uk   http://www.nhic.org.uk
    Exec Dir: Roman N Russocki
▲ Company Limited by Guarantee
○ *T; to be the home imrovement industry's principal interface
    with government, ensuring that housing policies & public
    funding are directed at home & environmental improvement
    & fuel policy issues; to promote to homeowners the benefits
    of renovating & maintaining houses to the highest possible
    standards of energy efficiency
● Mtgs - ET - Res - Comp - Stat - Inf - VE - LG
M 20 f, 20 org
¶ Progress - 2.

National Hop Association of England (NHA)
■ Parsonage Farm, Heath Rd, Boughton Monchelsea,
    MAIDSTONE, Kent, ME17 4JB.   (hsb)
    Sec: Tony Redsell
○ *F, *N; to represent the hop growers of England, through the 5
    producer groups
● Mtgs - Res - Stat - Expt - Inf - PL
M 5 gps

National Horse Brass Society (NHBS) 1975
■ 8 Cassiobury Park Avenue, WATFORD, Herts, WD18 7LB.
    (treas/p)
    01923 247619
    http://www.horse-brass-society.org.uk
    Treas: Brian O'Riordan
▲ Un-incorporated Society
○ *G; to bring together people interested in horse brasses
● Mtgs - VE - Archives
M c 450 i
¶ Jnl - 2;   NL - 2;   Directory - 1; all ftm.
    Reference works - 1½-2 yrly; c £10.

National Housing Federation (NHF) 1935
NR Lion Court, 25 Procter St, LONDON, WC1V 6NY.   (hq)
    020 7067 1010   fax 020 7067 1011
    email info@housing.org.uk   http://www.housing.org.uk
    Chief Exec: David Orr
▲ Company Limited by Guarantee
Br 10
○ *N; to support & promote the work that housing associations do
    & campaign for better housing & neighbourhoods
● Conf - Mtgs - ET - Res - Exhib - Stat - Inf - LG
< Intl Fedn Housing & Planning; Comité Européen Co-ordination
    de l'Habitat Social (CECODHAS Housing Europe)
M 1,200 housing assns
¶ Bulletin - 10; ftm, prices on application nm.

National Ice Skating Association of Great Britain & NI (NISA) 1879
NR Grains Building, High Cross St, Hockley, NOTTINGHAM,
    NG1 3ax.   (hq)
    0115-988 8060   fax 0115-988 8061
    email nisa@iceskating.org.uk
    http://www.iceskating.org.uk
    Chief Exec: Keith Horton
▲ Company Limited by Guarantee
○ *S; to develop ice skating in all its disciplines; to optimise
    individual achievement at every level
● Comp - Inf
< Intl Skating U (ISU)(Switzerland)
M 4,500 i, 84 clubs
¶ Ice Link (Jnl) - 6; free.

National Information Forum
    activities have been discontinued

National Infrastructure Planning Association (NIPA)
■ 4a Woodside Business Park, Whitley Wood Lane, READING,
    Berks, RG2 8LW.
    020 7783 3425
    email nipa@nipa.org.uk   http://www.nipa.org.uk
    Sec: Robbie Owen
○ *P; to bring together those involved in the planning &
    authorisation of nationally significant infrastructure projects in
    the UK, predominantly focusing on projects in the areas of
    energy, transport, water, waste & waste water

National Institute of Adult Continuing Education (England & Wales) (NIACE) 1949
■ Renaissance House, 20 Princess Road West, LEICESTER,
    LE1 6TP.   (hq)
    0116-204 4200   fax 0116-285 4514
    email enquiries@niace.org.uk   http://www.niace.org.uk
    Dir: Alan Tuckett
▲ Company Limited by Guarantee; Registered Charity
○ *E, *N; a national centre for cooperation, enquiry, research,
    information & consultation in the field of continuing
    education for adults
● Conf - Mtgs - Res - Exhib - SG - Stat - Inf - Lib - LG
< Eur Assn of Adult Educ; Intl Coun of Adult Educ
M c 250 i, 480 org
¶ Publications list available.

National Institute of Carpet & Floorlayers Ltd   (NICF)   1979
- ■ 4c St Mary's Place, The Lace Market, NOTTINGHAM, NG1 1PH.   (hq)
  0115-958 3077   fax 0115-941 2238
  email info@nicfltd.org.uk   http://www.nicfltd.org.uk
  Pres: Steve Ramsden
- ○ *T; to promote excellence in the field of carpet fitting & provide assurance of quality of workmanship to the public
- ● ET - Exam - Exhib - Inf - Conciliation of complaints
- M 500 i, 100 f (manufacturers as patrons, retailers as associates)
- ¶ Installation Manual; £50 m, £75 nm.

National Institute of Medical Herbalists Ltd   (NIMH)   1864
- ■ Elm House, 54 Mary Arches St, EXETER, Devon, EX4 3BA.   (hq)
  01392 426022   fax 01392 498963
  email info@nimh.org.uk   http://www.nimh.org.uk
  Hon Sec: Anne Varley
- ▲ Company Limited by Guarantee
- ○ *L, *P, *Q; a professional body of practising medical herbalists; research & education in herbal medicine
- ● Conf - Mtgs - ET - Res - Inf - Lib - LG
- < Eur Herbal Practitioners Assn; Brit Herbal Medicine Assn
- M 575 i, UK / 120 i, o'seas
- ¶ Herbal Thymes (NL) - 4; ftm only.   LM - 1; free.

National Insulation Association   (NIA)   2002
- ■ 2 Vimy Court, Vimy Rd, LEIGHTON BUZZARD, Beds, LU7 1FG.   (hq)
  0845 163 6363
  email info@nationalinsulationassociation.org.uk
  http://www.nationalinsulationassociation.org.uk
  Chief Exec: Neil Marshall
- ▲ Company Limited by Guarantee
- ○ *T; to represet the manufacturers, installers & associate members of cavity wall insulation, draught proofing & other innovative solutions
- Gp Installers; Manufacturers; Surveyors; Scheme managers
- ● Conf - Mtgs - Exhib - Inf - LG
- < Bldgs Efficiency Fedn (BEEF)
- M 99 i, 11 f, 5 associate
  (Sub: £1173.83 i, £3523.83 f & org)
- ¶ The Installer - 3;   In-House NL - 6/10; both ftm only.
  LM - updated; free.

National Insurance Repair Contractors Association   (NIRCA)
- NR Kingsley House, Ganders Business Park, Kingsley, BORDON, Hants, GU35 9LU.
  01420 471618
  http://www.nirca.org.uk
  Sec: John G Fairley
- ○ *T; to represent the interests of companies working in the insurance repair market

National Irish Safety Organisation   (NISO)
- IRL A11 Calmount Park, Ballymount, DUBLIN 12, Republic of Ireland.
  353 (1) 465 9760   fax 353 (1) 465 9765
  email info@niso.ie   http://www.niso.ie
  Operations Mgr: Ted O'Keeffe
- ○ *P; voluntary organisation dedicated to the prevention of occupational accidents & diseases
- < Electro-Technical Coun of Ireland

National Joint Utilities Group   (NJUG)   1977
- NR 111 Buckingham Palace Rd, LONDON, SW1W 0SR.   (hq)
  020 7340 8737
  email info@njug.org.uk
  Chief Exec: Richard Wakelen
- ○ *N, *T; the forum for objects of mutual interest in distribution engineering activities for the gas, electricity, water & cable telecommunications industries; to coordinate reports / responses on behalf of the utilities
- Gp Electricity industry; Gas industry; Telecommunications; Water industry
- ● Conf - Mtgs - Res - Exhib
- < Assn Geographic Inf
- M f & org
- ¶ Bulletin - 2; free.
  Specialist reports; prices vary (free to £10).   AR.

National Jousting Association
see **Knights of Royal England**

National Jumblers Federation   (NJF)
- NR 347 Kingston Rd, Ewell, EPSOM, Surrey, KT19 0BS.   (hsp)
  020 8393 3342
  email truedvd@aol.com
  Sec: David True
- ○ *G, *T; acts in the interests of autojumblers, bike jumblers & boat jumblers
- M i & f
- ¶ Jnl - 6.

National Karting Association Ltd   (NKA)   1993
- ■ Devonia, Long Road West, Dedham, COLCHESTER, Essex, CO7 6ES.   (hsp/b)
  01206 322726   fax 01206 322726
  email nka@nationalkarting.co.uk
  http://www.nationalkarting.co.uk
  Co Sec: Mrs Linda D Barton
- ▲ Company Limited by Guarantee
- Br USA
- ○ *S, *T; to help circuit owners in the aspects of health & safety & promotion
- Gp Safety coordination
- ● Mtgs - ET - LG
- < Motor Activities Trg Coun; [& a proposed Kart Forum body]
- M c 100 i
- ¶ NL - 4;   NKA Guideline; both ftm.

National Kidney Federation   1978
- NR The Point, Coach Rd, WORKSOP, Notts, S81 8BW.   (regd/office)
  01909 544999   fax 01909 481723
  email nkf@kidney.org.uk   http://www.kidney.org.uk
- ▲ Registered Charity
- ○ *W; to promote the welfare of persons suffering from kidney disease or renal failure & those relatives & friends who care for them
- ● Conf - Inf - LG
  Helpline: 0845 601 0209
- < Eur Kidney Patients' Assn (CEAPIR)
- M 500 i, 65 org
- ¶ Kidney Life - 4; £12.
  Conference Report - 1;   AR & Accounts - 1; both free.

© CBD Research Ltd · Beckenham · BR3 5JS · Tel 020 8650 7745 · E-mail cbd@cbdresearch.com · www.cbdresearch.com

National Landlords' Association (NLA) 1973
- ■ 22-26 Albert Embankment, LONDON, SE1 7TJ. (hq)
   020 7840 8900   fax 0871 237 7535
   email info@landlords.org.uk
   http://www.landlords.org.uk
   Chief Exec: David Salusbury
- ▲ Company Limited by Guarantee
- ○ *K; to protect & promote the interests of private residential
   landlords
- ● Conf - Mtgs - ET - Exhib - Inf - LG
- M 14,000 i, f
   (Sub: £88 i, £128 f)
- ¶ UK Landlord - 6; ftm, £50 nm.
   Landlord Development Manual - 1; ftm, £3 nm.
- × 2008 National Federation of Residential Landlords

National Library for the Blind
   since 2008 the national library service of the **Royal National
   Institute of Blind People**

National Limousine & Chauffeur Association (NLCA) 1997
- ■ Units 108-109 Middlemore Business Park, Middlemore Rd,
   SMETHWICK, W Midlands, B66 2PP. (mem/sb)
   07817 940185
   http://www.thenlca.co.uk
   Mem Sec: Jag Mann
   Chmn: Peter Wright (07957 856315)
- ▲ Company Limited by Guarantee
- Br 4
- ○ *T; to ensure the safe & legal operation of limousines &
   chauffeur driven cars throughout the UK
- ● Conf - Mtgs - ET - Res - Exhib - LG
- M i & f
   (Sub: £120 f)
- ¶ New items on web - 12; ftm only.
- × 2007 (January) National Limousine Association

National Literacy Association (NLA) 1993
- NR 87 Grange Rd, RAMSGATE, Kent, CT11 9QB. (hq)
   01843 239952
   email mail@nla.org.uk   http://www.nla.org.uk
   Dir & Sec: Jo Klaces
- ▲ Registered Charity
- ○ *K; a charity working to eliminate illiteracy amongst children &
   young people
- ● ET - Res - Stat - Inf - Lib - LG
- < Assn Educl Psychologists; Assn of Teachers & Lecturers; Brit
   Dyslexic Assn; Brit Educl Suppliers Assn [& 9 other
   educational bodies]
- M 64 i, 298 org
- ¶ NL - 4; free.   AR - 1; board members only.
   The Guide to Literacy Resources 7th ed - 1.
   Literacy & ICT: cutting edge practice in the primary school - 1.

National Market Traders Federation (NMTF) 1899
- ■ Hampton House, Hawshaw Lane, Hoyland, BARNSLEY, S Yorks,
   S74 0HA. (hq)
   01226 749021   fax 01226 740329
   email enquiries@nmtf.co.uk   http://www.nmtf.co.uk
   Gen Sec: Joe Harrison
- ▲ Un-incorporated Society
- Br 125
- ○ *T; representation of market traders at local, national &
   international level
- ● Conf - Exhib - LG - Promotion events
- < World U of Whls Market Retail Section (WUWM)
- M 35,000 i
   (Sub: £90-£225)
- ¶ Federation News - 6; free.

National Microelectronics Institute (NMI) 1997
- NR Innovation Centre (1st floor), Broad Quay, BATH, Somerset,
   BA1 1UD. (hq)
   email info@nmi.org.uk   http://www.nmi.org.uk
   Chief Exec: Derek Boyd
- ▲ Company Limited by Guarantee
- ○ *N, *T; to provide a mechanism for collaboration between
   members, educational organisations, regional bodies &
   government
- ● Mtgs - ET - LG
- M [not stated]

National Mining Memorabilia Association (NMMA) 1996
- NR Northcliffe Cottage, Newton Rd, Newton Solney, BURTON-ON-
   TRENT, Staffs, DE15 0TG. (mem/sp)
   http://www.mining-memorabilia.co.uk
   Mem Sec: Jeremy Winter
- ○ *G; for collectors of all materials connected with mining, tokens
   lamps, badges, tickets, tallies, blasting & related explosive
   equipment as well as local history research
- ● Mtgs - Inf - VE - Field trips
- M c 100 i
- ¶ NL - 4; ftm

National Motorcycle Council (NMC) 1985
- ■ Unit 4, 92-98 Vauxhall Walk, LONDON, SE11 5EL. (hq)
   http://www.nmc.org.uk
   Secretariat: Craig Carey-Clinch
- ○ *N; liaison between various sectional interests within
   motorcycling
- ● Inf - LG
- < Parliamentary Advisory C'ee on Transport Safety (PACTS)
- M i, f & org

National Mouse Club (NMC) 1895
- NR 260 Washway Rd, SALE, Cheshire, M33 4RZ. (hsp)
   http://www.thenationalmouseclub.co.uk
   Hon Sec: Mrs A Tomkins
- ▲ Un-incorporated Society
- ○ *B; to promote breeding & exhibition of fancy mice
- ● Mtgs - Exhib - Comp - Inf
- M 150 i, UK / 5 i, o'seas
- ¶ NMC News - 12; £20 yr m, £2 each nm.   Ybk; ftm only.

National Network of Assessment Centres (NNAC)
- ■ c/o ACCESSCENTRAL, Innovation Centre, 1 Devon Way,
   Longbridge, BIRMINGHAM, B31 2TS. (hq)
   0121-222 5362
   email admincentre@nnac.org   http://www.nnac.org
   Treas: Michael Trott
- ○ *N, *W; for physically or sensorily disabled people; to advise
   colleges & universities about teaching, learning strategies &
   enabling devices to ensure access to the curriculum for all
   students
- M centres

National Newspapers of Ireland (NNI)
- IRL Clyde Lodge, 15 Clyde Rd, DUBLIN 4, Republic of Ireland.
   353 (1) 668 9099   fax 353 (1) 668 9872
   email nni@cullencommunications.ie   http://www.nni.ie
- ○ *T; the representative body of Ireland's daily & weekly
   newspapers

National Obesity Forum (NOF) 2000
- NR PO Box 10131, NOTTINGHAM, NG2 9NH.
   0115-846 2109   fax 0115-846 2329
   email info@nof.uk.com
   http://www.nationalobesityforum.org.uk
- ○ *P; for health care professionals concerned in raising
   awareness of the growing impact of obesity on the National
   Health Service
- M i
- ¶ Via their webpage

National Off-Licence Association

IRL Block D - Unit 6, Nutgrove Office Park, Rathfarnham,
   DUBLIN 14, Republic of Ireland
   353 (1) 296 2326   fax 353 (1) 296 2451
   email admin@noffla.ie   http://www.noffla.ie
   Admin: Reggie Walsh
○ *T

National Office of Animal Health Ltd   (NOAH)   1986

■ 3 Crossfield Chambers, Gladbeck Way, ENFIELD, Middx,
   EN2 7HF.   (hq)
   020 8367 3131   fax 020 8363 1155
   email noah@noah.co.uk   http://www.noah.co.uk
   Chief Exec: Philip Sketchley
▲ Company Limited by Guarantee
○ *T, *V; for manufacturers of licensed animal medicines in the
   UK (incl pet & farm animals)
Gp Code of Practice C'ee for the Promotion of Animal Medicines
● Conf - Mtgs - ET - Res - Exhib - Stat - Inf - LG - Conducts
   research sales survey on behalf of members & non-members
   - Media relations on behalf of members
< Intl Fedn Animal Health (IFAH); Intl Fedn Animal Health (IFAH-
   Europe)
M 32 i, 12 f
¶ Compendium of Data Sheets IOC Animal Medicines - 1.
   (also available online: www.noahcompendium.co.uk).
   Poisoning in Veterinary Practice, 1992; £3.
   Animal Medicine Record Book, 1999; £3.50.
   Briefing documents & reports; free.

National Operatic & Dramatic Association   (NODA)   1899

NR NODA House, 58-60 Lincoln Rd, PETERBOROUGH, Cambs,
   PE1 2RZ.   (hq)
   01733 865790
   email everyone@noda.org.uk   http://www.noda.org.uk
   Chief Exec: Tony Gibbs
▲ Registered Charity
○ *A, *D, *N; 'national umbrella body for amateur operatic &
   dramatic societies'
● Conf - Mtgs - ET (Summer school for amateur operatic &
   dramatic students with professional tutors)
< Intl Theatre Exchange (UK branch of IATA)
M 2,500 i, 2,500 org
¶ NODA National News - 4; ftm, £2.50 each nm.

National Organisation of Beaters & Pickers Up   (NOBs)   2005

NR PO Box 292, FRAMLINGHAM, Suffolk, IP13 9FA.
   0845 634 5014
   http://www.nobs.org.uk
   Chief Exec: Neil Dale
○ *G; for those interested in working with gamekeepers & shoot
   captains as beaters, pickers-up or loaders

National Organisation for Phobias, Anxiety, Neuroses, Information & Care
   see **No Panic**

**National Organisation for Pupil Referral Units in England &
   Wales   2004**

NR Somerset County Council, County Hall, TAUNTON, Somerset,
   TA1 4DY.
   01823 358163
   email secretary@prus.org.uk   http://www.prus.org.uk
   Sec: Jacky Mackenzie
○ *E; the provision of suitable education for pupils of compulsory
   school age who, because of illness etc, are unable to attend
   a mainstream school
✕ 2009 National Organisation for Short Stay Schools

National Organisation for Short Stay Schools
   since 2009 **National Organisation of Pupil Referral Units**

**National Organisation for the Treatment of Abusers   (NOTA)
   1991**

NR PO Box 21, Skirlaugh, HULL, HU11 5WD.   (hq)
   email notaoffice@aol.com   http://www.nota.co.uk
▲ Registered Charity
Br 12; Eire
○ *K, *P; to protect potential victims of sexual aggression through
   developing & promoting professional practice with both sex
   offenders (regardless of their age or gender)... & by direct
   work with their victims & non-abusing family members
● Conf - Mtgs - ET - Res - LG
< Assn for the Treatment of Abusers (USA)
M c 1,200 i
¶ Jnl of Sexual Aggression - 2.   NOTA News - 4.
   Annual Conference Audio Tapes - 1.

National Orthophobics Group

■ 81 Park View, Collins Rd, LONDON, N5 2UD.
○ *W; for people with a fear of property
M 7 i

National Osteoporosis Society   (NOS)   1986

■ Manor Farm, Skinners Hill, Camerton, BATH, Somerset,
   BA2 0PJ.   (hq)
   01761 471771 (Mon-Thurs 0900-1630, Fri 0900-1600)
   fax 01761 471104
   email info@nos.org.uk   http://www.nos.org.uk
   Chief Exec: Mrs Claire L Severgnini
▲ Registered Charity
Br 130 regional support groups
○ *W; to provide help & support for sufferers of osteoporosis; to
   encourage the medical professions, government etc to work
   together towards improving treatment & prevention; to
   support research
● Conf - Mtgs - ET - Res - Inf - LG - Advice & reassurance to
   people with medical queries through the helpline staffed by
   specialised nurses, booklets etc
   Helpline: 0845 450 0230
< Eur Foundation for Osteoporosis & Bone Disease; Intl
   Osteoporosis Foundation; Nat Coun Women
M 25,000 i
   (Sub:£15)
¶ Osteoporosis News (NL) - 4; ftm only.
   Osteoporosis Review - 4; ftm only.   AR; free.

National Outdoor Events Association   (NOEA)   1979

■ PO Box 4495, WELLS, Somerset, BA5 9AS.   (hq)
   01749 674531
   email secretary@noea.org.uk   http://www.noea.org.uk
   Gen Sec: Susan Tanner
▲ Un-incorporated Society
○ *T; to enhance professionalism in the outdoor events industry
   through education, networking, lobbying, advice & creating
   business opportunities
● Conf - LG - Mtgs
M 362 f
¶ NL - by email;   Ybk; both ftm.

National Outsourcing Association   (NOA)

NR 44 Wardour St, LONDON, W1D 6QZ.   (hq)
   020 7292 8686   fax 020 7287 2905
   email admin@noa.co.uk   http://www.noa.co.uk
▲ Company Limited by Guarantee
○ *T; to develop experience & professionalism in all areas of
   business technology outsourcing - in particular outsourcing of
   telecommunications & computing networks; to promote the
   business advantages of outsourcing
● Conf - Mtgs - Res - Inf - LG - Promotion & lobbying
M f
¶ Business Technology Outsourcer - 2; free.

National Packaging Council
   no longer exists

National Park Homes Council
a division of the **National Caravan Council**

National Pawnbrokers Association of the UK (NPA) 1892
NR Chiltern Court 37 St Peters Avenue, Caversham, READING,
Berks, RG4 7DH.   (asa)
0118-947 7385
http://www.thenpa.co.uk
Sec Gen: Des Milligan
▲ Company Limited by Guarantee
○ *T
● Conf - Mtgs - Res - Exhib - Comp - Stat - Inf - VE - LG -
Insurance - Legal, financial, operations, publicity advice -
New business promotion & assistance
< Nat Cham Tr; Soc Assn Execs: Glasgow Pawnbrokers Assn
M c 450 f
¶ NPA Times - 4;   AR & Accounts - 1; both free.
Leaflets:
Pawnbrokers Guide;   Using a Pawnbroker; both ftm.

National Pensioners Convention (NPC) 1990
■ Walkden House, 10 Melton St, LONDON, NW1 2EJ.   (hq)
020 7383 0388
email info@npcuk.org   http://www.npcuk.org
Gen Sec: Dot Gibson
▲ Un-incorporated Society
Br 500 affiliated groups
○ *K, *N; umbrella organisation for pensioner organisations,
regional pensioner liaison forums, charities & trade union
retired members associations
● Mtgs - ET - Res - Inf - LG
< AGE: the Eur Older People's Platform
M 1,200 i, 100 f, 400 org
¶ The Message - 4; ftm, 10p per copy nm.
Pension credit for beginners; 50p.
Women - 'Wise-up' on Pensions; £1.

National Pest Technicians Association (NPTA) 1993
■ NPTA House, Hall Lane, Kinoulton, NOTTINGHAM,
NG12 3EF.   (hq)
01949 81133   fax 01949 823905
email officenpta@aol.com   http://www.npta.org.uk
Sec: John A Davison
Admin Officer: Mrs Julie Gillies
▲ Company Limited by Guarantee
○ *P; to promote the role of pest controller
● Conf - Mtgs - ET - Exhib - Inf
M c 900 i & f
¶ Today's Technician - 4; ftm, £4 each nm.

National Pharmacy Association (NPA) 1921
NR Mallinson House, 38-42 St Peter's St, ST ALBANS, Herts,
AL1 3NP.   (hq)
01727 858687
email npa@npa.co.uk   http://www.npa.co.uk
▲ Company Limited by Guarantee
○ *T; for community retail pharmacists
Gp NPA Insurance Ltd
M 11,000 f

National Philatelic Society (NPS) 1899
■ British Postal Museum & Archive, Freeling House, Phoenix Place,
LONDON, WC1X 0DL.   (hq)
020 7239 2571
email nps@ukphilately.org.uk
http://www.ukphilately.org.uk/nps
Hon Gen Sec: Peter Mellor
▲ Un-incorporated Society
○ *G; promotion & encouragement of philately
● Mtgs - Lib
< Assn of Brit Philatelic Socs
M 600 i, 1 org, UK / 50 i, o'seas
¶ The Stamp Lover - 6; ftm, £17 yr nm.

National Phobics Society
since 2009 **Anxiety UK**

National Piers Society (NPS) 1979
NR Flat 1 - 128 Gloucester Terrace, LONDON, W2 6HP.
(mem/sp)
email nationalpierssociety@googlemail.com
http://www.piers.org.uk
Mem Sec: Neville Taylor
Chmn: 01404 831335
▲ Company Limited by Guarantee; Registered Charity
○ *G, *K; promoting interest in the preservation & continued
enjoyment of seaside piers
● Res - Inf - PL - VE - LG
< Paddle Steamer Preservation Soc
M i & f
¶ Piers (Jnl) - 4; ftm.   Good Piers Guide.
Guide to British Piers, 3rd ed.

National Pig Association (NPA) 1999
NR Agriculture House, STONELEIGH PARK, Warks, CV8 2LZ.   (hq)
024 7685 8784   fax 024 7865 8786
email npa@npanet.org.uk   http://www.npa-uk.org.uk
Exec Dir: Stewart Houston
▲ Company Limited by Guarantee
○ *B, *T; for the UK pig industry
Gp Allied industry; Campaigns
● Conf - Mtgs - ET - LG
M 1,300 i, 100 f

National Pigeon Association (NPA) 1918
■ Churchbrook House, Church St, Barton St David, SOMERTON,
Somerset, TA11 6BU.   (hsp)
01458 851617
http://www.nationalpigeonassociation.co.uk
Sec: Graham Giddings
▲ Un-incorporated Society
○ *B, *G; organising body for issue of rings & exhibitions of fancy
pigeons (NOT racing pigeons)
● Mtgs - Exhib
< Entente Européenne d'Aviculture et de Cuniculture
M c 150 org
¶ Feathered World - 12; £21 yr.

National Pipe Organ Register
a group of the **British Institute of Organ Studies**

National Playbus Association 1974
■ Brunswick Court, Brunswick Square, BRISTOL, BS2 8PE.   (hq)
0117-916 6580   fax 0117-916 6588
email info@workingonwheels.org
http://www.workingonwheels.org
Chief Exec: Geoffrey Riddick
▲ Company Limited by Guarantee; Registered Charity
○ *N, *W, *Y; a national umbrella organisation which supports the
work of locally based community groups who make use of
covered vehicles to provide services
● Conf - ET - Inf - Project support & development
< Nat Coun Voluntary Orgs (NCVO); Scot Coun Voluntary
Orgs (SCVO); Nat Coun Voluntary Child Care
Orgs (NCVCCO)
M c 230 org
¶ Busfare - 3.   AR.
Information sheets & specialist publications; prices vary.
uses the title Working on Wheels

National Playing Fields Association   (NPFA)   1925
- ■ 15 Crinan St, LONDON, N1 9SQ.   (hq)
   020 7427 2110   fax 020 7247 2128
   email info@fieldsintrust.org   http://www.fieldsintrust.org
   Dir: Alison Moore-Gwyn
- ▲ Registered Charity
- Br 4
- ○ *K; charity committed to the protection & preservation of
   recreational space
- ● Conf - ET - Inf - LG
- M 600 i, f & org
- ¶ The Six Acre Standard; £25.   Taking a Lead; £12.95.
   Playwork - a guide for trainers; £10.
   Impact Absorbing Surfaces for Children's Playgrounds; £15.
   Play Safety Guidelines; £11.95.   NPFA Cost Guide; £25.
   Note: uses the operating name of Fields in Trust

National Pony Society   (NPS)   1893
- ■ Willingdon House, 7 The Windmills, St Mary's Close, ALTON,
   Hants, GU34 1EF.   (hq)
   01420 88333   fax 01420 80599
   email info@nationalponysociety.org.uk
   http://www.nationalponysociety.org.uk
   Chief Exec: Mrs Caroline Nokes
- ▲ Registered Charity
- ○ *B, *V; to encourage the breeding, registration & improvement
   of British riding ponies (incl mountain & moorland ponies); to
   foster the welfare of ponies in general
- Gp Breed societies; Veterinary & animal welfare gps
- ● Conf - Mtgs - ET - Comp - Inf - LG
- < Brit Driving Soc; Brit Show Pony Soc; Brit Equine Welfare C'ee;
   Central Prefix Register
- M 3,000 i
   (Sub: £35)
- ¶ Review - 1; ftm, £10 nm.   NL - 3; ftm only.
   Stud Book.   AR; free.   Judges List & Rules.
   Show Schedule; free.   Show Catalogue.

National Portage Association   (NPA)   1983
- NR Kings Court, 17 School Rd, BIRMINGHAM, W Midlands,
   B28 8JG.
   email npa@portageuk.freeserve.co.uk
   http://www.portage.org.uk
- ▲ Company Limited by Guarantee; Registered Charity
- Br Regional
- ○ *E, *W; to support families caring for children with special
   needs by promoting & supporting portage educational home
   visiting services
- Gp Ethics; Information & Publicity; Training & monitoring
- ● Conf - Mtgs - ET - Exhib - Inf
- M 400 i, 77 groups, UK / 3 i, 1 group, o'seas
- ¶ Portage Post NL - 3; ftm.   AR - 1; free.
   Conference Proceedings - 1; £11.74.
   Publications list available from:
      PO Box 3075, Yeovil, BA21 3FB or
      npa@portageuk.freeserve.co.uk

National Portraiture Association   (NPA)   1972
- NR 59-60 Fitzjames Avenue, LONDON, W14 0RR.   (hq)
   020 7602 0892   fax 020 7602 6705
   Dir: William H Deeves
- ▲ Un-incorporated Society
- ○ *A; acquisition of fine portrait commissions in all media
- ● Bursaries for talented children

National Pot Leek Society   1978
- NR 147 Sea Rd, Fulwell, SUNDERLAND, Tyne & Wear, SR6 9EB.
   (hsp)
   0191-549 4274
   Hon Sec: Derek Richardson
- ○ *H; culture, knowledge & research into growth & diseases of
   pot grown leeks
- ● ET - Res - Exhib - Stat - Inf
- M i
- ¶ Jnl - 4; ftm.   NL.

National Private Hire Association   (NPHA)   1993
- NR 8 Silver St, BURY, Lancs, BL9 0EX.   (hq)
   0161-280 2800   fax 0161-280 7787
   Gen Sec: Bryan M Roland
- ▲ Company Limited by Guarantee
- ○ *T; for private hire & hackney carriage companies & drivers; to
   raise standards in the trade, both actual & as perceived by
   the public
- Gp NPH QA - ISO 9002 consultancy
- ● Conf - ET - Exhib - Inf - LG - Legal guidance - Representations
   in court
- M 50 i, 600 f, 66 local org
- ¶ Private Hire & Taxi Monthly - 12.

National Pure Water Association   (NPWA)   1960
- ■ 42 Huntington Rd, YORK, YO31 8RE.   (hsp)
   020 8220 9168
   http://www.npwa.org.uk
   Vice-Chmn: Ian Packington
- ○ *K; to oppose the use of public water supplies for the purpose
   of mass medication, particularly fluoridation; to protect the
   public water supplies from any form of pollution or
   contamination, deliberate or accidental
- ● Inf - Supporting local groups witn similar aims
- M [not stated]
- ¶ NL - 2/3; free.

National Register of Access Consultants   (NRAC)   2000
- ■ 70 South Lambeth Rd, LONDON, SW8 1RL.   (hq)
   020 7735 7845   fax 020 7840 5811
   email info@nrac.org.uk   http://www.nrac.org.uk
   Chief Exec: Sarah Langton-Lockton
- ○ *P; accreditation of individuals in the access/inclusive
   environments sector who make improvements to the built
   environment
- Gp Countryside; Designer; Expert witness; Policy & strategy;
   Signage & wayfinding; Specialists for building types; Trainer;
   Transport; Web accessibility
- ● Conf - Accreditation of individuals - Services to members
- M 200 i, + 150 affiliates (i & org)
- ¶ email NL - m only.

**National Register of Hypnotherapists & Psychotherapists
(NRHP)   1985**
- ■ 18 Carr Rd (1st floor), NELSON, Lancs, BB9 7JS.   (hq)
   01282 716839
   email admin@nrhp.co.uk   http://www.nrhp.co.uk
   Chmn: Sir Bill Connor
- ▲ Company Limited by Guarantee
- ○ *P; a free referral service (by post, email, telephone) for
   members of the public seeking qualified
   hypnotherapists.   All members trained by a UKCP
   recognised training organisation, with on-going supervision,
   adhere to a code of practice & carry appropriate insurance
- ● Conf - ET
- < Eur Assn Hypno-Psychotherapy; UK Coun Psychotherapy; Brit
   Assn Counselling & Psychotherapy
- M 450 i, UK / 10 i, o'seas
   (Sub: £140, UK / £52 o'seas)
- ¶ NL - 3; ftm only.   LM (by area); free on request.
   Directory of Practitioners - 1; ftm, £7 nm.

National Register of Personal Trainers   (NRPT)   1991
- NR PO Box 870, SYWELL, Northants, NN6 0ZB.
   0844 848 4644
   email info@nrpt.co.uk   http://www.nrpt.co.uk
- ○ *P
- M c 600 i

© CBD Research Ltd · Beckenham · BR3 5JS · Tel 020 8650 7745 · E-mail cbd@cbdresearch.com · www.cbdresearch.com

National Register of Property Preservation Specialists
- ◼ 11 Greenland Rd, BARNET, Herts, EN5 2AL.
  07876 192249
  http://www.nrpps.co.uk
  Contact: Mr Smith
- ○ *P
- M c 180 i

National Register of Public Service Interpreters
  interpreters working in public services - health, legal, local
  government related (education, environmental health,
  housing, social services, welfare), is a wholly owned
  subsidiary of the **Chartered Institute of Linguistics**

National Rheumatoid Arthritis Society (NRAS) 2001
- NR Unit B4 Westacott Business Centre, Littlewick Green,
  MAIDENHEAD, Berks, SL6 3RT. (hq)
  01628 823524
  email enquiries@rheumatoid.org.uk
  http://www.rheumatoid.org.uk
  Chmn: Ailsa Bosworth
- ▲ Registered Charity
- ○ *G, *K; is patient-led & focuses on rheumatoid arthritis; to
  provide an advisory & information service on all aspects of
  the disease
- Gp Expert patient network
- ● Inf
  Helpline: 0800 298 7650
- M c 850 i

National Rifle Association (NRA) 1860
- ◼ c/o National Shooting Centre, Bisley Camp, Brookwood,
  WOKING, Surrey, GU24 0PB. (hq)
  01483 797777 fax 01483 797285
  email info@nra.org.uk http://www.nra.org.uk
  Chmn: John Jackman, Sec Gen: Glynn Algar
- ▲ Registered Charity
- ○ *S; to promote rifle & pistol shooting
- ● Mtgs - ET - Exhib - Comp - Stat - Inf - Lib - PL - LG
- < Brit Shooting Sports Coun; GB Target Shooting Fedn
- M 4,500 i, 1,100 org, UK / 42 org, o'seas
- ¶ Jnl - 3; ftm.

**National Roller Hockey Association of England Ltd (NRHA)
1909**
- ◼ Home Farm House, Marshide, CHISLET, Kent, CT3 3EG. (sp)
  email debpughenrha@btinternet.com
  http://www.nrha.co.uk
  Sec: Debbie Pughe
- ○ *S; governing body for roller hockey
- M i & clubs
- ¶ NL - 12. Coaching Manual. AR.

National Rounders Association
  since 2009 **Rounders England**

National School Band Association (NSBA) 1952
- ◼ c/o David Martin, Korina Associates, Pembroke Centre,
  Cheney Manor, SWINDON, Wilts, SN2 2PQ. (execoffr/b)
  http://www.nsba.org.uk
  Exec Officer: David Martin
- ▲ Registered Charity
- ○ *D; to encourage an interest in music, through the playing of
  brass & woodwind instruments in schools
- M i & schools

National Search & Rescue Dog Association (NSARDA)
- ◼ 3 Strawberry Hill Rd, The Haulgh, BOLTON, Lancs, BL2 1DP.
  email secretary@nsarda.org.uk
  http://www.nsarda.org.uk
- ○ *G; provision of dogs for searching for people in mountain
  areas, crime scenes & other emergencies

National Secular Society (NSS) 1866
- ◼ 25 Red Lion Sq, LONDON, WC1R 4RL. (hq)
  020 7404 3126 fax 0870 762 8971
  email admin@secularism.org.uk
  http://www.secularism.org.uk
  Exec Dir: Keith Porteus Wood
- ▲ Company Limited by Guarantee
- ○ *K; to campaign for secularism (incl free speech, freedom from
  religious discrimination & other civil liberties) & for an end to
  religious privilege (incl no public finding of an established
  church, of sectarian schools & of faith-based social services)
- ● LG - Campaigning
- < Intl Ethical & Humanist U; Liberty; Amnesty Intl; Abortion Law
  Reform Assn; Network for Peace
- M 2,090 i, 31 org, UK / 45 i, o'seas
- ¶ Bulletin - 3; Newsline (email) - 52; AR - 1; all free.

National Security Inspectorate (NSI) 2001
- ◼ Sentinel House, 5 Reform Rd, MAIDENHEAD, Berks, SL6 8BY.
  (hq)
  0845 006 3003 fax 01628 773367
  email nsi@nsi.org.uk http://www.nsi.org.uk
  Chief Exec: Andrew White
- ▲ Company Limited by Guarantee
- ○ *N; an independent regulatory & certification body approving &
  regulating firms concerned with installation, service &
  maintenance of security systems - intruder alarms, CCTV,
  access control & alarm receiving centres; inspection of
  companies providing 'people based' services in the security
  industry; inspection of companies designing, installing,
  commissioning & maintaining fire detection systems
- ● Conf - Mtgs - Exhib - Inf - LG - Inspection services
- < BSI; Security Ind Training Org; Security Ind Bd; Jt Security Ind
  Coun; Fedn of Brit Fire Orgs
- M 1,100 f
- ¶ Network NL - 3; free.
  Technical Memoranda - irreg; ftm only.
  Regulatory Documents - irreg; £9.

National Sewerage Association (NSA) 1995
- ◼ 42 Manor Drive North, NEW MALDEN, Surrey, KT3 5NY. (hsp)
  020 8330 0123
  email nsa@tinyonline.co.uk http://www.sewerage.org
  Sec: Mrs V A Gibbens
- ▲ Un-incorporated Society
- ○ *T; to improve the professional standards of firms carrying out
  sewer & drainage surveys, cleaning, monitoring, repairs &
  renovation
- Gp Contractors: Blockage clearance & cleaning, CCTV sewer
  inspection; Flow monitoring; Associated manufacturers
- ● Mtgs - ET - Inf - LG - Liaison with water companies & WRc on
  national standards for the industry
- M 32 f
- ¶ Members Directory - on request; free.

National Sheep Association (NSA) 1892
- NR The Sheep Centre, MALVERN, Worcs, WR13 6PH. (hq)
  01684 892661 fax 01684 892663
  http://www.nationalsheep.org.uk
  Chf Exec: Peter Morris
- Br 9
- ○ *B, *T; to promote & represent the sheep industry
- < Assn of Show & Agricl Orgs
- M f
- ¶ Sheep Farmer - 6.

National Small-bore Rifle Association   (NSRA)   1903
NR   Lord Roberts Centre, Bisley Camp, Brookwood, WOKING,
       Surrey, GU24 0NP.   (hq)
       01483 485505   fax 01483 476392
       email info@nsra.co.uk   http://www.nsra.co.uk
▲   Registered Charity
○   *S; promotion of .22 target shooting & air rifle shooting & .177
       airgun shooting
M   i & clubs
¶   The Rifleman - 4; ftm.

National Small Schools Forum   (NSSF)
NR   Old Sodbury School, 44 Church Lane, Old Sodbury, BRISTOL,
       BS37 6NB.   (treas/b)
       email cwilliams0@btinternet.com   http://www.nssf.co.uk
       Treas: Chris Williams
○   *E; promotes high quality education in small schools with
       primary pupils
M   c 1,000 i

**National Society of Allied & Independent Funeral Directors
   (SAIF)   1989**
■   SAIF Business Centre, 3 Bullfields, SAWBRIDGEWORTH, Herts,
       CM21 9DB.   (hq)
       0845 230 6777
       email info@saif.org.uk   http://www.saif.org.uk
       Chief Exec: Peter O'Neill
▲   Un-incorporated Society
○   *P, *T; to promote, project & assist the interests of independent
       funeral directors
●   Conf - Mtgs - ET - Res - Exhib - SG - LG
<   Independent Funeral Directors College
M   600 f
¶   SAIFinsight (NL) - 12; free.
       Note: also known as the Society of Allied & Independent
       Funeral Directors

**National Society of Allotment & Leisure Gardeners Ltd
   (NSALG)   1930**
■   O'Dell House, Hunters Rd, CORBY, Northants, NN17 5JE.
       (hq)
       01536 266576   fax 01536 264509
       email natsoc@nsalg.org.uk   http://www.nsalg.org.uk
       Sec: Geoff Stokes
○   *G, *H; to ensure that allotments & leisure gardens are
       available to all who require them
●   Conf - Inf
<   NCVO
M   85,000 i, 1,700 org
¶   Allotment & Leisure Gardener - 4; ftm, £2 nm.

**National Society (Church of England) for Promoting Religious
   Education   1811**
NR   Church House, Great Smith St, LONDON, SW1P 3NZ.   (hq)
       020 7898 1518
       http://www.natsoc.org.uk
       Gen Sec: Canon John Hall
▲   Registered Charity
○   *R; to support all involved in religious education in schools,
       colleges & churches in England & Wales
M   i & schools

National Society for Clean Air & Environmental Protection
   since October 2007 **Environmental Protection UK**

**National Society for Education in Art & Design   (NSEAD)
   1888**
■   3 Masons Wharf, Potley Lane, CORSHAM, Wilts, SN13 9FY.
       (hq)
       01225 810134   fax 01225 812730
       email johnsteers@nsead.org   http://www.nsead.org
       Sec: Dr John Steers
▲   Un-incorporated Society
○   *E, *P, *U; to promote & defend art & design education & the
       interests of teachers
Gp   Boards: Editorial, Teacher education, Information &
       communications technology
●   Conf - ET - Res - Inf - Empl
<   Intl Soc for Educ through Art
M   c 2,500 i
¶   International Jnl of Art & Design Education - 3; ftm.
       Start - 4; ftm (some categories); £30 nm.

National Society for Epilepsy   (NSE)   1892
■   Chesham Lane, CHALFONT ST PETER, Bucks, SL9 0RJ.   (hq)
       01494 601300   fax 01494 871927
       Chief Exec: Graham Faulkner
▲   Company Limited by Guarantee; Registered Charity
○   *W; to advance research, treatment, care, understanding &
       support for people with epilepsy
●   ET - Res - Exhib - Inf
       Helpline: 01494 601400
M   i
¶   Epilepsy Review (Jnl) - 3; ftm only.   AR - 1; free.

National Society of Hypnosis & Psychotherapy   (NSHP)
NR   PO Box 5779, LOUGHBOROUGH, Leics, LE12 5ZF.   (hq)
       0845 257 8735
       http://www.hypno-psychotherapy.net
       Chmn: Richard Nicholls
○   *P
<   UK Confedn of Hypnotherapy Orgs

National Society of Master Thatchers   (NSMT)   1967
■   Warringtons, Gelsmoor Rd, Coleorton, COALVILLE, Leics, LE67
       8JE.   (hsp)
       01530 222954
       email avraffle@gmail.com   http://www.nsmtltd.co.uk
       Sec: Andrew Raffle
▲   Company Limited by Guarantee
○   *T; the protection & promotion of thatch for the benefit of
       members & the thatch owning public
Gp   Thatched property ownership; Thatching; Thatching advice
●   Conf - Mtgs - ET
M   120 i, 3 f, 3 org
¶   The Thatcher's Standard - 4; ftm, £12.50 yr nm.
       Hbk: a practical guide to thatch & thatching in the 21st
       century; £12.50.
       Guidance Notes:
         Fire & Thatch; £5.50.
         Conservation Issues & the Maintenance of Cereal
           Varieties for Thatching; £5.50.

**National Society of Painters, Sculptors & Printmakers   (NS)
   1930**
■   122 Copse Hill, LONDON, SW20 0NL.   (hsp)
       020 8946 7878
       http://www.nationalsociety.org
       Hon Sec: Gwen Spencer
▲   Registered Charity
○   *A; 'formed in 1930 to meet a growing desire among artists of
       every creed & outlook for an annual exhibition in London
       which would embrace all aspects of art under one roof,
       without prejudice or favour to anyone'
●   Mtgs - Exhib
M   83 i, UK / 1 i, o'seas
¶   NL - 2; ftm only.

© CBD Research Ltd · Beckenham · BR3 5JS · Tel 020 8650 7745 · E-mail cbd@cbdresearch.com · www.cbdresearch.com

National Society for Phenylketonuria (United Kingdom) Ltd (NSPKU) 1973
- ■ PO Box 26642, LONDON, N14 4ZF.   (mail/address)
  020 8634 3010   fax 0845 004 8341
  email info@nspku.org   http://www.nspku.org
  Sec: Eric Lange
- ▲ Company Limited by Guarantee; Registered Charity
- ○ *W; the welfare of persons suffering from Phenylketonuria & allied (amino acid) disorders, their families & carers
- Gp Medical advisory panel (provides a link with the medical profession & a voice in decisions on standards on PKU treatment)
- ● Conf - Mtgs - Inf
- < Eur Soc for Phenylketonuria (ESPKU); Genetic Interest Gp (GIG)
- M 1,130 i, 5 f, 1 org, UK / 50 i, 10 org, o'seas
  (Sub: £17 i, £25 f, UK / £25 i, £33 f, o'seas)
- ¶ Publications on treatment, diet, & children; 25p - £30.

National Society for the Prevention of Cruelty to Children (NSPCC) 1884
- ■ 42 Curtain Rd, LONDON, EC2A 3NH.   (hq)
  020 7825 2500   fax 020 7825 2525
  email info@nspcc.org.uk   http://www.nspcc.org.uk
  Dir & Chief Exec: Mary Marsh
- ▲ Registered Charity
- ○ *K, *W; to prevent child abuse & neglect in all its forms
- ● ET - Res - Inf - Lib - LG
  Child protection helpline: 0800 800 5000
- M voluntary workers
- ¶ Publications catalogue & some full text publications available on website.

National Society of Professional Hypnotherapists (NSPH) 1990
- NR Kennard, Shawfield Lane, BLAIRGOWRIE, Perthshire, PH10 6GW.   (hq)
  01250 874384
  email nwblair@nsph-hypnotherapy.co.uk
  http://www.nsph-hypnotherapy.co.uk
  Hon Sec: Sandra Stewart
- ▲ Un-incorporated Society
- ● Mtgs - ET - Exam - Res - Exhib - SG - Inf
- M 100 i, UK / 6 i, o'seas
- ¶ NSPH Members Jnl - 4; ftm only.

National Society for the Promotion of Punctuality   (NSPP)
- ■ 81 Park View, Colins Rd, LONDON, N5 2UD.   (asa)
- ○ *K; to increase public awareness of the importance of punctuality; 'being late may be fashionable but it is also rude'
- ● Mtgs - Stat - VE
- M 50 i
- ¶ Stopwatch (Jnl) - 12.

National Society for Research into Allergy   (NSRA) 1980
- NR 2 Armadale Close, Hollycroft, HINCKLEY, Leics, LE10 0SZ.   (hsp/b)
  01455 250715
  email eunicerose@talktalk.net   http://www.all-allergy.org
  Hon Sec: Mrs Eunice L Rose
- ▲ Registered Charity
- Br New Zealand, USA
- ○ *K, *Q; to promote the awareness of allergic diseases; to research into the causes of allergic diseases & methods of safe treatment; to offer help & advice to people suffering from allergy-intolerance
- Gp Allergy; Asthma; Crohn's; Eczema; Food & chemical intolerance; ME; Migraine
- ● Mtgs - ET - Res
- M c 1,000 i, UK / c 100 i, o'seas
- ¶ Reaction - 3; ftm, £5 nm.
  Is it anything you ate? - 1; ftm (on joining), £10 nm.
  Publications list available.

National Society of Teapot & Kettle Collectors
- ■ 81 Park View, Collins Rd, LONDON, N5 2UD.
- ○ *G
- Gp Miniature teapots
- ● Mtgs - Exhib - PL
- M 53 i
- ¶ Spouting (Jnl) - 6; ftm only.
- ✕ 2008 National Society of Teapot Collectors

National Specialist Contractors Council   (NSCC) 1992
- NR Royal London House, 22-25 Finsbury Square, LONDON, EC2A 1DX.   (hq)
  0844 249 5351   fax 0844 249 5352
  http://www.nscc.org.uk
  Chief Exec Officer: Suzannah Nichol
- ▲ Company Limited by Guarantee
- Br Scottish section: PO Box 28011, Edinburgh, EH16 6WN.
  0131-448 0266   fax 0131-440 4032
  Sec: Alan McKinney
- ○ *T; the sub-contract sector of the construction industry
- ● Conf - Mtgs - ET - Res - SG - Stat - Inf - LG
- M 30 associations
- ¶ Bulletin - 2;   AR; both ftm only.
  Check It - 2; ftm, £10 nm.

National Sprint Association Ltd   (NSA) 1958
- NR 8 King George Gardens, Chapel Allerton, LEEDS, W Yorks, LS7 4NS.   (chmn/p)
  0113-295 6949
  Chmn: Tony Hodgson
- ○ *S; organisation of motorcycle & three-wheeler standing-start quarter-mile sprints (& record attempts) in a straight line, not circuits
- < Auto-Cycle U

National Stallion Association   (NaStA) 1981
- ■ Godlington Farm, Godlington, BICESTER, Oxon, OX27 9AF.
  01869 277562   fax 01869 277762
  email info@nationalstallion.org.uk
  http://www.nasta.fsnet.co.uk
  Sec: Roger Truelove
- ○ *V
- M 9 org

National Stoolball Association
  since 28 September 2008 **Stoolball England**

National Street Rod Association
- ■ c/o Mick Harle, H & B Motor Engineers Ltd, King St, LONDON, N2 8DL.   (chmn/b)
  020 8444 8615
  Chmn: Mick Harle
- ○ *G
- M 2,000 i

National Street Van Association   (NSVA) 1974
- NR 84 Melthorne Drive, RUISLIP, Middx, HA4 0TR.   (mem/sp)
  020 8582 0877
  http://www.nsva.co.uk
  Mem Sec: George Meacher
- ○ *G; for owners of vans

National Sugar Art Association
- ■ 24 Oaklands Avem WEST WICKHAM, Kent, BR4 9LF.
  020 8777 4445
  Chmn: Sheila Tasker
- ○ *A

National Sweet Pea Society   (NSPS)   1900
- 8 Wolseley Rd, Parkstone, POOLE, Dorset, BH12 2DP.   (hsp)
  01202 734088
  email bg.bulstrode@btinternet.com
  http://www.sweetpeas.org.uk
  Hon Sec: Janet Bulstrode
▲ Registered Charity
○ *H; to promote the growing of the sweet pea & to further its development
● Conf - Exhib - Comp
< R Horticl Soc
M 1,100 i, 10 f, 300 affiliated socs, UK / 50 i, o'seas
¶ NSPS Annual.   Bulletin (Spring & Autumn) - 2.
  Schedule of Exhibitions - 1.   Judges' Rules.
  Enjoy Sweet Peas.

National Taxi Association   (NTA)   1960
NR 60 Chesterholm, CARLISLE, Cumbria, CA2 7XX.   (hsb)
  01228 598740
  email secretary@national-taxi-association.co.uk
  Admin Officer: Wayne Casey
▲ Company Limited by Guarantee
○ *N, *P, *T; the Hackney carriage trade
● Conf - Mtgs - Exhib - LG
M c 70 trade org

National Tenant Voice   2009
NR Hays Executive, 1 Southampton St, LONDON, WC2R 0LR.
  (hq)
  020 7520 5973
  email david.cairncross@hays.com
  Contacts: David Cairncross,   Andre Timlin
○ *K; to give social housing tenants in England a voice so that they might better influence national policies & practices that affect their lives

National Tortoise Club of Great Britain   1975
- 2 Laith Close, Cookridge, LEEDS, W Yorks, LS16 6LE.
  (chief/exec/p)
  0113-267 7587
  Chief Exec: Mrs B Waller
Br worldwide
○ *B, *G; exchange of information on all aspects of tortoise keeping & breeding (incl the American Box, Greek & all Mediterranean & other species)
● Mtgs - ET - Helpline - Inf - SG - Talks - Box Tortoise (help & advice) - Speaker available for talks incl radio & TV
M i (numbers expanding)
¶ Care sheets & data; prices on application.   [NL under review].
  Note: this is a voluntary body run by experts, all enquiries must be accompanied by a pre-paid envelope &/or donation.
  NO visits at address - mail & phone calls ONLY

National Traction Engine Trust   1954
- South View, Hutton Roof, CARNFORTH, Lancs, LA6 2PF.   (hsp)
  01524 271584
  email ntet@ntet.co.uk   http://www.ntet.co.uk
  Gen Sec: Mrs Jenny Holt
▲ Registered Charity
○ *G; preservation, restoration & maintenance of steam driven traction engines & steam driven road vehicles; training in operation & maintenance of steam driven vehicles
● Conf - Mtgs - Res - Exhib - Comp - Inf - VE
< Fedn of Brit Historic Vehicle Clubs
M 3,100 i, 60 affiliated gps
¶ Steaming - 4; ftm, £22 nm.
  Code of Practice for the better organisation of Traction Engine rallies, incorporating the Rally Authorisation Scheme.
  Code of Practice for Traction Engines & Similar Vehicles.

National Trailer & Towing Association Ltd   (NTTA)   1976
- Plestowes Barnes, Hareway Lane, BARFORD, Warks, CV35 8DD.
  01926 335445   fax 01926 335445
  email info@ntta.co.uk   http://www.ntta.co.uk
  Exec Admin: David Millington
▲ Company Limited by Guarantee
○ *T; to represent the trailer & towbar industries on British, European & Industrial Standards Committees
Gp Training courses; NVQ qualifications; Consultancy; Expert witness; Inspection & report
● Conf - Mtgs - ET - Exhib - Inf - LG
< BSI; ISO; SMMT
M 170 f, 2 org
¶ NTTA News - 4; ftm only.

National Trainers Federation   (NTF)   1975
NR 9 High St, Lambourn, HUNGERFORD, Berks, RG17 8XN.   (hq)
  01488 71719   fax 01488 73005
  email info@racehorsetrainers.org
  http://www.racehorsetrainers.org
  Chief Exec: Rupert Arnold
○ *T; to promote the interests of racehorse trainers within the racing industry
M c 550 i

National TravelWise Association
  merged in 2008 with the Association for Commuter Transport to form
  ACT TravelWise

National Trolleybus Association   (NTA)   1963
NR 559 Reading Rd, Winnersh, WOKINGHAM, Berks, RG41 5HQ.   (chmn/p)
  0118-978 1821
  http://www.trolleybus.co.uk/nta/
  Chmn: Robin Helliar-Symons
▲ Company Linited by Guarantee; Registered Charity
○ *G; to promote the recording & study of trolleybus operations in the UK & throughout the world & the preservation of historic vehicles
● Mtgs
< Assn of Indep Museums; Transport Trust
M 500 i
¶ Trolleybus Magazine - 6; ftm,££22 nm.

National Trust for Ireland   (An Taisce)   1948
IRL Tailor's Hall, Back Lane, DUBLIN 8, Republic of Ireland.
  353 (1) 454 1786   fax 353 (1) 453 3255
  email info@antaisce.org   http://www.antaisce.org
○ *G

National Trust for Places of Historic Interest or Natural Beauty   1895
NR Heelis, Kemble Drive, SWINDON, Wilts, SN2 2NA.   (hq)
  01793 817400   fax 01793 817401
  email enquiries@thenationaltrust.org.uk
  http://www.nationaltrust.org.uk
  32 Queen Anne's Gate, LONDON, SW1H 9AB.
  Dir-Gen: Dame Fiona Reynolds
▲ Registered Charity
○ *G; to preserve places of historic interest or natural beauty permanently for the nation to enjoy; as a charity independent of government, the Trust cares for more than 350 houses, gardens, woodlands, monuments, nature reserves & parks, totalling 630,000 acres of land, much of it of outstanding natural beauty, & including 709 miles of coastline
< Intl Nat Trusts Org (INTO); Access to Farms Partnership
M 3,800,000 i

© CBD Research Ltd · Beckenham · BR3 5JS · Tel 020 8650 7745 · E-mail cbd@cbdresearch.com · www.cbdresearch.com

National Trust for Scotland for Places of Historic Interest or Natural Beauty   (NTS)   1931
NR   Hermiston Quay, 5 Cultins Rd, EDINBURGH, EH11 4DF.   (hq)
0844 493 2100   fax 0844 493 2102
email information@nts.org.uk   http://www.nts.org.uk
Chief Exec: Kate Mavor
▲   Registered Charity
○   *G; to protect & promote Scotland's national & cultural heritage
for present & future generations to enjoy
●   Care of properties & opening them to the public - Inf (on
matters relating to the Trust only) - VE
<   Europa Nostra
M   308,000 i
¶   Jnl - 4;   Ybk - 1; both ftm only.

National Tyre Distributors Association   (NTDA)   1930
NR   8 Temple Square, AYLESBURY, Bucks, HP20 2QH.   (hq)
0870 900 0600   fax 0870 900 0610
email mail@ntda.co.uk   http://www.ntda.co.uk
Dir: Richard Edy
○   *T; for companies in the tyre specialist & fast fit trade
Gp   Divisions: Training services; Technical services;
Specialist c'ees: Tyre Wholesalers Group; Approved tyre
repairers
●   Conf - Mtgs - ET - Exhib - Comp - Stat - Inf - LG
<   BIPAVER
M   450 f, UK / 1 f, o'seas
¶   NTDA News - 12;   AR; both ftm only.
Directory of Members & Ybk - 1; ftm, £25 nm.

National Union of Journalists   (NUJ)   1907
NR   Headland House, 308-312 Gray's Inn Rd, LONDON,
WC1X 8DP.   (hq)
020 7843 3705   fax 020 7837 8143
email info@nuj.org.uk   http://www.nuj.org.uk
Gen Sec: Michelle Stanistreet
○   *U; for staffers & freelances, writers & reporters, editors & sub-
editors, photographers & illustrators, working in
broadcasting, newspapers, magazines, books, public
relations & a variety of new media
<   Creators' Rights Alliance
M   29,930 i

National Union of Rail, Maritime & Transport Workers   (RMT)
NR   Unity House, 39 Chalton St, LONDON, NW1 1JD.
020 7387 4771   fax 020 7387 4123
email info@rmt.org.uk   http://www.rmt.org.uk
Gen Sec: Bob Crow
○   *U; represents almost every sector of the transport industry,
from maritime & underground rail to shipping & offshore,
buses & road freight
<   Trades U Congress (TUC)
M   79,499 i

National Union of Residents' Associations   (NURA)   1921
■   20 Park Drive, ROMFORD, Essex, RM1 4LH.   (chmn/p)
01708 749119   fax 01708 736213
Chmn: Ian Wilkes
○   *K
●   Mtgs - LG
M   c150 org
¶   NURA NL - irreg; ftm.
Simple Guide to Planning Applications; £5.25.

National Union of Students   (NUS)   1922
NR   184-192 Drummond St (4th floor), LONDON, NW1 3HP.   (hq)
0845 521 0262
email nusuk@nus.org.uk   http://www.nus.org.uk
Chief Exec: Matt Hyde
▲   Un-incorporated Society
Br   4
○   *U; to promote, defend & extend the rights of students & to
develop & champion strong students' unions
Gp   Business services; Campaigns & strategy; Communications;
Membership
●   Conf - Res - Inf - LG - Campaigns
M   5,000,000 i in 700+ student unions

National Union of Teachers   (NUT)   1870
NR   Hamilton House, Mabledon Place, LONDON, WC1H 9BD.
(hq)
020 7388 6191   fax 020 7387 8458
email enquiries@nut.org.uk
http://www.teachers.org.uk
Gen Sec: Christine Blower
▲   Un-incorporated Society
○   *U; to promote state education & protect & improve the
salaries, working conditions & status of the teaching
profession in England & Wales
●   Conf - ET - Res - Exhib - Inf - Empl - LG
<   Educ Intl; Trades U Congress (TUC)
M   295,124 i
¶   NUT News - 8.

National Vegetable Society   (NVS)   1960
NR   36 The Ridings, Ockbrook, DERBY, DE72 3SF.   (nat sec/p)
07778 622628
http://www.nvsuk.org.uk
Nat Sec: D V Thornton
Br   5
○   *H; to advance the education of the public in the cultivation &
improvement of vegetables
●   Mtgs - Exam - Exhib - Comp - Inf - Lib - Displays at shows
<   R Horticl Soc
M   2,500 i
¶   Bulletin - 4;   Directory - 1;   AR; all ftm.
Growing leaflets (13); 40p each m.
Judges Guide; £3.50 m.

National Vintage Tractor & Engine Club   (NVTEC)   1965
■   Eastfields, North Wheatley, RETFORD, Notts, DN22 9BK.   (hsp)
01427 880238
email p.scarborough@lineone.net
http://www.nvtec.co.uk
Sec: Pat Scarborough
▲   Un-incorporated Society
Br   33; France, Germany, Norway, USA
○   *G; study & preservation of agricultural tractors, machines &
implements & all associated equipment
●   Cobnf - Mtgs - ET - Exhib - Comp - Inf - VE - LG
<   Soc Ploughmen; Traction Engine Trust; Nat Farmers' U
M   61000 i
¶   Vaporising - 4; ftm only.

National Voices   1989
■   202 Hatton Square, 16 Baldwins Gardens, LONDON,
EC1N 7RJ.   (hq)
020 7813 3637   fax 020 7405 5300
http://www.nationalvoices.org.uk
▲   Company Limited by Guarantee; Registered Charity
○   *N, W; 'an umbrella body working with member organisations
towards better lives for people with long-term health
conditions; it aims to gain recognition of people's needs &
ensure resources are available to meet them'
●   Conf - Mtgs - ET - Res - LG
M   110 org
×   2009 Long-term Conditions Alliance
2007 Long-term Medical Conditions Alliance

National Women's Register (NWR) 1960
- ■ Unit 23 Vulcan House, Vulcan Road North, NORWICH, Norfolk, NR6 6AQ. (hq)
  01603 406767 fax 01603 407003
  email office@nwr.org http://www.nwr.org
  Admins: Angela Norman & Samantha Bushell
- ▲ Company Limited by Guarantee; Registered Charity
- Br c 450; Australia, Belgium, South Africa, Zimbabwe
- ○ *G; for women of all ages who wish to participate in wide-ranging discussions leading to friendship & other activities
- Gp Correspondence magazine; Penfriends; House exchange; Research bank; Postal Book
- ● Conf - Mtgs - ET - Res - Exhib - Comp
- M c 7,500 i
- ¶ Register - 2; ftm only.

National Wool Textile Export Corporation
closed 2010

National Workboat Associaton (NWA) 1994
- NR 21 Southcote Close, Bacchus Lane, South Cave, BROUGH, E Yorks, HU15 2BQ. (sp)
  01430 470013
  email secretary@workboatassociation.org
  Sec: Mark Ranson
- ○ *T; for owners, charterers & builders of workboats
- ● Mtgs - LG
- M c 19 f

National Youth Choirs of Great Britain (NYCGB) 1979
- NR Pelaw House, University of Durham, Leazes Rd, DURHAM, DH1 1TA. (sb)
  0191-334 8110 (weekdays 0900-1700)
  email office@nycgb.net
  Hon Sec: Carl Browning
- ▲ Registered Charity
- ○ *D
- ● Mtgs - ET - Exam - VE - Concerts
- M i

National Youth Council of Ireland (NYCI) 1967
- IRL 3 Montague St, DUBLIN 2, Republic of Ireland.
  353 (1) 478 4122 fax 353 (1) 478 3974
  email info@nyci.ie http://www.youth.ie
  Dir: Mary Cunningham
- ○ *Y; to represent & support the interests of voluntary youth organisations
- M c 40 orgs

National Youth Federation
- IRL 20 Lower Dominick St, DUBLIN 1, Republic of Ireland.
  353 (1) 872 9933 fax 353 (1) 872 4183
  email info@nyf.ie http://www.youthworkireland.ie
  Chief Exec: Diarmuid Kearney
- ○ *Y
  Note: Trades as Youth Work Ireland

Nationwide Association of Security Installation Companies (NASIC) 1995
- NR 329-333 Hale Rd, Hale Barns, ALTRINCHAM, Cheshire, WA15 8SS. (hq)
  0870 444 2055
  http://www.nasic.co.uk
- ▲ Private Limited Company with Share Capital
- ○ *T; a national network of independent security installation companies
- ● Mtgs
- M 38 f

Nationwide Caterers Association Ltd (NCASS) 1987
- ■ Association House, 89 Mappleborough Rd, Shirley, SOLIHULL, W Midlands, B90 1AG. (hq)
  0121-603 2524 fax 0121-474 3938
  email enq@ncass.org.uk http://www.ncass.org.uk
  Managing Dir: Bob Fox
- ▲ Company Limited by Guarantee
- ○ *T; for caterers & suppliers - mobile caterers, static caterers (sandwich bars, takeaways) & suppliers to the trade
- Gp Technical c'ee
- ● Conf - Exam - State - LG
- M 600 i, 100 f
  (Sub: £199 caterers, £480 suppliers)
- ¶ NL - 4; free.
  Profitable Mobile Catering - 1; £20.
  The Events Directory - 1; £20 m, £40 nm.
  Annual Industry Guide - 1; £20.

Natural Gas Vehicle Association (NGVA) 1992
- ■ Gould's House, HORSINGTON, Somerset, BA8 0EW. (hq)
  01963 371007 fax 01963 371300
  Contact: Christopher Maltin
- ▲ Company Limited by Guarantee
- Br Brussels
- ○ *T; to stimulate the use of natural gas & biomethane as vehicle fuels
- Gp C'ees: Government relations, Marketing, Technical
- ● Conf - Mtgs - ET - Res - Expt - Inf
- < Intl Natural Gas Vehicle Assn; Eur Natural Gas Vehicle Assn; Japan & USA Gas Vehicle Assn
- M 30 f
- ¶ NGV News - 4.

Natural History Society of Northumbria (NHSN) 1829
- ■ Great North Museum: Hancock, Barras Bridge, NEWCASTLE upon TYNE, NE2 4PT. (hq)
  0191-232 6386 fax 0191-232 2177
  email nhsn@ncl.ac.uk http://www.nhsn.ncl.ac.uk
  Dir: James Littlewood
- ▲ Registered Charity
- ○ *L; to encourage the study of natural history in all its branches; to protect the natural environment & local flora & fauna
- Gp Natural history library & archives
- ● Mtgs - Res - Lib (open for public access) - VE - LG - Field mtgs - Lectures
- M 900 i, UK / 4 i, o'seas
- ¶ Bulletin - 3. Transactions - 3 (2-yrly); AR; all ftm.

NAtural Materials Association
a group of the **Institute of Materials, Minerals & Mining**

Natural Physique Association (NPA) 2001
- NR 76A Station Rd, HOLMFIRTH, W Yorks, HD9 1AE. (mem/sp)
  01484 683685
  Mem Sec: Michael Phillips
- ○ *G, *S; promotion of the sport of bodybuilding
- ● Comp

Natural Sausage Casings Association (NSCA) 1953
- NR Wychwood Cottage, 38 High St, RISELEY, Beds, MK44 1DX. (asa)
  01234 709022 fax 01234 709749
  Sec: Digby Morgan-Jones
- ○ *T; for those involved in the natural casings industry in the UK; to cooperate with any other organisation worldwide with similar objectives
- ● Mtgs - LG - Statistical information for members
- < Eur Natural Casings Assn
- M 13 f + 1f (Eire)

© CBD Research Ltd · Beckenham · BR3 5JS · Tel 020 8650 7745 · E-mail cbd@cbdresearch.com · www.cbdresearch.com

Natural Sciences Collections Association (NatSCA) 2003

- ■ Dept of Entomology, The Natural History Museum, Cromwell Rd, LONDON, SW7 5BD. (chmn/b)
  020 7942 5196
  email p.brown@nhm.ac.uk   http://www.natsca.info
  Chmn: Paul A Brown
- ▲ Registered Charity
- ○ *N, *P; to represent natural science collections (particularly biological collections) & associated museum staff
- ● Conf - Mtgs - ET - VE - LG
- < Inst of Consvn (UK); Nat Biodiversity Network
- > Geology Curators Gp
- M c 200 i, c 50 org
  (Sub: £15 i, £30 org)
- ¶ NatSCA News - 4; ftm, £5 nm.

Nature in Art Trust 1982

- ■ Wallsworth Hall, Twigworth, GLOUCESTER, GL2 9PA. (hq)
  01452 731422   fax 01452 730937
  email enquiries@nature-in-art.org.uk
  http://www.nature-in-art.org.uk
  Dir: Simon Trapnell
- ▲ Company Limited by Guarantee; Registered Charity
- ○ *A; to collect & display fine, decorative & applied art inspired by nature in all media & from any period or culture; to provide learning opportunities for young people & adults
- ● Conf - Mtgs - ET - Exhib - Comp - SG - Inf - Lib - VE
- < Accredited by Museums, Libraries & Archives Council
- M c 1,200 i
- ¶ Nature in Art - 4; ftm.

Nautical Archaeology Society (NAS) 1972

- ■ Fort Cumberland, Fort Cumberland Rd, PORTSMOUTH, Hants, PO4 9LD. (hq)
  023 9281 8419   fax 023 9281 8419
  email nas@nasportsmouth.org.uk
  http://www.nasportsmouth.org.uk
  Chmn: George Lambrick
- ▲ Registered Charity
- Br 7; 20 countries
- ○ *G, *L, *Q; to further research into all aspects of nautical & maritime archaeology; to bring together all people interested in our maritime heritage
- Gp Ancient technologists; Archaeologists; Avocationals; Conservators; Historians; Naval architects; Researchers; Sports divers; Students
- ● Conf - Mtgs - ET - Res - Exhib - Comp - Inf - Lib - VE - LG
- < Inst of Naval Archaeology (INA)
- > The Dive Connection (TDC)
- M 500 i, 50 f, UK / 300 i, 25 f, o'seas
- ¶ International Jnl of Nautical Archaeology - 2; ftm.
  Nautical Archaeology NL - 4; ftm.   NAS Monograph series.

Nautical Heritage Association (NHA)

- ■ c/o The Secretary, PO Box 212, HASTINGS, E Sussex, TN35 5WT. (hsp)
  01424 200958
  http://www.nautical-heritage.org.uk
  Hon Sec: Angela Renno
- ▲ Registered Charity
- ○ *G, *L; to support, enhance & promote the work of the Nautical Museums Trust & the Shipwreck & Coastal Heritage Centre
- ● Res - Exhib - Restoration - Talks
- M 120 i

Nautical Institute (NI) 1972

- NR 202 Lambeth Rd, LONDON, SE1 7LQ. (hq)
  020 7928 1351   fax 020 7401 2817
  email sec@nautinst.org   http://www.nautinst.org
  Chief Exec: C P Wake
- ▲ Company Limited by Guarantee; Registered Charity
- Br 40 worldwide
- ○ *P; to promote a high standard of knowledge among those in control of sea-going vessels including non-displacement craft. Is open to all qualified mariners
- ● Conf - ET - Inf - Lib
- < Sea Vision UK; UK Maritime Forum
- M 6,500 i in 110 countries
- ¶ Publications list available.

Nautilus UK

in 2009 merged with Nautilus NL to form Nautilus International, & is therefore outside the scope of this directory

Naval Dockyards Society 1996

- NR School of Civil Engineering & Surveying, Portland Building, Portland St, PORTSMOUTH, Hants, PO1 3AH. (hsb)
  email ann.coats@port.ac.uk
  http://www.navaldockyards.moonfruit.com
  Sec: Dr Ann Coats
- ○ *G; to increase public awareness of & access to historic dockyards & related sites
- ● Conf - Mtgs - VE
- M 200 i
- ¶ NL - 2

Naval Historical Collectors & Research Association (NHCRA) 1988

- ■ 9 Lyngate Gardens, Lyngate Rd, NORTH WALSHAM, Norfolk, NR28 0NE. (mem/sp)
  email wilkinsonA44@hotmail.com
  http://www.nhcra-online.org
  Mem Sec: Anthony C Wilkinson
- ▲ Un-incorporated Society
- ○ *G; collecting naval medals & memorabilia; research into naval battles, ships & personnel
- ● Scientific, systematic research - PL
- M 400 i, 5 f, 12 org, UK / 40 i, o'seas
- ¶ The Review (Jnl) - 4; ftm, £15 nm (£17 EU) (£20 o'seas) or £3.50 each.
  Note: the association is a non-profit-making body in support of worthy naval causes & charities

Navy Records Society (NRS) 1893

- ■ c/o Pangbourne College, PANGBOURNE, Berks, RG8 8LA. (hsb)
  http://www.navyrecordssociety.com
  Hon Sec: R H A Brodhurst
- ▲ Registered Charity
- ○ *L; editing & publishing manuscripts & rare works illustrating the history, administration, organisation or social life of the Navy
- ● Publishing
- M c 650 i, c 150 org
- ¶ NL - 1;   AR - 1.   1 or 2 volumes each year.

Needleloom Underlay Manufacturers' Association (NUMA) 1957

- NR 269 Walmersley Rd, BURY, Lancs, BL9 6NX. (hq)
  0161-761 5231   fax 0161-761 3001
  email numa@felt-underlay.com
  http://www.numa-online.co.uk
  Chmn: Tim Cormack
- ▲ Un-incorporated Society
- ○ *T; to promote the benefits of felt underlay, allowing consumers to make a better informed choice when selecting a carpet & underlay combination
- ● Conf - Mtgs - Inf
- < BSI
- M 5 f

Neil Munro Society   1996

NR   4 Randolph Rd, GLASGOW, G11 7LG.   (chmn/p)
     0141-339 5452
     email ronnierenton@googlemail.com
     http://www.neilmunro.co.uk
     Chmn: Ronnie Renton
▲   Un-incorporated Society
○   *A; to promote interest in the life & works of Neil Munro (1863-
     1930) Scottish novelist, journalist & poet
●   Conf - Mtgs - Res - Exhib - Comp - Lib - VE
<   Alliance Literary Socs
M   160 i, 2 f, UK / 15 i, o'seas
¶   Paragraphs (NL) - 2; ftm only.

Nelson Society   1981

NR   87 Bromyard Rd, Sparkhill, BIRMINGHAM, W Midlands,
     B11 3AY.   (mem/sec)
     0121-624 6770
     Mem Sec: Phyll Proctor
▲   Registered Charity
Br   6
○   *G; to promote interest in, & appreciation of, the outstanding
     qualities of leadership & patriotism displayed by Admiral
     Lord Nelson
●   Conf - Mtgs - Res - Exhib - Lib - VE
M   c 1,000 i
¶   The Nelson Dispatch - 4.

Neonatal Society   (NNS)   1959

NR   c/o Dr Anoo Jain, Peter Dunn Intensive Care Nursery,
     St Michael's Hospital, Southwell St, BRISTOL, BS2 8EG.   (hsb)
     0117-928 5062
     Sec: Dr Anoo Jain
○   *Q; 'a research society with members from clinical & basic
     science disciplines relating to perinatology'
●   Conf - Mtgs - Res - Exhib
M   c 280 i, UK / c 90 i, o'seas
¶   NL - 3.   Hbk.

Nerine & Amaryllid Society   (NAAS)   1997

■   9 London Rd, Bozeat, WELLINGBOROUGH, Northants,
     NN29 7LZ.   (hsp)
     email mike.garrett@tesco.net   http://www.nerine.org.uk
     Sec: Dr Roger D Beauchamp
▲   Un-incorporated Society
○   *H; for the general study & promotion of interest in, the plant
     family Amaryllidaceae
●   Exhib - Inf - is the International Cultivar Registration
     Authority (ICRA) for Nerine
<   R Horticl Soc
     is an Agency of the Intl Soc for Horticl Science (ISHS)
M   c 130 i, UK / c 5 i, o'seas
¶   Amaryllids - 3;   LM - 1;   AR; all ftm only.

Netball Northern Ireland   (NINA)   1951

■   City of Lisburn Racquets Club, 36 Belfast Rd, LISBURN,
     Co Antrim, BT27 4AS.   (hq)
     07845 875802   fax 028 9266 8215
     email mckeown_392@hotmail.com
     http://www.netballnorthernireland.org
     Hon Sec: Louise McKeown
○   *S; to develop netball in NI
<   Intl Fedn Netball Assns (IFNA); Fedn Eur Netball Assns (FENA)
>   NI Clubs Netball Assn (NICNA); NI Schools Netball
     Assn (NISNA)
M   c 1,500 i, 30 clubs

Netball Scotland   1946

NR   Central Chambers (suite 196), 93 Hope St, GLASGOW,
     G2 6LD.   (hq)
     0141-572 0114   fax 0141-248 5566
     http://www.netballscotland.com
▲   Un-incorporated Society
○   *S; promotion & playing of netball in Scotland
M   c 2,000 i & org

Netherlands British Chamber of Commerce   1891

■   Imperial House, 15-19 Kingsway, LONDON, WC2B 6UN.
     (hq)
     020 7539 7960   fax 020 7836 6988
     email info@nbcc.co.uk   http://www.nbcc.co.uk
     Dir: Michiel van Deursen
Br   2; Netherlands
○   *C
●   Conf - Mtgs - Res - Exhib - Expt - Inf - VE
M   200 i, UK / 200 i, o'seas
¶   In Touch - 4; ftm.   Ybk; ftm.
     Other publications & directories.

**Network for Alternative Technology & Technology Assessment
(NATTA)   1976**

■   c/o EERU, Faculty of Technology, Open University, Walton Hall,
     MILTON KEYNES, Bucks, MK7 6AA.   (hq)
     01908 654638 (24-hr answering machine)
     fax 01908 654052
     email s.j.dougan@open.ac.uk
     http://www.eeru.open.ac.uk/natta/rol.html
     Coordinator: Ms Tam Dougan,
     Editor: Prof David Elliott
▲   Un-incorporated Society
○   *E; renewable energy (water, solar, wind power) & related
     energy issues
●   Conf - ET
M   500 i
¶   Renew (NL) - 6; prices vary.
     Renewables, Past, Present & Future: a review of government
     policy & the development of the UK Renewable Energy
     Programme 1994-97 by Dave Elliott; £10.
     Various other publications.

**Network of Government Library & Information Specialists
(NGLIS)   1925**

■   c/o Kate Pritchard, Defra, Ergon House, 17 Smith Square,
     LONDON, SW1P 3JR.   (sb)
     email k.pritchard@defra.gsi.gov.uk
     http://www.nglis.org.uk
     Sec: Kate Pritchard
▲   Un-incorporated Society
○   *P; to promote networking with colleagues working in the
     information sector
●   Conf - Mtgs - ET - Inf - VE
<   C'ee of Departmental Librarians (CDL); Govt Libaries & Inf
     Gp (GLIG)
M   494 i
¶   The Network (Jnl) - 2; ftm.

Network of Independent Forensic Accountants   (NIFA)   1999

■   4 Pavilion Court, 600 Pavilion Drive, Northampton Business
     Park, NORTHAMPTON, NN4 7SL.   (sb)
     0845 609 6091   fax 01604 662681
     email nifa@nifa.co.uk   http://www.nifa.co.uk
     Sec: Clive Adkins
▲   Company Limited by Guarantee
○   *P, *T; to provide accounting & litigation support
●   Conf
M   15 i, 15 f
¶   NIFA News - 4; free.

**Neuroanaesthesia Society of Great Britain & Ireland
(NASGBI)   1965**

NR   21 Portland Place, LONDON, W1B 1PY.   (mail/add)
     email info@nasgbi.org.uk
     Sec: Dr Nigel Huggins
▲   Registered Charity
○   *P
M   i

© CBD Research Ltd · Beckenham · BR3 5JS · Tel 020 8650 7745 · E-mail cbd@cbdresearch.com · www.cbdresearch.com

Neuroblastoma Society   1982
NR   53 Kennington Rd, Kennington, OXFORD, Oxon, OX1 5PB.
     (sp)
     0777 199 7277
     email secretary@neuroblastoma.org.uk
     http://www.nsoc.co.uk
     Hon Sec: Mrs Yvonne Boyd
     Chmn: Stephen Smith (01904 633744)
▲   Registered Charity
○   *K, *W; to raise funds for UK based research into
     neuroblastoma (a children's cancer); to offer support for
     families affected by neuroblastoma
●   Res - SG - Social fundraising events
     Helpline: 020 8940 4353
M   c 350-400 i
¶   Neuroblastoma News - 4.
     Neuroblastoma - a booklet for parents - every 3-4 years.

Neurofibromatosis Association   1981
NR   Quayside House, 38 High St, KINGSTON upon THAMES,
     Surrey, KT1 1HL.   (hq)
     020 8439 1234
▲   Registered Charity
○   *W; a self-help group providing advice & information; to
     establish & maintain a network of family support workers; to
     sponsor research through fund raising
M   i
¶   Factsheets & videos.   Publications list available.

Neurological Alliance   1994
■   Dana Centre, 165 Queen's Gate, LONDON, SW7 5HE.   (hq)
     020 7584 6457
     email admin@neural.org.uk
     Chief Execs: Katie Smith, Claire Moonan
▲   Company Limited by Guarantee; Registered Charity
○   *N, *W; unites charities working to raise the profile of
     conditions & needs of people with neurological conditions &
     their carers; to raise the standards of care & improve lives
●   Conf - Mtgs - LG - Lobbying/campaigning
M   c 60 org
¶   Publications list available.

Neutral Alcohol Producers Association
     since 1 January 2008 **National Alcohol Producers Association**

New Baxter Society
NR   c/o Reading Museum & Art Gallery, Blagrave St, READING,
     Berks, RG1 1QH.
     http://www.newbaxtersociety.org
○   *G; to promote interest in George Baxter (1804-1867) colour
     picture printer, his licensees & nineteenth century colour
     printing century colour printing

**New Canterbury Literary Society - Richard Aldington Society
(NCLS)   1973**
NR   2B Bedford Rd, ST IVES, Cornwall, TR26 1SB.   (hsp)
     http://www.imagists.org
     Editor: David Wilkinson
○   *A; to promote interest in the life & writings of the author
     Richard Aldington (1892-1962)

New English Art Club
     a member of the **Federation of British Artists**

New Forest Agricultural Show Society   1920
NR   The Showground, New Park, BROCKENHURST, Hants,
     SO42 7QH.   (hq)
     01590 622400   fax 01590 622637
     email info@newforestshow.co.uk
     http://www.newforestshow.co.uk
     Contact: Denis Dooley
▲   Company Limited by Guarantee; Registered Charity
○   *F, *H; to promote & encourage the development of agriculture,
     forestry, equestrianism & horticulture... & to encourage the
     breeding of stock
●   New Forest & Hampshire County Show
<   Assn of Show & Agricl Orgs

New Forest Pony Breeding & Cattle Society   (NFPB&CS)   1891
NR   Deepslade House, Ringwood Rd, BRANSGORE, Hants,
     BH23 8AA.   (hsp)
     01425 672775
     http://www.newforestpony.com
     Sec: Jane Murray
▲   Company Limited by Guarantee; Registered Charity
○   *B
●   Mtgs - Exhib - Comp - Expt
<   Stud Book Societies in: Australia, Belgium, Denmark, Finland,
     France, Germany, Holland, Norway, Sweden, USA
M   c 1,400 i
¶   Stud Book - 1.   Leaflets.   AR.
     Celebration of New Forest Ponies.

New Producers Alliance
closed 2010

New Schools Network   (NSN)   2009
§   89 Buckingham Palace RD, LONDON, SW1W 0QL.   (hq)
     020 7537 9208
     http://www.newschoolsnetwork.org
     Dir: Rachel Woolf
     Offers help & advice in setting-up an independent, innovative
     school within the state sector, particularly in the most
     deprived areas.

New Under Ten Fishermen's Association Ltd   (NUTFA)   2008
NR   42 Julian Rd, IVYBRIDGE, Devon, PL21 9BU.   (regd off)
     01752 893628
     email info@nutfa.org   http://www.nutfa.org
▲   Company Limited by Guarantee
○   *T; to support the under 10 metre & non sector fishing industry
●   Mtgs
M   300+ i

Newark & Nottinghamshire Agricultural Society   1799
■   The Showground, Lincoln Rd, Winthorpe, NEWARK, Notts,
     NG24 2NY.   (hq)
     01636 705796   fax 01636 675151
     email info@newarkshowground.com
     http://www.newarkshowground.com
     Chief Exec: Adrian Johnston
▲   Company Limited by Guarantee; Registered Charity
○   *F; to promote agriculture through the County Show, held
     annually on the 2nd weekend of May
●   Annual show - Hire of venue, halls & catering business
<   Assn of Show & Agricl Orgs; Nat Outdoor Events Assn;
     Derbyshire & Nottinghamshire Cham Comm
M   500 i, 40 f, 40 org
¶   NL - 2; free.   AR - 1; ftm only.

Newbury & District Agricultural Society   1909
NR   Newbury Showground, Priors Court, Hermitage, THATCHAM,
      Berks, RG18 9QZ.
      01635 247111   fax 01635 247227
      email office@newburyshowground.co.uk
      http://www.newburyshowground.co.uk
      Gen Mgr: Rebecca Elvin
▲   Registered Charity
○   *F; to promote agriculture, horticulture, forestry & rural crafts &
      skills
●   Royal County of Berkshire Show
<   Assn of Show & Agricl Orgs

**Newcomen Society for the Study of the History of Engineering &
Technology   (The Newcomen Society)   1920**
NR   Science Museum, LONDON, SW7 2DD.   (hq)
      020 7371 4445   fax 020 7371 4445
      email office@newcomen.com
      http://www.newcomen.com
      Exec Sec: R M Swann
○   *L; the study of the history of engineering & technology

Newman Association   1942
NR   20-22 Bedford Row, LONDON, WC1R 4JS.   (regd/office)
      email secretary@newman.org.uk
      http://www.newman.org.uk
      Contact: The Secretary
▲   Company Limited by Guarantee; Registered Charity
Br   20
○   *E, *R; educational & religious organisation
●   Conf - Mtgs
<   Pax Romana
M   830 i
¶   The Newman - 3; ftm, £1 nm.

*Newport & Gwent Chamber of Commerce, Enterprise & Industry
since October 2008 **South Wales Chamber of Commerce***

Newspaper Conference   1920
■   St Andrew's House, 18-20 St Andrew St, LONDON,
      EC4A 3AY.   (hq)
      020 7632 7400   fax 020 7632 7401
      http://www.newspapersoc.org.uk
      Sec: Paul Sinker
○   *P; comprises London editors & political correspondents of
      regional newspapers in membership of the Newspaper
      Society; meets 3 or 4 times a year with senior politicians
●   Conf - Mtgs
M   23 i

Newspaper Publishers Association Ltd   (NPA)   1906
■   St Andrew's House (8th floor), 18-20 St Andrew St, LONDON,
      EC4A 3AY.   (hq)
      020 7632 7430   fax 020 7632 7431
      Dir: David Newell
▲   Company Limited by Guarantee
○   *T; for British national newspaper publishers
M   f

Newspaper Society   1836
■   St Andrew's House, 18-20 St Andrew St, LONDON,
      EC4A 3AY.   (hq)
      020 7632 7400   fax 020 7632 7401
      email ns@newspapersoc.org.uk
      http://www.newspapersoc.org.uk
      Dir: David Newell
▲   Un-incorporated Society
○   *P, *T; 'the voice of Britain's regional press; to represent &
      promote the interests of over 1,300 local & regional titles'
Gp   Political, Editorial & Regulatory Affairs (PERA); Marketing;
      Communications; Finance & administration
●   Conf - Mtgs - ET - Res - Exhib - SG - Stat - Inf - LG - Legal
      advice - Issuing of press ID cards - Press/Rota passes
<   Wld Assn Newspapers (WAN); Eur Newspaper Publishers Assn
      (ENPA); Advertising Assn (AA); Newspaper Conf; Young
      Newspaper Executives Assn (YNEA)
M   f
¶   NS News (NL) - 52.   Commercial Update - 4.
      Production Jnl - 12.   Headlines - 6.
      Both above available by annual subscription.

Newstead Abbey Byron Society
NR   Acushla, Halam Rd, SOUTHWELL, Notts, NG25 0AD.
      (chmn/p)
      01636 813818
      Chmn: P K Purslow
○   *G; for all interested in the life & works of the poet Lord
      George Gordon Byron (1788-1824)
<   Mtgs - VE

NFU Scotland   (NFUS)   1913
■   Rural Centre, West Mains, Ingliston, NEWBRIDGE, Midlothian,
      EH28 8LT.   (hq)
      0131-472 4000   fax 0131-472 4010
      http://www.nfus.org.uk
      Chief Exec: James Withers
Br   72
○   *F, *H, *P; agriculture in all its branches
●   Conf - Mtgs - ET - Res - Exhib - Comp - SG - Stat - Inf - Lib - VE
      - Empl - LG
<   C'ee Agricl Orgs in the EU (COPA); Intl Fedn Agricl Producers
M   12,000 i
¶   Scottish Farming Leader Update - 4/6; ftm.

NHS Alliance   1998
NR   Rossington House, West Carr Rd, RETFORD, Notts,
      DN22 7SW.   (hq)
      01777 869080
      http://www.nhsalliance.org
○   *P; to represent primary care groups & trusts to government; to
      provide networking opportunities & develop & spread good
      practice

NHS Confederation
NR   29 Bressenden Place, LONDON, SW1E 5DD.
      020 7074 3200
      email enquiries@nhsconfed.org
      Chief Exec: Mike Farrar
○   *M, N; 'to represent over 95% of NHS organisations & provide
      a strong voice for NHS leadership to help improve patient
      health & care'
Gp   Ambulance Service Network (GB & Guernsey, Jersey, Isle of
      Man, Isle of Wight & Gibraltar)
×   2008 Ambulance Service Association (merged)

NHS Support Federation   1989
NR   113 Queens Rd, BRIGHTON, E Sussex, BN1 3XG.   (hq)
      01273 234822
      http://www.nhscampaign.org
○   *K; an independent organisation to protect & promote a
      comprehensive NHS
M   c 5,000 i in groups

© CBD Research Ltd · Beckenham · BR3 5JS · Tel 020 8650 7745 · E-mail cbd@cbdresearch.com · www.cbdresearch.com

NHS Trusts Association   (NHSTA)
NR   PO Box 45734, LONDON, SW16 5JW.
    020 8679 2471   fax 020 8765 4818
    http://www.nhsta.org.uk
    Chief Exec: Dr David Tod
○   *N
✕   2006 Association of Primary Care Groups & Trusts

NIAB   (NIAB)   1919
NR   Huntingdon Rd, CAMBRIDGE, CB3 0LE.   (hq)
    01223 342200   fax 01223 277602
    email info@niab.com   http://www.niab.com
Br   8 regional trials centres
○   *F, *H, *Q; improvement of crop varieties & seeds
●   Conf - Mtgs - ET - Exam - Res - Exhib - Stat - Inf - Lib - PL - LG
M   c 4,300 i
¶   Jnl.   AR.
    Publications list available.

NISA Today's (Holdings) Ltd   (NISA)   1978
NR   Waldo Way, Normanby Enterprise Park, SCUNTHORPE, Lincs,
    DN15 9GE.
    01724 282028
    http://www.nisa-todays.com
○   *T; to support independent retailers & wholesalers in food &
    drink markets, through buying power, marketing &
    distribution services
M   f

NO2ID   (NO2ID)   2004
NR   PO Box 412, 19-21 Crawford St, LONDON, W1H 1PJ.
    (mail/add)
    0700 580 0651
    email enquiries@no2id.net   http://www.no2id.net
▲   Un-incorporated Society
○   *K; 'to research, evaluate & raise public awareness of the issues
    around ID cards, identity registers & unique identifiers,
    including biometrics; to lobby & campaign against any such
    legislation or schemes that would prove detrimental to UK
    citizens, including initiatives that would involve
    comprehensive data sharing without the fully informed &
    explicit consent of the individual'
●   Conf - Mtgs - ET - Res - Exhib - Comp - Stat - Inf - LG
<   Eur Social Forum
M   20,000 i, 80 org

No Panic
■   93 Brands Farm Way, TELFORD, Shropshire, TF3 2JQ.   (hsp)
    01952 590005   fax 01952 270962
    email ceo@nopanic.org.uk   http://www.nopanic.org.uk
    Chief Exec: Colin M Hammond
▲   Registered Charity
Br   Ireland
○   *W; the relief & rehabilitation of those people suffering from
    panic attacks, phobias, obsessive compulsive disorder,
    related anxiety disorders & tranquilliser withdrawal; to
    provide support to sufferers & their families &/or carers
●   Conf - ET - Inf - Telephone recovery course - Advice & support
    Helpline: 0808 808 0545 (0010-2200 daily)
M   3,000 i, UK / 100 i, o'seas
¶   NL - 24; ftm.
    No Panic: the facts [about the charity].
    Information booklets [on specific problems]; £1.50 each.
    Books; £5 - £12 each.   Audio & Visual aids; £2 - £14.
✕   National Organisation for Phobias, Anxiety, Neuroses
    Information & Care

Noctis: the voice of the nighttime economy
    reverted in 2011 to the title **Bar Entertainment & Dance**
    Association

NOF Energy Ltd   (NOF Energy)   2006
■   Thames House (1st floor), Mandale Business Park,
    Belmont Industrial Estate, DURHAM, DH1 1TH.   (hq)
    0191-384 6464
    email business@nofenergy.co.uk
    http://www.nofenergy.co.uk
    Chief Exec: Geroge Rafferty
▲   Company Limited by Guarantee
○   *T; business support for the oil, gas, nuclear & offshore wind
    sectors in the UK
Gp   Sub-sea North East; Intl steering gp
●   Conf - Mtgs - Res - Exhib - Expt - Inf - VE
<   Aberdeen & Grampian Cham Comm
M   275 f, UK / 7 f, o'seas
¶   News 4 Energy - 4;   NOF Energy Directory - 1;
    NOF Energy North Sea Map (2007) - 1; all free.

Noise Abatement Society   (NAS)   1959
NR   26 Brunswick Terrace (flat 2), HOVE, E Sussex, BN3 1HJ.   (hq)
    01273 823850
    email info@noise-abatement.org
    http://www.noiseabatementsociety.com
▲   Registered Charity
○   *K; to reduce noise from all sources to tolerable & reasonable
    levels
●   Conf - Mtgs - ET - Res - Exhib - SG - Stat - Inf - LG
M   11,000 i, 128 f, 250 org
¶   NL - 4; ftm only.

Non-Administrative Receivers Association
    since 2008 **NARA - Association of Property & Fixed Charge**
    Receivers

Non-Executive Directors Association   (NEDA)   2006
NR   Crowthorne Business Estate, Old Wokingham Rd,
    CROWTHORNE, Berks, RG45 6AW.   (hq)
    01344 751672
    email info@nedaglobal.com
    http://www.nedaglobal.com
▲   Company Limited by Guarantee
○   *P; to represent non-executive directors & ensure they are
    properly trained & developed
●   ET - Inf
¶   Handbook (published in association with the Institute of
    Chartered Secretaries & Administrators); ftm.
    NL; ftm.

Non-Ferrous Alliance   (NFA)   1995
NR   National Metalforming Centre, 47 Birmingham Rd,
    WEST BROMWICH, W Midlands, B70 6PY.   (hq)
    0121-601 6363   fax 0870 138 9714
    http://www.nfalliance.org.uk
▲   Un-incorporated Society
○   *T; the Uk's non-ferrous metal industry - aluminium, copper,
    nickel, lead, zinc, magnesium, titanium, cobalt, molybdenum
    & tungsten, as well as UK-based precious metals & minerals
    companies
●   Conf - Mtgs - ET - Stat - LG
M   280 f in 9 org:
    Aluminium Federation
    British Non-Ferrous Metals Federation
    Cobalt Development Institute
    International Molybdenum Association
    International Tungsten Industry Association
    Lead Development Association International
    Nickel Institute
    Titanium Information Group
    Zinc Information Centre

Noonan Syndrome Association   (NSA)
NR   Newlife Center, Hemlock Way, CANNOCK, Staffs,
       WS11 7GF.   (sb)
       0800 083 2972
       http://www.noonansyndrome.co.uk
▲   Registered Charity
○   *W; for parents a& children with Noonam syndrome - a genetic
       disorder with range of clinical features
●   Mtgs -Inf

NORCAP
       see **Adults Affected by Adoption - NORCAP**

Norfolk Chamber of Commerce & Industry   1896
NR   9 Norwich Business Park, Whiting Rd, NORWICH, Norfolk,
       NR4 6DJ.   (hq)
       01603 625977   fax 01603 633032
       email info@norfolkchamber.co.uk
       http://www.norfolkchamber.co.uk
       Chief Exec: Caroline Williams
▲   Company Limited by Guarantee
○   *C

Norfolk Horn Breeders Group   1994
NR   The Close, Drayton Beauchamp, AYLESBURY, Bucks,
       HP22 5LU.   (hsp)
       07599 566657
       email info@norfolkhornbreeders.co.uk
       http://www.norfolkbreeders.co.uk
       Sec: Linda Rollason
○   *B; to promote & raise awareness of the Norfolk Horn breed of
       sheep
<   Nat Sheep Assn
M   100 i

Norfolk Naturalists' Trust
       see **Norfolk Wildlife Trust**

Norfolk & Norwich Archaeological Society   (NNAS)   1846
■   9 Church St, NEW BUCKENHAM, Norfolk, NR16 2BA.   (hsp)
       email secretary@nnas.info   http://www.nnas.info
       Hon Gen Sec: Alice Cattermole
▲   Registered Charity
○   *L; study of the archaeology, history, architecture & antiquities
       of Norfolk
Gp   Young archaeologists; Walking
●   Conf - Mtgs - ET - Lib - VE
<   Coun Brit Archaeology
M   400 i, 100 f, 10 org, UK / 50 org, o'seas
       (Sub: £16 i, UK / £20 instns)
¶   Norfolk Archaeology - 1; ftm, £20 nm.

Norfolk Record Society   (NRS)   1923
NR   29 Cintra Rd, NORWICH, Norfolk, NR1 4AE.   (hsp)
       01603 436046
       email nrs@norfolkrecordsociety.org.uk
       http://www.norfolkrecordsociety.org.uk
       Hon Sec: Dr G A Metters
▲   Registered Charity
○   *L; publication of historical record material relating to the
       County of Norfolk
●   Lectures to accompany launch of each new volume
<   Fedn of Norfolk Historical & Archaeol Socs
M   c 350 i
¶   1 publication each year; ftm, £18 nm.

Norfolk Wildlife Trust   (NWT)   1926
■   Bewick House, 22 Thorpe Rd, NORWICH, Norfolk, NR1 1RY.
       (hq)
       01603 625540
       http://www.norfolkwildlifetrust.org.uk
       Dir: Brendan Joyce
▲   Registered Charity
○   *E, *G; to protect & enhance Norfolk's wildlife & wild places;
       the trust looks after 40 nature reserves & owns 10 km of
       coastline, 9 Norfolk Broads & 5 ancient woodlands
●   Mtgs - ET - Exhib - Stat - Inf - VE
<   The Wildlife Trusts (R Soc Nature Consvn)
M   17,500 i, c 100 f
¶   Tern (NL) - 3;   Events Listings - 3;   AR; all free.
       Note: also uses registered name of Norfolk Naturalists' Trust

North Country Cheviot Sheep Society   1945
■   Wallacehall West, Waterbeck, LOCKERBIE, Dumfriesshire,
       DG11 3HR.   (sp)
       01461 600673
       email alison.brodie@nc-cheviot.co.uk
       http://www.nc-cheviot.co.uk
       Sec: Alison Brodie
▲   Registered Charity
○   *B
●   Mtgs - Exhib - Comp - Inf - Shows
<   Nat Sheep Assn
M   150 i
¶   Flock Book - 1; £5 m, £7.50 nm.   Brochures.

North Devon Agricultural Society   (NDAS)   1966
NR   13 George Arcade, Broad St, SOUTH MOLTON, Devon,
       EX36 3AB.   (hsp)
       01769 573852
       email secretary@northdevonshow.com
       http://www.northdevonshow.com
       Sec: Mrs Pat Sennett
▲   Company Limited by Guarantee; Registered Charity
○   *F
●   The North Devon Show
<   Assn of Shows & Agricl Orgs

North Devon Chamber of Commerce & Industry
       closed 2009

**North East Chamber of Commerce, Trade & Industry   (NECC)
1995**
NR   Aykley Heads Business Centre, Aykley Heads, DURHAM,
       DH1 5TS.   (hq)
       0191-386 1133   fax 0191-386 1144
       email enquiries@necc.co.uk   http://www.necc.co.uk
       Chief Exec: James Ramsbotham
▲   Company Limited by Guarantee
Br   Durham, Middlesbrough, Newcastle upon Tyne, Sunderland
○   *C
M   4,000 f

North East Hampshire Chamber of Commerce
       merged in 2010 with other chambers of commerce in Hampshire to
       form the **Hampshire Chamber of Commerce**

North of England Horticultural Society   (NEHS)   1911
NR   Regional Agricultural Centre, Great Yorkshire Show Ground,
       HARROGATE, N Yorks, HG2 8NZ.   (hq)
       01423 546158
       email info@flowershow.org.uk
       http://www.flowershow.org.uk
       Co Sec: Jane Kitchen
▲   Registered Charity
○   *G, *H; organisation of Harrogate spring & autumn flower
       shows
●   Exhib
M   150 i
¶   Show leaflet - 2; free.   Show Catalogue - 2.

© CBD Research Ltd · Beckenham · BR3 5JS · Tel 020 8650 7745 · E-mail cbd@cbdresearch.com · www.cbdresearch.com

North of England Institute of Mining & Mechanical Engineers (NEIMME) 1852

NR Neville Hall, Westgate Rd, NEWCASTLE upon TYNE, NE1 1SE. (hq)
    0191-232 2201   fax 0191-232 2201
    email office@mininginstitute.org.uk
    http://www.mininginstitute.org.uk
    Hon Sec & Treas: J S Porthouse
▲ Registered Charity
○ *L, *Q; to advance & promote the science & technology of mining engineering & other allied branches of engineering, particularly coal mining
● Conf - Mtgs - SG - Lib - VE
< Inst of Materials, Minerals & Mining (NE)
M c 400 i

North of England Mule Sheep Association (NEMSA) 1980

NR Albierigg Farm, CANONBIE, Dumfriesshire, DG14 0RY. (regd off)
    01387 371777
    email nemsa@btinternet.com   http://www.nemsa.co.uk
    Sec: Mrs Marion Hope
Br 9
○ *B; to promote the North of England mule ewe lamb as a breeding sheep (a cross of 2 contrasting pure breeds; a Bluefaced Leicester ram to either a Swaledale or Northumberland type Blackface dam)
● Mtgs - Exhib - Comp - Stat - Expt - Inf
< Nat Sheep Assn
M c 1,000 i
¶ Mule News (Jnl) - 1;   Sales booklet - 1; both free.

North of England Rosecarpe Horticultural Society (ROSECARPE) 1938

■ 11 Jones St, Birtley, CHESTER le STREET, Co Durham, DH3 1DZ. (hsp)
    0191-410 5895
    email jbell748@btinternet.com
    Sec: Mrs Dorothy Bell
▲ Un-incorporated Society
○ *H; to encourage, improve & extend the cultivation of flowers & the art of flower arranging, information on show exhibits & on all garden enquiries
Gp Carnations; Daffodils; Roses; Sweet peas
● Mtgs - Exhib - Inf - VE - Spring bulb show
    Show Sec: Morris Robinson, 0191-413 8026
< Nat Sweet Peas Soc; Brit Nat Carnation Soc; Nthn Daffodil Soc
M 150 i
    Sub: £3
¶ News Bulletin - 10;   Ybk; both ftm only.
✕ 2007 North of England Rose, Carnation & Sweet Pea Horticultural Society

North of England Zoological Society (Chester Zoo) 1934

■ Cedar House, Caughall Rd, UPTON by CHESTER, Cheshire, CH2 1LH. (hq)
    01244 380280   fax 01244 371273
    email marketing@chesterzoo.co.uk
    http://www.chesterzoo.org
    Chief Exec: Prof Gordon McGregor Reid
▲ Company Limited by Guarantee; Registered Charity
○ *B, *E, *V; a conservational & educational charity dedicated to breeding & supporting rare & endangered species & increasing knowledge of fauna & flora worldwide
● Conf - Mtgs - ET - Res - SG - Lib - VE
< Wld Assn Zoos & Aquariums (WAZA); Intl U Conservation of Nature (IUCN); Eur Assn Zoos & Aquaria (EAZA); Assn Leading Visitor Attractions (ALVA); Fedn Zoological Gardens GB & Ireland
M 10,000+ i
¶ Chester Zoo Life (Jnl) - 4; ftm, £1 nm.
    Guide Book & Map; £3 (£4 by post).   AR; ftm, £5 nm.

North Hampshire Chamber of Commerce & Industry
    merged in 2010 with other chambers of commerce in Hampshire to form the **Hampshire Chamber of Commrce**

North of Ireland Potato Marketing Association

    has closed

North London Chamber of Commerce

NR Enfield Business Centre, 201 Hertford Rd, ENFIELD, Middx, EN3 5JH.
    020 8443 4464   fax 020 8443 3822
    email chamber@nlcc.co.uk   http://www.nlcc.co.uk
○ *C

North Ronaldsay Sheep Fellowship (NRSF) 1997

NR Walmer Hall, Dob Lane, Little Hoole, PRESTON, Lancs, PR4 4SU. (hsb)
    01772 613928
    http://www.nrsf.moonfruit.com
    Sec: Anne Lane
○ *B

North of Scotland Grassland Society 1961

NR Ferguson Building, SAC Aberdeen, Craibstone, Aberdeen, AB21 9YA. (hsp)
    01224 711065
    Hon Sec: Chris Stockwell
▲ Registered Charity
○ *F; research into methods & management of grass & forage crops

North Somerset Agricultural Society 1840

NR Mutual Barn, Udley Farm, West Hay Rd, WRINGTON, Somerset, BS40 5NP. (sb)
    0845 634 2464   fax 01934 8636358
    email tim@nsas.org.uk   http://www.nsas.org.uk
    Sec: Tim Ledbury
▲ Company Limited by Guarantee; Registered Charity
○ *F; to promote agriculture & rural issues
Gp Annual agricultural show; Annual ploughing match & produce show
● Mtgs - ET - Exhib (agricultural & produce shows) - Comp (ploughing match)
< Assn of Show & Agricl Orgs (ASAO)
M 500 i
¶ NL - 12; ftm, £15 nm.

North Staffordshire Chamber of Commerce & Industry (NSCCI) 1861

■ Commerce House, Festival Park, STOKE-ON-TRENT, Staffs, ST1 5BE. (hq)
    01782 202222   fax 01782 202448
    email info@nscci.co.uk   http://www.nscci.co.uk
    Chief Exec: Bryan Carnes
▲ Company Limited by Guarantee
Br Stafford, Stoke-on-Trent
○ *C
Gp Export club; Manufacturing; Professional services network
● Mtgs - ET - Res - Expt - Inf - LG
< Brit Chams Comm
M 1,070 f
¶ Focus - 4; ftm, £30 nm.   International Trade News. Business Bulletin - 6.

North West London Chamber of Commerce Ltd (NWLCC)
- ■ Enterprise House, 297 Pinner Rd, HARROW, Middx, HA1 4HS. (hq)
  020 8427 2884   fax 020 8861 5709
  email info@nwlchamber.org.uk
  http://www.nwlchamber.org.uk
  Sec: Mrs Vandona Patel
- ▲ Company Limited by Guarantee
- ○ *C
- ● Conf - Mtgs - ET - Inf - Networking
- < London Cham Comm & Ind
- M f
- ¶ NL - 4; free.

North West Timber Trade Association (NWTTA) 1972
- ■ Forest View, Blakemere Lane, NORLEY, Cheshire, WA6 6NS. (hsp)
  email secretary@nwtta.org   http://www.nwtta.org
  Sec: Alison Cunningham
- ▲ Un-incorporated Society
- ○ *T; importers, agents & merchants for timber
- ● Mtgs - Stat - Inf - VE
- < Timber Tr Fedn
- M 64 f

North & Western Lancashire Chamber of Commerce (NWLCC) 1916
- NR 9-10 Eastway Business Village, Olivers Place, Fulwood, PRESTON, Lancs, PR2 9WT. (hq)
  01772 653000   fax 01772 655544
  email info@lancschamber.co.uk
  http://www.lancschamber.co.uk
  Chief Exec: Babs Murphy
- ▲ Company Limited by Guarantee
- Br Blackpool, Preston
- ○ *C
- < Brit Chams Comm; Chams Comm NW
- M f

** **North Western Model Railway Clubs Association**
  Organisation lost: see Introduction paragraph 3

North Yorkshire Moors Historical Railway Trust (NYMR) 1967
- NR Pickering Station, PICKERING, N Yorks, YO18 7AJ. (hq)
  01751 473799   fax 01751 476970
  email info@nymr.co.uk   http://www.nymr.co.uk
  Gen Mgr: Philip Benham
- ▲ Registered Charity
- ○ *G; to advance the education of the public in the history & development of railway locomotion by the maintenance, in working order, of the historic & scenic railway line between Grosmont & Pickering
- ● ET
- < Assn of Rly Presvn Socs
- M c 7,225 i, 50 f
- ¶ Moors Line - 4; ftm, £1.20 nm.

Northamptonshire Archaeological Society 1974
- NR Bolton House, Wootton Hall Park, NORTHAMPTON, NN4 8BE.
  01604 700493
  email achapman@northamptonshire.gov.uk
  http://www.northants-archaeology.org.uk
  Hon Sec: Andy Chapman
- ○ *L; to study of the archaeology of the County
- ● Mtgs - VE
- M i
- ¶ Northamptonshire Archaeology (Jnl).

Northamptonshire Chamber of Commerce 1991
- NR Opus House, Anglia Way, Moulton Park, NORTHAMPTON, NN3 6JA. (hq)
  01604 490490   fax 01604 670362
  email info@northants-chamber.co.uk
  http://www.northants-chamber.co.uk
  Chief Exec: Paul Griffiths
- ○ *C
- M c 1,300 i & f

Northamptonshire Natural History Society 1876
- NR The Humfrey Rooms, 10 Castilian Terrace, NORTHAMPTON, NN1 1LD. (hq)
  01604 602242
  Sec: C T Sampson
- ○ *G; to promote research into the natural history & allied sciences of the County
- ● Mtgs - Res
- M i & org
- ¶ Jnl.

Northamptonshire Record Society 1920
- NR Wootton Hall Park, Mereway, NORTHAMPTON, NN4 8BQ. (hq)
  01604 762297
  http://www.northamptonshirerecordssociety.org.uk
  Sec: Leslie C Skelton
- ▲ Registered Charity
- ○ *L, *Q; the pursuit of the history of Northamptonshire in all its forms
- ● Mtgs - Lib - Lectures
- M 500 i, 130 org, UK / 80 families, o'seas
- ¶ Northamptonshire Past & Present (Jnl) - 1; £3. Publications list available.

Northern Cricket Union of Ireland (NCU) 1886
- ■ 181 Belvoir Drive, BELFAST, BT8 7DS. (gsp)
  028 9064 7328
  email ncu.cricket@btinternet.com
  Gen Sec: Bryan Milford
- ▲ Un-incorporated Society
- ○ *S; the governing body for cricket in Belfast & Counties Antrim, Down & Armagh
- ● Mtgs - ET - Comp
- < Ir Cricket U
- M 50 clubs, 45 schools
- ¶ Hbk - 1;   AR - 1.

Northern Ireland Agricultural Producers' Association (NIAPA)
- NR 15 Molesworth St, COOKSTOWN, Co Tyrone, BT80 8NX.
  028 8676 5700
- ○ *T

Northern Ireland Amusement Caterer's Trade Association (NIACTA)
- ■ 696 Doagh Rd, NEWTOWNABBEY, Co Antrim, BT36 4TP. (hq)
  028 9334 5137
  Hon Sec: Jon H Sander
- ○ *T

Northern Ireland Archery Society (NIAS)
- NR PO Box 282, CRAIGAVON, Co Armagh, BT67 0YA. (mail add)
  email admin@nias.co.uk
  Hon Sec: Mrs Hazel CampbellChmn: Hugh Irvine (0713 174 9193)
- ○ *S; governing body of the sport of archery in NI

Northern Ireland Association for the Care & Resettlement of Offenders (NIACRO) 1971
- NR Amelia House, 4 Amelia St, BELFAST, BT2 7GS. (hq)
  028 9032 0157
- ○ *W; to assist with the rehabilitation of offenders; to work with those at risk of criminal involvement & thereby prevent crime

© CBD Research Ltd · Beckenham · BR3 5JS · Tel 020 8650 7745 · E-mail cbd@cbdresearch.com · www.cbdresearch.com

Northern Ireland Association of Christian Teachers   (NIACT)
NR   4 Bolea Park, LIMAVADY, Co Londonderry, BT49 0SH.
        email fred@capple.demon.co.uk   http://www.niact.org.uk
        Chmn: Fred Corscadden
○   *P, *R; to support Christians employed in education in Northern
        Ireland

Northern Ireland Association for Mental Health   1959
NR   80 University St, BELFAST, BT7 1HE.   (hq)
        028 9032 8474
        email info@niamh.co.uk
▲   Company Limited by Guarantee
○   *W; all aspects of mental health & mental illness

**Northern Ireland Association for the Study of Psychoanalysis
      (NIASP)   1988**
NR   131 Belmont Rd, BELFAST, BT4 2AD.
        028 9047 3254
        Sec: Ms Paddy Maynes
▲   Registered Charity
○   *P
Gp   Child psychotherapy; Group psychotherapy
●   Conf - Mtgs - ET - Res - SG
<   Brit Confedn Psychotherapy (BCP); Intl Psychoanalytic Assn (IPA)
M   c 20 i

Northern Ireland Athletic Federation   (NIAF)   1935
NR   Athletics House, Old Coach Rd, BELFAST, BT9 5PR.   (hq)
        028 9060 2707   fax 028 9030 9939
        email info@niathletics.org   http://www.niathletics.org
        Hon Sec: John Allen
○   *S; men's & women's athletics in NI
<   Intl Assn of Athletic Fedns; UK Athletics
M   45 clubs
¶   Ybk.   AR.

Northern Ireland Bat Group   (NIBG)   1985
NR   33 Glebe Manor, NEWTOWNABBEY, Co Antrim, BT36 6HF.
        (hsp)
        07989 354592
        email secretary@bats-ni.org.uk
        http://www.bats-ni.org.uk
        Hon Records Sec: James McCrory
        Hon Sec: Catherine Shields (07921 953727)
▲   Un-incorporated Society
○   *V; to promote bat conservation in Northern Ireland by
        educating & advising the public; to monitor numbers &
        investigate aspects of bat biology
●   ET - Res - Exhib - LG
M   71 i
¶   NL - 4; ftm only.

Northern Ireland Chamber of Commerce   1783
NR   22 Great Victoria St, BELFAST, BT2 7BJ.   (hq)
        028 9024 4113   fax 028 9024 7024
        email mail@northernirelandchamber.com
        http://www.northernirelandchamber.com
        Chief Exec: Ann McGregor
○   *C
M   c 1,100 f

Northern Ireland Childminding Association   1990
NR   16-18 Mill St, NEWTOWNARDS, BT23 4LU.
        028 9181 1015   fax 028 9182 0921
        http://www.nicma.org
        Dir: Bridget Nodder
○   *P
M   c 2,500 i

Northern Ireland Council for Voluntary Action   (NICVA)   1938
NR   61 Duncairn Gardens, BELFAST, BT15 2GB.   (hq)
        028 9087 7777   fax 028 9087 7799
        http://www.nicva.org
        Chief Exec: Seamus McAleavey
▲   Company Limited by Guarantee; Registered Charity
○   *N, *W; resource & development body serving the voluntary
        sector in Northern Ireland
M   i, f & org

** Northern Ireland Countryside Staff Association
        Organisation lost: see Introduction paragraph 3

Northern Ireland Cycling Federation   (NICF)   1949
■   10 Cairndore Avenue, NEWTOWNARDS, Co Down,
        BT23 8RF.   (hsp)
        028 9181 7396
        http://www.nicyclingfederation.com
        Hon Sec: Anthony Mitchell
▲   Un-incorporated Society
○   *S; sporting body for cyclists in Northern Ireland
●   Comp
<   Cycling Ireland
M   200 i
¶   Ybk; ftm.
×   2007 (1 Jan) Cycling Ulster (amalgamated)

Northern Ireland Deer Society
        a regional group of the **British Deer Society**

Northern Ireland Family History Society
NR   c/o School of Education, 69 University St, BELFAST, BT7 1HL.
        (mail/address)
○   *G

**Northern Ireland Federation of Housing Associations
      (NIFHA)   1977**
NR   6c Citylink Business Park, Albert St, BELFAST, BT12 4HB.   (hq)
        028 9023 0446   fax 028 9023 8057
        email info@nifha.org   http://www.nifha.org
        Chief Exec: Chris Williamson
▲   Company Limited by Guarantee
○   *N; to promote housing associations in Northern Ireland &
        speak authoritatively on their behalf
●   Conf - Mtgs - ET - Res - Exhib - SG - Stat - Inf - VE - LG
<   Intl Co-operative Alliance; Comité Européen Co-ordination de
        l'Habitat Social (CECODHAS Housing Europe)
M   37 housing assns
¶   AR.

Northern Ireland Food & Drink Association   (NIFDA)
NR   Belfast Mills, 71-75 Percy St, BELFAST, BT13 2HW.
        028 9024 1010   fax 028 9024 0500
        email mbell@nifda.co.uk   http://www.nifda.co.uk
○   *T

Northern Ireland Fruit Growers Association   (NIFGA)   1942
NR   100 Drumilly Rd, LOUGHALL, Co Armagh, BT61 8JH.
        (chmn/p)
        028 3889 1234
        Chmn: John Beggs
○   *T; promotion of fruit growing

Northern Ireland Grain Trade Association Ltd   (NIGTA)   1966
NR   Cuinne an Chaireil, 27 Berwick View, MOIRA, Co Down,
        BT67 0SX.   (hq)
        028 9261 1044   fax 028 9261 1979
        email info@nigta.co.uk   http://www.nigta.co.uk
        Sec: Doris Leeman
○   *T
M   30 f

Northern Ireland Hotels Federation   1922
NR   The McCune Building, 1 Shore Rd, BELFAST, BT15 3PG.   (hq)
    028 9077 6636   fax 028 9077 1899
    email office@nihf.co.uk
    Chief Exec: Janet Gault
▲   Un-incorporated Society
○   *T; private sector business in the hospitality industry - hotel,
    guesthouses, restaurants, commercial & trade suppliers

Northern Ireland Independent Retail Trade Association
(NIIRTA)   2000
■   261-263 Ormeau Road, BELFAST, BT7 3GG.   (hq)
    028 9022 0004   fax 021 9022 0005
    email info@niirta.com   http://www.niirta.com
    Chief Exec & Sec: Glyn Roberts
▲   Company Limited by Guarantee
○   *T; to lobby on behalf of the independent retail sector in
    Northern Ireland
●   Conf - Mtgs - Res - Exhib - Inf - LG
<   Assn of Convenience Stores; Assn of Town Centre Mgrs; Scot
    Grocers Fedn
M   1,300 i & f
    (Sub:£10,000 UK / £250 o'seas)

Northern Ireland Local Government Association   (NILGA)
1973
NR   Unit 5B Castlereagh Business Park, 478 Castlereagh Rd,
    BELFAST, BT5 6BQ.   (hq)
    028 9079 8972   fax 028 9079 1248
    email office@nilga.org   http://www.nilga.org
    Acting Chief Exec: Nora Winder
▲   Un-incorporated Society
○   *N; represents the interests of local authorities in Northern
    Ireland
●   Conf - Mtgs - SG - Empl - LG
<   LEIB; Local Authorities Coordinating Body on Food & Trading
    Standards (LACOTS)
M   c 150 councils
¶   The Councillors' Hbk - 4 yrly; free.
    NL - 4;   AR - 1; both free.

Northern Ireland Master Butchers Association   (NIMBA)
1937
■   38 Oldstone Hill, MUCKAMORE, Co Antrim, BT41 4SB.   (sp)
    028 9446 5180
    Sec: Harry Marquess
▲   Un-incorporated Society
○   *T
●   Mtgs - Comp - Inf - Empl - LG
M   200 i
¶   N.I. Master Butchers - 4.

Northern Ireland Master Plumbers' Association   (NIMPA)
1931
■   38 Hill St, BELFAST, BT1 2LB.   (asa)
    028 9032 1731   fax 028 9024 7521
    email crawfordsedgwick@excite.com
    Sec: W A Crawford
▲   Un-incorporated Society
○   *T
●   Conf - Mtgs - ET - Empl
<   Scot & NI Plumbing Employers' Fedn
M   118 f
¶   Plumbheat - 10; ftm only.

Northern Ireland Meat Exporters Association   (NIMEA)   1980
NR   Lissue House, 31 Ballinderry Rd, LISBURN, Co Down,
    BT28 2SL.   (hq)
    028 9262 2510
    email nimea@aol.com   http://www.nimea.co.uk
    Chief Exec: Philim O'Neill
▲   Company Limited by Guarantee
○   *T; to represent all EU approved meat exporting companies in
    Northern Ireland
Gp   Plants: Slaughter, Cutting, Processing
●   Conf - Mtgs - ET - Expt - Inf - LG
<   UECBV (Brussels, Belgium)
M   17 f

Northern Ireland Mixed Marriage Association   (NIMMA)
1974
NR   28 Bedford St, BELFAST, BT2 7FE.
    028 9023 5444   fax 028 9043 4544
    email nimma@nireland.com   http://www.nimma.org.uk
▲   Registered Charity
○   *W; for the mutual support & help of people involved in or
    about to be involved in a mixed (Catholic / Protestant)
    marriage
●   Inf - 'helping the clergy to understand the concept &
    practicalities of mixed marriage' - Influencing the attitudes of
    the community to mixed marriage
<   Assn Interchurch Families
M   80 i
¶   Newssheet / Update - 4; ftm only.
    Mixed Marriage in Ireland: A companion to those involved, or
    about to be involved, in a mixed marriage; £3.50.

Northern Ireland Oil Federation
NR   11 Ballyblack Road East, NEWTOWNARDS, Co Down,
    BT22 2BD.
    0845 600 2105   fax 028 9186 3459
    email david@nioil.com   http://www.nioil.com
    Contact: David Blevings
○   *T

Northern Ireland Orienteering Association
NR   31 Pond Park Avenue, LISBURN, Co Antrim, BT28 3HL.
    07797 725398
    http://www.niorienteering.org.uk
    Devt Officer: Helen Baxter
○   *S
M   i

Northern Ireland Polymers Association   (NIPA)   2002
NR   Canyon Europe Ltd, 4 Mallusk Rd, NEWTOWNABBEY,
    Co Antrim, BT36 4PR.
    028 9084 1917   fax 028 9084 4528
    http://www.nipa.net
    Chmn: Hugh Ross
○   *T

Northern Ireland Potato Breeders Association   (NIPBA)   1996
NR   38-40 Carnlea Rd, BALLYMENA, Co Antrim, BT43 6TS.   (hq)
    028 2568 5533
    Chmn: R J Cherry
▲   Company Limited by Guarantee
○   *T; interests of breeders of new varieties of potatoes for home &
    overseas markets

Northern Ireland Poultry Federation
NR   c/o O'Kane Poultry Ltd, 170 Larne Rd, BALLYMENA, Co Antrim,
    BT42 9XX.   (chmn/b)
    028 2564 1111   fax 028 2565 8498
    Chmn: Tony O'Neill
○   *T
M   f

© CBD Research Ltd · Beckenham · BR3 5JS · Tel 020 8650 7745 · E-mail cbd@cbdresearch.com · www.cbdresearch.com

Northern Ireland Public Service Alliance (NIPSA) 1971
NR 54 Wellington Park, BELFAST, BT9 6DP. (hq)
      028 9066 1831   fax 028 9066 5847
      http://www.nipsa.org.uk
      Gen Sec: John Corey
Br 250
○ *U; representing non-industrial grades of civil & public servants
● Conf - Mtgs - ET - Inf - Lib - Empl
M 44,000 i
¶ NIPSA News (newspaper) - 11;   Bulletins;
    Rule Book & Constitution - 1;   AR; all free.

Northern Ireland Self-Catering Holiday Association (NISCHA) 1989
NR Belfast Business Centre, Cathedral House, 23-31 Waring St,
      BELFAST, BT1 2DX. (hq)
      028 9043 6632   fax 028 9043 6699
      email info@nischa.com   http://www.nischa.com
○ *T; the voice of the self-catering holiday accommodation sector
    in Northern Ireland
< Fedn of Nat Self Catering Assns (FoNSCA)
M 110 i & f

Northern Ireland Shows' Association (NISA) 1983
■ The King's Hall Complex, Balmoral, BELFAST, BT9 6GW. (hsb)
      028 9066 5225   fax 028 9066 1264
      email karen@kingshall.co.uk
      Hon Sec: Colin McDonald
○ *F, *N; to represent all agricultural shows in Northern Ireland
● Conf - Mtgs - ET - Exhib - Comp
M 15 agricultural org (N Ireland)

Northern Ireland Timber Trade Association
has closed

Northern Ireland Transplant Association 1991
NR Eagle Lodge, 51 Circular Rd, BELFAST, BT4 2GA. (hq)
      028 9076 1394
      email nitransplants@email.com
      http://www.nitransplant.org
      Hon Sec: Beverly Robinson
▲ Registered Charity
○ *W; to give support, advice & aid to those concerned with
    organ transplantation; to promote the organ donor card &
    registration scheme
● Conf - Mtgs - ET - Inf - VE - LG
M 200 i
¶ NL - 2; ftm only.

Northern Ireland Volleyball Association (NIVA) 1970
NR Room 11D06B, Univerity of Ulster, Shore Rd,
      NEWTOWNABBEY, Co Antrim, B37 0QB. (mail address)
      028 9036 6373   fax 0870 432 2559
      http://www.nivb.com
      Pres: Patrick Murphy
○ *S; the organisation of the sport of volleyball in Ireland
¶ Hbk - 1; ftm.

Northern Ireland Women's Aid Federation (NIWAF) 1978
NR 129 University St, BELFAST, BT7 1HP. (hq)
      028 9024 9041   fax 028 9023 9296
      email info@womensaidni.org
      Dir: Annie Campbell
▲ Company Limited by Guarantee; Registered Charity
○ *K, *W; to challenge attitudes & beliefs which perpetuate
    domestic violence; it seeks to promote healthy & non-abusive
    relationships
Gp Advice; Aftercare; Education & awareness on domestice
    violence; Outreach; Refuge
● Conf - Mtgs - ET - Exhib - Stat - Inf - Lib - LG
    Helpline 0800 917 1414 (24-hr)
< Eur Women's Lobby (EWL); Women against Violence (WAVE);
    Women's Aid Fedn England / Scotland / Wales / Eire
M 11 groups
¶ List of publications on request.

Northern Irish Bridge Union
    see **Irish Bridge Union**

Northern Mill Engine Society (NMES) 1966
■ 84 Watkin Rd, Clayton-le-Woods, CHORLEY, Lancs, PR6 7PX.
      (hsp)
      01257 265003
      http://www.nmes.org
      Hon Sec: John Phillp
▲ Company Limited by Guarantee; Registered Charity
○ *G, *L; preservation of steam engines used to drive the textile
    mills of Lancashire & Yorkshire
● Mtgs - Exhib - Operation of Bolton Steam Museum
M 230 i, 4 f, 4 org, UK / 5 i, 1 org, o'seas
¶ The Flywheel - 3;   NL - 4; both ftm.

Northern Mine Research Society (NMRS) 1960
■ 36 Broadlake, Willaston, NESTON, Cheshire, CH64 2XB. (sp)
      http://www.nmrs.co.uk
      Sec: Ron Callender
▲ Registered Charity
○ *G, *L; encourages research & publication covering all aspects
    of mining history & related topics in Britain
● Conf - Mtgs - Res - Inf - Lib - VE
< Nat Assn of Mining History Orgs (NAMHO); Assn Indl
    Archaeology (AIA)
M 425 i, UK / 8 i, o'seas
¶ NL - 4; ftm only.
    British Mining Monograph - 1; ftm, £13 nm.
    British Mining Memoirs - 1; ftm, £13 nm.

Northumberland & Newcastle Society 1924
NR Jesmond Methodist Church, St George's Terrace, Jesmond,
      NEWCASTLE upon TYNE, NE2 2DL. (hq)
      0191-281 6266
      email secretary@nandnsociety.org.uk
      http://www.nandnsociety.org.uk
○ *G; conservation & preservation of buildings & the countryside

Northumbrian Pipers' Society (NPS) 1928
■ Park House, Lynemouth, MORPETH, Northumberland,
      NE61 5XQ. (hsp)
      01670 860215
      email secretary@northumbrianpipers.org.uk
      http://www.northumbrianpipers.org.uk
      Hon Sec: Julia Say
▲ Un-incorporated Society
○ *D; to foster & encourage the playing, study, manufacture &
    development of Northumbrian pipes & their music &
    traditional Northumbrian music in general
● Mtgs - ET - Res - Comp
M 650 i, UK / 150 i, o'seas
¶ NPS NL - 4; ftm only.   NPS Magazine - 1; ftm, £4 nm.

Norwegian-British Chamber of Commerce   1906
NR   Charles House, 5 Lower Regent St, LONDON, SW1Y 4LR.   (hq)
    020 7930 0181   fax 020 7930 7946
    http://www.norwegian-chamber.co.uk
    The General Manager
▲   Company Limited by Guarantee
○   *C
●   Conf - Mtgs
M   c 800 i & f
¶   Ybk & LM - 1; ftm, £25 nm.

Not Forgotten Association   1920
§   2 Grosvenor Gardens (4th floor), LONDON, SW1W 0DH.
    (hq)
    020 7730 2400   fax 020 7730 0020
    http://www.nfassociation.org
    A charity providing recreation for disabled ex-service men and
    women, such TV sets and licences, holidays and day trips,
    and in-house entertainment in care homes.

Notaries' Society   1907
NR   PO Box 226 Melton, WOODBRIDGE, Suffolk, IP12 1WX.   (hq)
    01394 380436
○   *P; for public notaries

Nottinghamshire Chamber of Commerce & Industry
    in 2008 merged with Derbyshire Chamber & Business Link to form
    Derbyshire & Nottinghamshire Chamber

Nottinghamshire Local History Association   (NLHA)   1953
■   Cratley, Back Lane, Eakring, NEWARK, Notts, NG22 0DJ.
    (chmn/p)
    Chmn: Derek Walker,   Hon Sec: Colin Whitham
    Hon Sec: Colin Whitham (0177 770 2475)
▲   Registered Charity
○   *G; to encourage interest in the local history of
    Nottinghamshire
●   Mtgs - Publishing works on Nottinghamshire local history
M   149 i, 51 org
¶   Nottinghamshire Historian (Jnl) - 2; ftm, £2 nm.

Nuclear Industry Association   (NIA)   1962
■   Carlton House, 22A St James's Sq, LONDON, SW1Y 4JH.
    (hq)
    020 7766 6640   fax 020 7839 1523
    email info@niauk.org   http://www.niauk.org
    Chief Exec: Keith Parker
▲   Company Limited by Guarantee
○   *T; UK civil nuclear industry
●   Conf - Mtgs - ET - Exhib - Expt - Inf - LG
<   Brit Energy Assn
M   87 f
¶   Industry Link (NL) - 4;   Trade Directory - 1;
    Educational Booklets;   AR; all free.

Nuclear Institute
NR   Allan House, 1 Penerley Rd, LONDON, SE6 2LQ.   (hq)
    020 8695 8220
    Exec Sec: Mark Andrew
○   *L; the application & advancement of nuclear engineering
    technology & allied fields
●   Conf - Mtgs - Inf
M   i
¶   Jnl - 6; ftm.
×   2009 (British Nuclear Energy Society
    (Institution of Nuclear Engineers (merged 1 Jan)

Nuclear Stock Association Ltd   (NSA)   1952
NR   15 Orchard Way, Cowbit, SPALDING, Lincs, PE12 6XA.   (hq)
    01406 380993   mob 07713 161153
    Sec: Sarah Troop
○   *H, *T; the maintenance & supply of high health status indexed
    propagation material for soft & tree fruit propagation
Gp   Working gps: Strawberry, rubus & ribes; Tree fruits c'ee
●   Mtgs - VE - LG
M   i
¶   AR - 1; ftm only.
    Note: is a limited company registered as a Friendly Society

Nurse Directors Association
    since 2008 **Association of Nurse Leaders**

Nurses Opposed to Euthanasia
    a group of the **Society for the Protection of Unborn Children**

Nursing Homes Ireland   (NHI)   2008
IRL   A5 Centrepoint Business Park, Oak Rd, DUBLIN 12,
    Republic of Ireland.
    353 (1) 429 2570
    http://www.nhi.ie
○   *N
×   2008 (Federation of Irish Nursing Homes
    (Irish Nursing Homes Organisation

Nutrition & Health Foundation   (NHF)
IRL   Confederation House, 84-86 Lower Baggot St, DUBLIN 2,
    Republic of Ireland.   (hq)
    353 (1) 605 1570   fax 353 (1) 638 1570
    http://www.nutritionandhealth.ie
    Manager: Dr Muireann Cullen
○   *P; to communicate evidence based information on nutrition,
    health & physical activity to encourage an improved &
    healthier society in Ireland
<   Ir Business & Emplrs Confedn (IBEC)

Nutrition Society   1941
NR   10 Cambridge Court, 210 Shepherds Bush Rd, LONDON,
    W6 7NJ.   (hq)
    020 7602 0228
    email office@nutsoc.org.uk
▲   Company Limited by Guarantee
○   *L, *P; to advance the scientific study of nutrition & its
    application to the maintenance of human & animal health

NWA an association of housing & support managers)
    has closed

Nystagmus Network   1984
■   5 Pen-y-Lan Terrace, CARDIFF, CF23 9EU.   (Inf/Offr/p)
    0845 634 2630
    email john.sanders@nystagmusnet.org
    http://www.nystagmusnet.org
    Information Officer: John Sanders
▲   Registered Charity
○   *W; to promote help, support & information to all those
    affected by the eye condition Nystagmus (characterised by
    jerky eye movements which nearly always impair vision)
●   Conf - ET - Res - Exhib - Inf
    Helpline: 01392 272573
<   Look; Contact a family; Albino Fellowship
M   500 i, 20 org
¶   Focus (NL) - 4;   Parent Pack; both ftm only.
    Understanding Nystagmus (booklet); ftm.
    Tales of Northwick (book).   Information sheets; ftm.
    Publications list available.

© CBD Research Ltd · Beckenham · BR3 5JS · Tel 020 8650 7745 · E-mail cbd@cbdresearch.com · www.cbdresearch.com

Observer's Pocket Series Collectors' Society   (OPSCS)   1993
NR   10 Villiers Rd, KENILWORTH, Warks, CV8 2JB.   (hsp)
  01926 857047
  http://www.observersbooksociety.co.uk
  Hon Sec: Alan Sledger
▲   Un-incorporated Society
○   *G; 'to promote the interest in & collecting of Observer's &
  other related books published by Frederick Warne'
●   Mtgs
M   550 i, UK / 15 i, o'seas
¶   OPSCS Magazine - 4; ftm only.

Obstetric Anaesthetists Association   (OAA)   1969
■   PO Box 3219, LONDON, SW13 9XR.   (regd off)
  020 8741 1311   fax 020 8741 0611
  email secretariat@oaa-anaes.ac.uk
  http://www.oaa-anaes.ac.uk
▲   Company Limited by Guarantee; Registered Charity
○   *P; highest standards of anaesthetic practice in the care of
  mother & baby
●   Conf - Mtgs - ET - Res - Exhib - Inf
M   1,925 i, UK / 343 i, o'seas
  (Sub: £110)
¶   Pencil Point (NL) - 4; ftm only.
  International Jnl of Obstetric Anesthesia - 4; ftm.

Occupational & Environmental Diseases Association
  has closed

Occupational Pensioners Alliance   (OPA)   2003
■   Unit 6 Imperial Court, Laporte Way, LUTON, Beds, LU4 8FE.
  (exec/b)
  01582 721652
  email rogerturner@pensioneronline.com
  http://www.opalliance.org.uk
  Exec Officer: Roger Turner
▲   Un-incorporated Society
○   *K; to develop & promote policies that are in the interests of
  occupational pension schemes; to influence national &
  European policy making
●   Mtgs - LG - Campaigning to government on all issues affecting
  occupational pensions
<   Nat Pensioners' Convention
M   c 2,000,000

OCD Action   1991
■   Davina House (suite 506-507), 137-149 Goswell Rd,
  LONDON, EC1V 7ET.   (hq)
  0870 360 6232   fax 020 7253 5277
  email info@ocdaction.org.uk
  http://www.ocdaction.org.uk
  Chmn: Peter Jennings
▲   Registered Charity
○   *W; to advance awareness, research, understanding &
  treatment of obsessive compulsive disorder & associated
  disorders; to offer support & advice to sufferers, their families
  & interested professionals
●   Conf - Inf
  Support & informaton helpline 0845 390 6232
M   1,200 i
¶   NL - 3;   Challenging OCD; free.

Ocean Liner Society   (OLS)   1987
NR   27 Old Gloucester St, LONDON, WC1N 3XX.   (hsp)
  http://www.ocean-liner-society.com
▲   Un-incorporated Society
○   *G; to promote interest in passenger ships past & present (incl
  line service or cruising, ferries with overnight accommodation
  & sailing or cargo ships carrying passengers)
●   Mtgs - Res - Exhib - Lib - PL - VE
M   400 i, 40 f, 10 org, UK / 200 i, 20 f, 5 org, o'seas
¶   Sea Lines (Jnl) - 4; ftm.

Ocean Modelling Group
  a group of the **Challenger Society for Marine Science**

Octavia Hill Society   1992
NR   c/o Octavia Hill's Birthplace House, 8 South Bank, WISBECH,
  Cambs, PE13 1JB.   (hq)
  01945 476358
  email info@octaviahill.org   http://www.octaviahill.org
○   *G; for those with an interest in Octavia Hill (1838-1912) who
  worked for the provision of public open spaces & better
  housing for the poor; she was a co-founder, in 1895, of the
  National Trust

Oesophageal Patients Association   1985
NR   22 Vulcan House, Vulcan Rd, SOLIHULL, West Midlands,
  B91 2JY.   (regd/office)
  0121-704 9860
  Chmn: David Kirby
○   *W; support group for people with oesophageal cancer

Offa's Dyke Association   (ODA)   1969
■   West St, KNIGHTON, Powys, LD7 1EN.   (hq)
  01547 528753
  Chmn: Sophie Andreas,   Hon Sec: Ian Bapty
▲   Registered Charity
○   *G; to provide a link between walkers, tourists, historians,
  conservationists & those who live & work on the Welsh
  Border; to provide visitors with information about the area &
  specifically the Offa's Dyke Path
●   Mtgs - ET - Exhib - Inf - PL - Footpath maintenance - Tourist
  Information centre (on behalf of Visit Wales)
<   None formal but close links with: local authorities, CADW
  (Welsh Historic Monuments), Countryside Coun for Wales,
  English Heritage, Natural England,
M   1,000 i & org
¶   NL - 3; ftm only.   Accommodation list - 1; ftm, £4.50 nm.
  Strip maps of Offa's Dyke Path; £5 a set of 10.
  Route Notes N to S, S to N; £2 each.
  List available of other publications.

Offenders Tag Association   (OTA)   1982
NR   128 Kensington Church St, LONDON, W8 4BH.   (hq)
  020 7221 7166   fax 020 7792 9288
  email ota@stacey-international.co.uk
  http://www.offenderstag.co.uk
  Chmn: Tom Stacey,   Sec: M A Carruthers
▲   Un-incorporated Society
○   *K; penal reform lobby group
●   Inf - LG
M   30 i

Office Agents Society (OAS)

NR The Old Farmhouse, Allaleigh, Blackawton, TOTNES, Devon,
TQ9 7DL
01803 712788
email abedggood@milmarproperties.co.uk
Mem Sec: Alyson Bedggood
○ *P
● Mtgs - Awards
M i, f
(Sub: £35.00)
¶ NL. LM.

Officers' Association (OA) 1920

§ Mountbarrow House (1st floor), 6-20 Elizabeth St, LONDON,
SW1W 9RB. (hq)
http://www.officersassociation.org.uk
A registered charity for the relief of distress amongst those who
have, or have had, a commission in HM Forces, or their
families

Offshore Contractors' Association (OCA) 1995

■ Heritage House, Grandholm Crescent, ABERDEEN,
AB22 8BH. (hq)
01224 747545   fax 01224 706400
email info@ocainternet.com
http://www.ocainternet.com
Chief Exec: Bill Murray
▲ Company Limited by Guarantee
○ *T; to represent the UK's oil & gas contracting industry
● Mtgs - Res - Exhib - Stat - Inf - Lib -Empl - LG
M c 70 f
¶ NL - 12;   Brochure; both free.
Guidance Notes - irreg; prices vary.

Offshore Engineering Society (OES) 1987

■ Institution of Civil Engineers, 1 Great George St, LONDON,
SW1P 3AA. (hq)
020 7665 2262   fax 020 7799 1325
email oes@ice.org.uk   http://www.oes.org.uk
Sec: Adam Kirkup
▲ Registered Charity
○ *P, *T; offshore engineering
● Conf - Mtgs
< is an associated society of the Institution of Civil Engineers
M i & f
(Sub: £17i, from £72 f)
¶ List of publications available.

Offshore Industry Liaison Committee (OILC) 1992

NR 49 Carmelite St, ABERDEEN, AB11 6NQ. (hq)
01224 210118   fax 01224 210095
email gensec@oilc.org   http://www.oilc.org
Gen Sec: Jake Molloy
○ *U; for offshore workers
● Conf - ET
M i [not stated]
¶ Blowout (Jnl) - 4; ftm, £1 nm.
Flareoff (supplement) - 4; free.
Note: Is the offshore energy branch of RMT - the Rail, Marine &
Transport Union

Oige
see **An Óige**

Oil & Colour Chemists' Association (OCCA) 1918

■ 3 Eden Court (1st floor), Eden Way, LEIGHTON BUZZARD,
Beds, LU7 4FY. (hq)
01525 372530   fax 01525 372600
http://www.occa.org.uk
Gen Sec: Chris Pacey-Day
▲ Company Limited by Guarantee; Registered Charity
Br 12; 7 o'seas
○ *L; for scientific & technical personnel in the surface coatings
industry
● Conf - Mtgs - ET - Exhib (SURFEX)
< Coating Socs Intl (CSI)
M 1,550 i, UK / 1,650 i, o'seas
¶ Surface Coatings International - 6.
UK Surface Coatings Hbk - 1.

Oil Firing Technical Association for the Petroleum Industry (OFTEC) 1991

■ Foxwood House, Dobbs Lane, Kesgrave, IPSWICH, Suffolk,
IP5 2QQ. (hq)
0845 658 5080   fax 0845 658 5181
email enquiries@oftec.org   http://www.oftec.org
Dir Gen: Jeremy Hawksley
▲ Company Limited by Guarantee
Br Republic of Ireland
○ *T; to provide technical services for the oil firing industry
Gp Oil: Companies, Distributors, Manufacturers
● Conf - Mtgs - ET - Exam - Exhib - Stat - LG - Testing & approval
of oil firing equipment - Register of approved technicians
< Eurofuel
M 150 f, UK / 1 f, o'seas

Oil & Gas UK
the trading name of the **United Kingdom Oil & Gas Industry
Association Ltd**

Oil Recycling Association (ORA) 1998

■ 62 Lower St, STANSTED, Essex, CM24 8LR. (hsp)
01279 814035   fax 01279 814035
email oilrecyclingasso@aol.com
Hon Sec: Roger Creswell
▲ Company Limited by Guarantee
○ *T; for those engaged in the recovery & recycling of lubricants,
fuels & other liquid wastes which are no longer fit for their
original purpose and arise mainly from the servicing of
automotive engines & other mechanical equipment;
The recovery & recycling of other garage wastes such as oil
filters, catalysts, batteries & other products
Gp Allied shipping services
● Mtgs - Res - Stat - Inf - LG
M 29 f
¶ NL - 4; ftm only.

Old Bottle Club of Great Britain (OBCofGB) 1975

NR Elsecar Heritage Centre, BARNSLEY, S Yorks, S74 8HJ. (hq)
01226 745156
Hon Sec: Alan Blakeman
Br 40
○ *G; recovery & study of antique bottles & containers pre 1911
● Conf - Mtgs - Res - ET - Exhib - Comp - Inf - VE
M c10,000 i
¶ British Bottle Review - 4.

Old Gaffers Association

NR 6 Chatham Place, RAMSGATE, Kent, CT11 7PT. (hsp)
01843 582997
Hon Sec: Robert Holden
○ *G; for owners of 'gaff-rigged' (mainly 19th century) sailing
craft

Old Lawn Mower Club   1990
NR   PO Box 5999 Apsley Guise, MILTON KEYNES, MK17 8HS.
         (mail address)
         email enquiry@oldlawnmowerclub.co.uk
         http://www.oldlawnmowerclub.co.uk
         Contact: Membership Secretary
▲   Un-incorporated Society
○   *G; promotes the collection, preservation & display of old
         lawnmowers
●   Mtgs - Exhib - Inf
M   300 i, UK / 15 i, o'seas
¶   Grassbox (NL) - 4; ftm only.

Old Time Dance Society   1984
■   35 Chestnut Garth, BURTON PIDSEA, E Yorks, HU12 9DA.
         (hsp)
         01964 670033
         http://www.oldtimedance.co.uk
         Sec: June Urquhart
▲   Un-incorporated Society
○   *D; to keep Old Time Dancing & its music alive; to help form
         new old time dance clubs
●   Conf
M   1,450 i, UK / 40 i, o'seas
         (Sub: £15 (couple) UK / £27 (couple) o'seas)
¶   NL - 8;   AR; both ftm only.

Omnibus Society   (OS)   1929
■   100-102 Sandwell St, WALSALL, W Midlands, WS1 3EB.   (hsb)
         http://www.omnibussoc.org
         Hon Sec: Tony Francis
▲   Registered Charity
Br   7
○   *G; study of passenger road transport; understanding of traffic,
         engineering & methods of operating buses, coaches,
         trolleybuses & tramcars
Gp   Photographic register; Central timetable collection; Ticket
         collection; Route recording schemes; Historical research
●   Mtgs - Res - SG - Inf - Lib - VE
M   960 i, UK / 10 i, o'seas
¶   The Omnibus Magazine - 6;   Members' Bulletin - 6; both ftm.

On Site Massage Association   (OSMA)   1992
■   34 Selsdon Avenue, Woodley, READING, Berks, RG5 4PG.
         (hq)
         0118-927 2750
         email info@aosm.co.uk   http://www.aosm.co.uk
         Principal: Pauline Baxter
○   *P; 'a form of acupressure massage where the client sits on a
         specially designed chair, with no clothes removed or aids
         used. The sequence takes just 20 minutes & leaves the client
         feeling relaxed & alert'
●   Conf - ET - Exhib - Work in therapy centres & offices
<   Brit Complementary Medicine Assn (BCMA); Complementary
         Medicine Assn (CMA); Embody, Complementary Therapists
         Assn
M   550 i
¶   In Touch (NL) - 4; £20 yr.

One Parent Families Scotland   (OPFS)   1944
■   13 Gayfield Sq, EDINBURGH, EH1 3NX.   (hq)
         0131-556 3899
         http://www.opfs.org.uk
         Dir: Sue Robertson
▲   Company Limited by Guarantee, Registered Charity
○   *W; to promote & provide support, information & services for
         single parent families within Scotland
●   Conf - ET - Res - Inf
         Helpline: 0800 018 5026
M   c 430 i & org
¶   Various factsheets; free.

One Voice Wales   (OVW)   2004
■   24 College St, AMMANFORD, Carmarthenshire, SA18 3AF.
         (hq)
         01269 595400   fax 01269 598510
         email admin@onevoicewales.org.uk
         http://www.onevoicewales.org.uk
         Chmn: Cllr Isgoed Williams,   Chief Exec: Simon White
▲   Un-incorporated Society
Br   13 area committees
○   *N; representative body for community & town councils in
         Wales
●   Conf - Mtgs - Empl - LG
M   509 councils
¶   The Voice - 4; £2. only, (discount on bulk purchase).

Online Content UK   2001
NR   Mayfair House, 14-18 Heddon St, LONDON, W1B 4DA.   (hq)
         0845 123 5717
         http://www.onlinecontentuk.org
         Dir: Elizabeth Varley
▲   Un-incorporated Society
○   *P; for UK based new media editorial professionals; to support
         the editorial community within the new media & technology
         industries
●   Conf - Mtgs - ET - Email discussion list - Industry job &
         resources lists
M   215 i, UK / 10 i, o'seas

Online User Group
    a group of **CILIP**

Onsite Communications Association   (OSCA)   1963
NR   25 Shelley Lane, HAREFIELD, Middx, UB9 6HP.   (sb/p)
         01895 473551   fax 0870 831 6161
         Sec Gen: Derek Banner
▲   Un-incorporated Society
○   *T; manufacturers & suppliers of radio paging & local
         communications equipment
●   Conf - Mtgs - Exhib - Inf - LG
M   i & f

Open Canoe Association   (OCA)
NR   12 De Verdun Avenue, BELTON, Leics, LE12 9TY.   (mem/sp)
         http://www.opencanoe.info
         Mem Sec: Alan Jones
○   *S

Open Canoe Sailing Group   (OCSG)
NR   Hampsfell, Keasdale Rd, Carr Bank, MILNTHORPE, Cumbria,
         LA7 7JZ.
         http://www.ocsg.org.uk
         Mem Sec: Malcolm Cox
○   *S; for those who use sails on canoes & kayaks

Open Spaces Society
    the working title of the **Commons, Open Spaces & Footpaths**
    Preservation Society

Operational Research Society   (ORSoc)   1948
- ■ Seymour House, 12 Edward St, BIRMINGHAM, W Midlands, B1 2RX.   (hq)
  0121-233 9300   fax 0121-233 0321
  email email@theorsociety.com
  http://www.theorsociety.com
  Sec & Gen Mgr: Gavin Blackett
- ▲ Company Limited by Guarantee; Registered Charity
- Br 10 regions
- ○ *L; the advancement of the knowledge & applications of operational research
- Gp Agricultural & natural resources; Community OR; Criminal justice; Decision analysis; Defence; Financial services; Forecasting; Health & social services; Independent consultants; Information systems; Local search; Mathematical programming; OR+strategy; OR for developing countries; Problem structuring methods; Productivity measurement; Simulation; System dynamics (SD+)
- ● Conf - Mtgs - ET - Res - Exhib - SG - Inf - Lib - Careers information - Publicity for OR grants
- < Intl Fedn of Operational Res Socs (IFORS); Assn of Eur OR Socs (EURO)
- M 2,290 i, UK / 310 i, o'seas
  (Sub: £69)
- ¶ Jnl - 12; ftm, institutional only nm.
  Inside OR - 12; ftm only.   O.R. Insight -4.
  European Jnl of Information Systems - 6.
  Knowledge Management Research & Practice - 4.
  Jnl of Simulation - 4.

Ophthalmic Lens Manufacturers', Assemblers' & Distributors' Association   (OLMADA)   1950
- ■ 199 Gloucester Terrace, LONDON, W2 6LD.   (hq)
  020 7298 5123   fax 020 7298 5120
  email info@fmo.co.uk
- ▲ Company Limited by Guarantee
- ○ *T; prescription spectacles
- ● Conf - Mtgs - Exhib - Inf - LG
- < Fedn Mfrg Opticians
- M 85 f
- ¶ AR; ftm only.

Ophthalmological Products Trade & Industry Conference   (OPTIC (UK))   1984
- ■ PO Box 540, WINCHESTER, Hants, SO23 3FA.   (hq)
  01962 870850
  http://www.opticuk.org
- ○ *N

Optical Confederation   2010
- ■ 199 Gloucester Terrace, LONDON, W2 6LD.
  http://www.opticalconfederation.org.uk
- ○ *N; to speak with a united voice for patients, professionals & the sector & for greater cohesion of the 5 optical bodies - the Association of British Dispensing Opticians, the Association of Contact Lens Manufacturers, the Association of Optometrists, the Federation of Manufacturing Opticians, & the Federation of Ophthalmic & Dispensing Opticians
- M 5 org

Optical Equipment Manufacturers' & Suppliers' Association   (OEMSA)   1990
- ■ 199 Gloucester Terrace, LONDON, W2 6LD.
  020 7298 5123   fax 020 7298 5120
  email info@fmo.co.uk
  Contact: the Hon Sec
- ▲ Un-incorporated Society
- ○ *T
- ● Mtgs
- < Fedn Mfrg Opticians
- M 18 f

Optical Frame Importers' & Manufacturers' Association   (OFIMA)   1983
- ■ 199 Gloucester Terrace, LONDON, W2 6LD.   (hq)
  020 7405 8101   fax 020 7831 2797
  email info@fmo.co.uk
  Contact: the Hon Sec
- ○ *T; companies importing & distributing spectacle frames manufactured outside the UK
- ● Mtgs
- < Fedn Mfrg Opticians
- M 45 f
- ¶ AR; ftm only.

Optra Exhibitions UK   (OEUK)   1968
- ■ 199 Gloucester Terrace, LONDON, W2 6LD.   (hq)
  020 7298 5123   fax 020 7298 5120
  email info@fmo.co.uk
  Contact: the Hon Sec
- ▲ Un-incorporated Society
- ○ *T; to formulate the ophthalmic optical trades policy on exhibitions
- ● Mtgs - Exhib
- < Fedn Mfrg Opticians
- M c 40 f

Oral History Society
- ■ c/o Dept of History, University of Essex, COLCHESTER, Essex, CO4 3SQ.   (hq)
  email rob.perks@bl.uk   http://www.oralhistory.org.uk
  Sec: Robert Perks
- ▲ Registered Charity
- ○ *L; study & writing of history through the words of people who experienced it
- Gp Archives; Care of the elderly; Local history; Reminiscence; Political history; Social history
- ● Conf - Mtgs - Res - Inf
- M 600 i, 300 org
- ¶ Oral History - 2.

Orchid Society of Great Britain   (OSGB)   1950
- NR 103 North Rd, Three Bridges, CRAWLEY, W Sussex, RH10 1SQ.   (hsp)
  01293 528615
  http://www.orchid-society-gb.org.uk
  Hon Sec: Mrs Val Micklewright
- ▲ Registered Charity
- Br 3
- ○ *H; support & encouragement in amateur orchid growing; orchid conservation
- ● Mtgs - Exhib - Comp - Inf - Lib - PL - VE - Conservation of orchids by redistribution of deceased members' plants
- < R Horticl Soc; American Orchid Soc; Barbara Everard Trust for Orchid Consvn
- M 1,011 i, 25 org, UK / 69 i, 45 org, o'seas
- ¶ Jnl - 4; ftm only.
  Orchid Cultivation Booklet; ftm, £3 nm.

Order of Malta   1174
- IRL St John's House, 32 Clyde Rd, DUBLIN 4, Republic of Ireland.
  353 (1) 614 0033   fax 353 (1) 668 5288
  email omac@orderofmalta.ie
  http://www.orderofmalta.ie
- ○ *W; care in the community

© CBD Research Ltd · Beckenham · BR3 5JS · Tel 020 8650 7745 · E-mail cbd@cbdresearch.com · www.cbdresearch.com

Order of Woodcraft Chivalry   (OWC)   1916
- ■ 22 West Moor Lane, Heslington, YORK, YO10 5ER.   (hsp)
  Recorder: Katherine Pringle
- ▲ Un-incorporated Society
- Br 3
- ○ *G; family outdoor activities as a means of character development, self-sufficiency & initiative in adults as well as children
- Gp Camping in adverse conditions for survival skills; Country dancing; Woodcraft
- ● Inf - VE
- ¶ Pine Cone (Jnl) - 4; ftm, £6 nm.

Orders & Medals Research Society   (OMRS)   1942
- ■ PO Box 1233, HIGH WYCOMBE, Bucks, HP11 9BW.   (hsb)
  01494 441207
  email generalsecretary@omrs.org.uk
  http://www.omrs.org.uk
  Gen Sec: Peter M R Helmore
- ▲ Un-incorporated Society
- Br 10; Australia, Canada, Hong Kong, New Zealand
- ○ *G; to foster an interest in orders, decorations & campaign medals; to publish the results of members' researches
- Gp Miniature medal collectors; Ribbon collectors
- ● Mtgs - Res - Lib - Annual convention
- M 1,850 i, 63 f, 39 org, UK / 753 i, 17 f, 22 org, o'seas
- ¶ Orders & Medals - 4;   LM - 2 yrly; both ftm only.

Ordnance Society   (OS)   1988
- NR 3 Maskell Way, FARNBOROUGH, Hants, GU14 0PU.   (mem/sp)
  01252 521201
  http://www.freespace.virgin.net/ordnance.society/
  Mem Sec: Iain McKenzie
- ▲ Un-incorporated Society
- ○ *G; to study all aspects of the history of ordnance, artillery & ammunition

Orff Society UK   1964
- ■ 7 Rothesay Ave, RICHMOND, Surrey, TW10 5EB.   (hsp)
  020 8876 1944   fax 020 8876 1944
  email orffsocuk@btconnect.com   http://www.orff.org.uk
  Hon Sec: Margaret Murray
- ▲ Un-incorporated Society
- ○ *D, *E; to promote the experience & understanding of Carl Orff's approach to music education; a creative way of teaching music to groups using voices in speech/singing, movement/dance & all percussion in early stages
- ● Conf - ET - Exam - Inf - Lib - Workshops
- < Carl-Orff & Orff-Schulwerk associations & societies worldwide
- M 135 i, 1 f, 8 universities, UK / 11 i, 2 universities, 9 schools, o'seas
- ¶ Orff Times - 2; ftm only.

The Organ Club   1926
- NR 92 The Hawthorns, Charvil, READING, Berks, RG10 9TS.   (mem/sp)
  http://www.organclub.org
  Mem Sec: Mark Jameson
- ○ *D; to promote & develop public education in organs & organ music; to promote study & research
- ● Mtgs - Inf - Lib - PL - VE
- M 500 i, UK / 60 i, o'seas
- ¶ Jnl - 3.   NL - 6;   AR - 1;   Hbks - irreg.

Organic Food Federation   (OFF)   1986
- NR 31 Turbine Way, Eco Tech Business Park, SWAFFHAM, Norfolk, PE37 7XD.   (hq)
  01760 720444
  http://www.orgfoodfed.com
  Exec Sec: Julian Wade
- ▲ Company Limited by Guarantee
- ○ *F, *T; for processors, producers & retailers of organic food
- ● Mtgs - ET - Exhib - Stat - LG
- < UK Register of Organic Food Standards ([UKROPS] A division of DEFRA)
- M c 380 f

Organic Living Association   1971
- ■ St Mary's Villa, Hanley Swan, WORCESTER, WR8 0EA.   (sp)
  fax 01684 310703
  Dir & Sec: Dennis C Nightingale-Smith
- ▲ Un-incorporated Society
- ○ *K; to integrate the production & consumption of food crops grown on healthy, naturally fertilised soil; to disseminate knowledge of nutrition, alternative medicine, conservation & self-sufficient community living
- ● Mtgs - Inf - VE
- M 200 i, UK / 10 i, o'seas
- ¶ NL - 6; free.
  Note: please send sae for information.

Organic Organisation
  an alternative title for the **Henry Doubleday Research Association**

Organisation of Horsebox & Trailer Owners
- NR Whitehill Farm, Hamstead Marshall, NEWBURY, Berks, RG20 0HP.   (hq)
  01488 657651
  email info@horsebox-rescue.co.uk
  http://www.horsebox-rescue.co.uk
- ○ *G; membership covers a road rescue/repair service & tyre network for horsebox breakdown problems

Oriental Ceramic Society   (OCS)   1921
- ■ PO Box 517, CAMBRIDGE, CB21 5BE.   (hq)
  01223 881328   fax 01223 881328
  email ocslondon@btinternet.com
  http://www.ocs-london.com
  The Society of Antiquaries, Burlington House, LONDON, W1J 0BF.   (regd/office)
  Admin: Mrs Mary Painter
- ▲ Company Limited by Guarantee; Registered Charity
- ○ *A, *G; to increase the knowledge & appreciation of ceramics & all the arts of Asia; to provide a link between collectors, curators, scholars & others with like interests
- ● Conf - Mtgs - Res - Exhib - SG - VE
- M 440 i, UK / 500 i, o'seas, & Libraries, museums & other ceramic societies
- ¶ Transactions - 1; ftm only.
  (Sub: £55 (home), £50 (o'seas), £100 (corporate), £100 (benefactor) £25 (under-25 & curators)).

Original Pearly Kings & Queens Association   (OPKA)   1975
- § 14 Shelton Avenue, WARLINGHAM, Surrey, CR6 9NE
  020 8556 5971; 020 8508 6467
  http://www.thepearlies.com
  Trustee: Louisa Hitchen
  a registered charity supporting the church of St Martin's-in-the-Fields; it also raises money for nominated charities to provide a better way of living & support those in need of help

Orkney Chamber of Commerce   1992
- NR PO Box 6202, KIRKWALL, Orkney, KW15 1YG.
- ○ *C

Orkney Heritage Society   1979
- ■ PO Box 6220, KIRKWALL, Orkney, KW15 9AD.   (hsp)
  email orkneyheritagesociety@gmail.com
  http://www.orkneycommunities.co.uk/OHS
  Hon Sec: Lynn Campbell
- ○ *G; to stimulate public interest in, & care for, the beauty, history & character of Orkney

Ornamental Aquatic Trade Association   (OATA)   1991
- NR Wessex House, 40 Station Rd, WESTBURY, Wilts, BA13 3TN.
  (hq)
  0870 043 4013   fax 01373 301236
  email info@ornamentalfish.org
  http://www.ornamentalfish.org
  Chief Exec: Keith Davenport
- ▲ Company Limited by Guarantee
- ○ *T; for the ornamental fish industry
- ● ET - Stat - Inf
- M c 700 f
- ¶ The Voice (NL) - 4;   OATA Worldwide NL - 12;
  LM - 1; all ftm only.   Handbooks.
  Publications list available.

Ornithological Society of the Middle East   (OSME)   1967
- NR c/o RSPB, The Lodge, SANDY, Beds, SG19 2DL.
  (mail/address)
  01636 703512   fax 01442 822623
  email secretary@osme.org   http://www.osme.org
  Sec: John Bartlet,   Chmn: Keith Betton
- ▲ Registered Charity
- ○ *G; recording, conservation study of wild birds in the Middle East
- ● Conf - ET - Res - SG - Lib - LG
- M 429 i, 3 f, 68 org, UK / 325 i, o'seas
- ¶ Sandgrouse - 2; ftm, £5 nm.

Orthodontic Technicians Association   (OTA)   1971
- ■ Centre for Dental Technology, Room T018 CSHS, UWIC,
  Western Ave, Llandaff, CARDIFF, CF5 2YB.   (chmn/b)
  029 2041 6899   fax 029 2041 6898
  email jlewis@uwic.ac.uk   http://www.ota-uk.org
  Chmn: Jeff Lewis
- ▲ Un-incorporated Society
- ○ *P; to encourage the study, improve the practice & advance the knowledge of the science of orthodontic laboratory techniques
- Gp Education sub-c'ee
- ● Conf - Mtgs - ET - Exhib - Comp - Inf - PL - Empl - LG
- < Brit Orthodontic Soc (BOS)
- M 250 i, UK / 5 i, 3 f, o'seas
- ¶ NL - 4;   Proceedings - 1; both ftm only.

Oscar Wilde Society   (OWS)   1990
- NR Kambah, Harcourt Hill, OXFORD, OX2 9AS.   (memsec/p)
  http://www.oscarwildesociety.co.uk
  Mem Sec: Cressida Battersby
- ▲ Un-incorporated Society
- ○ *A; to further interest in & knowledge of, the life & works of Oscar Wilde
- ● Conf - Mtgs - ET - Res - Exhib - Comp - Inf - VE - Lib
- < Alliance of Literary Socs
- M 210 i, UK / 75 i, o'seas
- ¶ The Wildean (Jnl) - 2.
  Intentions (NL) - 5.

Osteopathic Sports Care Association   (OSCA)   1995
- NR 1 Brewers Yard, Ivel Rd, SHEFFORD, Beds, SG17 5GY.
  07807 356485
  email oscasecretary@hotmail.co.uk
  http://www.osca.org.uk
- ▲ Un-incorporated Society
- ○ *M; osteopathic education, promotion & sports care
- Gp Sub-c'ees: Conferences, Periodical, Post graduate education
- ● Conf - Mtgs - ET - Res - Inf - VE
- < in partnership with Nat Sports Medicine Inst
- M c 250 i
- ¶ Still Improving Sport - 4.

Outdoor Advertising Association of Great Britain Ltd   (OAA)   1982
- NR Summit House, 27 Sale Place, LONDON, W2 1YR.   (hq)
  020 7973 0315   fax 020 7973 0318
  email enquiries@oaa.org.uk   http://www.oaa.org.uk
  Chief Exec: Alan James
- ○ *T; for UK poster contractors
- M f

Outdoor Advertising Council
    see **Outdoor Media Centre**

Outdoor Industries Association   (OIA)   2010
- NR ECIA Ratho, South Platt Hill, Newbridge, EDINBURGH,
  EH28 8AA.
  0131-333 4414
  email info@outdoorindustriesassociation.co.uk
  Chief Exec; Louise Ramsay
- ○ *T; for manufacturers, retailers & other organisations providing products & services for the outdoor leisure pursuits market in the UK
- ● ET - Inf
- M c 120 f

Outdoor Media Association
- IRL Arena House (office 201), Arena Road, Seaford Industrial
  Estate, DUBLIN 18, Republic of Ireland.
  353 (1) 201 6760
  http://www.oma.ie
  Dir: Su Duff

Outdoor Media Centre   1947
- ■ Summit House, 27 Sale Place, LONDON, W1 1YR.   (hq)
  020 7973 0318
  email enquiries@outdoormediacentre.org.uk
  http://www.ourdoormediacentre.org.uk
  Chief Exec: Chris Baker
- ▲ Un-incorporated Society
- ○ *N
- ● Conf - Mtgs - ET - LG
- M c 300 f

Outdoor Power Equipment Council
    a division of the **Agricultural Engineers' Association**

Outdoor Swimming Society   (OSS)
- ■ 10 Turners Tower, RADSTOCK, Somerset, BA3 5UP.
  http://www.outdoorswimmingsociety.com
- ○ *G, *S; for all who enjoy swimming in Britain's lakes, rivers, lidos & the sea

Outdoor Writers' & Photographers' Guild   (OWG)   1980
■   1 Waterside Close, GARSTANG, Lancs, PR3 1HJ.   (hsp)
    01995 605340   fax 0871 266 8621
    email info@owg.org.uk   http://www.owg.org.uk
    Hon Sec: Terry Marsh
▲   Un-incorporated Society
○   *P; to promote a high professional standard among writers who
    specialise in outdoor activities; to provide a forum for
    members to meet, includes writers, photographers,
    illustrators, broadcasters
●   ET - VE - Awards to members - Press trips
<   Creators' Rights Alliance
M   160 i, UK / 5 i, o'seas
¶   Outdoor Focus - 4;
    Electronic Media Bulletin - 6; both ftm only.
✕   2007 Outdoor Writers' Guild

Ovacome: the ovarian cancer support network   1996
■   PO Box 6294, LONDON, W1A 7WJ.   (hq)
    020 7299 6654   fax 020 7631 4674
    email ovacome@ovacome.org.uk
    http://www.ovacome.org.uk
    Trustee: Adrian Dickinson
▲   Registered Charity
○   *W; a nationwide support group for all those affected by
    ovarian cancer - sufferers, families, carers & health
    professionals
●   Conf - Mtgs - ET - Res - Inf - LG
    Support line: 0845 371 0554
M   1,700 i, 100 hospitals, care professionals
¶   NL - 3;   AR; both free.

Ovarian Cancer Support Network
    see **Ovacome: the ovarian cancer support network**

Over Fifties Association   (TOFFS)   1990
NR   29 Hill Court, Hanger Lane, LONDON, W5 3DF.   (hq)
    020 8998 2065
    Chmn: Eric Bellenie
○   *K; to abolish age discrimination; to establish training centres;
    to encourage cooperative commercial ventures
M   10,000 i, 50 f

Overeaters Anonymous   (OA)   1960
■   483 Green Lanes, LONDON, N13 4BS.   (mail address)
    0700 078 4985
    http://www.oagb.org.uk
Br   200; worldwide
○   *W; to help compulsive eaters & people with eating disorders to
    recover using the 12 steps adopted from Alcoholics
    Anonymous
●   Conf - Mtgs
M   i [unknown]
¶   Lifeline - 12.

Overseas Press & Media Association   (OPMA)   1965
NR   CRI-Media Ltd, PO Box 3345, COVENTRY, Warks, CV6 6YD.
    (asa)
    024 7636 1888   fax 024 7636 3916
    http://www.opma.co.uk
    Hon Sec: Sandrine Marchal
▲   Company Limited by Guarantee
○   *T; to promote the interests of advertising representatives of
    media from overseas
●   Mtgs - ET
M   c 150 f
¶   Overseas Press & Media Guide - 1.

Overseas Territories Association
    see **United Kingdom Overseas Territories Association**

** Owner Drivers Society
    Organisation lost: see Introduction paragraph 3

Oxford Down Sheep Breeders' Association   (ODSBA)   1889
NR   Meadow View, Kelby, GRANTHAM, Lincs, NG32 3AJ.   (hsp)
    01400 230142
    email secretary@oxforddownsheep.org.uk
    http://www.oxforddownsheep.org.uk
    Sec: Mrs Ruth Mawer
▲   Company Limited by Guarantee; Registered Charity
○   *B
●   Mtgs - Exhib - Comp - Stat - Inf
<   Nat Sheep Assn
M   70 i, 2 f, UK / 1 i, o'seas
¶   Flock Book - 1; £7.
    The Oxford Down - One Hundred Years of Breeding; £5.

Oxford Sandy & Black Pig Society   (OSB)   1985
NR   Field Farm, Church Rd, North Leigh, WITNEY, Oxon,
    OX29 6TX.   (hsp)
    01993 881207
    email barnsnap.pigs@btinternet.com
    http://www.oxfordsandypigs.co.uk
    Hon Sec: Peter Colson
○   *B; to promote one of the oldest British pig breeds
●   Mtgs - Exhib - Comp - Inf - Agricultural shows
M   c 100 i
¶   NL - 6/8; free.   Herdbook - 1; ftm.

Oxford University Archaeological Society   (OUAS)   1911
NR   Institute of Archaeology, 36 Beaumont St, OXFORD,
    OX1 2PG.   (mail address)
    Contact: The President
▲   Un-incorporated Society
○   *L; investigation of local antiquities
Gp   Excavations; Anglo-Saxon, Mediaeval & Roman archaeology
M   i

Oxfordshire Architectural & Historical Society   (OAHS)   1839
NR   99 Wellington St, THAME, Oxon, OX9 3BW.   (hsp)
    email secretary@oahs.org.uk   http://www.oahs.org.uk
    Hon Sec: Mrs Jill Hind
▲   Registered Charity
○   *L; study of local history, archaeology & architecture
Gp   Listed buildings c'ee; Oxford City & County Archaeological
    Forum; Victorian
●   Mtgs - Lib - VE
<   Coun Brit Archaeology
M   600 i, 150 org, UK / 10 i, 10 org, o'seas
¶   Oxoniensia (Jnl) - 1; ftm, £12 nm.

Oxfordshire Chamber of Commerce
    a local chamber of **Thames Valley Chamber of Commerce &
    Industry**

Oxfordshire Record Society   (ORS)   1919
NR   Tithe Corner, 67 Hill Crescent, Finstock, CHIPPING NORTON,
    Oxon, OX7 3BT.   (hsp)
    email morley.shaun@gmail.com
    Sec: Shaun Morley
▲   Registered Charity
○   *L; to publish edited texts of local history documents relating to
    the County of Oxford

P G Wodehouse Society (UK) 1995
NR 26 Radcliffe Rd, CROYDON, Surrey, CR0 5QE. (mem/sp)
     http://www.eclipse.co.uk/wodehouse
     Mem Sec: Christine Hewitt
▲ Un-incorporated Society
○ *A; to promulgate the enjoyment of the writings of
     P G Wodehouse (1881-1975)
M i
     (Sub: £15)
¶ Wooster Sauce - 4; ftm only.

**Pacific Islands Society of the United Kingdom & Ireland
(PISUKI) 1981**
NR 9 Pershore Rd, HALESOWEN, W Midlands, B63 4QJ.
     (mem/sp)
     Mem Sec: David Evans
▲ Un-incorporated Society
○ *X; for Pacific Islanders in the UK & Ireland & to bring together
     all those interested in, or concerned with, the islands
● Conf - Mtgs - Inf - Social activities especially for islanders
     temporarily in UK
M c 300 i & f, 16 org
¶ The Outrigger (NL) - 3/4; ftm.

Packaging Federation (PF) 1995
■ 1 Warwick Row, LONDON, SW1E 5ER. (regd/office)
     020 7808 7217   fax 020 7808 7218
     email dicksearle@packagingfedn.co.uk
     http://www.packagingfedn.co.uk
     Chief Exec: Dick Searle
▲ Company Limited by Guarantee
○ *T; to represent members, who are the major packaging firms,
     on economic & environmental issues
● Mtgs - LG
M f

Packaging & Films Association (PAFA) 1973
■ Gothic House (2nd floor), Barker Gate, NOTTINGHAM,
     NG1 1JU. (hq)
     0115-959 8389   fax 0115-959 9326
     email pafa@pafa.co.uk   http://www.pafa.co.uk
     Chief Exec: David Tyson
▲ Company Limited by Guarantee
○ *T; converters, producers,thermoformers & distributors of
     flexible packaging & industrial films
● Mtgs - ET - Stat - LG
< Plast Euro Film; Brit Plastics Fedn; Packaging Fedn
M 55 f, UK / 4 f, o'seas
¶ PIFA Annual review - 1; ftm, £25 nm.
     PIFA Annual Statistical Report - 1; £25 m, £50 nm.
× 2007 Flexible Packaging Association (merged
     2009 Packaging & Industrial Films Association (merged)

Packaging & Industrial Films Association
     in 2007 merged with the Flexible Packaging Association & in 2009
     became the **Packaging & Films Association**

Packaging Society
     see IOP: the Packaging Society, a division of the **Institute of
     Materials, Minerals & Mining**

Paddle Steamer Preservation Society   (PSPS) 1959
■ 17 Stockfield Close, HIGH WYCOMBE, Bucks, HP15 7LA.
     (regd/office)
     Hon Sec: John Anderson
▲ Company Limited by Guarantee; Registered Charity
Br 5
○ *G, *K; to encourage interest in paddle steamers; retention of
     existing services & preservation of the society's own steamers
Gp Models
● Conf - Mtgs - Res - Exhib - VE - Special cruises
< Transport Trust
M 3,400 i, UK / 100 i, o'seas
¶ Paddle Wheels - 4; ftm.

Paediatric First Aid Association   (PFAA) 2006
NR 178 Marlborough Way, ASHBY DE LA ZOUCH, Leics,
     LE65 2QH.
     020 8798 0766
     email info@pfaa.org.uk   http://www.pfaa.org.uk
     Secretariat: Ian Irwin
○ *P; approval body for paediatric first aid training
● ET

Paediatric Haematology Forum
     a group of the **Royal College of Paediatrics & Child Health**

Paediatric Intensive Care Society
     a group of the **Royal College of Paediatrics & Child Health**

Pagan Federation (PF) 1971
NR BM Box 7097, LONDON, WC1N 3XX.   (mail address)
     07986 034387
     http://www.paganfed.org
     Media Enquiries: Chris Cowley (0798 573 3441)
▲ Un-incorporated Society
○ *G; to promote & defend pagan traditions
● Conf - Mtgs - ET - Inf - VE - LG
M c 4,000 i, UK / 200 i, o'seas
¶ Pagan Dawn - 4;   AR; ftm.
     Various information packs.

Paget's Association 1973
NR 323 Manchester Rd, Walkden, Worsley, MANCHESTER,
     M28 3HH.   (hq)
     0161-799 4646   fax 0161-799 6511
○ *W; to support & inform sufferers of Paget's disease of bone, &
     their carers; to raise awareness of the disease among the
     medical profession & the public at large; to support & raise
     funds for research
× 2011 National Association for the Relief of Paget's Disease

Paget Gorman Society
     has closed.

Pain Association Scotland
■ Moncrieffe Business Centre (suite D), Friarton Rd, PERTH,
     PH2 8DG.   (hq)
     0800 783 6059 (Mon-Fri 0800-1630)
     email info@painassociation.com
     http://www.chronicpaininfo.org
Br 32 in Scotland
○ *W; to pioneer the development & delivery of the self-
     management training approach to chronic pain in Scotland

Paint & Powder Finishing Association
     a group of the **Surface Engineering Association**

© CBD Research Ltd · Beckenham · BR3 5JS · Tel 020 8650 7745 · E-mail cbd@cbdresearch.com · www.cbdresearch.com

Paint Research Association   (PRA)   1926
NR   14 Castle Mews, High St, HAMPTON, Middx, TW12 2NP.   (hq)
      020 8487 0800   fax 020 8487 0805
      http://www.pra.org.uk
▲   Company Limited by Guarantee
○   *Q; research, technology & information services for the
      coatings & related industries
●   Conf - Mtgs - ET - Res - Exhib - Stat - Inf - Lib
<   Assn Indep Res & Technology Orgs
M   100 f, UK / 75 f, o'seas

Painting & Decorating Association   2002
■   32 Coton Rd, NUNEATON, Warks, CV11 5TW.   (hq)
      024 7635 3776   fax 024 7635 4513
      http://www.paintingdecoratingassociation.co.uk
▲   Un-incorporated Society
○   *T; for professional painters & decorators in GB
●   Conf - Mtgs - ET - Exhib - Comp - LG
M   2,400 f

Palaeontographical Society   (PalSoc)   1847
■   Dept of Palaeontology, The Natural History Museum,
      Cromwell Rd, LONDON, SW7 5BD.   (hsb)
      020 7942 5552   fax 020 7942 5546
      http://www.palaeosoc.org
      Pres: Dr A B Smith
▲   Registered Charity
○   *L, *Q; promotion of study of geology through publication of
      monographs on British fossil fauna & flora
●   Mtgs - ET - Res - Publication of monographs
M   144 i, 210 f, 110 org
      (Sub: £33 i, £110 org)
¶   Monographs - 1; £33 m, £210 nm.

Palaeontological Association   1957
NR   c/o Dr T J Palmer, Institute of Geography & Earth Sciences,
      University of Wales Aberystwyth, ABERYSTWYTH, Ceredigion,
      SY23 3BD.   (exec/offr)
      http://www.palass.org
      Exec Officer: Dr T J Palmer
▲   Registered Charity
○   *L, *Q; to study palaeontology (life of the past) & its allied
      sciences
●   Conf - Mtgs - Res - Inf - PL
M   c 1,200 i, c 700 f, UK / c 500 i, o'seas
¶   Palaeontology - 6; £28 yr m, £55 per part nm.

Pali Text Society   (PTS)   1881
NR   c/o CPI Antony Rowe Ltd, Unit 4 Pegasus Way, Bowerhill
      Industrial Estate, MELKSHAM, Wilts, SN12 6TR.   (hq)
      0117-955 4100 (Mon/Wed/Fri 1900-1600)   fax 0117-
      955 4100
      email pts@palitext.com   http://www.palitext.com
▲   Registered Charity
○   *L, *Q, *R; promoting the study of Pali by publishing Pali texts in
      Roman characters, translations & ancillary work; funding
      research students
●   Res - Inf - Lib - Publishing
M   c 570 i
¶   Jnl - irreg.   List of Issues; free.
      NL - 2;   AR; both ftm only.

Palmerston Forts Society   (PFS)   1984
NR   Fort Nelson, Portsdown Hill Rd, FAREHAM, Hants,
      PO17 6AN.   (hq)
      http://www.palmerstonforts.org.uk
      023 9266 0261 (0900-1700 hrs)   (chmn/b)
      Vice-Chmn: Geoffrey M Salvetti
▲   Registered Charity; Un-incorporated Society
○   *G, *L; a forum for research into the field of Victorian
      fortification & artillery; to offer advice to government & local
      authorities on Victorian fortifications
Gp   Portsdown artillery volunteers
●   Conf - Mtgs - ET - Res - Exhib - SG - Inf - Lib - PL - Artillery re-
      enactment (authentic Victorian gun drills on period pieces)
M   i

Pancreatic Society of GB & Ireland
■   HPB Surgical Unit, Freeman Hospital, NEWCASTLE upon TYNE,
      NE7 7DN.   (sb)
      email jeremy.french@nuth.nhs.uk
      http://www.pancsoc.org.uk
      Sec: Jeremy French
▲   Registered Charity
○   *L
●   Conf - ET - Res - SG
M   180 i, UK / 20 i, o'seas

Paper Agents Association   (PAA)   1924
■   48 Courtmoor Ave, FLEET, Hants, GU52 7UE.   (dir/p)
      01252 680449   fax 07092 386132
      email info@paa.org.uk   http://www.paa.org.uk
      Dir: John R Paine
▲   Un-incorporated Society
○   *T; to promote a better & closer understanding among
      accredited agents & mill owned sales offices in the UK & Eire
      representing overseas paper & board makers; to represent
      legitimate overall best interests in the local market
Gp   Carton boards, industrial & other boards; Corrugated case
      materials; Packaging, industrial & other papers; Publications
      & fine paper
●   Mtgs - Stat - LG
<   Confedn Paper Inds
M   39 f

Paper Industry Technical Association Ltd   (PITA)   1920
■   5 Frecheville Court, BURY, Lancs, BL9 0UF.   (hq)
      0161-764 5858   fax 0161-764 5353
      email info@pita.co.uk   http://www.pita.co.uk
      Gen Enquiries: Barry Read
▲   Company Limited by Guarantee; Registered Charity
○   *P; for all involved in the pulp, paper, converting & allied
      industries
Gp   Coating; Engineering; Environmental; Finishing; Raw materials
●   Conf - Mtgs - ET - SG - Inf - VE
M   1.097 i, 138 f, UK / 150 i, o'seas
¶   Paper Technology - 12; ftm, £100 yr nm.
      PITA Ybk - 1; ftm only.
      The Essential Guide to Aqueous Coating of Paper & Board
      (textbook); £75 m, £85 nm.

Paper Makers' Allied Trades Association
      has closed

Paperweight Collectors Circle   (PCC)   1981
■   PO Box 941, Comberton, CAMBRIDGE PDO, CB23 7GQ.
      (mail)
      01223 264656
      http://www.paperweightcollectorscircle.org.uk
      Sec: Angela Faulkner
▲   Un-incorporated Society
○   *G; for collectors of paperweights; to promote the art of
      paperweight makers
●   Mtgs - Exhib - VE
<   Paperweight Collectors Assn (USA)
M   200 i, UK / 30 i, o'seas
¶   NL - 4; ftm only.

Parakart Association   (PKA)   1993
NR   1 Withington Avenue, Culcheth, WARRINGTON, Cheshire,
        WA3 4JE.   (mem/sp)
        email thepka@googlemail.com
        http://www.parakartassociation.co.uk
        Mem Sec: Adrian Lavelle
○   *S; the regulating body for kite buggying
●   Mtgs - Comp
M   i
        (Sub: £20)

Parallel Traders Association
NR   c/o Clintons, 55 Drury Lane, LONDON, WC2B 5SQ.   (asa)
        020 7379 6080
        Contact: Gary Lux
○   *T

Parity   1986
■   Constables, Windsor Rd, ASCOT, Berks, SL5 7LF.   (hsp)
        01344 621167
        http://www.parity-uk.org
        Hon Sec: David Yarwood
▲   Registered Charity
○   *K; to promote & protect the equal rights of men & women to
        the enjoyment of all civil, political, economic, social &
        cultural rights under the law
Gp   Human rights; Legal; Parliamentary; Pensions; Research
●   Mtgs - Res - Inf - Identifying & monitoring unequal treatment of
        men & women under law - Promoting legal activities
M   c 300 i, 2 trade unions, UK / c 5 i, o'seas
¶   NL - 4.   Information sheets - irreg.

Parkinson's Disease Society of the United Kingdom   (PDS)
1969
NR   215 Vauxhall Bridge Rd, LONDON, SW1V 1EJ.   (hq)
        020 7931 8080
        http://www.parkinsons.org.uk
        Chief Exec: Linda Kelly
▲   Company Limited by Guarantee; Registered Charity
Br   250
○   *W; welfare, research, education of the public & help to
        patients & their relatives
Gp   Support group: YAPPERS - Young Alert Parkinsonians, Partners
        & Relatives
●   Conf - Mtgs - ET - Res - Stat - Inf - Lib - PL
<   Eur Parkinson's Disease Soc (EPDA)
M   27,000 i

Parrot Society UK   1967
■   92a High St, BERKHAMSTED, Herts, HP4 2BL.   (hq)
        01442 872245   fax 01442 872245
        email les.rance@theparrotsocietyuk.org
        http://www.theparrotsocietyuk.org
        Sec: Les A Rance
▲   Registered Charity
○   *B, *G; to promote the breeding & keeping of all parrot-like
        birds
●   Conf - Mtgs - Exhib - Inf - VE - LG
<   Soc for the Protection of Aviculture
M   4,777 i, UK / 171 i, o'seas
¶   The Magazine of the Parrot Society UK - 12; m only.

Parson Woodforde Society   1968
■   22 Gaynor Close, WYMONDHAM, Norfolk, NR18 0EA.   (hsp)
        email editor@parsonwoodforde.org.uk
        http://www.parsonwoodforde.org.uk
        Mem Sec: Mrs A Elliott
▲   Registered Charity
○   *A; to extend & develop the knowledge of the life of the
        eighteenth century diarist James Woodforde (1740-1803) &
        of the society in which he lived
●   Mtgs - Res
<   Alliance of Literary Societies
M   390 i, UK / 10 i, o'seas
¶   Jnl - 4;   NL - 4; both ftm only.
        [15 volumes of diary material]; £20-£25 (available from the
        President).

Partially Sighted Society   (PSS)   1973
NR   7-9 Bennetthorpe, DONCASTER, S Yorks, DN2 6AA.   (hq)
        0844 477 4966   fax 0844 477 4966
        http://www.partsight.org.uk
        Sec: Norman Stenson
▲   Company Limited by Guarantee
Br   10
○   *W; to help visually impaired people to make the best use of
        remaining sight; to raise public awareness of the problems
        associated with visual impairment
●   Inf - Supply of aids & equipment to help in daily living
M   i, f & clubs
¶   Oculus - 4.   AR.

Passenger Boat Association   (PBA)   1970
NR   PO Box 453, FLEET, Hants, GU51 3PS.   (hsb)
        01252 560027
        http://www.passengerboats.co.uk
        Sec: Roger Flitter
○   *T; to promote the prosperity of companies operating boats on
        the rivers, canals, lakes & coastal waters, throughout the UK,
        providing scheduled transport services, pleasure trips, private
        hire & charter services
●   Mtgs
M   i, f & associates

Passenger Shipping Association
since 2007 **Association of Cruise Experts**

Passive Fire Protection Federation   (PFPF)   1995
■   Kingsley House, Ganders Business Park, Kingsley, BORDON,
        Hants, GU35 9LU.   (asa)
        01420 471621   fax 01420 471511
        http://www.pfpf.org
        Sec: John G Fairley
○   *T; 'the primary measure integrated within the constructional
        fabric of a biulding to provide inherent fire safety &
        protection by responding against heat, smoke & flame to
        maintain the fundamental requiremnets of building
        compartmentation, structural stability, fire separation & a safe
        means of escape'
M   14 f, 9 f liaison

Past Life Therapists Association   (PLTA)
NR   c/o Hypnotherapy South West, Virginstow, BEAWORTHY,
        Devon, EX21 5EA.
        01409 211559
        http://www.pastliferegression.co.uk/pltahome/html
        Chmn: Andrew Hillsdon
○   *P

Pastel Society
a member of the **Federation of British Artists**

© CBD Research Ltd · Beckenham · BR3 5JS · Tel 020 8650 7745 · E-mail cbd@cbdresearch.com · www.cbdresearch.com

Pathological Society of Great Britain & Ireland   (Path Society)   1906
■ 2 Carlton House Terrace, LONDON, SW1Y 5AF.   (sb)
   020 7976 1260   fax 020 7930 2981
   email admin@pathsoc.org   http://www.pathsoc.org
   Pres: Prof D A Levison,   Gen Sec: Prof C S Herrington
▲ Registered Charity
○ *L; 'dedicated to understanding disease'
● Conf - ET - Exhib
M 1,039 i, UK / 294 i, o'seas
   (Sub: £48 (full members), £10 (concessions))
¶ Jnl of Pathology - 12; £54 m, £678 nm.   NL - 2; ftm only.

Patient Information Forum   (PiF)   1997
■ 500 Chiswick High Rd, LONDON, W4 5RG.   (hq)
   07813 143384
   email secretary@pifonline.org.uk
   http://www.pifonline.org.uk
   Pres: Mark Duman (07824 605352)
▲ Un-incorporated Society
Br 13
○ *M, *N; for those producing, developing, disseminating &
   researching high quality information for patients, carers, their
   families & others
● Conf - Mtgs - ET - Res - Inf - LG - Quality, appraisal,
   accreditation - Consulting
M 778 i, UK / 2 i, o'seas
¶ [subscription, £50 yr].

Patients Association   1963
§ PO Box 935, HARROW, Middx, HA1 3YJ.   (hq)
   020 8423 9111   fax 020 8423 9119
   email mailbox@patients-association.com
   http://www.patients-association.com
● Helpline: 0845 608 4455
   Promotes the voice of patients by offering them an opportunity
   to share their experiences of health services, and uses this
   knowledge to work with the NHS and other healthcare
   providers in improving services.

Patients' Voice for Medical Advance
NR Healthcare Landscape, 100-104 Upper Richmond Rd,
   LONDON, SW15 2SP.
   020 3130 0630
   email info@healthcarelandscape.com
   http://www.patientsvoice.org.uk
   Dir: Katherine Murphy
○ *K; 'a patients' group which supports the humane use of
   animals & genetic technology, where necessary, in medical
   research'

Pattern Model & Mouldmakers Association   (PMMMA)   1954
NR National Metalforming Centre, 47 Birmingham Rd,
   WEST BROMWICH, W Midlands, B70 6PY.   (hq)
   0121-601 6976   fax 01544 340332
   email andrew@pmmma.co.uk
   http://www.pmmma.co.uk
   Sec: Andrew Turner
▲ Un-incorporated Society
○ *T
Gp Mould makers; Pattern makers
● Mtgs - Exhib - Inf - LG
< Wld Foundrymen Org; Inst Cast Metals Engrs
M 11 f
¶ Patternmaking News - 4.

Patton Historical Society
   is no longer active

Payroll Alliance   1985
NR Quadrant House (13th floor), The Quadrant, SUTTON, Surrey,
   SM2 5AS.   (hq)
   020 8401 1828
○ *P

Peace Pledge Union   (PPU)   1934
■ 1 Peace Passage, LONDON, N7 0BT.   (hq)
   020 7424 9444
   Admin: Annie Bebington
▲ Un-incorporated Society
○ *K; promotion of pacifism & nonviolent solution to
   international, national & local conflict

Peak District Mines Historical Society Ltd   (PDMHS)   1959
■ Peak District Mining Museum, The Pavilion, MATLOCK BATH,
   Derbys, DE4 3NR.   (regd office)
   01629 583834
   email mail@peakmines.co.uk   http://www.pdmhs.com +
   peakmines.com
   Hon Sec: Nigel Nix
▲ Company Limited by Guarantee; Registered Charity
○ *L; to promote, encourage & further the study of & research
   into the mines & mineralogy of the Peak district & adjacent
   areas in England; to catalogue, collect, collate, publish & sell
   material & inforamtion & service, or interest to the members
   & general public
Gp Archaeology & conservation; Mining museum
● Mtgs - Res - Exhib - Inf - Lib - VE - Preservation of artifacts -
   Peak District Mining Museum
< Nat Assn of Mining Hist Orgs (NAMHO)
M 450 i, 10 org, UK / 12, o'seas
¶ Mining History (Jnl) - 2; ftm, £8 nm.   NL - 4; ftm only.

Peak & Northern Footpaths Society   (PNFS)   1894
NR Taylor House, 23 Turncroft Lane, Offerton, STOCKPORT,
   Cheshire, SK1 4AB.   (hq)
   0161 480 3565   fax 0161 429 7279
   email mail@peakandnorthern.org.uk
   http://www.peakandnorthern.org.uk
   Chmn: Clarke Rogerson
▲ Registered Charity
○ *K; preservation, maintenance & defence of public rights of
   way, commons & open spaces in the Northern & Midland
   counties of England
● Conf - Mtgs - Inf - LG
< Brit Trust for Consvn Volunteers (BTCV); Open Spaces Soc;
   Ramblers Assn; NW Coun for Sport; Byways & Bridleways
   Trust
M c 1,000 i, 80 org
¶ Signpost - 4; ftm.   AR; ftm, £2 nm.

Pedestrians Association
   see **Living Streets**

Pedigree Welsh Pig Society   2009
NR Office 12 Enterprise Centre, Bryn Road, Tondu, BRIDGEND,
   Glams, CF32 9BS.   (hq)
   01656 724914
   http://www.pedigreewelsh.com
○ *B
M i
   (Sub: £15)

Peeblesshire Agricultural Society
NR Easter Happrew Old Farm, Stobo, PEEBLES, Scottish Borders,
   EH45 8NT.   (hsp)
   01721 760266
   email campbelljacqui@hotmail.com
   http://www.peebles-show.co.uk
   Sec: Jacqui Campbell
○ *F
● Peebles Show
< Assn of Show & Agricl Orgs

Peeblesshire Archaeological Society (PAS) 1994

- ■ 9 Glen Rd, PEEBLES, EH45 9AY. (hsp)
  01721 722203
  email robknox@9glenrd.freeserve.co.uk
  http://www.peeblesarchsoc.org.uk
  Hon Sec: R D Knox
- ▲ Un-incorporated Society
- ○ *L; to stimulate public interest in the history and archaeology of the Peebles area; to encourage the preservation & recording of features of general historic & archaeological interest by any appropriate action
- ● Conf - Mtgs - Res - Exhib
- < Archaeology Scotland
- M 40 i
- ¶ PAST; Peebles Archaeological Society Times - 4; ftm,nm (free (if attending lecture).

Peel Society

- NR 2 Sunningdale, TAMWORTH, Staffs, B77 4NW.
  http://www.thepeelsociety.org.uk
- ○ *G; Sir Robert Peel (1788-1850), founder of the Metropolitan Police; hence the names 'Bobbies' & 'Peelers'

Pelargonium & Geranium Society 1970

- ■ 8 Ingswell Avenue, Notton, WAKEFIELD, W Yorks, WF4 2NG. (hsp)
  01226 722187
  Hon Sec: David Steele
- ▲ Un-incorporated Society
- Br 11
- ○ *H; to promote interest in the cultivation & hybridisation of pelargoniums & geraniums by amateurs & professionals
- ● Conf - Mtgs - ET - Exhib - Comp - SG - Stat - VE - Lectures - Advisory panel for information
- × 2008 (British & European Geranium Society (British Pelargonium & Geranium Society (merged)

Pembrokeshire Agricultural Society (PAS) 1784

- ■ County Showground, Withybush, HAVERFORDWEST, Pembrokeshire, SA62 4BW. (hq)
  01437 764331   fax 01437 767203
  email info@pembrokeshireshow.co.uk
  http://www.pembsshow.org
  Gen Mgr: Alex Bruce
- ▲ Registered Charity
- ○ *F, *H; agricultural show
- ● Pembrokeshire County Show - Conf - Mtgs - Exhib
- < Assn of Show & Agricl Orgs
- M i

Pembrokeshire Chamber of Commerce
  see **Chamber of Commerce - Pembrokeshire**

Pembrokeshire Historical Society (PHS) 1983

- ■ Headlands, Broad Haven, HAVERFORDWEST, Pembrokeshire, SA65 9RN. (hsp)
  01437 781339
  Hon Sec: Rev Dr David Pusey
- ▲ Un-incorporated Society
- ○ *L, *Q; to promote interest in & research into subjects of historical, archaeological, artistic, genealogical & architectural importance in the heritage of Pembrokeshire
- ● Conf - Mtgs - VE
- > Pembrokeshire Family History Soc; Pembrokeshire local history societies
- M 250 i
- ¶ PHS Jnl - 1; £5 m, £6 nm.

Penguin Collectors' Society (PCS) 1974

- NR 31 Myddelton Sq, LONDON, EC1R 1YB. (regd/office)
  020 7278 8064
  Sec/Treas: Michael Fowle
- ▲ Company Limited by Guarantee
- Br Australia, Canada, USA etc
- ○ *G; to encourage the study, research & collection of Penguin books; to publish relevant material
- ● Conf - Res - Publication
- M 350 i, UK / 50 i, o'seas
- ¶ The Penguin Collector - 2.
  List of publications available on request.

Pennine Way Association 1971

- NR 49 Hedley Hill Terrace, WATERHOUSES, Co Durham, DH7 8AZ. (sp)
  http://www.penninewayassociation.co.uk
  Sec: Doug Moffatt
- ○ *G; to protect the Pennine Way; to campaign for upkeep & refurbishment of signs, sits & bridges

Pensions Action Group

- NR 36 Seaside Avenue, Minster on Sea, SHEERNESS, Kent, ME12 2NN.
  01795 875835
  Andrew Parr
- ○ *G, *K; a protest group on the wind-up of company pension schemes

Pensions Management Institute (PMI) 1976

- ■ PMI House, 4-10 Artillery Lane, LONDON, E1 7LS. (hq)
  020 7247 1452   fax 020 7375 0603
  email enquiries@pensions-pmi.org.uk
  http://www.pensions-pmi.org.uk
  Chief Exec: Vince Linnane
- ▲ Company Limited by Guarantee
- Br 9; Ireland
- ○ *P
- Gp Pensions professionals; Trustees
- ● Conf - Mtgs - ET - Exam - Res - Exhib - Inf - LG
- M 4,700 i, UK / 160 i, o'seas
- ¶ PMI News - 12;   PMI Technical News - 4; both ftm only.

Pentathlon GB
  see **Modern Pentathlon Association of Great Britain Ltd**

Penzance Chamber of Commerce

- NR Sycamores, Relubbus Lane, St Hilary, PENZANCE, Cornwall, TR20 9EG. (sb)
  01736 762888
  http://www.penzance.co.uk/chamber
  Sec: A Vinnac
- ○ *C

People & Dogs Society (PADS) 1988

- ■ Longwood, Carleton Close, PONTEFRACT, W Yorks, WF8 3NB. (hq)
  email pads@btinternet.com   http://www.padsonline.org
  Hon Sec: Mrs K Le Seelleur (0845 269 0093)
- ▲ Registered Charity
- ○ *V; to encourage high standards of dog ownership; to help people with problem dogs or dog-related problems
- ● ET - Exhib - Comp - Inf - Dog shows - Confidential advice line
- < Helplines Assn (associate mem)
- M [not stated]
- ¶ Pawprints - 3; m only.
  Code of Caring (leaflets on dog care);   Factsheets; both free.

PEP & ISA Managers' Association
  since 2007 **Tax Incentivised Savings Association**

PERA   1946

NR   Pera Innovation Park, MELTON MOWBRAY, Leics, LE13 0PB.
        (hq)
        01664 501501
        http://www.pera.com
▲   Company Limited by Guarantee
○   *Q; to promote innovation & productivity within technology &
        manufacturing led organisations through the application of
        current & future thinking & technology transfer practices
M   c 500 f
¶   Pera Abstracts - 5;   Technical Reports - irreg; both ftm only.

Percussive Arts Society   (PAS)

■   25 Copperfield Rd, Cheadle Hulme, CHEADLE, Cheshire,
        SK8 7PN.   (msp)
        0161-439 5757
        http://www.pas.org
        Mem Sec: Ron Baker
○   *D, *P; for teachers, instructors & players of percussive
        instruments
●   ET - Inf
<   Percussive Arts Soc (USA)
M   i
¶   Percussive Notes - 4; ftm.

Percy Grainger Society   (PGS)   1978

■   6 Fairfax Crescent, AYLESBURY, Bucks, HP20 2ES.   (hsp)
        01296 428609   fax 01296 581185
        email pgsoc@percygrainger.org.uk
        http://www.percygrainger.org.uk
        Sec: Barry P Ould
▲   Un-incorporated Society
○   *D; to promote & develop interest in the life & works of the
        Australian composer & pianist Percy Aldridge
        Grainger (1882-1961)
●   Inf - Lib (music & sound archives) - PL
<   Intl Percy Grainger Soc (USA); Friends of Percy Grainger
        Museum (Melbourne, Australia)
M   120 i, 10 f, UK / 300 i, 15 f, o'seas
¶   The Grainger Society Jnl - 2;   Random Round (NL) - 2;
        In a Nutshell - 4;   (subscription for all 3, £14 m, £18 nm).

Performance Textiles Association Ltd   (PTA/MUTA)   1919

■   c/o Luther Pendragon, Priory Court, Pilgrim St, LONDON,
        EC4V 6DR.   (asa)
        020 7618 9196   fax 020 7329 7301
        email info@muta.org.uk
        http://www.performancetextiles.org.uk
▲   Company Limited by Guarantee
○   *T; all facets of the textile industry from production, through
        conversion, manufacture & on to use (includes awnings,
        banners & flags, healthcare products, inflatables, load
        restraints, ropes, cords & slings, shower curtains, tarpaulins,
        tents, webbing, & welding curtains)
Gp   Association of Inflatable Manufacturers, Operators, Designers
        & Suppliers; Reusable Healthcare Textiles Association
        Coaters; Industrial textiles manufacturers; Marquee hire;
        Suppliers
●   Conf - Mtgs - ET - Res - Exhib - Inf - LG - British & European
        Standards
M   250 f
        (Sub: varies)
¶   Performance Textiles - 3;
        Safe Use of & Operation of Marquees & Temporary Structures;
        Business Guide & Ybk - 1;   all free.
        Note: Trades as MUTA

Performing Artists' Media Rights Association
        in 2007 merged with **Phonographic Performance Ltd**

Performing Right Society Ltd
        a member of the **MCPS-PRS Alliance**

Periodical Publishers Association - Interactive
        is no longer active

Periodical Publishers Association of Ireland
        since c 2010 **Magazines Ireland**

Periodical Publishers Association Ltd   (PPA)   1913

NR   Queens House, 28 Kingsway, LONDON, WC2B 6JR.   (hq)
        020 7404 4166   fax 020 7404 4167
        email barry.mcilheney@ppa.co.uk
        http://www.ppa.co.uk
        Chief Exec: Barry McIlheney
▲   Company Limited by Guarantee
○   *T; interests of the UK magazine publishing industry
Gp   Association of Publishing Agencies; Magazines Ireland;
        PPA Scotland
        C'ees: Ad marketing, B2B media, Copyright, Credit
        management, Editorial public affairs, Environmental,
        Finance, Newstrade, PPA Interactive, Parliamentary & legal
        affairs, Production & technology, Subscriptions
        Postal contract gp; Independent Publishers Advisory Council
●   Conf - Mtgs - ET - Res - Exhib - Comp - SG - Stat - Expt - Inf -
        Lib - PL - VE - LG
<   is linked with: Publishers Assn (books), Newspaper Soc
        (newspapers), Newspaper Pubrs Assn (daily newspapers) to
        form the UK Publishing Media
        Online Publishing Assn (US)
M   c 400 f
¶   List of publications available.

Permaculture Association (Britain)   (PcA)   1984

NR   BCM Permaculture Association, LONDON, WC1N 3XX.   (mail
        address)
        0845 458 1805 & 01132 307461
        Coordinator: Andrew Goldring
▲   Registered Charity
○   *F; sustainable design & implementation in agriculture, forestry,
        housing & energy
Gp   Designers' register; Permaculture design courses; Permaculture
        diploma; Projects network; Teachers' register
●   Conf - ET - Res - Exhib - Inf
M   800 i, UK / 50 i, o'seas
¶   Permaculture Works (Jnl) - 4; ftm.

Permanent Show Organisers Association
        is defunct

Permanent Way Institution   (PWI)   1884

■   4 Coombe Rd, FOLKESTONE, Kent, CT19 4EG.   (regd/office)
        01303 274534
        Sec: John Linkin
▲   Company Limited by Guarantee
Br   20; Australia, Ireland, Malaysia, S Africa
○   *L, *P; management, construction & maintenance of railway
        permanent way & works
Gp   Sub-c'ees: Technical (training & education), Textbooks
●   Conf - Mtgs - Exhib - VE
<   Verband Deutscher Eisenbahn-Ingenieure (VDEI); U of Eur
        Railway Engineer Assns (UEEIV)
M   c 4,000 i
¶   Jnl & Report of Proceedings - 4.   British Railway Track.
        The Permanent Way Institution - the first 100 years, 1884-1984.
        New Tracks to the Cities.   Evolution of Permanent Way.

Permit Trainers Association   1973
- ■ Drewitts, Warninglid, HAYWARDS HEATH, W Sussex, RH17 5TB.   (chmn/p)
  01444 461235   fax 01444 461485
  email freddie@pta.eclipse.co.uk
  Chmn: Frederick Gray
  Hon Sec: J Payne (01398 371244)
- ▲ Company Limited by Guarantee
- ○ *P; for racehorse owners & trainers who are training family-owned National Hunt racehorses
- M 300 i

Pernicious Anaemia Society
- NR Brackle House, Brackla St, BRIDGEND, Glam, CF31 1BZ.
  01656 769717
  http://www.pernicious-anaemia-society.org
- ○ *W

Personal Finance Society   (PFS)   1972
- NR 42-48 High Rd, South Woodford, LONDON, E18 2JP.
  020 8530 0852
- ○ *P
- M 22,000 i

Personal Injuries Bar Association   (PIBA)   1995
- NR Crown Office Chambers, 2 Crown Office Row, Temple, LONDON, EC4Y 7HJ.   (sb)
  email snowden@crownofficechambers.com
  http://www.piba.org.uk
  Sec: Steven Snowden
- ▲ Un-incorporated Society
- ○ *P; to represent the Personal Injury Bar of England & Wales; to provide education & training to barristers in the field of personal injuries
- ● Conf - Mtgs - ET - Inf - LG
- M c 1,100 i
- ¶ NL - 3/4; ftm.
  Personal Injuries Hbk (published by Sweet & Maxwell).

Personal Managers Association Ltd   (PMA)   1950
- ■ 27 College Gardens, BRIGHTON, E Sussex, BN2 1HP.   (hq)
  0845 602 7191
  email info@thepma.com
  Liaison Sec: Angela Adler
- ○ *P; for those variously operating in the entertainment & publishing industries as personal managers, theatrical agents, literary or authors' agents
- ● Mtgs
- M 125 f

Personal Safety Association
  believed to have closed - we should appreciate confirmation.

Personal Safety Manufacturers Association
  a group of the **British Safety Industry Federation**

Perthes Association   1976
- ■ PO Box 773, GUILDFORD, Surrey, GU1 1XN.   (hq)
  01483 534431
  email admin@perthes.org.uk   http://www.perthes.org.uk
  Dir: Lisa Grant
- ▲ Registered Charity
- ○ *W; to help & advise families with children suffering from Perthes disease (a potentially crippling disease of the hip) & other forms of osteochondritis as well as multiple epiphyseal dysplasia
- ● Comp - Inf - VE - Children's Christmas party - Contact register - Equipment loan for members (subject to availability)
- < Contact a Family
- M c 1,000 i
- ¶ NL - 4; ftm only.   Hbk; ftm.
  Layman's Guide to Osteochondritis; ftm.
  Your Child in an Immobilising Plaster: a few hints; ftm.
  Leaflets; ftm, one free copy nm.

Perthshire Agricultural Society   (PAS)   1867
- ■ 26 York Place, PERTH, PH2 8EH.   (hq)
  01738 623780   fax 01738 621206
  email secretary@perthshow.co.uk
  http://www.perthshow.co.uk
  Sec: Neil C Forbes
- ▲ Company Limited by Guarantee
- ○ *F; promotion of agriculture & organisation of 2-day agricultural show
- ● ET - Agricultural show
- M 750 i

Perthshire Chamber of Commerce   (PCC)   1871
- NR Algo Business Centre, Glenearn Rd, PERTH, PH2 0NJ.   (hq)
  01738 450401   fax 01738 450402
  email info@perthshirechamber.co.uk
  http://www.perthshirechamber.co.uk
  Chief Exec: Vicki Unite
- ▲ Company Limited by Guarantee
- ○ *C
- ● Mtgs - Expt - Inf - Lib - LG
- < Scot Chams Comm
- M c 400 f
- ¶ NL - 12;   AR; both ftm.

Perthshire Society of Natural Science   (PSNS)   1867
- ■ 29 Balhousie St, PERTH, PH1 5XX.   (treas/p)
  01738 626594
  email President@psns.org.uk   http://www.psns.org.uk
  Treas: David Perry
- ▲ Registered Charity
- ○ *L; to encourage, foster & further interest in a wide range of natural history subjects
- Gp Archaeological & historical; Botanical; Ornithological; Photographic
- M i

Pesticide Action Network UK   (PAN UK)
- ■ Development House, 56-64 Leonard St, LONDON, EC2A 4LT.   (hq)
  020 7065 0905   fax 020 7065 0907
  email admin@pan-uk.org   http://www.pan-uk.org
  Dir: Keith Tyrell
- ▲ Company Limited by Guarantee; Registered Charity
- ○ *K; to eliminate the use of hazardous pesticides & increase use of sustainable alternatives
- ● Res - Inf - LG
- < Pesticide Action Network Intl
- ¶ Pesticides News - 4; £25.
  Current Research Monitor - 4; £10.

Pet Care Trade Association   (PCTA)   2010
- ■ Bedford Business Centre, 170 Mile Rd, BEDFORD, MK42 9TW.   (hq)
  01234 273933   fax 01234 273550
  email info@petcare.org.uk   http://www.petcare.org.uk
  Chief Exec: Janet Nunn
- ▲ Company Limited by Guarantee
- ○ *T; membership body for pet retailers, dog groomers, kennels & catteries, manufacturers, wholesalers & professional services such as colleges, publishers, dog walkers & pet sitters
- Gp British Dog Groomers' Association; British Kennel & Cattery Association; Pet Care Trust (charity)
- ● Conf - Mtgs - ET - Exam - Exhib - Stat - Expt - LG
- M 1,500 f
- ¶ PS (PCTA NL) - 4.   Hbk.
  Grooming Snippets (BDGA NL) - 2.
  Paws for Thought (BKCA NL) - 2; all ftm

Pet Care Trust
  the charity group of the **Pet Care Trade Association**

Pet Food Manufacturers' Association Ltd   (PFMA)   1969
- 6 Catherine St (4th floor), LONDON, WC2B 5JJ.   (hq)
  020 7379 9009   fax 020 7379 8008
  email info@pfma.org.uk   http://www.pfma.org.uk
  Chief Exec: Michael Bellingham
- ▲ Company Limited by Guarantee
- ○ *T
- ● Mtgs - Inf - VE - LG - Seminars - Symposia
- < Eur Pet Food Mfrs Assn (FEDIAF)
- M 50 f

Pet Fostering Service Scotland   (PFSS)   1985
- PO Box 6, CALLANDER, Perthshire, FK17 8ZU.   (mail address)
  0844 811 9909
  Chmn: Anne Docherty
- ▲ Registered Charity
- ○ *G, *W; provision of short-term care of pets belonging to
  people who have to go into hospital or other short-term care
  in emergencies
- < SCAS; The Blue Cross
- M 300 i
- ¶ Booklet.

Pet Health Council   (PHC)   1979
- NR 6 Catherine St (4th floor), LONDON, WC1B 5JJ.   (hq)
  020 7379 6545
- ▲ Company Limited by Guarantee
- ○ *N; *V; to promote pet health in relation to human health
- ● Inf
- M 11 org:
    Associaton of Pet Behaviour Counsellors
    British Small Animal Veterinary Association
    British Veterinary Association
    National Office of Animal Health
    Peoples Dispensary for Sick Animals
    Pet Care Trade Association
    Pet Food Manufacturers Association
    Pets as Therapy
    Royal College of Nursing - Complementary Therapies
      Forum
    Royal Pharmaceutical Society of GB
    Society for Companion Animal Studies
- ¶ Leaflets.

Pet Product Retail Association   (PPRA)
- NR 225 Bristol Rd, Edgbaston, BIRMINGHAM, B5 7UB.   (hq)
  0121-446 6688   fax 0121-446 5215
  email info@bira.co.uk   http://www.bira.co.uk/ppra/
  Chmn: Debbie Keeling
- ○ *T; petshops & their suppliers
- ● Empl - ET - Inf - LG - Mtgs
- < Brit Indep Retailers Assn

Peter Warlock Society   1963
- NR 31 Hammerfield House, Cale St, LONDON, SW3 3SG.   (hsp)
  020 7589 9595   fax 020 7589 9595
  http://www.peterwarlock.org
  Hon Sec: Malcolm Rudland
- ▲ Registered Charity
- ○ *D; to increase the knowledge of all aspects of the life & works
  of composer Peter Warlock (1894-1930); Philip Arnold
  Heseltine, an Anglo-Welsh music critic & composer used the
  (now better known) name when he composed
- ● Mtgs - Comp - Inf - Lib - Publishing complete edition of
  Warlock's works
- M 250 i, UK / 35 i, o'seas
- ¶ NL - 2.   Society Edition of Songs, 9 vols.

Peterborough Chamber of Commerce
  a local chamber of **Cambridgeshire Chambers of Commerce**

Peterborough Royal Foxhound Show Society   (PRFSS)   1878
- East of England Showground, PETERBOROUGH, Cambs,
  PE2 6XE.   (hq)
  01733 234451   fax 01733 370038
  email dralleydavies@eastofengland.org.uk
  Sec: David Ralley Davies
- ○ *B; breeding & showing of foxhounds
- ● Peterborough Festival of Hunting
- < Assn of Show & Agricl Socs

Petrol Retailers Association
  a group of the **Retail Motor Industry Federation**

Petroleum & Drilling Engineering Division
  a group of the **Institute of Materials, Minerals & Mining**

**Petroleum Exploration Society of Great Britain   (PESGB)
1965**
- NR 9 Berkeley St (5th floor), LONDON, W1J 8DW.   (hq)
  020 7408 2000
  http://www.pesgb.org.uk
  Exec Dir: Guy Elliot
- ▲ Registered Charity
- ○ *L; to promote, for the public benefit, education in the scientific
  & technical aspects of petroleum
- ● Conf - ET - Exhib - Inf - VE
- < Amer Assn Petroleum Geologists (AAPG); SEG
- M 5,300 i, UK / 600 i, o'seas
- ¶ NL - 12; ftm only.

Pewter Society   1918
- 37 Hurst Lane, BOLLINGTON, Cheshire, SK10 5LT.   (hsp)
  email secretary@pewtersociety.org
  http://www.pewtersociety.org
  Hon Sec: John Swindell
- ▲ Un-incorporated Society
- ○ *A, *G; to stimulate interest in, & preservation of, old pewter
- ● Mtgs - Res - Inf - Lib
- M 150 i, 10 org, UK / 90 i, o'seas
- ¶ Jnl - 2;   NL - 2;   LM; all ftm only.

Pharmaceutical & Healthcare Sciences Society   (PHSS)   1981
- 6a Kingsdown Orchard, Hyde Rd, SWINDON, Wilts,
  SN2 7RR.   (hq)
  01793 824254   fax 01793 832551
  email info@phss.demon.co.uk   http://www.phss.co.uk
  Business Devt Mgr: Mrs June T Prout
- ▲ Un-incorporated Society
- ○ *L, *P; for research, development, manufacture & control of
  pharmaceutical & healthcare products; with representatives
  from academia, pharmaceutical industries, medical devices,
  pharmaceutical packaging, equipment suppliers &
  biotechnology
- Gp Aseptic process filtration; Autoclave validation; Cleanroom
  particle monitoring systems; Dry heat sterilisation; Freeze
  drying; LAL users; Parenteral GMP inspection;
  RABS (Restricted access barriers)
- ● Conf - ET - Exhib - Inf - LG
- M 700 i, UK / 289 i, o'seas
  (Sub: £90)
- ¶ European Jnl of Parenteral & Pharmaceutical Sciences - 4; ftm.
  NL - 4; free on website.   LM (on disc) - 1; ftm only.
  Technical monographs.   Publications Catalogue.

**Pharmaceutical Information & Pharmacovigilance Association
(PIPA)   1980**
- NR PO Box 254, HASLEMERE, Surrey, GU27 7XT.   (mail address)
  07531 899537
  email pipa@pipaonline.org
- ○ *P; to maintain & develop professional standards in all aspects
  of information work in the pharmaceutical industry
- M i

Pharmaceutical Society of Ireland   1875
IRL   18 Shrewsbury Rd, DUBLIN 4, Republic of Ireland.
    353 (1) 218 4000   fax 353 (1) 283 7678
    email info@pharmaceuticalsociety.ie
    Admin Sec: Dr Ambrose McLoughlin
○   *T

Pharmaceutical Society of Northern Ireland   (PSNI)   1925
■   73 University St, BELFAST, BT7 1HL.   (hq)
    028 9032 6927   fax 028 9043 9929
    email info@psni.org.uk   http://www.psni.org.uk
    Dir: Trevor Patterson,   Pres: Raymond Anderson
▲   Un-incorporated Society
○   *P; registration & regulatory body for the practice of Pharmacy
    in Northern Ireland
●   Mtgs - ET - Exam - LG
M   1,836 i, 539 f, UK / 87 i, o'seas
    (Sub: £345 i, £142 f UK / £158 i o'seas)

PharmaChemical Ireland
IRL   Confederation House, 84-86 Lower Baggot St, DUBLIN 2,
    Republic of Ireland.   (hq)
    353 (1) 605 1584   fax 353 (1) 638 1584
    email matt.moran@ibec.ie
    http://www.pharmachemicalireland.ie
    Dir: Matt Moran
○   *T: representative body for the pharmaceutical & chemical
    manufacturing sectors in Ireland
Gp   Chemical Distribution Ireland; Irish Bioindustry Association;
    Irish Cosmetics, Detergent & Allied Products Association
<   Ir Business & Emplrs Confedn (IBEC)
M   55 f

Philatelic Traders Society Ltd   (PTS)   1946
■   PO Box 371, FLEET, Hants, GU52 6ZX.   (hq)
    01252 628006   fax 01252 684674
    email info@philatelic-traders-society.co.uk
    http://www.philatelic-traders-society.co.uk
    Sec: J M Czuczman
▲   Company Limited by Guarantee
○   *G, *T; organisation of stamp dealers, auctioneers, philatelic
    publishers & philatelic accessory dealers; to promote the
    hobby of philately
●   organisation of two national stamp exhibitions in London by
    Stampex Ltd (a wholly owned subsidiary)
M   300 f, UK / 200 i, o'seas
¶   PTS News - 6; ftm only.   Directory - 1; ftm, £10 nm.

Philip Larkin Society   (PLS)   1995
■   PO Box 44, HORNSEA, E Yorks, HU18 1WP.   (sb)
    email plssecretary@philiplarkin.com
    http://www.philiplarkin.com
    Hon Sec: Andrew Eastwood
▲   Registered Charity
○   *A, *G; to promote awareness of the life & work of the poet,
    writer & Hull University librarian Philip Larkin (1922-1985) &
    his literary contemporaries
Gp   Publishing sub-c'ee
●   Conf - Mtgs - Res - Exhib - VE
<   Alliance Literary Socs
M   250 i, UK / 50 i, o'seas
¶   About Larkin - 2; ftm, £7 each nm.   Monographs.

Philological Society   1842
■   6 Craighall Dene Rd, NEWCASTLE upon TYNE,
    Northumberland, NE3 1QR.   (hsb)
    email m.c.bavidge@newcastle.ac.uk
    http://www.philsoc.org.uk
    Chmn: M C Bavidge
▲   Company Limited by Guarantee; Registered Charity
○   *L, *Q; the study of the structure, the affinities & the history of
    languages
●   Conf - Mtgs - Res
M   618 i
¶   Transactions - 3.
    Publications of the Philological Society - irreg.

Philosophical Society of England   (PhS)   1913
■   6 Craighall Dene Avenue, NEWCASTLE upon TYNE,
    NE3 1QR.   (hsb)
    0191-284 1223
    email thephilosophicalsociety@yahoo.co.uk
    http://www.philsoc.co.uk
    Chmn: Michael Bavidge
○   *L, *R; the study & discussion of the philosophy of religion &
    'English thought'
M   110 i, UK / 60 i, o'seas
¶   The Philosopher - 2; ftm, £15 m.

Phoenix Camping Club   1999
■   88 Charfield Drive, Eggbuckland, PLYMOUTH, Devon,
    PL6 5PS.   (hsp)
    01752 518669
    email enquiries@thephoenixcampingclub.co.uk
    http://www.thephoenixcampingclub.co.uk
    Sec: Sue Britten
▲   Un-incorporated Society
○   *G; a national singles camping club for anyone who lives &
    camps alone in motor caravan, caravan, tent or trailer tent
●   Mtgs
<   ACCEO
M   190 i
    (Sub: £10)
¶   NL - 6; ftm only.
    Note: Please enclose a large SAE with all enquiries

Phonographic Performance (Ireland) Ltd   (PPI)   1968
IRL   1 Corrig Avenue, DÚN LAOGHAIRE, Co Dublin, Republic of
    Ireland.
    353 (1) 280 5977   fax 353 (1) 280 6579
    email info@ppiltd.com   http://www.ppiltd.com
○   *T; collects royalties originating from the broadcasting of sound
    recordings

Phonographic Performance Ltd   (PPL)   1934
NR   1 Upper James St, LONDON, W1F 9DE.   (hq)
    020 7534 1000   fax 020 7534 1111
    email info@ppluk.com   http://www.ppluk.com
    Chief Exec: Fran Nevrkla
▲   Company Limited by Guarantee
○   *T; licenses recorded music & music videos for public
    performance, broadcast & new media use
Gp   Video Performance Ltd
M   i & f
×   2007 (Performing Artists' Media Rights Association
    (Association of United Recording Artists

© CBD Research Ltd · Beckenham · BR3 5JS · Tel 020 8650 7745 · E-mail cbd@cbdresearch.com · www.cbdresearch.com

Photo Imaging Council (PIC) 2002

- ■ Airport House, Purley Way, CROYDON, Surrey, CR0 0XZ. (hq)
  020 8253 4507   fax 020 8253 4510
  email pic@admin.co.uk   http://www.pic.uk.net
  Co Sec: Mrs Pamela Hyde
- ▲ Company Limited by Guarantee
- ○ *T; to represent & promote the interests of the photographic & imaging industry in the UK to government, the media, external organisations & the general public
- Gp Manufacturing; Marketing; Photo wastes; Export
- ● Conf - Mtgs - Exhib - Comp - Stat - Expt - LG
- < Brit Brands Gp
- M 110 f

Photographic Alliance of Great Britain (PAGB) 1930

- ■ 1 Orchard Close, PONTEFRACT, W Yorks, WF8 3NL.
  email hgtate@tesco.net
  http://www.pagb-photography-uk.co.uk
  Hon Sec: Howard G Tate
- ▲ Un-incorporated Society
- ○ *N; to coordinate the interests of the 15 photographic federations in the UK
- ● Mtgs - Exhib - Comp - SG- Inf - Provision of services & awards to the Federations - Confers patronage to exhibitions
- < Fédn Intle de l'Art Photographique (FIAP)
- > c 1,000 UK Camera Clubs
- M 25 i, 15 federations
- ¶ NL - 2; ftm, £5 nm.   Hbk - 2; ftm, £10 nm.

Photographic Collectors' Club of Great Britain (PCCGB) 1977

- ■ 5 Buntingford Rd, Puckeridge, WARE, Herts, SG11 1RT.
  (regd/office)
  01920 821611   fax 01920 821611
  email info@pccgb.com   http://www.pccgb.com
  Mem Sec: Diana Balfour
- ▲ Company Limited by Guarantee
- ○ *A, *G; to promote the study & collection of historical photographic equipment & images
- ● Mtgs - SG - Inf - VE - Major Fair (London, May)
- < Exacta Circle; Half Frame Gp; Voigtlander Verein; Kodak Brownie
- M 930 i, UK / 85 i, 5 org, o'seas
  (Sub: £32 i, UK / £34-£42, o'seas)
- ¶ Photographica World (Jnl) - 4;   Tailboard (NL) - 6;
  Postal Auction - 3;   Members' Hbk (LM) - 1; all ftm only, on application nm.

Photoluminescent Safety Products Association (PSPA) 1991

- NR PO Box 377, REDHILL, Surrey, RH1 2YZ. (mail add)
  01737 763400   fax 01737 728818
  email pspa@pspa.org.uk   http://www.pspa.org.uk
- ▲ Company Limited by Guarantee
- ○ *T; promotes use & knowledge of photoluminescent products in the field of safety
- M 16 f

Photonics Cluster

- NR Faraday Wharf, Holt St, Aston Science Pk, BIRMINGHAM, B7 4BB.
  0121-260 6020
  http://www.photonicscluster.org
- ○ *T; is the business network for the UK's photonics industry

Physical Education Association of Ireland (PEAI) 1968

- IRL University of Limerick, National Technology Park, LIMERICK, Republic of Ireland.
  353 (87) 648 0475
  email peai@peai.org   http://www.peai.org
  Sec: Catherine Kiely
- ○ *E, *P

Physics & Chemistry of Sea Ice Group
a group of the **Challenger Society for Marine Science**

Physio First 1952

- NR Minerva House, Tithe Barn Way, Swan Valley, NORTHAMPTON, Northants, NN4 9BA.
  01604 684960
  http://www.physiofirst.org.uk
  Gen Sec: Paul Donnelly
- ○ *P; to promote the highest standards of clinical practice in physiotherapy

Physiological Society 1876

- NR Peer House, Verulam St, LONDON, WC1X 8LZ. (hq)
  020 7269 5710
  http://www.physoc.org
  Pres: Mike Spyer
- ▲ Company Limited by Guarantee; Registered Charity
- ○ *L, *M; to promote the advancement of physiology; to contribute to the understanding of biomedical & related sciences; to aid the prevention & treatment of disease, disability & malfunction of physical processes in all forms of life
- ● Mtgs - ET - Res - SG - LG
- M c 2,000 i, UK / c 500 i, o'seas
- ¶ Jnl of Physiology - 24.   Experimental Physiology - 6.
  Magazine - 6;   AR;   Monographs;   Study guides;   Books; prices vary.

Pianoforte Tuners' Association (PTA) 1913

- ■ PO Box 1312, LIGHTWATER, Surrey, GU18 5UB.
  (mail/address)
  0845 602 8796   fax 0845 602 8796
  email secretary@pianotuner.org.uk
  http://www.pianotuner.org.uk
  Sec: Mrs Annette Summers
- ▲ Un-incorporated Society
- ○ *P
- ● Conf - Mtgs - ET - Exam - Inf - Lib - VE
- M 200 i, UK / 10 i, o'seas
- ¶ NL - 12; ftm.   Ybk; ftm, £2 nm.

Pick's Disease Support Group (PDSG) 1993

- ■ 3 Fairfield Park, LYME REGIS, Dorset, DT7 3DS. (hsp)
  01297 445488
  email penelope@pdsg.org.uk   http://www.pdsg.org.uk
  Hon Sec: Penelope K Roques
- ▲ Registered Charity
- ○ *W; for carers of people with frontotemporal dementia - Pick's disease, frontal lobe degeneration, corticostal degeneration & alcohol related dementia
- ● Conf - Mtgs - ET - VE
- < Nat Hospital Devt Foundation
- M 600 i, 50 org, UK / 700 i, 50 org, o'seas
- ¶ NL - 4; free.

Picon Ltd (Printing Industry Confederation) (PICON) 1993

- ■ PO Box 300, HITCHIN, Herts, SG4 8WJ. (hq)
  01438 832742   fax 01438 833812
  email info@picon.co.uk   http://www.picon.com
  Exec Dir: Tim Webb
- ▲ Company Limited by Guarantee
- ○ *T; for manufacturers & suppliers to the printing, publishing, paper making & paper converting industries (including plastics film)
- Gp Division: British Paper Machinery Suppliers Association
- ● Mtgs - Exhib - Stat - Expt - VE - LG
- < Eur C'ee of Printing & Paper Converting Machinery (EUMAPRINT); Paper Ind Technical Assn (PITA)
- M 150 f
- ¶ British Paper Machinery News - 2; free.
- × 2007 Association of Printing Machinery Importers (merged)

Pictish Arts Society (1988)
■ Pictavia, Haughmuir, BRECHIN, Angus, DD9 6RL.
  (visitor/centre)
  http://www.pictish-arts-society.org
  Hon Sec: Stewart Mowatt
▲ Registered Charity (Scotland)
○ *G; the study, research, development & preservation of Pictish
  arts, crafts & language; to advance the education of the
  public in all aspects of the early history of Scotland & in
  particular the Picts in Scotland
● Conf - Mtgs (Winter) - ET - Lib - VE
M 200 i, 10 org, UK / 18 i, o'seas
¶ Jnl - 1; ftm, £5 nm.   NL - 4; ftm only.

Picture Research Association (PRA) 1977
NR 10 Marrick House, Mortimer Crescent, LONDON, NW6 5NY.
   (mail/address)
   07771 982308
   Chmn: Veneta Bullen
○ *P; for all those involved in picture research, editing,
  management & supply
Gp Freelance register; Members advisory service
● Conf - Mtgs - ET - Inf
M 250 i, UK / 30 i, o'seas
¶ Montage - 4.   Bulletin (NL) - 12.

Pig Veterinary Society
   a group of the **British Veterinary Association**

Pigging Products & Services Association (PPSA) 1990
■ PO Box 30, Kesgrave, IPSWICH, Suffolk, IP5 2WY.   (hsb)
  01473 635863
  email ppsa@ppsa-online.com
  http://www.ppsa-online.com
  Exec Sec: Diane Cordell
▲ Company Limited by Guarantee
Br USA
○ *T; to promote the knowledge of pipeline pigging & its related
  products & services by providing a channel of
  communication between members themselves, users & other
  interested parties
  Pigs are devices inserted into & travel throughout the length of
  a pipeline driven by the product flow
● Conf - ET - Inf - PL
M 20 i, 67 f, UK / 5 i, 49 f, o'seas
¶ Pigging Industry News - 3; free.
  Buyers' Guide & Directory of Members - 1; free.
  An Introduction to Pipeline Pigging; ftm, £25 ($50 o'seas).

Pike & Shot Society (P&SS) 1973
NR 15 Victor St, YORK, YO1 6HQ.   (hsp)
   email secretary@pikeandshotsociety.org
   http://www.pikeandshotsociety.org
   Hon Sec: John Norris
▲ Un-incorporated Society
○ *L; to promote interest in the pike & shot period of warfare,
  from the first mass use of handguns by the Hussites of
  Bohemia in around 1400 to the end of the Great Northern
  War in 1721 & the demise of the pike
● Res
M 250 i, UK / 50 i, o'seas
¶ The Arquebusier - 6; ftm only.

The Pilgrims 1902
■ PO Box 1289, MAIDSTONE, Kent, ME18 5WQ.   (hq)
  01622 817780
  email sec@pilgrimsociety.org
▲ Un-incorporated Society
○ *X; promotion of Anglo-American good fellowship
● Dinners & receptions
< The Pilgrims of the USA
M 1,000 i, UK / 50 i, o'seas
¶ NL - 2;   LM & Rules - 2 yrly; free.

Pillbox Study Group (PSG) 1989
■ 12 Castle Close, KING'S LYNN, Norfolk, PE30 3EP.
  (memsec/p)
  01553 675053
  http://www.pillbox-study-group.org.uk
  Mem Sec: Tom Bell
▲ Un-incorporated Society
○ *G; the study & preservation of 20th century UK & international
  pillboxes & anti-invasion defences
● SG - Inf
M 300 i
  (Sub: £7.50 UK / £9.50 o'seas)
¶ Loopholes - 3; ftm only.
✕ 2008 UK Fortifications Club (merged)

Pinball Owners' Association (POA) 1976
■ Kilndown, 31 Earlsmead Crescent, Cliffsend, RAMSGATE, Kent,
  CT12 5LQ.   (mail address)
  email poa@dial.pipex.com   http://www.ds.dial.pipex.com/
  poa/
▲ Un-incorporated Society
○ *G, *S; to promote the playing, collecting & ownership of
  pinball & other coin operated machines
● Comp - Exhib (Annual show) - Inf - Spares & specialist goods
  sales
M 470 i, 15 f, UK / 50 i, 10 f, o'seas
¶ Pinball Player - 10; £16 m, £20 nm.

Piobaireachd Society 1902
NR 16-24 Otago St, GLASGOW, G12 8JH.   (hq)
   0141-334 3587   fax 0141-587 6068
   Hon Sec: Dugald MacNeill
▲ Un-incorporated Society
○ *D, *G; the encouragement & dissemination of the
  piobaireachd & its playing

Pipe Jacking Association (PJA) 1973
■ 10 Greycoat Place, LONDON, SW1P 1SB.   (hq)
  0845 070 5201   fax 0845 070 5202
  email secretary@pipejacking.org
  http://www.pipejacking.org
  Sec: Andrew K Marshall
▲ Company Limited by Guarantee
○ *T; to represent the leading contractors, pipe suppliers &
  machine manufacturers in the pipe jacking & microtunnelling
  industry in the UK
Gp Tunnelling; Tunnelling machinery; Pipe manufacture
● Conf - Mtgs - ET - Inf
M 21 f
¶ NL - 2.
  Guide to Best Practice for the Installation of Pipe Jacks &
  Microtunnels; £35 nm.
  An Introduction to Pipe Jacking & Microtunnelling
  Design £9.50 nm.

Pipe Roll Society 1883
■ c/o Prof N C Vincent, School of History, University of East
  Anglia, NORWICH, NR4 7TJ.
  http://www.piperollsociety.co.uk
  Sec: Prof N C Vincent
▲ Registered Charity
○ *L; 'the enlargement of the public knowledge of medieval
  English history by the publication of the Pipe Rolls &
  associated records of medieval English government & other
  manuscripts of national importance prior to 1350'

Pipedown
   see **Campaign for Freedom from Piped Music**

© CBD Research Ltd · Beckenham · BR3 5JS · Tel 020 8650 7745 · E-mail cbd@cbdresearch.com · www.cbdresearch.com

Pipeline Industries Guild Ltd   (PIG)   1957
■ F150 (1st floor), Cherwell Business Village, Southam Rd,
    BANBURY, Oxon, OX16 2SP.   (hq)
    020 7235 7938
    email hqsec@pipeguild.co.uk
    http://www.pipeguild.co.uk
    14-15 Belgrave Square, LONDON, SW1X 8PS.   (regd/
    office).
    020 7235 7938
    Dir Gen: Cheryl Burgess
▲ Company Limited by Guarantee
Br 7; Republic of Ireland
○ *T; science & practice of aspects of the pipeline engineering
Gp Technical panels: Offshore, Onshore, Utilities
● Conf - Mtgs - ET - Exhib - Comp/Awards - Expt - Inf - Lib - LG
< Fedn of Wld Pipeline Assns
M 900 i, 220 f, UK / 250 i, 20 f, o'seas
¶ Pipeline Industry Directory - 1; ftm, £50 nm.

Pipers' Guild   1932
■ 36 Ladysmith Rd, EDINBURGH, EH9 3EU.   (sp)
    email secdes@pipersguild.org
    http://www.pipersguild.org
    Sec: Des Truman
○ *G; for those interested in making, selling & playing bamboo
    pipes

Pira International   1929
■ Cleeve Rd, LEATHERHEAD, Surrey, KT22 7RU.   (hq)
    01372 802000   fax 01372 802238
    email infocentre@pira.co.uk   http://www.piranet.com
    Managing Dir: Michael Hancock
▲ Company Limited by Guarantee
○ *Q; consultancy & research into paper, packaging, printing &
    publishing
Gp Packaging; Paper & board; Printing & publishing
● Conf - ET - Res - Inf - Lib
¶ [Publications catalogue on website].
    Note: is a Smithers Group company of Akron (OH)

Pizza, Pasta & Italian Food Association   (PAPA)   1977
NR Association House, 18c Moor St, CHEPSTOW, Monmouthshire,
    NP16 5DB.   (hq)
    01291 636331   fax 01291 630402
    email enq@papa.org.uk   http://www.papa.org.uk
    Dir: Jim Winship
○ *T; to promote better standards & knowledge in the industry
● Mtgs - Inf - VE - Promotions - Insurance schemes - Financial
    advice
< Nat Assn of Pizza Operators (USA)
M 52 i, 680 f, UK / 13 i, 36 f, o'seas
¶ Magazine - 6; ftm, £48 nm.   PAPA Ybk - 1; ftm.

Plain English Campaign 1979   (PEC)
■ PO Box 3, New Mills, HIGH PEAK, Derbys, SK22 4QP.   (hq)
    01663 744409   fax 01663 747038
    email info@plainenglish.co.uk
    http://www.plainenglish.co.uk
    Mgr: Tony Maher
▲ Company Limited by Guarantee
○ *K; to persuade government departments, local councils &
    companies to write forms, leaflets, letters & agreements
    clearly & to set them out clearly & logically
● Conf - ET - Res - Exhib - Comp - LG
M 1,000 i, 500 f
¶ Plain English (Jnl) - 4; free.
    List available on request.

Plainsong & Mediæval Music Society   (PMMS)   1888
NR Bangor University, School of Music, College Rd, BANGOR,
    Gwynedd, LL57 2DG.   (hq)
    email admin@plainsong.org.uk
    http://www.plainsong.org.uk
    Chmn: Prof John Harper
▲ Registered Charity
○ *D, *L; the advancement of education in plainsong & mediæval
    music
● Publication of scholarly books & facsimiles
M i & libraries
¶ Plainsong & Medieval Music (Jnl) - 2; ftm.

Planning Disaster Coalition
NR c/o FOE, 26-28 Underwood St, LONDON, N1 7JQ.
    020 7566 1649
    http://www.planningdisaster.co.uk
○ *K; against the government's plans to remove community
    voices from the planning process
M 17 org

Planning & Environment Bar Association   (PEBA)
NR Landmark Chambers, 180 Fleet St, LONDON, EC4A 2HG.
    (sb)
    020 7430 1221
    http://www.peba.info
    Sec: Christopher Boyle
○ *P

Planning Officers Society   1997
NR The Croft, 81 Walton Rd, AYLESBURY, Bucks, HP21 7SN.   (sb)
    01296 422161
    http://www.planningofficers.org.uk
    Sec: Chris Swanwick
○ *P

Plant Heritage
    a title used by the **National Council for the Conservation of
    Plants & Gardens**

**Plantagenet Medieval Archery & Combat Society
(Plantagenet Society)   1976**
■ 37 Willowslea Rd, WORCESTER, WR3 7QP.   (mem/sp)
    01905 455192
    email mike@mkerslake.freeserve.co.uk
    http://www.plantagenet.org.uk
    Mem Sec: Jean Kerslake
▲ Un-incorporated Society
○ *G; re-enactment of medieval tourneys, sieges, foot combat,
    archery, music & dance
Gp Archers; Dancers; Knights; Musicians
● Re-enactments & entertainment
M 60 i

Plantlife International: the wild plant conservation charity
NR 14 Rollestone St, SALISBURY, Wilts, SP1 1DX.   (hq)
    01722 342730
    email enquiries@plantlife.org.uk
    http://www.plantlife.org.uk
    Devt Mgr: Lisa Clements
▲ Registered Charity
○ *K; 'the in-situ conservation of wild plants'
● Res - LG - Conservation of wild plants
M 125,000 i
¶ Plantlife - 3; ftm, on request nm.

Plastics & Board Industries Federation
    closed 2008

Plastics Historical Society   (PHS)   1986
- ■ c/o IOM3, 1 Carlton House Terrace, London, SW1Y 5DB. (mail/address)
  email memb.sec@plastiquarian.com
  http://www.plastiquarian.com
  Mem Sec: Deborah Jaffé,   Hon Sec: Jen Cruse
- ▲ Un-incorporated Society
- ○ *L; to study all historical aspects of plastics & other polymers; to record current developments
- ● Conf - Mtgs - Res - Exhib - Inf - Lib at the (Institute of Materials Minerals & Mining) - VE
- < Inst Materials, Minerals & Mining
- M 175 i, 25 org, UK / 50 i, o'seas
- ¶ Plastiquarian - 2; ftm, £10 nm.   NL - 6; ftm, £3 nm.

Plastics Ireland
- IRL Confederation House, 84-86 Lower Baggot St, DUBLIN 2, Republic of Ireland.   (hq)
  353 (1) 605 1574   fax 353 (1) 638 1574
  email marian.byron@ibec.ie
  http://www.plasticsireland.ie
  Dir: Marian Byron
- ○ *T; to promote the interests of all sectors of the plastics industry in Ireland & to encourage the growth & development of each to its full potential
- < Ir Business & Emplrs Confedn (IBEC)
- M 39 f

Plastics Window Federation
- NR Federation House, 85-87 Wellington St, LUTON, Beds, LU1 5AF.   (hq)
  01582 456147
  http://www.pwfed.co.uk
- ▲ Company Limited by Guarantee
- ○ *T; manufacturers & installers of plastics (PVCU) windows for domestic & commercial use

Platform 51
- from January 2011 the operating name of the **YWCA**

Play Matters
- see **National Association of Toy & Leisure Libraries   (Play Matters)**

Play Providers Association   (PPA)   2005
- ■ Federation House, STONELEIGH PARK, Warks, CV8 2RF.   (hq)
  024 7641 4999   fax 024 7641 4990
  http://www.playproviders.org.uk
- ▲ Company Limited by Guarantee
- ○ *T; for operators of indoor children's play centres
- ● Mtgs
- < a group of the Federation of Sports & Play Assns (FSPA)
- M f

Player Piano Group   (PPG)   1959
- ■ Strets, Church Rd, LINGFIELD, Surrey, RH7 6AH.   (hsp)
  Hon Sec: Steve Streatfield
- ▲ Un-incorporated Society
- ○ *D, *G; to foster interest in the player piano & the reproducing piano; their history, mechanisms & musical virtues
- ● Mtgs - VE
- < Automatic Musical Instrument Collectors Assn Intl (AMICA); Ned Pianola Vereniging; NW [& S Wales & the West] Player Piano Assn[s]; Gesellschaft Selbspielende Musikinstrumente eV; Australian Collectors Mechanical Musical Instruments; Perferons la Musique; Pianola Inst
- M 273 i, 5 org, UK / 26 i, 5 org, o'seas
  (Sub: £12)
- ¶ The Bulletin - 4; ftm only.

Player-Playwrights   1947
- ■ 7 Cain Court, Castlebar Mews, LONDON, W5 1RY.   (treas/p)
  http://www.playerplaywrights.co.uk
  Treas: Tony Diggle,   Hon Sec: Peter Thompson
- ▲ Un-incorporated Society
- ○ *A; to promote the writing & appreciation of theatre in all its forms
- ● Mtgs - Comp - Reading & performing new texts & trying to get them before the public
- M 125 i
  (Sub: £12 to join + £8 annually)
- ¶ NL & Programmes - 3.

Pleasure Horse Society Ltd
- has ceased - operations now tranferred to the Horse Passport Agency Ltd - 01494 601042 (enquiries)

Plymouth Chamber of Commerce & Industry   (PCCI)   1813
- NR 22 Lockyer St, PLYMOUTH, Devon, PL1 2QW.   (hq)
  01752 220471
  http://www.plymouth-chamber.co.uk
  Dir of Operations & Co Sec: Sally Perdrisat
- ▲ Company Limited by Guarantee
- ○ *C
- Gp Membership consultation, policy & representation; Membership services & marketing
- ● Mtgs - ET - Res - Exhib - Expt - Inf - VE - LG - Representation of members' views
- M 900 f
- ¶ NL - 12.   LM - 12.   Ybk.

POA: the Professional Trades Union for Prison, Correctional & Secure Psychiatric Workers   (POA)   1939
- NR Cronin House, 245 Church St, LONDON, N9 9HW.   (hq)
  020 8803 0255   fax 020 8803 1761
  http://www.poauk.org.uk
  Gen Sec: Steve Gillan
- Br 4
- ○ *U; to represent uniformed prison grades & staff working within the field of secure forensic psychiatric care
- Gp Nurses & ancillary staff in special hospitals; Prison officers
- ● Conf - Mtgs - ET - Res - Stat - Inf - Lib - VE - Empl
- < Coun Civil Service Us; EUROFEDOP; Trades U Congress (TUC)
- M 35,972 i
- ¶ Gatelodge - 6.
- ✕ 2007 Prison Officers Association

The Poetry Society (Inc)   (PS)   1909
- ■ 22 Betterton St, LONDON, WC2H 9BX.   (hq)
  020 7420 9880   fax 020 7240 4818
  email info@poetrysociety.org.uk
  http://www.poetrysociety.org.uk
- ▲ Company Limited by Guarantee; Registered Charity
- ○ *A; promotion of poets & poetry
- ● ET - Res - Exhib - Comp - Inf
- M c 4,000 i & org
- ¶ Poetry Review - 4.   Poetry News - 4.

Point-to-Point Owners & Riders Association   (PPORA)   1977
- NR The Coach House, 7 Mill Rd, Sturry, CANTERBURY, Kent, CT2 0AJ.   (hsb)
  01227 713080   fax 01227 713088
  http://www.ppora.co.uk
- ▲ Un-incorporated Society
- ○ *G, *S
- M i
  (Sub: £25)
- ¶ Between the Flags - 2.

© CBD Research Ltd · Beckenham · BR3 5JS · Tel 020 8650 7745 · E-mail cbd@cbdresearch.com · www.cbdresearch.com

Police Federation of England & Wales   (PFEW)   1919
- ■ Federation House, Highbury Drive, LEATHERHEAD, Surrey, KT22 7UY.   (hq)
    01372 352000   fax 01372 352039
    email polfed@polfed.org   http://www.polfed.org
    Gen Sec: Ian Rennie
- Br 43 branch boards
- ○ *U; a staff association to consult & negotiate on terms & conditions of service for police officers in the ranks of constable to chief inspector
- ● Conf - Empl
- M 125,000 i
- ¶ Police - 12; free to branches.

Police Federation for Northern Ireland   (PFNI)   2008
- ■ 77-79 Garnerville Rd, BELFAST, BT4 2NX.   (hq)
    028 9076 4200
    email secretary.pfni@btconnect.com
    Sec: Stevie McCann
- ▲ Un-incorporated Society
- ○ *P; representative body concerned with welfare & efficiency of police officers in Northern Ireland
- ● Conf - Mtgs - ET - Res - Inf - Empl - LG
- < Standing C'ee of Police in Europe
- M 8,000 i
    Sub: £15
- ¶ Police Beat - 4; ftm only.

Police History Society   (PHS)   1985
- ■ 64 Nore Marsh Rd, WOOTTON BASSETT, Wilts, SN4 8BH.
    (hsp)
    01793 853635
    email stevebridge100@btinternet.com
    http://www.policehistorysociety.co.uk
    Hon Sec: Steve Bridge
- ▲ Registered Charity
- ○ *G; promotion of interest in police history
- Gp Police museum curators
- ● Conf - Res - Re-publication of historical sources of police history
- M c350 i
- ¶ Jnl - 1; ftm, £5 nm.   NL - 4;   LM - 2/3 yrly; both ftm only. Monographs - irreg; prices vary.

Police Insignia Collectors Association of Great Britain   (PICA GB)   1975
- ■ 8 Foxon Lane Gdns, CATERHAM, Surrey, CR3 5SN.   (mem/sp)
    http://www.pica.co.uk
    Mem Sec: Tony Collman
- ○ *G; to foster comradeship through a mutual interest in police insignia; to instruct, inform & interest all collectors of police insignia
- ● Swap mtgs
- M 600 i, UK / 150 i, o'seas.
- ¶ PICA Magazine - 3; ftm only.

Police Professional Network
    a group of the **Chartered Management Institute**

Police Superintendents' Association of England & Wales   1921
- NR 67a Reading Rd, PANGBOURNE, Berks, RG8 7JD.   (hq)
    0118-984 4005   fax 0118-984 5642
    email enquiries@policesupers.com
    http://www.policesupers.com
    Pres: Derek Barnett
- Br 44
- ○ *P; for police superintendents & chief superintendents in England & Wales
- Gp Business Areas: BCU (Basic Command Unit) liaison; Command resilience; Crime; Diversity; Human resources; Operational policing; Panel of friends; Roads policing
- ● Conf - Mtgs - Res - Stat - Inf - Empl - LG
- M 1,510 i
- ¶ The Superintendent - 3; free.

Political Cartoon Society
- NR PO Box 3516, BARNET, Herts, EN5 9LF.
    07973 622371
    email info@politicalcartoon.co.uk
    http://www.politicalcartoon.co.uk
- ○ *G; to promote the political cartoon as an educational, amusing & informative force
- ● Exhib
- ¶ NL - 4; ftm.

Political Studies Association of the United Kingdom   (PSA) 1950
- NR Dept of Politics, University of Newcastle, NEWCASTLE-upon-TYNE, NE1 7RU.   (hq)
    0191-222 8021   fax 0191-222 3499
    http://www.psa.ac.uk
    Hon Sec: Prof Paul Carmichael
- ▲ Registered Charity
- ○ *L; promotion of the development of political studies
- ● Conf - Mtgs - ET - Res - SG - Stat - LG
- M i & f
- ¶ Many publications available

Politics Association
    closed 2009

Polymer Machinery Manufacturers' & Distributors' Association Ltd   (PMMDA)   1966
- ■ New Progress House, 34 Stafford Rd, WALLINGTON, Surrey, SM6 9AA.   (asa)
    020 8773 8111   fax 020 8773 0022
    email pmmda@pmmda.org.uk
    http://www.pmmda.org.uk
    Pres: Paul Goodhew
- ▲ Company Limited by Guarantee
- ○ *T; support to plastics machinery suppliers in the UK
- Gp Export; Technical; Health & safety
- ● ET - Exhib - SG - Stat - Expt - Inf - LG - Sponsorship of 'Modern Apprentice'
- < Brit Plastics Fedn
- M c 80 f
- ¶ Buyers Guide to...
    Chillers;   Dryers;   Granulators;   Robots; Temperature Control; all 2 yrly; free.

Polymer Society
    a group of the **Institute of Materials, Minerals & Mining**

Ponies Association (UK) Ltd   (P(UK))   1988
- ■ 56 Green End Rd, SAWTRY, Cambs, PE28 5UY.   (hq)
    01487 830278   fax 01487 832086
    email info@poniesuk.org   http://www.poniesuk.org
    Chmn: Mrs Davina Whiteman
- ▲ Company Limited by Guarantee; Registered Charity
- ○ *G; to promote equestrian events & the training of horse & rider
- ● Conf - ET - Comp
- < Assn of Show & Agricl Orgs
- M 4,500 i
- ¶ NL - 2 + by email; ftm only.

Pony Breeders of Shetland Association   (PBSA)   1971

- ■ 5 Dale Park, DUNROSSNESS, Shetland, ZE2 9JH.   (hsp)
  01950 461811
  email pbsa@btinternet.com
  http://www.shetlandponybreeders.com
  Hon Sec & Treas: Miss Sonja E Flans
- ▲ Un-incorporated Society
- ○ *B; to improve communication between Island breeders in Shetland; to improve the quality of Shetland's ponies; to promote the ponies worldwide
- ● Mtgs - ET - Stat - Inf - VE
- < Shetland Pony Stud-Book Soc
- M 82 i, UK / 1 i, o'seas
  (Sub: £10-15)
- ¶ NL -1-4; ftm only
  List of Shetland Pony Breeders in Shetland; irreg; free.
  List of all Registered Shetland Ponies in Shetland - irreg; p.o.a.

Pony Club   (Pony Club)   1929

- ■ Stoneleigh Park, KENILWORTH, Warks, CV8 2RW.   (hq)
  024 7669 8300
  http://www.pcuk.org
  Chief Exec: Mrs Judy E Edwards
- ▲ Registered Charity
- Br 347; 15 countries
- ○ *S, *Y; an international voluntary youth organisation for those interested in ponies & riding
- Gp Dressage; Eventing; Mounted games; Polo; Polocrosse; Racing; Show junping; Tetrathlon
- ● Conf - ET - Exam - Exhib - Comp - VE
- < Brit Equestrian Fedn
- M 36,000 i, UK / 104,500 i, o'seas
- ¶ Instructors Hbk.   Manual of Horsemanship.
  Ybk.   All Rule Books - 1.

Pony Riders Association   (PRA)   1991

- NR 131 The Butts, FROME, Somerset, BA11 4AQ.
  http://www.ponyriders.org.uk
  Mem Sec: Gina Coltman
- ○ *G; for adults with ponies

** Pool Promoters Association
Organisation lost: see Introduction paragraph 3

** Pop & Rock Fans' Association
Organisation lost: see Introduction paragraph 3

Popular Flying Association
  since 2007 **Light Aircraft Association**

Porcupine Marine Natural History Society   (PMNHS)   1977

- ■ c/o Dr Andrew Mackie, National Museum of Wales, Cathays Park, CARDIFF, CF10 3NP.   (chmn)
  email andrew.mackie@museumwales.ac.uk
  http://www.pmnhs.co.uk
  Chmn: Dr Andrew Mackie
- ▲ Un-incorporated Society
- ○ *L; marine natural history, taxonomy, biogeography particularly of the north east Atlantic & the Mediterranean Sea; (named after the first marine biology deep-sea research vessel, HMS Porcupine)
- ● Conf - Mtgs - ET - Res - Field survey
- M [not stated]
- ¶ NL - 3; ftm.

Pork Pie Appreciation Society   1982

- ■ Bridge Inn, Priest Lane, Ripponden, SOWERBY BRIDGE, W Yorks, HX6 4DF.   (hsb)
  01484 539715
  Sec: Peter Charnley
- ▲ Un-incorporated Society
- ○ *K; the tasting & judging of pork pies
- ● Mtgs - Comp - Fund raising
- M 12 i

Portable Electric Tool Manufacturers Association   (PETMA)   1942

- ■ PO Box 35084, LONDON, NW1 4XE.   (asa)
  020 7935 8532   fax 07006 065950
  email office@petma.org.uk
  Sec: Crispin Dunn-Meynell
- ○ *T
- ● Mtgs - Res - Inf
- < Eur Power Tool Assn (EPTA)
- M 2 f

Portland Sheep Breeders Group   (PSBG)

- NR 6 Clos-yr-Avon, KIDWELLY, Carmarthenshire, SA17 4TJ.   (hsp)
  07789 006401
  email croes-cade@hotmail.co.uk
  http://www.portlandsheepbreeders.org.uk
  Sec: Andrew Jenkins
- ○ *B
- < Nat Sheep Assn
- M c 200 i

Portman Group   (TPG)   1990

- ■ 20 Conduit St - 4th fl, LONDON, W1S 2ZW.   (hq)
  020 7290 1460
  email info@portmangroup.org.uk
  http://www.portmangroup.org.uk
  Chief Exec: David Poley
- ○ *K; a drinks industry initiative against alcohol misuse
- ● Conf - Mtgs - ET - Res - Stat - Inf
- M 8 f, 2 org

Ports & Terminals Group   (PTG)

- ■ 28-29 Threadneedle St, LONDON, EC2R 8AY.
  020 7628 2555   fax 020 7638 4376
  email info@maritimeindustries.org
  http://www.maritimeindustries.org
  Dir: Ken Gibbons
- ○ *T; port development, supply chain management & related security systems
- < Soc of Maritime Inds

Portsmouth & South East Hampshire Chamber of Commerce & Industry
  merged in 2010 with other chambers of commerce in Hampshire to
  form the **Hampshire Chamber of Commerce**

Portuguese Chamber - the Portuguese UK Business Network   1980

- ■ 11 Belgrave Square (4th floor), LONDON, SW1X 8PP.   (hq)
  020 7201 6638
  http://www.portuguese-chamber.org.uk
  Gen Mgr: Christina Hippisley
- ▲ Company Limited by Guarantee
- Br representative offices in Midlands & Scotland; Lisbon (Portugal)
- ○ *C
- Gp Constuction; Consultancy; Design; Financial; Freight/Transport; Import/export; Industry; Legal; Marketing; Services
- ● Conf - Mtgs - Res - SG - Stat - Expt - Inf - LG
- M 240 f & org, UK / 105 f & org, o'seas
- ¶ Tradewinds (NL) - 3; ftm.
  Directory & Ybk; ftm.

© CBD Research Ltd · Beckenham · BR3 5JS · Tel 020 8650 7745 · E-mail cbd@cbdresearch.com · www.cbdresearch.com

Post Office Vehicle Club   (POVC)   1962
- ■ 32 Russell Way, LEIGHTON BUZZARD, Beds, LU7 3NG.   (hsp)
    01525 382129
    email povehclub@aol.com   http://www.povehclub.org.uk
    Hon Sec: Francis J Weston
- ○ *G; for people interested the operations & fleets of the General
    Post Office & its successors, the Post Office, BT & Royal Mail
- Gp Modern fleet; Preservation & archives
- ● Inf - VE
- < Roads & Road Transport Hist Assn
- M 200 i
    (Sub: £19 Europe / £30 RoW)
- ¶ Post Horn - 12; £6 m, £12 nm.
    Books on various types of vehicle; c £10-14.

Post Tensioning Association   (PTA)   1984
- NR Riverside House, 4 Meadows Business Park, Station Approach,
    Blackwater, CAMBERLEY, Surrey, GU17 9AB.   (hq)
    01726 606800
    Chmn: Huw Jones
- ▲ Un-incorporated Society
- ○ *T; post-tensioned concrete
- ● Mtgs - SG - Technical developments in conjunction with other
    technical committees & bodies
- M 10 f

Postal History Society   (PHS)   1936
- ■ 22 Burton Crescent, Sneyd Green, STOKE-ON-TRENT, Staffs,
    ST1 6BT.   (hsp)
    Sec: Steve Ellis
- ▲ Un-incorporated Society
- ○ *G, *L, *Q; the study of written communication, with special
    emphasis on the postal services of the world
- ● Conf - Mtgs - Res - Exhib - Comp - Inf - Lib - Publications
- < British Philatelic Federation
- M 235 i
    (Sub: £24 GB, £27 (Europe), £30 (RoW))
- ¶ Postal History Jnl - 4; ftm only.

Postcard Traders' Association   (PTA)   1976
- NR 24 Parry Rd, Sholing, SOUTHAMPTON, Hants, SO19 0HU.
    (hsp)
    email ptasec@postcard.co.uk   http://www.postcard.co.uk
    Hon Sec: Derek Popplestone
- ▲ Un-incorporated Society
- ○ *T; to encourage the hobby of picture postcard collecting
    worldwide
- ● Exhib - Comp - Inf - Organisation of the Picture Postcard Show
- M 160 f, UK / 21 f, o'seas
- ¶ News - 4; ftm only.

Potato Processors' Association   (PPA)
- NR 6 Catherine St, LONDON, WC2B 5JJ.   (hq)
    020 7836 2460   fax 020 7836 0580
    email lucy.curzon@fdf.org.uk
- ▲ Un-incorporated Society
- ○ *T
- ● Mtgs
- < Eur Potato Processors' Assn (EUPPA); Food & Drink Fedn
- M 11 f, 1 org

Poultry Club of Great Britain   (PCGB)   1877
- ■ Keeper's Cottage, 40 Benvarden Rd, Dervock, BALLYMONEY,
    Co Antrim, BT53 6NM.   (gsp)
    028 2074 1056
    email info@poultryclub.org   http://www.poultryclub.org
    Gen Sec: Mrs A Bachmet
- ▲ Registered Charity
- ○ *B, *F; to promote high standards in the keeping & breeding of
    purebred poultry
- ● ET - Exhib - Inf
- M c 1,400 i & org
- ¶ NL - 4;   Ybk - 1; both ftm only.

Power Fastenings Association Ltd   (PFA)   1978
- ■ 42 Heath St, TAMWORTH, Staffs, B79 7JH.   (hq)
    01827 52337   fax 01827 310827
    email info@powerfastenings.org.uk
    http://www.powerfastenings.org.uk
    Sec: Alain Skelding
- ▲ Company Limited by Guarantee
- ○ *T; to represent the major manufacturers & suppliers of
    branded, power-driven tools & collated fasteners
- ● Mtgs - Res - Inf - LG - British & European Standards
- M 7 i
    (Sub: £750)
- ¶ Using Power Fastener Driving Tools Safely; 20p m,
    1 copy free nm.

Powys Society   1967
- NR Flat D, 87 Ledbury Rd, LONDON, W11 2AG.   (hsp)
    020 7243 0168
    http://www.powys-society.org
    Hon Sec: Chris Thomas
- ▲ Registered Charity
- ○ *A, *G; to establish public recognition of the writings, thought &
    contribution to the arts of the Powys family, particularly the
    brothers John Cowper, Theodore & Llewelyn & their close
    circle of friends: Louis Wilkinson, James Hanley, T E Lawrence
    & Sylvia Townsend Warner
- ● Conf - Mtgs - Lib
- < Powys Soc of N America
- M 200 i, UK / 150 i, o'seas
- ¶ The Powys Journal - 1.   The Powys NL - 3.   LM - 3 yrly.
    A Powys Checklist (list of publications by the Powys family &
    circle) - irreg.

Powysland Club   1867
- NR Cartref, 14 Berriew Rd, WELSHPOOL, Powys, SY21 7SS.   (sp)
    01938 552161
    email powyslandclub.co.uk
    Hon Sec: Rev R L Brown
- ○ *L; the study of the history of Montgomeryshire
- ● Mtgs - Lib - Lectures - VE
- M i
- ¶ Montgomeryshire Collections (Jnl) - Vol 99; £15-£25.
    Books.   Maps.

Prader-Willi Syndrome Association (UK)   (PWSA (UK))   1981
- ■ 125a London Rd, DERBY, DE1 2QQ.   (welfare/coord/p)
    01332 365676   fax 01332 360401
    email admin@pwsa.co.uk   http://www.pwsa.co.uk
    Chief Exec: Leigh Vallance
- ▲ Registered Charity
- Br 6
- ○ *W; to promote care, welfare & treatment of people with
    Prader-Willi syndrome; to offer support & information to
    carers & professionals
- ● Conf - Mtgs - ET - Inf - Lib
- < Intl Prader-Willi Syndrome Org
- M 1,500 i, UK / 130 i, o'seas
- ¶ Publications list available.

Prayer Book Society   (PBS)   1975
- ■ The Studio, Copyhold Farm, Lady Grove, Goring Heath,
    READING, Berks, RG8 7RT.   (chmn/b)
    0118-984 2582
    http://www.pbs.org.uk
    Chmn: Prudence Dailey
- ▲ Registered Charity
- Br 44; Portugal, S Africa
- ○ *R; to uphold the worship & doctrine of the Church of England
    as enshrined in the Book of Common Prayer; to spread the
    use of the Book of Common Prayer & to see that it is used
- ● Conf - Mtgs - ET - Comp - Inf
- M i
- ¶ NL - 4.   The Journal - 2.   Faith & Worship - 2.

Pre Basic Growers Association   (PBGA)
- ■ 1 St Fillans Grove, Aberdour, BURNTISLAND, Fife, KY3 0XG. (hsp)
  01383 860695
  email secretary@pbga.org.uk   http://www.pbga.org.uk
  Hon Sec: Bill Rennie
- ▲ Un-incorporated Society
- ○ *T; to maintain & improve the technical standards relating to the production, classification & marketing of Pre Basic seed potatoes & to liaise with official bodies & others in reviewing & modifying arrangements for the regulation of the production, classification & marketing of Pre Basic seed potatoes
- ● Conf - SG - LG
- M 40 f
- ✕ 2007 Virus Tested Stem Cutting Growers Association

Pre Eclampsia Society   (PETS)   1981
- NR Rhianfa, Carmel, CAERNARFON, Gwynedd, LL54 7RL. (trustee/p)
  01702 205088
  email dawnjames@clara.co.uk
  http://www.pre-eclampsia-society.org.uk
  Founder: Dawn James,   Trustee: Sharon Copping
- ▲ Registered Charity
- ○ *W; self-help & support group for women suffering from, or who have suffered from, pre-eclampsia / eclampsia, & others interested in the condition
- ● Res - Comp - Stat - Inf - Lib
- M 200 i
- ¶ NL - 4; ftm only.

Pre-Raphaelite Society   (PRS)   1988
- ■ 37 Larchmere Drive, Hall Green, BIRMINGHAM, B28 8JB. (sp)
  email info@pre-raphaelitesociety.org
  http://www.pre-raphaelitesociety.org
  Sec: Barry C Johnson
- ▲ Registered Charity
- ○ *A; the study of the lives & art of the Pre-Raphaelite Brotherhood
- ● VE - Lectures - Seminars
- M 350 i, UK & o'seas
- ¶ The Review of the PRS - 3.

Pre-School Learning Alliance   1961
- NR The Fitzpatrick Building, 188 York Way, LONDON, N7 9AD. (hq)
  020 7697 2534   fax 020 7700 0319
  email info@pre-school.org.uk
  http://www.pre-school.org.uk
  Chief Exec : Neil Leitch
- ▲ Registered Charity
- Br 78
- ○ *E; to deliver high quality, flexible & affordable childcare (from pre-schools & baby/toddler groups to full daycare opportunities in nurseries & children centres) to families throughout England
- ● Conf - Mtgs - ET - Exam - Res - Exhib - Comp - Stat - Inf - Lib - PL - VE - Empl - LG
- M 14,000 org
- ¶ Under Five (NL) - 10.   AR; free.
  Guide to Training [lists courses] - 1.
  Leaflets; free.   Publications list available.

Precast Concrete Paving & Kerb Association
  see Interpave, the Precast Concrete Paving & Kerb Association, a product association of the **British Precast Concrete Federation**

Precast Flooring Federation
  a product association of the **British Precast Concrete Federation**

Prefabricated Access Suppliers' & Manufacturers' Association (PASMA)   1978
- ■ PO Box 2699, GLASGOW, G3 9DR.   (hsp)
  0845 230 4041   fax 0845 230 4042
  email info@pasma.co.uk   http://www.pasma.co.uk
- ▲ Company Limited by Guarantee
- ○ *T; the safe use of alloy access towers
- ● Conf - Mtgs - ET - Exam - Exhib
- < Access Ind Forum
- M 40 i, 220 f
- ¶ Operators Code of Practice; £5.
  Guide to Safe Use of Mobile Access (DVD); £35.

Prehistoric Society   1935
- NR c/o Institute of Archaeology, 31-34 Gordon Sq, LONDON, WC1H 0PY.   (mail address)
  http://www.prehistoricsociety.org
  Admin Sec: Dr Tessa Machling
- ○ *L; study of prehistory & its interpretation & conservation

Premature Menopause Support Group
  see **Daisy Network**

Premenstrual Society
  has closed

Premium Rate Association
  since 2011 has been succeeded by **Action4**

Presbyterian Historical Society of Ireland   (PHSI)   1906
- ■ 26 College Green, BELFAST, BT7 1LN.   (hq)
  028 9072 7330
  email phslibrarian@pcinet.org
  Librarian: Valerie Adams
- ▲ Registered Charity
- ○ *L; to collect & preserve the materials & to promote knowledge of the history of the Presbyterian Church in Ireland & of its constituent congregations
- ● Mtgs - Lib
- M 400 i, UK / 50 i, o'seas
- ¶ Bulletin - 1; ftm, £2 nm.
  Fasti of the General Assembly of the Presbyterian Church in Ireland 1840-1910; 3 parts; £2 per part.
  Publications list available.

Press Standards Board of Finance Ltd   (PRESSBOF)   1990
- ■ 21 Lansdowne Crescent, EDINBURGH, EH12 5EH.   (sb)
  0131-535 1064   fax 0131-535 1063
  email info@pressbof.org.uk
  Sec & Treas: J B Raeburn
- ▲ Company Limited by Guarantee
- ○ *N, *T; coordination & finance of self-regulation in the newspaper & magazine publishing industry in the UK
- ● Mtgs - LG
- M 5 org
- ¶ Code of Practice; ftm.

Pressed Flower Guild   1983
- ■ Glan Ffrwd, Llanfihangel Talylynn, BRECON, Powys, LD3 7TL. (hsp)
  01874 658234
  Hon Sec: Mrs C Foster
- ▲ Un-incorporated Society
- ○ *H; to raise the standard of pressed flowers; to arrange teaching & seminar facilities
- ● Conf - Mtgs - ET - Exam - Res - Exhib - Comp - SG - Inf - Lib - VE
- < R Horticl Soc
- M c 150 i
  (Sub: £24-£33).
- ¶ NL - 4;   LM - 1; both ftm only.

Pressure Gauge & Dial Thermometer Association   (PGDT) 1951
- ■ 35 Calthorpe Rd, Edgbaston, BIRMINGHAM, B15 1TS.   (asa)
   0121-454 4141   fax 0121-207 7002
   email info@pgdt.org   http://www.pgdt.org
   Sec: Sharon Parker
- ▲ Un-incorporated Society
- ○ *T; to represent manufacturers & suppliers of pressure &
   temperature dial gauges & associated equipment
- ● Mtgs - Stat
- M 14 f

Prestressed Concrete Association
   a product association of the **British Precast Concrete Federation**

Primary Care Dermatology Society   (PCDS)   1994
- ■ Titan Court (2nd floor), 3 Bishop Square, HATFIELD,
   AL10 9NA.   (secretariat)
   01707 226024
   email pcds@pcds.org.uk   http://www.pcds.org.uk
   Chmn: Dr Stephen Kownacki
   Sec: Dr Elizabeth Ogden
- ▲ Company Limited by Guarantee
- Br Republic of Ireland
- ○ *M
- ● Conf - Mtgs - ET
- < Brit Assn Dermatologists
- M 580 i, 13 f, UK / 80 i, o'seas
- ¶ PCDS Bulletin - 4; free.

Primary Care Rheumatology Society
- NR PO Box 42, NORTHALLERTON, N Yorks, DL7 8YG.
   01609 774794   fax 01609 774726
   http://www.pcrsociety.org.uk

Primary Immunodeficiency Association   (PiA)   1989
- ■ Alliance House, 12 Caxton St, LONDON, SW1H 0QS.   (hq)
   020 7976 7640   fax 020 7976 7641
   email info@pia.org.uk   http://www.pia.org.uk
   Chief Exec: Chris Hughan
- ▲ Registered Charity
- ○ *W; to promote the wellbeing of people with primary
   immunodeficiencies
- Gp Medical advisory panel; Personal support
- ● Conf - Mtgs - Res - Inf - LG
- < Intl Patient Org for Primary Immunodeficiencies (IPOPI); AMRC
- M c 1,500
- ¶ Insight - 4; subscription only.
   Various publications; ftm, 50p - £2 nm.

Primate Society of Great Britain   (PSGB)   1967
- ■ c/o Dr Sarah Elton, The University of Hull, Loxley Building,
   Cottingham Rd, HULL, HU6 7RX.   (hsb)
   01482 463327
   email secretary@psgb.org   http://www.psgb.org
   Sec: Dr Sarah Elton
- ▲ Registered Charity
- ○ *L; research into & general awareness of primate biology,
   evolution, conservation & management
- Gp Working parties: Captive care, Conservation
- ● Conf - Mtgs - ET - Res - Inf - LG
- < Intl Primatological Soc; Eur Primatological Fedn; Soc Biology
- M 265 i, 10 f, UK / 20 i, 10 f, o'seas
- ¶ Primate Eye - 3; £25 m, £30 nm.

Princess Gwenllian Society   1996
- ■ 158 Lake Rd East, Roath Park, CARDIFF, CF23 5NQ.
   http://www.princessgwenllian.co.uk
   Sec: Mrs Mallt Anderson
- ○ *G; to commemorate Gwenllian (c1282-1337), daughter of
   Llewellyn the last ruling 'Prince of Wales'

Principals' Professional Council   1920
- ■ 1 Heath Sq, Boltro Rd, HAYWARDS HEATH, W Sussex,
   RH16 1BL.   (hsb)
   01444 472499
   Sec: Dr Michael Thrower
- ▲ Un-incorporated Society
- Br 9
- ○ *E, *P; committed to the strong mutual support of its members
   working with other organisations for the promotion &
   development of the further education sector
- Gp Colleges of Agriculture & Horticulture
- ● Conf - Mtgs - ET - LG
- < a council of the National Association of Head Teachers
- M 750 i
- ¶ Newslink (NL) - 5;   Life Members (NL) - 2;
   Hbk (incl LM) - 1; all ftm only.

Printed Postage Impression Study Circle
   a group of the **British Postmark Society**

Printing Historical Society   (PHS)   1964
- ■ c/o St Bride Library, Bride Lane, Fleet St, LONDON,
   EC4Y 8EE.   (hq)
   email secretary@printinghistoricalsociety.org.uk
   Hon Sec: Philip Wickens
- ▲ Registered Charity
- ○ *L; history of printing & preservation of historical printing
   equipment; history of the book
- ● Conf - Mtgs - ET - Res - VE - Recording & preserving antique
   equipment
- M i & libraries
- ¶ Jnl - 2;   NL - irreg; both ftm.

Printing Industry Confederation
   see **Picon (Printing Industry Confederation)**

Printmakers Council   (PMC)   1965
- NR Ground Floor Unit, 23 Blue Anchor Lane, LONDON,
   SE16 3UL.   (hq)
   020 7237 6789 (Wednsdays 1400-1800)
   email info@printmakerscouncil.com
- ▲ Registered Charity
- ○ *A; promotion of printmaking & the art & work of
   contemporary printmakers & new & experimental techniques;
   to aid young & unestablished artists

Prism - Association of Print Specialists & Manufacturers   1934
- ■ Innovation Way, BARNSLEY, S Yorks, S75 1JL.   (hq)
   01226 321202   fax 01226 294797
   email info@prismuk.org   http://www.prismuk.org
   Manager: John Keith
- ▲ Company Limited by Guarantee
- ○ *T; to improve the profitability & competitiveness of UK imaging
   specialists, serving the POS, graphics, industrial, garment &
   textile markets
- < Fedn of Eur Screen Printers Assns (FESPA)
- M 114 f
- × 2008 (23 April) [Digital &] Screen Printing Association

Prison Advice & Care Trust   (PACT)   1975
- § Park Place, 12 Lawn Lane, LONDON, SW8 1UD.   (hq)
   020 7735 9535
   Dir: Andy Keen-Downs
   a registered charity offering advice, information & emotional
   support to families & friends of prisoners

Prison Governors Association (PGA) 1987

NR   Clive House (1st floor), 70 Petty France, LONDON,
        SW1H 9HD.   (hq)
        030 0047 5281
        email contact@prisongovernors.org.uk
        http://www.prisongovernors.org.uk
        Pres: Eoin McLennan-Murray,   Gen Sec: Paddy Scriven
▲   Un-incorporated Society
Br   c 150
○   *P; to represent the industrial relations & professional interests
        of prison governors (operational managers & senior
        operational managers in England, Wales, Scotland &
        Northern Ireland)
Gp   Northern Ireland (separate prison services), Scotland
●   Conf - Mtgs - Empl - LG
M   1,200 i
¶   The Key - 4; ftm only.

Prison Officers Association
        since 2007 see **POA: the Professional Trades Union for Prison,
        Correctional & Secure Psychiatric Workers**

Prisoners Abroad 1978

■   89-93 Fonthill Rd, LONDON, N4 3JH.   (hq)
        020 7561 6820   fax 020 7561 6821
        email info@prisonersabroad.org.uk
        http://www.prisonersabroad.org.uk
        Chief Exec: Pauline Crowe
▲   Registered Charity
○   *W; to offer support for British citizens in prison outside the UK
        & their families. Information on foreign criminal justice
        systems, prison conditions & transfer
●   Inf - Practical support - Survival grants - Pen-pal scheme -
        Resettlement assistance
        Helpline: 0808 172 0098
¶   NL - 3;   AR - 1; both free.

Private Libraries Association (PLA) 1956

■   29 Eden Drive, HULL, E Yorks, HU8 8JQ.   (mem/sp)
        email dchambrs@aol.com   http://www.plabooks.org
        Hon Mem Sec: Jim Maslen
▲   Registered Charity; Un-incorporated Society
○   *A, *G; encouragement of buying & private ownership of
        books; publication of books of relevance to book collectors
●   Mtgs - VE
<   [in liaison with the Chart Inst of Library & Inf Profls]
M   370 i, 30 f, UK / 150 i, 100 f, o'seas
        (Sub: £30)
¶   The Private Library - 4; ftm, £25 nm.   NL - 4.
        Private Press Books (check list of work of private presses in the
            western world) - 1; £10 m, £16 nm.
        Members' Volume - 2/3 yrly; ftm, £30-£50 nm.
        Exchange List - 4.

Private Wagon Federation (PWF) 1977

NR   Homelea, Westland Green, Little Hadham, WARE, Herts,
        SG11 2AG.   (hsp)
        01279 843487
        email geoffrey.pratt@btconnect.com
        Sec Gen: Geoffrey Pratt
○   *T
Gp   Railway wagon: Building; Hiring; Owners; Repairers
M   5 org

Probation Association 2008

NR   29 Great Peter St, LONDON, SW1P 3LW.   (hq)
        020 7340 0970
        http://www.probationassociation.co.uk
        Chief Exec: Christine Lawrie
▲   Company Limited by Guarantee
○   *P, U; for members of probation boards in England & Wales
M   42 probation boards
✕   2008 (1 April) Probation Boards' Association

Probation Boards' Association
        since 1 April 2008 the **Probation Association**

Probation Managers' Association (PMA) 1980

■   Unite, Hayes Court, West Common Rd, HAYES, Kent, BR2 7AU.
        020 8462 7755   fax 020 8315 8234
        email info@probationmanagers.co.uk
Br   9
○   *P; to provide professional support & advice for members who
        hold management post within the National Probation Service
        an autonomous professional body within Unite the Union

Proceeds of Crime Lawyers Association (POCLA) 2008

NR   Watchmaker Court, 33 St John's Lane, LONDON,
        EC1M 4DB.   (hsp)
        020 7405 2000
        email warren.foot@bllaw.co.uk   http://www.pocla.co.uk
        Hon Sec: Warren Foot
○   *P; to advance, foster & encourage the exchange of
        information, education & training in all matters relating to the
        practice of law involving the recovery of the proceeds of
        crime
●   ET - Mtgs

Process Servers Association
        see **United Kingdom - Process Servers Association**

Processed Vegetable Growers Association
        since December 2011 **British Growers Association**

**Processing & Packaging Machinery Association (PPMA)
1987**

■   New Progress House, 34 Stafford Rd, WALLINGTON, Surrey,
        SM6 9AA.   (hq)
        020 8773 8111   fax 020 8773 0022
        email administrator@ppma.co.uk
        http://www.ppma.co.uk
        Chief Exec: Chris Buxton
▲   Company Limited by Guarantee
○   *T; for manufacturers of machinery used in processing &
        packaging food, cosmetics, pharmaceuticals, beverages etc
●   Conf - Mtgs - ET - Exhib - Stat - Expt - Inf - Lib - PL - LG
<   Confedn Packaging Machinery Assns (COPAMA); European
        Sector Gp (EUROPAMA)
M   310 f
¶   Machinery Update - 6;
        PPMA Machinery Directory - 1; both ftm only.

Processors & Growers Research Organisation (PGRO) 1944

■   The Research Station, Great North Rd, THORNHAUGH,
        Cambs, PE8 6HJ.   (hq)
        01780 782585   fax 01780 783993
        email info@pgro.org   http://www.pgro.org
        Dir & Sec: G P Gent
▲   Registered Charity
○   *H, *Q; research into the production & harvesting of peas &
        beans for both vegetable & protein use
Gp   Agronomy; Biology; Botany
●   Conf - ET - Res - SG - Inf - Lib - VE - Advisory & technical
        services
M   3,003 i, 135 f, 30 org, UK / 8 i, 33 f, 17 org, o'seas
¶   NL - 2; ftm.   AR; ftm, £2 nm.
        Information sheets - 8/10; m only.

Procurators Fiscal Society 1930

NR   c/o Emma Knox, Crown Office, 25 Chambers St, EDINBURGH,
        EH1 1LA.   (hsb)
        email fdasecretary@copfs.gsi.gov.uk
        Sec: Emma Knox
○   *P; [in Scotland the Procurator Fiscal is the name for the public
        prosecutor who also does the same work as a Coroner
        elsewhere]
        is a division of the Association of First Division Civil Servants

© CBD Research Ltd · Beckenham · BR3 5JS · Tel 020 8650 7745 · E-mail cbd@cbdresearch.com · www.cbdresearch.com

Producers Alliance for Cinema & Television (PACT) 1991
NR   Fitzrovia House (3rd Floor), 153-157 Cleveland St, LONDON,
     W1T 6QW.   (hq)
     020 7380 8230
     http://www.pact.co.uk
○   *P, *T; for independent film & television producers in the UK
M   f

Production Managers Association 1991
NR   Ealing Studios, Ealing Green, LONDON, W5 5EP.   (hq)
     020 8758 8699
     Admin: Caroline Fleming
○   *P; for film, TV & video production managers
<   Producers Alliance for Cinema & Television (PACT)
M   c 180 i
¶   The Bottom Line - 6.
     Directory of Members - 1.

Production Services Association (PSA) 1994
■   PO Box 2709, BATH, BA1 3YS.   (hq)
     01225 332668   fax 01225 332701
     email admin@psa.org.uk   http://www.psa.org.uk
     Gen Mgr: Andy Lenthall
▲   Company Limited by Guarantee
○   *T; to make representations to government & the EU on matters
     affecting the live music, events & entertainment industry
Gp   Training & qualification development in the BTEC award system
●   Conf - ET - Exhib - LG
M   c 500

Professional Anglers Association Ltd (PAA)
■   Federation House, STONELEIGH PARK, Warks, CV8 2RF.   (hq)
     024 7641 4999   fax 024 7641 4990
     email paa@sportsandplay.com   http://www.paauk.com
     Contact: Eileen Taylor
▲   Company Limited by Guarantee
○   *P;to represent accredited angling coaches
●   ET
<   a group of the Fedn of Sports & Play Assns (FSPA)
M   130 i

Professional Association of Alexander Teachers (PAAT) 1987
■   The Big Peg (room 706), 120 Vyse St, BIRMINGHAM,
     B18 6NF.   (hq)
     01743 236195
     http://www.paat.org.uk
     Hon Sec: Liz Tunnicliffe
▲   Un-incorporated Society
○   *P; to support members who are teachers of the Alexander
     Technique; to promote the Alexander Technique which
     provides a practical means for change by bringing about an
     improvement in physical balance & coordination
●   ET
M   48 i
¶   Pamphlets.

Professional Association for Catering Education (PACE) 2003
NR   c/o McCullough Moore Ltd, Meadow Court, Faygate Lane,
     FAYGATE, W Sussex, RH12 4SJ.   (sb)
     0870 777 9586   fax 01293 852375
     email info@keepinpace.org.uk
     http://www.keepinpace.org.uk
     Chief Exec: Jim Armstrong (0788 776 8524)
▲   Company Limited by Guarantee
Br   6 regional
○   *N, *P; to encourage catering educational institutions to work
     together to manage the challenges of continual change
     within hospitality & catering education
●   Conf - Mtgs - ET - Res - Exhib - Comp - Inf - LG
M   c 500 i, f & org
     Note: PACE is the trading name of Keep in Pace Ltd

*Professional Association for Children's Guardians & Children & Family
Reporters & Independent Social Workers*
     see **NAGALRO: Professional Association for Children's
     Guardians & Children & Family Reporters & Independent
     Social Workers**

Professional Association of Clinical Therapists
     a group of the **Federation of Holistic Therapists**

Professional Association of Legal Services (PALS) 2002
NR   9 Morston Court, Aisecombe Way, WESTON-SUPER-MARE, N
     Somerset, BS22 8NG.
     email secretary@thepals.org.uk
○   *P; to represent licensed agents & consultants in England &
     Wales
●   Inf
M   i

Professional Association of Nursery Nurses
     on 28 February 2008 merged with the Professional Association of
     Teachers and Professionals Allied to Teaching to become **Voice**

Professional Association of Teachers
     on 28 February 2008 merged with Professionals Allied to Teaching
     and the Professional Association of Nursery Nurses to become **Voice**

Professional Associations Research Network (PARN) 1998
■   16 Great George St, BRISTOL, BS1 5RH.   (hq)
     0117-929 4515   fax 0117-934 9623
     email info@parnglobal.com
     http://www.parnglobal.com
     Dir: Andy Friedman
▲   Company Limited by Guarantee
○   *N, *P; 'the centre of expertise on issues relating to
     professionalism & the professionalisation of professional
     bodies. To provide a research enriched network for
     professional associations & a range of specialist knowledge
     based services'
Gp   CPD Network; Consultancy & information services
●   Conf - ET - Res - Inf - Lib - Consultancy - Publications -
     Networking
M   150 org
¶   CPD Spotlight (NL) - 12; ftm only.
     PARN Members News Update - 12; ftm only
     PARN Research Publications - 2; ftm, £50-£95 nm.

Professional Boatmans Association 1991
NR   48 Loveys Rd, Yapton, ARUNDEL, W Sussex, BN18 0HG.   (hq)
     01243 551927
     http://www.pba.org.uk
○   *P

Professional Bodyguard Association (PBA) 1985
NR   484 Albany House, 324 Regent St, LONDON, W1B 3HH.   (hq)
     0845 519 4580
     http://www.the-pba.com
     Hon Sec: M J Tombs
▲   Un-incorporated Society
○   *P; for the training of bodyguards
●   ET
<   Amer Soc of Law Enforcement Trainers (ASLET)
M   1,000 i, UK / 300 i, o'seas

Professional Business & Technical Management
     since c 2011 **Faculty of Professional Business & Technical
     Management**

Professional Charter Association   (PCA)   1991
- ■ The Glass Works, Penns Rd, PETERSFIELD, Hants, GU32 2EW. (hq)
  01730 710425   fax 01730 710423
  email info@ybdsa.co.uk   http://www.ybdsa.co.uk
  Chmn: Robin Milledge
- ○ *T; to represent professional skippers & vessel owners whose principal activity is skippered charter in domestic waters
- ● Mtgs - LG - Social events
- < Yacht Brokers, Designers & Surveyors Assn
- M 25 f
- ¶ [in the YBDSA Ybk - 2 yrly.]

Professional Coarse Fisheries Association   (PCFA)   2005
- ■ Federation House, STONELEIGH, Warks, CV8 2RF.   (hq)
  024 7641 4999 ext 204   fax 024 7641 4990
  email enquiries@pcfa.co.uk   http://www.pcfa.co.uk
  Assn Mgr: Milly Durrant
- ▲ Un-incorporated Society
- ○ *T; professional coarse fisheries in the UK
- Gp Fishery managers
- ● Conf - Mtgs - ET - Res - SG - Stat - LG
- < Angling Foundation; Brit Disabled Anglers Assn; Nat Fedn of Anglers
- > Fedn of Sports & Play Assns
- M i, f & org
  (Sub: £100)
- ¶ FSPA Members' Directory - 1; free.
  (www.sportsandplay.com)

Professional Computing Association
in 2009 merged with the Mac Technologies Association to form the Technology Channels Association, which in turn merged with CompTIA, a USA association, and is therefore outside the scope of this directory.

Professional Contractors Group Ltd   (PCG)   1999
- NR Heathrow Boulevard, 280 Bath Rd, WEST DRAYTON, Middx, UB7 0DQ.   (hq)
  020 8897 9970   fax 020 8759 1946
  email admin@pcg.org.uk   http://www.pcg.org.uk
  Chmn: Chris Bryce
- ▲ Company Limited by Guarantee
- ○ *T; to represent the interests & to promote the use of independent contractors & consultants, & to ensure the sector retains a professional image; to make representations to Government for legislation affecting independent contractors; to help members cope with the burden of new legislation, particularly IR35; to oppose IR35
- Gp Aberdeen Working Party (AWP); Associate members
- ● Conf - Mtgs - LG - Legal / accounting / tax technical advice
- < Assn Technology Staffing Cos (ATSCO); Confedn Brit Ind (CBI); Fedn Small Businesses (FSB); Inst Chart Accountants (ICAEW); Inst Directors (IoD); Recruitment & Employment Confedn (REC); Tax Faculty / Inst Taxation
- M c 14,000 f
- ¶ NL (email only) - irreg; ftm.

Professional Council for Religious Education
since 2008 the **National Association of Teachers of Religious Education**

Professional Cricketers' Association   (PCA)   1967
- NR 3 Utopia Village, 7 Chalcot Rd, LONDON, NW1 8LH.   (hq)
  07584 262083
  email aporter@thepca.co.uk   http://www.thepca.co.uk
  Chief Exec: Angus Porter
- ○ *S; to promote & protect the interests of present & past first class cricketers
- < Profl Players Fedn
- M 420 i

Professional Darts Players Association   (PDPA)
- ■ Federation House, STONELEIGH PARK, Warks, CV8 2RF.   (hq)
  024 7669 3360   fax 024 7641 4990
  http://www.pdpa.co.uk
  Chmn: Peter Manley
- ○ *P
- < a group of the Fedn of Sports & Play Assns (FSPA)
- M i

Professional Drivers Association   (PDA)   2002
- NR 10 East Moor Lane, Doddington, MARCH, Cambs, PE15 0TD.
  0790 999 5615
  http://www.pda-uk.org
- ○ *P; for drivers of heavy commercial vehicles (trucks)
- ● Inf

Professional Flight Instructor Association
- NR 4 Highdown House, Shoreham Airport, SHOREHAM, E Sussex, BN43 5FF.   (chmn/b)
  0797 332 6559
  http://www.theflyinginstructor.com
  Chmn: Dorothy Pooley
- ○ *P

Professional Footballers Association   (PFA)   1907
- ■ 20 Oxford Court, Bishopsgate, MANCHESTER, M2 3WQ.   (hq)
  0161-236 0575   fax 0161-228 7229
  email info@thepfa.co.uk
  http://www.givemefootball.com
  Chief Exec: Gordon Taylor
- ○ *U; to protect, improve & negotiate the conditions, rights & status of all professional players by collective bargaining agreements
- ● Conf - Mtgs - ET - Res - Empl - LG
- < Intl Assn of Football Players Us (FIFPro); Trades U Congress (TUC)
- M 2,713 i
- ¶ The Players Jnl - 4;   The Players Club - 4;   AR; all ftm only.

Professional Footballers' Association Scotland   (PFA Scotland)   2007
- NR Woodside House, 20-23 Woodside Place, GLASGOW, G3 7QF.
  0141-582 1301   fax 0141-582 1303
  email info@pfascotland.co.uk
  http://www.pfascotland.co.uk
  Sec: Fraser Wishart
- ○ *U; to protect & promote the interests of members
- < Profl Players Fedn

Professional Garden Photographers' Association
a group of the **Garden Media Guild**

© CBD Research Ltd · Beckenham · BR3 5JS · Tel 020 8650 7745 · E-mail cbd@cbdresearch.com · www.cbdresearch.com

Professional Gardeners' Guild   (PGG)   1977
- 59 Main St, Great Gidding, HUNTINGDON, Cambs,
  PE28 5NU.   (hsp)
  01832 293236
  email secretary@pgg.org.uk
  Hon Sec: Margi Comeau
▲ Un-incorporated Society
Br 4; Ireland, USA, worldwide
○ *H, *P; to promote & encourage professional contact,
  communication & cooperation between gardeners,
  exchanging ideas & information on all aspects of
  professional gardening, including the use of both new
  technology & traditional skills; to promote gardening as a
  profession, & the better management & maintenance of
  gardens & designed landscapes, especially those of historic,
  horticultural & botanical value
● Conf - Mtgs - ET - Res - Exhib - Comp - SG - Stat - Inf - VE -
  Empl - LG - Training bursary - Job opportunities - Advice -
  Industry representation
< Historic Houses Assn; Nat Trust; English Heritage; Garland
M 800+ i, c 10 f, c 30 org, UK / 100+ i, o'seas
¶ The Professional Gardener (Jnl) - 4; £25 m, £36 nm,
  £40 companies, £48 libraries.

Professional Golfers' Association   (PGA)   1901
- Centenary House, The Belfry, SUTTON COLDFIELD,
  W Midlands, B76 9PT.   (hq)
  01675 470333   fax 01675 477888
  http://www.pga.info
  Chief Exec: Sandy Jones
Br 7 regions
○ *P, *S; to train & serve golf professionals whose principal aim is
  to offer a highly professional service to amateur golfers at a
  club, driving range or other golf establishment
Gp Women's Professional Golf Association
● Conf - Mtgs - ET - Exam - Comp - Stat - Inf - Lib - PL - Empl -
  Securing sponsorship for members tournaments
< Profl Players Fedn
M 7,000 i
¶ Profile (Jnl) - 12; ftm, £35 yr nm.
  The PGA Ybk - 1; ftm only.   Regional Hbks - 1; ftm only.

Professional Guild of After Dinner Speakers
  no longer in existence

Professional Jockeys Association   (PJA)   1969
- 39b Kingfisher Court, Hambridge Rd, NEWBURY, Berks,
  RG14 5SJ.   (hq)
  01635 44102   fax 01635 37932
  email info@thepja.co.uk   http://www.thepja.co.uk
  Chief Exec: Paul Struthers
▲ Company Limited by Guarantee
○ *P, *S; to promote, protect & represent the interests of
  professional jockeys both on & off the racecourse working
  with regulatory, industry & commercial bodies to secure
  agreements for the benefit of all & continually working in the
  best interest of British horseracing
< Profl Players Fedn
M i
✕ 1988 Jockeys Association

Professional Koi Dealers Association   (PKDA)   2000
- 88 Newark Avenue, PETERBOROUGH, Cambs, PE1 4NS.
  01733 561016
  http://www.pkda.co.uk
  Gen Sec: Marion Parker
○ *T;
● Inf - Comp
M 26 f

Professional Lighting & Sound Association   (PLASA)   1977
- Redoubt House, 1 Edward Rd, EASTBOURNE, E Sussex,
  BN23 8AS.   (hq)
  01323 524120   fax 01323 524121
  email info@plasa.org   http://www.plasa.org
  Exec Dir: Ruth Rossington
▲ Company Limited by Guarantee
○ *T; to serve the entertainment, leisure, communication &
  architectural industries
● Exhib - Expt - Inf - Lib - VE - LG - Members deliver technical &
  creative solutions to clients & projects worldwide
< Wld Entertainment Technology Fedn (WETF)
M 60 i, 457 f, 7 educational, 10 affiliates
¶ Lighting & Sound International - 11; ftm, £30 yr nm.
  Lighting & Sound America - 12; ftm, controlled nm.   AR; ftm.
  Membership News - 12;   Standards News - 12; both ftm only.

Professional Photographic Laboratories Association
  dissolved November 2006

Professional Plant Users Group   (PPUG)
NR c/o Landscape Institute, 33 Great Portland St, LONDON,
  W1W 8QG.
  020 7299 4500
○ *H, *P; professional & trade bodies using plants in landscaping

Professional Players Federation   (PPF)
NR 10 Bow Lane (3rd floor), LONDON, EC4M 9AL.   (hq)
  020 7236 5148   fax 020 7329 3355
  email admin@ppf.org.uk   http://www.ppf.org.uk
  Gen Sec: Simon Taylor
▲ Un-incorporated Society
○ *P, *S; to promote, protect & develop the collective interests of
  professional sports players
● Conf - Mtgs - Res - Stat - LG
< Eur Elite Athletes Assn (EU Athletes)
M 9 org
✕ 2007 Institute of Professional Sport

Professional Rugby Players Association
  since October 2009 **Rugby Players Association**

Professional Services Marketing Group
NR 28 Canonbury Rd, LONDON, N1 2HS.   (asa)
  0845 619 9886
  http://www.psmg.co.uk
  Admin: Gail Jaffa

Professional Speakers Association   (PSA)
NR 12 Russell Close, UTTOXETER, Staffs, ST14 8HZ.   (hq)
  0845 370 0504   fax 0845 370 0503
  http://www.professionalspeakers.org
  Admin Mgr: Sue Cliff
○ *T; to represent speakers for all occasions - business, after-
  dinner
● Mtgs
M i

*Professional Trades Union for Prison, Correctional & Secure Psychiatric
Workers*
  see **POA: the Professional Trades Union for Prison,
  Correctional & Secure Psychiatric Workers**

Professionals Allied to Teaching
  on 28 February 2008 merged with the Professional Association of
  Nursery Nurses amd the Professional Association of Teachers to
  become **Voice**

Promota (UK) Ltd (Promotional Merchandise Trade Association) 1958
- Concorde House, Trinity Park, SOLIHULL, W Midlands, B37 7UQ.   (asa)
  0845 371 4335   fax 0845 371 4336
  email info@promota.co.uk   http://www.promota.co.uk
  Sec: Annette Scott
- ▲ Company Limited by Guarantee
- ○ *T; 'to promote & further the interests of businesses engaged in the promotional merchandise trade'
- ● Conf - Exhib
- M 735 f, UK / 108 f, o'seas
- ¶ Promota Bulletin - 6; ftm.

Promotional Merchandise Trade Association
   see **Promota (UK) Ltd   (Promotional Merchandise Trade Association)**

Property Care Association   (PCA)   2006
- NR Lakeview Court, Ermine Business Park, HUNTINGDON, Cambs, PE29 6XR.   (hq)
  0844 375 4301   fax 01480 417587
  email pca@property-care.org
  http://www.property-care.org
  Gen Mgr: Stephen Hodgson
- ○ *T; represents specialists in damp control, flood restoration, structural repair, structural waterproofing & timber preservation
- Gp Structural waterproofing; Technical panel
- ✕ 2006 British Wood Preserving & Damp-proofing Association

Property Consultants Society Ltd   (PCS)   1954
- NR 1 Surrey St (basement office), ARUNDEL, W Sussex, BN18 9DT.   (hq)
  01903 883787   fax 01903 889590
  http://www.propertyconsultantssociety.org
  Sec: David J May
- ▲ Company Limited by Guarantee
- ○ *P; a central organisation for qualified surveyors, architects, valuers, auctioneers, land & estate agents, master builders & constructional engineers who practise as consultants
- ● Stat - Inf
- M 550 i, UK / 70 i, o'seas
- ¶ NL - 4;   LM - irreg;   AR - 1; all ftm only.

Property & Energy Professionals Association   (PEPA)
- NR The Old Rectory, Church Lane, THORNBY, Northants, NN6 8SN.   (regd/office)
  0870 950 7739
  email info@pepassociation.org
  http://www.pepassociation.org
- ▲ Company Limited by Guarantee
- ○ *T; represents businesses engaged in the provision of energy marketing performance certificates (EPCs) & display energy certificates (DECs), the companies that undertake to distribute them, the accreditation schemes that oversee the products, the energy assessors that produce them & the technology companies that support the industry
- ● Mtgs

Property Managers Association   (PMA)   1975
- The Dolls House, Audley End Business Centre, SAFFRON WALDEN, Essex, CM11 4JL.   (secretariat)
  01799 544904   fax 01799 542991
  email pma@orbsupport.co.uk
  http://www.propertymanagersassociation.co.uk
  Hon Sec: Louise Oliver
- ▲ Un-incorporated Society
- ○ *P; to represent the interests of retail organisations by enabling their property professionals to work together for mutual benefit
- ● Conf - Mtgs - Res - Exhib - SG
- M 400 i, 150 f
- ¶ NL.   LM.   Ybk.

Property Managers Association Scotland Ltd   1991
- NR 302 St Vincent St, GLASGOW, G2 5RZ.   (hq)
  0141-248 3434
  http://www.pmas.org.uk
- ▲ Company Limited by Guarantee
- ○ *P; 'all aspects of property management & the law relating to heritable property'
- ● Conf - Mtgs - ET
- M i, f

Proprietary Acoustic Systems Manufacturers   (PASM)
- NR Adam St, off Lever St, BOLTON, Lancs, BL3 2AP.
  01204 380074   fax 01204 380957
  email info@pasm.org.uk   http://www.pasm.org.uk
- ○ *T; for manufacturers of proprietary acoustic (sound-proofing & insulation) products
- M 9 f

Proprietary Association of Great Britain   (PAGB)   1919
- Vernon House, Sicilian Ave, LONDON, WC1A 2QS.   (hq)
  020 7242 8331   fax 020 7405 7719
  email info@pagb.co.uk   http://www.pagb.co.uk
  Co Sec: Marion Fergusson
- ▲ Company Limited by Guarantee
- ○ *T; to represent manufacturers of branded over-the-counter (OTC) medicines & food supplements
- ● Conf - Mtgs - ET - Exam - Res - Inf - LG
- M 40 f, 35 f associates
- ¶ This Week (NL) - 52; ftm only.   AR; free.

Prospect   2001
- NR New Prospect House, 8 Leake St, LONDON, SE1 7NN.   (hq)
  020 7902 6600   fax 020 7902 6667
  email enquiries@prospect.org.uk
  http://www.prospect.org.uk
  Connect Sector, 4 The Square, 111 Broad St, BIRMINGHAM, B15 1AS.
  Gen Sec: Paul Noon
- ○ *P, *U; to promote & protect the interests of professionals at work; members include engineers, scientists, managers & specialists in areas as diverse as agriculture, defence, energy, environment, heritage, shipbuilding & transport
- Gp Connect sector (telecommunications & information technology)
- ● Conf - Mtgs - ET - Res - Inf - Lib - Empl - Campaigning
- < Trades U Congress (TUC)
- M 123,409 i

Prostate Cancer Support Association
   no longer in existence

Prostate Cancer Support Federation   (PCSF)
- NR Mansion House Chambers, 22 High St, STOCKPORT, Cheshire, SK1 1EG.
  0161-474 8222
  http://www.prostatecancerfederation.org.uk
  Hon Chmn: Sandy Tyndale-Biscoe (01243 572223)
- ○ *N; 'an organisation of UK patient-led prostate cancer support groups'
- ● Conf - Mtgs - Wokshops - Campaigning
  National Helpline 0845 601 0766
- < Europa Uomo
- M org
- ¶ NL - 4.

Protestant Alliance   (PA)   1845
- NR 77 Ampthill Rd, FLITWICK, Beds, MK45 1BD.   (hsp/b)
  01525 712348   fax 01525 712348
  Sec: Dr S J Scott-Pearson
- ○ *R; Protestant theology & history
- M i
- ¶ The Reformer - 6; £10.   The Young Reformer - 6; £6.

Protestant Reformation Society   (PRS)   1827
NR   15 Grange Court, CAMBRIDGE, CB3 9BD.   (hsp)
     01843 580542
     Gen Sec: Dr D A Scales
○   *R; to promote the religious principles of the Reformation
M   i
¶   NL - 3.

Protestant Truth Society (Inc)   (PTS)   1889
NR   184 Fleet St, LONDON, EC4A 2HJ
     020 7405 4960
     email info@protestant-truth.org
     Sec: G Rae
▲   Company Limited by Guarantee; Registered Charity
○   *K, *R; 'for the promotion & protection of the Protestant
     reformed faith'
●   Conf - Mtgs - Exhib - Comp - VE - Providing preachers for
     church services & deputation meetings
M   55 i
¶   Protestant Truth - 6.

Provincial Booksellers Fairs Association   (PBFA)   1974
■   The Old Coach House, 16 Melbourn St, ROYSTON, Herts,
     SG8 7BZ.   (hq)
     01763 248400   fax 01763 248921
     email info@pbfa.org   http://www.pbfa.org
     Admin: Ms Becky Wears
▲   Un-incorporated Society
○   *T; to promote interest in the collection & sale of antiquarian &
     secondhand books by organising book fairs, exhibitions,
     lectures & seminars; to publish books on book collecting
●   Conf - Exhib - Inf - Book fairs
     Book fairs information: 01763 249212
M   703 f, UK / 47 f, o'seas
¶   NL - 10; ftm only.
     Calendar of Book Fairs - 1; Fair Catalogues; both free.
     Book Collecting; ABC of Book Collecting; both £12.95
     Directory of Antiquarian & Second Hand Booksellers - 1;
       ftm, £4.00 nm.

Provincial Hospital Services Association   (PHSA)   1919
§   14 St Cuthbert's Street, BEDFORD, MK40 3JU.   (hq)
     0800 389 4431
     http://www.phsa.org.uk
     is now part of Engage Mutual of Harrogate, & has been re-
     named Engage Mutual Health; it retains its acronym PHSA as
     a not-for-profit insurance company specialising exclusively in
     corporate & individual healthcare cash plans

Provincial Newspapers Association of Ireland
     in 2008 merged with the Irish Master Printers Association of Ireland to
     form the **Regional Newspapers & Printers Association of
     Ireland**

Provision Trade Federation   (PTF)   1976
■   17 Clerkenwell Green, LONDON, EC1R 0DP.   (hq)
     020 7253 2114   fax 020 7608 1645
     email info@provtrade.co.uk
     http://www.provtrade.co.uk
     Dir Gen: Mrs Clare Cheney
▲   Company Limited by Guarantee
○   *T; for the provision trade & allied trades in the UK
Gp   Bacon & pigmeat; Canned foods; Chilled & processed meats;
     Dairy products; Export; Speciality cheese; Yoghurt & short life
     dairy products
●   Mtgs - Stat - Inf - LG - Annual dinner
<   Food & Drink Fedn (FDF); EUCOLAIT; Tr Assn Forum
M   130 f
¶   Ybk; free.

PSHE Association   2007
NR   CAN Mezzanine, Downstream Building, London Bridge,
     LONDON, SE1 9BG.   (hq)
     020 7022 1911
     email info@pshe-association.org.uk
     http://www.pshe-association.org.uk
     Mgr: Sarah Smart
▲   Company Limited by Guarantee
○   *P; to raise the status, quality and impact of PSHE (Personal
     Social Health & Economic) education
Gp   Local authority advisers; Teachers
●   Conf - Mtgs - ET - Res - Inf - Lib - LG
<   DCSF - Dept for Children Schools & Families
M   226 i, 577 f, 112 org

Psoriasis Association   1968
■   Dick Coles House, 2 Queensbridge, NORTHAMPTON,
     NN4 7BF.   (hq)
     01604 251620   fax 01604 251621
     email mail@psoriasis.demon.co.uk
     Chief Exec: Mrs Gladys Edwards
▲   Registered Charity
Br   12
○   *W; all matters relating to psoriasis & psoriatic arthritis
●   Conf - Res - Inf - LG
<   Eur Psoriasis Assns (EUROPSO); Assn Med Res
     Charities (AMRC); Long Term Med Conditions Alliance
     (LMCA); Nat Coun Voluntary Orgs
M   5,020 i, 10 f, UK / 80 i, o'seas
¶   Psoriasis (Jnl) - 4; ftm.

Psoriasis & Psoriatic Arthritis Alliance   (PAPAA)   2007
NR   PO Box 111, ST ALBANS, Herts, AL2 3JQ.   (hq)
     0870 770 3212   fax 0870 770 3213
     email info@papaa.org   http://www.papaa.org
     Chief Exec: David Chandler
▲   Company Limited by Guarantee; Registered Charity
○   *W; to raise awareness of & help people with psoriatic arthritis
     & its associated skin disorder, psoriasis
●   Conf - ET - Exhib - Inf - LG
<   Intl Fedn Psoriasis Assns; All Party Parliamentary Gp for Skin;
     Brit League against Rheumatism
M   [subscribers]
¶   Skin 'n' Bones Connection (Jnl) - 2; £3.
     Psoriatic Care Fact File - ongoing; £9.50.
     Leaflets & booklets.
×   2007 (Psoriatic Arthropathy Alliance
       (Psoriasis Support Trust

Psoriatic Arthropathy Alliance
     in 2007 joined with the Psoriasis Support Trust to form the **Psoriasis
     & Psoriatic Arthritis Alliance**

PSP Association   1994
NR   PSP House, 167 Watling St West, TOWCESTER, Northants,
     NN12 6BX.
     01327 322410   fax 01327 322412
     email psp@pspeur.org   http://www.pspeur.org
     Chief Exec: Fergus Logan
○   *W; PSP - progressive supranuclear palsy, the progressive death
     of neurons in the brain

PSV Circle
NR   Unit 1R, Leroy House, 436 Essex Rd, LONDON, N1 3QP.   (hq)
     email post-office@psv-circle.org.uk
     http://www.psv-circle.org.uk
     Hon Sec: John Skilling
▲   Un-incorporated society
○   *G; all aspects of bus & coach operations in Great Britain &
     Ireland & in other parts of the world where British vehicles
     are in use
●   Facebook - Lib - Mtgs
¶   British Journal - 4;   Overseas Journal - 4;
     News sheets (9 area edns) - 12; Books & booklets.

Psychiatric Rehabilitation Association   (PRA)   1959
- 1A Darnley Rd, LONDON, E9 6QH.   (hq)
   020 8985 3570
   http://www.praservices.org.uk
   Chief Exec: Mirella Manni
▲ Registered Charity
Br   14
○ *W; to promote mental health & improve attitudes towards the
   mentally ill
Gp   Art training; Computer training; Counselling; European
   networking; Stress management
● ET - Exam - Res - Exhib - SG - Inf - VE - Provision of day
   centres, work programmes, residential care
M   2,000 i
¶   NL - 4; ftm, £10 yr nm.   AR - 1; free.

Psychological Society of Ireland   1970
IRL   Grantham House (floor 2), Grantham St, DUBLIN 2,
   Republic of Ireland.
   353 (1) 472 0105
   email info@psihq.ie   http://www.psihq.ie
○ *P

Psychologists Protection Society   (PPS)   1970
§   Inglewood House, Inglewood, ALLOA, Clackmannanshire,
   FK10 2HU.   (hsp/b)
   0845 053 1182
   http://www.ppsweb.info
   Contact: Ewan Murray
   a not-for-profit mutual association offering professional
   indemnity & advice for psychologists, counsellors,
   psychotherapists & others in the talking & listening therapies

Public & Commercial Services Union   (PCS)   1998
- 160 Falcon Rd, LONDON, SW11 2LN.   (hq)
   020 7924 2727   fax 020 7924 1847
   email info@pcs.org.uk   http://www.pcs.org.uk
   Gen Sec: Mark Serwotka
▲ Un-incorporated Society
Br   1,000
○ *U; to represent civil & public servants
● Conf - Mtgs - ET - Res - Inf - Empl - LG
< Public Services Intl (PSI); Trades U Congress (TUC)
M   301,562 i
¶   PCS View - 12; ftm only.   AR - 1; free.

Public Fundraising Regulatory Association   (PFRA)   2001
- Unit 11 Europoint, 5-11 Lavington St, LONDON, SE1 0NZ.
   (hq)
   020 7401 8452   fax 020 7928 2925
   email info@pfra.org.uk   http://www.pfra.org.uk
   Chief Exec: Michael Aldridge
▲ Company Limited by Guarantee
○ *K, *N; to regulate the 'face-to-face' fundraising by charities &
   professional fundraising organisations; works with local
   authorities to ensure that fundraising sites are used
   appropriately
● Mtgs - Res - SG - Stat - Inf - LG - Accreditation scheme -
   Monitoring of compliance - Complaints processing &
   resolution - Mystery shopping
M   1 i, 16 f, 114 org
¶   AR - 1; free.

Public Management & Policy Association   (PMPA)   1998
NR   3 Robert St, LONDON, WC2N 6RL.
   020 7543 5600
○ *P; for managers & policy-makers within the public services; is
   managed by the Chartered Institute of Public Finance &
   Accountancy

Public Monuments & Sculpture Association   (PMSA)   1991
- 70 Cowcross St, LONDON, EC1M 6EJ.   (hq)
   020 7490 5001
   email pmsa@pmsa.org.uk   http://www.pmsa.org.uk
   Chmn: Peter Brown
▲ Company Limited by Guarantee; Registered Charity
○ *A, *G, *L; to record, preserve, research & enhance public
   appreciation of all aspects of public sculpture & monuments
Gp   Custodians Handbook; Marsh award for public sculpture;
   National Recording Project (NRP); Save our Sculpture
   Campaign; The Sculpture Journal
● Conf - Mtgs - Res - Inf - VE
< Ancient Monuments Soc; Art & Architecture; Brit Sundial Soc;
   Fountain Soc; Historic Gardens Foundation; Landscape &
   Arts Network; R Brit Soc Sculptors; Soc of Portrait Sculptors;
   Twentieth Century Soc
M   228 i, UK / 10 i, 35 f, o'seas
¶   The Sculpture Jnl - 2; ftm, £35 nm.
   Public Sculpture of Britain (a series of volumes describing in
   detail the national heritage of public sculpture); £19.95 -
   £52.95.

Public Relations Consultants Association   (PRCA)   1969
NR   Willow House, Willow Place, LONDON, SW1P 1JH.   (hq)
   020 7233 6026
   http://www.prca.org.uk
   Chief Exec: Francis Ingham
▲ Company Limited by Guarantee
○ *P; the maintenance of ethics & standards throughout the
   industry
Gp   Scottish Public Relations Consultants Association
   Finance directors c'ee; Government; Market sector
● Conf - Mtgs - ET - Res - Comp - Inf - Lib - Empl
< Intl C'ee of Public Relations Consultancies Assns Ltd (ICO)
M   160 f
¶   Public Relations Consultancy (Ybk) - 1.

Public Relations Consultants Association (Ireland)   (PRCA)
IRL   8 Upper Fitzwilliam St, Dublin 2, Republic of Ireland.
   353 (1) 661 8004   fax 353 (1) 676 4562
   email info@prca.ie   http://www.prca.ie
   Chmn: Laurie Mannix
○ *P
M   34 f

Public Relations Institute of Ireland   (PRII)   1953
IRL   8 Upper Fitzwilliam St, DUBLIN 2, Republic of Ireland.
   353 (1) 661 8004   fax 353 (1) 676 4562
   email info@prii.ie   http://www.prii.ie
   Chief Exec: Gerry Davis
○ *P

Public Sector People Managers' Association   (PPMA)   1975
NR   154 Cleveland Way, GREAT ASHBY, Herts, SG1 6BY.   (hq)
   01438 742811
   email admin@ppma.org.uk   http://www.ppma.org.uk
   Contact: Carol Sands
▲ Un-incorporated Society
Br   17
○ *P
Gp   Equal opportunites; Industrial relations & conditions of service;
   Performance review organisation & planning; Recruitment
   training & development
● Conf - Mtgs - ET - Res - Exhib - Comp - SG - Stat - Inf - Empl
< Inst Personnel Managers Assn (USA)
M   500 i
¶   NL - 4;   AR; both free.   Various technical publications.

Public Services Network
   has closed

Publicity Club of London
   has closed

© CBD Research Ltd · Beckenham · BR3 5JS · Tel 020 8650 7745 · E-mail cbd@cbdresearch.com · www.cbdresearch.com

Publishers Association   (PA)   1896
■   29b Montague St, LONDON, WC1B 5BW.   (hq)
    020 7691 9191   fax 020 7691 9199
    email mail@publishers.org.uk
    http://www.publishers.org.uk
    Chief Exec: Richard Mollet
▲   Company Limited by Guarantee
○   *T; to represent interests of UK publishers in books, book
    related material & journals to governments, other bodies in
    the trade & the public at large
Gp Educational Publishers Council (EPC); Trade Publisher Council
    Academic & professional division; International
●   Conf - Mtgs - Exhib - Stat - Expt - Inf - LG
M   180 f
¶   LM (CAPP) - 1;   LM (EPC) - 1; both free.
    Book Trade Year Book - 1; £10 m, £50 nm.

Publishers Licensing Society   (PLS)   1981
■   55-56 Russell Square, LONDON, WC1B 4HP.   (hq)
    020 7079 5930
    email pls@pls.org.uk   http://www.pls.org.uk
    Chief Exec: Sarah Faulder
▲   Company Limited by Guarantee
○   *T; formed jointly by the Association of Learned & Professional
    Society Publishers, the Periodical Publishers Association & the
    Publishers Association to protect & enforce publishers' rights
    in copyright of all published works (by means of
    reprographic reproduction); to distribute royalties from such
    reproduction
<   Intl Fedn of Reproduction Rights Orgs; Copyright Licensing
    Agency
M   1,800 f
¶   PLS Plus (NL) - 3;   AR - 1; both ftm only.

Publishing Ireland   1970
IRL Guinness Enterprise Centre, Taylor's Lane, DUBLIN 8, Republic
    of Ireland.
    353 (1) 415 1210
    email info@publishingireland.com
    http://www.publishingireland.com
    Admin: Karen Kenny
○   *T
<   Fedn Eur Pubrs; Intl Pubrs Assn
×   2008 Clé: Irish Book Publishers Association

Publishing Scotland   1973
NR Scottish Book Centre, 137 Dundee St, EDINBURGH,
    EH11 1BG.   (hq)
    0131-228 6866   fax 0131-228 3220
    email enquiries@publishingscotland.org
    http://www.publishingscotland.org
    Chief Exec: Marion Sinclair
▲   Registered Charity
○   *T; to provide information, advice, consultancy, training,
    marketing & promotional services
Gp Scot Book Marketing Gp (publicity & marketing service for
    booksellers in Scotland)
●   ET - Inf - LG - Attending bookfairs, both domestic & overseas;
    Marketing & export advice; Promotional services
M   72 f
¶   Directory of Publishing in Scotland - 1; £9.99.
×   2007 Scottish Publishers Association

Pubs of Ulster
    the trading name of **Federation of the Retail Licensed Trade of
    Northern Ireland**

Pugin Gild   1974
■   157 Vicarage Rd, LONDON, E10 5DU.   (hq)
    020 8539 3876   fax 020 8539 3876
    email keys@fsmail.net
    Sec: Ronald King
▲   Un-incorporated Society
○   *L; to promote Christian architecture, crafts & guild system
●   Res - SG - Inf - Lib - PL

Pugin Society   1995
■   33 Montcalm House, Westferry Rd, LONDON, E14 3SD.   (hsp)
    020 7515 9474
    email pamcole@madasafish.com
    http://www.pugin-society.org
    Hon Sec: Pam Cole
▲   Registered Charity
○   *G; to study the work of Augustus Welby Pugin (1812-1852) &
    other designers of the Victorian period; to report on buildings
    at risk (eg churches being demolished or changed from
    original design)
●   Mtgs - Res - Exhib - Inf - VE - Annual 4-day study tour
<   Victorian Soc; Pugin Foundation (Australia)
>   Enniscorthy Pugin Soc (Ireland)
M   460 i, UK / 40 i, o'seas, also corporate
    (Sub: £15 i, 18 joint, UK / £25 i, o'seas / corporate)
¶   True Principles - 1; ftm, £5 nm.
    Present State - 1; ftm, £5 nm.

Pullet Hatcheries Association   (PHA)   1985
■   89 Charterhouse St (2nd floor), LONDON, EC1M 6HR.   (hq)
    020 7608 3760   fax 020 7608 3860
    email Louisa.Platt@britisheggindustrycouncil.com
    http://www.britegg.co.uk
    Sec: Louisa Platt
▲   Company Limited by Guarantee
○   *T
●   Mtgs - LG
M   8 f

Pullet Rearers Association   (PRA)   1983
■   89 Charterhouse St (2nd floor), LONDON, EC1M 6HR.   (hq)
    020 7608 3760   fax 020 7608 3860
    email Louisa.Platt@britisheggindustrycouncil.com
    http://www.britegg.co.uk
    Sec: Louisa Platt
▲   Company Limited by Guarantee
○   *T; for pullet rearers & shell egg producers
●   Mtgs - LG
<   Brit Egg Ind Coun; Pullet Hatcheries Assn
M   13 f

Pulmonary Hypertension Association   (PHA)
NR Unit 2 Concept Court, MANVERS, S Yorks, S63 5BD.
    01709 761450   fax 01709 760265
    http://www.phassociation.uk.com
○   *M

Pulp & Paper Fundamental Research Society   (FRC)   c1984
■   5 Frecheville Court, BURY, Lancs, BL9 0UF.   (hq)
    0161-764 5858   fax 0161-764 5353
    email frc@pita.co.uk   http://www.ppfrs.org.uk
▲   Company Limited by Guarantee; Registered Charity
○   *Q; to promote research & education in the pulp & paper
    industry; its principal activity is the organising of four-yearly
    symposia, alternately in the universities of Oxford &
    Cambridge
●   Conf
M   10 i, UK / 6 i, o'seas
¶   Proceedings of each symposia - 4 yrly; £135.

Pump Distributors Association   (PDA)   1985
■   5 Chapelfield, Orford, WOODBRIDGE, Suffolk, IP12 2HW.
    (dir/b)
    fax 01394 450181
    email pumps@the-pda.com   http://www.the-pda.com
    Dir: Ian Castle
▲   Un-incorporated Society
○   *T; to represent firms who distribute industrial pumps, install
    pumps & repair them
Gp Pump training in conjunction with the British Pump
    Manufacturers' Association
●   Conf - Mtgs - ET - Inf
M   28 f, UK / 1 f, o'seas
¶   NL - 2; free.

Punch & Judy College of Professors
- ■ 2 Pembury Road, WORTHING, W Sussex, BN14 7DN.
  01903 200 364
  email enquiries@punchandjudy.org
  http://www.punchandjudy.org
  Coordinator: Glyn Edwards
- ○ *D
- < Worldwide Friends of Punch & Judy
- M 12 i

Purine Metabolic Patients Association   (PUMPA)   1992
- ■ c/o Dr Bridget Bax, Child Health, Division of Clinical
  Developmental Science, Lanesborough Wing (3rd floor),
  St George's, University of London, Cranmer Terrace,
  LONDON, SW17 0RE.   (hq)
  020 8725 5898
  email info@pumpa.org.uk   http://www.pumpa.org.uk
- ▲ Registered Charity
- ○ *W; to increase awareness of the 28 genetic nucleotide
  disorders under the PUMPA umbrella which include
  compulsive self-biting, kidney disease & fatal infections; to
  improve diagnosis & develop treatments Europe-wide
- Gp Familial juvenile gout; Patient contact Lesch-Nyhan disease
- ● Conf - Mtgs - ET - Res
- < Intl Fedn of Clinical Chemists; Contact a Family; Lesch-Nyhan
  Action C'ee
- M i
- ¶ Publications list available on request.

Pushkin Club   1954
- ■ 5A Bloomsbury Sq, LONDON, WC1A 2TA.   (hq)
  020 7269 9770
  Co-Chmn: Lucy Daniels,   Richard McKane
- ▲ Un-incorporated Society
- ○ *A; the promotion of Russian culture; also provision of
  education & information on Russian language & literature
- ● Mtgs - Inf - ib - Lectures in English &/or Russian - Recitals
- M c 80 i
- ¶ Programme - 1; free.

Pygmy Goat Club   1982
- NR Solomons Farm, Latchley, GUNNISLAKE, Cornwall,
  PL18 9AX.   (sp)
  01822 834474
  http://www.pygmygoatclub.org
  Sec: Mrs Margaret Thompson
- ▲ Un-incorporated Society
- ○ *B
- ● Mtgs - Exhib - Inf - Shows
- M 500 i, org, UK / 4 i, o'seas
- ¶ Pygmy Goat Notes - 4; ftm only.   Herdbook - 1.
  Pygmy Goat Hbk.   Members Hbk - 1; ftm only.

Pylon Appreciation Society   2005
- NR 1 Davies Lane, LONDON, E11 3DR.
  http://www.pylons.org
  Contact: Flash Bristow (07939 579090 pm ONLY)
- ○ *G; for those interested in all aspects of power transmission
  pylons

Pyramus & Thisbe Club   1974
- ■ Rathdale House, 30 Back Rd, Rathfriland, NEWRY, BT34 5QF.
  (hq)
  028 4063 2082   fax 028 4063 2083
  email info@partywalls.org.uk
  http://www.partywalls.org.uk
  Admin: Ada Elliott
- ○ *P; for professionals specialising in party wall matters

© CBD Research Ltd · Beckenham · BR3 5JS · Tel 020 8650 7745 · E-mail cbd@cbdresearch.com · www.cbdresearch.com

Q Guild   1997

NR   Algo Business Centre, 24 Gleneam Rd, PERTH, PH2 0NJ.   (hq)
01738 450443   fax 01738 449431
email info@qguild.co.uk   http://www.qguild.co.uk
▲   Company Limited by Guarantee
○   *T; butchers with traditional craft skills who support the British farming industry
●   Mtgs - Comp - Promotion
M   136 f
✕   Guild of Q Butchers

Quad Racing Association UK   (QRA UK)

NR   74 Roman Way, ANDOVER, Hants, SP10 5JJ.
01264 354259
email tonynash@qrauk.com   http://www.qrauk.com
Sec: Tony Nash
○   *S; for all interested in quad bike racing
●   Mtgs

Quality British Celery Association   (QBC)

■   PVGA House, Nottingham Rd, LOUTH, Lincs, LN11 0WB.
(asa)
01507 602427   fax 01507 600689
email jayne.dyas@pvga.co.uk
Sec: Mrs Jayne Dyas
○   *T; to provide technical, commercial & marketing information for growers
●   Conf - Mtgs - Res - Exhib - Stat - Inf - LG
M   120 f

Quality Guild   (QG)   1994

■   Westwinds, Lambley Bank, Scotby, CARLISLE, Cumbria, CA4 8BX.   (hq)
01228 631681
email blightowler@qgbiz.co.uk   http://www.qgbiz.co.uk
Managing Dir: Brian Lightowler
▲   Company Limited by Guarantee
○   *T; a network of quality assessed businesses
●   Inf - Business advice
M   250 f
(Sub: £315-£500)

Quality Meat Scotland   (QMS)

■   Rural Centre, West Mains, Ingliston, NEWBRIDGE, Midlothian, EH28 8NZ.   (hq)
0131-472 4040
email info@qmscotland.co.uk
http://www.qmscotland.co.uk
Chief Exec: Uel Morton
▲   Non-Departmental Public Body
○   *T; marketing & development of Scottish red meat industry
●   Conf - Mtgs - ET - Res - Exhib - Comp - Stat - Expt - Inf - PL - VE - LG
¶   Corporate Plan - 3 yrly; free.

Quality Milk Producers Ltd   1954

NR   Scotsbridge House, Scots Hill, RICKMANSWORTH, Herts, WD3 3BB.   (hq)
01923 695866
▲   Company Limited by Guarantee
○   *T; marketing, advertising & representation for Gold Top milk producers
●   Conf - Exhib - Comp - Stat - Expt - Inf - Promotion
M   450 f
¶   Gold Top News - 3; m only.

Quarry Forum
a forum within **Stone Federation Great Britain**

Quarry Products Association
merged in June 2009 with the British Cement Association to form the
Mineral Products Association

Queen's English Society   (QES)   1972

NR   1 Oban Gardens, Woodley, READING, Berks, RG5 3RO.
(admin)
0797 947 4826
http://www.queens-english-society.com
Admin Sec: Ennis Killip
▲   Registered Charity
Br   4
○   *K; to promote & uphold the use of good English; to encourage the enjoyment of the language; to defend the precision, subtlety & richness of the language against debasement, ambiguity & other forms of misuse
●   Conf - Mtgs
M   695 i, UK / 84 i, o'seas
¶   Quest (Jnl) - 4.

Queen's Nursing Institute   (QNI)   1887

§   3 Albemarle Way, LONDON, EC1V 4RQ.
020 7490 4227   fax 020 7490 1269
email mail@qni.org.uk   http://www.qni.org.uk
An independent non-membership body promoting the highest standards of nursing for the benefit of the community & public health.

Quekett Microscopical Club   (QMC)   1865

■   90 The Fairway, SOUTH RUISLIP, Middx, HA4 0SQ.
(subn/manager/p)
email secretary@quekett.org   http://www.quekett.org
Subscription Manager: Peter Thomas
▲   Registered Charity
○   *L; all aspects of light microscopes
●   Mtgs
M   360 i, UK / 60 i, o'seas
¶   The Quekett Jnl of Microscopy - 2.   Bulletin - 2.

Quilling Guild   1982

■   33 Mill Rise, Skidby, COTTINGHAM, E Yorks, HU16 5UA.
(hsp)
01482 843721   fax 01482 840783
email guild@quilling.karoo.co.uk
http://www.quilling-guild.co.uk
Sec: Paul Jenkins
▲   Registered Charity
○   *A, *G; to promote the art form / craft (a.k.a. paper filigree or paper rollwork) where paper is rolled and applied to create pictures
●   Mtgs - Exhib - Comp - Inf - Archive of antique & modern work
M   600 i, UK / 100 i, o'seas
(Sub: £18 UK / £24 o'seas)
¶   Quillers Today (NL) - 3.

Quilt Art
a group of the **Quilters' Guild of the British Isles**

Quilt Association   1995

■   The Minerva Arts Centre, High St, LLANIDLOES, Powys,
    SY18 6BY.
    01686 413467
    email quilts@quilt.org.uk   http://www.quilt.org.uk
    Exhib Organiser: Mrs Doreen Gough
▲   Company Limited by Guarantee; Registered Charity
○   *G; the exhibition of Welsh quilts, both antique &
    contemporary; education connected with quilting, its history &
    artistry
●   Conf - Mtgs - ET - Exhib - SG - VE
>   Mid-Wales branch of Embroiderers' Gld; Welsh Heritage
    Quilters
M   150 i, UK / 25 i, o'seas
¶   NL - 2;   AR;   both ftm only.

Quilters' Guild of the British Isles   1979

■   St Anthony's Hall, Peaseholme Green, YORK, YO1 7PW.   (hq)
    01904 613242   fax 01904 632394
    email info@quiltersguild.org.uk
    http://www.quiltersguild.org.uk
    Admin: Carol Bowden
▲   Company Limited by Guarantee; Registered Charity
Br 17 regions
○   *G; to promote the study & art of the techniques & heritage of
    patchwork, quilting & appliqué & of their future use &
    development
Gp British Quilt Study Group; Quilt Art
●   Conf - ET - Res - Exhib - Comp - SG - Inf - Lib - VE
<   Eur Quilting Assn
M   c 6,500 i, UK / c 200 i, o'seas
¶   The Quilter - 4;   Hbk - 1;   NL (Regional) - 3; all ftm only.

Quoted Companies Alliance   (QCA)   1992

■   6 Kinghorn St, LONDON, EC1A 7HW.   (hq)
    020 7600 3745   fax 020 7600 8288
    email mail@quotedcompaniesalliance.co.uk
    http://www.quotedcompaniesalliance.co.uk
    Chief Exec: Tim Ward
▲   Company Limited by Guarantee
○   *N; for smaller quoted companies (SQCs) which are listed on
    the London Stock Exchange & are outside the FTSE 350
    Index, including those on AIM + FWS Market Group
¶   QCA Voice - 4.

© CBD Research Ltd · Beckenham · BR3 5JS · Tel 020 8650 7745 · E-mail cbd@cbdresearch.com · www.cbdresearch.com

R S Surtees Society (RSSS) 1983
■ Wheelwrights Cottage, Croscombe, WELLS, BA5 3QQ.
  01749 344338
  email support@rssurtees.com
  http://www.r.s.surteessociety.org
  Sec: Jeremy Lewis
▲ Un-incorporated Society
Br USA
○ *A, *L; for those interested in the life & works of Robert Smith
  Surtees (1803-64), the sporting writer of the 'Jorrocks' stories;
  to keep the works in print
● Exhib - Publishing
< Selwood Foundation
M c 4,000 i

Rabbit Welfare Association (RWA) 1996
NR PO Box 603, HORSHAM, W Sussex, RH13 5WL.
  (mail/address)
  0844 324 6090
  http://www.rabbitwelfare.co.uk
  Chief Exec: Rachel Todd
▲ Un-incorporated Society
○ *B; to promote the keeping of rabbits as house pets; to raise
  interest in rabbit medicine within the veterinary profession
Gp Coordinators: Houserabbits, Pets, Rabbits
● Conf - Mtgs - ET - Exhib - Inf
M 3,500 i, f & org
¶ Rabbiting On - 4; Hbk; both ftm.

Race Walking Association (RWA) 1907
■ Hufflers, Heard's Lane, Shenfield, BRENTWOOD, Essex,
  CM15 0SF. (hsp)
  01277 220687 fax 01277 212380
  email racewalkingassociation@btinternet.com
  http://www.racewalkingassociation.btinternet.co.uk
  Hon Gen Sec: Peter J Cassidy
▲ Un-incorporated Society
○ *S; organisation, management, control & development of race
  walking (within the territory of England Athletics - England,
  the Isle of Man & the Channel Islands)
● Conf - Mtgs - ET - Exam - Comp - SG - Stat - Inf - VE
< England Athletics
M 120 clubs & county org
¶ Race Walking Record - 12; £20 (UK), £30 (Europe),
  £40 (o'seas).
  Hbk.

Racecourse Association Ltd (RCA) 1907
NR Winkfield Rd, ASCOT, Berks, SL5 7HX. (hq)
  01344 625912
  Chmn: Ian Barlow
▲ Company Limited by Guarantee
○ *S, *T; to promote & represent the interests of racecourse
  owners
Gp Publicity & marketing
● Mtgs - Exhib - Inf
M 58 f (racecourses)
¶ AR; free.

Racehorse Owners Association Ltd (ROA) 1945
■ 75 High Holborn (1st floor), LONDON, WC1V 6LS. (hq)
  020 7152 0200 fax 020 7152 0213
  email info@roa.co.uk http://www.racehorseowners.net
  Chief Exec: Michael Harris
▲ Company Limited by Guarantee
○ *S; representation of all racehorse owners in negotiation with
  the British Horseracing Authority, Horserace Betting Levy
  Board, the government & other bodies in racing in the UK &
  abroad
● Conf - Mtgs - Res - SG - Stat - Inf - LG
M c 7,250 i & f
¶ Thoroughbred Owner & Breeder - 12; ftm, £42 nm.

Racehorse Transporters Association (RTA Ltd) 1967
■ Folly House, Lambourn, HUNGERFORD, Berks, RG17 8QG.
  (chmn/p)
  01488 71700 fax 01488 73208
  email info@racehorsetransporters.org
  Chmn: Merrick E D Francis,
  Sec: Miss Philippa Gillie (07870 947335)
▲ Company Limited by Guarantee
○ *T; 'the RTA is the trade association member of the British
  Horseracing Authority Industry Committee, which represents
  the majority of all UK & Irish transporters & shipping agents;
  the association is available to help & advise members on any
  subject of horse transport'
● Mtgs - ET - Inf - LG
< Brit Horseracing Auth Ind C'ee Ltd; Nat Trainers Fedn;
  Thoroughbred Breeders Assn
M 90 f, UK / 15 f, o'seas (Republic of Ireland)

Rachmaninoff Society 1990
■ Merton House, 4 Carlton Rd, KIBWORTH HARCOURT,
  Leics, LE8 0LZ (mem sec/p)
  email Charles@neilmac.co.uk
  http://www.rachmaninoff.org
  Mem Sec: Dr John Malpass
▲ Registered Charity
Br North America
○ *D; furtherance of public knowledge, interest & appreciation of
  the life, art & music of Sergei Vassilyevich
  Rachmaninoff (1873-1943)
● Conf - Res - Inf
M 200 i, UK / 200 i, o'seas
  (Sub: £15)
¶ The Bells - a music jnl - 2; Update (NL) - 1; both ftm only.

Racket Sports Association
  in 2006 merged with the **Sporting Goods Industry Association**

Radical Statistics Group 1975
■ 27/2 Hillside Crescent, EDINBURGH, EH7 5EF.
  email admin@radstats.org.uk http://www.radstats.org.uk
  Admin: Alistair Cairns
▲ Un-incorporated Society
○ *P; for statisticians & research workers with a common concern
  about the political assumptions & implications of much of
  their work & an awareness of the actual & potential use of
  statistics & its techniques. The group is independent from
  other organisations... members are radical in the sense of
  being committed to helping to build a more free, egalitarian
  & democratic society
Gp Radical Statistics Health Gp
● Conf - Res - SG - Stat
M c 300 i, 30 librarians
¶ Radical Statistics - 3; £12.
  Jnl; NL.

Radio Academy   1983
NR   5 Golden Square (2nd floor), LONDON, W1F 9BS.   (hq)
       020 3174 1180   fax 020 7990 8050
       email info@radioacademy.org
       http://www.radioacademy.org
       Chief Exec: John Myers
▲   Registered Charity
Br   11
○   *P; dedicated to the encouragement, recognition & promotion
       of excellence throughout the UK radio industry
Gp   Administers the Student Radio Association
●   Conf - Mtgs - ET - Res - Comp
>   Student Radio Assn
M   c 1,800 i & f
¶   Off Air (NL) - 4; ftm only.   AR - 1; free.
       Directory - 1; ftm.

**Radio, Electrical & Television Retailers' Association Ltd
(RETRA)   1942**
■   Retra House, St John's Terrace, 1 Ampthill St, BEDFORD,
       MK42 9EY.   (hq)
       01234 269110   fax 01234 269609
       email retra@retra.co.uk   http://www.retra.co.uk
       Chief Exec: Bryan Lovewell
▲   Company Limited by Guarantee
○   *T; for electrical & electronics retailers, renters & service
       businesses; to represent small independents together with
       regional & national multiples
Gp   Conference; Training; Legal; Advice; Representation; Lobbying;
       Visits & excursions; Stationery & business supplies;
       Information; Meetings
●   Conf - Mtgs - ET - Comp - Inf - VE - LG
<   Eur Fedn Electronics Retailers (EFER); Retailers' Forum
M   1,500 i, 4,000 f
¶   Alert (NL) - 10.   Ybk.   AR.
       Safety in Electrical Testing.   Directory - 1.

Radio Society of Great Britain   (RSGB)   1913
NR   3 Abbey Court, Fraser Rd, Priory Business Park, BEDFORD,
       MK44 3WH.   (hq)
       01234 832700 (0830-1630)   fax 01234 831496
       http://www.rsgb.org.uk
▲   Company Limited by Guarantee
○   *G; all activities concerned with the advancement of amateur
       radio & the science of communication
<   Intl Amat Radio U (IARU); Inst of Electrical Engrs
M   c 26,000 i, UK / c 2,500 i, o'seas, 700 affiliated clubs & org
¶   Radcom - 12.   Various other publications.

Radionic Association Ltd   (RA)   1943
■   Baerlein House, Goose Green, Deddington, BANBURY, Oxon,
       OX15 0SZ.   (hq)
       01869 338852   fax 01869 338852
       email secretary@radionic.co.uk
       http://www.radionic.co.uk
       Sec: Miss Rebecka Blenntoft
▲   Company Limited by Guarantee
○   *M, *P, *Q; to promote the study & practice of radionics
●   Con f- ET - Exam - Res - Inf - Lib
<   Confedn of Healing Orgs
M   i
¶   The Radionic Jnl - 4; ftm.

Radnorshire Society   1930
■   Pool House, Discoed, PRESTEIGNE, Powys, LD8 2NW.   (hsp)
       http://www.radnorshiresociety.org.uk
       Hon Sec: Mrs S Cole
▲   Registered Charity
○   *L; history & culture of Radnorshire (pre-1974 county, now part
       of Powys)
●   Mtgs - Lib
M   350 i, 20 org, UK / 10 i, o'seas
¶   Transactions - 1; ftm, back issues £1 m, £5 nm.

Rail Freight Group   (RFG)   1990
NR   7 Bury Place, LONDON, WC1A 2LA.   (hq)
       020 3116 0007   fax 020 3116 0008
       http://www.rfg.org.uk
       Admin Mgr: Phillippa O'Shea
▲   Company Limited by Guarantee
○   *K; promotion & development of freight by rail
●   Conf - Mtgs - Res - Inf - Lib - LG - Media relations - Press
       releases - Political lobbying
M   145 f, UK / 5 f, o'seas
¶   Rail Freight Group News - 6; free.   Hbk - 1; ftm.

Rail Industry Contractors Association   (RICA)   1999
NR   Gin Gan House, Thropton, MORPETH, Northumberland,
       NE65 7LT.
       01669 620569
       http://www.rica.uk.com
○   *T; to represent suppliers of labour & other suppliers & services
       to the railway industry
●   Mtgs - Liaison within rail industry - Lobbying
M   50 f
✕   2006 Association of On-Track Labour Suppliers

Rail Plant Association
       is a group of the **Construction Plant-hire Association**

Railfuture
       the campaigning title used by the **Railway Development Society**

Rails Bookmakers Association
NR   PO Box 42, TADWORTH, Surrey, KT20 5YT.
       01737 216376   fax 01737 356141
       email rba@frb.org.uk
       http://www.rba-bookmakers.co.uk
       Chmn: Robin Grossmith
○   *T; bookmakers who operate from the members' rail on British
       racecourses
<   Fedn Racecourse Bookmakers

Railway & Canal Historical Society   (R&CHS)   1954
■   17 Lovelace Rd, OXFORD, OX2 8LP.   (hsp)
       01865 240514
       email secretary@rchs.org.uk   http://www.rchs.org.uk
       Hon Sec: Matthew Searle
▲   Company Limited by Guarantee; Registered Charity
Br   6
○   *G, *L; to encourage the study of the history of transport, with
       particular reference to railways & canals but including
       associated modes of transport such as river navigations,
       roads, docks, coastal shipping, ferries & by air
Gp   Air transport; Pipelines; Railway chronology; Road transport;
       Tramroads; Waterways
●   Mtgs - Res - Inf - PL - VE
M   780 i, 2 f, 3 org, UK / 16 i, 1 org, o'seas
¶   Jnl - 3;   Bulletin - 6; both ftm.

Railway Correspondence & Travel Society   (RCTS)   1928
NR   23 Haig Drive, SLOUGH, Berks, SL1 9HA.   (mem/sp)
       http://www.rcts.org.uk
       Hon Sec: Alan Cooke
▲   Un-incorporated Society
Br   27
○   *G; railway history, operation & development
Gp   Photographic
●   Conf - Mtgs - Exhib - Stat - Inf - Lib - VE - Publication of
       specialist histories involving research on locomotives
<   6 railway socs in UK; 30 o'seas
M   3,000 i
¶   The Railway Observer - 12; ftm.
       A wide range of books on railway subjects.

© CBD Research Ltd · Beckenham · BR3 5JS · Tel 020 8650 7745 · E-mail cbd@cbdresearch.com · www.cbdresearch.com

Railway Development Society Ltd   (RDS)   1978
NR   33 Station Court, Aberford Rd, Garforth, LEEDS, LS25 2QQ.
　　　(hq)
　　　0113-286 4844
　　　email info@railfuture.org.uk　　http://www.railfuture.org.uk
　　　Chmn: Mike Crowhurst
▲　Company Limited by Guarantee
Br　17
○　*K; to gain improvements to the railways; to provide the public
　　　with a modern joined-up transport system; to fight for
　　　environmentally friendly transport
Gp　Freight; International; Passenger; Policy & lobbying; Reopenings
●　Conf - Mtgs - SG - Inf - VE - LG
<　Transport 2000
M　3,400 i, 10 f, 80 org, UK / 10 i, o'seas
¶　Railwatch - 4.
　　　Note: Uses title Railfuture for all campaigning purposes.

Railway Enthusiasts Society (Rail Europe)   1963
■　PO Box 1, Thornton, BRADFORD, W Yorks, BD13 3QD.　(hsb)
　　　07974 651105　fax 01274 830520
　　　email raileurope@blueyonder.co.uk
　　　http://www.rail-europe.co.uk
　　　Hon Sec: Dale W Fickes
▲　Un-incorporated Society
○　*G; to further an interest in railways, particularly modern
　　　traction, with similar enthusiasts throughout Europe
●　VE
<　Utd Travel Associates
M　80 i, UK / 2 i, o'seas
　　　(Sub: £25, UK / 40 ($60) o'seas)
¶　European Rail News (NL) - 5/6; £15 m (2004).

Railway Forum
　　　has closed

Railway Industry Association   (RIA)   1875
■　22 Headfort Place, LONDON, SW1X 7RY.　(hq)
　　　020 7201 0777　fax 020 7235 5777
　　　email ria@riagb.org.uk　　http://www.riagb.org.uk
　　　Dir Gen: Jeremy Candfield,　Dir: G Coomb
▲　Un-incorporated Society
○　*T; to promote the interests of British rail industry
　　　manufacturers, contractors & specialist service providers,
　　　both in the UK & overseas
●　Conf - Mtgs - Exhib - Expt - Inf - LG
<　Eur Fedn of Rly Trackworks Contrs; U des Inds Ferroviaires Eur;
　　　Confedn Brit Ind; Rly Forum
M　140 f
¶　UK Railway Suppliers Directory.　Technical Specifications.

Railway Preservation Society of Ireland   (RPSI)   1964
■　PO Box 461, NEWTOWNABBEY, Co Antrim, BT36 9BT.　(regd
　　　off)
　　　028 9337 3968 (Mon-Fri 0900-1330)
　　　email rpsitrains@hotmail.com
　　　http://www.steamtrainsireland.com
　　　Hon Sec: Paul McCann
▲　Company Limited by Guarantee; Registered Charity
Br　Republic of Ireland
○　*G, *K; to preserve, maintain & operate mainline steam
　　　locomotives & vintage rolling stock on the main line railways
　　　of Ireland
●　Mtgs
<　Heritage Rly Assn (HRA)
M　700 i, UK / 300 i, o'seas
¶　Five Foot Three (Jnl) - 1; ftm, £3 nm.

Railway Ramblers   (RR)   1978
■　27 Sevenoaks Rd, Brockley, LONDON, SE4 1RA.　(mem/sp)
　　　http://www.railwayramblers.org.uk
　　　Mem Sec: Peter Walker
○　*G; exploration & documentation of disused railways - mainly
　　　in the UK
●　VE
M　583 i, 2 org, UK / 3 i, o'seas
　　　(Sub: £8 i, £24 org, UK / £12 i, o'seas)
¶　Railway Ramblings - 4; ftm only.

Railway Study Association   (RSA)   1909
NR　PO Box 375, BURGESS HILL, W Sussex, RH15 5BX.　(hsp)
　　　email info@railwaystudyassociation.org
　　　http://www.railwaystudyassociation.org
　　　Hon Sec: Steven Saunders
▲　Un-incorporated Society
○　*G; 'to be the most effective forum in Great Britain for
　　　promoting a broad understanding of all aspects of the
　　　railway industry'
●　Conf - Mtgs - VE
M　830 i, 32 f, UK / 12 i, o'seas
¶　NL - irreg.　Ybk.

Ramblers' Association   (RA)   1935
■　Camelford House (2nd floor), 87-90 Albert Embankment,
　　　LONDON, SE1 7TW.　(hq)
　　　020 7339 8500　fax 020 7339 8501
　　　email ramblers@ramblers.org.uk
　　　http://www.ramblers.org.uk
　　　Chief Exec: Tom Franklin
▲　Registered Charity
Br　3
○　*G, *K, *S; to encourage walking; to protect footpaths; to
　　　campaign for freedom to roam in open country; to defend
　　　the beauty of the countryside
●　Conf - Mtgs - ET - Res - Exhib - Inf - Lib (maps) - LG
M　140,000 i, UK / 5,000 i, o'seas

Randolph Caldecott Society   1983
■　Blue Grass, Clatterwick Lane, Little Leigh, NORTHWICH,
　　　Cheshire, CW8 4RJ.　(hsb)
　　　01606 891303 & 781731 (evgs)
　　　Hon Sec: Kenneth N Oultram
○　*A, *G; to promote the work of Randolph Caldecott, the 19th
　　　century artist & illustrator; to liaise with the American-based
　　　society
●　Mtgs (at Caldecott's birthplace in Chester)

Ranulf Higden Society   1992
NR　Southerton, Hazier Rd, CHURCH STRETTON, Salop,
　　　SY6 7AQ.　(hsp)
　　　email ranulphhigden@btinternet.com
　　　http://www.ranulfhigden.org.uk
　　　Contact: The Secretary
○　*A; to promote interest, understanding & research into
　　　documents written in Medieval Latin & Anglo Norman (with
　　　particular emphasis on north western England - specifically
　　　Lancashire, Cheshire, Staffordshire & Derbyshire); Ranulf
　　　Higden was a Benedictine monk & English chronicler who
　　　died in 1364
M　c 75 i
　　　(Sub: £5).

Ranunculaceae Group   2003
- ■ Frith Old Farmhouse, Otterden, FAVERSHAM, Kent,
    ME13 0DD.   (hsp)
    01795 890556
    email gillian.regan@virgin.net
    http://www.hardy-plant.org.uk
    Admin Sec: Gilian Regan
- ○ *H; to foster interest in plants belonging to the buttercup family
    - Ranunculaceae
- ● Conf - Mtgs (irreg) - VE
- < Hardy Plant Soc
- M 15 i, 1 f, 1 org, Republic of Ireland / 65 i, o'seas
- ¶ NL - 4; ftm, £2 nm.

Rapid Prototyping & Manufacturing Association   1995
- NR Institution of Mechanical Engineers, Engineering Programmes,
    1 Birdcage Walk, LONDON, SW1H 9JJ.
    020 7304 6837
    Exec: Charlotte Newman
- ○ *T
- M 250 i

Rapra Technology Ltd
- ▲ Private Limited Company
    an independent research technology & information consultancy
    specialising in rubber, plastics & composites
    Is part of the Smithers Group (Smithers Rapra).

Rare Breeds Survival Trust   (RBST)   1973
- ■ Stoneleigh Park, KENILWORTH, Warks, CV8 2LG.   (hq)
    024 7669 6551   fax 024 7669 6706
    email enquiries@rbst.org.uk   http://www.rbst.org.uk
    Gen Mgr: David Leafe
- ▲ Company Limited by Guarantee; Registered Charity
- ○ *B, *K; the preservation, conservation & promotion of native
    breeds of British farm livestock
- ● Conf - Res - Exhib - SG - Stat - Inf - Lib - PL - LG
- < Rare Breeds Intl
- M 9,500 i, 114 org, UK / 260 i, o'seas
- ¶ The Ark - 4; ftm.

Rare Disease UK   (RDUK)   2008
- NR Unit 4D Leroy House, 436 Essex Rd, LONDON, N1 3QP.
    020 7704 3141   fax 020 7359 1447
    email info@raredisease.org.uk
    http://www.raredisease.org.uk
    Chmn: Alastair Kent,   Exec Offr: Stephen Nutt
- ○ *K; to campaign for the development & implementation of an
    effective strategy for rare diseases in the UK
- ● Conf - Inf - LG - Mtgs - Res
- M 900 i & org

Rare Poultry Society   (RPS)   1969
- ■ Common Farm Bungalow, Sustead Rd, Lower Gresham,
    NORWICH, Norfolk, NR11 8RE.   (hsp)
    01263 577843
    Hon Secs: Stuart Clark,   Crystal Cutting
- ▲ Un-incorporated Society
- ○ *G, *K; for the preservation of over 60 rare & endangered
    breeds of poultry
- ● Exhib - Inf
- < Poultry Club of GB; Fedn of Poultry Clubs
- M 204 i, UK / 3 i, o'seas
    (Sub: £10)
- ¶ NL - 4.

Rating Surveyors' Association   1909
- NR c/o Hartnell Taylor Cook, 12-13 Conduit St, LONDON,
    W1S 2XH.   (hsb)
    020 7788 3809
    email martin.davenport@htc.uk.com
    http://www.ratingsurveyorsassociation.org
    Hon Sec: Martin Davenport
- ▲ Un-incorporated Society
- ○ *P; to represent experienced Chartered Surveyors who
    specialise in the field of business rates, in both the public &
    private sector
- ● Mtgs - Inf - VE - LG
- < R Instn of Chart Surveyors
- M 350 i
- ¶ NL - 2;   LM;   President's Report (AR) - 1.

Rationalist Association   (RPA)   1899
- ■ Merchants House, 5-7 Southward St, LONDON, SE1 1RQ.
    (hq)
    020 3117 0630
    email info@newhumanist.org.uk
    http://www.newhumanist.org.uk
    Editor: Caspar Melville
- ▲ Registered Charity
- ○ *K; publishing & campaigning in the area of secular humanism
    & non-religious thought; for artists, non-religious, free
    thinkers - philosophy, science & culture
- ● Conf - Publishing
- M 2,190 UK / 310 i, o'seas
- ¶ The New Humanist (Jnl) - 6; £18.

Ray Society   1844
- ■ c/o Dept of Zoology, Natural History Museum, Cromwell Rd,
    LONDON, SW7 5BD.   (hsb)
    020 7942 5560
    email t.ferrero@nhm.ac.uk
    http://www.scientificbooks.co.uk
    Hon Sec: Dr Tim Ferrero
- ▲ Registered Charity
- ○ *L; publication of original texts of scientific interest & merit
    which would not otherwise be published because of lack of
    commercial interest; works usually (but not exclusively) relate
    to British flora & fauna
    Founded in memory of English naturalist John Ray (1627-1705)
- ● ET - Res - Publication of scientific books/monographs of
    original works, translations & facsimiles on natural history
- M c 200 i, UK / c 50 i, o'seas
- ¶ Volumes (bound books 700-900 pages) - c 1; prices vary.
    AR - 1; ftm, £1 nm.

Raynaud's & Scleroderma Association   1982
- ■ 112 Crewe Rd, Alsager, STOKE-on-TRENT, Staffs, ST7 2JA.
    (hq)
    01270 872776   fax 01270 883556
    email info@raynauds.org.uk
    http://www.raynauds.org.uk
    Dir: Mrs Anne H Mawdsley
- ▲ Registered Charity
- ○ *W; to promote better communication between doctors &
    patients; to put patients in touch with each other in order to
    exchange ideas; to raise funds for research
- Gp Sufferers; Health professionals; General public
- ● Conf - Mtgs - Res
- < Brit Soc of Rheumatology; Arthritis & Musculoskeletal
    Alliance (ARMA)
- M 6,000 i
- ¶ Hot News (NL) - 4; ftm.
    Raynaud's: your questions answered; £4.
    Journey of Discovery; £12.
    Scleroderma - The Inside Story; £5.99.

© CBD Research Ltd · Beckenham · BR3 5JS · Tel 020 8650 7745 · E-mail cbd@cbdresearch.com · www.cbdresearch.com

Re-Solv (the Society for the Prevention of Solvent & Volatile Substance Abuse) 1984
- ■ 30A High St, STONE, Staffs, ST15 8AW.
  01785 817885
  http://www.re-solv.org
  Dir: Stephen Ream
- ▲ Company Limited by Guarantee; Registered Charity
- Br 3 regions
- ○ *K; the only national charity dealing with all aspects of solvent & volatile substance abuse (VSA)
- ● Conf - ET - Res - Inf
- M c 30 i, 50 assns, 220 health authorities etc
- ¶ NL - 6; free.
  Publications & videos, list available.

REACH: the Association for Children with Hand or Arm Deficiency (REACH) 1978
- ■ PO Box 54, HELSTON, Cornwall, TR13 8WD. (hq)
  0845 130 6225 fax 0845 130 0262
  email reach@reach.org.uk http://www.reach.org.uk
  Nat Coordinator: Mrs Sue Stokes
- ▲ Registered Charity
- Br 15; Eire
- ○ *W; to support families of upper limb deficient children
- ● Conf - Mtgs - Exhib - Inf
- M 1,053 i, UK / 53 i, o'seas
- ¶ Within Reach - 4; Introductory Booklet;
  Guide to Artificial Arms; AR; all free.

Reading Association of Ireland
- IRL Education Research Centre, St Patrick's College, Drumcondra, DUBLIN 9, Republic of Ireland.
  353 (1) 806 5210
  http://www.reading.ie
  Mem Sec: Hilary Walshe
- ○ *K

Reading Chamber of Commerce
a local chamber of **Thames Valley Chamber of Commerce & Industry**

Real Bread Campaign
a campaign group of **Sustain**

Record Society of Lancashire & Cheshire (LCRS) 1878
- NR c/o Dept of Economic History, London School of Economics, Houghton St, LONDON, WC2A 2AE. (mail/address)
- ○ *L; publication of original documents relating to the two counties
  Note: The GMCRO hosts the society's site but staff cannot answer any queries regarding the Society's membership or publications.

Recorded Vocal Art Society 1953
- NR 2 Oaks Way, Long Ditton, SURBITON, Surrey, KT6 5DS. (sp)
  020 8224 5204
  email richard.nicholson57@ntlworld.com
  Hon Sec: Richard Nicholson
- ○ *D, *G; to encourage the enjoyment of opera & song
- ● Mtgs - Concerts
- M i
  (Sub: £20)
- ¶ The Record Collector - 4. CDs.

Records Management Society of Great Britain
since 2010 **Information & Records Management Society**

RECOUP - maximising efficient plastics recycling 1990
- NR 1 Metro Centre, Welbeck Way, Woodston, PETERBOROUGH, Cambs, PE2 7UH.
  01733 390021 fax 01733 390031
  email enquiry@recoup.org http://www.recoup.org
- ○ *K; a charity promoting best practice in the recycling of plastics - pots, tubs trays & film
- < Inf

Recruitment & Employment Confederation (REC) 2000
- ■ 15 Welbeck St, LONDON, W1G 9XT. (hq)
  020 7009 2100 fax 020 7935 4112
  email info@rec.uk.com http://www.rec.uk.com
  Chief Exec: Kevin Green
- ▲ Company Limited by Guarantee
- ○ *P, *T; to represent all the recruitment industry
- Gp Childcare; Construction; Drivers; Engineering; Healthcare; Hospitality; Interim management; IT & Communications; Media; Search & selection; Security
- ● Conf - Mtgs - ET - Exam - Res - Stat - Inf - LG
- M 5,000 i, 8,000 f
- ¶ Recruitment Matters - 4.

Recruitment Society 1978
- ■ 6 Bretland Rd, ROYAL TUNBRIDGE WELLS, Kent, TN4 8PB. (hsb)
  01892 557784
  email admin@recruitmentsociety.org.uk
  http://www.recruitmentsociety.org.uk
  Admin: Val Hiscock
  Chmn: Steve Huxham: 07774 128148
- ▲ Un-incorporated Society
- ○ *P; to provide a forum for discussion of best practice in recruitment
- ● Conf - Mtgs
- M 300 i

Recycling Association 1975
- ■ Heritage House, Vicar Lane, DAVENTRY, Northants, NN11 4GD. (hq)
  01327 703223 fax 01327 300612
  http://www.therecyclingassociation.com
  Sec: D J Symmers
- ▲ Un-incorporated Society
- ○ *T; to represent a significant part of the independent sector of waste paper merchants; to promote & widen the use of recovered paper, both within the UK & other world markets
- ● Mtgs - Expt - LG
- < Bureau of Intl Recycling (BIR); Eur Recovered Paper Assn (ERPA)
- M 83 f, UK / 4 f, o'seas
- × 2009 Independent Waste Paper Processors Association

Red Poll Cattle Society 1888
- ■ 1 Nabbott Road, CHELMSFORD, Essex, CM1 2SW. (hsp)
  01245 600032 fax 01245 600032
  email secretary@redpoll.co.uk http://www.redpoll.org
  Sec: Ray Bowler
- ▲ Registered Charity
- ○ *B
- ● Stat - Expt - Inf
- < Nat Beef Assn; Nat Cattle Assn (Dairy)
- M 314 i, f & org, UK / 31 i, f & org, o'seas
- ¶ NL - 4; m only. Herd Book - 1; ftm, £10 nm.

Redbridge Chamber of Commerce
- NR PO Box 330, RAINHAM, Essex, RM13 0BA. (hq)
  0845 270 2009
  email chamber@redbridgechamber.co.uk
  http://www.redbridgechamber.co.uk
  Sec: Mrs Vibeke Gardiner, Chmn: Julie Woodward
- ▲ Company Limited by Guarantee
- ○ *C
- ● Conf- Mtgs - ET- Stat - Inf
- M c 200 f

RedR UK: people & skills for disaster relief   (RedR)   1980

§   250A Kennington Lane, LONDON, SE11 5RD.   (hq)
    020 7840 6000
    http://www.redr.org.uk
    to relieve suffering in disasters by selecting, training & providing competent & effective personnel to humanitarian relief agencies worldwide

Referees' Association   (The RA)   1908

■   Unit 12 Ensign Business Centre, Westwood Way, Westwood Business Park, Westwood Heath, COVENTRY, Warks, CV4 8JA.   (hq)
    024 7642 0360
    email ra@footballreferee.org
    http://www.footballreferee.org
    Gen Sec: Arthur Smith
▲   Un-incorporated Society
○   *S; interests of all grades of Football Association registered referees & assistant referees
●   Conf - Mtgs - ET - Supplies - Members' insurance - Help & advice
<   Football Assn
M   c 35,000 i
    (Sub: £15 UK / £13 o'seas)

Referenda Society   1991

■   29 Cleves Walk, ILFORD, Essex, IG6 2NQ.   (regd office)
    020 8500 4074
    email info@directvotes.info
    Dir: G Munnery
○   *K; to campaign for the introduction of a referenda voting system by which the electorate can express an opinion on issues of public concern & interest & secure the appropriate legislation
●   Campaigning
<   Direct Votes
M   i
¶   Introducing Direct Democracy; free for sae.

Refined Bitumen Association Ltd   (RBA)   1968

■   Harrogate Business Centre, Hammerain House, Hookstone Avenue, HARROGATE, N Yorks, HG2 8ER.   (hq)
    01423 876361   fax 01423 873999
    http://www.bitumenuk.com
    Sec: Chris Southwell
▲   Company Limited by Guarantee
○   *T; to represent the bitumen supply industry in the UK; to increase knowledge of the engineering properties of bitumen & the development of the applications in which bitumens are used
Gp Technical c'ee
●   Mtgs - ET - Res - SG - Inf - LG - Sponsoring research into bituminous materials for use in the construction & maintenance of highways & airfields
<   Eurobitume; Quarry Products Assn; Road Surface Dressing Assn (RSDA)
M   f
¶   Technical bulletins on specific subjects - irreg; free.

Refined Sugar Association   (RSA)   1891

NR 154 Bishopsgate, LONDON, EC2M 4LN.   (hq)
    020 7377 2113   fax 020 7247 2481
    http://www.sugarassociation.co.uk
    Sec: N Durham
○   *T; rules & contract conditions for the white sugar trade
Gp Arbitrators; Rules & contract conditions
●   Mtgs - ET - Inf - Empl - LG
M   40 f, UK / 70 f, o'seas
¶   Rules & Regulations; £35 m, £60 nm.

Refractory Users Federation   (RUF)   1945

■   Broadway House (5th floor), Tothill St, LONDON, SW1H 9NS.   (asa)
    020 7799 2000
▲   Un-incorporated Society
○   *T; for contractors involved in refractory work of all types incl furnace installation & boiler setting
●   Mtgs - ET - Inf - Empl - LG
<   Engg Construction Ind Assn (ECIA)
M   10 f

Refrigerated Transport Information Society
    a group of **Cambridge Refrigeration Technology**

Regency Society of Brighton & Hove   1945

■   85 Furze Croft, Furze Hill, HOVE, E Sussex, BN3 1PE.   (hsp)
    01273 737434
    email john-small@waitrose.com
    http://www.regencysociety.org
    Hon Sec: John Small
▲   Registered Charity
○   *A, *K; preservation of historic architecture of Brighton & Hove; to promote interest in architecture & urban design
●   Mtgs - Res - Exhib - VE
<   Georgian Gp; Civic Trust; Fedn of Sussex Amenity Socs; 20th Century Soc; Victorian Soc
M   c 400 i, 5 org
¶   AR; free.

Regia Anglorum   (Regia)   1980

NR 9 Durleigh Close, Headley Park, BRISTOL, BS13 7NQ.   (hq)
    0117-964 6818
    email events@regia.org   http://www.regia.org
    Business Mgr: Kim Siddorn
▲   Un-incorporated Society
Br 40; Australia, Canada, Denmark, Germany, Italy, N Zealand, USA
○   *D, *G; to accurately re-create the life & times of the Saxons, Vikings, Cymru, Scots, Normans & other inhabitants of the islands of Britain between the reigns of Alfred the Great & Richard the Lionheart
Gp Permanent site in Kent
    Archery; Arms & armour; Battle re-enactment; Carpentry & house-building techniques; Early music; Folkdance; Hunting; Ships & the sea
●   Conf - Mtgs - ET - Res - Exhib - Inf - PL - LG
<   Nat Assn Re-enactment Socs; Engliscan Gesíðas; York Archaeological Trust
M   650 i, UK / 100 i, o'seas
¶   Chronicle (NL) - 4; ftm only.   Clamavi - irreg.

Regional Newspapers & Printers Association of Ireland (RNPAI)   1919

IRL Latti, CAVAN, Co Cavan, Republic of Ireland.
    353 (1) 677 9116
○   *T; the representative body of Ireland's weekly regional newspapers
×   2008 (Irish Master Printers Association of Ireland (Provincial Newspapers Association

Regional Studies Association   (RSA)   1965

■   PO Box 2058, SEAFORD, E Sussex, BN25 4QU.   (hq)
    01323 899698   fax 01323 899798
    email sally.hardy@rsa-ls.ac.uk
    http://www.regional-studies-assoc.ac.uk
    Chief Exec: Sally Hardy
▲   Registered Charity
Br 11; Hungary, Ireland, Poland
○   *E, *L; to promote education & studies in regional planning
Gp International regional research
●   Conf - Mtgs - SG - Inf
M   450 i, 170 org, UK / 110 i, 17 org, o'seas
¶   Regional Studies - 9;   NL - 6;   AR; all ftm.

© CBD Research Ltd · Beckenham · BR3 5JS · Tel 020 8650 7745 · E-mail cbd@cbdresearch.com · www.cbdresearch.com

Register of Apparel & Textile Designers   (RATD)   1985
NR   3 Queen Sq, Bloomsbury, LONDON, WC1N 3AR.   (hq)
      020 7843 9460   fax 020 7843 9478
      Mgr: Laurian Davies
○   *T; to assist manufacturers of clothing & textiles in the UK &
      overseas; to offer a help & advice service to designers by
      holding up-to-date lists of designers by speciality.
      The Register is jointly sponsored by the British clothing industry
      & UK Fashion Exports
●   Conf - Mtgs - ET - Res - Exhib - Expt - Inf - Lib - VE - Empl - LG
M   i
¶   NL - 12; ftm only.

Register of Chinese Herbal Medicine   (RCHM)   1987
■   1 Exeter St (office 5), NORWICH, NR2 4QB.   (hq)
      01603 623994   fax 01603 667557
      email herbmed@rchm.co.uk   http://www.rchm.co.uk
      Sec: Emma Farrant
○   *P; to register & regulate fully qualified practitioners of
      traditional Chinese herbal medicine across the UK; to
      safeguard & promote their interests
●   Conf - ET - Res - Exhib - Inf - LG
<   Eur Herbal & Traditional Medicine Practitioner Assn (EHPA)
M   450 i
¶   RCHM Jnl - 2; ftm, £25 yr nm.
      NL - c 6; ftm only.

**Register of Independent Professional Turfgrass Agronomists
      (RIPTA)   2002**
■   c/o Peter Jones Associates Ltd, 65 Crow Lane, HUSBORNE
      CRAWLEY, Beds, MK43 0XA.   (hsb)
      01525 280573
      email pjassociates@clara.co.uk   http://www.ripta.co.uk
      Register Administrator: Peter Jones
▲   Un-incorporated Society
○   *P; ; to give independent advice on growing & tending turf
●   Inf
M   22 i

Register of Professional Turners
NR   The Workshop, Moor Close Lane, Over Kellet, CARNFORTH,
      Lancs, LA6 1DF.   (chmn/p)
      01524 735882
      Chmn: Malcolm Cobb
○   *P; woodturners
M   215 i

Registered Nursing Home Association Ltd   (RNHA)   1968
■   John Hewitt House, Tunnel Lane (off Lifford Lane),
      Kings Norton, BIRMINGHAM, B30 3JN.   (hq)
      0121-451 1088   fax 0121-486 3175
      http://www.rnha.co.uk
      Chief Exec: Frank E Ursell
▲   Company Limited by Guarantee
Br   35
○   *P; improvement of standards of care & techniques in
      registered nursing homes
●   Conf - Mtgs - ET - Res - SG - Stat - Inf - VE - Joint efforts with
      DH & DSS.
M   1,600 nursing homes, clinics & hospitals
¶   Courier (NL) - 6;   Nursing Home News - 6; both ftm only.
      Reference Book - 1; ftm.
      Care Assistant Training Manual; ftm.
      Management Manuals; ftm only.

Reiki Association   (TRA)   1991
NR   Westgate Court, Spittal, HAVERFORDWEST, Pembrokeshire,
      SA62 5QP.   (coordinator/p)
      07704 270727
      email enquiries@reikiassociation.org.uk
      http://www.reikiassociation.org.uk
      Contact: Sonia Thornton
▲   Company Limited by Guarantee
○   *P, *W; for Reiki practitioners & masters with the focus of Usui
      Shiki Ryoho Reiki; to offer information to the public about
      Reiki treatments
●   Conf - Mtgs - ET - Exhib - Inf
M   936 i, UK / 31 i, o'seas
¶   Touch - 4; ftm only.
      Reiki Magazine International - 6; £26 yr m, £45 yr nm.

Relate Scotland
      on 1 April 2008 merged with Family Mediation Scotland to form
      Relationships Scotland

Relationships Scotland   2008
■   18 York Place, EDINBURGH, EH1 3EP.   (hq)
      0845 119 2020   fax 0845 119 6089
      email enquiries@relationships-scotland.org.uk
      http://www.relationships-scotland.org.uk
      Contact: Graeme Hutchinson
      Chmn: Jim Wallace,   Chief Exec: Stuart Valentine
▲   Company Limited by Guarantee
○   *N, *W; a coordinating body for 24 affiliated family mediation
      services operating throughout Scotland; responsible for the
      promotion & development of a confidential counselling
      service to those in marriage & other intimate relationships
●   Conf - Mtgs - ET - Res - Stat - Inf - Lib - LG
      Mon-Fri 0900-1700 - local services on website
<   Nat Family Mediation
M   24 org
¶   NL - 2.   AR.
      Various guidance leaflets & training videos.
×   2008 (Family Mediation Scotland
            (Relate Scotland (merged 1 April)

Relatives & Residents Association   (R&RA)   1992
■   1 The Ivories, 6-18 Northampton St, LONDON, N1 2HY.   (hq)
      020 7359 8148   fax 020 7226 6603
      email advice@relres.org   http://www.relres.org
      Chief Exec: Gillian Dalley
▲   Company Limited by Guarantee; Registered Charity
○   *W; to support & advise older people, & their relatives &
      friends, who are in, or considering, long term care; to
      promote good practice in homes through local groups,
      publications & training
●   Conf - Mtgs (local gps) - ET - Inf
      Advice line: 020 7359 8136
M   c 300 i
¶   NL - 2; ftm, £1 nm.
      Publications list available.

Relief Patterned Tile Research Group
      no longer in existence

Religious Drama Society   (Radius)   1929
■   50 Norris Rd, Blacon, CHESTER, Cheshire, CH1 5DZ.   (hq)
      email info@radius.org.uk   http://www.radius.org.uk
      Contact: Dilys Stone
▲   Registered Charity
○   *R; to promote drama which explores faith & the human
      condition
●   Conf - ET - Comp - Inf - Lib - VE
M   200 i, 30 org, UK / 20 i, o'seas
¶   Radius Performing (Jnl) - 4; ftm, £1 nm.

Religious Society of Friends (Quakers)   (Quakers)   1650
NR   173-177 Euston Rd, LONDON, NW1 2BJ.   (hq)
　　020 7663 1000
　　Recording Clerk: Elsa Dicks
▲   Registered Charity
Br   475; Worldwide
○   *R; pastoral work; witness to Quaker beliefs
●   Conf - Mtgs - Inf - Lib - Supporting international representatives
M   16,978 i, (13,309 attenders)
¶   Quaker News - 4.   Quaker Monthly - 12.
　　Quaker Projects - 2;   Books - irreg.

Remote Gambling Association   (RGA)   2005
■   High Holborn House (6th floor), 52-54 High Holborn,
　　LONDON, WC1V 6RL.
　　020 7831 2193
　　email chawkswood@rga.eu.com   http://www.rga.eu.com
　　Dir: Brian Wright
○   *T; for licensed gambling operators in the UK & Europe
M   34 online betting and poker sites

Remote Imaging Group   (RIG)
■   PO Box 2001, DARTMOUTH, Devon, TQ6 9QN.   (msp)
　　fax 01803 839498
　　email membership@rig.org.uk   http://www.rig.org.uk
▲   Company Limited by Guarantee
○   *G; to promote interest & disseminate information pertaining to
　　the reception & display of 'remote images' namely weather
　　satellites; to liaise with official bodies, eg AMSAT-UK, the
　　Dept of Trade & Industry, the European Space Agency, Nat
　　Oceanic & Atmospheric Administration (US), the Radio
　　Society of Great Britain, etc
●   Conf - Exhib - Inf
M   1,250 i, UK / 536 i, o'seas

Remote & Rural Paediatric Special Interest Group
　　a group of the **Royal College of Paediatrics & Child Health**

Remote Sensing & Photogrammetry Society   (RSPSoc)   2001
■   Dept of Geography, University of Nottingham, NOTTINGHAM,
　　NG7 2RD.   (hq)
　　0115-951 5435   fax 0115-951 5249
　　email rspsoc@nottingham.ac.uk   http://www.rspsoc.org
　　Exec Sec: Dr Philippa Mason
▲   Company Limited by Guarantee; Registered Charity
○   *L; to educate the public in remote sensing & photogrammetry
Gp   Special interest: Archaeology, Education, Geological remote
　　sensing, GIS, Modelling & advanced techniques, Ocean
　　colour, Synthetic aperture radar
●   Conf - Mtgs - ET - Inf
<   Intl Soc of Photogrammetry & Remote Sensing (ISPRS)
M   1,200 i, 65 f
¶   RSPSoc NL - 4;   AR; both ftm only.
　　International Jnl of Remote Sensing - 22.
　　The Photogrammetric Record - 4; ftm.
　　Annual Conference Proceedings (CD-ROM) - 1.

Renal Association   1950
■   Durford Mill, PETERSFIELD, Hants, GU31 5AZ.   (secretariat)
　　0870 458 4155   fax 0870 442 9940
　　Hon Sec: Dr Lorraine Harper
▲   Company Limited by Guarantee; Registered Charity
○   *L; to advance, collate & disseminate knowledge of renal
　　function & structure; to seek means for the prevention &
　　treatment of renal disorders
●   Conf - Mtgs - ET - Exhib
M   950 i, 16 f

Renewable Energy Association   (REA)   2001
■   Capital Tower, 91 Waterloo Rd, LONDON, SE1 8RT.   (hq)
　　020 7925 3570   fax 020 7925 2715
　　email info@r-e-a.net   http://www.r-e-a.net
　　Chief Exec: Gaynor Hartnell
▲   Company Limited by Guarantee
○   *T; to secure the best legislative & regulatory controls for
　　expanding renewable energy production in the UK
Gp   Biomass; Bioenergy; Solar; Ocean energy; Renewable transport
　　fuels
●   Conf - Mtgs - SG - Stat - LG
<   Construction Products Assn
M   400 i, f & org
¶   Renewables Ybk - 1.
×   2006 (British Association of Biofuels & Oils
　　　　(British Photovoltaic Association (merged April)

Renewable UK Association   1979
NR   Greencoat House, Francis St, LONDON, SW1P 1DH.   (hq)
　　020 7901 3000   fax 020 7901 3001
　　email info@bwea.com   http://www.bwea.com
　　Chief Exec: Marcus Rand
▲   Company Limited by Guarantee
○   *T; to represent companies in the UK wind & marine
　　renewables industries
Gp   Inshore & offshore; Small scale wind systems; Wave & tidal
　　stream; Wind energy development
　　Associated services from manufacturing through planning &
　　consultancy
●   Conf - ET - Res - Exhib - Stat - PL - LG
<   Eur Wind Energy Assn (EWEA); Scot Renewables Forum (SRF)
M   320 f
¶   Real Power (Jnl) - 4;   Annual Review - 1.
　　Specialist topic conference & seminar briefing sheets.
×   2009 (21 December) British Wind Energy Association

Renfrewshire Chamber of Commerce   1964
NR   Bute Court, St Andrews Drive, Glasgow Airport, PAISLEY,
　　Renfrewshire, PA3 2SW.
　　0141-847 5450   fax 0141-847 5499
　　email info@renfrewshirechamber.com
　　http://www.renfrewshirechamber.com
　　Chief Exec: Bob Davidson
▲   Company Limited by Guarantee
○   *C
<   Scot Chams Comm

Reptile & Exotic Pet Trade Association   (REPTA)   2004
NR   242-244 Havant Rd, Cosham, PORTSMOUTH, Hants,
　　PO6 1PA.   (regd/office)
　　023 9220 0990   fax 023 9220 0990
　　Chmn: Chris Newman
▲   Company Limited by Guarantee
○   *T; to represent the opinions of the reptile & exotic pet trade
　　with a view to ensuring that no unreasonable legislation is
　　made regarding the keeping & trading in exotic animals
●   LG
M   f

Rescare   1984
NR   Steven Jackson House, 31 Buxton Rd - Heaviley, STOCKPORT,
　　Cheshire, SK2 6LS.   (hq)
　　0161-474 7323   fax 0161-480 3668
　　email office@rescare.org.uk   http://www.rescare.org.uk
　　Chmn: Richard S Jacobson
○   *W; support & information for families of children & adults with
　　learning disabilities & their families
●   Helpline: 0161-477 1640
¶   Resnews - 4.

Rescue & Recovery Trainers Association
　　see **Institute of Vehicle Recovery**

Research Defence Society
2008 merged with the Coalition for Medical Progress to form
Understanding Animal Research

Research & Development Society   (R&D)   1962
■   c/o Octinver Ltd, 18 Grantchester Rd, CAMBRIDGE,
CB3 9ED.   (hq)
01223 5600323   fax 020 7930 2170
email randsociety@octinver.com   http://www.rdsoc.org
Admin Sec: Scott Keir
▲   Company Limited by Guarantee
○   *P; 'to promote networking between people involved in R & D
management & related professions over the whole range of
science, engineering & technology; to disseminate current
new ideas in science & technology, related management &
business development, & science policy'
●   Conf - Mtgs
M   150 i, 45 f, UK / 5 f, o'seas
(Subs: £60 i, £600 f)
¶   LM - 1; ftm only.   AR; free.
Note: the society was incorporated in 1961

Research Libraries UK
see **RLUK: Research Libraries UK**

Residential Boat Owners Association   (RBOA)   1963
■   NB Wasp, Off Barons Way, MOUNTSORREL, Leics,
LE12 7EA.   (mail add)
07710 029247
email secretary@rboa.org.uk   http://www.rboa.org.uk
Gen Sec: Beryl McDowall
▲   Un-incorporated Society
○   *K; to further the interests of boat dwellers on the coasts, rivers
& canals of Britain; to safeguard & increase the number of
residential moorings; to encourage high standards of safety
of boats & their moorings & good relations between
members & landlords & local authorities; to encourage
mobile boats to cruise
●   Mtgs
<   Nat Navigation Users Forum (NNUF)
M   i, f & org
(Sub: £21 i, £60 instns)
¶   Soundings (NL) - 4; ftm.   Living Afloat; £8.50.
A Home Afloat (leaflet); free.

Residential Landlords Association Ltd
NR   1 Roebuck Lane, SALE, Cheshire, M33 7SY.
0845 666 5000   fax 0845 665 1845
http://www.rla.org.uk

Residential Sprinkler Association   (RSA)   2007
■   Mill House, Mill Lane, Padworth, READING, Berks, RG7 4JX.
(hq)
0118-971 2322
email info@firesprinklers.org.uk
http://www.firesprinklers.org.uk
Sec Gen: Sir George Pigot
▲   Un-incorporated Society
○   *T; to provide support facilities to the residential sector of the
UK fire sprinkler industry in whatever manner is deemed
necessary by the membership
Gp   Technical c'ee
●   ET - Exam - Inf - LG
M   43 f
(Sub: £250)
×   2007 (March) Fire Sprinkler Association

Residential Ventilation Association   (RVA)   2000
■   2 Waltham Court, Milley Lane, Hare Hatch, READING, Berks,
RG10 9TH.   (hq)
0118-940 3416   fax 0118-940 6258
email info@feta.co.uk   http://www.feta.co.uk
Dir Gen: Cedric Sloan
○   *T; the responsible provision of suitable ventilation products for
all applications in the home
●   Mtgs - SG - Inf
<   Heating & Ventilating Mfrs' Assn (HEVAC); Fedn Envtl Trade
Assns (FETA)
M   19 f

Resin Flooring Association
see **FeRFA: the Resin Flooring Association**

Resolution   1982
NR   PO Box 302, ORPINGTON, Kent, BR6 8QX.   (hq)
01689 820272   fax 01689 896972
email info@resolution.org.uk
http://www.resolution.org.uk
Chmn: Godfrey Freeman
Br   40 regional groups
○   *P; solicitors working in the area of family law & marriage
breakdown, who have adopted a conciliatory, rather than a
litigious approach to family law
Gp   Child Support Act
Working parties & c'ees: Children, Education, Legal aid,
Mediation, Procedure, Training
M   5,000 i
¶   NL - 6.   Precedents for Consent Orders - updated.

Resource Use Institute Ltd   (RUI)   1969
NR   19 West End, Kinglassie, LOCHGELLY, Fife, KY5 0XG.   (hsb)
01592 882248
http://www.rui.co.uk
Sec: Miss Isabel Soutar
▲   Company Limited by Guarantee
Br   3
○   *L; to encourage new thinking, especially in science, technology
& economics; the management of innovation
Gp   Clay minerals; Land utilisation; Mathematical chemistry;
Resource economics
●   Res
M   18 i, UK / 1 i, o'seas

Restaurant Property Advisors Society   (RPAS)   1990
NR   c/o Restaurant Property, 58 Paddington St, LONDON,
W1U 4JA.   (sb)
020 7935 2222
http://www.rpas.org.uk
Sec: David Rawlinson
▲   Un-incorporated Society
○   *P; 'professionals specialising in the sale, acquisition, letting,
valuation, rent review & lease renewal advice on restaurants
& other licensed properties'
●   Conf - Mtgs
M   58 i

Restaurants Association of Ireland   1970
IRL   11 Bridge Court, City Gate, Saint Augustine St, DUBLIN 8,
Republic of Ireland.
353 (1) 677 9901   fax 353 (1) 671 8414
email info@rai.ie
Chief Exec: Henry O'Neill
○   *T

Restricted Growth Association   (RGA)   1970
NR   PO Box 15755, SOLIHULL, W Midlands, B93 3FY.
        (mail/address)
        0300 111 1970 (office & helpline)
        email office@restrictedgrowth.co.uk
        http://www.restrictedgrowth.co.uk
        Assn Mgr: Angela Belcher
▲   Registered Charity
○   *Q, *W; to promote the general welfare of persons of restricted
      growth; to investigate the causes & mitigate their medical
      condition
M   i

**Retail Book, Stationery & Allied Trade Employees Association
(RBA)**
NR   PO Box 3664, SWINDON, Wilts, SN3 9BR.
        01793 864848
        http://www.the-rba.org
○   *U
      Note: generally known as the Retail Book Association

Retail Bridalwear Association Ltd   (RBA)   1995
■   106 Broad Street Mall, READING, Berks, RG1 7QA.   (hq)
        0118-958 3560
        email rba@fsmail.net   http://www.rbaltd.org.uk
        Sec: Philip Rathkey
▲   Company Limited by Guarantee
○   *T; an association of independent bridal & formalwear retailers
      committed to the highest standards of customer service
      where the bride & groom can buy with confidence
●   Mtgs - ET - SG - VE - LG - Annual awards
>   Brit Bridalwear Assn
M   100 i
¶   LM on website

**Retail Confectioners & Tobacconists Association Ltd   (RCTA)
1976**
NR   c/o Levicks, 3 Lloyd Rd, BROADSTAIRS, Kent, CT10 1HY.   (hq)
        Contact: Michael Collier
○   *T; 'providing a distribution service of product to members;
      liaison with trade & industry on issues parochial to the CTN
      sector in tobacco, confectionery & ancillary fields'

Retail Grocery, Dairy & Allied Trades Association [IRL]
        see **RGDATA**

Retail Ireland
IRL   Confederation House, 84-86 Lower Baggot St, DUBLIN 2,
        Republic of Ireland.   (hq)
        353 (1) 605 1558
        email stephen.lynham@ibec.ie
        http://www.retailireland.ie
        Dir: Stephen Lynham
○   *T; the national representative body for the entire retail sector
<   Ir Business & Emplrs Confedn (IBEC)

Retail Markets Alliance
        members of the alliance represents wholesale, retail & specialist
        markets - & are the Association of London Markets; Association of
        Town Centre Management; Country Markets; National Association of
        British Market Authorities; National Farmer & Retail Markets'
        Association (qqv)

Retail Markets Alliance
        see the **Markets Alliance**

Retail Motor Industry Federation   (RMI)   1913
NR   201 Great Portland St, LONDON, W1W 5AB.   (hq)
        020 7580 9122
        http://www.rmif.co.uk
○   *T; interests of those selling & servicing new & used cars, trucks
      & motorcycles & other related activities
Gp   Cherished Numbers Dealers Association; Independent Garage
        Association; Motorcycle Retailers Association; Motorcycle
        Rider Training Association; National Franchised Dealers
        Association; Petrol Retailers Association; Society of Motor
        Auctions;
        Bodyshop Services Division
M   12,000 f
¶   Motor Retailer - 12.
      Forecourt - 12.
      Recovery Operator - 4.
×   2009 MVRA Ltd (merged)

Retailers against Smuggling   2009
IRL   PO Box 16126, Ballsbridge, DUBLIN 4, Republic of Ireland.
        353 (1) 800 727727
○   *K; to raise widespread awareness on the issue of tobacco
      smuggling in Ireland & its cost to retailers
      a campaign of the **Tobacco Alliance**

Rethink   1972
■   89 Albert Embankment (15th floor), LONDON, SE1 7TP.   (hq)
        0845 456 0455
        email info@rethink.org   http://www.rethink.org
        Chief Exec: Paul Jenkins
▲   Registered Charity
Br   9 in England, 1 Northern Ireland
○   *W; to help everyone affected by severe mental illness to
      recover a better quality of life
Gp   350 mental health services; 30 local support groups; National
        advice service
●   Mtgs - Res - Inf - LG
      Advice service: 020 7840 3188 (Mon-Fri 1000-1300)
<   Mental Health Providers' Forum; Mental Health Alliance; NHS
      Confedn
M   c 6,000 i
¶   Publications list on www.mentalhealthshop.org

Retread Manufacturers Association   (RMA)   1938
NR   PO Box 320, CREWE, Cheshire, CW2 6WY.   (hq)
        01270 561014   fax 01270 668801
        http://www.retreaders.org.uk
▲   Un-incorporated Society
○   *T; for the UK retread tyre industry & associated businesses
●   Conf - Mtgs - ET - Exam - Res - Exhib - SG - Stat - Inf - VE - LG
<   Intl Assn of Retreading & Dealer Assns (BIPAVER); Eur Tyre
      Recycling Assn (ETRA); Soc of Assn Execs (SAE); Tyre Ind
      Coun (TIC); Brit Tyre Ind Fedn (BTIF)
M   110 f, UK / 6 f, o'seas
¶   The Retreader (published in Tyres & Accessories) - 12.
      LM - updated.   AR.
      Manual of Operating Standards.

© CBD Research Ltd · Beckenham · BR3 5JS · Tel 020 8650 7745 · E-mail cbd@cbdresearch.com · www.cbdresearch.com

Retreat Association (RA) 1989
NR Kerridge House, 42 Woodside Close, AMERSHAM, Bucks,
    HP6 5EF. (hq)
    01494 433004 fax 0871 715 1917
    email info@retreats.org.uk http://www.retreats.org.uk
    Dir: Alison MacTier
▲ Registered Charity
○ *G, *N, *R; a federation of Christian retreat groups
● Conf - Mtgs - ET - Inf - Promoting retreats & offering advice
    about spiritual direction & training
M 7 retreat gps each with own members:
    Association for Promoting Retreats
    Baptist Union Retreat Group
    Catholic Network for Retreats & Spirituality
    Methodist Retreat & Spirituality Network
    Quaker Retreat Group
    United Reformed Church Silence & Retreat Network
    affiliates of the Retreat Associaton
¶ Retreats - 1. 2 copies ftm m, £5.50 nm.
    Information leaflets.

**Retroreflective Equipment Manufacturers' Association
(REMA) 1977**
NR 9 Cavendish Rd, LYTHAM ST ANNES, Lancs, FY8 2PX. (hsp)
    01253 722598 fax 01253 722598
    email info@rema.org.uk http://www.rema.org.uk
    Hon Sec: John Lloyd
▲ Un-incorporated Society
○ *T; manufacturers of road & other safety products that employ
    wholly retroreflective surfaces in their construction or form
Gp Barriers & temporary signs; High visibility clothing; Marker
    posts & street furniture; Retroreflective materials; Road cones
    & cylinders; Road danger lamps; Road studs; Temporary
    markings
● Mtgs - SG - Inf - LG
M 32 f
¶ LM - 1; free.

Rett Syndrome Association (RSA) 1985
■ Langham House West, Mill St, LUTON, Beds, LU1 2NA.
    01582 798910 fax 01582 724129
    email info@rettsyndrome.org.uk
    http://www.rettsyndrome.org.uk
    Hon Chmn: Linda Partridge
▲ Registered Charity
○ *M, *W; 'Rett syndrome is a complex neurological disorder that
    occurs mostly in females; the charity offers help & advice to
    all families & professionals; to raise funds for research'
● Fund raising - Specialist clinics - Facilitates local support groups
< Intl Rett Syndrome Assn
M i
¶ NL - 4.

Returned Volunteer Action
    incorporated by Action Village India & therefore outside the
    scope of this directory.

Reusable Healthcare Textiles Association
    a group of the **Performance Textiles Association**

RGDATA (RGDATA)
IRL Rock House, BLACKROCK, Co Dublin, Republic of Ireland.
    353 (1) 288 7584 fax 353 (1) 283 2206
    email rgdata@rgdata.ie http://www.rgdata.ie
    Dir Gen: Tara Buckley
○ *T; the representative body for the independent retail grocery
    sector in Ireland

Rhea & Emu Association (REA)
NR 31 Newbold Rd, KIRKBY MALLORY, Leics, LE9 7QG. (hsp)
    01455 823344 fax 01455 823344
    email margaret@leicestershireemus.com
    Sec: Margaret Dover
○ *B; for keepers of rhea (Pampas ostrich) & emus
● Mtgs
M 40 i, UK / 1 i, o'seas

Rheumatoid Arthritis Surgical Society
    a specialist society of the **British Orthopaedic Association**

Rhwyfo Cymru
    see **Welsh Amateur Rowing Association**

Rice Association (RA) 1989
NR 21 Arlington St, LONDON, SW1A 1RN. (hq)
    020 7493 2521 fax 020 7493 6785
    email info@riceassociation.org.uk
    http://www.riceassociation.org.uk
▲ Un-incorporated Society
○ *T; to promote the interests of members in all matters
    pertaining to the import, preparation, processing, packaging
    & marketing of rice
● Mtgs - LG
M 7 f

Richard Aldington Society
    see **New Canterbury Literary Society - Richard Aldington
    Society**

Richard III Society - Fellowship of the White Boar 1924
■ 23 Ash Rise, HALSTEAD, Essex, CO9 1RD. (hsp)
    01787 472512 fax 01787 472512
    email wells4r3@btinternet.com
    http://www.richardiii.net
    Jt Hon Secs: Susan & David Wells
▲ Un-incorporated Society
Br 23; Australia, Canada, New Zealand, US
○ *G, *L; 'In the belief that many features of the character &
    career of Richard III are neither supported by sufficient
    evidence nor reasonably tenable, the Society aims to
    promote in every possible way research into the life & times
    of Richard III, and to secure a reassessment of the material
    relating to this period & of the role in English history of this
    monarch'
Gp Richard III & Yorkist History Trust
● Conf - Mtgs - ET - Res - Exhib - SG - Inf - Lib - VE
M 2,108 i, UK & o'seas
¶ The Ricardian - 1; ftm, £15 nm.
    The Ricardian Bulletin - 4; ftm only.

Richard Jefferies Society 1950
■ Pear Tree Cottage, Longcot, FARINGDON, Oxon, SN7 7SS.
    (hsp)
    01793 783040
    email info@richardjefferiessociety.co.uk
    http://www.richardjefferiessociety.co.uk
    Hon Sec: Jean Saunders
▲ Registered Charity
○ *A; to promote study & interest in the life of [John] Richard
    Jefferies (1848-1887), naturalist & writer, & concern for
    places intimately connected wth him in Wiltshire, Sussex &
    Surrey
● Mtgs - Res - Inf - Lib - PL - VE - Book sales - Care of memorials
M c 300 i & org
¶ Jnl - 1; ftm, £1.50 nm. NL - 2; AR; both ftm.

Richard Strauss Society   1991
NR   104 Church Rd, RICHMOND, Surrey, TW10 6LW.   (treas/p)
        http://www.richard-strauss-society.co.uk
        Treas: Nigel Coles
▲   Registered Charity; Un-incorporated Society
○   *D; the life & works of Richard Strauss
●   Conf - SG - VE
M   100 i, UK / 2 i, o'seas
¶   NL - 3/4; ftm only.

Richmond Chamber of Commerce   1908
NR   1-3 Richmond Rd (1st floor), TWICKENHAM, Middx,
        TW1 3AB.   (hq)
        020 8891 7457
        http://www.richmondchamberofcommerce.co.uk
        Pres: Christina Jackson
○   *C
●   Conf - Mtgs - ET - Stat - Inf - LG
<   West London Enterprise Agency; Richmond in Business

Rider Haggard Society   (RHS)   1984
■   27 Deneholm, Monkseaton, WHITLEY BAY, Tyne & Wear,
        NE25 9AU.   (hsp)
        0191-252 4516
        email rb27allen@blueyonder.co.uk
        http://www.riderhaggardsociety.org.uk
        Hon Sec: Roger Allen
▲   Un-incorporated Society
○   *A; to futher the works of Rider Haggard (1856-1925) &
        provide access to his books, his life & his influence on others
●   Mtgs - Res - Comp - Inf - VE
<   Alliance of Literary Socs
M   70 i, UK / 30 i, o'seas
        (Sub: £10 UK / £12 o'seas
¶   The Haggard Jnl - 4; ftm.
        Illustrated Guide to Fiction of Rider Haggard; £15.
        Illustrated Guide to Non-Fiction of Rider Haggard; £16.
        Haggardiana (ephemera folder); £16 m, £25 nm.

Riding for the Disabled Association   1969
■   Norfolk House, 1a Tournament Court, Edgehill Drive,
        WARWICK, CV34 6LG.   (hq)
        0845 658 1082   fax 0845 658 1083
        email info@rda.org.uk   http://www.rda.org.uk
        Chief Exec: Ed Bracher
▲   Company Limited by Guarantee; Registered Charity
○   *W; to improve the lives of people with special needs, by
        enabling them to ride &/or carriage drive for the benefit of
        their health & general wellbeing
●   Conf - Mtgs - ET - Exam - Comp - LG
<   Brit Equestrian Fedn; Fedn of Riding for the Disabled Intl; Nat
        Equine Welfare Coun
M   18,500 i (volunteers), 25,000 i (riders)
¶   RDA News - 3; free (not Summer).

Riggit Galloway Cattle Society
NR   Sherberton Farm, Princetown, YELVERTON, Devon, PL20 6SF.
        01364 631276
        http://www.riggitgallowaycattlesociety.co.uk
        Sec: Anton Coaker
○   *B

Rights of Women   (ROW)   1975
§   52-54 Featherstone St, LONDON, EC1Y 8RT.   (hq)
        020 7251 6575   fax 020 7490 5377
        email info@row.org.uk
        http://www.rightsofwomen.org.uk
        Dir: Ranjit Kaur
        a campaign & telephone-only helpline, to attain justice &
        equality for women.
        Advice line 020 7251 6577
        Sexual violence legal advice line 020 7251 8887

Ring of Tatters   1980
■   20 Fairwater Close, FAIRWATER, Cumbran, NP44 4RA.
        (mem/sp)
        http://www.ringoftatters.org.uk
        Mem Sec: Jean Johnston
○   *G; to promote interest in & knowledge of the lacemaking craft
        of tatting
●   Mtgs - ET - Exhib - Comp - Lib
M   800 i, 400 i
¶   NL - 2; £6.75 m only.

**River Association for Freight & Transport (incorporating
AMLBO)   (RAFT)   2000**
NR   Tamesis House, 35 St Philip's Avenue, WORCESTER PARK,
        Surrey, KT4 8JS.   (hq)
        020 8330 6446   fax 020 8330 7447
        email raft@tamgroup.co.uk
        Sec: N Barry Jaynes
○   *T; for operation on & around the River Thames
Gp   Lighterage; Passenger boats; Wharves
●   Mtgs - Comp - LG
M   12 f

River Thames Alliance   2003
NR   c/o Environment Agency (SE Region), Kings Meadow House,
        Kings Meadow Rd, READING, Berks, RG1 8DQ.
        0370 850 6506
        http://www.riverthamesalliance.com
        Contact: Juliet King
○   *G, *K, *N; a partnership of public & private sector
        organisations working to help manage the future of the non-
        tidal Thames
M   82 org

River Thames Society   (RTS)   1962
■   23a Cuxham Rd, WATLINGTON, Oxon, OX49 5JW.   (admin p)
        01491 612456
        http://www.riverthamessociety.org.uk
        Admin: Mrs Helen Batten
▲   Company Limited by Guarantee; Registered Charity
Br   5
○   *G; encouragement of interest in the river & preservation &
        development of its amenities & natural beauty
●   Conf - Mtgs - Exhib - Lib (at River & Rowing Museum, Henley-
        on-Thames)
<   Inland Waterways Assn; Ramblers Assn
M   c 1,200 i, f & org, UK / 2 i, o'seas
¶   Thames Guardian - 4.

RLS-UK / Ekbom Syndrome Association   1988
NR   42 Nursery Rd, Rainham, GILLINGHAM, Kent, ME8 0BE.   (hsp)
        http://www.rsluk-esa.org.uk
        Coordinator: Mrs Beverley Finn
▲   Un-incorporated Society
○   *W; to support sufferers from Ekbom Syndrome (also known as
        Restless Legs Syndrome); to educate the medical profession;
        works with RLS UK a committee of professionals - doctors,
        consultants etc in the UK
●   Conf - Mtgs - Res - SG - Inf - Penfriend service
        Helpline: 01634 260483 (Mon-Thurs 0900-1100)
M   c 200 i. UK / 4 i, o'seas
¶   NL - 2; free.
✕   Ekbom Support Group

© CBD Research Ltd · Beckenham · BR3 5JS · Tel 020 8650 7745 · E-mail cbd@cbdresearch.com · www.cbdresearch.com

RLUK: Research Libraries UK (RLUK) 1985

- ■ Maugham Library, King's College London, Chancery Lane, LONDON, WC2A 1LR.   (dir b)
  020 7848 2137
  http://www.rluk.ac.uk
  Exec Dir: Anne Poulson
- ▲ Company Limited by Guarantee; Registered Charity
- ○ *P; to increase the ability of research libraries to share resources for the benefit of the local, national & international research community
- ● Res - Lib
- < Ligue des Bibliothèques Européennes de Recherche (LIBER); Digital Presvn Coalition; Counting Online use of Networked Electronic Resources (COUNTER)
- M 29 research libraries
- ¶ AR - 1.
- × 2008 CURL: Consortium of Research Libraries in the British Isles

RNID (RNID) 1911

- NR 19-23 Featherstone St, LONDON, EC1Y 8SL.   (hq)
  0808 808 0123 (voice)   0808 808 9000 (textphone)
  fax 020 7296 8199
  email informationline@rnid.org.uk
  http://www.rnid.org.uk
  Chief Exec: Jackie Ballard
- ▲ Registered Charity
- Br 7 offices
- ○ *W; works to provide services for deaf & hard of hearing people; seeks to raise public awareness of the issues surrounding deafness
- ● ET - Res - Exhib - Inf - Lib
  Services for deaf people: Typetalk, the national telephone relay service; Sound Advantage, providing assistive devices
- M 37,624 i & org
- ¶ One in Seven - 6
  trades as Action on Hearing Loss

Road Block
a group of the **Campaign for Better Transport**

Road Emulsion Association Ltd (REAL) 1928

- NR September House, Plantation Way, STORRINGTON, W Sussex, RH20 4JF.   (hq)
  01903 746584
  http://www.rea.org.uk
  Consultant & Sec: John Keayes
- ▲ Company Limited by Guarantee
- ○ *T; to promote the interests of producers & suppliers of road emulsion materials
- ● Conf - Mtgs - Inf - LG
- < Intl Bitumen Emulsion Fedn (IBEF); Asphalt Emulsion Mfrs Assn (AEMA)
- M 6 f

Road Haulage Association Ltd (RHA) 1945

- ■ Roadway House, Bretton Way, Bretton, PETERBOROUGH, Cambs, PE3 8DD.   (hq)
  01733 261131
  http://www.rha.net
  Chief Exec: Geoff Dunning
- ▲ Company Limited by Guarantee
- Br 4
- ○ *T; to represent Britain's professional hire-or-reward hauliers
- Gp Car transporters; Express parcels; Livestock carriers; Milk carriers; National agricultural, foods & tipping; Tankers
- ● Conf - Mtgs - ET - Exhib
- < Intl Road Transport U
- M 10,000 f
- ¶ Roadway - 12; ftm.   Road Haulage Manual - 2 yrly; ftm.

Road Locomotive Society (RLS) 1937

- NR PO Box 1878, ANDOVER, Hants, SP10 9AU.
  Hon Sec: W Wright
- ▲ Registered Charity
- ○ *G; to encourage education & research into the history of self propelling steam engines & vehicles (other than those running on rails) & portable engines

Road Records Association (RRA) 1888

- NR 135 Beaconsfield Rd, ENFIELD, Middx, EN3 6AY.   (chmn/p)
  01992 762121
  http://www.rra.org.uk
  Gen Sec: Brian Edrupt
- ○ *S; verification of road cycling records
- ● Dinner (triennial)
- M 500 i, UK / 6 i, o'seas
- ¶ 100 Years of Cycling Road Records; £7.

Road Rescue Recovery Association (RRRA) 1987

- ■ Hubberts Bridge Rd, Kirton Holme, BOSTON, Lincs, PE20 1TW.   (hq)
  01205 290622   fax 01205 290611
  email linda@recovery.co.uk   http://www.rrra.co.uk
  Chmn: Peter Cosby
- ▲ Company Limited by Guarantee
- ○ *T;
- ● Mtgs - ET - Exam - Res - Exhib - Inf - LG - Shows
- M 31 i, 448 f
- ¶ Jnl - 4; ftm, £2.95 nm.   NL - 2; ftm only.
  Ybk - 1; free.   LM - irreg.   AR; ftm only.

Road Roller Association (RRA) 1974

- NR Invicta, 9 Beagle Ridge Drive, Acomb, YORK, YO24 3JH.   (memsec/p)
  email info@r-r-a.org.uk   http://www.r-r-a.org.uk
  Mem Sec: Mrs D Rayner
- ○ *G; preservation, study of history & manufacture of road rollers & road making equipment, especially steam road rollers
- ● Mtgs - ET - Res - Exhib - Inf - Lib - PL - VE
- < Nat Traction Engine Trust; Transport Trust; Fedn British Historic Vehicles Clubs
- M 500 i, 8 f
- ¶ Rolling - 4; ftm.

Road Runners Club (RRC) 1951

- NR 7 Bellway Court, Grosvenor Rd, WESTCLIFF-on-SEA, Essex, SS0 8EP.   (treas/p)
  Hon Treas: Elaine Oddie
- ○ *S; road running & long distance running & racing
- ● Mtgs - Comp - Road running course measurement - Standards scheme for road runners - Insurance for road runners
- M i
- ¶ Roadrunner [NL] - 3; ftm only.

Road Safety GB (RSGB) 1974

- NR Stennik, The Thatched Barn, Low Rd, Wortham, DISS, Norfolk, IP22 1SH.   (hsb)
  01379 650112
  http://www.roadsafetygb.org.uk
  Contact: Sally Bartram
- ▲ Un-incorporated Society
- ○ *P; a national forum for road safety education, training, publicity & the School Crossing Patrol Service
- M all local authorities except London
- × 2009 (30 April) Local Authority Road Safety Officers Association

Road Safety Markings Association   (RSMA)   1976

■ Unit 35 Corringham Rd Industrial Estate, GAINSBOROUGH, Lincs, DN21 1QB.   (hq)
01427 610101   fax 01427 610106
email rsma@dial.pipex.com   http://www.rsma.co.uk
Nat Dir: George Lee

▲ Un-incorporated Society

○ *T; provision of road/traffic safety markings, both vertical & horizontal (incl: thermoplastic, paint, road studs, road tapes)
Is an NVQ assessment centre

Gp Ad hoc projects; Client/contractor partnership; Contracting; Health & safety forum; Marketing; Promoting health & safety to industry; Road marking forum; Technical

● Conf - Mtgs - ET - Res - Exhib - SG - Stat - Inf - LG - is an NVQ assessment centre

< Intl Road Fedn

M 75 f, 5 org

¶ Standard Issue (NL) - 4.
Update your Road Markings (CD); ftm.
Whose Job is it Anyway? (video).
Top Marks - 1;   Stanspec 2006 (CD).
RSMA Safety Code of Practice (CD) - 1.

Road Surface Dressing Association Ltd
in 2008 merged with the Slurry Surfacing Contractors Association & the High Friction Surfacing Association to form the **Road Surface Treatments Association**

Road Surface Treatments Association   (RSTA)   2008

■ Westwood Park, London Rd, Little Horkesley, COLCHESTER, Essex, CO6 4BU.   (hq)
01206 274052   fax 01206 274053
email enquiries@rsta-uk.org   http://www.rsta-uk.org
Chief Exec: Howard Robinson

▲ Company Limited by Guarantee

○ *T; highways maintenance - to promote quality, workforce competence & safe working practices

● Conf - Mtgs - ET - Exhib - Stat

< Road Users Alliance

M 67 f
(Sub: £1,000)

¶ Code of Practice for Surface Dressing; £30 m, £50 nm; and Code of Practice for Signing in at Surface Dressing Sites; both free to download.
Pocket Guide to Road Note 39; £5 m, £8 nm.

✕ 2008 (High Friction Surfacing Association
(Road Surface Treatments Association
(Slurry Surfacing Contractors Association

Road Transport Fleet Data Society   (Fleet Data)   1980

■ 18 Poplar Close, BIGGLESWADE, Beds, SG18 0EW.   (hsp)
email info@fleetdata.co.uk
Hon Sec: P Jarman

▲ Un-incorporated Society

○ *G; interest in vehicles of local & national government, public service fleets, power & water industries etc; research on vehicles & operators which no longer exist

● Res - SG - Inf - Lib - PL - VE - Compilation of photographic & related items

M 90 i

¶ Council Vehicle News - 4;   Ybk - irreg;
Public Utilities Bulletin - 4; all ftm only.
Vehicle Operator Lists - irreg.
British Military Serials - irreg.
Note: NO trade enquiries please!

Road Users' Alliance   (RUA)   2002

NR Delegate House, 30a Hart Street, Henley-on-Thames, Oxon, RG29 2AL.
01491 578761   fax 01491 579835
http://www.rua.org.uk

○ *K

RoadPeace, UK's charity for road crash victims   1992

■ G4b Shakespeare Business Centre, 245a Coldharbour Lane, LONDON SW9 8RR.   (hq)
0845 450 0355
email info@roadpeace.org   http://www.roadpeace.org

▲ Registered Charity

○ *K, *W; offers vital information & assistance to bereaved & injured road victims; advocates for their rights & justice; highlights road danger issues

● Conf - Mtgs - ET - Res - Exhib - Stat - Inf - Lib - LG

< Eur Fedn of Road Crash Victims (NGO of UN); PACTS; Transport 2000; Safer Streets Coalition, Slower Speeds Initiative

M 2,000 i, 300 f, 50 org, UK / 30 i, o'seas

Roads & Road Transport History Association Ltd   (RRTHA)   1992

■ 21 The Oaklands, DROITWICH, Worcs, WR9 8AD.   (hsp)
email enquiries@rrtha.org.uk   http://www.rrtha.org.uk
Hon Sec: P Jaques

▲ Company Limited by Guarantee

○ *G; to promote the study of the history of roads, road passenger transport & the carriage of goods

● Conf - Mtgs - Res - SG - Inf - VE

M 100 i, 16 org

¶ NL - 4; m only.   Symposium Papers - 1; £3.

RoadSafe

§ Forbes House, Halkin St, LONDON, SW1X 7DS.
020 7344 9236   fax 020 7235 7112
email info@roadsafe.co.uk   http://www.roadsafe.com
a forum for promoting & devising solutions to road safety problems

Robert Bloomfield Society   2000

NR 71 Spenser Rd, BEDFORD, MK40 2BE.   (sp)
Contact: Hugh Underhill

○ *A; English shoemaker & poet 1766-1823

Robert Burns World Federation Ltd   1885

■ Dower House, Dean Castle Country Park, KILMARNOCK, Ayrshire, KA3 1XB.   (hq)
01563 572469   fax 01563 572469
email admin@robertburnsfederation.com
http://www.robertburnsfederation.com
Chief Exec: Mrs Shirley Bell

▲ Company Limited by Guarantee; Registered Charity

○ *A, *E; to stimulate the teaching & study of Scottish literature, history, art, music & language through competitions; to conserve buildings & places associated with Robert Burns (1759-1796) & his contemporaries

● Conf - Mtgs - ET - Comp - Inf - LG

M 356 i, 6 f, 249 org, UK / 67 i, 54 org, o'seas

¶ Burns Chronicle - 3; ftm, £5 nm.   AR.

Robert Farnon Society   (RFS)   1956

■ 33 Bramleys, ROCHFORD, Essex, SS4 3BD.   (mem/sp)
http://www.rfsoc.org.uk
Mem Sec: Albert Killman

▲ Un-incorporated Society

○ *D; a musical appreciation society for lovers of light orchestral & film music; to keep members informed of all aspects of Robert Farnon's work (1917-2005) in radio, TV, films, records etc; to encourage & publicise the work of other similar musicians from light classics to jazz

● Mtgs (in London April & November) - Res - Stat - Inf

M 750 i, UK / 100 i, o'seas

¶ Journal into Melody - 4; £15 yr.

© CBD Research Ltd · Beckenham · BR3 5JS · Tel 020 8650 7745 · E-mail cbd@cbdresearch.com · www.cbdresearch.com

Robert Louis Stevenson Club   (RLS Club)   1920
- ■ 17 Heriot Row, EDINBURGH, EH3 6HP.   (hsp)
    0131-556 1896   fax 0131-556 1896
    email mail@stevenson-house.co.uk
    http://www.rlsclub.org.uk
    Correspondence Sec: John W S McFie
- ▲ Registered Charity
- ○ *A, *G; to foster an interest in the life & works of Robert Louis Stevenson (1850-94)
- ● Mtgs - Inf - VE
- M 282 i, 2 f, UK / 64 i, 2 org, o'seas
    (Sub: £20 i, £26 org UK / £26 i, £34 org o'seas)
- ¶ RLS Club News - 2; ftm only.

Robert Simpson Society   (RSS)   1980
- ■ 42 Tiverton Way, CAMBRIDGE, CB1 2TU.   (sp)
    01223 210552
    email d.jones3@btinternet.com
    http://www.robertsimpson.info
    Sec: David Jones
- ▲ Un-incorporated Society
- ○ *D; to promote the music of composer Robert Simpson (1921-1997) to the public
- ● Conf - Mtgs - Res - Inf - Lib
- M 91 i, UK / 12 i, o'seass
- ¶ Tonic (Jnl) - 1 ftm.
    Books on specific topics; prices vary.

Roller Coaster Club of Great Britain   (RCCGB)   1988
- ■ PO Box 235, UXBRIDGE, Middx, UB10 0TF.   (hq)
    01895 259802   fax 01895 259802
    email rccgb@rccgb.co.uk
    Chmn: Andy Hine
- ○ *G; to unite roller-coaster enthusiasts from all over the world; to encourage amusement parks & manufacturers to create & build new, exciting & daring rides
- Gp Historians photo library
- ● Mtgs - Res - Exhib - Comp - Stat - Inf - PL - Annual coach tour of coasters in Europe & the USA
- < Intl Assn of Amusement Parks & Attractions (IAAPA)
- M 1,300 i, 21 f, 1 org, UK / 100 i, 17 f, 1 org, o'seas
    (Sub: £27 i, £32 f, £25 org UK / £35 i, £40 f, £35 org o'seas)
- ¶ AIRtime (Jnl) - 6; ftm only.
    Yearly Survey (Report) - 1; ftm, £3 nm.

Roman Finds Group
- ■ English Heritage, Fort Cumberland, Fort Cumberland Rd, Eastney, PORTSMOUTH, Hants, PO4 9LD.
    023 9285 6716
    http://www.romanfinds.org.uk
    Gen Sec: Nicola Hembrey
- ○ *G; for all interested in Roman artifacts
- ● Mtgs
- M i
- ¶ NL - 2

Roman Society
see **Society for the Promotion of Roman Studies   (Roman Society)**

Romantic Novelists Association   (RNA)   1960
- NR Nevermore, Little Birch, HEREFORD, HR2 8BB.   (hsp)
    http://www.rna-uk.org
    Hon Sec: Evelyn Ryle
- ▲ Un-incorporated Society
- ○ *A; to raise the prestige of the genre & the professionalism of romantic novelists
- Gp New Writers Scheme (for unpublished writers)
- ● Conf - Mtgs - Comp - Inf
- M 700 i, UK / 20 i, o'seas
- ¶ RNA News - 4.

Romany Society   1996
- ■ 10 Haslam St, BURY, Lancs, BL9 6EQ.   (hsp)
    0161-764 7078   fax 01625 504515
    email romany@macclesfield.gov.uk
    Hon Sec: John Thorpe
- ▲ Un-incorporated Society
- ○ *G; to celebrate the life & work of the Rev George Bramwell Evens - 'Romany of the BBC'; to ensure that his ground-breaking natural history broadcasting is remembered by future generations; to promote interest in the natural world by all & particularly the young
- ● Mtgs - Res - Inf - Lib - VE
- < Alliance Literary Socs
- M 241 i, 3 org, UK / 2 i, o'seas
- ¶ Romany Magazine - 1;   NL - seasonal; both ftm only.

Romney Sheep Breeders Society   1895
- ■ 2 Woodland Close, WEST MALLING, Kent, ME19 6RR.   (sp)
    01732 845637
    email alan.t.west@btinternet.com
    http://www.romneysheepuk.com
    Sec: Alan West
- ▲ Company Limited by Guarantee
- ○ *B
- Gp Registration of members; Registration of animals; Official society records; Export promotion
- ● Mtgs - Exhib - Expt
- < Nat Sheep Assn
- M 120 i, 60 org
- ¶ The Romney Flock Book - 1;   The Romney Hbk - irreg; both free.

Ronald Stevenson Society   (RSS)   1993
- ■ 3 Chamberlain Rd, EDINBURGH, EH10 4DL.   (hsp)
    fax 0131-229 9298
    email info@ronaldstevensonsociety.org.uk
    http://www.ronaldstevensonsociety.org.uk
    Chmn: Philip Hutton,   Hon Sec: Iain Colquhoun
- ▲ Un-incorporated Society
- Br Luxembourg, Switzerland
- ○ *D; to publish & promote the performance & recording of the music of Ronald Stevenson, Scottish composer, pianist & writer
- Gp Pianists; Singers; Chamber players; Conductors
- ● Conf - Res - Summer symposium - Concerts & recitals - Publication of Stevenson's music
- < Scot Music Centre; Nat Lib Scotland; Scot Poetry Lib; Scot Arts Coun
- M 105 i, 3 org, UK / 25 i, o'seas
- ¶ NL - 3; ftm, subscribers only nm.
    Catalogue of Publications.

Roofing Industry Alliance   (RIA)   1997
- ■ Roofing House, 31 Worship St, LONDON, EC2A 2DX.   (hq)
    020 7448 3857   fax 020 7256 2125
    Exec Sec: Bennett Judson
- ▲ Company Limited by Guarantee
- ○ *N, *T; to provide an umbrella organisation to bring together the various associations within the roofing industry; to provide a collective forum to work with construction skills to improve training in the roofing industry
- ● ET - LG
- < Construction Products Assn

ROOM at RTPI   (ROOM)   1900
- NR 41 Botolph Lane, LONDON, EC3R 8DL.   (hq)
    020 7929 9494   fax 020 7929 9490
    email room@rtpi.org.uk   http://www.room.org.uk
- ▲ Registered Charity
- ○ *K, *N; to bring together all those involved in housing planning & regeneration on an equal footing, to share information, debate the issues, influence policy & contribute to best practice

Rotating Electrical Machines Association
an association of **BEAMA Ltd**

Rough Fell Sheep Breeders Association   (RFSBA)   1926
- ■ High Borrow Bridge, Selside, KENDAL, Cumbria, LA8 9LG. (hsp)
  01539 823270
  email jknowles666@gmail.com
  http://www.roughfellsheep.co.uk
  Sec: Jayne Knowles
- ○ *B
- ● Mtgs - Res - Exhib - Inf
- < Nat Sheep Assn
- M c 200 i
- ¶ Flock Book - 1.

Rough & Smooth Collie Training Association   (RSCTA)   1991
- ■ 1 Leigh Lane, Bramshall, UTTOXETER, Staffs, ST14 5DN.   (hsp)
  01889 568090
  email jean@rscta.co.uk   http://www.rscta.co.uk
  Hon Sec: Mrs Jean Tuck
- ▲ Un-incorporated Society
- ○ *B; to preserve, promote & enhance the Rough & Smooth Collie as a working breed through the establishment & support of working events & tests
- ● ET
- M 83 i
  (Sub: £5)
- ¶ NL - 3; ftm, £1 nm.   LM - 1; ftm only.

Round Tower Churches Society   (RTCS)   1973
- ■ Crabbe Hall, Burnham Market, KING'S LYNN, Norfolk, PE31 8EN.   (hsp)
  01328 738237
  http://www.roundtowers.org.uk
  Hon Sec: Mrs E M Stilgoe
- ▲ Registered Charity
- ○ *G; promotion of interest, research & preservation of round tower churches
- ● Res - Exhib - SG - Inf - Lib - VE - Lectures, slide shows & organised tours to churches
- M 520 i, 55 parochial church councils, UK / 6 i, o'seas
- ¶ Magazine - 4; ftm, 50p nm.

Rounders England   1943
- NR PO Box 4458, SHEFFIELD, S Yorks, S20 9DP.   (office/address)
  0114-248 0357
  email enquiries@roundersengland.co.uk
  http://www.roundersengland.co.uk
  Contact: Alan Fergus
- ▲ Voluntary Organisation
- ○ *S; national governing body for game of rounders; trustees of the rules of rounders worldwide
- Gp International teams at 8 age groups (ladies)
- ● Mtgs - ET - Exam - Res - Comp - Inf - LG
- < Cent Coun for Physical Recreation (CCPR); Sports Coach UK (SCUK)
- M c 10,000 i, c 800 org
- ¶ Publications list on request.
- ✕ 2009 National Rounders Association

Roundhead Association
a group of the **English Civil War Society Ltd**

Roussin Sheep Society   1989
- NR Mount Pleasant Farm, Deckport Cross, Hatherleigh, OKEHAMPTON, Devon, EX20 3LN.   (hsp)
  01837 810006
  email roussinsheep@tiscali.co.uk
  http://www.bohdgaya.net/roussinsheepsociety/
  Sec: Andrea Molyneux
- ○ *B
- < Nat Sheep Assn

Routemaster Operators & Owners Association   (Routemaster Association)   (RMOOA)   1988
- NR Unit 12dc, York Farm Business Centre, Watling St, TOWCESTER, Northants, NN12 8EU.   (hq)
  01327 830663
  email secretary@routemaster.org.uk
  http://www.routemaster.org.uk
  Sec: Graham Lunn
- ○ *G; for operators & owners of Routemaster buses, suppliers of parts or services & anyone else with a genuine interest in their operation or preservation
- M c 400
- ¶ Routemaster Magazine

Royal Academy of Arts   (RA)   1768
- NR Burlington House, Piccadilly, LONDON, W1J 0BD.   (hq)
  020 7300 8000   fax 020 7300 8001
  http://www.royalacademy.org.uk
  Sec & Chief Exec: Charles Saumarez Smith
- ▲ Registered Charity
- ○ *A; to promote the creation, enjoyment and appreciation of the visual arts through exhibitions, education and debate
- Gp Friends of the Royal Academy
- ● ET - Exhib - Lib
- < Amer Associates of the R Academy Trust; R Scot Academy; R Hibernian Academy
- M 80 i & c 85,000 friends
- ¶ R A Magazine - 4; ftm.   AR.

Royal Academy of Dance   (RAD)   1920
- NR 36 Battersea Sq, LONDON, SW11 3RA.   (hq)
  020 7326 8000   fax 020 7924 3129
  email info@rad.org.uk   http://www.rad.org.uk
  Chief Exec: Luke Rittner
- ▲ Registered Charity
- Br 83 o'seas
- ○ *D, *E, *P; to improve the standards of dance teaching worldwide; to provide the opportunity for largest number of children to learn & enjoy ballet
- Gp Benesh Institute
- ● Conf - ET - Exam - Comp - Inf - Lib - PL
- M 13,000 i, UK & o'seas
- ¶ Dance Gazette - 3.
  UK Diary (with Dance Gazette).   AR.

Royal Academy of Dramatic Art   (RADA)   1904
- § 62-64 Gower St, LONDON, WC1E 6ED.   (hq)
  020 7636 7076   fax 020 7323 3865
  http://www.rada.org
  To train actors, stage managers & technical staff for professional stage, film & television.

Royal Academy of Engineering   (RAEng)   1976
- ■ 3 Carlton House Terrace, LONDON, SW1Y 5DG.   (hq)
  020 7766 0600   fax 020 7930 1549
  email administrator@raeng.org.uk
  http://www.raeng.org.uk
  Chief Exec: P D Greenish
- ▲ Registered Charity
- ○ *L, *N; promotion of excellence in engineering in the UK; promotion of engineering education
- ● Conf - Mtgs - ET - Res - SG - VE - LG
- < Eur Coun of Applied Sciences & Engg (Euro-CASE); Coun of Academies of Engg & Technological Services (CAETS)
- M 1,259 i, UK / 87 i, o'seas
  (Sub: £210)
- ¶ Ingenia - 4;   NL - 4; both free.

Royal Academy of Medicine in Ireland   (RAMI)   1882
- IRL Frederick House, 19 South Frederick St, DUBLIN 2, Republic of Ireland   (hq)
  353 (1) 633 4820   fax 353 (1) 676 4918
  email secretary@rami.ie   http://www.rami.ie
  Gen Sec: Dr John O'Connor
- ○ *M, *P

Royal Academy of Music   (RAM)   1822
NR   Marylebone Rd, LONDON, NW1 5HT.   (hq)
    020 7873 7373   fax 020 7873 7374
    http://www.ram.ac.uk
    Principal: Prof Jonathan Freeman-Attwood
▲   Registered Charity
○   *D, *P; the further education & training of musicians
    (performers of classical music & jazz, opera & music theatre;
    composers)
●   ET - Res - Exhib - Inf - Lib - VE - Public concerts
<   University of London
M   i
¶   Diary of Events - 3; free.
    Prospectus (details of classes & entry arrangements); free.

Royal Aero Club Trust   1998
NR   Chacksfield House, 31 St Andrew's Rd, LEICESTER, LE2 8RE.
    (regd/off)
    0116-244 0028
    email administrator@royalaeroclubtrust.org
    http://www.royalaeroclubtrust.org
    Hon Treas & Sec: Peter Crispin
▲   Company Limited by Guarantee; Registered Charity
○   *G; to advance the course of air sport & aviation
Gp   Airsport information data bank; Bursary scheme; Conservation
    of memorabilia; Flying for Youth; National photographic
    competition
●   Conf - ET - Res - Comp - SG - PL
<   R Aero Club UK
¶   AR

Royal Aero Club of the UK
■   Chacksfield House, 31 St Andrews Rd, LEICESTER, LE2 8RE.
    (hq)
    0116-244 0028   fax 0116-244 0645
    email secretary@royalaeroclub.org
    http://www.royalaeroclub.org
    Gen Sec: David Phipps
▲   Company Limited by Guarantee
○   *G, *N, *S; the coordinating body of British airsport
●   Comp - LG
<   EAS; FAI
M   160 i, 6 f, 20 org, UK / 5 i, o'seas
¶   NL - 4; ftm.
    Annual Award Ceremony Report - 1; ftm (on application nm).

Royal Aeronautical Society   (RAeS)   1866
■   4 Hamilton Place, LONDON, W1J 7BQ.   (hq)
    020 7670 4300   fax 020 7499 6230
    email raes@aerosociety.com
    http://www.aerosociety.com
    Chief Exec: Keith Mans
▲   Registered Charity
Br   37; Australia, Cyprus, France, Germany, Hong Kong, Ireland,
    Kenya, Malaysia, New Zealand, Pakistan, Singapore,
    South Africa, UAE, Zimbabwe
○   *L, *P; for the global aerospace community; for the general
    advancement of aeronautical art, science & engineering &
    for promoting that species of knowledge which distinguishes
    the profession of aeronautics
Gp   Aerodynamics; Aerospace medicine; Air law; Air power; Air
    transport; Airworthiness & maintenance; Avionics & systems;
    Environment; Flight operations; Flight simulation; Flight test;
    General aviation; Historical; Human factors; Human
    powered; Licensed engineers; Management studies;
    Propulsion; Rotorcraft; Space; Structures & materials; UAV;
    Weapons systems & technology
●   Conf - Mtgs - ET - Res - Comp - Inf - Lib - PL - VE - LG -
    Careers service
M   15,000 i, 101 f, UK / 4,500 i, 15 f, o'seas
¶   Aeronautical Jnl - 12.   Aeronautical International 12.
    Aerospace Professional - 12; ftm only.

Royal African Society   1901
NR   36 Gordon Sq, LONDON, WC1H 0PD.   (hq)
    020 3073 8335   fax 020 3073 8340
    email ras@soas.ac.uk
    http://www.royalafricansociety.org
    Sec: Gemma Haxby
Br   3
○   *X; to spread information about the peoples & countries of
    Africa; to develop public interest in African problems; to
    serve as a link between the peoples of UK & Africa
●   Conf - Mtgs - Lib
M   599 i, 23 f, UK / 157 i, 2 f, o'seas
¶   African Affairs - 4.

Royal Agricultural Society of the Commonwealth   (RASC)   1957
■   Royal Highland Centre, Ingliston, EDINBURGH, EH28 8NF.
    (hq)
    0131-335 6200   fax 0131-335 6229
    email rasc@commagshow.org
    http://www.commagshow.org
    Hon Sec: Charles Runge
▲   Company Limited by Guarantee; Registered Charity
Br   1
○   *F, *N; a federation of national agricultural societies within the
    British Commonwealth, to encourage interchange of
    knowledge & experience in the practice & science of
    agriculture
●   Conf - Organising cooperation & exchange between member
    societies
M   12 org, UK / 31 org, o'seas
¶   NL - 4; ftm.   Biennial Conference Report - 2 yrly.

Royal Agricultural Society of England   (RASE)   1840
■   STONELEIGH PARK, Warks, CV8 2LZ.   (hq)
    024 7669 6969   fax 024 7669 6900
    email info@rase.org.uk   http://www.rase.org.uk
    Chief Exec: Denis Chamberlain
▲   Registered Charity
○   *F; dedicated to agriculture, land management, the well being
    of rural communities & to shaping a strong rural economy
●   Conf - ET - Res - Exhib - Lib - VE - LG
<   Assn of Show & Agricl Orgs
>   Farming & Countryside Educ (FACE)
M   5,935 i, UK / 8 i, o'seas
¶   Jnl - 1; ftm, £35 nm.
    Rural Matters - 4; ftm only.

Royal Air Force Historical Society   (RAFHS)   1986
■   Silverhill House, Coombe, WOTTON-under-EDGE, Glos,
    GL12 7ND.   (hsp)
    01453 843362
    Mem Sec: Dr Jack Dunham
▲   Registered Charity
○   *L; to serve as a focus of interest in the history of the Royal Air
    Force & its precursor services, their operations, policies &
    personalities
●   Seminars (2 a yr) - AGM
M   860 i, UK / 55 i, o'seas
¶   Jnl (proceedings of seminars & AGM) - 2/3; ftm.

Royal Air Forces Association   (RAFA)   1943
■   117½ Loughborough Rd, LEICESTER, LE4 5ND.   (hq)
    0116-266 5224
    http://www.rafa.org.uk
    Sec Gen: Edward Jarron
▲   Un-incorporated Society
Br   502; 27 countries o'seas
○   *W; the welfare of serving & ex-serving members of the RAF &
    Commonwealth Air Forces & their dependents
●   Conf - Mtgs - ET
M   100,000 i
¶   Air Mail - 4;   AR; both free.

Royal & Ancient Golf Club   (R&A)   1754
NR   St Andrews, FIFE, KY16 9JD.   (hq)
       01334 460000   fax 01334 460001
       http://www.randa.org
▲   Un-incorporated Society
○   *S; governing body for rules of golf & amateur status for all
       countries of the world apart from the USA & Canada
Gp Organisers of golf championships; Rules of golf seminars
●   Conf - Mtgs - Exam - Exhib - Comp - Lib - PL
<   Wld Amat Golf Coun
M   2,400 unions & assns worldwide
¶   R&A News Bulletin - 2; free.
       A Course for all Seasons: a guide to golf course management.
       Practical Greenkeeping (textbook) by J Arthur.

**Royal Anthropological Institute of Great Britain & Ireland
(RAI)   1843**
■   50 Fitzroy St, LONDON, W1T 5BT.   (hq)
       020 7387 0455   fax 020 7388 8817
       http://www.therai.org.uk
       Hon Sec: Dr Eric Hirsch
▲   Company Limited by Guarantee; Registered Charity
○   *L; to promote the study of the science of man
●   Conf - Res - Inf - Lib - PL - Fundraising
M   c 1,000 i, UK / c 500 i, o'seas
¶   Jnl - 4.   Anthropology Today - 6.
       Anthropological Index Online (free Internet bibliographic
       service).

Royal Archaeological Institute   (RAI)   1844
■   c/o Society of Antiquaries, Burlington House, Piccadilly,
       LONDON, W1J 0BE.   (hq)
       0116-243 3839   fax 0116-243 3839
       email admin@royalarchinst.org
       http://www.royalarchinst.org
       Admin: Sharon Gerber-Parfitt
▲   Registered Charity
○   *L; all aspects of archaeology & history of architecture but
       mainly that of GB
●   Conf - Mtgs - Res - Comp - VE
M   c 1,700 i, 384 libraries & org
¶   Archaeological Jnl - 1; ftm; £65 nm.   NL - 2; free.
       Index to Jnl; prices on application.

Royal Army Veterinary Corps Division
       a group of the **British Veterinary Association**

Royal Asiatic Society of Great Britain & Ireland   (RAS)   1823
NR   14 Stephenson Way, LONDON, NW1 2HD.   (hq)
       020 7388 4539   fax 020 7391 9429
       email ao@royalasiaticsociety.org
       http://www.royalasiaticsociety.org
       Dir: Alison Ohta
▲   Registered Charity
○   *L; to investigate subjects connected with science, literature &
       the arts in relation to Asia
●   Mtgs - Lib
M   c 500 i, UK / c 300 i, o'seas
¶   Jnl - 3; ftm.

Royal Association of British Dairy Farmers   (RABDF)   1876
■   Dairy House, Unit 31 Abbey Park, Stareton, KENILWORTH,
       Warks, CV8 2LY.   (hq)
       0845 458 2711   fax 0845 458 2755
       email office@rabdf.co.uk   http://www.rabdf.co.uk
       Chief Exec: Nick Everington
▲   Company Limited by Guarantee; Registered Charity
○   *F; to improve the status & well-being of dairy farmers & the
       dairy industry through the provision of technical information,
       training & lobbying activities
●   Conf - Mtgs - Exam - Exhib - Comp - SG - Inf - VE - LG
       Dairy Event & Livestock Show (http://www.dairyevent.co.uk)
M   2,000 i
¶   Milk Digest - 6;
       Dairy Farming Event Showguide - 1; both ftm.

Royal Association for Deaf People   (RAD)   1841
§   Century House South, Riverside Office Centre, North Station
       Rd, COLCHESTER, Essex, CO1 1RE.   (hq)
       0845 688 2525
       email info@royaldeaf.org.uk
       http://www.royaldeaf.org.uk
       Chief Exec: Tom Fenton
       A registered charity promoting the welfare and interests of deaf
       people whose first or preferred language is sign language.

**Royal Association for Disability & Rehabilitation   (RADAR)
1977**
NR   12 City Forum, 250 City Rd, LONDON, EC1V 8AF.   (hq)
       020 7250 3222
       email radar@radar.org.uk   http://www.radar.org.uk
       Chief Exec: Liz Sayce
▲   Registered Charity
○   *K, *N, *W; to promote change by empowering disabled
       people to achieve our rights and expectations and by
       influencing the way that we, as disabled people, are viewed
       as members of society
●   Inf
M   c 600 i & org
¶   Bulletin - 12.   A Guide to RADAR.   AR & Accounts.
       Publications list available.

Royal Astronomical Society   (RAS)   1820
NR   Burlington House, Piccadilly, LONDON, W1J 0BQ.   (hq)
       020 7734 4582; 3307   fax 020 7494 0166
       email info@ras.org.uk   http://www.ras.org.uk
       Exec Sec: David Elliott
▲   Registered Charity
○   *L; the leading UK body for astronomy & astrophysics,
       geophysics, solar & solar-terrestrial physics & planetary
       sciences
●   Conf - Mtgs - Res - Comp - Lib - PL - Empl - LG - Support for
       educational activities - Awards grants & prizes
<   IAU; EAS; Science Coun
>   Brit Sundial Soc; Brit Geophysical Assn (BGA)
M   2,037 i, UK / 1,236 i, o'seas
¶   Astronomy & Geophysics (Jnl) - 6; ftm.
       Monthly Notices - 36 [9 volumes of 4 issues each];
       Geophysical Journal International - 12 [4 volumes of
       3 issues each]; prices for both on application.

Royal Bath & West of England Society   1777
NR   The Showground, SHEPTON MALLET, Somerset, BA4 6QN.
       (hq)
       01749 822200   fax 01749 823169
       http://www.bathandwest.co.uk
       Chief Exec: Dr Jane Guise
▲   Company Limited by Guarantee; Registered Charity
○   *F, *H; for the encouragement of agriculture, arts, manufacture,
       commerce
●   Conf - Exhib (incl Nat Gardening Show; Royal Bath & West
       Show)
<   Assn of Show & Agricl Orgs
M   2,141 i
¶   NL - 2;   Annual Review & Report - 1; both free.
       Show Programme - 1;   Show Catalogue; both ftm.
       Note: commonly known as the Bath & West

Royal Birmingham Society of Artists   (RBSA)   1814
■   4 Brook St, St Paul's, BIRMINGHAM, B3 1SA.   (hq)
       0121-236 4353   fax 0121-236 4555
       email secretary@rbsa.org.uk   http://www.rbsa.org.uk
       Hon Sec: Simon Davis
▲   Registered Charity
○   *A; to advance the public education in (& the practice of) art,
       particularly painting, sculpture, ceramics & printing
●   Mtgs - ET - Res - Exhib - Inf
M   127 i & associates
¶   NL - 4; ftm & Friends.

© CBD Research Ltd · Beckenham · BR3 5JS · Tel 020 8650 7745 · E-mail cbd@cbdresearch.com · www.cbdresearch.com

Royal Botanical & Horticultural Society of Manchester & the Northern Counties (RBS) 1827
§ Hallidays Accountants LLP, Riverside House, Kings Reach Rd, STOCKPORT, Cheshire, SK4 2HD. (asa)
0161-476 8276
Sec: Anna Bennett
A grant making charity, also known as the Royal Botanical Society

Royal British Legion 1921
■ 199 Borough High St, LONDON, SE1 1AA. (hq)
020 3207 2100
Dir Gen: Chris Simpkins
▲ Registered Charity
Br 101
○ *K, *W; to assist needy ex-servicemen & women & their families; to ensure the maintenance of war pensions, war widows pensions & associated allowances
Gp Attendants company (security & car parking); RBL poppy factory; Poppy appeal; Training company
● Conf - Mtgs - Comp - Inf
< Brit C'wealth Ex-Services League; Wld Veterans Fedn; Coun of British Service & Ex-service Orgs
M 398,132 i, UK & o'seas
¶ The Legion (Jnl) - 12; AR; Publicity leaflets & posters; all free.

Royal British Legion Scotland (RBLS) 1921
NR New Haig House, Logie Green Rd, EDINBURGH, EH7 4HR. (hq)
0131-557 2782 fax 0131-557 5819
email lao@rblscotland.org http://www.rblscotland.org
Legion affairs officer: George Ross
▲ Registered Charity
Br 214 in Scotland
○ *K, *W; to safeguard the welfare, interests & memory of those who have served in the armed forces, & their dependents
Gp War pensions claims & appeals
● Conf - Mtgs - Inf - VE _ LG
< Brit C'wealth Ex-Services League; Earl Haig Fund (Scotland); Officers Assn Scotland; Scot Ex-Services Charitable Orgs
M 50,000 i, 88 private clubs
¶ Scottish Legion News - 4; ftm.

Royal British Society of Sculptors (RBS) 1904
NR 108 Old Brompton Rd, LONDON, SW7 3RA. (hq)
020 7373 8615
email info@rbs.org.uk http://www.rbs.org.uk
Dir: Anne Rawcliffe-King
▲ Registered Charity
○ *A, *P; to advance the art & practice of sculpture
● Mtgs - Exhib - Inf - Lib
M c 500 i

Royal Caledonian Curling Club (RCCC) 1838
■ Cairnie House, Avenue K Ingliston Showground, NEWBRIDGE, Midlothian, EH28 8NB. (hq)
0131-333 3003 fax 0131-333 3323
email office@royalcaledoniancurlingclub.org
http://www.royalcaledoniancurlingclub.org
Chief Exec Officer: Colin Grahamslaw
Finance & Admin Mgr: Alastair Hibbert
▲ Company Limited by Guarantee
Br Canada
○ *S; governing body for the sport of curling throughout Scotland & mother club of curling throughout the world
● Conf - Mtgs - ET - Comp - Stat - Lib
< Wld Curling Fedn (WCF); Eur Curling Fedn (ECF)
M 13,000 i, 562 clubs, UK / 20 assns, o'seas
¶ RCCC Annual - 1; £6. RCCC Rules of the Game - 1; £1.

Royal Caledonian Horticultural Society (RCHS) 1809
NR 17 Jordan Lane, EDINBURGH, EH10 4RA. (hsp)
0131-478 2141
http://www.rchs.co.uk
Sec: Alison Murison
▲ Registered Charity
○ *H; the encouragement & advancement of horticulture in all its forms
● Mtgs - Exhib - Comp - Inf - VE - Lectures - Awards
< R Horticl Soc (London)
¶ Preview - 3. Caledonian Gardener - 1.

Royal Cambrian Academy of Art (RCA) 1881
■ Crown Lane, CONWY, LL32 8AN. (hq)
01492 593413 fax 01492 593413
email rca@rcaconwy.org http://www.rcaconwy.org
Hon Sec: Tim Pugin, Curator: Gill Bird
▲ Company Limited by Guarantee; Registered Charity
○ *A; to promote the arts of painting, engraving & sculpture & other forms of art in Wales
● Mtgs - Exhib - Art classes
M 120 i
¶ Summer Exhibition Catalogue - 1; £1. AR 1; ftm, £1 nm.

Royal Celtic Society 1820
■ 23 Rutland St, EDINBURGH, EH1 2RN. (asa)
0131-228 6449 fax 0131-229 6987
email gcameron@stuartandstuart.co.uk
Hon Sec & Treas: J Gordon Cameron
▲ Registered Charity
○ *G; to promote interest in the history, traditions, arts & music of Scotland & in Scottish Gaelic
● Mtgs - One-off grants to assist with the aims of the society
M 200 i, UK / 10 i, o'seas
¶ AR; m only.

Royal Choral Society (RCS) 1872
NR Studio 9, 92 Lots Rd, LONDON, SW10 0QD. (hq)
020 7376 3718 fax 020 7376 3719
email virginia@royalchoralsociety.co.uk
http://www.royalchoralsociety.co.uk
Admin: Virginia Edwyn-Jones
▲ Registered Charity
○ *D; 'we are an amateur choir, singing to a professional standard; we work with professional orchestras & promoters'
● Mtgs - Concerts
< Making Music (Nat Fedn Music Socs)
M c 200 i
¶ Summer NL.

Royal College of Anaesthetists 1948
NR Churchill House, 35 Red Lion Square, LONDON, WC1R 4SG. (hq)
020 7092 1500
email info@rcoa.ac.uk
○ *L; advancement of art & science of anaesthetics
M 13,000 i

Royal College of General Practitioners (RCGP) 1952
■ 1 Bow Churchyard, LONDON, EC4M 9DQ. (hq)
020 3188 7400 fax 020 3188 7401
email info@rcgp.org.uk http://www.rcgp.org.uk
Hon Sec: Prof Amanda Howe
▲ Registered Charity
○ *L, *P; to encourage & maintain high standards of general medical practice
● Conf - Mtgs - ET - Exam - Res - Exhib - SG - Inf - Lib - LG
M 17,500 i, UK / 1,300 i, o'seas
¶ Jnl - 12; ftm, £124 nm. Members' Reference Book - 1; ftm.

Royal College of Midwives   (RCM)   1881
NR   15 Mansfield St, LONDON, W1G 9NH.   (hq)
     020 7312 3535   fax 020 7312 3536
     http://www.rcm.org.uk
     Gen Sec: Cathy Warwick
▲   Company Limited by Guarantee; Registered Charity
Br   5
○   *P, *U; to advance the art & science of midwifery
●   Conf - Mtgs - ET - Inf - Lib - VE - Empl - LG
<   Intl Confedn Midwives; WHO Collaborating Centre for
     Midwifery
M   c 36,000 i, UK / 7000 i, o'seas
¶   Jnl - 12.

Royal College of Nursing of the United Kingdom   (RCN)   1916
NR   20 Cavendish Sq, LONDON, W1G 0RN.   (hq)
     020 7409 3333
     http://www.rcn.org.uk
     Chief Exec & Gen Sec: Dr Peter Carter
▲   Registered Charity
○   *M, *P; to act as the voice of nursing in the UK; to campaign on
     behalf of nurses & nursing; to promote the interests of nurses
     & patients by working with government, the professional
     bodies, trade unions & voluntary organisations
●   Conf - Empl - ET - Exhib - LG - Lib - Res
<   Intl Coun of Nurses (ICN); Eur Fedn of Public Service Us (EPSU);
     C'wealth Nurses Fedn (CNF); Standing C'ee of Nurses (PCN)
M   390,000 i
¶   Nursing Standard - 52.   RCN Bulletin - 26; both ftm.

**Royal College of Obstetricians & Gynaecologists   (RCOG)
1929**
■   27 Sussex Place, LONDON, NW1 4RG.   (hq)
     020 7772 6200   fax 020 7772 6359
     email coll.sec@rcog.org.uk   http://www.rcog.org.uk
     Chief Exec: Ian Wylie
▲   Registered Charity
○   *L, *Q
●   Conf - Mtgs - ET - Exam - Res - Exhib - SG - Stat - Inf - Lib - LG
M   4,000 i, UK / 6,000 i, o'seas
     (Sub: £430 UK / £90 o'seas)
¶   BJOG: an international Jnl of Obstetrics & Gynaecology - 12.
     The Obstetrician & Gynaecologist - 4.

Royal College of Ophthalmologists   1988
NR   17 Cornwall Terrace, LONDON, NW1 4QW.   (hq)
     020 7935 0702   fax 020 7935 9838
     http://www.rcophth.ac.uk
     Hon Sec: Bernie Chang
○   *L; advancement of study & practice of ophthalmology
Gp   Ophthalmology; Medicine
●   Conf - Mtgs - ET - Exam
M   2,800 i, UK / 950 i, o'seas
¶   Eye (Jnl) - 6.   College News (NL) - 4.   LM - 1.

Royal College of Organists   (RCO)   1864
NR   PO Box 56357, LONDON, SW16 7XL.
     0560 076 7208
     email admin@rco.org.uk   http://www.rco.org.uk
▲   Registered Charity
Br   4
○   *D; to promote the arts of organ-playing, choir-training &
     related activities
●   Conf - Mtgs - ET - Exam - Res - Exhib - Comp - SG - Inf - Lib -
     PL - VE - Empl
     The College is open during term time Mon-Fri 1000-1700
<   Inc Soc of Musicians (corporate member); R School of Church
     Music
M   2,479 i, 102 f, UK / 836 i, o'seas
¶   RCO News (Jnl) - 4.

Royal College of Paediatrics & Child Health   (RCPCH)   1996
NR   5-11 Theobalds Rd, LONDON, WC1X 8SH.   (hq)
     020 7092 6000   fax 020 7092 6001
     email enquiries@rcpch.ac.uk   http://www.rcpch.ac.uk
     Chief Exec: Len Tyler
▲   Registered Charity
○   *L; to advance education in child health & paediatrics; to
     relieve sickness by promoting improvements in paediatric
     practice; to promote research & publish the results
Gp   Association of Paediatric Emergency Medicine; Association
     Paediatric Palliative Medicine; British Association of
     Community Child Health; British Association of Community
     Doctors in Audiology; British Association of General
     Paediatrics; British Association for Paediatric Nephrology;
     British Association of Paediatricians in Audiology; British
     Associaton of Perinatal Medicine; British Congenital Cardiac
     Association; British Inherited Metabolic Disease Group;
     British Paediatric & Adolescent Bone Group; British Paediatric
     Allergy, Immunity & Infection Group; British Paediatric Mental
     Health Group; British Paediatric Neurology Association;
     British Paediatric Pathology Group; British Paediatric
     Respiratory Society; British Society for the History of
     Paediatrics & Child Health; British Society for Paediatric &
     Adolescent Rheumatology; British Society for Paediatric
     Dermatology; British Society for Paediatric Endocrinology;
     British Society for Paediatric Gastroenterology; British Society
     of Paediatric Radiology; Child Protection Special Interest
     Group; Child & Public Health Special Interest Group;
     Children's Cancer & Leukaemia Group Clinical Genetics
     Group; International Child Health Group; Paediatric
     Haematology Forum; Paediatric Intensive Care Society;
     Remote & Rural Paediatric Special Interest Group
●   Conf - Mtgs - ET - Exam - Res
<   Intl Paediatric Assn; Conf of Eur Specialists in Paediatrics
M   7,194 i, UK / 1,625 i, o'seas
¶   NL - 4; ftm.   Hbk; ftm.
     Archives of Disease in Childhood - 12; ftm, p.o.a.
     Cherub Bulletin - 4;   Guideline Appraisal - irreg;   AR - 1;
     all free.
     British National Formulary for Children - 1: free to those
     prescribing to children.

Royal College of Pathologists   (RCPath)   1962
NR   2 Carlton House Terrace, LONDON, SW1Y 5AF.   (hq)
     020 7451 6700   fax 020 7451 6701
     email info@rcpath.org   http://www.rcpath.org
     Chief Exec: Daniel Ross
▲   Registered Charity
○   *P, *Q; to advance the science & practice of pathology
●   Conf - Exam
M   5,000 i, UK / 2,500 i, o'seas
¶   Bulletin - 4; ftm, £60 nm.   Hbk - 2 yrly; ftm only.

Royal College of Physicians of Edinburgh   (RCPE)   1681
NR   9 Queen St, EDINBURGH, EH2 1JQ.   (hq)
     0131-225 7324   fax 0131-220 3939
     http://www.rcpe.ac.uk
     Chief Exec: Elaine Tait
▲   Registered Charity
○   *L, *P; to promote the highest standards of practice in internal
     medicine & related specialities wherever its fellows, collegiate
     members & members practise
●   Conf - Mtgs - ET - Exam - Res - Exhib - Lib - VE - LG
M   2,168 fellows, 1,917 collegiate m, 73 affiliates, UK /
     2,623 fellows, 609 collegiate m, 7 affiliates, o'seas
¶   The Journal - 4;   The Bulletin (NL) - 12 (online); both ftm.

Royal College of Physicians of Ireland
IRL   Frederick House, 19 South Frederick St, DUBLIN 2, Republic of
     Ireland.
     353 (1) 863 9700   fax 353 (1) 672 4707
     email info@rcpi.ie   http://www.rcpi.ie
○   *M, *P

Royal College of Physicians of London   (RCP)   1518
■   11 St Andrews Place, Regent's Park, LONDON, NW1 4LE.
    (hq)
    020 7224 1539   fax 020 7487 5218
    email info@rcplondon.ac.uk
    http://www.rcplondon.ac.uk
    Chief Exec: Martin Else
▲   Registered Charity
Br 12
○   *L, *P; to set & improve standards in education & training; to
    ensure quality of care for patients; to influence the delivery of
    care; to provide professional leadership & influence
    government; to involve patients & the public
Gp Faculty of: Forensic Medicine; Occupational Medicine;
    Pharmaceutical medicine; Public Health
    Jt C'ee for Higher Medical Training
●   Conf - Mtgs - ET - Exam - Exhib - Inf - Lib - LG
<   Eur Assn of Med Specialists (EUMS)
M   18,900 i (fellows & members), UK / 2,700 i (fellows), o'seas
¶   Clinical Medicine (Jnl) - 6; ftm, £120 nm (UK).
    LM - 1; ftm, price on application nm.   AR; free.

**Royal College of Physicians & Surgeons of Glasgow
(RCPSGlasg)   1599**
■   232-242 St Vincent Street, GLASGOW, G2 5RJ.   (hq)
    0141-221 6072
    http://www.rcpsg.ac.uk
    Chief Exec: John Cooper
▲   Registered Charity
○   *L, *P; to set & maintain standards of practice in medicine,
    surgery & dental surgery; to conduct postgraduate
    examinations & organise training & educational events for
    physicians, surgeons & dentists at all stages of their careers
Gp Dental faculty; Faculty of travel medicine
●   Mtgs - ET - Exam - Res - Lib
<   Intl Assn of Coll & Academy Presidents; Fedn of R Colls of
    Physicians in the UK; Senate of Surgery of GB & Ireland
M   c 4,100 i, UK / 2,300 i, o'seas
¶   Bulletin - 3; ftm, on application nm.
    News & Views - 3;   AR; both free.

Royal College of Psychiatrists   (RCPsych)   1971
■   17 Belgrave Sq, LONDON, SW1X 8PG.   (hq)
    020 7235 2351   fax 020 7245 1231
    email rcpsych@rcpsych.ac.uk   http://www.rcpsych.ac.uk
    Registrar: Prof Sue Bailey
▲   Registered Charity
○   *L, *M, *P; to advance the science & practice of psychiatry &
    related subjects
Gp Faculties:
    Academic psychiatry; Addictions; Child & adolescent psychiatry;
    Forensic psychiatry; General & community psychiatry; Liaison
    psychiatry; Psychiatry of learning disability; Psychiatry of old
    age; Psychotherapy; Rehabilitation & social psychiatry
●   Conf - ET - Exam - Res - Inf - VE - LG
<   Wld Psychiatric Assn
M   6,941 i, UK / 1,729 i, o'seas
¶   British Journal of Psychiatry - 12.
    Psychiatric Bulletin - 12.
    Advances in Psychiatric Treatment - 6.

Royal College of Radiologists   1975
■   38 Portland Place, LONDON, W1B 1JQ.   (hq)
    020 7636 4432   fax 020 7323 3100
    email enquiries@rcr.ac.uk   http://www.rcr.ac.uk
    Pres: Dr Jane Barrett
○   *L, *M, *P; the science & practice of radiology & oncology
M   5,820 i, UK / 1,580 i, o'seas
¶   Clinical Radiology (Jnl) - 12.   Clinical Oncology (Jnl) - 8.
    NL - 4;   AR - 1.

**Royal College of Speech & Language Therapists   (RCSLT)
1945**
NR 2 White Hart Yard, LONDON, SE1 1NX.   (hq)
    020 7378 1200
    email postmaster@rcslt.org   http://www.rcslt.org
    Chief Exec: Kamini Gadhok
▲   Registered Charity
○   *P; the governing body for speech & language therapy in the
    UK
Gp all acquired or developmental conditions affecting
    communication
●   Conf - Mtgs - ET - Exam - Res - Exhib - SG - Stat - Inf - Lib - PL
    - Empl
<   Allied Health Professions Fedn; Intl Assn Logopedics &
    Phoniatrics (AILP); Standing Liaison C'ee EC Speech &
    Language Therapists & Logopedists (CPLOL)
M   10,031 i, UK / 418 i, o'seas
¶   European Journal of Disorders of Communication - 4; ftm.
    Communicating Quality (professional standards).   LM.
    Bulletin - 12 (supplements - 24); ftm.   AR; ftm only.
    Publications list available.

Royal College of Surgeons of Edinburgh   (RCSEd)   1505
NR Nicolson St, EDINBURGH, EH8 9DW.   (hq)
    0131-527 1600   fax 0131-557 6406
    email information@rcsed.ac.uk   http://www.rcsed.ac.uk
    Chief Exec: Alison Rooney
▲   Registered Charity
○   *L, *P; a body incorporated by royal charter, concerned with
    education & training for medical & surgical practice & the
    maintenance of high standards of professional competence
    & conduct; includes both surgery & dental surgery
Gp Faculty of: Dental surgery, Health informatics, Pre-hospital care,
    Sport & exercise medicine
●   Conf - ET - Exam - Inf - Lib - LG
M   7,800 i, UK / 5,500 i, o'seas
¶   Jnl - 6;   NL - 4.

Royal College of Surgeons of England   (RCS)   1800
NR 35-43 Lincoln's Inn Fields, LONDON, WC2A 3PE.   (hq)
    020 7405 3474
    http://www.rcseng.ac.uk
    Chief Exec: Alan Bennett
▲   Registered Charity
○   *L, *P; an independent professional body committed to
    promoting & advancing the highest standards of surgical
    care for patients
M   i

Royal College of Surgeons in Ireland   (RCSI)   1784
IRL 123 St Stephen's Green, DUBLIN 2, Republic of Ireland.   (hq)
    353 (1) 402 2100   fax 353 (1) 402 2460
    http://www.rcsi.ie
    Chief Exec: Michael Horgan
○   *P

Royal College of Surgeons in Ireland
IRL 123 St Stephen's Green, DUBLIN 2, Republic of Ireland.   (hq)
    353 (1) 402 2100
    http://www.rcsi.ie
○   *P
>   Professor Eoin O'Malley

Royal College of Veterinary Surgeons (RCVS) 1844
- ■ Belgravia House, 62-64 Horseferry Rd, LONDON, SW1P 2AF. (hq)
  020 7222 2001 fax 020 7222 2004
  email admin@rcvs.org.uk http://www.rcvs.org.uk
  Registrar: Miss Jane C Hern
- ▲ Incorporated Statutory Body
- ○ *L, *P, *V
- ● ET - Exam - Stat - Inf - Lib
- M 16,137 i, UK / 2,606 i, o'seas
- ¶ NL - 3; ftm & online. Register of Members - 1.
  Directory of Veterinary Practices - 1.
  Guide to Professional Conduct - 1; free online.
  List of Veterinary Nurses - 1; AR; free.

Royal Cornwall Agricultural Association (RCAA) 1793
- ■ Royal Cornwall Showground, WADEBRIDGE, Cornwall, PL27 7JE. (hq)
  01208 812183 fax 01208 812713
  email info@royalcornwall.co.uk
  http://www.royalcornwall.co.uk
  Sec: Christopher Riddle
- ▲ Registered Charity
- ○ *F; to promote agriculture
- Gp C'ees for: Bees, Cage birds, Dogs, Fur, Goats, Honey, Horticulture, Pigeons, Poultry
- ● Royal Cornwall Show - Mtgs - Exhib - Comp
- < Assn of Show & Agricl Orgs; most livestock breed societies
- M 6,500 i, c 750 f
- ¶ Show Catalogue - 1; £4.00. AR; ftm only.
  Souvenir Programme - 1; £3.00.

Royal Dublin Society (RDS) 1731
- IRL Ballsbridge, DUBLIN 4, Republic of Ireland. (hq)
  353 (1) 668 0866 fax 353 (1) 660 4014
  email info@rds.ie http://www.rds.ie
- ○ *L

Royal Economic Society (RES) 1890
- ■ School of Economics & Finance, University of St Andrews, ST ANDREWS, Fife, KY16 9AL. (hsb)
  01334 462479 fax 01334 462444
  email royaleconsoc@st-andrews.ac.uk
  http://www.res.org.uk
  Sec-Gen: Prof John Beath
- ▲ Registered Charity
- ○ *L
- ● Conf - ET - Res - Inf
- < Intl Economic Assn
- M 1,500 i, UK / 1,700 i, o'seas
- ¶ The Economic Jnl - 8. NL - 4; both ftm.
  New editions of economic classics.

Royal Entomological Society of London (REntSoc) 1833
- NR The Mansion House, Chiswell Green Lane, ST ALBANS, Herts, AL2 3NS. (hq)
  01727 899387 fax 01727 894797
  http://www.royensoc.co.uk
  Registrar: W H F Blakemore
- ○ *L
- M i

Royal Environmental Health Institute of Scotland (REHIS) 1983
- ■ 19 Torphichen St, EDINBURGH, EH3 8HX. (hq)
  0131-229 2968
  email contact@rehis.com http://www.rehis.org
  Sec & Chief Exec: Tom Bell
- ▲ Incorporated by Royal Charter
- ○ *P; covers food safety, housing, health & safety, pollution, public health, waste management
- ● Conf - Mtgs - ET - Exam - Res - Exhib - SG - Stat - Inf - Lib - VE - LG
- < Intl Fedn of Envtl Health
- M 1,000 i, UK / 100 i, o'seas
- ¶ Environmental Health Scotland - 6;
  Congress Proceedings - 1; AR- 1; all ftm only.

Royal Faculty of Procurators in Glasgow (RFPG) pre-1668
- ■ 12 Nelson Mandela Place, GLASGOW, G2 1BT. (hq)
  0141-332 3593 fax 0141-332 4714
  email library@rfpg.org http://www.rfpg.org
  Chief Exec: John McKenzie
- ▲ Royal Charter
- ○ *P; to provide a library, an education programme & auditing services for members
- ● Mtgs - ET - Comp - Lib - Management of charitable funds
- M 1,400 i, 200 f

Royal Forestry Society of England, Wales & Northern Ireland (RFS) 1882
- NR 102 High St, TRING, Herts, HP23 4AF. (hq)
  01442 822028 fax 01442 890395
  email rfshq@rfs.org.uk http://www.rfs.org.uk
  Chief Exec: Dr J E Jackson
- ▲ Company Limited by Guarantee; Registered Charity
- Br 21 divisions
- ○ *L; promoting the wise management of trees & woods; advancement of knowledge & practice of forestry & arboriculture; promotion of sustainable forestry
- ● Mtgs - Exam - Lib - VE
- M 4,235 i, 280 f
- ¶ Quarterly Jnl of Forestry - 4; ftm, £2.50 nm.

Royal Geographical Society (with the Institute of British Geographers) (RGS-IBG) 1830
- NR 1 Kensington Gore, LONDON, SW7 2AR. (hq)
  020 7591 3000 fax 020 7591 3001
  http://www.rgs.org
  Dir & Sec: Dr Rita Gardner
- ▲ Registered Charity
- ○ *L, *Q; to advance geographical science and support its practitioners
- M i, f & org

Royal Glasgow Institute of the Fine Arts (RGI) 1861
- ■ 5 Oswald St, GLASGOW, G1 4QR. (asa)
  0141-248 7411 fax 0141-221 0417
  email rgi@robbferguson.co.uk
  http://www.rgiscotland.co.uk
  Sec: Mrs Lesley Nicholl
- ▲ Company Limited by Guarantee; Registered Charity
- ○ *A; to encourage & promote contemporary art
- ● Exhib
- M 1,100 i

Royal Guernsey Agricultural & Horticultural Society
- NR PO Box 59, ST PETER PORT, Guernsey, GY1 3BR.
  0778 144 9110
  Sec: Joan de Garis
- ○ *F, *H
- M c 100 i

**Royal Highland & Agricultural Society of Scotland   (RHASS)
1784**
- ■   Royal Highland Centre, Ingliston, EDINBURGH, EH28 8NF.
      (hq)
      0131-335 6200   fax 0131-335 6229
      email info@rhass.org.uk   http://www.rhass.org.uk
      Chief Exec: Stephen Hutt
- ▲   Registered Charity
- ○   *F; promotion of agriculture & allied industries in Scotland
- ●   Conf - Mtgs - ET - Exhib - Comp - Inf - Lib - LG
- <   Assn of Show & Agricl Orgs; R Agricl Soc of the C'wealth
- M   14,000 i, UK / 50 i, o'seas
      (Sub: £48)
- ¶   Royal Highland Review - 3; ftm only.
      Royal Highland Show Guide - 1.
      Royal Highland Show Catalogue - 1.

Royal Highland Education Trust   (RHET)   1999
- ■   Royal Highland Centre, Ingliston, EDINBURGH, EH28 8NF.
      (hq)
      0131-335 6227   fax 0131-333 5236
      email rhetinfo@rhass.org.uk   http://www.rhet.org.uk
- ▲   Registered Charity
- ○   *F; information service for schools & the public about the
      economic & environmental realities of farming, forestry &
      food production in Scotland
- Gp   Local initiative bodies available for school-farm links
- ●   Inf
- ¶   Sprouts (NL) - 3.

Royal Historical Society   (RHistS)   1868
- NR   University College London, Gower St, LONDON, WC1E 6BT.
      (hq)
      020 7387 7532
      http://www.royalhistoricalsociety.org
      Exec Sec: Susan Carr
- ○   *L; promote the study of history by the publication of
      documentary, bibliographical & reference material
- M   i

Royal Horticultural Society   (RHS)   1804
- ■   80 Vincent Sq, LONDON, SW1P 2PE.   (hq)
      0845 260 5000
      http://www.rhs.org.uk
      Dir Gen: Sue Biggs
- ▲   Registered Charity
- Br   4 gardens: Harlow Carr (N Yorks); Hyde Hall (Essex); Rosemoor
      (Devon); Wisley (Surrey)
- ○   *H; the encouragement & improvement of the science, art &
      practice of horticulture in all its branches
- ●   Conf - Mtgs - ET - Exam - Res - Exhib - Comp - Inf - Lib
- <   Assn of Show & Agricl Orgs
- M   335,000 i, 3,000 org, UK & o'seas
- ¶   The Garden (Jnl) - 12; ftm, £3.50 each nm.
      Numerous manuals & reference works.

Royal Horticultural Society of Ireland   (RHSI)   1830
- IRL   Cabinteely House, The Park, Cabinteely, DUBLIN 18, Republic
      of Ireland.
      353 (1) 235 3912   fax 353 (1) 235 3912
      email info@rhsi.ie   http://www.rhsi.ie
- ○   *H

Royal Humane Society   (RHS)   1774
- NR   50-51 Temple Chambers, 3-7 Temple Avenue, LONDON,
      EC4Y 0HP.   (hq)
      020 7936 2942   fax 020 7936 2942
      email info@royalhumanesociety.org.uk
      http://www.royalhumanesociety.org.uk
      Sec: Dick Wilkinson
- ▲   Registered Charity
- ○   *W; to encourage the saving of human life; to present awards
      for bravery in so doing
- ●   Mtgs - Res - Lib
- <   R Humane Socs: Australasia, Canada, New South Wales, New
      Zealand
- M   i & f
- ¶   Short History of the Society;   Medals of the Society;
      Saved from a Watery Grave;   AR.

Royal Incorporation of Architects in Scotland   (RIAS)   1916
- ■   15 Rutland Sq, EDINBURGH, EH1 2BE.   (hq)
      0131-229 7545   fax 0131-228 2188
      email info@rias.org.uk   http://www.rias.org.uk
      Sec: Neil Baxter
- ▲   Registered Charity
- Br   6
- ○   *L, *P; for all chartered architects in Scotland
- Gp   Bookshop & gallery; Competitions; Exhibitions; Library;
      Professional section for architects & public
- ●   Conf - Mtgs - ET - Res - Exhib - Comp - Lib - PL - LG
- <   R Inst Brit Architects (RIBA)
- M   3,500 i, 500 f
- ¶   Chartered Architect - 4.   e-bulletins - 12.

Royal Institute of the Architects of Ireland   (RIAI)   1839
- IRL   8 Merrion Sq, DUBLIN 2, Republic of Ireland.
      353 (1) 676 1703   fax 353 (1) 661 0948
      email info@riai.ie   http://www.riai.ie
- ○   *P

Royal Institute of British Architects   (RIBA)   1834
- ■   66 Portland Place, LONDON, W1B 1AD.   (hq)
      020 7580 5533   fax 020 7255 1541
      email info@riba.org   http://www.architecture.com
      Chief Exec: Harry Rich
- Br   9
- ○   *L, *P; to champion better buildings, communities & the
      environment through architecture; to provide standards,
      training, support & recognition for architects
- ●   Conf - Exam - Exhib - Comp - Inf - Lib - PL - LG
- M   40,500 i
- ¶   RIBA Jnl - 12; ftm.   AR - 1; free.
      Architecture Periodicals Index - 4.
      RIBA Directory of Practices - 1 (printed & on-line).
      RIBA Directory of Members - 1; ftm (on-line only).
      RIBA International Directory of Practices - 1 (on-line only).

Royal Institute of International Affairs (RIIA) 1920
NR Chatham House, 10 St James's Sq, LONDON, SW1Y 4LE.
     (hq)
     020 7957 5700   fax 020 7957 5710
     email contact@chathamhouse.org.uk
     http://www.chathamhouse.org.uk
     Dir: Dr Robin Niblett
▲ Registered Charity
○ *L; for the discussion, research & analysis of international
     affairs; the provision of information on & analysis of
     international issues with the object of stimulating informal
     debate among decision-makers & the wider public
Gp Research programmes:
     Africa; Americas; Asia; Energy, environment & development;
     Europe; International economics; International law;
     International security; Middle East; Russia & Eurasia; Global
     trends - food supply project
● Conf - Mtgs - Res - SG - Lib
< Instns of international affairs
M 1,700 i, 300 f
¶ The World Today (Jnl) - 12.   Chatham House NL - 12.
     International Affairs (Jnl) - 6; ftm.   AR.
     Publications list available.
     Note: Chatham House is both the name of the building and the
     name by which the Institute is widely known.

Royal Institute of Navigation (RIN) 1947
NR 1 Kensington Gore, LONDON, SW7 2AT.   (hq)
     020 7591 3130   fax 020 7591 3131
     email admin@rin.org.uk   http://www.rin.org.uk
     Dir: Gp Capt D W Broughton
▲ Registered Charity
Br 2
○ *L; the advancement of the art & science of navigation by land,
     sea, air & in space (includes animal & bird navigation)

Royal Institute of Oil Painters
     a member of the **Federation of British Artists**

Royal Institute of Painters in Water Colours
     a member of the **Federation of British Artists**

Royal Institute of Philosophy 1925
NR 14 Gordon Sq, LONDON, WC1H 0AR.   (hq)
     020 7387 4130
     Sec: James Garvey
▲ Company Limited by Guarantee; Registered Charity
○ *L; to promote the study of philosophy & the encouragement of
     original work
M i

Royal Institute of Public Health
     in October 2008 merged with the Royal Society (for the Promotion) of
     Health to form the **Royal Society for Public Health**

Royal Institution of Chartered Surveyors (RICS) 1868
■ Parliament Square, LONDON, SW1P 3AD.   (hq)
     0870 333 1600   fax 020 7334 3811
     email contactrics@rics.org   http://www.rics.org
     Chief Exec: Sean Tompkins
▲ Un-incorporated Society
○ *P
< Soc for the Envt (SocEnv)
M i & f

Royal Institution of Cornwall (RIC) 1818
■ Royal Cornwall Museum, 25 River St, TRURO, Cornwall,
     TR1 2SJ.   (hq)
     01872 272205   fax 01872 240514
     email enquiries@royalcornwallmuseum.org.uk
     http://www.royalcornwallmuseum.org.uk
     Dir: Hilary Bracegirdle
▲ Registered Charity
○ *L; furtherance of Cornish studies; maintenance of the Museum
● Mtgs - ET - Exhib - Inf - Lib - PL - VE
M 714 i, UK / 25 i, o'seas
¶ RIC Jnl - 1;   NL - 2; both ftm.

Royal Institution of Great Britain (RI) 1799
NR 21 Albemarle St, LONDON, W1S 4BS.   (hq)
     020 7409 2992
     http://www.rigb.org
     Chief Exec: Chris Rofe
Br Davy Faraday Research Laboratory
○ *L, *Q; advancement of the public understanding of science; to
     research into solid state chemistry
M i & f
¶ Elements - 4.

Royal Institution of Naval Architects (RINA) 1860
NR 10 Upper Belgrave St, LONDON, SW1X 8BQ.   (hq)
     020 7235 4622   fax 020 7259 5912
     email hq@rina.org.uk   http://www.rina.org.uk
     Chief Exec: Trevor Blakeley
▲ Registered Charity
Br Europe (14), Asia Pacific, Australia, Middle East
○ *L, *P; advancement of the art & science of naval architecture,
     as applied to ship design & other related activities
Gp Small craft; High speed craft; Historical; Young members
● Conf - Mtgs - ET - Exhib - Comp - SG - Inf - Lib - LG
< W Confedn of Maritime Technology Socs (WEMT)
M 4,100 i, UK / 2,400 i, o'seas
¶ The Naval Architect - 10.   Ship & Boat Intl - 10.
     Offshore Marine Technology - 4.
     Warship Technology - 5 (included with The Naval Architect).
     Ship Repair & Conversion Technology - 4.
     Significant Ship - 1.   Significant Small Craft - 1.

Royal Institution of South Wales (RISW) 1835
■ c/o Swansea Museum, Victoria Rd, SWANSEA, Glam,
     SA1 1SN.   (hq)
     01792 653763   fax 01792 652585
     email swanseamuseum@swansea.gov.uk
     http://www.risw.org.uk
▲ Registered Charity
○ *L; created as a literary & philosophical institution; nowadays,
     acts as a friends group of Swansea Museum
Gp Collection; Education; Publication
● Conf - Mtgs - Et - Res - Exhib - Comp - Inf - PL - VE
M 400 i, 4 org
¶ Minerva: Jnl of Swansea History - 1.   NL - 3; ftm.

Royal Irish Academy (RIA) 1785
IRL 19 Dawson St, DUBLIN 2, Republic of Ireland.   (hq)
     353 (1) 676 2570   fax 353 (1) 676 2346
     email admin@ria.ie   http://www.ria.ie
     Exec Sec: PAtrick Buckley
○ *L
M 320

Royal Irish Academy of Music (RIAM) 1848
IRL 36-38 Westland Row, DUBLIN 2, Republic of Ireland.
     353 (1) 676 4412   fax 353 (1) 662 2798
     email info@riam.ie   http://www.riam.ie
     Sec: Dorothy Shiel
○ *D, *E

Royal Irish Automobile Club   (RIAC)   1901
IRL   34 Dawson St, DUBLIN 2, Republic of Ireland.
        353 (1) 677 5141 (Motor Sport Dept: 677 5628)
        fax 353 (1) 671 0793
        email info@riac.ie   http://www.riac.ie
○   *G

Royal Isle of Wight Agricultural Society   (RIWAS)   1882
NR   Central House, 48/49 High St, NEWPORT, Isle of Wight,
        PO30 1SE.   (hq)
        01983 826275   fax 01983 826275
        email riwas@aol.org   http://www.riwas.org.uk
        Hon Sec: Mrs Rosemary Edwards
▲   Company Limited by Guarantee; Registered Charity
○   *F; to promote farming & agriculture & organisation of the Isle
        of Wight County Show
●   Exhib - Shows
<   Assn of Shows & Agricl Studies
M   540 i, UK / 1 i, o'seas
¶   NL - 4;   AR; both ftm only.

**Royal Jersey Agricultural & Horticultural Society   (RJA&HS)
1833**
■   Royal Jersey Showground, La Route de la Trinité, TRINITY,
        Jersey, Channel Islands, JE3 5JP.   (hq)
        01534 866555   fax 01534 865619
        email society@royaljersey.co.uk
        http://www.royaljersey.co.uk
        Chief Exec: James W Godfrey
▲   Registered Charity
○   *B, *F, *H
●   Conf - Mtgs - Exhib - Comp - Expt - Inf - LG
M   1,000 i, 20 f, 10 org, UK / 200 i, o'seas
¶   Jersey at Home - 1; ftm, £5 nm.

Royal Lancashire Agricultural Society   (RLAS)   1767
■   52 Brookfield Rd, THORNTON-CLEVELEYS, Lancashire,
        FY5 4DT.   (hq)
        email info@rlas.co.uk   http://www.rlas.co.uk
        Hon Sec: Wendy George
▲   Company Limited by Guarantee; Registered Charity
○   *F; promotion of agriculture; to organise the annual show
●   Exhib (annual show)
M   450 i
¶   Rural Review (NL) - 2; m only.   Show Catalogue - 1.   AR.

Royal Life Saving Society UK   (RLSS UK)   1891
■   River House, High St, Broom, ALCESTER, Warks, B50 4HN.
        (hq)
        01789 773994   fax 01789 773995
        email lifesavers@rlss.org.uk
        http://www.lifesavers.org.uk
        Chief Exec: Di Standley
▲   Company Limited by Guarantee; Registered Charity
Br   50
○   *K, *W; educating people in preventing the loss of life through
        drowning, choking & heart attacks
●   ET - Comp - Inf - LG
<   Intl Lifesaving Fedn; Inst Sport & Recreational Mgt
M   13,000 i, 1,400 org
¶   Lifesavers Magazine - 4; ftm & supporters.

Royal Manx Agricultural Society   1858
■   Alpines, Curragh Rd, ST JOHNS, Isle of Man, IM4 3LN.   (hsb)
        01624 801850
        email royalmanx@manx.net   http://www.royalmanx.com
        Sec: Mrs Christine A Pain
▲   Company Limited by Guarantee
○   *F, *H; to organise an annual agricultural show
●   Mtgs - Exhib - Comp - VE - LG - Schools competition with
        'greenfingers' bias
<   Brit Show Jumping Assn; Clydesdale Horse Soc of GB &
        Ireland; Shire Horse Assn; Holstein UK Premier Show; R
        Gardeners Benevolent Assn
M   100 i

Royal Martyr Church Union   (RMCU)   1906
■   7 Nunnery Stables, ST ALBANS, Herts, AL1 2AS.   (hsp)
        01727 856626
        Hon Sec & Treas: E D Roberts
▲   Un-incorporated Society
○   *G, K; to promote the restoration of King Charles I's name to
        its proper place & fitting observance in the worldwide
        Anglican Communion's calendar; to maintain the principles
        of faith, loyalty & liberty for which the King died; open to
        anyone interested in the heroic & stirring times of King
        Charles I
●   Mtgs - Annual remembrance service on the nearest Thursday to
        30 January at St Mary's Cathedral, Palmerston Place,
        Edinburgh & on the nearest Saturday to 30 January in
        St Mary-le-Strand, London WC2
M   85 i, UK / 6 i, o'seas
¶   Royal Martyr Annual - 1; ftm, on application nm.

Royal Medical Society   (RMS)   1736
■   Potterrow, 5/5 Bristo Sq, EDINBURGH, EH8 9AL.   (hq)
        0131-650 2672   fax 0131-650 2672
        email enquiries@royalmedical.co.uk
        http://www.royalmedical.co.uk
        Sec: Mrs Elizabeth Singh
▲   Registered Charity
○   *L; the medical student society of Edinburgh
Gp   Learning resource centre; Library; Museum
●   Mtgs - ET - Comp - SG - Inf - Lib - PL
M   300 i
¶   Res Medica (Jnl) - 2.

Royal Mencap Society   (MENCAP)   1946
NR   123 Golden Lane, LONDON, EC1Y 0RT.   (hq)
        020 7454 0454   fax 020 7608 3254
        email information@mencap.org.uk
        http://www.mencap.org.uk
▲   Registered Charity
○   *W; 'Everything we do is about valuing and supporting people
        with a learning disability, and their families and carers'
Gp   Divn: National Federation of Gateway Clubs
●   Conf - Mtgs - ET - Res - Exhib - Inf - LG
M   i & org
¶   Publications list available.
✕   2009-10 Mencap Ltd
        Note: uses the operating title Mencap

Royal Meteorological Society   (RMetS)   1850
NR   104 Oxford Rd, READING, Berks, RG1 7LL.   (hq)
        0118-956 8500   fax 0118-956 8571
        email info@rmets.org   http://www.rmets.org
        Gen Sec: Bob Riddaway
▲   Registered Charity
○   *L; promotion of all aspects of the science of meteorology
        (including the application of the discipline to agriculture,
        aviation, hydrology, marine transport & oceanography)
<   Soc for the Envt (SocEnv)
M   i, f & org

Royal Microscopical Society   (RMS)   1839
NR   37-38 St Clements St, OXFORD, OX4 1AJ.   (hq)
        01865 254760   fax 01865 791237
        email info@rms.org.uk   http://www.rms.org.uk
        Admin: Karen Lonsdale
▲   Registered Charity
○   *L; 'publication & discussion of research in fields of
        improvement in construction & mode of application of
        microscopes, & those branches of science where microscopy
        is important'
Gp   Cell biology; Cytometry; Electron microscopy; Light microscopy;
        Materials science
●   Conf - Mtgs - ET - Exhib
<   Intl Fedn Socs Histochemistry & Cytochemistry; Intl Fedn Socs
        Electron Microscopy
M   c 900 i, UK / 500 i o'seas
¶   Jnl of Microscopy - 12.   In Focus - 4; ftm.

Royal Miniature Society
see **Royal Society of Miniature Painters, Sculptors & Gravers**

Royal Musical Association (RMA) 1874

- ■ 4 Chandos Rd, Chorlton-cum-Hardy, MANCHESTER,
  M21 0ST. (hsp/b)
  0161-861 7542   fax 0161-861 7543
  email jeffrey.dean@stingrayoffice.com
  http://www.rma.ac.uk
  Sec: Dr Jeffrey Dean
- ▲ Company Limited by Guarantee; Registered Charity
- Br 2
- ○ *D, *L; art, science & history of music
- ● Conf - Mtgs
- < Amer Musicological Soc; Soc for Musicology in Ireland
- M 900 i, UK / 85 i, o'seas
- ¶ Jnl - 2; ftm, £109 nm.
  NL - 2; ftm, £10 nm.
  RMA Research Chronicle - 1; price varies.
  RMA Monographs; price varies.

Royal National Institute of Blind People (RNIB) 1868

- NR 105 Judd St, LONDON, WC1H 9NE. (hq)
  020 7388 1266   fax 020 7388 2034
  http://www.rnib.org.uk
  Dir Gen: Lesley-Anne Alexander
- ▲ Registered Charity
- Br 9
- ○ *W; 'works for blind & partially sighted people throughout the
  UK. We have over 60 different services to help people at all
  stages of their lives'
- ● RNIB National Library Service (Talking book service);Inf - Tape
  & braille services - Holidays - Residential homes; Training,
  rehabilitation & help in finding jobs
  Helpline: 030 3213 9999
- M subscribers

Royal National Lifeboat Institution (RNLI) 1824

- NR West Quay Rd, POOLE, Dorset, BH15 1HZ. (hq)
  0845 122 6999
  http://www.rnli.org.uk
  Chief Exec: Paul Boissier
- ○ *W; to save lives at sea around the coasts of UK & Ireland
- ● Conf - Mtgs - Exhib - Inf - PL - VE
- < Intl Lifeboat Fedn
- M 200,000+ i
- ¶ The Lifeboat - 4; ftm.   AR; free.

Royal National Rose Society (RNRS) 1876

- NR Gardens of the Rose, Chiswell Green, ST ALBANS, Herts,
  AL2 3NR. (hq)
  01727 850461   fax 01727 850360
  http://www.rnrs.org
  Chief Exec: Roz Hamilton
- ▲ Company Limited by Guarantee; Registered Charity
- ○ *H
- ● Res - Exhib - Inf - Lib - PL
- M c 10,000 i & org
- ¶ The Rose (Jnl) - 3.   How to Grow Roses - irreg.

Royal Naval Association (RNA) 1950

- NR Semaphore Tower (room 209), PP70, HM Naval Base,
  PORTSMOUTH, Hants, PO1 3LT. (hq)
  023 9272 3747
  http://www.royal-naval-association.co.uk
- ▲ Registered Charity
- Br 450; 10 o'seas
- ○ *W; 'to further the efficiency of the Service in which members of
  the association have served or are serving, by fostering the
  esprit de corps & preserving the traditions of the Service; ...
  to relieve members of the association who are in conditions
  of real hardship or distress'
- ● Conf - Mtgs - VE
- M 47,000 i, UK / 1,000 i, o'seas
- ¶ NL - 4;   Circular - 11;   Ybk;   AR; all ftm.

Royal Naval Bird Watching Society (RNBWS) 1946

- ■ 20 Shepards Close, FAREHAM, Hants, PO14 3AJ. (hsp)
  http://www.rnbws.org.uk
  Hon Sec: S Copsey
- ▲ Registered Charity
- ○ *G; forum for exchange of information & observation of
  seabirds & land birds at sea & onboard ships whilst at sea
- Gp Seabird distribution database
- ● Res - PL of seabirds: c/o Lt Cmdr G D Lewis RN,
  40 Pondfield Rd, Saltash, Cornwall, PL12 4UA.
- M 180 i, org, UK / 60 i, org, o'seas
- ¶ NBWS Bulletin - 2; ftm, £1 each nm.
  Sea Swallow - 1; ftm, £8 nm.

Royal Navy Enthusiasts' Society (RNES) 1977

- ■ 7 Valley Rd, PEACEHAVEN, E Sussex, BN10 8AE. (hq)
  01273 589187
  Chmn: Dave Palmer
- ▲ Un-incorporated Society
- ○ *G; collectors of memorabilia & ephemera of the Royal Navy
  from 1600 to the present day
- Gp Collectors of: Branch badges, Cap tallies
  Historians: Nelson, his ships & men, World War I & II;
  Photographs of ships; the Royal Navy & other navies
- ● Mtgs - Res
- < Fedn of Naval Assns
- M 145 i, UK / 4 i, o'seas
- ¶ Excalibur (NL) - 12; free.

Royal Norfolk Agricultural Association (RNAA) 1847

- ■ Norfolk Showground, Dereham Rd, NORWICH, Norfolk,
  NR5 0TT. (hq)
  01603 748931   fax 01603 748729
  http://www.royalnorfolkshow.co.uk
  Chief Exec: John Purling
- ▲ Company Limited by Guarantee; Registered Charity
- ○ *F; to promote, through the Royal Norfolk Show & other events,
  the image, understanding & prosperity of agriculture & the
  countryside
- ● ET - Res - Exhib - Comp - Annual show covering large & small
  livestock, equine events, agricultural machinery & trade
  stands
- < Assn of Show & Agricl Orgs (ASAO); breed socs
- M 4,000 i
- ¶ Jnl;   Prize List - 1;   NL;   AR; all ftm.
  Catalogue - 1; £5.

Royal Northern Agricultural Society (RNAS) 1843

- ■ Auchcairnie Farm, LAURENCEKIRK, Aberdeenshire,
  AB30 1ER. (sp)
  01561 340221
  email secretary@rnas.org.uk   http://www.rnas.org.uk
  Sec: Alison M Argo
- ▲ Registered Charity
- ○ *F; to improve agricultural production & the rural economy in
  all its branches
- ● Conf - Res - Exhib - VE
- M 525 i

Royal Numismatic Society (RNS) 1836

- ■ Dept of Coins & Medals, British Museum, Great Russell St,
  LONDON, WC1B 3DG. (hsb)
  020 7323 8173   fax 020 7323 8267
  email info@numismatics.org.uk
  http://www.numismatics.org.uk
  Hon Sec: Jennifer Adam
- ▲ Registered Charity
- ○ *L; to promote & support numismatic research
- ● Mtgs - Lib
- M 420 i, 21 org, UK / 500 i, 54 org, o'seas
- ¶ The Numismatic Chronicle (Jnl) - 1; ftm.
  Special publications - irreg.

© CBD Research Ltd · Beckenham · BR3 5JS · Tel 020 8650 7745 · E-mail cbd@cbdresearch.com · www.cbdresearch.com

Royal Odonto-Chirurgical Society of Scotland   1867
NR   c/o Royal College of Surgeons of Edinburgh, Nicolson St,
        EDINBURGH, EH8 9DW.
        0131 527 1600   fax 0131 557 6406
        Sec: R A C Chate
○   *P

Royal Over-Seas League   (ROSL)   1910
■   Over-Seas House, Park Place, St James's St, LONDON,
        SW1A 1LR.   (hq)
        020 7408 0214   fax 020 7499 6738
        email info@rosl.org.uk   http://www.rosl.org.uk
        Dir Gen: Robert F Newell
▲   Royal Charter
Br   19; Australia, Canada, Hong Kong, New Zealand, Thailand &
        Switzerland
○   *X; private membership-based London club which encourages
        the arts in the youth of the Commonwealth; to increase the
        knowledge & interest in the Commonwealth
●   Conf - Mtgs - Comp (music & art) - Exhib - VE - Residential
        club-house - Lectures
M   12,814 i, UK / 10,038 i, o'seas
¶   Overseas - 4; ftm, £7.50 nm (£10 o'seas).

Royal Pharmaceutical Society of Great Britain   (RPSGB)   1841
NR   1 Lambeth High St, LONDON, SE1 7JN.   (hq)
        020 7572 2737
        email enquiries@rpsgb.org   http://www.rpsgb.org
        Chief Exec: Helen Gordon
▲   Un-incorporated Society
Br   Scotland
○   *L, *P; to lead, regulate, develop & represent the profession of
        pharmacy
¶   Pharmaceutical Jnl - 52.   Hospital Pharmacist - 10.
        Tomorrow's Pharmacist - 1.
        Communities - 12.
        International Jnl of Pharmacy Practice - 4.
        Publications list available of pharmacopoeia, textbooks &
        handbooks on various aspects of pharmacy practice.

Royal Philatelic Society London   (RPSL)   1869
■   41 Devonshire Place, LONDON, W1G 6JY.   (hq)
        020 7486 1044
        email secretary@rpsl.org.uk   http://www.rpsl.org.uk
        Hon Sec: Mrs Christine Earle
▲   Registered Charity
○   *L, *T; for collectors & philatelic traders interested in the
        advancement & study of philately & postal history
●   Mtgs - Lib
M   c 1,570 i
¶   The London Philatelist (Jnl) - 10; ftm.
        Books & booklets.

Royal Philharmonic Society   (RPS)   1813
■   10 Stratford Place, LONDON, W1C 1BA.   (hq)
        020 7491 8110   fax 020 7493 7463
        email admin@royalphilharmonicsociety.org.uk
        http://www.royalphilharmonicsociety.org.uk
        Gen Admin: Rosemary Johnson
▲   Registered Charity
○   *D; to promote excellence, creativity & understanding in
        classical music
●   Lectures - Scholarships - Awards - Commissioning new music
M   700 i, 8 f, UK / 30 i, o'seas
¶   RPS Annual Lecture Text - 1.

Royal Philosophical Society of Glasgow   (RPSG)   1802
■   160 Bothwell St (D12), GLASGOW, G2 7EL.   (sb)
        0141-564 3841 (admin)
        email info@royalphil.org   http://www.royalphil.org
        Pres: Dr Felicity Grainger
▲   Company Limited by Guarantee; Registered Charity
○   *L; lectures & discussion on all branches of arts & science
●   Mtgs
M   700 i
        (Sub: £20)
¶   Summaries of lectures published on website.

Royal Photographic Society of Great Britain   (RPS)   1853
NR   Fenton House, 122 Wells Rd, BATH, Somerset, BA2 3AH.   (hq)
        01225 325733
        email reception@rps.org   http://www.rps.org
        Dir Gen: Stuart Blake
▲   Company Limited by Guarantee; Registered Charity
Br   18
○   *L; to promote the art & science of photography in all aspects
Gp   Archaeology & heritage; Audio visual; Colour; Contemporary;
        Creative; Digital imaging; Film & video; Historical;
        Holography; Imaging science; Medical; Nature; Travel;
        Visual art; Visual journalism
●   Mtgs - ET - Res - Exhib - Comp - Inf
M   7,972 i, 102 f, UK / 1,271 i, 104 f, o'seas
¶   RPS Journal - 10; ftm, £65 yr nm (£70 o'seas).
        Imaging Science Journal - 4; ftm.
        Group & Regional NLs - 1/2; ftm only.

Royal Pigeon Racing Association   (RPRA)   1896
■   The Reddings, CHELTENHAM, Glos, GL51 6RN.   (hq)
        01452 858242   fax 01452 857119
        email dorothyhadley@rpra.org   http://www.rpra.org
        Gen Mgr: Davis Bills
Br   13
○   *B, *S; control & administration of long distance pigeon racing
●   Conf - Mtgs - Exhib - Comp - Stat - Inf - LG
<   Fédn Colombophile Intle (FCI)
M   33,000 i, 2,000 clubs
¶   British Homing World - 52; 55p m.

Royal School of Church Music   (RSCM)   1927
■   19 The Close, SALISBURY, Wilts, SP1 2EB.   (hq)
        01722 424848
        email enquiries@rscm.com   http://www.rscm.com
        Dir: Mr Lindsay Gray
▲   Company Limited by Guarantee; Registered Charity
Br   52; Australia, Canada, N Zealand, S Africa, USA
○   *D, *L; training, advice & resources for all concerned with music
        in worship - singers, organists, instrumentalists, clergy &
        congregation
●   ET - Exam - Comp - SG - Inf - Lib - Publishing & retailing
        church music & training material
M   2,158 i, 4,260 org, UK / 787 i, 1,137 org, o'seas
¶   Church Music Quarterly - 4; ftm.   AR.

Royal Scottish Academy   (RSA)   1826
■   The Mound, EDINBURGH, EH2 2EL.   (hq)
        0131-225 6671   fax 0131-220 6016
        email info@royalscottishacademy.org
        http://www.royalscottishacademy.org
        Academy Coordinator: Pauline Costigane
▲   Registered Charity
○   *A; promotion & furtherance of the fine arts in Scotland
        (painting, sculpture, architecture & printmaking)
●   Exhib - Comp - Lib
M   104 academicians, 30 hon mems
¶   Exhibition Catalogue - 1.

Royal Scottish Academy of Music & Drama (RSAMD) 1847
NR 100 Renfrew St, GLASGOW, G2 3DB. (hq)
    0141-332 4101   fax 0141-332 8901
    email registry@rsamd.ac.uk   http://www.rsamd.ac.uk
    Principal: John Wallace
▲ Company Limited by Guarantee; Registered Charity
○ *D; an international conservatoire for degree courses in music
    & drama; to act as an arts & conference venue
< St Andrews University; Glasgow University; The Piping Centre
M [none]
¶ Drama NL - 4;   Events Brochure - 4;
    Events Brochure - 4;   Prospectus - 1; all free.

Royal Scottish Country Dance Society (RSCDS) 1923
NR 12 Coates Crescent, EDINBURGH, EH3 7AF. (hq)
    0131-225 3854   fax 0131-225 7783
    email info@rscds.org   http://www.rscds.org
    Exec Officer: Elizabeth Foster
▲ Registered Charity
Br 170
○ *D; to preserve & further the practice of traditional Scottish
    country dancing
● Mtgs - Exam
M c 17,000 i
¶ Bulletin - 1; ftm.   Scottish Country Dancer - 2.

Royal Scottish Forestry Society (RSFS) 1854
■ Potholm, LANGHOLM, Dumfriesshire, DG13 0NE. (hq)
    01387 383945
    email rsfs@lumison.co.uk   http://www.rsfs.org
    Admin: Anne Wood
▲ Registered Charity
Br 6
○ *H, *L; to advance all areas of forestry
Gp Forest for a 1000 years; Silviculture; Trees, woods & people
● Conf - Mtgs - ET - Exhib - Comp - SG - Lib - VE - LG
< Forestry Ind Coun (FIC)
M 950 i, 50 f, UK / 50 i, 10 f, o'seas
¶ Scottish Forestry - 4; ftm.

Royal Scottish Geographical Society (RSGS) 1884
■ Lord John Murray House, 15-19 North Port, PERTH,
    PH1 5LU. (hq)
    01738 455050
    email enquiries@rsgs.org   http://www.rsgs.org
    Dir & Sec: Dr David M Munro
▲ Registered Charity
Br 14
○ *E, *L; to advance the science of geography & create a greater
    understanding of the wider world
● Conf - Mtgs - ET - Exhib - Comp - Inf - Lib - PL - VE - LG
M 2,500 i
¶ Scottish Geographical Jnl - 4; ftm, £44 nm (£95 instns).
    GeogScot (NL) - 3; ftm, £2 nm.   AR.

Royal Scottish Pipe Band Association (RSPBA) 1930
NR 45 Washington St, GLASGOW, G3 8AZ. (hq)
    0141-221 5414   fax 0141-221 1561
    http://www.rspba.org
▲ Registered Charity
Br 12
○ *D, *G
● Conf - ET - Comp - Lib
M c 650 pipe bands
¶ The Pipe Band - 4.

Royal Scottish Society of Arts (Science & Technology) (RSSA) 1821
■ 29 East London St, EDINBURGH, EH7 4BN. (hsp)
    0131-556 2161
    email secretary@rssa.org.uk   http://www.rssa.org.uk
    Hon Sec: Mrs Jane Ridder-Patrick
▲ Registered Charity
○ *L; 'for the promotion of the 'useful arts' - science, technology,
    engineering, manufacturing'
● Mtgs - VE
M 180 i

Royal Scottish Society of Painters in Water Colours (RSW) 1878
■ 5 Oswald St, GLASGOW, G1 4QR. (asa)
    0141-248 7411   fax 0141-221 0417
    email rsw@robbferguson.co.uk
    http://www.thersw.org.uk
    Sec: Mrs Lesley Nicholl
▲ Registered Charity
○ *A; to develop & encourage the art of painting in watercolour
● Exhib
M 120 i

Royal Scottish Society for Prevention of Cruelty to Children (Children 1st) 1884
■ 83 Whitehouse Loan, EDINBURGH, EH9 1AT. (hq)
    0131-446 2300   fax 0131-446 2339
    email info@children1st.org.uk
    http://www.children1st.org.uk
    Chief Exec: Anne Houston
▲ Registered Charity
Br 30 (Scotland)
○ *K, *W, *Y; to give every child in Scotland a safe & secure
    childhood; to support families under stress; to protect
    children from harm & neglect; to protect their rights &
    interests; to help them recover from abuse
● Conf - ET - Exhib - Inf
    ParentLine Scotland - 0808 800 2222 - helpline for parents &
    carers
¶ AR - 1; free.

Royal Smithfield Club (RSC) 1798
NR 95 Hillside View, Peasedown St John, BATH, Somerset,
    BA2 8EU. (hq)
    01225 837904   fax 01225 432444
    email sally@royalsmithfieldclub.co.uk
    http://www.royalsmithfieldclub.co.uk
    Sec: Geoff Burgess,   Admin: Sally Ball
▲ Company Limited by Guarantee; Registered Charity
○ *F; to improve & promote the breeding of cattle, sheep, pigs,
    poultry & other livestock
● Comp - Exhib - Inf
< Assn of Show & Agricl Orgs
¶ NL - 4.

© CBD Research Ltd · Beckenham · BR3 5JS · Tel 020 8650 7745 · E-mail cbd@cbdresearch.com · www.cbdresearch.com

The Royal Society   1660
- ■ 6-9 Carlton House Terrace, LONDON, SW1Y 5AG.   (hq)
  - 020 7451 2500
  - http://www.royalsociety.org
  - Exec Dir: Dr Julie Maxton
- ▲ Registered Charity
- ○ *L, *Q; 'to recognise excellence in science; to support leading edge scientific research & its applications: to stimulate international interaction; to further the role of science, engineering & technology in society; to promote education & the public's understanding of science; to provide independent authoritative advice on matters relating to science; to encourage research into the history of science
- ● Mtgs - Res - Exhib - SG - Stat - Inf - Lib - PL - Grants for research & travel overseas - Appointments
- < Intl Coun for Science (ICSU); Eur Science Foundation (ESF)
- M 1,200 i, UK / 100 i, o'seas
- ¶ Philosophical Transactions:
  - (Series A - Mathematical & Physical Sciences.
  - (Series B - Biological Sciences); prices vary.
  - Proceedings (Series A & B); prices vary.
  - Science & Public Affairs - 1.   NL; ftm.
  - Notes & Records - 2; ftm.   Ybk.
  - Biographical Memoirs of Fellows - 1.
  - List of Fellows 1660-2000.
  - Obituaries of Fellows 1830-2000.
  - Numerous reports & papers.

Royal Society of Antiquaries of Ireland   (RSAI)   1849
- IRL 63 Merrion Sq, DUBLIN 2, Republic of Ireland.
  - 353 (1) 676 1749   fax 353 (1) 676 1749
  - http://www.rsai.ie
  - Exec Sec: Colette Ellison
- ○ *L

Royal Society of Architects in Wales   (RSAW)
- NR 4 Cathedral Rd, CARDIFF, CF11 9LJ.   (hq)
  - 029 2022 8987   fax 029 2023 0730
  - email rsaw@riba.org   http://www.architecture.com
  - Dir: Liz Walder
- ▲ Registered Charity
- Br 4
- ○ *L, *P
- ● Conf - Mtgs - Comp - LG
- < is the regional branch of the R Inst of Brit Architects (RIBA) in Wales
- ¶ Touchstone - 2; £5.

Royal Society for the encouragement of Arts, Manufactures & Commerce   (RSA)   1754
- ■ 8 John Adam St, LONDON, WC2N 6EZ.   (hq)
  - 020 7930 5115   fax 020 7839 5805
  - email general@rsa.org.uk   http://www.thersa.org
  - Chief Exec: Matthew Taylor
- ▲ Registered Charity
- Br 11; 4 o'seas
- ○ *A, *E, *L, *P; the RSA's 21st century mission is to:
  - encourage enterprise
  - move towards a zero waste society
  - develop a capable population
  - foster resilient communities
  - advance global citizenship
- Gp Examples of projects: Design directions, Environment awards forum, Intellectual property charter, Opening minds
- ● Conf - Mtgs - Res - Exhib - Comp - SG - Lib - Archive (200 years of RSA history) - Lectures
- M 20,500 i, 15 f, UK / 2,500 i, o'seas
- ¶ The RSA Jnl - 5.
  - Note: Also known as the Royal Society of Arts.

Royal Society for Asian Affairs   1901
- ■ 2 Belgrave Sq, LONDON, SW1X 8PJ.   (hq)
  - 020 7235 5122
  - http://www.rsaa.org.uk
  - Sec: Neil Porter
- ▲ Registered Charity
- ○ *L; culture & current affairs of Asian countries, from the Near East to China & Japan
- ● Conf (occasional) - Mtgs - Lib - PL
- ¶ Asian Affairs (Jnl) - 3; ftm, £55 i (£125 instns), nm.

Royal Society of British Artists
  a member of the **Federation of British Artists**

Royal Society of Chemistry   (RSC)   1980
- ■ Burlington House, Piccadilly, LONDON, W1J 0BA.   (hq)
  - 020 7437 8656   fax 020 7437 8883
  - email library@rsc.org   http://www.rsc.org
- ▲ Registered Charity
- Br 35; 8 o'seas
- ○ *L; to advance the chemical sciences
- Gp Specialist subject groups are controlled by the following divisions:
  - Analytical, Dalton, Education, Faraday, Industrial, Perkin
- ● Conf - Mtgs - ET - Exam - SG - Stat - Inf - Lib
- < Intl U of Pure & Applied Chemistry; Fedn of Eur Chemical Socs; Eur Communities Chemistry Coun
- M 34,721 i, UK / 7,714 i, o'seas
- ¶ The Analyst.   Analytical Abstracts.
  - Annual Reports on the Progress of Chemistry:
    - Section A;   Section B;   Section C.
  - Catalysts & Catalysed Reactions.   Chemical Communications.
  - Chemical Hazards in Industry.
  - Physical Chemistry Chemical Physics.
  - Chemical Society Reviews.   Chemical World.
  - Chromatography Abstracts.   CrystEngComm.
  - Dalton Transactions.   Education in Chemistry.
  - Faraday Discussions.   Geochemical Transactions.
  - Green Chemistry.   Hazards in the Office.
  - Issues in Environmental Science & Technology.
  - Jnl of Analytical Atomic Spectrometry.
  - Jnl of Environmental Monitoring.
  - Jnl of Materials Chemistry.   Lab on a Chip.
  - Laboratory Hazards Bulletin.   Mass Spectrometry Bulletin.
  - Methods in Organic Synthesis.   Natural Products Reports.
  - Natural Products Updates.   New Jnl of Chemistry.
  - Organic & Biomolecular Chemistry.   New Pesticide Outlook.
  - Photochemical & Photobiological Sciences.
  - PhysChemComm.   Russian Chemical Reviews.
  - University Chemistry Education.
    - [Reduced member prices are available for all RSC publications].

Royal Society of Edinburgh   (RSE)   1783
- NR 22-26 George St, EDINBURGH, EH2 2PQ.   (hq)
  - 0131-240 5000   fax 0131-240 5024
  - http://www.rse.org.uk
  - Gen Sec: Prof Geoffrey Boulton
- ▲ Registered Charity
- ○ *L; the achievement of learning & useful knowledge in Scotland.
  - 'The Society is unique in the UK as it encompasses all branches of learning - science, arts, letters, the professions, technology, industry & commerce'
- ● Conf - Mtgs - SG - LG - Awards research fellowship, prizes & prize lectureships - Schemes to interest young people in science & technology
- M c 1,200 i (fellows by election only)
- ¶ Transactions: Earth Sciences - 4.
  - Proceedings Section A (Mathematics) - 6.
  - RSE News - 4;   AR.   Ybk (inc LM).

Royal Society of Health
  in October 2008 merged with the Royal Institute of Public Health to form the **Royal Society for Public Health**

Royal Society of Literature   (RSL)   1820
■   Somerset House, Strand, LONDON, WC2R 1LA.   (hq)
        020 7845 4676
        email info@rslit.org   http://www.rslit.org
        Sec: Maggie Fergusson
▲   Registered Charity
○   *A; to sustain & encourage all that is perceived as best, whether
        traditional or experimental, in English letters
●   Conf - Mtgs - Comp
M   450 fellows, 420 members, 10 org
¶   News from the RSL - 1.

Royal Society of Marine Artists
        a member of the **Federation of British Artists**

Royal Society of Medicine   (RSM)   1805
■   1 Wimpole St, LONDON, W1G 0AE.   (hq)
        020 7290 2900   fax 020 7290 2909
        email membership@rsm.ac.uk   http://www.rsm.ac.uk
        Chief Exec: Ian Balmer
▲   Registered Charity
○   *L; 'for the cultivation & promotion of physic & surgery & of the
        branches of science connected with them'
Gp   Sections:
        Accident & emergency medicine, Anaesthesia, Black & ethnic
        minority health, Cardiothoracic, Catastrophes & conflict,
        Clinical, Clinical forensic & legal medicine, Clinical
        immunology & allergy, Clinical neurosciences,
        Coloproctology, Communication in healthcare, Comparative
        medicine, Dermatology, Endocrinology & diabetes,
        Epidemiology & public health, Food & health, General
        practice with primary healthcare, Geriatrics & gerontology,
        History of medicine, Hypnosis & psychosomatic medicine,
        Laryngology & rhinology, Learning disability, Lipids in clinical
        medicine, Maternity & the newborn, Medical genetics,
        Nephrology, Obstetrics & gynaecology, Occupational
        medicine, Odontology, Oncology, Open, Ophthalmology,
        Orthopaedics, Otology, Paediatrics & child health, Palliative
        care, Pathology, Pharmaceutical medicine & research, Plastic
        surgery, Psychiatry, Quality in health care, Radiology,
        Respiratory medicine, Rheumatology & rehabilitation, Sexual
        health & reproductive medicine, Sleep medicine, Sports &
        exercise medicine, Surgery, Telemedicine & e-health,
        Transplantation, United services, Urology, Vascular medicine,
        Venous
●   Conf - Mtgs - ET - Lib
M   17,000 i, UK / 4,000 i, o'seas
¶   Jnl - 12;   Calendar - 1;   AR; all ftm only.

**Royal Society of Miniature Painters, Sculptors & Gravers
(RMS)   1895**
■   119 St Dustans Rd SE22 0HD.   (exec/sp)
        020 8693 9536
        email info@royal-miniature-society.org.uk
        http://www.royal-miniature-society.org.uk
        115 Vale Rd, CHESHAM, Bucks, HP5 3HP.
            01494 772362.   (hsp)
        Exec Sec: Patricia Houchell
        Hon Sec: Helen White
▲   Registered Charity
○   *A, *P; to esteem, protect & practice the traditional 16th century
        art of miniature painting, emphasising the infinite patience
        needed for its fine techniques
●   Exhib
M   c 120 i
¶   100th Anniversary Book; £40.
        Annual Exhibition Catalogue - 1; £3.50.
        Note: is more usually known as the Royal Miniature Society.

Royal Society of Musicians of Great Britain   (RSM)   1738
§   10 Stratford Place, LONDON, W1C 1BA.   (hq)
        020 7629 6137   fax 020 7629 6137
        http://www.royalsocietyofmusicians.co.uk
        A charity to provide assistance to those working in the music
        profession and their dependents, when in need, because of
        accident, illness or old age.

Royal Society of Painter-Printmakers   (RE)   1884
■   48 Hopton St, LONDON, SE1 9JH.   (hq)
        020 7928 7521
        http://www.banksidegallery.com
        Pres: Hilary Paynter
▲   Registered Charity
○   *A; to promote printmaking through exhibitions
●   ET - Exhib - SG - Inf - Lib
M   i

Royal Society of Portrait Painters
        a member of the **Federation of British Artists**

Royal Society for the Prevention of Accidents   (RoSPA)   1916
NR   RoSPA House, 28 Calthorpe Rd, Edgbaston, BIRMINGHAM,
        B15 1RP.   (hq)
        0121-248 2000   fax 0121-248 2001
        email help@rospa.com   http://www.rospa.com
        Chief Exec: Tom Mullarkey
▲   Company Limited by Guarantee; Registered Charity
Br   3
○   *E, *K; accident prevention
●   Conf - Mtgs - ET - Exam - Exhib - Stat - Inf - Lib - PL - LG
<   La Prévention Routière Intle
M   4,528 i, f & org
¶   Safety Connections - 26.
        Occupational Safety & Health - 12.
        Safety Express - 6.   Staying Alive - 4.
        Care on the Road - 6.   Safety Education - 3.

**Royal Society for the Prevention of Cruelty to Animals
(RSPCA)   1824**
NR   Wilberforce Way, Southwater, HORSHAM, W Sussex, RH13 9RS.
        030 0123 4555   fax 030 3123 0284
        http://www.rspca.org.uk
        Chief Exec: Mark Watts
○   *K; to, by all lawful means, prevent cruelty, promote kindness &
        alleviate suffering of animals
●   Cruelty Line: 030 0123 4999 (24-hour)
M   i

Royal Society for the Promotion of Health
        in October 2008 merged with the Royal Institute of Public Health to
        form the **Royal Society for Public Health**

Royal Society for the Protection of Birds   (RSPB)   1889
NR   The Lodge, SANDY, Beds, SG19 2DL.   (hq)
        01767 680541
        http://www.rspb.org.uk
        Chief Exec: Mike Clarke
▲   Registered Charity
○   *G, *K; conservation & protection of wild birds; 'RSPB works for
        a healthy environment rich in birds & wildlife'
●   Conf - Res - Lib - PL
<   Birdlife Intl
M   1,036,869 i
¶   Birds - 4.

© CBD Research Ltd · Beckenham · BR3 5JS · Tel 020 8650 7745 · E-mail cbd@cbdresearch.com · www.cbdresearch.com

Royal Society for Public Health   (RSPH)   2008
NR   John Snow House, 59 Mansell St, LONDON, E1 8AN.   (hq)
    020 7265 7300   fax 020 7265 7301
    email info@rsph.org.uk   http://www.rsph.org.uk
    Chief Exec: Prof Richard Parish
▲   Registered Charity
○   *E, *L; to improve public health & to support the public health
    workforce
●   Conf - Exam - LG
<   Intl U for Health Promotion & Educ; Eur Public Health Alliance;
    Wld Fedn of Public Health Assns; Amer Public Health Assn
M   6,000 i
¶   Perspectives in Public Health - 6.
    Essential Food Hygiene, 3rd ed (2006).
✕   2008 (Royal Institute of Public Health
       (Royal Society (for the Promotion) of Health
        (merged in October)

Royal Society of St George   1894
■   127 Sandgate Rd, FOLKESTONE, Kent, CT20 2BH.   (hq)
    01303 241795   fax 01303 211710
    email info@rssg.u-net.com
    http://www.royalsocietyofstgeorge.com
    Chmn: James Newton
▲   Registered Charity
Br   40; c 40
○   *K, *W; 'the premier patriotic society of England, standing for
    loyalty & patriotic service to our nation & within our
    communities, with duty to our sovereign who as head of state
    transcends all party, political & personal ego & ambitions'
Gp   C'ees: Charitable trust, Events, Policy
●   Conf - Mtgs - ET - Lib - VE
<   about 40 affiliated socs o'seas
M   10,000 i
¶   England's Standard - 3; ftm, £2.50 nm.

**Royal Society of Tropical Medicine & Hygiene   (RSTM&H)
1907**
■   Northumberland House, 303-306 High Holborn, LONDON,
    WC1V 7JZ.   (hq)
    020 7405 2628
    email mail@rstmh.org   http://www.rstmh.org
▲   Registered Charity
○   *L; 'study of diseases & hygiene of man & other animals in
    warm climates'
●   Mtgs
M   827 i, UK / 2,067 i, o'seas
¶   Transactions - 12;   Ybk - 1; both ftm.

Royal Society of Ulster Architects   (RSUA)   1901
NR   2 Mount Charles, BELFAST, BT7 1NZ.   (hq)
    028 9032 3760   fax 028 9023 7313
    email info@rsua.org.uk   http://www.rsua.org.uk
▲   Registered Charity
○   *P
●   Conf - Mtgs - ET - Exhib - Comp - VE
<   R Inst Brit Architects
M   750 i
¶   Perspective (Jnl) - 6; ftm, £4.50 nm.   Ybk; ftm, £25 nm.

Royal Society of Wildlife Trusts   (RSWT)   1912
■   The Kiln, Waterside, Mather Rd, NEWARK, Notts, NG24 1WT.
    (hq)
    01636 677711   fax 01636 670001
    http://www.rswt.org
    Chief Exec: Stephanie Hilborne
▲   Registered Charity
Br   47 wildlife trusts
○   *K, *N; to promote wildlife conservation in the UK
Gp   Programmes: Community recycling & economic development;
    Social, economic & environmental development
●   Conf - Mtgs - ET - Res - Stat - Inf - LG - Land management
<   Eur Envtl Bureau; NCVO; Wildlife Link
M   c 260,000 i in 47 trusts
¶   Natural World - 3;   Watchword - 3; both ftm only.   AR.

Royal Statistical Society   (RSS)   1834
NR   12 Errol St, LONDON, EC1Y 8LX.   (hq)
    020 7638 8998
    http://www.rss.org.uk
▲   Registered Charity
○   *L

Royal Stuart Society   1926
NR   Southwell House, Egmere Rd, WALSINGHAM, NR22 6BT.
    (hsp)
    email principal-secretary@royalstuartsociety.com
    http://www.royalstuartsociety.com
    Principal Sec: Thomas FitzPatrick
▲   Un-incorporated Society
○   *G; for all who have an interest in the members of the Royal
    House of Stuart, their descendants & supporters; to promote
    research in, & further knowledge of, Stuart history; to uphold
    rightful monarchy & oppose republicanism; to arrange
    commemorations, lectures & other activities as shall advance
    these objects
●   Conf - Mtgs - Res - VE - LG - Lectures - Commemorative &
    social events
<   Intl Monarchist League
M   i
¶   NL - 3; ftm only.
    Royal Stuart Papers - 2; ftm, £3 each nm.
    Royal Stuart Review - 1; ftm, £3 each nm.

Royal Surgical Aid Society   (RSAS)   1862
§   High Broom, Stone Cross, CROWBOROUGH, East Sussex,
    TN6 3RE.   (hq)
    01892 611542   fax 01892 613014
    http://www.agecare.org.uk
    operating as AgeCare, the charity is committed to the
    advancement of excellence in residential care for older
    people & ensuring that dignity, respect & individual choice is
    paramount in the care provided

Royal Television Society   (RTS)   1927
NR   Kildare House (5th floor), 3 Dorset Rise, LONDON,
    EC4Y 8EN.   (hq)
    020 7822 2810   fax 020 7822 2811
    http://www.rts.org.uk
○   *L

Royal Town Planning Institute   (RTPI)   1914
NR   41 Botolph Lane, LONDON, EC3R 8DL.   (hq)
    020 7929 9494   fax 020 7929 9490
    http://www.rtpi.org.uk
    Chief Exec: Trudi Elliott
▲   Registered Charity
Br   12
○   *L, *P; to advance the science & art of planning, including town
    & country & spatial planning, for the benefit of the public
Gp   Planning service; Historic Environment
●   Conf - Mtgs - ET - Res - SG - Inf - Lib - LG
<   Eur Coun of Town Planners; C'wealth Assn of Planners; Urban
    Design Alliance
M   22,156 i

Royal Ulster Academy of Arts
NR   Riverhouse (9th floor), 48 High St, BELFAST, BT1 2BA.
    028 9032 0819
    http://www.Royalulsteracademy.org
    Pres: Julian Friers
○   *A; 'an artist led organisation promoting traditional &
    contemporary approaches to visual art through its exhibition
    & education programme'
●   Exhib
M   c 54 i

Royal Ulster Agricultural Society   (RUAS)   1854
- ■ The King's Hall Complex, Balmoral, BELFAST, BT9 6GW.   (hq)
  028 9066 5225   fax 028 9066 1264
  email info@kingshall.co.uk
  http://www.balmoralshow.co.uk
  Chief Exec: Colin McDonald
- ▲ Registered Charity
- ○ *F; to promote agriculture in Northern Ireland by holding
  agricultural shows & giving agricultural instruction
- ● Conf - Exhib - Organisation of the Balmoral Show (the national
  agricultural show in NI) & Royal Ulster Winter Fair
  (predominantly dairy)
- < Assn of Show & Agricl Orgs; R Agricl Soc of the C'wealth
- M 3,500 i
- ¶ NL.   Hbk.   AR.

**Royal United Kingdom Beneficent Association   (RUKBA)
1863**
- § 6 Avonmore Rd, LONDON, W14 8RL.   (hq)
  020 7605 4200   fax 020 7605 4201
  http://www.independentage.org.uk
  Operating as Independent Age, the charity tackles older
  people's financial need & loneliness by offering information,
  advice & friendship. financial difficulties & thus enable them
  to remain independent with dignity & peace of mind

**Royal United Services Institute for Defence & Security Studies
(RUSI)   1831**
- NR Whitehall, LONDON, SW1A 2ET.   (hq)
  020 7930 5854   fax 020 7321 0943
  email defence@rusi.org   http://www.rusi.org
  Dir Gen: Prof Michael Clarke
- ▲ Registered Charity
- Br Qatar; USA (Washington DC)
- ○ *L, *P, *Q; the study, analysis & debate of matters concerning
  natural & international defence & security; is a professional
  association of the Armed Forces
- Gp International security studies; Military sciences & homeland
  security & resilience
- ● Conf - Mtgs - Res - SG - Inf - Lib - LG
- M 4,500 i, 300 f, 200 org, UK / 1,000 i, 50 f, 32 org, o'seas
- ¶ RUSI Jnl - 6.   HSR Monitor - 10;
  RUSI Defence Systems - 3.   Whitehall Papers - 6.
  Newsbrief - 12.   Various other publications.

Royal Warrant Holders Association   1840
- ■ 1 Buckingham Place, London, SW1E 6HR.   (hq)
  020 7828 2268   fax 020 7828 1668
  email warrants@rwha.co.uk
  http://www.royalwarrant.org
  Sec: Richard Peck
- ○ *T; to unite in one body all who hold a Royal Warrant of
  Appointment; the maintenance of the highest standards of
  craftsmanship & service
- M c 870 f

Royal Watercolour Society   (RWS)   1804
- ■ 48 Hopton St, LONDON, SE1 9JH.   (hq)
  020 7928 7521   fax 020 7928 2820
  email info@banksidegallery.com
  http://www.royalwatercoloursociety.co.uk
  Pres: Richard Sorrell
- ▲ Registered Charity
- ○ *A; to spread the knowledge of watercolour painting; to act as
  a showcase for the best of watercolour either by members or
  annually by non-members in open competition
- Gp Friends of the RWS
- ● ET - Exhib
- M 84 i
- ¶ NL - 3; ftm only.

**Royal Welsh Agricultural Society Ltd   (Cymdeithas Amaethyddol
Frenhinol Cymru Cyf)   (RWAS)   1904**
- ■ Royal Welsh Showground, Llanelwedd, BUILTH WELLS, Powys,
  LD2 3SY.   (hq)
  01982 553683   fax 01982 553563
  email requests@rwas.co.uk   http://www.rwas.co.uk
  Chief Exec: David Walters,   Sec: Barrie Jones
- ▲ Company Limited by Guarantee
- ○ *F, *H; to promote agriculture, horticulture, forestry &
  conservation in Wales
- Gp R Welsh Show; Winter Fair; Smallholder & Garden Festival
- ● Conf - Mtgs - Exhib - Comp - Agricultural shows
- < Assn of Show & Agricl Orgs
- M 17,000 i
- ¶ Jnl - 1;   Show Programme;   Show Catalogue.

Royal Yachting Association   (RYA)   1875
- NR RYA House, Ensign Way, HAMBLE, Hants, SO31 4YA.   (hq)
  023 8060 4100   fax 023 8060 4299
  email admin@rya.org.uk   http://www.rya.org.uk
- ▲ Company Limited by Guarantee
- ○ *S; for UK sailors, windsurfers, powerboat racers, motorboaters
  & personal watercraft users
- < Boating Alliance

Royal Yachting Association Scotland   (RYAS)
- NR Caledonia House, 1 Redheughs Rigg, South Gyle,
  EDINBURGH, EH12 9DQ.
  0131-317 7388   fax 0131-317 8566
  email admin@ryascotland.org.uk
  http://www.ryascotland.org.uk
  Hon Sec: Bob Forsyth
- ○ *S; the promotion of sailing in Scotland
- ¶ NL - 12.

Royal Zoological Society of Scotland   (RZSS)   1909
- NR 134 Corstorphine Rd, EDINBURGH, EH12 6TS.   (hq)
  0131-334 9171   fax 0131-314 0384
  email info@rzss.org.uk
  http://www.edinburghzoo.org.uk
  Chief Exec: David Windmill
- ▲ Registered Charity
- ○ *L, *V; 'to promote, facilitate & encourage the study of zoology
  & kindred subjects; to foster an interest in animal life'
- Gp Edinburgh Zoo; Highland Wildlife Park
- ● Mtgs - ET - VE - Care & conservation of wildlife
- < Intl U Consvn Nature & Natural Resources; World Assn Zoos &
  Aquariums; Eur Assn Zoos & Aquaria; Brit & Ir Assn Zoos &
  Aquariums
- M 15,000 i, 85 f
- ¶ Life Links (NL) - 3; free.   Guide Book; £5.   AR; free.

RSAC Motorsport Ltd   1982
- NR PO Box 3333, GLASGOW, G20 2AX.   (hq)
  0141-946 5045   fax 0141-946 5045
  email mail@rsacmotorsport.co.uk
  http://www.rsacmotorsport.co.uk
- ▲ Company Limited by Guarantee
- ○ *S; for the development of motor sport in Scotland;
  authorisation of motoring events on the public highway in
  Scotland
- Gp Development; Event organising c'ees
- ● Mtgs - Comp - Inf
- < Motor Sports Assn UK
- M 2 f, 40 clubs
- ¶ NL - 2.   Ybk.

Rubber Stamp Manufacturers' Guild   (RSMG)
- ■ Farringdon Point, 29-35 Farringdon Rd, LONDON, EC1M 3JF.   (hq)
   0845 450 1565   fax 020 7405 7784
   email info@rsmg.org.uk   http://www.rsmg.org.uk
   Sec: Philippa Morrell
- ▲ Company Limited by Guarantee
- ○ *T; rubber stamps, daters, marking devices
- ● Conf - Mtgs - Exhib - SG - Inf
- < an affiliate of the British Office Supplies & Services Fedn
- M f

Rudolf Kempe Society
- NR 58 Waterside, STRATFORD-upon-AVON, Warks, CV37 6BA. (dir/p)
   01789 298869
- ○ *D; for those interested in the life & work of Rudolf Kempe (1910-1976), the German conductor

Rugby Fives Association   (RFA)   1927
- ■ 23 Rose St, TONBIDGE, Kent, TN9 2BN.4 6AA.
   020 7627 8303
   http://www.rfa.org.uk
   Gen Sec: Ian Fuller
- ▲ Company Limited by Guarantee
- ○ *S; governing body of the game of Rugby fives
- ● Exhib - Comp - Inf - LG
- M 600 i, 100 org
- ¶ NL - 2;   Hbk - 1;   Pocket Book - 1; all ftm only.

Rugby Football League   (RFL)   1895
- NR Red Hall, Red Hall Lane, LEEDS, W Yorks, LS17 8NB.   (hq)
   0844 477 7113   fax 0844 477 0013
   email enquiries@rfl.uk.com   http://www.rfl.uk.com
   Chief Exec: Nigel Wood
- ○ *S; governing body of rugby league football in the UK
- Gp Brit Amat Rugby League Assn
- < Rugby League Intl Fedn
- M professional clubs
- ¶ Guide - 1; ftm.

Rugby Football Union   (RFU)   1871
- NR Rugby House / Twickenham Stadium, 200 Whitton Rd, TWICKENHAM, Middx, TW2 7BA.   (hq)
   0871 222 2120
   http://www.rfu.com
   Chmn: Martin Thomas
- ○ *S; promotion, encouragement & extension of Rugby Union football
- ● Conf - Mtgs - ET - Exam - Comp - Inf - Organisation of international matches
- < Intl Rugby Football Bd
- M 2,000 clubs, 3,500 schools, UK / 70 unions & clubs, o'seas
- ¶ RFU Hbk (incl Laws of the Game).   Laws of the Game. Numerous specialised publications.

Rugby Memorabilia Society
- NR PO Box 57, HEREFORD, HR1 9DR.   (mail/address)
   http://www.rugby-memorabilia.co.uk
   21 Coulston Close, NEWPORT, NP20 2RQ. (mem/sp).
   Contact: Hon Sec,   Mem Sec: Steve Bennet
- ○ *G, *S

Rugby Players Association   (RPA)   1998
- NR Regal House, London Rd, TWICKENHAM, Middx, TW1 3QS.   (hq)
   020 8831 7930   fax 020 8891 6078
   email info@therpa.co.uk   http://www.therpa.co.uk
   Chief Exec: Damian Hopley
- ○ *U, *S; to promote & protect the interests of past, present & future professional Rugby Union players in England
- ● Mtgs
- M i
- × 2009 (October) Professional Rugby Players Association

Rural Crafts Association   (RCA)   1970
- ■ Heights Cottage, Brook Rd, Wormley, GODALMING, Surrey, GU8 5UA.   (hq)
   01428 682292   fax 01428 685969
   email ruralcraftsassociation@btinternet.com
   http://www.ruralcraftsassociation.co.uk
- ▲ Company Limited by Guarantee
- ○ *A; to encourage men & women to make & sell their work & skills; to uphold the quality of work; to encourage the growth of small craft businesses & provide employment on a long-term basis
- ● Exhib - Inf - Provision of a forum for the sale members' work
- M 600 i, UK / 15 i, o'seas
- ¶ NL - 6.   Directory - 1.

Rural & Industrial Design & Building Association Ltd   (RIDBA)   1956
- ■ 5a Maltings Business Centre, Stowupland Rd, STOWMARKET, Suffolk, IP14 5AG.   (hq)
   01449 676049   fax 01449 770028
   email secretary@ridba.org.uk   http://www.ridba.org.uk
   Nat Sec: A M Hutchinson
- ▲ Company Limited by Guarantee
- Br 4
- ○ *F, *T; an independent organisation covering all aspects of rural building, both industrial & agricultural
- Gp Construction group
- ● Conf - Mtgs - SG - Inf - VE - LG
- < Nat Specialist Contractors Coun; Advy C'ee on Roofwork
- M 240 i, 60 f, UK / 4 i, o'seas
- ¶ Countryside Building - 4; ftm, £25 nm.

Rural Shops Alliance   (RSA)   2001
- NR Egdon Hall, Lynch Lane, WEYMOUTH, Dorset, DT4 9DN.   (hq)
   01305 752044   fax 01305 772949
   email info@rural-shops-alliance.co.uk
   http://www.rural-shops-alliance.co.uk
   Chief Exec: Ken Parsons
- ▲ Company Limited by Guarantee
- ○ *T; to be the campaigning voice of the independent rural retailer; to provide practical support, particularly in terms of retail best practice
- ● Mtgs - ET - Res - SG - Inf - LG
- M 7,200 f
- ¶ Rural Retailer - 4; ftm.

Rural Theology Association   (RTA)   1981
- ■ The Vicarage, 28 Park Avenue, WITHERNSEA, E Yorks, HU19 2JU.   (hsp/b)
   01964 611462
   email secretary@rural-theology.org.uk
   http://www.rural-theology.org.uk
   Sec: Stephen Cope
- ▲ Registered Charity
- ○ *R
- ● Conf - Res - SG - Inf
- M i, f & org
- ¶ Rural Theology (Jnl) - 2; ftm, £7.50 nm.
   NL - 2;   LM - 1; both ftm.

Ruskin Society   1997
- ■ 49 Hallam St, LONDON, W1W 6JP.   (hsp)
   020 7580 1894
   email c.gamble@zen.co.uk   http://www.lancs.ac.uk/fass/centres/ruskin/links.htm
   Chmn: Robert Whelan,   Sec: Allan Webb
- ▲ Un-incorporated Society
- ○ *A; to promote an interest in the life & ideals of John Ruskin (1819-1900) & to relate his thought to the present day
- ● Mtgs - VE
- < The Ruskin Foundation (Bowland College, University of Lancaster)
- M 130 i, UK / 5 i, o'seas
- ¶ NL - irreg; ftm only.

Ruskin Society of London   1985

NR   20 Parmoor Ct, Summerfield Rd, OXFORD, OX2 7XB.   (hsp/b)
     01865 310987
     Hon Sec: D Forbes
▲   Un-incorporated Society
○   *A, *L; to promote interest in John Ruskin (1819-1900); in his
     philosophy, artistic guidance & economic recommendations;
     his connection with his contemporaries
●   Res - SG - Inf - VE
<   Brit-Italian Soc; R Soc Literature
M   c 35 i
¶   The Ruskin Gazette - 1; ftm.
✕   Ruskin Society of London

Russell Society

NR   Dunstan Lodge, South St, Letcome Regis, WANTAGE, Oxon,
     OX12 9JY.   (sec/p)
     01235 762054
     http://www.russellsoc.org
     Gen Sec: Chris Finch
○   *L; named after Sir Arthur Russell (1878-1964) mineralogist;
     the principal aims are the study, recording & conservation of
     mineralogical sites & material
●   Mtgs
M   c 500 i
¶   Jnl - irreg.   NL - 2; ftm.

Russo-British Chamber of Commerce   (RBCC)   1916

■   11 Belgrave Rd, LONDON, SW1V 1RB.   (hq)
     020 7931 6455   fax 020 7232 9736
     email infolondon@rbcc.com   http://www.rbcc.com
     BC Regent Hall (office 705), Vladimirsky Prospect 23,
     RU-191002 St PETERSBURG, Russia.
     00 (7) 812 346 50 51.
     Chief Exec: Stephen Dalziel
▲   Company Limited by Guarantee
Br   Russia
○   *C; facilitation & promotion of trade between Russia & Britain
●   Conf - Mtgs - LG
<   Russian Fedn Cham Comm & Ind
M   250 f, UK / 300 f, Russia
¶   Bulletin - 10/12.   Observer - 52; both free.

Rutland Agricultural Society   1830

NR   Manor Farm, Moor Lane - Teigh, OAKHAM, Leics, LE15 7GE.
     (hq)
     01572 787567; (mobile: 07790 293443)
     email jo@rutlandshow.fsnet.co.uk
     http://www.rutlandcountyshow.co.uk
○   *F; organise Rutland county show
●   Mtgs
M   i

Rutland Boughton Music Trust   1978

■   25 Bearton Green, HITCHIN, Herts, SG5 1UN.   (sb/p)
     01462 434318 & 0770 358 4152 (mobile)
     email boughtontrust@aol.com
     http://www.rutlandboughtonmusictrust.org.uk
     Admin: Ian Boughton
▲   Registered Charity
○   *D; to promote an interest in the composer Rutland Boughton
     (1878-1960) by encouraging performances & sponsoring
     recordings of his finest works
●   Mtgs - Exhib - Lib
M   200 i
¶   NL - 1/2; free.

Rutland Local History & Record Society   1970

NR   Rutland County Museum, Catmose St, OAKHAM, Rutland,
     LE15 6HW.   (hq)
     01572 758440   fax 01572758445
     http://www.rutlandhistory.org
     Sec: Jill Kimber
○   *L; to promote the study of the history & archaeology of the
     ancient County of Rutland

Ryeland Flock Book Society   (RFBS)   1903

■   Ty'n y Mynydd Farm, Boduan, PWLLHELI, Gwynedd,
     LL53 8PZ.   (hsp)
     01758 721898
     http://www.ryelandfbs.com
     Sec: Mrs Dot Tyne
▲   Company Limited by Guarantee
○   *B; to promote & register pedigree Ryeland sheep
●   Mtgs - Exhib - Inf
<   Nat Sheep Assn
M   300 i, UK / 7 i, o'seas
¶   NL - 4;   AR - 1; both ftm only.
     Hbk; ftm, £5.10 nm.   Flock Books - 1; ftm, £5. nm.

© CBD Research Ltd · Beckenham · BR3 5JS · Tel 020 8650 7745 · E-mail cbd@cbdresearch.com · www.cbdresearch.com

SAA - the Society for All Artists   1992
- ■ PO Box 50, NEWARK, Notts, NG23 5GY.   (hq)
  0845 8770 775
  http://www.saa.co.uk
  Chmn: John Hope-Hawkins
- ▲ Un-incorporated Society
- ○ *A; to inform, encourage & inspire all who want to paint, from the complete beginner to those whose profession depends on it
- ● Exhib - Comp - Inf
- M 41,000 i, 923 clubs, UK / 1,244 i, o'seas
- ¶ Paint (NL) - 6;   SAA Home Shopping Catalogue - 4; both ftm only.

Sabine Baring-Gould Appreciation Society   (SBGAS)   1989
- NR Hampton Dene, 4 Ash Lane. WELLS, Somerset, BA5 2LU. (mem/sp)
  http://www.sbgas.org
  Mem Sec: Bill Oke
- ○ *A; to interest people in the life & works of the novelist, hymn writer & folklorist (1834-1924)
- ● Mtgs
- M i
- ¶ NL - 3; ftm.

Sacro   1971
- NR 29 Albany St, EDINBURGH, EH1 3QN.   (hq)
  0131-624 7270   fax 0131-624 7269
  http://www.sacro.org.uk
- ○ *K, *W; to make communities safer in Scotland by reducing conflict & offending & by influencing change in criminal justice & social policy
- M i

SAD Association   (SADA)   1987
- ■ PO Box 989, STEYNING, W Sussex, BN44 3HG. (mail address)
  http://www.sada.org.uk
- ▲ Registered Charity
- ○ *W; to offer advice & support for sufferers of Seasonal Affective Disorder (SAD)
- ● Inf
- < Mind; R Coll of Psychiatry
- M c 1,500 i, UK / i, o'seas
  (Sub: £12)
- ¶ NL - 3; ftm.

Safe Home Income Plans   (SHIP)   1994
- ■ 83 Victoria St, LONDON, SW1H 0HW.   (hq)
  020 3178 4395
  email info@ship-ltd.org   http://www.ship-ltd.org
  Dir Gen: Andrea Rozario
- ▲ Company Limited by Guarantee
- ○ *T; a non-profit trade association dedicated to safe equity release plans including lifetime mortgages & home reversions
- ● Mtgs - Stat - Inf - LG
- M 21 f

Safe Speed Campaign   (SS)   2001
- ■ Coast View, Hunting Hill, TAIN, Ross-shire, IV19 1PE. (founder/p)
  01862 893030; 0779 904 5553
  Contact: Claire Armstrong
- ○ *K; campaigning for the removal of speed cameras, for improved driving standards & safe speeds set by drivers
- ● ET - Res - SG - Stat - Inf
- M 300 i, UK / 30 i, o'seas

SAFE: Struggle against Financial Exploitation   (SAFE)
- § 69 Sutton Rd, Heston, HOUNSLOW, Middx, TW5 0PN.   (hq)
  020 8630 9990
  http://www.safe-online.org
  a Parliamentary Working Group highlighting the serious issues related to cases, concerned with fraud & deception, seemingly condoned by banks & other government institutions

Safety Assessment Federation   (SAFed)   1995
- NR Unit 4, 70 South Lambeth Rd (first floor), LONDON, SW8 1RL.   (hq)
  020 7582 3208   fax 020 7735 0286
  email info@safed.co.uk   http://www.safed.co.uk
  Chief Exec: Richard Hulmes
- ▲ Company Limited by Guarantee
- ○ *T; representing companies that undertake independent safety inspection & certification of engineering & manufacturing plant & equipment
- Gp SAFed Type Approval Service (STAS)
- ● Mtgs - Stat - LG
- < Eur Confedn of Orgs for Testing, Inspection, Certification & Prevention (CEOC)
- M 13 f, UK / 2 f, o'seas
- ¶ Guidelines on/for:
  the Thorough Examination & Testing of Lifts (LG1).
  Periodicity of Examinations of Pressure Systems (PSG1).
  the Periodic Testing & Examination of Fixed Low Voltage Electrical Installations at Quarries.
  Shell Boilers - Guidelines for the Examination of:
  Longitudinal Seams of Shell Boilers.
  Welding Procedures & Welding Guidelines on Approval Testing.

Safety Pass Alliance   (SPA)
- NR Unit 3 The Court, Holywell Business Park, Northfield Rd, SOUTHAM, Warks, CV47 0FS.
  01926 817450
- ○ *T; established, in response to the needs identified in industry, to develop & extend the safety passport culture across all interested industry sectors; to provide a nationally recognised standard of health & safety training & insurance

Safety & Reliability Society   1980
- NR 1 Central Park, Northampton Rd, MANCHESTER, Lancs, M40 5BP.   (hq)
  0161-918 6663
  Chief Exec: Jacqueline Christodoulou
- Br 5
- ○ *P; to provide a forum for the exchange of information on safety & reliability engineering; to establish professional & educational standards for safety & reliability engineers

Sailing Barge Association   (SBA)
- ■ PO Box 5191, BOURNEMOUTH, Dorset, BH1 3WZ. (mail/address)
  01202 552582
  email sba@ffbs.co.uk
  http://www.sailingbargeassociation.co.uk
  Sec: Frank Morris
- ▲ Un-incorporated Society
- ○ *T; to keep Thames sailing barges working
- M 28 i, 13 f, 3 org
- ¶ NL - 4; ftm only.

Sailing Smack Association   (SSA)   1991

NR 11 Butt Lane, MALDON, Essex, CM9 5HD.   (mem/sec)
email info@ssa-uk.org   http://www.ssa-uk.org
Mem Sec: Hilary Halajko
○ *G; to protect the historical fishing vessels used in Great Britian
from the great trawlers to the oyster dredgers
< RYA

Saint

In the entries below Saint is put in full (rather than St) in order
to keep them in their correct alphabetical order in the
directory.

Saint Albans District Chamber of Commerce   1907

■ Suite 19 STANTA Business Centre, 3 Soothouse Spring,
ST ALBANS, Herts, AL3 6PF.   (hq)
01727 863054   fax 01727 851200
email lisa@stalbans-chamber.co.uk
http://www.stalbans-chamber.co.uk
▲ Company Limited by Guarantee
○ *C
● Mtgs - Conf - Inf
M 250 f
¶ Chamber Bulletin - 6;   Ybk - 1; both ftm only.

Saint Albans & Hertfordshire Architectural & Archaeological Society   (SAHAAS) 1845

■ 24 Monks Horton Way, ST ALBANS, Herts, AL4 9AF.   (hsp)
01727 851734
email admin@stalbanshistory.org
http://www.stalbanshistory.org
Sec: Bryan Hanlon
▲ Registered Charity
○ *L; to preserve, record & disseminate information about sites &
buildings of archaeological & historical importance as well as
historical documents & records
Gp Archaeology; Architecture & local history; 17th century research
● Conf - Mtgs - Res - Exhib - SG - Inf - Lib - PL - VE
< Coun Brit Archaeology; Brit Assn Local History
M 500 i, 10 org, UK / 5 i, o'seas
¶ Hertfordshire Archaeology - 1; ftm, prices vary nm.
NL - 3; ftm only.
History of the Society 1845-1995; £2 m, £3 nm.
Research Reports - irreg; prices vary.

Saint Andrew's Ambulance Association   1882

■ St Andrew's House, 48 Milton St, GLASGOW, G4 0HR.   (hq)
0141-332 4031   fax 0141-332 6582
email firstaid@staaa.org.uk   http://www.firstaid.org.uk
▲ Registered Charity
Br 11
○ *W; first aid training & services in Scotland
Gp Volunteer Corps
● ET - Services for public events
M 1,600 i
¶ First Aid Manual (8th ed); £9.90.   AR - 1; free.

Saint Andrew Society   1902

NR PO Box 84, EDINBURGH, EH3 8LG.   (mail/address)
email secretary@st-andrew.org.uk
http://www.st-andrew.org.uk
○ *K, *N; to promote the study and celebration of all things
Scottish
M i

Saint Austell District Chamber of Commerce & Industry

NR Semball House, West Hill, ST AUSTELL, Cornwall, PL25 5ET.
01726 69094
○ *C

Saint Dunstan's   1915

§ 12-14 Harcourt St, LONDON, W1H 4HD.   (hq)
020 7723 5021   fax 020 7262 6199
email enquiries@st-dunstans.co.uk
http://www.st-dunstans.co.uk
Rehabilitation, training & settlement of ex-service men &
women with very significant loss of sight.

Saint Helens Chamber Ltd   1989

■ Salisbury St, off Chalon Way, ST HELENS, Merseyside,
WA10 1FY.   (hq)
01744 742000   fax 01744 742001
email info@sthelenschamber.com
http://www.sthelenschamber.com
Chief Exec: Kath Boullen
▲ Company Limited by Guarantee
Br 3
○ *C
● Conf - Mtgs - ET - Inf - Business advice
< Brit Chams Comm; Chams Comm NW
M 1,100 f
¶ Comment - 3;   Comment Extra - 6;   AR; all free.

Saint John Ambulance   1888

NR 27 St John's Lane, LONDON, EC1M 4BU.   (hq)
0870 010 4950   fax 0870 010 4065
http://www.sja.org.uk
Chief Exec: Sue Killen
▲ Registered Charity
○ *W; to provide an effective & efficient charitable first aid service
to local communities; to provide training & products to satisfy
first aid & related health & safety needs for all of society
● Comp - ET - Ambulance & first aid services
< Grand Priory of the Order of St John of Jerusalem
M 43,000 i
¶ AR - 1.   Handbooks & manuals.

Saintpaulia & Houseplant Society

has closed

Salers Cattle Society of the United Kingdom Ltd   1986

NR Ball Green Cottage, Well Head Lane, Hubberton, HALIFAX,
W Yorks, HX6 1NN.   (hsp)
01422 839170
http://www.salers-cattle-society.co.uk
Sec: Liz Wilde
▲ Company Limited by Guarantee
○ *B; a breed originating in the southern half of the Massif
Central in the Auvergne region of France
● Conf - Mtgs - Exhib - Comp - Inf - VE
< Intl Salers Fedn; Nat Beef Assn
M 180 i
¶ Salers Jnl - 1; free.
NL - 4;   Herd Book - 1; both ftm only.

Sales Institute of Ireland

IRL 68 Merrion Sq, DUBLIN 2, Republic of Ireland.
353 (1) 662 6904   fax 353 (1) 662 6968
email info@salesinstitute.ie   http://www.salesinstitute.ie
○ *P

© CBD Research Ltd · Beckenham · BR3 5JS · Tel 020 8650 7745 · E-mail cbd@cbdresearch.com · www.cbdresearch.com

**Salisbury & District Chamber of Commerce & Industry (1912)
1912**
- ■ Brewery House (ground floor suite 1), 36 Milford St, SALISBURY, Wilts, SP1 2AP>   (hq)
  01722 322708
  email loretta@salisburychamber.co.uk
  http://www.salisburychamber.co.uk
  Chief Exec: Loretta Lupi
- ▲ Company Limited by Guarantee
- ○ *C
- ● Mtgs - ET - Exhib - Inf - VE - LG - Networking - Economic partner with local government - Lobbying
- M 350 f
- ¶ Journal Business - 4;   enewsletter - 12; both free.

Salmon Processors & Smokers Group
  a group of the **Scottish Salmon Producers' Organisation**

Salmon & Trout Association (S&TA) 1903
- ■ Fishmongers' Hall, London Bridge, LONDON, EC4R 9EL.   (hq)
  020 7283 5838   fax 020 7626 5137
  email hq@salmon-trout.org
  http://www.salmon-trout.org
  Chief Exec: Paul Knight
- ▲ Company Limited by Guarantee; Registered Charity
- ○ *S; safeguarding the salmon & trout fisheries of the UK & game fishing & angling
- M 15,000 i, 100 f, 25 org, UK / 50 i, o'seas

Salonika Campaign Society (SCS)
- NR 4 Watson's Walk, ST ALBANS, Herts, AL1 1PA.   (chmn/p)
  email chair@salonikacampaignsociety.org.uk
  http://www.salonikacampaignsociety.org.uk
  Chmn: Alan Wakefield
- ○ *G; for all interested in the campaign fought in northern Greece, Serbia & Albania in 1915-1918
- × Salonika Society

Salt Association (SA) 1970
- NR PO Box 125, KENDAL, Cumbria, LA8 8XA.   (mail)
  01539 568005   fax 01539 568999
  email info@saltinfo.com   http://www.saltsense.co.uk
- ▲ Un-incorporated Society
- ○ *T; promoting the use of salt for domestic, catering, water-softening, industrial & de-icing uses; to monitor related medical & environmental issues
- ● Mtgs - Res - Stat - Inf - LG - Promoting the use of salt
- < Eur Salt Producers Assn; Salt Inst (USA); Food & Drink Fedn
- M 6 f
- ¶ Facts on Salt; free.

Saltire Society 1936
- ■ 9 Fountain Close, 22 High St, EDINBURGH, EH1 1TF.   (hq)
  0131-556 1836   fax 0131-557 1675
  email saltire@saltiresociety.org.uk
  http://www.saltiresociety.org.uk
  Admin: Mrs Kathleen Munro
- ▲ Registered Charity (Scotland)
- Br 9
- ○ *K; preservation of the best in Scottish tradition & encouragement of development of Scottish cultural life
- Gp Arts & crafts; Civil engineering; Education; Housing design; Literature; Publications; Science
- ● Conf - Mtgs - Exhib - SG - Scots Songs
- M 1,057 i, 35 f
- ¶ AR; ftm.

Salvation Army 1865
- § 101 Newington Causeway, LONDON, SE1 6BN.   (hq)
  020 7367 4500
  http://www.salvationarmy.org.uk
  A church demonstrating its Christian principles through social welfare provision, with programmes including homeless centres, drug rehabilitation centres, schools, hospitals and medical centres.

The Samaritans 1953
- § The Upper Mill, Kingston Rd, EWELL, Surrey, KT17 2AF.   (hq)
  020 8394 8300   fax 020 8394 8301
  email admin@samaritans.org
  http://www.samaritans.org
  Chief Exec: Dominic Rudd
  Helpline: 0845 790 9090. A 24-hour-a-day service of confidential & emotional support for people experiencing feelings of distress or despair, including those which might lead to suicide.

SANE (SANE) 1986
- ■ Cityside House (1st floor), 40 Adler St, LONDON, E1 1EE. (hq)
  020 7375 1002   fax 020 7375 2162
  email info@sane.org.uk   http://www.sane.org.uk
  Chief Exec: Marjorie Wallace
- ▲ Registered Charity
- ○ *K, *W; to raise awareness of mental illness & campaign to improve services; to initiate & fund research into the causes of serious mental illness; to provide information & support to those experiencing mental health problems through its helpline, SANELINE
- Gp SANELINE: 0845 767 8000 (1800-2300 hrs, every day) Prince of Wales International Centre for SANE Research, Warneford Hospital, Oxford
- ● Res - Inf - Helpline
- M 11,000 i, 2,000 f, 1,000 org
- ¶ SANE News - NL;
  Medical Methods of Treatment;   Talking Treatments;
  Anxiety;   Depression;   Manic Depression;   Phobias;
  Obsessions;   Schizophrenia;   all free.

**Sanitary Medical Disposal Services Association (SMDSA)
1993**
- NR 111 Wollaston Rd, IRCHESTER, Northants, NN29 7DD.   (hsb)
  01933 311223   fax 01993 311223
  email info@smdsa.com   http://www.smdsa.com
  Sec: Martin Foulser
- ▲ Company Limited by Guarantee
- ○ *T; interests of companies involved in the collection & disposal of sanitary, medical & clinical waste materials
- M 37 f

**SAPERE (Society for the Advancement of Philosophical Enquiry &
Reflection in Education) (SAPERE) 1992**
- NR Innovation House, Mill St, OXFORD, OX2 0JX.   (hq)
  01865 811184   fax 01865 793165
  email admin@sapere.org.uk   http://www.sapere.org.uk
  Chmn: Paul Cleghorn
- ▲ Registered Charity
- ○ *E; to promote philosophy for children; to train teachers
- Gp Citizenship education; Education; Emotional literacy; Teaching; Thinking skills
- ● Conf - ET - Res - Inf - Teacher training - Projects - Courses
- < Intl Coun for Philosophical Inquiry with Children
- M 650 i
- ¶ NL - 4; ftm only.

Sarcoidosis & Interstitial Lung Association (SILA) 1993

- ■ c/o Dept of Respiratory Medicine, Cheyne Wing (1st floor),King's College Hospital, Denmark Hill, LONDON, SE5 9RS. (mail/address)
  020 7237 5912
  email info@sila.org.uk   http://www.sila.org.uk
  Hon Sec: Heather Walker
- ▲ Registered Charity
- ○ *W; to raise public awareness of sarcoidosis & the effect it has on sufferers, patients & friends; to give support & practical advice to those affected; to promote research & to identify those most at risk
- ● Mtgs - Res - Inf
- < Eur Assn of Patients Orgs for Sarcoidosis & Other Granulomatous Disorders (EPOS); Long-term Conditions Alliance
- M 150 i, UK / 2 i, o'seas
  (Sub: £12)
- ¶ NL - 2; ftm, (free on website).
  So You Have Sarcoidosis! by Rose Bartholomew-Thomas; ftm, large sae nm.

Satellite & Cable Broadcasters' Group (SCGB) 1983

- ■ 5 Golden Square (4th floor), LONDON, W1F 9BS. (hq)
  020 7319 4264
  Exec Dir: Victoria Read
- ▲ Un-incorporated Society
- ○ *T; for satellite & cable programme providers
- ● Mtgs - Res - LG
- < Advertising Assn; Brit Screen Advy Coun; Skillset
- M 20 f

SATIPS - Support & Training in Prep Schools (SATIPS) 1953

- ■ Cherry Trees, Stebbing, GREAT DUNMOW, Essex, CM6 3ST. (admin/p)
  01371 856823   fax 01371 856823
  http://www.satips.com
  Admin: Mrs Pat Harrison
- ▲ Company Limited by Guarantee; Registered Charity
- ○ *E; professional support for staff in independent schools
- Gp Art; Classics; Design & technology; Drama; English; Geography; History; Information & communications technology; Maths; Modern languages; Music; Personal & social education with health; Physical education; Pre-prep & nursery; Religious studies; Science; Senior management; Special needs; Years 3 & 4 teachers
- ● Conf - Mtgs - ET - Exhib - Comp - SG - Inf
- M c 100 i, c 450 schools, UK / c 10 i/schools, o'seas
- ¶ Prep School - 3; ftm, £10 yr nm. (published with the Inc Assn of Preparatory Schools).
  NL - 3; ftm only.   Broadsheets - 3; ftm, £5 each nm.
- × c1908 Society of Assistants Teaching in Preparatory Schools Ltd

Saudi-British Society 1987

- ■ 1 Gough Square, LONDON, EC4A 3DE. (mail/addrress)
  01372 842788
  email secretary@saudibritishsociety.org.uk
  http://www.saudibritishsociety.org.uk
  Hon Sec: Mrs Ionis V Thompson
- ▲ Registered Charity
- Br Saudi Arabia
- ○ *X; to foster Saudi-British relations & promote closer friendship & understanding
- ● Mtgs - VE
- M 210 i, 2 f, UK / 50 i, 8 f, o'seas

Save Britain's Heritage (SAVE)]975

- NR 70 Cowcross St, LONDON, EC1M 6EJ. (hq)
  020 7253 3500   fax 020 7253 3400
  email office@savebritainsheritage.org
  http://www.savebritainsheritage.org
  Sec: William Palin
- ▲ Registered Charity
- ○ *K; to campaign for the preservation & re-use of historic buildings; to prevent their loss through demolition or neglect
- ● Res - Exhib
- M c 350 i
  (Sub: £25)
- ¶ NL - 2; ftm only.
  Publications list on website.

Save our Building Societies (SoBS) 2000

- NR 100 Albert St, ST ALBANS, Herts, AL1 1RU. (hsp)
  01727 847370
  email info@sobs.org.uk   http://www.sobs.org.uk
  Coordinator: Bob Goodall
- ○ *K
- ¶ NL - irreg;   Press releases; both free.
  'not currently active as mutual societies are safe for the time being'

Save our Parsonages (SOP) 1994

- ■ Flat Z / 12-18 Bloomsbury St, LONDON, WC1B 3QA. (dir/p)
  020 7636 4884
  email ajsjennings@hotmail.com
  http://www.saveourparsonages.co.uk
  Dir: Anthony J S Jennings
- ▲ Un-incorporated Society
- ○ *K; a support group for historic, or traditional, parsonages remaining in church use
- ● Conf - Mtgs - Res - Inf
- < Rural Theology Assn; Engl Clergy Assn
- M 150 i, UK / 1 i, o'seas
- ¶ NL - 1; ftm, £2 nm.

Saving Teeth Awareness Campaign

- NR The Harley Street Centre for Endodontics, 121 Harley St, LONDON, W1G 6AX.
  020 7935 6393
  http://www.savingteeth.co.uk
- ○ *K; to provide information to patients who may face losing a tooth due to infection

Saxifrage Society

- ■ 64 Stevenage Rd, Walkern, STEVENAGE, Herts, SG2 7NE. (sp)
  http://www.saxifraga.org
  Sec: Richard Ball
- ○ *H; for all interested in the growing of the genus Saxifraga

SBGI (SBGI) 1905

- ■ Camden House, Warwick Rd, KENILWORTH, Warks, CV8 1TH. (hq)
  01926 513777   fax 01926 511926
  email mail@sbgi.org.uk   http://www.sbgi.org.uk
  Chief Exec: John Stiggers
- ○ *T; operates in 2 divisions - Heating & Hot Water Industry Council & SBGI Utility Networks:
  HHIC (01926 513747) &
  SGBI Utility Networks (01926 513765)
- Gp Ancillary products; Appliance manufacturers; Distribution & transmission equipment manufacturers & contractors; Gas storage operators; Gas suppliers shippers & transporters; Metering & control manufacturers; Service providers
- ● Conf - Mtgs - Exhib - Stat - Expt - LG - Provides a wide range of support services
- < Construction Products Association
- M 170 f
- ¶ Gas Business - 4.   Review of Activities - 1.
  Directory of Products & Services - 1.
- × 2008 Society of British Gas Industries

© CBD Research Ltd · Beckenham · BR3 5JS · Tel 020 8650 7745 · E-mail cbd@cbdresearch.com · www.cbdresearch.com

Scala - serving construction & architecture in local authorities (SCALA)   1973
- ■ Hillside, St Mary Church, COWBRIDGE, Glamorgan, CF71 7LT.   (hq)
  01446 771209   fax 01446 772580
  email policy@scala.org.uk   http://www.scala.org.uk
  Sec: Stephen Dodsworth
- ▲ Company Limited by Guarantee
- ○ *P; development, design & management of the public sector estate
- Gp Design forum: design & related issues; Practice forum: professional & legal issues
- ● Conf - Mtgs - ET - LG
- M 290 i
- ¶ SCALAnews (NL) - 5; ftm only.
  Building Maintenance Expenditure by Local Authorities; £60 m, £80 nm.
  Appointment of Consultants Document; £30 m, £38 nm.
- × c 2008 Society of Chief Architects of Local Authorities

Scallop Association
a member association of the **Scottish Fishermen's Federation**

Schizophrenia Ireland
since 2009 **Shine - Supporting People Affected by Mental Ill-Health**

School Journey Association   (SJA)   1911
- § 48 Cavendish Rd, LONDON, SW12 0DH.   (hq)
  020 8675 6636   fax 020 8673 8763
  http://www.sjatours.org
  A travel organisation, run by teachers and ex-teachers, promoting educational travel for school pupils to centres in the UK and Europe.

School Leaders Scotland   (SLS)   1936
- ■ East Dunbartonshire Campus of Further & Higher Education, Southbank Business Park, KIRKINTIILLOCH, G66 1NH.   (hq)
  0141-404 2792   fax 0845 308 2600
  email info@sls-scotland.org.uk
  http://www.sls-scotland.org.uk
  Gen Sec: Ken Cunningham
- ▲ Un-incorporated Society
- ○ *E, *P; professional support for members in being effective leaders in the provision of the highest quality learning for young people; to influence the educational policies of the Scottish government & local authorities
- ● Conf - ET - Exhib - LG
- < Assn of School & College Leaders (ASCL)
- M 500 i
  (Sub: £318)
- ¶ Scottish Leader - 4;   Scottish Bylines - 4; both ftm.
- × 2008 (1 August) Headteachers' Association of Scotland

School Library Association   (SLA)   1937
- ■ Unit 2 Lotmead Business Village, SWINDON, Wilts, SN4 0UY.   (hq)
  01793 791787   fax 01793 791786
  email info@sla.org.uk   http://www.sla.org.uk
  Chmn: Ginette Doyle
- ▲ Registered Charity
- Br 15
- ○ *E; promotion of development of the school library as central to literacy & the curriculum
- ● Conf - Mtgs - ET - Llb - LG
- < Intl Assn School Libraries (IASL); Intl Fedn Library Assns (IFLA)
- M 3,200 i
  (Sub: £79.50)
- ¶ The School Librarian (Jnl) - 4; ftm, £95 nm.
  Practical Guidelines.   Booklists.

Schools Music Association   (SMA)   1938
- ■ Brook House, 24 Royston St, POTTON, Beds, SG19 2LP.   (regd off)
  01767 2608159   fax 01767 261729
  email secretary@schoolsmusic.org.uk
  http://www.schoolsmusic.org.uk
  Hon Sec: Carole Lindsay-Douglas
- ▲ Registered Charity
- Br 14 regions
- ○ *D, *E; to promote the musical education of young people by supporting those who work with them
- ● Conf - Mtgs - ET - Res - SG - Inf
- < Inc Soc Musicians (ISM), Music Educ Coun (MEC)
- M i, f & org
- ¶ Bulletin - 3;   Register of Members - 1;   AR; all ftm only.

Schoolwear Association   (SA)   2006
- ■ c/o AIS, Sheward House, Cranmore Ave, Shirley, SOLIHULL, W Midlands, B90 4LF.
  0121-683 1415
  email info@schoolwearassociation.co.uk
  http://www.schoolwearassociation.co.uk
  Sec: Joyce Daly
- ○ *T; for school uniform manufacturers, suppliers and retailers
- M 200 f

Schubert Society of Britain   1957
- ■ German YMCA, 35 Craven Terrace, LONDON, W2 3EL.   (sb)
  020 7723 5684
  email u.bauer@german-ymca.org.uk
  http://www.german-ymca.org.uk/schubert.htm
  Sec: Udo Bauer
- ▲ Registered Charity
- ○ *D; for those interested in the life & works of the Austrian composer Franz Schubert (1797-1828)
- ● Schubertiades - Gives young musicians an opportunity to perform in London
- < sponsored by the German YMCA in London
- M 60 i, 5 org
- ¶ Concert programmes.

Schumacher UK
see **Doctor E F Schumacher Society**

Science, Technology, Engineering, Medicine Public Relations Association   (STEMPRA)   1992
- ■ 38 Trinity Court, 254 Gray's Inn Rd, LONDON, WC1X 8JZ.   (treas/p)
  email info@stempra.org.uk   http://www.stempra.org.uk
  Treas: Dr Robert Walker
- ▲ Un-incorporated Society
- ○ *P; for press & public relations people who work in, with, or for, all the scientific societies
- ● Conf - Mtgs - ET - VE - LG
- M 88 i
  (Sub: £15)
- ¶ NL - 4.

Scientific Alliance   2001
- NR St John's Innovation Centre, Cowley Rd, CAMBRIDGE, CB4 0WS.
  01223 421242
  email info@scientific-alliance.org
  http://www.scientific-alliance.org
  Dir: Martin Livermore
- ○ *K; a campaign aiming to bring together scientists & non-scientists to have rational discussions & debates on the challenges facing the environment today

Scientific Exploration Society Ltd (SES) 1969

- ■ Exploration Base, Motcombe, SHAFTESBURY, Dorset, SP7 9PB. (hq)
  01747 853353
  email ses@ses-explore.org http://www.ses-explore.org
  Exec Dir: Mrs Yvonne Konieczna
  Hon Pres: Col John Blashford-Snell
- ▲ Registered Charity
- Br 1 (01494 722229)
- ○ *L; to enable advancement of knowledge through the initiation & support of challenging, scientific expeditions to remote areas of the world
- ● Mtgs - Expeditions overseas
- < Just a Drop (water aid charity)
- M 400 i, 10 f, UK / 150 i, o'seas
- ¶ Sesame (Jnl) - 2; ftm only.

Scientific Instrument Society (SIS) 1983

- ■ 90 The Fairway, SOUTH RUISLIP, Middx, HA4 0SQ. (hq)
  email sis@sis.org.uk http://www.sis.org.uk
  Exec Officer: Peter Thomas
- ▲ Registered Charity
- ○ *G, *L; for all interested in scientific instruments from antiques to the latest electronic devices (collectors, antiques trade, museum staff, professional historians & enthusiasts)
- ● Conf - Mtgs - VE - Lectures
- M 250 i, UK / 350 i, o'seas
- ¶ Bulletin - 4; ftm.

Scientists for Global Responsibility (SGR) 1992

- ■ Ingles Manor, Castle Hill Avenue, FOLKESTONE, Kent, CT20 2RD. (hq)
  01303 851965
  email info@sgr.org.uk http://www.sgr.org.uk
  Exec Dir: Dr Stuart Parkinson
- ▲ Un-incorporated Society
- ○ *K, *Q; promoting ethical science & technology
- Gp Built environment & sustainable development; Climate change & energy; Emerging technologies; Security & disarmament
- ● Conf - Res - SG - Inf
- < Intl Architects Designers Planners for Social Responsibility (ARC-PEACE);Intl Network of Engrs & Scientists for Global Responsibility (INES)
- M 950 i, UK / 15 i, o'seas
- ¶ SGR NL - 2; ftm, £3.50 nm. AR; ftm only.
  Publications list available.

Scleroderma Society 1982

- ■ PO Box 581, CHICHESTER, W Sussex, PO19 9EW.
  020 7000 1925
  http://www.sclerodermasociety.co.uk
  Sec: S Holloway
- ○ *W
- M 300 i
- ¶ NL - 4; ftm only.

Scoliosis Association (UK) (SAUK) 1981

- ■ 4 Ivebury Court, 325 Latimer Rd, LONDON, W10 6RA. (hq)
  020 8964 5343 fax 020 8964 5343
  email info@sauk.org.uk http://www.sauk.org.uk
  Chmn: Stephanie Clark
- ▲ Registered Charity
- Br Regional
- ○ *W; to put people with scoliosis (curvature of the spine) in touch with each other; to make available to parents of children with scoliosis the experience of others in this field
- ● Mtgs - Inf
  Helpline: 020 8964 1166
- M 3,000 i
- ¶ Backbone - 2. NL Index. AR.
  Scoliosis Hbk. Shona's Story.
  Clothes to Suit. A Twist of Fate.

Scope 1952

- NR 6 Market Rd, LONDON, N7 9PW. (hq)
  020 7619 7100
  http://www.scope.org.uk
  Chief Exec: David Prescott
- ▲ Company Limited by Guarantee; Registered Charity
- ○ *E, *W; the disability organisation in England & Wales whose focus is people with cerebral palsy; with the aim that disabled people achieve equality, and a society in which they are valued and have the same human & civil rights as everyone else
- ● Conf - Res - Exhib - Inf - Lib - Campaigns
  Helpline: 0808 800 3333
- < Capability Scotland; Cedar Foundation (NI)
- M 208 groups
- ¶ Disability Now - 12; ftm. Reports. AR; free.
  Publications list available.

Scotch Malt Whisky Society Ltd (SMWS) 1983

- NR The Vaults, 87 Giles St, EDINBURGH, EH6 6BZ. (hq)
  0131-554 3451 fax 0131-553 1003
  email vaults@smws.com http://www.smws.co.uk
- ▲ Company Limited by Guarantee
- ○ *G; club for anyone who enjoys single malt whisky
- M i

Scotch Mule Association 1986

- NR Bogside Cottage, Ochiltree, CUMNOCK, Ayrshire, KA18 2QF. (hsp)
  01292 591821
  email scotchmule.association@yahoo.co.uk
  http://www.scotchmule.co.uk
  Sec: George Allan
- ▲ Registered Charity
- ○ *B; to promote the breed of Mule sheep
- < Nat Sheep Assn

Scotch Whisky Association (SWA) 1942

- ■ 20 Atholl Crescent, EDINBURGH, EH3 8HF. (hq)
  0131-222 9200 fax 0131-222 9237
  email contact@swa.org.uk
  http://www.scotch-whisky.org.uk
  Chief Exec: Gavin Hewitt
- ▲ Company Limited by Guarantee
- Br 2
- ○ *T; protection promotion of Scotch whisky; including legal protection, public affairs, international trade issues & promoting responsible attitudes to alcohol
- ● Conf - Mtgs - ET - Res - Exhib - Stat - Expt - Inf - VE - LG
- < Confédn Eur des Producteurs de Spiritueux (CEPS); CBI; Scot Coun Devt & Ind; Scotland Europa
- M 54 f
- ¶ Scotch Whisky: questions & answers. Distillery Map.
  Scotch at a Glance. Statistical report - 1.
  Distilleries to Visit Guide. Annual Review - 1.
  Scotch Whisky: matured to be enjoyed responsibly.

Scotland Patients Association (SPA) 2007

- ■ PO Box 2817, GLASGOW, G61 9AY. (hsp)
  0141-942 0376
  email contact@scotlandpatients.com
  http://www.scotlandpatients.com
  Exec Dir: Dr Jean McG Turner
- ▲ Company Limited by Guarantee; Registered Charity
- ○ *G,*W; advocacy for patients with concerns about healthcare
- ● Conf - Exhib - VE - LG
- < Fundraising Standards Board (FRSB); Scottish Council for Voluntary Organisations (SCVO)
- M patients in Scotland

Scotland-Russia Forum   2003
- ■ 9 South College St, EDINBURGH, EH8 9AA.   (hq)
     0131-668 3635
     email info@scotlandrussiaforum.org
     http://www.scotlandrussiaforum.org
     Chmn: Jennifer Carr
- ▲ Registered Charity
- ○ *X; to promote mutual understanding between Scotland &
     Russia & its neighbours
- ● Mtgs - ET - Exhib - Lib
- M [not stated]
- ¶ SRF Review - 2; ftm, £1.50 nm.

ScotlandIS   2000
- ■ Geddes House (suite 47), Kirkton North, LIVINGSTON,
     W Lothian, EH54 6GU.   (hq)
     01506 472200   fax 01506 472209
     email info@scotlandis.com   http://www.scotlandis.com
     Exec Dir: Polly Purvis
- ▲ Company Limited by Guarantee
- Br 2
- ○ *T; design & development of Scottish quality software, IT &
     creative technology
- Gp Aberdeen area; Advanced technologies; Quality
- ● Conf - Mtgs - ET - Res - Exhib - Comp - SG - Stat - Expt - Inf -
     LG
- M 344 f

Scots Language Society   (SLS)   1972
- ■ c/o Scottish Language Dictionaries, 25 Buccleuch Place,
     EDINBURGH, EH8 9LN.   (mail/address)
     0131-650 4149
- ▲ Registered Charity
- Br 2
- ○ *L; celebration & preservation of the Scots language
- ● Conf - Mtgs - Res - Comp - Inf
- < Scot Poetry Lib Assn
- M 350 i, 30 org, UK / 50 i, 10 org, o'seas
- ¶ Lallans (Jnl, in Scots Language) - 2; ftm, £6.50 each nm.

Scottish Adoption Association Ltd   1923
- § 161 Constitution St, Leith, EDINBURGH, EH6 7AD.   (hq)
     0131-553 5060
     email info@scottishadoption.org
     http://www.scottishadoption.org
     A charity specialising in all aspects of adoption work

Scottish Aeromodellers Association   (SAA)   1943
- NR PO Box 1621, JOHNSTONE, Renfrewshire, PA9 1YN.
      (mail add)
      http://www.saaweb.org.uk
      Admin: Ken McCormick
- ○ *G; flying radio controlled model aircraft
- ● Mtgs - Exam - Exhib - Comp - Inf - VE
- < Brit Model Flying Assn; Scottish Sports Council
- M 1,700 i in 50 clubs
- ¶ Airtime - 4; ftm.

**Scottish Agricultural Arbiters & Valuers Association   (SAAVA)
1926**
- NR c/o Anderson Strathern LLP, 1 Rutland Court, EDINBURGH,
      EH3 8EY.   (asa)
      0131-625 8025
      email secretary@saava.org.uk   http://www.saava.org.uk
      Sec: John Mitchell
- ▲ Un-incorporated Society
- ○ *F, *P; professional interests of agricultural arbiters & valuers
- Gp Agricultural arbiters & valuers
- ● Conf - Mtgs - ET - LG
- M 243 i, 5 org
- ¶ LM - 1; ftm only.

Scottish Agricultural Organisation Society Ltd   (SAOS)   1905
- NR Rural Centre, West Mains, Ingliston, NEWBRIDGE, Midlothian,
      EH28 8NZ.   (hq)
      0131-472 4100   fax 0131-472 4101
      http://www.saos.co.uk
      Chief Exec: James Graham
- ○ *F, *N, *T; to promote agriculture & rural cooperation in
     Scotland
- M 15 i (personal), 80 i (business)
- ¶ NL - 4;   AR (incl LM) - 1.

Scottish Air Rifle & Pistol Association   (SARPA)   1984
- NR [contact by email only]
      email secretary@sarpa.org.uk   http://www.sarpa.org.uk
      Sec: Erna Macfarlane
- ○ *S; the national governing body for field target air rifle shooting
     in Scotland
- ● Comp - Mtgs
- M i, clubs

Scottish Amateur Football Association   (SAFA)   1909
- NR Hampden Park, GLASGOW, G42 9DB.   (hq)
      0141-620 4550
      http://www.scottishamateurfa.co.uk
      Sec: Hugh Knapp
- ○ *S
- Gp Association football as played by amateurs: Saturday, Sunday,
     Youth, Summer
- ● Mtgs - Comp - Inf
- < Scot Football Assn
- M 65,000 i, 3,000 clubs
- ¶ Hbk - 1.   AR; ftm only.

Scottish Amateur Music Association   (SAMA)   1956
- ■ 18 Craigton Crescent, ALVA, Clackmannanshire, FK12 5DS.
     (hsp)
     email secretary@sama.org.uk   http://www.sama.org.uk
     Sec: Margaret W Simpson
     Hon Sec: Joy M Mowatt
     Week-long courses offer the amateur musician, both of school
     age and adult years, tuition and experience of string
     orchestras and wind and brass bands. Chamber music and
     recorder ensemble playing are catered for on weekend
     courses. Indigenous Scottish music is encouraged and
     promoted by the Traditional Scots Fiddle School and the
     biennial Scots Song Recital Competition.

Scottish Amateur Rowing Association
     since 2009 **Scottish Rowing**

Scottish Amateur Swimming Association Ltd   (SASA)   1888
- NR National Swimming Academy, University of Stirling, STIRLING,
      FK9 4LA.   (hq)
      01786 466520   fax 01786 466521
      email info@scottishswimming.com
      http://www.scottishswimming.com
- ▲ Company Limited by Guarantee
- Br 4
- ○ *S; governing body for swimming, masters, diving, water polo,
     open water & synchronised swimming in Scotland
- Gp Swimming: Disability, Diving, Masters, Open water,
     Synchronised
- ● Mtgs - ET - Exam - Comp - Inf
- < Fédn Intle de Natation Amateur (FINA); League Eur de
     Natation (LEN); C'wealth Games Coun for Scotland (CGCS);
     Amat Swimming Fedn of GB (ASFGB); Sportscotland; Scot
     Sports Coun (SSC)
- M 160 clubs
- ¶ Bank of Scotland Learn to Swim Syllabus; £29.99.
     Bank of Scotland Learn to Swim (Adult & Child Syllabus); £35.
     National Swimming Award Pack; £10 m.
     Note: uses trading name Scottish Swimming

Scottish Anglers National Association Ltd   (SANA)   1880
- ■ The National Game Angling Centre, The Pier, Loch Leven,
KINROSS, KY13 8UF.   (hq)
01577 861116   fax 01577 864769
email admin@sana.org.uk   http://www.sana.org.uk
Sec: Alastair Wallace
- ▲ Company Limited by Guarantee
- ○ *S; governing body for game angling in Scotland
- ● Conf - Mtgs - ET - Exam - Exhib - Comp - Inf - LG
- < FIPS Mouche; Scot Sports Assn
- M 195 i, 20 f, 420 org
(Sub: £26 i, £65 f, £35 associates)
- ¶ SANACAST (NL) - 4;   Hbk & AR;   Information leaflets;
all free.

Scottish Archery Association   (SAA)   1949
- ■ Glenearn Cottage, Edinburgh Rd, Cockenzie, PRESTONPANS,
E Lothian, EH32 0HQ.   (regd off)
01875 811344
http://www.scottisharchery.org.uk
Admin: Mrs J Dunlop
- ▲ Un-incorporated Society
- ○ *S; to promote the sport of archery incl target, field, flight, clout
& all types of bow including Olympic, compound & longbow
- M i

Scottish Assessors' Association   (SAA)   1854
- ■ c/o 235 Dumbarton Rd, CLYDEBANK, G81 4XT.   (hsb)
0141-562 1260   fax 0161-562 1255
email david.thomson@dab-vjb.gov.uk
http://www.saa.gov.uk
Sec: David C Thomson
- ▲ Un-incorporated Society
- ○ *P; to promote uniformity in operating the provisions of the
Lands Valuation (Scotland) Acts & the Representation of the
People Acts
- ● Conf - ET - Mtgs - LG
- M 94 i

Scottish Association of Community Hospitals   (SACH)
- NR 28 Dundas St, EDINBURGH, EH1 1NJ.   (hsb)
0131-557 3374
email frances@scotcommhosp.org.uk
Dir: Mrs Frances Smith
- ○ *G, *K; to develop community hospitals in Scotland
- ● Symposium
- ¶ SACH NL.

Scottish Association for Country Sports   (SACS)   1994
- ■ Netherholme, Netherburn, LARKHALL, Lanarkshire,
ML9 3DG.   (hq)
01698 885206   fax 01698 885206
email sacs@netherholm.sol.co.uk
http://www.sacs.org.uk
Dir: Ian Clark
- ▲ Un-incorporated Society
- ○ *K, *S; To represent all who take part in country sports in the
UK; to protect the environment on which they depend
- ● Conf - Mtgs - ET - Exhib - Stat - Inf - LG
- M 15,000 i
- ¶ SACS Jnl- 4; ftm..

Scottish Association of Family History Societies   (SAFHS)   1986
- NR 22 Spey Terrace, EDINBURGH, EH7 4PL.
http://www.safhs.org.uk
Sec & Treas: Kenneth Nisbet
- ▲ Registered Charity
- ○ *G, *N; to promote the study of Scottish family history,
genealogy & local history; to coordinate the work of member
societies
- ● Conf - Mtgs - ET - Res - Exhib - Comp - LG
- M 45,000 i, org, UK / 39,000, org, o'seas
- ¶ Bulletin - 2; ftm only.

Scottish Association of Geography Teachers   (SAGT)   1970
- ■ 42 Culzean Crescent, Newton Mearns, GLASGOW,
G77 5TA.   (hsp)
0141-639 8134   fax 0141-943 0216
email ssmith@boclair.e-dunbarton.sch.uk
http://www.sagt.org.uk
Gen Sec: Sheree Smith
- ▲ Registered Charity
- ○ *E, *P; geographical education
- ● Conf - Comp - VE
- < Coun for Brit Geography
- M 670 i, UK / 10 i, 20 org, o'seas
- ¶ Jnl - 1.   NL - 3.   Occasional Papers - 1.

Scottish Association of Landlords
- ■ 22 Forth St, EDINBURGH, EH1 3LH.   (hq)
0131-270 4774
email info@scottishlandlords.com
http://www.scottishlandlords.com
- ▲ Company Limited by Guarantee
- ○ *T

Scottish Association of Law Centres   (SALC)   1993
- ■ c/o Renfrewshire Law Centre, 65-71 George St, PAISLEY,
PA1 2JY.   (sb)
0141-561 7266
Sec: Jon Kiddie
- ▲ Un-incorporated Society
- ○ *P
- ● Conf - Mtgs - ET - Inf - LG
- < Advice Services Alliance
- M 8 f
- ¶ SALC Briefing - 1; free.

Scottish Association of Local Sports Councils   (SALSC)   1979
- ■ Flat 2/L - 2 Lorne St, HELENSBURGH, Dunbartonshire,
G84 8TT.   (hsb)
0753 087 1456
email oliver@salsc.org.uk   http://www.salsc.org.uk
Admin: Oliver Barsby
- ○ *N, *S
- M district sports councils in Scotland

Scottish Association for Marine Science   (SAMS)   1885
- ■ Scottish Marine Institute, OBAN, Argyllshire, PA37 1QA.   (hq)
01631 559000   fax 01631 559001
email info@sams.ac.uk   http://www.sams.ac.uk
Sec: Alison Dawson
- ▲ Company Limited by Guarantee; Registered Charity
- ○ *Q; research & education in marine science
- M i, f, org

Scottish Association of Master Bakers   (SAMB)   1891
- ■ Atholl House, 4 Torphichen St, EDINBURGH, EH3 8JQ.   (hq)
0131-229 1401   fax 0131-229 8239
http://www.samb.co.uk
Chief Exec: Alan Clarke
- ▲ Company Limited by Guarantee
- ○ *T; craft bakery trade & employers association
- Gp Industrial relations; Member services; Technical; Training &
education
- ● Conf - Mtgs - ET - Res - Comp - SG - Inf - Lib - VE - Empl - LG
- < CBI; UK Baking Ind Consultative C'ee
- M 600 i, 400 f, UK / 10 i, o'seas
- ¶ NL - c17.   Ybk.

© CBD Research Ltd · Beckenham · BR3 5JS · Tel 020 8650 7745 · E-mail cbd@cbdresearch.com · www.cbdresearch.com

Scottish Association of Meat Wholesalers (SAMW) 1977
- ■ c/o BLP Consultancy, 38 North Meggetland, EDINBURGH, EH14 1XG. (asa)
  0131-443 2180   fax 0131-443 2180
  email ianranderson@btinternet.com
  http://www.samw.org.uk
  Exec Mgr: Ian Anderson
- ▲ Company Limited by Guarantee
- ○ *T; to represent the views of members, on issues affecting the Scottish meat industry, to government & other agencies
- ● Conf - Mtgs - Expt - Inf - LG
- < Eur Livestock & Meat Trading U (UECBV)
- M 39 f
- ¶ NL - 12; ftm only.

Scottish Association for Mental Health (SAMH) 1967
- § Brunswick House, 51 Wilson St, GLASGOW, G1 1UZ. (hq)
  0141-530 1000
  http://www.samh.org.uk
  Company Sec: Patricia Aniello
  Works to support people who experience mental health problems, homelessness, addictions and other forms of social exclusion.

Scottish Association for Metals (SAM) 1974
- NR 11 Craig's Court, TORPHICHEN, W Lothian, EH48 4NU. (hsp)
  01506 634184
  email haywood.jim@btinternet.com
  http://www.scottishmetals.org
  Hon Sec: Jim Haywood
- ▲ Registered Charity
- ○ *L; the development, performance & processing of metals & related materials
- ● Conf - Mtgs - VE
- < Inst of Materials
- M 180 i

Scottish Association for Music Education (SAME)
- ■ PO Box 2658, KIRKCALDY, Fife, KY2 9BP.
  email office.same@btinternet.com
  Sec: Graeme Wilson
- ○ *E; for all who are concerned in promoting music in education

Scottish Association of Painting Craft Teachers (SAPCT) 1955
- ■ 16 Riverside Gardens, MUSSELBURGH, E Lothian, EH21 6NW. (hsp)
  0131-665 2735
  email brownjeff178@aol.com   http://www.sapct.org
  Nat Sec: Jeff Brown
- ▲ Un-incorporated Society
- ○ *P; to advance education of painting & decorating; to liaise with other relevant bodies
- ● Mtgs - ET - Exhib - Comp - VE
- < Assn Painting Craft Teachers
- M 57 i
- ¶ Artisan - 3; ftm (in liaison with the PCTA in England).

Scottish Association of Psychoanalytical Psychotherapists 1972
- NR c/o SIHR, 172 Leith Walk, EDINBURGH, EH6 5EA.
  0131-454 3240   fax 0131-454 2341
  email info@sihr.org.uk   http://www.sihr.org.uk
  Office Mgr: Pamela Sinclair
- ○ *P; 'to facillitate the growth of individuals in their sense of themselves'

Scottish Association for Public Transport (SAPT) 1970
- ■ 11 Queens Crescent, GLASGOW, G4 9BL. (hq)
  0776 038 1729
  email mail@sapt.org.uk   http://www.sapt.org.uk
  Chmn: Dr John McCormick,   Sec: Alastair Reid
- ▲ Un-incorporated Society
- Br 2
- ○ *K; to promote an integrated, socially inclusive public transport
- ● Conf - Mtgs
- < Transport 2000; Transform Scotland
- M 120 i, 20 f, 10 org
- ¶ Scottish Transport Matters - 4; ftm.
  Transport Papers; £1.   AR - 1; ftm only.

Scottish Association of Sign Language Interpreters (SASLI) 1981
- NR Baltic Chambers (suite 404-408), 50 Wellington St, GLASGOW, G2 6HJ. (hq)
  0141-248 8159   fax 0141-221 1693
  email mail@sasli.org.uk   http://www.sasli.org.uk
  Dir: Iain Whyte
- ▲ Registered Charity
- ○ *P
- ● Conf - Mtgs - ET - Exam - Stat
- < Eur Forum of Sign Language Interpreters
- M 38 i

Scottish Association of Speech & Drama Adjudicators (SASDA)
- NR 104 Argyle Rd, SALTCOATS, Ayrshire, KA21 5NE.
  01294 552807   fax 01294 559274
  email admin@sasda.org.uk   http://www.sasda.org.uk
  Admin: Jim Gibson
- ○ *P

Scottish Association of Spiritual Healers (SASH) 1980
- ■ 46 Wood Place, Eliburn South, LIVINGSTON, W Lothian, EH54 6SZ. (hsb)
  01506 411801
  email maureennic@aol.com
  http://www.scottishhealers.bravehost.com
  Pres: Maureen Nicoll
- ▲ Registered Charity
- Br 10
- ○ *P, *W; to provide spiritual & hands-on healing
- ● Mtgs - ET - Exam - SG
- < Confedn of Healers Org; Alliance of Healers Assns
- M 149 i
  (Sub: £12, £10 concessions)

Scottish Association for the Study of Offending (SASO)
- NR Association Management Solutions, PO Box 2781, GLASGOW, G61 3YL.
  0141-560 4092
  email icameron@a-m-s-online.com
  http://www.sastudyoffending.org.uk
  Admin: Irene Cameron
- Br 10
- ○ *K, *L; to study & research the causes of delinquency & crime & its treatment & prevention
- < Mtgs - Res
- M i

Scottish Association of Teachers of History (SATH) 1968
- NR Ayr Academy Secondary School, 7 Fort St, AYR, S Ayrshire, KA7 1HX. (sb)
  http://www.sath.org.uk
  Contact: The Secretary
- ○ *P
- ● Conf - Mtgs - ET - LG
- M i & org

Scottish Association of Young Farmers Clubs (SAYFC) 1938

NR Young Farmers Centre, Ingliston, EDINBURGH, EH28 8NE. (hq)
0131-333 2445   fax 0131-333 2488
email natsec@sayfc.org   http://www.sayfc.org
○ *F, *Y

Scottish Athletics Ltd 2001

NR Caledonia House, South Gyle, EDINBURGH, EH12 9DQ.   (hq)
0131-539 7320   fax 0131-539 7321
email admin@scottishathletics.org.uk
http://www.scottishathletics.org.uk
Chief Exec: Nigel Holl
▲ Company Limited by Guarantee
○ *S; governing body for athletics in Scotland (incl track & field, road running, cross country & hill running)
Gp Athletes; Coaches; Officials
● Mtgs
< UK Athletics
M 150 clubs
¶ PB (NL) - 4.   AR - 1.

Scottish Auto Cycle Union (SACU) 1913

NR 28 West Main St, UPHALL, W Lothian, EH52 5DW.   (hq)
01506 858354   fax 01506 855792
email office@sacu.co.uk   http://www.sacu.co.uk
Sec: Robert Young
▲ Company Limited by Guarantee
○ *S; governing for motorcycle sport in Scotland

Scottish Badminton Union (SBU) 1901

■ Cockburn Centre, 40 Bogmoor Place, GLASGOW, G51 4TQ. (hq)
0141-445 1218   fax 0141-425 1218
email enquiries@badmintonscotland.org.uk
http://www.badmintonscotland.org.uk
Chief Exec: Anne Smillie
○ *S
Gp SBU coaching c'ee; Scottish Schools Badminton Union
● Mtgs - Comp
< Intl Badminton Fedn; Eur Badminton U
M c 12,000 i, 560 clubs
¶ Scottish Badminton - 4 (each season); free to clubs, £6 nm.
Note: uses the trading name Badminton Scotland

Scottish Basketball Association

Scottish Basketball Association
since 2007 **Basketball Scotland Ltd**

Scottish Basketmakers' Circle

NR Cardean Cottage, Boarhills, FIFE, KY16 8PP.   (mem/sec)
http://www.scottishbasketmakerscircle.org
Mem Sec: Lynne Mathews
○ *G; to promote basketmaking in Scotland
● Mtgs - Exhib
M i
¶ NL - 4.

Scottish Beekeepers Association (SBA) 1912

■ 20 Lennox Row, EDINBURGH, EH5 3JW.   (gensec/p)
0131-552 3439
email secretary@scottishbeekeepers.org.uk
http://www.scottishbeekeepers.org.uk
Gen Sec: Mrs Bron Wright
▲ Registered Charity
Br 40
○ *G; to promote beekeeping within Scotland
● Conf - Mtgs - ET - Exam - Res - Exhib - Comp - SG - Stat - Inf - Lib - VE - LG
< Coun of Nat Beekeepers Assns (CONBA)
M 1,200 i, UK / 40 i, o'seas
¶ The Scottish Beekeeper - 12; ftm only.

Scottish Beer & Pub Association (SBPA) 1906

NR 6 St Colme St, EDINBURGH, EH3 6AD.
0131-225 4681
http://www.scottishpubs.co.uk
Chief Exec: Patrick Browne
○ *T
< Brit Beer & Pub Assn
M 13 f

Scottish Borders Chamber of Commerce

NR 19 Buccleugh St, HAWICK, Roxburghshire, TD9 0HL.
01573 410607
email enquiries@borderschamber.org.uk
http://www.borderschamber.org.uk
Mgr: Sally Scott Aiton
○ *C
< Scot Chams Comm

Scottish Bowling Association

Scottish Bowling Association
merged in 2010 with the Scottish Women's Bowling Association to form **Bowls Scotland**

Scottish Brass Band Association (SBBA)

■ 71 Tantallon Drive, PAISLEY, Renfrewshire, PA2 9HS.   (sp)
http://www.sbba.org.uk
Sec: Tom Allan
▲ Registered Charity
○ *D; the development of brass bands in Scotland
● Mtgs - ET - Res - Exhib - Comp
< Eur Brass Band Assn
> Nat Youth Brass Bands of Scotland; Scot Borders Brass Band Assn; Nthn Counties Brass Band Assn
M 2,500 i, 80 brass bands, 15 youth bands
¶ SBBA Ybk - 1; £10 m.

Scottish Building Contractors Association (SBCA) 1869

NR 4 Woodside Place, GLASGOW, G3 7QF.   (hq)
0141-353 5050   fax 0141-332 2928
email sbca@btinternet.com
http://www.scottishcontractors.com
Pres: Craig McKillop
▲ Un-incorporated Society
○ *T
● Conf - Mtgs - Inf - VE
< Scot Construction Industry Gp
M 21 i, 37 f
¶ NL - 4;   AR; both ftm only.   LM; free.

Scottish Building Federation

■ Crichton House, 4 Crichton's Close, Holyrood, EDINBURGH, EH8 8DT.   (hq)
0131-556 8866   fax 0131-558 5247
email info@scottish-building.co.uk
http://www.scottish-building.co.uk
Chief Exec: Michael Levack
Br 17 local assns
○ *N, *T
● Conf - Mtgs - ET - Exhib - SG - Inf - Empl
< Construction Confedn
M c 800 f
¶ Magazine - 4;   Bulletin - 36;   Directory; all ftm;   AR.

© CBD Research Ltd · Beckenham · BR3 5JS · Tel 020 8650 7745 · E-mail cbd@cbdresearch.com · www.cbdresearch.com

Scottish Business in the Community (SBC) 1982

NR Livingstone House (1st floor east), 43a Discovery Terrace,
Heriot-Watt Research Park, EDINBURGH, EH14 4AP. (hq)
0131-451 1100 fax 0131-451 1127
email info@sbcscot.com   http://www.sbcscot.com
Chief Exec: Samantha Barber

▲ Company Limited by Guarantee; Registered Charity
○ *K, *T; to support, broker & challenge businesses to continually
improve their positive impact on society to ensure a
successful, sustainable economy & environment

Gp Community; Environment; Marketplace; Workplace
● Conf - ET - LG
< Business in the Community
M 80 f
¶ NL - 3;   LM;   AR - 1; all free.

Scottish Campaign for National Parks (SCNP) 1990

■ The Barony, Glebe Rd, KILBIRNIE, Ayrshire, KA25 6HX.
(chmn/p)
01505 682447 fax 0870 051 6410
email info@scnp.org.uk   http://www.scnp.org.uk
Chmn: Robert Maund,   Sec: Kate Walsham

▲ Registered Charity
○ *F, *K; to promote the establishment of National Parks in
Scotland with adequate powers & finance to ensure good
management of the landscape, tourism & the local economy
● Conf - ET - Res - Exhib - Inf - PL - LG
< Intl U for the Consvn of Nature; Campaign for National Parks:
Scot Environment Link
> Assn for the Protection of Rural Scotland; Camping & Caravan
Club; Friends of Loch Lomond & the Trossachs; Ramblers
Assn; Save Your Regional Park Campaign
M 71 i, 22 org, UK / 4 i, o'seas
Subs: £10 (single), £16 couple, UK / varies, o'seas
¶ NL - 4;   AR & Accounts; both free.
✕ 2008 Scottish Council for National Parks

Scottish Canoe Association (SCA) 1939

■ Caledonia House, South Gyle, EDINBURGH, EH12 9DQ. (hq)
0131-317 7314 fax 0131-317 7319
email general.office@canoescotland.com
http://www.canoescotland.com
Admin: Mrs Margaret Winter

○ *S; governing body of the sport of canoeing in Scotland
Gp Access; Canoe polo; Canoe sailing; Canoe surf; Coaching;
Marathon racing; Slalom; Sprint; Touring; White water racing
● Mtgs - ET - Comp - Inf - Coaching - Tests, proficiency
certificates & instructors' awards
< Brit Canoe U; C'wealth Canoe Fedn; Intl Canoe Fedn
M 2,200 i & org
¶ Scottish Paddler - 4; ftm.   Ybk.

Scottish Carriage Driving Association

NR Woodfield, Balmullo, ST ANDREWS, Fife, KY16 0AN.
0771 414 3243
email secretary@scda.co.uk   http://www.scda.co.uk
Sec: Simon Sanders
○ *S; carriage driving

Scottish Cashmere Producers Association
closed 2009

Scottish Catholic Historical Association (SCHA) 1950

NR c/o Dr A Newby, School of Divinity History & Philosophy,
Crombie Annexe, King's College, University of Aberdeen,
OLD ABERDEEN, AB24 3FX. (sb)
email a.newby@abdn.ac.uk
http://www.scottishcatholicarchives.org.uk
Sec: Dr Andrew G Newby

▲ Registered Charity
○ *L; to study the history of the Catholic church in Scotland
● Conf - Res
M 270 i, c 80 org, UK / c 30 i, o'seas
¶ Innes Review - 2.

Scottish Chambers of Commerce 1946

NR 30 George Square, GLASGOW, G2 1EQ. (hq)
0141-204 8316 fax 0141-204 8371
email admin@scottishchambers.org.uk
http://www.scottishchambers.org.uk
Chief Exec: Liz Cameron

▲ Un-incorporated Society
Br 20 chams
○ *C, *N; business support
● Conf - Mtgs - LG
< Scotland Europa
M 9,000 f
¶ Business Survey - 4; ftm, varies nm.   AR - 1; free.
National Directory - 1.

Scottish Childminding Association (SCMA) 1990

NR 7 Melville Terrace, STIRLING, FK8 2ND. (hq)
01786 445377 fax 01786 449062
email information@childminding.org
http://www.childminding.org
Chief Exec: Maggie Simpson

▲ Company Limited by Guarantee; Registered Charity
○ *P; 'to promote quality childminding; building confident
children within a family childcare experience'
● Conf - Mtgs - ET - Exhib - Stat - Inf - LG
< Intl Family Day Care Org
M i
¶ Childminding - 4;   AR; both free.

Scottish Chiropractic Association

NR 1 Chisholm Avenue, BISHOPTON, Renfrewshire, PA7 5JH.
0141-404 0260
email dmin@sca-chiropractic.org
http://www.sca-chiropractic.org
○ *P

Scottish Church History Society (SCHS) 1922

■ 16 Murrayburn Park, EDINBURGH, EH14 2PX. (hsp)
0131-442 3772
email virginia.russell@btopenworld.com
http://www.schs.org.uk
Hon Sec: Miss Virginia Russell

▲ Registered Charity
○ *L; to promote the study of the history of the Church in Scotland
& to publish the results
● Conf - Mtgs
M 175 i, 40 libraries, UK / 45 i, 45 libraries, o'seas
¶ Records of the Scottish Church History Society - 1; £15 ($32).

Scottish Clay Target Association Ltd (SCTA) 2000

■ PO Box 8168, DALRY, Ayrshire, KA25 9AA. (mail add)
0844 335 1698
http://www.scta.co.uk
Admin: Ian Dawson

▲ Company Limited by Guarantee
○ *S; 'to promote the art of clay target shooting in Scotland at all
levels, from novice to international'
● ET - Comp - Organised series of shoots & selection shoots for
team selection for national team
< Intl Coun Clay Pigeon Shooting GB & I; Brit Intl Clay Target
Shooting Fedn; Scot Target Shooting Fedn
M 1,080 i
¶ NL - 4;   Annual Bulletin; both ftm only.

Scottish Committee of Optometrists
since 2010 **Acuity**

Scottish Community Drama Association   (SCDA)   1926
- ■ Stirling Enterprise Park (suite 88), Springkerse, STIRLING,
  FK7 7RP.   (hq)
  01786 4400772
  email headquarters@scda.org.uk
  http://www.scda.org.uk
  Contact: The National Chair
- ▲ Un-incorporated Society
- Br   28
- ○ *G, *N; to act as the umbrella body for encouragement of
  amateur & community theatre in Scotland
- Gp Festivals; Playwriting; Youth activities
- ● Conf - Mtgs - ET - Exhib - Comp - Inf - Lib - LG - Theatre
  Maker
- < Intl Amat Theatre Assn (IATA); Intl Theatre Exchange (ITE); Indep
  Theatre Coun; Scot Coun for Voluntary Orgs (SCVO)
- M   700 i, 175 org
      (Sub: £25 i, £55 org)
- ¶ Scene Magazine - 4; free.

Scottish Consortium for Learning Disability
- NR   Adelphi Centre (Room 16), 12 Commercial Rd, GLASGOW,
  G5 0PQ.
  0141 418 5420   fax 0141 429 1142
- ○ *N
- M   13 org

Scottish Contaminated Land Forum   (SCLF)   1997
- ■ 7 Aberdour Place, Inverskip, GREENOCK, Renfreshire,
  PA16 0HZ.   (sb)
  email admin@sclf.co.uk   http://www.sclf.co.uk
  Sec: Alison McKay
- ▲ Un-incorporated Society
- ○ *G; to promote the effective & sustainable rehabilitation of
  contaminated land in Scotland & elsewhere
- ● Mtgs - ET - SG

Scottish Corn Trade Association Ltd   (SCTA)   1969
- ■ 77/2 Hanover St, EDINBURGH, EH2 1EE.   (asa)
  0131-225 7773   fax 0131-226 4448
- ▲ Company Limited by Guarantee
- ○ *T; promotion of the interests of the grain trade
- ● Mtgs - LG - Annual dinner
- < UKASTA; GAFTA
- M   80 f

SCOTTISH COUNCIL ...
  For details of bodies whose names begin thus, other than those
  entered below, see the companion volume **'Councils, Committees
  & Boards' (Introduction paragraph 6)**

Scottish Council on Deafness   (SCOD)   1927
- ■ Central Chambers (suite 62/1st floor), 93 Hope St, GLASGOW,
  G2 6LD.   (hq)
  0141-248 2474 & 0141-248 2477 (text)   fax 0141-
  248 2479
  email admin@scod.org.uk   http://www.scod.org.uk
  Dir: Lilian Lawson
- ▲ Registered Charity
- ○ *N, *W; to act on behalf of agencies & organisations working
  with deaf people in Scotland by forming strategic alliances,
  developing policy initiatives & using them to improve the
  human & civil rights of deaf people living in Scotland
- ● Conf - Mtgs - ET - Res - Inf - LG
- M   80 org
- ¶ NL - 4; ftm only.   Bulletin - 12; ftm, £5 yr nm.
  Directory; online only.   AR - 1; ftm.

Scottish Council for Development & Industry   (SCDI)   1931
- ■ 1 Cadogan Square, GLASGOW, G2 7HF.   (hq)
  0141-243 2667
  email enquiries@scdi.org.uk   http://www.scdi.org.uk
  Chief Exec: Dr Lesley Sawers
- ▲ Company Limited by Guarantee
- Br   4
- ○ *K; an independent, non-political membership network, which
  strengthens Scotland's competitiveness by influencing
  government policies to encourage sustainable, economic
  prosperity; membership is from manufacturing & service
  sectors, universities & colleges, trade associations, local
  enterprise companies, the churches & trade unions
- Gp Business information; Education/industry links; Public policy;
  Trade development
- ● Conf - Mtgs - Res - Stat - Expt - Inf - LG
- M   1,300 f
- ¶ Pointer - 10; £45 m, £90 nm.
  Indicator - 6; ftm only.   AR; free.
  Annual Survey of Scottish Export Sales - 1; ftm only.

Scottish Council for National Parks
  since 2008 **Scottish Campaign for National Parks**

Scottish Council for Single Homeless   (SCSH)   1974
- ■ Stanhope House (suite B), 12 Stanhope Place, EDINBURGH,
  EH12 5HH.   (hq)
  0131-337 8243
  email admin@scsh.org1uk   http://www.scsh.org.uk
  Dir: Robert Aldridge
- ▲ Registered Charity
- ○ *K, *W; to promote awareness about the causes, nature &
  extent of single homelessness; to identify means of
  preventing & alleviating homelessness & to collaborate with
  all appropriate agencies
- ● Conf - Mtgs - ET - Res - Exhib - Inf - Lib - LG
- < Fédn Eur des Assns Nationaux Travaillant avec les Sans-
  Abris (FEANTSA); Shelter; Age Concern Scotland
- M   90 i, 200 org, UK / 5 org, o'seas
- ¶ Briefing Papers; free.
  Publications list available.

Scottish Council for Voluntary Organisations   (SCVO)   1943
- ■ 15 Mansfield Place, EDINBURGH, EH3 6BB.   (hq)
  0131-556 3882   fax 0131-556 0279
  email enquiries@scvo.org.uk   http://www.scvo.org.uk
  Chief Exec: Martin Sime
- ▲ Company Limited by Guarantee; Registered Charity
- Br   3
- ○ *N, *W; an independent organisation working at a national
  level to provide services to voluntary & community groups
  throughout Scotland
- Gp Equal project strengthening the economy; IT services; New deal;
  Parliamentary information & advisory service; Policy officers
  network; Social inclusion partnership team; Voluntary
  management development unit
- ● Conf - Mtgs - ET - Res - Stat - Inf - Lib - LG
- < Scotland Europa; Civicus
- M   1,200 i & org
- ¶ Third Force News & Inform (jt information pack) - 48;
  ftm, £110 nm.
  Work packs;   Handbooks;   Directories;   AR.
  Publications list available.

Scottish Countryside Rangers' Association   (SCRA)   1974
- NR   Pitcairn Centre, Moidart Drive, Coul, GLENROTHES, Fife,
  KY7 6ET.
  http://www.scra-online.co.uk
- ▲ Un-incorporated Society
- ○ *P; countryside ranger services in Scotland
- M   i & f

© CBD Research Ltd · Beckenham · BR3 5JS · Tel 020 8650 7745 · E-mail cbd@cbdresearch.com · www.cbdresearch.com

Scottish Covenanter Memorials Association   1966
- ■ Lochnoran House, AUCHINLECK, Ayrshire, KA18 3JW.   (hsp)
     01290 425594
     email info@covenanter.org.uk
     http://www.covenanter.org.uk
     Hon Sec: Dane Love
- ▲ Registered Charity
- ○ *G; to preserve monuments & memorials to the Scottish
     Covenanters (mainly 1638-1689); to erect new memorials to
     commemorate Covenanters or events
- ● Lib - Annual mtg - Annual dinner - Irregular religious services
     (Conventicles)
- M 360 i, UK / 40 i, o'seas
- ¶ NL - 3; ftm only.

Scottish Crofting Federation   (SCF)   1986
- NR Unit 26 Kyle Industrial Estate, KYLE of LOCHALSH, IV40 8AX.
     (hq)
     01599 530005
     email hq@crofting.org   http://www.crofting.org.uk
     Chief Exec: Patrick Krause
- ▲ Un-incorporated Society
- ○ *F; to develop, promote & encourage crofting
- M i & f
- ¶ The Crofter - 4.
- × Scottish Crofting Foundation

Scottish Croquet Association   (SCA)   1974
- NR 2 (2F3) St Leonard's Bank, EDINBURGH, EH8 9SQ.
     (matchsec/p)
     0131-667 4216
     http://www.scottishcroquet.org.uk
     Match Sec: Fergus McInnes
- ▲ Un-incorporated Society
- ○ *S; promotion, development & organisation of croquet in
     Scotland
- ● ET - Comp
- < Wld Croquet Fedn; Eur Croquet Fedn
- M 130 i, 9 org
- ¶ Bulletin - 4.   Ybk.

Scottish Cycling   (SC)   1953
- NR Caledonia House, 1 Redheughs Rigg, South Gyle,
     EDINBURGH, EH12 9DQ.   (hq)
     0131-317 9704   fax 0131-339 9201
     email info@scottishcycling.com
     http://www.scuonline.org
- ▲ Company Limited by Guarantee
- ○ *S; governing body for cycle sport in Scotland
- Gp Coaching; Cycling; Mountain biking; Sports
- ● ET - Comp - Inf - Coaching & leadership - Scottish Mountain
     Bike Leader Award (SMBLA) Scheme
- < Brit Cycling Fedn; Sportscotland
- M c 2,4000 i, 100 clubs
- ¶ NL - 12; free.   Hbk - 1.   AR.
     Note: Scottish Cycling is the trading name of the Scottish
     Cyclists' Union

Scottish Daily Newspaper Society
     2010 merged with the Scottish Newspaper Publishers Association to
     form the **Scottish Newspaper Society**

Scottish Dance Teachers Alliance   (SDTA)   1934
- NR 101 Park Rd, GLASGOW, G4 9JE.   (hq)
     0141-339 8944   fax 0141-357 4994
     email info@sdta.co.uk   http://www.sdta.co.uk
     Pres: Mrs Betty Sutherland
- ○ *D, *P; for professional teachers of dancing: ballet, tap,
     modern, jazz, highland, Scottish national, sequence,
     ballroom, Latin American, line-dancing, baton twirling &
     cheerleading, disco; rock'n'roll
- ● Conf - Mtgs - ET - Exam - Comp - SG - Expt - Inf - Provision of
     examinations in all forms of [above] dancing
- < Scot Official Bd of Highland Dancing (SOBHD); Brit Dance
     Coun (BDC); Coun for Dance Educl Trg (CDET)
- M 500 i, UK / 450 i, o'seas
- ¶ Alliance News - 4;   AR; both ftm only.

Scottish Darts Association   (SDA)   1971
- NR 4 Burns Avenue, GLENROTHES, Fife, KY6 1EB.   (hsp)
     01592 757864
     email fifedarts@talk21.com
     http://www.scottishdarts.com
     Sec: Cliff Murray
- ○ *S

Scottish Decorators Federation   (SDF)   1878
- ■ Pavilion 2, Castlecraig Business Park, STIRLING, FK7 7SH.
     (hq)
     01786 448838   fax 01786 450541
     http://www.scottishdecorators.co.uk
     Chief Exec: Ian H Rogers
- ○ *T
- ● Conf - Mtgs - ET - Comp - Inf - Lib - Empl - LG
- M f
- ¶ NL - 4; free.   Ybk - 1; ftm.
     Wage agreement information - 1; free.

Scottish Disability Sport   (SDS)   1963
- ■ Caledonia House, South Gyle, EDINBURGH, EH12 9DQ.   (hq)
     0131-317 1130   fax 0131-317 1075
     email admin@scottishdisabilitysport.com
     http://www.scottishdisabilitysport.com
     Chief Exec: Gavin MacLeod,   Admin: Caroline Lyon
- ▲ Company Limited by Guarantee; Registered Charity
- Br 15 (Scotland)
- ○ *S, *W; national governing & coordinating body of all sports for
     all people with a disability in Scotland
- Gp C'ees: Athletes, Local development; Medical, Sports
- ● Conf - Mtgs - ET - Res - Comp - SG - Inf - LG
- M 5,500 i, 8 org
- ¶ Changing with the Times (NL) - 3;   AR; both free.

Scottish Dowsing Association
     reported to us as having closed - we should appreciate
     confirmation.

Scottish Ecological Design Association   (SEDA)   1991
- NR Rose Cottage, BIGGAR, Lanarks, ML12 6LZ.   (regd off)
     http://www.seda.uk.net
     Chmn: Robin Baker,   Admin: Sydny Brogan
- ▲ Company Limited by Guarantee; Registered Charity
- ○ *K; to promote the design of communities, environments,
     projects, systems, services, materials & products which
     enhance the quality of life of and are not harmful to living
     species and planetary ecology
- ● Mtgs - Res - VE
- M 350 i
- ¶ Jnl - 3; ftm.

Scottish Economic Society   (SES)   1954
NR   School of Accounting & Economics, Napier University,
     Craiglockhart Campus, EDINBURGH. EH14 1DJ.   (sec/b)
     http://www.scotecsoc.org
     Sec: Dr Linda Juleff
▲   Registered Charity
○   *L; to promote the study & teaching of economics on the widest
    basis, in accordance with the Scottish tradition of political
    economy inspired by Adam Smith, & to provide a forum for
    the discussion of Scottish economic problems & their
    relationship to the political & social life of Scotland
¶   Scottish Journal of Political Economy - 5.

Scottish Educational Research Association   (SERA)   1971
NR   Charteris5.05 Moray House School of Education, University of
     Edinburgh, Holyrood Rd, EDINBURGH, EH8 8AQ.   (hsb)
     0131-652 6403
     email zoe.williamson@ed.ac.uk   http://www.sera.ac.uk
     Admin: Dr Zoë Williamson
▲   Registered Charity
○   *E; to promote educational research; to debate about the
    contribution that research can make to enhanced practice

Scottish Egg Producer Retailers Association   (SEPRA)   1970
■   11 Meadowbank, Station Rd, Polmont, FALKIRK, FK2 0UG.
    (sp)
    01324 715337
    email dennissurgenor@compuserve.com
    http://www.scottisheggs.com
    Sec: Dennis Surgenor
▲   Un-incorporated Society
○   *T; to keep Scottish egg producers abreast of local & national
    demand & pricing of eggs, at retail & wholesale level
●   Conf - Mtgs - Stat - LG
M   143 i,
¶   Market Report - 52.

Scottish Employers' Council for the Clay Industries   (SECCI)
    the Council no longer meets

Scottish Engineering   1991
■   105 West George St, GLASGOW, G2 1QL.   (hq)
    0141-221 3181   fax 0141-204 1202
    email consult@scottishengineering.org.uk
    http://www.scottishengineering.org.uk
    Chief Exec: Dr Peter Hughes
○   *T; employers' association
Gp Representation;Employment information & statistics;
    Employment law; Health & safety advice &/or consultation;
    Industrial tribunal advice & representation; Personnel
    procedures & practices; Representation; Supervisor &
    management development
●   Mtgs - ET - SG - Stat - Inf - Lib - VE - Empl - LG - Forums &
    seminars
M   350 f
¶   Quarterly Review.   Hbk.   Information sheets.   AR.

Scottish Environment Link   1987
NR   2 Grosvenor House, Shore Road, PERTH, PH2 8BD.   (hq)
     01738 630804   fax 01738 643290
     email enquiries@scotlink.org   http://www.scotlink.org
     Chief Officer: Jen Anderson
▲   Registered Charity
○   *N; 'voluntary organisations working together to care for &
    improve Scotland's heritage for people & nature'
M   31 org
¶   The Link (NL) - 4.

**Scottish Environmental & Outdoor Education Centres Association
Ltd   (SOEC)   1947**
§   Loaningdale House, Carwood Rd, BIGGAR, Lanarks,
    ML12 6LX.   (hq)
    01899 221115   fax 01899 220644
    http://www.soec.org.uk
    Responsible for 4 Scottish Outdoor Education Centres in
    Scotland it is the country's largest provider of residential
    outdoor education

Scottish Environmental Services Association   (SESA)
NR   Excel House (2nd floor), 30 Semple St, EDINBURGH,
     EH3 8BL.   (hq)
     0131-220 1000
     Note: is a sectional association of the Environmental Services
     Association.

Scottish Equestrian Association
   2010 (6 May) rebranded as **Horsescotland**

**Scottish Esperanto Association   (Esperanto-Asocio de
Skotlando)   (SEA)   1908**
■   Tigh na Cnoc, Ardgay Hill, ARDGAY, Sutherland, IV24 3DH.
    (treas/p)
    01698 263199
    email secretary@skotlando.org   http://www.skotlando.org
    Treas: David Hannah
▲   Registered Charity
Br 2 clubs
○   *E, *K; to promote & teach Esperanto
●   Conf - Mtgs - ET - Exam - Res - Exhib - SG - Inf - Lib - LG
<   Wld Esperanto Assn; Esperanto Assn of Britain
M   100 i, 10 org, UK / 10 i, o'seas
¶   Scottish Esperanto Bulletin - 2; ftm.
    Esperanto en Skotlando - 2; ftm.

Scottish Federation of Baton Twirling
NR   55 Springkell Ave, Maxwell Park, GLASGOW, G41 4DP.
     0141-424 0109
     email secretary@sfbt.org.uk   http://www.sfbt.org.uk
     Sec: Tony Pratt
○   *S
<   Confédn Eur de Twirling Bâton

Scottish Federation for Coarse Angling   (SFCA)
NR   The Cottage, 6 The Pleasance, HALBEATH, Fife, KY12 0TT.
     (mem/sp)
     http://www.sfca.co.uk
     Contact: Membership Secretary
○   *S; the governing body for coarse angling in Scotland
M   8 clubs

Scottish Federation of Housing Associations Ltd   (SFHA)   1976
NR   Pegasus House, 375 West George St, GLASGOW, G2 4LW.
     (hq)
     0141-332 8113   fax 0141-332 9684
     email sfha@sfha.co.uk   http://www.sfha.co.uk
     Chief Exec: Mary Taylor
▲   Company Limited by Guarantee
○   *N; advisory & representative body for housing associations in
    Scotland
Gp Teams: Consultancy, Policy & practice, Training & events
    Lintel Trust (charitable)
●   Conf - Mtgs - ET - Exhib - Inf - LG
<   Comité Européen Co-ordination de l'Habitat Social
    (CECODHAS Housing Europe)
M   164 housing assns
¶   Federation Focus (Jnl) - 10.
    Federation Digest - 10.
    SFHA Directory - 1.   SFHA Diary - 1.

© CBD Research Ltd · Beckenham · BR3 5JS · Tel 020 8650 7745 · E-mail cbd@cbdresearch.com · www.cbdresearch.com

Scottish Federation of Meat Traders Associations   (SFMTA) 1917
- 8-10 Needless Rd, PERTH, PH2 0JW.   (hq)
  01738 637472   fax 01738 441059
  email info@sfmta.co.uk   http://www.sfmta.co.uk
  Chief Exec: Douglas Scott
▲ Company Limited by Guarantee
○ *T; for independent meat retailers in Scotland
  In 2000 the SFMTA Training organisation became Food Training Services, which in 2003 became Scottish Meat Training
● Conf - Mtgs - ET - Exam - Exhib - Comp - Inf - Empl - LG
M 420 f
¶ NL - 12; ftm only.

Scottish Federation of Sea Anglers   (SFSA)   1960
NR Unit 62 Evans Business Centre, Mitchelston Drive, Mitchelston Industrial Estate, KIRKCALDY, KY1 3NB.   (hq)
  01592 657520   fax 01592 657520
  http://www.fishsea.co.uk
  Sec/Admin: Mrs Margaret McCallum
▲ Un-incorporated Society
○ *S; governing body of the sport of sea angling in Scotland
Gp Coaching; Competitions; Conservation
● Mtgs - ET - Comp - Inf - LG
< Sportscotland
M 155 i, 30 clubs
¶ NL - 4; ftm.   SFSA Hbk - 1; ftm, £4 nm.

Scottish Fencing
NR Airthrey Castle, University of Stirling, STIRLING, FK9 4LA.   (regd off)
  01786 466248
  email admin@scottish-fencing.com
  http://www.scottish-fencing.com
  Exec Admin: Lorraine Rose
○ *S; the governing body in Scotland for the sport of fencing
M c 750 i

Scottish Fiddle Society   2002
NR 28 Arnott Gardens, EDINBURGH, EH14 2LB.
  0131-443 6631
  email watson-alan@tiscali.co.uk
  http://www.thescottishfiddlesociety.org.uk
  Admin: Alan Watson
○ *D; to support, enrich and encourage a burgeoning Scottish fiddle music scene

Scottish Field Archery Association   (SFAA)   1966
  Sec: Gordon Jackson
▲ Company Limited by Guarantee
○ *S; 'to foster & encourage good fellowship among those who take up the sport of IFAA based field archery'
● Mtgs - ET - Comp
< Intl Field Archery Assn
M 250 i, 12 clubs
¶ NL - 4; ftm only.

Scottish Field Studies Association Ltd
  has closed

Scottish Fishermen's Federation   (SFF)   1973
NR 24 Rubislaw Terrace, ABERDEEN, AB10 1XE.   (hq)
  01224 646944   fax 01224 647058
  email sff@sff.co.uk   http://www.sff.co.uk
  Chief Exec: Bertie Armstrong
▲ Un-incorporated Society
○ *N, *T; to preserve & promote the collective interests of fishermen's associations
Gp Anglo-Scottish Fishermen's Association; Fishermen's Association (Scotland) Ltd; Scallop Association; Scottish Pelagic Fishermen's Association; Scottish White Fish Producer's Association
< Assn Nat Fishing Orgs EEC (EUROPECHE)
M 8 org

Scottish Fishermen's Organisation   (SFO)   1973
NR 601 Queensferry Rd, EDINBURGH, EH4 6EA.
  0131-339 7972   fax 0131-339 6662
  email info@scottishfishermen.co.uk
  http://www.scottishfishermen.co.uk
  Chief Exec: Iain McSween
○ *N

Scottish Food & Drink Federation   (SFDF)   1999
NR 4a Torphichen St, EDINBURGH, EH3 8JQ.   (hq)
  0131-229 9415   fax 0131-229 9407
  email sfdf@sfdf.org.uk   http://www.sfdf.org.uk
  Dir: Flora McLean
○ *T; to represent the interests of the food & drink manufacturing industry in Scotland
● Conf - Mtgs - Inf - LG
< Food & Drink Fedn; Scot Civic Forum
M 75 f
¶ NL - 12;   AR; both ftm.

Scottish Food Trades Association   (SFTA)   1889
NR c/o Accredited Training, 40 Rhindmu Rd, GLASGOW, G34 9HY.   (hsb)
  0141-773 2100
  Sec: Mrs Mari McTear
▲ Un-incorporated Society
Br 4
○ *T; the networking platform for the Scottish food industry
● Mtgs
M 100 i, 50 f

Scottish Football Association Ltd   (SFA)   1873
- Hampden Park, GLASGOW, G42 9AY.   (hq)
  0141-616 6000   fax 0141-616 6001
  email info@scottishfa.co.uk   http://www.scottishfa.co.uk
  Chief Exec: Stewart Regan
▲ Company Limited by Guarantee
○ *S; to promote, foster & develop in all its branches the game of Association Football in Scotland
● Conf - Mtgs - ET - Exam - Comp - Stat - Inf
< FIFA; UEFA
M 77 clubs
¶ Hbk; ftm, £10 nm (£2p&p).
  Laws of the Game; ftm, £4 nm.   AR; ftm, £5 nm.

Scottish Football League   (SFL)   1890
- ■ The National Stadium, Hampden Park, GLASGOW, G42 9EB.   (hq)
  0141-620 4160   fax 0141-620 4161
  email info@scottishfootballleague.com
  http://www.scottishfootballleague.com
  Chief Exec: David Longmuir
- ▲ Un-incorporated Body
- ○ *S; to promote & extend the game of Association Football in Scotland
- ● Conf - Mtgs - ET - Res - Comp - Stat - Inf - Provision of League championships & League cup competitions
- < Intl Football League Bd; Scot Football Assn
- M 30 clubs
- ¶ Hbk (incl list of clubs & referees) - 1; £10. Fixture Book - 1; £3.

Scottish Freshwater Group   (SFG)
- ■ Dr Laurence Carvalho, Centre for Ecology & Hydrology, Edinburgh Bush Estate, PENICUIK, EH26 0QB.   (sb)
  0131-445 4343
  http://www.ceh.ac.uk/sci_programmes/water/scottish_freshwater_group.html
  Sec: Dr Laurence Carvalho
- ○ *P; an informal forum for the exchange of information on current issues & research related to Scottish freshwaters
- ● Conf - Mtgs
- M 350 i, 20 org

Scottish Gaelic Texts Society   (SGTS)   1934
- ■ c/o McLeish Carswell, 29 St Vincent Place, GLASGOW, G1 2DT.   (hsb)
  0141-248 4134   fax 0141-226 3118
  http://www.sgts.org.uk
  Hon Sec: Miss A F Wilson
- ▲ Registered Charity
- ○ *L; to promote the publication of texts in the Scottish Gaelic language, accompanied by introductions, English translations & glossaries
- ● Res
- M 120 i, 10 org, UK / 20 i, 10 org, o'seas
- ¶ Various publications.

Scottish Gamekeepers Association   (SGA)   1997
- NR Arran House, Arran Rd, PERTH, PH1 3DZ.   (hsp)
  01738 587515   fax 01738 587516
  email info@bscottishgamekeepers.co.uk
  http://www.scottishgamekeepers.co.uk
  Mem Sec: Sheila Beattie
- ▲ Un-incorporated Society
- ○ *P; to promote the work of gamekeepers, stalkers, ghillies & rangers; to educate them in good practice; to promote their welfare
- ● Conf - Mtgs - ET - Res - Comp - Inf - VE - LG
- M 2,500 i, 500 f, 25 org, UK / 500 i, o'seas
- ¶ Scottish Gamekeeper (Jnl) - 4.

Scottish Games Association
  see **Scottish Highland Games Association**

Scottish Genealogy Society   1953
- NR 15 Victoria Terrace, EDINBURGH, EH1 2JL.
  0131-220 3677   fax 0131-220 3677
  email enquiries@scottishgenealogy.com
  http://www.scottishgenealogy.com
  Hon Sec: Ken Nisbet
- ▲ Registered Charity
- ○ *L, *Q; to promote research into Scottish family history
- ● Mtgs - Inf - Lib
- M i, org
- ¶ The Scottish Genealogist - 4; ftm.
  Lists of pre 1855 Monumental Inscriptions.

Scottish Glass Society   1979
- ■ PO Box 29329, GLASGOW, G20 2BA.
  email sgssecretary@hotmail.co.uk
  http://www.scottishglasssociety.com
  Hon Sec: Siobhan Healy
- ▲ Registered Charity
- ○ *A, *G; to champion the work of glass artists in Scotland; to promote the development of the art and craftsmanship of glass making in its many variations
- M c 180 i

Scottish Gliding Union Ltd   (SGU)   1934
- ■ The Scottish Gliding Centre, Portmoak Airfield, Scotlandwell, by KINROSS, KY13 9JJ.   (hq)
  01592 840543
  http://www.portmoak.force9.co.uk
  Hon Sec: Bruce Marshall,   Chmn: John Williams
- ▲ Company Limited by Guarantee
- ○ *S; provision & promotion of gliding activities to members & the public
- Gp Disabled facilities; Flying for disabled
- ● ET (training of glider pilots) - Trial flight option for members of the public
- < Brit Gliding Assn
- M 250 i
  Note: uses the trading name The Scottish Gliding Centre.

Scottish Golf Union Ltd   (SGU)   1920
- NR The Duke's, ST ANDREWS, Fife, KY16 8NX.   (hq)
  01334 466477   fax 01334 462361
  email sgu@scottishgolf.org   http://www.scottishgolf.org
  Chief Exec: Hamish Grey
- ○ *S; governing body of amateur golf in Scotland
- ● Mtgs - ET - Comp - VE - LG
- < Intl Golf Fedn; Eur Golf Assn; Coun of Nat Golf Us
- > Scot Golf Envt Gp (wholly owned subsidiary)
- M 260,000 i, 650 clubs in Scotland
- ¶ Scottish Golfer - 8;   Ybk; both free.
- × 2004 (February) Scottish Golf Union

Scottish Grocers' Federation   (SGF)   1918
- ■ 222-224 Queensferry Rd, EDINBURGH, EH4 2BN.   (hq)
  0131-343 3300   fax 0131-343 6147
  email info@scotgrocersfed.co.uk
  http://www.scottishshop.org.uk
  Chief Exec: John Drummond
- ▲ Company Limited by Guarantee
- ○ *T; for independent convenience retailers in Scotland
- ● Conf - Mtgs - ET - SG - Stat - Inf - LG
- < Intl Fedn of Grocers' Assns (IFGA)
- M 600 f
- ¶ Retail News - 12;   Retail Outlook (Ybk) - 1.

Scottish Gymnastics Association   (SGA)   1890
- NR Airthrey Castle, University of Stirling, STIRLINF, FK9 4LA.   (hq)
  01786 446232
  email info@scottishgymnastics.com
  http://www.scottishgymnastics.com
  Chief Exec: Caitriona O'Shea
- ▲ Company Limited by Guarantee
- ○ *S
- M 7,000 i

Scottish Handball Association   (SHA)
- NR National Sports Centre Inverclyde, Burnside Rd, LARGS, N Ayrshire, KA30 8RW.   (sb)
  01475 687804
  http://www.scottishhandball.com
- ○ *S

© CBD Research Ltd · Beckenham · BR3 5JS · Tel 020 8650 7745 · E-mail cbd@cbdresearch.com · www.cbdresearch.com

Scottish Hang Gliding & Paragliding Federation (SHPF) 1973
NR 27 CAmus Avenue, EDINBURGH, EH10 6QY.   (hsp)
       0131-445 5249
       email bob@shpf.co.uk   http://www.shpf.co.uk
       Chmn: Mike Jardine,   Sec: Naomi Miskin
○   *S; to promote the sports of hang gliding & paragliding in
       Scotland
M   i & clubs
¶   The Flying Scot (NL) - 4.

Scottish Hazards Campaign Group   1993
NR 113 Kingsknowe Rd North, EDINBURGH, EH14 2DQ.   (hsp)
       0131-477 0817
       email info@scottishhazards.co.uk
       http://www.scottishhazards.co.uk
       Sec: Kathy Jenkins
▲   Un-incorporated Society
○   *K; to campaign for improved worker health & safety
       throughout Scotland
●   Conf - Mtgs - ET - Res
M   30 i, 10 org

Scottish Hereford Breeders' Association   1950
■   Cowbog, KELSO, Roxburghshire, TD5 8EH.   (hsp)
       email cowbog@aol.com   http://www.herefordcattle.org
       Sec: R B Wilson
○   *B; Hereford cattle in Scotland

Scottish Highland Games Association   (SHGA)   1946
NR 54 Crawford Gardens, ST ANDREWS, Fife, KY16 8XQ.   (sp)
       01334 476305
       http://www.shga.co.uk
       Sec: Ian Grieve
▲   Company Limited by Guarantee
○   *S; to encourage & foster the highest standards of ethics &
       performance in open athletics & traditional Highland games
●   Mtgs - Comp
M   65 full members, 5 associate members, 4 committees
¶   Ybk.

Scottish History Society   (SHS)   1886
■   School of History, St Katharine's Lodge, The Scores,
       ST ANDREWS, Fife, KY16 9AL.   (hsb)
       01337 831996
       email kcs7@st-andrews.ac.uk
       http://www.scottishhistorysociety.org
       Hon Sec: Dr Katie Stevenson
▲   Registered Charity
○   *L; 'to discover & print, in a series of annual volumes,
       unpublished documents illustrating the history of Scotland'
●   Conf - Mtgs - ET - Res - Comp
<   R Histl Soc (Brit Nat C'ee)
M   380 i, 175 f
       (Sub: £20 i, £25 f)
¶   Annual Volume (back copies available; prices vary).

Scottish Hockey Union   (SHU)   1989
■   589 Lanark Rd, EDINBURGH, EH14 5DA.   (hq)
       0131-453 9070   fax 0131-453 9079
       email info@scottish-hockey.org.uk
       http://www.scottish-hockey.org.uk
       Chief Exec: Robert Heatly
▲   Company Limited by Guarantee
○   *S; the national governing body for the sport of hockey in
       Scotland
Gp Youth Commission
●   Mtgs - ET - Exam - Exhib - Comp - Inf - LG
<   Intl Hockey Fedn (FIH); Eur Hockey Fedn (EHF)
M   6,000 i, 165 clubs
¶   Hockey Scotland - 2; free.
       Note: uses title Scottish Hockey

Scottish Homing Union   (SHU)
NR 386A Stewarton St, WISHAW, Lanarks, Ml2 8DU.   (hq)
       01698 768939
       email enquiries@shuonline.co.uk
       http://www.shuonline.co.uk
       Sec: Linda Brooks
○   *N, *S; the governing body for members who race & show
       racing pigeons in Scotland

Scottish Huntington's Association   1989
NR St James Business Centre (suite 135), Linwood Rd, PAISLEY,
       PA3 3AT.   (hq)
       0141-848 0308   fax 0141-887 6199
       email sha-admin@hdscotland.org
       http://www.hdscotland.org
       Sec: Ann Carruthers
▲   Company Limited by Guarantee; Registered Charity
Br 9
○   *W; to help sufferers of Huntington's disease & their families; to
       help people at risk of developing the disease
Gp Professional interest
●   Conf - Mtgs - ET - Res - Inf - Lib
<   Intl Huntington's Disease Assn
M   1,000 i
¶   Books:
       A Physician's Guide to the Management of Huntington's
          Disease.
       Behavioural Problems in Huntington's Disease.
       Huntington's Disease: What's it all about? A guide for young
          people (aged 14+).
       Other publications available.

Scottish Ice Skating Association
       has closed

Scottish Icelandic Horse Association
       company dissolved 4 March 2011

Scottish Independent Advocacy Alliance   (SIAA)   2002
■   Melrose House, 69a George St, EDINBURGH, EH2 2JG.   (hq)
       0131-260 5380   fax 0131-260 5381
       email enquiry@siaa.org.uk   http://www.siaa.org.uk
       Dir: Shaben Begum
▲   Company Limited by Guarantee; Registered Charity
○   *N; to promote, support & defend independent advocacy
       throughout Scotland
●   Conf - Mtgs - ET - Res - Stat - Inf - LG
M   100 org
       (Sub: £100)
¶   About Advocacy (Jnl) - 4;   AR - 1.

Scottish Indoor Bowling Association   (SIBA)   1936
■   1 Nursery Lane, MAUCHLINE, Ayrshire, KA5 6EH.   (hsp)
       01290 551067   fax 01290 551067
       email gordon.siba@o2mail.co.uk
       http://www.bowls-siba.co.uk
       Hon Sec: Gordon Woods
▲   Un-incorporated Society
○   *S
●   Mtgs - Comp
<   Wld Indoor Bowls Coun; Brit Isles Indoor Bowls Coun
M   60,000 i (Scotland only)
¶   Bowls International - 12.
       World Bowls - 12.   Scots Bowler - 12.
✕   2001 [merged] Scottish Women's Indoor Bowling Association

Scottish Industrial Heritage Society (SIHS) 1984
NR 58 Kenningknowes Rd, STIRLING, FK7 9JG. (sp)
   http://www.sihs.co.uk
   Contact: C D Bates
▲ Company Limited by Guarantee; Registered Charity
○ *L; the study of the history & development of industry in
   Scotland
● Conf - Mtgs - Inf - VE
< Assn for Indl Archaeology
M 120 i, 10 f, 5 org, UK / 1 i, 1 f, o'seas
¶ SIHS Review (NL) - 2.
   Guide to Scottish Industrial Heritage (Hbk).

Scottish Inland Waterways Association (SIWA) 1971
■ 5 Calder Rd, Bellsquarry, LIVINGSTON, W Lothian,
   EH54 9AA. (hsp)
   01506 417685
   http://www.siwa.org.uk
   Sec: Ann Street
▲ Registered Charity
○ *G, *K, *N; to preserve & rehabilitate Scottish inland
   waterways; to coordinate local canal societies; to promote
   the use of waterways for leisure & commercial purposes
● Mtgs - Exhib - Inf - VE
< Inland Waterways Assn
M 137 i, 18 org

Scottish Intensive Care Society (SICS) 1991
NR ICU, Aberdeen Royal Infirmary, Foresterhill Rd, ABERDEEN,
   AB25 2ZN. (hsb)
   http://www.scottishintensivecare.org.uk
   Hon Sec: Dr Roxanne Bloomfield
▲ Registered Society
○ *P

Scottish Ju-Jitsu Association (SJJA) 1979
NR 93 Douglas St, DUNDEE, DD1 5AZ. (hq)
   01382 201601
   http://www.scottishjujit.su
▲ Un-incorporated Society
Br 20; Spain, USA
○ *S; governing body for the sport in Scotland
Gp Ju Jitsu (un-armed combat); Ko-Ryu (traditional schoools of
   combat)
● Conf - Mtgs - ET - Exam - Res - Exhib - Comp - Inf - Lib - VE -
   LG
< Nippon Jujitsu & Kobudo Intl; Amer Self-Defence Assn; Hon Tai
   Yoshin Ryu; Scot Sports Coun; Sportscotland; Scot Sports
   Assn; Fedn of Scot School Sports Assn
M 800 i, 20 org, UK / 150 i, 3 org, o'seas
¶ Samuri NL - 6;   Scottish Jujitsu - 4; both ftm only.

Scottish Justices Association (SJA) 2007
■ c/o 3 The Steading, Smallholm Farm, Hightae, LOCKERBIE,
   DG11 1JY. (hsp)
   01387 810911
   email secretary@scottishjustices.org
   http://www.scottishjustices.org
   Sec: Johan Findlay
▲ Un-incorporated Society
○ *N, *P; to assist Justices of the Peace in Scotland in performing
   their judicial duties
● Mtgs - LG
< C'wealth Magistrates & Justices Assn
M 400+ i
¶ The Scottish Justice - 2/4; ftm only.

Scottish Kennel Club (SKC) 1881
NR Paterson House, Eskmills Park, Station Rd, MUSSELBURGH,
   E Lothian, EH21 7PQ. (hq)
   0131-665 3920 (Mon-Fri 1000-1600)   fax 0131-
   653 6937
   email info@scottishkennelclub.org
   http://www.scottishkennelclub.org
   Sec: Mrs Myra Orr
○ *B; to promote dogs, canine education & responsible dog
   ownership
M i

** Scottish Labour History Society
   Organisation lost: see Introduction paragraph 3

Scottish Ladies' Golfing Association (SLGA) 1904
NR The Den, 2 Dundee Rd, PERTH, PH2 7DW. (regd/office)
   01738 442357   fax 01738 442380
   email secretary@slga.co.uk   http://www.slga.co.uk
○ *S
● ET - Comp - Inf
< Ladies' Golf U
M 38,000 i, 420 org
¶ Ybk; £3.

Scottish Land & Estates 1906
■ Stuart House, Eskmills, MUSSELBURGH, E Lothian,
   EH21 7PB. (hq)
   0131-653 5400   fax 0131-653 5401
   email info@scottishlandandestates.co.uk
   http://www.scottishlandandestates.co.uk
   Chief Exec: Douglas McAdam
▲ Company Limited by Guarantee
Br 5
○ *F; 'working for: high standards of land management; the
   owners of rural land in Scotland; the rural economy & those
   who depend upon it'
● Conf - Mtgs - Inf - VE - LG
< Eur Landowners Org (ELO)
M 2,600 i, 200 f
¶ Land Business - 6; ftm only.   NL.   Ybk.
× 2011 Scottish Rural Property & Business Association

Scottish Language Dictionaries (SLD) 2002
■ 25 Buccleugh Place, EDINBURGH, EH8 9LN. (hq)
   0131-650 4149   fax 0131-650 4149
   email mail@scotsdictionaries.org.uk
   http://www.scotsdictionaries.org.uk
   Dir: Dr Christine Robinson
▲ Company Limited by Guarantee; Registered Charity
○ *L, *Q; 'we research Scots language as it is spoken & used in
   writing, & use our results to update the nation's record of one
   of Scotland's indigenous languages; we also support the use
   of Scots in the community & promote it internationally as part
   of Scottish culture'
● Res - Inf
M 135 i, 4 org, UK / 6 i, o'seas
¶ NL - 2.
   Compact Scottish National Dictionary (hardback) £157.50 m,
   £175 nm / (paper) £108 m, £120 nm.
   Concise Scots Dictionary (hardback) £22.50 m, £25 nm /
   (paper) £13.50 m, £14.99 nm.
   Scots Thesaurus (paper) £13.50 m, £14.99 nm.
   Pocket Scots Dictionary (paper); £5.40 m, £5.99 nm.
   Essential Scots Dictionary (paper); £7.20 m, £7.99 nm.
   Dictionary of the Scots Language (www.dsl.ac.uk); free.

© CBD Research Ltd · Beckenham · BR3 5JS · Tel 020 8650 7745 · E-mail cbd@cbdresearch.com · www.cbdresearch.com

Scottish Law Agents Society   (SLAS)   1884
- ■ 166 Buchanan St, GLASGOW, G1 2LW.   (sb)
  0141-332 3536   fax 0141-353 3819
  email secretary@slas.co.uk   http://www.slas.co.uk
  Sec: Michael Sheridan
- ▲ Un-incorporated Society
- ○ *P; for Scottish solicitors; central legal practice, legal policy & research
- Gp Conveyancing; Legal aid; Legal education & training; Litigation
- ● Conf - Mtgs - ET - Res - SG - Stat - Inf - Lib - VE - LG
- M 2,000 i, 30 org
  (Sub: £70 i, £40 org)
- ¶ The Scottish Law Gazette - 6; ftm, £10 nm.
  Memorandum Book - 1; ftm, £5 nm.

Scottish Legal Action Group   (SCOLAG)   1975
- NR 148 Muirdrum Ave, GLASGOW, G52 3AP.   (admin)
  056 0072 7138   fax 056 0072 7138
  email admin@scolag.org   http://www.scolag.org
  Convenor: Robert Sutherland
- ▲ Company Limited by Guarantee; Registered Charity
- ○ *P; to explain the law; to promote the use of legal services (& changes in the law & legal system) so as to benefit disadvantaged members of society & promote equal access to justice
- ● Conf - LG
- M [not stated]
- ¶ SCOLAG (Jnl) - 12.

Scottish Lettercutters Association   (SLA)   2001
- NR 2 West Park Place, EDINBURGH, EH11 2DP.   (hsp)
  0131-466 5194
  http://www.scottishlettercutters.co.uk
  Hon Sec: Jane Raven
- ○ *P

Scottish Library Association
a division of **CILIP**

Scottish Licensed Trade Association   (SLTA)   1880
- NR 21 Lansdowne Crescent (Suite 6), EDINBURGH, EH12 5EH.
  (hq)
  0131-535 1062   fax 0131-535 1069
  email enquiries@theslta.co.uk   http://www.theslta.co.uk
  Sec: Colin Wilkinson
- ▲ Un-incorporated Society
- Br 7
- ○ *T; represents all sections of the licensed trade in Scotland
- ● Conf - Mtgs - ET - Exam - Exhib - Inf - LG
- < UK & Ireland Licensed Tr Assn
- M 3,000 i, 40 f
- ¶ Scottish Licensee (Jnl) - 4; free.

** Scottish Local Authority Network of Physical Education
Organisation lost: see Introduction paragraph 3

Scottish Local History Forum
- ■ PO Box 103, 12 South Bridge, EDINBURGH, EH1 1DD.   (hq)
  http://www.slhf.org
  Admin: Doris Williamson
- ○ *N; for Scottish local history societies & local historians

Scottish Massage Therapists Organisation Ltd   (SMTO)   1992
- ■ 70 Lochside Rd, Bridge of Don, ABERDEEN, AB23 8QW.   (hsb)
  01224 822960   fax 01224 822960
  email smto@scotmass.co.uk
  http://www.scotmass.co.uk
  Chmn: Maggie Brooks-Carter,   Sec: Nicola Brooks
- ▲ Company Limited by Guarantee
- ○ *M, *P; for massage therapists, remedial & sports massage therapists, advanced remedial massage therapists, manipulative therapists, on-site massage therapists, clinical aromatherapists & reflexologists in the UK, primarily in Scotland
- ● Conf - Mtgs - ET - Res - Exhib - Inf - Continuing professional development for members
- < Gen Coun for Massage Therapies
- > Black Isle Complementary Therapies; Scottish Massage Schools Ltd; Western School of Massage
- M 500 i, 5 org, UK / 5 i, o'seas
- ¶ On the Massage Scene - 3; ftm, £2.50 nm.
  Directory of therapists.

Scottish Master Slaters & Roof Tilers Association   (SMSRTA)
- NR c/o Scottish Building Federation, Crichton House, 4 Crichton's Close - Holyrood, EDINBURGH, EH8 8DT.
  0131-556 8866   fax 0131-558 5247
  Sec: Ian McNaughton
- ○ *T
- M 21 f

Scottish Master Wrights & Builders Association   (SMWBA) 1885
- NR Blairtummock Lodge, Campsie Glen, GLASGOW, G66 7AR.
  (asa)
  01360 770583
  http://www.smwba.org.uk
  Sec/Treas: David Milliken
- ○ *T
- M i

Scottish Medievalists: the Colloquium for Scottish Medieval & Renaissance Studies   1958
- ■ c/o Dr Amanda Beam-Frazier, University of Glasgow, 9 University Gardens, GLASGOW, G12 8QH.   (hsb)
  0141-330 5934
  email amanda.beam-frazier@glasgow.ac.uk
  Hon Sec: Dr Amanda Beam-Frazier
- ▲ Scottish Charity
- ○ *L; to further the study of & promote interest in, Scottish history, particularly the period before 1707
- ● Conf - Res - Inf - SG
- M 201 i, UK / 24 i, o'seas
  (Sub: £5)

Scottish Microbiology Association
- NR Monklands Hospital, Monkscourt Avenue, AIDRE, Lanarkshire, ML6 0JS.   (hsb)
  http://www.scottish-micro-assoc.org.uk
  Sec: Liz Kilgour
- ○ *P

Scottish Microbiology Society
- NR Glasgow Dental School & Hospital, 378 Sauchiehall St, GLASGOW, G2 3JZ.
  0141-211 9752
  email g.ramage@dental.gla.ac.uk
  http://www.scottish-microbiology.org.uk
  Sec: Dr Gordon Ramage
- ○ *L

Scottish Modern Pentathlon Association   (SPMA)   1990
- ■ 4 Smeaton Grove, Inveresk, MUSSELBURGH, Midlothian, EH21 7TW.   (dir/b)
  http://www.pentathlon-scotland.org
  Dir/Admin: Rachel Caughey
- ▲ Company Limited by Guarantee
- ○ *S; the governing body in Scotland of the sport & the sports pursuits which comprise the modern pentathlon; to provide services to individuals, clubs & other bodies with an interest in such sports
- ● ET - Comp - Coaching
- < Modern Pentathlon Assn GB
- M i

Scottish Motor Neurone Disease Association   1981
- ■ 76 Firhill Rd, GLASGOW, G20 7BA.   (hq)
  0141-945 1077   fax 0141-945 2578
  email info@scotmnd.co.uk   http://www.scotmnd.org.uk
  Chief Exec: Craig Stockton
- ▲ Company Limited by Guarantee; Registered Charity
- Br 4 (Scotland)
- ○ *W; to help the motor neurone disease patient live as full & normal a life as possible
- ● Conf - Mtgs - ET - Res - Inf - Lib - Care research - Equipment loan service - Fundraising - Counselling service - Holiday caravan - Small grants scheme
- < Intl Alliance of MND Assns
- M 800 i
- ¶ Aware (NL) - 3;   AR; both ftm.   Infofact; free. Publications list available.

Scottish Motor Racing Club Ltd   (SMRC)   1946
- NR Birch House, Duncrievie, by Glenfarg, PERTH, PH2 9PD.   (sp)
  01577 830133
  http://www.smrc-uk.com
  Competition Sec: Chris Edwards
- ▲ Company Limited by Guarantee
- ○ *S; organisation of motor racing at Knockhill & Ingliston race circuits
- ● Mtgs - Comp
- M i

Scottish Motor Trade Association Ltd   (SMTA)   1903
- ■ Palmerston House, 10 The Loan, SOUTH QUEENSFERRY, EH30 9NS.   (hq)
  0131-331 5510   fax 0131-331 4296
  email info@smta.co.uk   http://www.smta.co.uk
  Chief Exec: Douglas Robertson
- ▲ Company Limited by Guarantee
- ○ *T
- ● Conf - LG
- M i & f
- ¶ Monthly Bulletin;   AR & Accounts;   both ftm only.

Scottish Museums Federation   1932
- NR National Galleries of Scotland, The Mound, EDINBURGH, EH2 2EL.
  http://www.scottishmuseumsfederation.org.uk
  Sec: Emma-Jane Wells
- ○ *P; for all who manage & work in museums in local authorities, universities, national & independent museums of Scotland
- ● Mtgs

Scottish Music Hall & Variety Theatre Society, incorporating the Sir Harry Lauder Society   (SMH&VTS)   1979
- ■ 69 Langmuirhead Rd, Auchinloch, KIRKINTILLOCH, G66 5DJ.   (hsp)
  0141-578 4108
  email bob.bain@ntlworld.com
  Hon Sec: Bob Bain
- ▲ Un-incorporated Society
- ○ *A; the Scottish variety theatre & music hall - past, present & future
- ● Exhib - VE - Staging shows
- M 260 i, UK / 16 i, o'seas
- ¶ Stagedoor - 4; ftm only.

Scottish Music Industry Association   (SMIA)   2007
- NR c/o Scottish Music Centre, City Halls, Candleriggs, GLASGOW, G1 1NQ.
  0141-553 2784
  email caroline@smia.org.uk
  Contact: Caroline Cooper
- ○ *T

Scottish National Federation for the Welfare of the Blind   (SNFWB)   1917
- NR 8 Netherlea, SCONE, Perthshire, PH2 6QA.   (hsp)
  email richard.mazur@virgin.net   http://www.snfwb.org.uk
  Sec & Treas: Richard Mazur
- ▲ Registered Charity
- ○ *W; to promote the education & social wellbeing of blind & partially sighted people throughout Scotland
- ● Conf - Mtgs - ET - Inf
- > most local authorities & volunteer organisations dealing with the visually impaired in Scotland
- M 52 org
- ¶ AR; free.

Scottish Neuroscience Group   (SNG)   1971
- NR School of Biology, St Andrews University, Bute Medical Building, Queens Terrace, ST ANDREWS, Fife, KY16 9TS.   (treas/b)
  01334 463503
  Treas: Prof Keith Sillar
- ○ *L, *P; incl neuroethology, electrophysiology, neuroanatomy, neurochemistry, pharmacology, muscle physiology

Scottish Newspaper Publishers Association
  2010 merged with the Scottish Daily Newspaper Society to form the
  Scottish Newspaper Society

Scottish Newspaper Society   (SNS)
- ■ 108 Holyrood Rd, EDINBURGH, EH8 8AS.   (hq)
  0131-620 8369
  Pres: Michael Johnston
- ○ *T; represents daily & Sunday newspapers in Scotland
- ● Mtgs - LG
- M 12 f
- × 2010 (Scottish Daily Newspaper Society (Scottish Newspaper Pubishers Association

Scottish & Northern Ireland Plumbing Employers' Federation   (SNIPEF)   1923
- ■ 22 Hopetoun St, EDINBURGH, EH7 4GH.   (hq)
  0131-556 0600
  http://www.snipef.org
  Dir & Sec: Robert D Burgon
- ▲ Company Limited by Guarantee
- ○ *T; the national trade association for all types of firms involved with the plumbing & domestic heating industry
- Gp Association of Installers of Unvented Hot Water Systems (Scotland & NI)
- ● Conf - Mtgs - ET - Exhib - Comp - Inf
- M 800 f
- ¶ Plumb Heat - 3.   SNIPEF Ybk.

© CBD Research Ltd · Beckenham · BR3 5JS · Tel 020 8650 7745 · E-mail cbd@cbdresearch.com · www.cbdresearch.com

Scottish Official Highland Dancing Association   (SOHDA) 1947
- 40 Dalbeattie Braes, Chapelhall, AIRDRIE, Lanarkshire, ML6 8GQ.   (sp)
  01698 7280983
  email admin@sohda.org.uk   http://www.sohda.org.uk
  Sec: Alex McGuire
- ○ *G, *P; for all interested in learning & teaching Highland dancing & keeping the dances alive

Scottish Optoelectronics Association   (SOA)   1994
- Geddes House, Kirkton North, LIVINGSTON, W Lothian, EH54 6GU.   (hq)
  01506 497228
  email soa@optoelectronics.org.uk
  http://www.optoelectronics.org.uk
  Chief Exec: Chris Gracie
- ▲ Un-incorporated Society
- ○ *T; to represent the optoelectronics community in Scotland
- Gp Displays; Measurement & instrumentation; Optical components, modules, systems
- ● Mtgs - Exhib - Stat - Expt - Inf - VE - LG
- < Optoelectronics Ind Devt Assn (USA); Optoelectronics Ind & Technology Devt Assn (Japan); Photonics Ind Devt Assn (Taiwan); Singapore Photonics Assn; Optech net Deutschland; Korean Assn Photonics Ind Devt; Optoelectronics Inds Australia
- M 50 f, 30 university depts
- ¶ Membership Directory; on-line.   AR - 1; ftm only.

Scottish Organic Producers Association   (SOPA)   1988
- NR SFQC - Royal Highland Centre, 10th Avenue, Ingliston, EDINBURGH, EH28 8NF.   (hq)
  0131-335 6606   fax 0131-335 6601
  email info@sopa.org.uk   http://www.sopa.org.uk
  Chmn: John Hamilton
- ○ *T; strengthening the prosperity & sustainability of members' businesses by being the champion of the development of organic food & farming in Scotland
- ● Mtgs
- M c 450 i

Scottish Organisation for Practice Teaching   (ScOPT)   1999
- NR PO Box 21163, ALLOA, Clackmannanshire, FK10 9BD.   (mail/address)
  0845 643 4061
  email enquiries@scopt.co.uk   http://www.scopt.co.uk
  Admin: Tara Hamilton
- ○ *P; to promote practice learning and teaching in social work practice

Scottish Orienteering Association   (SOA)   1962
- National Orienteering Centre, Glenmore Lodge, AVIEMORE, Inverness-shire, PH22 1QU.   (regd/office)
  01479 861374 (Tues & Thurs)
  http://www.scottish-orienteering.org
  Hon Sec: Kate Robertson
- ▲ Un-incorporated Society
- ○ *S; to promote & coordinate the sport of orienteering in Scotland
- ● Comp
- < Brit Orienteering Fedn; Intl Orienteering Fedn
- M 1,400 i, UK / 15 i, o'seas
- ¶ Score (NL) - 6.   AR.

Scottish Ornithologists' Club   (SOC)   1936
- Scottish Birdwatching Resource Centre, Waterston House, ABERLADY, W Lothian, EH32 0PY.   (hq)
  01875 871330
  http://www.the-soc.org.uk
  Office Mgr: Wendy Hicks
- ▲ Registered Charity
- Br 14
- ○ *L; study of Scottish ornithology & protection of rare birds
- ● Conf - Mtgs - Res - SG - Lib
- M 2,800 i, 100 org, UK / 300 i, 50 org, o'seas
- ¶ Scottish Birds (Jnl).   Scottish Bird News.
  Scottish Bird Report.
  Scottish Raptor Monitoring Scheme Report.

Scottish Otolaryngological Society   (SOS)   1910
- NR Gartnavel General Hospital, 1055 Great Western Rd, GLASGOW, G12 0XH.   (hsb)
  0141-211 3000
  http://www.scottish-otolaryngological-society.scot.nhs.uk
  Hon Sec/Treas: Fiona MacGregor
- ▲ Registered Charity
- ○ *P; the study & advancement of otology, rhinology & laryngology & all allied branches of medical science by the continuing education of members & their trainees
- ● Conf - Mtgs - ET - Acting as an advisory body on otolaryngological matters to other organisations
- M 90 i

Scottish Parent Councils Association
  has closed

Scottish Pelagic Fishermen's Association
  a member association of the **Scottish Fishermen's Federation**

Scottish Pensioners Forum   (SPF)   1992
- 333 Woodlands Rd, GLASGOW, G3 6NG.   (hq)
  0141-337 8113   fax 0141-337 8101
  http://www.scottishpensioners.org.uk
  Admin: Eileen Cawley
- ○ *K, *N; an umbrella body for groups & individuals campaigning on behalf of older people in Scotland

** Scottish Pensions Association
  Organisation lost: see Introduction paragraph 3

Scottish Pétanque Association   (SPA)   1985
- NR 288 Union Grove, ABERDEEN, AB10 6TP.   (hsp)
  07711 249616
  email scotland@fipjp.com
  http://www.scottishpetanque.org
  Sec: Lynn Jenkins
- ○ *S; the governing body in Scotland for the playing of pétanque
- ● ET - Inf
- < Fédn Intle de Pétanque et Jeu Provençal (FIPJP)
- M c 300 i
- ¶ NL - 3; free.

Scottish Pharmaceutical Federation
  merged 2006 with the Scottish Pharmaceutical General Council, since 2007 **Community Pharmacy Scotland**

Scottish Pharmaceutical General Council
  since 2007 **Community Pharmacy Scotland**

Scottish Pipers Association   (SPA)   1920

■ 2/3 69 Kirkland St, GLASGOW, G20 6SU.   (pres/p)
   0141-946 2137
   Pres: Miss J E Campbell
▲ Un-incorporated Society
○ *D; 'the study & practice of the great Highland bagpipe'
● Mtgs - Comp - Recitals of bagpipe music - Ceilidhs
M 120 i, UK / 20 i, o'seas

Scottish Piping Society of London   (SPSL)   1932

■ 49 Nursery Rd, TAPLOW, Berks, Sl6 0JX.   (mem/sp)
   email adam@scottishpipingsocietyoflondon.com
   http://www.scottishpipingsocietyoflondon.com
   Pres: Hugh Jamieson,   Mem Sec: Lynda Jamieson
▲ Registered Charity
○ *G; to further interest in solo piping of the great Highland
   bagpipe
● Mtgs - ET - Comp
M 250 i, 6 i, o'seas
¶ NL - 12; free.

Scottish Pistol Association   (SPA)   1964

NR Fairlie Quay Marina, FAIRLIE, Ayrshire, KA29 0AS.   (hsp)
   01475 560055
   email admin@scottishpistol.co.uk
   http://www.scottishpistol.co.uk
▲ Un-incorporated Society
○ *S; governing body for target pistol shooting in Scotland; to
   develop target pistol shooting as a sport, together with
   lightweight sport rifle & gallery rifle
< Scot Target Shooting Fedn

Scottish Place-Name Society   (SPNS)   1996

NR c/o SLD, 25 Buccleuch Place, EDINBURGH, EH8 9LN.   (hsb)
   http://www.spns.org.uk
▲ Registered Charity
○ *L; to advance & encourage research in & understanding of
   place-names & their essential contribution to the languages,
   history & culture of Scotland
M i
¶ NL

Scottish Plant Owners Association   (SPOA)   1950

NR 302 St Vincent St, GLASGOW, G2 5RZ.   (sb)
   0141-248 3434   fax 0141-221 1226
   email info@spoa.org.uk   http://www.spoa.org.uk
   Sec: Graham Bell
○ *T; for civil engineering, building & plant hire contractors
● Maintains a schedule of rates prepared from an annual survey
   of rates obtained in the market by members - Sponsors a
   form of agreement suitable for the transaction of plant hire
M 260 f
¶ Schedule of Rates & Handbook - 1.

Scottish Plastics & Rubber Association   (SPRA)   1993

■ 143 Lady Nairn Avenue, KIRKCALDY, Fife, KY1 2AT.   (hsp)
   01592 651269
   email c.geddes@blueyonder.co.uk
   http://www.spra.org.uk
   Hon Sec: Dr Charlie Geddes
▲ Company Limited by Guarantee
○ *T; to promote the advancement of plastics, rubber & related
   materials through education & training
● Mtgs - ET - Exhib - Comp - Inf - VE - LG
< Inst Materials, Minerals & Mining; Brit Plastics Fedn
M 216 i, 24 f
¶ NL - 4; free.

Scottish Poetry Library   (SPL)   1984

■ 5 Crichtons Close, Canongate, EDINBURGH, EH8 8DT.   (hq)
   0131-557 2876   fax 0131-557 8393
   email reception@spl.org.uk   http://www.spl.org.uk
   Dir: Dr Robyn Marsack
▲ Registered Charity
Br 13
○ *A, *E; a reference & lending library (free to public) for Scottish
   & international poetry, mainly of the 20th century
● Lib - Events during the Edinburgh International Festival - Visits
   to schools & other orgs - Monthly workshops for practising
   poets
< Scot Lib Inf Coun (SLIC)
M 700 i, 100 schools, colleges & libraries, UK / 50 i, o'seas
¶ NL - 2; ftm, (donation) nm.
   Scottish Poetry Index (ongoing series indexing poetry
   magazines) - irreg.

Scottish Police Federation   (SPF)   1919

NR 5 Woodside Place, GLASGOW, G3 7QF.   (hq)
   0141-332 5234   fax 0141-331 2436
   http://www.spf.org.uk
   Gen Sec: Calum Steele
Br 8
○ *P; staff association, covering constable to chief inspector
M 16,000 i

Scottish Potato Trades Association
   in 2006 merged with the National Association of Seed Potato
   Merchants to form the **British Potato Trade Association**

Scottish Potters' Association   (SPA)

NR 20 South St, CUPAR, Fife, KY11 3EA.   (hsp)
   07866 025491
   email secretary@scottishpotters.org
   http://www.scottishpotters.org
   Sec: Diane Cassidy
▲ Un-incorporated Society
○ *G, *P; the promotion of Scottish potters & ceramics; open to
   professional & amateur potters
● Mtgs - Exhib - VE - Workshops
M 60 i
¶ NL - 4; ftm.

Scottish Prayer Book Society   (SPBS)

■ 11 Melrose Gardens, GLASGOW, G20 6RB.   (hsp)
   0141 946 5045
   http://www.scottish-prayer-book.co.uk
   Hon Sec: Mr J C Lord
▲ Registered Charity
○ *G, *K, *R; to keep in print & promote the use of the 1929
   Scottish Prayer Book, one of the official service books of the
   Scottish Episcopal Church
● Mtgs
< Prayer Book Soc
M 175 i
¶ Scottish NL - 4.

© CBD Research Ltd · Beckenham · BR3 5JS · Tel 020 8650 7745 · E-mail cbd@cbdresearch.com · www.cbdresearch.com

Scottish Pre-School Play Association (SPPA) 1967

NR 21 Granville St, GLASGOW, G3 7EE. (hq)
     0141-221 4148   fax 0141-221 6043
     email info@sppa.org.uk   http://www.sppa.org.uk
     Chief Exec: Ian McLaughlan
▲ Company Limited by Guarantee; Registered Charity
Br 5
○ *W; to promote the development of quality care & education in
     pre-school groups which respect the rights, responsibilities &
     needs of all children & their parents
Gp Field staff; Grants; Information & advice; Insurance;
     Publications; Training
● Conf - Mtgs - ET - Res - Comp - Inf - Empl - LG
< Pre-school assns of England, Wales, Nthn Ireland & Ireland;
     Pre-School Learning Alliance
M 15 i, 26 f, 1,400 member gps
¶ First Five - 4; ftm.
     Learning & Development: an introduction to childcare in an
       early years setting; £38 m, £58 nm.
     Publications list available.

Scottish Print Employers Federation
     since 2009 **Graphic Enterprise Scotland**

Scottish Public Relations Consultants Association
     a group of the **Public Relations Consultants Association**

Scottish Publishers Association
     since 2007 **Publishing Scotland**

Scottish Quality Salmon
     since 2006 the **Scottish Salmon Producers' Organisation**

Scottish Rafting Association   (SRA)

NR The Coachyard, Chapel St, Aberfeldy, Perthshire, PH15 2AS.
     (hq)
     01887 829292
     http://www.scottish-rafting-association.org.uk
     Chmn: Alistair Leitch
○ *S

Scottish Railway Preservation Society   (SRPS) 1961

■ Bo'ness Station, Union St, BO'NESS, W Lothian, EH51 9AQ.
     (hq)
     01506 825855   fax 01506 828766
     http://www.srps.org.uk
▲ Company Limited by Guarantee; Registered Charity
○ *G; 'to obtain, restore, display & run a working railway; to
     preserve all aspects of Scottish railway history'
     The railway operates under title of Bo'ness & Kinnel Railway
● Mtgs - Exhib - SG - Operating the railway
< Heritage Rly Assn
M 1,200 i
¶ Blastpipe - 4; ftm.

Scottish Record Industry Association
     closed 2010

Scottish Record Society

■ The Old School House, Mordington, nr FOULDEN,
     Berwickshire, TD15 1XA. (treas/p)
     01289 386779
     Treas: Gregory Lauder-Frost
○ *L; to publish volumes relating to the history of Scotland
M c 900 i

Scottish Records Association   (SRA) 1977

NR Royal College of Physicians & Surgeons, 232-242 St Vincent St,
     GLASGOW, G2 5RJ.   (hsb)
     0141-227 3234   fax 0141-221 1804
     email carol.parry@rcpsglasg.ac.uk
     http://www.scottishrecordsassociation.org
     Sec: Mrs Carol Parry
▲ Registered Charity
○ *L; the preservation & use of historical records in Scotland
● Conf - Inf - VE
< Scot Coun on Archives; Nat Coun on Archives
M 276 i, 67 org, UK / 8 i, 11 org, o'seas
¶ Scottish Archives (Jnl) - 1; ftm, £25 nm.   NL - 2.

Scottish Reformation Society   (SRS) 1851

NR The Magdalen Chapel, 41 Cowgate, EDINBURGH, EH1 1JR.
     (hq)
     0131-220 1450   fax 0131-220 1450
     email info@scottishreformationsociety.org.uk
     http://www.scottishreformationsociety.org.uk
     Sec: Rev Douglas Somerset
▲ Registered Charity
Br 2
○ *R; 'to promote a witness to the Reformation in its history,
     theology & principles'
● Mtgs - ET - Res - SG - Inf - VE - Reformation tours
< Utd Protestant Coun
M 400 i, UK / 40 i, o'seas
¶ The Bulwark - 4.

Scottish Renewables Forum   (SRF) 1996

NR 49 Bath St (3rd floor), GLASGOW, G2 2DL.   (hq)
     0141-353 4980   fax 0141-353 4989
     email info@scottishrenewables.com
     http://www.scottishrenewables.com
     Chief Exec: Niall Stuart
▲ Company Limited by Guarantee
○ *T; renewable energy
● Conf - Mtgs - Exhib - LG
< Brit Hydropower Assn; Brit Wind Energy Assn
> Renewable Energy Gp(s): Aberdeen, Highland, Orkney,
     Shetland; Hebridean Renewable Energy Partnership
M 14 i, 252 f

Scottish Retail Consortium   (SRC) 1999

NR PO Box 13737, GULLANE, E Lothian, EH31 2WX.
     0870 609 3631   fax 0870 609 3631
     http://www.brc.org.uk/src_home.asp
     Chmn: Ken Mackenzie
○ *T
M f

Scottish Rifle Association   (SRA) 1886

NR 164 Ledi Drive, Bearsden, GLASGOW, G61 4JX.   (hsp)
     0141-942 2390
     email mabooonscotland@ntlworld.com
     http://www.scottishrifleassociation.org.uk
     Hon Sec: Allan Mabon
▲ Registered Charity; Un-incorporated Society
○ *S; the governing body for full-bore target rifle shooting in
     Scotland
● Comp
< Nat Rifle Assn; Scot Target Shooting Fedn
M 180 i, 20 org

Scottish Rights of Way & Access Society (ScotWays) 1845
- ■ 24 Annandale St, EDINBURGH, EH7 4AN.   (hq)
  0131-558 1222   fax 0131-558 1222
  email info@scotways.com   http://www.scotways.com
- ▲ Company Limited by Guarantee; Registered Charity
- ○ *G, *K; protection of public rights of way & outdoor access
  rights in Scotland
- Gp Fund-raising; Legal; Projects; Publicity; Walks
- ● Res - Stat - Inf - VE - LG - Maintain National Catalogue of
  Rughts of Way - Heritage Paths Project
- M 2,105 i, 463 org
- ¶ NL - 2;   AR - 1; both free.
  Access Rights & Rights of Way: a guide to the law in
  Scotland.   Scottish Hill Tracks.
  Rights of Way: the authority of case law; £5.

Scottish Rock Garden Club (SRGC) 1933
- ■ PO Box 14063, EDINBURGH, EH10 4YE.   (mail address)
  http://www.srgc.org.uk
  Sec: Carol Shaw
- ▲ Registered Charity
- Br affiliated groups
- ○ *H; to promote the cultivation of alpine & peat garden plants
- ● Conf - Mtgs - Exhib - Comp - SG - Inf - Lib - PL - VE
- < Amer Rock Garden Soc; Caledonian Horticl Soc; R Horticl Soc;
  Nthn Horticl Soc; Alpine Garden Soc
- M 4,500 i, UK / in 38 countries o'seas
- ¶ The Rock Garden (Jnl) - 2;   Secretary's Page - 2;   Ybk - 1;
  all ftm only.

Scottish Rowing 1881
- NR Tordarroch, Belmaduthy, MUNLOCHY, Ross-shire, IV8 8PG.
  01463 811747
  http://www.scottish-rowing.org.uk
  Contact: Roy Sinclair
- ▲ Un-incorporated Society
- ○ *S; governing body for rowing in Scotland
- ● Conf - Mtgs - Exam - Comp - VE
- < represented internationally by the Amateur Rowing Association
  (ARA)
- M 32 clubs
- ¶ Rowing Action - 4; free (donations from nm please).
- ✕ 2009 Scottish Amateur Rowing Association

Scottish Rugby Union plc (SRU) 1873
- NR Murrayfield, EDINBURGH, EH12 5PJ.   (hq)
  0131-346 5000   fax 0131-346 5001
  http://www.scottishrugby.org
  Sec: Graham Ireland
- ○ *S; administration of Rugby in Scotland; the development of the
  game at all levels in schools, clubs, district, national &
  international
- M 15,000 i, 276 org
- ¶ SRU Hbk - 1.   SRU Laws Book - 1.

Scottish Rural Property & Business Association
  in 2011 became **Scottish Land & Estates**

Scottish Salmon Producers' Organisation (SSPO)
- NR Durn, Isla Rd, PERTH, PH2 7HG.   (hq)
  01738 587000   fax 01738 621454
  email enquiries@scottishsalmon.co.uk
  http://www.scottishsalmon.co.uk
- ○ *T; salmon farming
- Gp Salmon Processors & Smokers Group
- M f
- ✕ 2006 Scottish Quality Salmon

Scottish Schoolsport Federation (SSF) 1988
- ■ 5 Mount Rich Place, DINGWALL, Ross-shire, IV15 9RU.   (hsp)
  01349 867924
  email alan.clark@highland.gov.uk
  http://www.scottishschoolsportfederation.org
  Sec: Alan Clark
- ○ *N, *S; concerned with school sports, extra-curricular activities
  & international school sport Federation (ISF) events
- Gp Education; Schools organisations; Sports organisations
- ● Conf - Mtgs - Comp - LG
- < Scot Sports Assn
- M 14 assns, 18 local authorities
  (Sub: £50)

Scottish Seafood Processors Federation Ltd 1986
- NR South Esplanade West, ABERDEEN, AB11 9FJ.   (hq)
  01224 897744
  http://www.scottishseafoodprocessors.org
- ▲ Company Limited by Guarantee
- Br 7
- ○ *T
- ● Mtgs - ET - LG
- M 180 f
- ¶ Ybk & Diary.

Scottish Secondary Teachers' Association (SSTA) 1946
- ■ 14 West End Place, EDINBURGH, EH11 2ED.   (hq)
  0131-313 7300   fax 0131-346 8057
  email info@ssta.org.uk   http://www.ssta.org.uk
  Gen Sec: Ann Ballinger
- Br 32
- ○ *E, *U
- ● Conf - Mtgs - ET - Res - SG - Inf - Empl - LG
- < Education Intl (EI); Eur Tr U C'ee for Education (ETUCE); Scot Tr
  U Congress
- M 9,500 i
- ¶ NL - 4/5;   Bulletin - 5/6.

Scottish Security Association
  Association dissolved summer 2011

Scottish Seed & Nursery Trade Association (SSNTA) 1917
- ■ 7 Preston Watson St, Errol, PERTH, PH2 7UR.
  01821 641048
  Sec: Donna McNicol
- ▲ Un-incorporated Society
- ○ *T; for all those involved in the Scottish seed trade (agricultural,
  horticultural, wholesale, retail, nursery traders & landscape
  contractors)
- ● Mtgs - VE
- < Attends mtgs of Agricl Industries Fedn (AIF) & UK Plant Varieties
  & Seeds Advisory Body (UKSAB)
- M f

Scottish Ship Chandlers Association (SSCA) 1955
- ■ McColl & Associates Ltd, 11 Burns Rd, ABERDEEN,
  AB15 4NT.   (sb)
  01224 313473   fax 01224 310385
  email roddy@mccollassociates.com
  http://www.shipchandlers.co.uk
  Secs: McColl & Associates Ltd
- ○ *T; trade protection
- ● Mtgs
- M 14 f

© CBD Research Ltd · Beckenham · BR3 5JS · Tel 020 8650 7745 · E-mail cbd@cbdresearch.com · www.cbdresearch.com

Scottish Ski Club (SSC) 1907
- ■ 44 Broomvale Drive, GLASGOW, G77 5NW.   (hsp)
       email secretary@scotski.org.uk   http://www.scotski.org.uk
       Hon Sec: Alan Forbes
- ▲ Un-incorporated Society
- ○ *S; promotion of skiing; support for competitive ski racing
- Gp Alpine; Racing; Touring
- ● Mtgs - ET - Comp - Inf - Lib - VE
- < Snowsport GB; Snowsport Scotland
- M 1,100 i, UK / 50 i, o'seas
       (Sub: £33)
- ¶ Jnl - 1;   NL - 4; both ftm only.

Scottish Smallbore Rifle Association (SSRA) 1966
- NR 27 Redwood Avenue, INVERNESS, IV2 6HA.   (mem/sp)
       http://www.ssra.co.uk
       Mem Sec: W H Allen
- ○ *S; the Scottish governing body for smallbore & air rifle
       shooting for the Olympic & Commonwealth Games
- M i, affiliate clubs
       (Sub:£30, £15 student)

Scottish Society for Autism 1968
- NR Hilton House, Alloa Business Park, Whins Rd, ALLOA,
       Clackmannanshire, FK10 3SA.   (hq)
       01259 720044   fax 01259 720051
       email autism@scottishautism.org
       http://www.scottishautism.org
       Chief Exec: Alan Somerville
- ▲ Registered Charity
- ○ *W; to provide care, support & education for peoples of all
       ages with autism throughout Scotland
- ● Conf - Mtgs - ET - Inf - Lib - Residential school for children -
       Respite care & family support - Adult accommodation &
       community houses
- M 662 i, 37 schools & housing org
- ¶ In Touch (Jnl) - 2; ftm, £3 nm.
       Jigsaw (NL) - 3;   AR - 1; both free.

Scottish Society for Contamination Control (S2C2) 1986
- NR 272 High Street, GLASGOW, G4 0QT.
       0141 552 8180
       email admin@s2c2.co.uk   http://www.s2c2.co.uk
- ▲ Registered Charity
- ○ *K; to advance the education of the public in matters relating to
       the practice & science of contamination control as applicable
       to a wide range of industries - cleanroom design, classroom
       suppliers, pharmaceutical & medical devices, biotechnology,
       hospitals etc
- M c 1,000 i

Scottish Society for Crop Research (SSCR) 1981
- NR c/o The James Hutton Institute, Invergowrie, DUNDEE,
       DD2 5DA.   (hq)
       01382 562731
       email bill.macfarlane.smith@scri.ac.uk
       http://www.sscr.scri.ac.uk
       Hon Sec: Dr Bill Macfarlane Smith
- ○ *F, *Q; crop research & plant breeding
- Gp Combinable crops; Potatoes; Soft fruit

Scottish Society of the History of Medicine (SSHM) 1948
- ■ 13 Craiglea Drive, EDINBURGH, EH10 5PB.   (hsp)
       0131-447 2572
       email nigel@michael-smith43.wanadoo.co.uk
       http://www.st-andrews.ac.uk
       Hon Sec: Dr Nigel Michael-Smith
- ▲ Registered Charity
- ○ *L; to further the general history of medicine, with special
       reference to Scottish medicine

Scottish Society for the History of Photography (SSHoP)
- NR 115 Clober Rd, Milngavie, GLASGOW, G62 7LS.
       http://www.sshop.arts.gla.ac.uk

Scottish Society for Northern Studies (SSNS) 1968
- NR Celtic & Scottish Studies, University of Edinburgh,
       27 George Sq, EDINBURGH, EH8 9LD.   (hq)
       http://www.northernstudies.org.uk
- ▲ Registered Charity
- ○ *L; the study the inter-relationships between the Scandinavian,
       Celtic & Scottish cultures
- M i & org
- ¶ Northern Studies (Jnl) - 1.

Scottish Society of Playwrights (SSP) 1973
- NR Flat 2/2, 5 Garrioch Quadrant, GLASGOW, G20 8RT.
       http://www.scottishsocietyofplaywrights.co.uk
       Treas: Alan McKendrick
- ○ *A; to develop & promote the interests & craft of professional
       playwrights & playwriting within Scottish theatre & also
       abroad

**Scottish Society for the Prevention of Cruelty to Animals
(ScottishSPCA) 1839**
- ■ Kingseat Rd, Halbeath, DUBNFERMLINE, Fife, KY11 8RY.   (hq)
       0300 099 9999   fax 0131-339 4777
       email enquiries@scottishspca.org
       http://www.scottishspca.org
       Chief Exec: Stuart Earley
- ▲ Company Limited by Guarantee; Registered Charity
- Br 12
- ○ *K, *V; to prevent cruelty to animals & to promote kindness in
       their treatment
- ● ET - Inf - PL - Inspectors investigate complaints of cruelty -
       Animal welfare & re-homing centres - Education officers give
       talks to schools
- < Wld Soc for the Protection of Animals
- M 33,150 i
       (Sub: £36)
- ¶ Friends Magazine - 2;   Information leaflets;   AR - 1.

Scottish Society for Psychical Research (SSPR) 1987
- ■ PO Box 2887, GLASGOW, G64 9BL.   (vp/p)
       0141 956 4516
       email ssprmail@aol.com   http://www.sspr.co.uk
       Sec: Tricia Robertson
- ▲ Registered Charity
- ○ *Q; investigating the paranormal in Scotland
- Gp Historical research; Investigation
- ● Mtgs - Res - SG - Inf - Library including audio & video tapes
- M 225 i, UK / 5 i, o'seas
- ¶ Psi Report - 9; ftm, £1 nm.

Scottish Solar Energy Group (SSEG) 1980
- NR School of Engineering & the Built Environment, Glasgow
       Caledonian University, Cowcaddens Rd, GLASGOW,
       G4 0BA.   (treas/b)
       0141-331 3897
       email s.burek@gcal.ac.uk   http://www.sseg.org.uk
       Treas: Dr Stas Burek
- ○ *P; to encourage the use of solar energy in Scotland
- ● Conf - Mtgs - VE - Seminars
- M i
- ¶ NL - 1.
       Published papers.

Scottish Spina Bifida Association (SSBA) 1964

NR   The Dan Young Building, 6 Craighalbert Way, CUMBERNAULD,
     G68 0LS.   (hq)
     01236 794500   fax 01236 736435
     email mail@ssba.org.uk   http://www.ssba.org.uk
     Chief Exec: Andrew H D Wynd
▲   Company Limited by Guarantee; Registered Charity
Br   5
○   *W; to increase public awareness & understanding of
     individuals with spina bifida, hydrocephalus & related
     disorders; to aim to secure provision for their special needs &
     those of their families
Gp   Spina bifida; Hydrocephalus
●   Mtgs - ET - Res - Exhib - SG - Inf - VE - Empl - LG
     Family support services: 0845 911 1112
<   Intl Fedn for Spina Bifida & Hydrocephalus; Assn for Spina
     Bifida & Hydrocephalus
M   3,800 i, 20 f, 10 org, UK / 20 i, o'seas
¶   talkBACK - 4; ftm, on request nm.
     Publications list available.

Scottish Sporting Car Club (SSCC) 1932

NR   18 Ayr Road, Giffnock, GLASGOW, G46 6RY.   (sp)
     http://www.scottishsportingcarclub.org.uk
     Company Limited by Guarantee
     Sec: Charles Turner
○   *S; organisation of motor sport events
M   i

Scottish Sports Association (SSA) 1983

■   Caledonia House, Redheughs Rigg, South Gyle, EDINBURGH,
     EH12 9DQ.   (hq)
     0131-339 8785
     email admin@info-ssa.org.uk
     http://www.scottishsportsassociation.org.uk
     Policy Director: Chris Robison
▲   Company Limited by Guarantee
○   *N, *S; to promote cooperation among governing bodies &
     organisations of sport in Scotland in consultation with (& as
     an independent consultative body to) Sportscotland
●   Conf - Mtgs - Res - Inf - LG
M   c 52 org
¶   Bulletin - 12; ftm.

Scottish Sports Horse

NR   Saline Shaw Farmhouse, Saline, DUNFERMLINE, Fife,
     KY12 9UG.   (admin/p)
     0844 846 5220
     http://www.scottishsportshorse.org
     Contact: Jackie Aird
○   *B; to promote the breeding of the very best sport horses and
     ponies for the Olympic disciplines of dressage, showjumping
     and eventing

Scottish Squash Ltd 1937

NR   Caledonia House, 1 Redheughs Rigg, South Gyle,
     EDINBURGH, EH12 9DQ.   (hq)
     0131-625 4425   fax 0131-317 7202
     email info@scottishsquash.org
     http://www.scottishsquash.org
     Chief Exec: John Dunlop
▲   Company Limited by Guarantee
○   *S; the national governing body for the sport of squash in
     Scotland
<   Wld Squash Fedn (WSF); Eur Squash Fedn (ESF); Scot Sports
     Assn (SSA)
M   10,500 i, 200 clubs

Scottish Stone Liaison Group (SSLG)

■   c/o Colin Tennant, Historic Scotland, Longmore House,
     Salisbury Place, EDINBURGH, EH9 1SH.   (hq)
     0131-668 8600
     email colin.tennant@scotland.gsi.gov.uk
     Chief Exec: Colin Tennant,   Admin: Jane Milroy
▲   Registered Charity
○   *G, *K; to advance the education of the public about the stone
     built heritage of Scotland; to assist in production of guidance
     on use of stone for specifiers
●   Conf - Mtgs - ET - Res - SG - Inf - LG
M   31 i, 15 f, 11 associates
¶   NL; free.

Scottish Sub Aqua Club (ScotSAC) 1953

NR   Caledonia House, 1 Redheughs Rigg, South Gyle,
     EDINBURGH, EH12 9DQ.   (hq)
     0131-625 4404   fax 0131-317 7202
     email hq@scotsac.com   http://www.scotsac.com
     Co Sec: Sandy McPherson
▲   Un-incorporated Society
Br   70+; Eire
○   *S; governing body for sub-aqua diving in Scotland
Gp   Boat handling (rigid inflatable boats)
●   Conf - Mtgs - ET - Exam - Comp - Lib
<   Scot Sports Coun
M   c 2,000 i
¶   Scottish Diver - 6; ftm, £2.50 nm.

Scottish Support for Learning Association (SSLA)

■   11 Mayshade Rd, LOANHEAD, Midlothian, EH20 9HJ.   (hsp/p)
     email info@ssla.org.uk   http://www.ssla.org.uk
     Sec: Sheena Richardson
▲   Registered Charity
○   *P; to support professionals working with children & young
     people
●   Conf - Mtgs - ET - Inf - LG
<   Ir Support for Learning Assn (ISLA); Scot Dyslexia Assn; Afasic
     Scotland; Enquire
M   c 200 i, c 16 f, 4 org

Scottish Swimming
     see **Scottish Amateur Swimming Association**

Scottish Table Tennis Association (STTA) 1935

NR   Caledonia House, Redheughs Rigg, South Gyle, EDINBURGH,
     EH12 9DQ.   (hq)
     0131-317 8077   fax 0131-317 8224
     http://www.tabletennisscotland.com
▲   Un-incorporated Society
○   *S; governing body for table tennis in Scotland
Gp   Veterans
●   ET - Comp - Stat - Inf
<   Intl Table Tennis Fedn; Eur Table Tennis U; C'wealth Table
     Tennis Fedn
M   1,500 i
¶   The Bulletin - 5/6.
     Note: trades as Table Tennis Scotland.

Scottish Target Shooting Federation 1886

NR   House of Sport, Caledonia House, South Gyle, EDINBURGH,
     EH12 9DQ.   (hq)
     email admin@stsf.org.uk   http://www.stsf.org.uk
     Admin: Jacqui Dunlop
○   *S
M   4 org:
     Scottish Clay Target Shooting Association
     Scottish Pistol Association
     Scottish Rifle Association (full-bore rifle)
     Scottish Small-Bore Rifle Association

Scottish Tenants Organisation (STO)
NR Claymore House (suite 633), 145 Kilmarnock Rd, Shawlands,
    GLASGOW, G41 3JA. (hq)
    0787 671 8111
    email contact@scottishtenants.org.uk
    http://www.scottishtenants.org.uk
○   *K, *W; campaigns for the rights of tenants
M   c 100 org

Scottish Text Society (STS) 1882
■   School of English Studies, University of Nottingham, University
    Park, NOTTINGHAM, NG7 2RD. (editorial/sb)
    0115-957 5922
    email editorialsecretary@scottishtextsociety.org
    http://www.scottishtextsociety.org
    Editorial Sec: Dr Nicola R Royan
▲   Registered Charity
○   *L; to further the study & teaching of Scottish literature by
    publishing editions of original texts (mediaeval period to the
    18th century)
●   AGM
M   45 i, 52 f, UK / 17 i, 120 f, o'seas
¶   Annual volume; ftm, £30 nm.   AR; ftm only.

Scottish Textile Industry Association (STIA)
NR 5 Lethame Gardens, STRATHAVEN, Lanarkshire, MD10 6DF.
    Sec: Peter Brook
○   *T; to promote the best in design, innovation & quality of textiles
    in Scotland
M   c 500 f
    Note: Uses brand name of Textiles Scotland

Scottish Timber Trade Association (STTA) 1910
NR Office 14 John Player Building, Stirling Enterprise Park,
    Springbank Rd, STIRLING, FK7 7RP. (asa)
    01786 451623   fax 01786 473112
    email mail@stta.org.uk   http://www.stta.org.uk
    Sec: David Sulman
○   *T
M   f
    Note: is a regional association of the Timber Trade Federation.

Scottish Tourism Forum (STF) 1994
■   29 Drumsheugh Gardens, EDINBURGH, EH3 7RN. (hq)
    0131-220 6321   fax 0131-220 5905
    email mail@stforum.co.uk   http://www.stforum.co.uk
    Chief Exec: Iain Herbert
▲   Company Limited by Guarantee
○   *N; to represent tourism industry interests with government &
    public agencies
●   Conf - Mtgs - Res - LG
M   165 f
¶   News Digest - 52;   NL - 4;   AR - 1; all ftm only.
    LM - on website; free.

Scottish Tourist Guides Association (STGA) 1960
■   Norie's House, 18b Broad St, STIRLING, FK8 1EF. (hq)
    01786 447784   fax 01786 451953
    email info@stga.co.uk   http://www.stga.co.uk
    Chmn: Norma Clarkson
▲   Company Limited by Guarantee
○   *P; for tourist guides in Scotland
Gp Blue Badge members; Regional affiliates; Site affiliates
●   Conf - ET - Exhib - SG - Inf - VE - Tourist guide accreditation
<   Wld Fedn Tourist Guide Assns; Eur Fedn of Tourist Guides
>   Scot Tourism Forum
M   475 i
¶   Guidelines - 12;   Guide List (guide directory) - 1.

Scottish Traction Engine Society (STES)
NR c/o 2 Denhead, Hillside, MONTROSE, Angus, DD10 9JR. (sp)
    01674 830606
    Sec: Heather Mair
○   *G; for all traction engine enthusiasts
●   Mtgs
M   i

Scottish Trades Union Congress (STUC) 1897
NR 333 Woodlands Rd, GLASGOW, G3 6NG. (hq)
    0141-337 8100   fax 0141-337 8101
    email info@stuc.org.uk   http://www.stuc.org.uk
    Gen Sec: Grahame Smith
○   *U; to coordinate, develop & articulate the views & policies of
    the trade union movement in Scotland
●   Conf
M   37 unions
¶   AR.   LM.   Agenda.

Scottish Tramway & Transport Society (STTS) 1951
NR PO Box 7342, GLASGOW, G51 4YQ. (mail/address)
    email stts.glasgow@virgin.net
    http://www.stts-glasgow.co.uk
    Gen Sec: Hugh McAulay
▲   Registered Charity
○   *G; recording of history of the development of public transport
    in Scotland, especially trams, trolleybuses & buses; to support
    preservation schemes
●   Mtgs - Res - Exhib - VE
<   Tramway Museum Soc
M   165 i, UK / 20 i, o'seas
¶   Scottish Transport - 1; £3.95.
    Occasional publications and videos.

Scottish Transport Studies Group (STSG) 1984
■   2 Dean Path, EDINBURGH, EH4 3BA. (chmn/b)
    0870 350 4202   fax 0871 250 4200
    email enquiries@stsg.org   http://www.stsg.org
    Chmn: Derek Halden
▲   Registered Charity
○   *G, *L, *N; to stimulate interest in, & awareness of, the
    transport function & its importance for the Scottish economy
    & society
Gp Publication
●   Conf - Mtgs - Res - SG - Stat - Inf
M   80 i, 20 f, 10 org
    (Sub: £30 i, £60-£500 org)
¶   Scottish Transport Review - 4; ftm £30 nm.
    Occasional Papers - irreg; ,ftm, £30 nm.

Scottish Tug of War Association (STOWA) 1981
NR 47 Finlay Avenue, EAST CALDER, W Lothian, EH53 0RP. (hsp)
    01506 881650
    http://www.scottishtugofwar.com
    Sec: Gary Gillespie
○   *S

**Scottish Vernacular Buildings Working Group (SVBWG)
1972**
NR National Museums of Scotland, Chambers St, EDINBURGH,
    EH1 1JF. (treas/b)
    email info@svbwg.org.uk   http://www.svbwg.org.uk
    Treas: D Kidd
▲   Registered Charity
○   *G; for all interested in the traditional buildings of Scotland
●   Conf - Mtgs - Res - VE
¶   Vernacular Building (Jnl) - 1.

Scottish Vintage Vehicle Federation (SVVF) 1973
■ 4 Plockton Terrace, DUNDEE, DD2 4TS.   (hsp)
01382 643083
http://www.svvf.org.uk
Sec: John Hyman
○ *N
M 100 orgs representing 6,700 individuals

Scottish Volleyball Association (SVA) 1963
NR 48 The Pleasance, EDINBURGH, EH8 9TJ.   (hq)
0131-556 4633   fax 0131-557 4314
http://www.scottishvolleyball.org
Chief Exec: Margaret Ann Fleming
○ *S; to promote, develop & control volleyball in Scotland
M i, schools & clubs

Scottish White Fish Producers' Association
a member association of the **Scottish Fishermen's Federation**

Scottish Wholesale Association (SWA) 1940
NR 30 McDonald Place, EDINBURGH, EH7 4NH.   (hq)
0131-556 8753   fax 0131-558 1623
email info@scottishwholesale.co.uk
http://www.scottishwholesale.co.uk
Exec Dir: Kate Salmon
○ *T; food, grocery & drink wholesale industry in Scotland
Gp Committee for Licensed Active Negotiations (CLAN); Scottish
Trade Activity Group (STAG); Scottish Wholesale Association
Security (SAS)
● Conf - Mtgs - ET - LG
< Fedn Whls Distbrs; Scot Grocers' Fedn; Scot Licensed Tr Assn
M 37 f, 80 associate members
¶ NL - 4; Ybk; both free.

Scottish Wild Land Group (SWLG) 1982
■ East Lodge, Crabstone, BUCKSBURN, Aberdeenshire,
AB21 9SJ.   (hsp)
01224 716709
email enquiries@swlg.org.uk   http://www.swlg.org.uk
Co-ordinator: Dr Robert McMorran
▲ Registered Charity; Un-incorporated Society
○ *K; to protect wild land in Scotland against intrusive
developments; to ensure any development is done sensitively
& sustainably
< Scot Envt Link
M 450 i, UK / 10 i, o'seas
¶ Wild Land News - 3; ftm, 50p nm.

Scottish Wildcat Association
NR c/o Shepherd & Wedderburn LLP, 1 Exchange Crescent,
Conference Square, EDINBURGH, EH3 8UL.   (asa)
email admin@scottishwildcats.co.uk
http://www.scottishwildcats.co.uk
▲ Registered Charity
○ *K; a campaign to save the Scottish wild cat
M i, (f & org - as affiliates)
(Sub: £25)
¶ NL - 4.

Scottish Wildlife Trust Ltd (SWT) 1964
NR Cramond House, 3 Kirk Cramond, EDINBURGH, EH4 6HZ.
(hq)
0131-312 7765   fax 0131-312 8705
email enquiries@swt.org.uk   http://www.swt.org.uk
Chief Exec: Simon Milne
▲ Company Limited by Guarantee; Registered Charity
Br 3 regional offices
○ *K; to conserve all forms of wildlife & habitats in Scotland
● ET - Res - Management of wildlife reserves
< UK Wildlife Trusts
M 19,000 i, 34 f, 51 org
¶ Scottish Wildlife - 3.   AR.

Scottish Wirework Manufacturers Association (SWMA) 1908
NR 162 Glenpark St, GLASGOW, G31 1PG.
0141-554 7081
○ *T

Scottish Women's Bowling Association 1936
NR Office 2 Commercial Centre, Stirling Enterprise Park, STIRLING,
FK7 7RP.   (hq)
01324 812351
http://www.scottishwomensbowling.co.uk
Sec: Mrs Anna Marshall
▲ Company Limited by Guarantee
○ *S; to foster, encourage, promote & develop the sport of
Outdoor Bowling for Women
M 42 clubs

Scottish Women's Football (SWF) 1972
■ Hampden Park, GLASGOW, G42 9DF.   (hq)
0141-620 4580   fax 0141-620 4581
email swf@scottish-football.com
http://www.scottishwomensfootball.com
Exec Admin: Maureen McGonigle
○ *S
Gp Leagues: Senior, Universities, Under 19, Under 17, Under 13,
Under 11
● Conf - Mtgs - ET - Comp
M 4,000 i
¶ NL - 2;   Club Secretary Lists - irreg; both free.

Scottish Women's Indoor Bowling Association
2011 merged with the **Scottish Indoor Bowling Association**

Scottish Women's Rural Institutes (SWRI) 1917
■ 42 Heriot Row, EDINBURGH, EH3 6ES.   (hq)
0131-225 1724   fax 0131-225 8129
email swri@swri.demon.co.uk
Gen Sec: Mrs Anne Peacock
▲ Registered Charity
Br 886
○ *G; non-political, non-sectarian organisation providing
educational, recreational & social opportunities for those who
live & work in the country or are interested in country life
● Conf - Mtgs - ET - Exhib - Comp - Lib
< Associated Countrywomen of the World
M 23,000 i
¶ Scottish Home & Country - 12; £1.

Scottish Working Trials Society
NR Greenside Cottage, LAUDER, Berwickshire, TD2 6PD.
01578 718861
http://www.workingtrials.co.uk
Contact: June McPhillips
○ *G; for all interested in sheep dog trials

Scottish Wrestling Association (SWA) 1930
NR c/o Athletes Lounge, Palace of Art. 1121 Paisley Rd,
GLASGOW, G52 1EQ.   (hsb)
email secretary@scottishwrestling.org
Sec: David Murray
▲ Un-incorporated Society
○ *S; to promote, organise, administer & coach wrestling
● Mtgs - ET - Comp
M 250 i
¶ Takedown (NL) - 6.
Rules of Wrestling.   Coaching course syllabus.   Clublist.

© CBD Research Ltd · Beckenham · BR3 5JS · Tel 020 8650 7745 · E-mail cbd@cbdresearch.com · www.cbdresearch.com

Scottish Youth Hostels Association   (SYHA)   1932

NR   7 Glebe Crescent, STIRLING, FK8 2JA.
    01786 891400   fax 01786 891333
    email info@syha.org.uk   http://www.syha.org.uk
    Gen Sec: Keith Legge
▲   Company Limited by Guarantee; Registered Charity
Br   5
○   *Y; to help all, but especially young people, to experience &
    appreciate the Scottish countryside & places of historic &
    cultural interest in Scotland, & to promote their health,
    recreation & education, particularly by providing low cost
    accommodation for them on their travels
●   Conf - Mtgs - Exhib - Comp - Stat - Inf - Empl - Activity holidays
    - Foreign travel
M   44,745 i, 1,000 org, clubs & schools
¶   AR; free.   Guides & books.   Publicity pamphlets.

Scout Association   1908

■   Gilwell Park, Bury Rd, LONDON, E4 7QW.   (hq)
    020 8433 7100   fax 020 8433 7103
    email info.centre@scout.org.uk
    http://www.scout.org.uk
    Sec: David Shelmerdine
▲   Registered Charity
Br   7,373
○   *Y; the purpose of scouting is to promote the development of
    young people in achieving their full physical, intellectual,
    social & spiritual potentials, as individuals, as responsible
    citizens & as members of their local, national & international
    communities
Gp   Beaver Scouts (6-8 years); Cub Scouts (8-10$\frac{1}{2}$); Scouts (10$\frac{1}{2}$-
    15); Explorer Scouts (15-18); Scout Network (18-25)
●   Conf - Mtgs - ET - Exhib - Comp - VE - Activities (camping,
    creative, faith)
<   Wld Scout Org
M   453,278 i
    (Sub: £30 scouts, £25 cub scouts, £20 beaver scouts)
¶   Scouting - 6; ftm.   AR - 1; free.

Scout & Guide Graduate Association   (SAGGA)   1957

■   33 Ward Rd, Northleach, GLOUCESTER, GL54 3RL.   (chmn/p)
    email chairman@sagga.org.uk   http://www.sagga.org.uk
    Chmn: Amy Lesley
▲   Registered Charity
Br   6
○   *N, *Y; to provide service to the scout & guide movements; to
    promote scout & guide cooperation
●   Conf - Mtgs - ET - SG - VE - Service work
<   Scout Assn; Girl Guiding UK
M   250 i, UK & o'seas
¶   News & Ideas - 4; ftm only.

Scouting Ireland   2004

IRL   Larch Hill, DUBLIN 16, Republic of Ireland.
    353 (1) 495 6300   fax 353 (1) 495 6301
    http://www.scouts.ie
    Nat Sec: Michael Devins
○   *Y
<   World Org of the Scout Movement
M   40,000 i

Scrabble Clubs (UK)   1993

■   Mattel House, Vanwall Business Park, Vanwall Rd,
    MAIDENHEAD, Berks, SL6 4UB.   (hq)
    01628 500000   fax 01628 500075
    email philip.nelkon@mattel.com
    Mgr: Philip Nelkon
○   *G
●   Conf - Comp - Inf
M   500 clubs, UK / 400 clubs, o'seas
¶   Scrabble Club News - 4; ftm.

Screen Printing Association (UK) Ltd
    since 23 April 2008 **Prism: association of print specialists &
    manufacturers**

Screen Producers Ireland   1987

IRL   77 Merrion Square, DUBLIN 2, Republic of Ireland.
    353 (1) 662 1114   fax 353 (1) 661 9949
    http://www.screenproducersireland.com
    Chief Exec: Sean Stokes
○   *T

SCTE - the Society for Broadband Professionals   (SCTE)   1945

NR   41A Market St, WATFORD, Herts, WD18 0PN.   (hq)
    01923 815500   fax 01923 803203
    http://www.scte.org.uk
    Sec: Mrs Beverley Walker
▲   Un-incorporated Society
○   *L, *P; to raise the standard of broadband engineering in the
    telecommunications industry
●   Mtgs - ET - Exam - Exhib - Inf
<   Intl SCTE (America)
M   c 700 i, 100 f
¶   Broadband (Jnl) - 4;   Ybk; both free.
✕   Society for Cable Telecommunications Engineers

Scuba Industries Trade Association   (SITA)

NR   382 Godstone Road, WHYTELEAFE, Surrey, CR3 0BB.
    http://www.sita.org.uk
    Admin: Pat Oates
○   *T; to represent the manufacturers, distributors, retailers,
    registered dive operators, dive boat charter operators & other
    bodies related to the scuba industry
M   23 f

Sculptors' Society of Ireland   (SSI)

IRL   Central Hotel Chambers, 7/9 Dame Court, DUBLIN 2, Republic
    of Ireland.
    353 (1) 672 9388
    email info@visualartists.ie   http://www.visualartists.ie
○   *A; to promote contemporary sculpture
M   420
    uses the trading name of Visual Artists Ireland

Scurry Driving Association   (SDA)

■   Willoughby House, 42 Church Lane, Manby, LOUTH, Lincs,
    LN11 8HL.   (sp)
    http://www.scurrydrivers.co.uk
    Sec: Carole Davenport
▲   Company Limited by Guarantee
○   *S; a competitive sport in which a driven pair of ponies
    complete a course of obstacles, the winner being the pair
    with the fastest overall time
●   ET - Exhib - Comp - Inf
M   40 i
¶   NL - 3; ftm, £3 nm.   Rules leaflet.

Sea Cadet Corps
    a group of the **Marine Society & Sea Cadets**

Sea of Faith Network (UK)   (SoF)   1989

NR   3 Belle Grove Place, Spital Tongues, NEWCASTLE upon TYNE,
    NE2 4LH.   (mail add)
    email john.pearson@unn.ac.uk   http://www.sofn.org.uk
    Chmn: John Pearson
▲   Un-incorporated Society
Br   26 groups
○   *L, *R; exploring & promoting religious faith as a human
    creation
●   Conf - Local group meetings for study & discussion
<   Sea of Faith Networks Australia, NZ
M   526 i, UK / 47 i, o'seas
¶   Sofia - 6.   NL - 6.
    Agenda of Faith.
    A Reasonable Faith: introducing the Sea of Faith Network.
    Time and Tide: Sea of Faith beyond the Millennium.

Seabed User & Developer Group (SUDG)

NR   Woodview, Southwick Road, Bulwick, CORBY, Northants, NN7 3DY.
    01780 450931
    email info@sudg.org.uk   http://www.sudg.org.uk
    Sec: Peter Barham
○   *T;
M   1 f, 8 org

Seabird Group 1966

■   c/o JNCC, Inverdee House, Baxter St, ABERDEEN, AB11 9QA.   (mail/address)
    email linda.wilson@jncc.gov.uk
    http://www.seabirdgroup.org.uk
    Sec: Linda Wilson
▲   Registered Charity
○   *L; to promote & help coordinate the study & conservation of seabirds
●   Conf - Res
M   331 i, 30 f, 4 org
    (Sub: £20 i, £15 f, £35 org)
¶   Seabird (Jnl) - 1.   NL - 3; both ftm only.

Seafood Group
    a group of the **Food & Drink Federation**

Seafood Scotland 1999

NR   18 Logie Mill, Logie Green Rd, EDINBURGH, EH7 4HG.
    0131-557 9344
    email enquiries@seafoodscotland.org
    http://www.seafoodscotland.org
    Chief Exec: Libby Woodhatch
○   *T

Seal Conservation Society (SCS) 1996

NR   c/o 14 Bridge Street, KILLYLEAGH, Co Down, BT30 9QN.
    028 4482 1107
    email info@pinnipeds.org   http://www.pinnipeds.org
○   *K; to protect & conserve pinnipeds (seals, sea-lions & walruses) worldwide

Sealed Knot Ltd (SK) 1968

■   Burlington House, Botleigh Grange Business Park, SOUTHAMPTON, Hants, SO30 2DF.   (hq)
    0845 209 1556
    email lesley.barnes@clarkewillmott.com
    http://www.thesealedknot.org.uk
    Chief Exec: Arthur Jackson
▲   Company Limited by Guarantee; Registered Charity
○   *G; promotes education & research into history
Gp   Artillery; Cavalry; Living history; Medical services
●   Exhib - Inf - Re-enactment of 17th century life & military displays
M   4,500 i
    (Sub: £20)
¶   Orders of the Day - 6; ftm, prices on application nm.

Seasonal Affective Disorder Association
    see **SAD Association**

Seasoning & Spice Association (SSA) 1992

NR   6 Catherine St, LONDON, WC2B 5JJ.   (hq)
    020 7836 2460   fax 020 7836 0580
    email ssa@fdf.org.uk
    http://www.seasoningandspice.org.uk
▲   Un-incorporated Society
○   *T; to be the leading voice of the UK seasoning & spice industry in the interests of members, food manufacturers & consumers alike
●   Mtgs
<   Eur Spice Assn (ESA); Food & Drink Fedn
M   21 f

SEBDA - the Social, Emotional & Behavioural Difficulties Association (SEBDA) 1952

NR   The Triangle (room 211), Exchange Square, MANCHESTER, M4 3TR.   (hq)
    0161-240 2418   fax 0161-240 5601
    email admin@sebda.org   http://www.sebda.org
    Exec Dir: Barbara Knowles
▲   Registered Charity
Br   6
○   *P; for all professionals working with children with emotional &/or behavioural difficulties & their families
●   Conf - Mtgs - ET - LG
<   Nat Children's Bureau; Young Minds
M   1,100 i, UK / 60 i, o'seas
¶   Emotional & Behavioural Difficulties (Jnl) - 3; ftm.
    Sebda News - 12.
    Publications list available.

Second World War Aircraft Preservation Society
    has closed

Secondary Heads Association
    since 2006 **Association of School & College Leaders**

Securities & Investment Institute
    since 2008-09 **Chartered Institute for Securities & Investment**

Security Institute of Ireland (SII) 1981

IRL   Unit W9G, Ladytown Business Park, NAAS, Co Kildare, Republic of Ireland.   (regd off)
    353 (045) 409222   fax 353 (045) 409354
    email sii@eircom.net   http://www.sii.ie
▲   Company Limited by Guarantee
○   *P
●   ET - Exam

Sedum Society 1987

■   8 Percy Gardens, CHOPPINGTON, Northumberland, NE62 5YH.   (sp)
    01670 817901
    email ray@sedumray.ndo.co.uk
    http://www.cactus-mall.com/sedum/
    Sec/Chmn/Editor: Ray Stephenson
▲   Un-incorporated Society
○   *H; to preserve as many species, sub-species, varieties, forms & cultivars in cultivation as possible
●   Res - Exhib - SG - Inf - Lib -PL
<   Brit Cactus & Succulent Soc
M   70 i, UK / 140 i, o;seas
    (Sub: £10 UK / £15 o'seas)
¶   NL - 4; ftm.   Occasional booklets.

Seed Crushers & Oil Processors Association

■   PO Box 259, BECKENHAM, Kent, BR3 3YA.   (hq)
    020 8776 2644; 020 8398 5955   fax 020 8249 5402
    http://www.scopa.org.uk
    Exec Sec: Lynda Simmons,   Sec Angela Bowden
▲   Un-incorporated Society
○   *T
<   Intl Assn Seed Crushers (IASC); Eur Seed Crushers & Oil Processors' Assn (FEDIOL); FOSFA; Food & Drink Fedn
M   13 f
¶   AR.

© CBD Research Ltd · Beckenham · BR3 5JS · Tel 020 8650 7745 · E-mail cbd@cbdresearch.com · www.cbdresearch.com

Seeing Dogs Alliance   1979
NR   116 Potters Lane, Send, WOKING, Surrey, GU23 7AL.   (hq)
      01483 765556
      email info@seeingdogs.org.uk
      http://www.seeingdogs.org.uk
      Sec: Chris Parker
▲   Registered Charity
○   *W; to train guide dogs for blind people; to give instruction in
      the use of alternative mobility aids where guide dogs are not
      suitable
M   i
¶   Lead On - 3.

Sefton Chamber of Commerce & Industry Ltd   1993
NR   150 Lord St, SOUTHPORT, Merseyside, PR9 0NP.   (hq)
      01704 531710   fax 01704 539255
      email mail@seftonchamber.org.uk
      http://www.seftonchamber.com
      Chief Exec: Steve Dickson
▲   Company Limited by Guarantee
○   *C
●   Conf - Mtgs - ET - Res - Exhib - SG - Stat - Expt - Inf - Lib - VE -
      LG
<   Brit Chams Comm; Chams Comm NW
M   600 f, 6 org
¶   Chamber News - 6; ftm only.
      Business to Business Flyer - 12.
      Sefton Business Directory - 2; ftm.

Selborne Society   1885
■   89 Daryngton Drive, GREENFORD, Middx, UB6 8BH.
      (regd/add)
      020 8840 3250
      http://www.biochem.ucl.ac.uk/~dab/selborne.html
      Hon Sec: R.J. Hall
▲   Company Limited by Guarantee; Registered Charity
○   *E, *G; to promote interest in conservation & natural history,
      especially among children; to maintain Perivale Wood Nature
      Reserve
●   Mtgs - Res - Exhib - Lib - VE
M   800 i
¶   Jnl Pioneers of Conservation (2004); £2 m, £3 nm.
      Wildlife in the Suburbs (3rd ed); £2 m,£3 nm.

Selden Society   1887
■   c/o Law Building, Queen Mary University of London,
      Mile End Rd, LONDON, E1 4NS.   (hq)
      020 7882 5136   fax 020 8981 8733
      email selden-society@qmul.ac.uk
      http://www.selden-society.qmul.ac.uk
      Sec: Victor Tunkel
▲   Registered Charity
○   *L, *Q; history of English law
●   Res - Inf - Advice to public bodies, libraries, the media &
      general public on questions of legal history, history of courts,
      the profession, institutions, manuscripts, family & local
      history, etc
<   Assn Intle de l'Histoire de Droit
M   380 i, 165 f & org, UK / 1,080 i, f & org, o'seas
¶   Main series - annual volume.
      Volumes in supplementary series - irreg; prices vary.
      Hbk (incl LM & Rules) - 5 yrly.
      Lectures - irreg.   AR - 1.

SELECT   1900
■   The Walled Garden, BUSH ESTATE, Midlothian, EH26 0SB.
      (hq)
      0131-445 5577   fax 0131-445 5548
      email admin@select.org.uk   http://www.select.org.uk
      Managing Dir: D N McGuiness
▲   Un-incorporated Society
Br   7
○   *T; to represent the electrical, electronic & communications
      systems industry in Scotland; membership categories incl
      electrical installation, safety & security systems, information
      technology, telecommunications, electronics & controls
●   Conf - Mtgs - ET - Exhib - Comp - SG - Inf - Empl - LG
<   Intl Assn of Electrical Contractors
M   550 f
¶   Cabletalk - 6.   NL - 12.   AR.   LM - 1.

Selective Mutism Information & Research Association   (SMIRA)
NR   13 Humberstone Drive, LEICESTER, LE5 0RE.
      0116-212 7411
      http://www.selectivemutism.co.uk
      Co-ordinator: Lindsay Whittington
○   *W; for sufferers & parents of the rare childhood condition
      characterised by 'a consistent failure to speak in specific
      situations in which there is an expectation for speaking'
●   Mtgs

Self Storage Association Ltd   (SSAUK)
■   Priestley House, The Gullet, NANTWICH, Cheshire,
      CW5 5SZ.   (hq)
      01270 623150   fax 01270 623471
      email admin@ssauk.com   http://www.ssauk.com
      Chief Exec: Rodney Walker
▲   Company Limited by Guarantee
○   *T
●   Conf - Mtgs - ET - Exhib - Stat - Inf - LG
M   229 f, UK / 12 f, o'seas
      (Sub: £650)
¶   Focus Magazine - 4; ftm, £4 nm.

Sense - National Deafblind & Rubella Association   1955
■   101 Pentonville Rd, LONDON, N1 9LG.   (hq)
      0845 127 0060   fax 0845 127 0062
      email info@sense.org.uk   http://www.sense.org.uk
      Chief Exec: Richard Brook
▲   Registered Charity
Br   11 regions
○   *K, *W; to support & campaign for children & adults who are
      deafblind & their families
●   ET - Inf - Lib
M   350 i
¶   Talking Sense - 3; ftm.

Sense about Science   2002
§   14A Clerkenwell Green, LONDON, EC1R 0DP.   (hq)
      020 7490 9590
      email enquiries@senseaboutscience.org
      http://www.senseaboutscience.org
      An independent charitable trust promoting good science &
      evidence in public debates; to help the public make sense of
      scientific & medical claims in the public area.
      It is supported by over 2,000 scientists/supporters.

Services, Industrial, Professional & Technical Union
      see **SIPTU (Services, Industrial, Professional & Technical
      Union)**

Sevenoaks & District Chamber of Commerce   1910
- ■ 54 High St, SEVENOAKS, Kent, TN13 1JG.   (hq)
    01732 455188   fax 01732 455188
    email info@sevenoakschamber.com
    http://www.sevenoakschamber.com
    Admin: Mrs Avril Ferguson
- ▲ Company Limited by Guarantee
- ○ *C
- ● Conf - Mtgs - Inf
- M 120 f
    (Sub: £100-£220)
- ¶ NL - 4; on website

Seventeen Fortyfive / 1745 Association   1946
- ■ Ferry Cottage, Corran, Ardgour, FORT WILLIAM, Highland,
    PH33 7AA.   (v-p/p)
    01855 841306
    http://www.1745Association.org.uk
    Vice-Pres: Miss C W H Aikman
- ▲ Registered Charity; Un-incorporated Society
- ○ *L; the study of Jacobite history; erection of memorials on
    historical sites
- ● Conf - VE
- M 350 i, 1 f, UK / 50 i, 1 org (Alliance France-Ecosse), o'seas
    (Sub: £15)
- ¶ The Jacobite - 3;   AR - 1; ftm only.

Seventeenth Century Life & Times   2000
- NR Fern Cottage, 91 High St, ALTON, Hants, GU34 1LG.
    01420 541731
    http://www.17thcenturylifeandtimes.com
    Events Coordinator: Geoffrey Thorne
- ▲ Un-incorporated Society
- ○ *G; 17th century (mainly English civil war) civilian & military
    living history re-enactment
- ● Mtgs - ET - Res - Exhib - SG - Inf - VE
- < Nat Assn of Re-enactment Socs
- M 130 i
- ¶ The Scrichowl - 2; ftm only.

Sewing Machine Trade Association Ltd   (SMTA)   1939
- ■ Claremont House, 70-72 Alma Rd, WINDSOR, Berks,
    SL4 3EZ.   (hq)
    0870 330 8610   fax 0870 330 8611
    email info@smta.org.uk
    http://www.sewingmachine.org.uk
- ○ *T; interests of sewing machine dealers & allied interests in the
    UK & Eire
- ● Conf - Mtgs - ET - Exhib - Inf - VE
- M 45 f
- ¶ Shuttle Plus - 4; free.

Sexaholics Anonymous   (SA)   1991
- NR PO Box 1914, BRISTOL, BS99 2NE.   (mail/address)
    07000 725463
    http://www.sauk.org
- ▲ Un-incorporated Society
- ○ *M, *W; offers a 12-step programme of recovery for those who
    want to stop their self-destructive sexual thinking & behaviour
- ● Mtgs

Sexual Advice Association   1995
- ■ Emblem House (suite 301), London Bridge Hospital,
    27 Tooley St, LONDON, SE1 2PR.   (asa)
    020 7486 7262
    email info@sda.uk.net   http://www.sda.uk.net
    Chmn: Dr Graham Jackson
- ▲ Registered Charity
- ○ *M, *W; to raise awareness of the causes & treatments of male
    & female sexual dysfunction
- ● Inf
- < Eur Sexual Dysfunction Alliance (ESDA)
- M i
    (Sub: £15)
- ¶ NL - 2; free.   AR; free.
- ✕ 2009-10 Sexual Dysfunction Association

Sexual Dysfunction Association
  see **Sexual Advice Association**

Sexual Freedom Coalition   (SFC)   1996
- ■ BCM Box Lovely, LONDON, WC1N 3XX.   (mail/address)
    0777 088 4985
    email mail@sfc.org.uk   http://www.sfc.org.uk
    Chmn: Dr Tuppy Owens
- ▲ Un-incorporated Society
- ○ *K; 'to represent supporters & campaign groups who revere sex
    & want to be free to enjoy seeing, hearing, reading & doing
    as we please, so long as nobody is exploiting anyone else'
- ● Conf - LG
- > TLC; Outsiders Trust; Leydig Trust

Shakespeare Reading Society   (SRS)   1874
- ■ 123 Lynton Rd, LONDON, W3 9HN.   (hsp)
    020 8992 0772
    Hon Sec: Mrs Frances J Hughes
- ▲ Un-incorporated Society
- ○ *A, *L; to read & study the works of Shakespeare
- ● Mtgs - Res - VE - Reading of plays - Lectures - Acting
    workshops
- M 50 i
- ¶ Annual programme; free.

Shared Care Network   1988
- ■ Units 34-36 Easton Business Centre, Felix Rd, BRISTOL,
    BS5 0HE.   (hq)
    0117-941 5361   fax 0117-941 5362
    email enquiries@sharedcarenetwork.org.uk
    http://www.sharedcarenetwork.org.uk
    Chief Exec: Candy Smith
- ▲ Registered Charity
- Br 8
- ○ *N, *W; to support the development of family based short-term
    care services in England, Wales & Northern Ireland
    Family based care services link disabled children to support
    families willing to offer occasional care. The network
    supports 300 schemes organising family based short breaks
- ● Conf - ET - Res - Inf - LG - Campaigning
- M 300 services
- ¶ Annual Review; free.

Shark Angling Club of Great Britain   (SACGB)   1953
- ■ Middletons Corner, The Quay, EAST LOOE, Cornwall,
    PL13 1DX.   (hq)
    01503 262642
    email sharkclublooe@gmail.com
     http://www.sharkanglingclubofgreatbritain.org.uk
    Sec: Linda Reynolds
- ○ *S; to promote shark angling in GB, including reef fishing,
    mackerel trips, evening conger trips
- ● Res - Comp - SG - Stat - Inf - Lib
- < Intl Game Fishing Assn
- M 500 i, UK / 50 i, o'seas
- ¶ NL - 2; ftm only.

© CBD Research Ltd · Beckenham · BR3 5JS · Tel 020 8650 7745 · E-mail cbd@cbdresearch.com · www.cbdresearch.com

Shaw Society   1941

NR   1 Buckland Court, 37 Belsize Park, LONDON, NW3 4EB.
　　　(mem/sp)
　　　020 7794 7014
　　　email shawsociety@blueyonder.co.uk
　　　http://www.shawsociety.org.uk
　　　Mem Sec: Evelyn Ellis
▲　Un-incorporated Society
○　*A, *L; study of the life & work of George Bernard Shaw; to
　　　promote interest in his work & provide 'a rallying point for
　　　the cooperation & education of kindred spirits & a forum for
　　　their irreconcilable controversies'
●　Mtgs - Inf - Performances at Shaw's house at Ayot St Lawrence
　　　(Herts)
M　c 90 i, 10 libraries, UK / c 40 i, 100 libraries, o'seas
¶　The Shavian - 2; ftm, donation nm.   NL - 3; ftm.
　　　News-sheet for meetings - 10; free to attendees.

Sheep Veterinary Society
　　　a group of the **British Veterinary Association**

Sheet Plant Association   (SPA)

NR   24 Grange St, KILMARNOCK, Ayrshire, KA1 2AR.   (hq)
　　　01563 570518   fax 01563 572728
　　　email office@sheetplantuk.com
　　　http://www.sheetplantassociation.com
○　*T; to represent the interests of corrugated converters
●　Conf - ET - Exhib - Comp - Inf
<　Fédn Français du Cartonnage; Assn of Indep Corrugated
　　　Converters (USA)
M　65 f, UK / 5 f, o;seas

Sheffield Chamber of Commerce & Industry   (SCCI)   1857

■　Albion House, Savile St, SHEFFIELD, S Yorks, S4 7UD.   (hq)
　　　0114-201 8888   fax 0114-272 0950
　　　email info@scci.org.uk   http://www.scci.org.uk
　　　Exec Dir: Richard Wright
▲　Company Limited by Guarantee
○　*C
●　Conf - ET - Res - Expt - Inf - VE
<　Brit Chams Comm
M　1,800 f

Sheila Kaye-Smith Society   (SK-S)   1987

■　Flat 3, 5 Villa Rd, ST LEONARDS-on-SEA, E Sussex,
　　　TN37 6EJ.   (hsp)
　　　01424 427886
　　　Hon Sec: Michael Bristow-Smith
○　*A; to stimulate & widen interest in the life & work of this
　　　English writer & novelist (1887-1956)
●　Mtgs - VE
<　Alliance of Literary Societies (ALS)
M　56 i
¶　The Gleam (Jnl) - 1;   NL - 1.
　　　Occasional papers & books.

Shellfish Association of Great Britain   (SAGB)   1908

NR   Fishmongers' Hall, London Bridge, LONDON, EC4R 9EL.   (hq)
　　　020 7283 8305
　　　email sagb@shellfish.org.uk   http://www.shellfish.org.uk
　　　Dir: Dr Tom Pickerell
○　*T; for the UK shellfish industry (catching, cultivating & selling)
M　f

Shellfish Working Group
　　　a group of the **Food & Drink Federation**

Shelter   1966

§　88 Old St, LONDON, EC1V 9HU.   (hq)
　　　0844 515 2000   fax 0844 515 2030
　　　email info@shelter.org.uk   http://www.shelter.org.uk
　　　Scotiabank House (4th floor), 6 South Charlotte St,
　　　EDINBURGH, EH2 4AW.
　　　Chief Exec: Adam Sampson
　　　gives advice, information & advocacy to people in housing
　　　need; campaigns for lasting political change to end the
　　　housing crisis for good.
　　　Helpline: 0808 800 4444

Sherlock Holmes Society of London   1951

■　41 Sandford Rd, CHELMSFORD, Essex, CM1 6DE.   (pro/p)
　　　01245 284006
　　　email shi@waitrose.com
　　　http://www.sherlock-holmes.org.uk
　　　PR Officer: Roger Johnson
▲　Un-incorporated Society
○　*A, *G; 'a spoof literary society devoted to the lives & works of
　　　Sherlock Holmes & Dr John Watson'
●　Mtgs - VE
M　c 1,000 i
¶　Sherlock Holmes Journal - 2; ftm only.

Shetland Cattle Breeders' Association   (SCBA)   2000

NR   Renwick Mill, Renwick, PENRITH, Cumbria, CA10 1JH.
　　　(mem/sp)
　　　http://www.shetlandcattle.org.uk
　　　Mem Sec: Barry Allen
○　*B

Shetland Cattle Herd Book Society

NR   Shetland Rural Centre, Staneyhill, LERWICK, Shetland,
　　　ZE1 0NA.
　　　01595 696300   fax 01595 696305
　　　Sec: Evelyn Leask
▲　Registered Charity
○　*B

Shetland Cheviot Marketing Society   1986

■　Lonabrek, Aith, BIXTER, Shetland, ZE2 9ND.   (hsp)
　　　01595 810343
　　　Sec: Jim Nicolson
▲　Un-incorporated Society
○　*B
●　Mtgs
<　Nat Sheep Assn
M　100 i

Shetland Flock Book Trust   1926

NR   Lonabrek, Aith, BIXTER, Shetland, ZE2 9ND.   (hsp)
　　　01595 810343
　　　Sec: Jim Nicolson
▲　Registered Charity
○　*B; the breed society for sheep bred on the Shetland Islands: to
　　　encourage the breeding of pure Shetland sheep; to ensure
　　　that all flock book sheep comply with the breed standards
●　Mtgs - Comp
<　Nat Sheep Assn
M　116 i
　　　for the breed on the UK mainland see the Shetland Sheep
　　　Society

Shetland Livestock Marketing Group   (SLMG)
- ■ Shetland Rural Centre, Staneyhill, LERWICK, Shetland, ZE1 0NA.   (hq)
  01595 696300   fax 01595 696305
  email hazel_slmg@hotmail.co.uk
  http://www.shetlandagriculture.com
  Sec: Peter Duncan
- ○ *F; to promote and market agriculture in Shetland
- ● Mtgs - Inf - LG
- < Shetland Flock Health Assn
- M 300 i

Shetland Pony Stud-Book Society   (SPSBS)   1890
- NR Shetland House, 22 York Place, PERTH, PH2 8EH.   (hq)
  01738 623471   fax 01738 442274
  http://www.shetlandponystudbooksociety.co.uk
  Pres: G N Hurst
- ▲ Company Limited by Guarantee; Registered Charity
- ○ *B
- Gp Pony Breeders of Shetland; Ridden & Driven Performance Award Schemes
- ● Expt - Inf
- M 2,200 i, UK / 120 i, o'seas
- ¶ Shetland Pony Stud Book - 1.   Magazine - 1.

Shetland Sheep Society   1985
- NR The Fold, East Torrington, MARKET RASEN, Lincs, LN8 5SE.   (hsp)
  01673 857363
  email secretary@shetland-sheep.org.uk
  http://www.shetland-sheep.org.uk
  Hon Sec: Mrs Maureen Turner
- ○ *B; the registration authority for the Shetland breed within the UK mainland
- ● Conf - Mtgs - ET - Exhib - Comp - Expt - Inf - VE
- < Nat Sheep Assn
- M 375 i, UK / 25 i, o'seas
- ¶ The Shetland Breed - 4; ftm only.
  for the breed in Shetland see the Shetland Flock Book Trust

Shiatsu Society (UK)   1981
- ■ PO Box 4580, RUGBY, Warks, CV21 9EL.   (hq)
  0845 130 4560   fax 01788 555052
  email admin@shiatsusociety.org
  http://www.shiatsusociety.org
- ▲ Company Limited by Guarantee
- ○ *P; for students, practitioners & teachers of Shiatsu - the use of finger &/or palm pressure - as a natural healing discipline
- ● Conf - Mtgs - ET - Exam - Res - Exhib - Comp - SG - Stat - Inf - Lib - PL - Empl - VE - LG
- < Eur Shiatsu Fedn
- M 1,850 i, UK / 52 i, o'seas
- ¶ NL - 4; £43 yr.   Guide to Shiatsu.   GP leaflet.
  Shiatsu in the NHS.   Schools Booklet.

Shine - Supporting People Affected by Mental Ill Health (Shine)
- IRL 38 Blessington St, DUBLIN 7, Republic of Ireland.
  353 (1) 860 1620   fax 353 (1) 860 1602
  http://www.shineonline.ie
  Dir: John Saunders
- ○ *W
- ✕ 2009 Schizophrenia Ireland

Shingles Support Society
- NR 41 North Rd, LONDON, N7 9DP.   (hq)
  0845 123 2305
- ○ *W; to supply information on shingles & post-herpetic neuralgia
- ¶ Information pack.

Ship Stamp Society   (SSS)   1970
- ■ 10 Heyes Drive, LYMM, Cheshire, WA13 0PB.   (hsp)
  01925 758435
  email brad666sss@freenetname.co.uk
  Hon Sec: T Broadley
- ▲ Un-incorporated Society
- Br 1
- ○ *G; for collectors of postage stamps with ship interest
- ● Mtgs - Res - Exhib - Inf
- < Intl Fedn of Maritime Philately; Brit Thematic Assn
- M 180 i, UK / 108 i, o'seas
- ¶ The Log Book - 12.   LM & Reports; m only.

Shipbuilders & Shiprepairers Association   (SSA)   1989
- ■ Marine House, Meadlake Place, Thorpe Lea Rd, EGHAM, Surrey, TW20 8BF.   (hq)
  01784 223770   fax 01784 223775
  email office@ssa.org.uk   http://www.ssa.org.uk
  Admin: Julie Robson
- Br 2
- ○ *T; to support UK shipbuilding, shiprepair, conversion, disposal, design, operation & key supply chain such as electical, propulsion, mechanical / pressure / fluid systems, naval architecture & safety
- Gp Marine Industries Leadership Council (MILC)
- ● Conf - Mtgs - Res - Exhib - SG - Stat - Inf - Lib - PL - VE - LG - Health & safety - Project management - Technology/ translation
- < C'ee of Eur Shipyard Assns; R Inst Naval Architects; Lloyds Register; Yorkshire Forward
- > Best Practice Club; Business Enterprise Regulations & Reform; Ministry of Defence; SEMTA
- M 144 f, UK / 2 f, o'seas
- ¶ Circular - 52; ftm only.   Reports - irreg; m only.
  NL - 4;   Ybk - 1;   LM - on web; all free.

Shire Horse Society   (SHS)   1878
- ■ East of England Showground, PETERBOROUGH, Cambs, PE2 6XE.   (hq)
  01733 234451   fax 01733 370038
  email dralleydavies@eastofengland.org.uk
  http://www.shire-horse.org.uk
  Sec: David Ralley Davies
- ○ *B; the protection, promotion & improvement of the Shire Horse
- ● Mtgs - ET - Exhib - Comp - Stat - Expt - Inf - VE - LG - Spring Show
- < Assn of Show & Agricl Orgs
- M i, f & org
- ¶ NL;   List of Shows - 1;   Panel of Judges.   AR.
  List of Breeders, Exhibitors & Local Societies - 2;
  Notes for Overseas Breeders - irreg; all free.

Shooters' Rights Association   (SRA)   1984
- ■ PO Box 3, CARDIGAN, Ceredigion, SA43 1BN.   (hq)
  01239 698607   fax 01239 698614
  Sec: Richard Law
- ▲ Un-incorporated Society
- ○ *K; provision of public liability & legal costs insurance; assistance in difficulties encountered with respect to gun licence grant or renewal
- ● Res - Exhib - Comp - Inf - Lib
- M 3,285 i, 85 f, 115 org, UK / 29 i, o'seas

© CBD Research Ltd · Beckenham · BR3 5JS · Tel 020 8650 7745 · E-mail cbd@cbdresearch.com · www.cbdresearch.com

Shop & Display Equipment Association   (SDEA)   1947
- ■ 24 Croydon Rd, CATERHAM, Surrey, CR3 6YR.   (hq)
     01883 348911   fax 01883 343435
     email enquiries@sdea.co.uk
     http://www.shopdisplay.org
     Dir: Lawrence Cutler
- ▲ Un-incorporated Society
- ○ *T; for manufacturers, distributors & importers of shop fittings &
     retail display equipment
- ● Conf - Mtgs - Exhib - Stat - Expt - Inf - LG
- M 202 f
- ¶ Shoptalk (NL) - 4;   LM - 1;   PR Planner - 1;
     Confidential Circulars - 52;   all ftm only.
     SDEA Directory of Shopfittings & Display - 1; ftm, £10 nm.

Shorthorn Society of the United Kingdom & Ireland   1875
- ■ 4th Street, Stoneleigh Park, KENILWORTH, Warks, CV8 2LG.
     (hq)
     024 7669 6549   fax 024 7669 6729
     email shorthorn@shorthorn.co.uk
     http://www.shorthorn.co.uk
     Sec: Frank Milnes
- ○ *B
- Gp Red Cattle Genetics (semen company)
- ● Mtgs - Res - Exhib - Comp - Stat - Expt - Inf - PL - VE - Empl -
     Breed societies
- < Assn of Show & Agricl Orgs; Wld Shorthorn Coun
- M 280 i, UK / 250 i, o'seas
- ¶ Shorthorn Jnl - 1.   NL - 4.
     Coates Herd Book - 1.

Showmen's Guild of Great Britain   1889
- NR 151A King St, Drighlington, LEEDS, W Yorks, BD11 1EJ.   (hq)
      01132 853341
      email denise@showmensguild.com
      http://www.www.showmensguild.com
      Sec: Mrs Denise Ablett
- ○ *T; interests of travelling showmen & protection of the industry
- M f

Shrievalty Association
      alternative name for the **High Sheriffs' Association of England &
      Wales**

Shropshire Archaeological & Historical Society   (SAHS)   1877
- ■ Glebe House, Vicarage Rd, SHREWSBURY, Shropshire,
     SY3 9EZ.   (hsp)
     01743 236914   fax 01743 351255
     email s.baugh@virgin.net
     http://www.discovershropshire.org.uk
     Sec: G C Baugh
- ▲ Registered Charity
- ○ *L; archaeological research, local history & publication of
     parish registers
- ● Mtgs - Lib - VE
- < Coun Brit Archaeology
- M 316 i, 33 universities & libraries, UK / 3 i, 11 org, o'seas
     (Sub: £14 UK / £18 o'seas)
- ¶ Shropshire History & Archaeology (Transactions) - 1;
     ftm, varies nm.
     NL - 2; ftm only.

Shropshire Chamber of Commerce & Enterprise Ltd   1962
- ■ Trevithick House, Stafford Park 4, TELFORD, Shropshire,
     TF3 3BA.   (hq)
     01952 208200   fax 01952 208208
     email enquiries@shropshire-chamber.co.uk
     http://www.shropshire-chamber.co.uk
     Man Dir: Richard Sheehan
- ▲ Company Limited by Guarantee
- ○ *C
- Gp Networking; Policy & representation
- ● Inf
- < Brit Chams Comm; Confedn W Midlands Chams Comm
- M i
- ¶ Shropshire Business Matters - 6; free.

**Shropshire Sheep Breeders Association & Flock Book Society
(SSBA)   1882**
- ■ 146 Chandlers Way, ST HELENS, Merseyside, WA9 4TG.   (hsp)
     01744 811124
     email simon.mackay1@virgin.net
     http://www.shropshire-sheep.co.uk
     Sec: Simon Mackay
- ▲ Registered Charity
- ○ *B
- ● Mtgs - ET - Exhib - Comp - Expt - Inf - PL - LG
- < Nat Sheep Assn
- M 110 i, UK / 1 i, o'seas
- ¶ Shroptalk (NL) - 4; ftm; £10 yr nm.

**Shropshire & West Midlands Agricultural Society   (SWMAS)
1875**
- ■ West Mid Agricultural Showground, Berwick Rd, SHREWSBURY,
     Shropshire, SY1 2PF.   (hq)
     01743 289831   fax 01743 289920
     email enquiries@shropshirecountyshow.com
     http://www.shropshirecountyshow.com
     Gen Mgr: Mary Hopkins
- ▲ Company Limited by Guarantee; Registered Charity
- ○ *F; to promote agriculture & industry
- Gp Horse; Cattle; Sheep; Machinery & arable farming;
     Horticulture; Conservation
- ● Exhib - Comp - 2 day county show
- < Assn of Show & Agricl Orgs
- M 4,000 i, 400 f, 50 org
- ¶ Show Programme - 1; ftm, £2 nm.   AR; ftm; £2 nm.
     Schedule(s) - 1; free.   Catalogue - 1; £2.50.

Sickle Cell Society   1979
- NR 54 Station Rd, LONDON, NW10 4UA.   (hq)
      020 8961 7795   fax 020 8961 8346
      email info@sicklecellsociety.org
      http://www.sicklecellsociety.org
      Chief Exec: Dr Philip Nortey
- ▲ Registered Charity
- ○ *W; to help & support families affected by sickle cell disorders;
     to educate the general public & health professionals about
     the problems of sickle cell disorders
- ● Conf - Exhib - Inf - Provides financial assistance, educational
     grants & holiday & recreational opportunities
- M 150 i
- ¶ News Review - 4.   AR.
     Information leaflets (publications list available); free.

Side Saddle Association   (SSA)   1974
- ■ Rhoades Farm, Main Rd, Sibsey, BOSTON, Lincs, PE2 0TW. (hsp)
  01205 751599
  email paulagolby@btinternet.com
  http://www.sidesaddleassociation.co.uk
  Hon Gen Sec: Mrs Paula Golby
- ▲ Un-incorporated Society
- Br 15; Australia, Austria, Belgium, Canada, Eire, France, Germany, Japan, Netherlands, New Zealand, Northern Ireland, South Africa, Spain, Sweden, USA
- ○ *G; to encourage & promote the art of riding side saddle, & the furtherance of the interests of side saddle riders all over the world
- ● Conf - Mtgs - ET - Exam - Exhib - Comp - Inf
- < Brit Horse Soc
- M 1,300 i
- ¶ NL - 3.   Shows & Fixture List - 1.
  Members' Hbk - 1.

Siegfried Sassoon Fellowship   2001
- NR PO Box 11, COWBRIDGE, Vale of Glamorgan, CF71 7XT. (mail/address)
  http://www.sassoonfellowship.org
  Hon Sec: Deborah Fisher
- ○ *G; for all interested in the llife & works of the poet & novelist Siegfried Sassoon (1886-1967) & the literature of the first World War
- M i

SIFA
  merged with the London Investment Banking Association to form the
  Association for Financial Markets in Europe

Signalling Record Society   1969
- NR 51 Queensway, WALLASEY, Cheshire, CH45 4PZ.   (hsp)
  http://www.s-r-s.org.uk
  Sec: Malcolm Atherton
- ○ *G; for those interested in railway signalling
- ● Mtgs - Archive
- ¶ SRS NL; + Back issues 1-101 (CD), £20; both ftm only.
  Great Western Telegraph Rule Book, 1878; £2.75.
  Midland Rule Book, 1904; £5.95.
  Accident & Collision Reports; £3.20 - £5.45.
  Other publications.

Silhouette Collectors Club   1965
- ■ Flat 5/13 Brunswick Sq, HOVE, E Sussex, BN3 1EH.   (hsp)
  01273 735760
  Hon Sec: Miss Diana B Joll
- ○ *A; for collectors & anyone interested in the silhouette from 1760 to the present
- ● Res - VE
- M 68 i, UK / 3 i, o'seas
- ¶ NL - 3; ftm only.

Silica & Moulding Sands Association
  is a product group of the **Mineral Products Association**

Silk Association of Great Britain   (SAGB)   1970
- NR 3 Queen Sq, Bloomsbury, LONDON, WC1N 3AR.   (hq)
  020 7843 9460   fax 020 7843 9478
  email sagb@dial.pipex.com   http://www.silk.org.uk
- ▲ Company Limited by Guarantee
- ○ *T; to promote the use of & knowledge of real silk
- ● Mtgs - Stat - Inf - LG
- < Intl Silk Assn; Brit Apparel & Textile Confedn
- M 35 f
- ¶ Serica (NL) - 4; ftm.

Silver Society
- NR Box 246 / 2 Landsdowne Row, LONDON, W1J 6HL. (mail/address)
  email secretary@the silversociety.org
  http://www.thesilversociety.org
- ○ *G; to widen the appreciation of silver of all periods, also gold & platinum
- ¶ Jnl - 1.

Silver Spoon Club of Great Britain   (SSC)   1989
- NR Daniel Bexfield Antiques, 26 Burlington Arcade, LONDON, W1J 0PU.   (ed/b)
  Jnl Editor: Daniel Bexfield
- ▲ Un-incorporated Society
- ○ *G; to assist & support connoisseurs & collectors of antique & other fine silver spoons & related table silver
- Gp Historical; Research; Marketing; Instruction
- ● Res - Comp - SG - Stat - Inf - Lib
- M 175 i, UK / 25 i, o'seas
- ¶ The Finial (Jnl) - 6.
  Note: all activities are carried out by post.

Simplified Spelling Society
  since 2011 the **Spelling Society**

Sing for Pleasure   (SfP)   1964
- NR Bolton Music Centre, New York, BOLTON, Lancs, BL3 4NG. (hq)
  01204 333540
  email admin@singforpleasure.org.uk
  http://www.singforpleasure.org.uk
  Sec/Treas: Nick Wilmer
- ▲ Registered Charity
- Br Regional c'ees
- ○ *D, *G; for conductors, teachers, singers & children interested in choral music
- ● Conf - Mtgs - ET - SG - Inf - VE
- < À Coeur Joie; Europa Cantat; Brit Fedn Young Choirs; NCVO; Tonsil
- M 650 i, 100 choirs
- ¶ NL - 2; ftm.   Sheet Music - 3; ftm.
  AR; ftm.   Summer & Weekend Course Brochures.

Singapore United Kingdom Association   (SUKA)   1988
- NR P O Box 6358, LONDON, W1A 6BF.
  email secretary@suka.org   http://www.suka.org
  Sec: Adeline Crouch
- ○ *X

Single Ply Roofing Association   (SPRA)   1994
- NR Roofing House, 31 Worship St, LONDON, EC2A 2DY.   (hq)
  0115-914 4445   fax 0115-974 9827
  email enquiries@spra.co.uk   http://www.spra.co.uk
  Dir: Jim Hooker
- ▲ Un-incorporated Society
- ○ *T; to provide independent technical advice to clients & designers on polymeric roofing membranes & to ensure the membership comply with membership criteria
- ● Mtgs - ET - Comp - Inf
- < Brit Flat Roofing Coun; Construction Products Assn; Nat Specialist Contrs Coun; Roofing Ind Alliance; RIBA CPD Providers Network
- M 75 f
- ¶ Brochure;   Design Guide; both free.

© CBD Research Ltd · Beckenham · BR3 5JS · Tel 020 8650 7745 · E-mail cbd@cbdresearch.com · www.cbdresearch.com

SIPTU (Services, Industrial, Professional & Technical Union) (SIPTU) 1990
IRL Liberty Hall, DUBLIN 1, Republic of Ireland.
353 (1) 858 6300   fax 353 (1) 874 9466
email info@siptu.ie   http://www.siptu.ie
Gen Sec: Joe O'Flynn
○ *U; to represent workers in both the public & private sector in almost every industry in Ireland & at virtually every level
M 276,000 i
Ireland's largest trade union

Sir Arthur Sullivan Society   (SASS)   1977
■ Captain's Post, The Old Rectory, Talland Hill, Polperro, LOOE, Cornwall, PL13 2RY.   (sp)
01503 272874
email shturnbull@aol.com
http://www.sullivansociety.org.uk
Sec: Stephen Turnbull
▲ Registered Charity
○ *A, *D, *G, *L; to advance the education of the public in & promote the performance of, the music of Sir Arthur Seymour Sullivan (1842-1900) & other contemporaneous British composers
● Conf - Mtgs - ET - Res - Exhib - Comp - SG - Inf - Lib - VE
M 400 i, 15 org, UK / 80 i, 5 org, o'seas
¶ Magazine - 3; ftm, £2 nm (back numbers only). NL - 1/2; ftm only.

Sir Harry Lauder Society
see the **Scottish Music Hall & Variety Theatre Society, incorporating the Sir Harry Lauder Society**

Sir Joseph Banks Society
NR 9-13 Bridge St, HORNCASTLE, Lincs, LN9 5ZH.
○ *G; to stimulate interest in the life & achievements of Sir Joseph Banks (1744-1820), English botanist & President of the Royal Society from 1778 to 1819; the genus Banksia commemorates his work in botany
● ET - Res - Inf
M i
¶ NL.   Publications.

Sira Ltd
No longer exists as an association

Sittingbourne & Kemsley Light Railway Ltd   (SKLR)   1969
■ PO Box 300, SITTINGBOURNE, Kent, ME10 2DZ.   (hq)
0871 222 1568
email info@sklr.net   http://www.sklr.net
Hon Sec: N G Widdows
▲ Registered Charity
○ *G; railway preservation & operation
● Exhib - Railway operation
< Heritage Rly Assn; Kent [& Swale] Museum[s] Gp; Swale Heritage Assn; Swale Tourism Assn
M 350 i
¶ NL - 6; ftm.

Sk8scotland
'we do not need to appear in directories since our members are well known to us'

Skates & Rays Producers Association   (SRPA)
NR c/o Sea Fish Industry Authority, 18 Logie Mill, Logie Green Rd, EDINBURGH, EH7 4HS.
0131-558 3331
○ *T; to preserve stocks of skates & rays as an endangered species
● Mtgs - Res - Stat - Inf
M 5 f
¶ Seafish I.D.Guide

Ski Club of Great Britain   1903
NR The White House, 57-63 Church Rd, LONDON, SW19 5SB.   (hq)
020 8410 2000   fax 020 8410 2001
email skiers@skiclub.co.uk   http://www.skiclub.co.uk
▲ Company Limited by Guarantee
○ *S; sport & recreation of skiing - cross-country, downhill, ski mountaineering & snowboarding
M 34,000 i

Ski Council of Wales   1994
■ Cardiff Ski & Snowsport Centre, Fairwater Park, Fairwater, CARDIFF, CF15 3JR.   (hq)
029 2056 1904   fax 029 2056 1924
email admin.snowsportwales@virgin.net
http://www.snowsportwales.net
Chief Exec: Robin Kellen
▲ Company Limited by Guarantee
○ *S; the governing body of skiing and snowboarding in Wales
● Mtgs - ET - Exam - Comp - VE - LG
< Brit Ski & Snowboard Ltd
> Ski Clubs in Wales; John Nike Ski Centre (Llandudno)
M 350 i, 1 f, 5 clubs schools, corporate support (Sub: £48 i, £70 f, £3 (per head) clubs)
¶ NL - 4;   AR - 1;   Website Updates - 12; all ftm.
Note: uses trading name of Snowsport Cymru/Wales

Skibob Association of Great Britain   (SAGB)   1966
NR 2-4 Langhorne Gardens, FOLKESTONE, Kent, CT20 2EA.   (regd off)
01303 251444   fax 01303 255167
email admin@skibob.org.uk   http://www.skibob.org.uk
Chmn: Richard Platt
▲ Un-incorporated Society
○ *S; promoting the sport of skibobbing
● ET - Comp - VE
< Fédn Intle de Skibob
M 500 i
¶ NL - 1; free.

Sleep Apnoea Trust Association   (SATA)
NR PO Box 60, CHINNOR, Oxon, OX39 4XE.
0845 606 0685
email sata.admin@tiscali.co.uk
http://www.sleep-apnoea-trust.org
Chmn: Brian Spires
○ *W; to improve the lives of sleep apnoea patients, their partners & their families
¶ Sleep Matters (NL) - 4.

Sleep Council   1995
NR High Corn Mill, Chapel Hill, SKIPTON, N Yorks, BD23 1NL.   (hq)
0845 058 4595   fax 0845 055 6407
email info@sleepcouncil.org.uk
http://www.sleepcouncil.com
▲ Company Limited by Guarantee
○ *T; 'promotes the benefits of a good bed to a good night's sleep to the consumer & media on behalf of bed manufacturers & retailers'
● Inf - Advertising
M 5,000 f
¶ Marketing Newz - 3; free.

Slough Chamber of Commerce
a local chamber of **Thames Valley Chamber of Commerce & Industry**

Slurry Surfacing Contractors Association
in 2008 merged with the Road Surface Dressing Association & the High Friction Surfacing Association to form the **Road Surface Treatments Association**

SMAE Fellowship (Association of British Physiotherapists) (SMAE)   1919
NR   New Hall, 149 Bath Rd, MAIDENHEAD, Berks, SL6 4LA.   (hq)
        01628 621100
        Principal: Michael J Batt
▲   Un-incorporated Society
○   *P; to promote professionalism & training in physiotherapy &
        sports injuries; covers surgical chiropody, podiatric medicine
        & complementary medicine
<   SMAE Institute
M   i

Small Abattoir Federation   1998
NR   Noel Chadwick Ltd, 51 High Street, Standish, WIGAN, Lancs,
        WN6 OHA.   (hb)
        01257 421137
        Sec: John Chadwick
○   *T

Small Animal Medical Society
        a group of the **British Small Animal Veterinary Association**

Small Charities Coalition   (SCC)
NR   24 Stephenson Way, LONDON, NW1 2DP.   (hq)
        020 7391 4812   fax 020 7391 4808
        email info@smallcharities.org.uk
        http://www.smallcharities.org.uk
        Chief Exec: Cath Lee
▲   Company Limited by Guarantee; Registered Charity
○   *N; to help small charities & trustees gain access to the skills,
        experience & resources they need to achieve their aims
Gp   Charity Trustee Networks

**Small Electrical Appliance Marketing Association   (SEAMA)
1981**
■   Airport House, Purley Way, CROYDON, Surrey, CR0 0XZ.
        (asa)
        020 8253 4508   fax 020 8253 4510
        email seama@admin.co.uk   http://www.seama.org.uk
        Sec: T Faithfull
▲   Un-incorporated Society
○   *T
●   Conf - Mtgs - SG - Stat - Inf - LG
M   12 f (22 brand names)
¶   LM; free.   Retailers Guide to Service - 1; ftm & retailers.

Small Farms Association   (SFA)   1987
■   Ley Coombe Farm, Modbury, IVYBRIDGE, Devon, PL21 0TU.
        (hq)
        01548 830302
        http://www.small-farms-association.org
        Chmn: David Trigger
▲   Un-incorporated Society
○   *F; for those who are interested in the conservation of the
        countryside, particularly farmers who farm less than 250
        acres, & also practise less intensive traditional methods of
        farming that are sympathetic to the needs of the environment
        & its wildlife
Gp   Steering group for marketing
●   Conf - Mtgs - ET - VE - LG
M   250 i
¶   NL - 12; ftm, on request nm.

Small Firms Association   (SFA)
IRL   Confederation House, 84-86 Lower Baggot St, DUBLIN 2,
        Republic of Ireland.   (hq)
        353 (1) 605 1602   fax 353 (1) 638 1602
        email info@sfa.ie   http://www.sfa.ie
        Dir: Patricia Callan
○   *T; national organisation exclusively representing the needs of
        enterprises with less than 50 employees
●   Comp - Conf - ET - Inf - LG - Mtgs - Res - Stat
<   Business Europe; Eur Assn of Craft, Small & Medium-Sized
        Enterprises (UEAPME); Ir Business & Emplrs Confed (IBEC)
M   8,000 f
¶   Owner Manager Magazine - 6; ftm.

Small Practices Association
        since September 2007 **Family Doctor Association**

Small Voices
        see **UK Federation of Smaller Mental Health Agencies**

Small Woods Association   (SWA)   1988
NR   Green Wood Centre, Station Rd, Coalbrookedale, TELFORD,
        Shropshire, TF8 7DR.   (hq)
        01952 432769   fax 01952 433082
        http://www.smallwoods.org.uk
        Contact: Diane Wood
▲   Company Limited by Guarantee; Registered Charity
○   *K, *N; to advance education in the conservation of small
        woodlands
Gp   Policy development; Training; Marketing; Information line
●   Conf - Mtgs - ET - Exhib - SG - Inf - VE - LG
M   700 i, 100 f, 50 org, UK / 10 i, 5 org, o'seas
¶   Smallwoods - 4.
        Small Woods Information Pack.
        Woodland Initiatives Register.

Smart Housing
        an association of **BEAMA Ltd**

Smoke Control Association   (SCA)
■   2 Waltham Court, Milley Lane, Hare Hatch, READING, Berks,
        RG10 9TH.   (hq)
        0118-940 3416   fax 0118-940 6258
        email info@feta.co.uk   http://www.feta.co.uk
        Dir-Gen: C Sloan
○   *T; specialist smoke control section of the HEVAC
        Association.   Develops & promotes high standards of
        quality, design, safety & workmanship in the industry &
        publishes standards for smoke control
Gp   Technical
●   Mtgs - Exhib - Stat - LG
<   Fedn Envtl Tr Assns (FETA)
M   22 f

Snack Food Association
        a group of **Food & Drink Industry Ireland**

**Snack, Nut & Crisp Manufacturers Association   (SNACMA)
1983**
NR   6 Catherine St, LONDON, WC2B 5JJ.   (hq)
        020 7420 7220   fax 020 7420 7221
        email esa@esa.org.uk   http://www.esa.org.uk
        Sec Gen: Steve Chandler
▲   Company Limited by Guarantee
○   *T; to collaborate with industry players & external stakeholders
        in order to develop & grow savoury snacks in the UK
Gp   Working groups: Commercial, PR task force, Technical
●   Mtgs - ET - Stat - Inf - LG
<   Eur Snacks Assn (ESA); Food & Drink Fedn
M   5 f
¶   NL - 12; ftm.

© CBD Research Ltd · Beckenham · BR3 5JS · Tel 020 8650 7745 · E-mail cbd@cbdresearch.com · www.cbdresearch.com

Snowsport Cymru/Wales
is the trading name of the **Ski Council of Wales**

Snowsport England
see **English Ski Council Ltd**

Snowsport GB
closed in February 2010, replaced by **British Ski & Snowboard Ltd**

Snowsport Industries of Great Britain   (SIGB)   1987
- ■   3 Coalhill, The Shore, EDINBURGH, EH6 6RH.   (asa)
      0131-555 3820   fax 0131-553 7488
      email sigb@raremanagement.co.uk
      http://www.snowlife.org.uk
      Mgrs (Rare Management): Mike Jardine & Lesley Beck
- ▲   Company Limited by Guarantee
- ○   *T; for the ski & snowboard industry
- Gp   Exhibition organisation
- ●   Res - Exhib - Stat - Inf
- M   200 f
- ¶   e NL - 12; ftm only.   Exhibition Catalogue - 1; ftm, £5 nm.

Snowsport Scotland   (SNSC)   1963
- ■   Caledonia House, South Gyle, EDINBURGH, EH12 9DQ.   (hq)
      0131-625 4405   fax 0131-317 7202
      email info@snowsportscotland.org
      http://www.snowsportscotland.org
      Chief Exec: Jane Harvey
- ▲   Company Limited by Guarantee
- ○   *S; national governing body for skiing & snowboarding in Scotland
- Gp   Clubs (include) Skiing: Disabled, nordic, alpine, freestyle; Snowboarding
- ●   Mtgs - ET - Exam - Comp - LG
- <   Fédn Intle de Ski; Brit Ski & Snowboard Ltd; Scot Sports Assn
- M   7,000 i, 10 f, 40 clubs, UK / 20 i, o'seas
- ¶   Snowsport News - 4.
      Scottish Snowsport Hbk - 1.   AR.

** Snuff Bottle Society
Organisation lost: see Introduction paragraph 3

Snuff - Narcotic Inhaler Followers & Aficionados
- ■   191 Westcombe Hill, LONDON, SE3 7DR.
- Gp   Snuff Users
- ●   Conf
- M   20 i
- ¶   The Sniffer (Jnl) - 6; ftm only.

Soay Sheep Society   2000
- NR   Back Forest Farm, Swythamley, MACCLESFIELD, Cheshire, SK11 0RF.
       01260 227643
       email secretary.jw@soaysheep.org
       http://www.soaysheep.org
       Sec: Julie Suffolk
- ○   *B; to support Soay & Boreray sheep & the people who breed them, keep them or just like them
- ¶   NL

Social Care Association   (SCA)   1949
- ■   350 West Barnes Lane, Motspur Park, NEW MALDEN, Surrey, KT3 6NB.   (hq)
      020 8949 5837   fax 020 8949 4384
      email sca@socialcaring.co.uk
      http://www.socialcaring.co.uk
- ▲   Company Limited by Guarantee
- Br   2
- ○   *P; to promote high standards in social care services
- ●   Conf - ET - Exhib - Inf - LG
- M   4,000 i, 100 f
- ¶   Social Caring - 4.

Social, Emotional & Behavioural Difficulties Association
see **SEBDA - the Social, Emotional & Behavioural Difficulties Association**

Social History Curators Group   (SHCG)   1975
- ■   c/o Museum of Croydon, Croydon Clocktower, Katharine St, CROYDON, CR9 1ET.   (sb)
      email enquiry@shcg.org.uk   http://www.shcg.org.uk
      Sec: Georgina Young
- ▲   Registered Charity
- ○   *P; to raise standards of curatorship in museums; interest in all aspects of social history
- ●   Conf - ET - SG - VE - LG
- <   Museums Assn; Collections Trust
- M   170 i, 123 f, UK / 8 i, o'seas
      (Sub: £18 i, £38 f, UK / £26 i, o'seas)
- ¶   Social History in Museums (Jnl) - 1; ftm, £7.50 nm.
      News - 3; ftm only.

Social History Society   (SHS)   1976
- ■   Centre for Social History, Furness College, LANCASTER, LA1 4YG.   (hq)
      01524 592547   fax 01524 846102
      email l.persson@lancaster.ac.uk
      http://www.socialhistory.org.uk
      Admin Sec: Linda Persson
- ▲   Registered Charity
- ○   *P; to encourage the study of the history of society
- ●   Conf
- M   250 i, UK / 100 i, o'seas
- ¶   Cultural & Social History - 3; ftm only.

Social Policy Association   (SPA)
- NR   c/o Prof C Glendinning, SPRU, University of York, Heslington, YORK, N Yorks, YO10 5DD.   (chmn/b)
       email cg20@york.ac.uk   http://www.social-policy.com
       Chmn: Prof Caroline Glendinning
- ○   *P; for academics & practitioners working in social policy

Social Research Association   (SRA)   1978
- ■   24-32 Stephenson Way, LONDON, NW1 2HX.   (hq)
      020 7388 2391
      email admin@the-sra.org.uk   http://www.the-sra.org.uk
      Dir: Nigel Goldie
- ▲   Company Limited by Guarantee; Registered Charity
- Br   3
- ○   *P; to advance the conduct, development & application of social research
- Gp   C'ees: Events, Training
       Working gps: Commissioning & funding, Dissemination
- ●   Conf - Mtgs - ET - Res
- M   1,000 i, UK / 30 i, o'seas
- ¶   SRA News (NL) - 4;   e-bulletin - 12; both ftm only.
      Ethical Guidelines; ftm, £10 nm.
      Data Protection Act 1998: guidelines for social research; ftm, £10 nm.
      Commissioning Social Research: a good practice guide; ftm, £10 nm.

Socialist Environment & Resources Association   (SERA)   1973
- NR   1 London Bridge, Downstream Bldg (2nd floor), LONDON, SE1 9BG.   (hq)
       020 7022 1985
       email enquiries@sera.org.uk   http://www.sera.org.uk
       Co Chmn: Leonie Cooper & Martin Tiedeman
- ▲   Company Limited by Guarantee
- ○   *K; 'an environmental pressure group, affiliated to the Labour Party'
- Gp   Energy; Transport; Waste
- ●   Conf - Mtgs - Inf - LG
- <   Labour Party
- M   992 i, 23 f, 45 org, UK
- ¶   New Ground - 2; ftm.

Socialist Health Association (SHA) 1930
■ 22 Blair Rd, East Chorlton, MANCHESTER, Lancs, M16 8NS.
     (hq)
     0161-286 1926
     email admin@sochealth.co.uk
     http://www.sochealth.co.uk
     Dir: Martin Rathfelder
▲ Un-incorporated Society
Br 6
○ *K; to defend & extend the NHS; to develop the Labour Party's
     health policies; to encourage debate about politics & health
● Conf - Mtgs - SG
< Brit Labour Party
M 800 i, 100 org, UK / 10 i, o'seas
¶ Socialism & Health (Jnl) - 2/3; free.

La Société Guernesiaise 1882
■ Candie Gardens, ST PETER PORT, Guernsey, GY1 1UG.   (hq)
     01481 725093   fax 01481 726248
     email societe@cwgsy.net   http://www.societe.org.gg
     Sec: Mrs Lawney Martin
▲ Incorporated Society
○ *L; all aspects of natural science, archaeology, history, folklore,
     language, geography, geology, genealogy, nature
     conservation, etc of Guernsey & its islands
Gp Archaeology; Astronomy; Botany; Climate change;
     Entomology; Family history; Geology & geography; Historic
     buildings; History & philology; Marine biology & zoology;
     Nature conservation; Ornithology
● Res - Lib - VE - LG
< Alderney Wildlife Trust; Bat Gp; Friends of Priaulx Library;
     Guernsey Conservation Volunteers; La Comité d'la Culture
     Guernésiase; La Société Sercquiaise; Meteorological
     Observatory; NCCPG (Guernsey gp), WEA
M 1,150 i, 65 f, (260, UK / 110, foreign)
¶ Transactions - 1; ftm, £10 nm.   NL - 3; ftm only.

Société Jersiaise 1873
■ 7 Pier Rd, ST HELIER, Jersey, Channel Islands, JE2 4XW.   (hq)
     01534 758314   fax 01534 888262
     email societe@societe-jersiaise.org
     http://www.societe-jersiaise.org
     Exec Dir: Mrs Pauline J Syvret
▲ Registered Charity
○ *L; the study of the history, language, geology, natural history &
     antiquities of Jersey
Gp Archives; Bibliography; Garden history; History; Numismatics
● Mtgs - ET - Res - Exhib - SG - Inf - Lib - VE - Preservation
< Museums Assn
M 3,500 i
¶ Bulletin - 1; ftm, £15 nm.

Society of Academic & Research Surgery (SARS) 1953
NR at the Royal College of Surgeons, 35-43 Lincoln's Inn Fields,
     LONDON, WC2A 3PE.   (hsb)
     020 7869 6640   fax 020 7869 6644
     email sars@rcseng.ac.uk
     http://www.surgicalresearch.org.uk
     Hon Sec: Frank Smith
○ *L; to provide for the interchange of information about research
     related to surgery & surgical disease
● Conf - Mtgs - Res
M 600 i
¶ Summaries of papers given at meetings are published in the
     British Journal of Surgery.

Society for Acute Medicine (SAM)
NR 9 Queen St, EDINBURGH, EH12 1JQ.   (hs/b)
     email sam@rcpe.ac.uk
     http://www.acutemedicine.org.uk
     Sec: Dr Mark Holland   Admin: Mrs Christina Berwick
○ *P

Society of Adhesion & Adhesives
     a group of the **Institute of Materials, Minerals & Mining**

Society for Advanced Legal Studies 1997
NR Charles Clore House, 17 Russell Square, LONDON,
     WC1B 5DR.   (hq)
     020 7862 5865   fax 020 7862 5855
     email sals@sas.ac.uk   http://www.ials.sas.ac.uk/sals/
     society.htm
     Sec: Julian Harris
○ *Q; to facilitate legal research at an advanced level; to
     engender collaboration between scholars & those involved in
     the practice of law
M 1,000+ i
¶ Amicus Curiae (Jnl) - 4; ftm, £75 nm.

**Society for the Advancement of Anaesthesia in Dentistry
(SAAD) 1957**
NR 21 Portland Place, LONDON, W1B 1PY.   (hq)
     020 7631 8893
     email saad@aagbi.org   http://www.saad.org.uk
     Exec Sec: Fiona Wraith
▲ Registered Charity
○ *L; to research into the applications of methods of pain &
     anxiety control in dentistry
● Conf - ET - Courses - Lectures
< Intl Fedn of Dental Anaesthesiology Socs
M 1,700 i, UK / 300 i, o'seas
¶ SAAD Digest - 4.

**Society for the Advancement of Games & Simulations in
Education & Training (SAGSET) 1970**
NR Staffordshire University Business School, College Road, STOKE-
     on-TRENT, Staffs, ST4 2DE.   (hsb)
     01782 294000
     http://www.sagset.org
     Sec: Peter J Considine
▲ Un-incorporated Society
○ *E; to develop games, simulations & all forms of interactive
     learning in education & training
● Conf - Mtgs - ET - Inf
< ISAGA, ABSEL
M 71 i, 26 f & org, UK / 26 i, 23 f & org, o'seas
¶ Interact - 3.
     International Simulation & Gaming Research Ybk.

Society for the Advancement of Management Studies Ltd 1963
NR Durham Business School, Durham University, Mill Hall Lane,
     DURHAM, DH1 3LB.   (admin/b)
     0191-334 5395
     email j.m.brudenell@durham.ac.uk
     Admin: J M Brudenell
     Chmn: Prof Richard Thorpe
▲ Registered Charity
○ *P; advancement of education in management studies
● Mtgs - ET - Exhib - Publishing

*Society for the Advancement of Philosophical Enquiry & Reflection in
Education*
     see **SAPERE (Society for the Advancement of Philosophical
     Enquiry & Reflection in Education)**

Society for All Artists
     see **SAA - the Society for All Artists**

Society of Allied & Independent Funeral Directors
     an alternative title for the **National Society of Allied &
     Independent Funeral Directors**

Society for Anaerobic Microbiology   1975
NR   Centre for Biomolecular Sciences, Clifton Boulevard, University
       Park, NOTTINGHAM, NG7 2RD.   (sb)
       0115 846 6287
       email jacqueline.minton@nottingham.ac.uk
       Sec: Jacqueline Minton
▲   Company Limited by Guarantee
○   *P
●   Conf - Mtgs - ET
M   200 i, UK / 68 i, o'seas
¶   NL - 2; free.
       Proceedings of Biennial Meetings - 1/2 yrly; free to
       delegates, £20.

Society of Analytical Psychology Ltd
§   1 Daleham Gardens, LONDON, NW3 5BY.   (hq)
       020 7435 7696
       a training institue offering psychotherapy, analysis & short-term
       work to people who are in distress, or who have emotional
       problems

Society of Ancients   (SOA)   1965
NR   Twin Oaks, The Drive, Ifold, LOXWOOD, W Sussex,
       RH14 0TE.   (hsp)
       01403 752973
       email davidedwards30@hotmail.com
       http://www.soa.org.uk
       Sec: David Edwards
▲   Un-incorporated Society
○   *G; to promote the study of ancient & mediæval military history
       & wargaming therein (3000 BC - 1500 AD)
●   Conf - Exhib - Comp
M   872 i, UK / 446 i, o'seas
¶   Slingshot - 6.

Society for Anglo-Chinese Understanding Ltd   (SACU)   1965
■   PO Box 179, BARROW IN FURNESS, Cumbria, LA14 9BQ.
       (hq)
       01229 472010
       email info@sacu.org   http://www.sacu.org
       Chmn: David Clare
▲   Company Limited by Guarantee; Registered Charity
Br   5
○   *X; to promote friendship & understanding between the peoples
       of Britain & China
●   Mtgs - ET - Lib - Inf on China related events in Britain - Inf
       about China for schools, playgroups & local groups
M   340 i, 4 org
       (Subs: £18 i, £22 org)
¶   China Eye - 4; ftm, £1 nm.   Hbk.   AR.
       Education pack on request.

Society of Antiquaries of London   1707
■   Burlington House, Piccadilly, LONDON, W1J 0BE.   (hq)
       020 7734 0193
       Gen Sec: John Lewis
▲   Registered Charity
○   *L; promotion of antiquarian interests, particularly
       archaeological investigation & the preservation of historic
       buildings
●   Conf - Mtgs - Res - Lib
M   1,700 i, UK / 300 i, o'seas
¶   Antiquaries Jnl - 1.
       Research reports;   Occasional papers; prices vary.

Society of Antiquaries of Newcastle upon Tyne   (SANT)   1813
■   Great North Museum: Hancock, Barras Bridge,
       NEWCASTLE UPON TYNE, NE2 4PT.   (hq)
       0191-231 2700
       email admin@newcastle-antiquaries.org.uk
       http://www.newcastle-antiquaries.org.uk
       Secs: Dr N Hodgson,   Derek Cutts
▲   Registered Charity
○   *L; the study & preservation of antiquities & historical records
       particularly relating to the old counties of Northumberland &
       Durham & Newcastle upon Tyne
●   Conf - Mtgs - Res - Lib - VE - One-day workshop (annual) -
       Workshops (10 evenings)
M   600 i, 100 f, UK / 20 i, 20 f, o'seas
¶   Archaeologia Aeliana - 1.
       Occasional research publications & guide books.

Society of Antiquaries of Scotland   1780
■   National Museums Scotland, Chambers St, EDINBURGH,
       EH1 1JF.   (hq)
       0131-247 4115   fax 0131-247 4163
       email administration@socantscot.org
       http://www.socantscot.org
       Dir: Dr Simon Gilmour
▲   Registered Charity
○   *L; archaeology, history & antiquities of Scotland
●   Conf - Mtgs - Res - VE - LG
<   Built Environment Forum Scotland; The Archaeology Forum
M   3,000 i, UK / 600 i, o'seas
       (Sub: £60)
¶   Proceedings - 1; ftm, £60 nm.   NL - 2; ftm only.
       Books - irreg; prices vary.

Society for Applied Microbiology   (Sfam)   1931
NR   Bedford Heights, Brickhill Drive, BEDFORD, MK41 7PH.   (hq)
       01234 326661
       email info@sfam.org.uk   http://www.sfam.org.uk
       Chief Exec: Philip Wheat
▲   Registered Charity; Un-incorporated Society
○   *L; to advance the study of microbiology, in its application to
       the environment, agriculture & industry
Gp   Special interest: Bioengineering, Educational development,
       Environmental, Food safety & technology, Infection,
       Molecular biology, Prevention &treatment
●   Conf - Publishing
<   Intl U Microbiology Socs; Fedn Eur Microbiology Socs; Inst of
       Biology; Foundation for Science & Technology; UK Nat C'ee
       for Microbiology
M   1300 i, UK / 500 i, o'seas
¶   Jnl of Applied Microbiology - 12; [with]
       Letters in Applied Microbiology - 12.
       Environmental Microbiology - 6.   NL - 4.

Society for Applied Philosophy   (SAP)   1982
■   c/o Jon Cameron, RIISS, 19 College Bounds, University of
       Aberdeen, ABERDEEN, AB24 3UG.   (admin)
       01224 272343
       Admin: Jon Cameron
       Hon Sec: Dr Kimberley Brownlee
▲   Registered Charity
○   *L; to promote philosophical research into practical problems of
       social & ethical concern
●   Conf - Funding academic activity
M   80 i, UK / 45 i, o'seas
       (Sub: £25)
¶   Jnl of Applied Philosophy - 4; ftm, £70 nm.

Society of Archer-Antiquaries (SAA) 1956
- 29 Batley Court, OLDLAND, S Glos, BS30 8YZ.   (hsp)
  0117-932 3276   fax 0117-932 3276
  email bogaman@btinternet.com
  http://www.societyofarcher-antiquaries.org
  Hon Sec: Hugh D Hewitt Soar
- ▲ Registered Charity
- Br Italy
- ○ *L; the study of the history & development of the bow & arrow across the world
- ● Mtgs - Res - Inf - Lib
- M 227 i, UK / 161 i, o'seas
- ¶ Jnl - 1;   NL - 3; both ftm only.

Society of Architectural Historians of Great Britain   (SAHGB) 1956
- NR RCAHMS, 16 Bernard Terrace, EDINBURGH, EH8 9NX.   (hsb)
  email honsecretary@sahgb.org.uk
  http://www.sahgb.org.uk
  Hon Sec: Simon Green
- ▲ Company Limited by Guarantee; Registered Charity
- ○ *L; to encourage an interest in the history of architecture
- ● Conf - Mtgs - Res - VE
- ¶ Architectural History - 1.   NL - 3.

Society of Architectural Illustration Ltd   (SAI) 1975
- Rosemary Cottage, Bletchinglye Lane, ROTHERFIELD, E Sussex, TN6 3NN.   (hq)
  01892 852578
  email info@sai.org.uk   http://www.sai.org.uk
  Admin: Heather Coe
- ▲ Registered Charity
- ○ *A, *P; for members of the design profession specialising in illustration of architectural subjects
- Gp Illustrators; Photographers; Model makers
- ● Conf - Mtgs - ET - Exhib - Comp
- M 178 i, UK / 8 i, o'seas
- ¶ Viewpoint - 2;   NL - 4; both free.
  LM; on application & by region.   AR.
- ✕ Society of Architectural Illustrators

Society of Archivists
  merged in 2010 with the National Council on Archives & the Association of Chief Archivists in Local Government to form the
  Archives & Records Association (UK & Ireland)

Society for Army Historical Research (SAHR) 1921
- NR c/o Colonel G N R Sayle OBE, c/o The Cavalry & Guards Club, 127 Piccadilly, LONDON, W1J 7PX.   (accom address)
  http://www.sahr.co.uk
  Mem Sec: Col G N R Sayle
- ▲ Registered Charity
- ○ *L; research into the history & traditions of the British Army, the land forces of the Empire, Dominions & Commonwealth & ancillary units attached thereto
- ● Mtgs - Res - VE - Publishing members' research - Lecture series
- M 930 i, 20 org, UK / 40 i, 10 org, o'seas
- ¶ Jnl - 4.   Special issues - irreg; ftm only.

Society of Artists' Agents (SAA) 1992
- 31 Eleanor Rd, LONDON, E15 4AB.   (admin/p)
  0845 050 7600
  http://www.saahub.com
- ▲ Un-incorporated Society
- ○ *T; to promote the use of illustration & improve the working practices between clients, agents & artists
- ● Mtgs
- < Pro-Action
- M 11 f
- ¶ Originals - 1; ftm.

Society of Assistants Teaching in Preparatory Schools Ltd
  see **SATIPS - Support & Training in Prep Schools**

Society of Authors (SoA) 1884
- 84 Drayton Gardens, LONDON, SW10 9SB.   (hq)
  020 7373 6642   fax 020 7373 5768
  email info@societyofauthors.org
  http://www.societyofauthors.org
  Gen Sec: Mark Le Fanu
- ○ *U
- Gp Translators' Association;
  Academic writers; Broadcasting; Children's writers & illustrators; Educational writers; Medical writers
- ● Conf - Mtgs - Inf - Empl - LG
- < Creators' Rights Alliance
- M 8,000 i
- ¶ The Author - 4.

Society of Authors in Scotland
- c/o The Society of Authors, 84 Drayton Gardens, LONDON, SW10 9SB.   (mail/address)
  020 7373 6642   fax 020 7373 5768
  email anguskonstam@aol.com
  Hon Sec: Caroline Dunford
- ▲ Company Limited by Guarantee
- ○ *A; the Scottish branch of the Society of Authors
- ● Mtgs - ET - VE
- < Soc Authors
- M 450 i
- ¶ Occasional NL - irreg.

Society for the Autistically Handicapped
  see **Autism Independent UK (Society for the Autistically Handicapped**

Society of Automotive Engineers - UK
  Company dissolved 2 August 2011

Society of Automotive Historians in Britain   (SAH) 1977
- 20 Mapperley Gardens, Moseley, BIRMINGHAM, W Midlands, B13 8RN.   (mem/sp)
  0121-449 9666
  Mem Sec: Anders Clausager
- ▲ Un-incorporated Society
- ○ *G; to encourage research, preservation, recording, compilation & publication of historical facts concerning the worldwide development of the automobile & related items
- ● Conf - Res - Res - Lib - PL
- < American Histl Soc
- > Veteran Car Club of GB
- M c 100 i, UK / c 900 i, o'seas
  (Sub: £30)
- ¶ SAHB Times - 4; free.
  Aspects of Motoring History - 1; ftm, £5 nm.
  in USA:
  SAH Jnl - 6;   SAH Review - irreg; both ftm only.

Society for Back Pain Research
  a specialist society of the **British Orthopaedic Association**

Society of Bariatric Anaesthetists   (SOBAUK) 2009
- NR 21 Portland Place, LONDON, W1B 1PY.   (mail/add)
  020 7631 8889
  email sec@sobauk.com   http://www.soba@aagbi.org
  SecL Mike Margarson
- ○ *P; a specialist society for anaesthetists interested in critical care for bariatric surgical & other morbidly obese patients
- ● Conf - Mtgs
- M i
  (Sub: £25)
- ¶ NL

© CBD Research Ltd · Beckenham · BR3 5JS · Tel 020 8650 7745 · E-mail cbd@cbdresearch.com · www.cbdresearch.com

Society of Batrachologists   1995
- ■ 3 Hughes Stanton Way, MANNINGTREE, Essex, CO11 2HQ.
  (hsp)
- ○ *L
- ● Conf - VE
- M 85 i, 1 org
- ¶ On the Hop (Jnl) - 4.

Society of Biology   1950
- ■ 12 Roger St, LONDON, WC1N 2JU.   (hq)
  020 7685 2550
  email info@iob.org   http://www.societyofbiology.org
  Chief Exec: Dr Mark Downs
- ▲ Registered Charity
- Br 17; Hong Kong
- ○ *L, *P; to advance the science & practice of the biological
  sciences; to advance education & encourage the study of the
  biological sciences & their applications
- ● Conf - Mtgs - ET - Exam - Exhib - Comp - Inf - VE - LG
- < Intl U of Biological Sciences (IUBS); Eur Countries Biologists
  Assn (ECBA); Science Coun; Royal Instn; Brit Assn for the
  Advancement of Science; Save Brit Science
- M 15,800 i, 6 f, 76 org, UK / 1,331 i, o'seas
- ¶ Jnl of Biological Education - 4.
  Biologist - 6.   AR - 1.
  Publications list available.
- × 2009 (Biosciences Federation
  (Institute of Biology (merged)

Society of Bookbinders   (SOB)   1974
- NR 102 Hetherington Rd, SHEPPERTON Middx, TW17 0SW.
  (mem/sp)
  http://www.societyofbookbinders.com
  Mem Sec: Hilary Henning
- ▲ Registered Charity
- Br 8; overseas
- ○ *L, *T; to advance the art, craft & science of bookbinding, book
  restoration & conservation
- ¶ Bookbinder (Jnl) - 1.   NL - 3.

Society of Border Leicester Sheep Breeders   1896
- ■ Rock Midstead, ALNWICK, Northumberland, NE66 2TH.   (hsp)
  07891 245870   fax 01665 579326
  email border@borderleicesters.co.uk
  http://www.borderleicesters.co.uk
  Sec: Ian J R Sutherland
- ▲ Registered Charity
- ○ *B
- ● Mtgs - Exhib - Expt - Inf
- < Nat Sheep Assn
- M 250 i, 10 f, UK / 5 i, o'seas
- ¶ Jnl - 1.   Flock Book - 1; £15.   AR.

Society of Botanical Artists   (SBA)   1985
- ■ 1 Knapp Cottages, Wyke, GILLINGHAM, Dorset, SP8 4NQ.
  (hq)
  01747 825718   fax 01747 826835
  email info@soc-botanical-artists.org
  http://www.soc-botanical-artists.org
  Exec Sec: Mrs Pamela Henderson
- ▲ Company Limited by Guarantee; Registered Charity
- ○ *A, *P; to paint & record for the benefit of art, botany,
  conservation & horticulture
- ● Exhib
- M 140 i, UK / 13 i, o'seas
- ¶ Annual Exhibitions Catalogue - 1; £5.

Society of British Aerospace Companies Ltd
  on 1 October 2009 merged with the Association of Police & Public
  Security Suppliers & the Defence Manufacturers Association to form
  ADS Group Ltd

Society of the British Battery Industry
  2011 merged with the Independent Battery Distributors Association to
  form the **British Battery Industry Federation**

Society of British Gas Industries
  since 2008 **SBGI**

Society of British Neurological Surgeons   (SBNS)   1926
- ■ at the Royal College of Surgeons, 35-43 Lincoln's Inn Fields,
  LONDON, WC2A 3PE.   (hq)
  020 7869 6892   fax 020 7869 6890
  email admin@sbns.org.uk   http://www.sbns.org
  Admin: Suzanne Murray
- ○ *P; interests of neurosurgery & neurosurgeons
- ● Conf - Mtgs - Exam - Res - LG
- < WFNS; EANS
- M c 400 i
- ¶ NL - 3.

Society of British Theatre Designers   (SBTD)   1971
- ■ Theatre Design Dept, Rose Bruford College, Burnt Oak Lane,
  SIDCUP, Kent, DA15 9DF.   (regd/office)
  020 8308 2664
  email admin@theatredesign.org.uk
  http://www.theatredesign.org.uk
  Jt Hon Secs: Sophie Jump & Iona McLeish
- ▲ Registered Charity
- ○ *P; to enhance the standing of British theatre design at home &
  abroad; to support designers in their working lives
- ● Conf - Exhib (4-yrly) - Inf
- < Intl Org of Scenographers (OISTAT); Assn of Brit Theatre
  Technicians (ABTT)
- M 300 i, 10 org, UK / 10 i, o'seas
  (Sub: £60 i, £200 org, UK / £67.50 i, o'seas)
- ¶ The Blue Pages (NL) - 4; ftm only.

**Society of British Water & Wastewater Industries   (SBWWI)
1986**
- ■ 38 Holly Walk, LEAMINGTON SPA, Warks, CV32 4LY.   (hq)
  01926 831530   fax 01926 831931
  email hq@sbwwi.co.uk   http://www.sbwwi.co.uk
  Exec Dir: Carol Hickman
- ▲ Un-incorporated Society
- ○ *T; for manufacturers, contractors, suppliers, consultants &
  other organisations involved in the UK water & wastewater
  industry
- Gp Sections: Commercial, Technical
  Groups: Export, Health & safety, Leakage, Specialist products
- ● Conf - Mtgs - Exhib - Stat - Inf - LG
- < Construction Products Assn
- M 90 f

Society for Broadband Engineers
  see **SCTE - the Society for Broadband Engineers**

Society of Business Economists   (SBE)   1953
- ■ Dean House, Vernham Dean, ANDOVER, Hants, SP11 0JZ.
  (sec/p)
  01264 737552
  email admin@sbe.co.uk   http://www.sbe.co.uk
  Sec: Katie Abberton
- ▲ Company Limited by Guarantee
- ○ *P; applications of economics in business & industry
- Gp Forecasting; Industrial economics; Statistics
- ● Conf - Mtgs - SG
- < Intl Fedn Assns Business Economists (IFABE); Assn Française
  Economistes d'Entreprise (AFEDE); Canadian Assn Business
  Economists (CABE); Nat Assn Business
  Economists (NABE)(USA)
- M 600 i, UK / 50 i, o'seas
- ¶ The Business Economist (Jnl) - 3; ftm, £38 nm (£45 outside
  Europe).

Society of Business Practitioners (SBP) 1956
- ■ PO Box 11, SANDBACH, Cheshire, CW11 3GE.   (hq)
  01270 526339   fax 01270 526339
  email info@mamsasbp.org.uk
  http://www.mamsasbp.org.uk
  Pres: M Whitaker
- ▲ Company Limited by Guarantee
- Br China, Hong Kong, New Zealand, Singapore
- ○ *P; professional qualifications for all aspects of management
- ● ET - Exam
- M 3,000 i, UK / 9,000 i, o'seas
- ¶ Nexus - 1.

Society of Cable Telecommunication Engineers
   see **SCTE - the Society for Broadband Engineers**

Society Campaigning for the Removal of Exasperating Automated Switchboards (SCREAMS) 2003
- NR 191 Westcombe Hill, LONDON, SE3 7DR.
- ○ *K
- M 153 i
- ¶ Human Voices (NL) - 4.

Society for Cardiological Science & Technology (SCST) 1948
- ■ Executive Business Support, City Wharf, Davidson Road, LICHFIELD, Staffs, WS14 9DS.   (admin)
  0845 838 6037   fax 0121-355 2420
  email admin@scst.org.uk   http://www.scst.org.uk
  Hon Sec: Mrs Catriona MacGregor
- ▲ Registered Charity
- ○ *P; to support clinical physiologists within cardiology
- ● ET - Exam - LG
- M 1,500 i

Society for Cardiothoracic Surgery in Great Britain & Ireland (SCTS) 1933
- ■ at the Royal College of Surgeons, 35-43 Lincoln's Inn Fields, LONDON, WC2A 3PE.   (asa)
  020 7869 6893   fax 020 7869 6890
  email sctsadmin@scts.org   http://www.scts.org
  Hon Sec: Graham Cooper
- ▲ Registered Charity
- ○ *P; cardiothoracic surgery
- ● Conf - ET - Exhib - Empl - LG
- M 492 i, UK / 53 i, o'seas

Society of Chartered Surveyors Ireland
- IRL 38 Merrion Sq, DUBLIN 2, Republic of Ireland.
  353 (1) 661 1794
  email info@scsi.ie   http://www.scsi.ie
  Hon Sec: Pauline Daly
- ○ *P
- × 2011 (Irish Auctioneers & Valuers Institute
  (Society of Chartered Surveyors

Society of Cheese Connoisseurs (SCC) 1985
- NR 76c The Avenue, BECKENHAM, Kent, BR3 5ES.   (mail address)
- ○ *G
- ● Mtgs - VE - Tastings
- M 25 i
- ¶ Mousetrap! (incl AR) - 1;   NL - 4; both ftm only.

Society of Chemical Industry (SCI) 1881
- NR 14-15 Belgrave Sq, LONDON, SW1X 8PS.   (hq)
  020 7598 1500   fax 020 7598 1545
  email secretariat@soci.org   http://www.soci.org
  Exec Dir: Joanne Lyall
- ▲ Registered Charity
- Br 8
- ○ *L; 'the society where science meets industry on independent and impartial ground'
- Gp Bioresources; Colloid & surface chemistry; Construction materials; Environment; Fine chemicals; Food; Health & safety; Horticulture; Lipids; Science & enterprise

Society of Chief Architects of Local Authorities
   since 2008 **Scala - Serving Construction & Architecture in Local Authorities**

Society of Chief Librarians (SCL) 1996
- ■ Public Libraries Advocacy Manager, The British Library, 96 Euston Rd, LONDON, NW1 2DB.
  020 7412 7114
  http://www.goscl.com
  Communications Mgr: Elizabeth Elford
- ▲ Un-incorporated Society
- ○ *P; to take a leading role in the development of public libraries through sharing best practices, advocating for continuous improvement on behalf of local people, & leading the debate on the future of the public library service
- ● Conf - Mtgs - Res - SG - Stat - LG
- < Quality Forum [for library & information services]; Share the Vision
- M 122 i
- ¶ Fines & Charges in Public Libraries in England & Wales - 1.

Society of Chief Officers of Trading Standards in Scotland (SCOTSS) 1975
- NR Trading Standards Service, John Muir House, HADDINGTON, E Lothian, EH41 3HA.   (hsb)
  01620 827365
  email tmcauley@eastlothian.gov.uk
  http://www.scotss.org.uk
  Sec: Tony McAuley
- ▲ Un-incorporated Society
- ○ *P; coordination of trading standards & consumer protection in Scotland
- < Trading Standards Inst
- M 33 i

Society for Children & Adults with Learning Disabilities & their Families
   see **Rescare - the Society for Children & Adults with Learning Disabilities & their Families**

Society of Chiropodists & Podiatrists (SCP) 1945
- NR 1 Fellmonger's Path, Tower Bridge Rd, LONDON, SE1 3LY.   (hq)
  020 7234 8620   fax 0845 450 3721
  email enq@scpod.org   http://www.feetforlife.org
  Chief Exec: Joanna Brown
- ▲ Un-incorporated Society
- Br 40
- ○ *P, *U; registered podiatrists
- < Allied Health Professions Fedn (AHPF); Trades U Congress (TUC)
- M 10,000 i
- ¶ Podiatry Now - 12.

Society of Chiropodists & Podiatrists of Ireland
- IRL 69 Granville Rd, DUNLAOGHAIRE, Co Dublin, Republic of Ireland.
  353 (1) 202 4939
  Admin Sec: Donald Maxwell
- ○ *P

Society for Church Archaeology 1996
- NR c/o CBA, St Mary's House, 66 Bootham, YORK, YO30 7BZ.   (hsb)
  01522 851340
  email churcharchaeology@gmail.com
  http://www.britarch.ac.uk/socchurcharchaeol
  Sec: Kevin Booth (kevin.booth@ebglish-heritage.org.uk)
- ○ *G; study & preservation of churches, chapels & their contents (monuments, stained glass, bells & furnishings) - as well as burial grounds, & earthworks

© CBD Research Ltd · Beckenham · BR3 5JS · Tel 020 8650 7745 · E-mail cbd@cbdresearch.com · www.cbdresearch.com

Society of Cirplanologists   1955
- ■ 26 Roe Cross Green, Mottram, HYDE, Cheshire, SK14 6LP.
  (hsp)
  01457 763485
  Sec: E A Rose
- ▲ Un-incorporated Society
- ○ *L; study, collection, preservation of circuit plans, mainly
  Methodist
- ● Informal annual mtg
- M 100 i, UK / 5 i, o'seas
- ¶ Cirplan - 2; £1.50.

**Society of Clinical Perfusion Scientists of Great Britain & Ireland
1974**
- ■ at the Royal College of Surgeons, 35-43 Lincoln's Inn Fields,
  LONDON, WC2A 3PE.   (hq)
  020 7869 6891
  http://www.sopgbi.org
  Admin: Ms Valerie Campbell
- ○ *P

Society of Clinical Psychiatrists   (SCP)   1958
- ■ Chapel Garth, Westway, Crayke, YORK, YO61 4TE.   (hsp)
  01347 823042
  email mthaslam@btopenworld.com
  http://www.scpnet.com
  Hon Sec: Dr M T Haslam
- ▲ Un-incorporated Society
- ○ *P; to promote good practice in psychiatry; to undertake studies
  in related matters
- Gp Suspended doctors support
- ● Conf - Mtgs - Res - SG - LG
- M 50 i, UK / 5 i, o'seas
  (Sub: £20)
- ¶ NL - updated on web.

Society of Coat Hook & Hanger Collectors   (SCHHC)   1976
- ■ 76c The Avenue, BECKENHAM, Kent, BR3 5EF.   (hsp)
- ▲ Un-incorporated Society
- ○ *G
- ● Conf - Mtgs
- M i
- ✕ 2010 Society of Coat Hook Collectors

**Society of College, National & University Libraries
(SCONUL)   1950**
- NR 102 Euston St, London, NW1 2HA.   (hq)
  020 7387 0317   fax 020 7383 3197
  email info@sconul.ac.uk   http://www.sconul.ac.uk
  Exec Dir: Ann Rossiter
- ▲ Company Limited by Guarantee; Registered Charity
- ○ *L; to promote excellence in library services in higher education
  & national libraries across the UK & Ireland
- ● LG - Mtgs
- M university & national libraries

Society for Companion Animal Studies   (SCAS)   1979
- NR The Blue Cross, Shilton Rd, BURFORD, Oxon, OX18 4PF.   (hq)
  01993 825597   fax 01993 825598
  email info@scas.org.uk   http://www.scas.org.uk
  Dir: Jo-Ann Fowler
- ▲ Registered Charity
- Br Australia, France, Japan, Netherlands, New Zealand,
  Singapore, Spain & USA
- ○ *E, *V, *W; to study the nature of the bond between people &
  companion animals
- Gp Pet bereavement support; Research advisory panel
- ● Conf - ET - Res - Exhib - Inf - Lib
- < Intl Assn of Human-Animal Interaction Orgs (IAHAIO)
- M 361 i, 58 f, UK / 25 i, o'seas
- ¶ Jnl - 4; ftm, £2.50 nm.
  When a Pet Dies [learning pack]; £58.
  Children & Pets; £5.99.

Society for Computers & Law   (SCL)   1973
- NR 10 Hurle Crescent, Clifton, BRISTOL, BS8 2TA.   (hq)
  0117-923 7393   fax 0117-923 9305
  http://www.scl.org
  Gen Mgr: Ruth Baker
- ▲ Company Limited by Guarantee; Registered Charity
- ○ *L; to study the development of the law and practice regulating
  IT
- M 1,676 i, 68 org
- ¶ Computers & Law - 3.

**Society for Computing & Technology in Anaesthesia   (SCATA)
1987**
- ■ 21 Portland Place, LONDON, W1B 1PY.   (hq)
  email mail@scata.org.uk   http://www.scata.org.uk
  Sec: Paul Cooper
- ▲ Registered Charity
- ○ *L, *M, *P; to promote research into the use of computing &
  technology in anaesthetic practice
- ● Conf - Mtgs - ET - Res - SG - LG
- < Eur Soc for Computing & Technology Anaesthesia & Intensive
  Care; Assn Anaesthetists GB & Ireland
- M 325 i, UK / 25 i, o'seas

Society of Construction Law   (SCL)   1983
- NR The Cottage, Bulfurlong Lane, Burbage, HINCKLEY, Leics,
  LE10 2HQ.   (hq)
  01455 233253   fax 01455 233253
  http://www.scl.org.uk
  Admin: Jill Ward
- ▲ Registered Charity
- ○ *L; to promote the study & advancement of education in the
  theory & practice & application of construction law
- < Eur Soc Construction Law
- M 2,090 i
- ¶ NL - 9; ftm only.   Papers (after meetings); ftm.

Society of Construction & Quantity Surveyors   (SCQS)   1973
- ■ 24 Pennine Rise, Scissett, HUDDERSFIELD, W Yorks, HD8 9JE.
  (ch/exec/p)
  01484 863686
  http://www.scqs.org.uk
  Chief Exec: Brian Kirkham
- ▲ Company Limited by Guarantee
- ○ *P; interchange of information on quantity surveying, building
  economics, types of contract, government regulations & all
  other matters affecting the built environment in the public
  sector
- ● Conf - Mtgs - ET - Res - SG - Stat - LG
- < Fedn Property Socs
- M 224 i
- ¶ NL - 4; free.   Ybk - 1; ftm, £5 nm.

Society of Consulting Marine Engineers & Ship Surveyors   1920
- ■ 202 Lambeth Rd, LONDON, SE1 7JW.   (hq)
  020 7261 0869   fax 020 7261 0871
  email sec@scmshq.org   http://www.scmshq.org
  Sec: Paul Owen
- ▲ Company Limited by Guarantee
- ○ *P; for consulting marine engineers, naval architects & ship
  surveyors
- ● Mtgs - Inf - Social events
- < Fedn of Eur Maritime Assns of Surveyors & Consultants
  (FEMAS)
- M 252 i, UK / 137 i, o'seas
- ¶ Jnl; m only.

Society for Cooperation in Russian & Soviet Studies (SCRSS) 1924
- ■ 320 Brixton Rd, LONDON, SW9 6AB.   (hq)
  020 7274 2282   fax 020 7274 3230
  email ruslibrary@scrss.org.uk   http://www.scrss.org.uk
  Sec: Jean Turner
- ▲ Registered Charity
- ○ *X; to promote studies in the language, culture & history of Russia & other republics of the former USSR
- Gp Art; History; Lawyers & architects; Music; Russian/Soviet literature; Visual aids
- ● Conf - Mtgs - ET - Res - Exhib - Inf - Lib - PL
- < Russian State Centre for Intl Co-operation in Science & Culture; St Petersburg Assn for Intl Co-operation
- M 400 i, 18 f, 4 org, UK / 2 i, o'seas
- ¶ SCRSS Information Digest - 3; ftm, £1+p&p nm. Publicity brochure.   AR.

Society of Cosmetic Scientists (SCS) 1948
- ■ Langham House East (suite 6), Mill St, LUTON, Beds, LU1 2NA.   (hq)
  01582 726661   fax 01582 405217
  email ifscc.scs@btconnect.com   http://www.scs.org.uk
  Sec Gen: Mrs Lorna Weston
- ▲ Un-incorporated Society
- ○ *P; to promote the scientific status of the cosmetic industry
- ● Conf - Mtgs - ET (courses) - Exam - Exhib
- < Intl Fedn Socs Cosmetic Chemists (IFSCC)
- M 950 i
- ¶ International Jnl of Cosmetic Science - 6; NL - 9/10;   AR;   all ftm only.

Society of County Treasurers (SCT) 1903
- NR Finance & Resources, Staffordhire County Council, St Chad's Place, STAFFORD, ST16 2LR.   (hsb)
  0300 111 8000
  http://www.sctnet.org
  Hon Sec: Andrew Burns
- ▲ Un-incorporated Society
- ○ *P; financial management, personnel & other matters affecting local government in England & Wales
- Gp Local government finance
- ● Mtgs - SG - Stat - LG
- M 37 i
- ¶ Standard Spending Indicators - 1. Precept Return - 1.   AR.

Society for Court Studies 1995
- ■ PO Box 57089, LONDON, EC1P 1RF.   (hq)
  email admin@courtstudies.org
  http://www.courtstudies.org
  Contact: Chemeck Slowik
- ▲ Un-incorporated Society
- Br USA
- ○ *L; to stimulate the study of royal courts from 1400 to the present
- ● Conf - Mtgs
- M 240 i & f
- ¶ The Court Historian (Jnl) - 2.

Society of Crisp Packet Collectors (SCPC)
- ■ 81 Park View, Collins Road, LONDON, N5 2UD.
  Hon Sec: V Salis
- ○ *G
- ● Mtgs - Exhib
- M 13 i
- ¶ Blue Bag - irreg, ftm only.

Society of Dairy Technology (SDT) 1943
- ■ PO Box 12, APPLEBY-in-WESTMORLAND, Cumbria, CA16 6YJ.   (hq)
  01768 354034
  http://www.sdt.org
  Exec Dir: Maurice Walton
- ▲ Company Limited by Guarantee; Registered Charity
- Br 15; 1
- ○ *L, *F, *P; the advancement of dairy science & technology
- Gp Dairy - education, advisory, research; Milk & milk products processing, manufacture & distribution; Supply of dairy plant & equipment
- ● Conf - Mtgs - ET
- < Intl Dairy Fedn (through the UK Dairy Assn)
- M 450 i, UK / 30 i, o'seas
- ¶ International Jnl of Dairy Technology - 4; ftm, £230 nm.NL - 4; AR; both ftm only

Society for Dance Research (SDR) 1983
- ■ c/o Helen Thomas, London College of Fashion, 20 John Princes St, LONDON, W1B 0BJ.   (hsb)
  http://www.dancebooks.co.uk/sdr-uk/
  Sec: Dr Helen Julia Minors
- ▲ Registered Charity
- ○ *D; to further research in dance history, anthropology, analysis & criticism in both theatre & social forms
- ● Conf - Mtgs - ET - Res - Inf
- M c 170 i, c 20 org, UK / c 40 i, o'seas
- ¶ Dance Research Jnl - 2; £30 m, £35 nm o'seas.

Society of Decorative Art Curators (SODAC)
- ■ c/o Caroline Alexander, Harris Museum & Art Gallery, Market Sq, PRESTON, Lancs, PR1 2PP.   (hsb)
  01772 258248
  http://www.sodac.org.uk
  Sec: Caroline Alexander
- ▲ Un-incorporated Society
- ○ *P; to promote the decorative arts & support those with a professional interest in the subject
- ● Mtgs - VE
- M i & org
- ¶ NL - 2; ftm.

Society of Designer Craftsmen (SDC) 1887
- NR 24 Rivington St, LONDON, EC2A 3DU.   (hq)
  020 7739 3663
  email info@societyofdesignercraftsmen.org.uk
  http://www.societyofdesignercraftsmen.org.uk
- ▲ Registered Charity
- ○ *A; to promote & support the work of creative thinkers, designers & makers who continue to innovate in the crafts through their exploration of materials & skills
- Gp Ceramics; Furniture & wood; Glass; Jewellery & metal; Textiles (constructed; felted; knitted; printed; stitched; woven); Other disciplines
- ● Conf - Res - Exhib - SG - Inf
- M 529 i
- ¶ The Designer Craftsman - 1;   NL - 4; both ftm only.

Society of Diagnostic Engineers
  a division of the **Institution of Diagnostic Engineers**

Society of District Council Treasurers
- NR c/o Jason Vaughan, Weymouth & Portland Borough Council, Council Offices, North Quay, WEYMOUTH, Dorset, DT4 8TA.
  01305 838000
  email ange.b100@yahoo.co.uk   http://www.socdct.co.uk
  Pres: Jason Vaughan
  Hon Sec: Angela Brown
- ○ *P; to represent the treasurers of district councils in England & Wales
- M 201 org

© CBD Research Ltd · Beckenham · BR3 5JS · Tel 020 8650 7745 · E-mail cbd@cbdresearch.com · www.cbdresearch.com

Society of Dyers & Colourists   (SDC)   1884
NR   Perkin House, 82 Grattan Rd, BRADFORD, W Yorks,
      BD1 2LU.   (hq)
      01274 725138   fax 01274 392888
      http://www.sdc.org.uk
      Chief Exec: Susie Hargreaves
Br   7; Bangladesh, China, India (Mumbai & Tirupur), Pakistan
      (Karachi & Lahore), Sri Lanka
○   *L, *P; science & technology of colour & colouration
¶   Coloration Technology - 6.   The Colourist - 4.
      Colour Index - online.
      Textbooks & technical publications.

Society for Earthquake & Civil Engineering Dynamics
(SECED)   1969
NR   Institution of Civil Engineers, One Great George St, LONDON,
      SW1P 3AA.   (hq)
      020 7222 7722   fax 020 7222 7500
      email secretary@seced.org.uk   http://www.seced.org.uk
      Chmn: Dr Ahmed Elghazouli
○   *L, *Q; the better design of structures subject to dynamic loads
      from earthquakes & other sources
M   i & org
¶   NL - 4.

Society for Economic Analysis Ltd   (SEAL)   1933
NR   46 Heddon Court Avenue, Cockfosters, BARNET, Herts,
      BN4 9NG.   (regd/office)
▲   Company Limited by Guarantee; Registered Charity
○   *L; research in economics
●   Conf - Mtgs - ET - Res
M   35 i
¶   The Review of Economic Studies - 4; ftm.

Society of Editors   1999
■   University Centre, Granta Place, Mill Lane, CAMBRIDGE,
      CB2 1RU.   (hq)
      01223 304080
      http://www.societyofeditors.co.uk
      Exec Dir: Bob Satchwell
▲   Company Limited by Guarantee
Br   11
○   *P; to represent editors in national, regional & local
      newspapers, magazines, broadcasting, new media,
      journalism, education & media law; to protect & promote the
      freedom of the media & the general right to the freedom of
      expression
●   Conf - Mtgs - ET - Res - LG
<   Wld Assn of Newspapers
M   475 i
¶   Briefing - 12; ftm only.

Society for Editors & Proofreaders   (SfEP)   1988
NR   Erico House, 93-99 Upper Richmond Rd, LONDON,
      SW15 2TG.   (admin)
      020 8785 5617   fax 020 8785 5618
      email administration@sfep.org.uk
      http://www.sfep.org.uk
      Exec Sec: Justina Amenu
▲   Un-incorporated Society
○   *P; to foster & encourage high standards of editing &
      proofreading
●   Conf - Mtgs - ET
M   1,315 i, 49 f, 30 org, UK / 35 i, 2 f, 5 org, o'seas
¶   NL - 6; ftm only.   Directory - 1; free.

Society of Education Consultants   (SEC)   1990
■   215 The Green House, The Custard Factory, Gibb St,
      BIRMINGHAM, B9 4AA.   (admin)
      0845 345 7932
      email administration@sec.org.uk   http://www.sec.org.uk
      Admin: Sandy Ghose
▲   Un-incorporated Society
○   *P; to support education management consultants
●   Conf - ET
M   140 i, 12 f, UK / 10 i, o'seas
¶   NL - 6;   Education - 52; both ftm only.

Society for Education, Music & Psychology Research
(SEMPRE)   1972
NR   University of Roehampton, (Room QB110) School of Education,
      Roehampton Lane, LONDON, SW15 5PJ.   (hsb)
      020 8392 3701
      http://www.sempre.org.uk
      Sec: Prof Adam Ockelford
○   *D, *N; to bring together researchers in the field of music
      education & similar fields
●   Conf - Res
M   157 i, 82 f, UK /130 i, 461 f, o'seas
¶   Psychology of Music (Jnl) - 2; ftm only.

Society of Electrical & Mechanical Engineers serving Local
Government   (SCEME)   1951
■   32 Discovery Rd, Bearsted, MAIDSTONE, Kent, ME15 8HF.
      (hsp)
      07884 342315
      email tanswellc@gmail.com   http://www.sceme.org
      Hon Sec: Charles Tanswell
▲   Un-incorporated Society
○   *P; representing profesional engineers working for public
      authorities, related organisations & commercial companies
      serving local government in England, Scotland & Wales
Gp   Sub-c'ees: Electrical, Energy, Maintenance, Professional matters
●   Conf - Mtgs - LG
M   25 i, 54 f
      (Subs: £30 i)

Society for Endocrinology   1946
■   22 Apex Court, Woodlands, Bradley Stoke, BRISTOL,
      BS32 4JT.   (hq)
      01454 642200   fax 01454 642222
      http://www.endocrinology.org
      Chmn: Prof John Wass
▲   Registered Charity
○   *L; advancement of public education in endocrinology
●   Conf - ET - Exhib - Publishing
<   Intl Soc of Endocrinology; Eur Soc of Endocrinology;
      BioScientifica Ltd
M   1,400 i, UK / 400 i, o'seas
¶   Jnl of Endocrinology - 12.   Endocrine Related Cancer - 4.
      Jnl of Molecular Endocrinology - 6.   The Endocrinologist - 4.

Society for the Environment   (SocEnv)   2004
NR   Denham House, 120 Long St, ATHERSTONE, Warks,
      CV9 1AF.   (hq)
      0845 337 2951   fax 01827 717064
      email enquiries@socenv.org   http://www.socenv.org.uk
      Chmn: Prof Raymond Clark,   Acting Chief Exec: Kerry Geldart
○   *P; to license & award the title Chartered Environmentalist
      (CEnv) to professional individuals through its 24 licensed
      members
●   Conf - Mtgs - Inf - Awards
M   24 org

Society of Environmental Engineers   (SEE)

■ The Manor House, High St, BUNTINGFORD, Herts,
  SG9 9AB.   (asa)
  01763 271209   fax 01763 273255
  email office@environmental.org.uk
  http://www.environmental.org.uk
  Chief Exec: Prof Raymond Clark
○ *P; engineering & technical aspects of the environment
< Soc for the Envt
M i & f
¶ Jnl - 4.   NL - 9/10.

Society for Environmental Exploration   1989

NR 50-52 Rivington St, LONDON, EC2A 3QP.   (hq)
  020 7613 2422   fax 020 7613 2992
  email info@frontier.ac.uk   http://www.frontier.ac.uk
  Managing Dir: Ms Eibleis Fanning
▲ Company Limited by Guarantee
○ *L, *N, *Q; an international environmental research,
  conservation & natural resource development non-
  governmental organisation (NGO), operating long-term
  biodiversity & socio-economic field programmes in important
  threatened tropical habitats
  Note: uses the operating title of Frontier

Society of Equestrian Artists   (SEA)   1978

■ 174 Henwood Green Rd, PEMBURY, Kent, TN2 4LR.   (sp)
  0754 934 1376
  email sec@equestrianartists.co.uk
  http://www.equestrianartists.co.uk
  Hon Sec: Alexander Hooton
▲ Registered Charity
○ *A
● Mtgs - ET - Exhib - Comp - Inf
M c 450 i, UK / c 25 i, o'seas
¶ NL - 3/4; ftm only.

Society of Euphobics   1997

■ 374 Bishopsford Rd, MORDEN, Surrey, SM4 6BU.   (mail/add)
○ *W; for people with a fear of good news
● Mtgs - Lib - VE
M 237 i

Society of Event Organisers   1996

■ 29a Market Sq, BIGGLESWADE, Beds, SG18 8AQ.   (hq)
  01767 316255   fax 01767 316430
  http://www.eou.org.uk
  Gen Mgr: Peter Cotterell
▲ Un-incorporated Society
○ *P, *T; for organisers of events in companies & associations;
  events include meetings, conferences, exhibitions, incentive
  travel, training, corporate hospitality etc
● Conf - Mtgs - ET - Inf - VE - Seminars
M 150 f
¶ Event Organisers Update - 10; free to anyone involved in
  events.

Society for Existential Analysis   1988

■ BM Existential, LONDON, WC1N 3XX.   (mail address)
  email info@existentialanalysis.co.uk
  http://www.existentialanalysis.co.uk
  Chmn: Paul McGinley
▲ Registered Charity
○ *L; a forum for the analysis of existence from philosophical &
  psychological perspectives (membership consists mostly of
  psychotherapists, counsellors, psychologists & philosophers)
● Conf - Inf - Directory of Existential Psychotherapists
M 350 i, UK / 25 i, o'seas
¶ Jnl - 2.

Society for Experimental Biology   (SEB)   1923

NR Charles Darwin House, 12 Roger St, LONDON, WC1N 2JU.
  (hq)
  020 7685 2600
  http://www.sebiology.org
  Chief Exec: Paul Hutchinson
▲ Company Limited by Guarantee; Registered Charity
Br 2
○ *L, *Q; to embrace all disciplines of experimental biology; to
  support & promote experimental biology in all its branches,
  to both the scientific community & the general public
● Conf - Mtgs - ET - Exhib - LG
M 1,350 i, UK / 450 i, o'seas
¶ Jnl of Experimental Botany.   The Plant Jnl.
  Bulletin (NL).   Plant Biotechnology.
  Publications list available.

Society of Expert Witnesses   (SEW)   1996

■ PO Box 345, NEWMARKET, Suffolk, CB8 7TU.   (hq)
  01638 6606844
  email helpline@sew.org.uk   http://www.sew.org.uk
  Sec: Richard Cory-Pearce
▲ Company Limited by Guarantee
○ *P; to promote excellence in all aspects of the service provided
  by expert witnesses; to cooperate with other bodies with
  similar aims
● Conf - SG - Inf
  Helpline: 0845 702 3014
M i

Society of Feed Technologists   (SFT)   1967

NR 2 Highmoor Rd, Caversham, READING, Berks, RG4 7BN.   (sp)
  http://www.sft.uk.com
  Sec: Mabel Foye
○ *L

Society of Fine Art Auctioneers & Valuers   (SOFAA)   1973

■ 2 Kingfisher Court, Bridge Rd, EAST MOLESEY, Surrey,
  KT8 9HL.   (hsp)
  07803 303125
  email secretary@sofaa.org   http://www.sofaa.org
  Sec: Robbie Barry
▲ Un-incorporated Society
○ *P; promotion & maintenance of standards in the valuation &
  sale of antiques & fine art
● Conf - LG
M i & f

Society of Floristry Ltd
  on 1 March 2010 became the Training & Education Committee of the
  British Florist Association Ltd

Society for Folk Life Studies   1961

■ Beamish Museum, BEAMISH, Co Durham, DH9 0RG.   (hsb)
  http://www.folklifestudies.org.uk
  Mem Sec: Seb Littlewood
○ *L; to study traditional & changing ways of life in Great Britain
  & Ireland with particular interest in regional culture
● Conf - Res - SG
M c 400 I & instns
¶ Folk Life: a jnl of ethnological studies - 1; ftm.   NL.

Society of Food Hygiene & Technology   (SOFHT)   1979

■ The Granary, Middleton House Farm, Tamworth Rd,
  MIDDLETON, Staffs, B78 2BD.   (hq)
  01827 872500   fax 01827 875800
  email admin@sofht.co.uk   http://www.sofht.co.uk
  Operations Dir: Su Werran
▲ Company Limited by Guarantee
Br 1
○ *L, *P
● Mtgs - ET - Exhib - Inf
M 700 i, 130 f, UK / 30 i, o'seas
¶ SOFHT Focus (Jnl) - 3;   Diary; both ftm only.   NL.

© CBD Research Ltd · Beckenham · BR3 5JS · Tel 020 8650 7745 · E-mail cbd@cbdresearch.com · www.cbdresearch.com

Society for French Studies (SFS) 1947
NR French Dept, University of Warwick, COVENTRY, Warks,
      CV4 7AL.   (hsb)
      email emma.campbell@warwick.ac.uk
      http://www.sfs.ac.uk
      Hon Sec: Dr Emma Campbell
○   *L; to promote French studies in universities & institutions of
      comparable standing in the British Isles & Commonwealth
M   i & org
¶   French Studies (with French Studies Bulletin) - 4.

Society of Friends of King Richard III
■   7 Askrigg House, Bouthwaite Drive, YORK, YO26 4TJ.   (sp)
      01904 790265
      email sandra.wadley@yahoo.co.uk
      http://www.silverboar.org
      Sec: Sandra Wadley
▲   Un-incorporated Society
○   *G; to support King Richard III, to clear & support his name in
      York, his city
●   Mtgs - Res - VE
M   300 i, UK / 50 i, o'seas
      (Sub: £10 i, UK / £15 i, o'seas)
¶   Silver Boar (Jnl) - 4; free.

Society of the Friends of St George's & Descendants of the
     Knights of the Garter   1931
NR 1 The Cloisters, Windsor Castle, WINDSOR, Berks, SL4 1NJ.
      (hsb)
      01753 860629   fax 01753 620165
      email friends@stgeorges-windsor.org
      http://www.stgeorges-windsor.org
▲   Registered Charity
Br Australia, Canada, New Zealand, USA
○   *G; to help maintain the fabric & beauty of St George's
      Chapel, Windsor Castle; to promote interest & knowledge of
      the history & traditions of the Order of the Garter
M   3,800 i, UK / 1,500 i, o'seas
¶   AR - 1; ftm, £2.

Society of Garden Designers (SGD) 1981
■   Katepwa House, Ashfield Park Ave, ROSS-ON-WYE, Herefs,
      HR9 5AX.   (asa)
      01989 566695   fax 01989 567676
      email info@sgd.org.uk   http://www.sgd.org.uk
      Admin: Gill Hinton
▲   Company Limited by Guarantee
Br 11 regional groups
○   *P; to promote professional standards in garden design
Gp Education policy c'ee
●   Conf - Mtgs - ET - Exhib - Inf - Lib - VE
<   R Horticl Soc
M   1,600 i, UK / 60 i, o'seas
¶   Garden Design Jnl - 10; ftm, £45 (£62 o'seas) nm.

Society of Garlic Growers, Processors & Packers (SGPP) 1998
■   191 Westcombe Hill, LONDON, SE3 7DR.
      Sec: Ali Sati
○   *T
●   Mtgs - Tastings - LG
M   i
¶   NL - 3; ftm only.

Society of Genealogists (SoG) 1911
NR 14 Charterhouse Buildings, Goswell Rd, LONDON,
      EC1M 7BA.   (hq)
      020 7251 8799   fax 020 7250 1800
      email events@sog.org.uk   http://www.sog.org.uk
      Chief Exec: June Perrin
▲   Company Limited by Guarantee; Registered Charity
○   *G, *L; to promote & foster the study of genealogy
Gp Computers in genealogy
●   Conf - Mtgs - ET - Lib - VE
<   Fedn of Family History Socs
M   13,500 i, UK / 1,500 i, o'seas
¶   Genealogists' Magazine - 4.
      Computers in Genealogy - 4.   AR.

Society for General Microbiology (SGM) 1945
■   Marlborough House, Basingstoke Rd, Spencers Wood,
      READING, Berks, RG7 1AG.   (hq)
      0118-988 1800   fax 0118-988 5656
      email admin@sgm.ac.uk   http://www.sgm.ac.uk
      Gen Sec: Prof David Blackbourn
▲   Company Limited by Guarantee; Registered Charity
Br Ireland
○   *L; to promote the art & science of microbiology
Gp Education; Eukaryotes; Irish; Prokaryotes; Virus
●   Conf - Mtgs - Exhib - Inf - LG
<   Intl U of Microbiological Socs; Fedn of Eur Microbiological
      Socs (FEMS); Fedn of Infection Socs (FIS)
M   3,925 i, UK / 1,380 i, o'seas
¶   Jnl of General Virology - 12; £106 m, £1,000 nm.
      Microbiology - 12; £106 m, £1,000 nm.
      Microbiology Today - 4; ftm, £76 nm.
      Jnl of Medical Microbiology - 12; £60 m, £780 nm.
      International Journal of Systematic & Evolutionary
      Microbiology - 6; £106 m, £715 nm.

Society for Genomics, Policy & Population Health
     a group of the **British Society for Human Genetics**

Society of Glass Technology (SGT) 1916
■   9 Churchill Way, Chapeltown, SHEFFIELD, S35 2PY.   (hq)
      0114-263 4455   fax 0114-263 4411
      email info@sgt.org   http://www.sgt.org
      Hon Sec: John Henderson
▲   Registered Charity
Br 6; India, USA
○   *L; all aspects of the history, art, science, manufacture, after-
      treatment & use of glass of any & every kind
Gp Technical c'ees - Analysis & properties; Basic science &
      technology; Engineering; Glass batch, furnaces &
      refractories; Handmade glassware
●   Conf - Mtgs - Lib - VE
<   Intl Cmsn on Glass; Eur Soc Glass Science & Technology
M   350 i, 70 f, UK / 150 i, 20 f, o'seas
¶   Glass Technology - 6.
      Physics & Chemistry of Glasses - 6.
      Monographs & Topical issues in glass.
      Specialist publications on aspects of glass technology.

Society of Graphic Fine Art (SGFA) 1919
NR The Woolstore Studio, 26 Western Barn Close, RYE, E Sussex,
      TN31 7EF.   (pres/b)
      email enquiries@sgfa.org.uk   http://www.sgfa.org.uk
      Pres: Will Taylor
○   *P; to promote fine drawing skills in both traditional &
      contemporary media
●   Exhib - Mtgs
M   100 i
      Note: also known as the Drawing Society

Society of Greeting & Visiting Card Collectors   (SGVCC)   1986
- ■ 76c The Avenue, BECKENHAM, Kent, BR3 5EF.
- ▲ Un-incorporated Society
- ○ *G
- Gp Audibles
- ● Mtgs - Exhib
- M i

Society of Greyhound Veterinarians
  a group of the **British Veterinary Association**

Society of Headmasters & Headmistresses of Independent Schools
  see **Society of Heads of Independent Schools**

Society of Heads of Independent Schools   (SHMIS)   1961
- ■ 12 The Point, Rockingham Rd, MARKET HARBOROUGH, Leics,
  LE16 7QU.   (hq)
  01858 433760   fax 01858 461413
  http://www.shmis.org.uk
  Gen Sec: Dr Peter Bodkin
- ▲ Company Limited by Guarantee
- ○ *E, *P; to provide an opportunity for the sharing of ideas &
  common concerns, to promote links with the wider sphere of
  higher education, to strengthen links with maintained sector
  & with local communities
- ● Conf - Mtgs - ET - Inf - LG
- < Indep Schools Coun (ISC)
- M 109 i
- ¶ NL - 1;   Hbk - 1.
- × c 2011 Society of Headmasters & Headmistresses of
  Independent Schools

** **Society of Health Education & Health Promotion Specialists**
  Organisation lost: see Introduction paragraph 3

Society of Heraldic Arts   (SHA)   1987
- NR 12 Ridgeway, OTTERY St MARY, Devon, EX11 1DT.   (hsp)
  01404 811091
  email sha.hon-sec@tiscali.co.uk
  http://www.heraldic-arts.com
  Hon Sec: Kevin Arkinstall
- ▲ Un-incorporated Society
- ○ *P; for heraldic artists & craftsmen
- ● Mtgs - Res - Inf - VE
- M i
- ¶ The Heraldic Craftsman - 4; ftm, £1.50 nm.

Society for the History of Alchemy & Chemistry   (SHAC)   1937
- ■ Dept of Science & Technology Studies, University College
  London, Gower St, LONDON, WC1E 6BT.   (hsb)
  email secretary@ambix.org   http://www.ambix.org
  Hon Sec: Dr Georgette Taylor
- ▲ Registered Charity
- ○ *L; all aspects of the history of alchemy & chemistry from the
  earliest times
- ● Mtgs - Res - Comp
- M 82 i, UK / 94 i, o'seas; 133 f, UK/o'seas
  (Sub: £27 i, £142 f)
- ¶ Ambix - 1 vol in 3 pts each yr

Society for the History of Astronomy
  is a group of the **Birmingham & Midland Institute**

Society for the History of Natural History   (SHNH)   1936
- NR The Natural History Museum, Cromwell Rd, LONDON,
  SW7 5BD.   (hsb)
  email info@shnh.org   http://www.shnh.org.uk
  Hon Sec: Mrs Lynda Brooks
- ▲ Registered Charity
- ○ *L; study of the history & bibliography of all branches of natural
  history
- ● Conf
- M 600 i
- ¶ Archives of Natural History - 2.   NL - 3.
  Sherborn Facsimiles (of rare natural history texts) - irreg; price
  varies.
  Special publications & conference papers.

Society of Homeopaths   1978
- ■ 11 Brookfield, Duncan Close, Moulton Park, NORTHAMPTON,
  NN3 6WL.   (hq)
  0845 450 6611   fax 0845 450 6622
  email info@homeopathy-soh.org
  http://www.homeopathy-soh.org
  Senior Mgr: Maria Apps
- ▲ Company Limited by Guarantee
- ○ *P; to promote homoeopathy in the Hahnemannian tradition
- ● Conf - Mtgs - ET - Res - Inf - LG
- < Coun for Complementary & Alternative Medicine; Eur Coun for
  Classical Homeopathy; Intl Coun for Classical Homeopathy
- M 2,250 i, UK / 85 i, o'seas
- ¶ Register of Homeopaths (LM).

**Society of Hospital Linen Service & Laundry Managers
(SHLSLM)   1951**
- ■ c/o The Willows, 109 Victoria Road East, THORNTON
  CLEVELYS, Lancs, FY5 5HQ.
  01253 869968
  email information@linenmanager.co.uk
  http://www.linenmanager.co.uk
  Hon Sec: Lynn Fort
- ▲ Un-incorporated Society
- Br 8; Republic of Ireland
- ○ *P
- ● Conf - Mtgs - ET - Exhib - Inf - LG
- M 74 i
  (Sub: £40)
- ¶ Ybk; ftm, 20 nm.

Society of Independent Brewers   (SIBA)   1980
- ■ PO Box 136, RIPON, N Yorks, HG4 5WW.   (asa)
  0845 337 9158
  email secretariat@siba.co.uk   http://www.siba.co.uk
  Chief Exec: Julian Grocock
- ▲ Company Limited by Guarantee
- Br 7 regions
- ○ *T; to represent the small independent brewers
- Gp Training; Marketing; Political; Commercial
- ● Conf - Mtgs - ET - Comp - Inf - LG
- < Food & Drink Fedn
- M 220 f
- ¶ SIBA Jnl - 6; ftm only.

Society of Independent Roundabout Proprietors   (SIRP)   1985
- ■ 66 Carolgate, RETFORD, Notts, DN22 6EF.   (hsb)
  01777 702872
  http://www.sirp.co.uk
  Sec: Jack Schofield
- ○ *G, *T; owners & operators (both professional & semi-
  professional) of vintage fairground equipment (wood-framed,
  hand-turned, steam driven, pre-war) & vintage slot-machines
- ● Mtgs
- M 100 i

© CBD Research Ltd · Beckenham · BR3 5JS · Tel 020 8650 7745 · E-mail cbd@cbdresearch.com · www.cbdresearch.com

Society of Indexers   (SI)   1957
NR   Woodbourn Business Centre, 10 Jessell St, SHEFFIELD, S Yorks, S9 3HY.   (hq)
0114-244 9561   fax 0114-244 9563
email info@indexers.org.uk
http://www.indexers.org.uk
Sec: John Silvester,   Office Mgr: Paul Machen
▲   Un-incorporated Society
○   *L, *P; promotes standards & instruction on techniques for all forms of indexing
●   Conf - Mtgs - ET - Exam - Inf - Register of Indexers
<   Soc of Indexers in: Australia / America / China / South Africa; Indexing & Abstracting Soc of Canada
M   850 i, 16 f, UK / 60 i, 1 f, o'seas
¶   The Indexer - 2; ftm, £50 yr nm.
SIdelights - 4;   LM - 1; both ftm only.
Indexers Available - 1; free to publishers, £4.50 nm.
Occasional papers on aspects of indexing - irreg; prices vary.

Society for Individual Freedom   (SIF)   1945
■   PO Box 744, BROMLEY, Kent, BR1 4WG.   (chmn/p)
01424 713737
http://www.individualist.org.uk
Chmn: Michael Plumbe (chairman@individualist.org.uk)
▲   Un-incorporated Society
○   *K; to campaign & lobby on issues of personal freedom
●   Conf - Mtgs
M   c 200 i
¶   The Individual - 3/4; ftm.
Books & tracts - irreg.

Society of Industrial Emeregency Services Officers   (SIESO) 1973
NR   8 Highbury Hill, LONDON, N5 1SU.   (pres)
email sieso@sieso.org.uk   http://www.sieso.org.uk
Pres: John D Rimington,   Sec: David Goodridge
▲   Un-incorporated Society
Br   4
○   *P; for managers & those involved in the prevention, of & response to, industrial & commercial emergencies
Gp   Industrial safety: health, safety & environment; Crisis management; Risk assessment; Statutory regulations; EU & government legislation
●   Conf - ET - Exhib - SG - Inf - VE - LG
<   Nat Steering C'ee for Warning & Informing the Public; Civil Contingencies Coordination Alliance
M   300 i, UK / 20 i, o'seas

Society of Information Technology Management   (SOCITM) 1986
NR   43 Temple Row, BIRMINGHAM, B2 5LS.   (hq)
email enquiries@socitm.gov.uk   http://www.socitm.gov.uk
Managing Dir: Doug Maclean
▲   Un-incorporated Society
○   *P; ICT managers working in and for the public sector
M   1,900 i

Society for International Folk Dancing   (Interfolk)   (SIFD) 1946
NR   5 South Rise, CARSHALTON, Surrey, SM5 4PD.   (hq)
020 8395 1400
email mail@sifd.org   http://www.sifd.org
Contact: Group Liaison Officer
▲   Registered Charity
○   *D: to preserve folk dances of all peoples & to make them known; to encourage the practice of them in traditional form
●   Mtgs - ET - Public dances - Day & summer schools
<   Cent Coun of Physical Recreation; English Folk Dance & Song Soc
>   Israel Dance Inst; Welsh Circle Dance Assn
M   400 i
¶   SIFD News - 12; ftm only.

Society of Irish Foresters   1942
IRL   Glenealy, Co Wicklow, Republic of Ireland.
353 (0) 404 44204
email sif@eircom.net
http://www.societyofirishforesters.ie
Sec: Clodagh Duffy
○   *P; to advance & spread the knowledge of forestry in all its aspects

Society of the Irish Motor Industry   (SIMI)
IRL   5 Upper Pembroke St, DUBLIN 2, Republic of Ireland.
353 (1) 676 1690   fax 353 (1) 661 9213
email info@simi.ie   http://www.simi.ie
○   *T

Society for Italian Studies
NR   Dept of Italian, University of Leeds, LEEDS, W Yorks, LS2 9JT. (hsb)
0113-343 7846
http://www.sis.ac.uk
Hon Sec: Dr Matthew Treherne
▲   Registered Charity
○   *L; to advance public education, in the UK, by furthering the academic study of Italy, its language, literature, thought, history, society & arts organisations

Society for Italic Handwriting   (SIH)   1952
■   203 Dyas Avenue, Great Barr, BIRMINGHAM, B42 1HM.
.   (hsp)
0121 244 8006
email secretary@italic-handwriting.org
http://www.italic-handwriting.org
Sec: Nicholas Caulkin
▲   Registered Charity
○   *A; to promote the use of Italic handwriting
●   Mtgs - Exhib - Comp - SG - Inf - Lib
M   500 i, 3 f, 30 schools, UK / 200 i, o'seas
¶   Jnl - 4.

Society of Jewellery Historians   (SJH)   1977
NR   Scientific Research, British Museum, LONDON, WC1B 3DG.
fax 01588 620558
http://www.societyofjewelleryhistorians.ac.uk
Sec: Mo Cerrone
▲   Registered charity
○   *L; to stimulate interest in jewellery of all ages & cultures
M   i, f & org
¶   Jewellery Studies - occasional.
Jewellery History Today - 3.

Society of King Charles the Martyr   (SKCM)   1894
■   22 Tyning Rd, Winsley, BRADFORD-on-AVON, Wilts, BA15 2JJ.   (hsp)
01225 862965
Chmn: Robin Davies
▲   Un-incorporated Society
Br   Australia, USA
○   *R; observance of 30 January in commemoration of King Charles I's martyrdom & upholding the principles (the prayer book & episcopacy) for which he died
●   Mtgs - Services
M   150 i, UK / 350 i, o'seas
¶   Church & King - 2; ftm.

Society for Landscape Studies (SLS) 1979
- ■ c/o Dept of Geography, University of Exeter, Amory Building, Rennes Drive, EXETER, Devon, EX4 4RJ. (hsp)
  01392 263330   fax 01392 264358
  email d.c.harvey@exeter.ac.uk
  http://www.landscapestudies.com
  Hon Sec: Dr David Harvey
- ▲ Registered Charity
- ○ *G, *L; 'to secure a more penetrating comprehension of landscape evolution & an overall narrative account of landscape, prehistory & history, together with an understanding of how this has influenced & may usefully guide the management of the present-day landscape'
- ● Conf
- < Coun Brit Archaeology
- M 370 i, 140 org, UK / 14 i, o'seas
- ¶ Landscape History - 1.

Society of Later Life Advisers (SOLLA)
- NR Arnold's Oak, Eastling, FAVERSHAM, Kent, ME13 0BD. (hq)
  0845 303 2909
  Dirs: Tish Hanifan, Jane Finnerty
- ○ *P; 'to assist consumers & their families to find trusted accredited fimancial advisers who understand financial needs in later life;' such as equity release, long term care options, annuities, investments & savings & inheritance tax planning

Society of Laundry Engineers & Allied Trades Ltd (SLEAT) 1907
- ■ Suite 7 Southernhay, 207 Hook Rd, CHESSINGTON, Surrey, KT9 1HJ. (asa)
  020 8391 2266   fax 020 8391 4466
  email admin@sleat.co.uk   http://www.sleat.co.uk
  Sec: David M Hart
- ▲ Company Limited by Guarantee
- ○ *T; to promote, support & protect the welfare & interest of laundry engineers & allied trades
- ● Exhib - LG
- < Eur Laundry & Dry Cleaning Machinery Mfrs Org
- M 43 f

Society of Law Accountants in Scotland (SOLAS)
- NR 17 Raith Gardens, KIRKALDY, Fife, KY2 5NJ. (hsp)
  01592 260021
  email solas.admin@hotmail.co.uk
  http://www.solas.co.uk
  Admin: Dorothy Nicholson
- ○ *P

Society of Leather Technologists & Chemists Ltd (SLTC) 1897
- NR 8 Copper Leaf Close, MOULTON, Northants, NN3 7HS. (mem/sp)
  01604 497569
  email office@sltc.org   http://www.sltc.org
  Mem Sec: Mrs Pat Potter
- ▲ Company Limited by Guarantee; Registered Charity
- Br 2; Australia, South Africa
- ○ *L; to promote the theoretical & practical interests of leather manufacturers, hide & skin trades, machinery, chemical & dye & finish manufacturers, & allied industries
- < Intl U Leather Technologists & Chemists Socs (IULTCS)
- ¶ Jnl - 6.

Society of Legal Scholars in the United Kingdom & Ireland (SLS) 1908
- ■ School of Law, University of Southampton, Highfield, SOUTHAMPTON, SO17 1BJ. (hsb)
  023 8059 4039   fax 023 8059 3024
  email s.j.thomson@soton.ac.uk
  http://www.legalscholars.ac.uk
  Hon Sec: Prof Stephen Bailey, Admin Sec: Mrs S J Thomson
- ▲ Registered Charity
- ○ *P; to advance legal research & education
- Gp Law: Company, Comparative, Competition, Consumer, Contract & commercial, Criminal justice, Environmental, European, Family, Human rights & civil liberties, Immigration & refugee, Information technology, Intellectual property, International, Jurisprudence, Labour, Legal education, Legal history, Maritime media, Medical, Practice, Profession & ethics, Property & trusts, Public, Restitution, Tax, Torts
- ● Conf - Mtgs - ET - Res - LG
- M 2,800 i, 33 f, UK / 190 i, o'seas
- ¶ Legal Studies (Jnl) - 4;   The Reporter (NL) - 2; both ftm only.

Society of Leisure Consultants & Publishers (SOLCAP) 1989
- ■ 1 Sandringham Close, Tarleton, PRESTON, Lancs, PR4 6UZ. (dir/b)
  01772 816046
  Dir: J B A Sharples
- ▲ Un-incorporated Society
- ○ *T; to represent consultants, publishers & commercial interests in the leisure industry (entertainment, recreation, tourism, hotels, catering, marketing, publicity, sport & public relations)
- ● Conf - Mtgs - Exhib - Inf - VE
- M 38 i, 10 f, UK / 1 i, 1 f, o'seas
- ¶ NL - 2; ftm, £2 nm.   LM - 1; ftm, £5 nm.

Society of Ley Hunters (SOL) 2000
- ■ 9 Mawddwy Cottages, Minllyn, Dinas Mawddwy, MACHYNLLETH, SY20 9LW. (hsp)
  01650 531354
  email leyhunter@googlemail.com
  http://www.leyhunter.org
  17 Victoria St, CHELTENHAM, Glos, GL50 4HV. (mem/sp)
  Hon Sec: Laurence Main,   Mem Sec: Gerald Frowley
- ▲ Un-incorporated Society
- ○ *G; the study of leys (straight alignments of ancient sites in the landscapes), their meanings & purposes & other related mysteries
- ● Mtgs - VE
- M c 170 i
- ¶ NL - 4; ftm only.

Society for Libyan Studies 1969
- ■ c/o Institute of Archaeology, 31-34 Gordon Sq, LONDON, WC1H 0PY. (pt-time)
  email shirleystrong@btconnect.com
  http://www.britac.ac.uk/institutes/libya
  Sec: Mrs S K Strong
- ▲ Registered Charity
- ○ *L; study & research into history, archaeology, geography & geology of Libya
- ● Conf - Mtgs - Res - Exhib - SG - Inf
- M 199 i, 38 org, UK / 66 i, 74 org, o'seas
  (Sub: £25)
- ¶ Libyan Studies (AR); ftm, £30 nm.

© CBD Research Ltd · Beckenham · BR3 5JS · Tel 020 8650 7745 · E-mail cbd@cbdresearch.com · www.cbdresearch.com

Society of Licensed Conveyancers 1988
- ■ SLC House, 42 Thornton Crescent, OLD COULSDON, Surrey, CR5 1LH. (hq)
  0845 459 2194
  Chief Exec: N F Ewert Evans
- ▲ Company Limited by Guarantee
- ○ *P; for licensed conveyancers in England & Wales
- ● Conf - Mtgs - Inf - LG - Referral of the public to a local licensed conveyancer - Provision of compulsory professional development courses
- M 400 i
- ¶ The Licensed Conveyancer - 4.

Society of Limners (SLm) 1986
- ■ 16 Tudor Close, HOVE, E Sussex, BN3 7NR. (admin/p)
  01273 770628
  email rgeast.limners@ntlworld.com
  Administrator: Richard East
- ▲ Un-incorporated Society
- ○ *A; to promote & encourage interest in miniature painting, calligraphy & silhouette painting
- ● Conf - ET - Exhib
- < Wld Fedn Miniaturists
- M 140 i, 2 org, UK / 5 i, 1 org, o'seas
- ¶ NL - 3, ftm, £1.50 nm.

Society for Lincolnshire History & Archaeology (SLHA) 1974
- ■ Jews' Court, Steep Hill, LINCOLN, LN2 1LS. (hq)
  01522 521337   fax 01522 521337
  email slha@lincolnshirepast.org.uk
  http://www.lincolnshirepast.org.uk
- ▲ Registered Charity
- Br 2
- ○ *L; local history, archaeology & industrial archaeology of Lincolnshire
- Gp Archaeology; Industrial archaeology; Local history; Publications
- ● Conf - Mtgs - Res - SG - Lib - VE
- < Coun for Brit Archaeology; Brit Assn for Local History; Assn for Indl Archaeology
- M 550 i, 65 f, UK / 3 i, 22 f, o'seas
- ¶ Jnl - 1; ftm, £10 nm.   Magazine - 4; ftm, £1.60 nm.
  Bulletin - 4;   AR - 1; both ftm only.

Society of Local Authority Chief Executives & Senior Managers (SOLACE) 1973
- NR Hope House, 45 Great Peter St, LONDON, SW1P 3LT. (hq)
  020 7233 0081
  email hope.house@solace.org.uk
  http://www.solace.org.uk
  Dir Gen: David Clark
- ▲ Company Limited by Guarantee; Registered Charity
- Br 12
- ○ *P; for senior managers in local government in the UK; to develop & strengthen the UK local government sector
- ● Conf - Mtgs - ET - Res - Exhib - SG - Empl - LG
- M i & f

Society of Local Council Clerks (SLCC) 1974
- ■ 8 The Crescent, TAUNTON, Somerset, TA1 4EA. (hq)
  01823 253646   fax 01823 253681
  email treasurer@slcc.co.uk   http://www.slcc.co.uk
  Chief Exec: Nick Randle
- ▲ Un-incorporated Society
- Br 45
- ○ *P, *U; for clerks & managers of town, parish & community coucils in England & Wales
- ● Conf - ET - Exam - Inf - Empl - LG
- < Intl Inst of Municipal Clerks
- M 3,500 i
- ¶ The Clerk (Jnl) - 6; ftm, £5 nm.

Society of London Art Dealers (SLAD) 1932
- ■ Ormond House, 3 Duke of York St, LONDON, SW1Y 6JP. (hq)
  020 7930 6137   fax 020 7321 0685
  email office@slad.org.uk   http://www.slad.org.uk
  Dir Gen: Christopher Battiscombe
- ▲ Un-incorporated Society
- ○ *T; to promote & protect the good name & interests of the art trade throughout the UK & to enhance public confidence in responsible art dealing
- ● Mtgs - ET - Exhib - Inf - LG - Seminars - VAT & Droit de Suite helpline
- < Confédn Intle Négociants en Oeuvres d'Art (CINOA); Fedn Eur Art Galleries Assns (FEAGA); Brit Art Market Fedn
- M 115 f
- ¶ NL - 4; ftm only.
  Society of London Art Dealers Directory - 1; free.
  Society of London Art Dealers Survey - 2 yrly; ftm only.

Society of Maritime Industries 1966
- NR 28-29 Threadneedle St, LONDON, EC2R 8AY. (hq)
  020 7628 2555   fax 020 7638 4376
  email info@maritimeindustries.org
  http://www.maritimeindustries.org
  Chief Exec: John C Murray
- ▲ Company Limited by Guarantee
- ○ *T; 'the voice of the UK maritime business sector, promoting & supporting companies which build, refit & modernise warships, & which supply equipment & services for all types of commercial & naval ships, ports & terminals infrastructure, offshore oil & gas, & marine science & technology
- Gp Association of British Offshore Industries; Association of Marine Scientific Industries; British Marine Equipment Association; British Naval Equipment Association; Maritime Security & Safety Group; Ports & Terminals Group
- ● Conf - Mtgs - ET - Exhib - SG - Stat - Expt - LG
- M 200 f

Society of Martial Arts
- NR 69 Piccadilly, MANCHESTER, M1 2BS.
  0161-702 1660
  http://www.societyofmartialarts.org
- ▲ Company Limited by Guarantee; Registered Charity
- ○ *E, *Q; to promote the educational & research aspects of martial arts; to offer degrees & postgraduate qualifications in martial arts

Society of Master Saddlers (UK) Ltd 1966
- ■ Green Lane Farm, Stonham, STOWMARKET, Suffolk, IP14 5DS. (hq)
  01449 711642   fax 01449 711642
  http://www.mastersaddlers.co.uk
  Chief Exec: Mrs H Morley
- ▲ Company Limited by Guarantee
- ○ *T; representing manufacturers, retail & craft saddlers without retail premises; training & apprenticeship
- Gp Registered qualified saddle fitters
- ● ET - Exhib - Comp - Inf
- M 300 f
- ¶ NL - 2.   Members List & Ybk - 1.
  Leaflets.

Society of Medical Writers (SOMW) 1985
- NR 30 Dollis Hill Lane, LONDON. NW2 6JE. (treas/p)
  http://www.somw.org.uk
  Finance Officer: Dr Richard Cutler
- ▲ Un-incorporated Society
- ○ *A; to encourage good standards of writing within the medical professions
- ● Conf - ET - Comp
- < Assn Broadcasting Doctors; Media Medics
- M 200 i, UK / 25 i, o'seas
- ¶ The Writer (Jnl) - 2; ftm only.

Society for Medicines Research   (SMR)   1966
NR   840 Melton Rd, Thurmaston, LEICESTER, LE4 8BN.   (asa)
0116-269 1048   fax 0116-264 0141
email secretariat@smr.org.uk   http://www.smr.org.uk
Hon Sec: Dr Phillip Cowley
▲   Registered Charity
○   *P; to provide a forum for those interested in medicines
research; to further the education of such persons to the
ultimate benefit of the general public in the field of the relief
of sickness
Gp   Medicinal chemistry; Biology; Pharmacology; Medicine;
Pharmacy; Toxicology; Clinical
●   Conf - Mtgs - ET (one-day scientific mtgs)
<   Eur Fedn of Medicinal Chemistry (EFMC)
M   525 i, UK / 25 i, o'seas
¶   SMR NL - 2; ftm only.

Society for Medieval Archaeology   (SMA)   1957
NR   Dept of Archaeology, University of Sheffield, Northgate House,
West St, SHEFFIELD, S Yorks, S1 4ET.   (hsb)
0114-222 2920
http://www.medievalarchaeology.org
Hon Sec: Prof Dawn Hadley
○   *L; archaeology in the British Isles in the post-Roman period
M   i & org

Society of Messengers-at-Arms & Sheriff Officers   1922
NR   11 Alva St, EDINBURGH, EH2 4PH.   (hq)
0131-225 9110   fax 0131-220 3468
email admin@smaso.ednet.co.uk
http://www.smaso.org
Admin Sec: Alan Hogg
○   *P; professional officers of court (messengers-at-arms or sheriff-
officers) who are employed by private firms dealing with
service & enforcement of court papers & decrees
<   U Intle des Huissiers de Justice & Officiers Judiciaires
M   25 f

Society of Metaphysicians Ltd   (SofM)   1944
■   Archers' Court, Stonestile Lane, The Ridge, HASTINGS,
E Sussex, TN35 4PG.   (hq)
01424 751577   fax 01424 751577
email newmeta@btinternet.com
http://www.metaphysicians.org.uk
Gen Sec: Carrie Yuen
▲   Company Limited by Guarantee
Br   Belgium, Nigeria, USA
○   *L; development & application of the science of fundamental
laws (infinitely based or absolute) - neometaphysics, electro-
imaging, radiesthesia, extra-sensory perception, Zener tests
Gp   Mnemonics - effect of mind on physical processes; Radiation
from living organisations (AURA)
●   ET - Res - SG - Inf - Lib - VE
>   Hasting Holistic Health Clinic
M   2,318 i, 6 org, UK / 1,500 i, o'seas
(Sub: £50 UK / £60 o'seas)
¶   Neometaphysical Digest - 1; ftm, £4 nm.

Society of Model Aeronautical Engineers Ltd
see under the registered title **British Model Flying Association**

Society of Model & Experimental Engineers   (SM&EE)   1898
NR   Marshall House, 28 Wanless Rd, LONDON, SE24 0HW.   (hq)
email secretary@sm-ee.co.uk   http://www.sm-ee.co.uk
▲   Company Limited by Guarantee
○   *G; to support & encourage builders of models & experimental
devices
¶   Jnl - 6.

Society of Model Sheep Collectors   (SMSC)   2010
■   3 Hughes Stanton Way, MANNINGTREE, Essex, CO11 2HQ.
○   *G
Gp   Concrete, knitted, plastic
●   Mtgs - Exhib
M   30 i
¶   Baa Humbug - irreg.

Society of Model Shipwrights   (SMS)   1975
■   5 Lodge Crescent, ORPINGTON, Kent, BR6 0QE.   (hsp)
01689 827213
Hon Sec: Peter Rogers
▲   Un-incorporated Society
○   *G; to promote research into & construction of true scale
models of ships & boats of all periods; to preserve the skills
of model shipwrightry
●   Mtgs - Res - Exhib - Comp
M   c 80 i, UK / 3 i, o'seas
¶   The Log (NL) - 12; ftm only.

Society of Motor Auctions
a group of the **Retail Motor Industry Federation**

Society of Motor Manufacturers & Traders Ltd   (SMMT)   1902
NR   Forbes House, Halkin St, LONDON, SW1X 7DS.   (hq)
020 7235 7000   fax 020 7235 7112
http://www.smmt.co.uk
Chief Exec: Paul Everitt
▲   Company Limited by Guarantee
○   *T; to support & promote the interests of the UK automobile
industry at home & abroad
M   f

**Society for Mucopolysaccharide Diseases   (MPS Society)
1982**
■   MPS House, Repton Place, White Lion Rd, AMERSHAM, Bucks,
HP7 9LP.   (hq)
0845 389 9901   fax 0845 389 9902
email mps@mpssociety.co.uk
http://www.mpssociety.co.uk
Chief Exec: Mrs Christine Lavery
▲   Registered Charity
○   *W; to support those affected by the disease, their families &
carers; to bring about public awareness of MPS & related
diseases; to support research
●   Conf - ET - Res - Exhib - Stat - Inf - VE
<   Nat Coun for Voluntary Orgs
M   800 families, 6 f, 12 org, UK / 100 i, 3 f, o'seas
¶   NL - 4.   AR.
Booklets on specific diseases: Hurler, Scheie & Hurler/Scheie,
Morquio, Sanfilippo, Maroteaux/Lamy etc.

Society of Museum Archaeologists   (SMA)   1976
■   c/o Caroline McDonald, Ipswich Museums, High St, IPSWICH,
Suffolk, IP1 3QH.   (hsb)
01473 433574
http://www.socmusarch.org.uk
Hon Sec: Caroline McDonald
Br   1 regional group in Scotland
○   *P; to promote the interests of archaeology in museums
throughout the UK
●   Conf - SG
<   Museums Assn
M   250 i, 60 org, UK / 2 i, 2 org, o'seas
¶   The Museum Archaeologist - 1; ftm.   NL - 2; ftm.
Publications list available.

© CBD Research Ltd · Beckenham · BR3 5JS · Tel 020 8650 7745 · E-mail cbd@cbdresearch.com · www.cbdresearch.com

Society for Music Analysis (SMA)
- ■ c/o Dr David Bretherton, Dept of Music, University of Southampton, Highfield, SOUTHAMPTON, Hants, SO17 1BJ. (admin/b)
  023 8059 3425 fax 023 8059 3197
  http://www.sma.ac.uk
  Treas & Admin: Dr David Bretherton
- ▲ Registered Charity
- ○ *D, *L, *P; is the leading organisation dedicated to the theory & practice of musical analysis
- ● Conf - Mtgs - ET
- M i
- ¶ NL - 2.

Society for Name Studies in Britain & Ireland (SNSBI) 1991
- NR c/o Arts & Social Sciences Library, University of Bristol, Tyndall Avenue, BRISTOL, BS8 1TJ. (hsb)
  email secretary@snsbi.org.uk http://www.snsbi.org.uk
  Hon Sec: Miss Jennifer Scherr
- ▲ Registered Charity
- ○ *L; to research into place names, personal names & surnames of GB & Ireland
- ● Conf - Res - Comp - SG - Inf
- M 200 i, 5 org, UK / i & org, o'seas
- ¶ NOMINA (Jnl) - 1. NL.

Society for Nautical Research (SNR) 1910
- ■ 6 Ashmeadow Rd, Arnside, CARNFORTH, Lancs, LA5 0AE. (hsb)
  01524 761616 fax 01524 761616
  email honsecretary.snr@btinternet.com
  http://www.snr.org.uk
  National Maritime Museum, Greenwich, LONDON, SE10 9NF. (regd office).
  Hon Sec: Peter Winterbottom
- ▲ Company Limited by Guarantee; Registered Charity
- ○ *L, *Q; to research into all matters relating to seafaring & shipbuilding in all ages & among all nations & into the language & customs of the sea & other subjects of nautical interest
- Gp Provides the Chairman of the HMS Victory Advisory Technical C'ee, & in partnership with the Royal Navy oversees the continuing preservation, restoration & conservation of the ship
- ● Conf (with the British Commission for Maritime History) - Res - EXhib - LG - Sponsorship of N A M Rodger's Naval History of Britain (in 3 vol) - The recording of small watercraft
- M 1,000 i, 95 org, UK / 300 i, 220 org, o'seas (Sub: £37, £46 instns)
- ¶ The Mariner's Mirror - 4; ftm, £12.95 each nm..
  NL - 4; ftm only.
  Bibliography of Mariner's Mirror (index) - 5 yrly.

Society of Numismatic Artists & Designers
has closed

Society of Nursery Nursing Practitioners (SNN) 1991
- ■ 40 Archdale Rd, LONDON, SE22 9HJ. (hq)
  020 8693 0555 fax 07092 342170
  email info@snn.uk.com http://www.snnp.org.uk
  Chief Exec: Prof Sir R A Herbert-Blankson
- ▲ Company Limited by Guarantee
- Br 6; 20 o'seas
- ○ *P; 'the only professional examining body for all those who look after children & young people'
- Gp Associates (ASNNP); Fellows (FSNNP); Graduates (SGSNNP)
- ● Conf - Mtgs - ET - Exam - Res - Exhib - Comp - SG - Stat - Expt - Inf - Lib - VE - LG
- M 60 i, UK / 210 i, o'seas
- ¶ Nursery Nursing Practitioner - 4; ftm, £1.50 nm. NL - irreg.

Society of Occupational Medicine (SOM) 1935
- NR Hamilton House, Mabledon Place, LONDON, WC1H 9BB. (hq)
  020 7554 8628 fax 020 7554 8526
  email admin@som.org.uk http://www.som.org.uk
  Chief Exec: Hilary Todd
- ▲ Registered Charity
- Br 11 regional gps
- ○ *L; for doctors working in any capacity in occupational health in any field (incl government agencies & the armed forces) concerned with the protection of the health of people at work & the prevention of occupational diseases & injuries
- ● Conf - Mtgs - Res - Exhib - Inf - VE - LG
- M 1,800 i, UK / 100 i, o'seas
- ¶ Occupational Medicine Journal - 8; ftm.
  NL - 4; Hbk - 2 yrly; AR - 1; all ftm only.

Society for Old Age Rational Suicide (SOARS) 1996
- § 9 Waverleigh Rd, CRANLEIGH, Surrey, GU6 8BZ.
  Coorinator: Dr Michael Irwin
  a non-membership body which publishes a newsletter recording the society's activities & reports, from around the world, relating to old age rational suicide

Society for Old Testament Study (SOTS) 1917
- ■ c/o Dr Francesca Stavrakopoulou, University of Exeter, Amory Building, Rennes Drive, EXETER, EX4 4RJ. (hsb)
  http://www.sots.ac.uk
  Hon Sec: Dr Francesca Stavrakopoulou
- ▲ Un-incorporated Society
- ○ *L; the promotion & coordination of Old Testament studies in GB & Ireland
- ● Conf
- M 301 i, UK/ 158 i, o'seas
- ¶ NL & LM - 1; ftm only. Book List - 1; ftm, £23 nm.

Society of Olympic Collectors (SOC) 1984
- ■ 19 Hanbury Path, Sheerwater, WOKING, Surrey, GU21 5RB. (hsp)
  Hon Sec: Miss P Burger
- ▲ Un-incorporated Society
- ○ *G; to collect, collate & distribute information about philatelic & other memorabilia items related to the Olympic games
- ● Res - Exhib - Inf - Lib - VE
- < Assn Brit Philatelic Socs
- M 91 i, UK / 117 i, o'seas
- ¶ Torch Bearer (Jnl) - 4; ftm.

Society of Operations Engineers (SOE) 2000
- NR 22 Greencoat Place, LONDON, SW1P 1PR. (hq)
  020 7630 1111 fax 020 7630 6677
  email soe@soe.org.uk http://www.soe.org.uk
  Chief Exec: Nick Jones
- ▲ Company Limited by Guarantee; Registered Charity
- ○ *P; for engineers in the road transport, plant & engineer surveying industries
- Gp Professional sectors: Bureau of Engineer Surveyors, Institute of Road Transport Engineers, Institution of Plant Engineers physical processes physical processes physical processes
- ● Conf - Mtgs - ET - Comp - Inf - VE
- < Engg Coun; NICEIC; NCSIIB; Soc for the Envt (SocEnv)
- M 4,862 i, 16 f, UK / 684 i, o'seas
- ¶ The Plant Engineer (Jnl) - 6.
  Transport Engineer (Jnl).
  Various guides. AR.

Society of Orthopaedic Medicine   1983

- ■ 151 Dale St (4th Floor), LIVERPOOL, Merseyside, L2 2AH. (hq)
  0151-237 2970
  email admin@somed.org   http://www.somed.org
- ▲ Company Limited by Guarantee; Registered Charity
- ○ *P; to promote orthopaedic medicine for public benefit through education & research
- ● Conf - Mtgs - ET - Res
- < Cyriax Org; Orthopaedic Medicine Intl; Ir Soc of Orthopaedic Medicine
- M 1,000 i, UK / 300 i, o'seas
  (Sub: £30 UK / £35 o'seas)
- ¶ International Musculoskeletal Medicine Jnl - 3;   NL - 2; Members Directory; all ftm only.

Society of Parliamentary Agents   (SPA)   1844

- ■ Bircham Dyson Bell, 50 Broadway, LONDON, SW1H 0BL. (hsb)
  020 7783 3425
  email robbieowen@bdb-law.co.uk
  Hon Sec: Robbie Owen
- ▲ Un-incorporated Society
- ○ *P

Society of Parsley Cultivators

- ■ 191 Westcombe Hill, LONDON, SE3 7DR.
- ○ *H
- ● Mtgs - Stat - VE
- M f

Society for Pattern Recognition
   see full title **British Machine Vision Association & Society for Pattern Recognition**

Society of Pension Consultants   (SPC)   1958

- ■ St Bartholomew House, 92 Fleet St, LONDON, EC4Y 1DG. (hq)
  020 7353 1688   fax 020 7353 9296
  email info@spc.uk.com   http://www.spc.uk.com
  Sec: John Mortimer
- ▲ Company Limited by Guarantee
- Br 3
- ○ *T; interests of organisations providing advice on & services to schemes & funds for the provision of retirement benefits
- Gp Compliance forum
- ● Mtgs - Inf - LG
- < Occupational Pension Schemes Jt Working Gp
- M 133 f
- ¶ SPC News - 6; ftm only.   LM - 1;   AR; both free.

Society of Personnel Directors Scotland   (SPDS)

- NR Angus House, Orchardbank Business Park, FORFAR, Angus, DD8 1AX.
  01307 476111   fax 01307 476140
  email robertsonh@angus.gov.uk
  http://www.spds.org.uk
  Sec: Hugh Robertson
- ○ *P; to represent personnel in local government in Scotland

Society of Pharmaceutical Medicine

   has closed

Society of Ploughmen Ltd   1972

- ■ Quarry Farm, Loversall, DONCASTER, S Yorks, DN11 9DH. (hq)
  01302 852469   fax 01302 859880
  email info@ploughmen.co.uk
  http://www.ploughmen.co.uk
  Exec Dir: Ken Chappell
- ▲ Company Limited by Guarantee
- ○ *F; to promote the art & skill of ploughing the land; to promote the annual British National Ploughing Championship
- ● Comp
- < Wld Ploughing Org
- M 1,000 i, 250 org
- ¶ NL - 2; ftm only.   Official Rules for Ploughing; £1.50.

Society for Popular Astronomy   (SPA)   1953

- ■ 36 Fairway, Keyworth, NOTTINGHAM, NG12 5DU.   (hsp)
  email info@popastro.com   http://www.popastro.com
  Hon Sec: Guy Fennimore
- ○ *G, *L; to promote the knowledge & study of astronomy in a popular manner
- Gp Sections; Aurorae, Comets, Deep sky objects, Lunar occultations, Meteors, Moon, Planets, Sun, Variable stars
- ● Mtgs - ET - Res - Comp - Stat - Inf - VE - Weekend courses
- < Brit Astronomical Assn
- M 3,100 i, 60 org, UK / 70 i, 4 org, o'seas
- ¶ Popular Astronomy (Jnl) - 4; ftm, price on application nm. Circular (NL) - 6; ftm only.

Society of Portrait Sculptors   (SPS)   1953

- ■ 50A Hyde St, WINCHESTER, Hants, SO23 7DY.
  01962 860904
  email sps@portrait-sculpture.org
  http://www.portrait-sculpture.org
  Hon Sec: Robert Hunt
- ▲ Registered Charity
- ○ *A; 'portrait & figurative sculpture'
- ● Exhib (annual)
- M 30 i, UK / 2 i, o'seas
- ¶ Catalogue - 1; ftm, £6 nm.

Society for Post-Medieval Archaeology   (SPMA)   1967

- NR School of Archaeology & Ancient History, University of Leicester, University Rd, LEICESTER, LE1 7RH.
  0116-252 2846
  http://www.spma.org.uk
  Hon Sec: Dr Audrey Horning
- ▲ Company Limited by Guarantee
- ○ *L; to study evidence of British & Colonial history of the post-medieval period before industrialisation
- ● Conf - Res - Lib - VE - LG
- < Soc Histl Archaeology (USA)
- M 462 i, 219 org
- ¶ Post-Medieval Archaeology (Jnl); ftm.   NL - 2; free.

Society of Practising Veterinary Surgeons
   a group of the **British Veterinary Association**

Society for the Preservation of Beers from the Wood   (SPBW)   1963

- ■ 46 The Fairway, DEVIZES, Wilts, SN10 5DX.   (chmn/p)
  01380 726378
  email chairman@spbw.com
  Chmn: Chris Callow
- ▲ Un-incorporated Society
- Br 20; Turkey, USA
- ○ *K; to stimulate the brewing & encourage the drinking of traditional draught beers, drawn direct from the cask by gravity or by handpump or other appropriate methods & to support those brewers who, by their policy, assist in the society's aims
- ● Conf - Mtgs - Exhib (at beer festivals) - Comp (London Pub of the Year) - Stat
- M 600 i, UK / 300 i, o'seas
- ¶ Pint in Hand - 4; ftm only.

© CBD Research Ltd · Beckenham · BR3 5JS · Tel 020 8650 7745 · E-mail cbd@cbdresearch.com · www.cbdresearch.com

Society for the Prevention of Solvent & Volatile Substance Abuse
see **Re-Solv (Society for the Prevention of Solvent & Volatile Substance Abuse)**

Society of Procurement Officers in Local Government (SOPO) 1997

■ SBV Ltd, Timber House, Sandford Place, Sandford Avenue, Church Stretton, SY6 6DY.   (Chief Exec/b)
  01694 723333
  http://www.sopo.org
  Chief Exec: Peter Howarth
▲ Company Limited by Guarantee
Br 12 regions
○ *P; to provide procurement guidance & promote strategic procurement within local government; to provide a forum & network
● Conf - Mtgs - ET - Exhib - Inf - LG
< Chart Inst of Purchasing & Supply
M 2,400 i, 13 f
¶ enewsletter - 52; free.   Annual Ybk - 1; ftm, £200 nm.

Society for Producers & Composers of Applied Music (PCAM) 1982

■ Birchwood Hall, Storridge, MALVERN, Worcs, WR13 5EZ.   (hq)
  01886 884204
  email info@pcam.co.uk   http://www.pcam.co.uk
  Admin: Bob Fromer
▲ Un-incorporated Society
○ *T; music producers &/or composers working primarily in commissioned film, advertising & television programme music
Gp Television c'ee
● Mtgs - ET - Res - Inf
  Helpline (090 6633 0070)
< Creators' Rights Alliance; sister organisations in Australia, Germany, Spain, USA Alliance
M 159 i & f
¶ NL via email.   PCAM Directory - 1.

Society of Professional Accountants (SPA) 1996

■ 95 High St, GREAT MISSENDEN, Bucks, HP16 0AL.   (hq)
  01494 864414   fax 01494 864454
  email mail@spa.org.uk   http://www.spa.org.uk
  Chmn: Peter J D Mitchell
▲ Un-incorporated Society
○ *P; for chartered accountants who have a qualification issued by a recognised professional accountancy institute (ICAEW, ICAI, IAS, ACCA, CIMA); such individuals in practice
● Inf - LG
< ICAEW
M 1,800 i, 1,500 f
¶ NL;   LM;   AR; all ftm.

Society of Professional Engineers Ltd (SPE) 1969

■ Lutyens House, Billing Brook Rd, Weston Favell, NORTHAMPTON, NN3 8NW.   (regd off)
  01604 415729   fax 01604 415729
  email christine.braybrook@abe.org.uk
  http://www.professionalengineers-uk.org
  Chief Exec: David R Gibson
▲ Company Limited by Guarantee
○ *P; 'to promote the concept of the professional engineer & to place on a register those deemed to be so qualified'
● Mtgs - Exhib
M 150 i, UK / 400 i, o'seas
¶ The Professional Engineer - 4; free.

Society for Promoting Christian Knowledge (SPCK) 1698

§ 36 Causton St, LONDON, SW1P 4ST.   (hq)
  020 7592 3900   fax 020 7592 3939
  http://www.spck.org.uk
  an Anglican mission agency working, both in the UK and around the world, to help people grow in the Christian faith through the ministries of Christain education and literature.

Society for Promoting the Training of Women (SPTW) 1859

■ The Old Dairy, Appledore, ASHFORD, Kent, TN26 2AJ.   (hsp)
  email sec.sptw@btinternet.com   http://www.sptw.org
  Hon Sec: Mrs Michelle Bennett
▲ Registered Charity
○ *W; to make interest free loans to women (18+) undertaking full time (very occasionally part-time) training for a career
● ET
M 50 i
¶ AR; ftm, free nm (for sae).

Society for the Promotion of Byzantine Studies (SPBS) 1983

NR c/o Dr Tim Greenwood, School of History, University of St Andrews, St Katharine's Lodge, The Scores, ST ANDREWS, Fife, KY16 9AR.   (hsb)
  http://www.byzantium.ac.uk
  Hon Sec: Dr Antony Eastmond
▲ Registered Charity
○ *L; to further the study & knowledge of the history of the Byzantine Empire & its neighbours
● Conf - Mtgs - Res - PL - VE
< Assn Intle des Études Byzantines (AIEB)
M i
¶ Bulletin - 1.

Society for the Promotion of Hellenic Studies (Hellenic Society) (SPHS) 1879

■ Senate House (South Block - room 245), Malet St, LONDON, WC1E 7HU.   (hq)
  020 7862 8730   fax 020 7862 8731
  email office@hellenicsociety.org.uk
  http://www.hellenicsociety.org.uk
  Pres: Prof Malcolm Schofield
  Hon Sec: Dr Pantelis Michelakis
▲ Registered Charity
○ *L; to study the Greek language, literature, history & art in the ancient, Byzantine & modern periods
● Conf - Res - Comp - Lib - PL
< Brit School at Athens
M 3,000 i, UK / 1,000 org, o'seas
  (Sub: £22 student, £41 full mem, £200 corporate, £60 libraries & schools)
¶ Jnl of Hellenic Studies - 1; ftm only.
  Archaeological Reports - 1; ftm, £11 nm.
  Note: the Library is owned in common with the Society for the Promotion of Roman Studies & the Institute of Classical Studies of the University of London.

Society for the Promotion of New Music

  in 2008 merged with the British Music Information Centre, the Contemporary Music Network & the Sonic Arts Network to form Sound & Music - an agency & is therefore outside the scope of this directory

Society for the Promotion of Roman Studies (Roman Society) 1910

■ Senate House (South Block - room 244), Malet St, LONDON, WC1E 7HU.   (hq)
  020 7862 8727   fax 020 7862 8728
  email office@romansociety.org
  http://www.romansociety.org
  Sec: Dr Fiona K Haarer
▲ Company Limited by Guarantee; Registered Charity
○ *L; to promote the study of the history, archaeology, literature & art of Italy & the Roman Empire, from the earliest times down to c AD 700
● Conf - Mtgs - Lib
< Fédn Intle des Assns d'Études Classiques
M 2,100 i, 250 org, UK / 650 i, 950 org, o'seas
¶ Jnl of Roman Studies - 1; ftm, £60 yr nm.
  Jnl of Roman Studies Monographs - irreg; prices vary.
  Britannia - 1; ftm, £60 yr nm.
  Britannia Monographs - irreg; prices vary.   AR; free.

Society of Property Researchers (SPR) 1987

- ■ St Mary's, Gandish Rd, EAST BERGHOLT, Suffolk, CO7 6UR. (mem/sp)
  01206 298205   fax 01206 298683
  email ftrott@sprweb.com   http://www.sprweb.com
  Mem Sec: Fiona Trott
- ▲ Un-incorporated Society
- ○ *P
- ● Mtgs - Res - VE
- M 500 i, UK / 30 i, o'seas
- ¶ LM - 1;   SPR Property Review & Digest No 1 & 2 (1993); both ftm only.
  The Adequacy & Accuracy of Commercial Property Data, Working Paper No 1: The Need for Property Data (1995); Local Area Analysis & Portfolio Construction (1994); Property Indices Report (1994);   all ftm, £20 nm. Survey of Salaries & Benefits - 2 yrly; ftm, £30 nm.

Society for the Protection of Ancient Buildings (SPAB) 1877

- ■ 37 Spital Sq, LONDON, E1 6DY.   (hq)
  020 7377 1644   fax 020 7247 5296
  email info@spab.org.uk   http://www.spab.org.uk
  Sec: Philip Venning
- ▲ Company Limited by Guarantee; Registered Charity
- ○ *K, *L; to promote the conservative repair of pre-1700 buildings; SPAB must be notified of applications to demolish listed biuldings in England & Wales
- Gp SPAB Mills; SPAB in Scotland
- ● Conf - Mtgs - ET - Exhib - Inf - Lib - VE - LG
- < Jt C'ee of the Nat Amenity Socs
- M 8,500 i
- ¶ Cornerstone - 4;   Mills News - 4; both ftm.

Society for the Protection of Aviculture
   merged in 2007 with the **National Council for Aviculture Ltd**

Society for the Protection of Life from Fire   1836

- § 15 Mallow Close, HORSHAM, W Sussex, RH12 5GA.   (hq)
  http://www.splf.org.uk
  Sec: Michael Gale
  The Society exists to give recognition to people who perform acts of bravery in rescuing others from the life-threatening effects of fires.

Society for the Protection of Unborn Children   (SPUC)   1967

- NR 3 Whitacre Mews, Stannary St, LONDON, SE11 4AB.   (hq)
  020 7091 7091   fax 020 7820 3131
  email information@spuc.org.uk
  http://www.spuc.org.uk
  Gen Sec: Paul Tully
- Br 141
- ○ *K; to affirm, defend & promote the existence & value of human life from the moment of conception
- Gp Conservative Group; Muslim Division; No Less Human; Nurses Opposed to Euthanasia; Patients First Network; Silent No More; SPUC Evangelicals
- ● Conf - Mtgs - ET - Res - Comp - Inf - LG
- M 45,000 i
- ¶ Pro-Life Times - 2.

Society for Psychical Research
   see registered title **Incorporated Society for Psychical Research**

Society of Radiographers   (SoR)   1920

- ■ 207 Providence Square, Mill St, LONDON, SE1 2EW.   (hq)
  020 7740 7200   fax 020 7740 7233
  email info@sor.org   http://www.sor.org
  Chief Exec: Richard Evans
- ▲ Company Limited by Guarantee
- ○ *P, *U; the Society & College exist to promote & develop the science & practice of radiography (including both diagnostic & therapeutic disciplines); it is the recognised trade union for those engaged in radiography & related activities
- Gp College of Radiographers (charitable non-membership subsidiary)
- ● Conf - Mtgs - ET - Exam - Res - Exhib - Comp - SG - Stat - Lib - VE - Empl - LG
- < Allied Health Professions Fedn; Intl Soc Radiographers & Radiological Technologists; Trades U Congress
- M 19,690 i
- ¶ Radiography (Jnl) - 4;   Synergy (NL) - 12; both ftm. Imaging & Oncology - 1; free to all in radiological & oncological communities.

Society for Radiological Protection   (SRP)   1963

- ■ PO Box 117, BUCKFASTLEIGH, Devon, TQ11 0WA. (admin/off)
  01364 644487   fax 01364 644492
  email admin@srp-uk.org   http://www.srp-uk.org
- ▲ Registered Charity
- ○ *L, *P; the scientific, technological, medical & legal aspects of radiological protection
- ● Conf - Mtgs
- < Intl Radiation Protection Assn
- M 1,491 i, f & org
- ¶ Jnl - 4; ftm, £340 yr nm.

Society of Recorder Players   (SRP)   1937

- NR 21 Bereweeke Avenue, WINCHESTER, Hants, SO22 6BH. (hsp)
  01962 868862
  email secretary@srp.org.uk   http://www.srp.org.uk
  Sec: Bob Whitmarsh
- ▲ Registered Charity
- Br 50; Ireland
- ○ *D; 'education of the public in the study, practice & appreciation of the art of music & in particular the repertoire & playing of recorders'
- ● Conf - Mtgs - ET - SG - Exams for certificate for teaching & conducting - Workshops - Biennial competition for young professionals
- M 1,250 i, 4 org, UK / 30 i, o'seas

Society of Registered Naturopaths
   see the **Incorporated Society of Registered Naturopaths**

Society for Renaissance Studies   (SRS)   1967

- ■ c/o Dr Gabriele Neher, Dept of Art History, Lakeside Arts Centre, University of Nottingham, NOTTINGHAM, NG7 2RD.   (hsb)
  email gabriele.neher@nottingham.ac.uk
  http://www.rensoc.org.uk
  Hon Sec: Dr Gabriele Neher
- ▲ Registered Charity
- ○ *L; study of all aspects of the Renaissance
- ● Conf - Mtgs - ET - Exhib
- < Renaissance Soc of America (RSA)
- M c 600 i
- ¶ Renaissance Studies (Jnl) - 5; £25-£38 m.

Society for Reproduction & Fertility   2001

- ■ Portland Customer Services, Commerce Way, COLCHESTER, Essex, HG1 5LT.   (regd off)
  01206 796351
  http://www.srf-reproduction.org
- ▲ Company Limited by Guarantee; Registered Charity
- ○ *L; to enhance the knowledge of reproductive processes in man & animals

© CBD Research Ltd · Beckenham · BR3 5JS · Tel 020 8650 7745 · E-mail cbd@cbdresearch.com · www.cbdresearch.com

Society for Reproductive & Infant Psychology   (SRIP)   1980
NR   School of Nursing, Midwifery & Physiotherapy, University of
     Nottingham, Academic Division of Midwifery, B Floor East
     Block, Queen's Medical Centre, NOTTINGHAM, Notts,
     NG7 2UH.   (hsb)
     0115-823 0983
     email anita.hughes@nottingham.ac.uk
     http://www.srip.ac.uk
     Sec: Anita Hughes
▲   Registered Charity
○   *M; to promote the scientific study, both pure & applied, of all
     psychological & behavioural matters related to human
     reproduction
●   Conf - Mtgs - ET - Res - Comp
M   140 i, UK / 38 i, o'seas
¶   Journal of Reproductive & Infant Psychology - 4.

Society for Research into Higher Education Ltd   (SRHE)   1964
NR   44 Bedford Row, LONDON, WC1R 4LL.   (hq)
     020 7447 2525   fax 020 7447 2526
     email srheoffice@srhe.ac.uk   http://www.srhe.ac.uk
     Dir: Helen Perkins
▲   Company Limited by Guarantee; Registered Charity
○   *L; to advance understanding of higher education

**Society for Research into Hydrocephalus & Spina Bifida
(SRHSB)   1957**
■   ASBAH House, 42 Park Rd, PETERBOROUGH, Cambs,
     PE1 2UQ.   (hsb)
     email srhsb@asbah.org   http://www.srhsb.org
     Hon Sec: Mrs Rosemary R Batchelor
▲   Registered Charity
○   *L, *Q; to advance education & promote research into
     hydrocephalus & spina bifida; to bring together workers in
     different fields so that they may be aided in their joint effort
     to prevent, cure or alleviate these conditions
●   Conf - Res
M   56 i, UK / 200 i, o'seas
¶   Cerebrospinal Fluid Research - 1;   NL - 3;   AR - 1;
     Prospectus - 1; m only, £60 yr (£30 yr senior members).

**Society for the Responsible Use of Resources in Agriculture & on
the Land   (RURAL)   1983**
■   Chester House, 12 Hillbury Rd, Alderholt, FORDINGBRIDGE,
     Hants, SP6 3BQ.   (hq)
     01425 652035
     http://www.rural.org.uk
     Dir: Brig H J Hickman
○   *F; to assist the policy makers in the field of land use,
     agricultural & rural management; to form opinions; to
     reconcile competing rural interests; information policy
     development
●   Conf - Mtgs - SG - Discussion groups
M   180 i, 29 f
¶   RURAL Briefing; £15 yr.   Network opportunities.

Society for Sailing Barge Research   (SSBR)   1963
■   5 Cox Rd, Alresford, COLCHESTER, Essex, CO7 8EJ.   (hsp)
     01206 825317
     email john.white6@talk21.com
     http://www.sailingbargeresearch.org.uk
     Hon Sec: John White
▲   Un-incorporated Society
○   *G; research into the sailing barge, the men who built & sailed
     them & the ports from which they sailed
●   Res - Exhib - PL
M   340 i, 10 org, UK / 10 i, o'seas
¶   Topsail (Jnl) - 1;   NL - 2; both ftm only.

Society of Sales & Marketing   (SSAM)   1980
■   40 Archdale Rd, LONDON, SE22 9HJ.   (hq)
     020 8693 0555   fax 07092 342170
     email info@ssam.co.uk   http://www.ssam.co.uk
     Chief Exec: Prof R A Herbert-Blankson
▲   Company Limited by Guarantee
Br   12; 70 o'seas
○   *P; to encourage the study & practice of selling, sales
     management, retail management, marketing & international
     trade & services
●   Conf - Mtgs - ET - Exam - Res - Exhib - Comp - SG - Stat - Expt
     - Inf - Lib - LG
<   Soc of Nursery Nursing Practitioners
M   500 i, UK / 4,000 i, o'seas
¶   Sales & Marketing Today; ftm, £1.50 nm.   NL.

Society of Schoolmasters & Schoolmistresses   (SOSS)   1798
■   c/o Miss Sarah Brydon, SGBI, Queen Mary House, Manor Park
     Rd, CHISLEHURST, Kent, BR7 5PY.   (hsb)
     020 8468 7997   fax 020 8468 7200
     email sgbi@fsmail.net
     Case Officer: Miss Sarah Brydon
▲   Registered Charity
○   *W; 'to give assistance to necessitous schoolmasters,
     schoolmistresses & their dependents'
●   Mtgs
M   14 i

Society of Scottish Artists   (SSA)   1891
NR   2 Wemyss Avenue, GLAGSGOW, G77 6AR.   (sp)
     0141-616 2566
     email ssa@tangledwebs.co.uk   http://www.s-s-a.org
     Sec: Noreen Sharkey Paisley
▲   Registered Charity
○   *A; to mount an annual exhibition reflecting the adventurous
     spirit of Scottish art; to promote international exhibition &
     exchange
●   Exhib
M   350 i, UK / 10 i o'seas
¶   SSA NL - 4; free.   Exhibition Catalogue (& LM) - 1.
     The SSA: the last 100 years; £15.

Society of Scribes & Illuminators   (SSI)   1921
■   6 Queen Sq, LONDON, WC1N 3AR.   (mail address)
     email gillianhazeldine@austwick.org
     http://www.calligraphyonline.org
     Sec: Gillian Hazeldine
▲   Un-incorporated Society
○   *A; to perpetuate a tradition of craftsmanship in the production
     of manuscript books & documents; to encourage the practice
     & influence of calligraphy & fine letterings
Gp   64 fellows; 28 advanced calligraphers on 3-yr scheme
●   Mtgs - ET - Exhib - SG - Inf - Lib
M   700 i, UK / 200 i, o'seas
¶   The Scribe (Jnl) - 1; ftm.   NL.   LM.

Society of Sexual Health Advisers   (SSHA)
■   Unite the Union, 128 Theobald's Rd, LONDON, WC1X 8TN.
     (hq)
     07919 324716
     email info@ssha.info   http://www.ssha.info
     Nat Officer: Carol English
▲   Company Limited by Guarantee
○   *P, *U; for health advisers working in NHS departments of
     genito-urinary medicine & sexual health
●   Conf - Mtgs - ET - Res - Empl - LG - Professional website
<   a professional section of Unite, the Union
M   300 i
¶   SSHA NL - 2; ftm only.

Society of Share & Business Valuers 1996
NR 1 Winchester Rd, BROMLEY, Kent, BR2 0PZ. (hsb)
    020 8466 7924 fax 020 8466 7637
    http://www.ssbv.org
    Sec: D Bowes
○   *P; specialists in valuation of shares & derivatives, businesses,
    intellectual property & other intangibles

Society of Shoe Fitters 1959
■   c/o The Anchorage, 28 Admirals Walk, HINGHAM, Norfolk,
    NR9 4JL. (hsp)
    01953 851171 fax 01953 851190
    email secretary@shoefitters-uk.org
    http://www.shoefitters-uk.org
    Sec: Laura West
▲   Un-incorporated Society
○   *P; training people to fit shoes correctly to a recognised
    qualification
●   Mtgs - ET - Exam - Exhib - Inf - VE - LG - Providing foot health
    education material - Helpline
M   223 i, 9 f, UK/ 10 i, o'seas
    (Suib: £10.50 i, £150 f, UK / £50 i, o'seas
¶   LM; on website, £5 nm.   Leaflets; £5 per 100.

Society for the Social History of Medicine (SSHM) 1969
■   School of History Classics & Archaeology, University of
    Edinburgh, Doorway 4 Teviot Place, EDINBURGH,
    EH8 9AG. (hsb)
    email gayle.davis@ed.ac.uk   http://www.sshm.org
    Sec: Dr Gayle Davis
▲   Registered Charity
○   *L; to promote the study of all aspects of the social history of
    medicine, having reference to the patients as well as the
    practitioner & to health as well as disease
●   Conf - Mtgs - ET - Res - Comp - SG - Inf
M   189 i, UK / 158 i, o'seas
¶   Social History of Medicine (Jnl) - 3; £37 m, £101 nm, (2005).

Society for Social Medicine (SSM) 1957
■   University College London, Health & Social Surveys Group,
    Dept Epidemiology & Public Health, 1-19 Torrington Place,
    LONDON, WC1E 6BT. (hsb)
    020 7679 1269
    email secretary.ssm@googlemail.com
    http://www.socsocmed.org.uk
    Hon Sec: Jenny Mindell
▲   Un-incorporated Society
○   *L; concerned with all aspects of social medicine including
    epidemiology & the study of medical & health needs of
    society, provision & organisation of health services &
    prevention of disease
●   Conf - Mtgs
<   Eur Public Health Assn
M   1,250 i, UK / 70 i, o'seas
¶   NL - 4;   AR; both ftm only.

**Society of Solicitors in the Supreme Courts of Scotland
(SSCSoc) 1784**
■   SSC Library, Parliament House, 11 Parliament Sq, EDINBURGH,
    EH1 1RF. (hq)
    0131 225 6268   fax 0131 225 2270
    email enquiries@ssclibrary.co.uk
    http://www.ssclibrary.co.uk
    Sec: Ian L S Balfour
○   *P; to maintain a practitioners' law library; to express opinions
    on current legal questions; to maintain a fund for widows &
    orphans
●   Inf - Lib
<   part of the College of Justice in Scotland
M   300 i, UK / 6 i, o'seas

Society for South Asian Studies
    on 1 October 2007 merged with the **British Association for South
    Asian Studies**

Society of Specialist Paralegals
NR 80 St Vincent St (5th floor), GLASGOW, G2 5UB. (hq)
    0141-225 6700
○   *P
¶   The Specialist Paralegal - 4.

Society of Sports Therapists 1990
■   16 Royal Terrace, GLASGOW, G3 7NY. (hq)
    0845 600 2613   fax 0141-332 5335
    email admin@society-of-sports-therapists.org
    http://www.society-of-sports-therapists.org
    Chmn: Prof Graham N Smith
▲   Company Limited by Guarantee
○   *P; *S
●   Mtgs - Exam - LG
M   3,500 i
¶   Sports Therapy (Jnl) - 1.   NL - 6.

Society of Stars 1995
■   55 Denham Lane, Chalfont St Peter, GERRARDS CROSS, Bucks,
    SL9 0EW. (hq)
    01494 872817
    email info@thebiggive.org.uk
    Sec: Carol Hehir
▲   Company Limited by Guarantee; Registered Charity
○   *W; celebrity support for children & adults with cerebral palsy

Society for Storytelling (SfS) 1993
■   Morgan Library, Aston ST, WEM, Shropshire, SY4 5AU.   (mail)
    0753 457 8386
    email admin@sfs.org.uk   http://www.sfs.org.uk
    Sec: David England
▲   Company Limited by Guarantee; Registered Charity
○   *A; to increase awareness of the art, practice & value of oral
    storytelling; to provide information of storytelling, storytellers
    & events
Gp Education; Health & therapy; Storytelling in organisations
●   Conf - ET - Inf - Lib - Co-ordination of events
<   Assn Festival Organisers; FATE; Lapidus; Mythstories Museum;
    Scottish Storytelling Centre; The Telling Place
>   ACE; Bit Crack; FATE; Fibs & Fables; Mythstories Museum; Scot
    Storytelling Centre; The Telling Place
M   569 i, 16 org, UK / 18 i, o'seas
¶   Storylines Magazine - 4; ftm only.
    Directory of Storytellers - 1 £7.50 m, £11.50 nm.
    Talkshop Catalogue - 1; free.
    Booklets on the theory & practice of storytelling - irreg.
    Factsheets of useful information & booklists - irreg; £1.35.

Society of Stress Managers
NR 10 Wimborne Ave, Chadderton, OLDHAM, Lancs, OL9 0RN.
    (hq)
    0161-652 2284
    email petermatthews@manageyourstress.co.uk
    http://www.manageyourstress.co.uk
    Sec: Peter Matthews
○   *P
<   UK Confedn of Hypnotherapy Orgs
M   24 i

© CBD Research Ltd · Beckenham · BR3 5JS · Tel 020 8650 7745 · E-mail cbd@cbdresearch.com · www.cbdresearch.com

Society for the Study of Addiction to Alcohol & other Drugs (SSA) 1884

- ■ 19 Springfield Mount, LEEDS, W Yorks, LS2 9NG. (hq)
  0113-295 2787   fax 0113-295 2787
  email membership@addiction-ssa.org
  http://www.addiction-ssa.org
  Exec Offr: Graham Hunt
- ▲ Company LImited by Guarantee; Registered Charity
- ○ *L; to expand & promote the scientific understanding of addiction & the problems related to it; to advance the use of the evidence-base in policy & practice
- ● Conf - Mtgs - ET - Res - Comp
- M 300 i, UK / 110 i, o'seas
  (Sub: £85)
- ¶ Addiction - 12; ftm, £335 nm.
  Addiction Biology - 4; ftm, £244 nm.

Society for the Study of Animal Breeding
a group of the **British Veterinary Association**

Society for the Study of Artificial Intelligence & Simulation of Behaviour (SSAISB) 1964

- NR Institute of Psychiatry, King's College London, Addictions Sciences Building B3.06, 4 Windsor Walk, Denmark Hill, LONDON, SE5 8AF.
  020 7848 0191
  http://www.aisb.org.uk
  Admin: Dr Katerina Koutsantoni
- ○ *L; to promote the study of artificial intelligence, simulation of behaviour & the design of intelligent systems

Society for the Study of Flies
see **Dipterists Forum - the Society for the Study of Flies**

Society for the Study of Human Biology (SSHB) 1958

- ■ Dept of Human Sciences, Loughborough University, LOUGHBOROUGH, Leics, LE11 3TU. (hsb)
  01509 228486
  email p.griffiths@lboro.ac.uk   http://www.sshb.org
  Hon Sec: Dr Paula Griffiths
- ▲ Company Limited by Guarantee
- ○ *L; to advance the study in all its branches, of the biology of human populations & of humans as a species, particularly human variability, adaptability & ecology, auxology, environmental physiology, epidemiology & ageing
- ● Conf - Mtgs - Symposium
- < Inst Biology
- M 114 i, UK / 66 i, o'seas
- ¶ Annals of Human Biology - 6; ftm, £36 yr nm.
  Symposium Proceedings - 1; price varies (published by Taylor & Francis).

Society for the Study of Labour History (SSLH) 1960

- ■ Room 316 Lipman Building, School of Arts & Social Sciences, Northumbria University, NEWCASTLE upon TYNE, NE1 8ST. (conf/s/b)
  email charlotte.alston@northumbria.ac.uk
  http://www.sslh.org.uk
  Conf Sec: Charlotte Alston
- ▲ Registered Charity
- ○ *L; 'an exploration into the working lives & politics of 'ordinary' people; the emphasis is on British labour history, though comparative & international studies are not neglected'; preservation of labour archives
- Gp Archives & resources c'ee; Editorial Advy Bd (Labour History Review)
- ● Conf - Mtgs - Res - Comp - SG
- ¶ Labour History Review - 3; £24 m.

Society for the Study of Nineteenth-Century Ireland

- NR School of English, Queen's University of Belfast, BELFAST, BT7 1NN. (treas/b)
  Treas: Dr Leon Litvack
- ○ *L; to promote research into nineteenth century Ireland
- ● Conf - Mtgs
- M i
- ¶ Books.

Society for the Study of Subterranean Survival (SSSS) 1982

- ■ 76 May's Hill Rd, BROMLEY, Kent, BR2 0HT. (hsp)
- ▲ Un-incorporated Society
- ○ *L
- ● Conf - Mtgs - SG - Lib - VE
- ¶ Survival Underground - 2; ftm only.

Society of Teachers of the Alexander Technique (STAT) 1958

- NR Linton House (1st floor), 39-51 Highgate Rd, LONDON, NW5 1RS. (hq)
  0845 230 7828   fax 020 7482 5435
  email office@stat.org.uk   http://www.stat.org.uk
- ▲ Registered Charity
- ○ *P; to ensure the highest standards of teacher training & professional practice of the Alexander Technique

Society of Teachers of Speech & Drama (STSD) 1951

- ■ 73 Berry Hill Rd, MANSFIELD, Notts, NG18 4RU. (regd/office)
  01623 627636
  email ann.k.jones@btinternet.com
  http://www.stsd.org.uk
- ▲ Company Limited by Guarantee
- Br 34; 16 countries o'seas
- ○ *E; the teaching of speech & drama & other theatrical skills; to support & encourage students in training
- Gp Teaching: Communication skills, Speech & drama, Theatre skills;
  Amateur theatre; Business communication & presentation; Conferences; Correction of speech problems; Lecturing; Workshops
- ● Conf - ET - Exhib - Comp - SG - Inf
- < Nat Campaign for the Arts; Central Coun of Amat Theatre
- > Voice Network; Engl Speaking Bd; Gld of S African Teachers of Speech & Drama; Australian Speech & Drama Assns; New Zealand Speech Assn
- M 750 i, 18 f, UK / 98 i, 1 f, o'seas
- ¶ Speech & Drama (Jnl) - 2; ftm, £7 nm.   NL - 3; ftm only.

Society of Technical Analysts Ltd (STA) 1969

- NR Dean House, Vernham Dean, ANDOVER, Hants, SP11 0LA. (hq)
  0845 003 9549
- ▲ Company Limited by Guarantee
- ○ *P; to promote the use & understanding of technical analysis amongst the public & investment community; to maintain professional standards in the subject & to set an examination to allow competency to be measured & proven

Society of Television Lighting & Design (STLD) 1974

- ■ 18 Cheyne Avenue, TWICKENHAM, Middx, TW2 6AN. (sec/p)
  07973 152682
  email secretary@stld.org.uk   http://www.stld.org.uk
  Sec: Richard Bowles
- ▲ Un-incorporated Society
- ○ *P; an apolitical society for the free exchange of ideas in all aspects of the television profession (incl techniques & reports on the use & design of equipment both to manufacturers & members)
- ● Mtgs (also regional) - ET - Exhib - VE
- M i
- ¶ Television Lighting - 4; ftm only.
- × 2009 Society of Television Lighting Directors

Society of Theatre Consultants   (STC)   1964
- ■ 27 Old Gloucester St, LONDON, WC1N 3XX.   (asa)
  020 7419 8767
  http://www.theatreconsultants.org.uk
  Chmn: Michael Houlden
- ▲ Un-incoporated Society
- ○ *P; for specialist consultants in the field of theatre building design & management & the design & integration of specialist theatre equipment
- ● Conf - Mtgs - ET
- M i
- ¶ Occasional.

Society for Theatre Research   (STR)   1948
- NR The National Theatre Archive, 83-101 The Cut, LONDON, SE1 8LL.   (mail/address)
  http://www.str.org.uk
  Hon Secs: Eileen Cottis,   Valerie Lucas
- ▲ Registered Charity
- Br Northern
- ○ *L, *Q; to foster research into the history & practice of the British theatre
- ● Mtgs - Res - SG - VE - Research awards (£4,000 yr) - Annual Theatre Book Prize - Administration of annual William Poel Festival & the Edward Gordon Craig memorial lecture
- < Intl Fedn for Theatre Res; Theatres Trust
- M 400 i, 80 f, UK / 150 i, 150 f, o'seas
- ¶ Theatre Notebook - 3; £18 m (£19.50 o'seas), £6 back issue nm.
  NL - 2;   AR; both ftm only.
  Books on various aspects of the British theatre.

Society of Ticket Agents & Retailers   (STAR)
- NR PO Box 43, LONDON, WC2H 7LD.   (mail/address)
  0870 603 9011
  email info@star.org.uk   http://www.star.org.uk
  Sec: Jonathan Brown
- ○ *T

Society of Trust & Estate Practitioners   (STEP)   1991
- ■ Artillery House (South), 11-19 Artillery Row, LONDON, SW1P 1RT.   (hq)
  020 7340 0500   fax 020 7340 0501
  email step@step.org   http://www.step.org
  Chief Exec: David Harvey
- ▲ Company Limited by Guarantee
- Br 29; 30
- ○ *P; for those involved at senior level with trusts & estates - from the legal, accountancy, corporate trust, banking, insurance & related professions
- ● Conf - Mtgs - ET - Inf - LG
- M 5,388 i, UK / 8,745 i, o'seas
- ¶ STEP Jnl - 4;   Trust Quarterly Review - 4;
  STEP USA Jnl - 3; all ftm, all £345 yr nm.

Society of Turnaround Professionals
   since 2008 **Institute for Turnaround**

Society for Underwater Technology Ltd   (SUT)   1966
- NR 1 Fetter Lane, LONDON, EC4A 1BR.   (hq)
  020 3440 5535   fax 020 3440 5980
  email info@sut.org   http://www.sut.org.uk
  Hon Sec: S Hall,   Chief Exec: Dr R L Allwood
- ▲ Registered Charity
- Br 2; Australia (Melbourne, Perth), Brazil, Malaysia, USA
- ○ *L; to promote the understanding & use of the underwater environment; the development of the techniques & tools to explore, study & exploit the oceans & the earth beneath
- Gp Diving & submersibles; Education & training; Environmental forces; Marine renewable energies; Ocean resources; Offshore site investigation & geotechnics; Policy advisory; Subsea engineering & operations; Underwater robotics; Underwater science
- ● Conf - Mtgs - ET - Inf - LG
- M 868 i, 109 f
- ¶ Underwater Technology (Jnl) - 4.   SUT News - 8.
  Conference proceedings - irreg.   Ybk - 2-yrly.

Society for Vascular Technology of Great Britain & Ireland (SVT)   1992
- ■ at the Royal College of Surgeons, 35-43 Lincoln's Inn Fields, LONDON, WC2A 3PE.
  020 7973 0306   fax 020 7430 9235
  email office@vascularsociety.org.uk
  http://www.svtgbi.org.uk
  Pres: Kerry Tinkler
- ▲ Registered Charity
- ○ *M, *P; to promote education, training & research in the field of vascular science
- Gp C'ees: Education; Executive standards; Professionals standards
- ● Conf - Mtgs - ET - Exam - Res - SG - Inf - LG
- M 398 i, UK / 6 i, o'seas
  (Sub: £45)
- ¶ NL - 4;   LM (website);   AR - 1; all ftm.

Society of Wedding & Portrait Photographers   (SWPP/BPPA) 1988
- ■ 6 Bath St, RHYL, Flintshire, LL18 3EB.   (hq)
  01745 356935
  email enquiries@swpp.co.uk
  Chief Exec: Phil Jones
- ▲ Company Limited by Guarantee
- ○ *P
- ● Conf - Mtgs - ET - Exam - Exhib - Comp - Inf
- M 6,500 i
- ¶ Professional Imagemaker.

Society for the Welfare of Horses & Ponies   (SWHP)   1973
- NR The Horse Hospital, Coxstone, St Maughan's, MONMOUTH, NP25 5QF.   (hq)
  01600 750233   fax 01600 750468
  email swhp@swhp.co.uk   http://www.swhp.co.uk
  Chmn: Jenny MacGregor
- ▲ Registered Charity
- ○ *G, *K; to take into care sick, injured & abused horses & ponies, returning them to health & loaning them to homes suitable for their age, fitness & capabilities
- ● SG - LG - Care of horses on site & on loan
- < Nat Equine Welfare Coun
- M 1,200 i, UK / 10 i, o'seas
- ¶ NL - 2; free.

Society of West Highland & Island Historical Research
   has closed

Society of Wildlife Artists
   a member of the **Federation of British Artists**

© CBD Research Ltd · Beckenham · BR3 5JS · Tel 020 8650 7745 · E-mail cbd@cbdresearch.com · www.cbdresearch.com

Society of Will Writers & Estate Planning Practitioners   1994
- ■ Newland House (ground floor), The Point, Weaver Rd,
  LINCOLN, LN5 3QN.   (hq)
  01522 687888   fax 01522 694666
  email info@willwriters.com   http://www.willwriters.com
  Dir Gen: Brian W McMillan
- ▲ Company Limited by Guarantee
- Br 13
- ○ *P; 'a non-profit-making self-regulatory organisation whose
  primary objects are the advancement, education & ethical
  standards within the will-writing profession'
- ● Conf - Mtgs - ET - Exam - Res - SG - Inf - LG
- M 1,600 i, UK / 10 i, o'seas
  (Sub: £250)
- ¶ Testament (NL) - 12; ftm only.

Society of Women Artists   (SWA)   1855
- NR 1 Knapp Cottages, Wyke, GILLINGHAM, Dorset, SP8 4NQ.
  (hq)
  01747 825718   fax 01747 826835
  email pamhenderson@dsl.pipex.com
  http://www.society-women-artists.org.uk
  Exec Sec: Mrs Pamela Henderson
- ▲ Company Limited by Guarantee; Registered Charity
- ○ *A; a non-political, non-feminist society for the encouragement
  of women artists
- Gp Ceramics; Drawing; Engraving; Lithography; Miniature work;
  Painting in all media; Sculpture in all media
- ● Exhib
- M 142 i
- ¶ Illustrated Exhibition Catalogue - 1; ftm, £3.50 nm.

Society of Wood Engravers   (SWE)   1920
- ■ The Old Governor's House, Norman Cross, PETERBOROUGH,
  Cambs, PE7 3TB.   (sec/p)
  01733 242833
  http://www.woodengravers.co.uk
  Gen Sec: Geraldine Waddington
- ▲ Un-incorporated Society
- Br 1 o'seas
- ○ *A; for those interested in all aspects of wood engraving
- ● Conf - Mtgs - ET - Res - Exhib - Inf - Publications
- M 70 i, UK / 10 i, o'seas
  (Sub: £25 UK / £35 o'seas)
  (subscribers: 350 i, 30 org, UK / 50 i, 30 org, o'seas)
- ¶ Multiples (NL) - 6.

Society of Writers to Her Majesty's Signet   (WSSociety)   1594
- NR Signet Library, Parliament Sq, EDINBURGH, EH1 1RF.   (hq)
  0131-225 4923 & 220 3426 (general enquiries)
  fax 0131-220 4016
  email library@wssociety.co.uk
  http://www.signetlibrary.co.uk
- ▲ Un-incorporated Society
- ○ *P; private society of qualified Scottish solicitors
- Gp Signet Library (mainly Scottish law); Training & education
  (courses & seminars for members & non-members); Function
  & conference facilities letting
- ● Conf - ET - SG - Inf - Lib (current & historical material, mainly
  appertaining to Scotland) - Liaison with other legal bodies
- M i UK & o'seas
- ¶ Signet NL - 3; ftm only.   AR.

Society of Young Mathematicians
the youth group of the **Mathematical Association**

Society of Young Publishers   (SYP)   1949
- NR c/o The Publishers Association, 29b Montague St, London,
  WC1B 5BW.   (mem/sb)
  Sec: Alice Herbert
- ○ *P; to bring together young publishers
- ● Conf - Mtgs - London Book Fair - Annual study tour
- M 300 i & f
- ¶ Inprint - (Jnl/NL) - 12; ftm, £2 nm.
  Young Publisher's Handbook - 1.

Socio-Legal Studies Association   (SLSA)   1989
- NR c/o Sally Wheeler, School of Law, Queen's University Belfast,
  BELFAST, BT7 1NN.   (hsb)
  Sally Wheeler
- ▲ Un-incorporated Society
- ○ *E, *L
- ● Conf - ET - SG
- M i
- ¶ Socio-legal NL - 3; ftm only.   LM - 1.

Sociological Association of Ireland
- IRL Department of Sociology, University College Cork, Safari,
  Donovan's Rd, Cork, Republic of Ireland   (pres/b)
  353 (0) 21 490 3756
  email sai@ucd.ie   http://www.sociology.ie
  Pres: Dr Ciaran McCullagh
- ○ *P; for all concerned with theoretical & empirical issues in the
  social sciences

Soil Association Ltd   1946
- ■ South Plaza, Marlborough St, BRISTOL, BS1 3NX.   (hq)
  0117-314 5000   fax 0117-314 5001
  email info@soilassociation.org
  http://www.soilassociation.org
  Dir: Helen Browning,   Sec: Roger Mortlock
- ▲ Registered Charity
- Br 5
- ○ *E, *F, *H; to transform attitudes to food & farming in the UK &
  internationally; to work with the public, farmers, growers,
  food processors, retailers, consumers & policy makers to
  bring about change by creating a growing body of public
  opinion that understands the links between farming practice
  & food, & between plant, animal, human & environmental
  health
- ● Conf - ET - Res - Stat - Inf - Lib - PL - LG
- < Intl Fedn Organic Agricl Movements; Access to Farms
  Partnership
- M 18,000 i, 4,500 f, UK / 100 f, o'seas
- ¶ Living Earth - 3; ftm, £2 nm.
  Organic Farming - 4; ftm only.

Soil & Groundwater Technology Association   (SAGTA)
- NR c/o GRM, 1 Bedford Row, Holborn, LONDON, WC1R 4BZ.
  07742 723507
  email dwlaidler@dwlenv.co.uk   http://www.sagta.org.uk
  Sec: Doug Laidler
- ○ *L; to address the technical challenges associated with the
  management of landholdings which are potentially
  contaminated

Solar Energy Society   (UK-ISES)   1974
- NR PO Box 489, ABINGDON, Oxon, OX14 4WY.   (hq)
  0776 016 3559   fax 01235 484684
  email info@uk-ises.org   http://www.uk-ises.org
- ○ *L, *P; as the UK section of the International Solar Energy
  Society it aims to further the use of all forms of renewable
  energy
- Gp all renewable energy technologies
- ● Conf - Mtgs - ET - Inf - LG
- < Intl Solar Energy Soc
- M i & f

Solar Trade Association Ltd   (STA)   1978

- ■ Capital Tower (7th floor), 91 Waterloo Rd, LONDON, SE1 8RT.   (hq)
  020 7925 3575   fax 020 7925 2715
  email enquiries@solar-trade.org.uk
  http://www.solartrade.org.uk
- ▲ Company Limited by Guarantee
- ○ *T; to promote widespread use of solar energy technology; to encourage excellence within the UK solar energy industry
- Gp Working groups: Technial; Training
- ● Conf - Mtgs - ET - Exhib - Stat - Inf - LG
- < Eur Solar Thermal Inf Fedn (ESTIF)
- M 168 f, UK / 1 f, o'seas
  (Sub: £100 - £1,600)
- ¶ e-NL - 12; ftm only.
  Code of Ethical Practice - irreg;
  The Sun's Abundant Energy (information sheet); both free.

Soldiers, Sailors, Airmen & Families Association   (SSAFA) 1885

- § 19 Queen Elizabeth St, LONDON, SE1 2LP.   (hq)
  0845 130 0975
  email info@ssafa.org.uk   http://www.ssafa.org.uk
  Chief Exec: Andrew Cumming
  provides support for the serving men & women in today's armed forces, those who have served, & their families & dependents.

Solicitor Sole Practitioners Group   (SPG)   1990

- ■ Buckland Manor, LYMINGTON, Hants, SO41 8NP.   (hsb)
  01590 672595   fax 01590 671466
  email solicitor@clive-sutton.co.uk
  http://www.spg.uk.com
  Hon Sec: Edmund Clive Sutton
- ▲ Un-incorporated Society
- ○ *P; o protect the interests of sole practitioner solicitors
- ● Conf - Mtgs - ET - LG - Liaison with The Law Society
- < The Law Soc
- M 4,000 i
- ¶ Solo Magazine - 3; free.
- ✕ 2006-08 National Association of Sole Practitioners

Solicitors' Criminal Bar Association
a group of the **Law Society of Northern Ireland**

Solid Fuel Association   (SFA)   1993

- ■ 7 Swanwick Court, ALFRETON, Derbys, DE55 7AS.   (hq)
  01773 835400   fax 01773 834351
  http://www.solidfuel.co.uk
  Gen Manager: Jim Lambeth
- ▲ Company Limited by Guarantee
- ○ *T; promotion of solid fuel
- Gp Approval Coal Merchants Scheme - coal trade code to guarantee service to domestic solid fuel customers
- ● Mtgs - ET - Exam - Res - Exhib - Stat - Inf - Lib - LG - Advice on solid fuel heating
- M 2 f
- ¶ Various technical publications & videos.

Solids Handling & Processing Association Ltd   (SHAPA)   1981

- ■ 20 Elizabeth Drive, Oadby, LEICESTER, LE2 4RD.   (hq)
  0116-271 3704   fax 0116-271 3704
  email shapaltd@aol.com   http://www.shapa.co.uk
  Gen Sec: John Whitehead
- ▲ Company Limited by Guarantee
- ○ *T; representing companies/universities involved in the handling & processing of particulate solids particularly in the process industries; members' interests incl: Abrasion resistant equipment; Blowers/compressors; Bulk storage & handling; Centralised vacuum cleaning; Control systems; Dryers/coolers; Dust filters; Feeders; Grinding & milling machinery; Instrumentation; Intermediate bulk containers; Load cells; Mechanical conveyors/elevators; Mixers; Pneumatic handling; Process plant; Sack/bag systems; Sieves/screens; Silos, hoppers, bins & tanks & dischargers; Valves; Weighing machinery
- Gp Marketing; Technical; Commercial
- ● Mtgs - Expt - LG - Scholarship award
- < permanent member of Intl Solids Handling Advy Bd (ISHAB)
- M 106 i & f, 3 universities
- ¶ NL - 3.

Solihull Chamber of Commerce   (SCC)   1990

- ■ Wellington House, Starley Way, SOLIHULL, W Midlands, B37 7HE.   (hq)
  0121-781 7384   fax 0121-781 7385
  email info@solihull-chamber.com
  http://www.solihull-chamber.com
- ▲ Company Limited by Guarantee
- ○ *C
- ● Mtgs - ET - Res - Stat - Expt - Inf - Lib - VE - LG
- < Birmingham Cham Comm; Brit Chams Comm
- M 450 f
- ¶ Chamberlink - 10;   AR; both ftm.

Solvents Industry Association   (SIA)   1986

- ■ 8 St George's Avenue, Dovercourt, HARWICH, Essex, CO12 3RR.
  email info@sia-uk.org.uk   http://www.sia-uk.org.uk
  Sec: Peter Davis
- ▲ Company Limited by Guarantee
- ○ *T; a technical organisation dealing with legislation relating to Customs & Excise, health, safety & the environment
- Gp European Chemical Industry - Hydrocarbon Solvent Producers Assn (CEFIC-HSPA); HSE group on classificationt; Responsible care (SIASHE)
- ● Conf - Mtgs - Stat - LG
- < Eur Solvents Ind Gp (ESIG); Hydrocarbon Solvents Producers Assn (HSPA)
- M 21 f

Somerset Archaeological & Natural History Society   (SANHS) 1849

- NR Somerset Heritage Centre, Brunel Way, Norton Fitzwarren, TAUNTON, Somerset, TA2 6SF.   (hq)
  01823 272429
- ▲ Registered Charity
- ○ *L
- Gp Archaeology; Local history; Historic buildings; Natural history
- ● Conf - Mtgs - ET - Res - SG - Lib - PL - VE
- M 654 i, 42 org, UK / 4 i, 14 org, o'seas
- ¶ Proceedings - 1.   NL - 2.

Somerset Chamber of Commerce & Industry Ltd

- NR Equity House, Blackbrook Park Avenue, TAUNTON, Somerset, TA1 2PX.
  01823 444924
  email manager@somerset-chamber.co.uk
  http://www.somerset-chamber.co.uk
  Chief Exec: Rupert Cox

© CBD Research Ltd · Beckenham · BR3 5JS · Tel 020 8650 7745 · E-mail cbd@cbdresearch.com · www.cbdresearch.com

Somerset Record Society   1889
■ c/o Somerset Heritage Centre, Brunel Way, Langford Mead,
    Norton Fitzwarren, TAUNTON, Somerset, TA2 6SF.   (hsb)
    01823 278805
    Hon Sec: David Bromwich
▲ Registered Charity; Un-incorporated Society
○ *L; publication of historical records (not parish registers) of
    Somerset
● Annual mtg
M 121 i, 53 org, UK / 4 i, 68 org, o'seas
    (Sub: £10)
¶ Occasional volume - c 1; ftm, prices vary nm.

Songbird Survival   (SBS)
■ PO Box 311, DISS, Norfolk, IP22 1WW.   (hq)
    01379 641715
    email dawn-chorus@songbird-survival.org.uk
    http://www.songbird-survival.org.uk
▲ Registered Charity
○ *K; to protect & enhance the population of UK songbirds &
    other small birds by research & education
● Mtgs - Res - Exhib - Stat - Inf - VE - LG
M 1,800 i
¶ Songbird Survival (NL) - 4; ftm only.

Sonic Arts Network
    in 2008 merged with the British Music Information Centre, the
    Contemporary Music Network & the Society for the
    Promotion of New Music, to form Sound &Music - an agency
    & threfore outside the scope of this directory

Sound Sense   1990
■ Riverside House, Rattlesden, BURY ST EDMUNDS, Suffolk,
    IP30 0SF.   (hq)
    email info@soundsense.org   http://www.soundsense.org
    Chief Exec: Kathryn Deane
▲ Company Limited by Guarantee; Registered Charity
○ *D, *G, *N; for community musicians
Gp Campaigns; Cultural diversity; Health
● Conf - Res - Inf - LG
< Intl Soc for Music Educ
M 380 i, 95 org, UK / 20 i, o'seas
    (Sub: £35 i, £90 org UK / £50 i o'seas)
¶ Sounding Board - 4; ftm [back issues £5].
    Bulletin Board - 12; ftm only.
    Publications list available.

Source Testing Association   (STA)   1996
■ Unit 11 Theobald Business Centre, Knowle Piece, Wilbury Way,
    HITCHIN, Herts, SG4 0TY.   (hq)
    01462 457535   fax 01462 457157
    email dave.curtis@s-t-a.org   http://www.s-t-a.org
    Dir: Dave Curtis
▲ Company Limited by Guarantee
○ *T; research into aspects of emission monitoring
Gp Task Groups: Health & safety, Management, Quality, Small
    business, Technical, Training & personal development
● Conf - Mtgs - ET - Res - Exhib - Inf - Seminars - Company
    endorsement
M 102 f, UK / 3 f, o'seas
¶ STA Communicator (NL) - 2; free.

**South Cheshire Chamber of Commerce & Industry Ltd
    (SCCCI)   2001**
NR Lyme Building, Westmere Drive, Crewe Business Park, CREWE,
    Cheshire, CW1 6ZL.   (hq)
    01270 504700   fax 01270 504701
    email info@sccci.co.uk
    http://www.southcheshirechamber.co.uk
    Chief Exec: John Dunning
○ *C
● Mtgs - ET - Exhib - Stat - Expt - Inf - Lib
< Brit Chams Comm; Chams Comm NW
M f

South Devon Chamber of Commerce   (SDCC)   1995
■ Torbay Innovation Centre, Vantage Point, PAIGNTON, Devon,
    TQ4 7EJ.   (chmn/b)
    01803 540683
    email info@southdevonchamber.co.uk
    http://www.southdevonchamber.co.uk
    Admin: Brenda Hooper,   Chmn: Christian Seiflow-Moran
▲ Company Limited by Guarantee
○ *C
Gp Branches: Brixham, Paignton, Torquay
● Conf - Mtg - Inf
M 200 f
¶ NL - 4;   Directory/Ybk - 5 yrly; both ftm, p.o.a nm.
    Note: is also known as Torbay Chamber of Commerce

South Devon Herd Book Society   (SDHBS)   1891
NR Westpoint, Clyst St Mary, EXETER, Devon, EX5 1DJ.   (hq)
    01392 447494   fax 01392 447495
    email info@sdhbs.org.uk   http://www.sdhbs.org.uk
    Breed Sec: Caroline Poultney
▲ Registered Charity
Br Australia, Canada, New Zealand, South Africa, USA
○ *B; cattle breed society
● Conf - Mtgs - Res - Exhib - Comp - Stat - SG - Expt - Inf - VE -
    LG
< Nat Beef Assn
M 630 i, UK / 10 i, o'seas
¶ Jnl - 1.   NL - 12.   Herd Book - 2 yrly.

South Downs Society   (SDS)   1923
NR 2 Swan Court, Station Rd, PULBOROUGH, W Sussex,
    RH20 1RL.   (hq)
    01798 875073   fax 01798 873108
    http://www.southdownssociety.org.uk
○ *G; preservation of character & beauty of the South Downs,
    including their ancient monuments & public rights of way
● Conf - Mtgs - Exhib - Lib - VE - Illustrated talks
M i

South East London Chamber of Commerce   2007
NR Unit TW/45 Harrington Way, Warspite Rd, LONDON,
    SE18 5NR.   (hq)
    020 8317 3365   fax 020 8854 8273
    http://www.selondonchamber.org
    Co Sec: Adrian Hollands
▲ Company Limited by Guarantee
○ *C; chamber of commerce for the London boroughs of Bexley,
    Bromley, Greenwich & Lewisham
● Conf - Mtgs - ET - Inf - LG
M 600 f
× 2007 (July) Greenwich, Bexley & Lewisham Chamber of
    Commerce

South of England Agricultural Society   (SEAS)   1967
NR The South of England Centre, ARDINGLY, W Sussex,
    RH17 6TL.   (hq)
    01444 892700   fax 01444 892888
    email seas@btclick.com   http://www.seas.org.uk
    Dir: Deborah Barber
▲ Registered Charity
○ *F, *H; to promote industry in general & agriculture in
    particular; to advance education, particularly education in
    agriculture & allied industries, in animal husbandry & forestry
● Spring Garden & Leisure Show - South of England Show -
    Autumn Show & Game Fair - Festive Food & Drink Fayre
< Assn of Show & Agricl Orgs
M 3,000 i, 1,000 f
¶ Four Seasons News - 2; ftm only.

South Gloucestershire Chamber of Commerce
NR   Leigh Court, Abbots Leigh, BRISTOL, BS8 3RA.   (hq)
        01275 373373
        email info@businesswest.co.uk
        http://www.businesswest.co.uk
○   *C
<   GWE Business West Ltd

South Place Ethical Society   (SPES)   1793
NR   Conway Hall, 25 Red Lion Sq, LONDON, WC1R 4RL.   (hq)
        020 7242 8031   fax 020 7242 8034
        http://www.ethicalsoc.org.uk
▲   Registered Charity
○   *L; study & dissemination of ethical principles based on
        humanism; the cultivation of a rational & humane way of life
M   i & org
¶   Ethical Record - 10; ftm.   AR.
        Conway Memorial Lecture - 1; ftm.

South Suffolk Agricultural Association
NR   35 Dalham Rd, Moulton, NEWMARKET, Suffolk, CB8 8SB.
        (hsp)
        01638 750879
        email geoff@southsuffolkshow.co.uk
        http://www.southsuffolkshow.co.uk
        Sec: Geoff Bailes
○   *F
●   South Suffolk Show
<   Assn of Show & Agricl Orgs

South Wales Chamber of Commerce   1870
NR   Orion Suite, Enterprise Way, NEWPORT, NP20 2AQ.   (hq)
        01633 222664   fax 01633 222301
        email info@southwaleschamber.co.uk
        http://www.southwaleschamber.org.uk
        Dir: Graham Morgan
▲   Company Limited by Guarantee
Br   Cardiff: The Maltings, East Tyndall St, CARDIFF, CF24 5EZ.
        029 2048 1532
        Swansea: Ethos, Kings Rd, SWANSEA, SA1 8ES.
        01792 653297
○   *C
●   Conf - Mtgs - ET - Exhib - Expt - Inf - Lib - VE - LG -
        Commercial services
<   Brit Chams Comm
¶   Chamber Chat - 4; free.
✕   2008 Newport & Gwent Chamber of Commerce
        2009 West Wales Chamber of Commerce (merged)

South Wales Mountain Sheep Society
■   40 Rhys Rd, BLACKWOOD, Gwent, NP12 3QR.
        01443 839234
        Hon Sec: Glyn Davies
▲   Un-incorporated Society
○   *B
<   Nat Sheep Assn

South West Chambers
NR   Leigh Court, Abbots Leigh, BRISTOL, BS8 3RA.   (hq)
        01275 370789
        email nigel.hutchings@businesswest.co.uk
        http://www.businesswest.co.uk
        Chief Exec: Nigel Hutchings
○   *C
Gp   132 chambers, large & small, located across the seven counties
        of the South West Region of England
<   GWE Business West Ltd

South West Coast Path Association   (SWCPA)   1973
■   Bowker House, Lee Mill Bridge, IVYBRIDGE, Devon, PL21 9EF.
        (hsp)
        01752 896237   fax 01752 893654
        email info@swcp.org.uk   http://www.swcp.org.uk
        Admin: Liz Wallis
▲   Registered Charity
○   *K; to promote the interests of users of the South West coast
        path, Britain's longest national trail
●   Mtgs - Exhib - Inf - PL - LG
M   5,000 i, 20 org, UK / 150 i, o'seas
¶   The South West Coast Path Guide - 1; ftm, £8 nm.
        NL - 2;   AR; both ftm only.

South Western Circle   1962
NR   43 Raymond Rd, PORTSMOUTH, Hants, PO6 4RB.   (mem/sp)
        email peterswiftderby@tiscali.co.uk   http://www.lswr.org
        Mem Sec: C Hooper
▲   Un-incorporated Society
○   *G; historical society for the London & South Western Railway &
        its successors
●   Mtgs - Res - Inf - PL
M   500 i, UK / 25 i, o'seas
¶   South Western Circular - 4;   Monographs; both ftm.

Southampton & Fareham Chamber of Commerce & Industry
        merged in 2010 with other chambers of commerce in Hampshire to
        form the **Hampshire Chamber of Commerce**

Southdown Sheep Society   1890
■   Meens Farm, Capps Lane, All Saints, HALESWORTH, Suffolk,
        IP19 0PD.   (hsp)
        01986 782251   fax 01986 782416
        email secretary@southdownsheepsociety.co.uk
        http://www.southdownsheepsociety.co.uk
        Sec: Mrs Gail Sprake
▲   Company Limited by Guarantee; Registered Charity
○   *B
●   Res - Exhib - Expt - Inf - LG
<   Nat Sheep Assn; Rare Breeds Survival Trust
M   300 i
¶   The Southdown Flock Book - 2 yrly; ftm, £15 nm.
        The Southdown Year Book - 1; ftm, £5 nm.
        The Southdown Sheep; £20+£5p&p

Southern Counties Folk Federation   (SCoFF)   1966
NR   3 Cranbury Rd, Woolston, SOUTHAMPTON, Hants,
        SO19 7HZ.   (treas/p)
○   *D, *G, *N

Southern Counties Heavy Horse Association   (SCHHA)   1970
■   125 Hop Garden Rd, HOOK, Hants, RG27 9ST.   (hsp)
        Hon Sec: Anne Dawson
▲   Un-incorporated Society
○   *B, *F, *G, *V; to promote the heavy horse & preserve the art of
        horse ploughing
Gp   Show horses & drays for promotional work; Working horses for
        ploughing & working demonstrations
●   Mtgs - Exhib - Working demonstrations - Members' events
<   Shire Horse Soc
M   c 400 i & org
¶   NL - 4.   AR.

© CBD Research Ltd · Beckenham · BR3 5JS · Tel 020 8650 7745 · E-mail cbd@cbdresearch.com · www.cbdresearch.com

Southern Counties Historic Vehicle Preservation Trust (SCHVPT) 1962
■ 41 Gadesdon Rd, WEST EWELL, Surrey, KT19 9LA.   (sp)
    http://www.brmmbrmm.com/schvpt/
    Sec: Mrs Sheila Urben
▲ Registered Charity
○ *G, *L; to preserve historic vehicles & machinery
● Mtgs - Exhib - Inf - Lib - PL
< Nat Traction Engine Trust; Transport Trust; Historic Vehicles
    Clubs Jt C'ee; Historic Comml Vehicles Soc
M 300 i, 2 f, 3 org, UK / 2 i, o'seas
¶ News Circular - 12; ftm only.
    Traction Engine Register - 3 yrly; £4 m only.

Southern Staffordshire Chamber of Commerce & Industry
NR Blakenhall Park, Barton under Needwood, BURTON ON
    TRENT, Staffs, DE13 8AJ.
    0845 071 0891
○ *C

Southwark Chamber of Commerce
NR South Bank Technopark, 90 London Rd, LONDON, SE1 6LN.
    0845 680 1946
    http://www.southwarkcommerce.com
○ *C

SOVA (SOVA) 1975
■ Lincoln House (Unit 201), 1-3 Brixton Rd, LONDON,
    SW9 6DE.   (hq)
    020 7793 0404
▲ Registered Charity
Br 41
○ *W; 'to train local volunteers & involve them in work with
    offenders, ex-offenders & their families; we believe that
    everybody is touched by crime & that members of the
    community have a contribution to make in preventing &
    reducing crime'
Gp Befriending; Enployment training; Literacy & numeracy tuition
● Conf - ET - Stat
M 644 i
¶ AR; free.

Soya Protein Association (SPA) 1973
NR 2 Swan Court, Cygnet Park, Hampton, PETERBOROUGH,
    Cambs, PE7 8GX.   (hq)
    01733 367219   fax 01733 355371
    email dominic@cropprotection.org.uk
    Exec Sec: Dominic Dyer
○ *T; to represent the interests of UK manufacturers of soya
    products
● Mtgs - Inf
< Food & Drink Fedn
M 5 f

Spa Business Association Ltd (SpaBA) 1921
■ Philpot House (suite 5-6), Station Rd, RAYLEIGH, Essex,
    SS6 7HH.   (hq)
    0870 780 0787   fax 01268 745881
    email info@spabusinessassociation.co.uk
    http://www.spabusinessassociation.co.uk
    Sec: Mike Fitch
▲ Company Limited by Guarantee
○ *T; for the mutual benefit of all persons employed in,
    dependent upon or supplying the spa industry
Gp Consultant, Day spas, Destination spas, Education provider,
    Hotel spas, Other, Product house, Recruitment, Salon, Spa
    towns, Spa travel, Suppliers
● Conf - Mtgs - ET - Res - Exhib - Comp - Stat - Inf
< Eur Spas Assn
M 10 i, 62 f
    (Sub: £246.75-£4935 f, by turnover)

Spanish Chamber of Commerce in Great Britain
NR 126 Wigmore St, LONDON, W1U 3RZ.
    020 7009 9071   fax 020 7009 9089
    email info@spanishchamber.co.uk
    http://www.spanishchamber.co.uk
○ *C
M 225 i & f, UK / 118 i & f, Spain

Sparsity Partnership for Authorities Delivering Rural Service
    a group of the **Local Government Association**

Speakability 1979
■ 1 Royal St, LONDON, SE1 7LL.   (hq)
    020 7261 9572   fax 020 7928 9542
    email speakability@speakability.org.uk
    http://www.speakability.org.uk
    Chief Exec: Melanie Derbyshire
▲ Registered Charity
Br 91
○ *K, *W; to support people & carers living with aphasia (loss of
    communication skills as a result of a stroke, head injury or
    other neurological condition)
● Mtgs - ET - Inf - Ve - LG - Campaigning for improved services
    for people with communication impairments
< Aphasia Alliance
M 3,953 i, 26 f, 509 org, UK / 38 i, o'seas
¶ Publications list on website.
    Annual Review; free.

Specialised Information Publishers Association   (SIPA UK)
NR Cliveden House, 19-22 Victoria Villas, RICHMOND, Surrey,
    TW9 2JX.   (hq)
    020 8288 7415   fax 020 8288 7415
    email uksipa@btconnect.com
    http://www.sipaonline.com
    Dir: Karen Hindle
▲ Un-incorporated Society
Br USA (New England, New York, N California, S California,
    Southeast, Washington DC)
○ *T; to advance the interests of for-profit subscription newsletter
    publishers & specialised information services
● Conf - Mtgs - ET - Inf
< is the UK branch of the Specialized Information Publishers Assn
    (USA)
M 70+ f

Specialist Access Engineering & Maintenance Association (SAEMA) 1972
■ c/o 19 Joseph Fletcher Drive, Wingerworth, CHESTERFIELD,
    Derbys, S42 6TZ.   (hsp)
    01246 224175
    email enquiries@saema.org   http://www.saema.org
    Sec: Trevor Fennell
▲ Un-incorporated Society
○ *T; for companies involved in the design, manufacture,
    installation & maintenance of facade access systems
● Mtgs
< Nat Access & Scaffolding Confedn
M 26 f
    (Sub: £1,500)
¶ Ybk - 1.

Specialist Anglers Alliance
    in 2009 merged with the Anglers Conservation Association, the
    Fisheries & Angling Conservation Trust, the National Association of
    Fisheries & Angling Consultatives, the National Federation of Anglers
    & the National Federation of Sea Anglers to form the **Angling Trust**

Specialist Cheesemakers' Association (SCA) 1989

- 17 Clerkenwell Green, LONDON, EC1R 0DP. (hq)
  020 7253 2114   fax 020 7608 1645
  email info@provtrade.co.uk
  http://www.specialistcheesemakers.co.uk
  Sec: Mrs Clare Cheney
- ▲ Company Limited by Guarantee
- ○ *T; to encourage excellence in cheesemaking, promote
  speciality cheeses & represent the interests of members to
  Government & the media
- ● Mtgs - Res - Exhib - Inf - VE - LG
- < Amer Cheese Soc; Ir Cheesemakers Assn; Stilton
  Cheesemakers Assn; Farmhouse Cheesemakers Assn
- M 235 f, UK / 20 f, o'seas
- ¶ SCA NL - 4; ftm only.
  Guide to the Finest Cheeses of Britain & Ireland; £5.95.

Specialist Engineering Alliance (SEA)

- c/o 34 Palace Rd, LONDON, W2 4JG.
  020 7313 4819
  a group formed 'to foster a relationship with other specialist
  engineering groups, within the specialist engineering supply
  chain, to develop a joint approach to industry sector issues,
  such as teamworking & supply chain integration at every
  level of the procurement process'.
  Members:
  Association for Consultancy & Engineering
  Building Services Research & Information Association
  Chartered Institution of Building Service Engineers
  Federation of Environmental Trade Associations Ltd
  Specialist Engineering Contractors' Group

Specialist Engineering Contractors Group (SEC group) 1992

- Esca House, 34 Palace Court, LONDON, W2 4JG. (hq)
  020 7313 4919   fax 020 7727 9268
  email pmattison@hvca.org.uk
  http://www.secgroup.org.uk
  Exec Sec: John Nelson
- ▲ Un-incorporated Society
- ○ *N, *T; represents six trade associations (with a total
  membership of 8,000 companies) in the specialist
  engineering sector of the construction industry (including
  mechanical, electrical, plumbing, steel & lifts) to the
  government & other industry bodies
- M 6 associations:
  Association of Plumbing & Heating Contractors
  British Constructional Steelwork Association
  Electrical Contractors Association
  Electrical Contractors Association of Scotland
    (trades as SELECT)
  Heating & Ventilating Contractors Association
  Lift & Escalator Industry Association
- ¶ Guides on contractual & legal matters (these can be obtained
  from HVCA Publications on 01768 860405).

Spectrum Alliance

- NR 27 Cameron Park, EDINBURGH, EH16 5LA. (admin/p)
  0131 662 1620
  http://www.spectrumalliance.co.uk
  Co-ordinator: Catherine Hessett
- ○ *K; for the approximately 2,000,000 people on the UK
  adversely affected by modern lighting
- ● Inf - LG
- M 12 org

Speedway Control Board (SCB) 1940

- NR ACU House, Wood St, RUGBY, Warks, CV21 2YX.
  01788 565603   fax 01788 552308
  email office.scb@lineone.net
  http://www.british-speedway.co.uk
- ○ *S; governing body of speedway motorcycle racing in GB
- M i & clubs

Spelling Society
  since 2011 see **English Spelling Society**

Spina Bifida Hydrocephalus Ireland
  see **National Association for Spina Bifida & Hydrocephalus Ireland**

Spinal Injuries Association (SIA) 1974

- NR SIA House, 2 Trueman Place, Oldbrook, MILTON KEYNES,
  MK6 2HH. (hq)
  0845 678 6633   fax 01908 608492
  email sia@spinal.co.uk   http://www.spinal.co.uk
- ▲ Company Limited by Guarantee
- ○ *W; the national charity for spinal cord injured people & their
  families; controlled & run by people who are themselves
  paralysed, its aim is to enable spinal cord injured people to
  control their lives & achieve their goals
- Gp Helpline service; Publications
- ● Conf - Inf - Lib - LG
  Helpline: 0800 980 0501
- < Brit Coun of Disabled People; Dial UK; ADAIP; RADAR; NCVO
- M 6,000 i, 500 org, UK / 400 i, o'seas
- ¶ Forward (NL) - 6.   AR.
  Moving Forward: a guide to living with spinal cord injury.
  Other publications available.

Spinal Injuries Scotland (SIS) 1962

- Festival Business Centre, 150 Brand St, GLASGOW,
  G51 1DH. (hq)
  0800 013 2305   fax 0141-427 9258
  email info@sisonline.org   http://www.sisonline.org
  Chmn: Adrian O'Donnell
- ▲ Registered Charity
- ○ *K, *W; to offer information, advice & education to those with
  spinal cord injuries, their families & carers
- ● Conf - ET - Exhib - Inf - VE - LG
- M 750 i
- ¶ Newsline - 4; free.

Spiral Staircase Manufacturers Association

- c/o Spiral Construction Ltd, Water-Ma-Trout Industrial Estate,
  HELSTON, Cornwall, TR13 0LW. (hsb)
  01326 574497   fax 01326 574760
  email eric.nicholls@spiral.uk.com
  Sec: Eric Nicholls
- ○ *T; for manufacturers of spiral stairs in steel, wood, concrete &
  other materials

Spiritual Workers' Association (SWA) 2008

- C5 Business Centre, North Road, Bridgend Industrial Estate,
  BRIDGEND, Glam, CF31 3TP. (hq)
  01656 762299
  email info@theswa.org.uk   http://www.theswa.org.uk
  Dir: Carole McEntee-Taylor,   Admin: Miranda Curwood
- ○ *P; for spiritual workers; to raise standards & awareness &
  driving change in the spiritualistic industry
- Gp Spiritual industry
- ● Inf
- M 3,102 i, UK / 338 i, o'seas
- ¶ Spiritual Voices - 12; ftm, 50p nm.
  Note: the SWA is the trading name of Spiritual Service Providers
  Ltd

Spiritualist Association of Great Britain (SAGB) 1872

- NR 11 Belgrave Rd, LONDON, SW1V 1RB. (hq)
  020 7931 6488   fax 020 7931 6489
  http://www.spiritualistassociation.org.uk
- ▲ Company Limited by Guarantee; Registered Charity
- ○ *R; spiritualist healing; proof of survival after death
- ● Mtgs - Res
- M c 900 i, UK / c 200 i, o'seas
- ¶ Service - 3; ftm, £1 nm.

© CBD Research Ltd · Beckenham · BR3 5JS · Tel 020 8650 7745 · E-mail cbd@cbdresearch.com · www.cbdresearch.com

Spiritualists' National Union   (SNU)   1890
NR   Redwoods, Stansted Hall, STANSTED, Essex, CM24 8UD.   (hq)
　　　0845 458 0768
　　　http://www.snu.org.uk
　　　Gen Sec: Charles S Coulston
▲   Company Limited by Guarantee; Registered Charity
Br   15
○   *R; to promote the religion & religious philosophy of
　　　Spiritualism
Gp   The Arthur Findlay College (residential training school);
　　　Spiritualists' Lyceum Union (youth movement)
●   Conf - Mtgs - ET - Exam - Res - SG - Inf - Lib
M   2,200 i, 382 churches, UK / 80 i, 8 churches, o'seas
¶   Ybk & Diary.

SPLINTA
NR   PO Box 398, STEVENAGE, Herts, SG1 9DR.
　　　07831 805455
　　　email info@splintacampaign.co.uk
　　　http://www.splintacampaign.co.uk
　　　Note: inactive since the announcement, in May 2010, of the
　　　abolition of HIPs

Spode Society   1986
NR   PO Box 14896, SOLIHULL, W Midlands, B91 9NE.   (editor/p)
　　　email contact@spode-society.co.uk
　　　http://www.spode-society.co.uk
○   *G; to increase knowledge of the Spode/Copeland factory & its
　　　wares
●   Mtgs - Res - VE
M   c170 i, the Museum, UK / c20 i, o'seas
¶   Spode Society Review - 2; ftm only.

Spohr Society of Great Britain   1969
■   123 Mount View Rd, SHEFFIELD, S Yorks, S8 8PJ.   (hq)
　　　0114-258 5420   fax 0114-258 5420
　　　email chtutt@yahoo.co.uk
　　　http://www.spohr-society.org.uk
　　　Chmn: Keith Warsop,   Sec: Chris Tutt
▲   Un-incorporated Society
○   *D; to promote the music of the German composer Louis Spohr
　　　(1784-1859) through recordings, broadcasts & live
　　　performances; to research into his life & music
●   Mtgs - Res - Inf - Loan of performing material - Promoting
　　　recordings
<   Intle Louis Spohr Gesellschaft (Germany)
M   47 i, UK / 25 i, o'seas
　　　(Sub: £6 UK / £10 o'seas)
¶   Spohr Jnl - 1; ftm, £1.50 nm.   NL - 4; ftm, 40p each nm.

Sport Horse Breeding of Great Britain   (SHB(GB))   1886
■   96 High St, EDENBRIDGE, Kent, TN8 5AR.   (hq)
　　　01732 866277   fax 01732 867464
　　　email office@sporthorsegb.co.uk
　　　http://www.sporthorsegb.co.uk
　　　Chmn: D Walters
▲   Registered Charity
○   *B; to maintain the SHB(GB) stud books; to promote British
　　　bred sport horses nationally & internationally; to oversee the
　　　governance of all Hunter & Sport Horse classes held at major
　　　UK shows
Gp   Brood Mare; Stallion; Show
●   Conf - Mtgs - ET - Exhib - Comp - Stat - Inf - Lib
<   Assn of Show & Agricl Orgs; Wld Breeding Fedn for Sport
　　　Horses
M   3,500 i
¶   NL - 1.   Hbk - 1.   Sales List - 12.
　　　Show List - 1.   Show Secretaries List - 1.   Judges List - 1.
　　　Stallion List - 1.   Rulebook - 1.

Sport and Recreation Alliance   (SRA)
NR   Burwood House, 14 Caxton Street, LONDON, SW1H 0QT.
　　　(hq)
　　　020 7976 3900
　　　http://www.sportandrecreation.org.uk
　　　Sec: Kate Lawrenson
○   *N
M   320 org

Sporting Goods Industry Association   (SGIA)   2006
NR   Federation House, STONELEIGH PARK, Warks, CV8 2RF.   (hq)
　　　024 7641 4999   fax 024 7641 4990
　　　email info@sgiauk.com   http://www.sgiauk.com
○   *T; to promote, develop & protect the interests of
　　　manufacturers, wholesalers & distributors of sporting goods
●   Mtgs - Inf - LG
<   a group of the Fedn of Sports & Play Assns (FSPA)
M   22 f
×   2007 Sports Manufacturers & Retailers Trade Association
　　　2006 (merged):
　　　Bowls Group
　　　Cricket & Hockey Association
　　　Cue Sports Association
　　　Darts Association
　　　Fitness Products Association
　　　Independent Sports Retailers Association
　　　Racket Sports Association
　　　Sports Textiles & Footwear Association

Sports Coach UK
NR   114 Cardigan Rd, Headingley, LEEDS, W Yorks, LS6 3BJ.
　　　0113-274 4082   fax 0113-275 5019
　　　email coaching@sportscoachuk.org
　　　http://www.sportscoachuk.org
　　　Chmn: Chris Baillieu
○   *S; to develop & implement a coaching system for all coaches
　　　at every level

Sports & Fitness Equipment Association   (SAFEA)   1990
■   Federation House, STONELEIGH PARK, Warks, CV8 2RF.   (hq)
　　　024 7641 4999   fax 024 7641 4990
　　　email safea@sportsandplay.com
　　　http://www.safea.co.uk
▲   Company Limited by Guarantee
○   *T; for companies engaged in the supply & installation of sports
　　　hall, games, fitness & gymnasium equipment (incl physical
　　　education in schools)
●   Conf - Mtgs - Exhib - Inf - Lib - LG
<   a group of the Fedn of Sports & Play Assns (FSPA)
M   20 f

Sports Journalists' Association of Great Britain   (SJA)   1948
NR   c/o Start2Finish Event Management, Unit 92 Capital Business
　　　Centre, 22 Carlton Rd, SOUTH CROYDON, Surrey,
　　　CR2 0BS.   (asa)
　　　020 8916 2234   fax 020 8916 2235
　　　http://www.sportsjournalists.co.uk
○   *P, *S; for journalists who specialise in sport
●   Conf - Mtgs - Educ - Inf - LG (through UK Sport & Sport
　　　England) - Careers advice - Promotion of annual Sports
　　　Journalists of the Year & Sportsman, Sportswoman & Sports
　　　Team of the Year Awards
<   Assn Intle de la Presse Sportive (AIPS); U Eur de la Presse
　　　Sportive (UEPS)
M   550 i
¶   Bulletin - 2;   NL - 3/4;   Hbk; all free.

Sports Manufacturers & Retailers Trade Association
　　　since 2007 the **Sporting Goods Industry Association**

Sports Massage Association   (SMA)   1999
NR   PO Box 70412, LONDON, NW1W 8XF.   (hq)
         0845 459 6031   fax 0845 459 6032
         email info@thesma.org   http://www.thesma.org
         Chmn: Rodger Davis
○   *P; to establish & maintain the ethical, professional &
         educational standards of practitioners so as to give
         confidence to the general & sporting public, the medical
         profession & government agencies that practitioners are
         suitably trained
●   Conf - Mtgs - ET - Exam - Res
<   Gen Coun for Massage Therapies
M   i

Sports & Play Construction Association   (SAPCA)   1997
NR   Federation House, STONELEIGH PARK, Warks, CV8 2RF.   (hq)
         024 7641 6316   fax 024 7641 4773
         email info@sapca.org.uk   http://www.sapca.org.uk
         Chief Exec: Christopher Trickey
▲   Company Limited by Guarantee
○   *T; 'the recognised UK trade association for the sports facility
         construction industry'
Gp   Principal contractors (inc multi-sport, natural sportsturf, pitch,
         play surfaces, tennis court, track divisions)
         Surfacing contractors; Ancillary contractors; Manufacturers &
         suppliers; Professional services
●   Conf - Mtgs - ET - Res - Exhib - SG - Stat - Expt - Inf - VE - LG
<   a group of the Sports Industries Federation
>   Brit Assn Landscape Inds (BALI); Brit Paralympic Assn (BPA);
         England & Wales Cricket Bd (ECB); Inst of
         Groundsmanship (IOG); Intl Assn for Sports & Leisure
         Facilities (IAKS); Intl Sports Engg Assn (ISEA); Intl Tennis
         Fedn (ITD); Lawn Tennis Assn (LTA); Mineral Products
         Assn (MPA); Nat Playing Fields Assn (NPFA); Nat Trainers
         Fedn (NTF); Oxford Playing Fields Assn (OPFA); Sports Coun
         of NI (SCNI); Sports Turf Res Inst (STRI); UK Athletics (UKA);
         Waste Resources Action Programme (WRAP)
M   170 f, 30 org, UK / 10 f, 4 org, o'seas

Sports Pony Studbook Society   (SPSS)
NR   Bernwode Stud, Sock Farm, Chilthorne Domer, YEOVIL,
         Somerset, BA22 8QZ.
         01935 840029
         http://www.sportpony.org.uk
○   *B

Sports Textiles & Footwear Association
         in 2006 merged with the **Sporting Goods Industry Association**

Sports Turf Research Institute   (STRI)   1929
■   St Ives Estate, BINGLEY, W Yorks, BD16 1AU.   (hq)
         01274 565131   fax 01274 561891
         email anne.wilson@stri.co.uk   http://www.stri.co.uk
         Chief Exec: Dr Gordon McKillop
▲   Company Limited by Guarantee
Br   13
○   *Q, *S; independent non-profit-making research & advisory
         service: sports field & golf course management &
         construction; research on sports turf surfaces
Gp   Golf course architecture & design; Golf course ecology &
         management; Sports turf construction & irrigation
●   Conf - ET - Res - Exhib - Inf - Lib - VE
<   Sports Coun; All sports governing bodies
M   Subscribers: 150 i, 200 f, 1,900 org, UK / 120 i, 15 f,
         200 org, o'seas
¶   Jnl of Turfgrass & Sports Surface Science - 1; ftm, £28 nm.
         International Turfgrass Bulletin - 4; ftm, £55 yr nm.
         STRI Green Pages Trade Directory; online only.
         Various publications on turf related issues, available from their
         specialist online & mail order book service.

**Sportsmans Association of Great Britain & Northern Ireland
(SAGBNI)   1996**
NR   2 Clockhouse Place, LONDON, SW15 2EL.   (hq)
         020 8789 1211   fax 020 8789 1211
         email mike.wells@sagbni.co.uk
         http://www.sportsmansassociation.org.uk
         Gen Sec: M B Wells
▲   Un-incorporated Society
○   *K; 'to campaign against the ban on target pistol shooting &
         for freedom of choice & fair & effective firearms legislation'
●   Res - Inf - LG
<   Brit Shooting Sports Coun
M   c 3,000 i, 14 f
¶   NL - 12; ftm only.

Spotted Horse & Pony Society
         closed 2010

Spotted Pony Breed Society
         no longer in existence, records of passports issued by the SPBS
         now held by **British Show Pony Society**

Sprayed Concrete Association   (SCA)   1976
■   Kingsley House, Ganders Business Park, Kingsley, BORDON,
         Hants, GU35 9LU.   (asa)
         01252 357842   fax 01252 357831
         email admin@sca.org.uk   http://www.sca.org.uk
         Sec: John G Fairley
○   *T; to promote & foster the use of sprayed concrete, otherwise
         known as 'gunite' or 'shotcrete'
●   Conf - Mtgs - ET - Res - Exhib
<   Eur Fedn of Nat Assns of Specialist Contrs & Material Suppliers
         for the Construction Ind (EFNARC)
M   40 f
¶   LM; free.   Technical Data Sheets; ftm, £1 each nm.
         An Introduction to Sprayed Concrete.
         EFNARC Specification for Sprayed Concrete; £10.
         Seminar Papers & other technical publications; list available.

Square Dance Callers Club of Great Britain   (SDCCGB)   1955
■   2 Crossbridge Cottages, Thornborough Rd, Thornton,
         MILTON KEYNES, Bucks, MK17 0HE.   (hsp)
         01280 816940
         email graybo@freenet.co.uk
         Hon Sec: Susie Kelly
▲   Un-incorporated Society
○   *D; to promote & further American square & round dancing by
         the provision & instruction of callers & teachers
●   Mtgs - ET - SG - Lib
<   Intl Assn of Square Dance Callers (CALLERLAB-USA)
M   170 i, UK / 10 i, o'seas
¶   NL - 6; ftm.

Squash Rackets Association
         in 2009 merged with English Racketball to form **England Squash &
         Racketball**

Squash Wales Ltd   2005
■   Sport Wales National Centre, Sophia Gardens, CARDIFF,
         Glamorgan, CF11 9SW.   (hq)
         0845 846 0027   fax 029 2023 2737
         email squashwales@squashwales.co.uk
         http://www.squashwales.co.uk
         Finance & Office Mgr: Sue Evans
▲   Company Limited by Guarantee
○   *S; the governing body of squash in Wales
●   ET - Regulation
<   Wld Squash Fedn; Eur Squash Fedn; C'wealth Games Coun for
         Wales; Welsh Sports Assn
M   3,170 i, 122 clubs
¶   NL - 3/4.   Fixture List - 1.

St ...
         see **Saint ...**

Stable Lads Association
since September 2007 **National Association of Stable Staff**

Staff & Educational Development Association   (SEDA)
■   Woburn House, 20-24 Tavistock Square, LONDON,
    WC1H 9HF.
    020 7380 6767   fax 020 7387 2655
    email office@seda.ac.uk   http://www.seda.ac.uk
○   *P; for staff & educational developers

Staffordshire Archaeological & Historical Society   (SAHS)
1959
■   29 Boldmere Drive, Boldmere, SUTTON COLDFIELD,
    W Midlands, B73 5ES.   (hsp)
    0121-350 3497
    email sahs@sahs.uk.net   http://www.sahs.uk.net
    Hon Gen Sec: James Debney
▲   Registered Charity
Br 1
○   *L, *Q; the study, investigation, description & preservation of
    antiquities & historical records, particularly of Staffordshire
Gp Sub-c'ees: Editorial, Survey & excavation
●   Mtgs - Res - SG - VE - Publishing results of research -
    Archaeological excavations - Standing historical buildings
    survey
<   Coun for Brit Archaeology
M   180 i, 70 org
¶   Annual Transactions - 1; ftm.

Staffordshire & Birmingham Agricultural Society   (SBAS)
1800
NR County Showground, Weston Rd, STAFFORD, ST18 0BD.   (hq)
    01785 258060   fax 01785 246458
    http://www.staffscountyshowground.co.uk
    Chief Exec: Richard Williams
○   *F; promotion of agriculture through the County Show & Winter
    Fair
●   Staffordshire County Show - English Winter Fair
<   Assn of Show & Agricl Orgs
M   1,500 i

Staffordshire Parish Registers Society   (SPRS)   1900
■   35 Middlefield Lane, Hagley, STOURBRIDGE, W Midlands,
    DY9 0PY.   (chmn/p)
    01562 882210   fax 01562 882210
    email chair@sprs.org.uk   http://www.sprs.org.uk
    Chmn: Dr Peter D Bloore
▲   Registered Charity
○   *L; publication in printed form of Staffordshire parish registers,
    mainly to 1837
●   Mtgs (AGM) - Res - Transcription & printing of parish registers
M   280 i, 10 libraries, UK / 5 i, 5 libraries, o'seas
¶   Registers (up to 1837) - 2/3; prices vary.

Staffordshire Record Society   1879
■   c/o William Salt Library, Eastgate St, STAFFORD, ST16 2LZ.
    (hsb)
    email matthew.blake@btinternet.com
    Hon Sec: Matthew Blake
▲   Registered Charity
○   *L; the editing & printing of original documents relating to the
    County of Stafford & the publication of articles relating to the
    history of the county
M   i, f & org
¶   Collections for a history of Staffordshire - irreg; ftm,
    prices vary nm.

Stage Management Association   (SMA)   1954
■   89 Borough High St, LONDON, SE1 1NL.   (hq)
    020 7403 7999
    email admin@stagemanagementassociation.co.uk
    http://www.stagemanagementassociation.co.uk
    Chmn: Liz Burton-King
▲   Company Limited by Guarantee
○   *P; to support & represent professional stage management in
    the UK
Gp Professionally working stage managers (full members); Recent
    graduates (provisional members); Student members (on
    NCDT accredited courses); Non-professional associates
●   ET - Inf - VE
<   Stage Mgrs Assn (USA); Indep Theatre Coun
M   620 i
¶   Cue Line (NL) - 6; ftm only.
    SMA Guide to Props & Propping; £4.50 m, £7 nm.
    Freelist (LM available for work) - 12; free.
    Stage Management: a career guide, free.
    Stage Management Notes.   Notes for Company Managers.
    [prices available on website].
    A Stage Manager's Guide to the...
        ... West End Agreement;
        ... Provincial Commercial Contract;
        ... Subsidised Repertory Agreement.

Stair Society   1935
■   6 The Glebe, Manse Road, DIRLETON, E Lothian, EH39 5FB.
    (hsp)
    01620 850264
    email stairsecretary@btinternet.com
    http://www.stairsociety.org
    Sec: Thomas H Drysdale
▲   Un-incorporated Society
○   *L; to encourage the study & to advance the knowledge of the
    history of Scots law
●   Mtgs - Publication of original documents - Reprinting & editing
    of works of sufficient rarity or importance
M   259 i, 66 f & org, 14 students, UK / 35 i, 78 f & org, o'seas
¶   AR; free.

Stalin Society   1991
■   BM Box 2521, LONDON, WC1N 3XX.   (mail/address)
    020 8571 9723   fax 020 8571 9723
    http://www.stalinsociety.org.uk
    Chmn: Harpal Brar
○   *G, *L; research into the history of the USSR under Joseph
    Stalin (1879-1953) [Iosif Vissarionovich Dzhugashvili]
●   Mtgs - Res
M   [not stated]
¶   List of research presentations; on request.

Standardbred and Trotting Horse Association of Great Britain &
Ireland   (STAGBI)
■   Little Craig, LLANDEGLEY, Powys, LD1 5UD.
    01597 850033
    http://www.standardbred.org
▲   Company Limited by Guarantee
○   *B

Standing Conference of Archaeological Unit Managers
since 2008 **Federation of Archaeological Managers &**
Employers

State Boarding Schools Association
a group of the **Boarding Schools Association**

Statewatch
NR PO Box 1516, LONDON, N16 0EW.   (hq)
    020 8802 1882
○   *K; a civil liberties group concerned with secrecy laws & the
    public's 'right to know'

Statistical & Social Inquiry Society of Ireland   (SSISI)   1847
IRL   c/o ESRI, Whitaker Square, Sir John Rogerson's Quay,
        DUBLIN 2, Republic of Ireland.   (hsb)
        email sean.lyons@esri.ie   http://www.ssisi.ie
        Hon Sec: Seán Lyons
○   *L; to promote the study of statistics, jurisprudence, & social &
        economic science

Statisticians in the Pharmaceutical Industry   (PSI)   1977
■   Durford Mill, PETERSFIELD, Hants, GU31 5AZ.   (regd/office)
        0845 180 0349   fax 0870 442 9940
        email admin@psiweb.org   http://www.psiweb.org
▲   Company Limited by Guarantee
○   *P; to promote professional standards of statistics in the
        pharmaceutical industry
●   Conf - Mtgs - ET - SG - Stat
<   Eur Fedn of Statisticians in the Pharmaceutical Ind
M   834 i, 306 f, UK / 211 i, 148 f, o'seas
¶   Pharmaceutical Statistics (Jnl) - 4; free (electronic).
        Spin (NL) - 4;   LM - 1;   AR; all ftm only.

Statute Law Society   1968
NR   21 Goodwyns Vale, LONDON, N10 2HA.   (hsb)
        020 8883 1700
        http://www.statutelawsociety.org
        Admin: Mary Block
▲   Registered Charity
○   *K, *L; to educate the legal profession & the public about the
        legislative process, with a view to encouraging improvements
        in statute law
●   Conf - Lectures
M   i & f
¶   The Statute Law Review - 4.

Steam Boat Association of Great Britain   (SBA)   1971
■   Awelon, 28 Colley Lane, SANDBACH, Cheshire, CW11 4HE.
        (hsp)
        01270 765837
        email secretary@steamboat.org.uk
        http://www.steamboat.org.uk
        Hon Sec: Dr Peter F Cuthbert
▲   Un-incorporated Society
○   *G, *L; to foster & encourage steam boating & the building,
        development, preservation & restoration of steam boats &
        steam machinery
Gp   Heritage Steam Boats Sub-Committee
●   Mtgs - Exhib - Inf - Cruising events throughout the year
<   Eur Steamboat Fedn; Inland Waterways Assn; R Yachting Assn
>   The SBA Heritage Steam Boat Trust
M   1163 i
        (Sub: £18 (£12 under 18s)
¶   The Funnel - 4; ftm only.
        The Steamboat Register (CD-ROM; £5.
        Catalogue Reprints:
        LIFU Engineering (1910); £3.50.
        A G Mumford (1900); £8.
        Lune Valley Engineering (1909); £5.
        Simpson Strickland (7th ed); £5.
        Escher Wyss & Co (extract); £2.   All +P&P.

Steam Car Club of Great Britain
NR   41 Bedhampton Hill, HAVANT, Hants, PO9 3JN.   (hsp)
        023 9248 4457
        email greg@rtd.gb.com   http://www.steamcar.net
        Sec: Christopher Busk
○   *G; for all owners of steam cars & steam cycles
M   i
¶   The Steam Car - 4; ftm.

Steam Plough Club   (SPC)   1966
■   Pant-y-Cae, Clyro, HEREFORD, HR3 6JU.   (hsp)
        01497 820750
        http://www.steamploughclub.org.uk
        Hon Sec: Dick Eastwood
▲   Un-incorporated Society
○   *G; to encourage & expand interest in the use of steam plough
        cultivation by demonstration, discussion & archive research
●   Mtgs - ET - Res - Comp - SG - Stat - Inf - Lib - PL - VE
<   Nat Traction Engine Club; Fedn Brit Historic Vehicle Clubs
M   400 i
¶   Steam Plough Times - 4; ftm, £1 nm.

Steel Construction Institute   (SCI)   1986
■   Silwood Park, ASCOT, Berks, SL5 7QN.   (hq)
        01344 636525
        http://www.steel-sci.org
▲   Company Limited by Guarantee
○   *L; to promote the proper & effective use of steel in
        construction, both offshore & onshore
Gp   Computing: Structural analysis, CAD/CAE technical information
        database; Multi-media, Internet site development
        Design development & advisory: Technical advice to industry,
        Offshore & onshore engineering;
        Education: organises courses on all aspects of steel design
●   Conf - ET - Res - Inf - Lib - VE
M   50 i, 800 f, UK / 30 i, 150 f, o'seas
¶   New Steel Construction - 6.   SCI News (NL) - 4.
        Range of technical publications; £15-£50.   Ybk.   AR.

Steel Lintel Manufacturers' Association   (SLMA)   1978
■   PO Box 10, NEWPORT, Monmouthshire, NP19 4XN.   (sb)
        01633 290022
        email info@slma.co.uk   http://www.slma.co.uk
        Sec: Dr Clive Challinor
○   *T; steel lintels used for construction applications
●   Mtgs
<   Construction Products Assn
M   4 f

Steel Window Association   (SWA)   1967
■   42 Heath St, TAMWORTH, Staffs, B79 7JH.   (hq)
        0844 249 1355   fax 0844 249 1356
        email info@steel-window-association.co.uk
        http://www.steel-window-association.co.uk
▲   Un-incorporated Society
○   *T; represents manufacturers of steel windows & associated
        products
M   f

Stephenson Locomotive Society   (SLS)   1909
■   1A Lostock Ave, POYNTON, Cheshire, SK12 1DR.   (mem/sec)
        http://www.stephensonloco.org.uk
        Mem Sec: M D Dickin
Br   15
○   *G, *L; study of railways, particularly locomotives
●   Mtgs - Lib - PL - VE
M   c 700 i & org
¶   SLS Jnl - 6; ftm.

© CBD Research Ltd · Beckenham · BR3 5JS · Tel 020 8650 7745 · E-mail cbd@cbdresearch.com · www.cbdresearch.com

STEPS   (STEPS)   1980

NR   Warrington Lane, LYMM, Cheshire, WA13 0SA.   (hq)
     01925 750271
     email info@steps-charity.org.uk
     http://www.steps-charity.org.uk
     Founder & Dir: Sue Banton,   Office Mgr: Anna Dorman
▲   Registered Charity
Br   25
○   *W; a charity which gives support, contact, help, advice &
     information to families with children with lower limb
     abnormalities (club foot, congenital dislocated hip (CDH),
     developmental dysplasia of the hip (DDH), lower limb
     deficiency)
●   Conf - Inf - Register of families for contact
<   Contact-a-Family (GB)
M   1,200 i, 10 org
¶   NL - 4; ftm.   AR; free.
     Handbooks for parents:
       CDH/DDH Splints.   CDH/DDH Plasters.
       Lower Limb Deficiency.   Talipes.

Stereoscopic Society   (Stereo Society)   1893

■   27 Somervelle Drive, FAREHAM, Hants, PO16 7QL.   (hsp)
     01329 236559
     http://www.stereoscopicsociety.org.uk
     Hon Sec: Martin Lovell
▲   Un-incorporated Society
○   *L; 3D photography, graphics & computer graphics; the
     advancement of stereo images
Gp   Computer; Prints; Transparencies
●   Conf - Mtgs - Exhib - Comp - Lib - VE - Workshops - Auctions
<   Intl Stereoscopic U; Photographic Alliance of GB; Photographic
     Soc of America (Stereo Divn)
M   527 i, UK / 81 i, o'seas
¶   Jnl of Stereo Imaging - 4; ftm, £2 each nm.

Stewart Society   1899

■   53 George St, EDINBURGH, EH2 2HT.   (asa)
     0131-220 4512   fax 0131-220 4512
     email info@stewartsociety.org
     Sec: Mrs I Crichton
▲   Registered Charity
Br   Australia, Canada, Europe, Far East, N Zealand, USA
○   *G, *L; research into the Stewart family & its history
●   Res - Lib - VE
M   320 i, UK / 391 i, o'seas
¶   The Stewarts (Jnl) - 1; ftm, £5 nm.   NL - 2; free.

Stickler Syndrome Support Group   (SSSG)   1989

■   PO Box 3351, LITTLEHAMPTON, E Sussex, BN16 9GB.
     (mail/address)
     01903 785771
     email info@stickler.org.uk   http://www.stickler.org.uk
     Hon Pres & Sec: Mrs Wendy Hughes
▲   Registered Charity
○   *W; to raise awareness of Stickler syndrome amongst the
     medical profession & the general public
●   Conf
<   Genetic Interest Gp; Long Term Conditions Alliance; Nat Coun
     for Voluntary Orgs
M   400 families, 160 profls, UK / 40 families, o'seas
¶   Information Booklets; ftm.
     Stickler Syndrome: the elusive syndrome; £16.99 m,
       £19.99 nm.

Stiff Man Syndrome Support Group   (SMS/SPS)   1998

■   75 Normandy Ave, BEVERLEY, E Yorks, HU17 8PF.   (hsp)
     01482 868881
     email liz.blows@smssupportgroup.co.uk
     http://www.smssupportgroup.co.uk
     Hon Sec: Liz Blows
▲   Registered Charity
○   *W; for sufferers with a compromised auto-immune system,
     causing rigidity, spasms, anxiety & startle response symptoms
●   Res - Stat - Inf
M   c 100 i
¶   NL - 6.

Stillbirth & Neonatal Death Society   (SANDS)   1978

■   28 Portland Place, LONDON, W1B 1LY.   (hq)
     020 7436 7940   fax 020 7436 3715
     email support@uk-sands.org   http://www.uk-sands.org
     Chief Exec: Neal Long
▲   Registered Charity
○   *M, *W; to provide support for anyone affected by the death of
     a baby; to improve quality of care & services to bereaved
     families; to promote research or change in practice that
     could help reduce the loss of babies' lives
●   ET - Inf - LG
     Helpline: 020 7436 5881
M   c 1,000 i, f
     (Sub: £8-£16 i, £40 f UK / £24 i, o'seas)
¶   NL - 3.   AR.   Support leaflets.
     Pregnancy Loss & the Death of a Baby (guidelines for
       professionals).
     Understanding Pregnancy Loss.   When a Baby Dies.
     Saying Goodbye to Your Baby.

Stilton Cheese Makers' Association   (SCMA)   1936

■   PO Box 384a, SURBITON, Surrey, KT5 9YL.   (asa)
     0161-923 4994
     email nigelwhite@msn.com
     http://www.stiltoncheese.com
     Sec: Nigel White
▲   Un-incorporated Society
Br   USA
○   *T; to promote marketing of Stilton cheese - to protect the use
     of the 'Stilton' trade name & device
●   Mtgs - ET - Res - Exhib - Stat - Expt - Inf - LG
<   Cheese Importers Assn of America; Dairy UK
M   6 f
¶   Recipe leaflets & information leaflets; free.

Stirling Engine Society   1997

NR   20 Pines Rd, CHELMSFORD, Essex, CM1 2DL.   (hsp)
     email helpline@stirlingengines.org.uk
     http://www.stirlingengines.org.uk
     Chmn: Ken Boak
○   *G; hot air engines
M   i
¶   Stirling News - 4.

**Stoke-on-Trent Museum Archaeological Society   (SOTMAS)
1959**

■   The Potteries Museum, Bethesda St, Hanley, STOKE-ON-TRENT,
     Staffs, ST1 3DW.   (hq)
     01782 232323
     Hon Sec: Mrs R Helen Outram
▲   Un-incorporated Society
○   *Q; to promote & encourage research into the archaeology in
     N Staffordshire
●   Mtgs - ET - Res - Inf - Lib - VE
<   Coun Brit Archaeology; Coun for Indep Archaeology
M   c 60 i, UK / 1 i, o'seas
¶   Staffordshire Archaeological Studies - irreg.
     NL - 3; free.

Stone Federation Great Britain   (SFGB)   1974
- ■ Channel Business Centre, Ingles Manor, Castle Hill Avenue, FOLKESTONE, Kent, CT20 2RD.   (hq)
  01303 856123   fax 01303 856117
  email enquiries@stonefed.org.uk
  http://www.stone-federationgb.org.uk
  Chief Exec: Jane Buxey
- ▲ Un-incorporated Society
- ○ *T; to promote the interests of members within the construction industry as a whole; to educate specifiers in the correct use & maintenance of stone; to provide professional quality services to members
- Gp British Slate Association; Contractors group; Marble & granite group; Quarry Forum; Stone cleaning & surface repair group
- ● Conf - Mtgs - ET - Res - Exhib - Comp - Inf - VE - LG - Courses & seminars (RIBA & CPD approved) on stone
- M 200+ f, UK / 5 f, o'seas
- ¶ Stone Specifiers Guide - 1; ftm, price varies nm.
  Codes of Practice on the design & installation of:
  Kitchen Worktops; £25 m, £45 nm.
  Internal Flooring; £30 m, £50 nm.
  Modern Practical Masonry by E G Warland; £22 m, £30 nm.

Stone Roofing Association   1995
- NR Ceunant, CAERNARFON, Gwynedd, LL55 4SA.   (hsb)
  01286 650402   fax 07092 307784
  email terry@slateroof.co.uk
  http://www.stoneroof.org.uk
  Chmn: Terry Hughes
- ▲ Un-incorporated Society
- ○ *T; to support the manufacturers of stone slates in the UK; to act as a point of reference for users & specifiers with the stone slate industry
- ● Mtgs - Inf
- M 20 f

Stonehenge Society
   see **Megalithic Society (incorporating the Stonehenge Society)**

Stoolball England   1979
- NR 53 Kings Rd, HORSHAM, W Sussex, RH13 5PP.   (hsp)
  01403 252419
  http://www.stoolball.co.uk
  Sec: Kay Price
- ○ *S
- ✕ 2008 (September) National Stoolball Association

Stop Climate Chaos Coalition
- NR c/o Oxfam, 232-242 Vauxhall Bridge Rd, LONDON, SW1V 1AU.   (mail/address)
  020 7802 9989
- ○ *K
- M org

Storage Equipment Manufacturers' Association   (SEMA)   1970
- NR National Metalforming Centre, 47 Birmingham Rd, WEST BROMWICH, W Midlands, B70 6PY.   (hq)
  0121-601 6350   fax 0121-601 6387
  email enquiry@sema.org.uk   http://www.sema.org.uk
  Sec: David B Corns
- ▲ Company Limited by Guarantee
- ○ *T
- Gp Technical
- ● Mtgs - ET - Exhib - Stat - Inf - Issuing codes of practice for the design, manufacture & use of storage equipment
- < Brit Materials Handling Fedn; Fédn Européenne de la Manutention; METCOM
- M 22 f
- ¶ Various codes of practice & guidelines on storage equipment - irreg; prices vary.

Storage & Handling Equipment Distributors' Association   (SHEDA)   1978
- ■ 35 Calthorpe Rd, Edgbaston, BIRMINGHAM, B15 1TS.   (hq)
  0121-454 4141   fax 0121-207 7002
  email info@sheda.org.uk   http://www.sheda.org.uk
  Sec: Sharon Parker
- ▲ Un-incorporated Society
- ○ *T; for companies in the UK & Ireland that provide a design, product supply & installation service within the storage & materials handling industry
- ● Mtgs - ET - Exhib
- < Storage Eqpt Mfrs Assn (SEMA)
- M 37 f
- ¶ SHEDA News - 4; free.   LM; ftm.

Stove Industry Alliance   (SIA)
- NR The Manor, Hasely Business Cente, Birmingham Road, WARWICK, CV35 7LS.
  024 7624 7246
  Chmn: Phil Wood
- ○ *T; to promote manufacturers, distributors & test houses of stoves & room heaters; also flue equipment, fuels & services
- M c 35 f

Strategic Planning Society   1967
- NR Mayfair House, 14-18 Heddon St, LONDON, W1B 4DA.   (hq)
  0845 056 3663   fax 0845 056 3663
  email membership@sps.org.uk   http://www.sps.org.uk
- ▲ Company Limited by Guarantee; Registered Charity
- ○ *P; to foster & promote research, innovation & best practice in strategic thought & action
- Gp Corporate strategy; Financial services; Innovation & corporate venturing; Knowledge economy; Public sector; Risk; SMEs; Technology, media &telecoms (TMT); Utilities; Voluntary sector
- ● Conf - Mtgs - ET - Res - Inf
- < Eur Strategic Planning Fedn (ESPLAF)
- M 1,300 i, 50 f, UK / 200 i, 20 f, o'seas
- ¶ Long Range Planning (Jnl) - 6;   Strategy - 4; both ftm only.
  Email NL - 12; free.

Strathspey Railway Association Ltd   (SRA)   1972
- NR Spey Lodge, Aviemore Station, Dalfaber Rd, AVIEMORE, Inverness-shire, PH21 1ET.   (hq)
- ▲ Company Limited by Guarantee
- ○ *G; to support the operation of the railway by provision of staff, maintenance of stock & restoration of relics
- Gp Carriage & wagon; Civil engineering works; Locomotive engineering; Marketing; Permanent way; Publicity; Signalling
- ● Mtgs - ET - Res - Exhib - Inf - Lib - VE
- M 730 i, 2 org, UK / 20 i, o'seas
- ¶ The Strathspey Express - 2; ftm.

Straw Bale Building Association
   has closed

Street Sled Sports Racers   (SSSprint)   1995
- ■ 33a Canal St, OXFORD, OX2 6BQ.   (chmn/b)
  01865 311179   fax 01865 426007
  email dingboston@oxfordstuntfactory.com
  http://www.streetluge.co.uk
  Chmn: David Boston
- ▲ Un-incorporated Society
- ○ *S; the regulation, safety, promotion & supply of all facets of street luging & land luging
- ● Mtgs - ET - Res - Comp - Inf - LG
- M i
- ¶ NL - 8/10.

© CBD Research Ltd · Beckenham · BR3 5JS · Tel 020 8650 7745 · E-mail cbd@cbdresearch.com · www.cbdresearch.com

Strict Baptist Historical Society (SBHS) 1960
- 33 Addison Rd, CATERHAM-on-the-HILL, Surrey, CR3 5LU. (hsp)
  01883 341909
  email thesecretary@sbhs.org.uk
  http://www.strictbaptisthistory.org.uk
  Hon Sec: Pauline Johns
- ▲ Registered Charity
- ○ *L; all matters of Particular Baptist & Strict Baptist history
- ● Mtgs - Inf - Lib
- M 125 i, UK / 3 i, o'seas
  (Sub: £7)
- ¶ Bulletin - 1; ftm, £1 nm.   NL - 1; free.

Stroke Association 1899
- § Stroke House, 240 City Rd, LONDON, EC1V 2PR.   (hq)
  020 7566 0300   fax 020 7490 2686
  email stroke@stroke.org.uk   http://www.stroke.org.uk
  Chief Exec: Jon Barrick
- ● Helpline: 0845 303 3100
  Funds research into prevention, treatment and better methods of rehabilitation, and helps stroke patients directly through its rehabilitation and support services.

Structural Precast Association
  a product association of the **British Precast Concrete Federation**

Structural Waterproofing Group
  a group of the **Property Care Association**

Struggle against Financial Exploitation
  since 2007 **SAFE: Struggle against Financial Exploitation**

Student Radio Association
  is administered by the **Radio Academy**

Sub-Aqua Association (SAA) 1976
- NR Space Solutions Business Centre, Sefton Lane, Maghull, LIVERPOOL, L31 8BX.   (hq)
  0151-287 1001
  email admin@saa.org.uk   http://www.saa.org.uk
  PRO: Sally Cartwright
- ▲ Registered Charity
- Br 350
- ○ *S
- Gp Boat handling; Chartwork & navigation; Marine life identification; Nautical archaeology
- ● Conf - Mtgs - ET - Exam - Res - Exhib - Inf
- < R Yachting Assn; Marine Conservation Soc; Nautical Archaeol Soc
- M 6,000 i
- ¶ Scuba World - 12.
  Introduction to SAA - on enrolment; free.

Subsea UK 2004
- The Innovation Centre, Aberdeen Science & Energy Park, Exploration Drive, ABERDEEN, AB23 8GX.   (hq)
  01224 355355
  email admin@subseauk.com   http://www.subseauk.com
  Co Sec: Trish Banks
- ▲ Company Limited by Guarantee
- ○ *T; to act as the focal point for the entire British sub-sea industry; to increase business opportunities in the sector
- ● Conf - Mtgs - Exhib - Expt - Inf - LG
- M c 800 f
  (Sub: see website)
- ¶ NL - 4; free.
  Publications on website.

Subsidence Forum
- Kingsley House, Ganders Business Park, Kingsley, BORDON, Hants, GU35 9LU.
  01252 357843   fax 01252 357831
  http://www.subsidenceforum.org.uk
- ○ *N, *T

Subterranea Britannica (SUB.BRIT) 1974
- NR 14 Maple Close, Sandford, WAREHAM, Dorset, BH20 7QD. (hsp)
  email info@subbrit.org.uk   http://www.subbrit.org.uk
  Sec: Roger Starling
- ▲ Company Limited by Guarantee
- ○ *L; to study & record man-made & man-used underground structures & spaces & associated above ground features (nuclear bunkers, submarine bases, London Underground stations, radar stations etc)
- Gp Cold War research
- ● Conf - Mtgs - Res - SG - Inf - PL - VE
- < Coun Brit Archaeology; Nat Assn Mining Hist Orgs; SE Region Indl Archaeol Conf
- M 930 i, 25 org, UK / 20 i, o'seas
  (Sub: £18 i & org, UK / £26, o'seas)
- ¶ Bulletin Subterranea Britannica - irreg;
  Subterranea - 2/3; both ftm, £4 each nm.

Sudden Death Support Association
  has closed

Suffolk Agricultural Association (SAA) 1831
- NR Trinity Park, Felixstowe Rd, IPSWICH, Suffolk, IP3 8UH.   (hq)
  01473 707110   fax 01473 707120
  email enquiries@suffolkshow.co.uk
  http://www.suffolkshow.co.uk
  Exec Dir: Christopher Bushby
- ▲ Registered Charity
- ○ *F; to raise the profile of the food & farming industry to the general public; to act as a route for communication between the Association, its members, the farming & non-farming communities & schools
- ● Suffolk Show - Trinity Park Conference & Events Centre
- < Assn of Show & Agricl Orgs
- M c 3,500 i

Suffolk Chamber of Commerce, Industry & Shipping Incorporated 1884
- NR Felaw Maltings, South Kiln, 42 Felaw St, IPSWICH, Suffolk, IP1 2DE.   (hq)
  01473 680600   fax 01473 603888
  email info@suffolkchamber.co.uk
  http://www.suffolkchamber.co.uk
  Chief Exec: John Dugmore
- ▲ Company Limited by Guarantee
- Br Haverhill, Ipswich, Lowestoft, Newmarket, Stowmarket
- ○ *C
- Gp Business Library; Home & economic affairs; International trade; Ipswich Port; Training; Transport
- ● Conf - Mtgs - ET - Exhib - Expt - Inf - Lib
- < Brit Chams Comm
- M f

Suffolk Horse Society 1877
- The Market Hill, WOODBRIDGE, Suffolk, IP12 4LU.   (hq)
  01394 380643
  email sec@suffolkhorsesociety.org.uk
  http://www.suffolkhorsesociety.org.uk
  Chmn: Christopher Bushby
- ▲ Company Limited by Guarantee; Registered Charity
- ○ *B; to promote the Suffolk breed of heavy horse
- ● Stat - Inf - Maintenance of stud book
- M 1500 i
- ¶ Suffolk Horse Magazine - 3; ftm, £3.50 nm.

Suffolk Institute of Archaeology & History   (SIA)   1848
- ■ 116 Hardwick Lane, BURY St EDMUNDS, Suffolk, IP33 2LE. (hsp)
  01284 753228
  http://www.suffolkarch.org.uk
  Hon Gen Sec: Jane Carr
- ▲ Registered Charity
- ○ *L; the study of the archaeology & history of Suffolk
- Gp Archaeological field gp
- ● Mtgs - ET - Res - Exhib - Inf - Lib - VE
- < Coun Brit Archaeology
- M 790 i, 61 org, UK / 8 i, 20 org, o'seas
- ¶ Proceedings - 1;   NL - 2; both ftm.

Suffolk Records Society   (SRS)   1958
- ■ Westhorpe Lodge, Westhorpe, STOWMARKET, Suffolk, IP14 4TA.   (hsp)
  01449 781078   fax 01449 780335
  email claire@ejbarker.co.uk
  http://www.suffolkrecordssociety.com
  Hon Sec: Claire Barker
- ▲ Registered Charity
- ○ *L; publication of documents relating to Suffolk & its people in all periods
- ● Publication
- M 348 i, 90 f
  (Sub: £12.50 i)
- ¶ Annual volume; ftm.

Suffolk Sheep Society   1886
- NR Unit B, Ballymena Livestock Market, 1 Woodside Park, BALLYMENA, Co Antrim, BT42 4HG.   (hq)
  028 2563 2342   fax 028 2563 2739
  email lewismcc@suffolksheep.org
  http://www.suffolksheep.org
  Sec: Lewis McClinton
- ○ *B
- < Nat Sheep Assn
- M i, f, org

Sugar Association of London   (SAOL)   1882
- NR 154 Bishopsgate, LONDON, EC2M 4LN.   (hq)
  020 7377 2113   fax 020 7247 2481
  http://www.sugarassociation.co.uk
  Sec: N Durham
- Br 2
- ○ *T; supervisors of raw sugar cargoes; provision of rules & contract conditions for the raw sugar trade
- Gp Arbitrators; Rules & contract conditions; Supervisors of raw sugar cargoes
- ● Mtgs - ET - Inf - Empl - LG
- M 40 f, UK / 60 f, o'seas
- ¶ Rules & Regulations; £35 m, £60 nm.

Sugar Traders Association of the UK   (STAUK)   1952
- ■ c/o C Czarnikow Sugar Ltd, 24 Chiswell St, LONDON, EC1Y 4SG.   (hsb)
  020 7972 6631   fax 020 7972 6699
  email sugartraders@sugartraders.co.uk
  http://www.sugartraders.co.uk
  Hon Sec: John Ireland
- ▲ Un-incorporated Society
- ○ *T; to promote, support, develop, protect & maintain the trade in sugar
- ● Mtgs - LG
- < Assn Profl Orgs Sugar Tr EU (ASSUC)
- M 12 f, 5 org

Sunbed Association   1995
- ■ Chess House, 105 High St, CHESHAM, Bucks, HP5 1DE.   (hq)
  01494 785941   fax 01494 786791
  email info@sunbedassociation.org.uk
  http://www.sunbedassociation.org.uk
  Sec: Kathy Banks
- ▲ Company Limited by Guarantee
- ○ *T; interests of sunbed manufacturers, operators & hirers
- ● Mtgs - ET - Stat - Inf - LG - Printed merchandise
- < Eur Sunlight Assn
- M 1,000 f
- ¶ NL - 2; ftm only.   LM - 12; free.

Sunday Shakespeare Society   (SSS)   1874
- ■ 308 Copperfield, CHIGWELL, Essex, IG7 5JZ.   (hsp)
  020 8500 3768
  http://www.sundayshakespeare.weebly.com
  Hon Sec: Susan E Taylor
- ▲ Un-incorporated Society
- ○ *A, *G; to encourage the study of Shakespeare's plays by dramatic readings by members on Sundays
- ● Mtgs
- M 41 i
- ¶ NL - 12;   Programme - 1; both free.

Superintendents' Association of Northern Ireland   (PSANI)   1972
- ■ PSNI College, Garnerville, Garnerville Rd, BELFAST, BT4 2NX.   (hq)
  028 9092 2201   fax 028 9092 2169
  email mail@psani.org   http://www.psani.org
- ▲ Un-incorporated Society
- ○ *P; representing the interests of superintendents in the police service of Northern Ireland
- ● Conf - Mtgs - Empl - LG
- M 100 i

Superyacht UK
  a group association of the **British Marine Federation**

Support Dogs
- ■ 21 Jessops Riverside, Brightside Lane, SHEFFIELD, S Yorks, S9 2RX.
  0114-261 7800   fax 0114-261 7555
  email supportdogs@btconnect.com
  http://www.support-dogs.org.uk
- ▲ Registered Charity
- ○ *W; the only organisation worldwide that trains dogs to help disabled people with everyday tasks & also to recognise & predict an epileptic seizure

Support after Murder & Manslaughter   (SAMM)
- § L&DRC Tally Ho!, Pershore Rd, Edgbaston, BIRMINGHAM, W Midlands, B5 7RN.   (hq)
  0121-471 1200
  email support@samm.org.uk   http://www.samm.org.uk
  'a national charity supporting families bereaved by murder & manslaughter; [it provides] advice & training to agencies on issues relevant to the traumatically bereaved.'
  Hotline: 0845 872 3440

Support & Training in Prep Schools
  see **SATIPS - Support & Training in Prep Schools**

Supporters of Nuclear Energy   (SONE)   1998
- NR 9 Monahan Avenue, PURLEY, Surrey, CR8 3BB.   (hq)
  020 8660 8970
  email sec@sone.org.uk   http://www.sone.org.uk
- ▲ Company Limited by Guarantee
- ○ *K; promotion of nuclear energy policy
- ● Conf - Mtgs - Inf - LG
- M 280 i
- ¶ NL - 12; free on website.

© CBD Research Ltd · Beckenham · BR3 5JS · Tel 020 8650 7745 · E-mail cbd@cbdresearch.com · www.cbdresearch.com

Supporting Adults affected by Adoption
since c 2008 **Adults Affected by Adoption - NORCAP**

Supporting People Affected by Mental Ill Health
see **Shine - Supporting People Affected by Mental Ill Health**

Surf Life Saving Great Britain Ltd   (SLSGB)   1955
■ 19 Southernhay West (1st floor), EXETER, Devon, EX1 1PJ.   (hq)
 01392 218007   fax 01392 217808
 email mail@slsgb.org.uk
 http://www.surflifesaving.org.uk
▲ Company Limited by Guarantee; Registered Charity
○ *K, *S; promotion of beach & surf safety; provision of
 community service by voluntary lifeguards on British beaches;
 promotion of surf life saving as a competitive sport
Gp Commissions: Technical, Powercraft, Sport, Youth development
● Conf - Mtgs - ET - Exam - Comp - Stat - Inf - LG
< Intl Life Saving
M 4,000 i, 25 f, 75 org
¶ Swim & Save - 12.
✕ 2008 Surf Life Saving Association of Great Britain

Surface Engineering Association   (SEA)   1997
■ Federation House, 10 Vyse St, BIRMINGHAM, B18 6LT.   (hq)
 0121-237 1123   fax 0121-237 1124
 email info@sea.org.uk   http://www.sea.org.uk
 Chief Exec: D Elliot
▲ Company Limited by Guarantee
○ *T
Gp British Surface Treatment Suppliers Association; Contract Heat
 Treatment Association; Metal Finishing Association (& its
 division the British Electroless Nickel Society); Paint & Powder
 Finishing Association
 Health, safety & environment; Organic coating equipment;
 Process technology
● Conf - Mtgs - ET - Res - Exhib - Comp - SG - Stat - Inf - VE - LG
< Aluminium Finishing Assn (AFA), Brit Allied Trs Fedn (BATF)
M c 400 f
¶ SEA News - 4;   Watchword - 4; both ftm.

Surface Engineering Division
a group of the **Institute of Materials, Minerals & Mining**

Surfers against Sewage   (SAS)
■ Unit 2 Wheal Kitty Workshops, ST AGNES, Cornwall,
 TR5 0RD.   (hq)
 01872 553001   fax 01872 552615
 email info@sas.org.uk   http://www.sas.org.uk
 Dir: Hugo Tagholm
▲ Company Limited by Guarantee
○ *K; campaign for clear, safe recreational waters
● ET - Res - Campaigning - Fundraising (including selling
 merchandise)
M c 9,000 i, 200 f, UK / 100 i, o'seas
¶ Pipeline (NL) - 4; ftm only.

Surfing GB   2010
NR International Surfing Centre, Fistral Beach, NEWQUAY,
 Cornwall, TR7 1HY.   (hq)
 01637 876474
 http://www.surfinggb.com
 Chmn: Chris Thomson
▲ Company Limited by Guarantee
○ *S; the national governing body for surfing; is the successor
 body to the British Surfing Association
● Mtgs - Courses
< Intl Surfing Assn (ISA)
M i & org

Surgical Dressings Manufacturers Association   (SDMA)   1936
■ Fernbank, 17 The Crescent, Holymoorside, CHESTERFIELD,
 Derbys, S42 7EE.   (sb)
 01246 568175   fax 01246 568175
 email sdma@nigelb.fsworld.co.uk
 http://www.sdma.org.uk
 Sec: Dr Nigel Brassington
▲ Un-incorporated Society
○ *T; operates in the area of wound care products & associate
 products, including bandages, hip protectors, first aid kits &
 disposable medical devices
● Mtgs - SG - Inf - LG - Consideration of legislative measures -
 Discussions with government departments - Networking
M 17 f
¶ Industry Code of Practice - irreg; free.

Surrey Archaeological Society   (SyAS)   1854
NR Castle Arch, GUILDFORD, Surrey, GU1 3SX.   (hq)
 01483 532454   fax 01483 532454
 email info@surreyarchaeology.co.uk
 http://www.surreyarchaeology.org.uk
 Hon Sec: David Calow
▲ Company Limited by Guarantee; Registered Charity
○ *L; archaeology, history & antiquities of Surrey (including those
 parts now in Greater London)
Gp Artefacts & Archives Research Group; Local History Group;
 Medieval Studies Forum; Prehistoric Group; Roman Studies
 Group; Surrey Industrial History Society; Villages Study Group
● Conf - ET - Res - SG - Lib - PL - VE
< Brit Assn Local History; Coun Brit Archaeology; Field Studies
 Coun
M 787 i, 126 org, UK / 5 i, 38 org, o'seas
¶ Surrey Archaeological Collections - 1.
 Bulletin - 9.   AR.

Surrey Chambers of Commerce Ltd
NR Unit 14A, Monument Way East, WOKING, Surrey, GU21 5LY.
 (hq)
 01483 735540   fax 01483 756754
 email info@surrey-chambers.co.uk
 http://www.surrey-chambers.co.uk
 Chief Exec: Louise Punter
▲ Company Limited by Guarantee
○ *C
● Conf - Mtgs - ET - Res - Exhib - SG - Stat - Expt - Inf - Lib - LG
< Brit Chams Comm
M 3,300 f

Surrey County Agricultural Society   (SCAS)   1954
■ 8 Birtley Courtyard, Bramley, GUILDFORD, Surrey, GU5 0LA.
 (hq)
 01483 890810   fax 01483 890820
 email scas@surreycountyshow.co.uk
 http://www.surreycountyshow.co.uk
 Chief Exec: Sonia Ashworth
▲ Company Limited by Guarantee; Registered Charity
○ *F, *H; the encouragement of agriculture & agricultural
 employees in their various crafts & to promote good farming;
 the advancement of breeding & rearing of livestock & horses
 & to maintain the public's interest in the agricultural industry
 generally within the county
Gp Agriculture; Breeding (animals); Farming; Horticulture
● Surrey County Show - Country Fair & Ploughing Match - Surrey
 Food & Farm Week
< Assn of Show & Agricl Orgs
M 379 i, 3 f, 1 school
¶ AR - 1; free.

Surrey Industrial History Society
a group of the **Surrey Archaeological Society**

Surrey Record Society (SRS) 1913

■ c/o Surrey History Centre, 130 Goldsworth Rd, WOKING,
Surrey, GU21 6ND.   (hsb)
01483 5187379
email shs@surreycc.gov.uk
Hon Sec: Michael Page
▲ Registered Charity
○ *L; to publish records relating to areas within the ancient county
of Surrey (including those parts now in Greater London)
● Publication
< Brit Records Assn
M 149 i, 55 org, UK / 4 i, 17 org, o'seas
(Sub: £5)
¶ Record volumes; ftm, prices vary nm.   AR; ftm.

Surtees Society (SS) 1834

■ Faculty Office, Elvet Riverside block 2, New Elvet, DURHAM,
DH1 3JT.   (hsb)
0191-334 2908   fax 0191-334 2911
email surtees.society@dur.ac.uk
http://www.surteessociety.org.uk
Hon Sec: Melanie Farrell
▲ Registered Charity
○ *L; publication of unedited historical manuscripts illustrative of
the intellectual, moral, religious or social condition of the
ancient Kingdom of Northumbria (those parts of England &
Scotland between the Humber & Firth of Forth in the east &
the Mersey & the Clyde to the west)
Named after Robert Surtees 1779-1834, antiquary &
topographer
● Publication
M 225 i & org
¶ Annual Volume - 1; ftm (subscription £25), £50 nm.

Survey Association
see **United Kingdom Land & Hydrographic Survey
Association**

Survivors of Bereavement by Suicide

§ The Flamsteed Centre, Albert St, ILKESTON, Derbys, DE7 5GU.
0115-944 1117
a charity offering help & advice to those affected by suicide

Suspended Doctors Support Group
a group of the **Society of Clinical Psychiatrists**

Sussex Archaeological Society 1846

NR Bull House, 92 High St, LEWES, E Sussex, BN7 1XH.   (hq)
01273 486260
http://www.sussexpast.co.uk
Chief Exec: Tristan Bareham
▲ Company Limited by Guarantee; Registered Charity
Br 6
○ *L; to further interest in & knowledge of the history &
archaeology of Sussex
Gp Archaeological excavations; Sussex archaeology forum; Sussex
history forum
● Conf - Mtgs - ET - Res - Exhib - SG - Inf - Lib - PL - VE - LG -
Opens to the public society-owned museums, sites &
properties
M 2,102 i, 123 org, UK / 12 i, 69 org, o'seas
¶ Sussex Past & Present - 3.
Sussex Archaeological Collections - 1.

Sussex Cattle Society 1879

NR Station Rd, ROBERTSBRIDGE, E Sussex, TN32 5DG.   (hq)
01580 880105
email enq@sussexcattlesociety.org.uk
http://www.sussexcattlesociety.org.uk
Sec: Sue Kennedy
▲ Company Limited by Guaranmtee; Registered Charity
○ *B; for breeders of Sussex Cattle
< Nat Beef Assn
M i

Sussex Chamber of Commerce & Enterprise 1945

NR Greenacre Court, Station Rd, BURGESS HILL, W Sussex,
RH15 9DS.   (hq)
0844 375 9550   fax 01444 259190
email info@sussexenterprise.co.uk
http://www.sussexenterprise.co.uk
Chief Exec: Mark Froud
▲ Company Limited by Guarantee
○ *C; as the Chamber of Commerce & Business Link for Sussex to
help Sussex business prosper & develop
Gp International services; Important advice services; Employee
development advice; Membership organisation
● Conf - Mtgs - ET - Res - Exhib - Stat - Expt - Inf - LG
< Brit Chams Comm
M 2,500 f
¶ Business Edge - 10.
Business Directory - 1.
Note: The chamber trades as Sussex Enterprise

Sussex Enterprise
the trading name of **Sussex Chamber of Commerce &
Enterprise**

Sussex Industrial Archaeology Society (SIAS) 1967

■ 42 Falmer Avenue, Saltdean, BRIGHTON, E Sussex,
BN2 8FG.   (hsp)
01273 271330
email sias@ronmartin.org.uk   http://www.sussexias.co.uk
Gen Sec: R G Martin
▲ Registered Charity
○ *L; recording, repairing & preserving documentary & other
recordings & sites of economic & industrial activity in Sussex
Gp Breweries & malthouses; Brickmaking; Fuel & power;
Icehouses; Limekilns; Mills; Railways; Water supply
● Conf - Mtgs - Res - Exhib - SG - Inf - VE - LG
< Assn for Indl Archaeology; British Brick Soc; S E Region Indl
Archaeology Conf; Sussex Archaeological Soc
M 340 i, 23 org, UK / 3 i, o'seas
(Sub: £10)
¶ Sussex Industrial History - 1; ftm, £4.25 nm.
NL - 4; ftm, 50p nm.

Sussex Record Society (SRS) 1901

■ Barbican House, High St, LEWES, E Sussex, BN7 1YE.   (hq)
01273 405739
http://www.sussexrecordsociety.org
Hon Sec: P M Wilkinson
▲ Registered Charity
○ *L; transcribing & publishing in book form documents relating
to the County of Sussex
● Publication
M 268 i, 47 org, UK / 11 i, 39 org, o'seas
¶ Sussex Record Society [volume...] - 1; ftm, prices vary nm.
NL - 1;   LM - irreg;   AR - 1; all ftm.

© CBD Research Ltd · Beckenham · BR3 5JS · Tel 020 8650 7745 · E-mail cbd@cbdresearch.com · www.cbdresearch.com

Sustain, the Alliance for Better Food & Farming   1999
- 94 White Lion St, LONDON, N1 9PF.   (hq)
  020 7837 1228   fax 020 7837 1141
  email sustain@sustainweb.org
  http://www.sustainweb.org
  Coordinator: Jeanette Longfield
▲ Company Limited by Guarantee; Registered Charity
○ *F, *K, advocates food & agricultural policies & practices that
  enhance the health & welfare of people & animals, improve
  the working & living environment, promote equity & enrich
  society & culture
  Represents about 100 national public interest organisations
  working at international, national, regional & local level
Gp Projects & campaigns:
  Capital Growth; Children's Food Campaign; City Harvest;
  Ethical Eats; Food & Climate Change; Food Co-ops; Food
  Facts; Food & Mental Health; Good Food for Our Money;
  Good Food on the Public Plate; Local Action on Food;
  London Food Link; Making Local Food Work; Olympic Food;
  Real Bread Campaign; Sustainable Fish City; Urban
  Agriculture; Well London - Buy Well
● Conf - ET - Res - Stat - Inf - LG
M 90 org
¶ Publication list available.

Sustainable Restaurant Association   (SRA)
NR 25 Gerrard St, LONDON, W1O 6JL.
  020 7479 4224   fax 020 7479 4220
  http://www.thesra.org
○ *K, *T; 'to change not only the food that people eat, but also
  the way it is sourced, transported & created'

**Sutherland Society (the UK organisation for cranial osteopathy)
1970**
NR Church Street Practice, 15a Church St, BRADFORD-on-AVON,
  Wilts, BA15 1LN.   (mem/sb)
  http://www.cranial.org.uk
  Mem Sec: Stephanie Brown
○ *P; named for W G Sutherland, founder of osteopathy in the
  cranial field

Sutton Chamber   1936
NR 236-238 High St, SUTTON, Surrey, SM1 1PA.   (hq)
  020 8642 9661
  email admin@suttonchamber.biz
  http://www.suttonchamber.biz
  Chmn: Paul Cawthorne
▲ Company Limited by Guarantee
○ *C; for the London Borough of Sutton
● Mtgs - ET - Exhib - Inf

Swaledale Sheep Breeders Association   (SSBA)   1920
NR Barnley View, Town Head, Eggleston, BARNARD CASTLE,
  Co Durham, DL12 0DE.   (sp)
  01833 650516
  email jstephenson@swaledale-sheep.com
  http://www.swaledale-sheep.com
  Sec: John Stephenson
○ *B
● Mtgs - Inf
< Nat Sheep Assn
M i
¶ Flock Book - 1; ftm only.

Swaziland Society   1991
NR 45 Mayfield Close, WALTON on THAMES, Surrey, KT12 5PR.
  http://www.swazisoc.com
  Sec: Vera Robbins
▲ Un-incorporated Society
○ *X; developing & strengthening educational, cultural, economic
  & social ties between Britain & Swaziland; to foster friendship
  & uderstanding between the peoples of the two countries
● Mtgs - VE - Social gatherings - Financial assistance to
  development projects in Swaziland
M 160 i, UK / 86 i, o'seas
¶ Focus on Swaziland - 3; ftm.
  [subscription £18 (double), £12 (single).]

Swedenborg Society   1810
- 20-21 Bloomsbury Way, LONDON, WC1A 2TH.   (hq)
  020 7405 7986   fax 020 7831 5848
  email richard@swedenborg.org.uk
  http://www.swedenborg.org.uk
▲ Company Limited by Guarantee; Registered Charity
○ *A, *L; printing & publication of works of Emanuel Swedenborg
  (1688-1772), the Swedish philosopher, scientist & theologian
● Conf - Mtgs - Res - Exhib - Lib - PL
< Swedenborg Publishers International
M 500 i, UK / 350 i, o'seas
  (Sub: £5)
¶ Journal of the Swedenborg Society - 1; £9.50.
  Things Heard & Seen (NL) - 3;   AR; both free.

Swedish Chamber of Commerce for the United Kingdom   1906
NR 5 Upper Montagu St, LONDON, W1H 2AG.   (hq)
  020 7224 8001
  http://www.scc.org.uk
○ *C; to promote trade between Great Britain & Sweden

**Swimming Pool & Allied Trades Association Ltd   (SPATA)
1961**
NR 4 Eastgate House, East St, ANDOVER, Hants, SP10 1EP.   (hq)
  01264 356210   fax 01264 332628
  email admin@spata.co.uk   http://www.spata.co.uk
▲ Company Limited by Guarantee
○ *T; interests of contractors & manufacturers of equipment &
  accessories for swimming pools & spas
● Conf - Mtgs - ET - Exhib - Inf - Lib
< is part of the British Swimming Pool Federation
M 220 f, UK / 14 f, o'seas
¶ Various publications on standards for installations, water
  treatment for swimming pools & spas.

Swimming Teachers' Association Ltd   (STA)   1932
NR Anchor House, Birch St, WALSALL, W Midlands, WS2 8HZ.
  (hq)
  01922 645097   fax 01922 720628
  email sta@sta.co.uk   http://www.sta.co.uk
▲ Company Limited by Guarantee; Registered Charity
Br 16; Australia, Hong Kong, Singapore, Taiwan
○ *E, *S; 'to save lives by the teaching of swimming, lifesaving &
  survival techniques'
● Conf - Mtgs - ET - Exam
< Intl Fedn of Swimming Teachers Assns (IFSTA)
M 5,000 i
¶ Swim & Save - 6; ftm, £18 yr nm (UK) (£24 Europe).

Swindon Chamber of Commerce
  a local chamber of **Thames Valley Chamber of Commerce &
  Industry**

Swiss Railways Society
NR   28 Appletree Lane, REDDITCH, Worcs, B97 6SE.   (mem/sec)
     Mem Sec: Martin Fisher
○   *G; for all interested in rail journeys, particularly through
       Switzerland
●   Mtgs - VE
M   i
       (Sub: £15)
¶   Swiss Express

Sydney Smith Association   1996
■   Waysfield, Kilmington, AXMINSTER, Devon, EX13 7ST.   (hsp)
     01297 35525
     email sydie.bones@btopenworld.com
     http://www.sydneysmith.org.uk
     Hon Sec: Mrs Sydness M Bones
▲   Registered Charity
○   *A, *G; for all interested in the life & works of Sydney
       Smith (1771-1845) clergyman, esaayist & wit; he was one of
       the founders of the Edinburgh Review
●   Mtgs
M   230 i, UK / 8 i, o'seas
¶   NL - 1.

Sylvia Townsend Warner Society   2000
NR   26 Portwey Close, WEYMOUTH, Dorset, DT4 8RF.
     0740 315 9621
     email stwsociety@btinternet.com
     http://www.townsendwarner.com
     Editors: Judith Stinton & Dr Helen Sutherland
○   *G; to widen the readership of the works of Sylvia Townsend
       Warner (1893 - 1978), writer of novels, short storoes &
       poems
<   Alliance of Literary Socs
M   135 i
¶   Jnl - 1.   NL - 2.   News Archive.

Synthetic Fibre Rug, Mat & Carpet Association   (SFRMA)   1965
■   Kingsway House, Wrotham Rd, Meopham, GRAVESEND, Kent,
     DA13 0AU.   (hsp)
▲   Un-incorporated Society
○   *T
●   Conf - Mtgs - Stat - Lib
M   8 f
¶   NL - 6;   AR; both ftm only.

Systematics Association   1937
NR   c/o Dr P Wilkie, Royal Botanic Garden, 20a Inverleith Row,
     EDINBURGH, EH3 5LR.   (hsb)
     Sec: Dr P Wilkie
○   *L; for the study of systematics (the classification of organisms)
       in relation to general biology & evolution
●   Conf - Mtgs - ET - Inf
M   i

© CBD Research Ltd · Beckenham · BR3 5JS · Tel 020 8650 7745 · E-mail cbd@cbdresearch.com · www.cbdresearch.com

T E Lawrence Society   (TELS)   1985
- ■ PO Box 728, OXFORD, OX2 6YP.   (mail address)
  email info@telsociety.org.uk   http://www.telsociety.org.uk
  Sec: Ian Heritage,   Chmn: Peter Leney
- ▲ Registered Charity
- Br 3; Japan, Netherlands, USA
- ○ *A; to promote interest & research into the life & works of
  T E Lawrence (Lawrence of Arabia), 1888-1935
- ● Conf - Mtgs - Res - Exhib - Inf - Lib - VE
- M 348 i, UK / 235 i, o'seas
- ¶ Jnl - 2; ftm, £8 nm.   NL - 4; ftm only.
  [subscription £18 UK]

Table Soccer Players Association
we understand this organisation has been replaced by the
English Subbuteo Table Football Association -
confirmation is requested

Table Tennis Association of Wales   (TTAW)   1921
- ■ 3 Parc Cwm Ystrad, Johnstown, CARMARTHEN, SA31 3NZ.
  (hsp)
  http://www.ttaw.co.uk
  Sec: Stan Eastwood
- ○ *S
- Gp Sub-c'ees: Coaching, Veteran, Selection, Umpires,
  Management, Computer ranking
- M i & org

Table Tennis Scotland
see **Scottish Table Tennis Association**

Tai Chi Union for Great Britain   (TCUGB)   1991
- NR 5 Corunna Drive, HORSHAM, W Sussex, RH13 5HG.   (hsp)
  01403 257918
  http://www.taichiunion.com
  Sec: Peter Ballam
- ○ *S; for instructors in the art of Tai Chi in all its aspects - self-
  defence, meditation & health
- ● inf
- M c 400 i
- ¶ Tai Chi Tuan & Oriental Arts - 4.

Talking Newspaper Association of the United Kingdom (TNAUK)   1974
- ■ National Recording Centre, HEATHFIELD, E Sussex,
  TN21 8DB.   (hq)
  01435 866102   fax 01435 865422
  email info@tnauk.org.uk   http://www.tnauk.org.uk
- ▲ Registered Charity
- ○ *M, *W; to provide 230 national newspapers & magazines on
  tape, e mail, CD-ROM & bulletin board service to blind,
  visually impaired & disabled people
- ● Inf
- M c 11,500 i

Tall Persons Club GB & Ireland   (TPC)   1991
- ■ 88-90 Hatton Garden, LONDON, EC1N 8PN.   (hq)
  0700 082 5512
  email admin@tallclub.co.uk   http://www.tallclub.co.uk
  The Director
- ▲ Company Limited by Guarantee
- Br Links with clubs in Europe & USA
- ○ *K; to provide information for & to promote the interests of
  those who are taller than average; includes practical,
  medical, psychological & social aspects
- Gp Little Big Ones (for tall children & their parents)
- ● Mtgs - ET - Stat - Inf - VE
- < Links with Tall Clubs in Europe & USA
- M 1,000 i
- ¶ 6 ft+ - 4; ftm.
  Tall Suppliers Directory - 2; ftm, £35 nm.

Tallis Group
- NR 51 Vernon Ave, LONDON, SW20 8BN.   (pres/p)
  020 8715 7659
  Pres: Edward W Clark
- ○ *D; interest in the music of Thomas Tallis (c1505-1585)

Talybont Welsh Sheep Society   2002
- ■ Montague Harris & Co, 16 Ship St, BRECON, Powys,
  LD3 9AD.   (hsb)
  01874 623200   fax 01874 623131
  email jal@montague-harris.co.uk
  Sec: John Lewis
- < Nat Sheep Assn
- M c 40

Talyllyn Railway Preservation Society   (TRPS)   1950
- ■ Wharf Station, TYWYN, Merioneth, LL36 9EY.   (hq)
  01654 710472   fax 01654 711755
  email secretary@talyllyn.co.uk
  http://www.talyllyn.co.uk
- ▲ Un-incorporated Society
- Br 8
- ○ *G; operation of the Talyllyn Railway as an example of a
  steam-operated narrow-gauge railway built in the 19th
  century
- ● Mtgs - ET - Exhib - VE - Practical work on railway by volunteers
- > Talyllyn Holdings Ltd; Talyllyn Rly Co; Narrow Gauge Rly
  Museum Trust
- M 3,700 i, UK / 110 i, o'seas
- ¶ Talyllyn News - 4; ftm.   AR.

Tamworth Breeders' Group
- NR Walnut Cottage, Common Rd, Wrangle, BOSTON, Lincs,
  PE22 9BY.
  01205 871792
  Sec: Carolyn MacInnes
- ○ *B; for breeders of Tamworth pigs

Tandem Club of the United Kingdom   (TC)   1971
- ■ 25 Hendred Way, ABINGDON, Oxon, OX14 2AN.
  01235 525161
  email secretary@tandem-club.org.uk
  http://www.tandem-club.org.uk
  Hon Sec: Peter Hallowell
- ▲ Un-incorporated Society
- Br 50; Holland
- ○ *S; to encourage & assist tandem cycling
- Gp Disabilities liaison; Techncal
- ● Mtgs - Comp - Inf
- < Cycling Time Trials
- M 3,500 i, UK / 500 i, o'seas
  (Sub: £10)
- ¶ Tandem Club Jnl - 6.

Tank Storage Association (TSA) 1978
NR Black Dog Farm, Waverton, CHESTER, CH3 7PB. (dir/p)
    01244 335627 fax 01244 332198
    email tsa@tankstorage.org.uk
    http://www.tankstorage.org.uk
    Dir: Dr K H M Bray
▲ Company Limited by Guarantee
○ *T; to represent companies operating in the UK whose main
    business is the storage of bulk liquids for third parties
● Mtgs - LG
< Fedn of Eur Tank Storage Assns (FETSA)
M 13 f

Tapestry Frame Manufacturers' Association (TFMA) 1991
■ 81 Park View, Collins Rd, LONDON, N5 2UD.
○ *T
● Mtgs
M 11 f
¶ In the Frame (NL) - 1.

Tarot Association of the British Isles (TABI) 1999
■ PO Box 4791, SHEFFIELD, S Yorks, S6 9FE. (treas/p)
    email treasurer@tabi.org.uk http://www.tabi.org.uk
▲ Un-incorporated Society
○ *G; to promote tarot in a positive, contructive way
● Conf - ET - Comp - SG - Inf
< Spiritual Workers Assn
M 300 i, UK / 50 i, o'seas
    (Sub: £10 UK)

Tattoo Club of Great Britain 1975
NR 389 Cowley Rd, OXFORD, OX4 2BS. (hq)
    01865 716877 fax 01865 775610
    email tcgb@tattoo.co.uk http://www.tattoo.co.uk
    Pres: Lionel Titchener
○ *G; for tattoo artists & enthusiasts interested in furthering
    greater understanding of tattoo art
Gp TCGB Engineering is the manufacturing division of tattooing
    equipment supplied to trade worldwide
● Mtgs - Res - Exhib
< Brit Tattoo Artists Fedn
M 2,500 i, UK / 1,500 i, o'seas
¶ Tattoo International - 6.

Taunton Chamber of Commerce
■ 12F Fore St (1st floor), TAUNTON, Somerset, TA1 3TP. (hq)
    01823 353353 fax 01823 353353
    email office@taunton-chamber.co.uk
    http://www.taunton-chamber.co.uk
    Admin Officer: J Burden
○ *C
● Mtgs - Exhib - Inf - VE - LG - Promotional services
< Brit Chams Comm; Bristol Cham Comm & Initiative
M c 200 f
¶ Business News (Jnl) - 12; ftm only.

Tax Incentivised Savings Association (TISA) 1998
NR Dakota House, 25 Falcon Court, Preston Farm Business Park,
    STOCKTON-on-TEES, Co Durham, TS18 3TX. (hq)
    01642 666999
    http://www.tisa.co.uk
    Dir Gen: Tony Vine-Lott
▲ Company Limited by Guarantee
○ *T; to encourage consultation on existing & future regulations
    with government, HM Treasury, Inland Revenue, statutory
    regulating authorities & other relevant organisations
● Conf - Mtgs - ET - Res - Stat - Inf - LG
M c 115 f
✕ 2007 PEP & ISA Managers' Association

TaxPayers' Alliance (TPA) 2004
■ 55 Tufton St, LONDON, SW1P 3QL.
    0845 330 9554
    email info@taxpayersalliance.com
    http://www.taxpayersalliance.com
    Chief Exec: Matthew Elliott
○ *K; for a lowering of the tax rates

Tay-Sachs & Allied Diseases Association
NR 14 Monarch Way, Pinewood, IPSWICH, Suffolk, IP8 3TA.
    01473 404156
○ *W

Teachers' Union of Ireland
IRL 73 Orwell Rd, Rathgar, DUBLIN 6, Republic of Ireland.
    353 (1) 492 2588 fax 353 (1) 492 2953
    email tui@tui.ie http://www.tui.ie
    Gen Sec: Peter MacMenamin

Ted Heath Musical Appreciation Society (THMAS)
NR Flat 15 Ynysderwe House, PONTARDAWE, Glamorgan,
    SA8 4AA. (memsec/p)
    01792 830691
    Mem Sec: Mrs Jackie Jones
○ *D; for all interested in the music of the bandleader Edward
    (Ted) Heath (1902-1969)
M i
¶ Jnl - 4.

Teeswater Sheep Breeders Association Ltd (TSBA) 1949
NR Meadowcroft Farm, Ugthorpe, WHITBY, N Yorks, YO21 2BL.
    (hsp)
    01947 840924
    email teeswatersheep@yahoo.co.uk
    http://www.teeswater-sheep.co.uk
    Sec: Mrs Denise Newey
▲ Company Limited by Guarantee
○ *B; registration of pedigrees & promotion of Teeswater sheep
● Mtgs - Exhib - Recording lambs for the Flock Book
< Nat Sheep Assn
M 80 i
¶ Flock Book - 1; ftm.

Telecare Services Association (TSA) 1994
NR Membership Services Centre, Wilmslow House (suite 8),
    Grove Way, WILMSLOW, Cheshire, SK9 5AG. (hq)
    01625 520320
    email admin@telecare.org.uk
    The Secretary
▲ Company Limited by Guarantee
○ *T; to set standards for providers; to improve the available
    hardware & software for development in telemedicine,
    telehealth & eHealth in the UK
Gp Education; Technical; Training
● Conf - Mtgs - ET - Exhib - Stat - LG
M 126 f
¶ NL - 8; ftm only.
✕ 2009 (merged) United Kingdom eHealth Association

Telecommunications Heritage Group (THG) 1986
■ Dalton House, 60 Windsor Avenue, LONDON, SW19 2RR.
    (mem/sp)
    0330 321 1844
    email membership@thg.org.uk http://www.thg.org.uk
    Mem Sec: Alex Clark
▲ Un-incorporated Society
○ *L; to bring together all those engaged in the study,
    preservation and collection of the heritage of
    communications
● Mtgs - ET - Res - Exhib - SG - Inf - Lib - VE
M 400 i
¶ Telecommunications Heritage Jnl - 4; ftm only.

© CBD Research Ltd · Beckenham · BR3 5JS · Tel 020 8650 7745 · E-mail cbd@cbdresearch.com · www.cbdresearch.com

Telecommunications & Internet Federation   (TIF)
IRL   Confederation House, 84-86 Lower Baggot St, DUBLIN 2,
         Republic of Ireland.   (hq)
         353 (1) 605 1582   fax 353 (1) 638 1582
         email tif@ibec.ie   http://www.tif.ie
         Dir: Shane Dempsey
○   *P; the representative body for leading industry & associated
         interest groups in the field of electronic communications
<   Ir Business & Emplrs Confedn (IBEC)
M   70 f

Telecommunications UK Fraud Forum Ltd   (TUFF)   2000
NR   PO Box 28353, LONDON, SE20 7WJ.   (hq)
         020 8778 9864   fax 020 8659 9561
         email tuff@tuff.co.uk   http://www.tuff.co.uk
         Chief Exec: Jack Wraith
▲   Company Limited by Guarantee
○   *G, *T; to provide a forum for the exchange of information
         between telecom companies in respect to fraud & crime; to
         provide training for the telecom professional
Gp   Communications & operations; Premium rate services;
         Technical research & programs; Training
●   Mtgs - ET - Exam - Res - SG - Inf - LG
<   Ir Telecommunications Fraud Forum
M   150 i, 45 f, 5 org
¶   The Jnl - 2; ftm only.   In the Frame (NL) - 5; free.

Telecommunications Users' Association
         in October 2007 merged with the **Communications Management
         Association**

Telephone Helplines Association
         since October 2009 **Helplines Association**

Television & Radio Industries Club   (TRIC)   1931
NR   Hill Farm, Margaretting Rd, GALLEYWOOD, Essex, CM2 8TS.
         (hq)
         01245 290480   fax 01245 265963
         email info@tric.org.uk   http://www.tric.org.uk
         Sec: George Stone
○   *P

Telework Association   (TA)   1992
NR   61 Charterhouse Rd, ORPINGTON, Kent, BR5 9EN.   (regd off)
         0800 616008
         http://www.telework.org.uk
         Devt Dir: Shirley Borrett
▲   Company Limited by Guarantee
○   *G; to promote flexible and remote working and provide
         services to individuals and organisations involved in telework
●   Conf - Res - Inf & advice line - Networking with mem
M   2,000 i, 100 f, UK / 100 i, 20 f, o'seas
¶   Teleworker (Jnl) - 6; £34.50 yr.
         Teleworking Handbook - 1; £16.
         (Sub: £34.50)

Ten Sixty Six Enterprise   1993
NR   Summerfields Business Centre, Bohemia Rd, HASTINGS,
         E Sussex, TN34 1UT.   (hq)
         01424 205500   fax 01424 205501
         http://www.1066enterprise.co.uk
         Chief Exec: Graham Marley
▲   Company Limited by Guarantee
○   *C; the chamber of commerce for the Hastings & St Leonards
         area, the enterprise agency for Hastings & Rother
M   f

Tenant Farmers' Association Ltd   (TFA)   1981
■   5 Brewery Court, Theale, READING, Berks, RG7 5AJ.   (hq)
         0118-930 6130   fax 0118-930 3424
         email tfa@tfa.org.uk   http://www.tfa.org.uk
         Chief Exec: George Dunn
▲   Company Limited by Guarantee
Br   9
○   *F
Gp   Listed land agents; Professional legal advice
●   Conf - Mtgs - Exhib - Stat - Inf - VE - LG
M   c 4,000 i
         (Sub: c£65-£370, dependent on size of farm)
¶   TFA News Sheet - 6;   Briefing Notes - 52;
         Information Sheets - irreg; all ftm only.

**Tenants & Residents Organisations of England   (TAROE)
1997**
NR   Jackson House, 2nd Avenue, RUNCORN, Cheshire,
         WA7 2PD.   (hsb)
         01928 701001
         http://www.taroe.org
         Sec: Cora Carter
▲   Company Limited by Guarantee
○   *N; the representative body of tenants & residents groups,
         associations & federations in England relating to housing
●   Conf - Mtgs - Inf - Lib - Support for tenants
<   Intl U of Tenants
M   10 i, 90 org
                @

Tennis & Rackets Association   (TandRA)   1907
NR   The Queen's Club, Palliser Rd, LONDON, W14 9EQ.   (hq)
         020 7835 6937   fax 020 7385 8920
         email office@tennisandrackets.com
         http://www.tennisandrackets.com
         Chief Exec: C S Davies
○   *S; to act as the national governing body in Great Britain in all
         matters connected with the games of real tennis & rackets
Gp   Rackets; 'Real' tennis

Tennis Scotland   1895
■   177 Colinton Rd, EDINBURGH, EH14 1BZ.   (hq)
         0131-444 1984   fax 0131-444 1973
         http://www.tennisscotland.org
         Chief Exec: David Marshall
▲   Registered Charity
○   *S; controlling body of the game in Scotland
●   Mtgs - ET - Comp
<   Lawn Tennis Assn
M   9 district org
¶   Scottish Tennis - 4/6; free.

Tennis Wales
NR   Welsh National Tennis Centre, Ocean Way, Ocean Park,
         CARDIFF, CF24 5HF.   (hq)
         029 2046 3335
         email info@tenniswales.org.uk
         Exec Dir: Peter Hybart
○   *S; to promote & develop tennis in Wales
●   Mtgs - ET - Exam - Comp - Coaching
<   Lawn Tennis Assn
M   85 clubs

TenniscoachUK
         is the trading name of the **British Tennis COaches Association**

Tennyson Society   1960
■ Tennyson Research Centre, Central Library, Free School Lane, LINCOLN, LN2 1EZ.   (hsb)
01522 552862   fax 01522 552858
email kathleen.jefferson@lincolnshire.gov.uk
http://www.tennysonsociety.org.uk
Hon Sec: Miss K Jefferson
▲ Registered Charity
Br USA
○ *A, *L; life & work of Alfred, Lord Tennyson
● Conf - Mtgs - Exhib - Res - Inf - Lib - VE
< City University, New York (Victorian C'ee)
M 150 i, 20 universities & academic bodies, UK / 200 i, 130 universities, o'seas
¶ Tennyson Research Bulletin - 1; ftm.   AR.
Monographs & Occasional Papers (2 series) - 1; ftm.
Tape recordings & gramophone records.

Tenpin Bowling Proprietors Association of Great Britain (TBPA)   1966
■ 4 Goodacre Drive, Chandlers Ford, EASTLEIGH, Hants, SO53 4LG.   (hsp)
023 8026 1313   fax 023 8026 1313
email jashbridge@tiscali.co.uk
http://www.gotenpin.co.uk
Gen Sec: John Ashbridge
▲ Un-incorporated Society
○ *S, *T; to promote & develop tenpin bowling; to ensure that members accept international standards of the sport
● Mtgs - SG - Inf - Lib - LG
M 44 f

Tertiary Research Group   (TRG)   1969
NR 81 Crofton Lane, ORPINGTON, Kent, BR5 1HB.   (hsp)
email david@fossil.ws   http://www.trg.org
Hon Sec: David Ward
○ *L; to bring together amateur and professional geologists with an interest in the Tertiary period worldwide

Tescopoly Alliance   2005
■ c/o Banana Link, 42-58 St George's Street, NORWICH, NR3 1AB.
01603 765670
email info@tescopoly.org.uk   http://www.tescopoly.org
○ *N; an alliance of organisations to challenge the negative impacts of Tesco's behaviour & supply chain; the need to curb the power of supermarkets
M 7 org

Test Card Circle   (TCC)   1989
NR 175 Kingsknowe Rd North, EDINBURGH, EH14 2DY.   (sp)
http://www.testcardcircle.org.uk
○ *G; researching & archiving non-needletime music (ie that NOT available to the public) specifically used on TV trade test transmissions; Researching & archiving slide/photographs & other visual material (test cards, captions etc) & engineering test films shown throughout trade test periods; study of musical & technical aspects relevant 1947-1983
● Conf - Mtgs - Res - Comp - SG - Inf - Lib
M 200 i
¶ The Test Card Circle - 4; ftm only.

Tetbury Chamber of Commerce & Industry
NR PO Box 65, TETBURY, Glos, GL8 8YW.   (hq)
email peter@sureteam.co.uk
http://www.tetburychamber.org.uk
Chmn: Peter Hodgson
○ *C; to promote, advance & protect the commerce, trade, manufacturing & general commercial interests of Tetbury town & district
< Gloucestershire Cham of Comm & Ind
¶ NL - 12; ftm.

Tewkesbury Chamber of Commerce & Industry
NR c/o Thompson & Bancks LLP, 27 Church St, TEWKESBURY, Glos, GL20 5RH.   (pres/b)
01684 299633
email dcsb@tandblawt.co.uk
http://www.tewkesburychamber.co.uk
Pres: David Bloxham
○ *C
< Gloucestershire Cham of Comm & Ind

Textile Finishers' Association
closed 2009

Textile Institute International   1910
■ St James's Buildings (1st floor), 79 Oxford St, MANCHESTER, M1 6FQ.   (Intl hq)
0161-237 1188   fax 0161-236 1991
email tiihq@textileinst.org.uk   http://www.texi.org
Hon Sec: Elizabeth Fox
▲ Registered Charity
Br 2; 7 worldwide
○ *L, *P; for people involved in the textile, clothing & footwear industries worldwide
Gp Design & product marketing; Engineering & technical; Fibre science; Finishing; Floorcoverings; Human resources; Industrial; Knitting; Management & economics; Marketing; Narrow fabrics; Quality; Textiles; Weaving; Yarn; Young members
● Conf - Mtgs - Res - Exhib - Comp - SG - Stat - Inf - Lib - VE - LG
M 1,601 i, 48 f UK / 1,495 i, 51 f, o'seas
¶ Journal of the Textile Institute - 6; £60 m, £99 nm.
Textile Progress - 4; c £30 m, £45 nm.
Textiles Magazine - 4; ftm, £45 nm.
TI News (NL) - 4;   Membership Directory - 1;
LM (web-based) - continuous;   AR; all ftm only.

Textile Recycling Association   (TRA)   1913
■ PO Box 965, MAIDSTONE, Kent, ME17 3WD.   (sp)
0845 600 8276   fax 0845 600 8276
email info@textile-recycling.org.uk
http://www.textile-recycling.org.uk
Nat Liaison Mgr: Alan Wheeler
○ *T; interests of persons trading in discarded textiles
Gp Recyclatex (bonded textile recycling scheme)
● Conf - Mtgs - Inf - LG
< Bureau of Intl Recycling
M 45 f, UK / 4 f, o'seas
¶ Bulletins; m only.   LM;   AR; both free.
Recyclatex leaflet for local authorities.
Recyclatex booklet for schools.

Textile Services Association   (TSA)   1886
NR 3 Queen Sq, Bloomsbury, LONDON, WC1N 3AR.   (hq)
020 7843 9490   fax 020 7843 9491
email tsa@tsa-uk.org   http://www.tsa-uk.org
Chief Exec: Murray Simpson
▲ Company Limited by Guarantee
○ *T; for the drycleaning, laundry & textile rental industry
M i & f

© CBD Research Ltd · Beckenham · BR3 5JS · Tel 020 8650 7745 · E-mail cbd@cbdresearch.com · www.cbdresearch.com

Textile Society: for the study of the history, art & design of textiles   1981
- ■ PO Box 1012, ST ALBANS, Herts, AL1 9NE.   (mail/address)
  020 7539 7678
  email info@textilesociety.org.uk
  http://www.textilesociety.org.uk
- ▲ Registered Charity
- ○ *A; to unite scholars, designers, teachers, practitioners, artists, collectors & others who share an interest in the study of textile art, design & history
- Gp Collectors (advice on private collections)
- ● Conf - Mtgs - ET - Inf - VE
- M 350 i, 61 universities & museums, UK / 25 i, o'seas
  (Sub: £18 i, £35 org)
- ¶ Text (Jnl) - 1; ftm, £6 nm.   NL - 3;   AR; both ftm only.

Thalidomide Society Ltd   1962
- ■ [communication by telephone/e-mail only]
  01462 438212
  email info@thalsoc.demon.co.uk
  http://www.thalidomidesociety.co.uk
  Coordinator: Vivien Kerr
  tel 01462 438212; info@thalsoc.demon.co.uk
- ▲ Company Limited by Guarantee; Registered Charity
- ○ *W; to provide support & information to thalidomide & similarly impaired people
- ● Mtgs - Inf
- M 300 i
- ¶ The Independence (NL) - 2; ftm, £10 nm.
  Note: contact by telephone or email only.

Thame & Oxfordshire County Agricultural Association   1855
- NR 55 North St (suite 3), THAME, Oxon, OX9 3BH.   (hq)
  01844 212737
  email info@thameshow.co.uk
  http://www.thameshow.co.uk
  Exec Sec: Mike Howes
- ▲ Company Limited by Guarantee; Registered Charity
- ○ *F
- ● The Oxfordshire County & Thame Show
- < Assn of Show & Agricl Orgs

Thames Boating Trades Association
  2010 merged with the Thames Hire Cruiser Association to form BMF Thames Valley, a group of the **British Marine Federation**

Thames & Chilterns Vineyards' Association   (T&CVA)   1988
- ■ c/o Brightwell Vineyard, Rush Court, WALLINGFORD, Oxon, OX10 8LJ.   (chmn/p)
  01491 836586
  http://www.thameschilternsvineyards.org.uk
  Chmn: Bob Nielsen
- ▲ Un-incorporated Society
- ○ *T; to promote public interest in & knowledge of the wines of the region; membership is open to people interested in English wine
- Gp Amateur growers; Commercial vineyards
- ● Conf - Mtgs - ET - Comp - SG - Inf - VE
- < Confédn Eur Viticulture Indep; UK Vineyards Assn; English Wine Producers
- M c 100 i, 25 f
- ¶ NL - 4;   AR; both ftm only.

Thames Gateway (Kent) Chamber of Commerce
  closed January 2011

Thames Hire Cruiser Association
  2010 merged with the Thames Boating Trades Association to form BMF Thames Valley, a group of the **British Marine Federation**

Thames & Medway Canal Association   (TMCA)
- ■ Meadow View, Hodsoll Street, SEVENOAKS, Kent, TN15 7LA. (chmn/p)
  01732 823725
  email info@thamesmedway.co.uk
  http://www.thamesmedway.co.uk
  Chmn: Brian Macknish
- ▲ Registered Charity
- ○ *G; to promote the use of the Thames & Medway Canal as a multipurpose amenity

Thames Valley Chamber of Commerce & Industry   (TVCCi)   1993
- NR 467 Malton Ave, SLOUGH, Berks, SL1 4QU.   (hq)
  01753 870500   fax 01753 870501
  email slough@thamesvalleychamber.co.uk
  http://www.thamesvalleychamber.co.uk
  Chief Exec: Paul Briggs
- ▲ Company Limited by Guarantee
- Br 8 local chambers: Bracknell Forest, Buckinghamshire, Oxfordshire, Reading, Slough, Swindon, West Berkshire, Wokingham
- ○ *C
- ● Conf - Mtgs - ET - Exhib - Stat - Expt - Inf - Lib - LG
- < Brit Chams Comm
- M c 2,500 f
- ¶ Business Jnl - 6.   CCi News - 12.
  Directory - 1.

Thanet & East Kent Chamber Ltd
- NR Kent Innovation Centre, Millennium Way, BROADSTAIRS, Kent, CT10 2QQ.
  01843 609289
  http://www.tekc.co.uk
  CEO: David Foley
- ○ *C

The . . .
  Except for a few exceptions the word **The** has not been used to start the title of any organisation as this controls the left-hand margin of the text and puts the emphasis on the first noun of the title.

Theosophical Society in England   (TS)   1888
- ■ 50 Gloucester Place, LONDON, W1U 8EA.   (hq)
  020 7563 9817   fax 020 7935 9543
  email office@theosoc.org.uk
  http://www.theosoc.org.uk
  Nat Pres: Eric McGough
- ▲ Un-incorporated Society
- Br 39 lodges
- ○ *L; to form a nucleus of the universal brotherhood of humanity without distinction of race, creed, sex, caste or colour; to encourage study of comparative religion, philosophy & science; investigation of unexplained laws of nature & the powers latent in man
- ● Conf - Mtgs - SG - Inf - Lib - VE
- M 900 i
- ¶ Insight - 4; ftm, £10 UK, £15 o'seas
  Note: is a section of the International Theosophical Society (1875), Adyar, Madras 20, India.

Therapy Lecturers Association   (TLA)
- NR Chiswick Gate (2nd floor), 598-608 Chiswick High Rd, LONDON, W4 5RT.   (hq)
  0845 202 2941   fax 0844 779 8898
  email info@ctha.com   http://www.ctha.com
- ○ *P
- M c 9,000 i

Thermal Insulation Contractors Association (TICA) 1957

NR TICA House, Allington Way, Yarm Road Business Park,
   DARLINGTON, Co Durham, DL1 4QB.   (hq)
   01325 466704   fax 01325 487691
   email enquiries@tica-acad.co.uk
   http://www.tica-acad.co.uk
   Chief Exec: Ralph Bradley
▲ Company Limited by Guarantee
○ *T; for companies involved in industrial thermal insulation &
   asbestos removal
Gp Asbestos control & abatement division (ACAD); Insulation &
   environmental training agency (IETA)
● Conf - Mtgs - ET - Inf - Empl - LG
< Wld Insulation & Acoustics Congress Org (WIACO); Fédn Eur
   des Syndicats d'Entreprises d'Isolation (FESI)
M 220 f, UK / 2 f, o'seas
¶ ACADdemy (asbestos removal) - 4; ftm, on application nm.
   FESI - European Insulation Standards; on application.
   Health & Safety Handbook for Operatives.
   Man-made Mineral Fibre (1990 IOM Report).

Thermal Insulation Manufacturers & Suppliers Association (TIMSA) 1978

■ Kingsley House, Ganders Business Park, Kingsley, BORDON,
   Hants, GU35 9LU.   (asa)
   01252 357844   fax 01252 357831
   email info@associationhouse.org.uk
   http://www.timsa.org.uk
   Sec: John G Fairley
○ *T; to improve standards of thermal insulation contributing to
   energy conservation & fuel efficiency
Gp Acoustics; Building insulation; Publicity; Technical
● Mtgs - LG
< Thermal Insulation Contractors Assn
M 18 i, 4 i (associates)
¶ Insulation (Jnl) - 6.   Hbk & Directory - 3; free.

Thermal Spraying & Surface Engineering Association (TSSEA) 1984

■ 38 Lawford Lane, Bilton, RUGBY, Warks, CV22 7JP.   (hq)
   0844 804 6898   fax 0844 404 6899
   email info@tssea.org   http://www.tssea.co.uk
▲ Company Limited by Guarantee
○ *T; to promote the use & development of thermal (metal)
   spraying techniques used 1: to provide corrosion resistant
   coatings to structural steelwork, 2: to confer specific surface
   properties (wear/corrosion resistance, thermal protection,
   restore size)
Gp Euro-International standards; Health & safety
● Conf - Mtgs - ET - Exhib - SG - Inf - LG
< Inst of Materials
M 10 i, 75 f, 2 org, UK / 10 f, 1 org, o'seas
¶ Coatings (NL) - 4; free.

Thermostatic Mixing Valve Manufacturers' Association
   an association of **BEAMA Ltd**

Thimble Society of London 1981

■ 1 Cathcart St, LONDON, NW5 3BL.   (hq)
   020 7419 9562
   http://www.thimblesociety.com
   Sec: Bridget McConnel
○ *G; collection of antique sewing articles & thimbles
● Conf - Mtgs - Res - Inf
M 600 i, UK / 100 i, o'seas
¶ Magazine - 3.

Think Global
   an alternative title for **Development Education Association**

Thomas Hardy Society Ltd 1968

■ c/o Dorset County Museum, High West St, DORCHESTER,
   Dorset, DT1 1XA.   (accom/address)
   01305 251501   fax 01305 251501
   email info@hardysociety.org
   http://www.hardysociety.org
   Sec: Mike Nixon (01305 837331)
   Chmn: Dr Anthony Fincham
▲ Company Limited by Guarantee; Registered Charity
○ *A; promotion, study & appreciation of the works of Thomas
   Hardy
● Conf - Mtgs - Res
M 800 i, UK / 400 i, o'seas; universities, UK & o'seas
¶ The Thomas Hardy Jnl - 3; ftm, £4 nm.

Thomas Lovell Beddoes Society

   no longer an active organisation

Thomas Merton Society of Great Britain & Ireland (TMS-GBI) 1993

NR 3 Seaview Cottages, Spittal, BERWICK upon TWEED,
   Northumbria, TD15 2QS.   (mem/sp)
   http://www.thomasmertonsociety.org
   Mem Sec: Stephen Dunhill
▲ Un-incorporated Society
○ *A; to encourage the study of the life & works of Thomas
   Merton (1915-1968) poet, monk & prophet

Thomas Paine Society UK (TPS) 1963

NR 19 Charles Rowan House, Margery St, LONDON,
   WC1X 0EH.   (hsp)
   020 7833 1395
   http://www.thomaspainesocietyuk.org.uk
   Sec: Barbara Jacobson
▲ Un-incorporated Society
○ *L; to promote the recognition of Thomas Paine (1737-1809) &
   his contribution to the cause of freedom; to spread a
   knowledge of his work & activities with a view to encouraging
   the growth of a similar spirit of constructive criticism in every
   aspect of public life
● Conf (lecture) - Mtgs
M i00 i, UK / 30 i, o'seas
   (Sub: £15)
¶ NL.   Books, Poems & other writings.

Thoresby Society 1889

NR Claremont, 23 Clarendon Rd, LEEDS, W Yorks, LS2 9NZ.   (hq)
   0113-247 0704
   http://www.thoresby.org.uk
▲ Registered Charity
○ *L; history of Leeds & its neighbourhood
● Mtgs - Lib - VE - Publishing
M 461 i, 54 libraries, UK / 6 i, 42 libraries, o'seas
¶ Annual Volume; ftm, price on application nm.

Thoroton Society of Nottinghamshire 1897

■ Little Dower House, Station Rd, BLEASBY, Notts, NG14 7FX.
   (hsp)
   01636 830284
   email bjcast@aol.com   http://www.thorotonsociety.org.uk
   Hon Sec: Barbara Cast
▲ Registered Charity
○ *L; to promote & foster study of the history, archaeology &
   antiquities of Nottinghamshire
Gp Archaeological; Record
● Mtgs - Res - VE
M c 500 i
¶ NL - 4;   Transactions - 1;   AR - 1; Record Series; all ftm.

© CBD Research Ltd · Beckenham · BR3 5JS · Tel 020 8650 7745 · E-mail cbd@cbdresearch.com · www.cbdresearch.com

Thoroughbred Breeders' Association (TBA) 1917
■ Stanstead House, 8 The Avenue, NEWMARKET, Suffolk,
   CB9 9AA. (hq)
   01638 661321
   http://www.thetba.co.uk
   Chief Exec: Louise Kemble
▲ Registered Charity
○ *B; the science of maintaining the thoroughbred horse in Great
   Britain
● Mtgs - ET - Res - Expt - Inf - Lib - VE - LG - Prizes & awards
< Eur Fedn of Thoroughbred Breeders' Assns (EFTBA);
   is a member of the Brit Horse Ind Confedn
M 2,400 i, UK / 400 i, o'seas
¶ Thoroughbred Owner & Breeder;
   Thoroughbred Stallion Guide; both ftm.

Three Counties Agricultural Society (TCAS) 1797
■ The Showground, MALVERN, Worcs, WR13 6NW. (hq)
   01684 584900
   email info@threecounties.co.uk
   http://www.threecounties.co.uk
▲ Company limited by Guarantee; Registered Charity
○ *F, *H; promotion of agriculture & horticulture in the
   Gloucestershire, Herefordshire & Worcestershire
Gp C'ees: Dog show, Flower, Livestock
● Conf - Mtgs - ET - Exhib - Comp - Shows
< Assn of Show & Agricl Orgs
M c 5,500 i & f
¶ Members' News;   AR; both ftm.

Three Counties Cider & Perry Association (3CCPA) 1993
■ Gregg's Pit, Much Marcle, LEDBURY, Herefords, HR8 2NL.
   (hsp)
   01531 660687
   email helen.woodman@hotmail.co.uk
   http://www.thethreecountiesciderandperry
   association.co.uk
   Hon Sec: Helen Woodman
▲ Un-incorporated Society
○ *T; for top quality cider & perry makers
● Mtgs - ET - Comp - VE
< Nat Assn of Cider Makers (NACM)
M c 80 i, f & org
¶ NL - 4;   Technical Bulletin - 1;   LM - 1; all ftm only.

THRIVE 1978
NR Geoffrey Udall Centre, Trunkwell Park, Beech Hill, READING,
   RG7 2AT. (hq)
   0118-988 5688   fax 0118-988 5677
   email info@thrive.org.uk   http://www.thrive.org.uk
   Chief Exec: Nicola Carruthers
▲ Company Limited by Guarantee; Registered Charity
Br 4 gardens
○ *W; to promote the use of horticulture & gardening in therapy,
   rehabilitation, vocational training, leisure & employment for
   all disabled people (includes people with mental health
   problems, sensory, physical or learning disabilities)
Gp Advisory committee of blind gardeners; Full-time volunteers;
   Garden advisoryservice; Service for projects; Training service
● ET - Exam - Res - Inf - Lib - PL
< R Horticl Soc
M 800 i, 40 org, UK / 120 i, o'seas
¶ Growth Point - 4; ftm, £10 nm.
   Come Gardening (braille & tape only) - 4; £5 m only.
   Leaflets; prices vary.

Thyroid Eye Disease Charitable Trust (TEDct) 1990
■ PO Box 1928, BRISTOL, BS37 0AX. (hq)
   0844 800 8133
   email ted@tedct.co.uk   http://www.tedct.co.uk
   Contact: Margaret Russell
▲ Registered Charity
Br 13 support groups
○ *M, *W; to provide information, care & support to those
   affected by the disease; to promote better awareness of the
   condition amongst the medical profession & the general
   public
Gp Medical helpline of consultants
● Conf - ET - Res - Inf
< Thyroid Fedn Intl; Brit Thyroid Assn
M c 700 i
¶ NL - 4; free.

Tiga: the Independent Games Developers Association (TIGA) 2001
NR 1 London Wall (6th floor), LONDON, EC2Y 5EB.
   0845 094 1095   fax 0845 094 1095
   email info@tiga.org   http://www.tiga.org
   Chief Exec: Dr Richard Wilson
○ *T; for the computer games industry
M 157 f

Tile Association (TTA) 2000
■ 83 Copers Cope Rd, BECKENHAM, Kent, BR3 1NR. (hq)
   020 8663 0946   fax 020 8663 0949
   email info@tiles.org.uk   http://www.tiles.org.uk
   Exec Officer: Mrs Lesley Day
▲ Company Limited by Guarantee
○ *T; to represent manufacturers, suppliers & tiling contractors in
   the UK wall & floor tile industry
Gp Distributors, retailers & agents of wall & floor tiles; Tile adhesive
   & accessory manufacturers; Tiling contractors
● Conf - Mtgs - Exam - Inf - Empl - LG
< Ceram-Unie; CET; EUF
M 750 f

Tiles & Architectural Ceramics Society (TACS) 1981
■ c/o Potteries Museum, Bethesda St, STOKE-ON-TRENT, Staffs,
   ST1 3DW. (mail)
   email info@tilesoc.org.uk   http://www.tilesoc.org.uk
▲ Registered Charity
○ *G, *L; to promote the study & conservation of tiles &
   architectural ceramics
● Conf - Res - Exhib - SG - Inf - VE - Tile location index
M c 420 i, f & org
¶ TACS Jnl - 1;   Glazed Expressions - 3;   both ftm,
   charged to nm.
   Tour Notes.   Tile Bibliography - up-dated.

** Timber Arbitrators Association
   Organisation lost; see Introduction paragraph 3

Timber Decking Association (TDA) 1999

■ 5c Flemming Court, CASTLEFORD, W Yorks, WF10 5HW. (hq)
01977 558147
email info@tda.org.uk   http://www.tda.org.uk
Dir: Steve Young
▲ Company Limited by Guarantee
○ *T; technical & advice organisation established to set standards for the quality of materials & installation good practice in the UK; operates 'Deckmark'- a quality assurance scheme for products & contractors involved in timber deck design & construction
Gp Design installation; Forest & sawmilling; Manufacturing; Preservatives & coating
● ET - Stat - PL - LG - Promotion of standards
< Wood Protection Assn
M 22 f, 2 org
¶ The Timber Decking Manual; ftm, £32 nm.
An Introduction to Creating Quality Decks; free.
Parapet Design; ftm, £5 nm.
Statutory Regulations; free.
Decking - the essential guide for DIY; £5.99.

Timber Packaging & Pallet Confederation (TIMCON) 1940

NR 840 Melton Rd, Thurmaston, LEICESTER, LE4 8BN. (asa)
0116-264 0579   fax 0116-264 0141
email timcon@associationhq.org.uk
http://www.timcon.org
▲ Company Limited by Guarantee
○ *T; to represent the timber packaging industry
● Conf - Mtgs - ET - Exhib - Stat - Inf
< Eur Fedn of Wooden Pallet & Packaging Mfrs (FEFPEB); Brit Nat C'ee for EPAL - Eur Pallet Assn)(BREPAL)
M 110 f, UK / 20 f, o'seas

Timber Research & Development Association
operates as **TRADA Technology Ltd**

Timber Trade Federation (TTF) 1893

NR The Building Centre, 26 Store St, LONDON, WC1E 7BT. (hq)
020 3205 0067   fax 020 7291 5379
email ttf@ttf.co.uk   http://www.ttf.co.uk
Chief Exec: John White
Br 7
○ *T; to promote the use of wood through innovative industry representation; to provide business support for TTF members
< Construction Products Assn

Time Haiku 1994

■ Basho-an, 105 King's Head Hill, LONDON, E4 7JG. (hsp)
020 8529 6478
email facey@aol.com
Sec: Erica Facey
▲ Un-incorporated Society
○ *A; to promote haiku & related forms (Japanese poetry & prose); to increase accessibility through education
● ET - Yearly reading
M 50-200 i
(Sub: £10 UK / £12 o'seas)
¶ Time Haiku - 2; ftm.

Timeshare Consumers Association (TCA) 1997

■ Nornay, BLYTH, Notts, S81 8HG. (hq)
01909 591100   fax 01909 591338
email info@timeshare.org.uk
http://www.timeshare.org.uk
○ *G; to help make timeshare an enjoyable, value-for-money form of holidaying for consumers

Tissue Viability Nurses Association
in 2009 the Tissue Viability Nurses Association & the Wound Care Society merged to form the **Wound Care Alliance**

Tissue Viability Society 1981

■ 210 Capella House, CARDIFF, Glamorgan, CF10 4RE. (hq)
email tissue.viability@btinternet.com
http://www.tvs.org.uk
Professional Adviser: Michael Clark
▲ Registered Charity
○ *L, *M; to disseminate information relating to the development of wound prevention & healing (tissue viability); to raise awareness of classic & contemporary research to tissue viability; to provide examples of all aspects of peer accepted best practice
● Conf - Mtgs - ET - Res - Exhib - Inf
< Eur Wound Mgt Assn
M 1,100 i, 100 f, UK / 50 i, 20 f, o'seas
(Sub: £30 i, £140 f, UK / £40 i, o'seas)
¶ Jnl of Tissue Viability - 4; ftm, £70 nm.

Toastmasters of England

no longer in existence

Toastmasters of Great Britain

no longer in existence

Toastmasters for Royal Occasions

no longer in existence

Tobacco Industry Employers' Association

closed in 2010

Tobacco Manufacturers' Association (TMA) 1940

■ Burwood House (5th floor), 14-16 Caxton St, LONDON, SW1H 0ZB. (hq)
020 7544 0100   fax 020 7544 0117
email information@the-tma.org.uk
http://www.the-tma.org.uk
Chief Exec: Christopher Ogden
▲ Un-incorporated Society
○ *T; for companies manufacturing tobacco products in the UK
● Mtgs - Inf - LG
< Confedn of the Eur Community's Cigarette Mfrs (CECCM)
M 3 f
¶ Briefing - 3 to 4; free.

Tobacco Retailers Alliance 1984

■ PO Box 61705, LONDON, SW1H 0XS. (hq)
0800 008282
http://www.tobaccoalliance.org.uk
Nat Spokesman: Ken Patel
○ *K; to raise awareness of the issue of tobacco smuggling & the detrimental effects this has on independent retailers
● Conf - Mtgs - Res - VE - LG
M 17,000 i

Together: working for wellbeing 1879

■ 12 Old St, LONDON, EC1V 9BE. (hq)
020 7780 7300   fax 020 7780 7301
email contactus@together-uk.org
http://www.together-uk.org
Chief Exec: Liz Felton
▲ Registered Charity
○ *W; provides high quality services in the community, hospitals & prisons for people with mental health needs & their carers
M c 150 i
¶ AR; free.

© CBD Research Ltd · Beckenham · BR3 5JS · Tel 020 8650 7745 · E-mail cbd@cbdresearch.com · www.cbdresearch.com

Token Corresponding Society   (TCS)   1972
- ■ 40 Woodlands Avenue, NEW MALDEN, Surrey, KT3 3UQ.   (sp)
    email tim.everson@btinternet.com
  Editor: David Young
- ▲ Un-incorporated Society
- ○ *G; for all interested in British tokens, tickets, tallies & checks
- ● Res
- M 180 i, UK / 12 i, o'seas
- ¶ Bulletin - 4; m only.

Tolkien Society   (TS)   1969
- ■ 655 Rochdale Rd, Walsden, TODMORDEN, Lancs,
    OL14 6SX.   (h/mem/sp)
    email tolksoc@tolkiensociety.org
    http://www.tolkiensociety.org
  Mem Sec: Marion Kershaw
- ▲ Registered Charity; Un-incorporated Society
- Br 23; Australia, Brazil, Canada, Germany, Italy, Malta, Mexico,
    Netherlands, Taiwan, USA
- ○ *A; to promote research into the life & works of J R R Tolkien
- Gp Nigglings (fiction); Quettar (linguistics); The Tolkien collector
    (book collecting)
- ● Conf - Mtgs - Exhib - Lib - Archives
- < Alliance of Literary Socs
- M 613 i, 3 org, UK / 502 i, 18 org, o'seas
    (Sub: £21 i, £23 f & org, UK / £24-29, o'seas airmail)
- ¶ Mallorn (Jnl) - 1;
    Anon Hen (NL) - 6; both ftm, £22 nm (UK).

Tools for Self Reliance   (TFSR)   1979
- ■ Netley Marsh, SOUTHAMPTON, Hants, SO40 7GY.   (hq)
    023 8086 9697
  Chief Exec: Janice Kidd
- ▲ Company Limited by Guarantee; Registered Charity
- Br 65
- ○ *K; volunteers refurbish & ship handtools & sewing machines to
    village development groups in some of the poorest
    communities in Africa
- ● Conf - Exhib - Collection of tools
- M 300 i, UK / 50 i, o'seas
- ¶ Forging Links - 3.   AR - 1.

Tools & Trades History Society   (TATHS)   1983
- ■ Woodbine Cottage, Budleigh Hill, EAST BUDLEIGH, Devon,
    EX9 7DT.   (mem/sp)
    01395 443030
    email membership@taths.org.uk   http://www.taths.org.uk
  Mem Sec: W Rose
- ▲ Registered Charity
- ○ *G, *L; 'to further the knowledge & understanding of hand-
    tools & the trades & persons that used them'
- ● Conf - Mtgs - Exhib - Inf - Lib - VE
- M 348 i, 21 org, UK / 58 i, 9 org, o'seas
- ¶ Tools & Trades (Jnl) - 1; ftm, £15 nm.   NL - 4; ftm.

Torbay Chamber of Commerce
    alternative name of the **South Devon Chamber of Commerce**

Tornado & Storm Research Organisation   (TORRO)   1974
- NR 20 Massey Avenue, LYMM, Cheshire, WA13 0PJ.   (hsp)
    07813 075509
    email sam.hall@torro.org.uk   http://www.torro.org.uk
  Hon Sec: Samantha Hall
- ▲ Un-incorporated Society
- ○ *L, *Q; to research into severe weather in the UK; to document,
    archive & research severe weather events: Tornadoes & other
    whirlwinds; Severe thunderstorms & hail; Heavy rain, floods,
    snowstorms & blizzards; Ball lightning & other lightning
    incidents
- Gp Divisions: Ball lightning, Blizzards & heavy snowfalls, Coastal
    impacts, Extreme rainfall, Flash floods, Hailstorm, Lightning
    impacts, Thunderstorm census, Tornadoes & other
    whirlwinds, Weather disasters
- ● Conf - Mtgs - ET - Res - Stat - Inf - Lib - PL
- < Intl Jnl of Meteorology
- M c 400 worldwide
- ¶ International Jnl of Meteorology - 10; ftm, £38 nm.
    Convection - 2;   Members' Hbk - 1; both ftm only.
    [subscription £39.50].

Tortoise Trust   1986
- ■ BM Tortoise, LONDON, WC1N 3XX.   (asa)
    email tortoisetrust@aol.com   http://www.tortoisetrust.org
- ○ *V; provides sanctuary & hospital facilities for tortoises;
    educational material relating to tortoise welfare &
    conservation; carries out conservation projects overseas
- M i, f & org
- ¶ Jnl - 4.   NL - 6.
    Guide to Tortoises & Turtles - 1.

Tory Reform Group   (TRG)   1975
- ■ 83 Victoria St, LONDON, SW1H 0HW.   (hq)
    020 3008 4991
    email trg@trg.org.uk   http://www.trg.org.uk
  Contact: The Director
- ○ *K, *Z; to influence Conservative Party policy
- ● Conf - Mtgs - Res - Inf - LG
- M 'confidential'
- ¶ Reformer (Jnl) - 2.   Policy Papers - irreg.

Tourette Syndrome (UK) Association   (TSA(UK))   1980
- ■ Southbank House, Black Prince Rd, LONDON, SE1 7SJ.   (hq)
    020 7793 2356
    email enquiries@tsa.org.uk   http://www.tsa.org.uk
- ▲ Company Limited by Guarantee; Registered Charity
- ○ *W; to support people with the neurological disorder Tourette
    Syndrome throughout their lives, delivering appropriate
    information, practical help & opportunities for social contact;
    to educate & inform health & social care & other statutory
    agencies
- ● Conf - Mtgs - ET - Res - Inf
- M 660 i
    (Sub: £20)
- ¶ NL - 4;   AR; both ftm only.   Leaflets; free.
    Note: Trades as Tourettes Action.

Tourism for All UK
- ■ c/o Vitalise, Shap Rd Industrial Estate, Shap Rd, KENDAL,
    Cumbria, LA9 6NZ.
    0845 124 9973
    email info@tourismforall.org.uk
    http://www.tourismforall.org.uk
  Information Officer: Carrie-Ann Fleming
- ○ *K; accessible tourism

Tourism Alliance   2001
NR   Centre Point, 103 New Oxford St, LONDON, WC1A 1DU. (hq)
       020 7395 8246   fax 020 7395 8178
       email kurt.janson@tourismalliance.com
       http://www.tourismalliance.com
       Policy Dir: Kurt Janson
▲   Company Limited by Guarantee
○   *T; to work with & lobby government on all issues related to the growth of tourism & its contribution to the British economy
●   Conf - Mtgs - LG
M   46 org
¶   NL - 12;   AR - 1; both free.

Tourism Concern   1989
NR   Stapleton House, 277-281 Holloway Rd, LONDON, N7 8HN.   (hq)
       020 7133 3800   fax 020 7133 3331
       email info@tourismconcern.org.uk
       http://www.tourismconcern.org.uk
▲   Company Limited by Guarantee; Registered Charity
○   *G, *K; 'a UK-based organisation campaigning worldwide for just & sustainable tourism - tourism that is fairly traded'
●   Conf - ET - Res - Exhib
<   Ecumenical Coalition on Third World Tourism (ECTWT); Third World European Network (TEN)
M   i
¶   Tourism in Focus - 4.   Being There.
     The Good Alternative Travel Guide.

Tourism Management Institute   (TMI)   1997
■   18 Cuninghill Avenue, INVERURIE, Aberdeenshire, AB51 3TZ.   (hsp)
       01467 620769
       email secretary@tmi.org.uk   http://www.tmi.org.uk
       Hon Sec: Cathy Guthrie
▲   Company Limited by Guarantee
○   *P; 'the professional voice for tourism destination managers'
Gp   Panels: Education & training, Marketing, ICT
●   Conf - ET - LG
M   230 i, 14 f, UK / 3 i, o'seas
¶   The Tourism Manager (NL) - 3;   LM (website);
     TMI online (email NL) - 4; all m only.

Tourism Society Ltd   1977
NR   Trinity Court, 34 West St, SUTTON, Surrey, SM1 1SH.   (hq)
       020 8661 4636
       email admin@tourismsociety.org
       http://www.tourismsociety.org
       Exec Dir: Flo Powell
▲   Company Limited by Guarantee
○   *P; networking organisation for professionals working, or interested in, tourism
Gp   Association Tourism Teachers & Trainers (ATTT); Tourism Society Consultants' Group (TSCG)
●   Conf - Mtgs - Comp - Expt - Journal production
M   1,110 i, 2 f, UK / 100 i, o'seas
¶   Tourism - 4; ftm, £85 nm.
     Membership Executive - 1; free; £85 nm.

Town & Country Planning Association   (TCPA)   1899
NR   17 Carlton House Terrace, LONDON, SW1Y 5AS.   (hq)
       020 7930 8903   fax 020 7930 3280
▲   Registered Charity
○   *K; to promote a national policy of land-use planning

Townswomen's Guilds   (TG)   1929
■   Tomlinson House (1st floor), 329 Tyburn Rd, BIRMINGHAM, B24 8HJ.   (hq)
       0121-326 0400   fax 0121-326 1976
       email tghq@townswomen.org.uk
       http://www.townswomen.org.uk
▲   Registered Charity
○   *G, *K; a charitable organisation to educate women
Gp   National events; Public affairs; Sports & creative leisure
●   Conf - Mtgs - ET - Exhib - Comp - Stat - Inf - Lib - VE
M   35,000 i
¶   Townswoman - 4.

Towpath Action Group
NR   23 Hague Bar, NEW MILLS, Derbyshire, SK22 3AT.   (hsp)
       email andy@towpathtag.org   http://www.towpathtag.org
       Sec: Andy Screen
○   *K; campaigns for access to & along canals & rivers. Although based in the north west the group offers help to others similarly concerned with towpath access
●   Inf - LG

Toy Retailers Association   (TRA)   1950
■   207 Mercury House, Willoughby Drive, Foxby Lane Business Park, GAINSBOROUGH, Lincs, DN21 1DY.   (hq)
       0870 753 7437   fax 0870 706 0042
       email enquiries@toyretailersassociation.co.uk
       http://www.toyretailersassociation.co.uk
       Sec: Derek Markie
▲   Company Limited by Guarantee
○   *T
●   Conf - Exhib - Inf - LG
M   f

Tracheo-Oesophageal Fistula Support   (TOFS)   1982
■   St George's Centre, 91 Victoria Rd, Netherfield, NOTTINGHAM, NG4 2NN.   (hq)
       0115-961 3092   fax 0115-961 3097
       email info@tofs.org.uk   http://www.tofs.org.uk
       Office Mgr: Diane Stephens
▲   Registered Charity
○   *W; 'to offer support & information to the families & carers of babies born with tracheo-oesophageal fistula (TOF), oesophageal atresia (OA) & related conditions; the group enables families to benefit from the friendship of other parents who have experienced the particular stresses of caring for these children - as well as the joy when problems have been overcome'
●   Conf - Res - Inf - Support
M   1,016 i, 40 f, UK / 120 i, 13 f, o'seas
¶   Chew (NL) - 4;   AR; both free.
     We Just Want Our Daughter to Live; £9.99 m, £14.99 nm.
     The TOF Child; £9.99 m, £14.99 nm.

TRADA Technology Ltd   (TRADA)   1995
■   Stocking Lane, Hughenden Valley, HIGH WYCOMBE, Bucks, HP14 4ND.   (hq)
       01494 569600   fax 01494 565487
       email information@trada.co.uk   http://www.trada.co.uk
       Chief Exec: Andrew Abbott
▲   Company Limited by Guarantee
○   *Q; technical advice relating to the correct use of timber in construction
●   Conf - ET - Res - Exhib - Inf - PL
M   i, f & org
¶   Ybk;   AR; both ftm.   Numerous technical publications.
     Note: carries out all the activities of the Timber Research & Development Association.

Trade Association Forum   (TAF)   1997
NR   Centre Point, 103 New Oxford St, LONDON, WC1A 1DU.
     (hq)
     020 7395 8283   fax 020 7395 8178
     http://www.taforum.org
     Manager: Linda Cavender
○   *N; promotion of trade associations & best practice in the UK
●   Conf - Mtgs - ET - Res - Comp - Inf - LG
<   CBI
M   300 trade associations
¶   Managing Trade Associations by Mark Boleat; £25.

Trade Marks, Patents & Designs Federation   1920
■   63-66 Hatton Garden (5th floor), LONDON, EC1N 8LE.   (hq)
     020 7242 3923   fax 020 7242 3924
     email admin@ipfederation.com
     http://www.ipfederation.com
     Pres: James Hayles
▲   Company Limited by Guarantee
○   *T; to express the views of industry on intellectual property
     matters
●   Mtgs - LG
<   CBI
M   36 f
¶   Trends & Events - 1; free.
     since 2009 has used the operating name IP Federation

Trade & Professional Publishers Association   1976
IRL 31 Deansgrange Rd, BLACKROCK, Co Dublin, Republic of
     Ireland.
     353 (1) 289 3305   fax 353 (1) 289 6406
     Chmn: David Markey
○   *T

Trade Publishers Council
     a group of the **Publishers Association**

Trade Union Badge Collectors Society   (TUBCS)   1985
■   30 Richmond Grove, NORTH SHIELDS, Tyne & Wear,
     NE29 7QZ.   (sp)
     email tabcs@yahoo.co.uk
     http://www.unionbadges.wordpress.com
     Sec: Andy Redpath
▲   Un-incorporated Society
○   *G; to promote a wider appreciation of trade union badges
     and ephemera
●   Res - Exhib - Inf - Lib
M   i
¶   Trade Union Badge Collectors News (NL).
     Symbols of Solidarity (Jnl).

Trades Union Congress   (TUC)   1868
NR   Congress House, Great Russell St, LONDON, WC1B 3LS.   (hq)
     020 7636 4030
     email info@tuc.org.uk   http://www.tuc.org.uk
     Gen Sec: Brendan Barber
Br   8
○   *U
M   58 unions

Trading Standards Institute   (TSI)   1892
■   1 Sylvan Court, Sylvan Way, Southfields Business Park,
     BASILDON, Essex, SS15 6TH.   (hq)
     0845 608 9400   fax 0845 608 9425
     email institute@tsi.org.uk   http://www.tsi.org.uk
     Chief Exec: Ron Gainsford
▲   Company Limited by Guarantee
○   *L, *P; to offer expertise & unique services to the wider
     consumer affairs sector & to businesses in consumer markets
Gp   History pen circle (historical metrology)
●   Conf - Mtgs - ET - Exam - Res - Exhib - Comp - SG - Stat - Inf -
     Lib - VE - LG
M   3,500 i
¶   Trading Standards Today - 12.
     Trading Standards Appointments - 12.

Traditional Cosmology Society   (TCS)   1984
■   c/o School of Scottish Studies, University of Edinburgh,
     27 George Sq, EDINBURGH, EH8 9LD.   (h/pres/b)
     0131-650 4152   fax 0131-650 4163
     email e.lyle@ed.ac.uk
     http://www.thisisthetcson.wordpress.co,
     Pres: Dr Emily Lyle
▲   Registered Charity
○   *L; to explore myth, religion & cosmology across cultural &
     disciplinary boundaries; to increase our understanding of
     world views past & present
●   Conf - Mtgs - Res
M   106 i, UK / 56 i, o'seas
¶   Cosmos (Jnl) - 2; ftm, £25 yr nm.

Traditional Farmfresh Turkey Association   (TFTA)   1984
■   PO Box 3041, EASTBOURNE, E Sussex, BN21 9EN.
     (admin/sp)
     01323 419671   fax 01323 419671
     http://www.totallytraditionalturkeys.com
     Sec: Emma Peters
○   *T; marketing & promoting slower growing breeds of turkey,
     reared to full maturity, dry plucked & hung like a game bird
     for at least seven days
M   48 f

Traditional Housing Bureau
     an affiliated association of the **British Precast Concrete
     Federation**

**Traditional Music & Song Association of Scotland   (TMSA)
1966**
■   The Drill Hall (office G43), 30-38 Dalmeny St, EDINBURGH,
     EH6 8RG.   (hq)
     0131-555 2224
     email office@tmsa.org.uk   http://www.tmsa.org.uk
     Convenor: Douglas Craik
▲   Company Limited by Guarantee; Registered Charity
Br   11
○   *A; to nurture & maintain the indigenous traditional music and
     song of Scotland by working with practitioners, promoters,
     audiences, organisations & venues to present activities &
     develop interest, understanding & participation
●   Mtgs - ET - Comp - Inf - Concerts, festivals & events promoting
     traditional music & song in Scotland
M   617 i, 24 org
     (Sub: £15-20 i, £500, £50 org)

** **Traditional Youth Marching Bands Association**
     Organisation lost; see Introduction paragraph 3

Traffic Management Contractors Association (TCMA) 1898

NR   c/o Aggregate Industries, MERSTHAM, Surrey, RH1 3ES. (hq)
      020 8973 1777   fax 020 8973 1777
      http://www.tmca.org.uk
      Sec: P Crickmay.   Chmn: R Pearson
▲   Company Limited by Guarantee
○   *T; traffic management on high speed roads
●   Conf - Mtgs - Exhib - LG
M   12 f
¶   Notes for Guidance - irreg; ftm, £2 nm.

Trail Riders Fellowship (TRF) 1970

■   c/o Business Accountancy Consultants Ltd, 2 London Rd,
      Headington, OXFORD, OX3 7PA.   (regd off)
      email secretary@trf.org.uk   http://www.trf.org.uk
      Sec: Polly Cody
Br   45
○   *G, *K; 'a national, voluntary & non-competitive body formed
      by motorcyclists to preserve our heritage of green lanes &
      our right to use them'
●   Mtgs - Res - Exhib - Inf - VE - LG
<   Brit Motorcycle Fedn (BMF); Land Access & Recreation
      Assn (LARA); Motorcycle Action Gp (MAG); Nat Motorcycle
      Coun (NMC)
M   3,000 i
¶   Trail (Jnl) - 12;   TRF Hbk - 1; both ftm only.

Train Collectors Society (TCS) 1978

NR   PO Box 1329, HEMEL HEMPSTEAD, Herts, HP1 9JZ.   (mail)
      email memsec@traincollectors.co.uk
      http://www.traincollectors.co.uk
      Mem Sec: Tony Stanford
▲   Un-incorporated Society
○   *G; collection & restoration of model trains of any make, any
      age, any gauge
●   Mtgs - Exhib - Gatherings in Biggleswade, Sandy & Leicester
M   470 i, UK / 30 i, 2 org, o'seas
¶   TCS News - 4; £18 yr (£22 Europe)(£25 world) m only.
      Spares Directory (loose-leaf or CD) 2003; ftm.
      Archive CDs TCS News; £10 m, £20 nm.

Trakehner Breeders Fraternity (TBF) 1989

NR   Northlands Farm, Boat Lane, Great Ouseburn, YORK,
      YO26 9SJ.   (sec/p)
      01423 330780
      email stud_depris@tiscali.co.uk
      http://www.trakehnerbreeders.com
      Co Sec: Bev Brown
▲   Company Limited by Guarantee
○   *B; registration & promotion of the Trakehner horse in the UK
●   Mtgs - Inf - VE
<   Trakehner Verband (Germany)
M   220 i
      Note: the Fraternity's marketing name is Trakehners UK.

Tramway & Light Railway Society (TLRS) 1938

■   6 The Woodlands, BRIGHTLINGSEA, Essex, CO7 0RY.
      (memsec/p)
      07053 484647
      email tlrs.membership@tramwayinfo.com
      http://www.tramwayinfo.com
      Mem Sec: H J Leach
▲   Registered Charity
Br   18; Austria
○   *G; to advance education & knowledge in all facets of
      tramways; to encourage tramway modelling & exhibiting
●   Comp - Inf - Exhib - Lib - Mtgs - VE
M   1,000 i
¶   Tramfare - 6.

Tramway Museum Society (TMS) 1955

■   Crich Tramway Village, Crich, MATLOCK, Derbys, DE4 5DP.
      01773 854321
      Hon Sec: I M Dougill
▲   Company Limited by Guarantee; Registered Charity
○   *G; preservation & demonstration of the tramcar for museum
      purposes (by mobile operation in a period setting) &
      associated historical research
●   Exhib - Res - Inf - Museum
<   Assn Indep Museums; Assn Brit Transport & Engg Museums;
      Transport Trust; Heart of England Tourist Bd
M   c 1,800 i
¶   Jnl - 4;   Contact (NL) - 12;   AR; all ftm.
      Tramway Museum Guidebook.

Trans-Antarctic Association 1960

NR   British Antarctic Survey, Madingley Rd, CAMBRIDGE,
      CB3 0ET.   (hsb)
      01223 221400 (switchboard)
○   *L, *Q; furthering research in subjects relating to Antarctica
●   Awarding grants
M   5 i (committee of management), UK / i, o'seas.

Transform Scotland

NR   5 Rose St, EDINBURGH, EH6 6RD.
      0131-243 2690
      email info@transformscotland.org.uk
      http://www.transformscotland.org.uk
      Dir: Colin Howden
○   *K; sustainable transport

Transfrigoroute UK Ltd (TUK) 1984

NR   Sanderum House, Oakley Rd, CHINNOR, Oxon, OX39 4TW.
      (hq)
      01844 355560
      email secretary@transfrigoroute.co.uk
      http://www.transfrigoroute.co.uk
      Sec: Liam E W Olliff
▲   Company Limited by Guarantee
Br   24 o'seas
○   *T; promotes & coordinates the interests of operators & users of
      temperature-controlled transport
●   Conf - Mtgs - Res - Stat - Expt - Inf - LG
<   Transfrigoroute Intl
M   c 120 f
¶   TUK Talk (NL).   Code of Conduct.

Translators Association (TA) 1958

■   84 Drayton Gardens, LONDON, SW10 9SB.   (hq)
      020 7373 6642   fax 020 7373 5768
      email info@societyofauthors.org
      http://www.societyofauthors.org
      Sec: Sarah Baxter
○   *P, *U; a specialist unit of the Society of Authors, exclusively
      concerned with the interests & problems of writers who
      translate foreign literary, dramatic or technical work into
      English for publication or performance
●   Mtgs - Inf
<   Fédn Intle des Traducteurs (FIT); Eur Coun of Literary Translators
      Assns (CEATL)
M   420 i, UK / 60 i, o'seas
¶   The Author - 4.   In Other Words - 2.

© CBD Research Ltd · Beckenham · BR3 5JS · Tel 020 8650 7745 · E-mail cbd@cbdresearch.com · www.cbdresearch.com

Transparency International (UK) (TI(UK)) 1994
- ■ CAN Mezzanine, 32-36 Loman St, LONDON, SE1 0EH.   (hq)
  020 7785 6356   fax 020 7785 6355
  email info@transparency.org.uk
  http://www.transparency.org.uk
  Chmn: Laurence Cockcroft
  Co Sec: Mrs J Lanigan
- ▲ Company Limited by Guarantee; Registered Charity
- ○ *K; a non-profitmaking, independent, non-governmental
  organisation dedicated to increasing government
  accountability & to curbing national & international
  corruption
- ● Conf - Mtgs - Res
- < Transparency International (Berlin)
- M c 150 i, c 25 f
- ¶ (for publications see website)

Transplant Support Network 1995
- NR 6 Kings Meadow Drive, WETHERBY, W Yorks, LS22 7FS.
  0800 027 4490   fax 01937 585434
  email tsnetwork@tiscali.co.uk
  http://www.transplantsupportnetwork.org.uk
- ▲ Registered Charity
- ○ *W; to provide support (usually over the telephone) for patients
  & families & all concerned with transplants & mechanical
  implants

Transport Association (TA) 1955
- NR PO Box 374, LEATHERHEAD, Surrey, KT22 2EY.   (sb)
  0750 778 5845
  email marion@transportassociation.org.uk
  http://www.transportassociation.org.uk
- ○ *T
- ● Conf - Mtgs
- M c 60 f

Transport 2000 Ltd
   since 2007 **Campaign for Better Transport**

Transport Salaried Staffs' Association (TSSA) 1897
- NR Walkden House, 10 Melton St, LONDON, NW1 2EJ.   (hq)
  020 7387 2101   fax 0141 332 9879
  email enquiries@tssa.org.uk   http://www.tssa.org.uk
  Gen Sec: Gerry Doherty
- ○ *U; for clerical, supervisory, professional & technical employees
  of rail, shipping & bus companies, travel agencies, airlines,
  call centres & IT companies
- < Trades U Congress (TUC)
- M 28,298 i

Transport Ticket Society (TTS) 1946
- NR 6 Breckbank, Forest Town, MANSFIELD, Notts, NG19 0PZ.
  (memsec/p)
  http://www.transport-ticket.org.uk
  Mem Sec: D Randell
- ▲ Un-incorporated Society
- ○ *G; for collectors of transport (principally bus, tram & train)
  tickets
- ● Mtgs - Res - Exhib - SG - Inf - Lib
- < Roads & Road Transport History Assn
- M 360 i
- ¶ Jnl - 12; ftm only.   Various occasional papers.

Transport Trust (TT) 1965
- ■ 202 Lambeth Rd, LONDON, SE1 7JW.   (hq)
  020 7928 6464   fax 020 7928 6565
  email nfo@transporttrust.com
  http://www.transporttrust.com
  Dir Gen: Col Anthony Walker
- ▲ Registered Charity
- ○ *G; to facilitate the preservation of items of transport of
  historical & technical interest (road, rail, air & water)
  including books, papers, ephemera & photographs
- Gp Air (civil & military); Inland waterways; Coastal waters;
  Railways; Road transport
- ● Conf - Res - Inf - Lib - VE
- < Heritage Railways (AIRPS); Assn Brit Transport Museums; The
  Maritime Trust; Vintage Sports-Car Club (VSCC); The
  Shuttleworth Trust
- M 600 i, 20 f, 150 org
- ¶ The Transport Digest (Jnl) - 3; ftm, 'normally free' nm.

Transport-Watch 2004
- ■ 12 Redland Drive, NORTHAMPTON, NN2 8QE.   (hq)
  01604 847438   fax 01604 455074
  email enquiries@transport-watch.co.uk
  http://www.transport-watch.co.uk
  Dir: Paul F Withrington
- ▲ Company Limited by Guarantee
- ○ *Q; 'research & development reference transport policy,
  particularly road & rail'
- Gp Congestion charging; Rail; Rapid transit; Traffic management;
  Transport policy
- ● Res - Stat
- M 10 i, UK / 1 i, o'seas

Transport on Water Association (TOW) 1975
- NR 11 Fairfield Ave, UPMINSTER, Essex, RM14 3AZ.   (contact/p)
  01708 221461
  Contact: Revd Canon F J Hackett
- ▲ Registered Charity
- ○ *K; to promote the use of river & canals for commercial traffic
- ● Inf - LG
- M 200 i, 21 f

Transverse Myelitis Society (TMS)
- NR 35 Avenue Rd, BRENTFORD, Middx, TW8 9NS.   (sec/p)
  020 8568 0350
  http://www.myelitis.org.uk
  Sec: Lew Gray
- ▲ Registered Charity
- ○ *W; to provide information & support to TM sufferers, their
  carers & families
- < Transverse Myetitis Assn (intl/US)
- M 750 i

Travel Retail Forum
   see **United Kingdom Travel Retail Forum**

Travel Trust Association Ltd (TTA) 1993
- ■ Albion House (3rd floor), High St, WOKING, Surrey,
  GU21 1BE.   (hq)
  0870 889 0577   fax 01483 730746
  email steve.clark@traveltrust.co.uk
  http://www.traveltrust.co.uk
  Dir: Stephen Jeffrey Clark
- ▲ Company Limited by Guarantee
- ○ *T; 'for the travel industry & regulatory body, coupled with
  commercial negotiations with suppliers'
- Gp Tour organisers; Travel agents
- ● Conf - Mtgs - ET - Res - Exhib - Stat - Inf - VE - LG
- < Inst Travel & Tourism (ITT)
- M 460 f
- ¶ NL - 4;   Fax Publications - 52; both ftm.

Treacher Collins Family Support Group
NR   114 Vincent Rd, NORWICH, Norfolk, NR1 4HH.
         01603 433736   fax 01603 433736
         http://www.treachercollins.net
         Sec: Sue Moore
○   *W; for sufferers of the syndrome which causes facial
         malformation & severe hearing loss

Trebuchet Society   1998
■   23 Viewside Close, Corfe Mullen, WIMBORNE, Dorset,
         BH21 3ST.   (hsp)
         01202 690224
         email richardbarton@caving5.freeserve.co.uk
         Sec: Richard Barton
▲   Un-incorporated Society
○   *G; research into early weaponry; designing & building replica
         weaponry; experiments into the effectiveness of early
         weaponry
Gp   Field research; Workshop; Research into trebuchet science;
         Computer database
●   Res - SG - Inf - PL - VE
<   Coalhouse Fort Project; Artillery Assn GB
M   6 i, 2 org

Tree Council of Ireland   1985
IRL   Seismograph House, Rathfarnham Castle, DUBLIN 14, Republic
         of Ireland.
         353 (1) 493 1313   fax 353 (1) 493 1317
         email trees@treecouncil.ie   http://www.treecouncil.ie
         Pres: Dorothy Hayden
○   *H

Tree & Hedging Group
         a group of the **Horticultural Trades Association**

Trefoil Guild
NR   17-19 Buckingham Palace Rd, LONDON, SW1W 0PT.   (hq)
         020 7834 6242
         email trefoilguilduk.org.uk
○   *G; for men & women who have been, & still are, connected
         with guiding & scouting; to offer practical help to Girlguiding
         UK
M   20, 000 i
¶   Trefoil Guild Hbk; £6.75.

Trekking & Riding Society of Scotland   (TRSS)   1992
■   Bruaich-na-h'Abhainne, Maragowan, KILLIN, Perthshire,
         FK21 8TN.   (hsp)
         01567 820909   fax 01567 820909
         email trss@btinternet.com
         http://www.ridinginscotland.com
         Chief Exec: Mrs Susan Howard
▲   Un-incorporated Society
○   *T; to encourage & assist in the development of all forms of
         equestrian tourism in Scotland; to set & maintain standards
         of excellence
●   Conf - Mtgs - ET - Exam - Res - Exhib - SG - Stat - Inf - LG
<   Brit Horse Soc (Scotland); Scot Equestrian Assn; Scot Tourism
         Forum
M   c 70 f
¶   Promotional brochure by Scottish Tourist Board.

Trevithick Society   1935
■   PO Box 62, CAMBORNE, Cornwall, TR14 7ZN.   (asa)
         01209 716811
         Hon Sec: George B Wilson
▲   Registered Charity
Br   2
○   *G, *L; the study of the history of technology in Cornwall & the
         preservation of buildings, machinery & sites connected with
         mining, engineering, china clay workings, transport, & any
         other industry carried on elsewhere where there are Cornish
         connections
●   Mtgs - ET - Res - PL - Organisation of King Edward Mine Ltd,
         which is responsible for the last group of remaining mine
         buildings at Camborne which are Grade II* listed; these are
         installed with historic tin extraction & separation machines &
         other relevant artifacts
<   Assn Indl Archaeology (AIA); Nat Assn of Mining History Orgs
M   400 i, 4 f, UK / 20 i, o'seas
¶   Jnl - 1; ftm, £5 nm.   NL - 4; ftm, £1.50 nm.

Triathlon England   2007
NR   PO Box 25, LOUGHBOROUGH, Leics, LE11 3WX.   (mail)
         01509 226161   fax 01509 226165
         email info@triathlonengland.org
         http://www.triathlonengland.org
         Chmn: Jem Lawson
▲   Company Limited by Guarantee
Br   9
○   *S; to govern, administer & develop the sport of triathlon by
         providing opportunities for athletes of all ages & abilities to
         compete at the highest level
<   Brit Triathlon Fedn
M   12,000 i in 555 clubs

triathlonscotland   2007
NR   Gannochy Sports Centre, University of Stirling, STIRLING,
         FK9 4LA.   (hq)
         01786 466921
         email admin@triathlonscotland.org
         http://www.triathlonscotland.org
         Chief Operating Offr: Jane Moncrieff
▲   Company Limited by Guarantee
○   *S; the national governing body for the sports of triathlon,
         duathlon & multi-sport in Scotland, providing a broad &
         comprehensive range of services to its members
<   Brit Triathlon Fedn
M   3,000 i in 46 clubs

Tricycle Association   (TA)   1928
NR   1 Meath Green Lane, HORLEY, Surrey, RH6 8EE.   (hsp)
         http://www.tricycleassociation.org.uk
         Nat Sec: Richard Bailey
○   *G, *S; to provide social & competitive activities for members.
         Membership is open to all past & present riders of the
         tricycle; defined as a humanly propelled machine making
         three tracks when in motion
●   Mtgs - Exhib - Comp - VE
<   Cycling Time Trials; Road Records Assn
M   400 i, UK / 35 i, o'seas
¶   Gazette - 4; ftm only.

© CBD Research Ltd · Beckenham · BR3 5JS · Tel 020 8650 7745 · E-mail cbd@cbdresearch.com · www.cbdresearch.com

Trigeminal Neuralgia Association United Kingdom   (TNA UK)   1999
- ■ PO Box 234, OXTED, Surrey, RH8 8BE.   (hq)
  01883 370214
  email tna@ntlbusiness.com   http://www.tna.org.uk
  Chmn: Jillie Abbott,   Sec: Cathy Fletcher
- ▲ Registered Charity
- ○ *W; to provide information & support to members; to raise awareness of TN (an extremely severe facial pain which tends to come & go without warning) amongst medical professionals and general public
- ● Conf - Mtgs - ET - Exhib - SG - Stat - Inf - Lib - LG
- < informal affiliation to TNS USA & TNSA Australia
- M 815 i, UK / 15 i, o'seas
- ¶ NL - 3;   Contact list (voluntary entries) - 1; both ftm only.
  Medical books; £17.50 each,   Information leaflets; free.

Trollope Society   1987
- ■ Maritime House, Old Town, Clapham, LONDON, SW4 0JW.
  (hq)
  020 7720 6789
  email info@trollopesociety.org
  http://www.trollopesociety.org
  Office Mgr: Pelham Ravenscroft
- ▲ Registered Charity
- ○ *A; to produce the first complete, uniform, edition of the novels of Anthony Trollope; to serve as a forum for discussions
- ● VE - Annual dinner - Lecture
- M 1,200 i, UK / 500 i, USA
- ¶ Trollopiana Jnl - 3;   Mailing - 3; ftm.

Tropical Agriculture Association   (TAA)   1979
- ■ 3 Sandy Mead, BOURNEMOUTH, Dorset, BH8 9JY.   (mem/sp)
  01202 397085
  email membership-secretary@taa.org.uk
  http://www.taa.org.uk
  Mem Sec: J B Davis
- ▲ Registered Charity
- Br Regions: Southwest, Scotland & Borders, London & South East, East Anglia
- ○ *F; the promotion, practice, education & research in tropical agriculture
- ● Conf - Mtgs - ET - Inf - VE
- M 1,150 i, 12 f, UK / 350 i, o'seas
- ¶ TAA(UK) NL - 4; ftm, £2 nm.

Tropical Growers' Association Ltd   (TGA)   1907
- ■ 20 St Dunstan's Hill (1st floor), LONDON, EC3R 8NQ.   (hq)
  020 7283 2707   fax 020 7623 1310
  email stuart.logan@fosfa.org
  Co Sec: Stuart Logan,   Hon Sec: Philip Gatland
- ▲ Company Limited by Guarantee
- ○ *T; for all concerned with tropical commodities & plantation interests
- Gp Council
- ● Mtgs
- < Fedn of Oils, Seeds & Fats Assns Ltd (FOSFA)
- > Malaysian Palm Oil Bd
- M 50 i, 5 f, 5 Associates, UK / 1 f, 3 associates, o'seas
  (Sub: £15 i, £50 f, £30 associates UK)
- ¶ [nil in public domain]

Trussed Rafter Association   (TRA)
- NR The Building Centre, 26 Store St, LONDON, WC1E 7BT.
  020 3205 0032
  http://www.tra.org.uk
- ○ *T; for trussed rafter manufacturers, industry suppliers & professionals involved in roof design & construction

Trust for Training & Education in Building Maintenance
   see **Upkeep - the Trust for Training & Education in Building Maintenance**

TT Riders Association   (TTRA)   1951
- ■ Mountain View, GLEN MAYE, Isle of Man, IM5 3BJ.   (hsp)
  01624 843695
  email francesthorp@manx.net   http://www.ttra.co.uk
  Hon Sec & Treas: Frances Thorp
- ▲ Registered Charity
- ○ *S; 'the continuance of the Isle of Man TT races; the creation of a social & charitable association of all those who take part, have taken part & those who race no more'
- Gp Isle of Man TT race riders; Sidecar passengers
- ● Conf - Stat - Inf - Lib
- < Intl Historic Racing Org; Auto-Cycle U; Fédn Intle Motocyclisme; Manx Grand Prix Riders Assn; Amer Historic Motorcycle Racing Assn
- M 1,270 i, UK / 411 i, o'seas
- ¶ NL - 2; ftm.

Tuberous Sclerosis Association   (TSA)   1977
- ■ PO Box 13938, BIRMINGHAM, B45 5BF.   (sb)
  05602 420809
  email diane.sanson@tuberous-sclerosis.org
  http://www.tuberous-sclerosis.org
  Head of Development & Support Services: Mrs Fiona McGlynn
- ▲ Company Limited by Guarantee; Registered Charity
- ○ *W; to support & help sufferers & their families; to raise awareness of & to encourage research into the causes of the disease
- ● Conf - ET - Res - Inf
- < Tuberous Sclerosis Intl (associations in 25 countries)
- M 1,500 i, UK / 100 i, 25 org, o'seas
- ¶ Scan (NL) - 3;   Medical Brochure;   Factsheets; all free.
  Publications list available.

Tue Iron Manufacturers' Association   (TIMA)   1994
- NR 81 Park View, Collins Rd, LONDON, N5 2UD.   (asa)
- ▲ Un-incorporated Society
- ○ *T; 'the tue iron is a nozzle attached to a bellows, used in a forge to fan flames to a high heat'
- ● Mtgs - ET - Exhib
- M 17 f
- ¶ Hot Air (NL) - 4.

Tug of War Association   (TOWA)   1958
- NR 57 Lynton Rd, CHESHAM, Bucks, HP5 2BT.   (hsp)
  01494 783057   fax 01494 792040
  email peter@tugofwar.co.uk   http://www.tugofwar.co.uk
  Sec: Peter Craft
- ○ *S; controlling body of the game of tug-of-war in Britain

Turfgrass Growers Association Ltd   (TGA)   1995
- ■ PVGA House, Nottingham Rd, LOUTH, Lincs, LN11 0WB.
  (asa)
  01507 607722   fax 01507 600101
  email tim.mudge@pvga.co.uk
  http://www.turfgrass.co.uk
  Sec: Tim Mudge
- ▲ Company Limited by Guarantee
- ○ *T; turf growers for domestic & commercial use
- Gp Producers; Suppliers of goods & services
- ● Conf - Mtgs - Exhib
- M 60 f

Turkey Club UK   2000

NR   Cults Farmhouse, Whithorn, NEWTON STEWART,
    Wigtownshire, DG8 8HA.   (hsb)
    01988 600763
    Hon Sec & Treas: Janice Houghton-Wallace
○   *B; to conserve & promote the standards breeds of turkey; to
    encourage & assist with advice anyone wishing to keep
    turkeys; to establish a higher profile for the turkey as an
    exhibition bird & utility species of poultry (provider of eggs &
    meat)
Gp   Breeders of the original standard breeds of turkey
●   ET - Exhib - Comp - Inf - VE
<   Poultry Club of GB
M   200 i
¶   NL - 4;   Ybk - 1; both ftm only.
    a turkey column in 'Fancy Fowl' - 12.

Turkish-British Chamber of Commerce & Industry

■   Bury House (2nd floor), 33 Bury St, LONDON, SW1Y 6AU.
    (hq)
    020 7321 0999
    http://www.tbcci.org
○   *C

Turner Society   1975

■   BCM Box Turner, LONDON, WC1N 3XX.   (mail address)
    http://www.turnersociety.org.uk
▲   Registered Charity
○   *A; to promote interest in the life, work & influence of the
    painter J M W Turner (1775-1851)
●   Mtgs - VE
M   c 500 i & org, UK / c 100 i & org, o'seas
¶   Turner Society News - 3; ftm only.

Turner Syndrome Support Society (UK)   (TSSS)   1979

NR   13 Simpson Court, 11 South Avenue, Clydebank Business Park,
    CLYDEBANK, G81 2NR.   (hq)
    0141-952 8006   fax 0141-952 8025
    email turner.syndrome@tss.org.uk
    http://www.tss.org.uk
    Exec Officer: Arlene Smyth
▲   Registered Charity
○   *W; information & support for those who have Turner syndrome
    (genetic abnormality incl short stature & lack of ovarian
    function, it affects only females & is caused by complete, or
    partial deletion, of the X chromosome in some, or all cells, of
    the body), their families & health professionals involved in
    their care
●   Conf - Mtgs - ET - Res - Comp - Inf
    Helpline: 0845 230 7520
M   750 i, 20 org, UK / 10 i, o'seas
¶   Turner Syndrome - lifelong guidance & support;
    Talking About Turner Syndrome (video);
        both minimum donation £5 (UK), £10 (o'seas).
    Talking About Turner Syndrome (booklet); minimum donation
    £1 (UK), £3 (o'seas).
    Information leaflets: publications list available.

Twentieth Century Society   1979

■   70 Cowcross St, LONDON, EC1M 6EJ.   (hq)
    020 7250 3857   fax 020 7251 8985
    email director@c20society.org.uk
    http://www.c20society.org.uk
    Dir: Catherine Croft
▲   Registered Charity
○   *G; to safeguard the heritage of architecture & design of post-
    1914 Britain
●   Conf - ET - Res - VE
<   Jt C'ee of the Nat Amenity Socs
M   1,950 i, 50 f, 50 org, UK / 60 i, o'seas
    (Sub: £35 i, £180 f, £90 org, UK / £42 i, o'seas)
¶   Jnl - 1; ftm, £20 nm.   NL - 3; ftm, £4.50 nm.

TWI Ltd
    see **Welding Institute**

Twins & Multiple Births Association   (TAMBA)   1978

■   2 The Willows, Gardner Rd, GUILDFORD, Surrey, GU1 4PG.
    (hq)
    0870 770 3305   fax 0870 770 3303
    email enquiries@tamba.org.uk
    http://www.tamba.org.uk
    CEO: Keith Reed
▲   Registered Charity
○   *W; to provide information & mutual support networks for
    families of twins, triplets & more, highlighting their unique
    needs to all involved in their care
Gp   Bereavement; Infertility; One parent families; Special needs;
    Supertwins; Support groups
●   Conf - Mtgs - ET - Res - SG - Inf - PL
<   Intl Soc for Twin Studies
M   6,000 families
¶   Twins, Triplets & More - 4; ftm, £2.50 nm.   AR.
    Specialist Support Group NLs - irreg.

Tyre Industry Council
    since 2008 **TyreSafe**

Tyre Industry Federation

NR   5 Berewyk Hall Court, White Colne, COLCHESTER, Essex,
    CO6 2QD.
    01787 226995
    http://www.tif.uk.com
    Sec: John Dorken
○   *T; tyre industry
●   Mtgs - LG
M   5 org
    British Tyre Manufacturers' Association
    Imported Tyre Manufacturers Association
    National Tyre Distributors' Association
    Tyre Recovery Association

Tyre Recovery Association   (TRA)   2004

NR   5 Berewyk Hall Court, White Colne, COLCHESTER, Essex,
    CO6 2QD.
    0845 301 6852
    email info@tyrerecovery.org.uk
    http://www.tyrerecovery.org.uk
    Sec: Peter Taylor
○   *T; to support the Tyre Industry Council's Responsible Recycler
    Scheme - that all tyres collected are disposed of, or re-used,
    in an environmentally acceptable methos
M   c 29 f

Tyre Wholesalers Group
    a group of the **National Tyre Distributors Association**

TyreSafe   1989

NR   5 Berewyk Hall Court, White Colne, COLCHESTER, Essex,
    CO6 2QD.   (hq)
    0845 301 6852
    http://www.tyresafe.org
▲   Un-incorporated Society
○   *T; improving tyre safety awareness
●   Mtgs - ET - Res - Stat - Inf - PL - LG
<   Brit Rubber Mfrs Assn; Imported Tyre Mfrs Assn
¶   Annual Report; free.
✕   2008 Tyre Industry Council

Tyrone Farming Society   1832

NR   The Showgrounds, 3 Gillygooley Rd, OMAGH, Co Tyrone,
    BT78 5PN.   (hq)
    028 8224 2500   fax 028 8224 0066
    email info@tyronefarmingsociety.co.uk
    http://www.tyronefarmingsociety.co.uk
    Sec: Edwin Cartwright
○   *F
●   Omagh Show
<   Assn of Show & Agricl Orgs

© CBD Research Ltd · Beckenham · BR3 5JS · Tel 020 8650 7745 · E-mail cbd@cbdresearch.com · www.cbdresearch.com

UK ...

see **United Kingdom** ...

[All organisations whose names begin with 'UK' or 'United Kingdom' are printed & filed as 'United Kingdom' to avoid the confusion of two separate sequences - except for those below using acronyms as a title]

UKinbound   1977

■ 388 Strand, LONDON, WC2R 0LT.   (hq)
020 7395 7500   fax 020 7240 6618
email info@ukinbound.org   http://www.ukinbound.org
Company Limited by Guarantee
Chief Exec: Mary Rance
○ *T; to represent the interests of the UK's inbound tourism sector
● Conf - Mtgs - ET - Exhib - Stat
M 250 f
¶ Hbk & LM - 1.

UKLPG Ltd   (UKLPG)   1970

■ Camden House, Warwick Rd, KENILWORTH, Warks,
CV8 1TH.   (hq)
email mail@uklpg.org   http://www.uklpg.org
Chief Exec: Robert Shuttleworth
▲ Company Limited by Guarantee
○ *T; to champion & guard safety & technical standards within the LPG (liquefied petroleum gas) industry & provide advice & guidance to members; to raise the profile of the benefits, good experience & qualities of LPG to specific & agreed audiences
● Conf - Mtgs - Exhib - Stat - Inf - LG
< Wld LPG Assn (WLPGA); Eur LPG Assn (AEGPL)
M 78 f (full), 23 f (affiliate)
¶ NL - 4; ftm only.   AR.
Codes of Practice (30 to date) - irreg; prices on application.
✕ 2008 (Association for Liquid Gas Equipment & Distributors (L P Gas Association (merged))

UKspace   1975

■ PO Box 423, FLEET, Hants, GU51 9BD.   (hsb)
01252 898792
email secgenukspace@btinternet.com
http://www.ukspace.org
Sec Gen: Paul Flanagan
▲ Un-incorporated Society
○ *N, *T; to grow the share of the global space market; to promote greater awareness of commercial space in government & media; to provide the primary forum for the space industry to dialogue with government & shareholders
Gp Sector c'ees: Earth Observation Applications & Missions (EOSC); Research & Technology (RTSC); Satellite Navigation (SNSC); Satellite Telecommunications (STSC); Security & Defence (SDSC); Space Science (S3C)
● Conf - Mtgs - SG - Expt - LG
< Eurospace; Intellect; ADS
M 19 f
¶ Brochures & policy papers - irreg; all ftm.

Ukulele Society of Great Britain

NR 43 Finstock Rd, LONDON, W10 6LU.   (sp)
020 8960 0459   fax 020 8964 0990
email m@gicman.com   http://www.usgb.co.uk
Chmn & Sec: Fred Pearson
▲ Un-incorporated Society
○ *D; for all interested in the playing of the ukulele & ukulele banjo
M i

Ulster Angling Federation   (UAF)   1937

NR 14 Harwood Gardens, CARRICKFERGUS, Co Antrim,
BT38 7US.   (sp)
028 9336 8952
Hon Sec: Mrs Dianne Archibald
▲ Company Limited by Guarantee
○ *S; representative body for game angling in Northern Ireland; to conserve the aquatic environment; to prevent water pollution
● Mtgs - ET - Inf - LG
< N Atlantic Salmon Consvn Org; Salmon & Trout Assn; Countryside Alliance
M 10,000 i, 80 clubs
¶ The Ulster Angler - 1; ftm.

Ulster Archaeological Society   (UAS)   1935

■ c/o School of Geography, Archaeology & Palaeoecology,
Queen's University Belfast, 42 Fitzwilliam St, BELFAST,
BT9 6AX.   (mail/add)
http://www.uarcsoc.org
Hon Sec: K Pullin
▲ Registered Charity
○ *L; to further in every way the study of the past, particularly in Ulster
Gp Field survey
● Mtgs - Lectures - Fieldtrips
M c 300 i
(Sub: £15)
¶ Ulster Jnl of Archaeology - 1; ftm, £15 nm.
NL - 4; ftm only.

Ulster Architectural Heritage Society   (UAHS)   1967

■ 66 Donegall Pass, BELFAST, BT7 1BU.   (hq)
028 9055 0213   fax 028 9055 0214
email info@uahs.org.uk   http://www.uahs.org.uk
Administrator: Louise O'Neill
▲ Company Limited by Guarantee; Registered Charity
○ *A, *K, *L; to promote the appreciation & enjoyment of architecture from the prehistoric to the present in the nine counties of Ulster, & to encourage its preservation & conservation
● Conf - Mtgs - ET - Res - SG - Inf - Lib - VE - LG
M 1,200 i
¶ List of publications available.

Ulster Automobile Club Ltd   (UAC)   1925

NR Unit 04 Ards Business Centre, Jubilee Rd, NEWTOWNARDS,
Co Down, BT23 4YH.   (hq)
email office@ulsterautomobileclub.co.uk
http://www.ulsterautomobileclub.co.uk
▲ Company Limited by Guarantee
○ *S; organisation promotion of motor sport events
Gp Communications team (radio); Competitions c'ee (event organisation)
● Comp - VE
< Fédn Intle des Véhicules Anciens (FIVA); Motor Sports Assn - UK (MSA-UK); Assn of NI Car Clubs (ANICC)
M 250 i, UK / 30 i, o'seas
¶ Wheelspin - 2; ftm, on request, nm.

Ulster Chemists' Association   (UCA)   1901

■ 5 Annadale Avenue, BELFAST, BT7 3JH.   (hq)
028 9069 0456   fax 028 9059 0457
http://www.uca.org.uk
▲ Un-incorporated Society
○ *P, *T; for retail pharmacy in Northern Ireland
● Conf - Mtgs - ET - Inf - Liaison with trade - Assistance to small businesses
< Nat Pharmaceutical Assn
M 487 i
¶ NI Pharmacy in Focus - 12; ftm only.

Ulster Coarse Fishing Federation (UCFF) 1975
NR 7 Knockvale Grove, BELFAST, BT5 6HL.
   028 9065 5373
▲ Un-incorporated Society
○ *S; to promote & develop coarse angling in Northern Ireland
● ET - Comp - LG
< Nat Coarse Fishing Fedn of Ireland

Ulster Farmers Union (UFU) 1918
■ 475 Antrim Rd, BELFAST, BT15 3DA.   (hq)
   028 9037 0222   fax 028 9037 1231
   email info@ufuni.org   http://www.ufuni.org
   Chief Exec: Clarke Black
▲ Un-incorporated Society
Br 25
○ *F; to defend the rights & promote the interests of farmers
● Conf - Mtgs - ET - Res - SG - Stat - Inf - Lib - LG
M 12,000 i
¶ Farming News - 5.

Ulster Federation of Rambling Clubs (UFRC) 1980
■ 23 Innisfayle Park, BANGOR, Co Down, Northern Ireland,
   BT19 1DR.   (sec/p)
   email administration@ufrc-online.co.uk
   http://www.ufrc-online.co.uk
   Admin: Simon Reardon
▲ Un-incorporated Society
○ *S; 'to encourage recreational walking, appreciation & respect
   for the countryside'
● Mtgs - ET - LG
< Ramblers' Assn
M 29 org

**** Ulster Folk Life Society**
   Organisation lost; see Introduction paragraph 6

Ulster Genealogical & Historical Guild
   the membershp body of the **Ulster Historical Foundation**

Ulster Historical Foundation (UHF) 1956
■ 49 Malone Rd, BELFAST, BT9 6RY.   (hq)
   028 9066 1988   fax 028 9066 1977
   email enquiry@uhf.org.uk
   http://www.ancestryireland.com
   Exec Dir: Fintan Mullan
▲ Registered Charity
○ *P, *Q; publishers of Irish historical, genealogical, educational
   & academic texts; also genealogical research professionals
   offering bespoke research services
Gp Genealogical researchers; GU membership, accounts &
   administration; Publications; Sales & marketing
● Conf - ET - Res - Inf - VE - Publishing
< Fedn of Families Hist Socs; Family Hist Coun (Republic of
   Ireland); Brit Assn of Ir Studies
M 800 i, 20 org, UK / 1,000 i, 25 org, o'seas
   (Sub: £30)
¶ Familia: Ulster Genealogical Review - 1; ftm, £5.99 m.
   Directory of Irish Family History - 1; ftm, £6.99 nm.
   Note: The foundation's mambership body is the Ulster
   Genealogical & Historical Guild

Ulster Hockey Union
■ The Pavilion, Stormont, Newtownards Rd, BELFAST, BT4 3TA.
   028 9076 5766
   http://www.ulsterhockey.com
   Exec Mgr: Angela Platt
○ *S; the governing body for hockey in Ulster
× 2009 (Ulster Branch Irish Hockey Association
   (Ulster Women's Hockey Union

Ulster Launderers Association
   has closed

Ulster Place-Name Society (UPNS) 1952
NR Irish & Celtic Studies, School of Languages Literatures & Arts,
   Queen's University, BELFAST, BT17 1NN.
   028 9097 3689   fax 028 9097 5298
   email townlands@qub.ac.uk
   http://www.ulsterplacenames.org
○ *L; to undertake a survey of Ulster place-names
¶ Ainm (jnl)

Ulster-Scots Language Society (USLS) 1992
NR 68-72 Great Victoria St (2nd floor), BELFAST, BT2 7BB.
   028 9043 6716
   email usls@ulster-scots.com
   http://www.ulsterscotslanguage.com
▲ Registered Charity
○ *L; to record, promote & uphold the use of Ulster-Scots
   language in writing, education & speech; to promote Ulster-
   Scots cultural traditions
M c 250 i, UK / c 50 i, o'seas
¶ Ullans (Jnl) - 1.

Ulster Society of Organists & Choirmasters 1918
NR 8c Beechwood House, Woodland Drive, NEWTOWNABBEY,
   Co Antrim, BT37 9SF.   (hsp)
   028 9084 1001
   email secretary@usoc.org.uk   http://www.phoenix-ni.org/
   usoc/
   Hon Secs: Stephen & Carolyn Hamill
▲ Un-incorporated Society
○ *D; to promote the interests of church musicians
● Conf - Mtgs - ET - VE
< Inc Assn Organists (UK)
M 180 i
¶ NL - 12; m only.

**Ulster Society for Prevention of Cruelty to Animals (USPCA)
1836**
■ Unit 6   Carnbane Industrial Estate, NEWRY, Co Down,
   Northern Ireland, BT35 6QH.   (hq)
   07739 948 516   fax 028 3025 1423
   email enquiries@uspca.co.uk   http://www.uspca.co.uk
   Chief Exec: Stephen Philpott
▲ Company Limited by Guarantee; Registered Charity
○ *K, *V; care & prevention of cruelty to animals through
   education & inspectorate vigilance
● ET - VE - Shelters for homeless animals
< Wld Soc Protection of Animals
M 1,000 i
   (Sub: £10)
¶ AR; free.

**Ulster Society for the Protection of the Countryside (USPC)
1937**
■ 22 Donegall Rd, BELFAST, BT12 5JN.   (hq)
   028 9024 9006
   email countryside@uspc.org.uk   http://www.uspc.org.uk
   Hon Sec: Ian Lamont
▲ Un-incorporated Society
○ *K, *N; to safeguard the amenities of Northern Ireland; to do
   everything possible to protect & enhance its beauty for future
   generations
● Conf - Mtgs - Exhib - Inf - LG
< NI Envt Link
> Cyclists' Touring Club of NI; Ulster Fedn of Rambling Clubs;
   Youth Hostel Assn of NI
M 240 i, 5 org
¶ The USPC Countryside Recorder (NL) - 2;   AR; both free.

© CBD Research Ltd · Beckenham · BR3 5JS · Tel 020 8650 7745 · E-mail cbd@cbdresearch.com · www.cbdresearch.com

Ulster Teachers' Union   (UTU)   1919
- ■ 94 Malone Rd, BELFAST, BT9 5HP.   (hq)
  028 9066 2216   fax 028 9066 3055
  email office@utu.edu   http://www.utu.edu
  Gen Sec: Avril Hall-Callaghan
- ○ *P, *U
- ● Conf - Mtgs - ET
- < ICTU
- M 6,500 i
- ¶ UTU News - 4;   NL - 12;   AR; all free.

Ulster Women's Hockey Union
   2009 merged with Ulster Branch of the Irish Hockey Union to form
   Ulster Hockey Union

Undeb Amaethwyr Cymru
   see **Farmers' Union of Wales   (Undeb Amaethwyr Cymru)**

Undeb Badminton Cymru
   see **Welsh Badminton Union   (Undeb Badminton Cymru)**

Undeb Cenedlaethol Athrawon Cymru   (UCAC)   1940
- ■ Ffordd Penglais, ABERYSTWYTH, Ceredigion, SY23 2EU.   (hq)
  01970 639950   fax 01970 626765
  email ucac@athrawon.com   http://www.athrawon.com
  Gen Sec: Elaine Edwards
- ○ *E, *U; to represent teachers in Wales, particularly Welsh
  speaking teachers
- < Trades U Congress (TUC)
- M 3,946 i
- ¶ Yr Athro - 3; ftm.   Blwyddlyfr (yearbook).

Underfloor Heating Manufacturers' Association
   an association of **BEAMA Ltd**

Understanding Animal Research   (UAR)   1908
- § Charles Darwin House, 12 Roger St, LONDON, WC1N 2JU.
  (hq)
  020 7685 2670
  http://www.understandinganimalresearch.org.uk
- ○ *L; 'to make known the facts about experimental research
  involving use of animals; to emphasise importance &
  necessity of such experiments; to give guidance on the
  prevention of suffering of experimental animals'
  formed by a merger of the Coalition for Medical Progress & the
  Research Defence Society it is now an Industrial & Provident
  Society, which offers information on all forms of animal
  research & is supported by associates who have no legal
  status & may not attend the AGM

Union of Country Sports Workers   (UCSW)   1977
- ■ PO Box 129, BANBURY, Oxon, OX17 2HX.   (hsp)
  01295 712719   fax 01295 712719
  email office@ucsw.org   http://www.ucsw.org
  Chmn: Alex Ford,   Sec/Admin: Phillippa White
- ○ *U; to represent anyone employed in country sports, either
  directly or indirectly, full-time or part-time
- ● Empl - LG - Stands at country fairs, game fairs - Lobbying
- M 4,500 i
- ¶ Livin' Country - 3; ftm, £2 nm.

Union for Education Professionals
   see **Voice - the union for education professionals**

Union of Shop, Distributive & Allied Workers   (USDAW)   1947
- ■ 188 Wilmslow Rd, MANCHESTER, M14 6LJ.   (hq)
  0161-224 2804   fax 0161-257 2566
  email enquiries@usdaw.org.uk
  http://www.usdaw.org.uk
  Gen Sec: John Hannett
- Br 23
- ○ *U; to recruit, organise & represent workers in the retail,
  distributive, manufacturing & service sectors
- < Trades U Congress (TUC)
- M 407,000 i
- ¶ Arena (Jnl) - 4.

Union of UK Unicyclists   (UUU)   2001
- ■ 43 Melrose Ave, Monkseaton, WHITLEY BAY, Tyne & Wear,
  NE25 8BA.
  email chairperson@unicycle.org.uk
  http://www.unicycle.org.uk
  Chmn: Joe Baxter
- ○ *S

Union of Women Teachers
   see **National Association of Schoolmasters Union of Women
   Teachers**

Unison   (UNISON)   1993
- NR UNISON Centre, 130 Euston Rd, LONDON, NW1 2AY.   (hq)
  0845 355 0845   fax 0800 096 7968
  http://www.unison.org.uk
  Gen Sec: Dave Prentis
- ○ *U; 'the public service union' - local government, health care,
  water, gas & electricity industries, further & higher education,
  schools, transport, voluntary sector, housing associations,
  police support staff
- < Trades U Congress (TUC)
- M 1,374,500 i

Unitarian Historical Society   (UHS)   1915
- NR 223 Upper Lisburn Rd, BELFAST, BT10 0LL.   (hq)
  Sec: Rev David Steers
- ○ *L; study of history of Unitarian & kindred movements;
  preservation of records & antiquities
- M i & libraries
- ¶ Transactions - 1.

Unite Federation
   since 2010 **National Federation of Occupational Pensioners**

Unite the Union   2007
NR   Unite House, 128 Theobald's Rd, LONDON, WC1X 8TN.   (hq)
       020 7420 8900
       http://www.unitetheunion.org
       Gen Sec: Len McCluskey
O   *U; to improve members' standard of living & quality of life
       through efficient relationships with employers & government
Gp   Sectors:
       Aerospace & shipbuilding; Chemicals, pharmaceuticals,
       process & textiles; Civil air transport; Community, youth
       workers & not for profit; Construction; Docks, rail, ferries &
       waterways; Education; Electrical engineering & electronics;
       Energy & utilities; Finance & legal; Food, drink & tobacco;
       Graphical, paper & media; Health sector; IT &
       communications; Local authorities; Metals, including foundry;
       MoD & government departments; Motor components;
       Passenger transport; Road transport commercial, logistics &
       retail distribution; Rural & agricultural; Servicing & general
       industries; Vehicle building & automotive.
       Autonomous professional bodies:
       Electrical & Engineering Staff Association; Guild of Healthcare
       Pharmacists; National Association of Fire Officers; Probation
       Managers Association; United Kingdom Association of
       Professional Engineers
<   Trades U Congress (TUC)
M   1,474,564 i
X   2007 (Amicus
       (Transport & General Workers' Union (merged)

United Chiropractic Association   (UCA)   2000
■   45 North Hill (1st floor), PLYMOUTH, Devon, PL4 8EZ.   (hq)
       01752 658785   fax 01752 659796
       email admin@united-chiropractic.org
       http://www.united-chiropractic.org
O   *M, *P; to represent principle-centred chiropractic (wellness
       based)
●   Conf - Mtgs - ET - Res
M   150 i, UK / 10 i, o'seas

United Counties Agricultural & Hunters Society   1895
■   The Showground, Nantyci, CARMARTHEN, SA33 5DR.   (hq)
       01267 232141   fax 01267 221884
       email enquiries@unitedcounties.co.uk
       http://www.unitedcounties.org
       Sec: Mair James
▲   Registered Charity
O   *F, *H; covers Carmarthenshire & surrounding areas
●   Exhibitions & shows
<   Assn of Show & Agricl Orgs

United East Lothian Agricultural Society   1804
NR   Garden Stirling Burnet, 39 High St, DUNBAR, E Lothian,
       EH42 1EW.   (asa)
       07872 817117
       email secretary@haddingtonshow.co.uk
       http://www.haddingtonshow.co.uk
       Sec: Gill Tait
O   *F
●   Haddington Agricultural Show
<   Assn of Show & Agricl Orgs

United Grand Lodge of England
NR   Freemasons' Hall, 60 Great Queen St, LONDON,
       WC2B 5AA.   (hq)
       020 7831 9811
O   *G
M   10,000 i

**United Kingdom Access Management Federation for Education &
Research   2005**
NR   JSC Collections, Brettenham House, 5 Lancaster Place,
       LONDON, WC2E 7EN.
       020 3006 6086
O   *G; to provide a single solution to accessing online resources &
       services for education & research
Gp   Schools sector
M   f, orgchools

**United Kingdom Acquired Brain Injury Forum   (UKABIF)
1998**
■   PO Box 355, PLYMOUTH, Devon, PL3 4WD.   (mail)
       01752 601318
       email ukabif@btconnect.com   http://www.ukabif.org.uk
       Chmn: Prof Mike Barnes,   Exec Dir: Chloë Hayward
▲   Registered Charity
O   *K, *L; the advancement of education in the subject of children
       & adults with acquired brain injury; the relief of disability of
       people with acquired brain injury, by education rather than
       as a provider of direct services
●   Conf - Mtgs - ET - Inf - LG
M   100 i, 150 f
       (Sub: £25 i, £100 non-profit org)
¶   NL - 4;   Directory of Rehabilitation Services;   AR;   all ftm.

United Kingdom Alliance
       is in the process of closing

United Kingdom Alliance of Dance Teachers
       see **UK Alliance of Professional Teachers of Dancing &
       Kindred Arts**

**United Kingdom Alliance of Professional Teachers of Dancing &
Kindred Arts   (UKA)   1902**
■   Centenary House, 38-40 Station Rd, BLACKPOOL, Lancs,
       FY4 1EU.   (hq)
       01253 408828   fax 01253 408066
       email info@ukadance.co.uk
       http://www.ukadance.co.uk
▲   Company Limited by Guarantee
O   *D; to further the development of dance & movement in all its
       forms; to provide a syllabus & examination service
●   Conf - Mtgs - ET - Exam - Exhib - Comp - SG - Inf - LG
<   Brit Dance Coun; Scot Official Bd Highland Dancing; Sport &
       Recreation Alliance
M   i

**United Kingdom Alliance of Wedding Planners   (UKAWP)
2006**
NR   7 Churchfield Rd, COGGESHALL, Essex, CO6 1QE.   (hq)
       01376 561544
       email info@ukawp.com   http://www.ukawp.com
       Training Director: Bernadette Chapman
▲   Company Limited by Guarantee
O   *P; to promote professionalism in wedding planning
M   22 f (full & associate)

United Kingdom Aluminium Packaging Recycling Organisation
       see **Aluminium Packaging Recycling Organisation**

United Kingdom eHealth Association
       2009 merged with **Telecare Services Association**

© CBD Research Ltd · Beckenham · BR3 5JS · Tel 020 8650 7745 · E-mail cbd@cbdresearch.com · www.cbdresearch.com

United Kingdom Association for Accessible Formats   (UKAAF) 2009

NR   PO Box 127, CWMBRAN, NP44 9BQ.   (hq)
　　 0845 608 5223
　　 http://www.ukaaf.org
　　 Pres: Lord Low of Dalston
○   *G; to set standards & promote the best practice, for quality
　　 accessible information, based on user needs for people with
　　 print impairments.　Accessible formats are alternatives to
　　 printed information used by the blind & partially sighted,
　　 such as large print, audio, braille, electronic text & accessible
　　 images
×   2009 (Braille Authority UK
　　　　 (Confederation of Transcribed Information Services
　　　　 (UK Association of Braille Producers
　　　　　 (merged 1 January)

United Kingdom Association of Braille Producers
　　 merged on 1 January 2009 with the Braille Authority & the UK
　　 Confederation of Transcribed Information Services to form the **United
　　 Kingdom Association for Accessible Formats**

United Kingdom Association of Cancer Registries   (UKACR) 1992

NR   National Cancer Intelligence Centre, ONS, Segensworth Rd,
　　 Titchfield, FAREHAM, Hants, PO15 5RR.　(asa)
　　 0845 601 3034
　　 http://www.ukacr.org
　　 Co Chmn: Dr Gill Lawrence,　David Meechan
○   *W; to bring together organisations with an interest in
　　 developing cancer registration as a resource for studying and
　　 controlling cancer in the UK & Ireland
M   13 org

United Kingdom Association for European Law　1974

■   King's College London, Strand, LONDON, WC2R 2LS.　(hq)
　　 020 7848 1768
　　 email eva.evans@kcl.ac.uk　 http://www.ukael.org
　　 Admin: Andrea Cordwell James
▲   Registered Charity
○   *P
●   Conf
<   Fédn Intle du Droit Européen (FIDE)
M   200 i, 20 f, UK / 35 i, o'seas
¶   Conference publications - irreg.

United Kingdom Association of Fish Meal Manufacturers (AFMM)　1917

NR   Greenwell Place, East Tullos Industrial Estate, ABERDEEN,
　　 AB12 3AY.　(hq)
　　 01224 854488
　　 email ukfishmeal@ufp.co.uk
　　 Sec: Alison Chree
○   *T; the production & use of fish meal & fish oil in the UK

United Kingdom Association of Fish Producer Organisations (UKAFPO)　1988

■   2 St Wilfred Rd, BRIDLINGTON, E Yorks, YO16 4DJ.　(hsp)
　　 07742 252033
　　 email sue.willson@fishproducers.org
　　 Sec: Mrs S J Willson
▲   Friendly Society
○   *N, *T; to promote & develop cooperation between & the
　　 interests of fish producer organisations, both in the UK &
　　 other parts of the EU
●   Mtgs - LG
M   9 f

United Kingdom Association of Frozen Food Producers
　　 in 2010 became a group of the **Food & Drink Federation**

United Kingdom Association for Gestalt Practitioners (UKAGP)　2010

NR   8 Lancaster Avenue, FARNHAM, Surrey, GU9 8JY.
　　 email claire@ukagp.org.uk　 http://www.ukagp.org.uk
　　 Sec: Claire Asherson Bartram
○   *P; the psychology of 'wholeness'

United Kingdom Association of Letting Agents   (UKALA) 1997

■   PO Box 10582, COLCHESTER, Essex, CO1 9JD.　(hq)
　　 01206 765456
　　 email ukala@hotmail.com　 http://www.ukala.org.uk
　　 Gen Sec: John Peartree
▲   Company Limited by Guarantee
Br   c 500
○   *T; for letting agents & managing agents
●   ET - Stat - LG
M   206 i, 206 f
¶   Letting Update (Jnl) - 4; ftm, £75 yr nm.

United Kingdom Association of Manufacturers of Bakers' Yeast (UKAMBY)　1973

■   6 Catherine St, LONDON, WC2B 5JJ.　(hq)
　　 020 7420 7109　 fax 020 7836 0580
　　 email harriet.green@fdf.org.uk
　　 Exec Sec: Harriet Green
▲   Un-incorporated Society
○   *T; to represent the industry's interests to Government &
　　 Whitehall
●   Mtgs
<   Comité des Fabricants de Levure de Panification de
　　 l'U Eur (COFALEC); Food & Drink Fedn
M   3 f

United Kingdom Association of Preservation Trusts   (APT) 1989

NR   Alhambra House (9th floor), 27-31 Charing Cross Rd,
　　 LONDON, WC2H 0AU.　(hq)
　　 020 7930 1629
　　 Chmn: Colin Johns
　　 Co-ordinator: Louise Bailey
▲   Registered Charity
Br   9
○   *N; to encourage & assist building preservation trusts; to
　　 expand their capacity to preserve the built heritage
●   Conf - Mtgs - SG - Inf - LG
M   c 275 trusts
¶   NL - 2.　Guidance Notes - irreg.

United Kingdom Association of Professional Engineers (UKAPE)　1969

■   Unite House, 128 Theobald's Rd, LONDON, WC1X 8TN.
　　 020 3371 2046　 fax 0870 731 5043
　　 email info@ukape.org.uk　 http://www.ukape.org.uk
　　 Sec: Kevin O'Callagham
○   *P; for engineers, technologists, managers & professional staff
¶   Engineer Today (NL) - 4; ftm.
　　 an autonomous professional body within Unite the Union

United Kingdom Association of Programme Directors   (UKAPD)

NR   Ebsworth Building, Durham University, Queens Campus
　　 Stockton, University Boulevard, STOCKTON on TEES,
　　 N Yorks, TS17 6BH.
　　 0191-334 0831
　　 email ukapdadmin@gmail.com　 http://www.ukapd.org
　　 Chmn: Dr Prit Chahal
○   *P; for general practitioner training programme directors

United Kingdom Association of Proposal Management Professionals (UKAPMP) 2001
- ■ 32 Valley Crescent, WOKINGHAM, Berks, RG41 1NP. (ceo/p)
  07736 387029
  email ceo@ukapmp.co.uk   http://www.ukapmp.co.uk
  Chief Exec: Nic Adams
- Br Austria/Germany/Switzerland, Australia/New Zealand, Canada, India, Ireland, Israel, Netherlands, South Africa, Spain, USA (19 chapters)
- ○ *P; 'to advance the arts, sciences & technology of new business acquisition & to promote the professionalism of those engaged in those pursuits'
- ● Conf - Mtgs - ET - Exam - Res - Exhib - Stat - Inf - LG
- < Assn of Proposal Mgt Profls (International)
- M c 200 i, UK / c 1,600 i, o'seas
- ¶ Jnl - 2; ftm only.

United Kingdom Athletics Ltd (UKA) 1999
- NR Athletics House, Central Boulevard, Blythe Valley Park, SOLIHULL, B90 8AJ. (hq)
  0121-713 8400   fax 0121-713 8452
  http://www.uka.org.uk
  Chief Exec: Niels de Vos
- ▲ Company Limited by Guarantee
- ○ *S; national governing body for athletics
- M 1,400 clubs

United Kingdom Bartenders Guild (UKBG) 1933
- ■ Rosebank, Blackness, LINLITHGOW, W Lothian, EH49 7NL. (admin/p)
  01506 834448   fax 01506 834373
  Admin Officer: Jim Slavin
- ▲ Un-incorporated Society
- Br 4; 1 o'seas
- ○ *P; interests of bartenders
- ● Mtgs - ET - Exam - Exhib - Comp
- < Intl Bartenders' Assn
- M 600 i, UK / 15 i, o'seas

United Kingdom Bodybuilding & Fitness Federation (UKBFF)
- NR PO Box 231, Waterloo, LIVERPOOL, L22 9WW. (admin)
  0151-931 4090
  email admin@ukbff.co.uk   http://www.ukbff.co.uk
  Admin: Wanda Tierney
- ▲ Company Limited by Guarantee
- ○ *S
- < Intl Fedn of Body Builders (IFBB)

United Kingdom Botswana Society (UKBS) 1980
- NR c/o Botswanian Embassy, 6 Stratford Place, LONDON, W1C 1AY. (mail)
  email gasamani@hotmail.com
  http://www.ukbotswanasociety.org
  Hon Sec: George Asamani
- ▲ Un-incorporated Society
- ○ *X; to encourage & strengthen ties between Britain & Botswana
- ● Mtgs
- M 380 i, 10 f, UK / 5 i, o'seas
- ¶ NL - 4; ftm only.

United Kingdom Bungee Club 1989
- NR Magna Science Adventure Centre, Sheffield Rd, Templeborough, ROTHERHAM, S Yorks, S60 1DX. (hq)
  0700 028 6433   fax 01924 849452
  email enquiries@ukbungee.co.uk
  http://www.ukbungee.co.uk
  Dir: Jon Nicholls
- Br 2
- ○ *G, *S; 'thrill-seeking, fun, overcoming your fears'; for all interested in bungee jumping (filming, stunt jumpers & riggers); the group does not accept people with high blood pressure, heart or neurological conditions, dizziness / epilepsy, pregnancy, asthma, or diabetes
- < CityPaintball.com
- M 30,000 i

United Kingdom Business Incubation (UKBI) 1999
- NR Faraday Wharf, Birmingham Science Park Aston, Holt St, BIRMINGHAM, B7 4BB. (hq)
  0121 250 3538   fax 0121 250 3542
  email 09>ukbi.co.uk
  Chief Exec: Peter Harman
- ○ *P; 'for professionals & organisations actively involved in enterprise, innovation & sustainable economic growth'
- ● Mtgs - Inf - Lib
- M i, f
- ¶ Good practice guides.

United Kingdom Cards Association 2009
- NR 2 Thomas More Square, LONDON, E1W 1YN. (hq)
  http://www.theukcardsassociation.org.uk
  Contact: Miss Quinn
- ○ *T; to be a forum for credit, debit & cxhangecard users & merchant acquiring banks; to prevent card fraud; to contimue the APACS tradition
- ● Stat - Inf
- M i, f
- × 2009 (April) Association for Payment Clearing Services

United Kingdom Cartridge Remanufacturers Association (UKCRA) 1994
- NR Cheetham Mill (1st floor), Park St, STALYBRIDGE, Cheshire, SK15 2BT. (asa)
  01706 525050   fax 01706 647440
  email info@ukcra.com   http://www.ukcra.com
  Sec: Laura Heywood
- ▲ Company Limited by Guarantee
- ○ *T; for remanufactures & component suppliers to the toner & inkjet industry; to provide laser printer users with proven high quality products that are cost effective & environmentally friendly alternatives to imported toner cartridges
- Gp Inkjet cartridge refillers; Laser toner cartridge re-manufacturers
- ● Mtgs
- M 2,000 i, 40 f

United Kingdom Cast Stone Association (UKCSA) 1991
- NR 15 Stone Hill Court, The Arbours, NORTHAMPTON, NN3 3RA. (hq)
  01604 405666
  http://www.ukcsa.co.uk
- ▲ Un-incorporated Society
- ○ *T; for manufacturers of cast stone construction materials
- M 8 f

United Kingdom Catamaran Racing Association (UKCRA) 2001
- NR 9 Daniels Court, Island Wall, WHITSTABLE, Kent, CT5 2AJ.
  01227 282625
  http://www.catamaran.co.uk
  Chmn: Nick Dewhirst
- ○ *S

United Kingdom Chasers & Riders Ltd 1999
- NR Upper Farm, Down Farm Lane, Headbourne Worthy, WINCHESTER, Hants, SO23 7LA. (hq)
  01962 886144
  email dt@ukchasers.com   http://www.ukchasers.com
- ▲ Company Limited by Guarantee
- Br 2
- ○ *G; 'to help you enjoy your horse more by providing riding which is as varied, safe & enjoyable as possible. We provide a nationwide network of xc courses & equestrian centres providing competitions, facilities & safe off road riding for all members'
- ● ET - Comp - Inf
- M 30,000+ i, 50 farms & equestrian centres, 10 riding clubs
- ¶ UK Chasers Handbook - 1; ftm only.
  NL & Competitions Calendar - 2; free.
  Holidays with your Horse; free.

© CBD Research Ltd · Beckenham · BR3 5JS · Tel 020 8650 7745 · E-mail cbd@cbdresearch.com · www.cbdresearch.com

United Kingdom Cheerleading Association   (UKCA)

NR   The Worthington Building, Fence Avenue, MACCLESFIELD,
        Cheshire, SK10 1LY.
        01625 838557 (Mon-Fri 1000-1700)
        http://www.ukca.org.uk
○   *G; for cheerleaders, teachers & coaches
●   Mtgs - ET
M   i

United Kingdom Cheese Guild
        a training programme of the **Guild of Fine Food**

United Kingdom Chrysanthemum Growers' Association
        closed April 2011

**United Kingdom Cleaning Products Industry Association
(UKCPI)**

■   Century House (1st floor), Old Mill Place, TATTENHALL,
        Cheshire, CH3 9RJ.   (hq)
        01829 770055   fax 01829 770101
        email ukcpi@ukcpi.org   http://www.ukcpi.org
        Dir Gen: Philip Malpass
▲   Un-incorporated Society
○   *T; for producers of cleaning, hygiene & surface care products
Gp   Technical; Packaging; Legal; Industrial & institutional products
●   Mtgs - Stat - Inf - LG - Detergent Industry Information Bureau
<   Assn Intle de Savonnerie, Détergence & Produits
        d'Entretien (AISE); Alliance of Ind Assns (AIA); Chemical Inds
        Assn (CIA)
M   c 45 f

**United Kingdom Clinical Pharmacy Association   (UKCPA)
1981**

■   Publicity House (1st floor), 59 Long St, WIGSTON, Leics,
        LE18 2AJ.   (hq)
        0116-277 6999   fax 0116-277 6272
        email admin@ukcpa.com   http://www.ukcpa.org
        Gen Mgr: Marie Matthews
▲   Un-incorporated Society
○   *M, *P; to foster the concepts & practice of pharmaceutical care
        for the benefit of patients & public
Gp   Cardiology; Community pharmacy; Critical care; Dermatology;
        Diabetes; Education & training; Elderly care; Electronic
        prescribing; Emergency care; Gastroenterology /
        Hepatology; Haemostasis, anticoagulation & thrombosis;
        Infection management; Leadership development; Medicines
        safety & quality; Neurosciences; Pain management;
        Pharmacoeconomics; Respiratory; Rheumatology; Senior
        pharmacy managers; Stroke; Surgery & theatres; Women's
        health
●   Conf - Mtgs - ET - Res - Exhib - SG - Inf - LG
M   2,000 i, 23 f, 4 hospitals, UK / 60 i, 1 hospital, o'seas
¶   In Practice (NL) - 4; ftm only.   Practice Guides; £2.50.
        Symposia Abstract Booklet - 2; ftm, £7 nm.

United Kingdom Coloured Pencil Society   (UKCPS)   2001

NR   39 Castle Park, Ceres, CUPAR, Fife, KY15 5NL.   (sp)
        email secretary@ukcps.co.uk   http://www.ukcps.co.uk
        Sec: Carol Bramley
○   *A; to promote coloured pencils as a fine art medium, and to
        support UK artists who use, or wish to use, coloured pencils,
        in any way

**United Kingdom Competitive Telecommunications Association
(UKCTA)**

NR   10 Fitzroy Square, LONDON, W1T 5HP.
        0870 801 8000
○   *T; 'to foster a more competitive fixed telecommunications
        market in the UK'
M   f

**United Kingdom Computer Measurement Group   (UKCMG)
1981**

■   Kebbell House (suite A1), Carpenders Park, WATFORD, Herts,
        WD19 5BE.   (asa)
        020 8421 5330   fax 020 8421 5457
        email ukcmg@ukcmg.org.uk   http://www.ukcmg.org.uk
        Sec: Steve Hurley
○   *P; with a strong focus on training & education, UKCMG
        provides a platform for IT professionals to learn from experts
        & to exchange information & ideas with experienced
        practitioners
M   i, f & org
¶   e NL.

**United Kingdom Confederation of Hypnotherapy Organisations
(UKCHO)   1998**

■   Albany House (suite 404), 324-326 Regent St, LONDON,
        W1B 3HH.   (hq)
        0800 952 0560
        http://www.ukcho.co.uk
        Sec: Peter Matthews
▲   Company Limited by Guarantee
○   *N, *P; to provide a non-political arena to discuss & implement
        changes to the profession of hypnotherapy
●   Conf - Mtgs - ET - Res - LG
M   8 org
¶   NL - irreg.

United Kingdom Consortium for Photonics & Optics

NR   Geddes House, Kirkton North, LIVINGSTON, W Lothian,
        EH54 6GU.   (hq)
        01506 497228
        Secretariat: Leigh-Ann Donoghue
▲   Un-incorporated Society
○   *T

United Kingdom Contractors Group   (UKCG)   2009

NR   Centre Point, 103 New Oxford St, LONDON, WC1A 1DU.
        (hq)
        email enquiries@ukcg.org.uk   http://www.ukcg.org.uk
        Contact: Stephen Ratcliffe
○   *T; for contractors/constructors working in the UK
●   Mtgs - ET - Apprentice scheme
M   30 f
¶   Construction's impact on the big society (report); free
        on website.

United Kingdom Council for Psychotherapy   (UKCP)   1992

NR   Edward House (2nd floor), 2 Wakley St, LONDON,
        EC1V 7LT.   (hq)
        020 7014 9955   fax 020 7014 9977
        email info@psychotherapy.org.uk
        http://www.psychotherapy.org.uk
        CEO: Valerie Tufnell
▲   Registered Charity
○   *P; to promote & maintain the profession of psychotherapy
Gp   Analytical psychology; Behavioural & cognitive psychotherapy;
        Experiential constructivist therapies; Family / couple / sexual
        & systemic therapy; Humanistic & integrative psychotherapy;
        Therapy with children
●   Conf - Mtgs - ET - Inf - LG
<   Eur Assn for Psychotherapy; Brit Assn for Counselling
M   6,500 i, 80 f
¶   The Psychotherapist (NL) - 2; ftm only.
        National Register of Psychotherapists - 1.
        Directory of Member Organisations & Training Courses - 1.

**United Kingdom Crowd Management Association   (UKCMA)
2001**

NR   EB Events & Safety Ltd, Unit 6 & 10 Cantech Park, REDDITCH,
      Worcs, B98 9NR.   (hsb)
      0844 800 1642
      http://www.ukcma.com
      Sec: Chris Woodford
○   *T; to improve standards of crowd safety at entertainm,ent &
      sports events
●   ET through training programmes - Inf
M   10 f, 4 associates

United Kingdom Dance & Drama Federation   (UKDDF)   1989

NR   56 Old Bedford Rd, LUTON, Beds, LU2 7PA.
      01582 411439
      email infoukddf@aol.com   http://www.ukddf.com
▲   Un-incorporated Society
○   *D; an examination body offering a syllabus in ballet, tap,
      modern stage, acrobatics & drama for qualified &
      professional teachers of dance
●   ET - Exam
<   Gld of Profl Teachers of Dance
M   c 55 i
¶   NL - 4; m only.

United Kingdom Egg Producers Association Ltd   (UKEP)   1972

■   Kings House, Maunsel Rd, North Newton, BRIDGWATER,
      Somerset, TA7 0BP.
      01278 661280   fax 01278 661009
      email ukep@chicken-doctor.demon.co.uk
      http://www.laidinbritaineggs.co.uk
      Sec: David Spackman
▲   Company Limited by Guarantee
○   *T; a consortium of independent egg producers who market
      their produce on a regional or local basis
●   Stat - Inf - LG
M   90 i
¶   UKEP/LIB Hotwire - 12; ftm only.

United Kingdom EInformation Group   (UKeiG)   1978

NR   Piglet Cottage, Redmire, LEYBURN, N Yorks, DL8 4EH.
      (admin/hq)
      01969 625751
      email cabaker@ukeig.co.uk   http://www.ukeig.co.uk
      Hon Sec: Christine A Baker
▲   Registered Charity
○   *P; to encourage communication & the exchange of knowledge
      about electronic information
●   Conf - ET - Inf
<   is a special interest group (SIG) of CILIP
M   1,650 i, 105 f, UK / 50 i, o'seas
¶   eLucidate (Jnl) - 6; ftm only.

**United Kingdom Employee Assistance Professionals Association
(UKEAPA)   1991**

NR   PO Box 7966, Wilson, DERBY, DE1 0XP.   (asa)
      email info@eapa.org.uk   http://www.eapa.org.uk
      Sec: Libby Payne
○   *P; the advancement of education in the field of employee
      assistance programmes (EAPs); the encouragement of growth
      & development of EAPs in all workplaces
M   100 i, 50 f

**United Kingdom Environmental Law Association   (UKELA)
1986**

■   PO Box 487, DORKING, Surrey, RH4 9BH.   (exec/dir)
      01306 500090
      email vicki.elcoate@ntworld.com   http://www.ukela.org
      Exec Dir: Vicki Elcoate
▲   Company Limited by Guarantee; Registered Charity
○   *L, *P; to promote the enhancement & conservation of the
      environment; to advance the education of the public relating
      to the development, teaching, application & practice of law
      relating to the environment
Gp   Climate change; Contaminated land; Environmental due
      diligence; Environmental litigation Northern Ireland;
      Insurance; Nature conservation; Water
●   Conf - Mtgs - ET - Res - SG - Inf
<   Eur Envtl Law Assn
M   [not stated]
¶   Environmental Law (Jnl) - 6; ftm only.   AR; free.

**United Kingdom Environmental Mutagen Society   (UKEMS)
1977**

NR   1 Atholl Place, EDINBURGH, EH3 8HP.   (asa)
      email info@ukems.org   http://www.ukems.org
      Sec: Peter Jenkinson
▲   Registered Charity
○   *L; the advancement of genetic toxicology by research,
      discussion & developing methodology

United Kingdom Fashion Exports
      since 2009 has been a division of **United Kingdom Fashion &
      Textile Association**

United Kingdom Fashion & Textile Association   (UKFT)   1981

NR   3 Queen Sq, Bloomsbury, LONDON, WC1N 3AR.   (hq)
      020 7843 9460   fax 020 7843 9478
      http://www.ukft.org
      Dir: John R Wilson,   Asst Dir: Elizabeth P Fox
○   *T; to encourage, promote, develop & protect the clothing
      industry of the UK
Gp   Export Division; Guild British Tie Makers; Knitting Industries
      Federation
      Sectors: Foundation & swimwear; Men's & boys' outerwear,
      Shirt; Tailoring; Women's & Girls' outerwear; Workwear
●   Mtgs - Stat - Inf - Empl - LG
<   Intl Apparel Fedn; CBI; Apparel, Knitting & Textiles Alliance; Brit
      Apparel & Textile Confedn
M   f (membership covers 70% of UK production)
¶   News Sheet - 12;   Fact Card - 1;   AR; all ftm.
×   2009 British Clothing Industry Association

United Kingdom Federation of Jazz Bands   (UKFJB)   1977

■   Byker Community Centre, 153 Hedlam St, NEWCASTLE UPON
      TYNE, NE6 2DX.   (sec/b)
      0191-265 4723
      http://www.ukjazzbands.com
      Office Sec: Mrs Carol Blackborough
▲   Registered Charity
Br   5
○   *D; 'to advance the musical education of children throughout
      the UK by helping to train them in the playing of marching
      band instruments & by means of concerts & exhibitions at
      which such children may perform as bands to advance the
      aesthetic education of the public'
●   Mtgs - ET - Exhib - Comp - VE - LG
M   6,940 i
¶   [on website only]

United Kingdom Federation of Smaller Mental Health Agencies 1996
■ Findon House, 110 Ellis Rd, CROWTHORNE, Berks, RG45 6PH.   (hsp)
01344 772025
email ukfed@ontheside.org   http://www.ukfed.org.uk
Hon Sec: Tony Heyes
▲ Company Limited by Guarantee; Registered Charity
○ *W; to support small mental health groups to work together by coordination & information
● Inf - LG
M 30 i, 2200 org
¶ Small Voices (NL).

United Kingdom Forest Products Association   (UKFPA)   1996
NR Office 14 John Player Building, Stirling Enterprise Park, Springbank Rd, STIRLING, FK7 7RP.   (hq)
01786 449029
email dsulman@ukfpa.co.uk   http://www.ukfpa.co.uk
Exec Dir: David Sulman
▲ Company Limited by Guarantee
○ *T; to represent the British timber industry - harvesting companies, sawmillers, merchants & other processors of British home grown timber & forest products
Gp Environmental; Health & safety; Harvesting & contracting; Technical & development; Training; Wood supply
● Mtgs - ET - Res - Exhib - SG - Inf - VE - LG
M 116 f
¶ LM;   AR - 1.

United Kingdom Fortifications Club
in 2008 amalgamated with the **Pillbox Study Group**

United Kingdom Forum for Environmental Industries   2000
NR c/o Envirolink Northwest, Spencer House, 91 Dewhurst Rd, Birchwood, WARRINGTON, Cheshire, WA3 7PG.   (asa)
01925 813200
email info@ukfei.co.uk
http://www.hosting.creativeconcern.com/ukfei/
Business Devt Mgr: Gill Nowell
▲ Company Limited by Guarantee
○ *T; to help build powerful partnerships between the public & private sector, demonstrating the skills & expertise of UK companies & supporting the new technologies & sustainable solutions being developed to address the major global challenges of our time
● Mtgs - Expt - Inf - LG
M RDA's/DA's, Trade Associations, Enabling bodies

United Kingdom Gift Card & Voucher Association   (UKGCVA) 1996
■ Atrium Court, The Ring, BRACKNELL, RG12 1BW.   (asa)
0870 241 6445   fax 01344 397070
http://www.ukgcva.co.uk
Dir Gen: Andrew Johnson
▲ Un-incorporated Society
○ *T; an information & reference point for any company in the gift voucher, gift card, or prepaid cards market
● Conf - Mtgs - ET - Res - Exhib - Stat - Inf - VE - LG
< Brit Promotional Merchandise Assn (BPMA); Direct Marketing Assn (DMA); Inst of Sales Promotion (ISP); Indep Print Inds Assn
M 80 f
(Sub: £2,200)
✕ 2008 Voucher Association

United Kingdom Golf Course Owners Association   (UKGCOA) 2011
NR Federation House, STONELEIGH PARK, Warks, CV8 2RF.   (hq)
024 7641 4999   fax 024 7641 4990
email jerry.kilby@ukgcoa.com
Exec Dir: Jerry Kilby
▲ Company Limited by Guarantee
○ *T; owners of golf courses
● Conf - Mtgs - inf
< Fedn of Sports & Play Assns (FSPA)
M c 100 courses
(Sub: £300-450)
¶ [Buyers Guide; to come]

United Kingdom Gout Society   2002
NR PO Box 527, LONDON, WC1V 7YP.
email info@ukgoutsociety.org
http://www.ukgoutsociety.org
○ *W; to provide information and increase public awareness of the causes, treatment and prevention of this metabolic disorder.

United Kingdom Hand Knitting Association   (UKHKA)   1991
■ Tree Tops, Otley Rd, Eldwick, BINGLEY, W Yorks, BD16 3DA.   (hq)
email ukhka.secretariat@hotmail.co.uk
http://www.ukhandknitting.com
Co Sec: Ann Thomson-Krol
○ *K, *T; to create a desire to knit
● Mtgs - ET - Res - Exhib
M 9 f
¶ LM.
✕ 2007 (January) British Hand Knitting Confederation

United Kingdom Harp Association   (UKHA)   1964
■ 118 Blanmerle Rd, New Eltham, LONDON, SE9 2DZ.   (memsec/p)
http://www.ukharp.net
Mem Sec: Julie Hodgskin
○ *P, *T; for harpists, harp makers & repairers & harp enthusiasts, includes players of non-pedal harps (the clarsach), Paraguayan harp & metal strung harps
● Mtgs - Inf
M c 400 i, UK / c 100 i, o'seas
¶ Magazine - 4; £15 yr m.   Directory - 2 yrly; ftm only.

United Kingdom Herbal Infusions Association   (UKHIA)
■ 6 Catherine St, LONDON, WC2B 5JJ.
020 7836 2460   fax 020 7836 0580
email harriet.green@fdf.org.uk
Un-incorporated Society
Exec Sec: Harriet Green
○ *T; to represent the interests of British manufacturers of herbal & fruit infusions on a wide range of issues of concern
● Mtgs
< Eur Herbal Infusions Assn (EHIA)

United Kingdom Home Care Association   (UKHCA)   1988
NR Group House (2nd floor), 52 Sutton Court Rd, SUTTON, Surrey, SM1 4SL.   (hq)
020 8288 5291   fax 020 8288 5290
email enquiries@ukhca.co.uk   http://www.ukhca.co.uk
Chief Exec: Lesley Rimmer
▲ Company Limited by Guarantee
○ *N, *W; professional association to promote highest standards of domiciliary care
● Conf - Mtgs - ET - Exhib - LG
< Jt Advy Gp on Domiciliary Care; Nat Coun Voluntary Orgs (NCVO); Continuing Care Conference (CCC); Care Forum Wales; Indep Care Orgs Network (ICON)
M 1,600 f
¶ The Homecarer (NL) - 6; ftm.

United Kingdom Horse Shoers Association (UKHSA) 2002
- ■ 3 Roughdown Villas Road, HEMEL HEMPSTEAD, Herts, HP3 0AX.
  01442 248657
  Sec: Martin Humphrey
- ○ *U
- ✕ 2008 (September) United Kingdom Horse Shoers Union

United Kingdom Housekeepers Association (UKHA) 1985
- ■ c/o Jean Roberts, Hotel Duvin Harrogate, Prospect Place, HARROGATE, N Yorks, HG1 1LB. (hsb)
  email housekeeping.harrogate@hotelduvin.com
  http://www.ukha.co.uk
  Sec: Jean Roberts
- Br 4
- ○ *P
- ● Conf - Mtgs
- < Intl Exec Housekeepers Assn
- M i
  (Sub: £30 i, £75 associates)

United Kingdom Industrial Sugar Users Group (UKISUG)
- ■ 20-22 Stukeley St, LONDON, WC2B 5LR.
  020 7430 0356   fax 020 7831 6014
  email info@ukisug.org.uk   http://www.ukisug.org.uk
  Sec: Richard Laming
- ○ *T; for industrial users of sugar: manufacturers of confectionery, chocolate, cakes, biscuits, soft drinks, fruit juices & ice cream
- ● Mtgs
- < C'ee Indl Users Sugar (CIUS)
- M f

United Kingdom Industrial Vision Association (UKIVA) 1992
- ■ New Progress House, 34 Stafford Rd, WALLINGTON, Surrey, SM6 9AA.
  020 8773 8111   fax 020 8773 0022
  email info@ukiva.org   http://www.ukiva.org
  Admin: Don Braggins
- ▲ Company Limited by Guarantee
- ○ *T; to promote the use of vision technology by the manufacturing industry in Britain
- < is a special interest group of the Processing & Packaging Machinery Assn
- M 40 f, UK / 3 f, o'seas
- ¶ NL - 2;   LM; both free.
  21 Financial Justifications for using Machine Vision.
  Guide to Machine Vision; free to qualifying applicants.

United Kingdom Interactive Entertainment Association Ltd (ELSPA) 1989
- ■ 167 Wardour St, LONDON, W1F 8WL. (hq)
  020 7534 0580   fax 020 7534 0581
  email info@ukie.info   http://www.ukie.info
  Chmn: Andy Payne
- ▲ Company Limited by Guarantee
- ○ *T; for interactive consumer software publishers, including computer & video games
- Gp Publishers; Developers; Distributors; Duplicators; Suppliers; Hardware Mfrs; Trade & Consumer Media; Legal
- ● Conf - ET - Res - Exhib - Stat - Expt - Inf - LG - Anti piracy (crime unit) - Accreditation (duplicators)
- < Video Standards Couns: VUD (Germany); SELL (France); ISF-E
- M 120 f, 4 org
- ¶ The Britsoft Book
- ✕ 2010 Entertainment & Leisure Software Publishers Association

United Kingdom & Ireland Society of Cataract & Refractive Surgeons (UKISCRS)
- NR 9 Haylemere Court, 4 Oxford Rd, SOUTHPORT, Merseyside, PR8 2JT. (hq)
  07951 599165
  email ukiscrs@onyxnet.co.uk   http://www.ukiscrs.org.uk
  The Secretary
- ▲ Company Limited by Guarantee
- ○ *P; promotion & dissemination of knowledge of cataract & refractive surgery to interested healthcare professionals
- ● Conf - Mtgs - ET
- < Eur Soc of Cataract & Refractive Surgeons (ESCRS)
- M 500 i
- ¶ Jnl of Cataract & Refractive Surgery - 12; ftm, priced nm.
  NL - 2; ftm only.

United Kingdom Irrigation Association (UKIA) 1980
- ■ Moorland House, 10 Hayway, RUSHDEN, Northants, NN10 6AG. (hq)
  01427 717627   fax 01427 717624
  email m.kay@ukia.org   http://www.ukia.org
  Exec Sec: Melvyn Kay
- ▲ Company Limited by Guarantee
- ○ *F, *H; to promote interest in, and a better understanding of, all aspects of irrigation in the UK; to raise standards of knowledge and competence in irrigation design, installation & management
- ● Conf - Mtgs - ET - Inf - LG
- M 350 i, UK / 50 i, o'seas
- ¶ UK Irrigation News (Jnl) - 1.
  NL - 2.
  Industry Directory.

United Kingdom Land & Hydrographic Survey Association (TSA) 1979
- ■ Northgate Business Centre, 38 Northgate, NEWARK-ON-TRENT, Notts, NG24 1EZ. (hq)
  01636 642840   fax 01636 642841
  email office@tsa-uk.org.uk   http://www.tsa-uk.org.uk
  Sec Gen: Rory Stanbridge
- ▲ Company Limited by Guarantee
- ○ *T; for private sector businesses in land & hydrographic survey
- ● Mtgs - Inf
- M 130 f
- ¶ NL;   Members Directory; both free.
  Note: is generally known as the Survey Association

United Kingdom Literacy Association (UKLA) 1961
- ■ Attenborough Building (4th floor), University of Leicester, LEICESTER, LE1 7RH. (hq)
  email admin@ukla.org   http://www.ukla.org
  Hon Sec: Lyn Overall
- ▲ Registered Charity
- ○ *E; for professionals interested in the teaching & learning of language, literacy & communication
- ● Conf - ET - Res - Exhib - LG - Book awards
- < Intl Reading Assn
- M 500 i, 100 f, 80 schools
- ¶ Journal of Research in Reading - 3;   Literacy - 3; Language & Literacy News - 3; all ftm.

United Kingdom Locksmiths Association (UKLA) 2005
- ■ 370 Cranbrook Rd, Gants Hill, ILFORD, Essex, IG2 6HY.
  020 8590 7111   fax 020 8550 7703
  email info@uklocksmithsassociation.co.uk
  Sec: Adam Jackson
- ▲ Company Limited by Guarantee
- ○ *P; training students to become qualified locksmiths
- ● ET - Inf
- M 200 i, 5 f
  (Sub: £175)
- ¶ via website.

© CBD Research Ltd · Beckenham · BR3 5JS · Tel 020 8650 7745 · E-mail cbd@cbdresearch.com · www.cbdresearch.com

United Kingdom Lubricants Association Ltd (UKLA) 1968
- ■ Berkhamsted House, 121 High St, BERKHAMSTED, Herts, HP4 2DJ. (hq)
  01442 230589 fax 01442 259232
  email enquiries@ukla.org.uk http://www.ukla.org.uk
  Exec Dir: Rod G Parker
- ▲ Company Limited by Guarantee
- ○ *T; for the UK lubricants industry
- Gp Metalworking Fluid Product Stewardship Gp
- ● Conf - Mtgs - Stat - Inf - VE - LG
- < Indep U of the Eur Lubricants Ind (UEIL)
- M 100 f, UK / 2 f, o'seas
- ¶ Lube (Jnl) - 6; free.

United Kingdom Magnetics Society
- NR Grove Business Centre, Grove Technology Park, WANTAGE, Oxon, OX12 9FA. (asa)
  01235 770652
- ○ *L; 'to represent both industrial & academic interests in all field of magnetics'

United Kingdom Maize Millers' Association 1997
- NR 21 Arlington St, LONDON, SW1A 1RN. (hq)
  020 7493 2521
- ▲ Un-incorporated Society
- ○ *T; for the UK maize milling industry
- ● Mtgs - LG
- < Euromaiziers
- M 4 f

United Kingdom Major Ports Group (UKMPG)
- NR 12 Carthusian St (4th floor), LONDON, EC1M 6EZ. (hq)
  020 7260 1785
  Exec Dir: Richard Bird
- ○ *T; to represent most of the large commercial ports in the UK
- ● Mtgs - Inf
- < Eur Sea Ports Org (ESPO)
- M 9f (operating 41 ports)

United Kingdom Maritime Pilots' Association (UKMPA) 1884
- ■ Transport House, 128 Theobald's Rd, LONDON, WC1X 8TN. (hq)
  020 7611 2568 fax 020 7611 2757
  email ukmpa@tgwu.org.uk http://www.ukmpa.org
- ▲ Un-incorporated Society
- ○ *P; interests of maritime pilots of ports of Great Britain & Northern Ireland
- < Intl Maritime Pilots' Assn; Eur Maritime Pilots' Assn; Unite - T & G section
- M 500 i

United Kingdom Metering Forum
- NR c/o Gemserv, 10 Fenchurch St, LONDON, EC3M 3BE.
  020 7090 1000
  Sec: Ryan Perry
- ○ *T

United Kingdom Metric Association (UKMA) 2000
- ■ 34 Wroxham Gardens, LONDON, N11 2BA. (hsp)
  020 8374 6997; 07880 542950
  email secretary@metric.org.uk http://www.ukma.org.uk
  Sec: Derek Pollard
- ▲ Un-incorporated Society
- ○ *K; a non-political organisation which supports the use of the international metric system (SI) for all official, trade, health, safety, educational, media, legal & contractual purposes in the UK.
  It believes that the universal adoption of the metric system is in the best interests of the British Public
- Gp Cookery; Education; PR; Retail; Transport
- ● Conf - Res - SG - Inf - LG
- < US Metric Assn (USMA)
- M 80 i, UK / 5 i, o'seas
- ¶ NL - 4; AR - 1; both ftm only.
  Technical Reports; £6.25 m, £12.50 nm.

United Kingdom Mineral Wool Association
   title now **Mineral Wool Insulation Manufacturers Association**

United Kingdom Money Transmitters Association (UKMTA) 2005
- NR 145-157 St John St (2nd floor), LONDON, EC1V 4PY.
  020 7635 6634 fax 020 7692 0244
  email dominic.thorncroft@ukmta.org
  http://www.ukmta.org
  Chmn: Dominic Thorncroft
- ▲ Company Limited by Guarantee
- ○ *T; to represent businesses registered with HM Revenue & Customs for the purposes of money transfer
- M 250 f

United Kingdom National Defence Association Ltd (UKNDA) 2007
- NR PO Box 819, PORTSMOUTH, Hants, PO1 9FF.
  http://www.uknda.org
  Gen Sec: David Robinson, Chief Exec: John Muxworthy
- ▲ Company Limited by Guarantee
- ○ *K; a campaign for the full funding of the UK's armed forces for the defence of this country & throughout the world
- M i, f & org
  (Sub: £12i, f & org varies, £100 life)

United Kingdom Noise Association (UKNA) 2000
- ■ PO Box 551, CHATHAM, Kent, ME4 9AJ. (hq)
  01634 8638524
  email info@ukna.org.uk http://www.ukna.org.uk
  Chmn: John Stewart
- ▲ Un-incorporated Society
- ○ *K; campaigns for action against noise
- ● Conf - Mtgs - Res - Exhib - Inf - LG
- M 200 i, 40,000 org
  (Sub: £15 i, £75 org)

United Kingdom Offshore Oil & Gas Industry Association Ltd 2007
- NR Portland House (6th floor east), Bressenden Place, LONDON, SE1E 5BH. (hq)
  020 7802 2400
  email info@oilandgasuk.co.uk
  http://www.oilandgasuk.co.uk
  Admin: Alexa Chaffer
- Br Aberdeen, Brussels
- ○ *T
- Gp Well Services Contractors Forum
- × 2010 (1 January) Well Services Contractors Association (merged)
  Note: Uses the trading name Oil & Gas UK

United Kingdom Offshore Operators Association Ltd
   since 2007 **Oil & Gas UK**

**United Kingdom One World Linking Association   (UKOWLA)
1992**

■   The Glade Centre, Frog Lane, ILMINSTER, Somerset,
    TA19 0AP.   (hq)
    01460 55449   fax 01460 55753
    email info@ukowla.org.uk   http://www.ukowla.org.uk
    Sec: Ian Croxford
▲   Company Limited by Guarantee; Registered Charity
○   *X; to support, promote & encourage communities in the UK to
    develop partnership links with communities in the South
    (Africa, Asia, Latin America, the Caribbean)
●   Conf - Mtgs - ET - Res - LG
M   [not stated]
    (Sub: £15 i, £95 f, £30 org)
¶   Owl - 4; ftm only.

United Kingdom Onshore Operators Group   (UKOOG)   1986

■   c/o Midmar Energy Ltd, 6 Dean Park Crescent (1st floor),
    BOURNEMOUTH, Dorset, BH1 1HL.   (hq)
    01202 780333   fax 01202 780444
    Chmn: Peter Redman
▲   Company Limited by Guarantee
○   *T; for UK onshore oil & gas operators licensed under UK
    Landward   Licences (Petroleum Production Act 1934)

**United Kingdom Onshore Pipeline Operators' Association
(UKOPA)**

■   Pipelines Maintenance Centre, Ripley Rd, AMBERGATE, Derbys,
    DE56 2FZ.
    01773 852003   fax 01773 856456
    http://www.ukopa.co.uk
    Sec: Phill Jones
▲   Company Limited by Guarantee
○   *T

United Kingdom Organisation for Cranial Osteopathy
    see the **Sutherland Society (the UK organisation for cranial
    osteopathy)**

**United Kingdom Overseas Territories Association   (UKOTA)
1998**

NR   c/o British Virgin Islands Government Office, 15 Upper
    Grosvenor St, LONDON, W1K 7PJ.   (hq)
    020 7355 9570   fax 020 7355 9575
▲   Un-incorporated Society
○   *N, *W; to provide a forum for discussion for residents of British
    overseas territories on issues of common interest in the
    relevant areas
●   Conf - Mtgs - Inf
M   9 territories

United Kingdom Paint Horse Association

NR   Olde Walnut Tree Farm, Pristow Green Lane, Tibenham,
    NORWICH, NR16 1PU.
    01379 674551
    http://www.ukpha.co.uk
○   *B

United Kingdom Paintball Sports Federation   (UKPSF)   1991

■   5 Waingap Crescent, Whitworth, ROCHDALE, Lancs,
    OL12 8PX.   (chief exec/p)
    0845 130 4252
    http://www.ukpsf.com
    Chief Exec: Steven Bull
▲   Un-incorporated Society
○   *S; to promote the sport of paintball (the firing of paint 'blobs')
Gp   Players' Council
●   Exhib - Comp - Inf - LG
M   850 i, 175 f, 2 org, UK / 50 i, 10 f, o'seas
¶   Paintball UK (NL) - 4.   Paintball Games in Woodlands.
    Millennium Site Guide - 1.
    Code of Practice.   Site Survey - 1.

**United Kingdom Pakistan Chamber of Commerce & Industry
(UKPCCI)   1979**

NR   Premier Business Centre, 47-49 Park Royal Rd, LONDON,
    NW10 7LQ.   (sb)
    020 8090 0429
    http://www.ukpcci.com.
    Gen Sec: A M Shaheen
○   *C; the development of bi-lateral trade between the UK &
    Pakistan

**United Kingdom Petroleum Industry Association   (UKPIA)
1978**

NR   Quality House, Quality Court, Chancery Lane, LONDON,
    WC2A 1HP.   (hq)
    020 7269 7600
    email info@ukpia.com   http://www.ukpia.com
    Dir Gen: Chris Hunt
▲   Company Limited by Guarantee
○   *T; represents oil companies involved in the supply, refining &
    distribution of oil in the UK
M   9 f
    Note: the correct title of the Association is - UK Petroleum
    Industry Association
    see general note under UK. . .

United Kingdom Polarity Therapy Association   (UKPTA)   1996

NR   Monomark House, 27 Old Gloucester St, LONDON,
    WC1N 3XX.   (mail/address)
    http://www.polarity.tk
▲   Un-incorporated Society
○   *P; to support member polarity therapists through providing
    postgraduate training, promotional material, business advice
    & representation at a national level
M   26 i

United Kingdom Polocrosse Association Ltd   (UKPA)   1986

■   4 Heol Bryn Glas, Meadow Farm, LLANTWIT FARDRE, Mid
    Glamorgan, CF38 2DJ.   (hsp)
    01443 208264
    email secretary@polocrosse.co.uk
    http://www.polocrosse.org.uk
    Sec: Jeff Parr
▲   Company Limited by Guarantee
○   *S; to control & administer the game of Polocrosse (a team
    game played on horseback)
●   Mtgs - ET - Comp - VE
<   Intl Polocrosse Coun; Brit Horse Soc
M   500 i
¶   NL - 4;   Magazine - 1;   Ybk - 1; all ftm.

**United Kingdom Practical Shooting Association   (UKPSA)
1977**

■   PO Box 7057, Preston, WEYMOUTH, Dorset, DT4 4EN.
    (mail/add)
    07010 703845   fax 0870 765 7721
    email secretary@ukpsa.org.uk   http://www.ukpsa.co.uk
    Sec: Alan Phillips
▲   Registered Charity
○   *S; to encourage skill in practical shooting by providing
    instruction & practice in the use of firearms amongst HM
    subjects so that they will be better fitted to serve their country
    in the Armed Forces, Territorial Army or any other
    organisation in which their services may be required in the
    defence of the realm
●   Comp - LG
<   Intl Practical Shooting Confedn (IPSC)
M   [not stated]
¶   DVC - 1;   eDVC - 9; both ftm only.

© CBD Research Ltd · Beckenham · BR3 5JS · Tel 020 8650 7745 · E-mail cbd@cbdresearch.com · www.cbdresearch.com

United Kingdom Public Health Association   (UKPHA)   1988
NR   94 White Lion St, LONDON, N1 9PF.   (hq)
        020 7713 8910   fax 020 3051 1769
        email info@ukpha.org.uk   http://www.ukpha.org.uk
        Chief Exec: Angela Mawle
▲   Company Limited by Guarantee; Registered Charity
Br   11
○   *K, *P; to eliminate inequalities in health, promote sustainable
        development & combat anti-health forces
Gp   Alcohol & violence; Devolution; Food & nutrition; Health &
        sustainable environments; Health visiting & public health
●   Conf - Mtgs - Res - Exhib - SG - LG
M   1,000 i, 200 org, UK / 100 i, o'seas

United Kingdom Pyrotechnics Society   (UKPS)   2006
NR   c/o 17 Manor Drive, MIRFIELD, W Yorks, WF14 0ER.   .
        email secretary@pyrosociety.org.uk
        http://www.pyrosociety.org.uk
        Sec: Phil Coopers
▲   Company Limited by Guarantee
○   *G; to represent the heritage, science, history and art of
        pyrotechnics in the UK
¶   Spark

United Kingdom Quality Ash Association   (UKQAA)   1997
■   Maple House, Kingswood Business Park, Holyhead Rd,
        Albrighton, WOLVERHAMPTON, W Midlands, WV7 3AU.
        01902 373365
        email enquiries@ukqaa.org.uk   http://www.ukqaa.org.uk
        Technical Dir: Dr Lindon Sear
▲   Un-incorporated Society
○   *T; to represent the interests of producers & users of fly ash
        from coal fired power stations, eg the construction industry -
        use of fly ash in concrete fill, grouting & road construction
●   Conf - Mtgs - ET - Res - Exhib - Inf - Lib
<   Eur Ash Assn (ECOBA)
M   17 f
¶   Datasheets;   Case Studies;   Best Practice Guides - all irreg;
        all free.

United Kingdom Rainwater Harvesting Association   (UK-RHA)   2004
■   Millennium Green Business Centre, Rio Drive, Collingham,
        NEWARK, Notts, NG23 7NB.   (hq)
        01636 894900   fax 01636 894909
        email info@ukrha.org   http://www.ukrha.org
        Co Sec: Terry Nash
▲   Company Limited by Guarantee
○   *T; to represent the rainwater harvesting industry in the UK
Gp   Best practice; Industry liaison; Marketing
●   Conf - Mtgs - ET - Res - Exhib - SG - Stat - Inf - LG
M   30 f
        (Sub: £750)

United Kingdom Renderers' Association   (UKRA)   1966
NR   c/o Engreen Environmental Consultants, Office 7
        Arkwright Suite, Coppull Enterprise Centre, Mill Lane,
        COPPULL, Lancs, PR7 5BW   (dir/b)
        01257 791155
        email info@ukra.co.uk   http://www.ukra.co.uk
        Un-incorporated Society
        Technical Dir: David Green
○   *T; to promote good practice & the raise the profile of the
        rendering industry & its efforts to produce products &
        renewable fuels in an environmentally friendly way
M   8 f

United Kingdom Resilient Flooring Association   (UKRFA)
■   c/o Bunkers LLP, 7 The Drive, HOVE, E Sussex, BN3 3JS.   (hsb)
        01273 329797
        Hon Sec: Richard Crawt
○   *T; manufacturers of vinyl & linoleum floorcoverings
●   Mtgs - Inf (on vinyl & linoleum only)
M   8 f

United Kingdom Revenue Protection Association   (UKRPA)   1997
NR   c/o Gemserv, 10 Fenchurch St, LONDON, EC3M 3BE.   (hsb)
        020 7090 1000
        http://www.ukrpa.org.uk
▲   Un-incorporated Society
○   *T; for companies involved in investigating & dealing with theft
        of electricity &/or interference with meters
Gp   C'ees: Publicity, Technical
●   Conf - Mtgs - ET - Inf - LG
<   Intl Utilities Revenue Protection Assn (IURPA)
M   16 f

United Kingdom Rocketry Association   (UKRA)   1996
NR   27-29 South Lambeth Rd, LONDON, SW8 1SZ.   (mail
        address)
        email enquiries@ukra.org.uk   http://www.ukra.org.uk
        Sec: Jonathan Rhodes
▲   Un-incorporated Society
○   *G; to promote amateur rocketry in the UK; to provide a link
        between groups & individuals interested in rocketry in the UK;
        to create a recognised safety code & certification &
        achievement programme
●   Mtgs - ET - Exam - Exhib - LG - Annual flying events - Monthly
        club meetings
<   Brit Model Flying Assn (BMFA)
M   200 i, 7 org
¶   UKRA Hbk - 1.   10.9.8 - 4.

United Kingdom Roundabout Appreciation Society   (UKRAS)   2003
■   PO Box 12810, Astwood Bank, REDDITCH, Worcs, B97 9BH.
        07815 630416   fax 01527 522545
        email info@roundaboutsofbritain.com
        http://www.roundaboutsofbritain.com
▲   Un-incorporated Society
○   *G; to collect data & other information on traffic islands,
        roundabouts & all traffic gyratory systems
●   Mtgs - VE
M   30 i
¶   Roundabouts of GB Calendar [for 26 towns] - 1; £5 m, £8 nm.
        Roundabouts of Britain (book); £7.99.
        Roundabouts from the Air (book); £8.99.

United Kingdom Science Park Association   (UKSPA)   1984
■   Chesterford Research Park, Little Chesterford,
        SAFFRON WALDEN, Essex, CB10 1XL.   (hq)
        01799 532050   fax 01799 532049
        email info@ukspa.org.uk   http://www.ukspa.org.uk
        Chief Exec: Anthony P Wright
▲   Company Limited by Guarantee
○   *L, *N; 'to assist in the planning, development, operation &
        management of science parks / technology parks &
        incubators linked to universities & other institutes of higher
        education; to stimulate the growth of technology &
        knowledge based firms through the transfer of technology'
●   Conf - Mtgs - ET - Res - Stat - Inf - LG
<   Intl Assn of Science Parks (IASP); World Alliance for
        Innovation (WAINOVA); Assn of Universities Res & Indl
        Links (AUKUL)
M   60,000 i, 2,600 f
¶   Innovation into Success (Jnl) - 4; ftm, £4.95 nm.
        Annual Directory of Science Parks; ftm (£25 2nd copy), £50 nm.
        Evaluation of the Past & Future Economic Contribution of the
        UK Science Park Movement; £35 m, £75 nm.
        Planning, Development & Operation of Science Parks; £20.
        Best Practice Guides - irreg; £20 each or £60 the set.

United Kingdom Screen Association   2003
NR   47 Beak St, LONDON, W1F 9SE.
       020 7734 6060
       http://www.ukscreenassociation.co.uk
○   *T; to represent the UK's post production & special effects
       industries
●   Mtgs - ET
M   c 140 f
¶   Online training directory.   LM.

**United Kingdom Security Shredding Association   (UKSSA)
1997**
■   Heritage House, Vicar Lane, DAVENTRY, Northants,
       NN11 4GD.   (hq)
       0800 634 0212
       email info@ukssa.org.uk   http://www.ukssa.org.uk
       Chmn: Steve Houghton
▲   Company Limited by Guarantee
○   *T; to stipulate & enforce the highest standards of confidential
       data destruction & the manner in which it is undertaken
       together with legal requirements at local & national levels
●   Conf - Mtgs - ET - Inf - LG - National industrial standards
M   11 f

United Kingdom Serials Group   (UKSG)   1978
NR   PO Box 5594, NEWBURY, Berks, RG20 0YD.   (admin p)
       01635 254292   fax 01635 253826
       email alison@uksg.org   http://www.uksg.org
       Business Manager: Alison Whitehorn
○   *L, *P; 'to promote & assist discussion & research on serials &
       their management between all interested parties in the
       information industry'
●   Conf - Mtgs - ET - Res - Exhib - Stat - Inf
M   c 600 org
¶   Serials (online Jnl) - 3; £72+VAT m only.

United Kingdom Shareholders' Association Ltd   (UKSA)   1992
■   Chislehurst Business Centre, 1 Bromley Lane, CHISLEHURST,
       Kent, BR7 6LH.   (hq)
       020 8468 1027
       email uksa@uksa.org.uk   http://www.uksa.org.uk
       Chmn: Martin White,   Dir: Roger Lawson
       Mem Sec: Elizabeth Baxter (membership@uksa.org.uk)
▲   Company Limited by Guarantee
Br   6
○   *K, *W; to promote improved standards of corporate
       governance for the benefit of the UK economy including all
       shareholders; to represent the interests of private
       shareholders; to assist private shareholders exercise their
       responsibilities as joint owners of their companies
Gp   Company activities group
●   Mtgs - ET - Res - SG - VE - LG
<   Euroshareholders (Eur Shareholders Gp)
M   500 i, 10 org, UK / 10 i, o'seas
       (Sub: £50 i)
¶   UKSA Update (NL) - 6; ftm only.
       Numerous policy papers available on website.

United Kingdom Sibelius Society   1984
NR   51 Vernon Ave, LONDON, SW20 8BN.   (pres/p)
       020 8715 7659
       http://www.sibeliussociety.info
       Pres: Edward W Clark
▲   Un-incorporated Society
○   *D; to explore & promulgate Sibelius' achievement in 20th
       century music
●   Conf - Mtgs - Concerts - Seminars
M   120 i, UK / 40 i, o'seas
¶   NL - 4; free.

United Kingdom Skateboarding Association   (UKSA)
NR   113 Broomstick Hall Rd, WALTHAM ABBEY, Essex, EN9 1LP.
       (hsp)
       Sec: Dave Carlin
○   *DS
●   Mtgs - Comp
M   i

United Kingdom Skeptics
       UK-Skeptics is now a non-membership website
       (www.ukskeptics.com)

United Kingdom Social Investment Forum
       since 2009 **UKSIF: the Sustainable Investment & Finance
       Association**

United Kingdom Society for Co-operative Studies   (SCS)   1967
NR   Holyoake House, Hanover St, MANCHESTER, M60 0AS.   (hq)
       0161-246 3553
       email richardbickle@cooptel.net
       http://www.co-opstudies.org
       Sec: Richard Bickle
▲   Registered Charity
○   *L, *Q; to promote the knowledge & study of the co-operative
       movement
●   Conf - Mtgs - Res
M   184 i, 42 org
¶   Jnl - 3; ftm, £10 nm.

United Kingdom Society of Investment Professionals
       since 30 November 2007 **CFA Society of the UK**

United Kingdom Society for Trenchless Technology   (UKSTT)
■   38 Holly Walk, LEAMINGTON SPA, Warks, CV32 4LY.   (hq)
       01926 330935
       http://www.ukstt.org.uk
▲   Company Limited by Guarantee; Registered Charity
○   *P; to advance the science & practice of trenchless technology
       for public benefit; to promote education, training, study &
       research in trenchless technology
●   Conf - Mtgs - ET - Exhib - Expt - Inf - LG
<   Intl Soc for Trenchless Technology
¶   UKSTT News (NL) - 6; ftm.

United Kingdom Software Metrics Association   (UKSMA)
■   c/o Xchanging (Attn: Rob Ratcliff), Walter Burke Way,
       Chatham Maritime, CHATHAM, Kent, ME4 4RQ.   (chmn/b)
       01634 887890
       email rob.ratcliff@xchanging.com
       http://www.uksma.co.uk
       Chmn: Rob Ratcliff
▲   Company Limited by Guarantee
○   *P; for organisations & individuals involved in the development,
       promotion or use of software metrics
●   Conf - Mtgs - ET - Exam - Res - Exhib - SG - Inf - Lib
M   i, f
¶   NL - 4; ftm, £10 nm.

United Kingdom Specialised Information Publishers Association
       see **Specialised Information Publishers Association**

United Kingdom Spill Association   (UKSPILL)   2004
■   61 Sevenhampton, CHELTENHAM, Glos, GL54 5SL.   (hsb)
       0845 625 9890
       email info@ukspill.org   http://www.ukspill.org
       Exec Dir: Roger M Mabbott
▲   Company Limited by Guarantee
○   *T; for the UK oil spill industry, spill contractors, equipment
       manufacturers & consulting companies
●   Conf - Mtgs - Exhib - Expt - Inf - LG
<   Soc of Marine Inds
M   10 i, 80 f, 10 org

© CBD Research Ltd · Beckenham · BR3 5JS · Tel 020 8650 7745 · E-mail cbd@cbdresearch.com · www.cbdresearch.com

United Kingdom Spoon Collectors Club   (UKSCC)   1980
- ■ 72 Edinburgh Rd, NEWMARKET, Suffolk, CB8 0QD.   (hsp)
    01638 665457
    email david.cross340@ntlworld.com
    Hon Sec: David S Cross
- ▲ Un-incorporated Society
- Br 6; Australia, N Zealand, South Africa, USA
- ○ *G; for those interested in collecting spoons (souvenir or antique)
- ● Mtgs - AGM (October)
- M 200 i
- ¶ Club Magazine - 4; subscription varies (£12- £1).

United Kingdom Sports Association for People with Learning Disability (UKSA)   1980
- ■ 12 City Forum (1st floor), 250 City Rd, LONDON, EC1V 2PU. (hq)
    020 7490 3057   fax 020 7251 8861
    email info@uksportsassociation.org
    http://www.uksportsassociation.org
- ▲ Registered Charity
- ○ *N; the National Governing Body of sport in the UK for people with learning disabilities; to co-ordinate, promote & develop sport & recreational opportunities for all people with learning disability in the UK
- ● Conf - Mtgs - Inf - VE - LG
- < Intl Paralympic C'ee; Intl Sports Fedn for Persons with Intellectual Disability (INAS-FID); Brit Paralympic Assn; Disability Sport NI; Mencap Sport; Scot Disability Sport; Welsh Sports Assn for People with Learning Disability
- ¶ Coaching People with Learning Disability; £8.

United Kingdom Spring Manufacturers Association   (UKSMA) 1948
- ■ Henry St, SHEFFIELD, S Yorks, S3 7EQ.   (hq)
    0114-276 0542   fax 0114-252 7997
    email uksma@uksma.org.uk   http://www.uksma.org.uk
    Managing Dir: Andrew Watkinson
- ▲ Company Limited by Guarantee
- ○ *T
- ● Conf - Mtgs - ET - Res - Inf - Lib - VE
- < Eur Spring Fedn
- M c 100 f
- ¶ Directory of British Spring Manufacturers - 1; free.

United Kingdom Steel   1967
- NR EEF House, Queensway North, Team Valley Trading Estate, GATESHEAD, Tyne & Wear, NE11 0NX.   (hq)
    0191-497 3240
    email enquiries@uksteel.org.uk
    http://www.uksteel.org.uk
    Dir: Ian Rodgers
- ○ *T; representation of UK steel producing & processing companies
- Gp Tubes product (incorporating members of the former British Welded Steel Tube Assn)
- ● Conf - Mtgs - Stat - Expt - Inf - LG - Provision of detailed information on steel specifications to specifiers & users of steel
- < is a division of EEF
- > Energy Intensive Users Gp; Brit Metallurgical Plant Constructors Assn
- M 30 f
- ¶ LM;   Annual Statistics; AR; all free.
    Steel specifications [book & On-line]

United Kingdom Sustainable Development Association   (UK-SDA)   2008
- ■ Millennium Green Business Centre, Rio Drive, Collingham, NEWARK, Notts, NG23 7NB.   (hq)
    0845 026 0240   fax 01636 894909
    email info@uk-sda.org   http://www.uk-sda.org
    Sec: Terry Nash
- ▲ Company Limited by Guarantee
- ○ *T; to represent the sustainable development industry in the UK
- ● Conf - Mtgs - ET - Res - Exhib - SG - Inf
- M 20 f
    (Sub: £250)
- ¶ E-NL - 12; free.

United Kingdom Sustainable Investment & Finance Association (UKSIF)   1991
- NR Holywell Centre, 1 Phipp St, LONDON, EC2A 4PS.
    020 7749 9950
    email info@uksif.org   http://www.uksif.org
    Chief Executive: Penny Shepherd,   Admin: Louise Hopper
- ▲ Company Limited by Guarantee
- ○ *L; to promote sustainable & responsible finance
- M 200 f, i & org
- × 2009 UK Social Investment Forum

United Kingdom Synaesthesia Association   (UKSA)
- ■ Old Chapel House, The Street, PLAISTOW, W Sussex, RH14 0PT.   (hsp)
    email uksynaesthesia@hotmail.com
    http://www.uksynaesthesia.com
    Mem Sec: Giles Hamilton-Fletcher
- ○ *L; helping the understanding of Synaesthesia in public contexts, through the media & in scientific disciplines; Synaesthesia - a cognitive condition that produces an unusual combining of the senses
- ● Conf - Inf - puts synaesthesia researchers & the media in contact with each other
- M c 200 i, UK / c 30 i, o'seas
- ¶ NL - 2; ftm only.

United Kingdom Tea Council   (UKTA)   1953
- NR Crown House (suite 10), One Crown Sq, WOKING, Surrey, GU21 6HR.   (hq)
    01483 750599
    email info@teacouncil.co.uk   http://www.tea.co.uk
- ▲ Company Limited by Guarantee
- ○ *T; to promote tea & its unique story for the benefit of those who produce, sell & enjoy tea
- Gp Tea Advisory Panel
- ● Mtgs - Res
- < Food & Drink Fedn
- M 52 f
- ¶ NL (for health profls) - free.

United Kingdom Textile Laboratory Forum   (UKTLF)   2001
- ■ 8 Wentworth Way, LEEDS, W Yorks, LS17 7TG.   (hsb)
    0113-225 0014
    email info@uktlf.com   http://www.uktlf.com
    Hon Sec: Alan Ross
- ▲ Un-incorporated Society
- ○ *N, *T; to provide a technical forum for UK based UKAS accredited textile laboratories; to provide a system of inter-laboratory correlations; to provide a professional interface with other relevant organisations
- Gp Fibre composition, Flammability, Uncertainty of measurement
- ● Mtgs - LG
- < Soc of Dyers & Colourists; ASBCI; UKAS
- M 27 f
    (Sub: £100)

United Kingdom Thalassaemia Society (UKTS) 1976
- ■ 19 The Broadway, Southgate Circus, LONDON, N14 6PH. (hq)
  020 8882 0011
  http://www.ukts.org
  Pres: M Michael,   Coordinator: Elaine Miller
- ▲ Registered Charity
- ○ *M,*W; to provide advice, information & counselling to sufferers & carriers of thalassaemia (a hereditary blood disorder)
- ● Conf - Mtgs - ET - Res - Inf
- < Thalassaemia Intl Fedn (TIF)
- M c 600 i, UK / c 130 i, o'seas
- ¶ News Review (NL) - 4.   AR.
  Various booklets & leaflets.

United Kingdom Timber Frame Association (UKTFA) 2002
- NR The e-Centre, Cooperage Way Business Village, ALLOA, Clackmannanshire, FK10 3LP. (chmn/b)
  01259 272140   fax 01259 272141
  email office@ukfta.com   http://www.uktfa.com
  Chief Exec: Andrew Carpenter
- ○ *T; to promote timber as the ultimate sustainable building material; to raise awareness of the proven advantages of timber frames across all sectors of the UK construction industry
- < Construction Products Assn
- M 300 f

United Kingdom Trades Confederation (UKTC) 1995
- NR Spendale House (1st floor), The Runway, RUISLIP, Middx, HA4 6SE. (hq)
  0844 804 4575   fax 0844 804 4575
  email membership@uktc.com   http://www.uktc.com
  Managing Dir: Derek Vaughan
- ▲ Company Limited by Guarantee
- ○ *N, *T; to protect business in the face of growing bureaucracy & the legal minefield; to grow business in the ever-changing business environment through recommendation & lead generation; to save business money through specially discounted services & products
- < Allied Trs Confedn
- M 3,500 f

United Kingdom Transplant Co-ordinators Association
has closed

United Kingdom Travel Retail Forum (UKTRF) 1988
- ■ c/o Sarah Branquinho, WDF, 4 New Square, BEDFONT LAKES, Middx, TW14 8HA. (hq)
  07964 666300
  email info@uktrf.co.uk   http://www.uktrf.co.uk
  Sec Gen: Sarah Branquinho
- ▲ Company Limited by Guarantee
- ○ *T; to improve trading conditions for companies involved in the supply & sale of duty paid goods to international travellers within the EU; to protect all duty & tax free sales where these still exist
- ● Mtgs - Stat - Expt - LG
- < Eur Travel Retail Coun
- M 26 f

United Kingdom Ultimate Association (UKU) 1981
- NR 27 Old Gloucester Rd, LONDON, WC1N 3AX. (hq)
  0844 804 5949
  http://www.ukultimate.com
- ▲ Un-incorporated Society
- ○ *S; for the seven-a-side team sport of ultimate - a game played indoors & outdoors by men & women using a flying disc
- M i

United Kingdom Vaccine Industry Group
- NR 12 Whitehall, LONDON, SW1A 2DY.   (hq)
  http://www.uvig.org
- ○ *T; companies concerned with vaccine research, development & manufacture
- < is a group within the Association of the British Pharmaceutical Industry
- M 6 f

United Kingdom Vineyards Association (UKVA) 1996
- ■ PO Box 1193, CAMBRIDGE, CB25 9UY.   (hq)
  01223 813786
  email robert@ukva.org.uk   http://www.ukva.org.uk
  Gen Sec: Robert Beardsmore
- ▲ Company Limited by Guarantee
- ○ *T; to promote viticulture & viniculture in the UK
- ● Conf - Comp - Inf - LG
- < Nat Farmers U; Wine & Spirit Assn of GB
- > Vineyard Assns: Thames & Chilterns, Wessex, South East, South West, Mercia; East Anglia Winegrowers Assn
- M 470 i, UK / 3 i, o'seas
  (Sub: variable UK / £51 o'seas)
- ¶ The Grape Press - 2; ftm only.
  Pesticides booklet - 1; ftm, £25 nm.

United Kingdom Warehousing Association (UKWA) 1944
- ■ Walter House, 418-422 Strand, LONDON, WC2R 0PT.   (hq)
  020 7836 5522   fax 020 7438 9379
  email dg@ukwa.org.uk   http://www.ukwa.org.uk
  Chief Exec Officer: Roger J Williams
- ▲ Un-incorporated Society
- ○ *T; represents logistics companies in the UK
- Gp Customs & tax warehousing; Operations & safety
- ● Conf - Mtgs - ET - Inf - VE - LG
- < Intl Fedn of Warehousing Logistics Assns; Eur Warehousing & Logistics Confedn
- M 680 f
- ¶ NL - 10; ftm.
  Directory of Members' Services - 2 yrly; ftm, £60 nm.
  Fire Precautions Guide to Risk Assessment; £10 m, £20 nm.

United Kingdom Weighing Federation (UKWF) 1920
- ■ Federation House, 10 Vyse St, BIRMINGHAM, B18 6LT.   (asa)
  0121-237 1130   fax 0121-237 1133
  email pres@ukwf.org.uk   http://www.ukwf.org.uk
  Pres: Jim Harper
- ▲ Company Limited by Guarantee
- ○ *T; to promote & improve the understanding of modern weighing technology; to act on regulatory matters emerging at UK, EU & international level
- ● Conf - Mtgs - Inf - LG
- < Eur Fedn Scale & Weighing Machine Mfrs & Repairers (CECIP)
- M 100 f
- ¶ NL - 4; ftm.   LM - 1;   AR.

United Kingdom Windsurfing Association (UKWA) 1976
- ■ PO Box 703, HAYWARDS HEATH, W Sussex, RH16 9EE.   (hq)
  0845 410 3311   fax 01444 401567
  http://www.ukwindsurfing.com
  Admin: Arabella Andrup
- Br 4 regions
- ○ *S; organisation of regional & national windsurfing, racing, wave sailing, freestyle & speed sailing events
- ● Mtgs - PL - Regional & national windsurfing events
- < Intl Windsurfing Assn (IWA); Royal Yachting Assn (RYA)
- M 700+ i

United Kingdom Youth   1911

NR   Avon Tyrell, BRANSGORE, Hants, BH23 8EE.   (hq)
    01425 672347   fax 01425 675108
    email info@ukyouth.org   http://www.ukyouth.org
    Chief Exec: John Bateman
▲   Registered Charity
Br   42
○   *Y; 'to support & develop high quality voluntary youth work &
    informal educational opportunities for & with young people
    through a range of projects, accredited learning
    programmes, events & publications'
●   Conf - ET - Inf - LG
<   Eur Confedn of Youth Clubs; Nat Coun of Voluntary Orgs; Nat
    Coun for Voluntary Youth Services
M   715,440 i, 8,000 org
¶   Publications list available.
    Note: the correct name of this organisation is UK Youth;
    see also note under UK. . .

United Nations Association of Great Britain & Northern Ireland (UNA-UK)   1945

NR   3 Whitehall Court, LONDON, SW1A 2EL.   (hq)
    020 7766 3444   fax 020 7930 5893
    http://www.una.org.uk
    Exec Dir: Sam Daws
▲   Company Limited by Guarantee
○   *X; to promote the principles of the UN charter & the role of the
    UN in international affairs

United Reformed Church History Society   (URCHS)   1972

■   c/o Westminster College, Madingley Rd, CAMBRIDGE,
    CB3 0AA.   (admin/b)
    01223 741300
    email mt212@cam.ac.uk   http://www.urc.org.uk
    Admin: Mrs M Thompson
▲   Registered Charity
○   *L, *Q, *R; research into the history of Congregational &
    Presbyterian churches
●   Annual lecture & meeting - Inf - Lib (Collection specialises in
    C17 - C19 Presbyterianism)
M   175 i, 5 churches, UK / 60 i, o'seas
¶   Jnl - 2; ftm.

United Road Transport Union   (URTU)   1890

NR   Almond House, Oak Green, Stanley Green Business Park,
    CHEADLE HULME, Cheshire, SK8 6QL.   (hq)
    0161-486 2100   fax 0161-485 3109
    email info@urtu.com   http://www.urtu.com
    Gen Sec: Robert Monks
○   *U; to advance the interests of professional drivers in the road
    haulage, distribution & logistics industry
<   Trades U Congress (TUC)
M   12,250 i
¶   Wheels (Jnl) - 6; ftm.

United Saddlebred Association   (USA UK)   1995

■   24 Coton Grove, Shirley, SOLIHULL, W Midlands, B90 1BS.
    (hsp)
    0121-430 4281
    http://www.american-saddlebred.co.uk
    Dorothy Hasty
▲   Un-incorporated Society
○   *B; to promote interest in & care of American Saddlebreds; to
    show their versatility in all spheres of equestrianism
Gp   5-gaited; Saddle seat equitation
●   Conf - Mtgs - ET - Res - Exhib - Comp - Stat - Expt - Inf - Lib -
    PL - VE
<   Amer Saddle Horse Assn; Brit Morgan Horse Soc; Brit
    Skewbald, Piebald Assn; Coloured Horse & Pony Soc
M   c 100 i
¶   NL - 3;   Ybk - 1; both ftm only.   LM;   AR.

United Society of Artists

NR   68 Springdale Rd, LONDON, N16 9NX.   (mem/sp)
    Acting Hon Sec: Eric Jobbins (0788 307 9300)
    Mem Sec: Ged Rumak
○   *A; 'a non-profit-making society that exhibits high quality works
    of art at its annual open exhibitions in London; it was
    founded to give artists living outside Londonan opprtunity to
    exhibit in the capital'
●   Exhib
M   i

Unity   1825

NR   Hillcrest House, Garth St, Hanley, STOKE-ON-TRENT, Staffs,
    ST1 2AB.   (hq)
    01782 272755   fax 01782 284902
    email contact@unitytheunion.org.uk
    http://www.unitytheunion.org.uk
    Gen Sec: Harry Hockaday
○   *U; ceramics industry
<   Trades U Congress (TUC)
M   4,953 i
¶   Unity News - 4; ftm.

Universal Spiritualists Association   (AUHS)   1992

■   99 Wealcroft, Leam Lane, GATESHEAD, Tyne & Wear,
    NE10 8LN.   (pres/p)
    0191-442 2109
    email secretary869-auhs@yahoo.co.uk
    http://www.auhs.co.uk
    Pres: Rev Stewart Robinson,
    Nat Sec: Mrs Catherine Greenup Dusa
▲   Registered Charity
Br   22
○   *P, *R; to further & unite the religion of spiritualism
●   Mtgs - ET - Inf
<   Brit Alliance of Healing Assns
>   UK Spiritualist Churches
M   200 i, church & gp affiliations
    Note: also uses title of Association of Universal Healers &
    Spiritualists

Universities Association for Lifelong Learning   (UALL)   1992

■   21 De Montfort St, LEICESTER, LE1 7GE.   (hq)
    0116-285 9702   fax 0116-204 6988
    email admin@uall.ac.uk   http://www.uall.ac.uk
    Admin: Lucy Bate
▲   Registered Charity
○   *P; to represent the continuing education community within
    higher education; to liaise with policy makers & policy
    making bodies
●   Conf - Mtgs - ET - Res - Inf - LG
M   8 i, 107 f, 1 org, UK / 15 f, o'seas
¶   Ybk & AR - 1; ftm.   LM - 3; free.
    Occasional Papers - 3/4; ftm, £3 nm.
    Working Papers - 1; ftm, £3 nm.
    Conference Proceedings - 1; ftm, £3 nm.

Universities & Colleges Employers' Association   (UCEA)   1994

■   Woburn House, 20 Tavistock Sq, LONDON, WC1H 9HU.   (hq)
    020 7383 2444   fax 020 7383 2666
    email enquiries@ucea.ac.uk   http://www.ucea.ac.uk
    Chief Exec Officer: Jocelyn Prudence
▲   Company Limited by Guarantee
○   *P; the employers association for universities & colleges in the
    UK; to provide a framework within which salaries, conditions
    of service employee relations can be discussed & advice &
    guidance sought
●   Conf - Mtgs - ET - Stat - Empl - Seminars
M   164 f

Universities & Colleges Information Systems Association   (UCISA)

NR   University of Oxford, 13 Banbury Rd, OXFORD, OX2 6NN.
    01865 283425   fax 01865 283426
    http://www.ucisa.ac.uk

Universities Federation for Animal Welfare   (UFAW)   1926
NR   The Old School, Brewhouse Hill, WHEATHAMPSTEAD, Herts,
      AL4 8AN.   (hq)
      01582 831818   fax 01582 831414
      email ufaw@ufaw.org.uk   http://www.ufaw.org.uk/
      Chief Exec: Dr James Kirkwood,
      Sec: Donald Davidson
▲   Company Limited by Guarantee; Registered Charity
○   *V; to develop & promote improvements in the welfare of all
      animals through scientific & educational activity worldwide
●   Conf - ET - Res - Inf - Lib - VE - LG
M   c 1,200 i & f
¶   Animal Welfare (Jnl) - 4.   NL - 1.   AR.
      Publications list available.

**Universities Psychotherapy & Counselling Association
(UPCA)   1993**
■   PO Box 142, St LEONARDS-on-SEA, E Sussex, TN38 1DN.
      01424 430431
      email upca@hotmail.co.uk
      Sec: Julia Croft
○   *P
●   ET
M   1,300 i

Universities Scotland
NR   53 Hanover St, EDINBURGH, EH2 2PJ.
      0131-226 1111   fax 0131-226 1100
      http://www.universities-scotland.ac.uk
      Dir: Alastair Sim
○   *N; to represent, promote & campaign for the Scottish higher
      education sector
M   21 org
¶   Books.

Universities UK   (UUK)   2000
■   Woburn House, 20 Tavistock Sq, LONDON, WC1H 9HQ.   (hq)
      020 7419 4111   fax 020 7388 8649
      email info@universitiesuk.ac.uk
      http://www.universitiesuk.ac.uk
      Chief Exec: Nicola Dandridge
▲   Company Limited by Guarantee; Registered Charity
Br   2
○   *N; to be the essential voice for the UK universities; to promote
      & support their work & provide services to members; to
      speak out for a thriving & diverse higher education sector
      which creates benefits for all
Gp   Higher education policy & research; Employability; Longer term
      strategy; Teacher education advisory group; Universities
      Policy c'ees: Business & industry, Funding & management,
      Health & social care, International & European, Research,
      Student experience
●   Conf - Mtgs - Res - Stat - Inf - Lib - LG
>   Higher Educ Wales; Universities Scotland; UK HE International
      Unit; UK Higher Educ Eur Unit; UK Res Integrity Office; Med
      Schools Coun
M   132 f
      (Sub: £4,050)
¶   [all publications are available as downloadable pdf files on
      website].

**University Association for Contemporary European Studies
(UACES)   1968**
■   School of Public Policy, University College London, 29-
      30 Tavistock Sq, LONDON, WC1H 9QU.   (hq)
      020 7679 4975
      http://www.uaces.org
▲   Registered Charity
○   *L; exchanges ideas on Europe; to provide a forum for debate
      & act as a clearing house for information about European
      issues; it is directly involved in promoting research &
      establishing teaching & research networks.
      Members include academics (economists, political scientists,
      lawyers & historians) & practitioners & graduate students
Gp   Graduate students of European studies
●   Conf - Mtgs - Workshops
M   900 i, 105 universities, UK / 300 i, 20 universities, o'seas
¶   Jnl of Common Market Studies (JCMS) - 5.   NL - 4.
      Research interests of UACES Members; £28 m,
      £38 (or £123 nm).
      Listing of Courses in European Studies in UK
      Universities; online.
      Listing of Interests (at www.expertoneurope.com)

University & College Union   (UCU)   2006
■   Carlow St, LONDON, NW1 7LH.   (hq)
      020 7756 2500   fax 020 7756 2501
      email hq@ucu.org.uk   http://www.ucu.org.uk
      Gen Sec: Sally Hunt
○   *E, *P, *U; trade union & professional association for
      academics, lecturers, trainers, researchers & academic-
      related staff working in further & higher education
      throughout the UK
<   Trades U Congress (TUC)
M   119,401 i

Unlock Democracy (incorporating Charter 88)   1988
NR   9 Cynthia St, LONDON, N1 9JF.   (hq)
      020 7278 4443
      http://www.unlockdemocracy.org.uk
▲   Company Limited by Guarantee
○   *K; political pressure group campaigning for a modern & fair
      democracy through a democratic parliament, a freedom of
      information act, a bill of rights, decentralisation of power, a
      proportional voting system & a written constitution
M   80,000 i, UK / 3,000 i, o'seas
¶   Citizen (NL).

**Unlock - National Association of Reformed Offenders
(UNLOCK)   1999**
■   35A High St, SNODLAND, Kent, ME6 5AG.   (hq)
      01634 247350   fax 01634 247351
      email enquiries@unlock.org.uk
      http://www.unlock.org.uk
      Chief Exec: Bobby Cummines
▲   Registered Charity
○   *K, *W; to improve facilities & opportunities for serving
      prisoners to prepare for release & to overcome social
      exclusion & discrimination hindering them from re-
      integration into society; to prevent offending & re-offending
      by young people especially at risk; to campaign for serving
      prisoners' right to vote
●   ET - Inf - LG
M   [not stated]

**Upkeep: the Trust for Training & Education in Building
Maintenance   (Upkeep)   1979**
■   Royal London House, 22-25 Finsbury Square, LONDON,
      EC2A 1DX.   (hq)
      020 7275 7646   fax 020 7022 1575
      email info@upkeep.org.uk   http://www.upkeep.org.uk
      Dir: Annette McGill
▲   Company Limited by Guarantee; Registered Charity
○   *E, *T; to promote good standards of repair, maintenance &
      improvement of buildings, particularly houses & flats
M   org

© CBD Research Ltd · Beckenham · BR3 5JS · Tel 020 8650 7745 · E-mail cbd@cbdresearch.com · www.cbdresearch.com

Urban Design Group (UDG) 1978

NR 70 Cowcross St, LONDON, EC1M 6EJ. (hq)
020 7250 0892
email admin@udg.org.uk   http://www.udg.org.uk
Dir: Robert Huxford

Br 10

○ *L; for all who care about the quality of life in our cities, towns & villages & believe that raising standards of urban design is central to its improvement

● Conf - Mtgs - VE

M i, f & org

¶ Urban Design (Jnl) - 4; ftm, £5 nm.
Urban Design Directory - alt yrs; ftm.

Urban Saints 1906

NR Kestin House, 45 Crescent Rd, LUTON, Beds, LU2 0AH. (hq)
01582 589850   fax 01582 721702
http://www.urbansaints.org
Exec Dir: Matt Summerfield

▲ Registered Charity

○ *R, *Y; committed to sharing the Christian gospel with young people through interdenominational youth groups, overseas projects & holidays

● Conf - ET - Exhib - Comp - SG - Inf

< Nat Youth Org; Evangelical Alliance

M 20,000 i

✕ 2006 Crusaders

Urdd Gobaith Cymru (yr Urdd) 1922

NR Ffordd Llanbadarn, ABERYSTWYTH, Ceredigion, SY23 1EY. (hq)
01970 613100   fax 01970 626120
email ywe@urdd.org   http://www.urdd.org
Chief Exec: Efa Gruffudd Jones

▲ Company Limited by Guarantee; Registered Charity

Br 900

○ *Y; to give children & young people the chance to learn & socialise through the medium of Welsh speaking

M 50,000 i

¶ Cip, Bore Da, iaw! (Jnls) - each 10.

Urostomy Association (UA) 1971

■ Central Office, 18 Foxglove Avenue, UTTOXETER, Staffs, ST14 8UN. (hq)
0845 241 2159 or 01889 563191
email info.ua@classmail.co.uk
http://www.urostomyassociation.org.uk
Nat Sec: Mrs Hazel Pixley

▲ Registered Charity

Br 16

○ *W; to assist those who are about to undergo (or have undergone) surgery resulting in diversion or removal of the bladder; to provide information, help & advice

● Conf - Mtgs - ET - Res - Inf - LG

< Intl Ostomy Assn

M 2,400 i, UK / 200 i, o'seas

¶ Magazine - 3; ftm.

Uveitis Information Group (UIG) 1998

■ South House, Sweening, VIDLIN, Shetland Isles, ZE2 9QE. (hq)
0845 604 5660
email info@uveitis.net   http://www.uveitis.net
Hon Sec: Annie Folkard

▲ Registered Charity

○ *W; to provide high quality information & support to patients & professionals. Uveitis is a name for several types of inflammation of the uvea (the middle of the three concentric layers of the eye).

● ET - Inf

M 350 i, UK / 100 i, o'seas

¶ NL - 3; ftm, £5 nm.

Vale of Glamorgan Agricultural Society   1772

- ■ Pancross Barn, Llancarfan, BARRY, Vale of Glamorgan, CF62 3AJ.   (hsp)
  01446 710099
  email vale.show@btinternet.com
  http://www.valeofglamorganshow.co.uk
  Hon Sec: Mrs Nicola Gibson
- ▲ Company Limited by Guarantee; Registered Charity
- ○ *F; to promote British agriculture & its related industries
- Gp Craft fair; Food hall; Horticulture; Kennel Club dog show; Livestock; Rural crafts; Tradestands
  Competitions: Home produce, Livestock
- ● Exhib - Comp - Inf
- < Assn of Show & Agricl Orgs; R Horticl Soc; R Nat Rose Soc; Breed socs; Horse socs
- M 500 i, 10 f
- ¶ Schedule - 1.   AR.   Catalogue - 1.

Valpak   1997

- ■ Stratford Business Park, Banbury Rd, STRATFORD-upon-AVON, Warks, CV37 7GW.   (hsb)
  0845 068 2572   fax 0845 068 2532
  email info@valpak.co.uk   http://www.valpak.co.uk
  Chief Exec: Steve Gough
- ▲ Company Limited by Guarantee
- ○ *T; the nationwide compliance scheme for the packaging waste regulations
- ● LG
- < Pro Europe
- M c3,000 f
- ¶ Ybk; ftm only.

Vascular Society of Great Britain & Ireland
a group of the **Association of Surgeons of Great Britain & Ireland**

VAT Practitioners Group   (VPG)   1982

- ■ 105 Oxhey Avenue, WATFORD, Herts, WD19 4HB.   (nat admin/p)
  01923 230788   fax 01923 240707
  email administrator@vpgweb.com
  http://www.vpgweb.com
  Nat Admin: Susan Holman
- ▲ Un-incorporated Society
- Br 28
- ○ *P; a discussion group on Value Added Tax which makes representation to HM Customs & Excise on VAT matters; also has interests in Insurance Premium Tax (IPT), Landfill Tax & Air Passenger Duty (APD)
- ● Conf - Mtgs
- M 520 i
- ¶ Bulletin - 10; ftm only.

Vegan Society Ltd   1944

- NR Donald Watson House, 21 Hylton St, Hockley, BIRMINGHAM, B18 6HJ.   (hq)
  0121-523 1730   fax 0121-523 1749
  email info@vegansociety.com
  http://www.vegansociety.com
  Media Officer: Amanda Baker
- ▲ Registered Charity
- ○ *K; 'to promote ways of living free from animal products, for the benefit of people, animals & the environment'
- ● ET - Res - Inf
- M c 5,000 i
- ¶ The Vegan Magazine - 4.
  The Animal-Free Shopper - 2 yrly.   Vegan Stories.
  Vegan Passport.   Plant Based Nutrition & Health.

Vegetable Consultants Association   (VCA)

- NR Manor Park Nursery, Wash Road, Kirton, BOSTON, Lincs, PE20 1QQ.   (hq)
  01205 723414
  Contact: David E O'Connor
- ○ *P; to provide advisory & development services to leading growers, produce marketing organisations & retailers
- ● Inf
- M 22 i
- ¶ LM with specific skills.

Vegetarian Society of Ireland   1978

- IRL c/o Dublin Food Coop, 12 Newmarket, DUBLIN 8, Republic of Ireland.
  353 (1) 48 80 250
  email vegsoc@ireland.com   http://www.vegetarian.ie
  Hon Sec: Patricia Timoney
- ○ *K

Vegetarian Society (UK) Ltd   (VegSoc)   1969

- ■ Parkdale, Dunham Rd, ALTRINCHAM, Cheshire, WA14 4QG.   (hq)
  0161-925 2000   fax 0161-926 9182
  email info@vegsoc.org   http://www.vegsoc.org
  Chief Exec: Annette Pinner
- ▲ Company Limited by Guarantee; Registered Charity
- Br 150 local groups
- ○ *G, *K, *V; to promote knowledge of the vegetarian diet for the benefit of human health, animal welfare & the environment
- Gp Cordon Vert Cookery School for professional & amateur chefs
- ● Conf - ET - Exhib - Inf - Lib
- < Intl Vegetarian U
- M 14, 00 i, UK / 500 i, o'seas
  (Sub: £21 UK / £31 o'seas)
- ¶ The Vegetarian - 4; ftm.   AR - 1; ftm only.

Vehicle Builders' & Repairers' Association   (VBRA)   1914

- ■ Belmont House, Finkle Lane, Gildersome, LEEDS, W Yorks, LS27 7TW.   (hq)
  0113-253 8333   fax 0113-238 0496
  email vbra@vbra.co.uk   http://www.vbra.co.uk
  Dir Gen: Malcolm Tagg
- ▲ Company Limited by Guarantee
- ○ *T; to represent the motor repair & body building industry; to support members by providing advice, information & training
- Gp National Repairers Council; National Manufacturers Council
- ● Conf - Mtgs - ET - Exhib - Inf - VE - Empl - LG
- < Assn Intle des Réparateurs en Carrosserie (AIRC)(Brussels)
- M 1,100 f, 1,000 i (subscribers to Body)
- ¶ Body (Jnl) - 10; ftm, £4.50 each nm.   Ybk.

Vehicle Restraint Manufacturers Association   (VRMA)   1997

- ■ 35 Calthorpe Rd, Edgbaston, BIRMINGHAM, B15 1TS.   (asa)
  0121-454 4141   fax 0121-207 7002
  email sparker@cvdfk.com   http://www.vrma.co.uk
  Sec: Sharon Parker
- ▲ Un-incorporated Society
- ○ *T; to provide a means whereby the industry may put forward, as a collective body, its views to Government departments & other relevant organisations on the development of vehicle restraint systems compliant to EN1317
- ● Mtgs
- M 5 f

Vernacular Architecture Group (VAG) 1954
■ 3 Church Row, Redwick, NEWPORT, Monmouthshire, NP26 2DE. (hsp)
01633 889019
http://www.vag.org.uk
Hon Sec: Mrs Linda Hall
▲ Registered Charity
○ *L; study of small traditional buildings in GB & abroad
● Conf - Res - Inf - Lib - VE
M 619 i, 18 org, UK / 48 i, o'seas
¶ Vernacular Architecture - 1; ftm, £20 nm.
NL - 2; ftm only.   Bibliography - 5 yrly; ftm, £9.50 nm.

Veteran-Cycle Club (V-CC) 1955
NR 31 Rosebery Rd, DURSLEY, Glos, GL11 4PT. (sp)
01453 548348
http://www.v-cc.org.uk
Hon Sec: Mike Sims
▲ Un-incorporated Society
Br 21 regional sections
○ *G; to promote the riding & restoration of old bicycles; to study & exchange information about the history of cycles & cycling
Gp Marque enthusiasts for 82 makes of machine
● Mtgs - Res - Exhib - Lib
< Intl Veteran Cycle Assn; Transport Trust
M 2,300 i
¶ News & Views - 6;   The 'Boneshaker' - 3;   Ybk - 1;
all ftm only.

Veteran Horse Society (VHS) 2000
■ Hedre Fawr, St Dogmaels, CARDIGAN, N Pembrokeshire, SA43 3LZ. (hq)
0870 242 6653
http://www.veteran-horse-society.co.uk
Dir: Miss Julianne Aston
▲ Company Limited by Guarantee
○ *V; dedicated to the health, welfare & profile of the horse & pony over the age of 15
● Conf - Mtgs - ET - Res - Exhib - Comp - SG - Stat - Expt - Inf - PL - VE - Empl - LG
< Nat Equine Welfare Coun (NEWC); Brit Equestrian Tr Assn (BETA)
M 4,000 i, UK / 50 i, o'seas
¶ Voice of the Veteran - 4.

Veteran Speedway Riders Association
since 2006 **World Speedway Riders Association**

Veterinary Association for Arbitration & Jurisprudence
since 2008 **British Veterinary Forensic & Law Association**

Veterinary Cardiovascular Society
a group of the **British Small Animal Veterinary Association**

Veterinary Deer Society
a group of the **British Veterinary Association**

Veterinary History Society 1962
■ 17 Anseres Place, WELLS, Somerset, BA5 2RT. (hsp)
01749 673558
Hon Sec: Jean Mann
▲ Un-incorporated Society
○ *L, *V; promotion of interest in veterinary history in the UK
● Mtgs - Inf - VE
M 100 i, 15 libraries, UK / 20 i, 15 libraries, o'seas
¶ Bulletin of Veterinary History - 2; ftm, £15 nm.

Veterinary Ireland 1888
IRL 13 The Courtyard, Kilcarbery Park, Nangor Rd, DUBLIN 22, Republic of Ireland.
353 (1) 457 7976   fax 353 (1) 457 7998
email vetireland@eircom.net
http://www.veterinary-ireland.org
○ *P, *V

Veterinary Public Health Association
a group of the **British Veterinary Association**

Vets Tennis GB 1974
■ G01 Mandel House, Eastfields Avenue, LONDON, SW18 1JU. (hsp)
020 8875 1773
email vw@vetstennisgb.org   http://www.vetstennisgb.org
Sec: Valerie Willoughby
▲ Un-incorporated Society
○ *S; to provide opportunites for veteran tennis players to compete in individual & team events
● Conf - Comp - Inf
< Lawn Tennis Assn
M 20 clubs
¶ e NL - 3;   AR - 1; free.

Victim Support 1979
■ Hallam House, 56-60 Hallam Street, LONDON, W1W 6JL. (hq)
020 7268 0200   fax 020 7268 0210
email contact@victimsupport.org.uk
http://www.victimsupport.org
Chief Exec: Gillian Guy
▲ Registered Charity
○ *N, *W; independent national charity which helps people cope with crime. Services are free & available to everyone, whether or not the crime has been reported & regardless of when it happened.
● Conf - ET - Res - Inf - Lib - LG
Support line: 0845 303 0900
< Eur Forum for Victims Orgs; Nat Coun for Voluntary Orgs (NCVO)
M 374 schemes, 86 crown court witness services
¶ Publications list available.

Victim Support Scotland (VSS) 1985
■ 15-23 Hardwell Close, EDINBURGH, EH8 9RX. (hq)
0131-668 4486   fax 0131-662 5400
email info@victimsupportsco.demon.co.uk
http://www.victimsupport.org
Chief Exec & Co Sec: David McKenna
▲ Company Limited by Guarantee
Br 32 affiliated services (Scotland)
○ *W; to offer practical help, emotional support & essential information to victims, witnesses & others affected by crime. The service is free & provided by trained volunteers through a network of community based victim & court based witness services
● Conf - Mtgs - ET - Res - Inf
Helpline: 0845 603 9213 (Mon-Fri 0900-1630); outside these hours call UK Victim Support on 0845 303 0900
¶ Voice [NL] - 4.   Generic inforamtion Pack; free.   AR.

Victoria Cross & George Cross Association (VC&GCAssn) 1956
■ Horse Guards, Whitehall, LONDON, SW1A 2AX. (hq)
020 7930 3506   fax 020 7930 4303
○ *G; to establish a central focus for all Victoria Cross & George Cross holders
● Conf - Inf
M 5 i (VC), 14 i (GC), UK / 6 i (VC), 7 i (GC), o'seas
¶ Rules.

Victorian Military Society (VMS) 1975

NR PO Box 5837, NEWBURY, Berks, RG14 7FJ.
     http://www.victorianmilitarysociety.org.uk
▲ Un-incorporated Society; Registered Charity
○ *L, *Q; to encourage & foster the study of military aspects of
     the Victorian era (nominally 1837-1901, the period has been
     extended to 1914 to include the campaigns of the earlier
     part of the 20th century); the principal interest is in the forces
     of the British Empire & its adversaries, but forces of other
     countries are not excluded
Gp Anglo-Boer Wars; Sudan Wars; Wargames; 'The Diehard
     Company' - re-enactment based on the 57th Foot (Middlesex
     Regiment)
● Mtgs - Res - Exhib - Comp - SG - Stat - Inf - VE - Recording of
     all memorials of the Anglo-Boer War of 1899-1902
M c 900 i
¶ Soldiers of the Queen (Jnl) - 4;
     Soldiers Small Book (NL) - 4; both ftm only.

Victorian Society 1958

■ 1 Priory Gardens, LONDON, W4 1TT.   (hq)
     020 8994 1019   fax 020 8747 5899
     email admin@victoriansociety.org.uk
     http://www.victoriansociety.org.uk
     Dir: Dr Ian Dungavell
○ *A, *L; to preserve & protect the best buildings of the 19th
     century; to study the arts & architecture of the period
< Jt C'ee of the Nat Amenity Socs
M c 3,500 i

Video Performance Ltd
     a section of **Phonographic Performance Ltd**

Viewing Facilities Association UK (VFA) 1995

■ Davey House, 31 St Neots Rd, Eaton Ford, ST NEOTS, Cambs,
     PE19 7BA.
     01480 211288   fax 01480 211267
     email info@viewing.org.uk   http://www.viewing.org.uk
     Chmn: Liz Sykes
○ *T; for viewing facilities, market research, qualitative research
● Conf - Inf
< Market Res Soc; Assn for Qualitative Res
M 41 f
¶ [on website]

Viking Society for Northern Research 1892

NR c/o Alison Finlay, Birkbeck College, University of London, Malet
     St, LONDON, WC1E 7HX.   (hsb)
     email a.finlay@bbk.ac.uk   http://www.vsnr.org
     Hon Sec: Alison Finlay
▲ Un-incorporated Society
○ *A, *Q; literature & antiquities of the Scandinavian north,
     including Iceland
● Conf - Mtgs - ET - Res - Lib
M 296 i, 47 org, UK / 120 i, 152 org, o'seas
¶ The Saga Book; £20.   Text Series - irreg; prices vary.
     Dorothea Coke Memorial Lecture - irreg.

The Vikings 1971

■ 3 Smock Meadow, Bildeston, IPSWICH, Suffolk, IP7 7TG.
     (memsec/p)
     http://www.vikingsonline.org.uk
     Mem Sec: Julie Luke
▲ Company Limited by Guarantee; Registered Charity
Br 48; Netherlands, USA (12)
○ *G; dark age re-enactment (primarily that of the Vikings) incl
     battles, homelife, crafts & skills
Gp Film extras
● Mtgs - Res - Exhib - Inf - Re-enactment shows - Banquets
< Nat Assn Re-enactment Socs
M 700 i, UK / 20 i, o'seas
¶ Runestaff (Jnl) - 6/8; ftm, £1 nm.
     Flyer (Broadsheet) - 6/8; free.   Ybk; £4.

Village Retail Services Association Educational Trust

     has been absorbed into the Plunkett Foundation, The
     Quadrangle, WOODSTOCK, Oxon, OX20 1LH.

Village Sign Society 1999

NR Michaelmas, Tyland Lane, Sandling, MAIDSTONE, Kent,
     ME14 3BL.   (mem/sp)
     http://www.villagesignsociety.org.uk
     Contact: The Membership Secretary
○ *G; for all interested in old & new village signs
● Photo library
¶ Village Sign Times - 3; ftm.

Vinegar Brewers' Federation (VBF) 1929

■ Crescent House, 34 Eastbury Way, SWINDON, Wilts,
     SN25 2EN.   (hsb)
     01793 727387   fax 01793 726485
     email vinegarbrewers@aol.com
     Sec: Walter J Anzer
▲ Un-incorporated Society
○ *T
● Mtgs - LG
< Permanent Intl Vinegar C'ee, Common Market (CPIV)
M 5 f

Vintage Arms Association (VAA) 1973

■ 47 Hearsall Avenue, STANFORD-le-HOPE, Essex, SS1 7EH.
     (hsp)
     01375 361973
     http://www.vintagearms.org.uk
     Hon Sec: G S Moseley
Br 6; Jersey
○ *G; to promote an interest in, and the use of, all vintage and
     modern firearms
● Conf - Mtgs - Res
< Nat Rifle Assn; London & Middx Rifle Assn
M i [not stated]
¶ The Primer - 6; ftm only.

Vintage Carriages Trust (VCT) 1964

■ The Railway Station, Haworth, KEIGHLEY, W Yorks,
     BD22 8NJ.   (mail add)
     01535 680425   fax 01535 610796
     email admin@vintagecarriagestrust.org
     http://www.vintagecarriagestrust.org
     Ingrow Railway Station Yard, Halifax Rd, Ingrow, KEIGHLEY,
     W Yorks, BD21 5AX.   (location)
     Hon Sec: David Carr
▲ Registered Charity
○ *G; the conservation & restoration of railway carriages & other
     railway artifacts, & the interpretation of these through
     museum display
Gp Railway carriage restoration & preservation
● ET - Operating the Museum of Rail Travel at Ingrow
< Fedn of Eur Rlys (FEDECRAIL); Heritage Rly Assn (HRA);
     Transport Trust (TT)
M 580 i, UK / 4 i, o'seas
¶ NL - 4.   All Aboard; £3.00p.   AR - 1; free.
     All Aboard: your guide to the story of rail travel for the ordinary
     passenger.

© CBD Research Ltd · Beckenham · BR3 5JS · Tel 020 8650 7745 · E-mail cbd@cbdresearch.com · www.cbdresearch.com

Vintage Glider Club of Great Britain   (VGC)   1973
NR   201 Bridge End Road, GRANTHAM, NG31 7HA.   (hsp)
         01476 564200
         email stephensons@talktalk.net
         http://www.vintagegliderclub.org
         Hon Sec: Bruce Stephenson
Br   Australia, Austria, Belgium, Czech Republic, Denmark, France,
         Germany, Holland, Hungary, New Zealand, Norway, Poland,
         Sweden, Switzerland, USA
○   *S; 'to preserve old gliders in flying condition, & to prevent their
         mass destruction, as has happened in the past; there is no
         museum for them as yet in the UK'
●   Mtgs - Aeromodelling - Archive (plans, photographs, films/
         videos) - Holding national & international rallies
<   Oldtime Gliding Club Wasserkuppe
M   450 i, UK / 450 i, o'seas
¶   VGC News - 3.

**Vintage Horticultural & Garden Machinery Club   (VHGMC)
1993**
■   54A Southlands, SWAFFHAM, Norfolk, PE37 7PF.   (sp)
         http://www.vhgmc.co.uk
         Club Sec: K Tooley
○   *G, *H; to collect, preserve, restore & use garden &
         horticultural machinery, including hand tools
●   Displays at vintage rallies & garden shows - Information service
         to members only
M   680 i
¶   The Cultivator (NL) - 5; ftm only.
         (Sub: £12).

Vintage Motor Cycle Club Ltd   (VMCC)   1946
■   Allen House, Wetmore Rd, BURTON upon TRENT, Staffs,
         DE14 1TR.   (hq)
         01283 540557   fax 01283 510547
         email hq@vmcc.net   http://www.vmcc.net
         Chief Exec: James Hewing
▲   Company Limited by Guarantee
Br   75
○   *G; to preserve, restore & use both for competition & pleasure,
         motorcycles, combinations & tricycles: veteran (pre 1914),
         vintage (1915-1930), post-vintage (1931-1944), post-war
         (1945-1960), & post-1960 (1961- & +25 yrs old)
Gp   Grasstrack; Racing; Sprint
●   Mtgs - Exhib - Inf - Lib - PL - Archives - Insurance scheme
<   Auto-Cycle U (ACU); Fedn of Brit Historic Vehicle
         Clubs (FBHVC); RAC
M   13,400 i, UK / 500 i, o'seas
¶   The Vintage Motor Cycle - 12; ftm only.

Vintage Sports Car Club Ltd   (VSCC)   1934
■   The Old Post Office, West St, CHIPPING NORTON, Oxon,
         OX7 5EL.   (hq)
         01608 644777   fax 01608 644888
         email info@vscc.co.uk   http://www.vscc.co.uk
         Sec: Mike Stripe
▲   Company Limited by Guarantee
○   *G, *S; for owners of historic racing cars: Edwardian (1905-
         1918), vintage (pre 1931), post-vintage thoroughbred (pre
         1941), & certain front engined cars (pre 1961)
Gp   Alfa Romeo; Delage; Frazer Nash; Light Car & Edwardian
●   Conf - Mtgs - Res - Comp - Inf - Lib - VE
<   RAC Motor Sports Assn; Fédn Intle des Automobiles Anciennes
M   c 7,500 i, 14 f, UK / 500 i, o'seas
¶   Bulletin - 4;   NL - 12;   Ybk; all ftm only.

Vintage Wooden Boat Association   (VWBA)
NR   14 West End Lane, POTTON, Beds, SG19 2RD.
         http://www.vwba.org
         Mem Sec: Sally Walsh
○   *G; to promote the use, maintenance & restoration of wooden
         boats
¶   The Log (Jnl)

Vintners' Federation of Ireland   (VFI)   1973
IRL   VFI House, Castleside Drive, Rathfarnham, DUBLIN 14,
         Republic of Ireland.
         353 (1) 492 3400   fax 353 (1) 492 3577
         email enquiries@vintners.ie   http://www.vfi.ie
         Chief Exec: Tadg O'Sullivan
○   *T
M   c 6,000 f

Viola da Gamba Society   (VdGS)   1948
NR   28 Freelands Rd, OXFORD, OX4 4BT.   (admin/p)
         01865 723778
         email admin@vdgs.org.uk   http://www.vdgs.org.uk
         Admin: Susanne Heinrich
▲   Registered Charity
○   *D; to advance the study of viols, their music, their playing &
         their making
●   Conf - Mtgs - Res - Exhib - Inf
<   Viola da Gamba Soc of America; Lute Soc (UK)
M   460 i, libraries & universities
¶   Music - 1; ftm.   Care of Viol (booklet).
         LM - 1; ftm.   AR.

Violet Needham Society   (VNS)   1985
■   Blunsden, Faringdon Rd, ABINGDON, Berks, OX14 1BQ.
         (hsp)
         email hilaryclare@kinquest.fsnet.co.uk
         http://www.violetneedhamsociety.org.uk
         Hon Sec: Mrs Hilary Clare
▲   Un-incorporated Society
○   *A; interest in the life & works of Violet Needham & other
         children's writers of the period (1940s & 50s) & in Ruritanian
         fiction in general
●   Mtgs - Res - Lib - VE
M   260 i, 3 org, UK / 27 i, 1 org, o'seas
¶   Souvenir (Jnl) - 3; ftm, £2.50 nm.   NL - 3; ftm only.

Virgil Society   1943
■   8 Purley Oaks Rd, SANDERSTEAD, Surrey, CR2 0NP.   (mem/sp)
         http://www.virgilsociety.org.uk
         Mem Sec: Jill Kilsby
▲   Registered Charity
○   *L; study & interpretation of Virgil as the symbol of the central
         educational tradition of Western Europe
●   Mtgs
M   c 120 i
¶   Proceedings - 3 yrly.   NL - 2.

Virginia Woolf Society of Great Britain   (VWSGB)   1998
■   106 Gloucester Rd, KINGSTON upon THAMES, Surrey,
         KT1 3QN.   (chmn/p)
         020 8546 5712
         email sbarkway@btinternet.com
         http://www.virginiawoolfsociety.co.uk
         Chmn: Stephen Barkway,   Sec: Lynne Newland
▲   Un-incorporated Society
○   *A; 'to present Virginia Woolf (1882-1941) in her true light as a
         great novelist, essayist, publisher & woman of letters'
●   Conf - Inf - VE
M   250 i, 6 org, UK / 150 i, 3 org, o'seas
¶   Virginia Woolf Bulletin - 3; ftm, £5 nm.
         Annual Birthday Lecture - 1; £4 (£5 o'seas).

Virus Tested Stem Cutting Growers Association
since 2007 **Pre Basic Growers Association**

Vision Mixers Guild   1984
NR   PO Box 15678, BROMSGROVE, W Midlands, B60 9GN.
▲   Un-incorporated Society
○   *P; promotion of the professional status of vision mixers, to
      maintain & improve technical & artistic standards in television
      production
●   Mtgs - ET - Exhib - VE
M   i
¶   On-line magazine.
      Freelance Directory of VMs in the UK & Ireland.

Visual Artists Ireland
      is the trading name of the **Sculptors Society of Ireland**

Visual Arts & Galleries Association   (VAGA)   1978
■   The Old Village School, High St, Witcham, ELY, Cambs,
      CB6 2LQ.   (hq)
      01353 776356   fax 01353 775411
      email admin@vaga.co.uk   http://www.vaga.co.uk
      Dir: Hilary Gresty
○   *A, *P; to improve the status of the visual arts within
      contemporary culture
●   Conf - Mtgs - Res - SG - Inf - LG
M   c 350 i, f & affiliates
¶   VAGA update - 6; free.

Visual Arts Scotland   (VAS)   1989
NR   12 Rosevale Place, EDINBURGH, EH6 8AP.   (admin/p)
      07979 924744
      email info@visualartsscotland.org
      http://www.visualartsscotland.org
      Admin: Rebecca Pollard
▲   Registered Charity
○   *A; to promote contemporary & applied arts
M   i

Vitiligo Society   1985
NR   125 Kennington Rd, LONDON, SE11 6SF.   (hq)
      0800 018 2631
      http://www.vitiligosociety.org.uk
▲   Registered Charity
Br   14
○   *W; to give support & advice to people with vitiligo (a skin
      condition in which patches of skin turn white, although
      neither painful nor infectious)
●   Mtgs - Res - Inf
M   c 2,000 i
¶   Dispatches (NL) - 4.
      Vitiligo: understanding the loss of skin colour (Hbk).

Vitreous Enamellers' Society
      since 2010 as IVE: the Vitreous Enamellers' Society, has beome a
      group within the Surface Engineering Division of the **Institute of
      Materials, Minerals & Mining**

Voice: the union for education professionals   2008
■   2 St James' Court, Friar Gate, DERBY, DE1 1BT.   (hq)
      01332 372337   fax 01332 290310
      email enquiries@voicetheunion.org.uk
      http://www.voicetheunion.org.uk
      Gen Sec: Philip Parkin
○   *E, *U; for educational professionals working in education,
      early years & childcare settings
●   Conf - Mtgs - ET - Res - Exhib - Stat - Inf - LG
M   38,000 i
¶   Your Voice - 4; ftm, £2 nm.
      Hbk for Members - 1; ftm only.
✕   2008 (Professional Association of Nursery Nurses
            (Professional Association of Teachers
            (Professionals Allied to Teaching

Voice Care Network UK   (VCN)   1993
■   10 Station Rd (office 2), KENILWORTH, Warks, CV8 1JJ.   (hq)
      01926 864000   fax 01926 864000
      email info@voicecare.org.uk
      http://www.voicecare.org.uk
      Admin: Angela Brooks
▲   Registered Charity
○   *P; promotion & development of healthy & effective use of the
      voice for all professional voice users & in particular, for
      teachers
●   Conf - ET - Res - SG - Stat - Inf - Practical workshops (group
      teaching & one-to-one teaching)
<   Assn Teachers Singing (AOTOS): Soc Teachers Speech & Drama
>   Brit Voice Assn
M   250 i, UK / c 30 i, o'seas
¶   Voice Matters (NL) - 3; ftm.
      Keeping a Young Voice (leaflet).
      Booklets:
          More Care for Your Voice.
          Voice Warm-up Exercises.
          A Voice Care Guide for Call Centre Managers.

**Voice of Chief Officers of Cultural, Community & Leisure
Services   (VOCAL)   1975**
■   c/o Dept of Community Services, E Lothian Council, 9-11
      Lodge St, HADDINGTON, E Lothian, EH41 3DX.   (hsb)
      01620 827576
      Sec: Margaret O'Connor
▲   Un-incorporated Society
○   *P; to promote recreation & leisure services in Scotland; to act
      as a support agency & forum for senior leisure professionals
●   Conf - Mtgs - Res - LG
M   50 i
✕   2007-08 Voice of Chief Officers of Culture, Community &
      Leisure Services in Scotland

Voice of the Listener & Viewer Ltd   (VLV)   1983
■   PO Box 401, GRAVESEND, Kent, DA12 9FY.   (hq)
      01474 338711   fax 01474 351112
      email info@vlv.org.uk   http://www.vlv.org.uk
      Chmn: Mrs Jocelyn Hay
▲   Company Limited by Guarantee; Registered Charity
○   *K; an independent non-profit making body which represents
      the citizen & consumer interest in broadcasting & works to
      ensure high quality, diversity & independence in British
      broadcasting; to represent the interests of listeners & viewers
      on all broadcasting issues; to maintain the 'principle of
      public service in broadcasting'
Gp   Children's & educational broadcasting; Older people's
      broadcasting
●   Conf - Mtgs - Conf - Inf - Lib - VE - LG
      Holds the archives of:
          British Action for Children's Television [ceased 1995]
          Broadcasting Research Unit [ceased 1991]
<   Eur Alliance of Listeners' & Viewers' Assns (EURALVA)
M   2,000 i, 28 org, c 50 universities & colleges, UK / 30 i, o'seas
      (Sub: £25 i, £60 org (etc), UK / £35 i, £60 org o'seas)
¶   VLV Bulletin - 4; ftm; £30 (£35 o'seas) nm.
      Conference Proceedings Reports - 3/4; on application.
      Submissions to Official Consultations - irreg; free online,
          (hardcopy price on application).
      Other ad hoc publications.

Volleyball England
      the working name of the **English Volleyball Association**

Voluntary Action History Society   (VAHS)   1991
NR   4 High Oaks Rd, WELWYN GARDEN CITY, Herts, AL8 7BH.
      (memsec/p)
      http://www.vahs.org.uk
      Mem Sec: Brenda Weeden
▲   Registered Charity
○   *G; to advance the historical study & understanding of
      voluntary action & of charitable & voluntary organisations

© CBD Research Ltd · Beckenham · BR3 5JS · Tel 020 8650 7745 · E-mail cbd@cbdresearch.com · www.cbdresearch.com

Voluntary Arts Network   (VAN)
- ■ 121 Cathedral Road, Pontcanna, CARDIFF, CF11 9PH.   (hq)
  029 2039 5395
  email info@voluntaryarts.org
  http://www.voluntaryarts.org
  Chief Exec: Robin Simpson
- ▲ Company Limited by Guarantee; Registered Charity
- Br 5 centres
- ○ *A, *N; a development agency for amateur & voluntary arts & crafts; aims to promote participation across the UK & the Republic of Ireland
- ● Conf - ET - Res - Inf - Help with starting a group - Support for umbrella bodies
- ¶ Update (NL) - 4, (with 4 Briefing sheets to each issue); £25-50.

Voluntary Euthanasia Society
      since 2006 **Dignity in Dying**

Voluntary Euthanasia Society of Scotland
      since 2000 **Exit**

Voluntary Service Overseas   (VSO)   1958
- ■ Carlton House, 27A Carlton Drive, LONDON, SW15 2BS. (hq)
  020 8780 7500
  email enquiry@vso.org.uk   http://www.vso.org.uk
  Chief Exec: Mark Goldring
- ▲ Registered Charity
- Br 35 in Africa & Asia
- ○ *W; a voluntary charity dedicated to assisting development in the Third World by sending experienced, practical people on 2-year projects to share their skills in Africa, Asia, the Caribbean & the Pacific
- ● ET - International development
- < [too many to list]
- M 25,000 i, 2,000 f, UK / 150 i, o'seas

Volunteering England
- NR Regent's Wharf, 8 All Saints Street, LONDON, N1 9RL.   (hq)
  020 7520 8900   fax 020 7520 8910
  email volunteerin@volunteering.org.uk
  http://www.volunteering.org.uk
  Chief Exec: Dr Justin Davis Smith
- ○ *K, *W; to promote volunteering as a force for change in the community
- Gp Institute for Volunteering Research
- M i

Von Hippel-Lindau Contact Group   (VHLCG)   2002
- ■ 27 Westgate Avenue, Holcombe Brook, RAMSBOTTOM, Lancs, BL0 9SS.   (coord/p)
  01204 886112
  email maryweetman@waitrose.com
  http://www.vhlcg.co.uk
  Coordinator: Mary Weetman
- ▲ Registered Charity
- ○ *W; to help families with Von Hippel-Lindau disease (an inherited genetic disease causing abnormal growth of tumours in various parts of the body)
- ● Conf - ET - Fund raising
- M 50 i

Voucher Association
      since 2008 **UK Gift Card & Voucher Association**

Vulval Pain Society   (VPS)   1996
- ■ PO Box 7804, NOTTINGHAM, NG3 5ZQ.   (mail/address)
  http://www.vulvalpainsociety.org
  Jt Secs: David Nunns,   Kay Thomas
- ▲ Un-incorporated Society
- ○ *W; to provide sufferers with an increase in understanding of their condition; to raise awareness of the condition as an important aspect of women's health
- ● Inf
  Helpline: 0776 594 7599
- M c 200 i
- ¶ NL - 4; ftm only.   Factsheets; free.

W H Auden Society   1988
- ■ 78 Clarendon Rd, LONDON, W11 3HW.   (mem/sp)
  email newsletter@audensociety.org
  http://www.audensociety.org/membership.html
  Mem Sec: Dr Katherine Bucknell
- ▲ Registered Charity
- ○ *A; for all interested in the work of Wystan Hugh Auden (1907-73) & in The Thirties, twentieth century literature, opera & drama
- ● Res - Inf
- M c 100 i, c 7 libraries, UK / c 100 i, c 15 libraries, o'seas
- ¶ NL - email; £9 (i), £5 (students), £18 (instns & paper copies).

W W Jacobs Appreciation Society   (WWJ)   1988
- ■ 3 Roman Rd, SOUTHWICK, W Sussex, BN42 4TP.   (hsp)
  01273 596217
  Hon Sec: A R James
- Br 2
- ○ *A; develop interest in literary, dramatic & filmed works of the author W W Jacobs (1863-1943)
- Gp Biographical; Bibliographical; Theatre & film
- ● Res - Inf - Lib - PL
- < Assn of Literary Socs
- M 40 i, UK / 15 i, o'seas
- ¶ Field Guide (bibliography); £6.
  Biography; £12.   Films Directory; £2.
  Bibliography (a specialist detailed work); £15.

Wagner Society   1953
- ■ 16 Doran Drive, REDHILL, Surrey, RH1 6AX.   (h/mem/p)
  email mm@misterman.freeserve.co.uk
  http://www.wagnersociety.org
  Mem Sec: Mrs Margaret Murphy
- ▲ Registered Charity
- ○ *D; the appreciation & study of the life & music of Richard Wagner (1813-1883) his music
- ● Mtgs - Res - Lib
- M i
- ¶ Wagner News - 6; ftm.

Wagon Building & Repairing Association   (WBRA)   1991
- NR Homelea, Westland Green, Little Hadham, WARE, Herts, SG11 2AG.   (hsp)
  01279 843487
  email geoffrey.pratt@btconnect.com
  Sec Gen: Geoffrey Pratt
- ○ *T; all aspects of manufacture & repair of freight rolling stock
- M 10 f

Wakeboard UK   1996
- NR Arden Croft, Forshaw Heath Lane, TANWORTH IN ARDEN, Warks, B94 5LD.   (hsp)
  07958 617121
  email info@wakeboard.co.uk
  http://www.wakeboard.co.uk
  Chmn: Graham Creedy
- ▲ Un-incorporated Society
- ○ *S; to promote & monitor the sport of wakeboarding
- Gp Competitions; Training for coaches to NVQ standard
- ● ET - Comp - Free 'come & try it days'
- < Intl Waterski Fedn; Brit Waterski Fedn
- M 150 i, UK / 10 i, o'seas
- ¶ NL - 4.
  a division of British Water Ski & Wakeboard

Wales-Argentine Society
  English name of **Cymdeithas Cymru-Ariannin**

Wales Association of Self Catering Operators   (WASCO)
- NR 28 Trem y Ffridd, BALA, Gwynedd, LL23 7DG.   (admin/p)
  01678 521480
  http://www.wasco.org.uk
  Admin: Keith Robinson
- ○ *T; for anyone who has a self-catering business in Wales, from one-property owner/managers to multi-property businesses & large agencies
- < Fedn of Nat Self Catering Assns (FoNSCA)

Wales Council for Voluntary Action   (Cyngor Gweithredu Gwirfoddol Cymru)   (WCVA)   1934
- ■ Baltic House, Mount Stuart Square, CARDIFF BAY, Glamorgan, CF10 5FH.   (hq)
  029 2043 1734   fax 029 2043 1701
  email help@wcva.org.uk   http://www.wcva.org.uk
  Chief Exec: Graham Benfield
- ▲ Company Limited by Guarantee; Registered Charity
- Br 2
- ○ *W; the voice of the voluntary sector in Wales.   It represents the interests of, & campaigns for, all voluntary organisations
- ● Conf - Mtgs - ET - Res - Exhib - Stat - Inf - Lib - LG
- < NCVO (sister org)
- M 20 i, 80 f, 1,700 org
- ¶ NL - 12.   Directory - 2/3 yrly.   Wales Funding Hbk - 1.
  publications list available.

Wales Craft Council   (Cyngor Crefft Cymru Cyf)   (WCC)   1977
- ■ London House, The Square, CORWEN, Denbighshire, LL21 0DE.   (chmn/b)
  01490 412911   fax 01938 556237
  email info@walescraftcouncil.co.uk
  http://www.walescraftcouncil.co.uk
  Henfaes Lane, WELSHPOOL, Powys, SY21 7BE. (regd off)
  Chmn: Philomena Hearn
- ▲ Company Limited by Guarantee
- ○ *P, *T; to help, advise, represent & promote full-time professional makers of craft, gift & textile products working in Wales
- ● Exhib
- M 81 f
- ¶ NL - 4; ftm.

Wales Pre-school Playgroups Association
  since 2009 **Wales Pre-school Providers Association**

Wales Pre-school Providers Association   (Wales PPA)   1987
- ■ Unit 1 The Lofts, 9 Hunter St, CARDIFF BAY, CF10 5GX.   (hq)
  029 2045 1242
  email info@walesppa.org   http://www.walesppa.org
  Sec: Sian Davies
- ▲ Company Limited by Guarantee; Registered Charity
- Br 22
- ○ *E; to enhance the development, care & education of pre-school children in Wales by encouraging parents to understand & provide for their needs, through high quality provision
- ● Conf - Mtgs - ET - Res - Exhib - Comp - Stat - Inf - Lib - LG
- M 1,000 org
- ¶ Small Talk - 4; ftm.
- ✕ 2009 Wales Pre-School Playgroups Association

Wales Trades Union Congress
  a region of the **Trades Union Congress**

© CBD Research Ltd · Beckenham · BR3 5JS · Tel 020 8650 7745 · E-mail cbd@cbdresearch.com · www.cbdresearch.com

Wales Trekking & Riding Association   (WTRA)
- ■ Sunny Bank, Felindre, BRECON, Powys, LD3 0ST.   (hsp)
   01497 847464
   http://www.ridingwales.com
   Sec: Cheryl Hyde
- ○ *G, *S; riding centres

Wall Tie Installers Federation   (WTIF)   1989
- NR Heald House, Heald St, LIVERPOOL, L19 2LY.   (hq)
   0151-494 2503   fax 0151-494 2511
   email admin@wtif.org.uk   http://www.wtif.org.uk
- ▲ Company Limited by Guarantee
- ○ *T; installation of remedial & replacement wall ties & related services
- ● Conf - Mtgs - ET - Exhib - Inf - Lib - PL
- M 41 f
- ¶ WTIF News - 12; ftm.

Wallcovering Distributors Association   (WDA)
- ■ c/o William Robinson Interiors, Daleside Rd, NOTTINGHAM, NG2 4DH.
   0115-979 9790   fax 0115-959 9590
   Pres: Stuart Thorne,   Hon Sec: William Robinson
- ○ *T; for British distributors of wallcoverings, fabrics & decorating products
- M f

Wallpaper History Society   1986
- NR Old Moat Barn, Ardenrun, LINGFIELD, Surrey, RH17 6LN.
   (mem/secp)
- ▲ Un-incorporated Society
- ○ *L; to encourage research & provide information on all aspects of wallpaper production, consumption & design. Encompasses not only the history of wallpaper, but also topics relating to other kinds of wallcoverings & interior design generally
- ● Conf - SG - VE
- M c 225 i, f & org
- ¶ Jnl - 2 yrly; ftm.

Walmsley Society   1985
- ■ April Cottage, 1 Brand Rd, Hampden Park, EASTBOURNE, E Sussex, BN22 9PX.   (hsp)
   01323 506447
   email walmsley@mabarraclough.f9.co.uk
   http://www.walmsleysoc.org
   Hon Sec: Fred W Lane
- ▲ Un-incorporated Society
- ○ *A; to promote & encourage an appreciation of the writings of Leo Walmsley (1892-1966) & the paintings of his father, James Ulric Walmsley (1860-1954)
- Gp Biography planning; Publicity; Research/archives
- ● Mtgs - Res - Inf - VE - Encouraging the reprinting of books by Leo Walmsley or concerning the Walmsleys
- < Alliance Literary Socs
- M 200 i, UK / 4 i, o'seas
- ¶ Jnl - 2; ftm, £3 nm.   NL - 4/5; ftm only.
   Books & booklets.

Walpole   1992
- ■ 1 Southwark Bridge, LONDON, SE1 9HL.   (hq)
   020 7873 3803
   email julia.carrick@thewalpole.co.uk
   http://www.thewalpole.co.uk
   Chief Exec: Julia Carrick
- ○ *T; to further the interests of the British luxury industry
- ● Mtgs - Seminars - Awards
- M 82 f
- ¶ Ybk.

Walpole Society   1911
- ■ Dept of Prints & Drawings, The British Museum, Great Russell St, LONDON, WC1B 3DG.   (regd off)
   020 7727 8739
   email chairman@walpolesociety.org.uk
   http://www.walpolesociety.org.uk
   Chmn: Simon Jervis
- ▲ Registered Charity
- ○ *A; to promote the study of the history of British art
- ● Res - Publications
- M 280 i, 85 org, UK / 50 i, 130 org, o'seas
   (Sub: £45 i, £60 org]
- ¶ Walpole Society Volume - 1; ftm only.   AR.

Walter de la Mare Society   1997
- ■ 3 Hazelwood House, New River Crescent, LONDON, N13 5RE.   (hsp)
   020 8886 1771
   email fguthrie@talktalk.net
   http://www.walterdelamare.co.uk
   Hon Sec & Treas: Frances Guthrie
- ○ *A; to honour the memory of novelist, poet & essayist Walter de la Mare (1873-1956); to promote the study & deepen the appreciation of his works
- ● Mtgs
- M 65 i, UK / 10 i, o'seas
- ¶ Jnl - 1; ftm (£15 subn).

War Memorials Trust   (WMT)   1997
- ■ 42A Buckingham PAlace Rd, LONDON, SW1W 0RE.   (hq)
   020 7233 7356
   email info@warmemorials.org
   http://www.warmemorials.org
   Trust Mgr: Frances Moreton
- ▲ Registered Charity
- ○ *K; for the protection & conservation of war memorials in the UK
- ● Inf
- M 1,500 i, UK / 100 i, o'seas
   (Sub: £20)
- ¶ Bulletin - 4.

War Poets Association   (WPA)   2004
- NR c/o Veale Wasbrough (DBMW), Orchard Court, Orchard Lane, BRISTOL, BS1 5WS.   (treas/b)
   01275 376916
   email treasurer@warpoets.org   http://www.warpoets.org
- ▲ Registered Charity
- ○ *A; to promote interest in the work, life & historical context of poets whose subject is the experience of war
- ¶ War Poetry Review; NL.

War Research Society
- § 27 Courtway Ave, BIRMINGHAM, B14 4PP.   (hq)
   0121-430 5348   fax 0121-436 7401
   http://www.battlefieldtours.co.uk
   Office Mgr: Mike Heaven
   Organises guided tours of WW1 & WW2 sites; has taken thousands of pilgrims, veterans, widows & children to visit the battlefields, memorials & last resting places of the fallen.

War Widows Association of Great Britain   (WWA)   1971
- ■ c/o 199 Borough High St, LONDON, SE1 1AA.   (hq)
   0845 241 2189
   email info@warwidowsassociation.org.uk
   http://www.warwidowsassociation.org.uk
   The Hon Secretary
- ▲ Registered Charity
- ○ *W; to care for the welfare of War Widows; to speak on their behalf with government ministers
- ● Inf
- M 5,500 i
- ¶ Courage (NL) - 3; ftm, donations welcomed nm.

Ward Union Staghounds
a constituent body of the **Hunting Association of Ireland**

Warmblood Breeders' Studbook - UK   (WBS-UK)   1977
NR   Goblaen House, RHOSGOGH, Powys, LD2 3JT.   (sec/p)
      01497 851318
      http://www.bwbs.co.uk
      Sec: Mrs L Crowden
▲   Company Limited by Guarantee
○   *B; the controlled breeding of warm-blood horses, particularly
      Hanoverians, Holsteins & Dutch, Swedish & Danish Warm-
      Bloods, Trakehners & cross breeds
●   2-yearly show with mare & stallion gradings - Registering &
      passporting horses
<   Brit Horse Soc; Nat Stallion Approval Scheme
M   400 i
¶   NL - 2.
×   2008 (January) British Warm-Blood Society

Warrington Chamber of Commerce & Industry   1876
NR   International Business Centre, Delta Crescent, Westbrook,
      WARRINGTON, Cheshire, WA5 7WQ.   (hq)
      01925 715150   fax 01925 715159
      email info@warrington-chamber.co.uk
      http://www.warrington-chamber.co.uk
      Chief Exec: Colin Daniels
▲   Company Limited by Guarantee
○   *C
<   Brit Chams Comm; Chams Comm NW

Waste Watch   1987
NR   Development House, 56-64 Leonard St, LONDON,
      EC2A 4LT.   (hq)
      020 7549 0300   fax 020 7549 0301
      email info@wastewatch.org.uk
      http://www.wastewatch.org.uk
      Exec Dir: Stewart Crocker
▲   Company Limited by Guarantee; Registered Charity
○   *K; to promote & support action for waste reduction & recycling
      by working with community groups, voluntary organisations,
      local authorities & businesses - providing practical support
      for local action; to encourage government & industry to
      support recycling; it is partly funded by DEFRA's
      Environmental Action Fund
●   Inf - LG - Operates Wasteline: a telephone & postal
      information service on what can be re-cycled & where
M   i, f & org
¶   Practical guides & specialist reports; list available.

Water Colour Society of Ireland   1870
IRL   c/o Visual Arts Office, University of Limerick, LIMERICK,
      Republic of Ireland.   (asa)
      353 (61) 213052   fax 353 (61) 330316
      http://www.watercoloursocietyofireland.ie
      Hon Sec: Pat McCabe
○   *A; to promote & develop nationally the use & appreciation of
      watercolour & associated media among artists, students &
      the general public

Water Feature   1981
NR   Kingsway House, Wrotham Road, MEOPHAM, Kent,
      DA13 0AV.   (hsp)
▲   Un-incorporated Society
○   *T
●   Conf - Mtgs - Inf - VE
M   1 i, 11 f.
×   Ornamental Pool & Fountain Constructors Association

Water for Health Alliance
■   1 Queen Anne's Gate, LONDON, SW1H 9BT.
      http://www.water.org.uk/home/water-for-health

Water Jetting Association   1980
■   Thames Innovation Centre, Vendon Way, ERITH, Kent,
      DA18 4AL.   (hq)
      020 8320 1090   fax 020 8320 1094
      http://www.waterjetting.org.uk
      Dir: Norman Allen
○   *T; high pressure water jetting contractors, manufacturers &
      training providers
M   120 f
¶   Pressure Points (Jnl) - 2.
      Codes of Practice for safe working.
      Medical notes.   Medical card.
      Training course manuals.

Water Management Society Ltd   (WM Soc)   1970
■   6 Sir Robert Peel Mill, Tolson's Enterprise Park, Fazeley,
      TAMWORTH, Staffs, B78 3QD.   (hsb)
      01827 289558   fax 01827 250408
      email wmsoc@btconnect.com
      http://www.wmsoc.org.uk
      Gen Sec: Mrs Sue Pipe
▲   Company Limited by Guarantee
○   *P; the safe & efficient use of water in industry & commerce
Gp   Technical c'ee
●   Conf - ET - LG
M   594 i, UK / 20 i, o'seas
¶   Waterline - 4; ftm, £75 nm.
      Site Log Book for Water Services; £30 m, £50 nm.
      Guide to Risk Assessment for Water Services; £50 m, £75 nm.

Water UK   1998
NR   1 Queen Anne's Gate, LONDON, SW1H 9BT.   (hq)
      020 7344 1844   fax 020 7344 1866
      http://www.water.org.uk
      Chief Exec: Pamela Taylor
○   *N; for water & wastewater service companies of the UK
M   f

Waterheater Manufacturers Association
      in 2007 merged with Manufacturers of Domestic Unvented Systems to
      form the **Hot Water Association**

waterskiscotland   1974
NR   Scottish National Water Ski / Wakeboard Centre, Townhill
      Country Park, DUNFERMLINE, Fife, KY12 0HT.   (hq)
      01383 620123   fax 01383 620122
      email info@waterskiscotland.co.uk
      Nat Co-ordinator: Alan G Murray
▲   Company Limited by Guarantee
○   *S; to act as the national governing body promoting water
      skiing in Scotland
Gp   Barefoot; Corporate; Disabled; Kneeboard; Racing;
      Recreational; Schools; Tournament; Wakeboarding; Youth
●   Conf - Mtgs - ET - Exam - Exhib - Comp - Inf - LG
<   Intl Water Ski Fedn; Brit Water Ski Fedn
M   c250 i
¶   NL - 4;   Rule Books;   Codes of Practice;   AR; all free.

Waterway Recovery Group Ltd   (WRG)   1970
NR   Island House, Moor Rd, CHESHAM, Bucks, HP5 1WA.   (hq)
      01494 783453
      http://www.wrg.org.uk
      Exec Dir: Neil Edwards
▲   Registered Charity
○   *G, *N; co-ordinating body for voluntary labour on the inland
      waterways of Britain; is a non-membership subsidiary
      company of the Inland Waterways Association interested in
      the conservation & restoration of the inland waterways of
      Britain
●   Mtgs - ET - Inf - LG
M   1,850 i, 20 f, 100 org, UK / 30 i, o'seas
¶   Navvies - 6.   Canal Camps Brochure - 1.
      Other occasional publications.

© CBD Research Ltd · Beckenham · BR3 5JS · Tel 020 8650 7745 · E-mail cbd@cbdresearch.com · www.cbdresearch.com

Watford & West Herts Chamber of Commerce & Industry   1895
NR   Unit 47 The Business Centre, Colne Way, WATFORD, Herts,
       WD24 7AA.   (hq)
       01923 442442
▲   Company Limited by Guarantee
○   *C

Way Foundation   (WAY)   1997
NR   St Loyes House (suite 35), 10 St Loyes St, BEDFORD,
       MK40 1ZL.   (hq)
       0870 011 3450
       email info@wayfoundation.org.uk
       http://www.wayfoundation.org.uk
▲   Registered Charity
○   *W; a self-help group for men & women who are 50, or under,
       at the time of losing their partner; to help them, rebuild their
       lives by helping each other
●   Inf - Support network
M   1,500 i
¶   NL - 4.

Welding Institute   (TWI)   1968
■   Granta Park, Great Abington, CAMBRIDGE, CB21 6AL.   (hq)
       01223 899000
       email twi@twi.co.uk   http://www.twi.co.uk
       Chief Exec: Dr Bob John
▲   Company Limited by Guarantee
Br   3
○   *L, *P, *Q; to carry out confidential contract work on all aspects
       of welding& materials joining for industrial member
       companies; to teach good practice in welding, joining & non-
       destructive testing
Gp   10 technical gps on specific aspects of joining
●   Conf - ET - Exam - Res - Inf - Lib
<   Intl Inst Welding; Eur Welding Fedn; Assn Indep Res &
       Technology Orgs
M   7,000 i, 3,500 f
¶   Welding Abstracts (print) - 12; £656.
       Welding Abstracts (PDF) - 12; £578.
          (Both above) - 12; £788.
       Note: trades as TWI Ltd

Welding Manufacturers Association
       an association of **BEAMA Ltd**

Well Drillers Association   (WDA)   1985
NR   PO Box 4595, NUNEATON, Warks, CV11 9DX.
       07736 364259
       email david.s.duke@gmail.com
       http://www.welldrillers.org
       Sec: David Duke
▲   Un-incorporated Society
○   *T; to promote the design & construction of water wells &
       boreholes
●   Mtgs - ET - Inf - LG
<   Brit Drilling Assn
M   32 f
¶   LM; free.

Well Services Contractors Association
       since 1 January 2010 a group of **Oil & Gas UK**

Welsh Agricultural Organisation Society Ltd   (WAOS)   1922
NR   Gorseland, North Rd, ABERYSTWYTH, Ceredigion,
       SY23 2HE.   (hq)
       01970 636688   fax 01970 624049
       Chief Exec: Don Thomas
○   *F; agricultural marketing & consultancy (incl horticulture)

Welsh Aikido Society
       is part of the **British Aikido Board**

Welsh Amateur Boxing Association   (WABA)   1910
NR   Marcross Court, Marcross, LLANTWIT MAJOR, Vale of
       Glamorgan, CF61 1ZD.   (ops mgr/b)
       01446 790099   fax 01446 792444
       email davidbfrancis1@btconnect.com
       http://www.welshboxingassociation.org
       Operations Mgr: David Francis
▲   Company Limited by Guarantee
○   *S; to promote amateur boxing in Wales
Gp   Training; Commissions
●   Conf - Mtgs - ET - Exam - Comp - Inf
M   115 clubs
¶   AR.

**Welsh Amateur Gymnastics Association   (Welsh Gymnastics)
1901**
NR   Sport Wales National Ccentre, Sophia Gardens, CARDIFF,
       CF11 9SW.   (hq)
       0845 043 1240
       Gen Sec: Mrs Annette Brown
○   *S; governing body of gymnastics in Wales
Gp   General recreational; Men's artistic; People with disabilities;
       Preschool; Rhythmic, Sports acrobatics; Sports aerobics;
       Women's artistic
●   Mtgs - ET - Comp
<   C'wealth Confedn; Brit Gymnastics
M   i & clubs
¶   NL - 4.

**Welsh Amateur Music Federation   (Ffederasiwn Cerddoriaeth
Amatur Cymru)   (WAMF/FfCAC)   1968**
■   Tŷ Cerdd, Wales Millennium Centre, Bute Place, CARDIFF,
       CF10 5AL.   (hq)
       029 2063 5640   fax 029 2063 5641
       email wamf@tycerdd.org   http://www.tycerdd.org
       Dir: Keith Griffin
▲   Registered Charity; Un-incorporated Society
○   *D, *N, Y; support for amateur music making organisations
       through advice, grants, workshops & courses
Gp   National Youth Brass Band of Wales; National Youth Choir of
       Wales;
       National Youth Jazz Orchestra of Wales; National Youth Wind
          Orchestra of Wales; National Youth Symphonic Brass Wales
       Bands; Choirs; Folk; Musical theatre societies
●   Conf - Mtgs - ET - Res - Comp - Stat - Inf - Lib - VE - LG - Youth
       activities, grants & guarantees for performance - Music
       promotion & support
M   c 400 societies (representing 25,000 amateur performers)
¶   Annual Review of Activities; ftm, £1 nm.
       Various pamphlets etc.

Welsh Amateur Rowing Association   (WARA)
NR   Elfred House, Oak Tree Court, Cardiff Gate Business Park,
       CARDIFF, CF23 8RS.   (regd off)
       email acwrowing@hotmail.com
       http://www.walesrowing.com
       Company Sec: Andrew Williams
▲   Un-incorporated Society
○   *S; to regulate & promote the sport of rowing for men &
       women in Wales, for recreation as well as for national &
       international competition
Gp   Coastal rowing; Welsh Longboat Association
●   Mtgs - ET - Exam - Comp - Liaison with Welsh Assembly &
       SportWales
M   1,200 i (Wales)
¶   [website only]
       Note: also uses title Rhwyfo Cymru

Welsh Amateur Swimming Association   (WASA)   1897
- ■ Wales National Pool, Sketty Lane, SWANSEA, SA2 8QG.   (hq)
     01792 513636   fax 01792 513637
     email secretary@welshasa.co.uk
     http://www.welshasa.co.uk
- ○ *S; the governing body for swimming in Wales
- Gp Diving; Masters swimming; Swimming; Water polo
- ● ET (national team training) - Comp
- < Amat Swimming Fedn GB (ASFGB)
- M 10,000 i
     trading as Swim Wales

Welsh Association of Sub Aqua Clubs   (WASAC)
- NR Iscoed, Tresaith, CARDIGAN, SA43 2JG.   (chmn/p)
     http://www.wasac.co.uk
     Chmn: David Wakelam
- ○ *S; to promote underwater sport (scuba diving, underwater
     hockey, snorkeling, etc) in Wales

Welsh Athletics   (Athletau Cymru)   1897
- NR Cardiff International Sports Stadium, Leckwith Rd, CARDIFF,
     CF11 8AZ.   (hq)
     029 2064 4870   fax 029 2064 4870
     email office@welshathletics.org
     http://www.welshathletics.org
     Chief Exec: Matt Newman
- ▲ Compant Limited by Guarantee
- ○ *S; to promote & develop athletics in Wales through a strong
     club network
- ● Mtgs - ET - Exam - Comp - Stat - Inf
- < UK Athletics; SportWales
- M 74 clubs
- ¶ NL - 2.   Ybk.   AR.

**Welsh Badminton Union   (Undeb Badminton Cymru)
(WBU)   1928**
- ■ Sport Wales National Centre, Sophia Gardens, CARDIFF,
     CF11 9SW.   (hq)
     029 2033 4940
     http://www.welshbadminton.net
     CEO: Eddie O'Neill
- ○ *S; governing body of sport for badminton
- Gp Coaching & technical committee, Events committee, Disability
     working group
- < Intl Badminton Fedn (IBF); Eur Badminton U (EBU)
- M i & clubs
     Note: The Welsh Badminton Union is known as Badminton
     Wales.

Welsh Beekeepers Association
- NR The Old Tannery, Pontsian, LLANDYSUL, Ceridigion,
     SA44 4UD.   (hsp)
     01945 590515
     email john-of-pontsian@tiscali.co.uk
     http://www.wbka.com
     Sec: John Page
- ○ *G, *T
- M 1,350 i

Welsh Black Cattle Society   (WBCS)   1904
- ■ 13 Bangor St, CAERNARFON, Gwynedd, LL55 1AP.   (hq)
     01286 672391   fax 01286 672022
     http://www.welshblackcattlesociety.com
     Chief Exec: Andrew James
- ▲ Registered Charity
- Br 2; Australia, Canada, Germany, N Zealand
- ○ *B
- ● Mtgs - Res - Exhib - Comp - Inf
- M 884 i, UK / 17 i, o'seas
- ¶ Jnl - 1; £7.50.   NL - irreg.   Herd Book - 1; £35.

Welsh Bowling Association
     see **Welsh Bowls Federation**

Welsh Bowls Coaching Association
     see **Welsh Bowls Federation**

Welsh Bowls Federation   (WBF)   2001
- NR 48 Forest Hill, The Bryn, Pontllanfraith, BLACKWOOD, Gwent,
     NP12 2PL.   (chmn/p)
     07974 212004
     email chair@welshbowlsfederation.org.uk
     http://www.welshbowlsfederation.org.uk
     Chmn: Noel Tippett
- ▲ Un-incorporated Society
- ○ *N, *S; to improve channels of communication between
     governing bodies & act as a centralised coordinating body
     for bowls in Wales
- Gp Governing bodies:
     Welsh Bowling Association; Welsh Women's Bowling
     Association; Welsh Indoors Bowls Association; Welsh Ladies
     Indoor Bowling Association; Welsh Short Mat Bowls
     Association
     Professional associations:
     Welsh Bowls Coaching Association; Welsh Bowls Umpires
     Association
- < World Bowls; Eur Bowls U (EBU); Brit Isles Bowling Coun (BIBC)
- M 7 org (25,000 i in 670 clubs)

Welsh Bowls Umpires Association
     see **Welsh Bowls Federation**

Welsh Bridge Union   (WBU)   1933
- NR Meadow View, Llanddewi, LLANDRINDOD WELLS, Powys,
     LD1 6SE   (chiefexec/p)
     01597 850050
     email wbu@wbu.org.uk   http://www.wbu.org.uk
     Chief Exec: Neville Richards
- ▲ Un-incorporated Society
- ○ *G; for players of Contract Bridge
- ● Mtgs
- < Wld Bridge Fedn; Eur Bridge League
- > East, Mid, North & West Wales Bridge Assns
- M c 2,000 i
- ¶ Competition & Masterpoint Journal - 1; ftm, £5 nm.

Welsh Canoeing Association
     sinc 2009 **Canoe Wales**

Welsh Chess Union   (WCU)   1960
- NR 4 Ovington Terrace, CARDIFF, CF5 1GF.   (exec/dir)
     029 2034 0631
     http://www.welshchessunion.org.uk
     Exec Director: Bill Harle
- ▲ Un-incorporated Society
- ○ *S; to foster the game of chess in Wales
- ● Exam
- < Fédn Intle des Echecs (FIDE)
- M 900 i
- ¶ NL - 4.   Ybk - 1; ftm.
     Pawns (junior NL) - 12; free to juniors.

Welsh Culinary Association   (WCA)   1994
- ■ c/o The Bungalow, Maes y Neuadd, TALSARNAU, Gwynedd,
     LL47 6YA.   (chmn/p)
     01766 780319   fax 01766 780211
     email info@welshculinaryassociation.com
     http://www.welshculinaryassociation.com
     Chmn: Peter Jackson,   Sec: Kevin Williams
- ▲ Company Limited by Guarantee
- ○ *P; to represent & promote the chefs of Wales
- ● Conf - Mtgs - ET - Res - Exhib - Comp - Expt
- < Wld Assn of Cooks Socs
- M 320 i, Wales / 2 i, o'seas

© CBD Research Ltd · Beckenham · BR3 5JS · Tel 020 8650 7745 · E-mail cbd@cbdresearch.com · www.cbdresearch.com

Welsh Cycling Union Ltd   (WCU)   1972

■   Wales National Velodrome, Newport International Sports
    Village, NEWPORT, Monmouthshire, NP19 4PT.   (hq)
    01633 670540   fax 01633 670540
    email info@welshcycling.co.uk
    http://www.welshcycling.co.uk
    Admin: Edith Clark
    Events & Communications Officer: Michael Heaven
▲   Company Limited by Guarantee
○   *G, *S; the governing body for cycling in Wales & covers: road
    racing, track racing, mountain bike, BMX, cyclo cross & cycle
    speedway
●   Mtgs - ET - Comp - Inf - LG
<   Brit Cycling Fedn; Sports Coun Wales; U Cycliste Intle
M   950 i, 70 org

Welsh Folk Dance Society
    see **Cymdeithas Ddawns Werin Cymru   (Welsh Folk Dance
    Society)**

Welsh Folk Song Society (Cymdeithas Alawon Gwerin Cymru) (CAGC)   1906

■   Coed y Berllan, Brynmor rd, ABERYSTWYTH, Ceredigion,
    SY23 2HX.   (hsp)
    01907 610160
    Sec: Dr Rhidian Griffiths
▲   Registered Charity
○   *D; to collect, preserve, interpret & perform Welsh folk-songs;
    to foster an interest in folk literature & music in general
●   Conf - Res - Inf
M   250 i, 10 org, UK / 5 org, o'seas
¶   Canu Gwerin (Folk Song) (Jnl) - 1; £10 yr m.

Welsh Golfing Union
    in 2007 merged with the Welsh Ladies' Golf Union to form the **Golf
    Union of Wales**

Welsh Halfbred Sheep Breeders Association Ltd   1955

■   Corriecravie, Cross Lane, Bignall Lane, STOKE-ON-TRENT,
    Staffs, ST7 8ND.   (hsp)
    01782 721165
    http://www.welshhalfbredsheep.co.uk
    Sec: Anna Johnson
○   *B; marketing of the Welsh Halfbred sheep (the cross of a
    Welsh Mountain ewe & a Border Leicester ram)
●   Exhib - Shows & five annual sales
<   Nat Sheep Assn
M   400 i
¶   Welsh Halfbred News - 2; ftm only.

Welsh Highland Railways Association   (WHR)   1964

■   Tremadog Rd, PORTHMADOG, Gwynedd, LL49 9DY.
    (hq/regd office)
    01766 513402   fax 01766 513402
    email info@whr.co.uk   http://www.whr.co.uk
    Chmn: James Hewett
▲   Company Limited by Guarantee; Registered Charity
○   *G; to recreate the Welsh Highland Railway of the 1920s &
    1930s; to provide a quality education, interactive, visitor
    attraction; to preserve & increase the skills involved in
    running a railway
Gp   Locomotives - steam & diesel; Carriage & wagon; Civils;
    Commercial; Museum; Telecommunications
●   Mtgs - ET - Exhib - Inf - PL - VE
<   Heritage Rly Assn; N Wales Tourism; Great Little Trains of Wales
M   800 i, UK / 150 i, o'seas
¶   The Jnl - 3; ftm, £1.75 nm.   The Russell - irreg; free.
X   2006 (Welsh Highland Railway Ltd
        (Welsh Highland Railway Society
        (Welsh Highland Railway Heritage Group

Welsh Hill Speckled Face Sheep Society   1968

NR   Morris Marshall & Poole, Bank House, Great Oak St,
    LLANIDLOES, Powys, SY16 6BW.   (asa)
    01686 440279
    Asst Sec: M George
▲   Un-incorporated Society
○   *B
●   Mtgs - Comp
<   Nat Sheep Assn

Welsh Hockey Coaches Association
    a group of **Welsh Hockey Union Ltd**

Welsh Hockey Umpires Association
    a group of **Welsh Hockey Union Ltd**

Welsh Hockey Union Ltd   (WHU)   1897

■   Sport Wales National Centre, Sophia Gardens, CARDIFF,
    Glamorgan, CF11 9SW.   (hq)
    029 2078 0735
    email info@welsh-hockey.co.uk
    http://www.welsh-hockey.co.uk
    Chief Exec: Helen Bushell
▲   Company Limited by Guarantee
○   *S; governing body for hockey in Wales
Gp   Welsh Hockey Coaches Assn; Welsh Hockey Umpires Assn
●   Conf - ET - Exam - Comp - Inf - VE - LG
<   Fédn Intle de Hockey (FIH); Eur Hockey Fedn (EHF)
M   6,100 i, 115 clubs, 550 schools
¶   NL - 1;   Circulars - 4; both ftm.

Welsh Hospitals & Health Services Association   (WHA)   1948

§   60 Newport Rd, CARDIFF, CF24 0YG.   (hq)
    029 2048 5461   fax 029 2048 8859
    email mail@whahealthcare.co.uk
    http://www.whahealthcare.co.uk
    Chief Exec: Huw L Cooke
    Operates a range of low cost schemes to help with the
    everyday costs of staying healthy. Opoerates under the
    trading name WHA.

Welsh Indoor Bowls Association
    see **Welsh Bowls Federation**

Welsh Jazz Society   1963

■   26 The Balcony, Castle Arcade, CARDIFF, Glamorgan,
    CF10 1BY.   (hq)
    029 2034 0591   fax 029 2066 5160
    email welshjazz@btconnect.com
    http://www.jazzwales.org.uk
    Chief Exec: B J Hennessey
▲   Company Limited by Guarantee; Registered Charity
○   *D; promotion, learning & presentation of jazz music
●   Mtgs - ET - Inf - PL - Concert performances
<   Jazz Services Ltd
M   800 i, 8 org
¶   Jazz UK - 6; free.

Welsh Judo Association   (WJA)   1964

NR   Sport Wales National Centre, Sophia Gardens, CARDIFF,
    CF11 9SW.   (hsb)
    029 2033 4945
    email office@welshjudo.com   http://www.welshjudo.com
    Office Mgr: Emily Brown
▲   Company Limited by Guarantee
○   *S; promotion of judo
●   Mtgs - ET - Exam - Comp
<   Brit Judo Assn; C'wealth Judo Assn
M   2,200 i
¶   NL - 12; free.

Welsh Ladies' Golf Union
    in 2007 merged with the Welsh Golfing Union to form the **Golf Union of Wales**

Welsh Language Society
    see **Cymdeithas yr Iaith Gymraeg (Welsh Language Society)**

Welsh Library Association
    a division of **CILIP**

Welsh Local Government Association   (WLGA)   1996
NR   Local Government House, Drake Walk, CARDIFF, Glamorgan,
       CF10 4LG.   (hq)
       029 2046 8600   fax 029 2046 8601
       http://www.wlga.gov.uk
○   *N; to promote local democracy & represent the interests of
       local government in Wales

Welsh Longboat Association
    a group of the **Welsh Amateur Rowing Association**

Welsh Mills Society   (Cymdeithas Melinau Cymru)   1984
NR   Y Felin, Tynygraig, YSTRAD MEURIG, Ceredigion, SY25 6AE.
       email hilary.milaws@btinternet.com
       http://www.welshmills.org.uk
       Sec: Hilary Malaws
○   *G, *L; to study, record, interpret & publicise the wind & water
       mills of Wales; to advise on their preservation & use; to
       encourage working millers
¶   Melin - 1.

**Welsh Mines Society   (Cymdeithas Mwyngloddiau Cymru)
       (WMS)   1979**
■   20 Lutterburn St, Ugborough, IVYBRIDGE, Devon, PL21 0NG.
       (hsp)
       01752 896432
       email secretary@welshmines.org
       http://www.welshmines.org
       Sec: David Roe
○   *G; for those interested in all aspects of Welsh mines, especially
       the mineralogy, history & archaeology; preservation of sites
<   Nat Assn Mining History Orgs (NAMHO)
M   i
¶   NL - 2.

Welsh Mountain Sheep Society - Hill Flock Section   1950
NR   Gorseland, North Rd, ABERYSTWYTH, Ceredigion,
       SY23 2HE.   (asa)
       01970 636688   fax 01970 624049
       Sec: W G M Jones
○   *B
<   Nat Sheep Assn

**Welsh Mountain Sheep Society - Registered Section   (WMSS)
       1905**
NR   Llais Afon, Llangwm, CORWEN, Clwyd, LL21 0RA.   (hsp)
       01490 420626
       email bjroberts@hotmail.com
       Sec: Brian Roberts
▲   Registered Charity
○   *B
●   Conf - Mtgs - Exhib - Comp - Inf - Production of a flock book
<   Nat Sheep Assn
M   60 i
¶   NL - 2.   Ybk - 1.   Sale Catalogue - 1.

Welsh Mule Sheep Breeders Association   1978
NR   Gorseland, North Rd, ABERYSTWYTH, Ceredigion,
       SY23 2HE.   (asa)
       01970 636688   fax 01970 624049
       http://www.welshmules.co.uk
       Field Officer: Marcus Williams
○   *B
<   Nat Sheep Assn

Welsh Music Guild   1954
NR   71 Broad St, BARRY, Vale of Glamorgan, CF62 7AG.   (sec/p)
       http://www.welshmusic.org.uk
       Sec: Christopher Painter
○   *D; to promote Welsh music in its composition, performance &
       the teaching of the same; emphasis on Welsh contemporary
       music & its composers
M   i

Welsh National Literature Promotion Agency
    see **ACADEMI - Welsh National Literature Promotion Agency**

Welsh Netball Association   (WNA)   1945
■   Sport Wales National Centre, Sophia Gardens, CARDIFF,
       Glamorgan, CF11 9SW.   (hq)
       0845 045 4302
       email welshnetball@welshnetball.com
       http://www.welshnetball.co.uk
       Chief Exec: Mike Fatkin
▲   Company Limited by Guarantee
○   *S; to promote & develop the game of netball within Wales
●   Mtgs - ET - Comp
<   Intl Fedn Netball Assns (IFNA); Fedn Eur Netball Assns (FENA)
M   2,500 i, 500 schools & colleges
¶   Netball News (Jnl) - 2; ftm, £1 nm.

Welsh Pétanque Associaton   (WPA)   2007
■   27 Fairoak Rd, CARDIFF, CF23 5HH.   (vp/p)
       029 2040 4795
       email wales@fipjp.com
       http://www.welshpetanque.org.uk
       Vice Pres: Jean-Yves Robic
○   *S; to promote the game of pétanque in Wales
●   Mtgs - Comp
<   Fédn Intle de Pétanque et Jeu Provençal (FIPJP)
M   250 i

Welsh Pony & Cob Society   (WPCS)   1901
NR   Bronaeron, Felinfach, LAMPETER, Ceredigion, SA48 8AG.   (hq)
       01570 471754   fax 01570 470435
       http://www.wpcs.uk.com
       Sec: Anna Prytherch
▲   Company Limited by Guarantee; Registered Charity
○   *B; registration of Welsh Ponies & Cobs & their part-breeds
●   Mtgs - ET - Exhib - Inf - Archive Museum
<   Brit Horse Soc; Nat Pony Soc
M   8,000 i
¶   Jnl - 1.   NL - 2.   Welsh Ponies & Cobs (magazine) - 4.
       Stud Book - 1.

Welsh Rowing
    this title was formed to create the Wales international rowing team;
    see also **Welsh Amateur Rowing Association**

Welsh Rugby Players Association   (WRPA)
NR   3 Assembly Square, Britannia Quay, Cardiff Bay, CARDIFF,
       CF10 4PL.   (hq)
       029 2067 4455
       email nmacleansmith@wrpa.co.uk
       http://www.wrpa.co.uk
       Gen Sec: Neil Maclean-Smith
○   *U, *S; to protect & promote the interests of rugby players in
       Wales
<   Profl Players Fedn

Welsh Rugby Union Ltd (WRU) 1881
■ Westgate Terrace, Millennium Stadium, Westgate St, CARDIFF, CF10 1NS. (hq)
0870 013 8600
http://www.wru.co.uk
Chief Exec: Steven M Lewis
▲ Company Limited by Guarantee
○ *S; governing body of Rugby Union football in Wales
● Conf - Mtgs - ET - Comp - Inf - Lib - VE - Arranging international matches
< Intl Rugby Football Bd (IRB)
> Welsh Districts Rugby U; Welsh Schools Rugby U
M 240+ clubs
¶ WRU Hbk - 1; ftm, £5 nm.

Welsh Salmon & Trout Angling Association (WSTAA) 1952
NR Swyn Teifi, Pontrhydfendigaid, YSTRAD MEURIG, Ceredigion, SY25 6EF.
01974 831316
email info@wtsaa.org   http://www.wstaa.org
Sec: Julia Morgan
○ *S; the governing body for game angling in Wales
¶ NL.

Welsh Sea Rowing Association   (Cymdeithas Rhwyfo Môr Cymru) (WSRA)
NR c/o Aberystwyth Boat Club, The Promenade, Marine Terrace, ABERYSTWYTH, Ceredigion, SY23 2BX.
email secretary@welshsearowing.org.uk
http://www.welshsearowing.org.uk
Sec: Jasmine Sharp
○ *S; the national governing body for coastal & ocean rowing in Wales
< Welsh Rowing
M 28 clubs

Welsh Triathlon 2007
NR c/o Sport Wales, Sophia Gardens, CARDIFF, CF11 9SW.   (mail)
0845 045 4305
email admin@welshtriathlon.org
http://www.welshtriathlon.org
Chmn: Steve Butler
▲ Company Limited by Guarantee
○ *S; to promote & develop the sports of triathlon & duathlon within Wales; to encourage communication & cooperation between clubs & individuals
< Brit Triathlon Fedn

Welsh Weight Training Association (WWTA) 1985
■ 13 Barquentine Place, CARDIFF, CF10 4NJ.   (hsp)
029 2049 3919   fax 029 2049 3919
email lorraine.gray@ukgateway.net
Sec: Lorraine Gray
▲ Un-incorporated Society
Br 5
○ *S; to promote weight training; to improve & standardise coaching & instruction throughout Wales
● Mtgs - ET - Exam (coaches)
M 2,000 i
¶ Basic Coaches Manual.

Welshpool & Llanfair Light Railway Preservation Co Ltd 1960
NR The Station, Llanfair Caereinion, WELSHPOOL, Powys, SY21 0SF.   (hq)
01938 810441
http://www.wllr.org.uk
▲ Company Limited by Guarantee; Registered Charity
○ *G; preservation & operation of narrow-gauge railway, using British, African, Caribbean & Continental steam locomotives & rolling stock

Wensleydale Longwool Sheep Breeders' Association (WLSBA) 1890
■ Coffin Walk, Sheep Dip Lane, Princethorpe, RUGBY, Warks, CV23 9SP.
01926 633439
http://www.wensleydale-sheep.com
Sec: Dr Lynn Clouder
▲ Company Limited by Guarantee
○ *B; to promote the Wensleydale breed & maintain a register of animals eligible for registration
● Expt - Inf - Displays at agricultural shows & sheep events
< Nat Sheep Assn
M 200 i
¶ Wensleydale World (Jnl) - Every 2-3 years.
Flock Book - 1; both ftm.

Wesley Historical Society (WHS) 1893
■ 7 Haugh Shaw Rd, HALIFAX, W Yorks, HX1 3AH.   (hsp)
01422 250780
email generalsecretary@wesleyhistoricalsociety.org.uk
http://www.wesleyhistoricalsociety.org.uk
Gen Sec: Dr John A Hargreaves
▲ Registered Charity
Br 17; Irish (North & Eire), New Zealand (both autonomous)
○ *R; to promote interest in and study of Methodism
● Conf - Mtgs - Res - Exhib - Lib - PL - VE
M 388 i, 57 f, UK / 49 i, 78 f, o'seas
(Sub: £12 i, £16 f UK / £21 i, £27 f o'seas)
¶ Proceedings - 3; ftm.

Wessex Association of Chambers of Commerce (WACC) 1994
■ Pentagon House, 52 Castle St, TROWBRIDGE, Wilts, BA14 8AU.   (hq)
01225 355553   fax 01225 355554
email info@wessexchambers.org.uk
http://www.wessexchambers.org.uk
Chief Exec: Mike Williams
▲ Company Limited by Guarantee
Br 17 towns in Wiltshire & Somerset
○ *C
Gp Networks: Environmental, International, Training, Womans
● Conf - ET - Exhib - Comp - Expt - Inf - LG
M 1,400 f
(Sub: £65 - £3,500)
¶ Wessex in Business - 12; ftm.

Wessex Heavy Horse Society (WHHS) 2004
NR Coombe Corner Farm, Salisbury Rd, Donhead St Mary, SHAFTESBURY, Dorset, SP7 9LT.   (sp)
01747 828469
http://www.wessexheavyhorsesociety.org.uk
Sec: Mrs E Hiscock
○ *B; for the heavy horse enthusiast in the Wessex & surrounding area
● Spring show, Show & country fayre, Hand & harness championships - Ploughing match

West Africa Business Association
   see Business Council for Africa West & Southern

West Berkshire Chamber of Commerce
   a local chamber of **Thames Valley Chamber of Commerce & Industry**

West Cheshire & North Wales Chamber of Commerce   1921
NR   Riverside Innovation Centre, 1 Castle Drive, CHESTER,
    CH1 1SL.   (hq)
    01244 669988   fax 01244 669989
    email info@cepnwchamber.org.uk
    http://www.west-cheshire-chamber.co.uk
    Gen Mgr: Colin Brew
▲   Company Limited by Guarantee
Br   North Wales, West Cheshire
○   *C
<   Brit Chams Comm; Chams Comm NW
✕   Chester, Ellesmere Port & North Wales Chamber of Commerce

West Kent Chamber of Commerce & Industry   1858
NR   Castle Lodge, Castle St, TONBRIDGE, Kent, TN9 1BH.   (hq)
    01732 366653
○   *C

West Lothian Chamber of Commerce
NR   Alba Centre, Alba Business Park, LIVINGSTON, W Lothian,
    EH54 7EG.   (hq)
    01506 414808
    email chamber@wlchamber.com
    http://www.wlchamber.com
    Chief Exec: Dave McDougall
▲   Company Limited by Guarantee
○   *C
<   Scot Chams Comm

West Wales Chamber of Commerce
    since 2009 is the Swansea branch of the **South Wales Chamber of
Commerce**

Western Equestrian Society   (WES)   1985
■   Twin Oaks Stables, Duddington Rd, Collyweston, STAMFORD,
    Lincs, PE9 3PE.   (memsec/p)
    email secretary@wes-uk.com   http://www.wes-uk.com
    Mem Sec: Ann Hughes
○   *S; to promote & stimulate interest & high standards in Western
    (American) style of horsemanship

Western Front Association   (WFA)   1980
NR   PO Box 1918, STOCKPORT, Cheshire, SK4 4WN.
    0161-443 1918
    http://www.westernfrontassociation.com
    Hon Sec: S Oram
▲   Registered Charity
○   *G; to educate the public in the history of the Great War with
    particular reference to the Western Front
●   Conf - Mtgs - ET - Comp
M   6,500 i, UK / 1,000 i, o'seas
¶   Stand To - 3;   Bulletin - 3; both ftm only.

**Western Horsemens Association of Great Britain   (WHA)
1968**
NR   Brookglen, 1 Brook Lane, Brookville, THETFORD, Norfolk,
    IP26 4RQ.   (memsec/p)
    01366 727376
    email caroljudge@btinternet.com
    http://www.whagb.co.uk
    Mem Sec: Carol Judge
▲   Un-incorporated Society
○   *G; to promote & further the cause of all types of western riding
    in the UK, from show classes to speed events & the controlled
    movement of cattle
M   i

Western Isles Chamber of Commerce   1995
NR   30 Francis St, STORNOWAY, Isle of Lewis, HS1 2ND.   (hq)
    01851 700055   fax 01851 700066
▲   Un-incorporated Society
○   *C

Westminster Property Owners Association   (WPOA)   1988
NR   St Albans House (5th floor), 57-59 Haymarket, LONDON,
    SW1Y 4QX.   (hq)
    020 7630 1782
    http://www.wpoa.co.uk
▲   Un-incorporated Society
○   *T; interests of owners of property in the City of Westminster
M   f

Westmorland County Agricultural Society   (WCAS)   1799
■   Lane Farm, Crooklands, MILNTHORPE, Cumbria, LA7 7NH.
    (hq)
    01539 567804   fax 01539 567011
    email manager@westmorland.org.uk
    http://www.westmorlandshow.co.uk
    Chief Exec: Christine Knipe
▲   Company Limited by Guarantee; Registered Charity
○   *F, *H; to encourage & support agriculture, horticulture & rural
    crafts
●   Conf - Mtgs - ET - Exhib - SG - Inf
<   Assn Show & Agricl Orgs; Nat Farmers U; R Agricl Soc
    England; Nat Sheep Assn
M   1,019 i, 10 org
¶   Field & Fell NL - 4; ftm.   AR - 1; free.

Westmorland Damson Association
NR   Lile Yaks, Cartmel Fell, WINDERMERE, Cumbria, LA23 3PD.
    (hsp)
    01539 568698
    email info@lythdamsons.org.uk
    http://www.lythdamsons.org.uk
    Hon Sec: Helen Smith
○   *H

Wey & Arun Canal Trust Ltd   (W&ACT)   1970
■   The Granary, Flitchfold Farm, Vicarage Hill, LOXWOOD,
    W Sussex, RH14 0RH.   (hq/hsb)
    01403 752403   fax 01403 753991
    email office@weyandarun.co.uk
    http://www.weyandarun.co.uk
    Hon Sec: Julian Morgan
▲   Company Limited by Guarantee; Registered Charity
○   *G; to restore the derelict Wey & Arun canal in Surrey & W
    Sussex, linking the Thames with the English Channel
●   Mtgs - Working parties - Exhib - Inf - Fund raising - Talks -
    Sales stalls - Public boat trips
<   Inland Waterways Assn
M   2,500 i, 30 f
    (Subs: £10 i, £25 f)
¶   Wey-South - 4; ftm only.
    Wey-Arun Canal News - 2; free.

**Weymouth & Portland Chamber of Commerce, Industry &
Tourism   (WPCCIT)   1928**
■   Basepoint, Jubilee Enterprise Centre, Jubilee Close,
    WEYMOUTH, Dorset, DT4 7BS.
    07967 362585
    email secretary@wpchamber.co.uk
    http://www.wpchamber.co.uk
    Pres: Nigel Reed
▲   Un-incorporated Society
○   *C
●   Mtgs - LG
<   Dorset Cham Comm & Ind (Poole)
M   128 f
¶   NL - 12 ftm only.

Whale & Dolphin Conservation Society   (WDCS)   1987
NR   Brookfield House, 38 St Paul St, CHIPPENHAM, Wilts,
       SN15 1LJ.   (hq)
       01249 449500   fax 01249 449501
       email info@wdcs.org   http://www.wdcs.org
▲   Registered Charity
○   *K; to promote public awareness of the threats facing whales &
       dolphins throughout the world
M   50,000 i

Wheeled & Urban Sports Association
NR   Federation House, STONELEIGH PARK, Warks, CV8 2RF.
       024 7641 4999
       NOTE: A purely working title for a possible new trade
       association for the wheeled sports industry. Manufacturers,
       suppliers, retailers, press & operators of any wheeled sport
       activity are asked to contact Eileen Taylor.

WheelPower - British Wheelchair Sport   1972
■   Stoke Mandeville Stadium, Guttmann Rd, STOKE MANDEVILLE,
       Bucks, HP21 9PP.   (hq)
       01296 395995   fax 01296 424171
       email info@wheelpower.org.uk
       http://www.wheelpower.org.uk
       Chmn: Kevan Baker
▲   Company Limited by Guarantee; Registered Charity
○   *S, *W; the national organisation for wheelchair sport in the
       UK; to provide, promote & develop opportunities for men,
       women & children with disabilities to participate in
       recreational & competitive wheelchair sport
Gp   Sports associations throughout UK
●   ET - Comp - Inf - Organises events at novice, junior, national &
       international level
M   c 3,000 i, 1 f, 20 org
¶   NL - 3/4; free.

White Ensign Association Ltd   1958
■   HMS Belfast, Tooley St, LONDON, SE1 2JH.   (hq)
       020 7407 8658   fax 020 7357 6298
       email office@whiteensign.co.uk
       http://www.whiteensign.co.uk
       Office Mgr: Miss Emma C Copland
▲   Company Limited by Guarantee; Registered Charity
○   *W; advisory service to serving & retired members of the Royal
       Navy & Royal Marines on employment, resettlement &
       financial matters
●   ET - Inf
M   115 i, 32 f
¶   LM;   AR; both free.

White Face Dartmoor Sheep Breeders Association   1950
NR   Beckaford Farm, Manaton, NEWTON ABBOT, Devon,
       TQ13 9XH.   (Chmn/p)
       01647 221251
       email info@whitefacedartmoorsheep.co.uk
       http://www.whitefacedartmoorsheep.co.uk
       Chmn: Mrs Clare Butcher
▲   Un-Incorporated Society
○   *B; to encourage people to breed the White Face Dartmoor, to
       further the interests of the breed & to produce an annual
       Flock Book
●   Mtgs - Comp
<   Nat Sheep Assn
M   40 i

White Faced Woodland Sheep Society   1986
NR   North Park Cottage, Rokeby, BARNARD CASTLE, Co Durham,
       DL12 9RZ.   (hsp)
       01833 627102
       email rachelgodschalk@whitefacedwoodland.co.uk
       http://www.whitefacedwoodland.co.uk
       Hon Sec: Rachel Godschalk
○   *B
¶   NL - 4.

White Goods Association   (WGA)   2004
IRL   Confederation House, 84-86 Lower Baggot St, DUBLIN 2,
       Republic of Ireland.   (hq)
       353 (1) 605 1500   fax 353 (1) 638 1500
       email paul.sweetman@ibec.ie   http://www.ibec.ie/wga
       Dir: Paul Sweetman
○   *T; to promote the development of the white goods sector in
       Ireland; to monitor the development of the EU Waste
       Electrical & Electronic Equipment (WEEE) Directive
<   Ir Business & Emplrs Confedn (IBEC)
M   11 f

White Park Cattle Society   (WPCS)   1972
NR   Hillfields Lodge, Lighthorne, WARWICK, CV35 0BQ.   (hsp)
       01926 650122
       email whiteparks@aol.com
       http://www.whiteparkcattle.org.uk
       Sec: Yvonne Froelich
○   *B
M   i

Whitebred Shorthorn Association Ltd   1962
■   High Green Hill, Kirkcambeck, BRAMPTON, Cumbria,
       CA8 2BL.   (hsp)
       01697 748228
       email secretary@whitebredshorthorn.com
       http://www.whitebredshorthorn.com
       Hon Sec: Mrs Rosie Mitchinson
▲   Registered Charity
○   *B
●   Mtgs - Sales - Shows
<   Nat Beef Assn
M   51 i
¶   Herd Book - 2; ftm, £10 nm.   AR.

Whitegoods Trade Association   (WTA)   2007
NR   Unit 6 Bonnyton Industrial Estate, Munro Place,   KILMARNOCK,
       E Ayrshire, KA1 2NP.   (hq)
       0845 172 8001
       email enquiries@whitegoodstradeassociation.org
       http://www.whitegoodstradeassociation.org
○   *T; for repairers of large domestic appliances (washing
       machines, dishwashers, fridge freezers etc)

Wholesale Markets Brokers' Association   (WMBA)   1994
■   St Clements House, 27-28 St Clements Lane, LONDON,
       EC4N 7AE.   (hq)
       020 3207 9741
       email wmba@wmba.org.uk   http://www.wmba.org.uk
       Chief Exec: Alex McDonald
▲   Un-incorporated Society
○   *P; to represent broking companies listed by the Financial
       Services Authority whose primary purpose is to facilitate
       cooperation in areas of mutual interest & benefit to members
●   Mtgs - ET - Exam - Comp - LG
M   9 f

Wholesome Food Association   (WFA)   1999
NR   18 Currier Drive, Neath Hill, MILTON KEYNES, Bucks,
       MK14 6HB.   (hq)
       http://www.wholesome-food.org
       Sec: Sky McCain
▲   Company Limited by Guarantee
○   *T; a network of producers of wholesome food, locally grown &
       processed using sustainable, non-polluting methods
Gp   Beekeepers
M   122 f

Wigtown Agricultural Society   1811
NR   Crailloch Farm, Port William, NEWTON STEWART, DG8 9RN.
        (hsp)
        01988 860233
        email secretary@wigtownshow.org.uk
        http://www.wigtownshow.org.uk
        Sec: Helen McColm
○   *F
●   Wigtown Agricultural Show
<   Assn of Show & Agricl Orgs

Wild Deer Association of Ireland   (WDA)   1981
IRL   PO Box 31, MIDLETON, Co Cork, Republic of Ireland.
        353 (087) 249 6987
        email wilddeerireland.com
○   *V

Wild Flower Society   (WFS)   1886
■   43 Roebuck Rd, ROCHESTER, Kent, ME1 1UE.   (mem/secp)
        email wildflowermembership@yahoo.co.uk
        http://www.thewildflowersociety.com
        Mem Sec: Sue Poyser,   Treas: R Blades (020 8368 5328)
▲   Registered Charity
○   *G, *L; increasing the understanding of field botany in the UK
●   Mtgs - Exhib - VE
M   900 i
¶   Wild Flower Society Magazine - 4; ftm only.

Wild Trout Trust   (WTT)   1997
NR   PO Box 120, WATERLOOVILLE, Hants, PO8 0WZ.
        023 9257 0985
        http://www.wildtrout.org
        Admin: Christina Bryant (Mon-Thur 1000-1400)
▲   Registered Charity
○   *K, *V; conservation of wild trout habitat & populations in the
        UK & Ireland
●   Conf
M   1,650 i, 5 org, UK / 55 i, o'seas
¶   Jnl - 1;   NL - 4; both ftm only.

Wildlife & Countryside Link
■   89 Albert Embankment, LONDON, SE1 7TP.
        020 7820 8600   fax 020 7820 8620
        http://www.wcl.org.uk
        Dir: Jodie Bettis
○   *N; for voluntary environmental organisations
M   org

Wildlife Sound Recording Society   (WSRS)   1968
■   Fuschia Cottage, Helperthorpe, MALTON, N Yorks,
        YO17 8TQ.   (mail add)
        020 7412 7402
        http://www.wildlife-sound.org
        Mem Sec: David Mellor
▲   Un-incorporated Society
○   *L; to encourage the recording of wildlife sounds & further the
        appreciation of animal language
●   Mtgs - Comp
M   300 i, UK / 30 i, o'seas
¶   Wildlife Sound (Jnl) - 2;   NL - 3;   LM - 3 yrly;
        CD magazine of members' work - 4; all ftm.
        Introduction to Wildlife Sound Recording; £2.50.

Wilfred Owen Association   1989
NR   21 Culverdon Avenue, TUNBRIDGE WELLS, Kent, TN4 9RE.
        (chmn/p)
        email woa@1914-1918.co.uk
        http://www.wilfredowen.org.uk
        Chmn: Meg Crane
▲   Registered Charity
○   *A; to commemorate & promote awareness of the life & work
        of Wilfred Owen, the First World War poet
●   Mtgs - Res - Exhib - Inf - VE
M   400 i
¶   Jnl - 1.   NL - 2.

Wilhelm Furtwängler Society UK   1967
■   6 Goodwin Court, Devonshire Rd, LONDON, SW19 2EQ.
        (chmn/p)
        Chmn: John Hunt
○   *D; liaison with record companies to obtain greater
        representation of Furtwängler's art on record; dissemination
        of news & matters relating to articles, books & records by &
        about Furtwängler as man & artist

Wilkie Collins Society   (WCS)   1980
NR   3 Merton House, 36 Belsize Park, LONDON, NW3 4EA.
        (chmn/p)
        email apogee@apgee.co.uk
        http://www.wilkiecollinssociety.com
        4 Ernest Gardens, LONDON, W4 3QU. (sec/p)
        email paul@paullewis.co.uk
        Chmn: Andrew Gasson,   Sec: Paul Lewis
▲   Un-incorporated Society
Br   USA
○   *A, *G; to promote research into the life & works of Wilkie
        Collins (1824-89); to foster original, critical studies of his
        novels, plays, stories & essays
●   Mtgs
<   Alliance of Literary Socs
¶   Jnl - 1.   NL - 3.   Reprints - 1.

William Barnes Society   1983
■   72 Spa Rd, WEYMOUTH, Dorset, DT3 5ER.   (chmn/p)
        01305 782279
        Chmn: Dr Alan Chedzoy
○   *A; for those interested in the Rev William Barnes (1801-1886),
        the Dorset dialect poet
●   Mtgs - VE
M   200 i, UK / c 8 i, o'seas
¶   NL - 2/3; ftm only.

William Cobbett Society   1976
■   3 Park Terrace, Tillington, PETWORTH, W Sussex, GU28 9AE.
        (hsp)
        01798 342008
        http://www.williamcobbett.org.uk
        Chmn: Barbara Biddell
▲   Un-incorporated Society
○   *L; to make known the life & writings of William Cobbett
        (1763-1835)
●   Mtgs - Inf - Lib - VE
<   Alliance of Literary Socs; Historical Assn; Thomas Paine Soc
M   120 i, 6 libraries, UK / 6 i, i;seas
        (Sub: £8)
¶   Cobbett's New Register - 1.
        Anne Cobbett: account of the family; £4.50.
        William Cobbett in America by Molly Townsend; £15.50.

© CBD Research Ltd · Beckenham · BR3 5JS · Tel 020 8650 7745 · E-mail cbd@cbdresearch.com · www.cbdresearch.com

William Herschel Society   1979

- ■ 19 New King St, BATH, BA1 2BL.   (hq)
  01225 446865
  email fredsch@tiscali.co.uk
  http://www.williamherschel.org.uk
  Chmn: Dr Peter Ford
- ▲ Registered Charity
- Br Germany, Japan
- ○ *L; for all interested in: the life & achievements of William Herschel, his family & immediate descendants; the history of science, astronomy & 18th century music; telescope making; links with modern space discovery
- ● Conf - Mtgs - Res - Public lectures on astronomy & space research
- < The Royal Soc; R Astronomical Soc
- > Herschel Soc of Japan
- M 178 i, 9 org UK / 18 i, 1 org, o'seas
  (Sub: £10 UK & Europe / £13 o'seas)
- ¶ The Speculum (Jnl) - 2; ftm, £13 nm.

William Morris Society   1955

- ■ Kelmscott House Museum, 26 Upper Mall, LONDON, W6 9TA.   (hq)
  020 8741 3735   fax 020 8748 5207
  email william.morris@care4free.net
  http://www.morrissociety.org
  Hon Sec: Phillippa Bennett
- ▲ Registered Charity
- ○ *A, *L; to promote the study of the life, work & influence of William Morris (1834-96) designer & poet; to make his life, work & ideas better known
- ● Mtgs - ET - Res - Exhib - Inf - Lib - VE
- M 2,000 i
- ¶ Jnl - 2.   NL - 4; both ftm only.

Williams Syndrome Foundation Ltd   (WSF)   1980

- NR 161 High St, TONBRIDGE, Kent, TN9 1BX.   (hq)
  01732 365152
  http://www.williams-syndrome.org.uk
  Chief Exec: John Nelson
- ▲ Company Limited by Guarantee
- ○ *W; to help parents & carers of children & adults who have Williams Syndrome (infantile hypercalcaemia - a rare non-hereditary genetic syndrome occurring at random); to stimulate interest, particularly among the medical profession
- Gp Families with affected children; Medical profession; Students; Care workers
- ● Conf - Mtgs - Res - Inf - Lib
- < Mencap; Genetic Interest Gp; Contact-a-Family
- M 900 i, UK / 100 i, o'seas
- ¶ NL - 2.   Video.
  Various Guideline publications.

** Willwriters' Association

Organisation lost: see Introduction paragraph 3

Wiltshire Archaeological & Natural History Society   (WANHS)   1853

- ■ Wiltshire Heritage Museum, 41 Long St, DEVIZES, Wilts, SN10 1NS.   (hq)
  01380 727369   fax 01380 722150
  email wanhs@wiltshireheritage.org.uk
  http://www.wiltshireheritage.org.uk
  Sec: Mrs W Lansdown
- ▲ Company Limited by Guarantee; Registered Charity
- ○ *L; to promote, research & publish on the archaeology, art, history & natural history of Wiltshire for the public benefit
- Gp Archaeology field gp
- ● Mtgs - ET - Res - Exhib - SG - Inf - Lib - PL - VE - Maintenance of a museum & library displaying designated collections
- M 1,041 i, 83 org
- ¶ Wiltshire Archaeological & Natural History Magazine (Jnl) - 1; ftm, £15 nm.
  NL - 2.   AR.

Wiltshire Horn Sheep Society   (WHSS)   1923

- ■ Stickle Heaton Farm, CORNHILL-ON-TWEED, Northumberland, TD12 4XG.   (hsp)
  0844 800 1029
  email info@wiltshirehorn.org.uk
  http://www.wiltshirehorn.org.uk
  Sec: Mrs C Cormack
- ▲ Company Limited by Guarantee
- ○ *B
- ● Mtgs - Exhib - Comp - Expt
- < Nat Sheep Assn
- M 125 i, UK / 5 i, o'seas
- ¶ Flock Book - 1.

Wiltshire Record Society   (WRS)   1937

- ■ Wiltshire & Swindon History Centre, Cocklebury Rd, CHIPPENHAM, Wilts, SN15 3QN.   (hsb)
  01249 705500
  Hon Sec: Dr James Lee
- ▲ Registered Charity
- ○ *L; to promote publication of documentary sources of Wiltshire history
- ● AGM & Lecture
- M 150 i, 63 universities & public libraries, UK / 10 i, 75 org, o'seas
- ¶ Volume of edited documents - 1; £15 m, £20 nm.
  AR; ftm only.

Winchester Chamber of Commerce
merged in 2010 with other chambers of commerce in Hampshire to form the **Hampshire Chamber of Commerce**

Wind Engineering Society   (WES)   1990

- ■ Institution of Civil Engineers, 1 Great George St, LONDON, SW1P 3AA.   (hq)
  020 7665 2262   fax 020 7799 1325
  email adamkirkup@ice.org.uk
  http://www.ukwes.bham.ac.uk
  Sec: Adam Kirkup
- ○ *P; to promote cooperation in the advancement & application of knowledge in all aspects of wind engineering
- ● Conf - Mtgs
- < is an affiliated society of the Institution of Civil Engineers
- M i & f
  (Sub: £30 i, £90-£180 f)

Wine & Spirit Trade Association   (WSTA)   1824

- ■ International Wine & Spirit Centre, 39-45 Bermondsey St, LONDON, SE1 3XF.   (hq)
  020 7089 3877   fax 020 7089 3870
  email info@wsta.co.uk   http://www.wsta.co.uk
  Chief Exec: Jeremy Beadles
- ▲ Company Limited by Guarantee
- ○ *T; to represent the interests of shippers & distributors of wine & imported spirits in the UK
- Gp Distance seller; Importers; Logistics; UK wine growers
- ● Conf - Stat - Inf - LG
- < Fédn Intle de Vin et Spiritueux (FIVS); Eur Fedn of Wine & Spirit Importers & Distributors (EFWSID); Office Intle de de Vigne et du Vin (OIV); Comité Vins
- M 320 f, UK & o'seas
- ¶ Trade Voice - 12; ftm only   AR - 1.
  Checklists (the sole commercial guide to European wine & spirit legislation) - 1.

Wire Products Association

no longer in existence

Wireless for the Bedridden Society Inc

since 2010 is the charity WaveLength & is outside the scope of this directory.

Wirral Chamber of Commerce & Industry   1912

NR   Lord Leverhulme Chambers, 16 Grange Rd West, Birkenhead,
    WIRRAL, Merseyside, CH41 4DA.   (hq)
    0151-647 8899   fax 0151-650 0440
    email info@wirralchamber.org.uk
    http://www.wirralchamber.org.uk
    Chief Exec: Ken Davies
▲   Company Limited by Guarantee
○   *C
Gp   Education link; Environment; Central traders; Finance
●   Conf - Mtgs - ET - Res - Exhib - Stat - Expt - Inf - VE - LG
<   Brit Chams Com; Chams Comm NW
M   f
¶   Newsletter - 12.   LM - 1.   Diary - 1.

Wokingham Chamber of Commerce
    a local chamber of **Thames Valley Chamber of Commerce &
Industry**

Wolverton & District Archaeological & Historical Society   1955

■   82 Clarence Rd, Stony Stratford, MILTON KEYNES, Bucks,
    MK11 1JD.   (hsp)
    01908 565481
    Hon Sec: Mrs Audrey Lambert
○   *L; archaeology & local history within the Milton Keynes area &
    adjoining villages of North Buckinghamshire & South
    Northamptonshire; preservation & recording of sites &
    buildings under threat of destruction
●   Mtgs - Exhib - Inf - Lib
<   Coun Brit Archaeology; Bucks Archaeol Soc; Northants
    Archaeol Soc
M   145 i
¶   NL - 6; ftm.

Wolves & Humans Foundation   (WAH)   2005

■   2 Blackrod Cottages, Compton Durville, SOUTH PETHERTON,
    Somerset, TA13 5EX.   (hsp)
    01460 242593
    email info@wolvesandhumans.org
    http://www.wolvesandhumans.org
    Sec: Richard Morley
▲   Registered Charity
○   *K; support & promotion of research & scientific study of wolves
    & other large carnivores; the education & training in methods
    of managing conflict between such animals & agriculture &
    other human interests
●   Conf - ET - Res - Exhib - Inf
M   200 i, UK / 20 i, o'seas
¶   Wolves & Humans NL - 4; ftm only (subscription £25).

Women's Aid Federation (England) Ltd   (WAFE)   1986

■   PO Box 391, BRISTOL, BS99 7WS.   (hq)
    0117-944 4411   fax 0117-924 1703
    email info@womensaid.org.uk
    http://www.womensaid.org.uk
    Chief Exec: Nicola Harwin
▲   Company Limited by Guarantee; Registered Charity
Br   250
○   *N, *W; to coordinate & resource refuge groups for women &
    their children in need of temporary accommodation because
    of mental, physical or sexual abuse
●   ET - Res - Inf - LG - Public information work on domestic
    violence - Seminars - Networking
    Helpline: 0800 200 0247 (freephone 24-hr) the national
    domestic violence helpline run in partnership between
    Women's Aid & Refuge
<   Fedn Indep Advice Centres (FIAC)
¶   NL - 12; ftm only.   Publications list available.

Women's Archive of Wales
    see **Archif Menywod Cymru (Women's Archive of Wales)**

Women's Cycle Racing Association
    no longer active

Women's Engineering Society   (WES)   1919

■   Michael Faraday House, Six Hills Way, STEVENAGE, Herts,
    SG1 2AY.   (hq)
    01438 765506
    email info@wes.org.uk   http://www.wes.org.uk
    Office Mgr: Suzanne Korn
▲   Company Limited by Guarantee; Registered Charity
Br   Student groups
○   *P; to inspire women to achieve their potential as scientists,
    engineers & technologists; to assist educators, managers &
    employers in making this happen
Gp   Mentor set
●   Conf - Mtgs - ET - Comp - Inf - PL - VE - LG - Student support -
    Dr Karen Burt Award - Young Woman Engineer Award
M   700 i, 20 f, 12 student groups, UK / 40 i, 1 f, o'seas
    (Sub: £40 i, varies f)
¶   The Woman Engineer - 4; ftm, £25 yr (UK), £28 yr (o'seas) nm.
    LM; m only.   AR - 1.

Women's Environmental Network   (WEN)   1988

■   20 Club Row (ground floor), LONDON, E2 7EY.   (hq)
    020 7481 9004   fax 020 7481 9144
    email info@wen.org.uk,09.wen.org.uk
    Admin: Shirley Abranches
▲   Company Limited by Guarantee; Registered Charity
Br   55 local gps
○   *K; to inform, educate & empower women who care about the
    environment
●   ET - Res - Exhib - Inf
    Office hours Mon-Thur 1000-1800
M   3,500 i, 30 f, 160 org, UK / 50 i, 5 f, 10 org, o'seas
¶   NL - 4; ftm only.

Women's Farm & Garden Association   (WFGA)   1899

NR   175 Gloucester St, CIRENCESTER, Glos, GL7 2DP.   (hq)
    01285 658339   fax 01285 642356
    email admin@wfga.fsbusiness.co.uk
    http://www.wfga.org.uk
▲   Registered Charity
○   *F, *H; to unite all involved in agriculture & horticulture in the
    UK & overseas
M   i

Women's Food & Farming Union   (WFU)   1979

■   c/o Cargill plc, WITHAM St HUGHES, Lincs, LN6 9TN.   (hq)
    0844 335 0342
    http://www.wfu.org.uk
    Pres: Helen Bower,   Nat Sec: Sue Archer
▲   Un-incorporated Society
Br   26
○   *F; to link the producer & the consumer by promoting demand
    for British farm produce; to encourage farmers & growers to
    practise better marketing; to ensure British produce is
    available & well marketed; to lobby against unfair
    competition
Gp   Crops; Dairy; Livestock
●   Conf - Mtgs - ET - LG
<   Nat Coun Women GB
M   800 i
¶   Update - 5; ftm only.   Annual Review - 1; free.

Women in Management Network
    a group of the **Chartered Management Institute**

Women's Professional Golf Association
    a group of the **Professional Golfers' Association**

© CBD Research Ltd · Beckenham · BR3 5JS · Tel 020 8650 7745 · E-mail cbd@cbdresearch.com · www.cbdresearch.com

Women's Royal Voluntary Service   (WRVS)   1938
- ■   Beck Court, Cardiff Gate Business Park, CARDIFF, CF23 8RP. (hq)
     029 2073 9111
     email info@wrvs.org.uk   http://www.wrvs.org.uk
     Chief Exec: David McCullough
- ▲   Company Limited by Guarantee; Registered Charity
- Br   'hundreds'
- ○   *W; voluntary welfare service to local communities in Britain, working alongside local authorities & hospital trusts; 'to help people maintain independence & dignity in their local communities, particularly later in life'
- ●   Hospital services; Emergency services; Services for older people
- <   NCVO
- M   95,000 i
- ¶   AR.

Wood Panel Industries Federation   (WPIF)   1996
- ■   28 Market Place, GRANTHAM, Lincs, NG31 6LR.   (hq)
     01476 563707   fax 01476 579314
     email enquiries@wpif.org.uk   http://www.wpif.org.uk
     Dir Gen: Alastair Kerr
- ▲   Company Limited by Guarantee
- ○   *T; for industrial manufacturers in the UK & Ireland of Wood Chipboard, Oriented Strand Board (OSB) & Medium Density Fibreboard (MDF)
- Gp   Environmental; Technical
- ●   Mtgs - Res - Inf - LG
- <   Eur Confedn Woodworking Inds; Eur Fedn Assns Particleboard Mfrs; Construction Products Assn
- M   13 f, 3 org

Wood Protection Association   (WPA)   2006
- NR   5c Flemming Court, CASTLEFORD, W Yorks, WF10 5HW.   (hq)
     01977 558274
     email info@wood-protection.org
     http://www.wood-protection.org
     Company Limited by Guarantee
     Dir: Steve Young
- ○   *T; to achieve & promote clear understanding & leadership in the field of enhancing the durability & performance of wood & wood based panel products
- M   38 f, UK / 4 f, o'seas
- ✕   2006 British Wood Preserving & Damp-proofing Association

Wood Technology Society
     see IWSc: The Wood Technology Society, a division of the **Institute of Materials, Minerals & Mining**

Woodcraft Folk   1925
- NR   Units 9-10, 83 Crampton St, LONDON, SE17 3BF.
     020 7730 4173   fax 020 7358 6370
     email info@woodcraft.org.uk
     http://www.woodcraft.org.uk
     Gen Sec: Kirsty Palmer
- Br   500
- ○   *Y; an educational movement for children & young people which aims to develop self confidence & activity in society
- Gp   Woodchips (under 6 years); Elfins (6-9); Pioneers (10-12); Venturers (13-15); DFs (District Fellows - older teenagers & young adults)

Wooden Boatbuilders Trade Association   1990
- NR   Y Bwthyn, High St, LLANDYSUL, Ceredigion, SA44 4DN   (hsp)
     01559 363201
     email info@wbta.co.uk   http://www.wbta.co.uk
     Sec: Jane Kerr
- ○   *T; formed for boatbuilders by boatbuilders & to encourage the public to buy wooden boats
- ¶   Soundings - 4; ftm.

Woodworking Machinery Suppliers Association   (WMSA)   1983
- ■   Cliff Farm, Plaistow Green, MATLOCK, Derbys, DE4 5GX.
     01629 530998   fax 01629 530999
     email info@wmsa.org.uk   http://www.wmsa.org.uk
- ○   *T
- ●   Conf - Mtgs - Exhib
- M   90 f
- ¶   NL - 4; m only.
     Directory of Members & Buyers' Guide - 2 yrly; free.

Woolhope Naturalists' Field Club   1851
- ■   60 Hafod Rd, HEREFORD, HR1 1SQ.   (hsp)
     01432 269766
     http://www.woolhopeclub.org.uk
     Hon Sec: D Whitehead
- ▲   Registered Charity
- ○   *L; archaeology, natural history & allied subjects of Herefordshire & the area immediately adjacent
- Gp   Archaeology; Natural history
- ●   Mtgs - SG - Lib - VE
- M   550 i, 38 org, UK / 3 i, 6 org, o'seas
- ¶   Transactions - 1; m only.

Worcestershire Archaeological Society   (WAS)   1860
- ■   26 Albert Park Rd, MALVERN, Worcs, WR14 1HN.   (hsp)
     01684 565190
     http://www.worcestershirearchaeologicalsociety.org.uk
     Hon Sec: Janet Dunleavey
- ▲   Registered Charity
- ○   *L; to promote study of archaeology & local history in the County of Worcestershire & the diocese of Worcester
- Gp   Architectural study
- ●   Mtgs - SG - Lib - VE
- M   180 i, c 60 org, UK / c 30 org, o'seas
- ¶   The Worcestershire Recorder - 2; ftm.
     Transactions - 2; ftm, £25 nm.

Worcestershire Chamber of Commerce
     see **Herefordshire & Worcestershire Chamber of Commerce**

Work Experience UK
     a group of **English UK**

The Work Foundation   1918
- NR   21 Palmer St, LONDON, SW1H 0AD.   (hq)
     020 7976 3565
     http://www.theworkfoundation.com
     Exec Vice-Chmn: Will Hutton
- ▲   Registered Charity
- ○   *K; 'to work with employees to improve the productivity & quality of working life in the UK'
- ●   Res - Inf - Lib - LG
- M   400 i, 1,450 f, UK

Work-based & Placement Learning Association
     see **ASET, the Work-based & Placement Learning Association**

Workers' Educational Association   (WEA)   1903
- ■   4 Luke St, LONDON, EC2A 4XW.   (hq)
     020 7426 3450   fax 020 7426 3451
     http://www.wea.org.uk
     Gen Sec: Richard Bolsin
- ▲   Registered Charity
- Br   650
- ○   *E; as the largest voluntary provider of adult education in the UK the WEA has particular concern for the socially, economically & educationally disadvantaged; the voluntary & democratic traditions have created an approach that is unique in adult education
- M   5,000 i

Workers' Music Association   (WMA)   1936

- 12 St Andrew's Square, LONDON, W11 1RH.   (hsp)
  020 7243 0920
  email mavcook@talktalk.net
  http://www.wmamusic.org.uk
  Hon Sec: Mavis Cook
- ▲ Company Limited by Guarantee
- ○ *D; 'to print, publish & sell (including for export) music & the
  literature of music, & to deal in musical instruments
  (including instruments for the reproduction of music); to
  produce & sell (including for export) recorded music & films;
  to encourage the composition & performance of music, with
  special regard to music. . .'
- Gp Summer school c'ee; WMA singers
- ● Mtgs - ET - Lib - Annual summer school - Weekend musical
  events - Performances by WMA singers - Concerts
- < Birmingham Clarion Singers; Côr Cochion Caerdydd; Calumet
  Singers
- M 119 i, 4 choirs, UK / 3 affiliates
  (Sub: £7 i, £25 affiliates)
- ¶ Bulletin - 4;   NL - irreg;   AR; all ftm.
  Peace Song Book.   Easter Rising in Song & Ballad.

Working Families   1985

- 1-3 Berry St, LONDON, EC1V 0AA.   (hq)
  020 7253 7243   fax 020 7253 6253
  email office@workingfamilies.org.uk
  http://www.workingfamilies.org.uk
  Chief Exec: Sarah Jackson
- ▲ Company Limited by Guarantee; Registered Charity
- ○ *W; to give advice to working parents & carers, whilst helping
  employers create workplaces which encourage work/life
  balance for everyone
- ● Conf - ET - Comp - Inf
  Disability & careers issues: Janet Mearns 020 7253 7243
  Helpline: 0800 013 0313
- M [not stated]
- ¶ [see website]

Working Men's Club & Institute Union Ltd   (CIU)   1862

- 253-254 Upper St, LONDON, N1 1RY.   (hq)
  020 7226 0221   fax 020 7354 1847
  email information@wmciu.org   http://www.wmciu.org
  Gen Sec: Kevin Smyth
- Br 29
- ○ *W; 'an advisory & defensive organisation for non-profit
  making members' clubs'
- ● Conf - Mtgs - ET - Exam - Res - Exhib - Comp - SG - Stat - Inf -
  VE - Empl - LG - Provision of convalescent homes, recreation
  & sporting facilities
- < C'ee of Registered Clubs Assns; Workers Educational Assn;
  Ruskin College
- M 6,000,000 i, 2,903 clubs
- ¶ Club Jnl - 12; 60p each.   AR.

Working on Wheels
  the working title of the **National Playbus Association**

World Orthopaedic Concern
  a specialist society of the **British Orthopaedic Association**

World Pheasant Association UK   (WPA)   1975

- Newcastle University Biology Field Stataion, Close House Estate,
  Heddon on the Wall, NEWCASTLE UPON TYNE,
  NE15 0HT.   (hq)
  0845 241 0929
  email office@pheasant.org.uk
  http://www.pheasant.org.uk
  Admin: Barbara Ingham
- ▲ Registered Charity
- Br Australia, Austria, Belelux, China, France, Germany, India,
  Nepal, Pakistan, Portugal, Taiwan
- ○ *K, *L; to ensure the survival of the individual species of
  pheasant & related gamebirds which are threatened with
  extinction; the maintenance of viable populations of these
  groups of birds in natural habitat in their countries of origin
- Gp Grouse; Megapose; Partridge, quail & francolin; Pheasants
- ● Conf - Mtgs - ET - Res - Exhib - SG - Inf - Lib - LG
- < species survival commission of the Intl U for the Consvn of
  Nature (IUCN); Birdlife Intl
- M 520 i, 5 f, UK / 107 i, 1 f, o'seas
  (Sub: £25 i, £100, UK / £30 i, £100 f o'seas)
- ¶ WPA News - 2; ftm.
  WPA Annual Review - 1; ftm, £6 nm.
  Publications list available.

World Speedway Riders Association   (WSRA)   1958

- 90 Ruskin Ave, Long Eaton, NOTTINGHAM, NG10 3HX.   (hsp)
  0115-973 6041   fax 0115-946 5005
  email legend3333@btinternet.com
  Sec & Treas: Vic White
- Br Australia, New Zealand
- ○ *S; 'to help former colleagues to keep in touch, to stage
  frequent reunions & to enjoy the pleasures of reliving old
  times in convivial company'
- ● Exhib - Lunches - Dinners - Golf tournaments
- M c 550 i, UK & o'seas
- ¶ Opposite Lock (NL) - 4; ftm only.
- × 2006 Veteran Speedway Riders Association

World War Two Living History Association   (LHA)   1978

- NR Adam House, Birmingham Road, KIDDERMINSTER, Worcs,
  DY10 2SA.   (mail address)
  08432 896987
  email lha@ww2lha.co.uk   http://www.ww2lha.co.uk
- ▲ Company Limited by Guarantee
- ○ *G; to mount public displays of battle re-enactment & private
  'living history' re-enactments for members only
- M i

World War Two Railway Study Group   (WW2RSG)   1990

- NR 25 Woodcote Rd, LEAMINGTON SPA, Warks, CV32 6PZ.
  (memsec/p)
  01926 429378
  http://www.saxoncourtbooks.co.uk/ww2rsg/
  Mem Sec: Mike Christensen
- ▲ Un-incorporated Society
- ○ *G, *Q; to collect, exchange & publish information on the
  operation of railways of the combatant nations during World
  War II
- ¶ Bulletin - 6, ftm

© CBD Research Ltd · Beckenham · BR3 5JS · Tel 020 8650 7745 · E-mail cbd@cbdresearch.com · www.cbdresearch.com

World-Wide Opportunities on Organic Farms   (WWOOF) 1971
- ■ PO Box 2154, Winslow, BUCKINGHAM, MK18 3WS.
  (co-ordinator/p)
  http://www.wwoof.org.uk
  Co-ordinator: Fran Whittle
- ▲ Company Limited by Guarantee
- Br 24 countries o'seas
- ○ *F; in return for work on organic farms, gardens & smallholdings, volunteers are given meals & a place to sleep. Participants get first hand experience of organic farming & growing as well as the opportunity to get into the countryside. WWOOF operates on the Continent & there are similar organisations worldwide
- ● Conf - Practical work on farms
- M 2,000 i, 5,000 i (independents), UK / i, o'seas
- ¶ WWOOF UK News - 6; ftm.
  WWINDY News (NL) - 6; free, online only.
  List of branches overseas with host names.

Worldchoice   1978
- NR Worldchoice House, Minerva Business Park, Lynch Wood, PETERBOROUGH, Cambs, PE2 6FT.   (hq)
  01733 390900   fax 01733 396823
  email info@worldchoice.co.uk
  http://www.worldchoice.co.uk
- ▲ Company Limited by Guarantee
- ○ *T; independent travel agent consortia
- ● Conf - ET
- M c 700 f

Worthing & Adur Chamber of Commerce   1938
- NR 17 Liverpool Gardens, WORTHING, W Sussex, BN11 1RY.
  (hq)
  01903 203484   fax 01903 504697
  email info@worthingandadurchamber.co.uk
  http://www.worthingandadurchamber.co.uk
  CEO: Tina Tilley
- ▲ Company Limited by Guarantee
- ○ *C
- ● Mtgs - Exhib - Inf - VE - LG - Corporate entertainment
- < Sussex Enterprise
- M c 300 f
- ¶ NL - 6.   Diary - 1.
- ✕ Worthing Chamber of Commerce & Industry

Wound Care Alliance UK   (WCA)   1989
- ■ c/o Louise Toner, Faculty of Health, Birmingham City University, Seacole 265 Westbourne Rd, Edgbaston, BIRMINGHAM, B15 3TW.   (hq)
  0121-331 7083
  http://www.wcauk.org
  Chmn: Louise Toner
- ▲ Registered Charity
- ○ *M, *P; to promote & further the best practice in the prevention, treatment & management of wounds through the provision of educational resources
- ● Conf - ET - Exhib - SG - Inf
- M 1,500 i, 37 f, 3 org, UK / 35 i, o'seas
- ¶ Wound Care Jnl - 4; ftm only.
  Educational booklets; all £2 m, £2.50 nm:
    Cavity Wounds.   Diabetic Foot.
    Eczema - Aetiology & Management.
    Equipment Selection.   Graduated Compression Hosiery.
    Management of Exuding Wounds.   Pain & Wound Care.
    Palliative Management of Fungating Malignant Wounds.
    Wounds & Infection.
  Educational booklets 4-hole punched:
    Anatomy & Physiology Wound Healing & Wound Assessment.
    Dressings Selection.
    Principles of Leg Ulcer Management & Prevention.
    Principles of Pressure Ulcer Management & Prevention.
    Standardised Assessment Tools & the Management of Complex Wounds.
    Silver in Wound Care & Management.
    Pressure Ulcer Prevention Manual; £5.
- ✕ 2009 (Tissue Viability Nurses Association (Wound Care Society

Wound Care Society
  the Wound Care Society & the Tissue Viability Nurses Association merged to form the **Wound Care Alliance**

** Woven Wire Association
  Sec: Peter Mills
- ○ *T
  Organisation lost: see Introduction paragraph 3

Writers' Copyright Association UK   (WCA)
- NR Ealing Studios, Ealing Green, LONDON, W5 5EP.
  0870 442 1513
  email admin@wcauk.com   http://www.wcauk.com
- ○ *G; to protect the copyright of scriptwriters
- < Musicians' Copyright Assn; Webmasters' Copyright Assn

Writers' Guild of Great Britain   (WGGB)   1959
- ■ 40 Rosebery Avenue, LONDON, EC1R 4RX.   (hq)
  020 7833 0777
  email admin@writersguild.org.uk
  http://www.writersguild.org.uk
  Gen Sec: Bernie Corbett
- ○ *P, *U; for professional writers in the spheres of television, radio, theatre, books, poetry, film, online & video games
- Gp Books; Children; Film & television; Radio; Theatre
- ● Mtgs - ET - Inf - Empl - LG - Legal & professional advice & representation of members over contracts, fees, rights & other issues connected with their work as writers
- < Intl Affiliation of Writers Guilds (IAWG); Creators' Rights Alliance; TUC
- M 2,000 i, 100 f, UK / 100 i, 10 f, o'seas
- ¶ UK Writer - 4; ftm, £25 yr nm.

Writers & Photographers unLimited   (WPU)   2003
- ■ PO Box 520, Bamber Bridge, PRESTON, Lancs, PR5 8LF.   (hsp)
  01772 321243   fax 07053 491743
  email info@wpu.org.uk   http://www.wpu.org.uk
  Mgr: Terry Marsh
- ▲ Un-incorporated Society
- ○ *P; to promote the work of members
- ● Inf - PL
- M 20 i

Writing Equipment Society   (WES)   1980

■ 53 Horsecroft Rd, BURY ST EDMUNDS, Suffolk, IP33 2DT.   (sp)
  http://www.wesonline.org.uk
  Mem Sec: Martin Roberts
○ *G; for all interested in the collection, conservation & study of
  writing instruments & accessories - including pens, pencils,
  inkpots, quills, letter scales & information & ephemera
  connected with the subject
● Mtgs - SG - VE
M 400 i, 20 f, UK / 150 i, 10 f, 5 org, o'seas
¶ Jnl (incl LM) - 3;   LM; both ftm only.

Writing Instruments Association   (WIA)

■ Farringdon Point, 29-35 Farringdon Rd, LONDON,
  EC1M 3JF.   (hq)
  0845 450 1565   fax 020 7405 7784
  Chmn: Chris Reynolds
▲ Company Limited by Guarantee
○ *T
● Conf - Mtgs - SG - Stat
< Eur Writing Instruments Assn; is an affiliate of the British Office
  Supplies & Services Federation
M f

WW2 HMSO Paperbacks Society   1994

■ 3 Roman Rd, SOUTHWICK, W Sussex, BN42 4TP.   (hsp)
  01273 596217
  Hon Sec: A R James
○ *G; interest & research in World War Two publications by the
  Ministry of Information &/or HM Stationery Office
● Res - SG - Inf - Lib - PL
M 20 i, 1 f (HMSO), UK / 5 i, o'seas
¶ WW2 HMSO Paperbacks Collectors' Guide; £5.
  Informing the People (HMSO) 1996; £10.

Wyndham Lewis Society   1972

■ Flat 9 Victory House, 64-68 Trafalgar Rd, Moseley,
  BIRMINGHAM, B13 8BU.
  email a.l.burrells@bham.co.uk   http://www.unirioja.es/
  wyndhamlewis/
  Contact: Dr Alan Munton
▲ Un-incorporated Society
○ *A; to promote interest in the works of Percy Wyndham Lewis
  (1882-1957), novelist, painter & critic
● Conf - Res - Exhib - VE
¶ Wyndham Lewis Annual (jnl) - 1; £15.
  Lewisletter (NL) - 2; ftm only.

X

Xenophon   1989

■ 98 Cambridge Gardens, LONDON, W10 6HS.   (hsp)
  020 8968 1360
  email wolstan-dixie@hotmail.co.uk
  Hon Sec: Regor J Nagrom
▲ Un-incorporated Society
○ *G; the study, for recreational & historical purposes, of secret
  communication & its recovery
● Res - Comp - SG - Inf - Lib
M 20 i
¶ Crypt - 1; ftm, £5 nm.

Yacht Brokers, Designers & Surveyors Association
the trading company for the **Association of Brokers & Yacht Agents** & the **Yacht Designers & Surveyors Association**

Yacht Designers & Surveyors Association   (YDSA)   1912
- ■ The Glass Works, Penns Rd, PETERSFIELD, Hants, GU32 2EW, (hq)
  01730 710425   fax 01730 710423
  email info@ybdsa.co.uk   http://www.ybdsa.co.uk
  Co Sec: Jane Gentry
- ▲ Company Limited by Guarantee
- ○ *P; for yacht surveyors & designers
- ● Conf - Mtgs - ET - Exam
- M 100 i, UK / 15 i, o'seas
- ¶ NL - 4; ftm only.
  Note: The Yacht Brokers, Designers & Surveyors Association is the management company for the YDSA & the Association of Brokers & Yacht Agents

Yacht Harbour Association Ltd
a group association of the **British Marine Federation**

Yachting Journalists' Association   (YJA)   1960
- NR 36 Church Lane, LYMINGTON, Hants, SO41 3RB.   (hsp)
  01590 673894
  email secretary@yja.co.uk   http://www.yja.co.uk
  Hon Sec: Rachel Nuding
- ▲ Un-incorporated Society
- ○ *P; to promote greater awareness of a wide range of leisure boating activities through the professional services offered by members
- ● Mtgs - Inf - Organisation of annual awards - Yachtsman of the Year & Young Sailor of the Year
- M 270 i, UK / 28 i, o'seas
- ¶ Hbk (incl LM) - 1.

YMCA England   (YMCA)   1844
- § 45 Beech St, LONDON, EC2Y 8AD.   (hq)
  020 7070 2160
- ▲ Registered Charity
  'a leading Christian charity committed to supporting all young people, particularly in times of need'.

YMCA Ireland
- § Donard Park, NEWCASTLE, Co Down, BT33 0GR.
  028 4372 1975
  email admin@ymca-ireland.org
  http://www.ymca-ireland.org
  'a cross denomination organisation committed to local youth need'.

Ymgyrch Diogelu Cymru Wledig
see **Campaign for the Protection of Rural Wales   (Ymgyrch Diogelu Cymru Wledig)**

York & North Yorkshire Chamber of Commerce
2008 merged with Leeds Chamber of Commerce to form **Leeds, York & North Yorkshire Chamber of Commerce**

Yorkshire Agricultural Society   1837
- ■ Regional Agricultural Centre, Great Yorkshire Showground, HARROGATE, N Yorks, HG2 8NZ.   (hq)
  01423 541000   fax 01423 541414
  email info@yas.co.uk   http://www.yas.co.uk
  Chief Exec: Nigel Pulling
- ▲ Registered Charity
- ○ *F, *H; to help improve & promote agriculture in the region, to encourage & support the development of rural businesses & to educate future generations
- ● Conf - Mtgs - ET - Res - Exhib - Comp - SG - VE - Great Yorkshire Show - Countryside Live
- < Assn of Show & Agricl Orgs
- M 10,000 i
- ¶ NL - 3;   AR - 1; both ftm only.
  Great Yorkshire Show: Programme £3 / Catalogue £5.

Yorkshire Archaeological Society   (YAS)   1863
- ■ Claremont, 23 Clarendon Rd, LEEDS, W Yorks, LS2 9NZ.   (hq)
  0113-245 7910   fax 0113-245 7922
  email yas.secretary@googlemail.com
  http://www.yas.org.uk
  Hon Sec: M J Heron
- ▲ Company Limited by Guarantee, Registered Charity
- ○ *L; to promote research into all aspects of the history & archaeology of the historic County of York
- Gp Prehistory
  Sections: Industrial history, Mediaeval, Roman history
  Publishing sections: Parish registers, Record series, Wakefield Court rolls
- ● Conf - Mtgs - ET - Res - Exhib - Inf - Lib - VE
- < CBA; Archaeological & historical groups, university & similar here & abroad
- M i & org
  (Sub: £45 i, £23 associates, £50 instns, £45 affiliate orgs)
- ¶ Yorkshire Archaeological Jnl - 1; ftm, £25 nm.
  Update (NL) - 3; free.
  Yorkshire Parish Registers - 1; £18m.
  Record Series - 1; £12 m.
  Wakefield Court Rolls - 1; £12 m.
  Yorkshire Archaeological Research; prices vary.
  Yorkshire Occasional Papers; prices vary

Yorkshire Dialect Society   (YDS)   1897
- ■ 19 Prospect Close, SWINEFLEET, East Riding of Yorkshire, DN14 8FB.   (hsp)
  01405 704838
  Publicity & Inf Offr: Dr B M Rhodes
- ▲ Un-incorporated Society
- ○ *L; study of Yorkshire speech & traditional life
- ● Mtgs - Res - Inf
- M 450 i, UK / 90 i, o'seas
- ¶ Transactions - 1.
  Summer Bulletin - 1;   LM - 5 yrly; both ftm only.

Yorkshire Geological Society   (YGS)   1837
- ■ 2a Compass Rd, LEICESTER, LE5 2HF.
  email P.Boylan@city.ac.uk
  http://www.yorksgeolsoc.org.uk
  Contact: Prof Patrick Boylan
- ▲ Registered Charity
- ○ *L; to promote & record the results of research in geology & its allied sciences, especially in Yorkshire & Northern England
- ● Conf - Mtgs - Exhib - Lib - VE
- < Geologists' Assn
- M 800 i, 80 f
- ¶ Proceedings - 2; £30 m.   Circular - 8; ftm only.

Yorkshire Philosophical Society (YPS) 1822
■   The Lodge, Museum Gardens, YORK, YO1 7DR. (hq)
    01904 656713   fax 01904 656713
    email info@yorksphilsoc.org.uk
    http://www.yorksphilsoc.org.uk
    Clerk: Miss Frances Chambers,   Hon Sec: William G Smith
▲   Registered Charity
○   *L; the study of natural science, archaeology & antiquities in the
    county
Gp York excavation; Woodland history
●   Conf - ET - VE
<   is the local branch of the British Association for the
    Advancement of Science
M   500 i, 10 org
¶   NL - 4;   AR; both ftm.

Young Bloods
    a group of the **Haemophilia Society**

Young Embroiderers
    a group of the **Embroiderers' Guild**

Young Explorers' Trust (YET) 1970
NR at the Royal Geographical Society, 1 Kensington Gore,
    LONDON, SW7 2AR.   (regd/address)
    email info@theyet.org   http://www.theyet.org
    Hon Gen Sec: Ted Grey
▲   Company Limited by Guarantee; Registered Charity
○   *E; to provide advice & support to schools, youth organisations,
    commercial expedition providers & groups of friends who
    intend to run their own youth expedition
M   29 i; 61 f/org

Young Women's Christian Association
    see **YWCA (Young Women's Christian Association)**

Youth Access 1975
■   1-2 Taylor's Yard, 67 Alderbrook Rd, LONDON, SW12 8AD.
    (hq)
    020 8772 9900   fax 020 8772 9746
    email admin@youthaccess.org.uk
    Dir: Barbara Rayment
▲   Registered Charity
○   *W, *Y; provision of a referrals line for young people, parents &
    carers, to obtain information of their most local advice,
    counselling & information services
●   ET - Inf - Consultancy
<   Young Minds; Nat Children's Bureau
M   i & agencies

Youth Action Network 1995
■   Unit 360B The Big Peg, 120 Vyse St, Jewellery Quarter,
    BIRMINGHAM, B18 6NF.   (hq)
    0121-236 2912   fax 0121-212 3221
    email info@youthactionnetwork.org.uk
    http://www.youthactionnetwork.org.uk
    Chief Exec: Davina Goodchild
▲   Company Limited by Guarantee; Registered Charity
○   *Y; supports & develops a range of youth volunteering projects
    across England; provides training, information & guidance
    on recruiting, supporting & recognising the achievements of
    young volunteers; develops youth action projects led by
    young people & engages young people in decision making
●   Conf - ET - Res - Inf - Lib - PL - VE - Development / start-up
    support for orgs - Promotion of youth action in the media
M   95 org
¶   Activate - 4; ftm, £30 nm.
    Reach Quality Assessment Framework; ftm (additional copies
    £66.50 each), £95 nm.
    VIP Kit; ftm (additional copies £28 each), £40 nm.
    TREaD (Training & Education Programme); £63 m, £90 nm.
    AR; free.

Youth Action Northern Ireland 1945
§   14 College Square North, BELFAST, BT1 6AS.   (hq)
    028 9024 0551   fax 028 9024 8556
    http://www.youthaction.org
    Dir: June Trimble
    Works to enable young people to achieve their full potential by
    providing services, information, training & support to
    community groups, youth groups, young people, their
    trainers & workers.

Youth Hostel Association of Northern Ireland
    since 2007 **Hostelling International Northern Ireland**

Youth Hostels Association (England & Wales) Ltd (YHA) 1930
NR Trevelyan House, Dimple Rd, MATLOCK, Derbys, DE4 3YH.
    (hq)
    01629 592600   fax 01629 592702
    email customerservices@yha.org.uk
    http://www.yha.org.uk
    Chief Exec: Caroline White
▲   Company Limited by Guarantee; Registered Charity
Br   217
○   *Y; 'to help all, especially young people of limited means, to a
    greater knowledge, love & care of the countryside, &
    appreciation of the cultural values of towns & cities,
    particularly by providing youth hostels or other
    accommodation for them in their travels, & thus to improve
    their health, recreation & education'
●   Exhib - VE - Accommodation provision
<   Intl Youth Hostelling Fedn (IYHF)
M   230,000 i
¶   Triangle Magazine - 2; ftm, £2 nm.   Escape To. . . - 1; free.
    Guidebook - 2 yrly; ftm, £3.99 nm.   AR; free.

Youth Scotland 1930
NR Balfour House, 19 Bonnington Grove, EDINBURGH,
    EH6 4BL.   (hq)
    0131-554 2561
    Chief Exec: Carol Downie
▲   Company Limited by Guarantee; Registered Charity
Br   14 area assns
○   *N, *Y; 'to support, develop & improve the range & quality of
    informal educational, social & leisure opportunities available
    to young people in Scotland'
●   Conf - Mtgs - ET - Comp - Inf - Lib - LG
<   UK Youth; Youthlink; Scot Coun Voluntary Orgs (SCVO)
M   53,000 i, 670 clubs & area assns
¶   Magnet (Jnl) - 4; free.   Area Association Newsletter - 6; ftm.
    Safe & Sound - Building a Safer Youth Work Environment; £5
    (first copy ftm).

Youth Work Ireland
    is the trading name of the **National Youth Federation** of Ireland

© CBD Research Ltd · Beckenham · BR3 5JS · Tel 020 8650 7745 · E-mail cbd@cbdresearch.com · www.cbdresearch.com

YWCA of Ireland
IRL 64 Lower Baggot St, DUBLIN 2, Republic of Ireland.
      353 (1) 644 9536   fax 353 (1) 644 9537
      email ywcaofireland@eircom.net
      http://www.ywcaofireland.ie
      Pres: Dr Lorna Carson
○ *R; to share our faith in the Lord Jesus Christ with women and
      all young people; to serve the whole community by
      encouraging spiritual, physical and social development

YWCA (Young Women's Christian Association)   (YWCA)   1855
NR Clarendon House, 52 Cornmarket St, OXFORD, OX1 3EJ.
      (hq)
      01865 304200   fax 01865 204805
      email info@ywca.org.uk   http://www.ywca.org.uk
      Chief Exec: Penny Newman
▲ Company Limited by Guarantee; Registered Charity
Br 18
○ *W, *Y; is a force for change for women who are facing
      discrimination & inequalities of all kinds; to enable young
      women who are experiencing disadvantage to identify &
      realise their full potential; to influence public policy in order
      to achieve equality & social justice for young women
M 30,000 i
¶ Members' NL - 2; ftm only.   AR - 1; free.
      Note: uses the trading name of Platform 51

Z

Zero Waste Alliance UK   (ZWA UK)
NR Far Pasture Cottage, Ninebanks, HEXHAM, Northumberland,
      NE47 8DB.   (dir/p)
      01434 345456   fax 01434 345456
      email info@zwallianceuk.org
      http://www.zwallianceuk.org
      Dir: Val Barton
▲ Company Limited by Guarantee; Registered Charity
○ *K; to protect, preserve & improve the environment for the
      benefit of the public by the development, provision &
      promotion of sustainable waste practices

Zionist Federation of Great Britain & Ireland   (ZF)   1899
NR BM Box 1948, LONDON, WC1N 3XX.   (hq)
      Exec Dir; Alan Iziz
○ *R; promotion of Zionism

Zipper Club
      see **British Cardiac Patients Association   (Zipper Club)**

Zoological Society of Ireland   1830
IRL Phoenix Park, DUBLIN 8, Republic of Ireland.
      353 (1) 474 8900   fax 353 (1) 677 1660
      email info@dublinzoo.ie   http://www.dublinzoo.ie
○ *L, *V

Zoological Society of London   (ZSL)   1826
NR Outer Circle, Regent's Park, LONDON, NW1 4RY.   (hq)
      020 7722 3333
      http://www.zsl.org
▲ Company Limited by Guarantee; Registered Charity
○ *L, *Q, *V; to promote worldwide conservation of animal
      species & their habitats by stimulating public awareness &
      concern
M 40,000 i, UK / 450 i, o'seas
¶ Journal of Zoology - 12.   Zoological Record - 1.

Zwartbles Sheep Association   (ZSA)   1995
■ Hillfields Lodge, Lighthorne, WARWICK, CV35 0BQ.   (hsp)
      01926 651147   fax 01926 651147
      email secretary@zwartbles.org
      http://www.zwartbles.org
      Sec: Yvonne Froehlich
▲ Company Limited by Guarantee; Registered Charity
○ *B
● Conf - Mtgs - ET - VE
< Netherlands Zwartbles Soc (NZS); Nat Sheep Assn
M 270 i
¶ NL - 4;   Ybk; both free.

ABBREVIATIONS INDEX

A

A&A	Art & Architecture
A-A	Arrhythmia Alliance
A-DS	Anglo Danish Soc
AA	Advertising Assn
	Alcoholics Anonymous
	Arboricultural Assn
	Arthritic Assn
	Automobile Assn
AAA	AAA - Action against Allergy
	Assn Air Ambulances
	Assn Authors' Agents
	Assn Average Adjusters
	Ayrshire Agricl Assn
AAA-NORCAP	Adults Affected Adoption
AAB	Assn Applied Biologists
AABA	Assn Accountancy & Business Affairs
AAC	Assn ATOL Companies
AAD	Assn Amer Dancing
AAE	Assn Astronomy Educ
AAGB	Astrological Assn
AAGBI	Assn Anaesthetists
AAH	Assn Art Historians
AAI	Assn Advertisers Ireland
	Assn Alabaster Importers & Whlsrs
AAI&S	Assn Archaeol Illustrators & Surveyors
AAIA	Assn Achievement &...Assessment
AAME	Assn Aviation Med Examiners
AAMRA	Aluminium Alloy Mfrg & Recycling Assn
AANHS	Ayrshire Archaeol & Natural Hist Soc
AAPA	Aromatherapy & Allied Practitioners Assn
	Assn Authorised Public Accountants
AAS	Anglesey Antiquarian Soc & Field Club
AASDN	Architectural & Archaeol Soc Durham & Northumberland
AAT	Assn Accounting Technicians
ABA	Antiquarian Booksellers Assn
	Assn Biomedical Andrologists
	Assn Burial Authorities
	Assn Business Administration
ABAC	Assn GB Athletics Clubs
ABAE	Amat Boxing Assn England
ABBA	Assn Business to Business Agencies
ABBC	Assn Brit Brewery Collectables
ABC	Assn Brickwork Contrs
	Assn Brit Climbing Walls
	Assn Brit Counties
	Austro-Brit Cham
ABCB	Assn Brit Certification Bodies
ABCC	Arab Brit Cham Comm
	Assn Brit Correspondence Colls
	Assn Brit Cycling Coaches
ABCD	Assn Bldg Cleaning Direct Service Providers
	Assn Brit Choral Dirs
	Assn Brit Clinical Diabetologists
ABCUL	Assn Brit Credit Us
ABD	Assn Brit Drivers
	Assn Broadcasting Doctors
ABDO	Assn Brit Dispensing Opticians
ABDS	Contemporary British Silversmiths
ABE	Assn Bldg Engrs
	Assn Business Executives
ABFA	Asset Based Finance Assn
ABFG	Assn Brit Fungus Gps
ABFI	Alcohol Beverage Fedn Ireland
ABHI	Assn Brit Healthcare Inds
ABI	Assn Brit Insurers
	Assn Brit Investigators
ABIA	Assn Brit Introduction Agencies
ABIM	Assn Bakery Ingredient Mfrs
ABIS	Assn Brit & Ir Showcaves

ABKC	Assn Brit Kart Clubs
ABLS	Assn Brit Language Schools
ABM	Assn Breastfeeding Mothers
ABMA	Assn Business Mgrs & Adminstrators
	Assn Business Mgt Academics
ABMEC	Assn Brit Mining Eqpt Cos
ABN	Assn Brit Neurologists
ABNC	Assn Brit Naturist Clubs
ABO	Assn Brit Orchestras
ABOI	Assn Brit Offshore Inds
ABP	Assn Business Psychologists
ABPC	Assn Brit Pewter Craftsmen
ABPCO	Assn Brit Profl Conf Organisers
ABPI	Assn Brit Pharmaceutical Ind
ABPN	Assn Brit Paediatric Nurses
ABPS	Assn Brit Philatelic Socs
ABPT	Assn Blind Piano Tuners
ABRS	Assn Brit Riding Schools
ABS	Amat Boxing Scotland
	Anglo Belgian Soc
	Assn Breast Surgery
	Assn Brit Sailmakers
	Assn Business Schools
ABSE	Assn Boat Safety Examiners
ABSP	Assn Brit Scrabble Players
ABSTD	Assn Basic Science Teachers Dentistry
ABSW	Assn Brit Science Writers
ABTA	ABTA
ABTAPL	Assn Brit Theological... Libraries
ABTEM	Assn Brit Transport & Engg Museums
ABTO	Assn Brit Tennis Officials
ABTOF	Assn Brit Tour Operators France
ABTT	Assn Brit Theatre Technicians
ABWAK	Assn Brit & Ir Wild Animal Keepers
ABYA	Assn Brokers & Yacht Agents
AC	Alpine Club
	Assn Coaching
ACA	Agricl Consultants Assn [IRL]
	Aircrewman's Assn
	Assn Consultant Architects
	Assn Consulting Actuaries
	Assn Continence Advice
ACA (UK)	Assn Celebrity Assistants (UK)
ACADEMI	ACADEMI
ACAI	Assn Consultant Approved Inspectors
ACAL	Assn Child Abuse Lawyers
ACAMH	Assn Child & Adolescent Mental Health
ACAS	Anglo Cent Amer Soc
ACAT	Assn Cognitive Analytic Therapy
ACAVA	Assn Cultural Advancement through Visual Art
ACB	Assn Clinical Biochemistry
ACCA	Assn Chart Certified Accountants
ACCC	Assn County & City Councils [IRL]
ACCD	Assn Certified Comml Diplomats
ACCE	Assn County Chief Executives
ACCEO	Assn Caravan & Camping Exempted Orgs
ACCI	Ayrshire Cham Comm & Ind
ACCM	Assn Computer Cable Mfrs
ACCS	Assn County Cricket Scorers
ACCU	ACCU
ACDM	Assn Clinical Data Mgt
	Assn Composite Door Mfrs
ACE	Assn Catering Excellence
	Assn Church Editors
	Assn Circulation Executives
	Assn Confs & Events
	Assn Consultancy & Engg
	Assn Consvn Energy
	Assn Cruise Experts
ACE UK	Alliance Beverage Cartons & Envt
ACEG	Assn Careers Educ & Guidance
ACES	Assn Cannibals' Eqpt Suppliers
	Assn Chief Estates Surveyors... Public Sector
ACET	Assn Computer Engrs & Technicians

ACEVO	Assn Chief Executives Voluntary Orgs	ADPH	Assn Directors Public Health
ACF	Assn Charitable Foundations	ADS	ADS Gp
ACFA	Army Cadet Force Assn	ADSA	Automatic Door Suppliers Assn
	Assn Certificated Field Archaeologists [Scotland]	ADSHG	Addisons Disease Self Help Gp
ACFM	Assn Cereal Food Mfrs	ADSW	Assn Directors Social Work [Scotland]
ACFO	ACFO	AEA	Academy Executives & Administrators
ACG	Anti Counterfeiting Gp		Agricl Engrs Assn
	Arts Centre Gp		Aluminium Extruders Assn
ACH	Academy Curative Hypnotherapists		Assn Educ & Ageing
ACID	Anti Copying Design		Assn Electoral Administrators
ACIE	Assn Charity Indep Examiners		Assn Envtl Archaeology
	Assn Consulting Engrs Ireland		Assn Erotic Artists
ACIFC	Assn Concrete Indl Flooring Contrs	AEC	Assn Engl Cathedrals
ACIS	Assn Contemporary Iberian Studies	AECB	Assn Envt Conscious Bldg
ACJ	Assn Contemporary Jewellery	AECI	Assn Electrical Contrs (Ireland)
ACLM	Assn Contact Lens Mfrs	Aedips	Assn Educl Devt & Improvement Profls Scotland
ACLS	Assn Comparative Legal Studies	AEF	Aviation Envt Fedn
ACM	Assn Coll Mgt	AEGIS	Assn Educ & Guardianship Intl Students
ACMC	Assn Cost Mgt Consultants	AEME	Assn Events Mgt Educ
ACO	Assn Charity Officers	AEMES	Ancient Egypt & Middle East Soc
ACOGB	Autograph Club	AEMT	Assn Electrical & Mechanical Trs
ACoRP	Assn Community Rail Partnerships	AEO	Assn Event Organisers
ACostE	Assn Cost Engrs	AEP	Assn Educl Psychologists
ACOSVO	Assn Chief Officers Scot Voluntary Orgs		Assn Electricity Producers
ACP	Assn Child Psychotherapists	AEPU	Assn Early Pregnancy Units
	Assn Circus Proprietors	AES	Agricl Economics Soc
	Assn Clinical Pathologists		Amat Entomologists' Soc
	Assn Computer Profls		Audio Engg Soc
ACPO	Assn Chief Police Officers [E&W&NI]	AESS	Assn Engl Singers & Speakers
ACPOS	Assn Chief Police Officers Scotland	AEV	Assn Event Venues
ACRA	Assn Company Registration Agents		Assn External Verifiers
ACRE	Action Communities Rural England	AEWM	Assn Educ Welfare Mgt
ACRIB	Air Conditioning & Refrigeration Ind Bd	AF	Albinism Fellowship
ACS	Additional Curates Soc		Audiovisual Fedn [IRL]
	Anglo Catalan Soc	AFA	Access Flooring Assn
	Assn Charity Shops		Aluminium Finishing Assn
	Assn Consulting Scientists		Amat Football Alliance
	Assn Convenience Stores	AFAA	Assn Families Adopted Abroad
	Assn Cricket Statisticians & Historians	Afasic	Afasic
ACSeS	Assn Coun Secretaries & Solicitors	AFB	Assn Foreign Banks
AcSS	Academy Social Sciences	AfC	Assn Charities
ACT	Aid Children with Tracheostomies	AFC	Assn Fundraising Consultants
	Assn Childrens Palliative Care	AFCMA	Aberdeen Fish Curers'…Assn
	Assn Christian Teachers	AFDEC	Assn Franchised Distbrs Electronic Components
	Assn Corporate Treasurers	AFHSW	Assn Family Hist Socs Wales
	Assn Cycle Traders	AFLS	Assn French Language Studies
ACTA	Animal Consultants & Trainers Assn	AFM	Assn Financial Mutuals
	Assn Cardiothoracic Anaesthetists	AFME	Assn Financial Markets Europe
ACTC	Assn Classic Trials Clubs	AFMM	UK Assn Fish Meal Mfrs
ACTCTC	Assn Charter Trustee Towns &… Couns	AFO	Assn Festival Organisers
ACTH	Assn Cushing's Treatment & Help	AfPE	Assn Physical Educ
ACU	Assn C'wealth Universities	AFS	Assn Football Statisticians
	Auto-Cycle U		Australian Finch Soc
ACVW	Assn Countryside Voluntary Wardens	AFT	Assn Family Therapy
ACW	Gwartheg Hynafol Cymru	AGB	Assn Guernsey Banks
ACWRT(UK)	American Civil War Round Table	AGBIS	Assn Governing Bodies Indep Schools
ADA	Antiquities Dealers Assn	AGCAS	Assn Graduate Careers Advy Services
	Assn Dental Anaesthetists	AGCC	Aberdeen & Grampian Cham Comm
	Assn Drainage Authorities	AGI	Assn Geographic Inf
	Assn Drama Adjudicators (Ireland)	AGIP	Assn Gp & Individual Psychotherapy
ADASS	Assn Directors Adult Social Services	AGR	Assn Graduate Recruiters
adba	Anaerobic Digestion Biogas Assn	AGRA	Assn Genealogists & Researchers in Archives
ADCA	Assn Diocesan Cathedral Architects	AGS	Alpine Garden Soc
ADCAS	Assn Ductwork Contrs & Allied Services		Assn Geotechnical & Geoenvironmental Specialists
ADCH	Assn Dogs & Cats Homes	AGSD(UK)	Assn Glycogen Storage Diseases
ADCS	Assn Directors Children's Services	AGT	Assn Gardens Trusts
ADEPT	ADEPT	AGW	Assn Golf Writers
ADES	Assn Directors Educ Scotland	AHBMT	Assn Holistic Biodynamic Massage Therapists
ADFAM	ADFAM	AHC	Assn Healthcare Communications
ADFP	Assn Dance Freestyle Profls	AHC-UK	Assn Hist & Computing
ADH	Assn Dental Hospitals	AHCP	Assn Healthcare Cleaning Profls
ADI	Assn Dental Implantology	AHDA	Animal Health Distbrs Assn
ADINJC	Approved Driving Instructors Nat Jt Coun	AHDS	Assn Headteachers & Deputes Scotland
ADISA	Asset Disposal Inf Security Alliance	AHEM	Brit Fluid Power Assn
ADLS	Assn Dunkirk Little Ships	AHG	Assn Hist Glass
ADMG	Assn Deer Mgt Gps	AHGBI	Assn Hispanists
ADMT UK	Assn Dance Movement Therapy	AHGTC	Ancient & Honourable Gld Town Criers
ADP	Assn Disabled Profls	AHI	Assn Heritage Interpretation

© CBD Research Ltd · Beckenham · BR3 5JS · Tel 020 8650 7745 · E-mail cbd@cbdresearch.com · www.cbdresearch.com

AHOEC	Assn Heads Outdoor Educ Centres	ALGAO	Assn Local Govt Archaeol Officers
AHP(B)	Assn Humanistic Psychology	ALIP	Assn Leisure Ind Profls
AHPF	Allied Health Professions Fedn	ALK	Assn Lighthouse Keepers
AHPMA	Absorbent Hygiene Products Mfrs Assn	ALL	Assn Language Learning
AHS	AHS		Assn Latin Liturgy
	Antiquarian Horological Soc		Astrological Lodge Lond
AHSS	Architectural Heritage Soc Scotland	ALLEF UK	Assn Learning Languages en Famille
AIA	Anglo Israel Assn	ALLMI	ALLMI
	Assn Indl Archaeology	ALM	Assn Lloyd's Members
	Assn Intl Accountants	ALMR	Assn Licensed Mult Retailers
AIAC	Advice NI	ALP	Assn Labour Providers
AIC	Agricl Inds Confedn		Assn Learning Providers
	Assn Investment Companies		Horticultural Trs Assn
AICA	Assn Indep Care Advisers	ALPSP	Assn Learned & Profl Soc Pubrs
	Assn Indep Construction Adjudicators	ALRC	Assn Land Rover Clubs
AICC	Assn Indep Crop Consultants	ALS	Alliance Literary Socs
AICES	Assn Intl Courier & Express Services		Assn Laparoscopic Surgeons
AICR	Assn Intl Cancer Res		Assn Lipspeakers
AICS	Assn Indep Computer Specialists	ALSP	Assn Laser Safety Profls
AIF	Assn Interchurch Families	ALT	Assn Law Teachers
AIFA	Assn Indep Financial Advisers		Assn Learning Technology
AIIC	Assn Indep Inventory Clerks	ALTO	ALTO [IRL]
AIJV	Assn Indep Jewellery Valuers	ALTT	Assn Light Touch Therapists
AIL	Assn Indep Libraries	Alupro	Aluminium Packaging Recycling Org
AILU	Assn Laser Users	ALVA	Assn Leading Visitor Attractions
AIM	Assn Indep Museums	AMA	Additive Mfrg Assn
	Assn Indep Music		Amat Martial Assn
AIME	Assn Interactive Media & Entertainment		Arts Marketing Assn
AIMH UK	Assn Infant Mental Health UK		Assn Mining Analysts
AIMS	A1 Motor Stores		Assn Model Agents
	Assn Improvements Maternity Services	AMABO	Assn Med Advisers Brit Orchestras
	Assn Indep Meat Suppliers	AMCA	Amat Motor Cycle Assn
	Assn Ir Musical Socs	AMDEA	Assn Mfrs Domestic Appliances
AIMUK	Assn Automatic Identification &. . . Data Capture	AMDIS	Assn Marketing & Devt Indep Schools
AINA	Assn Inland Navigation Authorities	AMEC	Assn Measurement & Evaluation Communication
AIOA	Assn Indep Organ Advisers	AMED	Assn Mgt Educ & Devt
AIPP	Assn Intl Property Profls	AMEM	Assn Miniature Engine Mfrs
AIRMIC	Assn Insurance & Risk Mgrs	AMES	Assn Media Educ Scotland
AIRSO	Assn Indl Road Safety Officers	AMHB	Assn Masters Harriers & Beagles
AIRTO	AIRTO	AMHSA	Automated Material Handling Systems Assn
AIS	Anglo Indonesian Soc	AMI	Assn Meat Inspectors
	Assn Insurance Surveyors		Assn Mortgage Intermediaries
	Assn Interior Specialists	amii	Assn Med Insurance Intermediaries
AISABE	Assn Inf Security Auditors & Business Exexs	AMIMB	Assn Members Indep Monitoring Bds
AISMA	Assn Indep Specialist Med Accountants	AMLBO	River Assn Freight & Transport
AISSG	Androgen Insensitivity Syndrome Support Gp	AMO	Assn Meter Operators
AIST	Assn Integrative Sandplay Therapists	AMONO	Assn Mainframe Operators & Network Administrators
AITA	Adult Ind Trade Assn		
AITO	Assn Indep Tour Operators	AMPS	Assn Member-Directed Pension Schemes
AITS	Assn Indep Tobacco Specialists		Assn Mfrs Power generating Systems
AITT	Assn Indl Truck Trainers		Assn Motion Picture Sound
AIVC	Assn Inter-Varsity Clubs	AMRC	Assn Med Res Charities
AJA	Amat Jockeys Assn	AMRCO	Assn Motor Racing Circuit Owners
	Anglo Jewish Assn	AMRO	Assn Med Reporting Orgs
AJEX	Assn Jewish Ex-Servicemen & Women	AMRSS	Assn Model Rly Socs Scotland
AJFB	Franco-Brit Lawyers Soc	AMS	Academy Multi Skills
AJS	Anglo Jordanian Soc		Ancient Monuments Soc
Al-Anon	Al-Anon Family Gps		Antique Metalware Soc
ALA	Agricl Law Assn	AMSI	Assn Marine Scientific Ind
	Auto Locksmiths Assn	AMSPAR	Assn Med Secretaries, Practice Managers. . .
	Mineral Products Assn	AMTRA	Animal Medicines Trg Regulatory Auth
ALACE	Assn Local Authority Chief Execs	AMUS	Assurance Med & Underwriting Soc
ALAE	Assn Licensed Aircraft Engrs	AMUSF	Assn Master Upholsterers & Soft Furnishers
ALARM	ALARM	An Taisce	Nat Trust Ireland
ALBUM	Assn Local Bus Co Mgrs	ANA	Assn Nanny Agencies
ALC	Assn Lawyers Children	ANAIS	Assn New Age Inds
	Assn London Clubs	ANBG	Assn Natural Burial Grounds
ALCD	Assn Law Costs Draftsmen	ANC	Assn Noise Consultants
ALCI	Assn Landscape Contrs Ireland (NI)	ANDISP	Assn Nat Driver Improvement Scheme Providers
ALCS	Assn Low Countries Studies	ANEC	Assn N E Couns
	Authors Licensing & Collecting Soc	ANEW	Assd Nat Electrical Whlsrs
ALD	Assn Lighting Designers	ANH	Alliance Natural Health
ALEM	Assn Loading & Elevating Eqpt Mfrs	ANHSO	Ashmolean Natural Hist Soc Oxfordshire
ALEP	Assn Leasehold Enfranchisement Practitioners	ANIC	Assn NI Colleges
ALERC	Assn Local Envtl Records Centres	ANIFPO	Anglo North Ir Fish Producers Org
ALERT	ALERT	ANLHS	Assn Northumberland Local Hist Socs
ALES(UK)	Assn Amusement & Leisure Eqpt Suppliers	ANLP	Assn Neuro-Linguistic Programming
ALFED	Aluminium Fedn	ANM	Assn Natural Medicine

© CBD Research Ltd · Beckenham · BR3 5JS · Tel 020 8650 7745 · E-mail cbd@cbdresearch.com · www.cbdresearch.com

ANMW	Assn Newspaper Magazine Whlsrs	APSE	Assn Public Service Excellence
ANP	Assn Nurse Prescribing	APSGB	Academy Pharmaceutical Sciences
ANPA	Assn Nat Park Authorities	APSI	Assn Profl Shooting Instructors
ANS	Assn Neurophysiological Scientists	APSS	Aviation Presvn Soc Scotland
ANSA	Assn Nurses Substance Abuse	APT	Assn Psychological Therapies
ANTC	Assn Nursery Training Colls		UK Assn Presvn Trusts
ANTOR	Assn Nat Tourist Office Representatives	APTG	Assn Profl Tourist Guides
ANTS	Anglo Norman Text Soc	AQHA-UK	American Quarter Horse Assn
AOA	Airport Operators Assn	AQR	Assn Qualitative Res
AoC	Assn Colls	ARA	Aircraft Res Assn
AoFA	Assn First Aiders		Amat Rowing Assn
AOHNP (UK)	Assn Occupational Health Nurse Practitioners		Assn Roman Archaeology
AoI	Assn Illustrators	ARBA	Amat Rose Breeders Assn
AOP	Assn Online Publishers	ARC	Alliance Religions & Consvn
	Assn Optometrists		Assn Real Change
AOPA	Aircraft Owners & Pilots Assn		Assn Revenue & Customs
AOPA Ireland	Aircraft Owners & Pilots Assn [IRL]		Assn Run-off Cos
AOR	Assn Organics Recycling		Assn Running Clubs
AoR	Assn Reflexologists	ARCA	Adult Residential Colls Assn
AoT	Assn Tutors		Asbestos Removal Contractors Assn
AOTI	Assn Occupational Therapists Ireland	ARCH	ARCH
AOTOS	Assn Teachers Singing	ARCISS	Assn Res Centres Social Sciences
AOVC	Assn Old Vehicle Clubs NI	ARCOS	Assn Rehabilitation Communication & Oral Skills
APA	Advertising Producers Assn	AREBT	Assn Rational Emotive Behaviour Therapy
	Army Parachute Assn	AREF	Assn Real Estate Funds
	Assn Police Authorities	AREIAC	Assn RE Inspectors, Advisors & Consultants
	Assn Practising Accountants	ARH	Alliance Registered Homeopaths
	Assn Public Analysts	ARHM	Assn Retirement Housing Mgrs
	Assn Publishing Agencies	ARKS	Assn Racing Kart Schools
APA(GBI)	Academic Paediatrics Assn	ARLA	Assn Residential Letting Agents
APAGBI	Assn Paediatric Anaesthetists	ARLIS	ARLIS/UK & Ireland
APAi	Assn Profl Astrologers Intl	ARLT	Assn Latin Teaching
APAP	Assn Profl Ambulance Personnel	ARM	Assn Radical Midwives
APAS	Assn Public Analysts Scotland	ARMA	Arthritis & Musculoskeletal Alliance
APB	Assn Property Bankers		Assn Residential Managing Agents
APBC	Assn Pet Behaviour Counsellors	ARNO	Assn R Navy Officers
APCC	Assn Private Crematoria & Cemeteries	AROS	Assn Registrars Scotland
APCI	Assn Police & Court Interpreters	ARP	Assn Relocation Profls
APCIMS	Assn Private Client Investment Mgrs & Stockbrokers	ARPMA	Aluminium Rolled Products Mfrs Assn
APCMH	Assn Pastoral Care Mental Health	ARR	Assn Radiation Res
APCO	Brit Marine Fedn	ARS	Anaesthetic Res Soc
APCT	Assn Painting Craft Teachers	ARTP	Assn Respiratory Technology & Physiology
APCTSG	Assn Profl Clay Target Shooting Grounds		Assn Rly Training Providers
APDO-UK	Assn Profl De-clutterers & Organisers	ARTSM	Assn Road Traffic Safety & Mgt
APDT	Assn Pet Dog Trainers	ARVAC	Assn Res Voluntary & Community Sector
APEA	Assn Petroleum & Explosives Admin	AS	Acupuncture Soc
APEC	Action Pre-Eclampsia		Alzheimer's Soc
APG	Account Planning Gp		Avicultural Soc
APGI	Assn Profl Genealogists Ireland	AS UK	Alström Syndrome UK
APHA	Animal & Plant Health Assn [IRL]	ASA	Advice Services Alliance
	Assn Port Health Authorities		Aluminium Stockholders Assn
APHC	Assn Plumbing & Heating Contrs		Amat Swimming Assn
APHP	Assn Profl Hypnosis & Psychotherapy		Assn Sealant Applicators
API	Assn Play Inds		Assn Social Anthropologists
APICS	Assn Profl & Indep Chimney Sweeps		Assn Subscription Agents & Intermediaries
APIL	Assn Personal Injury Lawyers	ASAO	Assn Show & Agricl Orgs
APL	Assn Pension Lawyers	ASAoGB	American Saddlebred Assn
	Horticultural Trs Assn	ASAP	Assn Serviced Apartment Providers
APM	Assn Palliative Medicine	ASAUK	African Studies Assn
	Assn Project Mgt	ASBAH	Assn Spina Bifida & Hydrocephalus
APMC	Assn Pioneer Motor Cyclists	ASBCI	ASBCI
APMM	Assn Policy Market Makers	ASC	Assn Scotland's Colls
APNI	Assn Postnatal Illness		Assn Security Consultants
APNT	Assn Physical & Natural Therapists		Assn Speakers Clubs
APP	Assn Psychoanalytic Psychotherapy NHS	ASC/NAWCH	Action Sick Children
APPA	Aluminium Primary Producers Assn	ASCC	Assn Scot Community Couns
APPC	Assn Profl Political Consultants	ASCCO	Assn Special Constabulary Chief Officers
APPCC	Assn Private Pet Cemeteries & Crematoria	ASCHB	Assn Studies Consvn Historic Bldgs
APR	Assn Promoting Retreats	ASCII	Assn Copyright Infringement Investigators
APRO	Airline Public Relations Org	ASCL	Assn School & College Leaders
	Assn Paediatric Resuscitation Officers	ASDC	Assn Separated & Divorced Catholics
	Assn Private Rly Wagon Owners	ASDMA	Architectural & Specialist Door Mfrs Assn
APRS	Assn Profl Recording Services	ASDW	Assn Small Direct Wine Merchants
	Assn Protection Rural Scotland	ASE	Assn Science Educ
APS	Assn Project Safety		Astronomical Soc Edinburgh
APSA	Assn Profl Sales Agents (Sports & Leisure Inds)	ASEASUK	Assn South-East Asian Studies UK
APSCEH	Assn Profl Staffs Colls Educ [IRL]	ASEN	Assn Study Ethnicity & Nationalism
APSCo	Assn Profl Staffing Cos	ASET	ASET

ASF	Assn Soft Furnishers
ASFB	Assn Salmon Fishery Bds
ASFCEW	Assn Sea Fisheries C'ees [E&W]
ASFP	Assn Specialist Fire Protection
ASG	Air Safety Gp
	Anorchidism Support Gp
ASGBI	Anatomical Soc
	Assn Surgeons
ASGFM	Assn Stillwater Game Fishery Mgrs
ASGRA	Assn Scot Genealogists & Researchers Archives
ASH	Action Smoking & Health
ASHTAV	Assn Small Historic Towns & Villages
ASI	Ambulance Service Inst
ASIIP	Adlerian Soc Inst Individual Psychology
ASIM	Assn Solicitors & Investment Mgrs
ASinGB	Anthroposophical Soc
ASiT	Assn Surgeons in Training
ASK	Assn Systematic Kinesiology
ASKE	Assn Skeptical Enquiry
ASL	Assn Supported Living
ASLEC	Assn Signals, Lighting... Highway Electrical Connections
aslib	Aslib
ASLS	Assn Scot Literary Studies
ASLTIP	Assn Speech & Language Therapists...
ASM	Assn Supervisors Midwives
ASMAA	All Styles Martial Arts Assn
ASMCF	Assn Study Modern & Contemporary France
ASMD	Assn Sewing Machine Distbrs
ASME	Assn Study Med Educ
ASMI	Assn Study Modern Italy
ASN	Assn Solicitor Notaries Greater London
ASO	Assn Study Obesity
ASP	Assn Service Providers
ASPE	Assn Study Primary Educ
ASPEC	Assn Studio & Production Eqpt Companies
ASPECT	Assn Profls Educ & Children's Trusts
ASPIRE	Assn Spinal Injury Res...
ASPROM	Assn Study & Presvn Roman Mosaics
ASPS	Assn Scot Philatelic Socs
	Assn Scot Police Superintendents
ASRA	Assn Student Residential Accommodation
ASSA	Assn Scot Schools Architecture
ASSAP	Assn Scientific Study Anomalous Phenomena
ASSC	Assn Scotland's Self Caterers
ASSG	Assn Scot Shellfish Growers
AssHFP	Assn Hot Foil Printers
AST	Assn Stress Therapists
ASTAUK	Assn Secondary Ticket Agents
ASTI	Assn Secondary Teachers, Ireland
ASTO	Assn Sea Training Orgs
ASTOS	Assn Specialist Techl Orgs Space
ASTRA	Assn Scotland Res Astronautics
ASUCplus	ASUCplus
ASVA	Assn Scot Visitor Attractions
ASYC	Assn Scot Yacht Charterers
ATA	Angling Trs Assn
ATA Assn	Air Transport Auxiliary Assn
ATaC	Asbestos Testing & Consultancy Assn
ATAXIA	Ataxia UK
ATBA-UK	All Terrain Boarding Assn
ATC	Aromatherapy Tr Coun
	Assn Therapeutic Communities
	Assn Translation Companies
ATCM	Assn Tank & Cistern Mfrs
	Assn Town Centre Mgt
	Assn Traditional Chinese Medicine
ATCO	Assn Transport Co-ordinating Officers
ATCU	Assd Train Crew U
ATH	Assn Therapeutic Healers
ATI	Accounting Technicians Ireland
ATL	Assn Teachers & Lecturers
ATLA	Assn Teachers Lipreading to Adults
ATLAS	Assn Technical Lighting & Access Specialists
ATM	Assn Teachers Mathematics
ATMA	Adhesive Tape Mfrs' Assn
ATOC	Assn Train Operating Companies
ATP	Assn Teaching Psychology

ATS	Ataxia-Telangiectasia Soc
ATSS	Assn Teaching Social Sciences
ATT	Assn Taxation Technicians
ATTP	Assn Thallophyte Treatment Plants
AUA	Assn University Administrators
AUHS	Universal Spiritualists Assn
AUKML	Assn UK Media Librarians
AUKOI	Downstream Fuel Assn
AUKVA	Alliance UK Virtual Assistants
AUMPC	Assn Unpasteurised Milk Producers
AUPHF	Assn University Professors & Heads French
AURA	Assn Users Res Agencies
AURIL	Assn University Res & Ind Links
AURPO	Assn University Radiation Protection Officers
AVA	Automatic Vending Assn
AVID	Assn Visitors Immigration Detainees
AVLP	Assn Valuers Licensed Property
AVM	Assn Volunteer Managers
AvMA	Action Med Accidents
AVRO	Assn Vehicle Recovery Operators
AWCC	Assn Waterways Cruising Clubs
AWD	Assn Welding Distbution
AWDC	All Wheel Drive Club
AWE	Assn Wine Educators
AWEBB	Assn Whls Electrical Bulk Buyers
AWFF	Animal Welfare Filming Fedn
AWG	Art Workers Gld
AWGB	Assn Woodturners
AWHEM	Assn Well Head Eqpt Mfrs
AWHS	Alfred Williams Heritage Soc
AXrEM	AXrEM
AYME	Assn Young People with ME
AYRS	Amat Yacht Res Soc

B

B MET A	Birmingham Metallurgical Assn
B&CCC	Brit & Colombian Cham Comm
B-AS	Britain-Australia Soc
BA	Basketmakers Assn
	Booksellers Assn
BAA	Brit Academy Audiology
	Brit Accounting Assn
	Brit Aggregates Assn
	Brit Archaeol Assn
	Brit Astronomical Assn
BAAC	Brit Assn Aviation Consultants
	Brit Aviation Archaeol Coun
BAAF	Brit Assn Adoption & Fostering
BAAL	Brit Assn Applied Linguistics
BAAM	Brit Assn Anger Mgt
BAAP	Brit Assn Academic Phoneticians
	Brit Assn Audiovestibular Physicians
BAAPS	Brit Assn Aesthetic Plastic Surgeons
BAAS	Brit Assn Amer Studies
BAASDC	Brit Assn Amer Square Dance Clubs
BAAT	Brit Assn Art Therapists
BAB	Brit Aikido Bd
BABA	Brit Amat Boxing Assn
	Brit Artist Blacksmiths Assn
BABC	Brit Amer Business Coun
BABCP	Brit Assn Behavioural... Psychotherapies
BABi	Brit Amer Business Inc
BABO	Brit Assn Balloon Operators
BABS	Brit Assn Barbershop Singers
BABTAC	Brit Assn Beauty Therapy & Cosmetology
BAC	Business Archives Coun
BACA	Baltic Air Charter Assn
	Brit Assn Clinical Anatomists
BAcC	Brit Acupuncture Coun
BACC	Brit Argentine Cham Comm
BACDT	Brit Assn Clinical Dental Technology
BACFI	Bar Assn Comm, Finance & Ind
BACG	Brit Assn Crystal Growth
BACM-TEAM	Brit Assn Colliery Mgt

BACP	Brit Assn Counselling & Psychotherapy	BAP	Brit Assn Psychopharmacology
BACPOP	Brit Assn Cold Pressed Oil Producers		Brit Assn Psychotherapists
BACR	Brit Assn Cancer Res	BAPAM	Brit Assn Performing Arts Medicine
BACS	Brit Assn Canadian Studies	BAPC	Brit Assn Print & Communication
	Brit Assn Chemical Specialities		Brit Aviation Presvn Coun
	Brit Assn Chinese Studies	BAPCA	Brit Assn Person-Centred Approach
	Brit Assn Cosmetic Surgeons	BAPCO	Brit Assn Public Safety Communications Officers
BACSA	Brit Assn Cemeteries S Asia	BAPCR	Brit Assn Paintings Conservator-Restorers
BACTA	Brit Amusement Catering Trs Assn	BAPEN	Brit Assn Parenteral Enteral Nutrition
BAD	Brit Assn Dermatologists	BAPH	Brit Assn Paper Historians
BADA	Brit Antique Dealers Assn	BAPLA	Brit Assn Picture Libraries & Agencies
	Brit Audio-Visual Dealers Assn	BAPM	Brit Assn Perinatal Medicine
BADA-UK	Borreliosis & Assd Diseases Awareness UK	BAPO	Brit Assn Paediatric Otorhinolaryngology
BADC	Brit Acad Dramatic Combat		Brit Assn Prosthetists & Orthotists
BADN	Brit Assn Dental Nurses	BAPRAS	Brit Assn Plastic, Reconstructive & Aesthetic
BADS	Brit Assn Day Surgery		Surgeons
BADT	Brit Assn Dental Therapists	BApS	Brit Appaloosa Soc
BADth	Brit Assn Dramatherapists	BAPS	Brit Assn Paediatric Surgeons
BAeA	Brit Aerobatic Assn		Brit Astrological & Psychic Soc
BAEPD	Brit Assn Eur Pharmaceutical Distbrs	BAPSH	Brit Assn Purebred Spanish Horse
BAES	Brit Aviation Enthusiasts Soc	BAPT	Brit Assn Play Therapists
BAETS	Brit Assn Endocrine & Thyroid Surgeons		Brit Assn Psychological Type
BAF	Brit Aerobiology Fedn	BAPTO	Brit Assn Pool Table Operators
	Brit Armwrestling Fedn	BAPW	Brit Assn Pharmaceutical Whlsrs
BAFA	Brit Amer Football Assn	BAR	Brit Assn Reinforcement
	Brit Arts Festivals Assn		Brit Assn Removers
BAFD	Brit Assn Fastener Distbrs	BARA	Brit Automation & Robot Assn
BAFE	Brit Approvals Fire Eqpt	BARB	Brit Assn Rose Breeders
BAFEP	Brit Assn Flower Essence Producers	BARC	Brit Assn Rehabilitation Cos
BAFM	Brit Assn Forensic Medicine	BARC Ltd	Brit Automobile Racing Club
	Brit Assn Friends Museums	BAREMA	Barema
BAFRA	Brit Antique Furniture Restorers Assn	BARG	Berkshire Archaeology Res Gp
BAFS	Brit Academy Forensic Sciences	BARLA	Brit Amat Rugby League Assn
BAFSA	Brit Automatic Fire Sprinkler Assn	BARMA	Boiler & Radiator Mfrs Assn
BAFSAM	Brit Assn Feed Supplement & Additives Mfrs	BARQA	Brit Assn Res Quality Assurance
BAFTA	Brit Academy Film & TV Arts	BARSC	Brit Alpine Racing Ski Clubs
BAFTS	Brit Assn Fair Tr Shops		Brit Assn Remote Sensing Companies
BAFUNCS	Brit Assn Former UN Civil Servants	BAS	Brit Alpaca Soc
BAGB	Bingo Assn		Brit Ambulance Soc
BAGCC	Brit Assn Golf Course Constructors		Brit Andrology Soc
BAGCD	Brit Assn Green Crop Driers		Brit Aphasiology Soc
BAGMA	Brit Agricl & Garden Machinery Assn		Brit Arachnological Soc
BAHA	Brit Activity Holiday Assn		Brit Assn Steelbands
	Brit Alliance Healing Assns		Brit Autogenic Soc
	Brit Assn Hospitality Accountants	BASA	Black & Asian Studies Assn
BAHID	Brit Assn Human Identification		Brit Adhesives & Sealants Assn
BAHM	Brit Assn Homoeopathic Mfrs		Brit Airgun Shooters' Assn
BAHNO	Brit Assn Head & Neck Oncologists		Brit Assn Seed Analysts
BAHREP	Brit Assn Hotel Representatives	BASAS	Brit Assn S Asian Studies
BAHS	Brit Agricl Hist Soc	BASBWE	Brit Assn Symphonic Bands & Wind Ensembles
BAHSHE	Brit Assn Health Services in Higher Educ	BASC	Brit Assn Shooting & Consvn
BAHVS	Brit Assn Homoeopathic Veterinary Surgeons		Brit Assn Skin Camouflage
BAILER	Brit Assn Inf & Library Educ & Res	BASCA	Brit Academy Songwriters, Composers & Authors
BAIML	Brit Assn Intl Mountain Leaders	BASCD	Brit Assn Study Community Dentistry
BAIS	Brit Assn Ir Studies	BASDA	Business Application Software Developers Assn
BAJS	Brit Assn Japanese Studies	BASE	Brit Assn Service Elderly
BAKS	Brit Assn Korean Studies		Brit Assn Supported Employment
BALGPS	Bar Assn Local Govt & Public Service	BASEA	Brit Airport Services & Eqpt Assn
BALH	Brit Assn Local Hist	BASEES	Brit Assn Slavonic & E Eur Studies
BALI	Brit Assn Landscape Inds	BASEM	Brit Assn Sport & Exercise Medicine
BALID	Brit Assn Literacy in Devt	BASES	Brit Assn Seating Eqpt Suppliers
BALPA	Brit Air Line Pilots Assn		Brit Assn Sport & Exercise Sciences
BALPPA	Brit Assn Leisure Parks, Piers & Attractions	BASH	Brit Assn Study Headache
BALR	Brit Assn Lung Research	BASHH	Brit Assn Sexual Health & HIV
BAMA	Brit Aerosol Mfrs Assn	BASI	Brit Assn Snowsport Instructors
	Brit Assn Martial Arts	BASICS	Brit Assn Immediate Care
BAMF	Brit Art Market Fedn	BASL	Brit Assn Sport & Law
BAMS	Brit Air Mail Soc		Brit Assn Study Liver
	Brit Art Medal Soc	BASMA	Boot & Shoe Mfrs Assn
BAMT	Brit Assn Music Therapy	BASO-ACS	BASO
BANA	Brit Acoustic Neuroma Assn	BASP	Brit Assn Ski Patrollers
BANC	Brit Assn Nature Conservationists	BASPCAN	Brit Assn Study & Prevention Child Abuse
BANS	Brit Assn Numismatic Socs	BASR	Brit Assn Study Religions
BANT	Brit Assn Nutritional Therapy	BASRT	College Sexual & Relationship Therapists
BAO-HNS	Brit Assn Otorhinolaryngologists	BASS	Brit Assn Ship Suppliers
BAOMS	Brit Assn Oral & Maxillofacial Surgeons	BASSAC	Brit Assn Settlements & Social Action Centres
BAOT/COT	Brit Assn Occupational Therapists	BASW	Brit Assn Social Workers
		BATA	Brit Air Transport Assn

BATB	Brit Assn Tissue Banking	BCCF	Brit Calcium Carbonates Fedn
BATC	Brit Amat TV Club	BCCG	Brit Cham Comm Germany
	Brit Apparel & Textile Confedn	BCCH	Brit Cham Comm Hungary
BATD	Brit Assn Teachers Dancing	BCCI	Birmingham Cham Comm
BATF	Brit Allied Trs Fedn		Brit Cham Comm Italy
BAThH	Brit Assn Therapeutical Hypnotists	BCCIB	Brit Cham Comm & Ind Brazil
BATOD	Brit Assn Teachers Deaf	BCCJ	Brit Cham Comm Japan
BATS	Brit Assn Tennis Supporters	BCCL	Brit Cham Comm Latvia
BAUN	Brit Assn Urological Nurses	BCCM	Brit Cham Comm Morocco
BAUS	Brit Assn Urological Surgeons	BCCMA	Brit Coun Chinese Martial Arts
BAVA	Brit Anti-Vivisection Assn	BCCS	Brit Compact Collectors' Soc
	Brit Assn Vedic Astrology	BCCT	Brit Cham Comm Taipei
BAVE	Bates Assn Vision Educ		Brit Cham Comm Thailand
BAWE	Brit Assn Women Entrepreneurs		Brit Cham Comm Turkey
BB	Boys' Brigade	BCDS	Brit Contact Dermatitis Soc
BBA	Better Brickwork Alliance	BCECA	Brit Chemical Engg Contrs Assn
	Brit Bankers' Assn	BCF	Brit Coatings Fedn
	Brit Bison Assn		Brit Cycling Fedn
	Brit Bobsleigh Assn		English Chess Fedn
	Brit Bodyguard Assn	BCFA	Brit Contract Furnishing Assn
	Brit Bridalwear Assn	BCG	Brit Chelonia Gp
	Brit Buddhist Assn	BCGA	Brit Compressed Gases Assn
	Brit Burn Assn	BCGBA	Brit Crown Green Bowling Assn
BBAA	Brit Business Angels Assn	BCGTMA	Brit Ceramic Gift & Tableware Mfrs' Assn
	Brit Business Awards Assn	BChA	Brit Chiropody & Podiatry Assn
BBAC	Brit Balloon & Airship Club	BCHS	Brit Camargue Horse Soc
BBC	Brit Bodyboard Club	BCI	Business Continuity Inst
BBCC	Brit Bulgarian Cham Comm	BCIA	Building Controls Ind Assn
BBCS	Brit Big Cats Soc	BCIS	Building Cost Infm Service
BBCT	Bumblebee Conservation Trust	BCLA	Brit Comparative Literature Assn
BBF	Brit Basketball Fedn		Brit Contact Lens Assn
BBFS	Brit Bulgarian Friendship Soc	BCMA	BEAMA
BBG	Brit Brands Gp		Brit Colour Makers Assn
BBGA	Brit Business & Gen Aviation Assn		Brit Complementary Medicine Assn
BBI	Brit Bottlers' Inst	BCMPA	Brit Contract Mfrs & Packers Assn
BBIF	Brit Battery Ind Fedn	BCO	Brit Coun Offices
BBKA	Brit Bee-Keepers' Assn		College Optometrists
BBMA	Brit Barometer Makers Assn	BCofC	Bradford Cham Comm & Ind
	Brit Battery Mfrs Assn	BCPA	Brit Cardiac Patients Assn
	Brit Bluegrass Music Assn	BCPS	Brit Connemara Pony Soc
BBN	Blue Badge Network	BCRA	Brit Cave Res Assn
BBO	Brit Ballet Org	BCRC	Brit Cave Rescue Coun
BBPA	Brit Beer & Pub Assn	BCS	BCS
	Brit Body Piercing Assn		Biblical Creation Soc
BBPCS	Brit Brewery Playing Card Soc		Black Country Soc
BBRS	Blair Bell Res Soc		Brit Cardiovascular Soc
BBS	Brit Biophysical Soc		Brit Carillon Soc
	Brit Boomerang Soc		Brit Cartographic Soc
	Brit Brick Soc		Brit Classification Soc
	Brit Bryological Soc		Brit Comedy Soc
	Brit Button Soc		Brit Conifer Soc
	Brittle Bone Soc	BCSA	Brit Constructional Steelwork Assn
BBSA	Brit Blind & Shutter Assn		Brit Cutlery & Silverware Assn
BBTS	Brit Blood Transfusion Soc		Brit Czech & Slovak Assn
BCA	Beauty Companies Assn	BCSC	Brit Coun Shopping Centres
	Brit Cables Assn	BCSS	Brit Cactus & Succulent Soc
	Brit Caving Assn		Brit Charollais Sheep Soc
	Brit Cheerleading Assn	BCT	Bat Consvn Trust
	Brit Chiropractic Assn	bctc	Bournemouth Cham Tr & Comm
	Brit Confectioners Assn	BCTGA	Brit Christmas Tree Growers Assn
	Brit Costume Assn	BCU	Brit Canoe U
	Brit Crystallographic Assn	BCURA	Brit Coal Utilisation Res Assn
bca	Business Centre Assn	BDA	Brick Devt Assn
BCA	Business Coun Africa W & Sthn		Brit Deaf Assn
BCAS	Brit Compressed Air Soc		Brit Dental Assn
BCBA	Brit Marine Fedn		Brit Dietetic Assn
BCBC	Brit Cattle Breeders' Club		Brit Dragon Boat Racing Assn
BCC	Badge Collectors Circle		Brit Drilling Assn
	Brit Ceramic Confedn		Brit Dyslexia Assn
	Brit Cham Comm Luxembourg	BDAA	Biodynamic Agricl Assn
	Brit Chams Comm	BDF	Ballroom Dancers Fedn
	Brit Cleaning Coun	BDFA	aeroBILITY
	Brit Cryogenics Coun		Batten Disease Family Assn
BCC CR	Brit Cham Comm Czech Republic	BDFPA	Brit Deer Farms & Parks Assn
BCCA	Brit Cheque & Credit Assn		Brit Drug Free Powerlifting Assn
	Brit Correspondence Chess Assn	BDGA	Brit Disc Golf Assn
BCCB	Brit Cham Comm Belgium	BDMA	Brit Damage Mgt Assn
BCCC	Brit Cham Comm China - Beijing	BDO	Brit Darts Org

BDOA	Brit Domesticated Ostrich Assn	BGA	Brassica Growers Assn
BDPMA	Brit Dental Practice Mgrs Assn		Brit Gear Assn
BDRS	Brit Double Reed Soc		Brit Geomembrane Assn
BDS	Brit Dam Soc		Brit Geotechnical Assn
	Brit Deer Soc		Brit German Assn
	Brit Display Soc		Brit Gliding Assn
	Brit Dragonfly Soc		Brit Glove Assn
	Brit Driving Soc		Brit Go Assn
BDSC	Brit Deaf Sports Coun		Brit Grooms Assn
BDTA	Brit Dental Tr Assn		Brit Growers Assn
BDWCA	Brit Decoy & Wildfowl Carvers Assn	BGAS	Bristol & Gloucestershire Archaeol Soc
BEA	Brit Egg Assn	BGCS	Brit Golf Collectors' Soc
	Brit Epilepsy Assn	BGIA	Brit Golf Ind Assn
BEAMA	BEAMA	BGJA	Brit-German Jurists' Assn
beat	Eating Disorders Assn	BGMA	Brit Generic Mfrs Assn
BECA	Brit Electrostatic Control Assn	BGS	Brit Geriatrics Soc
BECTU	Broadcasting Entertainment Cinematograph...U		Brit Gladiolus Soc
BEDA	Bar Entertainment & Dance Assn		Brit Goat Soc
BEEF	Buildings Energy Efficiency Fedn		Brit Grassland Soc
BEF	Brit Equestrian Fedn	BGSS	Brit Gotland Sheep Soc
BEFMG	Brit Educl Suppliers Assn	BGTW	Brit Gld Travel Writers
BEHA	Baby Eqpt Hirers Assn	BH&HPA	Brit Holiday & Home Parks Assn
BELMAS	Brit Educl Leadership, Mgt & Admin Soc	BHA	Brit Hawking Assn
BEMA	Brit Engg Mfrs Assn		Brit Homoeopathic Assn
	Brit Essence Mfrs Assn		Brit Horseball Assn
BENHS	Brit Entomological & Natural Hist Soc		Brit Hospitality Assn
BEOA	Brit Essential Oils Assn		Brit Humanist Assn
BEPA	Brit Edible Pulse Assn		Brit Hydropower Assn
	Brit Egg Products Assn		Brit Hypnotherapy Assn
BERA	Brit Educl Res Assn	BHAB	Brit Helicopter Advy Bd
BERSA	Brit Elastic Rope Sports Assn	BHBF	Briti Marine Fedn
BES	Brit Ecological Soc	BHBIA	Brit Healthcare Business Intelligence Assn
	Brit Endodontic Soc	BHCA	Brit Health Care Assn
BESA	Brit Educl Suppliers Assn	BHCC	Brit Hellenic Cham Comm
BESCA	Heating & Ventilating Contrs Assn	BHCF	Brit Marine Fedn
BETA	Brit Educl Travel Assn	BHDTA	Brit Horse Driving Trials Assn
	Brit Equestrian Tr Assn	BHECTA	Brit Hardmetal & Engineers' Cutting Tool Assn
BEVIP	BEAMA	BHETA	Brit Home Enhancement Tr Assn
BExA	Brit Exporters Assn	BHF	Brit Hardware Fedn
BFA	Bee Farmers Assn	BHGS	Brit Histl Games Soc
	Brit Fedn Audio	BHHS	Brit Hanoverian Horse Soc
	Brit Florist Assn		Brit Hosta & Hemerocallis Soc
	Brit Flyball Assn	BHI	Brit Horological Inst
	Brit Footwear Assn	BHIVA	Brit HIV Assn
	Brit Franchise Assn	BHMA	Brit Herbal Medicine Assn
BFAWU	Bakers Food & Allied Workers U		Brit Holistic Med Assn
BFBB	Brit Fedn Brass Bands	BHPA	Brit Hang Gliding & Paragliding Assn
BFBi	Brewing, Food & Beverage Ind Suppliers Assn	BHPR	Brit Health Profls in Rheumatology
BFC	Brit Falconers' Club	BHPS	Brit Hedgehog Presvn Soc
	Brit Fire Consortium	BHRC	Brit Harness Racing Club
BFCC	Brit Fedn Correspondence Chess	BHRS	Bedfordshire Histl Record Soc
BFCMA	Brit Flue & Chimney Mfrs' Assn	BHS	Brit Haiku Soc
BFDG	Brit Film Designers Gld		Brit Herpetological Soc
BFFF	Brit Frozen Food Fedn		Brit Horn Soc
BFFS	Brit Fedn Film Socs		Brit Horse Soc
BFHS	Brit Fedn Histl Swordplay		Brit Hydrological Soc
BFI	Brit Film Inst		Brit Hypertension Soc
BFIDA	Brit Food Importers & Distrbrs Assn	BHSMA	Brit Hay & Straw Mchts' Assn
BFJA	Brit Fruit Juice Assn	BHSS	Brit Banking History Soc
BFM	BFM Ltd	BHTA	Brit Healthcare Trs Assn
BFMS	Brit False Memory Soc		Brit Herb Tr Assn
BFPA	Brit Fluid Power Assn	BI	Badminton Ireland
BFPDA	Brit Fluid Power Distrbrs Assn	BIA	BioIndustry Assn
BFREPA	Brit Free Range Egg Producers Assn	BIAC	Brit Inst Agricl Consultants
BFS	Brit Fantasy Soc	BIALL	Brit & Ir Assn Law Librarians
	Brit Fertility Soc	BIAS	Bristol Indl Archaeol Soc
	Brit Flute Soc	BIAZA	Brit & Ir Assn Zoos & Aquariums
	Brit Fuchsia Soc	BIBA	Brit Insurance Brokers' Assn
BFSA	Brit Fire Services Assn		Brit Isles Backgammon Assn
BFSLYC	Brit Fedn Sand & Land Yacht Clubs	BIBBA	Bee Improvement & Bee Breeders Assn
BFSTD	Brit Fedn Sexually Transmitted Diseases	BIBC	Brit Isles Bowls Coun
BFTA	Brit Fur Tr Assn	BIBOA	Brit Inflatable Boat Owners Assn
BFVEA	Brit Flower & Vibrational Essences Assn	BIBTA	Brit Isles Baton Twirling Assn
BFWG	Brit Fedn Women Graduates	BICA	Brit Infertility Counselling Assn
BFWMSS	Badger Face Welsh Mountain Sheep Soc	BICSc	Brit Inst Cleaning Science
BFYMBB	Brit Fedn Youth Marching Brass Bands	BIDA	Brit Interior Design Assn
BG	Brit Gymnastics	BIDST	Brit Inst Dental & Surgical Technologists
		BIE	Brit Inst Embalmers

© CBD Research Ltd · Beckenham · BR3 5JS · Tel 020 8650 7745 · E-mail cbd@cbdresearch.com · www.cbdresearch.com

BIEE	Brit Inst Energy Economics
BIFA	Brit Intl Freight Assn
BIFCA	Brit Indl Furnace Construction Assn
BIFD	Brit Inst Funeral Directors
BIFGA	Brit Indep Fruit Growers Assn
BIFM	Brit Inst Facilities Mgt
BIG	Brit Inst Graphologists
BIGGA	Brit & Intl Golf Greenkeepers' Assn
BIHA	Brit Inflatable Hirers Alliance
BII	Brit Inst Innkeeping
BIIBC	Brit Isles Indoor Bowls Coun
BIICL	Brit Inst Intl & Comparative Law
BIIS	Breast Implant Inf Soc
BILA	Brit Insurance Law Assn
BILD	Brit Inst Learning & Devt
	Brit Inst Learning Disabilities
BILETA	Brit & Ir Legal Educ Technology Assn
BIMA	Brit Interactive Media Assn
BIMM	Brit Inst Musculoskeletal Medicine
BIMTA	Brit Indep Motor Tr Assn
BInstNDT	Brit Inst Non-Destructive Testing
BIOA	Brit & Ir Ombudsman Assn
BIOS	Brit Inst Organ Studies
	Brit & Ir Orthoptic Soc
BIPDT	Brit Inst Profl Dog Trainers
BIPHA	Brit Inline Puck Hockey Assn
BIPP	Brit Inst Profl Photography
BIPS	Brit Inst Persian Studies
BIR	Brit Inst Radiology
BIRA	Brit Indep Retailers Assn
BIS	Brit Inst Interlingua Soc
	Brit Interplanetary Soc
	Brit Iris Soc
	Brit Italian Soc
BISA	Brit Intl Studies Assn
BISGBG	Brit Icelandic Sheep Breeders Gp
BiSHA	Brit Inline Skater Hockey Assn
BISL	Business Sport & Leisure
BITA	Brit Indl Truck Assn
	Brit Interior Textiles Assn
BIVDA Ltd	Brit In Vitro Diagnostics Assn
BIVR	Brit Inst Verbatim Reporters
BJA	Boat Jumble Assn
	Brit Jewellers Assn
	Brit Judo Assn
BJJAGB	Brit Ju Jitsu Assn GB
BJPL	Brit Jigsaw Puzzle Library
BKA	Brit Kodály Academy
	Brit Korfball Assn
BKKPS	Brit Kune Kune Pig Soc
BKPA	Brit Kidney Patient Assn
BKSA	Brit Kite Surfing Assn
BKSTS	BKSTS
BLA	Brit Legal Assn
	Mineral Products Assn
BLC	BLC, Leather Technology Centre
BLCC	Belgian-Luxembourg Cham Comm GB
BLCS	Brit Limousin Cattle Soc
BLDSA	Brit Long Distance Swimming Assn
BLESMA	Brit Limbless Ex-Service Men's Assn
BLF	Brit Lace Fedn
BLISS	BLISS
BLKA	Brit Locksmiths & Keycutters Assn
BLMRA	Brit Lawn Mower Racing Assn
BLOS	Brit Lingual Orthodontic Soc
BLPS	Brit Lop Pig Soc
BLS	Branch Line Soc
	Brit Lichen Soc
	Brit Longevity Soc
	Brit Lymphology Soc
BLSA	Brit Land Speedsail Assn
	Brit Leafy Salads Assn
BLSBA	Bluefaced Leicester Sheep Breeders Assn
BMA	Bathroom Mfrs Assn
	Brit Med Assn
BMAA	Brit Microlight Aircraft Assn
BMAPA	Mineral Products Assn
BMAS	Brit Med Acupuncture Soc

BMC	Brit Mountaineering Coun
BMCRC	Brit Motor Cycle Racing Club
BMEA	Brit Marine Eqpt Assn
	Briti Marine Fedn
BMF	Brit Marine Fedn
	Brit Motorcyclists Fedn
	Builders Mchts Fedn
	Building Materials Fedn [IRL]
BMFA	Brit Model Flying Assn
BMFMS	Brit Maternal & Fetal Medicine Soc
BMG	Brit Assn Mountain Guides
	Brit Menswear Gld
BMHA	Brit Malignant Hyperthermia Assn
BMHF	Brit Materials Handling Fedn
BMHS	Brit Miniature Horse Soc
	Brit Morgan Horse Soc
	Brit Music Hall Soc
BMI	Birmingham & Mid Inst
BMIG	Brit Myriapod & Isopod Gp
BML&BS	Brit Matchbox, Label & Booklet Soc
BMLA	Brit Maritime Law Assn
	Brit Med Laser Assn
BMLDA	Brit Manual Lymph Drainage Assn
BMLSS	Brit Marine Life Study Soc
BMMC	Brit Motorsport Marshals Club
bMPA	Brit Meat Processors Assn
BMPCA	Brit Metallurgical Plant Constructors Assn
BMRA	Brit Metals Recycling Assn
BMS	Brit Magical Soc
	Brit Malaysian Soc
	Brit Menopause Soc
	Brit Mexican Soc
	Brit Microcirculation Soc
	Brit Moroccan Soc
	Brit Mule Soc
	Brit Museum Friends
	Brit Music Soc
	Brit Mycological Soc
BMSS	Brit Model Soldier Soc
BMTA	Brit Measurement & Testing Assn
BMUS	Brit Med Ultrasound Soc
BMVA	Brit Machine Vision Assn...
BNA	Brit Naturalists Assn
	Brit Naturopathic Assn
	Brit Neuroscience Assn
	Britain-Nigeria Educl Trust
BNARA	Brit N Amer Res Assn
BNBC	Britain Nigeria Business Coun
BNC	Berwickshire Naturalists Club
BNCC	Britain-Nepal Cham Comm
BNCS	Brit Nat Carnation Soc
BNE	Business New Europe
BNEA	Brit Naval Eqpt Assn
BNETS	Brit Educl Suppliers Assn
BNF	Brit Nutrition Foundation
BNFA	Brit Narrow Fabrics Assn
BNFMF	Brit Non-Ferrous Metals Fedn
BNHS	Birmingham Natural Hist Soc
	Brit Natural Hygiene Soc
BNMA	Brit Number Plate Mfrs Assn
BNMS	Brit Nuclear Medicine Soc
BNPA	Brit Neuropsychiatry Assn
BNRA	Britannia Naval Res Assn
BNS	Brit Neuropathological Soc
	Brit Neuropsychological Soc
	Brit Numismatic Soc
	Britain Nepal Soc
BNTA	Brit Numismatic Tr Assn
BNTL	Brit Nat Temperance League
BNTVA	Brit Nuclear Test Veterans Assn
BNZTC	Brit New Zealand Tr Coun
BOA	Brit Olympic Assn
	Brit Oncological Assn
	Brit Orthopaedic Assn
	Brit Osteopathic Assn
BOAS	Brit Ophthalmic Anaesthesia Soc
BOBMA	Brit Oat & Barley Millers Assn

BOC	Brit Orchid Coun	Britpave	Britpave
	Brit Ornithologists Club	BRMCA	Mineral Products Assn
BOF	Brit Orienteering Fedn	BROA	Brit Rig Owners Assn
	Brit Othello Fedn	BRPPA	Brit Rubber & Polyurethane Products Assn
BOGA	Brit Orchid Growers Assn	BRPS	Bluebell Rly Presvn Soc
BOHS	Brit Occupational Hygiene Soc		Brit Retinitis Pigmentosa Soc
BOMSS	Brit Obesity & Metabolic Surgery Soc	BRS	Bone Res Soc
BOOBA	Brit Olive Oil Buyers Assn		Brit Rebirth Soc
BOPA	Brit Oncology Patients Assn		Brit Renal Soc
	Brit Outdoor Profls Assn	BRSA	Brit Rope Skipping Assn
BORDA	Brit Off Road Driving Assn	BRSCC	Brit Racing & Sports Car Club
	Brit Oriental Rug Dealers Assn	BRSF	Brit Roller Sports Fedn
BOS	Brit Origami Soc	BRTMA	Brit Rootzone & Top Dressing Mfrs Assn
	Brit Orthodontic Soc	BRUFMA	Brit Rigid Urethane Foam Mfrs Assn
BOSPA	Brit Obesity Surgery Patient Assn	BS	Beaumont Soc
BOU	Brit Ornithologists U		Budgerigar Soc
BP&TUAA	Brit Pensioners & Tr U Action Assn	BSA	Bereavement Services Assn
BPA	Baby Products Assn		Beverage Standards Assn
	Brit Packaging Assn		Boarding Schools Assn
	Brit Parachute Assn		Brit Sandwich Assn
	Brit Paralympic Assn		Brit Shakespeare Assn
	Brit Parking Assn		Brit Soc Aesthetics
	Brit Pig Assn		Brit Soc Audiology
	Brit Porphyria Assn		Brit Sociological Assn
	Brit Ports Assn		Brit Stammering Assn
	Brit Psychodrama Assn		Building Socs Assn
	Brit Pyrotechnists Assn		Business Services Assn
BPC	Backpackers Club		Business Software Alliance
	Brit Peanut Coun	BSAC	Brit Soc Antimicrobial Chemotherapy
	Brit Polling Coun		Brit Sub-Aqua Club
	Brit Poultry Coun	BSACI	Brit Soc Allergy & Clinical Immunology
	Brit Psychoanalytic Coun	BSAS	Brit Sausage Appreciation Soc
BPCA	Brit Pest Control Assn		Brit Soc Animal Science
BPCC	Brit Polish Cham Comm [Lond]	BSAVA	Brit Small Animal Veterinary Assn
	Brit Polish Cham Comm [Warsaw]	BSBA	Brit Marine Fedn
	Brit Portuguese Cham Comm	BSBI	Botanical Soc Brit Isles
BPCF	Brit Precast Concrete Fedn	BSBMT	Brit Soc Bone & Marrow Transplantation
BPF	Brit Plastics Fedn	BSC	Brit Soc Cinematographers
	Brit Polio Fellowship		Brit Soc Criminology
	Brit Property Fedn	BSCAH	Brit Soc Clinical & Academic Hypnosis
BPGS	Brit Plant Gall Soc	BSCB	Brit Soc Cell Biology
BPHS	Brit Percheron Horse Soc	BSCC	Brit Shell Collectors Club
BPI	BPI		Brit Soc Clinical Cytology
BPIF	Brit Printing Inds Fedn		Brit Swedish Cham Comm Sweden
BPKA	Brit Power Kitesports Assn		Brit-Swiss Cham Comm [Zürich]
BPMA	Brit Promotional Merchandise Assn	BSCDA	Brit Stock Car Drivers Assn
	Brit Pump Mfrs Assn	BSCH	Brit Soc Clinical Hypnosis
BPMTG	Brit Puppet & Model Theatre Gld	BSCN	Brit Soc Clinical Neurophysiology
BPOA	Brit Protected Ornamentals Assn	BSCPIA	Brit Soluble Coffee Packers & Importers Assn
BPPA	Brit Precision Pilots Assn	BSCRA	Brit Slot Car Racing Assn
	Soc Wedding & Portrait Photographers	BSCS	Brit Simmental Cattle Soc
	Soc Wedding & Portrait Photographers	BSCW	Brit Soc Comedy Writers
BPS	Brit Palomino Soc	BSD	Brit Soc Dowsers
	Brit Pharmacological Soc	BSDA	Brit Sheep Dairying Assn
	Brit Postmark Soc		Brit Soft Drinks Assn
	Brit Printing Soc	BSDB	Brit Soc Developmental Biology
	Brit Psychological Soc	BSDH	Brit Soc Disability & Oral Health
	Brit Pteridological Soc	BSDHT	Brit Soc Dental Hygiene & Therapy
BPW UK Ltd	Business & Profl Women	BSDMFR	Brit Soc Dental & Maxillofacial Radiology
BQA	Brit Quadrathlon Assn	BSDR	Brit Soc Oral & Dental Res
BQF	Brit Quality Foundation	BSE	Brit Soc Echocardiography
BRA	Brit Records Assn	BSEM	Brit Soc Ecological Medicine
	Brit Reflexology Assn	BSES	BSES Expeditions
	Brit Refrigeration Assn	BSF	Brit Shogi Fedn
BRADA	Brit Resorts & Destinations Assn		Brit Soc Flavourists
BrAPP	Brit Assn Pharmaceutical Physicians	BSFA	Brit Science Fiction Assn
BRBA	Brit Marine Fedn	BSG	Birthmark Support Gp
BRBMA	Ball & Roller Bearing Mfrs Assn		Brit Soc Gastroenterology
BRC	Brit Rabbit Coun		Brit Soc Gerontology
	Brit Retail Consortium		Brit Stickmakers Gld
BRCA	Brit Radio Car Assn		Brit Sugarcraft Gld
BRCS	Brit Red Cross Soc	BSGA	Brit Sign & Graphics Assn
BRE	BRE Trust	BSGB	Bead Soc
BRGA	Brit Reed Growers Assn	BSGDS	Brit Soc Gen Dental Surgery
BRINDEX	Assn Brit Indep Oil Exploration Cos	BSGE	Brit Soc Gynaecological Endoscopy
BRISC	Biological Recording Scotland	BSGT	Brit Soc Gene Therapy
BRISMES	Brit Soc Middle Eastn Studies	BSH	Brit Soc Haematology
BritCham	Brit Cham Comm Singapore		Brit Soc Hypnotherapists

© CBD Research Ltd · Beckenham · BR3 5JS · Tel 020 8650 7745 · E-mail cbd@cbdresearch.com · www.cbdresearch.com

BSHA	Brit Show Horse Assn		Brit Tinnitus Assn
BSHAA	Brit Soc Hearing Aid Audiologists		Brit Toilet Assn
BSHG	Brit Soc Human Genetics		Brit Trout Assn
BSHM	Brit Soc Hist Mathematics		Brit Tugowners Assn
	Brit Soc Hist Medicine	BTAA	Brit Travelgoods & Accessories Assn
BSHP	Brit Soc Hist Pharmacy	BTBA	Brit Tenpin Bowling Assn
	Brit Soc Hist Philosophy	BTC	BTC Testing Advisory Gp
BSHS	Brit Soc Hist Science	BTCV	Brit Trust Consvn Volunteers
BSI	Brit Soc Immunology	BTDA	Brit Theatre Dance Assn
	Brit Suzuki Inst	BTG	Brit Tapestry Gp
BSIA	Brit Security Ind Assn		Brit Toymakers Gld
	Brit Starch Ind Assn	BTHA	Brit Toy & Hobby Assn
BSIF	Brit Safety Ind Fedn		Brit Travel Health Assn
BSKF	Brit Shorinji Kempo Fedn	BTHG	Birmingham Transport Histl Gp
BSM	Brit Soc Miniaturists	BTLIA	Brit Turf & Landscape Irrigation Assn
BSMA	BEAMA	BTMA	Brit Textile Machinery Assn
	Building Socs Mems Assn		Brit Turned Parts Mfrs Assn
BSME	Brit Soc Magazine Editors		Brit Tyre Mfrs Assn
BSMFD	Brit Soc Mercury Free Dentistry	BTMR	Brit Traditional Molecatchers Register
BSMGP	Brit Soc Master Glass Painters	BTO	Brit Trust Ornithology
BSMHD	Brit Soc Mental Health & Deafness	BTRA	Brit Truck Racing Assn
BSMM	Brit Soc Med Mycology	BTRDA	Brit Trials & Rally Drivers Assn
BSMT	Brit Soc Microbial Technology	BTS	Brit Tarantula Soc
BSN	Brit Soc Neuroendocrinology		Brit Technion Soc
BSNA	Brit Specialist Nutrition Assn		Brit Titanic Soc
BSNG	Brit Educl Suppliers Assn		Brit Transplantation Soc
BSNR	Brit Soc Neuroradiologists		Brit Trolleybus Soc
BSOE	Brit Soc Enamellers		Brit Trombone Soc
BSOM	Brit Soc Oral Medicine		Brit Tunnelling Soc
BSOP	Brit Soc Oral & Maxillofacial Pathology		Britain-Tanzania Soc
BSoUP	Brit Soc Underwater Photographers	BTSA	Brit Tensional Strapping Assn
BSP	Brit Soc Parasitology	BTSS	Brit Texel Sheep Soc
	Brit Soc Perfumers	BTTG	Brit Textile Technology Gp
	Brit Soc Periodontology	BU	Baptist U
	Brit Soc Phenomenology	BUAS	Border U Agricl Soc
BSPA	Brit Skewbald & Piebald Assn	BUAV	Brit U Abolition Vivisection
	Brit Speedway Promoters' Assn	BUCS	Brit Universities & Colleges Sport
BSPB	Brit Soc Plant Breeders	BUFCA Ltd	Brit Urethane Foam Contrs Assn
BSPFA	Brit Swimming Pool Fedn	BUFORA	Brit UFO Res Assn
BSPOGA	Brit Soc Psychosomatic Obstetrics...	BUFVC	Brit Universities Film & Video Coun
BSPP	Brit Soc Plant Pathology	BUIRA	Brit Universities Indl Relations Assn
BSpPS	Brit Spotted Pony Soc	BUPMSA	Brit Used Printing Machinery Supplrs Assn
BSPR	Brit Soc Proteome Res	BURISA	Brit Urban & Regional Inf Systems Assn
BSPS	Brit Show Pony Soc	BUSC	Brit Universities Snowsports Coun
	Brit Soc Philosophy Science	BUUK	Bus Users UK
	Brit Soc Population Studies	BVA	Brit Veterinary Assn
BSR	Brit Soc Rheology		Brit Video Assn
	Brit Soc Rheumatology		Brit Voice Assn
BSRA	Brit Soc Res Ageing	BVAA	Brit Valve & Actuator Assn
	Brit Sound Recording Assn	BVC	Brit Vacuum Coun
BSRD	Brit Soc Restorative Dentistry	BVCA	BVCA
BSRIA	Building Services Res & Inf Assn	BVCS	Brit Veterinary Camelid Soc
BSRM	Brit Soc Rehabilitation Medicine	BVF	Brit Volleyball Fedn
BSS	Botanical Soc Scotland	BVFLA	Brit Veterinary Forensic & Law Assn
	Brit Ski & Snowboard	BVHA	Brit Veterinary Hospitals Assn
	Brit Sleep Soc	BVMA	Brit Violin Making Assn
	Brit Standards Soc	BVNA	Brit Veterinary Nursing Assn
	Brit Sundial Soc	BVRLA	Brit Vehicle Rental & Leasing Assn
BSSA	Brit Shops & Stores Assn	BVS	Battery Vehicle Soc
	Brit Sjogren's Syndrome Assn	BVSF	Brit Vehicle Salvage Fedn
	Brit Skeet Shooting Assn	BVWS	Brit Vintage Wireless Soc
	Brit Stainless Steel Assn	BW	BasketballWales
BSSAA	Brit Snoring & Sleep Apnoea Assn	BWA	Bonded Warehousekeepers' Assn
BSSC	Brit Shooting Sports Coun		Bridge Deck Waterproofing Assn
BSSG	Brit Soc Scientific Glassblowers		Brit Waterbed Assn
BSSH	Brit Soc Surgery Hand		Brit Waterfowl Assn
BSSM	Brit Soc Sexual Medicine		Brit Westerners Assn
	Brit Soc Strain Measurement		Brit Woodcarvers Assn
BSSO	Brit Scooter Sport Org		Brit Wrestling Assn
BSSOA	Brit Ski Slope Operators Assn	BWAA	Brit Wheelchair Athletics Assn
BSSPD	Brit Soc Study Prosthetic Dentistry	BWAHDA	Brit Warm Air Hand Drier Assn
BSSS	Brit Soc Soil Science	BWARS	Bees, Wasps & Ants Recording Soc
BSSVD	Brit Soc Study Vulval Diseases	BWAS	Birmingham & Warwickshire Archaeol Soc
BSTP	Brit Soc Toxicological Pathologists	BWBA	Brit Wheelchair Bowls Assn
BSUK	BaseballSoftballUK	BWCA	Brit Water Cooler Assn
BSWA	Brit Structural Waterproofing Assn	BWCMG	Brit Watch & Clock Makers Gld
BTA	Birth Trauma Assn	BWCS	Brit White Cattle Soc
	Brit Thyroid Assn	BWDA	Best Western Dance Academy

BWF	Brit Walking Fedn
	Brit Woodworking Fedn
BWLA	Brit Weight Lifting
BWMA	Brit Weights & Measures Assn
BWPA	Brit Women Pilots Assn
	Brit Wood Pulp Assn
BWRA	Brit Wheelchair Racing Assn
	Brit Whippet Racing Assn
BWS	Brit Watercolour Soc
BWS Support	Beckwith-Wiedemann Support Gp
BWTA	Brit Wood Turners Assn
BWY	Brit Wheel Yoga
BYBA	Brit Youth Band Assn
BZA	Brit Zeolite Assn
BZS	Britain Zimbabwe Soc

C

C&I	Commerce & Ind Gp
CA	Camanachd Assn
	Classical Assn
	Consumers' Assn
	Croquet Assn
	Cruising Assn
CAA	Cathedral Architects Assn
	Cement Admixtures Assn
	Chess Arbiters Assn
	Cinema Advertising Assn
	Concert Artistes' Assn
CAAA	County Antrim Agricl Assn
CAABU	Coun Advancement Arab-Brit Understanding
CAAT	Campaign Arms Trade
CAAV	Central Assn Agricl Valuers
CAB	Coun Aluminium Bldg
CAC	Campaign Censorship
CADAS	Coventry & District Archaeol Soc
CADD	Campaign Drinking & Driving
CAEF	Campaign Euro-federalism
CAGC	Welsh Folk Song Soc
CAH	Campaign Hysterectomy &…Operations on Women
CAI	Confedn Aerial Inds
CAJ	C'ee Admin Justice [NI]
CALH	Cambridgeshire Assn Local Hist
CAMRA	Campaign Real Ale
CANI	Canoe Assn NI
CAPEL	Capel
CAPPA	Compulsory Annuity Purchase Protest Alliance
CAPS	Captive Animals' Protection Soc
CAS	Caithness Agricl Soc
	Cambridge Antiquarian Soc
	Catholic Archives Soc
	Cheshire Agricl Soc
	Chester Archaeol Soc
	Citizens Advice Scotland
	Contemporary Art Soc
	Cornwall Archaeol Soc
CASE	Campaign Science & Engg UK
	Campaign State Educ
CASH	Campaign Stage Hypnosis
CASS GB	Clarinet & Saxophone Soc
CASW	Contemporary Art Soc Wales
CATRA	Cutlery & Allied Trs Res Assn
CAWS	County Armagh Wildlife Soc
CBA	Brit Marine Fedn
	Chemical Business Assn
	Coun Brit Archaeology
	Criminal Bar Assn
CBBC	Caribbean-Brit Business Coun
	China-Britain Business Coun
CBC	Conservatoires UK
CBDG	Concrete Bridge Devt Gp
CBHS	Children's Books Hist Soc
	Cleveland Bay Horse Soc
CBI	Confedn Brit Ind

CBM	Confedn Brit Metalforming
CBOA	Comml Boat Operators Assn
CBS(UK)	Caspian Breed Soc
CCA	Chilled Beam & Ceiling Assn
	Company Chemists' Assn
	Consumer Credit Association
	Customer Contact Assn
CCAA	Children's Chronic Arthritis Assn
CCAB	Cámara Comercio Argentino Britanica
CCBN	Central Coun Brit Naturism
CCC	Cambridgeshire Chams Comm
	Club Cricket Conf
	Cumbria Cham Comm
CCCB	Cámara Comercio Colombo Britanica
CCCC	Canal Card Collectors Circle
	Clarice Cliff Collectors Club
CCCI	Chichester Cham Comm & Ind
	Cornwall Cham Comm & Ind
CCE	Conf Centres Excellence
CCFA	Combined Cadet Force Assn
CCFGB	Chambre Comm Française GB
CCG	Comics Creators Gld
CCGB	Cartoonists' Club
CCMAUK	Call Centre Mgt Assn
CCMM	Cornish Cham Mines & Minerals
CCN	Community Composting Network
CCRA	Clinical Contract Res Assn
CCS	Commemorative Collectors Soc
	Computer Consvn Soc
	Confedn Construction Specialists
CCSA	Carbon Capture & Storage Assn
	Cathedral & Church Shops Assn
CCT	Chesterfield Canal Trust
CCTA	Consumer Credit Tr Assn
CCUA	Civil Court Users Assn
CDA	Copper Devt Assn
	Country Doctors Assn
CDdWC/WFDS	Cymdeithas Ddawns Werin Cymru
CDET	Coun Dance Educ & Training
cdfa	Community Devt Finance Assn
CDI	Chemical Distbn Ireland
CDNA	Community & District Nursing Assn
CDS	Conf Drama Schools
CE	Christian Educ
CEA	Catering Eqpt Assn [IRE]
	Cinema Exhibitors Assn
	Combustion Engg Assn
	Construction Eqpt Assn
CECA	Civil Engg Contrs' Assn
CEDA	Catering Eqpt Distbrs Assn GB
	Central Dredging Assn
	Consumer Electronics Distbrs Assn [IRL]
CEDIA	CEDIA
CEF	Construction Emplrs Fedn
CEFF	Confedn Engl Fly Fishers
CEGV	Church England Gld Vergers
CEI	Cycle Engrs' Inst
CEM	College Emergency Medicine
CENTA	Combined Edible Nut Tr Assn
CERAM	CERAM Res
ceretas	Ceretas
CES	Christian Evidence Soc
CESA	Catering Eqpt Suppliers' Assn
CF	Carpenters Fellowship
CFA	CFA Soc
	Chilled Food Assn
	Circus Friends Assn GB
	Construction Fixings Assn
	Consumer Finance Assn
	Contract Flooring Assn
	Craft Gld Chefs
CFBA	Canine & Feline Behaviour Assn
CFDG	Charity Finance Directors' Gp
CfDS	Campaign Dark Skies
CFE	Campaign Farmed Envt
CFG	Comml Farmers Gp
CFHS	Catholic Family Hist Soc
CFMA	Chair Frame Mfrs Assn

© CBD Research Ltd · Beckenham · BR3 5JS · Tel 020 8650 7745 · E-mail cbd@cbdresearch.com · www.cbdresearch.com

CFOA	Chief Fire Officers Assn		CLP	Cornish Language Partnership
CFPF	Campaign Philosophical Freedom		CMA	Cardiomyopathy Assn
CGA	Country Gentlemen's Assn			Communications Mgt Assn
	Cucumber Growers Assn			Community Media Assn
CGF	Child Growth Foundation			Complementary Med Assn
CGGB	Cine Glds GB			Countryside Mgt Assn
	Colour Gp		CMAI	Concrete Mfrs Assn Ireland
CGS	Carnival Glass Soc		CMAS Ltd	Coal Mchts Assn Scotland
	Contemporary Glass Soc		CMBA	Classic Motor Boat Assn
	Cottage Garden Soc		CMDA	Cornish Mining Devt Assn
CGTBF	Craft Gld Traditional Bowyers & Fletchers		CMF	Cast Metals Fedn
CHA	Children's Heart Assn			Coal Mchts Fedn
	Comml Horticl Assn		CMI	Cement Mfrs Ireland
	Community Hospitals Assn			Chart Mgt Inst
	Cookshop & Housewares Assn		CML	Coun Mortgage Lenders
	Coun Hunting Assns		CMPE	Contractors Mechanical Plant Engrs
CHAPS(UK)	Coloured Horse & Pony Soc		CMS	Church Monuments Soc
CHCS	Chemical Hazards Communication Soc			Cricket Memorabilia Soc
CHE	Campaign Homosexual Equality		CMT	Commemoratives Museum Trust
CHEM	Container Handling Eqpt Mfrs Assn		CMYF	Charlotte M Yonge Fellowship
CHF	Crystal & Healing Fedn		CND	Campaign Nuclear Disarmament
CHO	Confedn Healing Orgs		CNHSS	Croydon Natural Hist & Scientific Soc
	Credit Hire Org		CNITA	Chart & Nautical Instrument Tr Assn
CHPA	Combined Heat & Power Assn		CNK	CNK Alliance
CHS	Caernarvonshire Histl Soc		CNS	Cardiff Naturalists Soc
	Caspian Horse Soc		COA	Cathedral Organists Assn
	Clarinet Heritage Soc		COA(UK)	Casino Operators' Assn
	Clydesdale Horse Soc		COALPRO	Confedn UK Coal Producers
CHSA	Cleaning & Hygiene Suppliers' Assn		CoBDO	Coun Brit Druid Orders
CIA	Chemical Inds Assn		COBIS	Coun Brit Intl Schools
CIArb	Chart Inst Arbitrators		COBSEO	Confedn Brit Service & Ex-Service Orgs
CIAT	Chart Inst Architectural Technologists		CODE	Confedn Dental Emplrs
CIB	Campaign Indep Britain		CODP	College Operating Dept Practitioners
CIBSE	Chart Instn Bldg Services Engrs		COF	Coach Operators Fedn
CIC	CIC Assn CIC		CofCS	Coun Cricket Socs
	Construction Ind Coun		COFPG	BEAMA
CICA	Chemical & Indl Consultants' Assn		COG	Component Obsolescence Gp
CICRA	Crohn's Disease Childhood Res Assn		COGDEM	Coun Gas Detection & Envtl Monitoring
CIEA	Chart Inst Educl Assessors		Cognition	Cognition
CIEH	Chart Inst Envtl Health		COMA	Coke Oven Mgrs Assn
CIF	Cork Ind Fedn		COMBAR	Comml Bar Assn
CIFE	CIFE		COMPASS	Central Org Maritime Pastimes...
CIG	Conf Interpreters Gp		ConFor	Confedn Forest Inds
CIHT	Chart Instn Highways & Transportation		Construct	Construct: Concrete Structures Gp
CII	Chart Insurance Inst		CoP	College Paramedics
CIIG	Construction Ind Inf Gp		COPROP	Assn Chief Corporate Property Officers Local Govt
CILA	Chart Inst Loss Adjusters		CoPSO	Coun Property Search Orgs
CILIP	CILIP		CORCA	C'ee Registered Clubs Assns
CILT(UK)	Chart Inst Logistics & Transport		CORDA	Coronary Artery Disease Res Assn
CIM	Chart Inst Marketing		CORE	Comment Reproductive Ethics
CIMA	Cereal Ingredient Mfrs Assn			Corporate Responsibility Coalition
	Chart Inst Mgt Accountants		CORGI	Coun Registered Gas Installers
CIOB	Chart Inst Bldg		COS	Cinema Organ Soc
CIoH	Chart Inst Housing		COSCA	COSCA [Scotland]
CIOT	Chart Inst Taxation		COSLA	Convention Scot Local Authorities
CIPA	Chart Inst Patent Attorneys		COT	Brit Assn Occupational Therapists
CIPD	Chart Inst Personnel & Devt		CP	Cats Protection
CIPFA	CIPFA		CPA	Charities' Property Assn
CIPHE	Chart Inst Plumbing & Heating Engg			Chiropractic Patients' Assn
CIPR	Chart Inst Public Relations			Christmas Prepayment Assn
CIPS	Chart Inst Purchasing & Supply			City Property Assn
	Choice Personal Safety			Competing Pipers Assn
CIRIA	Construction Ind Res & Inf Assn			Concert Promoters Assn
CITA	Construction Ind Tr Alliance			Construction Plant-hire Assn
CIU	Working Men's Club & Inst U			Construction Products Assn
CIVEA	Civil Enforcement Assn			Consumer Protection Assn
CIWEM	Chart Instn Water & Envtl Management			Cornish Pasty Assn
CIWM	Chart Instn Wastes Mgt			Corrosion Prevention Assn
CJA	Criminal Justice Alliance			Craft Potters Assn
CKS	Coble & Keelboat Soc			Credit Protection Assn
CL&CGB	Church Lads & Church Girls Brigade			Crop Protection Assn
CLA	Care Leavers Assn			Inst Certified Public Accountants Ireland
	Country Land & Business Assn		CPA UK	Assn Certified Public Accountants
CLAA	Cathedral Libraries & Archives Assn		CPAS	Car Park Appreciation Soc
CLAPA	Cleft Lip & Palate Assn		CPBF	Campaign Press & Broadcasting Freedom
CLAS	Calligraphy & Lettering Arts Soc		CPCC	Caithness Paperweight Collectors Club
CLIMB	Children Living Inherited Metabolic Diseases		CPDA	Clay Pipe Devt Assn
CLOA	Chief Cultural & Leisure Officers Assn		CPF	Crystal Palace Foundation

CPG	Customs Practitioners Gp
CPI	Confedn Paper Inds
CPMG	BEAMA
CPRE	Campaign Protect Rural England
CPRW/TDCW	Campaign Protection Rural Wales
CPS	Cambridge Philosophical Soc
	Carnivorous Plant Soc
CPSA	Clay Pigeon Shooting Assn
CPT	Confedn Passenger Transport
CQI	Chart Quality Inst
CR/Ea/	Composting Assn Ireland
CRA	Caledonian Rly Assn
	Chemical Recycling Assn
	Concrete Repair Assn
	Creators Rights Alliance
CRAE	Children's Rights Alliance England
CRC	Confedn Roofing Contrs
CRCA	Comml Radio Companies Assn
CRE	Campaign Real Educ
CReSTeD	Coun Registration Schools Teaching Dyslexic Pupils
CRM Soc	Charles Rennie Mackintosh Soc
CRN UK	Community Recycling Network
CROP	Coalition Removal Pimping
CRS	Cambridgeshire Records Soc
	Catholic Record Soc
	Conflict Res Soc
CRSA	Cold Rolled Sections Assn
CRT	Cambridge Refrigeration Technology
CRTC	Clay Roof Tile Coun
CRUSE	Cruse Bereavement Care
CS	Café Soc
	Chess Scotland
CSA	Channel Swimming Assn
	Choir Schools Assn
	Commissioning Specialists Assn
	Credit Services Assn
CSAG	Central Scotland Aviation Gp
CSAR	Cambridge Soc Application Res
CSAUK	Cued Speech Assn
CSC	Claims Standards Coun
CSD	Chart Soc Designers
CSGBI	Conchological Soc
CSJ	Confraternity Saint James
CSMA	Cementitious Slag Makers Assn
CSNA	Convenience Stores & Newsagents Assn [IRL]
CSO	Christian Social Order
CSP	Chart Soc Physiotherapy
CSPF	Channel Swimming & Piloting Fedn
CSS	Costume Soc Scotland
CSSA	Cleaning & Support Services Assn
CSTA	Craniosacral Therapy Assn
CSV	Community Service Volunteers
CTA	Cinema Theatre Assn
	Comml Trailer Assn
	Community Transport Assn
	Complementary Therapists Assn
CTC	Coach Tourism Coun
CTCC	Campaign Traditional Cathedral Choir
CTG	Charity Tax Gp
CTMA	Brit Civil Engg Test Eqpt Mfrs Assn
CTPA	Cosmetic, Toiletry & Perfumery Assn
CTS	Catholic Truth Soc
CTT	Cycling Time Trials
CU	Casualties Union
	Catholic U
CVBC	Cámara Venezolana Británica Comercio
CWA	Careers Writers Assn
	Crime Writers Assn
CWAAS	Cumberland & Westmorland Antiquarian. . . Soc
CWAUK	Comedy Writers Assn UK
CWU	Communication Workers U
CWW	Circle Wine Writers
CYP	Clubs Young People
	Clubs Young People (NI)
	Clubs Young People Scotland
	Clubs Young People Wales
CYWU	Community & Youth Workers U

D

D&AD	D&AD
D-UK	Depression UK
DA	Depression Alliance
	Design Assn
	Despatch Assn
DAAS	Dad's Army Appreciation Soc
DACS	Design & Artists Copyright Soc
DAE	Discovery Award England
DAHS	Derbyshire Agricl & Horticl Soc
DAS	Derbyshire Archaeol Soc
	Devon Archaeol Soc
	Dorchester Agricl Soc
DASA	Domestic Appliance Service Assn
DATA	Design & Technology Assn
DATS	Dress & Textile Specialists
DAW	Drama Assn Wales
DB	Designer Bookbinders
DBA	DBA
	Design Business Assn
DBS	Donkey Breed Soc
DCAA	Devon County Agricl Assn
DCBS	Devon Cattle Breeders Soc
DCCE	Doncaster Cham Ind & Enterprise
DCCI	Dorset Cham Comm & Ind
DCLHS	Durham County Local Hist Soc
DCRS	Devon & Cornwall Record Soc
DCS	Diecasting Soc
DDA	Dispensing Doctors Assn
DDS	Dawn Duellists' Soc
DDSBA	Dorset Down Sheep Breeders Assn
DEA	Devt Educ Assn
DebRA	Dystrophic Epidermolysis Bullosa Res Assn
DELTA	Deaf Educ Listening & Talking
DEMSA	Debt Mgt Standards Assn
DES	Drake Exploration Society
DFI	Disability Fedn Ireland
DFSG	Duchenne Family Support Gp
DGCC	Dumfries & Galloway Cham Comm
DGGB	Directors Gld
DGNHAS	Dumfriesshire & Galloway Natural Hist. . . Soc
DGSS	Derbyshire Gritstone Sheepbreeders Soc
DHAPS	Dun Horse & Pony Soc
DHDS	Dolmetsch Hist Dance Soc
DHF	Door & Hardware Federation
DHS	Design Hist Soc
DHSBA	Dorset Horn & Poll Sheep Breeders Assn
DIA	Design & Inds Assn
	Driving Instructors Assn
DISA	Defence Ind Security Assn
DJG	Designer Jewellers Gp
DLA	Dental Laboratories Assn
	Discrimination Law Assn
DMA	Direct Marketing Assn
DMF	Disabled Motorists Fedn
DNCC	Derbyshire & Nottinghamshire Cham Comm
DNHAS	Dorset Natural Hist & Archaeol Soc
DPA	Dartmoor Presvn Assn
	Data Pubrs Assn
	Dental Profls Assn
DPAA	Draught Proofing Advy Assn
DPIS	Derby Porcelain Intl Soc
DPS	Dales Pony Soc
	Dartmoor Pony Soc
DRS	Derbyshire Record Soc
	Design Res Soc
DSA	Devt Studies Assn
	Direct Selling Assn
	Down's Syndrome Assn
	Drilling & Sawing Assn
DSAUK	Dwarf Sports Assn
DSBA	Dartmoor Sheep Breeders Assn
DSFA	Diplomatic Service Families Assn
DSGB	Dozenal Soc
DSSA	Dental System Suppliers Assn

DSWA	Dry Stone Walling Assn
DTA	Dental Technologists Assn
	Devt Trusts Assn
DUCC	Danish-UK Cham Comm
DWT	Durham Wildlife Trust
DWTA	BEAMA

E

E-AG	Eur Atlantic Gp
EA	English Assn
EAA	Eastern Africa Assn
	Electricity Arbitration Assn
EAB	Esperanto Assn Britain
EADA	EADA
EAGB	Executives Assn
EAHC	Essex Archaeol & Histl Congress
EAMA	Engg & Machinery Alliance
EAP	English Apples & Pears
EASA	Ecclesiastical Architects & Surveyors Assn
EASB	English Assn Snooker & Billiards
EASCO	English Assn Self Catering Operators
EAUK	Evangelical Alliance
EBA	Electric Boat Assn
	English Baseball Assn
	English Boccia Assn
EBBA	England Basketball
EBCC	Egyptian Brit Cham Comm
EBEA	Economics, Business & Enterprise Assn
EBF	Equine Behaviour Forum
EBS	Edinburgh Bibliographical Soc
EBU	English Bridge U
ECA	Educl Centres Assn
	Electrical Contrs Assn
	English Clergy Assn
	English Curling Assn
ECB ACO	England & Wales Cricket Bd Assn Cricket Officials
ECB CA	England & Wales Cricket Bd Coaches Assn
ECCA	English Community Care Assn
	English Cross Country Assn
ECCI	Essex Chams Comm
ECHO	English Carp Heritage Org
ECIA	Engg Construction Ind Assn
ECO	Environmental Communicators Org
ECR	ECR Irelnad
ECSA	Estuarine & Coastal Sciences Assn
ECWS	English Civil War Soc
EDA	Electrical Distbrs Assn
	English Draughts Assn
EDC	Early Dance Circle
EDCC	Eastbourne & District Cham Comm
EDS	Ectodermal Dysplasia Soc
EEF	EEF
EEMUA	Engg Eqpt & Materials Users Assn
EES	Egypt Exploration Soc
EETS	Early English Text Soc
EFA	Employers Forum Age
	Eton Fives Assn
EFDS	English Fedn Disability Sport
EFDSS	English Folk Dance & Song Soc
EG	England Golf
EGB	Endurance GB
EGBA	English Goat Breeders Assn
EGCS	English Guernsey Cattle Soc
EGS	English Goethe Soc
EHA	England Handball Assn
EHAS	E Herts Archaeol Soc
EHOA	Event Horse Owners Assn
EHRSS	Edinburgh Highland Reel & Strathspey Soc
EHS	Ecclesiastical Hist Soc
EI	Energy Inst
	Evaluation Intl
EIA	Electrical Insulation Assn
	Engg Inds Assn
	Eur Inf Assn

EIBA	English Indoor Bowling Assn
EIC	Energy Industries Council
	Environmental Inds Commission
EIG	Explosives Ind Gp
EIQA	Excellence Ireland Quality Assn
EIS	Educl Inst Scotland
	Engg Integrity Soc
EISA	EIS Assn
EJO Society	Elsie Jeanette Oxenham Appreciation Soc
ELA	Employment Lawyers Assn
	English Lacrosse Assn
ELAFNS	E Lothian Antiquarian & Field Naturalists Soc
ELAS	Education Law Assn
eLN	eLearning Network
ELSPA	UK Interactive Entertainment Assn
EMCIA	EMC Ind Assn
EMDP	EMDP
EMRG	Early Mines Res Gp
EMS	Edinburgh Mathematical Soc
ENABLE	ENABLE Scotland
ENT.UK	Brit Assn Otorhinolaryngologists
EO	Education Otherwise Assn
EOA	Examining Officers Assn
EPA	English Pétanque Assn
	English Pool Assn
EPCS	English Playing-Card Soc
EPiC	Engineered Panels Construction
EPNS	English Place-Name Soc
EPS	Emergency Planning Soc
	Experimental Psychology Soc
EPSG	Epiphany Plant Study Gp
EPSS	English Poetry & Song Soc
Equity	Brit Actors Equity Assn
ERA	Energy Retail Assn
	Entertainment Retailers Assn
	Evacuees Reunion Assn
	Event Riders Assn
	Executive Res Assn
ERC	Economic Res Coun
ERoSH	Essential Role Sheltered Housing Nat Consortium
ERRVA	Emergency Response & Rescue Vessels Assn
ERS	Electoral Reform Soc
	Electric Rly Soc
ES	Epilepsy Scotland
	Ergonomics Soc
ESA	Environmental Services Assn
ESAH	Essex Soc Archaeology & Hist
ESB	Earthworm Soc Britain
ESC	English Ski Coun
ESG	Exhibition Study Gp
ESHSI	Economic & Social Hist Soc Ireland
ESITO	Events Sector Ind Trg Org
ESMA	Equine Sports Massage Assn
ESMBA	English Short Mat Bowling Assn
ESMG	Electric Steel Makers Gld
ESPA	Brit Educl Suppliers Assn
ESPG	BEAMA
ESR	England Squash & Racketball
ESRI	Economic & Social Res Inst [IRL]
ESSA	Emergency Social Services Assn
	Event Supplier & Services Assn
ESTA	Earth Science Teachers' Assn
	ESTA Energy Services & Technology Assn
ESTFA	English Subbuteo Table Football Assn
ESU	English Speaking U C'wealth
ETAPS	Environmental & Technical Assn Paper Sack Ind
ETCI	Electro Technical Coun Ireland
ETEMA	Brit Educl Suppliers Assn
ETHIC	Electric Trace Heating Ind Coun
ETI	Ethical Trading Initiative
ETTA	English Table Tennis Assn
ETwA	English Tiddlywinks Assn
EV Network	Electric Vehicle Network
EVA	English Volleyball Assn
EVENTIA	Eventia
EWI	Expert Witness Inst
EWP	English Wine Producers
EWS	English Westerners Soc

EWT	Essex Wildlife Trust
EYLHS	E Yorkshire Local Hist Soc

F

F of M	Friends Mendelssohn
F&PA	Flowers & Plants Assn
FA	Families Anonymous
	Football Assn
FAA	Fife Agricl Assn
	First Aid Assn
FAB	Fedn Awarding Bodies
	Futon Assn
FACE	Face Painting Assn
	Farming & Countryside Educ
FACE(UK)	Fedn Assns Country Sports Europe
FACT	Falsely Accused Carers & Teachers
	Fedn Copyright Theft
	First Aid Coun Training
FACTA	Fabricated Access Covers Trade Assn
FAEI	Fedn Aerospace Enterprises Ireland
FAGB	Fairground Assn
FAI	Football Assn Ireland
FAIA	Food Additives & Ingredients Assn
FAME	Fedn Archaeol Mgrs & Emplrs
FARA	Formula Air Racing Assn
FARMA	Nat Farmers' Retail & Markets Assn
FARS	Fedn Artistic Roller Skating
FAS	Fedn Astronomical Socs
FASET	Fall Arrest Safety Eqpt Training
FASI	Friedreichs Ataxia Soc Ireland
FASNA	Foundation, Aided Schools & Academies
FAST	Fedn Software Theft
FASTA	Farnborough Air Sciences Trust Assn
FATE	Fedn Automatic Transmission Engrs
FBA	Fedn Bloodstock Agents
	Fedn Brit Artists
	Foreign Bird Assn
	Freshwater Biological Assn
FBAF	Fédn Britannique Alliances Françaises
FBAS	Fedn Brit Aquatic Socs
FBCA	Fedn Burial & Cremation Authorities
FBCCI	Franco British Cham Comm & Ind
FBETM	Fedn Brit Engrs Tool Mfrs
FBGOA	Fedn Brit Greyhound Owners Assns
FBH	Fedn Brit Herpetologists
FBHTM	Fedn Brit Hand Tool Mfrs
FBHVC	Fedn Brit Historic Vehicle Clubs
FBLS/AJFB	Franco Brit Lawyers Soc
FBS	Fire Brigade Soc
FBSC	Fedn Bldg Specialist Contrs
FBU	Fire Brigades U
FBY Soc	Francis Brett Young Soc
FC&PMS	Fort Cumberland & Portsmouth Militaria Soc
FCA	FCA Membership Ltd
	Fedn Commodity Assns
	Fencing Contrs' Assn
FCBG	Fedn Children's Book Gps
FCC	Fedn Cocoa Comm
	Fedn Crafts & Comm
FCDE	Fedn Clothing Designers & Executives
FCDL	Fedn Community Devt Learning
FCFCG	Fedn City Farms & Community Gardens
FCM	Friends Cathedral Music
FCOT	Fellowship Cycling Old Timers
FCS	Fedn Chefs Scotland
	Fedn Clinical Scientists
	Fedn Communication Services
FCSI	Foodservice Consultants Soc Intl
FDA	Family Doctor Assn
	Film Distbrs' Assn
	First Division Assn
FDAP	Fedn Drug & Alcohol Profls
FDF	Food & Drink Fedn
FDII	Food & Drink Ind Ireland

FDP	Friends Dymock Poets
FDW	Friends Dr Watson
FDYW	Fedn Detached Youth Work
FEBL	Fedn Educ Business Link Consortia
FedPAG	Fedn Profl Assns Guidance
FEF	Forecourt Eqpt Fedn
FER	Fedn Engine Re-Mfrs
FERA	Fastener Engg & Res Assn
	Further Educ Res Assn
FeRFA	FeRFA
FESA	Foundry Eqpt Supplies Assn
FESH	Fedn Ethical Stage Hypnotists
FETA	Fedn Envtl Tr Assns
FEU	Fedn Entertainment Us
FEW	Freemen England & Wales
FFA	Family Farmers Assn
	Farmers Action
	Flying Farmers Assn
FFC	Friends Friendless Churches
FfCAC	Welsh Amat Music Fedn
FFHS	Fedn Family Hist Socs
FFLM	Fac Forensic & Legal Medicine
FFMA	Funeral Furnishing Mfrs Assn
FfS	Farms Schools
FFS	Flecker & Firbank Soc
FFVMA	Fire Fighting Vehicles Mfrs Assn
FGDP(UK)	Fac Gen Dental Practice
FGMA	Flat Glass Mfrs Assn
FHA	Family Holiday Assn
FHAGBI	Friesian Horse Assn
FHBF	Freelance Hair & Beauty Fedn
FHCS	Fedn Healthcare Science
FHNSAofGB	Fjord Horse Nat Stud Book Assn
FHS	Flintshire Histl Soc
	Friends Histl Soc
	Furniture Hist Soc
FHSS	Fedn Heating Spares Stockists
FHT	Fedn Holistic Therapists
FIA	Fibreoptic Ind Assn
	Fire Ind Assn
	Fitness Ind Assn
FIBI	Fedn Intl Banks Ireland
FIBKA	Fedn Ir Beekeepers Assns
FID	Fedn Indep Detectorists
FIEC	Fellowship Indep Evangelical Churches
FIF	Fedn Irish Fishermen
FIM	Fedn Indep Mines
FIPI	Fedn Image Consultants
FIPO	Fedn Indep Practitioner Orgs
FIRA	Furniture Ind Res Assn
FIRESA	Fire & Rescue Suppliers Assn
FIS	Fedn Infection Socs
	Fedn Ir Socs
FISS	Fedn Inline Speed Skating
FITA	Flooring Ind Training Assn
FJMI	Fedn Jewellery Mfrs Ireland
FLA	Family Law Assn Scotland
	Finance & Leasing Assn
FLBA	Family Law Bar Assn
FLD	Friends Lake District
Fleet Data	Road Transport Fleet Data Soc
FLTA	Fork Lift Truck Assn
FLVA	Fedn Licensed Victuallers Assns
FMA	Facilities Mgt Assn
	Family Mediators' Assn
	Fan Mfrs' Assn
FMA UK	Fibromyalgia Assn
FMB	Fedn Master Builders
FMC	Fire Mark Circle
FMD	Friends Medieval Dublin [IRL]
FMI	Family Matters Inst
FMO	Fedn Mfrg Opticians
FMPS	Farm Machinery Presvn Soc
FMS	Fedn Music Services
FNCI	Friends Nat Collections Ireland
FNF	Families Need Fathers
FNL	Friends Nat Libraries

© CBD Research Ltd · Beckenham · BR3 5JS · Tel 020 8650 7745 · E-mail cbd@cbdresearch.com · www.cbdresearch.com

FOA	Fire Officers Assn
	Futures & Options Assn
FOB	Fedn Bakers
	Friends Blue
FOBBS	Fedn Brit Bonsai Socs
FOBFO	Fedn Brit Fire Orgs
FoC	Friends Classics
FOCAL	Fedn Comml Audiovisual Libraries
FODO	Fedn Ophthalmic & Dispensing Opticians
FOE	Friends Earth
FOM RCP	Fac Occupational Medicine
FoMRHI	Fellowship Makers... Histl Instruments
FoNSCA	Fedn Nat Self Catering Assns
FOPS	Fair Organ Presvn Soc
FOREST	Freedom Org Right Enjoy Smoking Tobacco
FoRL	Friends Real Lancashire
FoRSTA	Fedn Road Surface Treatment Assns
FOSC	Fedn Sidecar Clubs
FOSFA	Fedn Oils, Seeds & Fats Assns
FOSSUK	Fedn Swiss Socs UK
FPA	Family Planning Assn
	Fire Protection Assn
	Flood Protection Assn
	Food Processors Assn
	Foodservice Packaging Assn
	Foreign Press Assn Lond
FPB	Forum Private Business
FPC	Fresh Produce Consortium
FPDC	Fedn Plastering & Drywall Contrs
FPFC	Fair Play for Children Assn
FPH	Fac Public Health
FPI	Friends Pianola Inst
FPM	Fac Pharmaceutical Med
	Fellowship Postgraduate Medicine
FPRA	Fedn Private Residents' Assns
FPS	Fedn Petroleum Suppliers
	Fedn Piling Specialists
	Fell Pony Soc
FRA	Fell Runners Assn
FRAME	Fund Replacement Animals Med Experiments
FRC	Pulp & Paper Fundamental Res Soc
FRG	Family Rights Gp
FRLTNI	Fedn Retail Licensed Tr NI
FRMS	Fedn Recorded Music Socs
FRSL	Ffestiniog Railway Society Ltd
FSB	Fedn Small Businesses
FSBI	Fisheries Soc
FSBL	Friends St Bride Library
FSC	Fedn Stadium Communities
	Field Studies Coun
FSDF	Food Storage & Distbn Fedn
FSF	Football Supporters Fedn
FSG	Fortress Study Gp
FSI	Financial Services Ireland
FSID	Foundation Study Infant Deaths
FSOA	Football Safety Officers Assn
FSPA	Fedn Sports & Play Assns
FSPG	Fire Service Presvn Gp
FSR	Fedn Specialist Restaurants
FSRH	Fac Sexual & Reproductive Healthcare
FSS	Feng Shui Soc
FSSA	Fedn Surgical Speciality Assns
FSSoc	Forensic Science Soc
FST	Fedn Scot Theatre
FTA	Fedn Tax Advisers
	Fibre Technology Assn
	Floatation Tank Assn
	Freight Transport Assn
FTL	Free Trade League
FTMTA	Farm Tractor & Machinery Tr Assn [IRL]
FULS	Fedn Ulster Local Studies
FUW	Farmers' U Wales
FWA	Family Welfare Assn
FWC	Fedn Window Cleaners
FWD	Fedn Whls Distbrs
FWINI	Fedn Women's Insts NI

G

G&SS	Gilbert & Sullivan Soc
GA	Galvanizers Assn
	Geographical Assn
	Geologists' Assn
GAFTA	Grain & Feed Tr Assn
GAG	Grandparents Action Gp
GAI	Gld Architectural Ironmongers
GAPAN	Gld Air Pilots & Air Navigators
GARDENEX	GARDENEX
GAS	Glasgow Agricl Soc
	Glasgow Archaeol Soc
	Group Analytic Soc
GATCO	Gld Air Traffic Control Officers
GAvA	Gld Aviation Artists
GBC	Gld Builders & Contrs
GBCT	Gld Brit Camera Technicians
GBD	Gld Brit Découpeurs
GBDF	Great Britain Diving Fedn
GBFTE	Gld Brit Film & TV Editors
GBG	Great Bustard Gp
GBPCC	Great Britain Postcard Club
GBRF	Great Britain Racquetball Fedn
GBS	Guillain Barre Syndrome Support Gp
GCA	Garden Centre Assn
	Gasket Cutters Assn
	Golf Consultants Assn
	Greeting Card Assn
GCCF	Governing Coun Cat Fancy
GCGB	Golf Club GB
GCL	Gld Cleaners & Launderers
GCM	Gld Church Musicians
GCMA	Golf Club Mgrs Assn
GCMT	Gen Coun Massage Therapies
GCRN	Gen Coun & Register Naturopaths
GCUK	GeoConservationUK
GDBA	Guide Dogs for Blind Assn
GE	Gld Enamellers
GEA	Garage Eqpt Assn
GEM	Group Educ Museums
Gem-A	Gemmological Assn
GEO	Glosa Educ Org
GF	Ground Forum
GFA	Game Farmers Assn
GFFR	Gld Fine Food
GFS	George Formby Soc
GFTU	Gen Fedn Tr Us
GFW	Gld Food Writers
gGA	Good Gardeners Assn
GGA	Guernsey Growers Assn
GGF	Glass & Glazing Fedn
GHA	Good Homes Alliance
GHC/ACW	Gwartheg Hynafol Cymru
GHP	Gld Healthcare Pharmacists
GHS	Garden Hist Soc
GIMA	Garden Ind Mrfs Assn
GKCSoc	Chesterton Soc
GLASS	Green Lane Assn
GLDA	Garden & Landscape Designers Assn [IRL]
GLIAS	Greater Lond Indl Archaeology Soc
GLM	Gld Letting & Mgt
	Gld Location Mgrs
GLTA	Glued Laminated Timber Assn
GLULAM/GLTA	Glued Laminated Timber Assn
GMA	Glasgow Mathematical Assn
	Growing Media Assn
GMC	Gld Master Craftsmen
GMG	Garden Media Gld
GNAS	Grand Nat Archery Soc
GNR Society	Great Nthn Rly Soc
GNSRA	Great N Scotland Rly Assn
GoCB	Gld Church Braillists
GODA	Gld Drama Adjudicators
GOMW	Gld Motoring Writers
GOONS	Gld One Name Studies

GOSPBC	Gloucestershire Old Spots Pig Breeders' Club
GP	Gld Photographers
GPBT	Gld Profl Beauty Therapists
GPDA	Gypsum Products Devt Assn
GPEA	Gld Profl Estate Agents
GPP	Gld Pastoral Psychology
GPTD	Gld Profl Teachers Dance & Movement
GPV	Gld Profl Videographers
GRA	Garda Representative Assn [IRL]
GRCA	Intl Glassfibre Reinforced Concrete Assn
GROUPAUTO	Group Auto U
GRS	German Rly Soc
GRTG	Gld Registered Tourist Guides
GSA	Girls Schools Assn
GSIA	Gloucestershire Soc Indl Archaeology
GSPS	Goon Show Preservation Soc
GTA	Greyhound Trainers Assn
	Gun Tr Assn
GTMA	Gauge & Tool Makers Assn
GTMC	Gld Travel Mgt Cos
GTOA	Group Travel Organisers Assn
GUW	Golf U Wales
GVA	Gin & Vodka Assn
GVCAC	Girls Venture Corps Air Cadets
GWS	Great Wstn Soc
GWT	Gwent Wildlife Trust

H

HA	Heritage Afloat
	Histl Assn
	Historic Artillery
	Honey Assn
HAA	Historic Aircraft Assn
HACSG	Hyperactive Childrens Support Gp
HAI	Humanist Assn Ireland
	Hunting Assn Ireland
HAS	Hawick Archaeol Soc
	History Anaesthesia Soc
HBA	Herring Buyers Assn
	Home Business Alliance
	Nat Assn Hospital Broadcasting Orgs
HBAA	Hotel Booking Agents Assn
HBF	Home Builders Fedn
HBS	Henry Bradshaw Soc
HBSA	Hairdressing & Beauty Suppliers Assn
	Histl Breechloading Smallarms Assn
HCA	Healthcare Communications Assn
	Heritage Crafts Assn
	History Curriculum Assn
	Holiday Centres Assn
	Hospital Caterers Assn
HCAUK	Handcycling Assn
HCC	Historic Caravan Club
HCCI	Hitchin Cham Comm & Ind
HCGB	Hovercraft Club
HCGI	Houses Castles & Gardens Ireland
HCKA	Historic Canoe & Kayak Assn
HCS	Highland Cattle Soc
HCSA	Health Care Supply Assn
	Hospital Consultants & Specialists Assn
HCVS	Historic Comml Vehicle Soc
HDA	Huntington's Disease Assn
HDRA	Henry Doubleday Res Assn
	Home Decoration Retailers Assn
HDS	Histl Diving Soc
HDSBA	Hampshire Down Sheep Breeders Assn
HEA	Horticultural Exhibitors Assn
HEAS	Home Educ Advy Service
HEFF	Heart of England Fine Foods
HELOA	Higher Educ Liaison Officers' Assn
HEMSA	Highway Electrical Mfrs & Suppliers Assn
HERO	Historic Endurance Rallying Org
HES(UK)	History Educ Soc
HEVAC	Heating, Ventilating & Air Conditioning Mfrs' Assn

HFBG	Historic Farm Bldgs Gp
HFC	Hampshire Field Club & Archaeol Soc
HFI	Health Food Inst
HFMA	Health Food Mfrs Assn
	Healthcare Financial Mgt Assn
HGA	Human Genetics Alert
HGS	Harness Goat Soc
	Hurdy Gurdy Soc
HGWS	H G Wells Soc
HHA	Historic Houses Assn
HINI	Hostelling Intl NI
HIS	Healthcare Infection Soc
HISHA	Highlands & Islands Sheep Health Assn
HLAI	Hedge Laying Assn Ireland
HLCC	Home Laundering Consultative Coun
HLCPA	Hemp Lime Construction Products Assn
HLRA	Handbag Liners & Repairers Assn
HMA	Homeopathic Med Assn
	Hop Mchts Assn
HMC	Headmasters & Headmistresses Conf
HMCA	Hospital & Med Care Assn
HMES	Histl Med Eqpt Soc
HMRS	Histl Model Rly Soc
HMS	Histl Maritime Soc
	Histl Metallurgy Soc
HMSA	Hose Mfrs & Suppliers Assn
	Hypermobility Syndrome Assn
HOS	Hardy Orchid Soc
HOT	Hawk & Owl Trust
HPA	Handley Page Assn
	Heat Pump Assn
	Hurlingham Polo Assn
HPMA	Healthcare People Mgt Assn
HPS	Hardy Plant Soc
	Highland Pony Soc
HPTH UK	Hypoparathyroidism UK
HRA	Heritage Rly Assn
	Horse Rangers Assn
HRAS	Harry Roy Appreciation Soc
HRFBS	Hill Radnor Flock Book Soc
HRGB	Handbell Ringers
HSA	Hillclimb & Sprint Assn
	Horseracing Sponsors Assn
	Humane Slaughter Assn
HSBA	Herdwick Sheep Breeders Assn
HSGB	Haflinger Soc
HSKI	Honorable Soc Kings Inns [IRL]
HSLC	Historic Soc Lancashire & Cheshire
HSR-UK	Hovercraft Search & Rescue UK
HSS	Humanist Soc Scotland
HSSA	Health & Safety Sign Assn
HTA	Heavy Transport Assn
	Horticultural Trs Assn
	Hound Trailing Assn
HTF	Historic Towns Forum
Hums	Humanities Assn
HUSH	Haemolytic Uraemic Syndrome Help [noMems 11
HVA	Herpes Viruses Assn
HVCA	Heating & Ventilating Contrs Assn
HWA	Hot Water Assn
HWPA	Horserace Writers & Photographers Assn
HWS	Henry Williamson Soc

I

IA	IA
IAA	Indep Academies Assn
IAAF	Indep Automotive Aftermarket Fedn
IAAH	Ir Assn Art Historians
IAAS	Inst Auctioneers & Appraisers Scotland
IAAT	Intl Assn Animal Therapists
IAB	Internet Advertising Bureau
IABA	Ir Amat Boxing Assn
IAC	Inst Amat Cinematographers
IACP	Ir Assn Counselling & Psychotherapy

IACT	Ir Assn Corporate Treasurers	ICMMA	Indl Cleaning Machine Mfrs Assn
IADT	Ir Assn Distributive Trs	ICMSA	Ir Creamery Milk Suppliers Assn
IAEA	Inst Automotive Engr Assessors	ICNM	Inst Complementary & Natural Medicine
IAEG	Ir Assn Economic Geology	ICOM	ICOM Energy Assn
IAgrE	Instn Agricl Engrs	Icon	Inst Consvn
IAgrM	Inst Agricl Mgt	ICorr	Inst Corrosion
IAgSA	Inst Agricl Secretaries & Administrators	ICOS	Ir Co-op Org Soc
IAI	Inst Archaeologists Ireland	ICPA	Ir Corrugated Packaging Assn
	Inst Architectural Ironmongers	ICPD	Inst Continuing Profl Devt
IAIEC	Ir Assn Intl Express Carriers	ICPEM	Inst Civil Protection & Emergency Mgt
IAIR	Ir Assn Indl Relations	ICR	Inst Clinical Res
IAL	Inst Art & Law	ICS	Inst Chart Shipbrokers
IALPA	Ir Airline Pilots Assn		Inst Customer Service
IAM	Inst Administrative Mgt		Instn Construction Safety
	Inst Advanced Motorists		Intensive Care Soc
IAMI	Intl Assn Marine Instns		Ir Computer Soc
IAO	Inc Assn Organists	ICSA	Inst Chart Secretaries & Administrators
IAP	Instn Analysts & Programmers		Ir Cattle & Sheep Farmers Assn
IAPF	Ir Assn Pension Funds	ICSF	Ir Cold Storage Fedn
IAPI	Inst Advertising Practitioners Ireland	ICSI	Inst Clay Shooting Instructors
IAPS	Indep Assn Preparatory Schools	ICT	ICT Ireland
IAS	Indl Agents Soc		Inst Concrete Technology
IASW	Ir Assn Social Workers	ICTU	Ir Congress Tr Us
IAT	Inst Animal Technology	ICW	Inst Clayworkers
	Inst Asphalt Technology		Inst Clerks Works
IAV	Inst Assessors & Internal Verifiers	IDA	Information Design Assn
IAVS	Ir Anti Vivisection Soc		Ir Dental Assn
IBA	Ir Bowling Assn	IDE	Inst Demolition Engrs
	Ir Brokers Assn	IDF	Indep Doctors Fedn
IBAS	Indep Banking Advy Service	IDFA	Infant & Dietetic Foods Assn
IBAT	Inst Bookbinding & Allied Trs	IDGTE	Instn Diesel & Gas Turbine Engrs
IBC	Inst Barristers' Clerks	IDHEE	Inst Domestic Heating... Engrs
IBD	Inst Brewing & Distilling	IDHS(GB)	Ir Draught Horse Soc
IBE	Inst Business Ethics	IDI	Inst Designers Ireland
IBEC	Ir Business & Emplrs Confedn	IDM	Inst Direct Marketing
IBF	Ir Banking Fedn	IDMA	Ir Direct Marketing Assn
IBI	Indep Broadcasters Ireland	IDS	Ir Deaf Soc
	Inst Biology Ireland	IDSc	Inst Decontamination Sciences
IBIA	Ir BioIndustry Assn	IDSCA	Ir Decorative Surface Coatings Assn
IBIS	Imaginative Book Illustration Soc	IEA	Inst Economic Affairs
IBMS	Inst Biomedical Science		Ir Exporters Assn
IBO	Inst Brit Organ Bldg	IEAM	Inst Entertainment & Arts Mgt
IBS	Inst Broadcast Sound	IED	Instn Economic Devt
IBSS	Intl Bond & Share Soc		Instn Engg Designers
IC	Inst Consulting	IEDP	Inst Equality & Diversity Practitioners
ICA	Ice Cream Alliance	IEEF	Ir Engg Enterprises Fedn
	Inst Consumer Affairs	IEEM	Inst Ecology & Envtl Mgt
	Inst Contemporary Arts	IEMA	Inst Envtl Mgt & Assessment
	Ir Countrywomen's Assn	IER	Inst Employment Rights
ICAEW	Inst Chart Accountants England & Wales	IES	Instn Envtl Sciences
ICAS	Inst Chart Accountants Scotland	IESIS	Instn Engrs & Shipbuilders Scotland
ICB	Inst Certified Book-Keepers	IET	Instn Engg & Technology
ICBA	Instn Comml & Business Agents	IExpE	Inst Explosives Engrs
ICBF	Ir Cattle Breeding Fedn	IFA	Indep Motor Tr Factors Assn
ICCA	Ir Contract Cleaning Assn	IfA	Inst Field Archaeologists
ICCL	Ir Coun Civil Liberties	IFA	Inst Financial Accountants
ICCM	Inst Cemetery & Crematorium Mgt		Ir Farmers Assn
ICCT	Islington Cham Comm & Tr		Ir Football Assn
ICDA	Ir Cosmetics Detergent & Allied Products Assn		Ir Franchise Assn
ICE	Indoor Cricket England	IFB	Inst Family Business
	Instn Civil Engrs	IFBB	Indep Family Brewers
ICEA	Inst Cost & Executive Accountants	IFE	Instn Fire Engrs
	Intl Consulting Economists Assn	IFEDA	Indep Fire Engg & Distrbrs Assn
ICES	Chart Instn Civil Engg Surveyors	IFFPA	Ir Forestry & Forest Products Assn
ICF	Inst Chart Foresters	IFHS	Ir Family Hist Soc
	Ir Concrete Fedn	IFIF	Ir Fashion Ind Fedn
ICFM	Inst Car Fleet Mgt	IfL	Inst Learning
ICG	Inst Career Guidance	IFLSA	Brit Marine Fedn
ICGP	Ir Coll Gen Practitioners	IFM	Inst Fisheries Mgt
ICHA	Indep Children's Homes Assn	IFMA	Inst Football Mgrs & Admin
ICHAWI	Inst Consvn Historic &... Works Ireland	IFON	Indep Fedn Nursing Scotland
IChemE	Instn Chemical Engrs	IFP	Inst Financial Planning
ICIA	Ir Cellular Industry Assn	IFPA	Ir Family Planning Assn
ICM	Inst Comml Mgt	IFPO	Ir Fish Producers Org
	Inst Conflict Mgt	IFRA	Indep Footwear Retailers Assn
	Inst Construction Mgt	IFRA UK	Intl Fragrance Assn UK
	Inst Credit Mgt	ifs	Inst Financial Services
ICME	Inst Cast Metals Engrs	IFS	Inst Fiscal Studies

IFSA	Instock Footwear Suppliers Assn		Investment Mgt Assn
	Intumescent Fire Seals Assn		Ir Museums Assn
	Ir Fedn Sea Anglers	IManf	Inst Mfrg
IFST	Inst Food Science & Technology	IMarEST	Inst Marine Engg, Science & Technology
IFT	Inst Turnaround	IMC	Ir Mortgage Coun
IFUT	Ir Fedn University Teachers	IMCA	Inst Mgt Consultants & Advisers [IRL]
IGA	Inst Gp Analysis		Intl Marine Contrs Assn
	Ir Geological Assn	IMDA	Ir Med Devices Assn
	Ir Grassland Assn	IMechE	Instn Mechanical Engrs
IGAP	Indep Gp Analytical Psychologists	IMEG	Ir Mining & Exploration Gp
IGC	Inst Guidance Counsellors [IRL]	IMF	Inst Metal Finishing
IGD	Inst Grocery Distbn		Ir Marine Fedn
IGEM	Instn Gas Engrs & Mgrs	IMHS	Indian Military Histl Soc
IGFA	Ir Grain & Feed Assn	IMI	Inst Med Illustrators
IGI	Inst Geologists Ireland		Inst Motor Ind
IGRS	Ir Genealogical Res Soc		Ir Mgt Inst
IGS	Ir Georgian Soc	IMIS	Inst Mgt Inf Systems
IHA	Ir Hockey Assn	IMIT	Inst Musical Instrument Technology
IHBC	Inst Historic Bldg Consvn	IMLA	Intermediary Mortgage Lenders Assn
IHBMA	Ir Hardware & Bldg Materials Assn		Ir Maritime Law Assn
IHCA	Ir Hospital Consultants Assn	IMO	Ir Med Org
IHE	Inst Highway Engrs	IMPACT	Ir Municipal Public & Civil Tr U
IHEEM	Inst Healthcare Engg & Estate Mgt	IMPT	Inst Maxillofacial Prosthetists...
IHF	Ir Hotels Fedn	IMQS	Ir Mining & Quarrying Soc
IHGS	Inst Heraldic & Genealogical Studies	IMRG	Interactive Media Retail Group
IHH	Indep Holiday Hostels Ireland	IMS	Inst Mgt Services
IHI	Inst Home Inspection		Inst Mgt Specialists
	Ir Hospitality Inst		Intl Masonry Soc
IHM	Inst Healthcare Mgt	IMSPA	Inst Mgt Sport & Physical Activity
IHPE	Inst Health Promotion & Educ	IMT	Inst Mgt & Technology
IHRIM	Inst Health Record & Inf Mgt	IMTD	Inst Master Tutors Driving
IHS	Inst Home Safety	IMUK	Indep Midwives
IHSGB	Icelandic Horse Soc	IMW	Inst Masters Wine
IHSM	Inst Hotel Security Mgt	IMWoodT	Inst Machine Woodworking Technology
IHU	Ir Homing U	INA	Ir Naturist Assn
IHUK	Ice Hockey UK	INCA	Inst Numerical Computation & Analysis [IRL]
IIA	Chart Inst Internal Auditors		Insulated Render & Cladding Assn
	Ir Internet Assn	INCPEN	Ind Coun Packaging & Envt
IIB	Inst Indep Business	INFACT	Ir Nat Fedn Copyright Theft
	Inst Insurance Brokers	INMO	Ir Nurses & Midwives Org
IICM	Ir Inst Credit Mgt	InstMC	Inst Measurement & Control
IIE	Inst Indl Engrs Ireland	InstP	Inst Piping
IIF	Ir Insurance Fedn	INTO	Ir Nat Teachers Org
IIFA	Ir Intl Freight Assn	IOA	Indep Operators Assn
IIHA	Ir Ice Hockey Assn	IoA	Inst Acoustics
III	Insurance Inst Ireland	IoBM	Inst Builders Mchts
IILP	Inst Intl Licensing Practitioners	IOC	Inst Carpenters
IIM	Inst Interim Mgt	IoC	Inst Couriers
	Inst Intl Marketing	IoCP	Inst Chiropodists & Podiatrists
IIPA	Inst Inc Public Accountants [IRL]	IOCS	Inst Construction Specialists
IIPM	Ir Inst Pensions Mgt	IoD	Inst Directors
IIPMM	Ir Inst Purchasing & Materials Mgt		Inst Directors Ireland
IIS	Ir Instn Surveyors	IOE	Inst Export
IISP	Inst Inf Security Profls	IoF	Inst Fundraising
IIT	Inst Indirect Taxation	IofAM	Inst Assn Mgt
IITD	Ir Inst Training & Devt	IOFGA	Ir Organic Farmers & Growers Assn
IITI	Inst Intl Tr [IRL]	IOG	Inst Groundsmanship
IKA	Ir Kidney Assn	IOH	Inst Horticulture
ILA	Insolvency Lawyers Assn	IoI	Inst Inventors
	Intl Law Assn	IoIC	Inst Internal Communication
ILAM	Inst Leisure & Amenity Mgt Ireland	IOJ	Chart Inst Journalists
ILCU	Ir League Credit Us	IoL	Chart Inst Linguists
ILEX	Inst Legal Executives	IOL	Inst Outdoor Learning
ILFM	Inst Legal Finance & Mgt	IOM	Inst Operations Mgt
ILGU	Ir Ladies Golf U	IOM3	Inst Materials, Minerals & Mining
ILHS	Ir Legal Hist Soc	IOMNHAS	Isle of Man Natural Hist...Soc
ILI	Ir Landscape Inst	ION	Inst Optimum Nutrition
ILM	Inst Leadership & Mgt	IOOA	Ir Offshore Operators Assn
ILP	Instn Lighting Profls	IoP	Inst Physics
ILPA	Immigration Law Practitioners Assn	IOR	Inst Operational Risk
ILS	Indl Law Soc	IoR	Inst Refrigeration
	Indl Locomotive Soc		Inst Roofing
	Inst Legal Secretaries & PAs	IOS	Inst Swimming
ILSGB	Intl Language Ido Soc	IOSF	Intl Otter Survival Fund
ILTSA	Inst Licensed Tr Stock Auditors	IOSH	Instn Occupational Safety & Health
IMA	Inst Mathematics & Applications	IoTA	Inst Transport Administration
	Intelligent Membrane Tr Assn	IOV	Inst Videography
	Interim Mgt Assn	IoW	Inst Welfare

© CBD Research Ltd · Beckenham · BR3 5JS · Tel 020 8650 7745 · E-mail cbd@cbdresearch.com · www.cbdresearch.com

IP3	Inst Paper Printing & Publishing
IPA	Indep Pilots Assn
	Indl Packaging Assn
	Indl & Power Assn
	Insolvency Practitioners Assn
	Inst Practitioners Advertising
	Inst Public Administration [IRL]
	Involvement & Participation Assn
IPAV	Inst Profl Auctioneers & Valuers [IRL]
IPCC	Ir Peatland Consvn Coun
IPCRA	Ir Profl Conservators & Restorers Assn
IPD	Inst Profl Designers
IPEM	Inst Physics & Engg in Medicine
IPF	Investment Property Forum
	Ir Printing Fedn
IPFMA	Ir Property & Facility Mgt Assn
IPG	Indep Pubrs Gld
	Inst Profl Goldsmiths
IPGS	Inst Parks & Green Space
IPHA	Ir Pharmaceutical Healthcare Assn
IPI	Inst Patentees & Inventors
	Inst Profl Investigators
	Ir Planning Inst
IPIA	Indep Print Inds Assn
IPLA	Inst Public Loss Assessors
	Intellectual Property Lawyers Assn
IPM	Inst Place Mgt
	Inst Promotional Marketing
IPP	Chart Inst Payroll Profls
IPPA	Ir Profl Photographers Assn
IPPMA	Ir Plastic Pipe Mfrs Assn
IPROW	Inst Public Rights Way Mgt
IPS	Inc Phonographic Soc
	Infection Prevention Society
IPSA	Ir ProShare Assn
IPSG	Ir Playwrights & Screenwriters Gld
IPSM	Inst Public Sector Mgt
IPSS	Inst Profl Soil Scientists
IPU	Ir Pharmaceutical U
IPW	Inst Profl Willwriters
IPWFI	Incorporation Plastic Window Fabricators & Installers
IQ	Inst Quarrying
IR Society	Investor Relations Soc
IRATA	Indl Rope Access Tr Assn
IRCH	Intl Register Consultant Herbalists & Homoeopaths
IRCS	Ir Red Cross Soc
IRDG	Ind Res & Devt Gp [IRL]
IRE	Inst Refractories Engrs
IRFU	Ir Rugby Football U
IRHA	Ir Road Haulage Assn
IRM	Inst Risk Mgt
IRMA	Ir Recorded Music Assn
IRMS	Information & Records Mgt Soc
IRO	Instn Rly Operators
IRPM	Inst Residential Property Mgt
IRR	Inst Race Relations
IRRV	Inst Revenues Rating & Valuation
IRS	Indl Rly Soc
IRSE	Instn Rly Signal Engrs
IRSO	Inst Road Safety Officers
IRTA	Ir Real Tennis Assn
IRTS	Ir Radio Transmitters Soc
ISA	Indep Schools Assn
	Ir Sailing Assn
	Ir Soc Archives
	Ir Soc Autism
	Ir Software Assn
ISAA	Ir Ship Agents Assn
ISBA	Inc Soc Brit Advertisers
	Indep Schools Bursars Assn
ISBE	Inst Small Business & Entrepreneurship
ISC	Indep Schools Coun
ISCA	Indep Safety Consultants Assn
ISCE	Inst Sound & Communications Engrs
ISecM	Inst Security Mgt
ISG	Ichthyosis Support Gp
ISIA	Ir Security Ind Assn

ISIDA	Ir Sudden Infant Death Assn
ISKB	Imperial Soc Knights Bachelor
ISM	Inc Soc Musicians
	Inst Spiritualist Mediums
ISMA UK	Intl Stress Management Assn UK
ISME	Inst Sheet Metal Engg
	Ir Small & Medium Enterprises Assn
ISMM	Inst Sales & Marketing Mgt
ISOB	Inc Soc Organ Builders
ISOM	Ir Soc Occupational Medicine
ISPA UK	Internet Service Providers' Assn
ISPCA	Ir Soc Prevention Cruelty Animals
ISPCC	Ir Soc Prevention Cruelty Children
ISPE	Inst Swimming Pool Engrs
ISPPG	BEAMA
ISRN	Inc Soc Registered Naturopaths
ISS	Inn Sign Soc
ISSE	Inst Specialist Surveyors & Engrs
ISSETA	Inflatable Safety & Survival Eqpt...Assn
IST	Inst Science & Technology
	Inst Spring Technology
ISTA	Intl Steel Tr Assn
	Ir Seed Tr Assn
ISTC	Inst Scientific & Technical Communicators
ISTD	Imperial Soc Teachers Dancing
	Intl Soc Typographic Designers
ISTR	Inst Safety Technology & Res
IStructE	Instn Structural Engrs
ISVA	Indep Surveyors & Valuers Assn
IT	Inst Trichologists
ITA	Inst Transactional Analysis
ITAA	Ir Travel Agents Assn
ITAI	Inst Traffic Accident Investigators
ITBA	Ir Thoroughbred Breeders Assn
ITC	Indep Theatre Coun
ITDN	Indep Tyre Distbrs Network
ITGA	Ir Timber Growers Assn
ITI	Inst Translation & Interpreting
	Ir Taxation Inst
ITIA	Ir Translators & Interpreters Assn
	Ir Tyre Ind Assn
ITIC	Ir Tourist Ind Confedn
ITM	Inst Transport Mgt
	Inst Travel & Meetings
ITMA	Imported Tyre Mfrs Assn
	Inst Tr Mark Attorneys
ITOL	Inst Training & Occupational Learning
ITPAC	Imported Tobacco Products Advy Coun
ITS	Ir Texts Soc
ITSSAR	Indep Training Standards Scheme & Register
ITT	Inst Travel & Tourism
IUA	Intl Underwriting Assn Lond
	Ir Universities Assn
IVEA	Ir Vocational Educ Assn
IVM	Inst Value Mgt
IVR	Inst Vehicle Recovery
IWA	Indep Warranty Assn
	Inland Waterways Assn
	Inst Welsh Affairs
	Ir Wheelchair Assn
IWAI	Inland Waterways Assn Ireland
IWBA	Ir Women's Bowling Assn
IWMA	Ir Waste Mgt Assn
IWPS	Inland Waterways Protection Soc
IWU	Ir Writers U
IYHA	An Oige

J

JABS	Justice Awareness & Basic Support
JACT	Jt Assn Classical Teachers
JAPTA	Jazz Piano Teachers Assn
JBAS	Jussi Bjorling Appreciation Soc
JBS	Josephine Butler Soc
JCCI	Japanese Cham Comm & Ind UK

JCNAS	Jt C'ee Nat Amenity Socs
JCS	Jersey Cattle Soc
JDA	Jewellery Distributors Assn UK
JFU	Jersey Farmers' U
JGS	Japanese Garden Soc
JHS	James Hilton Soc
	John Hampden Soc
JHSE	Jewish Histl Soc England
JIMA	John Innes Mfrs Assn
JKJ Society	Jerome K Jerome Soc
JPR	Inst Jewish Policy Res
JSL	Johnson Soc Lond
JSoS	Japan Soc Scotland
JSRA	Jet Sport Racing Assn
JSS	Jacob Sheep Soc

K

K&ESR	Kent & E Sussex Rly Co
KaBCA	Kaolin & Ball Clay Assn
KAS	Kent Archaeol Soc
KBSA	Kitchen Bathroom Bedroom Specialists Assn
KC	Kennel Club
KCAS	Kent County Agricl Soc
KCCC	Kensington & Chelsea Cham Comm
KCoC	Kingston Cham Comm
KEBS	Kmoch Eur Bands Soc
KF	Kinesiology Fedn
KFA	Keep Fit Assn
KIF	Knitting Inds Fedn
KSA	Klinefelter's Syndrome Assn
KSGB	Kite Soc
KSMA	Keats Shelley Memorial Assn
KWVRPS	Keighley & Worth Valley Rly Presvn Soc

L

LA	Libertarian Alliance
	Lighting Assn
LAA	Lancashire Authors Assn
	Light Aircraft Assn
	Livestock Auctioneers Assn
	London Anglers Assn
LABBS	Ladies Assn Brit Barbershop Singers
LABC	LABC
LACA	Local Authority Caterers Assn
LACEF	Local Authority Civil Enforcement Forum
LACS	League Cruel Sports
LAGB	Linguistics Assn
LAHS	Leicestershire Archaeol & Histl Soc
LAMAS	London & Middlesex Archaeol Soc
LANDEX	Landex
LANI	Landlords Assn NI
LAPADA	Assn Art & Antique Dealers
LAPG	Legal Aid Practitioners Gp
LARA	Motoring Orgs' Land Access & Recreation Assn
LARIA	Local Authorities Res & Intelligence Assn
LARO	London Assn Recovery Operators
LAS	Leicestershire Agricl Soc
	Lincolnshire Agricl Soc
LASA	Laboratory Animal Science Assn
LaSMA	Ladder Systems Mfrs Assn
LASSA	Licensed Animal Slaughterers... Assn
LBBA	Brit Marine Fedn
	Brit Marine Fedn
LBES	Lifeboat Enthusiasts Soc
LBMA	London Bullion Mkt Assn
LBSG	Letter Box Study Gp
LBSGB	Lusitano Breed Soc
LC	Lutheran Coun
LCA	Lead Contrs Assn
	Lizard Canary Assn
	London Cornish Assn

LCAS	Lancashire & Cheshire Antiquarian Soc
LCC	Liverpool Cham Comm
	London Cyclists
LCCI	London Cham Comm & Ind
LCF	Law Centres Fedn
	Librarians Christian Fellowship
LCGB	Locomotive Club
LCRS	Record Soc Lancashire & Cheshire
LCTC	Loyal Company Town Criers
LDCA	Land Drainage Contrs Assn
LDS	Lakeland Dialect Soc
LDSA	London Dist Surveyors Assn
LDU	Legal Defence U
LDWA	Long Distance Walkers Assn
LEA	Leasehold Enfranchisement Assn
LEAF	Linking Envt & Farming
LEEA	Lifting Eqpt Engrs Assn
LEIA	Lift & Escalator Ind Assn
LES B&I	Licensing Executives Soc
LFI	Let's Face It
LFMA	London Fish Mchts Billingsgate
LGA	Local Govt Assn
LGU	Ladies' Golf U
LHA	Left Handers Assn
	World War Two Living Hist Assn
LHC	Left Handers Club
LI	Landscape Inst
LIF	Lighting Ind Fedn
LIFE	LIFE
LIS	List & Index Soc
LITRG	Low Incomes Tax Reform Gp
LLSA	Leicester Longwool Sheepbreeders Assn
LMA	League Mgrs Assn
	Lloyds Market Assn
	London Mayors Assn
LMBBS	Laurence Moon Bardet Biedl Soc
LMCPA	London Motor Cab Proprietors Assn
LMMA	London Money Market Assn
LMS	Latin Mass Soc
	London Mathematical Soc
	London Medieval Soc
LNHS	London Natural Hist Soc
LOFA	Leisure & Outdoor Furniture Assn
LPI	Learning & Performance Inst
LPOC	Listed Property Owners Club
LPRS	Lancashire Parish Register Soc
LPSS	Local Population Studies Soc
LRBA	London Rice Brokers Assn
LRCS	Lincoln Red Cattle Soc
LRG	Landscape Res Gp
LRS	Lincoln Record Soc
LRSA	Local Registration Services Assn
LRTA	Light Rail Transit Assn
LRWA	Liquid Roofing & Waterproofing Assn
LSA	Lead Sheet Assn
	Leisure Studies Assn
	Lowe Syndrome Assn
LSARS	Life Saving Awards Res Soc
LSBA	Lonk Sheep Breeders Assn
LSDS	London Swing Dance Soc
LSGB	Lipizzaner Soc
LSN	Lymphoedema Support Network
LSRA	Lead Smelters & Refiners Assn
LSSA	Legal Software Suppliers Assn
	London Subterranean Survey Assn
LTA	Lawn Tennis Assn
	Livestock Traders Assn
LTDA	Licensed Taxi Drivers' Assn
LTG	Little Theatre Gld
LTN	Lone Twin Network
LTS	London Topographical Soc
LTWA	Lawn Tennis Writers Assn
LURS	London Underground Rly Soc
LVA	Licensed Vintners Assn [IRL]
LVTA	London Vintage Taxi Assn
LVTC	Land Value Taxation Campaign
LWA	London Welsh Assn

© CBD Research Ltd · Beckenham · BR3 5JS · Tel 020 8650 7745 · E-mail cbd@cbdresearch.com · www.cbdresearch.com

LYRPS	Lancashire & Yorkshire Rly Trust
LYRS	Lancashire & Yorkshire Rly Soc

M

M Her S	Military Heraldry Soc
M.A.R.S.	MARS
MA	Mathematical Assn
	Miscarriage Assn
	Museums Assn
MAA	Manufacturers Agents Assn
	Marketing Agencies Assn
	Marketing Assn Alliance
	Medical Artists Assn
MAARA	Midlands Asthma & Allergy Res Assn
MAC	Mastic Asphalt Coun
MACS	Micro & Anophthalmic Children's Soc
MAFVA	Miniature Armoured Fighting Vehicle Assn
MAG(UK)	Motorcycle Action Gp
MAGB	Maltsters Assn
MAMSA	Managing & Marketing Sales Assn
MARCH	Nat Assn Mental After-Care in. . . Homes
MARQUES	MARQUES
MAS	Merioneth Agricl Soc
MASS	Motor Accident Solicitors Soc
MATCH	Mothers Apart Children
MAUK	Mining Assn
MBA	Macrobiotic Assn
	Marine Biological Assn
	Mountain Bothies Assn
MBF	Multiple Births Foundation
MBHA	Masters Basset Hounds Assn
MBN	Milk Bottle News
MBSGB	Musical Box Soc
MCA	Mail Consolidators Assn
	Management Consultancies Assn
	Master Carvers Assn
	McTimoney Chiropractic Assn
	Medical Coun Alcohol
MCCA	Minor Counties Cricket Assn
MCCC	Midlands Club Cricket Conf
MCCE	Macclesfield Cham Comm
MCGB	Master Chefs GB
MCI	Mountaineering Coun Ireland
MCIA	Motor Cycle Ind Assn
MCofS	Mountaineering Coun Scotland
MCRMA	Metal Cladding & Roofing Mfrs Assn
MCS	Marine Consvn Soc
MCU	Modern Churchpeople's U
MDA	Mobile Data Assn
MDAS	Malt Distillers Assn Scotland
MDBA	Marching Display Bands Assn
MDDUS	Medical & Dental Defence U Scotland
MDF	MDF
MDHA	Masters Deerhounds Assn
MDS	Macular Disease Soc
MDSG	Myotonic Dystrophy Support Gp
MDU	Medical Defence U
MEA	Media Education Assn
	Medical Equestrian Assn
	Middle East Assn
	Milking Eqpt Assn
	Myalgic Encephalopathy Assn
MEC	Music Educ Coun
MeCCSA	Media, Communication & Cultural Studies Assn
MEDACT	Medical Action Global Security
MEDATS	Medieval Dress & Textile Soc
MEEMA	Brit Marine Fedn
MEG	Museum Ethnographers Gp
MELCC	Midlothian & E Lothian Cham Comm
MENCAP	R Mencap Soc
MERG	Model Electronic Rly Gp
MES	Minerals Engg Soc
MESF	Mobile Electronics & Security Fedn
MF	Morris Fedn

MFHA	Masters Foxhounds Assn
MGA	Maize Growers Assn
	Myasthenia Gravis Assn
MGAGB	Mounted Games Assn
MGMA	Metal Gutter Mfrs Assn
MGPRA	Manx Grand Prix Riders Assn
MGS	Manchester Geographical Soc
MHEA	Materials Handling Engrs Assn
MHRA	Modern Humanities Res Assn
MHS	Military Histl Soc
MIA	Maritime Inf Assn
	Meetings Ind Assn
	Mineral Products Assn
	Motorsport Ind Assn
	Music Inds Assn
MICAF	Mobile Ind Crime Action Forum
MIHS	Merseyside Indl Heritage Soc
MII	Maritime Inst Ireland
MIMA	Mineral Wool Insulation Mfrs Assn
MIND	Mind
MINSOC	Mineralogical Soc
MIPAA	Motor Ind Public Affairs Assn Ltd
MIRA	MIRA Ltd
MIRAD	Inst Registration Agents & Dealers
MIRO	Mineral Ind Res Org
MJA	Medical Journalists Assn
MKKM	Assn Men Kent & Kentish Men
MLA	Master Locksmiths Assn
MLAGB	Muzzle Loaders Assn
MLAMA	Brit Marine Fedn
MLSBG	Manx Loaghtan Sheep Breeders Gp
MLTA	Mountain Leader Training Assn
MMA	Maize Maze Assn
	Microtome Mfrs Assn
	Music Masters' & Mistresses' Assn
MMDA	Miniature Mediterranean Donkey Assn
MMF	Music Managers Forum
MMMA	Metalforming Machinery Makers' Assn
MMS	Manchester Med Soc
MMSA	Mobile Media Specialist Assn
MNA	Merchant Navy Assn
MNFU	Manx Nat Farmers U
MNLPS	Merchant Navy Locomotive Presvn Soc
MOA	Mobile Operators Assn
MOMENTUM	Momentum
Mont Soc	Montessori Soc
MOOS	Mechanical Organ Owners Soc
MOS	Men Stones
MOSA	Medical Officers Schools Assn
MPA	Major Projects Assn
	Master Photographers Assn
	Mineral Products Assn
	Music Pubrs' Assn
MPAGB	Modern Pentathlon Assn GB
MPBA	Model Power Boat Assn
	Modular & Portable Bldg Assn
MPG	Museum Profls Gp
	Music Producers Gld
MPGA	Metropolitan Public Gardens Assn
MPMA	Metal Packaging Mfrs Assn
MPS	Medical Protection Soc
MPS Society	Soc Mucopolysaccharide Diseases
MRA	Machinery Ring Assn
MRC	Model Rly Club
MRG	Media Res Gp
MRI	Meuse Rhine Issel Cattle Soc
MRQSA	Market Res Quality Standards Assn
MRS	Market Res Soc
	Medical Res Soc
MS	Media Soc
MS Society	Multiple Sclerosis Soc
MSA	Malvern Spa Assn
	Margarine & Spreads Assn
	Maritime Skills Alliance
	Modern Studies Assn
	Motor Schools Assn
	MultiService Assn
MSAUK	Motor Sports Assn

MSBA	Masham Sheep Breeders Assn
MSGB	Manorial Soc
MSHS	Medical Science Histl Soc
MSRG	Medieval Settlement Res Gp
MSSC	Marine Soc & Sea Cadets
MTA	Brit Marine Fedn
	Manufacturing Technologies Assn
	Microwave Technologies Assn
MU	Mothers U
	Musicians U
MUA	Machinery Users Assn
	Mail Users Assn
MUTA	Performance Textiles Assn
MVDA	Motor Vehicle Dismantlers Assn
MVT	Military Vehicle Trust
MVWGS	Multi Vintage Wine Growers Soc
MWF	Medical Women's Fedn
MWSA	Mixed Wood-chip Suppliers Assn
MYA	Model Yachting Assn
MYCCI	Mid Yorkshire Cham Comm & Ind

N

N.A.G.	Nat Assn Goldsmiths
NA	Napoleonic Assn
NAA	Nat Arenas Assn
NAAC	Nat Assn Agricl Contrs
Naace	Naace
NAAE	Nat Assn Advisers English
NAAIDT	Nat Assn Advisers… Design & Technology
NAAONB	Nat Assn Areas Outstanding Natural Beauty
NAAOSEN	Nat Assn Advy Officers Special Educl Needs
NAAPS	Nat Assn Adult Placement Services
NAAS	Nerine & Amaryllid Soc
NAB	Nat Assn Bookmakers
NABAS	NABAS
NABBA	Nat Amat Bodybuilders Assn
NABBC	Nat Assn Brass Band Conductors
NABCO	Nat Assn Bldg Co-ops [IRL]
NABD	Nat Assn Bikers Disability
NABIM	Inc Nat Assn Brit & Ir Millers
NABMA	Nat Assn Brit Market Authorities
NABO	Nat Assn Boat Owners
NAC	Nat Assn Choirs
	Nat Assn Councillors
NACAB	Nat Assn Citizens Advice Bureaux
NACB	Nat Assn Catering Butchers
NACC	Nat Assn Care Catering
	Nat Assn Colitis & Crohn's Disease
NACCC	Nat Assn Child Contact Centres
NACE	Nat Assn Able Children in Educ
	Nat Assn Chimney Engrs
NACFB	Nat Assn Comml Finance Brokers
NACHP	Nat Assn Counsellors, Hypnoterpists & Psychotherapists
NACM	Nat Assn Cider Makers
NACMO	Nat Assn Cigarette Machine Operators
NACO	Nat Assn Caravan Owners
	Nat Assn Co-operative Officials
NACOA	Nat Assn Children Alcoholics
NACRS	Nat Assn Community Run Shops
NACS	Nat Assn Chimney Sweeps
NACSA	Nat Assn Child Support Action
NACT	Nat Assn Clinical Tutors
NADA	Nat Acupuncture Detoxification Assn
NADFAS	Nat Assn Decorative & Fine Arts Socs
NADP	Nat Assn Deafened People
NAEA	Nat Assn Estate Agents
NAEE	Nat Assn Envtl Educ
NAEGA	NAEGA
NAFAE	Nat Assn Fine Art Education
NAFAO	Nat Assn Financial Assessment Officers
NAFAS	Nat Assn Flower Arrangement Socs
NAFBAE	Nat Assn Farriers…
NAFD	Nat Assn Funeral Directors

NAFLIC	Nat Assn Leisure Ind Certification
NAFSO	Nat Assn Field Studies Officers
NAG	Nat Acquisitions Gp
NAGALRO	NAGALRO
NAGC	Nat Assn Gifted Children
NAGS	Nat Assn NFU Gp Secretaries
NAHEMI	Nat Assn Higher Educ Moving Image
NAHFO	Nat Assn Healthcare Fire Officers
NAHPS	Nat Assn Hospital Play Staff
NAHS	Nat Assn Health Stores
NAHT	Nat Assn Head Teachers
NAKMAS	Nat Assn Karate & Martial Art Schools
NALA	Nat Assn Language Advisers
NALC	Nat Assn Ladies Circles
	Nat Assn Laryngectomee Clubs
	Nat Assn Local Couns
NALD	Nat Assn Literature Devt
NALEO	Nat Assn Licensing & Enforcement Offrs
NALI	Nat Assn Launderette Ind
NALP	Nat Assn Licensed Paralegals
NAMA	Nat Assn Mathematics Advisers
NAMB	Nat Assn Master Bakers
NAME	Nat Assn Music Educators
NAMEM	Nat Assn Med Educ Mgt
NAMHO	Nat Assn Mining Hist Orgs
NAMLC	Nat Assn Master Letter Carvers
NAMM	Nat Assn Memorial Masons
NAMMT	Nat Assn Massage & Manipulative Therapists
NAMSS	Nat Assn Mgrs Student Services Colleges
NAO	Nat Accordion Org
NAOMI	Nat Assn Ovulation Method Instructors
NAOPV	Nat Assn Official Prison Visitors
NAPA	Nat Acrylic Painters Assn
	Nat Alcohol Producers Assn
	Nat Approved Premises Assn
	Nat Assn Press Agencies
	Nat Assn Providers Activities Older People
NAPAC	Nat Assn People Abused Childhood
NAPAS	Nat Assn Private Ambulance Services
NAPC	Nat Assn Primary Care
NAPCE	Nat Assn Pastoral Care Educ
	Nat Assn Primary Care Educators
NAPE	Nat Assn Primary Educ
NAPF	Nat Assn Pension Funds
NAPFP	Nat Assn Pre-Paid Funeral Plans
NAPGC	Nat Assn Public Golf Clubs & Courses
NAPHR	Nat Assn Park Home Residents
NAPIT	Nat Assn Profl Inspectors & Testers
NAPLIB	Nat Assn Aerial Photographic Libraries
NAPLIC	Nat Assn Profls… Language Impairment Children
NAPM	Nat Assn Paper Mchts
NAPO	Nat Assn Probation Officers
NAPS	Nat Assn Premenstrual Syndrome
	Nat Auricula & Primula Soc (Mid & West)
NAPT	Nat Assn Percussion Teachers
NARA	Assn Property & Fixed Charge Receivers
	NARA
NARC	Nat Assn Rly Clubs
NAReS	Nat Assn Re-enactment Socs
NARM	Nat Assn Rooflight Mfrs
NARPO	Nat Assn Retired Police Officers
NARTM	Nat Assn Road Transport Museums
NAS	Nat Arabidopsis Soc
	Nat Assn Shopfitters
	Nat Autistic Soc
	Nautical Archaeology Soc
	Noise Abatement Soc
NASA	Nat Autograss Sport Assn
NASBM	Nat Assn School Business Mgt
NASC	Nat Access & Scaffolding Confedn
NASCH	Nat Assn Swimming Clubs H'capped
NASDU	Nat Assn Security Dog Users
nasen	nasen
NASGBI	Neuroanaesthesia Soc
NASGP	Nat Assn Sessional GP's
NASH	Nat Assn Support Victims Stalking & Harassment
NASIC	Nationwide Assn Security Installation Cos
NASMAH	Nat Assn Screen Makeup Artists & Hairdressers

© CBD Research Ltd · Beckenham · BR3 5JS · Tel 020 8650 7745 · E-mail cbd@cbdresearch.com · www.cbdresearch.com

NASPM	Brit Potato Tr Assn	
NASS	Nat Ankylosing Spondylitis Soc	
	Nat Assn Small Schools	
	Nat Assn Stable Staff	
	Nat Assn Steel Stockholders	
NaStA	Nat Stallion Assn	
NASUWT	Nat Assn Schoolmasters U Women Teachers	
NASWE	Nat Assn Social Workers Educ	
NAT	Nat Assn Toastmasters	
NATD	Nat Assn Teachers Dancing	
	Nat Assn Teaching Drama	
	Nat Assn Tripe Dressers	
NATE	Nat Assn Teaching Engl	
	Nat Assn Therapeutic Educ	
NATECLA	Nat Assn Teaching Engl &...Community Languages	
NATLL	Nat Assn Toy & Leisure Libraries	
NATN	Assn Perioperative Practice	
NATO	Nat Assn Tree Officers	
NATRE	Nat Assn Teachers Religious Educ	
NatSCA	Natural Sciences Collections Assn	
NATSPEC	Assn Nat Specialist Colls	
NATT+	Nat Assn Teachers Travellers	
NATTA	Network Alternative Technology &...Assessment	
NAVA	Nat Assn Valuers & Auctioneers	
NAVCA	Nat Assn Voluntary & Community Action	
NAVS	Nat Anti-Vivisection Soc	
NAVSM	Nat Assn Voluntary Service Mgrs	
NAW	Nat Assn Widows	
NAWB(A)	Nat Assn Wine & Beer Makers	
NAWC	Nat Assn Women's Clubs	
NAWCH	Action Sick Children	
NAWDO	Nat Assn Waste Disposal Officers	
NAWE	Nat Assn Writers in Educ	
NAWG	Nat Assn Writers' Gps	
NAWO	Nat Alliance Women's Orgs	
NAWP	Nat Assn Women Pharmacists	
NAYD	Nat Assn Youth Drama [IRL]	
NAYJ	Nat Assn Youth Justice	
NAYT	Nat Assn Youth Theatres	
NBA	Nat Beef Assn	
NBF	Nat Bed Fedn	
NBGA	Nat Bingo Game Assn	
NBS	Nat Begonia Soc	
NBTA	Nat Baton Twirling Assn England	
NBTVA	Narrow-bandwidth TV Assn	
NCA	Nat Campaign Arts	
	Nat Cancer Alliance	
	Nat Care Assn	
	Nat Coun Aviculture	
	Nat Courier Assn	
NCASS	Nationwide Caterers Assn	
NCC	Nat Caravan Coun	
	Nat Cavy Club	
NCCA	Nat Carpet Cleaners Assn	
NCCPG	Nat Coun Consvn Plants & Gardens	
NCDS	Nat Coun Divorced, Separated & Widowed	
NCF	Nat Consumer Fedn	
	Nat Cooperage Fedn	
NCFGB	Nat Crossbow Fedn	
NCFS	Nat Campaign Firework Safety	
NCH	Nat Coun Hypnotherapy	
NCIF	Nat Casino Ind Forum	
NCIT	Nat Coun Inland Transport	
NCIUA	Nat Cochlear Implant Users Assn	
NCLS	New Canterbury Literary Soc	
NCMA	Nat Childminding Assn	
NCMD	Nat Coun Metal Detecting	
NCNE	Nat Campaign Nursery Educ	
NCP	Nat Coun Psychotherapists	
NCPTA	Nat Confedn Parent-Teacher Assns	
NCS	Nat Chinchilla Soc	
	Nat Chrysanthemum Soc	
NCT	Nat Childbirth Trust	
NCU	Northern Cricket U Ireland	
NCWA	Nat Childrenswear Assn	
NCWJ	Nat Campaign Water Justice	
ND	Nat Drama	
NDAS	N Devon Agricl Soc	
NDCS	Nat Deaf Childrens Soc	
NDFA	Nat Drama Festivals Assn	
NDFTA	Nat Dried Fruit Tr Assn	
NDNA	Nat Day Nurseries Assn	
NDS	Nat Dahlia Soc	
NDTA	Nat Dance Teachers Assn	
NDWA	Nat Dog Wardens Assn	
NEA	Nat Energy Action	
	Nat Exhibitors Assn	
NECC	N E Cham Comm, Tr & Ind	
NEDA	Non-Executive Directors Assn	
NEHS	N England Horticl Soc	
NEIMME	N England Inst Mining & Mechanical Engrs	
NEMA	Nat Early Music Assn	
NEMAL	Nat Egg Marketing Assn	
NEMSA	N England Mule Sheep Assn	
NEODA	Nat Edible Oil Distbrs Assn	
NES	Nat Eczema Soc	
NFA	Non Ferrous Alliance	
NFAS	Nat Field Archery Soc	
NFB	Nat Fedn Builders	
NFBA	Nat Fedn Bridleway Assns	
NFBR	Nat Fedn Biological Recording	
NFBUK	Nat Fedn Blind	
NFCF	Nat Fedn Cemetery Friends	
NFDC	Nat Fedn Demolition Contrs	
NFEA	Nat Fedn Enterprise Agencies	
NFEC	Nat Forum Engg Centres	
NFER	Nat Foundation Educl Res E&W	
NFF	Nat Fedn Fishmongers	
NFFF	Nat Fedn Fish Friers	
NFFO	Nat Fedn Fishermens Orgs	
NFG	Nat Fedn Glaziers	
NFIWFM	Nat Fedn Inland Whls Fish Mchts	
NFM	Nat Family Mediation	
NFMS	Nat Fedn Music Socs	
NFOP	Nat Fedn Occupational Pensioners	
NFPB&CS	New Forest Pony... & Cattle Soc	
NFRC	Nat Fedn Roofing Contrs	
NFRS	Nat Fancy Rat Soc	
NFS	Nat Fedn Shopmobility	
	Nat Fedn SwimSchools	
NFSH	Nat Fedn Spiritual Healers	
NFSN	Nat Fire Sprinkler Network	
NFSP	Nat Fedn Sub-Postmasters	
NFTMMS	Nat Fedn Terrazzo, Marble & Mosaic Specialists	
NFU	Nat Farmers U	
NFUS	NFU Scotland	
NFWI	Nat Fedn Women's Insts	
NFWS	Nat Ferret Welfare Soc	
	Nat Fox Welfare Soc	
NFYFC	Nat Fedn Young Farmers Clubs (E&W)	
NGCAA	Nat Golf Clubs Advy Assn	
NGDA	Nat Game Dealers Assn	
NGLIS	Network Govt Library & Inf Specialists	
NGO	Nat Gamekeepers Org	
NGRS	Narrow Gauge Rly Soc	
NGS	Nat Gardens Scheme Charitable Trust	
	Nat Gerbil Soc	
NGSA	Nat Grammar Schools Assn	
NGVA	Natural Gas Vehicle Assn	
NH	Nat Heritage	
NHA	Nat Hop Assn England	
	Nautical Heritage Assn	
NHBS	Nat Horse Brass Soc	
NHCRA	Naval Histl Collectors & Res Assn	
NHF	Nat Hairdressers Fedn	
	Nat Housing Fedn	
	Nutrition & Health Foundation [IRE]	
NHI	Nursing Homes Ireland	
NHIC	Nat Home Improvement Coun	
NHL	Nat Harmonica League	
NHLS	Nat Hedgelaying Soc	
NHSC	Nat Historic Ships	
NHSN	Natural Hist Soc Northumbria	
NHSTA	NHS Trusts Assn	
NI	Nautical Inst	

© CBD Research Ltd · Beckenham · BR3 5JS · Tel 020 8650 7745 · E-mail cbd@cbdresearch.com · www.cbdresearch.com

NIA	Nat Insulation Assn	NPFA	Nat Playing Fields Assn
	Nuclear Ind Assn	NPHA	Nat Private Hire Assn
NIAB	NIAB	NPS	Nat Philatelic Soc
NIACE	Nat Inst Adult Continuing Educ (E&W)		Nat Piers Soc
NIACRO	NI Assn Care & Resettlement Offenders		Nat Pony Soc
NIACT	NI Assn Christian Teachers		Northumbrian Pipers' Society
NIACTA	NI Amusement Caterer's Tr Assn	NPS UK	Nail Patella Syndrome UK
NIAF	NI Athletic Fedn	NPTA	Nat Pest Technicians Assn
NIAPA	NI Agricl Producers' Assn	NPWA	Nat Pure Water Assn
NIAS	NI Archery Soc	NRA	Nat Rifle Assn
NIASP	NI Assn Study Psychoanalysis	NRAC	Nat Register Access Consultants
NIBG	NI Bat Group	NRAS	Nat Rheumatoid Arthritis Soc
NICF	Nat Inst Carpet & Floorlayers	NRHA	Nat Roller Hockey Assn
	NI Cycling Fedn	NRHP	Nat Register Hypnotherapists & Psychotherapists
NICVA	NI Coun Voluntary Action	NRPT	Nat Register Personal Trainers
NIFA	Network Indep Forensic Accountants	NRS	Navy Records Soc
NIFDA	NI Food & Drink Assn		Norfolk Record Soc
NIFGA	NI Fruit Growers Assn	NRSF	N Ronaldsay Sheep Fellowship
NIFHA	NI Fedn Housing Assns	NS	Nat Soc Painters, Sculptors & Printmakers
NIGTA	NI Grain Tr Assn	NSA	Nat Sewerage Assn
NIIRTA	NI Indep Retail Trade Assn		Nat Sheep Assn
NILGA	NI Local Govt Assn		Nat Sprint Assn
NIMBA	NI Master Butchers Assn		Noonan Syndrome Assn
NIMEA	NI Meat Exporters Assn		Nuclear Stock Assn
NIMH	Nat Inst Med Herbalists	NSALG	Nat Soc Allotment & Leisure Gardeners
NIMMA	NI Mixed Marriage Assn	NSARDA	Nat Search & Rescue Dog Assn
NIMPA	NI Master Plumbers Assn	NSBA	Nat School Band Assn
NINA	Netball NI	NSCA	Natural Sausage Casings Assn
NIPA	Nat Infrastructure Planning Assn	NSCC	Nat Specialist Contrs Coun
	NI Polymers Assn	NSCCI	N Staffs Cham Comm & Ind
NIPBA	NI Potato Breeders Assn	NSE	Nat Soc Epilepsy
NIPSA	NI Public Service Alliance	NSEAD	Nat Soc Educ in Art & Design
NIRCA	Nat Insurance Repair Contractors Assn	NSHP	Nat Soc Hypnosis & Psychotherapy
NISA	Nat Ice Skating Assn GB&NI	NSI	Nat Security Inspectorate
	NI Shows Assn	NSMT	Nat Soc Master Thatchers
	NISA Today's Holdings Ltd	NSN	New Schools Network
NISCHA	NI Self Catering Holiday Assn	NSPCC	Nat Soc Prevention Cruelty Children
NISO	Nat Ir Safety Org	NSPH	Nat Soc Profl Hypnotherapists
NIVA	NI Volleyball Assn	NSPKU	Nat Soc Phenylketonuria
NIWAF	NI Women's Aid Fedn	NSPP	Nat Soc Promotion Punctuality
NJF	Nat Jumblers Fedn	NSPS	Nat Sweet Pea Soc
NJUG	Nat Jt Utilities Gp	NSRA	Nat Small-bore Rifle Assn
NKA	Nat Karting Assn		Nat Soc Res Allergy
NLA	Nat Landlords Assn	NSS	Nat Secular Soc
	Nat Literacy Assn	NSSF	Nat Small Schools Forum
NLCA	Nat Limousine & Chauffeur Assn	NSVA	Nat Street Van Assn
NLHA	Nottinghamshire Local Hist Assn	NTA	Nat Taxi Assn
NMC	Nat Motorcycle Coun		Nat Trolleybus Assn
	Nat Mouse Club	NTDA	Nat Tyre Distbrs Assn
NMES	Northern Mill Engine Soc	NTF	Nat Trainers Fedn
NMI	Nat Microelectronics Inst	NTS	Nat Trust Scotland
NMMA	Nat Mining Memorabilia Assn	NTTA	Nat Trailer & Towing Assn
NMRS	Northern Mine Res Soc	NUJ	Nat U Journalists
NMTF	Nat Market Traders Fedn	NUMA	Needleloom Underlay Mfrs Assn
NNAC	Nat Network Assessment Centres	NURA	Nat U Residents' Assns
NNAS	Norfolk & Norwich Archaeol Soc	NUS	Nat U Students
NNI	Nat Newspapers Ireland	NUT	Nat U Teachers
NNS	Neonatal Soc	NUTFA	New Under Ten Fishermen's Assn
NO2ID	NO2ID	NVS	Nat Vegetable Soc
NOA	Nat Outsourcing Assn	NVTEC	Nat Vintage Tractor & Engine Club
NOAH	Nat Office Animal Health	NWA	Nat Workboat Assn
NOBs	Nat Org Beaters & Pickers Up	NWLCC	N W Lond Cham Comm
NODA	Nat Operatic & Dramatic Assn		N & Wstn Lancs Cham Comm
NOEA	Nat Outdoor Events Assn	NWR	Nat Women's Register
NOF	Nat Obesity Forum	NWT	Norfolk Wildlife Trust
NOF Energy	NOF Energy	NWTTA	N W Timber Tr Assn
NORCAP	Adults affected Adoption	NYCGB	Nat Youth Choirs GB
NOS	Nat Osteoporosis Soc	NYCI	Nat Youth Coun Ireland
NOTA	Nat Org Treatment of Abusers	NYMR	N York Moors Hist Rly Trust
NPA	Nat Pawnbrokers Assn		
	Nat Pharmacy Assn		
	Nat Pig Assn		
	Nat Pigeon Assn		
	Nat Portage Assn		
	Nat Portraiture Assn		
	Natural Physique Assn		
	Newspaper Pubrs Assn		
NPC	Nat Pensioners Convention		

O

OA	Officers' Assn
	Overeaters Anonymous

© CBD Research Ltd · Beckenham · BR3 5JS · Tel 020 8650 7745 · E-mail cbd@cbdresearch.com · www.cbdresearch.com

OAA	Obstetric Anaesthetists Assn
	Outdoor Advertising Assn
OAHS	Oxfordshire Architectural & Hist Soc
OAS	Office Agents Soc
OATA	Ornamental Aquatic Tr Assn
OBCofGB	Old Bottle Club
OCA	Offshore Contrs' Assn
	Open Canoe Assn
OCCA	Oil & Colour Chemists Assn
OCS	Oriental Ceramic Soc
OCSG	Open Canoe Sailing Gp
ODA	Offa's Dyke Assn
ODSBA	Oxford Down Sheep Breeders Assn
OEMSA	Optical Eqpt Mfrs & Suppliers Assn
OES	Offshore Engg Soc
OEUK	Optra Exhibitions UK
OFF	Organic Food Fedn
OFIMA	Optical Frame Importers' & Mfrs' Assn
OFTEC	Oil Firing Technical Assn Petroleum Ind
OIA	Outdoor Inds Assn
OILC	Offshore Ind Liaison C'ee
OLMADA	Ophthalmic Lens Mfrs', Assemblers' & Distrbrs' Assn
OLS	Ocean Liner Soc
OMRS	Orders & Medals Res Soc
OPA	Occupational Pensioners Alliance
OPFS	One Parent Families Scotland
OPKA	Original Pearly Kings & Queens Assn
OPMA	Overseas Press & Media Assn
OPSCS	Observers Pocket Series Collectors' Soc
OPTIC (UK)	Ophthalmological Products Tr. . .Conf
ORA	Oil Recycling Assn
ORS	Oxfordshire Record Soc
ORSoc	Operational Res Soc
OS	Omnibus Soc
	Ordnance Soc
OSB	Oxford Sandy & Black Pig Soc
OSCA	Onsite Communications Assn
	Osteopathic Sports Care Assn
OSGB	Orchid Soc
OSMA	On Site Massage Assn
OSME	Ornithological Soc Middle East
OSS	Outdoor Swimming Soc
OTA	Offenders Tag Assn
	Orthodontic Technicians Assn
OUAS	Oxford University Archaeol Soc
OVW	One Voice Wales
OWC	Order Woodcraft Chivalry
OWG	Outdoor Writers' & Photographers' Gld
OWS	Oscar Wilde Soc

P

P&SS	Pike & Shot Soc
P(UK)	Ponies Assn
PA	Protestant Alliance
	Publishers Assn
PAA	Paper Agents Assn
	Profl Anglers Assn
PAAT	Profl Assn Alexander Teachers
PACE	Profl Assn Catering Educ
PACT	Prison Advice & Care Trust
	Producers Alliance Cinema & TV
PADS	People & Dogs Soc
PAFA	Packaging & Films Assn
PAGB	Photographic Alliance
	Proprietary Assn
PALS	Profl Assn Legal Services
PalSoc	Palaeontographical Soc
PAN UK	Pesticide Action Network
PAPA	Pizza, Pasta & Italian Food Assn
PAPAA	Psoriasis & Psoriatic Arthritis Alliance
PARN	Profl Assns Res Network
PAS	Peeblesshire Archaeol Soc
	Pembrokeshire Agricl Soc

	Percussive Arts Soc
	Perthshire Agricl Soc
PASM	Proprietary Acoustic Systems Mfrs
PASMA	Prefabricated Access Suppliers' & Mfrs' Assn
Path Society	Pathological Soc
PBA	Passenger Boat Assn
	Profl Bodyguard Assn
PBFA	Provincial Booksellers Fairs Assn
PBGA	Pre Basic Growers Assn
PBS	Prayer Book Soc
PBSA	Pony Breeders Shetland Assn
PBTM	Fac Profl Business & Technical Mgt
PcA	Permaculture Assn
PCA	Profl Charter Assn
	Profl Cricketers Assn
	Property Care Assn
PCAM	Soc Producers & Composers Applied Music
PCC	Paperweight Collectors Circle
	Perthshire Cham Comm
PCCGB	Photographic Collectors' Club
PCCI	Plymouth Cham Comm & Ind
PCDS	Primary Care Dermatology Soc
PCFA	Profl Coarse Fisheries Assn
PCG	Profl Contrs Gp
PCGB	Poultry Club
PCS	Penguin Collectors' Soc
	Property Consultants Soc
	Public & Comml Services U
PCSF	Prostate Cancer Support Fedn
PCTA	Pet Care Tr Assn
PDA	Profl Drivers Assn
	Pump Distbrs Assn
PDMHS	Peak District Mines Hist Soc
PDPA	Profl Darts Players Assn
PDS	Parkinson's Disease Soc
PDSG	Pick's Disease Support Gp
PEAI	Physical Educ Assn Ireland
PEBA	Planning & Environment Bar Assn
PEC	Plain Engl Campaign
PELS	Locomotive 6201 Princess Elizabeth Soc
PEPA	Property & Energy Professionals Assn
PESGB	Petroleum Exploration Soc
PETMA	Portable Electric Tool Mfrs Assn
PETS	Pre Eclampsia Soc
PF	Packaging Fedn
	Pagan Fedn
PFA	Power Fastenings Assn
	Profl Footballers Assn
PFA Scotland	Profl Footballers Assn Scotland
PFAA	Paediatric First Aid Assn
PFEW	Police Fedn England & Wales
PFMA	Pet Food Mfrs Assn
PFNI	Police Fedn NI
PFPF	Passive Fire Protection Fedn
PFRA	Public Fundraising Regulatory Assn
PFS	Palmerston Forts Soc
	Personal Finance Soc
PFSS	Pet Fostering Service Scotland
PGA	Prison Governors Assn
	Profl Golfers Assn
PGDT	Pressure Gauge & Dial Thermometer Assn
PGG	Profl Gardeners' Gld
PGRO	Processors & Growers Res Org
PGS	Percy Grainger Society
PHA	Pullet Hatcheries Assn
	Pulmonary Hypertension Assn
PHC	Pet Health Coun
PHS	Pembrokeshire Histl Soc
PhS	Philosophical Soc England
PHS	Plastics Histl Soc
	Police Hist Soc
	Postal Hist Soc
	Printing Histl Soc
PHSA	Provincial Hospital Services Assn
PHSI	Presbyterian Hist Soc Ireland
PHSS	Pharmaceutical & Healthcare Sciences Soc
PiA	Primary Immunodeficiency Assn
PIBA	Personal Injuries Bar Assn

PIC	Photo Imaging Coun
PICA GB	Police Insignia Collectors Assn
PICON	Picon Ltd
PiF	Patient Inf Forum
PIG	Pipeline Inds Gld
PIPA	Pharmaceutical Inf & Pharmacovigilance Assn
Pipedown	Campaign Freedom Piped Music
PISUKI	Pacific Islands Soc
PITA	Paper Ind Technical Assn
PJA	Pipe Jacking Assn
	Profl Jockeys Assn
PKA	Parakart Assn
PKDA	Profl Koi Dealers Assn
PLA	Private Libraries Assn
PLASA	Profl Lighting & Sound Assn
PLS	Philip Larkin Soc
	Publishers Licensing Soc
PLTA	Past Life Therapists Assn
Plus	Nat Fedn Plus Areas
PMA	Personal Mgrs Assn
	Probation Mgrs Assn
	Property Mgrs Assn
PMC	Printmakers Coun
PMI	Pensions Mgt Inst
PMMDA	Polymer Machinery Mfrs & Distbrs Assn
PMMMA	Pattern Model & Mouldmakers Assn
PMMS	Plainsong & Mediæval Music Soc
PMNHS	Porcupine Marine Natural Hist Soc
PMPA	Public Mgt & Policy Assn
PMSA	Public Monuments & Sculpture Assn
PNFS	Peak & Nthn Footpaths Soc
POA	Pinball Owners Assn
	POA
POCLA	Proceeds Crime Lawyers Assn
Pony Club	Pony Club
POVC	Post Office Vehicle Club
PPA	Periodical Pubrs Assn
	Play Providers Assn
	Potato Processors Assn
PPF	Profl Players Fedn
PPG	Player Piano Gp
PPI	Phonographic Performance (Ireland)
PPL	Phonographic Performance
PPMA	Processing & Packaging Machinery Assn
	Public Sector People Mgrs' Assn
PPORA	Point-to-Point Owners & Riders Assn
PPRA	Pet Product Retail Assn
PPS	Psychologists Protection Soc
PPSA	Pigging Products & Services Assn
PPU	Peace Pledge U
PPUG	Profl Plant Users Gp
PRA	Paint Res Assn
	Picture Res Assn
	Pony Riders Assn
	Psychiatric Rehabilitation Assn
	Pullet Rearers Assn
PRCA	Public Relations Consultants Assn
	Public Relations Consultants Assn [IRL]
PRESSBOF	Press Standards Bd Finance
PRFSS	Peterborough R Foxhound Show Soc
PRII	Public Relations Inst Ireland
PRS	Pre-Raphaelite Soc
	Protestant Reformation Soc
PS	Poetry Soc
PSA	Political Studies Assn
	Production Services Assn
	Profl Speakers Assn
PSANI	Superintendents' Assn NI
PSBG	Portland Sheep Breeders Gp
PSG	Pillbox Study Gp
PSGB	Primate Soc
PSI	Statisticians Pharmaceutical Ind
PSNI	Pharmaceutical Soc NI
PSNS	Perthshire Soc Natural Science
PSPA	Photoluminescent Safety Products Assn
PSPS	Paddle Steamer Presvn Soc
PSS	Partially Sighted Soc

PTA	Pianoforte Tuners' Assn
	Post Tensioning Assn
	Postcard Traders' Assn
PTA/MUTA	Performance Textiles Assn
PTF	Provision Tr Fedn
PTG	Ports & Terminals Gp
PTS	Pali Text Soc
	Philatelic Traders Soc
	Protestant Truth Soc
PUMPA	Purine Metabolic Patients Assn
PWF	Private Wagon Fedn
PWI	Permanent Way Instn
PWSA (UK)	Prader-Willi Syndrome Assn

Q

QBC	Quality Brit Celery Assn
QCA	Quoted Companies Alliance
QES	Queen's Engl Soc
QG	Quality Gld
QMC	Quekett Microscopical Club
QMS	Quality Meat Scotland
QNI	Queen's Nursing Inst
QRA UK	Quad Racing Assn
Quakers	Religious Society of Friends (Quakers)
QuiTE	Assn Promotion Quality TESOL Educ

R

R&A	R & Ancient Golf Club
R&CHS	Rly & Canal Histl Soc
R&D	Res & Devt Soc
R&RA	Relatives & Residents Assn
R3	Assn Business Recovery Profls
RA	R Academy Arts
	Radionic Assn Ltd
	Ramblers' Assn
	Retreat Assn
	Rice Assn
RABDF	R Assn Brit Dairy Farmers
RAD	R Academy Dance
	R Assn Deaf People
RADA	R Academy Dramatic Art
RADAR	R Assn Disability & Rehabilitation
Radius	Religious Drama Soc
RAEng	R Academy Engg
RAeS	R Aeronautical Soc
RAFA	R Air Forces Assn
RAFHS	R Air Force Histl Soc
RAFT	River Assn Freight & Transport
RAI	R Anthropological Inst
	R Archaeol Inst
RAM	R Academy Music
RAMI	R Academy Medicine Ireland
RAS	R Asiatic Soc
	R Astronomical Soc
RASC	R Agricl Soc C'wealth
RASE	R Agricl Soc England
RATD	Register Apparel & Textile Designers
RBA	Refined Bitumen Assn
	Retail Book, Stationery... Employees Assn
	Retail Bridalwear Assn
RBCC	Russo-Brit Cham Comm
RBLS	R Brit Legion Scotland
RBOA	Residential Boat Owners Assn
RBS	R Botanical & Hortl Soc Manchester
	R Brit Soc Sculptors
RBSA	R Birmingham Soc Artists
RBST	Rare Breeds Survival Trust
RCA	R Cambrian Academy Art
	Racecourse Assn
	Rural Crafts Assn
RCAA	R Cornwall Agricl Assn

© CBD Research Ltd · Beckenham · BR3 5JS · Tel 020 8650 7745 · E-mail cbd@cbdresearch.com · www.cbdresearch.com

RCCC	R Caledonian Curling Club
RCCGB	Roller Coaster Club
RCGP	R Coll Gen Practitioners
RCHM	Register Chinese Herbal Medicine
RCHS	R Caledonian Horticl Soc
RCM	R Coll Midwives
RCN	R Coll Nursing
RCO	R Coll Organists
RCOG	R Coll Obstetricians & Gynaecologists
RCP	R Coll Physicians Lond
RCPath	R Coll Pathologists
RCPCH	R Coll Paediatrics & Child Health
RCPE	R Coll Physicians Edinburgh
RCPSGlasg	R Coll Physicians & Surgeons Glasgow
RCPsych	R Coll Psychiatrists
RCS	R Choral Soc
	R Coll Surgeons England
RCSEd	R Coll Surgeons Edinburgh
RCSI	R Coll Surgeons Ireland
RCSLT	R Coll Speech & Language Therapists
RCTA	Retail Confectioners & Tobacconists Assn
RCTS	Rly Correspondence & Travel Soc
RCVS	R Coll Veterinary Surgeons
RDS	R Dublin Soc
	Rly Devt Soc
RDUK	Rare Disease
RE	R Soc Painter Printmakers
REA	Renewable Energy Assn
	Rhea & Emu Assn
REACH	REACH
REAL	Road Emulsion Assn
REC	Recruitment & Employment Confedn
RedR	RedR UK
Regia	Regia Anglorum
REHIS	R Envtl Health Inst Scotland
REMA	BEAMA
	Retroreflective Eqpt Mfrs Assn
REntSoc	R Entomological Soc Lond
REPTA	Reptile & Exotic Pet Tr Assn
RES	R Economic Soc
RETRA	Radio, Electrical & TV Retailers' Assn
RFA	Rugby Fives Assn
RFBS	Ryeland Flock Book Soc
RFG	Rail Freight Gp
RFL	Rugby Football League
RFPG	R Fac Procurators in Glasgow
RFS	R Forestry Soc England, Wales & NI
	Robert Farnon Soc
RFSBA	Rough Fell Sheep Breeders Assn
RFU	Rugby Football U
RGA	Remote Gambling Assn
	Restricted Growth Assn
RGDATA	RGDATA [IRL]
RGI	R Glasgow Inst Fine Arts
RGS-IBG	R Geographical Soc
RHA	Road Haulage Assn
RHASS	R Highland & Agricl Soc Scotland
RHET	R Highland Educ Trust
RHistS	R Histl Soc
RHS	R Horticl Soc
	R Humane Soc
	Rider Haggard Soc
RHSI	R Horticl Soc Ireland
RI	R Instn GB
RIA	R Ir Academy
	Rly Ind Assn
	Roofing Ind Alliance
RIAC	R Ir Automobile Club
RIAI	R Inst Architects Ireland
RIAM	R Ir Academy Music
RIAS	R Incorporation Architects Scotland
RIBA	R Inst Brit Architects
RIC	R Instn Cornwall
RICA	Rail Ind Contrs Assn
RICS	R Instn Chart Surveyors
RIDBA	Rural & Indl Design & Bldg Assn
RIG	Remote Imaging Group
RIIA	R Inst Intl Affairs

RIN	R Inst Navigation
RINA	R Instn Naval Architects
RIPTA	Register Indep Profl Turfgrass Agronomists
RISW	R Instn S Wales
RIWAS	R Isle of Wight Agrl Soc
RJA&HS	R Jersey Agricl & Horticl Soc
RLAS	R Lancashire Agricl Soc
RLS	Road Locomotive Soc
RLS Club	Robert Louis Stevenson Club
RLSS UK	R Life Saving Soc
RLUK	RLUK
RMA	R Musical Assn
	Retread Mfrs Assn
RMCU	R Martyr Church U
RMetS	R Meteorological Soc
RMI	Retail Motor Ind Fedn
RMOOA	Routemaster Operators & Owners Assn
RMS	R Medical Soc
	R Microscopical Soc
	R Soc Miniature Painters…
RMT	Nat U Rail Maritime & Transport Workers
RNA	R Naval Assn
	Romantic Novelists Assn
RNAA	R Norfolk Agricl Assn
RNAS	R Nthn Agricl Soc
RNBWS	R Naval Bird Watching Soc
RNES	R Navy Enthusiasts' Soc
RNHA	Registered Nursing Home Assn
RNIB	R Nat Inst Blind People
RNID	RNID
RNLI	R Nat Lifeboat Instn
RNPAI	Regional Newspapers… Assn Ireland
RNRS	R Nat Rose Soc
RNS	R Numismatic Soc
ROA	Racehorse Owners Assn
ROOM	ROOM RTPI
ROSECARPE	N England Rosecarpe Horticl Soc
ROSL	R Over-Seas League
RoSPA	R Soc Prevention Accidents
ROW	Rights of Women
RPA	Rationalist Assn
	Rugby Players Assn
RPAS	Restaurant Property Advisors Soc
RPRA	R Pigeon Racing Assn
RPS	R Philharmonic Soc
	R Photographic Soc
	Rare Poultry Soc
RPSG	R Philosophical Soc Glasgow
RPSGB	R Pharmaceutical Soc
RPSI	Rly Presvn Soc Ireland
RPSL	R Philatelic Soc Lond
RR	Rly Ramblers
RRA	Road Records Association
	Road Roller Assn
RRC	Road Runners Club
RRRA	Road Rescue Recovery Assn
RRTHA	Roads & Road Transport Hist Assn
RSA	R Scot Academy
	R Soc … Arts
	Refined Sugar Assn
	Regional Studies Assn
	Residential Sprinkler Assn
	Rett Syndrome Assn
	Rly Study Assn
	Rural Shops Alliance
RSAI	R Soc Antiquaries Ireland
RSAMD	R Scot Academy Music & Drama
RSAS	R Surgical Aid Soc
RSAW	R Soc Architects Wales
RSC	R Smithfield Club
	R Soc Chemistry
RSCDS	R Scot Country Dance Soc
RSCM	R School Church Music
RSCTA	Rough & Smooth Collie Training Assn
RSE	R Soc Edinburgh
RSFS	R Scot Forestry Soc
RSGB	Radio Soc GB
	Road Safety GB

RSGS	R Scot Geographical Soc	SAGB	Shellfish Assn
RSL	R Soc Literature		Silk Assn
RSM	R Soc Medicine		Skibob Assn
	R Soc Musicians		Spiritualist Assn
RSMA	Road Safety Markings Assn	SAGBNI	Sportsman's Assn
RSMG	Rubber Stamp Mfrs' Gld	SAGGA	Scout & Guide Graduate Assn
RSPB	R Soc Protection Birds	SAGSET	Soc Advancement Games & Simulations Educ &
RSPBA	R Scot Pipe Band Assn		Training
RSPCA	R Soc Prevention Cruelty Animals	SAGT	Scot Assn Geography Teachers
RSPH	R Soc Public Health	SAGTA	Soil & Groundwater Technology Assn
RSPSoc	Remote Sensing & Photogrammetry Soc	SAH	Soc Automotive Historians
RSS	R Statistical Soc	SAHAAS	Saint Albans & Hertfordshire Architectural. . .Soc
	Robert Simpson Soc	SAHGB	Soc Architectural Historians
	Ronald Stevenson Soc	SAHR	Soc Army Histl Res
RSSA	R Scot Soc Arts	SAHS	Shropshire Archaeol & Histl Soc
RSSS	R S Surtees Soc		Staffordshire Archaeol. . .Soc
RSTA	Road Surface Treatments Assn	SAI	Soc Architectural Illustration
RSTM&H	R Soc Tropical Medicine & Hygiene	SAIF	Nat Soc Allied & Indep Funeral Directors
RSUA	R Soc Ulster Architects	SALC	Scot Assn Law Centres
RSW	R Scot Soc Painters in Water Colours	SALSC	Scot Assn Local Sports Couns
RSWT	R Soc Wildlife Trusts	SAM	Scot Assn Metals
RTA	Rural Theology Assn		Soc Acute Medicine
RTA Ltd	Racehorse Transporters Assn	SAMA	Scot Amat Music Assn
RTBI	Nat Assn Round Tables	SAMB	Scot Assn Master Bakers
RTCS	Round Tower Churches Soc	SAME	Scot Assn Music Educ
RTPI	R Town Planning Inst	SAMH	Scot Assn Mental Health
RTS	R Television Soc	SAMM	Support Murder Manslaughter
	River Thames Soc	SAMS	Scot Assn Marine Science
RUA	Arts Soc Ulster	SAMSA	Mineral Products Assn
	Road Users Alliance	SAMW	Scot Assn Meat Whlsrs
RUAS	R Ulster Agricl Soc	SANA	Scot Anglers Nat Assn
RUF	Refractory Users Federation	SANDS	Stillbirth & Neonatal Death Soc
RUI	Resource Use Inst	SANE	SANE
RUKBA	R UK Beneficent Assn	SANHS	Somerset Archaeol & Natural Hist Soc
RURAL	Soc Responsible Use Resources Agriculture. . .	SANT	Soc Antiquaries Newcastle upon Tyne
RUSI	R Utd Services Inst Defence. . . Studies	SAOL	Sugar Assn Lond
RVA	Residential Ventilation Assn	SAOS	Scot Agricl Org Soc
RWA	Rabbit Welfare Assn	SAP	Soc Applied Philosophy
	Race Walking Assn	SAPCA	Sports & Play Construction Assn
RWAS	R Welsh Agricl Soc	SAPCT	Scot Assn Painting Craft Teachers
RWS	R Watercolour Soc	SAPERE	SAPERE
RYA	R Yachting Assn	SAPT	Scot Assn Public Transport
RYAS	R Yachting Assn Scotland	SARPA	Scot Air Rifle & Pistol Assn
RZSS	R Zoological Soc Scotland	SARS	Soc Academic & Res Surgery
		SAS	Surfers against Sewage
		SASA	Scot Amat Swimming Assn
		SASDA	Scot Assn Speech & Drama Adjudicators
		SASH	Scot Assn Spiritual Healers
		SASLI	Scot Assn Sign Language Interpreters
		SASO	Scot Assn Study Offending
		SASS	Sir Arthur Sullivan Soc
		SATA	Sleep Apnoea Trust Assn
		SATH	Scot Assn Teachers History
		SATIPS	SATIPS
		SAUK	Scoliosis Assn
		SAVE	Save Britain's Heritage
		SAYFC	Scot Assn Young Farmers Clubs
		SBA	Sailing Barge Assn
			Scot Beekeepers Assn
			Soc Botanical Artists
			Steam Boat Assn
		SBAS	Staffordshire & Birmingham Agricl Soc

S

S&TA	Salmon & Trout Assn	SBBA	Scot Brass Band Assn
S2C2	Scot Soc Contamination Control	SBC	Scot Business Community
SA	Salt Assn	SBCA	Scot Bldg Contrs Assn
	Schoolwear Assn	SBE	Soc Business Economists
	Sexaholics Anonymous	SBGAS	Sabine Baring-Gould Appreciation Soc
SAA	Scot Aeromodellers Assn	SBGI	SBGI
	Scot Archery Assn	SBHS	Strict Baptist Histl Soc
	Scot Assessors Assn	SBNS	Soc Brit Neurological Surgeons
	Soc Archer Antiquaries	SBP	Soc Business Practitioners
	Soc Artists' Agents	SBPA	Scot Beer & Pub Assn
	Sub Aqua Assn	SBS	Songbird Survival
	Suffolk Agricl Assn	SBTD	Soc Brit Theatre Designers
SAAD	Soc Advancement Anaesthesia Dentistry	SBU	Scot Badminton U
SAAVA	Scot Agricl Arbiters & Valuers Assn	SBWWI	Soc Brit Water & Wastewater Inds
SABRITA	Brit Cham Business Sthn Africa	SC	Scot Cycling
SACGB	Shark Angling Club		
SACH	Scot Assn Community Hospitals		
SACS	Scot Assn Country Sports		
SACU	Scot Auto Cycle U		
	Soc Anglo-Chinese Understanding		
SADA	SAD Assn		
SAEMA	Specialist Access Engg & Maintenance Assn		
SAFA	Scot Amat Football Assn		
SAFE	SAFE		
SAFEA	Sports & Fitness Eqpt Assn		
SAFed	Safety Assessment Fedn		
SAFHS	Scot Assn Family Hist Socs		

© CBD Research Ltd · Beckenham · BR3 5JS · Tel 020 8650 7745 · E-mail cbd@cbdresearch.com · www.cbdresearch.com

SCA	Scot Canoe Assn
	Scot Croquet Assn
	Smoke Control Assn
	Social Care Assn
	Specialist Cheesemakers Assn
	Sprayed Concrete Assn
SCAG	Gld Stunt & Action Coordinators
SCALA	Scala
SCAS	Soc Companion Animal Studies
	Surrey County Agricl Soc
SCATA	Soc Computing & Technology Anaesthesia
SCB	Speedway Control Bd
SCBA	Shetland Cattle Breeders' Assn
SCC	Small Charities Coalition
	Soc Cheese Connoisseurs
	Solihull Cham Comm
SCCCI	S Cheshire Cham Comm & Ind
SCCI	Sheffield Cham Comm & Ind
SCDA	Scot Community Drama Assn
SCDI	Scot Coun Devt & Ind
SCEME	Soc Electrical &... Engrs Local Government
SCF	Scot Crofting Fedn
SCGB	Satellite & Cable Broadcasters' Gp
SCHA	Scot Catholic Histl Assn
SCHHA	Southern Counties Heavy Horse Assn
SCHHC	Soc Coat Hook & Hanger Collectors
SCHS	Scot Church Hist Soc
SCHVPT	Southern Counties Historic Vehicle Presvn Trust
SCI	Soc Chemical Ind
	Steel Construction Inst
SCL	Soc Chief Librarians
	Soc Computers & Law
	Soc Construction Law
SCLF	Scot Contaminated Land Forum
SCMA	Scot Childminding Assn
	Stilton Cheese Makers Assn
SCNP	Scot Campaign Nat Parks
SCOD	Scot Coun Deafness
SCoFF	Southern Counties Folk Fedn
SCOLAG	Scot Legal Action Gp
SCONUL	Soc College Nat & University Libraries
ScOPT	Scot Org Practice Teaching
ScotSAC	Scot Sub Aqua Club
SCOTSS	Soc Chief Officers Trading Standards Scotland
ScottishSPCA	Scot Soc Prevention Cruelty Animals
ScotWays	Scot Rights Way & Access Soc
SCP	Soc Chiropodists & Podiatrists
	Soc Clinical Psychiatrists
SCPC	Soc Crisp Packet Collectors
SCQS	Soc Construction & Quantity Surveyors
SCRA	Scot Countryside Rangers' Assn
SCREAMS	Soc Campaigning Removal Exasperating Automated Switchboards
SCRSS	Soc Cooperation Russian & Soviet Studies
SCS	Salonika Campaign Soc
	Seal Consvn Soc
	Soc Cosmetic Scientists
	UK Soc Co-operative Studies
SCSH	Scot Coun Single Homeless
SCST	Soc Cardiological Science & Technology
SCT	Soc County Treasurers [E&W]
SCTA	Scot Clay Target Assn
	Scot Corn Tr Assn
SCTE	SCTE
SCTS	Soc Cardiothoracic Surgery
SCVO	Scot Coun Voluntary Orgs
SDA	Scot Darts Assn
	Scurry Driving Assn
SDC	Soc Designer Craftsmen
	Soc Dyers & Colourists
SDCC	S Devon Cham Comm
SDCCGB	Square Dance Callers Club
SDEA	Shop & Display Eqpt Assn
SDF	Scot Decorators Fedn
SDHBS	S Devon Herd Book Soc
SDMA	Surgical Dressings Mfrs Assn
SDR	Soc Dance Res

SDS	S Downs Soc
	Scot Disability Sport
SDT	Soc Dairy Technology
SDTA	Scot Dance Teachers Alliance
SEA	Scot Esperanto Assn
	Soc Equestrian Artists
	Specialist Engg Alliance
	Surface Engg Assn
SEAL	Soc Economic Analysis
SEAMA	Small Electrical Appliance Marketing Assn
SEAS	S England Agricl Soc
SEB	Soc Experimental Biology
SEBDA	SEBDA
SEC	Soc Educ Consultants
SEC group	Specialist Engg Contrs Gp
SECED	Soc Earthquake & Civil Engg Dynamics
SEDA	Scot Ecological Design Assn
	Staff & Educl Devt Assn
SEE	Soc Envtl Engrs
SEMA	Storage Eqpt Mfrs Assn
SEMPRE	Soc Educ Music & Psychology Res
SEPRA	Scot Egg Producer Retailers Assn
SERA	Scot Educl Res Assn
	Socialist Envt & Resources Assn
SES	Scientific Exploration Soc
	Scot Economic Soc
SESA	Scot Envtl Services Assn
SEW	Soc Expert Witnesses
SFA	Scot Football Assn
	Small Farms Assn
	Small Firms Assn [IRL]
	Solid Fuel Assn
SFAA	Scot Field Archery Assn
Sfam	Soc Applied Microbiology
SFC	Sexual Freedom Coalition
SFCA	Scot Fedn Coarse Angling
SFDF	Scot Food & Drink Fedn
SfEP	Soc Editors & Proofreaders
SFF	Scot Fishermen's Fedn
SFG	Scot Freshwater Gp
SFGB	Stone Fedn
SFHA	Scot Fedn Housing Assns
SFL	Scot Football League
SFMTA	Scot Fedn Meat Traders Assns
SFO	Scot Fishermen's Org
SfP	Sing for Pleasure
SFRMA	Synthetic Fibre Rug, Mat & Carpet Association
SFS	Soc French Studies
SfS	Soc Storytelling
SFSA	Scot Fedn Sea Anglers
SFT	Soc Feed Technologists
SFTA	Scot Food Trs Assn
SFTAH	Autism Indep UK
SGA	Scot Gamekeepers Assn
	Scot Gymnastics Assn
SGD	Soc Garden Designers
SGF	Scot Grocers Fedn
SGFA	Soc Graphic Fine Art
SGIA	Sporting Goods Ind Assn
SGM	Soc Gen Microbiology
SGPP	Soc Garlic Growers, Processors...[dummy]
SGR	Scientists Global Responsibility
SGT	Soc Glass Technology
SGTS	Scot Gaelic Texts Soc
SGU	Scot Gliding U
	Scot Golf U
SGVCC	Soc Greeting Card Collectors
SHA	Scot Handball Assn
	Soc Heraldic Arts
	Socialist Health Assn
SHAC	Soc Hist Alchemy & Chemistry
SHAPA	Solids Handling & Processing Assn
SHB(GB)	Sport Horse Breeding
SHCG	Social Hist Curators Gp
SHEDA	Storage & Handling Eqpt Distbrs Assn
SHGA	Scot Highland Games Assn
Shine	Shine [IRL]
SHIP	Safe Home Income Plans

SHLSLM	Soc Hospital Linen Service & Laundry Mgrs
SHMIS	Soc Heads Indep Schools
SHNH	Soc Hist Natural Hist
SHPF	Scot Hang Gliding & Paragliding Fedn
SHS	Scot Hist Soc
	Shire Horse Soc
	Social Hist Soc
SHU	Scot Hockey U
	Scot Homing U
SI	Soc Indexers
SIA	Solvents Ind Assn
	Spinal Injuries Assn
	Stove Ind Alliance
	Suffolk Inst Archaeology & Hist
SIAA	Scot Indep Advocacy Alliance
SIAS	Sussex Indl Archaeol Soc
SIBA	Scot Indoor Bowling Assn
	Soc Indep Brewers
SICS	Scot Intensive Care Soc
SIESO	Soc Indl Emergency Service Officers
SIF	Soc Individual Freedom
SIFD	Soc Intl Folk Dancing
SIGB	Snowsport Inds
SIH	Soc Italic Handwriting
SIHS	Scot Indl Heritage Soc
SII	Security Inst Ireland
SILA	Sarcoidosis & Interstitial Lung Assn
SIMI	Soc Ir Motor Ind
SIPA UK	Specialised Inf Publishers Assn
SIPTU	SIPTU [IRL]
SIRP	Soc Indep Roundabout Proprietors
SIS	Scientific Instrument Soc
	Spinal Injuries Scotland
SITA	Scuba Inds Tr Assn
SIWA	Scot Inland Waterways Assn
SJA	School Journey Assn
	Scot Justices Assn
	Sports Journalists' Assn GB
SJH	Soc Jewellery Historians
SJJA	Scot Ju-Jitsu Assn
SK	Sealed Knot
SK-S	Sheila Kaye-Smith Soc
SKC	Scot Kennel Club
SKCM	Soc King Charles Martyr
SKLR	Sittingbourne & Kemsley Light Rly
SLA	School Library Assn
	Scot Lettercutters Assn
SLAD	Soc Lond Art Dealers
SLAS	Scot Law Agents Soc
SLCC	Soc Local Coun Clerks
SLD	Scot Language Dictionaries
SLEAT	Soc Laundry Engrs & Allied Trs
SLGA	Scot Ladies' Golfing Assn
SLHA	Soc Lincolnshire Hist & Archaeology
SLm	Soc Limners
SLMA	Steel Lintel Mfrs Assn
SLMG	Shetland Livestock Marketing Gp
SLS	School Leaders Scotland
	Scots Language Soc
	Soc Landscape Studies
	Soc Legal Scholars
	Stephenson Locomotive Soc
SLSA	Socio-Legal Studies Assn
SLSGB	Surf Life Saving GB
SLTA	Scot Licensed Tr Assn
SLTC	Soc Leather Technologists & Chemists
SM&EE	Soc Model & Experimental Engrs
SMA	Catholic Med Assn
	Schools Music Assn
	Soc Medieval Archaeology
	Soc Museum Archaeologists
	Soc Music Analysis
	Sports Massage Assn
	Stage Mgt Assn
SMAE	SMAE Fellowship
SMDSA	Sanitary Med Disposal Services Assn
SMH&VTS	Scot Music Hall & Variety Theatre Soc
SMIA	Scot Music Ind Assn

SMIRA	Selective Mutism Inf & Res Assn
SMMT	Soc Motor Mfrs & Traders
SMR	Soc Medicines Res
SMRC	Scot Motor Racing Club
SMS	Soc Model Shipwrights
SMS/SPS	Stiff Man Syndrome Support Gp
SMSC	Soc Model Sheep Collectors
SMSRTA	Scot Master Slaters & Roof Tilers Assn
SMTA	Scot Motor Tr Assn
	Sewing Machine Tr Assn
SMTO	Scot Massage Therapists Org
SMWBA	Scot Master Wrights & Builders Assn
SMWS	Scotch Malt Whisky Soc
SNACMA	Snack, Nut & Crisp Mfrs Assn
SNFWB	Scot Nat Fedn Welfare Blind
SNG	Scot Neuroscience Gp
SNIPEF	Scot & NI Plumbing Emplrs' Fedn
SNN	Soc Nursery Nursing Practitioners
SNR	Soc Nautical Res
SNS	Scot Newspaper Soc
SNSBI	Soc Name Studies Britain & Ireland
SNSC	Snowsport Scotland
SNU	Spiritualists Nat U
SOA	Scot Optoelectronics Assn
	Scot Orienteering Assn
	Soc Ancients
SoA	Soc Authors
SOARS	Soc Old Age Rational Suicide
SOB	Soc Bookbinders
SOBAUK	Soc Bariatric Anaesthetists
SoBS	Save our Bldg Socs
SOC	Scot Ornithologists Club
	Soc Olympic Collectors
SocEnv	Soc Envt
SOCITM	Soc Inf Technology Mgt
SODAC	Soc Decorative Art Curators
SOE	Soc Operations Engrs
SOEC	Scot Envtl & Outdoor Educ Centres Assn
SoF	Sea Faith Network (UK)
SOFAA	Soc Fine Art Auctioneers & Valuers
SOFHT	Soc Food Hygiene & Technology
SofM	Soc Metaphysicians
SoG	Soc Genealogists
SOHDA	Scot Official Highland Dancing Assn
SOL	Soc Ley Hunters
SOLACE	Soc Local Authority Chief Execs & Senior Mgrs
SOLAS	Soc Law Accountants Scotland
SOLCAP	Soc Leisure Consultants & Pubrs
SOLLA	Soc Later Life Advisers
Solo NFSC	Nat Fedn Solo Clubs
SOM	Soc Occupational Medicine
SOMW	Soc Medical Writers
SONE	Supporters Nuclear Energy
SOP	Save our Parsonages
SOPA	Scot Organic Prodrs Assn
SOPO	Soc Procurement Officers Local Govt
SoR	Soc Radiographers
SOS	Scot Otolaryngological Soc
SOSS	Soc Schoolmasters & Schoolmistresses
SOTMAS	Stoke-on-Trent Museum Archaeol Soc
SOTS	Soc Old Testament Study
SOVA	SOVA
SPA	Safety Pass Alliance
	Scot Pétanque Assn
	Scot Pipers Assn
	Scot Pistol Assn
	Scot Potters' Assn
	Scotland Patients Assn
	Sheet Plant Assn
	Soc Parliamentary Agents
	Soc Popular Astronomy
	Soc Profl Accountants
	Social Policy Assn
	Soya Protein Assn
SPAB	Soc Protection Ancient Bldgs
SpaBA	Spa Business Assn
SPATA	Swimming Pool & Allied Trs Assn

© CBD Research Ltd · Beckenham · BR3 5JS · Tel 020 8650 7745 · E-mail cbd@cbdresearch.com · www.cbdresearch.com

SPBS	Scot Prayer Book Soc	SSEG	Scot Solar Energy Gp
	Soc Promotion Byzantine Studies	SSF	Scot Schoolsport Fedn
SPBW	Soc Presvn Beers Wood	SSHA	Soc Sexual Health Advisers
SPC	Soc Pension Consultants	SSHB	Soc Study Human Biology
	Steam Plough Club	SSHM	Scot Soc Hist Medicine
SPCK	Soc Promoting Christian Knowledge		Soc Social Hist Medicine
SPDS	Soc Personnel Dirs Scotland	SSHoP	Scot Soc Hist Photography
SPE	Soc Profl Engrs	SSI	Sculptors' Soc Ireland
SPES	S Place Ethical Soc		Soc Scribes & Illuminators
SPF	Scot Pensioners Forum	SSISI	Statistical & Social Inquiry Soc Ireland
	Scot Police Fedn	SSLA	Scot Support Learning Assn
SPG	Solicitor Sole Practitioners Gp	SSLG	Scot Stone Liaison Gp
SPHS	Soc Promotion Hellenic Studies	SSLH	Soc Study Labour Hist
SPL	Scot Poetry Library	SSM	Soc Social Medicine
SPMA	Scot Modern Pentathlon Assn	SSNS	Scot Soc Nthn Studies
	Soc Post-Medieval Archaeology	SSNTA	Scot Seed & Nursery Tr Assn
SPNS	Scot Place-Name Soc	SSP	Scot Soc Playwrights
SPOA	Scot Plant Owners Assn	SSPO	Scot Salmon Producers' Org
SPPA	Scot Pre-School Play Assn	SSPR	Scot Soc Psychical Res
SPR	Inc Soc Psychical Res	SSRA	Scot Smallbore Rifle Assn
	Soc Property Researchers	SSS	Ship Stamp Soc
SPRA	Scot Plastics & Rubber Assn		Sunday Shakespeare Soc
	Single Ply Roofing Assn	SSSG	Stickler Syndrome Support Gp
SPRS	Staffordshire Parish Registers Soc	SSSprint	Street Sled Sports Racers
SPS	Soc Portrait Sculptors	SSSS	Soc Study Subterranean Survival
SPSBS	Shetland Pony Stud-Book Soc	SSTA	Scot Secondary Teachers' Assn
SPSL	Scot Piping Soc Lond	STA	Soc Technical Analysts
SPSS	Sports Pony Studbook Soc		Solar Tr Assn
SPTW	Soc Promoting Training Women		Source Testing Assn
SPUC	Soc Protection Unborn Children		Swimming Teachers Assn
SRA	Scot Rafting Assn	STAGBI	Standardbred & Trotting Horse Assn
	Scot Records Assn	STAR	Soc Ticket Agents & Retailers
	Scot Rifle Assn	STAT	Soc Teachers Alexander Technique
	Shooters' Rights Assn	STAUK	Sugar Traders Assn
	Social Res Assn	STC	Soc Theatre Consultants
	Sport Recreation Alliance	STEMPRA	Science, Technology, Engg... Public Relations Assn
	Strathspey Rly Assn	STEP	Soc Trust & Estate Practitioners
	Sustainable Restaurant Assn	STEPS	STEPS
SRC	Scot Retail Consortium	Stereo Society	Stereoscopic Soc
SRF	Scot Renewables Forum	STES	Scot Traction Engine Soc
SRGC	Scot Rock Garden Club	STF	Scot Tourism Forum
SRHE	Soc Res Higher Educ	STGA	Scot Tourist Guides Assn
SRHSB	Soc Res Hydrocephalus & Spina Bifida	STIA	Scot Textile Ind Assn
SRIP	Soc Reproductive & Infant Psychology	STLD	Soc TV Lighting & Design
SRP	Soc Radiological Protection	STO	Scot Tenants Org
	Soc Recorder Players	STOWA	Scot Tug of War Assn
SRPA	Skates & Rays Producers Assn	STR	Soc Theatre Res
SRPS	Scot Rly Presvn Soc	STRI	Sports Turf Res Inst
SRS	Scot Reformation Soc	STS	Scot Text Soc
	Shakespeare Reading Soc	STSD	Soc Teachers Speech & Drama
	Soc Renaissance Studies	STSG	Scot Transport Studies Gp
	Suffolk Records Soc	STTA	Scot Table Tennis Assn
	Surrey Record Soc		Scot Timber Tr Assn
	Sussex Record Soc	STTS	Scot Tramway & Transport Soc
SRU	Scot Rugby U	STUC	Scot Trs U Congress
SS	Safe Speed Campaign	SUB.BRIT	Subterranea Britannica
	Surtees Soc	SUDG	Seabed User & Developer Gp
SSA	Sailing Smack Assn	SUKA	Singapore UK Assn
	Scot Sports Assn	SUT	Soc Underwater Technology
	Seasoning & Spice Assn	SVA	Scot Volleyball Assn
	Shipbuilders & Shiprepairers Assn	SVBWG	Scot Vernacular Bldgs Working Gp
	Side Saddle Assn	SVT	Soc Vascular Technology
	Soc Scot Artists	SVVF	Scot Vintage Vehicle Fedn
	Soc Study Addiction Alcohol...	SWA	Scot Whls Assn
SSAFA	Soldiers, Sailors & Airmen's Families Assn		Scot Wrestling Assn
SSAISB	Soc Study Artificial Intelligence...		Scotch Whisky Assn
SSAM	Soc Sales & Marketing		Small Woods Assn
SSAUK	Self Storage Assn		Soc Women Artists
SSBA	Scot Spina Bifida Assn		Spiritual Workers' Assn
	Shropshire Sheep Breeders Assn		Steel Window Assn
	Swaledale Sheep Breeders Assn	SWCPA	S W Coast Path Assn
SSBR	Soc Sailing Barge Res	SWE	Soc Wood Engravers
SSC	Scot Ski Club	SWF	Scot Women's Football
	Silver Spoon Club	SWHP	Soc Welfare Horses & Ponies
SSCA	Scot Ship Chandlers Assn	SWLG	Scot Wild Land Gp
SSCC	Scot Sporting Car Club	SWMA	Scot Wirework Mfrs Assn
SSCR	Scot Soc Crop Res	SWMAS	Shropshire & W Midlands Agricl Soc
SSCSoc	Soc Solicitors Supreme Courts Scotland	SWPP/BPPA	Soc Wedding & Portrait Photographers

© CBD Research Ltd · Beckenham · BR3 5JS · Tel 020 8650 7745 · E-mail cbd@cbdresearch.com · www.cbdresearch.com

SWRI	Scot Women's Rural Insts
SWT	Scot Wildlife Trust
SyAS	Surrey Archaeol Soc
SYHA	Scot Youth Hostels Assn
SYP	Soc Young Publishers

T

T&CVA	Thames & Chiltern Vineyards Assn
TA	Telework Assn
	Translators Assn
	Transport Assn
	Tricycle Assn
TAA	Tropical Agriculture Assn
TABI	Tarot Assn
TAC	Aeroplane Collection
TACMA	BEAMA
TACS	Tiles & Architectural Ceramics Soc
TACT	Assn Corporate Trustees
taen	Age & Emplt Network
TAF	Trade Assn Forum
TAG	Arthrogryposis Gp
	Local Government Technical Advisers Group
TALES	Assn Library Eqpt Suppliers
TAMBA	Twins & Mult Births Assn
TandRA	Tennis & Rackets Assn
TAROE	Tenants & Residents Orgs England
TARS	Arthur Ransome Soc
TAS	Aviation Soc
TATHS	Tools & Trs Hist Soc
TBA	Thoroughbred Breeders' Assn
TBF	Trakehner Breeders Fraternity
TBPA	Tenpin Bowling Proprietors Assn
TC	Tandem Club
TCA	Timeshare Consumers Assn
TCAS	Three Counties Agricl Soc
TCC	Test Card Circle
TCF	Compassionate Friends
TCMA	Traffic Mgt Contrs Assn
TCPA	Town & Country Planning Assn
TCS	Token Corresponding Soc
	Traditional Cosmology Soc
	Train Collectors Soc
TCUGB	Tai Chi U
TDA	Timber Decking Assn
TDS	Dystonia Soc
TEAM	Eur Atlantic Movement
TEDct	Thyroid Eye Disease Charitable Trust
TEGAS	Electric Guitar Appreciation Soc
TEHVA	BEAMA
TELS	T E Lawrence Soc
tESA	Equine Shiatsu Assn
TESA	Event Services Assn
TESS	English Spelling Soc
TFA	Freedom Assn
	Tenant Farmers' Assn
TFMA	Tapestry Frame Mfrs Assn
TFSR	Tools Self Reliance
TFTA	Traditional Farmfresh Turkey Assn
TG	Townswomen's Glds
TGA	Brit Tomato Growers Assn
	Tropical Growers' Assn
	Turfgrass Growers Assn
THA	Helplines Assn
The BAF	Brit Abrasives Fedn
The GA	Giftware Assn
The RA	Referees' Assn
TheCEP	Campaign English Parliament
THG	Telecommunications Heritage Gp
THMAS	Ted Heath Musical Appreciation Soc
THYA	Brit Marine Fedn
TI(UK)	Transparency Intl (UK)
TICA	Thermal Insulation Contrs Assn
TIF	Telecommunications & Internet Fedn [IRL]
TIGA	Tiga

TIMA	Tue Iron Mfrs Assn
TIMCON	Timber Packaging & Pallet Confedn
TIMSA	Thermal Insulation Mfrs & Suppliers Assn
TISA	Tax Incentivised Savings Assn
TLA	Therapy Lecturers Assn
TLGA	Leek Growers Assn
TLRS	Tramway & Light Rly Soc
TMA	Tobacco Mfrs' Assn
TMCA	Thames & Medway Canal Assn
TMI	Movers Inst
	Tourism Mgt Inst
TMS	Micropalaeontological Soc
	Tramway Museum Soc
	Transverse Myelitis Soc
TMS-GBI	Thomas Merton Soc
TMSA	Traditional Music & Song Assn Scotland
TMVA	BEAMA
TNA UK	Trigeminal Neuralgia Assn
TNAUK	Talking Newspaper Assn
TOFFS	Over Fifties Assn
TOFS	Tracheo-Oesophageal Fistula Support
TORRO	Tornado & Storm Res Org
TOW	Transport Water Assn
TOWA	Tug of War Assn
TPA	TaxPayers' Alliance
TPC	Tall Persons Club
TPG	Portman Gp
TPS	Thomas Paine Soc UK
TRA	Reiki Assn
	Textile Recycling Assn
	Toy Retailers Association
	Trussed Rafter Assn
	Tyre Recovery Assn
TRADA	TRADA Technology
Treoir	Nat Fedn Services Unmarried Parents...[IRL]
TRF	Trail Riders Fellowship
TRG	Tertiary Res Gp
	Tory Reform Gp
TRIC	TV & Radio Inds Club
TRPS	Talyllyn Rly Presvn Soc
TRSS	Trekking & Riding Soc Scotland
TS	Theosophical Soc England
	Tolkien Soc
TSA	Tank Storage Assn
	Telecare Services Assn
	Textile Services Assn
	Tuberous Sclerosis Assn
	UK Land & Hydrographic Survey Assn
TSA(UK)	Tourette Syndrome (UK) Assn
TSBA	Teeswater Sheep Breeders Assn
TSI	Trading Standards Inst
TSSA	Transport Salaried Staffs Assn
TSSEA	Thermal Spraying & Surface Engg Assn
TSSS	Turner Syndrome Support Soc
TT	Transport Trust
TTA	Tile Assn
	Travel Trust Assn
TTAW	Table Tennis Assn Wales
TTF	Timber Tr Fedn
TTRA	TT Riders Assn
TTS	Transport Ticket Soc
TUBCS	Trade U Badge Collectors Soc
TUC	Trades U Congress
TUFF	Telecommunications UK Fraud Forum
TUK	Transfrigoroute UK
TVCCi	Thames Valley Cham Comm & Ind
TWI	Welding Inst

U

UA	Urostomy Assn
UAC	Ulster Automobile Club
UACES	University Assn Contemporary Eur Studies
UAF	Ulster Angling Fedn
UAHS	Ulster Architectural Heritage Soc

© CBD Research Ltd · Beckenham · BR3 5JS · Tel 020 8650 7745 · E-mail cbd@cbdresearch.com · www.cbdresearch.com

UALL	Universities Assn Lifelong Learning
UAR	Understanding Animal Res
UAS	Ulster Archaeol Soc
UCA	Ulster Chemists Assn
	Utd Chiropractic Assn
UCAC	Undeb Cenedlaethol Athrawon Cymru
UCEA	Universities & Colls Emplrs' Assn
UCFF	Ulster Coarse Fishing Fedn
UCISA	Universities & Colls Inf Systems Assn
UCSW	U Country Sports Workers
UCU	University & Coll U
UDG	Urban Design Gp
UFAW	Universities Fedn Animal Welfare
UFRC	Ulster Fedn Rambling Clubs
UFU	Ulster Farmers U
UHF	Ulster Histl Foundation
UHMA	BEAMA
UHS	Unitarian Hist Soc
UIG	Uveitis Inf Gp
UK-ISES	Solar Energy Soc
UK-RHA	UK Rainwater Harvesting Assn
UK-SDA	UK Sustainable Devt Assn
UKA	UK Alliance Profl Teachers Dancing. . .
	UK Athletics
UKAAF	UK Assn Accessible Formats
UKABIF	UK Acquired Brain Injury Forum
UKACR	UK Assn Cancer Registries
UKAFPO	UK Assn Fish Producer Orgs
UKAGP	UK Assn Gestalt Practitioners
UKALA	UK Assn Letting Agents
UKAMBY	UK Assn Mfrs Bakers Yeast
UKAPD	UK Assn Programme Dirs
UKAPE	UK Assn Profl Engrs
UKAPMP	UK Assn Proposal Mgt Profls
UKAWP	UK Alliance Wedding Planners
UKBFF	UK Bodybuilding & Fitness Fedn
UKBG	UK Bartenders Gld
UKBI	UK Business Incubation
UKBS	UK Botswana Soc
UKCA	UK Cheerleading Assn
UKCG	UK Contractors Gp
UKCHO	UK Confedn Hypnotherapy Orgs
UKCMA	UK Crowd Mgt Assn
UKCMG	UK Computer Measurement Gp
UKCP	UK Coun Psychotherapy
UKCPA	UK Clinical Pharmacy Assn
UKCPI	UK Cleaning Products Ind Assn
UKCPS	UK Coloured Pencil Soc
UKCRA	UK Cartridge Remanufacturers Assn
	UK Catamaran Racing Assn
UKCSA	UK Cast Stone Assn
UKCTA	UK Competitive Telecommunications Assn
UKDDF	UK Dance & Drama Fedn
UKEAPA	UK Employee Assistance Profls Assn
UKeiG	UK EInformation Gp
UKELA	UK Envtl Law Assn
UKEMS	UK Envtl Mutagen Soc
UKEP	UK Egg Producers Assn
UKFJB	UK Fedn Jazz Bands
UKFPA	UK Forest Products Assn
UKFT	UK Fashion & Textile Assn
UKGCOA	UK Golf Course Owners Assn
UKGCVA	UK Gift Card & Voucher Assn
UKHA	UK Harp Assn
	UK Housekeepers Assn
UKHCA	UK Home Care Assn
UKHIA	UK Herbal Infusions Assn
UKHKA	UK Hand Knitting Assn
UKHSA	UK Horse Shoers Assn
UKIA	UK Irrigation Assn
UKISCRS	UK & I Soc Cataract & Refractive Surgeons
UKISUG	UK Indl Sugar Users Gp
UKIVA	UK Indl Vision Assn
UKLA	UK Literacy Assn
	UK Locksmiths Assn
	UK Lubricants Assn
UKLPG	UKLPG
UKMA	UK Metric Assn

UKMPA	UK Maritime Pilots' Assn
UKMPG	UK Major Ports Gp
UKMTA	UK Money Transmitters Assn
UKNA	UK Noise Assn
UKNDA	UK Nat Defence Assn
UKOOG	UK Onshore Operators Gp
UKOPA	UK Onshore Pipeline Operators' Assn
UKOTA	UK O'seas Territories Assn
UKOWLA	UK One World Linking Assn
UKPA	UK Polocrosse Assn
UKPCCI	UK Pakistan Cham Comm [?dead 05
UKPHA	UK Public Health Assn
UKPIA	UK Petroleum Ind Assn
UKPS	UK Pyrotechnics Soc
UKPSA	UK Practical Shooting Assn
UKPSF	UK Paintball Sports Fedn
UKPTA	UK Polarity Therapy Assn
UKQAA	UK Quality Ash Assn
UKRA	UK Renderers Assn
	UK Rocketry Assn
UKRAS	UK Roundabout Appreciation Soc
UKRFA	UK Resilient Flooring Assn
UKRPA	UK Revenue Protection Assn
UKSA	UK Shareholders' Assn
	UK Skateboarding Assn
	UK Sports Assn People Learning Disability
	UK Synaesthesia Assn
UKSCC	UK Spoon Collectors Club
UKSG	UK Serials Gp
UKSIF	UK Sustainable Investment & Finance Assn
UKSMA	UK Software Metrics Assn
	UK Spring Mfrs Assn
UKSPA	UK Science Park Assn
UKSPILL	UK Spill Assn
UKSSA	UK Security Shredding Assn
UKSTT	UK Soc Trenchless Technology
UKTA	UK Tea Coun
UKTC	UK Trs Confedn
UKTFA	UK Timber Frame Assn
UKTLF	UK Textile Laboratory Forum
UKTRF	UK Travel Retail Forum
UKTS	UK Thalassaemia Soc
UKU	UK Ultimate Assn
UKVA	Alliance UK Virtual Assistants
	UK Vineyards Assn
UKWA	UK Warehousing Assn
	UK Windsurfing Assn
UKWF	UK Weighing Fedn
UNA-UK	Utd Nations Assn GB & NI
UNISON	UNISON
UNLOCK	Unlock
UPCA	Universities Psychotherapy & Counselling Assn
Upkeep	Upkeep
UPNS	Ulster Place-Name Soc
URCHS	Utd Reformed Church Hist Soc
URTU	Utd Road Transport U
USA UK	Utd Saddlebred Assn
USDAW	U Shop Distributive & Allied Workers
USLS	Ulster-Scots Language Soc
USPC	Ulster Soc Protection Countryside
USPCA	Ulster Soc Prevention Cruelty Animals
UTU	Ulster Teachers U
UUK	Universities UK
UUU	U UK Unicyclists

V

V-CC	Veteran-Cycle Club
VAA	Vintage Arms Assn
VAG	Vernacular Architecture Gp
VAGA	Visual Arts & Galleries Assn
VAHS	Voluntary Action Hist Soc
VAN	Voluntary Arts Network
VAS	Visual Arts Scotland
VBF	Vinegar Brewers Fedn

VBRA	Vehicle Builders & Repairers Assn
VC&GCAssn	Victoria Cross & George Cross Assn
VCA	Vegetable Consultants Assn
VCN	Voice Care Network
VCT	Vintage Carriages Trust
VdGS	Viola da Gamba Soc
VegSoc	Vegetarian Soc
VFA	Viewing Facilities Assn UK
VFI	Vintners Fedn Ireland
VGC	Vintage Glider Club
VHGMC	Vintage Horticl & Garden Machinery Club
VHLCG	Von Hippel-Lindau Contact Gp
VHS	Veteran Horse Soc
VLV	Voice Listener & Viewer
VMCC	Vintage Motor Cycle Club
VMS	Victorian Military Soc
VNS	Violet Needham Soc
VOCAL	Voice Chief Offrs Cultural... Services
VPG	VAT Practitioners Gp
VPS	Vulval Pain Soc
VRMA	Vehicle Restraint Mfrs Assn
VSCC	Vintage Sports Car Club
VSO	Voluntary Service Overseas
VSS	Victim Support Scotland
VWBA	Vintage Wooden Boat Assn
VWSGB	Virginia Woolf Soc GB

W

W&ACT	Wey & Arun Canal Trust
WABA	Welsh Amat Boxing Assn
WACC	Wessex Assn Chams Comm
WAFE	Women's Aid Fedn (England)
WAH	Wolves & Humans Foundation
Wales PPA	Wales Pre-school Providers Assn
WAMF/FfCAC	Welsh Amat Music Fedn
WANHS	Wiltshire Archaeol & Natural Hist Soc
WAOS	Welsh Agricl Org Soc
WARA	Welsh Amat Rowing Assn
WAS	Worcestershire Archaeol Soc
WASA	Welsh Amat Swimming Assn
WASAC	Welsh Assn Sub Aqua Clubs
WASCO	Wales Assn Self Catering Operators
WAY	Way Foundation
WBCS	Welsh Black Cattle Soc
WBF	Welsh Bowls Fedn
WBRA	Wagon Bldg & Repairing Assn
WBS-UK	Warmblood Breeders' Studbook - UK
WBU	Welsh Badminton U
	Welsh Bridge U
WCA	Welsh Culinary Assn
	Wound Care Alliance
	Writers' Copyright Assn
WCAS	Westmorland County Agricl Soc
WCC	Wales Craft Coun
WCS	Wilkie Collins Soc
WCU	Welsh Chess U
	Welsh Cycling U
WCVA	Wales Coun Voluntary Action
WDA	Wallcovering Distbrs Assn
	Well Drillers Assn
	Wild Deer Assn Ireland
WDCS	Whale & Dolphin Consvn Soc
WEA	Workers' Educl Assn
WEN	Women's Envtl Network
WES	Western Equestrian Soc
	Wind Engg Soc
	Women's Engg Soc
	Writing Eqpt Soc
WFA	Western Front Assn
	Wholesome Food Assn
WFDS	Cymdeithas Ddawns Werin Cymru
WFGA	Women's Farm & Garden Assn
WFS	Wild Flower Soc
WFU	Women's Food & Farming U
WGA	White Goods Assn [IRL]

WGGB	Writers Gld
WHA	Welsh Hospitals & Health Services Assn
	Western Horsemens Assn
WHHS	Wessex Heavy Horse Soc
WHR	Welsh Highland Rlys Assn
WHS	Wesley Histl Soc
WHSS	Wiltshire Horn Sheep Soc
WHU	Welsh Hockey U
WIA	Writing Instruments Assn
WJA	Welsh Judo Assn
WLGA	Welsh Local Govt Assn
WLSBA	Wensleydale Longwool Sheep Breeders' Assn
WM Soc	Water Mgt Soc
WMA	BEAMA
	Workers' Music Assn
WMBA	Whls Markets Brokers Assn
WMS	Welsh Mines Soc
WMSA	Woodworking Machinery Suppliers Assn
WMSS	Welsh Mountain Sheep Soc - Registered Section
WMT	War Memorials Trust
WNA	Welsh Netball Assn
WPA	War Poets Assn
	Welsh Pétanque Assn
	Wood Protection Assn
	World Pheasant Assn UK
WPCCIT	Weymouth & Portland Cham Comm...
WPCS	Welsh Pony & Cob Soc
	White Park Cattle Soc
WPIF	Wood Panel Inds Fedn
WPOA	Westminster Property Owners Assn
WPU	Writers & Photographers unLimited
WRG	Waterway Recovery Gp
WRPA	Welsh Rugby Players Assn
WRS	Wiltshire Record Soc
WRU	Welsh Rugby U
WRVS	Women's R Voluntary Service
WSF	Williams Syndrome Foundation
WSRA	Welsh Sea Rowing Assn
	World Speedway Riders Assn
WSRS	Wildlife Sound Recording Soc
WSSociety	Soc Writers Her Majesty's Signet
WSTA	Wine & Spirit Trade Assn
WSTAA	Welsh Salmon & Trout Angling Assn
WTA	Whitegoods Tr Assn
WTIF	Wall Tie Installers Fedn
WTRA	Wales Trekking & Riding Assn
WTT	Wild Trout Trust
WW2RSG	World War Two Rly Study Gp
WWA	War Widows Assn
WWJ	W W Jacobs Appreciation Soc
WWOOF	World-Wide Opportunities on Organic Farms
WWTA	Welsh Weight Training Assn

Y

YAS	Yorkshire Archaeol Soc
YDCW	Campaign Protection Rural Wales
YDS	Yorkshire Dialect Soc
YDSA	Yacht Designers & Surveyors Assn
YET	Young Explorers' Trust
YGS	Yorkshire Geological Soc
YHA	Youth Hostels Assn (E&W)
YJA	Yachting Journalists' Assn
YMCA	YMCA England
YPS	Yorkshire Philosophical Soc
YWCA	YWCA (Young Women's Christian Assn)

Y

ZF	Zionist Fedn
ZSA	Zwartbles Sheep Assn
ZSL	Zoological Soc London
ZWA UK	Zero Waste Alliance UK

© CBD Research Ltd · Beckenham · BR3 5JS · Tel 020 8650 7745 · E-mail cbd@cbdresearch.com · www.cbdresearch.com

PUBLICATIONS INDEX

A

Archaeological Jnl - Royal Archaeol Inst
The Archaeologist - Inst of Field Archaeologists
Archery UK - Grand Nat Archery Soc
Architectural Heritage Jnl - Architectural Heritage Soc of Scotland
Architectural History - Soc Architectural Historians GB
Architectural Ironmongery Jnl - Gld Architectural Ironmongers
Architectural Technology - Chart Inst Architectural Technologists
The Architectural Technology Careers Hbk - Chart Inst
    Architectural Technologists
Architecture Periodicals Index - R Inst Brit Architects
Archives of Disease in Childhood - R Coll Paediatrics & Child
    Health
Archives of Natural History - Soc Hist Natural Hist
Arena - Assn Electoral Administrators
    U Shop, Distributive & Allied Workers
Argus - Nat Auricula & Primula Soc (Midland & West Section)
The Ark - Rare Breeds Survival Trust
The Arquebusier - Pike & Shot Soc
Art Antiquity & Law - Inst Art & Law
Art Business Today - Fine Art Trade Gld
Art History - Assn Art Historians
Art Libraries Jnl - ARLIS/UK & Ireland: Art Libraries Soc
Art Quarterly - Nat Art Collections Fund
Art Treasures & War - Inst Art & Law
Arthritis & Waterbeds - Brit Waterbed Assn
Arthritis News - Arthritis Care
Artisan - Scot Assn Painting Craft Teachers
Artist Blacksmith - Brit Artist Blacksmiths Assn
The Artist's Guide to Selling Work - Fine Art Tr Gld
Aseasuk News - Assn of South-East Asian Studies UK
Asepsis: preventing healthcare associated infection - Infection
    Prevention Soc
ASGARD - Assn Scotland Res Astronautics Ltd
Asian Affairs - R Soc Asian Affairs
Aspects of Applied Biology - Assn Applied Biologists
Asphalt - Asphalt Ind Alliance
Asphalt Professional - Inst Asphalt Technology
Aspirations! - Assn Spinal Injury Research, Rehabilitation &
    Reintegration
Assn Executive - Inst Assn Management
Astrocalendar - Fedn Astronomical Socs
Astrological Jnl - Astrological Assn GB
Astrology - Astrological Lodge London
Astrology & Medicine - Astrological Assn GB
Astronomy & Geophysics - R Astronomical Soc
At the Sign ofÉ - Inn Sign Soc
A-T: an overview - Ataxia-Telangiectasia Soc
The Ataxia - Ataxia UK
ATCO News - Assn Transport Co-ordinating Officers
Audit of Political Engagement - Hansard Soc Ltd
The Author - Soc Authors
    Translators Assn
Autism News - Autism Indep UK
Automobile Abstracts - MIRA Ltd
Automotive Business News - MIRA Ltd
Automotive Recycling & Disposal UK - Motor Vehicle Dismantlers
    Assn GB
Aviation Archaeologist - Brit Aviation Archaeol Coun
The Avicultural Magazine - Avicultural Soc
Aware - Scot Motor Neurone Disease Assn
Ayrshire Dairyman - Ayrshire Cattle Soc GB & I
Ayrshire Jnl - Ayrshire Cattle Soc GB & I
Ayrshire Monographs - Ayrshire Archaeol & Natural Hist Soc
Ayrshire Notes - Ayrshire Archaeol & Natural Hist Soc

B

Baby Blues & Post Natal Depression - Assn Postnatal Illness
Baby Watch - Meningitis Research Foundation
Back Chat - Chiropractic Patients' Assn
Backaches & Waterbeds - Brit Waterbed Assn
Backbone - Scoliosis Assn (UK)
Background - McTimoney Chiropractic Assn
Backpack - Backpackers Club
Baconiana - Francis Bacon Soc Inc

The Badge Mag - Brit Badge Collectors Assn
The Badger - Badge Collectors Circle
Badminton Magazine - Badminton England
Balance - Diabetes UK
A Balanced View: Practical Tips for a Healthy Diet - Arthritic
    Assn
Balloonies - NABAS
Bandersnatch - Lewis Carroll Soc
Banking Matters to Me - Assn Real Change
Bankruptcy Explained - Bankruptcy Assn
Baptist Quarterly - Baptist Histl Soc
Baptist Times - Baptist U GB
Barge Buyers' Hbk - DBA - the Barge Assn
Base Thoughts - Antique Metalware Soc
Baseline - Assn Certificated Field Archaeologists
Basic Account of Plastic Surgery - Brit Assn Cosmetic Surgeons
Basic Letterpress for Beginners - Brit Printing Soc
Basic Steps - Assn Real Change
Bat Monitoring Post - Bat Conservation Trust
Bat News - Bat Conservation Trust
Battery Vehicle Review - Battery Vehicle Soc
Battle of Britain Remembered - Battle Britain Histl Soc
BATTLEguide - Gld Battlefield Guides
BDN British Deaf News - Brit Deaf Assn
Be My Parent Newspaper - Brit Assn Adoption & Fostering
The Beat - Brit Cham Comm China - Shanghai
Beating Anger - Brit Assn Anger Mgt
Beating the Odds [&] Moving Steel by Crane - Nat Assn Steel
    Stockholders
The Beckford Jnl - Beckford Soc
Becoming a Chartered Accountant - training with a medium
    sized firm - Assn Practising Accountants
Beef Farmer - Nat Beef Assn
Behaviour & Information Technology - Ergonomics Soc
Behavioural & Cognitive Psychotherapy - Brit Assn Behavioural
    & Cognitive Psychotherapies
Behavioural Problems in Huntington's Disease - Scot
    Huntington's Assn
Being There - Tourism Concern
BELUX - Belgian-Luxembourg Cham Comm GB
The Bells - Rachmaninoff Soc
Ben's Story: an introduction to child contact centres - Nat Assn
    Child Contact Centres
Bereavement Care Jnl - Cruse Bereavement Care
Berkshire Archaeological Jnl - Berkshire Archaeol Soc
Best Practice - Inst Assessors & Internal Verifiers
Best Practice Guide to Timber Fire Doors - Architectural &
    Specialist Door Mfrs Assn
Best Practice Guidelines for the Production of Chilled Foods -
    Chilled Food Assn
The Betjemanian - Betjeman Soc
Between a Rock & a Hard Place - Creators' Rights Alliance
Between the Flags - Point-to-Point Owners & Riders Assn
The BIAE Probe - Brit Inst & Assn Electrolysis Ltd
Bifocals without Tears - Assn Brit Dispensing Opticians
The Big Youth Theatre Manual - Nat Assn Youth Theatres
Biochemical Jnl - Biochemical Soc
Biodynamic Massage - Assn Holistic Biodynamic Massage
    Therapists
Biographical Portraits Vol IV - Japan Soc
Biological Jnl - Linnean Soc London
Biological Reviews - Cambridge Philosophical Soc
Biomedical Scientist - Inst Biomedical Science
Biotechnology & Applied Biochemistry - Biochemical Soc
Bird Study - Brit Trust Ornithology
Bird Table - Brit Trust Ornithology
Birds - R Soc Protection Birds
Bison Hbk - Brit Bison Assn
BJOG: an international Jnl of Obstetrics & Gynaecology - R
    Coll Obstetricians & Gynaecologists
Black Powder - Muzzle Loaders Assn GB
The Black Sheep - Hebridean Sheep Soc
Black & White Photography - Gld Master Craftsmen
The Blackcountryman - Black Country Soc
Blake Jnl - Blake Soc St James's
Blasmusik Bulletin - Kmoch European Bands Soc
Blastpipe - Scot Rly Presvn Soc
Blinds & Shutters - Brit Blind & Shutter Assn

© CBD Research Ltd · Beckenham · BR3 5JS · Tel 020 8650 7745 · E-mail cbd@cbdresearch.com · www.cbdresearch.com

Blink - Assn Optometrists
Blithe Spirit - Brit Haiku Soc
Blonde - Brit Blonde Soc
Blonde News - Brit Blonde Soc
Blood Royal - Manorial Soc GB
Blowout - Offshore Ind Liaison Céee
Blue Book - Brit Motor Sprint Assn
Blue Flag - DBA - the Barge Assn
The Blue Pages - Soc Brit Theatre Designers
Blue Print Magazine - Emergency Planning Soc
Bluebell News - Bluebell Railway Presvn Soc
Blwyddlyfr - Undeb Cenedlaethol Athrawon Cymru
Boarding School Magazine - Boarding Schools Assn
Boat Jumble Fixtures List - Boat Jumble Assn
Bodgers Gazette - Assn Polelathe Turners & Greenwood Workers
Body - Vehicle Builders' & Repairers' Assn
The 'Boneshaker' - Veteran-Cycle Club
Book Collecting - Provincial Booksellers Fairs Assn
Bookbinder - Soc Bookbinders
Bookmark - Bookmark Soc
The Bookplate Jnl - Bookplate Soc
Bookselling Essentials - Booksellers Assn UK & I
Bore Da - Urdd Gobaith Cymru
Botanical Jnl - Linnean Soc London
The Bottle Street Gazette - Margery Allingham Soc
The Bottom Line - Production Mgrs Assn
The Bousfield Diaries - Bedfordshire Histl Record Soc
The Boutonneur - Buttonhook Soc
Bowls for the Beginner - Bowls Scotland
Bowls International - Scot Indoor Bowling Assn
The Boys' Brigade Gazette - Boys' Brigade
B-Plus - Breast Implant Inf Soc
Bradleya - Brit Cactus & Succulent Soc
Branch Line News - Branch Line Soc
Brand Book - English Westerners Soc
Brazil Business Brief - Brazilian Cham Comm GB
Breaking & Production - Brit Egg Products Assn
The Brewer & Distiller - Inst Brewing & Distilling
Brewing & Distilling Directory - Inst Brewing & Distilling
Brick Bulletin - Brick Devt Assn Ltd
The Brick Issue - Brickish Assn
Brickline - Gld Bricklayers
The Brief - Brit Cham Comm Thailand
Brit Oz Bulletin - Britain-Australia Soc
Britain & Europe - Manorial Soc GB
Britain & Overseas - Economic Res Coun
Britain and the 're-opening ' of Japan: the Treaty of Yedo of 1858 & the Elgin Mission (2008) - Japan Soc
Britain Brasil - Brit Cham Comm & Ind Brazil
Britaly - Brit Cham Commerce Italy, Inc
Britannia - Soc Promotion Roman StudiesBritish Actuarial Jnl - Inst & Faculty of Actuaries
British American Business, the UK Hbk - Brit-American Business Inc
British Archaeology - Council of Brit Archaeology
British Bluegrass News - Brit Bluegrass Music Assn
The British Bobsleigh Annual - Brit Bobsleigh Assn Ltd
British Bottle Review - Old Bottle Club GB
British Bulletin of Publications on Latin America, Spain & Portugal - Hispanic & Luso Brazilian Council
British Business in China - Brit Cham Comm Hong Kong
British Business in China Directory - Brit Cham Comm China - Shanghai
British Cinematographer Magazine - Brit Soc Cinematographers
British Crematoria in Public Profile - Cremation Soc GB
British Dental Jnl - Brit Dental Assn
British Dental Nurses' Jnl - Brit Assn Dental Nurses
British Educational Research Jnl - Brit Educl Res Assn
British Equestrian Directory - Brit Equestrian Tr Assn
British Farmer & Grower - Nat Farmers U E & Wales
British-German Review - Brit-German Assn
British Go Jnl - Brit Go Assn
British Grooms - Brit Grooms Assn
British Herbal Compendium - Brit Herbal Medicine Assn
The British Herbal Pharmacopoeia - Brit Herbal Medicine Assn
British Homing World - Royal Pigeon Racing Assn
British Horse - Brit Horse Soc

British & Irish Archaeological Bibliography - Coun Brit Archaeology
British Jnl for the History of Philosophy - Brit Soc Hist Philosophy
British Jnl for the History of Science - Brit Soc Hist Science
British Jnl for the Philosophy of Science - Brit Soc Philosophy Science
British Jnl of Aesthetics - Brit Soc Aesthetics
British Jnl of Biomedical Science - Inst Biomedical Science
British Jnl of Canadian Studies - Brit Assn Canadian Studies
British Jnl of Clinical Pharmacology - Brit Pharmacological Soc
British Jnl of Clinical Psychology - Brit Psychological Soc
British Jnl of Dermatology - Brit Assn Dermatologists
British Jnl of Developmental Psychology - Brit Psychological Soc
British Jnl of Educational Psychology - Brit Psychological Soc
British Jnl of Haematology - Brit Soc Haematology
British Jnl of Health Psychology - Brit Psychological Soc
British Jnl of Learning Disabilities - Brit Inst Learning Disabilities
British Jnl of Mathematical & Statistical Psychology - Brit Psychological Soc
British Jnl of Middle Eastern Studies - Brit Soc Middle Eastern Studies
British Jnl of Music Therapy - Brit Assn Music Therapy
British Jnl of Orthodontics - Brit Orthodontic Soc
British Jnl of Pharmacology - Brit Pharmacological Soc
British Jnl of Psychology - Brit Psychological Soc
British Jnl of Social Work - Brit Assn Social Workers
British Jnl of Sports Medicine - Brit Assn Sport & Exercise Medicine
British Jnl - PSV Circle
British Jnl for Special Education - nasen
British Jnl of Occupational Therapy - Brit Assn Occupational Therapists
British Jnl of Oral & Maxillofacial Surgery - Brit Assn Oral & Maxillofacial Surgeons
British Jnl of Psychiatry - R Coll Psychiatrists
British Latvian Trade - Brit Cham Comm Latvia
British Medical Jnl - Brit Med Assn
British Military Serials - Road Transport Fleet Data Soc
British Mining Memoirs - Northern Mine Res Soc
British Mining Monograph - Northern Mine Res Soc
British National Formulary for Children - Royal Coll Paediatrics & Child Health
British Naturopathic Jnl - Brit Naturopathic Assn
British Numismatic Jnl - Brit Numismatic Soc
British Origami - Brit Origami Soc
British Orthopaedic News - Brit Orthopaedic Assn
British Orthoptic Jnl - Brit & Ir Orthoptic Soc
British Paper Machinery News - Picon
British Pensioner Jnl - Brit Pensioners & Tr U Action Assn
British Railway Track - Permanent Way Instn
British Railways Mark 1 Coaches - Histl Model Rly Soc
The British Sugarcraft News - Brit Sugarcraft Guild
British Tennis - Lawn Tennis Assn
The British Weightlifter - Brit Weight Lifting
The Britsoft Book - UK Interactive Entertainment Assn Ltd
Broadband - SCTE
Broadlines - Heritage Rly Assn
Brochure: Engineers' & Architects' Guide to Hot Dip Galvanizing - Galvanizers Assn
The Broker - Brit Insurance Brokers' Assn
The Buddhist Directory - Buddhist Soc
The Budgerigar - Budgerigar Soc
The Bugle Call Rag - Harry Roy Appreciation Soc
Building & Repairing Dry Stone Walls - Dry Stone Walling Assn GB
Building Engineer - Assn Bldg Engrs
Building Maintenance Expenditure by Local Authorities - Scala
Building Services Engineering Research & Technology - Chart Instn Bldg Services Engrs
Building Services Jnl - Chart Instn Bldg Services Engrs
Building Societies Yearbook - Building Societies Assn
Bulletin Board - Sound Sense
Bulletin of Veterinary History - Veterinary Hist Soc
The Bulwark - Scot Reformation Soc
Burney Jnl - Burney Soc
Burney Letter - Burney Soc
Burns Chronicle - Robert Burns Wld Fedn
The Bursar's Review - Indep Schools' Bursars Assn

Bus & Coach Preservation Handbook - Nat Assn Road Transport Museums
Bus Fare - Brit Trolleybus Soc
Bus User - Bus Users UK
Busfare - Nat Playbus Assn
The Business - Dundee & Angus Cham Comm
The Business - Nat Caravan Coun Ltd
The Business Economist - Soc Business Economists
Business Consultant - Inst Consulting
Business Edge - Sussex Cham Comm & Enterprise
Business Executives - Assn Business Executives
Business Info Beyond the Lens - Assn Photographers Ltd
Business Informer - Credit Protection Assn plc
Business Intelligence - Hull & Humber Cham Comm, Ind & Shipping
Business Jnl - Thames Valley Cham Comm & Ind
Business Management Manual - Registered Nursing Home Assn
Business News - Brit Assn Landscape Inds
Taunton Cham Comm
Business Plus - Bradford Cham Comm & Ind
Essex Chams Comm
Business South - Croydon Cham Comm & Ind
Business Survey - Scottish Chams Comm
Business Technology Outsourcer - National Outsourcing Assn
But - What do you do in the Winter? - Concert Artistes' Assn
Butterflies of Gower - Gower Soc
Button Lines - Brit Button Soc
Buying & Selling Reed - Brit Reed Growers' Assn
The Byron Jnl - Byron Soc

C

C Vu - ACCU: professionalism in programming
CA Magazine - Inst Chartered Accountants Scotland
Cabletalk - SELECT
Cactus World - Brit Cactus & Succulent Soc
Café Culture Magazine - Café Soc
Cahiers - Assn French Language Studies
Caledonian Gardener - R Caledonian Horticl Soc
Calendar of Book Fairs - Provincial Booksellers Fairs Assn
The Call Boy - Brit Music Hall Soc
Cambrian Line Magazine - Cambrian Railways Soc
Campaign - Brit Nuclear Test Veterans Assn
The Campaigner - Library Campaign
Camping & Caravanning Magazine - Camping & Caravanning Club Ltd
Canal Camps Brochure - Waterway Recovery Group Ltd
Canoe Focus - Brit Canoe Union
Canu Gwerin (Folk Song) - Welsh Folk Song Soc
Care - Leukaemia CARE
Care Assistant Training Manual - Registered Nursing Home Assn Ltd
Care on the Road - R Soc Prevention Accidents
The Care & Storage of Photographs: recommendations for good practice - Nat Assn Aerial Photographic Libraries
Care of Viol - Viola da Gamba Soc
Career Secretary - Inst Profl Administrators
Careers Education & Guidance - Assn Careers Educ & Guidance
Careers Guidance Today - Inst Career Guidance
Carefree Camping & Caravanning Guide to Europe - Camping & Caravanning Club
Cargo Companion - Cambridge Refrigeration Technology
Caribbean Airline News - Caribbean-Brit Business Coun
Caribbean Briefing - Caribbean-Brit Business Coun
Caring for Staff - Ceretas
Carnation Ybk - Brit Nat Carnation Soc
The Carrollian - Lewis Carroll Soc
The Cartographic Jnl - Brit Cartographic Soc
Cartographiti - Brit Cartographic Soc
Cartophilic Notes & News - Cartophilic Soc GB
Cascade - Action Sick Children
The Case for Customer Magazines - Assn Publishing Agencies
The Case for a Friendlier Tax System - Low Incomes Tax Reform Group

The Case against Hysterectomy - Campaign Hysterectomy & Unnecessary Operations on Women
The Case for Untreated Milk - Assn Unpasteurised Milk Producers & Consumers
Casebook - Medical Protection Soc Ltd
Casemate - Fortress Study Group
The Caspian - Caspian Horse Soc
The Castles of Gower - Gower Soc
Casualty Simulation - Casualties U
Catalysts & Catalysed Reactions - R Soc Chemistry
Catchword - Assn Teachers Lipreading to Adults
Catena - Catenian Assn
Cathedral Music Singing in Cathedrals - Friends Cathedral Music
Cathodic Protection of Reinforced Concrete: Status Report - Corrosion Prevention Assn
Catholic Ancestor - Catholic Family History Soc
Catholic Archives - Catholic Archives Soc
Catholic Medical Quarterly - Catholic Med Assn (UK)
Catnap - Narcolepsy UK
Cave & Karst Science - Brit Cave Res Assn
Cavies - Nat Cavy Club
Cavity Wounds - Wound Care Alliance UK
CDH/DDH Plasters - STEPS
CDH/DDH Splints - STEPS
Celebration of New Forest Ponies - New Forest Pony Breeding & Cattle Soc
Cemetery & Churchyard Regulations - Assn Burial Authorities Ltd
Centre Circle - Inst Football Mgt & Admin
League Mgrs Assn
A Century of Archaeology in East Herts - E Herts Archaeol Soc
Ceramic Review - Craft Potters' Assn GB
Cerebrospinal Fluid Research - Soc Res Hydrocephalus & Spina Bifida
Ceredigion - Cymdeithas Hanes Ceredigion
Ceska Muzika - Kmoch Eur Bands Soc
CFC Contract Furnishing Concepts - Assn Master Upholsterers & Soft Furnishers
CFC Contract Furnishing Concepts - Chair Frame Mfrs' Assn
Challenger Wave - Challenger Soc Marine Science
Chamberlink - Solihull Cham Comm
Chance or Choice - Risk Management - Soc Local Authority Chief Execs & Senior Mgrs
Changing the Future - Community Foundation Network
Changing with the Times - Scot Disability Sport
Chanter - Bagpipe Soc
Charity Finance Ybk - Charity Finance Dirs' Gp
Charles Williams Quarterly - Charles Williams Soc
Charolais News - Brit Charolais Cattle Soc Ltd
Chartered Architect - R Incorporation Architects Scotland
The Chartered Forester - Inst Chart Foresters
Chat - Children's Chronic Arthritis Assn
Deaf Educ Listening & Talking
Check It - Nat Specialist Contrs Coun
Checklists (the sole commercial guide to European wine & spirit legislation) - Wine & Spirit Tr Assn
Chemical Communications - R Soc Chemistry
The Chemical Engineer - Instn Chemical Engrs
Chemical Engineering Research & Design - Instn Chemical Engrs
Chemical Hazards in Industry - R Soc Chemistry
Chemical World - R Soc Chemistry
Cheque This Out - Brit Cheque & Credit Assn
Cherryburn Times - Bewick Soc
Cherub Bulletin - R Coll Paediatrics & Child Health
Chess Moves - English Chess Fedn
Chester Zoo Life - N England Zoological Soc
Chew - Tracheo-Oesophageal Fistula Support
Child & Adolescent Mental Health - Assn Child & Adolescent Mental Health
Child Abuse Review - Brit Assn Study & Prevention Child Abuse & Neglect
Childminding - Scot Childminding Assn
Children & Pets - Soc Companion Animal Studies
Children and the Media - mediawatch-uk
Children in Prison - Howard League Penal Reform
Chilled Ceilings - Chilled Beam & Ceiling Assn
Chimney Jnl - Nat Assn Chimney Sweeps
China Eye - Soc Anglo-Chinese Understanding

© CBD Research Ltd · Beckenham · BR3 5JS · Tel 020 8650 7745 · E-mail cbd@cbdresearch.com · www.cbdresearch.com

China-Britain Trade Review - China-Britain Business Coun
Chivalry - Imperial Soc Knights Bachelor
Choir Schools Today - Choir Schools Assn
Choosing a Boarding School - Boarding Schools Assn
Choreography as Work - Dance UK Ltd
Chowkidar - Brit Assn Cemeteries S Asia
Christian Librarian - Librarians' Christian Fellowship
Chromatography Abstracts - R Soc Chemistry
Chronicle - Regia Anglorum
Church & King - Soc King Charles the Martyr
Church Monuments - Church Monuments Soc
Church Music Quarterly - R School Church Music
The Churches & Chapels of Gower - Gower Soc
Cider - Nat Assn Cider Makers
The Cigarette Packet - Cigarette Packet Collectors' Club GB
Cip - Urdd Gobaith Cymru
The Circler - Nat Assn Ladies' Circles GB & I
The Circuit - Brit Bodyguard Assn
Circuit - Girls Venture Corps Air Cadets
Circuit Chatter - Brit Radio Car Assn
Circulation - Brit Hydrological Soc
Circus News - Circus Soc
Cirplan - Soc Cirplanologists
Citizen - Unlock Democracy
Civil Engineering Surveyor - Chart Instn Civil Engg Surveyors
Clarinet & Saxophone - Clarinet & Saxophone Soc GB
Classical Quarterly - Classical Assn
Classical Review - Classical Assn
Clay Technology - Inst Materials, Minerals & Mining
Clearing Blocked Crushers - Mineral Products Assn
The Clematis - Brit Clematis Soc
The Clerk - Soc Local Council Clerks
Clinical Anatomy - Brit Assn Clinical Anatomists
Clinical & Experimental Allergy - Brit Soc Allergy & Clinical Immunology
Clinical & Experimental Dermatology - Brit Assn Dermatologists
Clinical & Experimental Immunology - Brit Soc Immunology
Clinical Medicine - R Coll Physicians London
Clinical Oncology - R Coll Radiologists
Clinical Radiology - R Coll Radiologists
Clinical Research Focus - Inst Clinical Res
Clinical Science - Biochemical Soc
The Clinical Teacher - Assn Study Med Educ
Close Up - Mid Yorkshire Cham Comm & Ind
Clothes to Suit - Scoliosis Assn (UK)
Club Green News - Furniture Ind Res Assn
Coaching People with Learning Disability - UK Sports Assn People with Learning Disability
Coachline - TenniscoachUK
Coal Trader - Coal Merchants Fedn
Coastal Racing Construction Regulations - Hovercraft Club GB
Coatings - Thermal Spraying & Surface Engineering Assn
Cobbett's New Register - William Cobbett Soc
The Cobweb - Kentish Cobnuts Assn
Cochlear Implants: a collection of experiences of users of all ages - Nat Cochlear Implant Users Assn
Code of Practice for Safe Use of Lifting Equipment - Lifting Eqpt Engrs Assn
Code of Practice for Signing in at Surface Dressing Sites - Road Surface Treatments Assn
Code of Practice for Surface Dressing - Road Surface Treatments Assn
Code of Practice for the Better Organisation of Traction Engine rallies, incorporating the Rally Authorisation Scheme - Nat Traction Engine Trust
Code of Practice for the Soluble Coffee Industry in the UK - Brit Soluble Coffee Packers & Importers Assn
Code of Practice for Traction Engines & Similar Vehicles - National Traction Engine Trust
The Coleridge Bulletin - Friends Coleridge
Collateral Warranties - Assn Geotechnical & Geoenvironmental Specialists
Collections for a history of Staffordshire - Staffordshire Record Soc
Collections News - Collections Trust
College News - R Coll Ophthalmologists
Colombian Correspondent - Brit & Colombian Cham Comm
Coloration Technology - Soc Dyers & Colourists

Colour Index - Soc Dyers & Colourists
Coloured Sheep News - Brit Coloured Sheep Breeders Assn
The Colourist - Soc of Dyers & Colourists
Combatting Malnutrition - Brit Assn Parenteral & Enteral Nutrition
Come Gardening (braille & tape only) - THRIVE
Come Into Horticulture - Inst Horticulture
Comfort Engineering - Inst Domestic Heating & Envtl Engrs
Comment - CMT UK
Commentary on the Unidroit Convention - Inst Art & Law
The Commission Agent - Manufacturers' Agents' Assn GB & I
Commissioning Social Research: a good practice guide - Social Res Assn
Common Fisheries Policy - End or Mend? - Campaign Indep Britain
Communicate - Assn Translation Companies
Communicating Quality - R Coll Speech & Language Therapists
Communicator - Inst Scientific & Technical Communicators
Communities - R Pharmaceutical Soc GB
Community - Nat Fedn Community OrgsCommunity Audit Tool - Infection Prevention Soc
Community Extra - Nat Fedn Community OrgsCommunity Foundations & Community Needs Assessment - Community Foundation Network
Community Investment Relief Guide - Community Devt Finance Assn
Community Transport - Community Transport Assn UK
Compact Scottish National Dictionary - Scottish Language Dictionaries
Comparative Criticism - Brit Comparative Literature Assn
Compass - Garden & Landscape Designers Assn
Compendium of Buttonhooks - Buttonhook Soc
Competition & Masterpoint Journal - Welsh Bridge U
Complete Corpus of Kempe Glass in the UK - Kempe Soc
The Complete Guide to Starting & Running a Bookshop - Booksellers Assn UK & I
The Complete Guidebook to Avebury - Megalithic Soc
Composting News - Assn Organics Recycling
A Comprehensive History - Birmingham Transport Histl Gp
Compressed Air Condensate - Brit Compressed Air Soc
Computer Resurrection - Computer Consvn Soc
Computers in Genealogy - Soc of Genealogists
Concise Scots Dictionary - Scottish Language Dictionaries
Concord - English-Speaking U Commonwealth
Concrete - Concrete Soc
Concrete Cutter - Drilling & Sawing Assn
Concrete Engineers International Jnl - Concrete Soc
Concrete Mix Design - Assn of Concrete Indl Flooring Contrs
The Conductor - National Assn Brass Band Conductors
The Conduit - Cambridge Antiquarian Soc
Connect - Brit Inst Learning & Devt
The Conradian - Joseph Conrad Soc (UK)
Conservation Issues & the Maintenance of Cereal - Nat Soc Master Thatchers
Conserving Lakeland - Friends Lake District
Construction & Law Review - Chart Instn Civil Engg Surveyors
Construction History Jnl - Construction History Soc
Construction Industry Forecasts - Construction Products Assn
Construction Information Quarterly - Chart Inst Bldg
Construction Manager - Chart Inst Bldg
Construction Markets Trends - Construction Products Assn
Construction Products Briefing - Construction Products Assn
Construction Products Trade Survey - Construction Products Assn
Construction's impact on the big society - UK Contrs Group
Consultancy Resources Directory - Assn Security Consultants
Consumer Credit - Consumer Credit Tr Assn
Contact - Brit Chiropractic Assn
    Brit-Polish Cham Comm
    Guernsey Cham Comm
    Inst Traffic Accident Investigators
    Tramway Museum Soc
Contact News - Contact the Elderly
Contact Point - Brit Assn Dental Therapists
Contacto - Brit Interlingua Soc
Contemporary Hypnosis - BSCAH
Contemporary Social Science - Academy Social Sciences
Context - Inst Historic Building Consvn
Contract Catering Survey - Brit Hospitality Assn
Contracting Bulletin - Nat Assn Agricl Contractors

Contractors Directory - Nat Assn Agricl Contractors
Control - Inst Operations Mgt
The Controversy of John Hampden's Death - John Hampden Soc
Convection - Tornado & Storm Res Org
Cookshop, Housewares & Tabletop - Cookshop & Housewares Assn
Co-operative Official - Nat Assn Co-operative Officials
The Corker - Multi Vintage Wine Growers Soc
Cornerstone - Soc Protection Ancient Bldgs
Cornish Archaeology - Cornwall Archaeol Soc
Correlation - Astrological Assn GB
Correspondence Chess - Brit Correspondence Chess Assn
Corrosion Management - Inst Corrosion
Corrosion Science - Inst Corrosion
Cosmic Voice - Aetherius Soc
Cosmos - Traditional Cosmology Soc
Cosmos & Culture - Astrological Assn GB
Costings of Agricultural Operations - Central Assn Agricl Valuers
Costume - Costume Soc
Council Vehicle News - Road Transport Fleet Data Soc
The Councillor - Nat Assn Councillors
Counselling & Psychotherapy Research - Brit Assn Counselling & Psychotherapy
Counselling at Work - Brit Assn for Counselling & Psychotherapy
Counselling in Scotland - COSCA
Counterfoil - Brit Banking History Soc
The Counties - Assn Brit Counties
Country Sports - Countryside Alliance
Countryside Building - Rural & Indl Design & Bldg Assn Ltd
Courage - War Widows Assn GB
Courier - Registered Nursing Home Assn
A Course for all Seasons - R & Ancient Golf Club
The Court Historian - Soc Court Studies
Courtesy Call - Nat Campaign Courtesy
The Cover - Brit Assn Skin Camouflage
Covered - Brit Coatings Fedn Ltd
CPD Spotlight - Profl Assns Res Network
CQ-TV - Brit Amateur TV Club
Creating a Fountain - Fountain Soc
Creators Have Rights - Creators' Rights Alliance
Credit Management - Inst of Credit Mgt
Credit Union News - Assn Brit Credit Us Ltd
The Creel - Friends Alan Rawsthorne
The Cricket Statistician - Assn Cricket Statisticians & Historians
The Crier - Ancient & Honourable Gld Town Criers
The Crofter - Scot Crofting Fedn
Cromwelliana - Cromwell Assn
The Croquet Gazette - Croquet Assn
Crossbow UK - Nat Crossbow Fedn GB
Crossed Grain Magazine - Coeliac UK
Crossfire - American Civil War Round Table (UK)
Crossways - Assn Low Countries Studies GB & I
Crossword - Crossword Club
The Crown - Monarchist League
Croydon Church Townscape - Croydon Natural Hist & Scientific Soc
Cruising Construction Regulations - Hovercraft Club GB
Crypt - Xenophon
Crystallography News - Brit Crystallographic Assn
Crystals & Healing for Everyone - Crystal & Healing Fedn
Crystals Strong & Beautiful - Crystal & Healing Fedn
CSDF Business Continuity Guide - Food Storage & Distbn Federation
CSDF Fire Risk Minimisation Guidance - Food Storage & Distbn Federation
CSDF Material Handling Safety Guide - Food Storage & Distbn Federation
Cue Line - Stage Mgt Assn
Cued Speech Explained by People who use it - Cued Speech Assn UK
Cued Speech Instructional Booklet - Cued Speech Assn UK
Cued Speech Instructional Video - Cued Speech Assn UK
The Cued Speech Research Book - Cued Speech Assn UK
Cultivation of Hebes & Parahebes - Hebe Soc
The Cultivator - Vintage Horticl & Garden Machinery Club
Cultural & Social History - Social Hist Soc
Current Awareness Service - Brit Inst Learning Disabilities

Current Folklore - Folklore Soc
Current Research Monitor - Pesticide Action Network UK
Cushy - Assn Cushing's Treatment & Help
The Custodian - Brit Assn Shooting & Conservation
Customer First - Inst Customer Service
Cutting Edge - Brit Olympic Assn
Cuttings - Brit Lawn Mower Racing Assn
Cyclamen Jnl - Cyclamen Soc
Cycle - CTC
Cymry Llundain - London Welshman - London Welsh Assn
Czech Music - Dvořák Soc Czech & Slovak Music

D

Dairy Farming Event Showguide - R Assn Brit Dairy Farmers
Dales Despatch - Dales Pony Soc
Dams & Reservoirs - Brit Dam Soc
Dance Gazette - Royal Academy Dance
Dance Matters - Nat Dance Teachers Assn
Dance Research Jnl - Soc Dance Res
Dance Teaching Essentials - Dance UK Ltd
Dance UK News - Dance UK Ltd
The Dancer - Brit Ballet Org Ltd
Danceworld - Brit Theatre Dance Assn
Danny's Mum - Action Prisoners' Families
Dark Horizons - Brit Fantasy Soc
Dartmoor Diary - Dartmoor Pony Soc
Dartmoor Matters - Dartmoor Presvn Assn
DATA Jnl - Design & Technology Assn
DATA News - Design & Technology Assn
Database of Long Distance Paths - Long Distance Walkers Assn
The David Jones Jnl - David Jones Soc
Dawn - Drama Assn WalesDawns - Cymdeithas Ddawns Werin CymruDeadline - Assn UK Media Librarians
Deafness & Education - Brit Assn Teachers Deaf
Decking - the essential guide for DIY - Timber Decking Assn
The Declaration - Assn Indep Inventory Clerks
Dedicated - Inst Legal Secretaries & PAs
Deer Farming - Brit Deer Farms & Parks Assn
Deer News - Brit Deer Farms & Parks Assn
Definitive Guide to Racing - Jet Sport Racing Assn of GB
The Delphinium Garden - Delphinium Soc
Delphiniums - Delphinium Soc
Dementia - Ceretas
Dementia in Scotland - Alzheimer Scotland
The Democrat - Campaign Euro-federalism
Democratic Broadsheet - Campaign Euro-federalism
Demolition & Dismantling Jnl - National Fedn Demolition Contrs
Demolition Engineer - Inst Demolition Engrs
Dental Historian - Lindsay Soc Hist Dentistry
Dental Implant Summaries - Assn Dental Implantology UK
Dental Laboratory - Dental Laboratories Assn
Dental Therapy Update - Brit Assn Dental Therapists
The Dental Trader - Brit Dental Tr Assn
Departing Drugs - Exit
Depression - SANE
Derby Awards brochure - Horserace Writers & Photographers Assn
Derbyshire Archaeological Jnl - Derbyshire Archaeol Soc
Derbyshire Miscellany - Derbyshire Archaeol Soc
Descriptions of Plant Viruses - Assn Applied Biologists
Design - Inst Scientific & Technical Communicators
Design Research NL - Design Res Soc
Design Research Quarterly - Design Res Soc
Design Risk Management Guide - Assn Project Safety
The Designer - Chart Soc Designers
The Designer Craftsman - Soc Designer Craftsmen
Designing Magazine - Design & Technology Assn
Desirable Criteria for Pain Management Programmes - Brit Pain Soc
Despatches Magazine - Despatch Assn
Deutsch: Lehren und Lernen - Assn Language Learning
Development Education - Devt Educ Assn
Devon Archaeology - Devon Archaeol Soc
The Dexter Bulletin - Dexter Cattle Soc
Dhooraght - Cheshaght Ghailckagh

© CBD Research Ltd · Beckenham · BR3 5JS · Tel 020 8650 7745 · E-mail cbd@cbdresearch.com · www.cbdresearch.com

Diabetes Update - Diabetes UK
Diabetic Foot - Wound Care Alliance UK
Diabetic Medicine - Diabetes UK
Diagnostic Engineering - Instn Diagnostic Engrs
Diagnostics in Healthcare - Brit In Vitro Diagnostics Assn Ltd
Dialogue - Inst Gp Analysis
The Dickensian - Dickens Fellowship
Dictionary of Fire Technology - Instn Fire Engineers
Dictionary of International Marketing - Inst Intl Marketing
Dictionary of the Scots Language - Scot Language Dictionaries
Dictionary of Welsh Biography - Honourable Soc Cymmrodorion
Diecasting World - Inst Cast Metals Engineers
Dietetics Today - Brit Dietetic Assn
Digital Exchange - Helplines Assn
Direct News - Assn Public Service Excellence
Directory of Accredited Behavioural / Cognitive & REBT Psychotherapists - Brit Assn Behavioural & Cognitive Psychotherapies
Directory of Acquisitions Librarians - Nat Acquisitions Gp
Directory of Antiquarian & Second Hand Booksellers - Provincial Booksellers Fairs Assn
Directory of Book Publishers - Booksellers Assn UK & I
Directory of Booksellers - Booksellers Assn UK & I
Directory of British Crematoria - Cremation Soc GB
Directory of British Spring Manufacturers - UK Spring Mfrs Assn
Directory of Contracting Officers - Assn Dirs Adult Social Services
Directory of Insolvency Permit Holders - Inst Chart Accountants Scotland
Directory of Irish Family History - Ulster Histl Foundation
Directory of Pet Crematoria - Cremation Soc GB
Directory of Postgraduate Medical Centres - Nat Assn Clinical Tutors
Directory of Publishing in Scotland - Publishing Scotland
Directory of Restoration: a compendium of examples - Mineral Products Assn
Directory for Specifiers & Buyers - Brit Constructional Steelwork Assn Ltd
Directory of Storytellers - Soc Storytelling
Directory of Veterinary Practices - R Coll Veterinary Surgeons
Dirigible - Airship Heritage Trust
Disability Now - Scope
Discovery & Excavation in Scotland - Archaeology Scotland
Discrimination Law Briefings - Discrimination Law Assn
DISKUS - Brit Assn Study Religions
Dispatches - Vitiligo Soc
Dispensing Optics - Assn Brit Dispensing Opticians
Distilleries to Visit Guide - Scotch Whisky Assn
Distillery Map - Scotch Whisky Assn
The Distributor - Jewellery Distributors' Assn UK
Dodo - E F Benson Soc
Dog Trainer - Assn Pet Dog Trainers
Dog Warden News - Nat Dog Wardens Assn
Doing Business in Brazil - Brit Cham Comm & Ind Brazil
The Dolls' House Magazine - Gld Master Craftsmen
Domestic & commercial spas - Inst Swimming Pool Engrs
Domestic Sprinkler Systems - Brit Automatic Fire Sprinkler Assn
Doris Stockwell Memorial Papers - Brit Assn Numismatic Socs
Dorothea Coke Memorial Lecture - Viking Soc Nthn Res
Double Reed News - Brit Double Reed Soc
The Double Tressure - Heraldry Soc Scotland
Doula News - Brit Doula Assn
Dowsing Today - Brit Soc Dowsers
The Dozenal Jnl - Dozenal Soc GB
Dragon Line - Brit Dragon Boat Racing Assn
Dragonfly News - Brit Dragonfly Soc
The Drake Broadside - Drake Exploration Soc
The Drake NL - Drake Exploration Soc
Drama - Nat Drama
The Dramatherapy Jnl - Brit Assn Dramatherapists
Driving after Amputation - Brit Limbless Ex-Service Men's Assn
Driving Instructor - Driving Instructors Assn
Driving Magazine - Driving Instructors Assn
Drummers Call - Corps Drums Soc
Dry Shake Topping - Assn Concrete Indl Flooring Contrs
Drystock Farmer - Ir Cattle & Sheep Farmers' Assn
Duchenne News - Duchenne Family Support Gp
Due North - Fedn Ulster Local Studies
The Dun Thing - Dun Horse & Pony Soc

The Dun Thing Update - Dun Horse & Pony Soc
Durbar - Indian Military Histl Soc
Durham Archaeological Jnl - Architectural & Archaeol Soc Durham & Northumberland
Durham Biographies - Durham County Local Hist Soc
Durham City and its MPs - Durham County Local Hist Soc
The Durham Crown Lordships - Durham County Local Hist Soc
Durham Wildlife - Durham Wildlife Trust
Dutch Crossing: a Jnl of Low Countries studies - Assn Low Countries Studies GB & I
DVC - UK Practical Shooting Assn
Dymock Poets & Friends - Friends Dymock Poets

E

Early Education - Brit Assn Early Childhood Education
Early Music Performer - Nat Early Music Assn
Earth Sciences - R Soc Edinburgh
Easter Rising in Song & Ballad - Workers' Music Assn
The Eastern Africa NL - Eastern Africa Assn
Ecclesiology Today - Ecclesiological Soc
The Eckhart Review - Eckhart Soc
Economic Affairs - Inst Economic Affairs
Economic Development - Instn Economic Devt
Economic History Review - Economic Hist Soc
The Economic Jnl - R Economic Soc
Economic Trends UK - Japanese Cham Comm & Ind UK
Ecos: a review of conservation - Brit Assn Nature Conservationists
Eczema - Aetiology & Management - Wound Care Alliance UK
Edgar Evans of Gower - Gower Soc
The Edge - Calligraphy & Lettering Arts Soc
EDS (English Dance & Song) - English Folk Dance & Song Soc
Education - Soc Educ Consultants
Education 3-13 - Assn Study Primary Educ
Education Management & Administration - Brit Educl Leadership, Mgt & Admin Soc
Education in Science - Assn Science Educ
The Education Social Worker - Nat Assn Social Workers Educ
Education Today - Coll Teachers
Education & Training Courses in Horticulture - Inst Horticulture
Educational Gerontology - Assn Educ & Ageing
Educational Psychology in Practice - Assn Educl Psychologists
Educational Therapy & Therapeutic Teaching - Caspari Foundation Educl Therapy & Therapeutic Teaching
Effective Business in Taiwan - Brit Cham Comm Taipei
EFNARC Specification for Sprayed Concrete - Sprayed Concrete Assn
The Egg Crafter - Egg Crafters Gld GB
Egyptian Archaeology - Egypt Exploration Soc
Egyptian-British Trade - Egyptian Brit Cham Comm
El Hornero - Brit Uruguayan Soc
Elder Abuse - Ceretas
Electric Boat News - Electric Boat Assn
The Egg Crafter - Egg Crafters Gld GB
Electronic Letters - Instn Engg & Technology
Electronic Transfer of Geotechnical Data from Ground Investigations - Assn Geotechnical & Geoenvironmental Specialists
Elements - R Instn GB
The Elgar Jnl - Elgar Soc
The Elgar News - Elgar Soc
eLucidate - UK EInformation Gp
The Embalmer - Brit Inst Embalmers
Embroidery - Embroiderers' Guild
E-Motion - Assn Dance Movement Therapy UK
Emotional & Behavioural Difficulties - SEBDA
Endocrine Related Cancer - Soc Endocrinology
The Endocrinologist - Soc Endocrinology
Energy Action - Nat Energy Action
Engineer Today - UK Assn Profl Engrs
The Engineering Designer - Instn Engg Designers
Engineering in Emergencies: a practical guide - RedR UK
Engineering Integrity - Engineering Integrity Soc
Engineering & Technology - Instn Engg & Technology
England's Standard - R Soc St George

English - English Assn
English 4-11 - English Assn
English Bridge - English Bridge U
English Draughts Jnl - English Draughts Assn
English in the UK - English UK
English UK News - English UK
English, Drama, Media - National Assn Teaching English
Enteral Feeding - Infection Prevention Soc
Enterprise Communities - Community Devt Finance Assn
Enterprising Matters - Inst Small Business & Entrepreneurship
Environmental Archaeology: Jnl of Human Palaeoecology -
   Assn Envtl Archaeology
Environmental Education - Nat Assn Envtl Educ
Environmental Health Scotland - R Envtl Health Inst Scotland
Environmental Law - UK Envtl Law Assn
Environmental Microbiology - Soc Applied Microbiology
The Environmental Scientist - Instn of Envtl Sciences
Envirotech News - Envtl Inds Cmsn
The Ephemerist - Ephemera Soc
Epilepsy News - Epilepsy Scotland
Epilepsy Review - Nat Soc Epilepsy
Epilepsy Today - Brit Epilepsy Assn
Epiphytes - Epiphytic Plant Study Gp
Equestrian Trade News - Brit Equestrian Tr Assn
Equine Behaviour - Equine Behaviour Forum
Equipment Selection - Wound Care Alliance UK
Ergonomics - Ergonomics Soc
Ergonomics in design - Ergonomics Soc
The Ergonomist NL - Ergonomics Soc
Escape To... - Youth Hostels Assn (England & Wales)
Escaping the Leasehold Trap - Leasehold Enfranchisement Assn
Esperanto en Skotlando - Scottish Esperanto Assn
Essays in Biochemistry - Biochemical Soc
Essays & Studies - English Assn
Essence - Brit Flower & Vibrational Essences Assn
The Essential Guide to Aqueous Coating of Paper & Board -
   Paper Industry Technical Assn Ltd
Essential Scots Dictionary - Scottish Language Dictionaries
Essex Archaeology & History - Essex Soc Archaeology & History
Essex Archaeology & History News - Essex Soc Archaeology &
   History
Essex Jnl - Essex Archaeol & Histl Congress
Essex Wildlife - Essex Wildlife Trust
The Estate Agent - Nat Assn Estate Agents
Ethical Record - South Place Ethical Soc
Eureka - Kingston Cham Comm
EuroChoices - Agricl Economics Soc
The European Advertising & Media Forecast - Advertising Assn
European-Atlantic Jnl - European-Atlantic Group
European Eating Disorders Review - Eating Disorders Assn
European Jnl for Dental Implantologists - Assn Dental
   Implantology UK
European Jnl of Information Systems - Operational Res Soc
European Jnl of Parenteral & Pharmaceutical Sciences -
   Pharmaceutical & Healthcare Sciences Soc
European Jnl of Phycology - Brit Phycological Soc
European Jnl of Prosthodontics & Restorative Dentistry - Brit
   Soc Restorative Dentistry
European Jnl of Soil Science - Brit Soc Soil Science
European Jnl of Surgical Oncology - BASO
European Jnl of Disorders of Communication - R Coll Speech &
   Language Therapists
European Morgan Horse Magazine - Brit Morgan Horse Soc
European Rail News - Railway Enthusiasts Soc
Europos Lietuvis - Lithuanian Assn UK Ltd
The Evacuee - Evacuees Reunion Assn
**Evaluation of the Past & Future Economic Contribution of the
   UK Science Park Movement -** UK Science Park Assn
Event Organiser - The Event Services Assn
Event Organisers Update - Soc Event Organisers
Evolution of Permanent Way - Permanent Way Institution
Excalibur - Royal Navy Enthusiasts' Soc
Excel - Assn Healthcare Cleaning Professionals
Exchange - National Eczema Soc
Executive Accountant - Inst Cost & Executive Accountants
Exhibition Standard - Assn of Event Organisers
Experimental Physiology - Physiological Soc
The Expert - Academy Experts

Explaining Vending - Automatic Vending Assn
Explosives Engineering - Inst Explosives Engineers
Export News - Brit Allied Trades Federation
Eye - Royal College of Ophthalmologists

F

FAB - Fanderson
Fabian Review - Fabian Soc
Face Facts - Brit Compact Collectors' Soc
Face to Face - Face Painting Assn
face2face - Confedn Dental Employers
Fact & Fiction - Brit Waterbed Assn
FACTion - Falsely Accused Carers & Teachers
Facts & Figures - Incorporated National Assn Brit & Irish Millers Ltd
The Facts on the Performance of Timber Doors & Doorsets -
   Architectural & Specialist Door Manufacturers Assn
Fair Catalogues - Provincial Booksellers Fairs Assn
Faith & Worship - Prayer Book Soc
Falconer - Brit Falconers' Club
Familia: Ulster Genealogical Review - Ulster Historical
   Foundation
Family History - Inst Heraldic & Genealogical Studies
Family Magazine - Fibromyalgia Assn UK
Family Matters - Family Rights Group
Farming News - Ulster Farmers Union
**Fasti of the General Assembly of the Presbyterian Church in
   Ireland 1840-1910 -** Presbyterian Historical Soc of Ireland
Feathered World - National Pigeon Assn
The FED - National Fedn Retail Newsagents
Feedback - Confedn Aerial Industries Ltd
The Fell Runner - Fell Runners Assn
Feng Shui News - Feng Shui Soc
Fern Gazette - Brit Pteridological Soc
FESI - European Insulation Standards - Thermal Insulation
   Contrs Assn
Festival of Hymns - Hymn Soc
Fidelity - Nat Coun Psychotherapists
Field & Fell NL - Westmorland County Agricl Soc
Field Guide - W W Jacobs Appreciation Soc
Field Studies Magazine - Field Studies Coun
The Fifth Fuel - Assn Consvn of Energy
Fight Back - Nat Ankylosing Spondylitis Soc
Film & Video Maker - Inst Amat Cinematographers
Films Directory - W W Jacobs Appreciation Soc
Financial Controller - Assn Financial Controllers & Administrators
Financial Planner - Inst Financial Planning
Financial World - Inst Financial Services
Finding Dad - Action Prisoners' Families
Fine Food Digest - Gld Fine Food
Fines & Charges in Public Libraries in England & Wales - Soc
   Chief Librarians
Fingerprint Whorld - Fingerprint Soc
The Finial - Silver Spoon Club
Fire & Thatch - Nat Soc Master Thatchers
Fire Cover - Fire Brigade Soc
Fire Engineers Jnl - Instn Fire Engrs
Fire Precautions Guide to Risk Assessment - UK Warehousing
   Assn
Fire Prevention - Fire Protection Assn
Fire Protection for Structural Steel in Buildings - Assn Specialist
   Fire Protection
Fire Protection Ybk - Fire Protection Assn
Fire Technology - Instn Fire Engrs
First - Local Government Assn
First Aid Manual - Saint Andrew's Ambulance Assn
First Five - Scot Pre-School Play Assn
First Voice - Fedn Small Businesses
Fiscal Studies - Inst Fiscal Studies
Fish - Inst Fisheries Management
Fish Friers Review - Nat Fedn Fish Friers Ltd
Fishing Boats - Forty Plus (40+) Fishing Boat Assn
Five Foot Three - Rly Presvn Soc Ireland
Five Last Acts - Exit
Flagmaster - Flag Inst

Flareoff - Offshore Ind Liaison Céee
Fleet Operator - ACFO Ltd
Flipside - Instn Engg & Technology
The Flower Arranger - Nat Assn Flower Arrangement Socs
Flueways - Nat Assn Chimney Engineers Ltd
The Flydresser - Flydressers Gld
The Flying Scot - Scot Hang Gliding & Paragliding Fedn
The Flywheel - Northern Mill Engine Soc
Flyball Record - Brit Flyball Assn
Focus on Fives - Brit Assn Adoption & Fostering
Focus on Haflingers - Haflinger Soc GB
Focus on Italy - Brit Cham Comm Italy
Focus on Swaziland - Swaziland Soc
Folk Arts England News - Assn Festival Organisers
Folk Life: a jnl of ethnological studies - Soc Folk Life Studies
Folk Music Jnl - English Folk Dance & Song Soc
Folklore - Folklore Soc
Follies - Folly Fellowship
Follies Jnl - Folly Fellowship
FoMRHI Quarterly - Fellowship Makers & Researchers of Historical Instruments
Food & Bioproducts Processing - Instn Chemical Engrs
Food Hygiene - Ceretas
Food Science & Technology - Inst Food Science & Technology
Food Service Standards at Ward Level: good practice guide - Hospital Caterers Assn
Food Trader - Nat Fedn Meat & Food Traders
Foodworker - Bakers, Food & Allied Workers Union
Footprint - Brit Walking Fedn
Footprints - Brit Reflexology Assn
Forecourt - Retail Motor Ind Fedn
Foreign Birds - Foreign Bird Fedn
Forensic Human Identification - Brit Assn Human Identification
Forestry & Timber News - Confedn Forest Inds
Forestry Jnl - Inst Chart Foresters
Forge - Nat Assn Farriers, Blacksmiths & Agricultural Engrs
Forging Links - Tools Self Reliance
The Formation Sign - Military Heraldry Soc
The Formulary - Friends Dr Watson
Fort - Fortress Study Gp
Forty Years On - Assn Past Rotarians
Forum - Brit Fedn Brass Bands
Forward - Spinal Injuries Assn
Foster Care - Fostering Network
Foundry Trade Jnl - Inst Cast Metals Engrs
Foundry Ybk & Castings Buyers Guide - Inst Cast Metals Engrs
Four Four - Brit Academy Songwriters, Composers & Authors
Four Seasons News - South of England Agricl Soc
Framework - Construct: Concrete Structures Gp Ltd
Franchise Link - Brit Franchise Assn Ltd
Franchisee Guide - Brit Franchise Assn Ltd
Franchisor Guide - Brit Franchise Assn Ltd
Free Life - Libertarian Alliance
Free Press - Campaign Press & Broadcasting Freedom
The Free Trader - Free Trade League
Freedom Today - The Freedom Assn
The Freeman - Gld Freemen City of London
Freeway - Brit Nat Temperance League
Freight - Freight Transport Assn
French Studies - Soc French Studies
Freshwater Reviews - Freshwater Biological Assn
Friends Connect - Attend
Friends Magazine - Scot Soc Prevention Cruelty to Animals
Fritillary - Ashmolean Natural Hist Soc Oxfordshire
From Netley to Maiwand - Friends Dr Watson
From Rome to Maastricht - a reappraisal of Britain's membership of the EC - Campaign Indep Britain
Front-Line - Inst Career Guidance Ltd
The Fulcrum - Craniosacral Therapy Assn UK
The Funeral Director Monthly - Nat Assn Funeral Dirs
Funerals without God - Brit Humanist Assn
The Funnel - Steam Boat Assn GB
Fur & Feather (inc Rabbits) - Brit Rabbit Council
Furniture & Cabinetmaking - Gld Master Craftsmen
Furniture History - Furniture History Soc
Future & the Inventor - Inst Patentees & Inventors

G

G K Quarterly - Chesterton Soc
GA Magazine - Geographical Assn
The Gallipolian - Gallipoli Assn
Game Farming NL - Game Farmers' Assn
The Garden - R Horticl Soc
Garden Design Jnl - Soc Garden Designers
Garden History - Garden Hist Soc
Gardens Open Directory - Alpine Garden Soc
The Gargoyle - Malcolm Muggeridge Soc
Gas Business - SBGI
Gas Installer Magazine - Coun Regd Gas Installers
Gatelodge - POA: Profl Trs U Prison, Correctional & Secure Psychiatric Workers
Gauchers Newsfree - Gauchers Assn
The Gavel - Nat Assn Valuers & Auctioneers
Gazeteers of Industrial Archaeology - Derbyshire Archaeological Soc
Genealogists' Magazine - Soc Genealogists
General Dental Practitioner - Dental Profls Assn
Generations Review - Brit Soc Gerontology
Geoenvironmental Site Assessment: guide to the model report - Assn Geotechnical & Geoenvironmental Specialists
Geography - Geographical Assn
GeogScot - R Scot Geographical Soc
Geonews - Geographical Soc Ireland
Geophysical Jnl International - R Astronomical Soc
George Borrow Bulletin - George Borrow Soc
George Eliot Review - George Eliot Fellowship
German History - German History Soc
Get Cruisewise - Assn Cruise Experts
Get it Sussed - Meningitis Research Foundation
Getting Started: the common induction standards in adult social care - Assn Real Change
Gifted & Talented - Nat Assn Gifted Children
Gilbert & Sullivan News - Gilbert & Sullivan Soc
Giving Shares & Securities: information pack for financial advisers - Community Foundation Network
Glasgow Business Jnl - Glasgow Cham Comm
Glasgow Naturalist - Glasgow Natural Hist Soc
Glass Circle Jnl - The Glass Circle
Glass Circle News - The Glass Circle
Glass Networks - Contemporary Glass Soc
Glass News - Assn Hist Glass
Glass Technology - Soc Glass Technology
Glaucus - Brit Marine Life Study Soc
Glazed Expressions - Tiles & Architectural Ceramics Soc
Glazing Manual - Glass & Glazing Fedn
The Gleam - Sheila Kaye-Smith Soc
Global Youth Work - Devt Educ Assn
Globe Trotter - Brit Gld Travel Writers
Glossary of Printing Terms - Brit Printing Soc
GN News - Great Nthn Rly Soc
Gnomon - Assn Astronomy Educ
Gold Top News - Quality Milk Producers
Golf Club Management - Golf Club Mgrs' Assn
Gongoozler - Canal Card Collectors Circle
The Good Alternative Travel Guide - Tourism Concern
Good Beer Guide - Campaign Real Ale
Good Beer Guide to Germany - Campaign Real Ale
Good Bottled Beer Guide - Campaign Real Ale
Good Cheese - Gld Fine Food
Good Parks Guide - GreenSpace
Good Piers Guide - Nat Piers Soc
Good Practice in Boarding Schools: a resource handbook for all those working in boarding - Boarding Schools Assn
Gower in Focus - Gower Soc
Gower Walks - Gower Soc
Gower Way - Gower Soc
Graduated Compression Hosiery - Wound Care Alliance UK
Grandparent Times - Grandparents' Assn
The Grape Press - UK Vineyards Assn
The Grapevine - Care Leavers Assn
Grapevine NL - Nat Assn Co-operative Officials
Graphic Archaeology - Assn Archaeological Illustrators & Surveyors

The Graphologist - Brit Inst Graphologists
Grass & Forage Farmer - Brit Grassland Soc
Grass & Forage Science - Brit Grassland Soc
Grassbox - Old Lawn Mower Club
Great North Review - Great North of Scotland Rly Assn
Great Oxford Collection of Newsletter Essays 1996-2004 - De Vere Soc
Great Western Echo - Great Wstn Soc Ltd
Great Western Telegraph Rule Book, 1878 - Signalling Record Soc
Greece & Rome - Classical Assn
Green Building Magazine - Assn Envt Conscious Building
Green Lanes - Green Lane Assn
Green Leaves - Barbara Pym Soc
Green Places - GreenSpace
Green Places - Inst Parks & Green Space
Greensheet - Military Vehicle Trust
The Grieg Companion - Grieg Soc GB
Grooming Snippets - Pet Care Tr Assn
The Groundsman - Inst Groundsmanship
The Grower - Assn Scot Shellfish Growers
The Growing Heap - Community Composting Network
Growing Places - Fedn City Farms & Community Gardens
Growth Point - THRIVE
GSQ - GS1 UK
Guernsey Breeders NL - English Guernsey Cattle Soc
Guidance for the Design, Construction & Maintenance of Petrol Filling Stations - Assn Petroleum & Explosives Admin
Guidance on Alcohol & Drug Misuse in the Workplace - Fac Occupational Medicine
Guidance on Ethics for Occupational Physicians - Fac Occupational Medicine
A Guide to Anerobic Digestion + Directory of Suppliers - Assn Organics Recycling
Guide to Artificial Arms - REACH: Assn Children Hand or Arm Deficiency
Guide to Best Practice for the Installation of Pipe Jacks & Microtunnels - Pipe Jacking Assn
Guide to British Piers - Nat Piers Soc
Guide to Careers in Outdoor Learning - Inst Outdoor Learning
Guide to Community Composting - Community Composting Network
A Guide to Customer Publishing - Assn Publishing Agencies
A Guide to European Funding - Community Foundation Network
Guide to the Finest Cheeses of Britain & Ireland - Specialist Cheesemakers' Assn
Guide to Funerals & Bereavement - Assn Burial Authorities Ltd
Guide to Good Practice for Scaffolding with Tubes & Fittings - Nat Access & Scaffolding Confederation
Guide to Gower - Gower Soc
Guide to History of Science Courses in Britain - Brit Soc for Hist Science
Guide to Homesearch (for those starting a business) - Assn Relocation Professionals
A Guide to In-Vessel Composting + Directory of Suppliers - Assn Organics Recycling
Guide to the Independent Holiday Hostels of Ireland - Indep Holiday Hostels Ireland
Guide to Laboratory Testing - Assn Geotechnical & Geoenvironmental Specialists
The Guide to Literacy Resources - Nat Literacy Assn
Guide to Machine Vision - UK Indl Vision Assn
Guide to Making Model Hovercraft - Hovercraft Club of GB
A Guide to Marketing in Europe - Inst Intl Marketing
A Guide to Marketing in North America - Inst Intl Marketing
A Guide to Play Therapy - Brit Assn Play Therapists
Guide Post - Gld Registered Tourist Guides
A Guide to Private Equity - BVCA (Brit Private Equity & Venture Capital Assn)
Guide to Professional Conduct - R Coll Veterinary Surgeons
Guide to Quality Chinchilla - Nat Chinchilla Soc
Guide to Reach - Brit Adhesives & Sealants Assn
Guide to Risk Assessment for Water Services - Water Mgt Soc Ltd
Guide to Safety in Burial Grounds - Assn Burial Authorities Ltd
Guide to Scottish Industrial Heritage - Scot Indl Heritage Soc
Guide to the servicing of portable fire extinguishers - Fire Ind Assn

Guide to Shiatsu - Shiatsu Soc (UK)
Guide to Tortoises & Turtles - Tortoise Trust
A Guide to Traditional Herbal Medicines - Brit Herbal Medicine Assn
Guide to the UK - Assn Relocation Profls
Guidebook to Goddards - Lutyens Trust
Guidelines - Scot Tourist Guides Assn
Guidelines for Combined Geoenvironmental & Geotechnical Investigation - Assn Geotechnical & Geoenvironmental Specialists
Guidelines for Local Safety Officers - Brit Elastic Rope Sports Assn
Guideline to Safe Operation of Cruising Hovercraft - Hovercraft Club of GB
Guidelines for Preventing Intravascular Catheter related Infection - Infection Prevention Soc
Guidelines on Essence Production - Brit Assn Flower Essence Producers
Guidelines on the Regulation, Labelling, Advertising & Promotion of Aromatherapy Products - Aromatherapy Tr Coun
Guiding - Girlguiding UK
Gut - Brit Soc Gastroenterology
Gut Reaction - Gut Trust

H

The Haggard Jnl - Rider Haggard Soc
Haggardiana - Rider Haggard Soc
Hampshire Studies - Hampshire Field Club & Archaeological Soc
Hand Chain Blocks & Lever Hoists in the Offshore Environment - Lifting Eqpt Engrs Assn
Hand Decontamination Guidelines - Infection Prevention Soc
Handbook for Fire Engineers - Instn Fire Engrs
Handbook: a practical guide to thatch & thatching in the 21st century - Nat Soc Master Thatchers
Handbook of School Health - Medical Officers Schools Assn
Handling Service Users' Finances & Valuables - Ceretas
The Hardy Plant - Hardy Plant Soc
Harmonica World - Nat Harmonica League
Harmony Express - Brit Assn Barbershop Singers
Harness Goat Soc - Harness Goat Soc
Hazard Analysis & Critical Control Point for Composting - Assn Organics Recycling
Head to Head - Assn Headteachers & Deputes Scotland
Headline Earnings Definition - CFA Soc UK
Healing Today - Nat Fedn Spiritual Healers
Health & Homeopathy - Brit Homoeopathic Assn
Health & Safety at Composting Sites - a guide for managers - Assn Organics Recycling
Health & Safety Handbook for Operatives - Thermal Insulation Contrs Assn
Health Club Management - Fitness Ind Assn
Health Estate Jnl - Inst Healthcare Engg & Estate Mgt
Health Management - Inst Healthcare Mgt
Health Policy & Technology - Fellowship Postgraduate Medicine
Health Writer - Gld Health Writers
Healthcare Counselling & Psychotherapy Jnl - Brit Assn Counselling & Psychotherapy
Healthcare Finance - Healthcare Financial Mgt Assn
Health-Care Focus - Assn Brit Healthcare Inds
Healthy & Organic Living - Gld Master Craftsmen
Healthy Living Report - Soc Local Authority Chief Execs & Senior Mrs
Heart Beat - Children's Heart Assn
Heart Children - Heart Line Assn
Heat losses from indoor & outdoor pools - Inst Swimming Pool Engrs
Heat pumps - Inst Swimming Pool Engrs
HeavyTalk - Heavy Transport Assn
Hebe News - Hebe Soc
Hedgeline - Hedgeline
Help & Advice - Inst Consumer Affairs
The Heraldic Craftsman - Soc Heraldic Arts
The Heraldry Gazette - Heraldry Soc
Herbal Thymes - National Inst Med Herbalists

© CBD Research Ltd · Beckenham · BR3 5JS · Tel 020 8650 7745 · E-mail cbd@cbdresearch.com · www.cbdresearch.com

I

Information - Inst T Mark Attorneys
Informed - Investor Relations Soc
Ingenia - R Academy Engg
Inland Racing Competition Regulation - Hovercraft Club GB
Inland Waterways Guide - Inland Waterways Assn
Inner Wheel - Assn Inner Wheel Clubs GB & I
Innes Review - Scot Catholic Histl Assn
Innovation in Print - Indep Print Inds Assn
Innovation into Success - UK Science Park Assn
Innovations in Primary Health Care Nursing - Community & District Nursing Assn UK
InRoads - Inst Road Safety Officers
Inscape - International Jnl of Art Therapy - Brit Assn Art Therapists
Inside Churches - Nat Assn Decorative & Fine Arts Socs
Inside OR - Operational Res Soc
Inside Out - Community Devt Finance Assn
Inside the Industry Report - Credit Services Assn
Inside Track - Brit Olympic Assn
Inside Track - Green Alliance Trust
The Insider - Crohn's in Childhood Res Assn
Insight - Leukaemia CARE
Primary Immunodeficiency Assn
Theosophical Soc England
In-Situ Concrete Frames: a report - Construct: Concrete Structures Group
Insolvency Intelligence - Insolvency Lawyers' Assn
Inspire - Assn Respiratory Technology & Physiology
The Installer - Nat Insulation Assn
Installation Guide - Brit Compressed Air Soc
Insulation - Thermal Insulation Mfrs & Suppliers Assn
Intentions - Oscar Wilde Soc
Interact - Soc Advancement Games & Simulations Educ & Training
Interaction - Action ME
Interfaces - Forensic Science Soc
Interior Insight - Assn Interior Specialists
Interiors Focus - Assn Interior Specialists
Internal Auditing & Business Risk - Chart Inst of Internal Auditors - UK & I
International - Nat Acrylic Painters' Assn
International Accountant - Assn Intl Accountants Ltd
International Affairs - Royal Inst Intl Affairs
International Endodontic Jnl - Brit Endodontic Soc
International Exchange - Motor Neurone Disease Assn
International Gas Engineering & Management - Instn Gas Engrs & Mgrs
International Jnl of Art & Design Education - Nat Soc Educ Art & Design
International Jnl of Audiology - Brit Soc Audiology
International Jnl of Cosmetic Science - Soc Cosmetic Scientists
International Jnl of Dairy Technology - Soc Dairy Technology
International Jnl of Food Science & Technology - Inst Food Science & Technology
International Jnl of Iberian Studies - Assn Contemporary Iberian Studies
International Jnl of Injury Control & Safety Promotion - Ergonomics Soc
International Jnl of Market Research - Market Res Soc
International Jnl of Meteorology - Tornado & Storm Res Org
International Jnl of Nautical Archaeology - Nautical Archaeology Soc
International Jnl of Obstetric Anesthesia - Obstetric Anaesthetists Assn
International Jnl of Paediatric Dentistry - Brit Soc Paediatric Dentistry
International Jnl of Pharmacy Practice - R Pharmaceutical Soc of Great Britain
International Jnl of Project Management - Assn Project Mgt
International Jnl of Psychoanalysis - Brit Psychoanalytical Soc
International Jnl of Psychoanalysis - Inst Psychoanalysis
International Jnl of Remote Sensing - Remote Sensing & Photogrammetry Soc
International Jnl of Systematic & Evolutionary Microbiology - Soc Gen Microbiology
International Musculoskeletal Medicine Jnl - Soc Orthopaedic Medicine
International Simulation & Gaming Research Ybk - Soc Advancement Games & Simulations Educ & Training

The International Therapist - Fedn Holistic Therapists
International Turfgrass Bulletin - Sports Turf Res Inst
The Interrupter - Assn Police & Court Interpreters
Introducing Direct Democracy - Referenda Soc
An Introduction to Cochlear Implants - Nat Assn Deafened People
An Introduction to Creating Quality Decks - Timber Decking Assn
An Introduction to Pipe Jacking & Microtunnelling Design - Pipe Jacking Assn
An Introduction to Pipeline Pigging - Pigging Products & Services Assn
An Introduction to Sprayed Concrete - Sprayed Concrete Assn
An Introduction to Tensional Strapping - Brit Tensional Strapping Assn
Introduction to Wildlife Sound Recording - Wildlife Sound Recording Soc
Investigate - Assn Brit Investigators
Investment Property Focus - Investment Property Forum
Invoice - Inst Certified Book-Keepers
The Irish Genealogist - Irish Genealogical Res Soc
Irish Geography - Geographical Soc Ireland
Irish Mountain Log - Mountaineering Coun Ireland
Irish Studies Review - Brit Assn Ir Studies
Is it anything you ate? - National Soc Res Allergy
Island Business - Isle of Wight Cham Comm, Tourism & Ind
Isle of Wight Birds - Isle of Wight Natural Hist & Archaeological Soc
The ITC Practical Guide for Writers & Companies - Indep Theatre Coun

J

Jacob Jnl - Jacob Sheep Soc
The Jacobite - Seventeen Fortyfive / 1745 Assn
Jade - Gld Erotic Artists
James Hilton - James Hilton Soc
Japan Experiences - Japan Soc
Japan Forum - Brit Assn Japanese Studies
Jem - English Goat Breeders Assn
The Jester - Cartoonists' Club GB
The Jeweller - Nat Assn Goldsmiths GB & I
Jersey at Home - R Jersey Agricl & Horticl Soc
Jewellery History Today - Soc Jewellery Historians
Jewellery Studies - Soc Jewellery Historians
Jigsaw - Scot Soc Autism
Jnl of Adventure Education & Outdoor Learning - Inst Outdoor Learning
Jnl of Agricultural Economics - Agricl Economics Soc
Jnl of American Studies - Brit Assn American Studies
Jnl of Anatomy - Anatomical Soc GB & I
Jnl of Animal Technology & Welfare - Inst Animal Technology
Jnl of Applied Microbiology - Soc Applied Microbiology
Jnl of Applied Philosophy - Soc Applied Philosophy
Jnl of Applied Research in Intellectual Disabilities - Brit Inst Learning Disabilities
Jnl of Arts Marketing - Arts Marketing Assn
Jnl of Biological Education - Soc Biology
Jnl of Bone & Joint Surgery - Brit Orthopaedic Assn
Jnl of Bryology - Brit Bryological Soc
Jnl of Cataract & Refractive Surgery - UK & I Soc Cataract & Refractive Surgeons
Jnl of Child Health Care - Assn Brit Paediatric Nurses
Jnl of Child Psychology & Psychiatry - Assn Child & Adolescent Mental Health
Jnl of Classics Teaching - Joint Assn Classical Teachers
The Jnl of Clinical Periodontology - Brit Soc Periodontology
Jnl of Common Market Studies - University Assn Contemporary Eur Studies
Jnl of Conchology - Conchological Soc GB & I
Jnl of Dental Research - Brit Soc Oral & Dental Res
Jnl of Design History - Design Hist Soc
Jnl of Egyptian Archaeology - Egypt Exploration Soc
Jnl of Electro-physiology & Technology - Assn Neurophysiological Scientists
Jnl of Endocrinology - Soc Endocrinology

© CBD Research Ltd · Beckenham · BR3 5JS · Tel 020 8650 7745 · E-mail cbd@cbdresearch.com · www.cbdresearch.com

Jnl of Euroendocrinology - Brit Soc Neuroendocrinology
Jnl of Experimental Botany - Soc Experimental Biology
Jnl of Family Planning & Reproductive Healthcare - Fac Sexual & Reproductive Healthcare
Jnl of French Language Studies - Assn French Language Studies
Jnl of General Virology - Soc Gen Microbiology
Jnl of Hand Surgery - Brit Soc Surgery Hand
Jnl of Hellenic Studies - Soc Promotion Hellenic StudiesJnl of Hospital Infection - Healthcare Infection Soc
Jnl of Human Nutrition & Dietetics - Brit Dietetic Assn
Jnl of Infection - Brit Infection Assn
Jnl of Infertility Counselling - Brit Infertility Counselling Assn
Jnl of Interactive Marketing - Inst Direct Marketing
Jnl of International Development - Devt Studies Assn
Jnl of International Marketing - Inst Intl Marketing
The Jnl of Latin Teaching - Assn Latin Teaching
Jnl of Linguistics - Linguistics Assn of GB
Jnl of Medical Microbiology - Soc Gen Microbiology
Jnl into Melody - Robert Farnon Soc
Jnl of Micropalaeontology - Micropalaeontological Soc
Jnl of Microscopy - R Microscopical Soc
Jnl of Modern Italy - Assn Study Modern Italy
Jnl of Molecular Endocrinology - Soc Endocrinology
Jnl of Molluscan Studies - Malacological Soc London
Jnl of Museum Ethnography - Museum Ethnographers Gp
Jnl of Natural Medicine - Intl Register Consultant Herbalists & Homoeopaths
Jnl of Occupational & Organisational Psychology - Brit Psychological Soc
Jnl of One-Day Surgery - Brit Assn Day Surgery
Jnl of One-Name Studies - Guild Master Craftsmen
Jnl of Orthopaedic Medicine - Brit Inst Musculoskeletal Medicine
Jnl of Paediatric Surgery - Brit Assn Paediatric Surgeons
Jnl of Pathology - Pathological Soc GB & I
Jnl of Perioperative Practice - Assn Perioperative Practice
Jnl of Physics - Inst Physics
Jnl of Physiology - Physiological Soc
Jnl of Plastic, Reconstructive & Aesthetic Surgery - Brit Assn Plastic, Reconstructive & Aesthetic Surgeons
Jnl for Play Therapy - Brit Assn Play Therapists
Jnl of Psychopharmacology - Brit Assn Psychopharmacology
Jnl of Reproductive & Infant Psychology - Soc Reproductive & Infant Psychology
Jnl of Research in Reading - UK Literacy Assn
Jnl of Roman Studies - Soc Promotion Roman StudiesJnl of Sexual Aggression - Nat Org Treatment of Abusers
Jnl of Simulation - Operational Research Soc
Jnl of Small Animal Practice - Brit Small Animal Veterinary Assn
Jnl of Sports Sciences - Ergonomics Soc
Jnl of Stained Glass - Brit Soc Master Glass Painters
Jnl of Stereo Imaging - Stereoscopic Soc
Jnl of Tissue Viability - Tissue Viability Soc
Jnl of Turfgrass & Sports Surface Science - Sports Turf Res Inst
Jnl of Ultrasound - Brit Med Ultrasound Soc
Jnl of Visual Communication in Medicine (Vision) - Inst Med Illustrators
The Jnl for Weavers, Spinners & Dyers - Assn Glds Weavers, Spinners & Dyers
Jnl of Zoology - Zoological Soc of London
John Hampden & His Times - John Hampden Soc
John Hampden of Buckinghamshire: the people's hero - John Hampden Soc
Joint Code of Practice for Sprinklers in Schools - Brit Automatic Fire Sprinkler Assn Ltd
Joint Report - Children's Chronic Arthritis Assn
Jordaniana - Anglo-Jordanian Soc
Joseph Bouet's Durham - Durham County Local History Soc
Journey of Discovery - Raynaud's & Scleroderma Assn
Judo News - Judo Scotland
Justice Bulletin - National Campaign Water Justice

K

Keeping a Young Voice - Voice Care Network UK
Kennel Gazette - Kennel Club

Kent - Assn Men of Kent & Kentish Men
Kent View - Kent County Agricultural Soc
The Key - Prison Governors Assn
The Key Frame - Fair Organ Preservation Soc
Key Issues in District Nursing - Community & District Nursing Assn UK
Keynote - Inst Food Science & Technology
The Keys of Peter - Christian Social Order
Keyways - Master Locksmiths' Assn
Kidney Life - Nat Kidney Fedn
King Pole - Circus Friends Assn GB
King's Army NL - English Civil War Soc
The Kipling Jnl - Kipling Soc
The Kiteflier - Kite Soc
Knitstats - Knitting Inds' Fedn
Knitting - Gld Master Craftsmen
Knotting Matters - Intl Gld Knot Tyers
Knowing the Score 2 - Assn Brit Orchestras
Knowledge Management Research & Practice - Operational Research Soc
Korfball - Brit Korfball Assn

L

La Brita Esperantisto - Esperanto Assn Britain
Laboratory Animals - Laboratory Animal Science Assn
Labour History Review - Soc Study Labour History
Lace - Lace Guild
Lacemaking - Lace Soc
Lakeland Gems 1999 - Lakeland Dialect Soc
Lakeland Treasury 1998 - Lakeland Dialect Soc
Lallans - Scots Language Soc
Lamp - Assn Lighthouse Keepers
Lancashire Business View - Cham Comm East Lancashire
The Lancastrian - Friends Real Lancashire
Land Business - Scot Land & Estates
The Land Registration Act - Manorial Soc of GB
The Land Registration Bill - Manorial Soc of GB
Land Sailor - Brit Fedn Sand & Land Yacht Clubs
Land Tenures & Customs of Manors - Manorial Soc of GB
Landlord Development Manual - Nat Landlords' Assn
Landscape History - Soc Landscape Studies
Landscape News - Brit Assn Landscape Inds
Landscape Research Jnl - Landscape Res Gp
Landwards - Instn Agricl Engrs
Language & Literacy News - UK Literacy Assn
Language Issues - Nat Assn Teaching English & other Community Languages Adults
Language Learning Jnl - Assn Language Learning
Language World - Assn Language Learning
The Laser User - Assn Laser Users
Lasers in Medical Science - Brit Medical Laser Assn
The Last Word - Assn Brit Scrabble Players
Laudate - Gld Church Musicians
Launderette & Cleaning World - Nat Assn Launderette Ind
The Laurel & Hardy Magazine - Laurel & Hardy Appreciation Soc
Law Centres providing Equal Access for All - Law Centres Fedn
The Law Teacher - Assn Law Teachers
Layman's Guide to Osteochondritis - Perthes Assn
Lead On - Seeing Dogs Alliance
The Leader - Lead Sheet Assn
Leading Note - Brit Assn Music Therapy
Leaning Ladder & Stepladder User Guide - Ladder Assn
Learning & Development: an introduction to childcare in an early years setting - Scot Pre-School Play Assn
Learning Blitz - Brit Inst Learning & Devt
Learning Disability Bulletin - Brit Inst Learning Disabilities
Leather Technician's Hbk - Leather Producers' Assn
The Left-Hander - Left-Handers Assn
Legal Abacus - Inst Legal Finance & Mgt
Legal Aid Solicitors List - Law Soc NI
Legal Executive Jnl - Inst Legal Executives
Legal Information Management - Brit & Irh Assn Law Librarians
Legal Studies - Soc Legal Scholars UK & I
The Legion - Royal Brit Legion

Leisure Management - Fitness Ind Assn
Leisure Opportunities - Fitness Ind Assn
LENNUK - Brit Estonian Assn
Les Nouvelles - Licensing Executives Soc
Let's Square Dance - Brit Assn American Square Dance Clubs
Letters in Applied Microbiology - Soc Applied Microbiology
Letting Update - UK Assn Letting Agents
Lewis Carroll Review - Lewis Carroll Soc
Lewisletter - Wyndham Lewis Soc
Liberty - Liberty
The Library - Bibliographical Soc
Libyan Studies - Soc Libyan Studies
The Licensed Conveyancer - Soc Licensed Conveyancers
The Lichenologist - Brit Lichen Soc
Life Links - R Zoological Soc Scotland
The Lifeboat - R Nat Lifeboat Instn
Lifeline - Brit Red Cross Soc
Lifeline - Overeaters Anonymous
Lifesavers Magazine - R Life Saving Soc UK
Lifting Engineers Hbk - Lifting Eqpt Engrs Assn
Lifting Equipment - Lifting Eqpt Engrs Assn
Light Aviation - Aircraft Owners & Pilots Assn
   Light Aircraft Assn
Light Hovercraft - Hovercraft Club GB
Lighting & Sound America - Profl Lighting & Sound Assn
Lighting & Sound International - Profl Lighting & Sound Assn
Lighting Journal - Instn Lighting Profls
Lighting News - Lighting Assn Ltd
Lighting Research & Technology - Chart Instn Bldg Services Engrs
Lime Stabilisation Manual - Mineral Products Assn
Line Up - Inst Broadcast Sound
Lingua e Vita - Brit Interlingua Soc
The Linguist - Chart Inst Linguists
Link - Assn Spina Bifida & Hydrocephalus
The Link - Scot Envt Link
Link Magazine - Nat Assn Writers' Gps
The Linnean - Linnean Soc London
The Lipizzaner - Lipizzaner Soc GB
Lipservice - Assn Leisure Industry Profls
The List of French Investments in the UK - Chambre de Commerce Française de Grande-Bretagne
List of all Registered Shetland Ponies in Shetland - Pony Breeders Shetland Assn
List of Shetland Pony Breeders in Shetland - Pony Breeders Shetland Assn
Listed Heritage - Listed Property Owners Club
Listing of Courses in European Studies in UK Universities - University Assn Contemporary European Studies
Listing of Dials in UK - Brit Sundial Soc
Literacy - UK Literacy Assn
Literacy & ICT: cutting edge practice in the primary school - Nat Literacy Assn
Literature Professional - Nat Assn Literature Devt
Little Bliss - BLISS
Little People - Miniature Mediterranean Donkey Assn
Liturgical Studies - Alcuin Club
Livin' Country - U Country Sports Workers
Living Afloat - Residential Boat Owners Assn
Living Earth - Soil Assn Ltd
Living Will + Forms - Assn Natural Burial Grounds
Living Wills - Dignity in Dying
Living with Ankylosing Spondylitis - Nat Ankylosing Spondylitis Soc
Local Council Review - Nat Assn Local Couns
The Local Historian - Brit Assn Local History
Local History News - Brit Assn Local History
Local News - Gwent Wildlife Trust
Local Population Studies - Local Population Studies Soc
The Locomotives of the Stockton & Darlington Railway - Historical Model Railway Soc
The Log - Soc Model Shipwrights
The Log Book - Ship Stamp Soc
Logopedics, Phoniatrics & Vocology - Brit Voice Assn
London Bird Report - London Natural Hist Soc
London Business Matters - London Cham Comm & Ind
London Cyclist - London Cyclists
The London Naturalist - London Natural History Soc
The London Philatelist - R Philatelic Soc London

The London Practice - Friends of Dr Watson
London Topographical Record - London Topographical Soc
London's Industrial Archaeology - Greater London Indl Archaeology Soc
Long Range Planning - Strategic Planning Soc
Long Term Advertising Expenditure Forecast - Advertising Assn
Look Before You Leap - Dance UK Ltd
Look North - Acuity
Looking Ahead - Bluefaced Leicester Sheep Breeders Assn
Loopholes - Pillbox Study Gp
Lorry Loader Operator's Manual - ALLMI Ltd
Lottery Magazine - Lotteries Coun
The Lost Hills - history of papermaking in County Durham - Durham County Local Hist Soc
Low Grade Hodgkin Lymphomas - Lymphoma Assn
Lower Limb Deficiency - STEPS
Lube - UK Lubricants Assn
The Luing Jnl - Luing Cattle Soc
Luing News - Luing Cattle Soc
Luso News - Lusitano Breed Soc GB
The Lute - Lute Soc
The Lutheran Link - Lutheran Coun GB
Lymphoma Fundraising News - Lymphoma Assn
Lymphoma NL - Lymphoma Assn
Lymphomas (a general booklet for Hodgkin) - Lymphoma Assn
Lynes - Lithuanian Assn UK Ltd

M

The Mace-Bearer - Gld Mace-Bearers
Machinery Update - Processing & Packaging Machinery Assn
The Magic Circular - The Magic Circle
Magnet - Youth Scotland
Maize Grower - Maize Growers Assn
The Maiwand Dispatch No 1 - Friends Dr Watson
The Maiwand Luncheon Monograph - Friends Dr Watson
Make a Sundial - Brit Sundial Soc
Making sense of Psychotherapy and Psychoanalysis - Brit Psychoanalytic Coun
Making the Best of Amputation - Brit Limbless Ex-Service Men's Assn
Mallorn - Tolkien Soc
Mammal News - Mammal Soc
Mammal Review - Mammal Soc
Mammalaction News - Mammal Soc
Management of CDM Coordination - Assn Project Safety
Management in Education - Brit Educl Leadership, Mgt & Admin Soc
Management of Exuding Wounds - Wound Care Alliance UK
The Management Specialist - Inst Mgt Specialists
Manager: the British Jnl of Administrative Management - Inst Administrative Management
Managing Absence - Ceretas
Managing Trade Assns - Trade Assn Forum
Manchester Memoirs - Manchester Literary & Philosophical Soc
Manic Depression - SANE
Man-made Mineral Fibre - Thermal Insulation Contrs Assn
Manpower News - HR Soc Ltd
Manual of Horsemanship - Pony Club
The Manual of the Mace - Guild Mace-Bearers
Manual of Operating Standards - Retread Manufacturers Assn
Manual of Sealant Practice - Brit Adhesives & Sealants Assn
Maplines - Brit Cartographic Soc
Marine Conservation - Marine Consvn Soc
The Mariner's Mirror - Soc Nautical Res
Market Leader - Marketing Soc
the marketer - Chart Inst Marketing
Marketing Newz - Sleep Counl
The Marketing Pocket Book - Advertising Assn
The Marquetarian - Marquetry Soc
Martial Arts Code of Safety - Nat Assn Karate & Martial Art Schools
Masonry International - Intl Masonry Soc
Masterbuilder - Fedn Master Builders
Masterchefs - Master Chefs GB

Mastersinger - Assn Brit Choral Directors
Match Label News - Brit Matchbox, Label & Booklet Soc
Materials World - Inst Materials, Minerals & Mining
Mathematical Proceedings - Cambridge Philosophical Soc
Mathematics Today - Inst Mathematics & Applications
Matrix - Brit Science Fiction Assn Ltd
May Catholics choose Cremation - Cremation Soc GB
McKenzie Magazine - Families Need Fathers
Me & My Face - Let's Face It
Measurement & Control - Inst Measurement & Control
Meat Hygienist - Assn Meat Inspectors GB Ltd
The Medal - Brit Art Medal Soc
Medals of the Soc - R Humane Soc
Medau News - Medau Soc
The Media Education Jnl - Assn Media Educ Scotland
Medical Companion - Myasthenia Gravis Assn
Medical Education - Assn Study Med Educ
Medical Methods of Treatment - SANE
Medical Practitioners' Financial Hbk - Assn Indep Specialist Med Accountants
Medical Woman - Medical Women's Fedn
Medication - Ceretas
Medication for Narcolepsy - Narcolepsy UK
Medicine, Science & the Law - Brit Academy Forensic Sciences
Medico-Legal Jnl - Medico-Legal Soc
Medium sized firms of Chartered Accountants - the vital link between businesses & the City - Assn Practising Accountants
Meeting Houses in Britain - Friends Histl Soc
Melin - Welsh Mills Soc
Membership Executive - Tourism Soc Ltd
Memory Lane - Al Bowlly Circle
Mercury - Brit Astrological & Psychic Soc
Merkur - German Rly Soc
The Message - Nat Pensioners Convention
Microbiology - Soc Gen Microbiology
Microbiology Today - Soc Gen Microbiology
Microlight Flying - Brit Microlight Aircraft Assn
Microscope - Meningitis Res Foundation
The Middle Way - Buddhist Soc
Midland Rule Book, 1904 - Signalling Record Soc
Midwifery Matters - Assn Radical Midwives
Milestones & Waymarkers - Milestone Soc
Milk Digest - R Assn Brit Dairy Farmers
Mills News - Soc Protection Ancient Buildings
Minerva: Jnl of Swansea History - R Instn S Wales
Mines Database - Confedn UK Coal Producers
Mining Heritage Guide - Nat Assn Mining Hist Orgs
Mining History - Peak District Mines Histl Soc
Minor Counties Cricket Annual - Minor Counties Cricket Assn
Missing the Grade: Education for Children in Prison - Howard League Penal Reform
The Missing Link - Brit Sausage Appreciation Soc
Mitteilungsblatt - Anglo-German Family History Soc
Mixed Marriage in Ireland: A companion to those involved, or about to be involved, in a mixed marriage - NI Mixed Marriage Assn
Mixed Moss - Arthur Ransome Soc Ltd
Mobilise - Disabled Motoring UK
Modern & Contemporary France - Assn Study Modern & Contemporary France
Modern Believing - Modern Churchpeople's U
Modern Language Review - Modern Humanities Res Assn
Modern Management - Inst of Leadership & Mgt
MODUS - Design & Technology Assn
Molecular Plant Pathology - Brit Soc Plant Pathology
Mollusc World - Conchological Soc GB & I
Monarchy - Monarchist League
Money Laundering Guidelines - Brit Cheque & Credit Assn
Money-go-Round: recycling finances, realising capital - Community Devt Finance Assn
Monitoring & Evaluation; a practical guide for grant-making trusts - Assn Charitable Foundations
Monographs & Topical issues in glass - Soc Glass Technology
Montage - Picture Research Assn
Montessori Direction - Montessori Soc (AMI) UK
Montgomeryshire Collections - Powysland Club
Monthly Member Report - Brit Edible Pulse Assn
Monthly Rice Circular - London Rice Brokers' Assn

Mood Food Magazine - Fedn Specialist Restaurants
Moors Line - N Yorkshire Moors Histl Rly Trust
Moral Philosophy, from Hippocrates to the 21st Aeon - Inst of Mgt & Technology
More Care for Your Voice - Voice Care Network UK
More than meets the eye - Laurence-Moon-Bardet-Biedl Soc
Mortice & Tenon - Carpenters' Fellowship
Motor Caravanner - Motor Caravanners' Club Ltd
Motor Industry Magazine - Inst Motor Ind
Motor Retailer - Retail Motor Ind Fedn
Motorcycle Rider - Brit Motorcyclists' Fedn
Motorcycling GB - Auto-Cycle U Ltd
Movement, Dance & Drama - Laban Gld Movement & Dance
Moving Forward: a guide to living with spinal cord injury - Spinal Injuries Assn
Moving News - Movers Inst (TMI)
Moving on Up: a short guide for professionals - Assn Real Change
MQR - Minerals Engg Soc
MS Matters - Multiple Sclerosis Soc GB & NI
The Mule - Brit Mule Soc
Mule News - North of England Mule Sheep Assn
Multiples - Soc Wood Engravers
The Museum Archaeologist - Soc Museum Archaeologists
Museum News - National Heritage
Museum Practice - Museums Assn
Museums Jnl - Museums Assn
Museums Ybk - Museums Assn
Music - Viola da Gamba Soc
Music Albums (anthologies) for Carillon of 2 or 3 octaves - Brit Carillon Soc
The Music Box - Musical Box Soc GB
Music Copyright Matters - Music Publishers' Assn
Music Jnl - Inc Soc Musicians
Musician - Musicians' U
My Daughter & ME - Assn Young People ME

N

n:gauge - Nat Assn Goldsmiths GB & I
Name magazine - Nat Assn Music Educators
The Name & Nature of Poetry - Housman Soc
Napoleon - Napoleonic Soc
Narcolepsy: a layman's guide - Narcolepsy UK
Narcolepsy: care & treatment - Narcolepsy UK
Narrow Gauge - Narrow Gauge Rly Soc
Narrow Gauge News - Narrow Gauge Rly Soc
The National Plant Collections Directory - National Coun Consvn Plants & Gardens
National Register of Psychotherapists - UK Coun Psychotherapy
National Tobacconists Trade Exhibition Catalogue - Assn of Indep Tobacco Specialists
Nations & Nationalism - Assn Study Ethnicity & Nationalism
Natterjack - Brit Herpetological Soc
Natterjack News - Landlife
The Natural Death Hbk - Assn Natural Burial Grounds
Natural Medicine - Assn Natural Medicine
Natural World - R Soc Wildlife Trusts
Nature in Art - Nature in Art Trust
Nautical Archaeology NL - Nautical Archaeology Soc
The Naval Architect - R Instn Naval Architects
Navvies - Waterway Recovery Gp
The Nelson Dispatch - Nelson Soc
Neometaphysical Digest - Soc Metaphysicians
Netball News - Welsh Netball Assn
Network - Brit Sociological Soc
The Network - Network Government Library & Inf Specialists
Network for Regions - Motorcycle Action Gp
Network London - Brit-American Business Inc
Network New York - Brit-American Business Inc
Networking - Brit Dental Practice Mgrs Assn
Networks - Brit Manual Lymph Drainage Assn
Neuroblastoma - a booklet for parents - Neuroblastoma Soc
Neuroblastoma News - Neuroblastoma Soc

Neuropathology & Applied Neurobiology - Brit
Neuropathological Soc
New Approach to Latin for the Mass - Assn Latin Liturgy
New Arrivals - Brit Humanist Assn
The New Bookbinder - Designer Bookbinders
New Books in Folklore - Folklore Soc
New Comparison - Brit Comparative Literature Assn
New Crystal Palace Matters - Crystal Palace Foundation
New Direction - Herefordshire & Worcestershire Cham Comm
New Generation - National Childbirth Trust
New Ground - Socialist Environment & Resources Assn
New Horizons - Brit Fantasy Soc
The New Humanist - Rationalist Assn
The New Idler - Johnson Soc London
New Invention List - Inst Inventors
New Latin-English Sunday Missal - Assn Latin Liturgy
The New Rambler - Johnson Soc London
New Sjogren's Hbk - Brit Sjogren's Syndrome Assn
New Steel Construction - Brit Constructional Steelwork Assn
New Steel Construction - Steel Construction Inst
The New Technical Guide - Mastic Asphalt Coun
New Tracks to the Cities - Permanent Way Instn
New Vision - Assn Separated & Divorced Catholics
New Welsh Review - ACADEMI - Welsh National Literature
Promotion Agency
New Wetland Harvests - Brit Reed Growers' Assn
New Writing Scotland (Anthology) - Assn Scot Literary Studies
The Newman - Newman Assn
News & Ideas - Scout & Guide Graduate Assn
News & Views Magazine - Anglo-Danish Soc
News Direct - Nat Baton Twirling Assn (England)
News Exchange - Licensing Executives Soc Ltd
Newstime - A1 Motor Stores Ltd
Nexus - Managing & Marketing Sales Assn
Nexus - Soc Business Practitioners
NI Pharmacy in Focus - Ulster Chemists' Assn
The Nibbler - Nat Gerbil Soc
Niche Commercial - Nat Assn Comml Finance Brokers
Nigeria News Report - Britain Nigeria Business Coun
Night - Bar Entertainment & Dance Assn
**No Overall Control? the impact of a 'hung parliament' on
British Politics -** Hansard Soc Ltd
NOMINA - Soc Name Studies Britain & Ireland
Norfolk Archaeology - Norfolk & Norwich Archaeol Soc
Norfolk Reed Roofing Today - Brit Reed Growers' Assn
North Wind - George MacDonald Soc
Northamptonshire Archaeology - Northamptonshire
Archaeological Soc
Northamptonshire Past & Present - Northamptonshire Record
Soc
Northern Studies - Scot Soc for Nthn Studies
North-West Geography - Manchester Geographical Soc
Notes for Company Managers - Stage Mgt Assn
Notes for Guidance - Traffic Mgt Contrs Assn
NoticeBoard - Assn Chief Execs Voluntary Organisations
Nottinghamshire Historian - Nottinghamshire Local Hist Assn
Nuclear Medicine Communications - Brit Nuclear Medicine Soc
The Numismatic Chronicle - R Numismatic Soc
Nurse Prescribing - Community & District Nursing Assn UK
Nursery News - National Day Nurseries Assn
Nursery Nursing Practitioner - Soc Nursery Nursing Practitioners
Nursing Care - Community & District Nursing Assn UK
Nursing Home News - Registered Nursing Home Assn Ltd
Nursing Management Manual - Registered Nursing Home Assn
Ltd
Nursing Scotland - Indep Fedn Nursing Scotland
Nursing Standard - R Coll Nursing UK
Nutrition & Health - McCarrison Soc
The Nymph and the Grot - Friends St Bride Library

O

Obsessions - SANE
The Obstetrician & Gynaecologist - R Coll Obstetricians &
Gynaecologists

Occupational Medicine Journal - Soc Occupational Medicine
Occupational Safety & Health - R Soc Prevention Accidents
Occupational Therapy News - Brit Assn Occupational Therapists
Ocean Challenge - Challenger Soc Marine Science
Oculus - Partially Sighted Soc
Off Air - Radio Academy
Off Road Rider - Amateur Motor Cycle Assn
Off the Record - Brit Veterinary Assn
Off the Run - Fire Service Presvn Gp
Official Rules for Ploughing - Soc Ploughmen
Offsets - Nat Auricula & Primula Soc (Sthn)
Offshore Marine Technology - R Instn Naval Architects
OH Today - Assn Occupational Health Nurse Practitioners
Older People on Low Incomes: - Low Incomes Tax Reform Group
Omnibus Magazine - Joint Assn Classical Teachers
The Omnibus Magazine - Omnibus Soc
On Air - Nat Assn Hospital Broadcasting Orgs
On Display - Fair Organ Presvn Soc
On the Ground - Milestone Soc
On the Massage Scene - Scot Massage Therapists Org
On the Road - Assn Brit Drivers
On Trade Media Review - Assn Licensed Multiple Retailers
One in Seven - RNID
Onze Taal - Assn Language Learning
Open Book - Alliance Literary Socs
Open Hand Magazine - Deafblind UK
Open House - National Assn Bikers Disability
Open Space - Commons, Open Spaces & Footpaths Preservation
SocOperators Safety Code for Powered Industrial Trucks - Brit Indl
Truck Assn Ltd
Opportunities - Brit-Peruvian Cham
Opportunity - Milton Keynes & North Bucks Cham Comm
Opposite Lock - World Speedway Riders Assn
Opticians in Business - Fedn Ophthalmic & Dispensing Opticians
Optics - Assn Brit Dispensing Opticians
Optics at a Glance - Fedn Ophthalmic & Dispensing Opticians
Optimum Nutrition - Inst Optimum Nutrition
OR Insight - Operational Res Soc
Oracle - Inst Sheet Metal Engg
Oral History - Oral Hist Soc
Orbit - Domestic Appliance Service Assn
Orchid Cultivation Booklet - Orchid Soc GB
Order Order - Assn Former MPs
Orders & Medals - Orders & Medals Res Soc
Orders of the Day - Sealed Knot Ltd
Orff Times - Orff Soc UK
Organic Farming - Soil Assn Ltd
Organists' Review - Inc Assn Organists
Originals - Soc Artists' Agents
Origins - Biblical Creation Soc
Ornithological Bulletin - London Natural Hist Soc
Orts - George MacDonald Soc
Osteopathy Today - Brit Osteopathic Assn
Osteoporosis News - National Osteoporosis Soc
Osteoporosis Review - National Osteoporosis Soc
The Ostomy Book - IAOT (Optometry Today/OpticsToday) - Assn
Optometrists
Otis - Great Bustard Gp
Our Common Land - Commons, Open Spaces & Footpaths
Preservation SocOutdoor Focus - Outdoor Writers' &
Photographers' Gld
Outdoor Photography - Gld Master Craftsmen
Outdoor Sourcebook - Inst Outdoor Learning
Outlaw - Arthur Ransome Soc Ltd
Outlook - Chemical Business Assn
Federation Sidecar Clubs
The Outrigger - Pacific Islands Soc UK & I
Overload - ACCU: professionalism in programming
Overseas - Royal Over-Seas League
Overseas Jnl - PSV Circle
Overseas Press & Media Guide - Overseas Press & Media Assn
Owl - UK One World Linking Assn
The Oxford Down - One Hundred Years of Breeding - Oxford
Down Sheep Breeders' Assn
Oxoniensia - Oxfordshire Architectural & Historical Soc
Ozone - Inst Swimming Pool Engrs

P

The Packaging Professional - Inst Materials, Minerals & Mining
Paddle Wheels - Paddle Steamer Presvn Soc
Paddles Past - Historic Canoe & Kayak Assn
Pagan Dawn - Pagan Fedn
Pain & Wound Care - Wound Care Alliance UK
Paint - SAA - Soc for All Artists
Paintball Games in Woodlands - UK Paintball Sports Fedn
Paintball UK - UK Paintball Sports Fedn
Palaeontology - Palaeontological Assn
Palliative Management of Fungating Malignant Wounds -
    Wound Care Alliance UK
Pallidula - Brit Shell Collectors Club
Palomino - Brit Palomino Soc
Pan - Brit Flute Soc
Panpodium - Brit Assn Steelbands
Paper Technology - Paper Ind Technical Assn Ltd
Paragraphs - Neil Munro Soc
The Paralegal - Nat Assn Licensed Paralegals
Parallel Vision - Brit & Ir Orthoptic Soc
Paranormal Review Magazine - Soc Psychical Res
Parapet Design - Timber Decking Assn
Parents' Guide to Maintained Boarding Schools - Boarding
    Schools Assn
Parking News - Brit Parking Assn
Parliamentary NL - Green Alliance Trust
Parson & Parish - English Clergy Assn
Partners in Progress - Brit Cham Comm Thailand
Pastoral Care in Education - Nat Assn Pastoral Care Educ
Pathfinder Business - Inst Export
The Patriot - John Hampden Soc
Patternmaking News - Pattern Model & Mouldmakers Assn
Patterns of Prejudice - Inst Jewish Policy Res
Pawnbrokers Guide - Nat Pawnbrokers Assn UK
Pawns - Welsh Chess U
Pawprints - People & Dogs Soc
Paws for Thought - Pet Care Tr Assn
Payroll Professional - Chart Inst Payroll Profls
Peace Song Book - Workers' Music Assn
Peewit! - Malcolm Saville Soc
Pencil Point - Obstetric Anaesthetists Assn
Pendulum - MDF - the BiPolar Org
The Penguin Collector - Penguin Collectors' Soc
Pension credit for beginners - Nat Pensioners Convention
Pension Lawyer - Assn Pension Lawyers
People Management - Chart Inst Personnel & Devt
Per Annum - Assn Chief Estates Surveyors & Property Mgrs Public
    Sector
Percussive Notes - Percussive Arts Soc
Peregrine - Hawk & Owl Trust
Performance Bond - Confedn Construction Specialists
Performance Textiles - Performance Textiles Assn Ltd
Permaculture Works - Permaculture Assn (Britain)
The Permanent Way Institution - the first 100 years, 1884-
    1984 - Permanent Way Instn
Permission to Speak Sir! - Dad's Army Appreciation Soc
Personal & Professional Boundaries - Ceretas
Personal Experience - Narcolepsy UK
Personal Injuries Hbk - Personal Injuries Bar Assn
Personal Safety - Ceretas
Perspective - R Soc Ulster Architects
Perspectives - Assn University Administrators
    Brit-Swiss Cham Comm
    Myalgic Encephalopathy Assn
Perspectives in Public Health - R Soc Public Health
Pesticides News - Pesticide Action Network UK
The Pharmaceutical Historian - Brit Soc Hist Pharmacy
Pharmaceutical Jnl - R Pharmaceutical Soc GB
Pharmaceutical Statistics - Statisticians Pharmaceutical Ind
Pharos International - Cremation Soc GB
The Philosopher - Philosophical Soc England
Philosophic Counselling for People & their Governments - Inst
    Mgt & Technology
Phobias - SANE

The Photogrammetric Record - Remote Sensing &
    Photogrammetry Soc
The Photographer - Brit Inst Profl Photography
Photographica World - Photographic Collectors' Club GB
Phrysko - Friesian Horse Assn GB & I
Physical Chemistry Chemical Physics - Royal Soc Chemistry
Physical Education & Sports Pedagogy - Assn Physical Educ
Physical Education Matters - Assn Physical Educ
Physicians Guide to the Management of Huntington's
    Disease - Huntington's Disease Assn
Physics & Chemistry of Glasses - Soc Glass Technology
Physiotherapy - Chart Soc Physiotherapy
    Nat Ankylosing Spondylitis Soc
Picture House - Cinema Theatre Assn
The Picture Restorer - Brit Assn Paintings Conservator-Restorers
Piers - Nat Piers Soc
Pigging Industry News - Pigging Products & Services Assn
Pinball Player - Pinball Owners' Assn
Pine Cone - Order Woodcraft Chivalry
Pint in Hand - Soc Presvn Beers Wood
Pioneers & Pathfinders - Assn Past Rotarians
The Pipe Band - R Scot Pipe Band Assn
Pipe Joint Guide - Brit Compressed Air Soc
Pipeline - Surfers against Sewage
Pipeline Industry Directory - Pipeline Inds Gld
The Piping Times - Coll Piping
Pitkin Guide to George Eliot - George Eliot Fellowship
The Place Names of [county] - English Place-Name Soc
Plain English - Plain English Campaign 1979
Plainsong & Medieval Music - Plainsong & Mediæval Music Soc
Plangon - Doll Club GB
Planning for Memorials - Assn Burial Authorities
Planning for Memorials after Cremation - Assn Burial Authorities
Planning, Development & Operation of Science Parks - UK
    Science Park Assn
Plant Based Nutrition & Health - Vegan Soc Ltd
Plant Biotechnology - Soc Experimental Biology
Plant Ecology & Diversity - Botanical Soc Scotland
The Plant Engineer - Soc Operations Engrs
Plant Heritage - Nat Coun Consvn Plants & Gardens
The Plant Jnl - Soc Experimental Biology
Plant Pathology - Brit Soc Plant Pathology
Planting & Managing Amenity Woodlands - Arboricultural Assn
Plantlife - Plantlife Intl
Plastiquarian - Plastics Histl Soc
The Platelet - ITP Support Assn
The Platform - Fairground Soc
Play Matters - Nat Assn Toy & Leisure Libraries
Play Safety Guidelines - Nat Playing Fields Assn
Playaction - Fair Play Children Assn
Playaction Guides - Fair Play Children Assn
Playing a Part: a study of the impact of youth theatre on the
    personal, social & political development of young people
    - Nat Assn Youth Theatres
The Players Club - Profl Footballers Assn
The Players Jnl - Profl Footballers Assn
Playwork - a guide for trainers - Nat Playing Fields Assn
Plu Glosa Nota - Glosa Educ Org
Plumb Heat - Scot & NI Plumbing Employers' Fedn
Plumbheat - NI Master Plumbers' Assn
Plus News - Nat Fedn Plus Areas GB
The Pocket Guide to Hysterectomy - Hysterectomy Assn
Pocket Scots Dictionary - Scot Language Dictionaries
Podiatry Now - Soc Chiropodists & Podiatrists
Podiatry Review - Inst Chiropodists & Podiatrists
Poetry News - Poetry Soc (Inc)
Poetry Review - Poetry Soc (Inc)
Points per Second - Modern Pentathlon Assn GB
Poisoning in Veterinary Practice - Nat Office Animal Health
Police - Police Fedn E & W
Police Beat - Police Fedn NI
Political Digest - Assn Licensed Multiple Retailers
Pollution Control Hbk - Envtl Protection UK
Pony Express - Mounted Games Assn GB
Popular Astronomy - Soc Popular Astronomy
Port Health Hbk - Assn Port Health Authorities
Portage Post - Nat Portage Assn
Portfolio - Monumental Brass Soc

Post Horn - Post Office Vehicle Club
Post Natal Depression - Assn Postnatal Illness
Postal Auction - Photographic Collectors' Club GB
Postal History Jnl - Postal Hist Soc
Postbag - Nat Assn Music Educators
Postcard World - Great Britain Postcard Club
Postgraduate Medical Jnl - Fellowship Postgraduate Medicine
Post-Medieval Archaeology - Soc Post-Medieval Archaeology
Potters - Craft Potters' Assn GB
The Power Engineer - Instn Diesel & Gas Turbine Engrs
A Powys Checklist - Powys Soc
The Powys Jnl - Powys Soc
The Powys NL - Powys Soc
PPI News & Junk Mail - Brit Postmark Soc
Practical Greenkeeping - Royal & Ancient Golf Club
Practical Ophthalmic Lenses - Assn Brit Dispensing Opticians
Practice Notes - Assn Project Safety
Praxis Makes Perfect - Dyspraxia Foundation
Precedents for Consent Orders - Resolution
Precept Return - Soc County Treasurers
Pre-construction Information - Assn Project Safety
Pregnancy Loss & the Death of a Baby - Stillbirth & Neonatal Death Soc
Prep School - SATIPS - Support & Training in Prep Schools
Prep School Magazine - Indep Assn Preparatory Schools
Present State - Pugin Soc
Pressure Points - Water Jetting Assn
Preventing falls in scaffolding & falsework - Nat Access & Scaffolding Confedn
Prevention of Infection in the Home - Infection Prevention Soc
Preview - R Caledonian Horticl Soc
A Price not worth Paying - Campaign Indep Britain
Primary Dental Care - Fac Gen Dental Practice (UK)
Primary First - Nat Assn Primary Educ
Primary Geography - Geographical Assn
Primary History - Histl Assn
Primary Science Review - Assn Science Educ
Primate Eye - Primate Soc GB
Primed - Assn Brit Healthcare Inds
The Primer - Vintage Arms Assn
Principles of Fire Investigation - Instn Fire Engrs
Principles of Ophthalmic Lenses - Assn Brit Dispensing Opticians
Prism NL - Brit Fantasy Soc
Private Hire & Taxi Monthly - Nat Private Hire Assn
The Private Library - Private Libraries Assn
Proceedings of the European Otter Conference - Intl Otter Survival Fund
Process Safety & Environmental Protection - Instn Chemical Engineers
ProContractor - Nat Assn Agricl Contrs
The Professional Engineer - Soc Profl Engrs Ltd
The Professional Gardener - Profl Gardeners' Guild
Professional Imagemaker - Soc Wedding & Portrait Photographers
Professional Investor - CFA Soc of the UK
Professional Manager - Chart Mgt Inst
Professional Pest Controller - Brit Pest Control Assn
The Professional Remover - Nat Gld Removers & Storers
Professional Social Work - Brit Assn Social Workers
Profile - Chart Inst Public Relations
Profl Golfers' Assn
Profitable Mobile Catering - Nationwide Caterers Assn Ltd
Progress - Nat Home Improvement Council
Progressive Greetings - Greeting Card Assn
Project - Assn Project Management
Pro-Life Times - Soc Protection Unborn Children
Promotions Buyer - Brit Promotional Merchandise Assn
The Prompt - Brit Assn Dramatherapists
The Property Magazine - Guild Profl Estate Agents
Pro-rat-a - Nat Fancy Rat Soc
Prosper - Black Country Cham Comm
Protestant Truth - Protestant Truth Soc
Pruning Kentish Cobnuts - Kentish Cobnuts Assn
Psi Report - Scot Soc Psychical Research
Psoriasis - Psoriasis Assn
Psoriatic Care Fact File - Psoriasis & Psoriatic Arthritis Alliance
Psychiatric Bulletin - R Coll Psychiatrists
Psychoanalytic Psychotherapy - Assn Psychoanalytic Psychotherapy NHS

The Psychologist - Brit Psychological Soc
Psychology & Psychotherapy - Brit Psychological Soc
Psychology of Music - Soc Educ, Music & Psychology Res
Psychology Teaching - Assn Teaching Psychology
The Psychotherapist - UK Coun Psychotherapy
PTA - Nat Confedn Parent-Teacher Assns
Pteridologist - Brit Pteridological Soc
Public Address - Inst Sound & Communications Engineers
Public Relations Consultancy - Public Relations Consultants Assn
Public Sculpture of Britain - Public Monuments & Sculpture Assn
Public Service Magazine - First Division Assn
Public Utilities Bulletin - Road Transport Fleet Data Soc
Puerperal Psychosis - Assn Postnatal Illness
Pull! - Clay Pigeon Shooting Assn Ltd
Pumps from Britain - Brit Pump Mfrs' Assn
Puppet Master - Brit Puppet & Model Theatre Guild
Pura Raza Española - Brit Assn Purebred Spanish Horse
Pygmy Goat Hbk - Pygmy Goat Club
Pygmy Goat Notes - Pygmy Goat Club

Q

Q Review - Assn Private Client Investment Managers & Stockbrokers
QCA Voice - Quoted Companies Alliance
Quaker Monthly - Religious Soc Friends (Quakers)
Quaker News - Religious Soc Friends (Quakers)
Quaker Projects - Religious Soc Friends (Quakers)
Quality in Agency - Brit Assn Service Elderly
Quality World - Chartered Quality Inst
Quarry Management - Inst Quarrying
Quarrying in Depth - recycling - Mineral Products Assn
The Quarterly - Brit Assn Paper Historians
Quarterly Account - Inst Money Advisers
Quarterly Jnl of Experimental Psychology - Experimental Psychology Soc
Quarterly Jnl of Forestry - R Forestry Soc E, W & NI
Quartermation - Brit Automation & Robot Assn Ltd
Quasar Magazine - Brit Assn Res Quality Assurance
The Quekett Jnl of Microscopy - Quekett Microscopical Club
Quest - Queen's English Soc
Quillers Today - Quilling Gld
The Quilter - Quilters' Gld
Quo Vadis? - Land's End - John O'Groats Assn

R

Rabbiting On - Rabbit Welfare Assn
Race against Time - Meningitis Research Foundation
Race Walking Record - Race Walking Assn
Racing Construction Regulation - Hovercraft Club GB
Radcom - Radio Soc GB
Radical Statistics - Radical Statistics Gp
Radiography - Soc Radiographers
The Radionic Jnl - Radionic Assn
Radius Performing - Religious Drama Soc
Rail Freight Group News - Rail Freight Gp
Railwatch - Rly Devt Soc Ltd
The Railway Observer - Rly Correspondence & Travel Soc
Railway Ramblings - Railway Ramblers
Random Round - Percy Grainger Soc
Ranger - Brit Free Range Egg Producers Assn
Ranger - Countryside Mgt Assn
Rapport - Assn Neuro-Linguistic Programming (UK) Ltd
Rapport - Community & Youth Workers' U
The Ravilious Notebook - Friends St Bride Library
Raw Power - Brit Drug Free Powerlifting Assn
A Ray of Hope - Assn Young People ME
Raynaud's: your questions answered - Raynaud's & Scleroderma Assn
Re:View - Brit Assn Reinforcement
Reach Quality Assessment Framework - Youth Action Network
Reaching Out - Guillain Barré Syndrome Support Group

Reaction - National Soc Res Allergy
Real Lives - Albinism Fellowship
Real Power - Renewable UK Assn
Really Easy - English Bridge Union
Recommendations for Clinical Practice - Fac Sexual & Reproductive Healthcare
Recommended Practice for Troughed Belt Conveyors - Materials Handling Engrs Assn
The Record - Lancashire Authors' Assn
The Record Collector - Recorded Vocal Art Soc
Recorder News - Biological Recording Scotland
Recording News - Brit Sound Recording Assn
Records of Buckinghamshire - Architectural & Archaeol Soc County of Buckinghamshire
Records of Huntingdon - Huntingdonshire Local Hist Soc
Recovery - Assn Business Recovery Profls
Brit Damage Mgt Assn
Recovery Operator - Retail Motor Ind Fedn
Recovery Operator Magazine - Assn Vehicle Recovery Operators
Re-creating Communities: business, the arts & regeneration - Arts & Business
Recruitment Matters - Recruitment & Employment Confedn
Recusant History - Catholic Record Soc
Recyclatex booklet for schools - Textile Recycling Assn
Recyclatex leaflet for local authorities - Textile Recycling Assn
Recycling Health & Safety Manual - Brit Metals Recycling Assn
Red Herrings - Crime Writers Assn
Reedbed Management for Bitterns - Brit Reed Growers' Assn
Reedbed Management for Commercial & Wildlife Interests - Brit Reed Growers' Assn
Reference Manual for Construction Plant - Chart Instn Civil Engg Surveyors
Referendum - Forum Private Business
Reflections - Nat Early Music Assn
Reflexions - Assn Reflexologists
The Reformer - Protestant Alliance
Reformer - Tory Reform Gp
Refractories Engineer - Inst Refractories Engrs
Regional Studies - Regional Studies Assn
Register - National Women's Register
Register of Certificated Wallers/Dykers - Dry Stone Walling Assn GB
Register of Homeopaths - Soc Homeopaths
Register of Independent Midwives - Indep Midwives' Assn
Register of One-Name Studies - Gld Master Craftsmen
Register of Patent Agents - Chart Inst Patent Attorneys
Register of Professional Private Music Teachers - Incorporated Soc Musicians
Register of Psychotherapists - Brit Psychoanalytic Coun
Register of Schools that help Dyslexic Children - Council Registration Schools Teaching Dyslexic Pupils
Rehab Directory - Assn Personal Injury Lawyers
Reiki Magazine International - Reiki Assn
Reinforced Concrete: History, Properties & Durability - Corrosion Prevention Assn
Release - Captive Animals' Protection Soc
Removals & Storage - Brit Assn Removers
Renaissance Studies - Soc Renaissance Studies
Renew - Network Alternative Technology & Technology Assessment
Renewables Ybk - Renewable Energy Assn
Renewables, Past, Present & Future - Network Alternative Technology & Technology Assessment
Replacing the State - Assn Chief Executives of Voluntary Organisations
Report of Investment Activity - BVCA (Brit Private Equity & Venture Capital Assn)
Reporter - Brit Inst Organ Studies
The Reporter - Soc Legal Scholars UK & I
Representation: jnl of democracy & electoral systems - Electoral Reform Soc Ltd
Res Medica - R Med Soc
Research - Market Res Soc
Research Buyers Guide - Market Res Soc
Research Intelligence - Brit Educl Res Assn
Resnews - Rescare
Resource - Nat Assn Teachers Religious Educ
Restart - Assn Classic Trials Clubs
Resurgam - Fedn Burial & Cremation Auths

Retail Express - Nat Fedn Retail Newsagents
Retail News - Scot Grocers' Fedn
Retail Newsagent - Nat Fedn Retail Newsagents
Retail Outlook - Scot Grocers' Fedn
Retail Sales Garment Cleaning - Gld Cleaners & Launderers
The Retreader - Retread Mfrs Assn
Retreats - Assn Promoting Retreats
Retreats - Retreat Assn
Retrospection - Nat Assn Re-enactment Societies
Reverberations - Handbell Ringers GB
A Review of Hospitality Management Education in the UK - Coun Hospitality Mgt Educ
Revolutions - Motor Cycle Ind Assn
RFIC Fire Prevention Guide - Food Storage & Distbn Fedn
RFIC Guidance on the Assessment of Fire Risk - Food Storage & Distbn Fedn
RFIC Storage & Handling of Frozen Foods - Food Storage & Distbn Fedn
Rheology Abstracts - Brit Soc Rheology
Rheology Bulletin - Brit Soc Rheology
Rheology Reviews - Brit Soc Rheology
Rheumatic Review - Arthritic Assn
Rheumatology - Brit Soc Rheumatology
The Ricardian - Richard III Soc
The Ricardian Bulletin - Richard III Soc
The Rifleman - Nat Small-bore Rifle Assn
Rights of Way: the authority of case law - Scot Rights of Way & Access Soc
Ringing Migration - Brit Trust Ornithology
The Ringing World - Central Coun Church Bell Ringers
Rivista - Brit-Italian Soc
The Road - Motorcycle Action Gp
Road Haulage Manual - Road Haulage Assn
Roadrunner - Road Runners Club
Roadway - Road Haulage Assn
The Rock Garden - Scot Rock Garden Club
Rolling - Road Roller Assn
Romany Magazine - Romany Soc
The Roofing Trades Jnl - Confedn Roofing Contrs Ltd
The Rose - R Nat Rose Soc
The Rotorhead - Brit Helicopter Advy Bd Ltd
Roundabouts from the Air - UK Roundabout Appreciation Soc
Roundabouts of Britain - UK Roundabout Appreciation Soc
Roundabouts of GB Calendar - UK Roundabout Appreciation Soc
Roundhead Assn NL - English Civil War Soc Ltd
Round-Up - Brit Westerners Assn
Route to a Successful Concrete Repair - Concrete Repair Assn
Routemaster Magazine - Routemaster Operators & Owners Assn
Rowing Action - Scot Rowing
Royal Highland Review - R Highland & Agricl Soc Scotland
Royal Highland Show Catalogue - Royal Highland & Agricl Soc Scotland
Royal Highland Show Guide - Royal Highland & Agricl Soc Scotland
Royal Martyr Annual - R Martyr Church U
Royal Stuart Papers - R Stuart Soc
Royal Stuart Review - R Stuart Soc
RSMA Safety Code of Practice - Road Safety Markings Assn
Runestaff - The Vikings
Running Elections - Soc Local Auth Chief Executives & Senior Mgrs
Rupert Calendar - Followers Rupert
RURAL Briefing - Soc Responsible Use Resources in Agriculture & on the Land
Rural History Today - Brit Agricl Hist Soc
Rural Matters - R Agricl Soc England
Rural Retailer - Rural Shops Alliance
Rural Review - R Lancashire Agricl Soc
Rural Theology - Rural Theology Assn
Rural Wales / Cymru Wledig - Campaign Protection Rural Wales
The Ruskin Gazette - Ruskin Soc London
The Russell - Welsh Highland Railways Assn
Russistika - Assn Language Learning

S

Safe & Sound - Building a Safer Youth Work Environment - Youth Scotland

Safe Use of & Operation of Marquees & Temporary Structures - Performance Textiles Assn Ltd

Safety & Health Practitioner - Instn Occupational Safety & Health

Safety Connections - R Soc Prevention Accidents

Safety Education - R Soc Prevention Accidents

Safety Express - R Soc Prevention Accidents

Safety Guidelines for Steel Stockholders & Processors - Nat Assn Steel Stockholders

Safety in Electrical Testing - Radio, Electrical & TV Retailers' Assn Ltd

The Saga Book - Viking Soc Nhn Res

Sail to Adventure - Assn Sea Training Orgs

Salers Jnl - Salers Cattle Soc UK

Sales & Marketing Today - Soc Sales & Marketing

Salon Focus - Nat Hairdressers' Fedn

Samuri NL - Scot Ju-Jitsu Assn

SANACAST - Scot Anglers Nat Assn

Sandgrouse - Ornithological Soc Middle East

Sandwich & Snack News - Brit Sandwich Assn

Saved from a Watery Grave - R Humane Soc

Saying Goodbye to Your Baby - Stillbirth & Neonatal Death Soc

Scan - Tuberous Sclerosis Assn

Scene Magazine - Scot Community Drama Assn

Schizophrenia - SANE

The School Librarian - School Library Assn

School is Not Compulsory - Education Otherwise Assn Ltd

School Science Review - Assn Science Education

Schools News - Devt Education Assn

Schumacher Briefings - Doctor E F Schumacher Soc Schumacher NL - Doctor E F Schumacher Soc Science & Justice - Forensic Science Soc

Science & Public Affairs - Brit Science Assn

Science Technology - Inst Science & Technology

Scleroderma - The Inside Story - Raynaud's & Scleroderma Assn

Scoliosis Hbk - Scoliosis Assn (UK)

Score - Scot Orienteering Assn

Scotch at a Glance - Scotch Whisky Assn

Scotch Whisky: matured to be enjoyed responsibly - Scotch Whisky Assn

Scotch Whisky: questions & answers - Scotch Whisky Assn

Scotland's Finest Visitor Attractions - Assn Scot Visitor Attractions

Scotlit - Assn Scot Literary Studies

ScotLit - Assn Scot Literary Studies

Scotnotes - Assn Scot Literary Studies

Scots Bowler - Scot Indoor Bowling Assn

Scots Thesaurus - Scot Language Dictionaries

Scottish Air News - Central Scotland Aviation Gp

Scottish Archaeological Jnl - Glasgow Archaeol Soc

Scottish Archives - Scot Records Assn

Scottish Badminton - Scot Badminton U

The Scottish Beekeeper - Scot Beekeepers Assn

Scottish Bird News - Scot Ornithologists' Club

Scottish Bird Report - Scot Ornithologists' Club

Scottish Birds - Scot Ornithologists' Club

Scottish Bylines - School Leaders Scotland

Scottish Chess - Chess Scotland

The Scottish Club Huts List - Mountaineering Coun Scotland

Scottish Country Dancer - R Scot Country Dance Soc

Scottish Diver - Scot Sub Aqua Club

Scottish Educational Jnl - Educl Inst Scot

Scottish Esperanto Bulletin - Scot Esperanto Assn

Scottish Farming Leader Update - NFU Scotland

Scottish Forestry - R Scot Forestry Soc

Scottish Gamekeeper - Scot Gamekeepers Assn

Scottish Geographical Jnl - R Scot Geographical Soc

The Scottish Genealogist - Scot Genealogy Soc

Scottish Golfer - Scot Golf U

Scottish Hill Tracks - Scot Rights of Way & Access Soc

Scottish Home & Country - Scot Women's Rural Insts

Scottish Jnl of Political Economy - Scot Economic Soc

Scottish Jujitsu - Scot Ju-Jitsu Assn

The Scottish Justice - Scot Justices Assn

Scottish Language - Assn Scot Literary Studies

The Scottish Law Gazette - Scot Law Agents Soc

Scottish Leader - School Leaders Scotland

Scottish Legion News - R Brit Legion Scotland

Scottish Licensee - Scot Licensed Trade Assn

The Scottish Mountaineer - Mountaineering Coun Scotland

Scottish National Directory - Aberdeen & Grampian Cham Comm

Scottish NL - Scot Prayer Book Soc

Scottish Paddler - Scot Canoe Assn

Scottish Philately - Assn Scot Philatelic Societies

Scottish Poetry Index - Scot Poetry Library

Scottish Raptor Monitoring Scheme Report - Scot Ornithologists' Club

Scottish Register [of aircraft based in Scotland] - Central Scotland Aviation Gp

Scottish Snowsport Hbk - Snowsport Scotland

Scottish Studies Review - Assn Scottish Literary Studies

Scottish Tennis - Tennis Scotland

Scottish Transport - Scot Tramway & Transport Soc

Scottish Transport Review - Scot Transport Studies Gp

Scottish Wildlife - Scot Wildlife Trust Ltd

Scouting - Scout Assn

Scrabble Club News - Scrabble Clubs (UK)

Scramble - Battle of Britain Histl Soc

Screening for Malnutrition in Sheltered Housing - Brit Assn Parenteral & Enteral Nutrition

The Scribe - Soc Scribes & Illuminators

The Scrichowl - Seventeenth Century Life & Times

The Scroll - Loyal Company of Town Criers

Scuba World - Sub-Aqua Assn

The Sculpture Jnl - Public Monuments & Sculpture Assn

Sea Lines - Ocean Liner Soc

Sea Swallow - R Naval Bird Watching Soc

Seabird - Seabird Group

The Seafarer - Marine Soc & Sea Cadets

Seafish IDGuide - Skates & Rays Producers Assn

Securities & Investment Review - Chart Inst Securities & Investment

Security Direct - Brit Security Ind Assn Ltd

Seen & Heard - NAGALRO: Profl Assn Children's Guardians & Children & Family Reporters & Indep Social Workers

Self & Soc - Assn Humanistic Psychology Britain

Serials - UK Serials Gp

Serica - Silk Assn GB

Service - Spiritualist Assn GB

Sesame - Scientific Exploration Soc Ltd

The Sessional GP - Nat Assn Sessional GPs

Sex Reassignment Surgery - Gender Trust

Sexual & Relationship Therapy - Coll Sexual & Relationship Therapists

The Shadow NL - Fedn Stadium Communities

Sharing the Future - Brit Humanist Assn

The Shavian - Shaw Soc

Sheep Dairy News - Brit Sheep Dairying Assn

Sheep Farmer - Nat Sheep Assn

Sheetlines - Charles Close Soc Study Ordnance Survey Maps

Sherborn Facsimiles - Soc Hist Natural Hist

Sherlock Holmes Journal - Sherlock Holmes Soc London

The Shetland Breed - Shetland Sheep Soc

Shetland Pony Stud Book - Shetland Pony Stud-Book Soc

Shiatsu in the NHS - Shiatsu Soc (UK)

Shifting Ground - Mineral Products Assn

Ship & Boat Intl - R Instn Naval Architects

Ship Repair & Conversion Technology - R Instn Naval Architects

Shoe Service - MultiService Assn Ltd

Shona's Story - Scoliosis Assn (UK)

Shooting & Conservation - Brit Assn Shooting & Consvn

Shoptalk - Shop & Display Eqpt Assn

Shorewatch - Brit Marine Life Study Soc

Short History of the Soc - R Humane Soc

Short List - Assn Profl Staffing Companies

Shortcuts - Gld Brit Découpeurs

Shorthorn Jnl - Beef Shorthorn Cattle Soc Shorthorn Soc UK & I

The Shot - Brit Wheelchair Bowls Assn

Shropshire Business Matters - Shropshire Cham Comm & Enterprise Ltd

Shropshire History & Archaeology - Shropshire Archaeol & Histl Soc

Shroptalk - Shropshire Sheep Breeders Assn & Flock Book Soc

Shuttle Plus - Sewing Machine Tr Assn Ltd

Side View - Macular Disease Soc

SIdelights - Soc Indexers

Sidelights on Sayers - Dorothy L Sayers Soc

Sidelines - Heritage Rly Assn

Sight & Sound - Brit Film Inst

Sign Matters - Brit Deaf Assn

Signals - Arthur Ransome Soc Ltd

Signet NL - Soc Writers Her Majesty's Signet

Significant Ship - R Instn Naval Architects

Significant Small Craft - R Instn Naval Architects

Signpost - Peak & Northern Footpaths Soc

Signs of the Times - Modern Churchpeople's U

SIHS Review - Scot Indl Heritage Soc

Silver Boar - Soc Friends King Richard III

Simile - Fac Homeopathy

Sing When You're Winning - E-Government - Soc Local Auth Chief Executives & Senior Mgrs

Site Log Book for Water Services - Water Mgt Soc

Site Recorder - Inst Clerks of Works GB

Sitelines - LABC

The Six Acre Standard - Nat Playing Fields Assn

Sizzle - Fedn of Chefs Scotland

Sjogren's Today - Brit Sjogren's Syndrome Assn

The Skeptical Adversaria - Assn Skeptical Enquiry

The Skeptical Intelligencer - Assn Skeptical Enquiry

Skin 'n' Bones Connection - Psoriasis & Psoriatic Arthritis Alliance

Skydive - Brit Parachute Assn

Skypointer - Independent Pilots Assn

Skywings - Brit Hang Gliding & Paragliding Assn

Sleep Matters - Sleep Apnoea Trust Assn

Sleipnir - Icelandic Horse Soc GB

Slingshot - Soc Ancients

Slip Knot - Knitting & Crochet Gld

Slot Car Racing News - Brit Slot Car Racing Assn

Small Printer - Brit Printing Soc

Small Printing - Brit Printing Soc

Small Talk - Wales Pre-school Providers Assn

Small Voices - UK Fedn Smaller Mental Health Agencies

Small Woods Information Pack - Small Woods Assn

Smallwoods - Small Woods Assn

The Sniffer - Snuff - Narcotic Inhaler Followers & Aficionados

Snippets - Deafblind UK

Snowsport News - Snowsport Scotland

So You Have Sarcoidosis! - Sarcoidosis & Interstitial Lung Assn

Social Caring - Social Care Assn

Social History in Museums - Social History Curators Gp

Social History of Medicine - Soc Social Hist Medicine

Social Inventions Annual Book - Inst Social Inventions

Social Science Teacher - Assn Teaching Social Sciences

Socialism & Health - Socialist Health Assn

Soc Matters - Building Socs Assn

Socio-legal NL - Socio-Legal Studies Assn

Sociology - Brit Sociological Assn

Sofia - Sea of Faith Network (UK)

Soil Use & Management - Brit Soc of Soil Science

Soldier I Wish You Well - Housman Soc

Soldiers of the Queen - Victorian Military Soc

Soldiers Small Book - Victorian Military Soc

Solicitors of the Supreme Court of Northern Ireland - Law Soc NI

Solo Magazine - Solicitor Sole Practitioners Group

SORP Made Simple: a guidance for grant-making charities - Assn of Charitable Foundations

A Sound Ear - Assn of Brit Orchestras

Sound Track Audio Magazine - Brit Sound Recording Assn

Sounding Board - Sound Sense

Soundings - Hydrographic Soc UK
Inst Musical Instrument Technology
Residential Boat Owners Assn

The South West Coast Path Guide - South West Coast Path Assn

Southern Express - Merchant Navy Locomotive Preservation Soc Ltd

Souvenir - Violet Needham Soc

Spacereport - Assn Scotland Res Astronautics

Spark - UK Pyrotechnics Soc

Speak to the World - Brit Cham Comm Italy

The Speaker - Assn of Speakers Clubs

Speaking Out - Brit Stammering Assn

Special - nasen

Specialist Building Finisher - Federation of Plastering & Drywall Contractors

The Specialist Paralegal - Soc of Specialist Paralegals

Spectra - Management Consultancies Assn

Spectrum - Brit Security Industry Assn Ltd
Brit Wheel of Yoga

The Speculum - William Herschel Soc

Speech & Drama - Soc of Teachers of Speech & Drama

Speleology - Brit Caving Assn

SPHERE - Herpes Viruses Assn

Spin - Statisticians in the Pharmaceutical Ind

Spiritual Voices - Spiritual Workers' Assn

Spode Soc Review - Spode Soc

Spohr Jnl - Spohr Soc GB

The Sport & Exercise Scientist - Brit Assn Sport & Exercise Sciences

Sport & the Law Jnl - Brit Assn Sports & Law

Sports Therapy - Soc Sports Therapists

Sportslife - Fedn Sports & Play Assns

Spot Press - Gloucestershire Old Spots Pig Breeders' Club

Spotlight - HR Soc Ltd

Spouting - Nat Soc Teapot & Kettle Collectors

The Sprat - Friends of Alan Rawsthorne

Sprinkler Systems: the facts - Brit Automatic Fire Sprinkler Assn Ltd

Sprinklers for Safety - Brit Automatic Fire Sprinkler Assn Ltd

Sprouts - Royal Highland Education Trust

Stable Talk - National Assn of Stable Staff

Staffordshire Archaeological Studies - Stoke-on-Trent Museum Archaeological Soc

Stage Management Notes - Stage Management Assn

Stage Management: a career guide, free - Stage Management Assn

Stage Screen & Radio - Broadcasting Entertainment Cinematograph & Theatre Union

Stagedoor - Scottish Music Hall & Variety Theatre Soc, incorporating the Sir Harry Lauder Soc

Stain Removal Guide - Gld Cleaners & Launderers

Stained Glass - Brit Soc of Master Glass Painters

Stained Glass + Monograms - National Assn of Decorative & Fine Arts Societies

Stainless Steel Industry - Brit Stainless Steel Assn

Stand To - Western Front Assn

The Stamp Lover - National Philatelic Soc

The Standard - Assn of Scotland's Self-Caterers

Standard Issue - Road Safety Markings Assn

Standard Method of Measurement - Concrete Repair Assn

Standard Spending Indicators - Soc of County Treasurers

Standardised Protocol for the Sampling & Enumeration of Airborne Microorganisms at Composting Facilities - Assn of Organics Recycling

Standards of Environmental Cleanliness in Hospitals - Assn of Healthcare Cleaning Professionals

Stanspec 2006 - Road Safety Markings Assn

Star & Furrow - Biodynamic Agricultural Assn

Start - National Soc Educ Art & Design

Starting up a Gallery & Frame Shop - Fine Art Tr Gld

Startline - Brit Automobile Racing Club

The Statute Law Review - Statute Law Soc

Staying Alive - R Soc Prevention Accidents

The Steam Car - Steam Car Club GB

Steam Plough Times - Steam Plough Club

The Steamboat Register - Steam Boat Assn GB

Steaming - National Traction Engine Trust

Steel & Its Distribution - National Assn Steel Stockholders

Steel Construction News - Brit Constructional Steelwork Assn Ltd

Steel Fibre Reinforcement - Assn Concrete Industrial Flooring Contractors

Step Forward - Limbless Assn

The Stewarts - Stewart Soc

Stickler Syndrome: the elusive syndrome - Stickler Syndrome Support Gp

The Stickmaker - Brit Stickmakers Gld

Still Improving Sport - Osteopathic Sports Care Assn

The Stock Auditor - Inst Licensed Tr Stock Auditors

Stone Specifiers Guide - Stone Fedn GB

Stopwatch - Nat Soc Promotion Punctuality
The Story of the Knights Bachelor - Imperial Soc Knights Bachelor
Storylines Magazine - Soc Storytelling
Straight Talk - Alcohol Concern
Strain - Brit Soc Strain Measurement
Strands - Braid Soc
Strategy - Strategic Planning Soc
The Strathspey Express - Strathspey Rly Assn
Stress News - Intl Stress Mgt Assn UK
Strider - Long Distance Walkers Assn Ltd
The Structural Engineer - Instn Structural Engrs
Student Focus - Assn Intl Accountants
Studies in Anglesey History - Anglesey Antiquarian Soc & Field Club
Studies in Church History - Ecclesiastical Hist Soc
Studies in Ethnicity & Nationalism - Assn Study Ethnicity & Nationalism
The Subpostmaster - Nat Fedn Sub-Postmasters
Subterranea - Subterranea Britannica
Suffolk Horse Magazine - Suffolk Horse Soc
Suicide & Self Harm Prevention - Howard League Penal Reform
Summons - Medical & Dental Defence U Scotland
The Sun's Abundant Energy - Solar Tr Assn Ltd
Sundial Makers - Brit Sundial Soc
The Superintendent - Police Superintendents' Assn of England & Wales
Supply Management - Chart Inst Purchasing & Supply
Support for Learning - nasen
The Supporter - Cleaning & Support Services Assn
Surface Coatings International - Oil & Colour Chemists' Assn
Surrey Archaeological Collections - Surrey Archaeol Soc
Survival Underground - Soc Study Subterranean Survival
Survive - Assn Illustrators
Susannah Blamire (18th century poet) 1994 - Lakeland Dialect Soc
Sussex Archaeological Collections - Sussex Archaeol Soc
Sussex Industrial History - Sussex Indl Archaeology Soc
Sussex Past & Present - Sussex Archaeol Soc
Swim & Save - Surf Life Saving GB
Swim & Save - Swimming Teachers' Assn Ltd
Swimming Pool Industry Directory & Specifier (SPidas) - Inst Swimming Pool Enrs Ltd
Swimming Times - Inst Swimming
Swiss Chimes Jnl - Brown Swiss Cattle Soc (UK)
Swiss Express - Swiss Railways Soc
Symbols of Solidarity - Trade U Badge Collectors Soc
Synergy - Soc Radiographers

T

Table Tennis News - English Table Tennis Assn
Tackling Multiple Disadvantage - Community Foundation Network
Tag Talk - Arthrogryposis Gp
Tai Chi Tuan & Oriental Arts - Tai Chi U GBn
Tailboard - Photographic Collectors' Club GB
Tak Tent - Heraldry Soc Scotland
Taking a Lead - Nat Playing Fields Assn
Taking Stock Book - Inst Licensed Tr Stock Auditors
Tales of Northwick - Nystagmus Network
Tales of Uruguay - Brit Uruguayan Soc
Taliesin - ACADEMI - Welsh NatLiterature Promotion Agency
Talipes - STEPS
Talk - Nat Deaf Children's Soc
Talkback - Nat Backpain AssntalkBACK - Scottish Spina Bifida Assn
Talking About Turner Syndrome - Turner Syndrome Support Soc (UK)
Talking Sense - Sense - National Deafblind & Rubella Assn
Talking Treatments - SANE
Talkshop Catalogue - Soc for Storytelling
Tall Suppliers Directory - Tall Persons Club GB & Ireland
Tally Sheet - E Westerners Soc
Talyllyn News - Talyllyn Railway Presvn Soc
Tankette - Miniature Armoured Fighting Vehicle Assn
Tanzanian Affairs - Britain-Tanzania Soc

Target MD - Muscular Dystrophy Campaign
Taste Gold - Gld Fine Food
Tattoo International - Tattoo Club GB
Tax Adviser - Assn Taxation Technicians
Tax Advisers Practice Hbk - Assn Taxation Technicians
Teaching Business & Education - Economics, Business & Enterprise Assn
Teaching Deaf People to Drive - Inst Master Tutors Driving
Teaching Earth Sciences - Earth Science Teachers' Assn
Teaching Geography - Geographical Assn
Teaching History - Historical Assn
Teaching Today - Nat Soc Schoolmasters Women Teachers
Team in Practice - Fac Gen Dental Practice (UK)
Technical Specifications for Terrazzo & Marble - National Federation Terrazzo, Marble & Mosaic Specialists
Telecommunications Heritage Jnl - Telecommunications Heritage Group
Television Lighting - Soc TV Lighting & Design
Teleworker - Telework Assn
Teleworking Handbook - Telework Assn
Template - Brit Zeolite Assn
Tempo - Gld Profl Teachers Dance & Movement to Music & Dramatic Arts
Ten 26 - National Fedn Young Farmers' Clubs (E & W)
Tenanted Farm Survey - Central Assn Agricl Valuers
Tennyson Research Bulletin - Tennyson Soc
Tenterden Terrier - Kent & East Sussex Railway Co Ltd
The Terrier - Assn Chief Estates Surveyors & Property Managers Public Sector
The Test Card Circle - Test Card Circle
Testament - Soc Will Writers & Estate Planning Practitioners
Texel Bulletin - Brit Texel Sheep Soc
Text - Textile Soc
Textile Ideas - Embroiderers' Gld
Textile Progress - Textile Inst Intl
Textiles for Launderers & Drycleaners - Guild Cleaners & Launderers
Textiles Magazine - Textile Inst Intl
TGM a coherent dozenal metrology - Dozenal Soc GB
Thames - Japanese Cham Comm & Ind UK
Thames Guardian - River Thames Soc
The Thatcher's Standard - Nat Soc Master Thatchers
Theatre Notebook - Soc Theatre Research
Theoretical Issues in Ergonomics - Ergonomics Soc
Therapeutic Communities Jnl - Assn Therapeutic Communities
Therapeutic Philosophy for the Individual & the State - Inst of Mgt & Technology
Therapy Today - Brit Assn Counselling & Psychotherapy
There is an Alternative - Campaign Indep Britain
Things Heard & Seen - Swedenborg Soc
Third Force News & Inform - Scot Coun Voluntary Orgs
Thirst Choice - Can Makers
This Week - Proprietary Assn GB
The Thomas Hardy Jnl - Thomas Hardy Soc
Thoroughbred Owner & Breeder - Racehorse Owners Assn Thoroughbred Breeders' Assn
Thoroughbred Stallion Guide - Thoroughbred Breeders' Assn
Those of Us Who Loved Her: the men in George Eliot's life - George Eliot Fellowship
Three Bromsgrove Poets - Housman Soc
Three Villains? - Assn Young People ME
Through the Green - Brit Golf Collectors' Soc
Thumbprint - Motor Neurone Disease Assn
The Timber Decking Manual - Timber Decking Assn
Time Haiku - Time Haiku
Tobacco Index - Assn of Indep Tobacco Specialists
Today's Technician - Nat Pest Technicians Assn
The TOF Child - Tracheo-Oesophageal Fistula Support
Together - Fellowship Indep Evangelical Churches
Tommy's Dad - Action Prisoners' Families
Tomorrow's Pharmacist - R Pharmaceutical Soc GB
Tonic - Robert Simpson Soc
Tools & Trades - Tools & Trades Hist Soc
Top Marks - Road Safety Markings Assn
Topics - Inst Public Sector Mgt
Topsail - Soc Sailing Barge Res
Torch Bearer - Soc Olympic Collectors
Torpedo - Brit Marine Life Study Soc

© CBD Research Ltd · Beckenham · BR3 5JS · Tel 020 8650 7745 · E-mail cbd@cbdresearch.com · www.cbdresearch.com

Tot Watch - Meningitis Res Foundation
Touch - Reiki Assn
A Touch of GAS - Glasgow Archaeol Soc
Touchstone - Royal Soc Architects in Wales
Tourism - Tourism Soc
Tourism in Focus - Tourism Concern
The Tourism Manager - Tourism Mgt Inst
Tourist Guides' Directory - Assn Profl Tourist Guides
Towards Community Care - Assn Directors Adult Social Services
Towards Equality - Fawcett Soc
The Town Guide - Exmouth Cham Trade & Commerce
Townswoman - Townswomen's Guilds
The Toymaker - Brit Toymakers Guild
Trackside - Brit Motorsport Marshals Club
Traction Engine Register - Southern Counties Historic Vehicle Preservation Trust
Trade Fairs & Exhibitions in Turkey - Brit Cham Comm Turkey
Trade Leads - Engg Inds Assn
Trade Suppliers Directory - Brit Equestrian Trade Assn
Trade Voice - Wine & Spirit Trade Assn
Tradewinds - Portuguese Chamber
Trading Standards Appointments - Trading Standards Inst
Trading Standards Today - Trading Standards Inst
Trail - Trail Riders Fellowship
Train Times - Assn Community Rail Partnerships
Training & Education Jnl - Brit Inst Profl Dog Trainers
Training & Learning - Inst of Training & Occupational Learning
Training for the Caring Business - Assn Directors Adult Social Services
Training Your Harness Goat - Harness Goat Soc
Tramfare - Tramway & Light Rly Soc
Tramway Museum Guidebook - Tramway Museum Soc
Tramways & Urban Transit - Light Rail Transit Assn
Transfusion Medicine - Brit Blood Transfusion Soc
Transit Magazine - Astrological Assn
Transition Care Pathway - Assn Children's Palliative Care
Transmit - Gld Air Traffic Control Officers
The Transport Digest - Transport Trust
Transport Engineer - Soc of Operations Engrs
Transport Management - Inst of Transport Admin
The Transport of Perishable Foodstuffs - Cambridge Refrigeration Technology
Transportation Professional - Chart Instn Highways & Transportation
The Travel Business - Guild Travel & Tourism
Travelwise - Brit Travel Health Assn
TREaD (Training & Education Programme) - Youth Action Network
The Treasurer - Assn Corporate Treasurers
The Treasurers Hbk - Assn Corporate Treasurers
Treating Arthritis Naturally - Arthritic Assn
Trees & Bats - Arboricultural Assn
Trends & Events - Trade Marks, Patents & Designs Federation
Trends & Statistics - Brit Hospitality Assn
Triangle Magazine - Youth Hostels Assn (E & W)
The Trichologists - Inst Trichologists
Trolleybus - Brit Trolleybus Soc
Trolleybus Magazine - Nat Trolleybus Assn
Trollopiana Jnl - Trollope Soc
The Trombonist - Brit Trombone Soc
True Blue - Friends Blue
The True Line - Caledonian Railway Assn
True Principles - Pugin Soc
Trust & Foundation News - Assn Charitable Foundations
Turner Syndrome - lifelong guidance & support - Turner Syndrome Support Soc (UK)
Tuttitalia - Assn Language Learning
Twins, Triplets & More - Twins & Multiple Births Assn
A Twist of Fate - Scoliosis Assn (UK)
Tyne & Tweed - Assn of Northumberland Local Hist Socs
Typefounders London A-Z - Friends St Bride Library
Typographic - Intl Soc Typographic Designers

U

UK Allergy Clinic Database - Brit Soc Allergy & Clinical Immunology
The UK Consulting Industry Report - Management Consultancies Assn
UK Contract Furnishing Directory - Brit Contract Furnishing Assn Ltd
UK Excellence - Brit Quality Foundation
UK Irrigation News - UK Irrigation Assn
UK Landlord - Nat Landlords' Assn
UK Railway Suppliers Directory - Rly Industry Assn
UK Schools Survey on Budget & Resource Provision - Brit Educl Suppliers Assn
UK Surface Coatings Hbk - Oil & Colour Chemists' Assn
UK Writer - Writers' Gld of GB
Ullans - Ulster-Scots Language Soc
The Ulster Angler - Ulster Angling Fedn
Ulster Countrywoman - Fedn Women's Insts NI
Ulster Jnl of Archaeology - Ulster Archaeol Soc
The Ultimate Cleavage - Breast Implant Inf Soc
Under Five - Pre-School Learning Alliance
Underground News - London Underground Railway Soc
Understanding Medical Education - Assn Study Med Educ
Understanding non-Hodgkin lymphoma - Lymphoma Assn
Understanding Nystagmus - Nystagmus Network
Understanding PMS - Nat Assn Premenstrual Syndrome
Understanding Pregnancy Loss - Stillbirth & Neonatal Death Soc
Underwater Technology - Soc Underwater Technology
Unkind to Unicorns - Housman Soc
Upbeat - Eating Disorders Assn
Update your Road Markings - Road Safety Markings Assn
Upholsterer & Soft - Assn Master Upholsterers & Soft Furnishers
Uplift - Fork Lift Truck Assn
The Uruguayan Short Story - Brit Uruguayan Soc
The Use of English - English Assn
Using a Pawnbroker - National Pawnbrokers Assn UK
Using Power Fastener Driving Tools Safely - Power Fastenings Assn Ltd

V

Value Jnl - Inst Value Management
Valve Users Manual - Brit Valve & Actuator Assn Ltd
Vaporising - Nat Vintage Tractor & Engine Club
Varieties for Thatching - Nat Soc Master Thatchers
Varoom - Assn Illustrators
Vauxhall Motors & the Luton Economy - Bedfordshire Histl Record Soc
Vector - Brit Science Fiction Assn Ltd
The Vegan Magazine - Vegan Soc
Vegan Passport - Vegan Soc
Vegan Stories - Vegan Soc
The Vegetarian - Vegetarian Soc
Vehicle Operator Lists - Road Transport Fleet Data Soc
Vellum - George Formby Soc
VENDinform - Automatic Vending Assn
Vending Quality Standards - Automatic Vending Assn
Vernacular Architecture - Vernacular Architecture Group
Vernacular Building - Scot Vernacular Bldgs Working Group
Vernacular Gower - Gower Soc
Veterinary Nursing Jnl - Brit Veterinary Nursing Assn Ltd
The Veterinary Record - Brit Veterinary Assn
Vida Hispánica - Assn Language Learning
Vienna Music - Johann Strauss Soc GB
The View - Girls' Brigade E & W
Viewpoint - Inst Construction Mgt
    Nat Fedn Blind UK
    Soc Architectural Illustration
Village Sign Times - Village Sign Soc
The Vintage Motor Cycle - Vintage Motor Cycle Club Ltd
Virginia Woolf Bulletin - Virginia Woolf Soc GB
Vitiligo: understanding the loss of skin colour - Vitiligo Soc

Voice - Assn Teachers Singing
Communication Workers U
Victim Support Scotland
The Voice - Brit Cleaning Council
One Voice Wales
Ornamental Aquatic Trade Assn
A Voice for All Time - Assn Latin Liturgy
A Voice Care Guide for Call Centre Managers - Voice Care
Network UK
Voice for Change - Assn Children's Palliative Care
Voice Matters - Voice Care Network UK
Voice of the Quarrying Industry - Mineral Products Assn
Voices from the Vaults - Dracula Soc
Voice of the Veteran - Veteran Horse Soc
Voice Warm-up Exercises - Voice Care Network UK
Volatile Substance Abuse - be aware - Brit Aerosol
Manufacturers Assn
Vouchers at a Glance - Fedn Ophthalmic & Dispensing Opticians
Vox Humana - Mechanical Organ Owners Soc

W

Wagner News - Wagner Soc
Wakefield Court Rolls - Yorkshire Archaeol Soc
Wales Funding Handbook - Wales Coun Voluntary Action
Waller & Dyker - Dry Stone Walling Assn GB
Wallpaper - Max Wall Soc
Wanderer - Historic Caravan Club
The War Correspondent - Crimean War Res Soc
War Poetry Review - War Poets Assn
Warship Technology - Royal Instn of Naval Architects
Wastes Management - Chart Instn Wastes Mgt
Watchword - R Soc Wildlife Trusts
Surface Engg Assn
Water & Environment Manager - Chart Instn Water & Envtl Mgt
Water Quality Management - Chilled Food Assn Ltd
Water treatment for pool operators - Inst of Swimming Pool
Engrs Ltd
Waterbed Owners Manual - Brit Waterbed Assn
Waterbeds - the facts - Brit Waterbed Assn
Waterfowl - Brit Waterfowl Assn
Waterline - Water Mgt Soc Ltd
The Waterloo Jnl - Assn Friends Waterloo Céee
Waterski & Wakeboard - Brit Water Ski & Wakeboard
Waterways - Inland Waterways Assn
Watsonia - Botanical Soc Brit Isles
Watson's Wanderings - Friends Dr Watson
Watson's Wanderings Again - Friends Dr Watson
Watson's Weapons - Friends Dr Watson
The Way Ahead - Disabled Motorists Fedn
Way of Life - Gld Health
Waymark - Inst Public Rights of Way Mgt
We Just Want Our Daughter to Live - Tracheo-Oesophageal
Fistula Support
The Week in Europe - Caribbean-Brit Business Coun
Welcome Aboard: good practice - Bus Users UK
Welding Abstracts - Welding Inst
Welfare World - Inst Welfare
The Wellsian - H G Wells Soc
Welsh Halfbred News - Welsh Halfbred Sheep Breeders Assn
Welsh Ponies & Cobs - Welsh Pony & Cob Soc
Wensleydale World - Wensleydale Longwool Sheep Breeders' Assn
Wessex in Business - Wessex Assn Chams Comm
A Westerly Wanderer - Housman Soc
The Western Dancer Magazine - Best Wstn Dance Academy
Wey-Arun Canal News - Wey & Arun Canal Trust
Wey-South - Wey & Arun Canal Trust
What is A-T? - Ataxia-Telangiectasia Soc
What is Play Therapy? - Brit Assn Play Therapists
What is Psychoanalytic Psychotherapy? free - Brit
Psychoanalytic Coun
What to Wear - Brit Equestrian Tr Assn
What's Bottling - Assn Brit Brewery Collectables
What's Brewing - Campaign Real Ale
What's in a Quarry - Mineral Products Assn

Wheatsheaf - Kempe Soc
Wheel & Palette - Guild Rly Artists
Wheels - Brit Trolleybus Soc
Wheels - Utd Road Transport U
Wheelspin - Ulster Automobile Club
When a Baby Dies - Stillbirth & Neonatal Death Soc
When a Pet Dies - Soc Companion Animal Studies
Where to Find Harness & Carts - Harness Goat Soc
Which? - Consumers' Assn
Whispering Gallery - Dorothy Dunnett Soc
Who Minds - Nat Childminding Assn
Whose Job is it Anyway? - Road Safety Markings Assn
Why Rich People Give - Assn Charitable Foundations
WI Life - Nat Fedn Women's Insts
Wiðowinde (Bindweed) - Ða Engliscan GesíðasWild Flower Soc
Magazine - Wild Flower Soc
Wild Land News - Scot Wild Land Group
The Wildean - Oscar Wilde Soc
Wildfowling - Brit Assn for Shooting & Conservation
Wildlife in the Suburbs - Selborne Soc
Wildlife Sound - Wildlife Sound Recording Soc
William Cobbett in America - William Cobbett Soc
Wiltshire Archaeological & Natural History Magazine -
Wiltshire Archaeol & Natural Hist Soc
The Wind in the Willows Short Stories - Kenneth Grahame Soc
Window Talk - Fedn of Window Cleaners
Winds - Brit Assn Symphonic Bands & Wind Ensembles
Windscreen - Military Vehicle Trust
Winged Words - Aviation Soc
Winking World - English Tiddlywinks Assn
Winning Edge - Inst Sales & Marketing Mgt
Wiring Matters - Instn Engg & Technology
With Our Complements - Complementary Medical Assn
Within Reach - REACH: Assn Children Hand or Arm Deficiency
Wolves & Humans NL - Wolves & Humans Foundation
The Woman Engineer - Women's Engg Soc
Women - 'Wise-up' on Pensions - Nat Pensioners Convention
The Woodcarver Gazette - Brit Woodcarvers Assn
Woodcarving - Gld Master Craftsmen
Woodland Initiatives Register - Small Woods Assn
Woods & Jack - English Indoor Bowling Assn
Woodturning - Gld Master Craftsmen
Woodworking plans & projects - Gld Master Craftsmen
Woodworking Technology - Inst Machine Woodworking
Technology
Wooster Sauce - P G Wodehouse Soc (UK)
The Worcestershire Recorder - Worcestershire Archaeol Soc
Work & Stress - Ergonomics Soc
Work, Employment & Soc - Brit Sociological Assn
The Work of Subscription Agents - Assn Subscription Agents &
Intermediaries
The Workbook - Embroiderers' Guild
The Works - Brit Academy Songwriters, Composers & Authors
World Bowls - Scot Indoor Bowling Assn
A World of Colour - Coloured Horse & Pony Soc
The World of Emissions - Garage Eqpt Assn
The World Today - R Inst Intl Affairs
Worldlywise - Devt Educ Assn
Wound Care Jnl - Wound Care Alliance UK
The Writ - Law Soc NI
The Writer - Soc Medical Writers
Writing in Education - Nat Assn Writers Educ
WWINDY News - World-Wide Opportunities Organic Farms
Wyndham Lewis Annual - Wyndham Lewis Soc

Y

Y Mag - Fedn Museums & Art Galleries Wales
Yarak Jnl - Brit Hawking Assn
The Yardstick - Brit Weights & Measures Assn
The Yellow Book - Nat Gardens Scheme Charitable Trust
Year's Work in Critical & Cultural Theory - English Assn
Year's Work in English Studies - English Assn
Yoga the World Over - Brit Wheel Yoga

© CBD Research Ltd · Beckenham · BR3 5JS · Tel 020 8650 7745 · E-mail cbd@cbdresearch.com · www.cbdresearch.com

Yorkshire Archaeological Jnl - Yorkshire Archaeol Soc
Yorkshire Archaeological Research - Yorkshire Archaeol Soc
Yorkshire Parish Registers - Yorkshire Archaeol Soc
You - User guide to SG4:05 - Nat Access & Scaffolding Confedn
Young Batworker - Bat Conservation Trust
Young Lacemaker - Lace Guild
Your Big Sites Book - Camping & Caravanning Club
Your Body Your Risk - Dance UK
Your Child in an Immobilising Plaster: a few hints - Perthes
   Assn
Your Place in the Country - Camping & Caravanning Club
Your Retirement - Life Academy
Your Voice - Voice: u educ profls

Youth Justice - National Assn Youth Justice
Yr Athro - Undeb Cenedlaethol Athrawon Cymru

Z

Zimbabwe Review - Britain Zimbabwe Soc
Zipper News - Brit Cardiac Patients Assn
Zone Press - England Basketball
Zoological Jnl - Linnean Soc London
Zoological Record - Zoological Soc London

SUBJECT INDEX

Chambers of commerce & industry are included under the heading 'Chambers of commerce' and subdivided into general, local and overseas trade.

County agricultural societies are brought together under the heading 'Agriculture: county societies' and are listed in county order.

County archaeological societies are brought together under the heading 'Archaeology: county societies' and are listed in county order.

County record societies are brought together under the heading 'Records: historical - county societies' and are listed in county order.

Associations concerned with the teaching, technology, equipment & supplies and similar aspects of an activity are generally listed under the activity heading.

In general, headings relate to substantive groups rather than qualifying factors; thus the Society for Experimental Biology is listed under 'Biology'.

Unverified and lost associations are not indexed.

A

Abattoirs
>> Assn Indep Meat Suppliers
>> Licensed Animal Slaughterers. . . Assn
>> Nat Assn Brit Market Authorities
>> Small Abattoir Fedn

Abercrombie (Lascelles)
>> Friends Dymock Poets

Abnormal loads
>> Heavy Transport Assn
>> > + Road: haulage

Abortion
>> Abortion Rights
>> LIFE
>> Soc Protection Unborn Children

Abrasives
>> Brit Abrasives Fedn

Abuse (sexual)
>> Nat Org Treatment of Abusers
>> > + Sex & sexual law reform

Academic dress
>> Burgon Soc

Academies
>> Anti Academies Alliance
>> Foundation, Aided Schools & Academies
>> Indep Academies Assn

Access covers
>> Fabricated Access Covers Trade Assn

Access engineering
>> Nat Register Access Consultants
>> Prefabricated Access Suppliers' & Mfrs' Assn

Access floors/flooring
>> Access Flooring Assn
>> Assn Interior Specialists
>> > + Floors

Access scaffolding > Scaffolding

Accidents
>> Credit Hire Org
>> Inst Home Safety
>> Inst Traffic Accident Investigators
>> Medical Equestrian Assn
>> R Soc Prevention Accidents
>> > + Safety

Accidents: medical treatment > Medicine: accident & emergency

Accidents: victims
>> Action Med Accidents
>> Campaign Drinking & Driving
>> Motor Accident Solicitors Soc
>> Personal Injuries Bar Assn
>> RoadPeace

Accommodation > Hotels & restaurants; Self catering; Students

Accordions
>> Nat Accordion Org
>> Nat Assn Accordion & Fiddle Clubs

Accountancy
>> Accounting Technicians Ireland
>> Assn Accountancy & Business Affairs
>> Assn Accounting Technicians
>> Assn Authorised Public Accountants
>> Assn Certified Public Accountants
>> Assn Chart Certified Accountants
>> Assn Corporate Treasurers
>> Assn Financial Controllers & Administrators
>> Assn Indep Specialist Med Accountants
>> Assn Intl Accountants
>> Assn Practising Accountants
>> Brit Accounting Assn
>> Brit Assn Hospitality Accountants
>> Chart Accountants Ireland
>> Chart Inst Internal Auditors
>> Chart Inst Mgt Accountants
>> CIPFA
>> Healthcare Financial Mgt Assn
>> Hundred Gp Finance Directors
>> Insolvency Practitioners Assn
>> Inst Certified Public Accountants Ireland
>> Inst Chart Accountants England & Wales
>> Inst Chart Accountants Scotland
>> Inst Cost & Executive Accountants
>> Inst Financial Accountants
>> Inst Inc Public Accountants [IRL]
>> Ir Assn Corporate Treasurers
>> Network Indep Forensic Accountants
>> Soc Law Accountants Scotland
>> Soc Profl Accountants
>> > + Bookkeeping; Cost management; Insolvency

Acoustic music
>> Assn Festival Organisers
>> Folk Arts England

Acoustic neuromas
>> Brit Acoustic Neuroma Assn

Acoustics
>> Assn Noise Consultants
>> Heating, Ventilating & Air Conditioning Mfrs' Assn
>> Inst Acoustics
>> Inst Sound & Communications Engrs
>> Proprietary Acoustic Systems Mfrs
>> > + Hearing

Acquired immune deficiency syndrome > Genito-urinary medicine

Acquisitions > Business: mergers & acquisitions

Acrylic (painting in)
>> Brit Soc Painters (in Oil, Pastels & Acrylic)
>> Nat Acrylic Painters Assn
>> > + Art & artists

Activity holidays > Holiday camps & centres

Actors & actresses
>> Brit Actors Equity Assn
>> R Academy Dramatic Art
>> > + Theatre

Actuarial practice
>> Assn Consulting Actuaries
>> Inst & Faculty Actuaries
>> > + Insurance

Acupuncture
>> Acupuncture Soc
>> Brit Acupuncture Coun
>> Brit Med Acupuncture Soc
>> Nat Acupuncture Detoxification Assn
>> > + Complementary medicine

Addiction
>> ADFAM
>> Assn Nurses Substance Abuse
>> Families Anonymous
>> Fedn Drug & Alcohol Profls
>> Nat Acupuncture Detoxification Assn
>> R Coll Psychiatrists
>> Salvation Army
>> Sexaholics Anonymous

Soc Study Addiction Alcohol. . .
> + Alcoholism
Addison's disease
Addisons Disease Self Help Gp
Additives
Food Additives & Ingredients Assn
Adhesive tape
Adhesive Tape Mfrs' Assn
Adhesives
Brit Adhesives & Sealants Assn
Contract Flooring Assn
Inst Materials, Minerals & Mining
Adler (Alfred)
Adlerian Soc Inst Individual Psychology
Admiralty chart agents
Chart & Nautical Instrument Tr Assn
Adolescents > Youth headings
Adoption
Adoption UK
Adults Affected Adoption
Assn Families Adopted Abroad
Brit Assn Adoption & Fostering
Scot Adoption Assn
Adult education
Adult Educ Officers' Assn [IRL]
Adult Residential Colls Assn
ASET
Assn Colls
Assn Nat Specialist Colls
Assn Profl Staffs Colls Educ [IRL]
Assn Scotland's Colls
Brit Inst Learning & Devt
Educl Centres Assn
Fedn Awarding Bodies
Inst Continuing Profl Devt
Inst Learning
NAEGA
Nat Inst Adult Continuing Educ (E&W)
Principals' Profl Coun
Universities Assn Lifelong Learning
Workers' Educl Assn
Adult industry
Adult Ind Trade Assn
Adventure playgrounds > Play & playgroups
Advertising
Account Planning Gp
Advertising Assn
Assn Advertisers Ireland
Assn Business to Business Agencies
D&AD
Inc Soc Brit Advertisers
Inst Advertising Practitioners Ireland
Inst Practitioners Advertising
Internet Advertising Bureau
Ir Direct Marketing Assn
Overseas Press & Media Assn
Advertising: gifts > Incentive marketing
Advertising: music
Soc Producers & Composers Applied Music
Advertising: outdoor
Outdoor Advertising Assn
Outdoor Media Assn [IRL]
Outdoor Media Centre
Advertising: television & screen
Advertising Producers Assn
Cinema Advertising Assn
Advice centres & bureaux
Advice NI
Advice Services Alliance
AdviceUK
Citizens Advice Scotland
Nat Assn Citizens Advice Bureaux
Advocacy/advocates > Law: Scotland
Aerial navigation > Navigation
Aerial phenomena > Unidentified flying objects
Aerial survey & photography
Brit Assn Remote Sensing Companies
Gld Brit Camera Technicians
Nat Assn Aerial Photographic Libraries
> + Landscape; Photography
Aerials: radio, telephone & television
Confedn Aerial Inds
Aerobatics
Brit Aerobatic Assn
Aerobiology
Brit Aerobiology Fedn
Midlands Asthma & Allergy Res Assn

Aerodromes > Aviation
Aerodynamics
Aircraft Res Assn
MIRA Ltd
> + Aviation
Aeromodelling > Models: hobby
Aeronautical engineering > Aviation
Aerosols
Aerosol Soc
Brit Aerosol Mfrs Assn
Aerospace industry > Aviation
Aesthetic surgery > Plastic surgery
Aesthetics
Brit Soc Aesthetics
Aethelflaed, Lady of Mercia
Aethelflaed
Afghanistan
Middle East Assn
Africa
African Studies Assn
Black & Asian Studies Assn
Brit Cham Business Sthn Africa
Business Coun Africa
R African Soc
UK One World Linking Assn
African dancing
Dance UK
> + Dancing
After dinner speakers > Speakers
Age discrimination > Employment
Ageing > Geriatrics & ageing
Agents > under specific headings
Aggregates
Brit Aggregates Assn
Ir Concrete Fedn
Mineral Products Assn
Agriculture
Agricl Economics Soc Ireland
Agricl Inds Confedn
Agricl Science Assn [IRL]
Assn Show & Agricl Orgs
Biodynamic Agricl Assn
Brit Inst Agricl Consultants
Campaign Farmed Envt
Inst Agricl Mgt
Ir Farmers Assn
Linking Envt & Farming
Nat Assn Agricl Contrs
NI Agricl Producers' Assn
NI Shows Assn
Permaculture Assn
R Agricl Soc C'wealth
R Agricl Soc England
R Highland & Agricl Soc Scotland
R Highland Educ Trust
Scot Seed & Nursery Tr Assn
Soc Applied Microbiology
Soc Responsible Use Resources Agriculture. . .
Soil Assn
Sustain
Tropical Agriculture Assn
Women's Farm & Garden Assn
Women's Food & Farming U
> + Farmers' organisations; Horticulture; Organic growing &
farming
Agriculture: buildings
Rural & Indl Design & Bldg Assn
Agriculture: chemicals
Animal & Plant Health Assn [IRL]
Assn Applied Biologists
Assn Public Analysts
Assn Public Analysts Scotland
Crop Protection Assn
Instn Agricl Engrs
Pesticide Action Network
> + Fertilisers; Pest control & pesticides
Agriculture: cooperatives
Scot Agricl Org Soc
Welsh Agricl Org Soc
Agriculture: county societies
Aberdeenshire > R Nthn Agricl Soc
Anglesey Agricl Soc
Antrim > County Antrim Agricl Assn
Ayrshire Agricl Assn
Bedfordshire > E England Agricl Soc
Berwickshire Agricl Assn
Birmingham > Staffordshire & Birmingham Agricl Soc

© CBD Research Ltd · Beckenham · BR3 5JS · Tel 020 8650 7745   E-mail cbd@cbdresearch.com · www.cbdresearch.com

Border U Agricl Soc
Brecknockshire Agricl Soc
Bucks County Agricl Assn
Caithness Agricl Soc
Cambridgeshire > E England Agricl Soc
Cardigan County Agricl Soc
Carmarthenshire > Utd Counties Agricl & HuntersSoc
Cheshire Agricl Soc
Cornwall > R Cornwall Agricl Assn
County Antrim Agricl Assn
Cumberland Agricl Soc
Cumbria > Westmorland County Agricl Soc
Denbighshire & Flintshire Agricl Soc
Derbyshire Agricl & Horticl Soc
Devon County Agricl Assn
Devon > N Devon Agricl Soc
Dorchester Agricl Soc
Dorset > Dorchester Agricl Soc
Driffield Agricl Soc
Dublin > R Dublin Soc
Dumfries & Galloway > Wigtown Agricl Soc
Dumfries & Lockerbie Agricl Soc
E England Agricl Soc
E Lothian > Utd E Lothian Agricl Soc
Essex Agricl Soc
Fife Agricl Assn
Flintshire > Denbighshire & Flintshire Agricl Soc
Glamorgan > Vale Glamorgan Agricl Soc
Glasgow Agricl Soc
Gloucestershire > Three Counties Agricl Soc
Gwent > Monmouthshire Show Soc
Gwynedd > Merioneth Agricl Soc
Hampshire > New Forest Agricl Show Soc
Herefordshire > Three Counties Agricl Soc
Hertfordshire Agricl Soc
Isle of Man > R Manx Agricl Soc
Isle of Wight > R Isle of Wight Agricl Soc
Jersey > R Jersey Agricl & Horticl Soc
Kent County Agricl Soc
Lancashire > R Lancashire Agricl Soc
Leicestershire Agricl Soc
Lincolnshire Agricl Soc
Lockerbie > Dumfries & Lockerbie Agricl Soc
Lothian > Utd E Lothian Agricl Soc
Merioneth Agricl Soc
Mid Somerset Agricl Show Soc
Monmouthshire Show Soc
N Devon Agricl Soc
N Ireland > R Ulster Agricl Soc
N Somerset Agricl Soc
New Forest Agricl Show Soc
Newark & Nottinghamshire Agricl Soc
Newbury & District Agricl Soc
Norfolk > R Norfolk Agricl Assn
Northamptonshire > E England Agricl Soc
Nottinghamshire > Newark & Nottinghamshire Agricl Soc
Oxfordshire > Thame & Oxfordshire County Agricl Assn
Peeblesshire Agricl Soc
Pembrokeshire Agricl Soc
Perthshire Agricl Soc
R Bath & W England Soc
R Cornwall Agricl Assn
R Dublin Soc
R Guernsey Agricl & Horticl Soc
R Isle of Wight Agrl Soc
R Jersey Agricl & Horticl Soc
R Lancashire Agricl Soc
R Manx Agricl Soc
R Norfolk Agricl Assn
R Nthn Agricl Soc
R Ulster Agricl Soc
R Welsh Agricl Soc
Rutland Agricl Soc
S England Agricl Soc
S Suffolk Agricl Assn
Shetland Livestock Marketing Gp
Shropshire & W Midlands Agricl Soc
Somerset > Mid-Somerset Agricl Show Soc
Somerset > N Somerset Agricl Soc
Somerset > R Bath & W England Soc
Staffordshire & Birmingham Agricl Soc
Suffolk Agricl Assn
Suffolk > S Suffolk Agricl Assn
Surrey County Agricl Soc
Sussex > S England Agricl Soc
Thame & Oxfordshire County Agricl Assn
Three Counties Agricl Soc

Tyrone Farming Soc
Ulster > R Ulster Agricl Soc
Utd Counties Agricl & Hunters Soc
Utd E Lothian Agricl Soc
Vale Glamorgan Agricl Soc
W Midlands > Shropshire & W Midlands Agricl Soc
Westmorland County Agricl Soc
Wigtown Agricl Soc
Worcestershire > Three Counties Agricl Soc
Yorkshire Agricl Soc
Yorkshire > Driffield Agricultural Soc
Agriculture: economics
    Agricl Economics Soc
Agriculture: education
    Landex
    Principals' Profl Coun
Agriculture: history
    Brit Agricl Hist Soc
    Historic Farm Bldgs Gp
Agriculture: irrigation > Irrigation
Agriculture: journalism
    Gld Agricl Journalists
Agriculture: law
    Agricl Law Assn
Agriculture: machinery
    Agricl Engrs Assn
    Brit Agricl & Garden Machinery Assn
    Brit Indep Retailers Assn
    Farm Tractor & Machinery Tr Assn [IRL]
    Instn Agricl Engrs
    Machinery Ring Assn
Agriculture: machinery - history
    Farm Machinery Presvn Soc
    Nat Vintage Tractor & Engine Club
    Southern Counties Historic Vehicle Presvn Trust
    Steam Plough Club
Agriculture: merchants
    Grain & Feed Tr Assn
    Ir Grain & Feed Assn
Agriculture: secretaries
    Inst Agricl Secretaries & Administrators
    Nat Assn NFU Gp Secretaries
Agriculture: valuation
    Central Assn Agricl Valuers
    Scot Agricl Arbiters & Valuers Assn
Agrochemicals > Agriculture: chemicals
Agronomy
    Assn Indep Crop Consultants
AIDS (disease) > Genito-urinary medicine
Aikido > Martial arts

Air: ambulances > Ambulance services
Air: cargo > Aviation: freight
Air: charter industry > Travel & tourism
Air: conditioning & ventilating
    Air Conditioning & Refrigeration Ind Bd
    Assn Ductwork Contrs & Allied Services
    Brit Refrigeration Assn
    Building Services Res & Inf Assn
    Chart Instn Bldg Services Engrs
    Chilled Beam & Ceiling Assn
    Commissioning Specialists Assn
    Fan Mfrs' Assn
    Fedn Envtl Tr Assns
    Heating, Ventilating & Air Conditioning Mfrs' Assn
    Heating & Ventilating Contrs Assn
    Hose Mfrs & Suppliers Assn
    Nat Assn Profl Inspectors & Testers
    Residential Ventilation Assn
    Smoke Control Assn
    > + Heating
Air: courier services
    Assn Intl Courier & Express Services
Air: extraction > Dust control; Fans; Fumes & fume extraction
Air: guns & weapons > Arms & armour; Guns & ammunition; Shooting
Air: mail (collecting) > Philately & postal history
Air: pilots, officers & crew > Aviation: pilots, officers & crew
Air: pollution > Air: conditioning & ventilating;   Pollution & pollution control
Air: sport > Aviation: sport
Air: surveying > Aerial survey & photography
Air: traffic control > Aviation: safety, control & training
Air: transport > Aviation
Aircraft > Aviation
Aircraft: historic > Aviation: history
Aircraft maintenance > Aviation: aircraft maintenance
Aircraft models > Models: hobby
Aircraft noise > Noise

Aircrete
>> Brit Precast Concrete Fedn
Airfields noise > Noise
Airports > Aviation
Airports: services & equipment
>> Assn Port Health Authorities
>> Brit Airport Services & Eqpt Assn
Air-sea rescue
>> Goldfish Club
Airships > Balloons & airships
Alarms > Security
Albinism
>> Albinism Fellowship
Alchemy
>> Soc Hist Alchemy & Chemistry
Alcohol
>> Nat Alcohol Producers Assn
>> > + Drink & beverage industry
Alcoholism
>> ADFAM
>> Al-Anon Family Gps
>> Alcohol Concern
>> Alcoholics Anonymous
>> Fedn Drug & Alcohol Profls
>> Medical Coun Alcohol
>> Nat Assn Children Alcoholics
>> Portman Gp
>> Soc Study Addiction Alcohol...
>> > + Addiction
Aldington (Richard)
>> New Canterbury Literary Soc
Ale > Brewing; Real ale
Alexander technique
>> Profl Assn Alexander Teachers
>> Soc Teachers Alexander Technique
Algae
>> Brit Phycological Soc
Alice in Wonderland
>> Daresbury Lewis Carroll Soc
>> Lewis Carroll Soc
Alkan (Charles Henri Valentin Morhange)
>> Alkan Soc
Allergy
>> AAA - Action against Allergy
>> Allergy UK
>> Anaphylaxis Campaign
>> Brit Aerobiology Fedn
>> Brit Inst Allergy & Envtl Therapy
>> Brit Soc Allergy & Clinical Immunology
>> Brit Soc Ecological Medicine
>> Brit Soc Immunology
>> Food & Chemical Allergy Assn
>> Hyperactive Childrens Support Gp
>> Latex Allergy Support Gp
>> Midlands Asthma & Allergy Res Assn
>> Nat Soc Res Allergy
>> > + Immunology
Allingham (Margery)
>> Margery Allingham Soc
Allotments
>> Allotments & Gardens Coun
>> Nat Soc Allotment & Leisure Gardeners
>> > + Gardens & gardening
Alloy(s) > Metal;   Steel: special & alloy
Almonds
>> Combined Edible Nut Tr Assn
Almshouses
>> Nat Assn Almshouses
Alopecia
>> Hairline Intl
Alpacas > Camelids
Alpha-1 deficiency
>> Alpha-1 Awareness Alliance
Alpine gardening
>> Alpine Garden Soc
>> > + Rock gardens
Alpine guiding
>> Brit Assn Mountain Guides
Alström syndrome
>> Alström Syndrome UK
Alternative medicine > Complementary medicine; specific forms
Alternative technology > specific form of energy/technology
Altimetry
>> Challenger Soc Marine Science
Aluminium
>> Aluminium Alloy Mfrg & Recycling Assn
>> Aluminium Extruders Assn

Aluminium Fedn
Aluminium Finishing Assn
Aluminium Packaging Recycling Org
Aluminium Primary Producers Assn
Aluminium Rolled Products Mfrs Assn
Aluminium Stockholders Assn
>> Coun Aluminium Bldg
>> Inst Metal Finishing
Aluminium: foil
>> Assn Hot Foil Printers
>> Packaging & Films Assn
>> > + Packaging
Aluminium: powder
>> Aluminium Powder & Paste Assn
Aluminium: towers
>> Prefabricated Access Suppliers' & Mfrs' Assn
Alzheimer's disease
>> Alzheimer Scotland
>> Alzheimer's Soc
Amaryllid
>> Nerine & Amaryllid Soc
Amateur activities > specific activity
Ambulance services
>> Ambulance Service Inst
>> Ambulance Service Network
>> Assn Air Ambulances
>> Assn Profl Ambulance Personnel
>> Brit Ambulance Assn
>> College Paramedics
>> Nat Assn Private Ambulance Services
>> > + First aid & immediate care
Ambulances: collection & restoration
>> Brit Ambulance Soc
>> > + Motor vehicles: historic
Amenity management > Leisure, recreation & amenity management
America > Latin America; USA
American Civil War
>> American Civil War Round Table
American dancing
>> Assn Amer Dancing
>> Best Western Dance Academy
>> Gld Profl Teachers Dance & Movement
>> Nat Assn Teachers Dancing
>> > + Dancing
American football
>> Brit Amer Football Assn
American 'West'
>> Brit Westerners Assn
>> English Westerners Soc
>> Western Equestrian Soc
>> Western Horsemens Assn
Ammunition > Guns & ammunition
Amnesia
>> Headway
Amphibians > Herpetology
Amputation > Limbless persons
Amusements & coin operated machines
>> Assn Amusement & Leisure Eqpt Suppliers
>> Brit Amusement Catering Trs Assn
>> Brit Assn Leisure Parks, Piers & Attractions
>> Indep Operators Assn
>> > + Automatic vending
Amyotrophic lateral sclerosis > Motor neurone disease
Anaemia
>> Pernicious Anaemia Soc
Anaerobics
>> Anaerobic Digestion Biogas Assn
>> Renewable Energy Assn
>> Soc Anaerobic Microbiology
Anaesthesia
>> Anaesthetic Res Soc
>> Assn Anaesthetists
>> Assn Cardiothoracic Anaesthetists
>> Assn Dental Anaesthetists
>> Assn Paediatric Anaesthetists
>> Barema
>> Brit Malignant Hyperthermia Assn
>> Brit Ophthalmic Anaesthesia Soc
>> History Anaesthesia Soc
>> Neuroanaesthesia Soc
>> Obstetric Anaesthetists Assn
>> R Coll Anaesthetists
>> Soc Advancement Anaesthesia Dentistry
>> Soc Bariatric Anaesthetists
>> Soc Computing & Technology Anaesthesia
Analysts (computer) > Computers: professionals

© CBD Research Ltd · Beckenham · BR3 5JS · Tel 020 8650 7745   E-mail cbd@cbdresearch.com · www.cbdresearch.com

Analysts (technical)
    Soc Technical Analysts
    > + Investment
Analytical chemistry
    Assn Public Analysts
    Assn Public Analysts Scotland
    Chromatographic Soc
    R Soc Chemistry
Anaphylaxsis > Allergy
Anatomy
    Anatomical Soc
    Assn Anatomical Pathology Technology
    Brit Assn Clinical Anatomists
Ancient monuments > Historic buildings
Anderson (Gerry)
    Fanderson
Androgen insensitivity > Endocrinology
Andrology
    Brit Andrology Soc
    Brit Soc Psychosomatic Obstetrics. . .
Anger management > Conflict & anger management
Angling > Fishing (sport);   Fishing tackle
Anglo-Saxon era
    Engliscan Gesíþas
    Ranulf Higden Soc
    Regia Anglorum
    Vikings (The)
Angora wool
    Brit Angora Goat Soc
    Brit Goat Soc
Animal feed
    Agricl Inds Confedn
    Brit Assn Feed Supplement & Additives Mfrs
    Brit Assn Green Crop Driers
    Brit Equestrian Tr Assn
    Grain & Feed Tr Assn
    Ir Grain & Feed Assn
    N Scotland Grassland Soc
    Nat Assn Agricl Contrs
    Soc Feed Technologists
    > + Pets & pet trade
Animals
    Brit Veterinary Assn
    Primate Soc
    R Inst Navigation
    Rare Breeds Survival Trust
    Soc Companion Animal Studies
    > + Conservation; Nature conservation;   Veterinary headings;
    Zoology & zoos; & specific animals
Animals: in entertainment
    Animal Consultants & Trainers Assn
Animals: language
    Wildlife Sound Recording Soc
Animals: slaughtering > Abattoirs
Animals: training
    Assn Pet Behaviour Counsellors
Animals: transportation
    Humane Slaughter Assn
    Racehorse Transporters Assn
Animals: welfare
    Animal Welfare Filming Fedn
    Assn Dogs & Cats Homes
    Brit Soc Animal Science
    Brit U Abolition Vivisection
    Captive Animals' Protection Soc
    Cats Protection
    Humane Slaughter Assn
    Intl Assn Animal Therapists
    Ir Anti Vivisection Soc
    Ir Soc Prevention Cruelty Animals
    League Cruel Sports
    Nutrition Soc
    R Soc Prevention Cruelty Animals
    Scot Soc Prevention Cruelty Animals
    Ulster Soc Prevention Cruelty Animals
    Universities Fedn Animal Welfare
    > + Pets & pet trade; Veterinary headings; Vivisection; specific
    animal/trade
Ankylosing spondylitis
    Nat Ankylosing Spondylitis Soc
Annuities (compulsory)
    Compulsory Annuity Purchase Protest Alliance
Anodising
    Aluminium Finishing Assn
Anophthalmia
    Micro & Anophthalmic Children's Soc

Anorchidism
    Anorchidism Support Gp
Anorexia & bulimia nervosa > Eating disorders
Antarctic > Polar research
Anthropology
    Assn Social Anthropologists
    Brit Assn Biological Anthropolgy & Osteoarchaeology
    Primate Soc
    R Anthropological Inst
Anthroposophy
    Anthroposophical Soc
Anti > object opposed
Antiques
    Assn Art & Antique Dealers
    Brit Antique Dealers Assn
    Brit Antique Furniture Restorers Assn
    Meyrick Soc
    R Instn Chart Surveyors
Antiques: shippers & packers
    Assn Art & Antique Dealers
Antiquities
    Antiquities Dealers Assn
    Assn Study & Presvn Roman Mosaics
    Soc Antiquaries Scotland
    > + Archaeology; History
Antisepsis
    Pharmaceutical & Healthcare Sciences Soc
Ants
    Bees, Wasps & Ants Recording Soc
Anxiety attacks > Panic & anxiety attacks
Aphasia
    Afasic
    Brit Aphasiology Soc
    Speakability
    > + Speech
Apiculture > Bees & beekeeping
Apnoea > Snoring & apnoea
Apostrophe (the)
    Apostrophe Protection Soc
Apparel > Clothing
Apparitions > Paranormal & psychical research
Appearance (personal)
    Fedn Image Consultants
Appetite loss > Eating disorders
Apples
    English Apples & Pears
Applied. . . > basic discipline
Appliqué
    Quilters' Gld
Appraisers (property)
    Inst Auctioneers & Appraisers Scotland
Aquaculture > Fish: farming
Aquaria
    Brit & Ir Assn Zoos & Aquariums
    Brit Marine Life Study Soc
    > + Fish: tropical & ornamental
Aquatic science > Marine: biology & biochemistry
Aquatic trade > Fish: tropical & ornamental
Arab states & peoples
    Coun Advancement Arab-Brit Understanding
    Middle East Assn
    Saudi-Brit Soc
Arachnology > Spiders
Arbitration
    Brit Veterinary Forensic & Law Assn
    Chart Inst Arbitrators
    Electricity Arbitration Assn
Arboriculture > Forestry; Trees
Arc welding > Welding
Archaeology
    Archaeology Abroad
    Assn Archaeol Illustrators & Surveyors
    Assn Envtl Archaeology
    Assn Local Govt Archaeol Officers
    Brit Academy
    Brit Archaeol Assn
    Brit Assn Local Hist
    Brit Soc Dowsers
    Coun Brit Archaeology
    Coun Indep Archaeology
    Egypt Exploration Soc
    Fedn Archaeol Mgrs & Emplrs
    Histl Metallurgy Soc
    Inst Field Archaeologists
    Medieval Settlement Res Gp
    Oriental Ceramic Soc
    Pillbox Study Gp

Prehistoric Soc
R Archaeol Inst
Remote Sensing & Photogrammetry Soc
Soc Landscape Studies
Soc Medieval Archaeology
Soc Museum Archaeologists
Soc Post-Medieval Archaeology
Archaeology: country - England
Merseyside Archaeol Soc
Archaeology: country - Ireland
Inst Archaeologists Ireland
R Ir Academy
R Soc Antiquaries Ireland
Archaeology: country - Scotland
Archaeology Scotland
Glasgow Archaeol Soc
Soc Antiquaries Scotland
Archaeology: country - Wales
Cambrian Archaeol Assn
R Instn S Wales
Archaeology: county societies
Abertay Histl Soc
Anglesey Antiquarian Soc & Field Club
Architectural & Archaeol Soc County Bucks
Ashmolean Natural Hist Soc Oxfordshire
Assn Northumberland Local Hist Socs
Ayrshire Archaeol & Natural Hist Soc
Bedford Architectural, Archaeol & Local Hist Soc
Berkshire Archaeol Soc
Berkshire Archaeology Res Gp
Berwickshire Naturalists Club
Birmingham & Warwickshire Archaeol Soc
Bristol & Gloucestershire Archaeol Soc
Buckinghamshire > Architectural & Archaeol Soc County Bucks
Buckinghamshire > Wolverton & Dist Archaeol & Histl Soc
Caernarvonshire Histl Soc
Cambridge Antiquarian Soc
Cambridgeshire Assn Local Hist
Carmarthenshire Antiquarian Soc
Cheshire > Historic Soc Lancashire & Cheshire
Cheshire > Lancashire & Cheshire Antiquarian Soc
Chester Archaeol Soc
Cornwall Archaeol Soc
Cornwall > R Instn Cornwall
Coventry & District Archaeol Soc
Croydon Natural Hist & Scientific Soc
Cumberland & Westmorland Antiquarian. . . Soc
Cymdeithas Hanes Ceredigion
Cymdeithas Hanes Sir Ddinbych
Denbighshire > Cymdeithas Hanes Sir Ddinbych
Derbyshire Archaeol Soc
Derbyshire > Hunter Archaeol Soc
Derbyshire Record Soc
Devon Archaeol Soc
Dorset Natural Hist & Archaeol Soc
Dublin > Friends Medieval Dublin [IRL]
Dumfriesshire & Galloway Natural Hist. . . Soc
Durham > Architectural & Archaeol Soc of Durham & Northumberland
Durham County Local Hist Soc
Durham > Soc Antiquaries Newcastle upon Tyne
E Herts Archaeol Soc
E Lothian Antiquarian & Field Naturalists Soc
E Yorkshire Local Hist Soc
Essex Archaeol & Histl Congress
Essex Soc Archaeology & Hist
Flintshire Histl Soc
Friends Medieval Dublin [IRL]
Galloway > Dumfries & Galloway Natural Hist. . . Soc
Glamorgan Hist Soc
Glasgow Archaeol Soc
Gloucestershire > Bristol & Gloucestershire Archaeol Soc
Guernsey > Société Guernesiaise
Hampshire Field Club & Archaeol Soc
Hawick Archaeol Soc
Hertfordshire > E Herts Archaeol Soc
Hertfordshire > St Albans & Hertfordshire Architectural. . .Soc
Historic Soc Lancashire & Cheshire
Hunter Archaeol Soc
Huntingdonshire Local Hist Soc
Isle of Anglesey > Anglesey Antiquarian Soc
Isle of Man Natural Hist. . .Soc
Isle of Wight Natural Hist & Archaeol Soc
Jersey > Société Jersiaise
Kent Archaeol Soc
Kent > Croydon Natural Hist & Scientific Soc
Lancashire Archaeol Soc

Lancashire & Cheshire Antiquarian Soc
Lancashire > Cumberland & Westmorland Antiquarian & Archaeol Soc
Lancashire > Historic Soc Lancashire & Cheshire
Leicestershire Archaeol & Histl Soc
Lincolnshire > Soc Lincolnshire Hist & Archaeol
London & Middlesex Archaeol Soc
London Topographical Soc
Lothian > E Lothian Antiquarian &. . .Naturalists Soc
Middlesex > London & Middlesex Archaeol Soc
Monmouthshire Antiquarian Assn
Norfolk & Norwich Archaeol Soc
Northamptonshire Archaeol Soc
Northamptonshire > Wolverton & Dist Archaeol & Histl Soc
Northumberland > Architectural & Archaeol Soc Durham & Northumberland
Northumberland > Assn Northumberland Local Hist Socs
Northumberland > Berwickshire Naturalists' Club
Northumberland > Soc Antiquaries Newcastle upon Tyne
Nottinghamshire Local Hist Assn
Nottinghamshire > Thoroton Soc Nottinghamshire
Orkney Heritage Soc
Oxford University Archaeol Soc
Oxfordshire Architectural & Hist Soc
Oxfordshire > Ashmolean Natural Hist Soc
Peeblesshire Archaeol Soc
Pembrokeshire Histl Soc
Perthshire Soc Natural Science
Powys > Radnorshire Soc
Powysland Club
R Instn Cornwall
Radnorshire Soc
Roxburghshire > Hawick Archaeol Soc
Rutland Local Hist & Record Soc
Saint Albans & Hertfordshire Architectural. . .Soc
Shropshire Archaeol & Histl Soc
Soc Antiquaries Lond
Soc Antiquaries Newcastle upon Tyne
Soc Lincolnshire Hist & Archaeology
Société Guernesiaise
Société Jersiaise
Somerset Archaeol & Natural Hist Soc
Staffordshire Archaeol. . .Soc
Staffordshire > Stoke on Trent Museum Archaeol Soc
Stoke-on-Trent Museum Archaeol Soc
Suffolk Inst Archaeology & Hist
Surrey Archaeol Soc
Surrey > Croydon Natural Hist Scientific Soc
Sussex Archaeol Soc
Tayside > Abertay Histl Soc
Thoresby Soc
Thoroton Soc Nottinghamshire
Ulster Archaeol Soc
W Midlands > Birmingham & Warwickshire Archaeol Soc
Warwickshire > Birmingham & Warwickshire Archaeol Soc
Warwickshire > Coventry & District Archaeol Soc
Westmorland > Cumberland & Westmorland Antiquarian & Archaeol Soc
Wiltshire Archaeol & Natural Hist Soc
Wolverton & Dist Archaeol & Histl Soc
Worcestershire Archaeol Soc
Yorkshire Archaeol Soc
Yorkshire > E Yorkshire Local Hist Soc
Yorkshire > Hunter Archaeol Soc
Yorkshire Philosophical Soc
Yorkshire > Thoresby Soc
Archaeology: industrial
Arkwright Soc
Assn Indl Archaeology
Brewery Hist Soc
Bristol Indl Archaeol Soc
Early Mines Res Gp
Gloucestershire Soc Indl Archaeology
Greater Lond Indl Archaeology Soc
Indl Locomotive Soc
Merseyside Indl Heritage Soc
Peak District Mines Hist Soc
Scot Indl Heritage Soc
Subterranea Britannica
Sussex Indl Archaeol Soc
Tools & Trs Hist Soc
Trevithick Soc
> + specific field of interest
Archaeology: medical
Brit Assn Biological Anthropolgy & Osteoarchaeology
Archaeology: nautical
Nautical Archaeology Soc

© CBD Research Ltd · Beckenham · BR3 5JS · Tel 020 8650 7745   E-mail cbd@cbdresearch.com · www.cbdresearch.com

Nautical Heritage Assn
Sub Aqua Assn
Archery
    Craft Gld Traditional Bowyers & Fletchers
    Grand Nat Archery Soc
    Nat Field Archery Soc
    NI Archery Soc
    Plantagenet Medieval Archery. . . Soc
    Scot Archery Assn
    Scot Assn Country Sports
    Scot Field Archery Assn
    Soc Archer Antiquaries
Architecture
    Architectural Assn
    Art & Architecture
    Assn Bldg Engrs
    Assn Consultant Architects
    Assn Diocesan Cathedral Architects
    Assn Scot Schools Architecture
    Brit Earth Sheltering Assn
    Chart Inst Architectural Technologists
    Inst Profl Designers
    Property Consultants Soc
    Pugin Gld
    R Incorporation Architects Scotland
    R Inst Architects Ireland
    R Inst Brit Architects
    R Scot Academy
    R Soc Architects Wales
    R Soc Ulster Architects
    Scala
Architecture: history & preservation
    Alexander Thomson Soc
    Architectural & Archaeol Soc County Bucks
    Architectural & Archaeol Soc Durham & Northumberland
    Architectural Heritage Soc Scotland
    Campaign Protection Rural Wales
    Cathedral Architects Assn
    Charles Rennie Mackintosh Soc
    Georgian Gp
    Inst Historic Bldg Consvn
    Ir Georgian Soc
    Men Stones
    Nat Trust
    Nat Trust Ireland
    Nat Trust Scotland
    Pugin Soc
    R Archaeol Inst
    Regency Soc Brighton & Hove
    Saint Albans & Hertfordshire Architectural. . .Soc
    Save Britain's Heritage
    Soc Architectural Historians
    Twentieth Century Soc
    UK Assn Presvn Trusts
    Ulster Architectural Heritage Soc
    Vernacular Architecture Gp
    Victorian Soc
    > + Archaeology; Church: buildings
Architecture: illustration
    Soc Architectural Illustration
Architecture: metalcraft
    Gld Architectural Ironmongers
    Inst Architectural Ironmongers
Architecture: naval > Shipbuilding & ship repairing
Architecture: religious > Church: buildings
Archives
    Archives & Records Assn
    Assn Genealogists & Researchers in Archives
    Assn Local Govt Archaeol Officers
    Assn Scot Genealogists & Researchers Archives
    Brit Assn Friends Museums
    Business Archives Coun
    Cathedral Libraries & Archives Assn
    Catholic Archives Soc
    Historic Libraries Forum
    Ir Soc Archives
    > + Records: historical
Arenas
    Nat Arenas Assn
Argentina
    Anglo Argentine Soc
    Cámara Comercio Argentino Britanica
    Cymdeithas Cymru-Ariannin
Arithmetic
    Dozenal Soc
    > + Mathematics

Arkwright (Sir Richard)
    Arkwright Soc
Armed forces & veterans: welfare
    Soldiers, Sailors & Airmen's Families Assn
    UK Nat Defence Assn
    > + Ex-service organisations
Armorial bearings > Heraldry
Armoured fighting vehicles (miniature)
    Miniature Armoured Fighting Vehicle Assn
    > + Military vehicles
Arms & armour
    Arms & Armour Soc
    Histl Breechloading Smallarms Assn
    Historic Artillery
    Meyrick Soc
    Muzzle Loaders Assn
    Ordnance Soc
    Palmerston Forts Soc
    Pike & Shot Soc
    Trebuchet Soc
    Vintage Arms Assn
    > + Defence equipment; Shooting
Arms trade & control
    Campaign Arms Trade
Arm wrestling
    Brit Armwrestling Fedn
Army
    Army Cadet Force Assn
    Victorian Military Soc
    > + Armed forces & veterans: welfare; Cadets; Military history
Aromatherapy
    Aromatherapy & Allied Practitioners Assn
    Aromatherapy Tr Coun
    Scot Massage Therapists Org
Arrhythmia
    Arrhythmia Alliance
    > + Cardiology
Arrows (for archery) > Archery
Art & artists
    Art & Architecture
    Art Workers Gld
    Arts & Business
    Arts Centre Gp
    Arts Marketing Assn
    Arts Soc Ulster
    Assn Cultural Advancement through Visual Art
    Brit Soc Miniaturists
    Brit Soc Painters (in Oil, Pastels & Acrylic)
    Contemporary Art Soc
    Contemporary Art Soc Wales
    Fedn Brit Artists
    Fine Art Tr Gld
    Gld Aviation Artists
    Gld Rly Artists
    Hilliard Soc Miniaturists
    Inst Contemporary Arts
    Medical Artists Assn
    Nat Acrylic Painters Assn
    Nat Assn Fine Art Education
    Nat Campaign Arts
    Nat Portraiture Assn
    Nat Soc Painters, Sculptors & Printmakers
    Nature Art Trust
    Pre-Raphaelite Soc
    Public Monuments & Sculpture Assn
    R Academy Arts
    R Birmingham Soc Artists
    R Cambrian Academy Art
    R Glasgow Inst Fine Arts
    R Philosophical Soc Glasgow
    R Scot Academy
    R Soc . . . Arts
    R Soc Miniature Painters. . .
    R Ulster Academy Arts
    R Watercolour Soc
    SAA
    Soc Artists' Agents
    Soc Botanical Artists
    Soc Decorative Art Curators
    Soc Equestrian Artists
    Soc Graphic Fine Art
    Soc Heraldic Arts
    Soc Scot Artists
    Soc Women Artists
    UK Coloured Pencil Soc
    Utd Soc Artists
    Visual Arts Scotland

Voluntary Arts Network
> + Artist by name; specific form of art
Art: appreciation
Brit Soc Aesthetics
engage
Oriental Ceramic Soc
Art: auctioneers > Art: trade
Art: conservation
ArtWatch UK
Brit Assn Paintings Conservator-Restorers
Fine Art Tr Gld
Inst Consvn
Inst Consvn Historic &... Works Ireland
Ir Profl Conservators & Restorers Assn
Nat Assn Decorative & Fine Arts Socs
> + Historic buildings; Picture restoring
Art: education
Arts Devt UK
Manchester Literary & Philosophical Soc
Nat Soc Educ in Art & Design

Art: festivals > Festivals: art, drama & music
Art: galleries
Assn Leading Visitor Attractions
Brit Assn Friends Museums
Contemporary Art Soc
Contemporary Art Soc Wales
Fedn Museums & Art Galleries Wales
Fine Art Tr Gld
Museums Assn
Nat Art Collections Fund
Nat Heritage
Visual Arts & Galleries Assn
> + Museums
Art: history
Assn Art Historians
Brit Academy
Ir Assn Art Historians
Walpole Soc
Art: law &
Inst Art & Law
Art: libraries
ARLIS/UK & Ireland
Art: management > Leisure, recreation & amenity management
Art: shippers & packers
Assn Art & Antique Dealers
Art: therapy
Allied Health Professions Fedn
Assn Integrative Sandplay Therapists
Brit Assn Art Therapists
Art: trade
Assn Art & Antique Dealers
Brit Art Market Fedn
Fine Art Tr Gld
Inst Auctioneers & Appraisers Scotland
Soc Fine Art Auctioneers & Valuers
Soc Lond Art Dealers
Arthritis & rheumatism
Arthritic Assn
Arthritis Care
Arthritis & Musculoskeletal Alliance
Behçet's Syndrome Soc
Brit Coalition Heritable Disorders Connective Tissue
Brit Health Profls in Rheumatology
Brit Orthopaedic Assn
Brit Soc Rheumatology
Children's Chronic Arthritis Assn
Fibromyalgia Assn
Nat Ankylosing Spondylitis Soc
Nat Rheumatoid Arthritis Soc
Primary Care Rheumatology Soc
Psoriasis Assn
Psoriasis & Psoriatic Arthritis Alliance
Arthrogryposis
Arthrogryposis Gp
Article numbering > Automatic identification & data capture
Artificial intelligence
Soc Study Artificial Intelligence...
Artificial limbs > Prosthetics & orthoses
Artillery > Arms & armour
Artists > Art & artists
Asbestos
Asbestos Removal Contractors Assn
Asbestos Testing & Consultancy Assn
Indep Safety Consultants Assn
Thermal Insulation Contrs Assn

Ash
UK Quality Ash Assn
Asia
Assn South-East Asian Studies UK
Black & Asian Studies Assn
Oriental Ceramic Soc
R Asiatic Soc
R Soc Asian Affairs
UK One World Linking Assn
Asia: languages
Assn Language Learning
Asparagus
Asparagus Growers Assn
> + Vegetables: growing
Asphalt & coated macadam
Asphalt Ind Alliance
Inst Asphalt Technology
Mastic Asphalt Coun
Mineral Products Assn
> + Bitumen
Asphasia > Speech
Asset sales services
Nat Assn Valuers & Auctioneers
Assisted dying > Euthanasia
Association football > Football (Association)
Association management
Inst Assn Mgt
Profl Assns Res Network
Assurance > Insurance
Asthma
Asthma Soc Ireland
Asthma UK
Midlands Asthma & Allergy Res Assn
> + Allergy
Astrology
Assn Profl Astrologers Intl
Astrological Assn
Astrological Lodge Lond
Brit Assn Vedic Astrology
Brit Astrological & Psychic Soc
Fac Astrological Studies
Astronautics > Space research & exploration
Astronomy
Assn Astronomy Educ
Assn Scotland Res Astronautics
Astronomical Soc Edinburgh
Brit Astronomical Assn
Campaign Dark Skies
Fedn Astronomical Socs
Ir Astronomical Soc
R Astronomical Soc
R Inst Navigation
Soc Popular Astronomy
William Herschel Soc
Asylum seekers
Assn Visitors Immigration Detainees
Ataxia
Ataxia-Telangiectasia Soc
Ataxia UK
Friedreichs Ataxia Soc Ireland
Atheism
AHS
Atheism
> + Religion
Athletic clothing > Sportswear
Athletics
Assn GB Athletics Clubs
Athletics NI
Brit Quadrathlon Assn
Brit Triathlon Fedn
Brit Wheelchair Athletics Assn
Dwarf Sports Assn
England Athletics
NI Athletic Fedn
Scot Athletics
Scot Highland Games Assn
Triathlon England
Triathlon Scotland
UK Athletics
Welsh Athletics
Welsh Triathlon
> + Sports
Atomic > Nuclear energy
Attention deficiency
Nat Acupuncture Detoxification Assn
Au pairs > Nannies & au pairs

Auctioneering
    Inst Auctioneers & Appraisers Scotland
    Inst Profl Auctioneers & Valuers [IRL]
    Livestock Auctioneers Assn
    Nat Assn Valuers & Auctioneers
    Property Consultants Soc
    Soc Fine Art Auctioneers & Valuers
Auden W[ystan] H[ugh]
    W H Auden Soc
Audio engineering > Sound recording & reproduction
Audio visual: aids & equipment
    Audiovisual Fedn [IRL]
    Brit Inst Profl Photography
    Brit Universities Film & Video Coun
    > + Sound recording & reproduction
Audio visual: libraries
    Fedn Comml Audiovisual Libraries
Audiology > Hearing
Auditing > Accountancy
Auriculas
    Nat Auricula & Primula Soc (Mid & West)
    Nat Auricula & Primula Soc (Nthn)
    Nat Auricula & Primula Soc (Sthn)
Austen (Jane)
    Jane Austen Soc
Australia
    Australian Business
    Britain-Australia Soc
Austria
    Anglo Austrian Soc
    Austro-Brit Cham
    German Rly Soc
Authors > Writing & writers; individual by name
Authors' agents
    Assn Authors' Agents
    > + Writing & writers
Autism
    Autism Indep UK
    Hyperactive Childrens Support Gp
    Ir Soc Autism
    Nat Autistic Soc
    Scot Soc Autism
    > + Children: handicapped
Auto-immune diseases
    Stiff Man Syndrome Support Gp
Autogenic therapy
    Brit Autogenic Soc
Autograph collecting
    Autograph Club
Autojumbles
    Nat Jumblers Fedn
Automata > Musical boxes
Automatic gates
    Fencing Contrs' Assn
Automatic identification & data capture
    Assn Automatic Identification &... Data Capture
    GS1 Ireland
    GS1 UK
Automatic metering > Meters & metering
Automatic vending
    Automatic Vending Assn
    Nat Assn Cigarette Machine Operators
    > + Amusements & coin operated machines
Automation
    Brit Automation & Robot Assn
    GAMBICA Assn
    Inst Materials, Minerals & Mining
    > + Computers; Control engineering; Production engineering
Automobile > Car headings; Motor headings
Automotive engineers > Motor industry
Auxiliary languages > Languages: auxiliary
Avebury
    Megalithic Soc
Average adjusters
    Assn Average Adjusters
Aviation
    ADS Gp
    Air-Britain (Historians)
    Air League
    Air Transport Auxiliary Assn
    Aircraft Res Assn
    Airline Public Relations Org
    Airport Operators Assn
    Assn ATOL Companies
    Aviation Envt Fedn
    Aviation Soc
    Baltic Air Charter Assn

    Brit Air Transport Assn
    Brit Assn Aviation Consultants
    Brit Business & Gen Aviation Assn
    Britpave
    Fedn Aerospace Enterprises Ireland
    R Aeronautical Soc
    Royal Aero Club Trust
    > + Air: sport; Gliding & soaring; Helicopters
Aviation: aircraft maintenance
    Assn Licensed Aircraft Engrs
Aviation: airships > Balloons & airships
Aviation: art
    Gld Aviation Artists
Aviation: freight
    Brit Intl Freight Assn
    > + Freight transport
Aviation: history
    Aeroplane Collection
    Air-Britain (Historians)
    Aviation Presvn Soc Scotland
    Brit Aviation Archaeol Coun
    Brit Aviation Enthusiasts Soc
    Brit Aviation Presvn Coun
    Brooklands Soc
    Central Scotland Aviation Gp
    Farnborough Air Sciences Trust Assn
    Handley Page Assn
    Historic Aircraft Assn
    R Aeronautical Soc
    Rly & Canal Histl Soc
Aviation: medicine
    Assn Aviation Med Examiners
    R Aeronautical Soc
Aviation: pilots, officers & crew
    Aircraft Owners & Pilots Assn
    Aircraft Owners & Pilots Assn [IRL]
    Brit Air Line Pilots Assn
    Brit Precision Pilots Assn
    Brit Women Pilots Assn
    Flying Farmers Assn
    Gld Air Pilots & Air Navigators
    Indep Pilots Assn
    Ir Airline Pilots Assn
Aviation: safety, control & training
    Air Safety Gp
    Aircraft Owners & Pilots Assn
    Gld Air Pilots & Air Navigators
    Gld Air Traffic Control Officers
    Profl Flight Instructor Assn
Aviation: sport/hobby
    aeroBILITY
    Brit Aerobatic Assn
    Brit Microlight Aircraft Assn
    Formula Air Racing Assn
    Light Aircraft Assn
    R Aero Club UK
Aviculture > Birds

B

Babies > Cot deaths; Maternity; Obstetrics & gynaecology; Paediatrics
Baby goods > Nursery & baby products
Baby life-support systems
    BLISS
Bach flower remedies
    Brit Assn Flower Essence Producers
    Brit Flower & Vibrational Essences Assn
    Crystal & Healing Fedn
Back pain > Chiropractic; Spine & spinal injury
Backgammon
    Brit Isles Backgammon Assn
Backpacking
    Backpackers Club
Bacon
    Provision Tr Fedn
    > + Pigs
Bacon (Francis) Baron Verulam
    Francis Bacon Soc
Bacteriology > Microbiology
Badgers
    Badger Trust
Badges & insignia
    Badge Collectors Circle
    Brit Badge Collectors Assn

Police Insignia Collectors Assn
Trade U Badge Collectors Soc
> + Numismatics

Badminton
Badminton England
Badminton Ireland
Scot Badminton U
Welsh Badminton U

Bagpipes > Pipe bands & music

Bahrain
Bahrain Soc

Bailiffs
Assn Brit Investigators
Civil Enforcement Assn
Local Authority Civil Enforcement Forum

Baking
Assn Bakery Ingredient Mfrs
Bakers Food & Allied Workers U
Brit Confectioners Assn
Fedn Bakers
Food & Drink Fedn
Food & Drink Ind Ireland
Nat Assn Master Bakers
Scot Assn Master Bakers
UK Assn Mfrs Bakers Yeast

Ball clay
Kaolin & Ball Clay Assn
> + Clay & clay products

Ball & roller bearings
Ball & Roller Bearing Mfrs Assn

Ballet
Brit Ballet Org
Imperial Soc Teachers Dancing
Nat Assn Teachers Dancing
R Academy Dance
UK Dance & Drama Fedn
> + Dancing

Balloons & airships
Airship Assn
Airship Heritage Trust
Brit Assn Balloon Operators
Brit Balloon & Airship Club

Balloons (decorated/toy)
NABAS

Ballroom dancing
Ballroom Dancers Fedn
Dancesport Scotland
Gld Profl Teachers Dance & Movement
Nat Assn Teachers Dancing
> + Dancing

Baltic countries > individual country

Bamboo
Bamboo Soc

Bands > Brass & silver bands; Dance bands; Pipe bands & music; Steel bands

Banjos > Ukuleles & banjos

Bank customers > Banking: customers & users

Banking
Assn Foreign Banks
Assn Guernsey Banks
Assn Property Bankers
Brit Bankers' Assn
Chart Inst Bankers Scotland
Fedn Intl Banks Ireland
Financial Services Ireland
Futures & Options Assn
Indep Banking Advy Service
Inst Bankers Ireland
Ir Banking Fedn
SAFE
UK Cards Assn

Banking: customers & users
Campaign Community Banking Services

Banking: history
Brit Banking History Soc

Bankruptcy
Assn Business Recovery Profls
Bankruptcy Assn
Inst Money Advisers

Banks (Sir Joseph)
Sir Joseph Banks Soc

Banners > Flags, banners & bunting

Baptist church
Baptist Histl Soc
Baptist U
Strict Baptist Histl Soc

The Bar > Law

Bar dancers
Adult Ind Trade Assn

Bar football > Table football

Barbecues
Leisure & Outdoor Furniture Assn

Barbershop singing
Brit Assn Barbershop Singers
Ladies Assn Brit Barbershop Singers

Barbirolli (Sir John)
Barbirolli Soc

Barcodes & data synchronisation > Automatic identification & data capture

Barges
DBA
River Assn Freight & Transport
Sailing Barge Assn
Soc Sailing Barge Res

Baring-Gould (Sabine)
Sabine Baring-Gould Appreciation Soc

Barley
Brit Oat & Barley Millers Assn

Barnes (William)
William Barnes Soc

Barometers
Brit Barometer Makers Assn

Barrels > Cooperage

Barriers (safety) > Road: safety & control;   Safety barriers & fences;   Stairs:
gates & barriers (for)

Barristers > Law

Bars (management & staff)
Bar Entertainment & Dance Assn
UK Bartenders Gld

Baseball
BaseballSoftballUK
English Baseball Assn

Basements
ASUCplus

Basketball
Basketball Ireland
Basketball Scotland
BasketballWales
Brit Basketball Fedn
England Basketball

Baskets
Basketmakers Assn
Scot Basketmakers' Circle

Bassethounds > Hounds

Bassoons (musical instruments)
Brit Double Reed Soc

Bathing water quality
Marine Consvn Soc

Baths & bathrooms
Bathroom Mfrs Assn
Kitchen Bathroom Bedroom Specialists Assn

Baths: public > Swimming pools

Batik
Batik Gld

Baton twirling
Brit Isles Baton Twirling Assn
Nat Baton Twirling Assn England
Scot Dance Teachers Alliance
Scot Fedn Baton Twirling

Bats
Bat Consvn Trust
NI Bat Group

Batten disease
Batten Disease Family Assn

Battered wives > Domestic violence

Batteries
Brit Battery Ind Fedn
Oil Recycling Assn

Battery vehicles > Electric: transport

Battle of Britain > World War II

Battlefields
Battlefields Trust
Gallipoli Assn
Gld Battlefield Guides

Battles (re-enactment) > Fights (historic/re-enactment); specific period of interest

Baxter (George)
New Baxter Soc

Beads
Bead Soc

Beam engines
Trevithick Soc

Beams (concrete)
Brit Precast Concrete Fedn
> + Concrete & concrete products

© CBD Research Ltd · Beckenham · BR3 5JS · Tel 020 8650 7745   E-mail cbd@cbdresearch.com · www.cbdresearch.com

Bearings
>> Ball & Roller Bearing Mfrs Assn
Bears ('teddies') > Rupert Bear
Beaters & pickers-up
>> Nat Org Beaters & Pickers Up
Beauty specialists/treatment
>> Brit Assn Beauty Therapy & Cosmetology
>> Fedn Holistic Therapists
>> Freelance Hair & Beauty Fedn
>> Gld Profl Beauty Therapists
>> Hairdressing & Beauty Suppliers Assn
>> > + Cosmetology & cosmetic surgery; Electrolysis
Beckford (William)
>> Beckford Soc
Beckwith-Wiedmann syndrome
>> Beckwith-Wiedemann Support Gp
Bedrooms (fitted)
>> Kitchen Bathroom Bedroom Specialists Assn
Beds & bedding
>> Brit Shops & Stores Assn
>> Brit Waterbed Assn
>> Futon Assn
>> Nat Bed Fedn
>> Sleep Coun
Bedsores
>> Tissue Viability Soc
Beef > Cattle headings; Meat
Beekeeping > Bees & beekeeping
Beer > Brewing
Beer: bottles, cans, labels & mats
>> Assn Brit Brewery Collectables
>> Labologists Soc
Bees & beekeeping
>> Assn Bee Appliance Mfrs
>> Bee Farmers Assn
>> Bee Improvement & Bee Breeders Assn
>> Bees, Wasps & Ants Recording Soc
>> Brit Bee-Keepers' Assn
>> Buglife
>> Bumblebee Conservation Trust
>> Fedn Ir Beekeepers Assns
>> Scot Beekeepers Assn
>> Welsh Beekeepers Assn
>> Wholesome Food Assn
Beet sugar > Sugar headings
Begonias
>> Nat Begonia Soc
Behaviour simulation
>> Soc Study Artificial Intelligence. . .
Behavioural studies
>> Assn Rational Emotive Behaviour Therapy
Behçet's syndrome
>> Behçet's Syndrome Soc
Belgium
>> Anglo Belgian Soc
>> Assn Low Countries Studies
>> Belgian-Luxembourg Cham Comm GB
>> Brit Cham Comm Belgium
Bell (Adrian)
>> Adrian Bell Soc
Bellringing
>> Brit Carillon Soc
>> Central Coun Church Bell Ringers
>> Handbell Ringers
Bennett ([Enoch] Arnold)
>> Arnold Bennett Soc
Benson (Edward Frederic)
>> E F Benson Soc
Bereavement
>> Bereavement Services Assn
>> Campaign Drinking & Driving
>> Compassionate Friends
>> Cruse Bereavement Care
>> RoadPeace
>> Support Murder Manslaughter
>> Survivors Bereavement Suicide
>> Way Foundation
>> > + specific cause of bereavement
Berlioz ([Louis] Hector)
>> Berlioz Soc
Bespoke tailoring > Tailoring
Betjeman (Sir John)
>> Betjeman Soc
Betting > Bookmaking; Casinos; Gaming
Beverage industry > Drink & beverage industry; & specific beverages
Bewick (Thomas)
>> Bewick Soc

Biathlon
>> Brit Biathlon U
Bible
>> Biblical Creation Soc
>> Soc Old Testament Study
Bibliography
>> Bibliographical Soc
>> Cambridge Bibliographical Soc
>> Edinburgh Bibliographical Soc
>> Soc Hist Natural Hist
>> > + Book(s)
Bicross > Cycling
Bicycles > Cycles & motorcycles
Big cats
>> Brit Big Cats Soc
Billiards > Cue sports
Bingo
>> Bingo Assn
>> Nat Bingo Game Assn
Biochemistry & biotechnology
>> Anaerobic Digestion Biogas Assn
>> Assn Clinical Biochemistry
>> Assn Clinical Biochemists Ireland
>> Biochemical Soc
>> BioIndustry Assn
>> Brit In Vitro Diagnostics Assn
>> Brit Soc Proteome Res
>> Brit Soc Toxicological Pathologists
>> Fedn Clinical Scientists
>> Genetics Soc
>> Ir BioIndustry Assn
Biocides
>> Brit Assn Chemical Specialities
>> Chemical Inds Assn
Biodegradable resources
>> Assn Organics Recycling
>> > + Composts & composting
Biodynamic massage
>> Assn Holistic Biodynamic Massage Therapists
Bioenergy
>> Micropower Coun
>> Renewable Energy Assn
>> Soc Metaphysicians
>> > + Renewable energy
Biological engineering
>> Soc Applied Microbiology
Biology
>> Assn Applied Biologists
>> Biological Recording Scotland
>> Brit Soc Developmental Biology
>> Freshwater Biological Assn
>> Inst Biology Ireland
>> Natural Sciences Collections Assn
>> Scot Freshwater Gp
>> Soc Biology
>> Soc Experimental Biology
>> Soc Study Human Biology
>> Systematics Assn
>> > + Botany; Cell biology; Marine: biology & biochemistry; Plants
Biomass > Bioenergy; Forestry
Biometrics
>> Assn Automatic Identification &. . . Data Capture
Biophysics
>> Brit Biophysical Soc
Biotechnology > Biochemistry & biotechnology
Birds
>> Australian Finch Soc
>> Avicultural Soc
>> Birdcare Standards Assn
>> Brit Assn Shooting & Consvn
>> Brit Ornithologists Club
>> Brit Ornithologists U
>> Brit Trust Ornithology
>> Foreign Bird Fedn
>> Nat Coun Aviculture
>> Ornithological Soc Middle East
>> R Inst Navigation
>> R Naval Bird Watching Soc
>> R Soc Protection Birds
>> Scot Ornithologists Club
>> Seabird Gp
>> Songbird Survival
>> > + Natural history
Birds of prey > Hawks & hawking
Birth & birth control > Family planning; Maternity; Obstetrics & gynaecology
Birthmarks & disfigurement
>> Birthmark Support Gp

Brit Assn Skin Camouflage
Craniofacial Soc
Let's Face It
Treacher Collins Family Support Gp
> + Children: handicapped
Births > Population registration
Biscuits
Cereal Ingredient Mfrs Assn
Food & Drink Fedn
Food & Drink Ind Ireland
Bison
Brit Bison Assn
Bitumen
Inst Asphalt Technology
Refined Bitumen Assn
Road Emulsion Assn
> + Asphalt & coated macadam
Björling (Jussi)
Jussi Bjorling Appreciation Soc
Blacksmiths
Blacksmiths Gld
Brit Artist Blacksmiths Assn
Bladder disease > Urology
Bladder problems > Incontinence
Blades
Cutlery & Allied Trs Res Assn
Blake (William)
Blake Soc St James's
Blasting contractors
Inst Explosives Engrs
Bleach
Brit Assn Chemical Specialities
UK Cleaning Products Ind Assn
Bleeding disorders
Haemophilia Soc
Blind & partially sighted
Bates Assn Vision Educ
Behçet's Syndrome Soc
Brit Computer Assn Blind
Brit Retinitis Pigmentosa Soc
Deafblind UK
Gld Church Braillists
Guide Dogs for Blind Assn
LOOK
Macular Disease Soc
Micro & Anophthalmic Children's Soc
Nat Fedn Blind
Nystagmus Network
Partially Sighted Soc
R Nat Inst Blind People
Saint Dunstan's
Scot Nat Fedn Welfare Blind
Seeing Dogs Alliance
Talking Newspaper Assn
UK Assn Accessible Formats
Blinds > Windows: blinds & shutters
Blizzards > Snowfall & blizzards
Blokarting
Brit Land Speedsail Assn
Blood > Haematology; Haemophilia
Blood: circulation
Soc Vascular Technology
> + Haematology
Blood: pressure
Blood Pressure Assn
Blood: sports > Cruel sports
Blood: transfusion
Brit Blood Transfusion Soc
> + Haematology
Bloodhounds > Hounds
Bloodstock > Horse(s) headings
Bloomfield (Robert)
Robert Bloomfield Soc
Blues > Jazz & Blues
Blyton (Enid)
Enid Blyton Soc
Board > Paper & paper products
Board: games > Wargaming; name of specific game
Board: sailing > Surfing, board & speed sailing
Boarding kennels > Kennels
Boarding schools
Assn Boarding School Survivors
Boarding Schools Assn
Girls Schools Assn
> + Independent & public schools
Boats & boating
Assn Boat Safety Examiners

Boat Jumble Assn
Boating Alliance
Brit Dragon Boat Racing Assn
Brit Inflatable Boat Owners Assn
Brit Marine Fedn
Classic Motor Boat Assn
Cruising Assn
Electric Boat Assn
Ir Marine Fedn
Ir Sailing Assn
Nat Assn Boat Owners
Nat Community Boats Assn
Profl Boatmans Assn
Vintage Wooden Boat Assn
Wooden Boatbuilders Trade Assn
> + Sailing; Ship; Steam engines, boats & machinery; Yachts & yachting
Bob skeleton & bobsleighing > Toboggan & luge racing/riding
Boccia
English Boccia Assn
Body piercing
Adult Ind Trade Assn
Brit Body Piercing Assn
Bodyboarding > Surfing, board & speed sailing
Bodybuilding
Brit Natural Bodybuilding Fedn
Nat Amat Bodybuilders Assn
Natural Physique Assn
UK Bodybuilding & Fitness Fedn
> + Fitness
Bodyguards
Brit Bodyguard Assn
Profl Bodyguard Assn
Boilers & waterheaters
Boiler & Radiator Mfrs Assn
Hot Water Assn
ICOM Energy Assn
> + Heating
Boilers & boilersetting
Refractory Users Federation
Bond collecting > Scripophily
Bondage
Adult Ind Trade Assn
Bonded warehouses
Bonded Warehousekeepers' Assn
Bone
Bone Res Soc
Brit Soc Bone & Marrow Transplantation
Brittle Bone Soc
Nat Ankylosing Spondylitis Soc
Nat Osteoporosis Soc
Paget's Assn
> + Orthopaedics
Bonsai
Fedn Brit Bonsai Socs
Japan Soc
Book-keeping
Inst Certified Book-Keepers
Inst Financial Accountants
Payroll Alliance
> + Accountancy; Computers; Data processing
Bookmaking
Assn Brit Bookmakers
Fedn Racecourse Bookmakers
Nat Assn Bookmakers
Rails Bookmakers Assn
Bookmatch cover collecting > Matchbox labels
Bookmarks
Bookmark Soc
Books
Booktrust
Brit Printing Inds Fedn
> + Libraries/librarians; Printing; Publishing
Books: binding & print finishing
Brit Printing Inds Fedn
Designer Bookbinders
Inst Bookbinding & Allied Trs
Soc Bookbinders
Books: bookplates
Bookplate Soc
Books: collecting
Folio Soc
Observers Pocket Series Collectors' Soc
Private Libraries Assn
> + Paperback collecting
Books: illustrations
Imaginative Book Illustration Soc

© CBD Research Ltd · Beckenham · BR3 5JS · Tel 020 8650 7745   E-mail cbd@cbdresearch.com · www.cbdresearch.com

Books: secondhand
    Antiquarian Booksellers Assn
    Provincial Booksellers Fairs Assn
Bookselling
    Booksellers Assn
    Brit Educl Suppliers Assn
    Retail Book, Stationery. . . Employees Assn
Boomerangs
    Brit Boomerang Soc
Boots & shoes > Footwear headings
Boring > Drilling
Boroughs > Local government
Borrow (George Henry)
    George Borrow Soc
Botany
    Botanical Soc Brit Isles
    Botanical Soc Scotland
    Linnean Soc Lond
    Ray Soc
    Soc Botanical Artists
    Soc Experimental Biology
    Wild Flower Soc
    > + Horticulture; Nature conservation; Plants
Bothies > Mountain bothies
Botswana
    UK Botswana Soc
Bottle collecting
    Assn Brit Brewery Collectables
    Old Bottle Club
Bottle feeding (babies)
    Baby Milk Action
Bottled water
    Brit Soft Drinks Assn
    Brit Water Cooler Assn
    Spa Business Assn
    > + Soft drinks; Water: treatment & supply
Bottling
    Brewing, Food & Beverage Ind Suppliers Assn
    Brit Bottlers' Inst
Boughton (Rutland)
    Rutland Boughton Music Trust
'Bouncers' > Door supervisors
Bouncy castles > Inflatable toys & structures
Boundary hedges > Hedges & hedge-laying
Bowel disease > Colitis/colostomy
Bowel (problems with)
    Bladder & Bowel Foundation
    Gut Trust
Bowen technique
    Bowen Assn
Bowles (Edward Augustus)
    E A Bowles of Myddleton House Soc
Bowling
    Bowls England
    Bowls Scotland
    Brit Crown Green Bowling Assn
    Brit Isles Bowls Coun
    Brit Isles Indoor Bowls Coun
    Brit Tenpin Bowling Assn
    Brit Wheelchair Bowls Assn
    English Bowling Fedn
    English Indoor Bowling Assn
    English Short Mat Bowling Assn
    Ir Bowling Assn
    Ir Women's Bowling Assn
    Scot Indoor Bowling Assn
    Scot Women's Bowling Assn
    Tenpin Bowling Proprietors Assn
    Welsh Bowls Fedn
Bowlly (Al)
    Al Bowlly Circle
Bows & bowyers
    Craft Gld Traditional Bowyers & Fletchers
    > + Archery
Bows (for string instruments)
    Brit Violin Making Assn
Boxes
    Brit Packaging Assn
    > + Packaging
Boxing
    Amat Boxing Assn England
    Amat Boxing Scotland
    Brit Amat Boxing Assn
    Ir Amat Boxing Assn
    Welsh Amat Boxing Assn
Boys clubs > Youth organisations
Braces > Prosthetics & orthoses

Bradburne (John)
    John Bradburne Memorial Soc
Bradshaw (Henry)
    Henry Bradshaw Soc
Braids
    Braid Soc
Braille
    Gld Church Braillists
    R Nat Inst Blind People
    UK Assn Accessible Formats
Brain injury & research
    Brain Tumour UK
    Brit Neuropathological Soc
    Brit Neuroscience Assn
    Headway
    PSP Association
    UK Acquired Brain Injury Forum
    > + Children: handicapped; Head & neck injury & disease
Branded products
    Anti Counterfeiting Gp
    Brit Brands Gp
Brass
    Cast Metals Fedn
    Copper Devt Assn
Brass & silver bands
    Brit Assn Symphonic Bands & Wind Ensembles
    Brit Fedn Brass Bands
    Brit Fedn Youth Marching Brass Bands
    Brit Youth Band Assn
    Drum Corps UK
    Kmoch Eur Bands Soc
    Marching Display Bands Assn
    Nat Assn Brass Band Conductors
    Nat School Band Assn
    Scot Brass Band Assn
    UK Fedn Jazz Bands
    Welsh Amat Music Fedn
    > + individual instrument
Brasses & church monuments
    Church Monuments Soc
    Monumental Brass Soc
Brassicas
    Brassica Growers Assn
    > + Vegetables: growing
Brazil
    Anglo Brazilian Soc
    Brazilian Cham Comm GB
    Brit Cham Comm & Ind Brazil
    Hispanic & Luso Brazilian Coun
Brazil nuts
    Combined Edible Nut Tr Assn
Brazing & soldering
    Welding Inst
Bread > Baking
Breakfast cereals
    Assn Cereal Food Mfrs
Breast feeding
    Assn Breastfeeding Mothers
Breast implants
    Breast Implant Inf Soc
Breast surgery
    Assn Breast Surgery
Breathing
    Brit Rebirth Soc
    NARA
Breed societies > type of animal bred
Brewery collectables
    Assn Brit Brewery Collectables
Brewing
    Alcohol Beverage Fedn Ireland
    Brewery Hist Soc
    Brewing, Food & Beverage Ind Suppliers Assn
    Brit Beer & Pub Assn
    Brit Gld Beer Writers
    Campaign Real Ale
    Craft Brewing Assn
    Indep Family Brewers
    Inst Brewing & Distilling
    Labologists Soc
    Maltsters Assn
    Nat Assn Wine & Beer Makers
    Scot Beer & Pub Assn
    Soc Indep Brewers
    Soc Presvn Beers Wood
Brian (William Havergal)
Bribery > Corruption

Bricklaying
    Assn Brickwork Contrs
    Better Brickwork Alliance
    Gld Bricklayers
Bricks
    Brick Devt Assn
    Brit Brick Soc
    Brit Ceramic Confedn
    CERAM Res
    > + Clay & clay products; Refractories
Brides & bridalwear > Weddings
Bridge (card game)
    English Bridge U
    Ir Bridge Union
    Welsh Bridge U
Bridges > Civil engineering; Road: construction, repair & materials
Bridges: concrete
    Concrete Bridge Devt Gp
Bridleways
    Nat Fedn Bridleway Assns
    > + Footpaths & rights of way
British independence
    Campaign Indep Britain
British Telecom staff
    Communication Workers U
Broadband engineering > Cable & satellite communications
Broadcasting
    Assn Service Providers
    Assn UK Media Librarians
    Indep Broadcasters Ireland
    Inst Broadcast Sound
    Nat U Journalists
    Outdoor Writers' & Photographers' Gld
    Radio Academy
    Voice Listener & Viewer
    > + Radio; Television
Brokers > specific subject
Brontë family
    Brontë Soc
Bronze
    Cast Metals Fedn
    Copper Devt Assn
Brooke (Rupert)
    Friends Dymock Poets
Browning (Robert & Elizabeth Barrett)
    Browning Soc
Brushes
    Coir Assn
Bryology
    Brit Bryological Soc

Buchan (John) Lord Tweedsmuir
    John Buchan Soc
Buddhism
    Brit Buddhist Assn
    Buddhist Soc
    Pali Text Soc
Budgerigars
    Budgerigar Soc
    Nat Coun Aviculture
Builders' materials & supplies > Building materials & supplies
Builders & plumbers merchants
    Builders Mchts Fedn
    Inst Builders Mchts
Building
    Assn Bldg Engrs
    Assn Envt Conscious Bldg
    BRE Trust
    Building Controls Ind Assn
    Building Cost Infm Service
    Building Services Res & Inf Assn
    Buildings Energy Efficiency Fedn
    Chart Inst Architectural Technologists
    Chart Inst Bldg
    Chart Instn Bldg Services Engrs
    Confedn Construction Specialists
    Construction Emplrs Fedn
    Cut the VAT Coalition
    Fedn Bldg Specialist Contrs
    Fedn Master Builders
    Gld Builders & Contrs
    Home Builders Fedn
    Homes for Scotland
    Inst Clerks Works
    Intl Masonry Soc
    London Dist Surveyors Assn
    Nat Fedn Builders

    Nat Specialist Contrs Coun
    Property Consultants Soc
    Scot Bldg Contrs Assn
    Scot Bldg Fedn
    Scot Master Wrights & Builders Assn
    > + Construction industries
Building board & timber > Insulation
Building materials & supplies
    Brit Indep Retailers Assn
    Brit Precast Concrete Fedn
    Building Materials Fedn [IRL]
    Construction Products Assn
    Coun Aluminium Bldg
    Door & Hardware Federation
    Engineered Panels Construction
    Ir Hardware & Bldg Materials Assn
    > + specific items
Building societies
    Building Socs Assn
    Building Socs Mems Assn
    Ir Mortgage Coun
    Save our Bldg Socs
Building: survey & inspection > Surveying
Buildings: cleaning & maintenance
    Assn Bldg Engrs
    Cleaning & Support Services Assn
Buildings: conservation
    Architectural Heritage Soc Scotland
    Inst Historic Bldg Consvn
    Nat Register Property Presvn Specialists
    Scot Stone Liaison Gp
    UK Assn Presvn Trusts
    Upkeep
    Vernacular Architecture Gp
    Victorian Soc
    > + Historic buildings
Buildings: earth sheltered
    Brit Earth Sheltering Assn
Buildings: historic & listed > Historic buildings
Buildings: insulation > Insulation
Buildings: literary connections > Historic buildings
Buildings: open to the public > Historic buildings
Bulbs
    Brit Flower Bulbs Assn
    > + Flowers, flower arrangement & floristry
Bulgaria
    Brit Bulgarian Friendship Soc
Bulimia nervosa > Eating disorders
Bulk solids > Materials: management/handling
Bulk storage
    Solids Handling & Processing Assn
    Tank Storage Assn
Bullion dealing
    Brit Jewellers Assn
    London Bullion Mkt Assn
Bungee jumping > Elastic rope sports
Bunting > Flags, banners & bunting
Burghs > Local government
Burglary
    Assn Insurance Surveyors
    > + Security
Burial & cremation
    Assn Burial Authorities
    Assn Natural Burial Grounds
    Assn Private Crematoria & Cemeteries
    Brit Inst Embalmers
    Brit Inst Funeral Directors
    Cremation Soc
    Fedn Burial & Cremation Authorities
    Funeral Furnishing Mfrs Assn
    Inst Cemetery & Crematorium Mgt
    Nat Assn Funeral Directors
    Nat Assn Pre-Paid Funeral Plans
    Nat Soc Allied & Indep Funeral Directors
    Soc Church Archaeology
    > + Cemeteries & churchyards
Burney (Fanny)[Frances Burney d'Arblay]
    Burney Soc
Burns
    Brit Burn Assn
Burns (Robert)
    Robert Burns World Fedn
Bursars
    Indep Schools Bursars Assn
    Nat Assn School Business Mgt
    > + Independent & public schools

© CBD Research Ltd · Beckenham · BR3 5JS · Tel 020 8650 7745 · E-mail cbd@cbdresearch.com · www.cbdresearch.com

Bus & coach operators
    Assn Local Bus Co Mgrs
    Coach Operators Fedn
    Coach Tourism Coun
    Confedn Passenger Transport
    Gld Brit Coach Operators
    Routemaster Operators & Owners Assn
    > + Passenger transport
Business
    Alliance Business Consultants
    Brit Business Angels Assn
    Business Analysts Assn Ireland
    Business Continuity Inst
    Business Mgt Assn
    Business Services Assn
    CIC Assn CIC
    EIS Assn
    Executives Assn
    Fedn Crafts & Comm
    Fedn Educ Business Link Consortia
    Fedn Small Businesses
    Forum Private Business
    Inst Business Ethics
    Inst Directors
    Inst Family Business
    Inst Indep Business
    Inst Small Business & Entrepreneurship
    Ir Small & Medium Enterprises Assn
    Nat Fedn Enterprise Agencies
    Quality Gld
    Quoted Companies Alliance
    R Soc ... Arts
    Small Firms Assn [IRL]
    Soc Business Practitioners
    UK Business Incubation
    UK Trs Confedn
    > + Employers
Business: administration > Management
Business: advisers > Management
Business: aircraft
    Brit Business & Gen Aviation Assn
    > + Aviation
Business: archives > Archives
Business: awards
    Brit Business Awards Assn
Business: centres
    Business Centre Assn
Business: communications systems > Radio: mobile;   Telecommunications
Business: counselling > Management
Business: economists
    Soc Business Economists
Business: education
    Assn Business Mgrs & Adminstrators
    Assn Business Mgt Academics
    Assn Business Schools
    Economics, Business & Enterprise Assn
    > + Commerce
Business: equipment > Office equipment & systems
Business: graduates
    Assn MBAs
    > + Commerce
Business: law > Law: industrial
Business: mergers & acquisitions
    UK Assn Proposal Mgt Profls
Business: property agents
    Brit Coun Offices
    Indl Agents Soc
Business: sponsorship
    Arts & Business
    Scot Business Community
Business: systems > Office equipment & systems
Business: travel > Travel & tourism
Business: valuation
    Soc Share & Business Valuers
Butchers
    Nat Fedn Meat & Food Traders
    Q Gld
    > + Meat
Butter > Dairying
Buttercups (ranunculaceae)
    Ranunculaceae Gp
Butterflies & moths
    Butterfly Consvn
    > + Entomology
Buttonhook
    Buttonhook Soc

Buttons
    Assn Button Merchants
    Brit Button Soc
Buy to Let
    Nat Landlords Assn
Buying > Purchasing & supply
Byron (George Gordon, Lord)
    Byron Soc
    Newstead Abbey Byron Soc
Byzantium
    Soc Promotion Byzantine Studies

C

Cabbages > Brassicas
Cable & satellite communications
    Confedn Aerial Inds
    Nat Jt Utilities Gp
    Satellite & Cable Broadcasters' Gp
    SCTE
    Telecommunications & Internet Fedn [IRL]
    UKspace
    > + Telecommunications
Cables > Electric: cable & conduit
Cabs > Taxis & minicabs
Cacti & succulents
    Brit Cactus & Succulent Soc
    Mammillaria Soc
Cadets
    Army Cadet Force Assn
    Combined Cadet Force Assn
Cage birds > Birds; specific species
Cakes & cake mixes
    Food & Drink Fedn
Calcium carbonates
    Brit Calcium Carbonates Fedn
    > + Lime & limestone
Caldecott (Randolph)
    Randolph Caldecott Soc
Calibration > Measurement
Call centres
    Call Centre Mgt Assn
    Customer Contact Assn
Calligraphy > Handwriting
Camelids
    Brit Alpaca Soc
    Brit Llama Soc
    Brit Veterinary Camelid Soc
Camera technicians & crews
    Brit Soc Cinematographers
    Gld Brit Camera Technicians
    Gld TV Cameramen
    > + Film
Cameras
    UK Indl Vision Assn
    > + Photographic/photography headings
Campanology > Bellringing
Camping
    Assn Caravan & Camping Exempted Orgs
    Backpackers Club
    Brit Holiday & Home Parks Assn
    Camping & Caravanning Club
    Order Woodcraft Chivalry
    Phoenix Camping Club
Canada
    Brit Assn Canadian Studies
    Brit Canadian Cham Tr & Comm
    Brit N Amer Res Assn
    Canada-UK Cham Comm
Canals > Inland waterways
Canaries
    Lizard Canary Assn
    Nat Coun Aviculture
Cancer
    Assn Intl Cancer Res
    BASO
    Brain Tumour UK
    Brit Assn Cancer Res
    Ir Cancer Soc
    Nat Cancer Alliance
    Neuroblastoma Soc
    Oesophageal Patients Assn
    Ovacome: the ovarian cancer support network
    Paget's Assn

UK Assn Cancer Registries
> + Oncology
Candida
Nat Candida Soc
Candles
Brit Candlemakers Fedn
Canes (walking)
Brit Stickmakers Gld
Canned foods > Cans & canning
Canoes & canoeing
Backpackers Club
Brit Canoe U
Canoe Assn NI
Canoe Wales
Channel Swimming & Piloting Fedn
Historic Canoe & Kayak Assn
Open Canoe Assn
Open Canoe Sailing Gp
Scot Canoe Assn
Cans & canning
Brit Bottlers' Inst
Can Makers
Metal Packaging Mfrs Assn
Provision Tr Fedn
> + Food: packaging; specific commodity canned
Canvas & canvas goods > Tents & marquees; Sails & sailmaking
Capacitors
BEAMA
Car > Motor headings
Car: hire > Motor vehicle hire; Taxis & minicabs
Car: parks > Parking (car)
Car: radios/audio systems > Radio: mobile
Car: pollution > Pollution & pollution control
Car: transporters > Motor verhicle: transporters
Caravans & caravanning
Assn Caravan & Camping Exempted Orgs
Brit Holiday & Home Parks Assn
Camping & Caravanning Club
Caravan Club
Historic Caravan Club
Motor Caravanners Club
Nat Assn Caravan Owners
Nat Caravan Coun
Phoenix Camping Club
> + Motor vehicles: historic
Carbon management
Carbon Capture & Storage Assn
ESTA Energy Services & Technology Assn
Carbon monoxide
Assn Profl & Indep Chimney Sweeps
Carbon Monoxide & Gas Safety Soc
Coun Gas Detection & Envtl Monitoring
Card collecting (cigarette & trade)
Cartophilic Soc
Cardiology
Arrhythmia Alliance
Assn Cardiothoracic Anaesthetists
Brit Cardiovascular Soc
Brit Soc Echocardiography
Cardiomyopathy Assn
Children's Heart Assn
Coronary Artery Disease Res Assn
Heart Line Assn
Heart UK
Marfan Assn
Soc Cardiological Science & Technology
Soc Cardiothoracic Surgery
Cardiology: patients
Brit Cardiac Patients Assn
Care & carers
Assn Indep Care Advisers
Carers Assn [IRL]
Carers UK
Ceretas
Crossroads
Nat Assn Care Catering
Nat Care Assn
Relatives & Residents Assn
Shared Care Network
UK Home Care Assn
Youth Access
> + Geriatrics & ageing; Old peoples organisations
Care homes > Residential: homes
Care labelling
Home Laundering Consultative Coun
Careers
Assn Careers Educ & Guidance

Assn Graduate Careers Advy Services
Careers Writers Assn
Fedn Profl Assns Guidance
Inst Career Guidance
Inst Guidance Counsellors [IRL]
NAEGA
Carers > Care & carers
Cargo: handling > Freight transport; Transport
Cargo: health inspection
Assn Port Health Authorities
Caribbean > West Indies & the Caribbean
Carillons
Brit Carillon Soc
> + Bellringing
Carlyle (Thomas & Jane)
Carlyle Soc
Carnations
Brit Nat Carnation Soc
N England Rosecarpe Horticl Soc
Carnival bands > Brass & silver bands
Carnivals & carnival goods
Nat Carnival Gld
Carnivorous plants
Carnivorous Plant Soc
Carp fishing
Carp Soc
English Carp Heritage Org
Carpentry & joinery > Woodworking
Carpets
Brit Antique Furniture Restorers Assn
Brit Shops & Stores Assn
Brit Textile Technology Gp
Carpet Foundation
Contract Flooring Assn
Nat Carpet Cleaners Assn
Nat Inst Carpet & Floorlayers
> + Floors: floorcoverings
Carrier bags > Plastics: bags
Carroll (Lewis)
Daresbury Lewis Carroll Soc
Lewis Carroll Soc
Carrots
Brit Carrot Growers Assn
Cars > Motor headings
Cars: usage
Cartography
Brit Cartographic Soc
Charles Close Soc
R Inst Navigation
Cartons
Alliance Beverage Cartons & Envt
Brit Printing Inds Fedn
> + Packaging; Paper & paper products
Cartoons
Brit Cartoonists Assn
Cartoonists' Club
Political Cartoon Soc
Cartophily > Card collecting (cigarette & trade)
Cartridges (laser)
UK Cartridge Remanufacturers Assn
Carving
Brit Antique Furniture Restorers Assn
> + Stone masons & sculptors; Woodworking
Cases > Optical industry; Packaging; Travel goods & accessories
Cash & carry
Fedn Whls Distbrs
Scot Whls Assn
Cash: security handling
Brit Security Ind Assn
Cashew nuts
Combined Edible Nut Tr Assn
Cashmere
Brit Goat Soc
Casings > Sausage & food casings
Casinos
Casino Operators' Assn
Nat Casino Ind Forum
Cassettes > Sound recording & reproduction; Video
Cast stone
UK Cast Stone Assn
> + Stone
Casting (metal) > Metal: casting
Castles
Castle Studies Gp
Houses Castles & Gardens Ireland
> + Fortresses & forts; Historic buildings; Inflatable toys & structures

© CBD Research Ltd · Beckenham · BR3 5JS · Tel 020 8650 7745   E-mail cbd@cbdresearch.com   www.cbdresearch.com

Casualty simulation
>>Assn Casualty & Health Emergency Simulators
>>Casualties Union
Catalonia & Catalan language
>>Anglo Catalan Soc
Catapults (shooting)
>>Brit Catapult Assn
Cataracts (eyes)
>>UK & I Soc Cataract & Refractive Surgeons
Catering
>>Assn Catering Excellence
>>Brit Hospitality Assn
>>Consortium Caterers Educ Hospitality. . .
>>Food & Drink Ind Ireland
>>Foodservice Consultants Soc Intl
>>Hospital Caterers Assn
>>Inst Hospitality
>>Ir Hospitality Inst
>>Local Authority Caterers Assn
>>Nat Assn Care Catering
>>Nat Assn Catering Butchers
>>NI Amusement Caterer's Tr Assn
>>Profl Assn Catering Educ
Catering: equipment
>>Catering Eqpt Assn [IRE]
>>Catering Eqpt Distbrs Assn GB
>>Catering Eqpt Suppliers' Assn
>>Nat Assn Range Mfrs
Catering: mobile
>>Nationwide Caterers Assn
Cathedral archives
>>Cathedral Libraries & Archives Assn
Cathedral & church shops
>>Cathedral & Church Shops Assn
Cathedral & church music
>>Assn Latin Liturgy
>>Cathedral Organists Assn
>>Friends Cathedral Music
>>Gld Church Musicians
>>Hymn Soc
>>R School Church Music
>>Ulster Soc Organists & Choirmasters
>>> + Organs, organists & organ music

Cathodic protection
>>Corrosion Prevention Assn
Catholic > Roman Catholic
Cats
>>Assn Dogs & Cats Homes
>>Brit Big Cats Soc
>>Canine & Feline Behaviour Assn
>>Cats Protection
>>Governing Coun Cat Fancy
>>Scot Wildcat Assn
Catteries
>>Pet Care Tr Assn
Cattle breed societies
>>Aberdeen Angus Cattle Soc
>>Aubrac Cattle Soc
>>Ayrshire Cattle Soc
>>Beef Shorthorn Cattle Soc
>>Belted Galloway Cattle Soc
>>Black Simmental Soc
>>Brit Bazadais Cattle Soc
>>Brit Blonde Soc
>>Brit Blue Cattle Soc
>>Brit Charolais Cattle Soc
>>Brit Gelbvieh Cattle Soc
>>Brit Kerry Cattle Soc
>>Brit Limousin Cattle Soc
>>Brit Parthenais Cattle Soc
>>Brit Piemontese Cattle Soc
>>Brit Simmental Cattle Soc
>>Brit White Cattle Soc
>>Brown Swiss Cattle Soc
>>Chillingham Wild Cattle Assn
>>Devon Cattle Breeders Soc
>>Dexter Cattle Soc
>>English Guernsey Cattle Soc
>>Galloway Cattle Soc
>>Gascon Cattle Soc
>>Gloucester Cattle Soc
>>Gwartheg Hynafol Cymru
>>Hereford Cattle Soc
>>Highland Cattle Soc
>>Holstein UK
>>Ir Hereford Breed Soc

>>Ir Moiled Cattle Soc
>>Jersey Cattle Soc
>>Lincoln Red Cattle Soc
>>Longhorn Cattle Soc
>>Luing Cattle Soc
>>Marchigiana Cattle Breed Soc
>>Meuse Rhine Issel Cattle Soc
>>Murray Grey Beef Cattle Soc
>>Red Poll Cattle Soc
>>Riggit Galloway Cattle Soc
>>S Devon Herd Book Soc
>>Salers Cattle Soc
>>Scot Hereford Breeders Assn
>>Shetland Cattle Breeders' Assn
>>Shetland Cattle Herd Book Soc
>>Shorthorn Soc
>>Sussex Cattle Soc
>>Welsh Black Cattle Soc
>>White Park Cattle Soc
>>Whitebred Shorthorn Assn
Cattle & livestock
>>Assn Show & Agricl Orgs
>>Brit Cattle Breeders' Club
>>Brit Livestock Genetics Consortium Ltd
>>Brit Soc Animal Science
>>Ir Cattle Breeding Fedn
>>Ir Cattle & Sheep Farmers Assn
>>Livestock Traders Assn
>>Nat Assn Agricl Contrs
>>Nat Assn Cattle Foot Trimmers
>>Nat Beef Assn
>>Nat Cattle Assn (Dairy)
>>New Forest Pony . . . & Cattle Soc
>>R Smithfield Club
>>> + specific animals
Cattle & livestock food > Animal feed
Cattle markets > Markets: street, cattle & farmers'
Cattle troughs
>>Metropolitan Drinking Fountain &. . . Assn
Caves & caving
>>Assn Brit & Ir Showcaves
>>Brit Cave Res Assn
>>Brit Cave Rescue Coun
>>Brit Caving Assn
Cavies (guinea pigs)
>>Brit Rabbit Coun
>>Nat Cavy Club
Cavity insulation > Insulation
Cecidology
>>Brit Plant Gall Soc
Ceilings
>>Assn Interior Specialists
>>Chilled Beam & Ceiling Assn
>>Fedn Plastering & Drywall Contrs
Celebrity assistants
>>Assn Celebrity Assistants (UK)
Celery
>>Quality Brit Celery Assn
>>> + Vegetables: growing
Cell biology
>>Brit Soc Cell Biology
>>Brit Soc Clinical Cytology
>>Brit Soc Immunology
>>Comment Reproductive Ethics
>>R Microscopical Soc
>>Soc Gen Microbiology
Cement & cement products
>>Cement Admixtures Assn
>>Cement Mfrs Ireland
>>Cementitious Slag Makers Assn
>>Instn Civil Engrs
>>> + Concrete & concrete products
Cemeteries & churchyards
>>Assn Burial Authorities
>>Assn Private Pet Cemeteries & Crematoria
>>Brit Assn Cemeteries S Asia
>>Metropolitan Public Gardens Assn
>>Nat Fedn Cemetery Friends
>>> + Burial & cremation
Censorship
>>Campaign Censorship
>>mediawatch-uk
>>Nat Secular Soc
Census > Population: registration
Centipedes
>>Brit Myriapod & Isopod Gp

Central America
    Anglo Cent Amer Soc
Central heating > Heating
Ceramic sanitaryware > Sanitaryware
Ceramics
    Brit Ceramic Confedn
    Brit Ceramic Gift & Tableware Mfrs' Assn
    CERAM Res
    Clarice Cliff Collectors Club
    Craft Potters Assn
    Derby Porcelain Intl Soc
    Inst Materials, Minerals & Mining
    Oriental Ceramic Soc
    R Birmingham Soc Artists
    Scot Potters' Assn
    Soc Women Artists
    Tiles & Architectural Ceramics Soc
    Unity
    > + Clay & clay products; Pottery; Refractories; specific products
Ceramics & pottery collecting > specific type collected
Cereals
    Campden BRI
    Food & Drink Ind Ireland
    Ir Seed Tr Assn
    Scot Soc Crop Res
    > + Grain
Cerebral palsy
    CP Sport England & Wales
    Scope
    Soc Stars
Certification bodies
    Assn Brit Certification Bodies
    > + Quality assurance & control
Chains & chain testing
    Lifting Eqpt Engrs Assn
    > + Lifting & loading equipment
Chairmen/Chairmanship
    Assn Speakers Clubs
Chairs
    Basketmakers Assn
    Chair Frame Mfrs Assn
    > + Furniture
Chalet sites > Caravans & caravanning
Chalk > Lime & limestone
Chamber music > Music
Chambers of commerce: general
    Brit Chams Comm
    GWE Business West
    Harrogate Cham Tr & Comm
    Intl Cham Comm UK
    Lanarkshire Cham Comm
    Midlothian & E Lothian Cham Comm
    N E Cham Comm, Tr & Ind
    NI Cham Comm
    Scot Chams Comm
Chambers of commerce: local
    Aberdeen & Grampian Cham Comm
    Altrincham & Sale Cham Comm
    Angus > Dundee & Angus Cham Comm
    Ayrshire Cham Comm & Ind
    Banbury & District Cham Comm
    Barking & Dagenham Cham Comm
    Barnsley & Rotherham Cham Comm
    Bath Cham Comm
    Bedfordshire & Luton Cham Comm
    Berkshire (W) Cham Comm > Thames Valley Cham Comm & Ind
    Bexley > S E London Cham Comm
    Birmingham Cham Comm
    Black Country Cham Comm
    Boston Area Cham Comm
    Bournemouth Cham Tr & Comm
    Bourton Water Cham Comm
    Bracknell Forest Cham Comm > Thames Valley Cham Comm & Ind
    Bradford Cham Comm & Ind
    Bristol Cham Comm & Initiative
    Bristol Junior Cham Comm
    Bromley > S E London Cham Comm
    Buckinghamshire Cham Comm > Thames Valley Cham Comm & Ind
    Buckinghamshire > Milton Keynes & N Bucks Cham Comm
    Burton & District Cham Comm
    Bury St Edmunds Cham Comm & Ind
    Cairngorms Cham Comm
    Caithness Cham Comm
    Calderdale > Mid Yorks Cham Comm & Ind
    Cambridgeshire Chams Comm
    Cardiff > S Wales Cham Comm

Cham Comm E Lancs
Cham Comm Pembrokeshire
Chams Comm NW
Channel Cham Comm
Chase Cham Comm
Chelsea Cham Comm > Kensington & Chelsea Cham Comm
Cheltenham Cham Comm
Cheshire > E Cheshire Cham Comm & Enterprise
Cheshire > S Cheshire Cham Comm & Ind
Cheshire > W Cheshire & N Wales Cham Comm
Chichester Cham Comm & Ind
Confedn W Midlands Chams Comm
Cornwall Cham Comm & Ind
Coventry & Warwickshire Cham Comm
Croydon Cham Comm & Ind
Cumbria Cham Comm
Dagenham > Barking & Dagenham Cham Comm
Derbyshire & Nottinghamshire Cham Comm
Devon > S Devon Cham Comm
District Wigtown Cham Comm
Doncaster Cham Ind & Enterprise
Dorset Cham Comm & Ind
Dover Dist Cham Comm & Ind
Dudley > Black Country Cham Comm
Dumfries & Galloway Cham Comm
Dundee & Angus Cham Comm
E Cheshire Cham Comm & Enterprise
Ealing Cham Comm
Eastbourne & District Cham Comm
Edinburgh Cham Comm
Essex Chams Comm
Exeter Cham Comm
Exmouth Cham Tr & Comm
Fife Cham Comm & Enterprise
Fort William Cham Comm
Galloway > Dumfries & Galloway Cham Comm
Glasgow Cham Comm
Gloucester Cham Tr & Comm
Gloucestershire Cham Comm & Ind
Gloucestershire > S Gloucestershire Cham Comm
Grampian > Aberdeen & Grampian Cham Comm
Greater Manchester Cham Comm
Greenock Cham Comm
Greenwich > S E London Cham Comm
Guernsey Cham Comm
Halton Cham Comm & Enterprise
Hampshire Cham Comm
Hampshire > N Hampshire Enterprise
Harrow > N W Lond Cham Comm
Hastings > Ten Sixty Six Enterprise
Helensburgh & Lomond Cham Comm
Herefordshire & Worcestershire Cham Comm
Hertfordshire Cham Comm & Ind
Hertfordshire > Watford & W Herts Cham Comm & Ind
Hitchin Cham Comm & Ind
Hull & Humber Cham Comm...
Inverness Cham Comm
Iona > Mull & Iona Cham Comm
Isle of Man Cham Comm
Isle of Wight Cham Commerce, Tourism & Ind
Islington Cham Comm & Tr
Jersey Cham Comm
Kensington & Chelsea Cham Comm
Kent Invicta Cham Comm
Kent > Thanet & E Kent Cham
Kent > W Kent Cham Comm & Ind
Kingston Cham Comm
Knowsley Cham Ind & Comm
Lancashire > Cham Comm E Lancs
Lancashire > N & Wstn Lancashire Cham Comm
Lancaster Dist Cham Comm
Leeds York & N Yorks Cham Comm & Ind
Leicestershire Cham Comm
Lewisham > S E London Cham Comm
Lichfield & Tamworth Cham Comm
Lincolnshire Cham Comm
Lisburn Cham Comm
Liverpool Cham Comm
Lomond > Helensburgh & Lomond Cham Comm
London Cham Comm & Ind
London > N London Cham Comm
London > N W Lond Cham Comm
Londonderry Cham Comm
Lothian > W Lothian Cham Comm
Luton > Bedfordshire & Luton Cham Comm
Macclesfield Cham Comm
Maidenhead & Dist Cham Comm

© CBD Research Ltd · Beckenham · BR3 5JS · Tel 020 8650 7745   E-mail cbd@cbdresearch.com · www.cbdresearch.com

Merton Cham Comm
Mid Yorkshire Cham Comm & Ind
Milton Keynes & N Bucks Cham Comm
Moray Cham Comm
Mull & Iona Cham Comm
N London Cham Comm
N Staffs Cham Comm & Ind
N W Lond Cham Comm
N & Wstn Lancs Cham Comm
Newcastle > N E Cham Comm, Tr & Ind
Norfolk Cham Comm & Ind
Northamptonshire Cham Comm
Norwich > Norfolk Cham Comm
Nottinghamshire > Derbyshire & Nottinghamshire Cham Comm
Orkney Cham Comm
Oxfordshire Cham Comm > Thames Valley Cham Comm & Ind
Pembrokeshire > Cham Comm Pembrokeshire
Penzance Chamb Comm
Perthshire Cham Comm
Plymouth Cham Comm & Ind
Reading Cham Comm > Thames Valley Cham Comm & Ind
Redbridge Cham Comm
Renfrewshire Cham Comm
Richmond Cham Comm
Rotherham > Barnsley & Rotherham Cham Comm
S Cheshire Cham Comm & Ind
S Devon Cham Comm
S E London Cham Comm
S Gloucestershire Cham Comm
S W Chams
S Wales Cham Comm
Saint Albans District Cham Comm
Saint Austell Dist Cham Comm & Ind
Saint Helens Cham
Saint Leonards > Ten Sixty Six Enterprise
Sale > Altrincham & Sale Cham Comm
Salisbury & Dist Cham Comm & Ind
Sandwell > Black Country Cham Comm
Scot Borders Cham Comm
Sefton Cham Comm & Ind
Sevenoaks & District Cham Comm
Sheffield Cham Comm & Ind
Shropshire Cham Comm & Enterprise
Slough Cham Comm > Thames Valley Cham Comm & Ind
Solihull Cham Comm
Somerset Cham Comm & Ind
Southern Staffordshire Cham Comm
Southport > Sefton Cham Comm & Ind
Southwark Cham Comm
Staffordshire > N Staffordshire Cham Comm & Ind
Staffordshire > Southern Staffordshire Cham Comm & Ind
Suffolk Cham Comm
Surrey Chams Comm
Sussex Cham Comm & Enterprise
Sutton Cham
Swansea > S Wales Cham Comm
Swindon Cham Comm > Thames Valley Cham Comm & Ind
Tamworth > Lichfield & Tamworth Cham Comm
Taunton Cham Comm
Ten Sixty Six Enterprise
Tetbury Cham Comm & Ind
Tewkesbury Cham Comm & Ind
Thames Valley Cham Comm & Ind
Thanet & E Kent Cham
Torbay > S Devon Cham Comm
W Cheshire & N Wales Cham Comm
W Kent Cham Comm & Ind
W Lothian Cham Comm
Wakefield > Mid Yorks Cham Comm & Ind
Wales > S Wales Cham Comm
Wales > W Cheshire & N Wales Cham Comm
Walsall > Black Country Cham Comm
Warrington Cham Comm & Ind
Warwickshire > Coventry & Warwickshire Cham Comm & Ind
Watford & W Herts Cham Comm & Ind
Wessex Assn Chams Comm
Western Isles Cham Comm
Weymouth & Portland Cham Comm. . .
Wigton > District Wigton Cham Comm
Wirral Cham Comm & Ind
Wokingham Cham Comm > Thames Valley Cham Comm & Ind
Wolverhampton > Black Country Cham Comm
Worcestershire > Herefordshire & Worcestershire Cham Comm
Worthing & Adur Cham Comm
York > Leeds, York & N Yorkshire Cham Comm
Yorkshire > Leeds, York & N Yorkshire Cham Comm
Yorkshire > Mid Yorkshire Cham Comm & Ind

Chambers of commerce: overseas trade
Africa > Brit Cham Business Sthn Africa
Arab Brit Cham Comm
Argentina > Brit Argentine Cham Comm
Argentina > Cámara Comercio Argentino Britanica
Australian Business
Austro-Brit Cham
Belgian-Luxembourg Cham Comm GB
Belgium > Brit Cham Comm Belgium
Brazil > Brit Cham Comm & Ind Brazil
Brazilian Cham Comm GB
Brit Amer Business Coun
Brit Amer Business Inc
Brit Argentine Cham Comm
Brit Bulgarian Cham Comm
Brit Canadian Cham Tr & Comm
Brit Cham Business Sthn Africa
Brit Cham Comm Belgium
Brit Cham Comm China - Beijing
Brit Cham Comm China - Shanghai
Brit Cham Comm Czech Republic
Brit Cham Comm Germany
Brit Cham Comm Hong Kong
Brit Cham Comm Hungary
Brit Cham Comm & Ind Brazil
Brit Cham Comm Italy
Brit Cham Comm Japan
Brit Cham Comm Korea
Brit Cham Comm Latvia
Brit Cham Comm Luxembourg
Brit Cham Comm Morocco
Brit Cham Comm Singapore
Brit Cham Comm Slovak Republic
Brit Cham Comm Spain
Brit Cham Comm Taipei
Brit Cham Comm Thailand
Brit Cham Comm Turkey
Brit & Colombian Cham Comm
Brit-Estonian Cham Comm
Brit Hellenic Cham Comm
Brit New Zealand Tr Coun
Brit Peruvian Cham
Brit Polish Cham Comm [Lond]
Brit Polish Cham Comm [Warsaw]
Brit Portuguese Cham Comm
Brit Swedish Cham Comm Sweden
Brit-Swiss Cham Comm [Zürich]
Britain-Nepal Cham Comm
Britain Nigeria Business Coun
Bulgaria > Brit Bulgarian Cham Comm
Camara Chileno Britanica Comercio
Cámara Comercio Argentino Britanica
Camara Comercio Britanica [Mexico]
Cámara Comercio Colombo Britanica
Cámara Comercio Uruguayo Británica
Cámara Venezolana Británica Comercio
Canada > Brit Canadian Cham Tr & Comm
Canada-UK Cham Comm
Chambre Comm Française GB
Chams Ireland
Chile > Camara Chileno Britanica Comercio
China > Brit Cham Comm China - Beijing
China > Brit Cham Comm China - Shanghai
Colombia > Cámara Comercio Colombo Británica
Czech Brit Cham Comm
Czech Republic > Brit Cham Comm Czech Republic
Danish-UK Cham Comm
Dublin Cham Comm [IRL]
Egyptian Brit Cham Comm
Estonia - Brit-Estonian Cham Comm
Finnish-Brit Cham Comm
France > Chambre Comm Française GB
Franco British Cham Comm & Ind
German-Brit Cham Ind & Comm
Germany > Brit Cham Comm Germany
Greece > Brit Hellenic Cham Comm
Hong Kong > Brit Cham Comm Hong Kong
Hungary > Brit Cham Comm Hungary
Ireland > Chambers Ireland
Ireland > Dublin Cham Comm
Italian Cham Comm Ind UK
Italy > Brit Cham Comm Italy
Japan > Brit Cham Comm Japan
Japanese Cham Comm & Ind UK
Korea > Brit Cham Comm Korea
Latvia > Brit Cham Comm Latvia
Luxembourg > Belgian-Luxembourg Cham Comm GB

Luxembourg > Brit Cham Comm Luxembourg
Mexico > Cámara Comercio Británica AC
Morocco > Brit Cham Comm Morocco
Nepal > Britain-Nepal Cham Comm
Netherlands Brit Cham Comm
New Zealand > Australian Business
New Zealand > Brit New Zealand Tr Coun
Nigeria > Britain Nigeria Business Coun
Norwegian-Brit Cham Comm
Pakistan > UK Pakistan Cham Comm & Ind
Peru > Brit-Peruvian Cham
Poland > Brit-Polish Cham Comm [Lond]
Poland > Brit-Polish Cham Comm [Warsaw]
Portugal > Brit-Portuguese Cham Comm
Portuguese Cham
Russia > Russo-Brit Cham Comm
Russo-Brit Cham Comm
S Africa > Brit Cham Business Sthn Africa
Singapore > Brit Cham Comm Singapore
Slovakia > Brit Cham Comm Slovak Republic
Spain > Brit Cham Comm Spain
Spanish Cham Comm GB
Sweden > Brit Swedish Cham Comm Sweden
Swedish Cham Comm UK
Switzerland > Brit-Swiss Cham Comm [Zürich]
Taiwan > Brit Cham Comm Taipei
Thailand > Brit Cham Comm Thailand
Turkey > Brit Cham Comm Turkey
Turkish-Brit Cham Comm & Ind
UK Pakistan Cham Comm [?dead 05
Uruguay > Cámara Comercio Uruguayo-Británica
USA > Brit Amer Business Coun
USA > Brit Amer Business Inc
Venezuela > Cámara Venezolana Británica Comercio
Champagne
      Champagne Agents' Assn
      > + Wines & spirits: trade
Chandlers > Ships: stores & supplies
Channel Islands > individual island
Channel swimming (& crossing)
      Channel Crossing Assn
      Channel Swimming Assn
      Channel Swimming & Piloting Fedn
Channels (concrete) > Culverts & channels
Chapels > Church headings
Charcot-Marie-Tooth disease
      CMT UK
Charcuterie
      Gld Fine Food
Charities
      Assn Charitable Foundations
      Assn Charities
      Assn Charity Indep Examiners
      Assn Charity Officers
      Assn Charity Shops
      Assn Med Res Charities
      Charities' Property Assn
      Charity Christmas Card Coun
      Charity Finance Directors' Gp
      Charity Law Assn
      Charity Tax Gp
      Inst Fundraising
      Public Fundraising Regulatory Assn
      Small Charities Coalition
Charities: guidance & lists > Introduction paragraph 6
Charles I King of England
      R Martyr Church U
      Sealed Knot
      Soc King Charles Martyr
Charts (nautical)
      Chart & Nautical Instrument Tr Assn
Charter operators > Travel & tourism
Charter trustee towns
      Assn Charter Trustee Towns &. . . Couns
Chauffeurs
      Brit Chauffeurs Gld
      London Private Hire Car Assn
Cheerleading
      Brit Cheerleading Assn
      UK Cheerleading Assn
Cheese
      Brit Goat Soc
      Brit Sheep Dairying Assn
      Gld Fine Food
      Provision Tr Fedn
      Specialist Cheesemakers Assn
      Stilton Cheese Makers Assn

Chefs
      Brit Culinary Fedn
      Craft Gld Chefs
      Fedn Chefs Scotland
      Master Chefs GB
      Welsh Culinary Assn
      > + Catering
Chelonia
      Brit Chelonia Gp
      Brit Tortoise Soc
      Nat Tortoise Club
      Tortoise Trust
      > + Herpetology
Chemical allergy > Allergy
Chemical engineering
      Brit Chemical Engg Contrs Assn
      Instn Chemical Engrs
Chemical hazards
      Brit Occupational Hygiene Soc
      Chemical Hazards Communication Soc
Chemical industry & trade
      BTC Testing Advisory Gp
      Chemical Business Assn
      Chemical Distbn Ireland
      Chemical & Indl Consultants' Assn
      Chemical Inds Assn
      PharmaChemical Ireland
      Soc Chemical Ind
Chemical specialities
      Brit Assn Chemical Specialities
Chemical waste
      Chemical Recycling Assn
      > + Reclamation & recycling
Chemicals: packaging
      Indl Packaging Assn
Chemistry
      Inst Chemistry Ireland
      R Instn GB
      R Soc Chemistry
      Resource Use Inst
      > + specific applications
Chemistry: history
      Soc Hist Alchemy & Chemistry
Chemists & druggists > Pharmaceuticals; Pharmacy
Chemotherapy > Pharmacology & chemotherapy
Cheques
      Brit Banking History Soc
      Brit Cheque & Credit Assn
      > + Banking
Chess
      Brit Correspondence Chess Assn
      Brit Fedn Correspondence Chess
      Brit Shogi Fedn
      Chess Arbiters Assn
      Chess Scotland
      English Chess Fedn
      Welsh Chess U
Chest diseases > Thoracic diseases
Chesterton (Gilbert Keith)
      Chesterton Soc
Chickens > Poultry
Child abuse
      Assn Child Abuse Lawyers
      Brit Assn Study & Prevention Child Abuse
      Falsely Accused Carers & Teachers
      Nat Assn People Abused Childhood
      > + Children: welfare
Child contact centres
      Nat Assn Child Contact Centres
Child Support Agency
      Nat Assn Child Support Action
Childbirth > Maternity; Midwifery; Obstetrics & gynaecology
Childless > Fertility
Childminding (home/workplace)
      Nat Childminding Assn
      NI Childminding Assn
      Scot Childminding Assn
      > + Fostering & foster parents
Children: books
      Children's Books Hist Soc
      Fedn Children's Book Gps
      George MacDonald Soc
      Violet Needham Soc
      > + Bookselling; individual authors
Children: clothing > Clothing
Children: cot deaths > Cot deaths

© CBD Research Ltd · Beckenham · BR3 5JS · Tel 020 8650 7745   E-mail cbd@cbdresearch.com · www.cbdresearch.com

Children: death by accident/violence
    Compassionate Friends
    RoadPeace
Children: gifted
    Nat Assn Able Children in Educ
    Nat Assn Gifted Children
Children: handicapped
    Afasic
    Assn Spina Bifida & Hydrocephalus
    Assn Wheelchair Children
    Brit Assn Teachers Deaf
    Capability Scotland
    Children's Heart Assn
    Deaf Educ Listening & Talking
    nasen
    Nat Assn Profls... Language Impairment Children
    Nat Assn Toy & Leisure Libraries
    Nat Portage Assn
    R Mencap Soc
    REACH
    Rescare
    Scope
    SEBDA
    Sense
    Soc Stars
    STEPS
    > + specific types of handicap
Children: health > Paediatrics
Children: in hospital
    Action Sick Children
    Children Hospital Ireland
    Nat Assn Hospital Play Staff
Children: psychology
    Assn Child & Adolescent Mental Health
    Assn Child Psychotherapists
    Assn Infant Mental Health UK
    Soc Reproductive & Infant Psychology
Children: & the theatre > Theatre: young people
Children: welfare
    4Children
    ARCH
    Assn Children's Hospices
    Assn Childrens Palliative Care
    Assn Families Adopted Abroad
    Assn Profls Educ & Children's Trusts
    Assn Shared Parenting
    Brit Assn Study & Prevention Child Abuse
    Children Living Inherited Metabolic Diseases
    Children's Rights Alliance England
    Children Scotland
    Coalition Removal Pimping
    Early Childhood Ireland
    Families Need Fathers
    Family Rights Gp
    Foundation Study Infant Deaths
    Heart Line Assn
    Indep Children's Homes Assn
    Ir Soc Prevention Cruelty Children
    LOOK
    Nat Assn Child Contact Centres
    Nat Assn Child Support Action
    Nat Care Assn
    Nat Deaf Childrens Soc
    Nat Soc Prevention Cruelty Children
    One Parent Families Scotland
    R Scot Soc Prevention Cruelty Children
    Rett Syndrome Assn
    > + Fostering & foster parents; Social: service;   Welfare:
    administration
Chile
    Anglo Chilean Soc
Chilled beams & ceilings
    Chilled Beam & Ceiling Assn
Chilled food > Food: frozen & chilled
Chimneys
    Assn Profl & Indep Chimney Sweeps
    Brit Flue & Chimney Mfrs' Assn
    Nat Assn Chimney Engrs
    Nat Assn Chimney Sweeps
    Refractory Users Federation
China (ceramic) > Ceramics; Pottery
China (country)
    Brit Assn Chinese Studies
    Brit Cham Comm China - Beijing
    Brit Cham Comm China - Shanghai
    China-Britain Business Coun
    Soc Anglo-Chinese Understanding

China clay (kaolin)
    Cornish Cham Mines & Minerals
    Kaolin & Ball Clay Assn
    Trevithick Soc
Chinchillas
    Nat Chinchilla Soc
Chinese medicine
    Acupuncture Soc
    Assn Traditional Chinese Medicine
    Register Chinese Herbal Medicine
    > + Complementary medicine
Chippendale (Thomas)
    Chippendale Soc
Chips & crisps > Potatoes: products
Chiropody & podiatry
    Alliance Private...Chiropody & Podiatry Practitioners
    Allied Health Professions Fedn
    Brit Chiropody & Podiatry Assn
    Inst Chiropodists & Podiatrists
    SMAE Fellowship
    Soc Chiropodists & Podiatrists
    Soc Chiropodists & Podiatrists Ireland
Chiropractic
    Brit Chiropractic Assn
    Chiropractic Patients' Assn
    McTimoney Chiropractic Assn
    Scot Chiropractic Assn
    Utd Chiropractic Assn
Chivalry
    Heraldry Soc
Chocolate > Cocoa & chocolate; Confectionery
Choirs & choral music
    Assn Brit Choral Dirs
    Assn Ir Choirs
    Campaign Traditional Cathedral Choir
    Choir Schools Assn
    Friends Cathedral Music
    Gregorian Assn
    Nat Assn Choirs
    Nat Fedn Music Socs
    Nat Youth Choirs GB
    R Choral Soc
    R Coll Organists
    R School Church Music
    Sing for Pleasure
    Ulster Soc Organists & Choirmasters
    Welsh Amat Music Fedn
    > + Cathedral & church music
Cholesterol
    Heart UK
    > + Cardiology
Chopin (Frédéric)
    Chopin Soc (Lond)
Choral music > Choirs & choral music
Choreography
    Dance UK
    Laban Gld Movement & Dance
    R Academy Dance
Christian activities
    Arts Centre Gp
    Assn Denominational Histl Socs Cognate Libs
    Christian Evidence Soc
    Christian Social Order
    Librarians Christian Fellowship
    Mothers U
    Urban Saints
    > + Missionary organisations; Welfare organisations
Christian education
    Assn Christian Teachers
    Assn Christian Teachers Scotland
    Christian Educ
    Nat Assn Teachers Religious Educ
    Nat Soc (CofE) Promoting Religious Educ
Christmas cards
    Charity Christmas Card Coun

Christmas trees
    Brit Christmas Tree Growers Assn
    > + Trees
Chromatography
    Chromatographic Soc
Chrysanthemums
    Nat Chrysanthemum Soc
    > + Flowers, flower arrangement & floristry
Church: bells > Bellringing
Church: brasses & monuments > Brasses & church monuments

Church: buildings
    Assn Diocesan Cathedral Architects
    Brit Assn Friends Museums
    Capel
    Cathedral Architects Assn
    Chapels Soc
    Ecclesiastical Architects & Surveyors Assn
    Ecclesiological Soc
    Friends Friendless Churches
    Pugin Gld
    Round Tower Churches Soc
    Save our Parsonages
    Soc Church Archaeology
    Soc Friends St George's. . . [Windsor]
    > + Historic buildings
Church: editors
    Assn Church Editors
Church: of England
    Church England Gld Vergers
    Diaconal Assn Church England
    English Clergy Assn
    Modern Churchpeople's U
    Protestant Reformation Soc
Church: of England liturgy > Liturgy
Church: history & records
    Canterbury & York Soc
    Catholic Record Soc
    Church England Record Soc
    Ecclesiastical Hist Soc
    Scot Church Hist Soc
    > + Parish registers; individual churches
Church: monuments > Brasses & church monuments
Church: music > Cathedral & church music; Choirs & choral music; Liturgy
Church: services > Liturgy
Church: shops > Cathedral & church shops
Churchill (Sir Winston Leonard Spencer)
    Churchill Soc Lond
Churchyards > Cemeteries & churchyards
Cider & perry
    Alcohol Beverage Fedn Ireland
    Craft Brewing Assn
    Nat Assn Cider Makers
    Three Counties Cider & Perry Assn
CIDP > Guillain-Barré Syndrome
Cigars & cigarettes
    Imported Tobacco Products Advy Coun
    Nat Assn Cigarette Machine Operators
    > + Tobacco
Cigars & cigarettes: accessories
    Cartophilic Soc
    Cigarette Packet Collectors Club
Ciné equipment > Audio visual aids & equipment; Photographic industry & trade
Cinema > Film
Cinema buildings
    Cinema Theatre Assn
Cinema organs
    Cinema Organ Soc
    > + Organs, organists & organ music
Circles (in crops & corn) > Crop: circles
Circuit plans
    Soc Cirplanologists
Circuits > Printed circuits
Circuses & circus artistes
    Assn Circus Proprietors
    Captive Animals' Protection Soc
    Circus Friends Assn GB
    Circus Soc
Cisterns, drums & tanks
    Assn Tank & Cistern Mfrs
    Indl Packaging Assn
Citizens' Advice Bureaux > Advice centres & bureaux
Citizenship
    Assn Citizenship Teaching
City farms
    Fedn City Farms & Community Gardens
Civil aviation > Aviation
Civil defence & industrial emergencies
    Civil Defence Assn
    Emergency Planning Soc
    Inst Civil Protection & Emergency Mgt
    Soc Indl Emergency Service Officers
Civil engineering
    Bridge Deck Waterproofing Assn
    Brit Civil Engg Test Eqpt Mfrs Assn
    Chart Instn Civil Engg Surveyors
    Civil Engg Contrs' Assn

Confedn Construction Specialists
Construction Emplrs Fedn
Instn Civil Engrs
Instn Structural Engrs
Major Projects Assn
Pipe Jacking Assn
    > + Construction industries
Civil liberties > Individual freedom
Civil Service
    Assn Higher Civil & Public Servants [IRL]
    Assn Revenue & Customs
    Bar Assn Local Govt & Public Service
    First Division Assn
    NI Public Service Alliance
    Public & Comml Services U
    > + Public administration
Civil War (English)
    Cromwell Assn
    English Civil War Soc
    John Hampden Soc
    Sealed Knot
    Seventeenth Century Life & Times
Cladding
    Brit Precast Concrete Fedn
    Insulated Render & Cladding Assn
    Metal Cladding & Roofing Mfrs Assn
    > + Building materials & supplies
Claims (compensation)
    Claims Standards Coun
Clairvoyance
    Brit Astrological & Psychic Soc
    > + Paranormal & psychical research
Clare (John)
    John Clare Soc
Clarinets & saxophones
    Clarinet Heritage Soc
    Clarinet & Saxophone Soc
Classic/historic craft/vehicles > Motor vehicles: historic; Ships (& boats): history & preservation
Classical studies
    Assn Latin Teaching
    Brit Academy
    Brit Epigraphy Soc
    Classical Assn
    Friends Classics
    Horatian Soc
    Jt Assn Classical Teachers
    Soc Promotion Hellenic Studies
    Soc Promotion Roman Studies
    Virgil Soc
Classification
    Brit Classification Soc
Clay & clay products
    Brit Ceramic Confedn
    Clay Pipe Devt Assn
    Clay Roof Tile Coun
    Inst Materials, Minerals & Mining
    Intl Masonry Soc
    Kaolin & Ball Clay Assn
    Mineralogical Soc
    Resource Use Inst
    > + Bricks; Pottery; Tiles (floor & wall)
Clay target (pigeon) shooting
    Assn Profl Clay Target Shooting Grounds
    Brit Skeet Shooting Assn
    Clay Pigeon Shooting Assn
    Inst Clay Shooting Instructors
    Scot Clay Target Assn
    > + Shooting
Clean air > Air: conditioning & ventilating; Pollution & pollution control
Cleaners & launderers > Laundering & dry cleaning
Cleaning & cleaning science
    Assn Bldg Cleaning Direct Service Providers
    Assn Healthcare Cleaning Profls
    Brit Cleaning Coun
    Brit Inst Cleaning Science
    Ir Contract Cleaning Assn
    UK Cleaning Products Ind Assn
Cleaning equipment
    Assn Healthcare Cleaning Profls
    BEAMA
    Cleaning & Hygiene Suppliers' Assn
    Indl Cleaning Machine Mfrs Assn
    > + Soap & detergents
Cleanrooms
    Scot Soc Contamination Control

© CBD Research Ltd · Beckenham · BR3 5JS · Tel 020 8650 7745　E-mail cbd@cbdresearch.com · www.cbdresearch.com

Clearing services (banking)
    UK Cards Assn
Cleft lip & palate
    Cleft Lip & Palate Assn
Clematis
    Brit Clematis Soc
Clergy
    English Clergy Assn
    > + Church: of England; other individual churches
Clerks of local councils > Local government: officers
Clerks of works
    Inst Clerks Works
Cliff (Clarice)
    Clarice Cliff Collectors Club
Climate
    Campaign Climate Change
    Environmental Protection UK
    Scientists Global Responsibility
    Stop Climate Chaos Coalition
    > + Environment; Meteorology
Climbing
    Alpine Club
    Assn Brit Climbing Walls
    Assn Heads Outdoor Educ Centres
    Assn Mountaineering Instructors
    Brit Assn Mountain Guides
    Brit Mountaineering Coun
    Mountain Leader Training Assn
    Mountaineering Coun Ireland
    Mountaineering Coun Scotland
Climbing walls
    Assn Amusement & Leisure Eqpt Suppliers
Clinical biochemistry
    Assn Clinical Biochemistry
    Assn Clinical Biochemists Ireland
    > + Biochemistry & biotechnology
Clinical data management
    Assn Clinical Data Mgt
    Brit In Vitro Diagnostics Assn
Clinical immunology > Allergy
Clinical pathology
    Assn Clinical Pathologists
Clinical pharmacy > Pharmacy
Clinical trials
    Brit Assn Res Quality Assurance
    Clinical Contract Res Assn
    Fac Pharmaceutical Med
    HealthWatch
    Inst Clinical Res
Clocks > Horology
Close (Sir Charles Frederick Arden-)
    Charles Close Soc
Closed-circuit television > Television: closed circuit
Closures (cork, metal, plastic)
    Cork Ind Fedn
    Metal Packaging Mfrs Assn
Clothing
    ASBCI
    Brit Apparel & Textile Confedn
    Brit Shops & Stores Assn
    Fedn Clothing Designers & Executives
    Nat Childrenswear Assn
    Register Apparel & Textile Designers
    Schoolwear Assn
    Textile Inst Intl
    UK Fashion & Textile Assn
    > + Fashion; Protective clothing/equipment; specific items of clothing
Clouds
    Cloud Appreciation Soc
Clowns > Circuses & circus artistes
Club foot > Talipes
Clubs
    Assn Inter-Varsity Clubs
    Assn London Clubs
    Bar Entertainment & Dance Assn
    C'ee Registered Clubs Assns
    Nat Assn Rly Clubs
    Working Men's Club & Inst U
    > + specific activities or interests
Clumsy child syndrome
    Dyspraxia Foundation
Clutter (organising)
    Assn Profl De-clutterers & Organisers
CMV > Cytomegalovirus
Coaches > Bus & coach operators;   Passenger transport

Coaches: sports
    Sports Coach UK
    > + individual sports
Coaching (lifestyle)
    Assn Coaching
Coal: mining
    Brit Coal Utilisation Res Assn
    Confedn UK Coal Producers
    Fedn Indep Mines
    Minerals Engg Soc
    N England Inst Mining & Mechanical Engrs
Coal: trade
    Coal Mchts Assn Scotland
    Coal Mchts Fedn
    > + Solid fuel
Coarse fishing > Fishing (sport)
Coastal history
    Nautical Heritage Assn
Coastal waters > Estuaries; Water
Coastal lookout stations
    Nat Coastwatch Instn
Coastguards
    Coastguard Assn
Coated abrasives > Abrasives
Coated macadam > Asphalt & coated macadam
Coatings
    Brit Coatings Fedn
    Brit Textile Technology Gp
    Brit Urethane Foam Contrs Assn
    Inst Materials, Minerals & Mining
    Ir Decorative Surface Coatings Assn
    Oil & Colour Chemists Assn
    Paint Res Assn
    Performance Textiles Assn
    Sprayed Concrete Assn
    Thermal Spraying & Surface Engg Assn
Cobbett (William)
    William Cobbett Soc
Cobles & keelboats
    Coble & Keelboat Soc
    > + Ships (& boats): history & preservation
Cobnuts
    Kentish Cobnuts Assn
Cobs > Horses & ponies
Cochlea implants
    Brit Academy Audiology
    Nat Cochlear Implant Users Assn
Cocktails
    UK Bartenders Gld
Cocoa & chocolate
    Chocolate Soc
    Fedn Cocoa Comm
    Food & Drink Fedn
Coconut matting
    Coir Assn
Codes of practice: standardisation
    BSI
Coeliac disease
    Coeliac Soc Ireland
    Coeliac UK
Coffee
    Brit Coffee Assn
    Brit Soluble Coffee Packers & Importers Assn
    Café Soc
    Food & Drink Ind Ireland
Coffins
    Funeral Furnishing Mfrs Assn
    > + Burial & cremation
Coin operated machines > Amusements & coin operated machines; Automatic vending
Coins & medals > Numismatics
Coir
    Coir Assn
Coke
    Coke Oven Mgrs Assn
    > + Solid fuel
Cold pressed oils
    Brit Assn Cold Pressed Oil Producers
Cold rolled metal
    Cold Rolled Sections Assn
    > + Metal: working
Cold sores > Herpes
Cold storage > Refrigeration; Temperature controlled storage
Cold War
    Subterranea Britannica
Coleridge (Samuel Taylor)
    Friends Coleridge

Colitis/colostomy
        Crohn's Disease Childhood Res Assn
        IA
        Nat Assn Colitis & Crohn's Disease
Collecting hobbies > Object(s) collected
Collection agencies > Credit: reporting
Colleges > Adult education; Education; Universities
Colleges: heads > Heads of schools & colleges
Collieries > Coal: mining
Collins ([William] Wilkie)
        Wilkie Collins Soc
Coloboma
        Micro & Anophthalmic Children's Soc
Colombia
        Anglo Colombian Soc [lost 09
        Brit & Colombian Cham Comm
        Cámara Comercio Colombo Britanica
        Flower Import Tr Assn
Colon hydrotherapy
        Gld Colon Hydrotherapists
Colostomy > Colitis/colostomy
Colour
        Colour Gp
        > + Paint; Pigments
Colposcopy
        Brit Assn Sexual Health & HIV
Combat (dramatic) > Fights (stage & film)
Combustion engineering
        Combustion Engg Assn
        ICOM Energy Assn
Comedy & comedy writers
        Brit Comedy Soc
        Brit Soc Comedy Writers
        Comedy Writers Assn UK
Comics (strip illustration)
        Comics Creators Gld
Commemorative items & souvenirs
        Commemorative Collectors Soc
        Commemoratives Museum Trust
Commerce
        Assn MBAs
        Brit Chams Comm
        Fedn Crafts & Comm
        R Soc ... Arts
        R Soc Edinburgh
        > + Chambers of commerce
Commercial management > Management
Commercial property agents
        Indl Agents Soc
        Instn Comml & Business Agents
        > + Estate agents
Commercial travellers > Sales management & representation
Commercial vehicles
        Historic Comml Vehicle Soc
        Nat Assn Road Transport Museums
        > + Motor headings
Commission agents
        Manufacturers Agents Assn
Commissioning (construction industry)
        Commissioning Specialists Assn
Commodities
        Fedn Commodity Assns
        Futures & Options Assn
        > + names of specific commodities
Common Market > European Union
Common Prayer
        Alcuin Club
        Prayer Book Soc
Commons & open spaces > Open spaces; Parks & gardens
Commonwealth affairs
        English Speaking U C'wealth
        R Over-Seas League
Commonwealth (1649-1688)
        Cromwell Assn
        John Hampden Soc
Communication services
        ALTO [IRL]
        Communications Mgt Assn
        Fedn Communication Services
        ICT Ireland
        Momentum
        Onsite Communications Assn
        > + Cable & satellite communications
Communications
        Inst Internal Communication
        Inst Sound & Communications Engrs
        > + form of communication

Communications: fraud
        Telecommunications UK Fraud Forum
Community: care
        Nat Care Assn
Community: development
        Community Devt Finance Assn
        Devt Trusts Assn
        Devt Trusts Assn Scot
        Scot Business Community
Community: drama > Theatre
Community: education
        Fedn Community Devt Learning
Community: medicine > Medical: officers
Community: music
        Sound Sense
Community: organisations
        Assn Community Rail Partnerships
        Assn Scot Community Couns
        Campaign Community Banking Services
        Community Foundation Network
        Community Transport Assn
        Fedn City Farms & Community Gardens
        Fedn Educ Business Link Consortia
        Nat Fedn Community Orgs
Community: resources (mobile) > Mobile community resources
Community: service (voluntary)
        Assn Res Voluntary & Community Sector
        Attend
        Brit Red Cross Soc
        Community Service Volunteers
        Nat Assn Round Tables
        Scot Coun Voluntary Orgs
        Voluntary Service Overseas
        Volunteering England
        Women's R Voluntary Service
        > + Welfare headings
Community: shops
        Nat Assn Community Run Shops
Commuters > Passenger transport
Companies: independent > Business
Companies: mergers & acquisitions > Business: mergers & acquisitions
Companies: quoted/London Stock Exchange
        Quoted Companies Alliance
Company: directors
        Inst Directors
        Inst Directors Ireland
        > + Management
Company: registration agents
        Assn Company Registration Agents
Company: secretaries
        Inst Chart Secretaries & Administrators
        > + Secretaries & administrators
Comparative law > Law: comparative
Compasses & compass adjusting
        Chart & Nautical Instrument Tr Assn
Compensation (claims)
        Claims Standards Coun
Compères
        Gld Profl Toastmasters
        > + Toastmasters & masters of ceremonies
Complementary medicine
        Assn Physical & Natural Therapists
        Brit Complementary Medicine Assn
        Complementary Med Assn
        Complementary Therapists Assn
        Inst Complementary & Natural Medicine
        > + specific forms eg Osteopathy
Composers: music > individual by name
Composing > Music: composing
Composites
        Composites UK
        Inst Materials, Minerals & Mining
        Scot Plastics & Rubber Assn
Composts & composting
        Assn Organics Recycling
        Community Composting Network
        Composting Assn Ireland
        Growing Media Assn
        John Innes Mfrs Assn
Comprehensive education
        Campaign State Educ
        > + Education
Compressed air
        Brit Compressed Air Soc
Compressed gases
        Brit Compressed Gases Assn
Compulsive/obsessive disorders > Obsessive/compulsive disorders

© CBD Research Ltd · Beckenham · BR3 5JS · Tel 020 8650 7745   E-mail cbd@cbdresearch.com · www.cbdresearch.com

Computer & video games
    Brit Academy Film & TV Arts
    Entertainment Retailers Assn
    Tiga
    UK Interactive Entertainment Assn
Computers
    BCS
    Brit Computer Assn Blind
    Intellect
    Ir Computer Soc
    > + Software headings
Computers: application
    Assn Hist & Computing
    Assn Survey Computing
    Dental System Suppliers Assn
    eLearning Network
    Inst Numerical Computation & Analysis [IRL]
    Instn Engg & Technology
    Nat Outsourcing Assn
Computers: in education
    Naace
Computers: historic
    Computer Consvn Soc
Computers: professionals
    ACCU
    Assn Certified IT Profls
    Assn Computer Engrs & Technicians
    Assn Computer Profls
    Assn Indep Computer Specialists
    Instn Analysts & Programmers
    Soc Computers & Law
Computers: supplies for
    Indep Print Inds Assn
    Legal Software Suppliers Assn
    UK Cartridge Remanufacturers Assn
Computers: vision > Machine vision
Concentrates > Animal feed
Concerts
    Brit Assn Concert Halls
    Concert Artistes' Assn
    Concert Promoters Assn
    Halle Concerts Soc
    Nat Early Music Assn
    > + Music; Orchestras
Conchology
    Brit Shell Collectors Club
    Conchological Soc
    Malacological Soc Lond
Concrete & concrete products
    Assn Concrete Indl Flooring Contrs
    Brit Assn Reinforcement
    Brit Precast Concrete Fedn
    Britpave
    Concrete Bridge Devt Gp
    Concrete Mfrs Assn Ireland
    Concrete Repair Assn
    Concrete Soc
    Construct: Concrete Structures Gp
    Corrosion Prevention Assn
    Inst Concrete Technology
    Instn Civil Engrs
    Insulating Concrete Formwork Assn
    Intl Glassfibre Reinforced Concrete Assn
    Intl Masonry Soc
    Ir Concrete Fedn
    Ir Concrete Soc
    Post Tensioning Assn
    Sprayed Concrete Assn
    UK Quality Ash Assn
Concrete cutting
    Drilling & Sawing Assn
Concrete pumping
    Construction Plant-hire Assn
Conductors: music > individual by name
Cones & cylinders (road)
    Retroreflective Eqpt Mfrs Assn
    > + Road: lighting, markings & traffic signs
Confectionery
    Food & Drink Fedn
    Food & Drink Ind Ireland
    Retail Confectioners & Tobacconists Assn
Conferences & conventions
    Assn Brit Profl Conf Organisers
    Assn Confs & Events
    Conf Centres Excellence
    Eventia
    Hotel Booking Agents Assn

    Meetings Ind Assn
    > + Exhibitions
Confinements (childbirth) > Maternity
Conflict & anger management
    Brit Assn Anger Mgt
    Conflict Res Soc
    Inst Conflict Mgt
Congenital defects
    CHARGE Family Support Gp
    STEPS
    > + Birthmarks & disfigurement;   Children: Handicapped
Congestion charging
    Transport-Watch
Congregational Church
    Utd Reformed Church Hist Soc
Conifers
    Brit Christmas Tree Growers Assn
    Brit Conifer Soc
    Horticultural Trs Assn
    > + Trees
Conjuring & magic
    Brit Magical Soc
    Magic Circle
Connective tissue disorders
    Brit Coalition Heritable Disorders Connective Tissue
Conrad (Joseph)
    Joseph Conrad Soc
Conservation
    Alliance Religions & Consvn
    Assn Envt Conscious Bldg
    Assn Protection Rural Scotland
    Brit Assn Shooting & Consvn
    Brit Trust Consvn Volunteers
    Campaign Protect Rural England
    Countryside Mgt Assn
    Friends Earth
    GeoConservationUK
    Historic Towns Forum
    Inst Consvn
    Nat Assn Regional Game Couns [IRL]
    Nat Trust
    Nat Trust Ireland
    Nat Trust Scotland
    Scot Wild Land Gp
    Selborne Soc
    Soc Envtl Exploration
    > + specific subjects eg Architecture; Natural history
Conservation: area organisations
    Black Country Soc
    Campaign Protection Rural Wales
    Dartmoor Presvn Assn
    Gower Soc
    Northumberland & Newcastle Soc
    S Downs Soc
    Ulster Soc Protection Countryside
    > + Nature conservation: local reserves
Conservative politics
    Tory Reform Gp
Conservatories > Glasshouses & conservatories
Conservators (art) > Art: conservation
Constitutional reform
    Unlock Democracy
Construction equipment
    Brit Compressed Air Soc
    Construction Eqpt Assn
    Construction Fixings Assn
    Construction Plant-hire Assn
    Construction Products Assn
    Contractors Mechanical Plant Engrs
    Scot Plant Owners Assn
    > + Materials: management/handling; specific items of equipment
Construction history
    Construction Hist Soc
Construction industries
    Assn Indep Construction Adjudicators
    Assn Project Safety
    Brit Civil Engg Test Eqpt Mfrs Assn
    Brit Constructional Steelwork Assn
    Builders' Conf
    Building Cost Infm Service
    Chart Inst Architectural Technologists
    Chart Instn Civil Engg Surveyors
    Commissioning Specialists Assn
    Confedn Construction Specialists
    Construction Ind Coun
    Construction Ind Fedn [IRL]
    Construction Ind Inf Gp

Construction Ind Res & Inf Assn
Construction Ind Tr Alliance
Engg Construction Ind Assn
Gld Builders & Contrs
Inst Construction Mgt
Inst Construction Specialists
Inst Materials, Minerals & Mining
Instn Construction Safety
Major Projects Assn
Nat Fedn Builders
Specialist Engg Contrs Gp
Steel Construction Inst
UK Contractors Gp
> + Building
Construction law & control > Law: construction
Construction materials > Building materials & supplies
Construction surveying
Soc Construction & Quantity Surveyors
Consultants > field of consultancy
Consumer affairs & protection
Assn Public Analysts
Assn Public Analysts Scotland
Consumer Focus
Consumer Protection Assn
Consumers' Assn
Consumers Assn Ireland
ECR Irelnad
Inst Consumer Affairs
Nat Consumer Fedn
Trading Standards Inst
> + Trading standards
Consumer credit > Credit: trade
Contact lens
Assn Contact Lens Mfrs
Brit Contact Lens Assn
> + Optical industry
Containers > specific type of container
Containers: freight > Freight transport; Materials: management/handling
Contamination control > Cleanrooms; Land: contaminated
Contemporary art > Art & artists
Contemporary history > History
Continuing education > Adult education; Education
Continuing professional development
Inst Continuing Profl Devt
Contraception > Family planning
Contract services
Assn Catering Excellence
Brit Contract Furnishing Assn
Brit Vehicle Rental & Leasing Assn
Cleaning & Support Services Assn
Contract Flooring Assn
Contractors
Assn Contractors & Temporary Workers
Profl Contrs Gp
UK Contractors Gp
> + specific activity
Contractors plant > Construction equipment
Control engineering
Assn Electrical & Mechanical Trs
BEAMA
Brit Fluid Power Assn
Evaluation Intl
GAMBICA Assn
ICOM Energy Assn
Inst Measurement & Control
Instn Engg & Technology
Solids Handling & Processing Assn
> + Automation
Convenience stores
Assn Convenience Stores
Convenience Stores & Newsagents Assn [IRL]
Scot Grocers Fedn
Convent schools > Independent & public schools
Conventions > Conferences & conventions
Conveyancing
Soc Licensed Conveyancers
> + Property & land owners
Conveyors > Lifting & loading equipment
Cookery
Academy Culinary Arts
Craft Gld Chefs
Master Chefs GB
Welsh Culinary Assn
> + Catering; Chefs
Cookware > Catering: equipment; Hardware & housewares
Cooling towers
Water Mgt Soc

Cooperage
Nat Cooperage Fedn
Co-operative movement
Co-operatives UK Ltd
Ir Co-op Org Soc
Nat Assn Bldg Co-ops [IRL]
Nat Assn Co-operative Officials
UK Soc Co-operative Studies
> + Agriculture: cooperatives
Co-partnership: industrial > Industrial involvement & participation
Copper
Brit Non-Ferrous Metals Fedn
Copper Devt Assn
Copyright
Alliance Intellectual Property Theft
Anti Copying Design
Authors Licensing & Collecting Soc
Brit Assn Picture Libraries & Agencies
Brit Music Rights
Brit Soc Plant Breeders
Chart Inst Patent Attorneys
Creators Rights Alliance
Design & Artists Copyright Soc
Fedn Copyright Theft
Ir Nat Fedn Copyright Theft
MCPS-PRS Alliance
Phonographic Performance
Phonographic Performance (Ireland)
Publishers Licensing Soc
Writers' Copyright Assn
> + Intellectual property; Patents & trade marks
Copyshops > Quickprinters & copyshops
Copywriting (advertising)
Coracles
Coracle Soc
Cork
Cork Ind Fedn
Corn > Agriculture: merchants; Flour; Grain
Corn circles > Crop: circles
Corn dollies
Gld Straw Craftsmen
Cornish pasties
Cornish Pasty Assn
Cornwall & Cornish language
Cornish Language Partnership
Kesva Taves Kernewek
London Cornish Assn
R Instn Cornwall
Trevithick Soc
Coronary diseases > Cardiology
Coroners
Coroners Soc E&W
Corporate hospitality
Eventia
Soc Event Organisers
> + Catering; Shows & events
Corporate trustees > Trusts, trusteeship & estate planning
Correspondence colleges
Assn Brit Correspondence Colls
Corrosion
Corrosion Prevention Assn
Galvanizers Assn
Inst Corrosion
Inst Materials, Minerals & Mining
Thermal Spraying & Surface Engg Assn
Corrugated paper > Packaging
Corruption
Transparency Intl (UK)
Cosmetic items (collecting)
Brit Compact Collectors' Soc
Cosmetics
Beauty Companies Assn
Cosmetic, Toiletry & Perfumery Assn
Intl Fragrance Assn UK
Ir Cosmetics Detergent & Allied Products Assn
Soc Cosmetic Scientists
Cosmetology & cosmetic surgery
Brit Assn Aesthetic Plastic Surgeons
Brit Assn Cosmetic Doctors
Brit Assn Cosmetic Surgeons
Brit Assn Plastic, Reconstructive & Aesthetic Surgeons
> + Beauty specialists/treatment
Cosmology
Traditional Cosmology Soc
Cost management
Assn Cost Engrs
Assn Cost Mgt Consultants

© CBD Research Ltd · Beckenham · BR3 5JS · Tel 020 8650 7745 E-mail cbd@cbdresearch.com · www.cbdresearch.com

Costume history, design & conservation
  Brit Costume Assn
  Costume Soc
  Costume Soc Scotland
  Costume & Textile Soc Wales
  Dolmetsch Hist Dance Soc
  Dress & Textile Specialists
  Medieval Dress & Textile Soc
  Textile Soc
Cot deaths
  Foundation Study Infant Deaths
  Ir Sudden Infant Death Assn
Cottage gardens
  Cottage Garden Soc
  > + Gardens & gardening
Cotton > Textile headings
Councillors > Local government
Counselling
  Brit Assn Counselling & Psychotherapy
  COSCA [Scotland]
  Counselling
  Inst Guidance Counsellors [IRL]
  Ir Assn Counselling & Psychotherapy
  Nat Assn Counsellors, Hypnoterpists & Psychotherapists
  Psychiatric Rehabilitation Assn
  Universities Psychotherapy & Counselling Assn
  > + field of counselling
Counterfeiting
  Alliance Intellectual Property Theft
  Anti Counterfeiting Gp
Counties (British)
  Assn Brit Counties
Country dancing & music > Folk dance & song
Countryside preservation > Conservation; Nature conservation
County agricultural societies > Agriculture: county societies
County archaeological societies > Archaeology: county societies
County councils > Local government
County history > Archaeology;   Records: historical
Courier services
  Assn Intl Courier & Express Services
  Despatch Assn
  Inst Couriers
  Nat Courier Assn
Courtesy
  Nat Campaign Courtesy
Courts of law > Law headings; Magistrates & magistrates courts
Courts (royal)
  Soc Court Studies
  > + Monarchy
Covenanters (Scottish)
  Scot Covenanter Memorials Assn
Cowboys > American 'West'
Cradles & suspended platforms
  Indl Rope Access Tr Assn
  Nat Access & Scaffolding Confedn
  Specialist Access Engg & Maintenance Assn
Crafts & craftsmanship
  Art Workers Gld
  Brit Toymakers Gld
  Gld Master Craftsmen
  Heritage Crafts Assn
  Makers Guild Wales
  Nat Assn Advisers. . . Design & Technology
  Rural Crafts Assn
  Soc Designer Craftsmen
  Voluntary Arts Network
  Wales Craft Coun
  > + individual crafts
Cranes
  Construction Plant-hire Assn
  > + Lifting & loading equipment
Cranio- > Head entries
Craniosacral therapy
  Cranio Sacral Soc
  Craniosacral Therapy Assn
Cream > Dairying
Creationism
  Biblical Creation Soc
Credit & magnetic strip(e) cards
  Assn Automatic Identification &. . . Data Capture
Credit hire: vehicles > Motor vehicles: hire
Credit: reporting
  Civil Court Users Assn
  Consumer Credit Tr Assn
  Credit Services Assn
Credit: trade
  Brit Cheque & Credit Assn

Consumer Credit Association
  Credit Protection Assn
  Finance & Leasing Assn
  Inst Credit Mgt
  Ir Finance Houses Assn
  Ir Inst Credit Mgt
Credit: unions
  Ace Credit U Services
  Assn Brit Credit Us
  Ir League Credit Us
Cremation & crematoria > Burial & cremation
Creutzfeldt-Jakob disease > Alzheimers' disease
Cricket
  Assn County Cricket Scorers
  Assn Cricket Statisticians & Historians
  Club Cricket Conf
  Coun Cricket Socs
  Cricket Memorabilia Soc
  Cricket Scotland
  Cricket Soc
  England & Wales Cricket Bd Assn Cricket Officials
  England & Wales Cricket Bd Coaches Assn
  Indoor Cricket England
  Midlands Club Cricket Conf
  Minor Counties Cricket Assn
  Northern Cricket U Ireland
  Profl Cricketers Assn
Cricket: pitches & equipment
  Sports & Play Construction Assn
Cri du chat syndrome
  Cri du Chat Syndrome Support Gp
Criers > Town criers
Crime protection & prevention
  Catch 22 in Action
  Victim Support
  Victim Support Scotland
Crime writers
  Crime Writers Assn
Crimea War
  Crimean War Res Soc
Criminal law
  Criminal Bar Assn
  Criminal Law Solicitors' Assn
  Proceeds Crime Lawyers Assn
  > + Law
Criminology
  Brit Soc Criminology
  Howard League for Penal Reform
  Scot Assn Study Offending
Crisis management > Civil defence & industrial emergencies
Crisps > Potatoes: products
Critical incident de-briefing
  Nat Coun Psychotherapists
  > + Counselling
Criticism
  Critics' Circle
Crochet
  Knitting & Crochet Gld
Crocuses
  Brit Iris Soc
Crofters
  Scot Crofting Fedn
Crohn's disease > Colitis/colostomy
Crompton (Richmal)
  Just William Soc
Cromwell (Oliver)
  Cromwell Assn
Crop: circles
  Brit Soc Dowsers
  Crop Circle Connector
  Megalithic Soc
Crop: consultants
  Assn Indep Crop Consultants
Crop: drying
  Brit Assn Green Crop Driers
  Instn Agricl Engrs
Crop: research
  NIAB
  > + Agriculture; Seeds
Crop: spraying & protection
  Agricl Inds Confedn
  Nat Assn Agricl Contrs
Croquet
  Croquet Assn
  Scot Croquet Assn
Crossbow shooting
  Grand Nat Archery Soc

Nat Crossbow Fedn
> + Archery
Crosswords
Crossword Club
Crowd control
UK Crowd Mgt Assn
Crown green bowling > Bowling
Cruel sports
League Cruel Sports
Cruise lines (shipping)
Assn Cruise Experts
Crustacea > Shellfish
Cryogenics
Brit Cryogenics Coun
Cryptography
Xenophon
Crystal healing
Crystal & Healing Fedn
Crystal Palace
Crystal Palace Foundation
Crystallography
Brit Assn Crystal Growth
Brit Crystallographic Assn
Mineralogical Soc

Cue sports
English Assn Snooker & Billiards
Cued speech
Cued Speech Assn
> + Speech
Culverts & channels
Brit Precast Concrete Fedn
Curates (Church of England)
Additional Curates Soc
Curling
English Curling Assn
R Caledonian Curling Club
Curtains
Assn Soft Furnishers
Curtain track fitters
Assn Soft Furnishers
Curwen (John)
Curwen Inst
Cushing's Syndrome
Assn Cushing's Treatment & Help
Customer care
Inst Customer Service
Cutlery
Brit Cutlery & Silverware Assn
Cutlery & Allied Trs Res Assn
Cutters & reamers
Brit Hardmetal & Engineers' Cutting Tool Assn
Cutting tools > Tools
Cyclamen
Cyclamen Soc
Cycles & motorcycles
Assn Cycle Traders
Bicycle Assn
Cycle Engrs' Inst
Motor Cycle Ind Assn
Nat Motorcycle Coun
Retail Motor Ind Fedn
> + Motor cycling & scooter riding
Cyclical vomiting syndrome
Cyclical Vomiting Syndrome Assn
Cycling
Assn Brit Cycling Coaches
Audax UK
Brit Cycling Fedn
CTC
Cycling Ireland
Cycling Time Trials
Fellowship Cycling Old Timers
Handcycling Assn
London Cyclists
NI Cycling Fedn
Road Records Association
Scot Cycling
Tandem Club
Tricycle Assn
Veteran-Cycle Club
Welsh Cycling U
Cyclo-Cross > Cycling
Cylinders (gas)
Brit Compressed Gases Assn

Cystic fibrosis
Cystic Fibrosis Assn Ireland
Cystic Fibrosis Trust
Cystitis
Cystitis & Overactive Bladder Foundation
Cytology > Cell biology
Cytomegalovirus
Congenital CMV Assn
Czech Republic
Brit Cham Comm Czech Republic
Brit Czech & Slovak Assn
Czech Brit Cham Comm
Dvořák Soc Czech & Slovak Music

D

Dad's Army (TV programme)
Dad's Army Appreciation Soc
Daffodils
Daffodil Soc
Dahlias
Nat Dahlia Soc
Dairy cattle > Cattle headings
Dairying
Assn Unpasteurised Milk Producers
Brit Goat Soc
Brit Sheep Dairying Assn
Dairy Executives Assn [IRL]
Dairy UK
Food & Drink Ind Ireland
Ir Creamery Milk Suppliers Assn
Milking Eqpt Assn
Quality Milk Producers
R Assn Brit Dairy Farmers
Soc Dairy Technology
Damage management
Brit Damage Mgt Assn
Dampcourses & dampproofing
Inst Specialist Surveyors & Engrs
Property Care Assn
Dams & reservoirs
Brit Dam Soc
> + Water: treatment & supply
Damsons
Westmorland Damson Assn
Dance bands
Harry Roy Appreciation Soc
Ted Heath Musical Appreciation Soc
Dance notation > Choreography
Dancing
Assn Amer Dancing
Assn Dance Freestyle Profls
Assn Dance Movement Therapy
Ballroom Dancers Fedn
Best Western Dance Academy
Brit Assn Teachers Dancing
Brit Ballet Org
Brit Theatre Dance Assn
Coun Dance Educ & Training
Dance UK
Dancesport Scotland
Dolmetsch Hist Dance Soc
EADA
Early Dance Circle
EMDP
Eurythmy Assn
Gld Profl Teachers Dance & Movement
Imperial Soc Teachers Dancing
Inst Contemporary Arts
Laban Gld Movement & Dance
London Swing Dance Soc
Nat Assn Teachers Dancing
Nat Campaign Arts
Nat Dance Teachers Assn
Old Time Dance Soc
R Academy Dance
Scot Dance Teachers Alliance
Soc Dance Res
UK Alliance Profl Teachers Dancing...
UK Dance & Drama Fedn
> + Ballet; Choreography; Folk dance & song
Dark skies
Campaign Dark Skies

© CBD Research Ltd · Beckenham · BR3 5JS · Tel 020 8650 7745   E-mail cbd@cbdresearch.com · www.cbdresearch.com

Dartmoor
    Dartmoor Presvn Assn
Darts
    Brit Darts Org
    Profl Darts Players Assn
    Scot Darts Assn
Data capture/synchronisation > Automatic identification & data capture
Data processing
    Assn Clinical Data Mgt
    Information & Records Mgt Soc
    Inst Mgt Inf Systems
    > + Computers; Information: services & technology
Data protection
    BCS
    Fedn Software Theft
    > + Documents: confidential disposal
Day surgery
    Brit Assn Day Surgery
    > + Surgery
Deafness
    Assn Lipspeakers
    Assn Teachers Lipreading to Adults
    Brit Assn Teachers Deaf
    Brit Deaf Assn
    Brit Deaf Sports Coun
    Brit Soc Mental Health & Deafness
    Deaf Educ Listening & Talking
    Deafblind UK
    DeafHear [IRL]
    Hearing Link
    Ir Deaf Soc
    Nat Assn Deafened People
    Nat Cochlear Implant Users Assn
    Nat Deaf Childrens Soc
    R Assn Deaf People
    RNID
    Scot Assn Sign Language Interpreters
    Scot Coun Deafness
    Sense
    Treacher Collins Family Support Gp
    > + Hearing; Speech
Death & bodily-death > Bereavement; Burial & cremation; Paranormal & psychical research; Population registration
Debt
    Assn Property & Fixed Charge Receivers
    Bankruptcy Assn
    Civil Court Users Assn
    Credit Services Assn
    Debt Mgt Standards Assn
    Inst Money Advisers
Debt collection > Credit: reporting
Decking (timber)
    Timber Decking Assn
Decontamination
    Inst Decontamination Sciences
Decorating > Painting & decorating
Decorations (medals) > Numismatics
Decorative arts
    Nat Assn Decorative & Fine Arts Socs
    > + Art headings
Decorative lighting > Lighting
Découpage
    Gld Brit Découpeurs
Deer
    Assn Deer Mgt Gps
    Brit Deer Farms & Parks Assn
    Brit Deer Soc
    Brit Veterinary Assn
    Game & Wildlife Consvn Trust
    Ir Deer Soc
    Wild Deer Assn Ireland
Deerhounds > Hounds
Defence
    Brit Intl Studies Assn
    Defence Ind Security Assn
    R Utd Services Inst Defence... Studies
    UK Nat Defence Assn
    > + Civil defence & industrial emergencies; Fortresses & forts
Defence equipment
    ADS Gp
    Intellect
Delinquency > Criminology
Delius (Frederick)
    Delius Soc
Delphiniums
    Delphinium Soc

Dementia
    Alzheimer Scotland
    Alzheimer's Soc
    Pick's Disease Support Gp
    > + Mental health
Demolition & dismantling
    Brit Metals Recycling Assn
    Inst Demolition Engrs
    Inst Explosives Engrs
    Nat Fedn Demolition Contrs
Denmark
    Anglo Danish Soc
    Danish-UK Cham Comm
Dental hospitals
    Assn Dental Hospitals
Dental hypnosis > Medical: & dental hypnosis
Dental practice management
    Brit Dental Practice Mgrs Assn
Dental radiology
    Brit Soc Dental & Maxillofacial Radiology
Dentistry
    Assn Basic Science Teachers Dentistry
    Assn Dental Anaesthetists
    Assn Dental Implantology
    Assn Ir Dental Ind
    Brit Assn Clinical Dental Technology
    Brit Assn Dental Nurses
    Brit Assn Dental Therapists
    Brit Assn Forensic Odontology
    Brit Assn Study Community Dentistry
    Brit Dental Assn
    Brit Dental Tr Assn
    Brit Endodontic Soc
    Brit Homeopathic Dental Assn
    Brit Inst Dental & Surgical Technologists
    Brit Lingual Orthodontic Soc
    Brit Orthodontic Soc
    Brit Soc Dental Hygiene & Therapy
    Brit Soc Disability & Oral Health
    Brit Soc Gen Dental Surgery
    Brit Soc Mercury Free Dentistry
    Brit Soc Oral & Dental Res
    Brit Soc Paediatric Dentistry
    Brit Soc Periodontology
    Brit Soc Restorative Dentistry
    Brit Soc Study Prosthetic Dentistry
    Confedn Dental Emplrs
    Craniofacial Soc
    Dental Laboratories Assn
    Dental Profls Assn
    Dental System Suppliers Assn
    Dental Technologists Assn
    Fac Dental Surgery
    Fac Gen Dental Practice
    Ir Dental Assn
    Lindsay Soc Hist Dentistry
    Nat Assn Med Educ Mgt
    Orthodontic Technicians Assn
    R Coll Physicians & Surgeons Glasgow
    R Coll Surgeons Edinburgh
    R Odonto-Chirurgical Soc Scot
    Soc Advancement Anaesthesia Dentistry
Dentists: legal protection
    Confedn Dental Emplrs
    Medical & Dental Defence U Scotland
    Medical Protection Soc
Department stores > Retail trade
Dependent territories (British) > Overseas territories (British)
Depression
    Depression Alliance
    Depression UK
    MDF
    SAD Assn
    SANE
Dermatitis herpetiformis
    Coeliac UK
Dermatology
    Brit Assn Dermatologists
    Brit Contact Dermatitis Soc
    Primary Care Dermatology Soc
Design
    Anti Copying Design
    Art Workers Gld
    Chart Soc Designers
    D&AD
    Design Assn
    Design Business Assn

Design Hist Soc
Design Res Soc
Design & Technology Assn
Information Design Assn
Inst Designers Ireland
Inst Profl Designers
Instn Engg Designers
Nat Assn Advisers... Design & Technology
Nat Soc Educ in Art & Design
R Soc ... Arts
Register Apparel & Textile Designers
Scot Ecological Design Assn
Design: industrial > Industrial design
Design registration > Patents & trade marks
Despatch industry > Courier services
Desserts
Food & Drink Fedn
Detection dogs
Nat Assn Security Dog Users
Detectives > Investigators
Detergents > Soap & detergents
Developing countries > Development education & studies; Overseas development
Development education & studies
Devt Educ Assn
Devt Studies Assn
> + Education
Development trusts
Devt Trusts Assn
Devt Trusts Assn Scot
Developmental biology > Biology
de Vere (Edward) Earl of Oxford
De Vere Soc
Diabetes
Assn Brit Clinical Diabetologists
Diabetes Fedn Ireland
Diabetes UK
Diagnostic engineering
Instn Diagnostic Engrs
Ir Med Devices Assn
Dialects
Lakeland Dialect Soc
Lancashire Authors Assn
Yorkshire Dialect Soc
> + English language & literature
Dialysis
Brit Kidney Patient Assn
Brit Transplantation Soc
Diamond drilling
Drilling & Sawing Assn
Diamonds > Industrial diamonds; Gemstones; Jewellery
Dianthus
Brit Nat Carnation Soc
Dickens (Charles John Huffam)
Dickens Fellowship
Diecasting
Diecasting Soc
Diesel engines & fuel
Downstream Fuel Assn
Instn Diesel & Gas Turbine Engrs
Dietetics
Allied Health Professions Fedn
Brit Dietetic Assn
Brit Specialist Nutrition Assn
Infant & Dietetic Foods Assn
> + Nutrition
Digital print
Brit Printing Inds Fedn
Dinosaurs
Dinosaur Soc
Diplomatic Service
Assn Certified Comml Diplomats
Diplomatic Service Families Assn
Diptera
Dipterists Forum
Direct mail advertising > Advertising; Direct selling
Direct selling
Direct Marketing Assn
Direct Selling Assn
Ir Direct Marketing Assn
Directors (company)
Hundred Gp Finance Directors
Inst Directors
Inst Directors Ireland
Non-Executive Directors Assn
> + Management

Directory publishing
Data Pubrs Assn
> + Publishing
Disabled: road users
Blue Badge Network
Disabled Motoring UK
Disabled Motorists Fedn
Nat Assn Bikers Disability
Disablement
aeroBILITY
Assn Disabled Profls
Assn Supported Living
Brit Assn Supported Employment
Brit Inst Learning Disabilities
Brit Soc Rehabilitation Medicine
Capability Scotland
Disability Alliance
Disability Fedn Ireland
Employers Forum Disability
Hereditary Spastic Paraplegia Support Gp
Ir Wheelchair Assn
Limbless Assn
Nat Fedn Shopmobility
Nat Network Assessment Centres
Nat Register Access Consultants
R Assn Disability & Rehabilitation
R Mencap Soc
Riding Disabled Assn
Scope
Support Dogs
> + Mobility aids; specific area of disability
Disarmament
Campaign Nuclear Disarmament
Medical Action Global Security
Scientists Global Responsibility
Disasters & disaster relief
Planning Disaster Coalition
RedR UK
Tornado & Storm Res Org
> + Civil defence & industrial emergencies;   Fire & flood damage restoration;   Welfare: organisations
Disc golf (flying discs) > Flying: discs (sport)
Discotheques & equipment
Bar Entertainment & Dance Assn
Profl Lighting & Sound Assn
Discovery awards
Discovery Award England
Discrimination
Discrimination Law Assn
> + Race relations
Discs (music) > Sound recording & reproduction
Disease > Infection control & study;   Occupational health & hygiene;   Rare diseases
Disfigurement > Birthmarks & disfigurement;   Skin camouflage
Disinfectants
Brit Assn Chemical Specialities
UK Cleaning Products Ind Assn
> + Sterilising
Dismantling (waste trades) > Demolition & dismantling
Dispensing doctors
Country Doctors Assn
Dispensing Doctors Assn
Dispensing opticians > Optical practice
Display
Brit Display Soc
Shop & Display Eqpt Assn
Disposables
Absorbent Hygiene Products Mfrs Assn
Foodservice Packaging Assn
Distilling
Inst Brewing & Distilling
Maltsters Assn
Distribution
Chart Inst Logistics & Transport
Food Storage & Distbn Fedn
Freight Transport Assn
Inst Grocery Distbn
Ir Assn Distributive Trs
U Shop Distributive & Allied Workers
UK Warehousing Assn
Utd Road Transport U
> + Materials: management/handling; Retail trade; specific trade
District councils > Local government
District heating
Combined Heat & Power Assn
> + Heating
District nursing > Nursing

© CBD Research Ltd · Beckenham · BR3 5JS · Tel 020 8650 7745   E-mail cbd@cbdresearch.com · www.cbdresearch.com

Diving (professional & scientific)
      Histl Diving Soc
      Intl Marine Contrs Assn
      Nautical Archaeology Soc
      Scuba Inds Tr Assn
      Soc Underwater Technology
      > + Ocean industries
Diving (sport) > Swimming & diving
Divining > Dowsing
Divorced & separated people > Singles, divorced & separated
DIY > Do-it-yourself
Docks > Ports
Doctors > Medical: practice
Documents: historical > Records: historical
Documents: confidential disposal
      Asset Disposal Inf Security Alliance
      Brit Security Ind Assn
      UK Security Shredding Assn
Dodgson (Charles Lutwidge)
      Daresbury Lewis Carroll Soc
      Lewis Carroll Soc
Dogs
      Assn Dogs & Cats Homes
      Brit Flyball Assn
      Brit Whippet Racing Assn
      Dogs Trust
      Kennel Club
      Nat Assn Registered Petsitters
      Nat Assn Security Dog Users
      Nat Dog Wardens Assn
      Nat Search & Rescue Dog Assn
      Scot Kennel Club
      > + Hounds
Dogs: groomers > Grooms & grooming (pets)
Dogs: training
      Assn Pet Behaviour Counsellors
      Assn Pet Dog Trainers
      Brit Inst Profl Dog Trainers
      Canine & Feline Behaviour Assn
      People & Dogs Soc
      Rough & Smooth Collie Training Assn
      Scot Working Trials Soc
      Support Dogs
Do-it-yourself
      Brit Hardware Fedn
      Brit Indep Retailers Assn
      Ir Hardware & Bldg Materials Assn
Dolls & dolls' houses
      Doll Club GB
      > + Toys
Dolphins
      Whale & Dolphin Consvn Soc
Domestic appliances
      Assn Mfrs Domestic Appliances
      Domestic Appliance Service Assn
      White Goods Assn [IRL]
      Whitegoods Tr Assn
      > + Electrical industry & engineering
Domestic engineering > specific subjects, eg Heating
Domestic fowl > Poultry
Domestic heating > Heating
Domestic ventilation
      Residential Ventilation Assn
      > + Air: conditioning & ventilating
Domestic violence
      NI Women's Aid Fedn
      Women's Aid Fedn (England)
      > + Crime & crime prevention
Domiciliary care
      Nat Care Assn
      UK Home Care Assn
Donations (public)
      Donor Watch
Donizetti (Gaetano)
      Donizetti Soc
Donkeys
      Donkey Breed Soc
      Miniature Mediterranean Donkey Assn
Door supervisors
      Nat Doorwatch
Doors
      Architectural & Specialist Door Mfrs Assn
      Assn Composite Door Mfrs
      Automatic Door Suppliers Assn
      Brit Woodworking Fedn
      Door & Hardware Federation

Double glazing
      Glass & Glazing Fedn
      Incorporation Plastic Window Fabricators & Installers
      > + Insulation; Windows
Down's syndrome
      Down's Syndrome Assn
      Down's Syndrome Scotland
      > + Children: handicapped
Dowsing
      Brit Soc Dowsers
Draghounds > Hounds
Dragon boats
      Brit Dragon Boat Racing Assn
Dragonflies
      Brit Dragonfly Soc
Drainage
      Assn Drainage Authorities
      Clay Pipe Devt Assn
      Land Drainage Contrs Assn
      Nat Sewerage Assn
      > + Concrete & concrete products; Pipes; Water
Drake (Sir Francis)
      Drake Exploration Society
Drama
      Assn Drama Adjudicators (Ireland)
      Conf Drama Schools
      Drama Assn Wales
      Drama League Ireland
      Gld Drama Adjudicators
      Gld Profl Teachers Dance & Movement
      Nat Assn Teaching Drama
      Nat Drama
      Nat Operatic & Dramatic Assn
      R Academy Dramatic Art
      R Scot Academy Music & Drama
      Religious Drama Soc
      Scot Assn Speech & Drama Adjudicators
      Scot Community Drama Assn
      Soc Teachers Speech & Drama
      > + Theatre
Drama festivals > Festivals: art, drama & music
Dramatists
      Ir Playwrights & Screenwriters Gld
      Player-Playwrights
      Scot Soc Playwrights
      Soc Authors
      Soc Authors Scotland
      Writers Gld
      > + Writing & writers
Dramatherapy
      Allied Health Professions Fedn
      Brit Assn Dramatherapists
Draught proofing > Insulation
Draughts (board game)
      English Draughts Assn
Drawing > Art & artists
Dredging
      Central Dredging Assn
      Fedn Dredging Contrs
Dress > Costume history, design & conservation;   Fashion
Dressage
      Brit Equestrian Fedn
      > + Horses: riding & driving
Dried flowers > Flowers, flower arrangement & floristry
Dried fruit
      Nat Dried Fruit Tr Assn
Drilling
      Brit Drilling Assn
      Brit Rig Owners Assn
      Drilling & Sawing Assn
      Inst Materials, Minerals & Mining
      Well Drillers Assn
Drink & beverage industry
      Beverage Coun Ireland
      Beverage Standards Assn
      Brewing, Food & Beverage Ind Suppliers Assn
      Brit Soft Drinks Assn
      Campden BRI
      Can Makers
      Drinks Ind Gp Ireland
      Food & Drink Fedn
      Food & Drink Ind Ireland
      NI Food & Drink Assn
      Processing & Packaging Machinery Assn
      Scot Food & Drink Fedn
      > + Bottling

Drinking & driving
  Campaign Drinking & Driving
Drinking (compulsive) > Alcoholism
Drinking fountains
  Metropolitan Drinking Fountain &... Assn
Drinking straws & vessels
  Foodservice Packaging Assn
Drinkwater (John)
  Friends Dymock Poets
Drip mats > Beer: bottles, cans labels & mats
Driving (off-road)
  All Wheel Drive Club
  Brit Off Road Driving Assn
  Motoring Orgs' Land Access & Recreation Assn
Driving tuition
  ADI Fedn
  Approved Driving Instructors Nat Jt Coun
  Assn Indl Road Safety Officers
  Assn Nat Driver Improvement Scheme Providers
  Driving Instructors Assn
  Inst Advanced Motorists
  Inst Master Tutors Driving
  Motor Schools Assn
Dromedary camels > Camelids
Drug addiction > Addiction
Drugs > Pharmaceuticals; Pharmacology & chemotherapy
Drugs: detection
  Nat Assn Security Dog Users
Druids
  Coun Brit Druid Orders
  Pagan Fedn
Drums (containers) > Cisterns, drums & tanks
Drums (musical instruments)
  Corps Drums Soc
  > + Brass & silver bands
Dry cleaning > Laundering & dry cleaning
Dry rot
  Inst Specialist Surveyors & Engrs
  > + Dampcourses & dampproofing
Dry stone walling
  Dry Stone Walling Assn
Dry waste
  Container Handling Eqpt Mfrs Assn
  > + Waste disposal
Drylining > Drywalling
Drywalling
  Fedn Plastering & Drywall Contrs
Dublin
  Friends Medieval Dublin [IRL]
  R Dublin Soc
Duchenne disease > Dystrophy
Ducks
  Brit Poultry Coun
  Brit Waterfowl Assn
  > + Poultry
Ducks (decoy)
  Brit Decoy & Wildfowl Carvers Assn
Ducting
  Assn Ductwork Contrs & Allied Services
  Heating & Ventilating Contrs Assn
Duelling
  Dawn Duellists' Soc
Dumbness
  Selective Mutism Inf & Res Assn
  > + Speech
Dunkirk
  Assn Dunkirk Little Ships
Dunnett (Dorothy)
  Dorothy Dunnett Soc
Duodecimal system
  Dozenal Soc
Dust control
  Fan Mfrs' Assn
  Solids Handling & Processing Assn
  > + Air: conditioning & ventilating
Dutch > Netherlands: language & literature
Duty-free trade
  Brit Assn Ship Suppliers
  UK Travel Retail Forum
Dwarfism > Growth
Dyeing & finishing
  Assn Glds Weavers, Spinners & Dyers
  Soc Dyers & Colourists
Dyestuffs
  Chemical Business Assn
Dyking
  Dry Stone Walling Assn

Dymock poets
  Friends Dymock Poets
Dyslexia
  Brit Dyslexia Assn
  Coun Registration Schools Teaching Dyslexic Pupils
  Dyslexia Action
  Dyslexia Assn Ireland
  Dyslexia Scotland
  nasen
  Nat Network Assessment Centres
  > + Children: handicapped
Dysmenorrhea
  Nat Assn Premenstrual Syndrome
Dysphasia > Speech
Dysplasia (ectodermal)
  Ectodermal Dysplasia Soc
Dyspraxia
  Dyspraxia Foundation
Dystonia
  Dystonia Soc
Dystrophy
  Duchenne Family Support Gp
  Muscular Dystrophy Campaign
  Muscular Dystrophy Ireland
  Myotonic Dystrophy Support Gp
Dzhugashvili (Iosif Vissarionovich) > Stalin (Joseph)

E

Ear tags (animal)
  Assn Automatic Identification &... Data Capture
Earth sciences, structure & resources
  Earth Science Teachers' Assn
  Geological Soc
  Inst Materials, Minerals & Mining
  Mineralogical Soc
  Remote Sensing & Photogrammetry Soc
  Soc Underwater Technology
  UKspace
  Yorkshire Geological Soc
  > + Geology
Earth sheltered buildings
  Brit Earth Sheltering Assn
Earthenware > Ceramics; Clay & clay products; Pottery
Earthquake engineering
  Instn Civil Engrs
  Soc Earthquake & Civil Engg Dynamics
Earthworms
  Earthworm Soc Britain
East/Eastern Africa
  Eastern Africa Assn
Eastern Europe > individual countries
Eating disorders
  Eating Disorders Assn
  Overeaters Anonymous
  > + Obesity
EC > European Union
Ecclesiastical > Church headings; individual religions
Eckhart (Johannes)
  Eckhart Soc
Ecology
  Brit Ecological Soc
  Inst Ecology & Envtl Mgt
  > + Conservation; Environment
Economic development
  Honourable The Irish Soc
  Instn Economic Devt
  Scot Coun Devt & Ind
Economic history
  Economic Hist Soc
  Economic & Social Hist Soc Ireland
Economics
  Agricl Economics Soc
  Brit Academy
  David Hume Inst
  Economic Res Coun
  Economic & Social Res Inst [IRL]
  Economics, Business & Enterprise Assn
  Inst Economic Affairs
  Inst Fiscal Studies
  Intl Consulting Economists Assn
  R Economic Soc
  Resource Use Inst
  Scot Economic Soc

© CBD Research Ltd · Beckenham · BR3 5JS · Tel 020 8650 7745 E-mail cbd@cbdresearch.com · www.cbdresearch.com

Soc Business Economists
Soc Economic Analysis
Statistical & Social Inquiry Soc Ireland
Ectodermal dysplasia
Ectodermal Dysplasia Soc
Ectopic pregnancy > Miscarriage
Ecuador
Anglo Ecuadorian Soc
Eczema
Nat Eczema Soc
Edgings (concrete) > Concrete & concrete products
Edible nuts > Nuts (edible)
Edible oils & fats
Brit Assn Cold Pressed Oil Producers
Fedn Oils, Seeds & Fats Assns
Nat Edible Oil Distbrs Assn
Seed Crushers & Oil Processors Assn
UK Assn Fish Meal Mfrs
> + individual fats; Rendering
Edinburgh
Cockburn Assn
Editing & editors
Assn Church Editors
Assn Freelance Editors, Proofreaders & Indexers [IRL]
Brit Soc Magazine Editors
Picture Res Assn
Soc Editors
Soc Editors & Proofreaders
> + Publishing
Education
Assn Achievement &...Assessment
Assn Colls
Assn Community & Comprehensive Schools [IRL]
Assn NI Colleges
Assn Quality Education
Assn Study Primary Educ
Assn Tutors
Brit Assn Early Childhood Educ
Brit Educl Leadership, Mgt & Admin Soc
Brit Educl Res Assn
Campaign Learning
Campaign Real Educ
Campaign State Educ
Caspari Foundation Educl Therapy...
CIFE
Fedn Educ Business Link Consortia
Further Educ Res Assn
Group Educ Museums
Honourable The Irish Soc
Indep Academies Assn
Ir Vocational Educ Assn
Modern Studies Assn
Montessori Soc
nasen
Nat Assn Envtl Educ
Nat Assn Primary Educ
Nat Assn Therapeutic Educ
Nat Forum Engg Centres
Nat Foundation Educl Res E&W
Nat Small Schools Forum
New Schools Network
PSHE Assn
SAPERE
Scot Educl Res Assn
Scot Support Learning Assn
Soc Res Higher Educ
Staff & Educl Devt Assn
> + Adult education; Independent & public schools; Teachers;
specific subjects
Education: computers in
Naace
Education: equipment & supplies
Brit Educl Suppliers Assn
Education: games & simulation
Soc Advancement Games & Simulations Educ & Training
Education: guardians
Assn Educ & Guardianship Intl Students
Education: guidance
Inst Guidance Counsellors [IRL]
NAEGA
Education: history
History Educ Soc
Education: home based
Education Otherwise Assn
Home Educ Advy Service
Nat Portage Assn
Education: occupational > Occupational training & education

Education: outdoor
Assn Heads Outdoor Educ Centres
Inst Outdoor Learning
Scot Envtl & Outdoor Educ Centres Assn
Education: specialists
Assn Coll Mgt
Assn Directors Children's Services
Assn Directors Educ Scotland
Assn Educ Welfare Mgt
Assn Educl Devt & Improvement Profls Scotland
Assn Educl Psychologists
Assn Painting Craft Teachers
Assn University Administrators
Chart Inst Educl Assessors
College Teachers
Higher Educ Liaison Officers' Assn
History Curriculum Assn
Inst Health Promotion & Educ
Nat Assn Advy Officers Special Educl Needs
Nat Assn Mathematics Advisers
Nat Governors' Assn
Nat Org Pupil Referral Units [E&W]
Soc Educ Consultants
Education: technology
Assn Learning Technology
Brit Educl Suppliers Assn
Brit Inst Learning & Devt
EEC > European Union
Effluents > Sewers, sewage & effluents
Egg decoration
Egg Crafters Gld
Eggs & egg products
Brit Egg Assn
Brit Egg Products Assn
Brit Free Range Egg Producers Assn
Nat Egg Marketing Assn
Scot Egg Producer Retailers Assn
UK Egg Producers Assn
Egypt
Ancient Egypt & Middle East Soc
Egypt Exploration Soc
Egyptian Brit Cham Comm
Ekbom syndrome
RLS-UK
Elastic materials > Narrow fabrics; Health care: equipment & supplies; Surgical
equipment & supplies
Elastic rope sports
Brit Elastic Rope Sports Assn
UK Bungee Club
Elderly persons > Geriatrics & ageing; Old people's organisations
Elections & electoral legislation
Assn Electoral Administrators
Electoral Reform Soc
Scot Assessors Assn
Unlock
Unlock Democracy
Electric: cable & conduit
BEAMA
Brit Cables Assn
Electric: fencing
Fencing Contrs' Assn
Electric: heating > Heating
Electric: lighting > Lighting
Electric: motors
BEAMA
Electric Vehicle Network
Electric: tools
Portable Electric Tool Mfrs Assn
Electric: transport
Battery Vehicle Soc
Electric Boat Assn
Electric Rly Soc
Electrical goods trade
Assd Nat Electrical Whlsrs
Assn Electrical & Mechanical Trs
Assn Whls Electrical Bulk Buyers
Electrical Distbrs Assn
Small Electrical Appliance Marketing Assn
Electrical industry & engineering
Assn Electrical Contrs (Ireland)
Assn Mfrs Domestic Appliances
BEAMA
Chart Instn Bldg Services Engrs
Electric Trace Heating Ind Coun
Electrical Contrs Assn
Electro Technical Coun Ireland

EMC Ind Assn
SELECT
Electricity
    Assn Electricity Producers
    Assn Mfrs Power generating Systems
    BEAMA
    Electricity Arbitration Assn
    Energy Industries Council
    Energy Networks Assn
    Energy Retail Assn
    Indl & Power Assn
    Micropower Coun
    Nat Assn Profl Inspectors & Testers
    Nat Jt Utilities Gp
    UK Revenue Protection Assn
Electricity meters > Meters & metering
Electrochemistry
    R Soc Chemistry
Electrodiagnostic medicine
    Brit Soc Clinical Neurophysiology
Electroencephalography
    Assn Neurophysiological Scientists
    Brit Soc Clinical Neurophysiology
Electroheat
    BEAMA
Electrohydraulic control
    Brit Fluid Power Assn
Electro-imaging
    Soc Metaphysicians
Electrolysis
    Brit Inst & Assn Electrolysis
    > + Beauty specialists/treatment
Electromagnetics
    EMC Ind Assn
Electronic: components (obsolescence)
    Component Obsolescence Gp
Electronic: industry & engineering
    Assn Franchised Distbrs Electronic Components
    BEAMA
    Brit Marine Fedn
    Electro Technical Coun Ireland
    EMC Ind Assn
    GAMBICA Assn
    Inst Materials, Minerals & Mining
    Instn Engg & Technology
    Intellect
    > + Computers; Data processing; Optoelectronics; Radio
Electronic: organs > Organs, organists & organ music
Electronic: surveillance > Security
Electronic: trade & commerce
    CEDIA
    GS1 Ireland
    GS1 UK
    Radio, Electrical & TV Retailers' Assn
Electronic: traffic control
    ITS UK
    > + Road safety & control
Electro-optics > Optoelectronics
Electrophoresis
    Brit Soc Proteome Res
    > + Biochemistry & biotechnology
Electrophysiology
    Scot Neuroscience Gp
Electroplating
    Surface Engg Assn
Electro-static equipment
    Brit Electrostatic Control Assn
Elgar (Sir Edward)
    Elgar Soc
Elia
    Charles Lamb Soc
Eliot (George) [Mary Ann Evans]
    George Eliot Fellowship
Eliot (Thomas Stearns)
    Eliot (T S) Society
Embalming
    Brit Inst Embalmers
Embroidery
    Embroiderers Gld
Embryology
    Assn Clinical Embryologists
    Brit Soc Developmental Biology
Emergency medicine > Medicine: accident & emergency
Emergency planning/management > Civil defence & industrial emergencies
Emigration > Immigration & emigration

Emission monitoring
    BTC Testing Advisory Gp
    Source Testing Assn
Employee assistance programmes
    UK Employee Assistance Profls Assn
Employee involvement > Industrial involvement & participation
Employers
    Confedn Brit Ind
    Employers Forum Disability
    Ir Business & Emplrs Confedn
    London First
    > + specific industry
Employment
    Age & Emplt Network
    Brit Assn Supported Employment
    Employers Forum Age
    HR Soc
    Over Fifties Assn
    Recruitment Soc
    > + Careers
Employment agents & consultants
    Assn Graduate Recruiters
    Assn Profl Staffing Cos
    Executive Res Assn
    Recruitment & Employment Confedn
Emu
    Rhea & Emu Assn
    > + Ostrich farming
Enamel: vitreous > Vitreous enamel
Enamelling
    Brit Soc Enamellers
    Gld Enamellers
Encephalitis
    Encephalitis Soc
    > + Myalgic encephalitis/encephalopathy
Endocrinology
    Androgen Insensitivity Syndrome Support Gp
    Brit Assn Endocrine & Thyroid Surgeons
    Brit Soc Neuroendocrinology
    Soc Endocrinology
Endodontics > Dentistry
Endometriosis
    Endometriosis UK
Endoscopy
    Brit Soc Gastroenterology
    Brit Soc Gynaecological Endoscopy
Endowment policies (secondhand)
    Assn Policy Market Makers
    > + Insurance
Energy
    Assn Consvn Energy
    Brit Hydropower Assn
    Brit Inst Energy Economics
    Buildings Energy Efficiency Fedn
    Combined Heat & Power Assn
    Energy Industries Council
    Energy Inst
    Energy Intensive Users Gp
    Energy Networks Assn
    ESTA Energy Services & Technology Assn
    Indl & Power Assn
    Inst Domestic Heating… Engrs
    Inst Materials, Minerals & Mining
    Instn Civil Engrs
    Instn Engg & Technology
    Ir Hydro Power Assn
    Nat Energy Action
    Property & Energy Professionals Assn
    Renewable Energy Assn
    Resource Use Inst
    > + Renewable energy; specific form of energy
Enforcement agents
    Civil Enforcement Assn
Engineering
    AIRTO
    Assn Brit Transport & Engg Museums
    Assn Consultancy & Engg
    Assn Consulting Engrs Ireland
    Brit Engg Mfrs Assn
    Brit Interactive Gp
    Brit Science Assn
    Brit Turned Parts Mfrs Assn
    EEF
    Engg Inds Assn
    Engg Integrity Soc
    Inst Indl Engrs Ireland
    Inst Numerical Computation & Analysis [IRL]

Instn Civil Engrs
Instn Diagnostic Engrs
Instn Engg Designers
Instn Engg & Technology
Instn Engrs Ireland
Instn Engrs & Shipbuilders Scotland
Instn Mechanical Engrs
Intellect
Ir Engg Enterprises Fedn
Prospect
R Academy Engg
Royal Soc (The)
Science, Technology, Engg. . . Public Relations Assn
Scot Engg
Soc Operations Engrs
Soc Profl Engrs
Specialist Engg Alliance
UK Assn Profl Engrs
Women's Engg Soc
> + other branches of engineering
Engineering: bricks > Bricks
Engineering: education
Brit Educl Suppliers Assn
Nat Forum Engg Centres
Engineering: equipment & materials
Engg Eqpt & Materials Users Assn
Engineering: history
Newcomen Soc
Stephenson Locomotive Soc
Trevithick Soc
Engineering: plant > Plant: industrial
Engineers' tools > Tools
Engines > specific type of engine
England
Campaign English Parliament
Campaign Protect Rural England
R Soc St George
English language & literature
Aethelflaed
Anglo Norman Text Soc
Assn Brit Language Schools
Assn Promotion Quality TESOL Educ
Early English Text Soc
Engliscan Gesíþas
English Assn
English Poetry & Song Soc
English Spelling Soc
English UK
Modern Humanities Res Assn
Nat Assn Advisers English
Nat Assn Teaching Engl
Nat Assn Teaching Engl &. . .Community Languages
Plain Engl Campaign
Queen's Engl Soc
R Soc Literature
Ranulf Higden Soc
> + individual writers by name
Engravers
Hand Engravers Assn
MultiService Assn
R Soc Painter Printmakers
Soc Wood Engravers
> + Art & artists
Enterprise agencies
Nat Fedn Enterprise Agencies
Entertainment
Adult Ind Trade Assn
Agents Assn
Arts Centre Gp
Assn Interactive Media & Entertainment
Brit Magical Soc
Broadcasting Entertainment Cinematograph. . .U
Concert Artistes' Assn
Fedn Entertainment Us
Inst Entertainment & Arts Mgt
Personal Mgrs Assn
Production Services Assn
> + Leisure, recreation & amenity management;   specific forms of
entertainment
Entertainment: equipment
Profl Lighting & Sound Assn
Entomology
Amat Entomologists' Soc
Assn Applied Biologists
Birmingham Natural Hist Soc
Brit Entomological & Natural Hist Soc
Buglife

R Entomological Soc Lond
> + Nature conservation
Environment
Assn Brit Certification Bodies
Assn Envtl Archaeology
Assn Heritage Interpretation
Aviation Envt Fedn
Campaign Farmed Envt
Doctor E F Schumacher Soc
Environmental Communicators Org
Environmental Inds Commission
Environmental Protection UK
Friends Earth
Good Homes Alliance
Green Alliance Trust
Indl & Power Assn
Inst Ecology & Envtl Mgt
Inst Envtl Mgt & Assessment
Linking Envt & Farming
Nat Assn Envtl Educ
Nat Register Access Consultants
Planning & Environment Bar Assn
Regional Studies Assn
Scot Ecological Design Assn
Scot Envt Link
Soc Envt
Soc Envtl Exploration
Soc Responsible Use Resources Agriculture. . .
Socialist Envt & Resources Assn
UK Envtl Law Assn
UK Forum Envtl Inds
Valpak
Wildlife & Countryside Link
Women's Envtl Network
> + Conservation; Pollution & pollution control
Environment: engineering/health
Assn Public Analysts
Assn Public Analysts Scotland
Brit Soc Ecological Medicine
Chart Inst Envtl Health
Environmental Health Officers Assn [IRL]
Inst Domestic Heating. . . Engrs
Instn Envtl Sciences
Keep Britain Tidy
R Envtl Health Inst Scotland
Scientists Global Responsibility
Soc Envtl Engrs
Soc Indl Emergency Service Officers
UK Envtl Mutagen Soc
Environmental illness > Occupational health & hygiene
Environmental services
Environmental Services Assn
Enzootic abortion of ewes
Highlands & Islands Sheep Health Assn
Ephemera
Brit Matchbox, Label & Booklet Soc
English Playing-Card Soc
Ephemera Soc
Exhibition Study Gp
Epidermolysis bullosa
Dystrophic Epidermolysis Bullosa Res Assn
Epigraphy
Brit Epigraphy Soc
Epilepsy
Brainwave
Brit Epilepsy Assn
Epilepsy Scotland
Nat Soc Epilepsy
Epiphytes
Epiphytic Plant Study Gp
> + Plants
Equal opportunities
Inst Equality & Diversity Practitioners
Nat Alliance Women's Orgs
Over Fifties Assn
Parity
> + Employment
Equestrian trade
Brit Equestrian Tr Assn
> + Horse headings
Equiano (Olaudah)
Equiano Soc
Equipment > Mining: equipment; Office equipment & systems
Equity finance
BVCA
EIS Assn

Equity release plans
>   Safe Home Income Plans
Ergonomics
>   Ergonomics Soc
Eritrea
>   Middle East Assn
Erotic art
>   Assn Erotic Artists
>   Gld Erotic Artists
Escalators
>   Lift & Escalator Ind Assn
Esperanto
>   Esperanto Assn Britain
>   Scot Esperanto Assn
Essences > Flavourings; Flower essences
Essential oils
>   Aromatherapy Tr Coun
>   Brit Essential Oils Assn
>   Brit Soc Perfumers
Estate agents
>   Assn Residential Letting Agents
>   Gld Letting & Mgt
>   Gld Profl Estate Agents
>   Inst Auctioneers & Appraisers Scotland
>   Inst Profl Auctioneers & Valuers [IRL]
>   Nat Assn Estate Agents
>   Property Consultants Soc
>   UK Assn Letting Agents
>   > + Property & land owners
Estate management
>   Assn Chief Corporate Property Officers Local Govt
>   Country Gentlemen's Assn
>   Country Land & Business Assn
>   Inst Clerks Works
>   Inst Healthcare Engg & Estate Mgt
>   Manorial Soc
Estate & trust planning > Trusts, trusteeship & estate planning
Estonia
>   Brit Estonian Assn
Estuaries
>   Estuarine & Coastal Sciences Assn
Ethics
>   Comment Reproductive Ethics
>   S Place Ethical Soc
Ethiopia
>   Middle East Assn
Ethnic studies
>   Assn Study Ethnicity & Nationalism
Ethnography
>   Museum Ethnographers Gp
>   R Anthropological Inst
Eton Fives
>   Eton Fives Assn
Eugenics
>   Galton Inst
Eurhythmics
>   Dalcroze Soc
Europe
>   Brit Assn Slavonic & E Eur Studies
>   Eur Atlantic Gp
>   Eur Inf Assn
>   Eur Movement
>   University Assn Contemporary Eur Studies
European Union
>   Atlantic Coun
>   Brit Inst Intl & Comparative Law
>   Campaign Euro-federalism
>   Campaign Indep Britain
>   Democracy Movement
>   Freedom Assn
Eurythmy
>   Eurythmy Assn
Euthanasia
>   ALERT
>   CNK Alliance
>   Dignity in Dying
>   EXIT
>   Soc Protection Unborn Children
Evacuees (WWII)
>   Evacuees Reunion Assn
Evangelism
>   Evangelical Alliance
>   Fellowship Indep Evangelical Churches
>   > + Christian activities
Evens (Rev Gerge Bramwell)
>   Romany Soc

Eventing (horse)
>   Brit Equestrian Fedn
>   Event Horse Owners Assn
>   Event Riders Assn
Events management
>   Assn Event Venues
>   Assn Events Mgt Educ
>   Event Services Assn
>   Events Sector Ind Trg Org
>   Nat Outdoor Events Assn
>   Soc Event Organisers
>   > + Corporate hospitality; Exhibitions; Shows & events
Examining officers
>   Examining Officers Assn
Excavation & land clearance
>   Inst Explosives Engrs
Exchanges: international
>   Assn Learning Languages en Famille
Exchequer records
>   Pipe Roll Soc
Executive research
>   Executive Res Assn
>   Recruitment & Employment Confedn
Exercise > Fitness; Physical education
Exhibitions
>   Assn Brit Profl Conf Organisers
>   Assn Event Organisers
>   Event Supplier & Services Assn
>   Exhibition Study Gp
>   Nat Exhibitors Assn
>   > + Conferences & conventions
Exhumation
>   Inst Cemetery & Crematorium Mgt
>   > + Burial & cremation
Experts & expert witness
>   Academy Experts
>   Assn Consulting Scientists
>   Expert Witness Inst
>   Soc Expert Witnesses
Exploration
>   BSES Expeditions
>   Scientific Exploration Soc
>   Young Explorers' Trust
Exploration: history
>   Hakluyt Soc
Explosives
>   ADS Gp
>   Assn Petroleum & Explosives Admin
>   Brit Cave Res Assn
>   Explosives Ind Gp
>   Inst Explosives Engrs
>   Nat Assn Security Dog Users
Explosives: detection
>   Nat Assn Security Dog Users
Export & import
>   Brit Exporters Assn
>   China-Britain Business Coun
>   Customs Practitioners Gp
>   Free Trade League
>   Inst Export
>   Inst Intl Tr [IRL]
>   Ir Exporters Assn
>   > + Chambers of commerce: overseas trade
Export packers
>   Brit Intl Freight Assn
>   > + specific trade
Express courier services
>   Assn Intl Courier & Express Services
Ex-service organisations
>   Assn Jewish Ex-Servicemen & Women
>   Brit Limbless Ex-Service Men's Assn
>   Confedn Brit Service & Ex-Service Orgs
>   Not Forgotten Assn
>   Officers' Assn
>   R Brit Legion
>   R Brit Legion Scotland
>   R Naval Assn
>   Saint Dunstan's
Extra sensory perception > Paranormal & psychical research
Eyes > Blind & partially sighted; Ophthalmology; specific diseases
Eyewear > Contact lens; Optical industry

© CBD Research Ltd · Beckenham · BR3 5JS · Tel 020 8650 7745   E-mail cbd@cbdresearch.com · www.cbdresearch.com

F

Fabric care
>> Home Laundering Consultative Coun
Fabrics > Textile: industry & trade
Fabry disease
>> Soc Mucopolysaccharide Diseases
Face painting
>> Face Painting Assn
Facial disfigurement > Birthmarks & disfigurement
Facilities management
>> Brit Inst Facilities Mgt
>> Chart Inst Bldg
>> Facilities Mgt Assn
>> Ir Property & Facility Mgt Assn
>> R Instn Chart Surveyors
>> + Offices (serviced & agents)
Factoring (banking & finance)
>> Asset Based Finance Assn
>> Nat Assn Comml Finance Brokers
Factors: motor > Motor factors
Fair trade
>> Brit Assn Fair Tr Shops
Fairgrounds & equipment
>> Fair Organ Presvn Soc
>> Fairground Assn
>> Fairground Soc
>> Mechanical Organ Owners Soc
>> Roller Coaster Club
>> Showmen's Gld
>> Soc Indep Roundabout Proprietors
Fairs
>> Charity Fairs Assn
>> Nat Assn Brit Market Authorities
Faith healing > Spiritual healing
Falconry > Hawks & hawking
Falkland Islands
>> Falkland Islands Assn
>> Falklands Consvn
Falkner (John Meade)
>> John Meade Falkner Soc
Fall arrest equipment
>> Fall Arrest Safety Eqpt Training
False memory
>> Brit False Memory Soc
Falsework
>> Nat Access & Scaffolding Confedn
Familial hypercholesterolaemia
>> Heart UK
>> + Cardiology
Family history > Genealogy
Family law
>> Assn Family Therapy
>> Family Law Assn Scotland
>> Family Law Bar Assn
>> Family Mediators' Assn
>> Family Rights Gp
>> NAGALRO
>> Nat Family Mediation
>> Resolution
Family planning
>> Fac Sexual & Reproductive Healthcare
>> Family Planning Assn
>> Fertility Care Scotland
>> Ir Family Planning Assn
>> Nat Assn Nurses Contraception & Sexual Health
>> Nat Assn Ovulation Method Instructors
Family therapy
>> Assn Family Therapy
>> Family Matters Inst
Family welfare > Welfare organisations
Fan clubs > subject of interest
Fancy dress
>> Brit Costume Assn
>> + Costume history, design & conservation
Fancy goods > Giftware
Fans
>> Fan Mfrs' Assn
>> Heating, Ventilating & Air Conditioning Mfrs' Assn
>> + Air: conditioning & ventilating; Heating
Fantasy
>> Brit Fantasy Soc
>> Brit Science Fiction Assn
Fare collection
>> Transport Ticket Soc

Farm animals > Animals; specific animals
Farm buildings
>> Brit Constructional Steelwork Assn
>> Historic Farm Bldgs Gp
>> Instn Agricl Engrs
>> Rural & Indl Design & Bldg Assn
Farm machinery > Agriculture: machinery
Farm shops & food
>> Nat Farmers' Retail & Markets Assn
>> Wholesome Food Assn
>> Women's Food & Farming U
Farm visits
>> Farming & Countryside Educ
>> Farms Schools
Farmers' markets > Markets: street, cattle & farmers'
Farmers' organisations
>> Comml Farmers Gp
>> Family Farmers Assn
>> Farmers Action
>> Farmers Club
>> Farmers' U Wales
>> Flying Farmers Assn
>> Ir Farmers Assn
>> Jersey Farmers' U
>> Manx Nat Farmers U
>> Nat Assn NFU Gp Secretaries
>> Nat Farmers' Retail & Markets Assn
>> Nat Farmers U
>> Nat Fedn Young Farmers Clubs (E&W)
>> NFU Scotland
>> Scot Assn Young Farmers Clubs
>> Small Farms Assn
>> Tenant Farmers' Assn
>> Ulster Farmers U
Farming > Agriculture; Dairying; Organic growing & farming
Farnon (Robert)
>> Robert Farnon Soc
Farriers
>> Nat Assn Farriers...
>> UK Horse Shoers Assn
>> + Blacksmiths
Fashion
>> Assn Model Agents
>> Assn Photographers
>> Brit Shops & Stores Assn
>> Costume Soc
>> Ir Fashion Ind Fedn
>> Scot Textile Ind Assn
>> UK Fashion & Textile Assn
>> + Clothing; Costume history, design & conservation
Fasteners
>> Brit Assn Fastener Distbrs
>> Confedn Brit Metalforming
>> Fastener Engg & Res Assn
>> Power Fastenings Assn
Fat (obese) > Obesity
Fatigue (materials/metals) > Materials: technology & testing
Fatigue (physical)
>> Action ME
>> Assn Young People with ME
>> Myalgic Encephalopathy Assn
Fats, edible & processing > Edible oils & fats; Rendering; individual fats
Fauna > Animals; Nature conservation; specific animals
Feed (animal) > Animal feed
Feet > Chiropody & podiatry; Footwear; Orthopaedics
Fell running
>> Assn Running Clubs
>> Fell Runners Assn
>> + Running
Felt & flat roofing > Roofing
Fencing (enclosure)
>> Fencing Contrs' Assn
Fencing (sport)
>> Brit Fedn Histl Swordplay
>> Brit Fencing Assn
>> Scot Fencing
Feng shui
>> Feng Shui Soc
Ferns
>> Brit Pteridological Soc
Ferrets
>> Nat Ferret Welfare Soc
Ferries
>> Assn Cruise Experts
>> + Shipping
Fertilisers
>> Agricl Inds Confedn

Fertilizer Assn Ireland
> + Agriculture: chemicals
Fertility
Assn Biomedical Andrologists
Brit Andrology Soc
Brit Fertility Soc
Brit Infertility Counselling Assn
Brit Soc Psychosomatic Obstetrics...
Daisy Network
Foresight
Infertility Network UK
Soc Reproduction & Fertility
Festivals: art, drama & music
Assn Drama Adjudicators (Ireland)
Assn Festival Organisers
Brit Arts Festivals Assn
Brit & Intl Fedn Festivals Music, Drama & Speech
Nat Drama Festivals Assn
Fibre optics
Fibreoptic Ind Assn
Fibreboard > Packaging
Fibromyalgia
Fibromyalgia Assn
Fiddles
Nat Assn Accordion & Fiddle Clubs
Scot Fiddle Soc
Field archery
Nat Field Archery Soc
Scot Field Archery Assn
Field names
English Place-Name Soc
Field sports
Countryside Alliance
Countryside Alliance Ireland
Countryside Ireland
Fedn Assns Country Sports Europe
Scot Assn Country Sports
U Country Sports Workers
> + individual sport
Field study > Natural history; other subjects of field study
Fights (historic/re-enactment)
English Civil War Soc
Histl Maritime Soc
Historic Artillery
Knights R England
Medieval Siege Soc
Napoleonic Assn
Nat Assn Re-enactment Socs
Plantagenet Medieval Archery... Soc
Regia Anglorum
Sealed Knot
Seventeenth Century Life & Times
Victorian Military Soc
Vikings (The)
World War Two Living Hist Assn
> + Stunts & stunt coordination
Fights (stage/film)
Brit Acad Dramatic Combat
> + Stunts & stunt coordination
Filing systems > Office equipment & systems
Filling stations
Assn Petroleum & Explosives Admin
Fedn Petroleum Suppliers
Film
access CINEMA [IRL]
Brit Academy Film & TV Arts
Brit Fedn Film Socs
Brit Film Inst
Fedn Comml Audiovisual Libraries
Inst Amat Cinematographers
Inst Contemporary Arts
Ir Film Inst
Nat Assn Higher Educ Moving Image
Test Card Circle
> + Photography
Film: advertising > Advertising: television & screen
Film: educational > Audio-visual aids & equipment
Film: festivals > Festivals: art, drama & music
Film: locations
Gld Location Mgrs
Film: production & distribution
Advertising Producers Assn
Assn Studio & Production Eqpt Companies
BKSTS
Brit Film Designers Gld
Brit Soc Cinematographers
Broadcasting Entertainment Cinematograph...U

Cine Glds GB
Cinema Exhibitors Assn
Directors Gld
Film Distbrs' Assn
Gld Brit Camera Technicians
Gld Brit Film & TV Editors
Producers Alliance Cinema & TV
Production Mgrs Assn
Screen Producers Ireland
UK Screen Assn
> + specialists concerned; Radio & TV; Video
Film: special effects
Inst Explosives Engrs
> + Stunts & stunt coordination
Film: stunts > Stunts & stunt coordination
Filters
Heating, Ventilating & Air Conditioning Mfrs' Assn
Filtration
Filtration Soc
Finance/Financial services
Assn Financial Markets Europe
Community Devt Finance Assn
Consumer Finance Assn
Financial Services Ireland
Inst Financial Services
> + Accountancy; Banking; Investment; Management accountancy
Finance: brokers & agents
Nat Assn Comml Finance Brokers
Whls Markets Brokers Assn
Finance: hire purchase > Credit: trade;   Credit: unions
Finance: officers & controllers > Accountancy
Finance: planning
Inst Financial Planning

Fine arts > Art headings
Fingerprinting
Fingerprint Soc
Finishes/finishing > Coatings; Metal: finishing; Paint
Finland
Anglo Finnish Soc
Finnish-Brit Cham Comm
Firbank ([Arthur Annesley] Ronald)
Flecker & Firbank Soc
Fire & flood damage restoration
Brit Damage Mgt Assn
Nat Carpet Cleaners Assn
Property Care Assn
Fire loss adjusters
Chart Inst Loss Adjusters
Fire marks
Fire Mark Circle
Fire protection & prevention
Architectural & Specialist Door Mfrs Assn
Assn Bldg Engrs
Assn Fire Consultants
Assn Specialist Fire Protection
Brit Approvals Fire Eqpt
Brit Fire Consortium
Brit Textile Technology Gp
Brit Urethane Foam Contrs Assn
Fedn Brit Fire Orgs
Fire Protection Assn
Glass & Glazing Fedn
Indep Fire Engg & Distrbrs Assn
Instn Fire Engrs
Intumescent Fire Seals Assn
Nat Fire Sprinkler Network
Passive Fire Protection Fedn
Soc Protection Life Fire
Fire protection & prevention: equipment
Brit Automatic Fire Sprinkler Assn
Brit Fire Consortium
Fire Fighting Vehicles Mfrs Assn
Fire Ind Assn
Fire & Rescue Suppliers Assn
Nat Security Inspectorate
Residential Sprinkler Assn
Fire protection & prevention: history
Fire Brigade Soc
Fire Mark Circle
Fire Service Presvn Gp
Fire protection & prevention: personnel
Brit Fire Services Assn
Chief Fire Officers Assn
Chief Fire Officers Assn Ireland
Fire Brigades U

Fire Officers Assn
Nat Assn Healthcare Fire Officers
Firearms > Arms & armour; Guns & ammunition; Shooting
Firebricks > Refractories
Fires & fireplaces
Stove Ind Alliance
Fireworks
Brit Fireworks Assn
Brit Pyrotechnists Assn
Explosives Ind Gp
Inst Explosives Engrs
Nat Campaign Firework Safety
UK Pyrotechnics Soc
Firms > Business
First aid & immediate care
Allied Health Professions Fedn
Assn First Aiders
Brit Assn Immediate Care
Brit Red Cross Soc
Casualties Union
College Paramedics
First Aid Assn
First Aid Coun Training
Hovercraft Search & Rescue UK
Ir Red Cross Soc
Medical Equestrian Assn
Order Malta [IRL]
Paediatric First Aid Assn
Saint Andrew's Ambulance Assn
Saint John Ambulance
> + Medicine: accident & emergency
Fiscal studies
Inst Fiscal Studies
> + Taxation
Fish: biology > Ichthyology
Fish: curing
Aberdeen Fish Curers'...Assn
Fish: farming
Brit Trout Assn
Ir Farmers Assn
Scot Salmon Producers' Org
> + Salmon & trout
Fish: frying
Nat Assn Range Mfrs
Nat Fedn Fish Friers
Fish: meal & fish oil
UK Assn Fish Meal Mfrs
Fish: trade
Anglo North Ir Fish Producers Org
Fedn Irish Fishermen
Herring Buyers Assn
Ir Fish Processors & Exporters Assn
Ir Fish Producers Org
London Fish Mchts Billingsgate
Nat Fedn Fishmongers
Nat Fedn Inland Whls Fish Mchts
Scot Seafood Processors Fedn
Seafood Scotland
Skates & Rays Producers Assn
UK Assn Fish Producer Orgs
Fish: tropical & ornamental
Assn Aquarists
Fedn Brit Aquatic Socs
Ornamental Aquatic Tr Assn
Profl Koi Dealers Assn
Fishing
Anglo North Ir Fish Producers Org
Assn Salmon Fishery Bds
Assn Sea Fisheries C'ees [E&W]
Coracle Soc
Countryside Alliance Ireland
Fedn Irish Fishermen
Inst Fisheries Mgt
Ir Fishermen's Org
Marine Inst [IRL]
Nat Fedn Fishermens Orgs
New Under Ten Fishermen's Assn
Profl Coarse Fisheries Assn
Scot Fishermen's Fedn
Scot Fishermen's Org
Fishing (sport)
Angling Trs Assn
Angling Trust
Assn Stillwater Game Fishery Mgrs
Carp Soc
Confedn Engl Fly Fishers
Countryside Alliance

Ir Fedn Sea Anglers
London Anglers Assn
Profl Anglers Assn
Salmon & Trout Assn
Scot Anglers Nat Assn
Scot Assn Country Sports
Scot Fedn Coarse Angling
Scot Fedn Sea Anglers
Shark Angling Club
U Country Sports Workers
Ulster Angling Fedn
Ulster Coarse Fishing Fedn
Fishing tackle
Angling Trs Assn
Fishing vessels > Ships (& boats): history & preservation
Fitness
Body Control Pilates Assn
EMDP
Fedn Holistic Therapists
Fitness Ind Assn
Fitness League
Fitness NI
Gld Profl Teachers Dance & Movement
Keep Fit Assn
Medau Soc
Nat Amat Bodybuilders Assn
Nat Register Personal Trainers
Nutrition & Health Foundation [IRE]
Profl Assn Alexander Teachers
Soc Teachers Alexander Technique
> + Health headings
Fitness equipment
Sporting Goods Ind Assn
Sports & Fitness Eqpt Assn
Fives > Eton Fives; Rugby Fives
Fixing systems
Construction Fixings Assn
Flags, banners & bunting
Brit Sign & Graphics Assn
Flag Inst
Heraldry Soc
Flat glass > Glass & glazing
Flat green bowling > Bowling
Flat roofing > Roofing
Flats: maintenance/management
Assn Serviced Apartment Providers
Upkeep
Flavourings
Brit Essence Mfrs Assn
Brit Soc Flavourists
Flecker (James Elroy)
Flecker & Firbank Soc
Fleet Air Arm
Aircrewman's Assn
Fleet car operators & management
ACFO
Inst Car Fleet Mgt
Mobile Electronics & Security Fedn
> + Motor headings
Fletchers
Craft Gld Traditional Bowyers & Fletchers
Flexible hoses
Hose Mfrs & Suppliers Assn
Flexible packaging > Packaging;   Plastics: film
Flies
Dipterists Forum
Flight safety > Aviation: safety, control & training
Flight simulation
R Aeronautical Soc
Floatation
Floatation Tank Assn
Flood damage restoration > Fire & flood damage restoration
Flood protection
Assn Drainage Authorities
Flood Protection Assn
Flood research
Tornado & Storm Res Org
Floors
Access Flooring Assn
Assn Concrete Indl Flooring Contrs
Brit Precast Concrete Fedn
FeRFA
Metal Cladding & Roofing Mfrs Assn
Nat Inst Carpet & Floorlayers
Floors: floorcoverings
Brit Shops & Stores Assn
Carpet Foundation

© CBD Research Ltd · Beckenham · BR3 5JS · Tel 020 8650 7745 · E-mail cbd@cbdresearch.com · www.cbdresearch.com

Contract Flooring Assn
Nat Inst Carpet & Floorlayers
UK Resilient Flooring Assn
> + Carpets
Floors: tiles & quarries > Tiles (floor & wall)
Floristry > Flowers, flower arrangement & floristry
Flour
Inc Nat Assn Brit & Ir Millers
Flowers, flower arrangement & floristry
Brit Florist Assn
Flower Import Tr Assn
Flowers & Plants Assn
Fresh Produce Consortium
Nat Assn Flower Arrangement Socs
Pressed Flower Gld
> + Horticulture; specific varieties of flowers
Flower essences
Brit Assn Flower Essence Producers
Brit Flower & Vibrational Essences Assn
Flues > Chimneys
Fluid mechanics > Hydraulics & hydromechanics
Fluoridation
Brit Fluoridation Soc
Flute playing
Brit Flute Soc
Fly ash > Ash
Flyball
Brit Flyball Assn
Fly-dressing
Flydressers Gld
Flying > Aviation: sport/hobby
Flying: discs (sport)
Brit Disc Golf Assn
UK Ultimate Assn
Flying: training
Brit Business & Gen Aviation Assn
> + Aviation
Foam (plastic) > Plastics: foam
Foil: aluminium > Aluminium: foil
Folk dance & song
Assn Festival Organisers
Best Western Dance Academy
Brit Bluegrass Music Assn
Cymdeithas Ddawns Werin Cymru
Elsie Jeanette Oxenham Appreciation Soc
English Folk Dance & Song Soc
Folk Arts England
Musicians U
Order Woodcraft Chivalry
R Scot Country Dance Soc
Soc Intl Folk Dancing
Southern Counties Folk Fedn
Welsh Amat Music Fedn
Welsh Folk Song Soc
> + Highland dancing
Folk life & lore
Dracula Soc
Folklore Ireland Soc
Folklore Soc
Lakeland Dialect Soc
Soc Folk Life Studies
Follies
Folly Fellowship
> + Historic buildings
Food
Assn Applied Biologists
Bakers Food & Allied Workers U
Brewing, Food & Beverage Ind Suppliers Assn
Brit Nutrition Foundation
Campden BRI
Food & Drink Fedn
Gld Food Writers
Inst Food Science & Technology
Instn Agricl Engrs
McCarrison Soc
NI Food & Drink Assn
Soc Food Hygiene & Technology
Sustain
> + Health food; Organic growing & farming
Food: additives
Assn Public Analysts
Assn Public Analysts Scotland
Food Additives & Ingredients Assn
> + Animal feed
Food: allergy > Allergy
Food: casings > Sausage & food casings
Food: farm > Farm shops & food

Food: frozen & chilled
Brit Frozen Food Fedn
Chilled Food Assn
Food & Drink Fedn
Food Storage & Distbn Fedn
Provision Tr Fedn
Food: packaging
Alliance Beverage Cartons & Envt
Brit Bottlers' Inst
Campden BRI
Foodservice Packaging Assn
Metal Packaging Mfrs Assn
Processing & Packaging Machinery Assn
Food: processing
Food & Drink Ind Ireland
Food Processors Assn
Instn Chemical Engrs
Food: safety
Assn Port Health Authorities
Brit Pest Control Assn
R Envtl Health Inst Scotland
Soc Applied Microbiology
Food: speciality & fine foods
Brit Specialist Nutrition Assn
Cornish Pasty Assn
Experimental Food Soc
Gld Fine Food
Heart of England Fine Foods
Infant & Dietetic Foods Assn
Melton Mowbray Pork Pie Assn
Provision Tr Fedn
Rural Crafts Assn
Food: trade
Brit Food Importers & Distrbrs Assn
Campden BRI
Food & Drink Ind Ireland
Ir Assn Distributive Trs
Nat Fedn Meat & Food Traders
Organic Food Fedn
Scot Food & Drink Fedn
Scot Food Trs Assn
Wholesome Food Assn
> + Grocery & provision trade; Health food; Takeaway & fast food
Food: transport > Road: haulage; Temperature controlled transport
Foodservice
Foodservice Consultants Soc Intl
Foodservice Packaging Assn
Foosball > Table football
Foot > Footwear; Orthopaedics
Football (American) > American football
Football (Association)
Amat Football Alliance
Assn Football Statisticians
Football Assn
Football Assn Ireland
Football Assn Wales
Football League
Football Safety Officers Assn
Football Supporters Fedn
Football Writers Assn
Inst Football Mgrs & Admin
Ir Football Assn
League Mgrs Assn
Profl Footballers Assn
Profl Footballers Assn Scotland
Referees' Assn
Scot Amat Football Assn
Scot Football Assn
Scot Football League
Scot Women's Football
Football (Rugby)
Brit Amat Rugby League Assn
Ir Rugby Football U
Rugby Football League
Rugby Football U
Rugby Memorabilia Soc
Rugby Players Assn
Scot Rugby U
Welsh Rugby Players Assn
Welsh Rugby U
Football (table) > Table football
Footpaths & rights of way
Commons, Open Spaces. . . Presvn Soc
Green Lane Assn
Inst Public Rights Way Mgt
Motoring Orgs' Land Access & Recreation Assn
Offa's Dyke Assn

© CBD Research Ltd · Beckenham · BR3 5JS · Tel 020 8650 7745   E-mail cbd@cbdresearch.com · www.cbdresearch.com

Peak & Nthn Footpaths Soc
Ramblers' Assn
S Downs Soc
S W Coast Path Assn
Scot Rights Way & Access Soc
Towpath Action Gp
Trail Riders Fellowship
> + Conservation; Open spaces

Footwear: industry
Boot & Shoe Mfrs Assn
Brit Equestrian Tr Assn
Brit Footwear Assn
Textile Inst Intl

Footwear: repairs
MultiService Assn

Footwear: trade
Indep Footwear Retailers Assn
Instock Footwear Suppliers Assn
Soc Shoe Fitters

Forage > Animal feed; Grass & grassland

Forces > Armed forces & veterans: welfare;   Army; Royal Navy

Forensic accountancy
Network Indep Forensic Accountants
> + Accountancy

Forensic science
Assn Consulting Scientists
Brit Academy Forensic Sciences
Brit Assn Forensic Medicine
Brit Assn Forensic Odontology
Brit Assn Human Identification
Fac Forensic & Legal Medicine
Fingerprint Soc
Forensic Science Soc
> + Medicine: & the law

Forestry
Brit Inst Agricl Consultants
Confedn Forest Inds
FCA Membership Ltd
Horticultural Trs Assn
Inst Chart Foresters
Instn Agricl Engrs
Ir Farmers Assn
Ir Forestry & Forest Products Assn
Ir Timber Growers Assn
Permaculture Assn
R Forestry Soc England, Wales & NI
R Highland & Agricl Soc Scotland
R Scot Forestry Soc
R Welsh Agricl Soc
S England Agricl Soc
Soc Ir Foresters
Tropical Agriculture Assn
UK Forest Products Assn
> + Timber

Forestry: machinery
Agricl Engrs Assn

Forging > Metal: forming

Fork-lift trucks
Assn Indl Truck Trainers
Brit Indl Truck Assn
Fork Lift Truck Assn
Indep Training Standards Scheme & Register
> + Lifting & loading equipment

Formby (George)
George Formby Soc

Fortresses & forts
Fort Cumberland & Portsmouth Militaria Soc
Fortress Study Gp
Hillfort Study Gp
Palmerston Forts Soc
Pillbox Study Gp
Subterranea Britannica

Forwarding > Aviation; Shipping & forwarding

Fossils > Palaeontology

Fostering & foster parents
Brit Assn Adoption & Fostering
Fostering Network

Foundations (buildings)
ASUCplus
Fedn Piling Specialists
Ground Forum
Subsidence Forum
> + Building

Foundries
Foundry Eqpt Supplies Assn
Inst Cast Metals Engrs

Fountains
Fountain Soc

4x4s (4-wheel drive vehicles)
All Wheel Drive Club
Alliance Urban 4x4s
Motoring Orgs' Land Access & Recreation Assn

Fowl > Poultry

Foxes
Nat Fox Welfare Soc

Foxhounds > Hounds

Fragile X syndrome
Fragile X Soc

Fragrances
Intl Fragrance Assn UK

Frames > Concrete & concrete products; Picture framers

France
Assn Brit Tour Operators France
Assn Study Modern & Contemporary France
Fédn Britannique Alliances Françaises
Franco British Cham Comm & Ind
Franco British Soc
Franco Scottish Soc
Napoleonic Soc

France: language & literature
Anglo Norman Text Soc
Assn French Language Studies
Assn Language Learning
Assn University Professors & Heads French
Fédn Britannique Alliances Françaises
Soc French Studies

Franchising
Assn Franchised Distbrs Electronic Components
Brit Franchise Assn
Ir Franchise Assn

Free Churches > individual Churches

Free speech > Censorship

Free trade
Free Trade League

Freedom of the individual > Individual freedom

Freemasonry
Grand Lodge Antient... Masons Scotland
Utd Grand Lodge England

Freemen
Freemen England & Wales
Freemen & Glds City Chester
Gld Freemen City Lond

Freestyle dancing > Dancing

Freezing (& chilled) food > Food: frozen & chilled; Refrigeration

Freight transport
Brit Intl Freight Assn
Chart Inst Logistics & Transport
Freight Transport Assn
ICHCA Intl
Ir Intl Freight Assn
Rail Freight Gp
> + Road: haulage;   Transport

French > France: language & literature

Freshwater biology > Biology

Friedreich's Ataxia
Ataxia UK
> Ataxia

Friendly societies
Assn Financial Mutuals

Friends (Quakers)
Friends Histl Soc
Religious Society of Friends (Quakers)

Frisbees > Flying: discs (sport)

Frost (Robert)
Friends Dymock Poets

Frozen food > Food: frozen & chilled; Refrigeration

Fruit: growing
Brit Indep Fruit Growers Assn
Brit Summer Fruits
English Apples & Pears
Meiosis
NI Fruit Growers Assn
Nuclear Stock Assn
Scot Soc Crop Res

Fruit: juice
Beverage Coun Ireland
Brit Fruit Juice Assn
Brit Soft Drinks Assn

Fruit: machines > Amusements & coin operated machines

Fruit: trade
Fresh Produce Consortium
Nat Dried Fruit Tr Assn

Frying media
　　Nat Edible Oil Distbrs Assn
Fuchsias
　　Brit Fuchsia Soc
Fuel
　　Chemical Recycling Assn
　　Natural Gas Vehicle Assn
　　Renewable Energy Assn
　　> + specific fuels
Fuel ash > Ash
Fumes & fume extraction
　　Fan Mfrs' Assn
　　> + Air: conditioning & ventilation; Pollution & pollution control
Fundraisers
　　Assn Fundraising Consultants
　　Inst Fundraising
　　Public Fundraising Regulatory Assn
Funerals > Burial & cremation
Fungi > Mycology
Fur
　　Brit Fur Tr Assn
Furnace technology & construction
　　Brit Glass Mfrs Confedn
　　Brit Indl Furnace Construction Assn
　　Inst Refractories Engrs
　　Refractory Users Federation
Furnishing fabrics
　　Assn Soft Furnishers
　　Brit Interior Textiles Assn
Furniture
　　BFM Ltd
　　Brit Antique Furniture Restorers Assn
　　Brit Educl Suppliers Assn
　　Brit Furniture Confedn
　　Brit Shops & Stores Assn
　　Furniture Ind Res Assn
　　Leisure & Outdoor Furniture Assn
Furniture: contract > Contract services
Furniture: history
　　Archibald Knox Soc
　　Chippendale Soc
　　Furniture Hist Soc
Furniture: warehousing & removal
　　Brit Assn Removers
　　Movers Inst
　　Nat Gld Removers & Storers
Further education > Adult education; Education; Technical education; Universities
Furtwängler (Wilhelm)
　　Wilhelm Furtwängler Soc
Futons
　　Futon Assn
　　> + Beds & bedding
Futures & options
　　Futures & Options Assn

G

Gaelic language & culture
　　Cheshaght Ghailckagh (Yn)
　　Comunn Clàrsaich
　　Comunn Gaidhealach
　　Feisean Gaidheal
　　Gaelic Athletic Assn
　　R Celtic Soc
　　Scot Gaelic Texts Soc
　　> + Scotland: language & literature
Galliformes
　　World Pheasant Assn UK
　　> + Game & game birds
Gallipoli
　　Gallipoli Assn
Galls (plants)
　　Brit Plant Gall Soc
Galvanising
　　Galvanizers Assn
Game & game birds
　　Brit Assn Shooting & Consvn
　　Game Farmers Assn
　　Game & Wildlife Consvn Trust
　　Nat Assn Regional Game Couns [IRL]
　　Nat Game Dealers Assn
　　Nat Gamekeepers Org
　　Nat Org Beaters & Pickers Up

　　Scot Gamekeepers Assn
　　World Pheasant Assn UK
Games > Athletics; Highland games; Sports; individual sports & games
Games: equipment > Sports: equipment
Gaming
　　Casino Operators' Assn
　　Nat Casino Ind Forum
　　Remote Gambling Assn
　　> + Casinos
Garages (doors)
　　Door & Hardware Federation
Garages (equipment)
　　Forecourt Eqpt Fedn
　　Garage Eqpt Assn
　　Retail Motor Ind Fedn
　　> + Filling stations; Motor trade
Garages (waste recycling)
　　Oil Recycling Assn
Garden centres & shops
　　Garden Centre Assn
　　Ir Hardware & Bldg Materials Assn
Garden equipent & furniture > Horticulture & garden: equipment
Gardens & gardening
　　Allotments & Gardens Coun
　　Assn Gardens Trusts
　　Assn Leading Visitor Attractions
　　Brit Assn Landscape Inds
　　Cottage Garden Soc
　　E A Bowles of Myddleton House Soc
　　Fedn City Farms & Community Gardens
　　Garden Hist Soc
　　Garden Ind Mrfs Assn
　　Garden & Landscape Designers Assn [IRL]
　　Good Gardeners Assn
　　Houses Castles & Gardens Ireland
　　Japanese Garden Soc
　　Nat Coun Consvn Plants & Gardens
　　Nat Gardens Scheme Charitable Trust
　　Nat Soc Allotment & Leisure Gardeners
　　Profl Gardeners' Gld
　　R Bath & W England Soc
　　Soc Garden Designers
　　> + Horticulture; Parks & gardens
Gardens & gardening: for disabled
　　Gardening Disabled Trust
　　THRIVE
Gardens & gardening: writers
　　Garden Media Gld
Gas
　　Assn Brit Offshore Inds
　　Brit Compressed Gases Assn
　　Carbon Monoxide & Gas Safety Soc
　　Coun Registered Gas Installers
　　Energy Industries Council
　　Energy Networks Assn
　　Gas Forum
　　ICOM Energy Assn
　　Instn Gas Engrs & Mgrs
　　Nat Jt Utilities Gp
　　Offshore Contrs' Assn
　　SBGI
　　UK Offshore Oil & Gas Ind Assn
　　UK Onshore Operators Gp
　　UK Onshore Pipeline Operators' Assn
　　> + Ocean industries
Gas appliances > Domestic appliances; Gas detection
Gas chromatography
　　Chromatographic Soc
Gas detection
　　Coun Gas Detection & Envtl Monitoring
Gas engines & turbines
　　Instn Diesel & Gas Turbine Engrs
　　Natural Gas Vehicle Assn
Gaskell (Mrs Elizabeth Cleghorn)
　　Gaskell Soc
Gaskets
　　Gasket Cutters Assn
Gastroenterology
　　Brit Soc Gastroenterology
　　GIST Support UK
Gates > Automatic gates;　Stairs: gates & barriers (for)
Guarantees (home improvements) > Warranty against work under guarantee
Gaucher disease
　　Gauchers Assn
Gauges
　　Gauge & Tool Makers Assn

© CBD Research Ltd · Beckenham · BR3 5JS · Tel 020 8650 7745 · E-mail cbd@cbdresearch.com · www.cbdresearch.com

Pressure Gauge & Dial Thermometer Assn
> + Control engineering
Gay organisations > Homosexuality
Gears
Brit Gear Assn
Geese
Brit Poultry Coun
Brit Waterfowl Assn
> + Poultry
Gemstones
Brit Jewellers Assn
Gemmological Assn
Gender dysphoria > Transsexuality & transvestism
Genealogy
Anglo German Family Hist Soc
Assn Family Hist Socs Wales
Assn Genealogists & Researchers in Archives
Assn Profl Genealogists Ireland
Assn Scot Genealogists & Researchers Archives
Catholic Family Hist Soc
Fedn Family Hist Socs
Harleian Soc
Heraldry Soc
Inst Heraldic & Genealogical Studies
Ir Family Hist Soc
Ir Genealogical Res Soc
NI Family Hist Soc
Scot Assn Family Hist Socs
Scot Genealogy Soc
Soc Genealogists
Ulster Histl Foundation
> + Heraldry
General practitioners > Hospitals; Medical: practice
Generators (electrical power)
Assn Mfrs Power generating Systems
> + Electricity
Generic medicines
Brit Generic Mfrs Assn
> + Pharmaceuticals
Genetically modified crops & food
GeneWatch
GM Freeze
Genetics
BioIndustry Assn
Brit Livestock Genetics Consortium Ltd
Brit Soc Gene Therapy
Brit Soc Human Genetics
Genetic Alliance
Genetics Soc
Human Genetics Alert
Soc Gen Microbiology
Genito-urinary medicine
Brit Assn Sexual Health & HIV
Brit Fedn Sexually Transmitted Diseases
Brit HIV Assn
Soc Sexual Health Advisers
Genomics > Genetics
Geography
Assn Geographic Inf
Geographical Assn
Geographical Soc Ireland
Manchester Geographical Soc
R Geographical Soc
R Scot Geographical Soc
Scot Assn Geography Teachers
Systematics Assn
Geology
Earth Science Teachers' Assn
Edinburgh Geological Soc
GeoConservationUK
Geological Soc
Geologists' Assn
Inst Geologists Ireland
Ir Assn Economic Geology
Ir Geological Assn
Mineral Ind Res Org
Remote Sensing & Photogrammetry Soc
Tertiary Res Gp
Yorkshire Geological Soc
> + Earth sciences, structure & resources; Palaeontology
Geomembranes
Brit Geomembrane Assn
Geomorphology
GeoConservationUK
Geological Soc
> + Geography

Geophysics
R Astronomical Soc
George Cross
Victoria Cross & George Cross Assn
Geospatial engineering
Chart Instn Civil Engg Surveyors
Geotechnics
Assn Geotechnical & Geoenvironmental Specialists
Brit Geotechnical Assn
Ground Forum
Soc Underwater Technology
Geraniums & pelargoniums > Pelargoniums
Gerbils
Nat Gerbil Soc
Geriatrics & ageing
Assn Educ & Ageing
Brit Assn Service Elderly
Brit Geriatrics Soc
Brit Longevity Soc
Brit Soc Gerodontology
Brit Soc Gerontology
Brit Soc Res Ageing
Relatives & Residents Assn
> + Old people's organisations
German > Germany: language & literature
German measles (Rubella)
Sense
Germany
Anglo German Family Hist Soc
Brit Cham Comm Germany
Brit German Assn
German-Brit Cham Ind & Comm
German Hist Soc
German Rly Soc
Germany: language & literature
Assn German Studies
Assn Language Learning
Germany: law
Brit-German Jurists' Assn
Gestalt therapy
UK Assn Gestalt Practitioners
Ghosts
Assn Scientific Study Anomalous Phenomena
> + Paranormal & psychical research
Gibson (Wilfred)
Friends Dymock Poets
Gift vouchers & cards
UK Gift Card & Voucher Assn
Gifted children > Children: gifted
Gifts (public) > Donations (public)
Giftware
Brit Allied Trs Fedn
Brit Ceramic Confedn
Brit Ceramic Gift & Tableware Mfrs' Assn
Giftware Assn
Wales Craft Coun
Gilbert (Sir William Schwenk)
Gilbert & Sullivan Soc
Gilding
Brit Antique Furniture Restorers Assn
Gin & vodka
Gin & Vodka Assn
> + Wines & spirits trade
Gipsies > Gypsies & travelling people
Girls organisations > Youth organisation headings
Gladiolus
Brit Gladiolus Soc
Glamour items > Cosmetic items (collecting)
Glass & glazing
Brit Glass Mfrs Confedn
Flat Glass Mfrs Assn
Glass & Glazing Fedn
Nat Fedn Glaziers
Soc Glass Technology
Glass blowing/making/collecting
Brit Soc Scientific Glassblowers
Carnival Glass Soc
Contemporary Glass Soc
Glass Assn
Scot Glass Soc
Glass engraving
Contemporary Glass Soc
Gld Glass Engravers
Glass painting
Brit Soc Master Glass Painters
Glass & Glazing Fedn
Kempe Soc

Glassfibre
    Intl Glassfibre Reinforced Concrete Assn
Glasshouse crops > Horticulture
Glasshouses & conservatories
    Glass & Glazing Fedn
Glassware
    Assn Hist Glass
    Contemporary Glass Soc
    Glass Circle
Glassware: scientific
    Brit Soc Scientific Glassblowers
    > + Laboratory equipment & technology
Glazing > Glass & glazing
Gliding & soaring
    Brit Gliding Assn
    Scot Gliding U
    Vintage Glider Club
    > + Hang gliding
Global warming > Climate
Glosa
    Glosa Educ Org
Gloves
    Brit Glove Assn
Glue sniffing > Solvent abuse
Glulam (glued laminated timber)
    Glued Laminated Timber Assn
Glycogen storage disease
    Assn Glycogen Storage Diseases
GM crops & food > Genetically modified crops & food
Gnomonics > Sundials
Go
    Brit Go Assn
Goats
    Anglo Nubian Breed Soc
    Bagot Goat Soc
    Brit Angora Goat Soc
    Brit Goat Soc
    Brit Veterinary Assn
    English Goat Breeders Assn
    Golden Guernsey Goat Soc
    Harness Goat Soc
    Pygmy Goat Club
Goethe (Johann Wolfgang von)
    English Goethe Soc
Gold (dealing in) > Bullion dealing
Gold panning
    Brit Goldpanning Assn
Goldsmiths & silversmiths
    Brit Allied Trs Fedn
    Brit Cutlery & Silverware Assn
    Company Goldsmiths Dublin
    Contemporary British Silversmiths
    Inst Profl Goldsmiths
    Nat Assn Goldsmiths
Golf
    Assn Golf Writers
    Brit Golf Collectors' Soc
    England Golf
    Golf Club GB
    Golf Club Mgrs Assn
    Golf Consultants Assn
    Golf U Wales
    Golfing U Ireland
    Ir Ladies Golf U
    Ladies' Golf U
    Nat Golf Clubs Advy Assn
    Profl Golfers Assn
    R & Ancient Golf Club
    Scot Golf U
    Scot Ladies' Golfing Assn
Golf courses
    Brit Assn Golf Course Constructors
    Brit & Intl Golf Greenkeepers' Assn
    Nat Assn Public Golf Clubs & Courses
    Sports Turf Res Inst
    UK Golf Course Owners Assn
    > + Sportsgrounds & synthetic surfaces
Golf equipment
    Brit Golf Ind Assn
Goon Show
    Goon Show Preservation Soc
Gothic literature > Horror literature
Gout
    Purine Metabolic Patients Assn
    UK Gout Soc
Government > Parliamentary government

Government: accountability
    Transparency Intl (UK)
Graduates in business > Commerce
Graffiti
    Anti-Graffiti Assn
Grahame (Kenneth)
    Kenneth Grahame Soc
Grain
    Grain & Feed Tr Assn
    Ir Grain & Feed Assn
    NI Grain Tr Assn
    Scot Corn Tr Assn
    > + Agriculture: merchants;   Flour
Grainger (Percy Aldridge)
    Percy Grainger Society
Grammar schools
    Nat Grammar Schools Assn
    > + Education;   Independent & public schools
Grandparents
    Grandparents Action Gp
    Grandparents Assn
    > + Parents
Granite
    Stone Fedn
Grapes > Wines & viticulture
Graphic arts & design
    Brit Assn Print & Communication
    Chart Soc Designers
    Soc Graphic Fine Art
    > + Industrial graphics; Printing headings
Graphology & graphoanalysis
    Assn Qualified Graphologists
    Brit Astrological & Psychic Soc
    Brit Inst Graphologists
Grass & grassland
    Brit Grassland Soc
    Ir Grassland Assn
    N Scotland Grassland Soc
    > + Seeds; Sportsgrounds & synthetic surfaces; Turf
Gravel > Sand & gravel
Grease > Lubricants
Great Bustard
    Great Bustard Gp
Greece
    Anglo Hellenic League
    Brit Hellenic Cham Comm
    Greek Inst
    Soc Promotion Hellenic Studies
    > + Classical studies
Green lanes/roads > Footpaths & rights of way
Greenhouses > Glasshouses & conservatories
Greeting cards
    Greeting Card Assn
Greville (Fulke)
    Fulke Greville Soc
Greyhounds
    Brit Veterinary Assn
    Fedn Brit Greyhound Owners Assns
    Greyhound Action
    Greyhound Trainers Assn
Grief > Bereavement
Grieg (Edvard Hagerup)
    Grieg Soc
Grills & security shutters
    Brit Blind & Shutter Assn
    > + Doors; Windows: blinds & shutters
Grinding & milling machinery
    Solids Handling & Processing Assn
Grit > Aggregates
Grocery & provision trade
    Assn Convenience Stores
    Convenience Stores & Newsagents Assn [IRL]
    Fedn Whls Distbrs
    Inst Grocery Distbn
    NISA Today's Holdings Ltd
    Provision Tr Fedn
    RGDATA [IRL]
    Scot Food Trs Assn
    Scot Grocers Fedn
    Scot Whls Assn
    > + Food
Grooms & grooming (pets)
    Brit Grooms Assn
    Pet Care Tr Assn
Grottoes
    Folly Fellowship

Groundnuts
Fedn Oils, Seeds & Fats Assns
Groundsmen
Inst Groundsmanship
> + Sportsgrounds & synthetic surfaces
Group analysis
Group Analytic Soc
Inst Gp Analysis
Grouse > Game & game birds
Grouts & grouting
UK Quality Ash Assn
Growth
Child Growth Foundation
Prader-Willi Syndrome Assn
Restricted Growth Assn
Tall Persons Club
Turner Syndrome Support Soc
Guanacos > Camelids
Guarantee > Warranty protection
Guard & patrol services
Brit Security Ind Assn
Guardians (educational) > Education: guardians
Guernsey (Channel Islands)
Guernsey Cham Comm
Guernsey Growers Assn
Société Guernesiaise
Guide dogs
Guide Dogs for Blind Assn
Seeing Dogs Alliance
Guide lecturers > Travel & tourism: guides
Guides (girls) > Youth organisation headings
Guillain Barré syndrome
Guillain Barre Syndrome Support Gp
Guinea pigs > Cavies
Guitars
Electric Guitar Appreciation Soc
Gulf War veterans
Nat Gulf Veterans & Families Assn
Gums > Resins & gums
Guns & ammunition
Gun Tr Assn
Histl Breechloading Smallarms Assn
Ordnance Soc
> + Shooting
Guttering
Metal Gutter Mfrs Assn
Gwenllian (Princess of Wales)
Princess Gwenllian Soc
Gymnasium: equipment
Fitness Ind Assn
Sports & Fitness Eqpt Assn
Gymnastics
Brit Gymnastics
Scot Gymnastics Assn
Welsh Amat Gymnastics Assn
> + Physical education
Gynaecology > Maternity; Obstetrics & gynaecology
Gypsies & travelling people
Nat Assn Teachers Travellers
Gypsum
Gypsum Products Devt Assn

H

Hacks > Horse(s) headings
Haematology
Brit Blood Transfusion Soc
Brit Hypertension Soc
Brit Microcirculation Soc
Brit Soc Haematology
Haemochromatosis Soc
Haemophilia
Haemophilia Soc
Haggard (Sir (Henry) Rider
Rider Haggard Soc
Haiku
Brit Haiku Soc
Time Haiku
Hailstorms
Tornado & Storm Res Org
Hair & scalp treatment
Hairline Intl
Inst Trichologists

Hairdressing
Freelance Hair & Beauty Fedn
Hairdressing & Beauty Suppliers Assn
Inc Gld Hairdressers
Nat Assn Screen Makeup Artists & Hairdressers
Nat Hairdressers Fedn
Ham > Bacon
Hammer-throwing
Hammer Circle
Hampden (John)
John Hampden Soc
Hand driers (warm air)
Brit Warm Air Hand Drier Assn
Hand knitting > Knitting
Hand tools > Tools
Handbags
Brit Travelgoods & Accessories Assn
> + Leathergoods
Handball
England Handball Assn
Gaelic Athletic Assn
Scot Handball Assn
Handbell ringing
Handbell Ringers
> + Bellringing
Handcycling
Handcycling Assn
Handicapped persons > Children: handicapped;   Disablement
Handicraft > Crafts & craftsmanship
Handley Page
Handley Page Assn
Handling > Materials: management/handling
Hands
Brit Soc Surgery Hand
Handwriting
Calligraphy & Lettering Arts Soc
Soc Italic Handwriting
Soc Limners
Soc Scribes & Illuminators
> + Graphology & graphoanalysis
Hang gliding
Brit Hang Gliding & Paragliding Assn
Scot Hang Gliding & Paragliding Fedn
> + Gliding & soaring
Harassment
Nat Assn Support Victims Stalking & Harassment
Harbours > Ports; Yachts & yachting
Hardmetal > Metal
Hardware & housewares
Brit Hardware Fedn
Brit Home Enhancement Tr Assn
Brit Indep Retailers Assn
Cookshop & Housewares Assn
Cutlery & Allied Trs Res Assn
Door & Hardware Federation
Ir Hardware & Bldg Materials Assn
> + Building materials & supplies
Hardwoods
Timber Tr Fedn
> + Timber
Hardy (Thomas)
Dorset Natural Hist & Archaeol Soc
Thomas Hardy Soc
Hares
Game & Wildlife Consvn Trust
Harmonicas
Nat Harmonica League
Harness racing
Brit Harness Racing Club
Harps & harp playing
Comunn Clàrsaich
UK Harp Assn
Hat pins
Hat Pin Soc
Hatcheries
Pullet Hatcheries Assn
Haulage > Freight transport; Road: haulage
Hauntings > Paranormal & psychical research
Hawks & hawking
Brit Falconers' Club
Brit Hawking Assn
Hawk & Owl Trust
Scot Assn Country Sports
> + Birds
Hay & straw
Brit Hay & Straw Mchts' Assn

Haydn (Franz Joseph)
    Haydn Soc
Hayfever > Allergy
Hazards > Home: safety; Road: safety & control; Safety
Hazel nuts
    Combined Edible Nut Tr Assn
Head & neck injury & disease
    Brit Assn Head & Neck Oncologists
    Brit Assn Otorhinolaryngologists
    Brit Soc Oral & Maxillofacial Pathology
    Cranio Sacral Soc
    Craniofacial Soc
    Craniosacral Therapy Assn
    Headlines
    > + Brain injury & research
Headaches > Migraine & headaches

Heads of schools & colleges
    Assn Headteachers & Deputes Scotland
    Assn School & College Leaders
    Girls Schools Assn
    Headmasters & Headmistresses Conf
    Nat Assn Head Teachers
    School Leaders Scotland
    Soc Heads Indep Schools
    > + Teachers
Headwear > Protective clothing/equipment
Healing
    Assn Therapeutic Healers
    Brit Soc Dowsers
    Confedn Healing Orgs
    > + Complementary medicine; Medicine headings
Health
    Alliance Natural Health
    Brit Assn Sport & Exercise Sciences
    Gld Health Writers
    Inst Health Promotion & Educ
    McCarrison Soc
    UK Public Health Assn
    > + other aspects of health
Health administration
    Assn Healthcare Communications
    Inst Healthcare Mgt
    > + National Health Service
Health care
    Brit Healthcare Business Intelligence Assn
    CNK Alliance
    Fedn Healthcare Science
    HL7 UK Ltd
    Nat Assn Primary Care
    Telecare Services Assn
    Welsh Hospitals & Health Services Assn
Health care: equipment & supplies
    Assn Brit Healthcare Inds
    Brit Assn Pharmaceutical Whlsrs
    Brit Healthcare Trs Assn
    Health Care Supply Assn
    Ir Med Devices Assn
    Performance Textiles Assn
    Performance Textiles Assn
    Pharmaceutical & Healthcare Sciences Soc
Health & fitness > Fitness
Health food
    Consumers Health Choice
    Health Food Inst
    Health Food Mfrs Assn
    Nat Assn Health Stores
    > + Food
Health records
    Inst Health Record & Inf Mgt
Health resorts > Spas
Health & safety
    Health & Safety Sign Assn
    Indep Safety Consultants Assn
    Safety Pass Alliance
    > + subject concerned eg Health
Hearing
    Brit Academy Audiology
    Brit Assn Audiovestibular Physicians
    Brit Soc Audiology
    Brit Soc Hearing Aid Audiologists
    Brit Tinnitus Assn
    > + Deafness
Heart disease > Cardiology
Heat treatment
    Inst Materials, Minerals & Mining
    Surface Engg Assn

Heat pumps
    Heat Pump Assn
Heath (Edward) [Ted]
    Ted Heath Musical Appreciation Soc
Heaths & heathers
    Brit Heather Growers Assn
    Heather Soc
    Horticultural Trs Assn
Heating
    Assn Plumbing & Heating Contrs
    BEAMA
    Building Services Res & Inf Assn
    Chart Inst Plumbing & Heating Engg
    Chart Instn Bldg Services Engrs
    Combined Heat & Power Assn
    Commissioning Specialists Assn
    Fedn Heating Spares Stockists
    Heat Pump Assn
    Heating, Ventilating & Air Conditioning Mfrs' Assn
    Heating & Ventilating Contrs Assn
    Hose Mfrs & Suppliers Assn
    ICOM Energy Assn
    Inst Domestic Heating... Engrs
    Nat Assn Profl Inspectors & Testers
    Oil Firing Technical Assn Petroleum Ind
    SBGI
    Scot & NI Plumbing Emplrs' Fedn
    Stove Ind Alliance
    > + Air: conditioning & ventilating

Hebe
    Hebe Soc
Hedgehogs
    Brit Hedgehog Presvn Soc
Hedges & hedge-laying
    Hedge Laying Assn Ireland
    Hedgeline
    Horticultural Trs Assn
    Nat Hedgelaying Soc
Helicopters
    Brit Helicopter Advy Bd
    R Aeronautical Soc
    > + Aerial survey & photography; Aviation
Hellenic studies > Classical studies
Helplines
    Helplines Assn
    > + specific area of interest
Hemerocallis > Hostas & Hemerocallis
Hemp
    Hemp Lime Construction Products Assn
Hens > Poultry
Henty (George Alfred)
    Henty Soc
Heraldry
    Harleian Soc
    Heraldry Soc
    Heraldry Soc Scotland
    Inst Heraldic & Genealogical Studies
    Soc Heraldic Arts
    > + Genealogy
Herbal infusions
    UK Herbal Infusions Assn
Herbicides > Agriculture: chemicals
Herbs & herbal medicine
    Assn Master Herbalists
    Brit Herb Tr Assn
    Brit Herbal Medicine Assn
    Consumers Health Choice
    Herb Soc
    Intl Register Consultant Herbalists & Homoeopaths
    Nat Inst Med Herbalists
    Register Chinese Herbal Medicine
Herpes
    Congenital CMV Assn
    Herpes Viruses Assn
    Shingles Support Soc
Herpetology
    Brit Herpetological Soc
    Fedn Brit Herpetologists
    Reptile & Exotic Pet Tr Assn
Herring
    Herring Buyers Assn
    > + Fish headings; Fishing
Herschel (Sir [Frederick] William)
    William Herschel Soc

© CBD Research Ltd · Beckenham · BR3 5JS · Tel 020 8650 7745 · E-mail cbd@cbdresearch.com · www.cbdresearch.com

Hides & skins
>		Soc Leather Technologists & Chemists
>		> + Leather
Hi-fi > Radio & TV trade; Sound recording & reproduction
Higden (Ranulf/Ralph)
>		Ranulf Higden Soc
Higher education > Education; Technical education; Universities
Highland dancing
>		Brit Assn Teachers Dancing
>		Edinburgh Highland Reel & Strathspey Soc
>		Imperial Soc Teachers Dancing
>		R Scot Country Dance Soc
>		Scot Dance Teachers Alliance
>		Scot Official Highland Dancing Assn
>		UK Alliance Profl Teachers Dancing. . .
>		> + Dancing
Highland games
>		Scot Highland Games Assn
Highway > Road headings
Hill farming
>		Blackface Sheep Breeders Assn
>		> + Agriculture
Hill (Octavia)
>		Octavia Hill Soc
Hill running > Running
Hill walking > Walking
Hillclimbs (motorcycling)
>		Nat Hillclimb Assn
>		> + Motor cycling & scooter riding
Hillforts > Fortresses & forts
Hilton (James)
>		James Hilton Soc
Hip (diseases of)
>		Brit Orthopaedic Assn
>		Perthes Assn
>		STEPS
Hire purchase > Credit trade
Hispanists > Portugal; Spain
Historic aircraft > Aviation: history
Historic buildings
>		Ancient Monuments Soc
>		Architectural Heritage Soc Scotland
>		Assn Local Govt Archaeol Officers
>		Assn Studies Consvn Historic Bldgs
>		Brit Assn Friends Museums
>		Campaign Protection Rural Wales
>		Charles Rennie Mackintosh Soc
>		Fortress Study Gp
>		Heritage Alliance
>		Historic Houses Assn
>		Historic Towns Forum
>		Houses Castles & Gardens Ireland
>		Inst Consvn Historic &. . . Works Ireland
>		Inst Historic Bldg Consvn
>		Jt C'ee Nat Amenity Socs
>		Listed Property Owners Club
>		Medieval Settlement Res Gp
>		Nat Assn Field Studies Officers
>		Nat Trust
>		Nat Trust Ireland
>		Nat Trust Scotland
>		Save Britain's Heritage
>		Scot Vernacular Bldgs Working Gp
>		Soc Antiquaries Lond
>		Soc Protection Ancient Bldgs
>		UK Assn Presvn Trusts
>		Vernacular Architecture Gp
>		> + Archaeology: county societies; Architecture; Church:
>		buildings; Castles; Conservation: area organisations
Historic vehicles > Motor vehicles: historic
Historical documents & records > Archives; Record agents;   Records: historical
History
>		Assn Hist & Computing
>		Brit Academy
>		Fedn Local History Socs [IRL]
>		Histl Assn
>		History Curriculum Assn
>		London Medieval Soc
>		Oral Hist Soc
>		R Histl Soc
>		Scot Assn Teachers History
>		Scot Hist Soc
>		Soc Genealogists
>		Social Hist Curators Gp
>		Social Hist Soc
>		> + Archaeology; other headings with 'history' as a sub-heading
HIV positive > Genito-urinary medicine

Hobbies
>		Brit Toy & Hobby Assn
>		> + object of interest
Hockey
>		England Hockey
>		Ir Hockey Assn
>		Scot Hockey U
>		Ulster Hockey U
>		Welsh Hockey U
>		> + Ice hockey; Skating: board, inline & roller
Hodgkin's disease
>		Lymphoma Assn
Hoists
>		Construction Plant-hire Assn
>		Materials Handling Engrs Assn
Holiday camps & centres
>		Assn Heads Outdoor Educ Centres
>		Brit Activity Holiday Assn
>		Holiday Centres Assn
>		Indep Holiday Hostels Ireland
Holiday property owners > Self catering
Holiday resorts
>		Brit Resorts & Destinations Assn
>		Tourism Mgt Inst
Holiday timesharing > Timeshare industry
Holidays > Travel & tourism
Holistic medicine & therapy
>		Assn Holistic Biodynamic Massage Therapists
>		Assn Reflexologists
>		Brit Holistic Med Assn
>		Fedn Holistic Therapists
>		Holistic Healers Assn
>		> + Complementary medicine
Holland > Netherlands

Holmes (Sherlock)
>		Friends Dr Watson
>		Sherlock Holmes Soc Lond
Holography
>		R Photographic Soc
Home: care > Domiciliary care
Home: confinements > Maternity
Home: decoration
>		Home Decoration Retailers Assn
>		Nat Home Improvement Coun
>		> + Paint; Wallcoverings & wallpaper
Home: equity release schemes
>		Safe Home Income Plans
Home: laundering
>		Home Laundering Consultative Coun
>		> + Laundering & dry cleaning
Home: safety
>		Inst Home Safety
Home: shopping
>		Catalogue Exchange
>		> + Mail order trade
Home: working from
>		Home Business Alliance
>		Telework Assn
Homeless
>		Homeless Link
>		Salvation Army
>		Scot Coun Single Homeless
>		Shelter
Homes > Housing; Nursing homes; Social service
Homeworkers > Home: working from
Homing pigeons > Pigeons
Homoeopathy
>		Action Homeopathy
>		Alliance Registered Homeopaths
>		Brit Assn Homoeopathic Mfrs
>		Brit Assn Homoeopathic Veterinary Surgeons
>		Brit Homeopathic Dental Assn
>		Brit Homeopathic Assn
>		Fac Homeopathy
>		Homeopathic Med Assn
>		Intl Register Consultant Herbalists & Homoeopaths
>		Soc Homeopaths
Homosexuality
>		Campaign Homosexual Equality
>		Consortium Lesbian Gay. . . Community Orgs
Honey
>		Honey Assn
Hong Kong
>		Brit Cham Comm Hong Kong
>		Hong Kong Assn
>		Hong Kong Soc

Hoods (academical)
    Burgon Soc
Hoof trimmers
    Nat Assn Cattle Foot Trimmers
Hopkins (Gerard Manley)
    Hopkins Soc
Hoppers > Silos & hoppers
Hops
    Brewery Hist Soc
    Hop Mchts Assn
    Nat Hop Assn England
Horace [Quintus Horatius Flaccus]
    Horatian Soc
Hormone study & related diseases > Endocrinology
Hormone replacement therapy (HRT)
    Brit Menopause Soc
Horns (musical instruments)
    Brit Horn Soc
Horology
    Antiquarian Horological Soc
    Brit Allied Trs Fedn
    Brit Horological Inst
    Brit Jewellers Assn
    Brit Sundial Soc
    Brit Watch & Clock Makers Gld
    MultiService Assn
    Nat Assn Goldsmiths
Horror literature
    Brit Fantasy Soc
    Dracula Soc
Horse: brasses
    Nat Horse Brass Soc
Horse: racing
    Amat Jockeys Assn
    Brit Harness Racing Club
    Fedn Bloodstock Agents
    Fedn Racecourse Bookmakers
    Horserace Writers & Photographers Assn
    Horseracing Sponsors Assn
    Ir Thoroughbred Breeders Assn
    Nat Assn Stable Staff
    Nat Trainers Fedn
    Permit Trainers Assn
    Point-to-Point Owners & Riders Assn
    Profl Jockeys Assn
    Racecourse Assn
    Racehorse Owners Assn
    Racehorse Transporters Assn
Horses: riding & driving
    Assn Brit Riding Schools
    Brit Driving Soc
    Brit Equestrian Fedn
    Brit Horse Driving Trials Assn
    Brit Horse Soc
    Brit Show Horse Assn
    Brit Show Pony Soc
    Endurance GB
    Event Horse Owners Assn
    Event Riders Assn
    Horse Rangers Assn
    Horsescotland
    London Harness Horse Parade Soc
    Medical Equestrian Assn
    Mounted Games Assn
    Nat Fedn Bridleway Assns
    Point-to-Point Owners & Riders Assn
    Riding Disabled Assn
    Scot Assn Country Sports
    Scot Carriage Driving Assn
    Scot Sports Horse
    Scurry Driving Assn
    Side Saddle Assn
    Standardbred & Trotting Horse Assn
    Trekking & Riding Soc Scotland
    UK Chasers & Riders Ltd
    Wales Trekking & Riding Assn
    Western Equestrian Soc
    Western Horsemens Assn
    > + American 'West'
Horses & ponies
    Brit Equestrian Fedn
    Brit Equestrian Tr Assn
    Brit Horse Soc
    Equine Behaviour Forum
    Equine Shiatsu Assn
    Equine Sports Massage Assn
    Horse Sport Ireland

    Nat Pony Soc
    Ponies Assn
    Pony Club
    Pony Riders Assn
    Soc Welfare Horses & Ponies
    Thoroughbred Breeders' Assn
    Veteran Horse Soc
    > + Cattle & livestock; Pony trekking
Horses & ponies: breed societies
    Akhal Teke
    American Quarter Horse Assn
    American Saddlebred Assn
    Arab Horse Soc
    Brit Appaloosa Soc
    Brit Assn Purebred Spanish Horse
    Brit Camargue Horse Soc
    Brit Connemara Pony Soc
    Brit Hanoverian Horse Soc
    Brit Miniature Horse Soc
    Brit Morgan Horse Soc
    Brit Palomino Soc
    Brit Percheron Horse Soc
    Brit Skewbald & Piebald Assn
    Brit Spotted Pony Soc
    Brit Tersk Soc
    Caspian Breed Soc
    Caspian Horse Soc
    Cleveland Bay Horse Soc
    Clydesdale Horse Soc
    Coloured Horse & Pony Soc
    Connemara Pony Breeders Soc [IRL]
    Crabbet Org
    Dales Pony Soc
    Dartmoor Pony Soc
    Donkey Breed Soc
    Dun Horse & Pony Soc
    Eriskay Pony Mother Studbook Soc
    Eriskay Pony Soc
    Exmoor Pony Soc
    Fell Pony Soc
    Fjord Horse Nat Stud Book Assn
    Friesian Horse Assn
    Glasgow Agricl Soc
    Gypsy Cob Soc
    Hackney Horse Soc
    Haflinger Soc
    Highland Pony Soc
    Icelandic Horse Soc
    Ir Draught Horse Soc
    Lipizzaner Nat Stud Book Assn GB
    Lipizzaner Soc
    Lusitano Breed Soc
    Nat Stallion Assn
    New Forest Pony . . . & Cattle Soc
    Pony Breeders Shetland Assn
    Shetland Pony Stud-Book Soc
    Shire Horse Soc
    Southern Counties Heavy Horse Assn
    Sport Horse Breeding
    Suffolk Horse Soc
    Trakehner Breeders Fraternity
    UK Paint Horse Assn
    Utd Saddlebred Assn
    Warmblood Breeders' Studbook - UK
    Welsh Pony & Cob Soc
    Wessex Heavy Horse Soc
Horses & ponies: dentistry
    Brit Assn Equine Dental Technicians
Horses & ponies: grooms
    Brit Grooms Assn
Horseball
    Brit Horseball Assn
Horseboxes & trailers
    Org Horsebox & Trailer Owners
Horticulture
    Brit Inst Agricl Consultants
    Brit Protected Ornamentals Assn
    Cardigan County Agricl Soc
    Comml Horticl Assn
    Derbyshire Agricl & Horticl Soc
    Flowers & Plants Assn
    Garden Centre Assn
    Gld Horticultural Tr Display Judges
    Guernsey Growers Assn
    Horticultural Exhibitors Assn
    Horticultural Trs Assn
    Inst Horticulture

© CBD Research Ltd · Beckenham · BR3 5JS · Tel 020 8650 7745   E-mail cbd@cbdresearch.com · www.cbdresearch.com

Ir Farmers Assn
N England Horticl Soc
N England Rosecarpe Horticl Soc
Nat Coun Consvn Plants & Gardens
Nat Farmers U
Nuclear Stock Assn
R Bath & W England Soc
R Botanical & Hortl Soc Manchester
R Caledonian Horticl Soc
R Guernsey Agricl & Horticl Soc
R Horticl Soc
R Horticl Soc Ireland
R Welsh Agricl Soc
S England Agricl Soc
Scot Seed & Nursery Tr Assn
Shropshire & W Midlands Agricl Soc
Soc Botanical Artists
Westmorland County Agricl Soc
Women's Farm & Garden Assn
> + Agriculture: county societies; Gardens & gardening; Landscape

Horticulture: disabled > Gardens & gardening: for disabled
Horticulture: education
Landex
Principals' Profl Coun
Horticulture & garden: equipment
Agricl Engrs Assn
Brit Agricl & Garden Machinery Assn
Brit Indep Retailers Assn
Farm Machinery Presvn Soc
Fedn Brit Hand Tool Mfrs
Garden Ind Mrfs Assn
GARDENEX
Leisure & Outdoor Furniture Assn
Vintage Horticl & Garden Machinery Club
> + Agriculture: machinery
Hoses (flexible)
Hose Mfrs & Suppliers Assn
Hosiery
Knitting Inds Fedn
Hospices
Assn Children's Hospices
Hospitality
Assn Business Executives
Assn Events Mgt Educ
Brit Hospitality Assn
Consortium Caterers Educ Hospitality. . .
Foodservice Consultants Soc Intl
Inst Hospitality
Profl Assn Catering Educ
> + Catering, Corporate hospitality; Hotels & restaurants; Shows & events
Hospitals
Assn Dental Hospitals
Community Hospitals Assn
Scot Assn Community Hospitals
Hospitals: administrative staff
Hospital Caterers Assn
Nat Assn Healthcare Fire Officers
Soc Hospital Linen Service & Laundry Mgrs
UK Housekeepers Assn
> + National Health Service
Hospitals: broadcasting
Nat Assn Hospital Broadcasting Orgs
Hospitals: contributory schemes
Brit Health Care Assn
Hospitals: decontamination & cleaning
Assn Healthcare Cleaning Profls
Healthcare Infection Soc
Inst Decontamination Sciences
Hospitals: engineering & equipment
Inst Healthcare Engg & Estate Mgt
Hospitals: medical staff
Assn Perioperative Practice
College Emergency Medicine
College Operating Dept Practitioners
Hospital Consultants & Specialists Assn
Ir Hospital Consultants Assn
Hospitals: nursing staff > Nursing
Hospitals: patients > Patients
Hospitals: veterinary
Brit Veterinary Hospitals Assn
Hostas & hemerocallis
Brit Hosta & Hemerocallis Soc
Hardy Plant Soc
Hostels (bail) > Probation service
Hot air balloons > Balloons & airships

Hot air engines
Stirling Engine Soc
Hot tubs
Brit & Ir Spa & Hot Tub Assn
Hot water storage & supply > Heating
Hotel accountants
Brit Assn Hospitality Accountants
Hotels & restaurants
Assn Valuers Licensed Property
Brit Assn Hotel Representatives
Brit Hospitality Assn
Fedn Specialist Restaurants
Hotel Booking Agents Assn
Inst Hospitality
Inst Hotel Security Mgt
Ir Hospitality Inst
Ir Hotels Fedn
NI Hotels Fedn
Restaurant Property Advisors Soc
Restaurants Assn Ireland
Sustainable Restaurant Assn
Hound trailing
Hound Trailing Assn
Hounds
Assn Masters Harriers & Beagles
Masters Basset Hounds Assn
Masters Deerhounds Assn
Masters Draghounds & Bloodhounds Assn
Masters Foxhounds Assn
Peterborough R Foxhound Show Soc
> + Hunts & hunting
House alarm systems > Intruder alarms; Security
House building > Building
House/flat maintenance
Upkeep
House plants > Indoor & houseplants; Horticulture; individual plant
Household distribution
Direct Marketing Assn
Household textiles > Textile headings
Housekeepers
UK Housekeepers Assn
Houses open to the public > Historic buildings
Housewares > Hardware & housewares
Housewives
Nat Women's Register
> + Women's organisations
Housing
Chart Inst Housing
Community Housing Cymru
Confedn Co-operative Housing
Good Homes Alliance
Housing Inst Ireland
Nat Assn Bldg Co-ops [IRL]
Nat Housing Fedn
NI Fedn Housing Assns
R Envtl Health Inst Scotland
ROOM RTPI
Scot Fedn Housing Assns
> + Building societies; Tenants & residents
Housman (A E) & family
Housman Soc
Hovercraft
Hovercraft Club
Hovercraft Search & Rescue UK
Hovercraft Soc
Howells (Herbert)
Herbert Howells Soc
Huguenots
Huguenot Soc
Human identification
Brit Assn Human Identification
Human relationships
Soc Companion Animal Studies
Human rights > Individual freedom
Humanism
AHS
Brit Humanist Assn
Humanist Assn Ireland
Humanist Soc Scotland
Nat Secular Soc
Rationalist Assn
S Place Ethical Soc
Humanities
Humanities Assn
Humidity control
Heating, Ventilating & Air Conditioning Mfrs' Assn
> + Air: conditioning & ventilating

Hungary
    Brit Cham Comm Hungary
    Brit-Hungarian Soc
Huntington's disease
    Huntington's Disease Assn
    Scot Huntington's Assn
Hunts & hunting
    Coun Hunting Assns
    Countryside Alliance
    Countryside Alliance Ireland
    Hunting Assn Ireland
    Ir Coun Blood Sports
    U Country Sports Workers
    Utd Counties Agricl & Hunters Soc
    > + Hounds
Hurdy-gurdy
    Hurdy Gurdy Soc
Hurling (sport)
    Gaelic Athletic Assn
Hydraulics & hydromechanics
    Brit Fluid Power Assn
    Brit Fluid Power Distbrs Assn
Hydrocephalus > Spina bifida & hydrocephalus
Hydrogen fluoride
    Chemical Inds Assn
Hydrology > Water
Hydromechanics > Hydraulics & hydromechanics
Hydropower > Water: power; Renewable energy
Hydrotherapy > Spas
Hygiene > Cleaning; Health; Natural health & therapeutics; Occupational
    health & hygiene; Public health
Hymns
    Hymn Soc
Hyper active children
    Fragile X Soc
    Hyperactive Childrens Support Gp
    > + Children: welfare
Hypercalcaemia
    Williams Syndrome Foundation
Hypermobility Syndrome
    Hypermobility Syndrome Assn
Hypertension
    Brit Hypertension Soc
Hyperthermia
    Brit Malignant Hyperthermia Assn
Hypertrophic cardiomyopathy
    Cardiomyopathy Assn
Hypnosis & hypnotherapy
    Academy Curative Hypnotherapists
    Assn Profl Hypnosis & Psychotherapy
    Brit Assn Therapeutical Hypnotists
    Brit Hypnotherapy Assn
    Brit Inst Hypnotherapy
    Brit Soc Clinical & Academic Hypnosis
    Brit Soc Clinical Hypnosis
    Brit Soc Hypnotherapists
    Campaign Stage Hypnosis
    Fedn Ethical Stage Hypnotists
    Hydrotherapy Assn
    Inst Mgt & Technology
    Nat Assn Counsellors, Hypnoterpists & Psychotherapists
    Nat Coun Hypnotherapy
    Nat Coun Psychotherapists
    Nat Register Hypnotherapists & Psychotherapists
    Nat Soc Hypnosis & Psychotherapy
    Nat Soc Profl Hypnotherapists
    Past Life Therapists Assn
    Soc Stress Mgrs
    UK Confedn Hypnotherapy Orgs
Hypnotic regression
    Assn Scientific Study Anomalous Phenomena
    Past Life Therapists Assn
Hysterectomy
    Campaign Hysterectomy &...Operations on Women
    Hysterectomy Assn

I

Iberia > Portugal; Spain
IBS > Irritable bowel syndrome (disease)
Ice climbing > Climbing
Ice cream
    Food & Drink Fedn
    Ice Cream Alliance

Ice hockey
    Ice Hockey UK
    Ir Ice Hockey Assn
Ice skating
    Nat Ice Skating Assn GB&NI
Icehouses
    Sussex Indl Archaeol Soc
Ichthyology
    Ichthyosis Support Gp
    Marine Biological Assn
Ichthyosis
    Ichthyosis Support Gp
Identity cards
    NO2ID
Ido
    Intl Language Ido Soc
Ileostomy
    Assn Coloproctology
    IA
Illiteracy > Reading
Illuminated signs > Road lighting, markings & traffic signs;   Signs
Illumination > Lighting
Illuminators
    Soc Scribes & Illuminators
Illustration
    Assn Archaeol Illustrators & Surveyors
    Assn Illustrators
    Brit Cartoonists Assn
    Comics Creators Gld
    Imaginative Book Illustration Soc
    Inst Med Illustrators
    Nat U Journalists
    Outdoor Writers' & Photographers' Gld
    Picture Res Assn
    Randolph Caldecott Soc
    Soc Architectural Illustration
    Soc Artists' Agents
    > + Art & artists
Image development (personal)
    Fedn Image Consultants
Image processing
    Brit Assn Picture Libraries & Agencies
    Brit Machine Vision Assn...
    Photo Imaging Coun
    R Photographic Soc
    UK Indl Vision Assn
Immediate care > First aid & immediate care
Immigration & emigration
    Assn Visitors Immigration Detainees
    Immigration Law Practitioners Assn
Immunology
    Brit Soc Allergy & Clinical Immunology
    Brit Soc Immunology
    Brit Transplantation Soc
    Primary Immunodeficiency Assn
    > + Allergy
Impact absorbing surfaces
    Assn Play Inds
Imperial weights & measures
    Brit Weights & Measures Assn
    Metric Martyrs
    > + Measurement
Implants (medical)
    Breast Implant Inf Soc
    UK & I Soc Cataract & Refractive Surgeons
Import > Export & import
Impotence > Sexual dysfunction
Incentive marketing
    Brit Promotional Merchandise Assn
    Promota UK Ltd
Income tax > Taxation
Incontinence
    Absorbent Hygiene Products Mfrs Assn
    Assn Continence Advice
    Bladder & Bowel Foundation
    Cystitis & Overactive Bladder Foundation
Independent companies > Business
Independent further education > Adult education; Education
Independent & public schools
    Assn Educ & Guardianship Intl Students
    Assn Governing Bodies Indep Schools
    Assn Marketing & Devt Indep Schools
    Foundation, Aided Schools & Academies
    Girls Schools Assn
    Headmasters & Headmistresses Conf
    Indep Assn Preparatory Schools
    Indep Schools Assn

Indep Schools Bursars Assn
Indep Schools Coun
Soc Heads Indep Schools
Indexing
Assn Freelance Editors, Proofreaders & Indexers [IRL]
Soc Indexers
India & Indian people
Brit Assn S Asian Studies
India: armed forces history
Indian Military Histl Soc
Indirect taxation > Taxation
Individual freedom
Big Brother Watch
C'ee Admin Justice [NI]
Campaign Philosophical Freedom
Choice Personal Safety
Freedom Assn
Freedom Org Right Enjoy Smoking Tobacco
Inst Equality & Diversity Practitioners
Ir Coun Civil Liberties
Liberation
Libertarian Alliance
Liberty
Manifesto Club
Nat Secular Soc
NO2ID
Soc Individual Freedom
Statewatch
Indonesia
Anglo Indonesian Soc
Indoor bowling > Bowling
Indoor & houseplants
Brit Protected Ornamentals Assn
Flowers & Plants Assn
Garden Centre Assn
> + Horticulture; individual plants
Industrial agents
Indl Agents Soc
Industrial archaeology > Archaeology: industrial
Industrial biology > Biology
Industrial catering > Catering
Industrial cleaning > Cleaning equipment
Industrial containers > specific type of container, or material used in their
manufacture
Industrial copyright > Copyright;   Patents & trade marks
Industrial design
Chart Soc Designers
Design & Inds Assn
Fac R Designers Ind
> + Design
Industrial development > Industry
Industrial diamonds
Brit Abrasives Fedn
Industrial editors
Inst Internal Communication
> + Technical writing & publishing
Industrial education > Occupational training & education
Industrial emergencies > Civil defence & industrial emergencies
Industrial fasteners > Fasteners
Industrial finishing > Coatings; Metal: finishing
Industrial: Innovation > Invention & innovation
Industrial involvement & participation
Involvement & Participation Assn
Industrial law > Law: industrial
Industrial leather > Leather
Industrial management > Management
Industrial marketing > Marketing
Industrial participation > Industrial involvement & participation
Industrial plant > Plant: industrial
Industrial pollution > Pollution & pollution control
Industrial property > Copyright; Patents & trade marks
Industrial relations
Brit Universities Indl Relations Assn
Ethical Trading Initiative
Inst Employment Rights
Ir Assn Indl Relations
Industrial research
AIRTO
Cambridge Soc Application Res
Ind Res & Devt Gp [IRL]
Res & Devt Soc
> + specific industries
Industrial safety > Safety
Industrial security > Security
Industrial trucks
Assn Indl Truck Trainers
Industrial training & education > Occupational training & education

Industrial vision
UK Indl Vision Assn
Industry
Assn University Res & Ind Links
Chemical & Indl Consultants' Assn
Confedn Brit Ind
Ir Business & Emplrs Confedn
R Soc Edinburgh
Scot Coun Devt & Ind
Infant food
Brit Specialist Nutrition Assn
Food & Drink Ind Ireland
Infant & Dietetic Foods Assn
Infants > Children: welfare;   Cot deaths
Infection control & study
Brit Infection Assn
Fedn Infection Socs
Healthcare Infection Soc
Infection Prevention Society
John Snow Soc
Soc Applied Microbiology
Infertility > Fertility
Inflatable toys & structures
Assn Amusement & Leisure Eqpt Suppliers
Assn Play Inds
Brit Inflatable Hirers Alliance
Brit Toy & Hobby Assn
Performance Textiles Assn
Information: destruction > Documents: confidential disposal
Information: freedom of
Campaign Freedom Infm
Campaign Press & Broadcasting Freedom
Information: management > Data processing; Information services &
technology
Information: security
Inst Inf Security Profls
Information: services & technology
Aslib
Assn Geographic Inf
Brit Assn Inf & Library Educ & Res
Brit Urban & Regional Inf Systems Assn
Business Services Assn
CILIP
Communications Mgt Assn
Construction Ind Inf Gp
Eur Inf Assn
ICT Ireland
Information Design Assn
Information & Records Mgt Soc
Inst Mgt Inf Systems
Inst Scientific & Technical Communicators
Instn Engg & Technology
Intellect
Momentum
Network Govt Library & Inf Specialists
Prospect
SELECT
Soc Inf Technology Mgt
Specialised Inf Publishers Assn
UK Access Mgt Fedn Educ & Res
UK Computer Measurement Gp
UK EInformation Gp
Universities & Colls Inf Systems Assn
> + Data processing
Infra-red heating > Electroheat
Inkpots > Writing equipment & accessories
Inks > Printing inks
Inland waterways
Assn Inland Navigation Authorities
Assn Waterways Cruising Clubs
Campaign Better Transport
Canal Card Collectors Circle
Chesterfield Canal Trust
Comml Boat Operators Assn
Inland Waterways Assn
Inland Waterways Assn Ireland
Inland Waterways Protection Soc
Nat Assn Boat Owners
Passenger Boat Assn
Rly & Canal Histl Soc
Rly Ramblers
Scot Inland Waterways Assn
Thames & Medway Canal Assn
Towpath Action Gp
Transport Water Assn
Waterway Recovery Gp

Wey & Arun Canal Trust
> + Rivers
Inline skating & rollerblading > Skating: board, inline & roller
Innes (John)
John Innes Mfrs Assn
> + Composts & composting
Innovation > Invention & innovation
Inns of Court > Law
Inns & innkeeping
Brit Inst Innkeeping
Inn Sign Soc
> + Wines & spirits: trade
Insects > Entomology
Insignia > Badges & insignia; Numismatics
Insolvency
Assn Business Recovery Profls
Insolvency Lawyers Assn
Insolvency Practitioners Assn
> + Accountancy
Instrumentation & control > Control engineering; Measurement
Instruments: musical > Musical instruments
Insulation
Brit Rigid Urethane Foam Mfrs Assn
Brit Urethane Foam Contrs Assn
Chart Instn Bldg Services Engrs
Draught Proofing Advy Assn
Engineered Panels Construction
Hemp Lime Construction Products Assn
Insulated Render & Cladding Assn
Mineral Wool Insulation Mfrs Assn
Nat Insulation Assn
Property & Energy Professionals Assn
Proprietary Acoustic Systems Mfrs
Thermal Insulation Contrs Assn
Thermal Insulation Mfrs & Suppliers Assn
> + Building; Heating
Insulation: electrical
Electrical Insulation Assn
Insurance
Assn Average Adjusters
Assn Brit Insurers
Assn Consulting Actuaries
Assn Financial Mutuals
Assn Lloyd's Members
Assn Policy Market Makers
Assn Run-off Cos
Brit Insurance Law Assn
Chart Insurance Inst
Claims Standards Coun
Financial Services Ireland
Inst Risk Mgt
Insurance Inst Ireland
Intl Underwriting Assn Lond
Ir Insurance Fedn
Lloyds Market Assn
Personal Finance Soc
> + Warranty protection
Insurance: brokers
Brit Insurance Brokers' Assn
Inst Insurance Brokers
Ir Brokers Assn
Insurance: companies staff
Assn Insurance & Risk Mgrs
Insurance: history
Fire Mark Circle
Insurance: medicine
Assn Med Insurance Intermediaries
Assurance Med & Underwriting Soc
Insurance: private health > Hospitals: contributory schemes
Insurance: repair
Nat Insurance Repair Contractors Assn
Intellectual property
Alliance Intellectual Property Theft
Anti Copying Design
Intellectual Property Lawyers Assn
Licensing Executives Soc
Soc Share & Business Valuers
Trade Marks Patents & Designs Fedn
> + Copyright
Intelligence
Nat Assn Gifted Children
Intensive care
Intensive Care Soc
Scot Intensive Care Soc
Interchurch families
Assn Interchurch Families

NI Mixed Marriage Assn
> + Welfare: organisations
Interim management
Inst Interim Mgt
Interior decoration & design
Assn Interior Specialists
Brit Assn Landscape Inds
Brit Interior Design Assn
Chart Soc Designers
Inst Profl Designers
Kitchen Bathroom Bedroom Specialists Assn
Wallpaper Hist Soc
Interlingua
Brit Interlingua Soc
Intermediate bulk containers
Indl Packaging Assn
Internal auditors
Chart Inst Internal Auditors
> + Accountancy
Internal combustion engines > Motor industry
International affairs
Brit Pugwash Gp
R Inst Intl Affairs
International friendship > individual countries
International law > Law: international
International mail consolidators > Postal services
International studies
Brit Intl Studies Assn
Eur Atlantic Movement
Internet
Internet Advertising Bureau
Internet Service Providers' Assn
Ir Internet Assn
ScotlandIS
Telecommunications & Internet Fedn [IRL]
> + Online users & publishers; Website design
Interplanetary travel > Space research & exploration
Interpreters > Translation & interpretation
Intestinal disorders > specific illness
Introduction agencies & marriage bureaux
Assn Brit Introduction Agencies
Intruder alarms
Nat Security Inspectorate
> + Security
Invention & innovation
AIRTO
Ideas UK
Inst Intl Licensing Practitioners
Inst Inventors
Inst Patentees & Inventors
R Scot Soc Arts
Inventories
Assn Indep Inventory Clerks
> + Production control; Stocktaking/auditing
Investigators
Assn Brit Investigators
Inst Profl Investigators
Investment
Assn Consulting Actuaries
Assn Corporate Trustees
Assn Indep Financial Advisers
Assn Investment Companies
Assn Mining Analysts
Assn Private Client Investment Mgrs & Stockbrokers
Assn Real Estate Funds
Assn Solicitors & Investment Mgrs
Brit Insurance Brokers' Assn
BVCA
CFA Soc
Chart Inst Securities & Investment
Financial Services Ireland
Futures & Options Assn
Gld Shareholders
Investment Mgt Assn
Investment Property Forum
Investor Relations Soc
Ir Assn Investment Mgrs
Ir ProShare Assn
London Money Market Assn
Soc Later Life Advisers
Soc Technical Analysts
Tax Incentivised Savings Assn
UK Sustainable Investment & Finance Assn
> + Trusts, trusteeship & estate planning
Investment casting > Metal: casting
In Vitro diagnostics
Brit In Vitro Diagnostics Assn

Invoice discounting
    Asset Based Finance Assn
Iran
    Brit Inst Persian Studies
    Iran Soc
    Middle East Assn
Ireland
    Fedn Ir Socs
    Inst Public Administration [IRL]
    Ir Assn Cultural Economic & Social Relations
Ireland: history, language & literature
    Brit Assn Ir Studies
    Economic & Social Hist Soc Ireland
    Fedn Ulster Local Studies
    Friends Nat Collections Ireland
    Ir Texts Soc
    R Ir Academy
    R Soc Antiquaries Ireland
    Soc Study Nineteenth-Century Ireland
Irises
    Brit Iris Soc
Irish > Ireland
Irish dancing
    Gld Profl Teachers Dance & Movement
    > + Dancing
Iron
    Cast Metals Fedn
    Inst Materials, Minerals & Mining
    > + Steel
Iron & steel scrap > Metal: scrap
Iron & steel stockholders
    Nat Assn Steel Stockholders
Ironfoundries > Foundries
Ironmongery
    Brit Hardware Fedn
    Brit Indep Retailers Assn
    Gld Architectural Ironmongers
    Inst Architectural Ironmongers
    > + Hardware & housewares
Irrigation
    Brit Turf & Landscape Irrigation Assn
    UK Irrigation Assn
    > + Water
Irritable bowel syndrome (disease)
    Gut Trust
Isopods
    Brit Myriapod & Isopod Gp
Israel
    Anglo Israel Assn
    Brit Technion Soc
    > + Jewish organisations
Italian > Italy: language & literature
Italic hand > Handwriting
Italy
    Assn Study Modern Italy
    Brit Cham Comm Italy
    Brit Italian Soc
    Italian Cham Comm Ind UK
    Pizza, Pasta & Italian Food Assn
Italy: language & literature
    Assn Language Learning
    Soc Italian Studies

J

Jacobites
    R Stuart Soc
    Seventeen Fortyfive Assn
Jacobs (W[illiam] W[ymark]
    W W Jacobs Appreciation Soc
Japan
    Brit Assn Japanese Studies
    Brit Cham Comm Japan
    Japan Soc
    Japan Soc Scotland
    Japanese Cham Comm & Ind UK
Japan: literature
    Brit Haiku Soc
    Time Haiku
Japanese chess > Shogi
Japanese knotweed
    Japanese Knotweed Alliance

Japanning > Lacquer & japanning
Jazz & Blues
    Assn Brit Jazz Musicians
    Jazz Piano Teachers Assn
    Musicians U
    UK Fedn Jazz Bands
    Welsh Amat Music Fedn
    Welsh Jazz Soc
Jefferies (Richard)
    Richard Jefferies Soc
Jerome (Jerome K)
    Jerome K Jerome Soc
Jersey (Channel Islands)
    R Jersey Agricl & Horticl Soc
    Société Jersiaise
Jetting (water)
    Water Jetting Assn
Jewellery
    Archibald Knox Soc
    Assn Contemporary Jewellery
    Assn Indep Jewellery Valuers
    Bead Soc
    Brit Allied Trs Fedn
    Brit Jewellers Assn
    Designer Jewellers Gp
    Fedn Jewellery Mfrs Ireland
    Gld Enamellers
    Inst Profl Goldsmiths
    Jewellery Distributors Assn UK
    Nat Assn Goldsmiths
    Soc Jewellery Historians
Jewish history & lore
    Chapels Soc
    Jewish Histl Soc England
Jewish organisations
    Anglo Jewish Assn
    Assn Jewish Ex-Servicemen & Women
    Fedn Synagogues
    Inst Jewish Policy Res
    Zionist Fedn
Jigsaws
    Brit Jigsaw Puzzle Library
Jirds
    Nat Gerbil Soc
Jockeys > Horse: racing
John O'Groats
    Land's End John O'Groats Assn
Johnson (Dr Samuel)
    Johnson Soc
    Johnson Soc Lond
Joinery > Woodworking
Joints
    Arthrogryposis Gp
Jones (David Michael)
    David Jones Soc
Jordan
    Anglo Jordanian Soc
Journalism
    Assn Brit Science Writers
    Assn Regional City Editors
    Brit Assn Journalists
    Chart Inst Journalists
    Football Writers Assn
    Foreign Press Assn Lond
    Gld Food Writers
    Gld Motoring Writers
    Horserace Writers & Photographers Assn
    Media Soc
    Medical Journalists Assn
    Nat Assn Press Agencies
    Nat U Journalists
    Sports Journalists' Assn GB
    Yachting Journalists' Assn
    > + Media; Newspapers; Writing & writers
Jousting
    Knights R England
Judo
    Brit Judo Assn
    Judo Scotland
    Welsh Judo Assn
    > + Martial arts
Jujitsu > Martial arts
Jurisprudence > Law
Just William stories
    Just William Soc

Justices & justices clerks
>>>> Scot Justices Assn
>>>>>>> + Magistrates & magistrates courts
Juvenile > Children headings; Family Law

K

Kaolin > China clay (kaolin)
Karate > Martial arts
Karg-Elert (Sigfrid)
>>>> Karg Elert Archive
Karting
>>>> Assn Brit Kart Clubs
>>>> Assn Racing Kart Schools
>>>> Brit Superkart Assn
>>>> Motor Sports Assn
>>>> Nat Karting Assn
Kayaks
>>>> Historic Canoe & Kayak Assn
>>>> Open Canoe Sailing Gp
Kaye-Smith (Sheila)
>>>> Sheila Kaye-Smith Soc
Keats (John)
>>>> Keats Shelley Memorial Assn
Keelboats > Cobles & keelboats
Keep fit > Fitness
Kegs > Cisterns, drums & tanks
Kempe (Charles Eamer)
>>>> Kempe Soc
Kempe (Margery)
>>>> Margery Kempe Soc
Kempe (Rudolf)
>>>> Rudolf Kempe Soc
Kennels
>>>> Pet Care Tr Assn
Kent
>>>> Assn Men Kent & Kentish Men
Kerbs > Paving & kerbs
Keys
>>>> Brit Locksmiths & Keycutters Assn
>>>> MultiService Assn
>>>>>>> + Locks & latches
Kickboxing > Martial arts
Kidney structure & disease > Nephrology
Kilvert (Francis)
>>>> Kilvert Soc
Kinesiology
>>>> Assn Light Touch Therapists
>>>> Assn Systematic Kinesiology
>>>> Kinesiology Fedn
>>>>>>> + Complementary medicine
Kings > under individual's name
Kipling ([Joseph] Rudyard)
>>>> Kipling Soc
Kippers > Herring
Kitchen furniture, equipment & design
>>>> Brit Woodworking Fedn
>>>> Catering Eqpt Distbrs Assn GB
>>>> Cookshop & Housewares Assn
>>>> Cutlery & Allied Trs Res Assn
>>>> Foodservice Consultants Soc Intl
>>>> Kitchen Bathroom Bedroom Specialists Assn
Kite flying
>>>> Kite Soc
Kite sports
>>>> Brit Fedn Sand & Land Yacht Clubs
>>>> Brit Kite Surfing Assn
>>>> Brit Power Kitesports Assn
>>>> Parakart Assn
>>>>>>> + Surfing, board & speed sailing
Klinefelter's syndrome
>>>> Klinefelter's Syndrome Assn
Knacker industry
>>>> Licensed Animal Slaughterers... Assn
Knights bachelor
>>>> Imperial Soc Knights Bachelor
Knitting
>>>> Gld Machine Knitters
>>>> Knitting & Crochet Gld
>>>> UK Hand Knitting Assn
>>>>>>> + Wool & wool products
Knitwear
>>>> Knitting Inds Fedn

Knots (tying)
>>>> Intl Gld Knot Tyers
Knox (Archibald)
>>>> Archibald Knox Soc
Kodály (Zoltán)
>>>> Brit Kodály Academy
Korea
>>>> Brit Assn Korean Studies
>>>> Brit Cham Comm Korea
Korfball
>>>> Brit Korfball Assn

L

Labels
>>>> Brit Printing Inds Fedn
Labels: collecting
>>>> Brit Matchbox, Label & Booklet Soc
>>>> Labologists Soc
Laboratory animals
>>>> Fund Replacement Animals Med Experiments
>>>> Inst Animal Technology
>>>> Laboratory Animal Science Assn
>>>> Understanding Animal Res
>>>>>>> + Animals: welfare
Laboratory equipment & technology
>>>> Brit Assn Res Quality Assurance
>>>> GAMBICA Assn
>>>> Inst Biomedical Science
>>>> Inst Science & Technology
>>>> UK Textile Laboratory Forum
Labour politics
>>>> Inst Employment Rights
>>>> Soc Study Labour Hist
Labour (provision of)
>>>> Assn Labour Providers
Labour relations > Industrial relations
Lace
>>>> Brit Lace Fedn
>>>> Gld Needle Laces
>>>> Lace Gld
>>>> Lace Soc
Lacquer & japanning
>>>> Brit Antique Furniture Restorers Assn
Lacrosse
>>>> English Lacrosse Assn
Ladders
>>>> Ladder Assn
>>>> Ladder Systems Mfrs Assn
Ladies circles
>>>> Nat Assn Ladies Circles
>>>>>>> + also Women's organisations
Legacies (public) > Donations (public)
Lake District
>>>> Friends Lake District
Lamas > Camelids
Lamb (Charles)
>>>> Charles Lamb Soc
Lamb(s) > Meat; Sheep
Laminates
>>>> Brit Laminate Fabricators Assn
Lancashire
>>>> Friends Real Lancashire
Land: access & rights of way > Footpaths & rights of way
Land-based education
>>>> Landex
Land: contaminated
>>>> Assn Geotechnical & Geoenvironmental Specialists
>>>> Scot Contaminated Land Forum
>>>> Soil & Groundwater Technology Assn
Land: drainage
>>>> Assn Drainage Authorities
>>>> Fedn Dredging Contrs
>>>> Land Drainage Contrs Assn
>>>>>>> + Plastics: pipes; Pipes; Water
Land: owners > Estate management; Property & land owners
Land: survey > Earth sciences, structure & resources;   Surveying
Land: usage > Conservation; Town & country planning
Land: valuation > Valuation: land & property
Land: yachting > Surfing, board & speedsailing
Landlords > Property & land owners
Land's End
>>>> Land's End John O'Groats Assn

Landscape
 Assn Landscape Contrs Ireland (NI)
 Brit Assn Landscape Inds
 Brit Turf & Landscape Irrigation Assn
 Garden & Landscape Designers Assn [IRL]
 Horticultural Trs Assn
 Inst Place Mgt
 Inst Profl Designers
 Ir Landscape Inst
 Landscape Inst
 Landscape Res Gp
 Permaculture Assn
 Profl Plant Users Gp
 Scot Seed & Nursery Tr Assn
 Soc Landscape Studies
 Soc Ley Hunters
 > + Earth sciences, structure & resources
Language: impairment
 Nat Assn Profls... Language Impairment Children
 R Coll Speech & Language Therapists
Languages
 Assn Brit Language Schools
 Assn Language Learning
 Assn Learning Languages en Famille
 Assn University Language Centres
 Brit Academy
 Brit Assn Academic Phoneticians
 Brit Assn Applied Linguistics
 Chart Inst Linguists
 Cheshaght Ghailckagh (Yn)
 Linguistics Assn
 Modern Humanities Res Assn
 Nat Assn Language Advisers
 Philological Soc
 UK Literacy Assn
 Ulster-Scots Language Soc
 > + Dialects; individual country
Languages: auxiliary
 Brit Interlingua Soc
 Esperanto Assn Britain
 Glosa Educ Org
 Intl Language Ido Soc
 Scot Esperanto Assn
Laparoscopy
 Assn Laparoscopic Surgeons
Larkin (Philip)
 Philip Larkin Soc
Laryngology/Laryngectomy > Otolaryngology
Laser printer cartridges
 UK Cartridge Remanufacturers Assn
 > + Printing machinery & supplies
Lasers
 Assn Laser Safety Profls
 Assn Laser Users
 Brit Med Laser Assn
 Ophthalmological Products Tr...Conf
Latex allergy
 Latex Allergy Support Gp
 > + Allergy
Latin > Classical studies
Latin America
 Hispanic & Luso Brazilian Coun
 UK One World Linking Assn
Latin American dancing
 Ballroom Dancers Fedn
 EADA
 Imperial Soc Teachers Dancing
 Nat Assn Teachers Dancing
 Scot Dance Teachers Alliance
 > + Dancing
Latin Mass > Liturgy
Latvia
 Brit Cham Comm Latvia
Lauder (Sir Harry)
 Scot Music Hall & Variety Theatre Soc
Laundering & dry cleaning
 Gld Cleaners & Launderers
 Nat Assn Launderette Ind
 Soc Laundry Engrs & Allied Trs
 Textile Services Assn
Laurel & Hardy
 Laurel & Hardy Appreciation Soc
Laurence-Moon-Bardet-Biedl disease
 Laurence Moon Bardet Biedl Soc

Law
 Assn Comparative Legal Studies

 Assn Personal Injury Lawyers
 Bar Assn Local Govt & Public Service
 Brit Legal Assn
 Comml Bar Assn
 Criminal Bar Assn
 Family Law Bar Assn
 Law Soc
 Legal Aid Practitioners Gp
 Magistrates Assn
 Medico-Legal Soc
 Soc Advanced Legal Studies
 Socio-Legal Studies Assn
 Solicitor Sole Practitioners Gp
 > + headings below; Forensic science
Law: Ireland
 Brit & Ir Assn Law Librarians
 Honorable Soc Kings Inns [IRL]
 Law Soc Ireland
Law: Northern Ireland
 C'ee Admin Justice [NI]
 Law Soc NI
Law: Scotland
 Fac Advocates
 Law Soc Scotland
 Procurators Fiscal Soc
 R Fac Procurators in Glasgow
 Scot Indep Advocacy Alliance
 Scot Law Agents Soc
 Scot Legal Action Gp
 Soc Solicitors Supreme Courts Scotland
 Soc Writers Her Majesty's Signet
Law: art
 Inst Art & Law
Law: centres
 Law Centres Fedn
 Scot Assn Law Centres
Law: charity
 Charity Law Assn
Law: children
 Assn Child Abuse Lawyers
 Assn Lawyers Children
 Nat Assn Youth Justice
Law: clerks
 Inst Barristers' Clerks
Law: comparative
 Brit Inst Intl & Comparative Law
Law: construction
 Assn Consultant Approved Inspectors
 Instn Construction Safety
 Soc Construction Law
Law: costs
 Assn Law Costs Draftsmen
Law: court officers
 Scot Justices Assn
 > + Magistrates & magistrates courts
Law: education
 Assn Law Teachers
 Brit & Ir Legal Educ Technology Assn
 Education Law Assn
 Franco Brit Lawyers Soc
 Soc Legal Scholars
Law: employment
 Employment Lawyers Assn
Law: environment
 Planning & Environment Bar Assn
 UK Envtl Law Assn
Law: European
 Brit-German Jurists' Assn
 Franco Brit Lawyers Soc
 UK Assn Eur Law
 > + Law: international
Law: expert witness > Experts & expert witness
Law: family > Family law
Law: history
 Ir Legal Hist Soc
 Selden Soc
 Stair Soc
Law: immigration
 Immigration Law Practitioners Assn
Law: industrial
 Bar Assn Comm, Finance & Ind
 Commerce & Ind Gp
 Indl Law Soc
Law: insolvency
 Insolvency Lawyers Assn
Law: insurance
 Brit Insurance Law Assn

Law: international
　　　Brit Inst Intl & Comparative Law
　　　Intl Law Assn
Law: libraries
　　　Brit & Ir Assn Law Librarians
Law: maritime
　　　Brit Maritime Law Assn
　　　Ir Maritime Law Assn
　　　Maritime Inf Assn
Law: motor accidents
　　　Motor Accident Solicitors Soc
Law: paralegal
　　　Inst Legal Executives
　　　Inst Legal Secretaries & PAs
　　　Inst Paralegals
　　　Nat Assn Licensed Paralegals
　　　Soc Specialist Paralegals
Law: pension
　　　Assn Pension Lawyers
Law: reform > specific subject of reform
Law: secretaries
　　　Inst Paralegals
　　　> Law: paralegal
Law: Statute
　　　Statute Law Soc
Lawn bowling > Bowling
Lawn mowers
　　　Brit Lawn Mower Racing Assn
　　　Old Lawn Mower Club
　　　> + Horticulture & garden: machinery
Lawn tennis > Tennis
Lawrence (David Herbert)
　　　D H Lawrence Soc
Lawrence (Thomas Edward) 'of Arabia'
　　　T E Lawrence Soc
Lawyers > Law; Legal advisers
Laying on of hands > Spiritual healing
Lead
　　　Lead Contrs Assn
　　　Lead Sheet Assn
　　　Lead Smelters & Refiners Assn
Learned society publishing
　　　Assn Learned & Profl Soc Pubrs
Learning disability
　　　Assn Nat Specialist Colls
　　　Assn Real Change
　　　Brit Dyslexia Assn
　　　Brit Inst Learning Disabilities
　　　Caspari Foundation Educl Therapy...
　　　Nat Assn Toy & Leisure Libraries
　　　Scot Consortium Learning Disability
　　　Scot Support Learning Assn
　　　> + Children: handicapped
Learning resources > Education: technology
Leasing
　　　Assn Leasehold Enfranchisement Practitioners
　　　Finance & Leasing Assn
　　　Leasehold Enfranchisement Assn
Leather
　　　BLC, Leather Technology Centre
　　　Soc Leather Technologists & Chemists
Leathergoods
　　　Brit Menswear Gld
　　　Brit Travelgoods & Accessories Assn
　　　Soc Master Saddlers
Lebanon
　　　Brit Lebanese Assn
Lecturers
　　　Assn Teachers & Lecturers
　　　University & Coll U
　　　> + Adult education; Teachers
Leeks
　　　Leek Growers Assn
　　　Nat Pot Leek Soc
　　　> + Vegetable: growing
Left-handed people
　　　Left Handers Assn
　　　Left Handers Club
Legacies
　　　Assn Run-off Cos
Legacies (public) > Donations (public)
Legal > Law; & headings below
Legal advisers/services
　　　Profl Assn Legal Services
Legal cashiers
　　　Inst Legal Finance & Mgt
Legal secretaries > Law: paralegal

Legal studies > Law
Legionnaire's disease
　　　Chart Inst Plumbing & Heating Engg
Lego
　　　Brickish Assn
Leisure equipment & clothing
　　　Outdoor Inds Assn
Leisure parks
　　　Assn Leading Visitor Attractions
　　　Brit Assn Leisure Parks, Piers & Attractions
　　　> + Amusements
Leisure, recreation & amenity management
　　　Assn Heritage Interpretation
　　　Assn Profl Sales Agents (Sports & Leisure Inds)
　　　Business Sport & Leisure
　　　Chief Cultural & Leisure Officers Assn
　　　Fitness Ind Assn
　　　Inst Entertainment & Arts Mgt
　　　Inst Leisure & Amenity Mgt Ireland
　　　Leisure Studies Assn
　　　Nat Assn Agricl Contrs
　　　Nat Assn Leisure Ind Certification
　　　Scot Countryside Rangers' Assn
　　　Soc Leisure Consultants & Pubrs
　　　Voice Chief Offrs Cultural... Services
Leisure software > Software: leisure
Lending rights > Copyright
Lenses > Optical industry
Lepidoptera > Entomology
Lesch-Nyhan syndrome
　　　Purine Metabolic Patients Assn
Letter boxes
　　　Letter Box Study Gp
Letter carving > Stone masons & sculptors;　Wood carving
Letter files
　　　Brit Office Supplies & Services Fedn
　　　> + Office equipment & systems
Letter scales > Scales & weighing machines;　Writing equipment & accessories
Letting agents
　　　Assn Residential Letting Agents
　　　UK Assn Letting Agents
Lettuces
　　　Brit Leafy Salads Assn
　　　> + Vegetables: growing
Leukaemia
　　　Leukaemia CARE
Lewis ([Percy] Wyndham)
　　　Wyndham Lewis Soc
Leylandii hedges
　　　Hedgeline
Leylines
　　　Assn Scientific Study Anomalous Phenomena
　　　Soc Ley Hunters
Liberty > Individual freedom
Libraries/librarians
　　　ARLIS/UK & Ireland
　　　Aslib
　　　Assn Brit Theological... Libraries
　　　Assn Denominational Histl Socs Cognate Libs
　　　Assn Indep Libraries
　　　Assn UK Media Librarians
　　　Brit Assn Friends Museums
　　　Brit & Ir Assn Law Librarians
　　　Career Devt Gp
　　　Cathedral Libraries & Archives Assn
　　　CILIP
　　　Friends Nat Libraries
　　　Historic Libraries Forum
　　　Library Assn Ireland
　　　Library Campaign
　　　London Library
　　　Nat Acquisitions Gp
　　　Network Govt Library & Inf Specialists
　　　Private Libraries Assn
　　　RLUK
　　　School Library Assn
　　　Soc Chief Librarians
　　　Soc College Nat & University Libraries
　　　Voice Chief Offrs Cultural... Services
　　　> + Picture libraries
Library schools
　　　Brit Assn Inf & Library Educ & Res
Library suppliers
　　　Assn Library Eqpt Suppliers
Libya
　　　Soc Libyan Studies

© CBD Research Ltd · Beckenham · BR3 5JS · Tel 020 8650 7745　E-mail cbd@cbdresearch.com · www.cbdresearch.com

Licensed property (valuation)
>> Assn Valuers Licensed Property
>> Restaurant Property Advisors Soc
Licensed trade > Bars (management & staff); Wines & spirits: trade
Licensing laws
>> Campaign Real Ale
Licensing (product) > Product licensing
Lichen
>> Brit Lichen Soc
Life assurance > Insurance
Life coaching
Life saving
>> Assn Paediatric Resuscitation Officers
>> Brit Long Distance Swimming Assn
>> Life Saving Awards Res Soc
>> R Humane Soc
>> R Life Saving Soc
>> R Nat Lifeboat Instn
>> Surf Life Saving GB
>> Swimming Teachers Assn
>> + Safety
Lifeboats
>> Lifeboat Enthusiasts Soc
>> R Nat Lifeboat Instn
Lifting & loading equipment
>> ALLMI
>> Assn Loading & Elevating Eqpt Mfrs
>> Automated Material Handling Systems Assn
>> Fork Lift Truck Assn
>> Lifting Eqpt Engrs Assn
>> Solids Handling & Processing Assn
>> + Construction equipment; Fork-lift trucks; Materials: management/handling
Lifts
>> Chart Instn Bldg Services Engrs
>> Lift & Escalator Ind Assn
Light alloys & metals > Metal headings
Light (disorder sufferers)
>> SAD Assn
Light music > Music
Light railways > Railways: light; Tramways & trams
Lighter-than-air craft > Balloons & airships
Lighterage
>> River Assn Freight & Transport
Lighthouses & lightships
>> Assn Lighthouse Keepers
Lighting
>> Assn Interior Specialists
>> Chart Instn Bldg Services Engrs
>> Instn Lighting Profls
>> Lighting Assn
>> Lighting Ind Fedn
>> Spectrum Alliance
>> + Road: lighting, markings & traffic signs
Lightning
>> Tornado & Storm Res Org
Lightning conductors
>> Assn Technical Lighting & Access Specialists
Limbless persons
>> Limbless Assn
>> + Disablement
Lime & limestone
>> Brit Calcium Carbonates Fedn
>> Hemp Lime Construction Products Assn
>> Mineral Products Assn
Limekilns
>> Sussex Indl Archaeol Soc
Limousines
>> Nat Limousine & Chauffeur Assn
Line dancing
>> Best Western Dance Academy
>> Gld Profl Teachers Dance & Movement
>> Scot Dance Teachers Alliance
>> + Dancing
Linen
>> Ir Linen Gld
>> + Textile headings
Liners (ships) > Ships & (boats) : history & preservation
Linesmen > Referees
Linguistics > Languages
Linguists > Translation & interpretation
Linoleum
>> Contract Flooring Assn
>> UK Resilient Flooring Assn
Lintels
>> Steel Lintel Mfrs Assn
>> + Doors; Windows

Lipreading & lipspeaking
>> Assn Lipspeakers
>> Assn Teachers Lipreading to Adults
>> Cued Speech Assn
>> + Deafness
Liquefied petroleum gas
>> UKLPG
Liqueurs > Wines & spirits: trade
Liquid roofing > Roofing
Liquidators
>> Insolvency Practitioners Assn
>> + Insolvency
Liquids: packaging
>> Alliance Beverage Cartons & Envt
Liquids: storage/warehousing
>> Tank Storage Assn
>> + Cisterns, drums & tanks
List broking
>> Direct Marketing Assn
>> + Advertising
Listed property
>> Listed Property Owners Club
>> + Historic buildings
Liszt (Franz)
>> Liszt Soc
Literacy
>> Brit Assn Literacy in Devt
>> Nat Literacy Assn
>> UK Literacy Assn
>> + Reading
Literary agents > Authors' agents
Literary rights > Copyright
Literary societies > individual writer; [Country]: language & literature
Literature
>> Alliance Literary Socs
>> Brit Academy
>> Brit Comparative Literature Assn
>> Manchester Literary & Philosophical Soc
>> Nat Assn Literature Devt
>> + English language & literature; & individual countries
Lithuania
>> Brit Lithuanian Soc
>> Lithuanian Assn
Litigation > Law
Litigation: support
>> Network Indep Forensic Accountants
Litter
>> Keep Britain Tidy
Liturgy
>> Alcuin Club
>> Ecclesiological Soc
>> Henry Bradshaw Soc
>> Latin Mass Soc
>> Prayer Book Soc
>> Scot Prayer Book Soc
Liver & liver disease
>> Brit Assn Study Liver
>> Brit Soc Gastroenterology
Liverworts
>> Brit Bryological Soc
Livestock > Cattle & livestock; Poultry; Sheep
Living history
>> Engliscan Gesíþas
>> Regia Anglorum
>> Seventeenth Century Life & Times
>> Vikings (The)
>> + Fights (historic/re-enactment)
Living wills
>> ALERT
>> Dignity in Dying
>> EXIT
>> + Euthanasia

Llamas > Camelids
Load conveyors > Lifting & loading equipment
Load restraint
>> Performance Textiles Assn
Loading equipment > Lifting & loading equipment
Loans (short term)
>> Consumer Finance Assn
Lobbyists
>> Assn Profl Political Consultants
Local government
>> Action Communities Rural England
>> Assn Charter Trustee Towns &... Couns
>> Assn County & City Councils [IRL]
>> Assn Municipal Authorities Ireland

Assn N E Couns
Convention Scot Local Authorities
Local Authorities Res & Intelligence Assn
Local Govt Assn
London Councils
Nat Assn Councillors
Nat Assn Local Couns
NI Local Govt Assn
One Voice Wales
Welsh Local Govt Assn
Local government: officers
Assn Chief Estates Surveyors... Public Sector
Assn Coun Secretaries & Solicitors
Assn County Chief Executives
Assn Local Authority Chief Execs
Assn Local Govt Archaeol Officers
Assn Local Govt Communications
Assn Transport Co-ordinating Officers
Bar Assn Local Govt & Public Service
Chief Cultural & Leisure Officers Assn
CIPFA
County Educ Officers Two Tier Authorities
Inst Public Sector Mgt
Instn Economic Devt
Local Authority Caterers Assn
Local Government Technical Advisers Group
Planning Officers Soc
Public Mgt & Policy Assn
Public Sector People Mgrs' Assn
Road Safety GB
Soc Construction & Quantity Surveyors
Soc County Treasurers [E&W]
Soc District Coun Treasurers
Soc Electrical &... Engrs Local Government
Soc Local Authority Chief Execs & Senior Mgrs
Soc Local Coun Clerks
Soc Procurement Officers Local Govt
Local government: services
Assn Public Service Excellence
Nat Assn Financial Assessment Officers
Local government: vehicles
Road Transport Fleet Data Soc
Local history & topography
Brit Assn Local Hist
Fedn Ulster Local Studies
Orkney Heritage Soc
Scot Local History Forum
> + Archaeology: county societies;   Records: historical
Location managers > Film: locations
Locks
Assn Insurance Surveyors
Auto Locksmiths Assn
Brit Locksmiths & Keycutters Assn
Master Locksmiths Assn
UK Locksmiths Assn
> + Security
Locomotives > Railway headings
Locomotives: road
Road Locomotive Soc
Locums
Nat Assn Sessional GP's
Logistics > Materials: management/handling
London
London First
London & Middlesex Archaeol Soc
London Natural Hist Soc
London Soc
London Subterranean Survey Assn
London Topographical Soc
London boroughs > Local government
Long-bow archery > Archery
Long distance swimming
Channel Swimming Assn
Channel Swimming & Piloting Fedn
Long range planning > Strategic planning
Longevity > Geriatrics & ageing
Lords-of-the-Manor > Manors
Lorry drivers
Profl Drivers Assn
Lorry loaders
ALLMI
> + Lifting & loading equipment
Loss assessment
Chart Inst Loss Adjusters
Inst Public Loss Assessors
Lost wax casting > Metal: casting

Lotteries
Lotteries Coun
Lovespoon carving
Brit Woodcarvers Assn
Low Countries
Assn Low Countries Studies
> + Belgium; Netherlands
Low frequency noise
UK Noise Assn
> + Noise
Low temperatures > Cryogenics
Lowe syndrome
Lowe Syndrome Assn
Lower limb deficiency
STEPS
> + Disablement
Lubricants
Oil Recycling Assn
UK Lubricants Assn
Luge racing > Toboggan & luge racing/riding
Luggage & travel goods > Travel goods & accessories
Lumber > Timber
Lung(s), disease & research > Thoracic diseases
Lupus
Lupus UK
Lutes & lute playing
Lute Soc
Lutheran Church
Lutheran Coun
Lutyens (Sir Edwin)
Lutyens Trust
Luxembourg
Belgian-Luxembourg Cham Comm GB
Brit Cham Comm Luxembourg
Luxury goods
Walpole
Lymphoedema & lymphology
Brit Lymphology Soc
Brit Manual Lymph Drainage Assn
Lymphoedema Support Network
Lymphoma Assn

M

Macadam > Asphalt & coated macadam
MacDonald (George)
George MacDonald Soc
Macebearers
Gld Mace Bearers
Macedonia
Macedonian Soc
Machen (Arthur)
Friends Arthur Machen
Machine knitting
Gld Machine Knitters
Machine tools
Brit Hardmetal & Engineers' Cutting Tool Assn
Engg & Machinery Alliance
Gauge & Tool Makers Assn
Manufacturing Technologies Assn
Machine vision
Brit Machine Vision Assn...
UK Indl Vision Assn
Machinery
Woodworking Machinery Suppliers Assn
> + specific types of machinery
Machinery: safety
Safety Assessment Fedn
Mackerel
Herring Buyers Assn
> + Fish headings; Fishing
Mackintosh (Charles Rennie)
Charles Rennie Mackintosh Soc
Macrobiotics
Macrobiotic Assn
Macular disease
Macular Disease Soc
> + Blind & partially sighted
Madagascar
Anglo Malagasy Soc
Magazines > Newspapers & periodicals: distribution; Periodicals
Magic > Conjuring & magic
Magic lanterns
Magic Lantern Soc

© CBD Research Ltd · Beckenham · BR3 5JS · Tel 020 8650 7745   E-mail cbd@cbdresearch.com · www.cbdresearch.com

Magistrates & magistrates courts
    Magistrates Assn
Magnetic compasses > Compasses & compass adjusting
Magnetic strip(e) cards > Credit & magnetic strip(e) cards
Magnetism
    UK Magnetics Soc
Mail > Postal services
Mail order trade > Advertising; Direct selling
Maintenance > Buildings: cleaning & maintenance;   Plant: industrial
Maintenance products
    Brit Assn Chemical Specialities
Maize & maize starch
    Brit Starch Ind Assn
    Maize Growers Assn
    UK Maize Millers Assn
Majorettes > Baton twirling
Make-up (stage & screen)
    Nat Assn Screen Makeup Artists & Hairdressers
    > + Beauty specialists/treatment
Malacology > Conchology
Maladjusted children > Children: handicapped
Malaysia
    Brit Malaysian Soc
Malt & malt products
    Malt Distillers Assn Scotland
    Maltsters Assn
    > + Vinegar; Whisky
Mammals
    Mammal Soc
    Marine Consvn Soc
    > + Nature conservation
Mammography
    Brit Machine Vision Assn...
Management
    Academy Executives & Administrators
    Academy Multi Skills
    Assn Business Administration
    Assn Business Executives
    Assn Business Schools
    Assn Mgt Educ & Devt
    Brit Educl Leadership, Mgt & Admin Soc
    Business Mgt Assn
    Chart Mgt Inst
    Corporate Responsibility Coalition
    Ergonomics Soc
    Fac Profl Business & Technical Mgt
    Inst Administrative Mgt
    Inst Comml Mgt
    Inst Interim Mgt
    Inst Leadership & Mgt
    Inst Mgt Services
    Inst Mgt Specialists
    Inst Mgt & Technology
    Inst Turnaround
    Inst Value Mgt
    Interim Mgt Assn
    Ir Mgt Inst
    Soc Advancement Mgt Studies
    Strategic Planning Soc
    > + Project management
Management accountancy
    Chart Inst Mgt Accountants
Management consultancy
    Inst Consulting
    Inst Mgt Consultants & Advisers [IRL]
    Management Consultancies Assn
    > + Employment agents & consultants
Mangelwurzels
    Mangold Hurling Assn
Manhole covers
    Fabricated Access Covers Trade Assn
Manic depression > Depression
Manipulative medicine
    LCSP Register Remedial Masseurs...
    > + specific type
Manors
    Manorial Soc
Manpower > Employment
Manslaughter > Murder & manslaughter
Manufacturing
    Additive Mfrg Assn
    Brit Assn Res Quality Assurance
    Brit Contract Mfrs & Packers Assn
    Confedn Brit Ind
    Inst Mfrg
    PERA

Rapid Prototyping & Mfrg Assn
    > + specific industries
Manx language
    Cheshaght Ghailckagh (Yn)
Maps > Cartography
Marble
    Brit Antique Furniture Restorers Assn
    Nat Fedn Terrazzo, Marble & Mosaic Specialists
    Stone Fedn
Mare, de la (Walter)
    Walter de la Mare Society
Marfan syndrome
    Marfan Assn
Margarine
    Food & Drink Ind Ireland
    Margarine & Spreads Assn
Marinas
    Brit Marine Fedn
    Ir Marine Fedn
    > + Yachts & yachting
Marine: aggregates
    Mineral Products Assn
    > + Aggregates
Marine: biology & biochemistry
    Brit Marine Life Study Soc
    Challenger Soc Marine Science
    Fisheries Soc
    Linnean Soc Lond
    Marine Biological Assn
    Marine Consvn Soc
    Porcupine Marine Natural Hist Soc
    Scot Assn Marine Science
    Scot Sub Aqua Club
    Sub Aqua Assn
    > + Oceanography
Marine: contractors
    Intl Marine Contrs Assn
    > + Ocean industries
Marine: education
    Central Org Maritime Pastimes...
    Intl Assn Marine Instns
    Marine Soc & Sea Cadets
Marine: energy > Renewable energy
Marine: engineering & equipment
    Assn Marine Scientific Ind
    Brit Marine Eqpt Assn
    Brit Naval Eqpt Assn
    Inst Marine Engg, Science & Technology
    Instn Civil Engrs
    R Instn Naval Architects
    Shipbuilders & Shiprepairers Assn
    Soc Consulting Marine Engrs & Ship Surveyors
    Soc Maritime Inds
    > + Shipbuilding & ship repairing; Underwater engineering &
    research
Marine: safety & equipment
    Emergency Response & Rescue Vessels Assn
    Inflatable Safety & Survival Eqpt...Assn
Marine: trading > Ships stores & supplies
Marine: training
    Maritime Skills Alliance
Mariners
    Ir Inst Master Mariners
    Nautical Inst
    > + Merchant Navy
Marital studies > Family headings
Maritime law > Law: maritime
Marker posts
    Retroreflective Eqpt Mfrs Assn
    > + Road markings, lighting & traffic signs
Market gardening > Fruit: trade;   Horticulture; Vegetables: growing
Marketing
    Arts Marketing Assn
    Assn Users Res Agencies
    Catalogue Exchange
    Chart Inst Marketing
    Direct Marketing Assn
    Inst Direct Marketing
    Inst Intl Marketing
    Inst Promotional Marketing
    Ir Direct Marketing Assn
    Market Res Soc
    Marketing Agencies Assn
    Marketing Assn Alliance
    Marketing Inst [IRL]
    Marketing Soc
    Marketing Soc [IRL]

Profl Services Marketing Gp
   Soc Sales & Marketing
   > + Incentive marketing; Sales management & representation
Marketing: researchers & interviewers
   Assn Qualitative Res
   Brit Polling Coun
   Market Res Quality Standards Assn
   Viewing Facilities Assn UK
Markets: street, cattle & farmers'
   Country Markets
   Fedn Street Traders Us
   Humane Slaughter Assn
   Livestock Auctioneers Assn
   Nat Assn Brit Market Authorities
   Nat Farmers' Retail & Markets Assn
   Nat Market Traders Fedn
Marlowe (Christopher)
   Marlowe Soc
Marquees > Tents & marquees
Marquetry
   Marquetry Soc
Marriage bureaux > Introduction agencies & marriage bureaux
Marriage guidance
   Family Matters Inst
Marriages > Population registration
Marrow (transplants)
   Brit Soc Bone & Marrow Transplantation
Martial arts
   All Styles Martial Arts Assn
   Amat Martial Assn
   Brit Aikido Bd
   Brit Assn Martial Arts
   Brit Coun Chinese Martial Arts
   Brit Fedn Histl Swordplay
   Brit Ju Jitsu Assn GB
   Brit Judo Assn
   Brit Shorinji Kempo Fedn
   Judo Scotland
   Nat Assn Karate & Martial Art Schools
   Scot Ju-Jitsu Assn
   Soc Martial Arts
   Tai Chi U
   Welsh Judo Assn
Mary, Queen of Scots
   Marie Stuart Soc
Mary Rose (the)
   Mary Rose Soc
Masefield (John)
   John Masefield Soc
Masonry > Stone
Massage
   Assn Holistic Biodynamic Massage Therapists
   Equine Sports Massage Assn
   Gen Coun Massage Therapies
   LCSP Register Remedial Masseurs. . .
   Nat Assn Massage & Manipulative Therapists
   On Site Massage Assn
   Scot Massage Therapists Org
   Sports Massage Assn
Masters of ceremonies > Toastmasters & masters of ceremonies
Mastic asphalt > Asphalt & coated macadam
Masts (radio/telephone) > Aerials: radio, telephone & television
Matchbox labels
   Brit Matchbox, Label & Booklet Soc
Materials (fabrics) > type of material
Materials: control > Stock & materials control
Materials: management/handling
   Automated Material Handling Systems Assn
   Brit Intl Freight Assn
   Brit Materials Handling Fedn
   Chart Inst Logistics & Transport
   Chart Inst Logistics & Transport Ireland
   Container Handling Eqpt Mfrs Assn
   Inst Transport Mgt
   Materials Handling Engrs Assn
   Solids Handling & Processing Assn
   Storage & Handling Eqpt Distbrs Assn
   UK Warehousing Assn
   > + Freight transport
Materials: recycling > Reclamation & recycling
Materials: technology & testing
   Brit Civil Engg Test Eqpt Mfrs Assn
   Brit Inst Non-Destructive Testing
   Brit Measurement & Testing Assn
   Brit Soc Strain Measurement
   BTC Testing Advisory Gp
   Engg Integrity Soc

   Inst Materials, Minerals & Mining
   Lifting Eqpt Engrs Assn
   R Microscopical Soc
   Welding Inst
Maternity
   Action Pre-Eclampsia
   Assn Improvements Maternity Services
   Assn Postnatal Illness
   Assn Radical Midwives
   Assn Supervisors Midwives
   Birth Trauma Assn
   Brit Maternal & Fetal Medicine Soc
   Foresight
   Nat Childbirth Trust
   Neonatal Soc
   > + Midwifery; Obstetrics & gynaecology
Mathematics
   Assn Teachers Mathematics
   Brit Interactive Gp
   Brit Soc Hist Mathematics
   Dozenal Soc
   Edinburgh Mathematical Soc
   Glasgow Mathematical Assn
   Inst Mathematics & Applications
   Inst Numerical Computation & Analysis [IRL]
   London Mathematical Soc
   MatheMagic
   Mathematical Assn
   Nat Assn Mathematics Advisers
Mats & matting
   Coir Assn
Maxillofacial disease
   Craniofacial Soc
   > Oral medicine
Mayors
   London Mayors Assn
Mazes
   Maize Maze Assn
ME (disease) > Myalgic encephalomyelitis
Meals on wheels
   Ceretas
Measurement
   Brit Measurement & Testing Assn
   Brit Weights & Measures Assn
   Evaluation Intl
   GAMBICA Assn
   Gauge & Tool Makers Assn
   Inst Measurement & Control
   Metric Martyrs
   Scot Optoelectronics Assn
   Trading Standards Inst
   UK Metric Assn
   UK Weighing Fedn
   > + Scales & weighing machines
Meat
   Assn Indep Meat Suppliers
   Assn Meat Inspectors
   Brit Meat Processors Assn
   Food & Drink Fedn
   Food & Drink Ind Ireland
   Mutton Renaissance Campaign
   Nat Assn Catering Butchers
   Nat Fedn Meat & Food Traders
   NI Master Butchers Assn
   NI Meat Exporters Assn
   Provision Tr Fedn
   Quality Meat Scotland
   Scot Assn Meat Whlsrs
   > + Bacon; Poultry
Meat-free products
   Food & Drink Fedn
Meat substitutes
   Soya Protein Assn
Mechanical components: obsolescence
   Component Obsolescence Gp
Mechanical engineering
   Instn Engg & Technology
   Instn Mechanical Engrs
   N England Inst Mining & Mechanical Engrs
   > + Engineering
Mechanical handling > Materials: management/handling
Medals > Numismatics
Media
   Arts Centre Gp
   Assn Interactive Media & Entertainment
   Assn Measurement & Evaluation Communication
   Assn Media Educ Scotland

© CBD Research Ltd · Beckenham · BR3 5JS · Tel 020 8650 7745 E-mail cbd@cbdresearch.com · www.cbdresearch.com

Assn UK Media Librarians
Brit Interactive Media Assn
Community Media Assn
Directors Gld
Fedn Entertainment Us
Inst Internal Communication
Media, Communication & Cultural Studies Assn
Media Education Assn
Media Res Gp
Media Soc
Online Content UK
> + Newspapers & periodicals;   Radio; Television; Multimedia

Mediæval history
London Medieval Soc
Medieval Settlement Res Gp
Medieval Siege Soc
Ranulf Higden Soc
Scot Medievalists
Soc Ancients
> + Records: historical

Mediation
Mediators Inst Ireland

Medical: accidents
Action Med Accidents

Medical: accountants
Assn Indep Specialist Med Accountants

Medical: apparatus & appliances > Health care: equipment & supplies;
Sterilising; Surgical equipment & supplies

Medical: broadcasts
Assn Broadcasting Doctors

Medical: conditions: long-term
Nat Voices

Medical: & dental hypnosis
Brit Assn Med Hypnosis
Brit Soc Clinical & Academic Hypnosis
> + Hypnosis & hypnotherapy

Medical: education
Assn Study Med Educ
Fellowship Postgraduate Medicine
Nat Assn Clinical Tutors
Nat Assn Primary Care Educators
Sense Science

Medical: equipment & devices > Health care: equipment & supplies; Sterilising;
Surgical equipment & supplies

Medical: herbalists > Herbs & herbal medicine

Medical: illustration
Inst Med Illustrators
Medical Artists Assn
R Photographic Soc

Medical: insurance > Hospitals: contributory schemes;   Medical: practitioners'
legal defence

Medical: journalism > Medical: writing/journalism

Medical: laboratory technology > Medical: technology

Medical: officers
Assn Directors Public Health
Medical Officers Schools Assn
Soc Occupational Medicine

Medical: physics
Fedn Healthcare Science
Inst Physics & Engg in Medicine

Medical: practice
Balint Soc
Catholic Med Assn
Country Doctors Assn
Family Doctor Assn
Fedn Indep Practitioner Orgs
Indep Doctors Fedn
Medical Women's Fedn
Nat Assn Med Educ Mgt
Nat Assn Patient Participation
Nat Assn Sessional GP's
NHS Consultants' Assn
R Coll Gen Practitioners
> + Medicine

Medical: practice - administration
Assn Med Secretaries, Practice Managers. . .
NHS Alliance

Medical: practitioners' legal defence
Medical Defence U
Medical & Dental Defence U Scotland
Medical Protection Soc

Medical: records
Inst Health Record & Inf Mgt

Medical: research
Academy Medical Sciences
Anaesthetic Res Soc
Assn Med Res Charities

Fedn Healthcare Science
Inst Clinical Res
Medical Res Soc
Patients' Voice Med Advance
> + Medicine

Medical: secretaries
Assn Med Secretaries, Practice Managers. . .

Medical: technology
Assn Brit Healthcare Inds
Brit Med Laser Assn
Inst Biomedical Science
Inst Physics & Engg in Medicine
Ir Med Devices Assn
Medical Science Histl Soc
Pharmaceutical & Healthcare Sciences Soc
> + individual science

Medical: waste
Sanitary Med Disposal Services Assn

Medical: writing/journalism
Assn Brit Science Writers
Medical Journalists Assn
Soc Medical Writers

Medicinal preparations > Pharmaceuticals

Medicine
Assn Palliative Medicine
Brit Holistic Med Assn
Brit Med Assn
Brit Med Ultrasound Soc
Brit Nuclear Medicine Soc
Brit Soc Rehabilitation Medicine
Fac Pharmaceutical Med
Harveian Soc Lond
Hunterian Soc
Intensive Care Soc
Ir Coll Gen Practitioners
Ir Med Org
Manchester Med Soc
Medical Soc Lond
Medical Women's Fedn
R Academy Medicine Ireland
R Coll Physicians Edinburgh
R Coll Physicians Ireland
R Coll Physicians Lond
R Coll Physicians & Surgeons Glasgow
R Medical Soc
R Soc Medicine
R Soc Tropical Medicine & Hygiene
Royal Soc (The)
Soc Social Medicine

Medicine: accident & emergency
Assn Paediatric Resuscitation Officers
Brit Assn Immediate Care
College Emergency Medicine

Medicine: acute
Soc Acute Medicine

Medicine: alternative > Complementary medicine; & specific forms

Medicine: herbal > Herbs & herbal medicine

Medicine: history
Brit Soc Hist Medicine
Brit Soc Hist Science
Histl Med Eqpt Soc
Medical Science Histl Soc
Scot Soc Hist Medicine
Soc Social Hist Medicine

Medicine: & the law
Assn Med Reporting Orgs
Fac Forensic & Legal Medicine
Medico-Legal Soc
> + Forensic science

Medicine: & religion
Catholic Med Assn
Gld Health
Gld Pastoral Psychology

Medicine: sports > Sports: medicine & therapy

Medicine: travel > Travel & tourism: health

Meetings (conduct of)
Assn Speakers Clubs

Megaliths
Megalithic Soc

Megapodes > Game & game birds

Members of Parliament
Assn Former MPs
> + Parliamentary government

Membranes (intelligent)
Intelligent Membrane Tr Assn

Memorials
Brit Epigraphy Soc

Church Monuments Soc
Nat Assn Memorial Masons
Public Monuments & Sculpture Assn
> + Stone masons & sculptors
Memory
Brit False Memory Soc
Mendelssohn-Bartholdy (Felix)
Friends Mendelssohn
Ménière's disease
Meniere's Soc
Meningitis
Meningitis Assn Scotland
Meningitis Res Foundation
Menopause (the)
Brit Menopause Soc
Brit Soc Psychosomatic Obstetrics...
Daisy Network
Menswear
Brit Menswear Gld
Brit Shops & Stores Assn
> + Clothing; Tailoring
Mental health
Anxiety UK
Assn Child & Adolescent Mental Health
Assn Infant Mental Health UK
Assn Pastoral Care Mental Health
Assn Therapeutic Communities
Brit Soc Mental Health & Deafness
Eating Disorders Assn
ENABLE Scotland
Fragile X Soc
Inclusion Ireland
Mental Health Ireland
Mind
Nat Assn Mental After-Care in... Homes
Nat Network Assessment Centres
NI Assn Mental Health
Psychiatric Rehabilitation Assn
R Mencap Soc
Rethink
Scot Assn Mental Health
Together
UK Fedn Smaller Mental Health Agencies
> + Psychiatry; specific forms of mental illness
Mental stress > Stress (physical & mental)
Merchant Navy
Merchant Navy Assn
Nat U Rail Maritime & Transport Workers
> + Shipping
Mercury in dentistry
Brit Soc Mercury Free Dentistry
Mergers & acquisitions > Business: mergers & acquisitions
Merry-go-rounds > Fairgrounds & equipment
Merton (Thomas)
Thomas Merton Soc
Messaging > Mobile phones
Messengers-at-Arms
Soc Messengers-at-Arms & Sheriff Officers
Metabolic disorders
Children Living Inherited Metabolic Diseases
Metal
Aluminium Alloy Mfrg & Recycling Assn
Brit Hardmetal & Engineers' Cutting Tool Assn
Minor Metals Tr Assn
Non Ferrous Alliance
Scot Assn Metals
Metal: abrasives > Abrasives
Metal: boxes
Metal Packaging Mfrs Assn
Metal: casting
Cast Metals Fedn
Inst Cast Metals Engrs
Inst Materials, Minerals & Mining
Metal: detecting
Fedn Indep Detectorists
Nat Coun Metal Detecting
Metal: finishing
Aluminium Finishing Assn
Brit Allied Trs Fedn
Inst Metal Finishing
Surface Engg Assn
Metal: forming
Confedn Brit Metalforming
Metalforming Machinery Makers' Assn
Metal: mining > Mining

Metal: non-ferrous
Aluminium Stockholders Assn
Brit Non-Ferrous Metals Fedn
Metal: scrap
Aluminium Alloy Mfrg & Recycling Assn
Brit Metals Recycling Assn
> + Reclamation & recycling
Metal: sheet
Inst Sheet Metal Engg
Metal: spraying
Thermal Spraying & Surface Engg Assn
Metal: working
Blacksmiths Gld
Brit Artist Blacksmiths Assn
Brit Metallurgical Plant Constructors Assn
Cold Rolled Sections Assn
Metalforming Machinery Makers' Assn
UK Lubricants Assn
Metallurgy
Birmingham Metallurgical Assn
Histl Metallurgy Soc
Mineral Ind Res Org
Minerals Engg Soc
Metals: precious > Gemstones; Goldsmiths & Silversmiths; Jewellery
Metalware (antique)
Antique Metalware Soc
Brit Antique Furniture Restorers Assn
Metamorphic technique
Metamorphic Association
Metaphysics
Aetherius Soc
Soc Metaphysicians
Meteorology
R Meteorological Soc
Remote Imaging Group
Tornado & Storm Res Org
Meters & metering
Assn Meter Operators
BEAMA
Nat Campaign Water Justice
SBGI
Soc Brit Water & Wastewater Inds
UK Metering Forum
UK Revenue Protection Assn
Methane
UK Onshore Operators Gp
Methicillin-resistant Staphylococcus
MRSA Support Gp
Methodist Church
Soc Cirplanologists
Wesley Histl Soc
Metric system
Dozenal Soc
UK Metric Assn
> + Measurement
Metrology > Measurement
Mexico
Brit Mexican Soc
Camara Comercio Britanica [Mexico]
Mice
Nat Mouse Club
Microbiology
Assn Applied Biologists
Brit Occupational Hygiene Soc
Brit Soc Antimicrobial Chemotherapy
Brit Soc Microbial Technology
Pathological Soc
Scot Microbiology Assn
Scot Microbiology Soc
Soc Anaerobic Microbiology
Soc Applied Microbiology
Soc Gen Microbiology
Microcirculation > Haematology
Microelectronics
Nat Microelectronics Inst
Microlight aircraft
Brit Microlight Aircraft Assn
Microphthalmia
Micro & Anophthalmic Children's Soc
Microscopy
Quekett Microscopical Club
R Microscopical Soc
Microwave ovens
Microwave Technologies Assn
Middle East
Ancient Egypt & Middle East Soc

© CBD Research Ltd · Beckenham · BR3 5JS · Tel 020 8650 7745   E-mail cbd@cbdresearch.com · www.cbdresearch.com

Brit Soc Middle Eastn Studies
Middle East Assn
Midwifery
Assn Radical Midwives
Assn Supervisors Midwives
Indep Midwives
R Coll Midwives
> + Maternity; Obstetrics & gynaecology
Migraine & headaches
Brit Assn Study Headache
Migraine Action Assn
Milestones
Milestone Soc
Military bands > Brass & silver bands
Military history
Army Records Soc
Brit Cartographic Soc
Brit Model Soldier Soc
Corps Drums Soc
Military Heraldry Soc
Military Hist Soc Ireland
Military Histl Soc
Pike & Shot Soc
R Air Force Histl Soc
Soc Ancients
Soc Army Histl Res
Victorian Military Soc
Western Front Assn
> + Fortresses & forts
Military vehicles
Military Vehicle Trust
Miniature Armoured Fighting Vehicle Assn
> + Defence equipment
Milk (incl milk products) > Dairying; Unpasteurised milk
Milk cartons & bottles
Alliance Beverage Cartons & Envt
Milk Bottle News
> + Packaging
Milking equipment
Milking Eqpt Assn

Milling > Grinding & milling machinery; & product milled
Millipedes
Brit Myriapod & Isopod Gp
Mills & mill engines
Northern Mill Engine Soc
Soc Protection Ancient Bldgs
> + Steam engines, boats & machinery
Mineral water > Bottled water; Water treatment & supply
Mineral wool
Mineral Wool Insulation Mfrs Assn
> + Insulation
Minerals
Brit Aggregates Assn
Inst Materials, Minerals & Mining
Ir Mining & Exploration Gp
Mineral Ind Res Org
Mineralogical Soc
Russell Soc
> + Geology
Miniature painting
Brit Soc Miniaturists
Hilliard Soc Miniaturists
R Soc Miniature Painters...
Soc Limners
> + Art & artists
Minicabs > Taxis & minicabs
Mining
Assn Mining Analysts
Brit Aggregates Assn
Brit Assn Colliery Mgt
Cornish Cham Mines & Minerals
Cornish Mining Devt Assn
Inst Materials, Minerals & Mining
Ir Assn Economic Geology
Ir Mining & Exploration Gp
Ir Mining & Quarrying Soc
Mineral Ind Res Org
Minerals Engg Soc
Mining Assn
N England Inst Mining & Mechanical Engrs
> + Coal mining
Mining: equipment
Assn Brit Mining Eqpt Cos
Mining: history
Early Mines Res Gp
Nat Assn Mining Hist Orgs

Nat Mining Memorabilia Assn
Northern Mine Res Soc
Peak District Mines Hist Soc
Subterranea Britannica
Trevithick Soc
Welsh Mines Soc
Minkhounds > Hounds
Mire research
Brit Ecological Soc
Mirrors
Glass & Glazing Fedn
Miscarriage
Miscarriage Assn
> + Maternity
Missionary organisations
Soc Promoting Christian Knowledge
Mnemonics
Soc Metaphysicians
Mobile catering > Catering: mobile
Mobile communications > Communication services; Mobile phones; Paging
(radio); Radio: mobile
Mobile community resources
Nat Playbus Assn
Mobile data
Assn Automatic Identification &... Data Capture
Mobile Data Assn
Mobile homes
Nat Assn Park Home Residents
> + Caravans & caravanning
Mobile phones
Ir Cellular Industry Assn
Mobile Electronics & Security Fedn
Mobile Ind Crime Action Forum
Mobile Operators Assn
Telecommunications & Internet Fedn [IRL]
Mobile radio > Radio: mobile
Mobility aids
Brit Healthcare Trs Assn
Ir Wheelchair Assn
> + Blind & partially sighted; Disabled: road users; Health care:
equipment & supplies
Model making
Pattern Model & Mouldmakers Assn
Soc Architectural Illustration
Soc Model & Experimental Engrs
> + Models: hobby
Model theatre > Theatre: model
Models: fashion > Fashion
Models: hobby
Assn Model Rly Socs Scotland
Brit Model Flying Assn
Brit Model Soldier Soc
Brit Radio Car Assn
Brit Slot Car Racing Assn
Histl Model Rly Soc
Miniature Armoured Fighting Vehicle Assn
Model Electronic Rly Gp
Model Power Boat Assn
Model Rly Club
Model Yachting Assn
Scot Aeromodellers Assn
Soc Model Shipwrights
Train Collectors Soc
Modern dancing > Dancing
Modern languages > Languages; & specific countries
Modular & portable buildings
Modular & Portable Bldg Assn
Molecatchers
Brit Traditional Molecatchers Register
Molluscs > Conchology; Shellfish
Monarchy
Monarchist League
R Stuart Soc
Soc Court Studies
Money transmission
UK Cards Assn
UK Money Transmitters Assn
Monumental masonry > Stone masons & sculptors
Monuments > Brasses; Historic buildings; Memorials
Moon type
R Nat Inst Blind People
Moore (John) conservationist
John Moore Soc
Moorland
Moorland Assn
Scot Assn Country Sports

Morocco
>> Brit Cham Comm Morocco
>> Brit Moroccan Soc
Morris dancing
>> Morris Fedn
>> Morris Ring
>> > + Folk dance & song
Morris (William)
>> William Morris Soc
Mortar
>> Intl Masonry Soc
>> Mineral Products Assn
Mortgages
>> Assn Mortgage Intermediaries
>> Coun Mortgage Lenders
>> Indep Banking Advy Service
>> Intermediary Mortgage Lenders Assn
>> Ir Mortgage Coun
>> Nat Assn Comml Finance Brokers
>> Safe Home Income Plans
Mosaics
>> Assn Study & Presvn Roman Mosaics
>> Nat Fedn Terrazzo, Marble & Mosaic Specialists
Mosses > Bryology
Mothers > Maternity; Obstetrics & gynaecology; Women's organisations
Moths > Butterflies & moths; Entomology
Motor > entries below, & Car headings
Motor boats > Boats & boating
Motor cycles > Cycles & motorcycles
Motor cycles: historic > Motor vehicles: historic
Motor cycling & scooter riding
>> Amat Motor Cycle Assn
>> Assn Pioneer Motor Cyclists
>> Auto-Cycle U
>> Brit Motor Cycle Racing Club
>> Brit Motorcyclists Fedn
>> Brit Scooter Sport Org
>> Brit Speedway Promoters' Assn
>> Fedn Sidecar Clubs
>> Hillclimb & Sprint Assn
>> Inst Advanced Motorists
>> Manx Grand Prix Riders Assn
>> Motorcycle Action Gp
>> Nat Assn Bikers Disability
>> Nat Hillclimb Assn
>> Nat Sprint Assn
>> Scot Auto Cycle U
>> Speedway Control Bd
>> Trail Riders Fellowship
>> TT Riders Assn
>> Vintage Motor Cycle Club
>> World Speedway Riders Assn
Motor(s): electric > Electric motors
Motor engines: reconditioning
>> Fedn Engine Re-Mfrs
Motor factors
>> Group Auto U
>> Indep Motor Tr Factors Assn
Motor industry
>> BTC Testing Advisory Gp
>> Fedn Automatic Transmission Engrs
>> Fire Fighting Vehicles Mfrs Assn
>> Inst Automotive Engr Assessors
>> Inst Motor Ind
>> MIRA Ltd
>> Motor Ind Public Affairs Assn Ltd
>> Motor Vehicle Dismantlers Assn
>> Soc Ir Motor Ind
>> Soc Motor Mfrs & Traders
>> Vehicle Builders & Repairers Assn
>> > + Electric: transport
Motor insurance > Insurance
Motor neurone disease
>> Motor Neurone Disease Assn
>> Scot Motor Neurone Disease Assn
Motor sport
>> Assn Motor Racing Circuit Owners
>> Brit Automobile Racing Club
>> Brit Motor Sprint Assn
>> Brit Motorsport Marshals Club
>> Brit Off Road Driving Assn
>> Brit Racing & Sports Car Club
>> Brit Stock Car Drivers Assn
>> Brit Trials & Rally Drivers Assn
>> Brit Truck Racing Assn
>> Brooklands Soc
>> Hillclimb & Sprint Assn

>> Motor Sports Assn
>> Motoring Orgs' Land Access & Recreation Assn
>> Motorsport Ind Assn
>> Nat Autograss Sport Assn
>> RSAC Motorsport
>> Scot Motor Racing Club
>> Scot Sporting Car Club
>> Ulster Automobile Club
Motor trade
>> A1 Motor Stores
>> Brit Indep Motor Tr Assn
>> Nat Jumblers Fedn
>> Retail Motor Ind Fedn
>> Scot Motor Tr Assn
>> > + Garages
Motor vehicles: customised
>> Nat Street Rod Assn
>> Nat Street Van Assn
Motor vehicles: electronic equipment
>> Mobile Electronics & Security Fedn
>> Mobile Media Specialist Assn
Motor vehicles: fleet management
>> Inst Car Fleet Mgt
Motor vehicles: hire
>> Brit Vehicle Rental & Leasing Assn
>> Car Rental Coun Ireland
>> Credit Hire Org
>> London Private Hire Car Assn
>> Nat Assn Licensing & Enforcement Offrs
>> Nat Limousine & Chauffeur Assn
>> Nat Private Hire Assn
Motor vehicles: historic
>> Assn Classic Trials Clubs
>> Assn Land Rover Clubs
>> Assn Old Vehicle Clubs NI
>> Brit Ambulance Soc
>> Brooklands Soc
>> Classic Rally Assn
>> Farm Machinery Presvn Soc
>> Fedn Brit Historic Vehicle Clubs
>> Fire Service Presvn Gp
>> Historic Comml Vehicle Soc
>> Historic Endurance Rallying Org
>> London Vintage Taxi Assn
>> Military Vehicle Trust
>> Nat Assn Road Transport Museums
>> Nat Jumblers Fedn
>> Nat Traction Engine Trust
>> Nat Vintage Tractor & Engine Club
>> Post Office Vehicle Club
>> Road Locomotive Soc
>> Road Roller Assn
>> Road Transport Fleet Data Soc
>> Roads & Road Transport Hist Assn
>> Scot Vintage Vehicle Fedn
>> Soc Automotive Historians
>> Southern Counties Historic Vehicle Presvn Trust
>> Steam Car Club
>> Steam Plough Club
>> Transport Trust
>> Vintage Motor Cycle Club
>> Vintage Sports Car Club
Motor vehicles: lining & racking
>> Mobile Electronics & Security Fedn
Motor vehicles: number plates
>> Brit Number Plate Mfrs Assn
Motor vehicles: recovery
>> Assn Vehicle Recovery Operators
>> Inst Vehicle Recovery
>> London Assn Recovery Operators
>> Retail Motor Ind Fedn
>> Road Rescue Recovery Assn
Motor vehicles: salvage
>> Brit Vehicle Salvage Fedn
Motor vehicles: security
>> Auto Locksmiths Assn
>> Mobile Media Specialist Assn
Motor vehicles: taxation
>> Alliance Urban 4x4s
Motor vehicle: transporters
>> Road Haulage Assn
Motoring journalism
>> Gld Motoring Writers
Motoring organisations
>> All Wheel Drive Club
>> Assn Brit Drivers
>> Automobile Assn

© CBD Research Ltd · Beckenham · BR3 5JS · Tel 020 8650 7745   E-mail cbd@cbdresearch.com · www.cbdresearch.com

Blue Badge Network
Disabled Motoring UK
Disabled Motorists Fedn
Drivers' Alliance
Inst Advanced Motorists
R Ir Automobile Club
Motoring schools > Driving tuition
Moulding sand
    Mineral Products Assn
Moulds > Patternmaking
Mountain bothies
    Mountain Bothies Assn
Mountaineering > Climbing
Mountains (walking in)
    Brit Assn Intl Mountain Leaders
Mounted games/activities > Horses: riding & driving
Movable walls
    Assn Interior Specialists
Mowers > Lawn mowers
MSRA
    MRSA Support Gp
Mucopolysaccharidosis
    Soc Mucopolysaccharide Diseases
Muggeridge (Malcolm)
    Malcolm Muggeridge Soc
Mules
    Brit Mule Soc
Multiple births > Twins & multiple births
Multiple sclerosis
    Multiple Sclerosis Nat Therapy Centres
    Multiple Sclerosis Soc
    Multiple Sclerosis Soc Ireland
Multiple shops > Retail trade
Mumming > Folk dance & song
Municipal > Local government
Munro (Neil)
    Neil Munro Soc
Murder & manslaughter
    Support Murder Manslaughter
    > + Children: death by accident/violence
Murray (Keith)
    Keith Murray Collectors Club
Muscle disorders
    Arthrogryposis Gp
Muscular dystrophy > Dystrophy
Musculoskeletal medicine
    Arthritis & Musculoskeletal Alliance
    Brit Inst Musculoskeletal Medicine
    Soc Orthopaedic Medicine
    > + Arthritis & rheumatism
Museums
    Assn Brit Transport & Engg Museums
    Assn Indep Museums
    Assn Leading Visitor Attractions
    Brit Assn Friends Museums
    Brit Museum Friends
    Collections Trust
    Fedn Museums & Art Galleries Wales
    Group Educ Museums
    Heritage Rly Assn
    Ir Museums Assn
    Museums Assn
    Nat Art Collections Fund
    Nat Assn Road Transport Museums
    Nat Heritage
    Scot Museums Fedn
    Social Hist Curators Gp
Museums: staff
    Assn Art Historians
    Museum Profls Gp
    Soc Museum Archaeologists
Mushrooms > Mycology
Music
    Assn Indep Music
    Assn Ir Musical Socs
    Brit Music Soc
    Campaign Freedom Piped Music
    Dvořák Soc Czech & Slovak Music
    Entertainment Retailers Assn
    Fedn Recorded Music Socs
    Inst Contemporary Arts
    Ir Recorded Music Assn
    Light Music Soc
    Music Inds Assn
    Music Managers Forum
    Nat Assn Brass Band Conductors
    Nat Early Music Assn

    Nat Fedn Music Socs
    Plainsong & Mediæval Music Soc
    Production Services Assn
    R Musical Assn
    R Philharmonic Soc
    R Scot Academy Music & Drama
    Robert Farnon Soc
    Scot Amat Music Assn
    Scot Music Ind Assn
    Soc Music Analysis
    Sound Sense
    Test Card Circle
    Viola da Gamba Soc
    Welsh Amat Music Fedn
    Welsh Music Gld
    Workers' Music Assn
    > + Choirs & choral music; Church music; Orchestras
Music: composers & conductors > individual by name
Music: composing
    Brit Academy Songwriters, Composers & Authors
    Brit Music Rights
    Soc Producers & Composers Applied Music
Music: copyright > Copyright
Music: festivals > Festivals: art, drama & music
Music: hall
    Brit Music Hall Soc
    Scot Music Hall & Variety Theatre Soc
Music: psychology
    Soc Educ Music & Psychology Res
Music: recording > Sound recording & reproduction
Music: sheet
    Music Pubrs' Assn
Music: teaching
    Brit Kodály Academy
    Brit Suzuki Inst
    Conservatoires UK
    Curwen Inst
    Fedn Music Services
    Inc Soc Musicians
    Jazz Piano Teachers Assn
    Music Educ Coun
    Music Masters' & Mistresses' Assn
    Nat Assn Music Educators
    Nat Assn Percussion Teachers
    Percussive Arts Soc
    R Academy Music
    R Ir Academy Music
    Schools Music Assn
    Scot Assn Music Educ
Music: therapy
    Allied Health Professions Fedn
    Brit Assn Music Therapy
Musical boxes
    Musical Box Soc
Musical instruments
    Fair Organ Presvn Soc
    Fellowship Makers... Histl Instruments
    Galpin Soc
    Inst Musical Instrument Technology
    Music Inds Assn
    Nat Early Music Assn
    > + specific instruments
Musicians
    Gld Musicians & Singers
    Inc Soc Musicians
    Musicians U
    R Soc Musicians
Mussels > Shellfish
Mutism
    Selective Mutism Inf & Res Assn
    > + Speech
Mutton
    Mutton Renaissance Campaign
Muzak
    Campaign Freedom Piped Music
Myalgic encephalitis/encephalopathy
    Action ME
    Assn Young People with ME
    Myalgic Encephalopathy Assn
Myasthenia
    Myasthenia Gravis Assn
Mycology
    Assn Brit Fungus Gps
    Birmingham Natural Hist Soc
    Brit Mycological Soc
    Brit Soc Antimicrobial Chemotherapy
    Brit Soc Med Mycology

Myelitis
>> Transverse Myelitis Soc
Myositis
>> Myositis Support Gp
Myotonic dystrophy > Dystrophy
Myriapods
>> Brit Myriapod & Isopod Gp
Myths & legends
>> Traditional Cosmology Soc
>> > + Folk life & lore

N

Naevus > Birthmarks & disfigurement
Nail Patella Syndrome
>> Nail Patella Syndrome UK
Names
>> Gld One Name Studies
>> Soc Name Studies Britain & Ireland
>> > + Place names
Nannies & au pairs
>> Assn Nanny Agencies
>> Voice
Napoleon I, II & III
>> Assn Friends Waterloo C'ee
>> Napoleonic Assn
>> Napoleonic Soc
Nappies
>> Absorbent Hygiene Products Mfrs Assn
Narcissus
>> Daffodil Soc
Narcolepsy
>> Narcolepsy UK
Narrow fabrics
>> Braid Soc
>> Brit Narrow Fabrics Assn
National Health Service
>> Ambulance Service Network
>> Health Care Supply Assn
>> Healthcare Financial Mgt Assn
>> Healthcare People Mgt Assn
>> Inst Healthcare Mgt
>> Nat Assn Healthcare Security
>> Nat Assn Primary Care
>> Nat Assn Voluntary Service Mgrs
>> NHS Confedn
>> NHS Support Fedn
>> NHS Trusts Assn
>> Socialist Health Assn
National Parks
>> Assn Nat Park Authorities
>> Campaign Nat Parks
>> Scot Campaign Nat Parks
>> > + Parks & gardens
National vocational qualifications
>> Inst Assessors & Internal Verifiers
Nationalism
>> Assn Study Ethnicity & Nationalism
Natural energy > Renewable energy; Solar energy
Natural gas
>> Natural Gas Vehicle Assn
Natural health & therapeutics
>> Alliance Natural Health
>> Assn Natural Medicine
>> Assn Physical & Natural Therapists
>> Assn Systematic Kinesiology
>> Brit Natural Hygiene Soc
>> College Vibrational Medicine Practitioner Assn
>> Consumers Health Choice
>> Radionic Assn Ltd
>> > + Complementary medicine
Natural history
>> Brit Entomological & Natural Hist Soc
>> Brit Naturalists Assn
>> Field Studies Coun
>> Linnean Soc Lond
>> Nat Assn Field Studies Officers
>> Northamptonshire Natural History Soc
>> Ray Soc
>> Soc Hist Natural Hist
>> Somerset Archaeol & Natural Hist Soc
>> Wiltshire Archaeol & Natural Hist Soc
>> > + Archaeology: county societies;   Conservation: area organisations

Nature conservation
>> Assn Natural Burial Grounds
>> Brit Assn Nature Conservationists
>> Butterfly Consvn
>> Countryside Alliance
>> Landlife
>> Marine Consvn Soc
>> Nat Assn Areas Outstanding Natural Beauty
>> Nat Coun Consvn Plants & Gardens
>> Nat Fedn Biological Recording
>> R Soc Wildlife Trusts
>> Scot Envt Link
>> Scot Wildlife Trust
>> Small Farms Assn
>> > + Conservation
Nature conservation: local reserves
>> Armagh > County Armagh Wildlife Soc
>> Ashmolean Natural Hist Soc Oxfordshire
>> Birmingham Natural Hist Soc
>> County Armagh Wildlife Soc
>> Croydon Natural Hist & Scientific Soc
>> Durham Wildlife Trust
>> Essex Wildlife Trust
>> Falklands Consvn
>> Glasgow Natural Hist Soc
>> Gwent Wildlife Trust
>> Herefordshire > Woolhope Naturalists' Field Club
>> Isle of Wight Natural Hist & Archaeol Soc
>> London Natural Hist Soc
>> Natural Hist Soc Northumbria
>> Norfolk Wildlife Trust
>> Northumbria > Natural Hist Soc Northumbria
>> Woolhope Naturalists' Field Club
Naturism
>> Assn Brit Naturist Clubs
>> Central Coun Brit Naturism
>> Ir Naturist Assn
Naturopathy
>> Brit Naturopathic Assn
>> Gen Coun & Register Naturopaths
>> Inc Soc Registered Naturopaths
>> > + Natural health & therapeutics
Nautical archaeology > Archaeology: nautical
Nautical history
>> Britannia Naval Res Assn
>> Hakluyt Soc
>> Histl Maritime Soc
>> Maritime Inf Assn
>> Maritime Inst Ireland
>> Mary Rose Soc
>> Naval Dockyards Soc
>> Naval Histl Collectors & Res Assn
>> Navy Records Soc
>> Soc Nautical Res
Nautical instruments
>> Chart & Nautical Instrument Tr Assn
Nautical training > Marine: education; Sailing
Naval archaeology > Archaeology: nautical
Naval architecture & equipment > Marine: engineering & equipment; Shipbuilding & ship repairing
Naval history > Nautical history
Navigation
>> Assn Lighthouse Keepers
>> Gld Air Pilots & Air Navigators
>> Nautical Inst
>> R Inst Navigation
>> Sub Aqua Assn
Navy > Royal Navy
Neck injury & disease > Head & neck injury & disease
Needham (Violet)
>> Violet Needham Soc
Nelson (Admiral, Lord Horatio)
>> Histl Maritime Soc
>> Nelson Society
>> R Navy Enthusiasts' Soc
Nematology
>> Assn Applied Biologists
Neonatal death > Maternity
Nepal
>> Britain-Nepal Cham Comm
>> Britain Nepal Soc
Nephrology
>> Brit Kidney Patient Assn
>> Brit Renal Soc
>> Ir Kidney Assn
>> Nat Kidney Fedn

Purine Metabolic Patients Assn
Renal Assn
Nerine
Nerine & Amaryllid Soc
Nesbit (Edith)
Edith Nesbit Soc
Netball
All England Netball Assn
Netball NI
Netball Scotland
Welsh Netball Assn
Netherlands
Anglo Netherlands Soc
Assn Low Countries Studies
Netherlands Brit Cham Comm
Netherlands: language & literature
Assn Language Learning
Netsuke carving
Brit Woodcarvers Assn
Networking
Assn Interactive Media & Entertainment
Intellect
Nat Outsourcing Assn
Neuralgia
Trigeminal Neuralgia Assn
Neuroblastoma
Neuroblastoma Soc
> + Cancer
Neurofibromatosis
Neurofibromatosis Assn
Neurology
Assn Brit Neurologists
Assn Neuro-Linguistic Programming
Batten Disease Family Assn
Brit Neuropsychiatry Assn
Brit Neuropsychological Soc
Brit Soc Neuroendocrinology
Brit Soc Neuroradiologists
CMT UK
Guillain Barre Syndrome Support Gp
Neuroanaesthesia Soc
Neurological Alliance
Stiff Man Syndrome Support Gp
Neuropathology
Brit Neuropathological Soc
Neurophysiology
Assn Neurophysiological Scientists
Brit Soc Clinical Neurophysiology
Neuroscience
Brit Neuropsychiatry Assn
Brit Neuroscience Assn
Physiological Soc
Scot Neuroscience Gp
Neurosurgery
Soc Brit Neurological Surgeons
Neutral alcohol
Nat Alcohol Producers Assn
New Zealand
Australian Business
Brit New Zealand Tr Coun
Hebe Soc
Newsagents > Newspapers & periodicals: distribution
Newsletters
Specialised Inf Publishers Assn
> + Periodicals
Newspapers
Assn Circulation Executives
Assn Regional City Editors
Assn UK Media Librarians
Foreign Press Assn Lond
Nat Newspapers Ireland
Newspaper Conf
Newspaper Pubrs Assn
Newspaper Soc
Press Standards Bd Finance
Regional Newspapers. . . Assn Ireland
Scot Newspaper Soc
Soc Editors
Talking Newspaper Assn
Newspapers & periodicals: distribution
Assn Newspaper Magazine Whlsrs
Assn Subscription Agents & Intermediaries
Convenience Stores & Newsagents Assn [IRL]
Nat Fedn Retail Newsagents
Nickel
Surface Engg Assn

Nigeria
Britain Nigeria Business Coun
Britain-Nigeria Educl Trust
Noise
Assn Noise Consultants
Aviation Envt Fedn
Campaign Freedom Piped Music
Engg Integrity Soc
Environmental Protection UK
Fencing Contrs' Assn
Heating, Ventilating & Air Conditioning Mfrs' Assn
Inst Acoustics
MIRA Ltd
Noise Abatement Soc
Proprietary Acoustic Systems Mfrs
UK Envtl Law Assn
UK Noise Assn
> + Insulation
Non-destructive testing > Materials: technology & testing
Non-ferrous metal > Metal
Non-wovens
Brit Textile Technology Gp
> + Textile headings
Noonam syndrome
Noonan Syndrome Assn
Norman-French texts
Anglo Norman Text Soc
> + English language & literature
North America > USA; Canada
Norway
Anglo Norse Soc
Norwegian-Brit Cham Comm
Notaries public
Assn Solicitor Notaries Greater London
Notaries Soc [E&W]
Novelists > under individual name
Nuclear disarmament > Disarmament
Nuclear energy
Brit Nuclear Test Veterans Assn
Instn Civil Engrs
Nuclear Ind Assn
Nuclear Inst
Supporters Nuclear Energy
Nudism > Naturism
Number plates
Brit Number Plate Mfrs Assn
Inst Registration Agents & Dealers
Numeracy > Literacy & numeracy
Numerical analysis
Inst Mathematics & Applications
Numismatics
Brit Art Medal Soc
Brit Assn Numismatic Socs
Brit Numismatic Soc
Brit Numismatic Tr Assn
Orders & Medals Res Soc
R Numismatic Soc
Token Corresponding Soc
Nurseries & nursery schools
Brit Assn Early Childhood Educ
Nat Campaign Nursery Educ
Nat Day Nurseries Assn
Pre-School Learning Alliance
Scot Pre-School Play Assn
Voice
Wales Pre-school Providers Assn
Nursery & baby products
Absorbent Hygiene Products Mfrs Assn
Baby Eqpt Hirers Assn
Baby Milk Action
Baby Products Assn
Early Childhood Ireland
Nursery stock > Horticulture
Nursing
Assn Brit Paediatric Nurses
Assn Leaders Nursing
Assn Nurse Prescribing
Assn Nursery Training Colls
Assn Nurses Substance Abuse
Assn Occupational Health Nurse Practitioners
Assn Psychosexual Nursing
Brit Assn Dental Nurses
Brit Assn Urological Nurses
Community & District Nursing Assn
Indep Fedn Nursing Scotland
Ir Nurses & Midwives Org
Nat Care Assn

Queen's Nursing Inst
R Coll Nursing
Soc Nursery Nursing Practitioners
> + Veterinary medicine
Nursing homes
English Community Care Assn
Nursing Homes Ireland
Registered Nursing Home Assn
Nutrition
Brit Assn Nutritional Therapy
Brit Assn Parenteral Enteral Nutrition
Brit Dietetic Assn
Brit Nutrition Foundation
Brit Soc Ecological Medicine
Brit Specialist Nutrition Assn
Inst Optimum Nutrition
McCarrison Soc
Nutrition & Health Foundation [IRE]
Nutrition Soc
> + Food
Nuts (allergy to)
Anaphylaxis Campaign
> + Allergy
Nuts (edible)
Brit Peanut Coun
Combined Edible Nut Tr Assn
Fedn Oils, Seeds & Fats Assns
Kentish Cobnuts Assn
Snack, Nut & Crisp Mfrs Assn
NVQs > National vocational qualifications
Nystagmus
Nystagmus Network

O

Oatmeal
Brit Oat & Barley Millers Assn
Obesity
Assn Study Obesity
Brit Obesity & Metabolic Surgery Soc
Brit Obesity Surgery Patient Assn
Nat Obesity Forum
Prader-Willi Syndrome Assn
> + Eating disorders
Oboes (musical instruments)
Brit Double Reed Soc
Observer's Pocket Series
Observers Pocket Series Collectors' Soc
Obsessive/compulsive disorders
Anxiety UK
Nat Acupuncture Detoxification Assn
No Panic
OCD Action
Tourette Syndrome (UK) Assn
> + Mental health
Obsolescence (electronic & mechanical)
Component Obsolescence Gp
Obstetrics & gynaecology
Assn Early Pregnancy Units
Blair Bell Res Soc
Brit Assn Perinatal Medicine
Brit Maternal & Fetal Medicine Soc
Brit Soc Gynaecological Endoscopy
Brit Soc Psychosomatic Obstetrics. . .
Fac Sexual & Reproductive Healthcare
Obstetric Anaesthetists Assn
Ovacome: the ovarian cancer support network
R Coll Obstetricians & Gynaecologists
> + Maternity; Midwifery
Occultism
Aetherius Soc
Occupational health & hygiene
Assn Med Advisers Brit Orchestras
Assn Occupational Health Nurse Practitioners
Brit Occupational Hygiene Soc
Fac Occupational Medicine
Inst Safety Technology & Res
Instn Occupational Safety & Health
Ir Soc Occupational Medicine
Nat Ir Safety Org
Soc Occupational Medicine
Occupational safety > Safety
Occupational therapy
Allied Health Professions Fedn

Assn Occupational Therapists Ireland
Brit Assn Occupational Therapists
Occupational training & education
Assn Learning Providers
Inst Training & Occupational Learning
Ir Inst Training & Devt
Ir Vocational Educ Assn
Learning & Performance Inst
> + Education
Ocean energy > Renewable energy
Ocean industries
Assn Brit Indep Oil Exploration Cos
Assn Brit Offshore Inds
Assn Well Head Eqpt Mfrs
Brit Rig Owners Assn
Emergency Response & Rescue Vessels Assn
Energy Industries Council
Inst Marine Engg, Science & Technology
Intl Marine Contrs Assn
Ir Offshore Operators Assn
NOF Energy
Offshore Contrs' Assn
Offshore Engg Soc
Offshore Ind Liaison C'ee
Seabed User & Developer Gp
UK Offshore Oil & Gas Ind Assn
Oceanography
Challenger Soc Marine Science
Challenger Soc Marine Science
Hydrographic Soc
Marine Inst [IRL]
R Meteorological Soc
Remote Sensing & Photogrammetry Soc
Scot Assn Marine Science
> + Earth sciences, structure & resources
Odontology > Dentistry; Teeth
Oesophageal conditions > Tracheostomy
Offa's Dyke
Offa's Dyke Assn
Offenders > Prisoners: welfare & rehabilitation
Office equipment & systems
Brit Assn Removers
Brit Inst Facilities Mgt
Brit Office Supplies & Services Fedn
Indep Print Inds Assn
Information & Records Mgt Soc
Intellect
Storage Eqpt Mfrs Assn
> + Computers
Office management
Brit Inst Facilities Mgt
Facilities Mgt Assn
Inst Administrative Mgt
Offices (serviced & agents)
Brit Coun Offices
Business Centre Assn
Office Agents Soc
Off-licences > Wines & spirits: trade
Off-road driving > Driving (off-road); Four by fours
Offshore engineering > Ocean industries
Off-street parking > Parking (car)
Oil (industry)
Assn Brit Offshore Inds
UK Onshore Operators Gp
UK Onshore Pipeline Operators' Assn
> + Petroleum; & entries below
Oil: burners & appliances
ICOM Energy Assn
Oil Firing Technical Assn Petroleum Ind
> + Boilers & waterheaters
Oil: hydrocarbon > Petroleum
Oil: lubricating
UK Lubricants Assn
Oil: recovery/waste
Oil Recycling Assn
Oil: spills > Spill control (oil)
Oils: edible > Edible oils & fats
Oils: essential > Essential oils
Oils: painting in
Brit Soc Painters (in Oil, Pastels & Acrylic)
> + Art & Artists
Oilseed
Fedn Oils, Seeds & Fats Assns
Seed Crushers & Oil Processors Assn
Old people's organisations
Abbeyfield Soc
Contact Elderly

Discovery Award England
Nat Assn Almshouses
Nat Assn Providers Activities Older People
Nat Pensioners Convention
R Surgical Aid Soc
R UK Beneficent Assn
Relatives & Residents Assn
Scot Pensioners Forum
> + Retirement
Old Testament > Bible
Olympic games
Brit Olympic Assn
Modern Pentathlon Assn GB
Soc Olympic Collectors
Oman
Anglo Omani Soc
Ombudsman
Brit & Ir Ombudsman Assn
Oncology
BASO
Brain Tumour UK
Brit Acoustic Neuroma Assn
Brit Assn Head & Neck Oncologists
Brit Oncological Assn
Brit Oncology Patients Assn
Von Hippel-Lindau Contact Gp
> + Cancer
One parent families > Singles, divorced & separated
Onions
Brit Onion Producers Assn
Online retailers
Interactive Media Retail Group
Ir Internet Assn
Online users & publishers
Assn Online Publishers
Online Content UK
UK EInformation Gp
> + Internet
Onshore engineering
UK Onshore Operators Gp
UK Onshore Pipeline Operators' Assn
Open learning
Brit Inst Learning & Devt
> + Education
Open spaces
Commons, Open Spaces. . . Presvn Soc
Inst Parks & Green Space
Nat Playing Fields Assn
> + Conservation; Footpaths & rights of way; Parks & gardens
Opencast mining > Mining; Coal mining
Opera
Nat Operatic & Dramatic Assn
Recorded Vocal Art Soc
> + name of composer or singer
Operational research
Inst Operations Mgt
Operational Res Soc
Ophthalmic opticians > Optical practice
Ophthalmology
Brit Ophthalmic Anaesthesia Soc
Ophthalmological Products Tr. . .Conf
R Coll Ophthalmologists
UK & I Soc Cataract & Refractive Surgeons
Opinion polls
Brit Polling Coun
Market Res Soc
Optical character recognition
Assn Automatic Identification &. . .Data Capture
Optical industry
Assn Contact Lens Mfrs
Brit Contact Lens Assn
Fedn Mfrg Opticians
Ophthalmic Lens Mfrs', Assemblers' & Distrbrs' Assn
Optical Confedn
Optical Eqpt Mfrs & Suppliers Assn
Optical Frame Importers' & Mfrs' Assn
Optra Exhibitions UK
Optical practice
Acuity
Assn Brit Dispensing Opticians
Assn Optometrists
Assn Optometrists Ireland
College Optometrists
Fedn Ophthalmic & Dispensing Opticians
Optical Confedn
Options > Futures & options

Optoelectronics
Photonics Cluster
Scot Optoelectronics Assn
Oral medicine
Brit Assn Oral & Maxillofacial Surgeons
Brit Soc Dental Hygiene & Therapy
Brit Soc Disability & Oral Health
Brit Soc Oral & Dental Res
Brit Soc Oral & Maxillofacial Pathology
Brit Soc Oral Medicine
Inst Maxillofacial Prosthetists. . .
> + Dentistry
Orchestras
Assn Brit Orchestras
Assn Med Advisers Brit Orchestras
Halle Concerts Soc
Nat Fedn Music Socs
R Philharmonic Soc
Welsh Amat Music Fedn
> + Music
Orchids
Brit Orchid Coun
Brit Orchid Growers Assn
Hardy Orchid Soc
Orchid Soc
Orders (insignia) > Badges & insignia;   Numismatics
Ordnance > Arms & armour
Ordnance Survey
Charles Close Soc
Orff (Carl)
Orff Soc
Organ donors > Transplants & transplant surgery
Organic chemicals > Chemical industry & trade
Organic growing & farming
Assn Organics Recycling
Biodynamic Agricl Assn
Food & Drink Fedn
Henry Doubleday Res Assn
Ir Organic Farmers & Growers Assn
Organic Food Fedn
Organic Living Assn
Scot Organic Prodrs Assn
Soil Assn
World-Wide Opportunities on Organic Farms
Organisation & methods > Management
Organising clutter
Assn Profl De-clutterers & Organisers
Organs, organists & organ music
Assn Indep Organ Advisers
Brit Inst Organ Studies
Cathedral Organists Assn
Cinema Organ Soc
Fair Organ Presvn Soc
Inc Assn Organists
Inc Soc Organ Builders
Inst Brit Organ Bldg
Karg Elert Archive
Mechanical Organ Owners Soc
Organ Club
R Coll Organists
Ulster Soc Organists & Choirmasters
> + Musical instruments
Oriental carpets & rugs
Brit Oriental Rug Dealers Assn
> + Carpets
Orienteering
Brit Orienteering Fedn
NI Orienteering Assn
Scot Orienteering Assn
Origami
Brit Origami Soc
Ornamental fish > Fish: tropical & ornamental
Ornithology > Birds; Nature conservation
Orthodontics > Dentistry
Orthopaedics
Brit Coalition Heritable Disorders Connective Tissue
Brit Orthopaedic Assn
Soc Orthopaedic Medicine
Orthoptics
Allied Health Professions Fedn
Brit & Ir Orthoptic Soc
> + Ophthalmology
Orthoses > Prosthetics & orthoses
Osteopathy
Brit Osteopathic Assn
Cranio Sacral Soc

Osteopathic Sports Care Assn
     Sutherland Soc
Osteoporosis > Bone
Ostrich farming
     Brit Domesticated Ostrich Assn
     > + Emu; Rhea
Othello (board game)
     Brit Othello Fedn
Otolaryngology
     Brit Assn Otorhinolaryngologists
     Brit Assn Paediatric Otorhinolaryngology
     Brit Voice Assn
     Nat Assn Laryngectomee Clubs
     Scot Otolaryngological Soc
Otters
     Intl Otter Survival Fund
Outdoor advertising > Advertising: outdoor
Outdoor centres > Holiday camps & centres
Outdoor education > Education: outdoor
Outdoor events > specific type of event
Outdoor furniture > Furniture; Horticulture & garden: equipment
Outdoor equipment
     Outdoor Inds Assn
Outdoor professionals
     Brit Outdoor Profls Assn
Outsourcing
     Brit Contract Mfrs & Packers Assn
     Nat Outsourcing Assn
Ovens
     Microwave Technologies Assn
     > + Domestic appliances
Overalls & workwear > Protective clothing/equipment
Overeating > Eating disorders;   Obesity
Overseas development
     Devt Studies Assn
     Voluntary Service Overseas
Overseas property
     Assn Intl Property Profls
     Nat Assn Estate Agents
     > + Property & land owners
Overseas territories (British)
     UK O'seas Territories Assn
Ovulation
     Nat Assn Ovulation Method Instructors
     > + Family planning
Owen (Wilfred)
     Wilfred Owen Assn
Owls
     Hawk & Owl Trust
Oxenham (Elsie Jeanette)
     Elsie Jeanette Oxenham Appreciation Soc
Oysters
     Assn Scot Shellfish Growers
     Shellfish Assn

P

Pacific Islands
     Pacific Islands Soc
Packaging
     Alliance Beverage Cartons & Envt
     Brit Aerosol Mfrs Assn
     Brit Bottlers' Inst
     Brit Brands Gp
     Brit Packaging Assn
     Brit Plastics Fedn
     Brit Printing Inds Fedn
     Ind Coun Packaging & Envt
     Indl Packaging Assn
     Inst Materials, Minerals & Mining
     Ir Corrugated Packaging Assn
     Metal Packaging Mfrs Assn
     Packaging Fedn
     Packaging & Films Assn
     Paper Agents Assn
     Pira Intl
     Processing & Packaging Machinery Assn
     Sheet Plant Assn
     Timber Packaging & Pallet Confedn
     Valpak
Packers & shippers for various trades
     Brit Contract Mfrs & Packers Assn
     > + trade concerned
Packing & packing cases > Packaging

Paddle steamers
     Paddle Steamer Presvn Soc
Paediatrics
     Academic Paediatrics Assn
     Assn Brit Paediatric Nurses
     Assn Paediatric Anaesthetists
     Assn Paediatric Resuscitation Officers
     Brit Assn Paediatric Surgeons
     Brit Soc Gastroenterology
     Children's Chronic Arthritis Assn
     Neonatal Soc
     Paediatric First Aid Assn
     R Coll Paediatrics & Child Health
     > + Children headings
Paeonies
     Hardy Plant Soc
Paganism
     Pagan Fedn
Pagets disease
     Paget's Assn
Paging (radio)
     Fedn Communication Services
     Onsite Communications Assn
Pain
     Brit Pain Soc
     Brit Soc Hypnotherapists
     Pain Assn Scotland
     > + Anaesthesia
Paine (Thomas)
     Thomas Paine Soc UK
Paint
     Brit Coatings Fedn
     Home Decoration Retailers Assn
     Ir Decorative Surface Coatings Assn
     Oil & Colour Chemists Assn
     Paint Res Assn
     Surface Engg Assn
Paintball
     UK Paintball Sports Fedn
Painters > Art & artists
Painting & decorating
     Assn Painting Craft Teachers
     Painting & Decorating Assn
     Scot Assn Painting Craft Teachers
     Scot Decorators Fedn
Pakistan
     Brit Assn S Asian Studies
     UK Pakistan Cham Comm [?dead 05
Palaeontology
     Dinosaur Soc
     Micropalaeontological Soc
     Palaeontographical Soc
     Palaeontological Assn
     Systematics Assn
     Tertiary Res Gp
Palate > Cleft lip & palate
Pallets
     Timber Packaging & Pallet Confedn
     > + Materials: management/handling; Packaging
Palliative care
     Assn Palliative Medicine
     CNK Alliance
     > + Medicine & related headings
Palmistry
     Brit Astrological & Psychic Soc
Palsy > Head & neck injury & disease
Pancreas
     Pancreatic Soc
Panels (insulated)
     Engineered Panels Construction
Panels (wood)
     Timber Tr Fedn
Panic & anxiety attacks
     Anxiety UK
     No Panic
Paper & paper products
     Brit Assn Paper Historians
     Brit Packaging Assn
     Confedn Paper Inds
     Environmental & Technical Assn Paper Sack Ind
     Foodservice Packaging Assn
     Indep Print Inds Assn
     Inst Paper Printing & Publishing
     Ir Corrugated Packaging Assn
     Nat Assn Paper Mchts
     Paper Agents Assn
     Paper Ind Technical Assn

© CBD Research Ltd · Beckenham · BR3 5JS · Tel 020 8650 7745 E-mail cbd@cbdresearch.com · www.cbdresearch.com

Pira Intl
Pulp & Paper Fundamental Res Soc
Paper: conservation
Inst Consvn
Paper: folding > Origami
Paper: making equipment
Picon Ltd
Paper: recovered & waste
Confedn Paper Inds
Pulp & Paper Fundamental Res Soc
Recycling Assn
Paperback collecting
Penguin Collectors' Soc
WW2 HMSO Paperbacks Soc
> + Book: collecting
Paperweights
Caithness Paperweight Collectors Club
Paperweight Collectors Circle
Parachuting
Army Parachute Assn
Brit Hang Gliding & Paragliding Assn
Brit Parachute Assn
Scot Hang Gliding & Paragliding Fedn
Parakarting > Kite sports; Surfing, board & speed sailing
Parallel trading
Parallel Traders Assn
Paramedics > First aid & immediate care
Paranormal & psychical research
Assn Scientific Study Anomalous Phenomena
Assn Skeptical Enquiry
Brit Astrological & Psychic Soc
Inc Soc Psychical Res
Scot Soc Psychical Res
Soc Metaphysicians
Parapet fences
Vehicle Restraint Mfrs Assn
Paraplegia > Disablement; Spine & spinal injury;   Sports: disabled &
handicapped
Parasitology
Brit Soc Parasitology
Parent-teacher associations
Nat Confedn Parent-Teacher Assns
Parents
Assn Shared Parenting
Brit False Memory Soc
Compassionate Friends
Families Need Fathers
Galton Inst
Grandparents Assn
Mothers Apart Children
Nat Assn Child Contact Centres
Nat Coun One Parent Families
Nat Fedn Services Unmarried Parents...[IRL]
Working Families
> + Adoption;   Fostering & foster parents;   Singles, divorced &
separated
Parish registers
Harleian Soc
Lancashire Parish Register Soc
Staffordshire Parish Registers Soc
Yorkshire Archaeol Soc
> + Records: historical;   Church: history & records
Park homes
Nat Assn Park Home Residents
Nat Caravan Coun
Parking (car)
Brit Parking Assn
Car Park Appreciation Soc
Parkinson's disease
Brit Geriatrics Soc
Parkinson's Disease Soc
Parks & gardens
Inst Parks & Green Space
Metropolitan Public Gardens Assn
> + National Parks
Parliamentary agents
Soc Parliamentary Agents
Parliamentary government
Assn Former MPs
Campaign English Parliament
Hansard Soc
Unlock Democracy
> + Government: accountability
Parrots
Parrot Soc
> + Birds

Parsnips
Brit Carrot Growers Assn
Parsonages
Save our Parsonages
> + Church: buildings
Partially sighted > Blind & partially sighted
Partitioning
Assn Interior Specialists
Partridges > Game & game birds
Party walls
Pyramus & Thisbe Club
R Instn Chart Surveyors
> + Surveying
Passenger conveyors
Lift & Escalator Ind Assn
Passenger transport
Assn Transport Co-ordinating Officers
Bus Users UK
Coach Tourism Coun
Confedn Passenger Transport
Gld Brit Coach Operators
Ocean Liner Soc
Omnibus Soc
Passenger Boat Assn
PSV Circle
River Assn Freight & Transport
Routemaster Operators & Owners Assn
Scot Assn Public Transport
> + specific types of transport
Pasta
Pizza, Pasta & Italian Food Assn
Pastels (art)
Brit Soc Painters (in Oil, Pastels & Acrylic)
> + Art & artists
Pastoral care
Assn Pastoral Care Mental Health
Patchwork & quilting
Quilters' Gld
Patent glazing > Glass & glazing
Patents & trade marks
Chart Inst Patent Attorneys
Inst Intl Licensing Practitioners
Inst Patentees & Inventors
Inst Tr Mark Attorneys
MARQUES
Trade Marks Patents & Designs Fedn
> + Copyright
Pathology
Assn Anatomical Pathology Technology
Assn Clinical Pathologists
Brit In Vitro Diagnostics Assn
Brit Soc Toxicological Pathologists
Pathological Soc
R Coll Pathologists
Pathology (of plants)
Brit Soc Plant Pathology
> + Plants
Patients
Action Sick Children
Nat Assn Patient Participation
Nat Cancer Alliance
Patient Inf Forum
Patients Assn
Scotland Patients Assn
> + Medicine
Patio doors > Glass & glazing; Windows
Pattern recognition
Brit Machine Vision Assn...
> + Automatic identification & data capture
Pattern sensing
Remote Sensing & Photogrammetry Soc
Patternmaking
Gauge & Tool Makers Assn
Pattern Model & Mouldmakers Assn
Paving & kerbs
Brick Devt Assn
Brit Precast Concrete Fedn
Pawnbroking
Nat Pawnbrokers Assn
Pay-to-play > Amusements & coin operated machines
Payroll staff
Chart Inst Payroll Profls
Payroll Alliance
Peace
Brit Pugwash Gp
Medical Action Global Security
Peace Pledge U

Peal ringing
        Central Coun Church Bell Ringers
Peanuts
        Anaphylaxis Campaign
        Brit Peanut Coun
        > + Nuts (edible)
Pearls
        Brit Jewellers Assn
Pearly kings & queens
        Original Pearly Kings & Queens Assn
Pears
        English Apples & Pears
        > + Fruit: growing
Peas
        Processors & Growers Res Org
Peat
        Growing Media Assn
        Ir Peatland Consvn Coun
Pedestrians' safety
        Living Streets
        > + Road: safety & control
Peel (Sir Robert)
        Peel Soc
Pelagic fish > Fish headings; Fishing
Pelargoniums
        Hardy Plant Soc
        Pelargonium & Geranium Soc
Penal reform
        Howard League for Penal Reform
        Offenders Tag Assn
        Unlock
Pencils
        UK Coloured Pencil Soc
Penguin books (collecting)
        Penguin Collectors' Soc
Penine Way
        Pennine Way Assn
Pens & pencils > Writing equipment & accessories
Pensions
        Assn Consulting Actuaries
        Assn Member-Directed Pension Schemes
        Assn Pension Lawyers
        Brit Pensioners & Tr U Action Assn
        Chart Inst Payroll Profls
        Compulsory Annuity Purchase Protest Alliance
        Ir Assn Pension Funds
        Ir Inst Pensions Mgt
        Nat Assn Pension Funds
        Nat Fedn Occupational Pensioners
        Nat Pensioners Convention
        Occupational Pensioners Alliance
        Parity
        Pensions Action Gp
        Pensions Mgt Inst
        Scot Pensioners Forum
        Soc Pension Consultants
Pentathlon
        Modern Pentathlon Assn GB
        Scot Modern Pentathlon Assn
Percussion (playing)
        Nat Assn Percussion Teachers
        Percussive Arts Soc
Performing animals > Animals: welfare;   Circuses & circus artistes
Performing arts medicine
        Brit Assn Performing Arts Medicine
Performing right > Copyright
Perfumery
        Brit Soc Perfumers
        Cosmetic, Toiletry & Perfumery Assn
        Inc Gld Hairdressers
        Intl Fragrance Assn UK
Perfusion
        Soc Clinical Perfusion Scientists
Perinatal medicine
        Brit Assn Perinatal Medicine
Periodicals
        Assn Circulation Executives
        Assn Online Publishers
        Assn Publishing Agencies
        Brit Soc Magazine Editors
        Magazines Ireland
        Periodical Pubrs Assn
        Press Standards Bd Finance
        Specialised Inf Publishers Assn
        UK Serials Gp
        > + Newspapers & periodicals: distribution
Periodontology > Dentistry

Permaculture
        Permaculture Assn
Perry > Cider & perry
Persia > Iran
Personal: assistants & secretaries > Secretaries & administrators
Personal: injury
        Assn Personal Injury Lawyers
        Claims Standards Coun
        Personal Injuries Bar Assn
Personal: rights > Individual freedom
Personal: safety > Guard & patrol services; Protective clothing/equipment; Safety
Personal: trainers
        Nat Register Personal Trainers
Personnel management
        Chart Inst Personnel & Devt
        Learning & Performance Inst
        Soc Personnel Dirs Scotland
        Work Foundation
        > + Management
Personnel services > Employment agents & consultants
Perthes disease
        Perthes Assn
Peru
        Anglo Peruvian Soc
        Brit Peruvian Cham
Pest control & pesticides
        Assn Applied Biologists
        Brit Pest Control Assn
        Nat Pest Technicians Assn
        Pesticide Action Network
        > + Agriculture: chemicals
Pet > Pets & pet trade
Pet food > Pets & pet trade
Pétanque
        English Pétanque Assn
        Scot Pétanque Assn
        Welsh Pétanque Assn
Petrochemicals > Petroleum
Petrol pumps
        Forecourt Eqpt Fedn
Petroleum
        Assn Brit Indep Oil Exploration Cos
        Assn Petroleum & Explosives Admin
        BTC Testing Advisory Gp
        Downstream Fuel Assn
        Energy Industries Council
        Fedn Petroleum Suppliers
        Hydrographic Soc
        Inst Materials, Minerals & Mining
        NI Oil Fedn
        Offshore Contrs' Assn
        Petroleum Exploration Soc
        Retail Motor Ind Fedn
        UK Offshore Oil & Gas Ind Assn
        UK Petroleum Ind Assn
Petroleum gas
        UKLPG
Petrology
        Ir Assn Economic Geology
        Mineralogical Soc
Pets & pet trade
        Assn Pet Behaviour Counsellors
        Assn Pet Dog Trainers
        Brit Indep Retailers Assn
        Food & Drink Ind Ireland
        Nat Assn Registered Petsitters
        Pet Care Tr Assn
        Pet Food Mfrs Assn
        Pet Fostering Service Scotland
        Pet Health Coun
        Pet Product Retail Assn
        Soc Companion Animal Studies
        > + Animal headings; individual animal
Pets: burial & cremation
        Assn Private Pet Cemeteries & Crematoria
        Cremation Soc
Pewter
        Assn Brit Pewter Craftsmen
        Pewter Soc
Pharmaceuticals
        Academy Pharmaceutical Sciences
        Assn Brit Pharmaceutical Ind
        Assn Clinical Data Mgt
        Assn Comml Specials Mfrs
        Brit Assn Eur Pharmaceutical Distbrs
        Brit Assn Pharmaceutical Physicians
        Brit Assn Pharmaceutical Whlsrs

Brit Generic Mfrs Assn
Clinical Contract Res Assn
Fac Pharmaceutical Med
Healthcare Communications Assn
HealthWatch
Inst Clinical Res
Ir Pharmaceutical Healthcare Assn
Pharmaceutical & Healthcare Sciences Soc
Pharmaceutical Inf & Pharmacovigilance Assn
Pharmaceutical Soc Ireland
Pharmaceutical Soc NI
PharmaChemical Ireland
Proprietary Assn
Soc Medicines Res
Statisticians Pharmaceutical Ind
> + Pharmacy
Pharmacology & chemotherapy
Brit Assn Psychopharmacology
Brit Pharmacological Soc
Brit Soc Antimicrobial Chemotherapy
Scot Neuroscience Gp
Soc Medicines Res
Pharmacy
Assn Pharmacy Technicians
Community Pharmacy Scotland
Company Chemists' Assn
Gld Healthcare Pharmacists
Ir Pharmaceutical U
Nat Assn Women Pharmacists
Nat Pharmacy Assn
R Pharmaceutical Soc
UK Clinical Pharmacy Assn
Ulster Chemists Assn
Pharmacy: history
Brit Soc Hist Pharmacy
Pharology > Lighthouses & lightships
Pheasants
World Pheasant Assn UK
> + Game & gamebirds
Phenolic composites
Composites UK
Phenomena > Paranormal & psychical research;   specific type of phenomena
Phenomenology
Brit Soc Phenomenology
Phenylketonuria
Nat Soc Phenylketonuria
Philanthropy: history
Voluntary Action Hist Soc
Philately & postal history
Assn Brit Philatelic Socs
Assn Scot Philatelic Socs
Brit Air Mail Soc
Brit Postmark Soc
Letter Box Study Gp
Nat Philatelic Soc
Philatelic Traders Soc
Postal Hist Soc
R Philatelic Soc Lond
Ship Stamp Soc
Soc Olympic Collectors
Phillumeny > Matchbox labels
Philology
Philological Soc
> + Dialects; Languages
Philosophy
Aristotelian Soc
Assn Brit Theological... Libraries
Brit Soc Hist Philosophy
Brit Soc Phenomenology
Brit Soc Philosophy Science
Philosophical Soc England
R Inst Philosophy
R Philosophical Soc Glasgow
Soc Applied Philosophy
Soc Existential Analysis
Phobias
Anxiety UK
Brit Soc Hypnotherapists
No Panic
Phonetics
Brit Assn Academic Phoneticians
Brit Voice Assn
> + Speech
Phonography > Shorthand writing;   Sound recording & reproduction
Photogrammetry
Chart Instn Civil Engg Surveyors
Remote Sensing & Photogrammetry Soc

Photographic agencies
Brit Assn Picture Libraries & Agencies
Nat Assn Press Agencies
Photographic industry & trade
Photo Imaging Coun
Photographic waste
Photo Imaging Coun
Photography
Assn Photographers
Brit Cave Res Assn
Brit Inst Profl Photography
Brit Soc Underwater Photographers
Camera Club
Gld Photographers
Inst Med Illustrators
Ir Profl Photographers Assn
Master Photographers Assn
Nat Assn Aerial Photographic Libraries
Nat U Journalists
Outdoor Writers' & Photographers' Gld
Photographic Alliance
Photographic Collectors' Club
R Photographic Soc
Scot Soc Hist Photography
Scot Sub Aqua Club
Soc Wedding & Portrait Photographers
Stereoscopic Soc
Writers & Photographers unLimited
> + Film
Photoluminescent products
Photoluminescent Safety Products Assn
Photonics
Photonics Cluster
Scot Optoelectronics Assn
UK Consortium Photonics & Optics
Phycology
Brit Phycological Soc
Physical disability > Disablement
Physical education
Assn Physical Educ
Physical Educ Assn Ireland
Sports & Fitness Eqpt Assn
Physical fitness > Fitness
Physically handicapped > Children: handicapped; Disablement
Physicians > Medical: practice; Medicine
Physics
Inst Physics
Inst Physics & Engg in Medicine
Physiology
Physiological Soc
Soc Orthopaedic Medicine
Physiotherapy
Allied Health Professions Fedn
Chart Soc Physiotherapy
Ir Soc Chart Physiotherapists
Physio First
SMAE Fellowship
Pianolas & pianola rolls
Friends Pianola Inst
Player Piano Gp
Pianos & piano playing
Assn Blind Piano Tuners
Jazz Piano Teachers Assn
Pianoforte Tuners' Assn
Pick-your-own > Farm shops & food
Pick's disease
Pick's Disease Support Gp
Picts
Pictish Arts Soc
Picture dealers > Art: trade
Picture framers
Fine Art Tr Gld
Picture libraries
Brit Assn Picture Libraries & Agencies
Nat Assn Aerial Photographic Libraries
Picture researching
Picture Res Assn
Picture restoring
Brit Assn Paintings Conservator-Restorers
Fine Art Tr Gld
> + Art: conservation
Piercing > Body piercing
Piers
Brit Assn Leisure Parks, Piers & Attractions
Nat Piers Soc
Pigeons
Confedn Long Distance Racing Pigeon Us

Ir Homing U
Nat Pigeon Assn
R Pigeon Racing Assn
Scot Homing U
Pigging (pipeline)
Pigging Products & Services Assn
Pigments
Brit Colour Makers Assn
Pigs
Berkshire Pig Breeders Club
Brit Kune Kune Pig Soc
Brit Lop Pig Soc
Brit Pig Assn
Brit Saddleback Breeders Club
Brit Veterinary Assn
Food & Drink Ind Ireland
Gloucestershire Old Spots Pig Breeders' Club
Middle White Pig Breeders Club
Nat Pig Assn
Oxford Sandy & Black Pig Soc
Pedigree Welsh Pig Soc
Tamworth Breeders Group
> + Bacon; Cattle & livestock; Pigging (pipelines)
Pilates
Body Control Pilates Assn
Pilchard
Herring Buyers Assn
> + Fish; Fishing
Pilgrims
Confraternity Saint James
Piling
Fedn Piling Specialists
Pillboxes (fortifications) > Fortresses & forts
Pilots > Aviation: pilots, officers & crew;   Sea pilots
Pinball
Pinball Owners Assn
> + Amusements & coin operated machines
Pinks (flowers) > Dianthus
Pinnipeds
Seal Consvn Soc
Pipe bands & music
Bagpipe Soc
College Piping
Competing Pipers Assn
Edinburgh Highland Reel & Strathspey Soc
Inst Piping
Northumbrian Pipers' Society
Piobaireachd Soc
Pipers' Gld
R Scot Pipe Band Assn
Scot Pipers Assn
Scot Piping Soc Lond
Traditional Music & Song Assn Scotland
Pipe organs > Organs, organists & organ music
Pipejacking
Pipe Jacking Assn
Pipelines
Land Drainage Contrs Assn
Pigging Products & Services Assn
Pipeline Inds Gld
Rly & Canal Histl Soc
Soc Brit Water & Wastewater Inds
UK Onshore Pipeline Operators' Assn
Pipes
Brit Ceramic Confedn
Brit Precast Concrete Fedn
Clay Pipe Devt Assn
Soc Brit Water & Wastewater Inds
> + Plastics: pipes;   Steel: tubes
Piracy (copyrighted goods) > Copyright
Pistachios
Combined Edible Nut Tr Assn
Pistol shooting
Nat Rifle Assn
> + Shooting
Pizzas
Pizza, Pasta & Italian Food Assn
Place-names
English Place-Name Soc
Scot Place-Name Soc
Soc Name Studies Britain & Ireland
Ulster Place-Name Soc
> + Names
Placement services (adult)
Nat Assn Adult Placement Services
> + Social: service

Plainsong
Plainsong & Mediæval Music Soc
Planetary sciences
R Astronomical Soc
> + Astronomy
Planning > Town & country planning
Plant: construction > Construction equipment
Plant: industrial
Brit Metallurgical Plant Constructors Assn
Engg Construction Ind Assn
Instn Diagnostic Engrs
Nat Assn Valuers & Auctioneers
Safety Assessment Fedn
Soc Operations Engrs
Plants
Assn Applied Biologists
Assn Indep Crop Consultants
Brit Assn Rose Breeders
Brit Mycological Soc
Brit Protected Ornamentals Assn
Brit Soc Plant Breeders
Brit Soc Plant Pathology
Epiphytic Plant Study Gp
Hardy Plant Soc
Linnean Soc Lond
Nat Coun Consvn Plants & Gardens
Plantlife Intl
Profl Plant Users Gp
Scot Soc Crop Res
> + Flowers, flower arrangement & floristry; specific plants
Plants: galls
Brit Plant Gall Soc
Plaques
Brit Sign & Graphics Assn
> + Signs
Plaster & plastering
Fedn Plastering & Drywall Contrs
Gypsum Products Devt Assn
Plastic surgery
Brit Assn Aesthetic Plastic Surgeons
Brit Assn Plastic, Reconstructive & Aesthetic Surgeons
> + Surgery
Plastics
Brit Laminate Fabricators Assn
Brit Plastics Fedn
Composites UK
NI Polymers Assn
Plastics Histl Soc
Plastics Ireland
Scot Plastics & Rubber Assn
Plastics: bags
Carrier Bag Consortium
Plastics: drums > Cisterns, drums & tanks
Plastics: film
Packaging & Films Assn
Picon Ltd
Plastics: foam
Brit Rigid Urethane Foam Mfrs Assn
Brit Urethane Foam Contrs Assn
Plastics: machinery
Polymer Machinery Mfrs & Distbrs Assn
Plastics: pipes
Brit Plastics Fedn
Ir Plastic Pipe Mfrs Assn
Soc Brit Water & Wastewater Inds
Plastics: recycling
RECOUP
> + Reclamation & recycling
Platforms > Cradles & suspended platforms
Play & playgroups
Brit Assn Play Therapists
Early Childhood Ireland
Fair Play for Children Assn
Nat Assn Hospital Play Staff
Nat Playbus Assn
Play Providers Assn
Play equipment > Sports: equipment
Playing cards & games
Brit Brewery Playing Card Soc
English Playing-Card Soc
Playing fields > Sportsgrounds & synthetic surfaces
Playrights & plays > Dramatists; Theatre; Writing & writers
Pleasurecraft
Brit Marine Fedn
> + Boats & boating; Yachts & yachting

© CBD Research Ltd · Beckenham · BR3 5JS · Tel 020 8650 7745   E-mail cbd@cbdresearch.com · www.cbdresearch.com

Ploughing
>Soc Ploughmen
>Southern Counties Heavy Horse Assn
Plumbers' merchants > Builders' & plumbers' merchants
Plumbing
>Assn Plumbing & Heating Contrs
>Chart Inst Plumbing & Heating Engg
>Nat Assn Profl Inspectors & Testers
>NI Master Plumbers Assn
>Scot & NI Plumbing Emplrs' Fedn
Pneumatics
>Brit Compressed Air Soc
>Brit Fluid Power Assn
>Brit Fluid Power Distbrs Assn
>Solids Handling & Processing Assn
>> + Hydraulics & hydromechanics
Podiatry > Chiropody & podiatry
Poetry
>English Poetry & Song Soc
>Friends Dymock Poets
>Poetry Soc
>Scot Poetry Library
>War Poets Assn
>> + individual by name
Poisons > Toxicology
Poland
>Anglo Polish Soc
>Brit Polish Cham Comm [Lond]
>Brit Polish Cham Comm [Warsaw]
Polar research
>Trans-Antarctic Assn
Polarity therapy
>UK Polarity Therapy Assn
Polarography & polarology
>R Soc Chemistry
Police
>Assn Chief Police Officers [E&W&NI]
>Assn Chief Police Officers Scotland
>Assn Police Authorities
>Assn Scot Police Superintendents
>Assn Special Constabulary Chief Officers
>Garda Representative Assn [IRL]
>Nat Assn Retired Police Officers
>Police Fedn England & Wales
>Police Fedn NI
>Police Superintendents' Assn [E&W]
>Scot Police Fedn
>Superintendents' Assn NI
>> + Security
Police: history
>Peel Soc
>Police Hist Soc
>Police Insignia Collectors Assn
Policy research
>David Hume Inst
Poliomyelytis
>Brit Polio Fellowship
Polishes
>Brit Assn Chemical Specialities
Politeness
>Nat Campaign Courtesy
Political correctness
>Campaign Political Correctness
Political consultants
>Assn Profl Political Consultants
Political economy > Economics
Political parties > [Party] politics
Political studies & reform
>Fabian Soc
>Political Studies Assn
>Unlock Democracy
Pollen
>Brit Aerobiology Fedn
>> + Allergy
Pollution & pollution control
>ACT TravelWise
>Environmental Inds Commission
>Marine Biological Assn
>Marine Consvn Soc
>Source Testing Assn
>Surfers against Sewage
>UK Spill Assn
Polo
>Hurlingham Polo Assn
Polocrosse
>UK Polocrosse Assn
Polyethylene foam > Plastics: foam

Polymers
>Inst Materials, Minerals & Mining
>NI Polymers Assn
>Plastics Histl Soc
>Polymer Machinery Mfrs & Distbrs Assn
>Scot Plastics & Rubber Assn
Polytechnics > Adult education; Technical education; Universities

Ponies > Horse headings
Pony trekking
>Trekking & Riding Soc Scotland
>Wales Trekking & Riding Assn
Pool
>Brit Assn Pool Table Operators
>Brit Wheelchair Pool Players' Assn
>English Pool Assn
>> + Cue sports
Pools > Football pools;   Swimming pools
Population: registration
>Assn Registrars Scotland
>Local Registration Services Assn
Population: study of
>Brit Soc Population Studies
>Local Population Studies Soc
Porcelain > Ceramics; Pottery
Pork butchery > Meat
Pork pies
>Melton Mowbray Pork Pie Assn
>Pork Pie Appreciation Soc
Porphyria
>Brit Porphyria Assn
Portable buildings > Modular & portable buildings
Portable engines
>Road Locomotive Soc
Portage
>Nat Portage Assn
Portland Cement
>Mineral Products Assn
>> + Cement & cement products
Portraits > Art & artists; Weddings: photography
Ports
>Brit Ports Assn
>Maritime UK
>Naval Dockyards Soc
>Ports & Terminals Gp
>Soc Sailing Barge Res
>UK Major Ports Gp
Ports: health
>Assn Port Health Authorities
Portugal
>Anglo Portuguese Soc
>Assn Contemporary Iberian Studies
>Brit Portuguese Cham Comm
>Hispanic & Luso Brazilian Coun
>Portuguese Cham
Portugal: language & literature
>Assn Language Learning
Post Office staff
>Communication Workers U
>> + Sub-postmasters
Post Office (GPO & BT) vehicles
>Post Office Vehicle Club
Postal history > Philately & postal history
Postal services
>Mail Consolidators Assn
>Mail Users Assn
Postcards
>Canal Card Collectors Circle
>Great Britain Postcard Club
>Postcard Traders' Assn
Poster advertising > Advertising: outdoor
Postgraduate education
>Assn MBAs
>Fellowship Postgraduate Medicine
>Nat Assn Clinical Tutors
Postmarks > Philately & postal history
Post-natal depression
>Assn Postnatal Illness
Post-tensioning
>Concrete Bridge Devt Gp
>Post Tensioning Assn
Post-viral infection
>Action ME
>Assn Young People with ME
>Myalgic Encephalopathy Assn
Pot holing > Caves & caving
Pot plants > Horticulture; Indoor & houseplants; individual plants

Potatoes
>> Brit Potato Tr Assn
>> Fresh Produce Consortium
>> NI Potato Breeders Assn
>> Pre Basic Growers Assn
>> Scot Soc Crop Res
>> > + Vegetables: trade
Potatoes: products
>> Potato Processors Assn
>> Snack, Nut & Crisp Mfrs Assn
Potter (Beatrix)
>> Beatrix Potter Soc
Pottery
>> Brit Ceramic Gift & Tableware Mfrs' Assn
>> CERAM Res
>> Craft Potters Assn
>> Scot Potters' Assn
>> > + Ceramics
Pottery & ceramics collecting
>> Clarice Cliff Collectors Club
>> Friends Blue
>> Old Bottle Club
>> Spode Soc
>> > + specific type collected
Pottery: sanitary > Sanitaryware
Potting composts > Composts & composting
Poultry
>> Assn Meat Inspectors
>> Brit Poultry Coun
>> Brit Veterinary Assn
>> Domestic Fowl Trust
>> Henkeepers Assn
>> NI Poultry Fedn
>> Poultry Club
>> Pullet Hatcheries Assn
>> Pullet Rearers Assn
>> Rare Poultry Soc
>> Traditional Farmfresh Turkey Assn
>> > + Game & game birds; Meat
The Pound (Sterling)
>> Democracy Movement
Powder coatings
>> Brit Coatings Fedn
>> Surface Engg Assn
Powder compacts (collecting)
>> Brit Compact Collectors' Soc
Powder handling
>> Solids Handling & Processing Assn
Powell (Anthony Dymock)
>> Anthony Powell Soc
Power > specific type of power
Power boating & powercraft
>> R Yachting Assn
Power generation > Electricity
Power presses
>> Metalforming Machinery Makers' Assn
Power tools > Tools
Power track systems
>> BEAMA
Powered access
>> Assn Loading & Elevating Eqpt Mfrs
>> Construction Plant-hire Assn
>> Specialist Access Engg & Maintenance Assn
Powerlifting
>> Brit Drug Free Powerlifting Assn
Powys (John Cooper) & family
>> Powys Soc
Prader-Willi syndrome
>> Prader-Willi Syndrome Assn
Prams & pushchairs > Nursery & baby products
Prayer book(s) > Common Prayer; Liturgy
Precast concrete > Concrete & concrete products
Precious metals & stones > Gemstones; Goldsmiths & silversmiths; Jewellery
Precision casting > Metal: casting
Pre-conceptual care > Family planning; Maternity
Pre-eclampsia
>> Action Pre-Eclampsia
>> Pre Eclampsia Soc
Prefabricated buildings > Modular & portable buildings
Pregnancy > Family planning; Maternity; Obstetrics & gynaecology
Prehistory
>> Megalithic Soc
>> Prehistoric Soc
>> R Anthropological Inst
Premature ageing > Geriatrics & ageing
Premenstrual syndrome
>> Nat Assn Premenstrual Syndrome

Premium promotions > Incentive marketing
Preparatory schools
>> Indep Assn Preparatory Schools
>> SATIPS
>> > + Independent & public schools
Pre-Raphaelites
>> Pre-Raphaelite Soc
Presbyterian church: history
>> Presbyterian Hist Soc Ireland
>> Scot Covenanter Memorials Assn
>> Utd Reformed Church Hist Soc
Pre-school playgroups > Nurseries & nursery schools; Play & playgroups
Preservation > Conservation; object preserved
Press > Information: freedom of; Journalism; Media; Newspapers; Periodicals
Press agencies
>> Nat Assn Press Agencies
Pressure gauges > Gauges
Pressure sores
>> Tissue Viability Soc
Priestley (John Boynton)
>> J B Priestley Soc
Primary care > Health care
Primary education > Education
Primulas
>> Nat Auricula & Primula Soc (Mid & West)
>> Nat Auricula & Primula Soc (Nthn)
>> Nat Auricula & Primula Soc (Sthn)
Print finishing > Books: binding & print finishing
Print making
>> R Scot Academy
>> R Soc Painter Printmakers
>> Soc Graphic Fine Art
Printed circuits & wiring boards
>> Inst Metal Finishing
Printing
>> Assn Hot Foil Printers
>> Brit Printing Inds Fedn
>> Brit Printing Soc
>> D&AD
>> Friends St Bride Library
>> Graphic Enterprise Scotland
>> Indep Print Inds Assn
>> Inst Paper Printing & Publishing
>> Ir Printing Fedn
>> New Baxter Soc
>> Pira Intl
>> Printing Histl Soc
>> Printmakers Coun
>> R Birmingham Soc Artists
>> Regional Newspapers... Assn Ireland
>> UK Assn Accessible Formats
Printing inks
>> Brit Coatings Fedn
>> Oil & Colour Chemists Assn
Printing machinery
>> Brit Used Printing Machinery Supplrs Assn
>> Picon Ltd
Prison service
>> POA
>> Prison Governors Assn
Prisoners: welfare & rehabilitation
>> Assn Members Indep Monitoring Bds
>> Assn Visitors Immigration Detainees
>> Criminal Justice Alliance
>> Howard League for Penal Reform
>> NACRO
>> Nat Approved Premises Assn
>> Nat Assn Official Prison Visitors
>> NI Assn Care & Resettlement Offenders
>> Prisoners Abroad
>> Sacro
>> SOVA
>> Unlock
>> > + Penal reform
Prisoners: wives & families
>> Action Prisoners' Families
>> Prison Advice & Care Trust
Private business > Business
Private hire
>> Nat Private Hire Assn
>> > + Motor vehicles: hire; Taxis & minicabs
Private medicine > Hospitals: contributory schemes
Private schools > Independent & public schools
Private secretaries > Secretaries & administrators
Probation service
>> Nat Approved Premises Assn
>> Nat Assn Probation Officers

© CBD Research Ltd · Beckenham · BR3 5JS · Tel 020 8650 7745 E-mail cbd@cbdresearch.com · www.cbdresearch.com

Probation Assn
Probation Mgrs Assn
SOVA
Process control > Control engineering
Process engineering
Energy Industries Council
Instn Chemical Engrs
Processing & Packaging Machinery Assn
Solids Handling & Processing Assn
Process servers
Assn Brit Investigators
Proctology
Assn Coloproctology
Procurators-Fiscal
Procurators Fiscal Soc
R Fac Procurators in Glasgow
> + Law: Scotland
Produce packaging & processing
Fresh Produce Consortium
Product licensing
Inst Intl Licensing Practitioners
Licensing Executives Soc
Production control
Inst Operations Mgt
Production engineering
Engg & Machinery Alliance
PERA
> + Automation
Products: counterfeiting
Anti Counterfeiting Gp
Programme producers > Film: production & distribution; Television: production
Project management
Assn Project Mgt
Major Projects Assn
Promotion merchandise > Incentive marketing
Proofreading
Assn Freelance Editors, Proofreaders & Indexers [IRL]
Soc Editors & Proofreaders
Property & land owners
Brit Property Fedn
City Property Assn
Country Land & Business Assn
Landlords Assn NI
Nat Assn Estate Agents
Nat Landlords Assn
Residential Landlords Association Ltd
Scot Assn Landlords
Scot Land & Estates
Westminster Property Owners Assn
> + Estate management
Property: investment
Assn Property Bankers
Investment Property Forum
Property: maintenance/management
Assn Residential Letting Agents
Assn Residential Managing Agents
Inst Residential Property Mgt
Property Consultants Soc
Property Mgrs Assn
Property Mgrs Assn Scotland
UK Assn Letting Agents
> + Buildings: cleaning & maintenance
Property: market research
Soc Property Researchers
Property: marking (security)
Brit Security Ind Assn
Property: search
Coun Property Search Orgs
Property: unit trusts
Assn Real Estate Funds
Proportional representation > Elections & electoral administration
Proprietary medicines
Proprietary Assn
> + Pharmaceuticals
Prostate disease
Prostate Cancer Support Fedn
Prosthetics & orthoses
Allied Health Professions Fedn
Brit Assn Prosthetists & Orthotists
Brit Orthopaedic Assn
Brit Soc Study Prosthetic Dentistry
Inst Maxillofacial Prosthetists...
Let's Face It
Nat Cochlear Implant Users Assn
REACH

Prostitution
Coalition Removal Pimping
Josephine Butler Soc
Protective clothing/equipment
Brit Footwear Assn
Brit Safety Ind Fedn
Photoluminescent Safety Products Assn
Retroreflective Eqpt Mfrs Assn
UK Fashion & Textile Assn
Protectorate (1649-1688) > Commonwealth (1649-1688);   Fights (historic/re-enactment)
Protein (vegetable) > Vegetables: protein
Proteomics
Brit Soc Proteome Res
Protestants
Protestant Alliance
Protestant Reformation Soc
Protestant Truth Soc
Scot Reformation Soc
Prototype design & manufacture
Additive Mfrg Assn
Rapid Prototyping & Mfrg Assn
Provision trade > Grocery & provision trade
Psoriasis
Psoriasis Assn
Psoriasis & Psoriatic Arthritis Alliance
Psychiatry
Assn Therapeutic Communities
Brit Neuropsychiatry Assn
College Psychiatry Ireland
R Coll Psychiatrists
Soc Clinical Psychiatrists
Psychical research > Paranormal & psychical research
Psychoanalysis
Assn Jungian Analysts
Balint Soc
Brit Psychoanalytical Soc
Inst Psychoanalysis
NI Assn Study Psychoanalysis
Soc Analytical Psychology
Soc Existential Analysis
> + Group analysis
Psychology
Adlerian Soc Inst Individual Psychology
Assn Business Psychologists
Assn Educl Psychologists
Assn Humanistic Psychology
Assn Psychosexual Nursing
Assn Teaching Psychology
Brit Assn Person-Centred Approach
Brit Assn Psychological Type
Brit Inst Graphologists
Brit Neuropsychological Soc
Brit Psychological Soc
Brit Soc Psychosomatic Obstetrics...
Experimental Psychology Soc
Gld Pastoral Psychology
Indep Gp Analytical Psychologists
Nat Assn Therapeutic Educ
Psychological Soc Ireland
Psychologists Protection Soc
Soc Existential Analysis
Soc Reproductive & Infant Psychology
Psychopharmacology
Brit Assn Psychopharmacology
Psychotherapy
Assn Child Psychotherapists
Assn Cognitive Analytic Therapy
Assn Gp & Individual Psychotherapy
Assn Profl Hypnosis & Psychotherapy
Assn Psychoanalytic Psychotherapy NHS
Assn Psychological Therapies
Brit Assn Behavioural... Psychotherapies
Brit Assn Counselling & Psychotherapy
Brit Assn Psychotherapists
Brit Autogenic Soc
Brit Hypnotherapy Assn
Brit Psychoanalytic Coun
Brit Psychodrama Assn
Brit Psychological Soc
Gld Psychotherapists
Group Analytic Soc
Inst Gp Analysis
Inst Mgt & Technology
Inst Transactional Analysis
Ir Assn Counselling & Psychotherapy
Nat Assn Counsellors, Hypnoterpists & Psychotherapists

© CBD Research Ltd · Beckenham · BR3 5JS · Tel 020 8650 7745 · E-mail cbd@cbdresearch.com · www.cbdresearch.com

Nat Coun Psychotherapists
Nat Register Hypnotherapists & Psychotherapists
Nat Soc Hypnosis & Psychotherapy
R Coll Psychiatrists
Scot Assn Psychoanalytical Psychotherapists
UK Coun Psychotherapy
Universities Psychotherapy & Counselling Assn
Pteridology > Ferns
Public access > Footpaths & rights of way; Open spaces
Public administration
Inst Public Administration [IRL]
> + Civil Service; Local government
Public analysts
Assn Public Analysts
Assn Public Analysts Scotland
Public auditing > Accountancy
Public conveniences
Brit Toilet Assn
Public gardens > Parks & gardens
Public health
Assn Directors Public Health
Assn Port Health Authorities
Assn Public Health Observatories
Chart Inst Envtl Health
Chart Instn Water & Envtl Management
Community & District Nursing Assn
Fac Public Health
R Soc Public Health
Scot Soc Contamination Control
> + Health
Public houses
Assn Licensed Mult Retailers
Assn Valuers Licensed Property
Brit Beer & Pub Assn
Campaign Real Ale
Licensed Vintners Assn [IRL]
Scot Beer & Pub Assn
Public lighting > Lighting
Public relations
Assn Local Govt Communications
Chart Inst Marketing
Chart Inst Public Relations
Healthcare Communications Assn
Public Relations Consultants Assn
Public Relations Consultants Assn [IRL]
Public Relations Inst Ireland
Science, Technology, Engg... Public Relations Assn
Public safety
Brit Assn Public Safety Communications Officers
Public schools > Independent & public schools
Public sector information
ALARM
Locus Assn
Public sector officials > Local government headings
Public speaking > Speakers
Public transport > Passenger transport
Public utilities > individual utility
Publicity > Advertising
Publishing
Assn Learned & Profl Soc Pubrs
Assn Publishing Agencies
Brit Business Awards Assn
Chart & Nautical Instrument Tr Assn
Data Pubrs Assn
Folio Soc
Indep Pubrs Gld
Inst Paper Printing & Publishing
Ir Educl Pubrs Assn
Periodical Pubrs Assn
Personal Mgrs Assn
Pira Intl
Publishers Assn
Publishers Licensing Soc
Publishing Ireland
Publishing Scotland
Soc Leisure Consultants & Pubrs
Soc Young Publishers
Trade & Profl Pubrs Assn [IRL]
> + Books; & other aspects of publishing
Pubs > Public houses
Pugin (Augustus Welby)
Pugin Soc
Pullets > Poultry
Pulmonaria
Hardy Plant Soc

Pulmonary hypertension
Pulmonary Hypertension Assn
> + Thoracic diseases
Pulp > Paper headings; Wood pulp
Pulses: edible
Brit Edible Pulse Assn
Grain & Feed Tr Assn
Pumps & pumping
Assn Electrical & Mechanical Trs
Brit Pump Mfrs Assn
Fire Fighting Vehicles Mfrs Assn
Pump Distbrs Assn
Punch & Judy
Punch & Judy Coll Professors
Punctuation
Apostrophe Protection Soc
Puppetry
Brit Puppet & Model Theatre Gld
Purchasing & supply
Chart Inst Purchasing & Supply
Ir Inst Purchasing & Materials Mgt
Soc Procurement Officers Local Govt
Purine metabolic disorders
Purine Metabolic Patients Assn
Push chairs > Nursery & baby products
PVC
Brit Plastics Fedn
> + Plastics headings
Pylons (electricity)
Pylon Appreciation Soc
Pym (Barbara Mary Crampton)
Barbara Pym Soc
Pyrotechnics > Fireworks

Q

Quad bike racing
Quad Racing Assn
Quadrathlon
Brit Quadrathlon Assn
Quadricycling
Assn Pioneer Motor Cyclists
> + Cycles & motorcycles
Quail > Game & game birds
Quakers > Friends (Quakers)
Quality assurance & control
Assn Brit Certification Bodies
Assn External Verifiers
Brit Approvals Fire Eqpt
Brit Assn Res Quality Assurance
Brit Civil Engg Test Eqpt Mfrs Assn
Brit Quality Foundation
BSI
Chart Quality Inst
Excellence Ireland Quality Assn
Market Res Quality Standards Assn
> + Materials: technology & testing
Quantity surveying
Chart Instn Civil Engg Surveyors
Soc Construction & Quantity Surveyors
Quarries & quarrying
Brit Aggregates Assn
Inst Explosives Engrs
Inst Quarrying
Ir Mining & Quarrying Soc
Mineral Products Assn
Minerals Engg Soc
Stone Fedn
> + specific stone quarried
Quarry tiles > Tiles (floor & wall)
Quickprinters & copyshops
Brit Assn Print & Communication
Quilling
Quilling Gld
Quills (pens) > Writing equipment & accessories
Quilting
Assn Soft Furnishers
Quilt Assn
Quilters' Gld

© CBD Research Ltd · Beckenham · BR3 5JS · Tel 020 8650 7745   E-mail cbd@cbdresearch.com · www.cbdresearch.com

R

Rabbits
  Brit Rabbit Coun
  Rabbit Welfare Assn
Race relations
  Assn Jewish Ex-Servicemen & Women
  Discrimination Law Assn
  Inst Race Relations
Racecourses
  Assn Ir Racecourses
  Racecourse Assn
Rachmaninov (Sergei)
  Rachmaninoff Soc
Racing > Horse racing; Motor sport
Rackets (squash)
  England Squash & Racketball
  Great Britain Racquetball Fedn
  Scot Squash
  Squash Wales
Racking
  Storage Eqpt Mfrs Assn
  > + Storage equipment
Radiation > Radiology/radiation
Radiators
  Boiler & Radiator Mfrs Assn
Radiesthesia > Radionics & radiesthesia
Radio
  Assn Service Providers
  Brit Amat TV Club
  Comml Radio Companies Assn
  Intellect
  Radio Academy
  TV & Radio Inds Club
  > + Aerials: radio & television;   Telecommunications
Radio: amateur
  Ir Radio Transmitters Soc
  Radio Soc GB
Radio: control
  Brit Radio Car Assn
  > + Models: hobby
Radio: community
  Community Media Assn
Radio: engineering & industry > Electronic: industry & engineering
Radio: mobile
  Fedn Communication Services
  Mobile Electronics & Security Fedn
  > + Radio: amateur
Radio: paging > Paging (radio)
Radio & TV: actors & actresses > Actors & actresses; Theatre
Radio & TV: censorship
  mediawatch-uk
  Voice Listener & Viewer
Radio & TV: medical broadcasts
  Assn Broadcasting Doctors
Radio & TV: history
  Brit Vintage Wireless Soc
  Narrow-bandwidth TV Assn
Radio & TV: rental
  Radio, Electrical & TV Retailers' Assn
Radio & TV: script writing
  Ir Playwrights & Screenwriters Gld
  Soc Authors
  Soc Authors Scotland
  Writers Gld
Radio & TV: trade
  Brit Audio-Visual Dealers Assn
  Confedn Aerial Inds
  Consumer Electronics Distbrs Assn [IRL]
  Radio, Electrical & TV Retailers' Assn
Radiography > Radiology/radiation
Radiology/radiation
  Allied Health Professions Fedn
  Assn Radiation Res
  Assn University Radiation Protection Officers
  Brit Inst Radiology
  Brit Occupational Hygiene Soc
  Brit Soc Dental & Maxillofacial Radiology
  Brit Soc Neuroradiologists
  R Coll Radiologists
  Soc Radiographers
  Soc Radiological Protection
Radionics & radiesthesia
  Radionic Assn Ltd
  Soc Metaphysicians

Radiotherapy > Radiology/radiation
Rafters
  Trussed Rafter Assn
  > + Roofing
Rafting
  Brit Canoe U
  Scot Rafting Assn
  > + Canoes & Canoeing
Railways: development > Railways: promotion & development
Railways: engineering
  Britpave
  Rail Ind Contrs Assn
Railways: equipment & rolling stock
  Assn Private Rly Wagon Owners
  Locomotive & Carriage Instn
  Private Wagon Fedn
  Rly Ind Assn
  Wagon Bldg & Repairing Assn
Railways: history & preservation
  Branch Line Soc
  Campaign Better Transport
  German Rly Soc
  Gld Rly Artists
  Heritage Rly Assn
  Histl Model Rly Soc
  Indl Locomotive Soc
  Indl Rly Soc
  Locomotive Club
  Merchant Navy Locomotive Presvn Soc
  Narrow Gauge Rly Soc
  Nat Assn Rly Clubs
  Rly & Canal Histl Soc
  Rly Correspondence & Travel Soc
  Rly Enthusiasts Soc
  Rly Presvn Soc Ireland
  Rly Ramblers
  Swiss Rlys Soc
  Transport Trust
  Vintage Carriages Trust
  World War Two Rly Study Gp
Railways: history & preservation - local
  Bluebell Rly Presvn Soc
  Caledonian Rly Assn
  Cambrian Railways Soc
  Ffestiniog Railway Society Ltd
  Great N Scotland Rly Assn
  Great Nthn Rly Soc
  Great Wstn Soc
  Highland Rly Soc
  Keighley & Worth Valley Rly Presvn Soc
  Lancashire & Yorkshire Rly Soc
  Lancashire & Yorkshire Rly Trust
  Locomotive 6201 Princess Elizabeth Soc
  London Underground Rly Soc
  N York Moors Hist Rly Trust
  S Wstn Circle
  Scot Rly Presvn Soc
  Sittingbourne & Kemsley Light Rly
  Stephenson Locomotive Soc
  Strathspey Rly Assn
  Sussex Indl Archaeol Soc
  Talyllyn Rly Presvn Soc
  Welsh Highland Rlys Assn
  Welshpool & Llanfair Light Rly Presvn Co
Railways: light
  Colonel Stephens Soc
  Heritage Rly Assn
  Light Rail Transit Assn
  Tramway & Light Rly Soc
  > + Tramways & trams
Railways: model
  Assn Model Rly Socs Scotland
  Model Electronic Rly Gp
  Train Collectors Soc
Railways: operating
  Assn Rly Training Providers
  Assn Train Operating Companies
  Instn Rly Operators
  Locomotive & Carriage Instn
  Rly Study Assn
Railways: promotion & development
  Assn Community Rail Partnerships
  Electric Rly Soc
  HS2 Action Alliance
  Permanent Way Instn
  Rail Freight Gp

Rly Devt Soc
Transport-Watch
Railways: signalling
Instn Rly Signal Engrs
Signalling Record Soc
Railways: workers
Assd Train Crew U
Nat U Rail Maritime & Transport Workers
Transport Salaried Staffs Assn
Rainwater
UK Rainwater Harvesting Assn
> + Water: treatment & supply
Rambling
Long Distance Walkers Assn
Mountaineering Coun Ireland
Ramblers' Assn
Ulster Fedn Rambling Clubs
Rangers & wardens
Assn Countryside Voluntary Wardens
Countryside Mgt Assn
Scot Countryside Rangers' Assn
Ranges (cooking) > Catering: equipment
Ransome (Arthur Mitchell)
Arthur Ransome Soc
Rare breeds
Rare Breeds Survival Trust
> + Cattle; Sheep etc
Rare diseases
Rare Disease
Rating
Assn Chief Estates Surveyors... Public Sector
Inst Revenues Rating & Valuation
Machinery Users Assn
Rating Surveyors Assn
Scot Assessors Assn
Rats (pets)
Nat Fancy Rat Soc
> + Rodents (pests)
Raw sugar > Sugar
Rawsthorne (Alan)
Friends Alan Rawsthorne
Raynaud's disease
Raynaud's & Scleroderma Assn
Rays (fish)
Skates & Rays Producers Assn
Razors > Shaving equipment
Reading
Brit Dyslexia Assn
Dyslexia Action
Nat Literacy Assn
Reading Assn Ireland
UK Literacy Assn
Ready-mixed concrete
Mineral Products Assn
> + Concrete & concrete products
Real ale
Campaign Real Ale
Soc Presvn Beers Wood
> + Brewing
Real estate > Estate headings; Property headings
Real tennis > Tennis
Real time locating systems
Assn Automatic Identification &... Data Capture
Rebirth > Breathing
Receivers
Assn Property & Fixed Charge Receivers
Insolvency Practitioners Assn
Receptionists (medical)
Assn Med Secretaries, Practice Managers...
Reclamation & recycling
Aluminium Alloy Mfrg & Recycling Assn
Aluminium Packaging Recycling Org
Brit Metals Recycling Assn
Brit Plastics Fedn
Brit Vehicle Salvage Fedn
Campaign Real Recycling
Can Makers
Chart Instn Wastes Mgt
Community Recycling Network
Confedn Paper Inds
Environmental Services Assn
Indl Packaging Assn
Oil Recycling Assn
Textile Recycling Assn
UK Cartridge Remanufacturers Assn
Waste Watch
White Goods Assn [IRL]

Zero Waste Alliance UK
> + other waste trades
Reconstructive surgery > Plastic surgery
Record agents
Assn Genealogists & Researchers in Archives
Recorders (musical instruments)
Soc Recorder Players
Recording studios
Assn Profl Recording Services
> + Sound recording & reproduction
Records: historical
Brit Record Soc
Brit Records Assn
Business Archives Coun
Catholic Record Soc
Ephemera Soc
Friends Nat Libraries
Hakluyt Soc
Harleian Soc
List & Index Soc
Manorial Soc
Navy Records Soc
Pipe Roll Soc
Scot Record Soc
Scot Records Assn
> + Archives; Parish registers
Records: historical - county societies
Bedfordshire Histl Record Soc
Caernarvonshire Histl Soc
Cambridgeshire Records Soc
Cheshire > Chetham Soc
Cheshire > Record Soc Lancashire & Cheshire
Chetham Soc
Cornwall > Devon & Cornwall Record Soc
Derbyshire Record Soc
Devon & Cornwall Record Soc
Dugdale Soc
Durham > Soc Antiquaries Newcastle upon Tyne
Hertfordshire > St Albans & Hertfordshire Architectural...Soc
Lancashire > Chetham Soc
Lancashire > Record Soc Lancashire & Cheshire
Lincoln Record Soc
London Record Soc
Norfolk Record Soc
Northamptonshire Record Soc
Northumberland > Soc Antiquaries Newcastle upon Tyne
Northumbria > Surtees Soc
Oxfordshire Record Soc
Record Soc Lancashire & Cheshire
Rutland Local Hist & Record Soc
Saint Albans & Hertfordshire Architectural...Soc
Soc Antiquaries Newcastle upon Tyne
Somerset Record Soc
Staffordshire Record Soc
Surrey Record Soc
Surtees Soc
Sussex Record Soc
Warwickshire > Dugdale Soc
Wiltshire Record Soc
Records management
Information & Records Mgt Soc
Records: musical > Copyright;   Sound recording & reproduction
Recovery & recycling > Reclamation & recycling
Recreation > Leisure, recreation & amenity management
Recruitment services > Employment agents & consultants
Recycling trades > Reclamation & recycling
Reeds & sedges
Brit Reed Growers Assn
Reef fishing
Shark Angling Club
Re-enactment of battles, fights etc > Fights (historic/re-enactment)
Referees
Referees' Assn
Referenda
Referenda Soc
Reflexology
Assn Light Touch Therapists
Assn Reflexologists
Brit Reflexology Assn
Scot Massage Therapists Org
Reformed Church (Scottish)
Scot Reformation Soc
Refractive surgery
UK & I Soc Cataract & Refractive Surgeons
Refractories
Brit Ceramic Confedn
CERAM Res

Inst Refractories Engrs
Refractory Users Federation
Refreshment vending
Automatic Vending Assn
Refrigerated transport > Temperature controlled transport
Refrigeration
Air Conditioning & Refrigeration Ind Bd
Brit Refrigeration Assn
Food & Drink Ind Ireland
Inst Refrigeration
> + Cryogenics; Temperature controlled storage
Refugees
Assn Visitors Immigration Detainees
Immigration Law Practitioners Assn
Refuse disposal > Waste disposal
Refuse incineration
Combined Heat & Power Assn
Registered designs > Copyright; Industrial design; Patents & trade marks
Registration of births etc > Population: registration
Regression > Hypnotic regression
Rehabilitation
Brit Assn Rehabilitation Cos
Brit Soc Rehabilitation Medicine
English Community Care Assn
R Assn Disability & Rehabilitation
> + Disablement
Reiki healing
Assn Light Touch Therapists
Confedn Healing Orgs
Reiki Assn
Reinforcement
Brit Assn Reinforcement
Intl Glassfibre Reinforced Concrete Assn
UK Steel
Reinsurance > Insurance
Relaxation
Brit Autogenic Soc
Floatation Tank Assn
Religion
Alliance Religions & Consvn
Assn Brit Theological... Libraries
Assn Denominational Histl Socs Cognate Libs
Atheism
Brit Assn Study Religions
Eckhart Soc
Pagan Fedn
Rural Theology Assn
Sea Faith Network (UK)
Traditional Cosmology Soc
Religion & medicine > Medicine: & religion
Religious drama
Religious Drama Soc
Religious education
Assn RE Inspectors, Advisors & Consultants
> + individual religions
Relocation agents & consultants
Assn Relocation Profls
Remedial education > Education
Remote imaging/sensing
Brit Assn Remote Sensing Companies
Mineralogical Soc
R Meteorological Soc
Remote Imaging Group
Remote Sensing & Photogrammetry Soc
Removers > Furniture: warehousing & removal
Renaissance
Scot Medievalists
Soc Renaissance Studies
Renal structure & disease > Nephrology
Rendering
Food & Drink Ind Ireland
UK Renderers Assn
Renewable energy
Network Alternative Technology &...Assessment
Renewable Energy Assn
Renewable UK Assn
Scot Renewables Forum
Solar Energy Soc
> + specific types of energy
Rented accommodation
Nat Landlords Assn
Rents > Property & land owners;   Tenants & residents
Repertory theatres > Theatre
Repetitive strain injury > Occupational health & hygiene; Performing arts
medicine
Reporters > Journalism

Reproductive ethics
Comment Reproductive Ethics
Reptiles > Herpetology
Rescue dogs
Nat Search & Rescue Dog Assn
Rescue equipment > field of rescue
Rescue organisations > Civil defence & industrial emergencies; First aid &
immediate care;   Welfare organisations; & field of rescue
Research > subject of research
Reservoirs > Dams & reservoirs
Residential: boats
Residential Boat Owners Assn
> + Inland waterways
Residential: colleges
Adult Residential Colls Assn
> + Adult education
Residential: homes
Assn Indep Care Advisers
English Community Care Assn
Relatives & Residents Assn
> + Nursing homes
Residential: property > Property: maintenance/management
Residential: settlements
Brit Assn Settlements & Social Action Centres
Residential: social work > Social: service
Residents > Tenants & residents
Resins & gums
FeRFA
Resorts > Holiday resorts
Respiratory disease
Brit Thoracic Soc
Respiratory equipment
Assn Respiratory Technology & Physiology
Barema
Rest homes > Residential homes
Restaurants > Hotels & restaurants
Restaurants: engineering > Catering: equipment
Restless legs
RLS-UK
Restorative dentistry > Dentistry
Restorers/restoration > object(s) restored
Restricted growth > Growth
Resuscitation techniques > Life saving
Retail trade
Brit Assn Fair Tr Shops
Brit Retail Consortium
Brit Shops & Stores Assn
Consumer Credit Association
Inst Grocery Distbn
Interactive Media Retail Group
NI Indep Retail Trade Assn
Retail Ireland
RGDATA [IRL]
Rural Shops Alliance
Scot Retail Consortium
U Shop Distributive & Allied Workers
UK Travel Retail Forum
> + specific trades
Retina (diseases of)
Brit Retinitis Pigmentosa Soc
Retirement
Active Retirement Ireland
Brit Pensioners & Tr U Action Assn
Life Academy
Retirement homes &/or sheltered housing
Assn Retirement Housing Mgrs
Assn Supported Living
Essential Role Sheltered Housing Nat Consortium
> + Nursing homes
Retreats (religious)
Assn Promoting Retreats
Retreat Assn
Retroreflective equipment
Retroreflective Eqpt Mfrs Assn
Rett syndrome
Rett Syndrome Assn
Revenue protection (electricity)
UK Revenue Protection Assn
Rhea
Rhea & Emu Assn
> + Ostrich farming
Rheology
Brit Soc Rheology
Rheumatism > Arthritis & rheumatism
Rhinology > Otolaryngology
Ribbon
Brit Narrow Fabrics Assn

© CBD Research Ltd · Beckenham · BR3 5JS · Tel 020 8650 7745 · E-mail cbd@cbdresearch.com · www.cbdresearch.com

Rice
        Grain & Feed Tr Assn
        London Rice Brokers Assn
        Rice Assn
Richard III King of England
        Richard III Soc
        Soc Friends King Richard III
Riding > Horses: riding & driving
Rifle shooting
        Nat Rifle Assn
        Nat Small-bore Rifle Assn
        Scot Air Rifle & Pistol Assn
        Scot Rifle Assn
        Scot Smallbore Rifle Assn
        Scot Target Shooting Fedn
        > + Shooting
Rights of the individual > Individual freedom
Rights of way > Footpaths & rights of way
Rigs (drilling)
        Brit Rig Owners Assn
Risk management
        ALARM
        Inst Operational Risk
        Inst Risk Mgt
        > + Insurance
Rivers
        Assn Rivers Trusts
        Estuarine & Coastal Sciences Assn
        > + Inland waterways;   Water
Road: accidents > Accidents; Road: safety & control
Road: construction, repair & materials
        ADEPT
        Asphalt Ind Alliance
        Brit Precast Concrete Fedn
        Britpave
        Chart Instn Highways & Transportation
        Fedn Road Surface Treatment Assns
        Inst Highway Engrs
        Instn Civil Engrs
        Refined Bitumen Assn
        Road Emulsion Assn
        Road Surface Treatments Assn
        UK Quality Ash Assn
Road: haulage
        Freight Transport Assn
        Heavy Transport Assn
        Ir Road Haulage Assn
        Road Haulage Assn
        Soc Operations Engrs
        Transport Assn
        Utd Road Transport U
Road: lighting, markings & traffic signs
        Assn Road Traffic Safety & Mgt
        Assn Signals, Lighting... Highway Electrical Connections
        Highway Electrical Mfrs & Suppliers Assn
        Photoluminescent Safety Products Assn
        Retroreflective Eqpt Mfrs Assn
        Road Safety Markings Assn
        > + Signs
Road: locomotives & rollers > Steam engines, boats & machinery
Road: safety & control
        Assn Indl Road Safety Officers
        Brake
        Campaign Drinking & Driving
        Inst Road Safety Officers
        Inst Traffic Accident Investigators
        ITS UK
        R Soc Prevention Accidents
        Road Safety GB
        RoadPeace
        RoadSafe
        Safe Speed Campaign
        Traffic Mgt Contrs Assn
        Vehicle Restraint Mfrs Assn
        > + Motoring organisations; Safety
Road: signs > Road: lighting, markings & traffic signs;   Signs
Road: sweeping > Street cleaning
Road: transport > Road: haulage
Robotics
        BCS
        Brit Automation & Robot Assn
        Materials Handling Engrs Assn
        Soc Underwater Technology
Rock climbing > Climbing
Rock gardens
        Alpine Garden Soc

Hardy Plant Soc
        Scot Rock Garden Club
Rock mechanics > Soil & rock mechanics
Rocketry
        Assn Scotland Res Astronautics
        MARS
        UK Rocketry Assn
Rocking horses
        Gld Rocking Horse Makers
Rodents (pests)
        Brit Pest Control Assn
        > + Rats (pets)
Roller bearings > Ball & roller bearings
Roller coasters
        Roller Coaster Club
        > + Fairgrounds & equipment
Roller sports > Skating: board, inline & roller
Roman archaeology & antiquities
        Assn Roman Archaeology
        Assn Study & Presvn Roman Mosaics
        Roman Finds Gp
        Soc Promotion Roman Studies
        > + Archaeology
Roman Catholic Church
        Assn Latin Liturgy
        Assn Separated & Divorced Catholics
        Catenian Assn
        Catholic Archives Soc
        Catholic Family Hist Soc
        Catholic Med Assn
        Catholic Record Soc
        Catholic Truth Soc
        Catholic U
        Chapels Soc
        Latin Mass Soc
        Newman Assn
        Scot Catholic Histl Assn
        > + Liturgy
Roman Empire
        Soc Promotion Roman Studies
        > + Classical studies
Romanies > Gypsies & travelling people
Romantic novelists
        Romantic Novelists Assn
Romany of the BBC
        Romany Soc
Roofing
        Brit Precast Concrete Fedn
        Clay Roof Tile Coun
        Confedn Roofing Contrs
        Copper Devt Assn
        Inst Roofing
        Intelligent Membrane Tr Assn
        Liquid Roofing & Waterproofing Assn
        Metal Cladding & Roofing Mfrs Assn
        Nat Fedn Roofing Contrs
        Nat Soc Master Thatchers
        Roofing Ind Alliance
        Scot Master Slaters & Roof Tilers Assn
        Single Ply Roofing Assn
        Stone Roofing Assn
        Trussed Rafter Assn
Rooflights
        Nat Assn Rooflight Mfrs
        > + Windows
Rootzone materials
        Brit Rootzone & Top Dressing Mfrs Assn
        > + Composts & composting
Rope access (safety & usage)
        Indl Rope Access Tr Assn
Ropes
        Performance Textiles Assn
Ropework
        Intl Gld Knot Tyers
Roses
        Amat Rose Breeders Assn
        Brit Assn Rose Breeders
        Horticultural Trs Assn
        N England Rosecarpe Horticl Soc
        R Nat Rose Soc
Rotary
        Assn Inner Wheel Clubs
        Assn Past Rotarians
Rotating electrical machines
        Assn Electrical & Mechanical Trs
        BEAMA
Rotorcraft > Helicopters

© CBD Research Ltd · Beckenham · BR3 5JS · Tel 020 8650 7745   E-mail cbd@cbdresearch.com · www.cbdresearch.com

Round tables
  Nat Assn Round Tables
Roundabouts (fairground) > Fairgrounds & equipment
Roundabouts (traffic)
  UK Roundabout Appreciation Soc
Rounders
  Gaelic Athletic Assn
  Rounders England
Roundheads > Cromwell (Oliver);   Fights (historic/re-enactment)
Route guidance
  ITS UK
  > + Road: safety & control
Routemaster buses
  Routemaster Operators & Owners Assn
Rowing
  Amat Rowing Assn
  Scot Rowing
  Welsh Amat Rowing Assn
  Welsh Sea Rowing Assn
Roy (Harry)
  Harry Roy Appreciation Soc
Royal Air Force
  R Air Force Histl Soc
  R Air Forces Assn
  > + Armed forces & veterans: welfare
Royal Marines
  White Ensign Assn
Royal Navy
  Aircrewman's Assn
  Assn R Navy Officers
  Naval Dockyards Soc
  Navy Records Soc
  R Naval Assn
  R Navy Enthusiasts' Soc
  White Ensign Assn
  > + Armed forces & veterans: welfare
Royal warrant holders
  R Warrant Holders Assn
Rubber
  Brit Rubber & Polyurethane Products Assn
  Brit Tyre Mfrs Assn
  Scot Plastics & Rubber Assn
Rubber stamps
  Brit Office Supplies & Services Fedn
  Rubber Stamp Mfrs' Gld
Rubella > German measles
Rugby Fives
  Rugby Fives Assn
Rugby football > Football: Rugby
Rugs > Carpets; Oriental carpets & rugs
Running
  Assn Running Clubs
  English Cross Country Assn
  Fell Runners Assn
  Road Runners Club
  > + Athletics
Run-off companies
  Assn Run-off Cos
Rupert Bear
Rural interests
  Country Land & Business Assn
  R Agricl Soc England
  Scot Land & Estates
  Westmorland County Agricl Soc
  > + Conservation; Environment;   Local government
Rural life: history > Agriculture: history
Ruritanian fiction
  Violet Needham Soc
Ruskin (John)
  Ruskin Soc
  Ruskin Soc London
Rusks
  Cereal Ingredient Mfrs Assn
Russia & associated states
  Brit Assn Slavonic & E Eur Studies
  Russo-Brit Cham Comm
  Scotland-Russia Forum
  Soc Cooperation Russian & Soviet Studies
Russia: language & literature
  Assn Language Learning
  Brit Assn Slavonic & E Eur Studies
  Pushkin Club

S

Sacks
  Environmental & Technical Assn Paper Sack Ind
SAD (seasonal affective disorder)
  SAD Assn
Saddlery
  Brit Equestrian Tr Assn
  Soc Master Saddlers
  > + Leathergoods
Safes
  Brit Security Ind Assn
Safety
  Brit Assn Public Safety Communications Officers
  Brit Safety Ind Fedn
  Catch 22 in Action
  Indep Safety Consultants Assn
  Inst Safety Technology & Res
  Instn Occupational Safety & Health
  Nat Ir Safety Org
  Safety & Reliability Soc
  Scot Hazards Campaign Gp
  SELECT
  > + Home: safety;   Road safety & control
Safety: assessment
  Assn Boat Safety Examiners
  Safety Assessment Fedn
Safety: barriers
  Fencing Contrs' Assn
  Retroreflective Eqpt Mfrs Assn
  Vehicle Restraint Mfrs Assn
Safety: equipment
  Health & Safety Sign Assn
  Inflatable Safety & Survival Eqpt...Assn
  Photoluminescent Safety Products Assn
  Retroreflective Eqpt Mfrs Assn
  Safety Pass Alliance
Safety: personal
  Brit Safety Ind Fedn
  Choice Personal Safety
  Fall Arrest Safety Eqpt Training
Safety: rigging/nets
  Fall Arrest Safety Eqpt Training
Sailing
  Assn Sea Training Orgs
  Ir Sailing Assn
  Old Gaffers Assn
  Sailing Smack Assn
  > + Boats & boating;   Ships (& boats): history & preservation;
  Yachts & yachting
Sailors > Merchant Navy; Royal Navy
Sailplanes > Gliding & soaring
Sails & sailmaking
  Assn Brit Sailmakers
  Brit Marine Fedn
  Performance Textiles Assn
St James of Compostela
  Confraternity Saint James
Salads
  Brit Leafy Salads Assn
  > + Vegetable(s) headings
Sales agents (general)
  Brit Intl Freight Assn
Sales management & representation
  Inst Promotional Marketing
  Inst Sales & Marketing Mgt
  Managing & Marketing Sales Assn
  Sales Inst Ireland
  Soc Sales & Marketing
  > + Marketing
Salmon & trout
  Assn Salmon Fishery Bds
  Brit Trout Assn
  Salmon & Trout Assn
  Scot Anglers Nat Assn
  Scot Salmon Producers' Org
  Welsh Salmon & Trout Angling Assn
  Wild Trout Trust
  > + Fish: farming
Salonika campaign (1915-18)
  Salonika Campaign Soc
Salt
  Salt Assn
Salvage > Reclamation & recycling; Towage & salvage
Salvage (underwater) > Underwater engineering & research

Salvage corps
    Brit Fire Services Assn
Sand & gravel
    Mineral Products Assn
Sand yachting > Kite sports
Sandplay
    Assn Integrative Sandplay Therapists
Sandwiches & sandwich bars
    Brit Sandwich Assn
    Nationwide Caterers Assn
Sanitary protection
    Absorbent Hygiene Products Mfrs Assn
Sanitaryware
    Brit Ceramic Confedn
Sarcoidosis
    Sarcoidosis & Interstitial Lung Assn
    > + Thoracic diseases
Sassoon (Siegfried Louvain)
    Siegfried Sassoon Fellowship
Satellite communications > Cable & satellite communications
Satellite navigation
    Challenger Soc Marine Science
    ITS UK
    UKspace
Saunas
    Fedn Holistic Therapists
Sausage & food casings
    Natural Sausage Casings Assn
Sausages
    Brit Sausage Appreciation Soc
    > + Meat
Saville (Malcolm)
    Malcolm Saville Soc
Savoy Operas
    Gilbert & Sullivan Soc
Sawmilling > Timber
Saxifrages (Saxifraga)
    Saxifrage Soc
Saxophones > Clarinets & saxophones
Sayers (Dorothy L[eigh])
    Dorothy L Sayers Soc
Scaffolding
    Nat Access & Scaffolding Confedn
    Prefabricated Access Suppliers' & Mfrs' Assn
Scales & weighing machines
    Solids Handling & Processing Assn
    UK Weighing Fedn
    > + Measurement
Scallops > Shellfish
Scandinavia: literature & antiquities
    Regia Anglorum
    Scot Soc Nthn Studies
    Viking Soc Nthn Res
Scanning
    UK Indl Vision Assn
Schizophrenia
    SANE
    Shine [IRL]
School bands
    Nat School Band Assn
School governors
School heads > Heads of schools & colleges
School secretaries & administrators
    Nat Assn School Business Mgt
    > + Secretaries & personal assistants
School teachers > Teachers
School uniform
    Schoolwear Assn
Schools
    Anti Academies Alliance
    Coun Brit Intl Schools
    Nat Assn Small Schools
    Nat Small Schools Forum
    New Schools Network
    > + Education; Teachers; & individual type of school
Schools: hygiene
    Medical Officers Schools Assn
Schools: independent
    Indep Schools Coun
Schools: inspection
    Assn Profls Educ & Children's Trusts
Schools: meals service
    Local Authority Caterers Assn
Schubert (Franz Peter)
    Schubert Soc
Schumacher (Dr E F)
    Doctor E F Schumacher Soc

Science
    Assn Brit Science Writers
    Assn Science Educ
    Brit Interactive Gp
    Brit Science Assn
    Brit Soc Philosophy Science
    Cambridge Philosophical Soc
    Campaign Science & Engg UK
    Manchester Literary & Philosophical Soc
    R Instn GB
    R Ir Academy
    R Scot Soc Arts
    R Soc Chemistry
    R Soc Edinburgh
    Royal Soc (The)
    Science, Technology, Engg… Public Relations Assn
    Scientific Alliance
    Scientists Global Responsibility
    Sense Science
    > + specific disciplines
Science fiction
    Brit Fantasy Soc
    Brit Science Fiction Assn
Science: history
    Brit Soc Hist Science
    Natural Sciences Collections Assn
Science parks
    UK Science Park Assn
Science: technology > Laboratory equipment & technology
Scientific film > Film
Scientific instruments
    Scientific Instrument Soc
    > + Glassware: scientific
Scientists > Science; specific disciplines
Scleroderma
    Raynaud's & Scleroderma Assn
    Scleroderma Soc
Sclerosis
    Multiple Sclerosis Nat Therapy Centres
    Multiple Sclerosis Soc
    Multiple Sclerosis Soc Ireland
    Tuberous Sclerosis Assn
Scoliosis
    Brit Orthopaedic Assn
    Scoliosis Assn
Scooter riding > Motor cycling & scooter riding
Scorpions
    Brit Arachnological Soc
    Brit Tarantula Soc
Scotland
    Assn Protection Rural Scotland
    Assn Scot Visitor Attractions
    Saint Andrew Soc
    Saltire Soc
    Scot Envt Link
    Scot Stone Liaison Gp
    Scot Wild Land Gp
    Scotland-Russia Forum
Scotland: archaeology
    Assn Certificated Field Archaeologists [Scotland]
    Soc Antiquaries Scotland
    > + Archaeology: county societies
Scotland: history
    Dorothy Dunnett Soc
    Pictish Arts Soc
    R Celtic Soc
    Scot Catholic Histl Assn
    Scot Record Soc
    Seventeen Fortyfive Assn
Scotland: language & literature
    Assn Scot Literary Studies
    Robert Burns World Fedn
    Scot Language Dictionaries
    Scot Poetry Library
    Scot Text Soc
    Scots Language Soc
    Ulster-Scots Language Soc
    > + Gaelic language & culture
Scotland: law history
    Stair Soc
Scotland: music
    R Celtic Soc
    Robert Burns World Fedn
    Traditional Music & Song Assn Scotland
    > + Pipe bands & music
Scott (Sir Walter)
    Edinburgh Sir Walter Scott Club

© CBD Research Ltd · Beckenham · BR3 5JS · Tel 020 8650 7745   E-mail cbd@cbdresearch.com · www.cbdresearch.com

Scouts > Youth organisations
Scrabble
    Assn Brit Scrabble Players
    Scrabble Clubs (UK)
Scrap > Materials: management/handling; Reclamation & recycling
Screen (film & television) > Film; Television headings
Screen printing
    Prism
Screen writers > Dramatists
Screens > Sieves & screens
Scribes
    Soc Scribes & Illuminators
Scripophily
    Intl Bond & Share Soc
Scriptwriting
    Brit Soc Comedy Writers
    > + Writing & writers
Scuba diving
    Scot Sub Aqua Club
    Scuba Inds Tr Assn
    > + Diving (professional & scientific); Water: sports
Sculpture
    Brit Art Medal Soc
    Nat Soc Painters, Sculptors & Printmakers
    Public Monuments & Sculpture Assn
    R Birmingham Soc Artists
    R Brit Soc Sculptors
    R Cambrian Academy Art
    R Scot Academy
    Sculptors' Soc Ireland
    Soc Portrait Sculptors
    Soc Women Artists
    > + Stone masons & sculptors
Sea > Marine; Nautical; Sailing etc
Sea angling
    Assn Sea Fisheries C'ees [E&W]
    Scot Fedn Sea Anglers
    > + Fishing (sport)
Sea pilots
    Europilots
    Nautical Inst
    > + Navigation
Sea pollution > Pollution & pollution control
Sea-bed exploration > Ocean industries
Seabirds > Birds
Seafood
    Food & Drink Fedn
    > + Fish headings; individual type of fish
Sealants & sealing
    Assn Sealant Applicators
    Brit Adhesives & Sealants Assn
    Brit Fluid Power Assn
    Brit Textile Technology Gp
    Extruded Sealants Assn
    Gasket Cutters Assn
Seals
    Seal Consvn Soc
Seamanship > Marine training; Sailing
Seamen > Merchant Navy; Royal Navy
Seaside piers > Piers
Seasonal affective disorder
    SAD Assn
Seasonings > Spices & seasonings
Seat belts
    Baby Products Assn
    Choice Personal Safety
    > + Personal safety
Seating (audience/sports)
    Brit Assn Seating Eqpt Suppliers
Seaweed > Algae
Secondary metal > Metal: scrap
Secondary schools
    School Leaders Scotland
Secondary teachers > Teachers
Secret passages
    Subterranea Britannica
Secret writing
    Xenophon
Secretaries & administrators
    Alliance UK Virtual Assistants
    Assn Celebrity Assistants (UK)
    Assn Coun Secretaries & Solicitors
    Assn Med Secretaries, Practice Managers...
    Inst Agricl Secretaries & Administrators
    Inst Legal Secretaries & PAs
    Inst Paralegals
    Inst Profl Administrators

    Nat Assn NFU Gp Secretaries
    Nat Assn School Business Mgt
Secularism
    AHS
    Campaign Philosophical Freedom
    Nat Secular Soc
    > + Humanism
Securities > Investment; Stocks & shares
Security
    Assn Automatic Identification &... Data Capture
    Assn Inf Security Auditors & Business Exexs
    Assn Insurance Surveyors
    Assn Security Consultants
    Brit Blind & Shutter Assn
    Brit Machine Vision Assn...
    Brit Security Ind Assn
    Defence Ind Security Assn
    Fencing Contrs' Assn
    Fibreoptic Ind Assn
    Inst Hotel Security Mgt
    Inst Security Mgt
    Ir Security Ind Assn
    Mobile Electronics & Security Fedn
    Nat Assn Healthcare Security
    Nat Assn Security Dog Users
    Nat Security Inspectorate
    Nationwide Assn Security Installation Cos
    Security Inst Ireland
    Telecare Services Assn
    UK Indl Vision Assn
    > + Defence; Police
Security: shredding > Documents: confidential disposal
Sedges > Reeds & sedges
Sedums (Crassulaceae)
    Sedum Soc
Seed crushing > Oilseed
Seed potatoes > Potatoes
Seeds
    Agricl Inds Confedn
    Biodynamic Agricl Assn
    Brit Assn Seed Analysts
    Brit Assn Seed Producers
    Ir Seed Savers Assn
    Ir Seed Tr Assn
    Nat Assn Agricl Contrs
    NIAB
    Scot Seed & Nursery Tr Assn
Self catering
    Assn Scotland's Self Caterers
    Brit Holiday & Home Parks Assn
    English Assn Self Catering Operators
    Fedn Nat Self Catering Assns
    NI Self Catering Holiday Assn
    Wales Assn Self Catering Operators
    > + Caravans & caravanning; Travel & tourism etc
Self defence
    Tai Chi U
    > Martial arts
Self employment
    Fedn Small Businesses
    > + Business
Self harm
    Purine Metabolic Patients Assn
Self healing
    Metamorphic Association
Selling > Direct selling; Sales management & representation
Semi conductors > Electronics: industry & engineering
Sensing > Remote imaging/sensing
Separated & divorced people > Singles, divorced & separated
Separation techniques
    Chromatographic Soc
Sequence dancing > Dancing
Serials > Periodicals
Servicemen's welfare > Armed forces & veterans: welfare;   Ex-service
    organisations
Services (local government)
    Assn Public Service Excellence
Settlements > Archaeology; Residential: settlements; Welfare: organisations
Sewers, sewage & effluents
    Chart Instn Water & Envtl Management
    Nat Sewerage Assn
    Soc Brit Water & Wastewater Inds
Sewing articles (collecting)
    Thimble Soc Lond
Sewing machines
    Assn Sewing Machine Distbrs

Sewing Machine Tr Assn
Tools Self Reliance
Sex equality > Women: equal rights
Sex & sexual law reform
    Campaign Homosexual Equality
    Sexaholics Anonymous
    Sexual Freedom Coalition
Sexual dysfunction
    Androgen Insensitivity Syndrome Support Gp
    Assn Psychosexual Nursing
    Brit Soc Sexual Medicine
    College Sexual & Relationship Therapists
    Sexual Advice Assn
Sexually transmitted disease > Genito-urinary medicine
Shaft sinking > Tunnels & shaft sinking
Shakespeare (William)
    Brit Shakespeare Assn
    De Vere Soc
    Shakespeare Reading Soc
    Sunday Shakespeare Soc
Share certificates (collecting) > Scripophily
Shareholders
    UK Shareholders' Assn
    > + Investment; Stocks & shares
Sharks
    Shark Angling Club
Shaving equipment
    Cutlery & Allied Trs Res Assn
Shaw (George Bernard)
    Shaw Soc
Shaw (Thomas Edward) > Lawrence (Thomas Edward) 'of Arabia'
Sheep
    Brit Veterinary Assn
    Highlands & Islands Sheep Health Assn
    Ir Cattle & Sheep Farmers Assn
    Mutton Renaissance Campaign
    Nat Sheep Assn
Sheep: breed societies
    Badger Face Welsh Mountain Sheep Soc
    Balwen Welsh Mountain Sheep Soc
    Beltex Sheep Soc
    Black Welsh Mountain Sheep Breeders Assn
    Blackface Sheep Breeders Assn
    Bluefaced Leicester Sheep Breeders Assn
    Brecknock Hill Cheviot Sheep Soc
    Brit Berrichon du Cher Sheep Soc
    Brit Bleu du Maine Sheep Soc
    Brit Charollais Sheep Soc
    Brit Coloured Sheep Breeders Assn
    Brit Friesland Sheep Soc
    Brit Gotland Sheep Soc
    Brit Icelandic Sheep Breeders Gp
    Brit Ile de France Sheep Soc
    Brit Milksheep Soc
    Brit Rouge Sheep Soc
    Brit Texel Sheep Soc
    Brit Vendeen Sheep Soc
    Cambridge Sheep Society
    Castlemilk Moorit Sheep Soc
    Charmoise Hill Sheep Soc
    Cheviot Sheep Soc
    Clun Forest Sheep Breeders Soc
    Cotswold Sheep Soc
    Dalesbred Sheep Breeders Assn
    Dartmoor Sheep Breeders Assn
    Derbyshire Gritstone Sheepbreeders Soc
    Devon Closewool Sheep Breeders Soc
    Devon & Cornwall Longwool Flock Assn
    Dorset Down Sheep Breeders Assn
    Dorset Horn & Poll Sheep Breeders Assn
    Easy Care Sheep Soc
    Eppynt Hill & Beulah Speckled Face Sheep Soc
    Exmoor Horn Sheep Breeders' Soc
    Hampshire Down Sheep Breeders Assn
    Hebridean Sheep Soc
    Herdwick Sheep Breeders Assn
    Hill Radnor Flock Book Soc
    Jacob Sheep Soc
    Kerry Hill Flock Book Soc
    Leicester Longwool Sheepbreeders Assn
    Lincoln Longwool Sheep Breeders Assn
    Llanwenog Sheep Soc
    Lleyn Sheep Soc
    Lonk Sheep Breeders Assn
    Manx Loaghtan Sheep Breeders Gp
    Masham Sheep Breeders Assn
    N Country Cheviot Sheep Soc

    N England Mule Sheep Assn
    N Ronaldsay Sheep Fellowship
    Norfolk Horn Breeders Gp
    Oxford Down Sheep Breeders Assn
    Portland Sheep Breeders Gp
    Romney Sheep Breeders Soc
    Rough Fell Sheep Breeders Assn
    Roussin Sheep Soc
    Ryeland Flock Book Soc
    S Wales Mountain Sheep Soc
    Scotch Mule Assn
    Shetland Cheviot Marketing Soc
    Shetland Flock Book Trust
    Shetland Sheep Soc
    Shropshire Sheep Breeders Assn
    Soay Sheep Soc
    Soc Border Leicester Sheep Breeders
    Southdown Sheep Soc
    Suffolk Sheep Soc
    Swaledale Sheep Breeders Assn
    Talybont Welsh Sheep Soc
    Teeswater Sheep Breeders Assn
    Welsh Halfbred Sheep Breeders Assn
    Welsh Hill Speckled Face Sheep Soc
    Welsh Mountain Sheep Soc - Hill Flock
    Welsh Mountain Sheep Soc - Registered Section
    Welsh Mule Sheep Breeders Assn
    Wensleydale Longwool Sheep Breeders' Assn
    White Face Dartmoor Sheep Breeders Assn
    White Faced Woodland Sheep Soc
    Wiltshire Horn Sheep Soc
    Zwartbles Sheep Assn
    > + Cattle & livestock
Sheep: dairying
    Brit Friesland Sheep Soc
    Brit Milksheep Soc
    Brit Sheep Dairying Assn
Sheet metal > Metal: sheet
Sheet music > Music
Shelley (Percy Bysshe)
    Keats Shelley Memorial Assn
Shellfish
    Assn Scot Shellfish Growers
    Food & Drink Fedn
    Scot Fishermen's Fedn
    Shellfish Assn
Shells > Conchology
Sheltered housing > Retirement homes &/or sheltered housing
Shelving & racking > Storage equipment
Shepherds' crooks
    Border Stick Dressers Assn
    Brit Stickmakers Gld
Sheriffs & sheriff officers
    High Sheriffs' Assn
    Soc Messengers-at-Arms & Sheriff Officers
Shiatsu
    Equine Shiatsu Assn
    Shiatsu Soc
    > + Complementary medicine
Shingles
    Herpes Viruses Assn
    Shingles Support Soc
Shinty (sport)
    Camanachd Assn
Shipbroking
    Inst Chart Shipbrokers
    Ir Ship Agents Assn
Shipbuilding & ship repairing
    Amat Yacht Res Soc
    Brit Marine Fedn
    R Instn Naval Architects
    Shipbuilders & Shiprepairers Assn
    Steam Boat Assn
    > + Marine: engineering
Shippers & packers for specific trades > trade concerned
Shipping
    Assn Cruise Experts
    Assn Port Health Authorities
    Cambridge Refrigeration Technology
    Cham Shipping
    Freight Transport Assn
    Grain & Feed Tr Assn
    Ir Cham Shipping
    Ir Marine Fedn
    London Shipowners & River Users Soc
    Marine Inst [IRL]

© CBD Research Ltd · Beckenham · BR3 5JS · Tel 020 8650 7745 · E-mail cbd@cbdresearch.com · www.cbdresearch.com

Maritime Inf Assn
Maritime UK
Shipping & forwarding
    Brit Intl Freight Assn
    Ir Intl Freight Assn
    > + Freight transport
Ships (& boats): history & preservation
    Brit Titanic Soc
    Classic Motor Boat Assn
    Coble & Keelboat Soc
    Cutty Sark Trust
    Forty Plus Fishing Boat Assn
    Heritage Afloat
    Mary Rose Soc
    Nat Historic Ships
    Ocean Liner Soc
    Soc Sailing Barge Res
    Wooden Boatbuilders Trade Assn
Ships: stores & supplies
    Brit Assn Ship Suppliers
    Scot Ship Chandlers Assn
Ships: survey
    Soc Consulting Marine Engrs & Ship Surveyors
Shipwrecks > Ships (& boats): history & preservation
Shirts
    UK Fashion & Textile Assn
Shoehorns
    Buttonhook Soc
Shoes > Footwear
Shogi (Japanese chess)
    Brit Shogi Fedn
Shooting
    Assn Profl Shooting Instructors
    Brit Airgun Shooters' Assn
    Brit Assn Shooting & Consvn
    Brit Shooting
    Brit Shooting Sports Coun
    Countryside Alliance
    Countryside Alliance Ireland
    Scot Assn Country Sports
    Scot Pistol Assn
    Shooters' Rights Assn
    Sportsman's Assn
    U Country Sports Workers
    UK Practical Shooting Assn
    Vintage Arms Assn
    > + Arms & armour; Rifle shooting
Shopfitting
    Glass & Glazing Fedn
    Nat Assn Shopfitters
    Shop & Display Eqpt Assn
Shopmobility
    Nat Fedn Shopmobility
Shopping centres
    Brit Coun Shopping Centres
Shopping from home > Home: shopping
Shops & stores > Retail trade
Shoring technology
    Construction Plant-hire Assn
Shorinji kempo > Martial arts
Shorthand writing
    Brit Inst Verbatim Reporters
    Inc Phonographic Soc
Show jumping
    Brit Equestrian Fedn
    > + Horse headings
Showmen (fairground)
    Showmen's Gld
    Soc Indep Roundabout Proprietors
    > + Fairgrounds & equipment
Shows & events
    Assn Show & Agricl Orgs
    Horticultural Exhibitors Assn
    > + Agriculture: county societies; Events management
Shredders (scrap)
    Brit Metals Recycling Assn
Shredding (security) > Documents: confidential disposal
Shutters > Windows: blinds & shutters
Sibelius (Jean)
    UK Sibelius Soc
Sickle cell anaemia
    Sickle Cell Soc
Side saddle riding
    Side Saddle Assn
Sidecars
    Fedn Sidecar Clubs
    > + Motor cycling & scooter riding

Sieves & screens
    Solids Handling & Processing Assn
Sight > Blind & partially sighted;   specific disease
Sigillology > Badges & insignia
Sign language
    Brit Deaf Assn
    Ir Deaf Soc
    R Assn Deaf People
    Scot Assn Sign Language Interpreters
    > + Deafness
Signals (highway/road)
    Assn Signals, Lighting... Highway Electrical Connections
Signs
    Brit Sign & Graphics Assn
    Health & Safety Sign Assn
    Village Sign Soc
    > + Road: lighting, markings & traffic signs
Silhouettes
    Silhouette Collectors Club
    Soc Limners
Silica
    Mineral Products Assn
Silk
    Brit Throwsters Assn
    Silk Assn
Silos & hoppers
    Solids Handling & Processing Assn
Silver
    Silver Soc
Silver bands > Brass & silver bands
Silver (dealing in) > Bullion dealing
Silversmiths > Goldsmiths & silversmiths
Simpson (Robert Wilfred Levick)
    Robert Simpson Soc
Simultaneous translation
    Conf Interpreters Gp
    Ir Translators & Interpreters Assn
    > + Translation & interpretation
Singapore
    Brit Cham Comm Singapore
    Singapore UK Assn
Singing
    Assn Engl Singers & Speakers
    Assn Teachers Singing
    Brit Voice Assn
    Gld Musicians & Singers
    Recorded Vocal Art Soc
    Sing for Pleasure
    > + Choirs & choral music
Single transferable vote
    Electoral Reform Soc
    > + Elections & electoral legislation
Singles, divorced & separated
    Assn Separated & Divorced Catholics
    Assn Shared Parenting
    Families Need Fathers
    Nat Coun Divorced, Separated & Widowed
    Nat Coun One Parent Families
    Nat Fedn Solo Clubs
    One Parent Families Scotland
    Phoenix Camping Club
    Relationships Scotland
    > + Widows & widowers
Site investigation > Surveying
Sixth form colleges
    Assn Colls
    CIFE
Sjogren's syndrome
    Brit Sjogren's Syndrome Assn
Skate-boarding > Skating: board, inline & roller
Skates (fish)
    Skates & Rays Producers Assn
Skating: ice > Ice skating
Skating: board, inline & roller
    All Terrain Boarding Assn
    Brit Inline Puck Hockey Assn
    Brit Inline Skater Hockey Assn
    Brit Roller Sports Fedn
    Fedn Artistic Roller Skating
    Fedn Inline Speed Skating
    Ir Ice Hockey Assn
    Ir Roller Hockey Assn
    Nat Roller Hockey Assn
    UK Skateboarding Assn
Skeet shooting > Clay target (pigeon) shooting
Ski slopes
    Brit Ski Slope Operators Assn

Skibob
		Skibob Assn
Skiing > Snowsports; Water sports
Skills
Skin camouflage
		Brit Assn Skin Camouflage
		> + Birthmarks & disfigurement
Skin disease > Dermatology; individual diseases
Skin diving > Water: sports
Skins > Hides & skins; Leather
Skipping
		Brit Rope Skipping Assn
Sky (visibility of)
		Campaign Dark Skies
Skylights > Rooflights
Slag: cementitious
		Cementitious Slag Makers Assn
Slate(s)
		Scot Master Slaters & Roof Tilers Assn
		Stone Fedn
		Stone Roofing Assn
Slaughtering > Abattoirs
Slave trade
		Equiano Soc
Slavonic languages & culture
		Brit Assn Slavonic & E Eur Studies
Sleep
		Brit Sleep Soc
		Brit Snoring & Sleep Apnoea Assn
		Brit Waterbed Assn
		Narcolepsy UK
		Sleep Apnoea Trust Assn
		Sleep Coun
Sleepers (concrete)
		Brit Precast Concrete Fedn
		> + Railways: engineering
Sliding doors
		Assn Interior Specialists
		> + Doors
Slimming > Dietetics; Eating disorders; Obesity
Slot cars
		Brit Slot Car Racing Assn
Slot machines (vintage)
		Soc Indep Roundabout Proprietors
Slovak Republic
		Brit Cham Comm Slovak Republic
		Brit Czech & Slovak Assn
Slovakia: music
		Dvořák Soc Czech & Slovak Music

Small arms > Arms & armour; Shooting
Small business > Business; Self employment
Small claims
		Chart Inst Arbitrators
Small woods > Woodlands
Smart cards > Credit & magnetic strip(e) cards
Smith (Adam)
		Scot Economic Soc
Smith (Sydney)
		Sydney Smith Assn
Smoke & smoke control
		Intumescent Fire Seals Assn
		Smoke Control Assn
		> + Air: conditioning & ventilating
Smoking
		Action Smoking & Health
		Freedom Choose
		Freedom Org Right Enjoy Smoking Tobacco
Smoking: of food > type of food smoked
Snacks
		Food & Drink Ind Ireland
		Snack, Nut & Crisp Mfrs Assn
Snakes > Herpetology
Snooker > Cue sports
Snoring & apnoea
		Brit Snoring & Sleep Apnoea Assn
		NARA
Snow (John)
		John Snow Soc
Snowboarding > Snowsports
Snowfall & blizzards
		Tornado & Storm Res Org
Snowsports
		Alpine Club
		Backpackers Club
		Brit Alpine Racing Ski Clubs
		Brit Assn Mountain Guides

Brit Assn Ski Patrollers
		Brit Assn Snowsport Instructors
		Brit Ski Slope Operators Assn
		Brit Ski & Snowboard
		Brit Universities Snowsports Coun
		English Ski Coun
		Mountaineering Coun Scotland
		Scot Ski Club
		Ski Club
		Ski Coun Wales
		Skibob Assn
		Snowsport Inds
		Snowsport Scotland
Soap & detergents
		Ir Cosmetics Detergent & Allied Products Assn
		UK Cleaning Products Ind Assn
Soaring > Gliding & soaring
Social: history > History
Social: inventions
		Inst Social Inventions
Social: sciences/research
		Academy Social Sciences
		Assn Res Centres Social Sciences
		Assn Teaching Social Sciences
		Brit Sociological Assn
		Inst Social Inventions
		Market Res Soc
		Modern Studies Assn
		Social Policy Assn
		Social Res Assn
		Socio-Legal Studies Assn
		Sociological Assn Ireland
		Statistical & Social Inquiry Soc Ireland
Social: service
		Assn Directors Adult Social Services
		Assn Directors Social Work [Scotland]
		Assn Educ Welfare Mgt
		Brit Assn Social Workers
		Ceretas
		Emergency Social Services Assn
		Inst Welfare
		Ir Assn Social Workers
		NAGALRO
		Nat Assn Adult Placement Services
		Nat Assn Social Workers Educ
		Nat Fedn Community Orgs
		Scot Org Practice Teaching
		Social Care Assn
		> + Community service: voluntary; Welfare: administration
Social service: area organisations
		NI Coun Voluntary Action
		Wales Coun Voluntary Action
Socialism
		Fabian Soc
		Socialist Health Assn
Sociology > Social: sciences/research
Soft drinks
		Beverage Coun Ireland
		Brit Soft Drinks Assn
Soft furnishings
		Assn Master Upholsterers & Soft Furnishers
		Assn Soft Furnishers
		Nat Carpet Cleaners Assn
		> + Upholstery
Soft tissue > Tissue paper
Softball
		BaseballSoftballUK
Software
		Component Obsolescence Gp
		Intellect
		Ir Software Assn
		ScotlandIS
		> + Computers
Software: development
		Business Application Software Developers Assn
		HL7 UK Ltd
		UK Software Metrics Assn
Software: leisure
		UK Interactive Entertainment Assn
Software: protection
		BCS
		Business Software Alliance
		Fedn Software Theft
Softwoods
		Timber Tr Fedn
		> + Timber

Soil
 Brit Soc Soil Science
 Growing Media Assn
 Inst Profl Soil Scientists
 Instn Agricl Engrs
Soil & rock mechanics
 Brit Geotechnical Assn
 Instn Civil Engrs
Solar technology
 Micropower Coun
 R Astronomical Soc
 Renewable Energy Assn
 Scot Solar Energy Gp
 Solar Energy Soc
 Solar Tr Assn
 > + Renewable energy
Soldering > Brazing & soldering
Soldiers' welfare > Armed forces & veterans: welfare
Sol-fa > Tonic Sol-fa
Solicitors > Law
Solicitors: matrimonial law > Family law
Solid fuel
 ICOM Energy Assn
 Solid Fuel Assn
 > + Coal headings
Solid waste
 Chart Instn Wastes Mgt
Solids in bulk > Materials: management/handling
Solo musicians
 Inc Soc Musicians
 > + performer by name
Soluble coffee > Coffee
Solvent abuse
 Re-Solv
Solvents
 Chemical Recycling Assn
 Solvents Ind Assn
 > + Cleaning equipment
Songbirds > Birds
Songs & songwriting
 Brit Academy Songwriters, Composers & Authors
 Brit Music Rights
 English Poetry & Song Soc
Sound > Acoustics; Insulation; Noise
Sound recording & reproduction
 Assn Motion Picture Sound
 Assn Profl Recording Services
 Audio Engg Soc
 BPI
 Brit Fedn Audio
 Brit Sound Recording Assn
 Fedn Recorded Music Socs
 Friends Pianola Inst
 Inst Broadcast Sound
 Inst Sound & Communications Engrs
 Ir Recorded Music Assn
 Music Producers Gld
 Profl Lighting & Sound Assn
 > + Video
South Downs
 S Downs Soc
Southern Africa
 Brit Cham Business Sthn Africa
Souvenirs > Commemorative items & souvenirs
Soviet Union > Russia & associated states
Soya
 Soya Protein Assn
Space: research & exploration
 ADS Gp
 Assn Scotland Res Astronautics
 Assn Specialist Techl Orgs Space
 Brit Interplanetary Soc
 MARS
 R Aeronautical Soc
 UKspace
Space: visitors from > Unidentified flying objects
Spain
 Anglo Spanish Soc
 Assn Contemporary Iberian Studies
 Brit Cham Comm Spain
 Hispanic & Luso Brazilian Coun
Spain: language & literature
 Assn Hispanists
 Assn Language Learning
Spas
 Brit & Ir Spa & Hot Tub Assn
 Inst Swimming Pool Engrs

 Malvern Spa Assn
 Spa Business Assn
 Swimming Pool & Allied Trs Assn
Spastics > Cerebral palsy
Speakers
 Assn Engl Singers & Speakers
 Assn Speakers Clubs
 Profl Speakers Assn
Special constables
 Assn Special Constabulary Chief Officers
 > + Police
Special education > Education
Spectacles > Optical industry
Spectator seating
 Brit Assn Seating Eqpt Suppliers
Speech
 Afasic
 Allied Health Professions Fedn
 Assn Engl Singers & Speakers
 Assn Lipspeakers
 Assn Rehabilitation Communication & Oral Skills
 Assn Speech & Language Therapists. . .
 Brit Aphasiology Soc
 Brit Assn Academic Phoneticians
 Brit Stammering Assn
 Brit Voice Assn
 Craniofacial Soc
 Cued Speech Assn
 Nat Assn Profls. . . Language Impairment Children
 R Coll Speech & Language Therapists
 Scot Assn Speech & Drama Adjudicators
 Selective Mutism Inf & Res Assn
 Soc Teachers Speech & Drama
 Speakability
 Voice Care Network
 > + Deafness
Speedsailing > Surfing, board & speed sailing
Speedway > Motor cycling & scooter riding
Speleology > Caves & caving
Spelling reform
 English Spelling Soc
Spices & seasoning
 Seasoning & Spice Assn
 > + Flavourings
Spiders
 Brit Arachnological Soc
 Brit Tarantula Soc
 Buglife
Spill control (oil)
 UK Spill Assn
Spina bifida & hydrocephalus
 Assn Spina Bifida & Hydrocephalus
 Nat Assn Spina Bifida & Hydrocephalus Ireland
 Scot Spina Bifida Assn
 Soc Res Hydrocephalus & Spina Bifida
Spine & spinal injury
 Assn Light Touch Therapists
 Assn Spinal Injury Res. . .
 Brit Orthopaedic Assn
 Nat Ankylosing Spondylitis Soc
 Nat Backpain Assn
 Scoliosis Assn
 Spinal Injuries Assn
 Spinal Injuries Scotland
Spinning: hand
 Assn Glds Weavers, Spinners & Dyers
Spirits > Wines & spirits trade; Individual spirits
Spiritual healing
 Aetherius Soc
 Assn Therapeutic Healers
 Brit Alliance Healing Assns
 Confedn Healing Orgs
 Crystal & Healing Fedn
 Nat Fedn Spiritual Healers
 Scot Assn Spiritual Healers
 Universal Spiritualists Assn
 > + Healing
Spiritualism
 Inst Spiritualist Mediums
 Spiritual Workers' Assn
 Spiritualist Assn
 Spiritualists Nat U
Splints > Prosthetics & orthoses
Spode china
 Spode Soc
Spohr (Louis)
 Spohr Soc

© CBD Research Ltd · Beckenham · BR3 5JS · Tel 020 8650 7745 · E-mail cbd@cbdresearch.com · www.cbdresearch.com

Spondylitis > Ankylosing spondylitis
Spoons > Cutlery
Spoons: collecting
>> Silver Spoon Club
>> UK Spoon Collectors Club
Sporting guns & rifles > Shooting
Sports
>> Brit Assn Sport & Exercise Sciences
>> Brit Olympic Assn
>> Brit Outdoor Profls Assn
>> Brit Universities & Colleges Sport
>> Inst Mgt Sport & Physical Activity
>> Profl Players Fedn
>> Scot Assn Local Sports Couns
>> Scot Schoolsport Fedn
>> Scot Sports Assn
>> Sport Recreation Alliance
>> Sports Journalists' Assn GB
>> > + individual sports
Sports: country
>> Countryside Alliance
>> U Country Sports Workers
>> > + individual sport
Sports: disabled & handicapped
>> Brit Deaf Sports Coun
>> Brit Paralympic Assn
>> Brit Wheelchair Athletics Assn
>> Brit Wheelchair Pool Players' Assn
>> Brit Wheelchair Racing Assn
>> CP Sport England & Wales
>> English Boccia Assn
>> English Fedn Disability Sport
>> Nat Assn Swimming Clubs H'capped
>> Scot Disability Sport
>> UK Sports Assn People Learning Disability
>> WheelPower
Sports: equipment
>> Assn Play Inds
>> Fitness Ind Assn
>> Sporting Goods Ind Assn
>> Sports & Fitness Eqpt Assn
Sports: history
>> Brit Soc Sports Hist
Sports: law
>> Brit Assn Sport & Law
Sports: medicine & therapy
>> Brit Assn Sport & Exercise Medicine
>> Brit Orthopaedic Assn
>> Osteopathic Sports Care Assn
>> Scot Massage Therapists Org
>> SMAE Fellowship
>> Soc Sports Therapists
>> Sports Massage Assn
Sports: stadia
>> Fedn Stadium Communities
Sports: trade
>> Assn Profl Sales Agents (Sports & Leisure Inds)
>> Business Sport & Leisure
>> Fedn Sports & Play Assns
Sportsgrounds & synthetic surfaces
>> Brit Rootzone & Top Dressing Mfrs Assn
>> Land Drainage Contrs Assn
>> Nat Assn Agricl Contrs
>> Nat Playing Fields Assn
>> Sports & Play Construction Assn
>> Sports Turf Res Inst
>> > + Playgrounds & playgroups
Sportshall equipment > Sports: equipment
Sportswear
>> Fedn Sports & Play Assns
>> Sporting Goods Ind Assn
>> > + Clothing
Sprats
>> Herring Buyers Assn
>> > + Fish; Fishing
Sprayed concrete > Concrete & concrete products
Spreads & spreadable products
>> Margarine & Spreads Assn
Springs
>> Inst Spring Technology
>> UK Spring Mfrs Assn
Sprinklers: fire
>> Brit Automatic Fire Sprinkler Assn
>> Nat Fire Sprinkler Network
>> Residential Sprinkler Assn
>> > + Fire protection & prevention
Sprouts > Brassicas

Square dancing
>> Brit Assn Amer Square Dance Clubs
>> Nat Assn Teachers Dancing
>> Square Dance Callers Club
Squash rackets > Rackets (squash)
Squirrels (red)
>> Friends Red Squirrel
Stable staff
>> Nat Assn Stable Staff
>> > + Horse: racing
Stadia (sports)
>> Fedn Stadium Communities
Staff recruitment > Employment agents & consultants
Staffordshire blue & white ware
>> Friends Blue
>> Spode Soc
Stage > Theatre
Staged fights > Fights (stage & film)
Staging / gantries
>> Nat Access & Scaffolding Confedn
>> > + Construction equipment
Stained glass > Glass painting
Stainless steel > Steel: special & alloy
Stairs
>> Spiral Staircase Mfrs Assn
Stairs: gates & barriers (for)
>> Baby Products Assn
Stalin (Joseph)
>> Stalin Soc
Stalking & harassment
>> Nat Assn Support Victims Stalking & Harassment
Stammering
>> Brit Stammering Assn
>> > + Speech
Stamp collecting > Philately & postal history
Standardisation
>> Brit Standards Soc
>> BSI
>> Chart Quality Inst
Standby ships
>> Emergency Response & Rescue Vessels Assn
>> > + Ocean industries
Starch
>> Brit Starch Ind Assn
Static electricity > Electro-static equipment
Stationery
>> Brit Office Supplies & Services Fedn
>> Brit Printing Inds Fedn
Statistics
>> Brit Urban & Regional Inf Systems Assn
>> R Statistical Soc
>> Radical Statistics Gp
>> Statistical & Social Inquiry Soc Ireland
>> Statisticians Pharmaceutical Ind
Statute law
>> Statute Law Soc
>> > + Law headings
Statutory auditors
>> Assn Authorised Public Accountants
Steam engines, boats & machinery
>> Nat Traction Engine Trust
>> Northern Mill Engine Soc
>> Paddle Steamer Presvn Soc
>> Road Locomotive Soc
>> Road Roller Assn
>> Scot Traction Engine Soc
>> Soc Indep Roundabout Proprietors
>> Southern Counties Historic Vehicle Presvn Trust
>> Steam Boat Assn
>> Steam Car Club
>> Steam Plough Club
>> Transport Trust
>> Trevithick Soc
>> > + Archaeology: industrial;   Fairgrounds & equipment; Railways;
>> Shipbuilding & ship repairing
Steel
>> Cast Metals Fedn
>> Electric Steel Makers Gld
>> Inst Materials, Minerals & Mining
>> Intl Steel Tr Assn
>> Nat Assn Steel Stockholders
>> UK Steel
>> > + Iron
Steel: bands
>> Brit Assn Steelbands
Steel: construction > Construction industries
Steel: drums > Cisterns, drums & tanks

© CBD Research Ltd · Beckenham · BR3 5JS · Tel 020 8650 7745   E-mail cbd@cbdresearch.com · www.cbdresearch.com

Steel: foundries > Foundries
Steel: special & alloy
    Aluminium Stockholders Assn
    Brit Stainless Steel Assn
    Nat Assn Steel Stockholders
Steel: stockholders > Iron & steel stockholders
Steel: tubes
    Nat Assn Steel Stockholders
Steeplejacks
    Assn Technical Lighting & Access Specialists
Steiner (Rudolf)
    Anthroposophical Soc
    Biodynamic Agricl Assn
Stereoscopy
    Stereoscopic Soc
Sterilisation > Family planning
Sterilising
    Inst Decontamination Sciences
Stevenson (Robert Louis)
    Robert Louis Stevenson Club
Stevenson (Ronald)
    Ronald Stevenson Soc
Stickler syndrome
    Stickler Syndrome Support Gp
Stickmaking
    Border Stick Dressers Assn
    Brit Stickmakers Gld
    Brit Woodcarvers Assn
Stiff man syndrome
    Stiff Man Syndrome Support Gp
Stillbirth > Maternity; Obstetrics & gynaecology
Stock (animals) > Cattle & livestock
Stock & materials control
    Chart Inst Logistics & Transport
    Ir Inst Purchasing & Materials Mgt
    > + Materials management/handling
Stockings > Hosiery
Stocks & shares
    Assn Private Client Investment Mgrs & Stockbrokers
    Chart Inst Securities & Investment
    London Stock Exchange Gp
    Soc Share & Business Valuers
    > + Investment
Stocktaking/auditing
    Inst Licensed Tr Stock Auditors
Stoma > Colitis/colostomy; Ileostomy; Urology
Stone
    Brit Antique Furniture Restorers Assn
    Cornish Cham Mines & Minerals
    Men Stones
    Scot Stone Liaison Gp
    Stone Fedn
    Stone Roofing Assn
    UK Cast Stone Assn
    > + Quarries & quarrying; specific types of stone
Stone masons & sculptors
    Intl Masonry Soc
    Master Carvers Assn
    Nat Assn Master Letter Carvers
    Nat Assn Memorial Masons
Stonehenge
    Megalithic Soc
Stones (precious) > Gemstones
Stoolball
    Stoolball England
Storage
    Movers Inst
    Nat Gld Removers & Storers
    Self Storage Assn
Storage equipment
    Storage Eqpt Mfrs Assn
    Storage & Handling Eqpt Distbrs Assn
    > + Materials: management/handling
Store cards
    Finance & Leasing Assn
Stores: control > Stock & materials control
Stores: department/general > Retail trade
Storm research > Tornado & storm research
Storytelling
    Soc Storytelling
Stoves > Catering equipment;   Domestic appliances;   Fires & fireplaces
Strain injury > Repetitive strain injury;   Sports: medicine & therapy
Strain measurement
    Brit Soc Strain Measurement
    > + Materials: technology & testing
Strapping
    Brit Tensional Strapping Assn

Strategic planning
    ADEPT
    Strategic Planning Soc
Strauss (Johann) & family
    Johann Strauss Soc
Strauss (Richard)
    Richard Strauss Soc
Straw > Hay & straw
Straw: crafts
    Gld Straw Craftsmen
Street cleaning
    Chart Instn Wastes Mgt
    Construction Plant-hire Assn
Street furniture & lighting > Road: lighting, markings & traffic signs
Street luge
    Street Sled Sports Racers
Street markets > Markets: street, cattle & farmers'
Street organs > Organs & organists
Streptocarpus
    Brit Streptocarpus Soc
Stress (physical & mental)
    Assn Stress Therapists
    Brit Assn Anger Mgt
    Brit Autogenic Soc
    Floatation Tank Assn
    Intl Stress Management Assn UK
    Nat Acupuncture Detoxification Assn
    Nat Coun Hypnotherapy
    Soc Stress Mgrs
String instruments > Musical instruments; & individual instruments
Strokes
    Stroke Assn
Structural engineering
    Instn Structural Engrs
    > + Construction industries
Structural waterproofing
    Brit Structural Waterproofing Assn
Stuart, House of
    R Stuart Soc
    Stewart Soc
Students
    AHS
    Assn Educ & Guardianship Intl Students
    Assn Student Residential Accommodation
    Brit Assn Health Services in Higher Educ
    Brit Educl Travel Assn
    Nat Assn Mgrs Student Services Colleges
    Nat Network Assessment Centres
    Nat U Students
    > + Youth organisations
Stunts & stunt coordination
    Gld Stunt & Action Coordinators
    UK Bungee Club
Stuttering > Stammering
Sub-aqua > Underwater; Water: sports
Sub-contractors > Building
Sub-postmasters
    Nat Fedn Sub-Postmasters
Sub-sea > Underwater headings
Subbuteo > Table football
Submersibles
    Soc Underwater Technology
Subsidence > Foundations (buildings)
Substance abuse > Addiction
Succulents > Cacti & succulents
Sudden infant death syndrome > Cot deaths
Sugar
    Refined Sugar Assn
    Sugar Assn Lond
    Sugar Traders Assn
    UK Indl Sugar Users Gp
Sugar beet seed
    Brit Soc Plant Breeders
Sugarcraft
    Brit Sugarcraft Gld
    Nat Sugar Art Assn
Suggestion schemes
    Ideas UK
Suicide
    ALERT
    CNK Alliance
    Compassionate Friends
    Samaritans
    Soc Old Age Rational Suicide
    Survivors Bereavement Suicide
Suitcases > Travel goods & accessories

Sullivan (Sir Arthur Seymour)
        Gilbert & Sullivan Soc
        Sir Arthur Sullivan Soc
Sunbeds
        Sunbed Assn
Sunblinds > Windows: blinds & shutters
Sundials
        Brit Sundial Soc
Supervisory management
        Inst Leadership & Mgt
Supply > Purchasing & supply
Supply chain management
        Brit Intl Freight Assn
Surface coatings > Coatings
Surfactants
        Brit Assn Chemical Specialities
Surfing, board & speed sailing
        Brit Bodyboard Club
        Brit Fedn Sand & Land Yacht Clubs
        Brit Kite Surfing Assn
        Brit Land Speedsail Assn
        Brit Power Kitesports Assn
        R Yachting Assn
        Surfing GB
        UK Windsurfing Assn
Surgery
        Assn Surgeons
        Assn Surgeons in Training
        Brit Assn Day Surgery
        Brit Assn Endocrine & Thyroid Surgeons
        Brit Assn Plastic, Reconstructive & Aesthetic Surgeons
        Brit Soc Surgery Hand
        College Emergency Medicine
        Fedn Surgical Speciality Assns
        Medical Soc Lond
        R Coll Physicians & Surgeons Glasgow
        R Coll Surgeons Edinburgh
        R Coll Surgeons England
        R Coll Surgeons Ireland
        R Coll Surgeons Ireland
        Soc Academic & Res Surgery
        > + specific branches
Surgical appliances
        Assn Brit Healthcare Inds
        Brit Assn Prosthetists & Orthotists
        Brit Healthcare Trs Assn
        Brit Inst Dental & Surgical Technologists
Surgical equipment & supplies
        Cutlery & Allied Trs Res Assn
        Ir Med Devices Assn
        Surgical Dressings Mfrs Assn
Surnames > Names
Surtees (Robert Smith)
        R S Surtees Soc
Surveying
        Assn Bldg Engrs
        Assn Chief Estates Surveyors... Public Sector
        Assn Consultant Approved Inspectors
        Assn Geotechnical & Geoenvironmental Specialists
        Brit Cartographic Soc
        Chart Inst Bldg
        Chart Instn Civil Engg Surveyors
        Chief Bldg Surveyors Soc
        Ground Forum
        Hydrographic Soc
        Indep Surveyors & Valuers Assn
        Ir Instn Surveyors
        LABC
        London Dist Surveyors Assn
        Nat Assn Profl Inspectors & Testers
        Property Consultants Soc
        R Instn Chart Surveyors
        Rating Surveyors Assn
        Soc Chart Surveyors Ireland [IRL]
        UK Land & Hydrographic Survey Assn
Suspended access equipment & cradles > Cradles & suspended platforms
Sussex Downs
        S Downs Soc
Sustainable development
        UK Sustainable Devt Assn
Sutures > Surgical equipment & supplies
Suzuki (Dr Shinichi)
        Brit Suzuki Inst
Swaziland
        Swaziland Soc
Sweden
        Anglo Swedish Soc

Brit Swedish Cham Comm Sweden
        Swedish Cham Comm UK
Swedenborg (Emanuel)
        Swedenborg Soc
Sweet peas
        N England Rosecarpe Horticl Soc
        Nat Sweet Pea Soc
Sweets > Confectionery
Swimming & diving
        Amat Swimming Assn
        Brit Long Distance Swimming Assn
        Brit Swimming
        Great Britain Diving Fedn
        Halliwick Assn Swimming Therapy
        Inst Swimming
        Nat Assn Swimming Clubs H'capped
        Nat Fedn SwimSchools
        Outdoor Swimming Soc
        Scot Amat Swimming Assn
        Swimming Teachers Assn
        Welsh Amat Swimming Assn
        > + Water: sports
Swimming pools
        Brit Swimming Pool Fedn
        Inst Mgt Sport & Physical Activity
        Inst Swimming Pool Engrs
        Swimming Pool & Allied Trs Assn
Swing dance
        London Swing Dance Soc
        > + Dancing
Switchgear (electrical)
        BEAMA
Switzerland
        Brit-Swiss Cham Comm [Zürich]
        Fedn Swiss Socs UK
Swordplay > Fencing (sport)
Synaesthesia
        UK Synaesthesia Assn
Synagogues
        Fedn Synagogues
        > + Jewish organisations
Synchronised swimming
        Amat Swimming Assn
        Brit Swimming
        > + Swimming & diving
Synthetic surfaces > Sportsgrounds & synthetic surfaces
Syria
        Brit Syrian Soc
Systematics
        Systematics Assn

T

Table football
        Brit Foosball Assn
        English Subbuteo Table Football Assn
Table tennis
        English Table Tennis Assn
        Scot Table Tennis Assn
        Table Tennis Assn Wales
Table wines > Wines
Tableware > Cutlery; Glass; Pottery
Taekwondo > Martial arts
Tai chi chuan > Martial arts
Tailoring
        UK Fashion & Textile Assn
Taiwan
        Brit Cham Comm Taipei
Takeaway & fast food
        Nationwide Caterers Assn
Takeovers > Business: mergers & acquisitions
Talipes (club foot)
        STEPS
Tall people
        Tall Persons Club
        > + Growth
Tallis (Thomas)
        Tallis Gp
Tank storage
        Tank Storage Assn
        > + Cisterns, drums & tanks
Tankers
        Inst Chart Shipbrokers
        > + Shipping

© CBD Research Ltd · Beckenham · BR3 5JS · Tel 020 8650 7745   E-mail cbd@cbdresearch.com · www.cbdresearch.com

Tankers (road)
    Road Haulage Assn
Tanning > Leather headings; Sunbeds

Tanzania
    Britain-Tanzania Soc
Tape(s): adhesive
    Adhesive Tape Mfrs' Assn
Tape(s): recording > Sound recording & reproduction
Tape(s): woven
    Brit Narrow Fabrics Assn
Tapestry
    Brit Tapestry Gp
Tarantulas
    Brit Tarantula Soc
Target archery > Archery
Target shooting > Pistol shooting; Rifle shooting
Tarot
    Brit Astrological & Psychic Soc
    Tarot Assn
Tarpaulins
    Performance Textiles Assn
Tatting
    Ring of Tatters
Tatting
    Lace Soc
Tattooing
    Adult Ind Trade Assn
    Tattoo Club
Taxation
    Assn Corporate Trustees
    Assn Revenue & Customs
    Assn Taxation Technicians
    Charity Tax Gp
    Chart Inst Taxation
    EIS Assn
    Fedn Tax Advisers
    Inst Fiscal Studies
    Inst Indirect Taxation
    Ir Taxation Inst
    Land Value Taxation Campaign
    Low Incomes Tax Reform Gp
    Profl Contrs Gp
    Soc Later Life Advisers
    Soc Trust & Estate Practitioners
    TaxPayers' Alliance
    VAT Practitioners Gp
Taxidermy
    Gld Taxidermists
Taxis & minicabs
    Ir Taxi Drivers Fedn
    Licensed Taxi Drivers' Assn
    London Motor Cab Proprietors Assn
    London Private Hire Car Assn
    London Vintage Taxi Assn
    Nat Private Hire Assn
    Nat Taxi Assn
    > + Motor vehicles: hire
Tay-Sachs disease
    Tay Sachs & Allied Diseases Assn
Tea
    UK Tea Coun
Teachers
    Assn Achievement &...Assessment
    Assn Christian Teachers
    Assn Christian Teachers Scotland
    Assn Citizenship Teaching
    Assn Promotion Quality TESOL Educ
    Assn Secondary Teachers, Ireland
    Assn Teachers & Lecturers
    Brit Assn Local Hist
    Educl Inst Scotland
    Inst Learning
    Ir Fedn University Teachers
    Ir Nat Teachers Org
    Nat Assn Schoolmasters U Women Teachers
    Nat Assn Teachers Travellers
    Nat U Teachers
    NI Assn Christian Teachers
    SATIPS
    Scot Assn Teachers History
    Scot Secondary Teachers' Assn
    Soc Schoolmasters & Schoolmistresses
    Teachers' U Ireland
    Ulster Teachers U
    Undeb Cenedlaethol Athrawon Cymru
    University & Coll U

    Voice
    > + Education; for teachers of specific subjects see subject taught
Technical drawing
    Assn Illustrators
Technical education
    Design & Technology Assn
    Fedn Awarding Bodies
    Inst Scientific & Technical Communicators
    Nat Assn Advisers... Design & Technology
Technical information > Information: services & technology
Technical terminology
    BSI
Technical writing & publishing
    Assn Brit Science Writers
    Inst Scientific & Technical Communicators
The Technion (Israel Inst of Technology)
    Brit Technion Soc
Technology parks > Science parks
Technology transfer
    AIRTO
    Inst Intl Licensing Practitioners
    Licensing Executives Soc
    PERA
    UK Science Park Assn
Tectonics
    Geological Soc
Teeth
    Saving Teeth Awareness Campaign
    > + Dentistry
Tegestology > Beer: bottles, cans, labels & mats
Telecommunications
    Action4
    ALTO [IRL]
    Communication Workers U
    Communications Mgt Assn
    Customer Contact Assn
    Fedn Communication Services
    ICT Ireland
    Intellect
    Nat Jt Utilities Gp
    Prospect
    SCTE
    SELECT
    Telecommunications & Internet Fedn [IRL]
    UK Competitive Telecommunications Assn
    > + Electronic: industry & engineering
Telecommunications: history
    Telecommunications Heritage Gp
Telecottages
    Telework Assn
Telepathy > Paranormal & psychical research
Telephone cables > Electric: cable & conduit
Telephones > Mobile phones; Telecommunications
Telescopes
    William Herschel Soc
Television
    Animal Welfare Filming Fedn
    Assn Studio & Production Eqpt Companies
    BKSTS
    Brit Academy Film & TV Arts
    Brit Amat TV Club
    Brit Film Inst
    Broadcasting Entertainment Cinematograph...U
    Directors Gld
    Gld TV Cameramen
    R Television Soc
    Soc TV Lighting & Design
    TV & Radio Inds Club
    Vision Mixers Gld
    Voice Listener & Viewer
    > + Audio visual aids & equipment
Television: advertising > Advertising: television & screen
Television: cable > Cable & satellite communications
Television: closed circuit
    Brit Security Ind Assn
    Nat Security Inspectorate
Television: engineering
    Fibreoptic Ind Assn
    Narrow-bandwidth TV Assn
    > + Electronic: industry & engineering
Television: history > Radio & TV: history
Television: production
    Gld Brit Film & TV Editors
    Producers Alliance Cinema & TV
    Production Mgrs Assn
    Satellite & Cable Broadcasters' Gp
Television: rental > Radio & TV: rental

Television: trade > Radio & TV: trade
Teleworkers
 Telework Assn
Temperance
 Brit Nat Temperance League
Temperature controlled storage
 Assn Meat Inspectors
 Brit Refrigeration Assn
 Cambridge Refrigeration Technology
 Food Storage & Distbn Fedn
 Ir Cold Storage Fedn
 Nat Assn Brit Market Authorities
 UK Warehousing Assn
Temperature controlled transport
 Cambridge Refrigeration Technology
 Food Storage & Distbn Fedn
 Transfrigoroute UK
Temporary workers
 Assn Contractors & Temporary Workers
Tenants & residents
 Fedn Private Residents' Assns
 Nat Tenant Voice
 Nat U Residents' Assns
 Scot Tenants Org
 Tenant Farmers' Assn
 Tenants & Residents Orgs England
 > + Property & land owners
Tennis
 Assn Brit Tennis Officials
 Brit Assn Tennis Supporters
 Brit Tennis Coaches Assn
 Ir Real Tennis Assn
 Lawn Tennis Assn
 Lawn Tennis Writers Assn
 Tennis & Rackets Assn
 Tennis Scotland
 Tennis Wales
 Vets Tennis GB
Tennis courts & equipment
 Sports & Play Construction Assn
Tennyson (Alfred, Lord)
 Tennyson Soc
Tenpin bowling > Bowling
Tensional strapping > Strapping
Tents & marquees
 Performance Textiles Assn
Terminals (ports) > Ports
Terrapins > Chelonia
Terrazzo-mosaic
 Nat Fedn Terrazzo, Marble & Mosaic Specialists
Tertiary colleges > Adult education
Tertiary era geology
 Tertiary Res Gp
 > + Geology

Test pilots
 R Aeronautical Soc
 > + Aviation: pilots, officers & crew
Testing laboratories
 Assn Consulting Scientists
 > + Materials: technology & testing
Testing methods
 AIRTO
Testing (non-destructive) > Materials: technology & testing
Textile: conservation
 Brit Antique Furniture Restorers Assn
 > + Costume history, design & conservation
Textile: design
 Chart Soc Designers
 Register Apparel & Textile Designers
 Textile Inst Intl
 Textile Soc
Textile: industry & trade
 ASBCI
 Brit Apparel & Textile Confedn
 Brit Interior Textiles Assn
 Brit Narrow Fabrics Assn
 Brit Textile Machinery Assn
 Brit Textile Technology Gp
 Brit Throwsters Assn
 Performance Textiles Assn
 Scot Textile Ind Assn
 Textile Inst Intl
 UK Textile Laboratory Forum
 Wales Craft Coun
 Wallcovering Distbrs Assn
 > + specific textiles

Textile: rental
 Textile Services Assn
Thailand
 Anglo Thai Soc
 Brit Cham Comm Thailand
Thalassaemia
 UK Thalassaemia Soc
Thalidomide
 Thalidomide Soc
Thames (The)
 River Assn Freight & Transport
 River Thames Alliance
 River Thames Soc
Thatching (roofs)
 Nat Soc Master Thatchers
 > + Roofing
Theatre
 Assn Brit Theatre Technicians
 Broadcasting Entertainment Cinematograph...U
 Directors Gld
 Fedn Ethical Stage Hypnotists
 Fedn Scot Theatre
 Indep Theatre Coun
 Inst Contemporary Arts
 Little Theatre Gld
 Soc Brit Theatre Designers
 Soc Theatre Consultants
 Stage Mgt Assn
 > + Drama; Entertainment; Music: hall
Theatre: history
 Cinema Theatre Assn
 Malone Soc
 Soc Dance Res
 Soc Theatre Res
Theatre: lighting
 Assn Lighting Designers
 Profl Lighting & Sound Assn
Theatre: model
 Brit Puppet & Model Theatre Gld
Theatre: playrights > Dramatists
Theatre: young people
 Nat Assn Youth Drama [IRL]
 Nat Assn Youth Theatres
 Nat Drama
 Scot Community Drama Assn
Theology > Religion
Theosophy
 Theosophical Soc England
Therapeutic communities
 Assn Therapeutic Communities
 > + Mental health
Therapeutic education
 Nat Assn Therapeutic Educ
 > + Education headings
Therapy
 Assn Physical & Natural Therapists
 Assn Rational Emotive Behaviour Therapy
 Complementary Therapists Assn
 Therapy Lecturers Assn
 > + individual forms of therapy
Thermal insulation > Insulation
Thermal spraying
 Thermal Spraying & Surface Engg Assn
 > + Coatings
Thermal waters > Spas
Thermoplastics > Plastics
Thermometers
 Pressure Gauge & Dial Thermometer Assn
Thimbles
 Thimble Soc Lond
Thirkell (Angela)
 Angela Thirkell Soc
Thomas (Dylan Marlais)
 Dylan Thomas Soc
Thomas ([Philip] Edward)
 Edward Thomas Fellowship
 Friends Dymock Poets
Thomson (Alexander)
 Alexander Thomson Soc
Thoracic diseases
 Brit Assn Lung Research
 Brit Thoracic Soc
 Pulmonary Hypertension Assn
 Sarcoidosis & Interstitial Lung Assn
 Soc Cardiothoracic Surgery
Thrombocytopenia
 ITP Support Assn

© CBD Research Ltd · Beckenham · BR3 5JS · Tel 020 8650 7745 E-mail cbd@cbdresearch.com · www.cbdresearch.com

Throwsters
Brit Throwsters Assn
Throwsticks
Brit Boomerang Soc
Thunderstorms
Tornado & Storm Res Org
Thyroid disease
Brit Assn Endocrine & Thyroid Surgeons
Brit Thyroid Assn
Hypoparathyroidism UK
Thyroid Eye Disease Charitable Trust
Tickets
Assn Secondary Ticket Agents
Omnibus Soc
Soc Ticket Agents & Retailers
Token Corresponding Soc
Transport Ticket Soc
Ticks
Borreliosis & Assd Diseases Awareness UK
Tidal energy > Renewable energy
Tiddlywinks
English Tiddlywinks Assn
Ties
Brit Menswear Gld
Tights > Hosiery
Tiles (floor & wall)
Cork Ind Fedn
Nat Fedn Terrazzo, Marble & Mosaic Specialists
Tile Assn
Tiles & Architectural Ceramics Soc
Tiles & tiling (roof) > Roofing
Timber
Confedn Forest Inds
Glued Laminated Timber Assn
N W Timber Tr Assn
Scot Timber Tr Assn
Timber Tr Fedn
TRADA Technology
UK Forest Products Assn
> + Forestry; Wood
Timber buildings
Carpenters Fellowship
Modular & Portable Bldg Assn
TRADA Technology
UK Timber Frame Assn
Timber containers > Packaging
Timber decking
Timber Decking Assn
Timber preserving
Property Care Assn
Timber roofing > Roofing
Time recording > Horology
Timeshare industry
Timeshare Consumers Assn
> + Property & landowners
Tin boxes > Metal: boxes
Tin cans > Cans & canning
Tin mining > Mining
Tinnitus
Brit Tinnitus Assn
Tinplate
Metal Packaging Mfrs Assn
Tipping vehicles
Road Haulage Assn
Tissue banking
Brit Assn Tissue Banking
Tissue paper
Confedn Paper Inds
> + Paper & paper products
Tissue viability
Tissue Viability Soc
Titanic (the RMS)
Brit Titanic Soc
Toadstools > Mycology
Toastmasters & masters of ceremonies
Gld Profl Toastmasters
Nat Assn Toastmasters
Tobacco
Assn Indep Tobacco Specialists
Cigarette Packet Collectors Club
Imported Tobacco Products Advy Coun
Nat Assn Cigarette Machine Operators
Retail Confectioners & Tobacconists Assn
Retailers Smuggling [IRL]
Tobacco Mfrs' Assn
Tobacco Retailers Alliance
> + Smoking

Toboggan & luge racing/riding
Brit Bob Skeleton Assn
Brit Bobsleigh Assn
Great Britain Luge Assn
Street Sled Sports Racers
Toiletries
Cosmetic, Toiletry & Perfumery Assn
Ir Cosmetics Detergent & Allied Products Assn
Toilets (public)
Brit Toilet Assn
Tokens
Token Corresponding Soc
Tolkien (J R R)
Tolkien Soc
Tomatoes
Brit Tomato Growers Assn
> + Vegetables: growing
Tonic Sol-fa
Brit Kodály Academy
Curwen Inst
> + Music: teaching
Tools
Assn Woodturners
Brit Compressed Air Soc
Brit Hardmetal & Engineers' Cutting Tool Assn
Brit Hardware Fedn
Brit Indep Retailers Assn
Cutlery & Allied Trs Res Assn
Fedn Brit Engrs Tool Mfrs
Fedn Brit Hand Tool Mfrs
Gauge & Tool Makers Assn
Portable Electric Tool Mfrs Assn
Power Fastenings Assn
Tools Self Reliance
> + specific tool
Tools: historic
Tools & Trs Hist Soc
Vintage Horticl & Garden Machinery Club
Top dressing materials
Brit Rootzone & Top Dressing Mfrs Assn
Tornado & storm research
Tornado & Storm Res Org
Tortoises > Chelonia
Tourette syndrome
Tourette Syndrome (UK) Assn
Tourism > Travel & tourism
Tourist guides
Assn Profl Tourist Guides
Inst Tourist Guiding
Towage & salvage
Brit Tugowners Assn
Towbars
Nat Trailer & Towing Assn
Tower fabricators
Brit Constructional Steelwork Assn
Prefabricated Access Suppliers' & Mfrs' Assn
Towing equipment (motor)
Mobile Electronics & Security Fedn
Town & country planning
Assn Project Safety
Assn Small Historic Towns & Villages
Assn Town Centre Mgt
Historic Towns Forum
Inst Place Mgt
Ir Planning Inst
London Soc
Nat Infrastructure Planning Assn
Planning & Environment Bar Assn
Planning Officers Soc
R Town Planning Inst
Regional Studies Assn
ROOM RTPI
Town & Country Planning Assn
Urban Design Gp
Town criers
Ancient & Honourable Gld Town Criers
Loyal Company Town Criers
Townswomen
Townswomen's Glds
Towpaths > Footpaths & rights of way
Toxicology
Brit Soc Toxicological Pathologists
Brit Toxicology Soc
Fund Replacement Animals Med Experiments
Soc Medicines Res
UK Envtl Mutagen Soc
Toxophily > Archery

Toys
    Baby Products Assn
    Brit Toy & Hobby Assn
    Brit Toymakers Gld
    Doll Club GB
    Equitoy
    Nat Assn Toy & Leisure Libraries
    Toy Retailers Association

Trace heating
    Electric Trace Heating Ind Coun

Tracheostomy
    Aid Children with Tracheostomies
    Tracheo-Oesophageal Fistula Support

Track events > Athletics

Tracking (cars)
    Mobile Electronics & Security Fedn

Tracks (sport) > Sportsgrounds & synthetic surfaces

Traction engines > Steam engines, boats & machinery;   Fairgrounds & equipment

Tractors > Agriculture: machinery

Trade > Commerce; Export & import; individual trades

Trade associations
    Trade Assn Forum

Trade marks & names > Patents & trade marks

Trade unions
    Communication Workers U
    Community
    Fedn Entertainment Us
    Gen Fedn Tr Us
    Ir Congress Tr Us
    Ir Municipal Public & Civil Tr U
    Scot Trs U Congress
    SIPTU [IRL]
    Trades U Congress
    UNISON
    Unite U

Trading standards
    Soc Chief Officers Trading Standards Scotland
    Trading Standards Inst
    > + Consumer affairs & protection

Traffic: accidents > Accidents; Road safety & control

Traffic: control > Road safety & control

Traffic: gyratory systems
    UK Roundabout Appreciation Soc

Traffic: signs > Road: lighting, markings & traffic signs; Signs

Trail riding
    Trail Riders Fellowship

Trailers: motor vehicle
    Comml Trailer Assn
    Nat Trailer & Towing Assn
    Org Horsebox & Trailer Owners

Training (industrial) > Occupational training & education

Trains > Railways

Tramways & trams
    Heritage Rly Assn
    Light Rail Transit Assn
    Omnibus Soc
    Rly & Canal Histl Soc
    Scot Tramway & Transport Soc
    Tramway & Light Rly Soc
    Tramway Museum Soc
    > + Railways: light

Tranquiliser withdrawal
    No Panic

Transactional analysis
    Inst Transactional Analysis

Transformers > Electrical industry & engineering

Transfusion science > Haematology

Transit shed operators
    Brit Intl Freight Assn

Translation & interpretation
    Assn Police & Court Interpreters
    Assn Translation Companies
    Chart Inst Linguists
    Conf Interpreters Gp
    Inst Translation & Interpreting
    Ir Translators & Interpreters Assn
    Translators Assn
    > + Languages

Transmission towers > Tower fabricators

Transplants & transplant surgery
    Brit Assn Tissue Banking
    Brit Soc Bone & Marrow Transplantation
    Brit Transplantation Soc
    NI Transplant Assn
    Transplant Support Network

Transport
    Assn Brit Transport & Engg Museums
    Brit Intl Freight Assn
    Campaign Better Transport
    Chart Inst Logistics & Transport
    Chart Inst Logistics & Transport Ireland
    Chart Instn Highways & Transportation
    Community Transport Assn
    Freight Transport Assn
    Inst Highway Engrs
    Inst Transport Administration
    Inst Transport Mgt
    Instn Civil Engrs
    Instn Engg & Technology
    Ir Assn Intl Express Carriers
    Nat Coun Inland Transport
    Nat U Rail Maritime & Transport Workers
    Profl Drivers Assn
    Road Transport Fleet Data Soc
    Scot Transport Studies Gp
    Transform Scotland
    Transport Salaried Staffs Assn
    Transport Ticket Soc
    Transport-Watch
    > + individual forms of transport

Transport: (of animals) > Animals: transportation

Transport: history
    Birmingham Transport Histl Gp
    Rly & Canal Histl Soc
    Roads & Road Transport Hist Assn
    Scot Tramway & Transport Soc
    Transport Trust
    > + specific forms of transport

Transport: security
    Brit Security Ind Assn
    > + Security

Transsexuality & transvestism
    Beaumont Soc
    Gender Trust

Travel & tourism
    ABTA
    Advantage
    Assn Brit Tour Operators France
    Assn Business Executives
    Assn Indep Tour Operators
    Assn Leading Visitor Attractions
    Assn Leisure Ind Profls
    Assn Nat Tourist Office Representatives
    Assn Scot Visitor Attractions
    Baltic Air Charter Assn
    Brit Gld Travel Writers
    Brit Resorts & Destinations Assn
    Eventia
    Family Holiday Assn
    Gld Travel Mgt Cos
    Gld Travel & Tourism
    Group Travel Organisers Assn
    Inst Travel & Meetings
    Inst Travel & Tourism
    Ir Tourist Ind Confedn
    Ir Travel Agents Assn
    Outdoor Writers' & Photographers' Gld
    Scot Tourism Forum
    Tourism for All
    Tourism Alliance
    Tourism Concern
    Tourism Mgt Inst
    Tourism Soc
    Travel Trust Assn
    UKinbound
    Worldchoice
    > + individual modes of travel

Travel & tourism: educational
    Brit Educl Travel Assn
    School Journey Assn

Travel & tourism: guides
    Gld Registered Tourist Guides
    Scot Tourist Guides Assn

Travel & tourism: health
    Brit Travel Health Assn

Travel goods & accessories
    Brit Menswear Gld
    Brit Travelgoods & Accessories Assn
    R Coll Physicians & Surgeons Glasgow

Travelling people > Gypsies & travelling people

Treacher Collins
    Treacher Collins Family Support Gp

© CBD Research Ltd · Beckenham · BR3 5JS · Tel 020 8650 7745   E-mail cbd@cbdresearch.com · www.cbdresearch.com

Treasurers > Accountancy;   Local government: officers
Trees
Ancient Tree Forum
Arboricultural Assn
Brit Christmas Tree Growers Assn
Brit Conifer Soc
Horticultural Trs Assn
Nat Assn Tree Officers
Tree Coun Ireland
> + Forestry
Trenchless technology
Soc Brit Water & Wastewater Inds
UK Soc Trenchless Technology
Triathlon
Brit Triathlon Fedn
Triathlon England
Triathlon Scotland
Welsh Triathlon
Tribology > Friction
Trichology > Hair & scalp treatment
Trichotillomania > Hair & scalp treatment
Tricycling
Assn Pioneer Motor Cyclists
Tricycle Assn
> + Cycles & motorcycles
Tridentine Mass
Latin Mass Soc
Trigeminal neuralgia > Neuralgia
Tripedressing
Nat Assn Tripe Dressers
Trolleybuses
Brit Trolleybus Soc
Nat Trolleybus Assn
Omnibus Soc
Trollope (Anthony)
Trollope Soc
Trombones
Brit Trombone Soc
Tropical crops
Tropical Agriculture Assn
Tropical Growers' Assn
Tropical environment
Soc Envtl Exploration
Tropical fish > Fish: tropical & ornamental
Tropical medicine
R Soc Tropical Medicine & Hygiene
> + Medicine
Troughed belt conveyors
Materials Handling Engrs Assn
Trout > Salmon & trout
Trucks > Fork-lift trucks; Lifting & loading equipment
Trucks: racing
Brit Truck Racing Assn
Trusts, trusteeship & estate planning
Assn Corporate Trustees
Assn Member-Directed Pension Schemes
Insolvency Practitioners Assn
Soc Trust & Estate Practitioners
Soc Will Writers & Estate Planning Practitioners
> + Investment; Pensions
TT racing
TT Riders Assn
> + Motor cycling & scooter riding
Tuberculosis > Thoracic diseases
Tuberous sclerosis
Tuberous Sclerosis Assn
Tubes > Pipes; Steel tubes
Tug of war
Scot Tug of War Assn
Tug of War Assn
Tugs
Brit Tugowners Assn
Tumours & tumorous diseases > Oncology
Tunnel lining
Brit Precast Concrete Fedn
Tunnels & shaft sinking
Brit Tunnelling Soc
Ground Forum
Inst Explosives Engrs
Joseph Williamson Soc
Pipe Jacking Assn
Subterranea Britannica

Turbines > Gas engines & turbines
Turf
Agricl Engrs Assn
Brit Turf & Landscape Irrigation Assn

Land Drainage Contrs Assn
Register Indep Profl Turfgrass Agronomists
Turfgrass Growers Assn
> + Grass & grassland; Sportsgrounds & synthetic surfaces
Turkey
Anglo Turkish Soc
Brit Cham Comm Turkey
Middle East Assn
Turkeys
Brit Poultry Coun
Traditional Farmfresh Turkey Assn
Turkey Club
> + Poultry
Turnaround specialists
Assn Business Recovery Profls
Inst Turnaround
Turned parts
Brit Turned Parts Mfrs Assn
Turner (Joseph Mallord William)
Indep Turner SocIndep   Turner Soc
Turner Soc
Turner syndrome
Turner Syndrome Support Soc
Turning > Woodworking
Turtles > Chelonia
Tutors
Assn Tutors
Tweed > Wool & wool products
Twins & multiple births
Lone Twin Network
Multiple Births Foundation
Twins & Mult Births Assn
Typography
Intl Soc Typographic Designers
Tyres
Brit Tyre Mfrs Assn
Imported Tyre Mfrs Assn
Indep Tyre Distbrs Network
Ir Tyre Ind Assn
Nat Tyre Distbrs Assn
Retread Mfrs Assn
Tyre Ind Fedn
Tyre Recovery Assn
TyreSafe

U

UFOs > Unidentified flying objects
Ukuleles & banjos
Ukulele Soc
Ulcers
Leg Ulcer Forum
Tissue Viability Soc
Ulster-Scots language
Ulster-Scots Language Soc
Ultimate (sport) > Flying: discs (sport)
Ultrasound
Brit Med Ultrasound Soc
Umbrellas
Brit Menswear Gld
Umpires > Cricket
Underfloor heating > Heating
Underground (the London)
London Underground Rly Soc
Nat U Rail Maritime & Transport Workers
> + Railways: history & preservation
Underground machinery > Mining: equipment
Underground structures
Subterranea Britannica
Underlay
Needleloom Underlay Mfrs Assn
Underpinning > Foundations (buildings)
Underwater engineering & research
Histl Diving Soc
Inst Explosives Engrs
Inst Marine Engg, Science & Technology
Nautical Archaeology Soc
Soc Underwater Technology
Subsea UK
> + Marine: biology & biochemistry; Ocean industries
Underwater photography
Gld Brit Camera Technicians
Underwater sports > Water: sports; individual sport
Underwriting > Insurance

Unicycling
U UK Unicyclists
Unidentified flying objects
Assn Scientific Study Anomalous Phenomena
Brit UFO Res Assn
Uniforms & protective clothing > Protective clothing/equipment
Unions > Trade unions
Unit trusts > Investment
Unitarian Church
Unitarian Hist Soc
United Nations
Brit Assn Former UN Civil Servants
Utd Nations Assn GB & NI
United Reformed Church
Utd Reformed Church Hist Soc
United States of America > USA
Universities
Assn C'wealth Universities
Assn University Administrators
Assn University Res & Ind Links
Brit Universities & Colleges Sport
Ir Universities Assn
Universities & Colls Emplrs' Assn
Universities Scotland
Universities UK
University students > Students
Unpasteurised milk
Assn Unpasteurised Milk Producers
> + Dairying
Upholstery
Assn Master Upholsterers & Soft Furnishers
Nat Carpet Cleaners Assn
Urban studies > Environment
Urethane foam > Plastics: foam
Urology
Assn Continence Advice
Brit Assn Urological Nurses
Brit Assn Urological Surgeons
Cystitis & Overactive Bladder Foundation
Urostomy Assn
> + Genito-urinary medicine
Uruguay
Brit Uruguayan Soc
Cámara Comercio Uruguayo Británica
USA
Brit Assn Amer Studies
Brit N Amer Res Assn
English Speaking U C'wealth
Pilgrims (The)
USSR
Stalin Soc
> + Russia & associated states; Slavonic languages & culture
Uveitis
Uveitis Inf Gp

V

Vaccination
Justice Awareness & Basic Support
UK Vaccine Ind Gp
Vacuum technology
Brit Compressed Air Soc
Brit Vacuum Coun
Solids Handling & Processing Assn
Valuation: art & antiques
Assn Art & Antique Dealers
Nat Assn Valuers & Auctioneers
Soc Fine Art Auctioneers & Valuers
Valuation: land & property
Assn Chief Estates Surveyors... Public Sector
Assn Valuers Licensed Property
Central Assn Agricl Valuers
Inst Profl Auctioneers & Valuers [IRL]
Inst Revenues Rating & Valuation
Property Consultants Soc
Scot Assessors Assn
> + Rating
Value management
Inst Value Mgt
Valves & actuators
BEAMA
Brit Valve & Actuator Assn
Solids Handling & Processing Assn
> + Electronic: industry & engineering

Vampires > Horror literature
Vans: lining & racking
Mobile Electronics & Security Fedn
Variety theatre > Music: hall
Vascular technology
Soc Vascular Technology
> + Haematology
VAT (value added tax)
VAT Practitioners Gp
> + Taxation
Veganism > Vegetarianism & veganism
Vegetables: growing
Brit Growers Assn
Nat Vegetable Soc
Processors & Growers Res Org
Vegetable Consultants Assn
> + individual vegetable
Vegetables: oils > Edible oils & fats
Vegetables: preserving
Food & Drink Fedn
Vegetables: protein
Soya Protein Assn
Vegetables: trade
Fresh Produce Consortium
Vegetarianism & veganism
Food & Drink Fedn
Vegan Soc
Vegetarian Soc
Vegetarian Soc Ireland
Vehicles > Electric transport; Military vehicles; Motor headings
Vehicle number plates > Number plates
Vending machines > Automatic vending
Venereal disease > Genito-urinary medicine
Venezuela
Anglo Venezuelan Soc
Cámara Venezolana Británica Comercio
Venison
Assn Deer Mgt Gps
Brit Deer Farms & Parks Assn
> + Deer; Meat

Ventilating > Air: conditioning & ventilating
Venture capital
BVCA
Venues > Arenas; Corporate hospitality
Verbatim reporting
Brit Inst Verbatim Reporters
> + Shorthand writing
Vergers (Church of England)
Church England Gld Vergers
Verse > Poetry
Veteran cars > Motor vehicles: historic
Veteran horses & ponies
Veteran Horse Soc
Veterans > Ex-service organisations
Veterinary medicine
Animal Health Distbrs Assn
Animal Medicines Trg Regulatory Auth
Animal & Plant Health Assn [IRL]
Brit Veterinary Hospitals Assn
Equine Shiatsu Assn
Equine Sports Massage Assn
Intl Assn Animal Therapists
Nat Office Animal Health
> + specific animal
Veterinary science
Brit Assn Homoeopathic Veterinary Surgeons
Brit Small Animal Veterinary Assn
Brit Soc Immunology
Brit Veterinary Assn
Brit Veterinary Forensic & Law Assn
Brit Veterinary Nursing Assn
R Coll Veterinary Surgeons
Veterinary Hist Soc
Veterinary Ireland
Veterinary tranquiliser dart recovery
Fedn Indep Detectorists
Vexillology > Flags, banners & bunting
Vibration
Assn Noise Consultants
Engg Integrity Soc
Heating, Ventilating & Air Conditioning Mfrs' Assn
Vibration healing
Brit Flower & Vibrational Essences Assn
College Vibrational Medicine Practitioner Assn
Crystal & Healing Fedn
Victims of accidents > Accidents: victims

© CBD Research Ltd · Beckenham · BR3 5JS · Tel 020 8650 7745 · E-mail cbd@cbdresearch.com · www.cbdresearch.com

Victims of crime > Crime protection & prevention; Domestic violence
Victoria Cross
    Victoria Cross & George Cross Assn
Victuallers > Meat;   Wines & spirits: trade
Vicuñas > Camelids
Video
    Adult Ind Trade Assn
    Advertising Producers Assn
    Assn Motion Picture Sound
    Audiovisual Fedn [IRL]
    Brit Interactive Media Assn
    Brit Soc Underwater Photographers
    Brit Universities Film & Video Coun
    Brit Video Assn
    Gld Profl Videographers
    Inst Videography
    Nat Assn Higher Educ Moving Image
    Production Mgrs Assn
    > + Film;   Sound recording & reproduction;   Television
Video games > Computer & video games
Viewing facilities
    Viewing Facilities Assn UK
Vikings > Scandinavia: literature & antiquities
Villages: deserted
    Medieval Settlement Res Gp
Villages: shops
    Rural Shops Alliance

Vinegar
    Vinegar Brewers Fedn
Vintage vehicles > Motor vehicles: historic
Vintners > Wines & spirits: trade
Vinyl flooring
    Contract Flooring Assn
    UK Resilient Flooring Assn
Violins & violas
    Brit Violin Making Assn
    Viola da Gamba Soc
    > + Musical instruments
Violence (work-related)
    Inst Conflict Mgt
Virgil
    Virgil Soc
Virology > Microbiology
Vision
    Applied Vision Assn
    > + Blind & partially sighted; Ophthalmology; Orthoptics
Vision mixing
    Vision Mixers Gld
Vision technology > Machine vision
Visual aids > Audio visual aids & equipment
Visually impaired > Blind & partially sighted
Viticulture > Wines & viticulture
Vitiligo
    Vitiligo Soc
Vitreous enamel
    Inst Materials, Minerals & Mining
Vivisection
    Brit U Abolition Vivisection
    Fund Replacement Animals Med Experiments
    Ir Anti Vivisection Soc
    Nat Anti-Vivisection Soc
    Understanding Animal Res
Vocational guidance > Careers
Vodka
    Gin & Vodka Assn
    > + Wines & spirits trade
Voice
    Brit Voice Assn
    Voice Care Network
    > + Speech
Voice recognition
    Assn Automatic Identification &. . . Data Capture
Volcanoes
    Geological Soc
    > + Earth sciences, structure & resources; Geology
Volleyball
    Brit Volleyball Fedn
    English Volleyball Assn
    NI Volleyball Assn
    Scot Volleyball Assn
Voluntary organisations/service
    Assn Chief Officers Scot Voluntary Orgs
    Assn Voluntary Services Managers
    Assn Volunteer Managers
    Volunteering England

    > + Charities; Community service: voluntary; Social: service; Welfare headings
Voluntary service: history
    Voluntary Action Hist Soc
Vomiting
    Cyclical Vomiting Syndrome Assn
Voucher system
    UK Gift Card & Voucher Assn
Vulval disease & pain
    Brit Soc Study Vulval Diseases
    Vulval Pain Soc

W

Wagner ([Wilhelm] Richard)
    Wagner Soc
Wakeboarding > Water sports
Wales
    Campaign Protection Rural Wales
    Inst Welsh Affairs
    Welsh Local Govt Assn
Wales: archaeology, language & culture
    ACADEMI
    Archif Menywod Cymru
    Cambrian Archaeol Assn
    Capel
    Cardiff Naturalists Soc
    Cymdeithas Ddawns Werin Cymru
    Cymdeithas Iaith Gymraeg
    Honourable Soc Cymmrodorion
    London Welsh Assn
    R Instn S Wales
    Undeb Cenedlaethol Athrawon Cymru
    Urdd Gobaith Cymru
    Welsh Folk Song Soc
    Welsh Music Gld
    > + Archaeology: county societies
Walking
    Brit Assn Intl Mountain Leaders
    Brit Mountaineering Coun
    Brit Walking Fedn
    Long Distance Walkers Assn
    Mountaineering Coun Ireland
    Mountaineering Coun Scotland
    Pennine Way Assn
    Race Walking Assn
Walking sticks > Stickmaking
Wall (Max[well George Lorimer])
    Max Wall Soc
Wall(s): insulation
    Insulated Render & Cladding Assn
    > + Insulation
Wall(s): movable > Partitioning
Wall(s): ties
    Wall Tie Installers Fedn
Wall(s): tiles > Tiles (floor & wall)
Wallcoverings & wallpaper
    Brit Coatings Fedn
    Brit Indep Retailers Assn
    Home Decoration Retailers Assn
    Wallcovering Distbrs Assn
    Wallpaper Hist Soc
Walling
    Dry Stone Walling Assn
Walmsley ([James] Ulric & Leo)
    Walmsley Soc
Walnuts
    Combined Edible Nut Tr Assn
War(s) > under name of War
War memorials
    War Memorials Trust
Wardens > Rangers & wardens
Warehousing
    Bonded Warehousekeepers' Assn
    Chart Inst Logistics & Transport Ireland
    Ir Intl Freight Assn
    UK Warehousing Assn
    > + Materials: management/handling
Wargaming
    Brit Histl Games Soc
    Soc Ancients
    > + Fights (historic/re-enactment);   Models: hobby
Warlock (Peter)
    Peter Warlock Soc

Warm air hand driers
>   Brit Warm Air Hand Drier Assn
Warne (Frederick) publishers
>   Observers Pocket Series Collectors' Soc
Warner (Sylvia Townsend)
>   Sylvia Townsend Warner Soc
Warranty protection
>   Indep Warranty Assn
Wars of the Roses
>   Soc Friends King Richard III
Warships > Marine: engineering & equipment
Washing instruction & labelling
>   Home Laundering Consultative Coun
Wasps
>   Bees, Wasps & Ants Recording Soc
Waste disposal
>   ADEPT
>   Chart Instn Wastes Mgt
>   Chemical Recycling Assn
>   Combined Heat & Power Assn
>   Container Handling Eqpt Mfrs Assn
>   Environmental Inds Commission
>   Environmental Protection UK
>   Environmental Services Assn
>   Ir Waste Mgt Assn
>   Nat Assn Waste Disposal Officers
>   Oil Recycling Assn
>   R Envtl Health Inst Scotland
>   Valpak
>   Zero Waste Alliance UK
>   > + Water: treatment & supply
Waste disposal: medical
>   Sanitary Med Disposal Services Assn
Waste disposal: photographic
>   Photo Imaging Coun
Waste trades > Reclamation & recycling; specific type of waste
Watches > Horology
Water
>   Assn Drainage Authorities
>   Brit Cave Res Assn
>   Brit Hydrological Soc
>   Estuarine & Coastal Sciences Assn
>   Hydrographic Soc
>   Land Drainage Contrs Assn
>   R Meteorological Soc
>   UK Rainwater Harvesting Assn
>   Water Health Alliance
>   > + Hydraulics & hydromechanics; Water treatment & supply
Water: bottled > Bottled water; Spas
Water: divining
>   Brit Soc Dowsers
Water: jetting
>   Water Jetting Assn
Water: mills > Wind & water mills
Water: power
>   Brit Hydropower Assn
>   > + Renewable energy
Water: sports
>   Amat Swimming Assn
>   Brit Sub-Aqua Club
>   Brit Swimming
>   Brit Water Ski & Wakeboard
>   Brit Wave Ski Assn
>   Jet Sport Racing Assn
>   Scot Amat Swimming Assn
>   Scot Sub Aqua Club
>   Sub Aqua Assn
>   Wakeboard UK
>   waterskiscotland
>   Welsh Amat Swimming Assn
>   Welsh Assn Sub Aqua Clubs
Water: treatment & supply
>   Assn Public Analysts
>   Assn Public Analysts Scotland
>   Brit Assn Chemical Specialities
>   Brit Water
>   Brit Water Cooler Assn
>   Chart Instn Water & Envtl Management
>   Inst Water
>   Instn Civil Engrs
>   Nat Campaign Water Justice
>   Nat Jt Utilities Gp
>   Nat Pure Water Assn
>   Soc Brit Water & Wastewater Inds
>   Soil & Groundwater Technology Assn
>   Water Mgt Soc
>   Water UK

Well Drillers Assn
>   > + Bottled water
Waterbeds
>   Brit Waterbed Assn
>   > + Beds & bedding
Watercolour painting
>   Brit Watercolour Soc
>   R Scot Soc Painters in Water Colours
>   R Watercolour Soc
>   Water Colour Soc Ireland
>   > + Art & artists
Watercoolers
>   Brit Water Cooler Assn
Waterfowl
>   Brit Waterfowl Assn
Waterheaters > Boilers & waterheaters
Waterloo (Battle of)
>   Assn Friends Waterloo C'ee
Waterproofing
>   Brit Structural Waterproofing Assn
>   Intelligent Membrane Tr Assn
>   Liquid Roofing & Waterproofing Assn
>   Property Care Assn
Waterways: inland > Inland waterways
Watson (Dr John)
>   Friends Dr Watson
>   Sherlock Holmes Soc Lond
Wave energy
>   Renewable UK Assn
>   > + Renewable energy
Wealth management > Investment
Weapons
>   ADS Gp
>   Brit Pugwash Gp
>   > + Arms & armour; Defence equipment; Guns & ammunition
Weather > Meteorology
Weaving
>   Assn Glds Weavers, Spinners & Dyers
Webb (Mary Gladys)
>   Mary Webb Soc
Webbing
>   Brit Narrow Fabrics Assn
Website design
>   Inst Profl Designers
Weddings
>   Brit Bridalwear Assn
>   Retail Bridalwear Assn
>   UK Alliance Wedding Planners
Weddings: photography
>   Brit Inst Profl Photography
>   Gld Photographers
>   Gld Profl Videographers
>   Master Photographers Assn
>   Soc Wedding & Portrait Photographers
Weighing machines > Scales & weighing machines
Weight control (personal) > Obesity
Weight lifting & training
>   Brit Weight Lifting
>   Welsh Weight Training Assn
Weights & measures > Consumer affairs & protection; Measurement; Trading standards
Welding
>   Assn Welding Distbution
>   BEAMA
>   Welding Inst
Welfare: administration
>   Assn Chief Executives Voluntary Orgs
>   Inst Welfare
>   Nat Assn Voluntary & Community Action
>   Nat Assn Voluntary Service Mgrs
>   > + Social: services
Welfare: organisations
>   Brit Assn Settlements & Social Action Centres
>   Brit Red Cross Soc
>   Care Leavers Assn
>   Family Welfare Assn
>   Ir Red Cross Soc
>   Nat Assn Pastoral Care Educ
>   Nat Family Mediation
>   Relationships Scotland
>   Saint John Ambulance
>   Shared Care Network
>   SOVA
>   Women's R Voluntary Service
>   Youth Access
>   > + Community service; objects of welfare

© CBD Research Ltd · Beckenham · BR3 5JS · Tel 020 8650 7745 · E-mail cbd@cbdresearch.com · www.cbdresearch.com

Well drilling & equipment
    Assn Well Head Eqpt Mfrs
    UK Offshore Oil & Gas Ind Assn
    UK Onshore Operators Gp
    Well Drillers Assn
Wellington (Arthur Wellesley) Duke of
    Assn Friends Waterloo C'ee
Wells (Herbert George ['HG'])
    H G Wells Soc
Welsh > Wales: archaeology, language & culture
Wesley (John & Charles)
    Wesley Histl Soc
West Africa
    Business Coun Africa W & Sthn
West Indies & the Caribbean
    Black & Asian Studies Assn
    Caribbean-Brit Business Coun
    UK One World Linking Assn
Western Front
    Western Front Assn
    > + World Wars I & II
Wet garden plants
    Brit Hosta & Hemerocallis Soc
Whales
    Whale & Dolphin Consvn Soc
Wharves
    River Assn Freight & Transport
Wheelchairs
    Brit Wheelchair Racing Assn
    Ir Wheelchair Assn
    > + Health care: equipment & supplies
Whippets
    Brit Whippet Racing Assn
Whisky
    Malt Distillers Assn Scotland
    Scotch Malt Whisky Soc
    Scotch Whisky Assn
    > + Wines & spirits trade
White goods > Domestic appliances
White Star Line
    Brit Titanic Soc
Whole milk > Unpasteurised milk
Wholesale markets > Finance: brokers & agents
Wholesale trade > Cash & Carry; specific trade
Widows & widowers
    Cruse Bereavement Care
    Nat Assn Widows
    Nat Assn Widows Ireland
    Nat Coun Divorced, Separated & Widowed
    Nat Fedn Solo Clubs
    War Widows Assn
    Way Foundation
    > + Singles, divorced & separated; Women's organisations
Wigs
    Hairdressing & Beauty Suppliers Assn
    Inc Gld Hairdressers
    > + Hairdressing
Wild animals
    Assn Brit & Ir Wild Animal Keepers
    Brit Big Cats Soc
    Captive Animals' Protection Soc
    Scot Wildcat Assn
    Universities Fedn Animal Welfare
    > + Zoology & zoos; specific animal
Wild flowers
    Landlife
Wilde (Oscar Fingall O'Flahertie Wills)
    Oscar Wilde Soc
Wildfowl
    Brit Assn Shooting & Consvn
    Brit Decoy & Wildfowl Carvers Assn
    Brit Waterfowl Assn
    > + Birds
Wildlife: art
    Nature Art Trust
Wildlife: recording
    Nat Fedn Biological Recording
    Wildlife Sound Recording Soc
    > + Nature conservation
Williams (Alfred)
    Alfred Williams Heritage Soc
    Friends Alfred Williams
Williams (Charles Walter Stansby)
    Charles Williams Soc
Williams syndrome
    Williams Syndrome Foundation

Williamson (Henry)
    Henry Williamson Soc
Wills
    ALERT
    Inst Profl Willwriters
    Soc Trust & Estate Practitioners
    Soc Will Writers & Estate Planning Practitioners
Wind instruments > Brass & silver bands; Musical instruments
Wind energy/engineering
    Micropower Coun
    Renewable UK Assn
    Wind Engg Soc
    > + Renewable energy
Wind sports > Kite sports; Surfing, board & speedsailing; Yachts & yachting
Wind tunnel testing
    Aircraft Res Assn
Wind & water mills
    Soc Protection Ancient Bldgs
    Sussex Indl Archaeol Soc
    Welsh Mills Soc
Windows
    Brit Plastics Fedn
    Brit Woodworking Fedn
    Incorporation Plastic Window Fabricators & Installers
    Nat Assn Rooflight Mfrs
    Plastics Window Fedn
    Steel Window Assn
    > + Glass & glazing
Windows: blinds & shutters
    Brit Blind & Shutter Assn
    Door & Hardware Federation
Windows: cleaning
    Fedn Window Cleaners
Windsurfing > Surfing, board & speed sailing

Wines & spirits: trade
    Alcohol Beverage Fedn Ireland
    Assn Convenience Stores
    Assn Licensed Mult Retailers
    Assn Small Direct Wine Merchants
    Bonded Warehousekeepers' Assn
    Fedn Licensed Victuallers Assns
    Fedn Retail Licensed Tr NI
    Gin & Vodka Assn
    Inst Masters Wine
    Nat Off-Licence Assn [IRL]
    Scot Grocers Fedn
    Scot Licensed Tr Assn
    Scotch Whisky Assn
    Vintners Fedn Ireland
    Wine & Spirit Trade Assn
Wines & viticulture
    Assn Wine Educators
    Circle Wine Writers
    English Wine Producers
    Thames & Chiltern Vineyards Assn
    UK Vineyards Assn
Wire & wire products
    Scot Wirework Mfrs Assn
Wireless: history
    Brit Vintage Wireless Soc
Witchcraft
    Pagan Fedn
Witness (expert) > Experts & expert witness
Wodehouse (Sir P[elham] G[renville])
    P G Wodehouse Soc
Wolves
    Wolves & Humans Foundation
Women: employment
    Brit Assn Women Entrepreneurs
    Business & Profl Women
    Soc Promoting Training Women
    Working Families
    > + special occupations
Women: equal rights
    Fawcett Soc
    Nat Alliance Women's Orgs
    Rights of Women
Women's organisations
    Archif Menywod Cymru
    Brit Fedn Women Graduates
    Brit Women Pilots Assn
    Fedn Women's Insts NI
    Ir Countrywomen's Assn
    Mothers Apart Children
    Nat Alliance Women's Orgs
    Nat Assn Ladies Circles

Nat Assn Women's Clubs
Nat Fedn Women's Insts
Nat Women's Register
NI Women's Aid Fedn
Scot Women's Rural Insts
Townswomen's Glds
Women's Aid Fedn (England)
YWCA (Young Women's Christian Assn)
Women's wear > Clothing; Fashion
Wood
Inst Materials, Minerals & Mining
UK Forest Products Assn
> + Timber
Wood burning stoves
Stove Ind Alliance
Wood carving
Brit Decoy & Wildfowl Carvers Assn
Brit Woodcarvers Assn
Chippendale Soc
Master Carvers Assn
Wood floors > Floors
Wood panels
Wood Panel Inds Fedn
Wood preservation & care
Property Care Assn
Wood Protection Assn
Wood pulp
Brit Wood Pulp Assn
Woodforde (James)
Parson Woodforde Soc
Woodlands
Confedn Forest Inds
Small Woods Assn
> + Forestry
Woodlice
Brit Myriapod & Isopod Gp
Woodworking
Assn Polelathe Turners & Greenwood Workers
Assn Woodturners
Brit Wood Turners Assn
Brit Woodworking Fedn
Inst Carpenters
Inst Machine Woodworking Technology
Register Profl Turners
Soc Wood Engravers
Woodworking Machinery Suppliers Assn
Woodworm
Inst Specialist Surveyors & Engrs
Wool & wool products
Brit Textile Technology Gp
Cloth Merchants Assn
UK Hand Knitting Assn
Welsh Mills Soc
> + Sheep: breed societies
Woolf (Virginia)
Virginia Woolf Soc GB
Word blindness > Dyslexia
Work-related violence
Inst Conflict Mgt
Work sciences & study > Management
Workboats
Nat Workboat Assn
Worker participation > Industrial involvement & participation
Working dogs
Brit Inst Profl Dog Trainers
> + Dogs
Works management > Management
Workspaces (managed)
Business Centre Assn
Workwear > Protective clothing/equipment
World War I
War Research Soc
Western Front Assn
World War II
Battle Britain Histl Soc
War Research Soc
World War Two Living Hist Assn
World War Two Rly Study Gp
WW2 HMSO Paperbacks Soc
Wound care & equipment
Surgical Dressings Mfrs Assn
Tissue Viability Soc
Wound Care Alliance
Woven labels
Brit Narrow Fabrics Assn

Wrestling
Brit Wrestling Assn
Scot Wrestling Assn
Writers' agents > Authors' agents
Writers to the Signet > Law: Scotland
Writing equipment & accessories
Brit Office Supplies & Services Fedn
Writing Eqpt Soc
Writing Instruments Assn
Writing & writers
Alliance Literary Socs
Assn Freelance Writers
Assn Golf Writers
Brit Soc Comedy Writers
Gld Health Writers
Ir Playwrights & Screenwriters Gld
Ir Writers U
Keats Shelley Memorial Assn
Lancashire Authors Assn
Nat Assn Writers in Educ
Nat Assn Writers' Gps
Outdoor Writers' & Photographers' Gld
Romantic Novelists Assn
Soc Authors
Soc Authors Scotland
Writers Gld
Writers & Photographers unLimited
> + Journalism; & individual subjects
Writing & writers: authors > under individual author's name
Wurlitzers > Cinema organs

X

X-ray equipment
AXrEM

Y

Yachts & yachting
Assn Brokers & Yacht Agents
Boating Alliance
Brit Fedn Sand & Land Yacht Clubs
Cruising Assn
Ir Marine Fedn
R Yachting Assn
R Yachting Assn Scotland
UK Catamaran Racing Assn
Yachting Journalists' Assn
Yachts: building & designing
Amat Yacht Res Soc
Brit Marine Fedn
Model Yachting Assn
Yacht Designers & Surveyors Assn
Yachts: chartering
Assn Scot Yacht Charterers
Profl Charter Assn
Yarns
Brit Throwsters Assn
Coir Assn
> + Textile headings;   Wool & wool products
Yeast
UK Assn Mfrs Bakers Yeast
Yoga
Brit Wheel Yoga
Yoghurt
Food & Drink Fedn
Provision Tr Fedn
> + Dairying
Yonge (Charlotte Mary)
Charlotte M Yonge Fellowship
Young farmers clubs > Farmers organisations
Young (Francis Brett)
Francis Brett Young Soc
Youth employment > Careers
Youth hostels
An Oige
Hostelling Intl NI
Scot Youth Hostels Assn
Youth Hostels Assn (E&W)
Youth organisations
Brit Nat Temperance League

© CBD Research Ltd · Beckenham · BR3 5JS · Tel 020 8650 7745 · E-mail cbd@cbdresearch.com · www.cbdresearch.com

Central Org Maritime Pastimes. . .
Church Lads & Church Girls Brigade
Clubs Young People
Clubs Young People (NI)
Clubs Young People Scotland
Clubs Young People Wales
Horse Rangers Assn
Marine Soc & Sea Cadets
Nat Fedn Plus Areas
Nat Youth Coun Ireland
Scot Assn Young Farmers Clubs
Scout Assn
Scout & Guide Graduate Assn
Trefoil Gld
UK Youth
Urdd Gobaith Cymru
Woodcraft Folk
YMCA England
Young Explorers' Trust
Youth Access
Youth Action Network
Youth Action NI
Youth Scotland
Youth organisations: boys & young men
    Boys' Brigade
    YMCA Ireland
Youth organisations: girls & young women
    Girlguiding UK
    Girls' Brigade
    Girls Venture Corps Air Cadets
    Ir Girl Guides
    YWCA Ireland
Youth work
    Community & Youth Workers U

Fedn Detached Youth Work
Nat Assn Youth Justice
Nat Youth Fedn [IRL]

Z

Zen Buddhism > Buddhism
Zeolites
    Brit Zeolite Assn
Zimbabwe
    Britain Zimbabwe Soc
Zinc
    Cast Metals Fedn
Zinc coatings
    Galvanizers Assn
Zionism > Jewish organisations
Zoology & zoos
    Assn Brit & Ir Wild Animal Keepers
    Brit Herpetological Soc
    Brit & Ir Assn Zoos & Aquariums
    Captive Animals' Protection Soc
    Linnean Soc Lond
    N England Zoological Soc
    Natural Sciences Collections Assn
    R Zoological Soc Scotland
    Ray Soc
    Zoological Soc Ireland
    Zoological Soc London

Directory of BRITISH ASSOCIATIONS

*All entries in this Directory are **FREE** - you incur no financial obligation by completing & returning this form*

1. **Name of organisation** (as stated in Articles, Constitution or Rules):

2. **Abbreviation** by which the organisation is generally known:

3. **Year of formation:**

4. **Telephone:**

5. **Postal address**, including postcode:

6. **Fax:**

7. **Email:**

8. **Website:**

9. Is the above address that of:

Permanent headquarters with its own staff ☐   Honorary secretary's private house ☐

A firm of secretaries, accountants or solicitors ☐   Honorary secretary's business office ☐

Other:

10. **Name** of Secretary / Honorary Secretary / Chief Executive – please state office held:

11. **Branches** in the UK – give number only: Branches overseas – give countries only:

12. **Objects / Sphere of interest** – please state concisely the purpose of your organisation & its field of interest – this information is required for the subject index, therefore please explain any technical terms used:

13. **Specialist groups** or sections – please list fully:

14. **Subject index** – please suggest any specific subjects under which your organisation should be indexed:

15. **Affiliations:** to international & other organisations – please give names in **FULL**:

Affiliations: bodies affiliated to yours:

16. **Membership** – give present number in each category and relevant subscription:

	Individual persons		Companies / Firms		Other organisations (clubs, societies etc.)	
UK		£		£		£
Overseas		£		£		£

Please complete overleaf ⟩

ABBREVIATIONS: 1 – IN MAIN ALPHABETICAL DIRECTORY

Validity indicators:

■	entry based on questionnaire, or other document, returned by organisation
NR	No reply received for this edition
IRL	Irish entry - see introduction 3(b)
§	Organisation outside normal scope of DBA but included for convenience of users
**	Organisation unverified or lost

Address:

asa	official secretariat		hsp	honorary secretary's private address
hq	organisation's permanent headquarters		sb/p	secretary's business or private address
hsb	honorary secretary's business address		regd off	registered office

Name of secretary or chief executive, with designation of office held:

Chmn	Chairman	Sec	Secretary	Org Sec	Organising Secretary
Dir	Director	Gen Sec	General Secretary	Pres	President
Exec	Executive	Hon Sec	Honorary Secretary	Hon Treas	Honorary Treasurer
Mgr	Manager	Mem Sec	Membership Secretary	PRO	Public Relations Officer

▲   Type of constitution

Br   Branches

○   Type of organisation & sphere of interest: indicated by one or more of the following letters, with an amplification or explanation only where necessary; if an organisation's interests are obvious from its name, only the starred letter is given

*A	Art & Literature		*N	Co-ordinating bodies
*B	Breed Societies		*P	Professional
*C	Chambers of Commerce Industry or Trade		*Q	Research Organisations
			*R	Religious Organisations
*D	Dance, Music & Theatre		*S	Sports
*E	Educational		*T	Trade
*F	Farming & Agriculture		*U	Trade Unions
*G	General Interest & Hobbies		*V	Veterinary & Animal Welfare
*H	Horticultural		*W	Welfare Organisations
*K	Campaigns & Pressure Groups		*X	International Friendship
*L	Learned, Scientific & Technical Socs		*Y	Youth Organisations
*M	Medical Interest		*Z	Political Organisations

Gp(s)   Groups

●   Activities:

Comp	Competitions		LG	Liaison with Government
Conf	Conference(s)		Lib	Library
Empl	Negotiations of pay & conditions of employment		Mtgs	Regular Meetings
ET	Education &/or training for professional or other qualifications		PL	Picture Library
Exam	Examinations for professional or other qualifications		Res	Scientific or other systematic research
Exhib	Exhibitions & Shows		SG	Study Groups
Expt	Export promotion		Stat	Collection of Statistics
Inf	Information service available		VE	Visits & Excursions

<   Affiliations to international & other organisations
>   Bodies affiliated to the organisation

M   Membership Data

     i=individuals   f=firms   org=organisations

¶   Publications

AR	Annual Report		m	members
ftm	free to members		NL	Newsletter
hbk	Handbook		nm	non-members
Jnl	Journal		Ybk	Year book
LM	List of members		yr	per annum

X   Former name or names of organisation if changed during past five years (preceded by date of change, if known)